ATLAS OF BRITAIN

TIMES BOOKS
LONDON

THE TIMES ATLAS OF BRITAIN

Times Books, 77-85 Fulham Palace Road, London W6 8JB

First Edition 2010
reprinted 2012

Printed in China

British Library Cataloguing in Publication Data
A catalogue record for this book is available from the British Library

ISBN 978 0 00 790172 2
Imp 002

All mapping in this atlas is generated from Collins Bartholomew digital databases.
Collins Bartholomew, the UK's leading independent geographical information supplier, can
provide a digital, custom, and premium mapping service to a variety of markets.

For further information:
Tel: +44 (0) 208 307 4515
e-mail: collinsbartholomew@harpercollins.co.uk

or visit our website at: www.collinsbartholomew.com

If you would like to comment on any aspect of this atlas, please write to
Times Atlases, HarperCollins Publishers, Westerhill Road, Bishopbriggs, Glasgow G64 2QT

The world's most authoritative atlases
www.timesatlas.com

Follow us on twitter @timesatlas

Historical maps available to view and buy at
www.mapseeker.co.uk

THE TIMES
ATLAS OF BRITAIN

With special thanks to

FOREWORD

This *Times Atlas of Britain* continues a long tradition of what are commonly described as national atlases. The prominence of such products has ebbed and flowed over the centuries, and the debate over what actually constitutes a 'national atlas' appears no nearer to being resolved.

Several types of cartographic product have been described as national atlases, from Christopher Saxton's *Atlas of England and Wales* of 1579, through the *Statistical Atlas of the United States* of 1874 and Bartholomew's 1895 *Survey Atlas of Scotland*, to the *'Oxford' Atlas of Britain and Northern Ireland* of 1963 and many others published throughout the twentieth century. Yet these are incredibly diverse products, and any strict definition of the genre, such as that attempted by the criteria proposed in 1960 by a commission of the International Geographical Union, seems doomed to failure. The diversity of such products reflects changing ideas relating to their scope, purpose and content.

In a national atlas, a nation could be portrayed strictly as the area within its current political boundaries, or as a wider cultural or ethnic area based on historical origins. The atlas could aim to establish and portray (both to its own citizens and the outside world) the nation's identity and independence – perhaps not surprisingly, such products seem to have proliferated in the post-colonial, post-war, and post-Soviet eras. It could act as a symbol of national unity, as a cartographic showcase, as an administrative tool, or simply as a collection of material which defines the nation's character and culture. Whatever its scope, such a product will be judged by how it represents its subject, what opinions its users will form and whether it provides an accurate contemporary portrait of the nation.

This *Times Atlas of Britain* achieves these things through a great variety of content. It is aimed at a general audience – the needs of the academic and administrative communities seem well-served today by the proliferation of 'real-time' data available in many forms on-line – and its content reflects this perfectly. It builds up a comprehensive modern portrait of the constituent countries of Britain (taken here to be synonymous with the United Kingdom), their individual counties and the nation as a whole. Reflecting to some degree the style of the very earliest national atlases, it takes a distinctive local approach in putting together a national portrait. Profiles of each county are provided through topographic, thematic and historical maps, contemporary and historical accounts, facts, statistics and images. Origins of county names, what the areas are renowned for, famous local people and literary quotations all give more than just a static picture – they present a dynamic insight into the individual character of each part of the country.

The historical content is a distinctive and important part. It provides, through extracts from the *Bartholomew Gazetteer of the British Isles* of 1887, and beautiful reproductions of historical maps primarily from the late nineteenth century, a context for the contemporary information. It also caters for a continuing fascination amongst readers for old maps and for how things have changed over time. The nature of change is here discernible in both the content of the historical and modern elements, and in the cartographic and writing styles reflected in them.

The modern topographic maps are loyal to the standards expected of a *Times* atlas – accurate, clear and distinctive in their layer-coloured style for which Bartholomew and Times atlases are renowned. They provide a detailed and contemporary interpretation of the nation's landscape.

From this collection of maps and other information, both old and new, a clear portrait of Britain is presented, from which any user can form their own view on the current state of our nation.

CONTENTS

REFERENCE MAPS

CITIES AND TOWNS, COUNTY MAPS

Population	National capital	Administrative centre / County town	District centre	Other town
5 million to 10 million	**LONDON** ▣	…	…	…
1 million to 5 million	…	…	…	…
500 000 to 1 million	…	**Glasgow** ▣	…	…
100 000 to 500 000	**EDINBURGH** ▣	**Liverpool** ▣	**Huddersfield** ⊙	**West Bromwich** ⊙
50 000 to 100 000		**Warrington** ▣	**Wigan** ◎	**Runcorn** ◎
10 000 to 50 000		**Hamilton** ▣	Ashton-under-Lyne ⊙	**Fleetwood** ⊙
5 000 to 10 000		Ruthin ▫	Epping ○	Burley in Wharfedale ○
1 000 to 5 000		Conwy ▫	West Malling ○	Preesall ○
under 1000		Chicksands ▫	Thundersley ○	Staynall ○
Suburb				Blundellsands ○

⬭ Built-up area

RELIEF
Contour intervals used in layer-colouring for land height and sea depth

County maps, excluding Northern Ireland

Metres / Feet
- 1000 / 3280
- 900 / 2952
- 800 / 2624
- 700 / 2296
- 600 / 1968
- 500 / 1640
- 400 / 1312
- 300 / 4921
- 200 / 656
- 150 / 492
- 100 / 328
- 50 / 164
- 0 Land below sea level
- 50 / 164
- 200 / 656
- 1000 / 3281

County maps, Northern Ireland

Metres / Feet
- 700 / 2296
- 500 / 1640
- 400 / 1312
- 300 / 984
- 200 / 656
- 100 / 328
- 0 Land below sea level
- 50 / 164
- 200 / 656

National maps (pages 20–27)

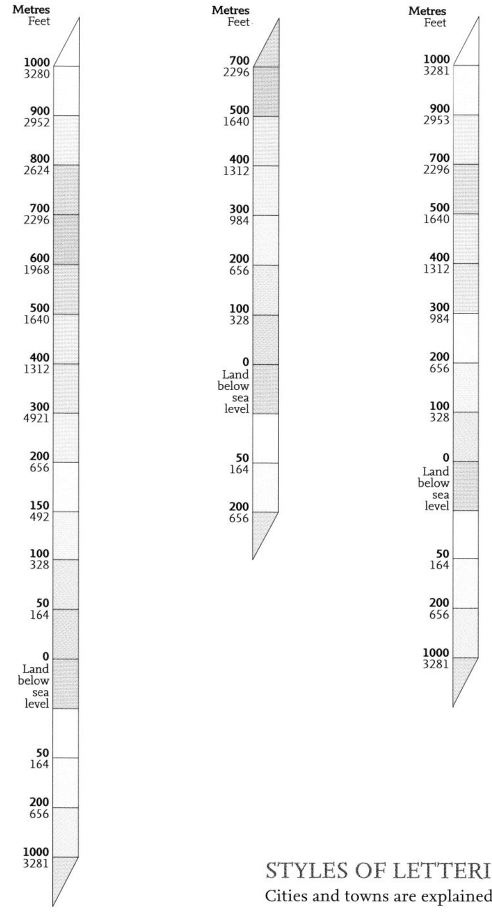

Metres / Feet
- 1000 / 3281
- 900 / 2953
- 700 / 2296
- 500 / 1640
- 400 / 1312
- 300 / 984
- 200 / 656
- 100 / 328
- 0 Land below sea level
- 50 / 164
- 200 / 656
- 1000 / 3281

PHYSICAL FEATURES

931 ▲	Summit
95 ·	Spot height
	Beach
⬭	Lake, Loch
—	River
‖	Waterfall

MISCELLANEOUS FEATURES COUNTY MAPS

-------	National Park
··········	Regional Park
◎	World Heritage Site
∴	Site of specific interest
∿∿∿∿	Wall
∣	Dam

TRANSPORT

under construction ▬▬ ▪▪▪▪ Motorway	▬▬ Railway	······ Canal
▬▬ Primary dual / primary single	→······· Railway tunnel	········ Minor canal
▬▬ Main	++++++++++ Private railway	)-------(Canal tunnel
——— Secondary / other	+++······+++ Private railway tunnel	⊕ International airport
-------- Track / private road	--------- Long distance footpath	✈ Regional airport
→······← Road tunnel (applies to all road classes)		

STYLES OF LETTERING
Cities and towns are explained separately

Country	**ENGLAND**
Administrative / county name	**DORSET**

Physical features

Island	*Rousay*
Lake, Loch	*Windermere*
Mountain	*Ben Nevis*
River	*Thames*
Region	*Strathblane*

BOUNDARIES

-·-·-·-	International boundary
-------	Administrative / County boundary
———	London borough boundary

NORTHERN IRELAND COUNTY MAPS

-·-·-·-	International boundary
-------	Historical county boundary
-------	Current administrative boundary
TYRONE	Historical county
OMAGH	Current administrative region

NORWAY

NORTH SEA

ATLANTIC OCEAN

SHETLAND

Lerwick

ORKNEY

Kirkwall

FAROE ISLANDS
(FAROYAR)
(Denmark)

WESTERN ISLES

Stornoway
Steornabhagh

HIGHLAND

Inverness

Elgin

MORAY

ABERDEENSHIRE

ABERDEEN
Aberdeen

SCOTLAND

ANGUS

Forfar

DUNDEE
Dundee

PERTH
AND
KINROSS

Perth

FIFE

Glenrothes

Alloa

8

EAST
LOTHIAN

Haddington

7 Edinburgh

WEST
LOTHIAN

10

Livingston

Dalkeith

MIDLOTHIAN

ARGYLL
AND BUTE

Lochgilphead

STIRLING

Stirling

5 Falkirk

Kirkintilloch

4 Glasgow

6

Dumbarton 2

1 Paisley

Greenock 3

RENFREWSHIRE

SCOTLAND
1. INVERCLYDE
2. WEST DUNBARTONSHIRE
3. EAST RENFREWSHIRE
4. GLASGOW CITY
5. EAST DUNBARTONSHIRE
6. NORTH LANARKSHIRE
7. FALKIRK
8. CLACKMANNANSHIRE
9. WEST LOTHIAN
10. EDINBURGH

Conic Equidistant Projection

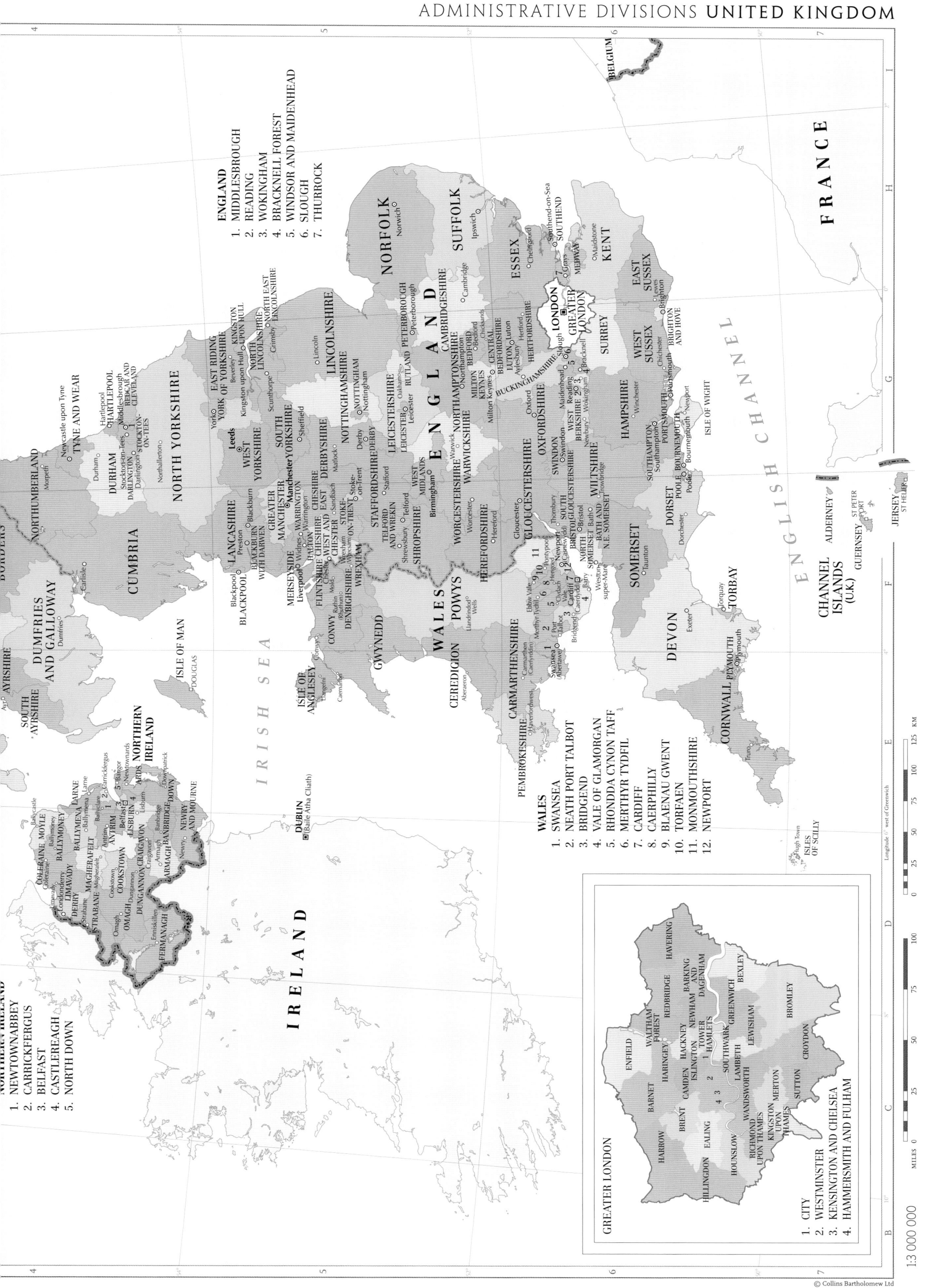

ENGLAND
1. MIDDLESBROUGH
2. READING
3. WOKINGHAM
4. BRACKNELL FOREST
5. WINDSOR AND MAIDENHEAD
6. SLOUGH
7. THURROCK

WALES
1. SWANSEA
2. NEATH PORT TALBOT
3. BRIDGEND
4. VALE OF GLAMORGAN
5. RHONDDA CYNON TAFF
6. MERTHYR TYDFIL
7. CARDIFF
8. CAERPHILLY
9. BLAENAU GWENT
10. TORFAEN
11. MONMOUTHSHIRE
12. NEWPORT

NORTHERN IRELAND
1. NEWTOWNABBEY
2. CARRICKFERGUS
3. BELFAST
4. CASTLEREAGH
5. NORTH DOWN

CHANNEL ISLANDS (U.K.)

FRANCE

BELGIUM

ENGLISH CHANNEL

IRISH SEA

IRELAND

ISLE OF MAN

GREATER LONDON
1. CITY
2. WESTMINSTER
3. KENSINGTON AND CHELSEA
4. HAMMERSMITH AND FULHAM

1:3 000 000

MILES 0   25   50   75   100

Longitude 0° west of Greenwich

0   25   50   75   100   125 KM

9

© Collins Bartholomew Ltd

CLIMATE

The United Kingdom has a temperate maritime climate, which usually means cool summers and mild winters and a relatively small annual temperature change, which in the UK is, on average, 10°C. The influence of the sea helps to keep the climate moderate, as it takes longer to heat up in summer but keeps its energy for some time after the land has cooled. The prevailing winds are south-westerly, from the Atlantic Ocean, which brings the benefits of the warming influence of the Gulf Stream.

Climate is a long-term view averaging weather events out over time, so while there are many weather extremes around the country and the climate is very changeable with many types of weather being experienced in a very short time scale, a longer term view shows a clearer pattern. The UK is generally wetter in the west where the land is higher, and drier in the east where a rain shadow effect is experienced.

Generally the west has mild maritime winters while the east is colder with a continental influence, but the north has cool summers while the south has warmer temperatures as these are influenced more by latitude.

Cumbria is a very wet part of the United Kingdom. Styhead Tarn has the highest annual average rainfall in the country.

The Cairngorm Mountains is a very exposed area which often experiences high winds.

TEMPERATURE AND CURRENTS, JANUARY

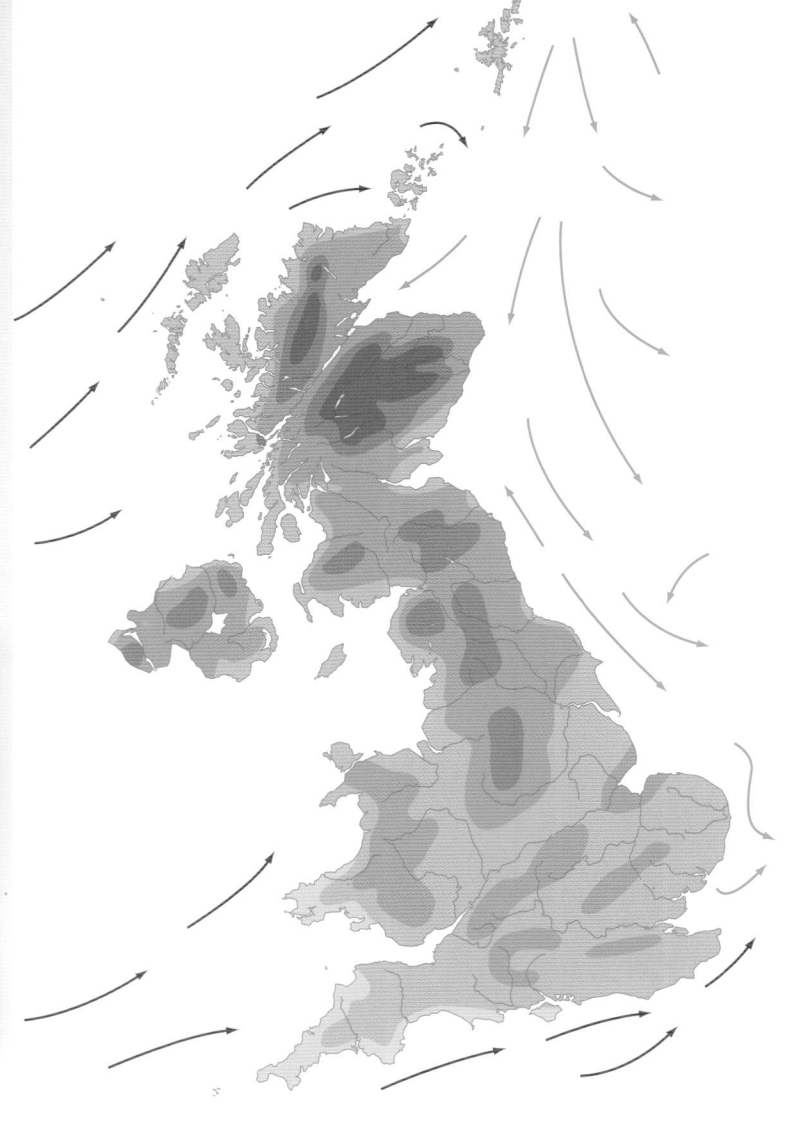

Temperature °C
6
4
2
0

Currents
→ Warm
→ Cold

Scale 1 : 8 000 000

TEMPERATURE AND CURRENTS, JULY

Temperature °C
16
14
12
10

Currents
→ Warm
→ Cold

Scale 1 : 8 000 000

TEMPERATURE EXTREMES

	Value	Date	Extreme
Faversham, Kent	38.5°C	10th August 2003	Highest
Braemar, Aberdeenshire	-27.2°C	10th January 1982 & 11th February 1895	Lowest
Altnaharra, Highlands	-27.2°C	30th December 1995	Lowest

RAINFALL EXTREMES

	Value	Date	Extreme
Sprinkling Tarn, Cumbria	6528 mm	1954	Highest in 1 year
St Osyth, Essex	513 mm		Lowest annual average
Styhead Tarn, Cumbria	4391 mm		Highest annual average

WIND EXTREMES

	Value	Date	Extreme
Fraserburgh, Aberdeenshire	123 knots	13th February 1989	Strongest low-level gust
Cairn Gorm, Highland	150 knots	20th March 1986	Strongest high-level gust

See map on opposite page for locations.

ANNUAL RAINFALL AND WINDS

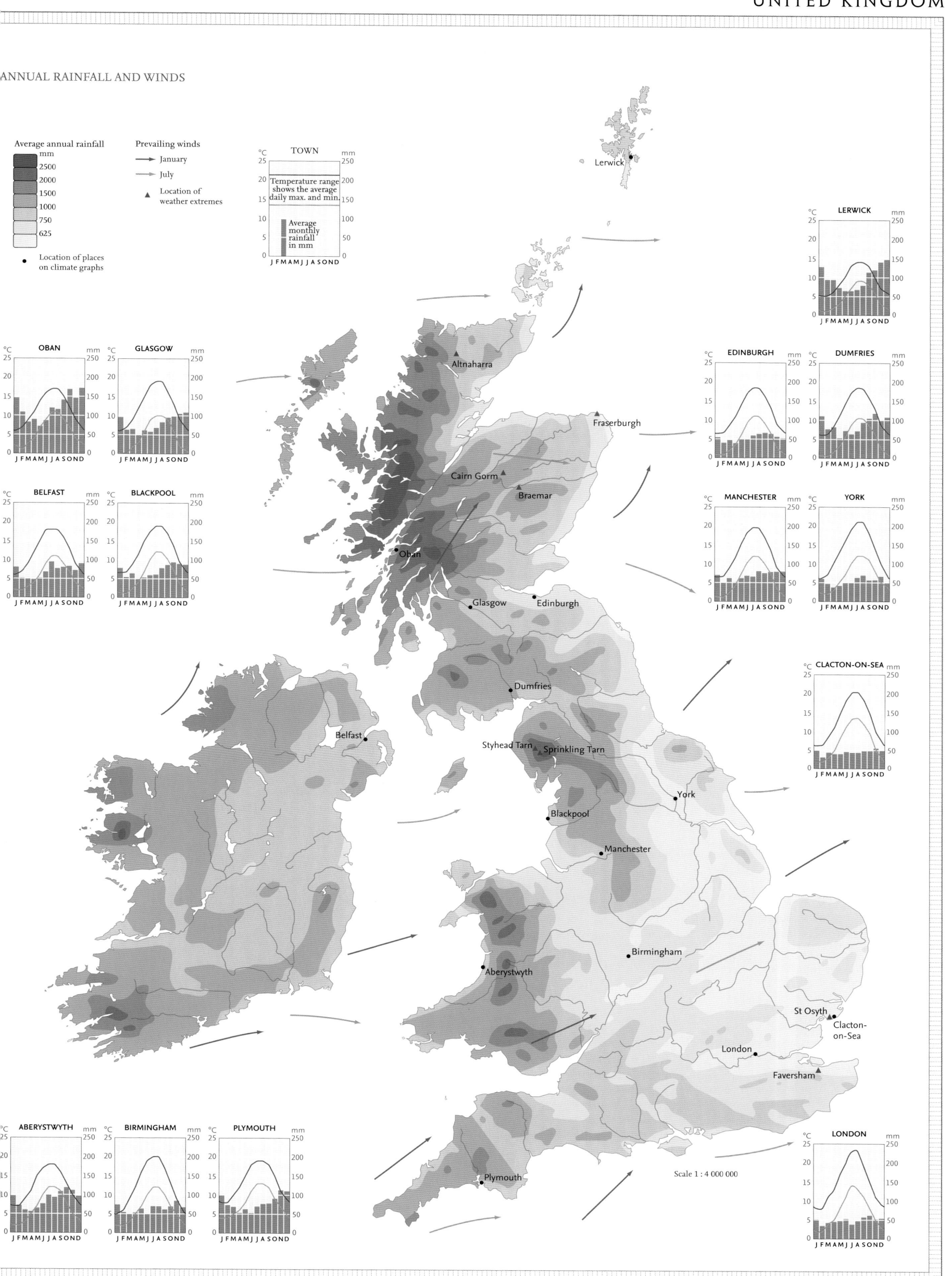

Average annual rainfall
mm
2500
2000
1500
1000
750
625

• Location of places
on climate graphs

Prevailing winds
→ January
→ July
▲ Location of
weather extremes

°C TOWN mm
25 250
20 200
Temperature range
15 shows the average 150
daily max. and min.
10 100
Average
5 monthly 50
rainfall
0 in mm 0
J F M A M J J A S O N D

OBAN
GLASGOW
BELFAST
BLACKPOOL
ABERYSTWYTH
BIRMINGHAM
PLYMOUTH
LERWICK
EDINBURGH
DUMFRIES
MANCHESTER
YORK
CLACTON-ON-SEA
LONDON

Altnaharra
Fraserburgh
Cairn Gorm
Braemar
Oban
Glasgow
Edinburgh
Dumfries
Belfast
Styhead Tarn • Sprinkling Tarn
Blackpool
York
Manchester
Lerwick
Aberystwyth
Birmingham
St Osyth
Clacton-on-Sea
London
Faversham
Plymouth

Scale 1 : 4 000 000

11

POPULATION

The United Kingdom population has increased steadily over the past century apart from a small plateau in the 1970s. Life expectancy at birth has increased from around 50 years a century ago to nearer 80 years, and while the birth rate has fallen from 151 births per 1000 population in 1901 to 10.65 in 2008, this has been compensated for by international migration where immigration is greater than emigration.

This is one of the world's more overall densely populated countries, but the population is unevenly distributed. The greatest concentration of people is in the southeast and Greater London area. Other densely populated areas are the West Midlands, Greater Manchester, West Yorkshire, Tyneside and Greater Glasgow.

Populations are much more mobile than they used to be. People will move much further to find work than in the past and there are also noticeable concentrations of retired peoples, and the non-white populations are often found in particular areas. London has the greatest ethnic mix of population in the UK.

East London is one of the more densely populated parts of the United Kingdom, it is also home to a large proportion of the non-white population.

Many parts of the Scottish highlands have small populations. Here at Lochinver on the north west coast the most frequent visitors are fishermen from French or Spanish trawlers.

Population fluctuation 1991–2008

People arriving (thousands)	Year	People leaving (thousands)	Balance (thousands)
329.0	1991	284.9	+44.1
268.1	1992	281.0	-12.9
265.6	1993	266.3	-0.7
315.0	1994	237.6	+77.4
312.4	1995	236.4	+76.0
318.4	1996	263.7	+54.7
326.7	1997	279.2	+47.5
391.0	1998	251.4	+139.6
453.8	1999	290.8	+163.0
478.7	2000	320.7	+158.0
480.7	2001	309.2	+171.4
515.8	2002	362.7	+153.1
511.0	2003	363.3	+147.6
589.0	2004	343.8	+245.2
566.7	2005	360.9	+205.9
596.0	2006	398.3	+197.7
573.8	2007	340.8	+233.0
590.2	2008	427.2	+163.0

POPULATION BY REGION

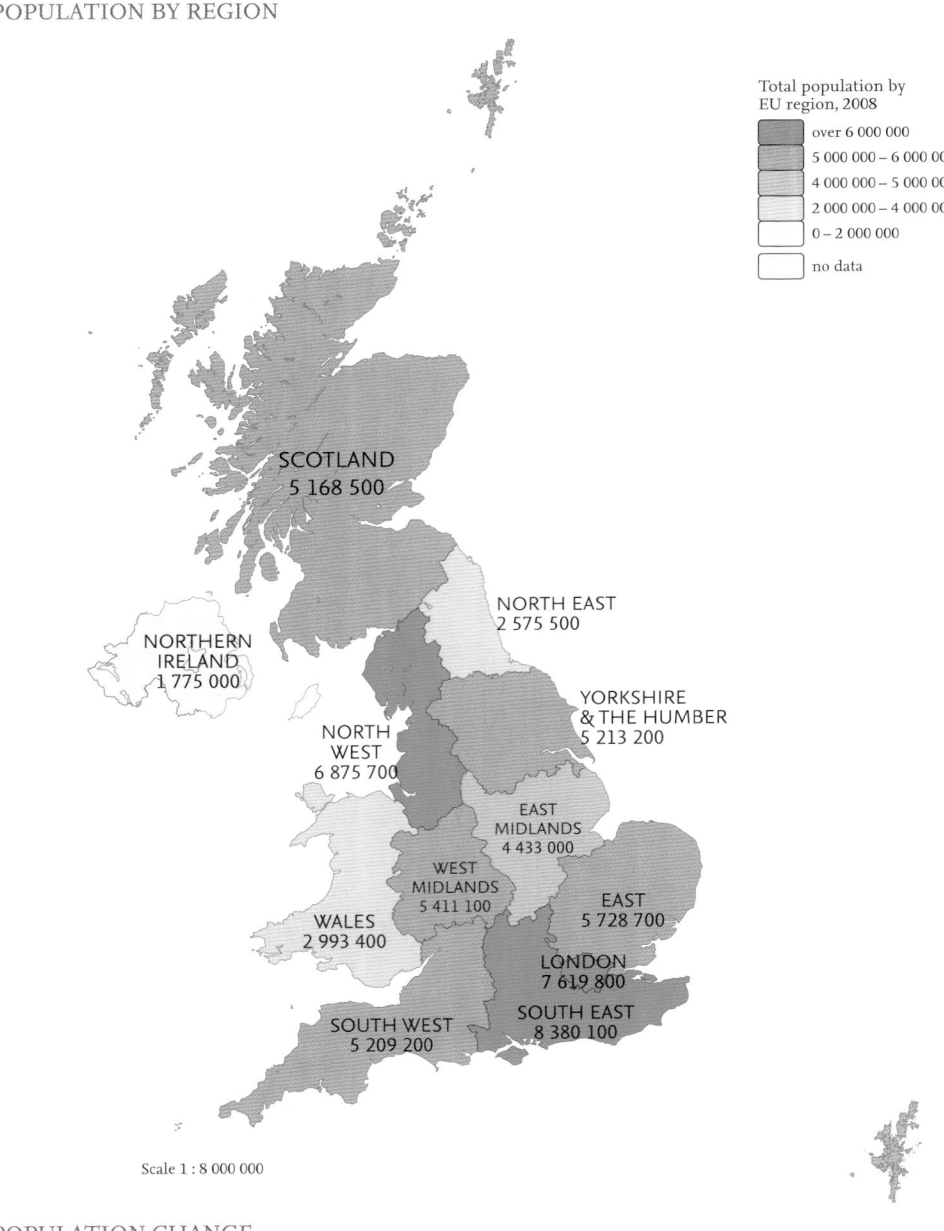

Total population by EU region, 2008

- over 6 000 000
- 5 000 000 – 6 000 000
- 4 000 000 – 5 000 000
- 2 000 000 – 4 000 000
- 0 – 2 000 000
- no data

SCOTLAND
5 168 500

NORTHERN IRELAND
1 775 000

NORTH EAST
2 575 500

YORKSHIRE & THE HUMBER
5 213 200

NORTH WEST
6 875 700

EAST MIDLANDS
4 433 000

WEST MIDLANDS
5 411 100

WALES
2 993 400

EAST
5 728 700

LONDON
7 619 800

SOUTH WEST
5 209 200

SOUTH EAST
8 380 100

Scale 1 : 8 000 000

POPULATION CHANGE

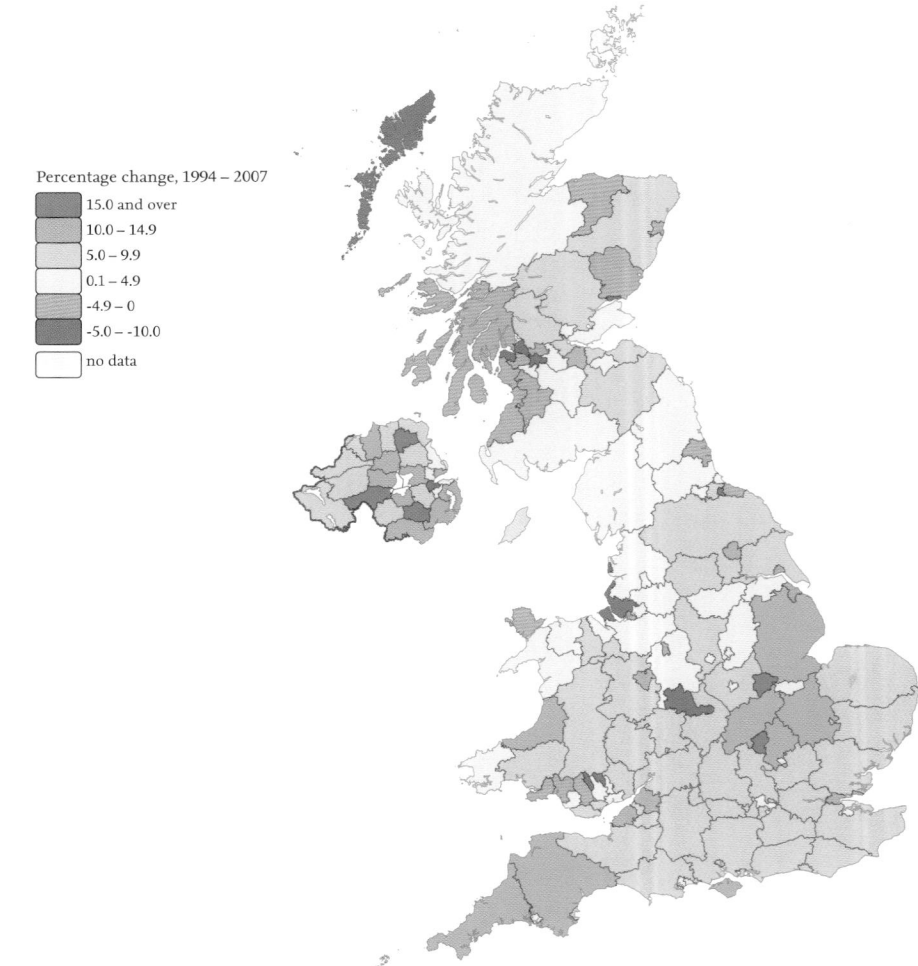

Percentage change, 1994 – 2007

- 15.0 and over
- 10.0 – 14.9
- 5.0 – 9.9
- 0.1 – 4.9
- -4.9 – 0
- -5.0 – -10.0
- no data

Scale 1 : 8 000 000

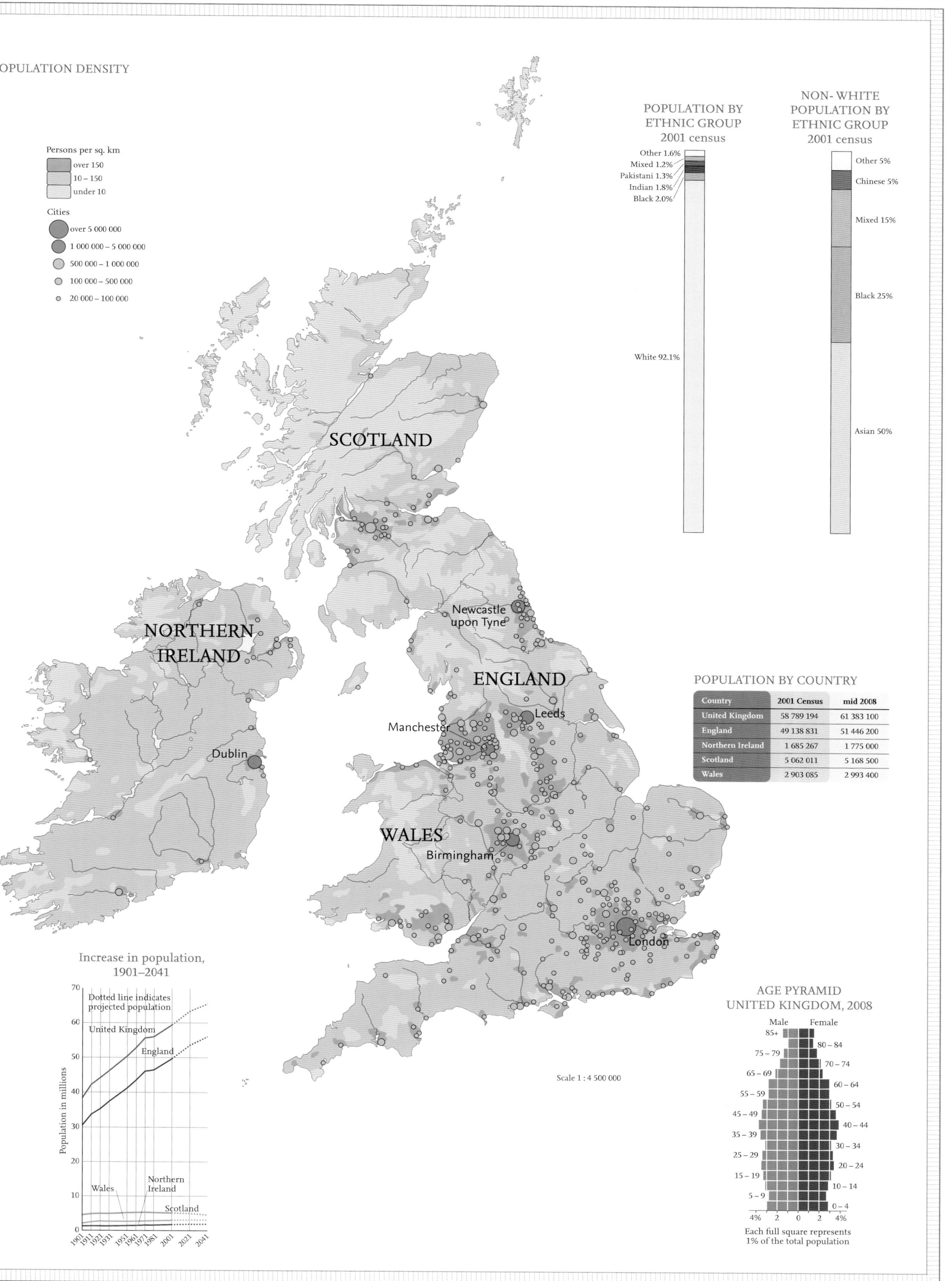

POPULATION DENSITY

Persons per sq. km
- over 150
- 10 – 150
- under 10

Cities
- over 5 000 000
- 1 000 000 – 5 000 000
- 500 000 – 1 000 000
- 100 000 – 500 000
- 20 000 – 100 000

POPULATION BY
ETHNIC GROUP
2001 census

Other 1.6%
Mixed 1.2%
Pakistani 1.3%
Indian 1.8%
Black 2.0%

White 92.1%

NON- WHITE
POPULATION BY
ETHNIC GROUP
2001 census

Other 5%
Chinese 5%
Mixed 15%
Black 25%
Asian 50%

SCOTLAND

NORTHERN
IRELAND

Dublin

Newcastle
upon Tyne

ENGLAND

Leeds

Manchester

WALES

Birmingham

London

POPULATION BY COUNTRY

Country	2001 Census	mid 2008
United Kingdom	58 789 194	61 383 100
England	49 138 831	51 446 200
Northern Ireland	1 685 267	1 775 000
Scotland	5 062 011	5 168 500
Wales	2 903 085	2 993 400

Increase in population,
1901–2041

Dotted line indicates
projected population

United Kingdom

England

Wales

Northern
Ireland

Scotland

Population in millions

70
60
50
40
30
20
10

1901 1911 1921 1931 1951 1961 1971 1981 2001 2021 2041

Scale 1 : 4 500 000

AGE PYRAMID
UNITED KINGDOM, 2008

Male   Female

85+
80 – 84
75 – 79
70 – 74
65 – 69
60 – 64
55 – 59
50 – 54
45 – 49
40 – 44
35 – 39
30 – 34
25 – 29
20 – 24
15 – 19
10 – 14
5 – 9
0 – 4

4%   2   0   2   4%

Each full square represents
1% of the total population

13

ECONOMIC ACTIVITY

Over the past thirty years the economy of the United Kingdom has changed. Employment in manufacturing industry has fallen to less than half the 1979 levels, while areas such as banking and finance have shown significant increases as have the sectors of public administration, education and health. The concentration of the banking and financial markets in London is also reflected in the higher average salaries to be found in the London and South East regions. However London has also suffered badly with unemployment, with east inner London being the worst hit area.

The housing market and the economy have been closely linked over the past fifty years with slumps and booms in one contributing to the other. Property transactions showed a marked rise in the 1980s as many owner-occupiers chose to move home and there was also a contribution from increasing numbers of first-time buyers and public sector tenants exercising their right to buy. The early 1980s also saw the credit market opening up which also contributed to the choice of many households to buy rather than rent. When interest rates rose in 1989 and an economic recession set in, transactions fell. The market did recover but recent events have precipitated another fall as prospective buyers have found it difficult to secure a mortgage.

The most recent economic problems have had a noticeable effect on the car manufacturing industry, which has experienced a worldwide slump. Registrations of new cars in the UK declined from mid-2008 and continued at around -20 to -30 per cent year on year until the government introduced the "scrappage" scheme which helped to reverse the trend, although sales were still down on the period two years previously. In April 2010 UK petrol prices reached a new record high, beating the previous record from May 2008, not a good sign for recovery in this area of the economy.

Houses for sale in Kensington, London.

New cars wait to be delivered in a vast parking area.

The Bank of England sets interest rates, issues banknotes in England and Wales, and works to maintain a stable financial system.

EMPLOYMENT BY SECTOR

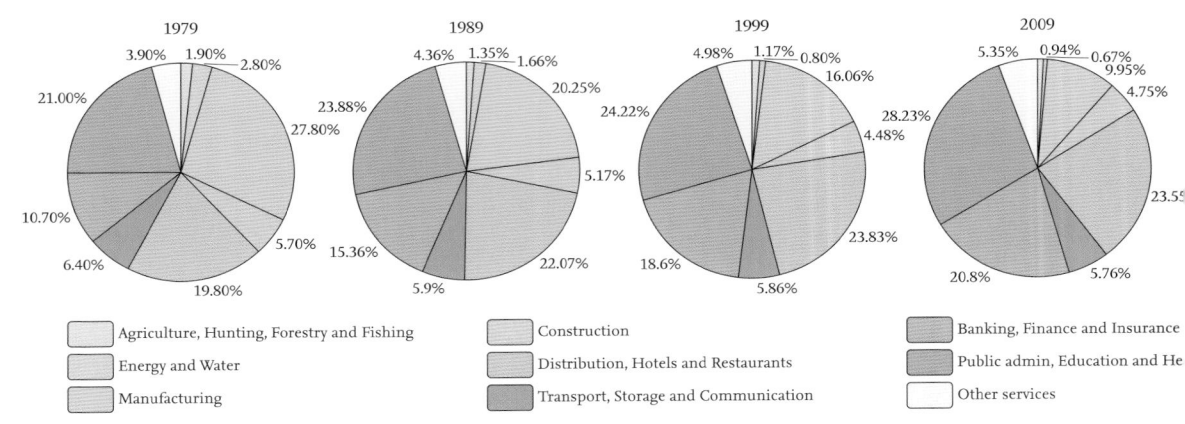

EMPLOYMENT CHANGE BY SECTOR

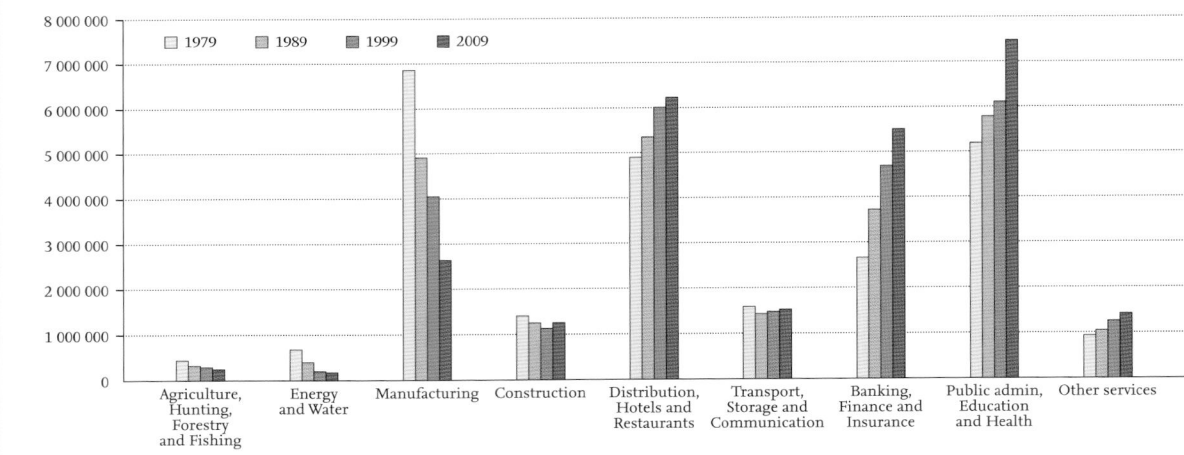

UNEMPLOYMENT, 2007, 2009

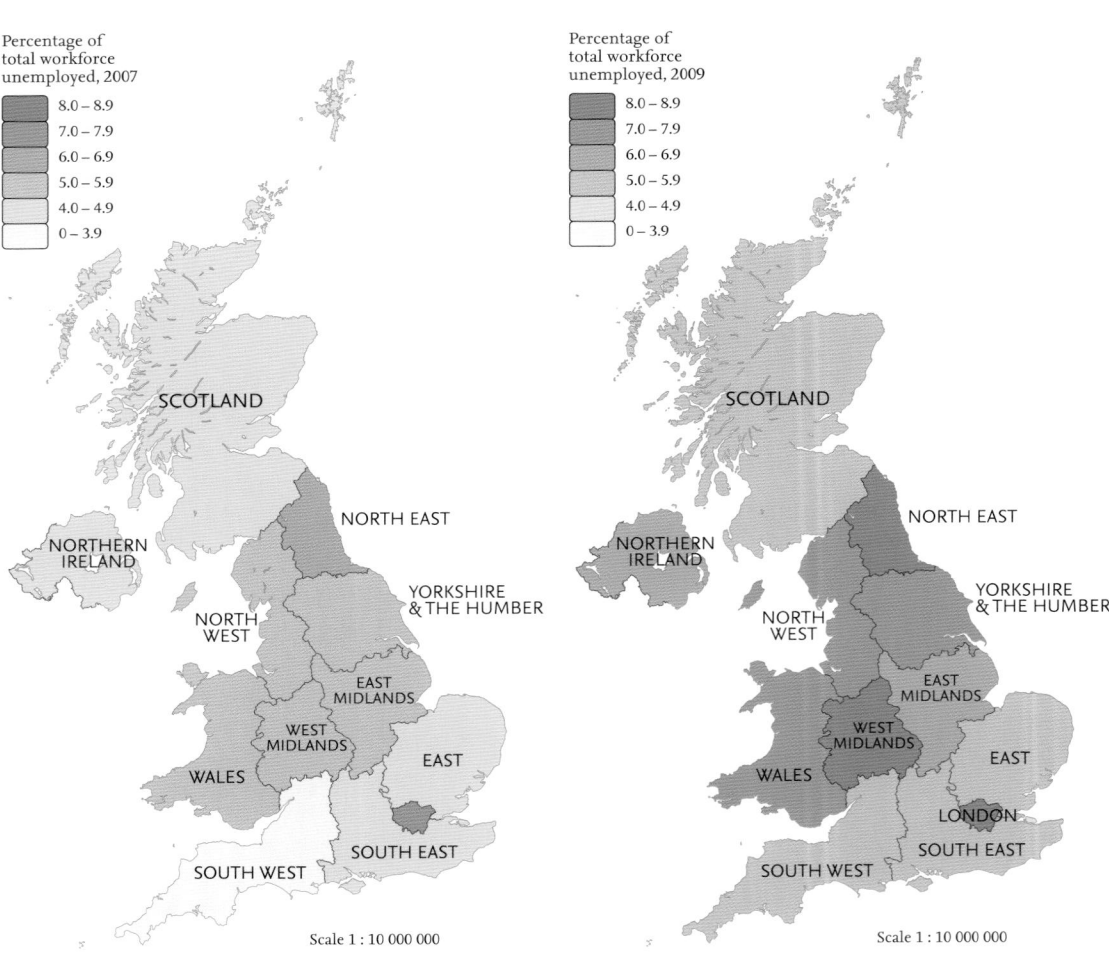

AVERAGE SALARY BY REGION, 2009

Average salary (pounds sterling)
- Over 27 000
- 26 000 – 26 999
- 25 000 – 25 999
- 24 000 – 24 999
- 23 000 – 23 999
- 22 000 – 22 999

Scale 1 : 10 000 000

AVERAGE SALARY VARIATION BY REGION, 2009

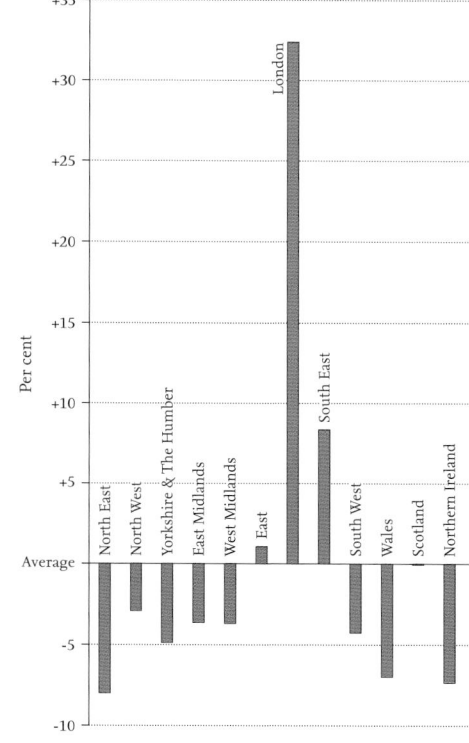

UK TRADE WITH EUROPEAN UNION, 2009

Country	% of total UK exports	% of total UK imports
Austria	1.01	1.40
Belgium	8.51	9.22
Bulgaria	0.16	0.11
Cyprus	0.47	0.04
Czech Republic	1.14	2.08
Denmark	1.95	2.30
Estonia	0.12	0.07
Finland	1.08	1.53
France	14.53	13.19
Germany	20.15	24.71
Greece	1.28	0.34
Hungary	0.67	1.32
Ireland	12.45	7.64
Italy	6.67	7.61
Latvia	0.08	0.17
Lithuania	0.14	0.23
Luxembourg	0.15	0.37
Malta	0.31	0.06
Netherlands	14.14	13.24
Poland	2.19	2.88
Portugal	1.20	0.87
Romania	0.54	0.47
Slovakia	0.30	0.96
Slovenia	0.14	0.15
Spain	7.28	5.68
Sweden	3.34	3.33

AVERAGE HOUSE PRICE, 1960–2009

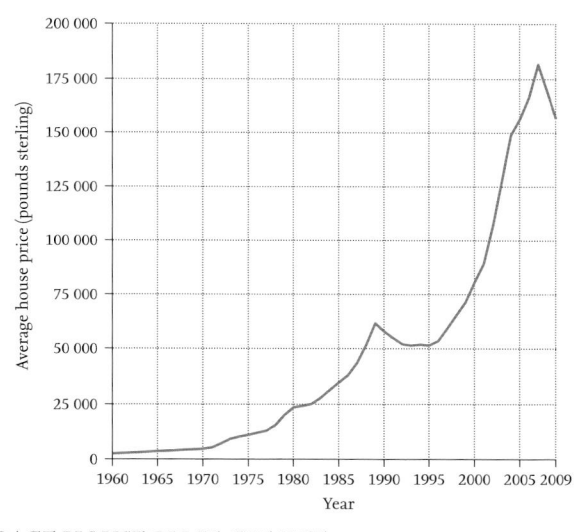

CAR PRODUCTION, 1980–2009

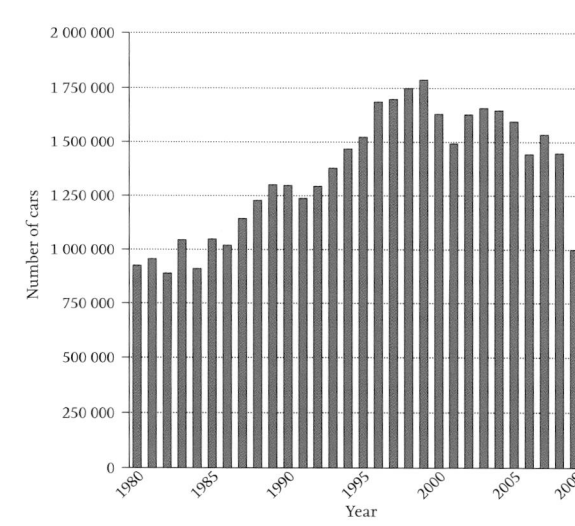

MANUFACTURING OUTPUT, 2008

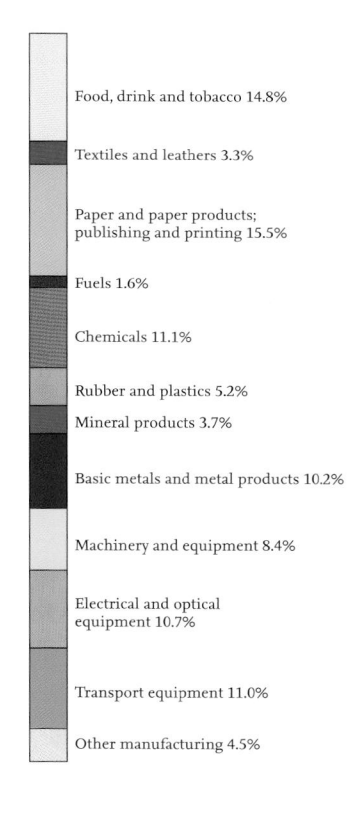

- Food, drink and tobacco 14.8%
- Textiles and leathers 3.3%
- Paper and paper products; publishing and printing 15.5%
- Fuels 1.6%
- Chemicals 11.1%
- Rubber and plastics 5.2%
- Mineral products 3.7%
- Basic metals and metal products 10.2%
- Machinery and equipment 8.4%
- Electrical and optical equipment 10.7%
- Transport equipment 11.0%
- Other manufacturing 4.5%

AVERAGE HOUSE PRICE CHANGE AND INFLATION, 1960–2009

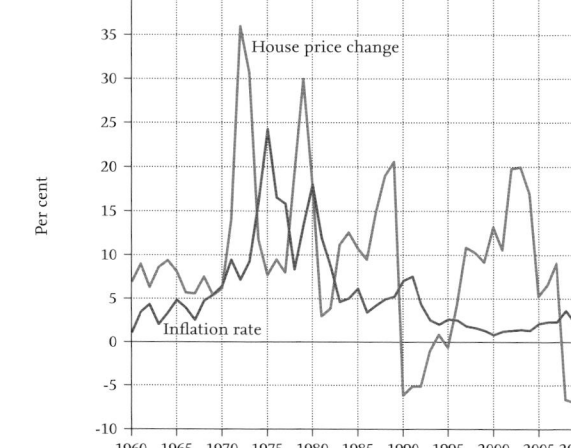

PETROL PRICES, 1980–2009

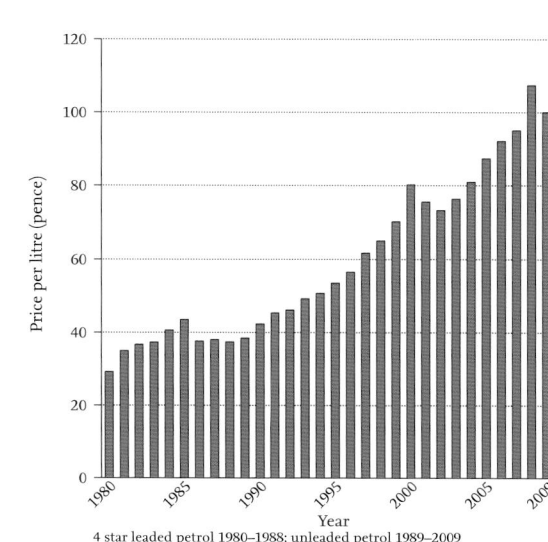

4 star leaded petrol 1980–1988; unleaded petrol 1989–2009

TRAVEL

In Britain car ownership has climbed steeply over the past fifty years and road traffic has grown by 85 per cent since 1980. The car is the preferred mode of transport for many people but the downside is busy roads, congestion, road works and road building work. Petrol prices have soared leading to more consideration being given to whether certain journeys are really necessary, but while the average number of trips has declined recently, the distance travelled is still similar and the time spent travelling has increased. Although, in and around London, train journeys are more popular and practical for many people for getting to and from work, more and more commuters travel further than ever each day to work and mostly use cars to do so.

UK airports are also very busy places, with Heathrow being one of the world's busiest. Growth in air travel accounts for most of the increases in visits to and from the UK with passengers using UK airports quadrupling between 1980 and 2008. There has also been a significant 27 per cent increase in freight traffic in the same period with many of the goods being moved by road. Air freight for high valued products has also increased and while this accounts for only around 1 per cent of traffic volume it is nearer 40 per cent of value.

As the car has increased in popularity congestion has become a daily problem on popular routes.

Many councils have set aside dedicated cycle lanes in their towns and cities to encourage cyclists.

TRANSPORT NETWORK

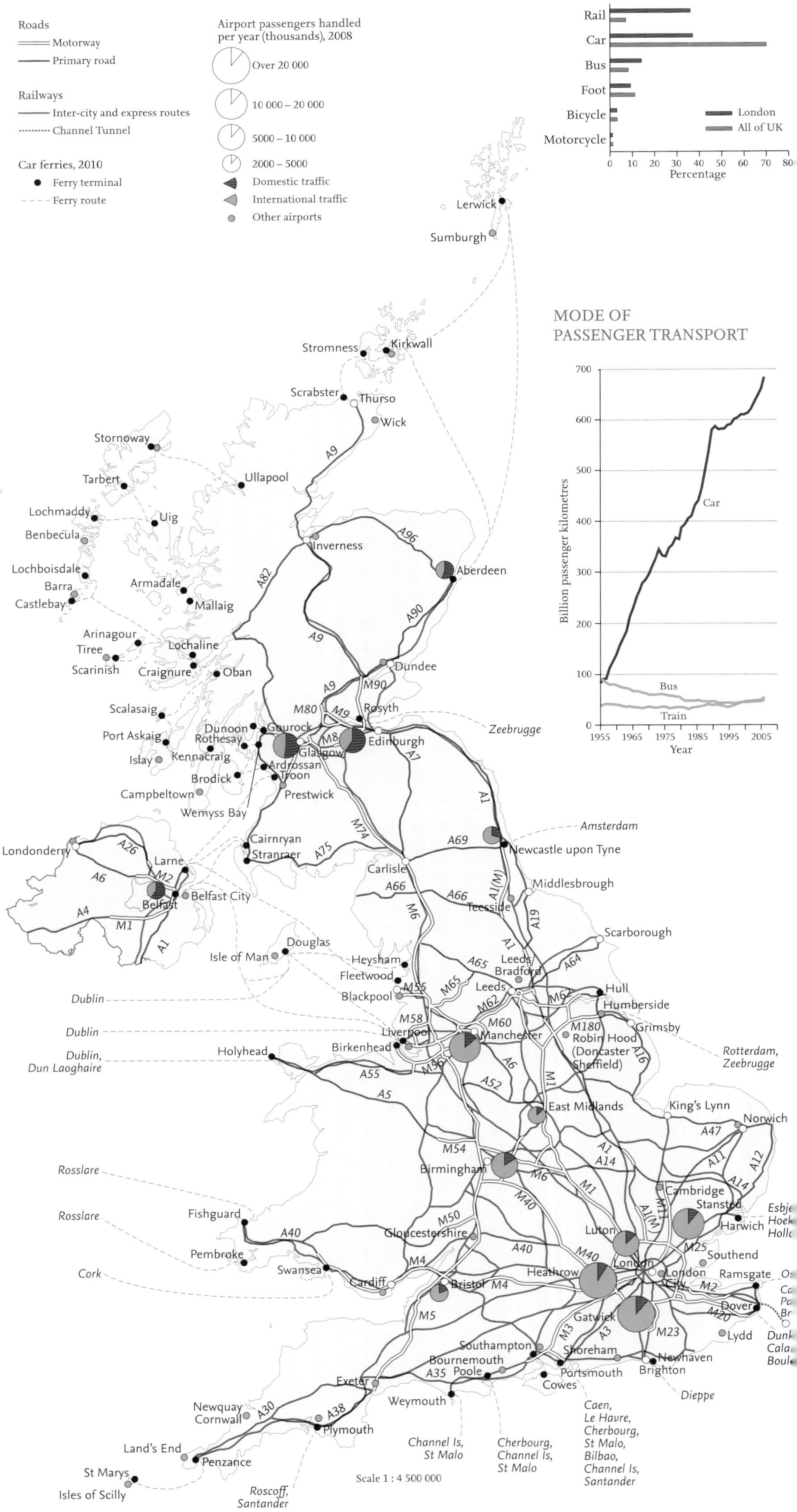

Roads
Motorway
Primary road

Railways
Inter-city and express routes
Channel Tunnel

Car ferries, 2010
● Ferry terminal
Ferry route

Airport passengers handled per year (thousands), 2008
Over 20 000
10 000 – 20 000
5000 – 10 000
2000 – 5000
◗ Domestic traffic
◖ International traffic
● Other airports

TRANSPORT TO WORK, 2006

Rail
Car
Bus
Foot
Bicycle
Motorcycle

Percentage
0 10 20 30 40 50 60 70 80

■ London
■ All of UK

MODE OF PASSENGER TRANSPORT

Billion passenger kilometres

700
600
500
400
300
200
100
0

1955 1965 1975 1985 1995 2005
Year

Car
Bus
Train

Scale 1 : 4 500 000

TOURISM

The United Kingdom has a wealth of places of interest for the visitor to enjoy. From Neolithic Orkney to the Eden Project in Cornwall, there is something to suit every taste, both old and new, and many are free to visit too. Museums and Galleries in London see the bulk of visitors from both home and overseas, but many other attractions are very popular and have helped revitalise tourism in other parts of the country.

Outdoor activities are popular and long distance footpaths, national parks and the numerous sections of fantastic coastline are the focus of many visits. Meanwhile, theme parks such as Alton Towers, and sites with multiple interactive experiences, compete with more traditional wildlife parks, historic houses, castles and museums.

Tourism visits from overseas have fluctuated due to economic conditions, rates of currency exchange and the development of other markets overseas. However more 'staycation' holidays have encouraged visits to UK attractions, boosting visitors and helping offset the downturn.

As the location of the world's largest greenhouse, which is part of a set of biomes containing plants from around the world, the Eden Project was opened in 2001 on the site of a former clay pit.

Hadrian's Wall is a World Heritage Site and a popular attraction for visitors of all ages with many locations to visit along its length. It is also a busy long distance footpath.

An exhibition at the Tate Modern, London. Opened in 2000, the Tate Modern houses a collection of international modern and contemporary art dating from 1900 in a former power station at Bankside.

TOURIST ATTRACTIONS

- National Park
- Area of Outstanding Natural Beauty (England, Wales & N. Ireland)
  National Scenic Areas (Scotland)
- Heritage Coast (England and Wales)
  Preferred Conservation Zone (Scotland)
- Long distance footpath
- ▲ World Heritage Site
- ● Major tourist attractions (over 1 million visitors)
- ○ Other tourist attractions

TOP TOURIST ATTRACTIONS, 2009

Attraction	Visitors
British Museum	5 569 981
The National Gallery	4 780 030
Tate Modern	4 747 537
Natural History Museum	4 105 106
Science Museum	2 793 930
Tower of London	2 389 548
National Maritime Museum	2 367 904
Victoria and Albert Museum	2 269 880
National Portrait Gallery	1 961 843
St Paul's Cathedral	1 821 321
Tate Britain	1 501 837
Westminster Abbey	1 449 593

Comparable figures are not available for Alton Towers and Madame Tussauds

London

London Zoo
Madame Tussauds
British Museum
National Portrait Gallery
Somerset House
St Paul's Cathedral
Royal Academy
National Gallery
Tate Modern
Tower of London
Science Museum
Victoria and Albert Museum
London Eye
Westminster Abbey
Natural History Museum
Tate Britain

Map labels

Shetland
The Heart of Neolithic Orkney ▲
Orkney
Lewis
Harris
St Kilda ▲
St Kilda
North Uist
Wester Ross
South Uist
Skye
Glen Affric
Loch Ness
Speyside Way
Kintail
Knoydart
Cairngorm Mountains
Cairngorms
Ben Nevis and Glen Coe
L. Shiel
Deeside and Lochnagar
L. Tummel
Mull
West Highland Way
Loch Lomond and The Trossachs
Antonine Wall
Fife Coastal Path
Edinburgh Castle
Jura
Kelvingrove Art Gallery & Museum
Old and New Towns of Edinburgh
Islay
Arran
New Lanark
St Cuthbert's Way
Southern Uplands Way
Giant's Causeway
Antrim Coast and Glens
Northumberland
New Metroland
Hadrian's Wall
Durham Cathedral and Castle
Sperrins
North Pennines
Cleveland Way
Ulster Way
Fermanagh Lakeland
Lagan Valley
Strangford Lough
Lake District
Windermere Lake Cruises
North York Moors
Flamingo Land
Mourne Mts
Arnside and Silverdale
Yorkshire Dales
Fountains Abbey
Studley Royal Park
Nidderdale
York Minster
Wolds Way
Forest of Bowland
Saltaire
The Deep
Blackpool Pleasure Beach
Pleasureland Southport
Lowry Centre
Pennine Way
Xscape Castleford
Lincolnshire Wolds
Liverpool
Albert Dock Liverpool
Chester Zoo
Peak District
Derwent Valley Mills
Anglesey
Chester Cathedral
Alton Towers
Norfolk Coast
Clwydian Range
Castles / Town Walls of King Edward
Pontcysyllte Aqueduct
Cannock Chase
Peddars Way and Norfolk Coast Path
Pleasure Beach Great Yarmouth
Llyn
Snowdonia
Ironbridge Gorge
Drayton Manor Park
The Broads
Offa's Dyke Path
Shropshire Hills
Suffolk Coast and Heaths
Pembrokeshire Coast Path
Malvern Hills
Dedham Vale
Wye Valley
Cotswolds
Blenheim Palace
River Lee Country Park
Pembrokeshire Coast
Brecon Beacons
Thames Path
Chilterns
Kew Gardens
Blaenavon Industrial Landscape
Ridgeway
Westminster Palace / Abbey
Tower of London
Gower
Ashton Court Estate
North Wessex Downs
Surrey Hills
Maritime Greenwich
Canterbury Cathedral
Bath
Roman Baths
N. Downs Way
Kent Downs
Mendip Hills
Stonehenge / Avebury
E. Hampshire
High Weald
Exmoor
Quantock Hills
New Forest
Sussex Downs
S. Downs Way
Flamingo Fun Park
Dorset
Poole Pottery
South Downs
Eastbourne Pier
Cornwall and West Devon Mining Landscape
East Devon Coast
Dorset and East Devon Coast
Isle of Wight
Tamar Valley
Dartmoor
Eden Project
South West Coast Path
Isles of Scilly

Scale 1 : 4 500 000

1. Windsor Castle
2. Legoland
3. Thorpe Park
4. Hampton Court
5. Chessington World of Adventures

ENERGY

Energy production in the United Kingdom has historically relied on coal, due to the significant deposits found around the country, with the remainder being supplied by oil. However by the 1950s a nuclear generating capacity was developed and at its peak in 1997 supplied around 26 per cent of electricity. Although oil started to flow from the North Sea in the 1970s this was not a factor in power generation and by the 1990s attention had turned to gas as coal production was reduced and North Sea gas became available. Also from the 1990s more attention was focused on renewable energy sources to add to the small existing hydroelectricity generation capacity.

Due to coal and nuclear power stations closing in the coming years a potential energy gap was identified. Some new coal- and gas-fired power stations were proposed but there are other options being developed. Of those, renewable energy has received a good deal of interest. As a result of its location Britain has many options for wind- and wave-power, and in Scotland and Wales there are already a number of hydroelectric schemes. In addition, attention is being paid to biofuel options where gas from sewage and landfill is utilised, and also to combined-power plants, where waste hot water is re-used for heating local housing or for industry.

This wind farm is one of many being developed in Wales and Scotland in areas with a high annual mean wind speed.

The Errochty hydro dam was constructed in 1957 to create a reservoir as part of the Tummel hydro-electric power scheme.

Heysham Nuclear Power Station in Lancashire began producing power in 1984. However, Heysham I and Heysham II reactors are expected to be decommissioned in 2014 and 2023 repectively. Nuclear power is seen by many as one of the potential solutions to global warming. However, it can take over a decade to build and bring these power stations into service. Although they produce no carbon dioxide, one of the main contributors to global warming, opponents argue that the radioactive waste they produce is a threat to the environment that lasts for hundreds of years.

POWER STATIONS

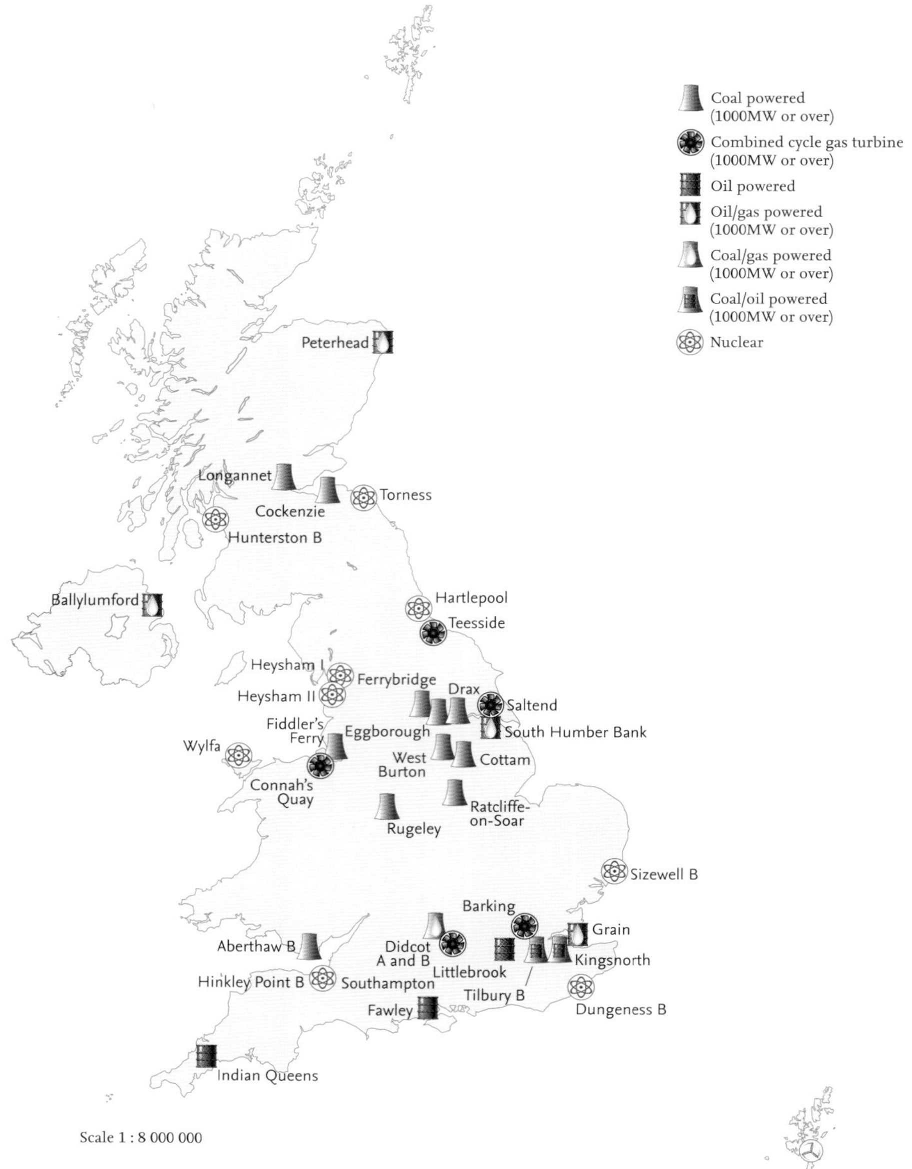

Coal powered (1000MW or over)
Combined cycle gas turbine (1000MW or over)
Oil powered
Oil/gas powered (1000MW or over)
Coal/gas powered (1000MW or over)
Coal/oil powered (1000MW or over)
Nuclear

Peterhead
Longannet
Cockenzie
Torness
Hunterston B
Ballylumford
Hartlepool
Teesside
Heysham I
Ferrybridge
Heysham II
Drax
Saltend
Fiddler's Ferry
Eggborough
South Humber Bank
Wylfa
West Burton
Cottam
Connah's Quay
Ratcliffe-on-Soar
Rugeley
Sizewell B
Barking
Grain
Aberthaw B
Didcot A and B
Kingsnorth
Hinkley Point B
Southampton
Littlebrook
Fawley
Tilbury B
Dungeness B
Indian Queens

Scale 1 : 8 000 000

RENEWABLE ENERGY

Pumped storage hydro-electric
Hydro-electric (40MW or over)
Wind farm
Offshore wind farm
Wave
Geothermal aquifer

Fasnakyle
Foyers
Rannoch
Errochty
Fort William
Clunie
Lochay
Cruachan
Sloy
Clachan
Islay
Dinorwig
Ffestiniog
Rheidol
Southampton

AVERAGE WIND SPEED

Metres per second
over 7
5 – 6.9
below 5

Scale 1 : 8 000 000

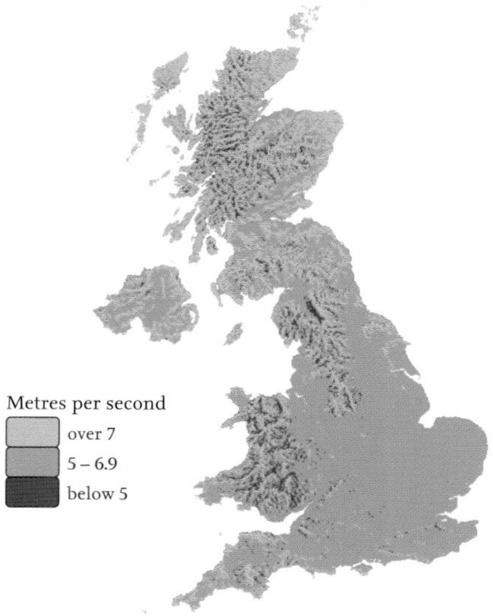

ENERGY PRODUCERS

SITES GENERATING ELECTRICITY FROM
RENEWABLE SOURCES, 2008

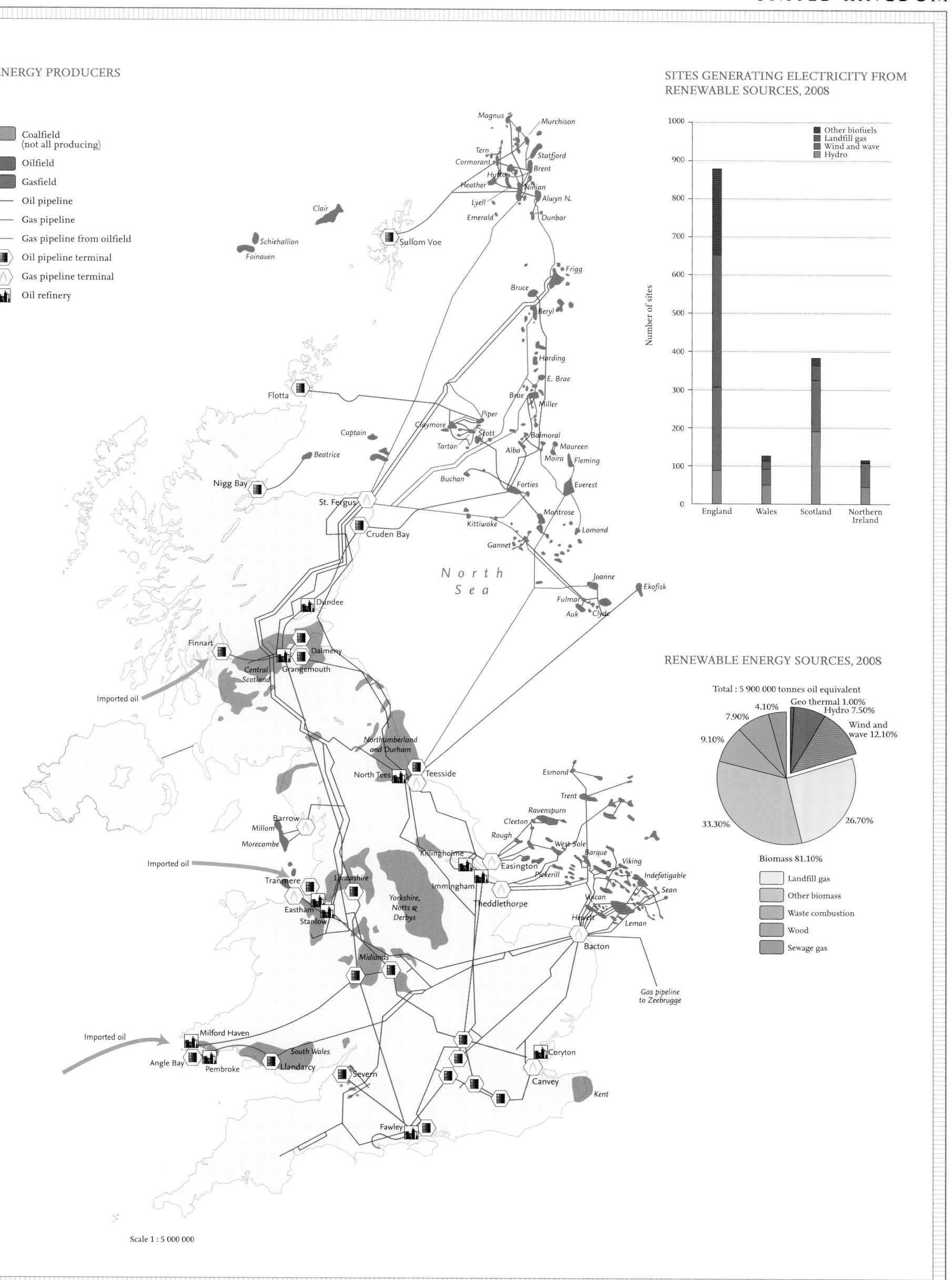

Coalfield
(not all producing)

Oilfield

Gasfield

Oil pipeline

Gas pipeline

Gas pipeline from oilfield

Oil pipeline terminal

Gas pipeline terminal

Oil refinery

RENEWABLE ENERGY SOURCES, 2008

Total : 5 900 000 tonnes oil equivalent

Geo thermal 1.00%
Hydro 7.50%
Wind and
wave 12.10%

4.10%

7.90%

9.10%

33.30%

26.70%

Biomass 81.10%

Landfill gas
Other biomass
Waste combustion
Wood
Sewage gas

Scale 1 : 5 000 000

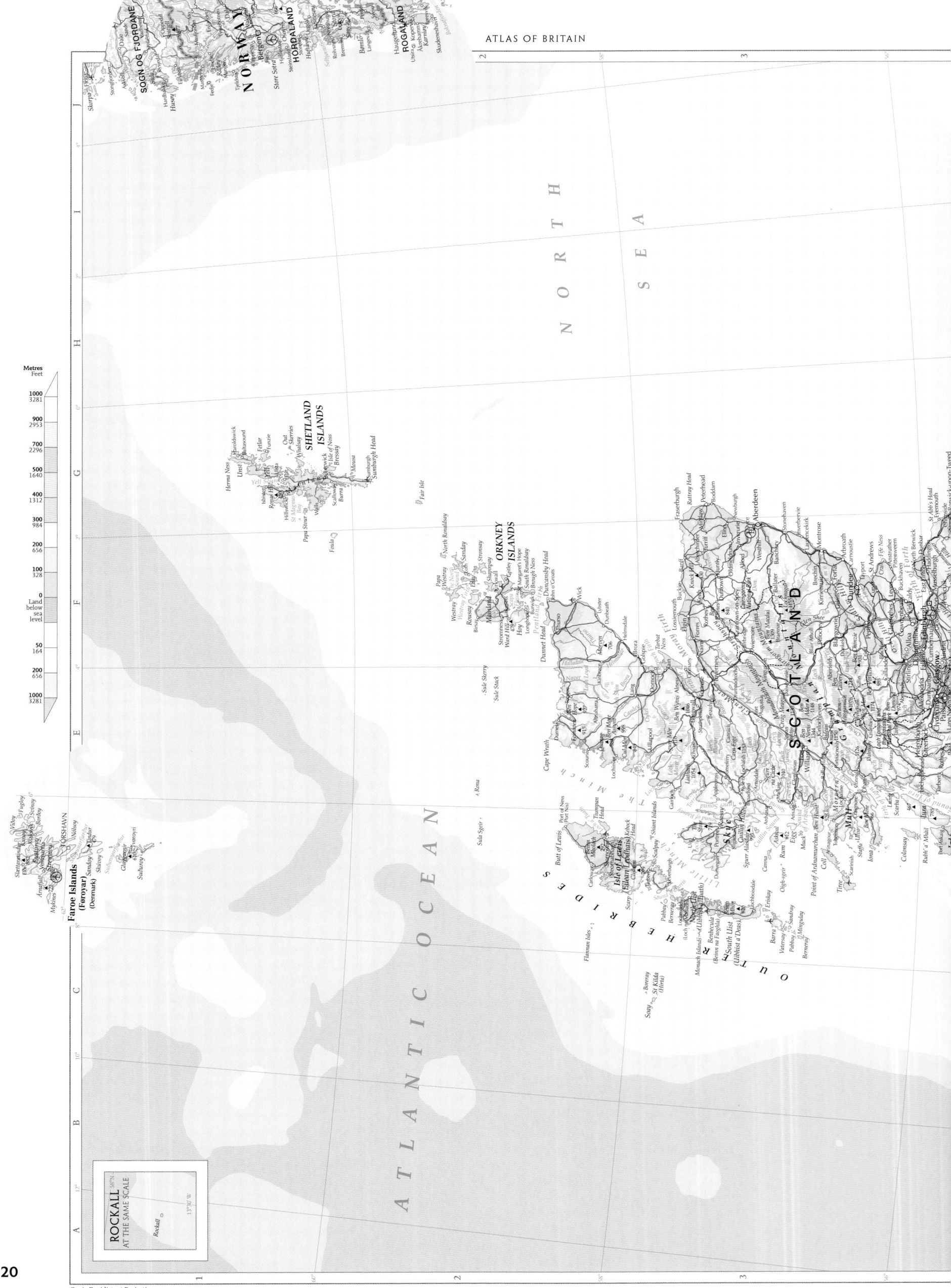

Metres
Feet

1000	3281
900	2953
700	2296
500	1640
400	1312
300	984
200	656
100	328
0	Land below sea level
50	164
200	656
1000	3281

NORWAY

SOGN OG FJORDANE

HORDALAND

ROGALAND

N O R T H   S E A

SHETLAND ISLANDS

Hermu Ness
Unst
Fetlar
Yell
Out Skerries
Isle of Noss
Bressay
Mousa
Sumburgh Head

Fair Isle

Foula

ORKNEY ISLANDS

North Ronaldsay
Papa Westray
Westray
Sanday
Stronsay
Rousay
Eday
South Ronaldsay
John o'Groats
Duncansby Head
Brough Ness

Wick

A T L A N T I C   O C E A N

Faroe Islands
(Føroyar)
(Denmark)

TÓRSHAVN

Sandoy
Suðuroy

Rona

Sula Sgeir

Sula Stack

Sule Skerry

Cape Wrath

Butt of Lewis
Port of Ness
(Port Nis)
Tiumpan Head

Flannan Isles

Isle of Lewis

St Kilda
(Hirta)
Borreray
Soay

O U T E R   H E B R I D E S

Monach Islands
(Heisker)
North Uist
Benbecula
South Uist
(Uibhist a Deas)
Barra
Vatersay
Pabbay
Sandray
Mingulay
Berneray

SCOTLAND

Fraserburgh
Rattray Head
Peterhead
Aberdeen
Stonehaven
Montrose
Arbroath
Carnoustie
Dundee
St Andrews
Anstruther
Firth of Forth
North Berwick

Skye
Mull
Coll
Tiree
Colonsay

The Minch

Little Minch

ROCKALL
AT THE SAME SCALE

Rockall

Conic Equidistant Projection

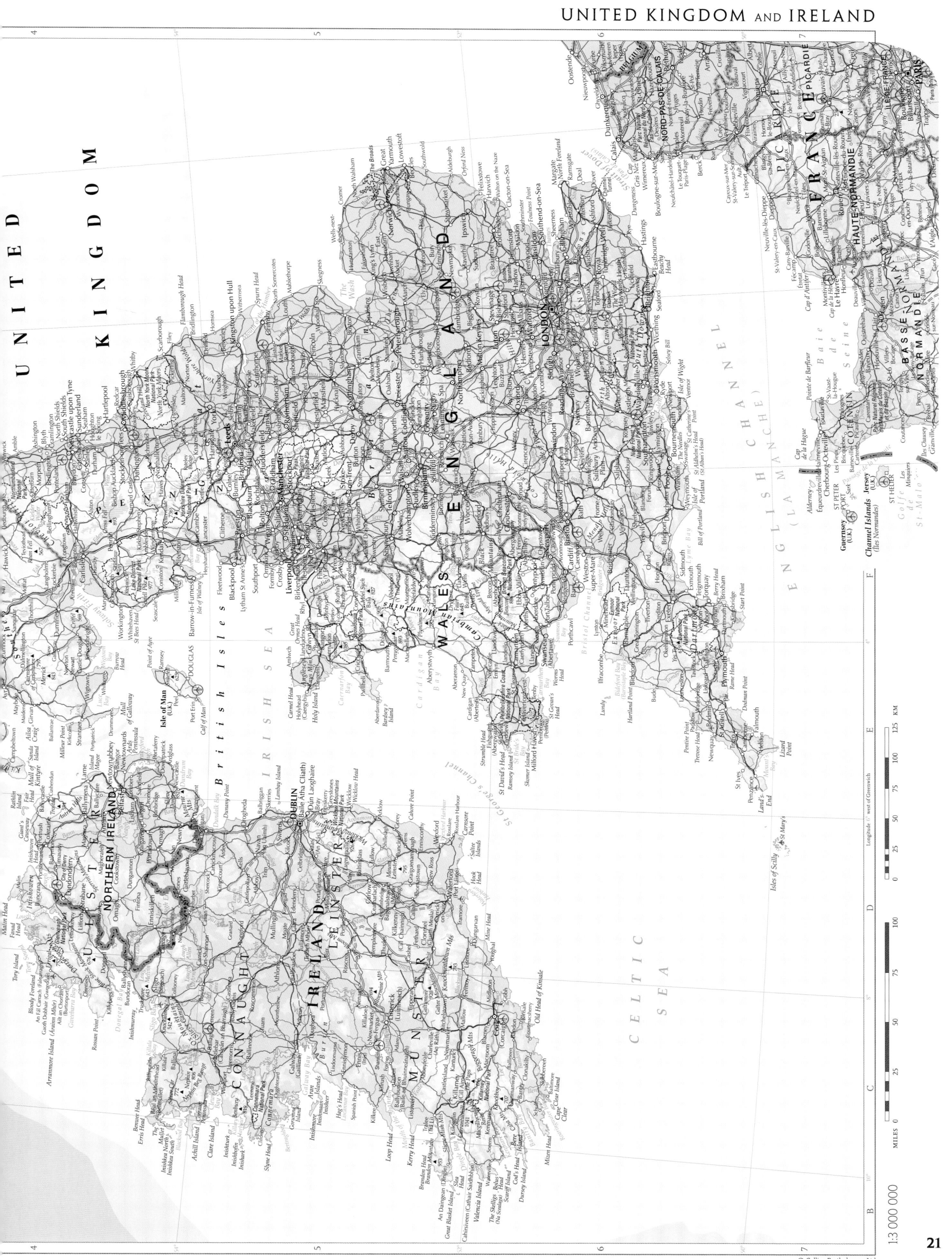

1:3 000 000

© Collins Bartholomew Ltd

SCOTLAND UNITED KINGDOM

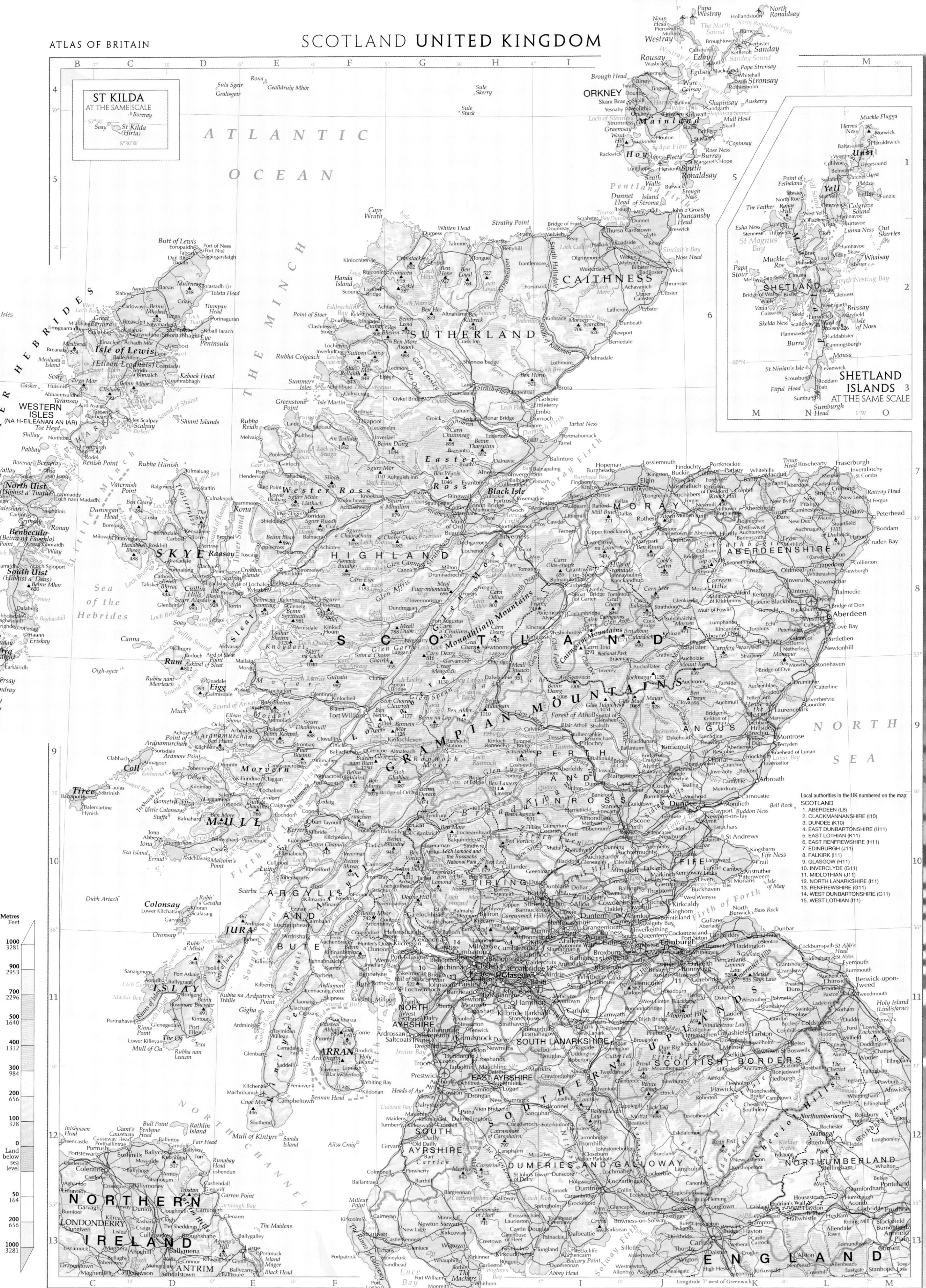

ST KILDA
AT THE SAME SCALE

Boreray
Soay   St Kilda
        (Hirta)
8°30'W

ATLANTIC

OCEAN

**SHETLAND
ISLANDS**
AT THE SAME SCALE

Local authorities in the UK numbered on the map:
SCOTLAND
1. ABERDEEN (L8)
2. CLACKMANNANSHIRE (I10)
3. DUNDEE (K10)
4. EAST DUNBARTONSHIRE (H11)
5. EAST LOTHIAN (K11)
6. EAST RENFREWSHIRE (H11)
7. EDINBURGH (J11)
8. FALKIRK (I11)
9. GLASGOW (H11)
10. INVERCLYDE (G11)
11. MIDLOTHIAN (J11)
12. NORTH LANARKSHIRE (I11)
13. RENFREWSHIRE (H11)
14. WEST DUNBARTONSHIRE (G11)
15. WEST LOTHIAN (I11)

Metres
Feet

1000 / 3281
900 / 2953
700 / 2296
500 / 1640
400 / 1312
300 / 984
100 / 328

Land below sea level

50 / 164
200 / 656
1000 / 3281

22

Conic Equidistant Projection

SCOTLAND

1:1 500 000

© Collins Bartholomew Ltd

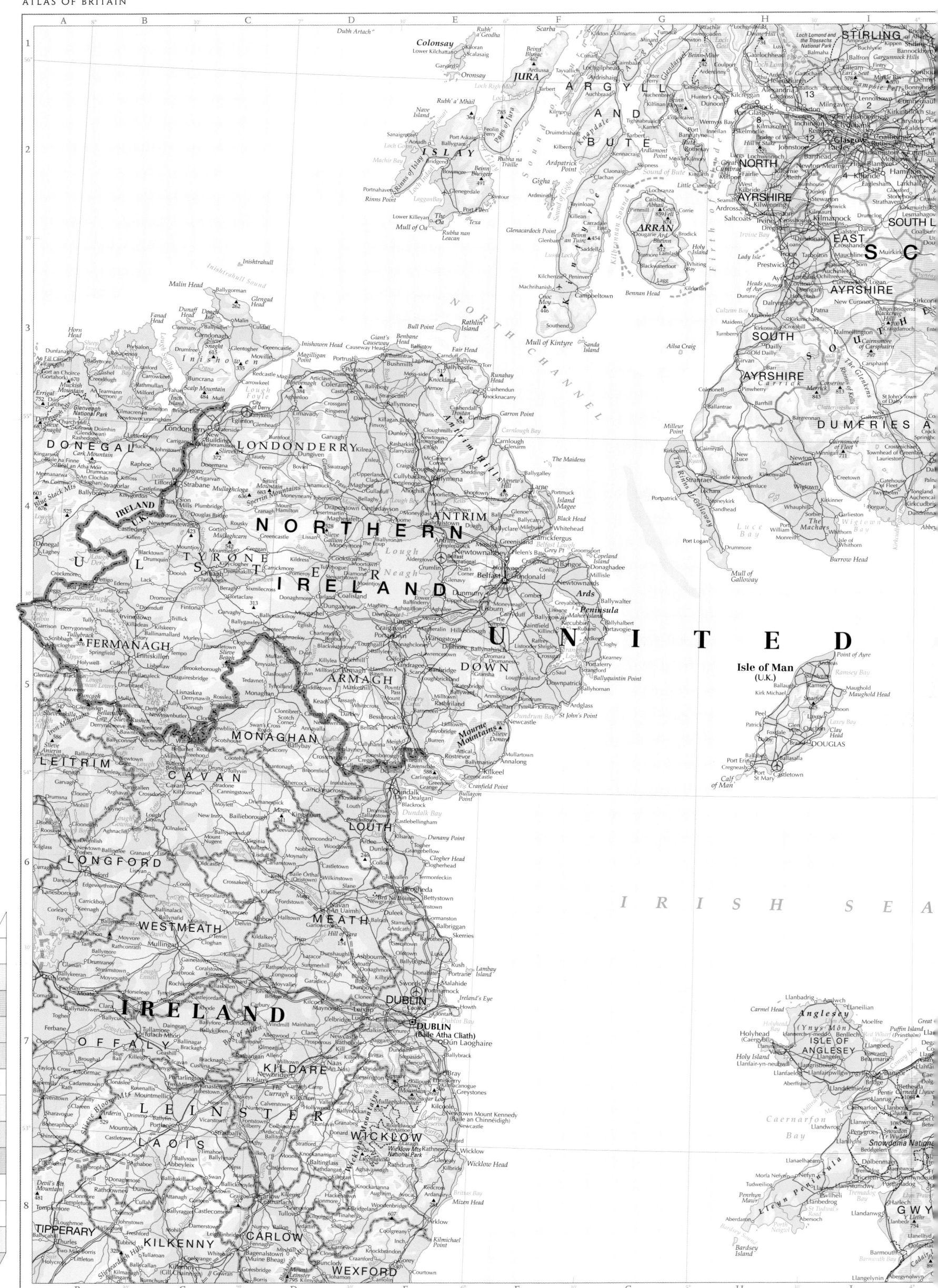

Conic Equidistant Projection

Local authorities in the UK numbered on the map:

ENGLAND
1. BATH AND N.E. SOMERSET (H5)
2. BRACKNELL FOREST (K5)
3. BRIGHTON AND HOVE (L6)
4. BRISTOL (G5)
5. BOURNEMOUTH (I6)
6. CENTRAL BEDFORDSHIRE (L3)
7. CHESHIRE EAST (H1)
8. CHESHIRE WEST & CHESTER (G1)
9. GREATER MANCHESTER (H1)
10. LUTON (L4)
11. MILTON KEYNES (K3)
12. NOTTINGHAM (J2)
13. PLYMOUTH (D7)
14. POOLE (I6)
15. PORTSMOUTH (J6)
16. READING (J5)
17. SLOUGH (K4)
18. SOUTHAMPTON (J6)
19. SOUTHEND (N4)
20. STOKE-ON-TRENT (H1)
21. SWINDON (I4)
22. THURROCK (M5)
23. TORBAY (E7)
24. WEST MIDLANDS (I3)
25. WINDSOR AND MAIDENHEAD (K5)
26. WOKINGHAM (K5)

WALES
27. BLAENAU GWENT (F4)
28. BRIDGEND (E4)
29. CAERPHILLY (F4)
30. CARDIFF (F5)
31. MERTHYR TYDFIL (F4)
32. NEWPORT (G4)
33. RHONDDA CYNON TAFF (F4)
34. TORFAEN (F4)

Metres / Feet

1000 / 3281
900 / 2953
700 / 2296
500 / 1640
400 / 1312
300 / 984
200 / 656
100 / 328
0 / Land below sea level
50 / 164
200 / 656
1000 / 3281

ISLES OF SCILLY
CONTINUATION AT THE SAME SCALE

26

Conic Equidistant Projection

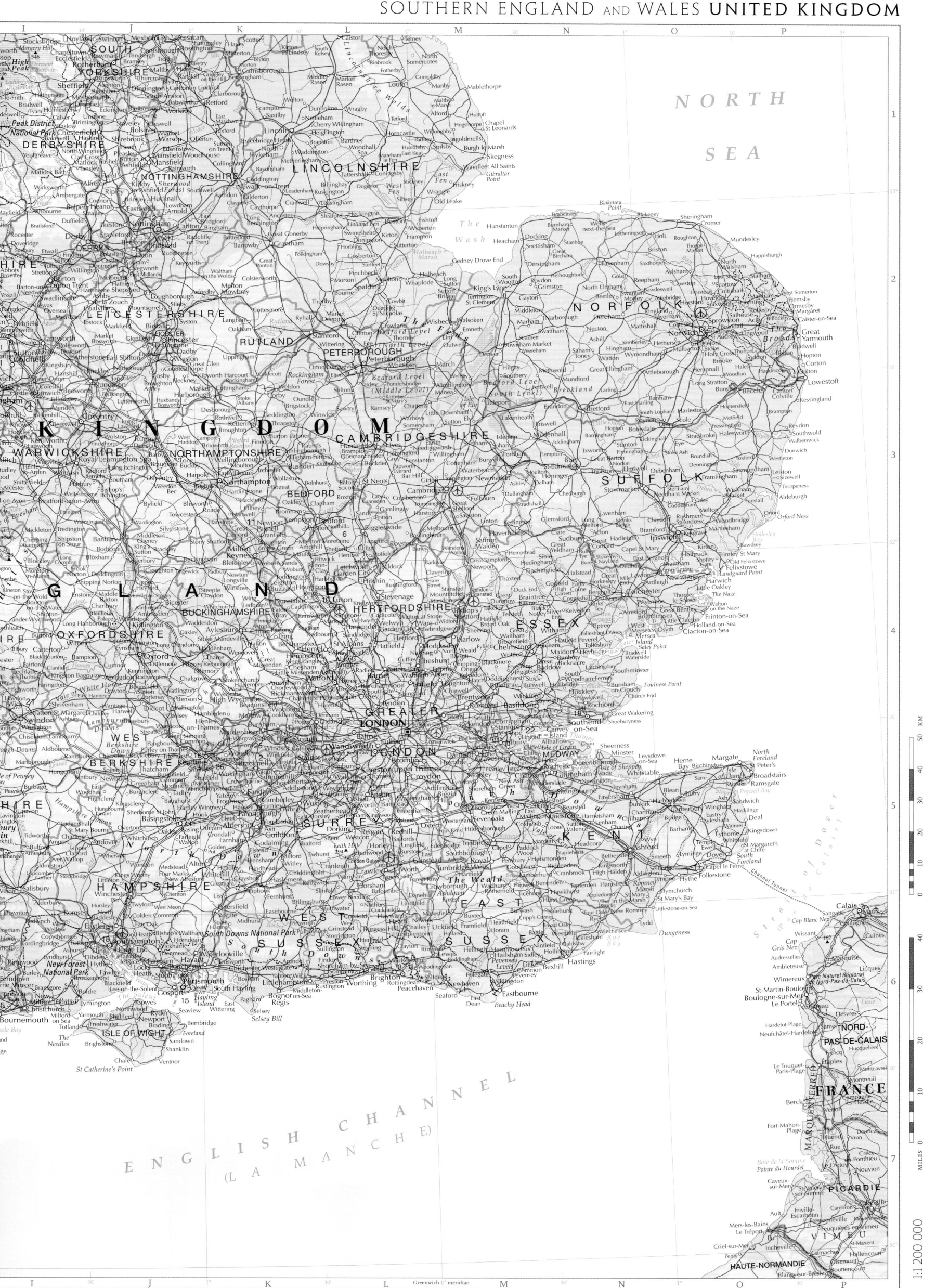

NORTH SEA

The Wash

NORFOLK

ENGLISH CHANNEL
(LA MANCHE)

FRANCE

NORD-PAS-DE-CALAIS

PICARDIE

HAUTE-NORMANDIE

1:1 200 000

© Collins Bartholomew Ltd

ENGLAND

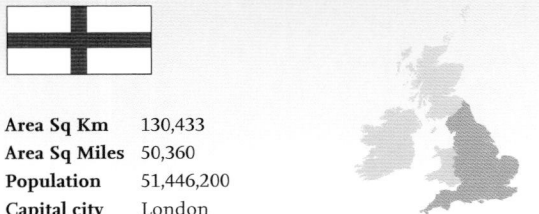

Area Sq Km	130,433
Area Sq Miles	50,360
Population	51,446,200
Capital city	London
Highest point	Scafell Pike (978 m)

Notting Hill Carnival, London.

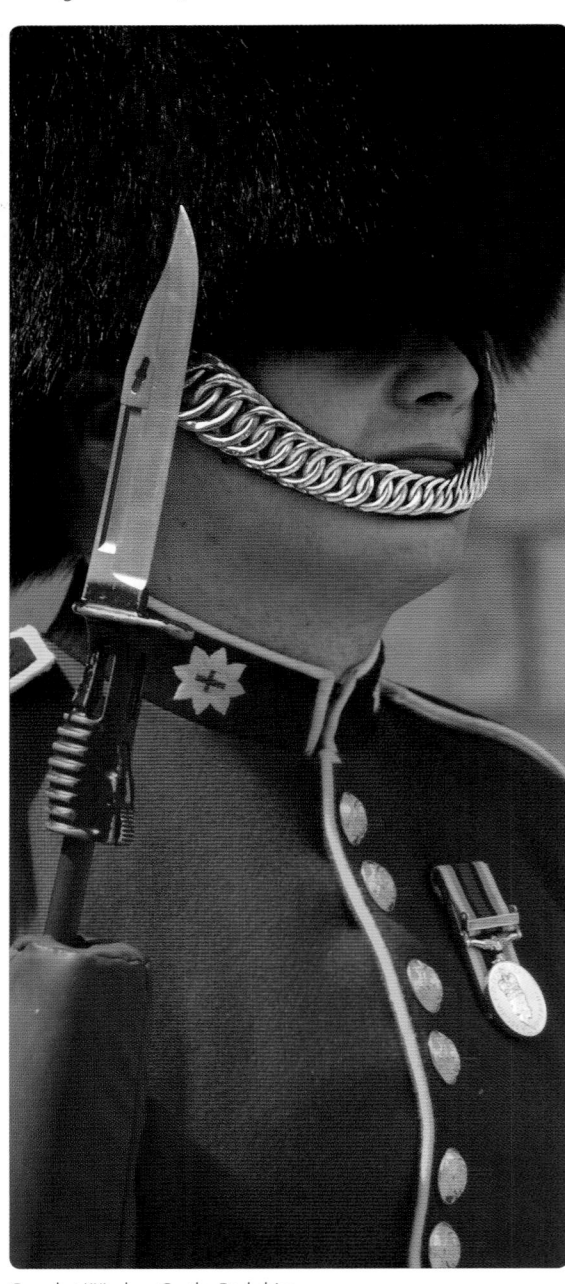

Guard at Windsor Castle, Berkshire.

England is the largest of the component parts of the United Kingdom of Great Britain and Northern Ireland and occupies a little less than two-thirds of the island of Great Britain. To the north its border with Scotland runs 96 km from the Solway Firth to just north of Berwick-upon-Tweed. In the west its border with Wales runs from where the River Wye flows into the Severn Estuary in the south around 260 km north to the marshes of the Dee Estuary. Since the opening of the Channel Tunnel there is now a physical link with France under the Strait of Dover, which, at its narrowest, separates England and France by 34 km. The Isle of Wight is the largest island in England (and the ninth largest in Britain). Most of the other English islands are low lying areas in southeast England, such as the Isle of Sheppey and Hayling Island, which are joined to the mainland by bridges or causeways. England's coastline is not greatly indented and stretches for 1,850 km, slightly less than half the length of Scotland's coastline. The highest point in England, at 978 m, is Scafell Pike in the Lake District, while the lowest point, around 3 m below sea level is at Holme Fen in Cambridgeshire. The most southerly point in England is Lizard Point, in Cornwall. The most westerly is at Land's End, also in Cornwall, while the most easterly is at Lowestoft Ness in Suffolk. The most northerly point is Marshall Meadows Bay, north of Berwick-upon-Tweed.

The south and east of England is characterized by low-lying hills and broad river valleys, such as those of the Thames and the Trent, England's two longest rivers at 346 and 297 km. The uplands include the chalk hills of the Chilterns and the South Downs and limestone hills that stretch up in a band from the Mendips through the Cotswolds to the Lincolnshire and Yorkshire Wolds. The east of England is particularly flat – the Fens have been drained and, as the soil has shrunk, the level of the land often falls below sea level. The southwestern peninsula has both a more rugged coast and landscape, the latter typified by the wild moors and granite tors of Dartmoor. The border with Wales is defined by hills and rivers. In the south the beautiful valley of the river Wye forms the boundary, then the border hills of Herefordshire and Shropshire rise up, reaching their highest point at Black Mountain (703 m) in Herefordshire. Flowing across the border and of great importance to the early industrialization of England is the river Severn, Britain's longest, that rises in Powys and flows 354 km to the Severn estuary. There are many important towns by the river – Shrewsbury, Ironbridge, Worcester and Gloucester. The northern part of England is much hillier. The Peak District, in Derbyshire, is the start of the Pennines that stretch up to the Cheviots on the border with Scotland. On either side of the Pennines lie the early mill towns of industrial England that used the power of the water flowing out of the Pennines to drive their machines. Towards the coast the land is flatter and cultivated, apart from the high lands of the North Yorkshire Moors to the east of the Pennines, and the great brooding mass of the Lake District to the west, the site of all ten of England's highest peaks.

The great variety of landscape is one of the defining features of England and it helps reinforce the regional differences within the country, whether that be in the type of building materials used, the variety of English accent spoken, the types of economic activity undertaken, or the variation in climate – colder and windier as you go north and wetter as you go northwest. In the south, communication has always been relatively easy, with wide river valleys and low, rolling countryside, but in the north the landscape provides much greater barriers with only a limited number of trans-Pennine routes.

The climate of England is maritime temperate with average temperatures in January ranging from around 0°C to 7°C and in July from around 11°C to 22°C. The highest temperature ever recorded was 38.5°C on 10 August 2003 at Faversham in Kent, while the coldest was –26.1°C on 10 January 1982 at Newport in Shropshire. One of the attractions of the south coast is the climate, and the highest monthly sunshine record was in July 1911 at Eastbourne, when the sun shone for 383.9 hours, nearly 100 hours more than the equivalent record for Northern Ireland. The highest daily total for rainfall was on 19 November 2009 at Seathwaite in Cumbria, when 316.4 mm fell (and 495 mm fell over four days), but there is great variation in rainfall – average annual rainfall in higher parts of the Lake District can be 3,200 mm compared with around 500 mm in the driest parts of East Anglia, while London itself receives less than 650 mm a year.

England's population in 2008 was estimated at 51,446,200, accounting for 84 per cent of the population of the United Kingdom. As well as having the greatest population, the population density, at around 400 people per sq km is greater than the other parts of the UK and all major European countries. England's population has been growing in recent years, both through natural increases and increased migration into England from other parts of the UK, from other countries in the European Union and from around the world. Between 1998 and 2007 migration was the largest single factor driving growth but since then natural change has again become most important. The population is expected to continue growing, reaching around 60 million in 2031, compared with 46.4 million in 1971. Reflecting the industrial decline that particularly affected the north of England, little growth is expected in northeast and northwest England, while significant growth will occur in the regions around London and in eastern and southwestern England.

There were known to be people in England from Palaeolithic times but we know little of them apart from the monuments they left behind – Stonehenge and Avebury in Wiltshire being two outstanding examples.

The Worcester and Birmingham canal at Tardebigge, Worcestershire.

Paul's Cathedral, London.

Celtic peoples arrived from around 600 BC, including a group called the Brythons, the origin of the name 'Britain'. Under pressure from later arrivals, the Celts retreated to Cornwall, Wales and Scotland. The Romans under Julius Caesar made preliminary incursions in 55 and 54 BC, but the main Roman invasion came in AD 43 under the direction of Emperor Claudius. Roman rule provided stability and saw the development of towns and roads, most radiating from London and some, such as the Fosse Way from Exeter to Lincoln, crossing the country. Even Hadrian's Wall, a physical northern boundary to England, remains a symbolic dividing line (even if most of Northumberland is north of the wall). With their empire collapsing, the Romans left in the early 5th century, and England was exposed to invasion from the Angles from Jutland and the Saxons from Germany. By the 7th century Anglo-Saxon kingdoms controlled much of England, reflected in the name 'England', meaning 'land of the Angles', first used to describe these kingdoms by Bede in 731. Viking incursions in the 9th century destroyed the power of Northumbria and Mercia and, at their peak, forced Alfred of Wessex to seek shelter among the marshes of Somerset. But Alfred regrouped and fought back. By 937 Alfred's grandson, Athelstan, had united the whole of England under his rule, and thereafter there would always be an identifiable kingdom of England, albeit for some time with fluctuating borders with Wales and Scotland. In 1066 William of Normandy defeated the Saxon King Harold at the Battle of Hastings. William's 'harrying of the north' forced the submission of areas that had remained aloof from an English kingdom, while the creation of marcher lords along the Welsh borders assisted the suppression of Welsh princely domains. Wales was subdued under Edward I and formally united with England only in 1538 under Henry VIII. The border with Scotland was disputed over many centuries and stability came when James VI of Scotland, became King of England, as James I, in 1603 on the death of Elizabeth I,

for he was the next in line to the English throne as the great grandson of Henry VIII's sister Margaret. Formal union of the two kingdoms did not happen until 1707.

The 18th century saw the emergence of the England we recognize today. The enclosure of agricultural land and revolutions in animal husbandry and arable farming enabled England to support a larger population. The Industrial Revolution from the late 18th century saw the transformation of areas in the Midlands, Lancashire, Yorkshire and the northeast into major manufacturing areas. By the 19th century England (and Scotland and Wales) had become the 'workshop of the world'. However, with international competition, industrial output declined and by the second half of the 20th century, many major industries had closed down. This de-industrialization led to widespread unemployment in the Midlands and the north, while the southern part of England became the economic driving force, as finance and other service industries began to dominate. The decline in manufacturing has continued into the 21st century – the percentage of total jobs that are in manufacturing shrunk from around 17 per cent in December 1997 to 10 per cent in June 2009, while jobs in financial and business services have increased from 19 per cent to approaching 22 per cent and in the public sector from over 23 per cent to over 27 per cent. There remains much regional disparity – financial and business services account for 33 per cent of jobs in London but only 16 per cent in the northeast, whereas 32.6 per cent of the jobs there are in the public sector compared with 22.6 per cent on London.

The division of England into administrative areas dates back to the creation of 'shires' in Wessex in the 9th century and many of the names and general areas of today's counties come from that period. In medieval times, many towns received royal charters granting them the status of 'borough' with certain local powers. A piecemeal system of boroughs, parishes and numerous boards developed and the system was overhauled in

1888 when county boroughs and county councils (mostly linked to existing shire areas) were established. Under a county council a network of urban and rural district councils delivered some services. In 1974 there was a major reform with the creation of a two-tier system across all of England, with counties and newly created metropolitan counties (such as Greater Manchester) at the strategic level and districts below them. In 1986, the metropolitan councils and the Greater London Council were abolished and the districts became responsible for providing all services. From 1996 there was further patchwork reform, which is still continuing, in the non-metropolitan areas. Some former districts, for example, Hartlepool, have become 'unitary authorities' responsible for all local government services. Some counties have, in local government terms, ceased to exist, so Berkshire has been replaced by six unitary authorities created from its former district councils, while other counties, such as Cornwall, have abolished all the districts and operate as a unitary authority across the whole county, and yet others such as Kent, retain the two-tier structure of a county council with districts beneath it. Such an individualistic approach has created problems in compiling the text in this atlas. We have provided entries on any area that is covered by a county council, unitary authority or metropolitan borough. Further changes are expected in the near future in Norfolk, Devon and Suffolk, and this is unlikely to be the end of change. One fixed point is the division of England into ceremonial counties, each served by a Lord Lieutenant, and these are primarily based on the counties and metropolitan counties that were established in 1974, though not entirely – the former county of Cleveland has been divided between Yorkshire and Co. Durham. Services may be delivered more efficiently under such arrangements but it has certainly made the recording of the current state of England less straightforward.

The Pennine Way in Derbyshire.

City of London

...atched roof in the Cotswolds.

...aditional terraced houses, Plymouth.

Ratcliffe-on-Soar coal fired power station, Nottinghamshire.

Angel of the North, Gateshead, Tyne and Wear.

...d Harry Rocks, Handfast Point, Dorset.

HISTORICAL MAPS OF ENGLAND

Blaeu Map of England & Wales, 1635.

These two maps of England and Wales, although published more than 250 years apart, show that traditional counties remained largely unchanged throughout that time. In fact many counties had been created in Saxon times, and still exist today in much the same form. The modern system of local government authorities has now diverged from this long-established system in many respects, though the old counties were the foundation of it. Even these traditional or 'ceremonial' counties were adjusted from time to time over the centuries, however – usually to iron out small enclaves and exclaves which had developed for odd geographical or political reasons.

The map on the left is a typical product of the Dutch cartographer Willem Blaeu, and was published in his *Atlas Novus* in 1635. The outline and place names were acquired from the English cartographer John Speed, who died not long before this map was published. Some of the 16th to 17th century county names now look slightly antiquated (e.g. Glocester, Lecester, Northamtonshire, Hantshire, Oxforde, The Ile of Wight, Darby, Yorkeshire, and particularly 'Chestershire'; and Lancashire is simply referred to as Lancaster, after its county town. The boundaries in those early days of mapping are of course not as precise as one would expect from a modern map, but even so it is remarkable how accurate the depiction of the coastline is – only the orientation of Cornwall, and the shape of the Isle of Man (and to a lesser extent the Isle of Wight) deviate significantly from how we now know them. Latin names are still used for the seas and also in *Scotiae Pars* ('Part of Scotland'). The mediaeval tradition to have pictures round a map as attractive space-fillers persists here to a restrained extent with the use of three sailing ships.

The 19th century map comes from the *Century Atlas and Gazetteer*, produced by John George Bartholomew for John Walker & Co. The atlas included a gazetteer of 35,000 place names, and cost 3s. 6d. It went through several editions until 1911, and judging by press reports at the time it was generally regarded as a magnificent production, as well as good value for money. It was printed about the time of the first major overhaul of the local government system. However, as with almost all maps published up until the 1970s, it continues to show the traditional counties – before the shapes and names of bodies responsible for local administration started to diverge significantly from the historic county boundaries. A map of traditional counties, as distinct from local authorities, in fact still looks much the same at this sort of scale even in the 21st century.

ENGLAND & WALES

English Miles

Railways thus

The Century Atlas & Gazetteer of the World, 1890.

CORNWALL

Area Sq Km	3,613
Area Sq Miles	1,395
Population	532,200
County town	Truro
Highest point	Brown Willy (420 m) on Bodmin Moor

Cornwall is named after its original Celtic inhabitants, whose Latin name was the *Cornovii*, from the Latin *cornu*, meaning 'horn' or 'promontory'. 'Wall' was added by the Anglo-Saxons, meaning 'foreigners', in that Cornwall was not peopled by Anglo-Saxons. In the Cornish language, the county's name is Kernow.

FAMOUS FOR
The most southerly point on mainland Britain is **The Lizard**, while the most westernmost point in England is **Land's End**. It is 1,249 km from Land's End to John o' Groats, Britain's most northerly settlement.

The first use of gas for domestic lighting by William Murdoch, a Scottish engineer, at his house in **Redruth** in 1794.

The **Eden Project**, which opened in 2001, is an extraordinary botanical garden in a disused china clay mine, 5 km from St Austell, with two domed greenhouses – the Rainforest Biome (the world's largest free-standing greenhouse, covering 1.5 ha and containing over 1,100 plant species) and the Mediterranean Biome.

In 1901, the first transatlantic radio transmission was made from **Poldhu**, near The Lizard, to Newfoundland, where the signal was received by Guglielmo Marconi.

According to legend, King Arthur was born at **Tintagel Castle** on the north coast of Cornwall.

In 2006 the **Cornwall and West Devon Mining Landscape** became a UNESCO World Heritage Site reflecting its contribution to Britain's industrial Revolution and its fundamental importance in the development of mining technology.

FAMOUS PEOPLE
William Bligh, captain of *HMS Bounty*, born Tinten Manor, St Tudy, 1754.
Andrew Pears, creator of Pears soap, born Mevagissey, 1768.
Richard Trevithick, inventor of first steam-powered vehicle (1801), born Tregajorran, 1771.
Humphrey Davy, chemist who discovered sodium and potassium and invented the miner's safety lamp, born Penzance, 1778.
Maria Branwell, mother of Charlotte, Patrick Branwell, Emily and Anne Brontë, born Penzance, 1783.
William Golding, Nobel laureate and author of *Lord of the Flies*, born St Columb Minor, 1911.
Michael John Kells (Mick) Fleetwood, drummer of Fleetwood Mac, born Redruth, 1947.

"The most impressive place I ever saw on the coasts of Britain." Thomas Carlyle on Land's End, 1882

"It is like the beginning of the world, wonderful: and so free and strong." D H Lawrence, 1916

"There are more saints in Cornwall than there are in heaven." old Cornish proverb

The coastline of Cornwall is wild and rocky; headlands and cliffs are interspersed with large sandy beaches in the north, and deeply indented with river estuaries in the south. The interior is dominated by areas of moorland, notably the granite mass of Bodmin Moor in the northeast. Rivers include the Tamar, forming the boundary with Devon, Fowey, East and West Looe, Fal, Camel, and Lynher. The boundaries of the county of Cornwall have remained unchanged for many years – the last boundary change was in 1890 when the Isles of Scilly became administratively distinct from Cornwall. The internal administration of the county has changed a number of times, most recently in 2009 when Cornwall became a single unitary authority with the abolition of the six district authorities of Caradon, Carrick, Kerrier, North Cornwall, Penwith and Restormel.

In 2008 the population of Cornwall was 532,200, and it is amongst the fastest-growing areas of Britain, with a net migration into the county of around 5,000 a year. The population of the county is scattered around a large number of small communities that initially developed to exploit natural resources (tin, granite, slate, china clay) or the sea. The largest settlement is the urban area of Camborne and Redruth (39,937), followed by St Austell (22,658), Falmouth (21,635), Truro (20,920), Penzance (20,255), Newquay (19,562), Saltash (14,124), Bodmin (12,778), Helston (10,578) and St Ives (9,866).

The economy of Cornwall, once dominated by the exploitation of natural resources, is now driven by tourism and public service – over 30 per cent of the employment is in retail, hotels and restaurants (with 14.5 per cent directly linked to tourist activity) and around 30 per cent in public administration, education and health. Finance, IT and other business activity provide around 11 per cent of jobs (about half the UK average).

Cornwall has always been slightly apart from the rest of England, and, indeed, it is not certain that it was ever entirely controlled by the Romans. Its importance was not in doubt, however, as it has been well known for over 3,000 years as a source of tin and copper and there was much trading with Europe. The people of Cornwall remained more Celtic that the rest of England and this was reflected in the survival of the Cornish language (linked to Welsh and Breton) and the presence of many Celtic saints, including the patron saint of Cornwall, St Piran, whose flag of black with a white cross is the flag of Cornwall. There is an active campaign to gain greater autonomy for Cornwall, and in the 2009 Council elections three members of Mebyon Kernow (Cornish for *Sons of Cornwall*) were elected.

Cornwall has a coastline of over 250 miles. The northern coast is very rugged with a limited number of safe anchorages, St Ives, which latterly became the haunt of artists, being most well-known. The south coast is more gentle – Falmouth is the third largest natural harbour in the world and there are many sandy beaches. Opposite Marazion, joined to the mainland by a causeway at low tide, is St Michael's Mount, whose former monastery was incorporated into a Tudor castle. Falmouth has long been an important port, being the most westerly harbour in Britain. Truro, now the county town, is dominated by its cathedral, built between 1880 and 1910, the first new Church of England cathedral built since the Reformation. It originally developed as a port, as did Penzance and Newquay (where there was a particularly important pilchard fishery).

Away from the coast, there are farmlands, providing rich cattle grazing, and moorlands. The climate is mild, and flower cultivation is carried on extensively. The many derelict tin mines are witness to the former importance of this industry. China clay is produced in large quantities in the St Austell area. The arrival of the railways over Brunel's magnificent bridge over the Tamar at Saltash, led to the development of the tourist industry, now a mainstay of the economy.

The Crowns Engine Houses at Botallack Tin Mine.

St Michael's Mount, opposite Marazion.

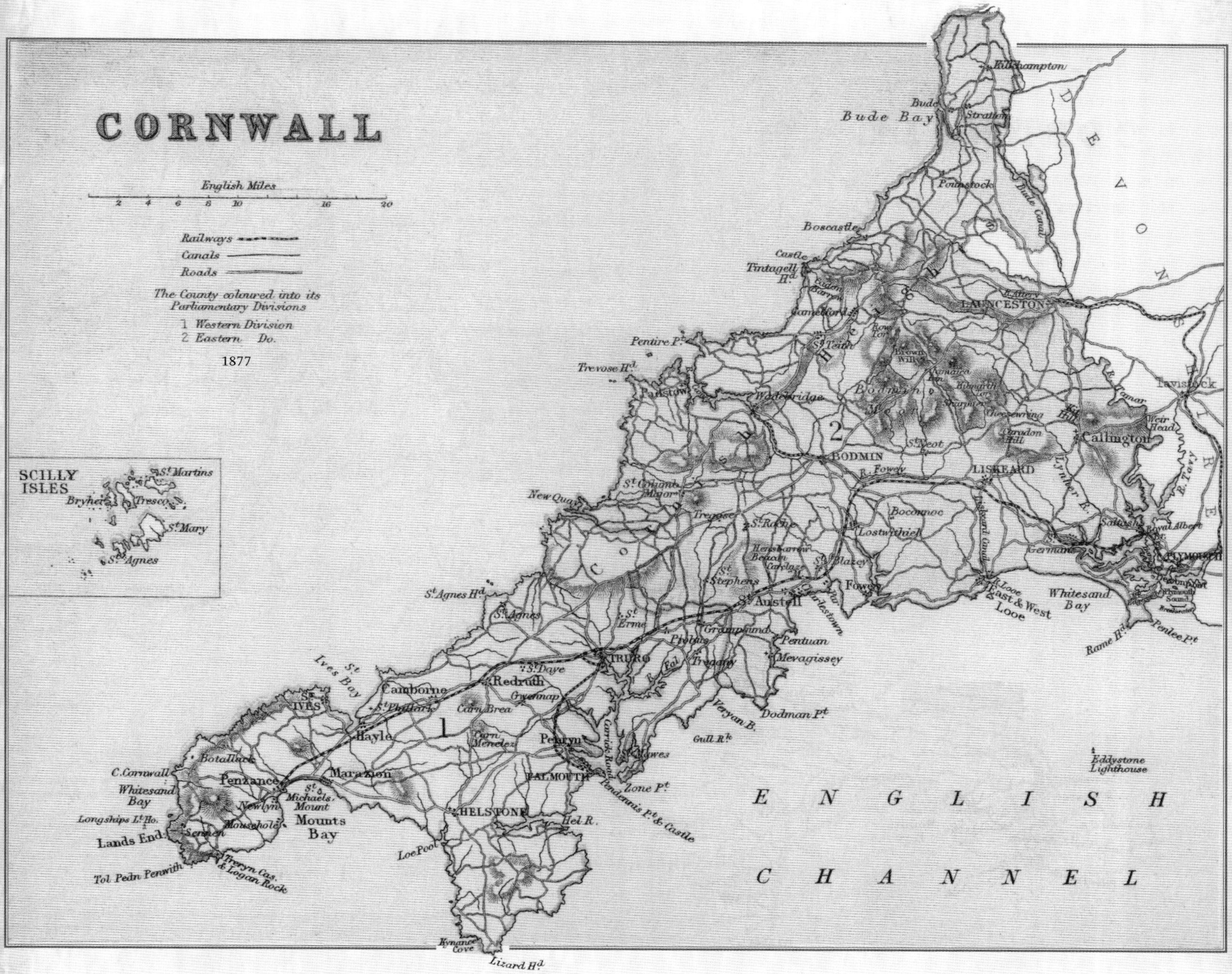

CORNWALL

English Miles

Railways
Canals
Roads

The County coloured into its
Parliamentary Divisions
1 Western Division
2 Eastern. Do.

1877

SCILLY
ISLES

Bartholomew Gazetteer of the British Isles, 1887

CORNWALL. – maritime co. of England, forming its SW.
extremity; is bounded by Devon on the E., and washed
on all the other sides by the sea; length, NE. and SW.,
75 miles; average breadth, 22 miles; coastline, about
200 miles; area, 863,665 ac., pop. 330,686. The S.
coast is much and deeply indented, and has some good
harbours. The principal openings from W. to E. are
Mounts Bay, Falmouth Bay and Harbour, St Austell
Bay, Fowey Harbour, Whitsand Bay, and Plymouth
Sound. Falmouth is one of the finest harbours in Britain.
The indentations on the N. consist of shallow bays with

few or no harbours. The chief promontories are Land's
End, where the granite cliffs are about 60 ft. high; and
the Lizard, the most S. point of England. The Scilly Isles
lie off Land's End, 25 miles to the SW. The Devonian
range extends NE. and SW., rising in Brown Willy to
an alt. of 1368 ft. The streams are numerous, but small.
The principal are the Tamar (which forms the boundary
with Devon), Lyhner, Fowey, and Camel. There is much
barren moorland, but the soil in the valleys is fertile. The
prevailing rock is granite, of a grey or bluish-grey colour,
which often rises above the surface in huge, rugged masses;
clay slate also abounds. The tin and copper mines of

Cornwall have been celebrated from remote ages,
having been known, it is supposed, to the Phoenicians.
Some of them are of very great depth, and have been
carried beneath the sea. Silver, lead, zinc, arsenic,
antimony, and bismuth are also found in considerable
quantities. The fisheries, especially of pilchard and
mackerel, are extensive and valuable. The co. comprises
9 hundreds, the Scilly Islands, 219 pars., and the mun.
bors. of Bodmin, Falmouth, Helston, Launceston,
Liskeard, Penryn, Penzance, St Ives, and Truro. It is
entirely in the diocese of Truro.

ISLES OF SCILLY

Area Sq Km	23
Area Sq Miles	9
Population	2,100
County town	Hugh Town
Highest point	Higher Newford (51 m), on St Mary's

The Isles of Scilly consist of some 140 islands 45 km
southwest of Land's End, Cornwall, of which five are
inhabited: Bryher, St Agnes, St Martin's, St Mary's and
Tresco. They make up the smallest unitary authority
in Britain. The majority of the population live on
St Mary's. The chief industries are tourism, fishing
and the growing of early flowers and vegetables due to
the exceptionally mild climate. On Tresco, the gardens
of its old abbey contain over 20,000 exotic species,
many of which cannot be grown elsewhere in Britain.
All of the Isles of Scilly are designated an Area of
Outstanding Natural Beauty. Regular sea ferry and
air services (including a helicopter service) link the
islands to the mainland.

Higher Town Bay Beach, St Martins.

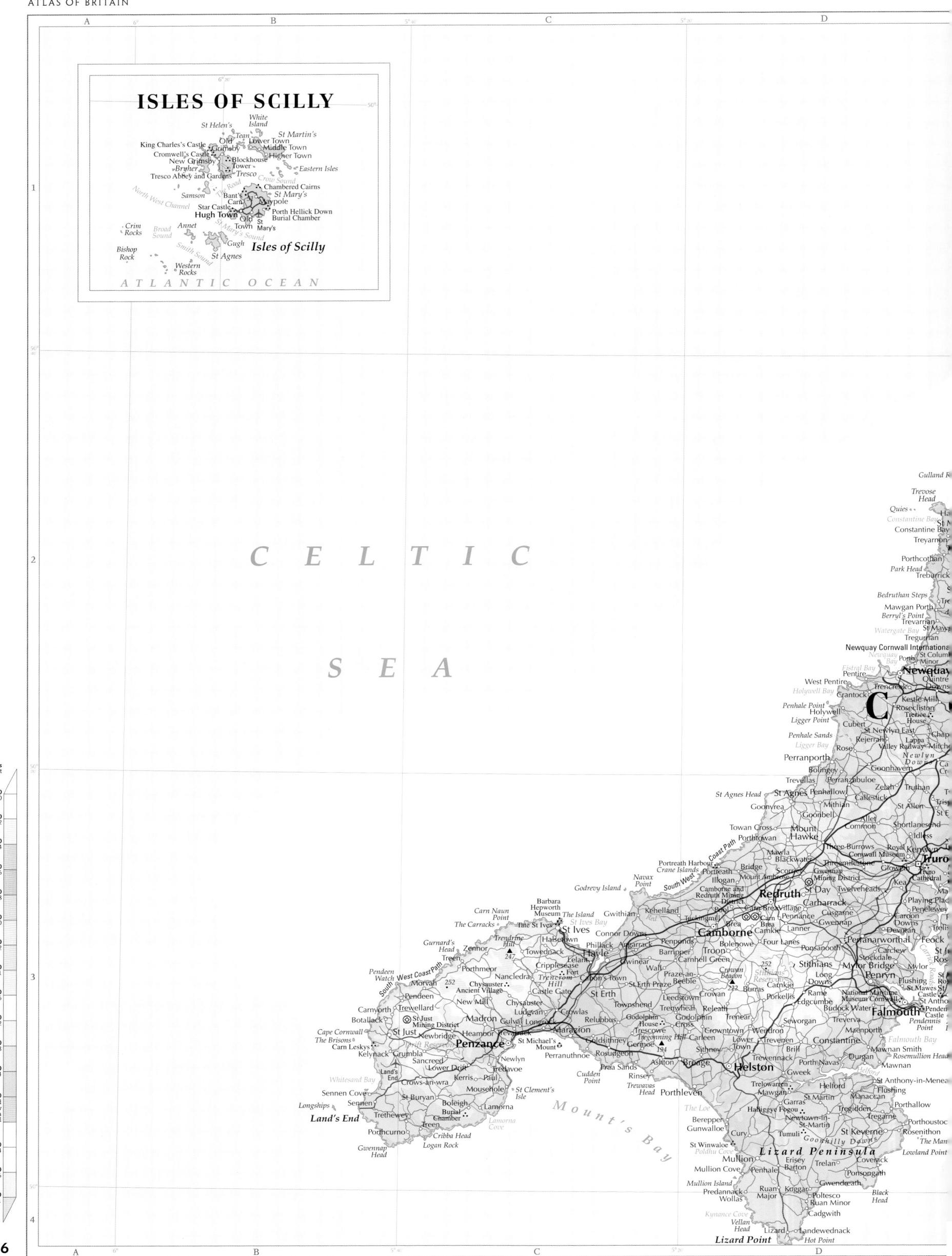

British National Grid projection

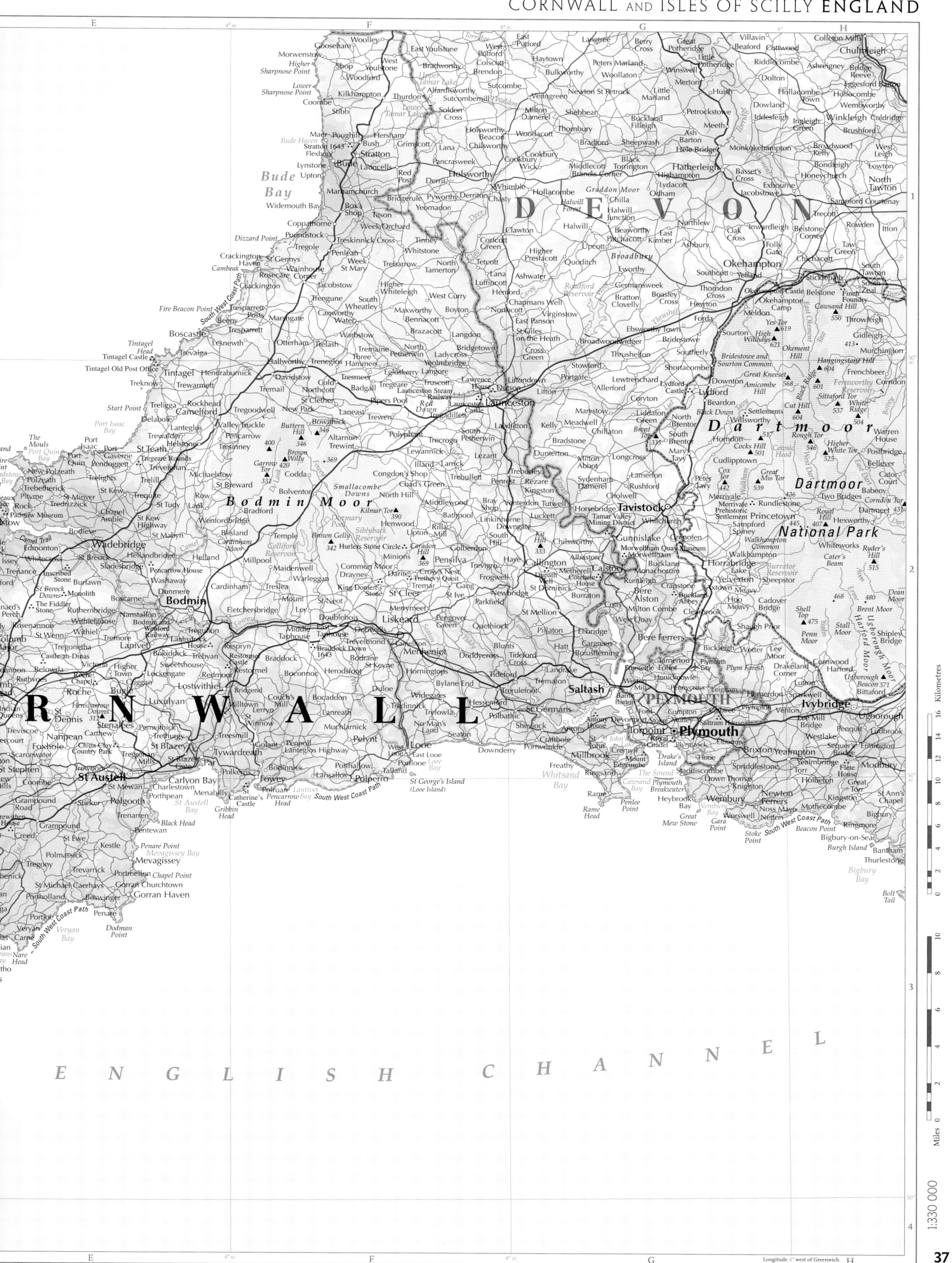

DEVON

Area Sq Km	6,636
Area Sq Miles	2,562
Population	754,700
County town	Exeter
Highest point	High Willhays (621 m), on Dartmoor
Districts	East Devon; Exeter; Mid Devon; North Devon; South Hams; Teignbridge; Torridge; West Devon

The county of Devon takes its name from the Celtic tribe that lived there – the *Dumnonii*, whose name means 'the deep ones' perhaps because they lived in the steep valleys of Devon or were known for their mining. The old English form of the tribal name was *Defnas*.

FAMOUS FOR
Devon is the only county in Britain with two separate coastlines.

The **Devonian Era** (416–360 million years ago) is named after the Old Red Sandstone rocks of Exmoor.

The foundation stone for **Dartmoor Prison** was laid in 1806. Originally the prison was to hold French prisoners of war. The prison is located near Princetown in Dartmoor National Park and now includes a museum that is open to the public.

Sir Arthur Conan Doyle wrote *The Hound of the Baskervilles* in 1901, a tale that highlights the mysteriousness of **Dartmoor**.

Lundy, an island of soaring granite cliffs in the Bristol Channel, was controlled by the Heaven family in the 19th century and was known as the 'Kingdom of Heaven'.

The **Tarka Trail** in North Devon is a 280-km network of paths and cycle tracks that follows the journeys of Tarka the Otter, as recounted in Hugh Williamson's book *Tarka the Otter* (1927).

On the edge of Dartmoor, near Sandypark, can be found the last castle built in Britain, **Castle Drogo**, designed by Edwin Lutyens and built in granite between 1911 and 1930.

FAMOUS PEOPLE
Sir Francis Drake, navigator, the first Britain to sail around the world, born Crowndale, near Tavistock, c.1540.
Sir Walter Raleigh, navigator and courtier, born Hayes Barton, near Sidmouth, 1552.
John Churchill, Duke of Marlborough, victor at the Battle of Blenheim (1704), born Exmouth, 1650.
Thomas Newcomen, inventor of the steam engine, born Dartmouth, 1663.
John Gay, author of *The Beggar's Opera* (1728), born Barnstaple, 1685.
Samuel Taylor Coleridge, poet, born Ottery St Mary, 1772.
Charles Babbage, mathematician and inventor of the 'Analytical Engine', the precursor of computers, born Teignmouth, 1791.
Sir Francis Chichester, yachtsman, the first person to sail single-handedly around the world from east to west (1966–7), born Barnstaple, 1901.
Christopher Anthony John (Chris) Martin, musician and lead singer, Coldplay, born Exeter, 1977.

*"When Adam and Eve were dispossess'd
Of the Garden hard by Heaven,
They planted another one down in the West,
'Twas Devon, glorious Devon."*
Sir Harold Edwin Boulton, 1902

Devon includes the western end of Exmoor and the whole of the granite mass of Dartmoor, the highest land in the county. Its principal rivers are the Exe, Teign, Dart, Avon, Erme, Tamar and Tavy in the south; and the Taw and Torridge in the north. Traditionally the county was the third largest in England, but in 1998 the city of Plymouth and the area of Torbay (primarily consisting of Torquay, Paignton and Brixham) became unitary authorities. The remainder of Devon, now covered by Devon County Council, was divided into eight district councils. The island of Lundy, in the Bristol Channel, is also administratively part of Devon.

The population of Devon in 2008 was 754,700 and it is growing at a faster rate than the national average. The area has a greater proportion of people over retirement age than the national average (over 30 per cent in East Devon). The largest conurbation in the area is Plymouth (see below), but within the County Council area the population is widely distributed over the many smaller market towns and seaports that make up the county. The largest centre of population is Exeter, with a population of 106,772, boosted by the presence of its university and an influx of new enterprises including the headquarters of the UK Meteorological Office. Other centres are significantly smaller and more reliant on the tourist industry and as centres for rural communities: Exmouth (32,972), Barnstaple (30,765), Newton Abbot (24,855), Tiverton (16,772), Bideford (16,262) and Teignmouth (14,799).

The economic development of Devon was based on agriculture, mining (especially tin) and a wide range of marine activities. With the coming of the railways, the county became much more accessible for tourism, which remains a key industry, particularly on the north and south coasts of the county, with around 11 per cent of all jobs being in this sector. The major employers are in public administration, education and health (30 per cent of all jobs), retail, hotels and restaurants (27.6 per cent) but only 10 per cent in manufacturing. The count has an above average number of self-employed workers and earnings significantly below the national average, Torridge and North Devon being very close to the bottom of UK rankings.

The south east of the county shares the UNESCO Jurassic Coast World Heritage Site with Dorset, stretching from Exmouth to the Dorset border. Inland the land is agricultural with some downland. Sidmouth and Exmouth developed as tourist towns ahead of the arrival of the railways and retain their Georgian charm. Exeter dominates this region; originally established by the Romans, the city became one of the most important settlements in medieval Britain, as shown by its magnificent cathedral, mainly dating from the 13th and 14th centuries.

The south of the county is an area of great contrast. The coast, with its many sheltered river estuaries and mild climate, is home to many seaside towns, including Teignmouth, Torbay and Salcombe, as well as the Royal Naval College at Dartmouth. Inland, however, is the Dartmoor National Park, covering around 1,000 sq km, about half of which is wild moorland. There is rough grazing for lifestock, some mining of china clay and, in the north around Okehampton, large areas are given over to military training.

The north of the county is more remote and less economically developed. The 100-m-high rocks at Hartland Point mark the point where the Bristol Channel joins the Atlantic. Heading west is the fishing village of Clovelly and the famous surfing beaches of Bideford Bay, while to the east of Barnstaple rises Exmoor and its National Park, most of which is in neighbouring Somerset.

Devon's regional dish: clotted cream tea.

The private fishing village of Clovelly.

Dartmoor

Boats at the mouth of the River Teign at Shaldon.

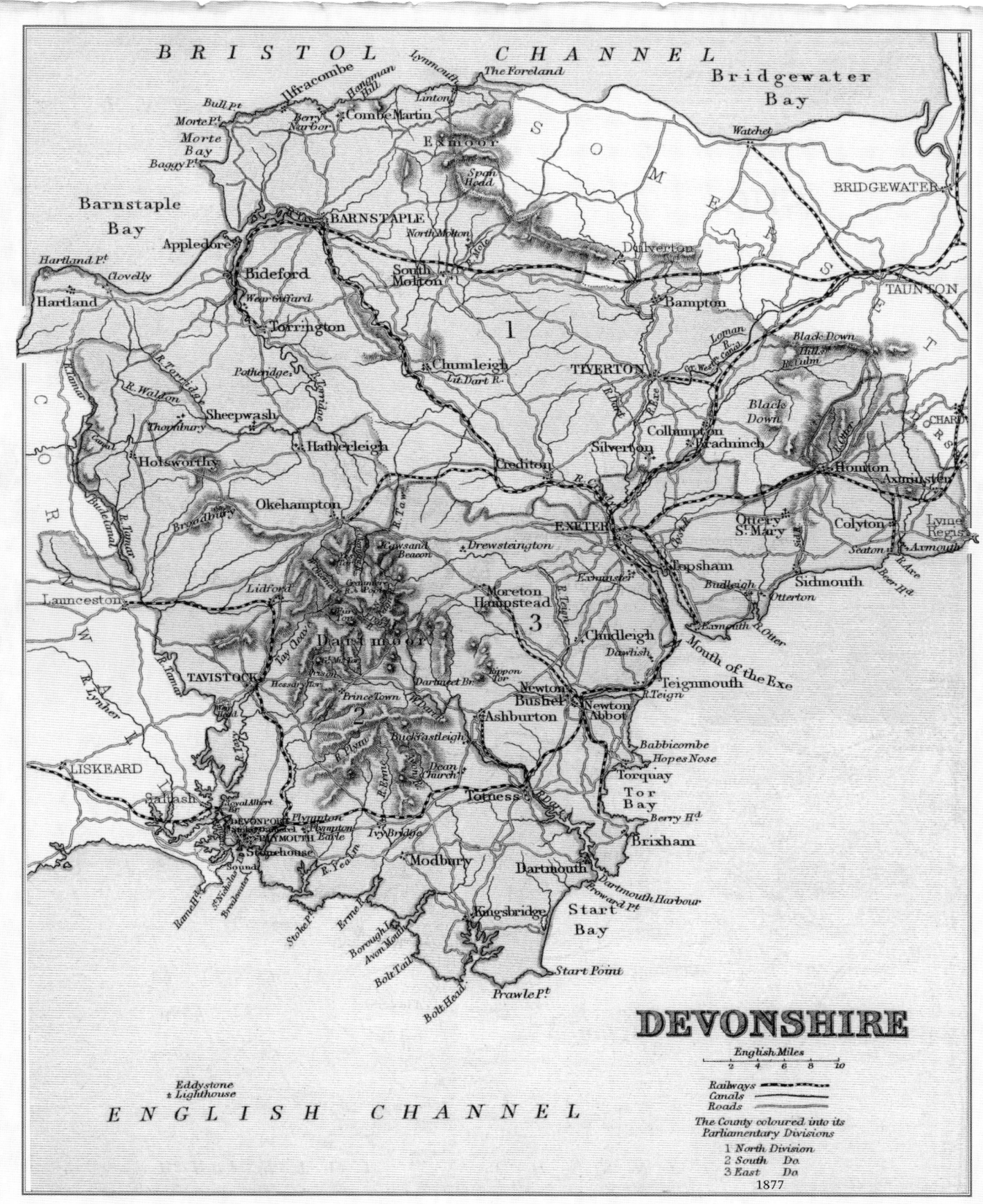

DEVONSHIRE

English Miles

2 4 6 8 10

Railways
Canals
Roads

The County coloured into its
Parliamentary Divisions

1 North Division
2 South   Do.
3 East   Do.

1877

Bartholomew Gazetteer of the British Isles, 1887

DEVON. – maritime co. in SW. of England; is bounded N. by the Bristol Channel, E. by Somerset and Dorset, S. by the English Channel, and W. by Cornwall; length, 69 miles; breadth, 65 miles; coast-line, about 143 miles; area, 1,655,208 ac., pop. 603,595. The surface is richly diversified; the prevailing scenery is beautiful; the climate is mild and salubrious. The coast-line is rocky and precipitous. In the S. is the fertile district called South Hams; in the centre is the bleak and rugged tract of Dartmoor, rising to a mean elevation of 1700 ft., and the rich and beautiful Vale of Exeter; in the N. of the co. moorland prevails. The principal rivers are the Taw and the Torridge, flowing into the Bristol Channel, and the Exe, Axe, Teign, Dart, Avon, and Tamar, flowing into the English Channel. The estuaries of all these rivers afford good harbours. The prevailing rocks are – granite on

Dartmoor, Devonian limestone in the N. and S., millstone grit in the centre and W., and new red sandstone, &c., in the E. The minerals are tin, copper, lead, iron, granite, limestone, marble, slate, &c. Potter's clay and pipeclay are also worked. Devon is celebrated for its orchards and dairy farms; butter, cheese, cider, and live stock are largely exported. The mfrs. are coarse woollen goods, lace, paper, gloves, and shoes. The fisheries are considerable. The co. comprises 33 hundreds, 481 pars, with 2 parts, the mun. bors. of Barnstaple, Bideford, Dartmouth, Devonport, Exeter, Honiton, Plymouth, South Molton, Tiverton, Torrington, and Totnes. It is mostly in the diocese of Exeter.

PLYMOUTH. – mun. bor., seaport, and naval station, Devon, on Plymouth Sound, between the estuaries of the Plym and Tamar, 53 miles SW. of Exeter by rail – mun. bor., 1395 ac., pop. 73,794, 7 Banks, 4 newspapers.

Market-days, Monday, Thursday, and Saturday. Plymouth, in the larger sense, consists of the "Three Towns" of Devon-port, Stonehouse, and Plymouth, the two first forming the borough of Devonport. Plymouth proper is built upon 2 eminences and the hollow between them. The southern eminence is called The Hoe, and is laid out as a promenade and recreation grounds. Plymouth was called Tamarworth by the Saxons, and Sudtone (i.e., South Town) by the Normans, and was a mere fishing hamlet until after the reign of Henry II., when its natural advantages as a seaport and naval station were perceived, and the town rapidly rose in importance. In 1346 it sent 26 ships and 600 men to the siege of Calais, and its contribution to the fleet on the threatened invasion by the Spanish Armada was second only to that of London. The name of Plymouth was taken in 1439, when it received its charter from Henry VI.

British National Grid projection

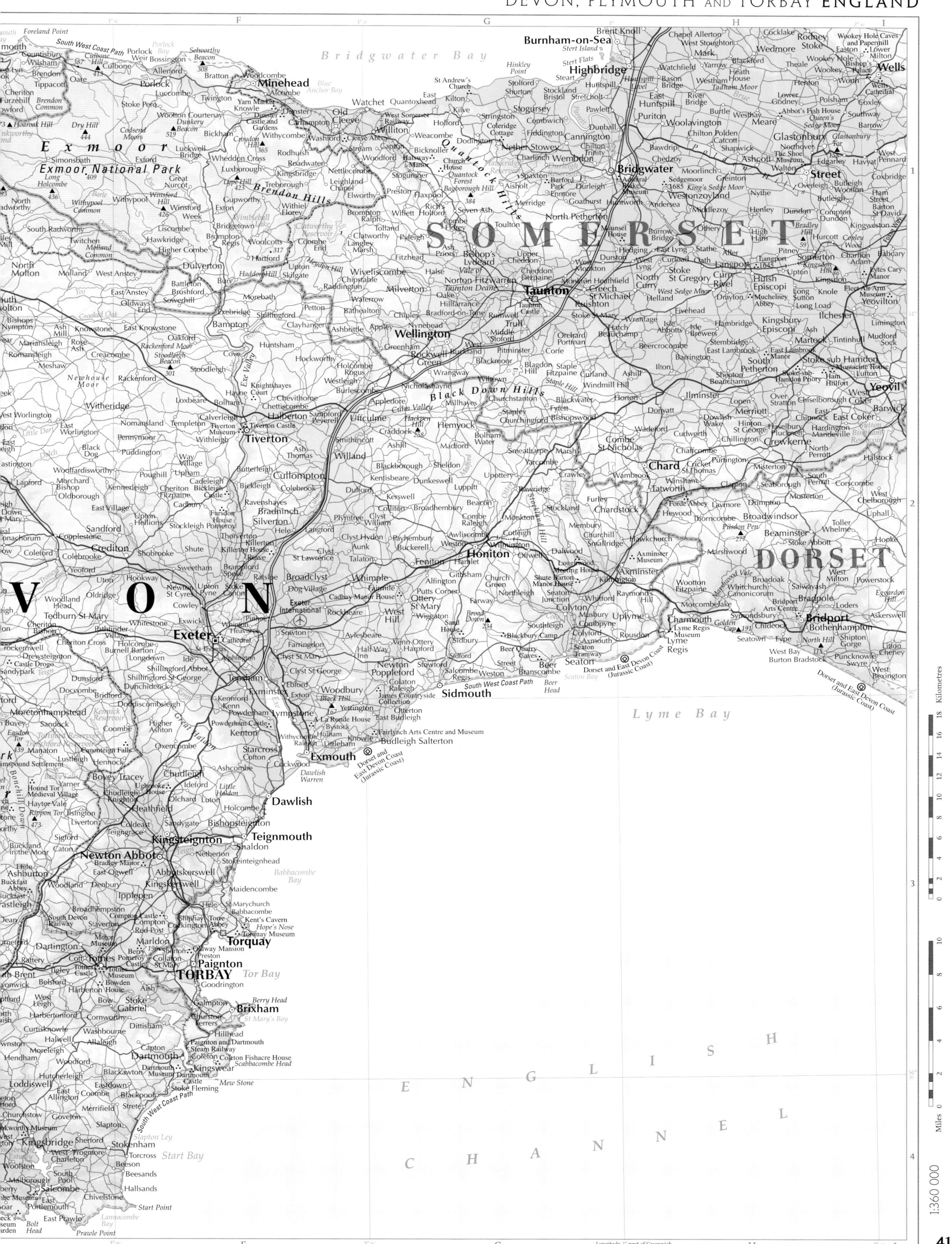

© Collins Bartholomew Ltd

1:360 000

PLYMOUTH

Area Sq Km 84
Area Sq Miles 33
Population 252,800
Highest point Woolwell Road (160 m)

FAMOUS FOR

In 1620, to escape religious persecution in Europe, the puritan **Pilgrim Fathers** sailed from Plymouth in the *Mayflower* to North America and established the first English settlement in New England, the Plymouth Colony.

FAMOUS PEOPLE

Sir Joshua Reynolds, artist and President of the Royal Academy, 1723.
Robert Falcon Scott (Scott of the Antarctic), 1868.
Guy Burgess, Russian spy, 1911.
George Passmore, of the artists Gilbert and George, 1942.
Wayne Sleep, dancer and choreographer, 1948.
Trevor Francis, footballer, 1954.

Plymouth, the largest city on the south coast, is on the sheltered estuary into which the Tamar and Plym flow. It developed as a port for exporting wool and its naval importance was sealed in the British imagination from the time of the Spanish Armada in 1588, when Sir Francis Drake allegedly completed his game of bowls on Plymouth Hoe before sailing forth to defeat the Armada. In the 1690s the first naval dockyards at Devonport were constructed and they have dominated Plymouth ever since. Today they are the largest naval dockyards in western Europe, employing over 12,000 civilian and military personnel. Their presence was the reason for the very heavy bombing of Plymouth in World War II, which resulted in the massive, and not always successful, reconstruction thereafter. The dockyards have brought many marine manufacturing businesses to the city, specialisms reflected in the University of Plymouth, established in 1992. Nearly 36 per cent of employment in public administration, education and health (9 per cent higher than the UK average) and manufacturing employment is also above the national average while finance, IT and other business employment is well below average.

Warship in Her Majesty's Naval Base Devonport in Plymouth.

TORBAY

Area Sq Km 119
Area Sq Miles 46
Population 134,000
Highest point Beacon Hill (196 m), near Maldon

FAMOUS FOR

In 1688 William of Orange landed at **Brixham** at the start of the Glorious Revolution that saw the peaceful overthrow of James II, the last Stuart king.

FAMOUS PEOPLE

Dame Agatha Christie, born Torquay 1890. She used the area in a number of her stories.
Peter Cook, comedian and actor, born Torquay, 1937.

Torquay lies in a very deep and well-sheltered spot,
And at first sight by strangers it won't be forgot;
'Tis said to be the mildest place in all England,
And surrounded by lofty hills most beautiful and grand.
William McGonagall, 1890

This area, situated on Tor Bay, is one of Britain's main holiday centres and is made up of the towns of Torquay (population 62,332), Paignton (43,658) and Brixham (15,678). They were brought together as the county borough of Torbay in 1968, which became a unitary authority in 1998. While Brixham had a long history as a fishing port, the area really developed at the start of the 19th century, for its coastline, dubbed the 'English Riviera', attracted those who could no longer travel to the French Riviera because of the Napoleonic Wars. The arrival of the railway in 1848 greatly stimulated this development and tourism is the main industry, with Torbay receiving over 1.5 million visitors per year. Excellent leisure, recreation and conference facilities are added attractions. Over 17 per cent of the employment in the area is directly linked to tourism while 34.5 per cent of employment is in public administration, education and health.

Torquay Harbour

DORSET

Area Sq Km	2,573
Area Sq Miles	993
Population	407,800
County town	Dorchester
Highest point	Lewesdon Hill (279 m)
Districts	Christchurch; East Dorset; North Dorset; Purbeck; West Dorset; Weymouth & Portland

The county of Dorset is named after its original pre-Roman inhabitants, the Durotriges, who lived around the town of Dorchester, most notably at Maiden Castle, the largest Iron Age fortress in Europe.

FAMOUS FOR

The **Cerne Abbas Giant** is a 55-m-high figure of an unashamedly naked man holding a club, cut into a chalk hillside. It may be a Romano-British image of Hercules or even a 17th century caricature of Oliver Cromwell.

The *Tolpuddle Martyrs* were six Dorset agricultural workers from the village of **Tolpuddle** who were sentenced in 1834 to transportation to Australia for engaging in trades union activities.

The **Fleet Lagoon**, sheltered by Chesil Beach, is home to 150 species of seaweed, 25 species of fish and 60 species of molluscs.

T. E. Lawrence (Lawrence of Arabia) lived at **Clouds Hill**, a small cottage near Bovington, at the time of his death in a motorcycle accident in 1935.

The largest onshore oilfield in Europe is at **Wytch Farm**, 3 km north of Corfe Castle. Production peaked in 1997.

Dorset abounds with unusual village names: **Iwerne Courtney, Piddletrenthide, Puddletown, Ryme Intrinsica, Sixpenny Handley.**

FAMOUS PEOPLE

Thomas Sydenham, the 'English Hippocrates', born Wynford Eagle, 1624.
Thomas Love Peacock, novelist, born Weymouth, 1785.
Mary Anning, fossil hunter who found the first complete *Ichthyosaurus*, born Lyme Regis, 1799.
William Fox Talbot, pioneer of photography, born Melbury, Dorset, 1800.
Thomas Hardy, novelist, born at Higher Bockhampton, near Stinsford, 1840.

"A man that coveted a retreat in this world might as agreeably spend his time, as well in Dorchester, as in any town that I know in England."
Daniel Defoe, 1727

The county of Dorset traditionally included Poole but not Bournemouth and Christchurch, which were in Hampshire. It now contains Christchurch and the area around it, but both Poole and Bournemouth have been unitary authorities since 1997. The population of the county is 407,800 and, in part reflecting its mild climate, it has the highest percentage of people over retirement age in Britain (28 per cent) and one of the lowest percentages of children. The two largest towns are Weymouth (56,043) and Christchurch (40,208), with the remainder of the population scattered between many smaller market towns and villages. The main urban areas that influence the county are Poole and Bournemouth at the eastern end of Dorset.

The county is not crossed by any major road or rail link and has remained predominantly rural. Traditionally, economic activity was centred around agriculture and activities linked to the sea, but the focus is now very different, with only 1 per cent of the working population being employed in agriculture. The main employers are now public administration, education and health (30 per cent), retail, hotels and restaurants (25 per cent), banking and finance (15 per cent) and manufacturing (12 per cent). The county is an important centre for marine and aviation technology, while tourism accounts for 11 per cent of the local economy. The employment mix results in incomes below the national average.

Most people's image of Dorset has been derived from the novels of Thomas Hardy, the county's most famous writer, who was born and lived near Dorchester, which he transformed into his fictional Casterbridge. Dorset is also renowned for its spectacular coastal scenery that provides evidence of the evolution of the earth over the last 185 million years. The 'Jurassic Coast' running from Old Harry Rocks near Studland Bay, close to Poole, to the county boundary beyond Lyme Regis and on towards Exmouth in Devon, was declared a World Heritage Site in 2001. The coastline contains the sublime Lulworth Cove, an almost circular bay surrounded by cliffs, and the great natural arch of Durdle Door. Chesil Beach is an extraordinary tombolo of shingle that stretches 28 km from Portland to West Bay. Behind the shingle bank is the Fleet Lagoon, a very important habitat for wading birds. The island of Portland is famed for its limestone, used to build many landmarks, including St Paul's Cathedral in London.

The coast remains a great magnet for visitors, and many of the coastal towns now rely greatly on the tourist trade, where once fishing, seafaring and all the related enterprises such as rope- and net-making provided the economic lifeblood of the communities – reflecting this, Bridport is still home to manufacturers of football and tennis nets. Lyme Regis, famed for the Cobb, a massive limestone breakwater originally built in the 13th century to protect the harbour, has featured in many stories, from Jane Austen's *Persuasion* to John Fowles' *The French Lieutenant's Woman*. Weymouth developed as a seaside resort, no doubt helped when George III started visiting in 1788 to bathe in the sea for his health. It is now a major centre for water sports and will be hosting the sailing competitions for the 2012 Olympic Games.

Inland the countryside is dominated by rolling downland punctuated by many villages and small market towns. In the centre of the county is Dorchester, the county town and administrative centre. Its population is growing with the building of Poundbury, a new community developed by the Prince of Wales to embody the virtues of traditional architectural and town planning ideals. Other major settlements are Christchurch, beyond Bournemouth at the far eastern end of the county, home to one of Britain's grandest parish churches, a former priory built between 1094 and 1520; Wimborne Minster, also dominated by its large church (the Minster); Blandford Forum, an unusual example of a Georgian planned town, having been rebuilt after a major fire in 1731; and, in the north of the county, Sherborne, a former capital of Wessex, with its grand Abbey and two castles, one built by Sir Walter Raleigh.

Thomas Hardy's cottage, Higher Bockhampton.

Sherborne Castle

Chesil Beach near Portland in Weymouth.

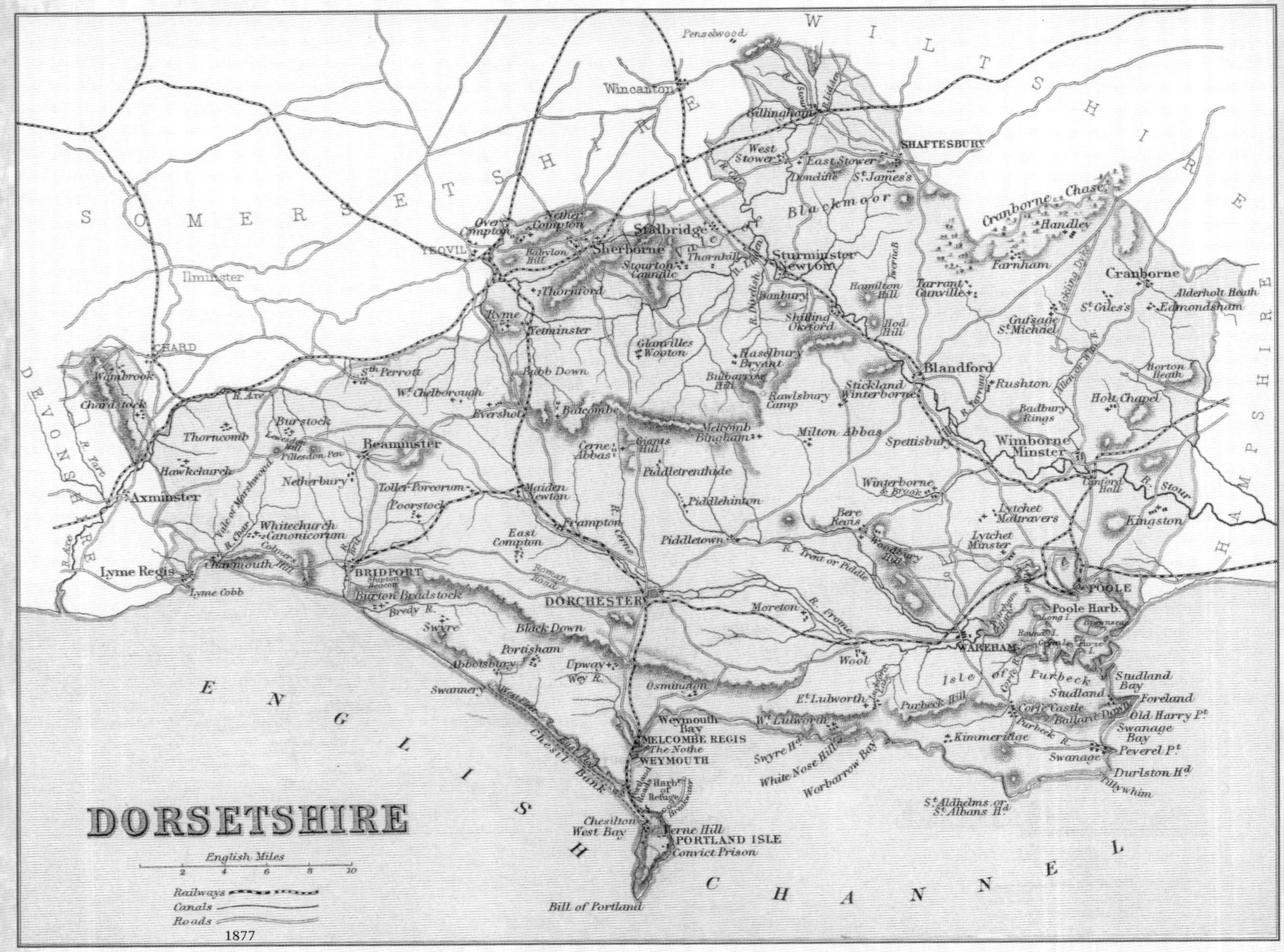

DORSETSHIRE

English Miles

2   4   6   8   10

Railways
Canals
Roads

1877

Bartholomew Gazetteer of the British Isles, 1887

DORSET, maritime co., on S. coast of England; is bounded N. by Somerset and Wilts, E. by Hants, S. by the English Channel, and W. by Devon; length, E. and W., 52 miles; breadth, N. and S., 37 miles; coastline, 75 miles; area, 627,265 ac.; pop. 191,028. The main features of the coast are Poole Harbour, St Alban's Head, and the singular projection called the Isle of Portland. The principal streams are the Stour and the Frome. Great part of the co. is traversed by the two ranges of chalk hills called the North and South Downs, and the soil consists mainly of chalk, gravel, and sand, but is very fertile in the valleys. Wheat and barley are grown in the W. and N. Immense flocks of sheep are pastured on the Downs. Dairy farms are generally large, and dairy husbandry is carried to a very high point of perfection. The only mineral of any importance is Portland stone, quarried in the Isle of Portland. There are mfrs., to some extent, of sailcloth, sacking, nets, paper, silk, &c., with malting and brewing, and iron-founding. The fisheries, especially of mackerel, are considerable, and ships and yachts are built at Poole. The co. comprises 34 hundreds, 22 liberties, 290 pars, and a part, and the mun. bors, of Blandford, Bridport, Dorchester, Lyme Regis, Poole, Shaftesbury, and Weymouth and Melcombe Regis. It is mostly in the diocese of Salisbury.

Durdle Door, with the Isle of Portland in the distance.

BOURNEMOUTH

Area Sq Km	47
Area Sq Miles	18
Population	163,900
Highest point	Ringwood Road (65 m)

FAMOUS FOR

The tomb of **Mary Shelley**, who was buried with the heart of her husband, Percy Bysshe Shelley, close to the final resting place of her parents (William Godwin and Mary Wollstonecraft), in the churchyard of St Peter's.

Robert Louis Stevenson, who wrote the *Strange Case of Dr Jekyll and Mr Hyde* at his house in Bournemouth, which he named 'Skerryvore', after the lighthouse built by his uncle, Alan Stevenson, on the Skerryvore reef off the west coast of Scotland.

Europe's first artificial surfing reef constructed off the shore at **Boscombe**.

"A Mediterranean lounging-place on the English Channel."
Tess of the d'Urbevilles, Thomas Hardy (he renamed Bournemouth as Sandbourne).

"This fashionable watering-place, with its eastern and its western stations, its piers, its groves of pines, its promenades, and its covered gardens, was, to Angel Clare, like a fairy place suddenly created by the stroke of a wand, and allowed to get a little dusty."
Tess of the d'Urbevilles, Thomas Hardy

The settlement of the heathland at the mouth of the Bourne river began in 1810 when the first holiday house was built by a retired army officer, Lewis Tregonwell. Originally in Hampshire, the town was transferred to Dorset in 1974 and in 1997 it became a unitary authority. The mild climate has encouraged many people to retire to Bournemouth. The growth of Bournemouth was due entirely to its attraction as a seaside resort, initially with Victorian villas by the chines (narrow valleys) that led from the heath to the sea. With the coming of the railway in 1870, the town boomed. Tourism has remained key to its economy, with Bournemouth also becoming a major conference centre. In the late 20th century, many financial services businesses based themselves in Bournemouth. There are few historical landmarks, the most noteworthy being the Russell Cotes Museum and two contrasting Victorian churches of national importance (St Peter's and St Stephen's). Bournemouth has a university and a symphony orchestra, but both are now primarily based in nearby Poole.

Bournemouth Beach and Pier.

POOLE

Area Sq Km	75
Area Sq Miles	29
Population	138,800
Highest point	Corfe Hills (78 m)

FAMOUS FOR

The **Sandbanks** district of Poole, which contains some of the most expensive houses in the world.

Brownsea Island, in Poole Harbour, one of the few remaining habitats of the red squirrel in England and the site of the first Scout camp run by Robert Baden Powell in 1907.

The **Poole logboat**, thought to date from around 300 BC, which was made from a single oak tree and is 10 m long and could carry 18 people. It was discovered in 1964 in Poole Harbour and can now be seen in Poole Museum.

FAMOUS PERSON

John le Carré, novelist, born Poole, 1931.

An important port from the Middle Ages, Poole is on the shores of Poole Harbour, the second largest natural harbour in the world with a sheltered coastline of 160 km. Originally in Dorset, Poole became a unitary authority in 1997. It has a more varied economy than its neighbour, Bournemouth, and the surrounding districts of Dorset, with an active manufacturing sector, particularly in marine engineering, and a busy commercial and ferry port. In the 18th century, Poole was one of Britain's busiest ports and it had particularly strong trading links with Newfoundland. After a long period of decline, the port is once again thriving, with cross-Channel ferries, much cargo handling, a fishing fleet, a Royal Marine base and pleasure boating. Poole is the main base for Bournemouth University, founded in 1992, and for the internationally renowned Bournemouth Symphony Orchestra, founded in 1893 in Bournemouth, but now based at the Lighthouse Centre for Performing Arts in Poole.

Low tide at Poole Harbour.

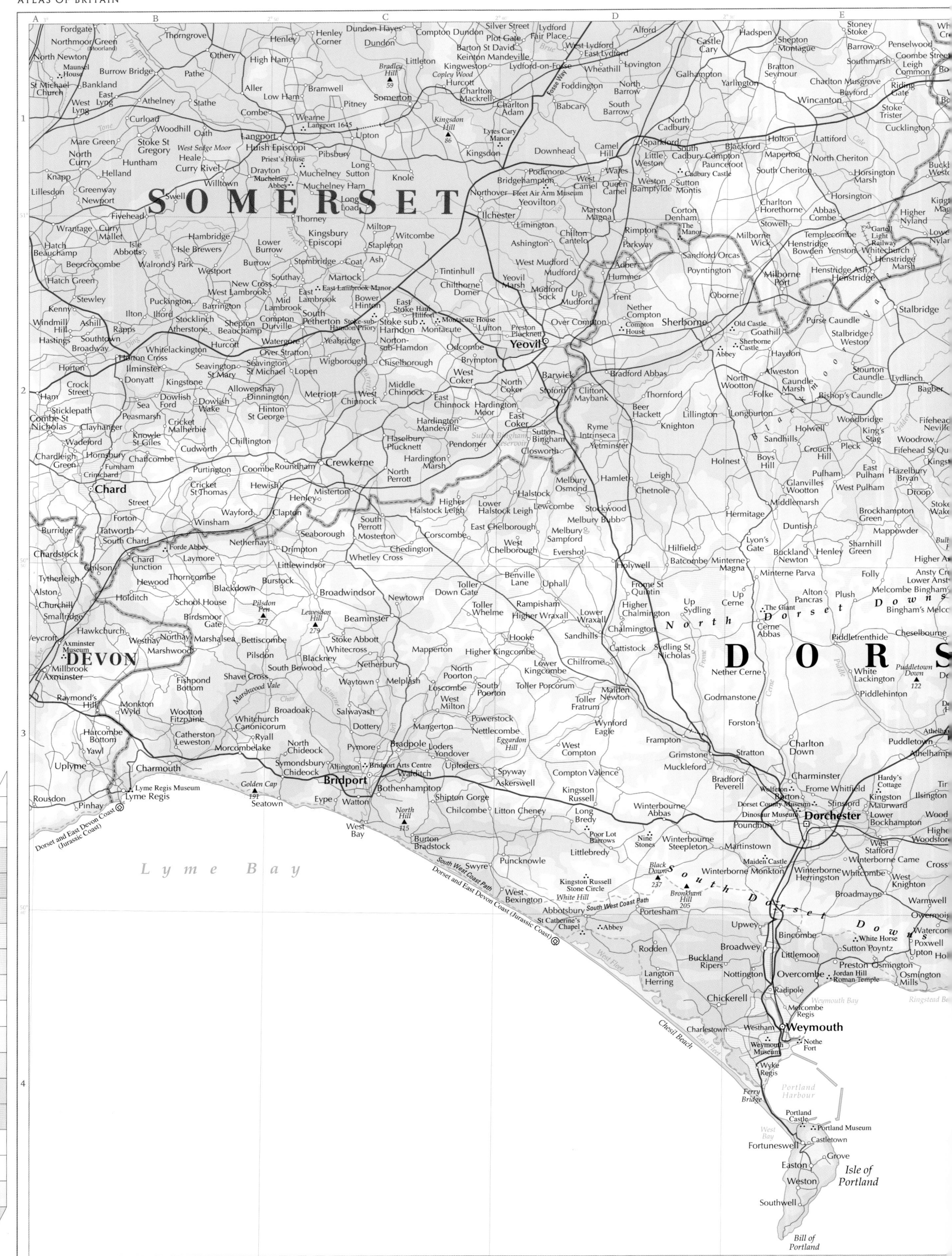

British National Grid projection

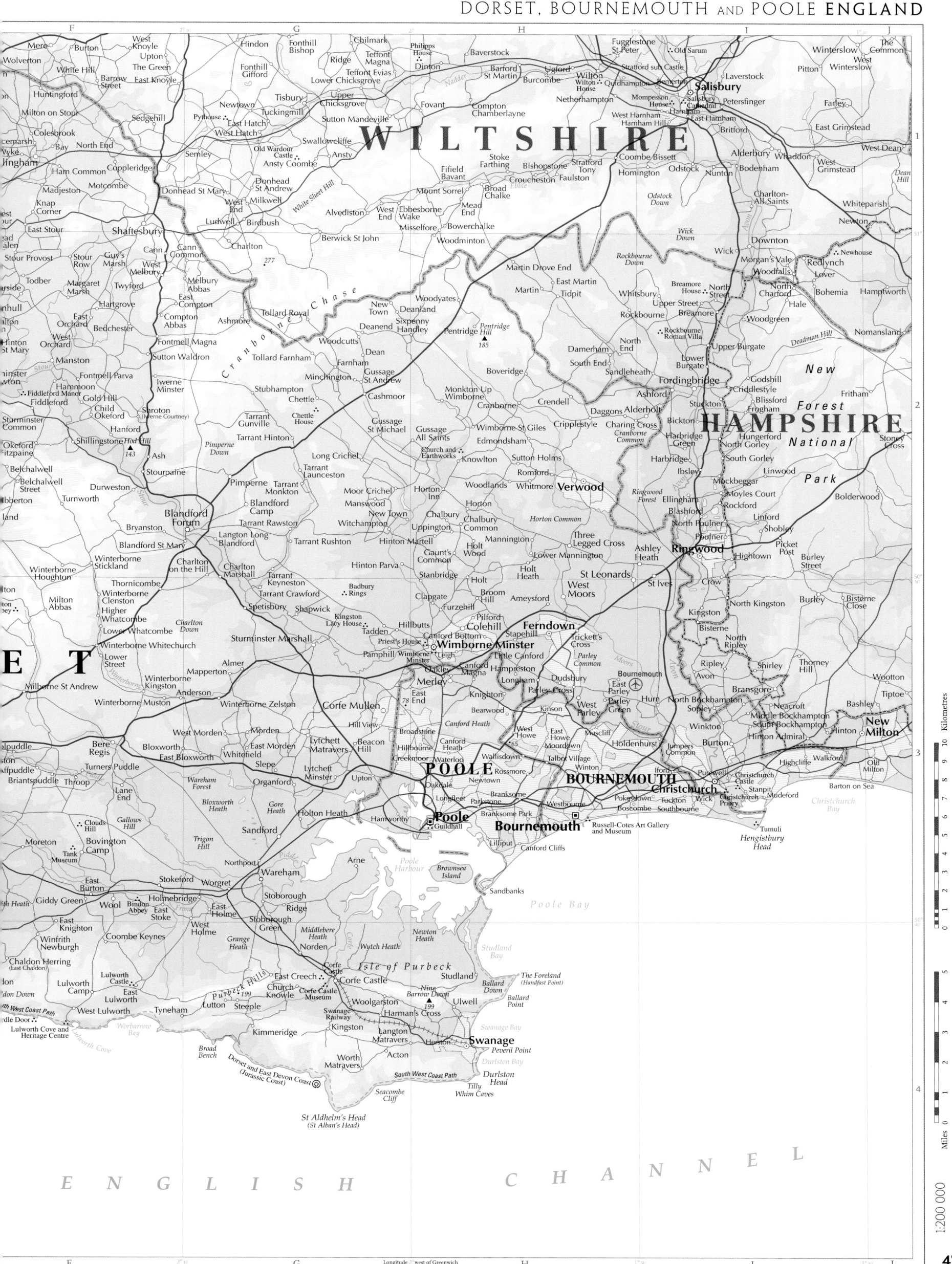

© Collins Bartholomew Ltd

1:200 000

HAMPSHIRE

Area Sq Km	3,738
Area Sq Miles	1,443
Population	1,285,900
County town	Winchester
Highest point	Pilot Hill (286 m), in North Hampshire Downs
Districts	Basingstoke and Deane; East Hampshire; Eastleigh; Fareham; Gosport; Hart; Havant; New Forest; Rushmoor; Test Valley; Winchester

Hampshire takes its name from 'Hampton', an early form of Southampton, the name now used to differentiate it from Northampton. Hampton itself means 'settlement on a promontory'. The abbreviation 'Hants' is derived from *Hantescir*, the name given to the county in the Domesday Book.

FAMOUS FOR

In 1382, William of Wykeham, Bishop of Winchester established 'St Mary College near Winchester', better known as **Winchester College**, one of the oldest schools in the country. Its motto is 'Manners makyth Man'.

The **Sandham Memorial Chapel**, near Burghclere, contains 19 spectacular murals featuring the daily life of World War I soldiers in Macedonia, created by the visionary painter Stanley Spencer between 1927 and 1933.

In the Great Hall, the only remaining part of the royal castle of **Winchester**, is a 600-year old representation of King Arthur's Round Table.

The **South Downs Way** starts near King Alfred's statue at City Mill in Winchester and finishes 160 km later in Eastbourne. The highest point on the walk is at Butser Hill (270 m).

In March 2010 the **South Downs National Park** was established, about one third of which is in Hampshire, stretching from the edge of Winchester to the Sussex borders.

Watership Down near Kingsclere in the North Hampshire Downs became immortalised in Richard Adams book, *Watership Down*.

In northern Hampshire are the remains of **Silchester**, an important Roman town that fell into ruins and was never built over. Its walls (over 2.5 km in length) survive, but little else above the ground. Excavation at the site has provided much information on how Roman towns were laid out.

FAMOUS PEOPLE

Henry III, King of England (1216–72), born Winchester, 1207.
Gilbert White, naturalist and clergyman, author of *The Natural History and Antiquities of Selborne* (1789), born Selborne, 1720.
Jane Austen, author, born Steventon, 1775.
John Arlott, cricket commentator, born Basingstoke, 1914.
Simon Gray, dramatist and writer, born Hayling Island, 1936.
Ian McEwan, author, born Aldershot, 1948.
Colin Firth, actor, born Grayshott, 1960.

"My admiration for the Forest is great; it is true old wild English Nature, and then the fresh heath-sweetened air is so delicious. The Forest is grand."
Alfred, Lord Tennyson, 1855

"This vale of Itchen is worthy of particular attention. There are few spots in England more fertile or more pleasant; and none, I believe, more healthy."
William Cobbett, 1830

The centre of Hampshire consists largely of chalk downs interspersed with fertile valleys. In the southwest is the New Forest, while in the northeast is the military area centred on Aldershot. The much indented coastline borders The Solent and looks across to the Isle of Wight. The principal rivers are the Itchen and Test, both chalk streams flowing into Southampton Water, and the Meon flowing into The Solent.

Hampshire is one of the oldest and largest counties in England. Traditionally the Isle of Wight was part of Hampshire, but it became a separate county in 1890. In 1974 Bournemouth, Christchurch and the area around them were transferred to Dorset. In 1997 the former county borough of Southampton and the district of Portsmouth became independent unitary authorities, and are described below. These changes have removed the main conurbations from the county. The northeast, around Basingstoke and Aldershot is the most densely populated and looks towards London, while the northwest is lightly populated downland and the New Forest in the southwest, bordering Dorset is a National Park. Its population has grown by about 10 per cent since 1991, ahead of the national average, to reach 1,285,900 in 2008, growing fastest in Winchester but actually declining in the Havant district. Its population is the third largest amongst the shire counties. The major towns are Basingstoke (90,171), Gosport (69,348), Waterlooville (63,558), Aldershot (58,170) and Farnborough (57,147). The county town of Winchester has a population of 41,420.

Economic activity within Hampshire reflects geographical differences in the county. The north east which initially grew in importance after the establishment of a military base at Aldershot in 1854, is also the base of various hi-tech industries, particularly in aerospace, based around Farnborough, where around a third of all workers are in hi-tech industries. The importance of the sea is most obvious in the development of Southampton and Portsmouth, but areas such as Havant and Gosport still owe some of their economic livelihood to the sea. Not every endeavour has lasted – Buckler's Hard, on the Beaulieu River in the New Forest saw major warship building during the Napoleonic War, drawing on the local supplies of timber but its prosperity was short-lived.

Winchester is the county town and has had a noble history. Originally a Roman base, it became capital of Wessex under King Alfred (AD 871–99), and it then became the capital of England until London displaced it in the 12th century. From this period come Winchester Cathedral, the longest medieval cathedral in Europe, and a jewel of Norman and Gothic style. The town now thrives as an administrative centre as well as the home of one of Britain's newest universities. Overall in the county, 25 per cent of employment is in retail, hotels and restaurants, 25 per cent in finance, IT and other business and nearly 23 per cent in public administration, education and health. Although much of the county is rural, fewer than 2 per cent of the population work on the land.

The most distinctive area of Hampshire is the New Forest, declared a National Park in 2005. It is the smallest National Park in Britain, but it has a long history – the area was originally established as a forest for hunting deer by the Norman kings, and, indeed, it saw the death in a hunting accident of William II (Rufus) in 1100. The area is a mixture of woodland, heathland and farmland. Because much of the land was poor, it was never intensively farmed and contains large expanses of unfenced grazing areas, home to over 4,000 New Forest ponies. The New Forest provides an example of how the English countryside looked before the Agricultural Revolution of the 18th century. As a reminder of more recent times, at Beaulieu within the New Forest, is the National Motor Museum.

Much of the county is open chalk downland that slopes gently down towards the coast. Within the downland are wooded valleys, particularly of the Test and Itchen rivers, famed for their trout fishing. In the east of the county, south of Alton, is Chawton, where Jane Austen worked on most of her books (her house is now a museum) and Selborne, where the detailed observations of nature by the rector, Gilbert White, helped establish the concept of the plants and animals depend upon each other, the basis of ecology.

King Alfred the Great statue, Winchester.

Winchester Cathedral

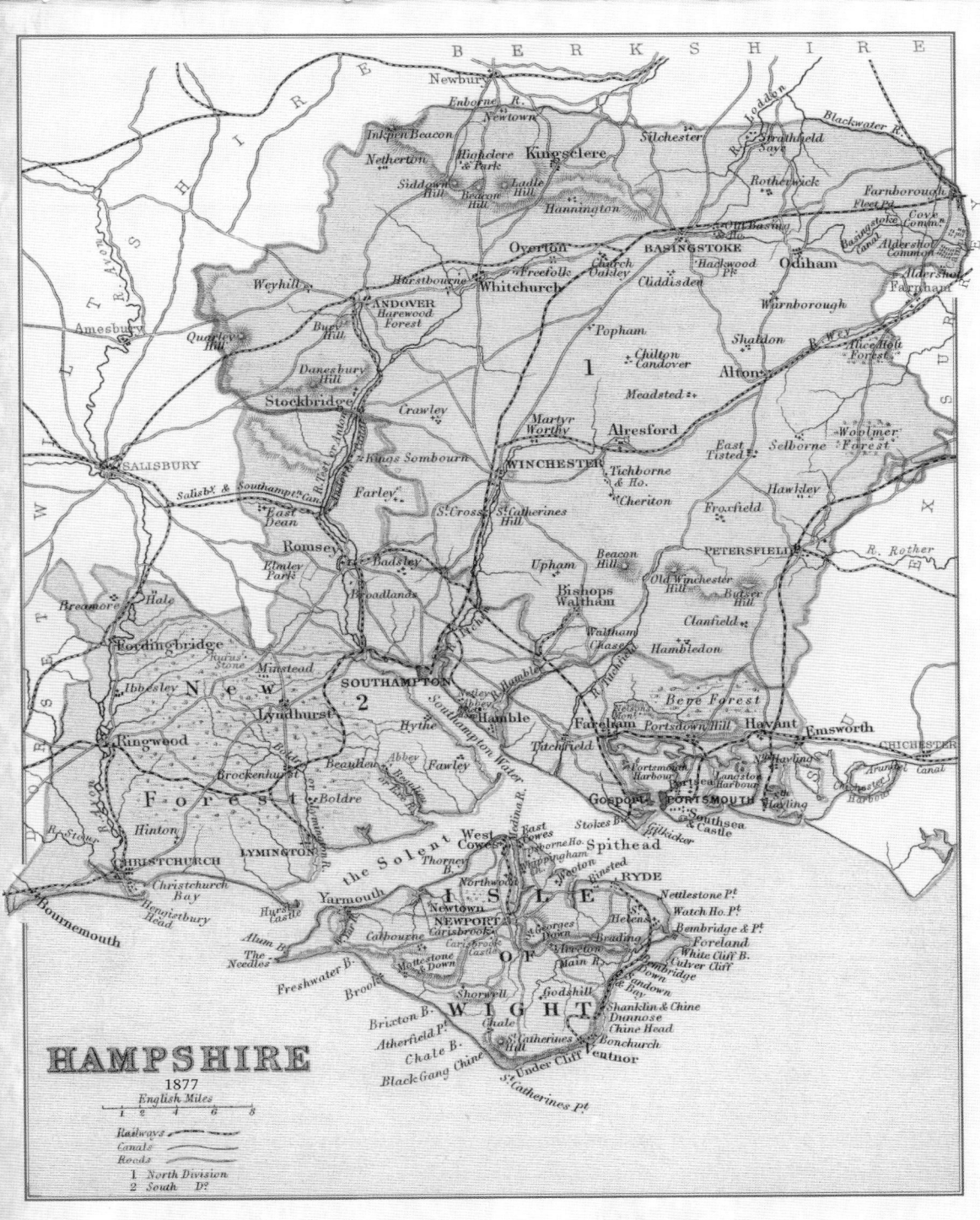

HAMPSHIRE
1877
English Miles

Railways
Canals
Roads
1 North Division
2 South D?

Bartholomew Gazetteer of the British Isles, 1887

HAMPSHIRE, *Hants, or Southampton, maritime co. (including the Isle of Wight), in S. of England; bounded N. by Berks, E. by Surrey and Sussex, S. by the English Channel, and W. by Wilts and Dorset; greatest length (exclusive of the Isle of Wight), N. to S., 46 miles; greatest breadth, E. to W., 46 miles; 1,037,764 ac., pop. 593,470. (The figures of ac. and pop. include the Isle of Wight.) Hampshire is undulating, finely wooded, and fruitful. Its coast line is very irregular, the principal indentation being Southampton Water. From Surrey and Sussex, NE. to Wilts and Berks, two ranges of chalk hills, known as the North and South Downs, traverse the co. In the W. is the New Forest, and in the SE. are the Forests of Bere and Waltham Chase. The Avon, Exe, Test, Itching, and Hamble are the chief rivers. The co. is noted for its agriculture, the wheat of Hampshire being especially prized. Upon the Downs are reared large flocks of the variety of sheep known as "Hampshire Downs", or "short wools". Pig breeding, and the curing of bacon, have long been large and lucrative branches of the county's industry.*

PORTSMOUTH.– *mun. bor., naval station, seaport, and par., Portsea Island, Hants, opposite the Isle of Wight, 18 miles SE. of Southampton and 74 SW. of London by rail – bor. 4320 ac. and 855 tidal water and foreshore, pop. 127,989; 3 Banks, 5 newspapers. Market-days, Tuesday, Thursday, and Saturday. Portsmouth is the largest naval establishment in the world, and the strongest fortified place in the kingdom, being protected by a complete chain of forts, including the forts at Spithead, the forts on the heights of Ports Down, and the lines of Hilsea. The harbour is 4 miles in length by nearly 2 miles in width, with an entrance 220 yards in breadth, permitting access to the largest vessels at low water.*

The New Forest National Park, Hampshire.

PORTSMOUTH

Area Sq Km   60
Area Sq Miles   23
Population   200,000
Highest point   Portsdown Hill (131 m)

FAMOUS FOR

Sir Arthur Conan Doyle wrote his first two Sherlock Holmes stories when he was practising as a doctor in **Southsea.**

The **Spinnaker Tower,** a viewing tower designed to represent the sailing heritage of the city, opened in 2005. It is 170 m tall – lifts will take you to the top in 30 seconds or you can walk up 570 steps

The *Mary Rose,* Henry VIII's flagship, capsized off Portsmouth on 19 July 1545, as the king watched. Its remains were brought back to the surface in 1982. A new museum housing the remains and thousands of artefacts will open in 2012.

FAMOUS PEOPLE

Isambard Kingdom Brunel, engineer and inventor, 1806.
Charles Dickens, author, 1812.
Leonard James (Jim) Callaghan, Baron Callaghan of Cardiff, Labour politician, Prime Minister (1976–9), 1912.
Richard Henry Sellers (Peter Sellers), comedian and actor, 1925.

Portsmouth is a unitary authority on the south coast of England surrounding the city of Portsmouth and bordered by Hampshire. Most of the city of Portsmouth is on Portsea Island, separated from the mainland by a narrow creek, crossed by a number of bridges, and so is the only British city built on an island. Only Inner London is more densely populated. The city of Portsmouth also includes Southsea. It was first granted a charter in 1194 and since 1997 the city has been a unitary authority. The value of its sheltered harbour was quickly recognised. The first docks were built in 1212 and it became the home of the Royal Navy. By World War I, the dockyards were the largest industrial site in Europe. It still remains a major dockyard for the Royal Navy as well as being a ferry and freight port. The Naval Dockyards are also a major tourist site for they contain HMS *Victory*, Nelson's flagship from the battle of Trafalgar, originally built in 1759–65, and HMS *Warrior*, the world's first iron-hulled, armoured and steam-powered warship. The city, badly bombed during World War II, has become a culturally diverse centre, attracting a wide range of industries which include financial services, distribution and hi-tech industries, as well as having its own university since 1992.

HMS *Warrior*

Spinnaker Tower, Gunwharf Quays.

SOUTHAMPTON

Area Sq Km   56
Area Sq Miles   22
Population   234,600
Highest point   Bassett Avenue, Bassett (82 m)

FAMOUS FOR

The **Old Bowling Green,** just outside the city walls is the oldest in the world, having been in regular use since 1299.

In 1912, the **RMS *Titanic*** sailed from Southampton on its fateful maiden voyage – 80 per cent of the crew came from the Southampton area and a third of all who perished when the ship struck an iceberg came from the city.

FAMOUS PEOPLE

Isaac Watts, author and hymn writer, 1674.
Sir John Everett Millais, artist, 1829.
Admiral John Jellicoe, 1st Earl Jellicoe, commander at the Battle of Jutland, the only World War I sea battle, 1859.
Alfred Hawthorne (Benny) Hill, comedian, 1924.
Ken Russell, film director, 1927.

Southampton is a unitary authority on the south coast of England surrounding the city of Southampton, and bordered by Hampshire. The city owes much to its position on a peninsula between the Itchen and the Test at the head of the deep Southampton Water. A port was established in the 8th century, and it gave its name to county of Hampshire. It has been a major port ever since the 11th century and it remains a key freight port for Britain as well as Northern Europe's busiest cruise port. The arrival of the railway from London in the 1840s saw it become the major transatlantic port, home to the Cunard Line. Water and the waterfront remain very important to the local economy, with marine technology, oceanography, boat shows and yacht races all prominent. The city is also a leading media, recreational, entertainment and retail centre, as well as the home of two universities, Southampton and Southampton Solent. The manufacturing base is more diverse than might be expected and major employers include the Ford Transit van factory and the Ordnance Survey. Even so, around 32 per cent of the population work in administration, education and health, 25 per cent higher than the regional average. The city was badly bombed in World War II and has suffered from much rebuilding, not always sympathetic. However about half of the city walls, completed around 1380, survive, including 13 towers and six gates.

Container and cruise ships in the busy port of Southampton.

ISLE OF WIGHT

Area Sq Km	395
Area Sq Miles	152
Population	140,200
County town	Newport
Highest point	St Boniface Down (241 m), near Ventnor

FAMOUS FOR

The 1970 **Isle of Wight Festival** was one of the largest rock festivals ever held, with upwards of 600,000 people attending. The Festival was revived in 2002 and is now held annually.

There are **red squirrels** but no grey squirrels or wild deer on the Isle.

In 1647, Charles I fled to the Norman castle of **Carisbrooke**, just south of Newport, initially hoping for protection but which instead turned into imprisonment leading up to his trial and execution in London in 1649. The castle is also famous for its donkey-powered water well.

The Needles are three 30 m tall chalk stacks in the sea at the tip of Alum Bay. None of them are needle-shaped – there used to be a fourth stack, called Lot's Wife, which was much more pointed, but it collapsed in a storm in 1764.

FAMOUS PEOPLE

Robert Hooke, scientist and architect born Freshwater, 1635.

Thomas Arnold, educationalist, headmaster, Rugby School, born East Cowes, 1795.

Sir Vivian Fuchs, polar explorer, born Freshwater, 1908.

Sheila Hancock, actress, born Blackgang, 1933.

Jeremy Irons, actor, born Cowes, 1948.

Anthony Minghella, playwright, and film director, born Ryde, 1954.

Its name is most likely derived from a Celtic word meaning 'place of the division', referring to the two arms of The Solent. It was known to the Romans as Vectis. It is the largest island in England and the ninth largest in Britain. Because of its defensive importance, it was considered as part of Hampshire from Saxon times until 1890, when it became a separate county, and today it is a unitary authority. The island is geologically diverse, composed of sedimentary rocks and contains many important fossil remains, and is almost divided in half by its main river, the Medina. Tourism flourishes owing to the mild climate and the natural beauty of the island. There are Royal associations as Queen Victoria lived and died at Osborne House in the north of the island. She and Prince Albert purchased Osborne in 1845, and Albert designed the Italian-style building that can be visited today. In 1856 the Royal Yacht Squadron was formed at Cowes, a place that is still renowned for its competitive yachting. There are ferries to Cowes from Southampton, to Ryde and Fishbourne from Portsmouth, and to Yarmouth from Lymington. There is also a hovercraft service from Southsea to Ryde, a crossing that takes 10 minutes – the first practical hovercraft was built at East Cowes in 1959 by Saunders-Rowe, under the guidance of Sir Christopher Cockerell.

The Needles, Alum Bay.

Red Squirrel

Isle of Wight hovercraft.

The southwest coast on the Isle of Wight.

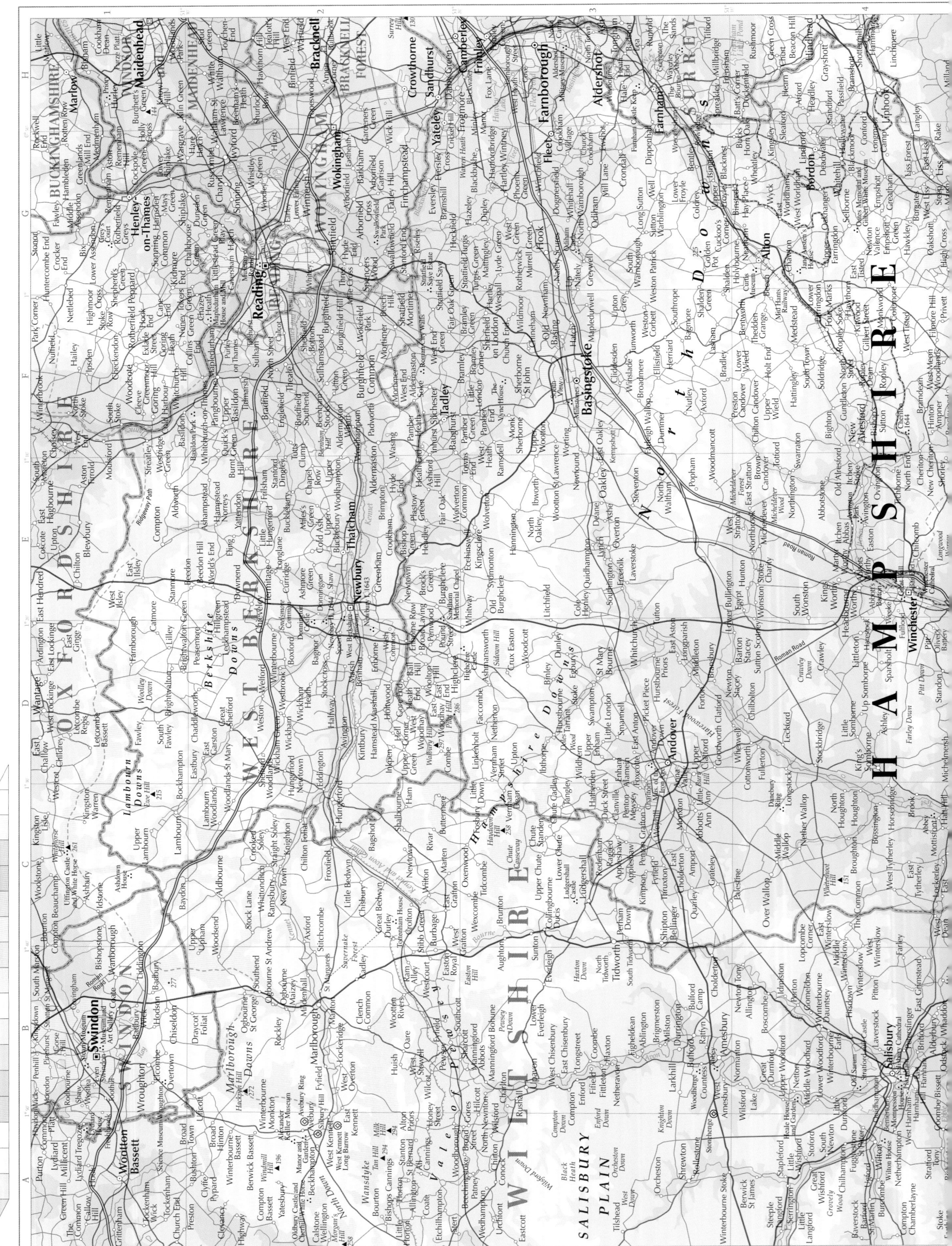

British National Grid projection

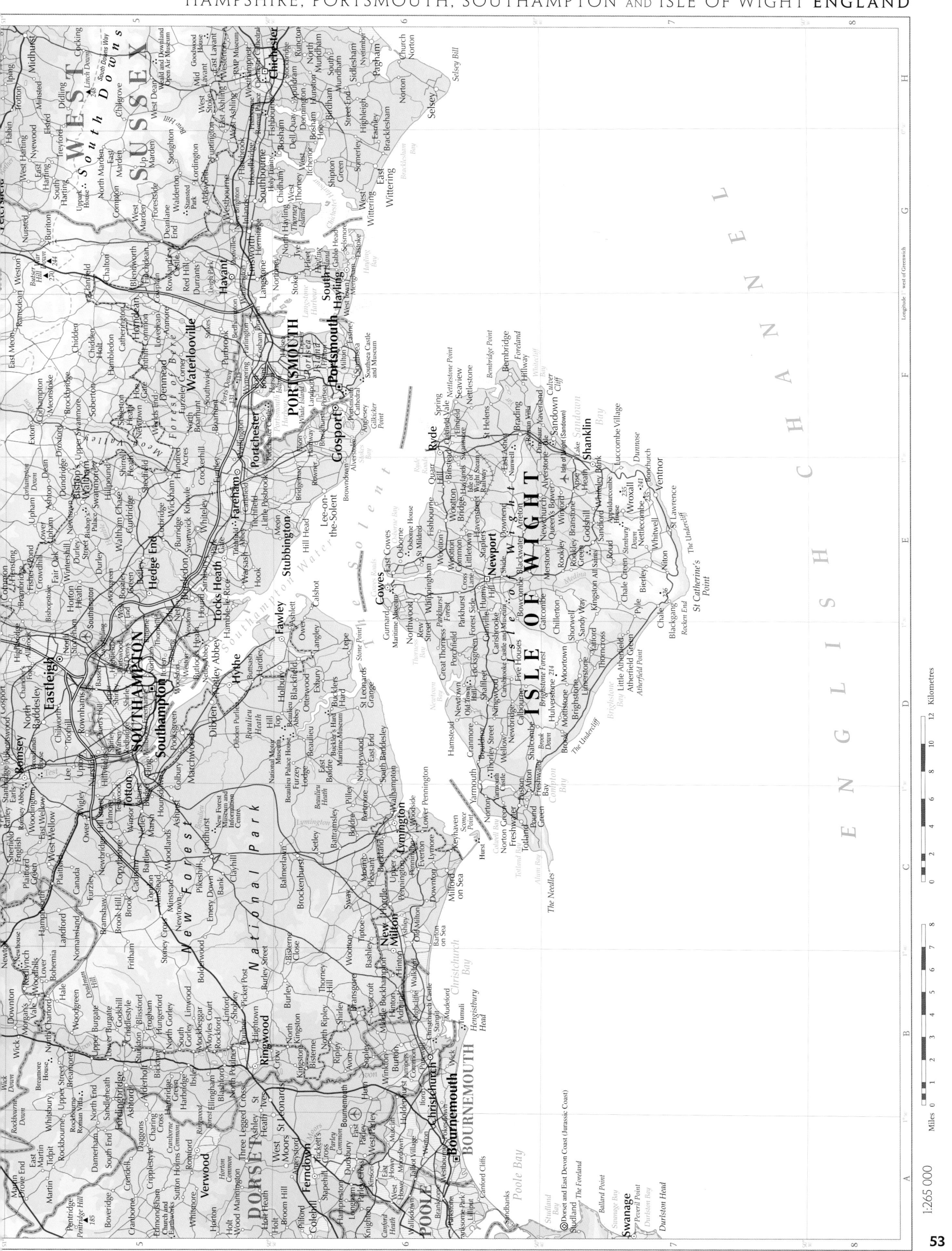

1:265 000

Miles 0 1 2 3 4 5 6 7 8

0 2 4 6 8 10 12 Kilometres

© Collins Bartholomew Ltd

WEST SUSSEX

Area Sq Km	2,025
Area Sq Miles	782
Population	781,500
County town	Chichester
Highest point	Black Down (280 m), near Haslemere
Districts	Adur; Arun; Chichester; Crawley; Horsham; Mid Sussex; Worthing

Sussex was the Anglo-Saxon name for the land of the South Saxons.

FAMOUS FOR

West Sussex's airport at **Shoreham**, is Britain's oldest airport still in use, having opened to flights in 1910, and it still has its Art Deco terminal building, opened in 1936.

Regis was only added to the name of **Bognor** in 1929 after George V had spent time there recovering from illness.

At **Bosham**, a village on Chichester Harbour, King Canute is alleged to have shown his nobles that even he could not hold back the sea, and from here in 1064 Harold Godwinson left to meet William in Normandy, an event illustrated in the Bayeux Tapestry.

Wakehurst Place just north of the village of Ardingly, is the country garden of the Botanic Gardens at Kew and is home to the Millennium Seed Bank, the project that aims to store seeds of 25 per cent of all the world's plants by 2020.

The church of St Mary at **Sompting** is one of the oldest in Britain and its unique tower, Germanic in its looks, is one of the greatest surviving achievements of Anglo-Saxon architecture.

The annual **Bognor** Birdman competition for human powered flying machines is held at the end of the pier – the 2009 record for the distance flown is 99.8 m.

FAMOUS PEOPLE

Percy Bysshe Shelley, Romantic poet, born Field Place, near Horsham, 1792.
Richard Cobden, economist and politician, born Heyshott, near Midhurst, 1804.
Dame Clara Butt, concert and opera singer, born Southwick, 1872.
Patrick Hamilton, novelist, born Hassocks, 1904.
Hammond Innes, author, born Horsham, 1913.
David Paul Schofield, actor, born Hurstpierpoint, 1922.
Anna Massey, actress, born Thakeham, 1937.
Dame Anita Roddick, founder of The Body Shop, born Littlehampton, 1942.
Jon Snow, television journalist, born Ardingly, 1947.

"Oh, Sussex, Sussex by the sea
Good old Sussex by the sea.
You may tell them all that we stand or fall
For Sussex by the sea."
W Ward-Higgs, 1907

"I had been training myself to see Chichester, the human city, the city of God, the place where life and work and things were all in one and all in harmony."
Eric Gill, 1940
Autobiography

"That part of England which is very properly called her Eden, that centre of all good things and home of happy men, the county of Sussex."
Hilaire Belloc, 1906

Sussex, the land of the South Saxons, was one of the earliest Anglo-Saxon kingdoms in the 6th century. It stretched along the south coast, but expansion northwards was limited by the heavily forested Weald. East-west communication has always been difficult, and, over time, the county divided into two areas, one based on Chichester in the west and one on Lewes, in the east. In 1888 the two counties of East Sussex and West Sussex were established. West Sussex has kept its county status since then, with seven district councils in the area. In 1974 Burgess Hill and Haywards Heath were moved from East to West Sussex.

North of a level coastal strip run the South Downs, a steep-sided chalk ridge, which is thickly wooded in parts. The remaining inland area, The Weald, is largely well-wooded farmland. The main rivers are the Adur and Arun, with its tributary the Rother; the Medway rises in the east of the county.

The population of West Sussex is 781,500 and is expected to grow by around 8 per cent by 2026. Overall, 23 per cent of the population is over 64 (compared with a national figure of 18 per cent), and this population is concentrated along the south coast, renowned for its mild climate and seaside towns – Shoreham (population 17,537), Worthing (96,964), Littlehampton (55,716) and Bognor Regis (62,141). The economic centre of the county is concentrated around Gatwick Airport, Britain's second largest airport, in the north east of the county, and the nearby towns of Crawley (100,547), Horsham (47,804) and Haywards Heath (29,110). While relatively slow communications from the coast to London have restricted commuting, the north of the county sees much greater movement of workers in and out of the county. At 23 per cent of jobs, employment in the public sector is significantly below the national average, while employment in transport and communications is over 60 per cent above the national average, indicating the major impact Gatwick has on the economy of West Sussex. Tourism provides around 9 per cent of employment, particularly along the coastal strip, while agriculture employs about 2 per cent of the workforce.

There are three major divisions in the county, the coastal strip, the South Downs and, beyond them, the Weald. The coastal strip is narrowest at the eastern end of the county, around Shoreham and widens to a broader area around Chichester, reaching down to Selse Bill, the southernmost part of the county, the site of the first cathedral in Sussex, founded by St Wilfrid around AD 680. Chichester, at the head of a large inshore harbour, was the Roman town of Regnum and the wealth of the area is shown by the substantial remains of a Roman palace at Fishbourne. The Roman street plan is still visible in part of the centre of Chichester, though the city is now dominated by its cathedral, construction of which began in 1075 with its spire completed in 1402. A beautiful and very English cathedral, it contains wonderful examples of modern art from Marc Chagall, Graham Sutherland, John Piper and Ceri Richards among others, all commissioned by its inspired Dean, Walter Hussey (1955–77). The city is also home to the county's only university.

The South Downs stretch across the county from the Hampshire border to East Sussex and now form part of the South Downs National Park. This rolling chalk downland is popular with walkers and the Weald and Downland Museum at Singleton, is home to over 50 historic buildings from the region that have been re-erected there. Close by is one of Britain's most famous racecourses – located on the top of the Downs, there have been horse races at Goodwood since 1802. Nearby is Goodwood House, surprisingly built of local flint, and home to a great private art collection.

North of the Downs lies the Weald, once a heavily forested area – its name meant wilderness. Timber from the forests was used in local ironworks until the early 18th century, and there are still large areas of ancient woodlands. Towards the Surrey border the land rises to its highest point in West Sussex at Black Down. Away from the woods, the landscape changes around Gatwick with all the industries and services needed to support the airport and the 35 million passengers who use it every year.

Chichester Cathedral

Triangulation point on the South Downs.

Wakehurst Place, near the village of Ardingly.

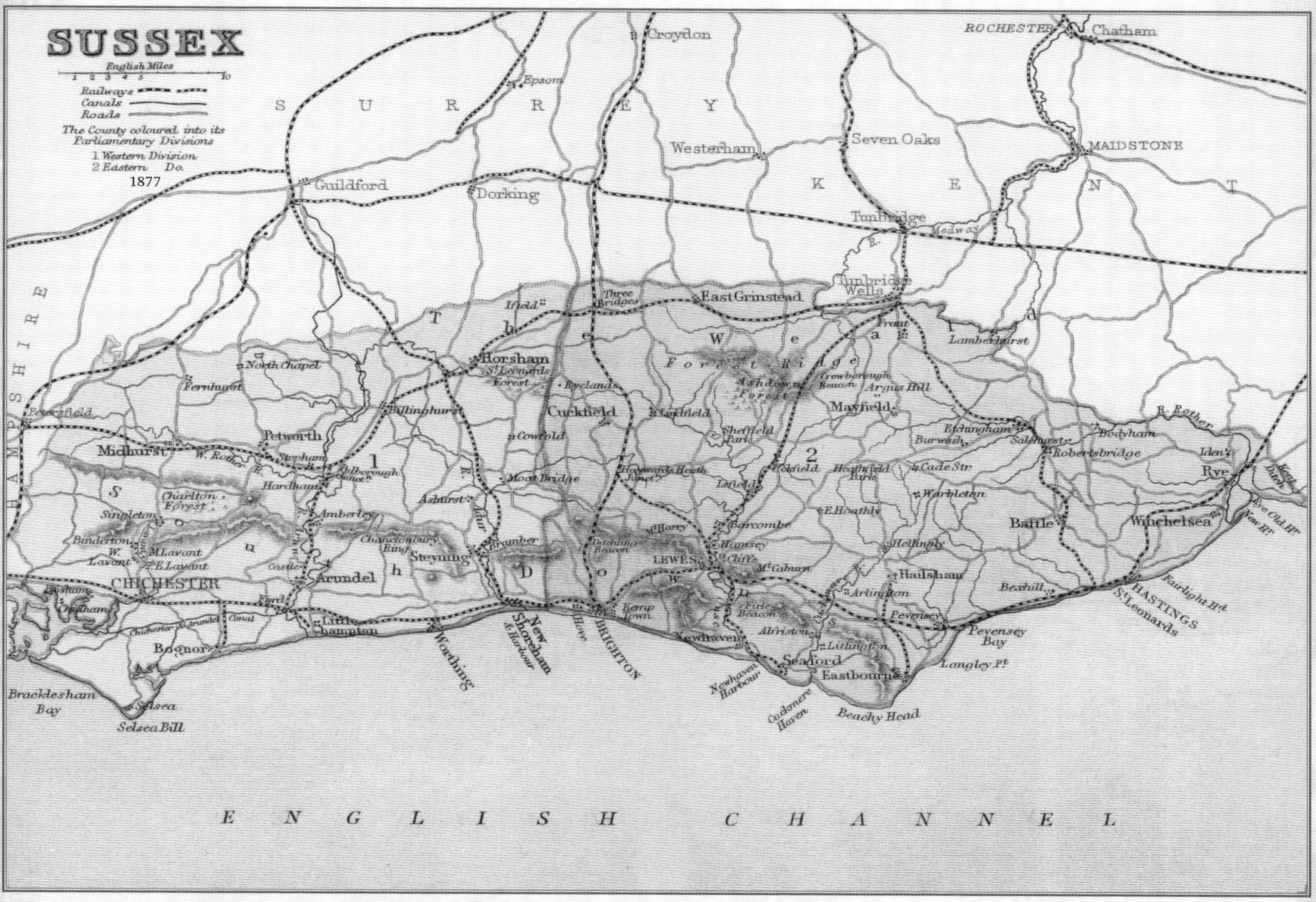

SUSSEX

English Miles
1 2 3 4 5   10

Railways
Canals
Roads
The County coloured, into its
Parliamentary Divisions
1 Western Division
2 Eastern   Do.
1877

Bartholomew Gazetteer of the British Isles, 1887

SUSSEX, maritime co. in SE. of England, bounded N. and NE. by Surrey and Kent, SE. and S. by the English Channel, and W. and NW. by Hants; greatest length, N. and S., 27 miles; greatest breadth, E. and W., 76 miles; area, 933,269 ac., pop. 490,505. From the Hants border, near Petersfield, to Beachy Head, the co. is traversed by the South Downs; to the N. of this range of chalk hills is the valley of the Weald, rising into the Forest Ridge on the NE., and sinking on the SE., towards the sea, into wide marshes. The rivers are not important; they are the Arun, Adur, Ouse, and Rother, all flowing S. to the English Channel. The principal means of communication are the railways; these belong chiefly to the London, Brighton,

and South Coast system, which has steamers running daily between Newhaven and Dieppe. The most fertile soil is the low land along the coast, which yields heavy crops of grain and hay; the South Downs are chiefly pastoral, and support a well-known breed of sheep to which they give name; the Weald consists generally of sandy or tenacious clays of a very indifferent description, but the clays produce a stiff soil, remarkably favourable to the growth of forest trees, particularly the oak, and about 150,000 acres are under wood; hops are grown in the eastern part of the co., which borders on the hop districts of Kent. Ironstone is abundant, and so long as wood only was used for smelting the co. was one of the chief seats of the British iron trade. "Sussex marble," a kind of limestone

containing fresh-water shells, is worked near Petworth. The mfrs. include woollens, paper, gunpowder, bricks and tiles, &c., but are not extensive. The seaports are now small and comparatively unimportant, but the mildness of the climate along the sea coast has led to the growth of numerous watering and bathing places and health resorts, including Brighton, Hastings, Eastbourne, Worthing, Seaford, Littlehampton, and Bognor. Sussex was the scene of much of the early history of the country, and is rich in archaeological remains. The co. contains 6 rapes, which comprise 68 hundreds, 2 liberties, the mun. bors. of Brighton, Hastings, Arundel, Chichester, Eastbourne, Lewes, and Rye. It is almost entirely in the diocese of Chichester.

Bognor Regis Pier

EAST SUSSEX

Area Sq Km	1,725
Area Sq Miles	666
Population	509,900
County town	Lewes
Highest point	Ditchling Beacon (248 m), on the South Downs
Districts	Eastbourne; Hastings; Lewes; Rother; Wealden

Sussex was the Anglo-Saxon name for the land of the South Saxons.

FAMOUS FOR

The most famous literary house in East Sussex is Lamb House in **Rye**, home to Henry James , E. F. Benson (the author of the *Mapp and Lucia* novels) and Rumer Godden. The house is now owned by the National Trust.

Bodiam Castle, built in 1385, is now one of the most picturesque castles in Britain, but it was a highly efficient defensive building, an early example of a castle built with gun ports.

On the side of Windover Hill is the 70-m-high **Long Man of Wilmington**, a figure of a man holding a stick in each outstretched hand. Its date is unknown and the cause of many theories. He won't vanish though, for the shape is now marked out in concrete blocks.

The model for Winnie the Pooh's '100 Aker Wood' was the ancient **Ashdown Forest**, an area of woods and heath in the north of the county, close to Hartfield, where A. A. Milne lived.

From west to east the chalk cliffs called the **Seven Sisters** are named Haven Brow, Short Brow, Rough Brow, Brass Point, Flat Hill, Bailey's Hill and Went Hill.

FAMOUS PEOPLE

John Fletcher, dramatist, born Rye, 1579.
Sir Frederick Gowland Hopkins, discoverer of vitamins and Nobel prize winner, born Eastbourne, 1861.
Frederick Soddy, discoverer of isotopes and Nobel prize winner, born Eastbourne, 1877.
Margaret Rumer Godden, novelist, born Eastbourne, 1907.
Elizabeth David, cookery writer, born Wootton Manor, near Folkington, 1913.
Sir Angus Wilson, writer, born Bexhill, 1913.
Charles Anthony Crosland, Labour politician and Cabinet minister, born St Leonards-on-Sea, 1918.
Angela Carter, novelist, born Eastbourne, 1940.
Sir David Hare, playwright, born Bexhill, 1947.
Josephine (Jo) Brand, comedian, born Hastings, 1957.

"On the road to Uckfield you cross Ashurst Forest, which is a heath with here and there a few birch scrubs upon it, verily the most villainously ugly spot I ever saw in England."
William Cobbett, 1822

"Choose ye your need from Thames to Tweed,
*   And I will choose instead*
Such lands as lie 'twixt Rake and Rye,
*   Black Down and Beachy Head."*
Rudyard Kipling, *Sussex*, 1900

Sussex, the land of the South Saxons, was one of the earliest Anglo-Saxon kingdoms in the 6th century. It stretched along the south coast, but expansion northwards was limited by the heavily forested Weald. East–west communication has always been difficult, and, over time, the county divided into two areas, one based on Lewes in the east and one on Chichester, in the west. In 1888 the two counties of East Sussex and West Sussex were established. In 1974 Burgess Hill and Haywards Heath were moved from East to West Sussex, and in 1997 Brighton and Hove became a unitary authority, leaving East Sussex divided into five districts.

The population of East Sussex is 509,870. Since 2001 the population has grown by 3.4 per cent, but it is expected to grow more slowly over the next 15 years. The mild climate and the attractive seaside towns of Eastbourne (population 106,562), Hastings (85,828), Bexhill (39,451), Seaford (21,851) and Peacehaven (17,541) make the area very attractive to pensioners, with over 23 per cent of the population over 64 and the highest percentage in Britain of people over 85, a trend which is only expected to continue over the coming years. Already there are three pensioners for every two children aged below 17.

The age profile of East Sussex influences its economic performance, allied with the fact that over 48,000 people commute out of the county to work. Over one third of the jobs are in the public sector compared with the national average of 27 per cent, while only 15 per cent work in finance, IT and other business compared with around 24 per cent in the region. Tourism provides nearly 10 per cent of jobs, with just 1 per cent in agriculture, for, while nearly 117,000 hectare are farmed, the land is not particularly fertile, with around 50 per cent of it being permanent grassland.

The South Downs provide the most dramatic landscape, cutting across to the north of Brighton, where Ditchling Beacon (248 m) is the highest point in the county, and reaching the sea at Beachy Head and the Seven Sisters. The cliffs rise to 162 m at Beachy Head, the highest chalk cliffs in Britain. To the east of Beachy Head is the resort and largest town in the county, Eastbourne, which developed as an archetypal Victorian resort after the arrival of the railway in 1849. To the east are the Pevensey Levels, flat land dominated by Pevensey Castle, a medieval castle built within the walls of a Roman fort, followed by the more modest sandstone cliffs between Bexhill and Hastings. The land drops again over the Brede Levels to the ancient port of Rye, once a Cinque Port, and now both a tourist attraction and the centre for Romney Marsh to the east.

Inland from the sea lies the farmland and woods of the Weald. The most famous place is Battle, about 10 km inland from Hastings, which is where the Battle of Hastings was actually fought. William of Normandy defeated Harold, the English king in 1066, one of the most important battles in European history. Lewes, originally a Saxon settlement, became a significant Norman town and was granted its charter in 1148. It effectively became the county town of eastern Sussex and this was formalised when the county was established in 1888, though, with a population of nearly 16,000 it is smaller than many other towns in the area.

Bodiam Castle, near Bodiam.

The Seven Sisters, South Downs.

BRIGHTON AND HOVE

Area Sq Km 85
Area Sq Miles 33
Population 256,600
Highest point West Hill (195 m)

FAMOUS FOR

Volk's Electric Railway, built in 1883 is the world's oldest operating electric railway. It runs for nearly 2 km along the edge of the beach.

The **Palace Pier** (now known as Brighton Pier) was opened in 1899 and is 524 m long. There have been many changes to it over the years, but it is now the only pier in Brighton in active use.

FAMOUS PEOPLE

Aubrey Beardsley, artist and illustrator, 1872.
Eric Gill, sculptor and artist, 1882.
Max Miller (*born* Thomas Henry Sargent), music hall comedian, 1894.
Gilbert Ryle, philosopher, 1900.
Sir Martin Ryle, astronomer and Nobel prize winner, 1918.
Steve Ovett, Olympic athlete, 1955.
Simon Cowell, television celebrity and entrepreneur, 1959.
Katie Price (also known as Jordan), celebrity, 1978.

"They must all go to Brighton. That is the place to get husbands."
Jane Austen (Lydia in *Pride and Prejudice*), 1813

"The Pavilion at Brighton is like a collection of stone pumpkins and pepper-boxes."
William Hazlitt, 1826

This unitary authority encompasses the seaside resort of Brighton, which is a major commercial and conference centre, and the surrounding area which includes Hove, Portslade-by-Sea, Portslade, Rottingdean, Saltdean and part of the South Downs. Brighton itself was a small fishing village, then called Brighthelmstone, which began to develop in the 18th century after a local doctor, Dr Richard Russell, recommended the healthy air and the virtues of sea bathing. The success of the town was sealed when the Prince of Wales started visiting in 1783 and had built the Royal Pavilion, initially a restrained building which was then rebuilt in an extravagant oriental design by John Nash between 1815 and 1822 – a building that has divided opinion ever since. With the arrival of the railway in 1841 its position as the most desirable seaside resort for London was secured and it has prospered ever since, not only as a commercial, conference and tourist centre but also as the home to two universities. It was granted city status in 2000.

Starlings over the disused, fire-damaged West Pier at Brighton.

Brighton Pier

The Royal Pavilion, Brighton.

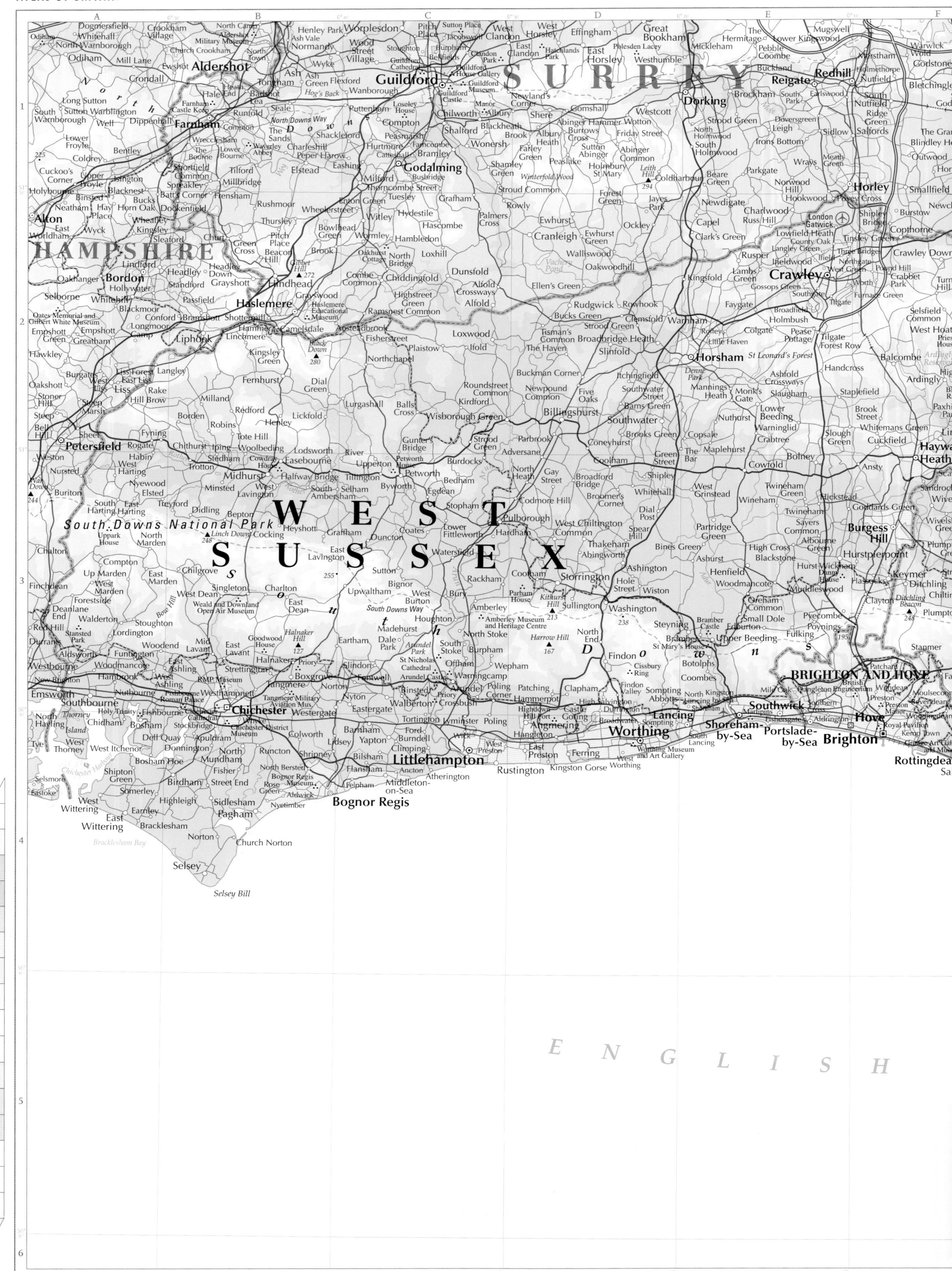

British National Grid projection

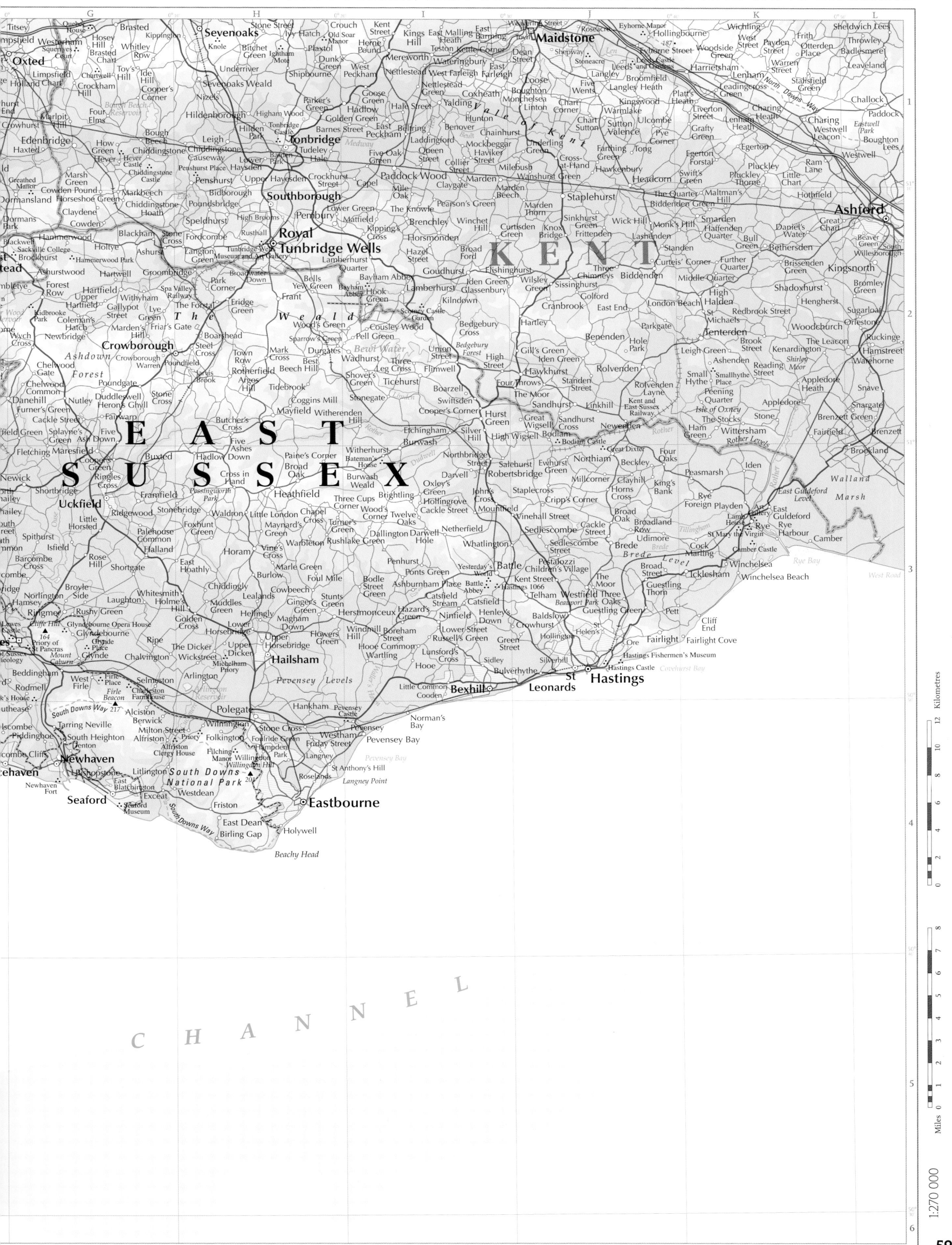

© Collins Bartholomew Ltd

Kilometres

12

1:270 000

Miles

CHANNEL

KENT

Area Sq Km	3,639
Area Sq Miles	1,405
Population	1,406,600
County town	Maidstone
Highest point	Betsom's Hill (251 m), near Tatsfield
Districts	Ashford; Canterbury; Dartford; Dover; Gravesham; Maidstone; Sevenoaks; Shepway; Swale; Thanet; Tonbridge and Malling; Tunbridge Wells

Kent is named after the Cantiaci, the tribes who lived here before the Roman invasion – indeed the name Cantium dates back to the 4th century BC. Their name may be derived from the Celtic word for 'border' or 'coastal land'.

FAMOUS FOR

A **Man of Kent** lives to the east of the Medway, whilst a **Kentish Man** lives to the west of the Medway.

In **Canterbury**, the Cathedral, St Martin's (in origin a 6th-century building and the oldest church in continuous use in Britain) and the ruins of St Augustine's Abbey form a UNESCO World Heritage Site.

Britain's only high speed railway link passes through the county from the Channel Tunnel at **Folkestone** 109 km to St Pancras Station in London, with trains travelling at 300 km per hour. It cost £5.8 billion to build and was the first new mainline route built since 1899.

Knowle, near Sevenoaks , was originally built by Thomas Bourchier, Archbishop of Canterbury, between 1456 and 1486, and over the centuries has been enlarged, especially by the Sackville family who lived there for over 400 years. It is sometimes called the 'Calendar House' because it 'has a room for every day, a stairway for every week and a courtyard for every day of the week'.

Mineral waters containing iron salts were discovered in **Tunbridge Wells** in 1606 and it quickly became fashionable because of its health-giving properties. The town prospered greatly in the 18th century, but did not receive its 'Royal' moniker until 1909.

The **Romney, Hythe and Dymchurch Railway** runs for 22 km between Hythe and Dungerness. It opened in 1926 and for many years was the smallest public railway in the world, with a track gauge of 381 mm (15 in).

FAMOUS PEOPLE

William Caxton, first British printer, born in the Weald, possibly Hadlow or Tonbridge, c.1415–22.
Christopher Marlowe, poet and playwright, born Canterbury, 1564.
William Harvey, discoverer of the circulation of the blood, born Folkestone, 1578.
Aphra Behn, writer and adventurer, born near Canterbury, 1640.
General James Wolfe, hero of the capture of Quebec, born Westerham, 1727.
William Pitt, the Younger, Prime Minister 1783–1801, born Hayes, 1759.
Siegfried Sassoon, poet and novelist, born Matfield, 1886.
Sir Edward Heath, Conservative politician, Prime Minister 1970–74, born Broadstairs, 1916.
Sir David Frost, broadcaster, born Tenterden, 1939.
Sir Michael (Mick) Jagger, lead vocalist the Rolling Stones, born Dartford, 1943.
Dame Kelly Holmes, Olympic athlete, born Pembury, 1970.

The traditional county of Kent, one of the early Anglo-Saxon kingdoms, used to stretch further into London. In 1889 the areas of Greenwich, Deptford, Woolwich, Eltham and Lewisham were moved into London, while in 1965 Bromley and Bexley were made London boroughs, and, in 1998, the area around Rochester and Chatham became the Medway unitary authority (which remains part of the ceremonial county of Kent). Even with these reductions, Kent is the most populous county in Britain with a population of 1,406,600, and it is also fast-growing – in the ten years from 1998, its population increased by nearly 100,000 (7.6 per cent). The west of the county is greatly influenced by London – over 80,000 people from Kent commute into London every day. Compared with other areas in the South East, employment within the public services is higher but lower in finance, IT and other business activity.

Kent has always been the gateway to Britain. The Roman invasion of AD 43 started at Richborough (where there are still remains of a Roman lighthouse). By the time of the Norman invasion, Dover was the pre-eminent port, a position confirmed by the imposing castle built by Henry II, greatly reinforced during the Napoleonic Wars and equipped with a major underground control centre during World War II. Today it looks out over the passenger and freight port, a port that has become less busy since the opening of the 50-km long Channel Tunnel (with its terminus near Folkestone). Kent's reputation as the 'Garden of England' is earned from its productive market gardening, fruit and hop production (the hops are dried in oast houses, so typical of the Kent landscape, and are then used in flavouring beer). Romney Marsh is used for extensive sheep-grazing.

The chalk ridge of the North Downs runs along the north side of the county, then southeast to Folkestone and Dover, ending in the iconic White Cliffs. The river Medway cuts through the chalk in the vicinity of Maidstone, and there are low lying areas to the east of Canterbury (here the area called the Isle of Thanet was once an island), on Romney Marsh in the south, and bordering the Thames estuary in the north, at Dartford and Gravesend and on the Isle of Sheppey, with its increasingly important port of Sheerness.

Whilst Maidstone, in the west of the county, is the county town, Canterbury was the capital of the ancient kingdom of Kent. It was to here that Augustine came bringing Christianity to the Saxons and founding his first church in 597 and establishing the Archbishopric of Canterbury, which has remained the pre-eminent position in the Church of England. Augustine's cathedral at Canterbury was destroyed by fire in 1067 and the current magnificent building was built in various stages from the 12th century until the completion of Bell Harry Tower in 1498. After the murder of Thomas Becket in the cathedral in 1170, his shrine became a major centre for pilgrimage until the Reformation. The city is home to three universities, dominating higher education in Kent.

The Kent coast has always been popular with Londoners. On the north coast is Whitstable (30,195), once famed for its oysters, Herne Bay (34,747) and Margate (58,465). After the coast turns south at North Foreland come the resorts of Broadstairs (22,712), a favourite of Charles Dickens, Ramsgate (37,967) and Deal (29,248), and then beyond the ports of Dover (34,087) and Folkestone (45,273), are Hythe (14,766) and then Dymchurch (5,693) and finally the isolated beach of Dungeness, shared with two nuclear power stations, one no longer active.

White Cliffs of Dover.

The keep of Dover Castle was built in the 12th century, on the site of earlier fortifications.

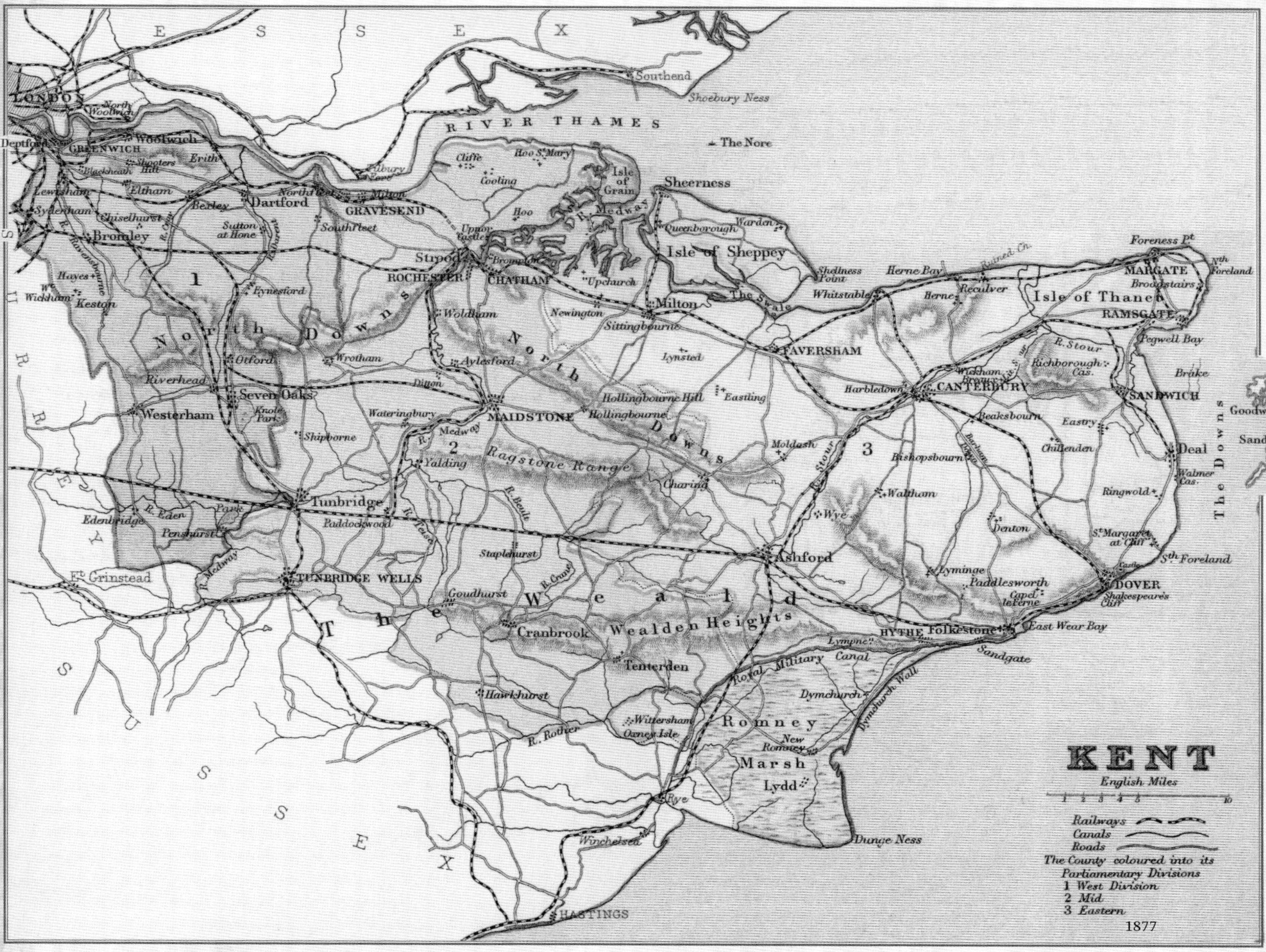

KENT
English Miles

Railways
Canals
Roads
The County coloured into its
Parliamentary Divisions
1 West Division
2 Mid
3 Eastern
1877

Bartholomew Gazetteer of the British Isles, 1887

KENT, *an important maritime county in SE. of England, bounded N. by the Thames and the North Sea, E. and SE. by the Strait of Dover, S. by the English Channel, SW. by Sussex, and W. by Surrey; greatest length, W. to E., 65 miles; greatest breadth, N. to S., 35 miles; 995,392 ac., pop. 977,706. The surface of the co. is hilly, being traversed E. and W. by the North Downs, a chalk range from 3 to 6 miles in breadth. On the N., along the shores of the Thames and Medway, there is a belt of marshland, which extends over a mile inland. The greater portion of the seaboard is washed by tidal water. Besides the Thames and Medway, the chief rivers are the Stour and the Darent. The soil is varied and highly cultivated, more especially in the valley of the Medway. All classes of cereals and root produce are abundant, as is also fruit of choice quality, and more hops are grown in Kent than in all the rest of England. The woods are extensive. The chief mfr. of the co. is paper, most of the mills being on the banks of the Medway, Cray, and Darent. The Government works and dockyards at Woolwich, Chatham, Sheerness, &c., employ an immense number of the inhabitants. Fishing is extensively prosecuted along the coast and in the estuaries of the rivers Thames and Medway, of which the oyster beds are especially famous. Historically Kent has greater associations than any other co. in England. The co. contains 5 lathes, 73 hundreds, 435 pars., and parts of 6 others, the Cinque Port Liberties of Dover, Hythe, and New Romney, the parl. bors. of Chatham, Deptford, Greenwich, Lewisham, and Woolwich, and the mun. bors. of Canterbury, Dover, Gravesend, Hythe, Maidstone, Rochester, Deal, Faversham, Folkestone, Margate, Sandwich, and Tenterden. It is almost entirely in the dioceses of Canterbury and Rochester.*

MEDWAY

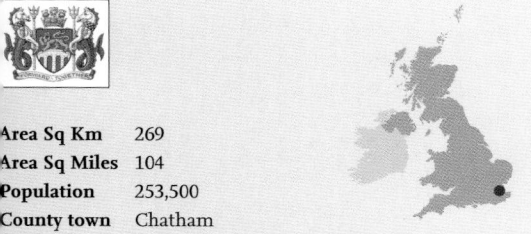

Area Sq Km	269
Area Sq Miles	104
Population	253,500
County town	Chatham
Highest point	Holy Hill (170 m) in the North Downs

FAMOUS FOR
Charles Dickens grew up in Rochester and Chatham, and many local places feature in his books. In 1857, he returned to the area when he moved to **Gad's Hill**, at Higham, just outside Rochester, and wrote many of his later books there.

HMS *Victory*, Nelson's flagship at Trafalgar, was built at the **Chatham** dockyard.

FAMOUS PEOPLE
William Adams, first Britain to reach Japan, born Gillingham, 1564.
Richard Dadd, artist, born Chatham, 1817.
Zandra Rhodes, fashion designer, born Chatham, 1940.

The unitary authority of Medway was formed in 1998 when the city of Rochester, with Chatham, Strood and Gillingham were merged together, in the process of which the cathedral city of Rochester lost its city status. It is the largest urban area in southeast England outside London, and its population is expected to grow to 300,000 by 2021. With good motorway and railway links and as part of the Thames Gateway Regeneration Programme, its economy is expected to grow at twice the national average. The history of the area is intimately connected to its location around the Medway estuary. Rochester is the site of the Roman crossing over the Medway and in AD 604 it became the second bishopric in England. Its importance was reinforced by its substantial Norman cathedral and castle. Neighbouring Chatham was the site of a Royal Dockyard by 1547 and it became essential for building and repairing ships for the Royal Navy until its closure in 1984. With many historic buildings the dockyard is now a major tourist attraction and is also the site of the Universities at Medway complex. The marshland to the north includes Kingsnorth Power Station and the Isle of Grain, but is mostly rural, and contains Northward Hill Nature Reserve, which is a haven for birds.

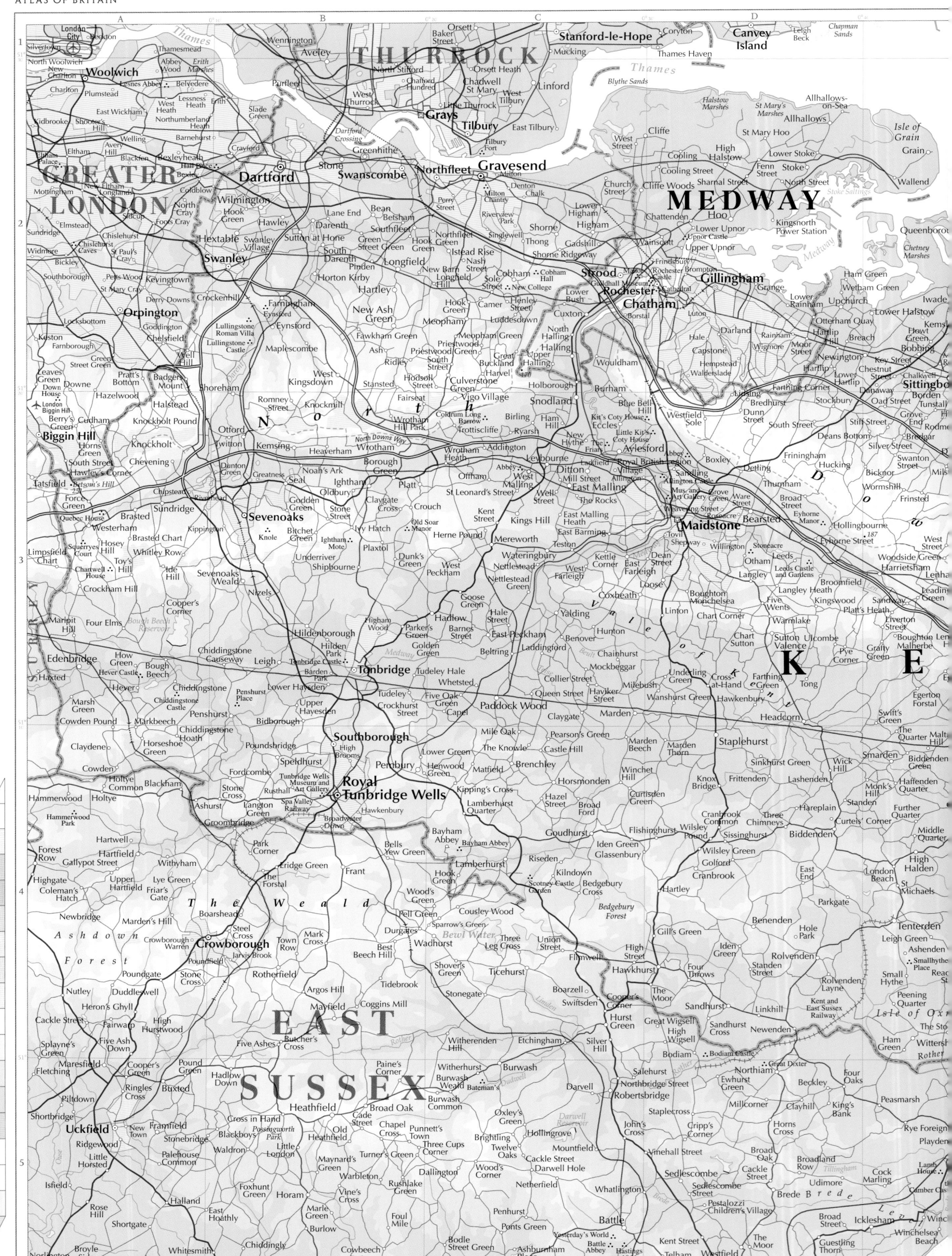

British National Grid projection

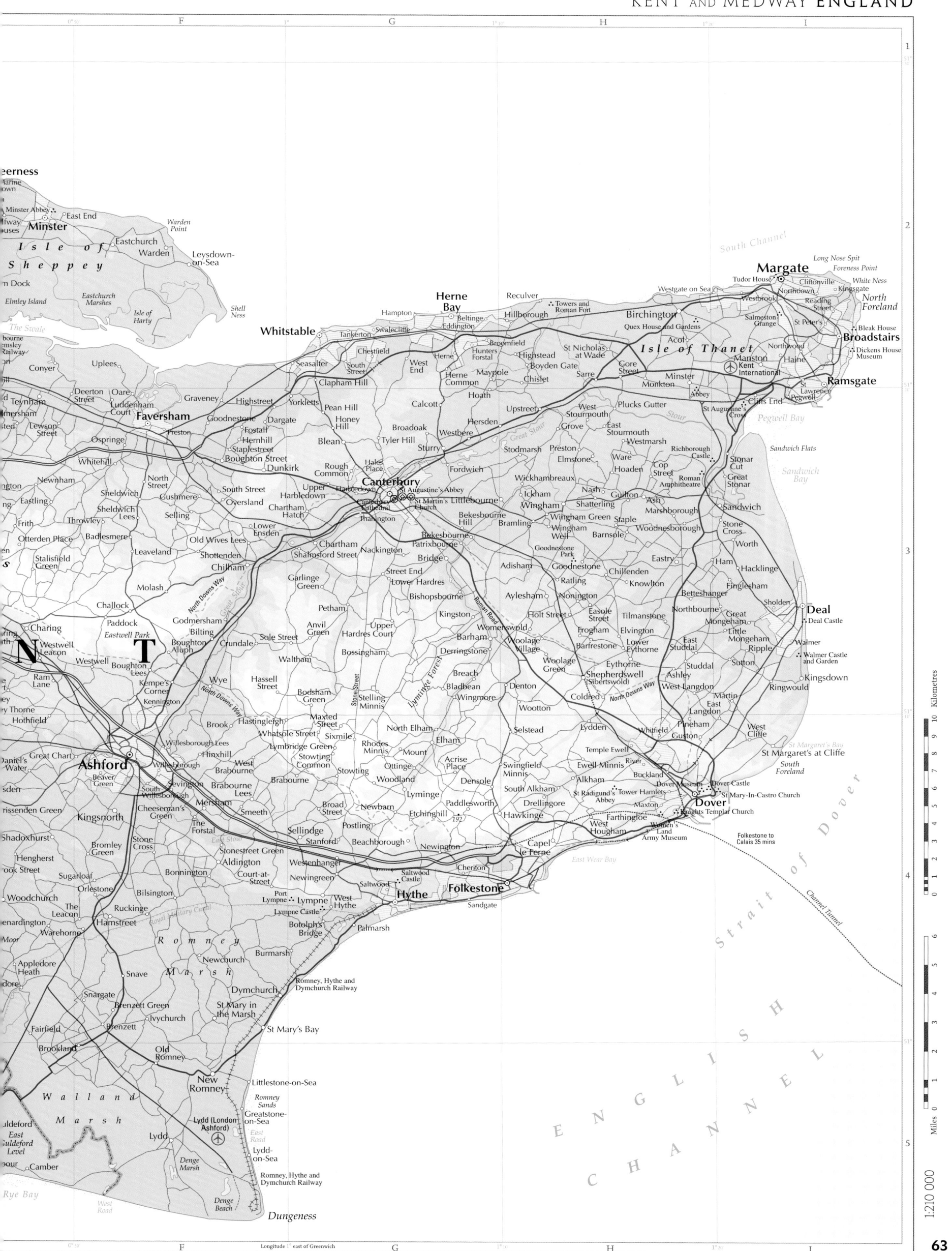

1:210 000

Longitude 1° east of Greenwich

© Collins Bartholomew Ltd

GREATER LONDON

Area sq. km	1,573
Area sq. miles	616
Population	7,619,800
Highest point	Westerham Hill (245 m) in the borough of Bromley
Highest point in Inner London	North End, Hampstead Heath (134 m) in the borough of Camden

City of London and London Borough Populations

Inner London	**3,029,600**
Camden	235,700
City of London	7,900
Hackney	212,200
Hammersmith and Fulham	172,200
Haringey	226,200
Islington	190,900
Kensington and Chelsea	180,300
Lambeth	274,500
Lewisham	261,600
Newham	249,500
Southwark	278,000
Tower Hamlets	220,500
Wandsworth	284,000
City of Westminster	236,000
Outer London	**4,590,200**
Barking and Dagenham	168,900
Barnet	331,500
Bexley	223,300
Brent	270,600
Bromley	302,600
Croydon	341,800
Ealing	309,000
Enfield	287,600
Greenwich	222,900
Harrow	216,200
Havering	230,100
Hillingdon	253,200
Hounslow	222,600
Kingston upon Thames	160,100
Merton	201,400
Redbridge	257,600
Richmond upon Thames	180,100
Sutton	187,600
Waltham Forest	223,200

The origin of the name of London is uncertain. Tacitus, the Roman historian, referred to *Londinium* around AD 115 but it is now thought that the name may have pre-Celtic origins, describing the location of the early settlement downriver from the last ford across the Thames at Westminster, and possibly meaning 'place at the unfordable river'.

Quotations

"When a man is tired of London, he is tired of life."
Samuel Johnson, 1777, as reported by James Boswell

"I don't know what London's coming to – the higher the buildings, the lower the morals."
Noel Coward, 1928

"That monarch of the road,
Observer of the Highway Code,
That big six-wheeler
Scarlet-painted
London Transport
Diesel-engined
Ninety-seven horsepower
Omnibus!"
Michael Flanders, 1956, *A Transport of Delight*

FAMOUS FOR

There have been royal palaces in London for nearly 1,000 years, starting with Edward the Confessor's **Palace of Westminster**. Today the official royal residences in London are **Buckingham Palace**, **St James's Palace**, **Clarence House** and **Kensington Palace**. Historic royal palaces, now no longer lived in by the royal family, include **Hampton Court Palace**, **The Tower of London**, **The Banqueting House** (all that remains of Whitehall Palace), **Kew Palace**, **Eltham Palace** and **The Queen's House** at Greenwich (all that survives of the Royal Palace of Greenwich), while Henry VIII's greatest palace, **Nonsuch**, on the London/Surrey border is no more – just the park survives.

The Palace of Westminster is now more commonly referred to as the **Houses of Parliament**. Edward the Confessor first built a palace at Westminster in the 11th century and it became the centre of royal power until the early 16th century, when Henry VIII moved to Whitehall Palace. The main survivor of the medieval palace is Westminster Hall, a magnificent great hall, first built by William II in 1097–99 and reconstructed by Richard II 200 years later. The remainder of the palace was destroyed in a fire in 1834, and the current building was built between 1840 and 1870.

Big Ben was originally the name given to the largest of the bells (which weighs in at 13.7 tonnes) in the clock tower of the Houses of Parliament. It is now used to describe the clock and even the whole tower. The chiming of the bells on the hour is one of the iconic sounds of London.

The **Royal Parks** provide London with over 2,000 ha of open green space, some of it right in the heart of Westminster and the West End, including St James's Park, Green Park, Hyde Park, Kensington Gardens and The Regent's Park (including Primrose Hill). The other Royal Parks are Richmond Park, Greenwich Park and Bushy Park.

London has many **covered markets** and **street markets**, some with histories that go back hundreds of years. Among the most well known are Bermondsey Market, Borough Market in Southwark, Brick Lane Market in Spitalfields, Brixton Market, Camden Lock Market in Camden, Camden Passage Market in Islington, Columbia Road Flower Market, Leadenhall Market in the City, Petticoat Lane Market, Portobello Road Market in Notting Hill, Shepherd's Bush Market, Spitalfields Market and Strutton Ground in Victoria. Some markets specialize in food, clothes or antiques and most have special opening times and days.

Covent Garden, originally a 'Convent Garden' owned by Westminster Abbey, used to be the site of London's main fruit and vegetable market, which moved to Nine Elms in 1973. The market building, sitting in the middle of a square at the back of the Royal Opera House is now a very popular shopping area and meeting place.

The **Thames** provides a natural division between the historic centre of London on the north bank and the less familiar areas south of the river, and is crossed by a number of important road and rail bridges.

London Bridge is close to the site of the Roman bridge across the Thames. In medieval times the old London Bridge was lined with houses. A new stone bridge was built in 1831. It was demolished in 1967 and sold to Lake Havasu City in Arizona, where it was rebuilt. The current London Bridge opened in 1973.

The **Millennium Bridge**, a pedestrian bridge between St Paul's and Tate Modern, the former Bankside power station, had a most inauspicious opening in 2000 – its innovative suspension design could not manage the large number of people crossing the bridge and it started to wobble. Within days it closed but it has since been modified and now provides a great way to cross the rive

The **London Eye** on the south bank of the Thames was the world's largest Ferris wheel when it opened in 2000. affords panoramic views over the city.

The **Millennium Dome** was built to house the Millennium Exhibition but now covers The O2, an entertainments area including an indoor arena.

The most historically important church in London is **Westminster Abbey**, founded in 960 by King Edgar. It has been used for coronations since 1066 and today's building was rebuilt in the soaring French gothic style by Henry III in the mid-13th century. Since Henry's burial there in 1272 it has become the principal place for royal burials and, more recently, for remembering the great public servants, artists, writers and scientists of the nation.

The great Christian religious buildings of London include **Westminster Abbey**, **Southwark Cathedral**, **St Paul's Cathedral**, **Westminster Cathedral** (Roman Catholic), **Wesley's Chapel** (the mother church of Methodism worldwide), **St Martin-in-the-Fields** by Trafalgar Square, the medieval round **Temple Church** Holborn, and over twenty-five surviving whole or in pa churches designed by Sir Christopher Wren

The **London Underground** is the oldest underground railway in the world, the first line having opened in 1863 between Paddington and Farringdon Street. It no carries 1,073 million passengers a year over a network of 400 km of track with 275 stations; 45 per cent of the network is in tunnels.

There are many **national museums** in London, includin the British Museum, the British Library, the Imperial War Museum, the National Gallery, the National Portrai Gallery, the Natural History Museum, the Science Museum, Tate Britain, Tate Modern and the Victoria an Albert Museum, as well as scores of more specialized museums, art galleries and exhibition venues.

The main airport for London is **Heathrow Airport**, to the west of the city but still within Greater London. Grass runways were first used in World War I and it was developed in 1930 by Richard Fairey to test the aeroplanes he built. At the end of World War II, it was being converted into a major RAF airfield, and became a civil airport in 1946, with 63,000 passengers using it i its first year. In 2009 nearly 66 million passengers pass through the airport, using 90 different airlines and flying to or from 179 different destinations.

The **Metropolitan Police Service** was formed in 1829 b Sir Robert Peel (hence the early nickname of 'Peelers'). Its headquarters were in Whitehall Place and a police station was established at the back of the building, wit an entrance on **Scotland Yard**, a name now synonymou with the organization. In 1890 'the Met' moved to a ne building on the Embankment, 'New Scotland Yard' an they moved again in 1967 to their current headquarter still called New Scotland Yard, just off Victoria Street.

Many of the famous names in **London shops** have had a long history: Fortnum and Mason was founded in 1707, William Hamley's toyshop, then called 'Noah's Ar was founded in 1760, Benjamin Harvey founded a stor in 1813, and in 1820 his daughter and her husband, Colonel Nichols began to run Harvey Nichols; Harrods was founded in 1849, John Lewis in 1863, Peter Jones in 1871 in Hackney and in 1877 at its present site, Liberty's in 1874 and Selfridges in 1909.

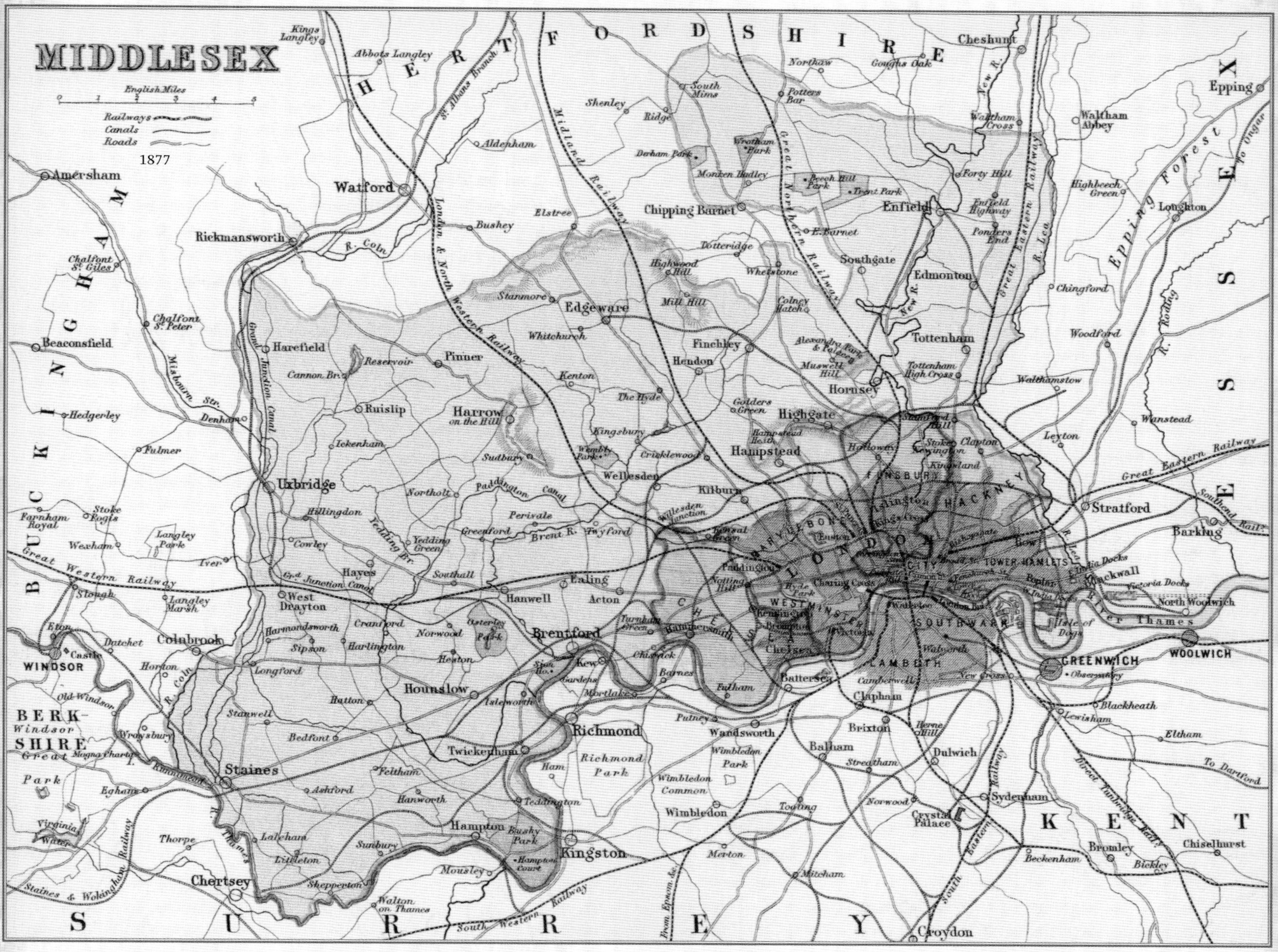

MIDDLESEX

English Miles

Railways
Canals
Roads

1877

Bartholomew Gazetteer of the British Isles, 1887

MIDDLESEX, south-midland co. of England, bounded N. by Herts, E. by Essex, W. by Bucks, and S. by the river Thames, which separates the county from Surrey; greatest length, NE. to SW., 24 miles; greatest breadth, N. to S., 18 miles; area, 181,317 ac.; pop. 2,920,485. Excepting Rutland, this is the smallest of the English counties; but as it contains the greater part of London, its population is second only to Lancashire, which has the highest position in point of numbers. It is the metropolitan county of England. The appearance of the country is generally flat, with slight elevations on the Herts border and in the N. suburbs of London. The Thames, and its affluents the Colne, Lea, and Brent, are the only rivers, although there are several smaller streams in the co. Middlesex is likewise traversed by the Grand Junction, Paddington, and Regent Canals, also by the New River; an artificial watercourse constructed in the reign of James I. in connection with the water supply of the metropolis. The London clay forms the greater part of the soil, so that it is generally poor for farming operations except in some places on the banks of the Thames. Farming is carried on with much spirit, and with scientific attention. A large number of market-gardens, in connection with the metropolitan supplies are to be found in the co. The co. comprises 6 hundreds, 222 pars., the parl. bors. of London City, Bethnal Green, Chelsea, Finsbury, Fulham, Hackney, Hammersmith, Hampstead, Islington, Kensington, Marylebone, Paddington, St Pancras, Shoreditch, Tower Hamlets, and Westminster. It is mostly in the diocese of London.

O2, formerly the Millennium Dome, Greenwich.

Tower of London

The settlement of London is thought to have started with the arrival of the Romans, who, by AD 50, had established themselves on the low-rising hills now known as Ludgate Hill and Cornhill. The city appears to have been deserted after the Romans left in the 5th century, with a new settlement constructed to the west, around the site of Covent Garden, in the 7th century. This new settlement was abandoned after Danish attacks in the 9th century, but by 886 King Alfred was encouraging the re-establishment a town within and protected by the old Roman walls. At the time of the Norman Conquest, London was well established, and, in addition, King Edgar had already built the first Westminster Abbey and a royal palace at Westminster, then a settlement distinct from London. William the Conqueror reinforced Norman rule by building the main keep (the White Tower) of the Tower of London. By 1200 its population may have been 40,000 and perhaps up to 100,000 a century later. The rule of the Tudors and Stuarts saw prodigious growth, the population reaching 200,000 in 1600 and over half a million in 1700. The growth of a colonial empire and of worldwide trading stimulated by the Industrial Revolution saw the population reach 1,117,000 in the first census in 1801 and 6,686,000 by 1901. Before World War II it had reached 8,700,000, after which it fell back to

6,700,000 by 1988. Since then it has grown again, and has become a most cosmopolitan city of 7,620,00 in 2008 with a predicted population of 8,390,000 in 2021 and 8,857,900 in 2031.

The government of London was initially focused on the City of London, within its Roman walls, and various forms of local government existed before the Norman Conquest. William I granted a charter to the city and greatest power was vested in elected Aldermen from whose number a mayor (from around 1280, a Lord Mayor) was selected. With the rapid growth of London, however, increasing numbers of people lived outside the restricted area of the City of London in parishes in the counties of Essex, Middlesex, Hertfordshire, Surrey, and Kent. While the City of London expanded into Southwark in 1327, various villages and related bodies administered the rest of London. These patchwork arrangements were thoroughly overhauled in 1888 when London County Council was created and, by 1900, twenty-eight boroughs operated within the council area. In 1965 the Greater London Council was created with thirty-three authorities underneath it. Primarily for political rather than administrative reasons the Greater London Council was abolished by the Conservative government in 1986 and all the boroughs effectively became unitary authorities. In 2000 the Labour

government established a Greater London Authority with strategic responsibilities in policing, transport and economic planning. There is a small elected Assembly headed by a Mayor, directly elected by the people of Greater London. It is based at City Hall, on the south bank of the Thames in Southwark.

Inner London

This term is used loosely to describe the boroughs of the core area of London. During the lifetime of the Greater London Council there was a formal grouping of inner London boroughs, who, for example, worked together in the Inner London Education Authority. The slightly different categorization used here is that of the Office for National Statistics.

The borough of **Camden** stretches from the central London area of Holborn up to the open expanses of Hampstead Heath. It contains some of the most desirable residential accommodation in inner London and some great poverty – a boy born in Hampstead has a life expectancy eleven years longer than a boy born near St Pancras. Among places within the borough are Lincoln's Inn Fields (including the Sir John Soane's Museum), the British Museum, the British Library, and the central buildings of the University of London in the Bloomsbury area, the national and international train termini at Euston, St Pancras and King's Cross, and, north of Regent's Park, the areas of Camden Town, Kentish Town and Hampstead.

The **City of London** claims to be the oldest continuous municipal democracy in the world. Its residential population is that of a small town but its working population is over 320,000, more than 80 per cent of whom work in finance, IT and other business. The City of London is home to one of the world's major financial centres and includes the Bank of England, the London Stock Exchange and the headquarters of many financial institutions, although some have left the City and moved into redeveloped areas of London dockland at Canary Wharf. The City (the 'Square Mile') is based on the area of the original Roman city and has been at the heart of the development of London ever since. The area was devastated by the Great Fire of London in 1666 from which emerged its great architectural treasures including St Paul's Cathedral and many parish churches designed by Sir Christopher Wren, the Monument, close to London Bridge (marking the spot where the fire began), the Mansion House and the Guildhall. It contains the rail termini of Liverpool Street, Fenchurch Street and Cannon Street.

Buckingham Palace

e borough of **Hackney** is northeast of the City of
ndon and is one of the more deprived London
roughs. It includes the areas of Hackney itself,
oxton, Shoreditch, Stoke Newington and the open
ea of Hackney Marshes in the Lea Valley, site of some
the 2012 Olympic Games venues. The borough has a
ry diverse population, with under half the population
ing of white British ethnicity. There are large
mmunities of ethnic Black, South Asian, Chinese and
rkish people. The public sector is a larger employer
an the average for London. The borough is home to
e Geffrye Museum of decorative arts, housed in the
rly 18th century Ironmongers' Company Almshouses,
e Hackney Empire, the greatest surviving music
ll, opened in 1901, and, in Hoxton, a very lively
ntemporary art scene.

e borough of **Hammersmith and Fulham** has
rontage along the Thames from Fulham to
mmersmith and also includes Shepherds Bush,
d Oak Common and West Kensington. The area is
pular with students and young adult workers and is
t as racially diverse as some London boroughs. The
ployment mix is fairly typical of London apart from
media, influenced by the BBC's Television Centre at
ite City, the home of BBC Television. Three major
otball teams (Chelsea at Stamford Bridge, Fulham
Craven Cottage and Queen's Park Rangers at Loftus
ad) are based in the borough, while the stadium at
ite City was host to the 1908 Olympic Games – its
e is now part of the BBC's Media Centre. The most
portant historic building is Fulham Palace, built in
95 for the Bishop of London and now a museum.
e Dove, a 17th century pub by the Thames in
mmersmith, is one of London's oldest and has been
quented by literary figures over the centuries.

e borough of **Haringey,** to the north of central
ndon, includes Highgate, Hornsey, Tottenham and
ood Green and stretches from the affluent areas
se to Hampstead Heath eastwards to the low-lying
d of Tottenham Hale in the Lea Valley. The borough
one of the most diverse in London, and just over
per cent of the population of white British ethnic
igin; over 130 different languages are used in the
mes of the borough's school pupils. It is also one of
e most deprived boroughs, with higher than average
employment and with nearly half as many jobs in the
ance, IT and other business (18 per cent) as
London average. Tottenham Hotspur's football
ound at White Hart Lane and the Alexandra Palace
Ally Pally), opened in 1873 as a great centre for
pular entertainment, and from where in 1936
e world's first television service was broadcast,
both in the borough.

e borough of **Islington** stretches from Farringdon
d Finsbury, close to the City of London, through
ington itself and Highbury and up to Holloway and
fnell Park. The business activities of the City flow over
to the borough and over 43 per cent of all jobs are in
ance, IT and other business, well over the average
London as a whole. With a resident population of
0,000 and nearly 188,000 jobs in the borough, many
rkers commute into Islington to work. Around
per cent of the population come from Black and
nic minority communities and there are also
nificant populations of Turks, Kurds and Cypriots.
e borough is home to the Sadler's Wells theatre in
erkenwell, the Almeida theatre in Islington, the City
iversity, the Holloway Road campus of London
etropolitan University, with its graduate centre,
signed by Daniel Libeskind, and the Emirates
adium, home of the Arsenal football club. Two of
ndon's prisons, at Pentonville and Holloway, are also
the borough.

e **Royal Borough of Kensington and Chelsea** extends
m the Thames at Chelsea, through Kensington to
olland Park and Notting Hill and beyond to North
nsington and Kensal Town. It is the most densely
pulated local authority area in Britain, with some of

Tower Bridge

Britain's most expensive housing in Chelsea and South
Kensington and with areas of real deprivation in the
north of the borough. Tourism accounts for around
20 per cent of jobs (nearly three times the London
average), influenced by the Victoria and Albert Museum,
the Natural History Museum and the many hotels in
the borough. It is also home to the Royal Hospital,
whose noble building designed by Sir Christopher
Wren welcomed its first military veterans ('Chelsea
Pensioners') in 1689, the royal palace of Kensington,
and internationally renowned Imperial College, the
Royal College of Music and the Royal College of Art.
In the 19th and first half of the 20th century, Chelsea
was home to many famous artists and writers. Europe's
largest street party, the Notting Hill Carnival, is held at
the end of August every year.

The borough of **Lambeth** takes in the south bank of the
Thames from Vauxhall to the South Bank Centre and
then stretches south in a narrow strip incorporating
Kennington, Stockwell, Clapham, Brixton and
Streatham. It is one of London's most diverse boroughs –
at the 2001 census around 38 per cent of the population
were from Black and ethnic minorities. It was classed as
the nineteenth most deprived local authority in England
in 2007 and contains great disparities of wealth within it.
The largest employment sector is public administration,
education and health, providing nearly 35 per cent of
all jobs. Lambeth Palace, the official residence of the
Archbishop of Canterbury, is by the Thames at Lambeth
Bridge. Many visitors to the borough go to the South
Bank Centre, home to the Hayward Gallery and the

Royal Festival Hall, to the neighbouring London Eye, the
world's largest Ferris wheel when it opened in 2000, or to
the Old Vic Theatre. The railway terminus of Waterloo is
in Lambeth, as is the Oval Cricket Ground.

The borough of **Lewisham** is to the south of the river,
with a short river frontage at Deptford. It then extends
south to include New Cross, Lewisham, Blackheath,
Catford, Forest Hill and Sydenham. It has a growing and
diverse population, with one in four of the population
aged under 19 and over 40 per cent of residents from
Black or ethnic minority communities. The largest
employment sector is public administration, education
and health, which provides nearly 39 per cent of all
jobs (compared with a London average of 22 per cent).
The borough is primarily residential and many of its
residents work in other areas of London. Goldsmiths'
College, internationally renowned for its creative art
courses, and the Laban, one of the world's finest dance
training institutions, housed in a stunning new building
at Creekside, are in the borough.

The borough of **Newham** is to the east of Tower
Hamlets. Its southern limits are by the Thames, where,
at Silvertown, is the Thames Barrier, built to protect
London from tidal surges. The huge Royal Docks were
built here between 1855 and 1921 on former marshland.
Once central to the economic life of the area, they
finally closed in 1981. There was space for the runway of
London City Airport on the site of old warehouses. The
main areas of the borough are East Ham, West Ham and
Stratford, the gateway to the 2012 Olympics Park, which

The London Eye

The Queen's House at Greenwich, now part of the National Maritime Museum, the former Royal Naval Hospital and, across the river, the tower blocks of Canary Wharf.

Outer London

There are sixteen outer London boroughs whose fringe incorporate open countryside. Whilst some areas have major concentrations of jobs, such as in Croydon or around Heathrow Airport, far more people live here than work here (4,590,200 people and 1,682,600 jobs) compared with inner London (3,029,600 and 2,485,300). Many people who live in outer London work in inner London and there is an extensive public transport system including buses, trains, trams (in south London) and the London Underground (particularly north of the Thames). The most populous borough in Greater London is Croydon (341,800), while the smallest (excluding the City of London) is Kingston upon Thames (160,100). Both are in outer London.

The borough of **Barking and Dagenham** remains distinctive for the importance of its manufacturing sector (over 16 per cent of jobs) compared with a London average of around 4 per cent. Dagenham was the home of Ford's integrated car plant, where the first vehicle rolled off the production line in 1931. No longer a site for vehicle production, it is Ford's major centre for diesel engine manufacture, producing over a million engines a year and employing 4,000 people.

The borough of **Barnet** is named after the old market town of Barnet, formerly in Hertfordshire and scene in 1471 of the battle of Barnet when Edward IV defeated the rebellious peer, Richard Neville (Warwick the Kingmaker). The borough stretches down to the northern end of Hampstead Heath and contains Hampstead Garden Suburb, an influential planned new housing development, dating from 1907, as well as the communities of Finchley and Golders Green. The borough also houses the Royal Air Force Museum at Colindale.

The borough of **Bexley** was formed from part of Kent in 1965. The area mostly developed from the 19th century onwards as suburbs for London. Erith was a small port from medieval times and most recently has benefited from some regeneration under the auspices of the Thames Gateway project. One of the most influential Victorian houses in Britain was built at Bexleyheath – the Red House built for William Morris by Philip Webb in 1859–60; it stimulated the development of the Arts and Crafts movement, and is now cared for by the National Trust.

The borough of **Brent** is based around Wembley and includes Harlesden and Willesden. Over half the population of Brent comes from the Black and ethnic minority communities, with over 18 per cent of the population of South Asian origin. Its most well known feature is the new Wembley Stadium, with its soaring arch to support part of the roof. It can accommodate up to 90,000 spectators. The stadium it replaces was built in 1923 as the British Empire Exhibition Stadium. It had a capacity of 127,000 (although it is thought that up to 200,000 watched the first FA Cup final played in the stadium in 1923).

The borough of **Bromley** has the largest area of the London boroughs and incorporates Penge, Beckenham, Chislehurst, Orpington and Biggin Hill. The borough is built up in the north and much more rural in the south. Down House, near the village of Downe, was the home of Charles Darwin, where he wrote *On the Origin of Species*. Sydenham Hill, near Penge, is where the Crystal Palace, originally built in Hyde Park for the 1851 Great Exhibition, was reconstructed and enlarged, opening in 1854. It was completely destroyed in a massive fire in 1936, leaving its park, complete with thirty-three full-scale model dinosaurs

The borough of **Croydon** includes Norwood, Selsdon, Purley, Coulsdon and the town of Croydon, a major commercial and retail centre in its own right. Croydon Airport was the original airport for London, opening in 1920. Up to the start of World War II, all international

is transforming this part of Newham. The borough is one of the most ethnically diverse areas in Britain: in a 2005 survey, it was estimated that 34 per cent of the population was ethnically white, 36 per cent South Asian, and 25 per cent Black. It is also one of the most deprived areas of London and Britain.

The borough of **Southwark** has a long boundary along the south bank of the Thames from the National Theatre to Rotherhithe, which contains Tate Modern and the Millennium Bridge, the newest, and pedestrian-only, bridge across the Thames, HMS *Belfast*, the reconstructed Globe Theatre, the medieval Southwark Cathedral, Tower Bridge and the former wharves and dockland of Bermondsey and Rotherhithe. To the south lie Camberwell, Peckham and Dulwich. Southwark's population is diverse, with nearly 20 per cent of the population of Black African or Black Caribbean origin, while in the borough's schools only one quarter of pupils are white British. The area close to the Thames and to the major commuting terminus of London Bridge Station, has had a major influence on 43 per cent of the borough's jobs being in finance, IT and business. Additional tourist attractions include the Imperial War Museum London and the Dulwich Picture Gallery. This was Britain's first public art gallery, opening in 1814, in a building designed by Sir John Soane that has influenced gallery design ever since.

The borough of **Tower Hamlets** contains much of London's traditional East End – Bethnal Green, Shoreditch, Whitechapel, Stepney, Poplar and Bow – but it has also seen immense change. The former docklands around the Isle of Dogs have become a major financial centre, centred around Canary Wharf and linked to the City by the Docklands Light Railway, while areas like Spitalfields, once occupied by French Huguenots and then by Jewish immigrants, is now home to a large Bangladeshi community. The borough is ethnically diverse with 44 per cent of the population white British and around 30 per cent Bangladeshi (two-fifths of London's Bangladeshi population live here). Many commute into Tower Hamlets to work, with over 55 per cent of all jobs in the borough in finance, IT and other business, but those who live in the borough are amongst the most deprived in Britain. The Tower of London is its most well-known landmark, while other significant buildings include the Royal Mint

and the Baroque churches of Nicholas Hawksmoor at Spitalfields, Wapping and Limehouse. It is a host borough for the 2012 Olympics.

The borough of **Wandsworth** on the south bank of the Thames from the edge of Richmond Park to Vauxhall is inner London's most populous borough, with many of the people living in Putney, Wandsworth, Tooting, Balham and Battersea working elsewhere in London. More than 40 per cent of residents are in the age range 25–39, the highest proportion in the country, while it is less ethnically diverse than many inner London boroughs. The borough contains a great range of housing stock, both in terms of size and quality. One quarter of the borough is open green space, such as Wandsworth Common, while one third is given over to residential accommodation. Its most symbolic building is the former Battersea Power Station, a legacy from the past still awaiting a secure future. Clapham Junction railway station (really in Battersea) is one of Europe's busiest stations, with commuting trains using its sixteen platforms.

The **City of Westminster** covers much of central London including Pimlico, Westminster, Covent Garden, Marylebone and Paddington. The heart of Westminster is around the UNESCO World Heritage Site of Westminster Abbey and the Houses of Parliament, the centre of royal and then parliamentary power for around 1,000 years. It has a cosmopolitan population and some of the most exclusive housing in London, but there is deprivation in West Kilburn and parts of North Paddington. More people come in to work in Westminster than live there, with approaching 600,000 jobs of which 39 per cent are in finance, IT and other business but only 17 per cent in public administration, education and health (even as the heart of government with senior civil servants and with seven major higher education institutions). Tourism provides 13 per cent of jobs, for the area includes galleries, the Royal Palaces, the Royal Parks and the shopping areas of Mayfair (including Bond Street), Oxford Street and Covent Garden. The Lord's Cricket Ground in St John's Wood and the rail termini of Paddington, Charing Cross, Victoria and Marylebone are also in the city.

ghts left from Croydon, and Art Deco buildings from
at time survive. It soon became too small, and its last
ght was in 1959. Tramlink, based around Croydon,
ened in 2000 and now has thirty-nine stations with
tions for further expansion being considered to
prove the transport infrastructure of south London.

e borough of **Ealing** in west London covers Ealing,
anwell, Acton, Southall, Greenford, Perivale and
rtholt. A popular residential area, it also has twice the
ndon average of manufacturing jobs, notably in food
ocessing and pharmaceuticals. In 1950 immigrants
om South Asia started to arrive in Southall and this
ea now has a majority South Asian population, while
e borough also has large communities of Poles,
ghanis, Iraqis, Iranians and Somalis. Bedford Park was
e of the world's first planned suburbs, started in 1875,
d it quickly became the fashionable home of artists
d writers.

e borough of **Enfield** is in north London bordering
ertfordshire. In the east is the Lea Valley while in the
rthwest is Enfield Chase, a reminder of Enfield's
story as a medieval royal hunting forest. The area is
w primarily residential, having developed greatly
en the Piccadilly line of the London Underground
rived in the 1930s, with its distinctive Art Deco
tions. Enfield was the home of the Royal Small Arms
ctory, established in 1816 and source of the
e-Enfield rifles, as well as the Bren gun and the Sten
n; manufacturing ceased in 1988.

e borough of **Greenwich**, on the south bank of the
ames, was the site of a royal palace from the
th century onwards; the Queen's House, a
volutionary building designed by Inigo Jones in 1616,
rvives. After the Restoration, Greenwich became home
both the Royal Naval Hospital and the Greenwich
oservatory and the buildings and their setting are
such significance that they form a UNESCO World
eritage Site. In the borough is also The O2, originally
ilt as the Millennium Dome in 1999, the *Cutty Sark*
d Eltham Palace, an extraordinary combination of
edieval royal palace and Art Deco house. In 2012
eenwich will become a royal borough reflecting the
ng royal associations with the area.

e borough of **Harrow** shares a rural boundary with
ertfordshire. Primarily a residential area, the borough
one of the most ethnically diverse in Britain. In 2001
er 41 per cent of the population belonged to an ethnic
nority and nearly 30 per cent of the population have
uth Asian origins. The area is best known for Harrow

School, the public school founded in 1572. Among its
pupils have been six prime ministers, a prime minister
of India, scientists, poets and novelists.

The borough of **Havering** is a based around Romford, the
main population and commercial centre, Hornchurch,
Upminster and Rainham. About half its area is open
green belt land. Havering is less ethnically diverse that
other outer London boroughs and also has the oldest
population. Havering takes its name from the Royal Liberty
of Havering, based around the royal palace at Havering-
atte-Bower. The Royal Liberty provided the administration
for the area from 1465 until it was incorporated into Essex
in 1888.

The borough of **Hillingdon** is dominated by Heathrow
Airport – over 35 per cent of the jobs in Hillingdon are
in transport and communication, nearly five times the
average for London. Heathrow is at the southern end
of the borough that also includes Hayes, West Drayton,
Uxbridge, Hillingdon and Ruislip. Brunel University is
at Uxbridge while the village of Harmondsworth, close to
Heathrow, has a 12th-century church and a magnificent
early 15th-century tithe barn, one of the largest timber-
framed medieval barns in Britain, both potentially
threatened by the airport's expansion.

The borough of **Hounslow** is adjacent to Heathrow
Airport and is also strongly influenced by it. To its east
are Hounslow, Brentford and Chiswick, and many large
companies are based here because of the good location.
The borough also contains three of the most important
country houses in Britain, Chiswick House, the great
Palladian-style building designed by its owner, the Earl
of Burlington, in 1729, and two dramatic alterations
of earlier buildings by Robert Adam, at Syon Park and
Osterley House.

The royal borough of **Kingston upon Thames** includes
Surbiton, New Malden and Chessington. The town
of Kingston upon Thames has a long history – the
Coronation Stone, now outside the Guildhall, may have
been used in the coronation of seven Saxon kings, and
the oldest surviving Royal Charter was granted by King
John in 1208. Once a centre for aircraft manufacture, the
area is now populated by service industries. New Malden
is thought to have the largest South Korean community
in Europe.

The borough of **Merton** covers Mitcham, Morden and
Wimbledon, the home of English tennis. It is named
after Merton the site of an Augustinian priory, founded
in 1117, where Thomas Becket was educated and

Henry IV's coronation was held in 1437. In the 17th
century the area became a textile centre and, in 1881,
William Morris established the Merton Abbey Works,
which produced textiles, wallpapers, carpets and stained
glass until 1940. The Baitul Futuh mosque in Morden,
inaugurated in 2003, is the largest purpose-built mosque
in western Europe.

The borough of **Redbridge** is centred around Ilford
and includes Wanstead, Woodford and Hainault. It
takes its name from the Redbridge, an old redbrick
bridge that once crossed the river Roding between
Ilford with Wanstead. The eponymous photographic
film manufacturer was founded in Ilford in 1879 and
from 1919 the innovative electronics company Plessey
was based there. Nowadays, however, the borough
is primarily a residential base for its very diverse
population, with only just over a third of residents
working in the borough.

The borough of **Richmond upon Thames** is the only
borough to straddle the Thames. Primarily a residential
borough, tourism provides over 12 per cent of jobs. Its
attractions include the great royal palace of Hampton
Court, the Royal Botanic Gardens at Kew, the royal Kew
Palace, Richmond Park, London's largest, complete
with herds of wild deer, Ham House, Marble Hill at
Twickenham, built for Henrietta Howard, mistress
of George II, and Twickenham Stadium, the home of
English Rugby Football. These attractions will soon be
joined by the restored Strawberry Hill, Horace Walpole's
18th century gothic fantasy.

The borough of **Sutton** is based around Sutton,
Carshalton, Cheam and Wallington. The development
of the area for residential use was linked to the arrival
of the railways – the first reached Sutton in 1847. The
area used to support a commercial lavender-growing
industry. On the borders with Surrey are the grounds of
Nonsuch Palace, Henry VIII's great royal palace that has
long since been demolished.

The borough of **Waltham Forest** borders the Lea Valley
in the west and in the north it contains the start of
Epping Forest – Queen Elizabeth I's hunting lodge
still survives in Chingford as a reminder of this once
great royal forest that stretches into Essex. One of the
most ethnically diverse in Britain, it is one of the host
boroughs for the 2012 Olympics. The great designer and
writer William Morris was born in Walthamstow and his
former family home is now a world-renowned museum.

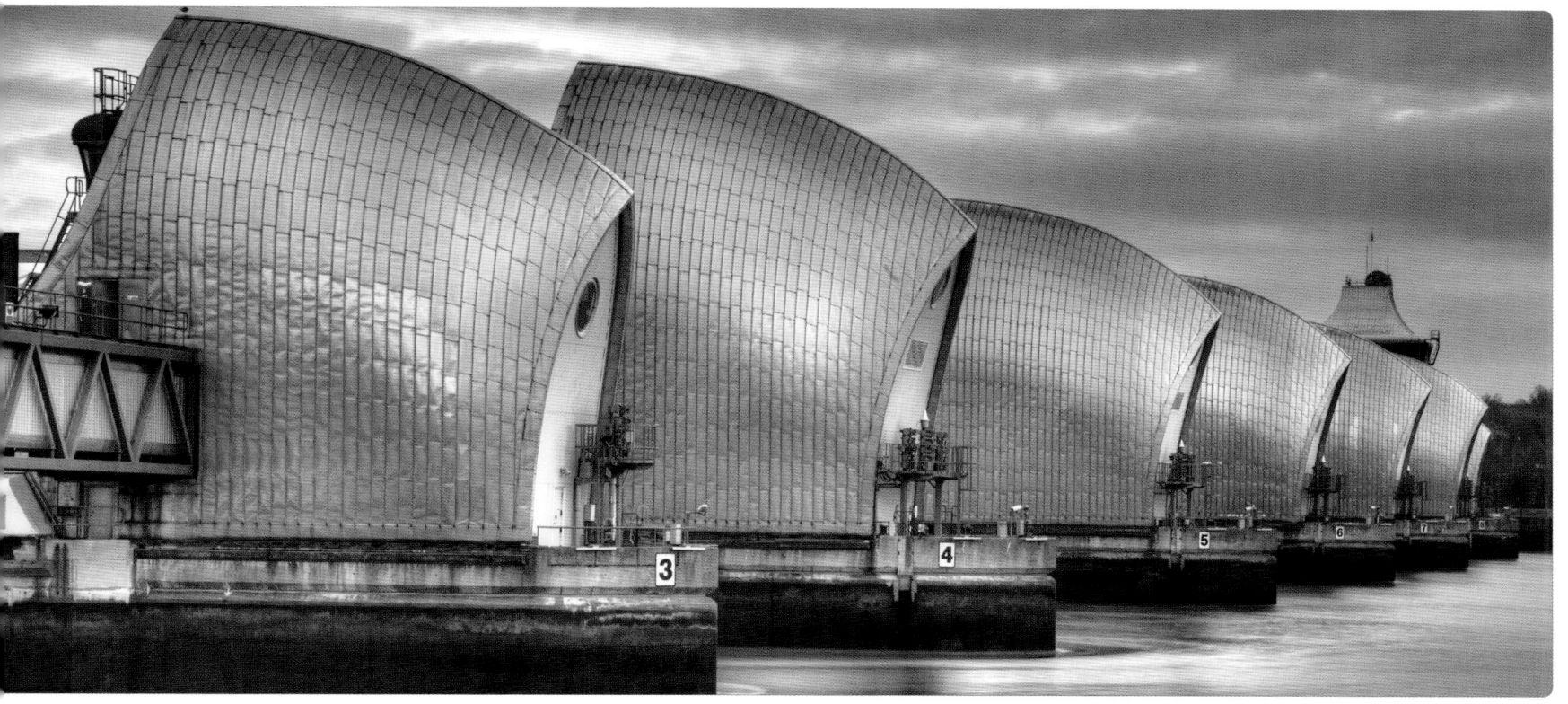

mes Flood Barrier

FAMOUS PEOPLE

Thomas Becket, Archbishop of Canterbury, martyr and saint, born Cheapside, c. 1118.

Thomas Cromwell, Earl of Essex, statesman and adviser to Henry VIII, born Putney, c. 1485

Francis Bacon, Viscount St Albans, philosopher, scientist and statesman, born York House, Strand, 1561.

John Donne, poet, Dean of St Paul's, born Bread Street, City of London, 1572.

John Milton, poet, born Bread Street, City of London, 1608.

Samuel Pepys, civil servant, politician and diarist, born Salisbury Court, Fleet Street, 1633.

Sir Edmond Halley, astronomer, born Shoreditch, 1656.

William Hogarth, artist and satirist, born Smithfield, 1697.

William Blake, artist and poet, born Soho, 1757.

Mary Wollstonecraft, feminist, author, *A Vindication of the Rights of Women*, born Spitalfields, 1759.

Joseph Mallord William Turner, artist, born Covent Garden, 1775.

Michael Faraday, chemist, physicist and inventor, born Southwark, 1791.

John Keats, poet, born Moorfields, 1795.

Benjamin Disraeli, Viscount Beaconsfield, author, Conservative politician and Prime Minister (1868, 1874–80), born Bedford Row, 1804.

Sir Joseph Lister, surgeon, founder of antiseptic medicine, born Upton, 1827.

William Morris, artist, designer and writer, born Walthamstow, 1834.

Dr Elizabeth Garrett Anderson, first female English physician, born Whitechapel, 1836.

Helen Beatrix Potter, author and illustrator, born South Kensington, 1866.

Herbert George (H.G.) Wells, author, born Bromley, 1866.

Clement Attlee, Earl Attlee, Labour politician and Prime Minister (1945–51), born Putney, 1883.

Bernard Montgomery ('Monty'), Viscount Montgomery of Alamein, army commander, born Kennington, 1887.

Sir Charles ('Charlie') Chaplin, comic actor and Hollywood star, born Walworth, 1889.

Sir Noël Coward, playwright and composer, born Teddington, 1899.

Sir Alfred Hitchcock, film director, born Leytonstone, 1899.

Sir John Gielgud, actor, born South Kensington, 1904.

Dame Edith Margaret (Peggy) Ashcroft, actress, born Croydon, 1907.

Alan Turing, mathematician and computing pioneer, born Paddington, 1912.

Sir Alec Guinness, actor, born Marylebone, 1914.

Dame Vera Lynn, singer, born East Ham, 1917.

Sir Alfred ('Alf') Ramsey, football player and England World Cup manager, born Dagenham, 1920.

Dame Elizabeth Taylor, actress, born Hampstead, 1932.

Dame Margaret Natalie Smith Cross (known as Maggie Smith), actress, born Ilford, 1934.

Mary Quant, fashion designer, born Blackheath, 1934.

Dudley Moore, comedian and actor, born Dagenham, 1935.

Sir Robert (Bobby) Moore, footballer, captain, England's winning World Cup team, 1966, born Barking, 1941.

David Bowie (born David Robert Jones), musician, born Brixton, 1947.

Tracy Emin, artist, born Croydon, 1963.

David Beckham, footballer, born Leytonstone, 1975.

Quotations
"A duller spectacle this earth of ours has not to show than a rainy Sunday in London."
Thomas de Quincey, 1822, *Confessions of an English Opium Eater*

"Forget the spreading of the hideous town;
Think rather of the pack-horse on the down,
And dream of London, small and white and clean,
The clear Thames bordered by its gardens green."
William Morris, 1868–70, *The Earthly Paradise*

"London: a nation, not a city."
Benjamin Disraeli, 1870, *Lothair*

Bartholomew Gazetteer of the British Isles, 1887
LONDON, *the capital of England and the principal town of the British Empire, on river Thames, mostly in Middlesex, but also occupying parts of Surrey, Kent, and Essex, 60 miles (by the river's course) from the sea at the Nore; the centre of the dome of St Paul's is in lat. 50° 30' 48" W.*

The centre of the Government and commerce of the British Empire, London is the greatest city of any age or country. Politically, financially, and commercially, as well as on account of its immense size and population, its progress and pre-eminence form a very remarkable feature in the history of civilisation. Without entering upon the vague traditions which have survived from more obscure eras, we find that as early as A.D. 61 the 'Lundinium' of the Romans was a place of importance; 'Colonia Augusta' being another of its Roman designations. One of the principal evidences, however, of a much earlier existence of the town is found in the etymology of the name, which comes from the Celtic 'Llyn-Din'. Three important events have especial prominence in the pre-Norman history of London; namely, the foundation of the bishopric, supposed to have taken place in A.D. 179; the rebuilding and fortifying of the town by the Romans in 306; and the founding of St Paul's by Ethelbert in the year 597. Coming upon the firmer ground of authentic history, it is seen that in 1079 the Tower was built by William I., who, in the same year, granted the city its first charter, a document which is still extant. A charter granted by King John in 1189 authorised the annual election of a mayor and corporation.

Conspicuous landmarks in the subsequent course of the city's history are – Wat Tyler's Rebellion, 1381; Jack Cade's Rebellion, 1450; the foundation of Christ's Hospital, 1533; numerous pestilences, culminating in the Great Plague of 1665; and the Great Fire of 1666. The latter, although in itself a disaster of terrible magnitude, had one good effect, in so far that it swept away the old haunts of disease, and left room for the erection of the present city, the history of which, in a large measure, is the history of the progress of the British nation. Modern London has no clearly defined limits, and the determination of its unofficial boundaries is yearly becoming more difficult through its rapid and wide suburban extension. Roughly speaking, the whole metropolis may be estimated to cover, E. to W., 14 m., and N. to S. 10m.

As the seat of the government of the Empire, the commercial emporium of Britain, the home of British literature, art and science, and the place of residence, at special seasons, of the wealthier classes from all parts of the country, it is natural that London should abound with interesting, stately, and imposing buildings of all descriptions. Among the greatest of these are the Houses of Parliament, Westminster Abbey, Buckingham Palace, St James' Palace, St Paul's Cathedral, Lambeth Palace, the Tower of London, the Guildhall, the Mansion House, the Royal Exchange, the Bank of England, the General Post-Office, the British Museum, and the National Gallery. The Government departments, such as the Home and Foreign Offices, the Education Office, Somerset House (Inland Revenue), &c., are also important. There are over 1400 churches and chapels, 45 theatres, and 400 music halls concert rooms, &c. Thirteen bridges, besides 5 railway bridges, span the Thames; London Bridge being the most easterly, and Hammersmith Bridge that most westerly.

The metropolis is singularly fortunate in the possession of public parks, which for the extent and beauty are unsurpassed by any open spaces belonging to other large cities. The chief are:- In the W., St James' Park (80 ac.), the Green Park (70 ac.), Hyde park (390 ac.), and Kensington Gardens (360 ac.); in the N., the Regent's Park (470 ac.), containing the gardens of the Zoological Society and the Botanical Society; in the SW., Battersea Park (180 ac.); and in the E., Victoria Park (300 ac.).

London is the supreme seat of the judicature of the country. The principal courts are concentrated in the magnificent range of buildings known as the New Law Courts. The Inns of Court are to some extent colleges for law students, and include the Inner Temple, Midd Temple, Lincoln's Inn, and Gray's Inn. Altogether the different courts give employment to over 3000 barriste and 5000 solicitors. Exclusive of the Mansion House and Guildhall, in the City, there are 13 police courts i various parts of the metropolis, and the whole police f is about 14,000.

All the military affairs of the country are manage from the War Office and Horse Guards; the actual ga of the metropolis mostly consisting of the Household cavalry, and Chelsea and Wellington barracks for inf The chief offices of the Admiralty, the Customs, and the mercantile marine service, are likewise situated in Lo.

Education is represented by many well-known institutions. London University is purely an examinin body for conferring degrees, the tests being open to all comers, and certificates are obtainable by women. Of colleges, University College and King's College are the principal, but there are also a number of others; nota the denominational institutions for the training of sch teachers. Medical education, at the head of which stan the Royal College of Physicians and the Royal College Surgeons, is actively carried on in the hospital, especi at Bartholomew's, St Thomas', Guy's, St George's, an the Middlesex Hospital. In all there are about 35 gene hospitals and infirmaries in the metropolis, besides a large number of kindred institutions for the treatment special diseases.

The chief public schools are Westminster; St Paul's, Christ Church (Bluecoat), Merchant Taylor (Charterhouse), City of London Schools, and Univers College Schools. The School Board has in operation 368 schools, accommodating 334,309 children.

The water-supply of the town is drawn, and after filtration distributed, from the Thames and the New The gas-supply is in the hands of joint-stock companie

Markets exist for almost every commodity that ha sufficient mercantile importance; those for food suppl being chiefly the London Central Market (meat and poultry), Billingsgate Market (fish), Covent Garden Market (fruit and vegetables), Borough Market (fruit and vegetables), Columbia Market (fish and general). A distinguished feature in metropolitan enterprise is t number and variety of means adopted for the conveya of passengers and goods. It is impossible to describe th labyrinth of the rail system; but some conception of its intricacy and extent may be formed from the fact that greater railway lines have 11 termini. The Metropoli and the Metropolitan District Railways, popularly k as the "Underground," are the most convenient, and about 136 millions of passengers every year. The "In Circle," which completed the circuit, was opened in 1 A gigantic traffic is also sustained by an immense nur of omnibuses, tramway cars, and cabs. Of the latter i estimated that there are about 10,000, while the cab-number about 13,000. Hundreds of steamers ply upo the river, and a large goods traffic is carried on upon Regent, Grand Junction, and the other canals. The tr London comprises every department of active comme enterprise that is usually associated with a great city. particularly, however, it is known as the headquarter finance, and the greatest emporium for merchandise i world, rather than as a place of special manufacturi industry.

Financial interests have their chief centre in the b of England, which in November 1884 had notes to th value of £24,795,670 in circulation; at the same tim unemployed notes amounted to the sum of £9,741,69 and gold and silver in all the branches to £19,752,9.

LONDON, c.1870

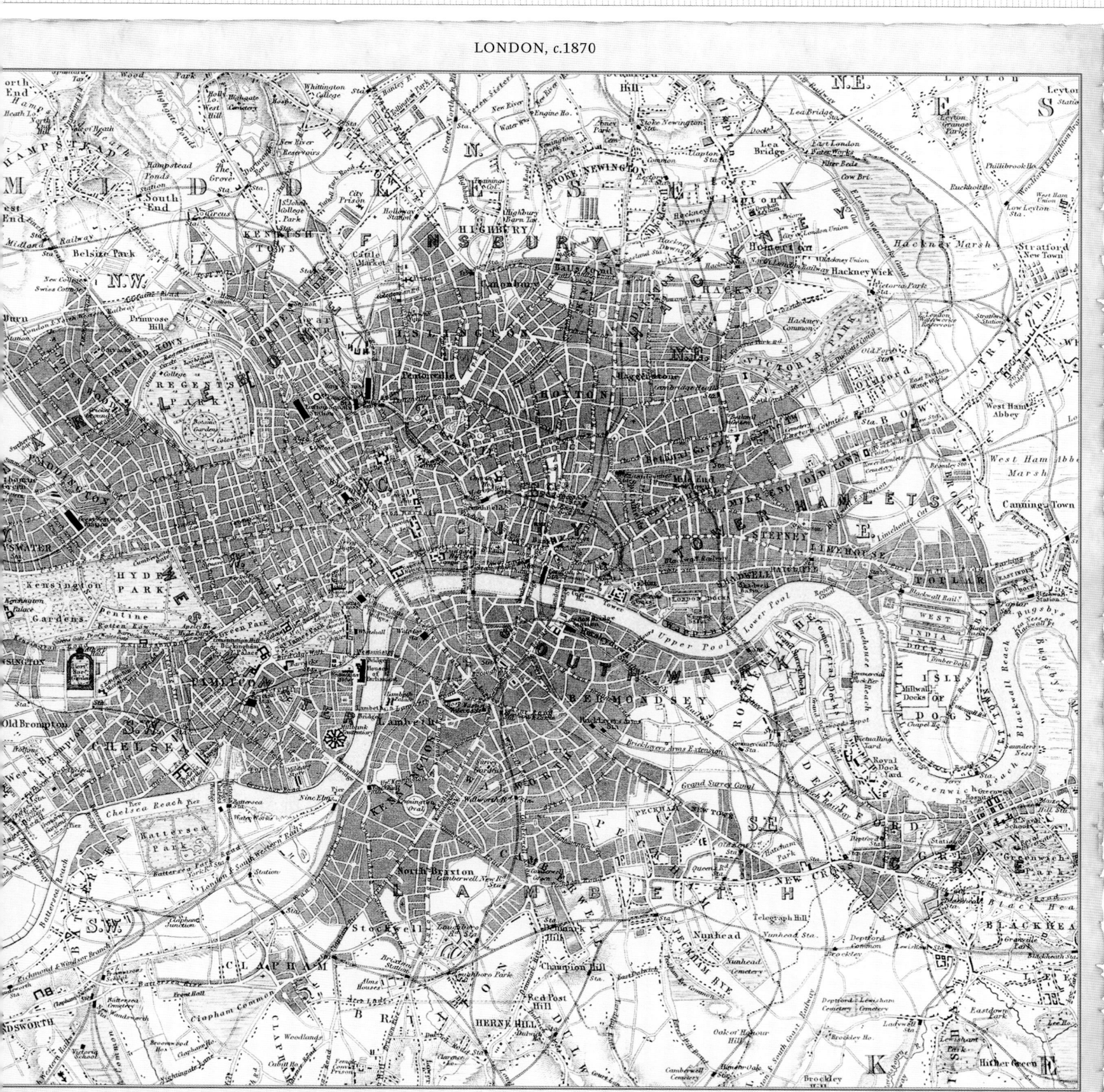

e number of private and joint-stock banks in London *60. Their inter-official accounts are adjusted and *led through the medium of the Bankers' Clearing *use, a splendidly organised establishment, dealing with *rmous transactions, which average £1,000,000 a week, *d which for the year ending April 1884 represented * aggregate sum of £5,838,158,000. The great centre *business is the Royal Exchange, which was founded *Sir Thomas Gresham in 1570. Other great exchanges, * special purposes, are the Corn Exchange, the Wool *change, the Coal Exchange, and an exchange for *ded property.

In its purely mercantile aspects London shows *excess of imports over exports. This is due to the *cumstance of its being a market for all descriptions of *oduce from every quarter of the globe; its especial trade *h the East Indies and China almost amounting to *onopoly. To meet the exigencies of this multifarious

traffic, a vast amount of dock accommodation has been provided. The chief docks are, the East and West India Docks, Blackwall; the London Docks, East Smithfield; Millwall Docks, Isle of Dogs; St Katherine's Docks, East Smithfield; Surrey and Commercial Docks, Rotherhithe; Regent Dock, Limehouse and the Royal Victoria and Albert Docks, North Woolwich. The new docks at Tilbury, constructed under the auspices of the East and West India Dock Company, have a water space of nearly 80 acres, with 12,000 ft. of quay room. With the completion of its railway system, this will be one of the most important undertakings connected with London shipping.

Brewing is, perhaps, the leading industry of London, which, however, may be said to carry on, more or less, nearly every mfr. known in the kingdom. Its potteries, glass works, tanneries, and chemical works are well known. Shipbuilding, which at one time showed a remarkable degree of industrial vitality, has seriously declined; the

work now conducted on the Thames being almost confined to the construction of boats, barges, and yachts.

London has long been the great seat of the British publishing trade. Many of the book-publishing offices are situated in the neighbourhoods of Paternoster Row and Covent Garden, while newspaper offices are nearly all concentrated in Fleet Street and its vicinity. The number of newspapers published in London in 1884 was over 400, of which 24 were daily papers, morning and evening.

Central London

The Wigmore Hall
OXFORD STREET
REGENT STREET
NEW BOND STREET
Palladium
Royal Academy of Arts
Soho
CHARING CROSS ROAD
SHAFTESBURY AVE
Royal Opera House
Theatre Royal
National Gallery
PICCADILLY CIRCUS
HAYMARKET
Mayfair
St James's
Admiralty Arch
St James's Palace
TRAFALGAR SQUARE
Charing Cross Station
PALL MALL
ST JAMES'S ST
PICCADILLY
Green Park
Marlborough House
THE MALL
Government Buildings
Banqueting House
WHITEHALL
Buckingham Palace
CONSTITUTION HILL
BIRDCAGE WALK
St James's Park
DOWNING ST
Treasury
PARLIAMENT SQUARE
GROSVENOR PLACE
WESTMINSTER
New Scotland Yard
VICTORIA STREET
Palace of Westminster
Westminster Abbey
Victoria Station
British Museum
Dominion Theatre
HIGH HOLBORN
Holborn
Lincoln's Inn Fields
Lincoln's Inn
KINGSWAY
Royal Courts of Justice
ALDWYCH
Temple Church
STRAND
Harrow
London Transport Museum
STRAND
Somerset House
King's College
WATERLOO BRIDGE
VICTORIA EMBANKMENT
HUNGERFORD BRIDGE
Queen Elizabeth Hall
Royal National Theatre
Royal Festival Hall
WATERLOO RD
Thames
London Eye
Waterloo Station
London Aquarium
Old County Hall
WESTMINSTER BR
WESTMINSTER BRIDGE ROAD
Big Ben
Houses of Parliament
LAMBETH
Lambeth Palace Gardens
Lambeth Palace

0   M   500
0   YARDS   500

Queensbury
Kingsbury
RAF Museums
GREAT N WAY
Holders Hill
EDGWARE ROAD
Hendon
M1
HINDON
Golders Green
Cricklewood
Fryent Country Park
Northwick Park
Wembley Park
BRENT
Brent Reservoir
NORTH CIRCULAR ROAD
Dollis Hill
A41
Gladstone Park
Wembley Stadium
Wembley
Willesden
A406
Willesden Green
Sunbury Golf Course
Alperton
EALING ROAD
Park Royal
Harlesden
Kilbu
Grand Union Canal
HARROW ROAD
Perivale
HANGER LANE
North Acton
WESTERN AVENUE
Perivale Park Golf Course
Ealing Golf Course
A40
EALING
Ealing
Wormwood Scrubs
North Kensington
WESTWAY
A40
A40
A4020
Notting Hill
A402
Hayes
Southall
Hanwell
Acton
THE VALE
East Acton
Shepherd's Bush
Holland Park
Yiewsley
Gunnersbury
HAMMERSMITH
Olympia
AND FULHAM
West Drayton
Norwood Green
M4
Gunnersbury Park
CHISWICK HIGH ROAD
Hammersmith Bridge
Earls Court Exhibition Centre
Earls Court
Grand Union Canal
North Hyde
Osterley Park
Brentford
A4
Chiswick
Chiswick House
A316
Castelnau
Barn Elms Wildfowl Reserve
Harmondsworth
Harlington
BATH ROAD
A4
GREAT WEST ROAD
Osterley
Royal Botanic Gardens Kew
KEW ROAD
Barnes
Football Stadium
FULHAM R
Heston
Syon House
Syon Park
Mortlake
Putney Bridge
Cranford
Heathrow Airport (London)
A30
Hounslow West
Osterley
Isleworth
SOUTH CIRCULAR ROAD
A205
Putney
ROEHAMPTON LANE
Crane
GREAT SOUTH WEST ROAD
Hounslow
Richmond
Putney Heath
Stanwell
HOUNSLOW
Rugby Ground
A316
Richmond
W
Sou
Staines Reservoirs
Hounslow Heath
RICHMOND UPON
Richmond Park
East Bedfont
Twickenham
Thames
THAMES
A3
Feltham
Crane
Teddington
All England Lawn Tennis and Croquet Club
Wimbledon Park
A30
A308
Ashford
Hanworth
Bushy Park
Wimbledon Common
Wimble
KINGSTON HILL
Coombe Hill Golf Course
KINGSTON
Kempton Park Racecourse
Hampton
M3
COOMBE BYPASS
Sunbury
Molesey Reservoirs
A308
Norbiton
New Malden
Bushy Mead
Queen Mary Reservoir
West Molesey
East Molesey
Hampton Court Palace
Hampton Court Park
Kingston Upon Thames
West Barnes
KINGSTON UPON THAMES
Queen Elizabeth II Reservoir
Shepperton
Thames Ditton
A309
Motspur Park
Morden Park

Terminal 5, Heathrow Airport.

Twickenham rugby stadium.

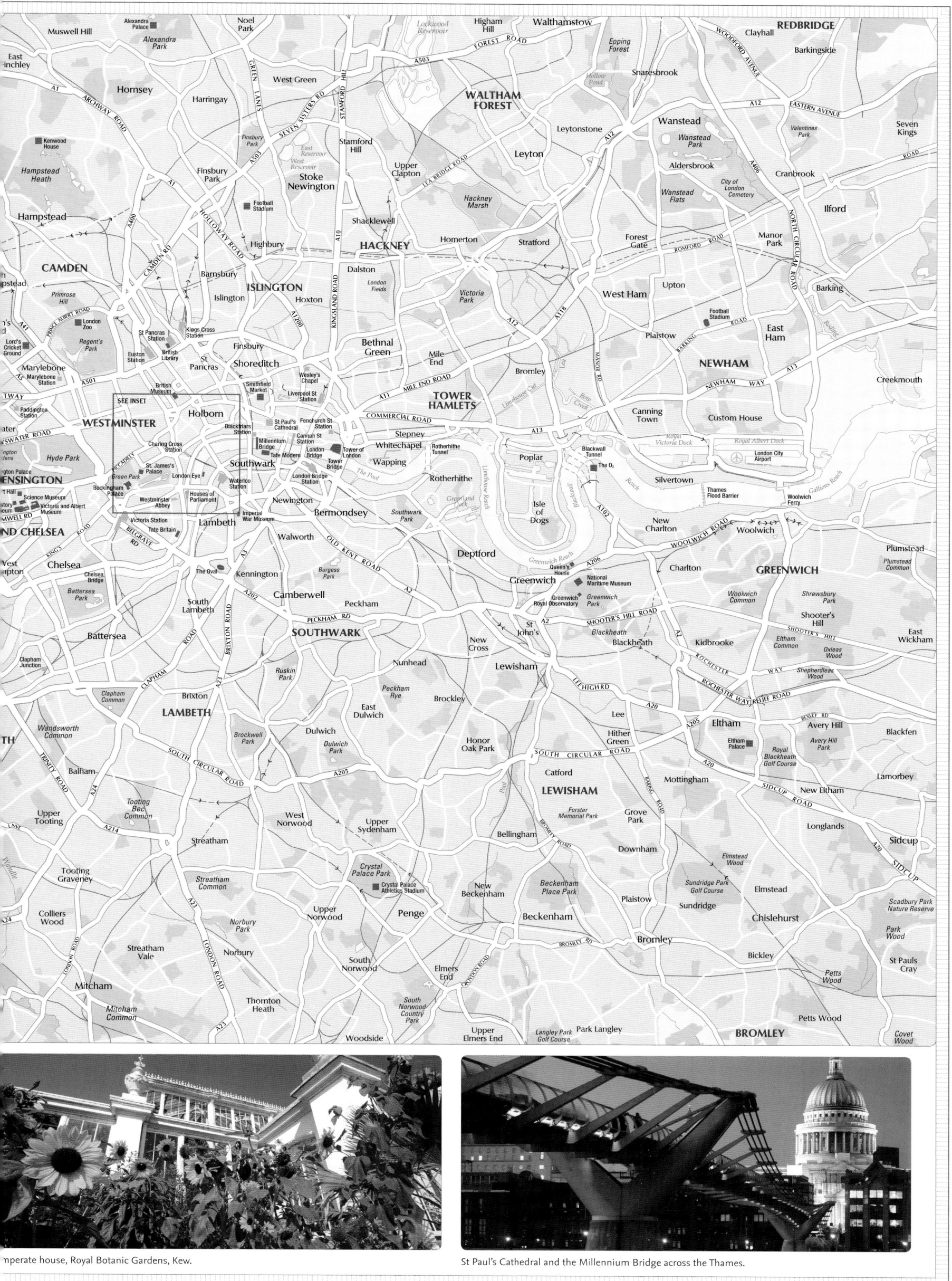

mperate house, Royal Botanic Gardens, Kew.

St Paul's Cathedral and the Millennium Bridge across the Thames.

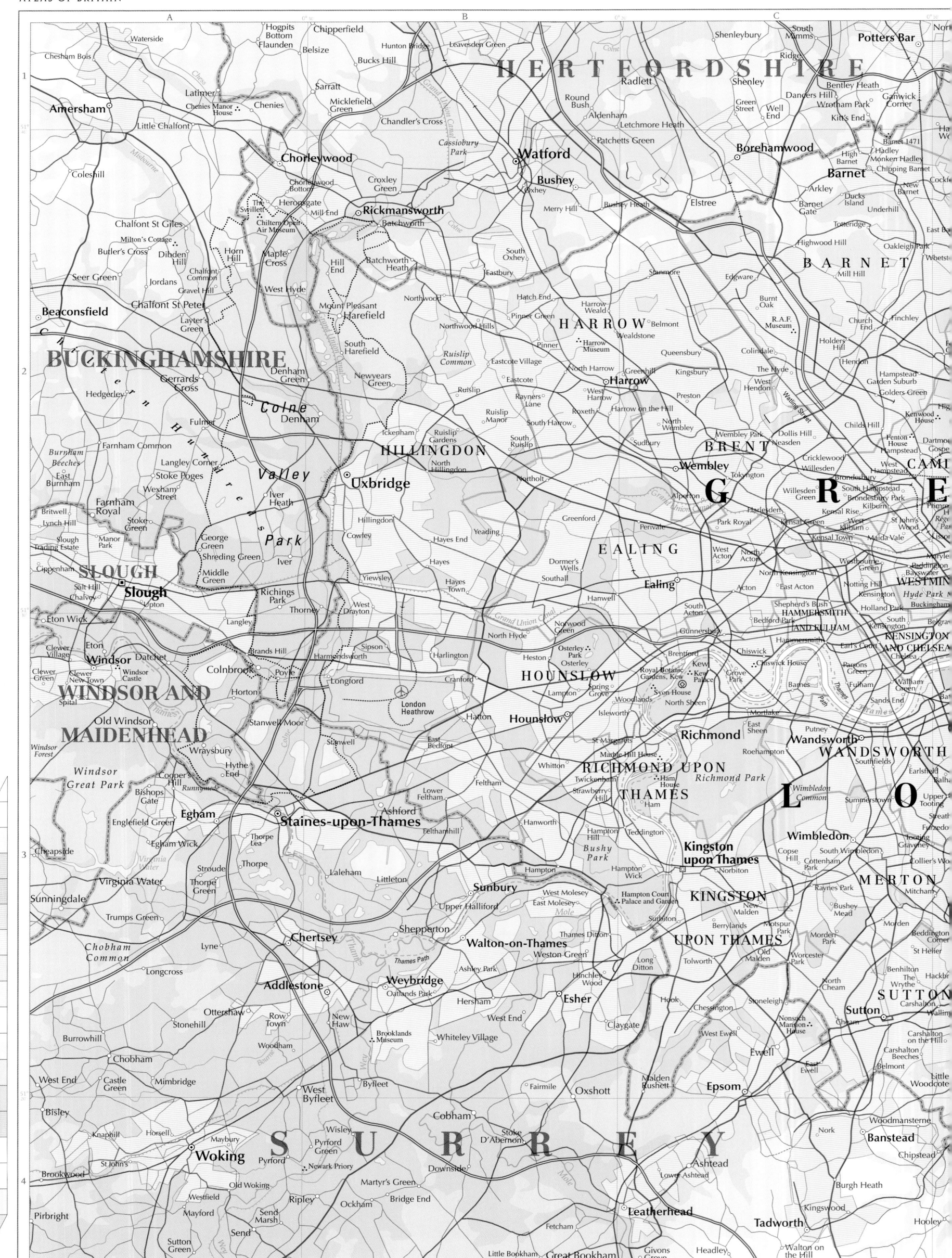

British National Grid projection

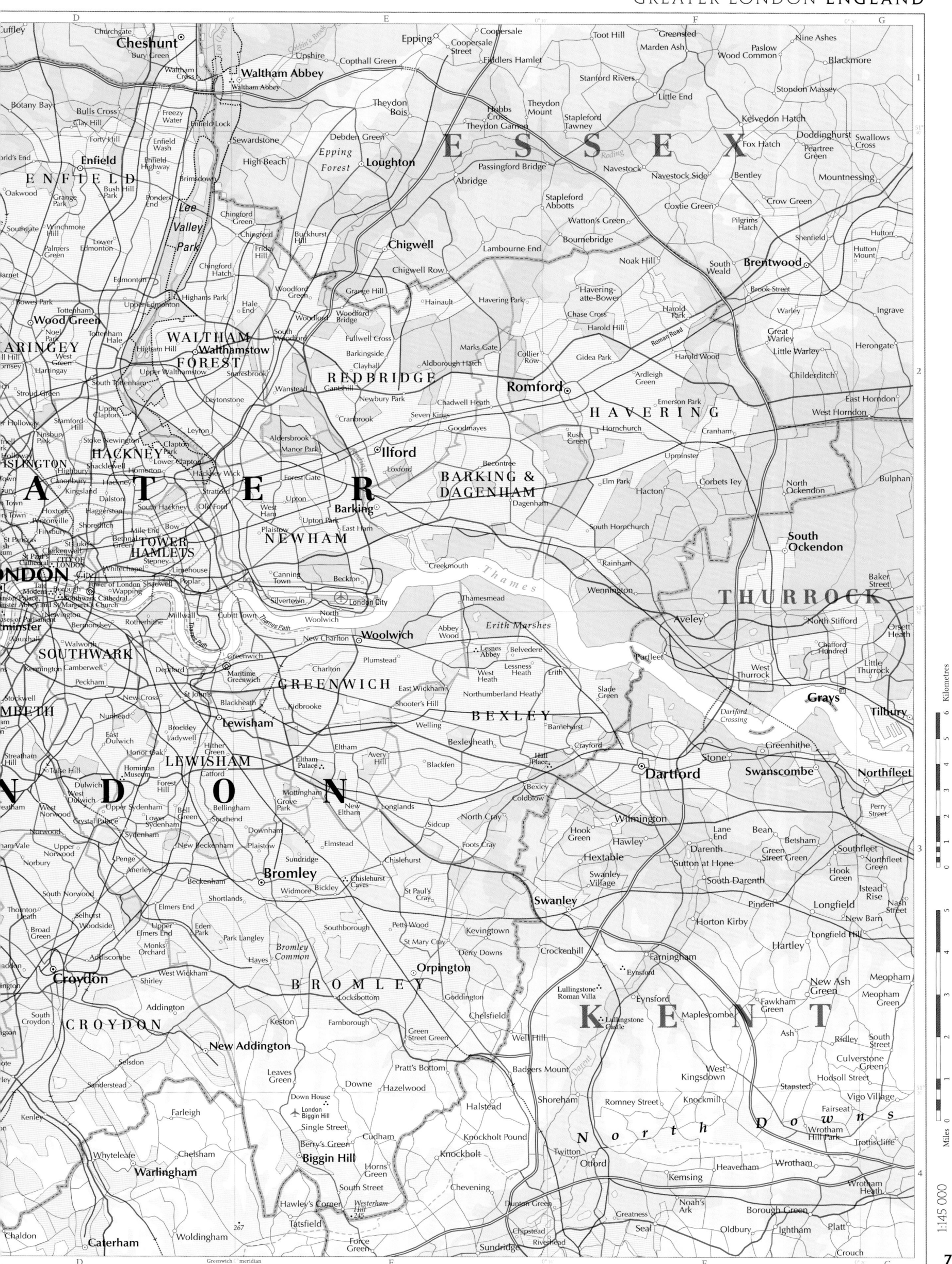

1:145 000

© Collins Bartholomew Ltd

SURREY

Area Sq Km	1,670
Area Sq Miles	645
Population	1,109,700
Admin centre	Kingston upon Thames
Highest point	Leith Hill (294 m), near Dorking
Districts	Elmbridge; Epsom and Ewell; Guildford; Mole Valley; Reigate and Banstead; Runnymede; Spelthorne; Surrey Heath; Tandridge; Waverley; Woking

The name of Surrey comes from the Old English meaning 'southern district', used to describe the area south of the Thames settled by the Middle Saxons, who also gave their name to Middlesex.

FAMOUS FOR

Richard Hull of Leith Hill Place wanted to make Leith Hill (at 294 m or 965 feet) over 1,000 feet high, and so, in 1765, he built **Leith Hill Tower**. The viewing point on its roof is 313.6 m (1,029 feet) above sea level, and from there you can see 13 counties (and the Urals, some say).

One of the great 'vanished' royal palaces of Britain was built near **Cheam** by Henry VIII. It was built over the church and village of Cuddington and was without equal in size and sumptuousness – and named Nonsuch Palace, for there was 'nonsuch like it'. Its demise was less glorious. Charles II gave it to his mistress, Barbara Villiers, who sold it for building materials to help cover her gambling debts.

The Anglican diocese of **Guildford** was created in 1927 to serve the growing population of Surrey. Its cathedral was designed by Sir Edward Maufe, and the predominantly brick building on Stag Hill above Guildford was built between 1936 and 1961.

The first known horse race on **Epsom Downs** took place in 1661. Two classic flat races are held here – the Oaks was first run in 1779 and the Derby in 1780. Both races were initially encouraged by the Earl of Derby who had an estate at nearby Carshalton called 'The Oaks'.

It is said that a farmer discovered **Epsom salts** in the early 17th century, when his cows refused to drink from a particular spring in the middle of a drought. When analysed the water was found to contain magnesium sulphate, a bitter laxative, a property valued by some as Epsom became a fashionable spa.

Waverley Abbey near Farnham was the first Cistercian house in England, built in 1138, though it never achieved the wealth of later Cistercian establishments such as Fountains or Tintern. Nor did Sir Walter Scott name his hero of the Waverley novels after the abbey, so it cannot be said the main railway station in Edinburgh is actually named after an abbey in Surrey.

J. M. Barrie wrote *Peter Pan* in the pine woods behind his country home Blacklake Cottage near **Farnham**, where his Newfoundland dog, the original of Nana, is buried.

Camberley was originally called Cambridge Town in 1862, after the Duke of Cambridge, Commander-in-Chief of the army, but it produced confusion with the other Cambridge, and the invented name of Camberley was created to get over this problem.

On the water meadows on the south bank of the Thames at **Runnymede**, the Magna Carta was signed by King John.

In 1889 Britain's first purpose-built mosque was opened at Woking by the orientalist Dr Leitner, and is now known as the **Shah Jahan Mosque**.

FAMOUS PEOPLE

John Evelyn, author and diarist, born Wotton, 1620.
William Cobbett, author, born Farnham, 1763.
Revd Thomas Malthus, population economist, born Westcott, near Dorking, 1766.
Sir Pelham Grenville (P G) Wodehouse, comic author, born Guildford, 1881.
Aldous Huxley, author, born Godalming, 1894.
John Piper, artist, born Epsom, 1903.
Sir Laurence Olivier, Lord Olivier of Brighton, actor, born Dorking, 1907.
Sir Peter Neville Luard Pears, tenor singer and co-founder, Aldeburgh Festival, born Farnham, 1910.
Mary Wesley, author, born Englefield Green, 1912.
Dame Margot Fonteyn, ballerina, born Reigate, 1919.
Donald Campbell, world speed record holder, born Horley, 1921.
Beryl Cook, painter, born Egham, 1926.
Dame Julie Andrews, singer and actress, born Walton-on-Thames, 1935.
Delia Smith, cookery writer, born Woking, 1941.
Eric Clapton, rock and blues guitarist, born Ripley, 194

The chalk ridge of the North Downs, gently sloping on the north side but forming a steep escarpment on the south, crosses the county from east to west. There are extensive sandy heaths in the west. The chief river, on the northern boundary of the county is the Thames, into which flow the Wey and the Mole.

The historic county of Surrey originally stretched into the heart of London – in 1888 the county lost Lambeth, Southwark and Wandsworth to London while Croydon became an independent borough. With the formation of the Greater London Council in 1965, Kingston, Merton, Sutton and part of Richmond were lost to the county, while in 1974 the county lost Gatwick to West Sussex. However, it still remains one of the most populous counties in Britain, and, while Guildford is the traditional county town, unusually the administrative headquarters are in Kingston, which is now no longer part of the county.

With many of those living in Surrey working in London, the population of the county has risen markedly in recent years, benefiting from the enhanced economic growth in the southeast. Its population increased by nearly 100,000 between 1991 and 2008 and it is expected to grow by over 200,000 by 2031. It is the most densely populated shire county in Britain. Around 90 per cent of the population live in urban areas, with the major centres of population being Guildford (69,400), Woking (62,796), Epsom and Ewell (64,493),

Farnham (36,298) and Camberley (30,155). The county is economically prosperous, with average salaries being 30 per cent higher than the national average for men and 20 per cent higher for women. This wealth is reflected not only in high house prices but also by the fact that there are more cars per mile of road than in any other shire county. Its close proximity to London means that a large number of residents commute into London, and, indeed only 64 per cent of residents actually work within the county. In Elmbridge district, around 11 per cent of residents actually work in central London. Within the county, nearly 30 per cent of jobs are within the finance, IT and other business sector (compared with a UK average of 21.6 per cent) while public administration, education and health accounts for around 25 per cent of jobs, while employment in manufacturing (at 5.6 per cent) is about half the national average.

However, Surrey is more than just a dormitory for London workers and a centre of the business services sector. It is home to three universities – Royal Holloway, part of the University of London, is based near Egham in an astounding Victorian building, created in 1876 as a college for women and funded by Thomas Holloway, a philanthropic patent medicine manufacturer; the University of Surrey, founded in 1966 at Guildford and with a strong reputation in advanced technology; and two campuses for the University for the Creative Arts in Epsom and Farnham.

In the west of the county, the sandy heaths are much used for military training, particularly around Camberley, Chobham, Pirbright and Deepcut, while the Royal Military Academy at Sandhurst straddles the border with Berkshire. Overall the county is surprisingly rural, with over 70 per cent of the land area being protected 'green belt', and around 22 per cent of the county is wooded, making it the most wooded county in Britain. These woods contain many traces of the iron industry that flourished here before the Industrial Revolution. The natural woodlands around Box Hill are some of the oldest natural woodlands in the country, and the importance of woodlands to Surrey is shown in the County Council's logo of two intertwined oak leaves. The county also contains much rolling downland which can be explored along the North Down Way that starts at Farnham, in the west of the county and crosses the county to Reigate and then on into Kent, ending at Dover, over 200 km away.

Tourism and recreation are also important, with Surrey containing numerous stately homes, Wentworth golf course, four horseracing courses (Epsom, Sandown, Kempton and Lingfield), the evocative remains of the international motor racing circuit of Brooklands, opened in 1907 and famed for its banked corners, the Royal Horticultural Society's gardens and research centre at Wisley (a horticulturalist's dream), and a theme park at Thorpe Park.

Horse racing at Sandown Park, Esher.

Leith Hill Tower, near Coldharbour village.

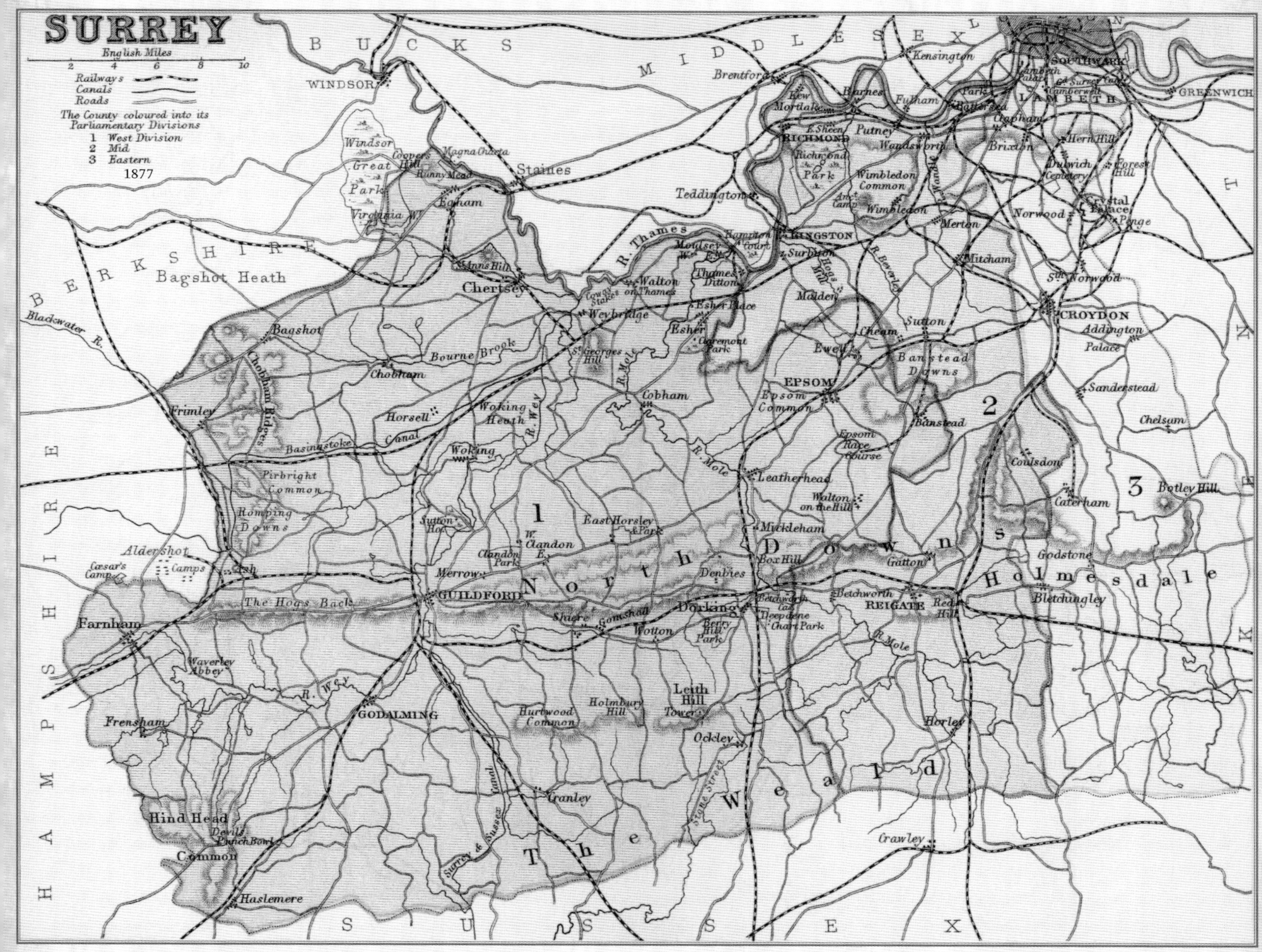

SURREY

English Miles
2 4 6 8 10

Railways
Canals
Roads
The County coloured into its
Parliamentary Divisions
1 West Division
2 Mid
3 Eastern
1877

Bartholomew Gazetteer of the British Isles, 1887

SURREY, co. in SE. of England, bounded N. by the Thames, which separates it from Bucks and Middlesex, E. by Kent, S. by Sussex, W. by Hants, and NW. by Berks; greatest length, N. and S., 26 miles; greatest breadth, E. and W., 40 miles; area, 485,129 ac., pop. 1,436,899. The co. is traversed from E. to W. by the North Downs range, from which the surface slopes gently down towards the Thames on the N., while on the S. it descends into an extensive flat plain (partly also in the cos. of Kent and Sussex) called the Weald. Except a small portion in the SW., and another small portion in the SE., the whole of the co. is drained by the Thames and its tributaries, the Wey, Mole, and Wandle. There are many varieties of soil, including plastic and alluvial clays, rich vegetable loam, calcareous earth, and almost barren heath. On the plastic clays the crops are wheat and beans; the alluvial soils, particularly in the vicinity of the metropolis, are chiefly occupied by orchards, market gardens, and farms for the culture of medical and aromatic plants; on the loamy soils the crops are barley, oats, and pease, carrots and parsnips; while the chief products of the calcareous soils are hops and clover. There are some industries in oil, paper, calicoes, woollen goods, &c., and those places situated on the Thames share in the trade of the port of London, but (except in that part of the co. included within the limits of the metropolis) the trade and mfrs, are not of great importance. The amenities of climate and scenery, the vicinity of the metropolis, and the complete means of railway communication, have caused many parts of Surrey to be studded over with mansions and villas. The co. contains 14 hundreds, 152 parishes with parts of 2 others, the metropolitan bors. of Battersea and Clapham, Camberwell, Lambeth, Newington, Southwark, and Wandsworth – and the mun. bors. of Croydon, Godalming, Guildford, Kingston upon Thames, and Reigate. The co. is in the dioceses of Canterbury, Rochester, and Winchester.

Hampton Court Palace

WINDSOR AND MAIDENHEAD

WOKINGHAM

BRACKNELL

FOREST

HAMPSHIRE

North

Downs

South Downs National Park

SURR

WES

British National Grid projection

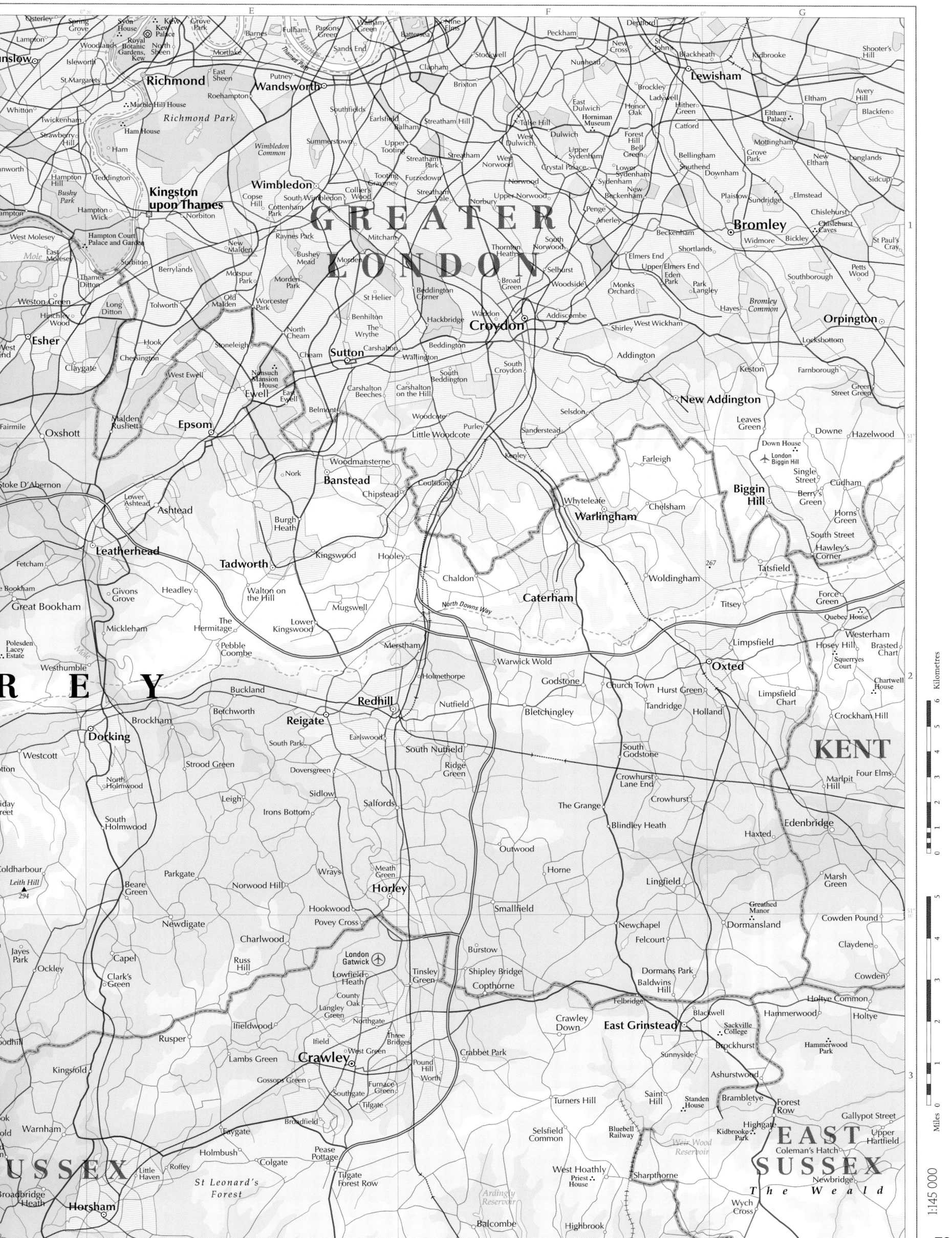

GREATER LONDON

REY

KENT

USSEX

EAST SUSSEX
The Weald

1:45 000

© Collins Bartholomew Ltd

BERKSHIRE'S UNITARY AUTHORITIES

Bracknell Forest	**Area** sq. km 109; sq miles 42 **Population** 114,700 **County town** Bracknell
Reading	**Area** sq. km 40; sq miles 16 **Population** 145,700 **County town** Reading
Slough	**Area** sq. km 33; sq miles 13 **Population** 121,200 **County town** Slough
West Berkshire	**Area** sq. km 704; sq miles 272 **Population** 152,800 **County town** Newbury
Windsor and Maidenhead	**Area** sq. km 198; sq miles 77 **Population** 142,800 **County town** Maidenhead
Wokingham	**Area** sq. km 179; sq miles 69 **Population** 159,100 **County town** Wokingham
Highest point of Ceremonial County	Walbury Hill (297 m) close to the Hampshire border

The name of Berkshire comes from the Celtic *berroc* meaning 'hilly place'. It is the only royal county in England, officially sanctioned since 1958. It is now just a ceremonial county, administered by six unitary authorities.

FAMOUS FOR

Queen Victoria made her first railway journey in 1842, travelling in a special Royal train from **Slough** to Paddington Station in London.

The Cox's Orange Pippin apple was first grown by Richard Cox at his nursery at **Colnbrook**, near Slough, in 1857.

T. E. Lawrence lost his 1919 draft of the *Seven Pillars of Wisdom* at Reading Railway Station, and had to rewrite the text from memory, while **Oscar Wilde** was the most famous resident of Reading Gaol from 1895–7, while serving his sentence of two years for 'gross indecency' relating to his homosexuality.

The Prehistoric **Ridgeway** that runs along the northern ridge of the Downs is part of the Ridgeway Trail that runs from Overton Hill near Avebury in Wiltshire to Ivinghoe Beacon in Buckinghamshire.

Greenham Common to the south of Newbury used to be a major American airbase. In the 1980s it was the focus of major demonstrations as nuclear-armed Cruise missiles were based there. The airbase is now closed, and the area has been returned to traditional open heathland, albeit with reminders of its military past still there.

Slough has always suffered from its somewhat unfortunate name – the use of the word 'slough' goes back to around 1190, when the name 'Slo' was recorded; most accept it describes the original site of Slough as a muddy or miry place.

FAMOUS PEOPLE

Edward III, King of England (1327–1377), born Windsor Castle, 1312.
Henry VI, King of England (1422–61, 1470–71), the last Lancastrian king, born Windsor Castle, 1421
Jethro Tull, inventor of the seed drill, born Basildon, 1674.
Sir John Herschel, astronomer and son of Sir William Herschel, born Slough 1792.
Sir Stanley Spencer, artist, born Cookham, 1891.
Sir Sydney Camm, aircraft designer, whose work includes the Hawker Hurricane, born Windsor, 1893.
Lord Louis Mountbatten, Admiral of the Fleet, last Viceroy of India and uncle of Prince Philip, Duke of Edinburgh, born Frogmore House, Windsor, 1900.
Humphrey Lyttleton (known as Humph), jazz musician and broadcaster, born Eton, 1921.
Michael Bond, creator of Paddington Bear, born Newbury, 1926.

Berkshire, now just a ceremonial county, was one of the oldest counties in Britain, being first mentioned in the *Anglo-Saxon Chronicle* in 860. William the Conqueror built one of his royal castles at Windsor shortly after the Norman Conquest and a more substantial stone castle was built there by Henry II (1165–79); it is the oldest royal palace still in active use. Berkshire's northern boundary used to follow the river Thames to the Wiltshire border. However, in the 1974 local government changes, it lost the Vale of the White Horse along with the towns of Faringdon, Wantage, Abingdon, Didcot and Wallingford to Oxfordshire, while gaining Slough and Eton from Buckinghamshire. With the growth of the new town of Bracknell, the focus of the county changed, with the bulk of its population concentrated close to London. In 1996 it ceased to be a county at all, apart from ceremonial functions, as it was divided into six separate unitary authorities that stretch from east to west – Slough, Windsor and Maidenhead, Bracknell Forest, Wokingham, Reading and West Berkshire.

Slough (population 121,200) began to develop when the Great Western Railway arrived in 1840, and it started to become a manufacturing centre – next to the station is the Horlicks factory, built in 1906 to make the famous malted drink. In the 1920s, Britain's first industrial estate was developed and it attracted many new businesses – the very first Mars bar was made there in 1932. While the service sector has grown significantly in recent years, manufacturing provides over 12 per cent of the jobs, compared with a regional average of 8.5 per cent, while transport, influenced by Slough's proximity to Heathrow airport, provides 14 per cent of jobs. Slough is the most ethnically diverse area outside of London, and Britain's first black mayor was appointed there in 1984.

The **Royal Borough of Windsor and Maidenhead** (population 142,800) is centred around the two towns of Windsor (population 30,568) and Maidenhead (58,848), while other settlements include Datchet, Eton, Ascot and Sunningdale. The river Thames forms the northern boundary, and, with 83 per cent of the area designated as green belt, the area is lush and green, albeit that there is a danger of flooding by the river Thames, with 19 per cent of the land area at high risk. The service sector provides over 90 per cent of the jobs in the area, of which 10 per cent are in tourism. Tourist attractions include Windsor Castle and the former Royal hunting estate of Windsor Great Park, Ascot racecourse, Windsor Legoland and Eton College.

Bracknell Forest (population 114,700) is centred on its main settlement, Bracknell (70,795). Designated as a new town in 1949, Bracknell was originally designed to have a population of 25,000; it is now almost triple that size. To the north of Bracknell are the villages of Winkfield and Binfield. To the south lies forest and heathland, and the town of Crowthorne, home both to the public school, Wellington College, founded in 1859 as a national monument to the Duke of Wellington, and Broadmoor Hospital, a high-security psychiatric hospital, established in 1863, and the town of Sandhurst famous for the Royal Military Academy.

Wokingham authority (population 159,100) includes riverside villages in the north, with undulating ridges covered by woodlands, and commons in the south. Wokingham (39,544) is a growing centre for hi-tech and computer industries. The river Thames forms the northern border, and the river Blackwater forms the border to the south.

Reading (population 145,700) developed as a crossing point of the River Thames and its tributary, the River Kennet. Traditional industries include brewing and food production, notably biscuits. These industries are accompanied by an increasing sector of hi-tech and computer-based companies, including Microsoft, the largest private-sector employer, attracted by Reading's location in the M4 corridor. Reading's university was established in 1926, with its origins going back to 1860. It is also known as an entertainments centre, with the Reading Festival, an annual event since 1971, leading the way.

West Berkshire (population 152,800) occupies over half the land area of Berkshire. The main towns are Newbury, the administrative centre, Thatcham and Hungerford. The West Berkshire countryside is dominated by the rolling North Wessex Downs, with a major centre of racehorse training at Lambourn and a renowned racecourse at Newbury. The M4 motorway makes it a major transport artery, while the historically significant Kennet and Avon Canal linked Reading to Bristol.

"Windsor stood out in the evening light: I think there can be no place like it." Gerard Manley Hopkins, 1874

"Probably the battle of Waterloo was won on the playing-fields of Eton, but the opening battles of all subsequent wars have been lost there." George Orwell, 1941

"[St George's Chapel, Winsdor Castle] has stood out the injury of time to admiration; the beauty of the building remains without any addition, and, indeed, requiring none." Daniel Defoe, 1724

Windsor Castle, Windsor.

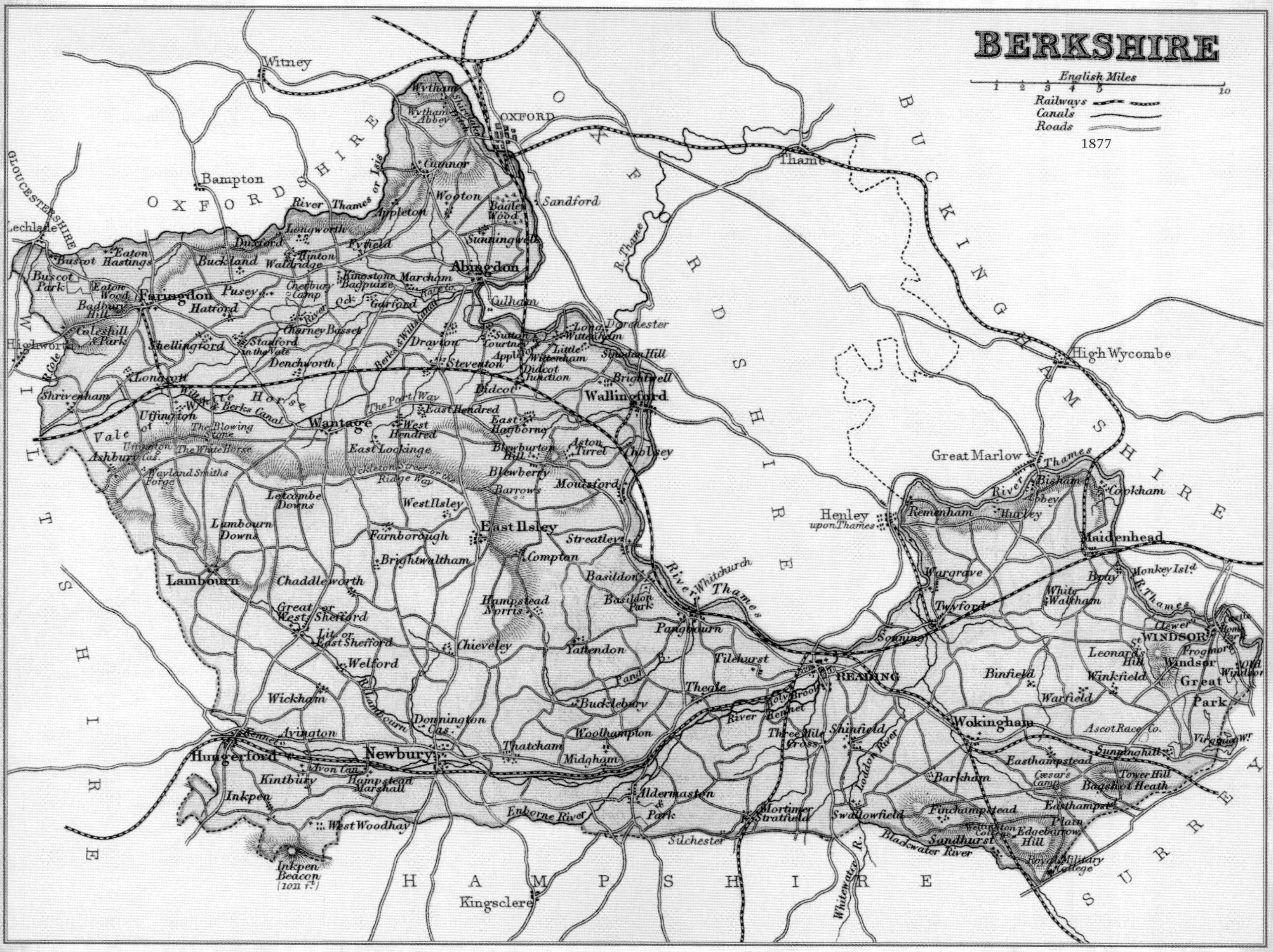

BERKSHIRE

English Miles

Railways
Canals
Roads

1877

Bartholomew Gazetteer of the British Isles, 1887

BERKSHIRE, one of the inland cos. of England, lying between Hants and the river Thames, bounded on the N. by Gloucestershire, Oxfordshire, and Bucks, E by Surrey, S. by Herts, and W. by Wilts; greatest length, E. and W., 53 miles; greatest breadth, N. and W., 30 miles; area 462,210 ac., pop. 218,363. It is intersected in a westerly direction by a line of chalk hills, a continuation of the Chilterns, the highest elevation being White Horse Hill, alt. 893 ft. N. Of this is the White horse Vale (so called from the figure of a horse cut out on the hillside), and to the S. lies the Vale of Kennet, watered by the Kennet stream. These tracts are well cultivated, and produce good crops of grain &c., especially in the Vale of the

White Horse. Dairy farms and commons abound; much of the surface in under woods, chiefly of oak and beech. Windsor Forest, covering upwards of 50,000 ac., lies in the E.. the Thames flows along the entire N. boundary (100 miles in extent); its tributaries are the Kennet, Lambourn, Ock, and Loddon. Reading.– mun. bor., and co. town of Berks, on river Kennet, near its confluence with the Thames, 36 miles W. of London by rail – mun. bor., 2186 ac., pop. 42,054; 4 Banks, 4 newspapers. Market-days, Wednesday and Saturday. Reading was a town in Saxon times, was occupied by the Danes in 871, and has remains of a magnificent abbey founded by Henry I., who was buried within the precincts in 1135; was the frequent meeting-place of church councils and

parliaments until 1466; and was fortified by the royalists, and besieged and taken by Essex, during the Civil War. The town is well laid out, and has some fine public buildings. Reading is the centre of a large agricultural district, and is also a great railway centre, while it has extensive water conveyance by the Thames and Kennet navigations; and it carries on an important trade in all kinds of agricultural produce, and in supplying the surrounding towns with goods. The industrial establishments include iron foundries, engine works, agricultural implement manufactories, flour mills, breweries, potteries, boat-building yards, a biscuit factory, and a seed emporium. Archbishop Laud (1573–1645) was a native.

cky Gervais, comedian and actor, born Reading, 1961.

Eton College, near Windsor.

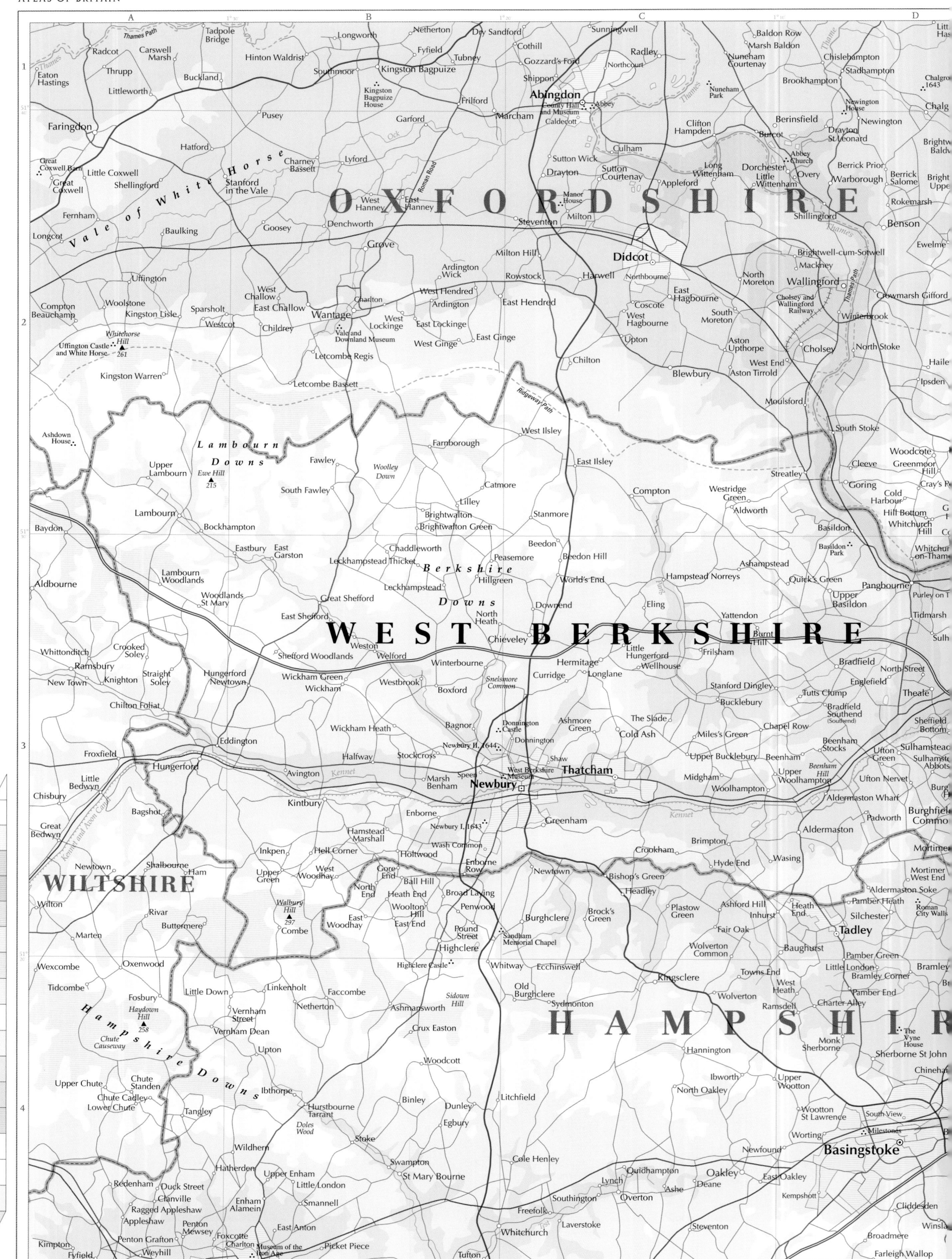

Metres Feet
1000 3280
900 2952
800 2624
700 2296
600 1968
500 1640
400 1312
300 4921
200 656
150 492
100 328
50 164
0 Land below sea level
50 164
200 656
1000 3281

82

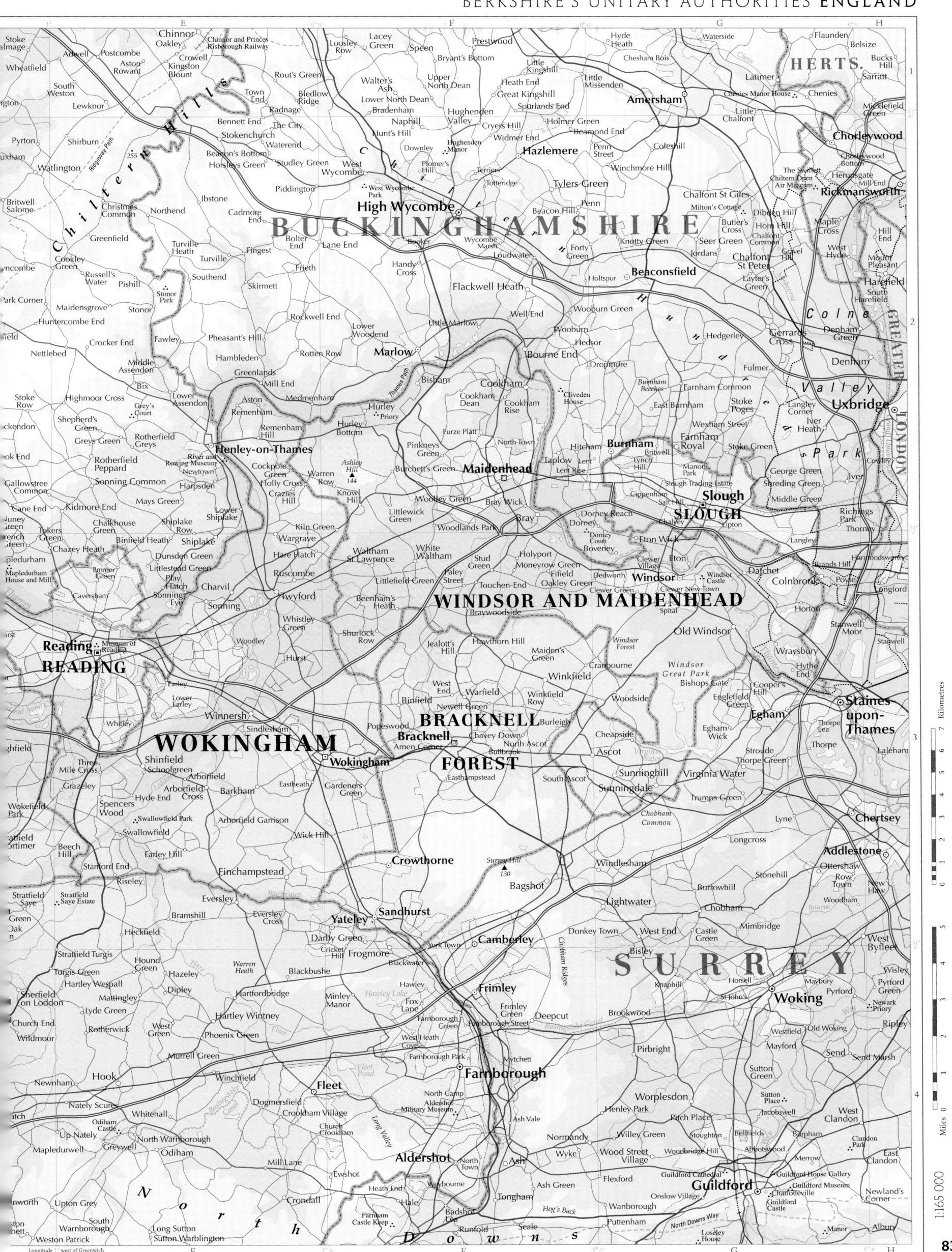

1:165 000

WILTSHIRE

Area Sq Km	3,255
Area Sq Miles	1,257
Population	455,500
County town	Trowbridge
Highest point	Milk Hill (294 m), near Alton Priors

Wiltshire takes its name from Wilton, near Salisbury – the shire of the people of Wilton, itself derived from the River Wylye, a Celtic name indicating a river liable to flood.

FAMOUS FOR

Salisbury Cathedral was built in a uniform Early English style between 1220 and 1320, to replace an older cathedral at Old Sarum, just to the north of Salisbury. Its spire, at 123 m high, is the tallest surviving medieval spire in Europe.

Near Devizes, at **Caen Hill**, is an extraordinary flight of canal locks that take the Kennet and Avon canal up 72 m in 29 locks over a distance of just over 3 km. The steepest flight contains 16 locks that follow immediately after each other straight up the hill.

Just south of Marlborough lies **Savernake Forest**, first referred to in a charter from King Athelstan in 934. After the Norman Conquest, care of the forest was given to Richard Esurmy, a victorious knight, and it has remained in his family ever since, the only privately owned ancient forest in Britain.

One of the most remarkable country houses ever built in Britain was **Fonthill Abbey**, at Fonthill Gifford, designed by James Wyatt for William Beckford, reputedly Britain's richest commoner. Built in the Gothic style, its main octagonal tower was 90 m tall and the main doors were over 11 m high. Beckford lived there alone for 20 years until he sold it in 1823. Shortly after that the main tower collapsed and now nothing remains.

One of the finest Saxon churches in Britain is **St Laurence** at Bradford on Avon, dating from the 10th century – but it was only rediscovered in 1856, for it had been converted into a school and a cottage and was surrounded by other buildings.

Maud Heath's Causeway near Chippenham, which was built in the 15th century, enabled travellers to walk across the water meadows of the Avon and keep their feet dry; it is over 6 km long.

FAMOUS PEOPLE

Thomas Hobbes, political philosopher author of *The Leviathan*, born Malmesbury, 1588.
Edward Hyde, Earl of Clarendon, Restoration statesman and author of *The History of the Rebellion and Civil Wars in England*, born Dinton, 1609.
Sir Christopher Wren, architect and scientist, born East Knoyle, 1632.
Joseph Addison, essayist, politician and co-founder of *The Spectator*, born Milston, 1672.
Henry Shrapnel, Army officer and inventor of the 'Shrapnel shell', born Bradford-upon-Avon, 1761.
Sir Isaac Pitman, educationalist and inventor of shorthand, born Trowbridge, 1813.
Robert Morley, actor, born Semley, 1908.
Michael Crawford, actor, born Salisbury, 1942.
William (Will) Carling, rugby union player, born Bradford-on-Avon, 1965.
James Blunt, popular musician, born Tidworth, 1974.

Wiltshire consists of extensive chalk uplands scattered with prehistoric remains, notably at Avebury and Stonehenge, and interspersed with wide, well-watered valleys. The north of the county is dominated by the Marlborough Downs which are much used for racehorse training, while in the south the chalk plateau of Salisbury Plain is an important military training area. Between these two upland areas lies the fertile Vale of Pewsey. Rivers include the so-called Bristol and Wiltshire Avons, Ebble, Kennet, Nadder, Wylye, and the upper reaches of the Thames.

In prehistoric times, the area was one of the most heavily populated in Britain, but it was not widely settled by the Romans, and the basic form of Wiltshire did not emerge until the 10th century. The County Council was formed in 1888, but it was not until 1940 that a County Hall was finally opened in Trowbridge, which became the administrative centre. In 1997 Swindon became an independent unitary council and, in 2009, the rest of Wiltshire became a unitary authority when the districts of Kennet, North Wiltshire, Salisbury and West Wiltshire were abolished.

The population of Wiltshire is 455,500, and in the ten years to 2008 it had grown by 7.9 per cent, over 40 per cent above the average for England. The population is distributed among many towns and villages scattered across this large county. The main centres of population are Salisbury (43,355), Trowbridge (34,401), Chippenham (33,189), Warminster (17,486), Devizes (14,379) and Melksham (14,372). Over half the jobs in the county are either in administration, health and education or in finance, IT and other business activities while other industries include electronics, computing, pharmaceuticals, plastics and telecommunications, though the industrial centre of the area is in Swindon.

Wiltshire contains some of the most important prehistoric remains in Britain – indeed Avebury, Stonehenge and their surrounding sites make up a UNESCO World Heritage Site. The enormous stone circle at Avebury was constructed around 2100 BC and contains an outer stone circle of 98 massive stones and two smaller inner circles. Much of the medieval village of Avebury is within the circle. Heading south from Avebury is an avenue of standing stones leading to Silbury Hill, the largest prehistoric mound in Europe. The scale is immense – the base covers 2.1 ha and it is 40 m high, but, despite excavations, its purpose has not been established. Stonehenge, around 30 km to the south on Salisbury Plain is the most sophisticated prehistoric monument in Europe. It was constructed over a period of about 1500 years from 2900 BC, using not just the local sarsen stones, some weighing up to 45 tonnes, but also bluestones, some up to 4 tonnes, that were transported from Pembrokeshire. While we will never know how it was used, the alignment of the stones to greet the rising sun on midsummer's day must be of significance.

Stained-glass windows in Salisbury Cathedral.

Caen Hill Locks, near Devizes.

Stonehenge, Salisbury Plain.

"To Stonehenge over the plain and some prodigious great hills even to fright us. Came thither and them find as prodigious as any tales I ever heard of them and worth going this journey to see. God knows what their use was."
Samuel Pepys, 1668

As many days as in one year there be,
So many windows in one church we see;
As many marble pillars there appear,
As there are hours throughout the fleeting year;
As many gates as moons one year do view;
Strange to tell, yet not more strange than true.
Traditional rhyme about Salisbury Cathedral

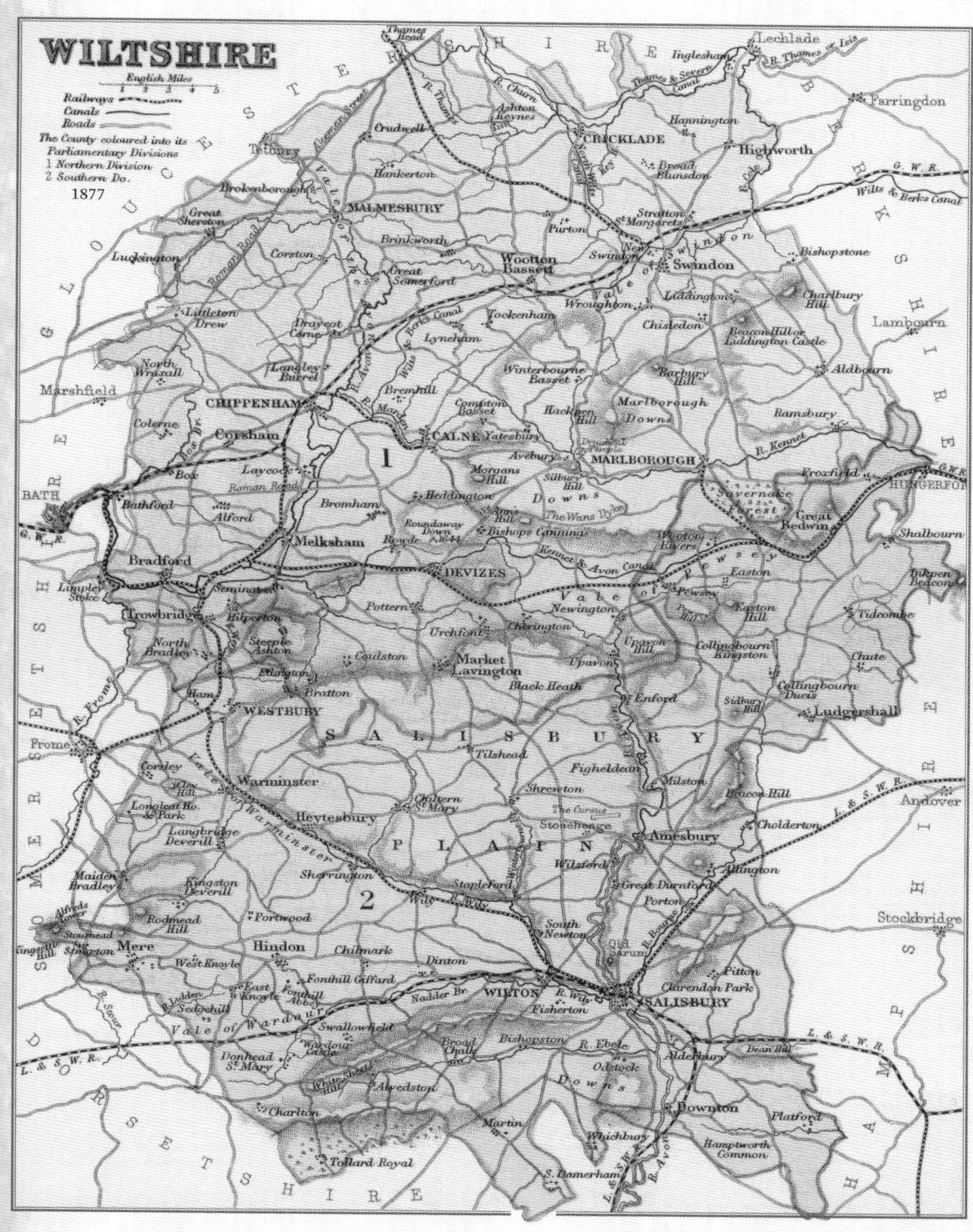

WILTSHIRE

English Miles

Railways
Canals
Roads
The County coloured into its
Parliamentary Divisions
1 Northern Division
2 Southern Do.
1877

Bartholomew Gazetteer of the British Isles, 1887
WILTSHIRE (or Wilts), co. in SW. of England, bounded NW. and N. by Gloucestershire, E. by Berks and Hants, S. by Hants and Dorset, and W. by Somerset; greatest length, N. and S., 53 miles; greatest breadth, E. and W., 37 miles; area, 866,677 ac., pop. 258,965. The county is divided into 2 divisions by the Vale of Pewsey extending E. and W., the northern principally a fertile flat rising near the N. border in the direction of the Cotswold Hills, the southern a varied district broken by downs and intersected by fertile and well-watered valleys. To the northern division belong the Marlborough Downs, and in the southern division is Salisbury Plain. The principal rivers are the Upper Avon, flowing SW. to the Bristol Channel; the Lower Avon (with its tributaries the Wiley, Nadder, and Bourne), flowing S. to the English Channel; and the Kennet, flowing E. to the Thames. The greater part of the surface is kept in pasture, devoted in the northern division to grazing and dairy farming, and in the southern division to the rearing of sheep. Wiltshire is famous for its bacon and cheese. The geological strata are principally cretaceous, forming part of the central chalk district of England. Ironstone is abundant. The principal mfrs. are woollens and carpets at Bradford, Trowbridge, Westbury, and Wilton; cutlery and steel goods at Salisbury; ironfounding at Devizes; and ropes and sacking at Marlborough. The locomotive and carriage works of the Great Western Railway are at Swindon, and near Downton is the College of Agriculture. Wiltshire is especially remarkable for the number and variety of the memorials of antiquity left by Britons, Romans, Saxons, and Danes, the chief of these being the megalithic remains of Stonehenge and Avebury.

SWINDON

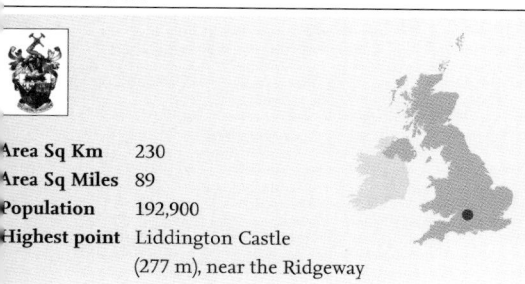

Area Sq Km 230
Area Sq Miles 89
Population 192,900
Highest point Liddington Castle
(277 m), near the Ridgeway

Swindon and the area around it, traditionally part of Wiltshire, latterly as the district of Thamesdown, became a unitary authority in 1997. As well as the major centre of Swindon, it includes the towns of Stratton St Margaret, Highworth and Wroughton. The area is located between the Cotswold Hills and Wiltshire Downs, on the fringes of the Thames Valley. The river Thames borders the area to the north and the river Cole to the east. Originally a railway town, selected by Isambard Kingdom Brunel to be the main railway workshops for the Great Western Railway in 1840, Swindon has experienced rapid recent growth and is now a centre for car manufacture and for many commercial and distribution operations. The impact on employment is clear as fewer than 20 per cent of the jobs in Swindon are in the public sector.

FAMOUS FOR
The railway works closed in 1986, and now part of the workshops have become STEAM, the **Museum of the Great Western Railway** – 'God's Wonderful Railway', as it was known.

In 2009, to the surprise of many, **Swindon** became the first town in Britain to be twinned with Disney World in Florida.

FAMOUS PEOPLE
Richard Jefferies, naturalist and novelist, born 1848
Diana Dors, actress, born 1931.
John Francome, champion national Hunt jockey, born 1952.
Billie Piper, (born Leanne Piper) singer and actress, born 1982.

Close up of the 'Caerphilly Castle', one of the steam locomotives on display at the Museum of the Great Western Railway.

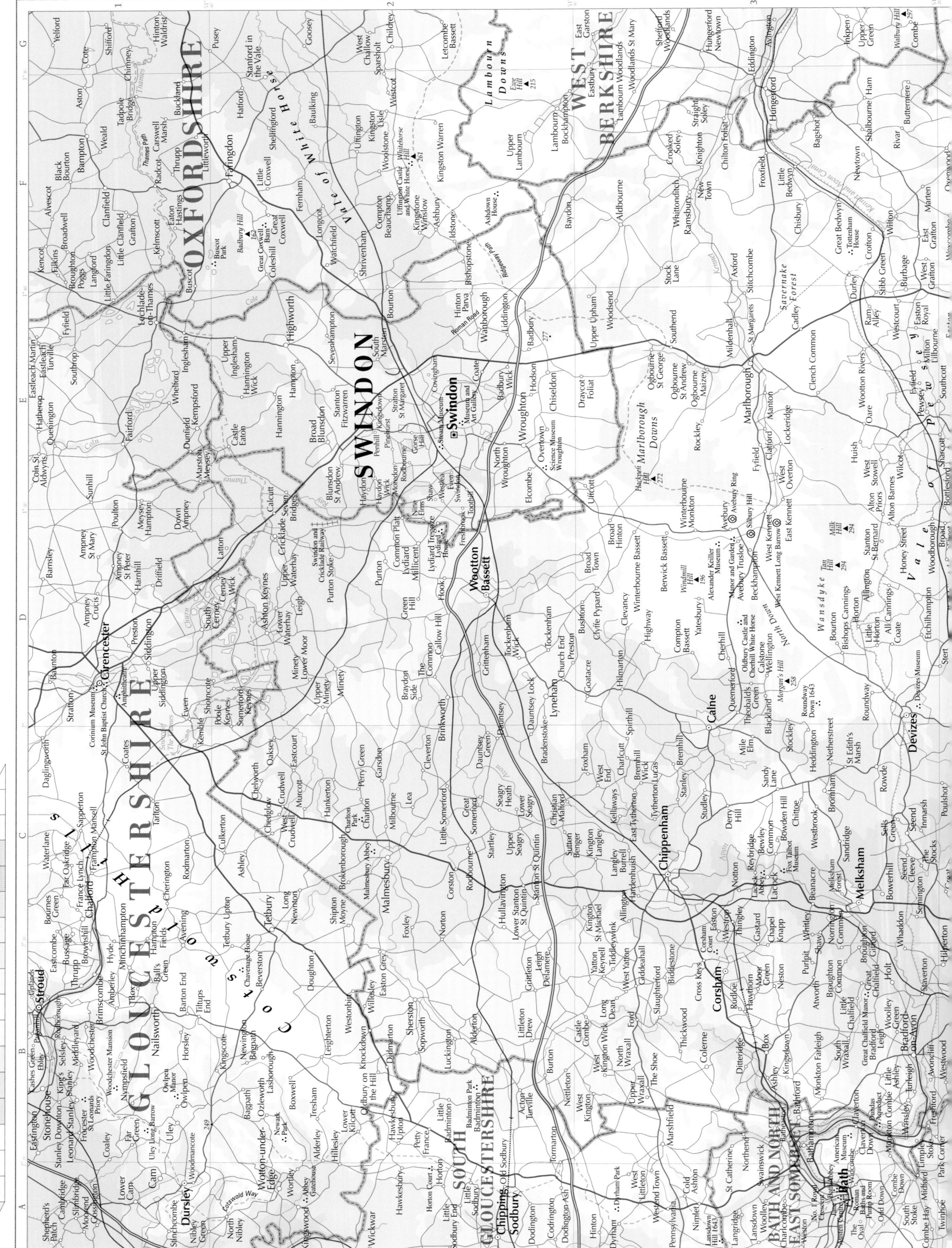

British National Grid projection

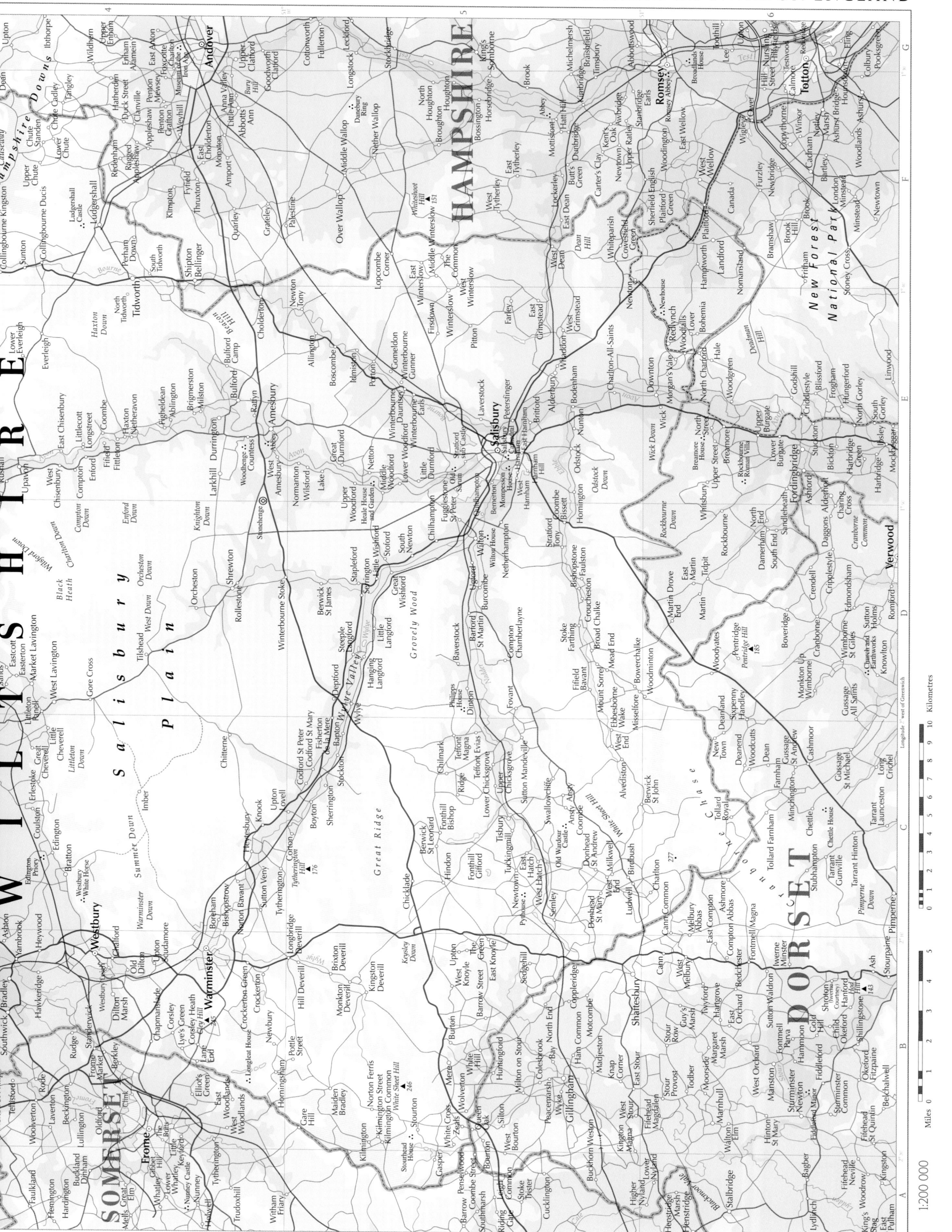

© Collins Bartholomew Ltd

SOMERSET

Area Sq Km	3514
Area Sq Miles	1357
Population	525,800
County town	Taunton
Highest point	Dunkery Beacon (519 m), on Exmoor
Districts	Mendip; Sedgemoor; South Somerset; Taunton Deane; West Somerset

The name of Somerset originally described the people who lived around Somerton, a former capital of Somerset, sited on the edge of Sedgemoor. Somerton itself means 'summer farm'.

FAMOUS FOR

The **Willow Man** is a 12-m-high sculpture in willow that was created by the artist Serena de la Hay, by the side of the M5 motorway near Bridgwater.

Castle House in **Bridgwater**, built by John Broad, a local brickmaker in 1851, was one of the first houses in the world to make extensive structural and decorative use of precast concrete.

King Alfred the Great created a stronghold at **Athelney** in Sedgemoor in 878 during the Danish invasion of Wessex prior to his defeat of the Danes at Edington in May 878. It was at Athelney that he allegedly burnt the cakes.

The oldest Neolithic timber trackway in Europe is **Sweet Track** in the Somerset Levels near the village of Westhay; it was built from oak planks around 3807 BC.

Shepton Mallett prison is the oldest prison still in use, its first buildings having been erected in 1610.

Arthur Wellesley, the first Duke of **Wellington**, took his title from the Somerset town of Wellington, close to the Blackdown Hills, where there is a large monument to him.

The hilltop **Cadbury Fort**, near Yeovil, is the legendary site of King Arthur's Camelot. Its formidable earthen ramparts were first built around 600 BC and were significantly improved around AD 500, by Arthur, some have argued.

The plum that '**Little Jack Horner**' pulled out of the pie is thought to be the deeds of the Manor of **Mells**; Thomas Horner was steward of the Abbey at Glastonbury around the dissolution of the monasteries. The Abbot sent him to see the King with a present of the deeds of the Abbey's estates hidden in a pie (to stop them being stolen). Temptation, it is thought, proved too much, and he took one of the deeds from the pie.

FAMOUS PEOPLE

Roger Bacon, philosopher and scientist, born Ilchester, c. 1214–20.
John Pym, leading Parliamentary opponent to Charles I, born Brymore House, near Bridgwater, 1584.
William Dampier, navigator and explorer, born East Coker, near Yeovil, 1651.
Henry Fielding, author and joint founder of the Bow Street Runners, London's first police force, born Sharpham Park, near Glastonbury, 1707.
Sir Henry Irving (born John Henry Brodribb), actor, born Keiton Mandeville, 1838.
Ernest Bevin, trade union leader and Labour politician, born Winsford, 1881.
Sir Arthur Charles Clarke, science fiction author and inventor, born Minehead, 1917.
Mary Rand, first British woman to win an athletics Olympic Gold, in the long jump (1964), born Wells, 1940.
Jenson Button, world-champion racing driver, born Frome, 1980.

Somerset consists of several hill ranges, including the Mendip, Polden, Quantock and Brendon Hills, along with most of Exmoor. These uplands are separated by valleys, or, on either side of the river Parrett, by the extensive marshy flats of Sedgemoor. The chief rivers are Axe, Brue, Parrett and Tone, draining into the Bristol Channel; and Barle and Exe, rising on Exmoor and flowing into Devon and the English Channel.

The county of Somerset traditionally stretched from Exmoor to the outskirts of Bristol. In the 1974 local government changes a new county of Avon was created, centred on Bristol, and the north and north east of Somerset was lost to it. In further reforms in 1996 Avon was abolished and the area that was in Somerset became two new unitary authorities, North Somerset, based around Weston-super-Mare, and Bath and North East Somerset, based on Bath. The ceremonial county of Somerset includes these two authorities.

The county, with a population of 525,800, is predominantly rural, with the main population in the villages and towns of central and eastern Somerset. Taunton, the county town is also the largest (58,241), with employment much focused on public service, education and the Ministry of Defence's UK Hydrographic Office. Other significant towns are Yeovil (41,871), home of the UK's only helicopter manufacturer, Augusta Westland, Bridgwater (36,563), Frome (24,171), Burnham on Sea and Highbridge (21,476), Chard (12,008), Street (11,669) and Wells (10,406). As in other areas of the southwest, population is growing at a faster rate than the rest of the UK, growth led by inward migration into the area, including a large number of retired people, so that the working age population is a lower percentage of the total than many places in the UK.

The economy of Somerset still has a major agriculture and food production sector – including the making of Cheddar cheese and the production of cider, for which the county is renowned. There is a surprisingly large manufacturing sector, particularly linked to aeronautics, defence and building materials. The largest sector for employment is in distribution, retail, hotels and restaurants (28 per cent), followed by public administration, education and health (27 per cent). Manufacturing provided 14 per cent of jobs, well above the national average. The main

London to Penzance railway cuts across the bottom of the county and Taunton and Bridgwater are close to the motorway system.

Tourism is becoming more important for the area, particularly in the west of Somerset, dominated by the Exmoor National Park, 71 per cent of which lies in Somerset. The park includes the highest sea cliffs in England, at 250m, found just into Devon at Great Hangman near Combe Martin. Indeed, the shoreline of Exmoor is very remote, with few places on the 55 km length of the coastline where a boat can land. The smallest church in England is at Culbone, a church with Saxon origins only accessible on foot. The market town of Dunster and the seaside resort of Minehead mark the end of Exmoor.

The Quantock Hills divide the Vale of Taunton from the Somerset Levels, an area of flat land, now drained but once peaty, inaccessible marshland. Near Westonzoyland is the site of the last battle fought on English soil – the Battle of Sedgemoor (1685), which saw the defeat of the Duke of Monmouth's rising against James II, followed by the 'Bloody Assizes' in the region when over 320 men were sentenced to death by Lord Chief Justice George Jeffreys, 144 alone at the Taunton Assizes. The Levels are divided by the Polden Hills and to their north lies Glastonbury, in legend the place where Joseph of Arimathea brought Christianity to Britain, and the site of one of the largest medieval monasteries. Nearby is Glastonbury Tor, a hill with many pagan associations, marked by the tower of the ruined church at its top. Beyond the Levels rise the bare Mendip Hills, where erosion of the limestone has produced many gorges and caves including Wookey Hole and Cheddar Gorge, in whose caves evidence of human settlement from 25,000 years ago has been found. The Mendips have also provided the stone for one of Britain's most beautiful cathedrals, built in the 13th and 14th centuries, in the very small city of Wells. The inside is dominated by extraordinary 'scissor' arches added to support the tower in 1338.

The major town in the south of the county is Yeovil and it is the centre both for this area and north Dorset. While Yeovil is surprisingly industrial, the remainder of the area features smaller market towns such as Chard, Crewkerne, Ilminster and Wincanton.

St Michael's Tower on Glastonbury Tor.

Wild Exmoor ponies are the oldest British native breed.

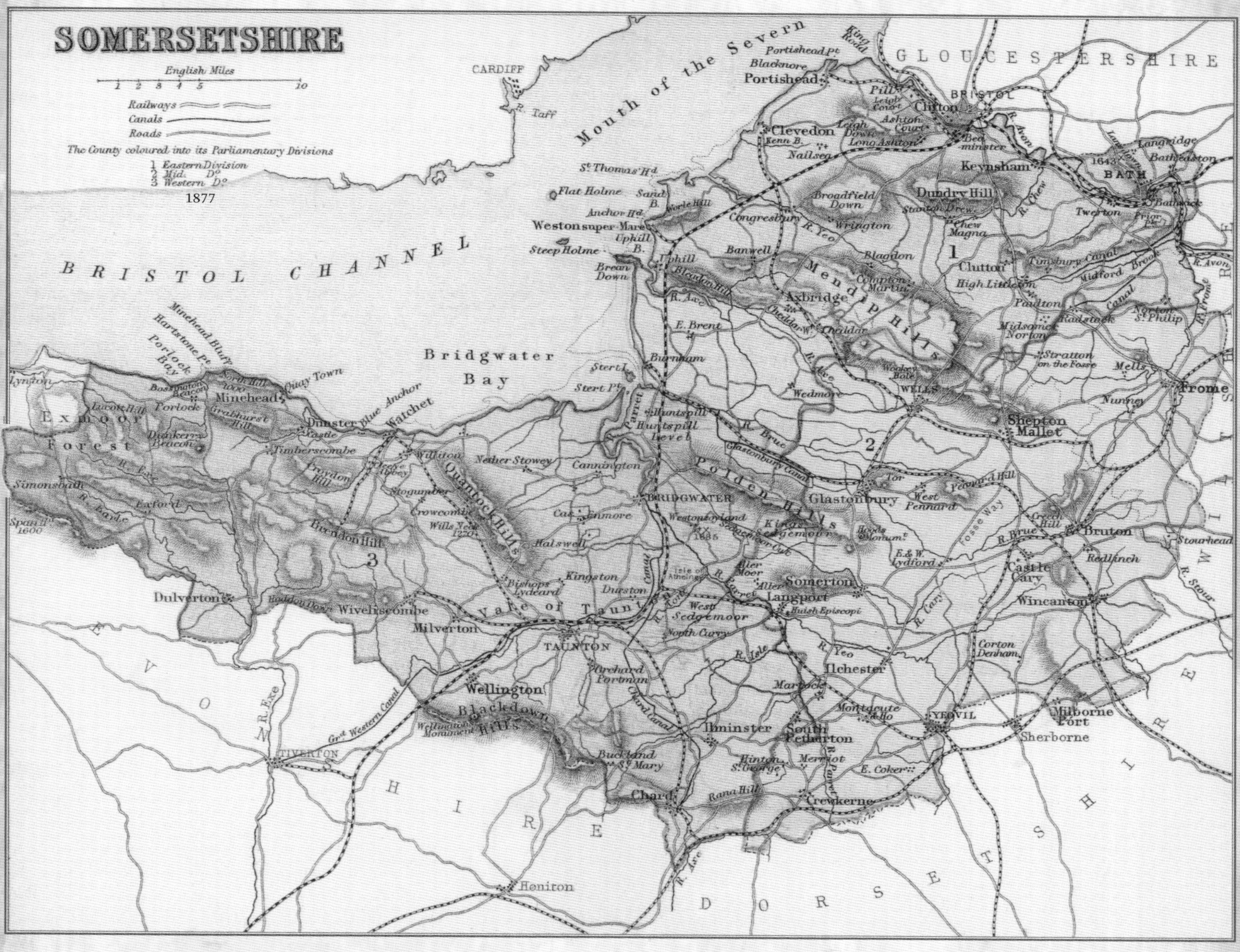

SOMERSETSHIRE

English Miles

Railways
Canals
Roads

The County coloured into its Parliamentary Divisions
1 Eastern Division
2 Mid. Do
3 Western Do

1877

MOUTH OF THE SEVERN

GLOUCESTERSHIRE

BRISTOL CHANNEL

Bridgwater Bay

Exmoor Forest

Vale of Taun

DORSETSHIRE

DEVONSHIRE

Bartholomew Gazetteer of the British Isles, 1887

SOMERSET, *maritime co. in SW. of England, bounded N. and NE. by the Bristol Channel and the estuary of the Severn, and from NE. round to S W. by the counties of Gloucester, Wilts, Dorset, and Devon; greatest length, N. and S., 43 miles; greatest breadth, E. and W., 67 miles; area, 1,049,812 ac., pop. 469,109. The coast line is generally low and marshy in the E., but lined with lofty slate cliffs in the W. The interior consists of ranges of hills separated by valleys, or by extensive low marshy flats. The principal ranges are the Mendip Hills, the Polden Hills, the Quantock Hills, the Brendon Hills, and Exmoor. The chief rivers are the Avon and the Parret (with its tributaries the Yeo or Ivel, Isle, and Tone), the former forming the boundary on the NE., the latter traversing the centre of the co.; the other streams are the Yeo, Ax, and Brue. Both soil and climate are well adapted for agriculture, particularly in the low alluvial tracts; and in the Vale of Taunton heavy crops of the finest wheat are raised. The rich meadows rear large numbers of cattle, and the hilly grounds are pastured with numerous flocks of sheep. In the E. of the co. are some small isolated coalfields, the most southerly in England, the quarries which furnish the famous Bath stone, and a large development of magnesian limestone; the W. of the co. consists chiefly of slaty rocks, forming the wild moorlands of Exmoor. The chief minerals worked are lead, iron, and slate. The principal mfrs. are woollen and worsted goods, gloves, lace, linen, crape, silk, paper, glass, and bath-bricks. There are salmon, herring, and other fisheries in the Bristol Channel. An important chain of internal communication is formed by the Yeo and Parret navigation and the Glastonbury Canal. The co. contains 40 hundreds, 2 liberties, 489 pars, with parts of 3 others, and the mun. bors. of Bath, Bridgwater, Chard, Glastonbury, Taunton, Wells, and Yeovil. It is nearly co-extensive with the diocese of Bath and Wells.*

e interior of Wells Cathedral, Wells.

Cheddar Gorge, Mendip Hills.

NORTH SOMERSET

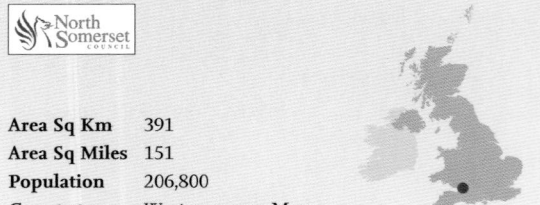

Area Sq Km	391
Area Sq Miles	151
Population	206,800
County town	Weston-super-Mare
Highest point	Blagdon Hill (240 m)

FAMOUS FOR

Bob Hope's father was a stonemason from Weston-super-Mare, and the young Bob Hope spent some time there before the family emigrated to the USA.

Jeffrey Archer, novelist and politician, was brought up in Weston-super-Mare from 1940, two weeks after he was born in London.

Tyntesfield House, near Wraxhall, is an exuberant Victorian Gothic country house, started in 1863 and now owned by the National Trust. It contains an amazing record of the life and tastes of four generations of the Gibbs family who created it.

FAMOUS PEOPLE

John Locke, philosopher and author of *An Essay Concerning Human Understanding*, born Wrington, 1632.

John Cleese, comedian and actor, born Weston-super-Mare, 1939.

Jill Dando, broadcaster and journalist, born Weston-super-Mare, 1961.

The unitary authority was created in 1996, prior to which, from 1974, it had been the Woodspring district of Avon, and before that, part of the county of Somerset. Originally an agricultural area, the tourist industry developed along the coast, particularly at Weston-super-Mare (population 68,830), while the northern end of the area was greatly influenced by its proximity to Bristol, with deepwater port facilities for the city being build first at Portishead and then at Portbury. Bristol International Airport is located in the east of the area.

Weston-super-Mare, the administrative centre for the council, really developed after the arrival of the railway in 1841, as seaside holidays grew in popularity. There were also many visitors who came across the Bristol Channel from South Wales for their holidays. The distribution, retail, hotel, and restaurant sector is the largest employer, reflecting both the tourist trade and the importance of distribution companies in the make up of the local economy.

John Cleese

The Drawing Room at Tyntesfield House, 1878.

BATH AND NORTH EAST SOMERSET

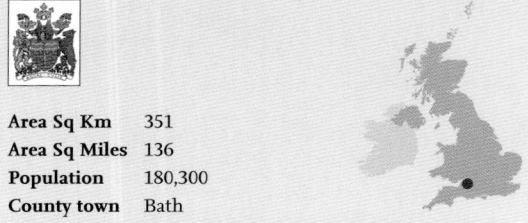

Area Sq Km	351
Area Sq Miles	136
Population	180,300
County town	Bath
Highest point	Niver Hill (260 m), in the Mendip Hills

FAMOUS FOR

Construction of **Bath Abbey** began in 1499; the story goes that Bishop Oliver King had a dream of ladders ascending from an olive tree and an instruction to restore the church and stone ladders can be seen ascending the West front of the Abbey today!

A **Bath Oliver** is a plain, unsweetened biscuit, in the centre of which is an image of its creator, Dr William Oliver (1695–1764), a Bath doctor.

The North Somerset coalfield was based around **Radstock**; the last pit closed in 1973.

Pulteney Bridge, in the centre of Bath, is a unique 18th-century bridge; designed by Robert Adam and completed in 1773; both sides of the bridge are lined with shops.

FAMOUS PEOPLE

Henry Cole, designer of the Penny Black and the first Christmas card, and organiser of the 1851 Great Exhibition, born Bath, 1808;

Charles Prestwich (C P) Scott, Editor and latterly owner, *Manchester Guardian* (1872–1929) born, Bath, 1846.

"Oh! who can ever be tired of Bath?"
Jane Austen (in *Northanger Abbey*, 1818)

The unitary authority was created in 1996, prior to which, from 1974, it had been the Wansdyke and Bath districts of Avon, and before that, part of the county of Somerset. Centred on the World Heritage Site city of Bath (population 83,900), the area also includes part of the Mendip Hills and the southern end of the Cotswold Hills. The fame of Bath rests upon the hot water springs close to the River Avon, first dedicated to the Celtic god Sulis before the arrival of the Romans. The baths were then developed by the Romans (who named the town *Aquae Sulis*), and substantial remains of the baths survive, incorporated into today's bath buildings. The medicinal

value of the baths was rediscovered in the late 17th century and in the 18th century Bath developed not on as a spa town but also as a fashionable social centre, under the guidance of Richard 'Beau' Nash. It became a model of Georgian town architecture, with many buildings designed by the local architects John Wood (both father and son), all built in the honey-coloured local limestone, including the Royal Crescent and the Circle. While its social importance declined in the 19th century, the city has remained a prosperous centre and it is now home to two universities and thriving publishing and communications industries.

The Great Bath at the Roman Baths with the abbey in the background.

Stained-glass windows in Bath Abbey.

teney Bridge, Bath.

anorama of Royal Crescent, Bath.

BRISTOL

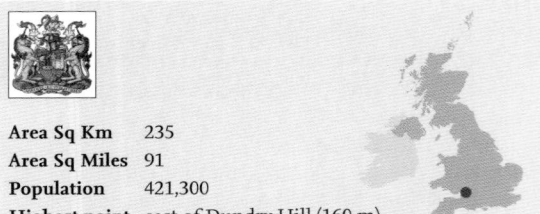

Area Sq Km 235
Area Sq Miles 91
Population 421,300
Highest point east of Dundry Hill (160 m)

Bristol, originally Brycgstow, takes its name from the Old English for 'meeting place by the bridge'.

FAMOUS FOR

Isambard Kingdom Brunel left his mark on the city with the **Clifton Suspension Bridge** (completed in 1864, it crosses the Avon Gorge in a single span of 214 m, 75 m above the level of the river), the **SS *Great Britain*** (the world's first propeller-driven iron steamship, and, at the time the largest ship in the world, an amazing 98 m long, was launched in Bristol in 1843 and 'relaunched' in 2005 as a brilliantly restored visitor attraction), and the original **Bristol Temple Meads Station** (the world's oldest surviving purpose-built railway terminus, opened in 1840 and now an exhibition space).

The phrase **'All shipshape and Bristol fashion'** to describe things in good order comes from the well-maintained ships of the Bristol trading fleet.

The iconic supersonic passenger aeroplane, **Concorde**, was built at Filton on the outskirts of Bristol. The first British prototype was rolled out on 19 September 1968.

Queen Elizabeth I declared that the **Church of St Mary**, **Redcliffe** was 'the most famous, absolute and goodliest parish church in England'.

The Italian **John Cabot** sailed with 18 men from Bristol in May 1497 in the *Matthew* in search of China, but reached North America, most likely Newfoundland in June. His second expedition, of six ships, left Bristol in 1498 but never returned.

FAMOUS PEOPLE

Thomas Longman, bookseller and founder of the eponymous publisher, born 1699.
Thomas Chatterton, poet, born 1752.
Sir Thomas Lawrence, painter, mostly of portraits, born 1769.
Robert Southey, poet, Poet Laureate (1813–43), born 1774.
Samuel Plimsoll, social reformer after whom the Plimsoll line is named, born 1824.
William Slim, Viscount Slim, Field Marshal, Governor-General of Australia (1953–60), born 1891.
Sir Allen Lane, founder of Penguin Books and creator of the paperback, born 1902.
Cary Grant (born Archibald Leach), actor, born 1904.
Christopher Fry (born Christopher Harris), dramatist, born 1907.
Sir Michael Redgrave, actor, born 1908.
Robin Cousins, Olympic champion figure skater, born 1957.
Damien Hirst, artist, born 1965.

Bristol was established where the rivers Avon and Frome join. To the west of the city the Avon then cuts through limestone hills at the Avon Gorge and flows into the Severn Estuary at Avonmouth, 11 km from the city centre. Bristol first became an important settlement after the Norman Conquest and was granted the status of a county in 1373 by Edward III, a position it has maintained ever since, apart from the period 1974–96, when it was subsumed into the former county of Avon. In 1542 it also became a cathedral city. Bristol's prosperity grew on colonial expansion in the West Indies and North America and in the 18th century it became the second-wealthiest city in Britain, built on the profits of the slave trade and the importing of tobacco and sugar. Its importance declined in the 19th century, though it was helped by the arrival of the Great Western Railway in 1840, and the building of new docks at Avonmouth in 1868. In the 20th century its prosperity revived, and is now built on a wide and varied industrial base, including aerospace and hi-tech industries, banking and finance, distribution and the creative industries. There are two universities and it has an international reputation as a good place to live and do business.

Clifton Suspension Bridge

Damien Hirst with 'Away from the Flock'.

SS *Great Britain*

Bartholomew Gazetteer of the British Isles, 1887

BRISTOL, *city, mun. bor., seaport, and co. of itself, chiefly in Gloucestershire but partly in Somerset, at the confluence of the rivers Avon and Frome, 6 miles from the Bristol Channel at Avonmouth and 120 miles W. of London by rail, the port being 29 miles from Cardiff, 70 from Swansea, 245 from Dublin, 255 from Cork, and 325 from Liverpool; mun. bor., 4632 ac., pop. 206,874. Bristol is built on a number of eminences, and has a fine appearance. It contains important institutions, religious, educational, and charitable. It has several fine churches, notably the Cathedral (1142–1160), and the church of St Mary Redcliffe. It includes the suburbs of Clifton, Redland, and Cotham. At Clifton Down a magnificent suspension bridge spans the river Avon, having an elevation of 245 ft. above high-water mark. From an early date B. has been a seaport of great importance, its position being very favourable to commerce. In the reign of Henry II it carried on trade with the N. of Europe, and between 1239 and 1247 there was occasion for enlarging and improving the accommodation for the shipping. There are now extensive docks, not only within the city itself, but also at Avonmouth on the N. side of the mouth of the river, and at Portishead on the S. side; both these harbours being in direct communication with the city by railway. The coasting trade is of great magnitude, steamers plying regularly between B. and Cardiff, Swansea, London, Cork, Dublin, Liverpool, and Glasgow; while the foreign trade extends to nearly all parts of the world. B. has mfrs. of glass, soap, and earthenware; shipbuilding, tanning, and sugar-refining; and extensive chemical and engineering works.*

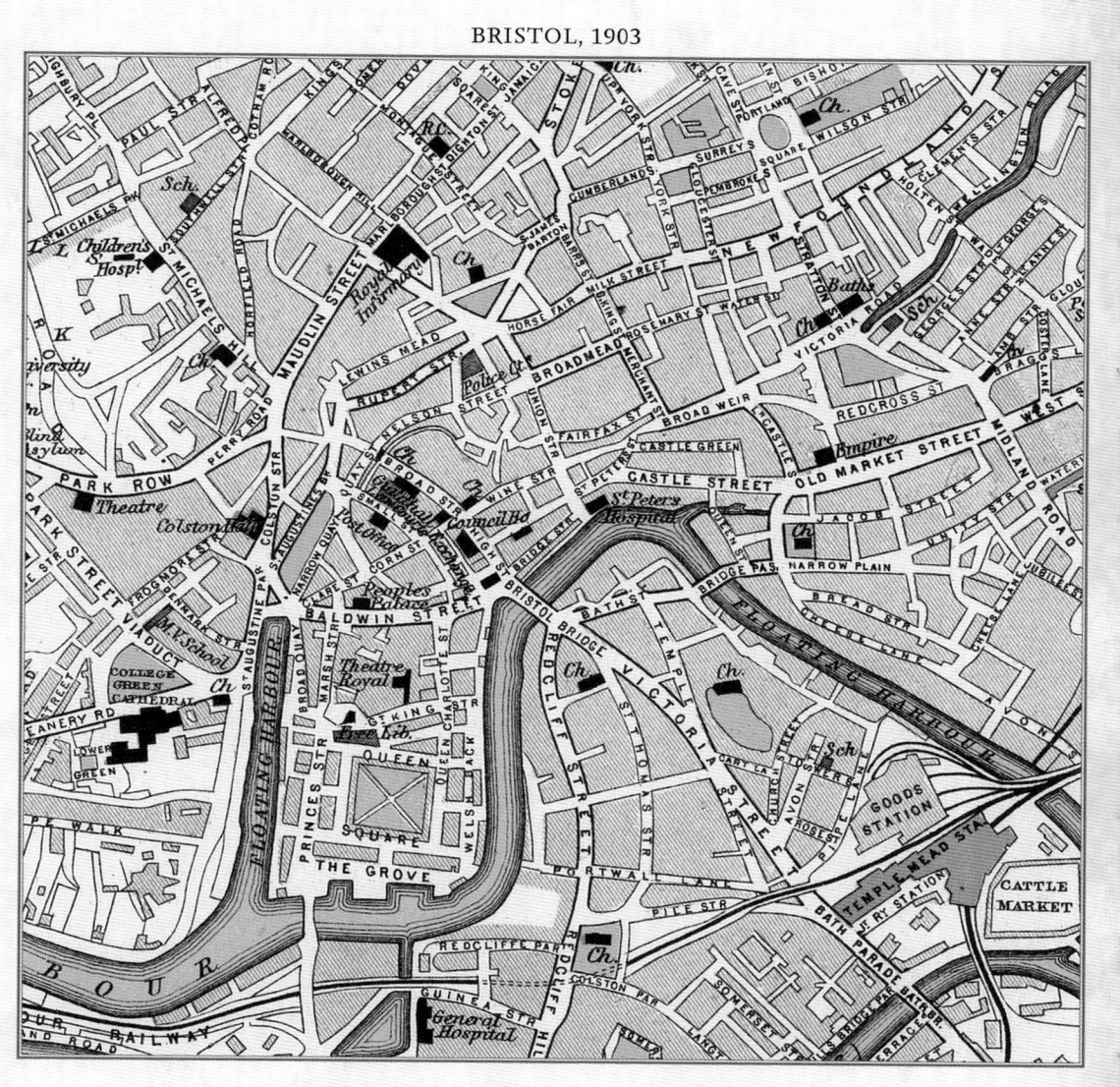

BRISTOL, 1903

...ot Tower which was built (1897–98) in memory of John Cabot.

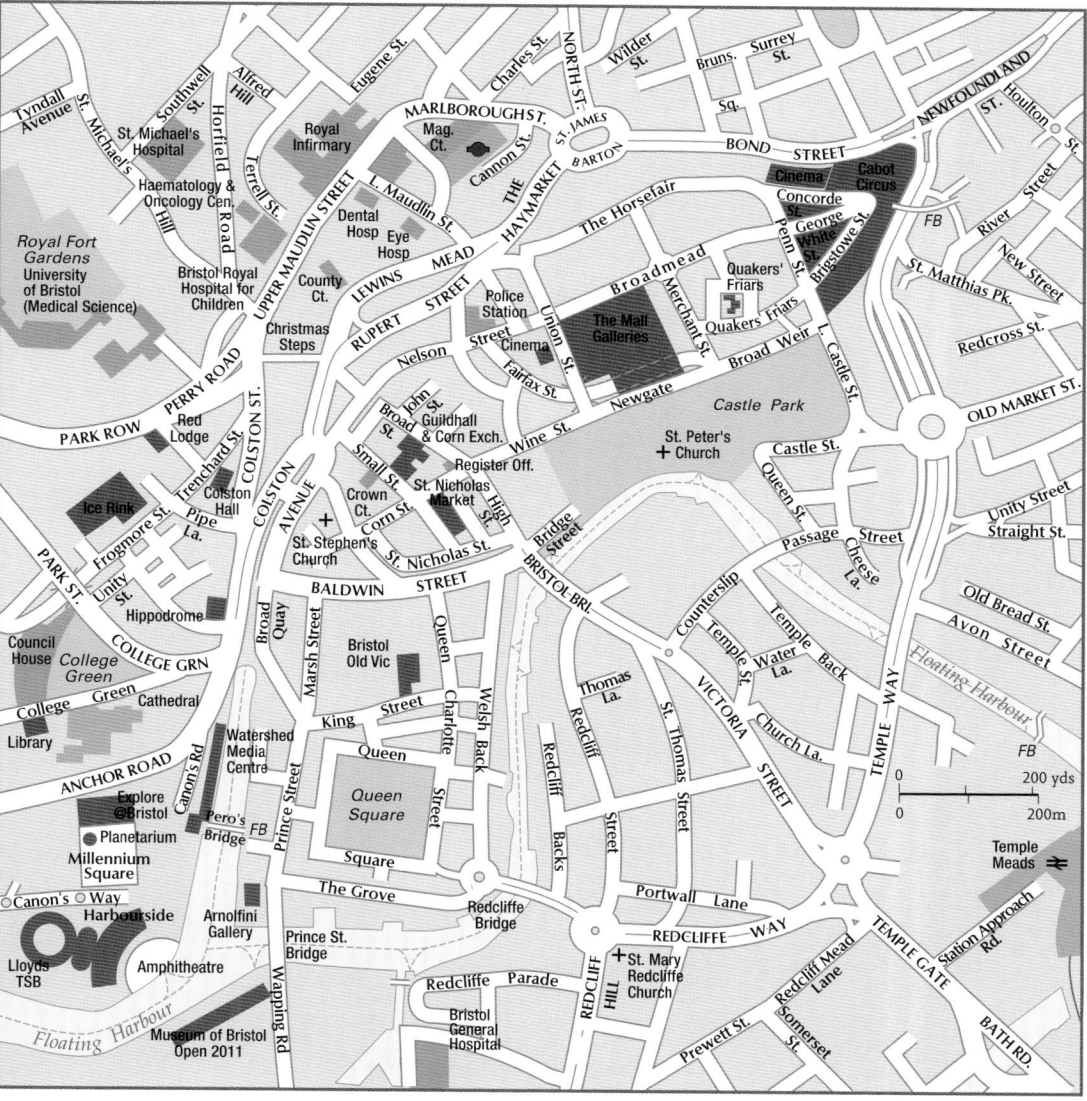

Modern Bristol

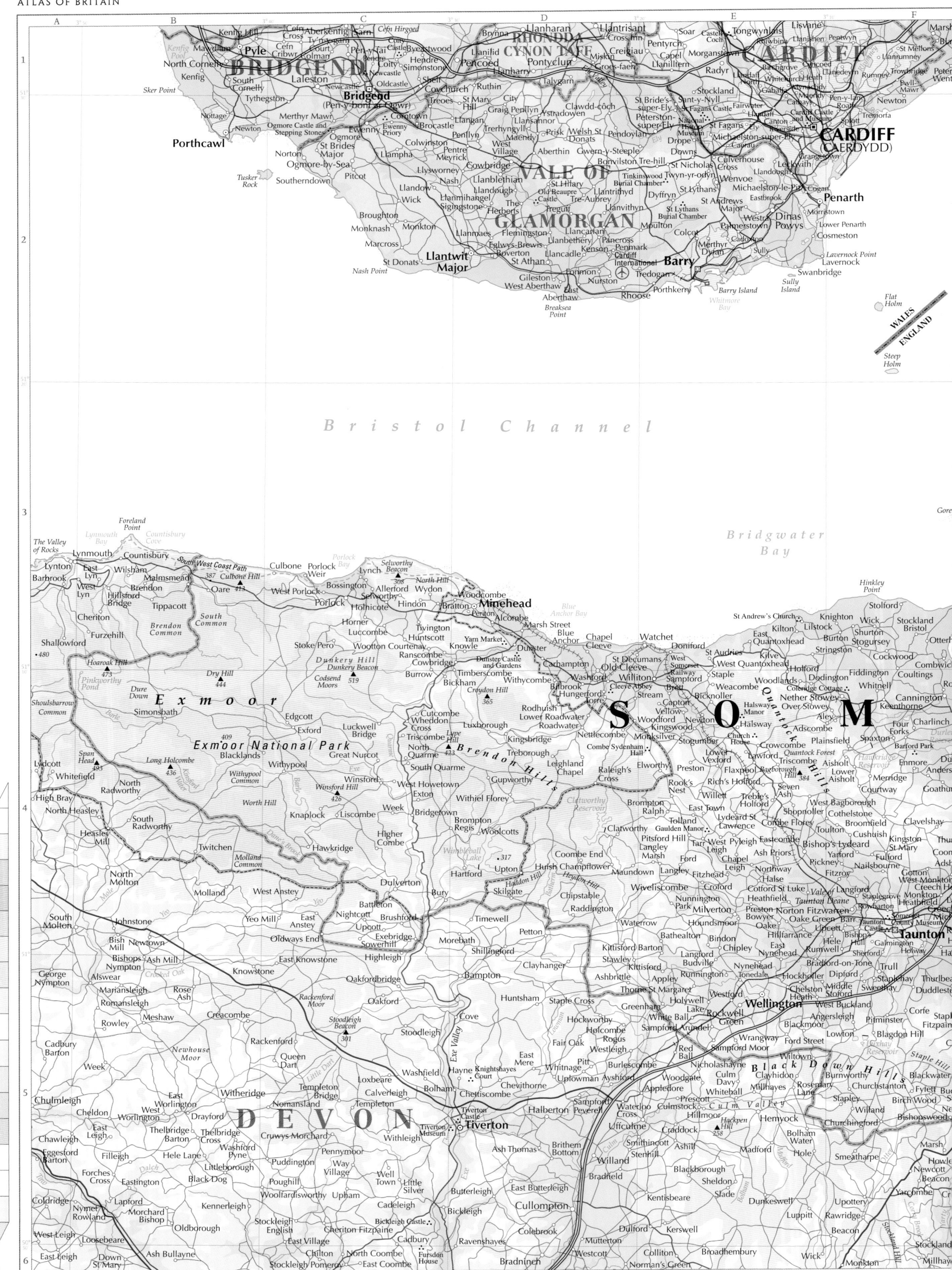

British National Grid projection

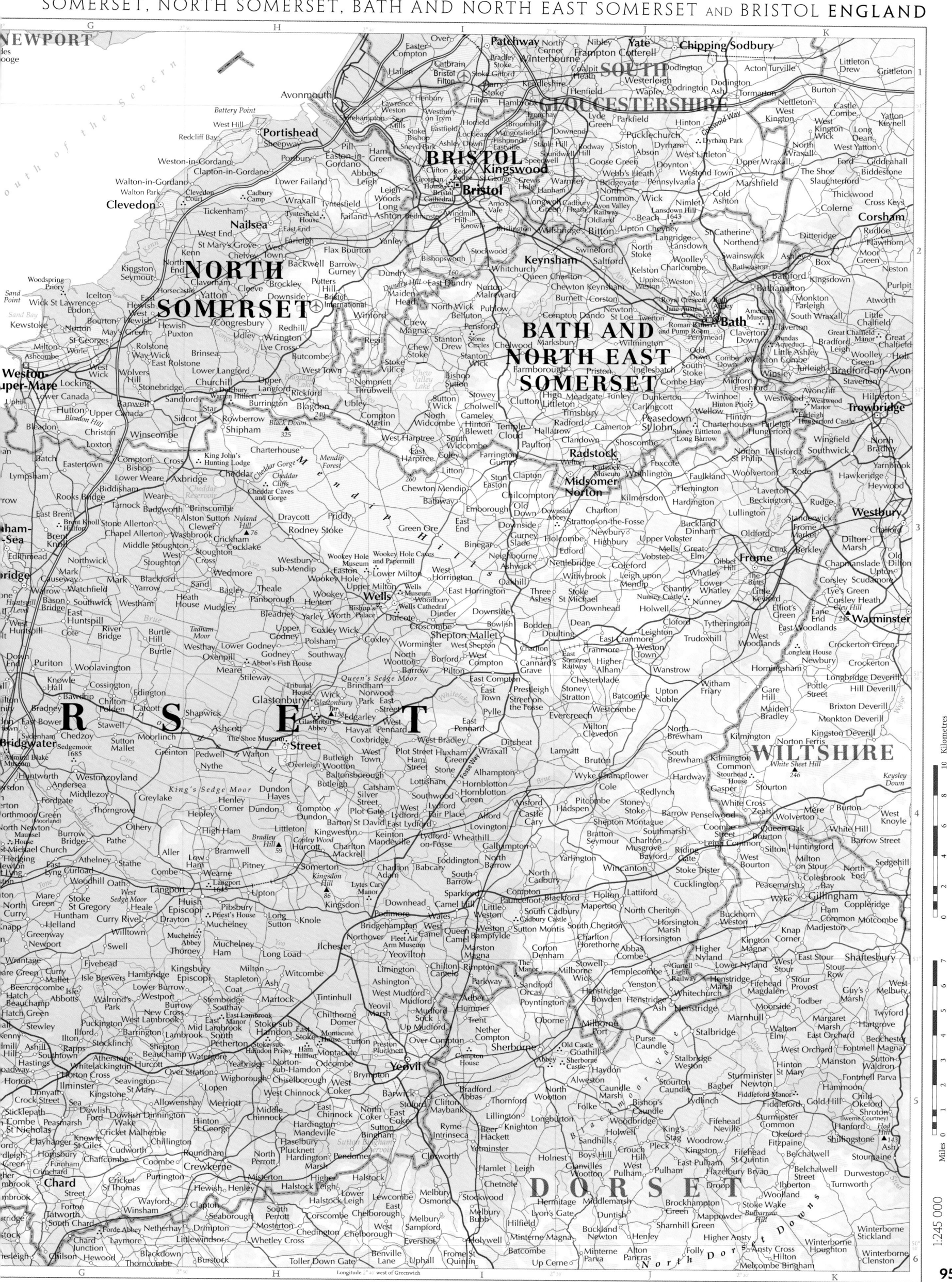

1:245 000

GLOUCESTERSHIRE

Area Sq Km	2,705
Area Sq Miles	1,044
Population	582,600
County town	Gloucester
Highest point	Cleve Common (330 m)
Districts	Cheltenham; Cotswold; Forest of Dean; Gloucester; Stroud; Tewkesbury.

Gloucestershire is named after its county town of Gloucester, originally the Roman town of Glevum, which is derived from the Celtic for 'bright place'.

FAMOUS FOR

The **Cheltenham Festival** is the pre-eminent National Hunt racing meeting in Britain. Spread over four days in March, the Festival was established in 1902 and includes the Cheltenham Gold Cup Steeplechase. It is estimated that 18,000 bottles of champagne and 214,000 pints of Guinness are consumed during the Festival.

Berkeley Castle was completed in the 12th century and is still lived in by the same family. Its fame grew after Edward II died there in 1327 after he had been forced to abdicate – though there is no evidence to support the accounts of some of the more extreme methods by which it is suggested he was murdered.

The **Slimbridge Wetland Centre** was founded in 1946 by Peter Scott (the son of 'Scott of the Antarctic'), the first reserve in the world to protect the wetland environment so essential for wildfowl. It now has the world's largest collection of swans, geese and ducks.

The **Severn Estuary** has the second highest tidal range in the world of up to 15 m. At high tide this water can be funnelled up the Severn to produce a wave (the **Severn Bore**) that travels quickly upstream from Awre to Gloucester and can be up to 2 m high.

FAMOUS PEOPLE

Edward Jenner, discovered principle of vaccination, born Berkeley, 1749.
John Keble, Anglican priest, founder of the Oxford Movement, born Fairford, 1792.
Sir Charles Wheatstone, physicist and inventor, born Gloucester, 1802.
Beatrice Webb, social reformer, born Gloucester, 1858.
Ralph Vaughan Williams, composer, born Down Ampney, 1872.
Gustav Holst, born Cheltenham, 1874.
Sir Arthur (Bomber) Harris, Commander-in-Chief, Bomber Command (1942–5), born Cheltenham, 1892.
Sir Ralph Richardson, actor, born Cheltenham, 1902.
Laurie Lee, writer, born Stroud, 1914.
Frederick Sanger, biochemist and Nobel Prize winner, born 1918, Rendcombe.
Dennis Potter, playwright, born Berry Hill, near Coleford, 1935.
Brian Jones, founding member of Rolling Stones, born Cheltenham, 1942.
David Hemery, Olympic athlete, born Cirencester, 1944.

The limestone mass of the Cotswold Hills dominates the centre of Gloucestershire and provides the characteristic pale golden stone of many of its buildings. The river Severn forms a wide valley to the west, ending in a long tidal estuary, beyond which are the hills of the Forest of Dean. The river Thames rises in the county, and forms part of its southern boundary in the vicinity of Lechlade. Apart from the Severn and the Thames, there is the river Wye, which forms part of the boundary with Monmouthshire, and many smaller rivers, among them the Chelt, Coln, Evenlode, Leach, Leadon, and Windrush.

The county of Gloucestershire was first so named in 1016. The fertile lands of the area soon brought wealth to the county, which also included the city of Bristol, until it gained independent status in 1373. Gloucester, which became a bishopric in 1541, became the centre of the county. In the 1974 local government changes, the area of the county close to Bristol became part of the new county of Avon. With Avon's abolition in 1996, this area became the new unitary authority of South Gloucestershire. The population of Gloucestershire is now 582,600. The main centres are the cathedral city and county town of Gloucester (population 123,205) and the towns of Cheltenham (98,875), Stroud (32,052), Cirencester (15,861) and Dursley (13,355). Industry is centred on the fertile Severn Vale, with aerospace, light engineering, food production, and service industries in and around the towns; in rural areas market gardening and orchards dominate. About 15 per cent of jobs in the area are in manufacturing, nearly 50 per cent above the national average, a figure belying the rural image of the county, while just under 80 per cent of the jobs are in the service sector.

The east of the county is dominated by the Cotswolds. While Cirencester (as *Corinium*) was the second largest Roman town in the country, the wealth this area in medieval times came from sheep farming and the woollen industry, as shown in some of the most beautiful parish churches in the country, most notably Fairford, Cirencester, Chipping Camden and Northleach. The mineral springs of Cheltenham were discovered in 1716, and the fame of Cheltenham Spa was established after George III visited in 1788; it became the most celebrated Regency spa town in Britain.

The centre of the county is based around the Severn valley, for a long period, a wealthy agricultural region, as shown by the magnificence of the Norman Tewkesbury Abbey, but it is also a region at the mercy of the Severn. In 2007 the area suffered the worst recorded floods in its history and there are increasing concerns over the viability of some of the settlements on the banks of the river. The western part of the county beyond the Severn contains the Forest of Dean, one of the ancient woodlands of Britain and an early centre of industrialisation – coal has been mined here since prehistoric times whilst the making of charcoal from forest trees led to development of iron smelting and, in the 19th century, to new breakthroughs in steel manufacture by the Mushet family in Coleford. Those born within the Hundred of St Briavels, in the Forest of Dean have the ancient rights of a Forester, which include the right to keep sheep in the Forest, to have their pigs forage in the Forest in autumn, and, if they have worked in a mine for a year and a day, to become Freeminers, with the right to mine coal within the Forest.

Cheltenham Racecourse

The village of Snowshill.

Bartholomew Gazetteer of the British Isles, 1887

GLOUCESTERSHIRE, *a west Midland co., situated upon the estuary of the Severn. and bounded N. and NE. by Herefordshire, Worcestershire, and Warwickshire; E. by Oxfordshire; S. by Berks, Wilts, and Somerset; and W. by Monmouthshire, Herefordshire, and the estuary of the Severn; greatest length, SW. to NE., 54 miles; greatest breadth, NW. to SE., 33 miles; area, 783,699 ac.; pop. 572,433. The face of the county shows varied aspects, of which the most distinctive are the Cotswold Hills, in the E.; the valley of the Severn, in the middle; and the Forest of Dean, in the W. Besides the Severn there are numerous important rivers, such as the Avon, Lower Avon, Wye, Thames, and Windrush. The canal system has been largely developed, and several important water-ways of that description pass through the county. Agriculture forms the leading occupation of the rural population; in the hills sheep-farming receives attention; while the rich valley of the Severn has long been famed for the superiority of its products. Its luxuriant pastures especially have originated and supported a great industry in the shape of dairy farms which produce the celebrated Glo'ster cheese. In the W. of the county are 2 great coal-fields – the Forest of Dean on the N., and the Bristol coal-field on the W. Other minerals are gypsum, barytes, quartz, limestone, and freestone. The mfrs. are mostly woollen and cotton stuffs, but at Bristol there are also large hardware mfrs. Gloucestershire comprises 29 hundreds, 387 pars. and parts of 4 others, the greater part of the mun. bor. of Bristol, the mun. bors of Cheltenham, Gloucester, and Tewkesbury. It is mostly in the diocese of Gloucester and Bristol.*

SOUTH GLOUCESTERSHIRE

Area Sq Km	537
Area Sq Miles	207
Population	257,700
County town	Thornbury
Highest point	Hanging Hill (237 m)

FAMOUS FOR

South Gloucestershire includes the English side of both Severn road bridges – the suspension bridge (the **Severn Bridge**) was opened in 1966 and the cable-stayed bridge (the Second Severn Crossing) in 1996. Tolls are only charged in one direction when leaving England for Wales.

FAMOUS PEOPLE

William Gilbert (W.G.) Grace, cricketer, born Downend, 1848.

Sir Bernard Lovell, astronomer, born Oldland Common, 1913.

[The forest of Dean] was a wonderfull thicke forrest, and in former ages so darke and terrible, by reason of crooked and winding waies, as also the grisly shade therein, that it made the inhabitants more fierce and bolder to commit robberies."
William Camden, 1610

South Gloucestershire became a unitary authority in 1996. Before that it was a district of the county of Avon (1974–96) and prior to that part of Gloucestershire. The southern part of the area lies on the northern and eastern fringes of Bristol. The Cotswold Hills are in the east, and the Severn Vale in the west. The river Severn borders the area to the northwest. Many of its communities are suburbs of Bristol, including Kingswood, Longwood Green, Downend, Filton and Patchway, while Chipping Sodbury with Yate (population 35,000) and Thornbury (14,000) are the largest self-contained settlements. With population growth of 8.5 per cent in the ten years up to 2008, it is one of the fastest growing areas in Britain. As well as being the home to many who work in Bristol, South Gloucestershire is a major centre for aerospace engineering and for the Ministry of Defence's Defence Equipment and Support operation.

The Second Severn Crossing.

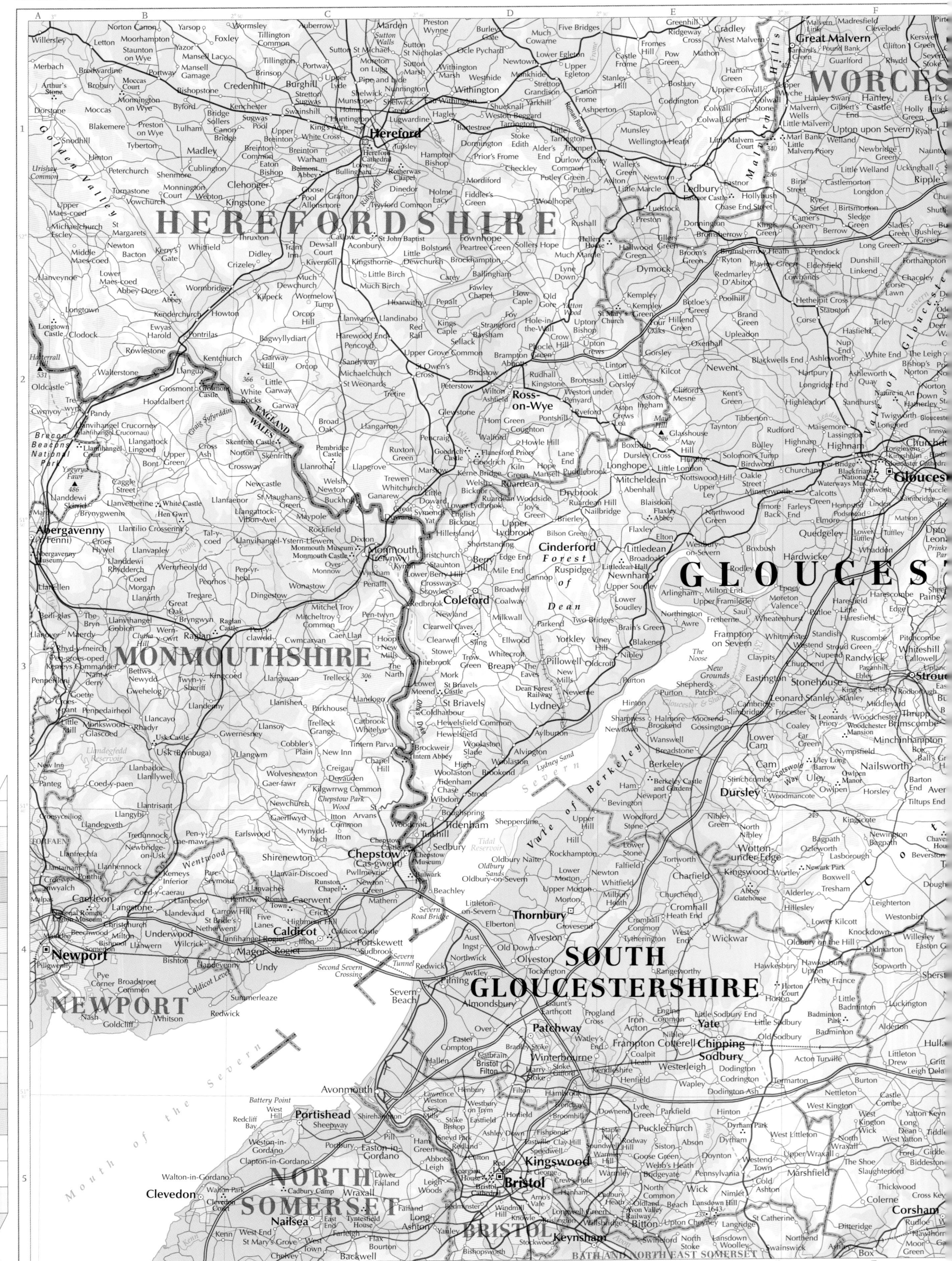

HEREFORDSHIRE

WORCES

GLOUCES

MONMOUTHSHIRE

GLOUCES

Hereford

Ross-on-Wye

Gloucester

Great Malvern

Upton upon Severn

Ledbury

Abergavenny

Monmouth
(Trefynwy)

Coleford

Cinderford

Chepstow
(Cas-gwent)

NEWPORT

Newport

Caldicot

SOUTH
GLOUCESTERSHIRE

Thornbury

Dursley

Nailsworth

Wotton-under-Edge

Yate

Chipping
Sodbury

Bristol

Kingswood

NORTH
SOMERSET

Clevedon

Portishead

Nailsea

BRISTOL

Metres
Feet

1000
3280

900
2952

800
2624

700
2296

600
1968

500
1640

400
1312

300
4921

200
656

150
492

100
328

50
164

0
Land
below
sea
level

50
164

200
656

1000
3281

British National Grid projection

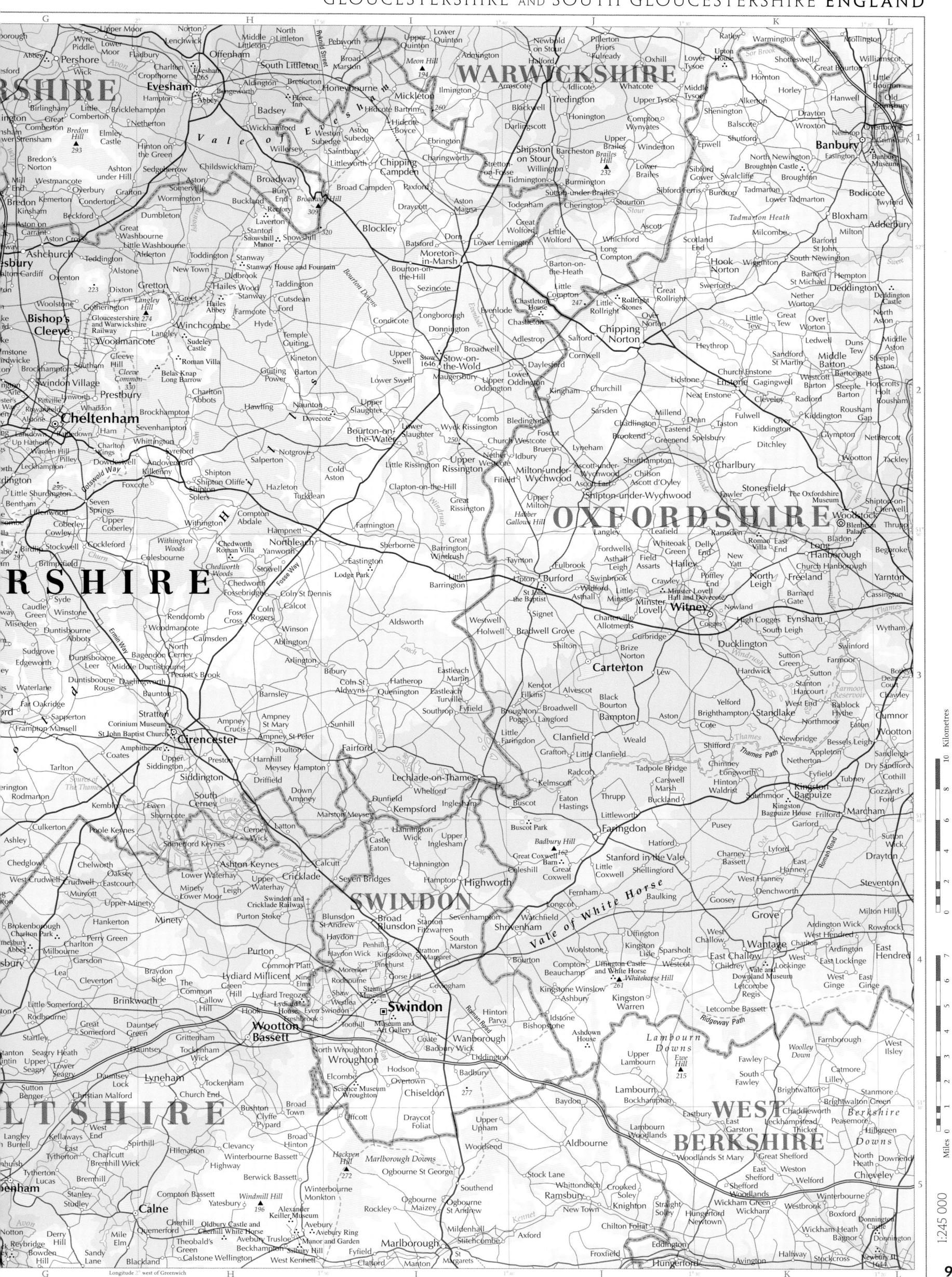

OXFORDSHIRE

Area Sq Km	2,606
Area Sq Miles	1,006
Population	639,800
County town	Oxford
Highest point	White Horse Hill (261 m) near Uffington
Districts	Cherwell; Oxford; South Oxfordshire; Vale of White Horse; West Oxfordshire

Oxfordshire takes its name from the city of Oxford, the place where there was a ford across the river Thames for oxen.

FAMOUS FOR

The **Rollright Stones**, on the border with Warwickshire, near Little Rollright, date back to around 1500 BC and are thought to have had ceremonial purposes, although tradition will have it that the stones are a king and his warriors who were turned to stone by Mother Shipton, a local witch.

The **Botanic Gardens** in Oxford were the first botanic gardens in Britain, established in 1621 on the banks of the river Cherwell, close to Magdalen College, to provide plants for students to study.

The **White Horse** near Uffington, an abstract horse-shape 110 m long, is thought to be the oldest figure carved into a chalk hillside in Britain, perhaps dating from 1000 BC. The best view of it is from the air, which only increases the uncertainty as to its purpose.

The **Ashmolean Museum** in Oxford is the oldest public museum in England originating in the 'Cabinet of Curiosities' given by Elias Ashmole to the University in 1675. The collection has grown greatly since, and in 2009 a spectacular extension was opened to display more treasures.

Chastleton House, near Moreton-in-Marsh was built between 1607 and 1612 by Walter Jones, a wealthy wool merchant. The family's fortune declined thereafter, and very little has changed in the following 400 years – it was only in 1991 that the family handed the house to the National Trust. It was here in 1865 that the rules of croquet were codified.

FAMOUS PEOPLE

Alfred the Great, King of Wessex (871–99), born Wantage, 849.
Edward the Confessor, King of England (1042–66), born Islip, c.1005.
Richard I (the Lion-heart), King of England (1189–99), born Oxford, 1157.
King John, King of England (1199–1216), born Oxford, 1167.
Edward, Prince of Wales (the Black Prince), heir apparent to Edward III and military commander, born Woodstock, 1330.
Warren Hastings, first Governor-General of India (1773–85), born Churchill, 1732.
Sir Winston Churchill, politician, Prime Minister (1940–45, 1951–55), born Blenheim Palace, Woodstock, 1874.
Dorothy L. Sayers, novelist, playwright and essayist, born Oxford, 1893.
Sir Alan Hodgkin, physiologist and Nobel Prize winner, born Banbury, 1914.
John Kendrew, molecular biologist and Nobel Prize winner, born Oxford, 1917.
Phyllis Dorothy (P.D.) James, Baroness James, novelist and civil servant, born Oxford, 1920.
Mike Hailwood, motorcycle road racer, winner of 14 Isle of Man TT races, born Great Milton, 1940.
Stephen Hawking, theoretical physicist, born Oxford, 1942.

The landscape of Oxfordshire is predominantly flat or gently undulating, forming part of the Thames Valley. High ground occurs where the Chiltern Hills enter the county in the southeast and the Cotswold Hills in the northwest, while the highest point, at White Horse Hill, forms part of the Berkshire Downs in the south of the county. Chief rivers are the Thames (or Isis as it is frequently called around the city of Oxford), Cherwell, Ock, Thame and Windrush.

The historic county of Oxfordshire was formed in the 11th century, following the burning of Oxford by the Danes in 1009. The southern boundary of the county was along the river Thames, but this changed in the local government reorganization in 1974, when the Vale of the White Horse along with the towns of Faringdon, Wantage, Abingdon, Didcot and Wallingford were added from Berkshire, significantly increasing the size of the county. The population is now 639,800, and the chief centres are Oxford (population 143,016), Banbury (43,867), Abingdon (36,101), Bicester (31,113), Witney (22,765) and Didcot (25,231), where future developments are being concentrated, so keeping the character of the smaller towns such as Thame and Henley-on-Thames. The county's population is expected to grow by 8.3 per cent between 2006 and 2016, an increase in 50,000 people.

The county is the most rural in the southeast of England, with industries centred on the towns. Scientific and medical research establishments are based both in Oxford and at major research establishments at Harwell and Culham (the home of the Joint European Torus, Europe's largest nuclear fusion research laboratory). Printing and publishing industries have a long history in Oxford (the first book was printed there in 1478) and the city now has the greatest concentration of publishing outside London. The motor industry developed out of a motorcycle business that William Morris (later Lord Nuffield) started in 1901, which grew into the Morris Motors Limited at Cowley, on the outskirts of Oxford, now the home of the Mini. The county also has the world's largest concentration of performance car development and manufacturing. With its many educational and research institutions, the administration, education and health sectors provide over 30 per cent of jobs, significantly above the regional average, as is employment in manufacturing, at approaching 10 per cent of jobs.

Oxford is a name known around the world for its university. The city itself was established in Saxon times and it was the sixth largest town in Britain at the time of the Norman Conquest. The University of Oxford is the oldest university in the English-speaking world, but its exact origins are unclear. It is known that teaching was already established in 1096 and that it developed rapidly from 1167. University and college buildings from the 13th century onwards dominate the centre of the city. Oxford Brookes University, founded in 1992, has its main campus at Headington, away from the city centre.

Tourism is important to the whole county and not just to the centre of Oxford, with its university buildings, churches and museums. The countryside, particularly to the west of Oxford, has many attractions, including Blenheim Palace, which was declared a World Heritage Site in 1987. This amazing Baroque palace was built between 1705 and 1724 by Sir John Vanbrugh for the Duke of Marlborough as a gift from the nation in thanks for his victory at the Battle of Blenheim fought in 1704 in Bavaria. Sheep farming and the resulting wool industry brought great wealth to the Cotswolds in the medieval period, and many splendid churches bear witness to this, for example Burford and Chipping Norton.

The Radcliffe Camera Reading Room of Oxford University's Bodleian Library.

All Souls College, Oxford.

Rollright Stones, near Little Rollright.

Bartholomew Gazetteer of the British Isles, 1887

OXFORDSHIRE, *south-midland co. of England, bounded N. by Warwickshire and Northamptonshire, E. by Bucks, S. by Berks, from which it is separated by the Thames, and W. by Gloucestershire; greatest length, 60 miles; greatest breadth, 30 miles; area, 483,621 ac., pop. 179,559. Most of the co. is level, but there are gentle undulations of surface, rising to 836 ft. at Broom Hill in the NW., which is the highest point of land. In the S. the Chiltern Hills stretch across the co. from Bucks to Berks. The chief rivers are the Windrush, Evenlode, Cherwell, and Thame, all being tributaries of the Thames, or Isis, which flows for about 70 miles along the S. border of the co. The Oxford Canal, in conjunction with the Coventry Canal, connects the Thames with the Severn, Mersey, and Trent. The soil is a light loam, which is exceedingly fertile and in a high state of cultivation, agriculture receiving so much attention that the co. is justly held to be one of the most productive districts in England. Excepting the N. district, Oxfordshire may be considered a well wooded co. It has many antiquities, and is likewise noted for the beauty of its ecclesiastical buildings and the number of its mansions. The mfrs. are not important. The co. comprises 14 hundreds, 292 pars, with parts of 7 others, the greater part of the mun. bor. of Oxford, and the mun. bors. of Banbury and Chipping Norton. It is almost entirely in the diocese of Oxford.*

[On Oxford] "Beautiful city! so venerable, so lovely, so unravaged by the fierce intellectual life of our century, so serene! ... Home of lost causes, and forsaken beliefs, and unpopular names, and impossible loyalties!"
Matthew Arnold, *Essays on Criticism*, 1865

"Oxford lends sweetness to labour and dignity to leisure."
Henry James, *Portraits of Places*, 1883

"Oxford is on the whole more attractive than Cambridge to the ordinary visitor; and the traveller is therefore recommended to visit Cambridge first, or to omit it altogether if he cannot visit both."
Karl Baedeker, *Great Britain*, 1887

Blenheim Palace, near Woodstock.

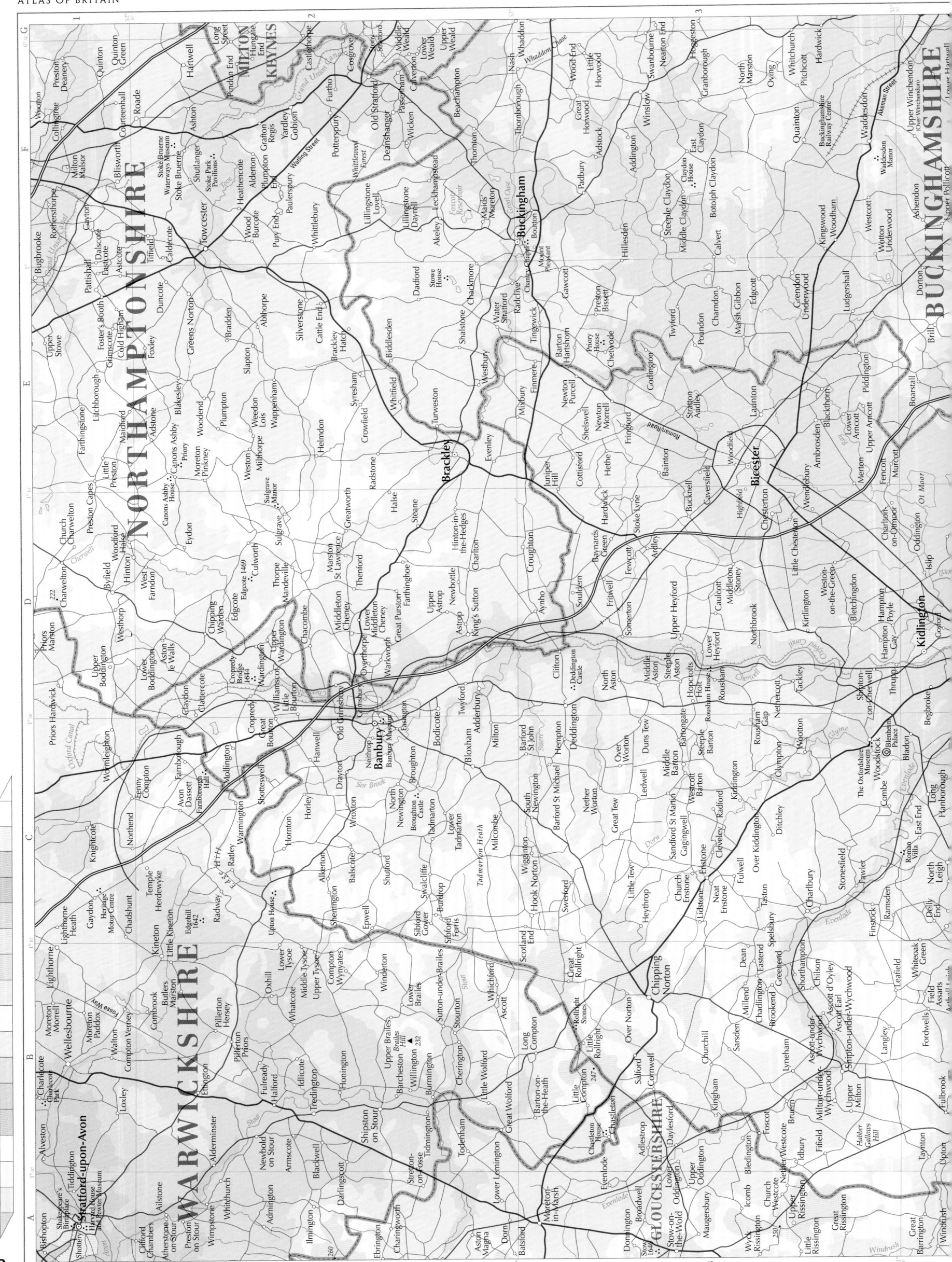

British National Grid projection

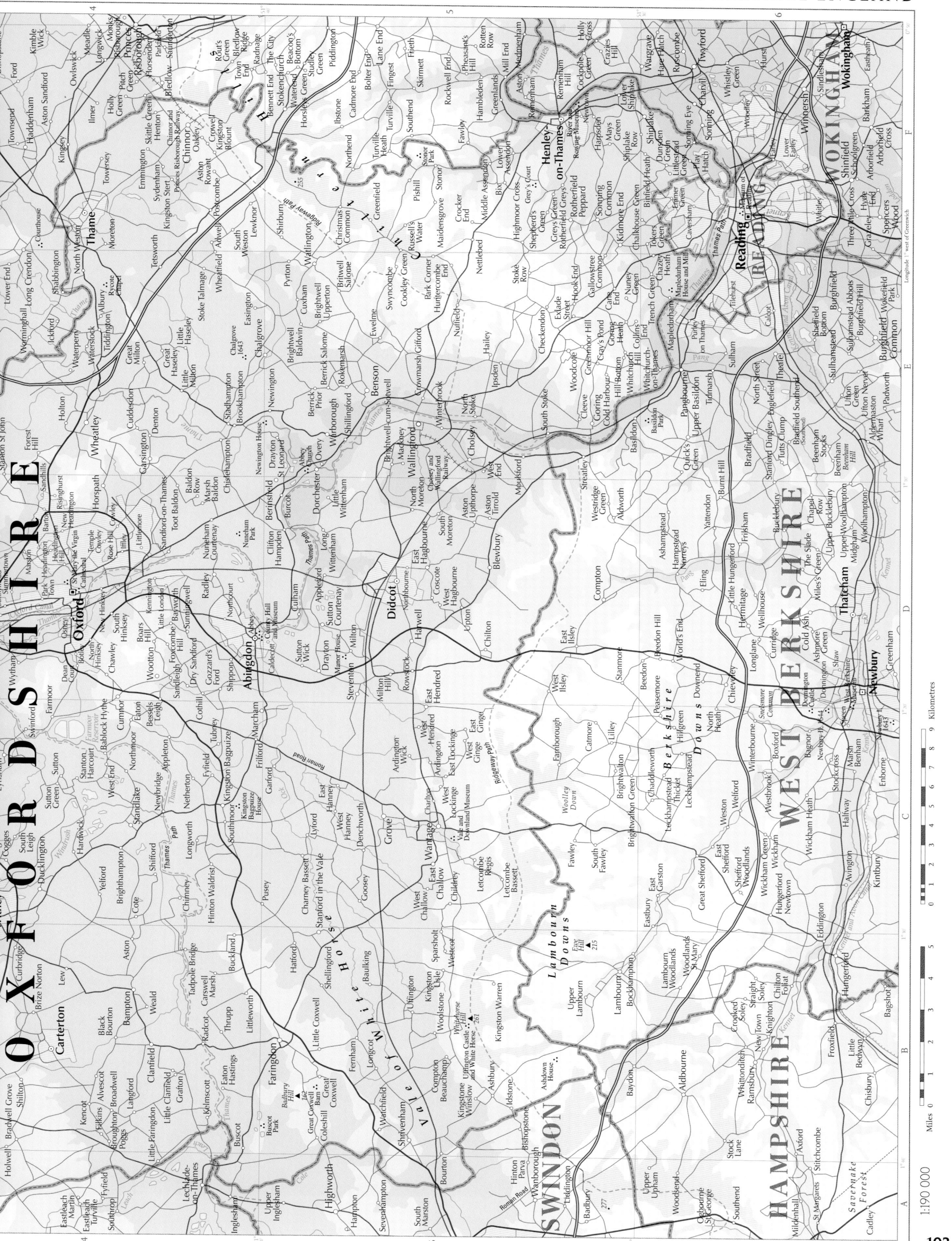

1:190 000

© Collins Bartholomew Ltd

BUCKINGHAMSHIRE

Area Sq Km	1,565
Area Sq Miles	604
Population	493,300
County town	Aylesbury
Highest point	Haddington Hill (267 m), in the Chilterns
Districts	Aylesbury Vale; Chiltern; South Bucks; Wycombe

Buckinghamshire is named after its former county town, Buckingham, derived from the Old English for 'land in a river bend belonging to Bucca's people'.

FAMOUS FOR

In **High Wycombe** there is a unique tradition of 'Weighing in the Mayor' – the winner of the annual mayoral elections is weighed in public at the start and finish of the period of office. If the mayor's weight has increased during the period of office, the crowd jeers, for it is considered that the weight gain must have been at the expense of the town's citizens.

Hughenden Manor, near High Wycombe, was the home from 1848 to his death in 1881 of Benjamin Disraeli, Queen Victoria's favourite prime minister and distinguished novelist, who she made Earl of Beaconsfield. It is now owned by the National Trust.

Chequers, a Tudor country house at the northern foot of the Chilterns near Aylesbury, has been the country home of British prime ministers since 1921, when it was given to the state by its previous owners.

The world's first model village called **Bekonscot**, was opened in 1929 in Beaconsfield. Created by Roland Callingham, it now contains over 3,500 models, model railways and much more besides, creating a unique image of 1930s England – and it is all outside.

William Penn, one of the founders of Quakerism, established the American colony of Pennsylvania in 1681. He returned to Britain in 1701 and worshipped at the Quaker Meeting House at **Jordans**, founded in 1688, where he is buried.

On the river Thames the monarch shares ownership of the swans with the Vintners' and Dyers' Companies. In July each year the Queen's Swan Marker and the Swan Uppers of the Vintners' and Dyers' spend five days in rowing boats going up a stretch of the Thames recording all the swans they see. They stop at **Marlow** on their way. This Swan Upping ceremony started in the 12th century, when swans used to be eaten as a great delicacy at Royal banquets.

Buckinghamshire is home to Britain's only private university, the **University of Buckingham**, founded in 1976, and one of Britain's newest universities, **Buckinghamshire New University**, founded in 2007.

FAMOUS PEOPLE

John Hampden, parliamentarian and leading opponent of Charles I, born Great Hampden, 1594.
James Brudenell, 7th Earl of Cardigan, Commander of the Light Brigade, Crimea, born Hambleden, 1797.
Sir George Gilbert Scott, Victorian architect, born Gawcott, 1811.
Sir Herbert Austin, Lord Austin, pioneering car manufacturer, born Little Missenden, 1866.
Rosamond Lehmann, novelist, born Bourne End, 1901.
Kenneth More, actor, born Gerrards Cross, 1914.
Michael York, actor, born Fulmer, 1942.
Sir Tim Rice, lyricist, born Amersham, 1944.
Sir Terence (Terry) Pratchett, author, born Beaconsfield, 1948.
Sir Steven Redgrave, Olympic rowing champion, born Marlow, 1962.

Buckinghamshire is a county divided in two by the chalk hills of the Chilterns, with their distinctive natural beech woodlands. To the north of the Chilterns is the flat land of the Vale of Aylesbury and the valley of the Ouse, this part of the county looks towards the Midlands. To the south of the Chilterns the land drains towards the river Thames, with economic activity focused towards London, with the London Underground system reaching out to Chesham and Amersham, making southern Buckinghamshire a popular commuter area.

Records suggest that the county of Buckinghamshire was formed in the 10th century. While Buckingham, in the north of the county, was the only town separately assessed in the Domesday Book, over the centuries it lost its pre-eminence to Aylesbury in the centre. It was Aylesbury that became the county town in 1889 when the new County Council was created. In 1974, the county lost Slough and Eton, both to the north of the Thames, to Berkshire, and in 1998 the new town of Milton Keynes and the surrounding area became a separate unitary authority (see below). The chief towns are High Wycombe (77,718), Aylesbury (69,021), Amersham (21,470), Chesham (20,357), Marlow (17,522) and Beaconsfield (12,292).

The population of Buckinghamshire is 493,300 and is estimated to grow to 530,800 by 2026, with the bulk of this growth in the north of the county – in the south there are restrictions over development from green-belt land and the Chilterns Area of Outstanding Natural Beauty. Overall Buckinghamshire is a prosperous county with average household income 24 per cent higher than the national average, and the proximity to London means that 13 per cent of its residents commute to London. Within the county, over 86 per cent of the jobs are in the services sector, with around a third of these in retail, hotels and restaurants. The proximity to London has seen a growth of hi-tech and finance businesses in the south of the county, while the traditional furniture making industry of High Wycombe survives, though not at the level it achieved in the 19th century – in 1875, it was estimated that 4,700 chairs were made in the town every day.

The county has attracted many writers over the years mostly to the Chilterns or to their south. John Milton came to Chalfont St Giles in 1665 to escape the plague in London, and here wrote *Paradise Lost*, while at Stoke Poges, Thomas Gray was inspired to write his 'Elegy Written in a Country Churchyard', completed in 1750. Mary Shelley completed *Frankenstein* while living in Marlow and Roald Dahl wrote most of his books at Great Missenden.

Hughenden Manor, near High Wycombe.

Chilterns

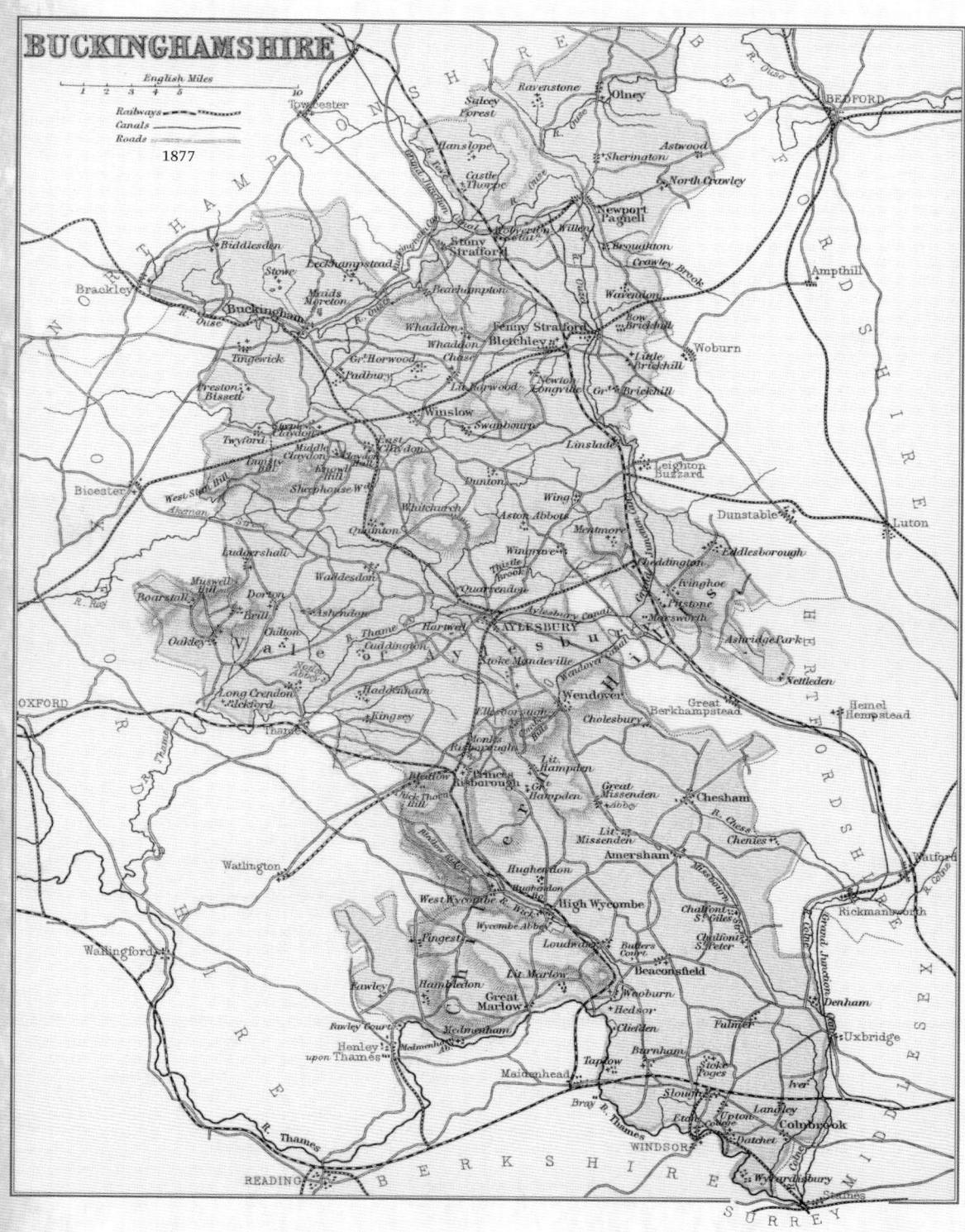

BUCKINGHAMSHIRE

English Miles
1 2 3 4 5 10

Railways
Canals
Roads

1877

Bartholomew Gazetteer of the British Isles, 1887

BUCKINGHAMSHIRE, or Bucks, an inland co. of England, bounded N. by Northamptonshire, E. by Bedfordshire, Herts, and Middlesex, S. by Surrey (for the distance of about 1 mile) and Berks, and W. by Oxfordshire; greatest length, N. and S., 50 miles; greatest breadth, E. and W., 24 miles; average breadth, 17 miles; area 477,151 ac., pop. 176,323. It is intersected by the chalk range of the Chiltern Hills, which extend NE. from Oxfordshire to Bedfordshire, the highest point being Wendover Hill, 905 ft. The country here is beautifully wooded, chiefly with oak and beech. To the S. there is much excellent grazing land. The fertile "Vale of Aylesbury," lies in the centre of the co., verdant with rich meadows and pasturage. Further N. the heavy arable land is now being brought under steam cultivation, and excellent crops of wheat, beans, &c., are produced. Farms are generally of small size, and are leased on a yearly tenure. Pigs and calves are largely reared on the numerous dairy-farms, and great numbers of ducks are sent yearly to the metropolis from the neighbourhood of Aylesbury. The quantity of butter, besides cream cheese, &c., sent annually to the London market, averages between 4,000,000 and 5,000,000 lbs. The making of wooden spades, brush-handles, bowls, &c., from beech is a considerable industry. Numbers of the female population are employed in the mfr. of thread-lace and straw-plaiting. The co. is traversed by the London and North-Western Ry. and its branches; the Grand Junction Canal extends about 24 miles through the NE. B. comprises 8 hundreds, – those of Stoke, Burnham, and Desborough being called the "Chiltern Hundreds"; – 224 pars.; and the mun. bors. of Buckingham and Chipping Wycombe. It is almost entirely in the diocese of Oxford.

MILTON KEYNES

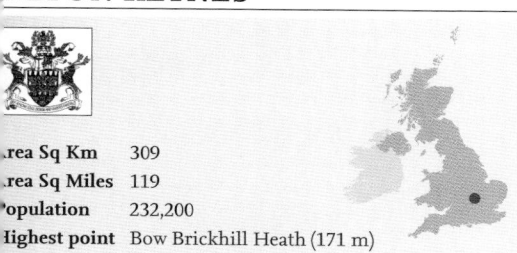

Area Sq Km	309
Area Sq Miles	119
Population	232,200
Highest point	Bow Brickhill Heath (171 m)

FAMOUS FOR

The headquarters of the **Open University**, the world's first distance learning university opened in 1970 at Walton Park in Milton Keynes. It currently has around 189,000 students studying a wide range of courses.

In 1978, the Canadian sculptor Liz Leyh created a sculpture of three cows and three calves in Milton Keynes, universally known as the **Concrete Cows**, and the cause of much debate ever since.

Bletchley Park became a code-breaking centre during World War II. It was here that the German 'Enigma' code was broken and much work was done that led directly to the development of the computer.

In 1764, John Newton a former slave-ship captain became curate of **Olney**. Here he wrote many hymns, including 'Amazing Grace'. He was a friend of poet William Cowper, who also settled in Olney.

The area includes Milton Keynes, Bletchley, Newport Pagnell, Great Linford, Stony Stratford and Wolverton. Originally a district within Buckinghamshire, this northern tip of the county became an independent unitary authority in 1997. Milton Keynes was the last major new town to be created in England. It was selected in 1967, based both on the recent growth of Wolverton and Bletchley and by its position half way between London and Birmingham. It took its name from a small village in the development area. The plan was to create a grid city with a central area and many neighbourhood centres. It has proved popular, with its population rising from around 60,000 to a projected 258,000 in 2016.

The curfew tolls the knell of parting day,
The lowing herd winds slowly o'er the lea,
The ploughman homeward plods his weary way,
And leaves the world to darkness and to me.

Some village-Hampden, that with dauntless breast
The little tyrant of his fields withstood,
Some mute inglorious Milton here may rest,
Some Cromwell, guiltless of his country's blood.
Thomas Gray, 'Elegy Written in a Country Churchyard', 1750

Clock tower at Bletchley Park – World War II code-breaking HQ in UK.

British National Grid projection

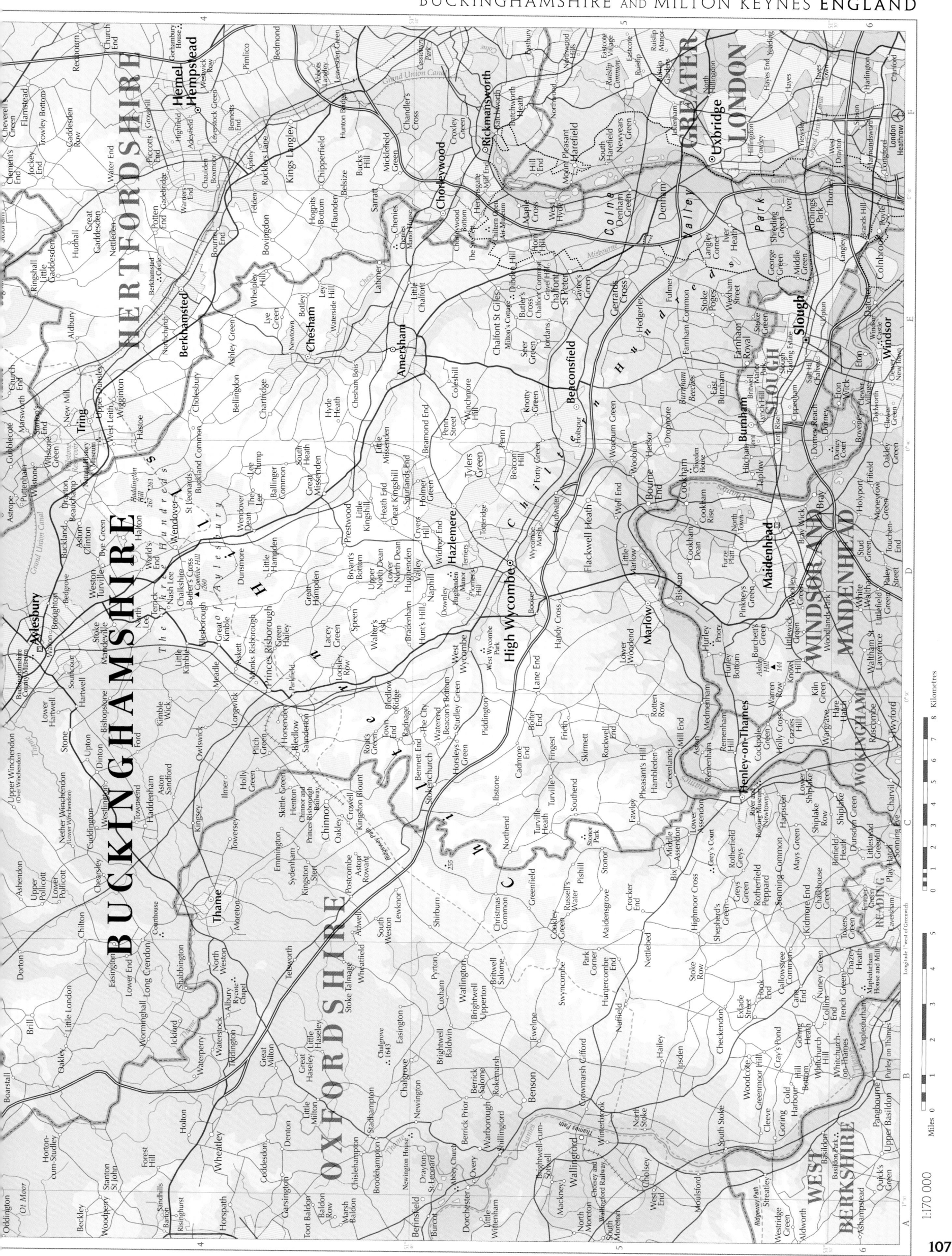

1:170 000

© Collins Bartholomew Ltd

BEDFORDSHIRE'S UNITARY AUTHORITIES

Bedford	**Area** sq. km 476; sq, miles 184 **Population** 155,700 **County town** Bedford
Central Bedfordshire	**Area** sq. km 1854; sq, miles 716 **Population** 255,000 **County town** Chicksands
Luton	**Area** sq. km 43; sq. miles 17 **Population** 191,800 **County town** Luton
Highest point of Ceremonial County	Dunstable Downs (243 m)

Bedfordshire takes its name from the town of Bedford, which most likely means 'the ford (across the River Ouse) of Beda', an otherwise unknown Saxon chief. It is now just a ceremonial county administered by three unitary authorities.

FAMOUS FOR

While he was in **Bedford** Jail between 1660 and 1672 for preaching without a licence, **John Bunyan** wrote *The Pilgrim's Progress: from This World to That Which is to Come. Delivered under the similitude of a dream*, the beautifully written Christian allegory that remains eternally popular and has been extensively translated into many languages. He lived in Bedford until his death in 1688.

At **Old Warden**, near Biggleswade is the **Shuttleworth Collection** of vintage and veteran aircraft, including the oldest aeroplane still flying in the world, the Bleriot XI from 1909.

Woburn Abbey is the stately home of the Dukes of Bedford. The abbey has been in the family since 1547, and the present building, with its superb art collection, mainly dates from the 1750s. **Woburn Safari Park** was opened in 1970, partly to provide funds to restore the abbey.

Whipsnade, near Dunstable is famous for its zoo (part of London Zoo) and also for the **Tree Cathedral**, planted with a wide variety of carefully chosen trees by E K Blyth in 1931–9 in the shape of a medieval cathedral.

Cardington, near Bedford, was the home of the Royal Airship Works, and two enormous hangers designed to contain airships still survive. It was here that Airship R101, which was 237 m long, was built, and from here that it departed on 4 October 1930 on its first flight to India, only to crash eight hours later near Beauvais in France ending the dream of airship travel.

The first section of the **M1 Motorway** was opened by the Transport Minister, Ernest Sharples at the Slip End junction, just to the south of Luton on 2 November 1959.

FAMOUS PEOPLE

Margaret Beaufort, mother of Henry VII, born Bletsoe Castle, near Bedford, 1443.
John Bunyan, author of *The Pilgrim's Progress*, born Elstow, 1628.
Nicholas Rowe, Poet Laureate, 1715–18, born Little Barford, 1674.
Sir Joseph Paxton, gardener and architect of the Crystal Palace, born Milton Bryan, near Woburn, 1803.
Harold Abrahams, athlete, Olympic 100 m champion 1924, born Bedford, 1899.
John Elton Le Mesurier De Somerys Halliley (John Le Mesurier), actor, born Bedford, 1912.
Archbishop Trevor Huddleston, a founder of the Anti-Apartheid Movement, born Bedford, 1913.
Arthur Hailey, novelist, born Luton 1920.
Ronald (Ronnie) Barker, comedian, born Bedford, 1929.

Bedfordshire is a predominantly agricultural county. In the north, the low-lying clay lands contain the meandering Great Ouse river, that flows north to the Wash, and its tributaries, the Ouzel and the Ivel, into which flow the Flit and Hiz. In the south, the eastern end of the chalky Chilterns can be seen on Dunstable Downs and around Luton, the source of the river Lea that flows south into the Thames (as the river Lee).

The traditional county of Bedfordshire has its origins in the early 11th century. Prior to that the area had been much fought over and divided between different kingdoms. Bedford became the most important settlement, with its strategic position on the river Ouse at the highest point that barges could navigate to. In the south, Dunstable's position at the junction of the Roman Watling Street and the Prehistoric Icknield Way ensured its early importance. Henry I built a hunting lodge here and founded Dunstable Priory in 1131. In 1889 Bedfordshire County Council was formed. With various changes to the districts with in the county, it remained the authority until 2009, although Luton became a unitary authority in 1997. In 2009 the County Council ceased to exist, and traditional Bedfordshire was divided into three unitary authorities; Bedford, Central Bedfordshire and Luton. The ceremonial county of Bedfordshire includes all three unitary authorities and Bedford and Central Bedfordshire work together to provide certain services.

The **Bedford** unitary authority is centred around the town of Bedford with agricultural land stretching up to the borders with Northamptonshire and Cambridgeshire. The population of the area is 155,700 and the main settlements are Bedford (80,230 in 2007) and Kempston (19,820 in 2007), a suburb of Bedford. Bedford and the surrounding area used to be a centre for the lace-making industry from the 1560s, remaining a significant activity until the early 20th century. To the south of Bedford in the Marston valley was a great concentration of brickworks. In the 1930s the London Brick Company works at Stewartby were the largest in the world, producing around 500 million bricks a year. Demand slowed in the late 1960s, and the works closed in 2008, leaving a legacy of clay pits. Now 85 per cent of jobs are in the service sector, with around a third being in administration, education and health. Bedford contains a campus of the University of Bedfordshire.

Central Bedfordshire has a population of 255,000, with the largest centres of population, such as Dunstable (34,600) and Leighton Buzzard and Lindale (36,000), in the south and within commuting distance of London, while Biggleswade (16,520) in the northeast of the area is closer to Cambridge but still only a 35-minute train journey to London. The population is expected to grow by 10 percent by 2020, one of the fastest growing areas in the country. The area is well served by the M1 motorway and major trunk roads and by mainline railway services. Fewer than 24 per cent of the jobs are in the public sector and there is a diverse range of businesses in the area from aero-engineering to food processing. Cranfield University, a post-graduate institution specializing in technology and management, has an international reputation.

Luton, at the southeastern corner of the county has a population of 191,800 and is one of the major centres of employment and manufacturing in southeast England, with automotive, electrical and retail industries among the most important. The Vauxhall Motor Company headquarters are in the town – the company moved from the Vauxhall area of London in 1905 and vans are still made in the town although car production moved away in 2002. The production and export of high-fashion and straw hats remains a feature of the local economy, having been an important industry since the 17th century. London Luton Airport situated to the southeast of the urban area was opened in 1938. It is now a major centre for low-cost and charter flights, with over 10.2 million passengers in 2008, employing 500 people directly and a further 8,000 indirectly. Luton is also the main base of the University of Bedfordshire.

Woburn Abbey, near Woburn.

Luton

Asian elephant show at Whipsnade Zoo, near Dunstable.

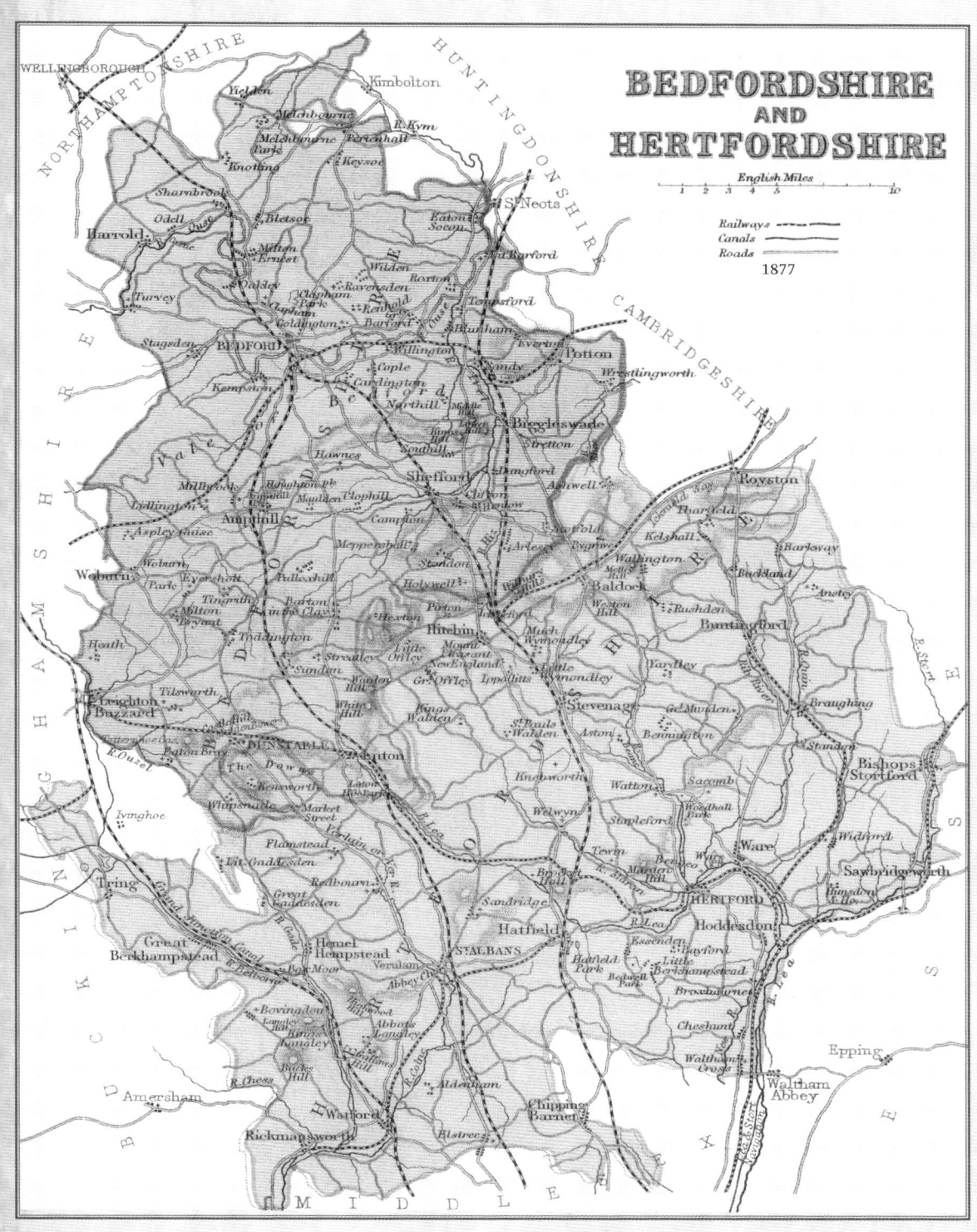

BEDFORDSHIRE
AND
HERTFORDSHIRE

English Miles
1 2 3 4 5 10

Railways
Canals
Roads
1877

Bartholomew Gazetteer of the British Isles, 1887

BEDFORDSHIRE, or Beds, a midland co. of England, bounded by the cos. of Northampton, Cambridge, Herts, and Bucks. Greatest length, N. and S., 30 miles; greatest breadth, E. and W., 20 miles; area, 29,983 ac.; pop. 149,473. The surface is mostly flat, varied in the S. by a spur of the Chiltern Hills, and in the NW. by a range of chalk hills. The chief river is the Great Ouse, with its affluent the Ivel. The country along the banks of the Ouse and other streams is highly verdant and luxuriant. The greater part of the surface is under tillage; indeed, agriculture, it is said, is further advanced here than in any other English county. On the heavy soils the principal crops are wheat and beans. The sandy and chalky soils of the middle districts are well adapted for horticultural husbandry, and vegetables are extensively grown for the markets of London, Cambridge, &c. There is excellent grazing ground in the SE., this co. being noted for its breeds of sheep and cattle. The principal mfrs. are agricultural implements and straw-plait for hats. Bedfordshire contains 9 hundreds, 134 pars. and 2 parts, and the mun. bors. of Bedford Dunstable and Luton. It is almost entirely in the diocese of Ely.

HERTFORDSHIRE (or Herts), an inland co. in SE. of England, bounded N. by Cambridgeshire, E. by Essex, S. by Middlesex, W. by Bucks, and NW. by Bedfordshire; greatest length, NE. and SW., 35 miles; greatest breadth, E. and W., 26 miles: 465,141 ac., pop. 203,069. In appearance the co. is hilly, but interspersed with fine pasture lands, arable farms, and picturesque parks and woods. The Lea, the Colne, and the Ivel are the principal rivers; the Grand Junction Canal likewise passes through a part of the co. A large number of the inhabitants are employed in husbandry, and in addition to grain of choice quality, hay, vegetables, and numerous fruits and flowers are extensively cultivated, especially for the London market. The greater portion of the commerce of the co. is supported by the trade in corn and malt. Mfrs. are few; paper-making, silk-weaving, and straw-plaiting being the principal industries. Railways penetrate to all parts of the co.; no place is at a greater distance than 5 miles from a station. Geologically the greater part of Herts consists of Lower, Middle, and Upper Chalk; in the S. is the London clay. The minerals are of no commercial importance. Herts comprises 8 hundreds, 138 pars., and parts of 3 others, and the mun. bors. of Hertford and St Albans. It is almost entirely in the diocese of St Albans.

...he of the airship hangers at Cardington, near Bedford.

An Arvo Triplane which is part of the Shuttleworth Collection, at Old Warden, near Biggleswade.

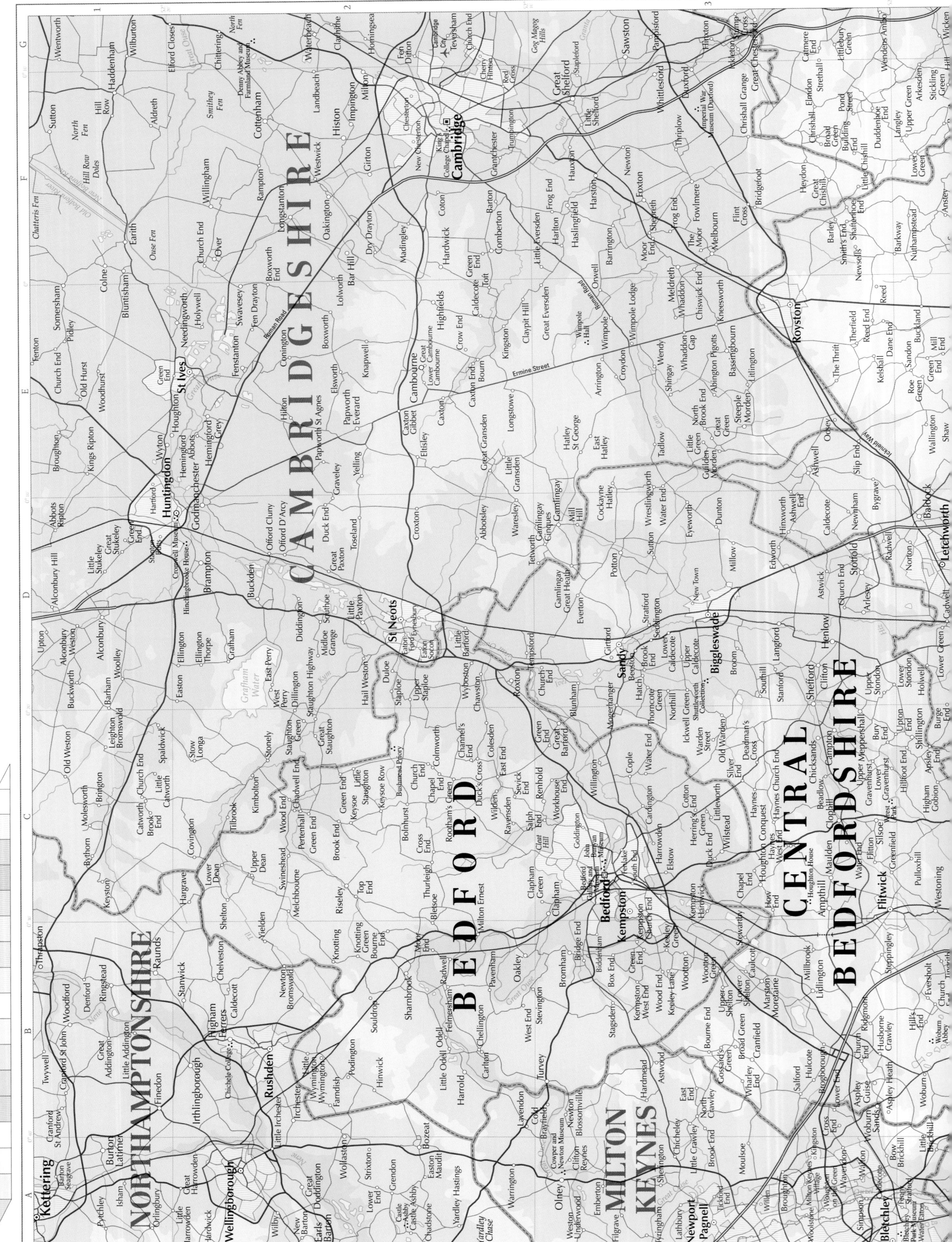

British National Grid projection

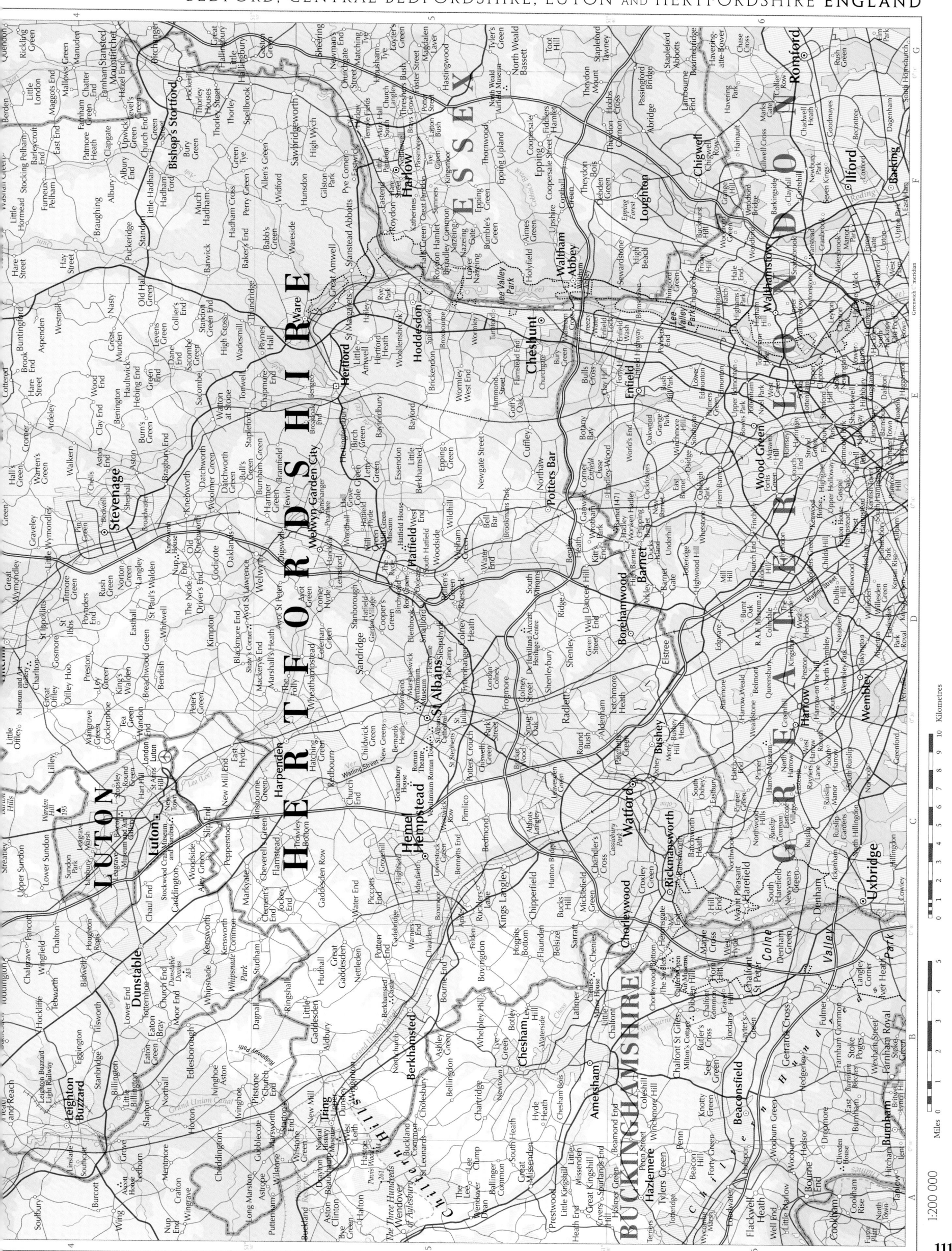

1:200 000

Miles 0   1   2   3   4   5

0 1 2 3 4 5 6 7 8 9 10 Kilometres

© Collins Bartholomew Ltd

HERTFORDSHIRE

Area Sq Km	1,643
Area Sq Miles	634
Population	1,078,400
County town	Hertford
Highest point	Pavis Wood (244 m) in the Chilterns near Tring
Districts	Broxbourne; Dacorum; East Herts; Hertsmere; North Hertfordshire; St Albans; Stevenage; Three Rivers; Watford; Welwyn Hatfield.

Hertfordshire takes its name from Hertford, the ford where harts (stags) crossed the River Lea.

FAMOUS FOR

The **Elstree Film Studios** (actually in **Borehamwood**) were opened in 1925, and, with some interruptions, major films have been made there ever since including the first British 'talkie' in 1929 (Alfred Hitchcock's *Blackmail*) and the first three *Star Wars* films as well as television series such as *Who Wants to be a Millionaire?*.

The Natural History Museum at **Tring** was once the private collection of Lord Lionel Walter Rothschild, one of the great collectors of specimens and live animals – in the museum grounds he kept a tame wolf, rheas, kangaroos, kiwis, cassowaries and giant tortoises, and had a carriage pulled by zebras.

The Nobel Prize author, George Bernard Shaw, lived at **Ayot St Lawrence** for 44 years until his death in 1950, and his house and writing 'retreat' in the garden have been preserved as he left them.

After the Battle of Hastings in 1066, William the Conqueror marched to **Berkhamsted**, where bishops, earls and the chief men of London swore allegiance to him ahead of his coronation in London on Christmas Day 1066.

The **Great Bed of Ware** is an enormous carved oak four-poster bed made around 1590, most likely for the White Hart Inn at Ware – it is over 3 m wide, twice the normal size of beds at that time.

The renowned sculptor Henry Moore moved to **Perry Green**, near Bishop's Stortford, during World War II and remained there until his death. His house, studio and grounds are now looked after by the Henry Moor Foundation, with regular exhibitions of their large collection of his sculptures and drawings.

Sunset Song, one of the classic novels of 20th century Scotland was actually written in **Welwyn Garden City**, which was the home of Lewis Grassic Gibbon from 1931–35.

FAMOUS PEOPLE

Sir Henry Bessemer, inventor of the Bessemer steel-making process, born Charlton, 1813.
Robert Cecil, 3rd Marquess of Salisbury, politician and Prime Minster (1885–92, 1895–1902), born Hatfield House, 1830.
Cecil Rhodes, British imperialist and diamond magnate, born Bishop's Stortford, 1853.
Graham Greene, novelist, born Berkhamsted, 1904.
Brian Johnston, cricket player and commentator, born Berkhamsted, 1912.
James Lovelock, scientist and creator of the Gaia theory, born Letchworth Garden City, 1919.
Georgios Kyriacos Panayiotou (George Michael), singer, born Bushey, 1963.
Lewis Hamilton, Formula One motor racing champion, born Stevenage, 1985.

The Chilterns rise along the western border of Hertfordshire, and there are chalk hills in the north around Royston; otherwise the landscape is mostly flat or gently undulating. By contrast, the south of the county merges into the urban sprawl of North London. The main river is the Lea (or Lee), which flows through Welwyn and Hertford before turning south through the Lee Valley to the Thames. Other rivers include the Ivel, flowing north into the Great Ouse and the Colne and the Ver, which meet near Watford and also flow down to the Thames.

The first reference to the county of Hertfordshire was in 903, to designate the area around a fort at Hertford. The county boundaries were finally fixed in 1844, only to be amended in 1965, when Barnet was transferred to the new London borough of Barnet and Potters Bar was added from Middlesex. Its area has since remained unchanged. With a population of 1,078,400, it is one of the most populous counties. The chief centres are Watford (population 120,960), Hemel Hempstead (83,118), Stevenage (81,482), the cathedral city of St Albans (82,429), Welwyn Garden City (43,512), Cheshunt (55,275), Bishop's Stortford (35,325), Hitchin (33,352), Letchworth (32,932), Borehamwood (31,172) and Hatfield (32,281). Between 2006 and 2031, the population of Hertfordshire is estimated to grow by 18.4 per cent, a figure similar to Greater London and lower than other counties in Eastern England. The Welwyn and Hatfield area is expected to see the greatest growth, at 33.2 per cent.

The economy of Hertfordshire is greatly influenced by the proximity of London. Over 160,000 residents of the county work elsewhere, mainly in London, while many businesses have settled in Hertfordshire to be close to London – the county is home to the head offices of major retailers, including Tesco. There is also significant hi-tech, aeronautics and pharmaceutical manufacturing in the county, though what was once the site of the major de Havilland aircraft manufacturing facility at Hatfield is now the main campus of the University of Hertfordshire, the only university in the county. There are also major film and television studies at Elstree, Borehamwood and Leavesden. Over 85 per cent of jobs are in the service sector, with the largest sector being Finance, IT and other business (27.2 per cent) followed by retail, hotels and restaurants at 26.5 per cent and administration, education and health at 21.1 per cent, well below the UK average.

Within this business-like county there are places to detain the visitor. St Albans stands on the site of *Verulamium*, originally the capital of the pre-Roman *Catuvellauni*, and, after being burnt by Boudicca in AD 60 it became a major Roman settlement, remains of which can still be seen. In the early 3rd century, Alban, a Roman officer, sheltered a Christian priest at a time of persecution, and as a result, became the first known Christian martyr in Britain. Around 793 King Offa endowed a monastery in his honour. It was rebuilt by the Normans, becoming the Cathedral and Abbey Church of St Albans in 1877.

Close to St Albans is Hatfield House, one of the finest Jacobean houses in Britain. It was built between 1608 and 1612 by Robert Cecil, close adviser to Elizabeth I and James I, and its grandeur reflects the power of the Cecil family. Further north, near Stevenage is Knebworth, originally a Tudor house but romantically rebuilt in the 1840s in a Jacobean style. Hertfordshire is also home to two important new towns – Letchworth Garden City was the first such settlement ever designed (in 1902) while Welwyn Garden City (from 1919) was the first 'garden city' designed to incorporate residential and industrial areas. Both were significant in the development of new towns in Britain and across the world.

"Oh, a mighty large bed, bigger by half than the great bed of Ware – ten thousand people may lie in it together, and never feel one another."
George Farquhar, *The Recruiting Officer*, 1706

"England was not like other countries, but it was all a planted garden. They had there on the right hand, the town of St Albans in their view; and all the spaces between, and further beyond it, looked indeed like a garden."
Daniel Defoe, noting comments made by two foreign travellers on Bushey Heath, 1725

The Cathedral and Abbey Church of St Alban.

[ES]SEX

[Are]a Sq Km	3,695
[Are]a Sq Miles	1,427
[Po]pulation	1,396,400
[Co]unty town	Chelmsford
[Hi]ghest point	Chrishall Common (147 m) near Saffron Walden
[Di]stricts	Basildon; Braintree; Brentwood; Castle Point; Chelmsford; Colchester; Epping Forest; Harlow; Maldon; Rochford; Tendring; Uttlesford.

[Es]sex takes its name from the kingdom of the East [Sa]xons (Old English '*Seaxe*') who settled in the area [in] the fifth century.

[FA]MOUS FOR

[Aft]er his death at the Battle of Hastings in 1066, King [Ha]rold was buried at **Waltham Abbey**. The current [bu]ilding is the magnificent nave of a Norman church [bu]ilt around 1120; the great abbey built by Henry II as [pa]rt of his penance for the murder of Thomas Becket [wa]s demolished after 1540.

[Ep]ping Forest was originally a royal forest, [wh]ere kings hunted deer and other animals while [co]mmoners had certain rights to gather wood. In [18]78, its administration was taken over by the City [of] London Corporation and, when Queen Victoria [vi]sited in 1882, she said 'it gives me the greatest [sa]tisfaction to dedicate this beautiful forest to the [us]e and enjoyment of my people for all time'.

[Fy]xta-Ongar is home to Britain's only wooden Saxon [ch]urch, **The Church of St Andrew (Greensted-juxta-[On]gar)** with its original nave walls of split oak, [th]ought to date from just before the Norman [Co]nquest.

[Th]e nursery rhyme 'Old King Cole' is based on a story [ab]out the naming of **Colchester**, apparently after the [my]thical 'King Coel', whose daughter, so the story [go]es, was Helena, the mother of the first Christian [Ro]man Emperor Constantine.

[Th]e town of **Saffron Walden** took its exotic name [fr]om the preparation of saffron from crocus flowers [th]at was its main business in the 16th century. [Th]e town also contains an extraordinary turf maze, [pr]obably dating from the 17th century – it is 35 m [in] diameter and the route to the centre is over [1,5]00 m long.

[F]AMOUS PEOPLE

[Wi]lliam Gilbert, physician and scientist, author of [D]e Magnete, born Colchester, 1544.
[Ma]rgaret Cavendish, Duchess of Newcastle (born [Ma]rgaret Lucas), writer and natural philosopher, [bo]rn Colchester, 1623.
[Jo]hn Ray, naturalist, born Black Notley, near [B]raintree, 1627.
[D]ick Turpin, highwayman, born Hempstead, 1705.
[Jo]hn Strutt, Lord Rayleigh, physicist and Nobel Prize [w]inner, born Langford Grove, Maldon, 1842.
[Ch]arlotte Rampling, actress, born Sturmer, 1946.
[Jo]hn Whitaker (Jack) Straw, politician, born [B]uckhurst Hill, 1946.
[S]ally Gunnell Olympic champion athlete, born [C]higwell, 1966.
[Ja]mie Oliver, chef and cookery writer, born Clavering, [1]975.

The landscape of Essex is mostly flat or gently undulating, and the low-lying coast is deeply indented with river estuaries and small islands, the most isolated area of southern England. The southwest of the county merges into the east of Greater London. Rivers include the Stour, forming part of the boundary with Suffolk, the Stort and the Lea (or Lee), forming part of the boundary with Hertfordshire, the Colne, the Blackwater and the Crouch.

The origins of the county lie with the Kingdom of Essex, created by the Saxons who colonized the area from the sea in the 5th century. The kingdom was never as strong as its neighbours and *c.* 825 Wessex gained control over it. After a Danish invasion in 878 and reconquest by English, it emerged as a shire in the early 11th century with roughly its historical boundaries. Its southwestern boundary included the settlements of Dagenham, Barking, Ilford, Walthamstow and East and West Ham. Essex County Council was formed in 1889, by which time these settlements had become the most populous part of the county. In 1965, with the creation of the Greater London Council, Essex lost much of its outer London area to the new London boroughs of Barking, Havering, Newham, Redbridge, and Waltham Forest. In 1998 the unitary authorities of Southend-on-Sea and Thurrock were created. Even with all these reductions, its population is 1,396,400 and its chief towns are Colchester (104,390), Basildon (99,976), the county town of Chelmsford (99,962), Harlow (88,296), Clacton-on-Sea (51,284), Brentwood (47,493), Braintree (42,393), Loughton (41,078), Canvey Island (37,479) and Billericay (33,687). The overall population is expected to grow by nearly 24 per cent between 2006 and 2031, but this growth is much slower than that seen in the second half of the 20th century, for the population of the current county council area in 1951 was around 600,000. Part of this growth came with the creation of new towns to house people from the East End of London, at Harlow in the west of the county and at Basildon, just inland from the Thames.

With its proximity to London, a great many residents of Essex commute into London, most relying on a railway network that cannot always manage the demand. Of those who work in Essex, 82.7 per cent of jobs are in the service sector, with 26 per cent of those jobs in public admin, education and health, but, for an area so close to London, only just under 20 per cent in finance, IT and other business. Major businesses are mainly in the south of the county, with electronics centred on Chelmsford and pharmaceuticals on Harlow. Brentwood is the European headquarters for the Ford Motor Company. Colchester has a major army garrison while the University of Essex is sited just outside the town at Wivenhoe Park. Anglia Ruskin University has one of its campuses at Chelmsford. Harwich remains a busy port for ferries to northern Europe but it lost out on container business to Felixstowe in Suffolk on the opposite side of the Orwell Estuary.

Before the Roman invasion Colchester was the seat of Cunobelinus (better known in literature as Cymbeline), and as Camulodunum became the first Roman capital of Britain, and the Normans incorporated some of the Roman remains into their castle. The estuaries of the Essex coast are all shallow, and, apart from Harwich provide no easy harbours. The Colne estuary is famed for its oyster beds, while the Blackwater near Maldon, is the site of the battle of Maldon at which the Vikings defeated the men of Essex under their leader Byrhtnoth, commemorated in an Old English poem, probably written around 1000. On the southern shore of the Blackwater, at Bradwell, is one of the oldest churches in Britain, St Peter-on-the-Wall, probably built by the Northumbrian missionary, St Cedd, around 654. It now shares this lonely spot with Bradwell Nuclear Power Station.

Inland from Manningtree, on the border with Suffolk flows the Stour through a landscape made famous by the great landscape painter John Constable. Further west are many beautiful villages and small towns – Fichingfield, Thaxted, Castle Hedingham and Saffron Walden. Some of the tranquillity is lost with Stansted Airport on the western boundary of the county and close to the M11 motorway. A civilian airport only since 1957, Stanstead is now London's third airport and used by over 22 million passengers a year.

Statue of Victory, Colchester.

Hadleigh Castle, the most important late-medieval castle in Essex.

SOUTHEND-ON-SEA

Area Sq Km 68
Area Sq Miles 26
Population 164,300
Highest point London Road (61 m)

FAMOUS FOR
Southend Pier dates from 1830 and is the longest pier in the world, stretching 2,158 m out into the Thames Estuary. Long a destination for London visitors, it has a lifeboat station and restaurant at the Pier Head, reached by a railway
that runs along the pier.

FAMOUS PEOPLE
Trevor Bailey, cricketer and commentator, born Westcliff-on-Sea, 1923.
John Fowles, novelist, born Leigh-on-Sea, 1926.
Sir Peter Cook, architect, with Populous, of the 2012 Olympic Stadium, born Southend-on-Sea, 1936.
John Lloyd, tennis player, born Leigh-on-Sea, 1954.

"You could not have a softer clime or sunnier skies than at abused Southend."
Benjamin Disraeli, 1834

"Southend. At low water a stranger would suppose that the sea had totally abandoned the place."
Anon., c. 1810

Southend became a unitary authority in 1996 and is a commercial, residential, shopping and holiday centre, with tourism among its main industries. It also contains a significant HM Revenues and Customs facility. Reflecting this, nearly 91 per cent of jobs in Southend are in the service sector. It has an 11 km shoreline from Leigh-on-Sea in the west to Shoeburyness in the east.

Southend developed as a seaside resort in the late 18th century and it really came into its own with the arrival the railway in 1856, becoming a magnet for day-trippe from London. It forms part of the Thames Gateway; the UK's largest regeneration project, stretching 64 km along the Thames estuary.

Adventure Island Fun Park.

THURROCK

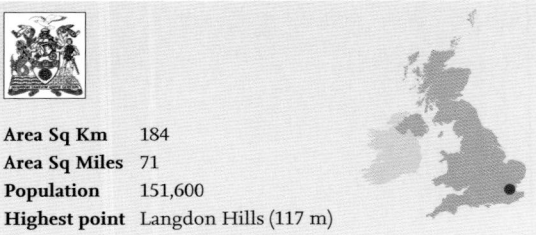

Area Sq Km 184
Area Sq Miles 71
Population 151,600
Highest point Langdon Hills (117 m)

FAMOUS FOR
In 1588, as the Spanish Armada approached, Queen Elizabeth I addressed her troops at **Tilbury**, near the fort originally built by Henry VIII and rebuilt and enlarged in 1670.

When it opened in 1991, the **Queen Elizabeth II Bridge** across the Thames was Europe's largest cable-stayed bridge with a central span of 450 m. It is the last bridge to cross the Thames before it flows into the sea.

On 22 June 1948 the MV *Empire Windrush* arrived at **Tilbury Docks** from Kingston, Jamaica, with 492 Jamaicans who had paid £28 for the trip to Britain. Its arrival became the symbol of the start of immigration from the West Indies.

Thurrock became a unitary authority in 1996. It has 29 km of Thames riverfront and the main centres are Grays and Tilbury. The area is a mix of old and modern, rural and urban, with 70 per cent of the land area classified as Green Belt. In the north there are historic villages, while in the south, there are the modern urban developments, and industrial activities surrounding oil

refining and the container port of Tilbury. Grays is the commercial centre of Thurrock, with the major retail centre being Thurrock Lakeside. The area includes the northern stretch of the Dartford Tunnel and Queen Elizabeth II Bridge, both of which cross the river Thames.

Queen Elizabeth II Bridge.

"How unjust the world is to Essex."
Matthew Arnold, 1853

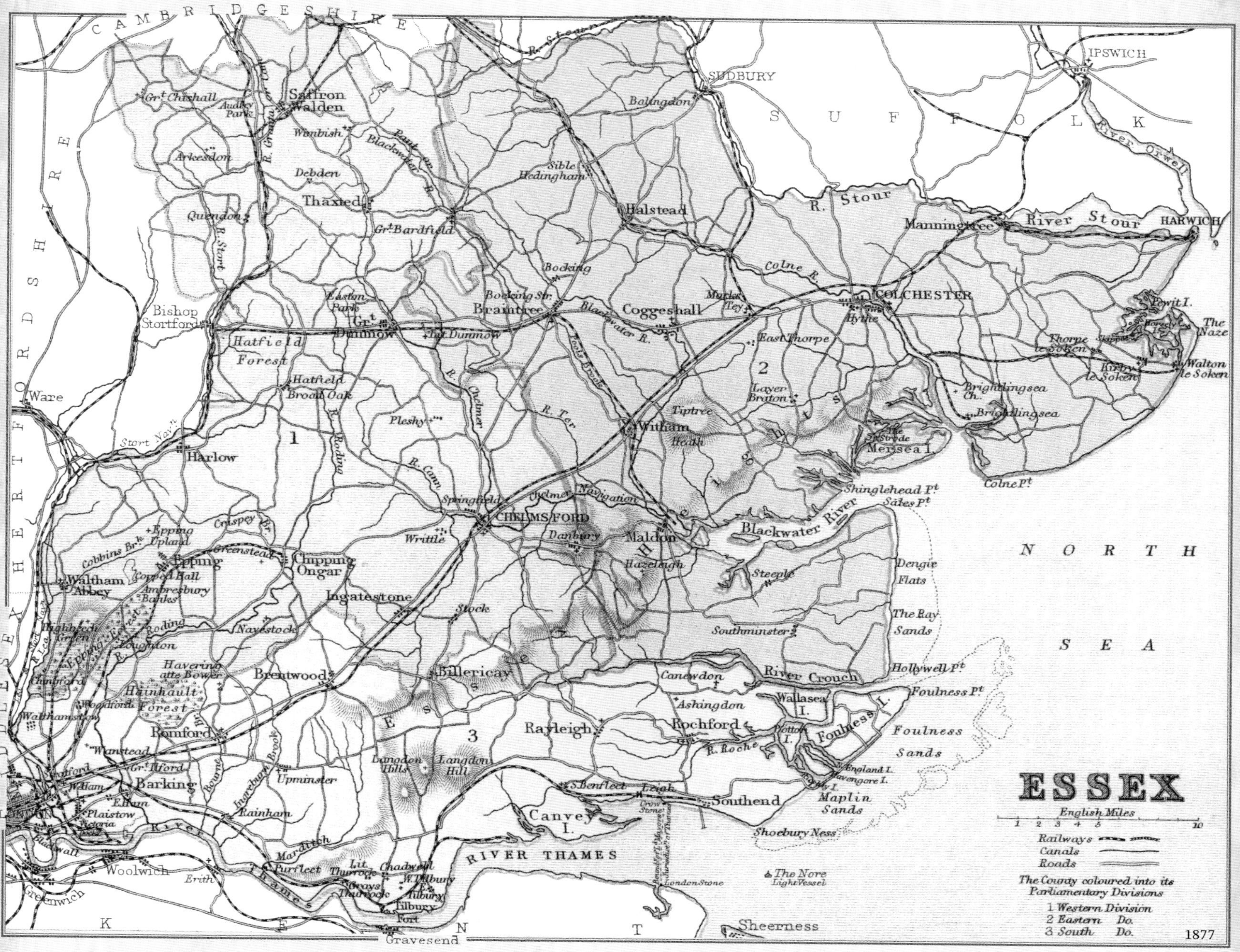

The map of ESSEX showing towns, rivers, railways, canals and roads. Key includes the county coloured into its Parliamentary Divisions: 1 Western Division, 2 Eastern Do., 3 South Do. Dated 1877.

Bartholomew Gazetteer of the British Isles, 1887

ESSEX, maritime co. in SE. of England; is bounded N. by Cambridgeshire and Suffolk, E. by the North Sea, S. by the river Thames, and W. by Middlesex and Herts; greatest length, N. and S., 44 miles; greatest breadth, E. and W., 57 miles; 987,032 ac.; pop. 576,434. On the coast are several marshy islands, such as Canvey, Foulness, Wallasea, Mersea, &c. Essex is one of the Metropolitan shires, or "Six Home Counties", and took its name from the East Saxons. It rests upon the London clay, and is watered by the Stour, Colne, Chelmer, Crouch, Thames, Roding, and Lea; the surface, flat near the coast and the rivers, is undulating and sometimes hilly towards the NW.; the soil is generally fertile. Wheat and barley of fine quality are largely grown in the NW. and the centre; the marshes on the coast have for the most part been drained and converted into fertile grazing lands. Essex had at one time a great extent of forest, which has almost entirely disappeared. Hainault Forest was disforested in 1851; Epping Forest was preserved by the Act of 1871. The co. has no mineral wealth, with the exception of chalk for lime, septaria for Roman cement, and clay for bricks. Its mfrs. are of no great extent – ironworks for the local supply of agricultural implements; crape, damasks and satins, &c. The Barking fishing smacks carry on an active industry; and there are very productive oyster beds in the estuaries of the Crouch, the Blackwater, and the Colne. Essex comprises 19 hundreds, 1 liberty, and 413 pars., with parts of 3 others, the parl. bor. of West Ham, and the mun. bors. of Colchester, Harwich, Maldon, and Saffron Walden. It is mostly in the diocese of St Albans.

don, Blackwater Estuary , Essex.

Turf maze, Saffron Walden, Essex.

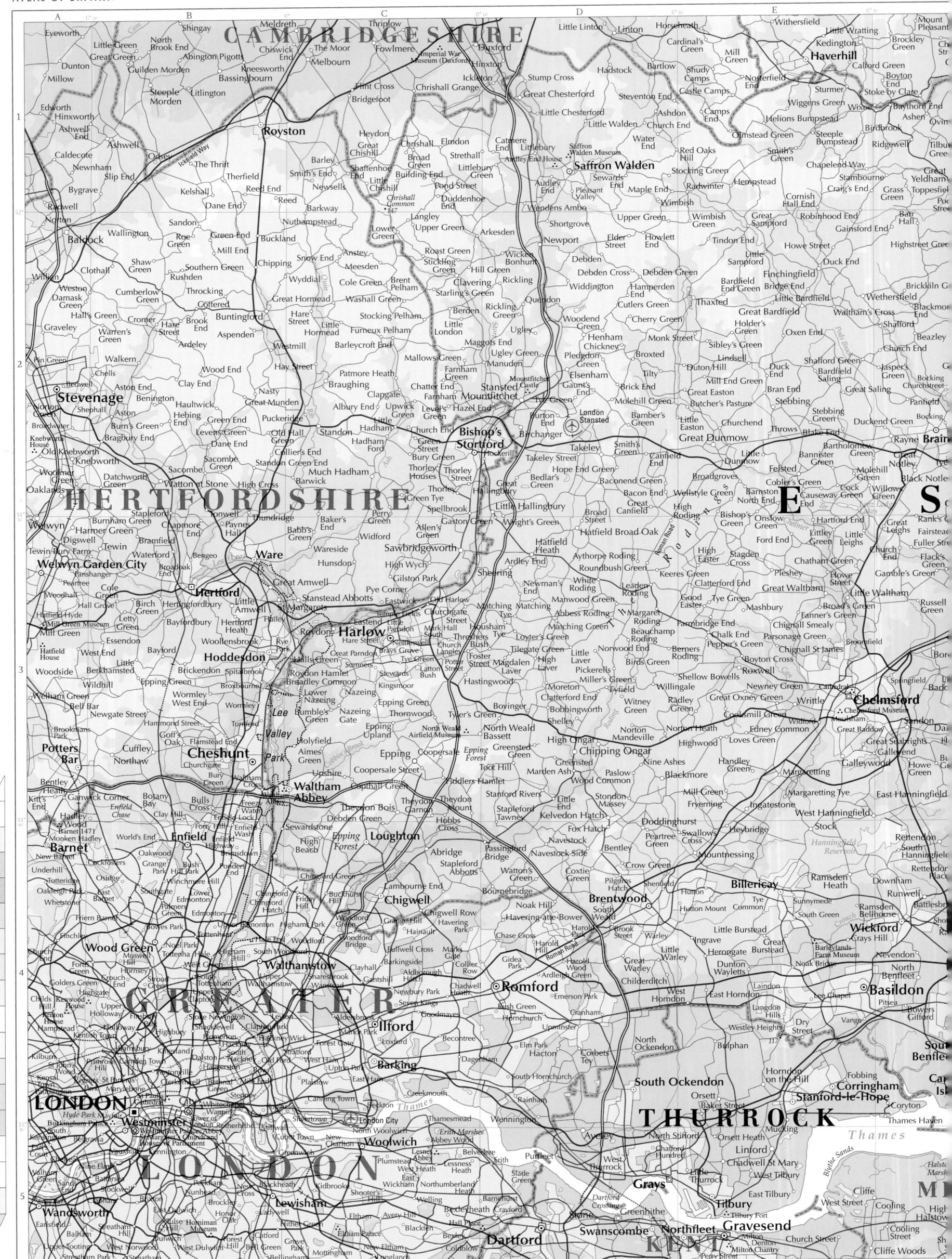

British National Grid projection

G · H · I · J · K

SUFFOLK

Brook Street · Glemsford · Kentwell Hall · Little Hall · Monks Fleigh Tye · Monks Eleigh · Nedging · Naughton · Somersham · Nettlestead · Claydon · Akenham · Culpho · Woodbridge · Melton · Rendlesham Forest

High Street · Long Melford · Melford Hall · Brent Eleigh · Chelsworth · Semer · Ash Street · Whatfield · Elmsett · Blakenham · Flowton · Whitton · Westerfield · Boot Street · Little Bealings · Playford · Sutton Hoo Tumuli

Liston · Foxearth · Newman's Green · Great Waldingfield · Little Waldingfield · Milden · Lindsey · Kersey · Bramford · Sproughton · Ipswich · Christchurch Mansion · Kesgrave · Martlesham Heath · Sutton

Sudbury · Chilton · Edwardstone · Groton · Horner's Green · St James's Chapel · Kersey Vale · Hadleigh · Hintlesham · Burstall · Copdock · Belstead · California · Brightwell · Newbourne · Waldringfield · Shottisham

Great Cornard · Cornard Tye · Newton · Sherbourne Street · Boxford · Hadleigh Heath · Bower House Tye · Polstead Heath · Chattisham · Wherstead · Woolverstone · Nacton · Kirton · Ramsholt

Bulmer · Middleton · Sackers Green · Assington · Polstead · Shelley · Raydon · Great Wenham · Little Wenham · Capel St Mary · Freston · Pin Mill · Levington · Stratton Hall · Trimley St Martin · Felixstowe Ferry · Falkenham

Henny Street · Alphamstone · Leavenheath · Honey Tye · Stoke-by-Nayland · Thorington Street · Higham · Holton St Mary · East Bergholt · Upper Street · Holbrook · Stutton · Lower Holbrook · Shotley Street · Erwarton · Trimley Lower Street · Trimley St Mary · Walton · Felixstowe

Twinstead · Twinstead Green · Lamarsh · Bures Green · Wissington · Nayland · Boxted · Stratford St Mary · Flatford Mill and Bridge Cottage · Cattawade · Brantham · Harkstead · Shop Corner · Shotley Gate · Felixstowe Museum

Great Maplestead · Little Maplestead · Cross End · Pebmarsh · Mount Bures · Little Horkesley · Boxted Cross · Dedham · Langham · Lamb Corner · Dedham Heath · Mistley · New Mistley · Parkeston · Harwich Harbour · Landguard Point

Halstead · Colne Engaine · White Colne · Wakes Colne · Rose Green · Horkesley Heath · Great Horkesley · Langham Moor · Lawford · Manningtree · Bradfield · Wrabness · Ramsey · Upper Dovercourt · Harwich · Dovercourt

Earls Colne · Chappel · Swan Street · Fordham · West Bergholt · Mile End · Fox Street · Ardleigh · St Mary's Church (remains of) · Bradfield Heath · Wix · Great Oakley · Little Oakley · Stone Point

Burton's Green · Colne Valley · Fordstreet · Fordham Heath · Colchester · Crockleford Heath · Elmstead · Horsley Cross · Goose Green · Tendring Green · Horsey Island · The Naze

Great Tey · Gallows Green · Aldham · Seven Star Green · Castle Museum · St Botolph's Priory · Greenstead · Elmstead Market · Cowey Green · Great Bromley · Raven's Green · Tendring · Goose Green · Beaumont · Flanders Water

Pattiswick · Little Tey · Marks Tey · Stanway · Beacon End · Shrub End · Old Heath · Balls Green · Hare Green · Great Bentley · Weeley · Thorpe Green · Kirby le Soken · Walton on the Naze

Bradwell · Broad Green · Long Green · Coggeshall · Pott's Green · Copford Green · Stanway Green · Heckfordbridge · Maypole Green · Rowhedge · Wivenhoe · Frating · Aingers Green · Weeley Heath · Thorpe-le-Soken · Kirby Cross · Frinton-on-Sea

Perry Green · Coggeshall Hamlet · Paycocke's · Skye Green · Langley Green · Easthorpe · Hardy's Green · Birch · Gryme's Dyke · Blackheath · High Park · Fingringhoe · South Green · Great Bentley · Row Heath · Little Clacton · Great Holland

Silver End · Notley · Feering · Gore Pit · Messing · Smythe's Green · Birch Green · Layer de la Haye · Malting Green · Abberton · Alresford · Thorrington · Eastend Green · Priory · Great Clacton · Holland-on-Sea

ESSEX

Rivenhall · Kelvedon · Inworth · Layer Breton · Layer Marney Tower · Layer Marney · Abberton Reservoir · Langenhoe · Brightlingsea · Hurst Green · St Osyth · Sandy Point

Rivenhall End · Little Braxted · Tiptree · Tiptree Heath · Tiptree Museum · Peldon · Point Clear · St Osyth Marsh · Jaywick · Clacton-on-Sea

Witham · Great Braxted · Oxley Green · Virley · Great Wigborough · East Mersea · Cudmore Grove · Seawick

Beacon Hill · Totham Plains · Salcott · Salcott Channel · West Mersea · Mersea Island · Mersea Flats · Colne Point

Wickham Bishops · Little Totham · Tolleshunt Knights · Tolleshunt D'Arcy · Cobmarsh Island · Gunfleet Sand

Great Totham · Tolleshunt Major · Virley Channel · Great Cob Island · The Nass

Langford · Broad Street Green · Goldhanger · Tollesbury · Tollesbury Fleet

Ulting · Heybridge · Maldon · Heybridge Basin · Osea Island · Northey Island · Blackwater · Bradwell Waterside · Sales Point · St Peter's Flat · East End · Bradwell-on-Sea

Curling Green · Woodham Walter · Maldon 991 · Ramsey Island · St Lawrence · Tillingham · Dengie Flat

Hazeleigh · Woodham Mortimer · Mundon · Steeple · Dengie · Dengie Marshes

Rudley Green · Purleigh · Maylandsea · Mayland · Asheldham · Ray Sand

Cock Clarks · Farther Howegreen · Latchingdon · Northend · Southminster · Stoneyhills · Old Montsale

Great Canney · Cold Norton · Stow Maries · Mangapps Railway Museum · Eves Corner

South Woodham Ferrers · North Fambridge · Ostend · Burnham-on-Crouch · Deal Hall · Holliwell Point · Foulness Sands · Foulness Point

South Fambridge · Bridgemarsh Island · Crouch · Canewdon · Courtsend

Hullbridge · Ashingdon · Paglesham Churchend · Wallasea Island · Ballards Gore · Paglesham Eastend · Churchend · Roach

Hawkwell · Great Stambridge · Potton Island · Foulness Island

Rayleigh · Stroud Green · Rochford · Barling · Havengore Island · Maplin Sands

Prittlewell Priory · Little Wakering · Great Wakering

Hadleigh · Prittlewell · **SOUTHEND-ON-SEA** · Central Museum · North Shoebury · Shoeburyness · Cambridge Town

Leigh-on-Sea · Southchurch · Thorpe Bay · Shoebury Ness

Westcliff-on-Sea · Chapman Sands

NORTH SEA

Allhallows-on-Sea · Allhallows · Isle of Grain · Grain · Hoo · Lower Stoke · Wallend · Sheerness · Mile Town · Marine Town · West Minster · Isle of Sheppey · Stoke Saltings

1:230 000

Kilometres 0 1 2 3 4 5 6 7 8 9 10

Miles 0 1 2 3 4 5 6 7

SUFFOLK

Area Sq Km	3,854
Area Sq Miles	1,488
Population	715,700
County town	Ipswich
Highest point	Great Wood Hill (128 m) on the Newmarket Ridge near Rede
Districts	Babergh; Forest Heath; Ipswich; Mid Suffolk; St Edmundsbury; Suffolk Coastal; Waveney

Suffolk takes its name from the Old English 'Suthfolch', the 'southern folk' of the East Angles, in contrast to Norfolk.

FAMOUS FOR

Today **Dunwich** is a small village threatened by the sea, and yet in the 12th century it was one of the largest and wealthiest towns in East Anglia before its harbour was destroyed and much of the town fell into the sea as its sandy cliffs were eroded.

The first horse race recorded at **Newmarket** was in 1622, and there was no looking back after Charles II started to visit in 1660. By an Act of Parliament he established the Town Plate race, first run in 1666, which is the oldest horse race in the world with written rules.

Sutton Hoo, by the River Deben near Woodbridge, is the site of an Anglo-Saxon royal burial ground. An excavation in 1938–9 uncovered spectacular objects from the 4th to the 7th centuries that had come from all over Europe and beyond.

The **Aldeburgh Festival** of classical music was founded in 1948 by the composer, Benjamin Britten, the singer, Peter Pears, and the writer, Eric Crozier. Initially concerts were held in local halls and churches, but, since 1967, the concert hall converted from the disused Snape Maltings has become its centre.

The great abbey at **Bury St Edmunds** was founded in 1020 by King Cnut to honour the last king of East Anglia, King Edmund, killed in a Danish attack in 869 and later canonized. Substantial remains still exist, next to Britain's most recently completed cathedral – the former 15th century parish church of St James became St Edmundsbury Cathedral in 1914 and a choir and tower were added, the 45 m tower being completed in 2005.

FAMOUS PEOPLE

Thomas, Cardinal Wolsey, Lord Chancellor to Henry VIII, born Ipswich, c. 1475.
Thomas Gainsborough, artist, baptized Sudbury, 1727.
Humphrey Repton, landscape gardener and designer, born Bury St Edmunds, 1752.
George Crabbe, poet, born Aldeburgh, 1754.
John Constable, artist, born East Bergholt, 1776.
Edward Fitzgerald, poet and translator of the *Rubaiyat of Omar Khayyam*, born Bredfield, 1809.
Sir Joseph Dalton Hooker, botanist, director Kew Gardens (1865–85), born Halesworth, 1817.
Charles Doughty, explorer and author of *Travels in Arabia Deserta*, born Theberton, 1843.
Dame Millicent Garrett Fawcett, suffragette, born Aldeburgh, 1847.
George Lansbury, politician, leader of the labour party (1931–5), born near Halesworth, 1859.
Edward Benjamin Britten, Baron Britten, composer, born Lowestoft, 1913.

"Still I should paint my own places best; painting is with me but another word for feeling, and I associate "my careless boyhood" with all that lies on the banks of the Stour; those scenes made me a painter, and I am grateful."
John Constable, 1821

Suffolk, one of the largest shire counties, is low-lying and gently undulating. The most easterly point in Britain is at Ness Point, close to Lowestoft. The low coastline, behind which are areas of heath and marsh, afforested in places, is subject to much erosion; it is deeply indented with long river estuaries which provide good sailing. The northwest corner of the county forms part of Breckland. The central region is almost entirely agricultural, with cereal crops and oil seed rape in abundance. The river Stour forms the southern boundary with Essex, and the Little Ouse and Waveney form most of the northern boundary with Norfolk. The many other small rivers include the Alde, Deben and Gipping, with its estuary the Orwell, in the east and Lark in the west.

The East Angles settled in this area from the 6th century and the kingdom of the East Angles lasted until it crumbled under Danish attack in the 9th century. Over time two centres developed for the county, Ipswich in the east and Bury St Edmunds in the west, and this division was formally recognized in 1888 when two county councils (East Suffolk and West Suffolk) were created. In 1974, the county was reunited as a single unitary authority. Discussions continue about revising this structure, the most recent proposal having been rejected in February 2010.

The population of Suffolk is 715,700 and the main towns are Ipswich (population 138,718), Lowestoft (68,340), Bury St Edmunds (36,218), Felixstowe (29,349), Sudbury (20,188), Haverhill (22,010), Newmarket (16,947), Stowmarket (15,059) and Woodbridge (10,956). A large proportion of the population live in smaller towns and villages scattered throughout the county, with the lowest population density being in the Breckland area in the northwest of the county. Between 2001 and 2008 the population grew by 6.8 per cent, with the fastest growth being in the Suffolk Coastal district.

The Moot Hall at Aldeburgh, now a museum.

St Edmundsbury Cathedral

Apart from agriculture and related support industries, from food processing to the manufacture of agricultural equipment, industries include electronics, telecommunications, printing and port facilities. Lowestoft is still a prominent fishing port (but less significant than in its heyday in the early 20th century) and is an operating base for offshore wind farms and the southern North Sea oil and gas fields. Felixstowe is Britain's largest container port and accounts for around 40 per cent of the country's import and export trade; it has had a significant impact on the road and rail infrastructure in the area. Employment in manufacturing and transport, at nearly 19 per cent of all jobs, is above the national average, while jobs in finance, IT and business are below. Tourism accounts for around 9.5 per cent of jobs and is important in the coastal area.

The coast of Suffolk is ever-changing – while erosion eats into the sandy cliffs at Covehithe and Dunwich, in other places, such as Orford Ness, the shingle banks grow. The area is a haven for birds and there are many nature reserves, including the renowned reserve of Minsmere, next to the nuclear power stations of Sizewell. In medieval times the wealth of Suffolk came from wool and wool trading. Along the coast there are majestic churches at Blythburgh and Southwold. Further west is the real wool country, where towns like Lavenham, with its many half-timbered buildings, and Long Melford provide physical evidence of their wealth in Tudor times.

Ipswich is the county town, and owes its importance to its position on the Orwell as a trading port with Europe, still a significant activity. It is the commercial centre of the county, but is not a particularly beautiful place, whereas Bury St Edmunds to the west, with its Medieval and Georgian buildings, is a different story. In the far west of the county is Newmarket, sitting on the down land almost encircled by Cambridgeshire.

Martello Tower, Aldeburgh. One of a series of small defensive forts built in British Empire countries during the Napoleonic Wars in the 19th century.

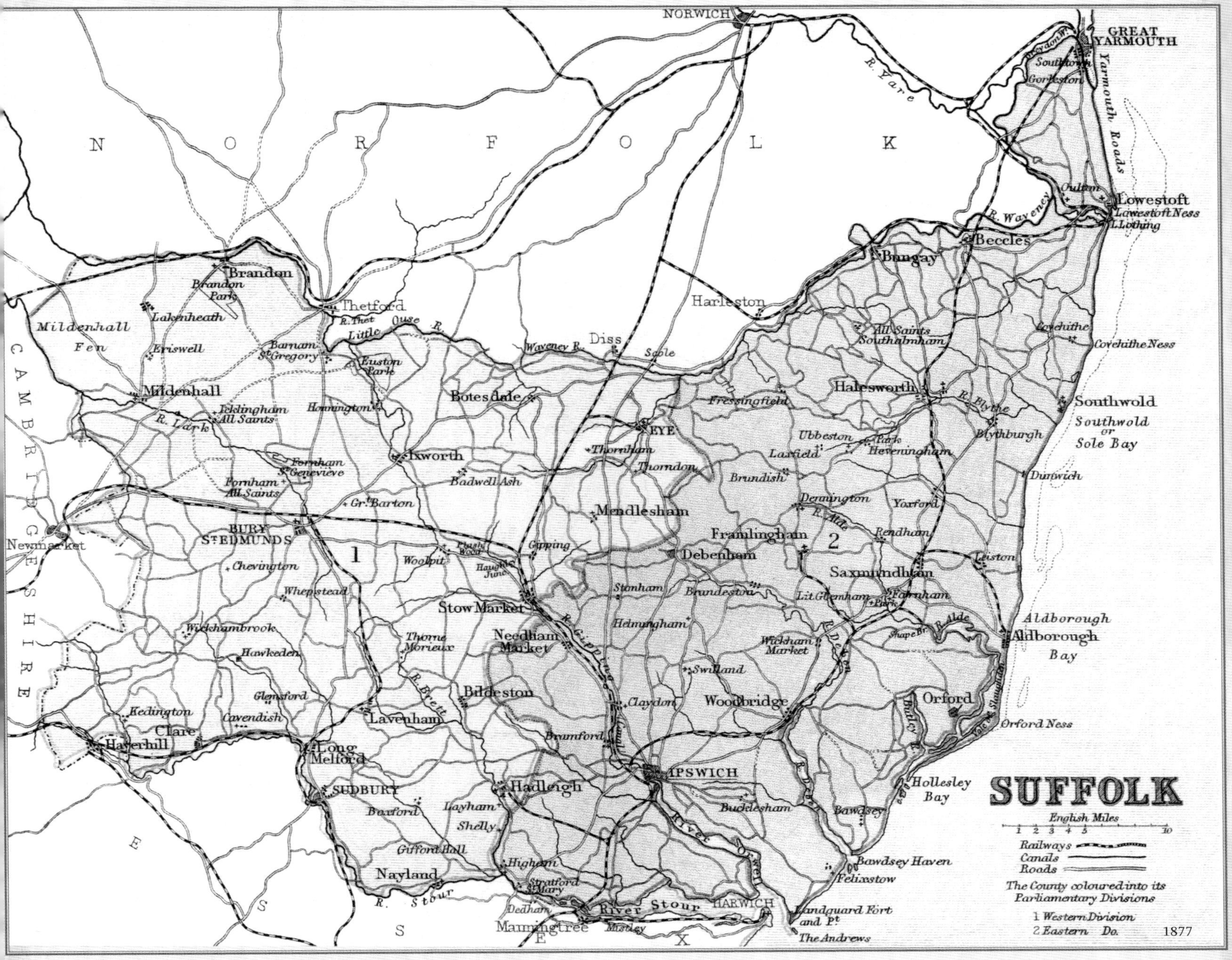

SUFFOLK

The County coloured into its Parliamentary Divisions

1 Western Division
2 Eastern Do.

1877

Bartholomew Gazetteer of the British Isles, 1887

SUFFOLK, *maritime co. in E. of England, bounded N. by Norfolk, from which it is separated by the Waveney and Little Ouse, E. by the North Sea, S. by Essex, from which it is separated by the Stour, and W. by Cambridgeshire, from which it is separated by the Lark; area, 944,060 ac., pop. 356,893. The coast line (of about 50 miles), broken by the estuaries of the Stour, Orwell, Deben, and Aide, is generally low, and the sea has made great encroachments, particularly in the neighbourhood of Dunwich and Aldeburgh. The surface is generally level,* and the soil is very varied – occasional fen, loam on the borders of the rivers, sand on the eastern and western borders, and clay in the centre. This last is fertile, and large crops are grown of wheat, barley, pease, and beans, the barley in particular being in high repute with brewers. Butter is extensively made for the London markets. Sheep are reared in the NW., which is hilly; and the Suffolk cart-horse, esteemed for its power of draught, is raised in considerable numbers. The mfrs.- principally agricultural implements and artificial manure – are limited. Fine sea-salt is made on the coast. The trade of the seaports *is chiefly in corn and malt. The herring and mackerel fisheries are extensively prosecuted at Lowestoft and other places, and oysters are found in the Orwell and Orford. Most of the towns have river communication, and the co. is traversed in all directions by the railways of the Great Eastern system. It comprises 21 hundreds, 517 pars, with parts of 7 others, the mun. bors. of Beccles, Bury St Edmunds, Eye, Ipswich, Lowestoft, and Southwold, and part of the mun. bor. of Sudbury. It is mostly in, the diocese of Norwich.*

thwold Pier

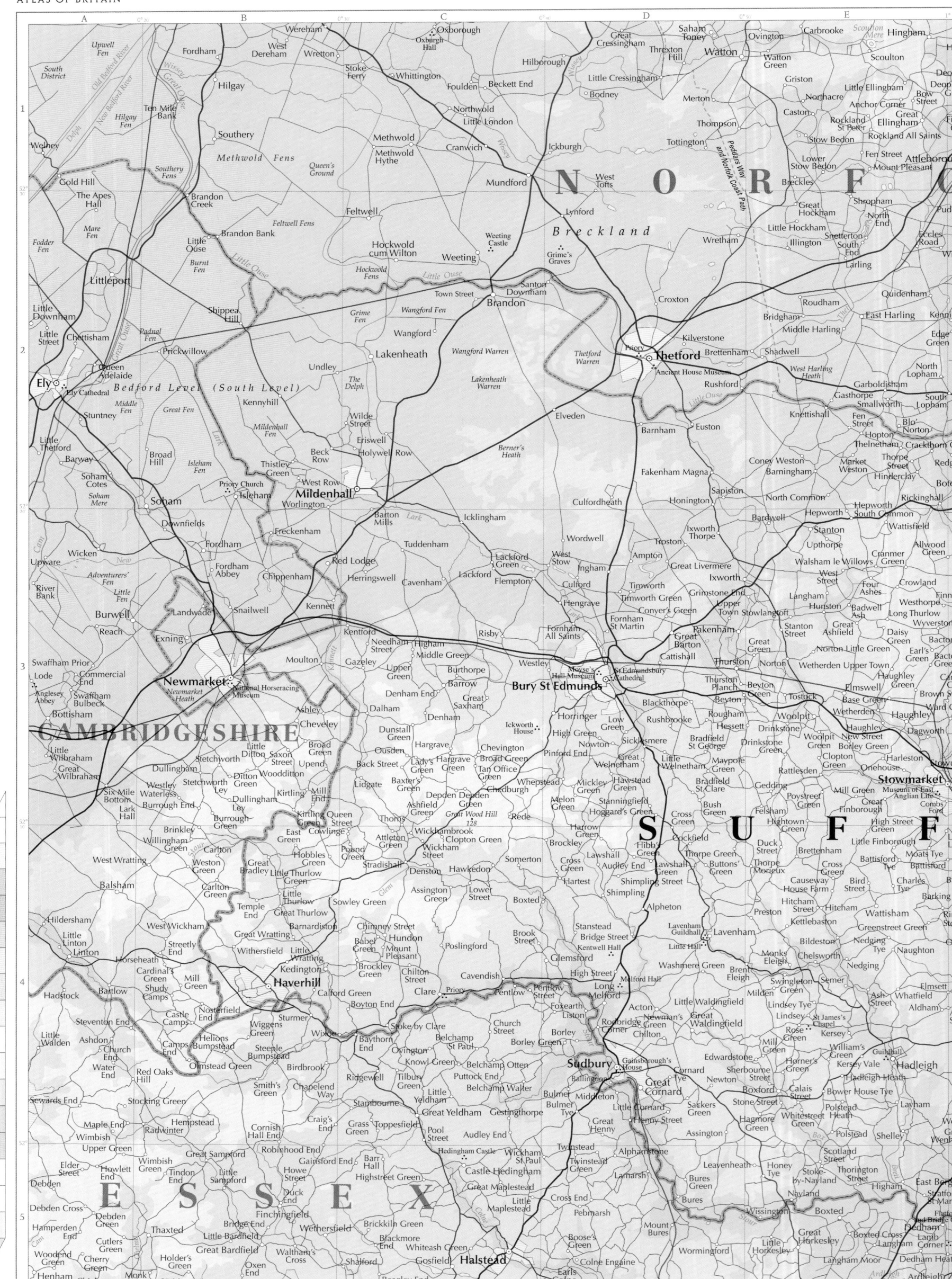

British National Grid projection

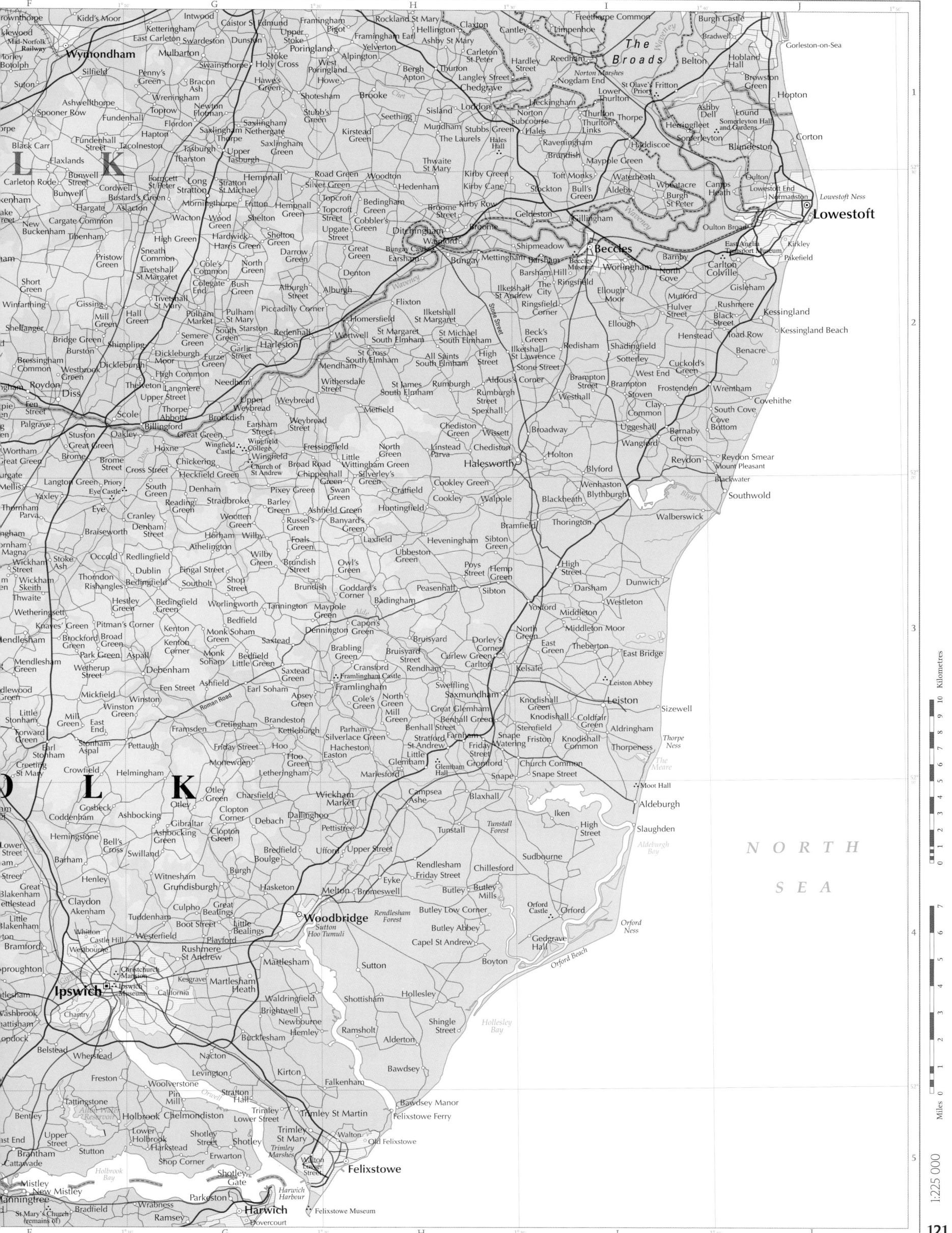

NORTH

SEA

1:225 000

© Collins Bartholomew Ltd

CAMBRIDGESHIRE

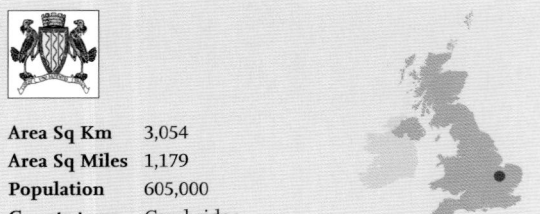

Area Sq Km	3,054
Area Sq Miles	1,179
Population	605,000
County town	Cambridge
Highest point	Great Chishill (146 m) close to the Essex and Hertfordshire borders
Districts	Cambridge; East Cambridgeshire; Fenland; Huntingdonshire; South Cambridgeshire

Cambridgeshire takes its name from Cambridge whose earliest Old English form was *Grantacaetir*, a Roman fort or '*caster*' by the river Granta, later becoming *Grontabricc* or 'bridge over the Granta'. Granta is a Celtic word of unknown origin. In Norman times, the town became Cambridge and then, after this change the river Granta was renamed the Cam.

FAMOUS FOR

In 1852 a cast-iron column was sunk into the peat in **Holme Fen**, south of Peterborough. Drainage of the Fens has caused the peat to dry out and the level of the land has dropped; the top of the column now stands 4 m above the ground and the farmland close by is now the lowest point in Britain.

The **Cambridge Rules** of football, originally drawn up in 1863 by football enthusiasts at Trinity College to provide some uniformity to the game, became the basis of rules adopted by the Football Association after its foundation in the same year.

The **University of Cambridge** claims to have had more Nobel Prize winners than any other institution in the world, with 87 people affiliated to the university winning a Nobel Prize since their foundation in 1904.

The **Imperial War Museum** at **Duxford**, has Europe's largest collection of military and civilian aircraft, with nearly 200 on display – Duxford was an RAF base in both World Wars and the runways are still used by the museum.

FAMOUS PEOPLE

Oliver Cromwell, Parliamentarian leader in the Civil War, Lord Protector (1653–58), born Huntingdon, 1599.
William Godwin, philosopher, writer and publisher, born Wisbech, 1756.
Octavia Hill, social reformer, co-founder of the National Trust, born Wisbech, 1838.
Sir John Berry (Jack) Hobbs, cricketer, born Cambridge 1882.
John Maynard Keynes, Baron Keynes, economist, born Cambridge, 1883.
Sir George Paget Thomson, physicist and Nobel laureate, born Cambridge, 1892.
Leslie Poles (L.P.) Hartley, novelist, born Whittlesey, 1895.
Ronald George Wreyford Norrish, chemist and Nobel laureate, born Cambridge, 1897.
Arthur Michael Ramsey, Baron Ramsey of Canterbury, Archbishop of Canterbury 1961–74, born Cambridge, 1904.
Sir Christopher Cockerell, inventor of the hovercraft, born Cambridge, 1910.
Ronald Searle, cartoonist, born Cambridge, 1920.
Richard Attenborough, Baron Attenborough, actor and director, born Cambridge, 1923.
Sir Harold (Harry) Kroto, chemist and Nobel laureate, born Wisbech, 1939.
Olivia Newton-John, singer, born Cambridge, 1948.
Douglas Adams, novelist, author of *The Hitch Hiker's Guide to the Galaxy*, born Cambridge, 1952.

Cambridgeshire is, typically, flat, with fenland to the north and east, although there are low chalk hills in the south, on the border with Hertfordshire and Essex, and southeast, along the Suffolk border. Rivers include the Cam, Nene, and Great Ouse, and in the heart of the fens, the two manmade drainage rivers, designed to take some of the waters of the Great Ouse, the Old Bedford River and the New Bedford River, both created in the 17th century. The scale of the enterprise was immense – the Old Bedford River is over 33.5 km long. One result was that the peat lands shrank as they dried, and much of the drained fenland is now below sea level.

The current county of Cambridgeshire is of recent origin. Traditionally Cambridge was the centre for the south of the county, while Ely, built on a low rise in the Fens with its spectacular cathedral from the 11th century, became the focus of the Isle of Ely. In 1888 two separate county councils were formed for Cambridgeshire and the Isle of Ely, which were then united in 1965. The new county of Cambridgeshire formed in 1974 also took in Huntingdon and Peterborough, itself formed from two authorities in 1965, the county of Huntingdonshire and the Soke of Peterborough. In 1998 Peterborough became a unitary authority separate from Cambridgeshire.

The population of Cambridgeshire is 605,000 and it is expected to grow to 673,000 by 2021, with almost all that growth being in Cambridge and South Cambridgeshire. Chief centres are Cambridge (117,717), St Neots and Eaton Socon (27,372), Wisbech (26,536), Huntingdon (20,600), March (18,040), St Ives (15,811) and Ely (13,954).

The Fens provide highly fertile agricultural land and there is much intensive farming of vegetables, sugar beet, potatoes and cereals; food processing and canning are also significant rural industries, served by the communities of Wisbech and March. Economic growth is centred on Cambridge – over 10,000 jobs are directly linked to research and development within private business in the area around Cambridge. Known as 'Silicon Fen' there are many electronics and IT businesses as well as medical and pharmaceutical companies. Overall in Cambridgeshire 30.7 per cent of all jobs are in public administration, education and health, while in Cambridge itself this figure rises to 43.5 per cent, showing the impact of two universities (the University of Cambridge and Anglia Ruskin University) and a major teaching hospital.

The attraction to hi-tech industries of Cambridge, is of course, proximity to Cambridge University, one of the world's leading universities, and one of its oldest, its origins going back to 1209 when some scholars settled in Cambridge from Oxford. Peterhouse was the first college to be founded, in 1284 by the Bishop of Ely. Over the centuries, many wonderful college buildings, especially King's College Chapel, built between 1446 and 1515 and one of the great late Gothic buildings in Britain, have brought visitors to the city. To the west lie Huntingdon and the Great North Road, and East Anglia begins to merge into the southern Midlands of Northamptonshire.

Eastern Gate to King's College, Cambridge.

Imperial War Museum at Duxford.

"Three years I was at Cambridge, three quiet years with little of disturbance in them, moving slowly on like the sluggish Cam."
Jawaharlal Nehru, 1936

"The Isle of Ely lying in the fens is like a starfish lying on a flat stone at low tide."
Hilaire Belloc, 1906

"All that I have seen of Huntingdon I like exceedingly. It is one of those pretty, clean, unstenched, unconfined places that tend to lengthen life and make it happy."
William Cobbett, 1822

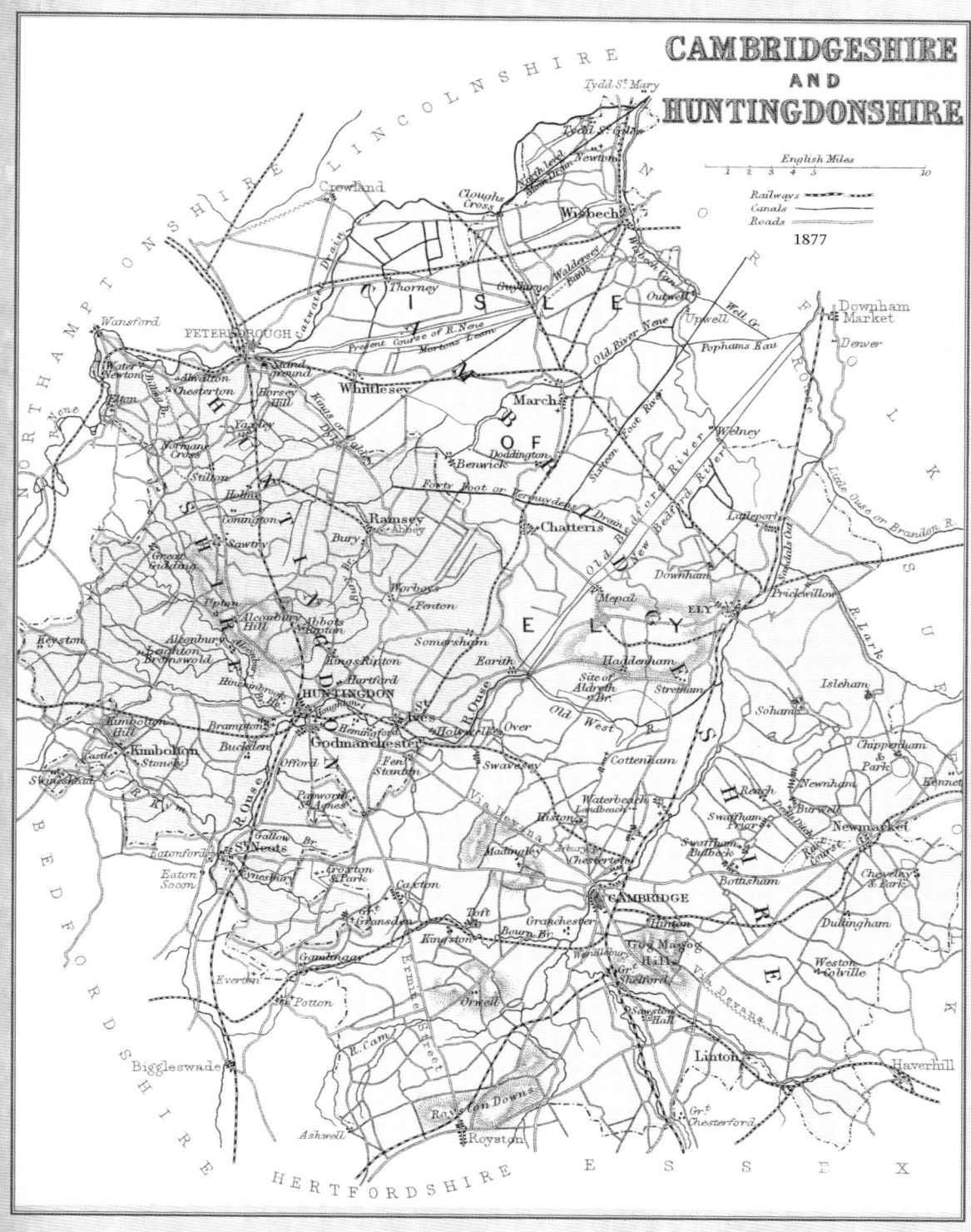

Bartholomew Gazetteer of the British Isles, 1887

CAMBRIDGESHIRE, *inland eastern co. of England; bounded N. by Lincolnshire, E. by Norfolk and Suffolk, S. by Essex and Herts, W. by Bedfordshire, Huntingdonshire, and Northamptonshire; greatest length, N. and S., 48 miles; greatest breadth, E. and W., 28 miles; average breadth, 16 miles; area, 524,935 ac.; pop. 185,594. The N. section of the county, including the Isle of Ely and part of the Great Bedford Level, is a large flat expanse of country, which, for the most part, formerly consisted of fen and marsh. It is now intersected in all directions by wide trenches or canals. The land, thus drained and reclaimed, is a rich, black soil, and bears excellent crops. From this tract the pleasant vale of the Cam stretches away to the SW., and contains a great number of excellent dairy farms. Cambridgeshire comprises 17 hundreds, 172 pars. with parts of 7 others, the mun. bosr. of Cambridge and Wisbech. It is almost entirely in the diocese of Ely. HUNTINGDONSHIRE, Huntingdon, or Hunts, inland co., South Midland District, England; is bounded W. and N. by Northamptonshire, E. by Cambridgeshire, and S. by Bedfordshire; greatest length, N. and S., 30 miles; greatest breadth, E. and W., 23 miles; 229,515 ac.; pop. 59,491. About a fourth of the co. (in the NE.) forms a portion of the great "fen" district, the remainder consisting of a succession of gentle hills and dales. Huntingdonshire is almost wholly devoid of trees, and may be described as an agricultural and pastoral co. Scientific farming has of late greatly stimulated the productiveness of the soil, and the arable farms of the upland districts are peculiarly noted for superior grain. Green crops, also of excellent quality, are obtained, while market gardening and cattle rearing form profitable employments. Willows are the chief product of the fen district. The Nen, in the N. and NW., and the Ouse, in the interior, are the chief rivers; both are navigable for barges. The geology of Huntingdonshire belongs to the Oolite system: many fossils are found, and the hills on the W. abound with stone brash, or forest marble. With the exception of papermaking and the preparation of parchment, there are no mfrs. of more than local importance. The co. is almost entirely in the diocese of Ely. It contains 4 hundreds; 103 pars., with parts of 6 others; the mun. bors. of Huntingdon, Godmanchester, and St Ives; and a part of the city of Peterborough.*

PETERBOROUGH

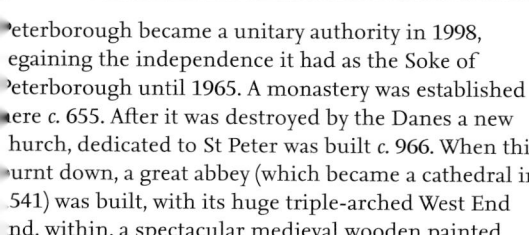

Area Sq Km	343
Area Sq Miles	133
Population	164,000
Highest point	Racecourse Road (81m)

Peterborough became a unitary authority in 1998, regaining the independence it had as the Soke of Peterborough until 1965. A monastery was established here c. 655. After it was destroyed by the Danes a new church, dedicated to St Peter was built c. 966. When this burnt down, a great abbey (which became a cathedral in 1541) was built, with its huge triple-arched West End and, within, a spectacular medieval wooden painted ceiling and the tomb of Katharine of Aragon, Henry VIII's first wife. With the coming of the railways in 1845–50, Peterborough developed rapidly, its key industries including brickworks, diesel engines and agricultural equipment. In 1967 it was declared a new town and its population has continued to grow, with further growth of around 50,000 expected by 2021. As manufacturing has declined financial services have become significant. With excellent north-south and east-west communications, it has also become a major distribution centre, and an attractive home for London commuters.

FAMOUS FOR
Burghley House, close to Stamford, is one of the grandest 16th-century houses in Britain; built between 1555 and 1587 by William Cecil, Lord High Treasurer to Elizabeth I. The house remains in the Cecil family and the grounds are home to the internationally renowned Burghley Horse Trials.

Excavations since 1982 at **Flag Fen**, near Peterborough, have revealed a major Bronze age site dating from around 3,500 years ago – a wooden causeway and platform that stretches for 1 km and required around 60,000 upright timbers have been found, along with many artefacts, including England's oldest known wheel.

FAMOUS PEOPLE
John Clare, poet, born Helpston, 1793; **Sir Henry Royce**, co-founder of Rolls-Royce, born Alwalton, 1863; and, possibly, the Anglo-Saxon defender of the Fens, **Hereward the Wake**.

Burghley House

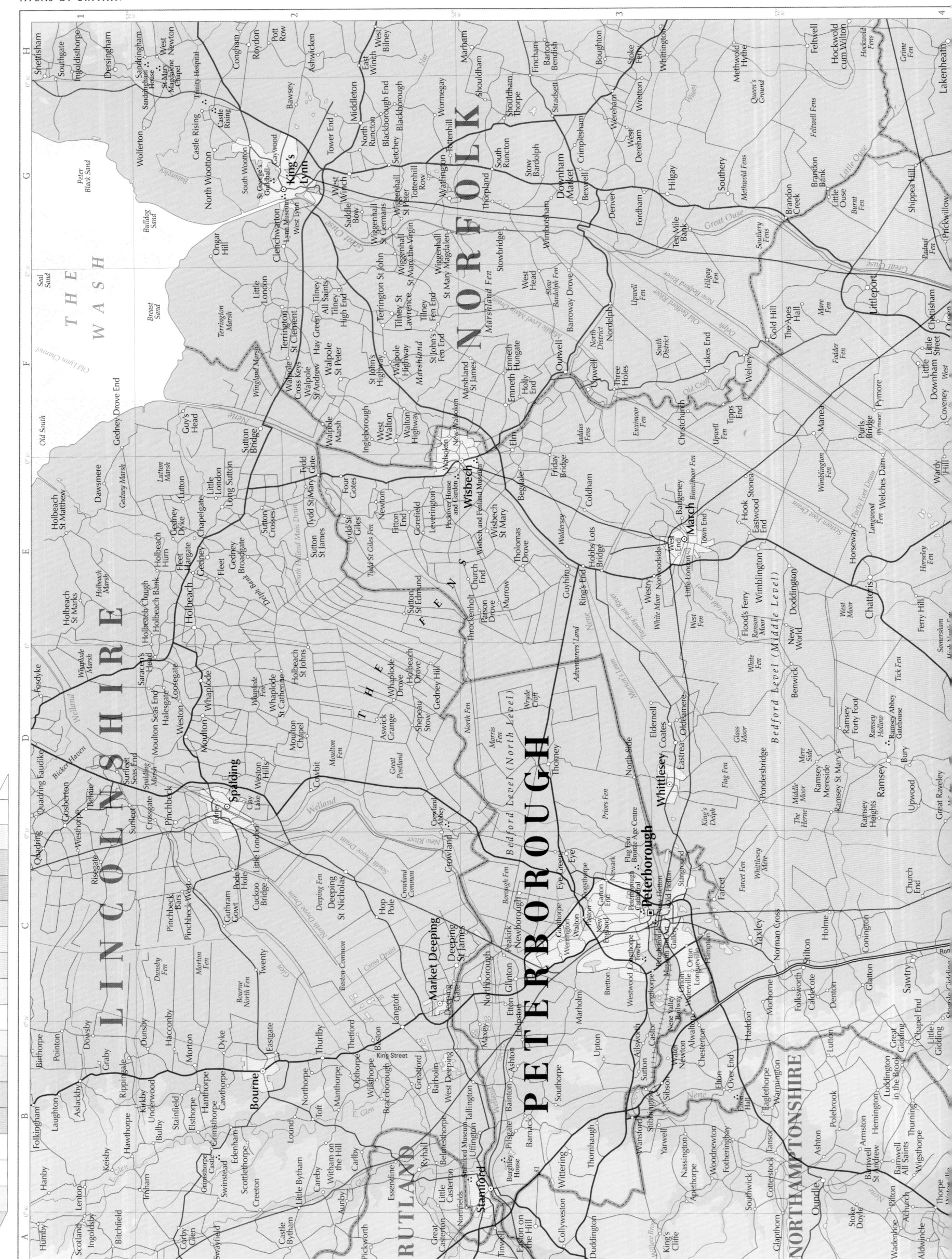

British National Grid projection

1:225 000

© Collins Bartholomew Ltd

NORTHAMPTONSHIRE

Area Sq Km	2,367
Area Sq Miles	914
Population	685,000
County town	Northampton
Highest point	Arbery Hill (224 m) near Daventry
Districts	Corby; Daventry; East Northamptonshire; Kettering; Northampton; South Northamptonshire; Wellingborough

Northamptonshire takes its name from the town of Northampton, originally '*Hamtun*' from the Old English '*ham*' and '*tun*' , 'home farm or homestead'. 'North' was added to distinguish it from (South) Hampton.

FAMOUS FOR

Silverstone, in the south of the county, is home to the British Grand Prix and other motorsport events – once a World War II airfield, the first motor race was held here in 1948.

The most prominent landmark in **Northampton** is the 127 m tall Express (now National) Lift Tower, built in 1980, originally designed to test lifts for the Express Lift Company. The factory is now closed, but the tower remains and is a Listed Building.

In the centre of the village of **Geddington**, is a remarkable Eleanor Cross – Eleanor was Queen to Edward I. In 1290 she died unexpectedly at Harby, near Lincoln. Her body was brought back to London and Edward ordered that a cross be built at each of the 12 places where her coffin rested over night on the journey, which ended at Charing Cross. Three survive and the one at Geddington is the finest.

The Triangular Lodge at **Rushton** was built between 1593 and 1597 by Sir Thomas Tresham, a convert to Roman Catholicism. It is devoted to the concept of the Trinity (God the Father, God the Son and God the Holy Spirit) for not only is it triangular in shape, it has three floors, each side has three triangular windows and there are many other references to the number three in its construction.

The National Waterways Museum at **Stoke Bruerne** near Towcester brings to life the history of the canal system. The museum is in an old cornmill near a lock on the Grand Union Canal, which goes between London and Birmingham.

FAMOUS PEOPLE

Elizabeth Woodville, future queen to Edward IV, born Grafton Regis, c.1437.
Richard III, King of England, born Fotheringhay, 1452.
Anne Bradstreet (born Anne Dudley), America's first noted poet, born Northampton, c.1612.
John Dryden, poet, born Aldwinkle, 1631.
Charles Montague, 1st Earl of Halifax, founder of the Bank of England and statesman, born Horton, 1661.
Edmund Rubra, composer, born Northampton, 1901.
Herbert Ernest (H E) Bates, novelist, born Rushden, 1905.
Francis Crick, biochemist, one of the discoverers of the structure of DNA, born Northampton, 1916.
Sir Malcolm Arnold, composer, born Northampton, 1921.
Nanette Newman, actress and author, born Northampton, 1934.
Thomas (Thom) Yorke, lead singer, Radiohead, born Wellingborough, 1968.

"Northamptonshire … is a clay pudding stuck full of villages."
Horace Walpole, 1763

Northamptonshire consists largely of undulating agricultural country rising locally to low hills, especially along the western border. Large fields, scattered woods, stone-built historic villages and a succession of elegant church spires typify this landscape of middle England which still retains its rural and agricultural charm, despite undergoing rapid population growth recently. The principal rivers are the Nene, which flows across the county from Daventry to Fotheringhay and then on to Peterborough and the Wash, the Welland, which flows along its northern border with Leicestershire, and the Cherwell, which rises in the south of the county and flows down to join the Thames.

The historic county of Northamptonshire was first mentioned in the 9th century to describe an area around Northampton captured by the Danes. By the end of the century, once recaptured by the English, this area stretched up to the Welland, and it has remained with its basic historic boundaries ever since. The main change was the creation of a separate status within the county for the Soke of Peterborough in 1888, now a unitary authority within the enlarged county of Cambridgeshire.

The population of Northamptonshire is 685,000 and it is the fastest growing non-metropolitan county in England, with at least a further 100,000 people expected to live there by 2023, a rate of growth that will put further strain on the main urban communities. The chief towns are Northampton (population 189,474), Kettering (51,063), Corby (49,222), Wellingborough (46,959), Rushden (25,331) and Daventry (21,731).

Agriculture and the related food processing industries (such as the making of potato crisps and breakfast cereals) remain a part of the economy but the traditional footwear industry that used to be based around Northampton and Wellingborough has markedly declined, though some limited manufacture continues, and the headquarters of the Dr Martens shoes remains at Wollaston. From 1935 until 1981 there was an integrated steelworks at Corby, the site selected because of the ready availability of iron ore, but since then the economy of the town has had to diversify into distribution and light industry. Now in Northamptonshire 80.5 per cent of jobs are in the service sector, with nearly a quarter of all jobs in the retail, distribution and hotel and restaurant sector and nearly 15 per cent in manufacturing.

Although Northamptonshire is in the centre of England, it has rarely been at the centre of events. The Roman road of Watling Street cuts across the south of the county while Ermine Street passes just beyond its borders in the north. Northampton developed as an important settlement with a large castle (all signs of which were demolished when the main railway station was built), and the town was the site of a victory for the Yorkists in the War of the Roses in 1460. Close the Leicestershire border, the last major battle of the Civil War was fought at Naseby in 1645, a convincing victory for the Parliamentarians and the first success c Cromwell's New Model Army. Thereafter the county developed only slowly, with both the canals and railwa arriving later than in the rest of the Midlands.

There is much of interest scattered through this quintessential shire county. In the north, by the Nene Fotheringhay, where once there was a royal castle that saw the birth of Richard III and the imprisonment an execution of Mary, Queen of Scots. The castle is no more, but there is a beautiful church with a startling octagonal lantern tower built in the 15th century. To th north are two important houses – Deene Park, the hor of the Brudenell family since 1514, whose most famou occupant was the 7th Earl of Cardigan, who led the Charge of the Light Brigade in the Crimean War. Near is the mysterious ruin of Kirby Hall, once one of the grandest Elizabethan and 17th century houses in Brita but now mainly a roofless shell.

In the centre of the county are two of the finest Anglo-Saxon churches in Britain, at Earls Barton, whe the tower mimics in stone a wooden construction, and at Brixworth, once described as 'perhaps the most imposing architectural monument of the 7th century surviving north of the Alps'. Both were originally missionary churches of the great abbey at Peterboroug Close to Northampton is Althorp, home of the Spence family since at least 1508, where, on an island in the estate is buried Diana, Princess of Wales, while toward the Oxfordshire border is Sulgrave Manor, ancestral home of George Washington, first president of the United States.

The Triangular Lodge at Rushton.

Canal boats in Aynho Wharf.

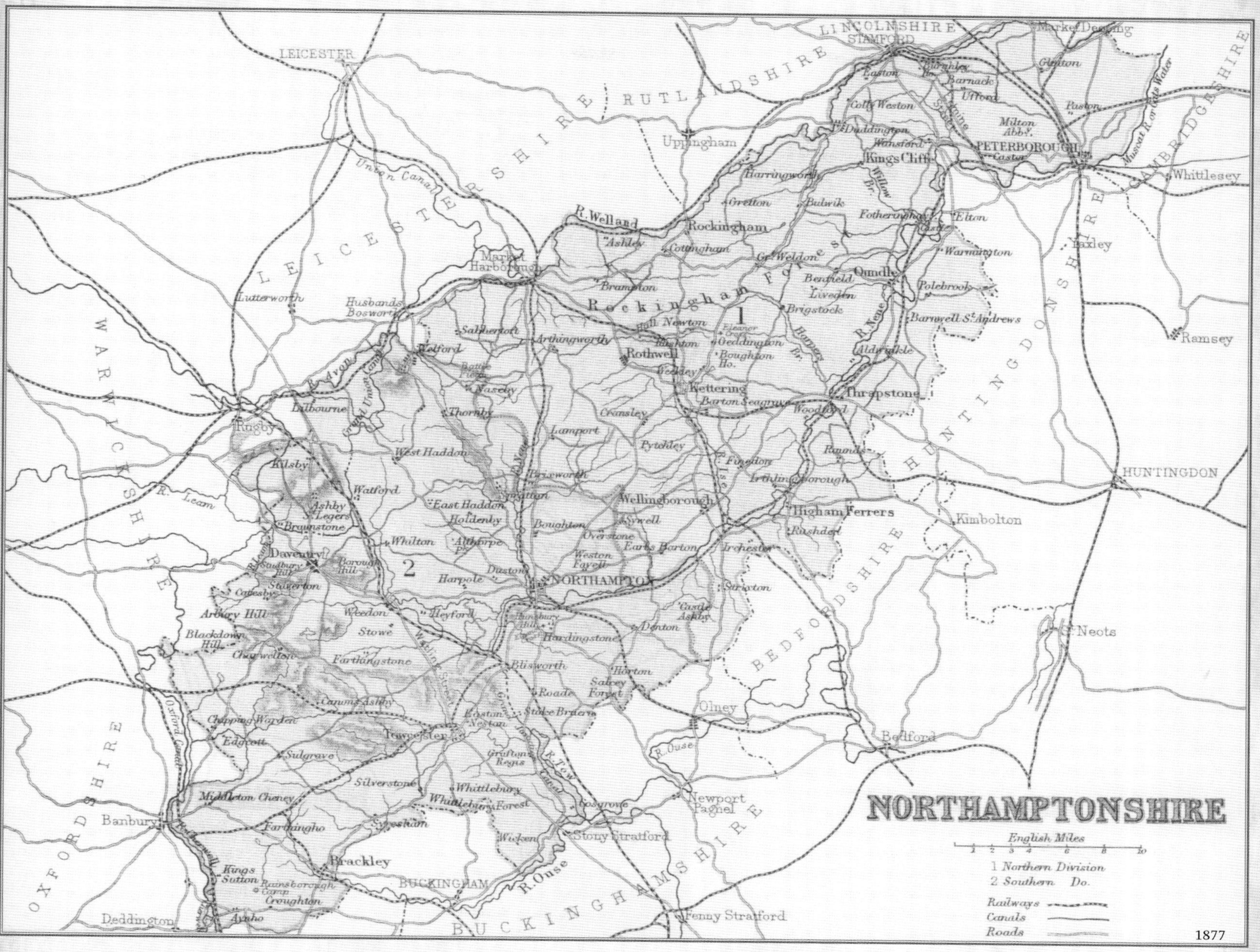

NORTHAMPTONSHIRE

English Miles

1 Northern Division
2 Southern   Do.

Railways
Canals
Roads

1877

Bartholomew Gazetteer of the British Isles, 1887

NORTHAMPTONSHIRE (or Northampton), south-midland county of England, bounded N. by Leicestershire, Rutland, and Lincolnshire, E. by Cambridgeshire, Huntingdonshire, and Bedfordshire, S. by Bucks and Oxfordshire, and W. by Warwickshire; greatest length, NE. to SW., about 70 miles; greatest breadth, E. to W., about 26 miles; area, 629,912 ac., pop. 272,555. Although the surface appearance of the county is generally hilly there are no elevations of considerable altitude, the highest being near Daventry, where Arbury Hill reaches 804 ft. The NE. part of the county belongs to the Fen district. In some localities, particularly the W. and SW., the scenery is especially attractive; while here and there throughout the co. rich woods and well-watered vales afford pleasing aspects. The chief rivers are the Nen and the Weiland; the Avon forms a part of the N. boundary of the co., the Cherwell of the SW. boundary, and the Learn of the W. boundary; the Ouse has its rise near Brackley in the S. The canal system includes the Union and Grand Junction Canal, besides other similar waterways. On the uplands the soil is a fine brown loam, but the richest portion is found in the black mould of the Fen district. Throughout the whole co. farming is successfully prosecuted, all kinds of cereal and green crops being raised; while upon the splendid pastures large numbers of cattle are reared, principally for the London market. Northampton is celebrated for its ash trees, old oaks, and elm avenues. Lias and oolite are the prevailing geological formations. Iron is largely found, and although worked as early as the time of the Roman occupation, its modern mfr. dates only from 1850, since which year remarkable progress has been made by the encouragement of the industry and its consequent productiveness. Apart from ironworking, the great industry of the co. is centred in the mfr. of boots and shoes in the town of Northampton and the towns of the middle of the co. Northamptonshire contains 20 hundreds, 344 pars, with parts of 4 others, the mun. bors. of Daventry, Northampton, part of the mun. bor. of Peterborough, and part of the mun. bor. of Stamford. It is almost entirely in the diocese of Peterborough.

Hall, near Corby.

British Grand Prix, Silverstone, 2007.

British National Grid projection

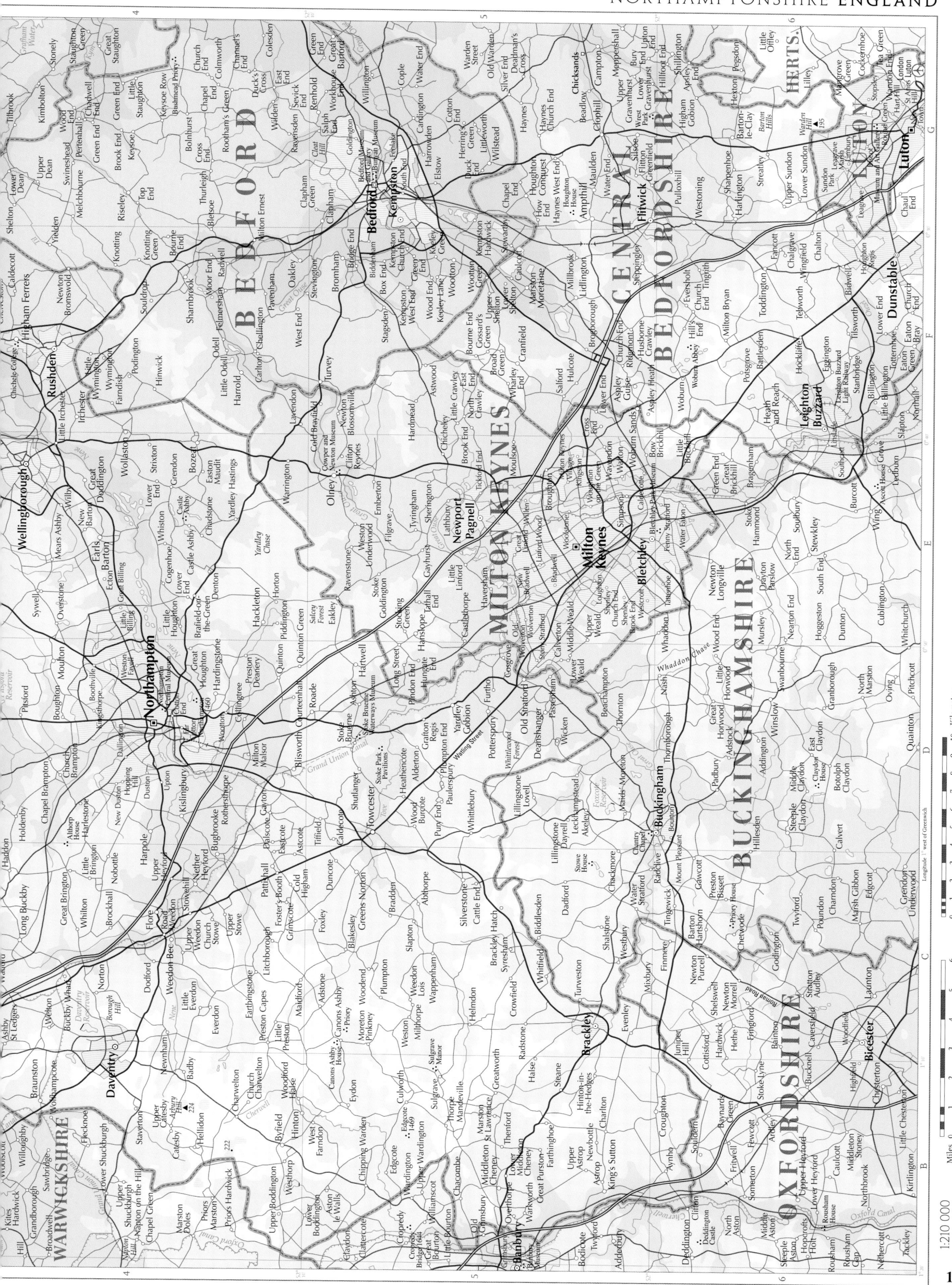

1:210 000

Miles 0 1 2 3 4 5 6

Kilometres 0 1 2 3 4 5 6 7 8 9 10

© Collins Bartholomew Ltd

WARWICKSHIRE

Area Sq Km	1,978
Area Sq Miles	764
Population	530,700
County town	Warwick
Highest point	Ebrington Hill (260 m)
Districts	North Warwickshire; Nuneaton and Bedworth; Rugby; Stratford-on-Avon; Warwick

The county of Warwickshire is named after the county town of Warwick, from the Old English 'settlement by the weir'.

FAMOUS FOR

The first lawn tennis club in the world was formed in **Leamington Spa** in 1872, and its rules form the basis of today's rules.

Guy of Warwick was a legendary hero of medieval literature – the son of the earl of Warwick's steward, he rescues a princess, fights the Saracens and defeats a Danish giant to win the hand of the earl's daughter, and then continues his mighty deeds, slaying the monstrous Dun Cow and killing a dragon. He then returns as a hermit and lives in a cave near Warwick castle, cared for but unrecognised by his wife.

In 1823, **William Webb Ellis**, a 16-year-old pupil at Rugby School, picked up the ball in a football game and ran with it, so creating a new game, now known as Rugby football.

On 23 October 1642 at **Edgehill**, in southern Warwickshire, the first major battle of the English Civil War between the Royalists and Parliamentarians was fought, but the outcome was inconclusive.

The village of **Gaydon** is home to the Heritage Motor Centre. With over 300 cars, it is the world's largest collection of British cars.

The **Belfry Golf Course**, established in 1977 at Wishaw in north Warwickshire, has already hosted the Ryder Cup three times.

Thomas Arnold, the headmaster of Rugby School described the purpose of education: 'First religious and moral principle, second gentlemanly conduct, third academic ability.'

The beautiful house of **Compton Wynyates**, near Upper Brailes, with around 100 rooms and 300 windows, was completed around 1520 and would have been demolished in the 1770s by order of its owner, Lord Northampton, had not his steward, John Berrill, disobeyed and just bricked up all the windows. The house was restored 60 years later.

Rugby became one of the stations on the original London to Birmingham railway line in 1838. At the height of the railway boom, railway lines from nine different directions converged on Rugby.

FAMOUS PEOPLE

Saint Wulfstan, Bishop of Worcester, born Long Itchington, 1008.
William Shakespeare, playwright, born Stratford-upon-Avon, 1564.
Sir Robert Catesby, leader of the Gunpowder Plot, born Lapworth, 1573.
Sir William Dugdale, English antiquary and Garter King of Arms, born Shustoke, near Coleshill, 1605.
Mary Anne Evans (pen name George Eliot), novelist, born Arbury Farm, near Nuneaton, 1819.
Sir Henry Parkes, Prime Minister, New South Wales 1872–95, born Stoneleigh, 1815.

Warwickshire consists of mostly flat or undulating farmland, although the foothills of the Cotswold Hills spill over its southwest border. The principal river is the Avon and other rivers include the Leam and Tame. The county traditionally included Coventry, Solihull and much of Birmingham, the original county boundaries predating the industrialisation of the Midlands, when much of these areas was covered by the forest of Arden. They became parts of the county of the West Midlands in 1974.

Now Warwickshire is primarily rural in the south and west, where it borders on to the Cotswolds, and more industrial in the north and east. Its population in 2008 was 530,700, having grown about 15 per cent since the 1970s, much of the this increase caused by people moving out of the Birmingham conurbation. The largest towns are Nuneaton (70,721) and Rugby (61,988), along with Bedworth (30,001), in the north and east of the county, while smaller towns are found further south – Leamington Spa (61,595), Warwick (23,350) and Stratford-upon-Avon (22,187).

Positioned in central England, the county has always been crossed by a number of major transport routes, from the Roman Fosse Way and Watling Street to canals, the West Coast Main Line railway and major motorways. Economic activity in the south and east is focused on tourism (particularly around Warwick and Stratford-upon-Avon), finance, light industry and agriculture. The north and east has a long history of industry, particularly focused around the railway towns of Rugby and Nuneaton. The main employers in the county are now hotels, catering and distribution (25 per cent), banking and finance (23 per cent), public administration, education and health (19 per cent) and manufacturing (12 per cent). The motor industry is important for the county – the headquarters of Aston Martin, Jaguar and Land Rover are at Gaydon while BMW have an engine plant at Hams Hall near Coleshill. Rugby is an important centre for the cement industry and also has a thriving electrical engineering sector. In the south of the county economic activity concentrates more on the service industries, although Leamington's manufacturing businesses range from car parts through cast-iron stoves to video games.

The south of the county is typified by the half-timbered houses of Stratford-upon-Avon, a centre of tourism ever since David Garrick organised a celebration of the bicentenary of Shakespeare's birth 1769. Stratford was a prosperous medieval market tow on the banks of the river Avon. Shakespeare was born here and educated at Stratford Grammar School and, although much of his adult life was spent in London, his connections with Stratford remained. He married Anne Hathaway (her family cottage can still be seen at Shottery, just outside Stratford) and is buried in the parish church. His birthplace, a building from the 16th century survives and, indeed, has been welcomin visitors for over 250 years. A memorial theatre was bu in 1879, rebuilt in 1932 and comprehensively refurbish in 2010. It is the home of the Royal Shakespeare Company. Leamington Spa is the largest town in sout Warwickshire, but its development only started after s waters were rediscovered in 1784 (having been found the Romans). When, in 1814 the Royal Pump Rooms were opened, Leamington became a popular spa reso and many elegant houses were built. Its 'Royal' title w granted in 1838 by the young Queen Victoria, who ha visited before she became Queen. The attraction of th spa waters declined in the late nineteenth century, an Leamington then attracted both people in retirement and a wide variety of light industries.

The county town of Warwick was an important medieval town, dominated by Warwick Castle, origina built by William the Conqueror in 1068 and home of powerful earls of Warwick until 1978. It was one of th largest inhabited castles in Europe and is now a majo tourist attraction. Nearby, Kenilworth Castle was not lucky – once a royal castle and then enlarged by Rober Dudley, Earl of Leicester, to impress Elizabeth I, it fell into ruins after the English Civil War. Near Kenilwort (and nearer Coventry than Warwick), is the campus of the University of Warwick, founded in the 1965 and n one of Britain's top universities.

The north and east of the county is less well-knov although the name of Rugby is, of course, recognised around the world, having given its name to the game rugby football. Thomas Arnold, Head Master of Rugb School (1828–42), established the style of English Pub School education, and his influence is still felt today.

Anne Hathaway's cottage, Shottery, Stratford-upon-Avon.

Henley-in-Arden village High Street.

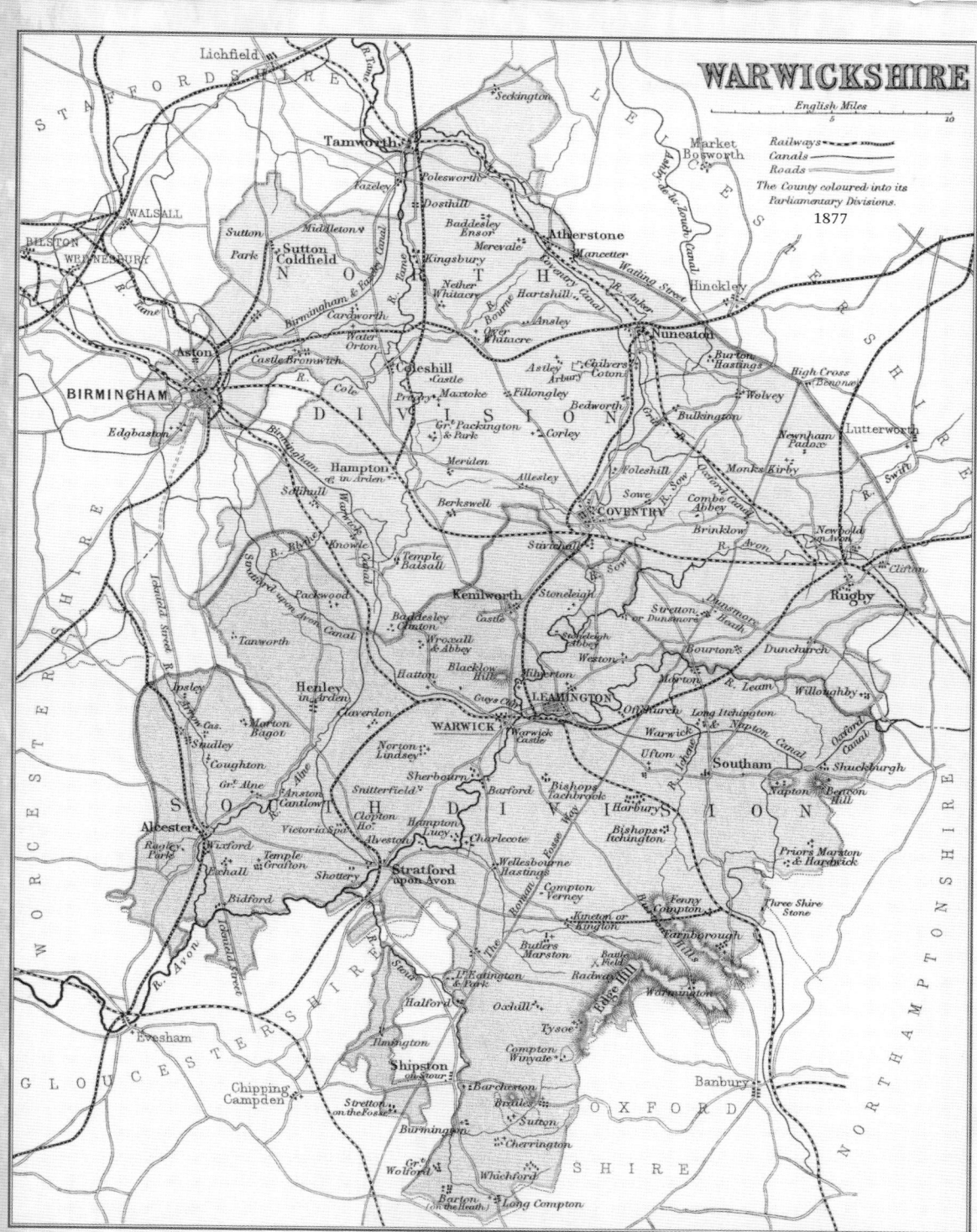

WARWICKSHIRE

English Miles

Railways
Canals
Roads

The County coloured into its
Parliamentary Divisions.
1877

Bartholomew Gazetteer of the British Isles, 1887

WARWICKSHIRE, *co. in west-midlands of England; bounded N. by Staffordshire, Derbyshire, and Leicestershire, E. by Northamptonshire, S. by Oxfordshire and Gloucestershire, and W. by Worcestershire; greatest length, N. and S., 52 miles; greatest breadth, E. and W., 32 miles; area, 566,271 ac., pop. 737,339. Warwickshire presents a pleasant undulating surface of hill and dale, watered by the Avon, Learn, and Tame. The climate is mild and healthy, and the soil, except some cold stiff clays on the higher grounds, is fertile. It consists chiefly of a strong red loam adapted for wheat and beans, or a sandy loam for barley and turnips. Much land is kept in permanent pasture for grazing. Formerly the co. was thickly wooded (that part N. of the Avon being called the Forest of Arden), and fine timber is still abundant. Geologically it mainly belongs to the secondary formation. A coal field, 16 miles by 3 miles, extends from the neighbourhood of Coventry to the border of Staffordshire, E. of Tamworth. The principal minerals are coal, ironstone, limestone, freestone, blue flagstone, and fire-clay. The mfrs. are carried on chiefly at Birmingham (hardware and silk goods) and Coventry (watches and ribbons). There are mineral springs at Leamington, Stratford on Avon, Umington, Southam, Willoughby, King's Newnham, &c. The co. is traversed in all directions by canals and railways. Warwickshire comprises 4 hundreds, 256 pars, with parts of 7 others, the parl. bor of Aston Manor, and the mun. bors. of Birmingham, Coventry, Leamington, Stratford on Avon, and Warwick. It is mostly in the diocese of Worcester.*

iam Shakespeare's cottage, Stratford-upon-Avon.

Warwick Castle

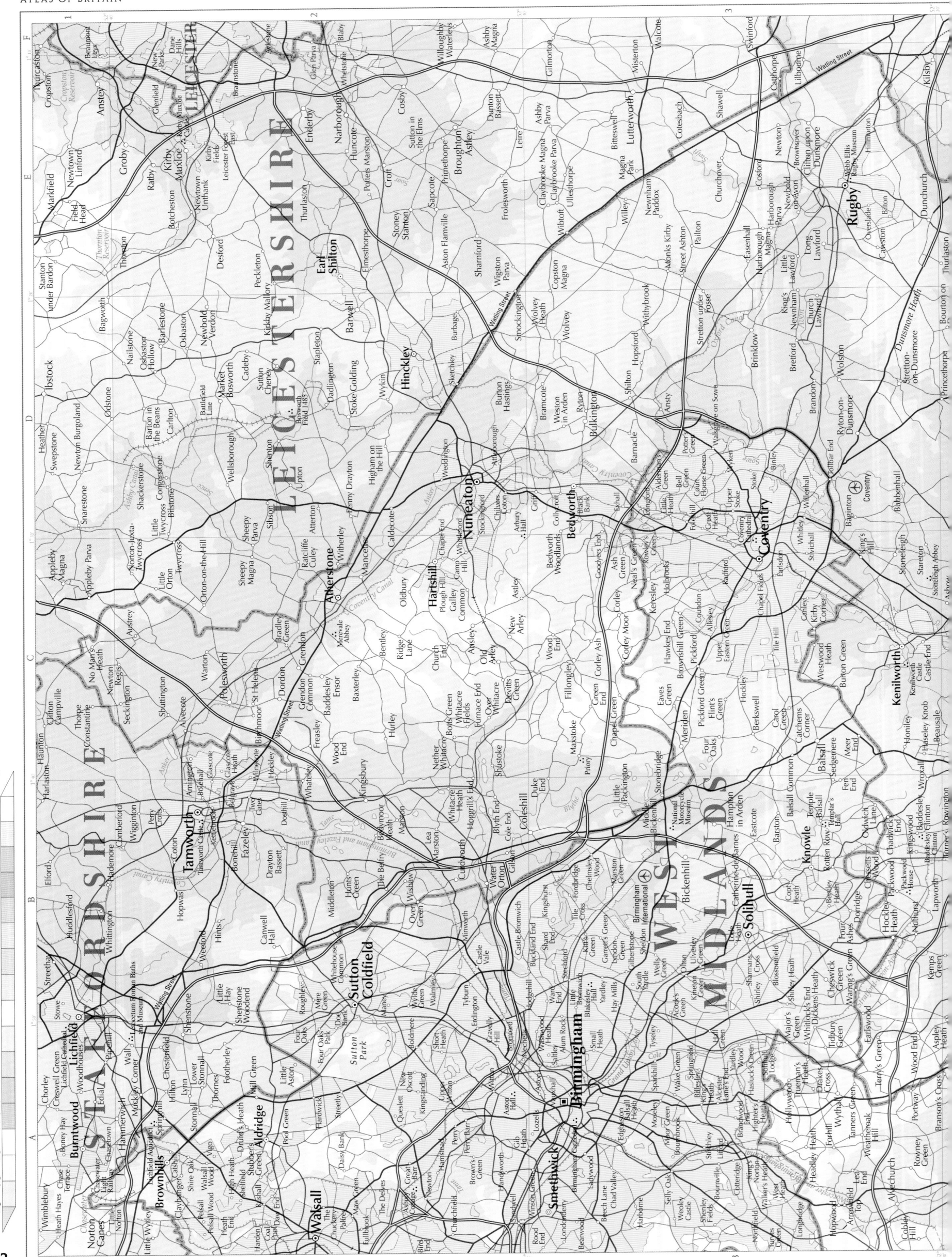

British National Grid projection

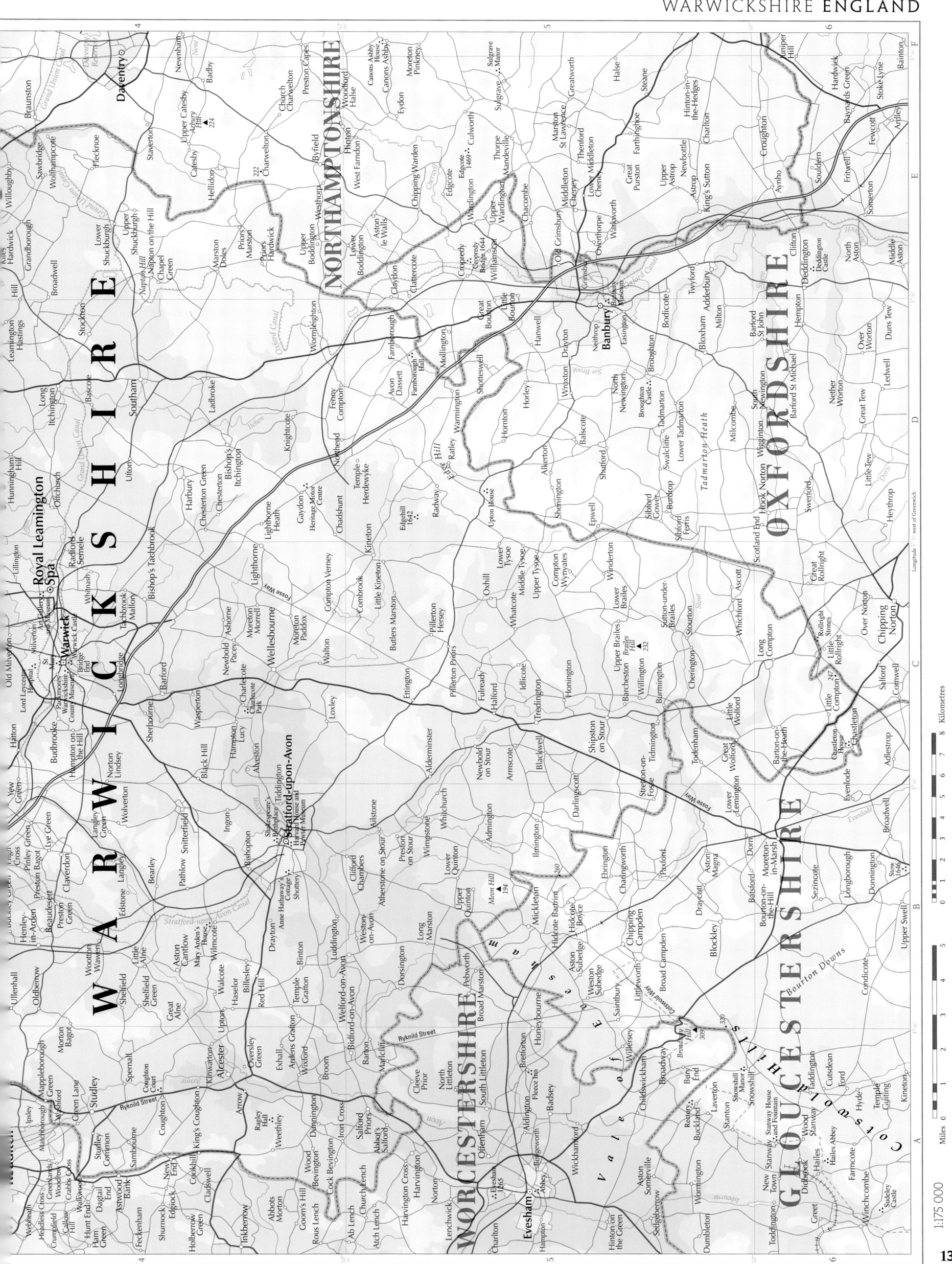

1:175 000

© Collins Bartholomew Ltd

WORCESTERSHIRE

Area Sq Km	1,741
Area Sq Miles	672
Population	557,600
County town	Worcester
Highest point	Worcestershire Beacon (425 m) in the Malvern Hills
Districts	Bromsgrove; Malvern Hills; Redditch; Worcester; Wychavon; Wyre Forest

Worcestershire takes its name from Worcester, once *Weogorna civitas*, 'Roman town of the Weogora tribe'. Weogara may be derived from a Celtic river-name, meaning 'winding river'.

FAMOUS FOR

Worcestershire Sauce was originally created by Sir Marcus Sandys upon his return from India and made for him by his local Worcester grocers, Lea and Perrins. It was first sold commercially in 1838.

The church at **Great Witley** brings the Italian baroque to rural Worcestershire – it is the most elaborate baroque church in Britain, created in the 1750s by Lord Foley, whose wealth came from making nails. It sits next door to the immense and ostentatious ruins of **Witley Court**, built with another industrial fortune by the Earl of Dudley.

Evesham Abbey was founded in the 8th century by Egwin, Bishop of Worcester. One story goes that before travelling to Rome to see the Pope, he had his legs manacled and the key thrown into the river Avon, which flows through Evesham. The key then reappeared in a fish he was served in Rome. On his return he founded Evesham Abbey, one of the greatest in Britain, the bell tower of which remains.

Brine has been extracted from under **Droitwich** since Roman times to produce salt, but it was only in the 19th century that it developed as a spa, the treatment being to bathe in brine. The development of the Brine Baths increased the fortune of the 'Salt King', John Corbett, who built Chateau Impney to remind his young wife of her Parisian upbringing.

Sir Edward Elgar, one of Britain's greatest composers, was born at **Lower Broadheath** near Worcester, and the local countryside, particularly the **Malvern Hills**, were an inspiration to him throughout his life. His birthplace is now a museum dedicated to his life and work.

FAMOUS PEOPLE

John Baskerville, printer and typographer, born Wolverley, 1706.

Sir Roland Hill, creator of the Penny Post, born Kidderminster, 1795.

Mrs Henry Wood (Ellen Wood), novelist, born Worcester, 1814.

Sir Edward Elgar, composer, born Lower Broadheath, 1857.

Alfred Edward (A E) Housman, poet and classicist, born Fockbury, near Bromsgrove, 1859.

Laurence Housman, novelist, dramatist and illustrator, born Bromsgrove, 1865.

Stanley Baldwin, 1st Earl Baldwin of Bewdley, politician, Prime Minister (1923–4, 1924–9, 1935–7), born Bewdley, 1867.

William Morris, 1st Viscount Nuffield, car manufacturer and philanthropist, born Worcester, 1877.

Sir John Vane, pharmacologist and Nobel laureate, born Tardebigge, 1927.

Sheila Scott, aviator, with many solo flight records, born Worcester, 1922.

Geoffrey Hill, poet, born Bromsgrove, 1932.

Nicola James (Jim) Capaldi, drummer, songwriter, member of Traffic, born Evesham, 1944.

Worcestershire is bisected by the river Severn, which enters the county by Bewdley and leaves in the south near Tewkesbury. On its western borders rise the Malvern Hills, which run for around 13 km parallel to the Severn. The Cotswolds enter the county briefly around the village of Broadway, while Bredon Hill lies to the south of the Vale of Evesham. The main river is the Severn, while the Avon flows west through the Vale of Evesham to join it at Tewkesbury and the Teme flows from the northwest to join it just south of Worcester. The Severn Valley suffers regularly from serious flooding, and many riverside areas have been inundated over recent years.

From earliest times Worcester was important as a crossing of the Severn and it provided one of the routes into Wales. The area was ruled by the Hwicce and then, in the 7th century, it became part of the Kingdom of Mercia. The county of Worcestershire is first referred to in the 11th century. Worcestershire County Council was established in 1888, with its population concentrated around Birmingham. By 1911, the county had lost the areas of Quinton, Northfield, Kings Norton and Yardley to Birmingham, by 1966 the major industrial centre of Dudley was lost and in the 1974 reforms, Halesowen and Stourbridge joined Dudley in the West Midlands, while, with much opposition, the remainder of Worcestershire was merged with Herefordshire, a union that was reversed in 1998.

The population of Worcestershire is now 557,600 and it is expected to grow by only around 4 per cent by 2026, the greatest increase being for Worcester itself but with Bromsgrove seeing a decline. The major settlements in the county are Worcester (population 94,029), Redditch (74,803), Kidderminster (55,348), Great Malvern (35,588), Bromsgrove (29,239), Droitwich Spa (22,585), Evesham (22,179) and Stourport-on-Severn (18,889). The urban areas in the north of the county form part of the periphery and commuter belt of the West Midlands conurbation.

Agriculture continues to play an important part in the economy of the county, particularly in the Vale of Evesham and the Severn Valley, while manufacturing, which provides 16.7 per cent of jobs, significantly above the national average, is more concentrated towards the north, close to the West Midlands, with the making of car parts a key business. Malvern is home to two contrasting businesses, the Morgan Motor Company with its traditionally made sports cars and QinetiQ, the privatized part of the Telecommunications Research Establishment, initially located in Malvern in 1942 to develop radar and with many other inventions to its credit.

The most significant building in Worcester is its cathedral by the banks of the Severn, built from the 11th to the 14th century. Within its walls are buried two saints (Oswald and Wulfstan) and one king (King John). Worcester was also the scene of the last battle of the English Civil War, in 1651, when Cromwell defeated Charles II and his Scottish army. The city was badly damaged and Charles had to flee from Britain. Thereafter it made its way from glove making and porcelain – Worcester porcelain was made from 1751 until 2009. The impact of the Industrial Revolution was felt in the north of the county. Kidderminster became famous for textiles and then carpet manufacture, Stourbridge (then in the county) for nail making and glass, and Redditch for needle making, all helped by the arrival of the canals (Stourport developed where the Staffordshire and Worcester canal joined the Severn). Droitwich, known for its saltpans, developed as a spa in the 19th century, and the landscape of north Worcestershire continues to show the impact of this early industrialisation.

To the south of Worcester, the Vale of Evesham, with its great abbey sites at Evesham and Pershore, remains agricultural, while, Great Malvern, on the other side of the Severn, also prospered in the 19th century as a spa, with Malvern Spring water still a popular drink.

Worcester Cathedral and surrounding buildings.

Malvern Hills, southwest Worcestershire.

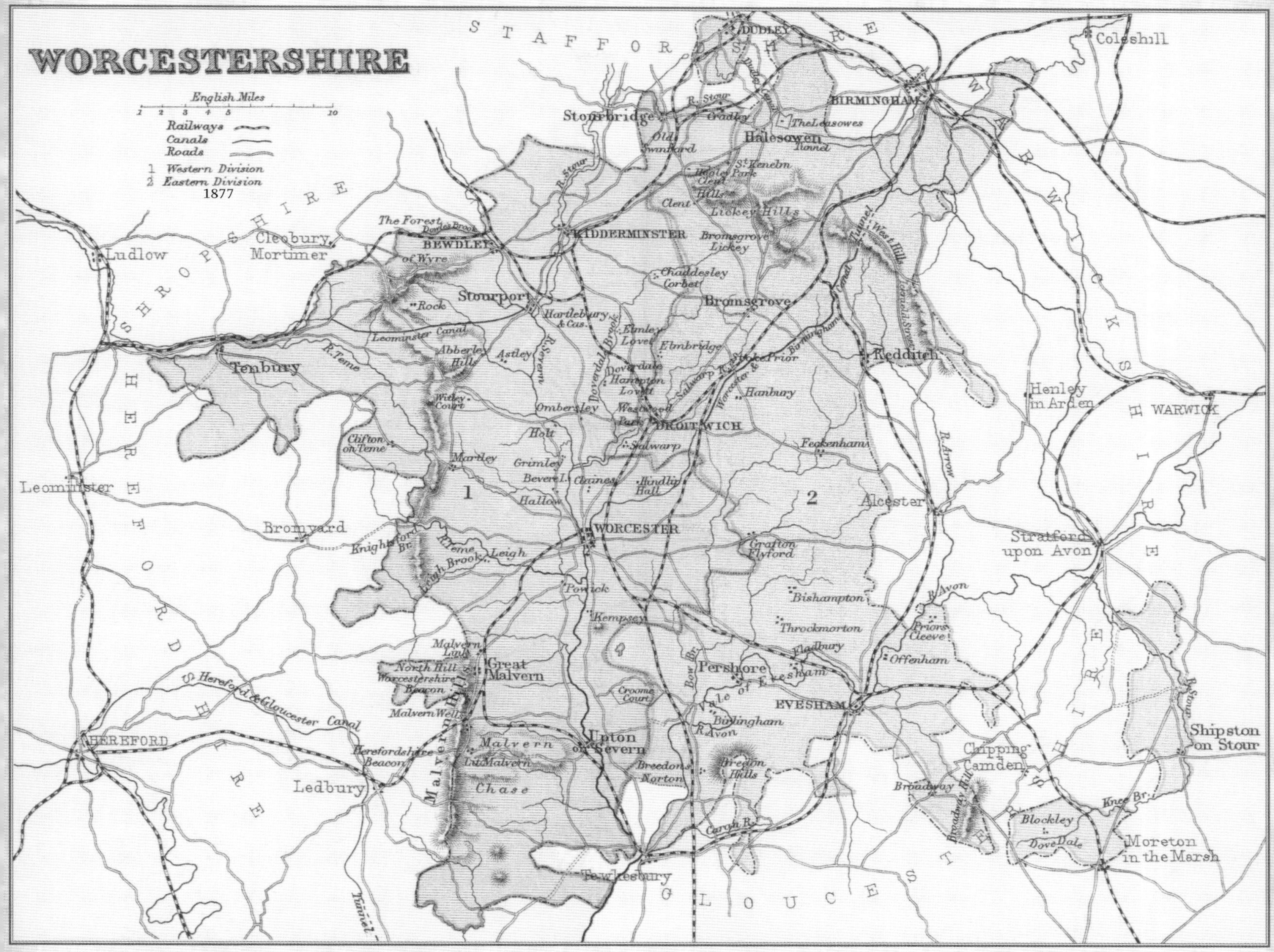

WORCESTERSHIRE

English Miles
1 2 3 4 5 10 20

Railways
Canals
Roads
1 Western Division
2 Eastern Division
1877

Bartholomew Gazetteer of the British Isles, 1887

WORCESTERSHIRE, *west-midland co. of England, bounded N. by Shropshire and Staffordshire, E. by Warwickshire, S. by Gloucestershire, and W. by Herefordshire; greatest length (not including the detached parts), NW. and SE., 36 miles; greatest breadth, NE. and SW., 45 miles; area, 472,453 ac., pop. 380,283. Worcestershire lies almost entirely in the basin of the Severn, which receives the Stour, Teme, and Avon. The surface is a broad undulating plain, broken in the NE. by hills of moderate height, and in the SW. by the Malvern*

Hills, which reach an altitude of 1395 ft. The soil, chiefly clay and loam, is very fertile. Wheat is extensively grown, and there are numerous hop-gardens and orchards. Large quantities of cider and perry are made. There are several extensive and beautiful valleys (notably that of the Severn), with rich pastures, and great numbers of cattle and sheep are fattened. The strata consist for the most part of new red sandstone, lias, and oolite; other formations are visible in the Malvern Hills and some other districts. Coal and iron are found in the Dudley district, and the mfr. of iron and steel and of hardware is

extensive. Carpets and rugs are made at Kidderminster, glass at Dudley and Stourbridge, gloves and porcelain at Worcester, and needles and fish-hooks at Redditch and Feckenham. Immense quantities of salt are obtained from the brine springs at Droitwich. The Birmingham and Worcester and other canals connect the Severn basin with those of the Trent and Mersey. The county contains 5 hundreds, 243 pars., part of the mun. bor. of Dudley, and the mun. bors. of Bewdley, Droitwich, Evesham, Kidderminster and Worcester. It is almost entirely in the diocese of Worcester.

...ey Court, near the village of Great Witley.

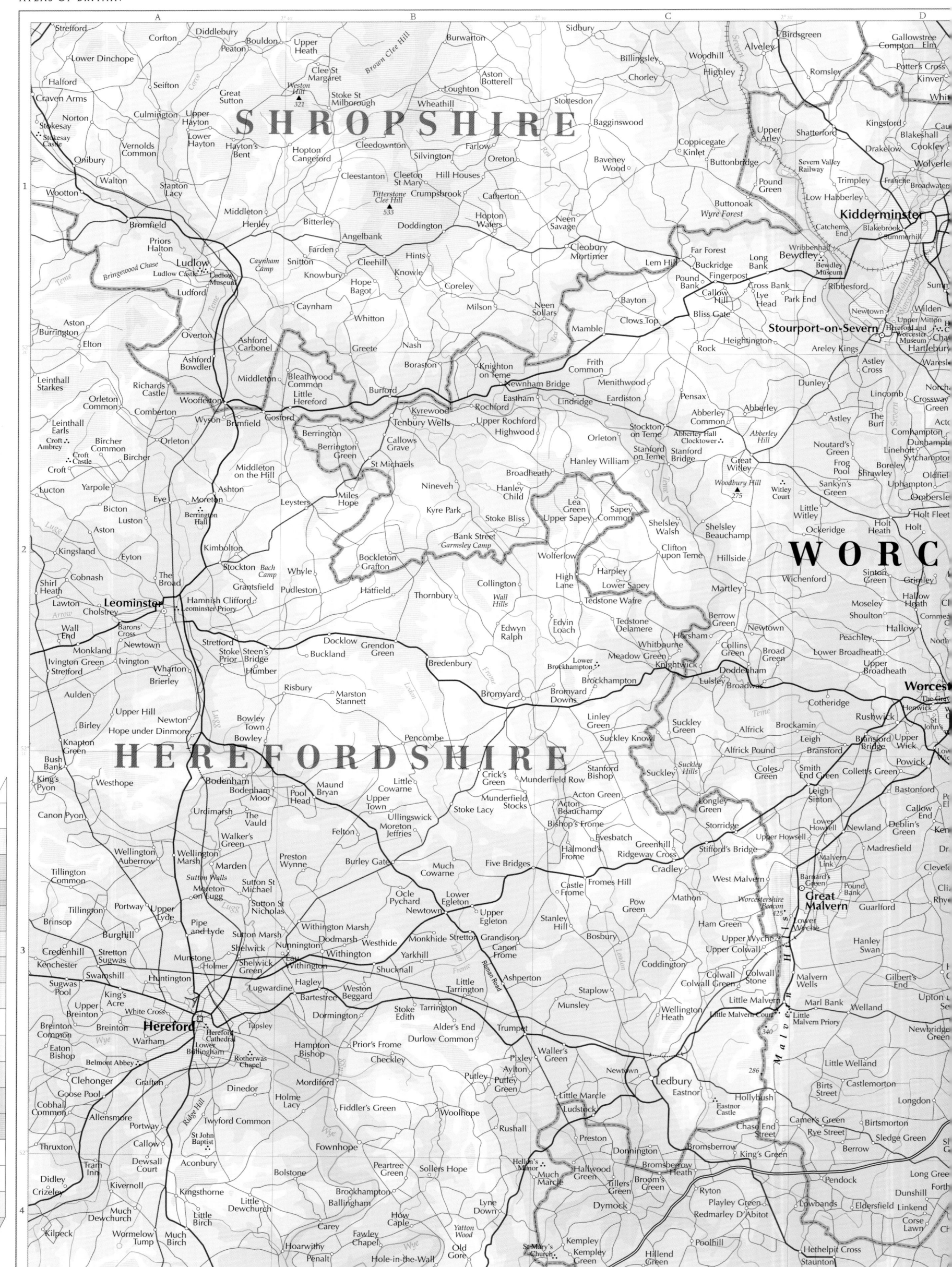

SHROPSHIRE

HEREFORDSHIRE

WORC

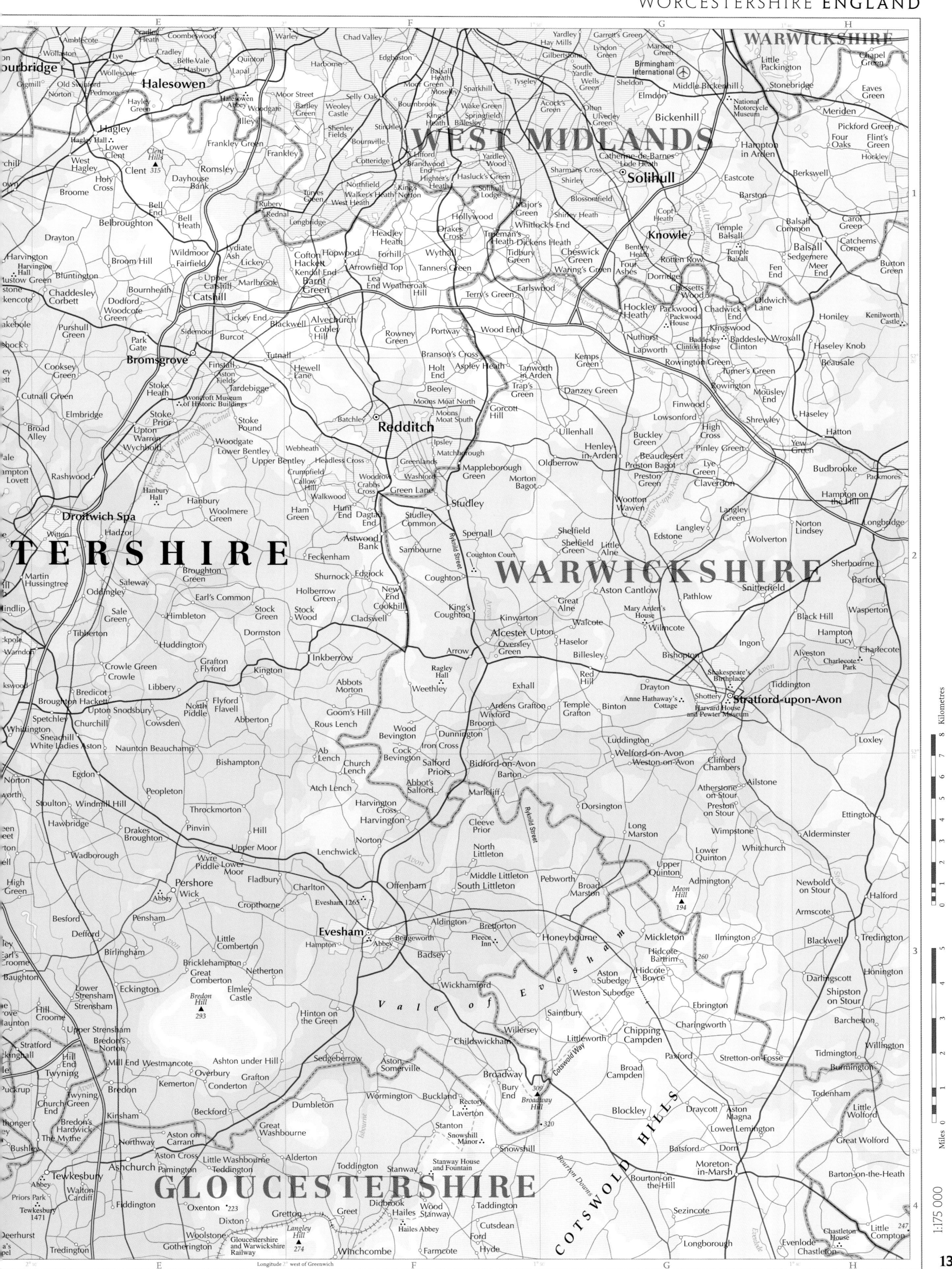

1:175 000

© Collins Bartholomew Ltd

HEREFORDSHIRE

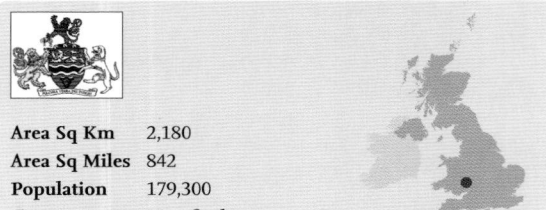

Area Sq Km	2,180
Area Sq Miles	842
Population	179,300
County town	Hereford
Highest point	Black Mountain (703 m) on the Welsh border

Herefordshire takes its name from Hereford, from the Old English 'here' and 'ford, meaning 'army ford', so a suitable place for marching soldiers to cross the River Wye.

FAMOUS FOR

One of Hereford Cathedral's prize possessions is the **Mappa Mundi**, a map of the world drawn on a single sheet of vellum that shows, within a 1.3 m diameter circle, the world around 1300, with Jerusalem at its centre, and illustrated with drawings of cities, people, plants and the occasional mythical creature.

Hereford cattle, a breed of beef cattle that originated in the 18th century in Herefordshire, is now common in most parts of the world, instantly recognizable with its white face and red body. They were first exported to the USA in 1817 and to Australia in 1825.

The thatched **Brockhampton Church** is a small jewel of the Arts and Crafts Movement, built by W R Letherby in 1902. In 2009 a facsimile of it was built within a tower block in Osaka for use in Japanese marriages.

Inside the Priory at **Leominster** is the last ducking stool ever used in England – in 1809 Jenny Pipes was ducked into the river Kenwater for causing a public nuisance. The stool was first wheeled through the town and then into the river, when the culprit, sitting at the end of its 4 m pole was unceremoniously lowered into the water.

The Bulmer's cider company was founded in 1887 by Percy Bulmer, the 20-year-old son of the rector of **Credenhill**, who used apples from the rectory orchard to produce his first cider.

FAMOUS PEOPLE

William Langland, author of *Piers Plowman*, probably born Ledbury, 1332.
Sir John Oldcastle, soldier, leader of the Lollards, born Almeley, c. 1378.
Saint John Kemble, Catholic priest and martyr, born St Weonards, 1599.
Thomas Traherne, cleric and poet, born Hereford, 1637.
Eleanor (Nell) Gwyn, actress and mistress to Charles II, born Hereford, 1650.
David Garrick, actor and theatre manager, born Hereford, 1717.
John Masefield, Poet Laureate (1930–67), born Ledbury, 1878.
Dora Carrington, (known as Carrington) painter, member of the Bloomsbury Group, born Hereford, 1893.
Beryl Reid, actress, born Hereford, 1920.
Frank Oz, (born Richard Frank Oznowicz) puppeteer with The Muppets and film director, born Hereford, 1944.
Peter Scudamore, champion National Hunt jockey, born Hereford, 1958.

"The lovely valley gleaming bright in the clear shining after rain … when the evening sun struck out jewels of gold where he lit upon the upland slopes and hill meadows … and the river blazed below the grey bridge with a sparkle of a million diamonds."
Francis Kilvert, on Bredwardine, 1876

Herefordshire lies between the Black Mountains on the Welsh border in the west and the Malvern Hills in the east, a land of rolling hills and remote valleys. The River Wye flows through the county, entering from Wales by Hay-on-Wye, then past Hereford and turning south through the Wye valley to leave the county by Symonds Yat.

Herefordshire became part of the kingdom of Mercia in the 7th century. The arrival of the Normans saw the strengthening of this border area with the construction of a major castle at Hereford. The county of Herefordshire was first mentioned in the 11th century, but it was not until Tudor rule that peace descended on the county. Herefordshire County Council was formed in 1888, but then, in 1974, with much opposition, it was merged with its much larger neighbour to form the county of Hereford and Worcester. In 1998, Herefordshire again became a unitary authority, this time with no district councils. The population of Herefordshire is 179,300, having grown by 3 per cent between 2001 and 2008, below the national average. It is expected to grow to 193,600 by 2026. The county has one of the lowest population densities in England and around 43 per cent of the population live in rural villages or the countryside. Already a quarter of the county's population is over retirement age and this is expected to increase. By far the largest settlement is Hereford, with a population of 56,373, while the significant market towns are Leominster (10,440), Ross-on-Wye (10,085), Ledbury (8,491), Bromyard (4,400) and Kington (2,597). Kington is the only settlement of any size in the west of the county.

Herefordshire's economy has been based on agriculture, which currently provides 9 per cent of jobs compared with 1 per cent nationally. Around 70 per cent of jobs are in the service sector, significantly less than the national figure, while manufacturing accounts for 15 per cent of jobs. Tourism employs 8 per cent of the working population and is an area of the economy that is being greatly encouraged, although the unspoilt

remoteness that appeals to visitors is hard to reach because communications are more limited than in m[...] counties – the only stretch of motorway links Ross-on[...] Wye to the M5 in the south of the county and there ar[...] few rail links.

Hereford developed on the east bank of the River Wye, centred around the castle and the Cathedra[...] The Norman castle, described in the 16th century as 'one of the fairest, largest and strongest in all England' was dismantled in the 17th century for its stone. The cathedral site was originally the burial spot for King Ethelbert of the East Angles, beheaded by King Offa in AD 792 when he came to Hereford to marry Offa's daughter. He was later canonized and his tomb becam[...] place of pilgrimage. The current building was started [...] the late 11th century with modifications and additions continuing until the 15th century. There has been muc[...] restoration, especially after the west front collapsed o[...] Easter Day in AD 1786. Hereford is now the administrative, educational and medical centre of the county as well as the home of the Herefordshire cider industry and the Cider Museum – there are over 5,500 ha of apple orchards that provide apples for the count[...] cider producers. Credenhill, just outside Hereford is t[...] base for the Special Air Services (SAS) Regiment.

To the south of Hereford, the Wye meanders down[...] to Ross on Wye and beyond to the border, where the valley becomes steeper. Along the Welsh border are numerous quiet valleys, the most scenic being the Golden Valley through which the river Dore flows. In this remote spot is Abbey Dore, founded by the French Cistercians in the 12th century, with the surviving church still feeling French. Close by is the small Norman church at Kilpeck, built in the 12th century and unchanged, with over 80 vigorously carved corbels on the outside ('all the busy and bawdy life of a Herefordshire village', as described by Simon Jenkins), along with heavily carved door and window openings [...] the outside and more saintly carvings within. Along th[...] border area runs Offa's Dyke, built by King Offa to delineate the western limits of his Mercian kingdom.

The Mappa Mundi in Hereford Cathedral.

Hereford Cathedral

"The hills that encompass [Golden Valley] on both sides are clothed with woods, under the woods lie corn-fields on each hand, and under those fields, lovely and gallant meadows. In the middle, between them, glides a clear and crystal river."
William Campden, 1586

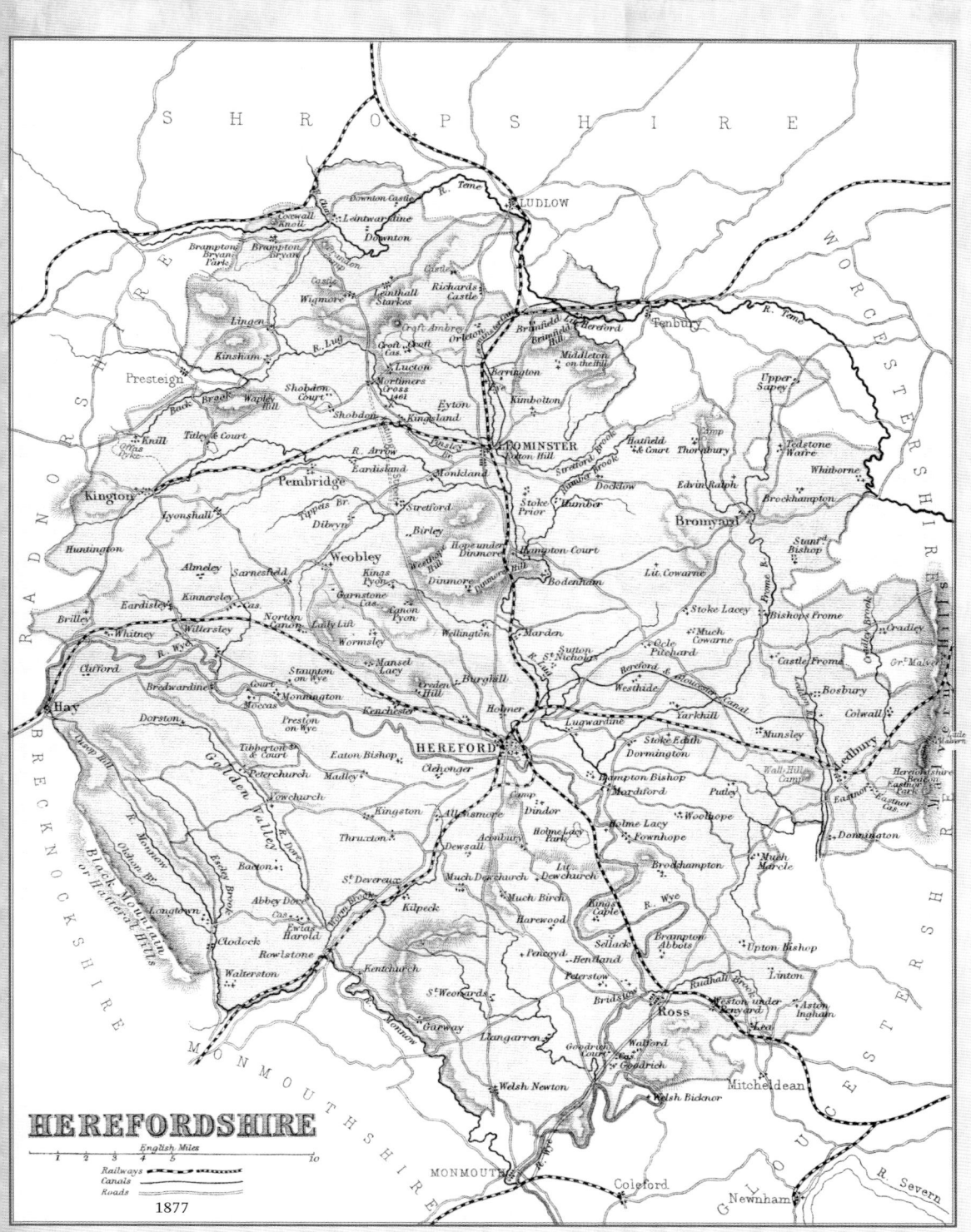

HEREFORDSHIRE

English Miles
1 2 3 4 5 10

Railways
Canals
Roads

1877

Bartholomew Gazetteer of the British Isles, 1887
HEREFORDSHIRE, *an inland co. on the SE. border of Wales, and bounded N. by Shropshire and Worcestershire, E. by Worcestershire and Gloucestershire, S. by Gloucestershire and Monmouthshire, and W. by Monmouthshire, Radnorshire, and Brecknockshire; greatest length N. and S. 38 miles, greatest breadth E. and W. 35 miles; 532,918 ac., pop. 121,062. The co. is almost circular in form, and its surface shows a series of quiet and beautiful undulations. It is watered by the Wye, Lugg, Monnow, Arrow, and Frome, also the Teme, which flows on the NE. boundary. All these streams are well stocked with fish. Of late agriculture has been greatly improved in the co.: the soil peculiarly suitable for the growth of timber, which is very abundant. The pear and apple orchards of Herefordshire are famous; while the luxuriant meadow-land affords pasture for a well-known breed of oxen. Marl and clay form the chief part of the soil; the subsoil is mostly limestone. There are no valuable minerals, and the mfrs. are insignificant. The co. comprises 11 hundreds, 258 pars., and parts of 3 others, the mun. bors. of Hereford, and Leominster. It is mostly in the diocese of Hereford.*

The Old House, High Town, Hereford, is now a museum.

Hereford Cattle

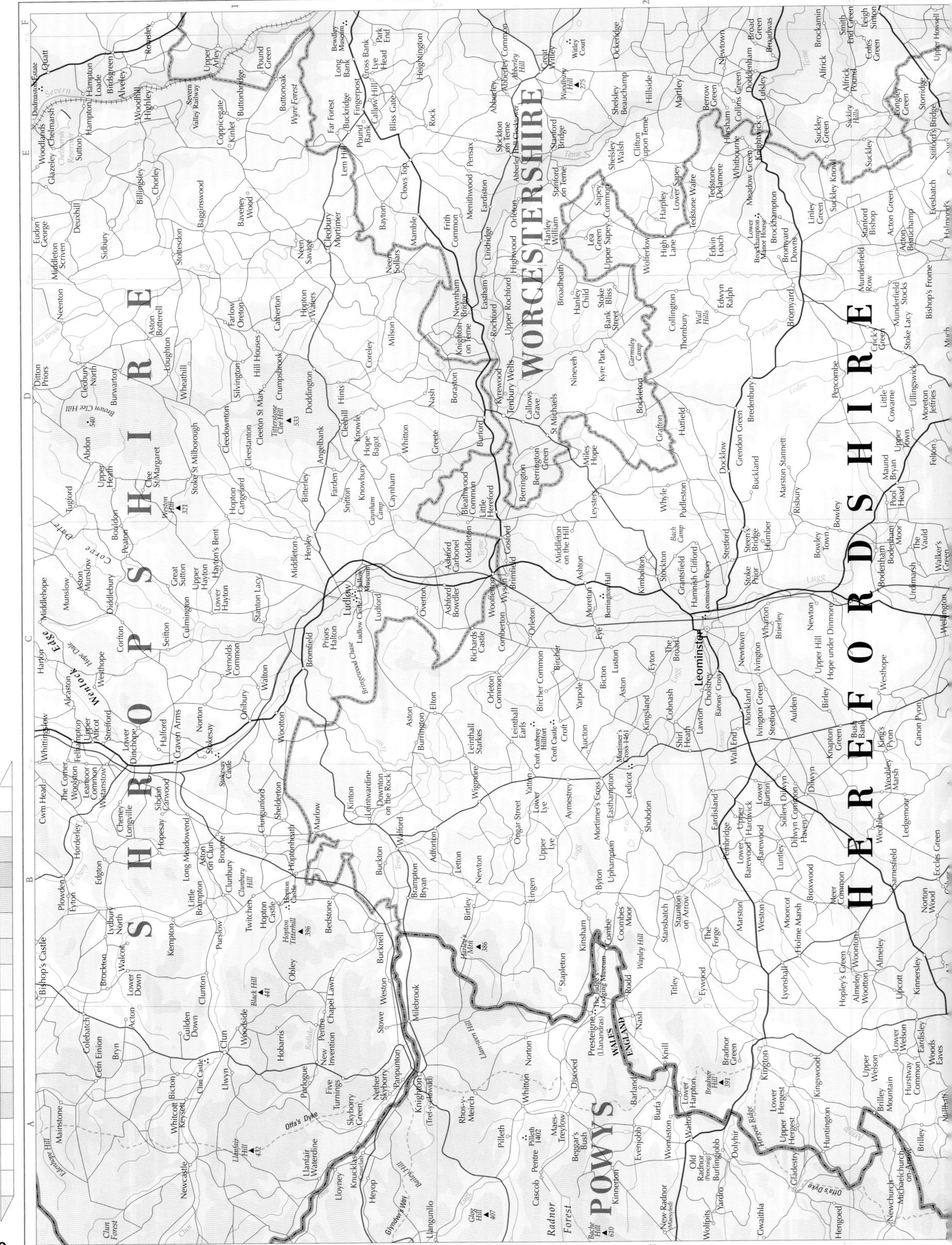

British National Grid projection

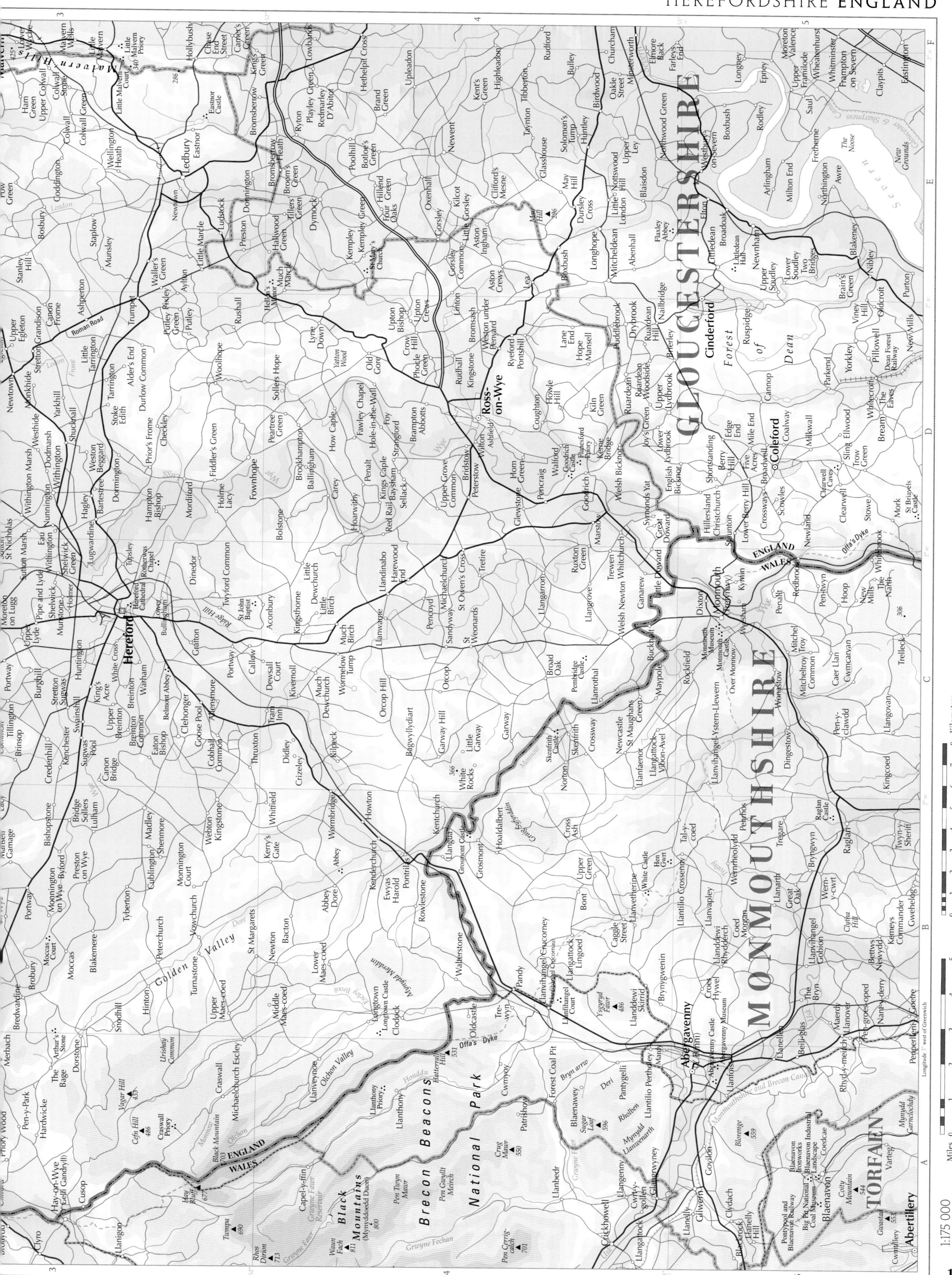

1:175 000

© Collins Bartholomew Ltd

SHROPSHIRE

Area Sq Km	3,197
Area Sq Miles	1,234
Population	292,800
County town	Shrewsbury
Highest point	Brown Clee Hill (540 m) in the Clee Hills

Shropshire takes its name from an old spelling of Shrewsbury. The abbreviation 'Salop' comes from the Norman spelling of the shire 'Salopescira'. Shrewsbury comes from the Old English 'Scrobbesbyrig', meaning a 'fortified place in scrubland'.

FAMOUS FOR

At **Wroxeter**, on the banks of the Severn are the remains of *Viroconium*, Britain's fourth largest Roman city. Excavations began in 1859 and there are extensive remains to be seen including part of the baths complex, the largest free-standing Roman ruin in Britain.

The **Chirk Aqueduct**, designed by Thomas Telford, was built over the river Ceiriog between 1796 and 1801. It is 21 m tall, 220 m long and has 10 spans. Half in Shropshire and half in Wales it carries the Llangollen Canal and is the start of a UNESCO World Heritage Site.

In a valley near Wenlock Edge is the remarkable **Stokesay Castle**, a fortified manor house completed around 1291 for Lawrence of Ludlow, a wealthy wool merchant, and little changed apart from the timber framed gatehouse that was built in 1641.

Thomas Parr is said to have been born in 1483 and died in 1635, at the age of 152. He was born at **Winnington** and lived there all his life until taken to London by Thomas Howard, Earl of Arundel, in 1635, a visit from which he did not return. He is buried in Westminster Abbey.

After his defeat at the Battle of Worcester in 1651, Charles II fled. At **Boscobel**, he first hid in an oak tree (the Royal Oak) and then in a priest's hole in the house before moving on.

FAMOUS PEOPLE

Richard Gough, author, *History of Myddle*, born Myddle, 1635.
William Wycherley, Restoration dramatist, born Clive, near Wem, 1640.
Admiral John Benbow, navy commander and popular hero, born Shrewsbury, 1653.
Francis Moore, astrologer, author of *Old Moore's Almanac*, born Bridgnorth, 1657.
Robert Clive (known as Clive of India),Baron Clive of Plassey, soldier and Governor of Bengal, born Moreton Say, 1725.
Charles Darwin, naturalist, author of *On the Origin of Species* (1859), born Shrewsbury, 1809.
Mary Webb (born Gladys Hary Meredith), novelist and poet, born Leighton-under-Wrekin, 1881.
Wilfrid Owen, World War I poet, born Oswestry, 1893.
Barbara Pym, novelist, born Oswestry, 1913.
Alexander (Sandy) Lyle, golfer, born Shrewsbury, 1958.
Ian Woosnam, golfer, born Oswestry, 1958.

The south and west of Shropshire is hilly, with large areas of open moorland, including the Long Mynd, Wenlock Edge and the Clee Hills. Elsewhere the county undulates towards the Severn Valley, which provides fertile agricultural land served by prosperous market towns. In the north the county merges with the Cheshire plain. The most important river is the Severn, which flows across the county from the Powys border east to Shrewsbury and then southeast to Bridgnorth and the Worcestershire border. Other rivers include the Clun, Corve, Perry, Rea Brook, and Teme.

After the Romans, the Shropshire area became part of the Welsh kingdom of Powys until annexed by Offa of Mercia in the 7th century – and Offa's Dyke still marks much of the western boundary of the county. The area was reinforced after the Norman Conquest, but the current border with Wales was not fixed until the 16th century, and since then there has been little change. The county was little affected by the 1974 local government changes but in 1998 the area around Telford became the Telford and Wrekin unitary authority and in 2009 the remaining part of Shropshire was made a unitary authority with the abolition of the districts of Bridgnorth, North Shropshire, Oswestry, Shrewsbury and Atcham, and South Shropshire.

The population of Shropshire is 292,800, and is one of the most sparsely populated counties in England. The population has grown by 7 per cent since 1991, all this growth coming from people moving into the county, and it is estimated to grow by a further 17 per cent by 2031. The population is already older th the national average and this trend will continue. The main urban centres are Shrewsbury (67,126), Oswestry (16,660), Bridgnorth (11,891), Market Drayton (10,407), Ludlow (9,548) and Whitchurch (8,673).

Agriculture and related food processing remain a vital part of the county's economy. Over a third of the county is given over to grassland, with another third devoted to cereal and horticultural use. Meat and milk processors are among the large employers in the coun The service sector accounts for 81.5 per cent of jobs, with public administration, education and health takin over 31 per cent and tourism 9.5 per cent.

As the former heart of the Marches of Wales, Shropshire contains the remains of numerous border defences, with major castles at Shrewsbury, sited on a defensive loop in the Severn, and closer t the Welsh border at Bishop's Castle and Clun. There a also the remains of several monasteries, for instance, a Much Wenlock and Buildwas. Ludlow, with its romant castle ruins and wealth of historic buildings has becor a popular tourist destination, assisted by the town's gastronomic reputation. Bridgnorth, on the Severn, ha been built on an unlikely site, with the Low Town at river level on one side and High Town built on cliffs o the other side and accessible by a funicular cliff railwa

The timber-framed gatehouse for Stokesay Castle, near Wenlock Edge.

Shrewsbury Castle

SHROPSHIRE

English Miles

0 1 2 3 4 5 6 10

Railways

Canals

Roads

The County coloured into its Parliamentary Divisions
1 Northern Division
2 Southern D?
1877

Bartholomew Gazetteer of the British Isles, 1887
SHROPSHIRE *(or Salop), co. in west-midlands of England, bounded N. by Cheshire and detached part of Flintshire, E. by Staffordshire, S. by Worcestershire, Herefordshire, and Radnorshire, and W. by Montgomeryshire and Denbighshire; area, 844,565 ac., pop. 248,014. The river Severn, running SE., divides the co. into 2 nearly equal parts. The northern, occupied by the new red sandstone, is generally level; the southern, belonging to the old red sandstone, is of a more elevated and rugged character, reaching in the Clee Hills a height of 1805 ft. The soil is various, but generally fertile and well cultivated; there are, however, considerable tracts of waste land. The principal crops are wheat, barley, oats, pease, beans, vetches, turnips, and potatoes. The co. is famous for its breed of sheep. Cattle-breeding and dairy-farming are carried on in the S. and W. The principal mineral products are coal and iron, with limestone, freestone, and lead. The mfrs., besides those connected with iron, include carpets, flannels, gloves, glass, stoneware, paper, and malt. Shropshire is connected by the river with Gloucester and Bristol, and by canals with Chester and Liverpool, while Shrewsbury is a railway centre. The co. contains 14 hundreds, 252 pars, with parts of 6 others, the mun. bors. of Bridgnorth, Ludlow, Oswestry, Shrewsbury, and Wenlock. It is in the dioceses of Hereford, Lichfield, and St Asaph.*

TELFORD AND WREKIN

Area Sq Km	290
Area Sq Miles	112
Population	162,100
County town	Telford
Highest point	The Wrekin (407 m)

FAMOUS FOR

A prominent landmark, **The Wrekin** has an Iron Age hill fort on its summit, as well as a transmitting station and the 'Wrekin Beacon' night beacon.

The world's first bridge using cast iron (the **Iron Bridge**) was built across the Severn at **Coalbrookdale**, opening in 1781. The main span is around 30 m and around 390 tonnes of cast iron was used in its construction.

FAMOUS PEOPLE

Abraham Darby II, iron founder, born Coalbrookdale, 1711.

William Withering, doctor, who first used digitalis in treatment of heart failure, born Wellington, 1741.

Abraham Darby III, builder of the Iron Bridge, born Coalbrookdale, 1750.

Matthew Webb, the first person to swim the English Channel, born Dawley, 1848.

Sir Gordon Richards, jockey, born Donnington Wood, 1904.

Edith Pargeter (pen name Ellis Peters), crime fiction writer, born Horsehay, 1913.

Lionel (Len) Murray, Baron Murray of Epping Forest, General Secretary, TUC, born Hadley, 1922.

William Ambrose (Billy) Wright, footballer, born Ironbridge, 1924.

Since 1998 Telford and Wrekin has been a unitary authority, centred on the new town of Telford, which incorporated Dawley, Oakengates and Wellington, and was named after Thomas Telford, the great canal and road engineer, who was County Surveyor for Shropshire (1788–1834). The area also includes Newport, many small villages and the Wrekin, at 407 m, a dominating part of the landscape. Coalbrookdale can claim to be the home of the Industrial Revolution, built on Abraham Darby's innovative use of coke in making iron. This and much more is celebrated in the UNESCO World Heritage Site of Ironbridge Gorge. With direct motorway links to Birmingham, the area has seen much recent inward investment – 15,000 people work for over 150 foreign companies with key industries being electronics and polymers. The population is younger than the national average and is expected to grow by nearly 25 per cent by 2026.

"We … looked at the Iron Bridge with Admiration, at the nightly Fires with Astonishment – artificial Stromboli! strange imitation of Nature's Volcanoes."
Mrs Thrale on Coalbrookdale, 1791

What are those blue remembered hills,
What spires, what farms are those?
That is the land of lost content,
I see it shining plain,
The happy highways where I went
And cannot come again.
A E Housman, *A Shropshire Lad* (1896)

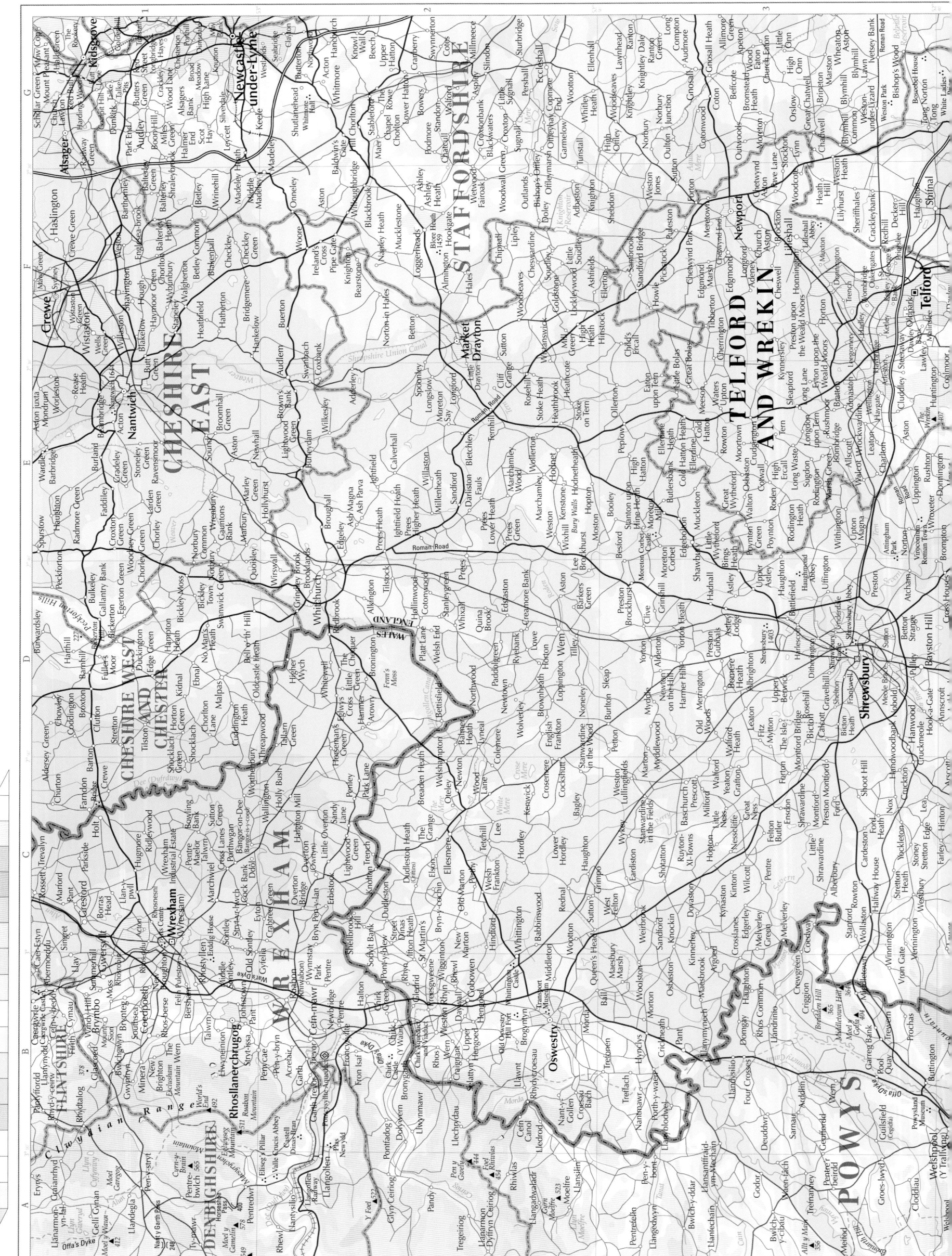

British National Grid projection

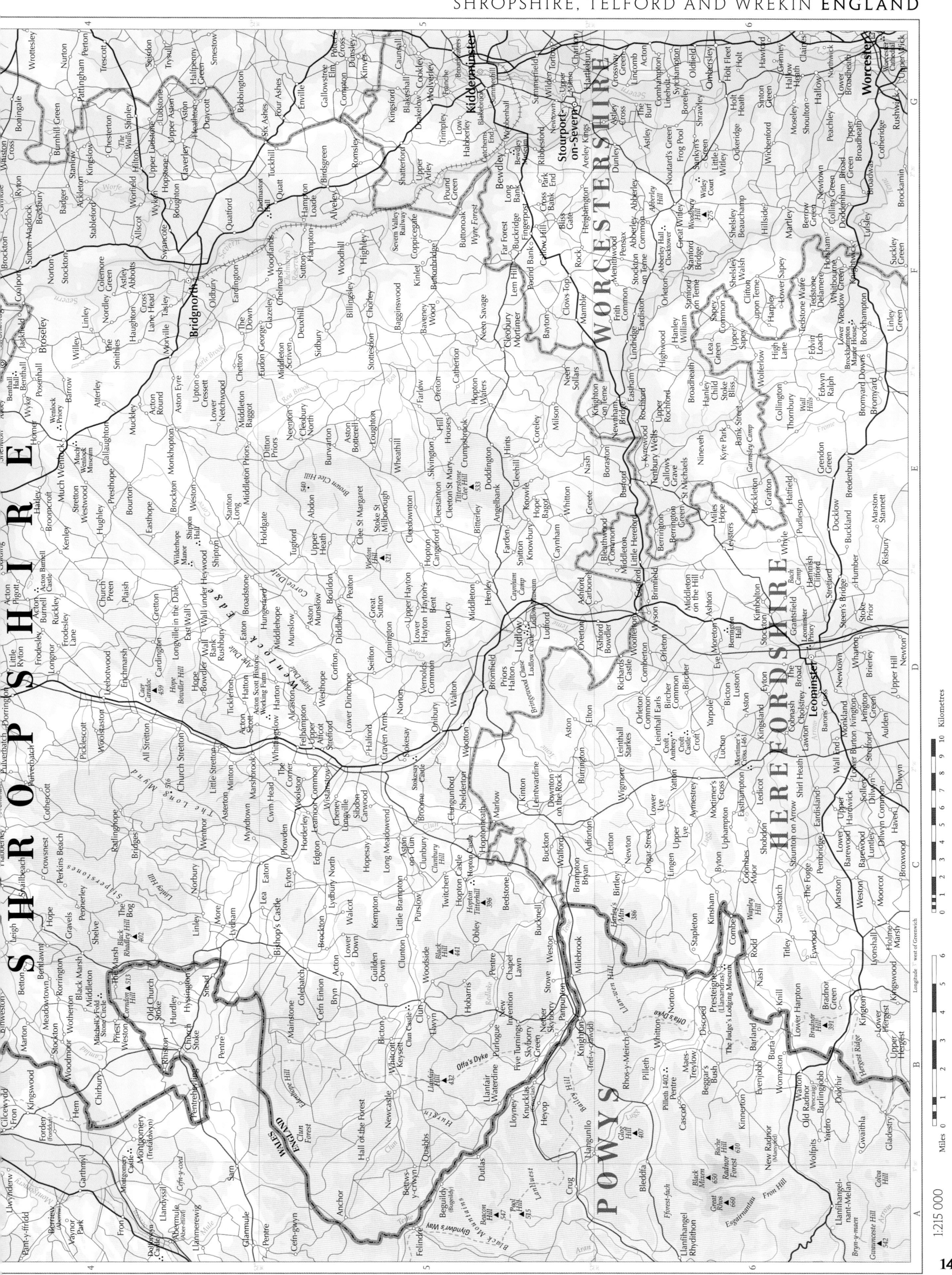

1:215 000

© Collins Bartholomew Ltd

STAFFORDSHIRE

Area Sq Km	1,263
Area Sq Miles	1,013
Population	828,900
County town	Stafford
Highest point	Cheeks Hill (520 m) in the Peak District
Districts	Cannock Chase; East Staffordshire; Lichfield; Newcastle-under-Lyme; South Staffordshire; Stafford; Staffordshire Moorlands; Tamworth

Staffordshire takes its name from the town of Stafford, from the Old English for 'ford by a landing place' on the River Sow.

FAMOUS FOR

The village of **Flash** is England's highest village, 463 m above sea level. It is close to the border with Cheshire and Derbyshire and was a haunt of thieves and forgers.

The Roman Catholic Church of St Giles at **Cheadle** is an early Victorian gem designed by A W N Pugin and was built with no expense spared for the Earl of Shrewsbury. Pugin also designed the nearby **Alton Towers** for him, though that building is now a shell in the grounds of the well-known theme park.

The National Memorial Arboretum at **Alrewas**, in the National Forest, was created in 1997 as a living tribute to the personal sacrifices made by the armed and civil services. With over 50,000 trees and 160 memorials, it is a place dedicated to peace and beauty.

The **Staffordshire Hoard**, was discovered in a field near the village of Hammerwich in 2009. It contains 1,500 7th-century items of gold and silver, including helmets, sword hilts and crests, provides dramatic evidence as to how rich and powerful the Mercian Kingdom was.

FAMOUS PEOPLE

Reginald Pole, last Roman Catholic Archbishop of Canterbury (1556–58), born, Stourton, near Stourbridge, 1500.
Izaak Walton, author of *The Compleat Angler*, born Stafford, 1593.
Elias Ashmole, antiquary and Oxford University benefactor, born Lichfield, 1617.
Samuel Johnson, writer and lexicographer, born Lichfield, 1709.
William Worthington, brewer, born Burton upon Trent, 1723.
Admiral John Jervis, 1st Earl St Vincent, naval commander, born Meaford, near Stone, 1735.
Peter de Wint, artist, born Stone, 1784.
Michael Thomas Bass, brewer, born Burton upon Trent, 1799.
Vera Mary Brittain, writer and pacifist, born Newcastle-under-Lyme, 1893.
Andrew Norman (A N) Wilson, writer and journalist, born Stone, 1950.

"They told us there [at Lichfield] a long story of St Chad, formerly bishop of this church, and how he lived in a little hovel or cell in the church-yard, instead of a bishop's palace. But the bishops, since that time, have, I suppose, thought better of it, and make shift with a very fine palace in the close."
Daniel Defoe, 1725

The ancient hunting forest Cannock Chase is in the centre of Staffordshire. In the northeast is part of the Peak District National Park and to the east of Leek, moorland broken up by limestone walls extends across the Manifold valley to the Derbyshire border. The rest of the county is predominantly agricultural, dominated by the river Trent, which rises near Biddulph on the moors north of Stoke-on-Trent, flows south through Stoke and Stone, then tracks eastwards through Rugeley and Burton upon Trent into Derbyshire. Other rivers include the Blithe, Manifold, Sow and Tame. The river Dove forms the boundary with Derbyshire.

Staffordshire became the centre of the Kingdom of Mercia, with Tamworth the site of King Offa's palace, and Lichfield its bishopric, founded by St Chad in AD 669. By the late 10th century the traditional boundary of Staffordshire was being established. After the Industrial Revolution, areas close to Birmingham came under its influence, ultimately leading to the creation of the county of West Midlands in 1974, which took in Walsall, Wolverhampton and West Bromwich, historically all in Staffordshire. In 1997 Stoke-on-Trent became a unitary authority, and the remainder of Staffordshire is now administered by Staffordshire County Council and eight district councils.

The population of Staffordshire is 828,900, and it is expected to grow to around 909,100 by 2026. About three-quarters of the population live in the urban areas around the West Midlands conurbation in the south, where main industries include engineering, iron and steel, rubber goods and leather production. The main centres are Newcastle-under-Lyme (74,427), Tamworth (71,650), Cannock (65,022), Stafford (63,681), Burton upon Trent (43,784), Burntwood (29,205) and Lichfield (28,435).

Staffordshire's industrial base grew out of the engineering, brewing and pottery industries and coal mining. While the latter is no more, all the other industries continue. Engineering businesses include the manufacture of industrial power transformers, domestic boilers and the iconic Bamford Excavators, the JCB diggers, while Burton upon Trent is still noted for brewing and for one of its by-products, Marmite. Over 46,500 jobs (14.5 per cent) are in manufacturing while the service sector provides just under 80 per cent of jobs. Around 10,200 people work in agriculture and 30,000 in tourism, where the top attraction is the Alton Towers theme park, with over 2.5 million visitors every year.

Lichfield is still dominated by the 'Three Ladies of the Vale', the spires of Lichfield Cathedral, a beautiful Gothic building (1190–1350) and the burial place of St Chad. In the Market Square is the Samuel Johnson Birthplace Museum that celebrates the town's most famous son. One of the wildest areas close to the West Midlands conurbation is Cannock Chase, an area of heathland and woodland covering 68 sq km and designated as an Area of Outstanding Natural Beauty; once a Royal hunting ground it is now carefully managed and easy to explore.

Air Rollercoaster, Alton Towers.

Three different types of Marmite, with the original in the middle.

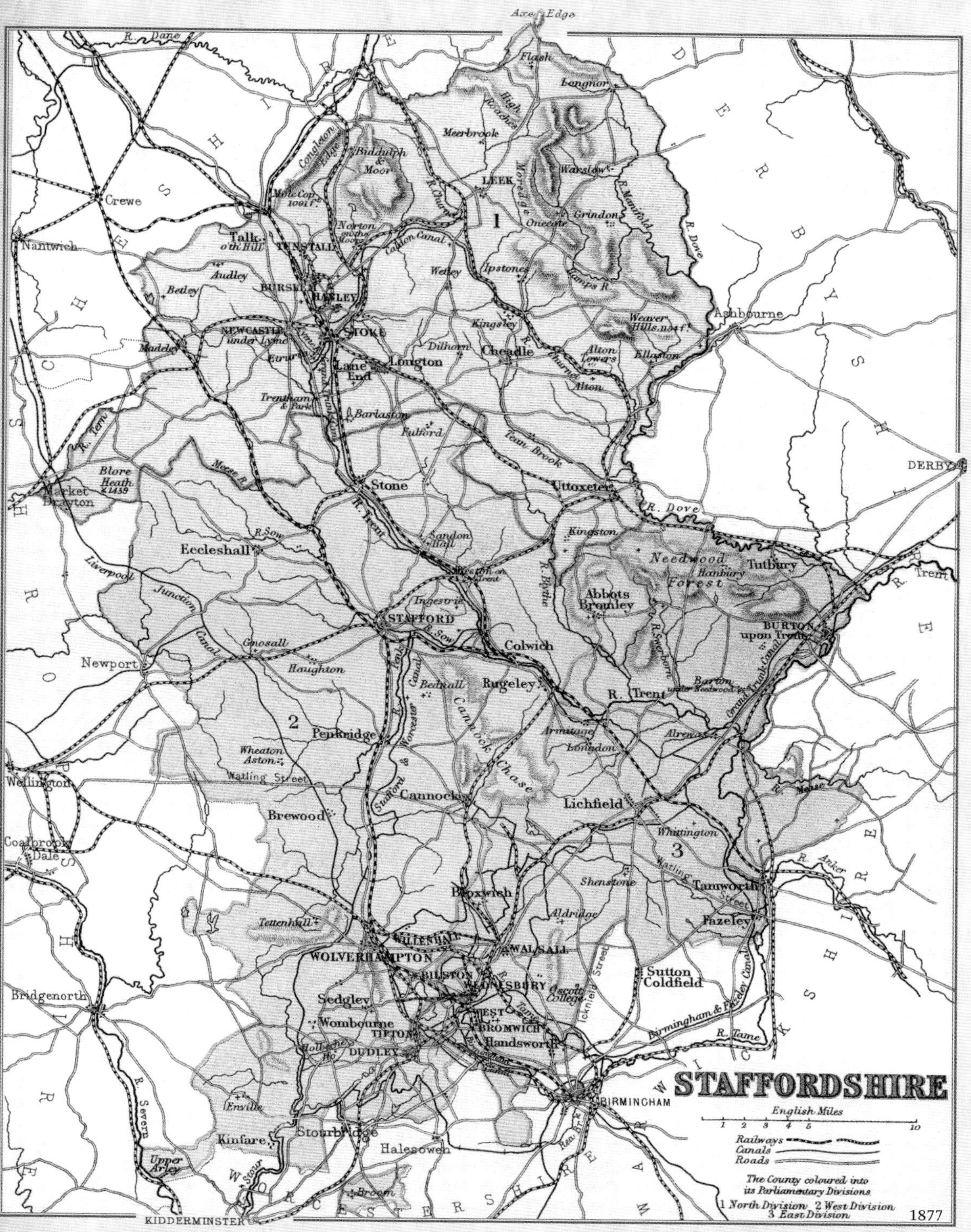

Bartholomew Gazetteer of the British Isles, 1887

STAFFORDSHIRE, *co. in west-midlands of England; bounded NW. and N. by Cheshire, NE. and E. by Derbyshire, SE. by Warwickshire, S. by Worcestershire, and W. by Shropshire; greatest length, N. and S., 50 miles; greatest breadth, E. and W., 34 miles; area, 748,433 ac., pop. 981,013. Staffordshire lies in the basin of the Trent, which traverses the co. from NW. to SE., receiving the Sow (with its tributary the Penk), Tame, Blythe, and Dove. Except in the north, which is chiefly wild moorland, the surface is generally level or gently undulating. About three-fourths of the surface is arable, but much of the soil is of a cold clayey nature; the best land is in the south. Along the banks of the streams are many rich meadows. The new red sandstone occupies the whole of the centre of the co., but in the N. and S. are 2 valuable coal fields – the Pottery coal field and the Dudley coal field, the latter of which is celebrated for the extraordinary thickness of one of its seams, for the excellence of its coal for ironmaking, and the number and richness of its iron ores. Its mineral wealth has given Staffordshire rank as the third co. in England for manufacturing industry, North Staffordshire being the chief seat of the earthenware mfr. in the kingdom, and South Staffordshire one of the chief seats of the iron mfr. The whole county is covered with a network of railways and canals. Staffordshire contains 5 hundreds, 247 pars, and parts of 5 others, the parl. bor. of Wednesbury, the mun. bors. of Burslem, Hanley, Lichfield, and Longton, Newcastle under Lyme, Stafford, Stoke upon Trent, Walsall, West Bromwich, and Wolverhampton, and parts of the mun. bors. of Burton on Trent and Tamworth. It is mostly in the diocese of Lichfield.*

STOKE-ON-TRENT

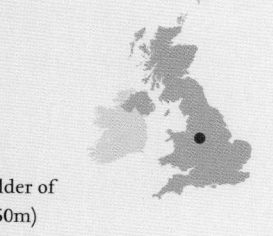

Area Sq Km	93
Area Sq Miles	36
Population	240,100
Highest point	The west shoulder of Meir Heath (250m)

FAMOUS FOR
Arnold Bennett, whose best novels are based here, insisted on calling the area **'the Five Towns'** for he never thought Fenton counted as a town. In his books he renamed the towns as Bursley, Hanbridge, Longshaw, Knype and Turnhill.

FAMOUS PEOPLE
Josiah Wedgwood, potter, born Burslem, 1730.
Josiah Spode, potter, born Lane End, 1733.
Edward John Smith, Captain of the RMS *Titanic*, born Hanley, 1850.
Sir Oliver Joseph Lodge, physicist and inventor, born Penkhull, 1851.
Arnold Bennett, writer, born Hanley, 1867.
Havergal Brian, composer, born Dresden, Stoke, 1876.
Clarice Cliff, pottery designer, born Tunstall, 1899.
Sir Stanley Matthews, footballer, born Hanley, 1915.
Charles Tomlinson, poet, born Stoke, 1927.
Robert Peter (Robbie) Williams, singer, born Tunstall, 1974.

Stoke-on-Trent was formed in 1910 as a federation of six towns: Burslem, Fenton, Hanley, Longton, Stoke and Tunstall, and it took the name Stoke-on-Trent. It gained 'city' status in 1925 and became a unitary authority in 1997. Hanley is where most current city centre activities are located. The area forms 'The Potteries', and is the largest claywear producer in the world, although now it is largely a finishing centre for imported pottery. Josiah Wedgwood built his Etruria works in 1769, soon to be powered by steam engines and mass-producing his elegant designs, now displayed in the award-winning Wedgwood Museum. The pottery industry prospered from around the opening of the Trent and Mersey Canal in 1777, an obvious boon for the safe transport of fragile goods. There are a wide variety of other industries, including steel, engineering, paper, glass and furniture. Stoke-on-Trent is a centre of employment, leisure and shopping for the surrounding areas of north Staffordshire and south Cheshire. It is noted for its land reclamation, which accounts for around 10 per cent of the city area; sites include Festival Park, Central Forest Park and Westport Lake.

"For Hanbridge, though it is the chief of the Five Towns – that vast, huddled congeries of boroughs devoted to the manufacture of earthenware – is a place where the art of attending to other people's business still flourishes in rural perfection."
Arnold Bennett, *Tales of the Five Towns*, 1905

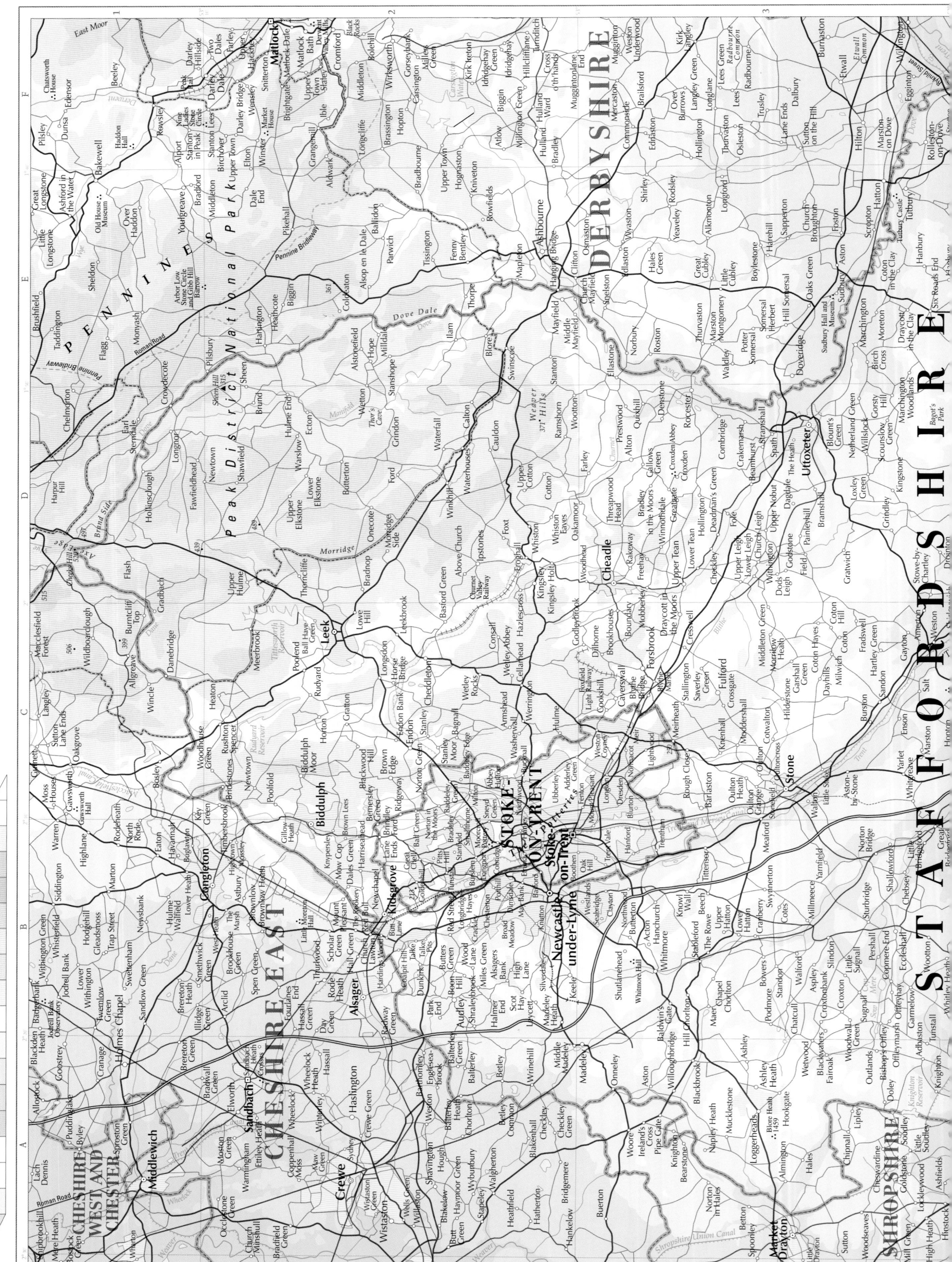

British National Grid projection

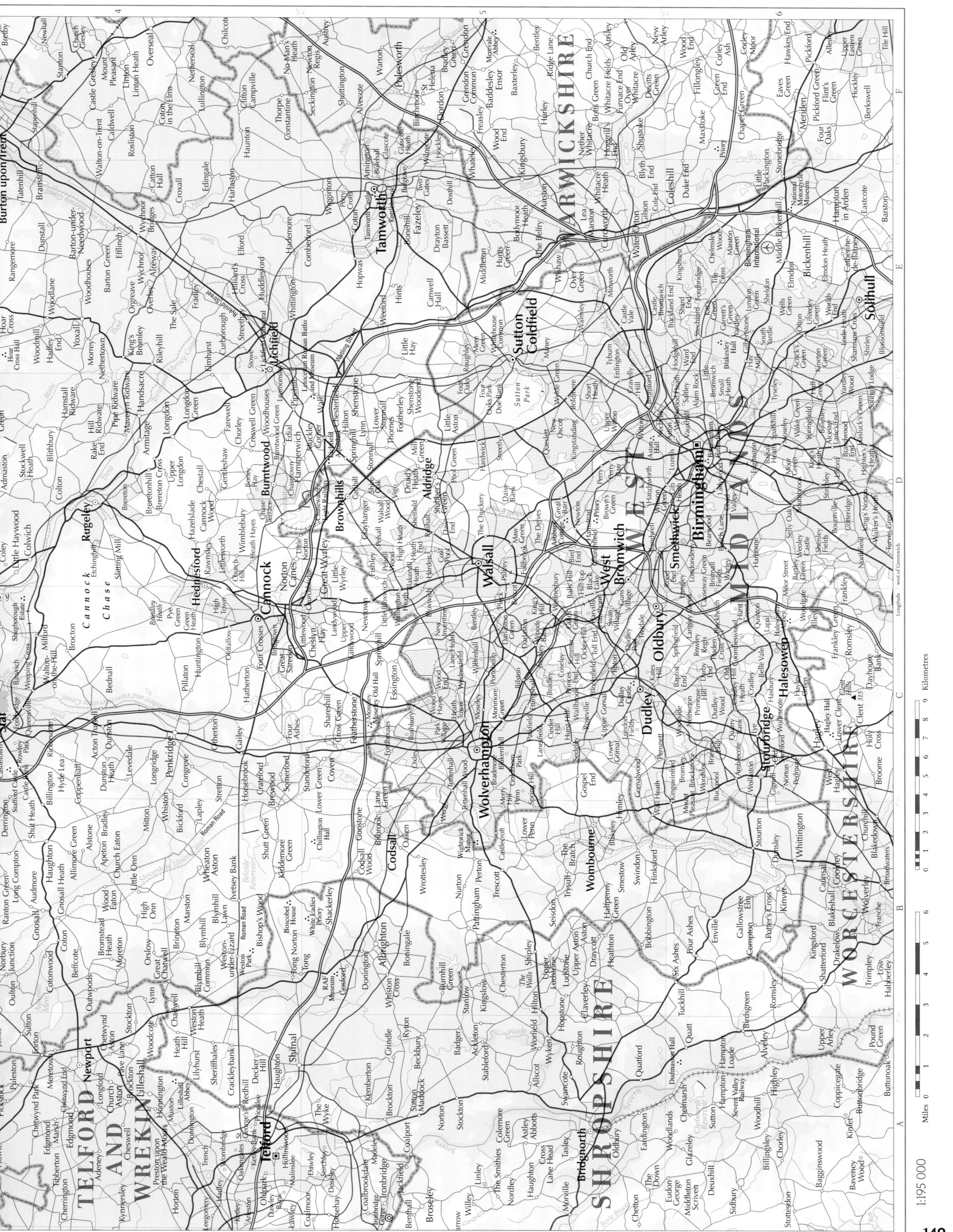

1:195 000

Miles 0   1   2   3   4   5   6

Kilometres 0 1 2 3 4 5 6 7 8 9

WEST MIDLANDS METROPOLITAN COUNTY

Area Sq Km	902
Area Sq Miles	348
Population	2,619,600
Highest point	Turner's Hill (271 m)

Metropolitan Borough Areas

City of Birmingham	268 sq km; 103 sq miles
City of Coventry	99 sq km; 38 sq miles
Dudley	98 sq km; 38 sq miles
Sandwell	86 sq km; 33 sq miles
Solihull	178 sq km; 69 sq miles
Walsall	104 sq km; 40 sq miles
City of Wolverhampton	69 sq km; 27 sq miles

Metropolitan Borough Populations

City of Birmingham	1,016,800
City of Coventry	309,800
Dudley	306,500
Sandwell	289,100
Solihull	205,500
Walsall	255,400
City of Wolverhampton	236,400

Before the Industrial Revolution, the West Midlands were divided between Warwickshire, Staffordshire and Worcestershire. Over the years Birmingham and Coventry and the neighbouring towns began to expand their boundaries at the expense of the surrounding counties. Some rationalization took place in 1966, and then in 1974, the new metropolitan county of West Midlands was created. Within this county were the following metropolitan boroughs: Birmingham (incorporating Sutton Coldfield), Coventry, Solihull (incorporating Meriden), Sandwell (incorporating West Bromwich and Warley), Dudley (incorporating Stourbridge and Halesowen), Wolverhampton, and Walsall (incorporating Aldridge and Brownhills). In 1986 central government removed all the powers of metropolitan counties in England and gave those powers to the boroughs, which then effectively became unitary authorities. The West Midlands continues as a ceremonial county with its own Lord Lieutenant, and some services (such as the police) operate across the whole West Midland region.

The West Midlands has a total population of 2,619,600, and is one of the most urbanized areas in Britain. There are some areas of open countryside, particularly between Coventry and the rest of the conurbation. The highest point in the county is Turner's Hill in Sandwell, with a height of 271 m. Rivers include the Tame and the Cole.

FAMOUS PEOPLE

City of Birmingham
Matthew Boulton, pioneer of the Industrial Revolution, born Birmingham, 1728.
John Cadbury, founder of the Cadbury chocolate business and social reformer, born Birmingham, 1801.
Alexander Parkes, scientist and inventor of the first plastic, born Birmingham, 1813.
Sir Francis Galton, scientist and founder of eugenics, born Sparkbrook, 1822.
Sir Edward Burne-Jones, Pre-Raphaelite painter, born Birmingham, 1833.
Arthur Neville Chamberlain, Conservative, Prime Minister (1937–40), born Edgbaston, 1869.
Dame Barbara Cartland, romantic novelist, born Edgbaston, 1901.
Enoch Powell, politician and classicist, born Birmingham, 1912.
Antony (Tony) Hancock, comedian, born Hall Green, 1924.
Jasper Carrott (*born* Robert Davis), comedian, born Acocks Green, 1945.
John Michael (Ozzy) Osbourne, musician, member of Black Sabbath, born Aston, 1948.
Benjamin Zephaniah, poet, born Handsworth, 1958.

City of Coventry
Dame Ellen Terry, actress, born 1847.
Sir Frank Whittle, inventor of the jet engine, born 1907.
Philip Larkin, poet, born 1922.
Sir Nigel Hawthorne, actor, born 1929.
Frank Ifield, singer, born 1937.
Vincent (Vince) Hill, singer, born 1937.

Pete Waterman, songwriter and musical entrepreneur, born 1947.
Laura Davies, golfer, born 1963.

Dudley
Abraham Darby, iron master first to smelt iron with coke, born 1678.
Francis Brett Young, novelist, born 1884.
Dorothy Round, Wimbledon Ladies Tennis Champion (1934 and 1937), born 1908.
Sir Maurice Wilkes, pioneering computer scientist, born 1913.
Lenworth (Lenny) Henry, comedian, born 1958.

Sandwell
William Perry, boxer, the 'Tipton Slasher', born 1819.
Robert Plant, musician, member of Led Zeppelin, born 1948.
Julie Walters, actress, born 1950.
Frank Skinner, comedian, born 1957.
Denise Lewis, athlete, born 1972.

Solihull
John Wyndham Harrish, science fiction writer, born 1903.
Felicity Kendal, actress, born 1946.
Martin Johnson, rugby player and manager, born 1970.

Walsall
Sir Harry Parkes, diplomat in China and Japan, born 1828.
Jerome Klapka Jerome, author of *Three Men in a Boat*, born 1859.
Neville John (Noddy) Holder, musician, member of Slade, born 1946.
Mark Lewis-Francis, Olympic champion sprinter, born 1982.

City of Wolverhampton
Sir William Bayliss, physiologist, born 1860.
Sir Henry Newbolt, poet, born 1862.
Evelyn Underhill, poet, born Wolverhampton, 1875.
Alfred Noyes, poet, born 1880.
Dame Maggie Teyte (*born* Margaret Tate), opera singer, born 1888.

Victoria Square and Council House, Birmingham.

City of Birmingham

The name of Birmingham comes from the Old English for a 'village of Beorma's (or Beonmund's) people', but who Beorma was history cannot relate.

FAMOUS FOR

Soho House, near Lozells, now a museum, was the home of Matthew Boulton from 1766 to 1809. It was here that meetings of the Lunar Society – a group of prominent scientists, engineers and thinkers – were held. The house was close to the long-since demolished Soho Manufactory, where Boulton pioneered the mass production of a wide range of items, including buttons, buckles and enamelled goods.

Sarehole Mill is a 200-year-old water mill in Hall Green. Over the years it has been used for grinding corn, rolling sheet metal, grinding blades and wire rolling. Once used by Matthew Boulton, it later inspired J R R Tolkien, who was brought up nearby.

The city is home to two of the oldest professional football teams in the country – **Aston Villa**, founded in 1874 and **Birmingham City** in 1875, while the **Edgbaston Cricket Ground** of Warwickshire County Cricket Club opened in 1886.

The **Balti** style of food originated in Birmingham in the 1970s, created by local Pakistanis and Kashmiris and distinguished by the cooking and serving of curries in a cast-iron pan (or balti).

A hamlet at the time of the Domesday Book, Birmingham became known for the manufacture of cutlery in the 16th century. By 1700, it had a population of over 10,000 and was involved a range of manufacturing. It was incorporated as a town in 1838, and just over 50 years later, in 1889, it was raised to the status of a city, and the first Lord Mayor was appointed in 1896. In the decades that followed, neighbouring areas were added to the city, and in 1974, the borough of Sutton Coldfield was merged with the city within the new county of the West Midlands. When the county was abolished in 1986, Birmingham District Council became Birmingham City Council, responsible for all local government services within its area (apart from the emergency services which remain West Midland services).

Birmingham's population is 1,016,800. In the second half of the 20th century its population declined, but this trend was reversed at the start of the 21st century and growth of a further 100,000 by 2026 is estimated. The city's age profile is much younger than the English average – nearly 46 per cent of Birmingham's population is under 30 compared with a national average of just under 37 per cent. Migration has played an important part in the make-up of Birmingham's population, which is now ethnically diverse, with large Pakistani, Indian, Caribbean, African and Bangladeshi communities. It is estimated that by 2024 the ethnic white population will be less than half the total population.

The economy of Birmingham was built on manufacturing – it had the reputation of being the 'city of a thousand trades' – but its economy is now focused on the service sector, which provides 86 per cent of jobs in the city (the highest percentage in the West Midlands). Just 10 per cent are employed in manufacturing. Over a third of those in the service sector work for public bodies, a figure influenced by the three universities based in the city, who between them provide education to over 60,000 students. Finance and other business remains important in the city which saw the founding of Lloyds Bank in 1765 and the Midland Bank (now HSBC) in 1836, while the International Convention Centre and the nearby National Exhibition Centre bring many visitors to the city. Major manufacturing activity includes Jaguar Cars at Castle Bromwich, and Cadbury chocolate at the factory and model village of Bourneville. Birmingham's thriving business centre attracts people from the whole region – over 163,000 people travel into the city to work – while 79,000 Birmingham residents work outside the city, at times stretching the local public transport system. The centre of Birmingham has undergone many recent improvements including the redevelopment of the Bull Ring shopping area, originally the home of Birmingham's market and the site of an unloved 1960s shopping centre.

"They came from Birmingham, which is not a place to promise much, you know. One has not great hopes from Birmingham. I always say there is something direful in the sound."
Jane Austen, *Emma*, 1816

"While neighbouring cities waste the fleeting hours, Careless of art, and knowledge, and the smile Of every Muse, expanding BIRMINGHAM, Illum'd by intellect, as gay in wealth, Commands her aye-accumulating walls From month-to-month, to climb the adjacent hills."
Anna Seward, 1784

Birmingham War Memorial

Part of Birmingham at night.

Bartholomew Gazetteer of the British Isles, 1887

BIRMINGHAM, *mun. bor. and par., on NW. border of Warwickshire, 88 miles SE. of Liverpool and 113 NW. of London by rail – par., 2955 ac., pop. 246,353; mun. bor. (comprising also Edgbaston par. and part of Aston par.), 8400 ac., pop. 400,774. Birmingham is situated on the verge of a great coal and iron dist., nearly in the centre of England, and built on a rising ground, the workshops and warehouses being in the lower parts of the city. Among the principal public buildings are the Town Hall, erected for public meetings and festivals as well as municipal purposes, and containing one of the largest and finest organs in the world; the County Court Buildings (1883); the Institute; the Exchange; the Post Office; and Corporation buildings; a new public gallery of art; a free library, which, with its branches, possesses over 70,000 vols.; Queen's College, for the study of theology, medicine, and arts; the Royal College, for medicine, arts, engineering, and law; Springhill College, for the education of clergymen of the Independents; the Wesleyan College, opened 1881: the College of Science and Art, founded by Sir Josiah Mason and opened in 1880; the Free Grammar School, founded by Edward VI; the R.C. College at Oscott; the R.C. Cathedral of St Chad, &c. It is the principal centre of metal mfrs., consisting of articles in iron, gold, silver, brass, steel, &c., valued at over £5,000,000 per annum. Of these the most important are the mfr. of fire-arms and swords, in some recent years as many as 500,000 gun-barrels being tested annually; the mfrs. of boilers and engines, the largest works, founded in 1757, being at Soho; the steel pen mfr., 900,000,000 pens being annually produced; the making of railway carriages and waggons; jewellery and electro-plate mfrs., which are continually on the increase; iron casting of all kinds; galvanised ironware; fancy-goods in leather, wood, papiér-maché, &c. Erasmus Darwin, poet and naturalist (1731–1802), resided here. Prior to the great civil war, B. had no prominent place in history, and only since 1832 has it taken a conspicuous part in politics.*

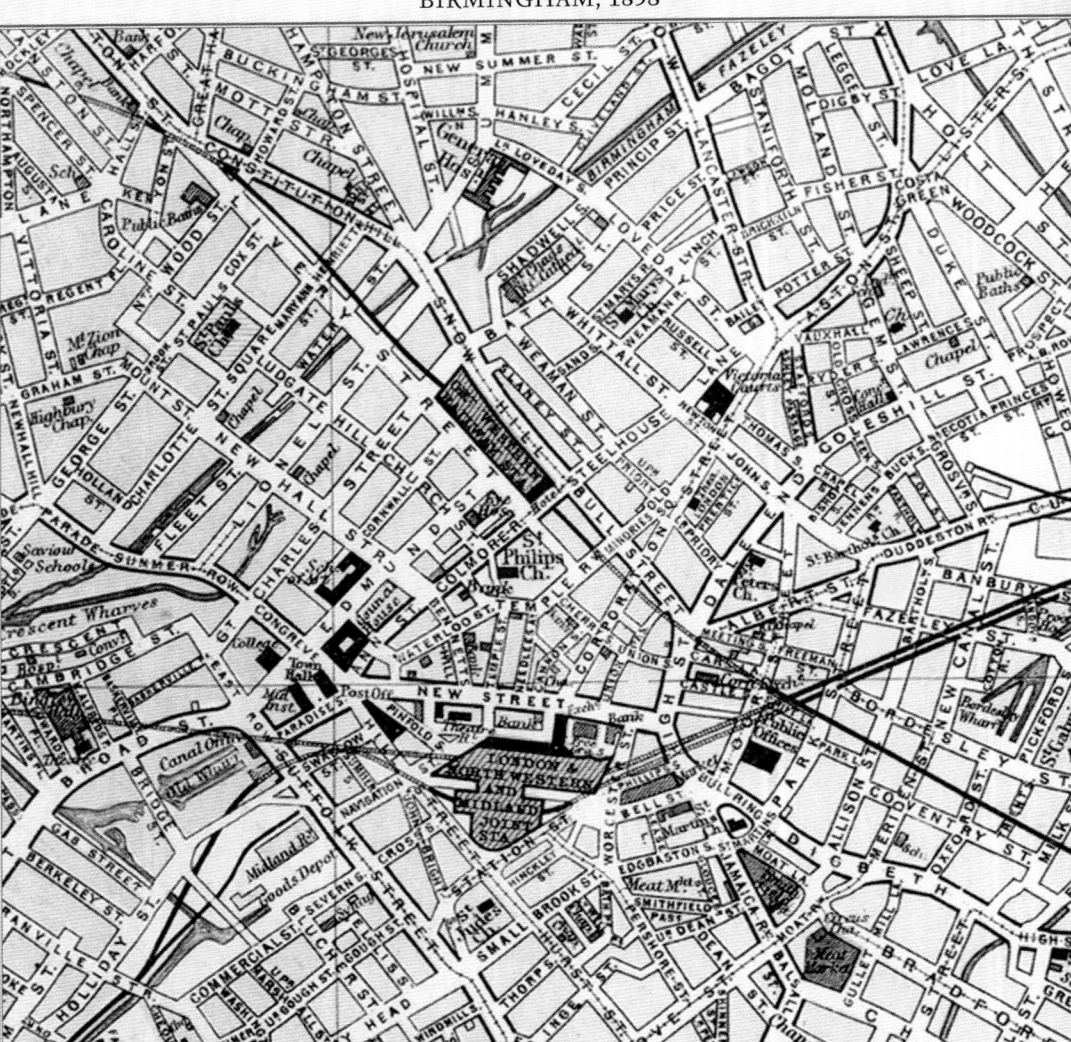
BIRMINGHAM, 1898

Entrance to the Bullring Shopping Centre, Birmingham.

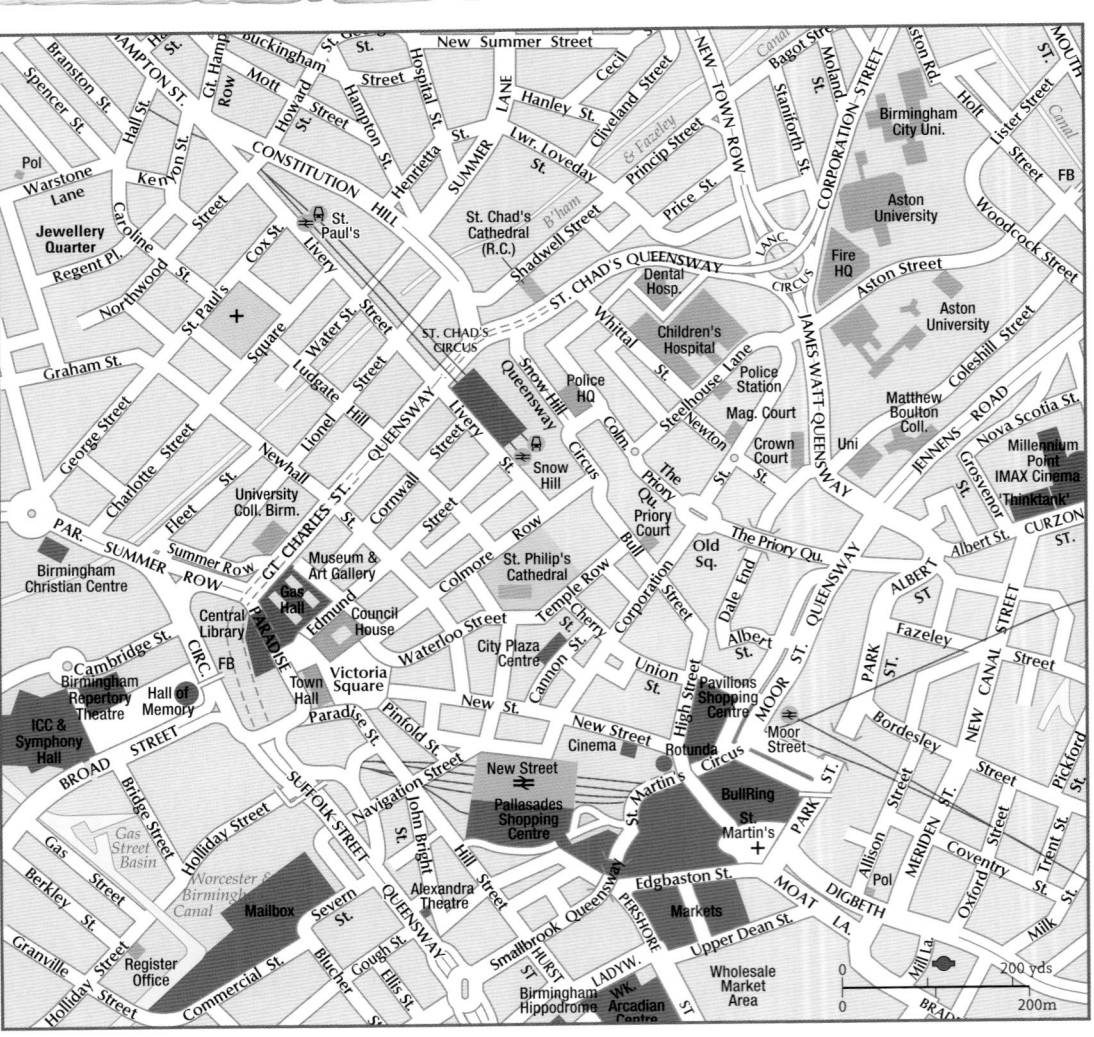
Modern Birmingham

Bartholomew Gazetteer of the British Isles, 1887

COVENTRY, *mun. bor. and market town, N.
Warwickshire, on the Sherbourne and Radford Brook,
18 miles SE. of Birmingham and 94 NW. of London
by rail – mun. bor., 1430 ac., pop. 42,111; 3 Banks, 6
newspapers. Market-day, Friday. C. is an ancient city
(the bishopric, founded in 656, was in 1121 united to the
see of Lichfield), with numerous fine old churches, schools,
and hospitals. It derives its name (Conventre, or convent
town) from a priory built (or rebuilt) in 1043 by Leofric
and his wife Lady Godiva, of whom there is a curious
and well-known legend. Of its fortifications (dismantled
at the Restoration, the town having espoused the side of
the Parliament), two gates and some portions of the wall
still remain. C. was early celebrated for its mfrs. In the
15th century it was noted for its woollens; then for its
dyeing; then for its weaving of camlets, shalloons, &c.
At present its staples are ribbons, silk, and watches; but
it has also woollens, carpets, cotton, art metalwork, and
ironfounding. Numerous fairs are held, and are generally
well attended.*

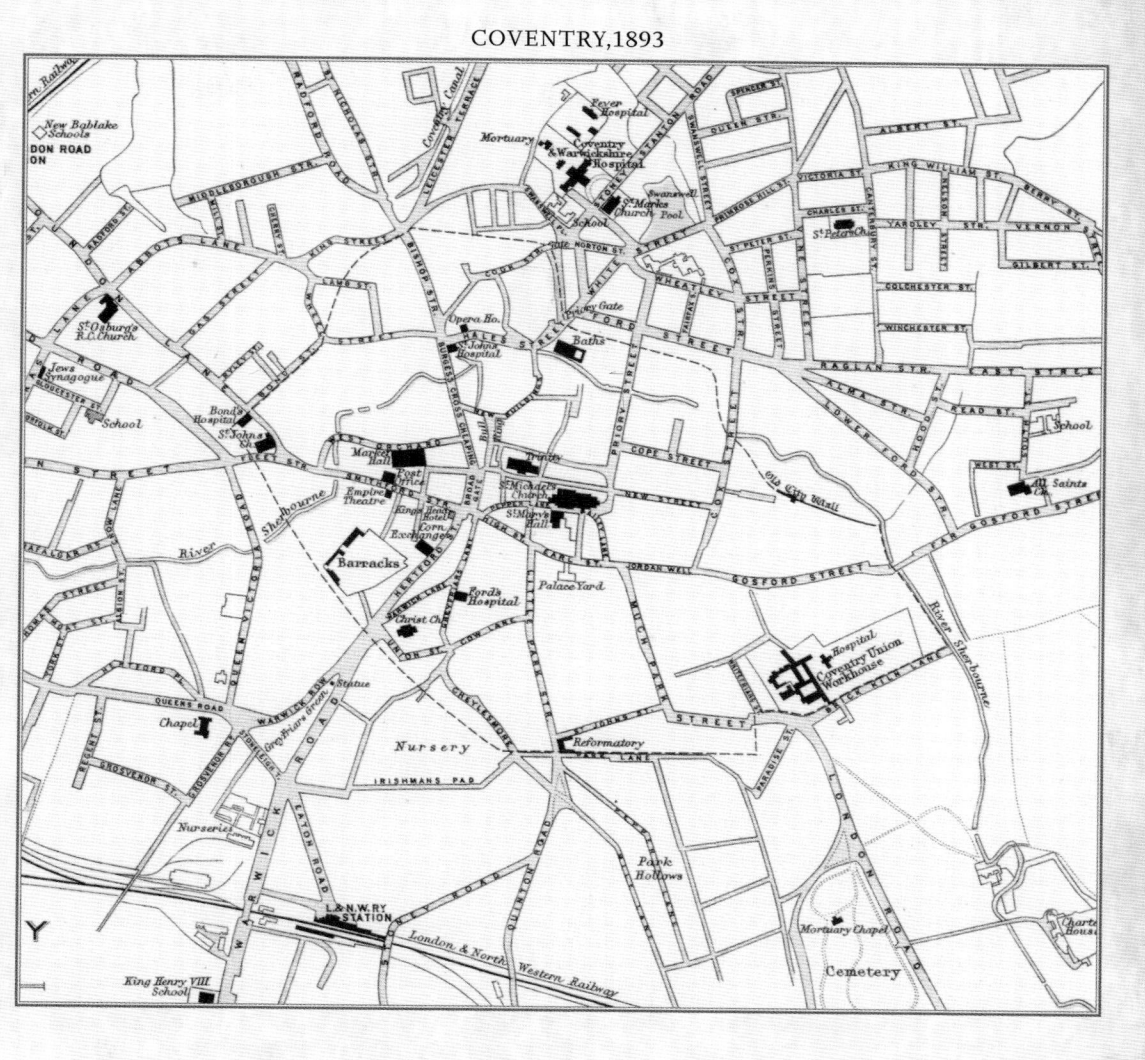

COVENTRY, 1893

Michael's Victory over the Devil' sculpture by Sir Jacob Epstein,
Coventry Cathedral.

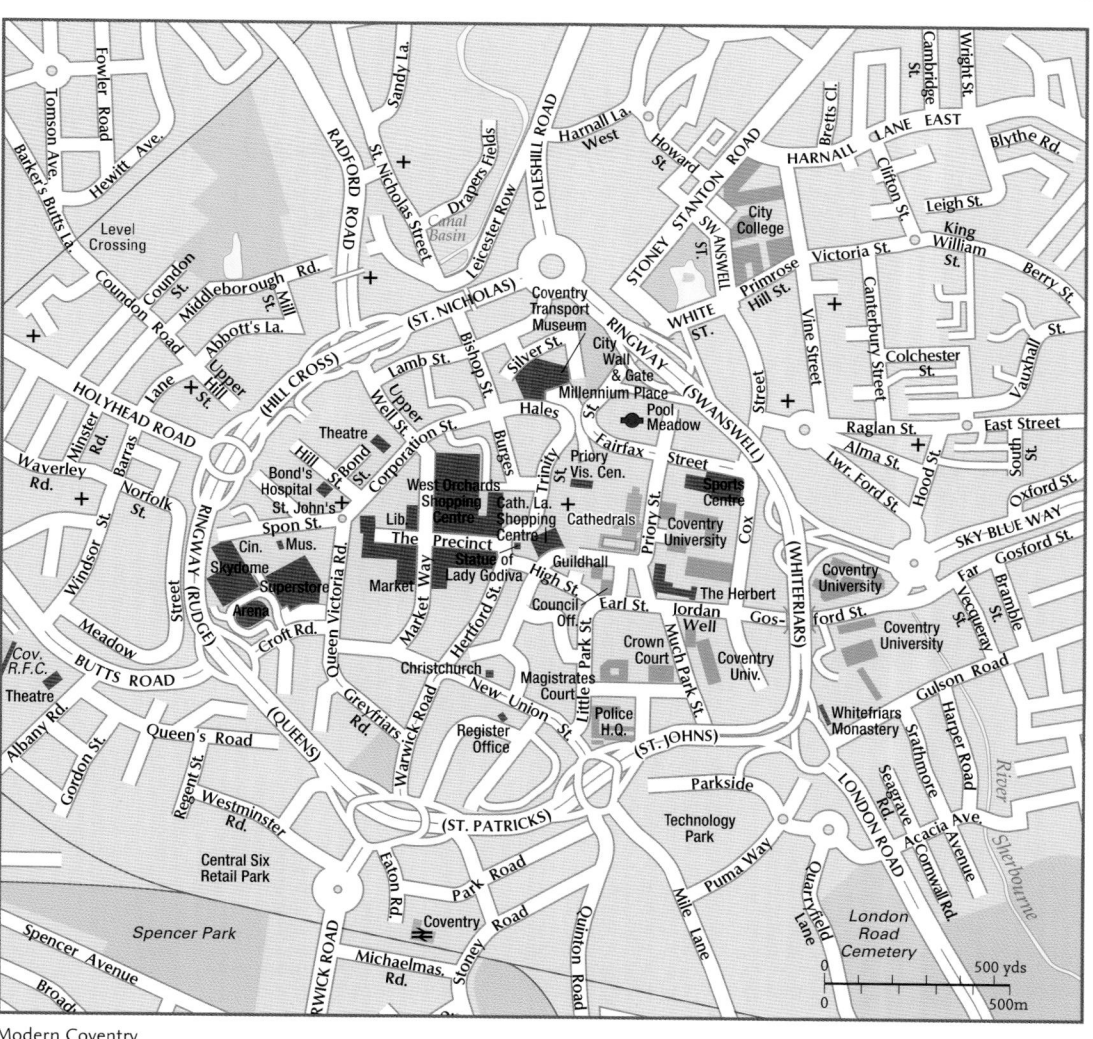

Modern Coventry

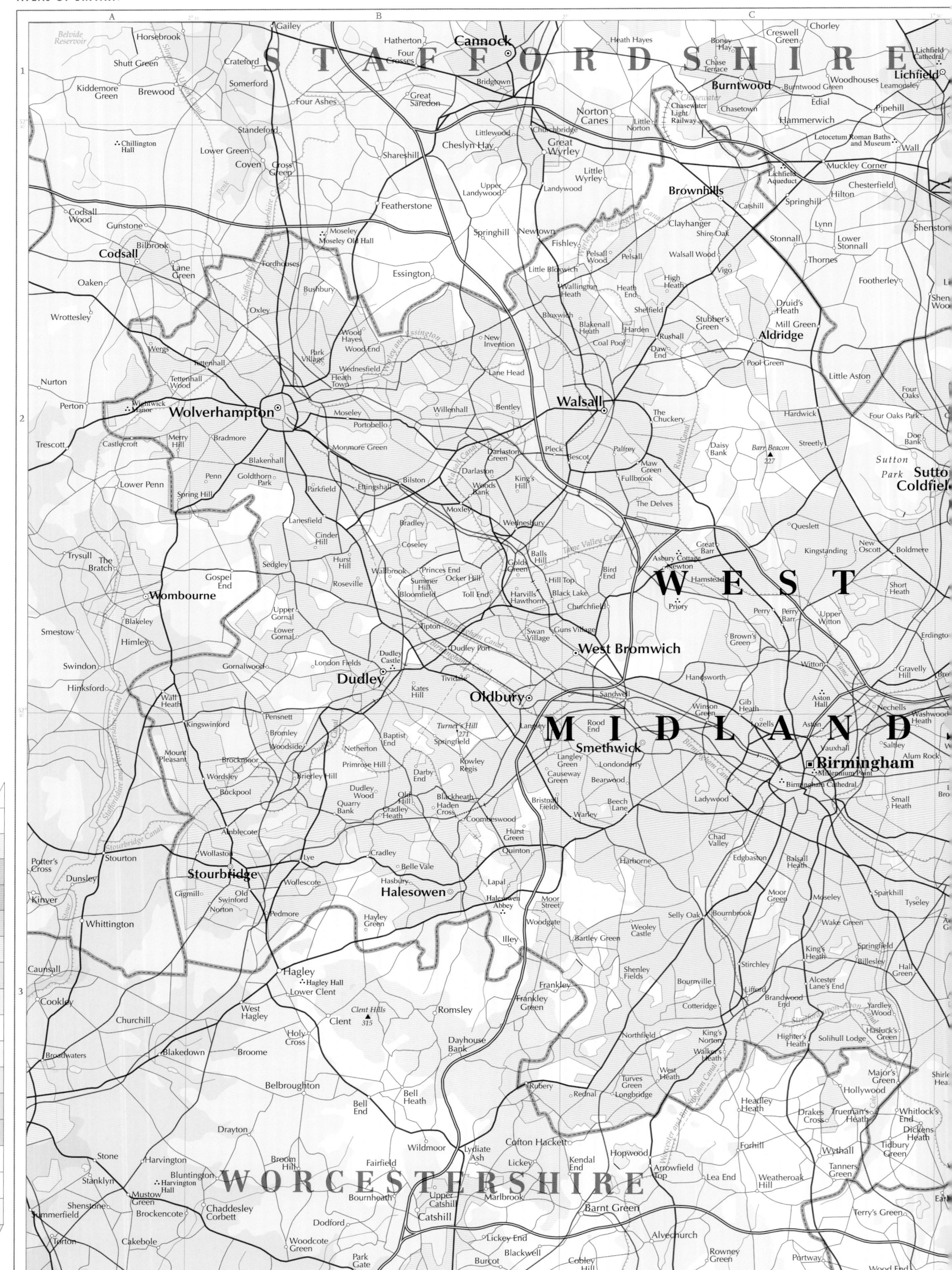

British National Grid projection

1:120 000

City of Coventry

The name of Coventry is thought to come from the old English meaning 'Cofa's Tree', though who Cofa was is unknown.

The city's origins go back to the 7th century but are most closely linked to the foundation of a monastery there by Leofric of Mercia and his wife Godgifu (better known to everyone as Godiva) in 1043. In medieval times it prospered greatly from the cloth trade and it became the fourth largest English city. Industrialization brought it wealth again in the 19th century, with the manufacture of bicycles, sewing machines and, in 1897, the first car made in Britain. This was produced by the Daimler Motor Company, founded the previous year by Harry Lawson. The car industry then dominated Coventry's economic growth until the 1970s. The city suffered from some of the worst bombing of World War II. The raid on the night of 14/15 November 1940 killed 380 people and destroyed many buildings, including the 14th-century cathedral. The new Coventry Cathedral, completed in 1962, was built next to the old cathedral's ruins, and was designed by Sir Basil Spence. The city, while still making London taxis and being home to the design centre for Jaguar cars, now has no mass production of cars; the Peugeot car plant at Ryton was the last to close in 2006. It has diversified, with nearly 83 per cent of jobs in the service sector and 13 per cent in manufacturing. It is home to two universities, for, confusingly, Warwick University, one of Britain's leading universities, is mostly within the city boundaries. Coventry University is in the city centre. Coventry is the second most populous area in the West Midlands. It has an ethnically diverse and relatively young population – and in term time is home to 48,950 full- or part-time university students.

"Not only we, the latest seed of Time,
New men, that in the flying of a wheel
Cry down the past, not only we, that prate
Of rights and wrongs, have loved the people well,
And loathed to see them overtax'd; but she
Did more, and underwent, and overcame,
The woman of a thousand summers back,
Godiva, wife to that grim Earl, who ruled
In Coventry."
Alfred Lord Tennyson, from Godiva, 1842

Coventry Cathedral: on the left are the ruins of the gothic church destroyed during World War II, with Basil Spence's modern building (1956–62) to the right.

London Taxis, the Coventry-made black hackney carriage.

Dudley

Dudley, from the Old English 'a woodland clearing belonging to Dud', is a long-established Black Country town.

The ruins of its Norman castle, enlarged in the 13th and 16th centuries, tower above Dudley Zoological Gardens, established in 1937. The town developed rapidly in the Industrial Revolution, and coal mining, metalworking, glass making and other manufacturing industries flourished in the area. These industries have declined in recent years, but over 18,000 jobs are still in manufacturing. The Black Country Living Museum, near Dudley Castle, relates the story of this area's industrialization, using rebuilt historic buildings. The nearby Wren's Nest is a limestone ridge renowned as a source of Silurian coral reef fossils. Over 700 different types of fossil have been discovered here, of which eighty-six are unique to the site. There are many species of trilobites including *Calymene blumenbachii*, or the 'Dudley Bug', which used to feature on the town's coat of arms. Wren's Nest shows physical evidence of the limestone quarrying industry (limestone is used to make iron) and it was Britain's first National Nature Reserve for geology. The Red House Glass Cone in Stourbridge is a further reminder of the industrial heritage of the area. This is an 18th-century cone furnace which was used in glass making for 140 years until 1936, and is now a museum.

Dudley Castle

One of the many trilobite fossils found near Dudley.

"Our earth was designed to be a seminary for young angels, but the devil has certainly fixed upon this spot for his own nursery garden and hot-house."
Robert Southey, 1807

Sandwell

o the west of Birmingham the metropolitan borough
Sandwell includes West Bromwich, Smethick,
...pton, Wednesbury, Oldbury and Rowley Regis. The
...me Sandwell (after the ruined Sandwell Priory in the
...ndwell Valley, an area of 720 hectares of open land
...the borough) was chosen for the district rather than
...at of any of the individual settlements. The towns
...Sandwell are typical 'Black Country' towns with a
...anufacturing history stretching back over 200 years.
...ey have an envied reputation for producing objects
...all sizes and for all purposes from iron and steel.
...methick is the site of the Soho Foundry, where Matthew
...oulton and James Watt produced the first steam
...gines that powered the factories of the Industrial
...volution. The towns of Sandwell have suffered
...sproportionately from the decline in manufacturing
...dustry, but over 21 per cent of jobs are still in this
...ctor, the highest figure in the West Midlands. In West
...omwich, Oak House, a black-and-white half-timbered
...ilding dating from 1450, is a museum reflecting
...e period in which it was constructed. Bishop Asbury
...ottage in Great Barr is the birthplace of Francis Asbury
...745–1816), who established Methodism in America.

Oak House, West Bromwich.

Solihull

...lihull, whose name probably comes from the Old
...glish for 'muddy hill', is the least urban of the West
...idlands boroughs, with 70 per cent of the area being in
...e Green Belt.
...hen it was created the town of Solihull gained the
...lage of Meriden and the strip of open countryside

between Coventry and the rest of the West Midlands
conurbation. Solihull, while primarily a residential area,
is home to the main Land Rover factory. It is also the site
of Birmingham International Airport – serving over 9
million passengers a year – and the National Exhibition
Centre – the major national and international exhibition

facility for the whole of Britain. The largest employment
sector, providing 26 per cent of jobs, is finance, IT and
other business activities. For centuries the village of
Meriden was claimed as the centre of England, but in
2002 the Ordnance Survey gave this honour to Lindley
Hall Farm near Fenny Drayton in Leicestershire.

Walsall

...alsall's name comes from the Old English 'nook of
...d of a person called Wahl'.
...s the most northerly metropolitan borough in the
...est Midlands and, as well as Walsall, the borough
...cludes Willenhall, Bloxwich, Brownhills and Aldridge.
...small medieval market town, Walsall quickly
...veloped in the Industrial Revolution as coal, iron
...d steel and the local speciality of leather working
...rticularly the making of saddles – the nickname
...the local football team is 'The Saddlers') industries
...veloped. The leather industry survives, together
...h a wide range of manufacturing and distribution
...sinesses. Many motorway travellers will be familiar
...h the RAC control centre situated here, next to
...e M6 motorway. Walsall's New Art Gallery opened
...2000 in an award-winning building. It houses an
...ernationally renowned collection of 20th century art
...nated by the widow of the sculptor Jacob Epstein.

A canal-side cottage in Walsall.

City of Wolverhampton

...olverhampton – the name meaning 'Wulfrum's high
...m' – owes its origin to Wulfruna, a Mercian lady who
...unded a monastery here in 944.
...medieval times the cloth industry brought wealth to
...e town, shown by the large parish church of St Peter's.
...1848 it was incorporated as a borough and, in 2000,
...was raised to 'city' status as a Millennium City. Like
...neighbouring towns, it developed in the Industrial
...volution through coal mining, iron, steel and
...gineering, and it also boasted a major lock-making
...dustry – Chubb locks are still made in the city. While
...re is also significant aerospace, construction and
...wing, the service sector is now the most important
...t of the economy, helped by the staffing of the
...iversity of Wolverhampton. This was established
...1992, but its origins date back to 19th century
...chanics Institutes. The city is close to the national
...otorway system and has good railway and Midland
...tro connections. As with most of the West Midlands,
...lverhampton's population has only recently started
...rise, having declined since the 1970s, and a 5 per
...nt increase is expected by 2031. The city is ethnically
...erse; over 7.5 per cent of the population are Sikhs,

The Red Arrows in flight at the 2009 Cosford Air Show,
Wolverhampton.

Wightwick Manor, Wolverhampton.

making it one of Britain's largest Sikh communities. On
the outskirts of Wolverhampton is Wightwick Manor,
a late Victorian house built for Theodore Mander, a
local paint manufacturer. This is probably Britain's best

surviving Arts and Crafts home, having decorations by
William Morris, Edward Burne-Jones, Dante Gabriel
Rossetti, glass by Charles Kempe and ceramics by William
de Morgan, compete with a period garden design.

LEICESTERSHIRE

Area Sq Km	2,084
Area Sq Miles	805
Population	645,800
County town	Leicester
Highest point	Bardon Hill (278 m), near Coalville
Districts	Blaby; Charnwood; Harborough; Hinckley and Bosworth; Melton; North West Leicestershire; Oadby and Wigston

Leicestershire takes its name from Leicester, 'Roman town of the Ligore', who were the local inhabitants whose name may come from the river Leire. More fanciful was the idea that it was named after the mythical King Leir, whose story was the inspiration behind Shakespeare's King Lear.

FAMOUS FOR

On 22 August 1485, near the town of Market Bosworth was fought the **Battle of Bosworth Field**, where the Yorkists, under Richard III, were defeated by the Lancastrians, under Henry Tudor. Richard III was killed on the battlefield and Henry Tudor, as Henry VII, became the first Tudor monarch.

The **National Forest** was established in 1990 linking the ancient Charnwood Forest in Leicestershire with Needwood Forest in Staffordshire. Forest cover has increased from 6 per cent in 1991 to 18 per cent in 2009 by the planting of 7 million trees.

There are two delicacies that can only be made in parts of Leicestershire and neighbouring counties – **Melton Mowbray Pork Pies** and **Stilton Cheese** (which is named after a village in Cambridgeshire, where Stilton cheese now can not be made).

Since 1784, **Loughborough** has been home to the Taylor bell foundry, now the largest in the world. The largest bell in Britain, 'Great Paul' at St Paul's Cathedral, weighing 17 tonnes, was cast here in 1881.

Sir Frank Whittle made his first jet engines at **Lutterworth**, and one of these engines powered the first jet-powered flight of the Gloster E.28/39 at Cranwell in Lincolnshire on 15 May 1941.

Stony Cove in Stoney Stanton was originally a granite quarry, but when production ceased, the quarry filled with water and it is now the National Diving Centre, with diving taking place to a depth of 36 m.

FAMOUS PEOPLE

Hugh Latimer, Protestant cleric burnt at the stake (1555), born Thurcaston, c.1485.
Lady Jane Grey, Queen of England for nine days in 1553, born Bradgate, 1537.
Robert Burton, author, *The Anatomy of Melancholy*, born Lindley, 1577.
George Villiers, 1st Duke of Buckingham, statesman and Royal favourite, born Brooksby, 1592.
John Cleveland, Cavalier poet, born Loughborough, 1613.
George Fox, founder the Society of Friends (the Quakers), born Fenny Drayton, 1624.
Robert Bakewell, agricultural reformer, born Dishley 1725.
John Ferneley, animal painter, born Thrussington, 1782.
Jenny Pitman, racehorse trainer and novelist, born Hoby, 1946.

Leicestershire is mostly a county of low, rolling hills. East and west of Leicester are areas of higher ground, notably Charnwood Forest, which includes the county's highest point, Bardon Hill. The river Soar, which rises near Hinckley, traverses the county from south to north, to join the Trent, while the river Welland forms part of the boundary with Northamptonshire to the south.

Leicestershire grew up around Leicester, at the heart of the shire. The town was mentioned in the Anglo-Saxon Chronicle and the shire in the Domesday Book. Its basic borders have remained very similar ever since. In 1974, Rutland became part of Leicestershire, but in 1997 it became a separate county again, and, at the same time, Leicester became a unitary authority.

The population of Leicestershire is 645,800 and it is expected to grow by just over 10 per cent by 2029, with the greatest growth in the districts of Harborough and North West Leicestershire. Leicester is by far the largest settlement (330,574) and has seen many people move out of the city to live in the surrounding areas. The major settlements in Leicestershire are Loughborough (55,258), Hinckley (43,246), Wigston, a suburb of Leicester (33,116), Coalville (32,124), Melton Mowbray (25,554), Oadby, also a suburb of Leicester (22,679), Market Harborough (20,127), Shepshed (12,882) and Ashby de la Zouch (11,409).

The west of the county is largely industrial with light engineering, hosiery and footwear. Around Loughborough, drawing on its prestigious university, significant industrial research activity, including Cen – the UK's first Centre of Excellence for low carbon ar fuel cell technologies. The county also hosts fashion design studios for major retailers and significant food production. Over 15 per cent of the jobs in the county are in manufacturing and 76.5 per cent in the service sector, over a quarter of whom work in public administration, education and health.

Part of the legacy left by the Roman occupation of Leicestershire are Watling Street and the Fosse Way which dissect the county. More recently the M1 cut across the county. Close to the motorway in the south Lutterworth has become a major distribution centre, while in the north Castle Donnington is the site of Ea Midlands Airport, used by 5 million passengers a year

The east of the county is rural, once the home to much sheep farming that provided wool for the weavi industry that initially started Leicestershire's industri development. It was at Dishley, near Loughborough, t Robert Bakewell in the late 18th century undertook hi work in animal breeding that revolutionized the qual of Britain's livestock and was instrumental in feeding the rapidly growing population.

Loughborough Carillon and War Memorial. The bells were made at the Taylor foundry.

Tornado steam train at Loughborough on the Great Central Railway, the UK's only double track main line heritage railway.

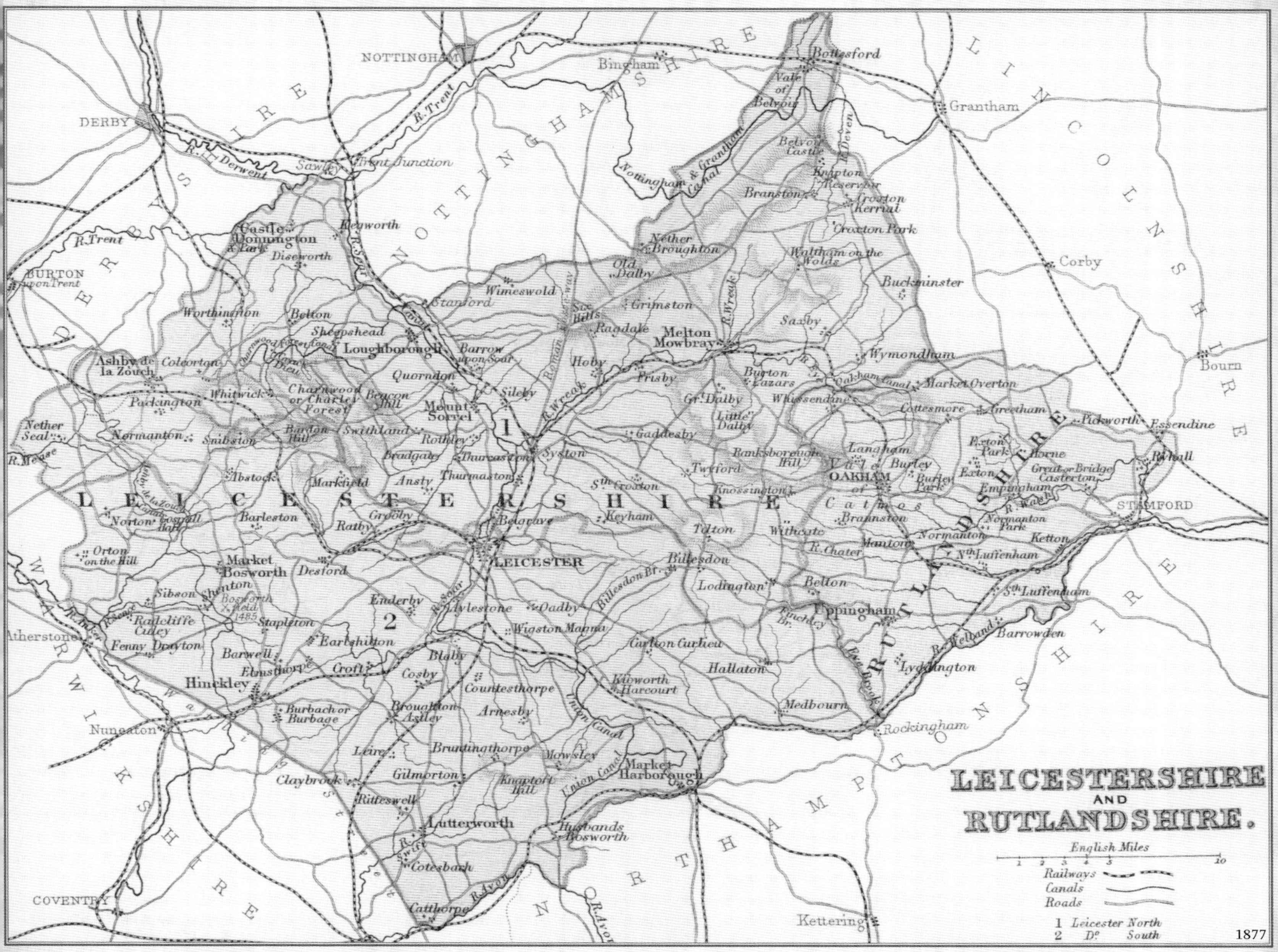

LEICESTERSHIRE
AND
RUTLANDSHIRE.

English Miles

Railways
Canals
Roads

1 Leicester North
2 Do South

1877

Bartholomew Gazetteer of the British Isles, 1887

LEICESTERSHIRE, inland co. of England, bounded N. by Notts, E. by Lincolnshire and Rutland, SE. by Northamptonshire, SW. by Warwickshire, and NW. by Derbyshire; greatest length, about 44 miles; greatest breadth, about 40 miles; area, 511,907 ac., pop. 321,258. Low undulating hills cover the surface of the county, the highest elevation being Bardon Hill (902 ft.), in the Charnwood range. Charnwood Forest, in the NW., is now nearly destitute of trees. The principal rivers are tributaries of the Trent, which flows in the NW. of the county; these are the Soar, Wreak, Anker, Devon, and Mease. The Avon and Welland flow in the S. Two canals, the Union and the Grand Union, are connected with the Grand Junction Canal. Much of the soil is loamy, and the richest districts are kept in pasture, upon which are reared the varieties of sheep and cattle for which the county is famous. Dairy farms are numerous, especially in the vicinity of Melton Mowbray where the well-known Stilton cheese is largely produced. Leicestershire consists mostly of the new reel sandstone formation. The coal measures have a total area of about 15 square miles, the most productive mines being in the neighbourhood of Ashby de la Zouch. Hosiery is the leading mfr., the wool employed being that of Leicestershire sheep. The county has 6 hundreds, 332 pars, and 8 parts, and the municipal bor. of Leicester. It is almost entirely in the diocese of Peterborough.

RUTLAND (or Rutlandshire), inland co. of England, bounded W. and N. by Leicestershire, NE. by Lincolnshire, and SE. by Northamptonshire; greatest length, N. and S., 18 miles; greatest breadth, E. and W., 17 miles; area, 94,889 ac., pop. 21,434. Rutland is the smallest county in England. The surface is diversified by gently rising hills and fine valleys, and is watered by the Eye Brook, the Chater, and the Gwash, flowing into the Welland, which forms the south-eastern boundary. The soil is in general loamy and fertile; in the east part it is chiefly in tillage, and in the west part under grass. The chief crops are wheat and barley. Great attention is paid to rearing choice breeds both of cattle and sheep. In the Vale of Catmose, round Oakham, are tracts of woodland, the remains of old forests. The prevailing rock is limestone. Rutland was made a county by Henry III., and gives the title of duke to the family of Manners. It contains 5 hundreds, 57 pars, and part of another, and the market-towns of Oakham (where the assizes are held) and Uppingham. It is in the diocese of Peterborough.

dge of Stilton Cheese.

Battle of Bosworth 1485 model, Bosworth Battlefield Heritage Centre and Museum.

A Melton Mowbray Pork Pie.

LEICESTER

Area Sq Km 73
Area Sq Miles 28
Population 294,700
Highest point Nether Hall (110 m)

FAMOUS FOR

Leicester was the home of **Daniel Lambert**.
His epitaph records his fame:
In Remembrance of that PRODIGY in NATURE
DANIEL LAMBERT a native of LEICESTER who
was possessed of an exalted and convivial Mind and,
in personal Greatness had no COMPETITOR: He
measured three Feet one Inch round the LEG and
nine Feet four Inches round the BODY and weighed
FIFTY TWO STONE ELEVEN POUNDS! He departed
this Life on the 21st of June 1809 AGED 39 YEARS.

FAMOUS PEOPLE

Joseph Merrick, 'the elephant man', born 1862;
Charles Percy (CP) Snow, scientist, administrator
and novelist, born 1905; **Joe Orton**, playwright, born
1933; **Graham Chapman**, comedian and writer, born
1941; **Julian Barnes**, writer, born 1946; **Sue Townsend**,
writer, born 1946; **Gary Lineker**, footballer, born 1960.

*"Leicester is an ancient large and populous town.
They have considerable manufacture carried on here, and
in several of the market towns round for the weaving of
stockings by frames; and one would scarce think it possible
so small an article of trade could employ such multitudes
of people as it does."* Daniel Defoe, 1725

The Romans first settled on the site of modern-day
Leicester establishing the important town of *Ratae
Corieltavorum*, and some remains of the public baths
remain as the Jewry Wall. In Norman times it came
under control of the earls of Leicester, based at its
castle. The most renowned earl was Simon de Montfort,
and, although one of the city's universities is named
after him, he had little connection with the place. Its
industry was based on hosiery and footwear. In 1889 it
became a county borough and over time its boundaries
spread out into the surrounding countryside. It became
a unitary authority in 1997. Its traditional industries
attracted many immigrants immediately after World
War II, and it is now Britain's most ethnically diverse
city, with over 40 per cent of the population coming
from ethnic minorities – 28 per cent of the population
are Gujarati Indians. Around 81.5 per cent of jobs in the
city are in the service sector, of which around 40 per cent
are in the public sector, influenced by the presence of
two universities and national institutions such as the
National Space Centre.

Jewry Wall and St Nicholas Church.

Bridge over the River Soar, Abbey Park.

RUTLAND

Area Sq Km 934
Area Sq Miles 152
Population 39,200
County town Oakham
Highest point East of Cold Overton Park Wood (197 m)

**The name of Rutland comes from the Old English
'Roteland', the estate of an unknown person called
Rota.**

FAMOUS FOR

Titus Oates was born in **Oakham** in 1649. An
inveterate liar and conspirator, he fabricated a
Catholic plot to murder Charles II. The so-called
'Popish Plot' led to the execution of innocent
Catholics before Oates was exposed.

The village of **Stoke Dry** was the ancestral home of
the Digby family. St Andrew's Church, which dates
from the 13th century, contains rare medieval wall
paintings, but there is no evidence that Sir Everard
Digby and his co-conspirators met in the room above
the porch to plan the Gunpowder Plot of 1605.

Normanton Church was the private chapel of the
Normanton Estate, and was threatened with flooding
when Rutland Water was created. Funds were raised
to build a protective bank around the building and
the floor was raised to the bottom of the windows
to bring it above the waterline. It is now a museum
about Rutland Water.

*"Rutlandshire, remarkable for being the least county in
England."*
Daniel Defoe, 1725

Rutland is Britain's smallest shire county, but it gained
this status rather later than the surrounding counties.
After the Norman Conquest, it became the personal
possession of the queen, first being described as a
county when King John granted the lands to Queen
Isabella in 1204. In 1974, amid much protest, Rutland
became a district in the enlarged Leicestershire
County Council, an arrangement which lasted until
1997, when Rutland once again became independent
as a unitary authority and ceremonial county, even
though its population was regarded as being too small
for such a status. The motto of the county 'Multum in
Parvo' (Much in Little) is singularly appropriate for a
county that is at most 29 km by 27 km. The population
of Rutland is 39,200, which is expected to grow to
49,200 by 2031. The two towns in Rutland are Oakham

(9,620) and Uppingham (3,947). Nearly 80 per cent of
jobs are in the service sector, while nearly 14 per cent
are in manufacturing, including engineering, cement
making, plastics and the clothing industries. Tourism
is also a significant employer. The centre of Rutland
is dominated by Rutland Water, a huge reservoir – in
England only Windermere has a greater surface area –
completed in the late 1970s to meet the growing need
of Peterborough and the East Midlands. It is now much
used for recreation and also provides an important
nature reserve – ospreys have been breeding here
since 2001. The county is home to two public schools,
at Uppingham and Oakham, both founded in 1584
by Robert Johnson, Archdeacon of Leicester, as free
grammar schools.

Great Hall of Oakham Castle.

Bartholomew Gazetteer of the British Isles, 1887

LEICESTER, *mun. bor., market town, and co. town of Leicestershire, on river Soar, 29 m. NW. of Northampton and 99 m. NW. of London by rail, 3200 ac., pop. 122,376; 5 Banks, 8 newspapers. Market-days, Wednesday and Saturday. It has been supposed that Leicester derived its name from the British King Lear. As a Roman station it was known as Rates or Ratiscorim. The first charter of incorporation was granted by King John. Leicester is the chief seat of the English worsted hosiery trade; besides which there are iron foundries, mfrs. of elastic webbing, sewing cotton, boots and shoes, lace, &c., also agricultural implements. The town has water communication by the Leicestershire and Northamptonshire Union Canal and the river Soar. At the Blue Boar Inn (now demolished) Richard III. slept on the night before the battle of Bosworth Field (1485); and at Leicester Abbey (now in ruins) Cardinal Wolsey died in 1530.*

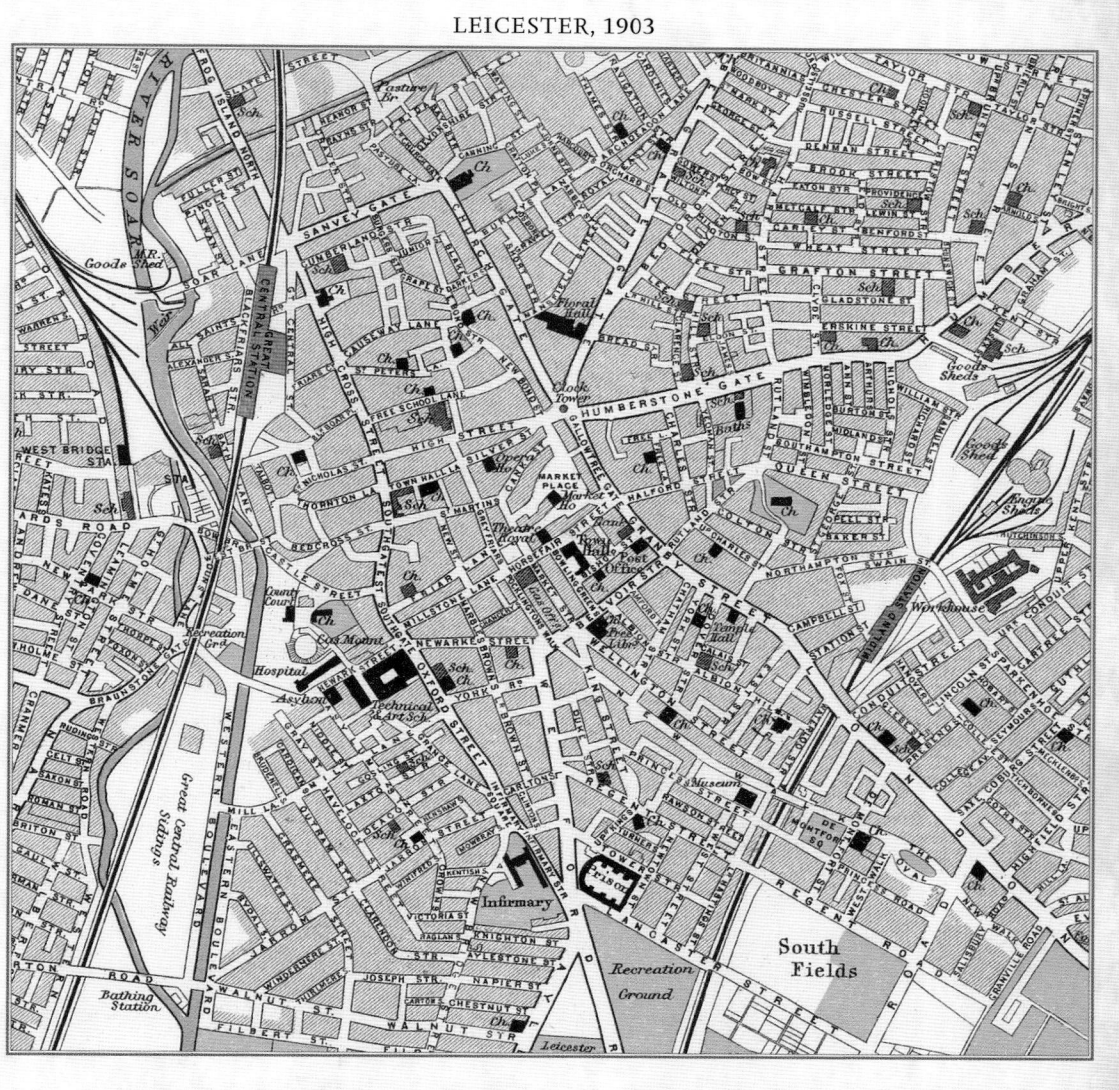

LEICESTER, 1903

ter-spotted woodpecker, Rutland Water.

anton Church, Rutland Water.

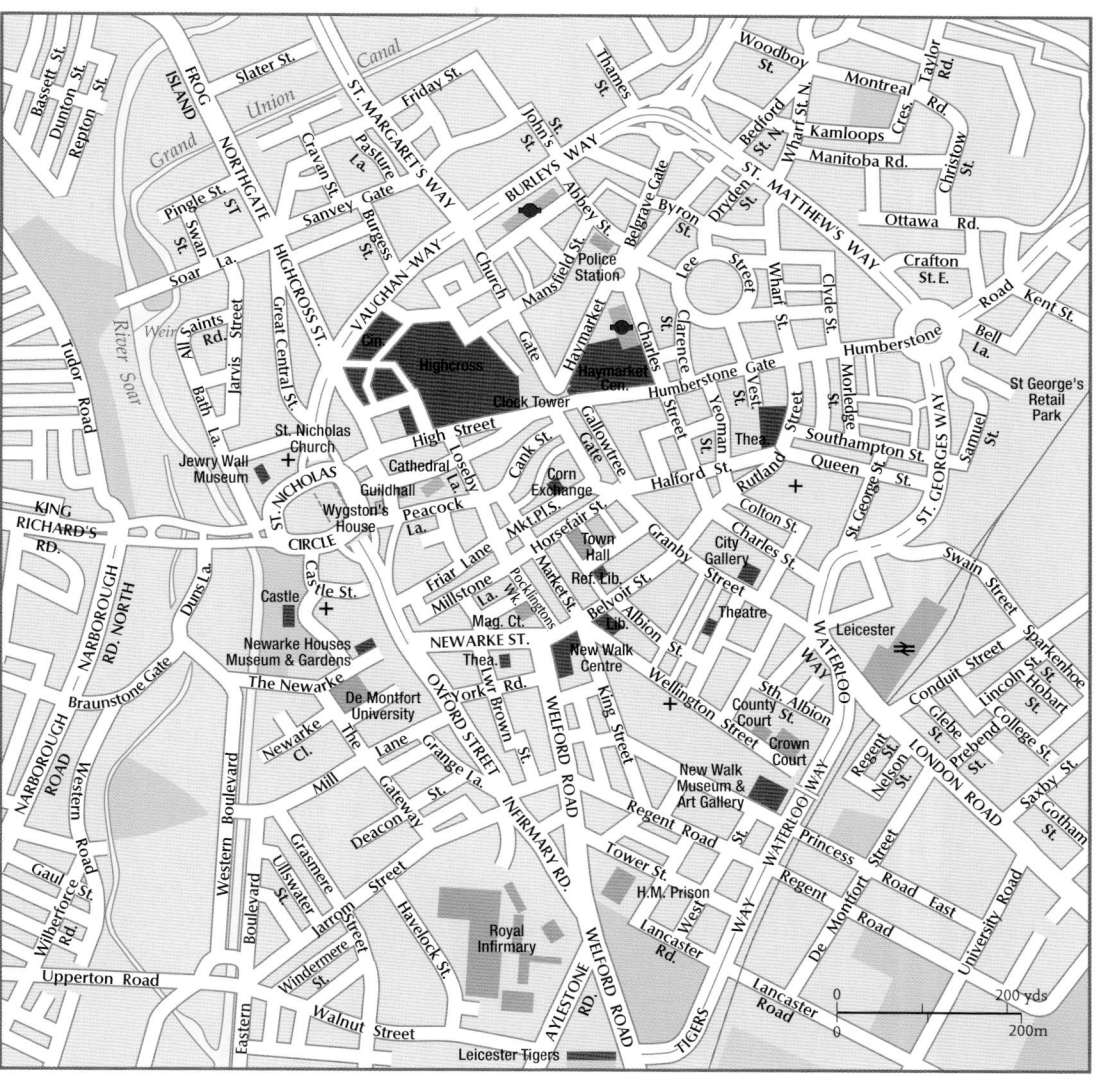

Modern Leicester

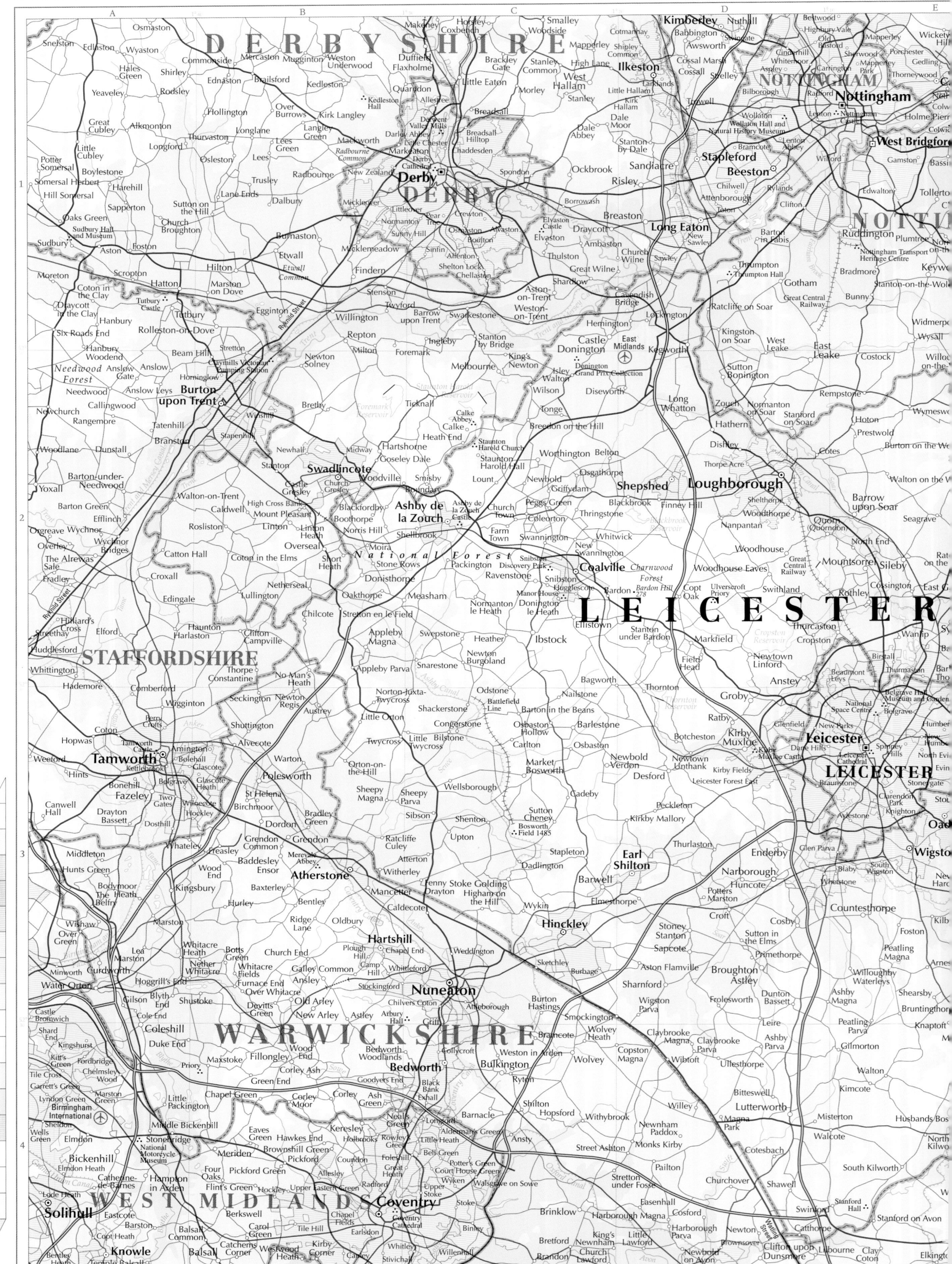

British National Grid projection

NORFOLK

Area Sq Km	5,498
Area Sq Miles	2,123
Population	850,800
County town	Norwich
Highest point	Beacon Hill (103 m) near West Runcton
Districts	Breckland; Broadland; Great Yarmouth; King's Lynn and West Norfolk; North Norfolk; Norwich; South Norfolk

Norfolk takes its name from the Old English 'Nordfolc', the 'northern folk' of the East Angles, in contrast to Suffolk.

FAMOUS FOR

An aspect of prehistoric life can be explored in the Breckland of southern Norfolk at **Grimes's Graves**, a series of Neolithic flint mines, some with shafts up to 12 m deep.

In medieval **Norwich**, with its wealth built on the wool trade, there were 57 parish churches, and today there remain 32 medieval churches, the greatest concentration in Britain.

The **Sandringham Estate**, near King's Lynn, has been a private home of the Royal Family since 1862, initially for the Prince of Wales, to provide him with a country retreat away from the attractions of the big city. The original house soon was too small and the present building dates from 1870.

An unknown anchoress (or hermit) at the church of St Julian (and now known as **Julian of Norwich**, c.1342 – c.1416), recorded her visions in *The Revelations of Divine Love*, her optimistic theology encapsulated in the saying: 'All shall be well, and all shall be well, and all manner of things shall be well.'

Samuel Lincoln, great-great-great-great-grandfather of the US President Abraham Lincoln, came from **Hingham**. In 1637, at the age of 15, he sailed to America, settling in Hingham, Massachusetts.

The world's largest sugar beet factory is at **Wissington**, near Downham Market– as well as producing sugar, bio-ethanol is made, and the waste heat used to warm an 11-ha glasshouse containing over a quarter of a million tomato plants, whose growth is also stimulated by receiving waste carbon dioxide.

FAMOUS PEOPLE

Margery Kempe, Christian mystic, born Bishop's (now King's) Lynn, c.1373.
Sir Robert Walpole, Britain's first Prime Minister (1721–42), born Houghton, 1676.
Thomas Paine, radical and author of *The Rights of Man* (1791), born Thetford, 1737.
Frances (Fanny) Burney, novelist, playwright and diarist, born Kings Lynn, 1752.
Horatio Nelson, 1st Viscount Nelson, Admiral and victor at Trafalgar, born Burnham Thorpe, 1758.
Elizabeth Fry, Quaker, prison and social reformer, born Norwich, 1780.
Edith Cavell, nurse, shot in Belgium in 1915 for helping British prisoners, born Swardeston, 1865.
Anna Sewell, author of *Black Beauty*, born Great Yarmouth, 1820.
King George VI, born York Cottage, Sandringham, 1895.
Sir James Dyson, inventor and entrepreneur, born Cromer, 1947.
Diana, Princess of Wales, born Park House, Sandringham, 1961.
Sir Matthew Pinsent, Olympic rowing champion, born Holt, 1970.

Norfolk, the fifth largest non-metropolitan county by area, is mainly flat or gently undulating, with fenland in the west, the sluices at Denver controlling the flow of water from the Fens into the Wash. In the southwest is the Breckland, an expanse of heath and conifer forest. Rivers include the Great Ouse, and its tributaries the Wissey and Nar; the Wensum, which rises near Fakenham, joins the Yare and, with the Bure flows out at Yarmouth; the Little Ouse and Waveney both enter the county briefly, but mainly form the boundary with Suffolk.

The East Angles settled in this area from the 6th century and their kingdom lasted until it crumbled under Danish attack in the 9th century. However, by 673 a separate diocese was established at North Elmham to cover the northern section of the kingdom, and, by the Norman Conquest, the historic boundaries of Norfolk were established. Norfolk County Council was formed in 1888, and there have only been small changes in the overall area covered (although significant changes in the organization of districts).

The population of Norfolk is 850,800 and it is predicted to grow to 1,058,000 by 2031, the increase largely coming from people moving into Norfolk from other parts of England. The chief centres are Norwich (population 174,047), Great Yarmouth (58,032), King's Lynn (40,921), Thetford (21,760), East Dereham (17,7879) and Wymondham (11,420). Overall, almost a third of the population lives in Norwich or in its immediate area.

The economy of Norfolk is strongly influenced by agriculture, agricultural research (such as the John Innes Centre) and related food processing industries (Norwich is the home of Colman's Mustard, for example). The county is the land base for many southern North Sea oil and gas operations (the Bacton Gas Terminal handles 30 per cent of Britain's gas) and for the growing service needs of offshore wind farms. Overall, however, approaching 82 per cent of all jobs are in the service sector, with over 28 per cent being in public administration, education and health and 9 per cent in tourism.

Norwich has always been the most important city East Anglia and up until the Industrial Revolution, wa one of the wealthiest towns in Britain. The Normans built both the large castle and the magnificent cathed with its great spire, later completed in the 15th centur The University of East Anglia was built on a new camp just outside the city from the 1960s and houses, withir an iconic Norman Foster building, the Sainsbury Cen for Visual Arts.

East from Norwich are the Broads, Britain's larges area of protected wetlands, and since 1989, with a similar status to a National Park. The Broads are mad up of lakes ('broads') and interlinking rivers, giving over 200 km of navigable waterways. For long thought to be natural, the Broads are now recognized as flood peat excavations. The rivers of the Broads flow out to sea at Great Yarmouth, for long one of Britain's most important fishing centres (and home to the largest medieval parish church in Britain), but now a port an seaside resort that has seen better times.

Some of Britain's worst coastal erosion happens along the Norfolk coast, where sandy cliffs, such as th at Happisburgh, are washed into the sea, along with farmland and houses. The north Norfolk coastline is Area of Outstanding Natural Beauty and includes the popular resorts of Cromer and Sheringham. Further around the coast is the offshore barrier island of Scol Head near Burnham Overy Staithe. Inland, Norfolk is primarily agricultural, and contains over 600 medieva churches and a number of great houses including the late medieval Oxburgh, the Elizabethan Blickling (home of the Boleyn family), and the Palladian Holkha (set in an estate improved by the great agricultural reformer 'Coke of Holkham').

Burgh Castle roman fort just west of Great Yarmouth.

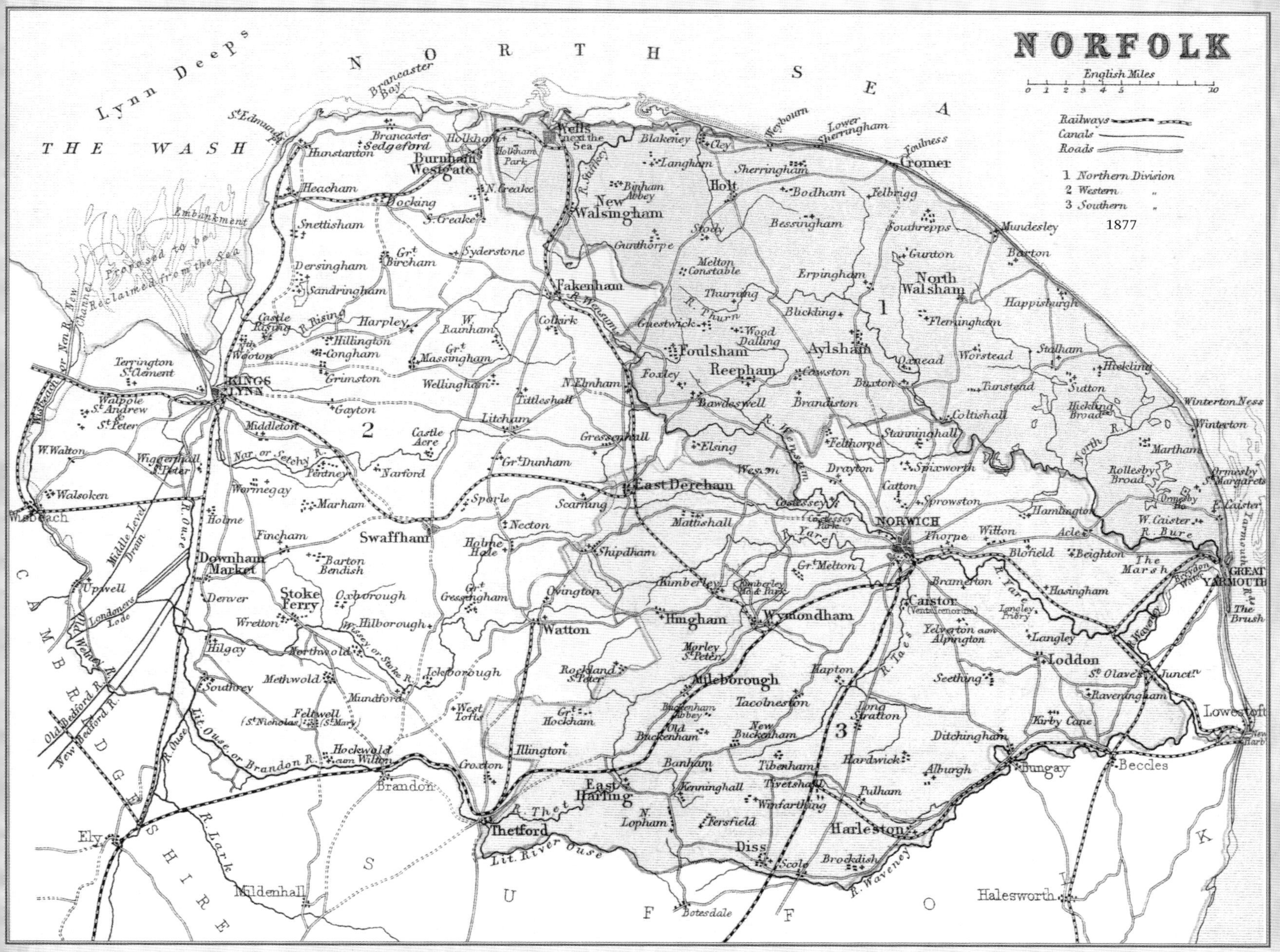

NORFOLK

English Miles

Railways
Canals
Roads

1 Northern Division
2 Western "
3 Southern "

1877

Bartholomew Gazetteer of the British Isles, 1887

NORFOLK, *a maritime co. in E. of England, bounded N. and E. by the North Sea, S. by Suffolk, and W. by Cambridgeshire; greatest length, 70 miles; greatest breadth, 43 miles; area, 1,356,173 ac., pop. 444,749. The coast line is about 90 miles in extent. All along the seaboard the land is low, and has suffered greatly from encroachments of the sea. Many thousands of acres however have been reclaimed from the waters of the Wash,* and the work is still being prosecuted. A level surface characterises the appearance of the co., which is watered by the Yare, with its tributaries the Wensum, Waveney, and Bure, and by the Ouse and its tributaries. Light sand and loam is the prevailing character of the soil, which generally has been rendered productive through the excellence of the system of farming that has been pursued during recent years. The barley of the co. has especial celebrity. Great attention is paid to live stock, and the cobs and cart horses of the co. are well known. Large numbers of geese and turkeys are supplied to city markets. Besides the great herring fishery of Yarmouth, there is all along the coast an important and valuable fishing industry, which employs many thousands of the people. Norfolk comprises 33 hundreds, 736 pars, with parts of 9 others, the mun. bors. of Great Yarmouth, King's Lynn, and Thetford. It is mostly in the diocese of Norwich.

cey Arms Wind Pump, Norfolk Broads.

Sandringham Estate, near King's Lynn.

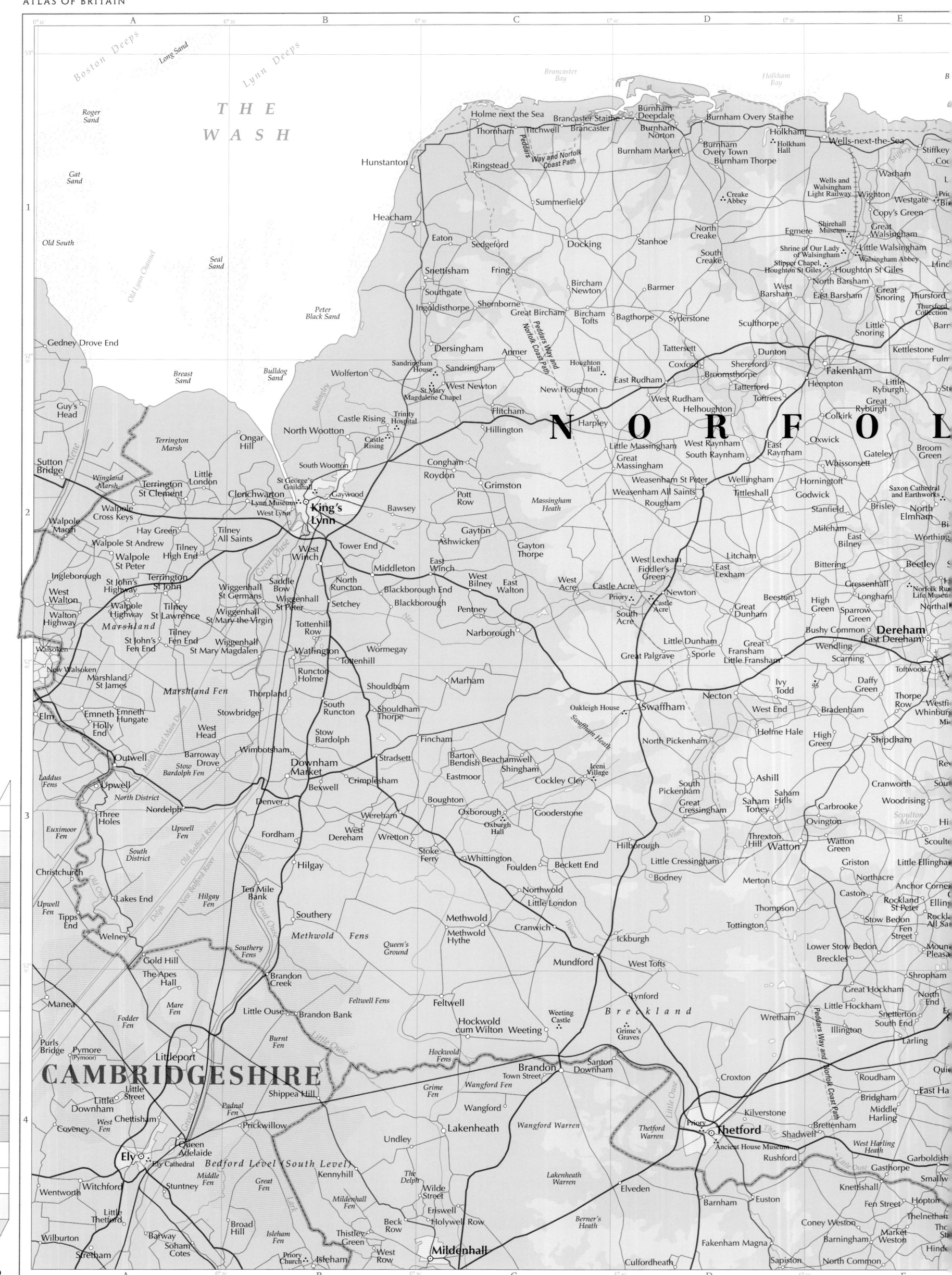

THE
WASH

NORFOL

CAMBRIDGESHIRE

Metres Feet
1000 3281
900 2952
800 2624
700 2296
600 1968
500 1640
400 1312
300 4921
200 656
150 492
100 328
50 164
0 Land below sea level
50 164
200 656
1000 3281

LINCOLNSHIRE

Area Sq Km	6,103
Area Sq Miles	2,356
Population	698,000
County town	Lincoln
Highest point	Wold Top (168 m) near Normanby-le-Wold
Districts	Boston; East Lindsey; Lincoln; North Kesteven; South Holland; South Kesteven; West Lindsey

Lincolnshire is named after the county town of Lincoln, whose name was adapted from the Roman *Lindum Colonia*, 'colony (for retired legionaries) by the pool', *Lindum* coming from the Celtic *lindo* meaning 'pool'. There is a large pool, now called Brayford Pool, formed by the River Witham at Lincoln.

FAMOUS FOR

The Newport Arch in **Lincoln** is the only Roman gateway in Britain through which a public road still passes. It had to be carefully restored in the 1970s after it was hit by a lorry that was too tall to fit under the arch.

The flat land of Lincolnshire made it attractive for siting RAF bases – **RAF Scampton** just north of Lincoln was the home of the Dambuster Squadron and is now home to the Red Arrows display team while **RAF Coningsby** is home to the Battle of Britain Memorial Flight.

In the centre of **Crowland** is a most unusual bridge, built by the monks of nearby Crowland Abbey in the 14th century. It consists of three intersecting arches designed to span the River Welland at a point where a tributary joined. The rivers have been diverted, and Trinity Bridge now merely crosses dry land.

The **High Bridge** (or **Glory Hole**) across the river Witham in the centre of Lincoln is the oldest bridge in Britain still to have buildings on it, which date from the 16th century.

FAMOUS PEOPLE

Henry IV, King of England (1399–1413), born, Bolingbroke Castle, 1366.
William Cecil, Baron Burghley, statesman and adviser to Elizabeth I, born Bourne, 1520.
John Smith, leader of the Jamestown Settlement, first British colony in America, born Willoughby, 1580.
Sir Isaac Newton, physicist and mathematician, born Woolsthorpe, 1642/1643.
Sir John Franklin, Arctic explorer, born Spilsby, 1786.
Alfred Tennyson, 1st Baron Tennyson, poet, Poet Laureate (1850–92), born Somersby, 1809.
George Boole, mathematician, creator of Boolean logic, born Lincoln, 1815.
Dame Sybil Thorndike, actress, born Gainsborough, 1882.
Margaret Thatcher, Baroness Thatcher, first female Prime Minister (1979–90), born Grantham, 1925.
Colin Dexter, author of Inspector Morse books, born Stamford, 1930.
Jennifer Saunders, actress and comedian, born Sleaford, 1958.

"Lincoln Cathedral is, I believe, the finest building in the whole world."
William Cobbett, 1830

"Passing through the Stonebow [in Lincoln], as the city gate close by is called, we ascend a street which grew steeper and narrower as we advanced; till at last it got to be the steepest street I ever climbed … Being almost the only hill in Lincolnshire the inhabitants seem disposed to make the most of it."
Nathaniel Hawthorne, 1863

The county has a reputation for being flat, and, indeed, three-quarters of the land lies below 30 m, especially in the Fens in the south, where some land is below sea level. However, there are two ranges of hills: the narrow limestone ridge, the Lincoln Edge, a continuation of the Cotswold Hills, runs from Stamford and Grantham through Lincoln to Scunthorpe; and the chalk Lincolnshire Wolds, about 20 km wide, running north from Spilsby and Horncastle to Caistor. Between them is a vale of clay land and to the east of the Wolds is a low-lying area of sand dunes and salt marshes. The river Witham rises in the southwest of the county and from Lincoln is largely incorporated into the extensive land-drainage system, as is the river Welland, in the south of the county. The river Trent forms part of the county boundary with Nottinghamshire.

The area of Lincolnshire was readily settled by the Saxons (and this Danish heritage is shown in the many placenames ending in '-by'), and the area became divided into three regions Lindsey, Kesteven and Holland. The county of Lincolnshire was first recognized in the 11th century. In 1888 three County Councils were established to administer the shire, using the old divisions of Lindsey, based in Lincoln and administering the northern half of the county, Kesteven, based at Sleaford and administering the centre of the county and Holland, based at Boston and administering the Fens. In 1974 these counties were combined into a single county of Lincolnshire, but the far north of the county (around Scunthorpe and Grimsby) became part of a new county of Humberside. In 1996 Humberside was abolished and two unitary authorities were established in north Lincolnshire covering Scunthorpe and Grimsby.

The population of Lincolnshire is 698,000 and has one of the fastest growing populations in Britain, having increased by nearly 20 per cent since 1991 and it is expected to grow to 782,000 by 2020. The county has also seen an influx of many migrant workers, particularly providing labour for the intensive vegetable cultivation in the Fens. The main settlements are Lincoln (85,963), Boston (35,124), Grantham (34,592), Spalding (22,081), Stamford (19,525), Gainsborough (19,110) and Skegness (16,806).

Agriculture and related food processing industries are central to the economy of the county. Two-thirds of the land area is intensively used, mainly for vegetable and cereal growing. The making of agricultural equipment and the servicing of the whole industry provides further employment. The single largest employment sector is public administration, education and health, providing 28 per cent of jobs, while tourism provides just below 9 per cent, a sector focused on historic Lincoln, and the coastal resorts of Skegness and Mablethorpe.

Roman Lincoln (*Lindum Colonia*) was one of the largest settlements in Roman Britain. After the conquest the Normans constructed a major castle and a cathedral. Much of the Norman cathedral was destroyed by an earthquake, leaving just parts of the west front, and most of the cathedral was rebuilt between 1190 and 1280. One of the finest medieval cathedrals in the world, it dominates the town and can be seen for miles around. In the 19th century Lincoln became a centre for the manufacture of agricultural equipment, and engineering is still an important industry, now boosted by the service sector, including the thriving University of Lincoln, established in the 1990s.

South of Lincoln, following the Lincoln Edge, the land is dominated by cereal cultivation, with the attractive stone-built towns of Grantham and Stamford both benefitting from proximity to the Great North Road (A1). To the southeast of Lincoln lies the rich agricultural lands of the Fens and the towns of Boston, once a wealthy wool port and still dominated by the 83-m-high tower (Boston Stump) of its parish church and Spalding, the centre of the daffodil and tulip business. To the east of Lincoln the land begins to rise into the undulating Lincolnshire Wolds, once heavily used for sheep farming that provided the wool for the shire's medieval prosperity. It is an area of scattered communities and small market towns such as Louth, with perhaps the most beautiful church spire in the country, Horncastle and Spilsby. Beyond the Wolds is the low-lying land close to the sea, home to the seaside resorts of Skegness and Mablethorpe and major nature reserves such as Gibraltar Point.

Lincoln Cathedral; view from the Lincoln Castle walls.

Statue of Alfred Lord Tennyson, outside Lincoln Cathedral.

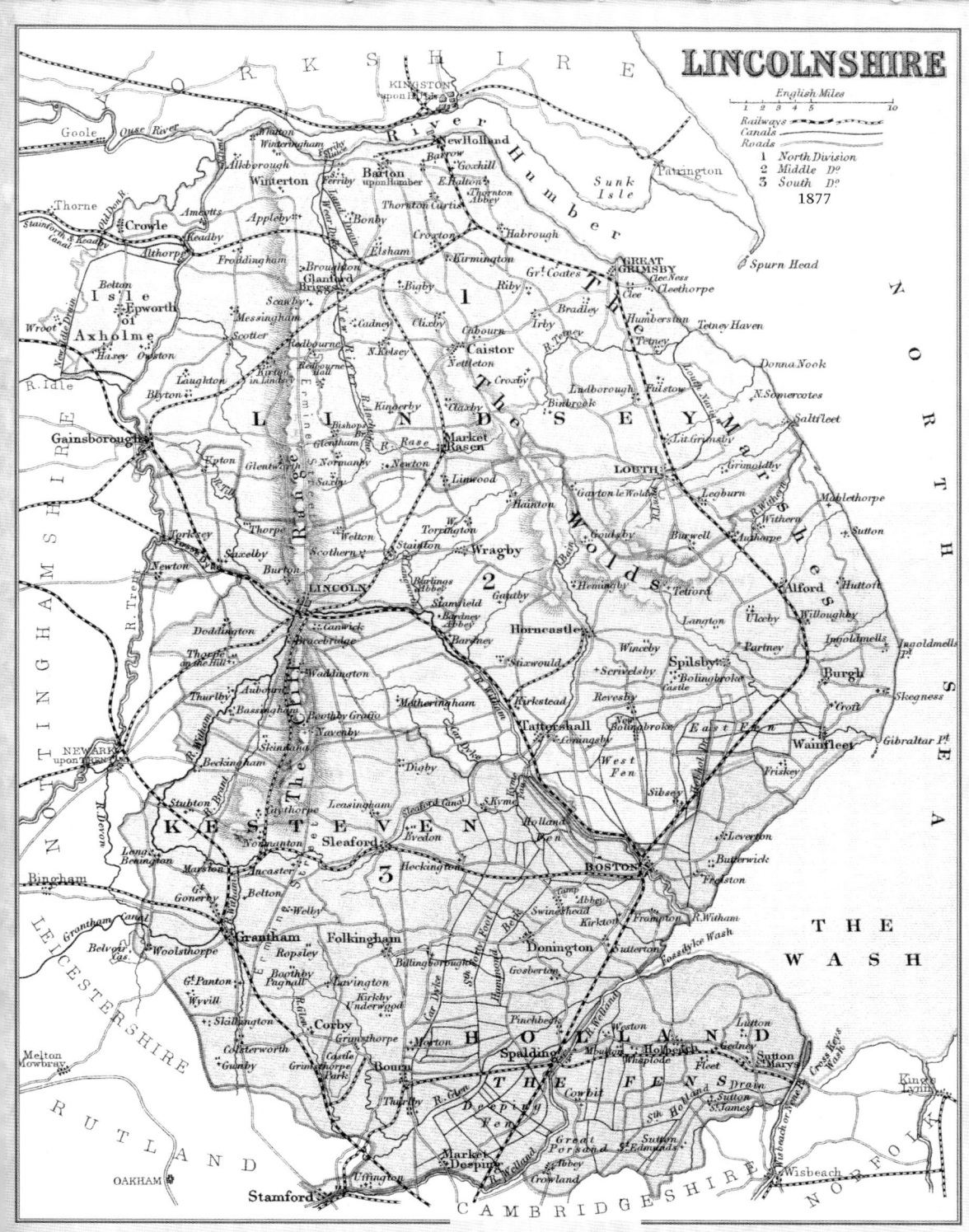

LINCOLNSHIRE

English Miles
1 2 3 4 5 10

Railways
Canals
Roads

1 North Division
2 Middle D°
3 South D°

1877

Bartholomew Gazetteer of the British Isles, 1887

LINCOLNSHIRE, *maritime county in E. of England, bounded N. by Yorkshire, from which it is separated by the Humber; E. by the North Sea; S. by Northamptonshire, Cambridgeshire, and Norfolk; and W. by Notts, Leicestershire, and Rutland; greatest length, N. to S., 75 miles; greatest breadth, E. to W., 45 miles; area, 1,767,879 ac., pop. 469,919. Lincolnshire is the second largest co. in England. For a very long time it has been divided into 3 "parts" – namely, the Parts of Lindsey, the Parts of Kesteven, and the Parts of Holland. Generally speaking the land is flat and low, especially on the coast, which in some parts requires an embankment to check the encroachments of the sea. The Wolds, or Chalk Hills, in the NE., are about 47 miles long and 6 miles broad. Most of the co. is watered by the rivers Trent, Witham, Ancholme, and Welland, with their tributaries. The co. is intersected by an intricate network of canals and dykes, the latter being cut for the purposes of drainage. The soil is varied and generally fertile, being especially rich in pasture, upon which splendid breeds of oxen, horses, and sheep are reared. The coast fisheries, especially at Grimsby, are of immense value. Inland the inhabitants are mostly employed in agriculture. Shipbuilding, cordage and net mfr., and machine-making are carried on. Lincolnshire is divided into 3 divisions, viz., the Parts of Holland, the Parts of Kesteven, and the Parts of Lindsey, and comprises 31 wapentakes, hundreds, liberties, and sokes, 757 pars, and 4 parts of pars., and the mun. bors. of Boston, Grantham, Great Grimsby, Lincoln , Louth and Stamford (part). It is almost entirely in the diocese of Lincoln.*

...oln Crown Court which is located within the grounds of Lincoln Castle.

Grey seal pup at Donna Nook on the Lincolnshire coast.

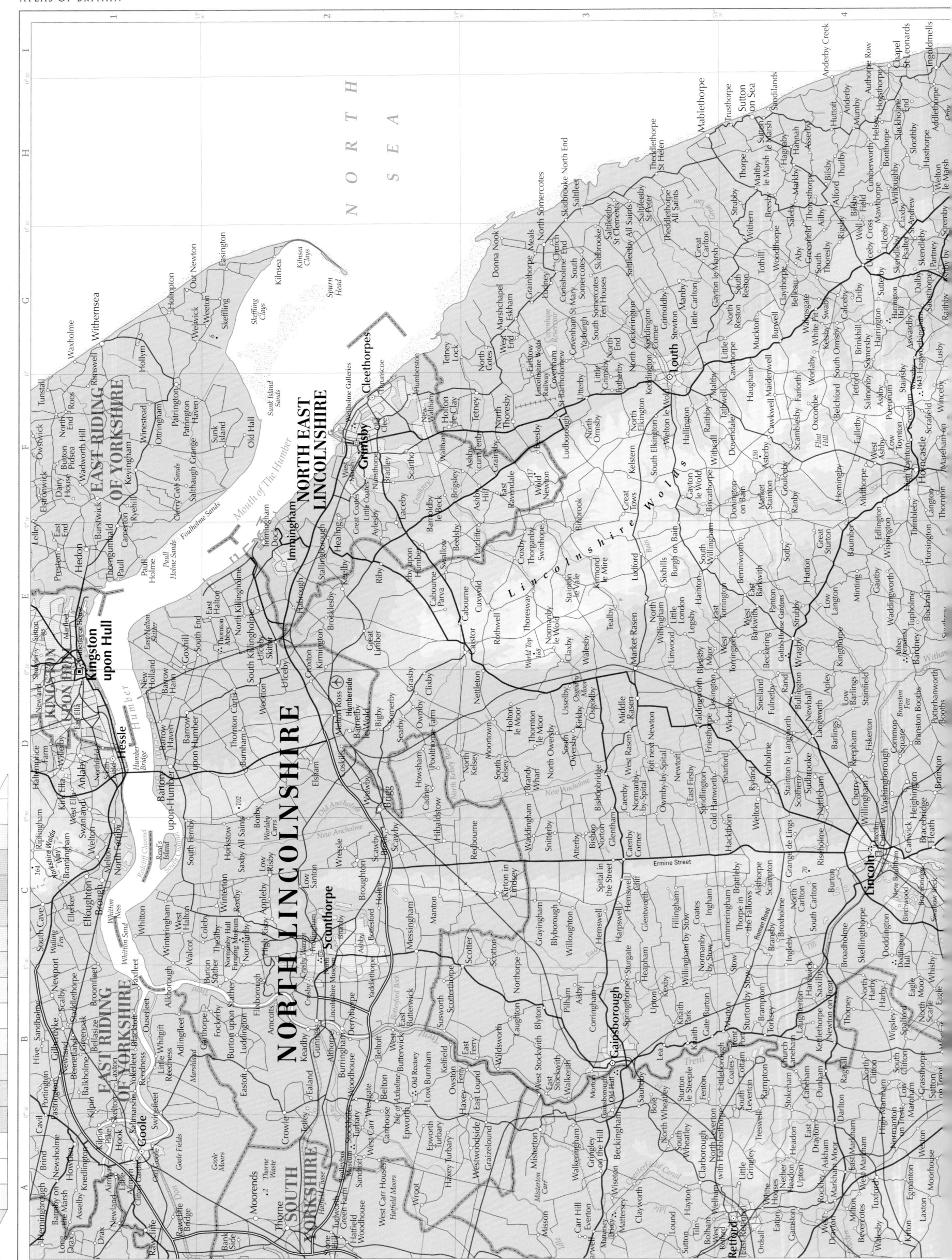

NORTH SEA

EAST RIDING OF YORKSHIRE

NORTH EAST LINCOLNSHIRE

NORTH LINCOLNSHIRE

KINGSTON UPON HULL

Kingston upon Hull

Lincolnshire Wolds

EAST RIDING OF YORKSHIRE

SOUTH YORKSHIRE

Grimsby

Cleethorpes

Immingham

Scunthorpe

Gainsborough

Lincoln

Goole

Thorne

Retford

Metres	Feet
1000	3280
900	2952
800	2624
700	2296
600	1968
500	1640
400	1312
300	4921
200	656
150	492
100	328
50	164
0	Land below sea level
50	164
200	656
1000	3281

British National Grid projection

1:280 000

Miles 0 1 2 3 4 5 6 7 8

Kilometres 0 2 4 6 8 10 12

© Collins Bartholomew Ltd

NORTH EAST LINCOLNSHIRE

Area Sq Km	204
Area Sq Miles	79
Population	158,200
County town	Grimsby
Highest point	Wold Newton (117 m) in the Lincolnshire Wolds

FAMOUS FOR

Grimsby takes its name from an unknown Dane called Grim ('-by' means 'village of').

Towering above Grimsby docks is the **Grimsby Dock Tower**. This 94-m-high tower was built in 1852 to provide hydraulic power for the lock at the entrance of the harbour – based on Sienna's town hall, it provides an overblown touch of Italy on the North Sea.

Originally part of Lincolnshire, this area was taken into the new county of Humberside in 1974 and then became a unitary authority in 1996 when Humberside was abolished. It lies on the south bank of the Humber Estuary and is based around the Grimsby and Cleethorpes conurbation. The port and petrochemical centre of Immingham and a small rural hinterland stretching into the edge of the Lincolnshire Wolds completes the area. Its population is 158,200 and has been virtually static since the 2001 census. The traditional economy of the area was driven by the fishing industry, for Grimsby in the 1950s was one of the largest fishing ports in the world. Although the fishing

fleet has greatly declined Grimsby still remains a maj fish market and fish-processing centre. At the start of the 20th century a deep-water port was developed at Immingham and it now handles over 50 million tonn of goods, primarily coal, oil and iron-ore imports. Th major petrochemical works are immediately adjacent North Lincolnshire. Over 22 per cent of jobs are eithe in manufacturing or in transport, reflecting the key importance of these sectors. Grimsby and Cleethorpe together are the shopping and commercial centres of the area, and the beaches at Cleethorpes attract some tourist business.

Grimsby Dock Tower.

Grimsby Indoor Market.

NORTH LINCOLNSHIRE

Area Sq Km	876
Area Sq Miles	338
Population	160,300
County town	Scunthorpe
Highest point	Saxby Wold (102 m) in the Lincolnshire Wolds

FAMOUS FOR

St Peter's Church at **Barton-upon-Humber** has one of the finest Anglo-Saxon towers in Britain, dating from the 10th century. Nearby are the ruins of **Thornton Abbey**, its power implied by its monumental fortified gatehouse, built in the late 14th century.

FAMOUS PEOPLE

Famous people born in North Lincolnshire include:
John Wesley (born 1703) and **Charles Wesley** (born 1707) founders of Methodism, at Epworth.
Dame Joan Ann Olivier, Baroness Olivier, (*born* Joan Plowright), actress, born Scunthorpe, 1929.
Anthony (Tony) Jacklin, golfer, born Scunthorpe, 1944.

Originally part of Lincolnshire, this area was taken into the new county of Humberside in 1974 and then became a unitary authority in 1996 when Humberside was abolished. Centred on Scunthorpe, the area is dominated by heavy industry, with one of Britain's two remaining working integrated iron and steelworks at Scunthorpe, oil and petrochemical works on the banks of the Humber and the Trent, and power stations. It was in the mid-19th century that the development of ironworks started, based on the discovery of iron ore

in the area. Before then, it was a remote area of poor agricultural land. To the west of the Trent is the Isle o Axholme, an area of fen drained in the 17th century, and now most well-known for Epworth, where John and Charles Wesley were born. Over 22 per cent of the population is employed in manufacturing, over twice the national average. The major settlements are Scunthorpe (72,660) Barton-upon-Humber (9,334) Brigg (5,860).

Gatehouse of Thornton Abbey, Barton-upon-Humber.

NOTTINGHAMSHIRE

Area Sq Km	2,087
Area Sq Miles	806
Population	776,500
County town	Nottingham
Administrative centre	West Bridgford
Highest point	Silverhill Millennium Point (205 m), reclaimed mine spoil heap
Districts	Ashfield; Bassetlaw; Broxtowe; Gedling; Mansfield; Newark and Sherwood; Rushcliffe

Nottinghamshire takes its name from the county town of Nottingham, the Norman version of its Old English name of *Snotingeham*, 'homestead of Snot's people'.

FAMOUS FOR

The **Major Oak** stands in the middle of the Sherwood Forest Country Park and is the biggest oak tree in Britain, with a girth of 10 m and a spread of 28 m. It could be anything between 800 and 1,000 years old. Its name comes from Major Hayman Rooke, who described it in a local history in 1790 – and any connection with Robin Hood is indeed the stuff of legend.

Newstead Abbey, originally an Augustinian priory founded in 1170, was the ancestral homes of the Byrons from 1540. The poet, Lord Byron, inherited it in a ruinous state from his great uncle in 1798. Never able to afford to restore it, he lived an eccentric life there from 1808, along with a tame bear, a few large dogs, tortoises and a wolf. He left the Abbey in 1814 and finally sold it in 1818.

Hucknall Airfield saw the first vertical take-off and hovering by a jet-lift aircraft in 1954 – officially it was a flight of the Rolls-Royce Thrust Measuring Rig, unofficially it was much more descriptively known as 'the Flying Bedstead'.

FAMOUS PEOPLE

Thomas Cranmer, first protestant Archbishop of Canterbury, born Aslacton, 1489.

John Blow, organist and composer of church music, born Newark-on-Trent, 1649.

Samuel Butler, author, born Langar, 1835.

David Herbert (DH) Lawrence, author, born Eastwood, 1885.

Eric Coates, musician and composer, born Hucknall, 1886.

Frank Cousins, Trade Union official and Labour politician, born Bulwell, 1904.

Harold Larwood, cricketer (bodyline tour, 1932–3), born Nuncargate, 1904.

Godfrey Hounsfield, electrical engineer and Nobel laureate, born Newark, 1919.

John Ogdon, concert pianist and composer, born Mansfield Woodhouse, 1937.

Graham Taylor, football player and manager (England manager 1990–93), born Worksop, 1944.

Rebecca Adlington, Olympic champion swimmer, born Mansfield, 1989.

"But this forest [Sherwood] does not add to the fruitfulness of the county, for 'tis now, as it were, given up to waste; even the woods which formerly made it so famous for thieves, are wasted; and if there was such a man as Robin Hood … he would hardly find shelter for a week, if he was now to have been there." Daniel Defoe 1725

"Through thy battlements, Newstead, the hollow winds whistle; Thou, the hall of my fathers, art gone to decay; In thy once smiling garden, the hemlock and thistle Have choked up the rose which late bloom'd in the way." Lord Byron, 'On Leaving Newstead Abbey', 1803

The defining feature of Nottinghamshire is the river Trent, which enters the county near Long Eaton, flows through Nottingham then up to Newark, from where it forms the boundary with Lincolnshire until it leaves the county near Walkeringham. Much of the county is rural, with extensive woodlands. In addition to the Trent, the Erewash forms part of the boundary with Derbyshire and the Soar joins the Trent from Leicestershire in the south of the county.

The shire developed around Nottingham in Saxon times and was occupied by the Danes in the late 9th century – Nottingham was one of the five boroughs of the Danelaw. Nottinghamshire was first mentioned in the 10th century, and, until the 16th century it was administered jointly with Derbyshire. Amidst all the later changes in local government, it has been little changed. Nottinghamshire is now a two-tier authority with six districts, while, since 1996, Nottingham has been a unitary authority, restoring the status it had prior to 1974. Nottingham is the historic county town of the shire, but the administrative headquarters of Nottinghamshire County Council are at West Bridgford, on the opposite bank of the Trent to Nottingham.

The population of Nottinghamshire is 776,500 and it is growing at a slower rate than the national average. The greatest concentration of population (373,958) is in the greater Nottingham conurbation, for most of the city's suburbs are in the county, including Beeston, Arnold, West Bridgford and Hucknall. The other main settlements are Mansfield (69,987), Sutton in Ashfield (41,951), Worksop (39,072), Newark-on-Trent (35,454) and Kirkby in Ashfield (27,067).

Originally an agricultural county, its industrialization began with the arrival of canals from the 1770s onwards, which saw the development of the Nottinghamshire coalfields. The largest pits were only developed at the beginning of the 20th century and, at their peak in the middle of the century, around 30 pits were producing 25 million tonnes of coal a year. Now just three deep mines are in use and the industry is no longer the key driver of the county's economy. The service sector now accounts for 77 per cent of jobs and manufacturing provides over 14 per cent, while many people also work in the city of Nottingham.

The coalfields were to the north of Nottingham and it is here that former mining towns, such as Hucknall and Eastwood, have suffered from the loss of their pits. Over much of the coalfields lies Sherwood Forest, once a major forest and royal hunting ground (and hiding place of Robin Hood, as the story goes). The forest lies in an area called the Dukeries, so called because of the dukes who had country houses here – the Duke of Northumberland at Clumber, the Duke of Portland at Welbeck and the Duke of Rutland at Kelham. A church was founded at Southwell around 630 by St Paulinus of York and the current building, Southwell Minster, is mainly Norman with a 13th-century choir and a chapter house which features wonderfully naturalistic carving of leaves. Nearby is Newark-on-Trent, whose castle, strategically positioned next to the bridge across the Trent, witnessed the death of King John in 1216, and, as a Royalist garrison in the Civil War, was much besieged and then reduced to its current ruined state after the Parliamentarian victory in 1645.

Newstead Abbey and Spanish Gardens, near Newstead.

Newark Castle, Newark-on-Trent.

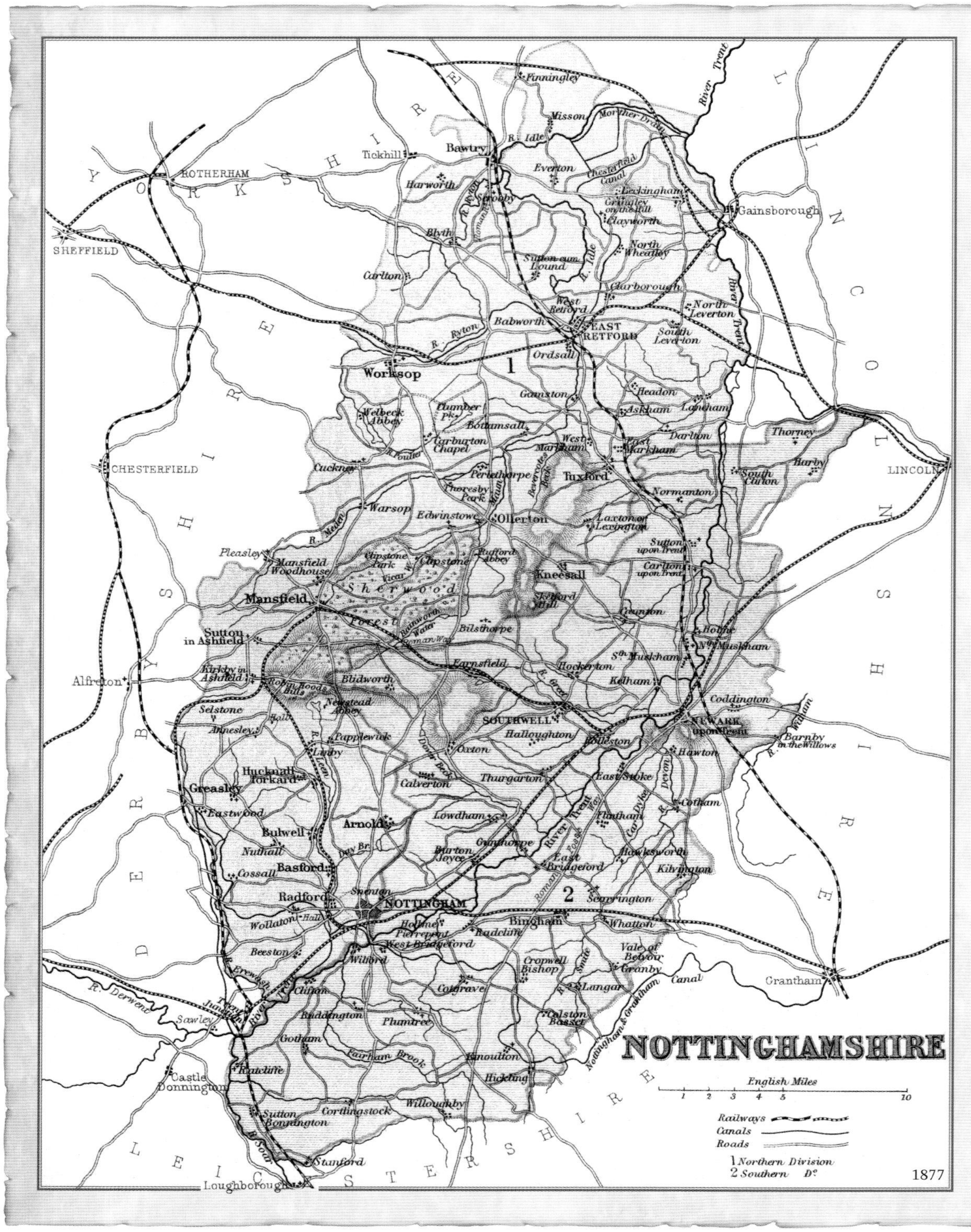

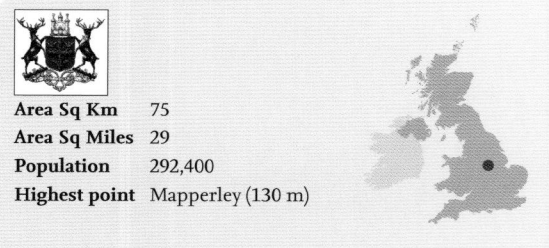

NOTTINGHAMSHIRE

Bartholomew Gazetteer of the British Isles, 1887
NOTTINGHAMSHIRE, *Nottingham, or Notts, north-midland county of England, bounded N. by Yorkshire, E. by Lincolnshire, S. by Leicestershire, and W. by Derbyshire; greatest length, N. to S., about 50 miles; greatest breadth, E. to W., about 25 miles; area, 527,752 ac., pop. 391,815. Towards the E., Nottinghamshire has a level surface; while westwards it is marked by gentle hills of no great elevation, which tend to impart some variety to the scenery. The eastern portion comprises the vales of the Trent and Belvoir; in the S., between the Soar and the Smite, are the Wolds, consisting of level tracts of moor and pasture; while in the W. are the remains of the royal forest of Sherwood. The Trent flows through the co. from SW. to NE., and is navigable for river vessels. All the other streams are tributaries of the Trent; they include the Soar, Erwash, and Idle. By the Nottingham and Grantham Canal, and the Fosse Dyke Canal, there is connection between the Trent and the Witham. The soil is varied, but cannot be spoken of as being highly productive. Green crops are the principal growth, and the common cereals are cultivated. Hop plantations are numerous, while in proximity to Nottingham and Newark there are many market gardens. Magnesian limestone and old red sandstone overlying coal prevail in the W.; in the other districts are formations of marl, new red sandstone, and lias, with quartz and gravel in the Forest. In a few places coal is worked. The principal mfrs. are laces of various descriptions, in recent years a great development being apparent in the production of lace curtains. Hosiery mfrs., woollen mills, cotton mills, and iron foundries are also actively productive. Nottinghamshire comprises 6 wapentakes, 273 pars. with parts of 5 others, the mun. bors. of East Retford, Newark, and Nottingham. It is almost entirely in the diocese of Southwell.*

NOTTINGHAM

Area Sq Km	75
Area Sq Miles	29
Population	292,400
Highest point	Mapperley (130 m)

FAMOUS FOR
'Ye Olde Trip to Jerusalem', built into the side of the rock on which Nottingham Castle stands is one of the oldest pubs in Britain and is associated with the knights who set out to Jerusalem on the Third Crusade in 1189.

In 2004 a new tram service (**Nottingham Express Transit**) opened. It runs 14 km from Hucknall to the city centre. It took twelve years to plan and then four years to build.

FAMOUS PEOPLE
William Booth, founder of Salvation Army, born 1829.
Sir Jesse Boot, who transformed a family shop into a nationwide pharmaceutical business, born 1850.
Alan Sillitoe, writer, born 1928.
Kenneth Clarke, Conservative politician, born 1940.
Doug Scott, mountaineer, born 1941.
Jayne Torvill, born 1957, and **Christopher Dean**, born 1958, Olympic champion ice dancers.

Originally a Saxon settlement, Nottingham became an important Norman town, with a castle built on the sandstone outcrop that made it a strategic site for crossing the Trent. At the start of the Civil War in 1642 Charles I raised his standard at Nottingham Castle. In the 18th century Nottingham became the centre for lace making and its rapid development left it with a legacy of some of the worst slums in Britain. In 1889 it became a county borough and was also awarded city status as part of the celebration of Queen Victoria's diamond jubilee. Since then its boundaries have grown to include some of its suburbs, but the boundary is tightly drawn and only around 40 per cent of the population of the greater Nottingham area actually live in the city. The city is now heavily dependent on the service sector – nearly 34 per cent of jobs are in public administration, education and health. The city is home to two universities (Nottingham and Nottingham Trent) as well as to Her Majesty's Revenue and Customs and the Driving Standards Agency. Manufacturing has now shrunk to 7 per cent of jobs – Raleigh Bicycles were made in the city from 1886 until 2003 while Boots no longer make their own pharmaceuticals here.

Jayne Torvill and Christopher Dean.

Bartholomew Gazetteer of the British Isles, 1887
NOTTINGHAM, *mun. bor., market town, co. town of Notts, and co. in itself, on the N. bank of the Trent, 15 miles E. of Derby and 126 NW. of London by rail, 9960 ac., pop. 186,575; 6 Banks, 6 newspapers. Market-days, Wednesday and Saturday. Little is known concerning the early history of the town. A stronghold was built by William the Conqueror, during whose reign also the town was fortified. During the Barons' Wars Nottingham was a centre of turbulence, and was taken several times, being partially destroyed in the reign of Stephen. Edward IV. was proclaimed here in 1460. Charles I. was besieged in Nottingham in 1642, and in the following year the town surrendered to Colonel Hutchinson, the Parliamentarian commander. Its public buildings do not call for special remark. The castle, founded by William I., was dismantled in the time of the Commonwealth, and after being rebuilt as a dwelling-house was burnt by the Reform rioters in 1830. It is now restored, and contains the "Midland Counties Art Museum", the property of the corporation. Lacemaking and the mfr. of cotton hosiery are very important industries, nearly all the supply of British laces being made in the town. Silk, flax, and woollen mills are also in operation; the mfr. of weaving and netting machinery is largely carried on; and iron-foundries, breweries, and tanneries are successful seats of industry. A picturesque feature of the town is its arboretum, 18 acres in extent.*

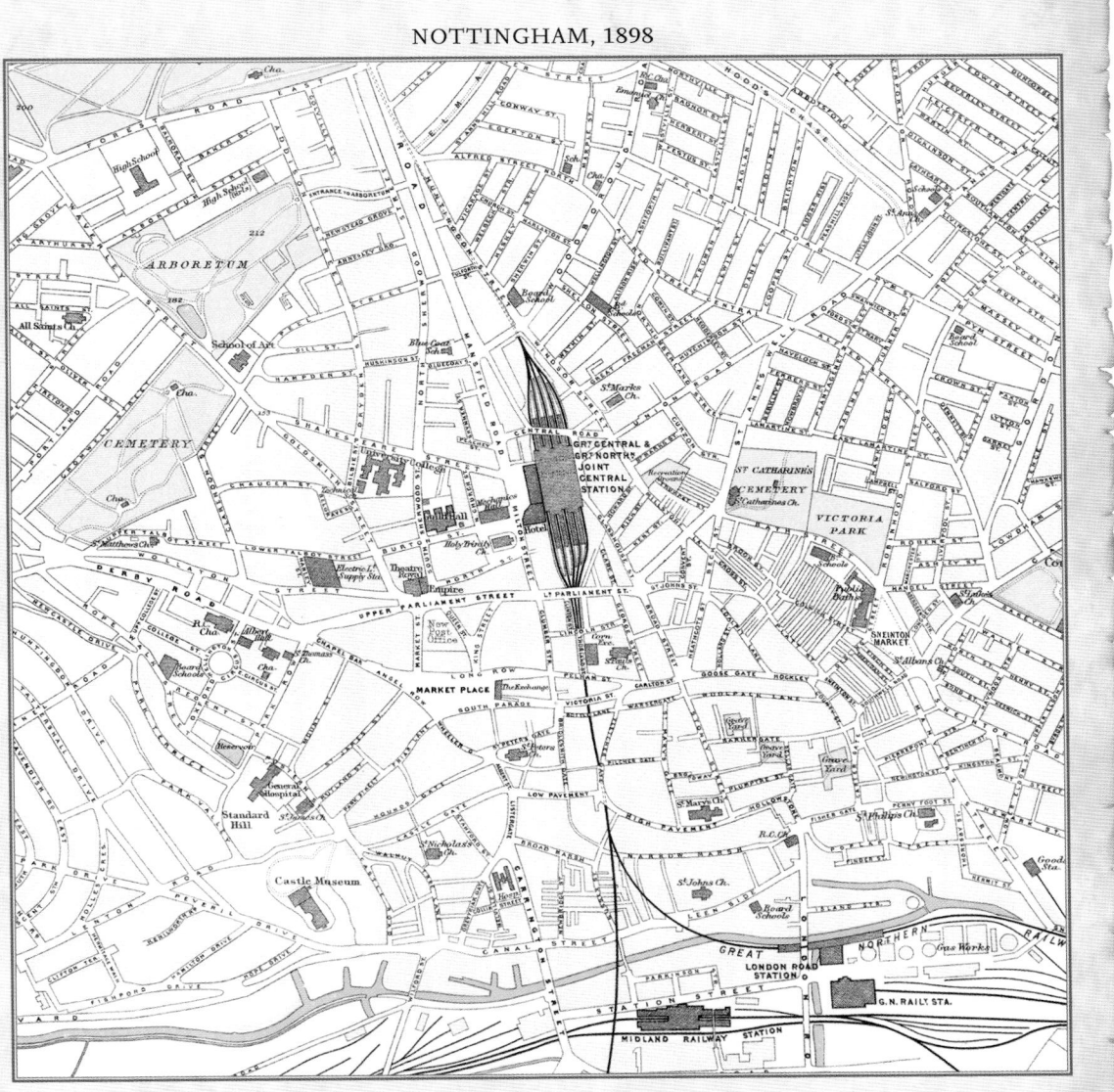

NOTTINGHAM, 1898

...tue of Robin Hood outside Nottingham Castle.

...Olde Trip to Jerusalem Inn, Nottingham.

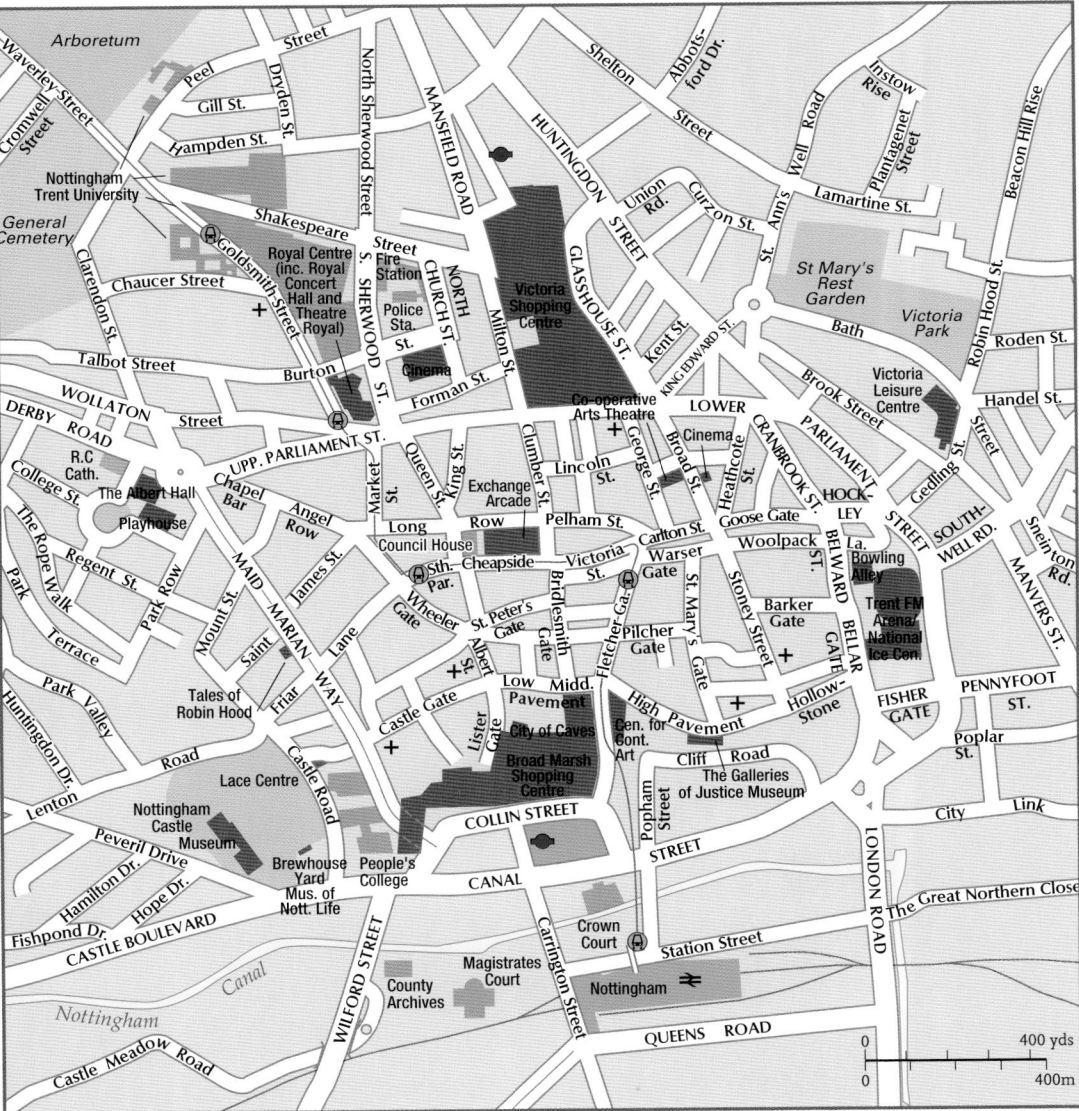

Modern Nottingham

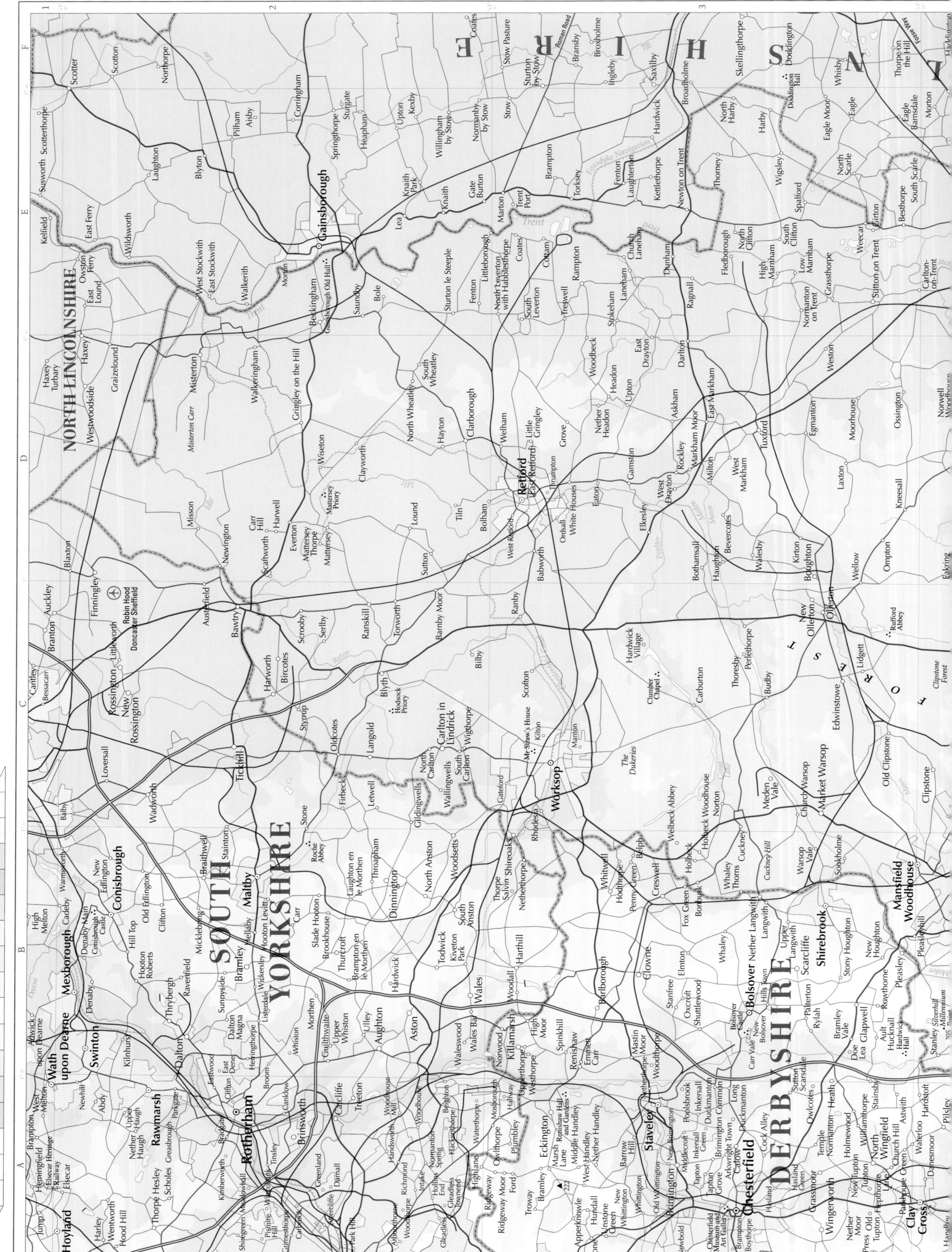

British National Grid projection

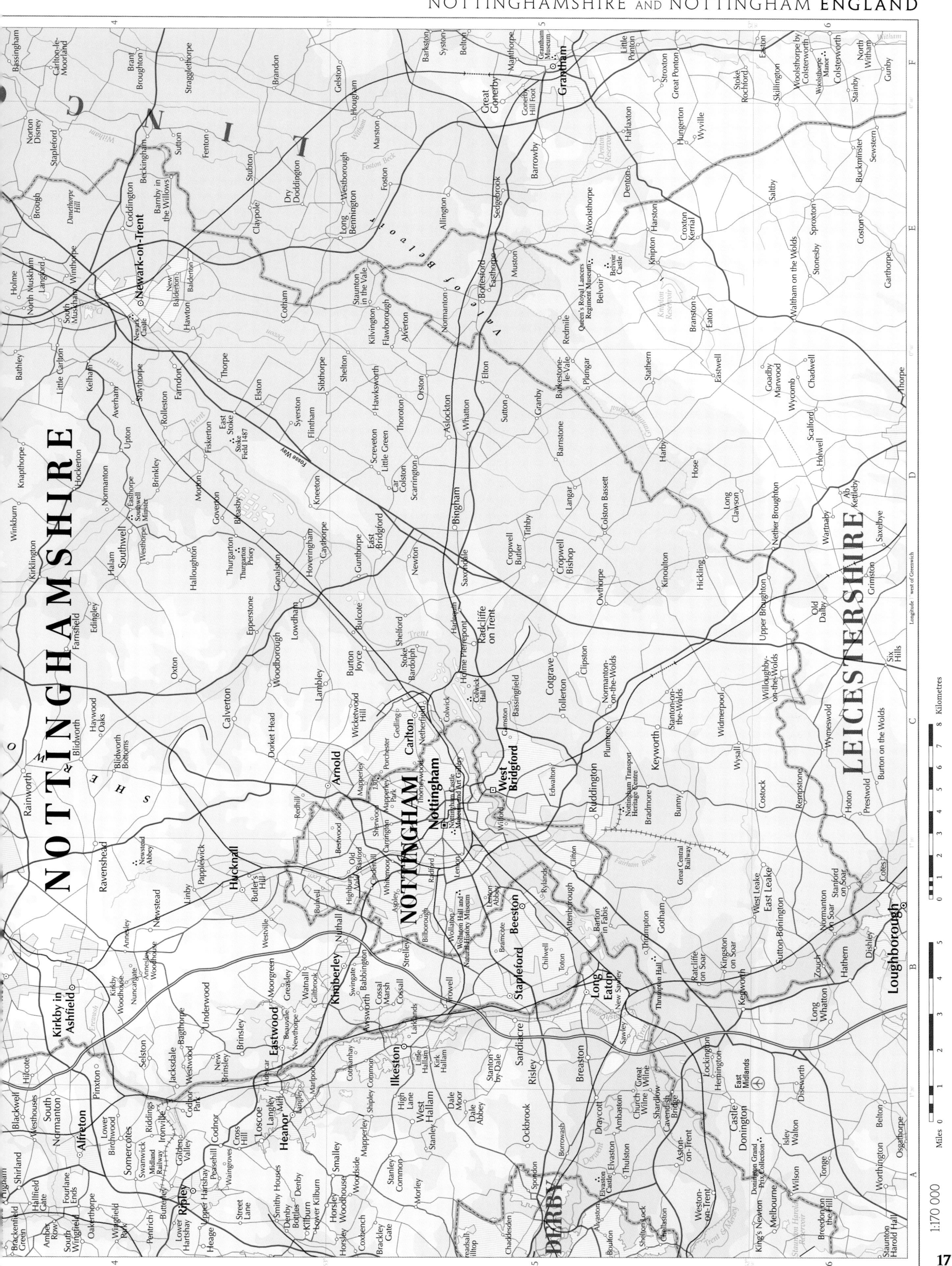

LINCOLNSHIRE

NOTTINGHAMSHIRE

LEICESTERSHIRE

DERBY

Loughborough

1:170 000

Miles 0 1 2 3 4 5

Kilometres 0 1 2 3 4 5 6 7 8

DERBYSHIRE

Area Sq Km	2,551
Area Sq Miles	985
Population	762,100
County town	Matlock
Highest point	Kinder Scout (636 m) in the Peak District
Districts	Amber Valley; Bolsover; Chesterfield; Derbyshire Dales; Erewash; High Peak; North East Derbyshire; South Derbyshire

Derbyshire takes its name from Derby, which comes from the Danish, 'village where deer were seen'.

FAMOUS FOR

The defining feature of **Chesterfield** is the crooked spire of the 14th-century church of St Mary and All Saints. The spire has a wooden frame that is covered in lead. Unfortunately the carpenters used unseasoned wood and, as the wood dried out, the structure twisted by about 45° at its base.

On 24 April 1932 there was a mass trespass at **Kinder Scout** to campaign for the right to roam. Around 400 ramblers from Manchester set off from Bowden Bridge Quarry for the top of Kinder Scout, then part of the Duke of Devonshire's estate and protected by the duke's gamekeepers.

Swarkestone Bridge, over the Trent a few kilometres south of Derby, was the southernmost point reached by the Jacobite Army when Bonnie Prince Charlie decided to turn around and return to Scotland, his army retreating from Derby on 6 December 1745.

The area around **Castleton** in the Peak District is full of underground limestone caverns with stalactites, stalagmites, subterranean rivers, and the semiprecious Blue John mineral, a blue and yellow banded fluorite. Its distinctive banding is unique to the Castleton area.

FAMOUS PEOPLE

Samuel Richardson, novelist, born Mackworth, 1689.
James Brindley, engineer and canal builder, born Tunstead, near Buxton, 1716.
Anna Seward, poet and novelist born Eyam, 1747.
Thomas Cook, founder of Thomas Cook travel agency born Melbourne, 1808.
Catherine Booth, 'The Army Mother' wife of William Booth, founder of Salvation Army, born Ashbourne, 18
Sir Robert Robinson, chemist, Nobel laureate, born Rufford, 1886.
Sir Barnes Wallis, aeronautical engineer and inventor of 'bouncing bomb', born Ripley, 1887.
Arthur Lowe, actor, born Hayfield, 1915.
Sir Alan Bates, actor, born Allestree, 1934.
Tim Brooke-Taylor, comic actor and entertainer, born Buxton, 1940.
Dame Vivienne Westwood, fashion designer, born Tintwistle, near Glossop, 1941.
Dame Ellen MacArthur, record-breaking yachtswoman born Whatstandwell, near Matlock, 1976.

Derbyshire straddles the north and midlands of England. In the far south, it borders the lush rolling countryside of Leicestershire while in the north, it is dominated by the Peak District, the southern end of the Pennines, and the hinterlands of Manchester and Sheffield. Church Flatts farm, near Coton in the Elms in southern Derbyshire is regarded as the furthest point from the sea of any place in Britain (around 113 km). The principal rivers are the Dove, forming much of the boundary with Staffordshire and the Derwent; the Trent flows through the southern corner of the county.

The Romans valued Derbyshire for its minerals and the south of the county was much disputed with the Danes until the start of the 11th century. Until the 16th century it was jointly administered with Nottinghamshire, but since then its boundaries have remained little changed, losing a little to Sheffield in the north but gaining parts of Longdendale from Cheshire in 1974. Derbyshire with its administrative centre at Matlock administers the shire in conjunction with eight districts, while Derby itself is a unitary authority.

The population of Derbyshire is 762,100, and between 2008 and 2029 it is estimated to grow by just under 11 per cent, a slower rate than the East Midlands. The main settlements are Chesterfield (70,260), Staveley (25,763) and Dronfield (17,456) close to Sheffield, Long Eaton (46,490) and Ilkeston (37,270) close to Nottingham, Alfreton (22,302) and Heanor (22,620) in the centre, Buxton (20,836) and Matlock (11,265) in the Peak District and Swadlincote (39,322) in the far south of the county.

Only around 15 per cent of the population live in villages and the countryside.

The raw materials that originally attracted the Romans still play an important part in Derbyshire's economy, particularly the quarrying of limestone and building stone. Coal mining was until recently an important industry, particularly in the area around Chesterfield and Bolsover, but now no mining takes place, though chemical and metal working industries still operate in this area. A limited textile industry remains in and around Belper, while at Burnaston, near Derby, is the Toyota car plant. Over 20 per cent of jobs in Derbyshire are in manufacturing, significantly above the national average, while the service sector provides 73 per cent of jobs. Tourism based on the attractions of the Peak District National Park, most of which is in Derbyshire and covers a third of the county's land area, provides 8.5 per cent of jobs

Derbyshire played a crucial role in the Industrial Revolution. In 1771 Richard Arkwright built the world's first water-powered (and later, steam-powered) cotton spinning factory at Cromford. Not only did he build mills but he also provided accommodation for his workers and managers, creating the world's first industrial town. So significant is this area of Derbyshire that the Derwent Valley Mills (from Cromford down the Derwent to Belper and on to the Derby silk mill) is a UNESCO World Heritage Site

Cromford is on the edge of the Peak District, a rugged and wild area, with houses and field walls built from the dark millstone grit. Health-giving spring waters led to the development of Buxton and Matlock as spas whilst, near Bakewell, is one of Britain's most spectacular and opulent country houses, Chatsworth, the home of the Duke of Devonshire, built at the turn of the 18th century.

Twisted spire of St Mary and All Saints Church, Chesterfield.

DERBY

Area Sq Km	78
Area Sq Miles	30
Population	239,200
Highest point	Allestree Park (135 m)

FAMOUS FOR

The **Arboretum** at Derby was the first public park in England, given to the people of Derby by Joseph Strutt, the Mayor of Derby, in 1840. Four days before the opening of the Arboretum, Franz Liszt gave a recital in the Derby Mechanics Institute hall.

FAMOUS PEOPLE

Joseph Wright, (Wright of Derby), romantic painter of the Industrial Revolution, born 1734.
Herbert Spencer, philosopher and proponent of social Darwinism, born 1820.
Constance Spry, designer, home maker and social reformer, born 1886.
Sir Richard John Roberts, molecular biologist, Nobel laureate, born 1943.

The Romans first settled in the Derby area, establishing their fort of *Derventio* at Chester Green and the town was one of the five boroughs of the Danelaw. From Britain's first water-powered silk mill, built in 1717, to its railway engineering works and the great aero-engine works of Rolls-Royce, Derby has had a long industrial history. As a result, manufacturing provides nearly 19 per cent of the jobs, while public administration, education and health provides around 29 per cent, including the staff of Derby University, established in 1992, but with a history going back to the 1850s. Derby became a county borough in 1888 and in 1968 its boundaries were considerably extended into its surrounding hinterland. Although it became a cathedral city in 1927 when the parish church of All Saints became the cathedral for the diocese of Derby, it was not given 'city' status until 1977. It became a unitary authority in 1996. The cathedral is built on the site of a church founded in 943, though no part of this remains, the tower dating from the early 16th century and the remainder from 1725 in an elegant and, for churches, unusual classical design.

Derbyshire landscape.

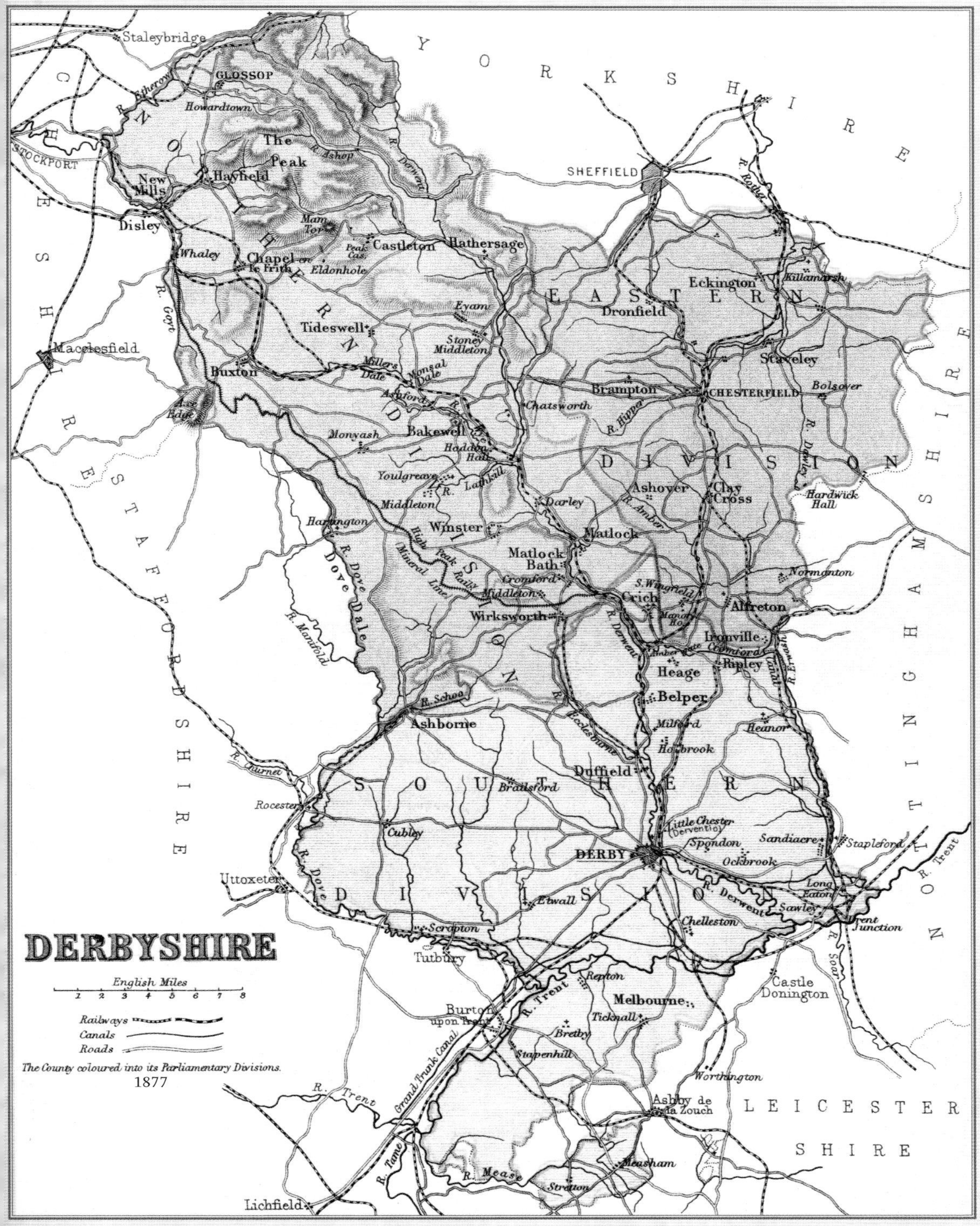

DERBYSHIRE

Bartholomew Gazetteer of the British Isles, 1887

DERBYSHIRE, midland co. of England, having Yorkshire on the N., Notts on the E., Leicestershire, Warwickshire, and Staffordshire on the S., and Staffordshire and Cheshire on the W.; length, N. and S., 52 miles; greatest breadth, 35 miles; average breadth, 20 miles; area, 658,624 ac.; pop. 461,914. The surface in the S. is either flat or undulating, irregular in the middle and NE., and picturesquely mountainous in the NW. or Peak district. The principal rivers are the Trent, Derwent, Dove, and Wye; river communication is supplemented by the Erewash and Grand Trunk Canals. The road and railway systems are highly developed. The soil in the Vale of the Trent is alluvial and very productive. In the hilly districts the land is mostly in pasture; much of it is rocky and unproductive. Oats, barley, potatoes, and wheat are cultivated; and there are many excellent dairy-farms. Warm mineral springs are numerous, the most popular being those at Buxton, Matlock, and Bakewell. Coal is abundant; iron ore and lead are worked; among the other mineral products are zinc, manganese, and barytes. There are numerous and extensive quarries of limestone and marble; fluor-spar is found in the caverns, and is manufactured into a great variety of ornamental articles. Silk, cotton, and lace are the chief mfrs., but malting and brewing are also carried on, and there are some extensive iron foundries. The co. comprises 6 hundreds, 314 pars, with parts of 8 others, the mun bors. of Chesterfield, Derby, and Glossop. It is mostly in the diocese of Southwell.

English Miles

1 2 3 4 5 6 7 8

Railways
Canals
Roads

The County coloured into its Parliamentary Divisions.
1877

Chatsworth House, near Baslow.

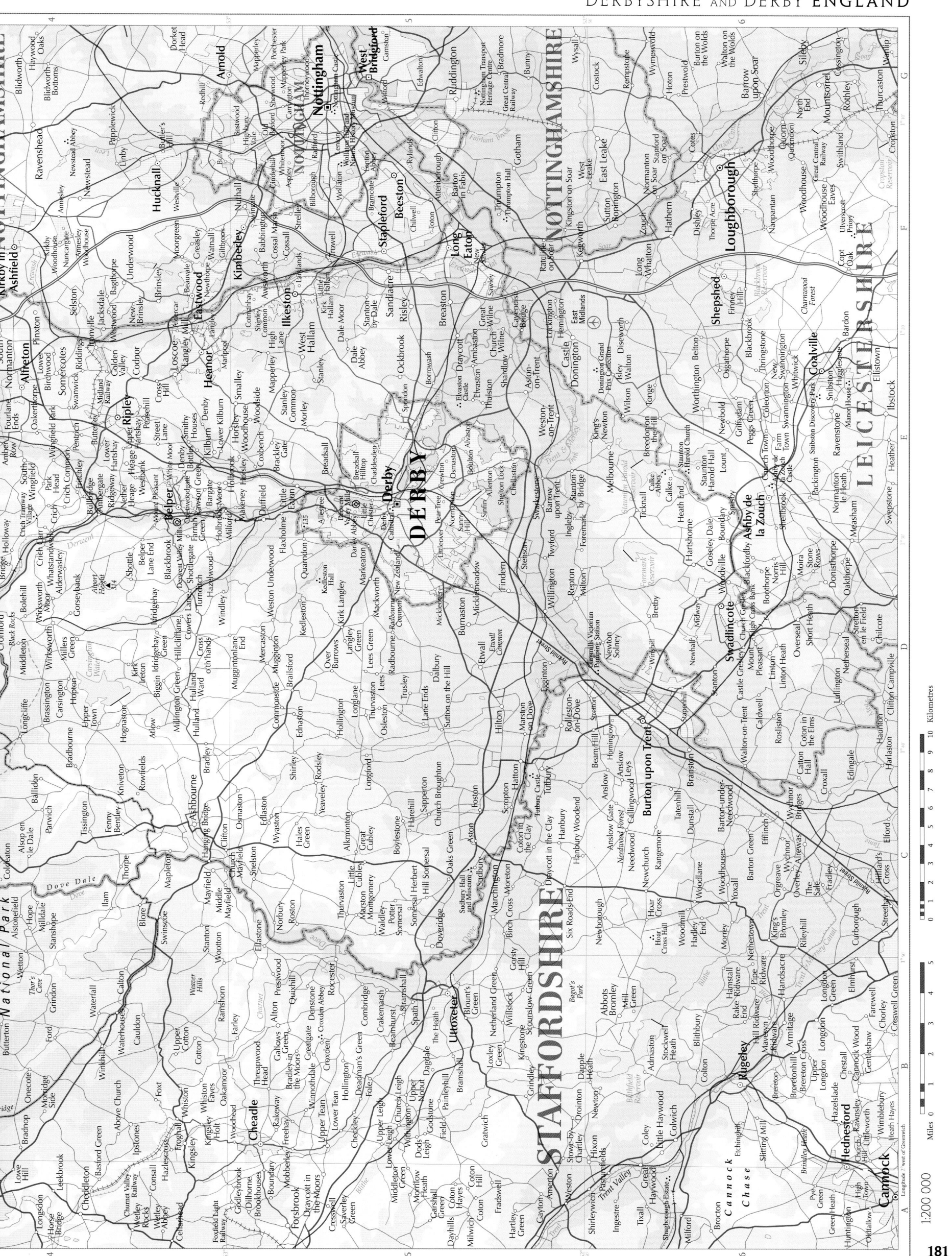

1:200 000

© Collins Bartholomew Ltd

CHESHIRE'S UNITARY AUTHORITIES

Cheshire East	**Area** sq. km 1167; sq. miles 451 **Population** 361,500 **County town** Sandbach
Cheshire West and Chester	**Area** sq. km 917; sq. miles 354 **Population** 328,600 **County town** Chester
Halton (see page 189)	**Area** sq. km 90; sq. miles 35 **Population** 119,800 **County town** Widnes
Warrington (see page 189)	**Area** sq. km 182; sq. miles 70 **Population** 196,200 **County town** Warrington
Highest point of Ceremonial County	Shining Tor (559 m) in the Peak District

Cheshire is a contraction of the old Chestershire, named after the town of Chester, from the Latin 'castra' or Old English 'caester' meaning 'camp of the Legions'.

FAMOUS FOR

Alderley Edge is a rocky outcrop covered in beech trees near the village of the same name. With many old mining tunnels it is an area of mystery, the alleged home of a wizard and knightly sleepers who would one day save England, and in more fanciful versions, linked to Merlin and Arthur and his Knights of the Round Table.

The **Jodrell Bank Centre for Astrophysics** is home to the Lovell Telescope, first operated in 1957 and still one of the world's biggest and most powerful radio telescopes, its massive white bowl a major feature of the south Cheshire landscape.

The moated manor house of **Little Moreton Hall**, near Congleton was built in the 16th century and is one of the finest examples of a black-and-white timber framed building in Britain.

The novelist Elizabeth Gaskell was brought up by her aunt, Hannah Lamb, in the small town of **Knutsford**, which became the basis for the setting of her novel *Cranford*, published in 1851.

The water-powered cotton mill, **Quarry Bank Mill**, at Styal near Wilmslow was founded by Samuel Greg in 1784. Now owned by the National Trust, it still makes cotton calico.

FAMOUS PEOPLE

John Gerard, herbalist, author of *The Herball*, born Nantwich, 1545.
John Speed, mapmaker, born Farndon, 1552.
Emma, Lady Hamilton, mistress of Admiral Lord Nelson, born Great Neston, 1765
Randolph Caldecott, artist and illustrator, born Chester, 1846.
David Beatty, Admiral of the Fleet (1916–19) and First Sea Lord (1919–27), born Nantwich, 1871.
Sir Adrian Boult, conductor, born Chester, 1889.
Sir James Chadwick, physicist, Nobel laureate, born Bollington, 1891.
Leonard Cheshire VC, World War II RAF pilot, founder Leonard Cheshire Disability charity, born Chester, 1917.
David Coleman, sports commentator, born Alderley Edge, 1926.
John Mayall, blues musician, born Macclesfield, 1933.
Daniel Craig, actor, born Chester, 1968.
Paula Radcliffe, marathon runner, born Northwich, 1973.
Michael Owen, footballer, born Chester, 1979

"The grasse and fodder there, is of that goodnesse and virtue that cheeses be made here in great number of a most pleasing and delicate taste, such as all England againe affourdeth not the like."
William Camden, 1610

The historic county of Cheshire started in the foothills of the Peak District in the east. West of the Peak District is the flat Cheshire plain that stretches to the border with Wales. The estuaries of the Mersey and Dee are to the north and west of the county.

The area covered by the county of Cheshire has varied significantly over the years. Originally part of Mercia, the outlines of the historical county were established in the 10th century and were consolidated in the 12th century, particularly along the Welsh border. Cheshire County Council was formed in 1888 and remained the senior tier of local government for the area until 1974, when major changes were made. Cheshire lost Stockport, Altrincham, Hyde and Stalybridge to Greater Manchester, parts of Tintwistle to Derbyshire, and much of the Wirral peninsula to Merseyside, while gaining Warrington and Widnes from Lancashire. In 1996 Warrington and Halton (including Widnes) became unitary authorities (see page 189) with a reduced Cheshire County Council operating with six districts. Further change came in 2009 when Cheshire was divided into two unitary authorities: Cheshire East and Cheshire West and Chester, and all the district councils were dissolved.

Cheshire East, with a population of 361,500, has its administrative headquarters at Sandbach. The population is expected to grow slowly to around 380,000 by 2026. No one settlement dominates East Cheshire, and the most important towns are Crewe (67,683), Macclesfield (50,688), Wilmslow and Alderley Edge (34,087), Congleton (25,400) and Sandbach (17,630). The northeast of the area is a prosperous commuter area for the greater Manchester conurbation and has become an increasingly popular place for administrative headquarters for companies as well as a centre for pharmaceutical research and manufacture. The southwest is more rural with industrialized towns such as Crewe and Sandbach, where manufacturing includes car making (Bentley motors at Crewe), railway engineering and maintenance (Crewe), china sanitary ware (Middlewich) and salt (Middlewich). Some manufacturing has been lost over recent years, including both the Foden and ERF lorry plants that had been based in Sandbach since their foundation. Manufacturing now accounts for over 13 per cent of jobs, while the service sector provides over 80 per cent of jobs – and the largest section is finance, IT and other business with the public sector providing nearly 22 per cent of employment, including staff on the Crewe campus of Manchester Metropolitan University.

Cheshire West and Chester, with a population of 328,600, has its administrative headquarters at Chester. The population has grown modestly over recent years but is expected to grow by around 9 per cent by 2026, double the rate of its neighbour. The main settlements are Chester (80,120), Ellesmere Port (51,330), Northwich (39,570) and Winsford (29,440). The industrial base of the area is in the north with car manufacturing (Vauxhall at Ellsemere Port), pharmaceuticals at Chester and chemicals and oil refining at Northwich and Ellesmere Port. Overall around 10 per cent of jobs are in manufacturing and over 83 per cent in the service sector, with Chester a centre for financial services and Chester University. The south of the county is rural, with much dairy farming, and is the home of Cheshire cheese.

Chester was established around AD 75 as the Roman town of *Deva*, a secure base to take the Roman conquest into Wales. Important as the last major settlement before the Welsh Marches, the city is unusual in that it still has a complete ring of city walls that can be walked on. Within the city is the cathedral originally built as a monastery to St Werburgh. Building started in 1092, under the guidance of St Anselm, and was completed around 1250, by which time the design was considered old-fashioned and most of the building was rebuilt between then and 1520. The famous Rows, the unique covered arcades of shops in the centre, date from the 13th century, though some of the more ornate black-and-white half-timbered buildings are from the 19th century.

Eastgate Street, Chester.

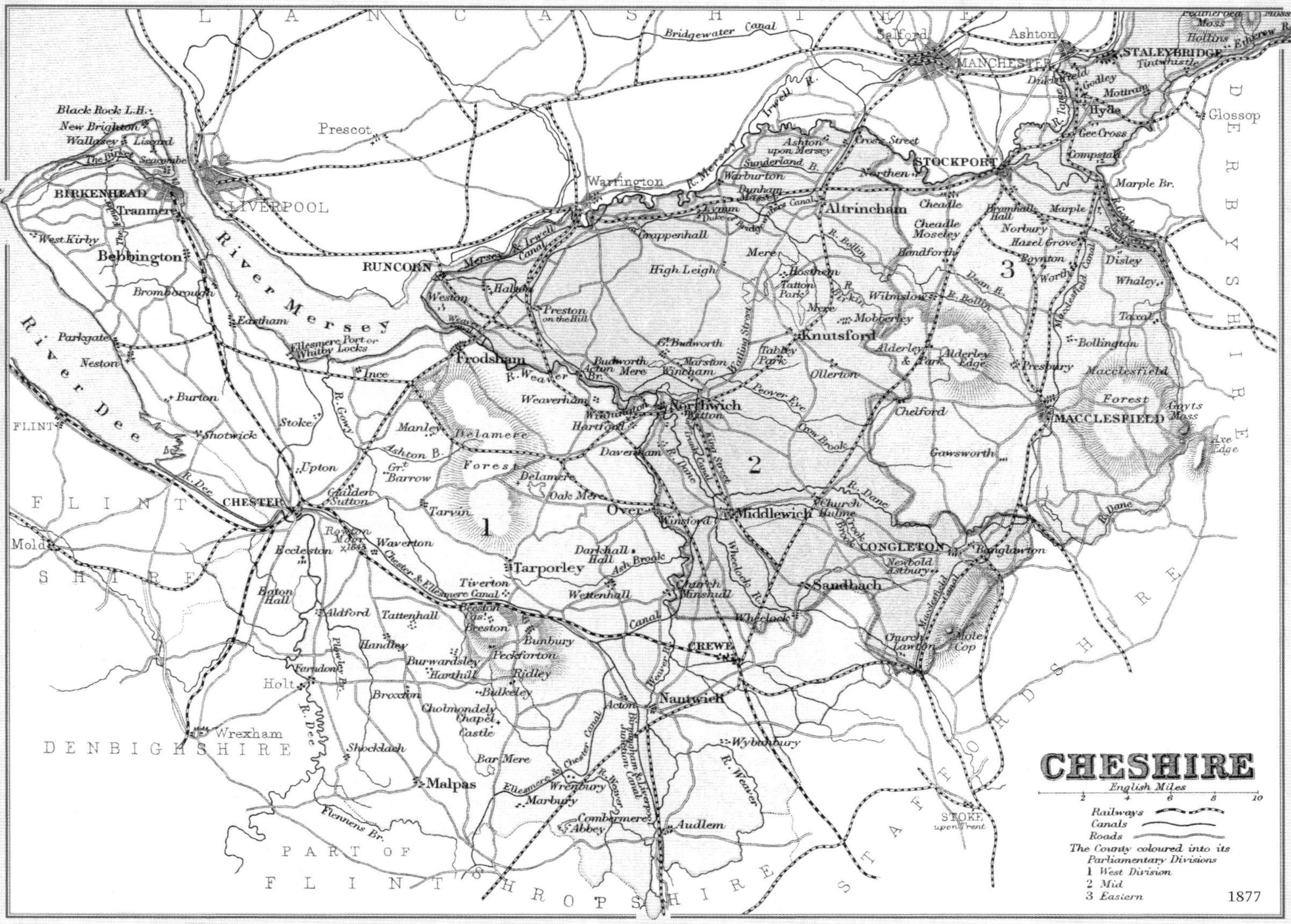

CHESHIRE

English Miles

Railways
Canals
Roads
The County coloured into its
Parliamentary Divisions
1 West Division
2 Mid
3 Eastern

1877

Bartholomew Gazetteer of the British Isles, 1887

CHESHIRE, or Chester, co. palatine and maritime co. of England, bounded on the NW. by the Irish Sea, and bordering on the cos. of Lancaster, York, Derby, Stafford, Salop, Denbigh, and Flint; extreme length, NE and SW., 58 miles; extreme breadth, 40 miles; average breadth, 18 miles; area, 657,123 ac.; pop. 644,037. C. forms, towards the Irish Sea, a flat peninsula, the Wirrall (12 miles by 7 miles), between the estuaries of the Mersey and the Dee, and inland a vast plain separating the mountains of Wales from those of Derbyshire. This plain is diversified with fine woods of oak, &c., and is studded with numerous small lakes or meres. A low ridge of sandstone hills runs N. from Congleton, near the E. border, and another extends from the neighbourhood of Malpas to Frodsham, near the estuary of the Mersey. The chief rivers are the Mersey with its affluent the Bollin, the Weaver, and the Dee. The soil consists of marl, mixed with clay and sand, and is generally fertile. There are numerous excellent dairy farms, on which the celebrated Cheshire cheese is made; also extensive market gardens, the produce of which is sent to Liverpool, Manchester, and the neighbouring towns. Salt has been long worked; it is obtained from rock salt and saline springs; the principal works are at Nantwich, Northwich, and Winsford. Coal and ironstone are worked in the districts of Macclesfield and Stockport. There are mfrs. of cotton, silk, and ribbons, carried on chiefly in the towns of the E. div.; and shipbuilding, on the Mersey. Cheshire contains 7 hundreds, 503 pars. the mun. bors. of Birkenhead, Chester, Congleton, Crewe, Hyde, Macclesfield, Stalybridge, and Stockport. It is mostly in the diocese of Chester.

...iel Craig

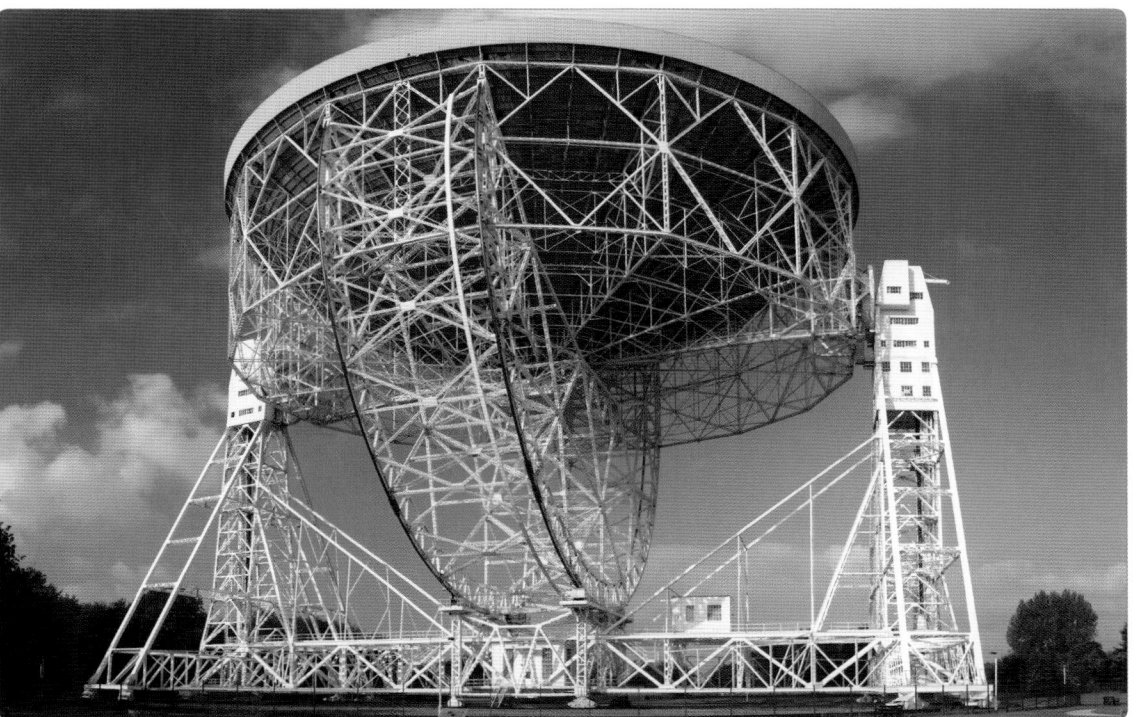

The Lovell Telescope, Jodrell Bank Centre for Astrophysics.

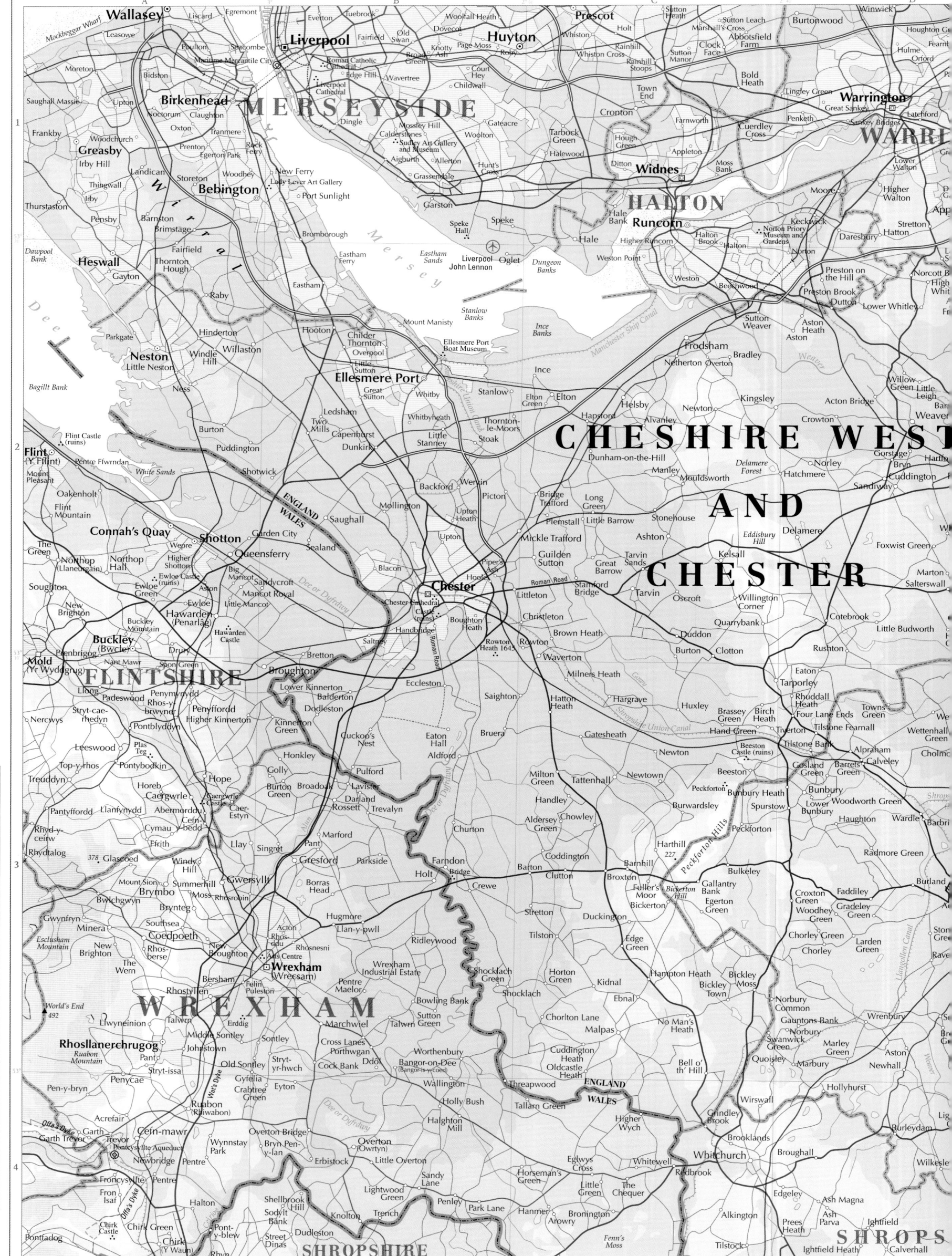

British National Grid projection

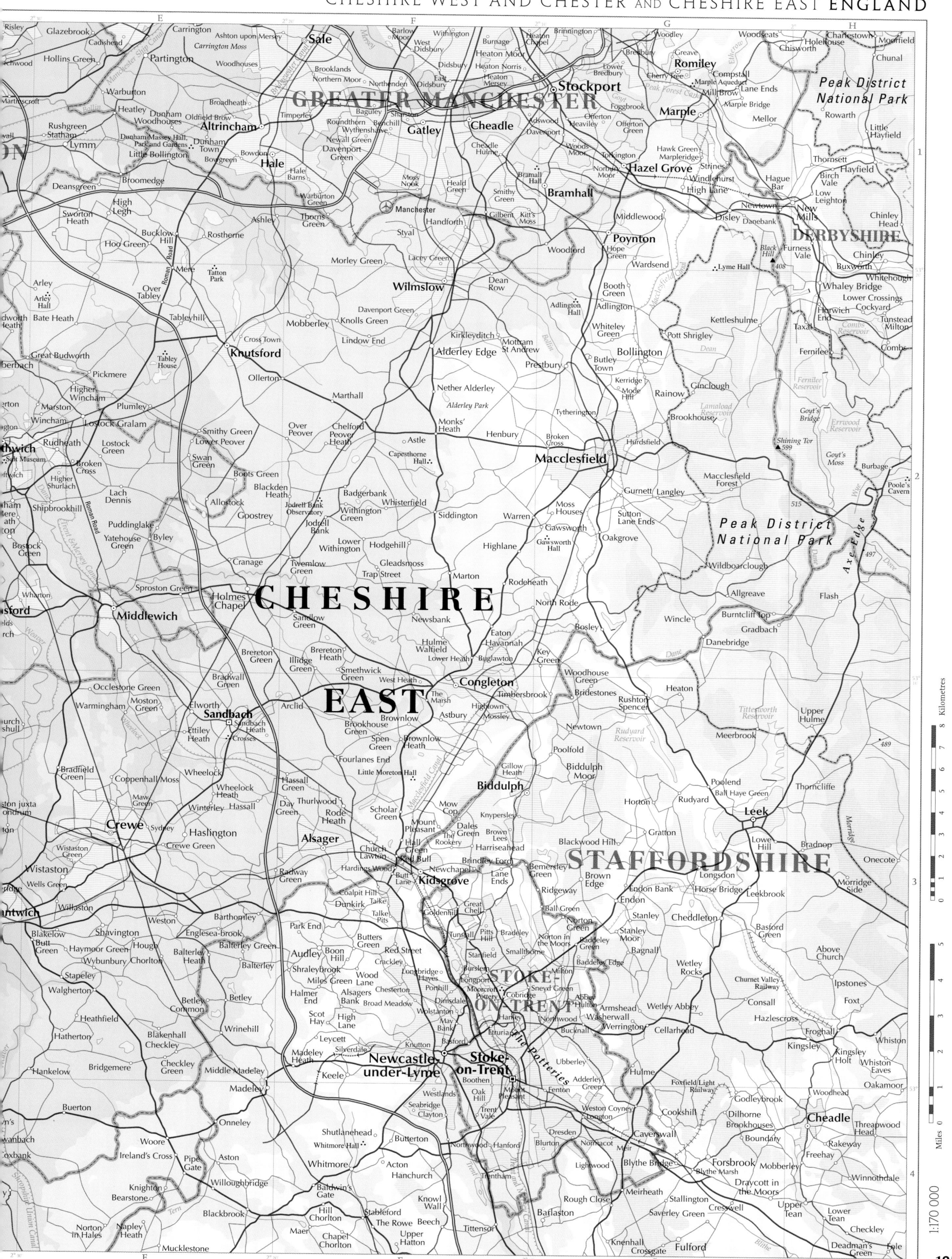

MERSEYSIDE METROPOLITAN COUNTY

Area Sq Km	818
Area Sq Miles	316
Population	1,347,900
Highest point	Billinge Hill (179 m) near St Helens

Metropolitan Borough Areas

City of Liverpool	134 sq km; 52 sq miles
Knowsley	86 sq km; 33 sq miles
St Helens	136 sq km; 53 sq miles
Sefton	205 sq km; 79 sq miles
Wirral	256 sq km; 99 sq miles

Population Borough Areas

City of Liverpool	434,900
Knowsley	150,800
St Helens	177,500
Sefton	275,100
Wirral	309,500

Merseyside, a name long used informally to describe the area around the Mersey estuary, was selected as the name of the metropolitan county formed in 1974 from existing county boroughs and parts of Lancashire and Cheshire. The five boroughs of Merseyside are the City of Liverpool, Knowsley, Sefton, St Helens and, to the south of the Mersey, Wirral. The metropolitan county was abolished by Parliament in 1986 along with all the other metropolitan counties in England and each borough then effectively became a unitary authority. Merseyside remains a ceremonial county distinct from Cheshire and Lancashire, with its own Lord Lieutenant and all the authorities share certain services including police, fire services and public transport.

The population of Merseyside is 1,347,900, making it the fifth largest metropolitan area after London, West Midlands, Manchester and West Yorkshire. The area has had a long history of population decline. Over the coming years this is expected to stabilize and then to increase slightly by 2031 overall, but with slight declines in Liverpool and Sefton. Merseyside is predominantly urban and low lying. The highest point is Billinge Hill (179 m) near St Helens.

In the pages that follow there are also descriptions of two unitary authorities on the Mersey that fall between Merseyside and Greater Manchester, Warrington and Halton (whose major towns are Runcorn and Widnes) but which remain within the ceremonial county of Cheshire. For areas and populations see page 182.

FAMOUS PEOPLE
City of Liverpool
George Stubbs, artist, born, 1724.

William Ewart Gladstone, Prime Minister of Britain four times, born 1809.
Arthur Clough, poet, born 1819.
Charles Booth, social reformer, born 1840.
John Brunner, founded Brunner Mond chemical company, born 1842.
Frank Hornby, inventor of Meccano, Hornby trains and Dinky toys, born 1863.
Arthur Askey, comedian, born 1900.
Nicholas Monsarrat, novelist (*The Cruel Sea*), born 1910.
Richard Laurence Millington (RLM) Synge, biochemist, Nobel laureate, born 1914.
George Melly, jazz singer, critic and writer, born 1926.
Kenneth (Ken) Dodd, comedian, born Knotty Ash, 1927.
Cilla Black, (*born* Pricilla White) singer, born 1943.
Kenny Everett, (*born* Maurice Cole) disc jockey and entertainer, born 1944.
Lynda La Plante, author and screenwriter, born 1946.
Alexei Sayle, writer, comedian and actor, born 1952.
Sir Simon Rattle, conductor, born 1955.
John Parrott, snooker player and presenter; World Snooker Champion in 1991, born 1964.
Wayne Rooney, footballer, born 1985.

Halton
Richard Bancroft, Archbishop of Canterbury (1604–10), born Farnworth.
Charles Lutwidge Dodgson (pseudonym Lewis Carrol), mathematician, author of *Alice in Wonderland*, born Daresbury, 1832.
Alfred Mond, 1st Baron Melchett, industrialist and politician, born Farnworth, 1868.
Charles Glover Barkla, physicist, Nobel laureate, born Widnes, 1877.

Knowsley
John Kemble, actor; manager of Drury Lane and Covent Garden theatres, born Prescot, 1757.
Edward Stanley, 14th Earl of Derby, British prime minister, leader of Conservative party 1846–68, born Knowsley Hall, 1799.
Sir Reginald (Rex) Harrison, actor, born Huyton, 1908.
John McCabe, composer and pianist, born Huyton, 1939.
Mary Peters, Olympic gold medal winning pentathlete, born Halewood, 1939.
Freddie Starr (*born* Frederick Fowell), comedian, impressionist, born Huyton, 1943.
Alan Bleasdale, television dramatist, born Kirkby, 1946.
Willy Russell, playwright and novelist, born Whiston, 1947.
John Conteh, boxer, born Kirkby, 1951.
Stephen Gerrard, footballer, born Whiston, 1980.

Sefton
Sir Edmund Whittaker, mathematician, born Southport, 1873.
Alan John Percival (AJP) Taylor, historian, born Birkdale, Southport, 1906.
Sir Anthony Quayle, actor, born, Ainsdale, 1913.

Robert Runcie, Archbishop of Canterbury (1980–91), born Crosby, 1921.
Roger McGough, poet, born Litherland, 1937.
Anne Robinson, journalist and television quiz show host, born Crosby, 1944.
Miranda Richardson, actress, born Southport, 1958.

St Helens
John Rylands, industrialist, benefactor and book collector, born Parr, St Helens, 1801.
Richard Seddon, Prime Minister of New Zealand (1893–1906), born St Helens, 1845.
Sir Thomas Beecham, conductor, born St Helens, 187
Sir John Randall, physicist and biophysicist, born Newton-le-Willows, 1905.
Rodney Porter, biochemist, Nobel laureate, born Newton-le-Willows, 1917.
Johnny Vegas (*born* Michael Joseph Pennington), comedian and actor, born St Helens, 1971.

Warrington
Kathleen Ferrier, contralto, born Higher Walton, 1912
Timothy Curry, actor and musician, born Grappenhal 1946.
Ian Brown, former lead singer of the Stone Roses, bor Warrington, 1963.
Christopher (Chris) Evans, radio and television presenter, born Warrington, 1966.

Wirral
May Sinclair, novelist and supporter of women's suffrage, born Rock Ferry, 1863.
Frederick Smith, Earl of Birkenhead, politician, Lord Chancellor, born Birkenhead, 1872.
Cyril Scott, composer, born Oxton, 1879.
Saunders Lewis, Welsh writer and nationalist, born Wallasey, 1893.
Siddonie Goossens, harpist, born Liscard, Wallasey, 189
John Selwyn Booke Lloyd, Baron Selwyn-Lloyd, Conservative politician, born West Kirby, 1904.
Malcolm Lowry, poet and novelist (*Under the Volcano*), born New Brighton, 1909.
Norman Thelwell, cartoonist, born Birkenhead, 1923.
Shirley Hughes, children's author and illustrator, born West Kirby, 1927.
Patricia Routledge, actress, born Birkenhead, 1929.
Adrian Henri, poet, born Birkenhead, 1932.
Glenda Jackson, Oscar winning actress and Labour politician, born Birkenhead, 1936.
Ralph Steadman, cartoonist, born Wallasey, 1936.
John Ravenscroft (known professionally as John Peel), disc jockey and radio presenter, born Heswell, 1939.
Sir Ian Botham, Test cricketer, all rounder, born Oldfield, Heswell, 1955.
Christopher (Chris) Boardman, Olympic medal winni cyclist, born Hoylake, 1968.
Matthew Dawson, rugby union player, England captai born Birkenhead, 1972.

Southport Pier

Bartholomew Gazetteer of the British Isles, 1887

LIVERPOOL, *mun. bor., city, seaport, and par., SW. Lancashire, on estuary of river Mersey, 31 m. W. of Manchester and 201 m. NW. of London by rail – mun. bor., 5210 ac., pop. 552,508. Markets, daily. Lyrpoole and Litherpoole were ancient names of this celebrated seaport, these designations being supposed to be derived from the Celtic Llerpwll, the "place on the pool." It is very doubtful whether the town existed at the time of the Conquest. Camden (1551–1623) refers to it as being more famous for its beauty and populousness than for its antiquity. In 1172 the military operations in Ireland gave it great importance as a convenient point of embarkation for troops. With this exception the early history of Liverpool contains little that is interesting or important. The first charter was granted in 1173 by Henry II.; in 1207 the charter was confirmed by King John, and 20 years later the town was constituted a free borough by Henry III. During the reign of Elizabeth a quay and breakwater were erected, the latter being intended to act as a winter protection for shipping. Commercial intercourse is maintained with every part of the world. Several lines of splendid steamships keep up regular communication with New York; others with Boston, Philadelphia, New Orleans, Halifax, the Canadian ports, and the East and West Indies. Extending along both shores of the Mersey are immense lines of docks, which form the principal feature of the city. Inland water communication is kept up with Yorkshire and all parts of Lancashire, chiefly by the Leeds and Liverpool Canal. The city is justly celebrated for its fine buildings. The Town Hall (1754) is the oldest and the most interesting; but the finest building, from an architectural point of view, is St George's Hall (1854), a superb edifice, which cost £250,000. At the head of the educational institutions stands University College (affiliated to the Victoria University), opened by Lord Derby in 1882; and among middle-class schools are the Royal Institution School, Collegiate Institution, and Liverpool Institute High School. Cotton is the staple of the* imports of Liverpool, which otherwise include goods from all parts of the world. Recently an enormous trade has arisen through the importation of provisions, including live stock, from America and the colonies. The port, too, is the principal place in the kingdom for the departure of emigrants. Mfrs. are not extensive. Shipbuilding has fallen off greatly owing to the competition at the Clyde and in the north of England. The mfrs. of engines for marine navigation, however, have a worldwide renown. Sugar refining, iron and brass founding, ropemaking, brewing, chemical works, iron chain cable and anchor making, and the distilling of tar and turpentine, form other leading industries. A large source of trade exists in the produce of neighbouring collieries. Liverpool was created a diocese in 1880, at which time it was transformed into a city by royal charter.

LIVERPOOL, 1903

Needle'. Hardshaw Centre, St Helens.

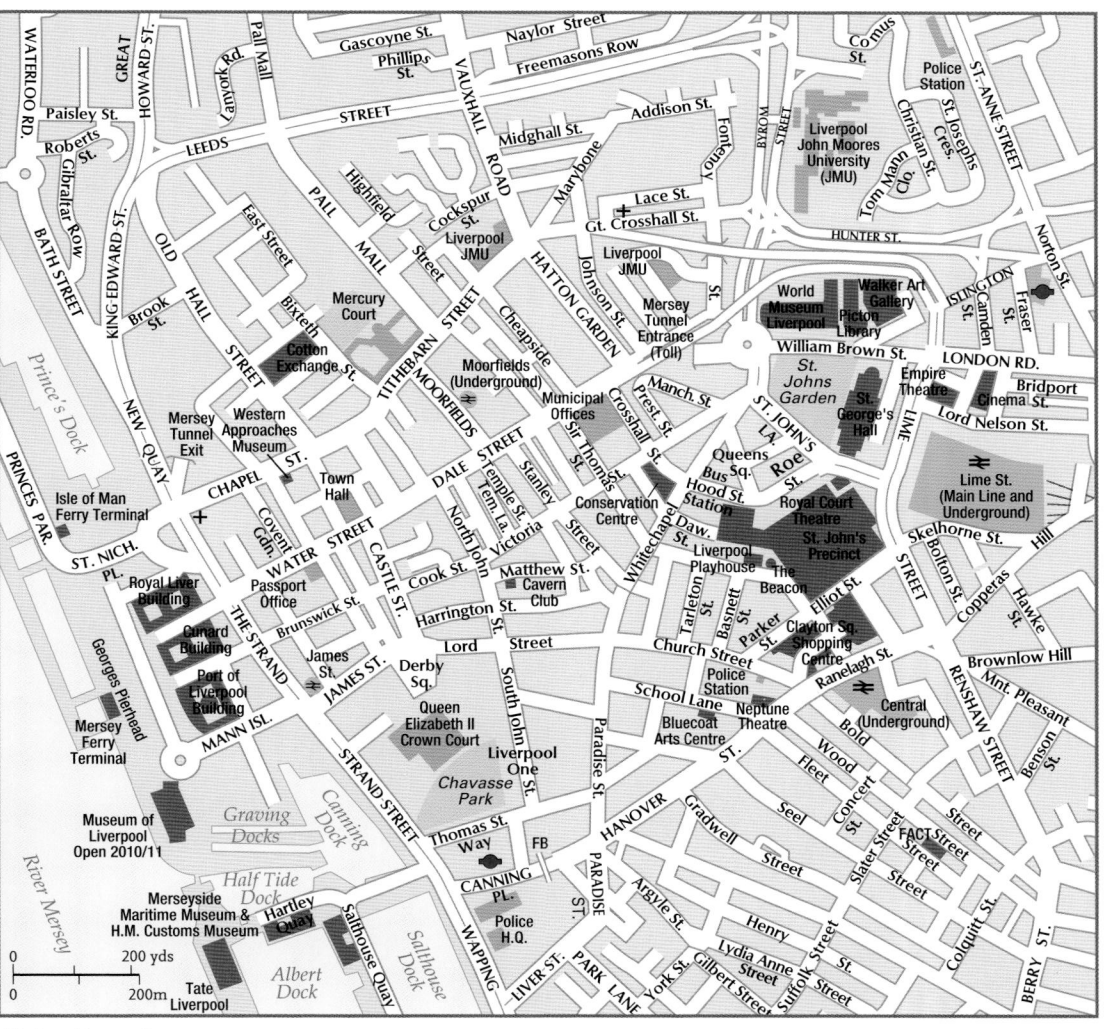

Modern Liverpool

City of Liverpool

The name of Liverpool comes from the Old English meaning 'pool or creek of muddy water'. The Liver bird is a heraldic bird rather than a real bird, although it is now often linked to the cormorant.

FAMOUS FOR

The Mersey sound, the great blossoming of pop music in the 1960s, and Liverpool's greatest group, The Beatles: John Lennon, born 1940; Ringo Starr (born Richard Starkey), born 1940; Sir Paul McCartney, born 1942; and George Harrison, born 1943.

The Three Graces is the name given to three imposing commercial buildings on Liverpool Pier Head – the Royal Liver Building (1911), the Cunard Building (1916) and the Mersey Docks and Harbour Board offices (1907). They now form part of the Liverpool Maritime Mercantile City UNESCO World Heritage Site.

Liverpool is home to two of Britain's great football teams – **Liverpool** and **Everton**. Overall Liverpool has had greater success, particularly in European football, but it has also suffered greater tragedies, particularly the Hillsborough Stadium disaster in Sheffield in 1989 when 96 fans died in a crowd crush.

Two of the most prominent buildings in Liverpool are the **Anglican Cathedral** (built between 1904 and 1978), the largest cathedral building in Britain, and the **Roman Catholic Cathedral**, built between 1962 and 1967 adjacent to the crypt of a building even bigger than the Anglican Cathedral, which was designed in the 1930s but never completed.

A person from Liverpool is called a **scouser** and speaks **scouse**. Somewhat surprisingly 'scouse' is the name of a sailor's meat stew, originally brought to Liverpool from northern Europe, where it was called lobscouse.

Liverpool is situated on the north bank of the Mersey Estuary, at this point about 1 km wide, with Birkenhead on its southern bank. The site of Liverpool has been settled since the 12th century. A castle was built around 1235, and about it were laid out the original seven streets of Liverpool. Very little of the city prior to the 18th century remains. The most significant building from that period is Speke Hall, a very fine timber-framed house primarily from the 16th century, once in open countryside but now close to Liverpool John Lennon Airport. In 1667 the first Liverpool ship returned from the West Indies with a cargo of sugar and thus began the city's trading with the Americas. In 1715 the first dock opened and in the 18th century the trade was primarily with Virginia and the West Indies and concentrated on sugar, tobacco and cotton. It also played a significant part in the slave trade – Liverpool ships controlled around 80 per cent of the British slave trade before its abolition in 1807.

Around 1700 its population was about 6,000. By 1801 it was nearly 80,000, and by 1901, 685,000. It had become, in the words of Benjamin Disraeli, the Second City of the Empire. It also became a cosmopolitan city, with Britain's oldest Black African and Chinese communities.

At the start of the 20th century, there were 14 km of docks through which a third of Britain's exports and a quarter of its imports flowed, and a seventh of the registered shipping in the world was owned by Liverpool companies. Its position began to decline after World War I as passenger lines moved away, the Depression directly reduced the quantity of goods moving through the docks, and commercial business moved to London. During the World War II, the city and its docks were heavily bombed and afterwards it never recovered its former glory. Its population declined rapidly from its peak of over 846,000 in 1931 and it became better known for its music, its poets, its comedians and its football teams rather than as a great trading city.

The port of Liverpool moved to Seaforth (in nearby Sefton) but, as a result of containerization, only needs to employ a small workforce. Sugar refining and engineering continue to provide manufacturing employment, but only just over 5 per cent of jobs are in this sector. Over 39 per cent of jobs are in public administration, education and health, nearly 45 per cent above the national average. The figures are boosted by three universities in the city (Liverpool, Liverpool John Moores and Liverpool Hope) and renowned medical facilities including one of Britain's two specialist institutions on tropical medicine. The Toxteth riots of 1981, born out of the intense economic decline of the city, led to the beginning of a revival, building on the creative industries. In 1984 there was the International Garden Festival and in 1988 The Tate North Gallery opened in the iconic Albert Docks buildings, once threatened with demolition but now part of the UNESCO World Heritage Site (Liverpool Maritime Mercantile City). In 2008, after a shaky start Liverpool had a successful year as European City of Culture.

"Liverpool is one of the wonders of Britain … What it may grow to in time I know not … The town has now an opulent, flourishing and increasing trade; in a word, they are almost become like Londoners, universal merchants."
Daniel Defoe, 1726

"Maritime commerce brought Liverpool not just wealth and employment, but an air of cosmopolitanism that few cities in the world could rival, and it still has that sense about it. In Liverpool you still feel like you are some place."
Bill Bryson, 1995, *Notes from a Small Island*

Liverpool FC photowall

Canning Docks

River Mersey with Birkenhead to the bottom and Liverpool to the top.

ALTON

Halton was created as a new district within Cheshire in 1974 and in 1998 became a unitary authority in its own right. It was named after the medieval barony of Halton (ruins of Halton Castle can still be seen). It is best known for its two major settlements, Runcorn and Widnes, which sit on opposite s of the Mersey and are now joined by the Silver Jubilee Bridge, one of the largest arch bridges in Europe. Up until the mid-19th century the area was a rural kwater. Widnes, on the northern bank was the first to be industrialized, prompted he construction of the first combined railway, canal and dock complex in 1845. years later the first chemical works were opened, and Widnes rapidly became a or and heavily polluted centre for the chemical industry. Runcorn, too, started to ome to the chemical industry and to tanneries. Its economy was further boosted he arrival of the Manchester Ship Canal. The chemical industry remains important oth places to this day. Food processing, metal-working and furniture making are significant. Manufacturing accounts for nearly 15 per cent of jobs while public inistration, education and health provides 17.6 per cent of jobs, over a third less the national average. The village of Daresbury has two claims to fame – as the hplace of Lewis Carroll and as the site of the Daresbury Laboratory, an international icle physics research facility and its related Science and Innovation Campus.

Helens

metropolitan borough of St Helens covers St Helens and also includes Haydock, vton-le-Willows and Rainford. The area was at the heart of the South Lancashire field. Coalmining was recorded from the late 16th century and its exploitation assisted by the Sankey Navigation, a canal opened in 1762; the last pit to close was kside colliery in 1992. The ready availability of coal and sand led to the industry has defined St Helens, that of glassmaking. In 1773 the British Cast Plate Glass npany was founded at Ravenhead, but it was in the 19th century that glassmaking ly thrived here. Although many companies have moved their manufacturing away, ington's, founded in 1826, still makes glass here, now using its innovative float glass nique. The World of Glass museum opened in 2000. The other major settlement ewton-le-Willows, which developed as a railway town, and was the scene of the accident at the opening of the Liverpool and Manchester Railway in 1830, when liam Huskisson, a Liverpool MP, was knocked down by the 'Rocket' locomotive died later of his injuries. Manufacturing now accounts for over 11 per cent of jobs the service sector takes 79 per cent of jobs (with 25 per cent of all jobs being in the lic sector).

owsley

wsley is a metropolitan borough formed in 1974 from a number of smaller orities. It lies immediately to the east of Liverpool and many of its settlements ffectively suburbs of Liverpool. Knowsley is named after the historic village of wsley, which is where the Stanleys (who became earls of Derby) built Knowsley which dates from the 15th century onwards. No longer a family home, the house d for events and the grounds now contain a safari park. In addition to Knowsley, settlements include Halewood, Huyton, Kirkby, Prescot, and Whiston. Kirkby developed after World War II as housing overspill for Liverpool, its population asing rapidly from around 3,00 in 1951 to nearly 60,000 in 1971 but then back a to 40,470 in 2001. The Kirkby industrial estate was short-lived as a manufacturing e and now hosts a range of service industries, including call centres. Coal mining to be important and the last mine, Sutton Manor, only closed in 1991. Halewood w the main manufacturing centre in the district with both a large car plant and or gear box manufacturer, while at Whiston, electrical appliances are made. result manufacturing accounts for nearly 20 per cent of all jobs while public nistration, education and health provides 32 per cent of jobs.

ton

metropolitan borough of Sefton stretches along the coast from Liverpool up to nport. Major settlements include Bootle, Litherland, Maghull, Crosby, Formby Southport. It is named after the old village of Sefton; the late 15th-century church Helen's Sefton is one of the finest in Merseyside. The communities of Sefton nainly strung out along the coast and have distinctive identities. Bootle is almost tinguishable from its immediate neighbour of Liverpool. Originally a seaside t at the start of the 19th century, its shoreline was taken over by docks. The main s for Liverpool have now moved a little further up the coast to Seaforth, the important docks for northwest England, but with containerization, no longer jor employer. Sandy beaches then stretch from here past Crosby and Formby to hport, originally developed in 1792 for its sea bathing and still a major resort Britain's second-longest pier). Also within Sefton is Aintree Racecourse, home e Grand National. Along Crosby Sands is Antony Gormley's installation, 'Another ', consisting of 100 cast-iron life-size figures of the artist placed along a 3 km ch of Crosby beach. Nearly 40 per cent of jobs are in public administration, ation and health (boosted by national government offices in Bootle) and 9 per cent tourism, compared with 6 per cent in manufacturing.

WARRINGTON

Warrington was created as a new district within Cheshire in 1974 and in 1998 became a unitary authority in its own right. The main settlement is Warrington and the area straddles the Mersey and the Manchester Ship Canal. Once ideally located for transport by water, it is now at the heart of the motorway system, with the M6 bisecting the area from north to south and the M62 and M56 both travelling east–west through the area. Warrington can trace its origins back to a Roman fort at a crossing point over the Mersey and it developed in medieval times as an important river crossing. Its parish church dedicated to an unknown saint called St Elphin dates from this time. In the 18th century copper smelting and weaving developed and industrialization really began with the arrival of Sankey and Bridgewater canals. The first mill in the northwest to be powered by a steam engine was built at Warrington in 1787 and further industrialization followed. In 1968, Warrington was granted New Town status, leading to traditional industries such as chemicals, brewing and food processing being joined by hi-tech industries and research and development facilities. Warrington retains its importance as a regional shopping, leisure and commercial centre. The service sector now provides nearly 85 per cent of jobs, the largest sector being business, IT and other business, while manufacturing accounts for only 7.5 percent of jobs.

Wirral

The metropolitan borough of Wirral was formed in 1974 out of part of Cheshire. It occupies most of the Wirral peninsula between the Mersey and the Dee. The main settlements are Birkenhead, Wallasey, New Brighton, Hoylake, Heswell and Bebington. The origins of Birkenhead go back to a priory founded at the end of the 12th century by monks from Chester on the headland of birch trees that give the town its name. Wirral remained an isolated and sparsely populated area until the 19th century. In 1817 the first steam ferry across the Mersey started and in 1824 William Laird founded his shipyard, which still operates today (as Cammell Laird), and began building a new town, inspired by the look of Edinburgh's New Town. Birkenhead Park was the first free municipal park in Britain, designed by Joseph Paxton and opened in 1847. Its design influenced that of New York's Central Park. In 1847 the first docks were opened and the area rapidly saw the growth of docks and related processing industries (sugar refining, flour milling, rubber manufacture). The regular Mersey ferries encouraged many Liverpool merchants to settle in Wirral, and the trend was enhanced by the Mersey rail tunnel, built in 1886, and the two road tunnels, built in 1934 and 1971. Wallasey developed along similar lines while New Brighton became a popular seaside resort for workers in the northwest, but now much declined. Port Sunlight, on the banks of the Mersey is a remarkable workers' village built by Lord Leverhulme for workers at his soap and detergents factory. Ship building and other manufacturing industries have declined during the late 20th century, and the area has increasingly become a dormitory area for Liverpool. Just over 10 per cent of jobs are in manufacturing (the national average for Britain) while over 36 per cent are in public administration, health and education.

Palm House at Sefton Park, Liverpool.

A   B   C   D

I R I S H

S E A

L i v e r p o o l

B a y

Horse Bank

Angry Brow

Southport Pier

Southport

Banks

Crossens

Marshside

Churchtown

Blowick

Birkdale

Brown Edge

Pool Hey

Snape Green

Carr Cross

Bescar

Lane En

Shirdley Hill

Scarisbrick

Smi

Heat

Bri

Ainsdale-on-Sea

Ainsdale

Pinfold

Hurlston Green

Woodvale

Halsall

Bangor's Green

Barton

Haskayne

Downholland Cross

Mad Wharf

Formby Point

Formby Hills

Freshfield

Formby

Little Altcar

Great Altcar

Aughton

Holt Green

Lydiate

Ince Blundell

Carr Houses

Maghull

Hightown

Homer Green

Lunt

Mos

Side

Little Crosby

Thornton

Sefton

Mell

Mou

Netherton

Melling

Wa

Blundellsands

Great Crosby

Buckley Hill

Ford

Crosby

Brighton le Sands

Aintree

Waterloo

Crosby Channel

Seaforth

Orrell

Litherland

Fazakerley

Walton

Norris Green

Crox

and Cou

Bootle

Kirkdale

New Brighton

West Derby

Clubmoor

Mockbeggar Wharf

M E R S

Anfield

Everton

Toebrook

Wallasey

Liscard

Egremont

East Hoyle Bank

Leasowe

Poulton

Seacombe

Liverpool

Fairfield

Old Swan

Broad G

Maritime Mercantile City

Roman Catholic Cathedral

Edge Hill

Wavertree

West Hoyle Bank

Moreton

Bidston

Liverpool Cathedral

Hoylake

Saughall Massie

Upton

Noctorum

Birkenhead

Dingle

Mossley Hill

Hilbre Island

Grange

Frankby

Woodchurch

Oxton

Claughton

Sudley Art Gallery and Museum

West Kirby

Greasby

Tranmere

Aigburth

Prenton

Rock Ferry

Grass

Irby Hill

Egerton Park

Caldy

Irby

Landican

Woodhey

New Ferry

Lady Lever Art Gallery

Thurstaston

Thingwall

Storeton

Bebington

Port Sunlight

Barnston

W

i

Brimstage

Fairfield

Bromborough

Pensby

Point of Ayr

Talacre

Mostyn Bank

Gayton

Heswall

Thornton Hough

Eastham Ferry

Llawndy

Raby

Eastham

Eastham Sands

Prestatyn

Gronant

Gwespyr

Ffynnongroyw

Pen-y-ffordd

Mostyn Quay

Dawpool Bank

Parkgate

Hooton

Mc

Ma

Llanasa

Picton

Meliden

(Galtt Melyd)

Gwaenysgor

Gyrn

Trelogan

Mostyn

Holywell Bank

Neston

Windle Hill

Willaston

Childer Thornton

Little Sutton

Overp

Tan-yr-allt

Gop Hill

Axton

Cwm

FLINTSHIRE

Ochr-y-foel

Trelawnyd

Maen Achwyfaen

Downing

Glan-y-don

Llannerch-y-Môr

Mertyn

CHES

Marian Cwm

Offa's Dyke

Whitford

(Chwitffordd)

Hinderton

Cwm

Llyn Helyg

Lloc

Pantasaph Friary

Carmel

Basingwerk Abbey

Greenfield

(Maes-Glas)

DENBIGHSHIRE

Gorsedd

St Winifred's

Holy Well and Chapel

Ellesmere Po

Longitude west of Greenwich

Metres	Feet
1000	3280
900	2952
800	2624
700	2296
600	1968
500	1640
400	1312
300	4921
200	656
150	492
100	328
50	164
0	Land below sea level
50	164
200	656
1000	3281

Welsh Channel

Dee

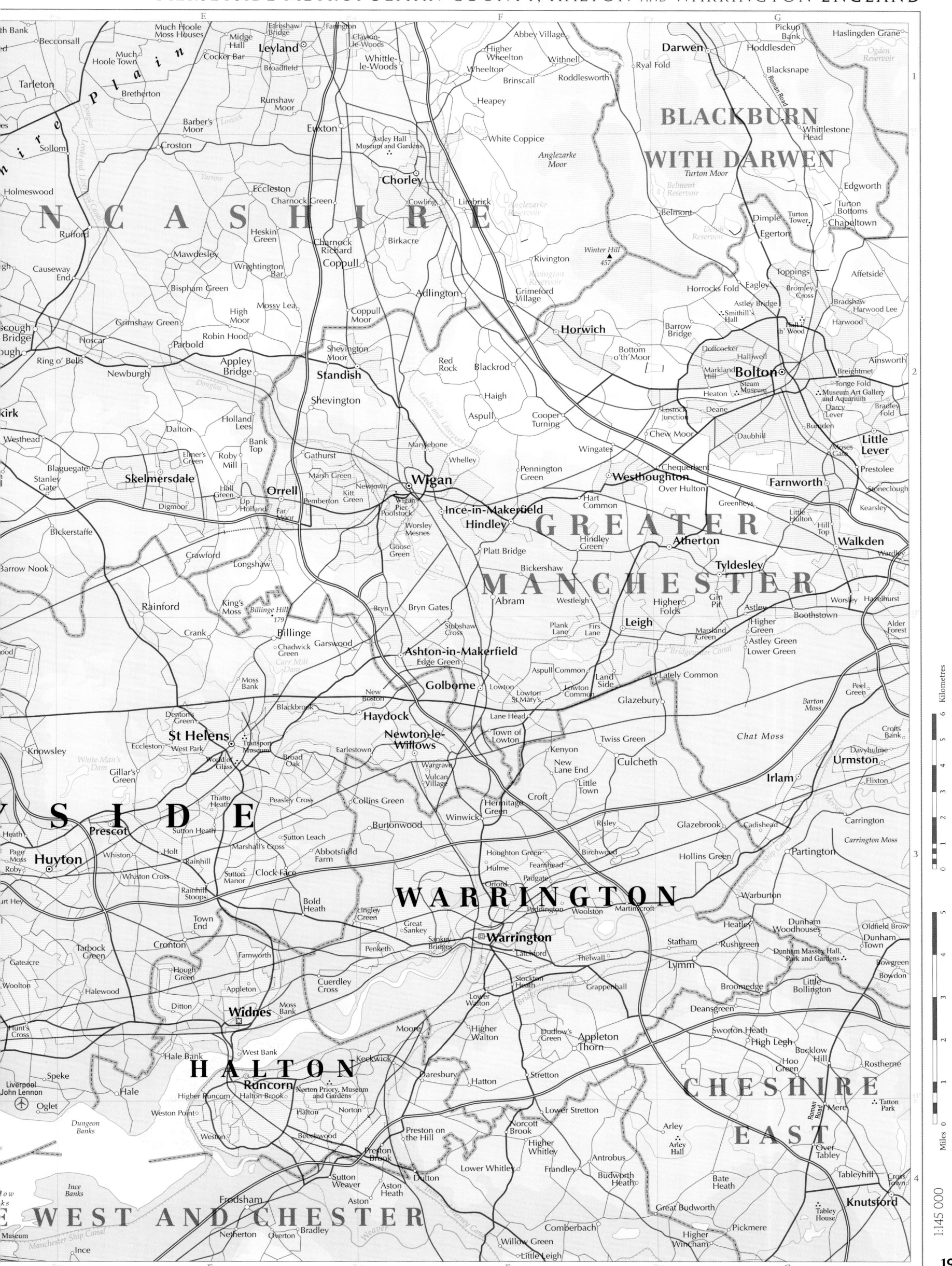

1:145 000

© Collins Bartholomew Ltd

GREATER MANCHESTER METROPOLITAN COUNTY

Area Sq Km	1,276
Area Sq Miles	493
Population	2,573.500
Highest point	Black Chew Head (542 m)
	on Saddleworth Moor above Oldham

Metropolitan Borough Areas

City of Manchester	116 sq km; 45 sq miles
Bolton	140 sq km; 54 sq miles
Bury	99 sq km; 38 sq miles
Oldham	142 sq km; 55 sq miles
Rochdale	158 sq km; 61 sq miles
City of Salford	97 sq km; 38 sq miles
Stockport	126 sq km; 49 sq miles
Tameside	103 sq km; 40 sq miles
Trafford	106 sq km; 41 sq miles
Wigan	188 sq km; 73 sq miles

Metropolitan Borough Populations

City of Manchester	464,200
Bolton	262,800
Bury	183,100
Oldham	219,700
Rochdale	206,300
City of Salford	221,300
Stockport	281,000
Tameside	215,500
Trafford	212,800
Wigan	306,800

Greater Manchester was established as a metropolitan county in 1974. After London and the West Midlands it is the third most populous conurbation in Britain. It was created to bring a little more order to the local government of the area which was divided between a large number of authorities and crossed a number of county boundaries. Centred on Manchester, it took in significant parts of Lancashire and Cheshire as well as a section of the old West Riding of Yorkshire. It was established with 10 metropolitan boroughs: City of Manchester, Bolton, Bury, Oldham, Rochdale, City of Salford, Stockport, Tameside, Trafford and Wigan. The metropolitan county was abolished by Parliament in 1986 along with all the other metropolitan counties in England and each district then effectively became a unitary authority. Greater Manchester remains a ceremonial county with its own Lord Lieutenant and all the authorities share certain services including police, fire services and public transport.

The total population of Greater Manchester is 2,573,500 and it is predicted to grow to around 2,950,000 by 2031. This growth is expected to be disproportionate with Manchester alone accounting for 36 per cent of the growth, while the old mill towns of Bury, Bolton, Oldham and Rochdale will see much lower growth. Across the area between 1981 and 2001 the population declined (and especially in the main urban areas) making Manchester's transformation all the more dramatic. Although the boundaries are quite tightly drawn around the urban areas, the land does rise into the Pennines in the east and the north. The highest point in the county is Black Chew Head (542 m) on Saddleworth Moor above Oldham. The main rivers are the Mersey and its many tributaries including the Bollin, Irwell, Medlock, Tame, Goyt and Roch.

FAMOUS PEOPLE

City of Manchester
Thomas De Quincey, author of *Confessions of an English Opium-Eater*, born 1785.
Frances Hodgson Burnett, author of *The Secret Garden*, born 1849.
Sir Joseph John (J J) Thomson, physicist, discovered the electron, Nobel laureate, born 1856.
Emmeline Pankhurst (born Emmeline Goulden), Suffragette and women's rights campaigner, born 1858.
David Lloyd George, 1st Earl Lloyd-George of Dwyfor, Liberal politician, Prime Minister (1916–22), born 1863.
Sir Arthur Harden, biochemist, Nobel laureate, born 1865.
Laurence Stephen (L S) Lowry, artist, born 1887.
John William Alcock, aviator, first nonstop flight over the Atlantic with Arthur Brown (1919), born 1892.
Les Dawson, comedian, born Collyhurst, 1934.
John Thaw, actor, born Gorton, 1942.
Chris Ofili, Turner prize-winning artist, born 1968.

Bolton
William Hesketh Lever, Viscount Leverhulme, manufacturer and philanthropist, born Bolton, 1851.
Roy Chadwick, aeronautical engineer; designed Lancaster bomber, born Farnworth, 1893.
Frank Finlay, actor, born Farnworth, 1926.
Robert Shaw, actor, born Westhoughton, 1927
Peter Kay, comedian, born Bolton, 1973.
Amir Khan, Olympic medal winning boxer, born Bolton, 1986.

Bury
Sir Robert Peel, prime minister; associated with formation of Metropolitan Police, born Bury, 1788.
Daniel Boyle, film director, born Radcliffe, 1956.
Victoria Wood, comedian and writer, born Prestwich, 1953.

Oldham
Dame Eva Turner, operatic soprano singer, born Werneth, 1892.
Sir William Walton, composer, born Oldham, 1902.
Roy Fuller, poet and novelist, born Failsworth, 1912.
Eric Sykes, comedian, born Oldham, 1923.
Michael Atherton, cricketer, England captain, born Failsworth, 1968.

Rochdale
Sir James Kay-Shuttleworth, education and public health reformer, born Rochdale, 1804.
John Bright, politician; co-founder of Anti-Corn Law League, born Rochdale, 1811.
Dame Gracie Fields, music hall comedienne and sing born Rochdale, 1898..

City of Salford
William Webb Ellis, instigator of the game of rugby, born Salford, 1806.
Alliott Verdon Roe, aircraft manufacturer (Avro aeroplanes), born Patricroft, Eccles, 1877.
Kenneth Wolstenholme, football commentator, born Worsley, 1920.
Michael Vaughan, cricketer, England captain, born Eccles, 1974.

Stockport
Sir Joseph Whitworth, engineer and industrialist, born Stockport, 1803.
Frederick (Fred) Perry, three times Wimbledon single tennis champion, born Stockport, 1909.
Sir Frederic Williams, electrical engineer and compu pioneer, born Stockport, 1911.
Dame Joan Bakewell, television presenter, born Stockport, 1933.

Tameside
Sir Geoffrey Hurst, footballer, 1966 World Cup winne born Ashton-under-Lyne, 1941.
Margaret Beckett, Labour politician; first woman Foreign Secretary, born Ashton-under-Lyne, 1943.

Trafford
John Ireland, composer, born Bowdon, 1879.
Robert Bolt, playwright, born Sale, 1924.

Wigan
George Formby Jr (born George Hoy Booth), entertai and comedian, born Wigan, 1904.
Eric Laithwaite, inventor, electrical engineer, born Atherton, 1921.
Roy Kinnear, actor, born Wigan, 1934.

Manchester Town Hall

"Ah! but the Mediterranean!" exclaimed Coningsby
"What I would not give to see Athens!"
"I have seen it" said the stranger, slightly shrugging his shoulders, "and more wonderful things. Phantoms and spectres! The Age of Ruins is past. Have you seen Manchester?"
Benjamin Disraeli, 1844, *Coningsby*

"One day I missed a train from Pendlebury – (a place) I had ignored for seven years – and as I left the station I saw the Acme Spinning Company's mill ... The huge black framework of rows of yellow-lit windows standing up agair the sad, damp charged afternoon sky. The mill was turning out ... I watched this scene – which I'd looked at many time without seeing – with rapture."
L S Lowry

Bartholomew Gazetteer of the British Isles, 1887

MANCHESTER, *mun. bor., city, par., and township, SE. Lancashire, on rivers Irk, Irwell, and Medlock, 31 miles E. of Liverpool and 186 miles NW. of London by rail – par. (including the greater part of the sister town of Salford, separated from Manchester by the Irwell, which is spanned by a series of bridges), 35,248 ac., pop. 720,481; township, 1646 ac., pop. 148,794; mun. bor., 4293 ac., pop. 341,414; 12 newspapers. Although the particulars regarding its early existence are scanty, and by no means indubitable, there are reasonable grounds for the conjecture that Manchester was the seat of a British stronghold, situated at the place which is still called Castlefield. A portion of its Roman wall still exists, and other relics of a Roman occupation have been disinterred in abundance. Its Roman name (supposed to be derived from the British Mancenion, the "place of tents") was Mancunium, hence the Saxon Manceastre. When the woollen mfrs. were introduced into England during the reign of Edward III. (1327–1377) Lancashire became the centre of the industry, and from that period the prosperity of Manchester may be dated. In an account of Manchester of date 1650 its mfrs. are described as comprising "woollens, frizes, fustians, sack cloths, mingled stuffs, inkles, tapes, and prints." Conspicuous events in its subsequent annals are: – Cheetham College founded (1653); cotton goods first exported (1760); Bridgwater Canal opened (1761); Manchester and Liverpool Ry. opened (1832); Manchester made a parl. bor. (1832) and a mun. bor. (1838); bishopric founded (1847); Owens College opened (1852); Manchester declared a city (1853); New Town Hall opened (1877). Three circumstances especially gave power and direction to the trade of the city: – (1.) The success of the great work of the Duke of Bridgwater (assisted by James Brindley), who in 1758 began the system of inland navigation, and gave Manchester a splendid waterway for traffic; (2.) the introduction of machinery in cotton spinning, which occurred late in the 18th century; and (3.) the opening of the Manchester and Sheffield Railway in 1830 – the*

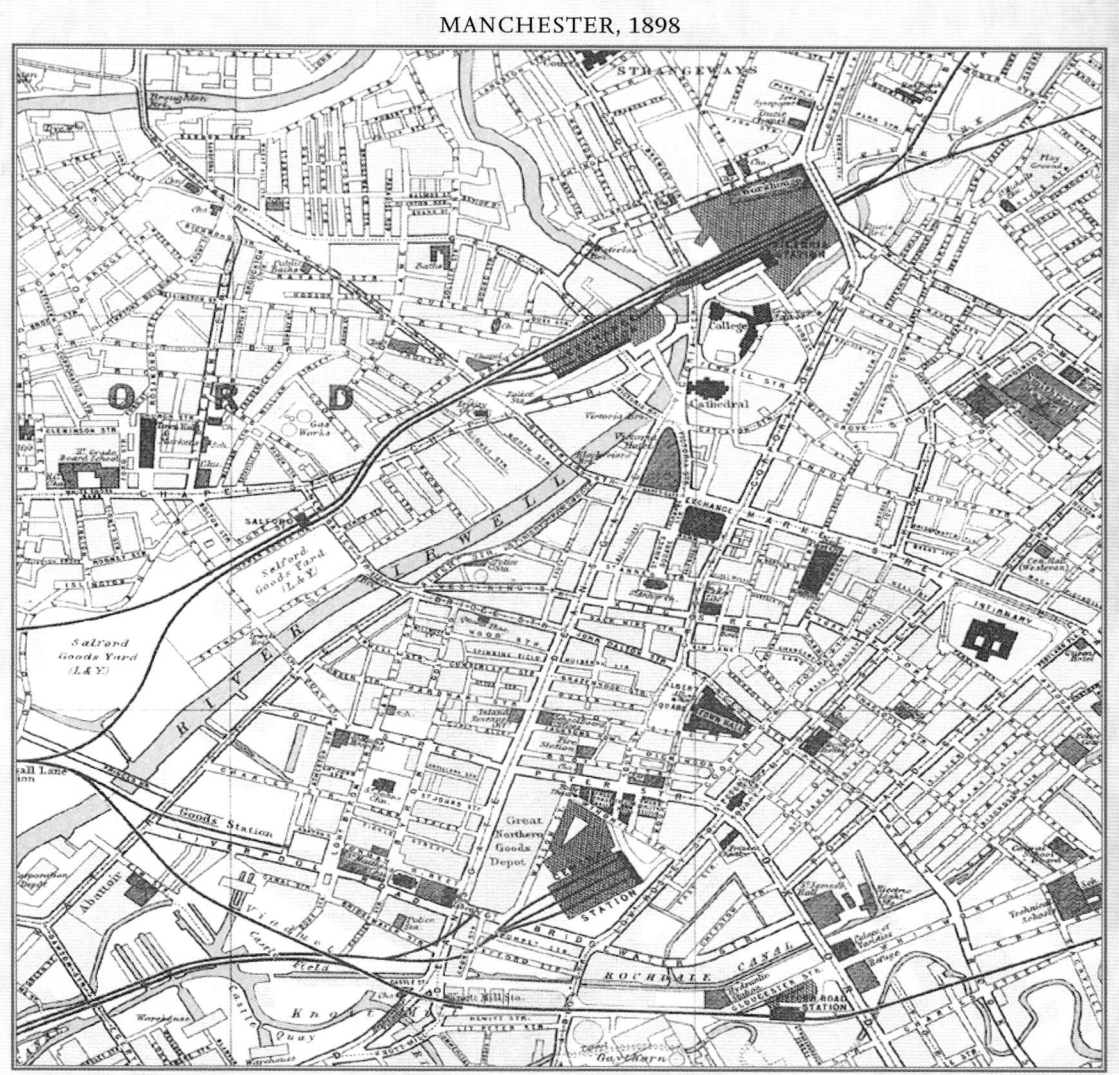

MANCHESTER, 1898

second in the kingdom. It is estimated that there are 250 cotton factories in the neighbourhood. Woollen and silk fabrics are manufactured in vast quantities.

Engineering, and the making of machinery of all descriptions, employ thousands of the people, as also do various large chemical works.

Manchester Central Convention Centre uses the former train shed of Manchester Central railway station, a Grade II listed building.

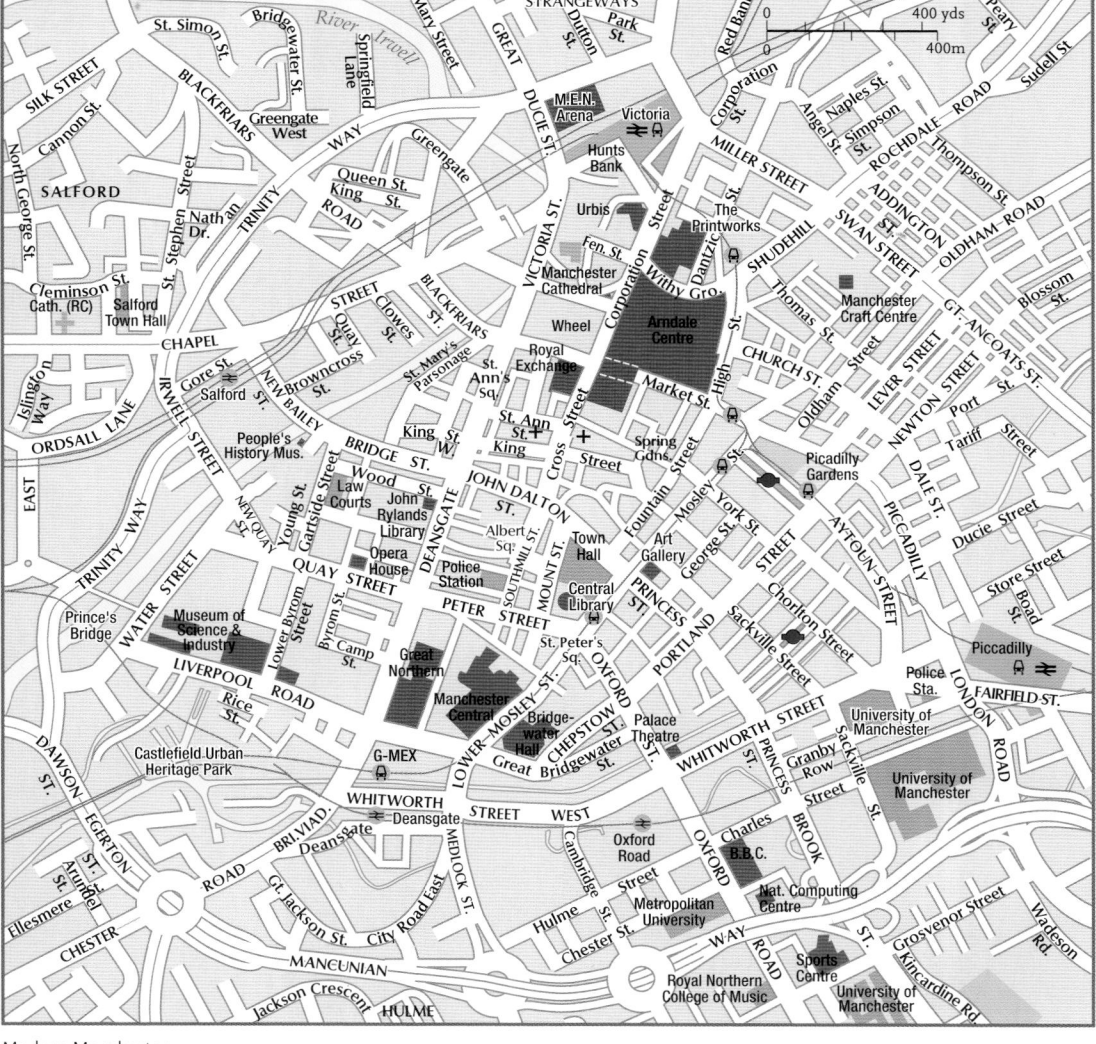

Modern Manchester

City of Manchester

The name of Manchester comes from the Roman fort ('chester') of *Mamucium* or *Mamucio*, a name probably derived from the Celtic *mamm* which means 'breast' and so named because the fort was built on a breast-shaped hill.

FAMOUS FOR

The buildings of **Chetham's School and Library** are remarkable survivors. The buildings date from the 15th century and were originally built to house a college of priests (the best preserved examples of this type of building in Britain). They were acquired by the executors of Humphrey Chetham and converted in 1654–8 to provide a school and the oldest free public library in Britain.

The **Bridgewater Canal** was the first modern canal in Britain. Designed by James Brindley, it was completed in 1765 and brought coal from the Duke of Bridgewater's pit at Worsley into Manchester.

Sport has played a part in the regeneration of the city. In 2002 the city hosted the very successful **Commonwealth Games**. The main stadium is now used by **Manchester City** football club. Their great rivals, **Manchester United** have their stadium at Old Trafford (actually in the neighbouring authority of Trafford).

On 16 August 1819, a huge crowd gathered at St Peter's Fields under the banners of 'Reform', 'Universal Suffrage', 'Equal Representation' and 'Love'. The local magistrates ordered them to disperse and used mounted militia to enforce this – up to 18 protestors were killed and over 500 injured in what is now known as the **Peterloo Massacre**.

Manchester's origins go back to the Roman fort built by the Irwell in Castlefield, now partially reconstructed in an improbable landscape of canals and railways. In medieval times Manchester developed as a market town for the surrounding agricultural area. Manchester Cathedral (originally the parish church) and Chetham's School and Library are the only two buildings that survive from this period. In Tudor and Stuart times, weaving began, using wool, linen and a little cotton. The much moved and reconstructed 'Old Wellington Inn' in the city centre is from this period. Around 1700 Manchester's population may have reached 10,000. During the 18th century canals brought coal and cotton direct to the city, and Manchester, and the towns around, saw the rapid development of cotton mills. By 1801 its population was around 70,000 and it became the main trading centre for cotton goods made in the surrounding towns. In the 19th century the development quickened and the urban area spread rapidly, creating great wealth for the merchant princes, shown in some of the confident buildings in the city, such as the former Free Trade Hall (whose name alone says much about Manchester business), the imposing Victorian Gothic Town Hall and the great cotton merchants' warehouses. The city also had terrible slums that inspired Friedrich Engels to write *The Condition of the Working Classes*, published in 1844.

At the end of the 19th century the Manchester Ship Canal was completed. It enabled ocean-going ships to dock in Manchester and saw new industries develop around the docks in Trafford and Salford. Th industrialization encouraged those who could afford live outside the city, which started to impoverish it. A World War II, with the decline in the textile industry and in heavy manufacturing, the city's economy shran and it has since reinvented itself as a major financial, service and educational centre. It has two universities (Manchester and Manchester Metropolitan), both just to the south of the city centre on Oxford Road, with over 58,000 full-time students and redevelopments ha brought people back to live in the city centre. The ser sector now provides nearly 94 per cent of jobs in the city, with over 31 per cent being in finance, IT and ot business and over 29 per cent in public administratio education and health. Only just over 4 per cent are in manufacturing, almost half the number employed in tourism. The vibrant cultural scene and night life of t city brings in many visitors, assisted by the closeness of Manchester International Airport, located within the southern boundaries of the city. After World War II, there was significant immigration, particularly fro South Asia, and around 20 per cent of the population comes from Asian, black or other ethnic minorities. The 'Curry Mile' in the Rusholme district, is the large concentration of South Asian restaurants in Britain, a development of the last 40 years.

Civil Justice Centre, Manchester.

Bridgewater Canal

Chetham's School and Library

lton

metropolitan borough of Bolton is based around the former cotton town of
on, and includes Farnworth, Westhoughton and Horwich. Bolton was a medieval
ket town and cotton weaving was taking place there from the 17th century. After the
ntion locally of the spinning mule by Samuel Crompton and many other advances,
on spinning, weaving, dyeing and printing began to dominate the rapid growth of
own. In 1801 its population was 17,000, in 1901 160,000 but, reflecting the impact
he decline in the textile industry, in 2001 it was 140,000. In the area there was also
mining at Westhoughton and a major locomotive works at Horwich. Now, however,
t of the textile trade and the heavy engineering have gone. Aerospace, the food
stry, paper manufacture, steel fabrication and the service sector (such as call
res) have helped to fill the gap. Manufacturing and construction provide nearly
er of jobs while public administration, education, and health provide nearly
er cent. Bolton University, established in 2005, is one of Britain's newest
ersities, with roots going back to the Bolton Mechanics Institute, founded in 1824.
ook sportswear is a local firm and the Reebok stadium, in Horwich, is where Bolton
derers football team play. Memorable buildings include the Hall i' th' Wood,
ch restored 16th century timber house (where Crompton invented his 'mule')
the wonderfully confident classical Town Hall, opened in 1873.

Bury

The metropolitan borough of Bury is based around Bury, a former cotton weaving and
cotton printing town, and also includes some outer suburbs of Manchester (Prestwich,
Whitefield and Radcliffe) and Ramsbottom, up the narrowing Irwell valley. Bury was a
small medieval town built around Bury Castle, a fortified manor house built in 1485,
whose recently excavated ruins can now be seen in Castle Square. Bury's industrial
development came in the late 18th century when Robert Peel (father of Sir Robert
Peel, the first British prime minister with a manufacturing background) established
a calico printing works here. In the 19th century Bury was dominated by mills and
their chimneys, and the decline in the industry has been marked by their demolition.
Ramsbottam and Radcliffe were both heavily industrialized but now, too, have lost most
of their industry. Prestwich is a commuting town for Manchester and has a large Jewish
community. Bury is at the end of one line of the Manchester Metrolink tram system.
Around 16 per cent of jobs are in manufacturing or construction and nearly 35 per cent
are in public service, education and health. The restored East Lancs Railway runs steam
trains up the valley from Bury to Ramsbottom and Rawtenstall. Above Ramsbottom
looms the Peel Tower, on Holcombe Hill, a memorial to Sir Robert Peel. The site is
335 m above sea level and the tower is then 39 m tall and visible over a wide area.

way to Bolton' bridge

All that remains of Bury Castle are the ruins that can be seen to the front of the the Castle Armoury.
The design of it's facade took inspiration from the old medieval castle and was built in the late 1800's.

Wheel of Manchester and city centre scene. On the left is the 'Old Wellington Inn', one of the oldest buildings in Manchester.

Oldham

The metropolitan borough of Oldham is based around Oldham, and also includes Chadderton, Failsworth, Royton and Shaw. The land rises steeply above Oldham to Saddleworth Moor on the edge of the Pennines, the highest land in the Greater Manchester area. Oldham was a hamlet before the first cotton mill was built there in 1788; 100 years later there were 265 mills and at its peak in the early 20th century there were 360 mills and a population of over 147,000. It was the greatest cotton-spinning town in the world, but now there is no cotton spinning remaining and the population of the town has shrunk to 103,540. Most of the mills have been demolished though some remain as distribution centres or for small businesses. Industries in the area today include aerospace, electronics, electrical goods and significant distribution operations. Over 22 per cent of jobs are in manufacturing or construction while distribution and retail provides 27 per cent and public administration, health and education 28 per cent. In the 1950s there was significant immigration from South Asia to work in the cotton mills, and now around 12 per cent of the Oldham district is of South Asian origin (over 58 per cent of the Werneth ward is non-white). The area has become a dormitory town for Manchester.

Rochdale

The metropolitan borough of Rochdale is based around the town of Rochdale and includes Middleton (a northern suburb of Manchester), Heywood, Milnrow, Wardle and Littleborough. The area rises into the Pennines in the north. Rochdale was a medieval market town whose initial wealth came from woollen textiles before the Industrial Revolution. In the 18th century cotton replaced wool and its industrialization began. It is a town of civic pride, which saw John Bright, the great free trade campaigner, as its MP and in 1844 the establishment of the Rochdale Society of Equitable Pioneers, generally regarded as the first co-operative retail shop in the world. Its Town Hall is one of the best Victorian Gothic town halls in the country ('it has panache and it is picturesque' according to Pevsner). The textile industry has virtually gone from the area now, replaced by light industry, national distribution centres, a growing service sector and, particularly in the south of the area, residential accommodation for Manchester workers. Over 22 per cent of jobs are in manufacturing and construction and 23 per cent in distribution and retail. Middleton has a late medieval church, which has a contemporary memorial window to the 17 archers of Middleton who were at the battle of Flodden in 1513. In 2003 the cross-Pennine Rochdale Canal was reopened, for pleasure use rather than the vital link that it once was. In 2012 the Manchester Metrolink trams will start from Rochdale Railway station.

Lowry Centre, Salford.

Rochdale Canal, between Todmorden and Hebden Bridge.

City of Salford

The City of Salford district is based on Salford, and also includes Eccles, Irlam, Pendlebury, Walkden and Worsley. Divided from Manchester by the River Irwell, now an almost indistinguishable barrier, Salford used to be more important than Manchester, but it lost this position long before the end of the 18th century. A reminder of Salford's early history can be found in Ordsall Hall, a timber-framed house dating from the 16th century and one of the finest in Greater Manchester. The development of Salford was first dictated by coal and textiles and then, with the arrival of the Manchester Ship Canal, with the docks on the southern edge of the city. In recent times Salford has changed greatly – around Salford Quays (as the docks were renamed) shops, offices, residential accommodation, the BBC's northern headquarters and the Lowry Art and Entertainment Centre have emerged. These changes are reinvigorating the Salford economy, which was very hard-hit by the decline in textiles, in coal mining (the last pit in the area, Agecroft, closed in 1990) and by the closure of the docks themselves. As a result the largest single employment sector is now finance, IT and other business (nearly 30 per cent). Once readily defined by 'Coronation Street', based on the now demolished Archie Street in Ordsall, Salford is becoming indistinguishable from Manchester. The Manchester Metrolink trams run through the area, one line finishing at Eccles. The most isolated community is Irlam on the other side of the large Chat Moss peat bog, which covers around 30 per cent of the city's area.

Stockport

The borough of Stockport, much of which was in Cheshire before 1974, is based around Stockport and includes Cheadle, Cheadle Hulme, Hazel Grove, Bramhall, Marple and Romiley. The eastern fringes of the area start to rise into the Peak District. Stockport, positioned where the Goyt and Tame rivers join to create the Mersey developed as a silk weaving centre in the 18th century, using the water power of the rivers. Cotton soon overtook silk, and became the basis of the industrial growth of Stockport and the neighbouring communities. It also developed a special niche in hat making – in the 1890s it was exporting 6 million hats a year but 100 years later the last hat factory closed. These industries have been replaced by hi-tech businesses including electronics and medical equipment and by financial services and IT companies. In addition the area has become a significant commuter zone for Manchester. Manufacturing and construction provide 20 per cent of jobs and banking, IT and other business over 22 per cent. Notable landmarks include the Stockport Railway Viaduct, a 27-arch brick viaduct over the Mersey that completely dominates that centre of Stockport. From an earlier age is Bramhall Hall, a magnificent 16th-century timber-framed manor house.

...ord Quays

...meside

...neside is based around Ashton-under-Lyne and includes Audenshaw, Denton, ...oylsden, Dukinfield, Hyde, Mossley and Stalybridge, and the start of Longdendale, ...ch reaches into the Peak District. Ashton is the largest settlement and dates back to ...dieval times – its main church which dates from the 15th century onwards is on an ...site – but the town only really developed in the early 19th century with the arrival ...he cotton mills in all the major settlements in Tameside. Coal was also mined ...he area, but its peak passed at the start of the last century. The textile industry ...lined earlier than is some parts of the northwest and there was some diversification ...o a range of lighter industries. Over 25 per cent of jobs are in manufacturing and ...struction. The area remained depressed until the regional economy began to pick ...in the 1980s and it has now become a popular commuting area for Manchester, ...nks to its good communications, soon to be improved with the arrival of the ...nchester Metrolink trams to Droylsden and then to Ashton by 2013. Some urban ...ewal is also following the reopening of the Huddersfield Light Canal that runs from ...re to Ashton. Denton was once famed for its hat-making. In the 1840s two Denton ...ters, Thomas and William Bowler, set up business in London, their names forever ...ked to the hat they designed. In 1919 Ada Summers became Mayor of Stalybridge ...l also the first women magistrate in Britain.

...igan

...e borough of Wigan is the most westerly in Greater Manchester. It is based around ...gan and includes Ashton-in-Makerfield, Hindley, Leigh and Orrell. Both Wigan and ...gh, the two largest settlements, were medieval market towns and weaving was an ...portant industry before the Industrial Revolution. Wigan had its own cloth hall in ...4. The powered mechanization of the cotton industry saw mills arriving in this part ...Lancashire in the early 19th century. At the same time coalmining developed first at ...gan and then it spread to Leigh. The last pit, Bickershaw, closed in 1992. The area has ...ays had a more diversified industry than the cotton towns closer to Manchester and ...nufacturing businesses including H J Heinz at Wigan, the largest food processing ...tory in Europe, while the Chinese are investing in a large trading estate for textiles ...Wigan. As a result over 22 per cent of jobs in the area are in manufacturing and ...struction, much higher than the national average. In the 19th century Wigan was ...l-served by canals, and it was a wharf on the Leeds and Liverpool Canal that George ...mby Senior (the father of the better known George Formby Jr) nick-named Wigan ...r. The building is still there, once exploited as a visitor attraction but currently ...sed. The image portrayed by George Orwell's *The Road to Wigan Pier* has been ...g-lasting – Bill Bryson wrote in 1995 that 'such was the picture of appalling squalor ...well painted that even now I was startled to find how neat and well maintained ...gan appeared to be'.

Trafford

The borough of Trafford borders Salford and western Manchester and contains many Manchester suburbs including Stretford, Urmston, Sale, Hale and Altrincham, as well as Trafford Park, the major industrial estate on the south side of Manchester Ship Canal docks that opened in 1897. It was the world's first planned industrial estate, and, at its peak, in 1945, employed 75,000 workers. It declined until the late 1980s since when its fortunes have revived and over 35,000 people work there for over 1,400 companies, many attracted by the excellent road network close by. To sports enthusiasts Trafford is the home of Manchester United Football Club and Lancashire Cricket Club, in separate grounds both referred to as Old Trafford. To shoppers it is the home of the Trafford Centre, the northwest's largest indoor shopping centre. The deindustrialization of the area has radically changed the employment profile with now only 9 per cent of jobs in manufacturing but 30 per cent in finance, IT and other business, the largest single sector in Trafford's economy. The Manchester Metrolink serves the area. The Imperial War Museum North, in a dramatic building composed of three interlocking shards designed by Daniel Libeskind, is on the south side of Salford Quays and opened in 2002.

Old Trafford Stadium, home of Manchester United Football Club.

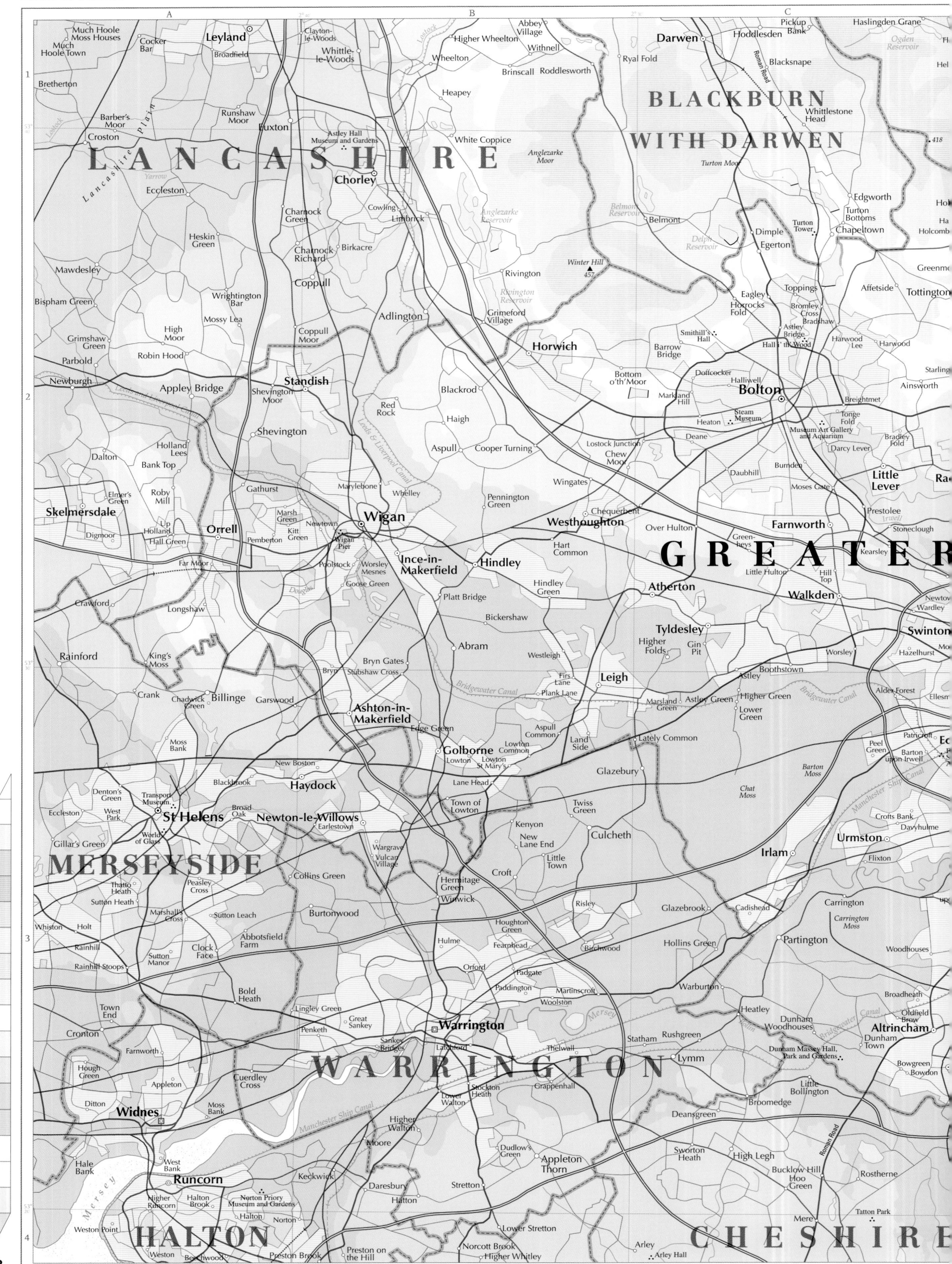

British National Grid projection

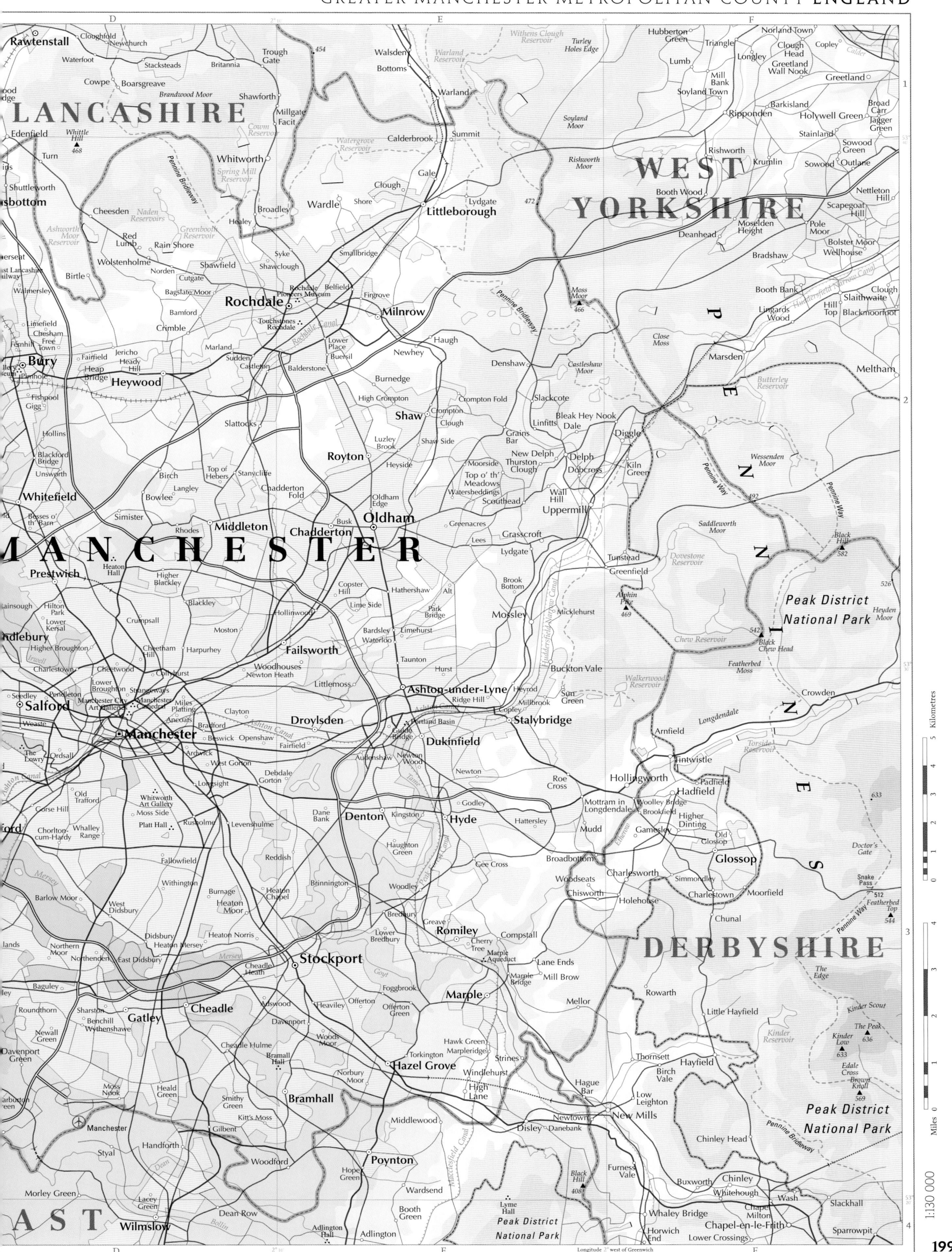

1:130 000

© Collins Bartholomew Ltd

SOUTH YORKSHIRE METROPOLITAN COUNTY

Area Sq Km	1,552
Area Sq Miles	599
Population	1,305,900
Highest point	Margery Hill (546 m)
	or High Stones (548m)

Metropolitan Borough Areas

City of Sheffield	368 sq km; 142 sq miles
Barnsley	329 sq km; 127 sq miles
Doncaster	569 sq km; 220 sq miles
Rotherham	287 sq km; 111 sq miles

Metropolitan Borough Populations

Sheffield	534,500
Barnsley	225,900
Doncaster	291,600
Rotherham	253,900

South Yorkshire was newly created as a metropolitan county in 1974 out of parts of the former West Riding of Yorkshire and some small areas from Nottinghamshire. It consisted of four district authorities: Barnsley, Doncaster, Rotherham and the City of Sheffield. In 1986 all the metropolitan counties in England were abolished by Parliament and the districts effectively became unitary authorities. South Yorkshire remains as a ceremonial county, with its own Lord Lieutenant, and the districts work together on joint boards to provide fire and police services and on the South Yorkshire Passenger Transport Executive.

The total population of South Yorkshire is 1,305,900 and it is expected to grow to around 1,489,400 by 2031, with the greatest growth being in Sheffield and Barnsley

and the slowest growth in Doncaster. The highest point in South Yorkshire is Margery Hill (546 m) on Howden Moors in the Peak District and within the boundaries of the City of Sheffield.

FAMOUS PEOPLE

City of Sheffield

Sir William Sterndale Bennett, composer, conductor and pianist, born 1816.
Sir John Fowler, railway engineer, co-designer of Forth Railway bridge, born 1817.
Harry Brearley, inventor of stainless steel, born 1871.
David Mellor, silversmith and industrial designer, born 1930.
Sir Malcolm Bradbury, novelist and critic, born 1932.
Roy Hattersley, Baron Hattersley, Labour politician, born 1932.
Antonia Byatt, novelist and critic, born 1936.
Margaret Drabble, novelist and critic, born 1939.
Bruce Chatwin, writer, born Sheffield, 1940.
Michael Palin, comedian and writer, born 1943.
John (Joe) Cocker, singer, born 1944.
John Krebs, zoologist and former chairman, Food Standards Agency, born 1945.
David Blunkett, Labour politician, born 1947.
Sean Bean, actor, born 1959.
Jarvis Cocker, singer (formerly of *Pulp*), born 1963.
Helen Sharman, first British citizen to be an astronaut, born 1963.

Barnsley

Joseph Bramah (born Bramma), locksmith and inventor of the hydraulic press, born Stainborough, 1748.
Harry Worth (born Harry Illingsworth), comedian, born Hoyland Common, 1917.
John Arden, playwright, born 1930.
Harold Dennis (Dickie) Bird, cricket umpire, born 1933.

Sir Michael Parkinson, television presenter, born Cudworth 1935.
Arthur Scargill, president of National Union of Mineworkers; formed Socialist Labour Party, born 193
Barry Hines, writer (*A Kestrel for a Knave*), born 1939.
Ian McMillan, poet and broadcaster, born Darfield, 19

Doncaster

Thomas Crapper, sanitary engineer, born Thorne, 183
Sir George Porter, chemist, Nobel laureate, born Stainforth, 1920.
John Michael (Mike) Hawthorn, racing driver, born Mexborough, 1929.
Fred Trueman ('Fiery Fred'), cricketer, fast bowler, born Stainton, 1931.
Brian Blessed, actor, born Mexborough, 1937.
Dame Diana Rigg, actress, born Doncaster, 1938.
Tony Christie (born Antony Fitzgerald), singer, born Conisbrough, 1943.
Kevin Keegan, football player and manager, born Armthorpe, 1951.
Lesley Garrett, opera singer, born Thorne, 1955.
Jeremy Clarkson, broadcaster and journalist, born Doncaster, 1960.
James Toseland, superbike world champion, born Doncaster, 1980.

Rotherham

Thomas Rotherham, cleric and statesman, Archbishop of York (1480–1500), born Rotherham 1423.
Sir Raymond Unwin, town planner and creator of the garden city, born Whiston 1863.
Gordon Banks, footballer, goalkeeper 1966 World Cup winners, born Catcliffe, 1937.
William Hague, Conservative politician, born Rotherham, 1961.

City of Sheffield

The name of Sheffield means 'open land by the river Sheaf'. 'Sheaf' is derived from an Old English word for 'border', for the river used to form the boundary between Derbyshire and Yorkshire.

FAMOUS FOR

Mary, Queen of Scots was held prisoner for 14 years between 1570 and 1584, under the supervision of George Talbot, Earl of Shrewsbury, and his wife, Bess of Hardwick. Much of her time was spent at Sheffield Castle (now the site of Castle Market) or Sheffield Manor (whose ruins can be seen in the Manor Estate).

Sheffield FC was the world's first official football club, formed in 1857. The club still plays, but has not reached the heights of Sheffield's two better-known teams, Sheffield United and Sheffield Wednesday.

One of the more unlikely new buildings in Sheffield is the **Winter Gardens**, a vast timber-arched temperate greenhouse right in the centre of the city. Opened in 2003, it contains over 2,500 different plants from around the world.

Sheffield has one of Britain's few **district energy systems**, whereby domestic waste is converted to heat and energy that is supplied to buildings in the city centre and to some residential developments.

The origins of Sheffield go back to the 12th century, when a castle was built where the river Sheaf joined the Don. It was not, however, any military significance of the site that brought prosperity to Sheffield, but the ready availability of iron ore, coal and water power that led to its pre-eminence in iron and steel long before the Industrial Revolution. In the 14th century Chaucer alludes to a Sheffield whittle (a short dagger). Its reputation for cutlery grew and by 1624 the Company of Cutlers in Hallamshire, headed by the Master Cutler, was granted a charter. By the start of the 19th century

Sheffield was the 10th largest town in England, with a population in 1801 of 60,100. It gained a town council in 1843 and became a city in 1893. By 1901 its population was 451,200. Sheffield has seen many innovative developments including the invention of Sheffield plate (silver plate), Huntsman's crucible steel, the Bessemer converter, stainless steel and modern high-strength alloy steels. Its peak population was in 1951, at 577,050. With the decline in heavy industry, so the population declined, but that has been reversed in recent years and it is predicted that the 1951 peak will be passed around 2021. Since that peak the city has also become more ethnically diverse, with around 14 per cent of its population coming from black or minority ethnic groups. Around 11 per cent of the jobs in the city are in manufacturing,

particularly in hi-tech uses of steel, but nearly 20 per cent were employed in this sector in 1995. Employment growth has come in public administratio health and education, particularly influenced by the growth of the city's two universities (Sheffield and Sheffield Hallam). Retail (exemplified by the Meadowh centre, built on the site of a former steelworks), and professional services (such as law) provide significant employment. Sheffield became the first National City o Sport and has superb indoor and outdoor stadiums an facilities. In addition there is much open countryside i the Peak District National Park, which occupies over a third of the land area of the city. Sheffield is well serve by the road system but less well served by rail. A new tram system was completed in 1995.

View from Stanage Edge, near Sheffield.

Bartholomew Gazetteer of the British Isles, 1887

SHEFFIELD, *mun. bor., manufacturing town, par., and township, S. div. West-Riding Yorkshire, on river Don, 157 miles NW. of London by rail, 42½ SE. of Manchester, and 53 SW. of York – township, 3028 ac., pop. 91,806; bor. and par., 19,651 ac., pop. 284,508; 6 newspapers. Market-days, Tuesday and Saturday. Sheffield has long been famous for its cutlery. It has also manufactures of almost every description, of iron, steel, and brass; and in connection with these it has numerous extensive iron and brass foundries, grinding, tilting, rolling, and slitting mills, &c. The branches of manufacture include steel, mostly made from Swedish iron; armour-plates for ships of war; rails, wheels, and all other castings for fixed or rolling stock; stoves, grates, fenders; plated goods; Britannia-metal goods; and optical instruments, including spectacles. Sheffield is picturesquely situated in an amphitheatre of wooded hills, traversed by the river Don. which here receives the Sheaf, Rivelin, Loxley, and Porter. It has several fine public buildings, and in the older parts of the town great street improvements have in recent years been made by the corporation. Among the educational and literary institutions is the Firth College, erected in 1879, in connection with the movement for the extension of university education. There are three public parks – Norfolk Park, Weston Park, and Firth Park. Sheffield is a very ancient place, supposed to have been originally a Roman station, but has few relics of antiquity. Its castle, probably of 13th century, and for many years the prison of Mary Queen of Scots, was demolished by order of Parliament in 1648. A part of the magnificent manor-house which was built in the time of Henry VIII., and where Cardinal Wolsey rested several days on his last journey, is still standing, and in 1873 was restored by the Duke of Norfolk, the lord of the manor.*

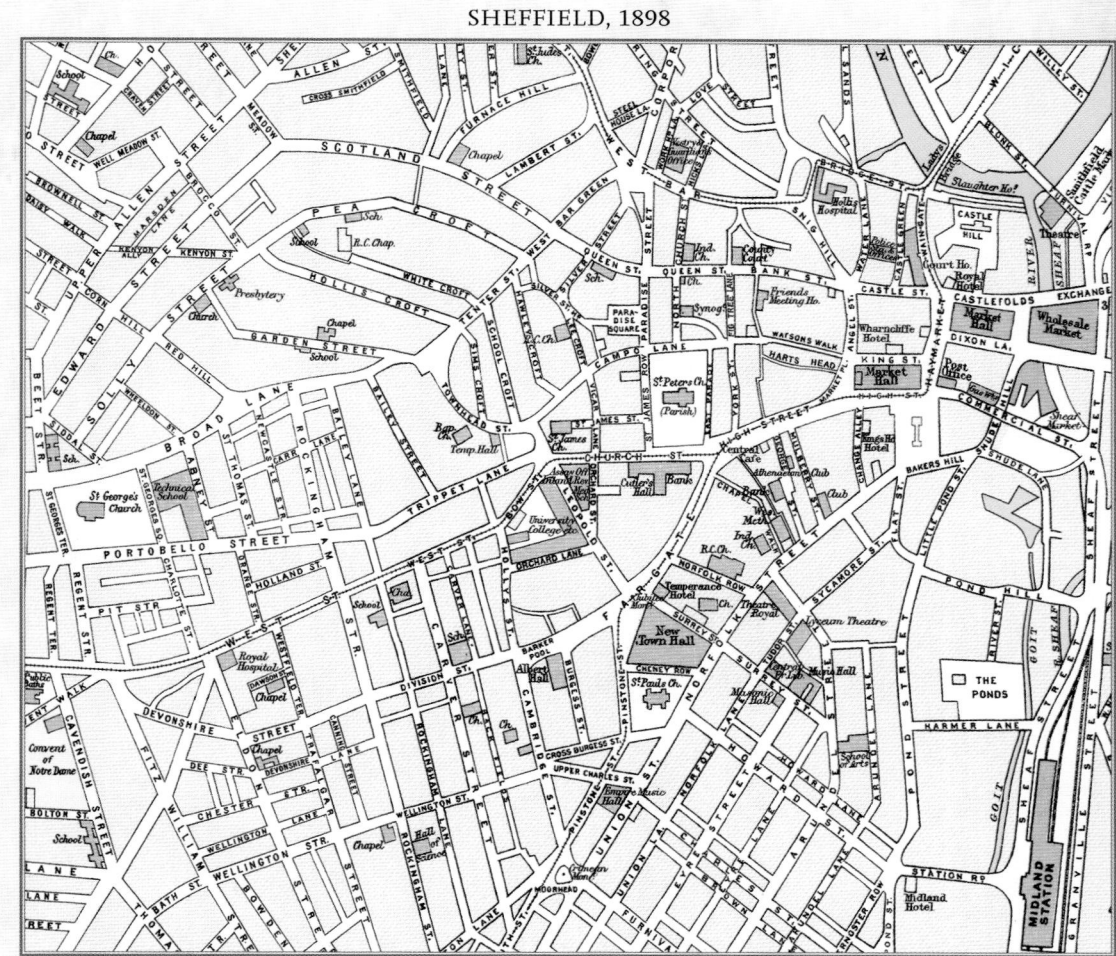

SHEFFIELD, 1898

The modern history of Sheffield is closely connected with that of Trades Unions. It narrowly escaped being burned by the Chartists in 1840, and was the scene of a terrible calamity in 1864, caused by the bursting of the Bradfield Reservoir. Sheffield had already become noted for its cutlery in the time of Chaucer, but for many centuries its progress as a town was slow. It is only since the middle of the 18th century, or even later, that it has risen to be one of the great manufacturing towns of the kingdom.

"It might have been Pluto's own metropolis, shrouded in sulphurous vapour."
Nathaniel Hawthorne, 1863

"Sheffield, I suppose, could justly claim to be the ugliest town in the Old World: its inhabitants, who want it pre-eminent in everything, very likely do make that claim for it."
George Orwell, *The Road to Wigan Pier*, 1937

"We will try to take some small piece of English ground, beautiful, peaceful and fruitful. We will have no steam-engines upon it, and no railroads; we will have no untended or unthought-of creatures on it; none wretched, but the sick; none idle, but the dead."
John Ruskin, on founding the St George's Guild that established a museum and the Totley Commune in Sheffield, 1878

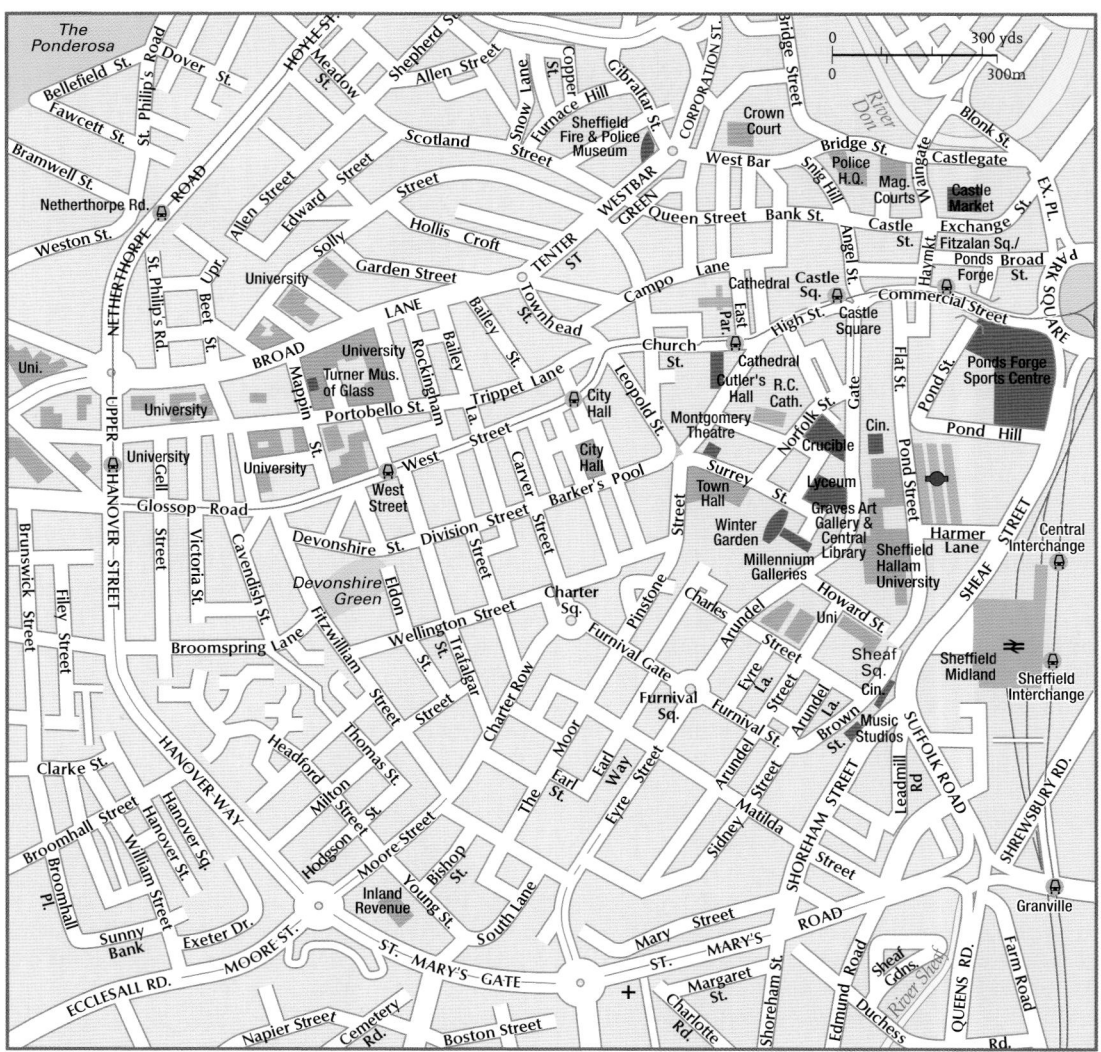

Modern Sheffield

Sheffield Winter Gardens

Sheffield Town Hall

Barnsley

The metropolitan borough of Barnsley covers the town of Barnsley, the nearby mining villages of the South Yorkshire coalfield, and west into the Pennines. Barnsley was first recorded in the Domesday Book. In the 18th and 19th centuries it was a centre of linen weaving. Glassmaking was also established in the 18th century and continues in the area today. The major development of Barnsley and its surrounding communities came with the exploitation of the South Yorkshire coalfield. Coal had been mined for local use since at least the 14th century. By the start of the 20th century, it was the dominant industry in the area, but the most accessible seams started to be worked out from the 1950s. The

area was one of the heartlands of the 1984–5 miners' strike and the industry never recovered. Goldthorpe, on the eastern boundaries of the borough, was the last pit to close, in 1994. Manufacturing is still a vital part of Barnsley's economy, providing over 16 per cent of jobs while 33 per cent are provided in public administration, health and education. To the north is the Elsecar Heritage Centre, which contains the only Newcomen steam engine still in its original location. To the south is Wentworth Castle, the 18th-century home of the Earls of Strafford. The grounds, which include Stainborough Castle, a mock ruin of 1730, are being restored to some of their former grandeur.

"If a model is sought of the most perfect taste in architecture, where grace softens dignity and lightness attempers magnificence; where proportion removes every part from peculiar observation and delicacy of execution recalls every part to notice; where the position is the most happy, and even the colour of the stone most harmonious; the virtuoso should be directed to the new front of Wentworth castle."
Horace Walpole, 1780, *The History of the Modern Taste in Gardening*

"Towards the City, a pit chimney and the pit-head winding gear showed above the rooftops, and at the back of the estate was a patchwork of fields, black, and grey, and pale winter green; giving way to a wood, which stood out on the far slope as an ink blot."
Barry Hines, 1968, *A Kestrel for a Knave*

Sir Michael Parkinson

oncaster

e town of Doncaster is the major settlement in
e metropolitan borough. Its hinterland contains a
mber of smaller towns and villages. Doncaster, as
name suggests, was originally a Roman fort on the
er Don. Situated on the Great North Road, it became
rosperous market town from medieval times. Horse
ing was recorded here from the 17th century and
ncaster racecourse, based at Town Moor since 1776,
sts important classic races including the Doncaster
p, first run in 1766 and the St Leger, established in
76 and named after its founder Colonel Anthony
Leger. The town changed dramatically in the
h century with the arrival of the railways and the
velopment of the South Yorkshire coalfield. Doncaster
came a major railway centre and locomotive workshop
e 'Flying Scotsman' was built here), while coal-
ning transformed the local landscape and brought in
er industries including glassmaking, iron and steel
cluding wire making) and tractor manufacture, all of
ich still continue, though now there is only open-cast
ning. The last deep pit to close was Hatfield in 2001
it may yet reopen to provide coal for a new clean
wer station. Overall manufacturing and construction
vide over 17.5 per cent of jobs while, with its good
nsport links, it has become a major distribution
tre. St George's Minster, a massive Victorian Gothic
urch completed in 1858, with a tower 52 m high,
minates the town. To the west is the great medieval
tle of Conisbrough, built around 1185. Its massive
ep is the oldest and best of its kind in Britain.

Conisbrough Castle

entworth Castle, near Barnsley.

otherham

e metropolitan borough of Rotherham is based
und the town of Rotherham, on the river Rother.
e towns and villages that surround it have all been
ked to the South Yorkshire coalfield; Maltby is the
e remaining deep mine in the coalfield. Rotherham
veloped as a medieval market town from which time
me the fine 15th-century Rotherham Minster, whose
ire rises up above All Saints Square, and the chapel of
r Lady of Rotherham Bridge, one of the few bridge
apels remaining in Britain. Thomas Rotherham,
o became Archbishop of York, had hoped to make
therham the Oxford of the North. In 1480 he founded
e College of Jesus', based on an Oxford college, but it
ly survived until 1547. In the 18th century Rotherham
came a major centre for cast iron after John Walker

had established the first ironworks in 1746. In the 19th
century came large iron and steel works – the Park Gate
works employed 10,000 at its peak and now part of it has
become the Magna Science Adventure Centre. The whole
area has suffered greatly from the decline of coal mining
and heavy industry. Rotherham still produces special
steels and also has glass and precision engineering
industries, and manufacturing and construction
provides 22 per cent of jobs while public administration,
education and health provides 28 per cent. To the north
of the town is Britain's greatest but saddest Georgian
country house, Wentworth Woodhouse, which reached
its apogee at the start of the 20th century, since when it
has suffered from many family, political and business
intrigues.

Fire Twister display at the Magna Science Adventure Centre.

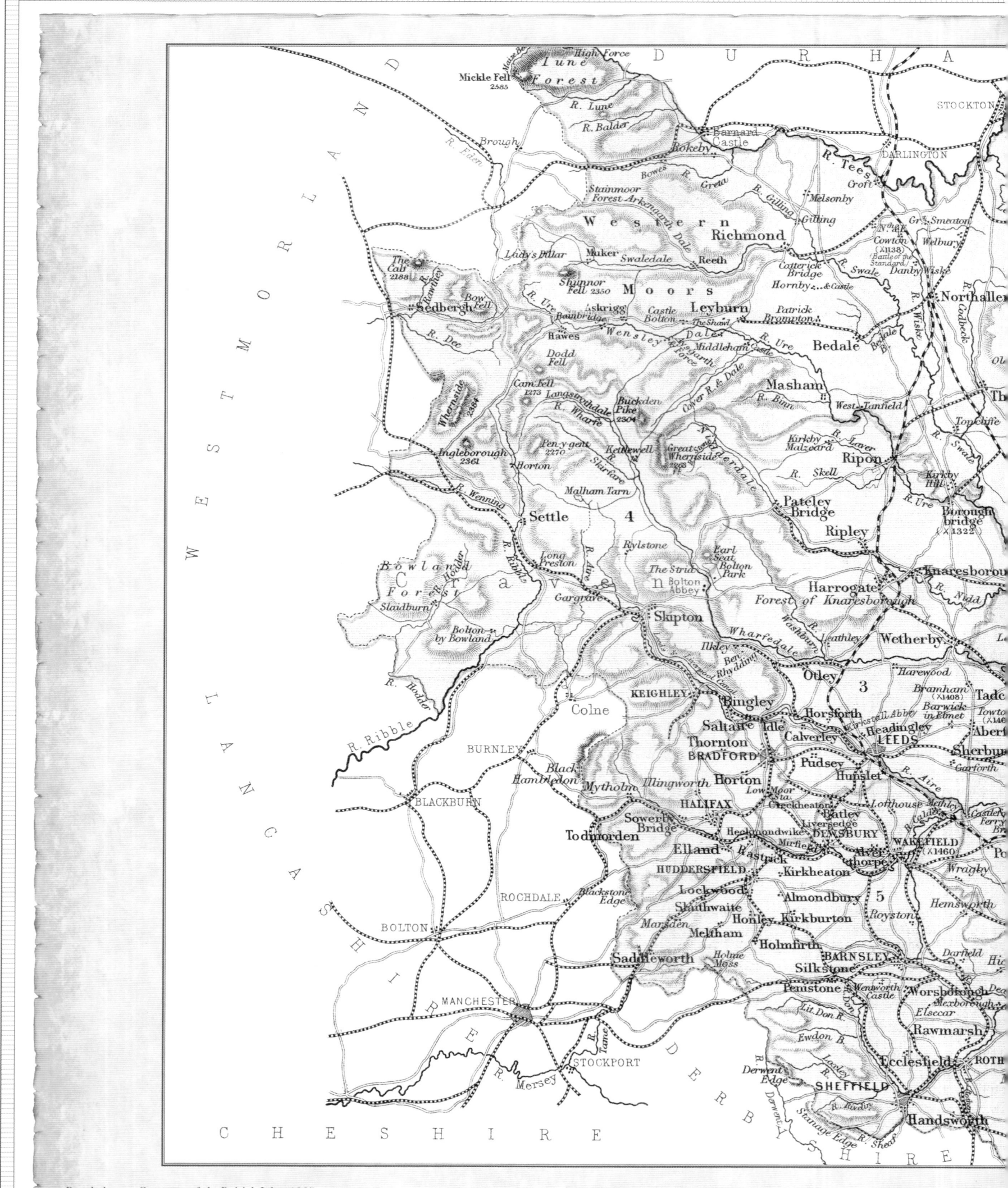

Bartholomew Gazetteer of the British Isles, 1887

YORKSHIRE, *maritime county of England; bounded N. by Durham and the Tees, NE. and E. by the North Sea, S. by the Humber and Lincolnshire, Notts, and Derbyshire, SW. by Cheshire, W. by Lancashire, and NW. by Westmorland; length, E. and W., 96 miles; breadth, 80 miles; area, 3,882,851 ac., pop. 2,886,564. Yorkshire is the first county of England in point of size, and the third in point of population. From the* *mouth of the Tees to Flamborough Head the coast is bold and rocky; from Flamborough Head to Spurn Head it lies low. The interior presents the appearance of a great central valley stretching SE. to the Humber, and flanked on either side by heights – on the E. by the Cleveland Hills and the Wolds, and on the W. by the Pennine chain. The Humber receives almost all the drainage of the county by the Ouse, with its tributaries the Swale, Ure, Derwent, Wharfe, Aire, and Don. A small part of the west is drained by the*

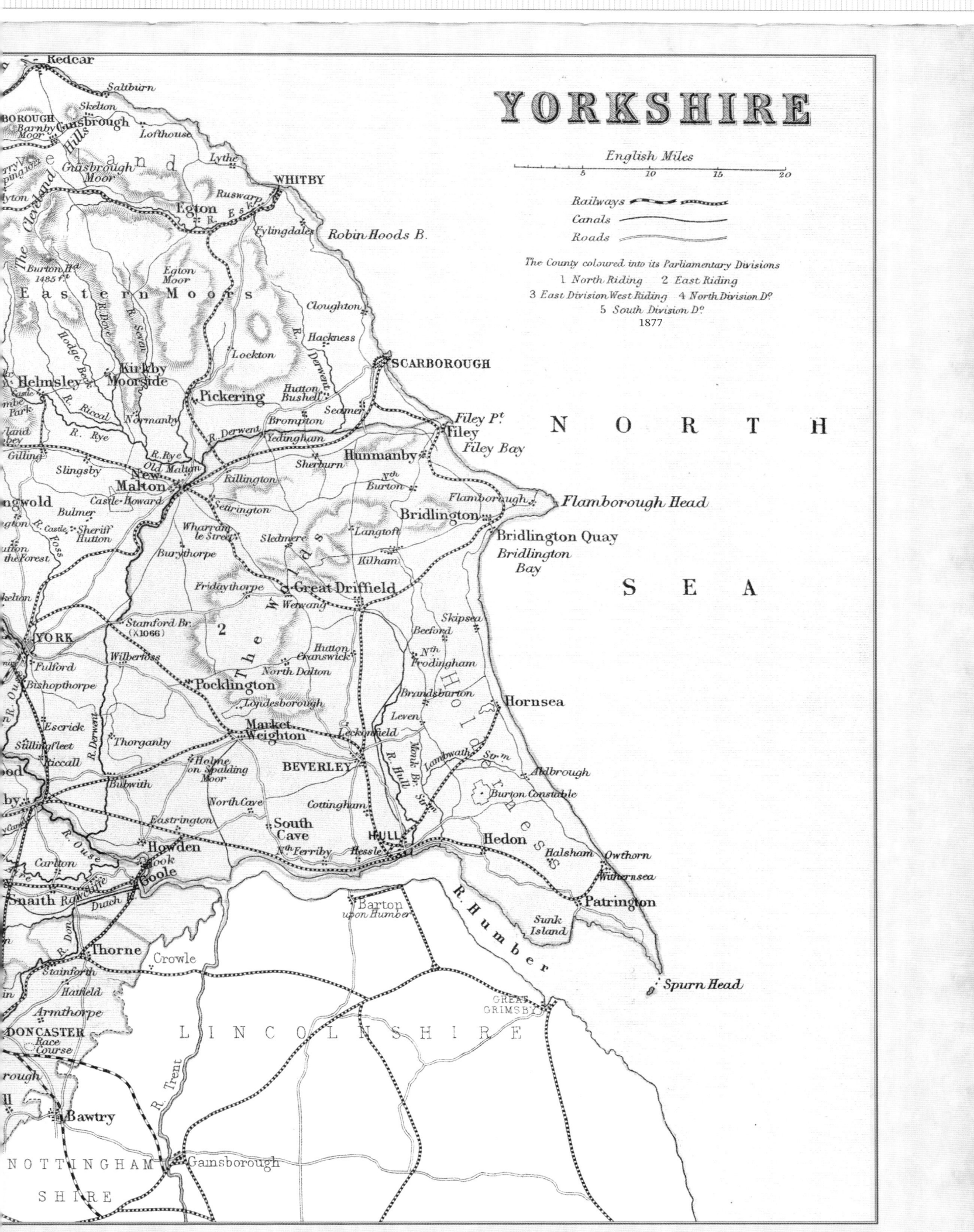

YORKSHIRE

English Miles

0   5   10   15   20

Railways
Canals
Roads

The County coloured into its Parliamentary Divisions
1 North Riding   2 East Riding
3 East Division West Riding   4 North Division D.º
5 South Division D.º
1877

N O R T H

S E A

Ribble, of the north by the Tees, and of the east by the North Sea. The general geological formation is limestone and coal in the west, succeeded towards the east by lias, oolite, and chalk. Yorkshire takes high rank as an agricultural, manufacturing, and mining county. It is well supplied with every means of communication. It has from an early period been divided into 3 Ridings – viz., East, North, and West, besides the Ainsty or Liberty of the city of York. Each Riding has a lord-lieutenant and a separate court of quarter sessions and a commission of the peace, and statistically is treated as a distinct county. It contains 26 wapentakes; 3 liberties; 1636 pars, with parts of 2 others; and the mun. bors. of Barnsley, Batley, Beverley, Bradford, Dewsbury, Doncaster, Halifax, Hedon, Huddersfield, Kingston upon Hull, Leeds, Middlesbrough, Morley, Pontefract, Richmond, Ripon, Rotherham, Scarborough, Sheffield, Wakefield, and York. It is in the dioceses of York, Ripon, and Manchester.

EAST RIDING OF YORKSHIRE

Area Sq Km	2,497
Area Sq Miles	964
Population	335,000
County town	Beverley
Highest point	Garrowby Hill (246 m) near Pocklington

Yorkshire takes its name from the city of York, a name that has been through many transformations since the Romans called it *Eboracum*, a Celtic word in origin, meaning either 'Eburos' land' or 'land of yew trees'. The Danes then modified the name to *Eorvik* and then to *Jorvik* and eventually to York. A Riding is the traditional name for one of the divisions of the historic county of Yorkshire.

FAMOUS FOR

Dick Turpin, the infamous 18th-century highwayman, fleeing from his exploits in Epping Forest in 1737, settled in the village of **Brough** in the south of the county, under the name of John Palmer. Arrested for drunken behaviour, he ended up in York prison, where he inadvertently gave away his real identity, and on 22 March 1739 he was sentenced to death.

Stamford Bridge, on the borders with York, was the scene of Harold II's great victory on 25 September 1066 over the Vikings under Harald Hardrada, King of Norway and Tostig, Harold II's brother. The victory was short-lived, for he was defeated by William the Conqueror at Hastings on 14 October 1066.

When it opened in 1981 the **Humber Bridge** was the longest suspension bridge in the world, with a span of 1,410 m. It links **Hessle** in East Yorkshire with **Barton-upon-Humber** in North Lincolnshire.

FAMOUS PEOPLE

Andrew Marvell, poet, born Winestead, 1621.
William Kent, architect and designer, born Bridlington, c.1685.
Winifred Holtby, novelist (*South Riding*), born Rudston, Driffield, 1898.

KINGSTON UPON HULL

Area Sq Km	81
Area Sq Miles	31
Population	258,700
Highest point	East Mount (11m) and Bransholme (11m)

FAMOUS PEOPLE

William Wilberforce, politician and anti-slavery campaigner, born 1759; **Joseph Arthur Rank**, 1st Baron Rank, motion picture pioneer, born, 1888; **Stevie Smith** (*born* Florence Margaret Smith), poet, born, 1902; **Amy Johnson**, aviator, born, 1903; **Ian Carmichael**, actor, born, 1920; **Maureen Lipman**, actress, born, 1946.

Hull, perhaps surprisingly, has been an inspiration to many poets from the 17th century **Andrew Marvell** to the 20th century **Philip Larkin**.

"Nor have the merchants of any port in Britain a fairer credit, or fairer character, than the merchants of Hull, as well as for the justice of their dealings as the greatness of their substance or funds for trade."
Daniel Defoe, 1725

The East Riding is mostly low-lying, except for the central ridge that forms the southern part of the Wolds. The river Derwent runs through the Riding and the Humber forms its southern border.

The historic East Riding of Yorkshire (which became a County Council in 1889) covered a slightly different area from that of the current riding and included Filey and an area to the east of Selby. In 1974 the new county of Humberside was created that took in all of the East Riding (except the areas mentioned above) along with Goole, previously in the West Riding. The county of Humberside was never a success, as the two sides of the Humber estuary had little in common, even when the Humber Bridge was opened in 1981. In 1996 a new unitary authority was created called the East Riding of Yorkshire, with Hull, the major settlement in the area, becoming its own unitary authority.

The population of the East Riding is 335,000, and is expected to reach 430,000 by 2031, a rate of growth significantly above regional and national trends. There are no major settlements, with over half the population living in rural communities. It has become an attractive area for people to commute into Hull and, in the northwest, to York. The largest settlements are Bridlington (33,589), Beverley (29,110), Goole (18,741) and Driffield (11,245).

The East Riding has historically been an important agricultural area, and while it still remains significant, other industries include aerospace, caravan manufacture, general engineering and the gas industry (Easington gas terminal is one of three in Britain receiving gas from

the North Sea). Overall, manufacturing and construction accounts for 20 per cent of jobs, while the service sector provides over 76 per cent, with 33 per cent of jobs in public administration, education and health.

Beverley is the administrative centre of the county. The town grew prosperous on the medieval cloth trade, a wealth most demonstrably shown by Beverley Minster, built between 1220 and 1425 on the site of the tomb of St John of York who founded a monastery here and died in 721. The Minster is grander than many a cathedral and is considered one of the finest Gothic buildings in Europe. On a slightly smaller scale is the parish church of St Mary's, itself one of Britain's finest parish churches ('the best late medieval money could buy' as described by Simon Jenkins).

It is the coast of the East Riding that provides real distinctiveness. At the northern end of the county is Flamborough Head, an 11-km-long chalky promontory that sticks out into the North Sea, with cliffs rising up to 135 m. It is home to one of the largest groupings of nesting seabirds in England. To the south, the land falls away and the chalk is replaced by the soft boulder clay of the Holderness region, where the land is retreating on average 1.5 to 2 m a year. Since Roman times, a number of villages and farms have been lost to the sea. Some of the land washed away is driven down the coast to Spurn Head, at the entrance to the Humber, a long, narrow spit of land that keeps growing and moving.

Sewerby Hall and Gardens, Bridlington.

Kingston upon Hull (usually shortened to Hull), is a unitary authority 40 km up the Humber Estuary from Spurn Head. It is a major sea port and a great industrial city, with key industries including chemicals, food processing, pharmaceuticals and engineering. The river Hull passes through the city. The population of 258,700 is over 44,000 less than its peak in 1962. Hull's origins go back to the monks of the nearby Cistercian Meaux Abbey who wanted a port to export their wool from. Edward I granted it a royal charter in 1299, renaming the settlement as Kingston upon Hull. It prospered greatly as a port and Henry VIII fortified it. By 1800 it was the third-largest trading port in Britain after

London and Liverpool and it also became a major fishing port. It was made a city in 1897, but its somewhat isolated position, severe blitz damage during World War II and the demise of its fishing industry has seen the city suffer economically. Its low lying location has also exposed it to serious flooding. While flooding from the sea is partially protected by the River Hull tidal barrage, in 2007 it suffered from severe flooding caused by unseasonably high rainfall. In recent years much has been done to regenerate Hull, including The Deep, a stunning underwater aquarium, that tells the story of the oceans and the creatures that live there.

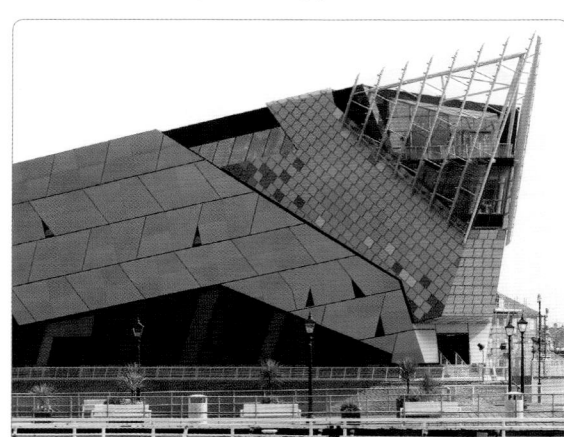

The Deep, Hull.

Humber Bridge, Hull.

Bartholomew Gazetteer of the British Isles, 1887

HULL.– or Kingston-upon-Hull, mun. bor., seaport, and co. in itself, East-Riding Yorkshire, on a low plain at the influx of the river Hull to the estuary of the Humber, 55½ miles SE. of Leeds and 173½ miles (by New Holland) from London, 7916 ac., pop. 165,690; 8 Banks, 12 newspapers. Market-days, Tuesday, Friday, and Saturday. Hull received its charter from Edward I., but was a place of some consequence long before the reign of that monarch. The marked progress and prosperity of the town in recent times may be attributed to the opening of docks, of which the chief are the Old Dock, and the Humber, Junction, Railway, and Victoria docks. Through the great maritime enterprise of the inhabitants, Hull has become one of the largest ports of the United Kingdom, having shipping commerce with all parts of the world. Regular lines of steamers ply between the town and the chief ports of the Continent. Sea-fishing is very extensively prosecuted by an immense fleet of trawlers and drifters belonging to the port. The other industries of Hull comprise shipbuilding, rope and sail works, chemical works, mfrs. of oil, paint, and colours, flax and cotton mills, engineering works, breweries, foundries, &c. There is a fine Town Hall and many other handsome and large public buildings. Near the docks is a monument to William Wilberforce (1759–1833), the philanthropist, who was a native.

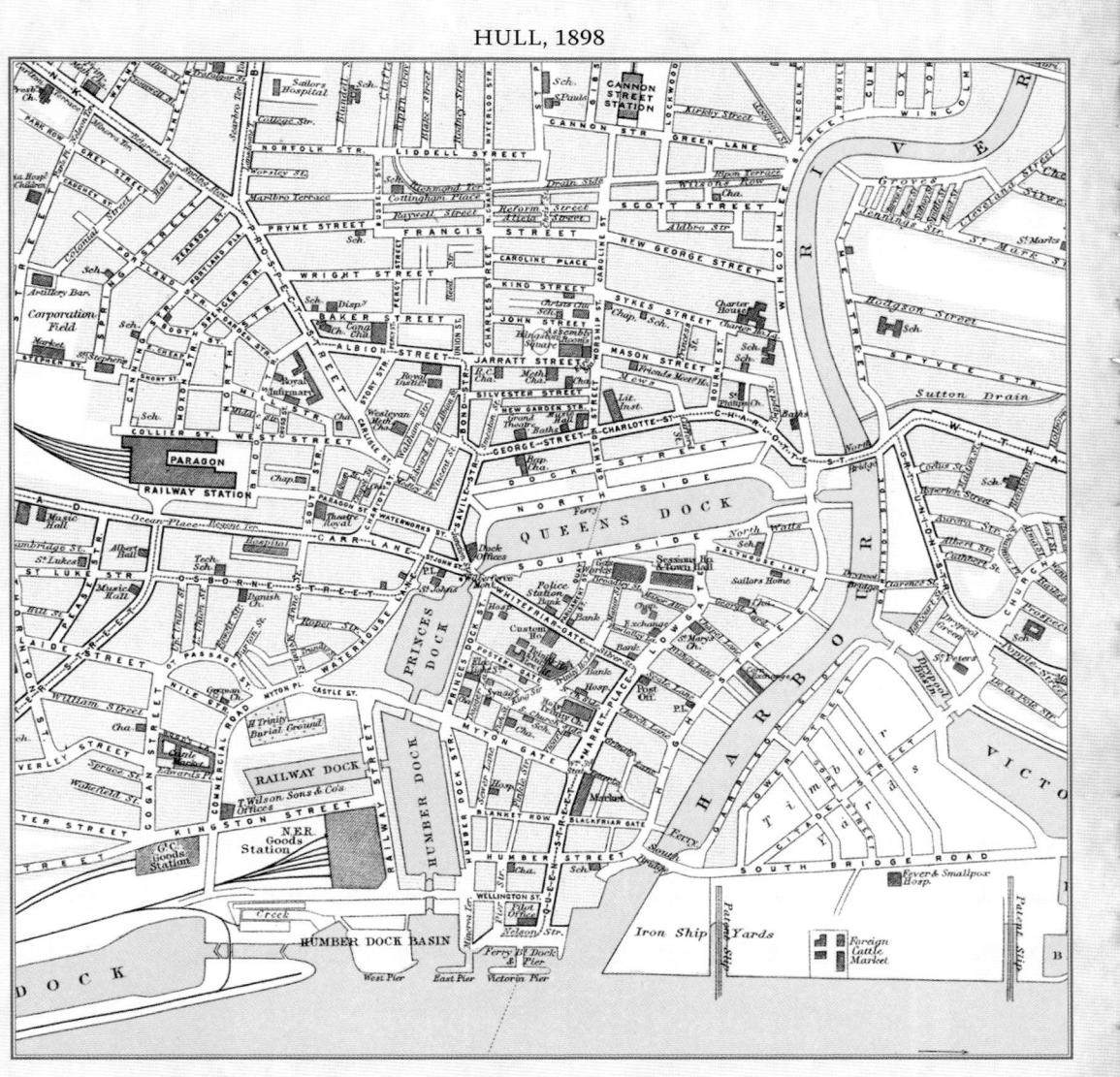

HULL, 1898

mborough Head

e interior of Beverley Minster.

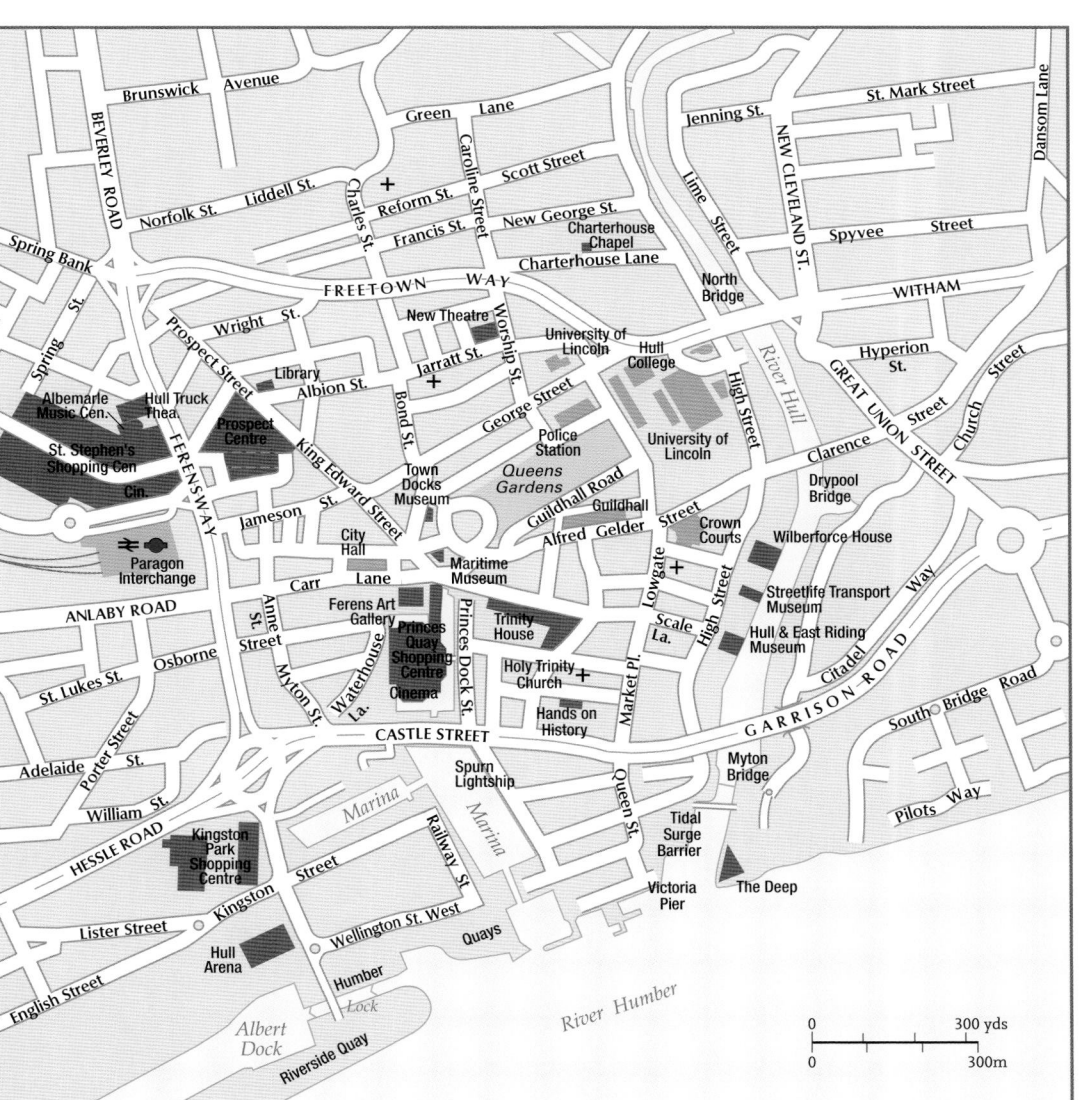

Modern Hull

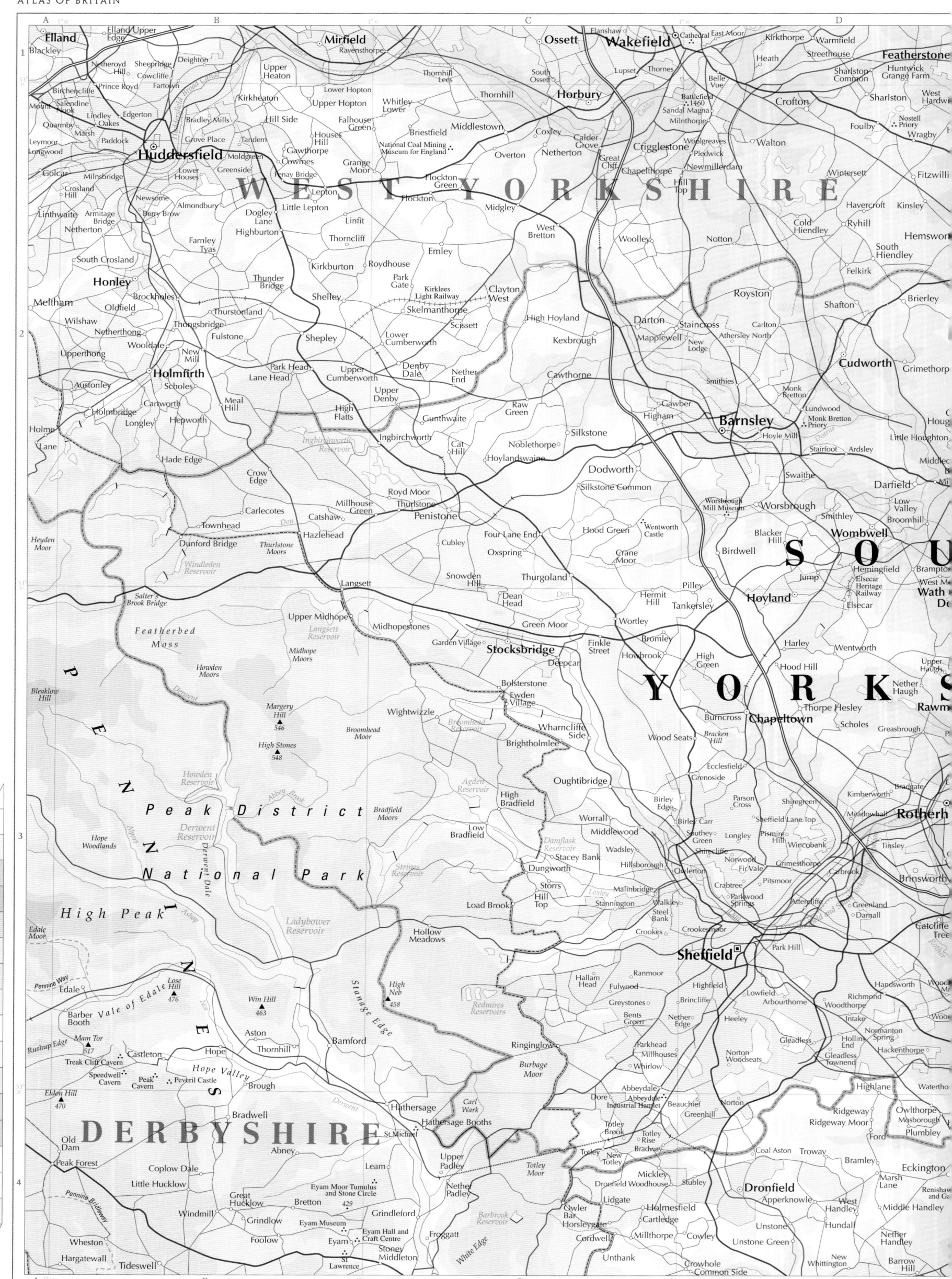

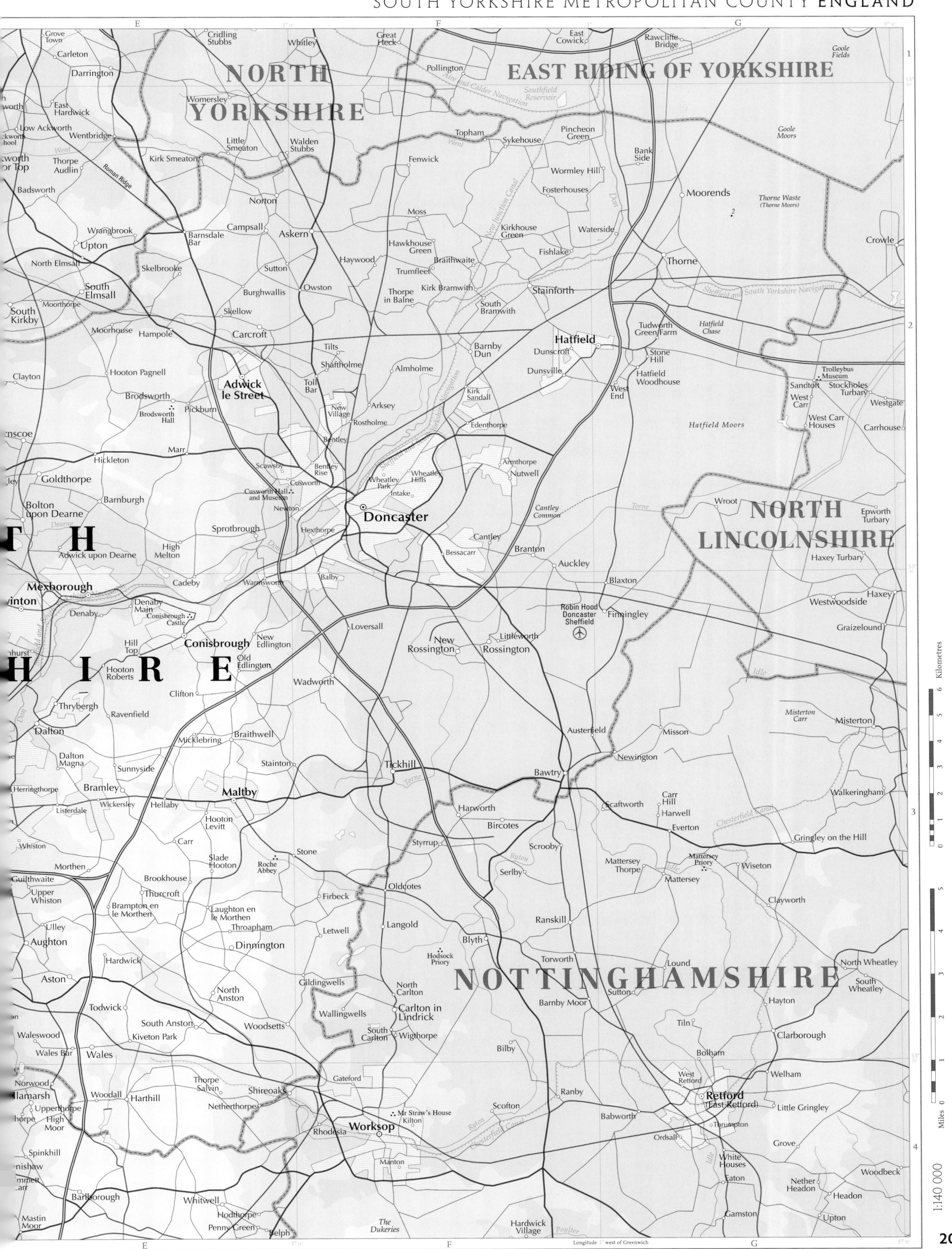

NORTH YORKSHIRE

EAST RIDING OF YORKSHIRE

NORTH LINCOLNSHIRE

NOTTINGHAMSHIRE

1:140 000

© Collins Bartholomew Ltd

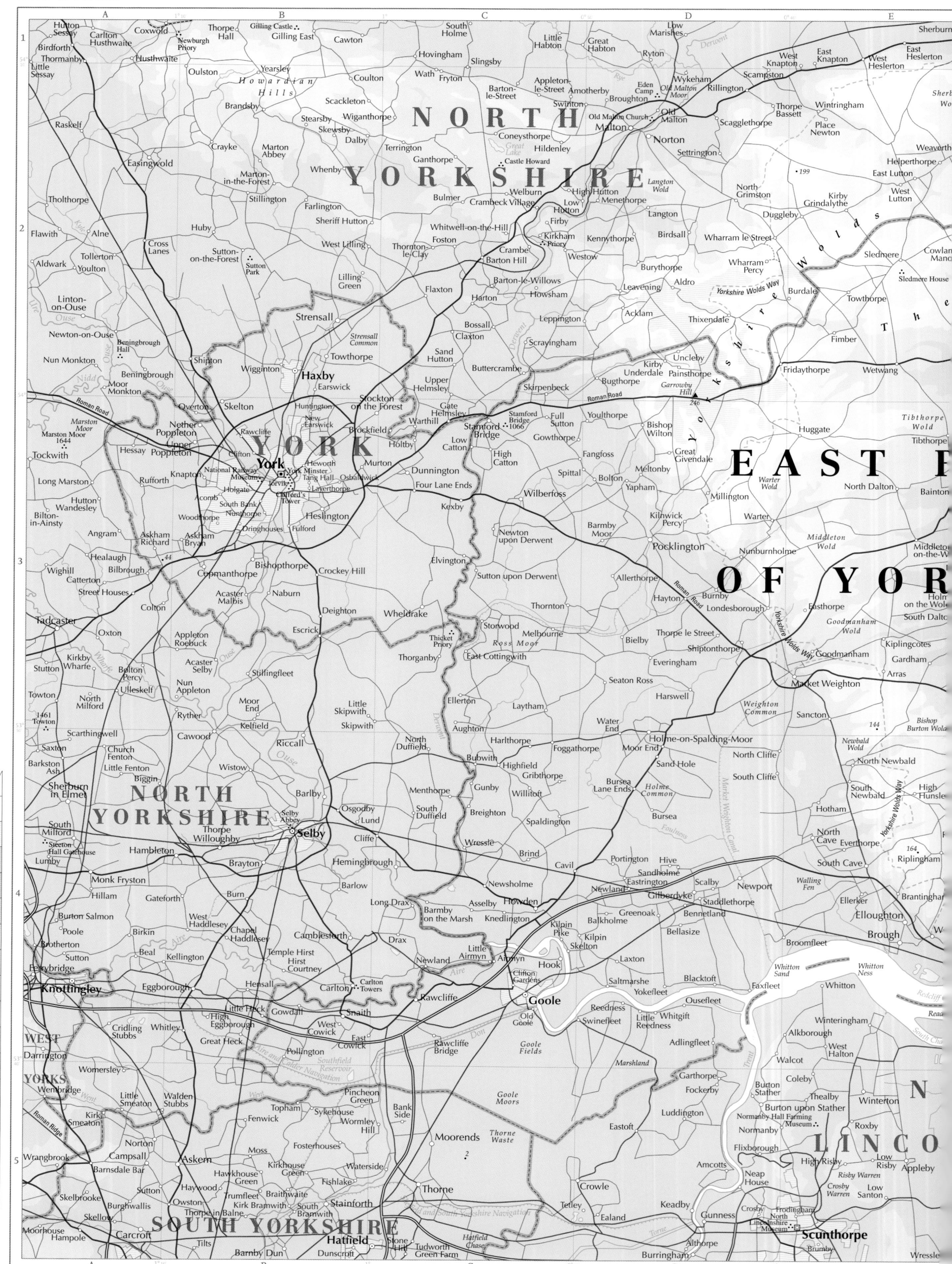

British National Grid projection

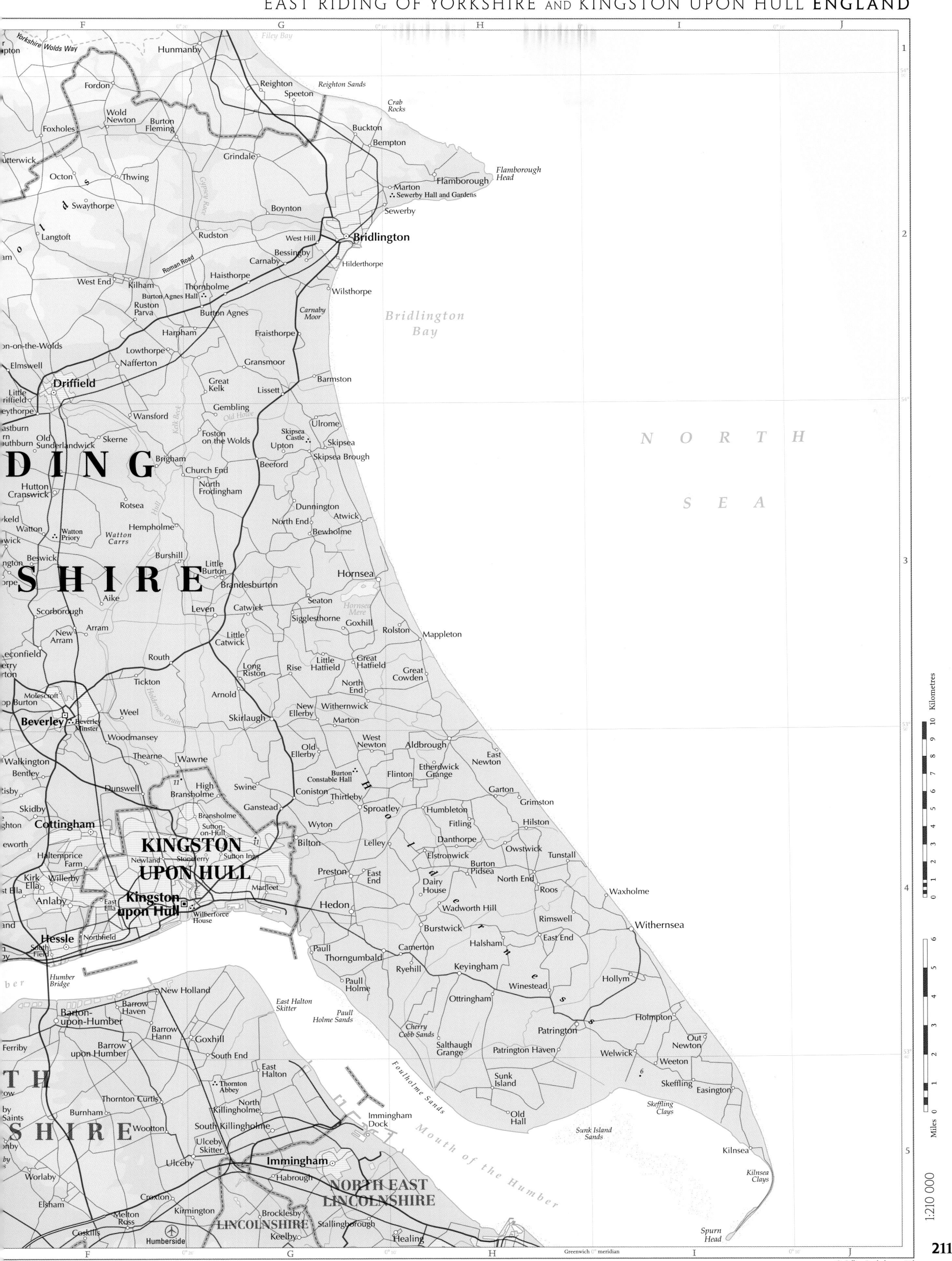

NORTH YORKSHIRE

Area Sq Km	8,053
Area Sq Miles	3,109
Population	559,200
County town	Northallerton
Highest point	Whernside (736 m) in the Yorkshire Dales near the Cumbrian border
Districts	Craven; Hambleton; Harrogate; Richmondshire; Ryedale; Scarborough; Selby

Yorkshire takes its name from the city of York, a name that has been through many transformations since the Romans called it _Eboracum,_ a Celtic word in origin, meaning either 'Eburos' land' or 'land of yew trees'. The Danes modified the name to _Eorvik_ and then to _Jorvik_ and eventually to York.

FAMOUS FOR

Some of the most spectacular limestone scenery can be seen in the southern Yorkshire Dales close to the village of **Malham** – Malham Cove, a 80-m-high and 300-m-wide curving limestone cliff that was once a massive waterfall; Malham Tarn, a large lake formed by a dam of glacial moraine; and Gordale Scar, a winding gorge with vertical sides over 100 m high.

Castle Howard, near Malton, is one of Britain's most spectacular country houses. Designed by Sir John Vanbrugh with assistance from Nicholas Hawksmoor, it was built between 1700 and 1737.

Knaresborough, built on a bluff above the River Nidd, was home to Mother Shipton, a 15th-century prophet and soothsayer, allegedly born in a cave near the Petrifying Well (or Dropping Well), whose mineral-laden waters turn objects to stone.

The **Selby coalfield** was the last to be exploited in Britain. Work started in 1976 and its deep mines were producing 12 million tonnes of coal a year in the 1990s, but closed completely in 2004 as the reserves became more difficult to mine.

The Georgian Theatre at **Richmond** in Britain's most complete Georgian theatre. It was built in 1788 and, from one of its 214 seats, you can really experience what it was like to see a play performed 200 years ago.

FAMOUS PEOPLE

Henry I, King of England (1100–35), son of William the Conqueror, born Selby, c. 1069.
Sir George Cayley, inventor of first glider to carry a person, born Scarborough, 1773.
William Bateson, biologist, coined the term 'genetics', born Whitby, 1861.
Charles Laughton, actor, born Scarborough, 1899.
Dame Honor Fell, biologist, born Filey, 1900.
Sir Ben Kingsley, (_born_ Krishna Pandit Bhanji) actor, born Scarborough, 1943.

"Was the aim frustrated by force or guile,
When giants scooped from out the rocky ground,
Tier under tier, this semicirque profound?"
William Wordsworth, '_Malham Cove_', 1819

"They have a legend here [Whitby] that when a ship is lost bells are heard out to sea. I must ask the old man about this. 'I wouldn't fash masel' about them, miss. Them things be all wore out… They be all very well for comers and trippers, an' the like, but not for a young lady like you. Them feet-folks from York and Leeds, that be always eatin' cured herrin's an' drinkin' tea an' lookin' out to buy cheap jet would creed aught."
I wonder masel' who'd be bothered tellin' lies to them."
Mina Murray's Journal in '_Dracula_', Bram Stoker, 1897

North Yorkshire is the largest shire county by area. Apart from the wide plain around York and the smaller Vale of Pickering, the county is dominated by two ranges of hills: the Pennines (mostly in the Yorkshire Dales National Park) in the west and the Cleveland Hills (included in the North York Moors National Park) in the northeast. The more gentle Wolds lie to the south of the Vale of Pickering. Principal rivers are the Ouse, fed by the Derwent, Swale, Ure, Nidd and Wharfe, and draining into the Humber; the Esk, flowing into the North Sea at Whitby; the Tees, on its northern boundary; and in the west, the Ribble, flowing into Lancashire and the Irish Sea.

The current North Yorkshire is significantly different from the old North Riding of Yorkshire, whose origins went back to the Danish division of Yorkshire. When the new county of North Yorkshire was formed in 1974, in the north, Middlesbrough and Redcar moved to the new county of Cleveland while the county gained Filey from the East Riding and large areas of the former West Riding including Harrogate, Ripon, Skipton and Selby, in the south of the county. The City of York became a unitary authority in 1996, as did Middlesbrough and Redcar with the abolition of Cleveland in that year. The ceremonial county of North Yorkshire includes all these unitary authorities plus those parts of Stockton-on-Tees that are on the south bank of the Tees.

The population of North Yorkshire is 559,200, and it is predicted to grow by 24 per cent by 2031. The population is very scattered with 56 per cent of people living in areas with less than 4 people per hectare, while only 21 per cent live in the two largest settlements, Harrogate and Knaresborough (85,128) and Scarborough (38,364). Other settlements include the cathedral city of Ripon (16,468), Selby (15,807), Northallerton (15,517), Skipton (14,313) and Whitby (13,594).

Agriculture and food processing play an important part in the economy – in the rural uplands this sector can provide over half of all jobs. Tourism is important in the resorts of Scarborough and Whitby, and in the North York Moors and Yorkshire Dales national parks.

Other economic activities include light engineering, power generation and hi-tech industries. The Army an the Royal Air Force have a number of bases, including Catterick garrison, the largest in Britain. In all, over 13 per cent of jobs are in manufacturing and 12 per ce in tourism. Public administration, education and heal account for nearly 25 per cent of all jobs.

Its coastal landscape is characterized by rocky cliff sheltered inlets and bays, as at Staithes, Runswick Bay and Robin Hood's Bay, and more sheltered beaches, as Sandsend, Filey and Scarborough, Britain's first seasid resort whose heyday was in late Victorian times. Whitb provides the best-sheltered harbour. With its ruined abbey on the cliffs above the town, its narrow streets and its connections with the original Dracula story an with Captain Cook, it is a popular place to visit. Inland is the wild area of the North York Moors. The sheltere valleys within the moors provided opportunities for sheep farming in medieval times. The Cistercian monks at Rievaulx Abbey excelled, pouring their wealt into their great Abbey building, now a romantic ruin, especially when seen from the 18th-century Terrace that overlooks it. Across the Vale of York the Yorkshire Dales start to rise. Again the Cistercians were active, this time at Fountains Abbey near Ripon, now a World Heritage Site, where they built the largest abbey in Britain. The magnificent Swaledale and Wensleydale a valleys that reach into the heart of the Pennines. Near the head of Wensleydale is the town of Hawes, home to the creamery that makes Wensleydale cheese. Just to the east of the Dales is Harrogate, whose prosperity wa built on mineral springs discovered in 1571. It became a great spa resort in the 18th and 19th centuries and now thrives as a conference centre and a tourist base f exploring the region (and as a commuter town for Lee and the West Yorkshire conurbation). The southern part of the county, to the south of York is flat and mor industrial. Selby, with its fine medieval Abbey, is the main settlement, but the most dominant feature in the landscape is Drax power station, the biggest in Britain providing 7 per cent of the country's electricity.

Sir Ben Kingsley

Swaledale

South Bay, Scarborough.

Whalebone arch, Whitby.

Bartholomew Gazetteer of the British Isles, 1887

YORK, *mun. bor., archiepiscopal city, county town of Yorkshire, and county in itself, 188 miles NW. of London by rail – mun. bor., pop. 60,683; 5 Banks, 5 newspapers. Market-days, Tuesday, Thursday, and Saturday. The city of York is pleasantly situated in a wide and fertile vale, at a point where the 3 Ridings meet, and where the Foss joins the Ouse, which is here navigable. The ancient part of the city is enclosed by walls, and entered by 4 principal gates. The walls, originally Roman, but restored by Edward I., are still for the most part in good preservation, and have been converted into promenades. The chief architectural feature of York is the minster or cathedral, the largest and finest ecclesiastical edifice in England. As it now exists, it was begun in 1171 and completed in 1472. It is cruciform in shape, with central tower and 2 western towers. Besides the cathedral there are numerous ancient churches and chapels, some of them worthy of notice, as are also the Roman Catholic pro-cathedral of St Wilfrid (1864), and the ruins of the mitred abbey of St Mary (11th century). Among other buildings are the castle, occupied as assize courts and county prison, and the new station of the Great Northern Ry. (1877), one of the finest in the kingdom. York is an important railway centre. There are large cavalry barracks near Fulford, and York has been made the centre of the northern military district. The only public recreation ground is the common of Knavesmire, where the races are held. The trade of York is now mostly local, and the industries are not important, but they include to some extent iron-castings, bottles, combs, gloves, leather, and confectionery. York was the capital of the Brigantes, and then called Caer Effroc; the capital of Roman Britain, and then called Eboracum; and the capital of Northumbria, and then called Eoforwic. In 624 Edwin, king of Northumbria, made it an archiepiscopal see.*

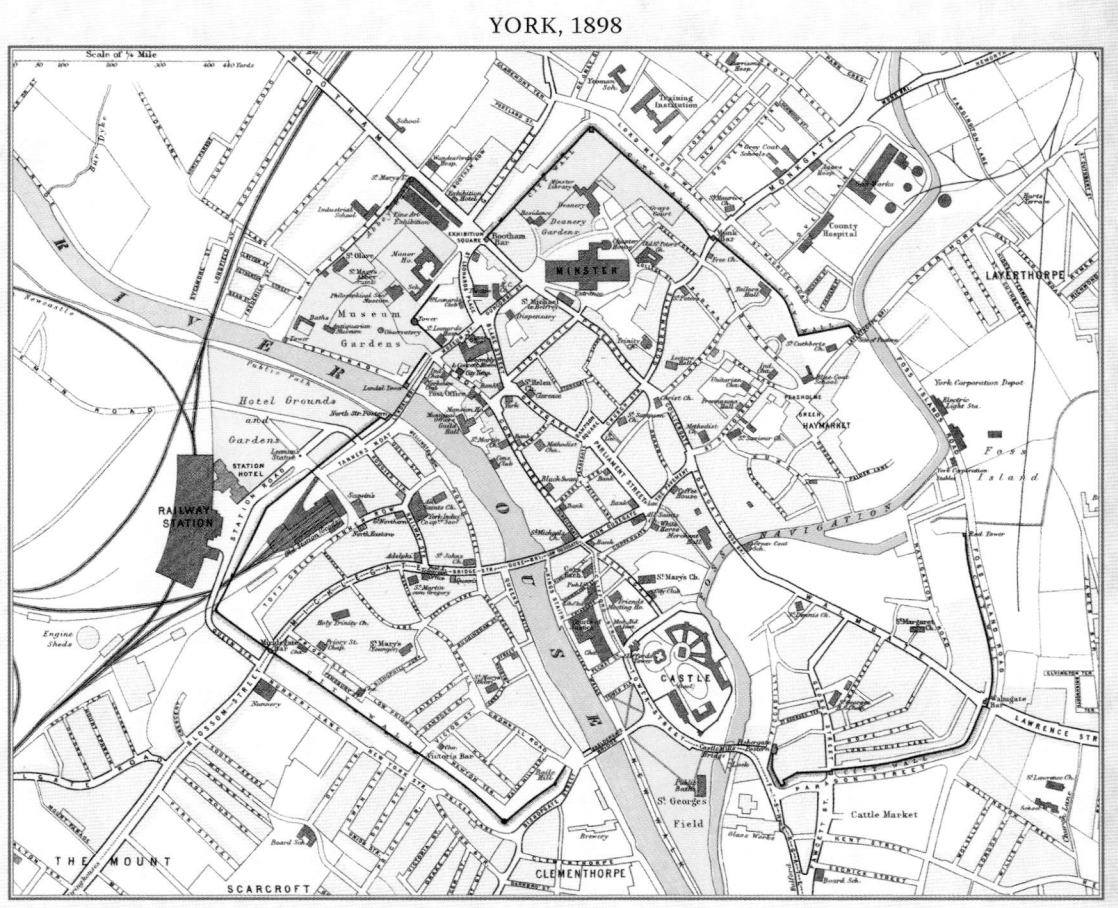

YORK, 1898

In the 8th century it was famous for its diocesan school, and it continued to make a distinguished figure in English history until the Civil War, when it was taken by the Parliamentarians after a siege of 13 weeks. Its decline commenced with the Wars of the Roses and the Pilgrimage of Grace, but it still ranks second among English cities, and gives its chief magistrate the title of Lord Mayor. Its first charter of incorporation was granted by Henry I., and the last important event in its municipal history is the extension of the city boundaries by an Act obtained in 1884.

Whitby Beach

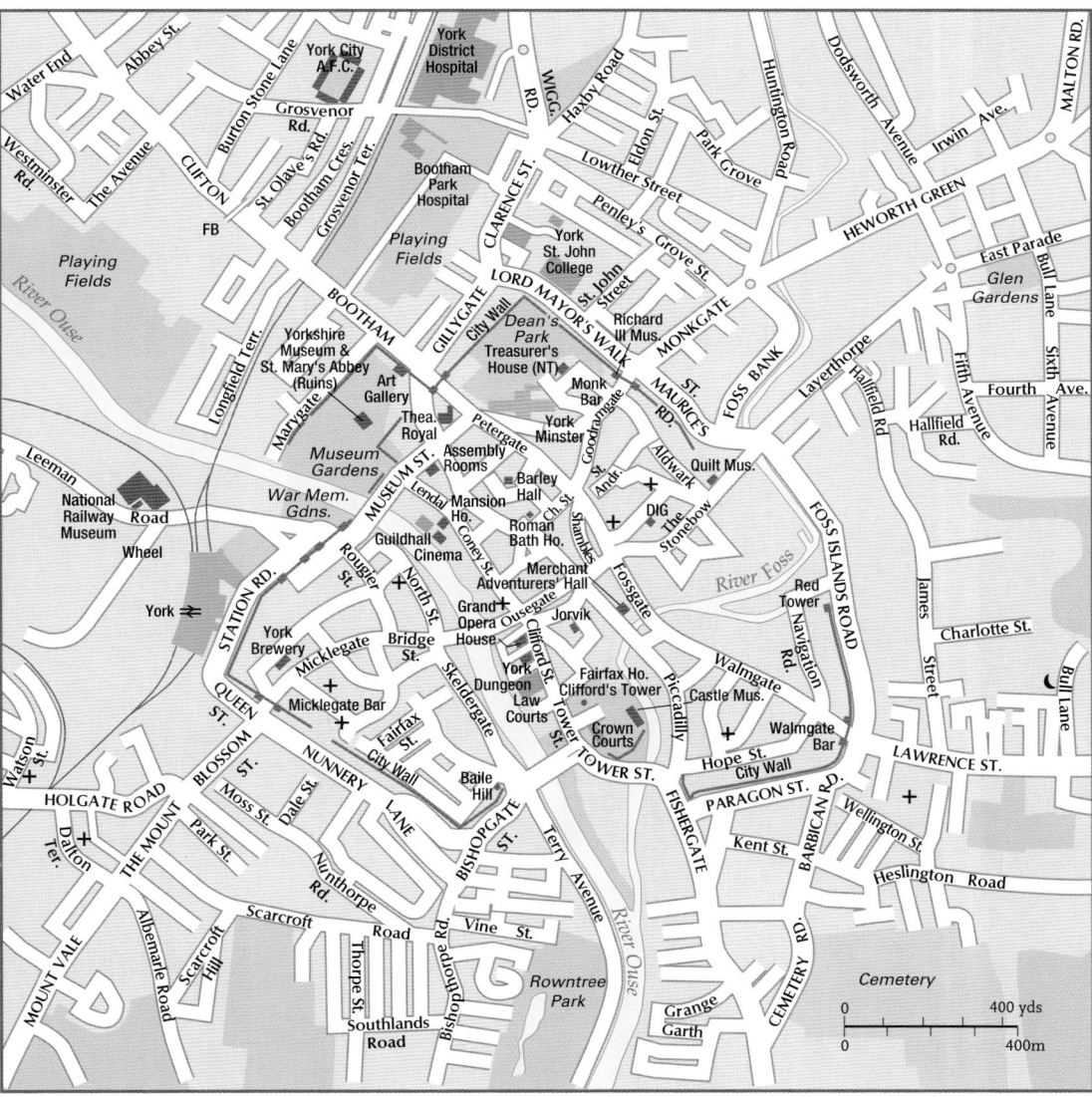

Modern York

YORK

Area Sq Km	272
Area Sq Miles	105
Population	195,400
Highest point	Stock Hill (44 m)

FAMOUS FOR

The Shambles, a narrow winding street leading to the Minster, is lined by medieval buildings, some dramatically overhanging the street. One poll in 2010 voted it Britain's most picturesque street.

FAMOUS PEOPLE

Guy Fawkes, born 1570.
John Flaxman, sculptor, born 1755.
William Etty, artist, born 1787.
Joseph Hansom, hansom cab inventor, born 1803.
Wystan Hugh (WH) Auden, poet, born 1907.
Dame Judi Dench, actress, born 1934.

York, sited where the river Foss joins the river Ouse, was founded by the Romans, as *Eboracum*, in AD 71. Abandoned in the early 5th century, a bishopric was established here in 627. Between 866 and 954 it was held by the Vikings, as *Jorvik*. By the late 14th century it was the second city of England after London, a wealth built on the wool trade. In 1888 it became a county borough and in 1974, a district within the new county of North Yorkshire. In 1996, it again became an independent unitary authority, with increased boundaries that brought in the rural hinterland. The city's heritage has made it a major museum and tourist centre, attracting over 4 million visitors a year. The historic core, situated around the imposing medieval Minster (the largest Gothic cathedral in northern Europe), is well preserved. Other major attractions include the Jorvik Viking Centre, the 3-km-long medieval city walls, the Castle Museum and the National Railway Museum. Economic sectors include the confectionery industry, the railways, insurance, research and development establishments and two universities (York and York St John).

"York Minster, with the sun new-washed for bed shining full on the west window, looked lovelier than I have ever seen it. Yellow, crisp, and eatable, like a crust of apple-pie."
James Agate, 1935

Dame Judi Dench

The Shambles

View from the central tower of York Minster.

Clifford's Tower, the Keep of York Castle.

MIDDLESBROUGH

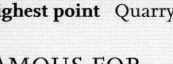

Area Sq Km   55
Area Sq Miles   21
Population   138,600
Highest point   Quarry Hill (100 m)

FAMOUS FOR

The steel in the **Sydney Harbour Bridge** was made in Middlesbrough, as was the steel in the **Middlesbrough Transporter Bridge**, built across the Tees, which opened in 1911 and is still working today.

FAMOUS PEOPLE

Captain James Cook, naval explorer, born, 1728.
Ernest William Hornung, novelist (*Raffles*), born 1866.
Don Revie, footballer and manager, born 1927.
Brian Clough, football manager, born 1935.

"This remarkable place [Middlesbrough], the youngest child of England's enterprise, is an infant, but if an infant, an infant Hercules."
William Gladstone, 1862

Middlesbrough, on the south bank of the Tees, is a unitary authority, formed from the district of Middlesbrough when the county of Cleveland was abolished in 1996. Prior to the 1974 creation of Cleveland, it was a borough within the North Riding of Yorkshire. The area is almost entirely urbanized and has a population of 138,600, which continues to decline from a peak of around 165,000 in the late 1960s. Middlesbrough developed in the 1830s as a port to ship out coal from the Durham coalfield. It used to be a major steel-making centre, upon which its initial wealth was based, after the discovery in the 1850s of iron ore in the nearby hills. Steel from the Dorman Long works was exported round the world, but the steelworks moved down river to Redcar to make it easier to ship in coal and iron ore (after local reserves were exhausted). The remaining industries include chemicals and petrochemicals. Since 1992 it has been the base for the University of Teesside. Manufacturing now only provides 5.6 per cent of jobs, while nearly 43 per cent of all jobs are in public administration, education and health.

Middlesbrough Transporter Bridge.

REDCAR AND CLEVELAND

Area Sq Km   254
Area Sq Miles   98
Population   139,500
Highest point   Guisborough Moor (329 m)

FAMOUS FOR

The cliff lift (actually an inclined tramway) at **Saltburn** links the seashore with the town on the cliff above. Opened in 1884, it is water-powered – water is added to a tank on the carriage at the top, which is then heavier than the carriage at the bottom. It descends and the other carriage ascends. The water is then pumped out of the carriage at the bottom and returned to the carriage at the top.

Redcar and Cleveland is a unitary authority, formed from the district of Langbaurgh-on-Tees, when the county of Cleveland was abolished in 1996. Prior to the creation of Cleveland, which straddled the river Tees, the area was in the North Riding of Yorkshire. Its population is 139,500 and is forecast to remain roughly static for the next 20 years. The main centres are Redcar (36,443), Eston and South Bank (32,788) and Guisborough (17,186). The area contains the northern edge of the North York Moors National Park with its small villages, market towns such as Guisborough, and a heavily populated urban area, heavy industry and port facilities, based around Redcar and Eston, along the south bank of the Tees. Industries include steel-making, chemicals and process engineering. The giant iron and steelworks at Lackenby by Redcar, was one of three integrated steelworks in Britain up to 2010, when the plant was moth-balled, bringing to an end iron-making on Teesside, which started when iron ore was found in the Cleveland Hills in the 1850s. The coastal towns attract some tourism to the great expanse of sandy beaches – indeed Saltburn was specifically built as a seaside resort in the 1860s, when its main hotel, the Zetland Hotel, had a private railway platform attached to the building.

The pier at Saltburn.

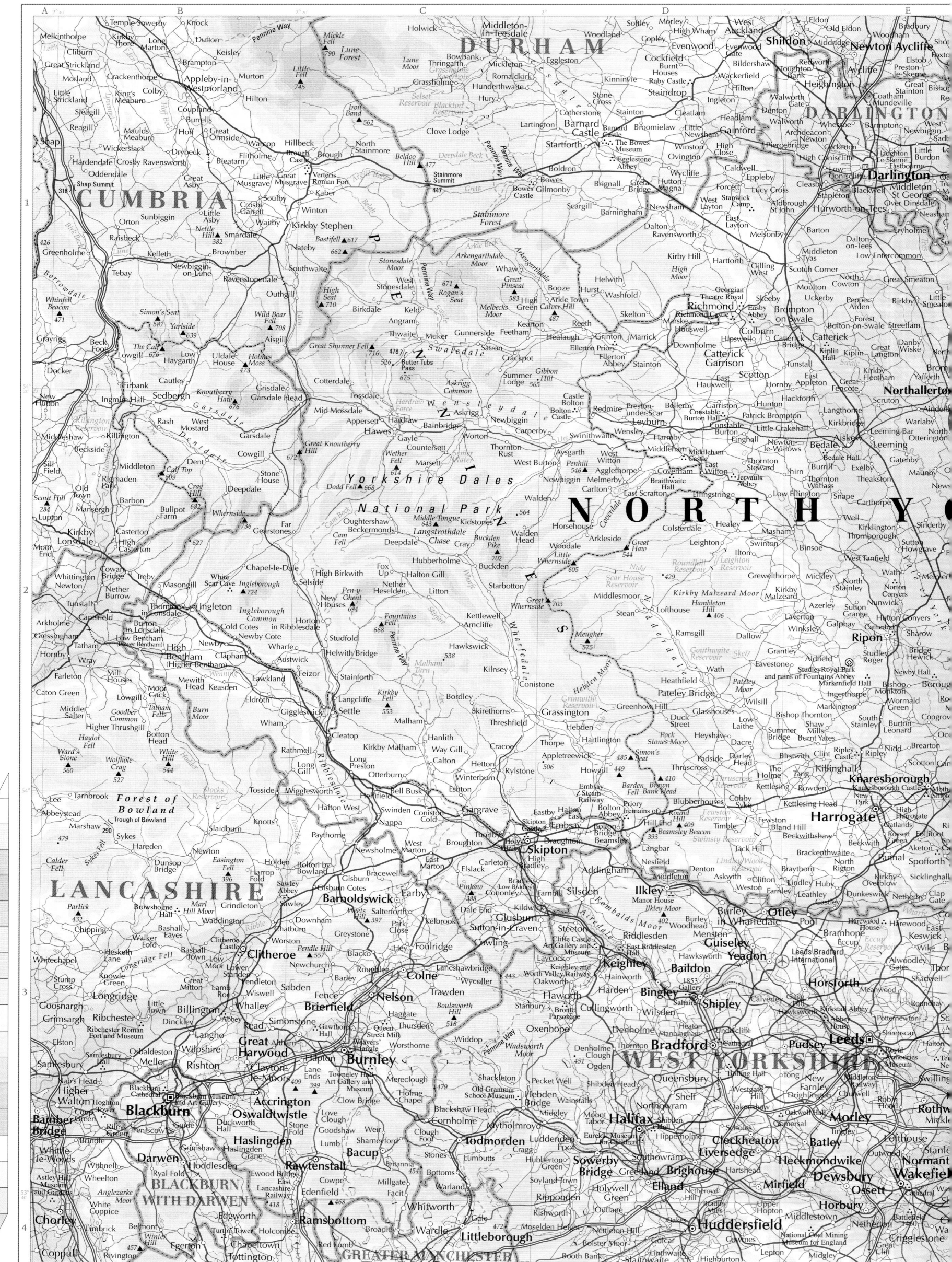

British National Grid projection

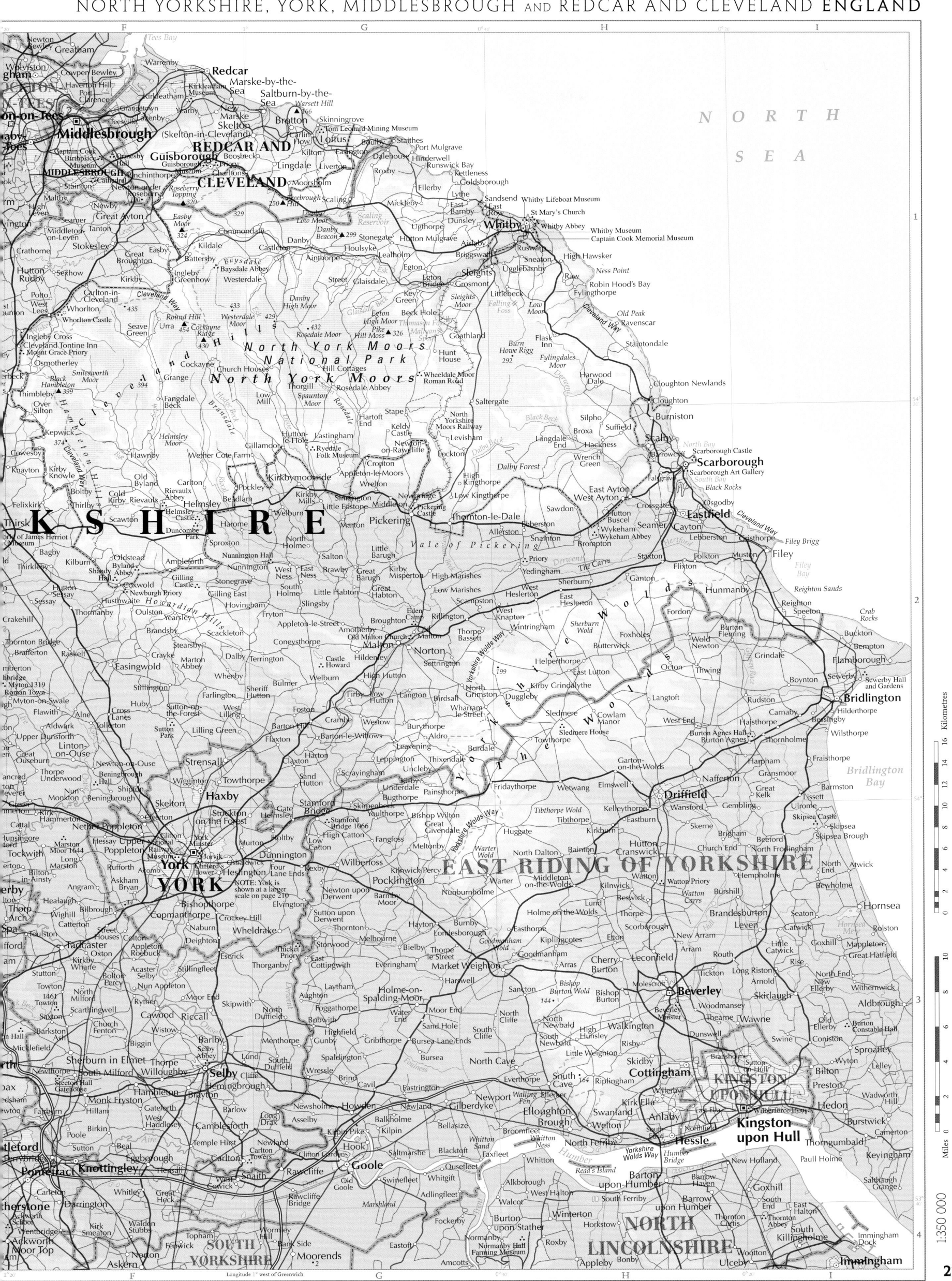

© Collins Bartholomew Ltd

1:350 000

WEST YORKSHIRE METROPOLITAN COUNTY

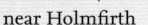

Area Sq Km	2,029
Area Sq Miles	784
Population	2,200,600
Highest point	Black Hill (582 m) near Holmfirth

Metropolitan Borough Areas

City of Bradford	366 sq km; 141 sq miles
Calderdale	364 sq km; 141 sq miles
Kirklees	409 sq km; 158 sq miles
City of Leeds	552 sq km; 213 sq miles
City of Wakefield	339 sq km; 131 sq mile

Metropolitan Borough Populations

City of Bradford	501,700
Calderdale	201,8000
Kirklees	403,900
City of Leeds	770,800
City of Wakefield	322,300

West Yorkshire was a new metropolitan county formed out of part of the old West Riding of Yorkshire in 1974. It consisted of five district authorities: City of Bradford, Calderdale, Kirklees, City of Leeds, and City of Wakefield. Each district contains a considerable rural area around the main conurbations, Bradford, Kirklees and Calderdale all stretching up into the Pennines and bordering the Greater Manchester conurbation on the western side of the Pennines. The metropolitan county was abolished by Parliament in 1986 along with all the other metropolitan counties in England and each district then effectively became a unitary authority. West Yorkshire remains a ceremonial county with its own Lord Lieutenant and all the authorities share certain services including police, fire services and the West Yorkshire Passenger Transport Executive.

The population of West Yorkshire is 2,200,600, and it is predicted to grow to 2,723,700 by 2031. The greatest growth, of around 30 per cent, is predicted for Bradford, followed by Leeds at 26 per cent. The slowest growth is expected in Wakefield. As the area includes a section of the Pennines, there are significant areas of high land in the county. The highest point in West Yorkshire is Black Hill (582 m) in Kirklees on the border with Derbyshire.

FAMOUS PEOPLE

City of Bradford
Charlotte Brontë, born 1816, **Emily Brontë**, born 1818 and **Anne Brontë**, born 1820, all novelists, born Thornton.
Sir Frederick Delius, composer, born Bradford, 1862.
Sir Edward Appleton, physicist, Nobel laureate, born Bradford, 1892.
John Boyton (JB) Priestley, novelist born Bradford, 1894.
Sir Fred Hoyle, astronomer, born Bingley, 1915.
Mollie Sugden, actress , born Keighley, 1922.
David Hockney, artist, born Bradford, 1937.

Calderdale
Percy Shaw, inventor of 'cats eyes', born Halifax, 1890.
Sir John Cockcroft, physicist, Nobel laureate, born Todmorden, 1897.
Sir Geoffrey Wilkinson, chemist, Nobel laureate, born Todmorden, 1921.
Oliver Smithies, geneticist, Nobel laureate, born Halifax, 1925.
Ted Hughes, poet, Poet Laureate (1984–98), born Mytholmroyd, 1930.
Professor Sir John Ernest Walker, chemist, Nobel laureate, born Halifax, 1941.

Kirklees
Joseph Priestley, clergyman and scientist, born Fieldhead, Birstall, 1733.
Sir Owen Richardson, physicist, Nobel laureate, born Dewsbury, 1879.

Sir David Brown, entrepreneur, owner, Aston Martin Cars (the 'DB' series), born Huddersfield, 1904
James Mason, actor, born Huddersfield, 1909.
Harold Wilson, (Baron Wilson), Labour politician, Prime Minister (1964–70, 1974–76), born Huddersfield, 1916
Betty Boothroyd (Baroness Boothroyd), first female Speaker of House of Commons, born Dewsbury, 1929
Roy Castle, entertainer, born Scholes, near Holmfirth, 1932.
Sir Patrick Stewart, actor, born Mirfield, 1940.
Anita Lonsbrough, Olympic champion swimmer, born Huddersfield, 1941.

City of Leeds
Henry Stuart, Lord Darnley, husband of Mary, Queen of Scots, born Temple Newsam House, 1545.
William Congreve, playwright and poet, born Bardsey, 1670.
Thomas Chippendale, furniture designer, born Otley, c. 1718.
Sir Titus Salt, industrialist, philanthropist and creator of Saltaire, born Morley, 1803.
Alfred Austin, poet, Poet Laureate (1896–1913), born 1835.
Herbert Henry Asquith (Earl of Oxford), Liberal politician, Prime Minister (1908–16), born Morley, 1852.
Arthur Ransome, journalist and author, born 1884.
Ernest Wiseman, (Ernie Wise), comedian (double act with Eric Morecambe), born 1925.
Sir James (Jimmy) Savile, DJ and charity worker, born 1926 .
Alan Bennett, playwright and author, born 1934.

City of Wakefield
Sir Martin Frobisher, sailor and explorer, born Altofts near Wakefield, c. 1535.
John Radcliffe, physician, benefactor of Oxford University, born Wakefield, 1652.
Henry Moore, sculptor, born Castleford, 1898.

City of Leeds

The name of Leeds comes from the Celtic meaning 'people living by a strong-flowing river', a description of how the river Aire once was.

FAMOUS FOR
The most distinguished of the Victorian and Edwardian shopping arcades that are such a distinctive feature of Leeds is the **County Arcade**, built between 1898 and 1900, designed by Frank Matcham, who usually designed the inside of theatres, and it shows!

In 1884 a Polish emigrant, who had originally settled in Stockton-on-Tees, rented a stall in Leeds' Kirkgate market and used the selling line 'Don't ask the price – it's a penny.' He was **Michael Marks** and ten years later he went into partnership with **Tom Spencer**.

The Royal Armouries, the national museum of arms and armour, opened in 1996 in a new building by the river Aire in the Clarence Dock area, close to Leeds city centre, a rather different setting from the Tower of London, its other main home.

To the north of Leeds city centre are the ruins of **Kirkstall Abbey**, founded by the Cistercians in 1152 as a daughter house of Fountains Abbey. It is one of Britain's best-preserved medieval abbeys.

"Leeds is a large, wealthy and populous town, it stands on [both banks] of the river Aire … and the whole is joined by a stately and prodigiously strong stone bridge, so large, and so wide, that formerly the cloth market was kept in neither part of the town, but on the very bridge itself."
Daniel Defoe, 1726

The County Arcade, Leeds.

Bartholomew Gazetteer of the British Isles, 1887

LEEDS.- *mun. bor., par., and township, E. div. West-Riding Yorkshire, on river Aire, 25 miles SW. of York, 42½ NE. of Manchester, and 164½ NW. of London by rail – township, 2736 ac., pop. 160,019; bor. and par., 21,572 ac., pop. 309,119; 10 newspapers. Market-days, Tuesday and Saturday. Lord Clarendon, in his History of the Rebellion (written in 1642), refers to Leeds as being one of three "very populous and rich towns, depending wholly upon clothiers." From this it will appear that the town has for centuries been known for its mfr. of woollen goods, an industry of which it is now the chief centre. Little is known regarding the early history of the town, which is supposed to have Norman, Saxon, and even Roman associations. It was incorporated by Charles I. in 1626. About a fifth of the population was carried off by the plague in 1644. Besides the woollen mfrs., with their immense variety of fabrics, Leeds carries on nearly all the employments common to a large industrial town. Here are large flax-mills, canvas and rope works, mfrs. of linen, thread, and worsted, also of boots and shoes, glass and earthenware. Of late the working of iron has been largely developed; engine works are numerous, also railway plant works, steam saw mills, breweries, tanneries, &c. St Peter's church is an interesting and beautiful building, containing a monument by Flaxman. The splendid Town Hall, built 1853–58, at a cost of £140,000, is 250 ft. long by 200 in breadth, and is about 67 ft. high; its tower rises to the height of 225 ft. Five bridges span the river Aire (which here becomes navigable); while by the Leeds and Liverpool Canal, and other waterways, traffic is maintained with both Eastern and Western seaports.*

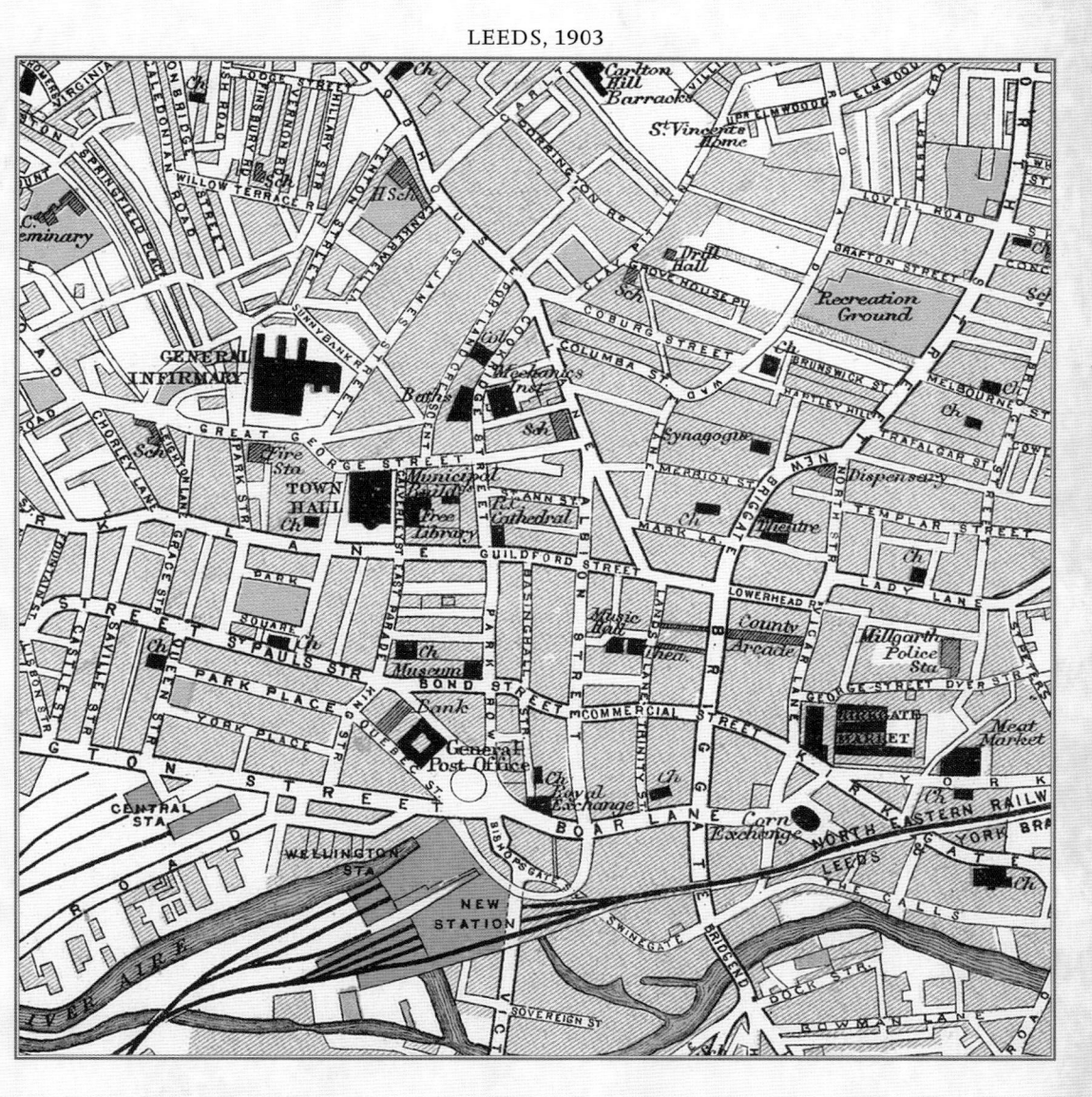

LEEDS, 1903

...iversity of Leeds campus.

...e authority now called the City of Leeds covers an area ...ch wider than just the historical city of Leeds. When ... district was established in 1974, in addition to the ...nty borough of Leeds, the areas of Rothwell, Garforth, ...dley, Pudsey, Yeadon, Guisley, Otley and Wetherby ...e incorporated into the new authority. The main ...rs flowing through the area are the Aire and the ...arfe. The highest point is on Ilkley Moor, in the ...thwest, at a height of 340 m.

...A settlement at Leeds is first mentioned in the ...mesday Book. It developed as a trading place for ...ollen cloth produced in the surrounding countryside. ...s trade grew significantly when the Aire and Calder ...rigation was completed in 1699, giving a direct link ...he North Sea, and the Leeds and Liverpool Canal, ...mpeted in stages between 1770 and 1816, which gave ...ess to the Atlantic.

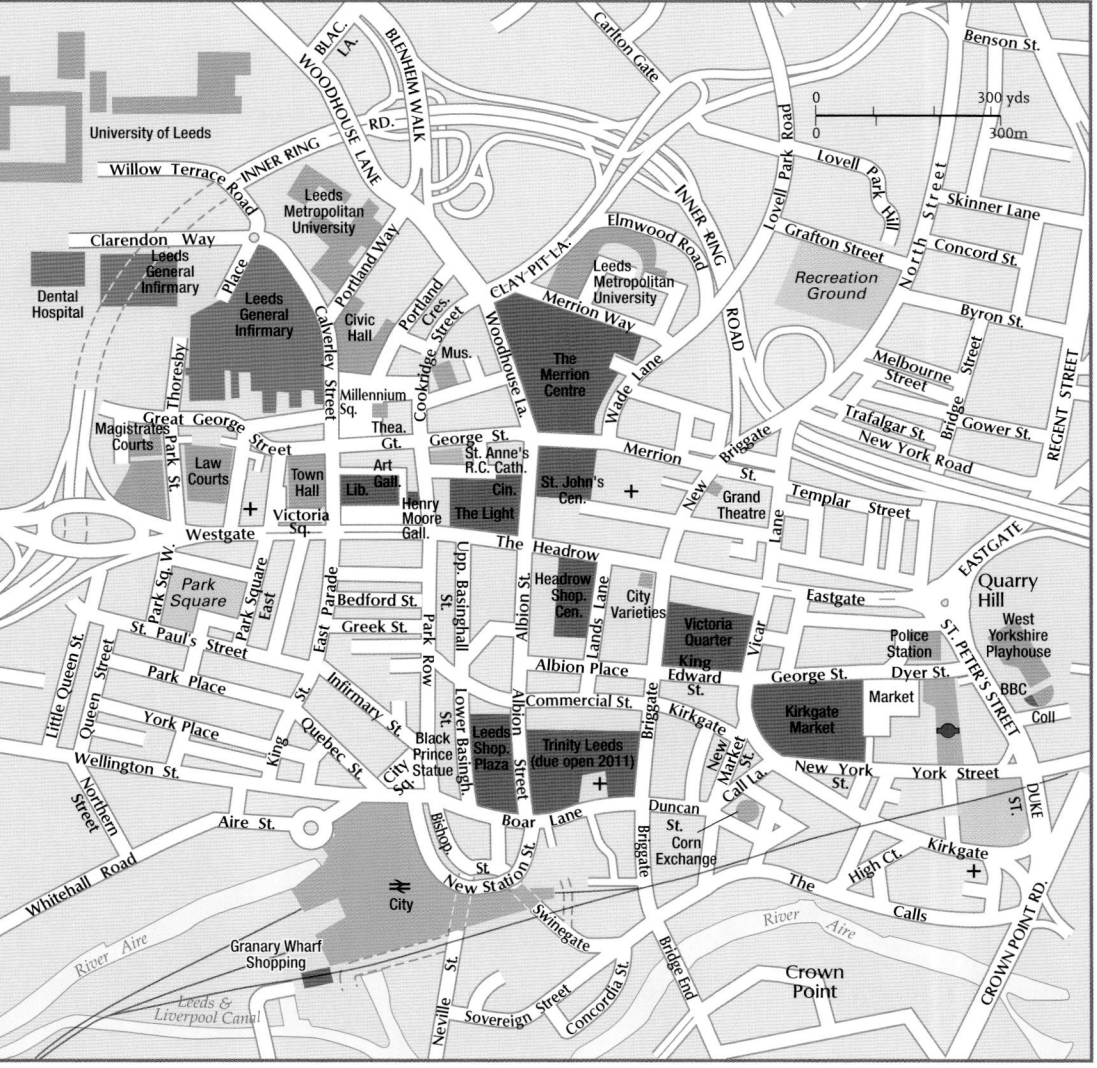

Modern Leeds

Leeds (*cont.*) With the Industrial Revolution came the woollen mills and woollen finishing works, and further improved communications with the railways. By the 20th century the focus of the woollen industry had moved to neighbouring Bradford, and Leeds became the commercial centre for the area as well as a major manufacturing centre for textile machinery, heavy engineering and chemicals, supported by locally mined coal. By 1801 the population of Leeds was 53,000, by 1841 it was 150,000 and by 1901 178,000. It became a city in 1893.

As manufacturing has declined the city has become the major business and financial centre for the West and South Yorkshire conurbation. The redevelopment and restoration of the city centre has also made it a major retail destination, epitomized by the resurgence of its elegant arcades. In 1858 one of the grandest town halls in the country, designed in a classical style by Cuthbert Broderick, opened, followed in 1863 by his equally original and impressive Corn Market. The city's housing has also been overhauled, with the demolition or conversion of the poorly built and unhealthy Victorian back-to-back terraces. The city is also a major

student centre with two universities (Leeds and Leeds Metropolitan, both with origins going back to the 19th century – Leeds School of Medicine was founded in 1831) which have over 46,000 full-time students, while the related hospitals provide specialist medical care for much of the region. The most important employment sector is finance, IT and other business (29 per cent) reflecting its major economic role in the region. Manufacturing now provides over 8.5 per cent of jobs. Leeds is now at the centre of north–south and east–west motorway links, but, unlike Sheffield, has not built a tram system to enhance public transport.

Beyond the historic city of Leeds are a number of towns, such as Guisley, whose original business was in the woollen trade, and they have found it harder to adapt than has metropolitan Leeds. In the far northeast of the area is Wetherby, now a dormitory town for Leeds and York, but once an important staging post on the Great North Road, with as many as 40 coaching inns, and where, in 1891 Wetherby racecourse opened. Close by is Boston Spa. Its waters were discovered in 1744 but Harrogate proved more attractive and now it is best known for housing part of the British Library.

Leeds Civic Hall

Kirkstall Abbey, Kirkstall, Leeds.

Leeds Town Hall

Bradford

The City of Bradford district is based around Bradford but also stretches up into the Pennines (including Haworth, home of the Brontë sisters for much their lives) and the Yorkshire Dales (including the former spa town of Ilkley). Bradford itself was a small medieval town (Bradford Cathedral, originally the parish church, dates from the 15th century) and its growth did not start until the 19th century. In 1801 its population was around 6,300; in 1831 it was 97,200 and by 1851 it was 181,960. This extraordinary growth was on the back of

the textile industry. By 1897, when Bradford became a city, it was the world centre of the woollen textile trade. The trade declined in the 20th century, though a small resurgence after World War II, led to an influx of workers from southern Asia (ethnic minorities now make up over 18 per cent of the population). The most significant reminder of the 19th century boom is Saltaire, the textile mills and workers village built by Sir Titus Salt from 1851 to 1853, and now a UNESCO World Heritage Site. The city is home to the National Media

Museum (covering film and television primarily) and the headquarters of Morrisons supermarkets, Britain's fourth largest, which grew from William Morrison's egg and butter stall in Bradford market in 1899. Even with industrial decline, over 15 per cent of jobs are in the manufacturing sector while 31 per cent are in public administration, education and health, a sector which includes the University of Bradford founded in 1966, whose roots go back to Bradford Technical College, founded in 1882.

Salts Mill in Saltaire.

A view of the town of Ilkley from the Ilkley Moors.

ty of Wakefield

City of Wakefield district is an area more influenced
oal mining than the textile industry. It is based
und Wakefield and other important towns are
tleford, Pontefract, Knottingley and Ossett. Wakefield
eloped as a market town in the medieval period,
from this time remain the Cathedral (originally
parish church), Kirkgate Bridge and its bridge
pel and the ruins of Sandal Castle. The Aire and
der Navigation brought more goods to Wakefield
it flourished as an 18th-century market town.
ustrialization came in the 19th century, and as
century developed coal-mines opened up around
kefield and across the whole district, becoming the
minant employer. The coal industry went into a rapid
line in the second half of the 20th century, and only
substantial elements remain, the one working deep
mine at Kellingley, and the National Coal Mining
seum at Caphouse Colliery near Overton. In addition,
iles, chemicals, machine tools, glassmaking and food
nufacture provide employment as does distribution
vices, benefitting from the good motorway access.
very local industries are the growing of Yorkshire
ced Rhubarb in the 'Rhubarb Triangle' around
kefield (granted EC protection in 2010) and liquorice
nufacture in Pontefract. Around 12 per cent of jobs are
manufacturing and 26 per cent in distribution, retail
hotels. Attractions include the open-air Yorkshire
lpture Park at Bretton and Nostell Priory, a Palladian
use designed by James Paine in 1733 which has a
ctacular collection of Chippendale furniture designed
the house by the Otley-born Thomas Chippendale.

Chippendale chair

Yorkshire Sculpture Park at Bretton.

lderdale

district of Calderdale is centred on Halifax and
tches right into the Pennines, where a number
ormer mill towns, such as Todmorden, Hebden
dge and Sowerby Bridge, are squeezed into narrow
eys. Halifax was a centre of the cloth trade before
Industrial Revolution, as shown by the most
arkable building in the town, the Piece Hall. Built
779 around a large square the Hall contained over
rooms where merchants could trade cloth pieces
ated on handlooms throughout the area. Textiles,
narily in the form of carpets still play a part in
ay's Halifax, which has a diverse industrial base
uding toffee manufacture (in 1890 John Mackintosh
rted a confectionery business, now part of Nestlés)

and financial services, for the town is home to the
Halifax Bank (formerly Halifax Building Society), now
part of the Lloyds Banking Group. As a result of this
mix, manufacturing accounts for 18 per cent of jobs
and finance, IT and other business for 25 per cent of
jobs, both well above regional averages. Much of Halifax
is built in a steep valley, which has resulted in one
dramatic landmark. John Wainhouse owned a dyeworks
and thought it would be a good idea to build a chimney
at the top of a hill and link it with a flue to his works.
The chimney, now called the Wainhouse Tower, was
completed in 1875, a highly decorative affair that is 77 m
tall – but it was never actually used as a chimney; instead
a climb of 403 steps to its top does give an amazing view.

rklees

klees district is named after Kirklees Abbey, an
ged burial place of Robin Hood. The district
tches from Batley and Dewsbury through the major
lement of Huddersfield and up into the Pennines
ond Holmfirth, the setting of the TV serial 'Last of
Summer Wine'. The development of the whole area
nked to the textile industry whether in Dewsbury
se to Leeds or in the hill settlements of the Pennines.
ddersfield is mentioned in the Domesday Book
was a medieval market town and a formal cloth
rket was established in 1672. It took full advantage
he industrialization of cloth making and became a
jor 19th-century manufacturing town whose wealth
hown in its public buildings, especially its railway
ion, a classical *tour de force*. Textiles still remain
portant in the area, and general engineering and the
mical industry are also significant manufacturing
tors. Over 20 per cent of jobs are in manufacturing,
ce the national average, while nearly 28 per cent
employed in public administration, education and
lth, including the staff of Huddersfield University,
ablished in 1992 from older institutions. In the
rtheast of Kirklees much is being done to revitalize
ley, Dewsbury, Cleckheaton and Heckmondwike, all
ns badly affected by the decline in the textile industry
l in less attractive settings than the towns closer to
Pennines.

Sir Patrick Stewart, born in Kirklees.

The Wainhouse Tower, Halifax.

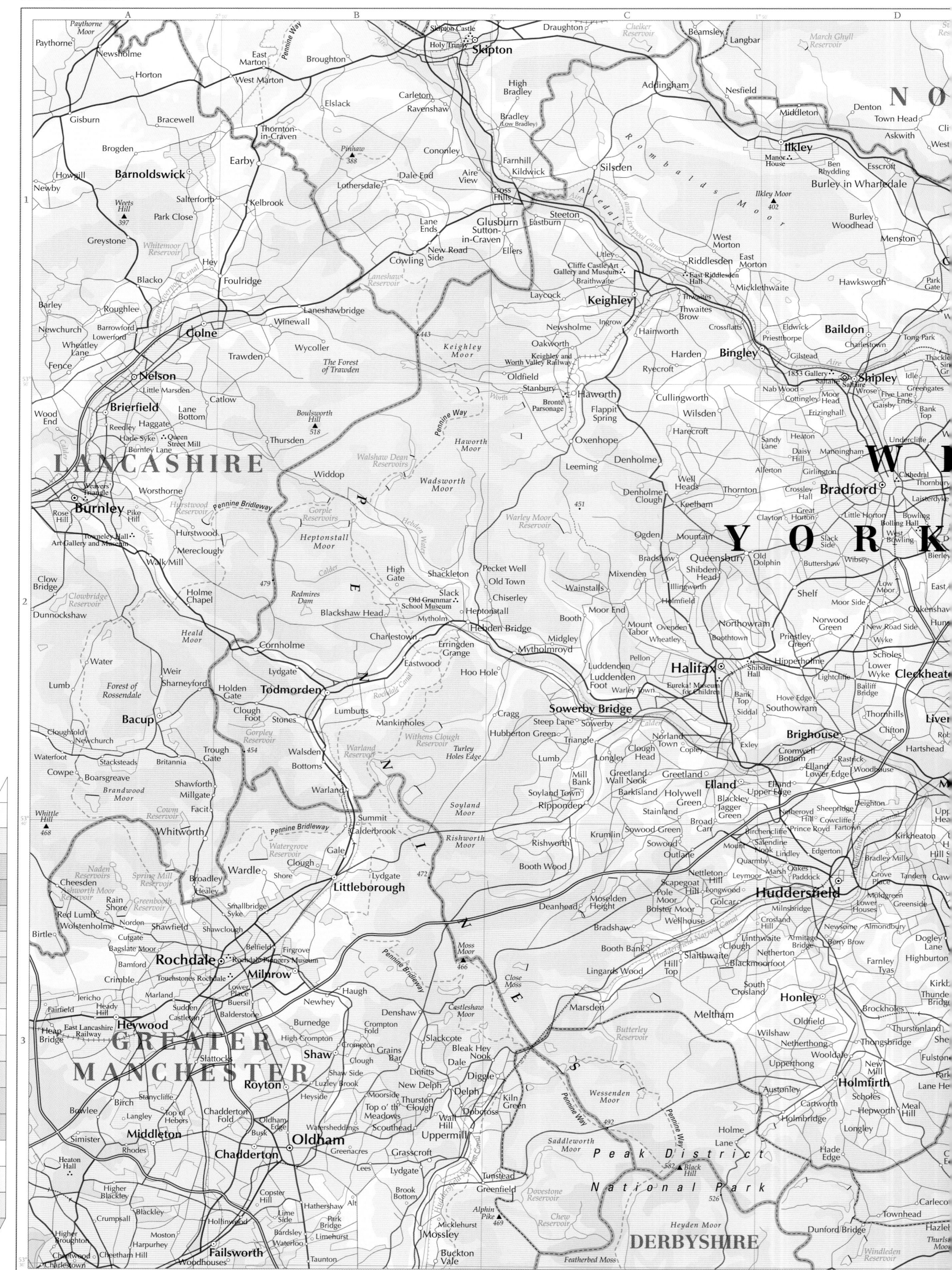

British National Grid projection

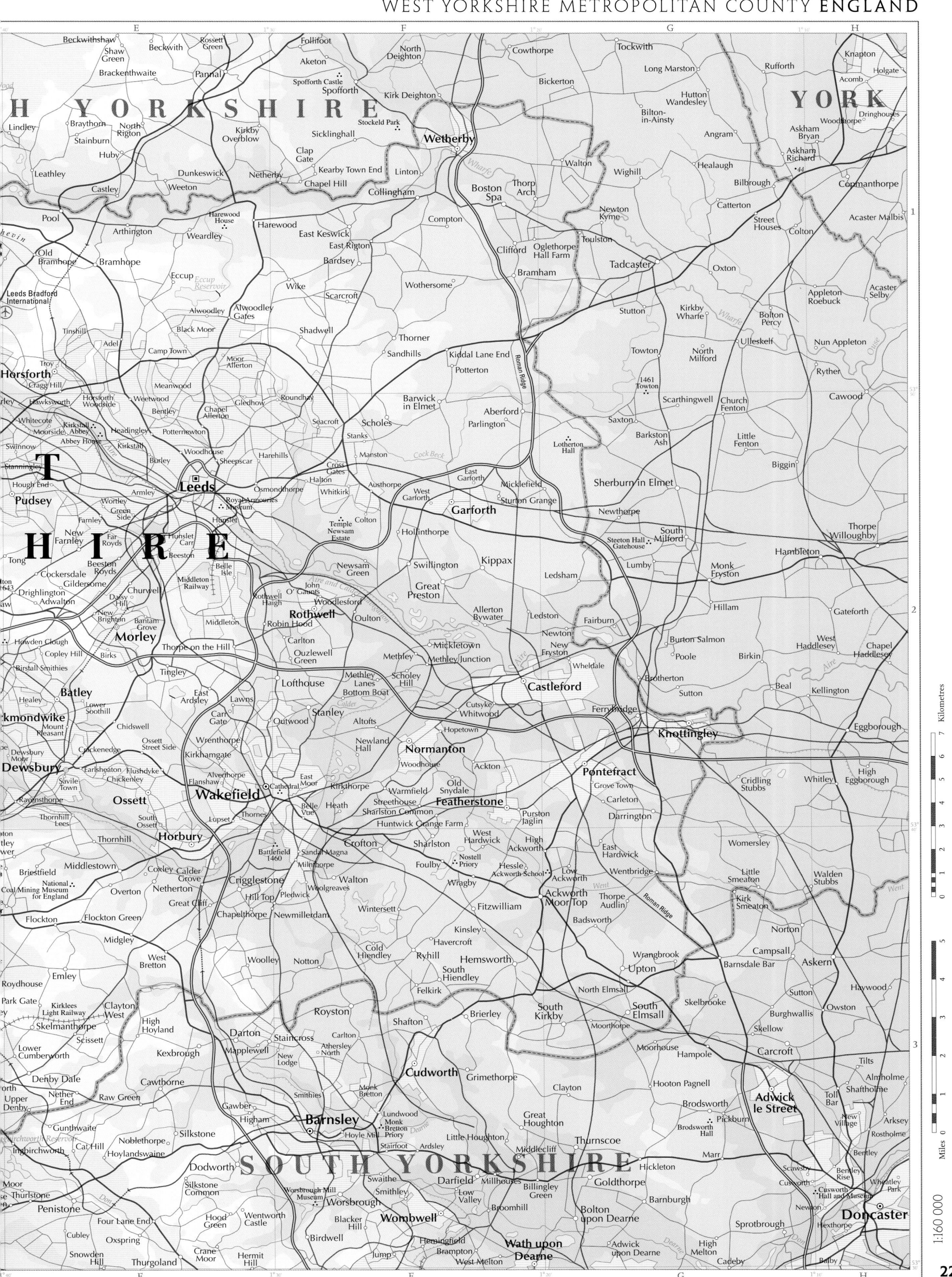

1:160 000

© Collins Bartholomew Ltd

LANCASHIRE

Area Sq Km	3,083
Area Sq Miles	1,191
Population	1,169,000
County town	Lancaster
Highest point	Green Hill (628 m) on Leck Fell, above Cowan Bridge
Districts	Burnley; Chorley; Fylde; Hyndburn; Lancaster; Pendle; Preston; Ribble Valley; Rossendale; South Ribble; West Lancashire; Wyre

Lancashire is a contracted form of the 14th-century 'Lancastreshire', named after the town of Lancaster, 'Roman fort on the River Lune'. The river's name is Celtic in origin, probably meaning 'healthy' or 'pure'.

FAMOUS FOR

In 1617, James I, when visiting the fortified medieval manor house of **Hoghton Tower**, near Preston, is reputed to have knighted the loin of beef that was served – 'Sir Loin'.

The area around **Pendle Hill** became infamous for its witches – in 1612 twelve people (ten women and two men) were accused of committing ten murders by the use of witchcraft. Eleven of them were taken by cart over the wild Forest of Bowland to Lancaster where they were tried. One died while awaiting trial, one was found not guilty, and nine were hanged in public on 20 August 1612.

The Great Hall of **Rufford Old Hall** was built by Sir Thomas Hesketh around the start of the 16th century – and the inside of the Hall is the most exuberant of any timber-framed building in England – fittingly theatrical for the likely performances here of William Shakespeare around 1583.

Accrington's wealth came from the cotton-printing factory of Robert Peel built in the 1760s. Robert Peel's grandson, also Robert Peel, became the first British Prime Minister to come from a manufacturing background.

The south front of Astley Hall in **Chorley**, built in the 1660s, is a bit of a shock – the front appears to have more windows than walls and the interior decoration was described as 'barbaric in its very excesses'.

FAMOUS PEOPLE

James Hargreaves, inventor of the spinning jenny, born Oswaldtwistle, 1720.
Sir Richard Arkwright, industrial pioneer; inventor of the water frame, born Preston, 1732.
Sir Henry Tate, sugar refiner and art collector; founder of the Tate Gallery, born Chorley, 1819.
Francis Thompson, poet, author of *The Hound of Heaven*, born Preston, 1859.
Angela Brazil, children's author, born Preston, 1868.
Sir Norman Haworth, chemist, Nobel laureate, born Chorley, 1883.
Dame Thora Hird, actress, born Morecambe, 1911.
Eric Morecambe (born Eric Bartholomew), comedian, born Morecambe, 1926.
Sir Harrison Birtwistle, composer, born Accrington, 1934.
John Inman, comedy actor, born Preston, 1935.
Sir Ian McKellen, actor, born Burnley, 1939.
Nick Park, Oscar-winning animator; creator of Wallace and Gromit, born Preston, 1958.
Wayne Hemingway, fashion designer, born Morecambe, 1961.
Andrew Flintoff, cricketer, born Preston, 1977.

The eastern side of the county lies along the edge of the Pennines and includes the Forest of Rossendale and the Forest of Bowland, not wooded forests but former Royal hunting grounds of high and wild heather moorland and bog. The Trough of Bowland is a high pass that connects Mashaw with Dunsop Bridge. Brennand farm, 7 km from Dunsop is the geographic centre of Britain. The western side of Lancashire contains the coastal plain and a coastline of dunes, marshes and part of the great tidal mudflats of Morecambe Bay. The principal rivers are the Lune, the Ribble and the Wyre.

The historic county of Lancashire was much larger than the current county, for it included the metropolitan areas of Manchester and Liverpool, and the Furness district, based around Barrow-in-Furness that lies across Morecambe Bay. In 1974 the Furness district became part of Cumbria; the metropolitan county of Merseyside took in Liverpool, St Helens, Knowsley and Southport; Warrington and Widnes were moved to Cheshire; and the county of Greater Manchester took in Manchester, Salford, Bolton, Bury, Oldham, Rochdale and Wigan. In further changes in 1998, Blackpool and Blackburn became unitary authorities so that, today, the population of Lancashire is 1,169,000 compared with over 5 million for the old county in 1971. From 1991 to 2008 the population grew by around 4.5 per cent. By 2031 the population is expected to have grown by around 17 per cent, ahead of the northwest regional average of 12.3 per cent. The growth, though, is expected to be uneven, ranging from nearly 33 per cent in Lancaster to 3.5 per cent in Burnley. The chief centres of population are Preston (184,836), Burnley (73,021), Morecambe (49,569), Lancaster (45,952), Skelmersdale (39,279), Lytham St. Anne's (41,327), Leyland (37,100), Accrington (35,203) and Chorley (33,424).

Lancashire was one of the centres of the Industrial Revolution, with the industrialization of cotton spinning aided by the inventions of the Lancastrians James Hargreaves and Richard Arkwright. The Pennine valleys to the east became the home to many mill towns – Blackburn, Accrington, Burnley, Nelson and Colne among many. However, the decline in the textile industry started with World War I – in 1912 Britain was producing 12 billion metres of cotton cloth, but the war restricted the export trade that did not recover thereafter. There was a slight resurgence after World War II, and many workers were recruited from the Indian subcontinent, but by the 1960s the industry started its rapid decline. In 1928, 239,000 worked in the textile industry, in 1951, 131,000, in 1971, 61,000 and today around 5,600 (7 per cent of the manufacturing employment in the area). Key industries now include the defence industries (particularly aerospace) and lorry manufacture at Leyland. Manufacturing accounts for nearly 16 per cent of jobs, while public administration, health and education provides 30 per cent of jobs. This sector includes the universities of Lancaster, Central Lancashire (based at Preston) and Edge Hill (based at Ormskirk).

Lancaster is the traditional county town of the county, positioned in the north of the county, on the banks of the Lune. The Normans built a castle on the site of a Roman fort, and their impressive stone keep and later major fortifications survive. The buildings are still used as a court and prison so public access is limited. Lancaster merges into Morecambe, which thrived in the 20th century as a more refined seaside resort than Blackpool, but which has now seen better days. One step in its revitalisation has been the restoration of the Art Deco Midland Hotel, a classic period piece from the 1930s. The hotel looks out across Morecambe Bay, the treacherous tidal mudflats that stretch from Morecambe across the bay to Barrow-in-Furness. The tide can come in at the speed of nine knots and while it is possible to cross the sands at low tide, this should only be done in the company of official guides – the Duchy of Lancaster has employed such guides since 1536. Preston is the administrative centre for Lancashire and gained city status in 2002. The origins of its wealth lie in the textile industry that existed here from the 13th century onwards and it was in the vanguard on the industrialisation of cotton industry and the related engineering industries. Since their decline it has faced many challenges in generating new employment.

Pendle Hill

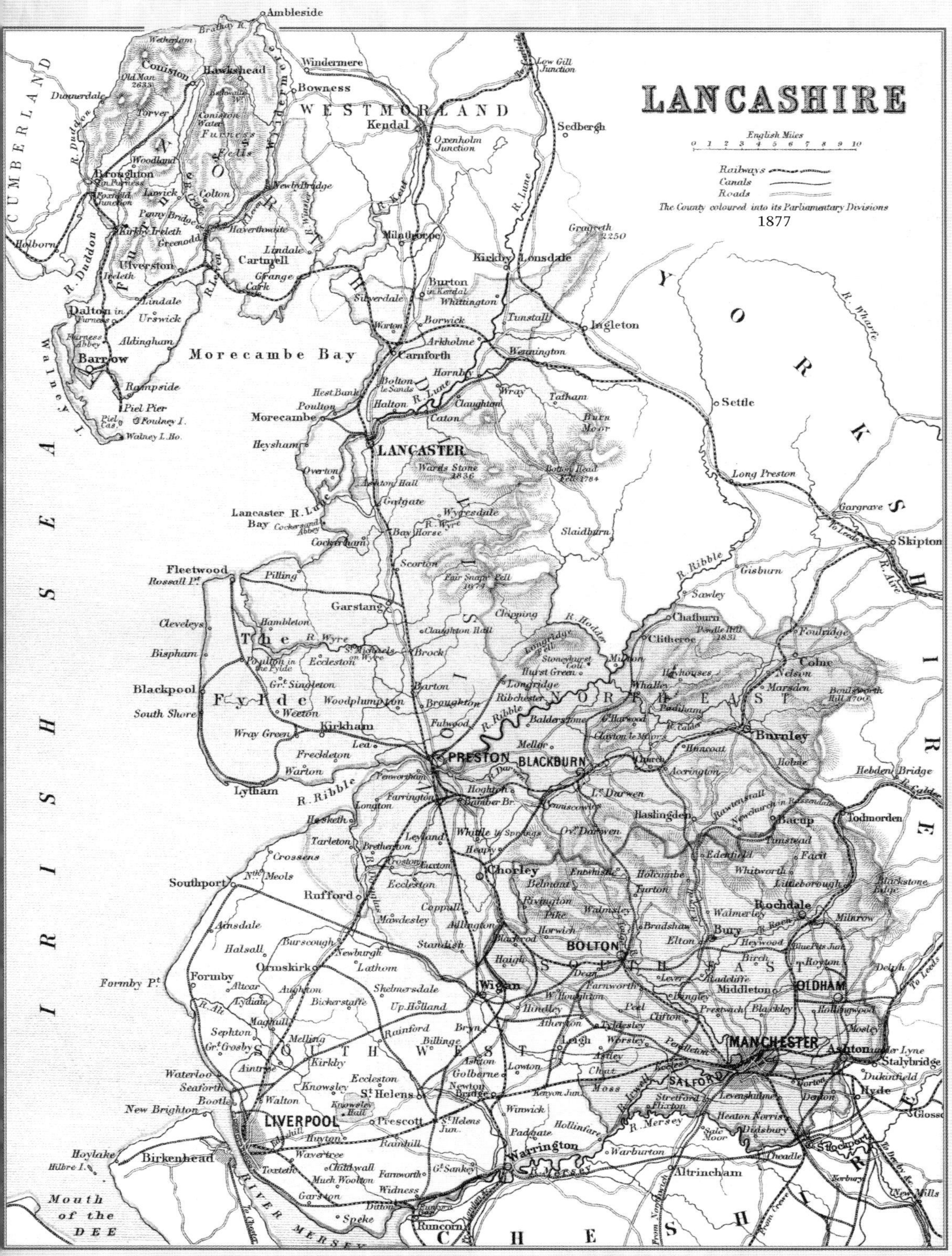

LANCASHIRE

The County coloured into its Parliamentary Divisions
1877

Bartholomew Gazetteer of the British Isles, 1887

LANCASHIRE, or Lancaster, co. palatine and maritime shire, in NW. of England. bounded N. by Westmorland and Cumberland, E. by Yorkshire, S. by Cheshire, and W. by the Irish Sea; greatest length, 76 miles; greatest breadth, 45 miles; area, 1,208, 154 ac.; pop. 3,454,441. A detached part of the co., known as Furness (25 miles long, 23 miles broad), is separated from the main portion by Morecambe Bay and a part of Westmorland co. The coast line of Lancashire is very irregular, the chief inlets being Morecambe Bay, Lancaster Bay, and the estuaries of the Mersey and the Ribble. Towards the shore, which comprises great stretches of sand, the land has generally a flat appearance. In the N. and E.. it becomes more elevated, but the chief heights are in Furness, where an alt. of 2633 ft. is reached at Coniston Old Man. The principal rivers are the Mersey, Ribble, Lune, Wyre, Winster, and Leven. Peat prevails in the soil of the upland districts, while much of the low lying land consists of a rich loam. The chief crops are oats, wheat, and potatoes. Carboniferous limestone abounds in the N. part of the co.; on the coast is the old red sandstone. The great coalfield of Lancashire, the existence of which has greatly contributed towards establishing its pre-eminence as a manufacturing co., covers an area of about 217 sq. miles between the Ribble and the Mersey. Iron is abundant in Furness. Lancashire is intersected by an intricate network of canals and railways. Its immense cotton mfrs. have a world-wide fame, while other textile fabrics are largely produced. Its mfrs. of machinery of all descriptions are also extensive. Lancashire comprises 6 hundreds, 453 pars., the mun. bors. of Barrow in Furness, Blackburn, Bolton, Burnley, Bury, Liverpool, Manchester, Salford, Oldham, Preston, Rochdale, St Helens, Wigan, the greater part of the mun. bors. of Accrington, Ashton under Lyne, Bacup, Blackpool, Bootle cum Linacre, Clitheroe, Heywood, Lancaster, Over Darwen, Southport, and Warrington. It is comprised in the dioceses of Liverpool, Manchester, Carlisle, and Ripon.

...ue of Eric Morecambe on the seafront at Morecombe, ...ome town.

Wallace and Gromit, two characters created by Nick Park who was born in Preston.

BLACKPOOL

Area Sq Km 43
Area Sq Miles 17
Population 141,900

FAMOUS FOR
In 1889 the Mayor of Blackpool visited Paris and was greatly impressed with the newly constructed Eiffel Tower, and quickly raised enthusiasm for an equivalent in Blackpool – **Blackpool Tower**, with a height of 158 m opened in 1894. As well as the tower, there is a ballroom, circus, aquarium and much more in the building at the tower's base.

FAMOUS PEOPLE
Michael Smith, biochemist and Nobel laureate, born 1932.
David Atherton, conductor, born 1944.
Zoe Ball, television presenter, born 1970.

"After you have visited the menagerie, and ascended to the top of the Tower in order to be badgered by rather nice girl-touts with a living to make and a powerful determination to make it, and see the blue turn deep purple over the sea, you reach at length the dancing-halls, which are the justification of Blackpool's existence. Blackpool is an ugly town, mean in its vastness, but its dancing halls present a beautiful spectacle."
Arnold Bennett, 1913

Blackpool became a unitary authority in 1998. From 1974 it had been a district of Lancashire County Council and before that, from 1908, an independent county borough. Its boundaries are tightly drawn around the town of Blackpool and it does not include neighbouring Lytham St Annes or Fleetwood. Its population is 141,900 and has declined by nearly 5 per cent since 1981, a trend yet to be reversed. Blackpool started as a holiday resort for healthy sea bathing in the late 18th century, but it was the coming of the railways in 1846 that saw it become the pre-eminent British seaside holiday resort. In the 1950s it attracted 17 million visitors annually and it still brings in over 14 million visitors, albeit only 10 per cent of those visitors stay overnight. Its many attractions include the Golden Mile, Blackpool Tower, Blackpool Pleasure Beach, which draws nearly 6 million people to its roller-coasters and many other hair-raising rides, the Winter Gardens, the Illuminations (between September and November) and three piers. The tramway that opened on Blackpool front in 1885 was the first electric tramway in Britain and it now runs 18 km between Blackpool and Fleetwood and carries around 7 million passengers every year.

Central Pier, Blackpool.

BLACKBURN WITH DARWEN

Area Sq Km 137
Area Sq Miles 53
Population 140,700

FAMOUS FOR
In 1931, Mahatma Gandhi visited **Darwen** and stayed in a cotton worker's house to see the plight of workers suffering from the boycott of British cotton in India that he led. Thousands turned out to warmly welcome him.

FAMOUS PEOPLE
John Morley, Viscount Morley, politician and biographer of W.E. Gladstone, born 1838.
Alfred Wainwright, fell walker, born 1907.
Ian McShane, actor, born 1942.
Alison Wilding, sculptor, born 1948.
Michael Winterbottom, film-maker, born 1961.
Carl Fogarty, World Superbike Champion, born 1965.

Blackburn with Darwen became a unitary authority in 1998 having previously been a district within Lancashire County Council. It consists of Blackburn (population 105,085), Darwen (population 31,570) and some moors to the south. The population of the area has grown very slowly since 2001 and by 2020 is expected to reach 153,800. The need for textile industry workers in the 1950s led to the arrival of many workers from the Indian subcontinent and now over 20 per cent of the population comes from Asian ethnic groups. It is the youngest area in Britain, with nearly a third of the population aged 19 or under. Blackburn is a manufacturing centre with over 20 per cent of jobs in this sector, double the national average. Blackburn's history is linked to the textile industry: by the start of the 20th century over 60 per cent of jobs in the town were directly linked to the textile industry. This over-reliance soon created problems and the decline started shortly thereafter. In 1907 there were 79,400 looms in the town, by 1976 there were 2,100. Industries that have replaced textiles include general engineering, plastics, paints and electronics.

Moorland above Blackburn, looking west across Preston to Blackpool.

kpool Tower and Promenade during a storm.

l locks in Blackburn.

Abandoned boat at Morecambe Bay.

ric rock-hewn graves and chapel ruins of St Patrick on the cliff edge overlooking Morecambe Bay at Heysham.

British National Grid projection

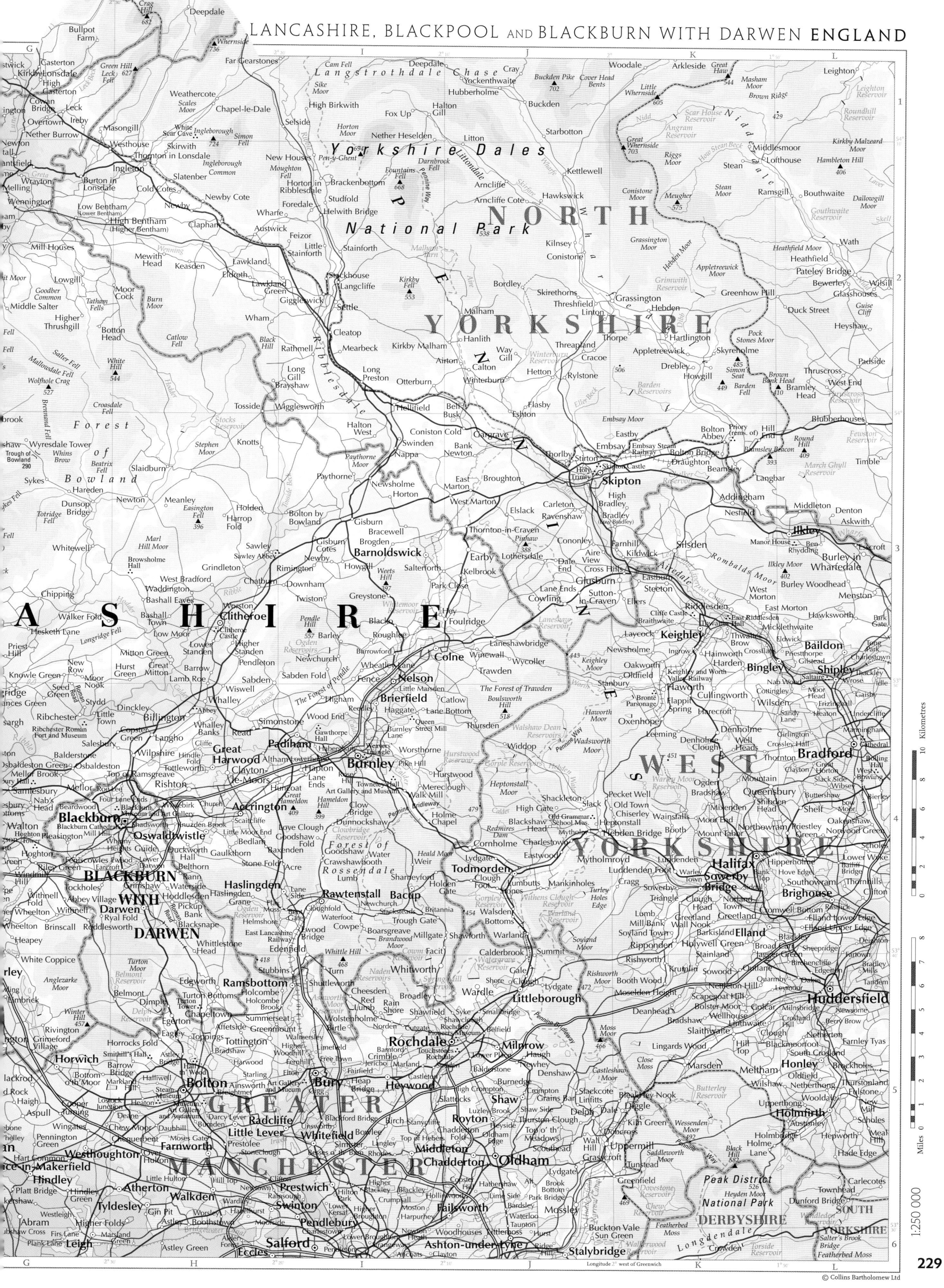

CUMBRIA

Area Sq Km	7,185
Area Sq Miles	2,774
Population	496,600
County town	Carlisle
Highest point	Scafell Pike (978 m)
Districts	Allerdale; Barrow-in-Furness; Carlisle; Copeland; Eden; South Lakeland

Cumbria was the name of an ancient north British kingdom, derived from a latinization of '*Cymry*' ('the Welsh'), which was adopted by the new county in 1974. Cumberland means 'land of the Welshmen' and Westmorland 'land of the people who live west of the moors (the Pennines)'.

FAMOUS FOR
In December 1799 William Wordsworth and his sister Dorothy settled in **Grasmere** at a former inn called the Dove and Olive Bough, and now known the world over as Dove Cottage. They lived there until 1808, and, during that time, William Wordsworth produced some of his greatest poetry.

Levens Hall, in southern Cumbria, is a lavishly decorated late Elizabethan House, with an even more fantastic garden, complete with amazing topiary, which was designed in 1694 by Guillaume Beaumont, who had trained at Versailles.

The **Appleby Horse Fair**, held in early June in Appleby-in-Westmorland, attracts around 10,000 travelling people (and many more visitors) to buy and sell horses and to celebrate their way of life. It is the largest such celebration in Europe.

Windermere is the largest lake in England – it is nearly 18 km long and its maximum depth is 67 m. The first steamer to sail on Windermere was the *Lady of the Lake*, launched in 1845. Many pleasure steamers now sail on the lake. The oldest is the *Tern*, launched in 1891.

Cartmel Priory, across the sands from Morecambe, was founded in 1188. It has been much modified over the years, and is, in Simon Jenkins' view, 'the most beautiful church in the northwest'.

FAMOUS PEOPLE
John 'Iron Mad' Wilkinson, industrialist; pioneer in use of cast iron, born Clifton, 1728.
George Romney, artist, born Dalton-in-Furness, 1734.
Fletcher Christian, leader of the mutiny on the *Bounty*, born Cockermouth, 1764.
John Dalton, scientist, born Eaglesfield, 1766.
William Wordsworth, poet, born Cockermouth, 1770.
Dorothy Wordsworth, poet and diarist, born Cockermouth, 1771.
George Routledge, publisher, born Brampton, 1812.
Sir William Bragg, physicist, Nobel laureate, born Wigton, 1862.
Sir Arthur Eddington, astronomer and astrophysicist, born Kendal, 1882.
Stan Laurel (*born* Arthur Stanley Jefferson), comedian, born Ulverston, 1890 .
Margaret Forster, biographer and novelist, born Carlisle, 1938.
Melvyn Bragg, broadcaster and writer, born Wigton, 1939.
David Starkey, historian and broadcaster, born Kendal, 1945.

A narrow strip of flat country along the coast of Cumbria widens to a plain in the north and around Carlisle. Otherwise the county is composed of mountains, moorland and lakes, and includes the renowned and dramatic scenery of the Lake District. Scafell Pike is the highest point not just in Cumbria but in the whole of England. The area is noted for its radial drainage, with Windermere and Ullswater being the largest of the lakes and the Eden and Derwent the chief of many rivers.

Cumbria is a new county created in the local government reorganization of 1974. It was formed from the historic counties of Cumberland and Westmorland, along with the Furness district of Lancashire (around Barrow-in-Furness, Cartmel and Grange-over-Sands) and Sedburgh and Dentdale from the old West Riding of Yorkshire. Its population is 496,600, and this is expected to grow to around 560,000 by 2031. The main settlements are Carlisle (71,773), Barrow-in-Furness (47,194), Whitehaven (24,978), Workington (21,514), Kendal (28,030), Penrith (14,471) and Ulverston (11,210).

Cumbria is mostly rural and uncultivated, with industry centred on Carlisle and the other towns. Whitehaven, Workington, and Maryport all once relied on coal, while Barrow-in-Furness developed due to shipbuilding and heavy industry. There are links with nuclear technology: Calder Hall, north of Seascale, was Britain's first atomic power station, while the adjacent site of Sellafield is Britain's major nuclear reprocessing plant and Trident nuclear-powered submarines were built at Barrow-in-Furness. Tourism in the Lake District and sheep farming are also important industries. As a result of the heavy industry, what appears to be a rural county has over 17 per cent of jobs in manufacturing, compared with a national average of just over 10 per cent. The service sector provides 75 per cent of jobs, with 25 per cent in public administration, health and education and nearly 13 per cent in tourism.

The county town of Carlisle, once the major Roman settlement of *Luguvalium*, is in the north of the county, close to the Scottish border. With the flat land around the edge of the Solway Firth, there is no clearly defined border. It was here that Hadrian's Wall, built by the Romans, established a division, starting at Bowness-on-Solway, passing close to Carlisle and leaving the count at Gilsland. The area was strongly contested between England and Scotland, and by the independent-minde border families who undertook raids against each oth Carlisle itself became an important military centre. The Normans first controlled it in 1092 and started to build Carlisle Castle, which was regularly modernized to include the latest in military defence, last seeing action when it was captured by Bonnie Prince Charlie in 1745. The city's cathedral, one of the smallest ancie cathedrals in Britain, dates from the early 12th centur Engineering, food processing and transport now prov its industrial base, though textiles once played a majo part. As Carlisle is 135 km south of Glasgow and 200 k north of Manchester, its fast motorway and mainline railway links are essential.

To the south of Carlisle the hills start to rise. The northern gateway to the Lake District is at Penrith, at junction of the major north-south and east-west route To the west of Penrith is the Lake District National Pa In the north of the park are the lakes of Ullswater and Derwent Water and the major settlements of Keswick and, just outside the park, Cockermouth. In the south are the great lakes of Windermere and Coniston Wate and the settlements of Ambleside, Windermere and, j outside the park, Kendal. The great beauty of the Lake District has attracted visitors for the last two centuries from the Romantic poets onwards (before then the are was more usually regarded as wild and forbidding). Tourism is crucial to the economy here, and in the South Lakeland and Eden districts, 20 per cent of all jobs are directly tourist-related.

East of the Lake District, the land rises either side of the Eden valley towards the Pennines, an area of sheep farming and of military training grounds, and great medieval castles at Brougham, Appleby (the former county town of Westmoreland) and Brough. The main cross-Pennine route (the A66) rises from Brough up to the border with Co. Durham at Stainmo Summit, at 477 m.

Windermere in the Lake District.

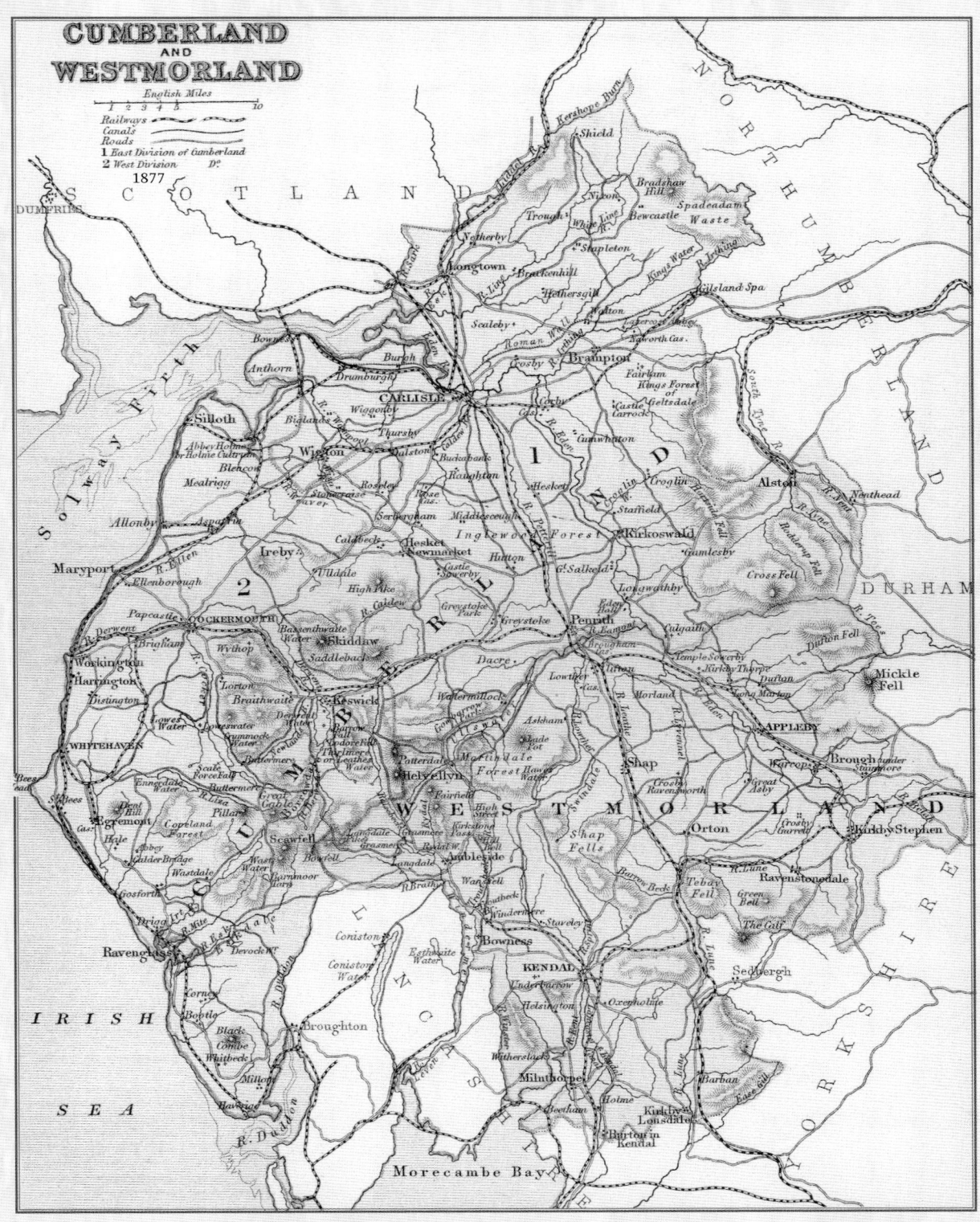

CUMBERLAND
AND
WESTMORLAND

English Miles
Railways
Canals
Roads
1 East Division of Cumberland
2 West Division D?
1877

Bartholomew Gazetteer of the British Isles, 1887

CUMBERLAND.– *a maritime and border co. of England, having the cos. of Dumfries and Roxburgh on the N., Northumberland and Durham on the E., Westmorland and Lancashire on the S., the Irish Sea on the W., and the Solway Firth on the NW.; length, NE. and SW., 75 miles; extreme breadth, E. and W., 45 miles; average breadth, 22 miles; coast line, about 75 miles; area, 970,161 ac., pop. 250,647. The coast on the Solway is low and sandy, but on the Irish Sea it is lofty and rugged; chief promontory, St Bees Head. In the NW. the country is open and flat; it is watered by the Eden and other streams, and consists chiefly of verdant meadows and good arable land. From this plain the surface rises towards the E. and S. into a region with deep denies or dales, which form the mountainous district of "The Lakes", the scenery of which is generally picturesque, and attracts great numbers of tourists. The principal summits are Scafell Pikes (3210 ft.), Scafell (3162 ft.), Helvellyn (3118 ft.), Skiddaw (3058 ft.) The largest lakes are Ullswater, Derwentwater, Bassenthwaite Water, Thirlmere, Buttermere, Wast Water, and Ennerdale Water. The*

Eden and the Derwent are the two longest rivers. Coal and iron are extensively worked in the W., the coalfield stretching from the neighbourhood of Whitehaven to that of Maryport. Numerous blast furnaces are constantly at work. Plumbago or black lead is obtained in considerable quantities near Keswick. Slate, limestone, and sandstone are abundant. Copper, cobalt, antimony, manganese, and gypsum are also found. Owing to the general elevation of the land, and the moisture of the climate, the cultivation of the soil is less attended to than the rearing of sheep and cattle. The dairy produce is very considerable. Woollen mfrs. are carried on to some extent at Carlisle and some other places. The co. comprises 5 wards, 208 pars., the mun. bor. of Carlisle, and the parl. bor. of Whitehaven. It is mostly in the diocese of Carlisle.

WESTMORLAND, *co. in N. of England; bounded NW. and N. by Cumberland, NE. by Durham, E. by Yorkshire, and S. and SW. by Lancashire and Morecambe Bay; greatest length, N. and S., 32 miles; greatest breadth, E. and W., 40 miles; area, 500,906 ac., pop. 64,191. Westmorland presents a continuous succession of*

mountain, moor, and fell, intersected by deep winding vales, traversed by numerous streams. The principal of these are the Eden, Lowther, Lune, and Kent, the last forming the broad estuary which terminates in Morecambe Bay. The mountains consist of various ridges belonging to the Pennine and Cumbrian chains. Helvellyn, on the Cumberland border, rises to a height of 3118 ft. The western part of the co. is within the Lake District, and contains Hawes Water, Grasmere, Rydal Water, and Ullswater on the Cumberland border, and Windermere on the Lancashire border. The arable land is mostly confined to the valleys, where the soil usually consists of a dry gravelly loam, well adapted for turnips, but the greater part of the co. is natural pasture. The mineral productions include graphite, marble, roofing slate, and some coal, lead, and copper. The county has good communications by railway. It comprises 4 wards, 109 pars., the mun. bor. of Kendal, and the towns of Ambleside, Appleby (the co. town), Brough, Kirkby Lonsdale, Kirkby Stephen, and Orton. It is entirely in the diocese of Carlisle.

British National Grid projection

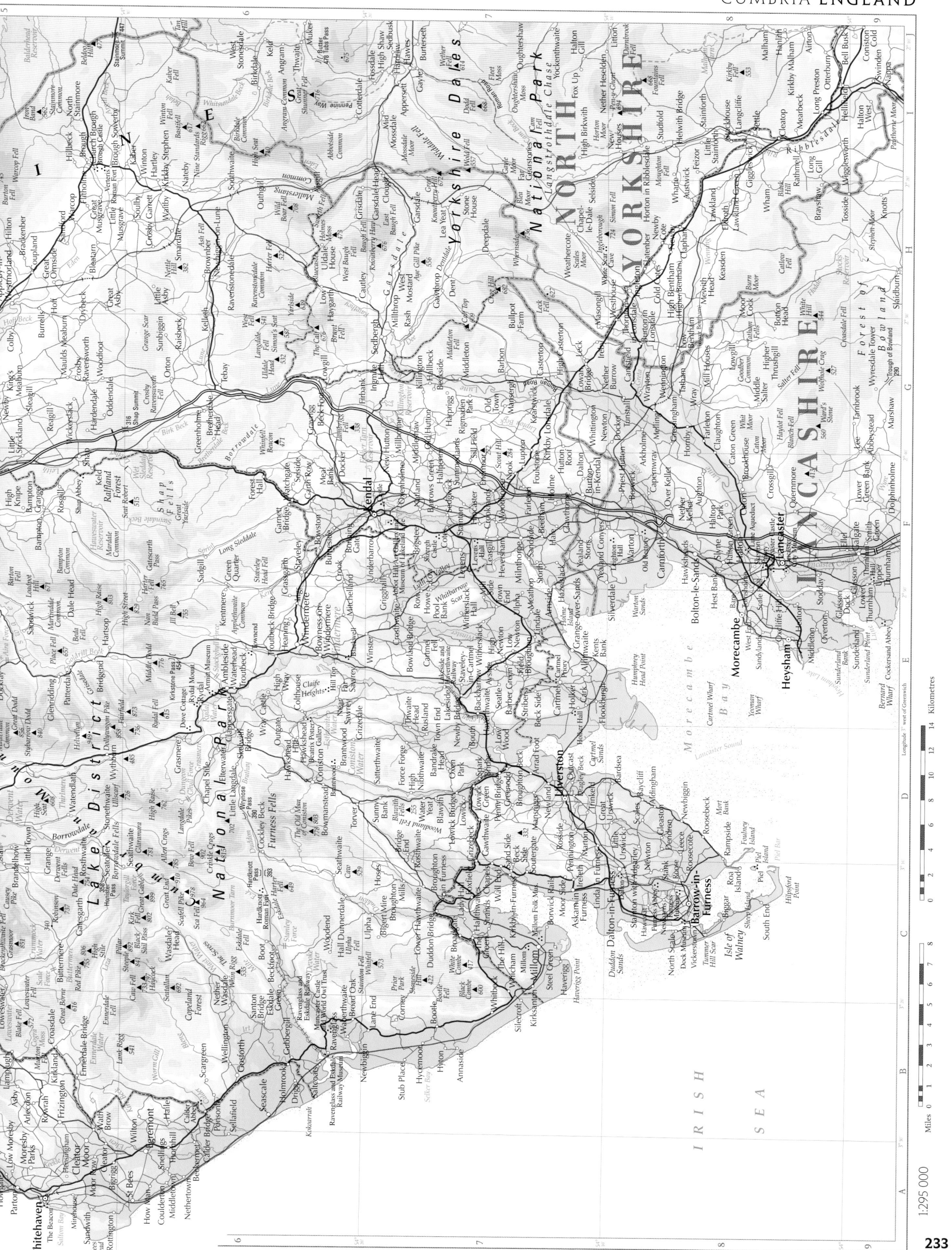

1:295 000

© Collins Bartholomew Ltd

COUNTY DURHAM

Area Sq Km	2,233
Area Sq Miles	862
Population	508,500
County town	Durham
Highest point	Mickle Fell (788 m) in the Pennines

The name Durham comes from the Old Scandinavian 'dun holm', or hill island, descriptive of the site of the city on a rocky promontory almost encircled by the river Wear.

FAMOUS FOR

Beamish, near Chester-le-Street, is the home of an amazing open-air museum devoted to life in the northeast around 1825 and 1913 told through the homes, shops and other regional buildings that have been brought here.

The river Tees cascades down 20 m of near vertical cliff at **High Force** above Middleton-in-Teesdale. Further upstream, on the boundary with Cumbria, is **Cauldron Snout**, a series of eight waterfalls within 370 m, in which the Tees drops 60 m.

On the edge of **Barnard Castle** is the unlikely view of a large French chateau that contains the Bowes Museum. Founded by John Bowes and his French wife, Joséphine, it was built between 1869 and 1892 to contain their internationally renowned art collection, with a mission to bring great art to the people of Co. Durham.

The church of St John the Evangelist at **Escomb** was built around 670 and, in the words of Nikolaus Pevsner 'is one of the most important and most moving survivals of the architecture of the time of Bede'.

FAMOUS PEOPLE

Granville Sharp, instrumental in abolition of slave trade, born Durham, 1735.
Sir Henry Taylor, dramatist, born Bishop Middleham, Durham, 1800.
Elizabeth Barrett Browning (born Elizabeth Barrett), poet, born Coxhoe Hall, Durham, 1806.
Sir Anthony Eden, foreign secretary and prime minister, born Windlestone, Bishop Auckland, 1897.
Roger Charles Blunt, cricketer, born Durham, 1900.
Cyril Northcote Parkinson, political scientist (Parkinson's Law), born Barnard Castle, 1909.
Sir Robert (Bobby) Robson, football player and manager, born Sacriston, Chester-le-Street, 1933.
Wendy Craig, actress, born Sacriston, Chester-le-Street, 1934.
Tommy Simpson, cyclist, born Haswell, 1937.
Craig Raine, poet, born Bishop Auckland, 1944.
Rowan Atkinson, actor and comedian, born Consett, 1955.
Bryan Robson, footballer, born Chester-le-Street, 1957.
Paul Collingwood, cricketer, born Shotley Bridge, Consett, 1976.

"Grey towers of Durham ...
Yet well I love thy mixed and massive piles,
Half Church of God, half castle 'gainst the Scot."
Sir Walter Scott, 1817, Harold the Dauntless

The western part of County Durham (usually abbreviated to Co.) includes part of the Pennines and consists mostly of open moorlands that provide rough sheep-grazing and water for the urban areas from a number of large reservoirs. There is lowland in the east, bordering the North Sea. The principal rivers flow east out of the Pennines, the Tees in the south of the county and the Wear in the north.

The Normans had to forcibly subdue the area and they then gave the Bishop of Durham 'palatinate' powers, which meant he had full jurisdiction over the area – the bishop was so powerful he was known as the 'Prince-Bishop'. The bishop lost his legal authority in 1536, but the remainder of the palatine authority lasted until 1836, when Co. Durham started to be used to describe the area. Durham County Council was established in 1888, administering an area from the Tees in the south to the Tyne in the north. The county was much reduced in size in 1974 when Gateshead, South Tyneside and Sunderland became part of the new metropolitan county of Tyne and Wear, while Hartlepool and Stockton in the south became part of the new county of Cleveland. In 1996 Cleveland was abolished, and Hartlepool and Stockton-on-Tees became unitary authorities, as did Stockton's neighbour, Darlington. The reduced Durham County Council initially had seven district councils, but in 2009 these districts were abolished and the county became a single unitary authority.

The population of Co. Durham is 508,500 and is expected to rise slowly over the coming years. The major settlements in the region are in the unitary authorities to the north and south of the county. The main settlements are Durham (42,939), Chester-le-Street (36,049), Peterlee (29,936), Newton Aycliffe (25,655),

Seaham (21,153) and Consett (20,659). Both Peterlee and Newton Aycliffe are new towns built to provide better accommodation for former miners.

Durham's economy was traditionally built on mining, lead and tin in the Pennines and coal in the coastal plain, with pits, such as those at Seaham, going out under the North Sea. Coal was actively mined from the 13th century onwards. The industry reached a peak in the 1920s (in 1923 there were 170,000 miners) but, from the 1950s, many pits closed, the last pit to close being Vane Tempest at Seaham in 1993. Other industrial closures included the Consett steelworks in 1980 and the Shildon railway wagon works in 1984. Manufacturing still remains an important part of the economy with around 17 per cent of jobs (with companies, such as makers of car-parts for Nissan's plant in Sunderland and chemical and pharmaceutical companies, encouraged to come to the area to provide work for former miners) but the service sector now provides nearly 77 per cent of jobs with over 32 per cent being in public administration, health and education.

Durham, on its rocky outcrop surrounded by a loop of the river Wear, was seen as a safe refuge in 995 for the remains of the great Northumbrian saint, St Cuthbert. It became a place of pilgrimage and the site of Britain's greatest Norman cathedral. With the Norman castle, the power-base of the Prince Bishop, next to it, both now form a UNESCO World Heritage Site. Heading west from Durham the Pennines here are starker and wilder than the Yorkshire Dales. At the top of Weardale is the Killhope lead mine, an early industrial site in the wildest of landscapes. To the south is Teesdale with Barnard Castle at the bottom of the Dale, with its vast 12th-century castle sitting on rocks above the Tees.

Durham Castle viewed from the tower of Durham Cathedral.

High Force waterfall.

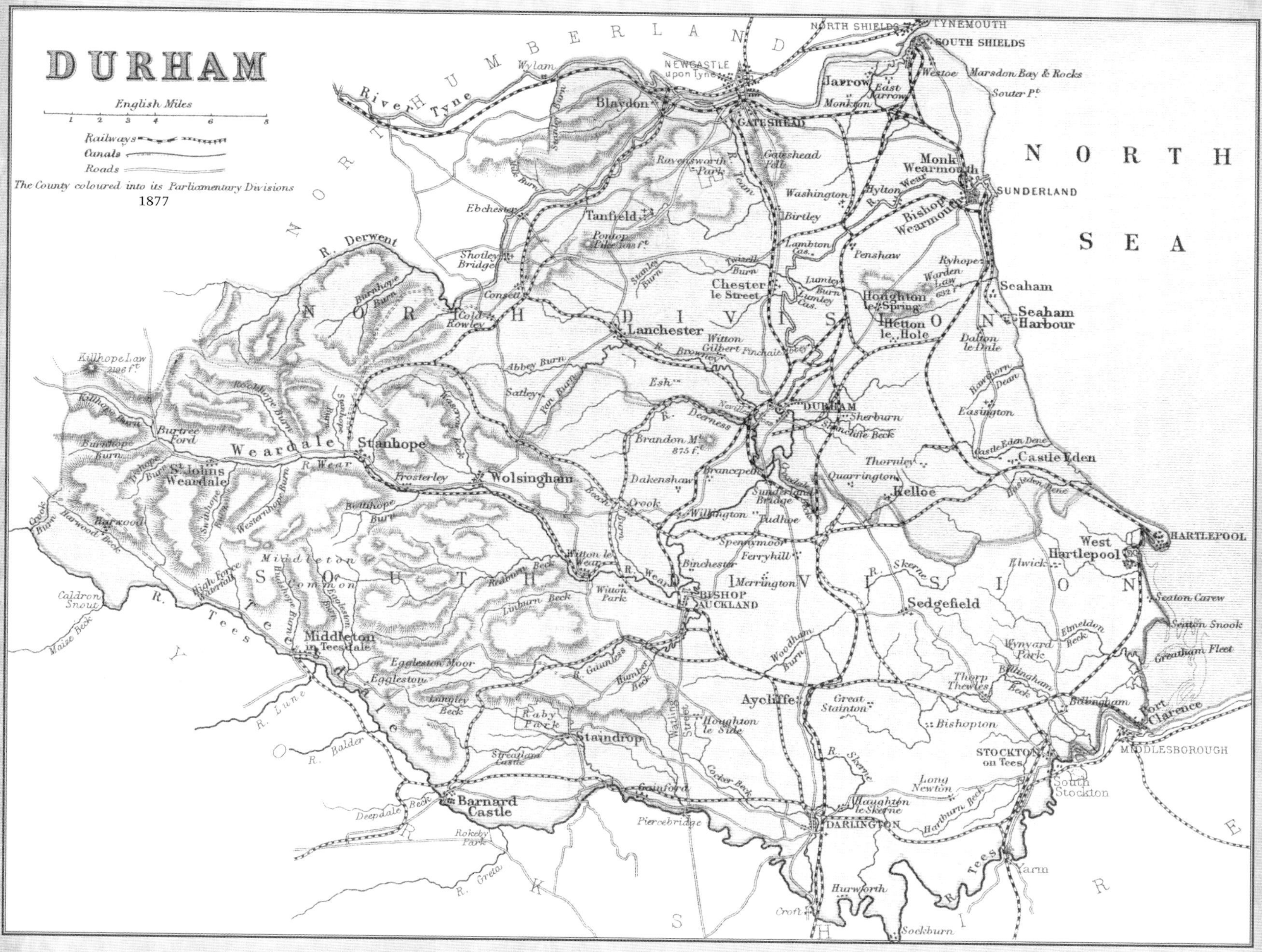

DURHAM

English Miles

Railways
Canals
Roads

The County coloured into its Parliamentary Divisions
1877

Bartholomew Gazetteer of the British Isles, 1887

DURHAM.– co. palatine and maritime co., in N. of England; is bounded N. by the Derwent and the Tyne, beyond which is Northumberland; E. by the North Sea; S. by the Tees, beyond which is Yorkshire; and W. by Cumberland and Westmorland; greatest length, 48 miles; greatest breadth, 40 m.; length of coast line, 32 m.; area, 647,592 ac.; pop. 867,258. The western portion of the co. consists of hill-ranges, enclosing fertile valleys; the eastern portion, in which the prevailing rocks are magnesian limestone and new red sandstone, is more level; in the central districts are the coal measures. In the valleys, and in the neighbourhood of the rivers, especially the Tees, the soil is very fertile. The chief corn crops are wheat and oats; the chief green crops are potatoes and turnips. A hardy breed of horses is raised on the moors in the west, and in the fertile pastures of the valleys a breed of cattle which is unsurpassed for dairy purposes. The principal mineral products are lead, iron, millstone, and coal. The coalfields are the most important in the kingdom. The principal mfrs. are chemicals, glass, and earthenware; shipbuilding and sail-making; paper-making; woollen and worsted stuffs, &c. There are also large ironworks and machine factories. Durham has great facilities of transport. The co. comprises 4 wards, 269 pars., mun. bors. of Darlington, Durham, Gateshead, Hartlepool, Jarrow, South Shields, and Sunderland, the greater part of the mun. bor. of Stockton. It is entirely in the diocese of Durham.

DARLINGTON

Area Sq Km	197
Area Sq Miles	76
Population	100,500
Highest point	East Shoulder of Redmires Hill (218 m)

FAMOUS FOR
The **Head of Steam** museum in the North Road Railway Station contains 'Locomotion No. 1', George Stephenson's locomotive that pulled the first train in the world to carry fare-paying passengers in 1825.

To celebrate Darlington's railway heritage, the sculptor David Mach created **'The Brick Train'** in 1997. The sculpture, which was modelled on the streamlined locomotive 'Mallard' coming out of a tunnel, used 185,000 bricks.

FAMOUS PEOPLE
Edward Pease, co-founded the Stockton and Darlington Railway company, born 1767.
Sir Edmund Backhouse, oriental scholar, born 1873.
Sir John Summerson, architectural historian, born 1904.
Mark Gatiss, writer and actor (*The League of Gentlemen*), born Darlington, 1966.

Darlington became a unitary authority in 1997, and is one of the smallest in England. Between 1974 and 1997 it was a district within Durham County Council and before that a county borough. The administrative area included the villages surrounding the town of Darlington as well at Durham Tees Valley Airport at Middleton St George. Originally an Anglo-Saxon settlement on the banks of the Skerne, a tributary of the Tees, it was a prosperous market town. The parish church of St Cuthbert's is one of the finest Early English churches in the northeast. Its population is 100,500, nearly all of whom live in the town of Darlington. Its population is expected to rise to 115,300 by 2031. Darlington's prosperity was based on the railways, central to its development since the opening of the Stockton and Darlington Railway in 1825. It was home to two locomotive works and Faverdale Wagon Works, all closing in the 1960s. Engineering and construction companies provide 20 per cent of jobs, but the service sector now dominates employment, in logistics and telecommunications and in public administration, health and education.

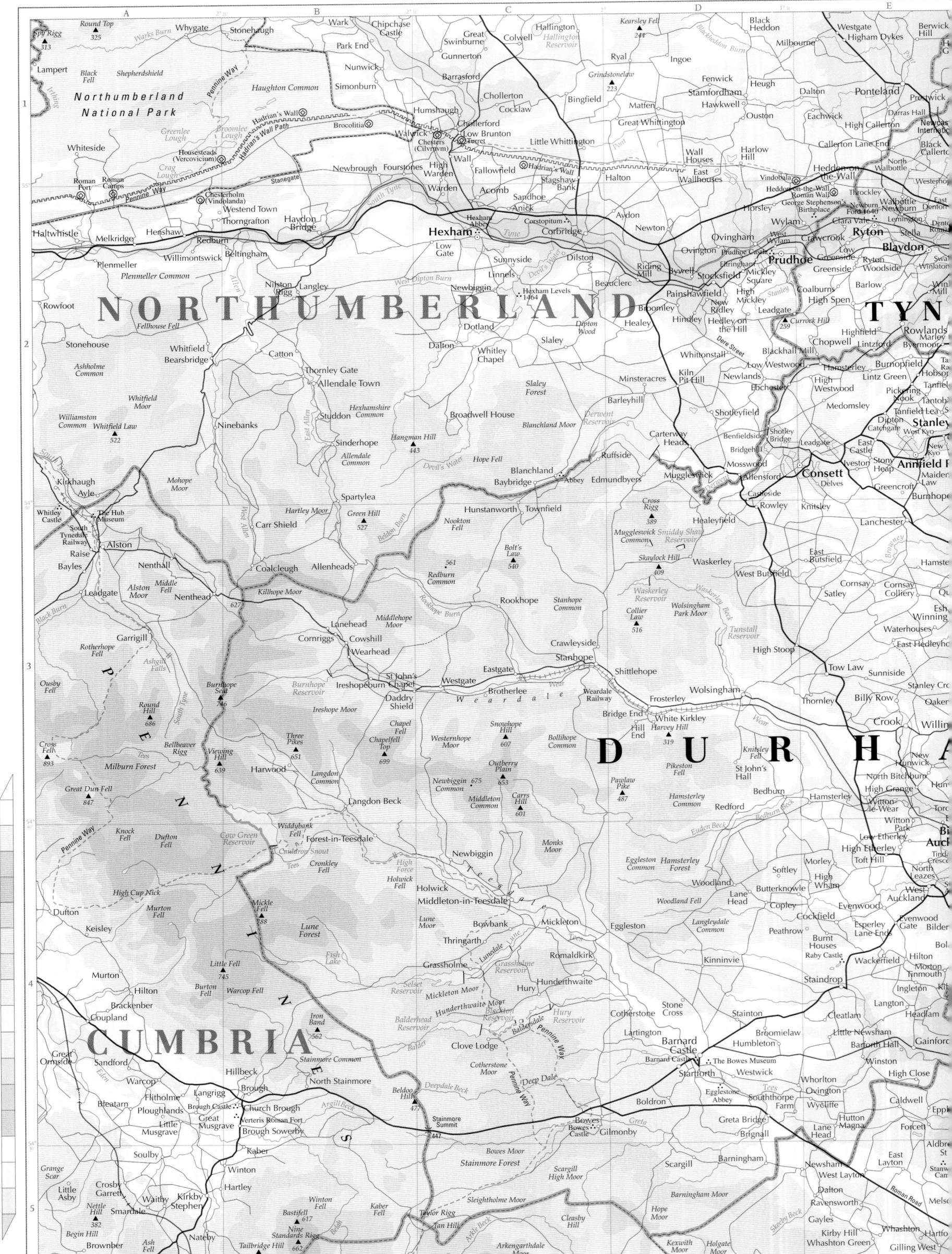

NORTH SEA

NORTH YORKSHIRE

DARLINGTON

STOCKTON-ON-TEES

HARTLEPOOL

REDCAR AND CLEVELAND

MIDDLESBROUGH

North York Moors National Park

1:220 000

© Collins Bartholomew Ltd

HARTLEPOOL

Area Sq Km 98
Area Sq Miles 38
Population 91,700
Highest point Whelly Hill (142 m)

FAMOUS FOR

A Hartlepool legend is that, during the Napoleonic Wars local fishermen found that the only survivor from a French warship that had foundered was a pet monkey dressed in navy uniform. Being simple, they thought the monkey must be a French spy, so hanged it, and for ever after, people from Hartlepool have been nick-named **'monkey hangers'**.

On the morning of 16 December 1914, the German Navy bombarded Hartlepool and in 40 minutes over 1100 shells were fired and 127 people were killed and 400 wounded, the first people killed on British soil in **World War I**.

FAMOUS PEOPLE

Sir Compton Mackenzie, author, born 1883.
Sir Edward Mellanby, doctor and scientist, researched role of vitamin D in rickets, born, 1884.
Reginald Hill, author, born 1936.

"I have been for two days [to Hartlepool] to taste the water, and do assure you that nothing could be salter and bitterer and nastier and better for you … I am delighted with the place; there are the finest walks and rocks and caverns…"
Thomas Gray, in a letter to Dr Wharton, 1765

Hartlepool is a unitary authority, formed in 1996 when the county of Cleveland was abolished. In 1974 the town of Hartlepool was joined with its surrounding villages to create the district of Hartlepool. Hartlepool has a history going back to the 7th-century foundation of a monastery; St Hilda was abbess there before she founded Whitby Abbey around 657. In 1200 the town received its charter from King John, and the large parish church dates from this period. From the 1830s new docks were built to ship coal out from the Durham coalfield. The West Hartlepool docks, which competed with Hartlepool docks, were opened in 1847 and a new town of West Hartlepool was built, which remained a separate borough until 1967. The docks have now gone to be replaced by a marina and Hartlepool's Marine Experience, a re-creation of an 18th century port and home to the warship HMS *Trincomalee*, built in Bombay in 1817. It has become a major visitor attraction in Hartlepool. The economy of the town is reviving, but the area still has 25 per cent of its resident workforce claiming benefits. Manufacturing and construction provide 22 per cent of jobs, including employment in the chemical industry and at Hartlepool's nuclear power station, while 33 per cent of the jobs are in public administration, health and education.

Sunset at the war memorial in 'Old' Hartlepool.

STOCKTON-ON-TEES

Area Sq Km 210
Area Sq Miles 81
Population 191,900
Highest point Boy Hill (82 m)

FAMOUS FOR

John Walker ran a chemist's shop in Stockton High Street, and it was there, in 1827, he invented and sold the first **friction match** (with the name Sulphurata Hyper-Oxygenata Frict), but he did not patent the idea and others exploited it.

FAMOUS PEOPLE

Thomas Sheraton, furniture designer, born Stockton-on-Tees, 1751.
Richard Griffiths, actor, born Thornaby-on-Tees, 1947.
Paul Smith, singer with the band Maxïmo Park, born Billingham, 1979.

"[On Billingham] This is one of the most extraordinary of experiences, a sight almost unique in England. On either side of the road are the works. Steaming, sizzling – tall steel towers, great cylinders, pipes everywhere."
Henry Thorold, *Shell Guide to Durham*, 1980

Stockton-on-Tees is a unitary authority that straddles the Tees. It was formed in 1996 when the county of Cleveland was abolished and includes Stockton-on-Tees, Billingham and Eaglescliffe and the surrounding countryside on the north side of the Tees, and Thornaby-on-Tees and Yarm on the south side of the Tees. The area to the south of the Tees is in the North Yorkshire ceremonial county while that to the north is in the Co. Durham ceremonial county. Its population of 191,900 makes it the largest of the authorities on Teesside. The population has been growing over recent years and is expected to reach around 221,000 by 2031. Stockton was originally a market town, and, after the arrival of the Stockton and Darlington railway in 1825, it developed as a port for shipping out Durham coal. Other industries followed, and neighbouring Billingham became a centre of the chemicals industry. The area has recently undergone major renewal and regeneration, with new employment in electronics and food technology. Manufacturing and construction provide 20 per cent of jobs, while public administration, health and education supply nearly 26 per cent, including staff on the Queen's Campus of Durham University at Thornaby-on-Tees. The main river is the Tees, which is controlled by the Tees Barrage, which has created Britain's largest purpose-built white-water canoeing course.

Tees Barrage White-Water Course.

TYNE AND WEAR METROPOLITAN COUNTY

Area Sq Km	551
Area Sq Miles	213
Population	1,093,500
Highest point	Currock Hill (259 m) near Chopwell

Metropolitan Borough Areas

City of Newcastle	119 sq km; 44 sq miles
North Tyneside	85 sq km; 33 sq miles
Gateshead	144 sq km; 56 sq miles
South Tyneside	67 sq km; 26 sq miles
City of Sunderland	140 sq km; 54 sq miles

Metropolitan Borough Populations

City of Newcastle	273,600
North Tyneside	197,300
Gateshead	190,600
South Tyneside	151,600
City of Sunderland	280,300

Tyne and Wear was created as a new metropolitan county in 1974 to bring together the industrial areas on both sides of the River Tyne. Prior to then all places to the north of the Tyne were in Northumberland and all areas south of the river in Co. Durham. Five metropolitan districts were created. North of the river were the City of Newcastle and North Tyneside and south of the river Gateshead and South Tyneside. The fifth area, Sunderland, straddles the river Wear to the south of the Tyne. In 1986 all the metropolitan counties in England were abolished by Parliament, and each district effectively became a unitary authority. The county of Tyne and Wear still exists for ceremonial purposes independent of Northumberland and Co. Durham, and some services (including, transport, museums and the fire service) are organized across Tyne and Wear.

The total population of the county of Tyne and Wear is 1,093,500 and it is expected to grow slowly to 1,152,000 by 2031, with the greatest growth in Newcastle and North Tyneside, while the population of Sunderland is expected to decline slightly. The county contains area of rural land, which to the south rises to the highest point at Currock Hill (259 m) near Chopwell in the borough of Gateshead.

FAMOUS PEOPLE

City of Newcastle upon Tyne

Admiral Cuthbert Collingwood, Baron Collingwood, Nelson's second in command at Trafalgar, born 1748.

Sir William Armstrong (Baron Armstrong), inventor and industrialist, born 1810.

Lewis Fry Richardson, physicist and meteorologist, born 1881.

Lesslie Newbigin, Church of Scotland missionary and bishop in Church of South India, born 1909.

Cardinal Basil Hume (*born* George Hume), Archbishop of Westminster, born 1923.

Harry Patterson (main pseudonym is Jack Higgins), thriller writer, born 1929.

Peter Higgs, theoretical physicist who predicted elementary particle the 'Higgs boson', born 1929.

Miriam Stoppard, physician, writer and broadcaster, born 1937.

Alan Shearer, footballer, born Gosforth, 1970.

Anthony McPartlin ('Ant') and **Declan Donnelly** ('Dec'), entertainers, both born 1975.

City of Sunderland

Sir Joseph Wilson Swan, inventor (photographic paper, light bulb, etc.), born Sunderland, 1828.

Gertrude Bell, explorer, writer, Arabist and founder of the Iraq Museum, born Washington, 1868

James Alfred Wright (pseudonym James Herriot), vet and author, born Sunderland, 1916.

Robert (Bob) Paisley, football manager, born Hetton-le-Hole, 1919.

Kate Adie, television journalist, born Sunderland, 1945.

David A. Stewart (often known as Dave Stewart), formed *Eurythmics* with Annie Lennox, born Sunderland, 1952.

Gateshead

Sir George Elliot, mining engineer, colliery owner, maker of first transatlantic cable, born 1815.

Paul Gascoigne, footballer, born Dunston, 1967.

Graham Onions, cricketer, born 1982.

North Tyneside

Thomas Addison, doctor, discovered Addison's Disease, born Longbenton, 1793.

Sting (born Gordon Sumner), musician and campaigner, born Wallsend, 1951.

Jimmy Nail (born James Bradford), actor and singer, born Benton, 1954

South Tyneside

St Bede (the Venerable Bede), scholar and historian, born Monkton in Jarrow, c.673.

Elinor M. Brent-Dyer, prolific children's author, born South Shields, 1894.

Dame Flora Robson, actress, born South Shields, 1902.

Dame Catherine Cookson, author, born Jarrow, 1906.

Ridley Scott, Oscar winning film director, born South Shields, 1937.

Eric Idle, actor, author and comedian, born South Shields, 1943.

Steve Cram, athlete, middle distance runner, born Jarrow, 1960.

City of Newcastle upon Tyne

Newcastle is named after the new castle that was started by Robert Curthose, William the Conqueror's son, in 1080.

FAMOUS FOR

The expression **'to carry coals to Newcastle'** for something unnecessary (because there was already plenty of coal there) has been in use since the middle of the 17th century, long before the Industrial Revolution.

The **Town Moor** is a 400 hectare area of common land that reaches into the centre of the city. In June every year it is the site of the Hoppings, Europe's largest travelling fairground, originally established as a Temperance festival in 1882, a tradition it still maintains.

The **Byker Wall** is part of a controversial housing development designed by the architect Ralph Erskine in the early 1970s. The Wall itself is a continuous building of three to twelve stories that contains 600 maisonettes and is now a listed building. It is also very close to Hadrian's Wall.

The city's origins date back to when the Romans built a bridge across the Tyne (around where the low-level swing bridge is today); a fort was built on the site of the current castle. Both bridge and fort were called *Pons Aelius*. The fort was the eastern end of Hadrian's Wall for a while until a further fort was built at Wallsend. Sections of Hadrian's Wall are still visible, particularly along West Road as it leaves the city. Renamed Monkchester in Anglo-Saxon times, the area was devastated in the Norman subjugation of the north, and the site was chosen for a new castle by Robert Curthose, son of William the Conqueror. His wooden castle was replaced in 1168 by Henry II's stone keep that can be seen today. A town soon formed around the castle and by the 14th century it was protected by massive city walls, some remnants of which still survive. By the 15th century it had become one of the most important towns in Britain, its prosperity based on coal exports from the many local

Bridges of the river Tyne connecting Newcastle, shown on the left, to Gateshead.

mines. In the 19th century, engineering and shipbuilding thrived and the centre of the city was elegantly developed in the 1830s and 1840s by the architect John Dobson and the speculative builder Richard Grainger, and is now wonderfully restored and bringing vibrant life to the city centre. The city, with two universities (Newcastle and Northumbria), has become the regional shopping and entertainment centre, with nearly 92 per cent of jobs in the service sector and only around 5 per cent in manufacturing. The riverside, spanned by a dramatic collection of bridges, including Robert Stephenson's High Level Bridge, opened in 1849 and still carrying both road and rail at two different levels, and the Tyne Bridge, a smaller version of the Sydney Harbour bridge and also built by Dorman Long of Middlesbrough, has become a thriving cultural quarter.

A fans' memorial to the late Sir Bobby Robson, former manager of Newcastle United football team.

NEWCASTLE, 1898

Bartholomew Gazetteer of the British Isles, 1887
NEWCASTLE UPON TYNE, *mun. bor., city, seaport, market town, and county of itself, Northumberland, on river Tyne, 10 miles from its mouth, 117 miles SE. of Edinburgh and 276 miles NW. of London by rail, 5371 ac., pop. 145,359; 8 Banks, 11 newspapers. Market-days, Tuesday and Saturday. Newcastle was originally called Pons Flii, from a bridge erected (120) by the Emperor Hadrian; its modern name originated from a fortress built (1080) by Robert Curthose, son of William the Conqueror. It was an important strategic key during the old Border feuds between England and Scotland, and suffered in the Civil War. Modern Newcastle, through the rich mineral products of the neighbourhood, and the industrial genius and activity of the inhabitants, has attained a first position among the great centres of British business enterprise. Being in the midst of one of the largest coalfields in England, it exports immense quantities of that commodity; also iron, chemicals, hardware, glass, earthenware, and machinery. Important industries are shipbuilding, the mfr. of locomotive and marine engines, cannon, patent shot, tools, fire-bricks, hemp and wire ropes, cables, anchors, sails, &c. The port (which is one of the Tyne Ports) has a very extensive traffic, greatly facilitated by the Northumberland and Tyne Docks, which cost £2, 500,000. Among its public works a great feature of the town is its series of fine bridges across the Tyne to Gateshead. The famous High Level Bridge (1846–50) of Robert Stephenson has an extreme length of 1375 ft., the upper part being 112 ft. above high water. The Swing Bridge (opened 1876), constructed by Sir W. Armstrong, is one of the largest of the kind in the world, and allows free navigation of the river. St Nicholas' Church (1359, restored 1879) is a very fine building, with a pointed spire (194 ft.), a peal of 8 bells, and an altar piece by Tintoretto. The central railway station and the general market are remarkable for their commodiousness and convenience. The Town Hall and offices form a large and imposing range of buildings. Richard Grainger, a builder*

in the town, is credited with the great improvements effected in the construction of new streets and buildings. Connected with the educational state of the town, it may be mentioned that the school system both for elementary and secondary pupils is excellent; special institutions are an institute of mining, a college of medicine, and a

college of physical science attached to Durham University. Several public grounds have been supplied for the inhabitants; they include Elswick Park, Armstrong Park, and Brandling Park. A bishopric was founded for Newcastle in 1882, and on the 13th June of that year the place was created a city.

"It was not long before, round these two last communities [Jarrow and Monkwearmouth monasteries] all the light and learning of England was to revolve, and not only England, but of the whole of Europe, during one of the darkest periods in the history of man."
Sir Timothy Eden, *History of Durham*, 1948

"The Walrus and the Carpenter
Were walking close at hand;
They wept like anything to see
Such quantities of sand:
'If this were only cleared away,'
They said, 'it would be grand!'"
Lewis Carroll, inspired by Whitburn Sands, 1871

The Sage Gateshead

Modern Newcastle

City of Sunderland

This administrative area, which formally became a city in 1992 in celebration of the Queen's 40th anniversary, is centred around Sunderland, built on either side of the river Wear. The first evidence of habitation is at Monkwearmouth (on the north bank of the Wear) where Benedict Biscop established St Peter's Monastery in 674, and part of the tower and nave from this period are incorporated into the current church. The monastery was linked to Benedict's slightly later foundation at Jarrow, and the two sites are jointly being considered for World Heritage Site status. With the coming of the Industrial Revolution, Sunderland began to flourish on coalmining and the establishment of a major shipbuilding industry. After World War II the industry went into a major decline and the last shipyard on the Wear closed in 1994.

Coal mining, too, has seen a great decline, with the last mine, Wearmouth, closing in 1993; on its site now stands the Stadium of Light, home to Sunderland's football team. The economy has diversified, however, most significantly with the arrival of car manufacturer Nissan. Their plant opened in 1986 and is now the largest in Britain and one of the most productive in Europe. In 2010 it started to produce Nissan's first mass-produced electric car. Over 15 per cent of the jobs in Sunderland are in manufacturing and around 29 per cent in public administration, education and health, including the staff of Sunderland University, established in 1992, and now with a new campus next to St Peter's Church and the National Glass Centre (7th century glass, some of Britain's earliest, have been discovered at St Peter's).

St Peter's Church

Gateshead

Always seen as a poor relation of Newcastle across the river, Gateshead was a centre for mining, iron works and heavy industry. Innovations developed here included the making of steel cables and wires (such as the first cross-Channel telephone cable) and electric light (Joseph Swan's house in Gateshead was the first domestic house in the world wired for electricity). Most of the heavy industry has gone. In the Depression the Team Valley Trading Estate, one of the first in Britain, was created for many smaller companies to use and it

continues to thrive. Towards the end of the 20th century came the real change in image, typified by the iconic Angel of the North sculpture, the development of the Metro Centre as Europe's largest covered shopping centre, and the rejuvenation of the Tyne waterfront with the Baltic Centre for Contemporary Art (in the former Baltic Flour Mills building), The Sage Gateshead music venue and the pedestrian Gateshead Millennium Bridge, with its unique tilting mechanism. The administrative area includes countryside to the south of the town where

the beautiful 18th-century chapel at Gibside, begun in 1760 by James Paine for the Bowes family, can be found. Sadly the Bowes-Lyon family let the rest of this grand estate fall into ruin, apart from a column, slightly taller than Nelson's column dedicated to 'British Liberty'. Manufacturing and construction still remain key parts of the economy, providing 21.5 per cent of jobs, while public administration, education and health and retail, hotels and restaurants both provide just over 26 per cent.

North Tyneside

North Tyneside brings together a number of communities along the northern banks of the Tyne and then up the North Sea coast to Whitley Bay. Wallsend was named because it was just that, the end of Hadrian's Wall, marked by the excavated Roman fort of *Segedunum*. Coal mining at Wallsend started in the 18th century and shipbuilding in the 19th century, with Swan Hunter, the last ship builder at Wallsend closing in 2007. *Turbinia*, the first steam-turbine powered ship was launched in 1894 by Charles Parsons at Wallsend, and its design was revolutionary. On a headland at the entrance to the Tyne stands Tynemouth Priory and Castle. The site of a monastery since the 7th century, the current building dates from 1090 and the site was fortified at the start of the 14th century. The fortress played a part in coastal defences until after World War II. North Shields was originally a fishing village that supplied Tynemouth Priory and developed into a port and shipbuilding centre; it is now a dormitory town for Newcastle. Whitley Bay developed as a seaside resort in the 19th century. Its charms no longer attract people from the Northeast and Scotland for their annual holidays and it has become another dormitory town for Newcastle, to which it is linked by the fast Tyneside Metro service. The demise of shipbuilding and coal mining in the area has caused high levels of unemployment and deprivation, from which it is slowly recovering.

The service sector now accounts for nearly 83 per cent of jobs (over a third of which are in public administration, education and health), while manufacturing provides just over 10 per cent.

Part of Tynemouth Priory.

South Tyneside

South Tyneside stretches along the southern bank of the Tyne from Gateshead to the sea. Its communities in the 19th century thrived on coal mining, shipbuilding, heavy engineering, glassworks, brickworks and chemical plants. In the 20th century these industries first started to decline during the Great Depression. An iconic event of that period was the Jarrow Crusade, the march of 200 unemployed men from Jarrow to London in 1936. The decline continued after World War II and by the start of the 21st century the area had the highest unemployment rate in all of England and Wales. New employment has been attracted in the service sector and such manufacturing, from ship repairing to electronics and waterproof clothing, continues. Over 12 per cent of jobs are in manufacturing and 82 per cent in the service

sector. In and amongst this industrial landscape is one of the most important early Christian sites in Britain, for in Jarrow are the substantial remains of St Paul's Church and Monastery founded by Benedict Biscop in 684, and home to the Venerable Bede for many years. The chancel and tower of the church date from this period. South Shields, a town that developed from the 18th century, is the site of the major Roman fort of *Arbeia*, built to hold supplies for Hadrian's Wall. A gateway to the fort has been reconstructed. South of the Tyne, the coast is a mixture of sandy dunes, beaches and cliffs. Lying just offshore is Marsden Rock, home to many seabirds, but which is now smaller, as a natural arch in the rock collapsed in 1996 and some of the rock had to be demolished for safety reasons.

Marsden Rock

NORTHUMBERLAND

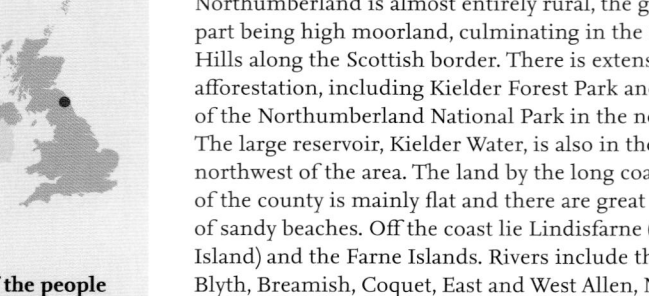

Area Sq Km	7,185
Area Sq Miles	2,774
Population	311,000
County town	Morpeth
Highest point	The Cheviot (815 m)

Northumberland means the 'territory of the people living north of the Humber', the name coming from the Anglo-Saxon Kingdom of Northumbria.

FAMOUS FOR

The Lindisfarne Gospels, one of the most magnificent illuminated books in the world, was created at Lindisfarne in honour of St Cuthbert by Eadfrith, Bishop of Lindisfarne (698–721). The sumptuous, highly-coloured illuminations, which reflect both Celtic and Anglo-Saxon traditions, are considered to be all Eadfrith's work rather than created by a team of illuminators.

Cragside, near Rothbury was designed by Norman Shaw in 1870 for the great Newcastle industrialist and inventor, William (later Lord) Armstrong. The house was the first in the world to use electricity generated by a hydroelectric turbine and to have a hydraulic lift. It even had a hydraulically-driven roasting spit.

Near Cornhill on Tweed is the site of the **Battle of Flodden**, where James IV of Scotland and many of his nobles were slain by an English army in 1513, a loss lamented in the ballad *'The Flowers of the Forest'.*

Seaton Delaval Hall, near Blyth, is a spectacular Baroque country house, the last designed by Sir John Vanbrugh and built between 1718 and 1728. Its future was secured in 2009 when it was purchased by the National Trust.

FAMOUS PEOPLE

Nicholas Ridley, Bishop of London (1550–3), Protestant martyr, born Willimontswick Castle, Haltwhistle, c.1500.
Lancelot Brown (known as 'Capability' Brown), landscape gardener, born Kirkharle, Ponteland, 1716.
Thomas Bewick, wood engraver and naturalist, born Cherryburn, Mickley, Stocksfield, 1753.
Charles Grey (2nd Earl Grey), British Prime Minister (1830–34) and tea connoisseur, born Falloden, 1764.
George Stephenson, engineer, inventor of the first steam locomotive, born Wylam, 1781.
Timothy Hackworth, railway locomotive engineer, born Wylam, 1786.
John Martin, painter, born Haydon Bridge, 1789.
Sir George Airy, astronomer (Astronomer Royal 1835–81), born Alnwick, 1801.
Grace Darling, daughter of lighthouse keeper, took part in heroic ship rescue, born Bamburgh, 1815.
Sir Daniel Gooch, engineer, laid first transatlantic cable, born Bedlington, 1816.
Sir William Coldstream, artist, born Belford, 1908.
Dame Veronica Wedgwood, historian, born Stocksfield, 1910.
Hugh Trevor-Roper, Lord Dacre, historian, born Glanton 1914.
John (Jackie) Milburn, footballer, born Ashington, 1924.
John (Jack) Charlton, footballer, born Ashington, 1935.
Sir Robert (Bobby) Charlton, footballer, born Ashington, 1937.

Heathland and bent-land –
Black land and white,
God bring me to Northumberland,
The land of my delight.
Wilfrid Wilson Gibson, c.1943

Northumberland is almost entirely rural, the greater part being high moorland, culminating in the Cheviot Hills along the Scottish border. There is extensive afforestation, including Kielder Forest Park and part of the Northumberland National Park in the northwest. The large reservoir, Kielder Water, is also in the northwest of the area. The land by the long coastline of the county is mainly flat and there are great expanses of sandy beaches. Off the coast lie Lindisfarne (Holy Island) and the Farne Islands. Rivers include the Aln, Blyth, Breamish, Coquet, East and West Allen, North and South Tyne, Till and Wansbeck. The Tweed forms part of the Scottish border and flows out to sea at Berwick-upon-Tweed.

Northumberland is but a part of the great Anglo-Saxon kingdom of Northumbria, which stretched from the Forth to the Humber. It suffered much from Danish attacks in the 9th century and in the 10th century it submitted to the kingdom of Wessex. The Normans forcibly suppressed the area and early governance was through powerful marcher lords. There was a long history of cross border incursions with Scotland and also between rival border families, which only settled down after the Union of the Crowns of England and Scotland in 1603. When Northumberland County Council was created in 1888, the southern border of the county was along the Tyne and included Newcastle, Wallsend and Tynemouth. In the 1974 local government reorganization, a new metropolitan county of Tyne and Wear was created, which includes Newcastle and North Tyneside. The reduced county of Northumberland, with headquarters at Morpeth, became primarily rural in character. It was originally divided into six districts (Blyth Valley, Wansbeck, Castle Morpeth, Tynedale, Alnwick and Berwick-upon-Tweed), but these were abolished in 2009, with the county becoming a single unitary authority.

The population of Northumberland is 311,000, and it is very unevenly distributed, with over 50 per cent of the population living in just 5 per cent of the county, in the south, near Newcastle. For the rest of the county population density is less than 0.4 people per hectare, with most people living in small rural market towns. The population is growing slowly, and is predicted to

reach 337,900 by 2031. The principal towns are Blyth (35,691), Ashington (27,335), Cramlington (28,653), Bedlington (16,464), Morpeth (13,555), Berwick-upon-Tweed (12,870) and Hexham (10,682).

Coal mining was critical to the economy of southe Northumberland. At its peak in the 1950s, the industr employed over 30,000 miners, but the last deep mine, Ellington, closed in 2005. Opencast mining continues and new sites are being developed. Industries that hav moved in to the area include aluminium smelting, pharmaceuticals, paint and paper products. Overall 13 per cent of jobs are in manufacturing, with nearly 36 per cent of jobs in public administration, educatio and health, while a growing tourism industry now provides approaching 12 per cent of jobs. Agriculture remains important close to the coast while more limit hill farming is practised in the high inland areas. Nea a third of the county's employed residents work outsi the county, primarily in Tyne and Wear.

Northumberland is defined by being a border county. Across the south from the Cumbria border ru Hadrian's Wall, that first, very solid attempt to define the border, built between AD 122 and 133. There is mu to see as it tracks across the wild land of the northern Pennines, including the major forts at Housesteads, on the exposed escarpment of Whin Sill, Chesters, by the banks of the Tyne, the fort at *Vindolanda* that predates the Wall, and *Corstopitum* near Corbridge, the main garrison town for the area. Hadrian's Wall is a UNESC World Heritage Site. The period of greatest stability wa during the ascendency of the kingdom of Northumbri which saw the arrival of Christianity in the northeast with the establishment of the monastery at Lindisfarn (Holy Island) by St Aidan, a monk from Iona, in c.635. Cuthbert, the great northeastern saint, was here from 664 until his death in 687 and the island remains a pla of pilgrimage. Because of the border disputes, great castles were built along the coast, including Warkwort Dunstanburgh, Alnwick and Bamburgh, while Berwic upon-Tweed, the only part of England north of the riv Tweed, changed sides many times, with English rule finally established in 1482. It then became a heavily fortified garrison town, protected by the impressive Elizabethan ramparts and walls.

Lindisfarne Castle on Holy Island.

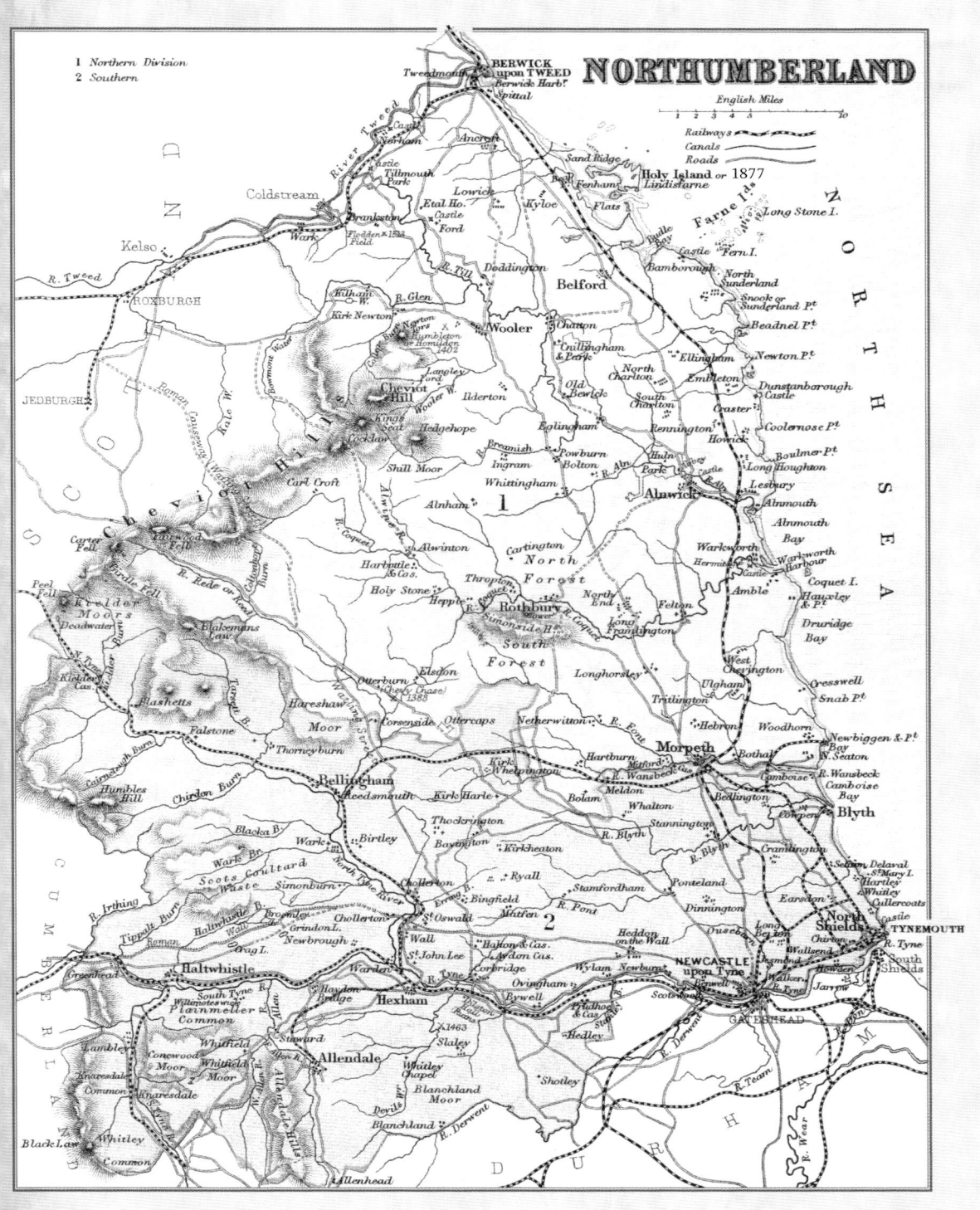

NORTHUMBERLAND

Bartholomew Gazetteer of the British Isles, 1887

NORTHUMBERLAND, *the most northerly co. of England, bounded N. by the river Tweed, which separates it from Berwickshire, NW. by the Cheviot Hills, separating it from Roxburghshire, E. by the North Sea, S. by Durham, and W. by Cumberland; greatest length, N. to S., 70 miles; greatest breadth, E. to W., 53 miles; area, 1,290,312 ac., pop. 434,086. Somewhat triangular in outline, Northumberland possesses a varied surface, principally rugged, and rising gradually from the coast to the hill ranges of the Cheviots on the borders of Scotland and Cumberland. In the centre of the co. the hills are undulating, and clad with green; in the W. and SW. they are bleak, and covered with moss and heather. On the coast are the Coquet, Farne, and Holy Islands. Allenhead, in the extreme S. of the co., is the highest inhabited district in England, its altitude being 1400 ft. Fertile valleys stretch from spurs of the Cheviots eastward towards the coast, and the co. is well watered by several celebrated rivers, the Alne, Coquet, Wansbeck, Till, Tyne, and Tweed. In those localities where farming is most diligently pursued – i.e., near the coast and in the valleys – the soil is a rich clayey loam. Barley, wheat, and beans form the chief crops; and a considerable and lucrative employment is found in the rearing of the famous Cheviot sheep, also of short-horned Durham cattle. Among anglers the Northumberland rivers and their estuaries are held in high repute for the excellence of their sport, and their fisheries also have a high commercial value. A large number of boats are employed in the sea fisheries. Geologically the conspicuous feature of the co. is its immense coal formation, producing about 20,000,000 tons a year; other districts consist of various sandstones, and the porphyry, trap, and limestone of the Cheviots. The lead mining district is in the S., in S. Tynedale and Allendale, but of late the industry has suffered through foreign competition. In addition to coal and lead works, with their auxiliary employments, Northumberland has an enormous industrial system, shown most prominently by the ironworking, ship-building, ropemaking, chemical mfr., glass making, pottery making, &c., on the Tyne. The co. is divided into 9 wards and 541 pars., and includes the mun. bors. of Berwick upon Tweed, Morpeth, Newcastle upon Tyne, and Tynemouth.*

tic terns on the Farne Islands.

'Sycamore Gap', Hadrian's Wall, which is commonly referred to as 'Robin Hood's Tree' as it featured in a famous scene in the 1991 film *'Robin Hood, Prince of Thieves'*.

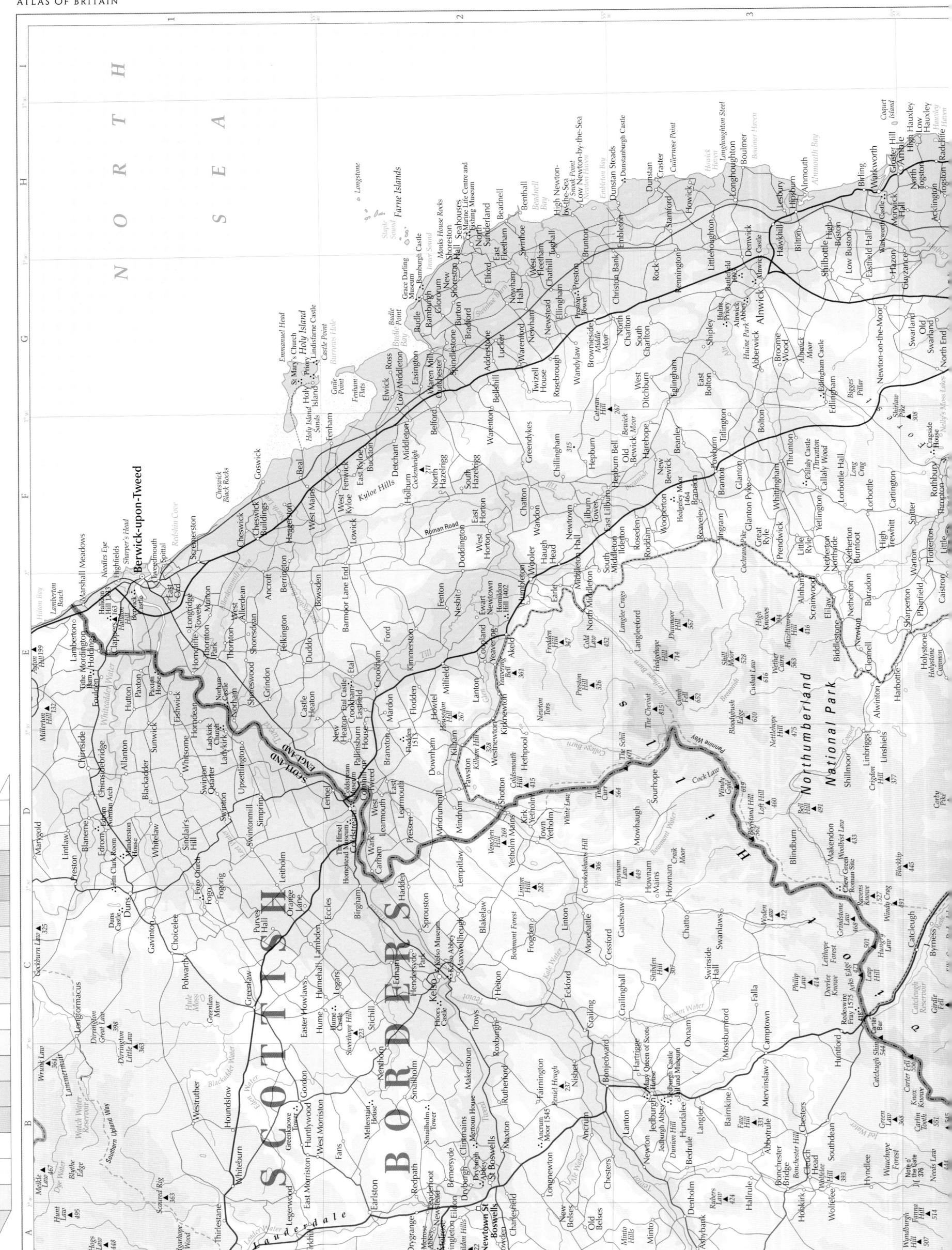

British National Grid projection

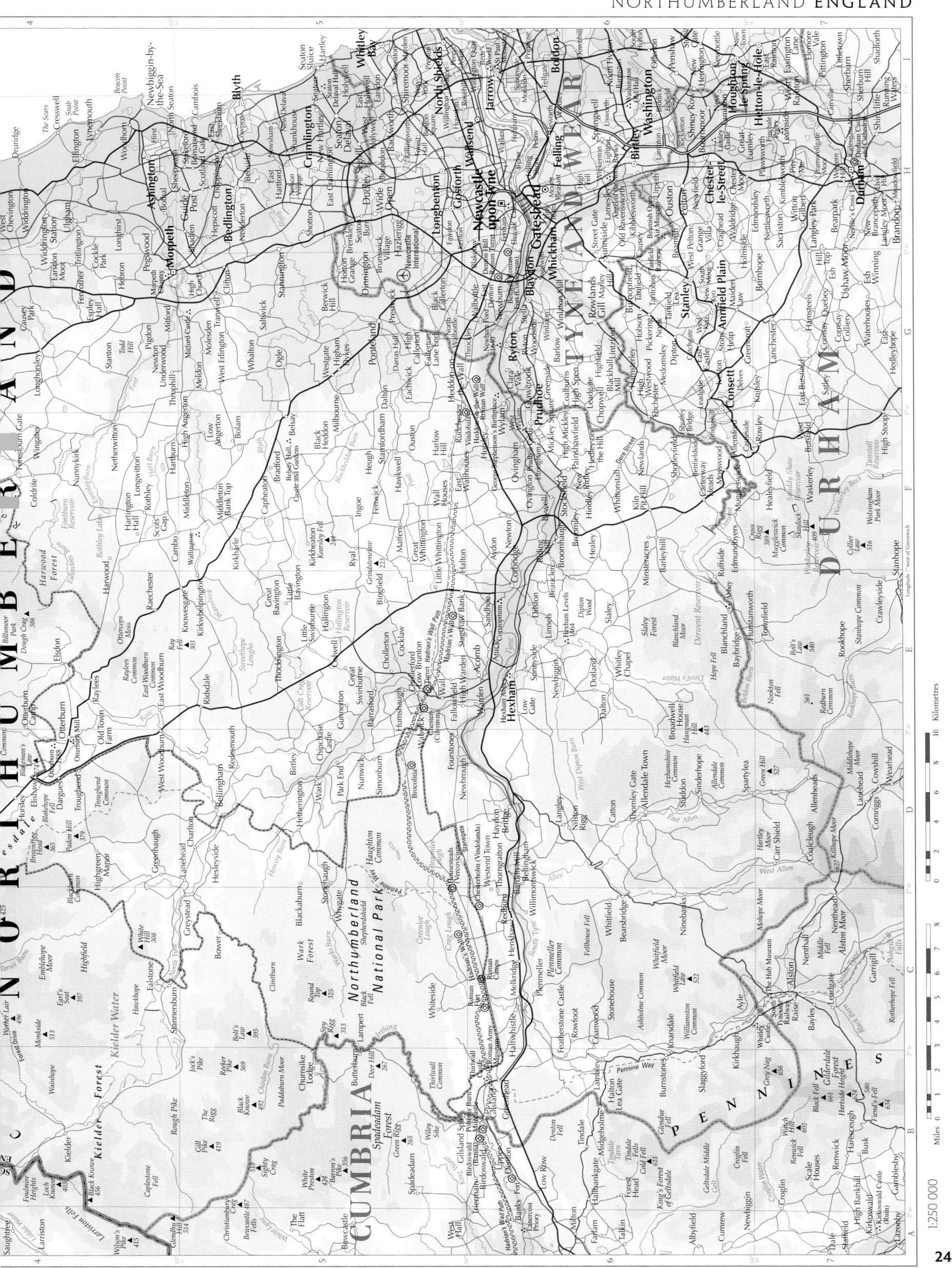

1:250 000

Scotland

Area Sq Km	78,822
Area Sq Miles	30,433
Population	5,168,500
Capital city	Edinburgh
Highest point	Ben Nevis (1,344m)

Whisky and tartan!

Ben Nevis, Scotland's and Britain's highest mountain.

Gairloch in Wester Ross, Highlands.

Scotland is surrounded by the North Sea to the east, the Atlantic Ocean to the northwest and the Irish Sea to the southwest. Scotland's only land border is with England which runs for 154 km from the Solway Firth to just north of Berwick-upon Tweed. Three large island groups surround the mainland to the north and west containing around 800 islands (about 130 of which are inhabited). The Hebrides, of which St Kilda is the most westerly outpost in the Atlantic, are themselves divided into two groups. The Outer Hebrides and Inner Hebrides are separated from each other and the mainland by a body of water known as The Minch. To the north, across the Pentland Firth lie the Orkney Islands and, further still, Shetland, and the most northerly inhabited island of the group, Unst. Scotland covers an area of 78,772 sq. km, roughly two-thirds the size of England and Wales. It is 248 km across at its widest point, and 440 km in length from Cape Wrath to the Mull of Galloway. The most westerly mainland point, both for Scotland and Great Britain, is at Ardnamurchan Point. Its deeply indented coastline is 3,900 km long.

Scotland is divided between Lowlands and Highlands. The Highland Boundary Fault runs roughly from the Isle of Arran in the southwest to Stonehaven in the northeast. To its north lie the Highlands, including the Grampian and Cairngorm Mountains, and all the land and islands north and west of Inverness. The Highlands itself is split in two by the rift valley of the Great Glen and its bodies of freshwater, Loch Lochy, Loch Oich and Loch Ness, that separate the Grampians from the Northwest Highlands.

The Lowlands are also divided geologically into two sections by the Southern Uplands Fault, which runs from the Rhinns of Galloway to Dunbar. The hills and valleys of the Southern Uplands run roughly in a line between South Ayrshire and West Lothian. North of the Southern Uplands is the Central Lowlands, a great vale between the Highland Boundary Fault to the north and the Southern Upland Fault to the south. This area of hills and valleys is not entirely synonymous with the 'Central Belt', the densely populated area in the Forth-Clyde valleys from Greenock to Edinburgh.

The longest Highland rivers are the Tay (193 km) which rises on the slopes of Beinn Laoigh and runs to the North Sea, and the Spey (172 km). The longest Lowland river is the Clyde, rising in the Lowther Hills and flowing 171 km to the Firth of Clyde and the Irish Sea. Other important Lowland rivers include the Tweed (156 km) and the Forth and its tributaries (105 km). The ten highest peaks in Britain are all to be found in Scotland, of which the greatest is Ben Nevis (1,344 m).

Scotland's climate is maritime temperate. Lying between 55°N and 60°N, Scotland's climate is colder and wetter than the rest of Great Britain. The west coast and Northern Isles benefit from the North Atlantic Drift, which carries warm water up from the Caribbean to the North Atlantic. Winter mean temperatures vary from –3°C to –5°C in the Cairngorm Mountains to 7°C in the Western Isles. Even summer mean temperatures are relatively low in the eastern Cairngorm at 5.5°C while in the west the mean is 7°C–15°C. The coldest recorded temperature was –27.2°C on 30 December 1995 at Altnaharra in Sutherland (Highlands). Scotland is also wetter than England or Wales, with an average 200 days of rain a year, but 250 days in the west, where on average at least 70 days see more than 10 mm of rainfall. Loch Sloy Main Adit (Argyll & Bute) recorded a record 238 mm of rain in 24 hours on 17 January 1974. The east coast is significantly drier than the west or north. At such a northern latitude, the winter days are short, but summer ones are long with a twilight 'gloaming'. On the longest day of the year, Orkney and Shetland experience the 'simmer dim', when it does not become completely dark at all.

The population of Scotland in 2008 was 5,168,500, a drop of 11,700 since 1981, but with a projected rise to 5,540,000 in 2033. Life expectancy for children born around 2006 is 74.8 years (men) and 79.7 years (women). The number of births in 2007 was the highest since 1997, but relatively low fertility rates since the 1960s mean that Scotland's population is an ageing one, and the number of people aged over 75 is projected to increase by 81 per cent by 2031. Since 1997, both West and East Lothian have increased most in population while Inverclyde and Dundee City have seen the greatest declines.

The Scottish Government recognizes three official languages: English, Gaelic and Scots. Gaelic was once the language of the great majority of people living on the Scottish mainland and Hebrides. Figures from the 2001 census show that 92,000 people (or just under 2 per cent) had some Gaelic language ability, and half of these were in the Western Isles. The report, however, also suggested that whereas use of Gaelic was declining in its traditional strongholds, it was increasing in other parts of the country, particularly among the young. The Scots language, and its variations, such as Doric, was and still is spoken widely in the Lowlands areas. Scholars might disagree as to whether it is a distinct language or only an ancient variety of English, but an extensive body of literature exists and five main dialects have been analysed. Scots, along with Gaelic, has been recognized and protected under the European Charter for Regional or Minority Languages (1992).

The peoples of Scotland were originally an amalgamation of Celtic peoples, particularly the Picts, the Gaels and the Britons. The Romans called the area from eastern Argyll to the Moray Firth 'Caledonia' after the main Pictish tribe that ruled it. The Gaels were, in fact, from Ireland and confusingly called Scotti by later commentators. They extended their own kingdom, Dalriada, to coastal Argyll in the 5th century A

...a Beach, Ardnamurchan Peninsula, Argyll and Bute.

...burgh, from the castle, with Scott Monument, Princes Street, Calton Hill, Waverley Station and the National Gallery all in view.

Tron clock tower in the Merchant City district, Glasgow.

...e Brythons, or Britons of the Kingdom of Strathclyde ...e related to Welsh Celtic groups.

The Romans marched north as part of their ...quest of Britain and constructed the Antonine Wall ...AD 139 between the rivers Clyde and Forth. Their ...tively brief colonization did not have the same ...th of influence felt in the south of England, however. ...ween the 4th and 6th centuries, tribal kings were ...verted by Irish missionaries to Christianity, and ...ough the shifting alliances and warfare, Kenneth ...cAlpine (the son of a Pictish princess and himself ...ng of the Scotti) and his descendants managed to ...trol most of the mainland, known as Alba. Norse ...ings in the 8th and 9th centuries took control of the ...brides and much of the northwest until the ...century. It was not until the reign of Alexander III ...t Scotland assumed its familiar shape (although ...ney and Shetland would not be incorporated until ...8).

The War of Independence, which culminated in ...crowning of Robert the Bruce in 1306 and the ...eat of Edward II at Bannockburn in 1314 was only ...mporary cessation in attempts by English monarchs ...laim sovereignty over Scotland. Ironically, the ...ions were to be unified by the Scottish James VI, ...at-great-nephew of Henry VIII, who claimed ...throne of England as James I in 1603. That he ...a suitable candidate had as much to do with ...gion as family ties. James was a Protestant, and ...Reformation, established in law in Scotland in ...0, was to have profound repercussions in all walks ...ife. The personal union of the crown became an ...of Union in 1707, although revolts challenged ...status quo in 1715, and especially 1745 when ...dominantly Highland Jacobite forces hoping to ...ce Charles Edward Stuart on the British throne were ...lly defeated in 1746 by a British army at Culloden, ...side Inverness. Although some Lowland areas were ...proved' to maximize rental income, it was in the

Highlands between 1785 and 1850 that the Clearances were the most brutal. The forced removal of large populations from areas in Sutherland, Caithness, Lewis, Skye and elsewhere, culminated in Scots migrating to the colonies or the industrial cities of the Lowlands in search of work. The Clearances overlapped with the acceleration of industrialization in Scotland. The Lowlands, especially the Central Belt, became the centre of heavy industry and engineering, particularly coal, copper, iron and lead mining, shipbuilding and textile manufacture. At its peak at the beginning of the 20th century, 40 million tonnes of coal a year was mined, but the same century saw the contraction and eventually cessation of most of these industries, replaced by the rise of a service economy.

By far the largest sector of the Scottish economy is in public administration, education and health, which accounts for 30 per cent of employment (ahead of the UK average of 27 per cent). Retail, hotels and restaurants employ 22 per cent (23 per cent for the UK) and finance, IT and other business activities employ 19 per cent (22 per cent for the UK). Tourism is a major employer almost uniformly throughout Scotland, providing 9 percent of jobs (the UK average is 8 per cent), but it is particularly important in the Highlands and Islands, providing 13 per cent of jobs. Manufacturing employs 8.7 per cent (the UK average is 10 per cent). Most of the traditional heavy industry is still found in the Central Belt, particularly in Falkirk, North Lanarkshire, West Lothian and Renfrewshire, but modern manufacturing, ranging from engineering for the oil industry to hi-tech businesses, is more widely distributed. Nationally, 8 per cent of the workforce is directly employed in agriculture in Scotland. Around 85 per cent of the land is classed as Less Favoured Area, an EU classification recognizing natural and geographic disadvantage. On this marginal land, sheep and beef cattle are reared, making this industry the single largest sector of Scottish agriculture.

Historically the government of Scotland was

handled by the Scottish Office, a part of the Westminster government. The Scottish National Party (SNP), formed in 1934, campaigns for Scottish independence and won its first parliamentary seat in 1945. A referendum on devolution was held in 1979, but failed to gain more than 40 per cent of the vote. A second referendum in 1997 overwhelmingly supported devolution of power from Westminster, and two years later the Scottish parliament reconvened (it had technically been adjourned in 1707). The Scottish Government has devolved powers to legislate in a wide range of areas including health, education, law, policing, the environment and planning. Other issues reserved to Westminster include foreign policy, defence, immigration, social security and constitutional issues.

The Scottish government sits in the new Parliament building in Edinburgh's Old Town. There are 129 Members of the Scottish Parliament (MSPs) elected according to a complicated proportional representation system with a mixture of constituency and regional MSPs, designed to ensure the number of seats each party receives closely mirrors the level of support each party enjoys with the voters. In 2010 the SNP forms a minority administration, with forty-seven seats. In addition, fifty-nine Scottish MPs represent the country's interests in Westminster.

Whether increased powers for the Scottish Government or the novel experience of an SNP administration have taken the urgency out of the desire for independence in Scotland remains a matter of conjecture. Having dispersed its countrymen all over the globe in previous centuries to develop industries and found nations, there are indications that Scotland is increasingly prepared to stop defining itself by what it is not – England – and trying to find its own way in the world. Perhaps its citizens are beginning to believe, with Henry James, that 'Once you get the hang of it, and apprehend the type, it is a most beautiful and admirable little country'.

HISTORICAL MAPS OF SCOTLAND

John Speed's map of Scotland, 1610.

Unlike the other pairs of historic national maps in this atlas, the 17th century map of Scotland shown here is not a county map as such. Instead, area naming is restricted to a fairly sparse selection of physical regions, some of which show antique spellings such as Louthiane, Muray, Buquhan and Loquhaber, while others such as Galloway and Sutherland have remained unchanged. What we now know as Assynt is named very prominently as 'Affin Shire' (the old style 's' looking like an 'f') – its designation as a 'shire' is long since disused. Breadalbane is rendered as Broad Albayn, and Strathnaver is Stranavern.

This map is also interesting in the way many of the islands are shown. It is clear that Scotland's coastal outline had not really been as thoroughly surveyed as that of England and Wales by this time – Skye for instance is not very accurate even by the standards technically feasible at the time, and nor are Mull, Kintyre, Islay, Coll and Tiree. The Outer Hebrides look

bigger than we now know they are. Accurate coastal mapping must have been delayed for a long time by the sheer remoteness of these parts, to an extent hard to believe these days – combined with the difficulty of sailing in often treacherous waters. The fact that the remoter parts of Scotland had by no means yet been brought under full national control must also have played a part.

Some maps of this era continue the mediaeval tradition of using Latin for sea names and some other features, but here we have the North Sea referred to in English – as The Germane Sea. With regard to the subject of sea names, there are probably few people nowadays who would recognise the quite prominent designation of the Atlantic north of the Hebrides as 'The Deucalidon Sea'.

The county map dating from the late 19th century is a complete contrast in many ways, although in its own way it also attempts to portray the hills and mountains

in a diagrammatic form. It could be said, though, that the more naïve techniques in the much older map are actually rather more successful in showing where the main hills are. The producer of this map, John Bartholomew & Son Ltd of Edinburgh, was in fact much lauded as the creator of a quite different technique of showing the lie of the land on maps: this was layer colouring (or 'hypsometric tints'), in which lowland is green, and heights are graded through browns and perhaps greys, finally to purple and even white. This now very familiar method was a relatively new idea at this time (1890) and had evidently not been universally adopted even by the company which seems to have pioneered it.

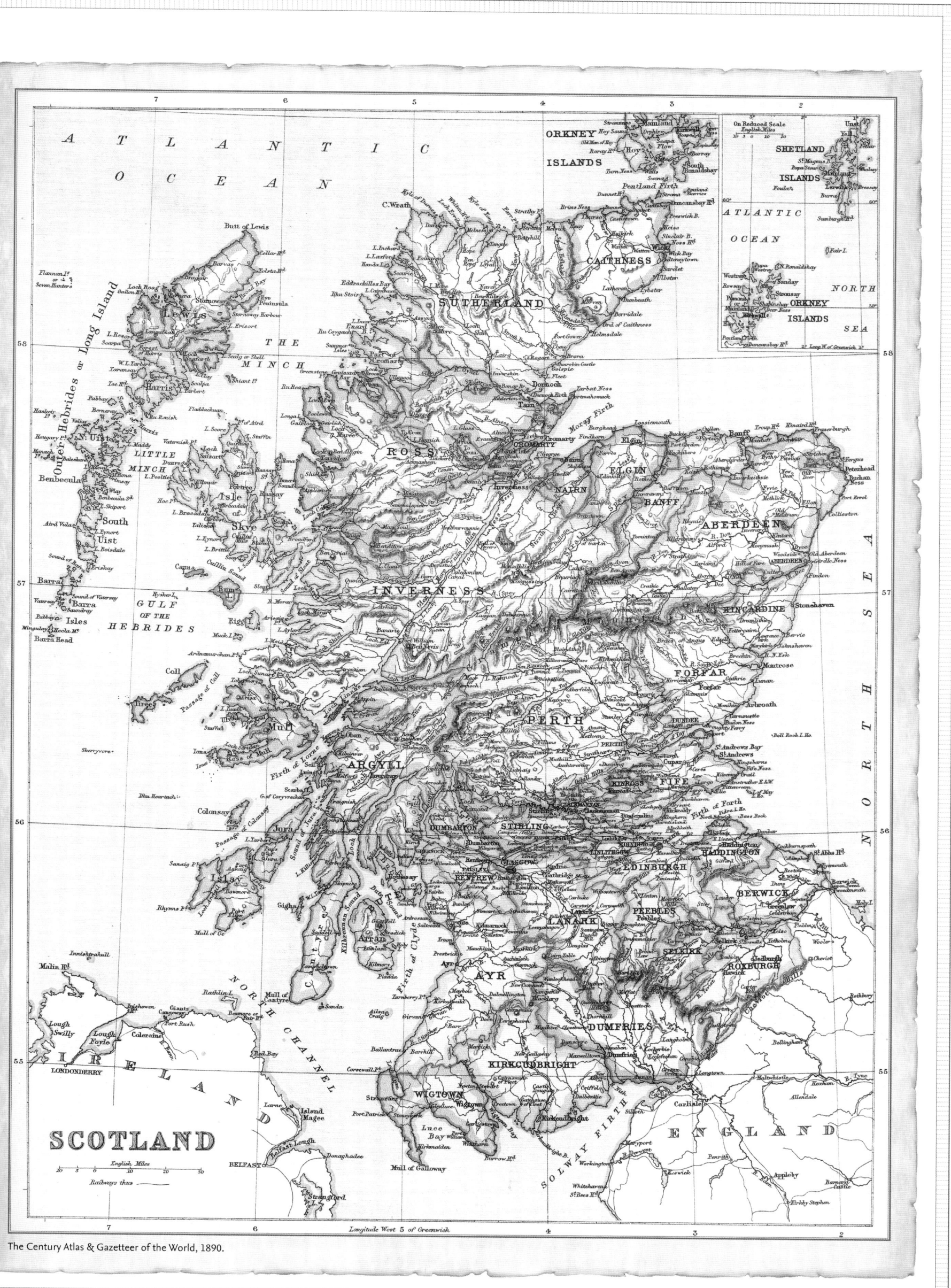

SCOTLAND

English Miles

Railways thus

The Century Atlas & Gazetteer of the World, 1890.

DUMFRIES AND GALLOWAY

Area Sq Km	6,673
Area Sq Miles	2,576
Population	148,600
Admin HQ	Dumfries
Highest point	The Merrick (843 m), in the Southern Uplands

Dumfries takes its name from the town of Dumfries derived from the Gaelic *dùn preas*, the 'woodland fort' and Galloway (*Gall Ghaidhealaibh*) means 'land of the foreign Gaels', probably those who came to the area in the 9th century.

FAMOUS FOR

Britain's first Buddhist temple was founded at **Eskdalemuir** near Langholm in 1967, and officially opened in 1988. It is the Tibetan Samye Ling, now the largest Buddhist monastery and centre in the western world, named after the first monastery to be founded in Tibet.

Distinctive red sandstone quarried from **Locharbriggs** has been used in the building of Glasgow and Edinburgh, as well as nearby Dumfries. It also was used to make the steps of the Statue of Liberty on Liberty Island in New York.

Gretna Green, a small village just north of the border, became famous in the 18th and 19th centuries for the numbers of eloping English couples married there. In Scotland, after 1754, couples only had to declare before witnesses their wish to marry, a ceremony which could be taken by anyone (traditionally the blacksmith). Over the years, residency requirements were put in place (1856), the rule on who could officiate was tightened (1940) although the age of consent is still not harmonized across the border. Still Gretna remains the venue for about 5,000 weddings a year and a whole industry has sprung up in the village to cater for them.

Sanquhar is home to Britain's oldest Post Office, opened in 1763 and still operating to this day.

Sweetheart Abbey (the Cistercian Abbey of Dulce Cor) was founded by Lady Dervorgilla of Galloway in 1273 as a memorial to her husband, John Balliol, who died in 1268. She had his heart embalmed and placed in a silver and ivory casket, which she took everywhere, and was buried in the abbey, clasping the casket.

The Roman emperor **Antoninus Pius** invested all the members of the Caledonian tribes in this region with the rights of Roman citizens, which held until their retreat in the 4th century AD.

FAMOUS PEOPLE

William Paterson, financier and founder of the Bank of England, born Tynwald, 1658.
John Paul Jones, founder of US Navy, born Kirkbean, 1747.
Thomas Telford, stonemason, architect and civil engineer, born Westerkirk, 1757.
William Jardine, surgeon, opium smuggler and Chinese trader, born Lochmaben, 1784.
Thomas Carlyle, historian and essayist, born Ecclefechan, 1795.
Hugh MacDiarmid (pseudonym of Christopher Murray Grieve), poet, born in Langholm in 1892.
John Laurie, actor, born Dumfries, 1897.
John Maxwell, painter, born Dalbeattie, 1905.
Sir James Mirrlees, economist and Nobel Prize winner, born Minnigaff, 1936.
David Coulthard, Formula 1 racing driver, born Dumfries, 1971.

Extending from the Rhins of Galloway in the west, the northern part of Dumfries and Galloway is mainly moorland and forested upland hills, sloping gently down to fertile farmlands on the Solway estuarine plain drained by the Nith, Annan and Esk rivers in the east.

The ruins of Whithorn Abbey mark the place where Christianity was brought to Galloway by St Ninian in around AD 397. Once a Gaelic-speaking kingdom, Galloway was also part of rich trading routes that brought luxury goods by sea from as far away as the Mediterranean. Since the 19th century, 'Dumfries and Galloway' has been used to describe this part of southwest Scotland, but the region was only formally created in 1975 when the traditional counties of Wigtownshire, Kirkcudbrightshire and Dumfries-shire were united in a single council area that remained unchanged following local administrative reorganisation in 1996. The administrative centre is Dumfries (31,530). Other important towns include Stranraer (10,440) and Annan (8,480), Locharbriggs (6,020), Dalbeattie (4,310), Locherbie (4,060), Castle Douglas (3,870).

The area has been invaded and settled by many groups, including the Romans, Scots (who actually came from Ireland) and Vikings, and was only really incorporated into Scotland by Alexander II in 1234. Geographically remote from the capital in Edinburgh, Dumfries and Galloway's proximity to a constantly shifting border with England meant that for nearly three centuries these 'debatable lands' along the Solway Firth were controlled by rapacious border clans, the Border 'reivers' with predictable results.

Situated at the most southerly crossing point of the river Nith, the market town of Dumfries received its charter as a royal burgh in 1186 from William the Lio The town once had a castle and several monasteries, including the Franciscan friary where Robert the Bruce infamously murdered John Comyn in 1306. Its strategic location meant that Dumfries suffered th attentions of more than the usual number of invadin English armies over the course of several centuries, headed by leaders ranging from Edward I to the Duke of Cumberland. Undeterred, the town took advantage of the Union of 1707 to trade in tobacco to England and across the Atlantic and in livestock, including the famous Belted Galloway breed. Although the 19th-century heavy industrialisation, which characterised much of central Scotland mostly, bypassed the county, textile mills were established, particularly for tweed.

The population of 148,600 is modest for the third largest administrative area in Scotland, but this reflec its mainly rural nature. Much of the local economy is based on forestry and agriculture, predominantly dairying. Service industries, however, provide the greatest employment in the area, particularly in publi administration, education and health (30.9 per cent). The area has a number of nature reserves as well as the Galloway Forest Park, where there is so little light pollution that it has been designated Britain's first Dark Sky Park, neatly combining two key industries. Employment in tourism (12 per cent) reflects the ma attractions in the area, but the industry is hindered by limited communications, with the West Coast mainli and the M74 motorway passing along the eastern frin while the ferry routes to Ireland from Stranraer and Cairnryan are somewhat isolated.

Belted Galloway calves

The Old Blacksmith's shop, Gretna Green.

Bridge across the river Nith at Dumfries.

DUMFRIES AND GALLOWAY, 1885

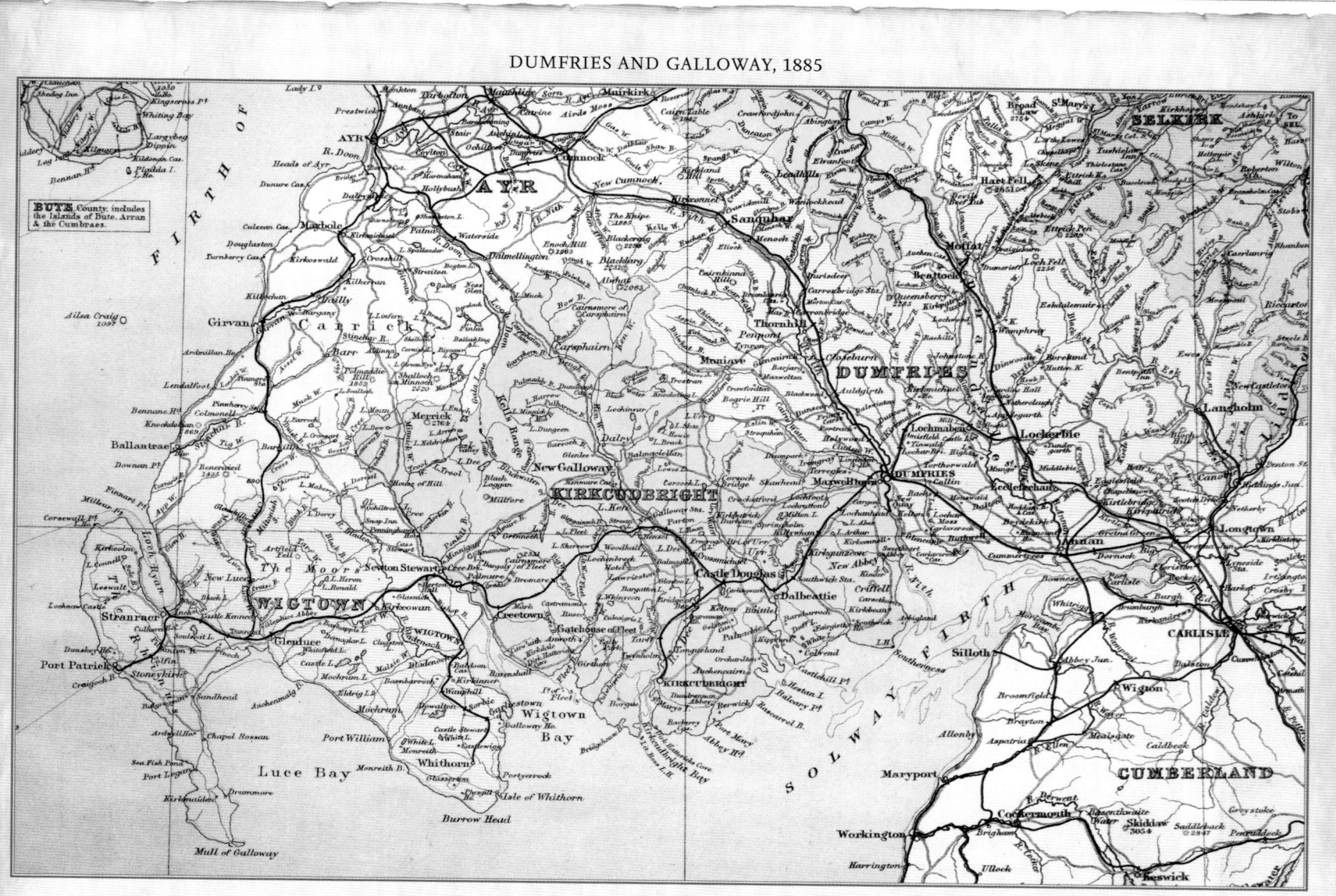

Bartholomew Gazetteer of the British Isles, 1887

WIGTOWNSHIRE, *a maritime co. in SW. extremity of Scotland, forming the W. division of Galloway; is bounded N. by Ayrshire and the mouth of the Firth of Clyde, E. by Kirkcudbrightshire, S. by the Irish Sea, and W. by the Irish Channel; greatest length, E. and W., 30 miles; greatest breadth, N. and S., 28 miles; area, 310,742 ac., pop. 38,611. The coast, about 120 miles in extent, is for the most part bold and rocky; the chief headlands are Burrow Head, the Mull of Galloway (the most southerly land in Scotland), and Corsewall Point. The interior is divided into three great districts – the double peninsula W. of Loch Ryan and Luce Bay, known as the Rhinns of Galloway; the peninsula between Luce Bay and Wigtown, called the Machers; and the Moors, in the N. of the co. The surface is mostly low and moderately level, except in the Moors, which are hilly, and abound in mosses. There is much excellent arable land in the Rhinns and the Machers. The chief streams are the Cree, which flows along the E. boundary, the Bladenoch, and Luce Water. Lochs are numerous, but small. Agriculture, dairy-farming, and sheep-farming afford the chief employments. The co. comprises 17 pars., the police burghs of Newton-Stewart, Stranraer, and Whithorn, and the royal burgh of Wigtown.*

KIRKCUDBRIGHTSHIRE, *maritime co. in S. of Scotland; is bounded NW. by Ayrshire, NE. by Dumfriesshire, SE. by the Solway Firth, and SW. by Wigtownshire; greatest length, NW. and SE., 46 miles; greatest breadth, NE. and SW., 31 miles; 574,587 ac., pop. 42,127. Kirkcudbrightshire is also known as the "Stewartry of Kirkcudbright" and "East Galloway." The coast line, which extends, in semicircular form, from the head of Wigtown Bay to the mouth of the Nith, a distance of 45 miles, is in general bold and precipitous, but is broken by the estuaries of the Nith, the Urr, the Dee, the Fleet, and the Cree, which form natural harbours, the principal seaports being Kirkcudbright, Gatehouse-of-Fleet, and Creetown. In the NW. the co. is mountainous, with deep glens, and numerous small lochs; in the SE. – except in the extreme SE. corner – it is for the most part level but undulating. Most of the soil in the higher regions is moorland and marsh; in the lower it is better suited for grass and green crops than for grain, and great attention is paid to the rearing of cattle. Granite is quarried, and lead, iron, and copper exist, but are little worked. The mfrs. comprise linen, cotton, and woollen goods, and paper. Deep-sea fishing is carried on in the Solway Firth, and salmon-fishing at the mouths of the rivers, especially the Dee and the Urr. The co. contains 28 pars., the royal burgh of Kirkcudbright, the royal burgh of New Galloway, and the police burghs of Castle Douglas, Dalbeattie, Gatehouse, and Maxwelltown.*

DUMFRIES-SHIRE, *maritime co., on S. border of Scotland; adjoins the cos. of Lanark, Peebles, and Selkirk on the N., and on the S. is washed by the Solway Firth; extends about 53 miles NW. and SE. between Ayrshire and Cumberland, and about 32 miles NE. and SW. between Roxburghshire and Kirkcudbrightshire; coast-line, about 20 miles; area, 680,217 ac., pop. 76,140, or 72 persons to each sq. mile. The surface in general is bare and hilly. The dales of the Nith, Annan, and Esk, however, are rich in beauty, and contain fine holms for pasture and some good arable land. The rivers are numerous, and yield splendid salmon and trout fishing. The coast and S. region is low and sandy; much of it is covered with morass, and lochs are numerous around Lockerbie; but there is also much excellent corn-growing land. The Lowther or Lead Hills along the N. boundary are upwards of 2000 ft. in height, and abound in lead ore. These and the other hills round the borders are mostly smooth in outline, and afford excellent pasturage. Red sandstone is a prevailing rock, and limestone, coal, and lead, are worked. The co. comprises 41 pars, with 2 parts, the parl. burghs of Annan, Dumfries (greater part), Lochmaben and Sanquhar; and the police burghs of Annan, Dumfries, Lochmaben, Lockerbie, and Moffat.*

"Oh the Galloway" hills are covered wi' broom,
Wi' heather bells, in bonnie bloom;
Wi' heather bells an' rivers a',
An' I'll gang oot ower the hills to Galloway".
Traditional

"Burns has been cruelly used, both dead and alive…
It is worse than ridiculous to see the people of Dumfries
coming forward with their pompous mausoleum."
William Wordsworth

"That last mentioned castle [Caerlaverock] has been
a very magnificent structure though now, like its owner,
in a state of ruin and decay."
William Defoe, 1726

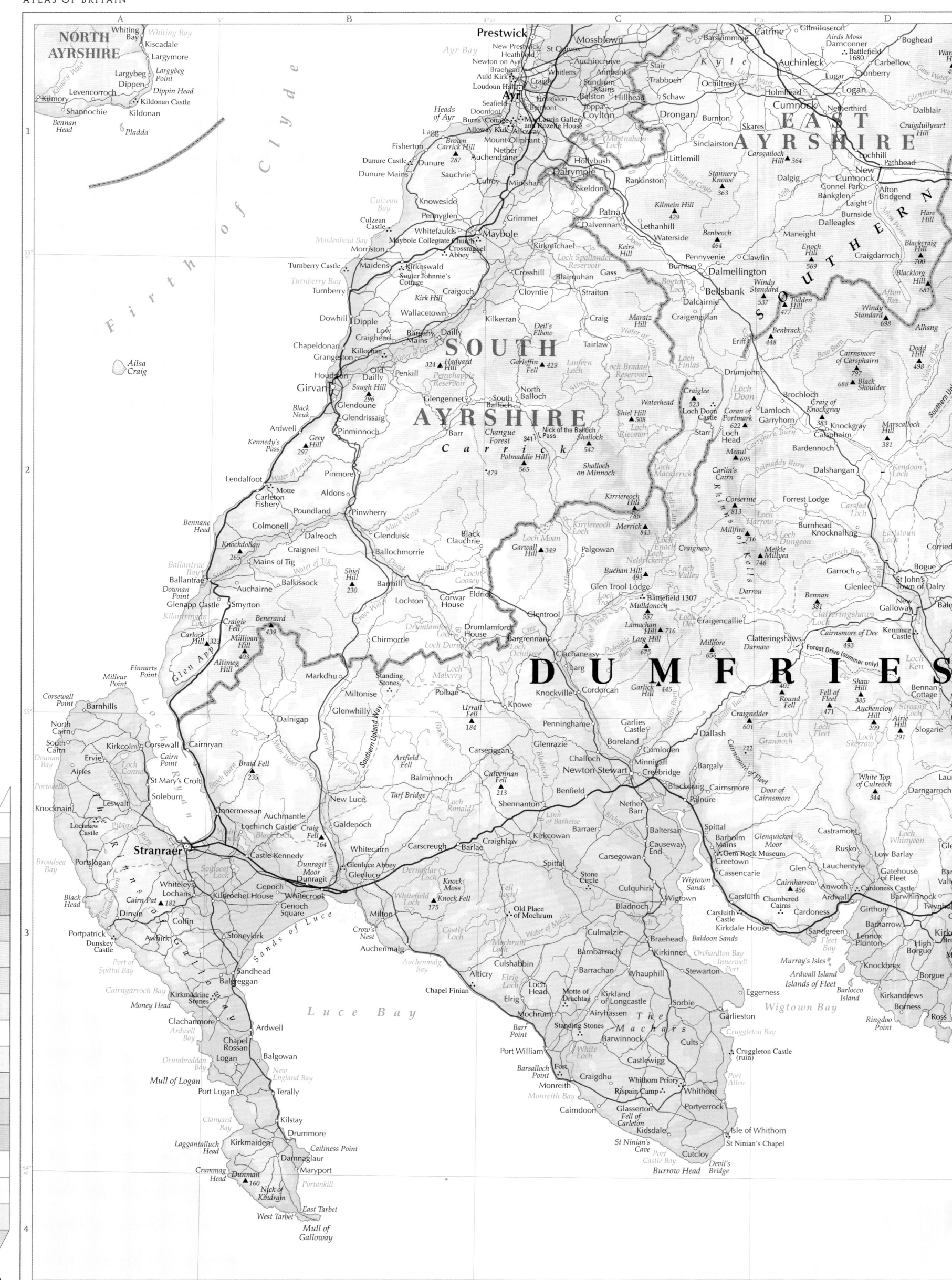

NORTH AYRSHIRE

Whiting Bay
Kiscadale
Largymore
Largybeg Point
Levencorroch Dippen
Dippin Head
Kilmory Shannochie Kildonan Castle Kildonan
Bennan Head
Pladda

Firth of Clyde

Prestwick
New Prestwick
Heathfield
Newton on Ayr St Quivox
Braehead
Auld Kirk
Loudoun Hall
Ayr
Seafield
Doonfoot
Burns Cottage
Alloway Kirk Alloway
Mount Oliphant
Nether
Heads of Ayr
Lagg
Fisherton
Carrick Hill 287
Dunure Castle Dunure
Dunure Mains Sauchrie
Culzean Bay
Culzean Castle
Whitefaulds
Morriston Maybole Collegiate Church
Maybole
Maidenhead Bay
Turnberry Castle Maidens
Kirkoswald
Souter Johnnie's Cottage
Turnberry Bay
Turnberry
Dowhill
Dipple
Chapeldonan Low Craighead
Grangeston Killochan
Houdston
Girvan Old Dailly
Saugh Hill 296
Penkill
Glendoune
Black Neuk
Ardwell
Grey Hill 297
Glendrissaig
Pinminnoch
Kennedy's Pass
Lendalfoot
Motte
Carleton Fishery
Bennane Head
Colmonell
Poundland
Knockdolian 265
Craigneil
Ballantrae Bay
Ballantrae
Mains of Tig
Downan Point
Auchairne Balkissock
Glenapp Castle Smyrton
Kilantringan
Craigie Fell
Benneraird 439
Carlock Hill 323
Milljoan Hill 403
Altimeg Hill
Milleur Point
Corsewall Point
Barnhills
North Cairn
South Cairn
Downan Bay
Ervie Airies
Portobello
Knocknain
Lochnaw Castle
Leswalt
Kirkcolm Corsewall
Cairn Point
St Mary's Croft
Soleburn
Innermessan
Stranraer
Loch Connell
Portslogan
Whiteleys Lochans
Black Head
Cairn Pat 182
Dinvin
Colfin
Portpatrick
Dunskey Castle
Awhirk
Port of Spittal Bay
Sandhead
Balgreggan
Kirkmadrine Stones
Money Head
Clachanmore
Chapel Rossan
Logan
Mull of Logan
Port Logan
Broadsea Bay
Cairngarroch Bay
Ardwell Bay
Drumbreddan Bay
New England Bay
Clanyard Bay
Laggantalluch Head
Crammag Head
Dunman 160
Kirkmaiden
Drummore
Damnaglaur
Maryport
Portankill
West Tarbet East Tarbet
Mull of Galloway
Nick of Kindram

SOUTH AYRSHIRE

Knoweside
Pennyglen
Crossraguel Abbey
Crosshill
Craigoch
Kirk Hill
Wallacetown
Bargany Mains Dailly
Hadyard Hill 324
Penwhapple Reservoir
Barr
Changue Forest
Glengennet
Polmaddie Hill 565 341
Pinmore
Aldons
Pinwherry
Dalreoch
Glenduisk
Ballochmorrie
Shiel Hill 230
Barnhill
Lochton
Corwar House
Chirmorrie
Markdhu
Miltonise
Glenwhilly
Dalnigap

Carrick

Penkill
South Balloch
North Balloch
Garleffin Fell 429
Linfern Loch
Loch Bradan Reservoir
Deil's Elbow
Black Clauchrie
Garwally Hill 349
Palgowan
Glen Trool Lodge
Glentrool
Bargrennan
Clachaneasy
Larg
Drumlamford House

Southern Upland Way

Standing Stones
Polbae
Urrall Fell 184
Knowe
Knockville
Cordorcan
Penninghame
Carseriggan
Artfield Fell
Balminnoch
New Luce
Tarf Bridge
Galdenoch
Whitecairn
Castle Kennedy
Dunragit Moor
Dunragit
Glenluce Abbey
Glenluce
Kildrochet House
Whitecrook
Genoch Square
Milton
Crow's Nest
Auchenmalg
Chapel Finian
Elrig
Barsalloch Point
Monreith
Monreith Bay

EAST AYRSHIRE

Mossblown
Auchincruive
Stair
Annbank
Sundrum Mains
Belston
Coylton
Hollybush
Rankinston
Skeldon
Grimmet
Dalrymple
Minishant
Sauchrie
Kirkmichael
Cloyntie
Straiton
Tairlaw
Maratz Hill
Craigengillan
Dalmellington
Bellsbank
Dalcairnie
Craig
Eriff
Shalloch on Minnoch 542
Waterhead
Shiel Loch 508
Loch Doon Castle
Starr
Loch Head
Meaul 695
Carlin's Cairn
Corserine 813
Forrest Lodge
Millfire 716
Burnhead
Knocknalling
Merrick 843
Kirriereoch Hill 786
Kirriereoch Loch
Meikle Millyea 746
Loch Enoch
Neldricken
Craignaw
Buchan Hill 493
Loch Valley
Glen Trool
Battlefield 1307
Mulldonoch 557
Lamachan Hill 716
Larg Hill 675
Millfore 656
Millfore
Clatteringshaws Darnaw
Forest Drive (summer only)
Craignelder 601
Garlick Hill 445
Round Fell
Fell of Fleet 471
Shaw Hill 385
Auchencloy Hill 209
Airie Hill 291
Slogarie
Cordorcan
Garlies Castle
Boreland
Cumloden
Dallash
Glenrazie
Newton Stewart
Creebridge
Minnigaff
Bargaly
Culvennan Fell 213
Benfield
Shennanton
Nether Barr
Barraer
Challoch
Cairnsmore
Blackcraig
Palnure
Cassencarie
Benfield
Kirkcowan
Craiglaw
Barlae
Craighlaw
Spittal
Carscreugh
Barnbarroch
Knock Fell 175
Whitefield Loch
Dernaglar Loch
Old Place of Mochrum
Bladnoch
Culmalzie
Barrachan
Whauphill
Stewarton
Kirkinner
Wigtown
Causeway End
Carsegowan
Stone Circle
Culquhirk
Braehead
Kirkland of Longcastle
Airyhassen
Mochrum
Elrig
Motte of Druchtag
Port William
Barwinnock
Fort
Craigdhu
Rispain Camp
Cairndoon
Glasserton
Fell of Carleton
Kidsdale
St Ninian's Cave
Cults
Sorbie
Garlieston
Cruggleton Castle (ruin)
Castlewigg
Whithorn Priory
Whithorn
Portyerrock
Cutcloy
Isle of Whithorn
St Ninian's Chapel
Burrow Head
Devil's Bridge

Loch Doon
Loch Riecawr
Loch Macaterick
Loch Dee
Loch Trool
Loch Ochiltree
Loch Maberry
Loch Ronald
Loch Moan
Loch Goosey
Loch Dornal
Loch Maberry
Loch Ken
Clatteringshaws Loch
Carsfad Loch
Earlstoun Loch
Loch Harrow
Loch Dungeon
Loch Grannoch
Loch Fleet
Loch Skerrow
Loch Whinyeon
Wigtown Sands
Wigtown Bay
Baldoon Sands
Luce Bay
Sands of Luce
Sea of Moyle
Rhins of Galloway
Machars
The Machars
Orchardton Bay
Innerwell Port
Ardwall Island
Islands of Fleet
Barlocco Island
Murray's Isles
Ringdoo Point
Cruggleton Bay
Rhins of Kells

DUMFRIES

Ailsa Craig

Metres Feet

1000	3280
900	2952
800	2624
700	2296
600	1968
500	1640
400	1312
300	4921
200	656
150	492
100	328
50	164
0	Land below sea level
50	164
200	656
1000	3281

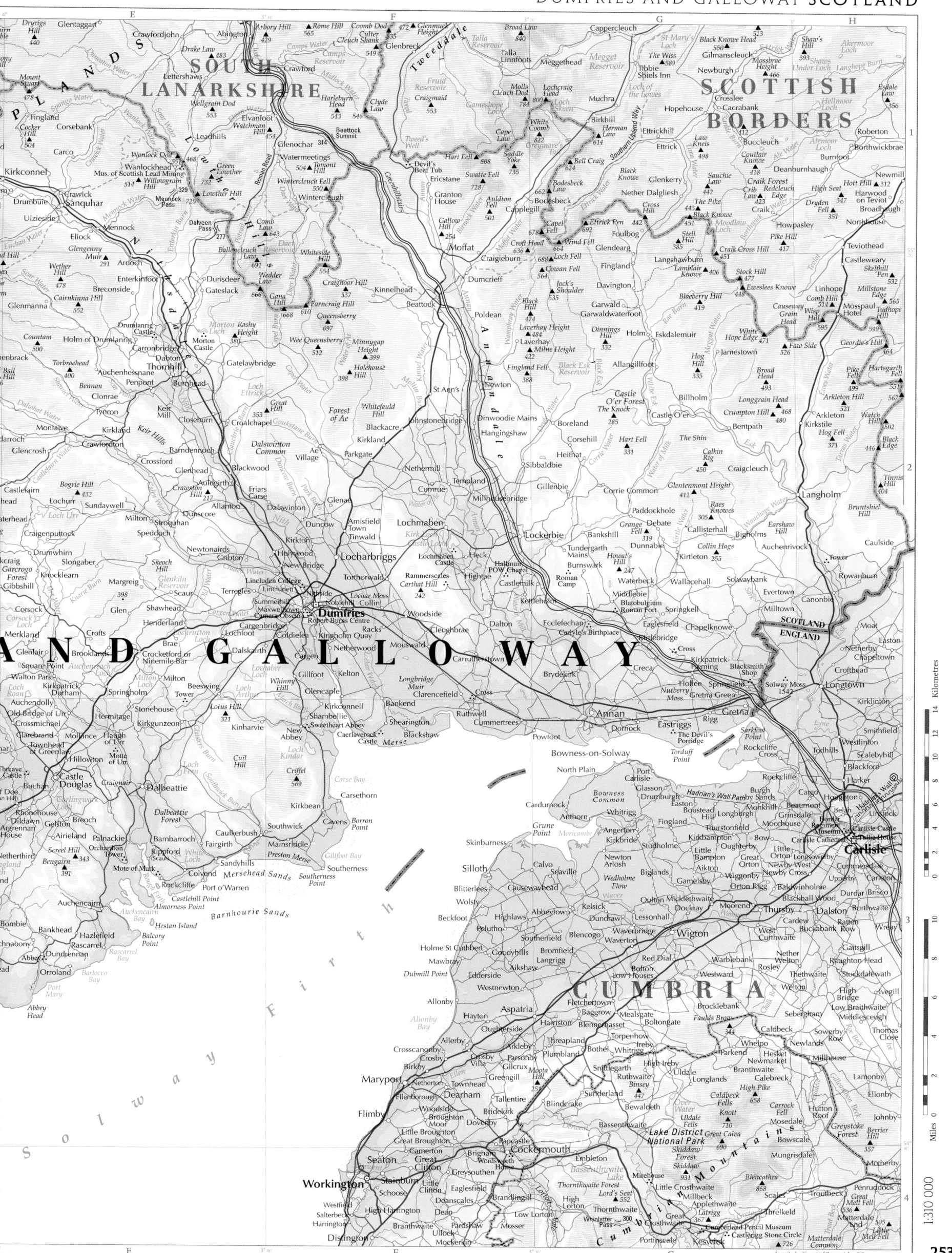

1:310 000

© Collins Bartholomew Ltd

SCOTTISH BORDERS

Area Sq Km	4,743
Area Sq Miles	1,831
Population	112,400
Admin HQ	Newtown St Boswells
Highest point	Broad Law (840 m) near Tweedsmuir

The Scottish Borders incorporates historical counties redolent of Scotland's history: Berwickshire, Selkirkshire, Roxburghshire and Peeblesshire, all of which were incorporated into this administrative unit in 1975 and left intact in the later reorganisation of 1996.

FAMOUS FOR

King Robert I was buried with other Scottish kings at Dunfermline Abbey in 1326. It was always alleged that his heart was taken on crusade against the Moors in Spain with Sir James Douglas. Traditionally, it was then returned to Scotland and buried at **Melrose Abbey**. Excavations in the abbey's Chapter House by Historic Scotland in 1996 revealed a small lead container inside a larger heart-shaped casket. An engraved copper plaque recorded that a 1921 excavation had opened it and discovered it contained 'a heart'.

A long tradition of independence in the traditional counties is expressed in the **Common Ridings** which take place each year, often to re-establish territorial boundaries or to mark particular historical occasions. In 1996, the **Hawick Common Riding** allowed women to participate on horseback for the first time.

Just south of Melrose are the triple peaks of the **Eildon Hills**. There was a fort at the top of North Eildon over 3,000 years ago and the Romans built the fort of Trimontium (three peaks) at their foot. It is said that Thomas the Rhymer met the Fairy Queen here and the hills are the entrance to the Fairy Kingdom and that King Arthur and his Court are asleep under the hill.

Traquair House, near Peebles, dates from the early 12th century and is one of Scotland's oldest inhabited houses. The Stuarts of Traquair supported the Jacobite cause, and tradition has it that a set of gates closed after Bonnie Prince Charlie left the house in 1745 would only be reopened when there was a Stuart king crowned in London.

When the Edinburgh & Hawick Railway company were deciding the route along the Tweed valley in 1849, the original plan was to bring the train through **St Boswells**, and to build a station on the famous Green, reputedly the largest in Scotland. However, the Buccleuch Hunt objected strongly, because their foxhound kennels overlooked the Green, so the company re-routed the tracks through **Newtown St Boswells** instead, guaranteeing the village's prosperity for generations.

FAMOUS PEOPLE

Sir John Pringle, physician and reformer, born Roxburgh, 1701.
James Hogg (also called the 'Ettrick Shepherd'), poet, born near Ettrick, 1770.
Mungo Park, African explorer, born Foulshiels, 1771.
Mary Somerville, mathematician and astronomer, born Jedburgh, 1780.
William Chambers, publisher, born Peebles, 1800.
Andrew Lang, writer and collector of fairy tales, born Selkirk, 1844.
Sir Charles (Chay) Blyth, yachtsman, born Hawick, 1940.

The Borders is a hilly region at the eastern end of the Southern Uplands, much of which is upland moorland, with river valleys running mainly north to south, draining into the river Tweed, which form a flat plain (the 'Merse') running towards the North Sea coast in the east. The principal rivers are the Tweed and its major tributaries, especially Ettrick Water and the Teviot.

The Borders, with its low population density is administered from a small centre at Newtown St Boswells (1,200). Other important towns include Eyemouth (3,320), Coldstream (2,050) and Duns (2,710) in the east, Hawick (14,120) and Jedburgh (3,860) to the south west, and Peebles (8,120), Innerleithen (2,910), Galashiels (14,090), Selkirk (5,610), Melrose (2,080) and Kelso (5,380), a cluster of central and northern towns roughly following the course of the Tweed.

'The Borders' or 'Marches' referred to lands in both Scotland and England on either side of a fluid divide that has been much contested. The Romans established a fort, Trimontium, in the lee of the Eildon Hills, in the 1st century AD, territory they held for a century. This fertile area with its salmon rivers and forests proved irresistible to the Danes in the 9th century, and was constantly fought over, or through. By the 12th century, it was not uncommon for nobles to own land on both sides of the border, and this was equally true of the princes of the Church. Different monastic orders established the four great Border abbeys: Jedburgh (1118), Kelso (1128), Melrose (1136) and Dryburgh (1152). All were patronised by the leading nobles of the day, and eventually brought to ruin principally by English armies. Local families, many famous as Border 'reivers' and making a living cattle thieving, have left a legacy of castles and tower houses.

Newtown St Boswells is, typically, not 'new' at all – there has been a community on this site since the Middle Ages, and it has also thrived under a number of different names such as Newtown of Eildon and Newtown of Dryburgh. It is, unsurprisingly, often confused with St Boswells, 1.5 km to the west, and bo[th] were connected to the great abbey of Melrose. The monks of the monastery patronised the grain mills a[t] Newtown powered by the local burns, including the Bowden Burn. Originally a small agricultural village, the advent of the railway in the 19th century created a railway junction here for transporting the goods, including livestock, produced in this fertile area. It is also the railway that gave the village its modern name, calling its station 'St Boswells', to which custo[m] appended its original appellation. By the turn of the century, due to its excellent rail links, it became a tow[n] of increasing importance in Roxburghshire, although not the county seat (which was at Jedburgh). Modern reorganisations in 1975 made it the centre of the loca[l] district in Borders Region.

Fishing remains a principal activity in the county['s] coastal villages, and Eyemouth received EU funding in 1997 to facilitate the construction of a deep-water extension to the harbour. Forestry and farming are also important in this predominantly rural economy. Traditionally, many of the larger towns, like Galashie[ls] and Hawick, developed in association with the manufacture of textiles and knitwear. More recently, electronics and light engineering have contributed to the local economy. Overall, the service industries are the greatest employers. Public administration, education and health (31.1 per cent) and retail, hotels and restaurants (24.7 per cent) account for nearly half of these, but transport and communications (currentl[y] 3.3 per cent) may experience a boost when the Waverl[ey] Railway from Edinburgh to Tweedbank opens in 2014 reconnecting the Borders to Edinburgh by train for t[he] first time since 1969.

Melrose Abbey

Floors Castle, Kelso.

River Tweed at Coldstream

SCOTTISH BORDERS, 1885

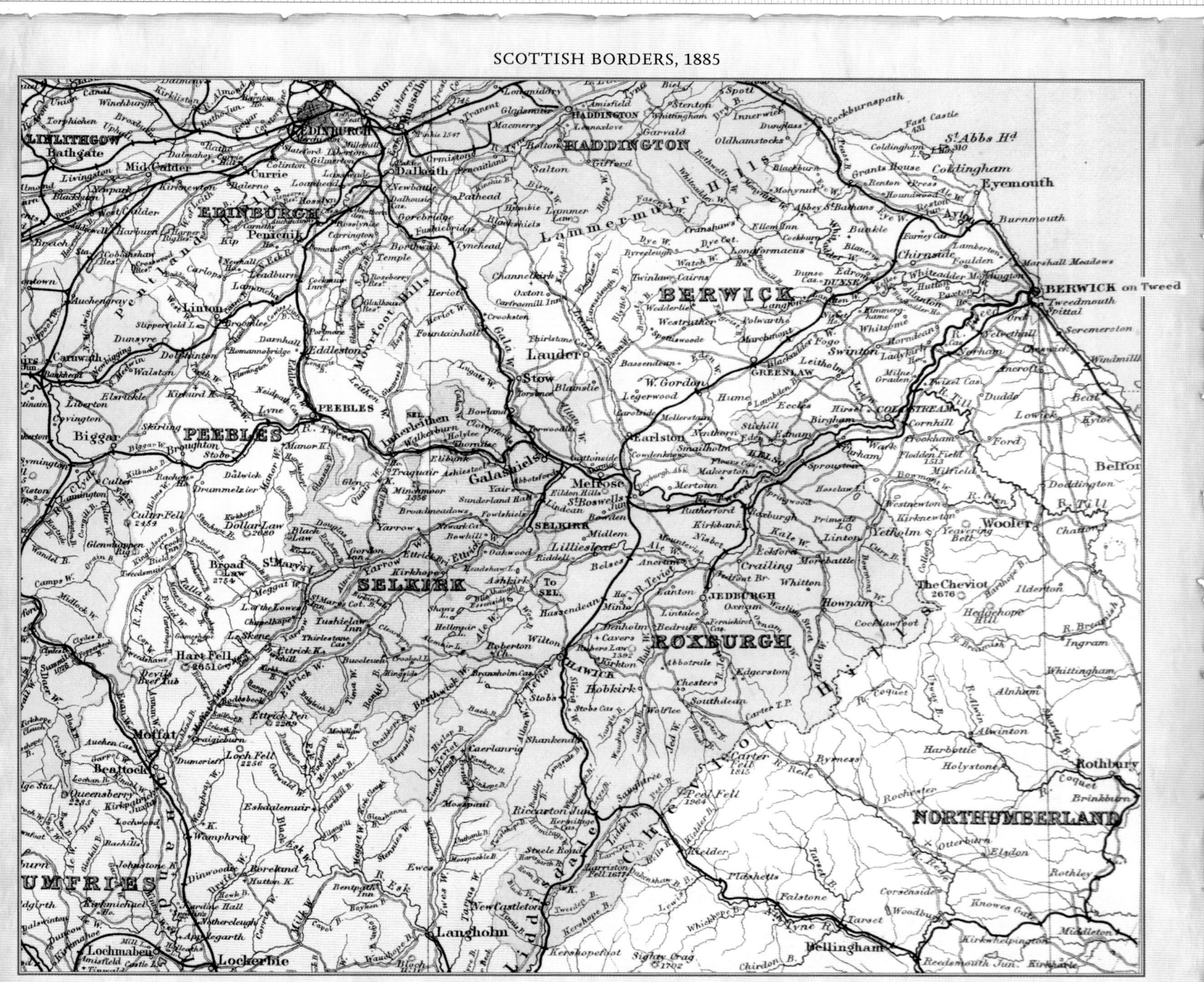

Bartholomew Gazetteer of the British Isles, 1887

PEEBLESSHIRE (or Tweeddale), an inland co. in the SE. of Scotland, bounded N. and NE. by Edinburghshire, E. and SE. by Selkirkshire, S. by Dumfriesshire, and W. by Lanarkshire; greatest length, N. and S., 29 miles; greatest breadth, B. and W., 21 miles; area, 226,890 ac., pop. 13,822. From the narrow central valley of the Tweed the surface rises into hills and mountains, with fertile valleys or deep gorges between the ridges. The hills for the most part are grassy and softly rounded. The highest summit is Broad Law, 2723 ft., near the S. border. The streams in the glens and valleys afford good angling. Blue clay slate has been extensively worked, limestone is abundant, and coal is mined to some extent in the N. of the co. Sheep-farming is the main industry. The woollen mfr. is carried on at Peebles, Innerleithen, and Walkerburn. The co. comprises 12 pars., with parts of 4 others, and the police burghs of Peebles and Innerleithen.

SELKIRKSHIRE, an inland co. in the SE. of Scotland; is bounded N. by Edinburghshire, E. by Roxburghshire, S. by Dumfriesshire, and W. by Peeblesshire; greatest length, NE. and SW., 28 miles; greatest breadth, NW. and SE., 17 miles; area, 164,545 ac., pop. 25,564. The surface, rising in a succession of verdant uplands or heath-clad hills, is from 300 to 2433 ft. above sea-level. The country in early times was covered with woods, and, known as Ettrick Forest, was long a royal hunting-ground. The river Tweed flows through the N. part of the co., and affords good salmon fishing. Ettrick Water and Yarrow Water flow from SW. to NE. in parallel courses, and unite before entering the Tweed. The vales of these streams are rich in beauty and historical associations. The lochs are numerous but small; the largest is St Mary's Loch, at the head of Yarrow Water. Selkirkshire is more pastoral than agricultural, and has a light soil on the arable land. The woollen manufacture is the great industry of Selkirk and Galashiels. The co. comprises 2 pars, with parts of 9 others, the police burgh of Selkirk and the greater part of the police burgh of Galashiels.

ROXBURGHSHIRE, inland co., in S. of Scotland, bounded N. by Berwickshire, NE. and SE. by Northumberland and Cumberland, SW. by Dumfriesshire, and NW. by Selkirkshire and Edinburghshire; greatest length, N. and S., 42 miles; greatest breadth, E. and W., 30 miles; area, 425,657 ac., pop. 53,442. The main body of the co., or three-fourths of the whole area, belongs to the basin of the Teviot; hence the general name of Teviotdale is sometimes used for Roxburghshire. The upper portions of Teviotdale and its tributary vales, rising by gently sloping and well rounded ridges from the banks of the streams to the watershed of the Cheviots, are chiefly bare and pastoral, but the lower portions consist of rich and well wooded valleys. The district in the N., lying between Gala Water and Leader Water, is partly upland, but is nearly all cultivated; the tract immediately N. of the Tweed is almost level, and belongs to the Merse; while the district in the extreme SW., known as Liddesdale, is chiefly pastoral, and is bounded by lofty hill ridges. Every vale abounds in rich and lovely scenery, and there is scarcely a spot without some interesting historical association. The principal streams which flow to the Teviot are the Borthwick, Ale, Slitrig, Rule, Jed, Oxnam, and Kale. The Liddel joins the Esk before it enters the Solway Firth. Farming is the great industry, and is in a highly advanced state. The woollen mfr. is extensively carried on at Hawick. The co. comprises 29 pars, with parts of 6 others, the police burgh of Hawick, and the police burghs of Jedburgh and Kelso.

BERWICKSHIRE, a maritime co. in the extreme SE. of Scotland, extending in extreme breadth about 20 m. between Haddingtonsh. and the English border, and in extreme length about 33 m. between Roxburgsh. and the German Ocean; coast-line about 20 miles; area, 460.6 sq. m., or 296,362 ac.; pop. 35,392, or 77 persons to each sq. m. The coast is high and rocky, and the few but important fishing harbs. are much exposed. St Abbs Head is the main projection. The Lammermuir Hills, to the average breadth of 7 m., occupy all the N.; a bleak and mostly moorland tract of 5 m. in breadth, but somewhat diversified towards the E., succeeds; and the luxuriant and fertile district, called the Merse, slopes from this to the banks of the Tweed. The district of Lauderdale, on the W., is chiefly upland. The Tweed traces about half of the S. boundary, and receives the Leader, Eden, Leet, and the Whiteadder (with its affl. the Blackadder). The Eye enters the German Ocean at Eyemouth. The lands on Tweedside are in a very high state of cultivation; the rest of the co. is chiefly pastoral. The fisheries, both on the coast and in the Tweed, are among the most important in Scotland. The co. comprises 31 pars. and parts of 2 others, and the police burghs of Coldstream, Duns, Eyemouth, and Lauder.

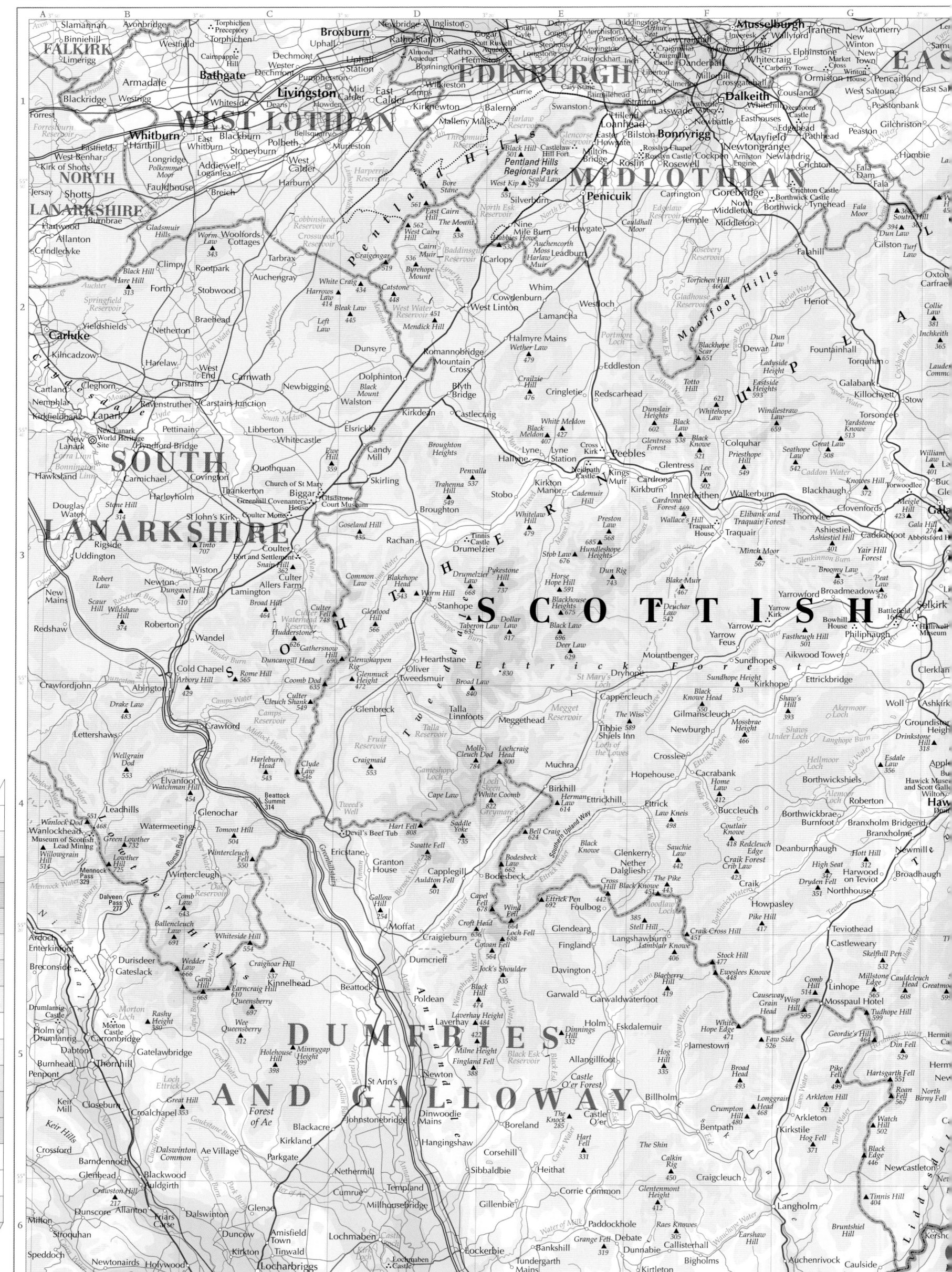

British National Grid projection

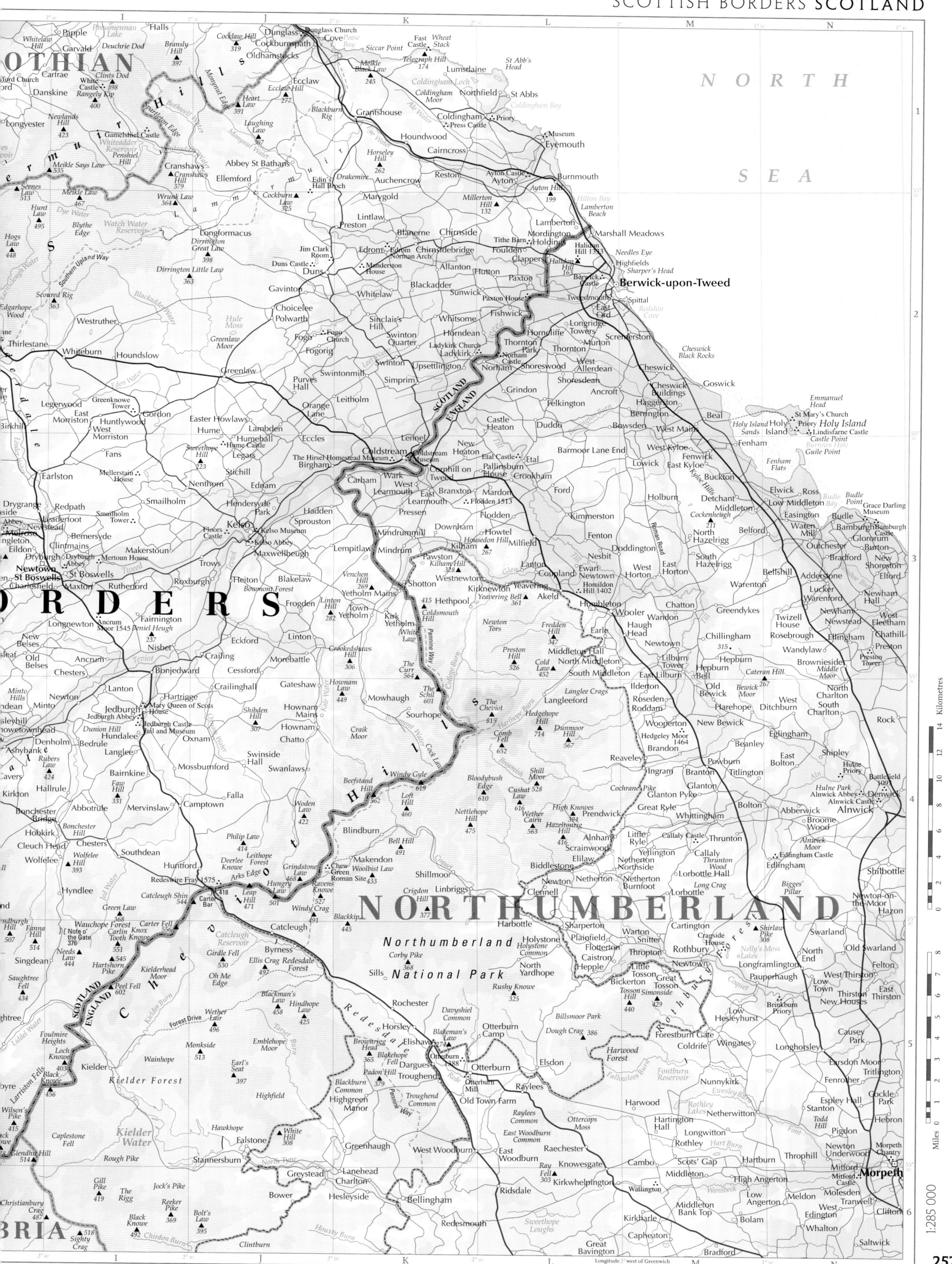

EAST AYRSHIRE

Area Sq Km	1,270
Area Sq Miles	490
Population	119,900
Admin HQ	Kilmarnock
Highest point	Blackcraig Hill (700 m)

East Ayrshire or *Siorrachd Inbhir Àir an Ear* ('the territory by the Ayr estuary') is the eastern section of the historic county of Ayrshire.

FAMOUS FOR

The first edition of the poems of Robert Burns was printed in **Kilmarnock** in 1786. The four-legged inspiration for his 'To a Mouse' was turned up when ploughing his field in Mossgiel Farm, outside **Mauchline**.

Cumnock was once home to a rather unusual industry, the making of snuffboxes. Around 100 people made these tiny decorated wooden boxes for storing ground tobacco.

When the north end of **Loch Doon** was dammed, the 8 m rise in water level threatened historic Loch Doon Castle, originally built on a rocky island. Rather than have it submerged, much of this ancient monument was relocated onto the shore.

Dumfries House, just outside Cumnock is one of the finest early works of the Adam brothers and was built in 1754–60. It still contains the original Chippendale furniture purchased for the house, which has been open to the public since 2007, when it was bought by the Great Steward of Scotland's, Dumfries House Trust.

FAMOUS PEOPLE

John Dalrymple, 1st Earl of Stair, born in Kyle in 1648.
Charles Tennant, chemist and industrialist, born Ochiltree in 1768.
John Boyd Orr (later Lord Boyd Orr), physician and Nobel Peace Prize winner, was born in Kilmaurs in 1880.
Sir Alexander Fleming, physician and discoverer of penicillin, born near Darvel in 1881.
John Grierson, documentary film maker, born in Kilmarnock in 1898.
William McIlvanney, poet and novelist, born Kilmarnock in 1936.

"But when I came roun' by Mauchline town,
Not dreadin anybody,
My heart was caught, before I thought,
And by a Mauchline lady."
Robert Burns

I'm gaun to Mauchline Holy Fair,
To spend an hour in daffin:
Robert Burns

East Ayrshire is a predominantly rural, agricultural, and in some cases remote, area, stretching from the moorlands around Loch Doon and the Galloway Forest in the Southern Uplands, north to rolling agricultural landscapes in the Central Lowlands. The principal rivers are the Irvine with its tributary Annick Water, the river Doon, and river Ayr. It is the eastern part of the traditional county of Ayrshire. After 1975, this area covered two districts of Strathclyde Region (Kilmarnock and Loudoun and Cumnock and Doon Valley), only becoming a separate administrative unit in 1996. Its population of 119,900 has shown a steady decrease since the 1981 census. Kilmarnock (44,030) is the administrative centre, and by far the largest town, and other important towns are Stewarton (6,590) Galston (4,900), Darvel (3,620) and Newmilns (3,070) towards the north, with Cumnock (9,020), Mauchline (4,020) and Auchinleck (3,650) in the central part of the area.

Kilmarnock received its charter as a burgh in 1591 under the auspices of the Boyd family, but it was not until the 18th century that it became closely associated with the manufacture of textiles, particularly woollens, as well as knives and shoes. Other industries followed engineering and iron founding, building of locomotives and carpet making. Whisky distilling under the Johnnie Walker label was established in 1820, while malting, blending and bottling was well established by 1907. The parent company's decision to move the bottling plant away from Kilmarnock was a blow to employment in the town.

Many of the villages and towns in East Ayrshire developed in the 19th century, particularly in association with coal mining, iron founding and textile manufacturing. There are still open-cast coal mines in operation near Cumnock. The majority of the heavy industry is gone, but manufacturing and construction are still important employers (15.7 per cent). Stewarton and other northern villages benefit from both a railway and trunk road link to Glasgow. By far the largest number of jobs in the area are found in the service industries, particularly public administration, education and health (34.1 per cent). Further south, Mauchline has associations with Robert Burns, who was a tenant farmer in the area, and agriculture, particularly dairy farming, continue to be important locally.

Loch Doon Castle

Dumfries House, Cumnock.

OUTH AYRSHIRE

rea Sq Km	1,235
rea Sq Miles	477
opulation	111,700
dmin HQ	Ayr
ighest point	Kirriereoch Hill (786 m) in the Southern Uplands

outh Ayrshire or *Siorrachd Inbhir Àir a Deas* ('the rritory by the Ayr estuary') is the southern section f the historic county of Ayrshire.

AMOUS FOR

am 'O Shanter and Souter Johnnie were real men, eighbours in **Kirkoswald** by the names of Douglas raham and John Davidson, well known for enjoying arket days in **Ayr** and arriving home late, worse for ear. Davidson was a 'souter' or shoemaker.

restwick golf course was the location of the very first pen Championship in 1860.

lvis Presley touched down briefly at **Prestwick irport** in 1960 on his way back to the United States the end of his army service, the only time he ever sited Britain.

ulzean Castle was originally a tower house built r the Kennedy family in the 12th century. The agnificent building now occupying the site was esigned by Robert Adam between 1777 and 1792, nd its parkland was laid out by Alexander Nasmyth. hen it was donated to the National Trust for cotland it was on the understanding that President isenhower, who had stayed there during World War , should continue to have a suite available to him for e remainder of his life, in recognition of his role as upreme Allied Commander.

AMOUS PEOPLE

obert the Bruce, king of Scotland (1306–29), rn Turnberry, 1274.
obert Burns, poet, born Alloway, 1759.
hn Loudon McAdam, inventor and engineer, rn Ayr, 1756.
illiam (Willie) Ross, Baron Ross of Marnock, acher and politician, born Ayr, 1911.

"On a sudden we turned a corner upon the immediate unty of Ayr – the sight was as rich as possible – I had no nception that the native place of Burns was so beautiful – e Idea I had was more desolate, his rigs of barley always emed to me but a few strips of Green on a cold hill – Prejudice! it was as rich as Devon."
hn Keats

"e banks and braes o' bonnie Doon, ow can ye bloom sae fresh and fair?"
obert Burns

auld Ayr, whom ne'er a toon surpasses, r honest men and bonny lasses."
obert Burns

Lying entirely within the historic county of Ayrshire, which was swallowed whole in 1975 with the creation of Strathclyde Region, its former Kyle and Carrick district became, as South Ayrshire, an independent administrative unit in 1996. It stretches along the Firth of Clyde and rises from a coastal plain towards the western Southern Uplands and Galloway Forest. The principal rivers are the river Ayr and river Doon. Its population of 111,700 has only declined slightly since the 1981 census. The administrative centre is in Ayr (46,050) and other important towns include Prestwick (14,680), Troon (14,510), Girvan (6,790) on the coast and Maybole (4,710) further inland.

Ayr was originally called Inverayr or St John's Town of Ayr, and a castle was built here by William I in 1197 near a fording place on the river. The oldest part of the town's layout dates back to this time. Little remains of the castle, although the walls of the Citadel with which Cromwell replaced it in 1654 are extant. A prosperous port in the 14th century, Ayr had links to Ireland, England and Europe, and 400 years later was trading in North America, importing in tobacco, as well as salt from Spain. By the 19th century, Ayr had become a fashionable tourist resort thanks to, initially, a ferry service and, later, the railway linking it to Glasgow.

South Ayrshire is probably best known for Robert Burns, its famous golf courses at Turnberry and Troon, and racecourse at Ayr, so it is not surprising that tourism is a vital employer (13 per cent). Other services, particularly public administration, education and health (33.5 per cent) are almost as important. The same mild climate that is an asset to the tourist trade also allows market gardening, especially of vegetables. The A77 trunk route to Glasgow connects the densely populated northern crescent between Troon and Ayr with Maybole and the rest of the coastal district, while arterial roads serve more rural districts, where livestock, particularly cattle and sheep, are raised. Manufacturing and construction are also main employers in the area (15 per cent) and many of the jobs in aircraft servicing and engineering are based at the international airport at Prestwick, also Scotland's international air freight hub.

The lighthouse and Ailsa golf course at Turnberry

The ruined Alloway Kirk, the setting for Robert Burns' poem 'Tam O' Shanter'.

Culzean Castle

Haggis is traditionally served on Burns night, 25th of January, to celebrate the poet's birthday.

NORTH AYRSHIRE

Area Sq Km 904
Area Sq Miles 349
Population 135,900
Admin HQ Irvine
Highest point Goat Fell (874 m) on the Isle of Arran

North Ayrshire or *Siorrachd Inbhir Àir a Tuath* ('the territory by the Ayr estuary') is the northern-most section of the historic county of Ayrshire.

FAMOUS FOR

Irvine is a 'New Town' with ancient roots: its burgh charter may have been conferred as early as the reign of David I, and the town certainly had this status by 1308. It was the main port for Glasgow until the 18th century, and one of the busiest in the country.

For seven years until 1848, the fastest route from London to Glasgow was by train to Fleetwood in Lancashire, and then by packet steamer to **Ardrossan** before finishing the journey by rail.

Holy Isle in Lamlash Bay off the east coast of Arran has associations with the 6th-century Irish missionary, St Mo Las. In 1991 it was purchased by the Samye Ling Tibetan community in Eskdale, and a Centre for World Peace and Health established.

FAMOUS PEOPLE

Thomas Brisbane, general and astronomer, born Largs, 1773.
John Galt, novelist and Canadian pioneer, born Irvine, 1779.
Daniel MacMillan, publisher, born Upper Corrie, Isle of Arran, 1813.
John Kerr, FRS, physicist, born Ardrossan, 1824.
John Boyd Dunlop, inventor of pneumatic tyre, born Dreghorn, 1840.
Henry Faulds, pioneer of fingerprint identification, born Beith, 1843.
James MacMillan, composer, born Kilwinning, 1959.
Nicola Benedetti, violinist, born West Kilbride, 1987.

"Prayer of the minister of the two Cumbrays, two miserable islands in the mouth of the Clyde: 'Oh Lord, bless and be gracious to the Greater and the Lesser Cumbrays, and in thy mercy do not forget the adjacent islands of Great Britain and Ireland.'"
Sir Walter Scott, *Journal*

"You feel, even if you cannot explain exactly why, that you are on a peculiar island."
Moray McLaren about Arran

"The end of the world is near when the MacBrayne's ship will be on time."
Iain Crichton Smith

North Ayrshire is a maritime county along the Firth of Clyde coast, with fertile arable cropland in the south and east, and hill farming in the more upland north. The local government reorganisation in 1996 combined the former district of Cunninghame with the Isle of Arran, Great and Little Cumbrae in the Firth of Clyde which had been traditionally been a part of Buteshire in the 19th century. The population of 135,900 has only decreased slightly since the 1991 census. Irvine is the administrative centre (33,060). Other important towns include Kilwinning (16,470), Saltcoats (11,730), Largs (11,400), Ardrossan (10,520), and Stevenson (8,990) on the mainland and Millport (1,280) on Great Cumbrae, and Lamlash (1,050) and Brodick (920) on Arran.

Many of the ports along the Firth of Clyde coast have long histories. Over several centuries, the Vikings used the Irish Sea as a highway connecting their possessions, but their defeat at the Battle of Largs in 1263 was a turning point, and gave control of the Hebrides and

Isle of Man to Scotland. Most of the towns along the coast have similar histories of trade and of then becoming resort towns connected to Glasgow by steam and, later, the railway. Saltcoats was a burgh of barony with a thriving port and shipyard trading in coal, salt and fish. Ardrossan was a centre of shipbuilding, railw engineering and oil refining, and retains ferry links with Arran.

There is quite a contrast, however between the urbanized coastal plain and rural interior on the mainland where dairy and potato farming are import business. Livestock is also raised on Arran, and a new whisky distillery was opened in 1995 at Lochranza. Th manufacturing sector is an important employer whet on Arran or the mainland (13.6 per cent). Tourism is a major employer in the area (11.8 per cent), especially in the islands, and good transportation links are vital. CalMac ferries run from Ardrossan to Arran; Wemyss ferries run to Bute; Largs ferries run to Great Cumbra

Caledonian MacBrayne ferry 'Caledonian Isles' near Isle of Arran.

Lochranza Castle, Arran, dates from the 14th century.

A 20th century memorial to the Battle of Largs, 1263.

View from Goat Fell, Arran.

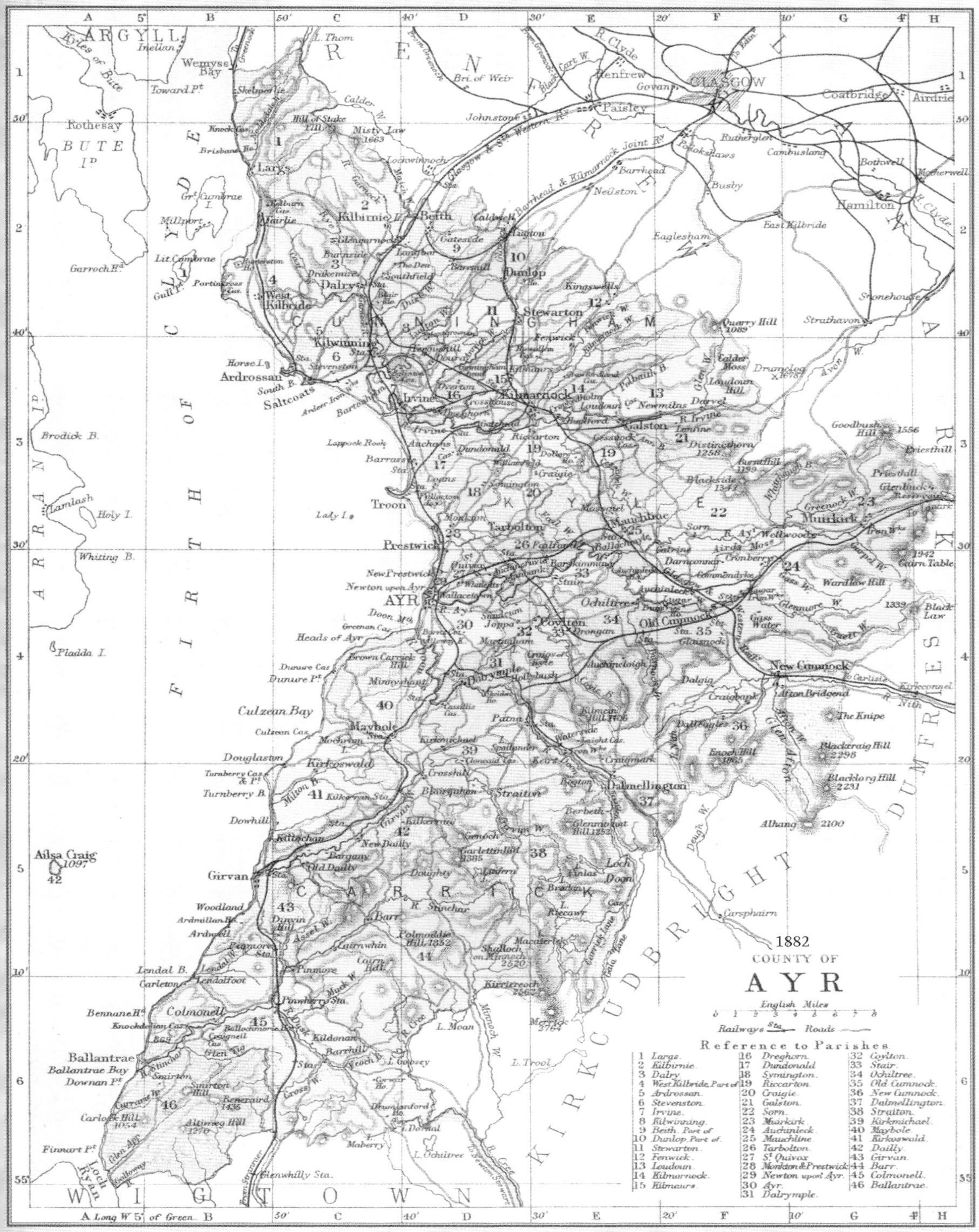

Bartholomew Gazetteer of the British Isles, 1887

AYRSHIRE, *a maritime co. in the SW. of Scotland, adjoining the cos. of Renfrew, Lanark, Dumfries, Kirkcudbright, and Wigtown. It is in the shape of a crescent, with the concave side, measuring about 70 miles, adjacent to the Firth of Clyde. Its greatest breadth, across the middle, is 30 miles. Area, 1128.5 sq. m., or 729,186 ac. Pop. 217,519, or 193 persons to each sq. m. The coast in the S. is rocky and destitute of natural harbours, but becomes low and sandy northwards from Ayr. The lofty islet of Ailsa Craig is comprised in this co. The surface slopes with slight undulations from the landward border, which is hilly in most parts, and is mountainous in the SE. The soil is various, sandy near the coast, of a rich clay in the middle parts, and moor in the uplands. The rivers are the Garnock, Irvine, Ayr, Doon, Girvan, and Stinchar. The largest lake is Loch Doon, on the SE. border. The minerals are coal, iron, limestone, and sandstone, all of which are extensively worked. The co. is famous for dairy produce and a fine breed of cows. The mfrs. are valuable, and include woollen, cotton, iron, and earthenware. The co. comprises 43 pars. and 3 parts, the police burghs of Ardrossan, Ayr, Darvel, Galston, Irvine, Kilmarnock, Largs, Maybole, Newmilns and Greenholm, Cumnock, and Stewarton.*

mountains of the island of Arran, viewed from Largs.

British National Grid projection

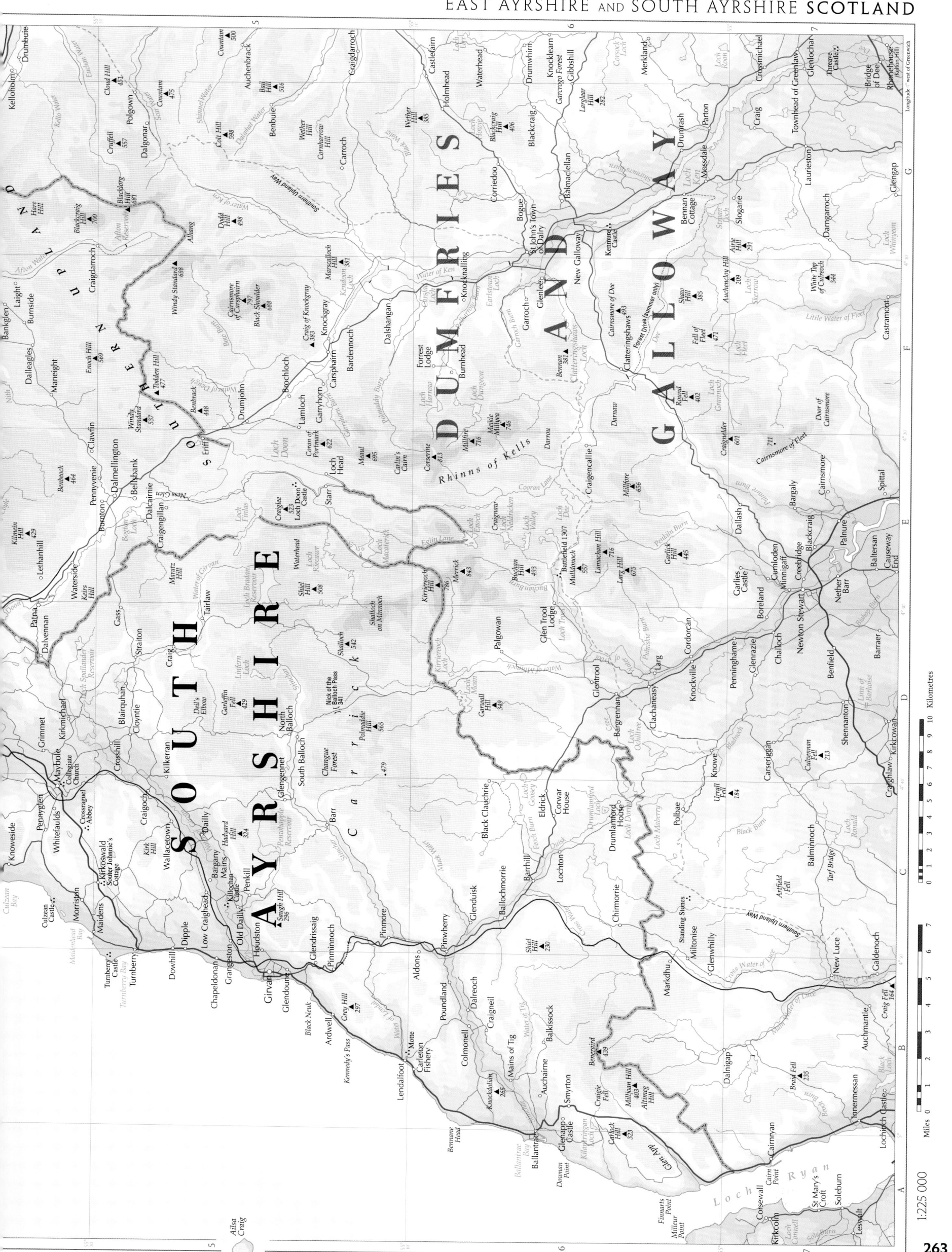

1:225 000

© Collins Bartholomew Ltd

British National Grid projection

1:65 000

© Collins Bartholomew Ltd

SOUTH LANARKSHIRE

Area Sq Km	1,774
Area Sq Miles	685
Population	310,100
Admin HQ	Hamilton
Highest point	Culter Fell (748 m) in the Southern Uplands

South Lanarkshire (*Siorrachd Lannraig a Deas*) takes its name from the historic county of Lanarkshire (named after the county town of Lanark, from the Celtic *lannarc* or *lannerch*, meaning 'glade').

FAMOUS FOR

New Lanark, the 18th-century cotton mill village built by David Dale and Robert Owen and whose workings epitomised the social reform movement of the time, is now a UNESCO World Heritage site, one of only five in Scotland.

Rutherglen is the oldest royal burgh in Scotland, having received its charter from David I in 1126.

East Kilbride might be Scotland's first 'New Town', established in 1947, but its origins are much earlier. The name is a Celtic one, hinting the old village had links to St Bride or Brigit, and historical records go back to at least as far as the 12th century, making it one of the country's oldest inhabited places.

FAMOUS PEOPLE

Allan Ramsey, poet, born Leadhills, 1686.
William Symington, engineer, born Leadhills, 1763.
Thomas Cochrane, 10th Earl of Dundonald, naval commander, born Annesfield, 1775.
John Claudius Loudon, horticulturalist, born Cambuslang, 1783.
David Livingstone, missionary and traveller, born in Blantyre in 1813.
Robert Giffen, economist, born Strathraven, 1837.
Robin Jenkins, novelist, born Cambuslang, 1912.
John (Jock) Stein, football player and manager, born Burnbank, 1922.
Colin McRae, rally driver, born in Lanark in 1968.

One of the traditional counties of Scotland, Lanarkshire was swallowed whole by Strathclyde Region in 1975, to be later disgorged in the local reorganisations of 1996 in two parts. South Lanarkshire lies entirely within the traditional county and includes commuter towns and some southern suburbs of Glasgow that account for its population of 310,100. Despite this population density, the majority of the county is rural in character stretching down to the mainly upland pasture and moorland the Lowther Hills. The principal river is the river Clyde. The administrative centre is Hamilton (48,850) and other important towns include East Kilbride (73,320), Rutherglen (32,120), Cambuslang (24,580), Blantyre (19,210), Larkhall (15,730) and the Glasgow suburbs (68,780) in the north, as well as Carluke (13,430), Lanark (8,200) and Strathaven (7,950) in the rural central and southern portions of the county.

The town of Hamilton was founded around the home of the eponymous Scots baronial family and their castles and palaces. Originally called Cadzow, it changed its name around the same time it was created a royal burgh (1455). Initially a centre for textile manufacture, especially lace, its fortunes were to be connected with the noble family's, although coalmining was the foundation of the town's real wealth, along with iron smelting. The arrival of the railways in the 19th century superseded the turnpike that previously connected Hamilton to Glasgow, Edinburgh and Carlisle.

Most of the northern towns have a similar history small local craft workings, such as weaving, transform or overtaken by the introduction of heavy industry, particularly coal mining, iron and steel working, and textile manufacture powered by the Clyde. Lead minin to the south in the Lowther Hills, known to have been carried out as early as the 12th century continued unti 1928 in Leadhills, and was profitable enough to justify improving the roads, and introducing a narrow gauge railway. Gold was also found in the area.

Sandwiched between, fruit growing, both as orchar or soft fruit, was established in the rural Clydesdale districts. So important was this industry that local growers in the 19th century complained that inferior Continental imports were ruining their reputations and insisted that only jam using local fruit could be labelled 'home-made'. Although the heavy industry has been lost, manufacturing still accounts for 12.7 per cent of employment, a higher percentage than the rest of Britain on average. The wide range of service industries from retail, hotels and restaurants (22.4 per cent) to public administration, education and health (25.4 per cent) and including finance, IT and other business activities (16.6 per cent) account for the lion's share of employment in South Lanarkshire. Excellent communications to Glasgow and the south along the A74(M) which bisects the area are duplicated by the We Coast Main Line rail service.

A stamp printed in Burundi shows David Livingstone, *c*.1970s.

Blantyre Weir, between Blantyre and Bothwell on the River Clyde, formerly used to power a mill.

New Lanark

"Hamilton is notoriously a dull place; if a joke finds its way into our neighbourhood, it is looked upon with as much surprise as a comet would be."
The Hamilton Hedgehog (October 1856)

"The pure and immaculate royal burgh of Rutherglen."
Job Galt

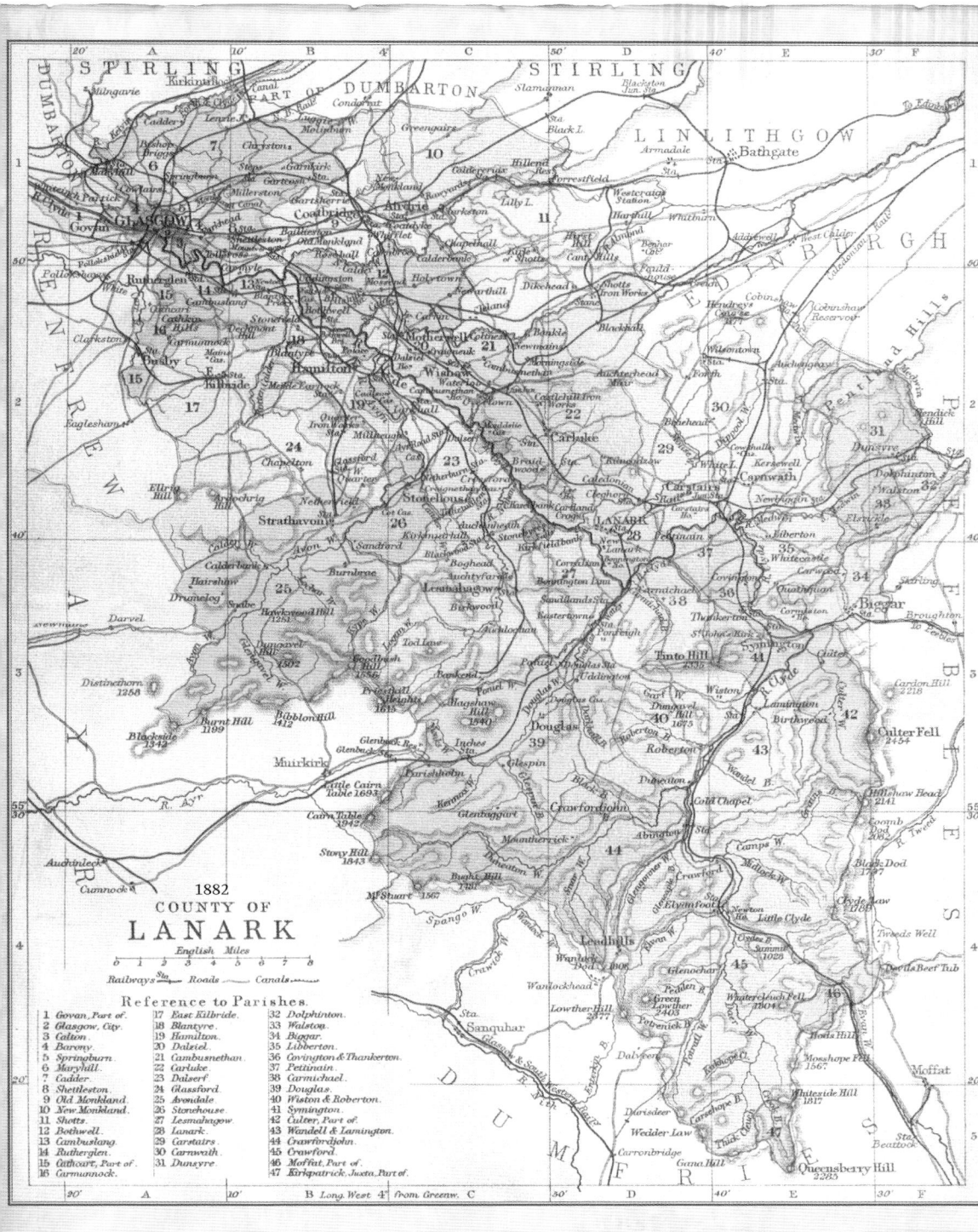

Bartholomew Gazetteer of the British Isles, 1887

LANARKSHIRE, *inland co. in SW. of Scotland; is bounded N. by Dumbartonshire and Stirlingshire, E. by Linlithgowshire, Edinburghshire, and Peeblesshire, S. by Dumfriesshire, and W. by Ayrshire and Renfrewshire; greatest length, NW. and SE., 52 miles; greatest breadth, NE. and SW., 34 miles; area, 564,284 ac., pop. 904,412. Lanarkshire is often called Clydesdale, occupying, as it does, the valley of the Clyde, which traverses the county from SE. to NW., and receives numerous tributary streams, including the Douglas, Avon, and Calder. The surface rises towards the S., where the Lowther or Lead Hills reach an alt. of 2403 ft. The Upper Ward is chiefly hill or moorland, affording excellent pasture for sheep; the Middle Ward contains the orchards for which Clydesdale has long been famous; and in the Lower Ward are some rich alluvial lands along the Clyde; but all over the county a considerable proportion of the soil is moist, marshy, and barren. Dairy-farming is prosecuted with success. The minerals are very valuable; coal and iron are wrought to such an extent that Lanarkshire is one of the principal seats of the iron trade; lead is mined in the Upper Ward. The co. comprises 40 pars. and 4 parts, the mun. burgh of Glasgow, the police burghs of Airdrie, Biggar, Govan, Govanhill, Hamilton, Hillhead, Lanark, Maryhill, Motherwell, Partick, Rutherglen, and Wishaw.*

t Kilbride Parish Church in the old village.

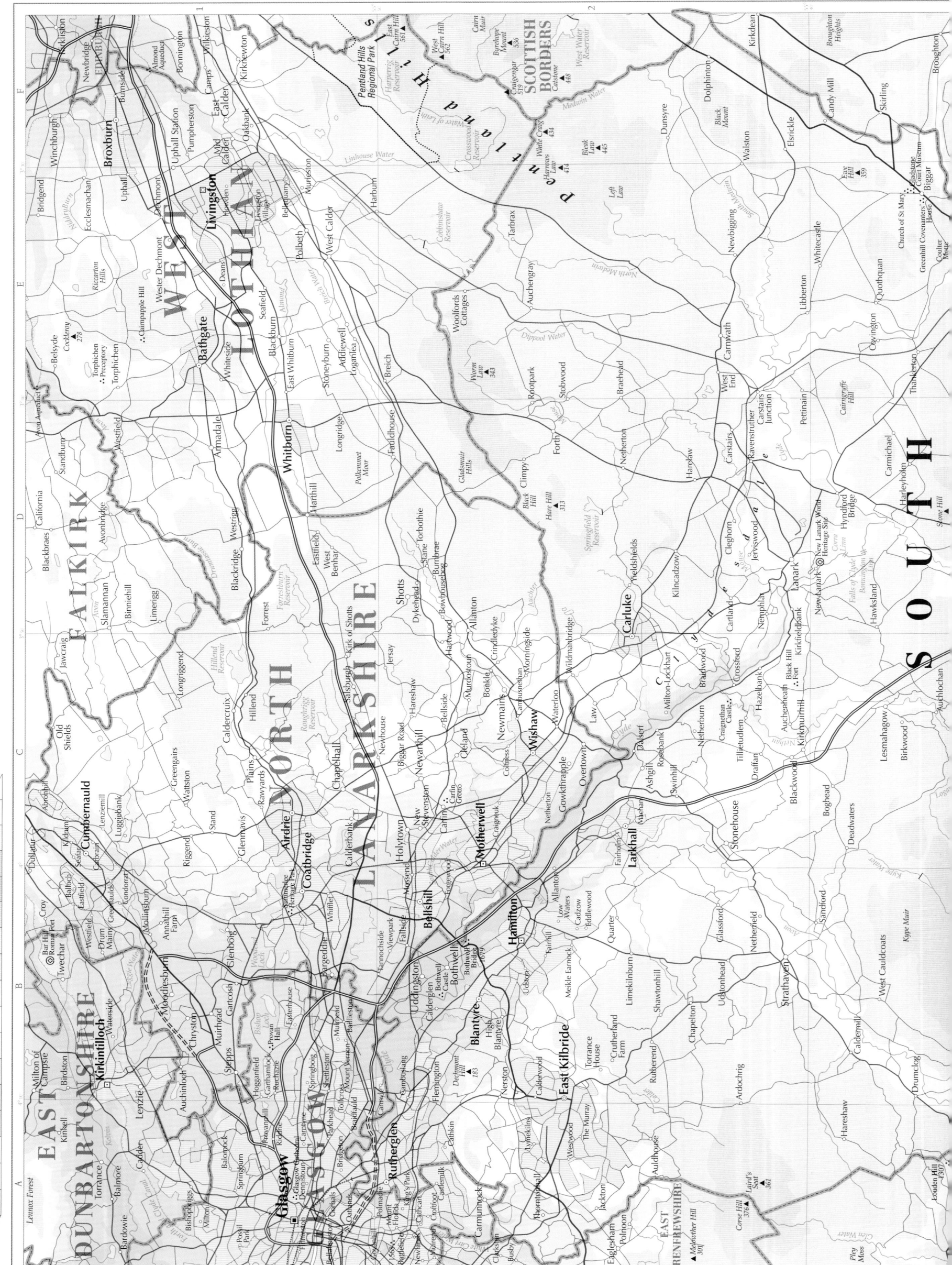

British National Grid projection

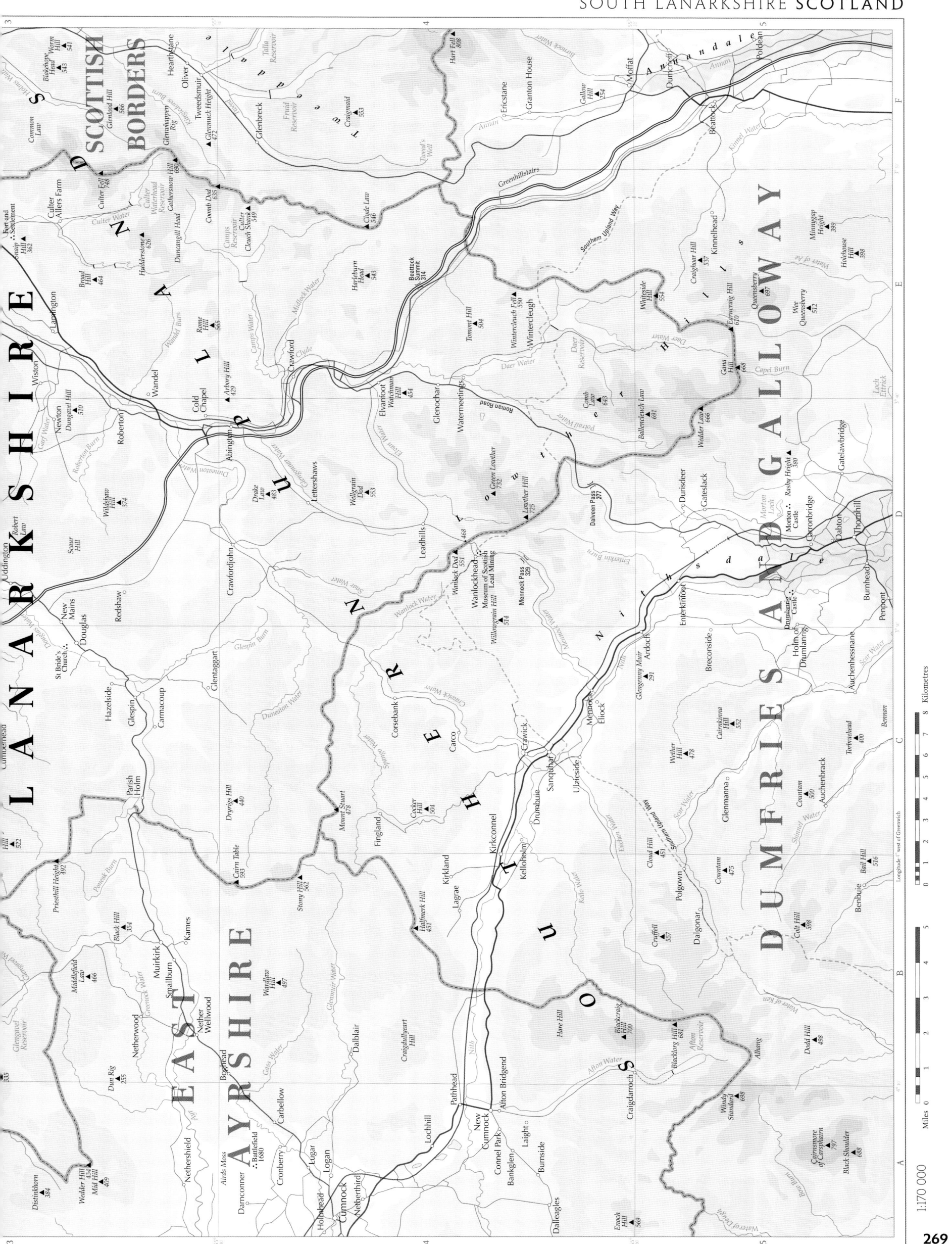

1:170 000

Miles 0   1   2   3   4   5

0   1   2   3   4   5   6   7   8 Kilometres

© Collins Bartholomew Ltd

INVERCLYDE

Area Sq Km	174
Area Sq Miles	67
Population	80,800
Admin HQ	Greenock
Highest point	Creuch Hill (441 m)

Inverclyde (or *Inbhir Chluaidh*, means 'the mouth of the Clyde').

FAMOUS FOR
Quarrier's Village, originally the Orphan Homes of Scotland, was by the 1890s a self-contained community including a school, church and fire station, to complement the 34 cottages. By the 1930s, 1,500 children were looked after here by house fathers and mothers, and there were also facilities for epileptics as well as a TB sanatorium, the first in Scotland.

Prior to 1996, Inverclyde was a western district of Strathclyde Region, having been created from a group of burghs and territory once part of historic Renfrewshire. In that year it became Scotland's third smallest authority with a population of 80,800, much reduced from 101,200 in 1981, primarily due to the collapse of heavy construction and manufacturing. Greenock is the administrative centre (43,820) and other towns on the Clyde include Port Glasgow (15,290) and Gourock (11,730), with Wemyss Bay (2,560) and

'**Granny Kempock's Stone**' in Gourock is a prehistoric monolith resembling a cloaked figure. Legends about its ability to bring good luck were common. Sailors would circle the stone before a voyage to solicit good luck, and newlyweds also visited the stone to ensure a long and happy marriage.

During World War II, Greenock was a naval base for the Free French, and was bombed and heavily damaged. A memorial cross, featuring the **Cross of Lorraine**, was built in the hills above the town in honour of the French seamen who died during the war.

Port Glasgow was the original deep-water port for its namesake further upstream.

FAMOUS PEOPLE
James Watt, engineer and inventor, born at Greenock in 1736.
Robert Campbell, merchant and Australian politician, born Greenock in 1769.
William Laird, shipbuilder, born Greenock in 1780.

Inverkip (2,640) further along the estuary, while inland Kilmacolm (3,860) is a now commuter town for Glasgow.

This coastal district was once a hive of industrial activity. Rope, paper, barrels, pottery and glass were all made here, copper mining, weaving and herring fishing – Greenock harbour boasted several hundred boats by the mid 18th century – were major employers, even sugar from Barbados was refined in Greenock. Gourock and Wemyss Bay also offered ferry services to holidaymakers, particularly sailings to Dunoon and Bute. Most of the

William Quarrier, merchant and philanthropist, born Greenock in 1829.
James Thomson, poet, born Port Glasgow in 1834.
James Guthrie, painter, born Greenock in 1859.
Neil Paterson (James Edmund Neil Paterson), author and screenwriter, born Greenock in 1916.
Charles (Chic) Murray, comedian, born Greenock, 191
Jimmy Mack (James F. McRitchie), broadcaster, born Greenock in 1934.
Bill Bryden, director and dramatist, born Greenock 1942.

"The law knows it can either say "it's against the law to go on strike", and jail the lot of us; or it can say "But then there will be no-one left to build ships", and leave us alone. What decision the law takes depends on how much the coun needs what you've got."
Chris Hannan, from his play *Elizabeth Gordon Quinn*

"Inverkip is so rough they put a date stamp on your head wh they mug you so they don't do you twice in the one day."
Chic Murray, quoted by A. Yule

towns in Inverclyde have ancient origins, and both Kilmacolm and Inverkip were religious centres. The area's reputation and prosperity, however, were focused on shipbuilding: John Scott established a shipbuilding yard in 1711, but the heyday of 'Clyde built' vessels was between 1875 and 1914, and by 2010 only one yard remained. The service sector is now the primary employer in the area (88 per cent) particularly public administration, education and health (37.3 per cent), and retail, hotels and restaurants (23.6 per cent).

RENFREWSHIRE

Area Sq Km	270
Area Sq Miles	104
Population	169,800
Admin HQ	Paisley
Highest point	Hill of Stake (522 m)

Renfrew takes its name from the Gaelic *rinn* ('point') and *friù* ('current'), the place where the river Gryfe meets the Clyde and gives its name to the entire area.

Once part of the historic county of Renfrewshire, today's Renfrewshire was, from 1975, a district of Strathclyde Region, and since 1996, has been a separate unitary authority. The area emerges west from the Greater Glasgow periphery into a contrasting countryside of highlands, lochs and glens, but with most of its important towns little more than Glasgow suburbs: Paisley (population 73,190), Renfrew (20,020), Johnstone (15,640), Erskine (15,580), and Linwood (8,420), while

FAMOUS FOR
Robert III, in his own words 'the worst of kings and the most wretched of men' was buried at **Paisley Abbey** because he felt himself unworthy to be placed near his father at Scone Abbey. The splendid marble tomb is not original, but was a gift of Queen Victoria in 1888.

The origins of the University of the West of Scotland, with its four campuses spread over as many counties, began as a Philosophical Institution, founded in 1808 by Peter and Thomas Coats, of the famous sewing thread manufacturers in **Paisley**.

Bridge of Weir (4,650) and Lochwinnoch (2,790) are more rural. Much of the area is heavily urbanised, and owed its initial industrialisation to the cotton textile industry – Paisley gave its name to the famous pattern. Coal mining for the growing iron and steel works was also associated with shipbuilding along the Clyde. The numbers working in heavy industrial jobs have collapsed with the closure of local industries like the Linwood car plant, but has benefited from being the

FAMOUS PEOPLE
Robert II, King of Scots, born Paisley, 1316.
Robert Tannahill, the 'Weaver Poet', born Paisley, 1774
David Stow, educational pioneer, born Paisley, 1793.
Jane Arthur (*née* Glen), women's rights advocate, born Paisley, 1827.
Fulton Mackay, actor and comedian, born Paisley, 192
Kenyon Wright, clergyman and Chairman, Scottish Constitutional Convention (1989–99), born Paisley, 19
Tom Conti, actor, born Paisley, 1941.
John Byrne, dramatist and stage designer, born Paisley 1940.
Archie Gemmill, footballer, born Paisley, 1947.

location of Glasgow International Airport at Abbotsin It was not the original airport for the area. Renfrew Airport, a former military airport near Renfrew, becam the third busiest civilian British airport with a futurist terminal building designed by Sir William Kininmont in 1954. Continued expansion of air traffic forced the move to the current airport location, and the last fligh from Renfrew was in 1966. Its main runway is now beneath part of the M8 motorway.

EAST RENFREWSHIRE

Area Sq Km	174
Area Sq Miles	67
Population	89,200
Admin HQ	Giffnock
Highest point	Corse Hill (376 m)

Once part of the historic county of Renfrewshire, East Renfrewshire was, from 1975, a district of Strathclyde Region and, since 1996, has been a separate unitary authority. East Renfrewshire is dominated by Glasgow, and the principal centres are all suburbs, including Newton Mearns (23,460), Clarkston (18,900), Barrhead (17,170), and Giffnock (16,260). Over two-thirds of

FAMOUS FOR
On 10 May 1941 Rudolf Hess, Adolf Hitler's deputy in the Nazi Party, parachuted on to **Eaglesham Moor**, and was detained by a local farmer, David McLean. It is thought that Hess was flying to meet the Duke of Hamilton at Dunvagel House to negotiate peace and lost his way. He remained in captivity for the rest of his life, dying in Spandau prison in Berlin in 1987.

East Renfrewshire is farmland, the rest being mostly residential, with some light industry. The Whitelee Wind Farm, with 140 turbines was the largest windfarm in Europe when it opened in 2009, capable of a maximum output of 322 MW. Its site straddles East Renfrewshire, South Lanarkshire and East Ayrshire.

FAMOUS PEOPLE
William Gemmel, sculptor, born Eaglesham, 1814.
Edward Arthur Walton, painter and 'Glasgow Boy', born Glanderston House, near Neilston, 1860.
Professor Kenneth Mellanby, ecologist and entomologist, born Barrhead, 1908.
Alexander (Alex) McLeish, football player and Scotland team manager, born Barrhead, 1959.

*Her cutty sark, o' Paisley harn,
That while a lassie she had worn,
In longitude tho' sorely scanty,
It was her best, and she was vauntie.*
Robert Burns, "Tam o' Shanter"

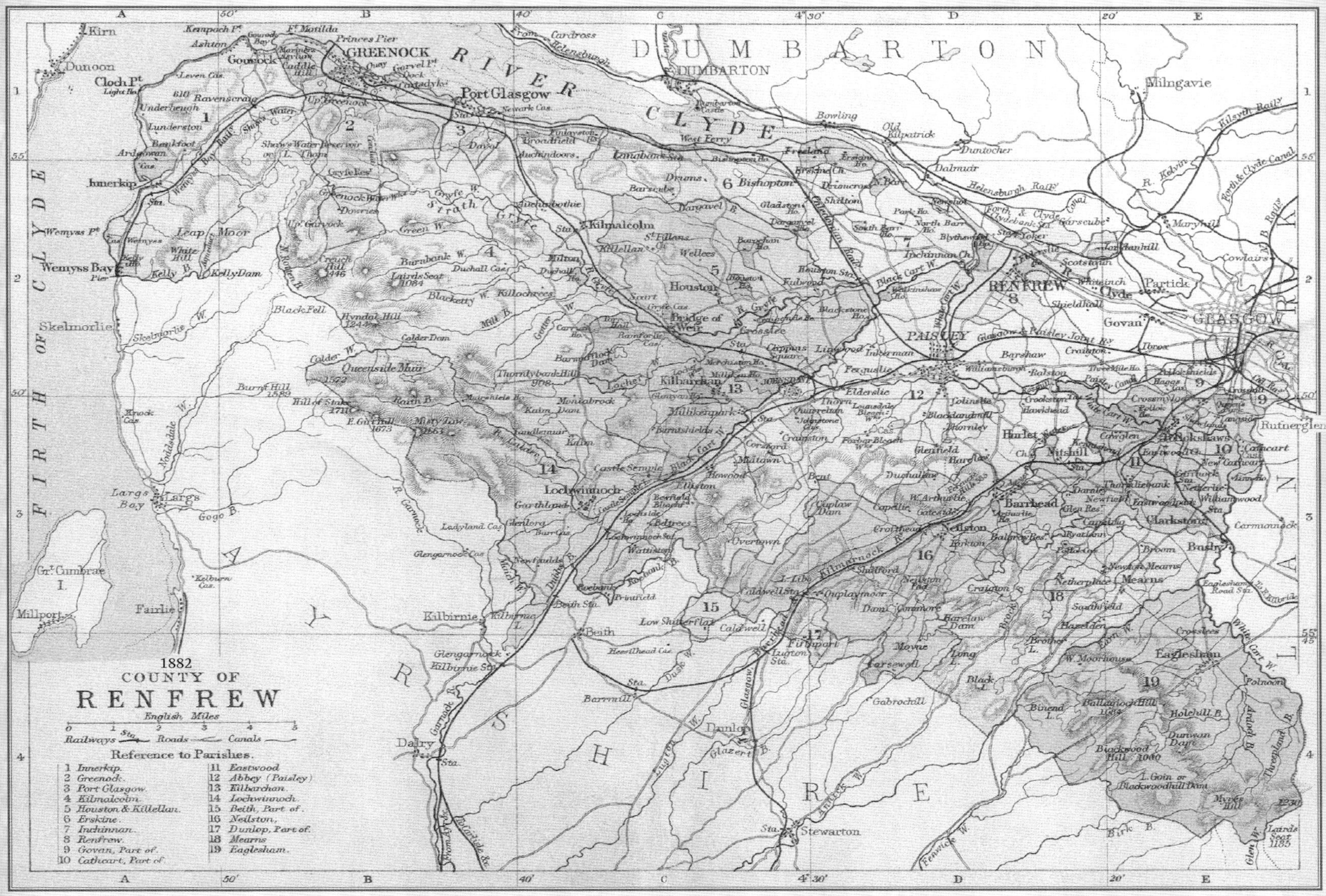
1882
COUNTY OF
RENFREW
English Miles
Railways Roads Canals
Reference to Parishes.
1 Innerkip.
2 Greenock.
3 Port Glasgow.
4 Kilmalcolm.
5 Houston & Killellan.
6 Erskine.
7 Inchinnan.
8 Renfrew.
9 Govan, Part of.
10 Cathcart, Part of.
11 Eastwood.
12 Abbey (Paisley)
13 Kilbarchan.
14 Lochwinnoch.
15 Beith, Part of.
16 Neilston.
17 Dunlop, Part of.
18 Mearns.
19 Eaglesham.
DUMBARTON
RIVER CLYDE
FIRTH OF CLYDE
AYRSHIRE
GREENOCK
Port Glasgow
Gourock
PAISLEY
RENFREW
GLASGOW
Kilbarchan
Lochwinnoch
Barrhead
Neilston
Eaglesham
Kilmalcolm
Houston
Wemyss Bay
Largs
Skelmorlie
Millport
Beith
Kilbirnie
Stewarton
Rutherglen
Milngavie
Partick
Govan

Bartholomew Gazetteer of the British Isles, 1887

RENFREWSHIRE, *maritime co., in SW. of Scotland, bounded N. by the river Clyde and Dumbartonshire, E. by Lanarkshire, S. by Ayrshire, and W. by the Firth of Clyde; greatest length, NW. and SE., 31 miles; greatest breadth, NE. and SW., 14 miles; area, 150,785 ac., pop. 263,374. The principal streams, all flowing to the Clyde, are the Black Cart, the White Cart, and the Gryfe. The surface in the S. and SW. parts of the co. is hilly, and somewhat bleak and moorish; it thence undulates to the banks of the Clyde, along which there is some rich and lowlying land. Coal, ironstone, and lime-stone are abundant; copper ore occurs near Gourock and Lochwinnoch. The principal industries, besides mining and agriculture, are the mfr. of cotton and thread, sugar-refining, and shipbuilding. The co. comprises 20 pars, with parts of 4 others, the police burghs of Greenock, Gourock, Johnstone, Paisley, Pollokshaws, and Port Glasgow and Renfrew, the police burghs (suburban of Glasgow) of Crossbill, Kinning Park, Pollokshields, and Pollokshields East.*

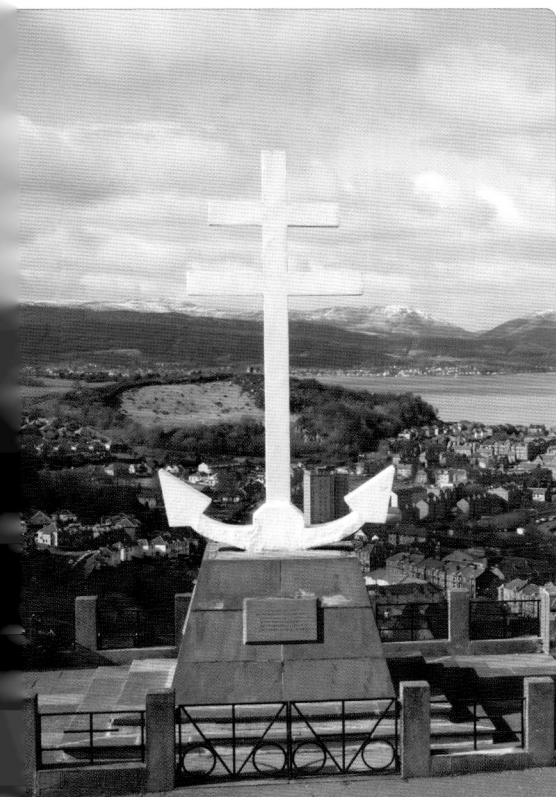

e Free French Memorial on Lyle Hill, Greenock, erlooking Gourock and the river Clyde.

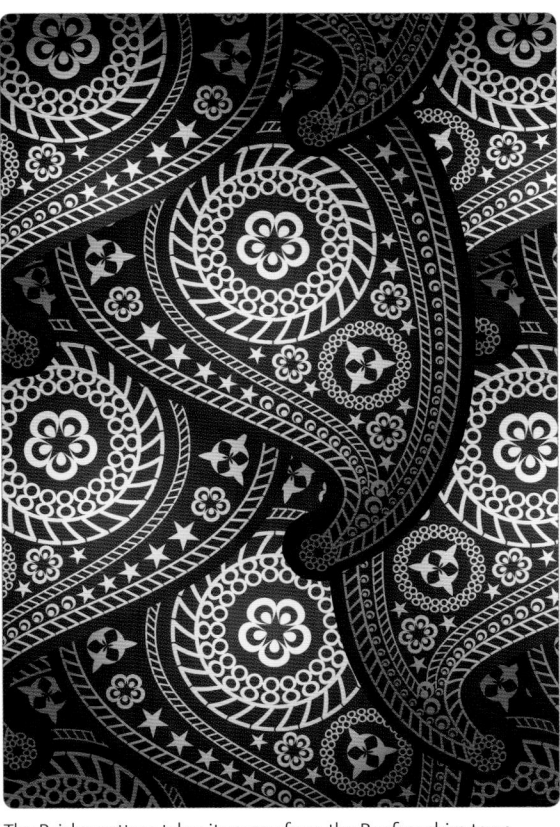

The Paisley pattern takes its name from the Renfrewshire town but is Asian in origin.

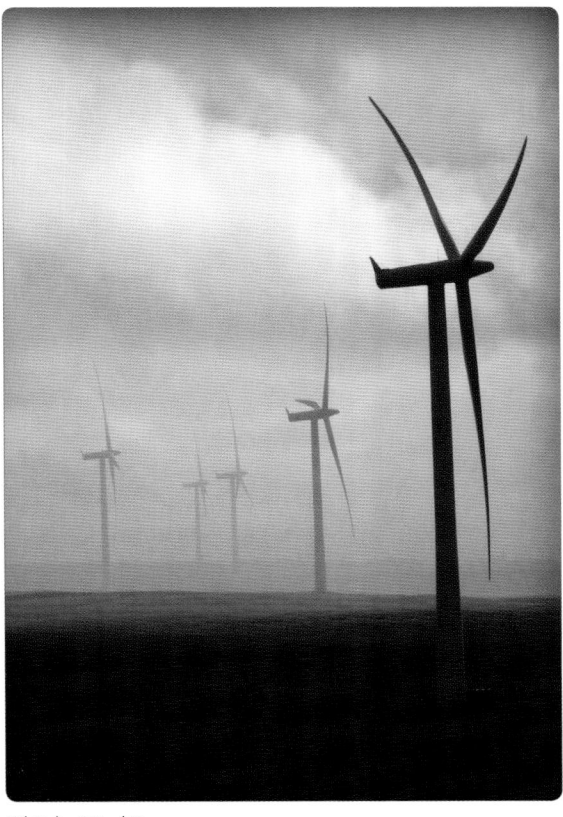

Whitelee Wind Farm

GLASGOW

Area Sq Km	176
Area Sq Miles	68
Population	584,200
Highest point	Cathkin Braes (200 m), 8 km southeast of the city centre

Glasgow's name, it is commonly accepted, comes from the Gaelic *Glas-* + *cau* 'green hollow' referring to the site's original wooded valley through which a series of streams flowed. It is known popularly as the 'dear green place'.

FAMOUS FOR
The curious assortment of emblems which make up Glasgow's coat of arms – a bird, a tree, a fish, and a bell – all have to do with the miracles of **St Mungo** (or Kentigern), the patron saint of the city.

The right to hold a fair in the city was established in the 12th century, and it still survives today.

Rutherglen, just upstream from Glasgow, was a royal burgh with a castle where parliament was occasionally held. In the 13th century, it was arguably more important than its neighbour down river.

Glasgow candlemakers were removed from inside to just outside the city gates as a result of several severe fires, including that of 1652 which destroyed a third of the city. They settled on the **Candleriggs**.

The **Athenaeum** was opened in 1847 with a banquet presided over by Charles Dickens.

1,090,380 people lived in Glasgow in 1926, including descendents of immigrants from Ireland and the Highlands, as well as Italians, East Europeans and Jews.

The **Finnieston** crane, still a Glasgow landmark, was built in 1931 to load boilers and engines, and later locomotives, onto ships for export around the world.

Glasgow's annual folk and world music festival, **Celtic Connections**, brings international performers to the city and is one of a growing number of festivals hosted in the city each year.

Two million people, almost two fifths (38.6 per cent) of the entire Scottish population live in the **Greater Glasgow** conurbation.

FAMOUS PEOPLE
Robert Stevenson, engineer, lighthouse designer, born Glasgow, 1772.
Henry Campbell-Bannerman, Liberal politician and Prime Minister, born Glasgow, 1836.
Sir William Ramsay, chemist and Nobel Prize winner, born Glasgow, 1852.
Sir William Burrell, shipowner and collector, born Glasgow, 1861.
Charles Rennie Mackintosh, architect and artist, born Glasgow, 1868.
Edwin Morgan, poet and critic, born Glasgow, 1920.
Alistair MacLean, novelist, born Glasgow, 1922.
Ronald David Laing, psychiatrist, born Glasgow, 1927.
Alaisdair Gray, writer and artist, born Glasgow, 1934.
Donald Dewar, labour politician first First Minister of Scotland, born Glasgow, 1937.
Sir Alexander (Alex) Ferguson, football player and coach, born Glasgow, 1941.
William (Billy) Connolly, comedian, born Glasgow, 1942.
Bill Forsyth, film-maker, born Glasgow, 1946.
Kenneth (Kenny) Dalglish, footballer, born Glasgow, 1951.

Said to be built on seven hills, Glasgow's first foundations were not along the Clyde at all, but about a mile away along the Molendinar Burn where traditionally, St Mungo built a church in the 6th century. This foundation would, under the patronage of kings and bishops, become the Glasgow Cathedral. As the ecclesiastical and scholastic centre expanded, so the original settlement spread down the hill towards the north bank of the Clyde below the tidal reach where the river was easily fordable. The first stone bridge across the river was built in 1345 approximately where the Victoria Bridge is today.

In these early days, the village was unimportant militarily: no Roman fort has ever been excavated, the Kingdom of Strathclyde's stronghold was at Dumbarton and the Clyde valley lacked any other defensible position. The river was too shallow to accommodate even the draughts of medieval ships. It was only in the late 17th century that a port for the city would be built further down river. The trans-Atlantic trade with the colonies, particularly the importation of sugar, tobacco and cotton and export of linen, would form the foundations of the city's wealth, and the first tobacco cargo arrived at the Broomielaw Quay in 1674. Glasgow gained a great deal from the 1707 Act of Union, and the Industrial Revolution that followed made Glasgow the second city of empire. Exploitation of coal deposits, and the development of heavy manufacturing, especially shipbuilding and iron founding, transformed Glasgow into an international powerhouse.

Glasgow is by far the largest city in Scotland with a population of 584,200 in the City of Glasgow council area and approaching 2 million in the Greater Glasgow area. The city expanded in phases in the 19th and early 20th centuries along both sides of the Clyde, and Glasgow was the county town of historic Lanarkshire. By 1975 Strathclyde Region, administered from Glasgow, comprised 19 districts – by far the largest political unit in Scotland. Further local reorganisation in 1996 pared the super-region down and Glasgow became a single unitary authority.

This growth and industrialisation created both great wealth and terrible poverty. Glasgow's slums were some of the worst in Britain even before the long collapse of the manufacturing industries along the Clyde following World War I. Serious attempts to address this involved knocking down entire areas of the city, and building high-rise tower blocks or moving people to nearby 'New Towns', not always successfully. Life expectancy rates are still the lowest in the country. The loss of skilled employment has only partially been rectified by the introduction of modern light industry. Service industries are now the major employers, especially public administration, education and health (31.3 per cent), finance, IT and other business activities (27.5 per cent), and retail, hotels and restaurants (20.2 per cent). Manufacturing (5.3 per cent) and construction (4.3 per cent) are low by national standards.

The city is revisiting its earlier cultural roots as a centre of culture and learning. Glasgow is now home to three universities: Glasgow University, founded in 1451, Strathclyde University, and Glasgow Caledonian University, with a combined student population of 44,600. It has recently refurbished museums, opened concert halls and literally cleaned itself up, revealing architectural gems under centuries of coal soot.

The Finnieston Crane and the Clyde Auditorium, popularly called 'The Armadillo'.

The Glasgow Science Centre

GLASGOW, 1895

Bartholomew Gazetteer of the British Isles, 1887

GLASGOW, *royal burgh, partly in Renfrewshire but chiefly in Lanarkshire, on river Clyde, 14 miles SE. of Dumbarton (at the commencement of the Firth of Clyde), 47½ (by rail) W. of Edinburgh, and 401½ (by West Coast route) NW. of London – royal burgh (co-extensive with City par.), pop. 166,128; municipal burgh, pop. 511,415; town (municipal and suburban), pop. 674,095; 13 newspapers. Market-day, Wednesday. Glasgow is the commercial and industrial metropolis of Scotland, and claims to be the second city of the British Empire. It is an ancient place, but almost the only monument of antiquity which it contains is the Cathedral (1179), dedicated to St Mungo, or Kentigern, the apostle of Strathclyde, who is said to have settled at Glasgow about 580. The old University buildings in High Street have been converted into a railway station; the new University buildings (1870), on Gilmore Hill, in the NW. of the city, are probably the finest modern specimen of secular architecture in Scotland. The University (1450) had in 1882-1883 professors to the number of 27, and students to the number of 2275, of whom 1307 were Arts students. The commercial importance of Glasgow is of comparatively modern date. At the Reformation the population was about 5000, at the Union about 12,000, and at the beginning of the 19th century about 77,000; it is now, including the neighbouring burghs, which are essentially parts of Glasgow, about 750,000. The chief natural cause of the rapid growth of Glasgow is its position within the richest coal and ironstone field in Scotland, and on the banks of a river which has been rendered, by almost incredible labour, navigable for vessels of the largest tonnage. Its industries, which are characterised by their immense variety, include textile mfrs. (principally cotton, woollen, and carpets): bleaching, printing, and dyeing; chemical mfrs.; the iron mfr., engineering, and shipbuilding. All the iron trade* of Scotland is controlled by Glasgow, which is also the headquarters of the great shipbuilding industry of the Clyde. Glasgow has 4 distilleries and 6 paper mills. It is one of the three principal seaports of the United Kingdom. The harbour extends along the river for over 2 miles, and includes 2 tidal docks, one of them (the Queen's Dock) the largest in Scotland. The foreign trade is with all parts of the world, but chiefly with India, the United States, Canada, and South America, Belgium, France, and Spain. Glasgow contains terminal stations of the 3 great trunk lines of Scotland; and its railway communications *are assisted by the City Union Railway and the Underground Railway. Tramways penetrate into every suburb, and the Clyde is crossed by numerous bridges and ferries. There are 4 parks – the Green, the Kelvingrove or West End Park, the Queen's Park, and the Alexandra Park. The health of the city has been greatly benefited by the Loch Katrine water supply, completed in 1859, and by the Improvement Act of 1866. The New Municipal Buildings, at the E. end of George Square, were founded October 1883. Glasgow is a brigade depôt; the barracks (1876) are at Maryhill.*

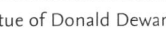
Statue of Donald Dewar

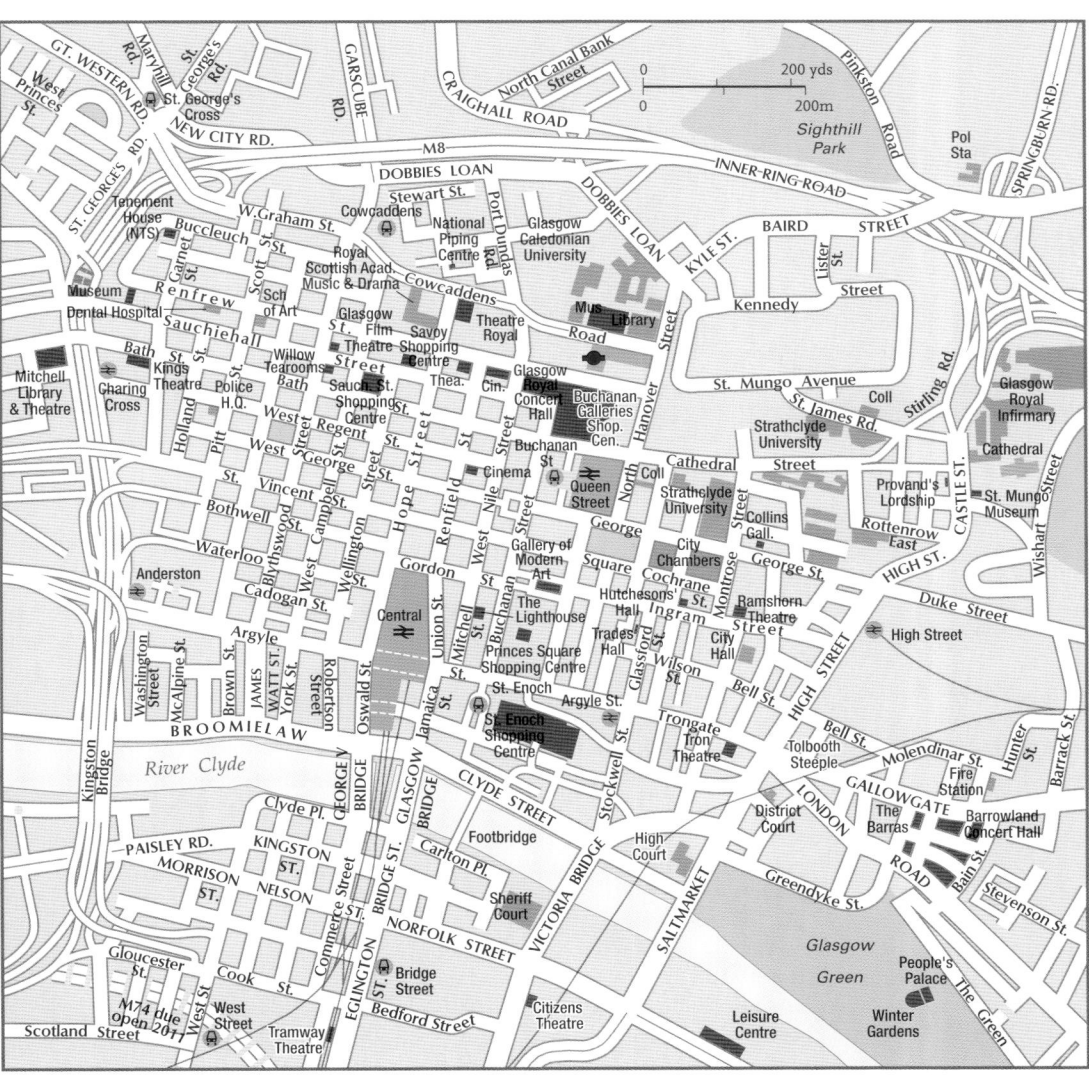
Modern Glasgow

WEST DUNBARTONSHIRE

Area Sq Km	183
Area Sq Miles	71
Population	90,900
Admin HQ	Dumbarton
Highest point	Duncolm (401 m)

West Dunbartonshire is the western part of the old county of Dunbartonshire, named after the town of Dumbarton, from the Gaelic *Dun Breattainn* meaning 'the fort of the Britons'.

FAMOUS FOR
Balloch is one of the many legendary birthplaces of **St Patrick** in AD 397.

The western end of the **Antonine Wall**, the Roman Empire's northernmost boundary, is situated at Old Kilpatrick.

West Dunbartonshire borders the north bank of the river Clyde and extends to the southern shore of Loch Lomond (including the island of Inchmurrin), and as well as the Kilpatrick Hills to the southeast. As part of the historic county of Dunbartonshire, the area was amalgamated into Strathclyde Region in 1975, and local reorganisation in 1996 created the authority from the districts of Dumbarton and Clydebank.

The current population of 90,900 represents a gradual decline of almost 15 per cent since the 1981 census. West Dunbartonshire includes Clydebank (29,200), part of the greater Glasgow conurbation, and the administrative centre at Dumbarton (19,990). The Vale of Leven connects Loch Lomond with the Clyde and became a continuation of the

RMS *Queen Mary* (launched in 1934) and RMS *Queen Elizabeth* (launched in 1938), both owned by Cunard, were built by John Brown & Co in Clydebank. Designed to see service between Southampton, Cherbourg and New York, the ships' availability for troop transport duties were said by Winston Churchill to have shortened World War II by a year.

The former **Argyll Motor Works** in Alexandria was built in 1905 and was then the largest factory of its kind in the world. After a transition to torpedo manufacture for the Ministry of Defence, the Grade A listed building, complete with marble staircase, is today a shopping mall.

FAMOUS PEOPLE
Matthew Stewart, Earl of Lennox and regent of Scotland, born Dumbarton Castle, 1516.
Tobias George Smollett, novelist, born Alexandria, 1721.
Robert Napier, marine engineer, born Dumbarton, 1791.
Sir Archibald Denny, shipbuilder and engineer, born Dumbarton, 1860.

industrial powerhouses of the district in towns like Alexandria (13,210).

Once the capital of the kingdom of Strathclyde, Dumbarton flourished as a port for sugar and tobacco, as well as building a reputation for glassmaking, particularly bottles and windows. Its 19th-century shipyards built the tea clipper *Cutty Sark*.

The 19th century saw the expansion of industry both along the Clyde and up through the Vale of Leven. The Forth and Clyde Canal linked Clydebank to Grangemouth in the east. Alexandria, Bonhill and Renton were famous for their textile industries, which included bleaching, printing and dyeing. In the early 20th century, a spectacular automobile plant for Argyll Motors was built in Alexandria and Singer located its

Sir John Young (Jackie) Stewart, OBE, born Dumbarton 1939.
Duncan Bannatyne, entrepreneur, born Clydebank, 1949.

"Waves of bombers… droned overhead relentlessly, heading for the vital shipyards strung out along the banks of the Clyde When morning came, news was sparse, but there was an eer glow to the north. Rumour had it that Clydebank had taken the full force of the blitz."
Lady Marion Fraser

"We now crossed the water of Leven which, though nothing near so considerable as the Clyde, is much more transparent, pastoral and delightful."
Tobias Smollett

"One of Scotland's misfortunes is that she was not conquered by the Roman cohorts who bequeathed to Western Europe th basic civilisation."
Arnold Fleming

largest European factory in Clydebank in 1885, but the town became almost synonymous with shipbuilding. The relocation or collapse of these industries has caus high unemployment and social deprivation.

Service industries now account for nearly 9 out of 10 jobs (88 per cent), almost half of them in public administration, education and health (42.5 per cent) an nearly another quarter in retail, hotels and restaurants (21.8 per cent). The tourism sector has been a relatively steady employer at 9.6 per cent, assisted by upgrading amenities and access to Loch Lomond at Balloch, including the headquarters of the Loch Lomond and Trossachs National Park. The great Titan crane from th John Brown Shipyard in Clydebank is also now a touri attraction.

EAST DUNBARTONSHIRE

Area Sq Km	175
Area Sq Miles	67
Population	104,700
Admin HQ	Kirkintilloch
Highest point	The Earl's Seat (578 m), in the Campsie Fells

East Dunbartonshire is the eastern part of the old county of Dunbartonshire, named after the town of Dumbarton, from the Gaelic *Dun Breattainn* meaning 'the fort of the Britons'.

FAMOUS FOR
The Antonine Wall, the extreme northern boundary of the Roman empire, marched through this area from Bar Hill fort near **Twechar** to **Bearsden**, where the remains of a bath house were excavated in 1973. It became a World Heritage Site in 2008.

A lowland county of Scotland within the broad Clyde valley; the urban south is distinct from the northern uplands, which includes the Campsie Fells and the eastern reaches of the Kilpatrick Hills. The principal waterway is the river Kelvin, a tributary of the Clyde.

This area of Dunbartonshire was part of the earldom of Lennox, created by William the Lion in 1174, and eventually stretching from the Clyde to Loch Lomond. In 1975 it became a northern outpost of Strathclyde Region but the local government reorganisation of 1996 replaced two former districts – Bearsden and Milngavie and Strathkelvin – with one administrative authority. As well as a large section of traditional Dunbartonshire, the present county also includes sections of historic

Many stories and superstitions surround the three stones of the Auld Wives' Lift just north of **Baldernock**, and local legend tells of three women who carried the huge stones up the hill as a bet. More prosaically, they are probably erratics left by glaciation.

The West Highland Way, Scotland's first long-distance footpath, begins its 152 km journey to Fort William in **Milngavie**.

Kirkintilloch had a strong Temperance Movement in the late 19th century. Eight years after the passage of the Temperance Act, the town voted in 1921 to ban the sale of alcohol, and this ban was only overturned in 1968.

FAMOUS PEOPLE
Macvey Napier, lawyer and editor of *Encyclopaedia Britannica*, born Kirkintilloch, 1776.
Archibald Scott Couper, chemist, born Kirkintilloch, 1803.
Sir William Stirling Maxwell, 9th baronet, art historian, born Kirkintilloch, 1818.

Lanarkshire and Stirlingshire. The population of 104,700 includes the administrative centre at Kirkintilloch (19,360), Lenzie (8,630) and the commuter towns of Bearsden (27,070), Bishopbriggs (23,370) and Milngavie (12,780) to the west and southwest. Milton of Campsie (3,870) and Lennoxtown (3,730) are in the north of the area.

Kirkintilloch is situated along the central section of the Forth and Clyde canal as it passes through East Dunbartonshire from Twechar to Bishopbriggs. Its origins are closely connected to the nearby Roman fort on the Antonine Wall. Kirkintilloch was a burgh of barony in the 12th century, but its development was based on textile industries (hand-loom weaving and

David Gray, poet, born Kirkintilloch, 1838.
Thomas (Tom) Johnston, politician and Secretary of State for Scotland, born Kirkintilloch, 1881.
Dame Emily Mathieson Blair, nurse and nursing administrator, born Lenzie, 1890.
Jessie Marion King, painter and illustrator, born Bearsden, 1875.
Sir Andrew McCance, metallurgist, born Cadder, 1889.
Sir Hugh Fraser, businessman, born Bearsden, 1936.
Lulu (Lulu Kennedy-Cairns) singer, born (Marie McDonald McLaughlin Lawrie) Lennoxtown, 1948.

"I'll take a rum.
"Rum it shall be, Mr Todd."
"I thought this was a temperance hotel?" I said.
"Oh, aye, it is. That way we get no trouble frae the polis."
William Boyd from *The New Confessions*.

bleaching), and later on transporting materials like coa iron and quarried stone from the works in surroundin villages, taking advantage of the development of turnpike roads, canals and railways.

The most populous towns in the county are today commuter suburbs for Glasgow, expanding from small settlements to fashionable suburbs in part due to excellent rail and later road links. However, manufacturing jobs in East Dunbartonshire have held up well (10.8 per cent), as has employment from touris (10 per cent), but the service industry provides the greatest number of jobs, particularly in public administration, education and health (28.9 per cent).

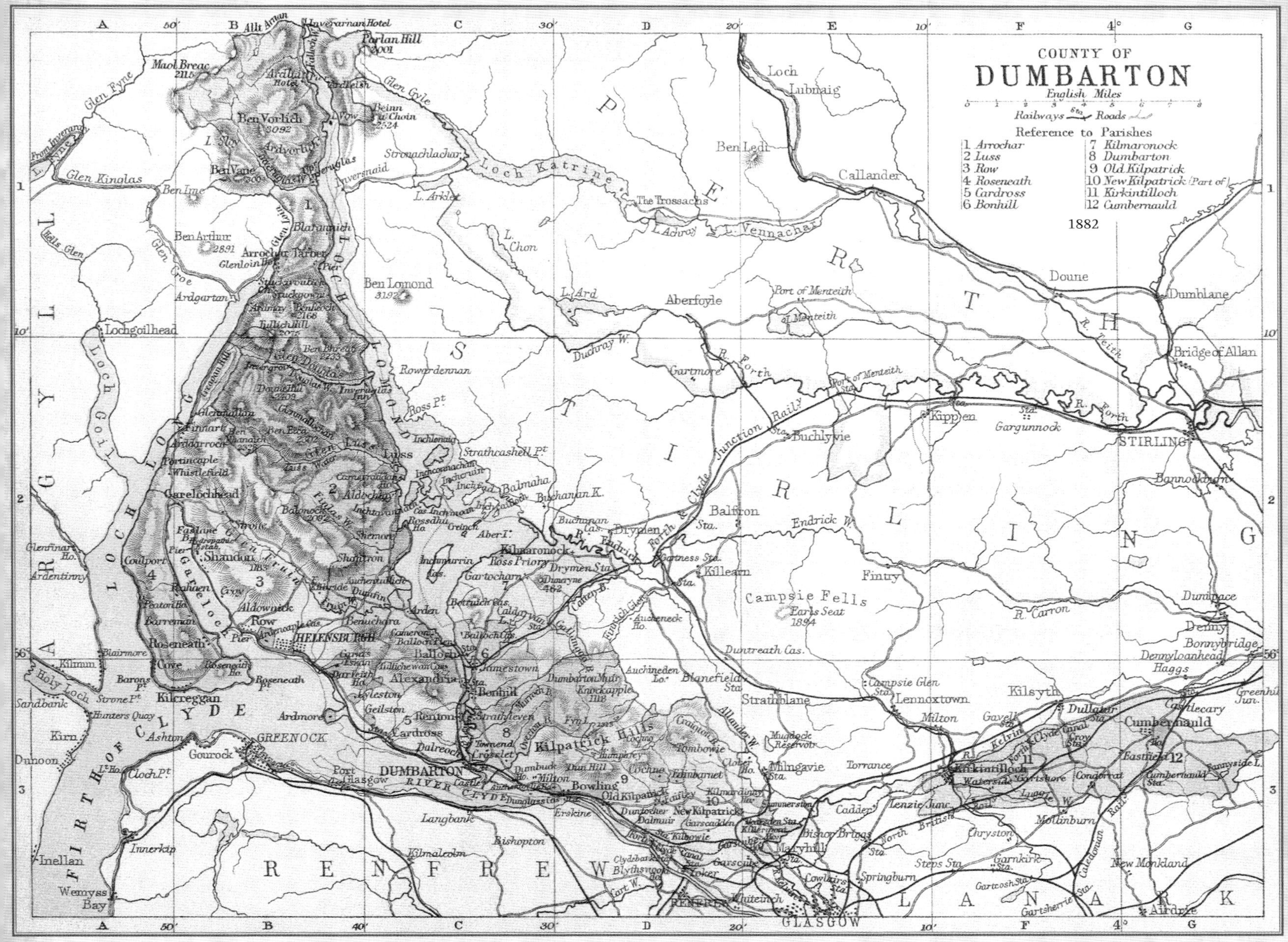

COUNTY OF
DUMBARTON
English Miles
Railways   Roads

Reference to Parishes

1	Arrochar	7	Kilmaronock
2	Luss	8	Dumbarton
3	Row	9	Old Kilpatrick
4	Roseneath	10	New Kilpatrick (Part of)
5	Cardross	11	Kirkintilloch
6	Bonhill	12	Cumbernauld

1882

Bartholomew Gazetteer of the British Isles, 1887

DUMBARTONSHIRE, co., partly maritime but chiefly inland, in W. of Scotland, comprising a main body and a detached portion; area, 154,542 ac.; pop. 75,333, or 312 persons to each sq. m. The main body is in the shape of a crescent, having the convex side adjacent to the estuary of the Clyde, and measures 1½ to 14 miles in breadth, and about 38 miles between its extreme points. The N. section (about two-thirds of the entire area), projecting between Loch Long and Loch Lomond, is wholly mountainous, and is celebrated for its picturesque and sublime scenery. Ben Vorlich and Ben Vane, in the extreme N., are 3092 and 3004 ft. high. The lower district along the Clyde is flat, and in general under excellent cultivation. The peninsular par. of Roseneath separates Loch Long and the Gare Loch, offshoots of the Firth of Clyde. The detached section (12 miles by 4 miles) lies 4½ miles E. of the nearest point of the main body. The rivers, besides the Clyde, are the Leven, Allander, Kelvin, and Endrick. The mfrs. are very important; numerous bleachfields, dye, print, and other works line the banks of the Leven; and there are extensive shipbuilding yards along the Clyde. D. in former times formed part of the territory of Lennox. Vestiges of the Roman wall of Antoninus still exist. The co. comprises 11 pars. and a part, the royal burgh of Dumbarton, and the police burghs of Cove and Kilcreggan, Helensburgh, and Kirkintilloch.

r Hill Roman Fort on the Antonine Wall near Twechar.

Loch Lomond

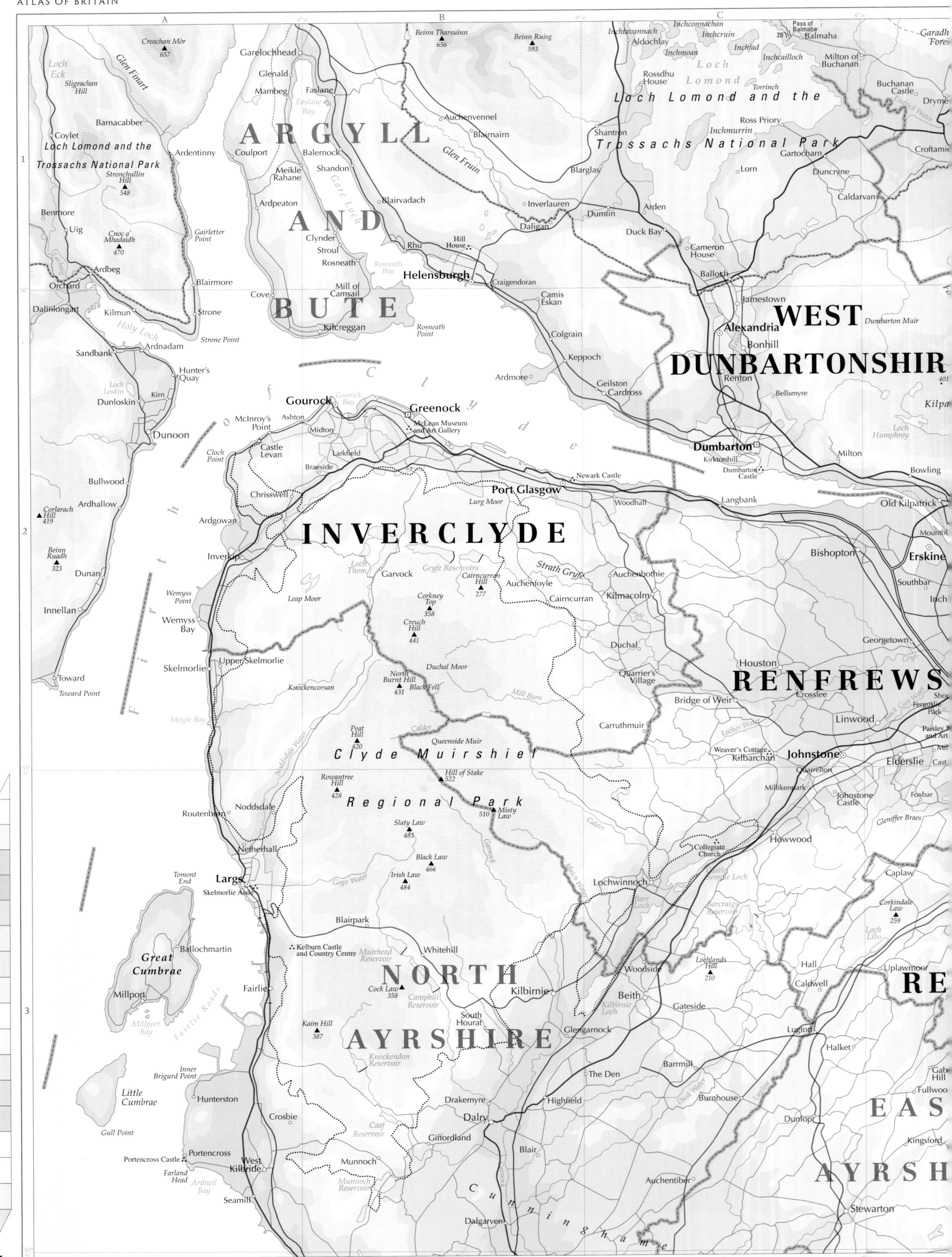

Metres
Feet

1000
3280

900
2952

800
2624

700
2296

600
1968

500
1640

400
1312

300
4921

200
656

150
492

100
328

50
164

0
Land
below
sea
level

50
164

200
656

1000
3281

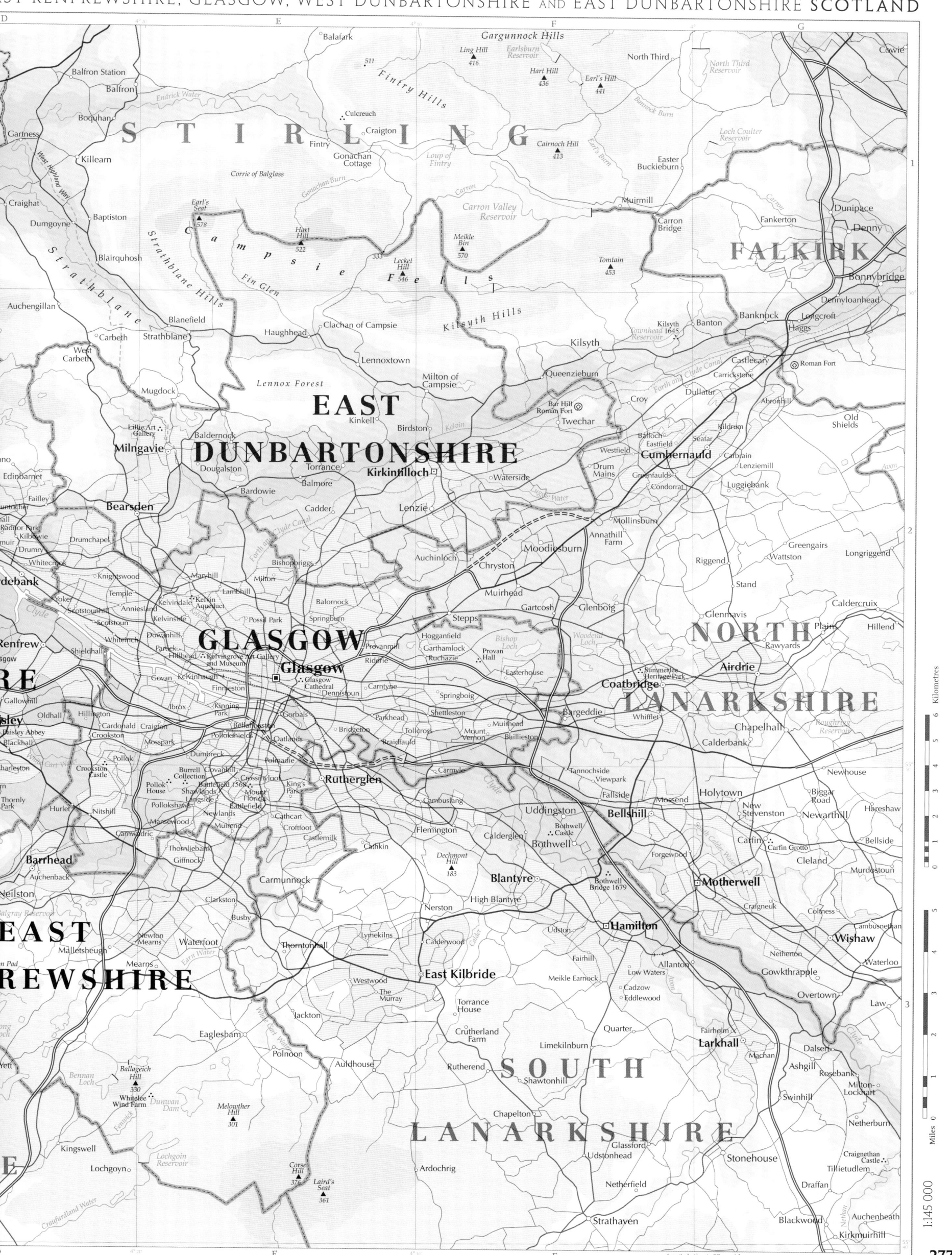

STIRLING

FALKIRK

EAST DUNBARTONSHIRE

GLASGOW

NORTH LANARKSHIRE

EAST RENFREWSHIRE

SOUTH LANARKSHIRE

1:145 000

Kilometres
0 1 2 3 4 5 6

Miles
0 1 2 3 4 5

Longitude west of Greenwich

© Collins Bartholomew Ltd

NORTH LANARKSHIRE

Area Sq Km	472
Area Sq Miles	182
Population	325,500
Admin HQ	Motherwell
Highest point	Garrell Hill (459 m) in the Kilsyth Hills

North Lanarkshire (*Siorrachd Lannraig a Tuath*) takes its name from the historic county of Lanarkshire (named after the county town of Lanark, from the Celtic, meaning 'glade').

FAMOUS FOR

Motherwell, prior to World War I, was home to the largest steelworks in Britain, and it was here that the plates for the Cunard liners RMS *Queen Mary* and RMS *Queen Elizabeth* were made.

Sir Robert McAlpine was known as **'Concrete Bob'** for his extensive use of the material to build both the Borrowdale and iconic Glenfinnan viaducts on the West Highland Railway at the turn of the 20th century.

The **Ravenscraig Steelworks**, a greenfield site in 1954, was by 1991 the largest hot strip steel mill in Europe. Its closure in 1992 marked the end of steelmaking in Scotland. In its place is a planned new town; with over 160 ha to be developed, it is one of the largest regeneration projects in Europe.

Unfortunately for **Cumbernauld**, it has twice won the 'Plook on a Plinth' *Prospect Magazine* Carbuncle Award for the Most Dismal Town in Scotland. It first won the award in 2001, when the town centre was described as 'a rabbit warren on stilts'. It fared little better in 2005: 'the Lego fantasy of an unhappy child'.

FAMOUS PEOPLE

Sir Robert McAlpine, builder and public works contractor, born Newarthill, 1847.
James Keir Hardie, politician, first leader of the Labour Party, born Newhouse, 1856.
Sir Alexander Matthew (Matt) Busby, football player and manager, born Bellshill, 1909.
George MacBeth, novelist and poet, born Shotts, 1932.
Liz Lochhead, poet and playwright, born Motherwell, 1947.

"What's Motherwell famous for? Coal and steel. What's Hamilton famous for? Stealin' coal."
Old Motherwell saying

In 1974, Lanarkshire was subsumed into Strathclyde Region, and then in 1996 Strathclyde was broken up into a group of new unitary authorities. North Lanarkshire, with a population of 325,500, includes the eastern section of the former Lanarkshire with additions from Stirlingshire in the very north and Dunbartonshire to the northwest. A highly urbanised district, the major towns are Cumbernauld (50,670), Coatbridge (41,700), Airdrie (35,520), Motherwell (30,790), Wishaw (29,220), Bellshill (20,200), Kilsyth (9,920) and Shotts (8,080).

It is a central lowland area extending from the Kilsyth Hills in the north – with rolling agricultural land to the north and east – to the Clyde River border in the south. Dairy farming, pork and poultry farms are situated in the north and east, and there are forests on the high grounds around the Campsie Fells to the far north. The river Almond rises in the hills north of Shotts and flows through the district eastwards, as does the river Avon. South Calder Water takes a western course as a tributary to the Clyde, as does North Calder Water. The heavily urbanised southern and western towns and villages could not provide a more stark contrast, with many inhabitants commuting either into Glasgow or one of the area's other centres for work. Coal mining and iron ore production in Coatbridge and Motherwell, which once included the massive Ravenscraig steel works, have given way to lighter industries like electronics, chemical and food processing, and account for a relatively high number of manufacturing jobs (11.5 per cent).

Originally a village of hand-loom weavers in the 19th century, modern Cumbernauld was built as a new town in 1956, and is today the largest conurbation in North Lanarkshire. Cumbernauld's local economy is centred on hi-tech industries and retail in an area where the service sector is by far the largest employer overall (79 per cent). Public administration, education and health accounts for nearly a third of that total. Businesses have been attracted here by the Eurocentral road–rail interchange and distribution hub at Mossend that opened in 1994.

The RMS *Queen Mary*

Statue of Sir Matt Busby outside Manchester United's football stadium.

Cumbernauld shopping centre

FALKIRK

Area Sq Km	315
Area Sq Miles	122
Population	151,600
Admin HQ	Falkirk
Highest point	Darrach Hill (357 m), near Carron Bridge

Falkirk, in Gaelic '*an Eaglais Bhreac*' or Scots '*Faw Kirk*', means 'the speckled church' and refers to the stone used to build the original church, erected sometime around AD 600.

FAMOUS FOR

The **Falkirk Wheel** is the world's only rotating boat-lift and was built in 2002 to lift vessels 35 m between the Forth and Clyde Canal and the Union Canal to re-establish the link between these two canals, broken in 1933 when a flight of 11 locks was dismantled. It necessitated an extension of the Union Canal, and was the pivotal project in the Millennium Link which re-connected Edinburgh and Glasgow by canal.

Falkirk has one of the shortest streets in Britain: **Tolbooth Street** is only 1.5 m (5ft) long.

The curious name of **Bo'ness** is actually a contraction of 'Borrowstounness' or 'the burgh's town on the ness'. It was the port for the royal palace at Linlithgow, one of the four most important burghs in Scotland until the Act of Union in 1707.

The **Carron Ironworks** were established on the banks of the river Carron near Falkirk in 1759. By the start of the 19th century, they were the largest ironworks in Europe, famed for the production of the 'Carronade', a very successful naval cannon – and later they manufactured pillarboxes and telephone boxes.

The *Charlotte Dundas*, the world's first practical steamship, was built at **Grangemouth** to the designs of William Symington, and it first sailed on the Forth and Clyde Canal in Glasgow in 1803. There were fears that it would damage the banks of the canal, and it was never used commercially.

FAMOUS PEOPLE

John Aitken, physicist and meteorologist, born Falkirk, 1839.
Thomas Clement (Tommy) Douglas, Baptist minister and Canadian politician, born Falkirk, 1904.
Andrew Greig Barr, soft drinks manufacturer and creator of Irn Bru, born Falkirk, 1872.
Elizabeth Blackadder, artist, born Falkirk, 1931.

The skilled manual worker, with a powerful union at his back, the owner of his own cottage and possibly enjoying a large joint family income, has a high sense of his own value and considers himself as good as any other man in the town. This attitude, which is an important local aspect of the social revolution, makes it difficult for any class to assume a position of recognised and effective superiority."
Rev. Wilson S. Leslie, *Third Statistical Account*, Falkirk, Stirlingshire (1953; revised 1961)

Falkirk District is a low-lying area along the south bank of the river Forth with agricultural land to the north and south, and a heavily industrialised area focused on the river. The river Forth forms one of Falkirk's boundaries and its tributary, the river Carron, bisects the district and enters the Forth at Grangemouth.

Originally part of the historic county of Stirlingshire, it became one of the three districts of Central Region in 1974 and a unitary authority in 1996. With a population of 151,600, it has more than recovered the population lost to the decline in heavy industry in the 1980s and 1990s. Falkirk (33,700) is the administrative centre, and other important towns include Polmont (20,720), Grangemouth (17,020), Stenhousemuir (17,190), Bo'ness (14,340) and Denny (10,100).

The Antonine Wall, built by the Romans in around AD 142 between the rivers Forth and Clyde, marked the Empire's northern limits. From the banks of the Forth near Bo'ness, its route can be traced across the district, with the most impressive remains at Rough Castle. It became a UNESCO World Heritage Site in July 2008.

Since the 18th century, this relatively small but populous area along the south bank of the Forth has been a hive of industrial activity. Coal and ironstone mining, steel and textile manufacture, distilling and brewing, food processing, paper making and book binding were all carried out here. Steeped in history, it is still a crossroads, with motorway links and two bridges spanning the Forth to Fife, the Kincardine Bridge and the Clackmannanshire Bridge, which opened in 2008.

Grangemouth, located just a few kilometres downstream from its rivals in Stirling and Alloa, was able to berth larger trading vessels in the 19th century. When the port became the link connecting the Forth and Clyde Canal with the Firth of Forth, trade boomed. The modern port is now Scotland's main container terminal and petrochemical complex, receiving North Sea oil by pipeline from Aberdeen (Cruden Bay). Falkirk has more people working in manufacturing and construction (22 per cent) than the average for either Scotland or Great Britain, but the public sector and the service industries now provide the majority of jobs.

The Falkirk Wheel and visitor centre.

Grangemouth Oil Refinery at night.

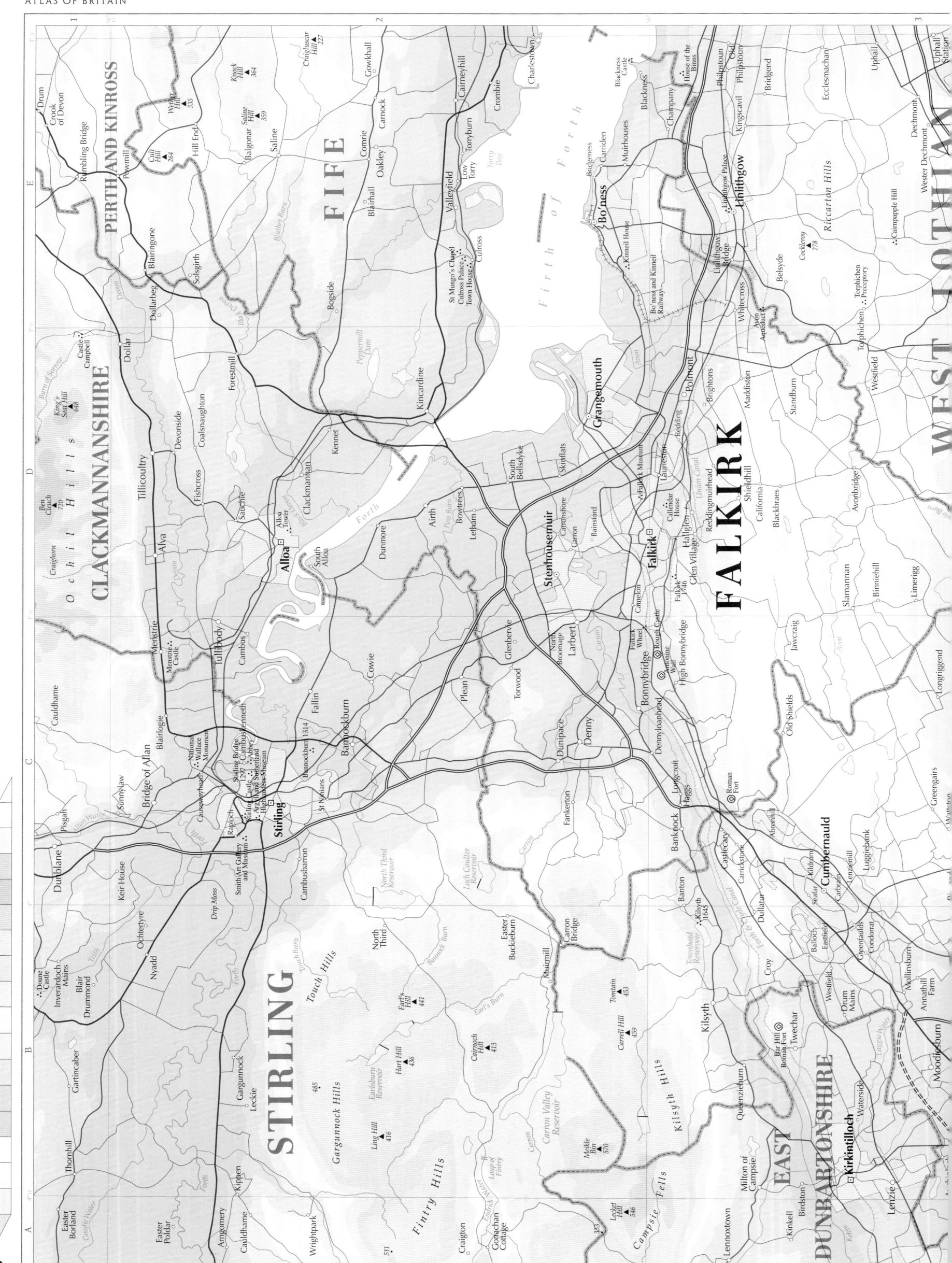

Metres
Feet

1000	3280
900	2952
800	2624
700	2296
600	1968
500	1640
400	1312
300	4921
200	656
150	492
100	328
50	164
0 Land below sea level	
50	164
200	656
1000	3281

British National Grid projection

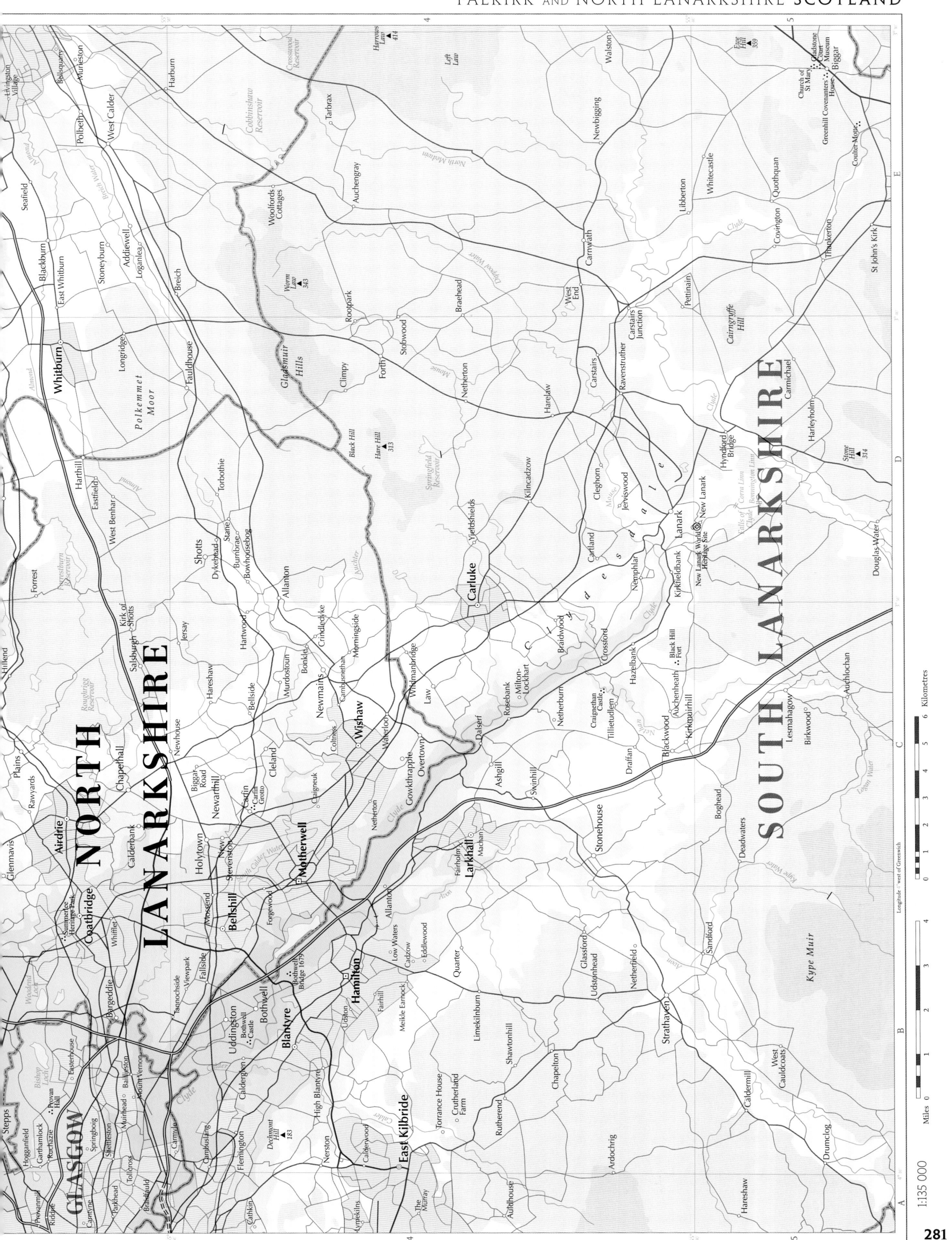

CITY OF EDINBURGH

Area Sq Km 273
Area Sq Miles 105
Population 471,700
Highest point Allermuir (493 m);
Arthur's Seat (250.5 m) is the highest point
within the city

An early form of Edinburgh's name was Din Eidyn (hence the Gaelic name of *Dun Eideann*), and, while '*Din*' means 'fort', the meaning of '*Eidyn*' is uncertain, although it may mean '*ridge*' (so the '*fort on the ridge*'). It does not mean, as sometimes asserted, 'Edwin's fort', after King Edwin of Northumbria (AD 616–632).

FAMOUS FOR

Its nickname of **'Auld Reekie'**, when the air was heavily polluted with smoke from coal and wood fires needed by residents to keep warm and cook upon.

The **Scottish Enlightenment** in the late 18th century when Edinburgh was the intellectual centre of Europe, home to the philosopher David Hume, the economist Adam Smith, the geologist James Hutton, and the chemist Joseph Black among many others.

The **Honours of Scotland** (the earliest surviving set of crown jewels in Britain, from the 15th and 16th centuries) and the **Stone of Destiny** (used in Scottish coronations since the 9th century), on display in Edinburgh Castle.

Mary King's Close, a 17th-century alley off the Royal Mile that still survives, deserted and ruined, underneath the City Chambers, which were built over the close in the 1750s.

Greyfriars Bobby, who was, so the story goes, the Skye terrier of Edinburgh police night watchman, 'Auld Jock' Gray. Gray was buried in Greyfriars churchyard in 1858 and Bobby remained near his grave for the next 14 years, until his own death, and is commemorated in a statue for his 'affectionate fidelity'.

Calton Hill, which contains many monuments, including one to Nelson that looks like an upturned telescope and an unfinished reproduction of the Parthenon in Athens.

The former Royal Yacht, HMY *Britannia*, which can now be visited at the Ocean Terminal in Leith.

Its world-renowned **festivals** – including the Edinburgh International Festival, Edinburgh Festival Fringe, Edinburgh International Book Festival, Edinburgh Military Tattoo, Edinburgh Science Festival, Edinburgh International Film Festival and Edinburgh's Hogmanay. In 2008 over 4 million people attended festival events.

Deacon Brodie, by day a respectable town councillor and deacon (head) of the Incorporation of Wrights and Masons, but by night leader of a burglary gang, which broke into properties where he was carrying out work during the day. He was exposed after one of his gang was caught, and, in 1788, was hung from a gibbet that he had once modified. His life influenced Robert Louis Stevenson's tale *Dr Jekyll and Mr Hyde*.

FAMOUS PEOPLE

John Napier, inventor of logarithms, born Merchiston Castle, 1550.
David Hume, philosopher, born Edinburgh, 1711.
James Hutton, the 'father' of modern geology, born Edinburgh, 1726.
Sir Henry Raeburn, portrait artist, born Edinburgh, 17??
Sir Walter Scott, novelist, born Edinburgh, 1771.
Alexander Graham Bell, inventor of the telephone, bo?? Edinburgh, 1847.
James Clerk Maxwell, physicist, born Edinburgh, 1831
Robert Louis Stevenson, writer, born Edinburgh, 1850
Sir Arthur Conan Doyle, writer and doctor, born Edinburgh, 1859.
Sir Henry (Harry) Lauder, music hall entertainer, bor?? Portobello, 1870.
Dame Muriel Spark, novelist, born Edinburgh, 1918.
Sir Eduardo Paolozzi, artist and sculptor, born Leith, 192??
Sir Thomas Sean Connery, actor, born Edinburgh, 193??
Ronald Balfour (Ronnie) Corbett, comedian, born Edinburgh, 1930.
Tony Blair, British Prime Minister (1997–2007), born Edinburgh, 1953.
Irvine Welsh, novelist, born Leith, 1958.
Sir Christopher Andrew (Chris) Hoy, Olympic and wo?? champion cyclist, born Edinburgh, 1976.

The original settlement of Edinburgh grew up around the Castle Rock from the 11th century onwards. The city spread and incorporated a number of the surrounding settlements, most importantly in 1920, the port of Leith, on the Firth of Forth. In 1975 the city became a district within Lothian Regional Council, at which point South Queensferry and Kirkliston were brought into the city from West Lothian and Cramond, Currie and part of the Pentland Hills were taken from Midlothian. With further local government reforms in 1996, Edinburgh once again became a unitary authority. Its population in 2008 was 471,700, having grown by 5.7 per cent over the previous 10 years, in contrast to population declines seen in all other major Scottish cities. Edinburgh has the highest percentage of working-age residents in Scotland, and it continues to be a magnet for those migrating to Scotland.

Edinburgh is capital of Scotland, the home of the Scottish Parliament and a major administrative, judicial, cultural, educational, financial and tourist centre. Employment is very much focused on the service industries, with 31.6 per cent of employment being in the banking, finance and business sector, 30.5 per cent in public administration, education and health, and 19 per cent in retail, hotels and restaurants, with a mere 3.7 per cent in manufacturing. Tourism-related employment accounts for around 10 per cent of all jobs. The financial crisis of 2008 particularly affected the banking sector, but it remains the powerhouse behind Edinburgh's economy, the top four businesses employing over 27,000 people in the city.

The setting of Edinburgh is one of the most dramatic of any major city. Castle Rock and Arthur's Seat are the remains of a major volcano that erupted over 350 million years ago, while Calton Hill and other areas were formed from lava flows. During the ice age, glaciers gouged out the low-lying areas of the Grassmarket to the south of the Castle Rock and Princess Street Gardens (once the Nor' Loch) to the north. Castle Rock is now an imposing crag right in the centre of the city, with its tail sloping down to Holyrood, forming the Royal Mile. Long a prized defensive site, Castle Rock became a royal castle under Malcolm II towards the end of the 11th century. In 1502 James IV moved the royal palace to Holyroodhouse, next to the Abbey of Holyrood at the other end of the Royal Mile. The castle is now one of the most visited tourist attractions in Scotland.

The city developed in a very dense fashion along the Royal Mile, leading to buildings of unprecedented height – Robertson's Land built in 1684 had 14 storeys. By the 18th century the 'Old Town' was becoming very over-populated and the city council finally agreed to the development of the 'New Town' in 1767, to the north of the Nor' Loch. Its elegant Georgian townscape soon became the centre of social and professional Edinburgh. The startling contrast between the Old and New Towns has led Edinburgh to becoming one of the world's favourite tourist destinations – a UNESCO World Heritage Site, UNESCO's first 'City of Literature' and, in August, the home since 1947 of the world's largest arts festival. The extension of the city boundaries in 1975 brought into the city South Queensferry and its two iconic bridges across the Firth of Forth, the massive cantilever Forth Railway Bridge, completed in 1890 and the suspension Forth Road Bridge, opened in 1964. A further cable-stayed road bridge is planned for completion in 2016.

Edinburgh is a major intellectual centre. Edinburgh University was founded in 1583 and is now the largest university in Scotland. The city is also home to Heriot-Watt University, Edinburgh Napier University and, until it moved to a new campus just outside the city at Musselburgh, Queen Margaret University. In all there are more than 50,00 full-time and part-time students studying in Edinburgh.

Edinburgh Castle

Scottish Parliament, Holyrood.

artholomew Gazetteer of the British Isles, 1887

DINBURGH, *ancient capital of Scotland, royal burgh, and
. town of Mid-Lothian, 1½ mile from its seaport Leith on
. shore of Firth of Forth, 42 E. of Glasgow, and 396¼ N. of
ondon by East Coast route – mun. burgh, 17,028 ac., pop.
36,032; 7 Banks, 10 newspapers. Market-day, Wednesday.
The municipal limits were extended in 1882). Edinburgh
one of the most picturesque of cities, and its beauties and
istorical associations attract a constant influx of visitors. It
built on 3 ridges running E. and W., and is surrounded on
ll sides, except the N., by lofty hills. The Old Town occupies
e central ridge, terminated by the Castle on the W., and by
Iolyrood on the E.; the Castle Rock is 437 ft. high. The Castle
as built in the 7th century by Edwin of Northumbria, on a
te previously occupied, in all probability, by the Romans and
e Southern Picts. Edinburgh was added to the kingdom of
e Scots in the 10th century, and was made a burgh by David
, who, in 1128, founded the Abbey of Holyrood. From 1437
when James I. was murdered at Perth) until the Union in
603, it was the favourite capital of the Stuart kings. It was
alled and fortified by James II. in 1450. The Old Town
ontains many buildings of historical interest, notably the
ncient Parliament House (now forming part of the supreme
ourts of law) and the collegiate church or cathedral of
t Giles (built 1110, restored 1883). The New Town, which
ccupies the N. ridge, took its rise towards the end of the 18th
entury. It presents a splendid assemblage of streets, squares,
ardens, and monuments. More recently the city has extended
apidly towards the S. and the W. The principal industries
f Edinburgh are printing, type-founding, bookbinding,
ithographing, and engraving; machine-making and brass-
ounding; coach-building; mfrs. of glass and jewellery;
nning, brewing, and distilling There are 3 distilleries.
Edinburgh is the seat of the Government departments for
Scotland, and is a garrison town. It is also the centre of the
 railway and the banking systems of Scotland. A railway, 7
niles long, round the S. suburbs, was begun in 1881 and
pened in 1884. It has railway and tramway communication
with Leith, which at one point it conjoins. Edinburgh,
owever, depends for its prosperity chiefly on its courts of law,
olleges, and schools, on its attractions for visitors, and its*

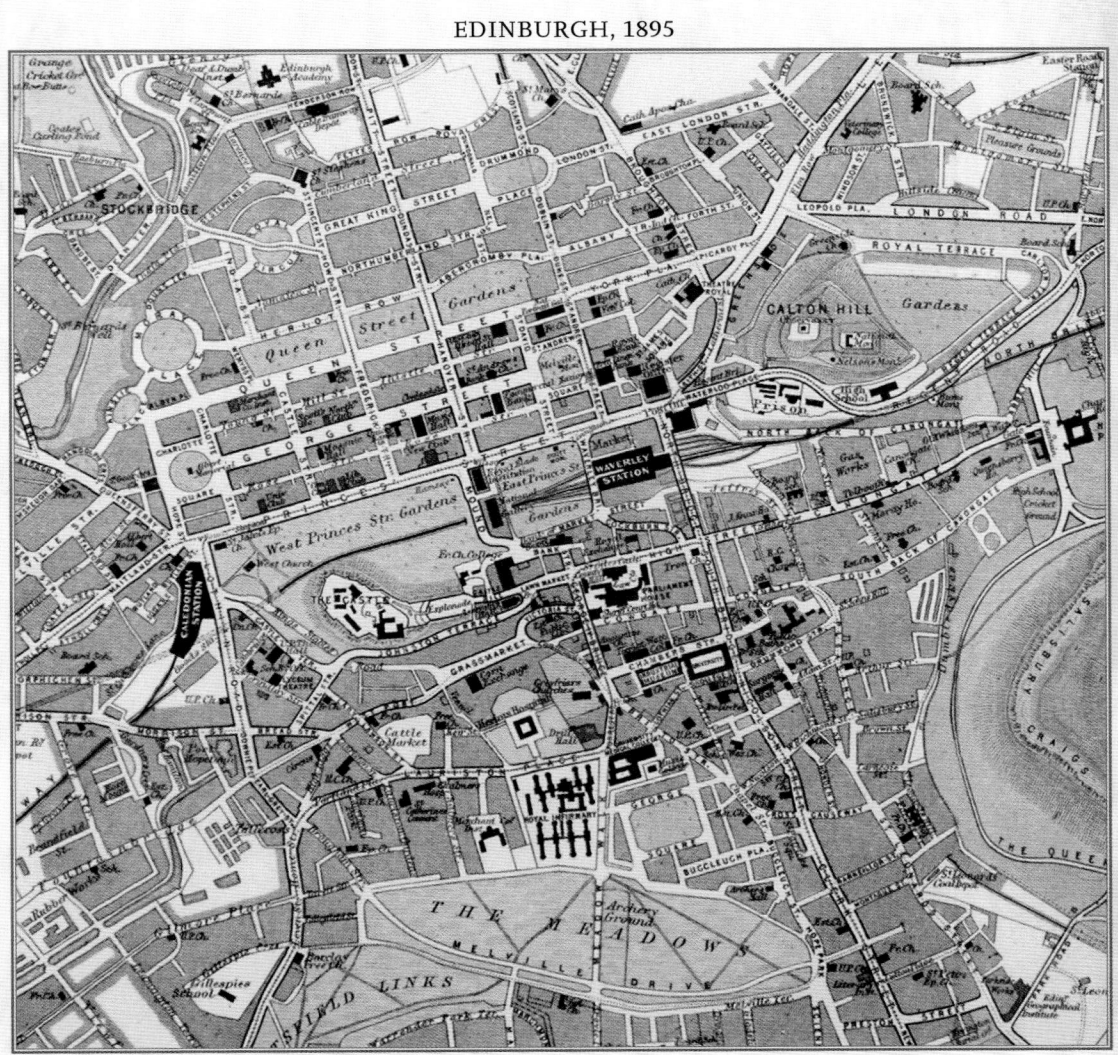

EDINBURGH, 1895

*amenity as a place of residence. The University (1582) had
in 1883-1884 professors to the number of 41, and students
to the number of 3408, of whom 1559 were medical students.
Edinburgh has long been famous for its medical schools, which
have attracted students from all parts of the world. The new
Medical School, adjacent to the new Royal Infirmary, was
built in 1878-1883. Of the other educational institutions the*

*more prominent are the Theological Colleges, the Training
Colleges, the High School, the Merchant Company's Schools,
Fettes College (modelled after the great public schools of
England), the Royal Scottish Academy of Painting, Sculpture,
and Architecture, and the School of Arts. There are also
numerous hospitals (Heriot's, Donaldson's, &c.) for the
maintenance and education of poor children.*

ces Street from Calton Hill.

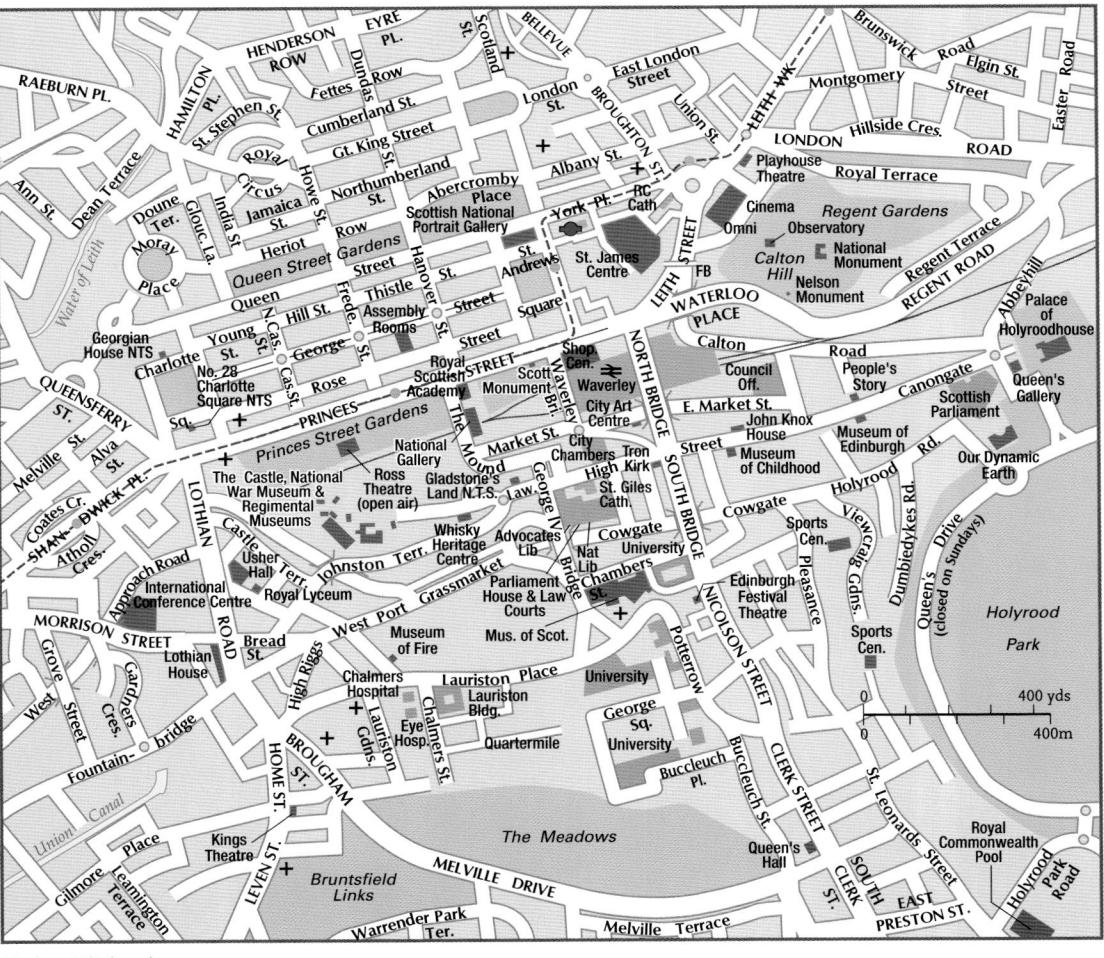

Modern Edinburgh

EAST LOTHIAN

Area Sq Km	701
Area Sq Miles	271
Population	96,100
Admin HQ	Haddington
Highest point	Meikle Says Law (535 m)

Siorrachd Lodainn an Ear (the Council of East Lothian) is more a transliteration than translation because the area's name probably had Welsh or Brythonic origins rather than Gaelic antecedents. Called *Louthion* c. 1200, and possibly named after a person, 'Leudonus', it also includes *'ear'*, the Gaelic direction 'east'.

FAMOUS FOR
After the defeat at the battle of Bannockburn in 1314, Edward II fled back to the stronghold at **Dunbar** for refuge.

The **'Lamp of the Lothians'**, was originally a title given to Haddington's Franciscan friary which was destroyed in 1356, and later to the 14th-century Church of St Mary.

Musselburgh was famous for its harvests of the bivalve molluscs located on banks at the mouth of the river Esk. Nowadays, the town is probably better known for horse racing than mussels.

Gullane is home to Muirfield Golf Course, which hosted its first Open Championship in 1892, a mere nine months after the course had been built. It is one of four 18-hole courses in the town.

The **Preston Mill** at East Linton is the latest mill to occupy the site, on which there has been a working watermill since 1599.

The 16th-century doocot (pigeon house) at **Dirleton Castle** west of North Berwick has nest boxes for 1,000 birds, an important food source for inhabitants of the castle.

The Bass Rock, off North Berwick was once the home of St Baldred in the 7th century, and now is the largest single-rock gannetry in the world, with approximately 80,000 birds.

Haddington Post Office, one of the first in Scotland, can trace its origins back to 1603, when James VI and I became king of both Scotland and England.

FAMOUS PEOPLE
Alexander II, King of Scotland, born Haddington in 1198.
John Knox, religious reformer and founder of the Church of Scotland, born near Haddington c. 1513.
John Heriot, newspaper editor and writer, born Haddington in 1760.
John Rennie, civil engineer and bridge builder, born near East Linton in 1761.
Robert Cadell, bookseller and publisher, born Cockenzie in 1788.
Robert Moffat, missionary in Africa and linguist, born Ormiston in 1795.
Samuel Smiles, author and social reformer, born Haddington in 1812.
Francis Cadell, riverine explorer and trader in Australia, born Cockenzie in 1822.
George Harley, physician and physiological chemist, born Harley House (Haddington) in 1829.
Walter Runciman, first Baron Runciman, ship owner, born Dunbar in 1847.
Arthur James Balfour, philosopher and Prime Minister, born Whittingehame House (East Linton) in 1848.

East Lothian is a south-eastern county of Scotland on the southern shore of the Firth of Forth, with an undulating coastal plain extending inland to the upland areas around the Lammermuir Hills, part of the Southern Upland Fault, and which form the county's southern boundary. The highest point in the area is found in these hills at Meikle Says Law (535 m). The area is bisected by the river Tyne, and the river Esk is also an important local waterway.

Part of the much larger ancient Lothian region, more recently the area was synonymous with the traditional county of Haddingtonshire until its abolition in 1921. East Lothian was a district of Lothian Region from 1975, but further reorganisation in 1996 liberated it once again, and added Musselburgh to its territory in the west. East Lothian's population (96,100) has risen steadily since 1981, undoubtedly due to its excellent road and rail communications with Edinburgh. Haddington (8,600) is the administrative centre. The western towns include Musselburgh (21,840), Tranent (9,440), Prestonpans (7,310) and Cockenzie (5,750) and are little more than residential suburbs for the capital, while Dunbar (7,700), North Berwick (6,430) and Gullane (2,390) have developed as holiday resorts.

Once part of the kingdom of Northumbria, it was only in the 10th century that the Lothians became part of Scotland. The same roads which brought the invading English armies into the region exist today in the form of the 'Great North Road' (A1), which sweeps up the eastern coast and across the north of the county towards its terminus in Edinburgh. In fact, proximity to the royal court and rich agricultural lands and ports meant that this area was always heavily contested in the wars between England and Scotland.

Haddington straddles the river Tyne and was one of Scotland's first royal burghs. It suffered more than most at the hands of contesting armies, being burnt to the ground in 1356 by Edward III, and left in ruins again in 1549. Despite these setbacks, the town was the site of Scotland's most important grain market by the 18th century, and was a staging post along the original route of the Great North Road. That wealth built homes designed by, for example, William Adam and allowed the restoration of many others so that today there are more than 200 listed or scheduled buildings in the town.

Fishing, mining and agriculture were traditional occupations in East Lothian, and just over half of the land is still designated for arable farming. Only one coal mine is currently in operation (Blindwells at Tranent), and the fishing ports at Musselburgh, Cockenzie, North Berwick and Dunbar are no longer active. Modern light industry and manufacturing jobs (7 per cent), particularly food processing, precision engineering and electronics have partially taken the place of heavier industry. However, service industries are major employers, particularly public administration, education and health (29 per cent), boosted by the removal of Queen Margaret University from Edinburgh to a new site at Musselburgh. Distribution, hotels and restaurants (21 per cent) together with tourism (11 per cent) are significant employers, unsurprisingly in a landscape crammed with castles, golf courses and seaside resorts.

Tantallon Castle and Bass Rock, North Berwick.

Preston Mill

EDINBURGH AND ENVIRONS, 1885

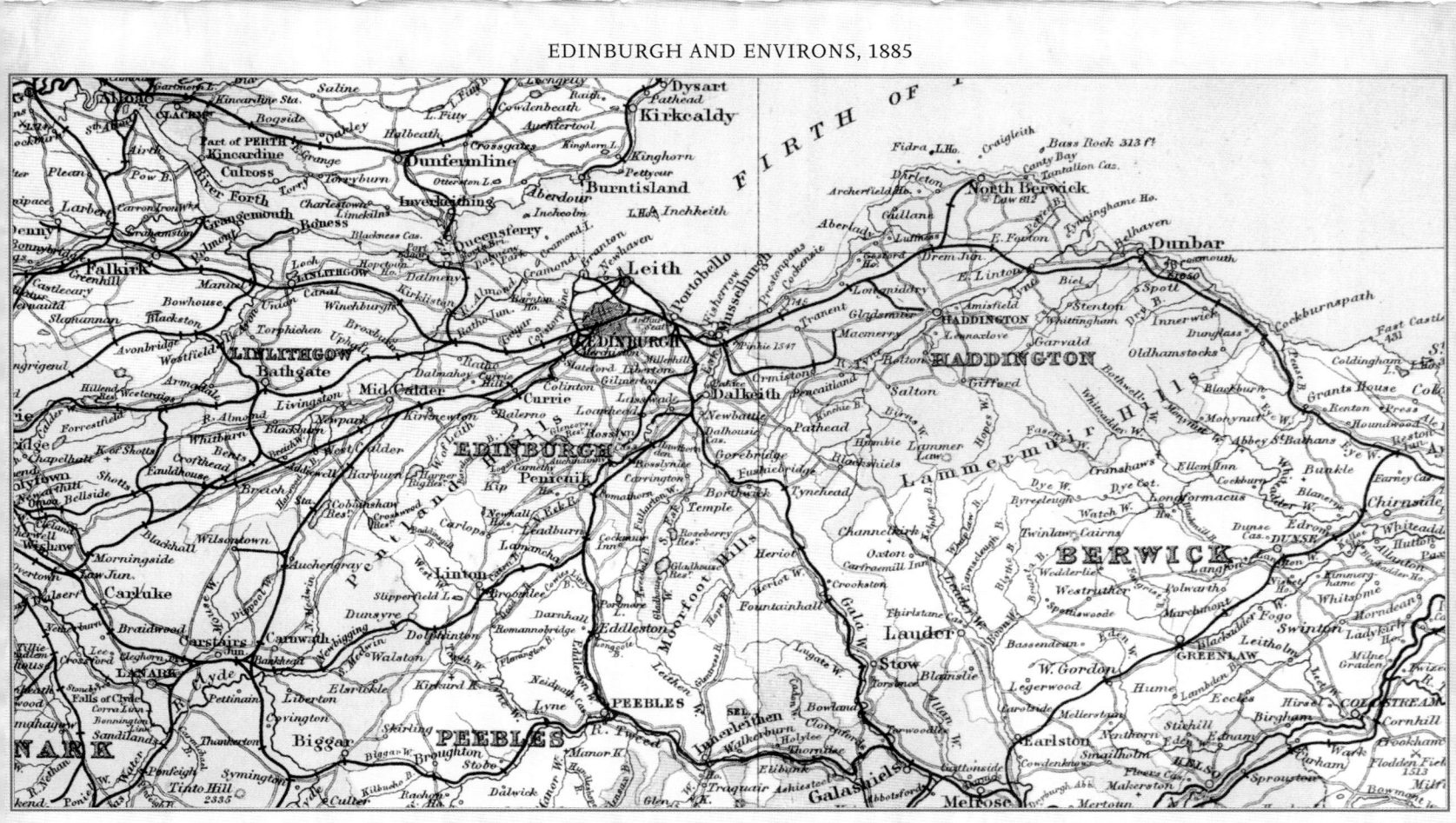

Bartholomew Gazetteer of the British Isles, 1887

LINLITHGOWSHIRE *(or West Lothian), maritime co. in SE. of Scotland; is bounded N. by Firth of Forth, SE. by Edinburghshire, and W. by Lanarkshire and Stirlingshire; greatest length, NE. and SW., 19 miles; greatest breadth, E. and W., 14 miles; area, 76,806 ac., pop. 43,510. The coast is low; the surface is varied, but there are few hills of any height; the chief rivers are the Avon on the W. and the Almond on the E. border. Much of the soil is fertile, and agriculture is in an advanced condition. Linlithgowshire is one of the richest mineral counties in Scotland, coal, shales, ironstone, freestone, limestone, &c., being very abundant. Paraffin oil is largely manufactured at Bathgate, Broxburn, and Uphall. The co. contains 12 pars, and 2 parts, the royal burghs of Linlithgow and Queensferry, and the police burghs of Armadale, Bathgate, Borrowstounness, and Whitburn.*

EDINBURGHSHIRE *(or Mid-Lothian), maritime co. in SE. of Scotland; is bounded E. by Haddington (or East-Lothian), Berwick, and Roxburgh; S. by Selkirk and Peebles; SW. by Lanark; and NW. by Linlithgow (or West-Lothian); coast-line, 12 miles; 231,724 ac., pop. 389,164. The surface is finely diversified. The Moorfoot Hills, a continuation of the Lammermuirs, occupy the SE.; the Pentland Hills stretch across the co. from the SW. All the streams, with the exception of the Tyne and Gala, in the E. and the SE., run to the Firth of Forth; the principal are the North Esk, the South Esk, the Water of Leith, and the Almond; the North Esk especially is noted for its picturesque scenery. The lowlands towards the Forth are the most fertile; the hilly parts of the S. are chiefly under pasture; in the W. are dairy-farms; in the vicinity of the city of Edinburgh are extensive nursery grounds and market gardens. The principal crops are oats and barley, turnips and potatoes. The co. consists chiefly of carboniferous strata; and coal, shale, ironstone, limestone, and freestone, are extensively worked. There are valuable herring fisheries in the Firth of Forth. The mfrs. are limited; but (beyond Edinburgh and Leith) there are numerous paper mills, oil-works, and several iron foundries and brick and tile works. Gunpowder is made at Roslyn. The co. is traversed by the North British and Caledonian Rys., and by the Union Canal. It contains 28 pars, and 4 parts, the parl. burgh of Edin., the Leith Burghs (Leith, Portobello, and Musselburgh, and the police burghs of Bonnyrigg, Dalkeith, Loanhead, and Penicuik.*

HADDINGTONSHIRE, *royal and police burgh, par., and co. town of Haddingtonshire, on river Tyne, 18¼ miles E. of Edinburgh, 44 NW. of Berwick on Tweed, and 388 NW. of London by rail – par., 12,113 ac., pop. 5660; burgh and town, pop. (including Nungate), 4043; 4 Banks, 2 newspapers. Market-day, Friday. Haddington has one of the largest grain markets in Scotland. Among the chief buildings are the church, a Gothic edifice of the 12th or 13th century, – it is surmounted by a square tower 90 ft. high, and its nave is used as the parish church; the Corn Exchange (1854); and the Knox Memorial Institute (1880), an educational foundation (with which the old grammar school is incorporated) in memory of John Knox (1505-1572), the Scottish Reformer, who was a native. Haddington gives the title of earl to the Hamiltons of Innerwick.*

e Welsh Carlyle, diarist, born Haddington in 1801.
n Muir, naturalist and conservationist, born nbar in 1838.
trick George Thomas Buchan-Hepburn, Baron iles, governor-general of the West Indies, born at eaton Hepburn in 1901.
° Horace Algernon Fraser Rumbold, civil servant d historian, born North Berwick in 1906.
° Matthew Alistair Grant, businessman, born ddington in 1937.

sselburgh was a burgh when Edinburgh was nane d Musselburgh will be a burgh when Edinburgh has gane. aditional

as my native place! That Goddess of dullness has strewed it all her poppies."
e Welsh Carlyle on Haddington

View from Byres Hill, one of the Garleton Hills, north across to Fife.

MIDLOTHIAN

Area Sq Km	355
Area Sq Miles	137
Population	80,600
Admin HQ	Dalkeith
Highest point	Blackhope Scar (651 m) in the Moorfoot Hills

Meadhan Lodainn is the Gaelic translation of the area's name which probably had Welsh or Brythonic origins rather than Gaelic antecedents. Called *Louthion* c. 1200, and possibly named after a person, 'Leudonus', or even the legendary British King Lot, to which has been added the Gaelic 'meadhan', a variation of 'meadhón' or 'middle'.

FAMOUS FOR
The Heart of Midlothian is no longer located within the district at all, since boundary changes have separated the city of Edinburgh from its former landward territories.

Rosslyn Chapel, founded in the 15th century by Sir William St Clair, is renowned for the exuberance of its carved interior, particularly the 'Apprentice Pillar', it gained the reputation of 'a Bible in stone'. Speculation as to its connection with the Knights Templar and stories about the Holy Grail, have been woven into the best-selling book and movie, *The Da Vinci Code*.

Borthwick Castle, built by Sir William Borthwick in 1430, was described centuries later as perhaps the finest example of its kind. Mary, Queen of Scots and her unfortunate third husband, James Hepburn, Earl of Bothwell fled here for safety in 1567. It is constructed of an estimated 30,000 tons of masonry with very thick walls, undoubtedly the rationale behind the removal of the public records of Scotland from Edinburgh during World War II and storing here for safekeeping.

Gunpowder was manufactured at Roslin Glen, just outside **Roslin** from the early 19th century until 1954.

FAMOUS PEOPLE
William Drummond of Hawthornden, poet, born Hawthornden Castle, in 1585.
Henry Dundas, 1st Viscount Melville, jurist and politician, born Dalkeith in 1742.

Sir Samuel Chisholm, temperance campaigner, born Dalkeith in 1836.
Peter Borthwick, newspaper editor, born Cornbank (Penicuik) in 1804.
James Ormiston McWilliam, epidemiologist, born Dalkeith in 1808.
John Lawson Johnston, nutrition promoter and food manufacturer, born Roslin in 1839.
Sir William Paterson, mechanical engineer, born Ros[...] in 1874.
Sir John Anderson, 1st Viscount Waverley, administra[...] and politician, born Eskbank (Dalkeith) in 1882.
Sir William MacTaggart, painter, born Loanhead in 19[...]
Annette Crosbie, actress, born Gorebridge in 1934.
Darren Fletcher, professional footballer, born Dalkeit[...] in 1984.

"It is so large and high that a man on horseback could turn[...] spear in it with all the ease imaginable."
Alexander Nisbet on the Great Hall at Borthwick Cast[...]

"The Right Honourable Gentleman is indebted to his mem[...] for his jests, and to his imagination for his facts." Richard Brinsley Sheridan on Henry Dundas

Landlocked Midlothian in south-eastern Scotland encompasses the suburban and rural areas south and southeast of Edinburgh. The Pentland Hills to the northwest and Moorfoot Hills to the southeast sandwich this part of the fertile coastal plain that rises from the Firth of Forth. Blackhope Scar (651 m) in the Moorfoot Hills is the highest point. The North Esk and South Esk, which flow northeast through the area, and Tyne Water in the south, are the most important waterways.

Once part of much larger Lothian in the Middle Ages, by the 19th century it was known as the County of Edinburgh (or, worse, Edinburghshire) until its abolition in 1921. By 1975, Lothian Region had subsumed the counties directly south of the Firth of Forth, of which Midlothian became a district. Further reorganisation in 1996 left Midlothian as a smaller unitary authority than either the original county or the district. Villages to the south were transferred to Scottish Borders Council,

and Edinburgh, Musselburgh and Inveresk with their links to the Forth were also shorn away: the population of 80,600 is less than in 1981, and one of the smallest in Scotland. The administrative centre is at Dalkeith (pop. 11,200). Other important towns include Penicuik (15,680), Bonnyrigg (14,080), Mayfield (12,950), Loanhead (6,290), in the north and west, and Gorebridge (5,510) to the southeast of the district.

An area much prized in the past, the Romans built a road to the Forth that skirted the Pentland Hills. It was part of the great kingdom of Northumbria until the 10th century, and, in common with the whole area, was never primarily Gaelic speaking. Access to the capital and rich farmland left its mark with many fine houses, castles and ecclesiastical foundations.

Pastoral and arable farming in the region still produce staple crops including oats, barley and wheat, as well as some dairy farming and sheep rearing.

Traditional industries once included coal mining and other heavy engineering, plus paper and carpet making, lime burning and glassmaking. Crystal glass is still made in Penicuik. The colliery at Newtongrang[...] is now the home of the Scottish Mining Museum, although curiously tourism is not as prominent an industry in the area (7 per cent of jobs) as might be expected. Construction and manufacturing still make[...] up almost 20 per cent of jobs, but it is in the service industries that provide the greatest employment. Pub[...] administration, education and health (32 per cent) an[...] distribution, hotels and restaurants (24 per cent) are the most important employers. Midlothian's fortunes may be directly related to the success of the Borders Railway project, which will connect Newtongrange an[...] Gorebridge to the Edinburgh suburban lines.

CLACKMANNANSHIRE

Area Sq Km	164
Area Sq Miles	63
Population	50,500
Admin HQ	Alloa
Highest point	Ben Cleuch (721 m) in the Ochil Hills

It takes its name from the town of Clackmannan (Gaelic *Chlach Mhannainn*), derived from *chlach* – the 'King's Stone' (a glacial rock preserved in the centre of Clackmannan) – in the district of Manau (possibly the ancient name of the lands around the upper reaches of the Forth).

FAMOUS FOR
A descendant of King Robert I, Catherine Bruce, 'knighted' Robert Burns when he was a guest in her home, **Clackmannan Tower**, allegedly using the king's two-handed sword.

In a rare revival, the rail service between **Kincardine** and **Stirling** reopened in May 2008, replacing the one closed 40 years earlier.

The **Clackmannanshire Bridge**, a 1.2 km crossing of the Forth near Kincardine, was opened on 19 November 2008. It reduces the traffic pressure on the nearby Kincardine Bridge, opened in 1936.

FAMOUS PEOPLE
William Alexander, Lord Stirling, poet and courtier, born Alva, c.1567.
John Erskine, Earl of Mar (Bobbing John), promoter of t[...] Act of Union and then Jacobite leader, born Alloa, 1675.
Sir George Younger, brewer and Conservative politici[...] born Alloa, 1851.
Alan Hansen, professional football player, born Alloa, 19[...]

"O Alva Hills is bonny
Tillicoultry hills is fair,
But to think on the Braes o' Menstrie
It maks my heart fu' sair"
Anonymous

Clackmannanshire is roughly divided between the Ochil Hills to the north and the lowland plains in the valleys of the Forth and Devon rivers to the south. The river Forth forms the district's southwest border, and its tributary, the river Devon joins it near Cambus. Once the smallest shire in Scotland, Clackmannanshire was incorporated into Central Region in 1975 and only reappeared on the map in the local government reorganisations of 1996, simply as Clackmannan. One of the first acts of the re-formed Council was to restore its original appellation: Clackmannanshire, albeit with Alloa as the county town. It remains one of the smallest unitary authorities, with a population of 50,500, an increase of 9 per cent since 1981. The Hillfoots mill villages of Tillicoultry (5,130), Alva (4,960) and Menstrie (2,290) lie in the shadow of the

Ochil Hills. To the southeast, Alloa (19,330) Tullibody (7,800) and Clackmannan (3,420) occupy strategic positions along the river Forth, and northeast is Dollar (2,860), at the mouth of Dollar Glen, overlooked by Castle Campbell in the hills above.

Until the 1960s, the backbone of Clackmannanshire's economy was coal mining, heavy engineering and textile manufacture. Manufacturing, including glassware and textiles, and distilling and brewing are still important employers (10.8 per cent). However, employment is concentrated in the service sector, particularly public administration, education and health (33.6 per cent). Retail, hotels and restaurants (23.6 per cent) dovetail with the tourism sector (8.3 per cent) as another major jobs provider.

Alloa's position along the Forth has been the source of the town's prosperity for centuries. The Erskine earls of Mar built Alloa Tower in the 14th century and the town grew up around it. As well as a thriving shipbuilding industry, Alloa became a major trading port for local coal, and the re-exportation of Caribbean sugar and American tobacco to Europe. In 1710 a Customs House was built to regulate trade alon[...] this stretch of the river, and in 1850 a railway station was opened. By the start of the 21st century most of these industries had dramatically declined, replaced by electronics and service industries, but rail and road links, including the new Clackmannanshire bridge across the Forth, remain good.

EST LOTHIAN

rea Sq Km	432
rea Sq Miles	167
opulation	169,500
dmin HQ	Livingston
ighest point	West Cairn Hill (562 m)

odainn an Iar is the Gaelic translation of the area's ame which probably had Welsh or Brythonic origins ther than Gaelic antecedents. Called *Louthion* c. 200, and possibly named after a person, 'Leudonus', even the legendary British King Lot, to which has en added '*iar*', the Gaelic direction 'west'.

AMOUS FOR

inlithgow Palace was a favourite royal residence of cottish monarchs in the 15th and 16th centuries, though it was first built sometime in the 12th ntury and, typically, much fought over and novated in following centuries. It might have riginally stood on an island, as it is estimated water vels of Linlithgow Loch were once much higher an they are today.

he **'West Lothian Question'** is a thorny problem oncerning voting rights between MPs in estminster and Edinburgh. It revolves around e propriety of Scottish MPs voting in Parliament issues solely relevant to English constituencies, hile unable to vote on the same issue in Scotland it concerned one of the areas 'devolved' to the cottish government (education, health, agriculture d justice). In fact, it is possible for the Scottish vernment to allow the UK Parliament to legislate devolved matters, using a procedure known as the wel Motion.

espite **Livingston** being a 'New Town' it was built the site of an older village, Livingston Peel. long with a village green and 18th-century church, derstone House includes part of a 16th-century wer.

ing George IV knighted the Scottish artist Henry aeburn during a visit to **Hopetoun House** in 1822.

y 2001, **'Silicon Glen'** had a 15 per cent share of tal European semiconductor capacity, producing per cent of branded PCs in Europe, 65 per cent of urope's ATMs, and nearly 80 per cent of Europe's orkstations, according to the then Minister for urope, Keith Vaz.

r James Young Simpson established the world's rst oil refinery in **Bathgate** to extract paraffin from ale oil.

AMOUS PEOPLE

ames V, king of Scotland, born Linlithgow in 1512.
Mary, Queen of Scots, born Linlithgow in 1542.
ir James Young Simpson, obstetrician and pioneer the use of anaesthetics, born Bathgate in 1811.
Henry Moubray Cadell, geologist, born at Torphichen 1860.
ngus McGillveray, nationalist politician, born East hitburn in 1930.
usan Magdalane Boyle, singer, born Blackburn in 061.
avid Tennant (pseudonym of David McDonald), tor, born in Bathgate in 1971.
aul Dickov, professional footballer, born Livingston 1972.

Every school needs a debating society far more than it eeds a computer."
r Malcolm Rifkind

West Lothian is a south central administrative area of Scotland, lying west of Edinburgh and south of the Firth of Forth. The short coastline rises southwards to a coastal plain towards the Pentland Hills in the southeast and moorland in the south and west. The highest point is West Cairn Hill (562 m) above the Harperrig Reservoir in the Pentland Hills. The river Almond, flowing through the centre of the county, and the river Avon are the most important natural waterways. The rich arable farmland associated with the Central Belt is to be found in the north and west of the area where wheat, barley, fodder crops and potatoes are grown. There is also some dairying and sheep farming on higher ground in the south.

The westernmost lands of the ancient region of Lothian, the modern area was known as Linlithgowshire until 1975, when it was subsumed into Lothian Regional Council. Further reorganisation in 1996 created West Lothian, which occupies a slightly different area than the original county, having lost both Bo'ness and South Queensferry to other authorities. The population of West Lothian (169,500) has increased since 1981 by almost 20 per cent, probably as a result of the opportunities presented by the 'dot-com' boom. The administrative centre is in Livingston (54,530). Other important towns include Bathgate (16,300), Broxburn (14,140), Linlithgow (13,180), Whitburn (10,780) and Armadale (10,830).

Livingston, the administrative centre, was designated Scotland's fourth 'New Town' in 1962 and specifically laid out to facilitate motor transport. The town with its five industrial parks, is an important player in the 'Silicon Glen' phenomenon, the Scottish hi-tech computer business sector. Computer software and hardware firms located to the area because of its excellent communication links alongside the M8 motorway and within a stone's throw of Edinburgh airport.

The Romans constructed roads and fortlets to hold the rural areas of Lothian, but away from the coastal fringe, with its busy little ports, the upland countryside was not easily accessible throughout the medieval and early modern periods. The impact of the Industrial Revolution was to change this dramatically, as demand for coal, shale oil and iron ore precipitated a population boom. Armadale, Broxburn, West Calder and Whitburn all grew from hamlets to towns during the 19th century. Within 100 years, however, most of the mining and heavy industries were played out, to be partially replaced by the entirely new electronics and computer hardware manufacturing industries. West Lothian had become part of 'Silicon Glen'. The bust of the dot-com boom in the early 21st century saw retrenchment in the industry, with an emphasis more on computer software development. The manufacturing and construction sectors remain strong, providing just over a quarter of local jobs, better on average than either Scotland or Great Britain as a whole. The largest employers in the area are the service industries, which together account for most of the remaining employment, particularly in distribution, hotels and restaurants (24 per cent), public administration, education and health (23 per cent) and finance, IT and other business activities (15 per cent).

Communication has been the key to West Lothian's recent expansion: the Forth Rail bridge (1890), the Forth Road Bridge (1964), and the completion of the links between Glasgow and Edinburgh along the M8 and M9 motorways have made accessible hitherto remote rural areas. Consultative talks are currently in progress with the view of building a third crossing of the Forth. The Airdrie–Bathgate rail link upgrade via Armadale would also connect Glasgow and Edinburgh through West Lothian.

Rosslyn Chapel, Roslin, Midlothian.

Castle Campbell, Dollar Glen, Clackmannanshire.

Linlithgow Palace, West Lothian.

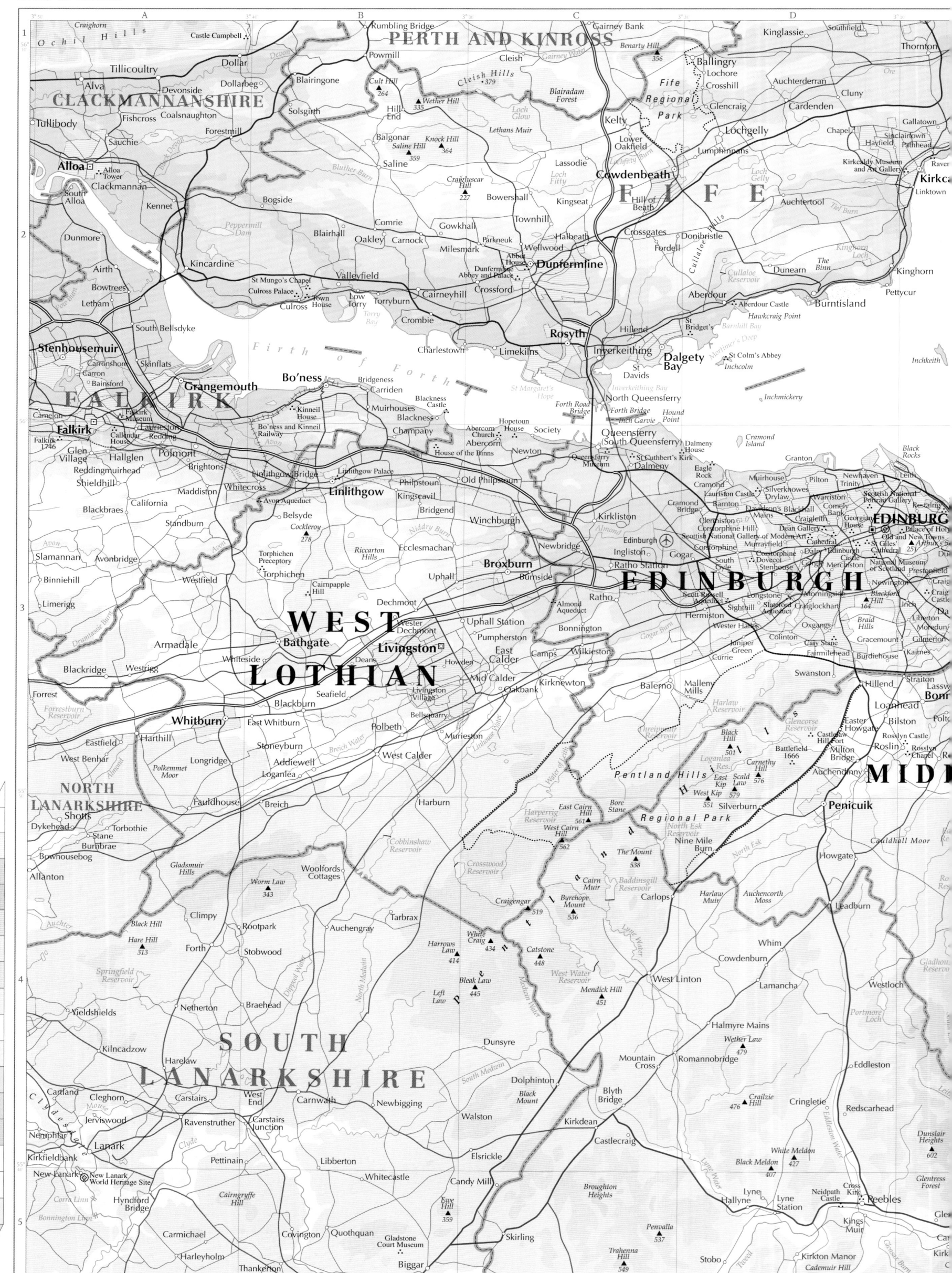

British National Grid projection

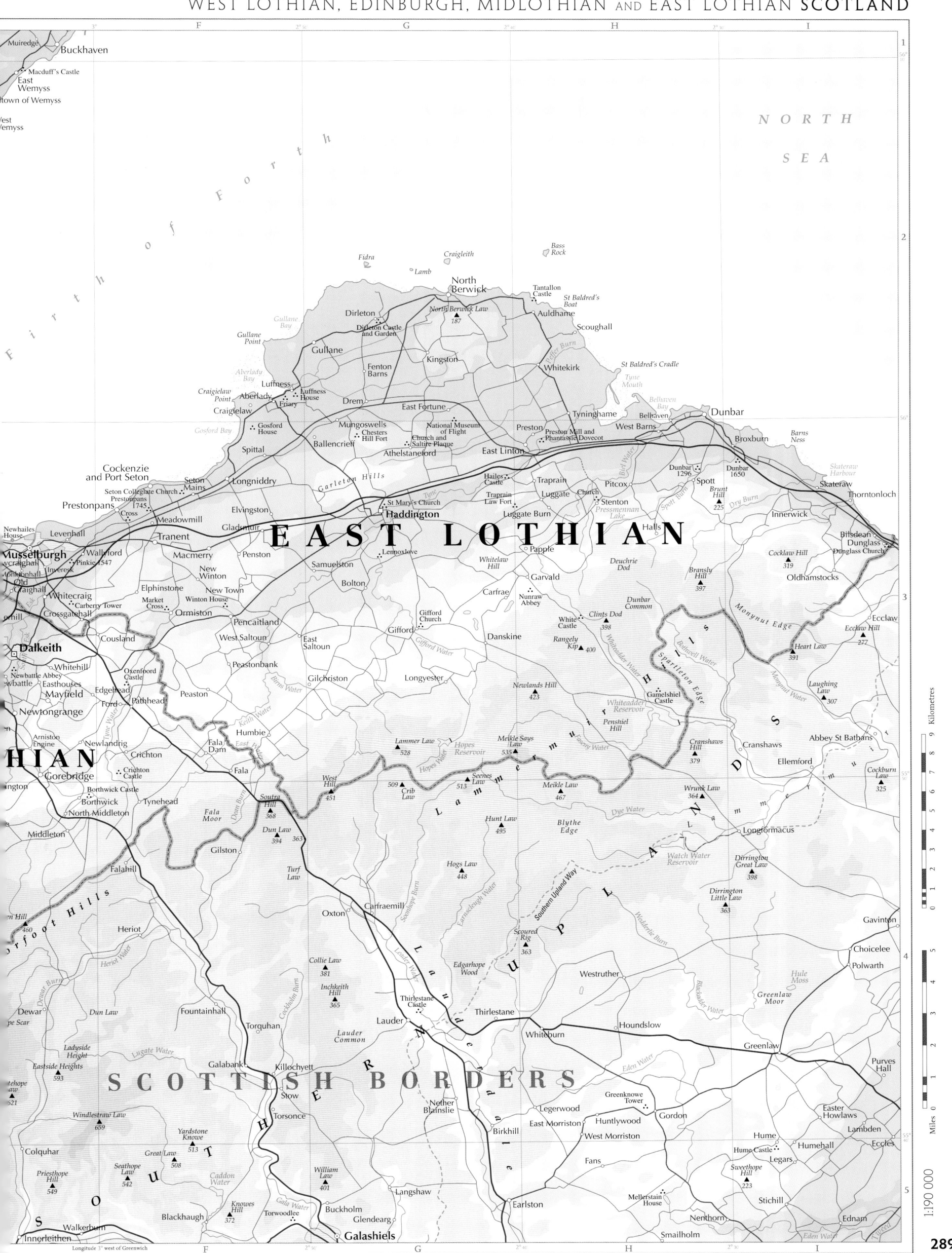

EAST LOTHIAN

HIAN

SCOTTISH BORDERS

NORTH

SEA

Muiredge
Buckhaven
Macduff's Castle
East Wemyss
Town of Wemyss
West Wemyss

Firth of Forth

Fidra
Craigleith
Lamb
Bass Rock

North Berwick
Dirleton
North Berwick Law 187
Tantallon Castle
St Baldred's Boat
Auldhame
Scoughall

Gullane Bay
Dirleton Castle and Garden
Gullane
Fenton Barns
Kingston
Whitekirk
St Baldred's Cradle

Gullane Point
Aberlady Bay
Luffness
Craigielaw Point
Aberlady
Luffness House
Drem
East Fortune
Tyninghame
Bellhaven Bay
Dunbar

Craigielaw
Friary
Gosford Bay
Gosford House
Mungoswells
National Museum of Flight
Preston
Preston Mill and Phantassie Dovecot
West Barns
Broxburn

Cockenzie and Port Seton
Spittal
Ballencrieff
Chesters Hill Fort
Church and Saltire Plaque
East Linton
Dunbar 1296
Dunbar 1650
Barns Ness
Skateraw Harbour

Seton Mains
Longniddry
Athelstaneford
Hailes Castle
Traprain
Pitcox
Stenton
Spott
Brunt Hill 225
Innerwick
Skateraw
Thorntonloch

Seton Collegiate Church
Prestonpans 1745
Elvingston
St Mary's Church
Tyne
Traprain Law Fort
Luggate
Church
Pressmennan Lake
Dunbar 1650
Dunglass
Dunglass Church

Prestonpans
Cross
Meadowmill
Gladsmuir
Haddington
Luggate Burn
Halls
Deuchrie Dod
Bransly Hill 397
Cocklaw Hill 319
Bilsdean
Oldhamstocks

Newhailes House
Levenhall
Tranent
Penston
Lennoxlove
Papple
White Castle
Clints Dod 398
Dunbar Common
Ecclaw
Ecclaw Hill 277

Musselburgh
Wallyford
Pinkie 1547
Macmerry
New Winton
Samuelston
Whitelaw Hill
Garvald
Nunraw Abbey
Rangely Kip 400
Whiteadder Water
Gamelshiel Castle
Heart Law 391
Monynut Edge

Inveresk
Old
Craighall
Whitecraig
Elphinstone
New Town
Bolton
Carfrae
Gifford Church
Danskine
Newlands Hill 423
Whiteadder Reservoir
Penshiel Hill
Spartleton Edge
Laughing Law 307

Carberry Tower
Market Cross
Winton House
Gifford
Longyester
Cranshaws Hill 379
Cranshaws
Abbey St Bathans
Cockburn Law 325

Crossgatehall
Ormiston
Pencaitland
West Saltoun
East Saltoun
Lammer Law 528
Hopes Reservoir
Meikle Says Law 535
Meikle Law 467
Wrunk Law 364
Ellemford

Dalkeith
Cousland
Peastonbank
Gilchriston
Binns Water
Hopes Water
Seenes Law
Blythe Edge
Dye Water
Longformacus

Newbattle
Whitehill
Oxenford Castle
Peaston
Humbie
Crib Law
509
Seenes Law 513
Hunt Law 495
Watch Water Reservoir
Dirrington Great Law 398

Newbattle Abbey
Easthouses
Edgehead
Keith Water
West Hill 451
Dirrington Little Law 363

Mayfield
Ford
Pathhead
Fala Dam
Soutra Hill 368
Gavinton

Newtongrange
Arniston Engine
Newlandrig
Crichton
Fala
Dun Law 394
363
Hogs Law 448
Choicelee

Gorebridge
Crichton Castle
Tynehead
Fala Moor
Gilston
Turf Law
Carfraemill
Oxton
Lammermuir
Scoured Rig 363
Southern Upland Way
Westruther
Polwarth

Borthwick Castle
Borthwick
North Middleton
Heriot
Collie Law 381
Lauder Water
Edgarhope Wood

Middleton
Falahill
Heriot Water
Inchkeith Hill 365
Thirlestane Castle
Thirlestane
Hule Moss

Moorfoot Hills 460
Dewar Burn
Fountainhall
Torquhan
Lauder
Whitburn
Houndslow
Greenlaw
Purves Hall

Dun Law
Cockholm Burn
Galabank
Killochyett
Stow
Nether Blainslie
Legerwood
Greenknowe Tower
Huntlywood
Gordon
Eden Water
Easter Howlaws

Ladyside Height
Eastside Heights 593
Windlestraw Law 659
Torsonce
Birkhill
East Morriston
West Morriston
Hume
Lambden

521
Colquhar
Yardstone Knowe 513
Great Law 508
Caddon Water
William Law 401
Langshaw
Fans
Hume Castle
Legars
Humehall
Eccles

Priesthope Hill 549
Seathope Law 542
Knowes Hill 372
Torwoodlee
Buckholm
Glendearg
Earlston
Mellerstain House
Sweethope Hill 223
Nenthorn
Stichill
Ednam

Walkerburn
Innerleithen
Blackhaugh
Galashiels
Smailholm
Eden Water

SOUTHERN UPLANDS

Longitude 3° west of Greenwich

289

© Collins Bartholomew Ltd

1:190 000

Kilometres

Miles

FIFE

Area Sq Km	1,374
Area Sq Miles	530
Population	361,900
Admin HQ	Glenrothes
Highest point	West Lomond (522 m), an extinct volcano

Fife was originally known as *Fib* or *Fif*, the 'Territory of Fib', one of seven subdivisions of Pictland. In legend Fib was one of the seven sons of the founder of the Picts, Cruithe.

FAMOUS FOR
William IV conferred the title of **'The Royal and Ancient Golf Club'** on the Society of St Andrews golfers in 1834, and in 1897 the 'R & A' was recognised as the governing body for the rules of the game.

In 1874, there were five companies in **Kirkcaldy** making floorcloths, or linoleum, mostly situated around the railway tracks. The smell of boiling linseed oil was all pervasive and could be smelled for miles.

The novelist Daniel Defoe based the character of Robinson Crusoe on Alexander Selkirk from **Largo** in Fife, who was marooned on Juan Fernandez Island for more than four years.

Kirkcaldy was nicknamed the 'Lang Toun' as early as the 16th century and its main street has grown since then from 1.4 km to 6.4 km.

St Andrews is the home of the oldest university in Scotland (1413) and the third oldest in Britain.

The lighthouse on the **Isle of May** was first lit in 1636 using coal beacons atop a tower.

The **St Andrews Sarcophagus**, an 8th-century Pictish sandstone burial kist, was discovered in several pieces in 1833. Its elaborate carvings depict lions and hunters, and a royal figure dressed like a Roman emperor, reminiscent of a mosaic of the Emperor Justinian at San Vitale in Ravenna.

FAMOUS PEOPLE
David II, Scottish king, born Dunfermline, 1324.
David Beaton, Roman Catholic cardinal and archbishop, born Balfour, 1494.
Alexander Selkirk, sailor and inspiration for Robinson Crusoe, born Largo, 1676.
Adam Smith, economist and philosopher, born Kirkcaldy, 1723.
Robert Adam, architect and designer, born Kirkcaldy, 1728.
Archibald Constable, bookseller and publisher, born Carnbee, 1774.
Thomas Chalmers, theologian and founder of the Free Church of Scotland, born Anstruther, 1780.
Andrew Carnegie, industrialist and philanthropist, born Dunfermline, 1835.
Jimmy Shand, musician, born East Wemyss, 1908.
Joseph (Jo) Grimond, Baron Grimond, Liberal politician, born St Andrews, 1913.
Gordon Brown, Labour politician and former Prime Minister (from 2007–2010), born Kirkcaldy, 1951.
Jack Vettriano (originally Jack Hoggan), painter, born Methil, 1951.
Ian Rankin, author, born Cardenden, 1960.

"I ken mysel' by the queer-like smell
That the next stop's Kirkcaddy!"
M.C. Smith

"Old tales, old customs, and old men's dreams
Obscure this town ... the past sleeps in the stones."
(about St Andrews) Edwin Muir

Fife is a peninsula of undulating farmland between the Firth of Forth and the Firth of Tay. Its principal rivers are the Eden and Leven. Once a Pictish kingdom and later an integral part of the kingdom of Alba, Fife has been one of the least altered areas in Scotland. A successful campaign in the 1970s prevented it from being divided between Tayside and Lothian Regions and further local government reorganisation in 1996 made similarly little impact. The population of Fife is 361,900, a rise of over 20,000 since 1981, probably linked with its proximity to Edinburgh. The two largest towns, Kirkcaldy (48,090) and Dunfermline (44,950), both border the Firth of Forth. Glenrothes (38,800), the administrative centre, is in Fife's geographical centre. St Andrews (16,640), Buckhaven (16,240), Rosyth (12,900) and Cowdenbeath (11,680) are important smaller population centres.

Fife was one of the favourite playgrounds of the kings of Scotland, who hunted boar and other game through its oak forests. James VI and I famously characterised Fife as a 'beggar's mantle fringed with gold', and the legacy of the thriving fishing and trading ports all along the coastline, and especially in the 'East Neuk' can still be glimpsed in their tall Dutch-influenced crow-stepped gable buildings and pan-tiled roofs. Wool, linen, sheepskin fleeces and leathers, salt and coal were traded with the Netherlands, the Baltic and eastern Mediterranean. Ease of access by ship and ferry meant that Fife was also one of the most important areas in the kingdom, with the royal residence at Falkland, the intellectual and ecclesiastical centre at St Andrews, and the former capital and royal burial place at Dunfermline.

Barely 80 km wide, there is a marked contrast between the rural north and east and the industrial central and south. North East Fife is characterised by rolling hills and arable farmland running down to picturesque villages, rocky shores and sandy beaches. Coal mining in the west and central areas was increasingly important from the 19th century, spurred on by the advent of the Edinburgh to Perth railway line that sliced through the centre of the county, and facilitated the construction of rail bridges over both the rivers Forth and Tay. At its height, 51 coalmines were operating in Fife, but the last two, the Frances and Seafield collieries, closed in 1988.

Glenrothes has been the administrative centre since 1996, and is a 'new town' built in 1948 partly to house miners working at the new Rothes Colliery (forced to close due to flooding in 1961). The town had links to papermaking in Leslie and distilling in Markinch, and successful efforts to encourage light industries in the 1960s resulted in high-profile computing, electronics and related technologies moving into the area. Glenrothes is now considered part of central Scotland's 'Silicon Glen'. Although manufacturing and construction still account for 17.6 per cent of jobs in Fife, public administration, education and health (31.8 per cent), and retail, hotels and restaurants (22.5 per cent) employ a majority of people. Quick road and rail links, with the abolition of tolls on the bridges and the promise of a new crossing on the Forth, mean that commuters can easily work in either Edinburgh or Dundee.

The Clubhouse of the Royal and Ancient Golf Club, St Andrews.

Crail harbour

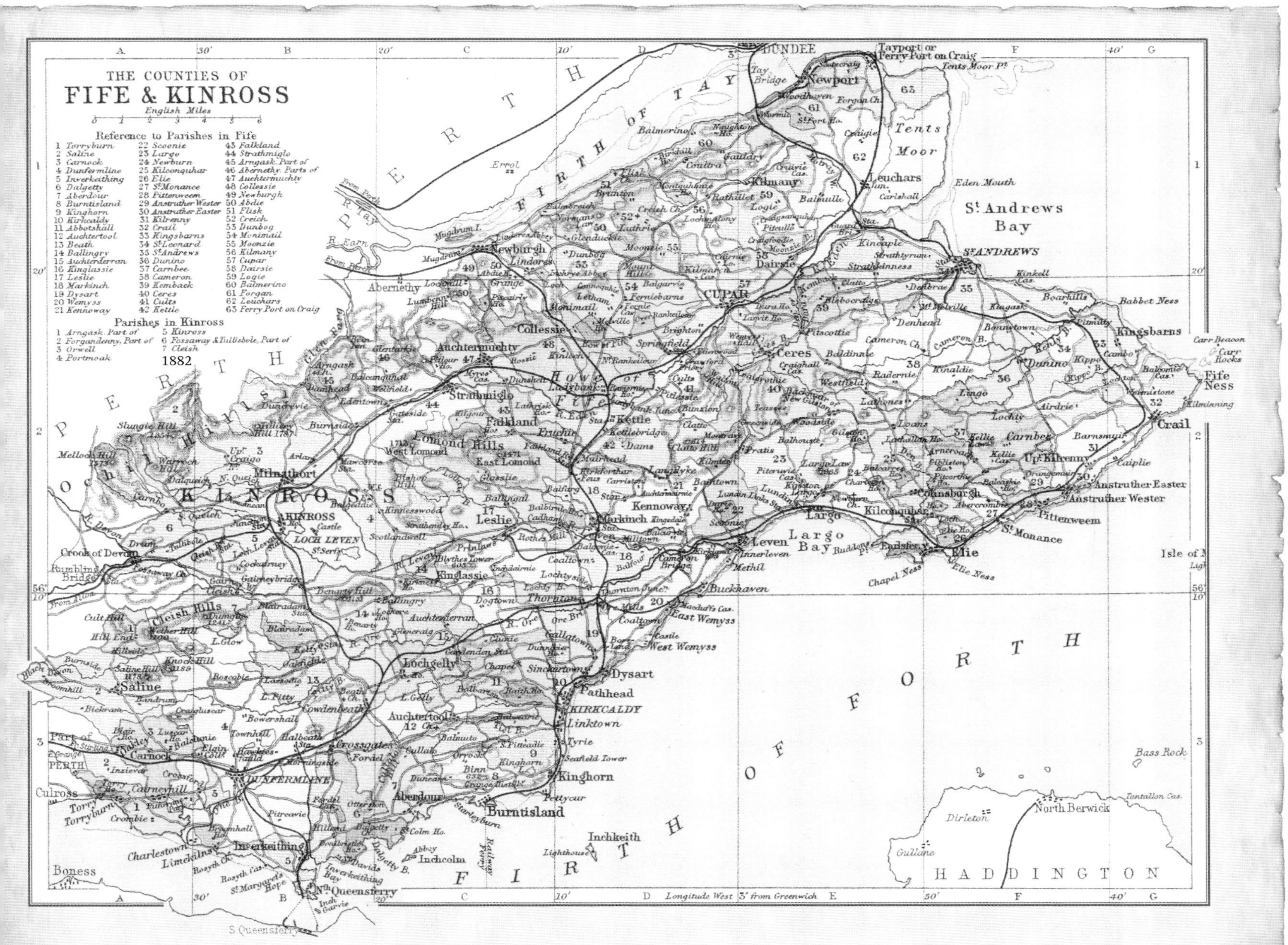
THE COUNTIES OF
FIFE & KINROSS
English Miles
Reference to Parishes in Fife
1 Torryburn
2 Saline
3 Carnock
4 Dunfermline
5 Inverkeithing
6 Dalgetty
7 Aberdour
8 Burntisland
9 Kinghorn
10 Kirkcaldy
11 Abbotshall
12 Auchtertool
13 Beath
14 Ballingry
15 Auchterderran
16 Kinglassie
17 Leslie
18 Markinch
19 Dysart
20 Wemyss
21 Kennoway
22 Scoonie
23 Largo
24 Newburn
25 Kilconquhar
26 Elie
27 St Monance
28 Pittenweem
29 Anstruther Wester
30 Anstruther Easter
31 Kilrenny
32 Crail
33 Kingsbarns
34 St Leonard
35 St Andrews
36 Dunino
37 Carnbee
38 Cameron
39 Kemback
40 Ceres
41 Cults
42 Kettle
43 Falkland
44 Strathmiglo
45 Arngask. Part of
46 Abernethy. Parts of
47 Auchtermuchty
48 Collessie
49 Newburgh
50 Abdie
51 Flisk
52 Creich
53 Dunbog
54 Monimail
55 Moonzie
56 Kilmany
57 Cupar
58 Dairsie
59 Logie
60 Balmerino
61 Forgan
62 Leuchars
63 Ferry Port on Craig
Parishes in Kinross
1 Arngask. Part of
2 Forgandenny, Part of
3 Orwell
4 Portmoak
5 Kinross
6 Fossaway & Tulliebole, Part of
7 Cleish
1882
PERTH
FIRTH OF TAY
FIRTH OF FORTH
KINROSS
DUNDEE
Newport
St Andrews Bay
ST ANDREWS
CUPAR
Kingsbarns
Fife Ness
Crail
Anstruther Easter
Anstruther Wester
Pittenweem
St Monance
Elie
Largo Bay
Leven
Buckhaven
KIRKCALDY
Kinghorn
Burntisland
Aberdour
Inverkeithing
N. Queensferry
DUNFERMLINE
Culross
Saline
Lochgelly
Cowdenbeath
Auchtermuchty
Falkland
Leslie
Markinch
Kennoway
Milnathort
Loch Leven
Lomond Hills
Cleish Hills
Ochil Hills
Inchkeith
Inchcolm
Bass Rock
North Berwick
HADDINGTON
Longitude West 3° from Greenwich

Bartholomew Gazetteer of the British Isles, 1887

FIFE *(or Fifeshire), maritime co. in E. of Scotland; is bounded N. by the Firth of Tay, E. by the North Sea, S. by the Firth of Forth, and W. by the cos. of Perth, Kinross, and Clackmannan; greatest length, 43 miles; greatest breadth, 18 miles; area, 314,952 ac., pop. 171,931. Fife forms the peninsula between the Firths of Forth and Tay. The coast is varied and picturesque; that part of it bordering on the Firth of Forth is lined with a succession of towns and villages, for the great number of which Fife is remarkable. The surface is pleasantly undulating. A ridge of high ground, commencing with the Lomond Hills, runs from W. to E.; to the N., between the Lomonds and a spur of the Ochils, lies an extensive plain called Strath Eden, or the Howe of Fife; to the S. is another stretch of low land, broken by Saline Hill, Knock Hill, the Hill of Beath, and the Cullalo Hills. The principal rivers are the Eden and the Leven. In the NW. the soil is moss, moor, and rock; in the NE. it consists of wet clay; the most fertile tracts are the Howe of Fife and the belt of loam which fringes the Firth of Forth. The formation is chiefly Carboniferous, and Fife is the third largest coal-producing county in Scotland. Limestone and freestone abound. Blackband ironstone is worked at Lochgelly and Oakley (where there are smelting furnaces); oil shale is worked near Burntisland. The principal mfr. is linen-damasks and diapers at Dunfermline, checks and ticks at Kirkcaldy. The co. comprises 61 pars. and 2 parts, the Kirkcaldy Burghs, the St Andrews Burghs, the parl. burghs of Dunfermline and Inverkeithing, and the police burghs of Anstruther Easter, Auchtermuchty, Burntisland, Cupar, Dunfermline, Dysart, Elie (Liberty and Williamsburgh), Inverkeithing, Kilrenny, Kinghorn, Kirkcaldy, Ladybank (and Monkston), Leslie, Leven, Lochgelly, Newburgh, Pittenweem, and St Andrews.*

KINROSS-SHIRE, *inland co. of Scotland; is bounded W. and N. by Perthshire, and E. and S. by Fifeshire; greatest length, N. and S., 10 miles; greatest breadth, E. and W., 12 miles; 46,485 ac.; pop. 6697. After Clackmannan, Kinross is the smallest co. in Scotland. The surface presents the appearance of a level plain almost surrounded by hills–the Ochil Hills in the NW., the Lomond Hills in the E., Benarty Hill in the S., and the Cleish Hills in the SW.; in the centre of this plain is Loch Leven. The higher regions are principally devoted to cattle and sheep farming; the low-lying lands are well sheltered and tolerably fertile. Limestone and sandstone are abundant, and coal is found in the S. The mfrs. are woollens (including plaids, shawls, &c.) and linens. Loch Leven is famous for its trout fishing. The co. contains 4 pars. and 3 parts, the police burgh of Kinross, the vil. of Milnathort, and part of the vil. of Kelty.*

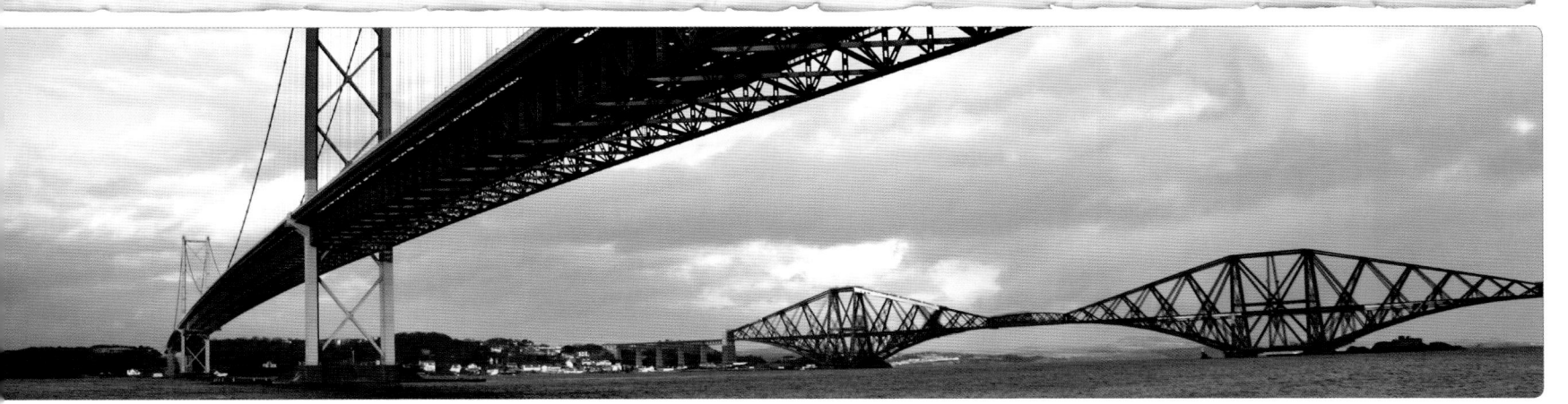

Forth road and rail bridges.

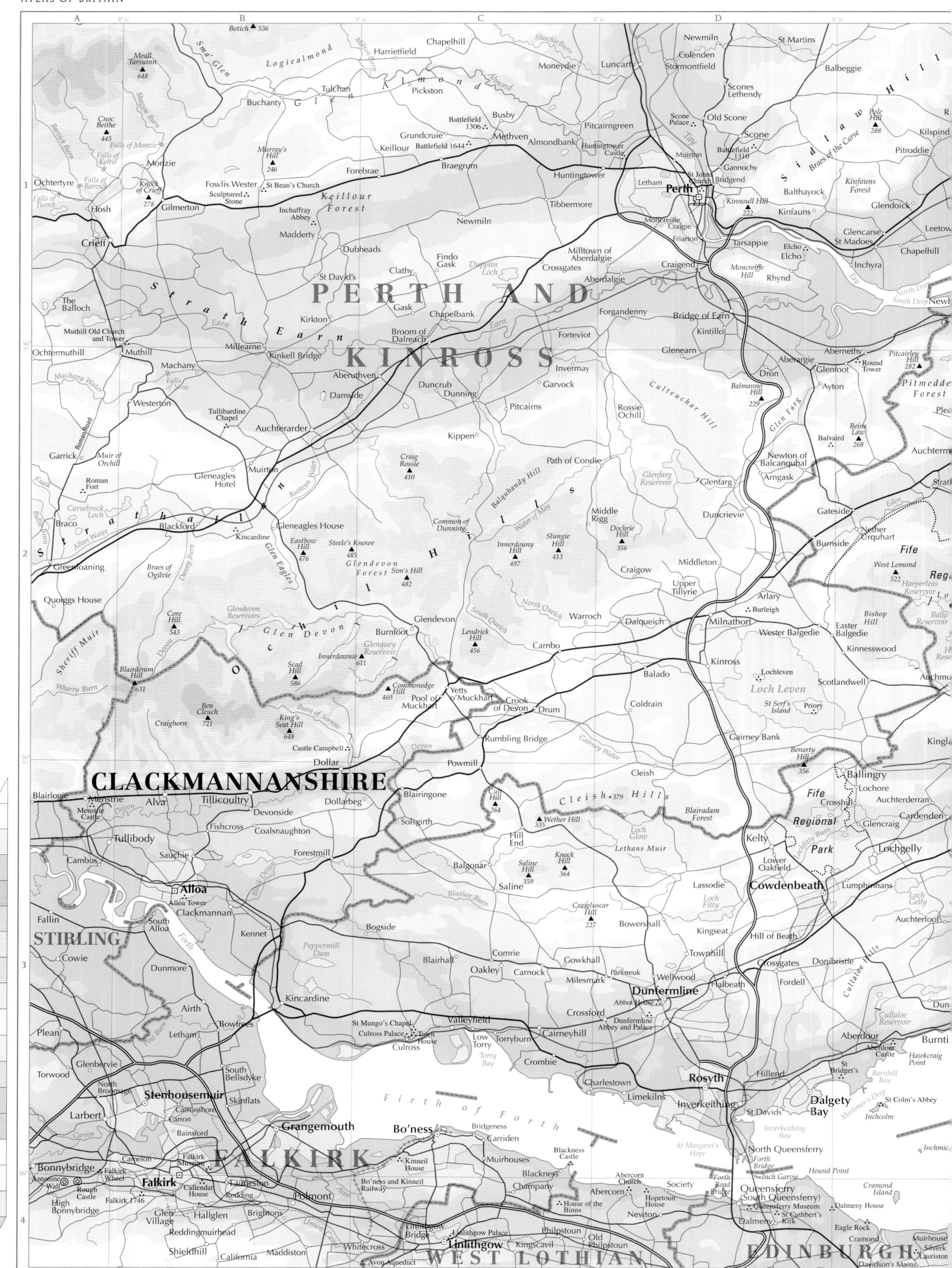

British National Grid projection

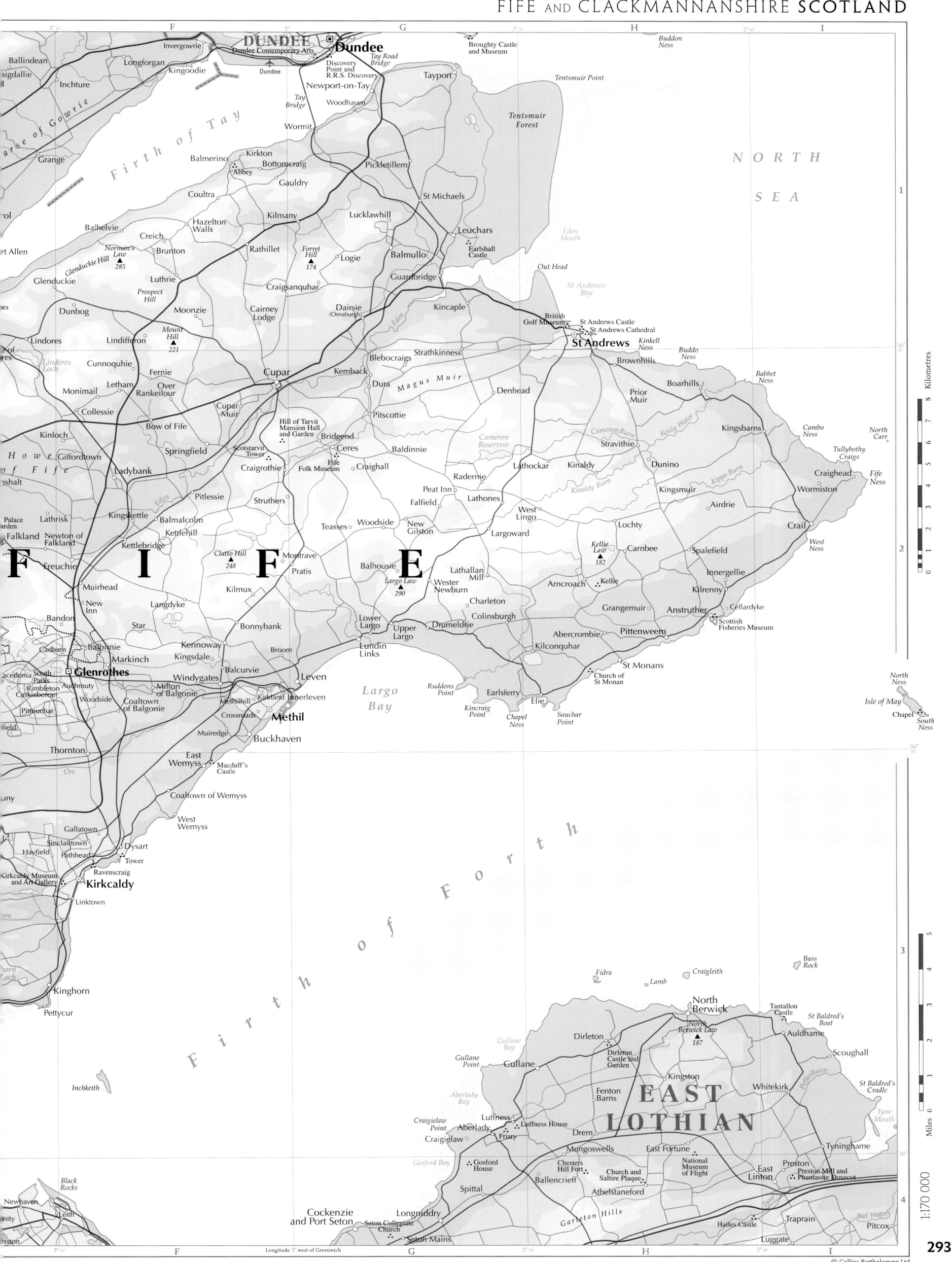

1:170 000

STIRLING

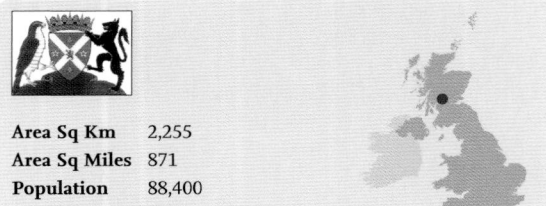

Area Sq Km	2,255
Area Sq Miles	871
Population	88,400
Admin HQ	Stirling
Highest point	Ben More (1,174 m) near Crianlarich

The origins of Stirling's name (Gaelic *Sruighlea*) name is unclear, and in many medieval documents it appears as a variation on 'Strevelin' which might contain a reference to its situation along the river Forth (from Celtic *forthin*), but by about 1420, it was widely known as 'Sterling'.

FAMOUS FOR

Although a royal burgh since around 1124, Queen Elizabeth II presented letters patent in 2002, making **Stirling** Scotland's newest city.

Frank and Harold Barnwell designed and flew the first powered aircraft in Scotland in a field in the Causewayhead area of Stirling in 1909. Frank Barnwell went on to design both the Bristol F.2 Fighter and the Bristol Blenheim aircraft.

Loch Lomond, 39 km long and 8 km wide, is the largest expanse of fresh water by surface area in Britain. It contains around 60 islands, some of which might be crannogs (ancient man-made islands) and one, Inchconnachan, is home to a colony of wallaby.

The Trossachs, and especially the Breadalbane area to the north, has been the backdrop for many major Hollywood films including *Rob Roy* which was filmed using locations in the area in three different versions (1922, 1953 and 1995); *The 39 Steps* and *Casino Royale* included scenes shot by the Falls of Dochart; and Doune Castle figured in *Monty Python and the Holy Grail*.

The **Glengoyne Distillery**, near Blairquhosh between Killearn and Strathblane, is the most southerly highland malt distillery in Scotland. Its property straddles the Highland line, so the whisky is distilled in the Highlands, and matured in the Lowlands.

Just to the north of Stirling on top of a rocky outcrop called Abbey Craig stands a 67 m tower completed in 1869 as a national monument to **William Wallace**, the victor at the Battle of Stirling Bridge, later captured and executed by the English.

Tyndrum, in the far northwest of Stirling is home to the Coronish gold mine, the only commercial gold mine in Scotland.

FAMOUS PEOPLE

George Buchanan, scholar and historian, born Killearn, 1506.
Robert Roy (Rob Roy) MacGregor, outlaw and folk hero, born Glengyle, 1671.
John Smith, bookseller, born Strathblane, 1724.
Sir Thomas Mitchell, surveyor and explorer of Australia, born Craigend, 1792.
Alexander 'Greek' Thomson, architect, born, Balfron 1817.
John Grierson, documentary film producer, born Kilmadock, 1898.
Norman McLaren, animator, born Stirling, 1914.
Archibald David Stirling, founder of the Special Air Service, born Lecropt (formerly in Perthshire), 1915.
Billy Bremner, footballer, born Stirling, 1942.

The old county of Stirlingshire was subsumed into Central Region in 1974 and the local government reorganisation of 1996 established Stirling as the administrative area based on the Central Region district rather than the old county of Stirlingshire, and so includes what was traditionally south Perthshire, but not Falkirk and southern Stirlingshire, which became its own authority. Stirling's population of 88,400 has risen by about 9 per cent since 1981. Stirling is the principal town (33,060) and the other largest are the ancient cathedral city of Dunblane (8,840), Bridge of Allan (5,120), Callander (3,130), Fallin (2,770) and Cowie (2,520).

The fertile agricultural lands of the Forth valley are in the centre of the area, bounded by mountains: The Trossachs and the mountain peaks of Ben Lomond, Ben More and Ben Lui are in the north, while in the south are the Campsie Fells. There are many lochs, including Loch Lomond, which forms part of the western border, and Loch Katrine. Scotland's only lake named as such, Lake of Menteith, is also in Stirling. The main river is the Forth and its tributaries, the Teith and the Allan. The Blane and the Endrick flow into Loch Lomond.

Edinburgh and Perth may have contended with each other over their claims to be the country's capital, but it was in and around Stirling that Scotland's history was often made. The royal castle, perched on its extinct volcano, commanded the only route north between the bogs of Flanders Moss to the west, the Campsie Fells to the south, and the tidal reach of the river Forth. Major battles were fought in the district, most notably Stirling Bridge (1297), Bannockburn (1314), Sauchieburn (1488) and Sheriffmuir (1715), but following the Act of Union in 1707, Stirling was forced to reinvent itself. Modern Stirling is a light industrial and commercial centre with excellent rail and road links to the north and to Glasgow and Edinburgh. The city and its satellite villages dominate the district, and as the administrative centre, Stirling's economy is primarily dependent on the service industries. Coupled with 42 primary and seven

secondary schools plus Stirling University at Bridge of Allan, which is the headquarters for the Scottish Institute of Sport, it is clear why public administration, education and health are important job providers (32.6 per cent). Finance, IT, and the business sector (19.5 per cent) are also important employers in Stirling town.

The Highland Boundary Fault cuts across the Stirling area, dividing it geologically into two. The lowland south and east features both pastoral and arable farming, and many smaller villages are strung out to the west along the Carse of Stirling and south towards the Campsie Fells. In the 19th century, the quarries and coal mines of the southeast, especially around Plean and Cowie, provided both the building material and energy to push forward the industrialization of the Forth valley. For a time Stirling was an important port, before ships increased in size and were no longer able to sail so far up the increasingly shallow and winding Forth. Kildean (the site of the Battle of Stirling Bridge) was the site of possibly the largest livestock market in Europe, replacing the former trysts at Falkirk and Crieff. The market has recently moved to a new site to the west of Stirling.

In the southern Highlands area, northwest of the Boundary Fault, from Callander in the east to Crianlarich, Tyndrum and Killin in the northwest, employment is connected with tourism (11 per cent) as well as farming and forestry. The West Highland Way, the first official long-distance footpath in the UK, runs through the area for a majority of its 152 km length, supporting many small businesses along the route. The Trossachs, which lie across the northern section of the Stirling area have often been called 'the Highlands in miniature', and Loch Katrine, were made famous as a tourist destination by Sir Walter Scott's *The Lady of the Lake*. More recently, the Loch Lomond and the Trossachs National Park, Scotland's first, opened in 2002. It covers 1,865 sq km across four administrative areas, of which majority is within Stirling Council.

Monument to Robert the Bruce, near the Bannockburn Heritage Centre.

"Stirling, like a huge brooch, clasps Highland and Lowlands together."
Alexander Smith

"[On Loch Lomond] This country is justly stiled the Arcadia of Scotland and I don't doubt but that it may vie with Arcadia in every thing but climate."
Tobias Smollett in *The Expedition of Humphry Clinker*, 1771.

"A crook of the Forth Is worth an earldom o' the north".
Traditional

Loch Achray, The Trossachs.

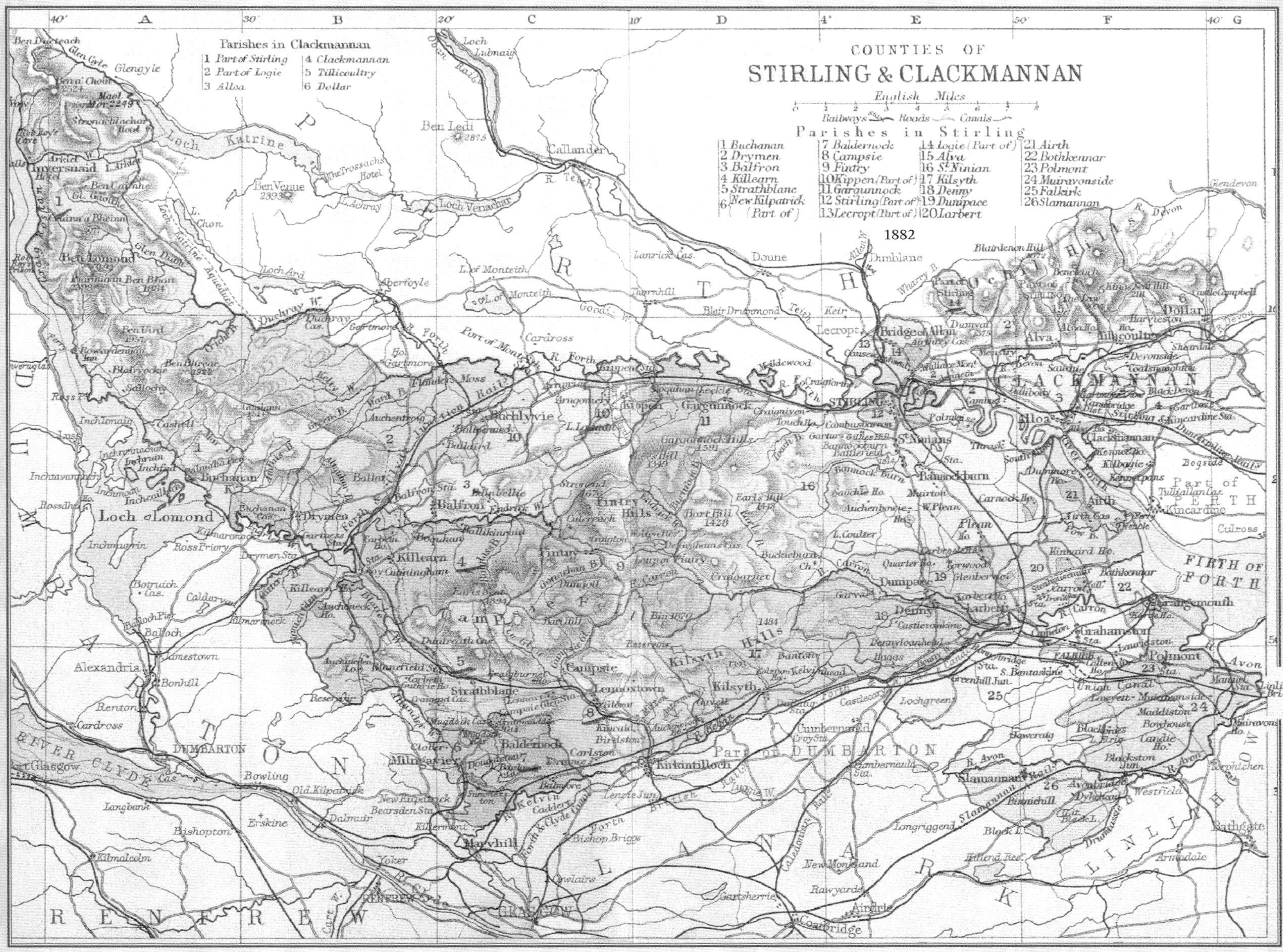

COUNTIES OF
STIRLING & CLACKMANNAN

English Miles

Railways ··· Roads ─── Canals ═══

Parishes in Stirling

1 Buchanan	7 Baldernock	14 Logie (Part of)	21 Airth
2 Drymen	8 Campsie	15 Alva	22 Bothkennar
3 Balfron	9 Fintry	16 St.Ninian	23 Polmont
4 Killearn	10 Kippen (Part of)	17 Kilsyth	24 Muiravonside
5 Strathblane	11 Gargunnock	18 Denny	25 Falkirk
6 New Kilpatrick (Part of)	12 Stirling (Part of)	19 Dunipace	26 Slamannan
	13 Lecropt (Part of)	20 Larbert	

1882

Parishes in Clackmannan
1 Part of Stirling   4 Clackmannan
2 Part of Logie   5 Tillicoultry
3 Alloa   6 Dollar

Bartholomew Gazetteer of the British Isles, 1887

STIRLINGSHIRE, *west-midland county of Scotland; consists of a main portion and two detached sections to the NE. included in Perthshire and Clackmannanshire; is bounded N. by Perthshire, NE. by Clackmannanshire and a detached portion of Perthshire, E. by the Firth of Forth and Linlithgowshire, S. by Linlithgowshire, Lanarkshire, and detached part of Dumbartonshire, and W. by Dumbartonshire; greatest length, NW. and SE., 46 miles; greatest breadth, NE. and SW., 22 miles; area, 286,338 ac., pop. 112,443. The E. part of the co. is flat, finely wooded, and well cultivated; and the valley of the Forth along the N. boundary includes some of the finest land in Scotland. The middle and S. are occupied with hills and valleys – the principal ridges being the Campsie Fells and Kilsyth Hills, and the Fintry Hills and Gargunnock Hills. On the W. a long projection extends north-wards, including a mountainous district in which Ben Lomond rises to an alt. of 3192 ft., and parts of Loch Lomond and Loch Katrine. Besides the Forth, the chief streams are the Avon, Carron, Bannock, Allan, Endrick, and Blane. Coal and ironstone are extensively worked; limestone and sandstone are abundant. There are important manufactures of woollens, cotton, and iron; and there are several large chemical works and distilleries. The co. comprises 21 pars, with parts of 5 others, and the police burghs of Alva, Bridge of Allan, Denny and Dunipace, Falkirk, Grangemouth, Kilsyth, Milngavie, and Stirling.*

CLACKMANNANSHIRE, *the smallest co. of Scotland, extending 10 miles N. and S. between the main body of Perthshire and the river Forth, and 11 miles E. and W. between the cos. of Stirling and Fife; area, 30,477 ac.; pop. 25,680, or 539 persons to each sq. m. The surface rises from the Forth by an easy ascent, broken by gentle undulations and by the valley of the river Devon, to the Ochil Hills, which extend along the N. border. These hills afford excellent pasturage; the low grounds are well cultivated. Coal is raised in the Devon valley; the towns of Alloa and Tillicoultry have woollen mfrs. The co. comprises 4 pars., parts of 2 other pars. and also the police burghs of Alloa and Tillicoultry.*

rling Castle

British National Grid projection

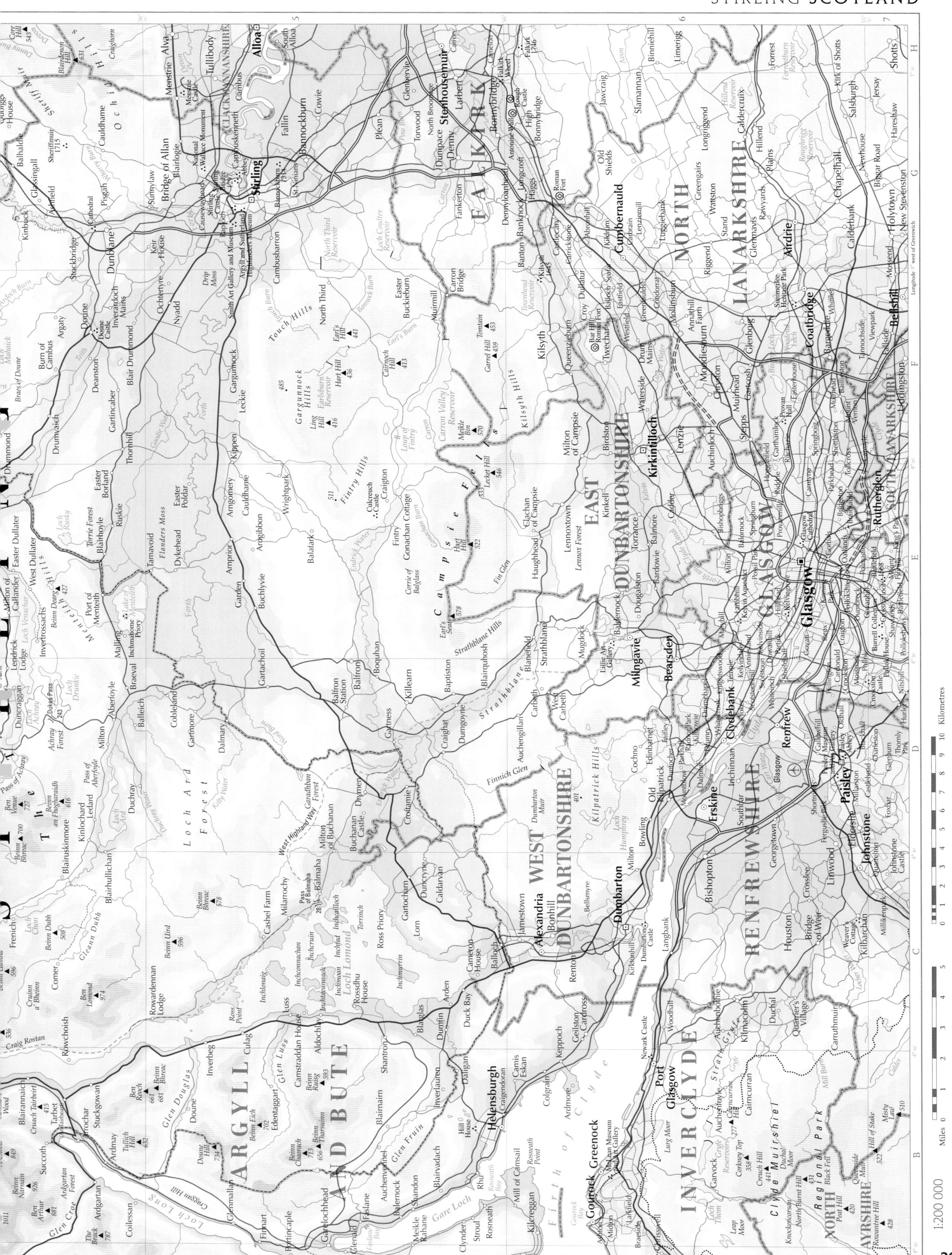

1:200 000

ARGYLL AND BUTE

Area Sq Km	7,163
Area Sq Miles	2,766
Population	90,500
Admin HQ	Lochgilphead
Highest point	Ben Cruachan (1,126 m)

Argyll (*Earra-Ghaidheal*) is 'the coastline of the (eastern or Irish) Gaels' and Bute (*Bòd*) is the 'fire' island, where signal fires were lit, neatly illustrating the importance of this maritime county and group of strategic Inner Hebridean islands.

FAMOUS FOR

Argyll and Bute's boundary with Stirling runs right down the middle of **Loch Lomond**. This is only a small section of the boundary of the county, though. When the coastline of all the islands is included, it is estimated to be about 4,800 km long.

Both the building and much of the furniture of The Hill House at **Helensburgh** was designed by Charles Rennie Mackintosh for the publisher Walter Blackie in 1902 and is internationally recognized as the finest example of his domestic work.

McCaig's Tower, on the hillside above **Oban**, was commissioned in 1895 by John Stuart McCaig to keep local stonemasons in work during the winter months.

Originally intended to house a museum and art gallery, McCaig died in 1902 before it could be completed, and so only the outer walls were built – in the style of the Coliseum in Rome.

Cruachan power station, the first reversible pump storage hydro station to be built in the world, was constructed inside Ben Cruachan between 1959 and 1965, and is generally used to help meet peak demand for electricity. Access tunnels go 1 km into the mountain to the turbine hall, where it is warm enough to grow tropical plants under artificial light.

The sea lochs emptying into the Firth of Clyde are both deep and easily navigable, having excellent access to open water. During World War II, the Royal Navy used **Holy Loch** as a base for submarine trials. During the 'Cold War' the US Navy used the loch for submarines on duty with its Atlantic squadron. **Gare Loch** is the site of Faslane Naval Base, home to the UK's controversial Trident nuclear submarine fleet as well as other Navy units, and a major employer in the area.

Helensburgh was founded in 1776 by Sir James Colquhoun of Luss, and named after his wife, Lady Helen Sutherland.

In **Lochawe** village is the extraordinary St Conan's Church, designed by Walter Campbell who was not a professional architect but knew what he liked and was able to afford to turn his ideas into reality. It was built between 1881 and 1930, and the result is a magical and moving building.

In about 1093, The Norwegian king Magnus Barelegs reached an agreement with King Malcolm III of Scotland that he could have control over any island off the west coast around which he could sail his boat. Wanting to control the rich Kintyre peninsula, Magnus duly sailed around the land and then, sails furled and sitting with his hand on the rudder, had his men portage the longboat between **East Loch Tarbert** and **West Loch Tarbert**, 'sailing' across the narrow isthmus.

FAMOUS PEOPLE

Colin MacLaurin, mathematician, born Kilmodan, 1698.
Duncan Ban Macintyre, (Donnchadh Ban Macan t-Saoi) Gaelic poet, born Glen Orchy, 1724.
Neil Munro (pseudonym of Hugh Foulis), novelist, creator of *Para Handy*, born Inveraray, 1864.
John Logie Baird, electrical engineer and television pioneer, born Helensburgh, 1888.
Donald MacKenzie MacKinnon, philosopher and theologian, born Oban, 1913.
Deborah Kerr, Hollywood film star, born Helensburgh, 1921.
John Smith, politician, born Dalmally, 1938.

"Iona of my heart, Iona of my love, instead of monks' voices shall be lowing of cattle, but ere the world comes to an end, Iona shall be as it was." Saint Columba

*"Cold is the wind in Islay
That blows on them in Kintyre."*
George Campbell Hay

This Atlantic coastal area of Scotland is characterised by fjord-like sea lochs and mountains divided by the Highland Boundary Fault, and stretches along the mainland from the southwestern Grampian Mountains in the north to the Kintyre peninsula in the south. It includes Mull, Iona, Coll, Tiree, Colonsay, Jura, Islay, Gigha and Lismore, and 17 other inhabited Inner Hebridean islands. Most of the local rivers are short and fast-flowing, emptying into the numerous lochs in the area.

One of the historic counties of Scotland, Argyll was central to the kingdom of Dalriada, and the later earls of Argyll were so powerful that they had their own navy. The county of Argyllshire became part of Strathclyde Region in 1974, and with the breakup of Strathclyde in 1996, Argyll and Bute became a unitary authority, gaining the section of Dunbartonshire west of Loch Lomond and north of the river Clyde, while separating Bute from its companion islands of Arran, and Great and Little Cumbrae. It is the second largest administrative area in Scotland, but its population of 90,500 (2008), a slight drop of 400 on the 1981 Census return, is relatively sparse. The major towns include Helensburgh (14,020), Dunoon (8,310), Oban (8,050), Campbeltown (5,040) and Lochgilphead (2,370) on the mainland, with Rothesay (4,850) and Port Bannatyne (1,400) on Bute.

Lochgilphead was originally a planned settlement laid out in a grid pattern in 1790 along the new road from Inveraray to Campbeltown (now the A83). The Crinan Canal, completed in 1816 under the direction of Thomas Telford, was opened just to the south at Ardrishaig, connecting Loch Fyne with the Sound of Jura at Crinan. It shortened a long and sometimes hazardous trade route from the Clyde around the Kintyre peninsula to 14.5 km. These good early communication links – a pier was built in 1831 – and its central location explain why Lochgilphead has remained the area's administrative centre despite numerous reorganisations and a modest population.

Just north of Lochgilphead is Kilmartin Glen, with more than 350 ancient monuments, half of them prehistoric, as well as Dunadd, once the fortress capital of Dalriada, many of whose kings were buried on Iona. Most of the region's islands and mainland territories share a similar broad history: prehistoric settlement followed by waves of immigration or conquest, particularly Irish and Viking, before being absorbed into the Scottish kingdom. When the sea was considered a road and not a barrier, trade united the islands and the mainland with Ireland and England. Subsistence farming and fishing once supported a much larger population, particularly in the islands, but a disastrous combination of crop failures and improvement programmes in the 19th century lead to emigration, both abroad and to other towns in the region.

Ferries and shipping remain the life-blood of the islands, although modern transportation is also part of the mix: Tiree, Islay and Campbeltown have their own airports. Pastoral farming, forestry, fishing (including fish farming) and whisky are traditional industries – currently Islay alone has eight working distilleries. The service sector, however, remains the greatest overall employer. Public administration, education and health provide the lion's share of the jobs (38 per cent) while tourism provides 15 per cent of jobs. In an area of stunning scenery, long-distance footpaths and outdoor pursuits, it is no surprise that tourism is an important industry, but it is not a modern invention. From the 19th century, towns along the Firth of Clyde such as Dunoon and Rothesay, on Bute, were magnets for city folk going 'doon the watter' for their annual holidays, and collectively gained the unlikely sobriquet of the 'Glaswegian Riviera'.

Ardbeg whisky distillery on Islay.

Tobermory, Isle of Mull.

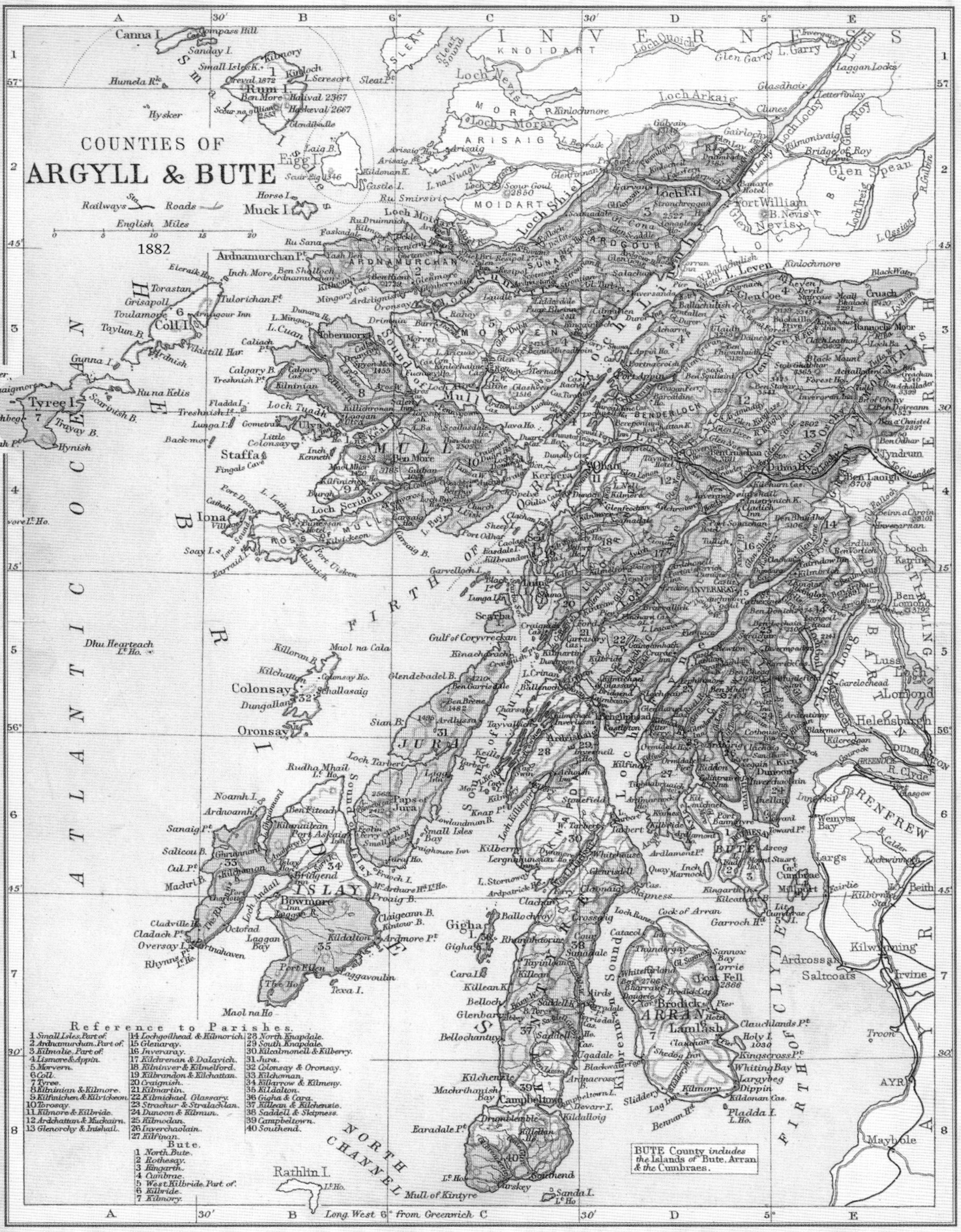

COUNTIES OF ARGYLL & BUTE

Railways ___ Roads ___

English Miles

1882

Reference to Parishes

1 Small Isles, Part of
2 Ardnamurchan, Part of
3 Kilmalie, Part of
4 Lismore & Appin
5 Morvern
6 Coll
7 Tyree
8 Kilninian & Kilmore
9 Kilfinichen & Kilvickeon
10 Torosay
11 Kilmore & Kilbride
12 Ardchattan & Muckairn
13 Glenorchy & Inishail
14 Lochgoilhead & Kilmorich
15 Glenaray
16 Inveraray
17 Kilchrenan & Dalavich
18 Kilninver & Kilmelford
19 Kilbrandon & Kilchattan
20 Craignish
21 Kilmartin
22 Kilmichael Glassary
23 Strachur & Strachlachlan
24 Dunoon & Kilmun
25 Kilmodan
26 Inverchaolain
27 Kilfinan
28 North Knapdale
29 South Knapdale
30 Kilcalmonell & Kilberry
31 Jura
32 Glenaray & Oronsay
33 Kildalton
34 Killarow & Kilmeny
35 Kildalton
36 Gigha & Cara
37 Killean & Kilchenzie
38 Saddell & Skipness
39 Campbeltown
40 Southend

Bute

1 North Bute
2 Rothesay
3 Kingarth
4 Cumbrae
5 West Kilbride, Part of
6 Kilbride
7 Kilmory

BUTE County includes
the Islands of Bute, Arran
& the Cumbraes.

Bartholomew Gazetteer of the British Isles, 1887

ARGYLLSHIRE, *a maritime co. in the W. of Scotland, including nearly all the islands of the Inner Hebrides. In extreme length the mainland extends about 112 miles S. from the boundary with Inverness-shire to the North Channel, and approaches the opposite coast of Ireland within a distance of 13 miles. Area, 3213.1 sq. m., or 2,092,458 ac. Pop. 76,468, or 24 persons to each sq. m. The mainland is much indented by picturesque and far-reaching sea-lochs, which render its coast-line proportionately very great. The peninsula of Kintyre extends about 55 miles S. from the Crinan Canal to the Mull of Kintyre, and is from 5 miles to 10 miles broad. Ardnamurchan Point is the most westerly projection on the mainland of Scotland. The principal sea-lochs are Eil, Linnhe, Leven, Etive, and Firth of Lorne in the NW.; and Fyne, Striven, Long, and Goil branching from the Firth of Clyde. The sea views along the W. coast and among the islands are magnificent, while the loch and mountain scenery is everywhere grand and picturesque. The surface is nearly all rugged and mountainous, the low and arable land lying chiefly round the coasts. The highest summit is Ben Cruachan, alt. 3611 ft., in the NW. of the mainland; another lofty summit, Ben More, in the isl. of Mull, rises to an alt. of 3185 ft. The largest lake is Loch Awe, which stretches for upwards of 20 miles S. from the base of Ben Cruachan. The chief islands are Mull, Islay, Jura, Tyree, Coll, Rum, Colonsay, and many smaller. The arable land constitutes about one-eighth of the entire area. Slate is extensively quarried and exported. The fisheries are very important, especially the herring fishery on Loch Fyne. There are several large distilleries in Islay and at Campbeltown. Railway communication extends through Perthshire to Oban, on the NW. of Argyllshire. The co. comprises the dists. of Lochiel, Ardgour, Sunart, Ardnamurchan, and Morven in the NW. detached section; Lorn, Argyll, Cowal, Knapdale, and Kintyre in the main body; 37 pars., parts of 3 other pars., the police burghs of Campbeltown, Dunoon, Inveraray, Lochgilphead, Oban and Tobermory.*

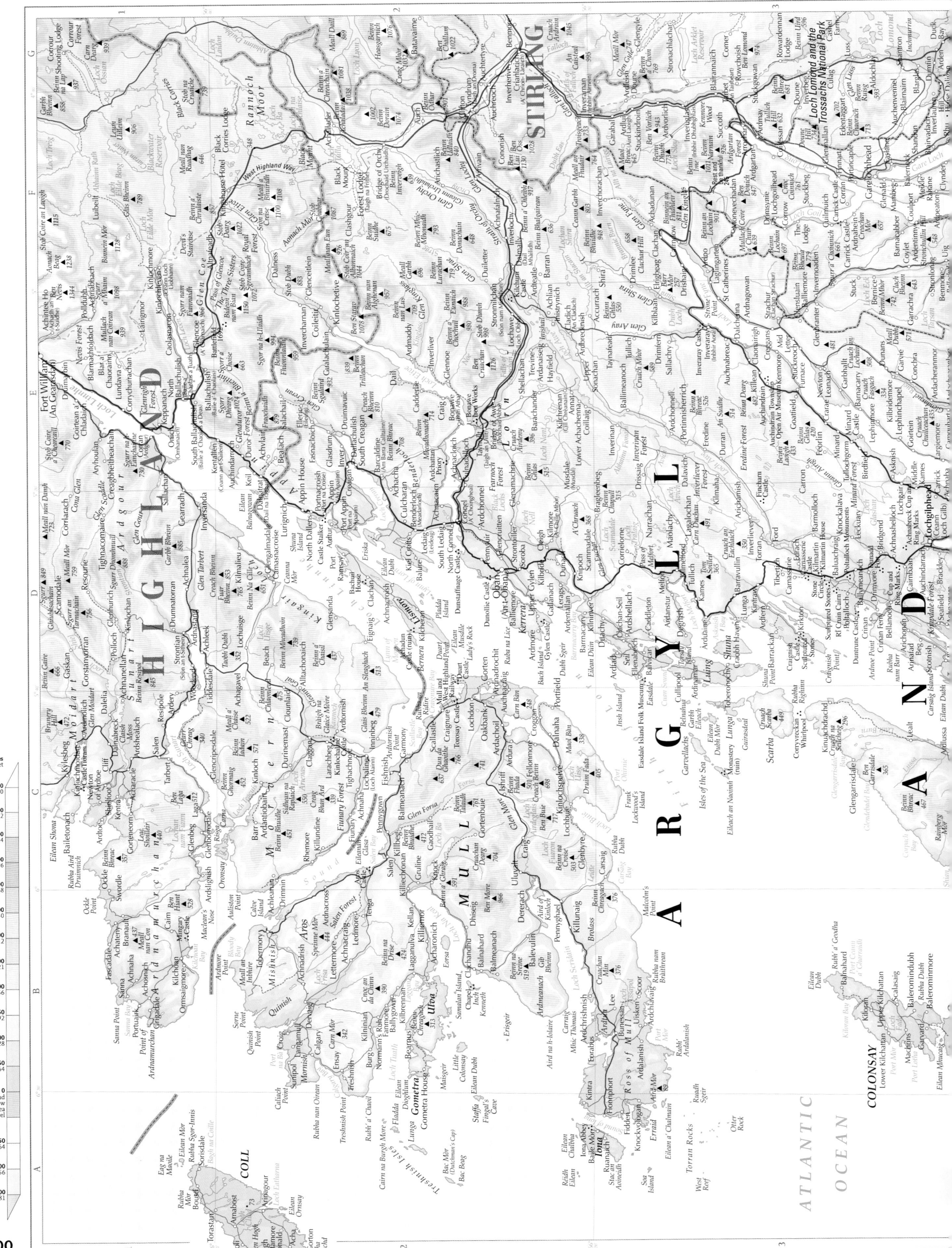

British National Grid projection

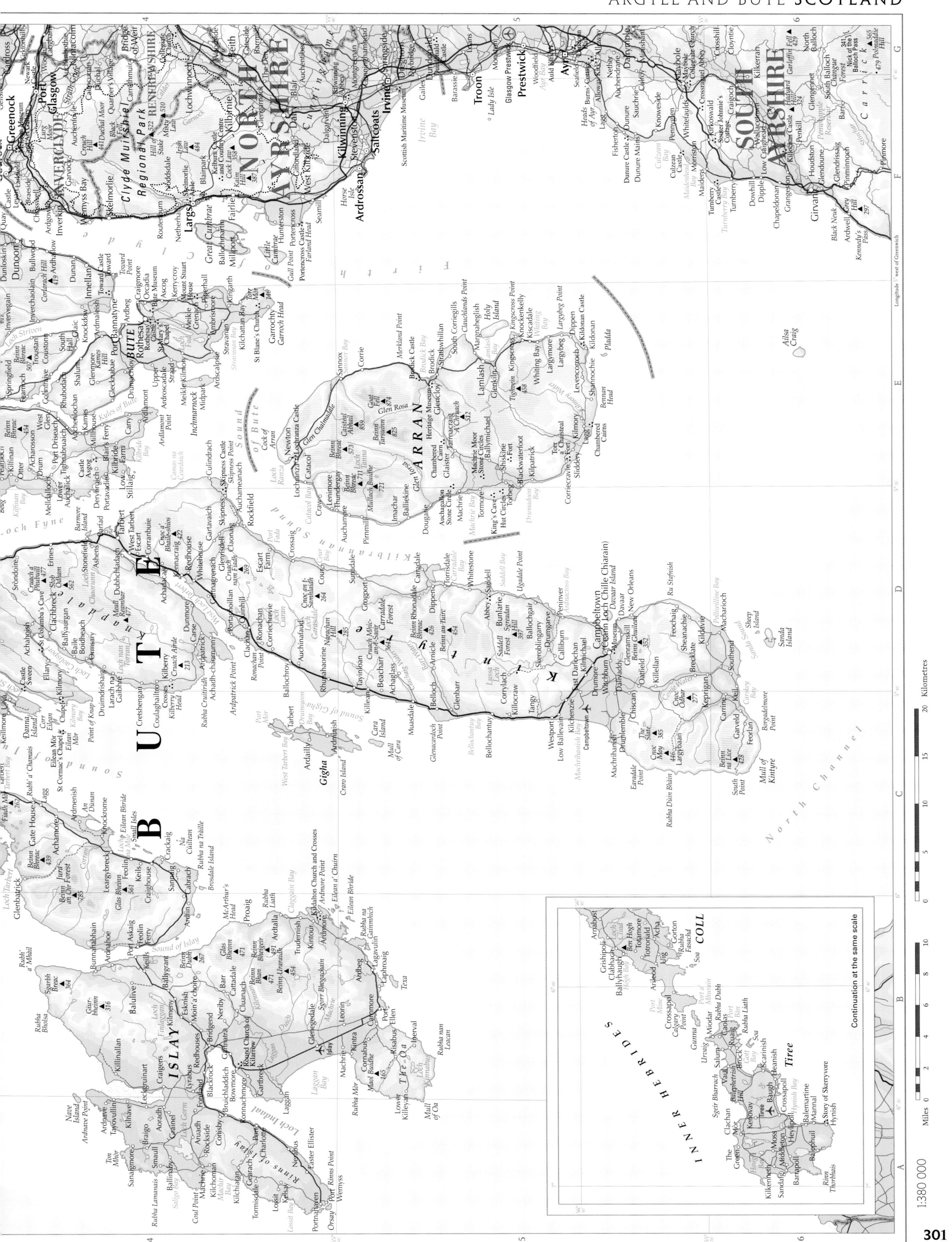

© Collins Bartholomew Ltd

PERTH AND KINROSS

Area Sq Km	5,419
Area Sq Miles	2,092
Population	144,200
Admin HQ	Perth
Highest point	Ben Lawers (1,214 m)

Kinross (*Ceann Rois*) possibly refers to 'the end of the promontory' due to its location at the southeastern end of the Ochils and next to Loch Leven. The name of **Perth**, an ancient settlement on the banks of the river Tay, might designate a '(place by a) thicket or copse', possibly from Pictish *perta* – but another, rather simpler, explanation is the corruption of *aber-tha* (at the mouth of the Tay) which lead the Romans to name this place 'Bertha', to Gaelic *Peairt*, and modern Perth.

FAMOUS FOR
Perth celebrated its 800th anniversary in 2010.

Sometime capital of Scotland, **Perth** was nearly the site of its first university, when the academics at St Andrews almost relocated there in the late 17th century.

Glen Lyon is the longest glen in Scotland: from Fortingall to the head of Loch Lyon, it is 40 km long.

The **Tummel-Garry Hydro-Electric Scheme** includes 10 power stations and is the largest in Scotland, producing 245 MW of power. The final reservoir is at **Loch Faskally** outside Pitlochry, built in the 1950s and which famously included a fish ladder to allow salmon up the river Tummel to spawn.

The Duke of Atholl commands the **Atholl Highlanders**, the only legal private army in Europe. Created from the defunct 77th Foot in 1839, the 6th duke took his men to a tournament the same year. Later, they acted as a bodyguard for Queen Victoria in 1842 and 1844, and she was so impressed that she presented them with colours, confirming their status as an official regiment. They have never seen active service.

The **Fortingall Yew** is the oldest tree in Europe, with an approximate age of around 2,000 years. In 1769, the tree's girth was 16 metres, but souvenir hunters and natural decay have reduced the original trunk to ground level. However, numerous separate branches are flourishing, and the whole tree is now protected by a wall. Fortingall is also reputedly the birthplace of Pontius Pilate.

FAMOUS PEOPLE
Neil Gow, violinist and songwriter, born near Dunkeld, 1727.
John Buchan, 1st Lord Tweedsmuir, author and statesman, born Perth, 1875.
Professor J. J. R. Macleod, physiologist and Nobel Prize winner (medicine), born Clunie, 1876.
William Soutar, poet, born Perth, 1898.
Ewan MacColl, author and folk singer, born Auchterarder, 1915.
Hamish Henderson, composer and folklorist, born Blairgowrie, 1919.

St Johnstoun is a merry toun
Whaur the water rins sae schire;
And whaur the leafy hill looks doun
On steeple and on spire.
William Soutar

Perth and Kinross is a central highland area of Scotland bisected by the Highland Boundary Fault, with fertile alluvial lowland farmland to the south and east and a highland plateau rising to the Grampian Mountains in the north and west. The highest peak is Ben Lawers to the north of Loch Tay, but there are many other Munros (peaks over 914 m) including Schiehallion (1,083 m), Carn Mairg (1,041 m), Meall Garbh (968 m) and Cairn Gorm (924 m). The principal river is the Tay with its tributaries, the Earn and the Tummel.

Prior to the 1996 local government reorganisation, Perth and Kinross comprised a single district of Tayside Region. The creation of the modern administrative area not only restored historic Perthshire – though without southern Perthshire that once reached down to the north bank of the Forth – and added to it Kinross-shire, plus a small area to the west of Dundee. Its population in 2008 was 144,200, a slow but steady increase from 121,900 in 1981.

Perth, at the head of the Tay's tidal estuary, has a population of 43,680 and is both the economic and administrative centre. Other important towns are Blairgowrie (8,090), Crieff (7,050), Kinross (4,680), New Scone (4,490), Auchterarder (4,450) and Pitlochry (2,610).

Long considered the gateway to the Highlands, Perth straddled both land and sea routes and was a very busy trading port. The layout of the oldest part of the city is thought to echo the Roman fort known to have been established here in AD 83. Seven sieges, Cromwell's army and a reputation for iconoclasm mean that few buildings remain from earlier periods, but documentary evidence shows that Perth was a royal burgh in 1210. It was also known by the alternative name of St Johnstoun, partly in reference to the grand burghal church, one of the few ancient building still standing and in use. Scottish kings were crowned nearby at Scone, and the establishment of Dunkeld Cathedral combined with t peripatetic nature of medieval monarchy allowed Pert to rival Edinburgh as the nation's capital.

Fertile areas like the Carse of Gowrie and the southern end of Strathmore encouraged arable agriculture in lowland Perth and Kinross to include wheat, sugar beet and potatoes (especially seed potatoe and an increasing variety of soft fruits for which the a is famous. Past ice ages have scoured the terrain here, leaving behind deep glens, lochs and rivers running mostly in either an east–west or southeast–northwest direction. Employment in tourism (13 per cent) is especially important in the northern upland areas, where the rivers and lochs support sporting estates and salmon and trout fisheries, as well as ski resorts and related outdoor pursuits in the Cairngorms. The Forestry Commission is an important employer, along with whisky distilling, knitwear, food manufacturing and crafts. Together with finance, IT and other busine activities, these account for around 19.8 per cent of the region's jobs. However, the service sector is the largest employer in the area as a whole, divided betwee retail, hotels and restaurants (29 per cent) and public administration, education and health (24 per cent).

Much of the mountainous north of Perth and Kinross was part of the ancient earldom of Atholl, centred on the seat of the earls (and later dukes) of Atholl at Blair Castle. The estate is approximately 48,5 ha, accrued as much by strategic marriages with rival clans like the Campbells and Stewarts as by warfare. Both the railway and the major trunk route of the A9 follow a much older and established route through this picturesque and much contested landscape. They maintain long-established links between Perth and Inverness in the north and with Edinburgh and Englan in the south.

Scone Palace

Blair Castle

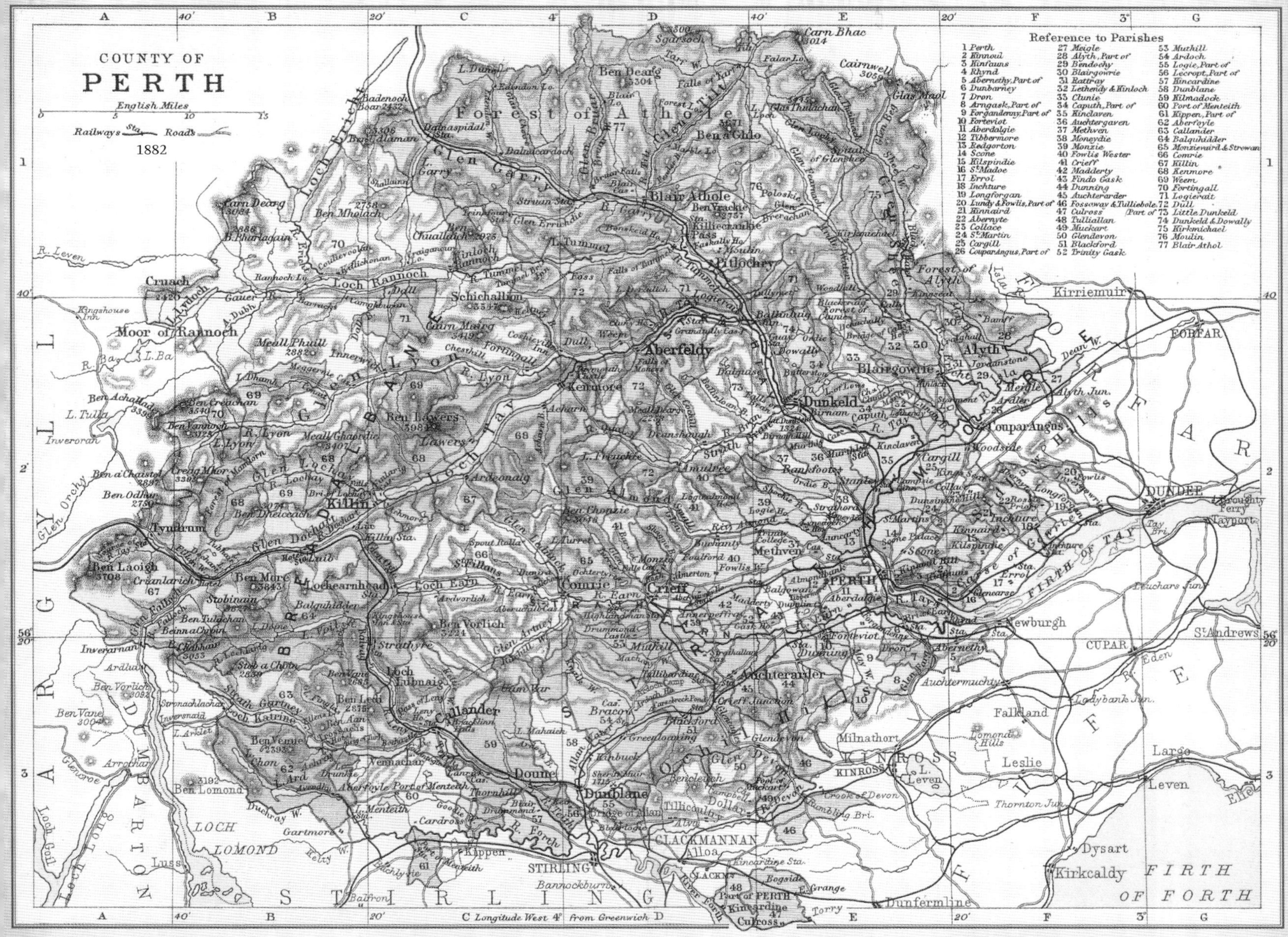

COUNTY OF PERTH

English Miles

Railways ⊷ Roads

1882

Reference to Parishes

1 Perth	27 Meigle	53 Muthill
2 Kinnoul	28 Alyth, Part of	54 Ardoch
3 Kinfauns	29 Bendochy	55 Logie, Part of
4 Rhynd	30 Blairgowrie	56 Lecropt, Part of
5 Dunbarney	31 Rattray	57 Kincardine
6 Aberuthven	32 Lethendy & Kinloch	58 Dunblane
7 Dron	33 Clunie	59 Kilmadock
8 Arngask, Part of	34 Caputh, Part of	60 Port of Menteith
9 Forgandenny, Part of	35 Kinclaven	61 Kippen, Part of
10 Forteviot	36 Kinclaven	62 Aberfoyle
11 Aberdalgie	37 Methven	63 Callander
12 Tibbermore	38 Moneydie	64 Balquhidder
13 Redgorton	39 Monzie	65 Monzievaird & Strowan
14 Scone	40 Fowlis Wester	66 Comrie
15 Kilspindie	41 Crieff	67 Killin
16 St Madoes	42 Madderty	68 Kenmore
17 Errol	43 Findo Gask	69 Weem
18 Inchture	44 Dunning	70 Fortingall
19 Longforgan	45 Auchterarder	71 Logierait
20 Lundy & Fowlis, Part of	46 Fossoway & Tullibole, Part of	72 Dull
21 Kinnaird	47 Culross	73 Little Dunkeld
22 Abernyte	48 Tulliallan	74 Dunkeld & Dowally
23 Collace	49 Muckart	75 Kirkmichael
24 St Martin	50 Glendevon	76 Moulin
25 Cargill	51 Blackford	77 Blair Athol
26 Couparangus, Part of	52 Trinity Gask	

Bartholomew Gazetteer of the British Isles, 1887

PERTHSHIRE, *east-midland co. of Scotland, bounded N. by Inverness-shire and Aberdeenshire, E. by Forfarshire, SE. by Fife and Kinross-shire, S. by Clackmannanshire and Stirlingshire, SW. by Stirlingshire and Dumbartonshire, and W. by Argyllshire; greatest length, E. and W., 72 miles; greatest breadth, N. and S., 60 miles; the detached portion (lying along the upper reach of the Firth of Forth, and separated from the main body by a belt of Fife and Clackmannanshire) is 6½ miles by 4½ miles; area, 1,617,808 ac.; pop. 129,007. Perthshire includes some of the grandest and most beautiful scenery in Scotland, combining features characteristic both of the Highlands and the Lowlands. The ranges of the Ochils and the Sidlaw Hills, which are parted by the estuary of the Tay, occupy the SE.; while the N. and NW. districts, to the extent of more than one-half of the entire county, are occupied with the mountains of the Grampian system, this Highland region being intersected by numerous lochs and glens. The rich and beautiful valley of Strathmore, extending from the SW. to the NE. across the whole co., lies between the base of the mountains in the N. and NW. and the lower ranges in the SE.; the fertile alluvial tract known as the Carse of Gowrie stretches between the Sidlaw Hills and the Firth of Tay; while the Carse of the Forth lies along the S. border. The general slope of the co. is towards the SE. The principal rivers are the Forth and the Tay. The largest tributaries of the Forth within the co. are the Teith, the Allan, and the Devon; while those of the Tay are the Tummel, the Lyon, the Isla, the Bran, the Almond, and the Earn. The largest lochs are Lochs Ericht and Rannoch in the N., Lochs Tay and Earn in the NW., and Lochs Katrine, Achray, Vennachar, and Menteith in the SW. The soils of this co. are of the most varied character, – rich deep clay or loam in the straths, a light sandy or gravelly soil in the hill valleys, and moorland on the higher lands. Coal and ironstone are wrought in the detached section of the co.; roofing slate is obtained near Alyth, Comrie, and Dunkeld; and limestone is quarried at various places. Agriculture and sheep-farming are the chief industries. There are extensive deer forests, and the fisheries on the Tay are of very considerable value. The mfrs. of woollen and tartan stuffs, cotton, and coarse linens are carried on to some extent. The ancient divisions of Perthshire, now only of local significance, were Athole, Breadalbane, Gowrie, Menteith, Methven, Perth, and Stormont. The co. comprises 68 pars, with parts of 13 others, the parl. burgh of Culross, and the police burghs of Abernethy, Alyth, Blairgowrie, Callander, Coupar Angus (part of), Crieff, Dunblane, Perth, and Rattray.*

er Tay and Perth

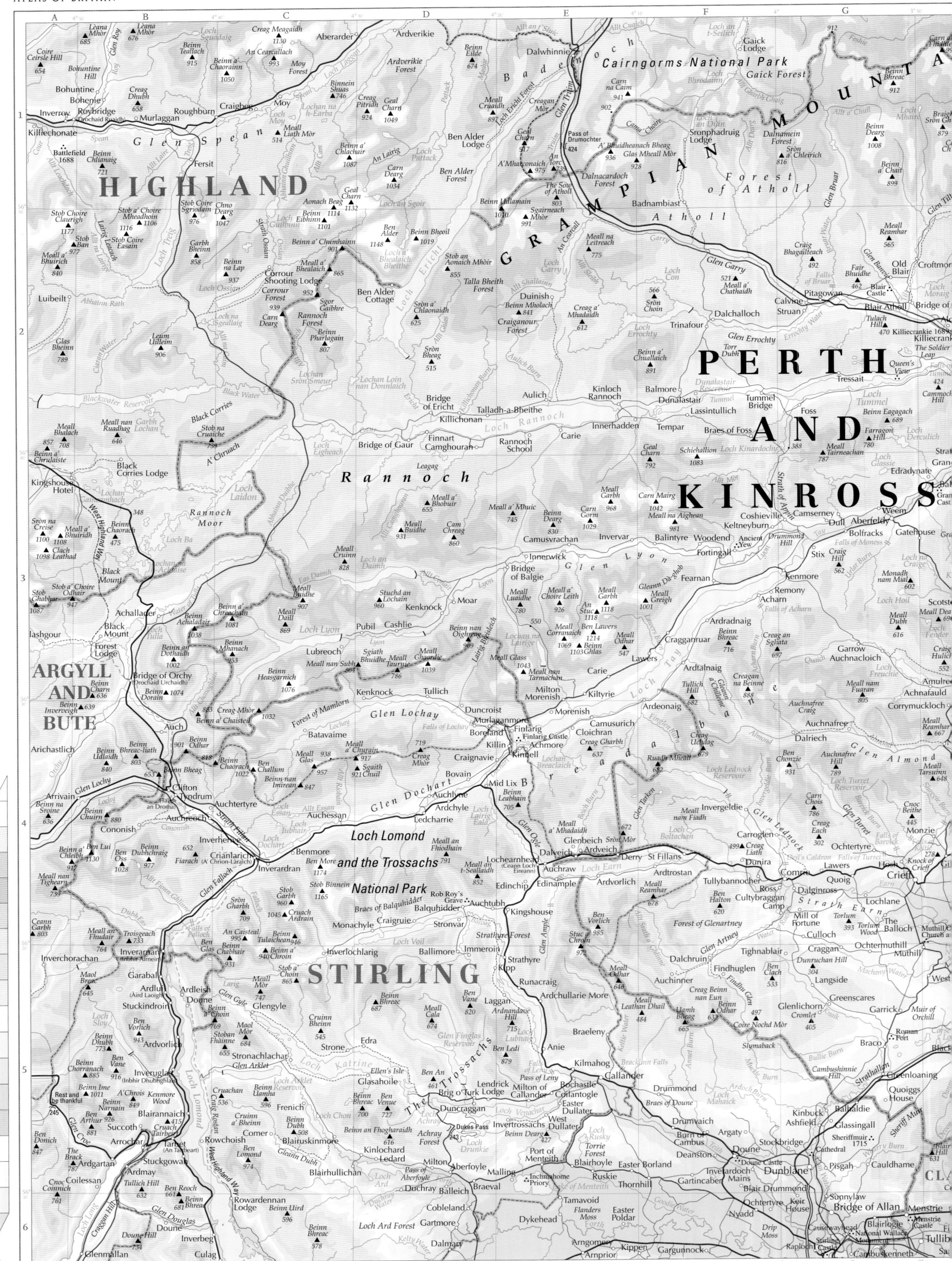

HIGHLAND

GRAMPIAN MOUNTAINS

Cairngorms National Park

Gaick Forest

Forest of Atholl

Atholl

PERTH
AND
KINROSS

ARGYLL
AND
BUTE

Rannoch Moor

Rannoch

Loch Lomond
and the Trossachs
National Park

STIRLING

Metres	Feet
1000	3280
900	2952
800	2624
700	2296
600	1968
500	1640
400	1312
300	4921
200	656
150	492
100	328
50	164
Land below sea level	
50	164
200	656
1000	3281

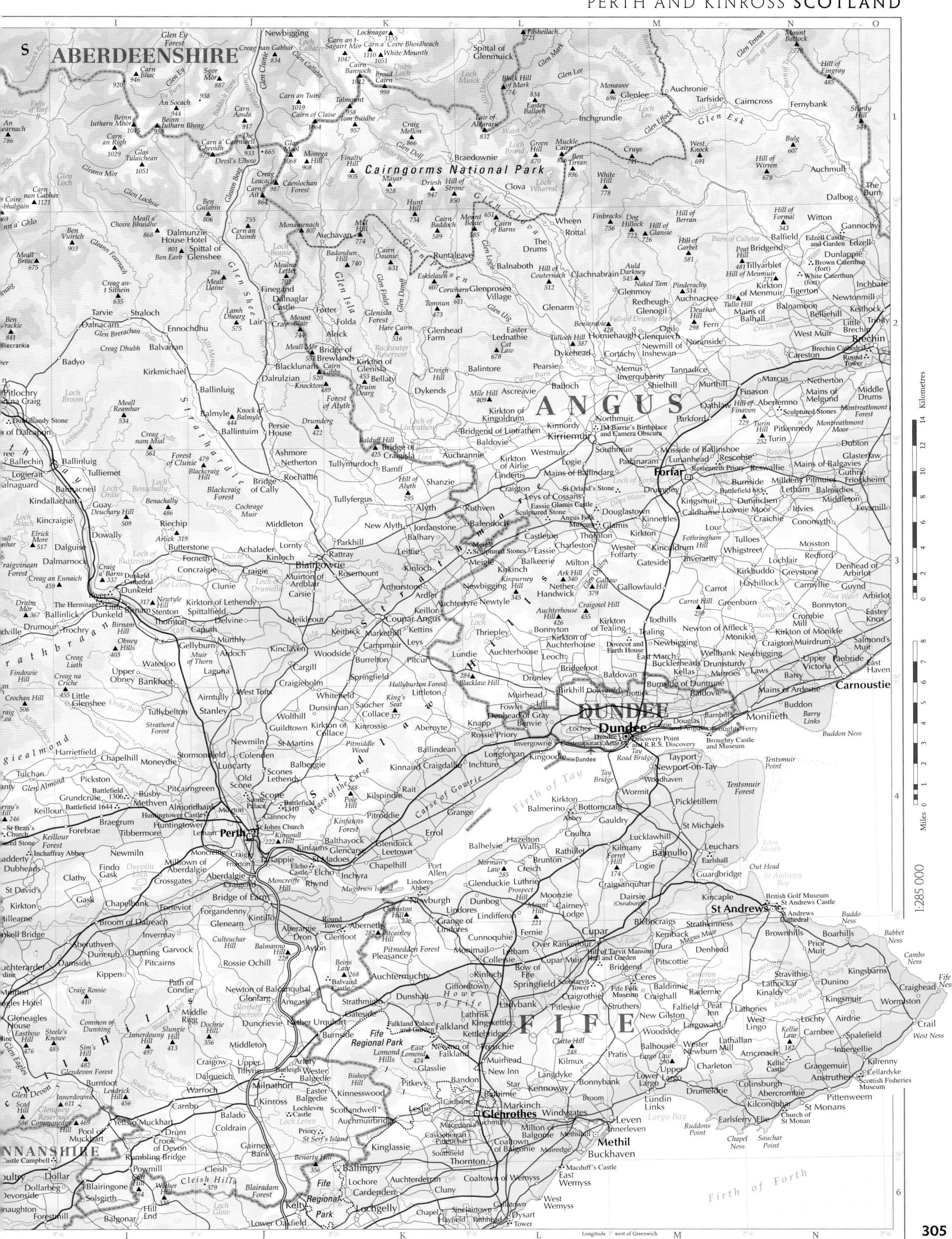

© Collins Bartholomew Ltd

DUNDEE

Area Sq Km	62
Area Sq Miles	24
Population	142,500
Highest point	Dundee Law (174 m)

The Gaelic name for Dundee (*Dun Dèagh*) denotes a hillfort (*dun*) along the river Tay, although there are suggestions that the second element might refer to a local ruler.

FAMOUS FOR

A common folk legend regarding the city's name concerns the King William I's brother, **David, Earl of Huntingdon** who was nearly lost at sea off the Scottish coast when returning from the Crusades. Once safely on dry land near the town, he is said to have renamed it *Donum Dei* (gift of God).

Dundee Law was once the site of an Iron Age hill fort, but it is now occupied by the city's war memorial.

The original **Tay Bridge**, built to carry the railway from Edinburgh to Aberdeen, was the longest in the world when completed in 1878. It notoriously collapsed during a storm on 28 December 1879. Along with sections of ironwork reused in the 'new' bridge, the engine was also salvaged and repaired. Unofficially nicknamed 'The Diver', it remained in service until 1919.

By the 1830s Dundee was supplying so much linen and sailcloth to the market it was known as '**Juteopolis**'.

Predominantly south facing, **Dundee** has the highest number of sunshine hours of any place in Scotland.

FAMOUS PEOPLE

John Playfair, mathematician, physicist and geologist, born Benvie, 1748.
David Coupar (DC) Thomson, newspaper and comic publisher, born 1861.
Sir Alexander Gibb, civil engineer, born 1872.
John Gordon, Editor, *Sunday Express*, published first newspaper crossword, born 1890.
Brian Cox, actor and director, born 1946.
George Galloway, politician, born 1954.
Elizabeth (Liz) McColgan, athlete, born 1964.

"It's an east coast town with a west coast temperament." George Blake

"Dundee, a frowsy fisherwife addicted to gin and infanticide." Lewis Grassic Gibbon

Dundee is surrounded by Angus, and Perth and Kinross. Broughty Ferry (population 13,155) is within its boundaries. It is a seaport and manufacturing centre situated along the north shore of the Firth of Tay. Prior to 1996, the city was a district of Tayside Region, but local government reorganisation of that year separated the city from the surrounding rural area.

The medieval harbour lies under modern developments, but there has been settlement on the banks of the Tay here for much longer, and possibly since the Mesolithic era. After a first mention in 1054, its town charter was granted in the 12th century, and royal burgh status followed in 1292. Its location made it an obvious strategic target: Dundee has been razed to the ground by invading armies at least four times.

Known traditionally for jute, jam and journalism, only the latter remains, under the auspices of D. C. Thomson, publisher of *The Courier*, the *Sunday Post*, *The Beano* and *The Dandy*. Although it is still possible to buy Keiller's marmalade, first created in the city in 1797, it is no longer manufactured here. The jute factories went hand-in-hand with the city's thriving shipbuilding and whaling industries in the 19th century. Robert Falcon Scott 's ship *RSS Discovery* was one of hundreds built in its docks, and at one time over half the population, including many women and children, worked in the jute mills, the last of which closed in the 1970s. In more recent times, Dundee has taken advantage of the discovery of North Sea oil as well as the digital revolution to increase its manufacturing sector (14 per cent), but public administration, education and health (30 percent) are major employers, unsurprising in a city with two universities (Dundee and Abertay).

ANGUS

Area Sq Km	2,204
Area Sq Miles	851
Population	110,300
Admin HQ	Forfar
Highest point	Glas Maol (1,068 m)

Angus (Gaelic *Aonghas*) takes its name from Angus, an 8th-century Pictish king.

FAMOUS FOR

The **Montrose Basin** covers 750 ha and had the largest mussel beds in Scotland in the 19th century. More poetically, it was called the 'Sea of Swans' because of the migratory Mute Swan population there.

Arbroath Abbey, founded in 1178 by William the Lion, was dedicated to the martyred Thomas Becket, Archbishop of Canterbury. It became the wealthiest abbey in Scotland. Abbot Bernard of Arbroath is considered to have drafted the Declaration of Arbroath in 1320, a powerful statement of Scottish independence.

The **Carnoustie Ladies Golf Club**, founded in 1873, was one of the first of its kind in the world.

According to myth, the last dragon in Scotland was killed at **Balkello**, near Bridgefoot, having devoured nine sisters. A carved Pictish stone stands at the legendary spot.

Arbroath Smokies are a distinctive form of smoked haddock, originally from Auchmithie, a fishing village near Arbroath. Following EU protection in 2004, an Arbroath Smokie can only be produced within 8 km of Arbroath.

FAMOUS PEOPLE

Andrew Melville, Protestant reformer, born Baldowie, 1545.
John Ogilby, topographer and map-maker, born Kirriemuir, 1600.
James Tytler, editor of *Encyclopaedia Britannica*, and the first Scot to fly a hot-air balloon in 1784, born Fern, 1747.
Robert Brown, botanist and discoverer of Brownian movement, born Montrose, 1773.
Sir Charles Lyell, geologist, author of *Principles of Geology*, born Kirriemuir, 1797.
Sir James Matthew (JM) Barrie, novelist, author of *Peter Pan*, born Kirriemuir, 1860.
Alex Sutherland (AS) Neill, educator, founder, Summerhill School, born Kingsmuir, 1883.
The Princess Margaret, Countess of Snowdon, sister of Queen Elizabeth II, born Glamis Castle, 1930.

"As long as but a hundred of us remain alive, never will we on any conditions be brought under English rule. It is in truth not for glory, nor riches, nor honours, that we are fighting, but for freedom – for that alone, which no honest man gives up but with life itself." Declaration of Arbroath, 1320

"The men of Angus do not understand a nature-lover's ecstasies. They have been growing potatoes so long that the Golden Wonder has entered into their souls." John R. Allan

Once part of the Pictish kingdom of Circinn, the fertile lands and excellent anchorages of Angus have proven irresistible to Roman, Viking, Scots and Norman invaders. It is one of the historic counties of Scotland (known for a time as Forfarshire) and was incorporated into Tayside Region in 1975, until 1996, when it was again established as an independent council area. Angus's population is 110,300, an increase of nearly 10 per cent since 1981. The largest towns are the administrative centre of Forfar (13,500), Arbroath (22,140), Carnoustie (10,630) and Montrose (10,830) along the North Sea coast, and further inland Brechin (6,950) and Kirriemuir (5,910).

Angus enjoys a base in skilled trades occupations higher than the national average, and the manufacturing sector is strong (14.6 per cent). The proximity of Dundee also supports the area's employment with public administration, education and health (29.4 per cent) and retail, hotels and restaurants (23.7 per cent) accounting for over half of all jobs.

Angus can be divided into three main geographical areas. The mountainous northwest runs up to the south of the Grampian Mountains and including the Angus glens. The Cairngorms National Park, established in 2003, takes in much of this area. To the southeast, rolling hills and upland farms run down to the ports and villages along the North Sea coast. Between lies Strathmore ('the big valley', stretching from south of Aberdeen to north of Perth), very fertile agricultural area, especially known for potatoes, cattle and soft fruit. The two main roads in the area underline the division: the coastal fishing ports are served by the A92, while the main A90 drives through the rural centre.

Glamis Castle, Forfar.

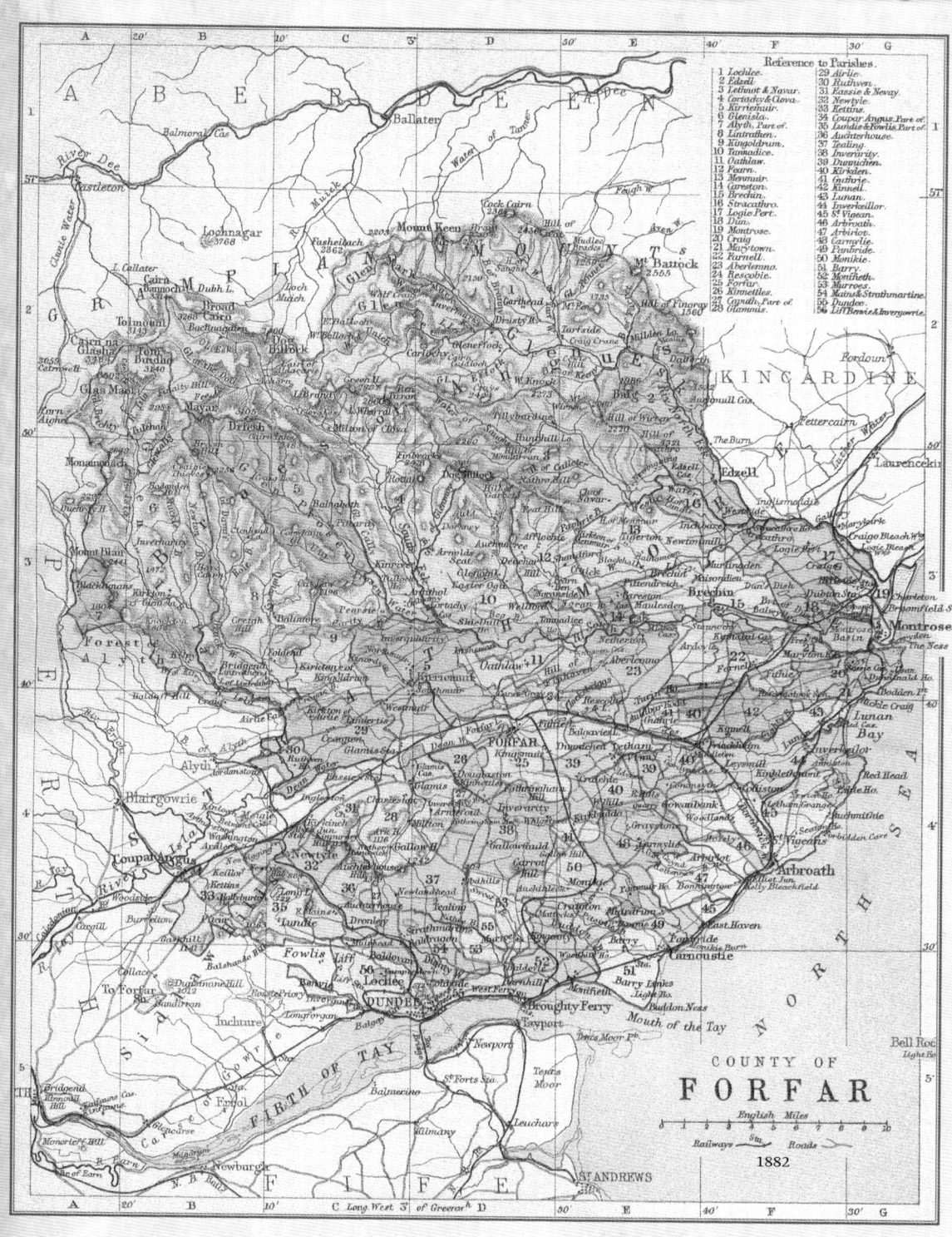

Bartholomew Gazetteer of the British Isles, 1887

FORFARSHIRE *(or Angus), maritime co. in E. of Scotland; is bounded N. by the cos. of Aberdeen and Kincardine, E. by the North Sea, S. by the Firth of Tay, and W. by the co. of Perth; greatest length, 37 miles; greatest breadth, 27 miles; area, 560,087 ac., pop. 266,360. The surface presents great variety. In the NW. are the Braes of Angus, a group of spurs of the Grampians, intersected by romantic glens; in the SW., 8 miles from and parallel to the Firth of Tay, are the Sidlaw Hills; between the Braes of Angus and the Sidlaw Hills is the fertile valley of Strathmore (Great Valley) or Howe of Angus; from the Sidlaw Hills to the coast on the E. and S. the land is level and highly cultivated. From Dundee to Arbroath the coast consists of sand; from Arbroath to Lunan Bay it is formed of sandstone cliffs, culminating in the Red Head. The chief rivers are the Isla, a tributary of the Tay, and the North Esk and South Esk, which flow SE. to the North Sea. Agriculture has the advantage of the most approved methods, and cattle rearing is carried to great perfection; the polled Angus cattle, however, are now raised chiefly in the county of Aberdeen. Nearly the whole of the NW. of the co. is either waste land, or is occupied as sheep-walks or deer-forests. Granite is the prevailing rock in the N. portion of the Grampians, and sandstone in the neighbourhood of the Sidlaw Hills; sandstone flags are quarried in the Carmylie district, and there are limeworks in the neighbourhood of Montrose. The principal industry is the mfr. of linen and jute, Dundee being the chief seat of those trades in Britain.*

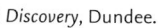

S Discovery, Dundee.

An early edition of the Dandy comic.

Arbroath Abbey

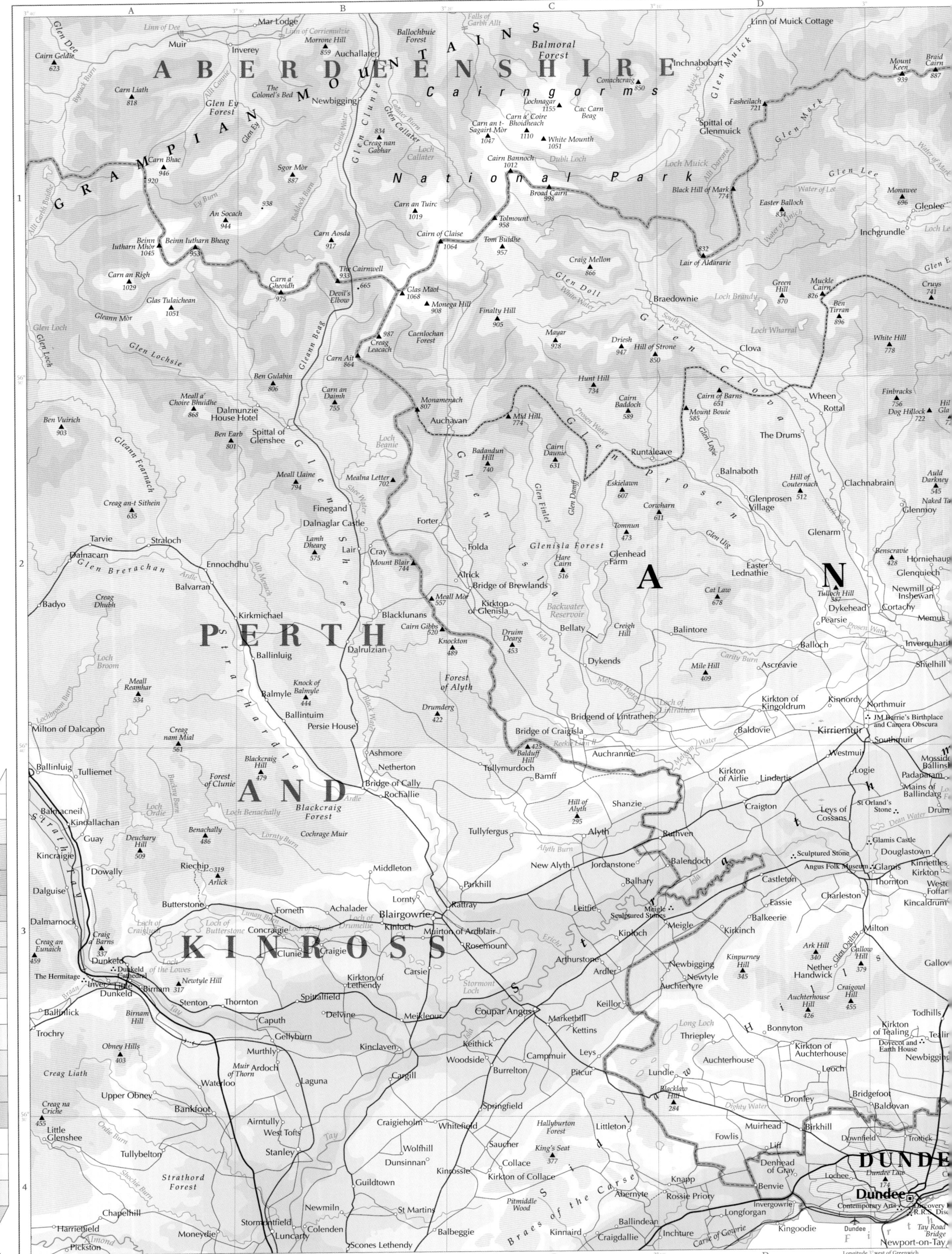

British National Grid projection

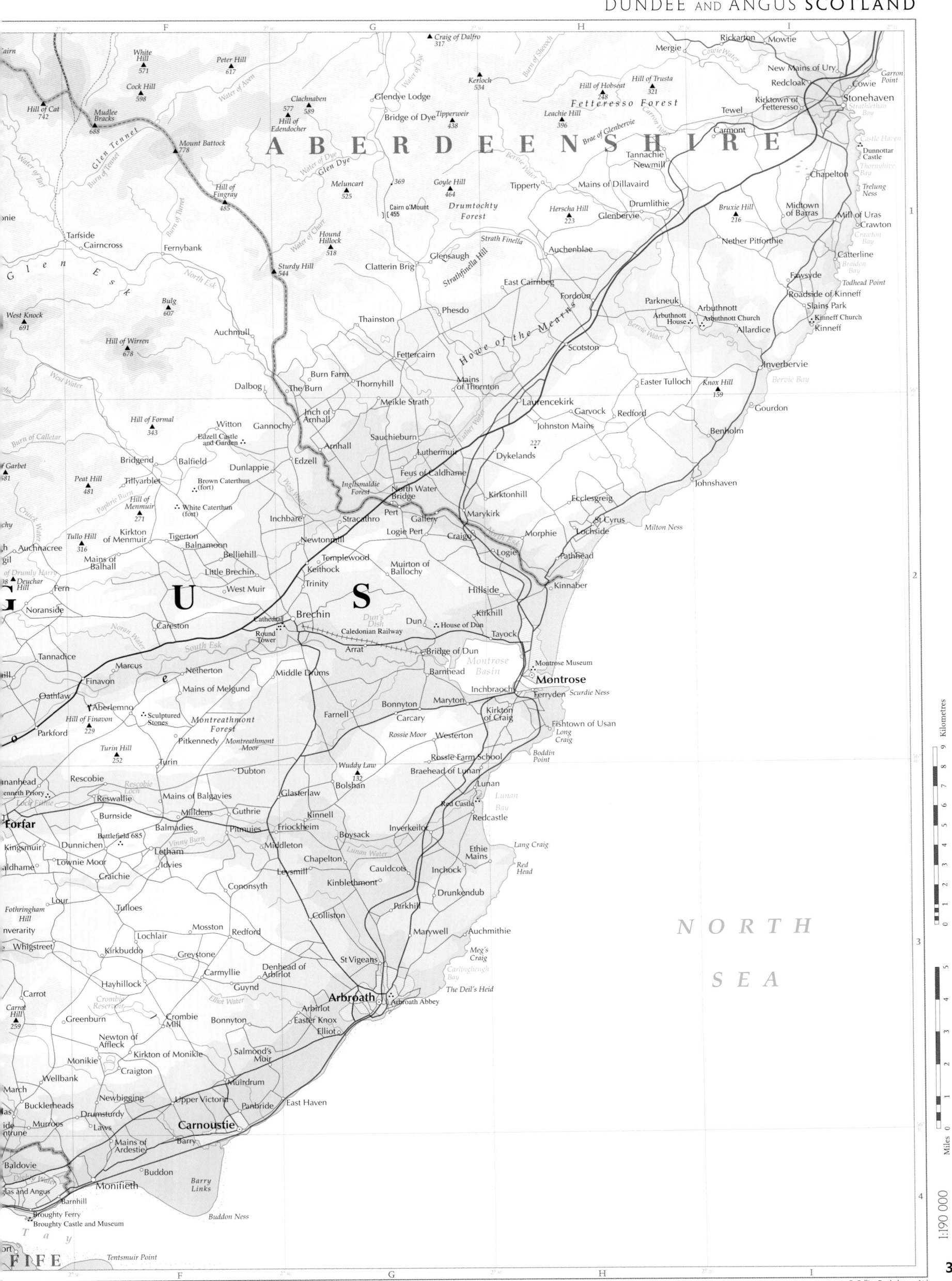

Cairn

Hill of Cat
742

Mudlee
Bracks
688

White
Hill
571

Cock Hill
598

Peter Hill
617

▲ Craig of Dalfro
317

Mergie

Rickarton

Mowtie

Cowie Water

New Mains of Ury

Redcloak

Garron
Point

Cowie

Stonehaven

Strathiethan
Bay

Hill of Hobseat
248

Hill of Trusta
321

Clachnaben
577
589

Hill of
Edendocher

Glendye Lodge

Bridge of Dye

Tipperweir
438

Leachie Hill
396

Fetteresso Forest

Kirktown of
Fetteresso

Tewel

Carmont

Castle Haven

Dunnottar
Castle

Thornyhive
Bay

Chapelton

Trelung
Ness

Glen Tennet

Mount Battock
778

Hill of
Fingray
485

Glen Dye

Meluncart
525

369

Goyle Hill
464

Cairn o'Mount
) (455

Drumtochty
Forest

Tipperty

Tannachie
Newmill

Mains of Dillavaird

Drumlithie

Bruxie Hill
216

Midtown
of Barras

Mill of Uras

Crawton

Craton
Bay

Herscha Hill
223

Glenbervie

Nether Pitforthie

Catterline

Braiden
Bay

Tarside

Cairncross

Fernybank

Hound
Hillock
518

Sturdy Hill
544

North Esk

Glensaugh

Strath Finella

Strathfinella Hill

Clatterin Brig

Auchenblae

East Cairnbeg

Parkneuk

Arbuthnott
House

Arbuthnott
Church

Allardice

Roadside of Kinneff

Slains Park

Kinneff
Church

Kinneff

Fawsyde

Todhead Point

West Knock
691

Bulg
607

Auchmull

West Water

Fordoun

Scotston

Bervie Water

Inverbervie

Bervie Bay

Hill of Wirren
678

Phesdo

Thainston

Mains
of Thornton

Easter Tulloch

Knox Hill
159

Gourdon

Hill of Formal
343

Witton

Gannochy

Burn Farm

Thornyhill

Fettercairn

Meikle Strath

Laurencekirk

Garvock

Redford

Benholm

Garbet
581

Edzell Castle
and Garden

Dalbog

The Burn

Inch of
Arnhall

Johnston Mains

227

Milton Ness

Bridgend

Balfield

Dunlappie

Arnhall

Sauchieburn

Luthermuir

Dykelands

Johnshaven

Peat Hill
481

Tillyarblet

Brown Caterthun
(fort)

Edzell

Feus of Caldhame

Kirktonhill

Ecclesgreig

Hill of
Menmuir
271

White Caterthun
(fort)

Inglismaldie
Forest

North Water
Bridge

Marykirk

St Cyrus

Kirkton
of Menmuir

Tigerton

Inchbare

Stracathro

Pert

Gallery

Logie Pert

Morphie

Lochside

Tullo Hill
316

Balnamoon

Newtonmill

Craigo

Logie

Pathhead

Auchnacree

Mains of
Balhall

Belliehill

Little Brechin

Keithock

Templewood

Trinity

Muirton of
Ballochy

Hillside

Kinnaber

Fern

Deuchar
Hill

West Muir

Kirkhill

Noranside

Careston

Cathedral

Brechin

Round
Tower

Dun's
Dish

Dun

House of Dun

Tayock

Noran Water

Marcus

Netherden

South Esk

Caledonian Railway

Arrat

Bridge of Dun

Montrose Museum

Tannadice

Finavon

Netherton

Middle Drums

Barnhead

Inchbraoch

Montrose
Basin

Montrose

Ferryden

Scurdie Ness

Oathlaw

Mains of Melgund

Hill of Finavon
229

Aberlemno

Sculptured
Stones

Montreathmont
Forest

Farnell

Bonnyton

Carcary

Maryton

Kirkton
of Craig

Fishtown of Usan

Long
Craig

Parkford

Turin Hill
252

Pitkennedy

Montreathmont
Moor

Rossie Moor

Westerton

Boddin
Point

Turin

Dubton

Wuddy Law
132

Rossie Farm School

Braehead of Lunan

Rescobie

Reswallie

Rescobie
Loch

Mains of Balgavies

Glasterlaw

Bolshan

Lunan

Lunan
Bay

enneth Priory

Loch Fithie

Burnside

Milldens

Guthrie

Kinnell

Red Castle

Redcastle

Forfar

Dunnichen

Battlefield 685

Balmadies

Pitmuies

Friockheim

Boysack

Inverkeilor

Kingsmuir

Letham

Idvies

Middleton

Ethie
Mains

Lang Craig

aldhame

Lownie Moor

Chapelton

Lunan Water

Red
Head

Craichie

Leysmill

Cauldcots

Inchock

Drunkendub

Lour

Cononsyth

Kinblethmont

Parkhill

Fothringham
Hill

Tulloes

Mosston

Redford

Colliston

Marywell

Auchmithie

nverarity

Lochlair

Greystone

Denhead
of Arbirlot

St Vigeans

Meg's
Craig

Carlinheugh
Bay

Whigstreet

Kirkbuddo

Carmyllie

Guynd

NORTH

Carrot

Hayhillock

The Deil's Heid

Carrot
Hill
259

Greenburn

Crombie
Reservoir

Crombie
Mill

Bonnyton

Arbroath

Arbirlot

Arbroath Abbey

SEA

Elliot Water

Easter Knox

Elliot

Newton of
Affleck

Monikie

Kirkton of Monikie

Salmond's
Muir

March

Wellbank

Craigton

Muirdrum

las

Bucklerheads

Newbigging

Upper Victoria

East Haven

ide

Murroos

Drumsturdy

Panbride

ntrune

Laws

Carnoustie

Barry

Baldovie

Buddon

Barry
Links

Barnhill

Buddon Ness

s and Angus

Broughty Ferry

Monifieth

Broughty Castle and Museum

ort

Tay

Tentsmuir Point

FIFE

© Collins Bartholomew Ltd

1:190 000

Kilometres

0 1 2 3 4 5 6 7 8 9

Miles 0 1 2 3 4 5

ABERDEENSHIRE

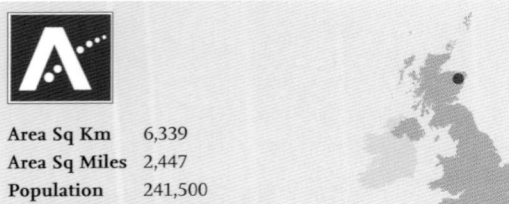

Area Sq Km	6,339
Area Sq Miles	2,447
Population	241,500
Admin HQ	Aberdeen
Highest point	Ben Macdui (1,309 m) on the border with Moray

Aberdeenshire takes its name from the city of Aberdeen, 'at the mouth of the Don'.

FAMOUS FOR

The annual **Stonehaven Fireballs Festival** has been held every year since at least 1908. Local people swing flaming wire cages around their heads as they walk the streets of the town. The idea is to burn away the bad spirits of the old year and create good luck for the new year.

Prince Albert paid £31,000 for the **Balmoral** estate in 1848. It now covers more than 50,000 acres and is centred on its new castle (completed in 1856). The Queen stays at Balmoral in the late summer.

Braemar, 339 m above sea level, holds the record for the UK's lowest recorded temperature: -27.2 °C on 10 January 1982.

Doric, a particular dialect of Lowland Scots, is spoken with a number of variations, throughout Aberdeenshire. It contains loanwords from both Gaelic and Norse, but curiously – except for place names – there are no Pictish words.

When Parliament passed the Act of 1786 for building lighthouses, **Kinnaird Head Light House** became Scotland's first 'official' lighthouse. It was built on top of a towerhouse (castle) and was manned until 1992.

Fraserburgh's Royal Charter of 1592 also established a university, but by 1607 it had closed, only to be revived briefly when King's College retreated to the town in 1647 to avoid an outbreak of plague in Aberdeen.

FAMOUS PEOPLE

Saint John Ogilvie, Jesuit priest, born in Banff, 1579.
James Legge, missionary and Chinese scholar, first professor of Chinese at Oxford University, born Huntly, 1815.
Robert William Thomson, inventor of the pneumatic tyre, born in Stonehaven, 1822.
Thomas Blake Glover, Japanese trader, known as the Scottish Samurai, born Fraserburgh, 1838.
Sir James Cantlie, co-founder of the Royal Society of Tropical Medicine and Hygiene, born in Dufftown, 1851.
Cosmo Gordon Lang, Anglican priest and Archbishop of Canterbury, born in Fyvie, 1864.
John Reith, 1st Baron Reith, engineer and first Director-General of the BBC, born in Stonehaven, 1889.
Lewis Grassic Gibbon, (pseudonym of James Leslie Mitchell) novelist, born in Auchterless, 1901.

"Here on fine days the Highlands wear a perpetual smile. It is true that there are wild places, but you are never quite deceived by them: you know that every pine-tree near Balmoral has its own valet, and that no matter how cold the wind, how cruel the mountainside, how bleak the rolling moor, there is a hot bath at the end of every day… . There is a charm about Deeside which is the charm of an armchair after a storm."
H V Morton, *In Search of Scotland*, 1929

Aberdeenshire rises from eastern coastal fringes, rocky in the north and sandy in the south, through rolling countryside to the Cairngorm mountains in the south and west. Aberdeenshire is crossed by both the rivers Don and Dee.

Named after the traditional county, modern Aberdeenshire, created in 1996, takes in three former Grampian Region districts – Banff and Buchan, Gordon, and Kincardine and Deeside – but not the city of Aberdeen. It has the curious distinction of being the only Scottish council area whose headquarters are outside its own borders. Aberdeenshire's population is 241,500, up almost 8 percent from 1981, undoubtedly due to the continuing exploitation of North Sea Oil. The largest towns are Peterhead (17,330), Fraserburgh (12,630), Inverurie (10,970), Westhill (10,750) and Stonehaven (10,090).

Aberdeen city supports much of the employment in the area, and services provide the lion's share of these. Public administration, education and health (24 per cent) and retail, hotels and restaurants (23.7 per cent) account for nearly half of all jobs. Manufacturing (14 per cent) and tourism-related industries (9 per cent) are also important. Aberdeenshire has 151 state primary and 17 state secondary schools. The Cairngorms National Park, established in 2003, includes southern areas of Aberdeenshire such as Ballater, Crathie and Braemar. Skiing and outdoor winter sports centres at the Lecht near Strathdon and Glenshee, which is the largest Scottish skiing resort, provide much seasonal employment and tourist income, and all the resorts are expanding their off-season facilities.

While all the major transport links lead to Aberdeen, the inland areas are predominantly rural, with the northern end of Strathmore and the Mearns being amongst Scotland's richest agricultural areas. *Sunset*

Song, a novel by Lewis Grassic Gibbon and one of the most popular Scottish novels of the 20th century, is set in a fictitious farm on an estate in the Kincardineshire Mearns. Fishing and trade have also traditionally been important in Aberdeenshire. Peterhead was a planned town, founded in 1593 around its port. Best known, perhaps, as the site of a prison, it is also an oil industry service centre. Almost 550 boats are registered in the harbour, although contractions in both the fishing industry and oil sector have led to attempts to diversify. Around the headland at the end of the Moray Firth lies Fraserburgh. Originally known as Faithlie, and a burgh of barony in 1546, Faithlie was renamed Fraserburgh in 1592. Always an important port, by 1894 there were over 800 boats registered there.

Aberdeenshire has been inhabited, and fought over, for thousands of years. The Brandsbutt Pictish standing stone is now to be found in the middle of a modern housing estate in Inverurie. The *Book of Deer*, a pre-Norman Gospel book, is the oldest known written Gaelic, possibly copied in the 10th century by the predecessors of the Cistercian monks who were known to own land around the site of the now ruined Deer Abbey. The Grampian Mountains to the south and west, known locally as the Mounths, were a considerable barrier to trade and armies in past ages. The Romans, using the Elsick Mounth trackway to cross the mountains, fought the battle of Mons Graupius here, defeating the native commander Calgacus, in 84 AD. Another trackway, the Causey Mounth, connected Bridge of Dee in Aberdeen with the fortress of Dunnottar at Stonehaven. More than a thousand castles, from medieval towerhouses to the Victorian rebuilding of Balmoral, attest to the historical importance of this land divided by the Highland Boundary Fault at Stonehaven between the Lowlands and Highlands.

Ruins of Dunnottar Castle

Glenshee Ski Centre

ABERDEENSHIRE, 1885

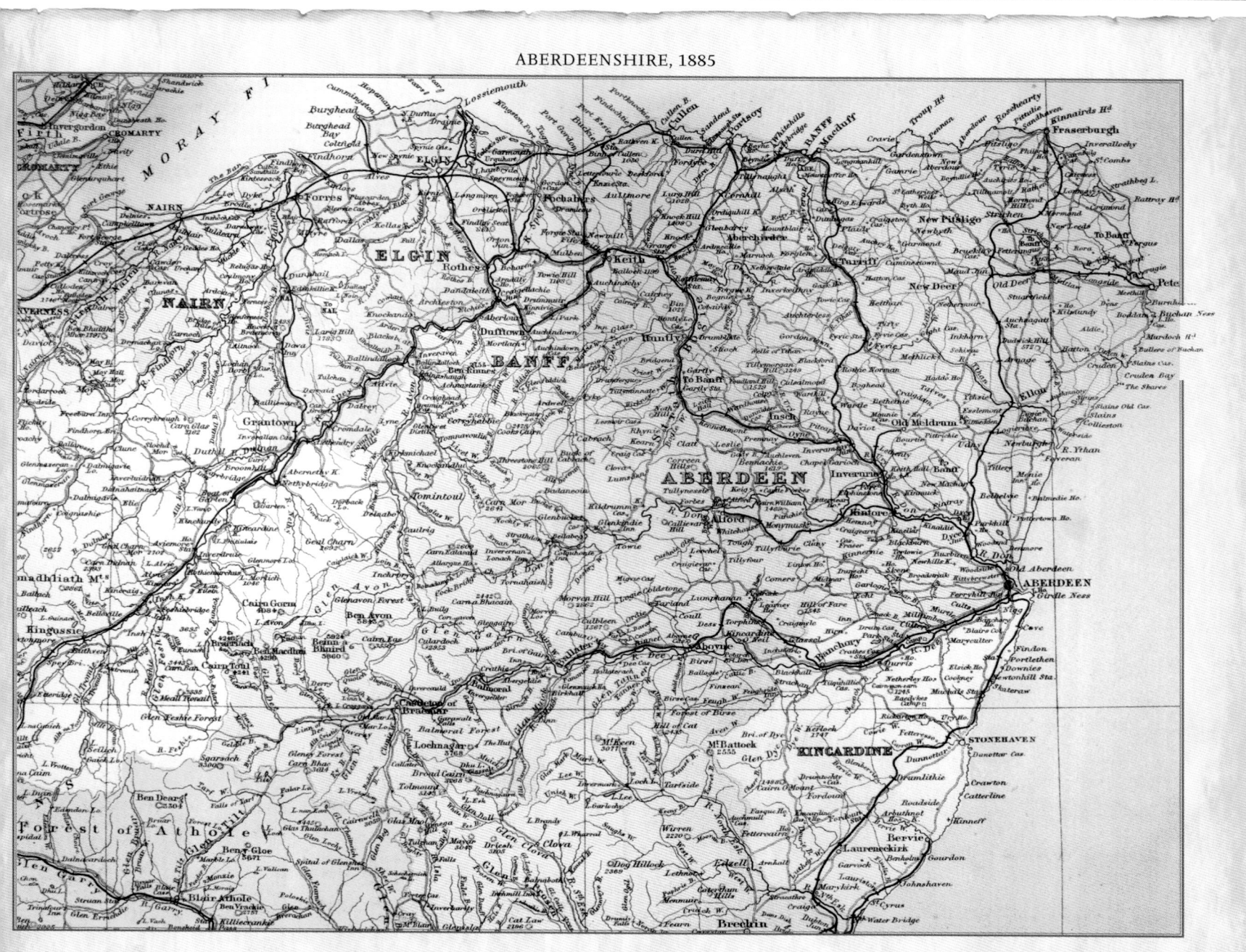

Bartholomew Gazetteer of the British Isles, 1887

NAIRNSHIRE, *a maritime co. in the NE. of Scotland, bounded N. by the Moray Firth, E. by Elginshire, and S. and W. by Inverness-shire; consists of a main body and 5 detached portions, 3 of which are in Elginshire, 1 in Inverness-shire, and 1 in Ross and Cromarty; the main body has an extreme length, N. and S., of 18 miles, and an average breadth, E. and W., of 11 miles; the coast, which is flat and sandy, has an extent of 10 miles; area, 127,905 ac.; pop. 10,455. The low ground near the coast is fertile and well-wooded, the soil consisting of a rich free loam over sand or gravel. The surface gradually rises thence into mountains in the S. Granite is abundant. The rivers are the Nairn and the Findhorn. Agriculture and the fisheries are the chief industries. The county comprises 3 pars, and 7 parts, and the royal burgh of Nairn.*

ELGINSHIRE *(or Morayshire), maritime co., in NE. of Scotland; is bounded N. by the Moray Firth, E. and SE. by Banff, SW. by Inverness, and W. by Nairn; coast-line, 30 miles; 304,606 ac.; pop. 43,788. Along the sea-coast the surface is mostly low and sandy; inland it consists of fertile valleys, divided by low hills, which gradually rise to the mountains on the S. border. The principal rivers are the Spey, Lossie, and Findhorn; the Spey and the Findhorn have salmon and grilse, large quantities of haddock, cod, and ling are caught in the Moray Firth. In the lower part of the co. farming and stock-raising are prosecuted with great success. The principal crops are wheat, oats, potatoes, and turnips, Granite occurs in the S., and red sandstone in the N. There are large quarries of freestone; whisky is distilled; and there is some shipbuilding at the mouth of the Spey. Corn, timber, salmon, and whisky are the chief exports. The co. comprises 15 pars, and 7 parts, the royal burghs of Elgin and Forres.*

BANFFSHIRE, *a maritime co. in the NE. of Scotland, stretching about 56 miles between Aberdeenshire and the cos. of Elgin and Inverness, and comprising a small detached section in Aberdeenshire. It is very narrow in proportion to its length, and is broadest along the N., where the coast on the Moray Firth measures about 30 miles. Area, 640.8 sq. m., or 412,258 ac. Pop. 62,736, or 98 persons to each sq. m. The greater part of the S. section (about three-fourths of the entire length) is occupied with lofty mountains, mainly wooded hills, and picturesque glens. The N. district is beautifully diversified with low hills, fine valleys, and small tracts of rich plain. The highest mountains, Ben Macdhui (4296 ft.) and Cairn Gorm (4080 ft.), are grouped on the SW. border. The rivers are the Spey, with its affluent the Fiddich; the Deveron, with its affluent the Isla; and the Boyne. There are quarries of slate and marble. The co. comprises 19 pars., with parts of 11 others, the police burghs of Banff and Cullen, Dufftown and Macduff.*

ABERDEENSHIRE, *a maritime co. in the NE. of Scotland; bounded N. and E. by the German Ocean; S. by the cos. of Kincardine, Forfar, and Perth; and W. by the cos. of Inverness and Banff. Greatest length, NE. and SW., 85 miles; greatest breadth, NW. and SE., 42 miles; coast-line, 60 miles. Area, 1955.4 sq. m., or 1,251,451 ac. Pop. 267,990, or 137 persons to each sq. m. The coast is mostly bold and rocky, and with little indentation. The chief promontories are Kinnaird's Head, Rattray Head, and Buchan Ness, the last being the most easterly point of Scotland. The surface, on the whole, is hilly and mountainous. It is lowest in the districts bordering on the coasts; and grandly mountainous in the SW., where numerous summits, including Ben Macdhui (4296 ft.), rise above 3000 ft. Much of the country is well-wooded. The chief rivers are the Dee, Don, Ythan, Ugie, and Deveron. Granite is the principal rock, and is extensively quarried for exportation. The soil has been rendered highly productive under skilful farming. Large numbers of fat cattle are annually reared and sent to the principal markets of Scotland and England. The coast and river fisheries are extensive and valuable. The co. comprises 76 pars. and 9 parts, the parl. burghs of Aberdeen, Inverurie, Kintore, and Peterhead, and the police burghs of Fraserburgh, Huntly, Inverurie, Peterhead, Turriff, &c.*

KINCARDINESHIRE *(or Mearns), maritime co. in NE. of Scotland; is bounded NW. and N. by Aberdeenshire, E. by the North Sea, and SW. by Forfarshire; greatest length, N. and S., 25 miles; greatest breadth, E. and W., 22 miles; coast-line, from the mouth of the North Esk to the mouth of the Dee, 31 miles; 245,346 ac., pop. 34,464. The coast is, in general, bold and rocky, but its indentations form fine natural harbours for numerous fishing villages. In the NW. the co. is occupied by the Grampian Mountains, which reach in Mount Battock an alt. of 2558 ft.; towards the N. it slopes into the valley of the Dee, and towards the S. into the Howe of the Mearns, a part of the great valley of Strathmore. The mountainous region is occupied chiefly by deer forests and grouse moors; the valley of the Dee and the Howe of the Mearns are both productive, but the most fertile part of the co. is that along the sea coast. There are no minerals of commercial importance. Fishing – including salmon fishing, both on the coast and on the rivers – is actively prosecuted, and there is some shipping at Stonehaven. The co. comprises 17 pars. and 4 parts, the royal burgh of Inverbervie, the seaport of Stonehaven, and the vils. of Auchinblae, Banchory, Cove, Fettercairn, Johnshaven, Laurencekirk, &c.*

ABERDEEN

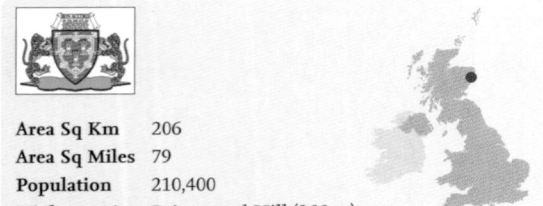

Area Sq Km	206
Area Sq Miles	79
Population	210,400
Highest point	Brimmond Hill (266 m)

Aberdeen (Gaelic, *Obar Dheathain*) means 'at the mouth of the Don' (the site of Old Aberdeen), the Don being named after the Celtic goddess Devona.

FAMOUS FOR

Aberdeen is the home of **water polo**. It was first played on the river Dee in around 1863.

Aberdeen's **Rowett Research Institute** has produced three Nobel prizewinners: J. J. R. Macleod (Physiology or Medicine) in 1923, Lord John Boyd Orr (Peace) in 1949, and Dr R. L. M. Synge in 1952 (Chemistry).

The Shore Porter's Society of Aberdeen is the oldest documented transport company in the world. It was established in 1498.

The building of **Union Street**, which required bridges to be built and land to be levelled off along its mile length, bankrupted the City Council by the time it was completed in 1817.

Until they were united in 1860, **King's College** (founded 1495) and **Marischal College** (founded 1593) were rival institutions. For 267 years, Aberdeen had as many universities within the city as were to be found in the whole of England.

FAMOUS PEOPLE

Robert Gordon, merchant trader, born 1668.
Charles Hamilton Sorley, poet, born 1895.
Flora Sadler, astronomer, born 1912.
Denis Law, professional footballer, born 1940.
Ann (Annie) Lennox, singer, born 1954.
Michael Clark, dancer and choreographer, born 1962.
Paul Lawrie, professional golfer, born 1969.

"Aberdeen is the Gaelic for hypothermia."
Billy Connolly

"Aberdeen impresses the stranger as a city of granite palaces, inhabited by people as definite as their building material... . The beauty of Aberdeen is the beauty of uniformity and solidity. Nothing so time-defying has been built since the Temple of Karnak."
H V Morton, *In Search of Scotland*, 1929

Aberdeen, called the 'Granite City' in honour of its main building stone, was one of five districts in Grampian Region prior to local government reorganisation in 1996. Its population is 210,400, a decrease of 2,100 since 1981, which may reflect a contraction in the off-shore oil industry. The city is the third largest in Scotland. Torry, a former royal burgh has been incorporated into the Aberdeen City Council area as have Kingswells and Peterculter.

There have been human settlements in the region for thousands of years. Old Aberdeen, at the mouth of the Don, and 'new' Aberdeen, on the banks of the Dee, were originally separate burghs. The city's earliest charter was granted by William the Lion in about 1179, but Aberdeen's importance has always been linked to its harbour. Medieval trade in wool with Germany and the Baltic states expanded over time to include shipping around Britain and the Orkney and Shetland Islands, and shipbuilding was another growth industry. Whaling in the 1820s gave way to herring fishing, and by 1870 there were around 200 boats based in Aberdeen. Discovery of North Sea oil in the 20th century increased the importance of the city and its harbour.

More than half of working people in Aberdeen are involved in the finance, IT and other business activities (24.6 per cent) or public administration, education and health (26.4 per cent). There are two universities in the city – Aberdeen University (founded in 1495) and The Robert Gordon University (formed from older institutions in 1992). In 2009, it was estimated that between a third and two fifths of jobs were related in some way to the oil and gas sector. Aberdeen is the centre of Europe's oil industry, with one of the busiest heliports in the world.

Aberdeen's skyline from the docks.

Aberdeen harbour

New King's College, Aberdeen University.

MORAY

Area Sq Km	2,257
Area Sq Miles	871
Population	87,800
Admin HQ	Elgin
Highest point	Ben Rinnes (840 m)

Moray (*Moireibh* or *Moireabh* in Gaelic) means 'sea settlement'.

FAMOUS FOR

Speyside whisky comes from a triangular area roughly 32 km long and 50 km wide, which includes the river Spey and its tributaries, the rivers Avon, Livet, Fiddich, Dullan and Lossie. However, none of the distillers draw their production water directly from the Spey.

The **Tugnet Ice House**, the largest structure of its kind, was built in 1830 near Spey Bay, to store ice cut from the river Spey and used to preserve the salmon catches. The fish were then sent by sea and later by rail as far south as London.

A resident population of bottlenose dolphins lives in the **Moray Firth**, one of only two pods in the UK.

A New Year celebration in **Burghead**, known as the 'Burning of the Clavie', still takes place on 11 January – the date of New Year in the old (Julian) calendar replaced in 1752.

Distilling whisky was a thriving – but illegal – industry all over **Moray** and many clandestine distillers regularised their operations only when the Excise Act of 1824 came into force.

Fashion icon Coco Chanel used fabrics woven by **Johnstons of Elgin** for her designs in the 1920s.

FAMOUS PEOPLE

Alexander Milne, businessman and philanthropist, born Fochabers, 1742.

William Marshall, composer and fiddler, born Fochabers, 1748.

Hugh Falconer, botanist and palaeontologist, born Forres, 1808.

James Ramsay MacDonald, politician and Prime Minister, born Lossiemouth, 1866.

George Stephen, 1st Baron Mount Stephen, co-founder of the Canadian Pacific Railway, born Dufftown, 1829.

William Grant, distiller, born Dufftown, 1839.

It would be no true – or, at least, no very discerning – lover of whisky who could enter this almost sacred zone without awe."

Aeneas Macdonald, 1930

Moray is a predominately rural area of farmland, fishing villages and moorland. While Ben Rinnes is the highest point, the much higher Ben Macdui (1,309 m) straddles Moray and Aberdeenshire. The principal river is the Spey and other rivers include the Findhorn and Lossie.

Originally part of a Pictish region, for centuries Moray was its own kingdom. Macbeth was probably its most famous ruler, and became a Scottish king himself. Modern Moray Council contains most of the historic counties of Banffshire and Elginshire. It was created in 1996 from districts of Grampian Regional Council. Its population in 2008 was 87,800, an increase of just over 4,000 from 1981. The largest towns are Elgin (20,330), Forres (8,990), Buckie (8,100), Lossiemouth (6,640), and Keith (4,580).

The sheltered southern coastline of the Moray Firth gives this area the name Laich of Moray with the reputation of being the 'garden of Scotland'. The winters can be harsh, however: routes to Tomintoul, the highest village in the area at 354 m, are routinely snow-bound. Coastal forests give way to a mainly agricultural landscape and moorland rising up in the south to the foothills of the Grampian Mountains. Predominantly rural in nature, the main employers are in education, health and public administration (32.9 per cent) and hotels, restaurants and retail (23.7 per cent). Gordonstoun School, where several generations of British royals have been educated, is located just outside the village of Duffus. Military connections continue in the form of the two Royal Air Force bases at Lossiemouth and Kinloss. Manufacturing is also an important sector manufacturing (15.2 per cent) and includes many household names. Food manufacturers *Baxters of Speyside* was established in Fochabers in 1868, *Johnstons of Elgin* cashmere mills have been operating since 1797, and *Walkers* bakery moved to Aberlour in 1898. Moray is home to many of the famous Strathspey whiskies, with the largest concentration of malt distillers in northeast Scotland.

Elgin, situated on the river Lossie, was a naturally defensible situation, and an important medieval centre. It is a city – being the site of the smallest and reputedly the most splendid cathedral in Scotland (the 'Lantern of the North'), which was built here in 1224. The ruins of two important medieval abbeys, Kinloss and Pluscarden, Pictish standing stones and castles make it clear why tourism is also an important area employer (9.3 per cent). The Speyside Way, first opened in 1981, is one of four long-distance footpaths in Scotland, running 100 km from near Buckie to Aviemore (in Highland), mostly along the river Spey. The unique Malt Whisky Trail also follows the Spey valley through the centre of Moray and on into Highland to the south. Golf links in Spey Bay opened in 1907, as did many grand hotels, as the railways brought in tourists. More recently, skiing (developed from the 1960s onwards), and outdoor activities of all sorts have been increasingly important for the local economy.

Ruins of Elgin Cathedral.

River Spey near Aberlour.

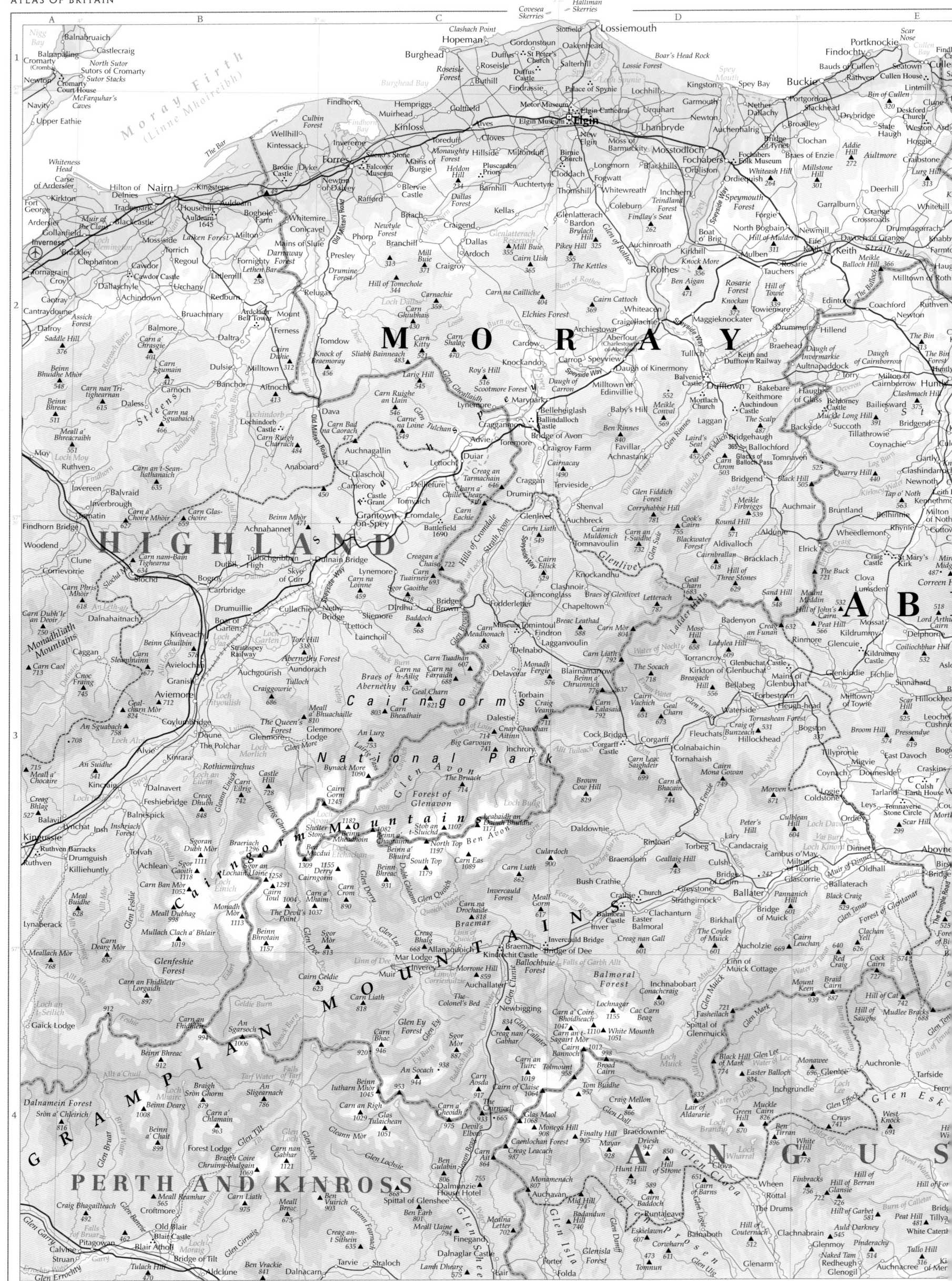

British National Grid projection

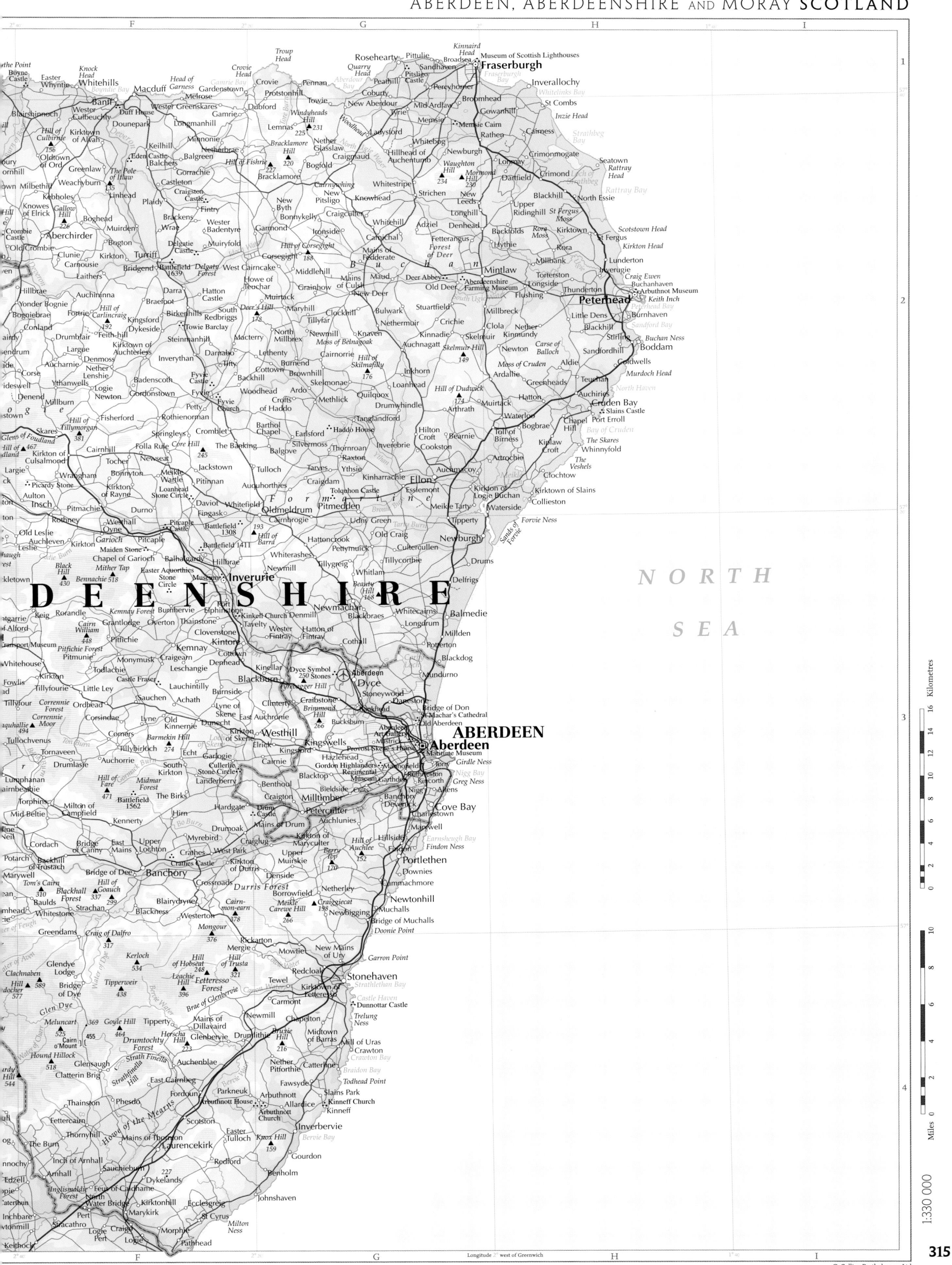

NORTH

SEA

ABERDEEN

D E E N S H I R E

Fraserburgh

Peterhead

Stonehaven

1:330 000

Kilometres

Miles

Longitude west of Greenwich

HIGHLAND

Area Sq Km	26,484
Area Sq Miles	10,226
Population	219,400
Admin HQ	Inverness
Highest point	Ben Nevis (1,344 m)

The name 'Highland' reflects the landscape, while the Gaelic *Comhairle na Gàidhealtachd* means the 'Council of Gaelic-speaking people'.

FAMOUS FOR

The only free-grazing herd of reindeer is to be found in the **Cairngorm Mountains** outside Aviemore.

Cape Wrath, in the far northwest, does have treacherous seas at it base, but the placename is Norse, 'hvarf', meaning turning point, because it was here the Viking longboats headed south to their settlements in the Hebrides and Ireland.

Paving for the streets of Paris in the 1890s came from flagstones quarried outside **Thurso**.

The battle of **Culloden** in 1746, fought between the British government and supporters of the Stuart claimant to the throne, Prince Charles Edward Stuart 'Bonnie Prince Charlie', was the last to be fought on the UK mainland.

The **Caledonian Canal**, begun in 1803 and finally finished in 1847 to a design by Thomas Telford, has 29 locks running north connecting Loch Linnhe to the Beauly Firth. The most spectacular of these is 'Neptune's Staircase', a series of eight locks which raise boats 21.3 m above sea level over a distance of 457 m at **Banavie**.

In 1997, the island of **Eigg** was bought by the local inhabitants in one of several famous 1990s Highland buy-out campaigns. The first community buy-out, by the **Assynt Crofters' Trust** in 1992, succeeded with a bid of £300,000 for the North Lochinver Estate of 8,620 ha to prevent it being broken up and sold. It is now known as the North Assynt Estate.

FAMOUS PEOPLE

Macbeth, *mórmaer* (chief) of Moray and king of Scotland, born Dingwall, c.1005.
Simon Fraser, 11th Lord Lovat, sometime Jacobite supporter, born Tomich, c.1667.
James Macpherson, poet and 'translator' of Ossian, born Ruthven, 1736.
Alexander Bain, clockmaker and inventor, born Watten, 1811.
Neil Miller Gunn, novelist, born Dunbeath, 1891.

"As for the Highlands, I shortly comprehend them all in two sorts of people: the one, that dwelleth in our mainland, that are barbarous for the most part, and yet mixed with some show of civility; the other, that dwelleth in the Isles, and are utterly barbarians."
King James VI

"… There is a great peculiarity about the Highlands and the Highlanders; and they are such a chivalrous, fine, active people."
Queen Victoria

"There is still something of an Odyssey up there, in among the islands and the silent lochs: like the twilight of the morning of the world, the herons fishing undisturbed by the water, and the sea running far in, for miles between the wet trickling hills, where the cottages are low and almost invisible, built into the earth. It is still out of the world like the very beginning of Europe."
D. H. Lawrence, 1926

Highland covers almost two-fifths of the entire Scottish mainland area, extending from Duncansby Head in the northeast to Loch Linnhe in the south, as well as taking in all of the Isle of Skye and many Inner Hebridean islands, including Eigg, Rum and Muck. Bisected by the Great Glen, it is a mountainous upland area of moorland and peatlands, rocky, fjord-like coastlines and deep glens. Not only is Ben Nevis (1,344 m) the highest peak in the area, it is the highest mountain in Britain. Numerous rivers run through this area either entirely or in part, including the Spey, Findhorn, Garry, Naver and Ness.

Highland is the largest council area in Britain. Five of Scotland's traditional post-1890 mainland counties – Caithness, Sutherland, Ross and Cromarty, Inverness-shire and Nairnshire – are subsumed into it, as well as parts of Argyll and Morayshire. Highland remains thinly populated relative to its size. The administrative headquarters are in Inverness, which is the largest town (42,400). Other major towns include Fort William (9,680), Nairn (8,830), Alness (5,180) Culloden (4,390), and Dingwall (5,080), while Invergordon (3,900), Aviemore (2,440) and Portree, on Skye, (2,070) are also important centres of population in an area generally described as very remote.

Despite its northerly latitude, the western coast enjoys a relatively mild although very damp climate due to the influence of the Gulf Stream. With little more than 2 per cent of the land in use for arable farming, it would be simple to underestimate the importance of both arable and pastoral agriculture, particularly crofting, in this region. Depopulation in modern times is due not only to the general harshness of the environment, but also to the historical consequences of the Highland Clearances in the 18th and 19th centuries and subsequent mass emigration. Despite a population increase of around 12 per cent since 1981, there are an average of about ten people per square km in Highland.

Inverness is not only the administrative centre of the area, but also the 'capital of the Highlands', for centuries a focus of trade and communications at the northern end of the Great Glen with access to the Mo Firth. Once a Pictish stronghold and thriving port, its original castle was eventually replaced in 1769 with F George, the finest 18th-century military fortification and garrison in Britain, still used by the army today. modern times, oil rig fabrication for North Sea fields has given way to rig maintenance. The aluminium smelter in Invergordon closed in 1981, but distilling still an important regional industry. However, the ma area employers are service industries, particularly in retail, hotels and restaurants (26 per cent) and public administration, education and health (32 per cent).

Digging peat is still practised in many Highland areas, but fuel poverty is a significant problem. A variety of solutions, principally to provide electricity, are being implemented, and there are more than 80 hydro-power stations operating in the area, the newe of which opened in 2009 at Glendoe near Loch Ness, as well as wind and wave demonstrators in the Moray Firth. Famously, the country's first experimental fast-breeder nuclear reactor was established at Dounreay, opened in 1955 by the UK Atomic Energy Authority with hopes of providing enough energy to supply a ci the size of Aberdeen. In its 1970s heyday, 3,500 people were employed there. Latterly dogged by controversy, the site was closed in 1998. There are no plans to buil more nuclear power facilities in the Highlands, but t long decommissioning period is expected to contribu significantly to the local economy.

Unsurprisingly for an area of outstanding natural beauty, tourism is also a healthy, if seasonal, employe (13.6 per cent). Outdoor pursuits, including deer stalking, fishing, skiing and mountaineering support local communities. A good example of this is the Caledonian Canal, 35.4 km of man-made waterway connecting Fort William and Inverness via four lochs (which themselves provide 61.2 km of navigable inlan waterway), including Loch Ness. What was originally a important improvement on an old trade route is now major tourist attraction.

Black Cuillin, Isle of Skye.

Highland dancing at the Highland Games near Aviemore.

Bartholomew Gazetteer of the British Isles, 1887

INVERNESS-SHIRE, *maritime co. in NW. of Scotland; is bounded N. by Ross and Cromarty and the Inner Moray Firth, NE. by Nairnshire and Elginshire, E. by Banffshire and Aberdeenshire, SE. by Perthshire, S. by Argyllshire, and W. by the Atlantic; area, 2,616,498 ac.; pop. 90,454. Inverness-shire is the largest county in Scotland. It consists of 2 portions, insular and mainland. The insular portion embraces the island of Skye, the St Kilda group, and the whole chain of the Outer Hebrides, except Lewis. The mainland portion – intersected NE. and SW. by Glen More nan Albin and the Caledonian Canal – consists almost entirely of mountain, loch, and glen. Ben Nevis (4406 ft.), in the SW., at Fort William, is the highest mountain in Great Britain. The principal lochs are Loch Ness, Loch Arkaig, Loch Lochy, Loch Laggan, and Loch Ericht. The W. coast is indented by Loch Hourn, Loch Nevis, and Loch Moidart. The principal rivers are the Spey, the Ness, and the Beauly, on all of which are valuable salmon fisheries. With the exception of the northern seaboard, the glens contain nearly all the fertile land, and only about one-twentieth of the total acreage is under tillage, all the rest being wood and forest, heath, and stony waste. There are nearly 300,000 ac. of deer forests, and about 1,700,000 ac. of heath, one-half of which affords pasturage for sheep; the other half serves only for grouse shooting. Inverness-shire is traversed by splendid military roads (constructed in the 18th century), by the Caledonian Canal, and in the N. and E. by the Highland Ry. The prevailing language is Gaelic. The county (insular and mainland) contains 26 pars. and parts of 10 others; the royal burgh of Inverness, and the police burghs of Fort William and Kingussie.*

ROSS AND CROMARTY, *maritime co., in NW. of Scotland; area, 2,003,065 ac., pop. 78,547. It consists of a mainland portion which comprises all the detached sections of Cromarty, and an insular portion properly called Ross-shire which includes Lewis island (excluding Harris) and a number of smaller islands in the Outer Hebrides. The mainland portion extends 67 m. N. and S. between Sutherland and Inverness-shire, and 75 miles E. and W. between the Moray Firth and the Atlantic Ocean. On the E. coast, which affords good harbours, are the Dornoch Firth, Cromarty Firth, and Beauly Firth; and of numerous indentations along the W. coast the largest are Loch Broom, Gruinard Bay, Loch Ewe, Loch Torridon, Loch Carron, and Loch Alsh. The largest streams are the Oykell, the Alness, and the Conon, which flow to the Moray Firth. The chief inland lochs are Maree, Fannich, Luichart, Sheallag, and Bosyne. Of the 3 great divisions of the co., Easter Ross, including all the low land between the Dornoch and Cromarty Firths, is fertile and well cultivated; Mid. Ross, including the district (known as the Black Isle) between the Cromarty Firth and the Moray and Beauly Firths, is mostly under good cultivation; while Wester Ross, including by far the greater portion of the co., is altogether of a highland character, and abounds in rugged mountains, beautiful lochs, and wild glens. Sheep farming and cattle grazing are extensively pursued. The distilling of whisky is the sole mfr. The fisheries, coast and inland, are extensive and valuable. The co. comprises 31 pars, with parts of 2 others, the police burghs of Cromarty, Dingwall, Fortrose, Invergordon, Stornoway, and Tain.*

SUTHERLAND, *maritime co. in the extreme N. of Scotland; is bounded W. and N. by the Atlantic Ocean, E. by Caithness and the Moray Firth, and S. by the Dornoch Firth and Ross and Cromarty; greatest length, NW. and SE., 63 miles; greatest breadth, NE. and SW., 60 miles; area, 1,297,846 ac., pop. 23,370. The N. and NW. coasts are bold and rocky, some of the cliff scenery being remarkably grand, but along the Moray Firth the ground is generally low and sandy. The surface consists chiefly of mountainous moorland, varied by numerous straths or narrow valleys which open towards the sea. The highest summit is Ben More Assynt, alt. 3273 ft. The principal streams are the Oykell Brora, Helmsdale, Halladale, Naver, and Hope. Of numerous lochs the largest are Lochs Shin, Assynt, Naver, Laoghal, Hope, and More. The angling in the lochs and streams is good, especially for trout. The coast fisheries are considerable. The amount of arable land is comparatively very small. There are extensive deer forests, and sheep are grazed in great numbers. The co. comprises 13 pars, with part of 1 other, and the parl. burgh of Dornoch.*

CAITHNESS-SHIRE, *a maritime co., in the extreme NE. of the mainland of Scotland. The side adjoining Sutherlandshire measures about 33 miles; the coast on the Pentland Firth about 41 miles; and the coast on the North Sea about 43 miles; area, 438,878 ac.; pop. 38,865, or 57 persons to each square mile. The coast along the N. and partly on the E. is bold and precipitous; between Wick and the Ord of Caithness, in the SE., it is mostly low and sandy. The chief promontories are Duncansbay Head and Dunnet Head, the latter being the most northerly point of the mainland. The surface in general is slightly undulating, and is much interspersed with small lakes and tracts of morass. It rises into mountains along the landward border, the chief summit of which, Morven, has an alt. of 2313 ft. The streams are numerous, but small; the principal are the Berridale and the Wick Water, flowing to the North Sea, and the Thurso and the Forss, flowing to the Pentland Firth. Flagstone is extensively quarried for exportation. The soil, though generally poor, is well cultivated. The coast fisheries are among the most important in the country; great quantities of herrings are annually cured and exported. The river Thurso is famed for its splendid salmon-fishing. There is railway communication to Thurso, in the extreme N. The co. comprises 9 pars. and part of 1 other, the royal burgh of Wick, and the police burgh of Thurso.*

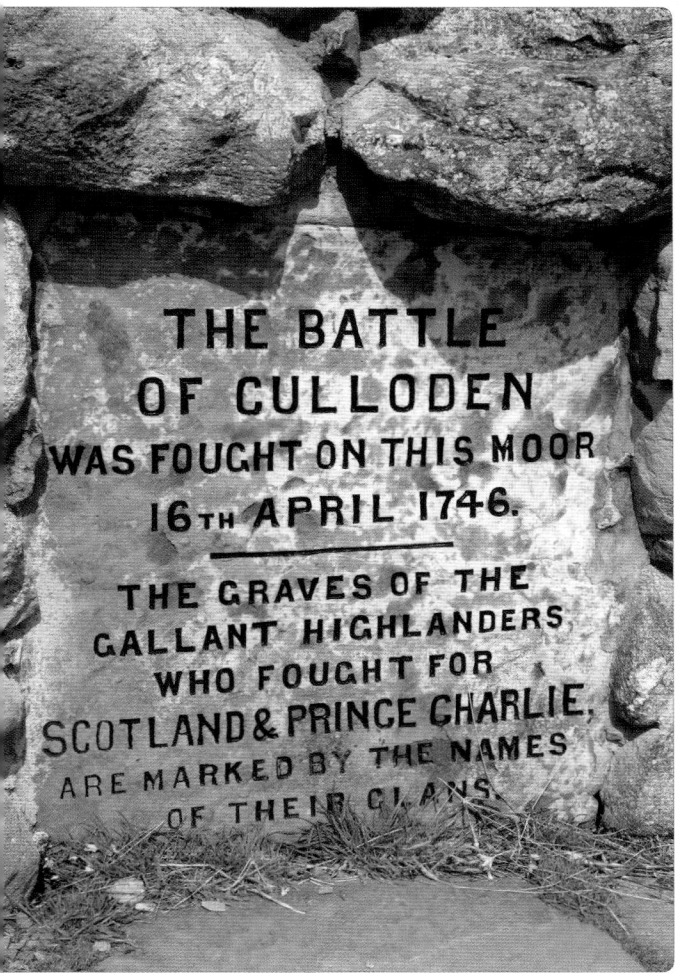

THE BATTLE OF CULLODEN WAS FOUGHT ON THIS MOOR 16TH APRIL 1746.

THE GRAVES OF THE GALLANT HIGHLANDERS WHO FOUGHT FOR SCOTLAND & PRINCE CHARLIE ARE MARKED BY THE NAMES OF THEIR CLANS.

Battle of Culloden monument

Eilean Donan Castle

Infirmary Bridge, Inverness.

THE HIGHLANDS, 1885

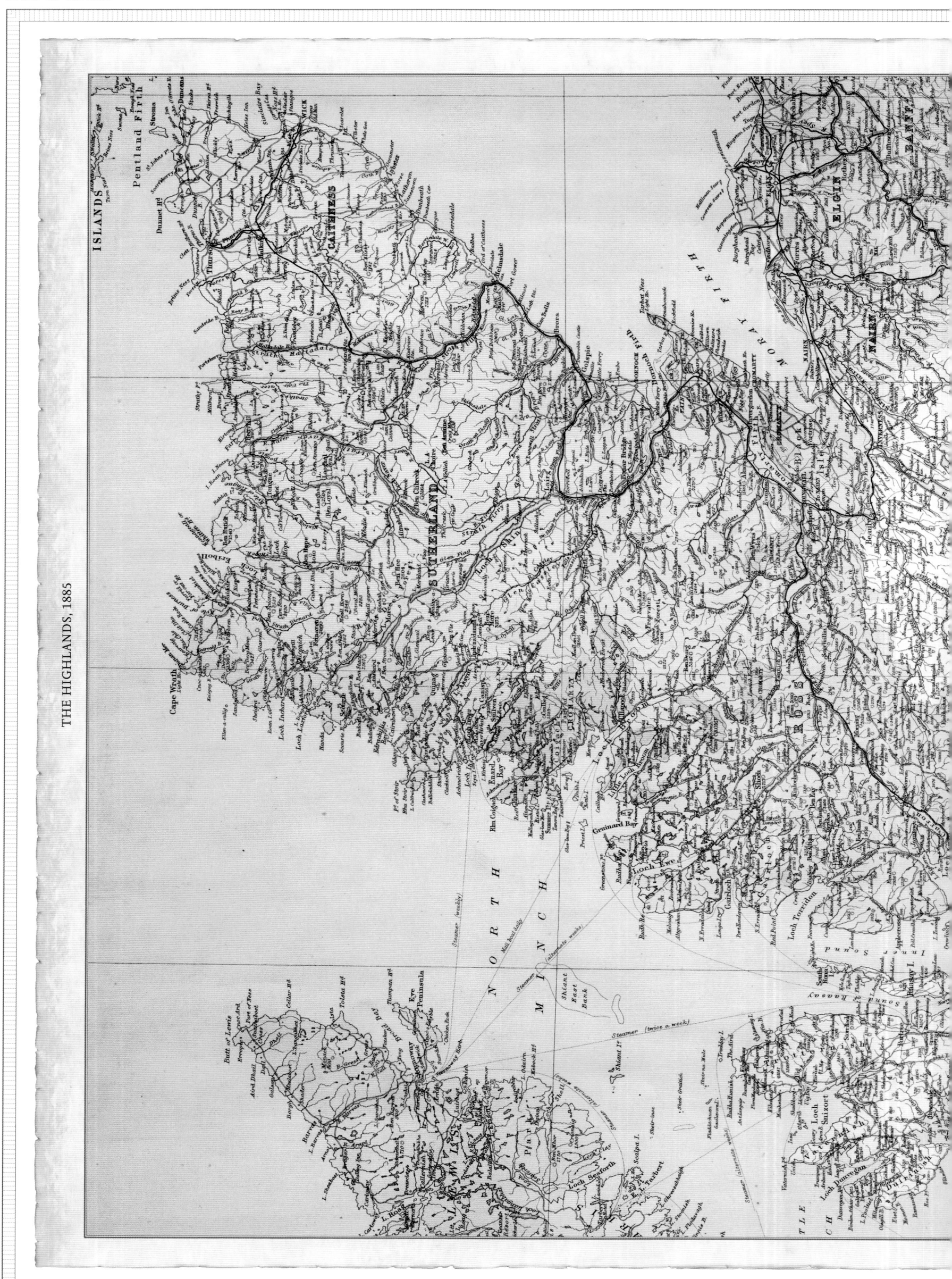

Walker descending Ben Nevis

ATLANTIC OCEAN

Isle of Lewis (Eilean Leodhais)

Butt of Lewis (Rubha Robhanais)
Eoropaidh
Teampull Mholuidh
Cóig Peighinnean
Lionel (Lional)
North Dell (Dail Bho Thuath)
Aird Dhail
Port of Ness (Port Nis)
Sgiogarstaigh
Cross (Cros)
Toa Galson
Gabhsunn Bho Dheas
Cuidhaseadair
Melbost Borve (Mealabost)
Broch
North Borve
Ness (Niss)
Cellar Head
Siadar Uarach
Steinacleit Cairn and Standing Stones
Loch Langavat
Baile an Truiseil
Upper Barvas
Brue (Brù)
Barvas (Barabhas)
Blackhouse
Lower Barvas
Arnol
Muirneag 248
Tolastadh Úr
Tolastadh
Tolsta Head
ISLE OF LEWIS (EILEAN LEODHAIS)
Loch Mòr Sandavit
Loch a Bhreòil
Beinn Mholach 292
Col Uarach
Col
Breibhig
Gress (Griais)
Bac
Creag Fhraoch
Gleann Tholastaidh

Tiumpan Head
Portnaguran (Port nan Giùran)
Aird Thunga
Newmarket
Tunga
Flesherin
Aird
Siulaisiadar
Seisiadar
Laxdale (Lacasdal)
Garrabost
Eye Peninsula (An Rubha)
Stornoway (Steòrnabhagh)
Stornoway
St Columba's Church
Knoc
Upper Bayble (Pabail Uarach)
Sandwick (Sanndabhaig)
Lower Bayble (Pabail Iarach)
Ceann na Circ
Achadh Mòr

WESTERN ISLES (EILEAN SIAR)

Achadh M
Leurbost (Liurbost)
Loch Erisort
Grimshader (Griomsiadar)
Ranish (Ranais)
Crosbost
Lacasaigh
Keose
Cromore
Talbot
Cearsiadar
Cabharstadh
Calbost
Marbhig
Glen Ouirn
Grabhair
Ceann Loch Shiphoirt
Feirihisval 326
Tom an Fhuadain
Kebock Head
Park
Orasaigh
Leumrabhagh
Eisgean
Eilean Iubhard
Srianach
Crionaig 470
Uisenis 371
Mulhagery
Mol Truisg
Gob Rubh' Uisenis
Bhalamus
Garbh Eilean
Eilean Mhuire 161
Eilean an Tighe
Shiant Islands

THE MINCH

Sound of Shiant

Priest Island
Summer Isles

Greenstone Point
Opinan
Mellon Udrigle
Achgarve
Mellon Charles
Laide
Coast
Gruinard Island
Gruinard Bay
Rubha Reidh
An Cuaidh 296
Cove
Bualnaluib
Aultbea (An t-Allt Beithe)
Second Coast
Little Gruinard
Melvaig
Inverasdale
Midtown
Aultgrishan
Peterburn
Naast
Tournaig
Boor
Londubh
North Erradale
Big Sand
Poolewe
Gairloch (Geàrrloch)
Gairloch Heritage Museum
Carn Dearg
Charlestown
Gair Loch
Badachro
Kerrysdale
Port Henderson
Slattadale
Opinan
Shieldaig
South Erradale
Red Point
Loch Maree
Letterewe
Talladale
Red Point!
Maol Ruadh
Furnace
Victoria Falls
Dubh Loch
Port Henderson
Loch na h-Oidhche

Fladda-chuain
Eilean Trodday
Rubha Hunish
The Aird
Duntulm Castle
Skye Cottage Museum
Rubha na Fearn
Fearnmore
Kilmaluag
Duntulm
Flodigarry
Eilean Flodigarry
Quiraing
Meall na Suiramach 543
Digg
Staffin Island
Borniskitaig
Kilvaxter
Staffin
Balgown
Linicro
Stenscholl
Monkstadt
Blishader
Marishader
Ascrib Islands
Totscore
Ben Gorm
Garros
Linicro
Flashader
Treaslane
Culnacnoc
Idrigil
Uig
Borve
Lealt
Earlish
Balnaknock
Ben Edra 611
Rubha Idrigil
Uig Bay
Loch Snizort
Cuidrach
Trotternish
Glenuachdarach
The Storr 719
Rona
Dry Harbour
Gillen
Greshornish Point
Kingsburgh
Romesdal
Eyre
Lusta
Lyndale House
Greshornish
The Storr
Rigg
Beinn Chreagach 326
Flashader
Treaslane
Skeabost
Bernisdale
Tote
Peinmore
Edinbane
Borve
Ben Dearg 552
Poolmore
Ben Sca 286
Carbost
Skeabost
Drumuie
Roskhill
Vatten
Harlosh
Glengrasco
SKYE (AN T-EILEAN SGITHEANACH)
Torvaig
Portree (Port Righ)
Penifiler
Beinn na Greine 417
Raasay
Glame
Balachuirn

Cape Wrath
Kearvaig
Scribhis-bheinn
Inshore
Old Ba
Bay of Keisgaig
Sandwood Loch
Creag Riabhach 485
Achiemore
Sandwood Bay
Sheigra
Strath Shinary
Farrmheall 521
Oldshoremore
Kinlochbervie
Badcall
Achresgill
Fanagmore
Tarbet
Foindle
Laxford Bridge
Arkle 787
Handa Island
Badnabay
Scourie Bay
Scourie More
Scourie
Badcall
Foinaven 911
Ben Stack 721
Achfary
Reay Forest
Point of Stoer
Clashnessie Bay
Eddrachillis Bay
Drumbeg
Ardvar
Kylestrome
Kylesku
Unapool
426 Glendhu Forest 547
Quinag 808
Culkein
Raffin
Clashnessie
Achnacarnin
Stoer
Nedd
Newton
Balchladich
Clachtoll
Rhicarn
Little Assynt
Ardvreck Castle
Glas Bheinn 776
Inchnadamph
Glencanisp Forest
Suilven 731
Canisp 846
Stronechrubie
Breabag 814
Achmelvich Bay
Achmelvich
Ardroe
Lochinver (Loch an Inbhir)
Beinn Garbh 540
Inchnadamph Forest
Rubha Coigeach
Baddidarach
Badnaban
Inverkirkaig
Falls of Kirkaig
Cam Loch
Reiff
Brae of Achnahaird
Enard Bay
Rhegreanoch
Inverpolly Forest 849
Ledbeg
Cùl Mòr 849
Elphin
Ledmore
Altandhu
Polbain
Achiltibuie (Achd-Ille-Bhuidhe)
Stac Pollaidh 613
Cùl Beag 769
Knockan
Drumrunie Forest
Ardnagoine
Garadheancal
Polglass
Achvraie
Ben Mòr Coigach 743
Drumrunie
Cremalt Hills
Meall an Fhuarain 578
Ardmair
Strathcanaird
Strath Canaird
Na Dromannan 408
Rhidorroch Forest
Rappach
Isle Martin
Ardmair
Rappach Water
Rhidorroch 548
Knockdamph
Sàil Mhòr 767
Achmore
Beinn Ghobhlach 635
Ullapool (Ullapul)
Beinn Eilideach 558
Leckmelm (Leac-Mailm)
Meall Dubh
Meall nan Ceapraichean 977
Freevater Forest
Scona Bhraigh 927
Gruinard Forest
An Teallach 1062
Bidein a' Ghlas Thuill 1059
Sgurr Fiona
Ardessie
Dundonnell House
Inverlael
Inverbroom
Glackour
Inverlael Forest
Eididh nan Clach Geala
Cona Mheall 980
Beinn Dearg 1084
Beinn Dearg 954
Strathvaich
Fisherfield Forest
Strathnasheallag Forest
Dundonnell Forest
Braemore
Fionn Loch
Beinn a' Chlaidheimh 908
Beinn Dearg Mhòr
Beinn a' Chaisgein Mòr
Beinn a' Chlaidheimh 914
Loch a' Bhraoin
Fain
Dirie More
Lochdrum
Beinn Airigh Charr 791
Ruadh Stac Mòr
A' Mhaighdean 967
Mullach Coire Mhic Fhearchair 1018
A'Chailleach
Sgurr Breac 999
934
1110
1093
Beinn Liath Mhòr Fannaich 954
Sgùrr Mòr
Sgùrr nan Clach Geala 923
Meall Gorm
Kinlochluichart Forest
Corriemoillie
Baosbheinn 875
Beinn a' Mhuinidh 692
Beinn Eighe 993
Beinn an Eoin 855
Slioch 980
Loch Fada
Fannaich Forest
An Coileachan 923
Leckie
Kinlochewe Forest
Jaagan Heights
Kinlochewe
Meall a' Ghiubhais 879
Meall a' Chrasgaidh 934
Corrievoulin
Fionn Bheinn 911
Lochrosque Forest
Loch Fannich
An Cabar 558
Lochluich
Shieldaig Forest
Craig
Sgorr Mhòr 516
Beinn Dearg 914
Liathach 1010
Spidean a' Choire Leith 1054
Loch Clair
Meall a' Chaorainn 705
Carn Loisgte 446
Carn Beag 550
Rubha na Fearn
Fearnmore
Craig
Lower Diabaig
Upper Diabaig
Beinn Alligin 985
Mullach an Rathain 1023
Torridon
Loch Torridon
Glen Torridon
Carn na Ba
Coulin Forest
Badavanich
Sgurr a' Mhuilinn 879
Meall na Faochaig 680
Milton
Arinacrinachd
Allligin Shuas
Fasag
Upper Loch Torridon
Beinn Liath Mhòr 782
Sgorr Ruadh 960
Fuar Tholl 907
Carn Gorm 733
Sgùrr nan Ceannaichean 913
Moruisg 928
Maoile Lunndaidh 1007
Sgurr a' Chaorachain 999
Beinn a' Chearcaill
Cuaig
Kenmore
Kishorn
Shieldaig
Balgy
Ben-damph Forest
Glenshieldaig Forest
Beinn Damh 902
Beinn Maol Cheandearg 925
Coulags
Strathcarron
Bidein a' Choire Sheasgaich 945
West Monar Forest
Meall Mòr 891
Meall Gorm
Callakille
Inverbain
Shieldaig
Ben Shieldaig 516
Lonbain
Meall na Fhuaid 518
Loch Lundie
Craig
An Staonach 513
Beinn Bhàn 896
Applecross Forest
Bealach na Ba 626
Applecross
Sgurr a' Chaorachain 776
Russel
Lochcarron (Loch Carann)
Ardaroch
Loch Kishorn
New Kelso
Balnacra
Achintee
Attadale Forest
Sgùrr Choinnich 999
Bidein a' Choire Sheasgaich
Maoile Lunndaidh
Sgùrr a' Mhuilinn
East Monar Forest
Sgùrr Coire nan Eun 789
Meallan Odhar
Carn Carnoch
Inchvuilt
Camusteel
Milton
Culduie
Camusterrach
Loch Monar

Sound of Raasay
Eilean Tigh
Dry Harbour
Manish Point
Torran
Arnish
Fladday
Eilean Fladday
Rona
Brochel
Eilean Trodday
Sound of Raasay
Inner Sound
Raasay

British National Grid projection

Metres / Feet
1000 / 3280
900 / 2952
800 / 2624
700 / 2296
600 / 1968
500 / 1640
400 / 1312
300 / 4921
200 / 656
150 / 492
100 / 328
50 / 164
0 / Land below sea level
50 / 164
200 / 656
1000 / 3281

1:450 000

© Collins Bartholomew Ltd

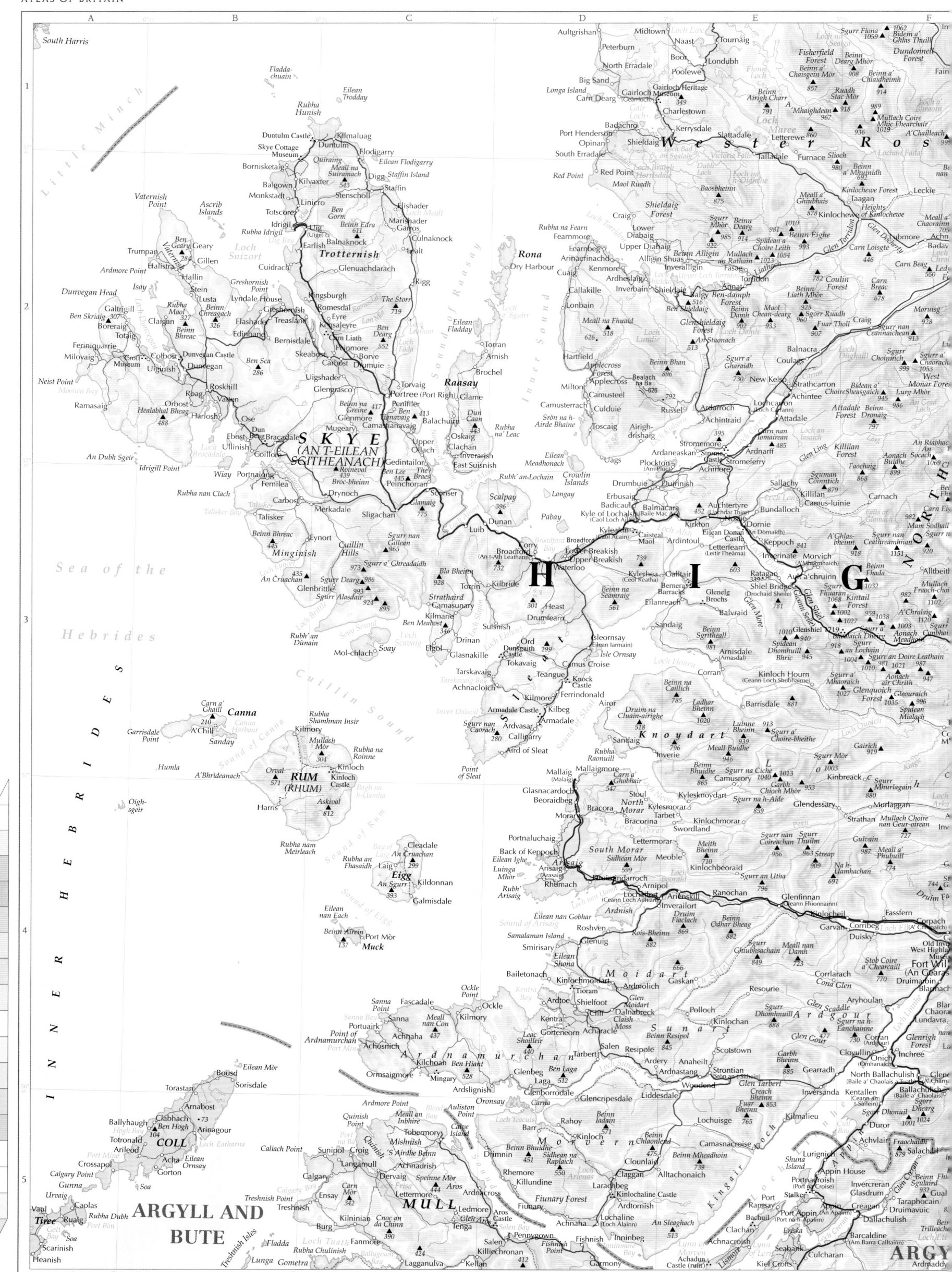

British National Grid projection

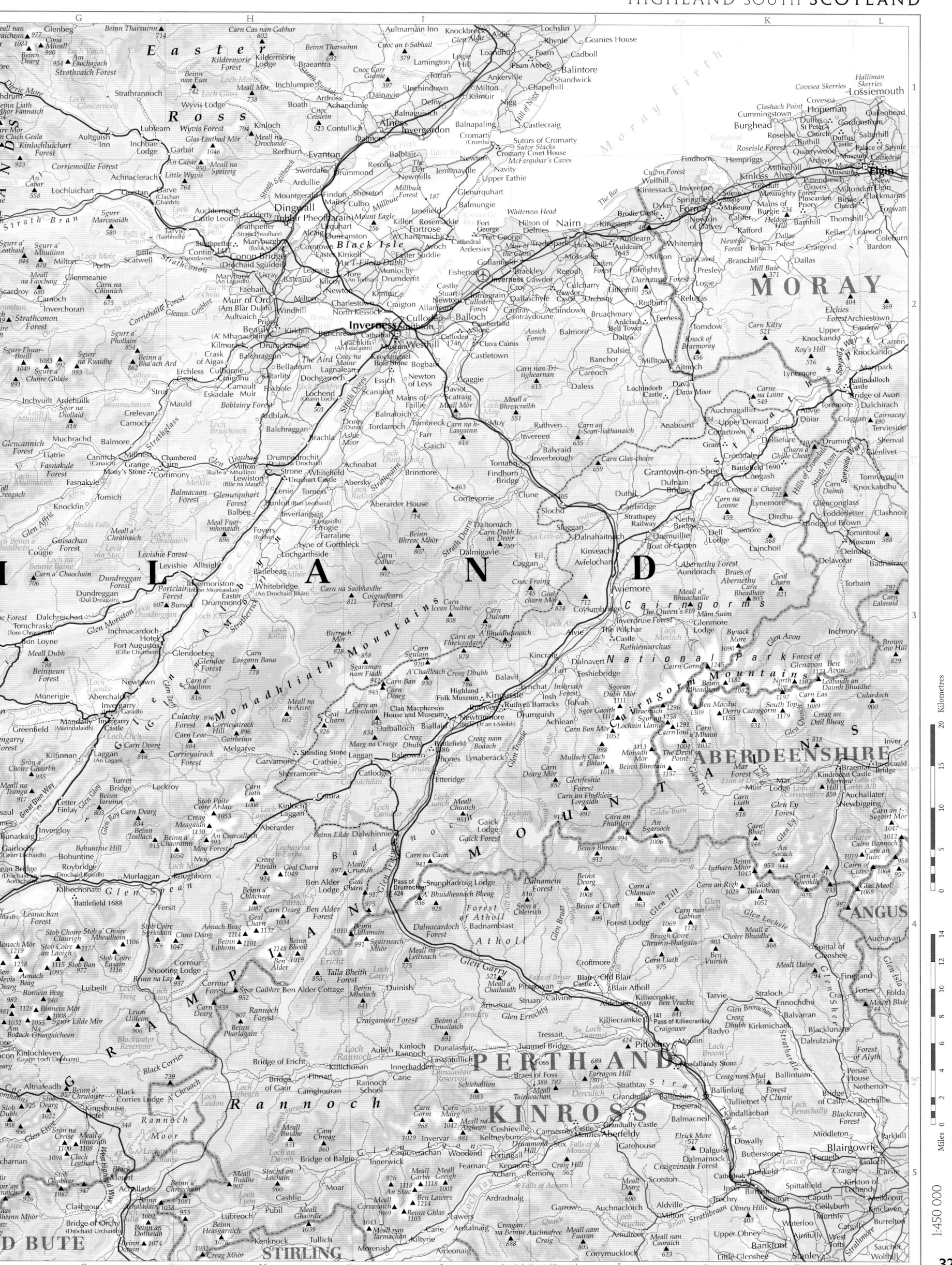

© Collins Bartholomew Ltd

WESTERN ISLES (EILEAN SIAR)

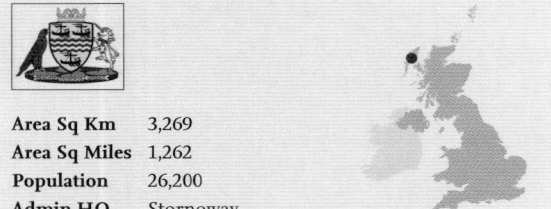

Area Sq Km	3,269
Area Sq Miles	1,262
Population	26,200
Admin HQ	Stornoway
Highest point	Clisham or *An Cliseam* (799 m) on north Harris

Eilean Siar is Gaelic for 'Western Islands', the unitary authority made up of the Outer Hebridean group of islands. The Gaelic name for the islands is *Na h-Eileanan an Iar*, 'The Islands of the West'.

FAMOUS FOR

The bedrock of these islands is mostly Lewisian Gneiss, some of the oldest in the world. **Roineabhal**, a mountain on Harris, is formed in part by a certain kind of granite, anorthosite, which is similar in composition to rocks retrieved from mountains on the Moon.

Vatersay is the southernmost permanently inhabited Hebridean island, and was linked to Barra by a causeway in 1991.

Sir James Matheson (who bought Lewis from the MacKenzies of Kintail in 1844 for £190,000) built **Lews Castle** just west of Stornoway from the profits of the tea and opium trades.

Harris Tweed is one of the last true cottage industries. Only authentic Harris Tweed bears the marque of the orb and cross, and has been woven from virgin Scottish wool on handlooms in the weaver's home.

Modern religious observance in the Western Isles has its roots in clan history. Lewis, Harris and North Uist tend to be Protestant. The more southerly islands, Benbecula, Barra, South Uist, remained Roman Catholic following the **Reformation** in 1560.

In 2005, **St Kilda** was awarded dual UNESCO World Heritage Status for both its natural habitats, including the surrounding marine environment, and its cultural significance.

FAMOUS PEOPLE

Flora Macdonald, Jacobite heroine, born Milton (South Uist), 1722.
Alexander MacDonald, vicar apostolic for the Roman Catholic Church in the Highlands, born Bornish, South Uist, 1736.
Colin Mackenzie, military engineer and surveyor, born Stornoway, Lewis, 1753.
Sir Alexander Mackenzie, explorer, born Stornoway, Lewis, 1763/4.
Agnes Mure Mackenzie, historian and novelist, born Stornoway, Lewis, 1891.
Malcolm (Callum) Macdonald, publisher, born Breaclete, Great Bernera, 1912.
Donald MacLeod, player and composer of highland bagpipe music, born Stornoway, Lewis, 1916.
Derick Smith Thomson, poet, academic and publisher, born Upper Bayble, Lewis, 1921.
Anne Frater, Gaelic writer, born Upper Bayble, Lewis, 1967.

"When a man gives out much, he must absorb much; and it is good to live with the gods for a bit; that is why some folk made pilgrimage to the Western Isles of Scotland."
Jessie Matthay

"What about the glamorous Hebrides, you ask? You think you will find a wonderful sensitiveness to nature – and to the supernatural – there? Not a bit of it. That is the bunkum of the Celtic Twilight. There is nothing more detestable, perhaps, than this Tiberization of the Hebrides."
Hugh MacDiarmid

The terms 'Hebrides' and 'Western Isles' are not synonymous. The Western Isles only cover the Outer Hebrides. The 'Long Island' is composed of two parts: the larger is Lewis, thought to be a pre-Norse name whose origins are now forgotten, although modern Gaelic *Leodhais* means 'marshy'. The smaller part of the large island is Harris (Gaelic *Na-h-Eareadh*) that is related to the Old Scandinavian *herath* or 'district'. Both North and South Uist were known by 1282 as *Iuist*, 'Inner Abode', possibly a Scandinavian interpretation of a pre-Celtic name. In common with many of the islands, Barra (Gaelic *Barraigh*), Mingulay and Eriskay display their Viking heritage with -'a(y)' endings, which in Old Scandinavian denotes an island.

Although each island has its own distinct characteristics, they broadly share fundamentals: deeply indented coastlines, small inland lochs and extensive peatland. In general their eastern shores tend to be moorland or mountainous. Beinn Mhor in South Uist is 620 m, but Clisham or *An Cliseam* (799 m) on Harris is the highest point, one of about 30 peaks over 300 m in the island. The western coasts tend to be generally more fertile, with shell sand beaches, and sometimes fringed with machair – ecologically fragile dune pastureland. The area also includes many other smaller islands stretching out into the Atlantic, most notably Vatersay and St Kilda, 66 km west of Benbecula. All are separated from the Inner Hebrides and the mainland by The Minch, a sea channel varying between 24 and 72 km in width. The influence of the Gulf Stream creates a much milder maritime climate than the area's northerly latitude might suggest.

There has been human settlement in the Western Isles for thousands of years. Archaeologists have found Neolithic houses and artefacts from the Beaker peoples, and it is assumed that Celtic groups settled the islands as they had the rest of Scotland. The Calanais (or Callanish) Stones on Lewis provide the most outstanding example of prehistoric megaliths. Known as 'Hyperborea' to the Greeks, the first written records arrived with Christianity in the 6th century AD. Norse control was formalized in 1098, when Magnus III of Norway became King of the Isles, and ended in 1266, when the Outer Hebrides and Man became part of

Scotland. By the 18th and 19th centuries, the struggling economies of the islands saw increases in emigration to Australia, New Zealand and Canada, which was only made worse by Clearances. Lewis alone lost more than 1,000 men in World War I, proportionally more than anywhere else in Britain.

The population of 26,200 (2008) has steadily declined since 1981. There are 14 populated islands, and although the majority of people live in Lewis and Harris, Flodaigh had 11 inhabitants in 2001. Gaelic language and culture survive throughout the Western Isles (62 per cent of the population speak, read or write the language). Prior to 1975, Lewis was part of Ross-shire, but Harris and the rest of the Outer Hebrides were designated as Inverness-shire. By 1975 the Western Isles authority had been established as a unitary authority, and government reorganization in 1996 had little impact.

Stornoway is the administrative centre with 5,740 inhabitants and by some margin the most populous town in the Isles. Its natural deep-water harbour is reflected in the Norse origins of its name: 'Steering Bay'. The original castle was built in the 12th century, and the town became a burgh of barony in 1607. Stornoway grew in the 19th century as a response to the herring fishery, and when that declined, weaving provided employment. Today, the harbour is still home to a fishing fleet, as well as freight and ferry traffic, linking the Western Isles to the Inner Hebrides and the mainland.

Traditionally, the economic mainstay has been crofting, although briefly in the 18th century an industry for burning seaweed for alkalis needed in the production of soap and glassmaking supplemented incomes. Arable farmland is scarce, and crofts, typically organized in townships, are small (on average about 3 hectares). Peat is still cut for fuel, and a 33-turbine windfarm has been approved for development. Fishing still contributes to the local economy. Tourism is increasingly important to the Western Isles, but, compared to the national average, public administration, education and health provide a disproportionate number of jobs (43 per cent). Road bridges connect many of the smaller islands today, and the ferry service are good, and in 2009 Sunday sailings were added, in the face of much controversy.

Cut peat drying, North Uist.

Deserted village, St Kilda.

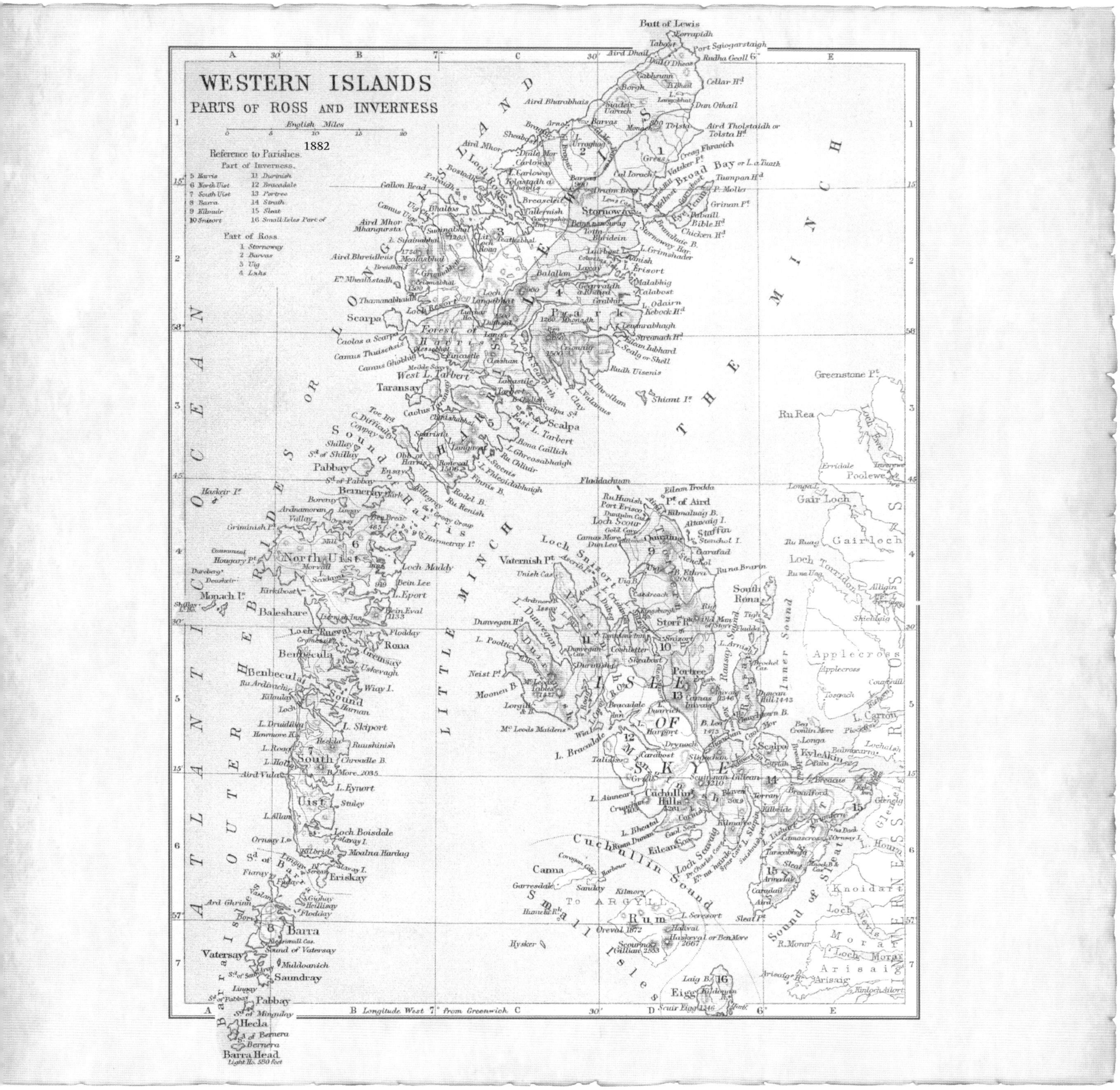
WESTERN ISLANDS
PARTS OF ROSS AND INVERNESS
English Miles
1882
Reference to Parishes.
Part of Inverness.
5 Harris
6 North Uist
7 South Uist
8 Barra
9 Kilmuir
10 Snizort
11 Durinish
12 Bracadale
13 Portree
14 Strath
15 Sleat
16 Small Isles Part of
Part of Ross.
1 Stornoway
2 Barvas
3 Uig
4 Lochs
Longitude West 7° from Greenwich

rnoway harbour

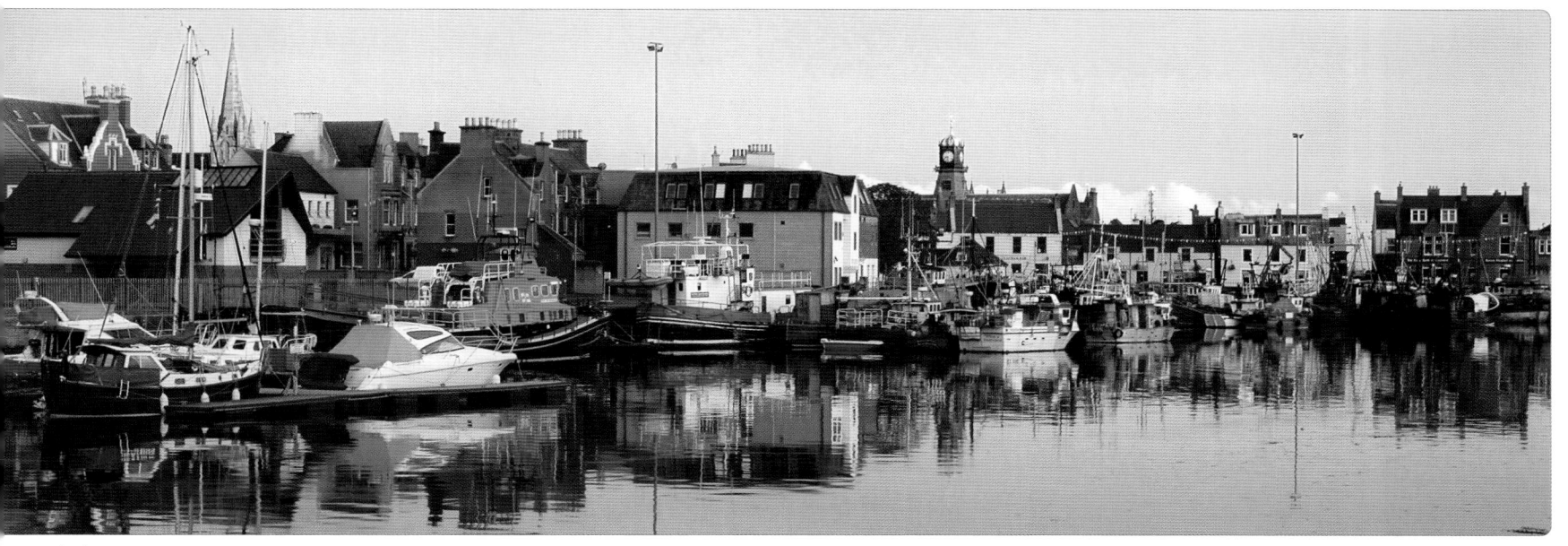

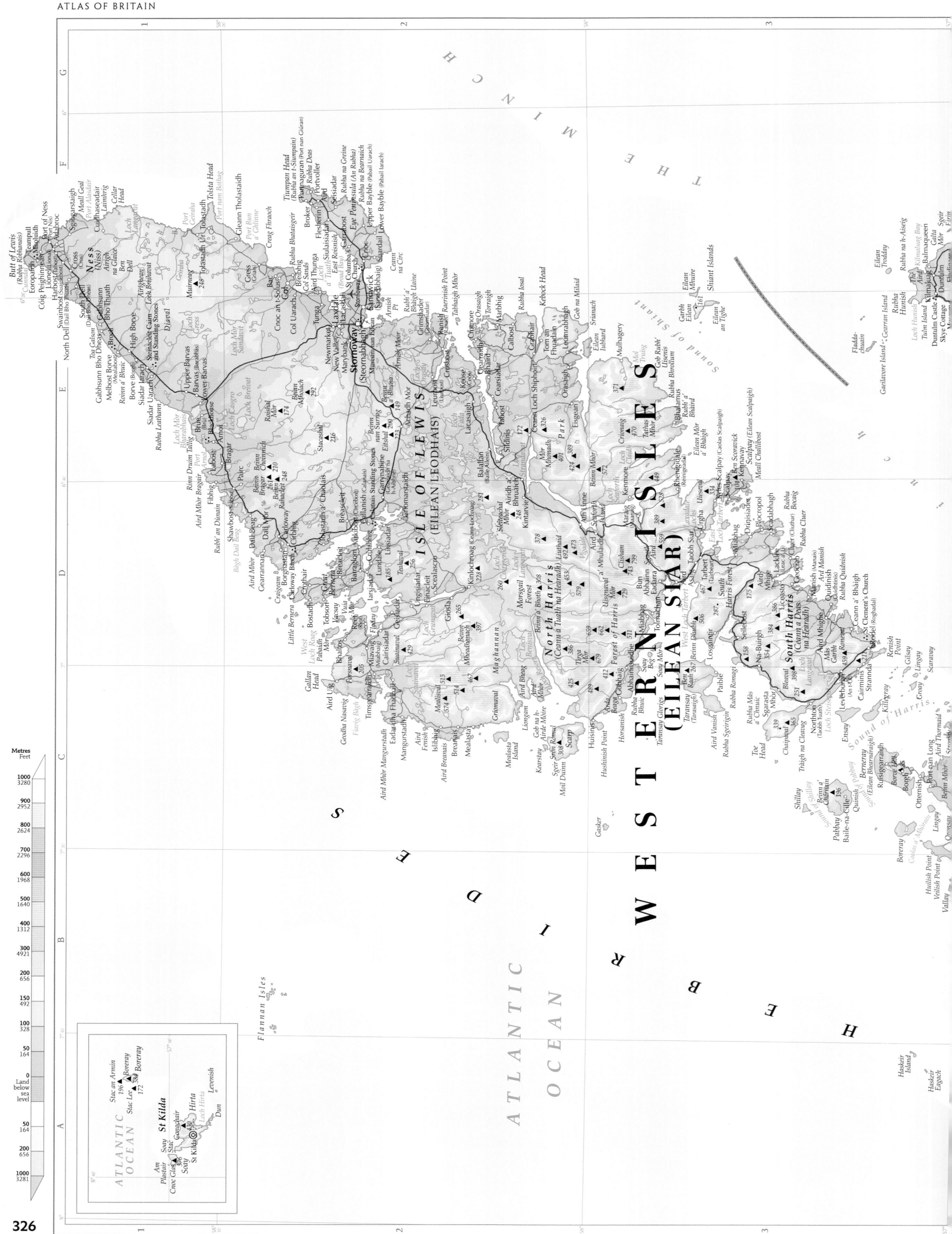

British National Grid projection

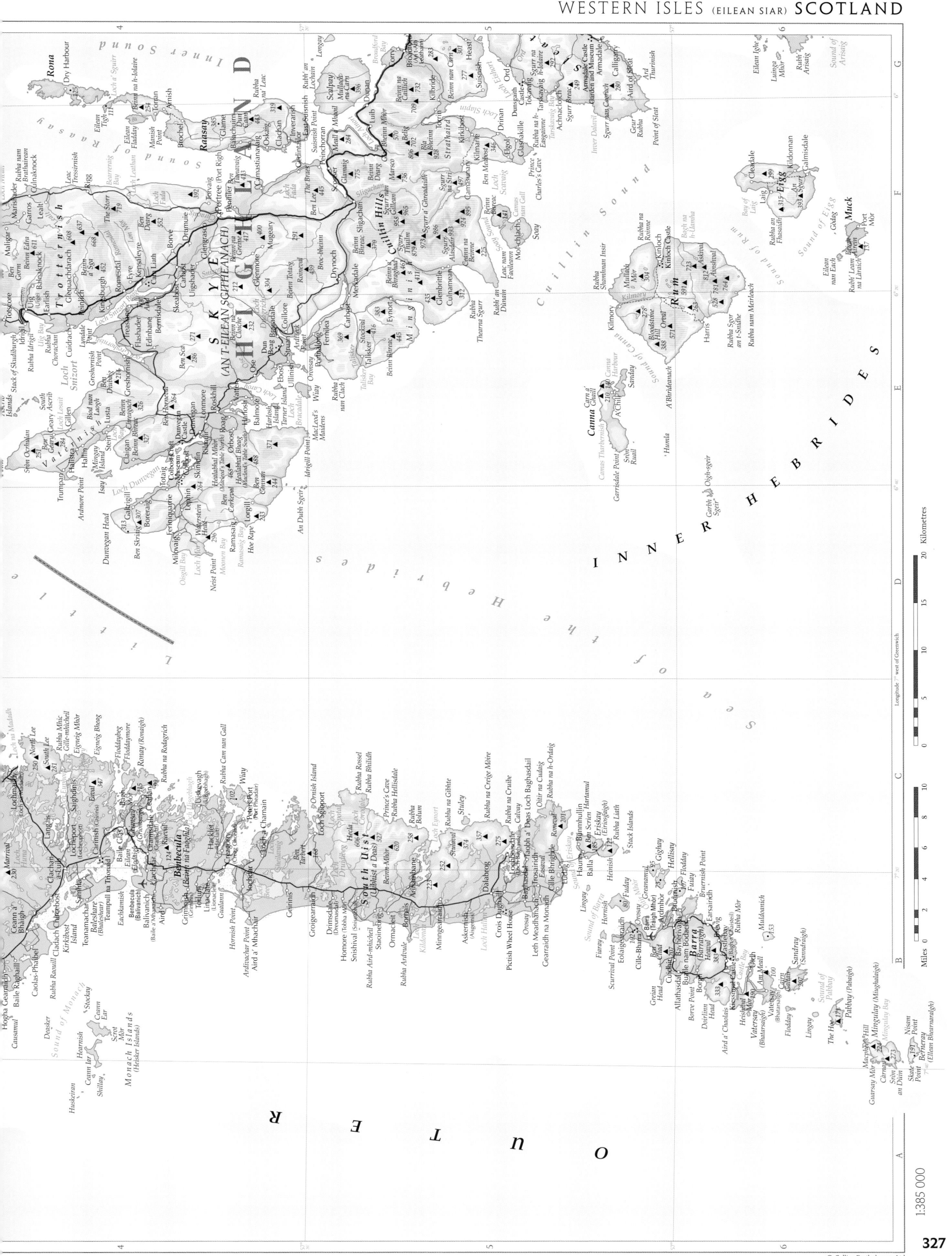

1:385 000

© Collins Bartholomew Ltd

ORKNEY

Area Sq Km	1,086
Area Sq Miles	419
Population	19,900
Admin HQ	Kirkwall
Highest point	Ward Hill (479 m) on Hoy

The *Orcades* was the name given by the Roman geographer Pomponius Mela, but by AD 970 Norse influence had incorporated the Old Scandinavian '*ey*' (island), *Orkaneya*. It is possible that the islands had a Pictish tribal name *orc* meaning 'young boar', so 'Boar (or Pig) Islands', which the Vikings mistook as *orkn* 'seal' (Seal Islands).

FAMOUS FOR

Orkney has its own **flag**: a blue and yellow Nordic cross on a red background.

Gaelic was never spoken in the Orkney Islands, and when the **Vikings** settled here in the 8th century, they brought Old Norse with them, which later developed into Norn. Most of the placenames have Old Norse roots.

The Big Tree, a sycamore, stands in the centre of Main Street in Kirkwall, and it was alleged to have been the largest tree in the islands at one time. Probably centuries old, and not large by mainland standards, it is a rarity on wind-swept and mainly treeless Orkney.

A conservation project on **North Ronaldsay** begun in the 1970s protects a seaweed-eating ancient breed of sheep. DNA shows the endangered animals to be virtually unchanged since the Bronze Age, and akin to the bones of sheep found by archaeologists at Skara Brae.

FAMOUS PEOPLE

[Saint] Magnús Erlendsson, Earl of Orkney and martyr, born 1075/6.
James Aitken, churchman and bishop, born Kirkwall, 1612/13.
John Rae, Arctic explorer, born Stromness, 1813.
William Balfour Baikie, explorer of Africa, born Kirkwall, 1824.
Marian (Florence) McNeill, folklorist, born St Mary's, Holm, 1885.
Edwin Muir, poet and literary critic, born Ayre, 1882.
George Mackay Brown, poet and novelist, born Stromness, 1921.
Magnus Linklater, journalist and newspaper editor, born Harray, 1942.

Skara Brae

"What struck me in these islands was their bleakness, the number of ridiculous little churches, the fact that bogs do not require a level surface for their existence but can also run uphill, and that ponies sometimes have a black stripe like the wild ass."
Norman Douglas

The Orkney Islands are an archipelago of 67 islands (one third are inhabited) located off the most northeasterly point on the Scottish mainland where the North Sea and Atlantic Ocean meet. In addition to the Mainland, these are roughly divided into a north and a south grouping of gently rolling, low-lying islands of fertile farmland, moorland and bog, enjoying a relatively mild climate due to the influence of the Gulf Stream. Sheer cliffs dominate the north and west coasts of the islands.

The population of 19,900 (2008) has hardly changed since the 1981 census. The administrative centre is at Kirkwall (6,460), and Stromness (1,560) is another important town; both are on the Mainland.

There is evidence that the islands have been inhabited for more than eight millennia, and it has some of the most extraordinary Neolithic monuments in the world, four of which – Maeshowe, the Stones of Stenness, Skara Brae and the Ring of Brodgar on the Mainland – were made a UNESCO World Heritage Site in 1999. The Tomb of the Eagles, another Neolithic site, is on South Ronaldsay. Known to the Romans, these islands were settled by Scandinavians during the first millennium AD and for centuries the islands were a Norse colony. Orkney only became part of Scotland when, in 1468, the islands were offered as surety for a dowry pledge when Margaret of Norway married James III.

Kirkwall, the administrative centre, first appears in the *Orkneyinga Saga* as *Kirkjuvag* (Church Bay), a possib[le] reference to St Olaf's church built around 1035, rather than the splendid red sandstone St Magnus Cathedral begun in 1137. Kirkwall is the only town of any size in the islands, and is the centre of most services and commerce in Orkney.

Agriculture is the most important economic secto[r] and the majority of the land is farmed as grazing for sheep and, particularly, beef cattle. Traditional industr[y] also include fishing, and exports of lobsters, crabs and other seafood compliment the rise in salmon fish farming. Services provide most employment, especiall[y] public administration, education and health (34 per cent). Tourism in Orkney is an increasingly important employment sector (11 per cent). Manufacturing on th[e] island is relatively small employer (6 per cent), but includes crafts, including textiles and jewellery makin[g], and one whisky distillery, Highland Park.

In the 1970s, the Flotta oil terminal was built in Scapa Flow to service the Piper and Claymore fields, while the European Marine Energy Centre is currently testing full-scale renewable wave and tidal technology prototypes in Orkney. Transport between Orkney and Scottish mainland as well as within the archipelago itself is mainly by ferries. The seven airports in the islands operate services between Orkney and Shetland [and] the rest of Scotland and Norway.

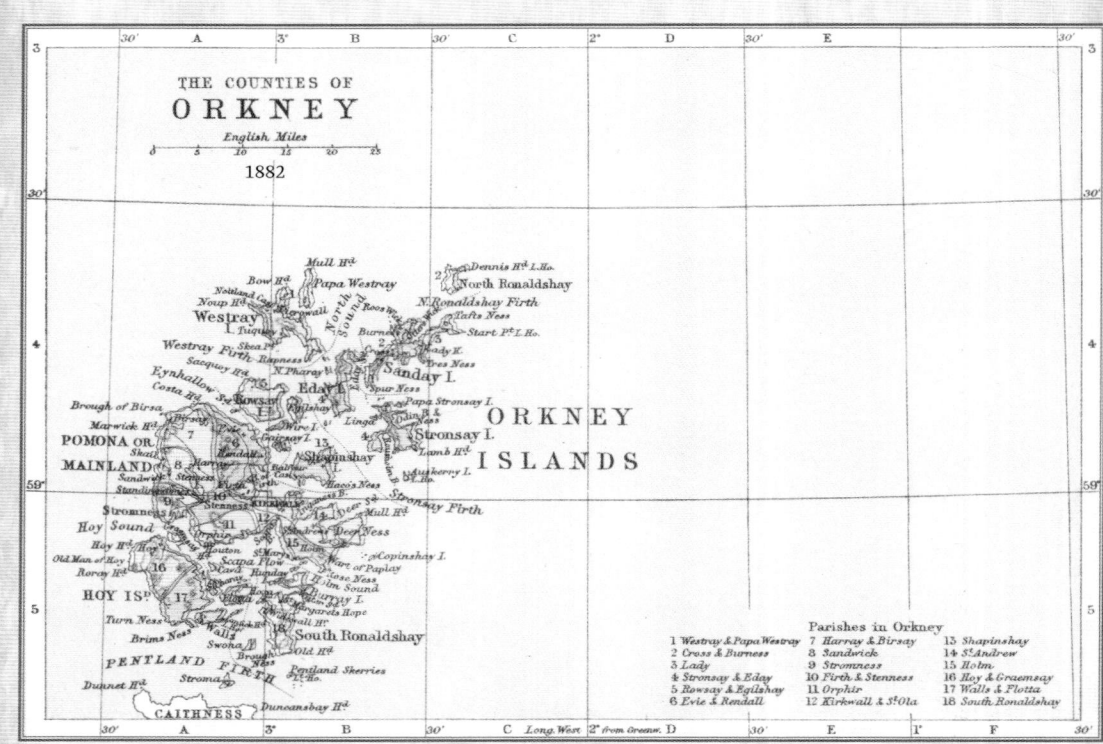

Bartholomew Gazetteer of the British Isles, 1887
ORKNEY, *insular co. of Scotland, separated from Caithness by the Pentland Firth (6½ to 8 miles broad); area, 240,476 ac., pop. 32,044; pop. of Pomona, or Mainland, 17,165. The Orkneys comprise 67 islands, 28 of which are inhabited, besides a large number of rocky islets or skerries. They are divided into 3 groups – the South Isles, comprising the large islands of Hoy, South Ronaldshay, and many smaller ones; Pomona, or Mainland, the largest island of the Orkneys; and the North Isles, comprising Rousay, Shapinshay, Westray, Papa Westray, Eday, Stronsay, Sanday, and North Ronaldshay. Except on the S. and W. sides, where the cliffs are bold and precipitous, the coasts of the islands are extremely irregular, abounding in bays and headlands. The surface – most elevated in Hoy, which is hilly – is generally low, and much interspersed with rocks, swamps, and lochs. The climate, prevailingly moist, is mild and equable for the latitude. The soil mostly consists of peat or moss, but is either sandy or of a good loam where the land is arable. The farms are usually of small size; oats, barley, and turnips are grown. Live stock, poultry, and eggs are largely exported. There is regular steam communication between Leith and Kirkwall, an active trade being kept up. Orkney forms one of the great Scottish fishery districts. Fishing and agriculture are the chief industries. There are two distilleries in Pomona. The Orkneys were known to the Romans as the Orcades, and seem to have been originally peopled by Celts. About the beginning of the 4th century the islands were visited by the Norse sea-rovers, who ultimately settled upon them. They were annexed to Norway in the latter part of the 9th century, and in 1468 were attached to Scotland as a pledge for the dowry of the Princess of Denmark who married James III. The people still retain some traces of their Scandinavian descent. Orkney comprises 18 pars., the police burghs of Kirkwall and Stromness.*

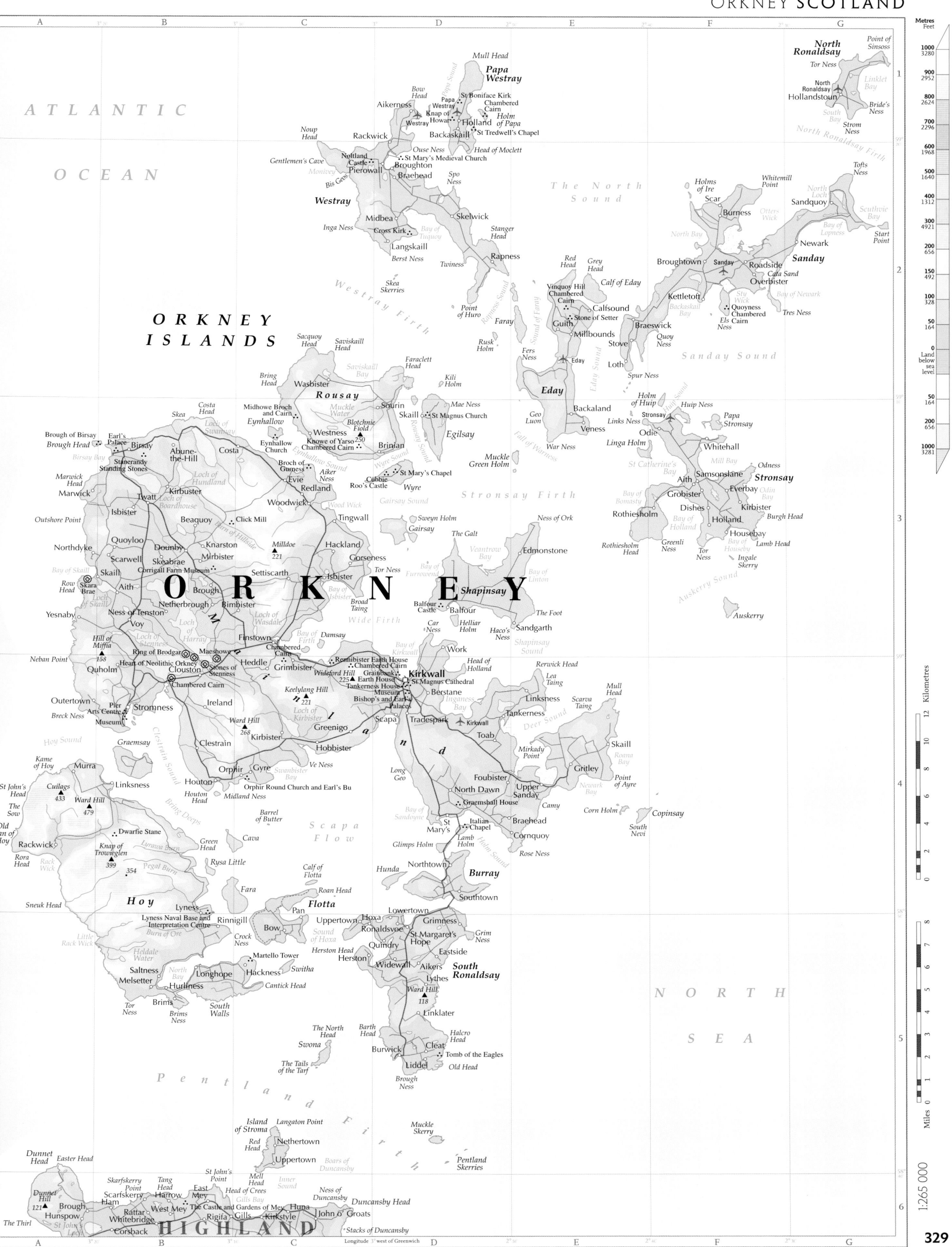

© Collins Bartholomew Ltd

tish National Grid projection

1:265 000

SHETLAND

Area Sq Km	1,657
Area Sq Miles	640
Population	22,000
Admin HQ	Lerwick
Highest point	Ronas Hill (450 m) on the Mainland

Most experts consider the name a variation of the Old Norse *Hjaltland* ('High Land') such as Hetland and Yetland. In around 1100, it appears in sources as 'Haltland' and, by 1289, 'Shetland', although it still is described in some modern sources as Zetland.

FAMOUS FOR

Jarlshoff, rediscovered in 1905 after a violent storm, has been shown by archaeologists to have been inhabited since around 2000 BC, and housed, at various times, Bronze Age, Iron Age, Pictish and Viking dwellers.

Fair Isle gave its name to a particular technique of creating patterns of multiple colours in hand-knitted jumpers. Traditional patterns have a palette of about five colours, and use only two colours in each row. Most importantly, they are knitted in the round.

Muckle Flugga is the most northerly point in the United Kingdom and constitutes little more than rocks with a lighthouse.

Up-Helly-Aa (Fire Festival) every January involves dragging a full-sized replica of a Viking longship through the town and setting fire to it. It has no connection to the Vikings at all, but seems to be a modern festival with some older links to rural Shetland celebrations.

FAMOUS PEOPLE

Arthur Anderson, ship-owner, founder of the Peninsular and Oriental Steam Navigation Company (P&O), born Grimista, Lerwick, 1792.
Thomas Barclay, minister and Glasgow University principal, born Unst, 1792.
Laurence Edmondston, ornithologist and physician, born Lerwick, 1795.
Thomas Edmondston, botanist, born Buness, Unst, 1825.
Sir Robert Stout, lawyer and prime minister of New Zealand, born Lerwick, 1844.
Laurence Williamson, crofter and antiquary, born Linkshouse, Mid Yell, 1855.
Norman Lamont, Conservative politician, born Lerwick, 1942.
Alexander (Aly) Bain, fiddler and composer, born Lerwick, 1946.

Scalloway Castle

The Shetland Islands are a group of around 100 low-lying islands strung out into the North Sea 280 km southeast of the Faroe islands, of which about 20 are inhabited. Rocky and steep-cliffed, the inlets (voes) rise to humped but low hills set in undulating moorland. The maritime climate is milder than the latitude might suggest, but winds are strong, stunting vegetation.

The Shetland population of 22,200 has dropped by 16 per cent since 1981, due to the decline of the North Sea oil industry. Lerwick (6,560) is the administrative centre while Scalloway (780) and Brae (690), both on Mainland, are important settlements.

Mousa Broch is the best preserved of over 100 examples of Iron Age Pictish fortifications. Christianity arrived in Shetland during the 6th century AD, but the pagan Vikings swept this new faith away. The Norse used these islands as stepping stones to their larger holdings in the Western Isles, Ireland and Iceland.
The islands were annexed to Scotland in 1472 as part of the dowry of Margaret of Norway when she married James III.

Lerwick, the most northerly town in Britain, was a fishing village until well into the 19th century, when whaling and, especially, the demand for herring exploded. In the single year 1905, a million barrels of pickled herring were exported to Europe. The collapse of one traditional industry after another by the early 1960s meant that the exploitation of North Sea oil beginning in the 1970s was welcomed as a lifeline. It increased the importance of Lerwick as a port and as a supply and service base for the industry, particularly associated with engineering. It is the commercial and social centre of the islands.

Crofting remains an important way of life in Shetland, although few crofts can support a family without additional income. Most crofters also fish, especially for lobster and crab, and salmon farming is an increasingly important industry. Traditionally the men also found work in the Royal or Merchant Navy and, more recently, in the oil industry. Sullom Voe was built in the 1970s to service the newly opened North Sea oil fields. In the late 1990s, it handled a quarter of the UK's petroleum production, employing around 500. Manufacturing and construction still account for about 16 per cent of jobs on the islands, but the service sector provide just over three quarters of jobs. A significant part of Shetland's economy is taken up by tourism (11 per cent of jobs). Ferries between the islands and from mainland Scotland as well as five airports provide the backbone of Shetland communication with Orkney, Scotland and Norway.

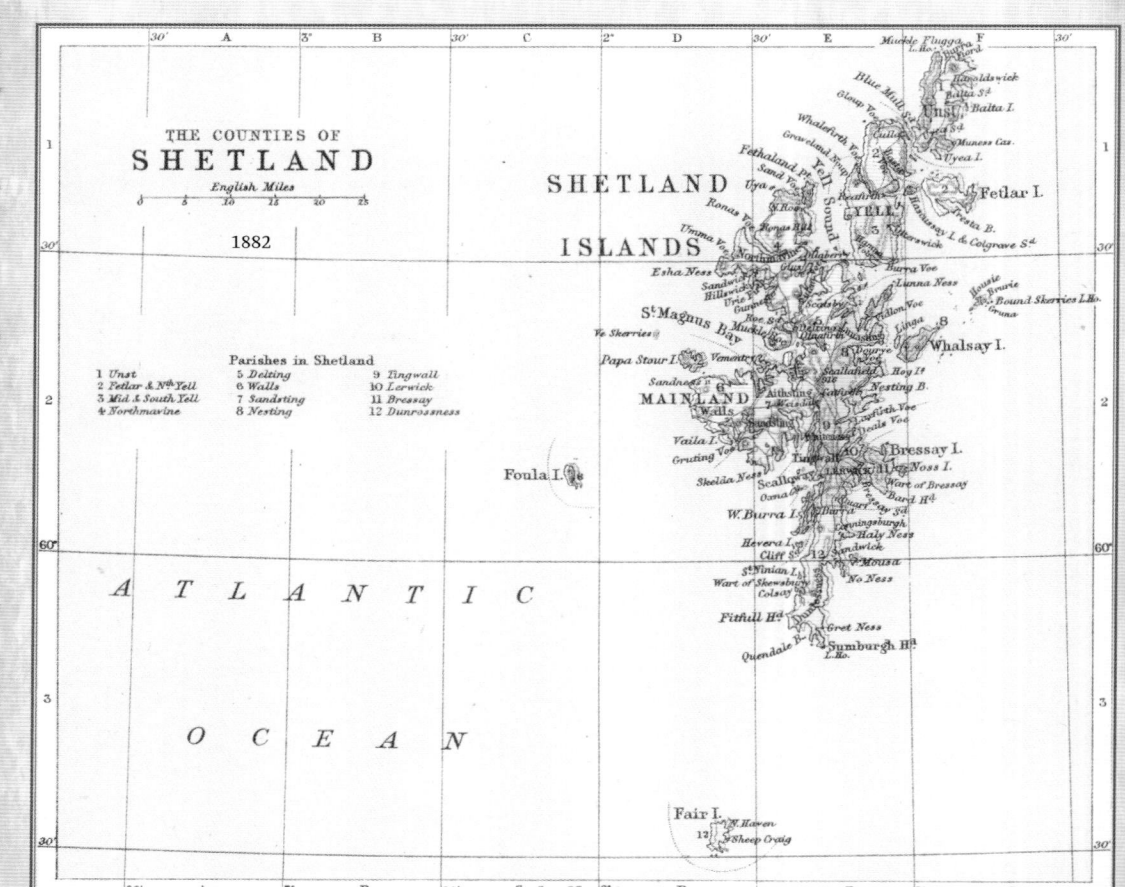

Bartholomew Gazetteer of the British Isles, 1887
SHETLAND, *insular co. of Scotland, 50 miles NE. of Orkney, 352,876 ac., pop. 29,705; Mainland, pop. 20,821; it consists of about 100 islands, 29 of which are inhabited – Mainland, Yell, Unst, Fetlar, Whalsay, and Bressay being the largest. Mainland, comprising more than half the area of the whole group, extends N. and S. for 54 miles, and has an extreme, breadth of 21 miles, but the coast-line is so irregular and deeply indented that no spot is 4 miles from the sea. The surface of Shetland is generally bleak and moorish, and rises to a maximum alt. of 1475 ft., but only in a few places higher than 500 ft. The rock scenery around the coasts is exceedingly grand and interesting. The climate is humid and comparatively mild, but severe storms are frequent. Large numbers of cattle and sheep of native breeds are reared, and the small Shetland ponies are remarkable for their strength and hardiness. Barley, oats, turnips, and potatoes are grown. The fisheries, especially the herring fishery, are of the greatest importance, and afford the chief employment. The knitting of woollen articles is also a great industry. Shetland comprises 12 pars., and the police burgh of Lerwick.*

'After all, my mind turns with most liking to the Norse type, in spite of their want of philosophic thinking and their terrible persistence. Their simplicity, frankness, sincerity, and their depth and persistence of affections, their firmness and bravery when need is all are most precious, and their independence and love of freedom.'
Laurence Williamson

WALES

Area Sq Km	20,778
Area Sq Miles	8,022
Population	2,993,400
Capital city	Cardiff
Highest point	Snowdon (1,085m)

The Millennium Centre, Cardiff.

One of the four countries that make up the United Kingdom, the Principality of Wales forms a wide peninsula on the western side of Great Britain. It is bounded on the east by England, on the south by the Bristol Channel, on the West by St George's Channel and on the north by the Irish Sea. Its most westerly point is St David's Head, in Pembrokeshire. Large areas of Wales are mountainous, with much of the land over 150 m, the highest peaks being in Snowdonia in the northwest (Snowdon is the highest point in Wales at a height of 1,085 m). The Cambrian Mountains stretch down to the southwest while in the southeast are the Brecon Beacons (reaching 885 m) and the Black Mountains, straddling the border with England and rising to a height of 811m. There are lowland areas around the Bristol Channel and along the coastal margins and most of the border with England, the so-called Welsh Marches. The main rivers in Wales are the Wye and the upper reaches of the Severn in the south and the Conwy and the upper reaches of the Dee in the north. The country is about 225 km from north to south and between 60 and 160 km from west to east. Its coastline is about 1,200 km long, with Anglesey its largest island.

The nature of the Welsh landscape has had a major impact upon its development – with lowlands only at the coastal margins and in the far east, communication between north and south Wales has always been difficult. It was a major reason for why no successful unified Welsh kingdom was able to survive – and even today, north–south communications are most effectively achieved by travelling into England and out again.

The climate of Wales is maritime temperate, often being cloudy, wet and windy, though not particularly cold. Coastal areas and the eastern borders tend to be warmer and less prone to rain and wind, while the upland mountains can see very wet and stormy weather. Overall, it tends to be wetter and slightly cooler than England. The January mean temperature ranges between 0°C and 3°C while in July the range is 17°C to 21°C. The coldest temperature recorded was –23.3 °C at Rhyader, in Powys, on 21 January 1940 and the hottest temperature was 35.2°C at Hawarden Bridge, in Flintshire, on 2 August 1990. A common perception is that Wales is always wet, but the rainfall varies greatly, with over 3,000 mm in Snowdonia down to under 1,000 mm in the Welsh Marches, with October to January being the wettest months of the year.

The population of Wales in 2008 was 2,993,400 an increase of around 90,000 since 2001 and it is projected to reach 3.3 million by 2031. While the birth rate in 2008 was at its highest level since 1973, the population of Wales continues to age – in the 10 years between 1997 and 2007, the number of people under 35 fell by 4.5 per cent while those aged over 65 increased by 5.5 per cent. The economically deprived South Wales valleys suffer from depopulation, with fewer people living in Merthyr Tydfil and Blaenau Gwent than in 2001, while the greatest increases were seen in Pembrokeshire and Powys.

One distinctive feature of the Welsh population is the use of the Welsh language, regarded as the oldest spoken language in Europe. In the 2001 Census 21 per cent of the population were able to speak Welsh (and studying the language is compulsory in schools), but there appears to be a decline in Welsh language speak in its traditional heartlands in the north and west whi there is an increase in the southeast. There is an active bilingual policy by the government and there has been long campaign to promote Welsh language and cultur (such as the 19th-century revival of eisteddfodau of poetry and music, most notably the National Eisteddf of Wales held annually since 1880 that traces its roots back to an Eisteddfod held at Cardigan Castle in 1176)

The population of Wales was Celtic in origin, reflected in the name Cymru, from the Celtic 'cymry', meaning 'fellow countrymen' (with the other Celtic peoples of western Britain and Ireland). By contrast, the name of Wales comes from the Old English 'walh', meaning 'foreigners', for the Celts of Wales were seen foreigners by the Anglo-Saxon invaders, and so Wales, them, was the 'land of foreigners'.

Sometime after 500 BC Celtic peoples began to settle in Wales, but they were unable to hold back the Romans, who controlled Wales by AD 78 from major forts at Caerleon and Chester. As well as colonizing th land along the Seven Estuary, they also mined copper in Anglesey and gold in Dyfed. After the Romans left, Wales split into many small kingdoms and by the 7th century its eastern borders were frequently attacke by the Saxon invaders of England. In the 8th century King Offa of Mercia built Offa's Dyke, a major earthwo that effectively established a border between England and Wales, stretching around 130 km from Wrexham t the Wye valley. Between the 9th and the 13th centuries Wales remained primarily a divided territory and only a few rulers were able to establish a more united country, most notably Hywel Dda in the 9th century a Gruffydd ap Llywelyn in the 10th. With no long-lasting united kingdom, Wales could not resist continuing attacks from England, and Edward I had established English dominance by 1282, defeating the last Welsh Prince of Wales, Llywelyn ap Gruffydd. Edward aggressively asserted his power in a series of spectacul castles, including those and Conwy and at Harlech, an also proclaimed his son and heir as Prince of Wales. T last serious resistance to the English was led by Owain Glendŵr at the start of the 15th century. Although he managed to capture Harlech Castle in 1404, support fo his rising waned and it was suppressed by 1410. Welsh influence on England was asserted in a different way, when Henry Tudor was declared king, as Henry VII, af the battle of Bosworth Field in 1485, the Welsh Tudor family became the royal family of England. Formal

'People like us' statue celebrates the people who lived and worked locally, Mermaid Quay, Cardiff.

One of the first of its kind in the world, the Menai Suspension Bridge was completed in 1826, linking Anglesey to the mainland.

...ales versus Italy in the annual Six Nations rugby tournament, Millennium Stadium, Cardiff.

...ild Welsh ponies on Anglesey.

Cricceith Castle overlooking Cardigan Bay, Gwynedd.

...nion with England was completed by 1543 under a ...ries of Acts of Union, which, among other measures, ...nposed English law on Wales and made English the ...nguage of the administration.

The 18th century saw the emergence of Methodism ...s a distinctive Welsh phenomenon, encouraging ...oth literacy (in Welsh and English) and the singing ...f hymns. Non-conformism became the dominant ...xpression of religion, with only the wealthy ...aintaining their allegiance to the Anglican Church. ...he 19th century saw the industrial exploitation of ...Vales' resources – coal in the South Wales valleys and ...ate in the north. Such was the demand for labour in ...ne coal industry that nearly four-fifths of the people ...f Wales were settled around the mines in the valleys ...nd the associated iron and steelworks nearby. Such ...ndustries were particularly vulnerable to economic ...ownturn and many jobs were lost in the depressions ...f the 1930s and the 1980s. The last deep coal mine, the ...ower Colliery at Hirwaun in the Cynon Valley, closed ...n January 2008 – 90 years earlier there had been over ...00 active mines in the valleys, employing over quarter ...f a million miners.

The economy of Wales now presents a rather ...ifferent picture as the country adapts to a post- ...ndustrial future. The largest sector of the economy ...n terms of employment is in public administration, ...ealth and education, accounting for 30 per cent of ...mployment (compared with a UK average of 25 per cent).

Retail, hotels and restaurants account for 23 per cent (22 per cent for the UK), finance and business activities 14 per cent (21 per cent for the UK) and manufacturing 13 per cent (ahead of the UK average of 11 per cent). Within Wales there are major differences – while nationally only 3 per cent of the employment is in agriculture, in Ceredigion and Powys it reaches 12 per cent, while Denbighshire has the highest percentage employed in public administration, health and education, at 44 per cent. The largest manufacturing locations include the Port Talbot integrated iron and steelworks, one of only two active in the UK, the oil refineries of Milford Haven which account for 20 per cent of UK production and the Ford engine plant at Bridgend, while tourism is a major industry, bringing money into cities such as Cardiff and the resorts of the north Wales coast and helping to provide alternative income in rural areas. Overall, however, the Welsh economy is performing less well than the UK economy as a whole and is most successful in northeast and south Wales where there are good transport links to England.

Plaid Cymru ('The Party of Wales') was established in 1925 to campaign for Welsh independence, gaining its first MP in 1966. A referendum on limited devolution was defeated in 1979 but in 1997 a referendum was just in favour of limited devolution of power. A Welsh Assembly was established in 1999 and, from 2007, has limited law-making powers. The Assembly and the Welsh Assembly Government are provided with a

financial settlement from London and have powers to use these funds in the areas of health, education, local government, transport, housing, economic development, agriculture and culture, but they have no powers over taxation, social security, defence, foreign policy, the legal system and policing. There are sixty Assembly members (AMs) – forty are elected to represent individual constituencies and a further twenty are elected by proportional representation to cover a region of Wales. The Assembly meets in the Senedd, a new building designed by the internationally renowned British architect Richard Rogers, on the waterfront in Cardiff. Welsh MPs continue to be elected to the UK parliament at Westminster to ensure that there is Welsh representation on matters that are the responsibility of the UK parliament. Local government is administered through twenty-two unitary authorities that cover the whole of Wales in a system introduced in 1996.

Devolution has increased local Welsh control of the way many services are delivered and in 2007 Plaid Cymru had its first taste of government in coalition with the Labour party, much reduced in power, reflecting the changing industrial landscape of the country. There is certainly a greater pride and confidence in Wales, with a real wish to throw off Dylan Thomas's unkind comment – 'Wales is the land of my fathers. And my fathers can have it.'

HISTORICAL MAPS OF WALES

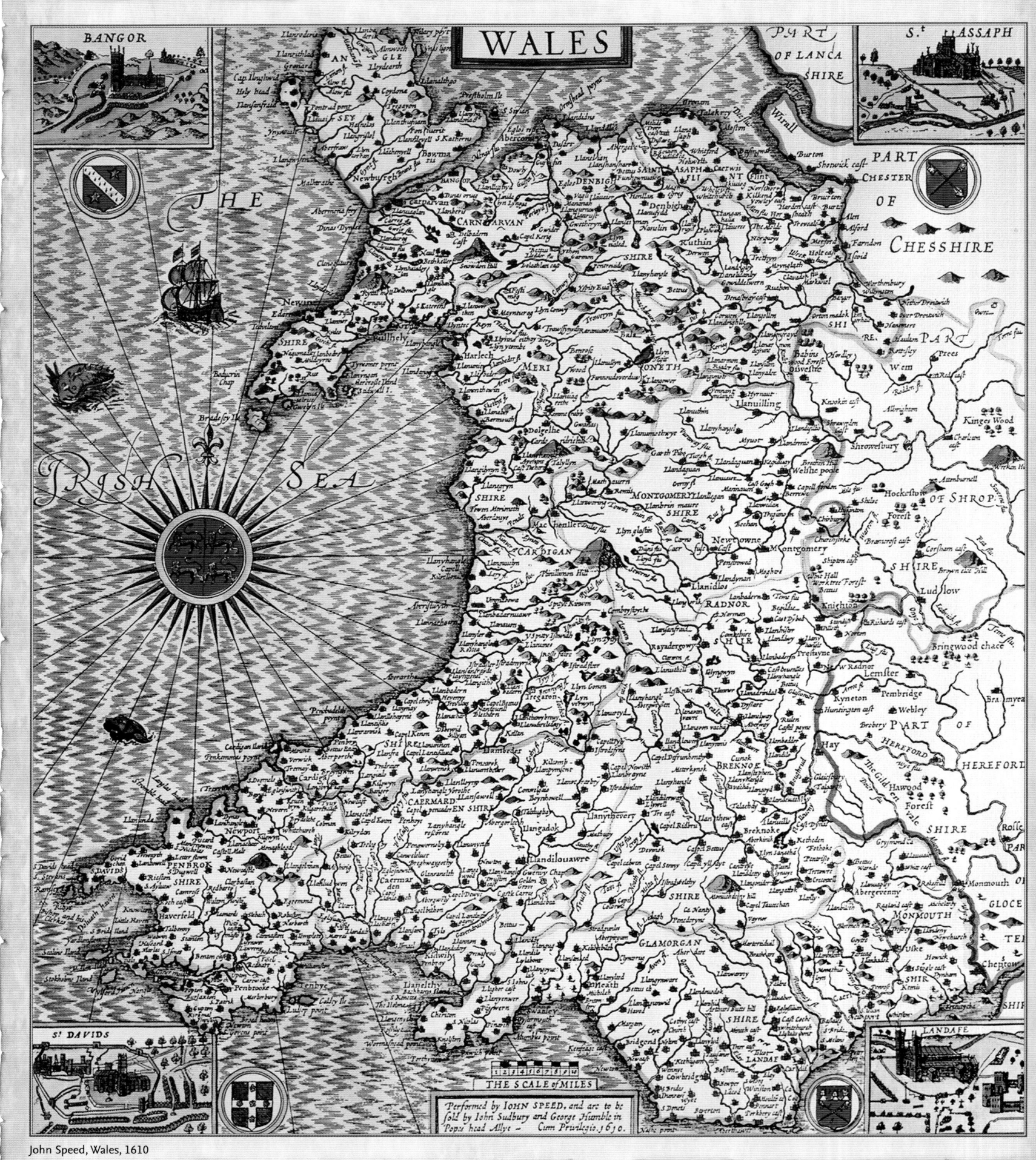

John Speed, Wales, 1610

There is a striking contrast between the appearance and design of these two maps, dating from 1610 and 1890 – although here, as in the rest of the UK, the traditional county boundaries scarcely changed in the meantime. The older map seems to be attempting more detail, especially as regards place names, though this is misleading because the right-hand map is actually an enlarged version of Bartholomew's original.

The more recent map is true to its era in being more earnest and factual, while the older preference is to throw in some entertainment and information

value, with tiny aerial views of the cathedrals of Wales, heraldic shields, and a decorative compass rose and a ship. Monstrous sea life leaps out of the dramatically-hachured water, which must have been extremely tedious to engrave. On land, there are some frankly rather overblown hill illustrations – Plynlimon, which in reality has a low profile, looks more like the Matterhorn, though the artist had presumably seen a picture of Snowdon.

County names have remained unchanged even to the present day, with a few exceptions. Brecknock

(usually Brecon in more recent times) is on both maps, Speed spelling it Breknokshire. The 19th-century map has Carnarvon (it reverted to the more correct spelling Caernarfon in the 20th century), while the older map has the less common 'Carnarvan' and gives Pembrokeshire 'Penbrokshire'.

John Speed's name is on the bottom of the 17th-century map, and one wonders if he or his staff just forgot to colour in the boundary between Radnor and 'Breknokshire'.

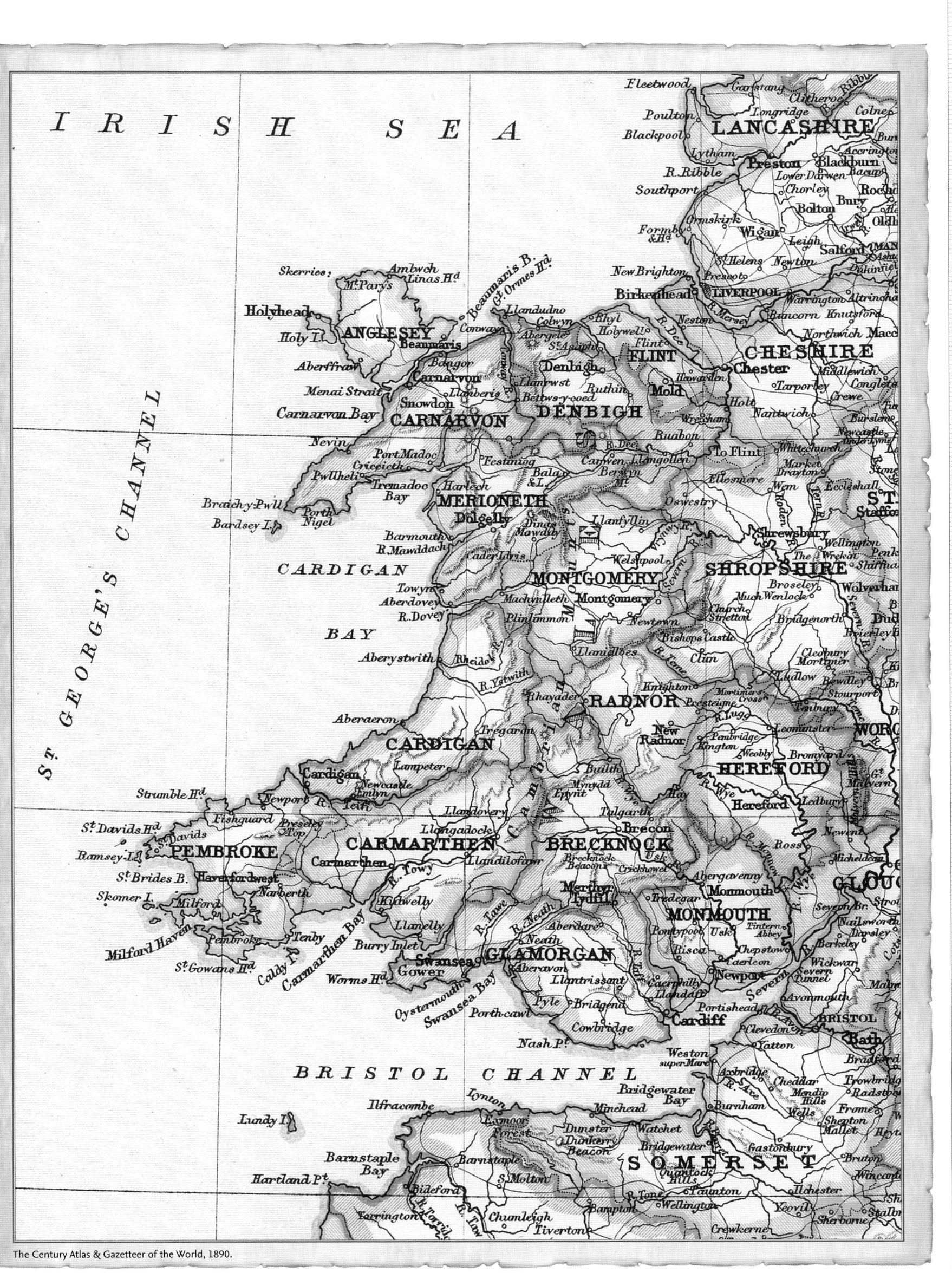

IRISH SEA

ST GEORGE'S CHANNEL

BRISTOL CHANNEL

LANCASHIRE

CHESHIRE

FLINT

ANGLESEY

CARNARVON

DENBIGH

MERIONETH

CARDIGAN BAY

MONTGOMERY

SHROPSHIRE

RADNOR

HEREFORD

CARDIGAN

CARMARTHEN

BRECKNOCK

MONMOUTH

GLAMORGAN

PEMBROKE

SOMERSET

The Century Atlas & Gazetteer of the World, 1890.

MONMOUTHSHIRE

Area Sq Km	886
Area Sq Miles	342
Population	88,400
Admin Centre	Cwmbrân (in Torfaen)
Highest point	Chwarel y Fan (679 m) in the Black Mountains

Once known as Munwi Mutha and Monemude, the Welsh is *Trefynwy* ('homestead on the Mynwy'). The Mynwy (or Monnow) River, which flows through the town of Monmouth, may mean 'swift flowing'.

FAMOUS FOR

Gobannium was the Roman fort built at the strategic point where the river Gavenny met the river Usk (now Abergavenny), enabling the defence of valley communications between the Black Mountains and the Brecon Beacons.

The **River Usk** is famous for its fishing, especially salmon, making sense of the fact that the Celtic origins of the name may mean 'abounding in fish'.

The abbey at **Tintern** (1131–1537) was the first Cistercian monastery to be built in Wales, and only the second established by that order in Britain.

FAMOUS PEOPLE

Henry of Lancaster, 1st Duke of Lancaster, soldier and diplomat, born Grosmont Castle, *c*.1310.
Adam of Usk, priest and chronicler, born Usk, *c*.1352.
Henry V, King of England, born Monmouth Castle, 1387.
William Bedloe, informer and adventurer, born Chepstow, 1650.
William Cadogan, physician, born Usk, 1711.
Alfred Russel Wallace, zoogeographer and pioneer of Natural Selection, born Usk, 1823.
Bertrand Russell, 3rd Earl Russell, philosopher, born Trelleck, 1872.

The Gwent Levels of Monmouthshire along the Severn estuary rise inland to the Gwent plain, the fertile basin of the river Usk, which flows through the county in the west. It rises to the north in the Black Mountain range, which forms the county's northern border. In the east is the deep valley of the other important waterway, the river Wye.

Modern Monmouthshire, created in 1975, was one of the districts of Gwent, a name still used for ceremonial purposes. Its population of 88,400 has risen steadily since 1981 (76,500). The 1996 local government reorganization combined over half of the historical county plus Llanelly to create the modern area. Important towns include Abergavenny (14,055), Caldicot (11,248), Chepstow (10,821) and Monmouth (8,547).

Romans, Anglo-Saxons and Normans in turn took and lost control over this district from about AD 75. The Normans built Raglan and Caldicot castles, and rebuilt Chepstow Castle on the site of a Roman fort. The Marcher lords ruled quasi-independently until

Five years have past; five summers, with the length
Of five long winters! and again I hear
These waters, rolling from their mountain-springs
With a soft inland murmur. —Once again
Do I behold these steep and lofty cliffs,
Which on a wild secluded scene impress
Thoughts of more deep seclusion; and connect
The landscape with the quiet of the sky.
William Wordsworth, *Lines Written a Few Miles above Tintern Abbey*, 1798

1536, when Henry VIII stripped them of most of their power. Today many of the southern villages in the county are commuter dormitories for workers in Newport and other urban centres, putting pressure on farmland for housing and commercial developments.

The administrative centre of Monmouthshire is no in Monmouthshire at all, but in the west at Cwmbrân, just across the border in Torfaen, occupying the buildin of the former Gwent County Council.

Monmouthshire is predominantly agricultural, especially in the Usk valley, with market gardening and light industries near Abergavenny. However, nearly 82 per cent of jobs are now in the service sector, with 34 per cent in public administration, education and health. Tourism is also an important industry, given th attraction of castles, Tintern Abbey, the southern Wye Valley and part of the Brecon Beacons National Park. Two bridges span the Bristol Channel taking the M4 through the south, and trunk roads up the Usk and Wye valleys provide good links to the West Midlands.

The first Severn Bridge was completed in 1966.

Tintern Abbey on the Welsh bank of the river Wye.

NEWPORT

Area Sq Km	218
Area Sq Miles	84
Population	140,700
County town	Newport
Highest point	Wentwood (309 m)

Newport's straightforward name comes from the Latin *novus burgus* first mentioned in 1138. The 12th century castle built here was 'new' in comparison to the Roman fort at Caerleon.

FAMOUS FOR

The amphitheatre built at *Isca Silurum* (**Caerleon**) for the entertainment of the 2nd Augustan Legion around

AD 80 later became known as King Arthur's Round Table. **Caerleon** is believed by some to be the Camelot of the Arthurian legends.

Newport Cathedral, dedicated to St Gwynllyw or Woolos, encapsulates most of the vagaries of local history: a wooden Saxon church built over the site of a 6th century warrior-prince's hermitic cell and grave, burnt down and replaced in Norman stone to which 15th-century Gothic was appended. When Rowan Williams became Archbishop of Wales in 2000, it became the Metropolitan cathedral.

Many of the **Chartists** of Newport backed up their demands for parliamentary reform in November 1839 with rioting, which was quickly suppressed. Their leaders were transported to Australia.

Newport Transporter Bridge, opened in 1906, is a rare example of this type of bridge. A platform suspended from a high beam conveyed people and vehicles across the river Usk until 2007 when it closed to traffic.

FAMOUS PEOPLE

John Frost, tailor and draper, and Chartist leader, born Newport, 1784.
Griffith J Griffith, mining millionaire and Los Angeles city father, born Bettws, 1850.
Arthur Machen, novelist, born Caerleon-on-Usk, 1863.
William Henry (WH) Davies, poet, born Newport, 1871.
Kenneth Baker, Baron Baker of Dorking, Conservative politician, born Newport, 1934.

The city of Newport and its surrounding villages have expanded along the mouth of the river Usk and the northern shore of the Severn estuary. It was historically part of the county of Monmouthshire and, by 1975, a district of Gwent; it became a unitary authority in 1996. The population of 140,700 has risen slightly since 1981, and most people live in the city itself (116,143), Caerleon (9,392), Marshfield (2,636) and Langstone (2,180). In 2002 it was granted 'city' status.

The great Roman fortress built at *Isca Silurum* or Caerleon 'City of the Legions' in AD 75 following the defeat of the native Silures tribe, was one of three permanent legionary bases in Britain. After the Roman retreat, Caerleon was a Welsh stronghold and

a commercial centre. Following their conquest of England, the Normans reached Newport around 1088 and built a castle. Newport's commercial reputation was sealed by a charter dating from 1385, and it eventually replaced Caerleon as the local port.

It was the Industrial Revolution that transformed Newport. The port prospered as it became a major coal exporter, until economic decline set in during the 1930s. A modern integrated steelworks opened in 1962 at Llanwern near Newport. However, steel making stopped in 2001 and the hot strip mill was mothballed in 2009, further reducing steel working activity. Newport is now home to offices for a number of government agencies, and the University of Wales, Newport, has further raised

the town's profile. The post-industrial economy in Newport is illustrated by the rise of the service sector, which now provides over 81 per cent of jobs, compared with 15 per cent in manufacturing.

"From the top of this eminence, the wild and beautiful environ of Caerleon are seen to the greatest advantage. The principal objects are the town, gently rising at the extremity of an oval vale; the bridge, supported by lofty and slender piles; the rapid Usk, flowing through fertile meadows; the sloping hills, richly clothed with wood; and Christchurch, towering like a cathedra on the brow of an overhanging eminence."
William Coxe, 1801

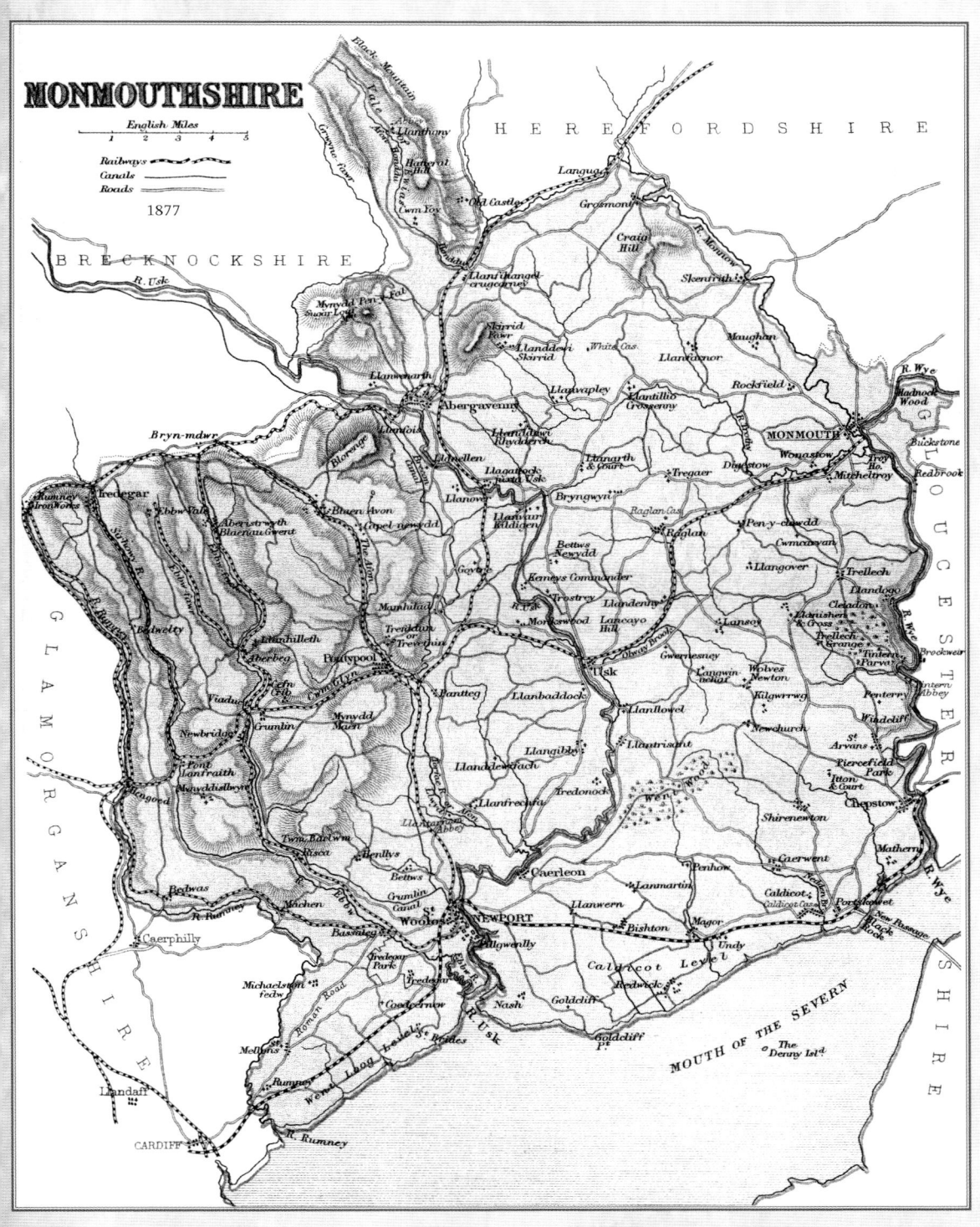

MONMOUTHSHIRE

1877

TORFAEN

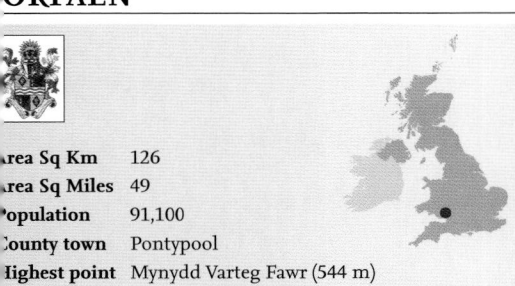

Area Sq Km 126
Area Sq Miles 49
Population 91,100
County town Pontypool
Highest point Mynydd Varteg Fawr (544 m)

**Torfaen combines the Welsh *tor* and *maen* meaning
'stone gap', a reference to the river Llwyd's course
through the steep valley.**

FAMOUS FOR
Welsh immigrants from **Pontypool** are said to have
built the first forge in the American colonies in 1652.

The river **Llwyd** was once called the Torfaen,
remembered in the name of this region.

Blaenavon World Heritage Site includes the Big Pit
National Coal Museum, dug under Coity Mountain.
It was called the Big Pit (*Pwll Mawr*) because it was
large enough for two tramways to service it.

FAMOUS PEOPLE
Roy Jenkins, Baron Jenkins of Hillhead, politician and
author, born Abersychan, 1920.
Kenneth (Ken) Jones, Olympic sprinter and rugby player,
born Blaenavon, 1921.
Dame Gwyneth Jones, soprano opera singer, born
Pontnewynydd,1936.
Joan Ruddock, politician and anti-nuclear campaigner,
born Pontypool, 1943.

The narrow unitary authority of Torfaen centres around
the valley of the river Llwyd and the surrounding
hills and moorlands extending from the border with
Newport north to the Black Mountains of the Brecon
Beacons. Torfaen was historically part of the county of
Monmouthshire and, by 1975, one of the five districts of
Gwent; in 1996 it became a unitary authority. Torfaen's
population of 91,100 has remained virtually static since
1981 (90,100). Pontypool is the administrative centre
(35,447) and Cwmbrân (47,254) and Blaenavon (5,626)
are other important towns.

Pontypool's reputation for iron smelting dates
back to the 16th century. However, it was the Industrial
Revolution and the area's location on the eastern edge
of the South Wales coalfields that encouraged the
development of heavy industry, initially iron founding
and then coal mining. Iron ore was mined at Blaenavon,
and a railway was built in the 1860s to transport coal
from the northern end of the valleys to Newport.
Despite diversification into aluminium smelting and
steel in the 20th century, heavy industry in this area
was mostly replaced by light and hi-tech industries
by the 1990s. Cwmbrân is a 'New Town' established in
1949 to encourage new industries in the area of older
industrial villages within the South Wales coalfield.
Factories producing car components, biscuits and

nylon yarns were established here; a brewery opened
in 1996.

While manufacturing has declined, over 20 per
cent of all jobs are still in this sector, double the
British average. Over 36 per cent of jobs are in public
administration, education and health, significantly
higher than average, but unemployment also remains
high. Southern Torfaen's communications are excellent,
including rail links as far north as Pontypool. Further
up the Llwyd valley, however, the road changes from a
major trunk road to a 'B' road until connecting with the
'Heads of the Valleys Road', the A465.

Tredegar House, in Newport, was home to the Morgan family until 1951.

The Newport Transporter Bridge was built in 1906 and is a rare example of the transporter bridge concept.

The Big Pit Mining Museum is part of the Blaenavon Industrial Landscape World Heritage site, Torfaen.

Raglan Castle, in Monmouthshire, was subjected to the longest siege of the English Civil War, in 1646.

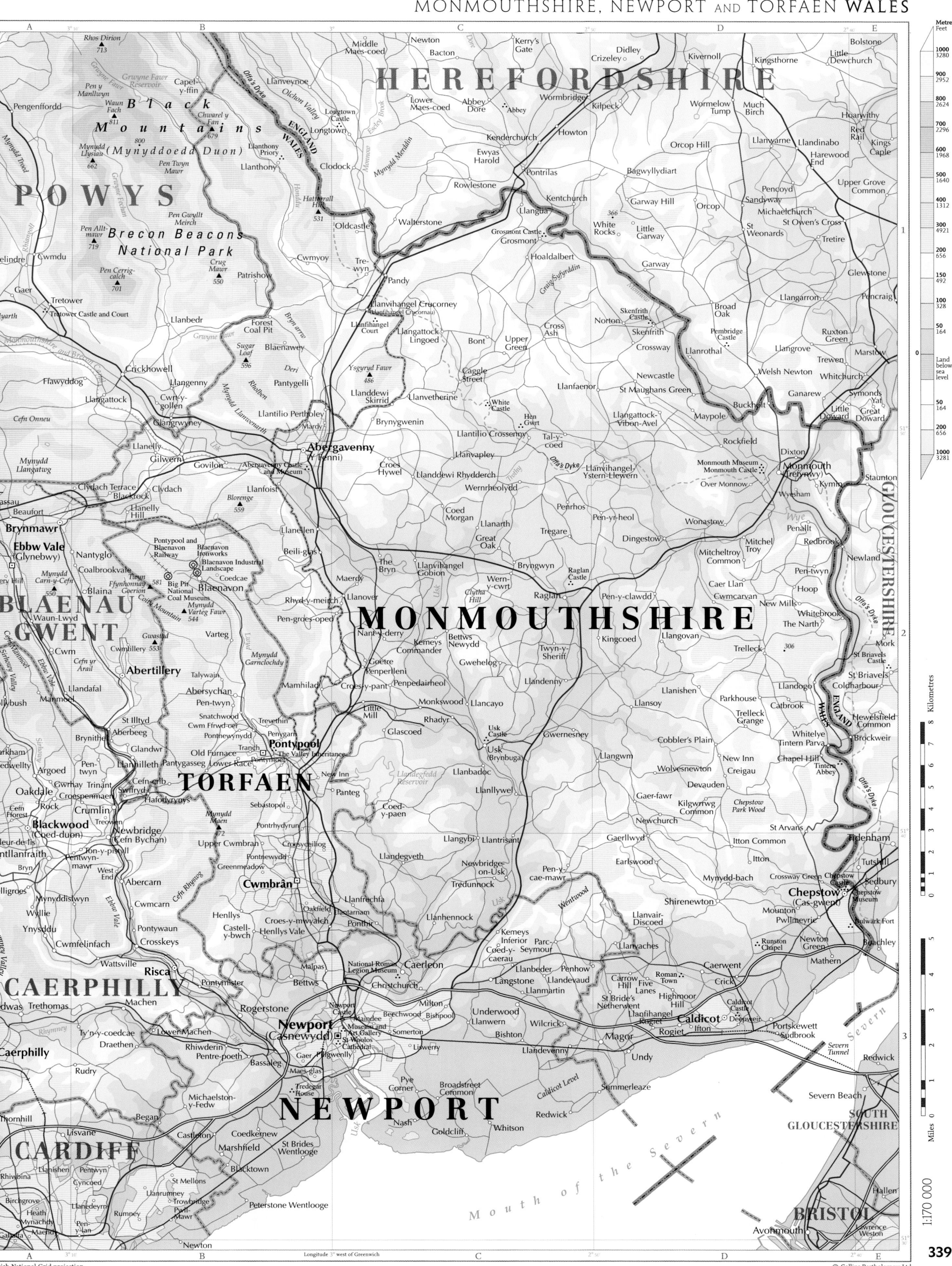

1:170 000

© Collins Bartholomew Ltd

CARDIFF

Area Sq Km	149
Area Sq Miles	58
Population	324,800
County town	Cardiff
Highest point	Garth Hill (307 m)

Known as *Caerdydd* in 1106, it incorporates the Welsh '*caer*' or 'fortress' with the name of the river Taff, so 'fortress on the River Taff'.

FAMOUS FOR

Cardiff Castle, on the site of the Roman fort, acquired a Norman stone keep in around 1140. The romantic restoration of the castle from 1865 onwards by flamboyant Victorian architect William Burgess was undertaken for the Marquess of Bute, whose fortune was built on the prosperity of Cardiff docks. Burgess also built **Castell Coch**, a fairytale castle on the edge of the city, for him.

Coal exports from Cardiff peaked in 1913 at 10.7 million tonnes.

The **University College of South Wales and Monmouthshire** was established in Cardiff in 1883, and was celebrated in the city by fireworks and cheering crowds.

St Fagans, on the outskirts of the city, is home to the award-winning National History Museum, which literally provides a walk around Wales as it houses over 40 traditional Welsh buildings that have been reconstructed here.

Although the people of Cardiff narrowly rejected the 1997 referendum proposition for self-government in Wales, the city successfully promoted itself, and not without controversy, as the natural home of the new **National Assembly for Wales**.

The **Millennium Stadium** is the home of Welsh rugby; built on the site of the National Stadium at Cardiff Arms Park in the centre of the city, it is Europe's largest stadium with a retractable roof, and can seat 74,500 spectators.

FAMOUS PEOPLE

Sir Henry Morgan, buccaneer, born Llanrhymney, *c*.1635.
Ivor Novello (originally David Ivor Davies), composer and actor, born Cardiff, 1893.
Roald Dahl, children's author, born Llandaff, 1916.
Terry Nation, science fiction writer and creator of the Daleks for *Doctor Who*, born Cardiff, 1930.
Dame Shirley Bassey, singer, born Tiger Bay, 1937.
Hywel Rhodri Morgan, Labour politician, First Minister (2000–09), born Cardiff, 1939.
John Humphrys, broadcaster, born Cardiff, 1943.
Griff Rhys Jones, actor, born Cardiff, 1953.
Ryan Giggs, professional footballer, born Ely, 1973.
Charlotte Church, singer, born Llandaff, 1986.

"We have no coal exported from this port, nor ever shall, as it would be too expensive to bring it down here from the internal part of the country."
Unnamed Cardiff customs official in 1782

"Though Cardiff has been termed the Welsh Chicago, it is a place of considerable antiquity."
Samuel Lewis

Located at the mouth of the river Taff, Cardiff is built on estuarine silt and marshlands only averaging about 50 m above sea level. As the city grew, it took in higher and firmer ground to the north near Garth Hill (307 m).

Cardiff was the county town of historic Glamorgan until 1975, when this large county was divided into three parts. One part, South Glamorgan, consisted of two districts, Cardiff and Vale of Glamorgan. In 1996, these districts in turn became two separate unitary authorities. (South Glamorgan remains as a 'Preserved County' for ceremonial purposes.) With a population of 324,800, Cardiff is the most populous authority in Wales, and has steadily increased in population since 1981 (286,900). As the city grew in the 19th and 20th centuries, it absorbed many of the small villages that had once existed independently around it. Llandaff, for example, with a population of 8,990 and a 13th-century cathedral, is now part of the capital. Other towns include Radyr (4,658), Creigiau (2,534) and Pentyrch (2,411) in the northwest.

Archaeologists have shown that Neolithic people lived in the area as long ago as 4,000 BC and Bronze Age people buried their dead on Garth Hill. Cardiff was a site of Roman fortification from about AD 75, probably an outpost associated with Caerleon (Newport). Roman garrisons left Britain in AD 383, and the later history of the area is hazy, although it was incorporated into the Welsh kingdom of Glywysing, later known as Morgannwg, and eventually came under Norman rule in the decades following the conquest of England in 1066. Cardiff received its borough charter as early as 1125, and a series of further royal charters bolstered its prosperity, despite being burnt to the ground by Owain Glyndwr in 1404.

Still a small town in the 18th century, Cardiff was utterly transformed by the Industrial Revolution. Previously, three private quays had shipped grain and livestock across the channel to Bristol. As early as 1767, a road brought iron from Merthyr Tydfil to the city for export, and then, after 1798, the Glamorganshire Canal linked both places. Cardiff gained a reputation for exporting cast and wrought iron to London and beyond. Once the new docks, completed in 1839, were

linked to the Taff Vale Railway in 1841, Cardiff became the main port for coal from the Taff, Cynon, Rhondda and Rhymney valleys, shipping 438,780 tonnes in 1846 alone. Additional docks were added in 1859, and just prior to World War I, Cardiff exported more coal than any other port in the world. The population expanded to around 160,000 in 1900, and included people from all over Britain and Ireland. A temporary boom after World War I preceded a decline in heavy industry and in the demand for coal from the South Wales valleys. Cardiff's industrial position was eroded by this decline, despite some recovery between 1939 and 1945.

Curiously, Cardiff's position as *de facto* capital of Wales seemed to strengthen as its industrial base faded. In part, this may have been due to the fact that, as rival docks opened along the Bristol Channel, the administration and organization of trade remained firmly in Cardiff. Other 'national' accoutrements followed the University College (1883): the National Museum of Wales (1907), the National War Memorial (1928), BBC Broadcasting Centre (1937) and the 1958 Commonwealth Games. Recognized in 1955 as the capital of Wales, any final quibbles were put to rest by the siting of the Welsh Assembly here, opening in 1999 and moving to the purpose-built Y Sennedd in 2005, one of a number of major new buildings in the revitalized Cardiff Docks area.

Unsurprisingly, the service industries have stepped into the breach left by heavy industry in the local economy, providing 88 per cent of all jobs, high even by national standards. These are divided between three main sectors: public administration, education and health (31 per cent), finance, IT and other business activities (26 per cent) and retail, hotels and restaurants (20 per cent). Tourism is increasingly important (8 per cent) with a gain of over 5,000 jobs in the sector since 1995. Due in part to developments such as the Millennium Centre arts complex and the Cardiff Bay Barrage (which created a 200 ha freshwater lake by trapping the waters of the rivers Taff and Ely as they entered Cardiff Bay), Cardiff is one of the most popular tourist destinations in Wales.

The Norman Keep of Cardiff Castle.

Cardiff Bay is Europe's largest waterfront development.

Bartholomew Gazetteer of the British Isles, 1887
CARDIFF, *mun. bor., seaport, and co. town of Glamorgan, at the mouth of the river Taff and on the estuary of the Severn 29 miles W. of Bristol by water and 170 miles W. of London by rail – municipal borough, pop. 82,761; 4 Banks, 5 newspapers. Market-days, Wednesday and Saturday. In 1801 the pop. was only 1018; in 1841 it was 10,077; and 59,494 in 1871. The rapid prosperity of the town is due to the abundance of minerals in the district. Its exports of coal and iron from the valleys of Taff, Rhymney, &c., are among the most important in the kingdom. The docks have become very extensive, and a tidal harbour and low-water pier have been constructed. There are also very large iron foundries, tin-plate works, and iron-shipbuilding yards. The South Wales University College was opened at C. in 1883. Cardiff Castle, originally founded in 1080, is the property of the Marquis of Bute, who has converted part of it into a modern seat. On the pier-head, Bute Dock, is a lighthouse, with fixed light (Cardiff) seen 10 miles.*

CARDIFF, 1896

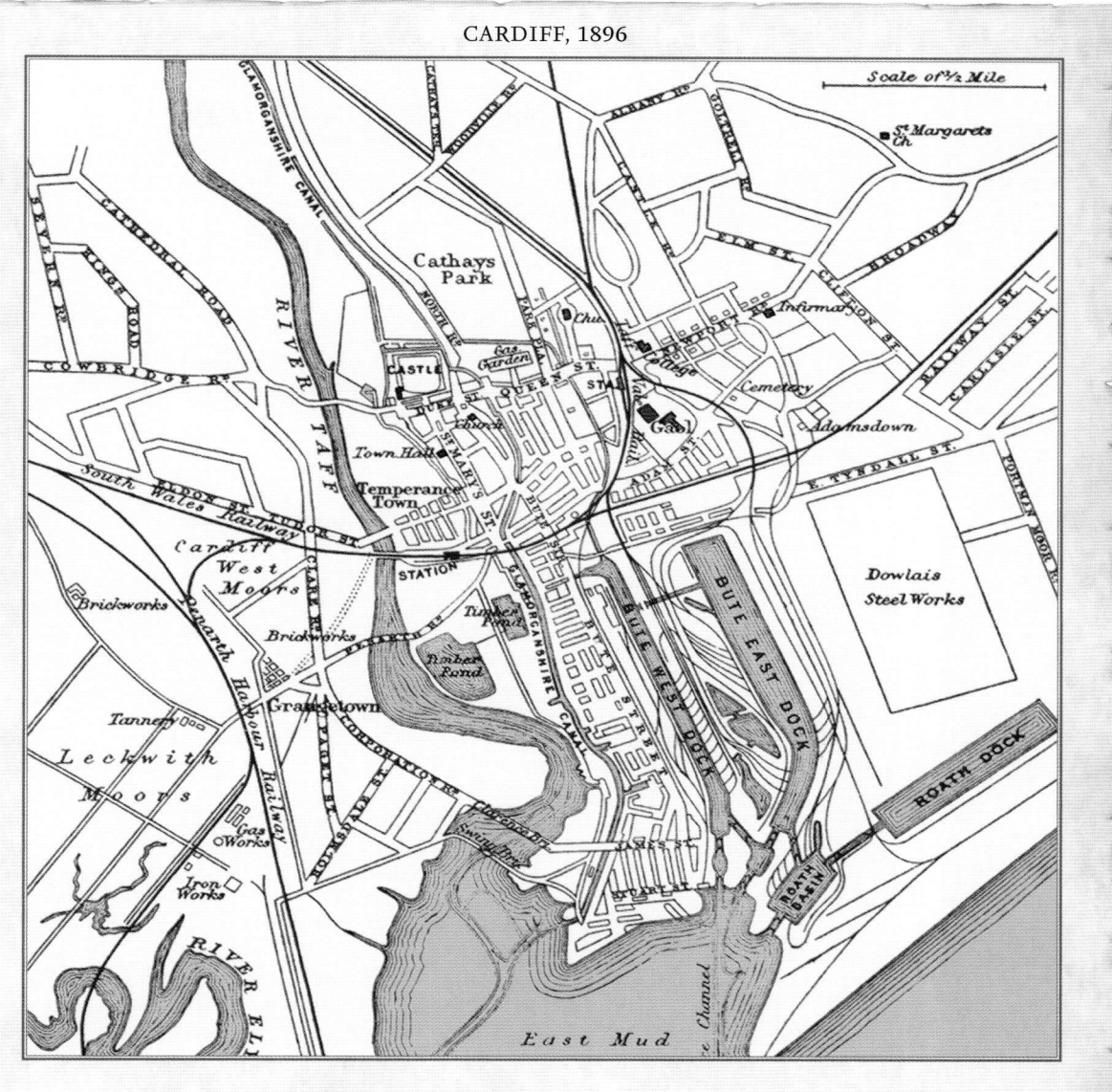

Millennium Stadium, Cardiff.

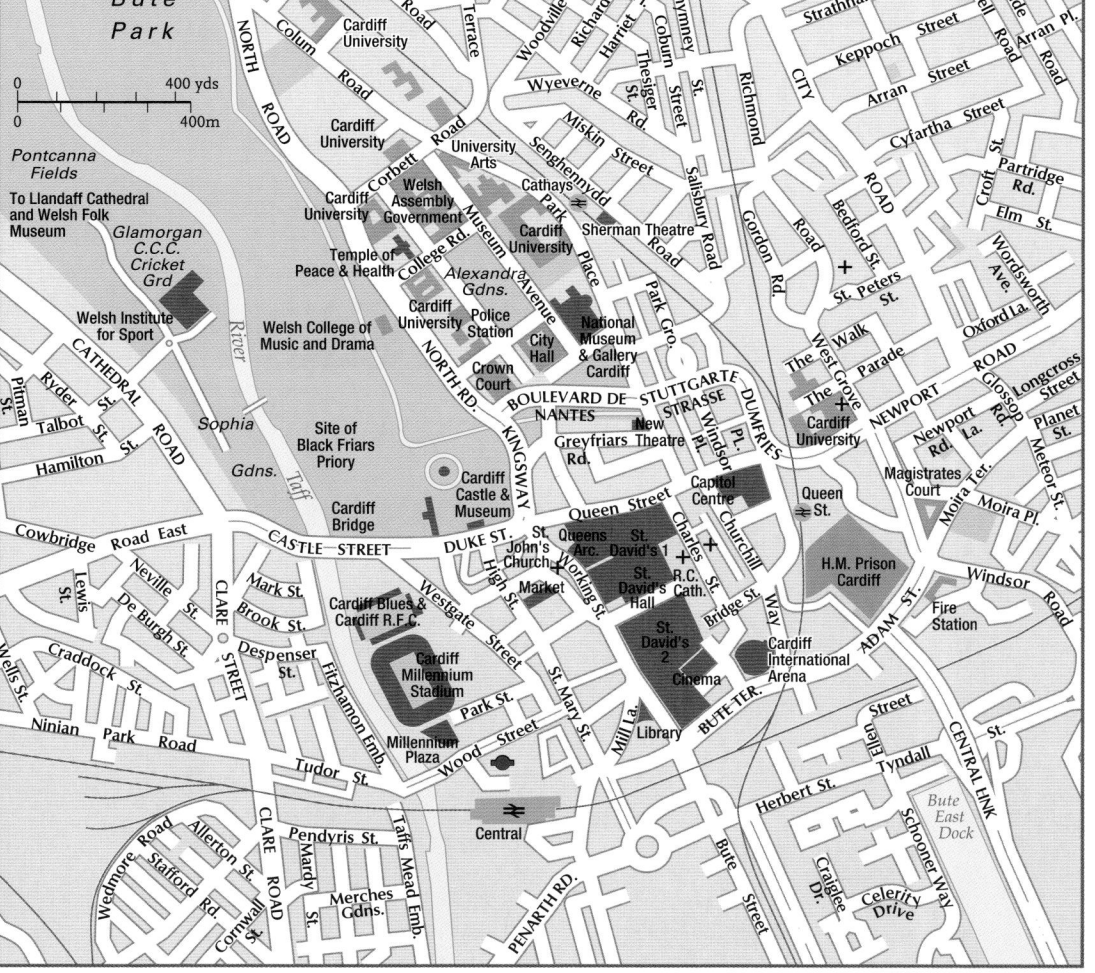

Modern Cardiff

BLAENAU GWENT

Area Sq Km	109
Area Sq Miles	42
Population	69,100
County town	Ebbw Vale
Highest point	Twyn Ffynhonnay Goerion (581 m) on the eastern border with Torfaen

The county's name is descriptive; Blaenau (or *Blaina*) is the Welsh for 'uplands' and the name Gwent comes from the British '*venta*' or 'trading place'.

FAMOUS FOR
During World War II, the steelworks at **Ebbw Vale** survived German attempts to demolish it because the valley was too deep and difficult to bomb.

The **National Garden Festival** was held on the site of the former steel mills in Ebbw Vale in 1992. The reclaimed area is now a retail centre and tourist attraction as well as the site of 1,000 new homes.

FAMOUS PEOPLE
Thomas Jones, administrator and writer, born Rhymney 1870.
Aneurin (Nye) Bevan, Labour politician, born Tredegar, 1897.
Victor Spinetti, comic actor, born Cwm, 1933.
Neil Kinnock (Baron Kinnock), Labour politician, born Tredegar, 1942.
Jeff Banks, fashion designer, born Ebbw Vale, 1943.

Blaenau Gwent is defined by three distinct narrow valleys and plateau uplands which run roughly north-south from the Brecon Beacons to form a wedge between Caerphilly and Torfaen. The Ebbw and its tributary, the Ebbw Fawr, and the Sirhowy are the most important rivers. Originally part of the traditional county of Monmouthshire, from 1975 it was one of five districts of Gwent. Further reorganization in 1996 created the present unitary authority. Although Llanelly, in the northeast, was retained by Monmouthshire, the new county gained Brynmawr in the north from Powys. Blaenau Gwent's population of 69,100 has fallen gradually by about 10 per cent since 1981. Ebbw Vale (18,558) is the administrative centre, and other important towns include Tredegar (14,802), Brynmawr (14,722) and Abertillery (11,194).

The northern uplands of Monmouthshire were remote and sparsely populated throughout most of their early history as part of the kingdom of Glywysing and, later, Gwent. The small villages with their ribbon pattern of settlement in the valley bottoms were transformed, however, by the exploitation of coal, and the development of railways and roads to move it out of the valleys. Coal had probably been used on a small industrial scale since the Middle Ages, but there was an upsurge in the demand for the fuel from the start of the Industrial Revolution. Demand for coal necessitated increasingly deeper shafts to be sunk, and encouraged related industries such as iron-ore smelting and steel-making in the area. Mining also created a huge demand for labour, employing the majority of the local male population and encouraging immigration. By the late 1930s, however, these industries were in economic decline, and by the end of the century had virtually ceased altogether.

Ebbw Vale's experience is broadly typical of the area as a whole. A tiny farming community of 120 people in 1775, it had become a district of 35,381 by 1921, due almost entirely to employment provided by the Ebbw Vale Steel, Iron and Coal Company. Their plant was partially closed in the 1980s, ceasing production in 2002. There have been successful initiatives to bring in replacement employment, and manufacturing is the second most important economic sector, providing 28 per cent of local jobs, but that represents a loss of almost 3,000 jobs since 1995. The service sector, particularly public administration, education and health is now the most important employment sector (31 per cent). Newly established business parks and industrial estates for modern light industry benefit from the good road links down the valleys to Newport and Cardiff, as well as the east-west link of the 'Heads the Valleys Road' (A465). A new rail route links Ebbw Vale to Cardiff.

CAERPHILLY

Area Sq Km	277
Area Sq Miles	107
Population	172,400
County town	Caerphilly
Highest point	Twyn Pwll Morlais (c.535 m) where Powys, Merthyr Tydfil and Caerphilly meet.

The county name is a straightforward combination of '*caer*' meaning 'fort' and the Celtic personal name of 'Ffili', so 'Ffili's fort'.

FAMOUS FOR
The southwest tower of **Caerphilly Castle** has a perpendicular lean of 10°, greater than the Leaning Tower of Pisa.

The cable stayed **Chartist Bridge,** linking the east and west sides of the Sirhowy valley, is 230 m long and 30 m above the valley floor. Its completion means that it is no longer necessary to travel along the steep road in the valley, locally known as the Rhiw (meaning 'slope' or 'hillside').

Artie Moore from Pontillanfraith, using his home-made wireless equipment, was the first person to hear the distress Morse code signals sent by **RMS *Titanic*** in 1912 nearly 3,000 miles away. He went on to work for Marconi and was involved in many important advances in transmitter development.

FAMOUS PEOPLE
William Price, physician and self-styled archdruid, born Ty'nycoedcae, 1800.
William Thomas, poet, born Ynysddu, 1832.
Gwyn Jones, scholar and writer, born New Tredegar, 1907.
Thomas Frederick (Tommy) Cooper, comedian and magician, born Caerphilly, 1921.
Alun Haddinott, composer, born Bargoed, 1929.
Grenfell (Gren) Jones MBE, cartoonist, born Hengoed, 1934.
Dame Margaret Price, opera singer, born Blackwood, 1941.

Occupying the basins of both the Rhymney and Sirhowy rivers, Caerphilly extends from the Brecon Beacons in the north almost to Cardiff in the south. The modern county of Caerphilly was formed in 1996 by combining the former Mid-Glamorgan borough of Rhymney Valley in the west with Islwyn, then part of Gwent, in the east. The area's population of 172,400 has changed little since 1981. The town of Caerphilly (31,060) is the administrative centre, and important settlements are Risca (20,219), Gelligaer (17,185), Blackwood (15,306), Bargoed (13,721) and Pontllanfraith (13,012).

The Romans invaded and settled this strategic area around AD 75, and built a fort near Gelligaer in the Rhymney valley. However, it is the defensive bulk of Caerphilly Castle, begun in 1268 by Gilbert de Clare as a defence against Llywelyn ap Gruffudd, which still dominates the landscape. By the 14th century, the town established around the castle had borough status, and had become the market for produce from the Rhymney Valley, and was famous for its cheese.

The upland villages of the county were small farming communities until the advent of the Industrial Revolution, after which many villages were founded to house those working in the local coal mines, such as Wyllie and Penallta mines. Rhymney, founded in 1802, provided housing for employees at the Bute ironworks, which also used locally sourced coal, iron ore and limestone. In common with the surrounding counties, mining was all but gone by the end of the 20th century. Although manufacturing remains important for local jobs (24 per cent), it nevertheless represents a loss of around 2,900 jobs since 1995.

Typically, services have expanded in the area, especially in public administration, education and health (31 per cent), and retail, hotels and restaurants (19 per cent), although the county's service sector is smaller than the national average. Tourism is expanding, providing around 3,600 jobs, possibly related to the number of former colliery sites now reclaimed as parkland, such as Parc Cwm Darran, once the Ogilvie Colliery north of Bargoed.

'Being a Welsh speaker in the Rhymney Valley is like being a tourist abroad or living in a parallel universe. When I was young we would speak English at home but at night I would count in Welsh in my sleep as if secretly exploring my other self... . In our predominantly English-speaking village we were called Welshies. I thought everyone was Welsh but obviously you can be Welsh with a difference.'
Lowri Pugh, 2002

The Aneurin Bevan Memorial above Tredegar, near Ebbw Vale, Blaenau Gwent.

Caerphilly Cheese, first sold in the town around 1830.

Caerphilly Castle is the largest castle in Wales and the second largest in Britain after Windsor Castle.

VALE OF GLAMORGAN

Area Sq Km   340
Area Sq Miles   131
Population   124,900
County town   Barry
Highest point   Pantylladron (137 m)

Morgan is from the Welsh personal name *Morgann*, and *gwlad* or *glan* meaning territory, land or shore, giving 'land of Morgan' or, slightly more poetically, 'Morgan's shore', with possible reference to a 7th- or even 10th-century prince.

FAMOUS FOR

A hoard found at Boverton in 2005, which included two Bronze Age palstaves (axes), was declared treasure trove in 2010. Another hoard, including more palstaves, was found in 2009 near **Llantwit Major** and dates from 1350–1250 BC.

Cardiff International Airport is not in Cardiff at all, but at **Rhoose**, a former Royal Air Force base, established in 1942 for training Spitfire pilots.

Breaksea Point near Aberthaw is the most southerly land in mainland Wales.

FAMOUS PEOPLE

Edward Williams (the pseudonym of Iolo Morganwg), poet and forger of literary manuscripts, born Llancarfan, 1747.
Mary Catherine Pendrill Llewelyn (née Rhys), writer and translator, born Cowbridge, 1811.
Sir Edgeworth David, geologist, born St Fagans, 1858.
Harold Stanley (Jim) Ede, museum curator and art collector, born Penarth, in 1895.
Dame Dorothy Mary Rees (née Jones), Labour politician, born Barry, 1898.
Eric Linklater, Scottish novelist, born Penarth, 1899.
Leslie Gilbert Illingworth, cartoonist and illustrator, born Barry, 1902.
Richard Gwynfor Evans, politician, first Plaid Cymru MP, born Barry, 1912.

The Vale of Glamorgan is mainly a low lying but gently rolling plateau, which gradually rises to the north of the county. There are cliffs along the shore of the Bristol Channel. The river Ely flows through the county on its way to Cardiff Bay to the east of the county and the river Thaw flows through Cowbridge to the sea at Aberthaw.

Originally part of historic Glamorgan, this large county was divided into three parts in 1975, of which South Glamorgan consisted of two districts, Cardiff and Vale of Glamorgan. In a further government reorganization of 1996, Vale of Glamorgan became a single unitary authority. Its population of 124,900 has increased by about 10 per cent since 1981. The administrative centre is Barry (50,611), and other important towns include Penarth (23,245), Dinas Powys (7,653) and Rhoose (4,211), which are predominantly dormitory towns for Cardiff, and Llantwit Major (13,366) and Cowbridge (3,616).

In common with most of south Wales, this fertile area was inhabited during the Bronze and Iron Ages. The Romans established forts, including one at Cowbridge (possibly the site of *Bovium*), and built roads to link their outposts. Following the withdrawal of the legions in the 4th century, the area was dominated by the Welsh kingdom of Morgannwg. The Welsh kings were ultimately unsuccessful in repelling the Anglo-Saxons and the Normans. Incorporated into the 'Union' of 1536 with England, it remained a region of farms, small ports and strategic castles until the Industrial Revolution.

Barry is the most easterly port along the Severn where shipping could dock or sail regardless of the tide. By 1922, Barry docks included two wet and three dry docks as well as 105 km of railway. It overtook its rival, Cardiff, in tonnage of coal shipped, before its decline in the later 20th century. Barry Island became a tourist attraction when a Butlin's Camp (now demolished) was built there in the 1960s.

Most of the outlying county is rural and agriculture has been an important employer, with Cowbridge as the market town. A majority of the county's manufacturing output, which provides 11 per cent of the area's employment, continues to be located around Barry. The service sector is the largest employer, particularly in public administration, education and health (34 per cent) while a rising tourism sector (10 per cent of jobs) hopes to attract visitors to the picturesque rural areas.

"All which things being put together make the land of Glamorgan in all its twelve Cantons a very plentiful and Goodly Country, insomuch that for Corn and good fruits they Call it in England the Garden of Wales, and for good Cattle of all kinds the nursery of the West, and for its good fires we have a saying by way of proverb, in calling a good fire Glamorgan Sun, there being so great a fullness of Wood and Coal."
Sir Edward Mansel, 1591

RHONDDA CYNON TAFF

Area Sq Km	424
Area Sq Miles	164
Population	234,100
County town	Clydach Vale
Highest point	Craig y Llyn (c.595 m) near the border with Neath Port Talbot

Rhondda Cynon Taf is named after local rivers. Rhondda is from the Welsh *rhoddni*, 'noisy one'. Cynon is possibly derived from a personal name. *Taf* may mean 'dark' or simply 'stream'.

The rivers Rhondda Fawr and Rhondda Fach, Ely, Cynon and Taff form a series of northwest to southeast running valleys situated at the centre of the South Wales coalfield, the largest continuous coalfield in Britain. The three major river valleys that give the county its name are steep sided with wooded tops, and were famed for their remoteness and beauty in the past. The county's northern borders are in the foothills of the Brecon Beacons.

Originally these three valleys were part of the historic county of Glamorgan, and later Mid Glamorgan. In 1996 the two districts of Cynon Valley and the Rhondda were combined with a third, Taff–Ely (minus the communities of Creigiau and Pentyrch) to create the new unitary authority. Its population of 234,100 has fallen by over 4,000 since 1981, continuing a general decline in numbers over many decades as a result of contraction of the coal industry. The administrative centre is the town of Clydach Vale (3,164). The major settlements are Rhondda (59,602), Aberdare (31,619) and Pontypridd (29,781).

FAMOUS FOR

Welsh longbow-men were often to be found in medieval English armies. The bowmen of **Llantrisant** fought with John, the Black Prince, Edward III's son, at the famous victory at Crècy in 1346.

'Steam' coal from the Cynon Valley was successfully trialled by the British Admiralty in 1845, which showed that it lit quickly, burned hot and cleanly, and left little clinker. It is said that both sides in the 1905 Russo-Japanese conflict used Welsh coal to fuel their ships.

The militancy of Maerdy coalminers during the **General Strike** of 1926 led to the village being known as 'Little Moscow'.

Although coal had been used locally in small amounts, surface mining only began in earnest at Dinas in the early 19th century. The first steam coal colliery in the Rhondda Fawr was Bute Merthyr, in 1855. The exploitation of this natural resource, as well as abundant iron ore, transformed a rural backwater into the industrial powerhouse that quite literally fuelled the British Empire. In an area almost wholly dependent on coal, the slow collapse of the industry during the 20th century caused terrible economic dislocation. Tower Colliery in Hirwaun, the last deep mine not only in the county, but in the whole of Wales, closed in 2008.

Hirwaun now has a modern industrial park, and there have been many other initiatives to bring in industries to replace coal mining. Even so, manufacturing has contracted since 1995, and while still providing 18 per cent of local employment, this represents almost 6,000 fewer jobs. The service sector provides 76 per cent of jobs, 37 per cent of which is from

FAMOUS PEOPLE

David Alfred Thomas, 1st Viscount Rhondda, politician and industrialist, born Ysguborwen, 1856.
Rosina Davies, evangelist, born Treherbert, 1863.
Elizabeth Andrews (née Smith), political organizer and women's rights campaigner, born Hirwaun, 1882.
Stephen Owen Davies, miners' leader and politician, born Abercwmboi, 1886.
Sir John Bailey, politician and co-operative movement activist, born Mountain Ash, 1898.
Tommy Farr, boxer, born Clydach Vale, 1913.
Sir Geraint Evans, opera singer, born Cilfynydd, 1922.
Sir Stanley Baker, actor, born Ferndale, 1928.
Thomas Jones Woodward (Tom Jones), pop singer, born Treforest, 1940.
David Christopher Kelly, microbiologist and weapons inspector, born Llwynypia, 1944.

public administration, education and health. Efforts to clean polluted waterways have been rewarded by the return of salmon to the lower reaches of the Taff and Rhondda rivers.

"Those who know the banks of the two Rhonthas and the wilds of Ystradyfodwg have seen such woods and groves as are rarely seen… The sides of many of the rocks and hills are clothed with an apparently inexhaustible opulence of timber."
Rev. B.H. Malkin in 1803

"The River Rhondda is a dark, turgid, and contaminated gutter, into which is poured the refuse of the host of collieries which skirt the thirteen miles of its course."
Arthur Morris in 1908

MERTHYR TYDFIL

Area Sq Km	111
Area Sq Miles	43
Population	55,700
County town	Merthyr Tydfil
Highest point	Waun Llysiog (c.515 m)

This name is in two parts. Tudful is a personal name, while '*merthyr*' is a grave, although it might also come from the Latin *martyrium*, so 'Tudful's grave'.

FAMOUS FOR

St Tudful or Tydfil, who graces the heraldic arms of the county, has been immortalized at the place of her apparent martyrdom. Legend has it that Tudfil, the daughter of King Brychan of Brycheiniog, was martyred at the hand of pagans around AD 480.

The landscape of Merthyr has had a profound effect on its history. The deep and steep-sided valley of the upper river Taff rises gradually from around 100 m in the south to over 400 m in the north on the edge of the Brecon Beacons. With heavy rainfall and thin soils, it was the county's geological wealth of limestone, iron ore and coal that was the foundation of local prosperity.

Originally Merthyr Tydfil was part of the historic county of Glamorgan, and later Mid Glamorgan. In 1996 it became a unitary authority, to which was added Vaynor, once part of Breconshire. Its population of 55,700 has fallen since 1981, and is 30 per cent less than its 1911 maximum of 80,900, directly as a result of the collapse of heavy industry in the area. The administrative centre and largest settlement is the town of Merthyr Tydfil (30,483).

The **Dowlais Ironworks** were the first to take full advantage of the technology of the age. In 1845, they were operating 18 blast furnaces and produced 88,400 tonnes of iron, employing 7,300 men. The works closed in 1987.

John Hughes, an engineer, emigrated to Imperial Russia in 1870. He founded the steelworks and town at **Hughesovka** (Yuzovka). The steel mills are still operating today, although after many name changes, the town is now called Donetsk, in Ukraine.

A spoil-heap used by the Merthyr Vale Colliery catastrophically collapsed in October 1966 onto the tiny village of **Aberfan** destroying a farm, 20 terraced houses and the north side of the Pantglas Junior School as well as a section of the Senior School. Of the 144 people killed, 116 were children.

Some industrial enterprises, such as textile weaving, charcoal burning and iron smelting, were in place in the 16th century, but the small local population were mainly farmers or shepherds. All this changed with the Industrial Revolution. The Dowlais Ironworks rapidly expanded after 1760 once coal was used in the smelting process instead of the less efficient charcoal. Transporting Merthyr Tydfil's iron to the port at Cardiff was made commercially possible by the Glamorganshire Canal, opened in 1794, and later by the opening of the railways in 1841. Demand for iron dropped in the late 19th century but the development of steel mills and deep coalmines replaced it. By the late 20th century most of this industry was gone.

Manufacturing still provides a significant proportion of jobs (17 per cent) in new light industries,

FAMOUS PEOPLE

Joseph Edwards, sculptor, born Ynysgau, 1814.
John Hughes, ironmaster and engineer, born Merthyr Tydfil, 1815.
Robert Thompson Crawshay, ironmaster, born Cyfarthfa, 1817.
William Thomas Lewis, 1st Baron Merthyr, mineral agent and mine owner, born Merthyr Tydfil, 1837.
Joseph Parry, composer, born Merthyr Tydfil, 1841.
Sir Samuel Walker Griffith, lawyer and Australian politician, born Merthyr Tydfil, 1845.
Jack Jones, novelist, born Merthyr Tydfil, 1884.
Charles 'Charlie' Jones, footballer, born Troed-y-rhiw, 1889.
Glyn Jones, writer, born Merthyr Tydfil, 1905.
Laura Ashley, fashion designer, born Merthyr Tydfil, 1925.

although in 1995, 26 per cent of jobs were in this sector. The service sector has helped to create new employment providing 80 per cent of jobs. Regeneration plans have included investments to attract tourists to the Brecon Beacons and to the Taff Valley. Many residents now commute to work in Cardiff and Newport.

"The Welsh population of Merthyr is gathered in large part from the mountains and wildish valleys hereabouts … To hear a poor and grimy Welshman, who looks as if he might not have a thought above bread and beer, talk about the poets and poetry of his native land, ancient and modern, is an experience which, when first encountered, gives the stranger quite a shock of agreeable surprise."
Wirt Sikes, *Rambles and Studies in Old South Wales*, 1881

gmore-by-Sea in the Vale of Glamorgan has an interesting bay with lots of fossils and rock-climbing opportunities.

unraven Bay, part of the Glamorgan Heritage Coast.

he Brecon Mountain Railway, Merthyr Tydfil.

The Rhondda Heritage Park is based at the former Lewis Merthyr Colliery, Trehafod, Rhondda Cynon Taff.

Pontsticill Reservoir in the Brecon Beacons National Park near Merthyr Tydfil.

BRIDGEND

Area Sq Km	255
Area Sq Miles	99
Population	134,800
County town	Bridgend
Highest point	Werfa (568 m) near the border with Rhondda Cynon Taf

Pen-y-bont ar Ogwr is the poetic and descriptive Welsh name, meaning 'head of the bridge on the Ogmore', while the prosaic Old English *brycg* (bridge) and *ende* means the 'end of the bridge'.

FAMOUS FOR
The dunes of **Kenfig Burrows** north of Porthcawl are gradually engulfing the remains of the castle and village of Kenfig in shifting sands, a process that was underway by around 1400.

Porthcawl was originally a small port shipping agricultural products and, later, coal, but the dock closed in 1907 because rough weather often made it impossible for shipping to dock. As a result, the town began to reinvent itself as a seaside resort, complete with pavilion and esplanade.

The munitions factory at **ROF Bridgend** employed more than 40,000 workers on three sites, and was the largest of sixteen such sites in the UK.

It was not only Allied soldiers who tried to make 'great escapes' during World War II. In March 1945, seventy German POWs tunnelled out of **Island Farm** (POW camp number 198) near Bridgend. All were recaptured, but a few managed to cover quite long distances before they were caught.

FAMOUS PEOPLE
George Cadogan Morgan, dissenting minister and scientist, born Bridgend, 1754.
John Thomas (the pseudonym of Pencerdd Gwalia), harpist, born Bridgend, 1826.
George Jeffreys, minister and founder of Elim Pentecostal Church, born Nantyffyllon (Maesteg), 1889.
Vernon Phillips Watkins, poet, born Maesteg, 1906.
Sir Morien Bedford Morgan, aeronautical engineer, born Bridgend, 1912.
Arthur Mervyn Stockwood, Anglican bishop of Southwark, born Bridgend, 1913.
Molly Parkin (née Thomas), novelist, born Ponycymer, 19
John James (JJ) Williams, rugby internationalist, born Nantyffyllon (Maesteg), 1948.
Huw Edwards, journalist and newsreader, born Bridgend, 1961.

Bridgend rises from the long coastline and, sometimes, steep cliffs along the Bristol Channel northwards through the fertile lowlands to the valleys of the river Ogmore and its tributaries, the Llunfi, Garw and Ewenny. Originally Bridgend was part of the historic county of Glamorgan, and later Mid Glamorgan. In 1996 the majority of the former Ogwr district in Mid Glamorgan became the new unitary authority of Bridgend. Its population of 134,800 has risen slowly but steadily since 1981. The administrative centre is in Bridgend town (39,429), and other important settlements include Maesteg (18,395), Porthcawl (15,640) and Pyle (12,466).

Bridgend is situated at the site of an old ford across the river Ogmore, below its meeting point with the Llynfi and Garw rivers. In around 1435, a stone bridge was built across the ford. Bridgend initially developed as a market town, and, although coal was never mined in the town, it benefited from being on the London to Fishguard railway, which also had branches up the valleys that were used to bring coal and steel to the port at Barry. Originally a fertile agricultural area, it was the county's location within the south Wales coalfield that transformed it to one known for mining, iron founding and steelmaking.

The Llynfi valley and the area around Maesteg, was developed from the early 19th century, and by 1870 wrought iron production had been replaced by steel. As well as mining, brickworks were established further down the valley at Tondu. The collapse of the coal industry during the 20th century was alleviated only briefly by the demand for coal during the world wars. Some opencast mining continues.

Concerted attempts to rebuild an engineering base in Bridgend saw the opening of the Ford automotive engine factory 1989. The percentage of manufacturing jobs has steadily contracted since the county's coal mining height, but 18 per cent of the county's employment is in this sector, healthy compared to Britain as a whole. Service sector jobs have risen by about a third since 1995, with public administration, education and health (34 per cent) supplying the large number of the jobs. Agriculture remains important in the southern part of the county, and jobs in tourism have gradually increased, bolstered by the reopening of several of the old valley railway lines and the reclamation of the old pit workings.

Porthcawl viewed across Ogmore Bay.

"This town [Bridgend] … is pleasantly situated, about three-quarters of a mile to the north of the turnpike road from Cardiff to Swansea, on the banks of the river Ogmore… .
It stands in a beautiful and fertile district, nearly in the centre of the county… . A rail-road from the iron-works at Maes Teg to the little harbour of Porthcawl, a distance of sixteen miles, has recently been completed".
Samuel Lewis, 1833

WANSEA

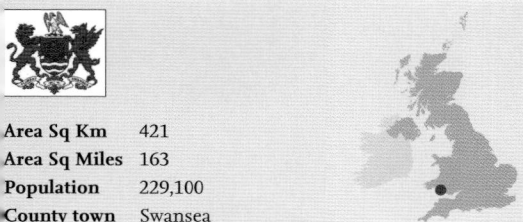

Area Sq Km	421
Area Sq Miles	163
Population	229,100
County town	Swansea
Highest point	Mynydd y Betws (374 m)

Swansea is from an Old Scandinavian personal name, probably *Sveinn*, and the word for island, '*ey*'. The Welsh, Abertawe, means 'mouth of the River Tawe', referring to the town's location. '*Tawe*' might simply be a Celtic word for 'water'.

FAMOUS FOR

By 1720 it was clear that **Swansea's** future lay in heavy industry, so the town fathers took the decision that industrial plants should be built to the east of the city along the lower Tawe, allowing the prevailing winds to blow the noxious fumes towards Neath.

The notion of trustworthiness captured in the phrase 'copper-bottomed guarantee' initially referred to ships sheathed in the metal as a result of the new **'Welsh method'** of copper smelting, developed by Swansea coppersmiths in the 18th century.

The city is home to two universities. **Swansea University** was established as part of the University of Wales in 1920 and became an independent institution in 2007. **Swansea Metropolitan University** was awarded its charter in 2008, having begun as three separate institutions founded in the 19th century.

In 1935, the **Swansea Rugby Club's** 'All Whites' defeated the 'All Blacks', 11–3, the first British club side ever to defeat a New Zealand full touring team.

FAMOUS PEOPLE

Richard Nash (Beau Nash), dandy, self-proclaimed 'King of Bath', born Swansea, 1674.
John Dillwyn Llewelyn, pioneer photographer, born Swansea, 1810.
Sir William Grove, physicist, fuel-cell pioneer, born Swansea, 1811.
George Grant Francis, antiquarian and civic leader, born Swansea, 1814.
Wynford Vaughan Thomas, journalist and broadcaster, born Swansea, 1908.
Dylan Thomas, poet, born Swansea,1914.
Sir Harry Secombe, singer and entertainer, born Swansea, 1921.
Michael Heseltine, Baron Heseltine of Thenford, Conservative politician, born Swansea, 1933.
Michael Howard, Conservative politician, born Gorseinon, 1941.
Rowan Williams, theologian and Archbishop of Canterbury, born Swansea, 1950.
Ieuan Evans, Welsh international rugby player, born Pontarddulais, 1964.
Rob Brydon, actor and comedian, born Swansea, 1965.
Catherine Zeta Jones, actress, born Swansea, 1969.

"… an ugly, lovely town … crawling, sprawling … by the side of a long and splendid curving shore."
Dylan Thomas

The county of Swansea includes the Swansea metropolitan area, the Gower peninsula, the lower reaches of the rivers Tawe and Loughor, which drain alluvial lowlands as they flow south, and part of the Lliw uplands, which reach the foothills of the Black Mountain. Mynydd y Betws (374 m) on the border with Carmarthenshire is the highest point.

Swansea lies entirely within the historic county of Glamorgan and formed one of four districts of West Glamorgan. The government reorganization in 1996 added part of Lliw Valley district to create the unitary authority. Its population of 229,100 has shown considerable fluctuation since 1981, but is now almost equal to its 1991 high of 229,700. Swansea, the second largest city in Wales, is the administrative centre (169,800). Other important towns include Gorseinon (19,264), Pontarddulais (7,925) and Clydach (7,500). Oystermouth (4,315) is the largest village in the Gower Peninsula.

From its beginnings as a Viking trading post, the town of Swansea received its earliest charter in around 1184, as a craft centre and port, dealing in wine, wool, hides and coal, which was first mined in the area around 1306. Within 300 years, it was probably the third largest coal port in Britain, and a 500 per cent population rise by 1801 was due to the success of both the port and industries, such as copper smelting, for which it became famous, as well as in tinplate manufacture. Swansea's port and factories were the target of bombing raids in 1941, and although most of the city centre was destroyed, the Guildhall, only completed in 1936 and located near the docks, survived.

Manufacturing is no longer the dominant economic sector, and many former mining centres in the county are now commuter suburbs for Swansea. The service sector provides 89 per cent of the area's jobs, principally in public administration, education and health (39 per cent), boosted by the presence of two universities (Swansea and Swansea Metropolitan) and government agencies, such as the Driver and Vehicle Licensing Agency (DVLA). The Gower Peninsula remains primarily an agricultural area, and has been designated an Area of Outstanding Natural Beauty with its limestone cliffs and sandy beaches, popular with surfers and many other visitors.

The statue of Dylan Thomas in Swansea.

The Mumbles Lighthouse was built in 1794.

Swansea Sail Bridge

NEATH PORT TALBOT

Area Sq Km	452
Area Sq Miles	174
Population	137,600
County town	Port Talbot
Highest point	Craig y Llyn (600 m) on the border with Rhondda Cynon Taf

Neath takes its name from the river Neath, possibly 'shining one'. The Welsh name for the town is *Castell-Nedd*, 'castle on the Nedd' in reference to the Norman castle built *c*.1114. Port Talbot, founded in 1836, takes its name directly from the Talbot family on whose land the town was built.

FAMOUS FOR

Hard Old Red Sandstone lying on top of softer limestones and shales have eroded over time to create an unusually high number of beautiful waterfalls along the **Vale of Neath**, giving the county the reputation of 'Waterfall Country'.

In the 1960s, the **Abbey Steelworks** at Port Talbot was not only the largest steelworks in Europe, but the largest single employer in Wales, with a workforce of 18,000.

The **Welsh Rugby Union** was established in March 1881 at the Castle Hotel in Neath following a match with England the previous month which featured the first truly Welsh team, picked to include players from all over the country. (They were comprehensively defeated.)

The **Cefn Coed Colliery** near Crynant was sunk in 1926 to the depth of 732 m and it was the world's deepest anthracite mine. Although it closed in 1968, its steam winding gear is the centrepiece of the local mining museum.

FAMOUS PEOPLE

Llywelyn ap Rhisiart, master poet (*pencerdd*), born at Tir Iarll, before 1520.
Richard Lewis (better known as Dic Penderyn), Chartist and industrial martyr, born Aberafon, 1808.
David Watts Morgan, miners' leader and politician, born Skewen, 1876.
Hugh Dalton, Labour politician, Chancellor of the Exchequer (1945–47), born Neath, 1887.
Ray Milland (*born* Reginald Truscott-Jones), Hollywood actor, born Neath, 1907.
Thomas George Thomas, Viscount Tonypandy, Speaker of the House of Commons, born Port Talbot, 1909.
Richard Burton (*born* Richard Walter Jenkins), actor, born Pontrhydyfen, 1925.
Sir Geoffrey Howe, Conservative politician, born Port Talbot, 1926.
Sir Anthony Hopkins, actor, born Port Talbot, 1937.
Katherine Jenkins, classical and popular singer, born Neath, 1980.

"As I proceeded I sometimes passed pleasant groves and hedgerows, sometimes huge works; in this valley there was a singular mixture of nature and art, of the voices of birds and the clanking of chains, of the mists of heaven and the smoke of furnaces."
George Borrow, 1854

Neath Port Talbot borders the Bristol Channel at Swansea Bay with its narrow, sandy coastal plain. The upland countryside is very hilly, with three rivers, the Tawe, the Neath (with its tributary, the Dulais) and the Afan forming broad valleys. The northwest of the county reaches to the western foothills of the Brecon Beacons. Originally Neath and Port Talbot were part of the historic county of Glamorgan, and later Mid Glamorgan. In 1996 the two districts were combined into one unitary authority. Its population of 137,600 has contracted by about 3 per cent since 1981. The major settlements are Neath (45,898) and Port Talbot (35,633).

Port Talbot's origins are linked to the Cistercian Margam Abbey founded in 1147. With industrialization from the 1770s, copper works were established, followed by collieries, and the original Port Talbot docks were opened in 1839. Coal mining declined after World War I, but the steelworks opened in 1916, and continue in operation. The docks have been rebuilt several times in order to cater for the increased volume and size of ships using the harbour.

It was the Romans who built the first fort, Nidum, at the crossing of the Neath in the 1st century AD, and the Normans fortified the area in the 12th century. The industrialisation of all three river valleys in the county were a feature of the 18th and 19th centuries. Although it suffered from the collapse of the coal industry by the end of the 20th century, Aberpergwm drift, near Glynneath, closed by British Coal in 1985, was reopened in 1996, and remains in operation.

Manufacturing jobs still provide 24 per cent of all employment, and it is once again a growing sector. Tourism is also a growing industry, employing almost 1,000 more people since 1995. Services are also a strong sector, with public administration, education and health providing 31 per cent of jobs.

Katherine Jenkins, born in Neath, is a classical and popular singer

The Gnoll Estate Country Park, Neath, is set in an 18th-century landscaped garden.

The Steel Works at Margam, Port Talbot.

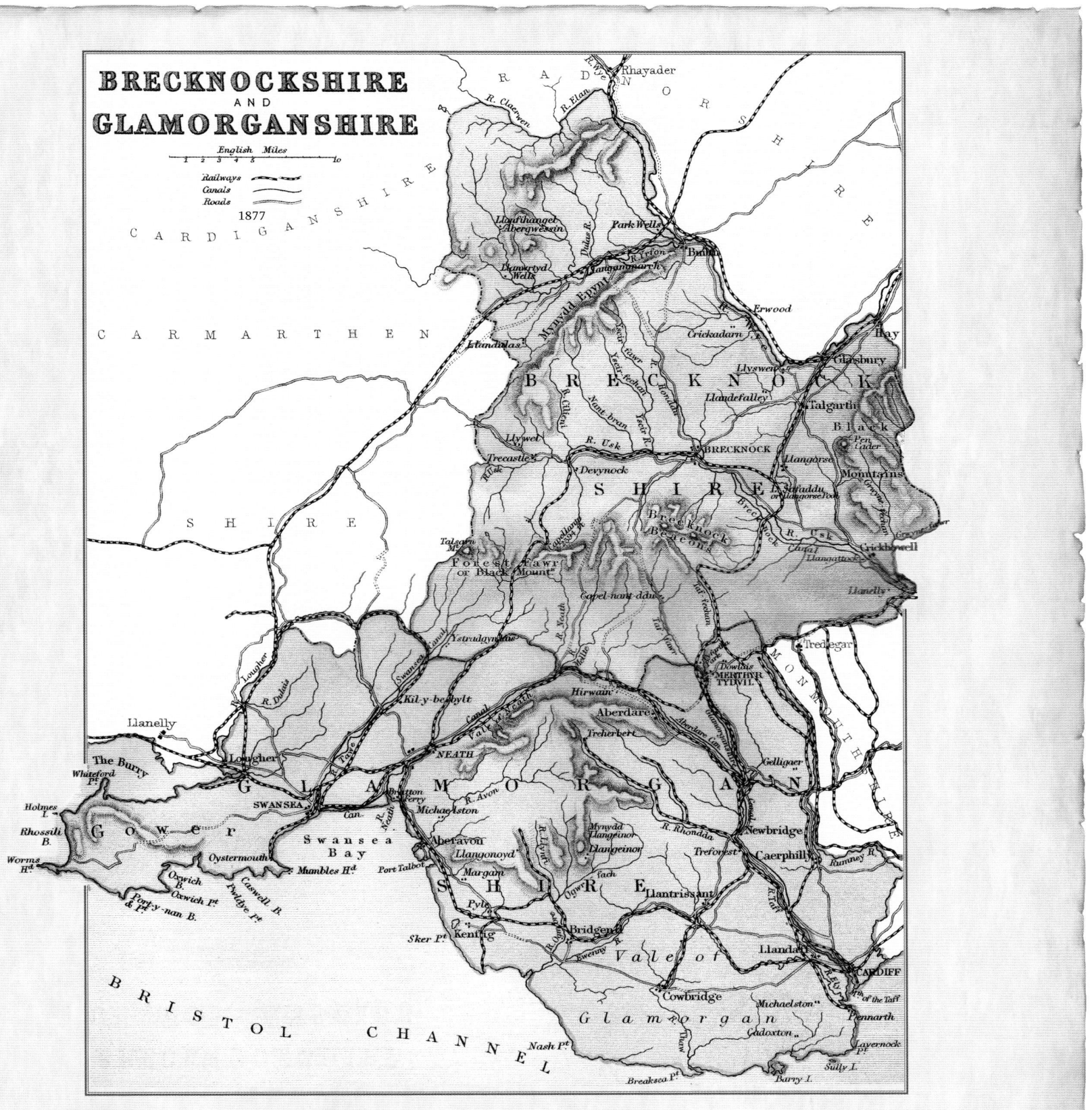

BRECKNOCKSHIRE
AND
GLAMORGANSHIRE

Bartholomew Gazetteer of the British Isles, 1887

BRECKNOCKSHIRE, *or Brecon, an inland co. of S. Wales, bounded N. by Radnorshire, E. by Herefordshire and Monmouthshire, S. by Monmouthshire and Glamorgan, and W. by Carmarthenshire and Cardiganshire; greatest length, N. and S., 38 miles; greatest breadth, E. and W., 33 miles; area, 460,158 ac., pop. 57,746. B. is one of the most mountainous of the Welsh counties, abounding in grand and picturesque scenery. A range of mountains, running E. and W., culminates about 4 miles S. of the centre of the co. in the Van or Beacon (2862 ft.), the highest summit of South Wales; its rocks belong to the old red sandstone or Devonian system. Part of the S. lies within the great Welsh coal-field, where ironstone is also abundant; limestone occurs in the W. Less than one-half of the surface is under cultivation, and the mountain land is generally bare. The river Wye traces nearly the whole of the N. boundary, and the Usk flows in an easterly direction through the central valley. There are mfrs. of coarse woollens and worsted hosiery. The Brecon Canal, 33 miles long, extends to the Monmouth Canal at Pontypool. The co. comprises 6 hundreds, 91 pars., with part of one other, and the mun. bor. of Brecknock. It is mostly in the diocese of St David's.*

GLAMORGAN, *a maritime co. of South Wales, bounded N. by Carmarthen, Brecknock, and Monmouth, E. by Monmouth and the estuary of the Severn, S. by the Bristol channel, and W. by Carmarthen and Carmarthen Bay; greatest length, N. and S., 28 m.; greatest breadth, E. and W., 48 m.; area, 516,959 ac., pop. 511,433. Glamorgan is, commercially, the most important co. in Wales, chiefly owing to its great mineral resources, the fertility of its soil, and the extent and convenience of its seaboard. The surface of the co. in the N. is mountainous; but towards the S. it becomes more level, especially in the fertile expanse known as the Vale of Glamorgan. It is watered by various rivers, of which the more important are the Taff, Taw, Neath, and Rhymney; all the streams flow S. to the Bristol Channel. Mining is the principal industry, the co. having one of the largest coalfields in Britain, while its supply of ironstone and limestone is said to be inexhaustible. The soil yields abundant and excellent crops of the usual cereals, and large quantities of dairy produce are exported. Some of the largest ironworks in the world are in Glamorgan, notably those at Merthyr Tydfil and Dowlais; and the co. likewise contains very important copper, tin, and lead works. Glamorgan comprises 10 hundreds, 166 pars., the greater part of the parl. bor. of Merthyr Tydfil, and the mun. bors. of Aberavon, Cardiff, Neath, and Swansea.*
It is mostly in the diocese of Llandaff.

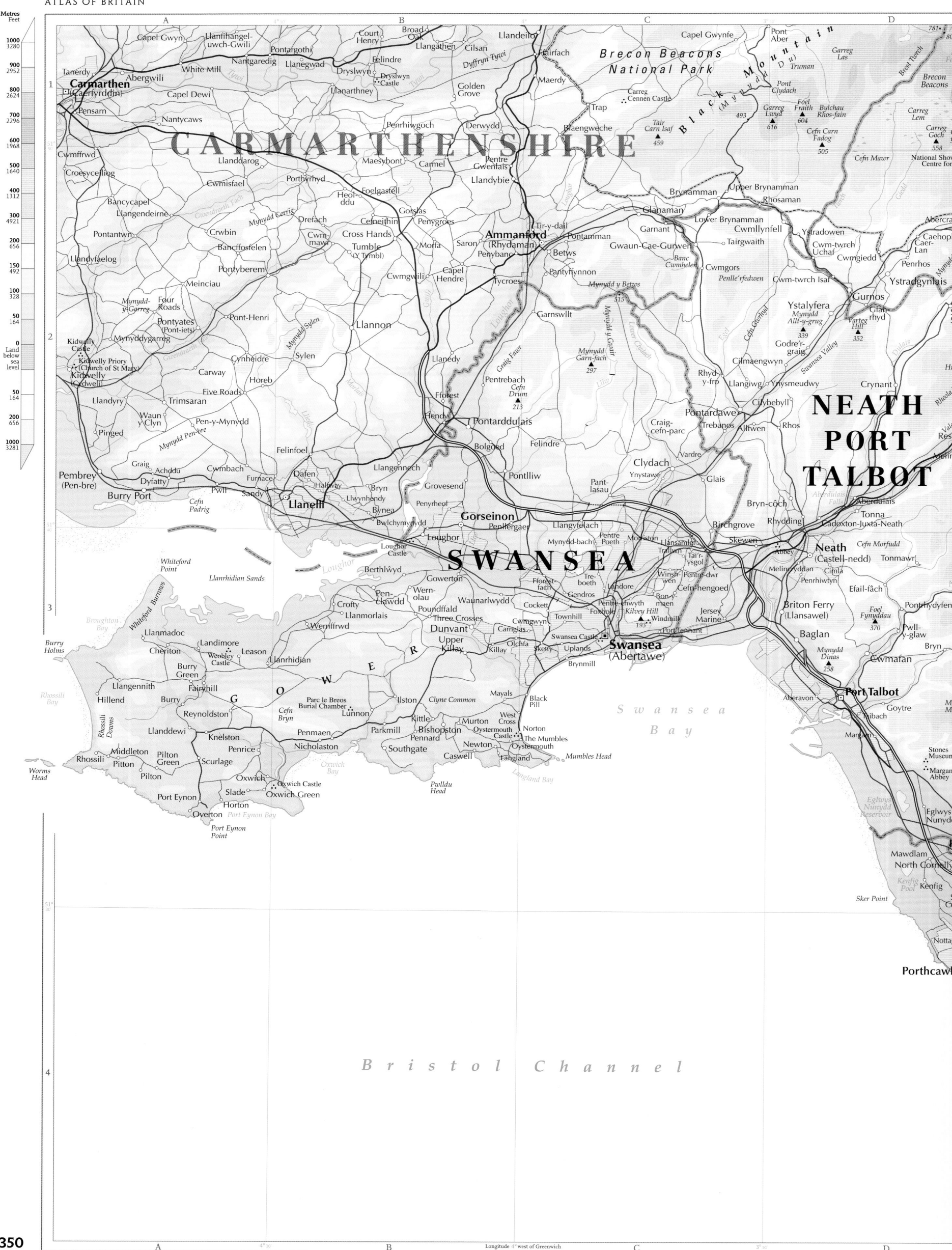

British National Grid projection

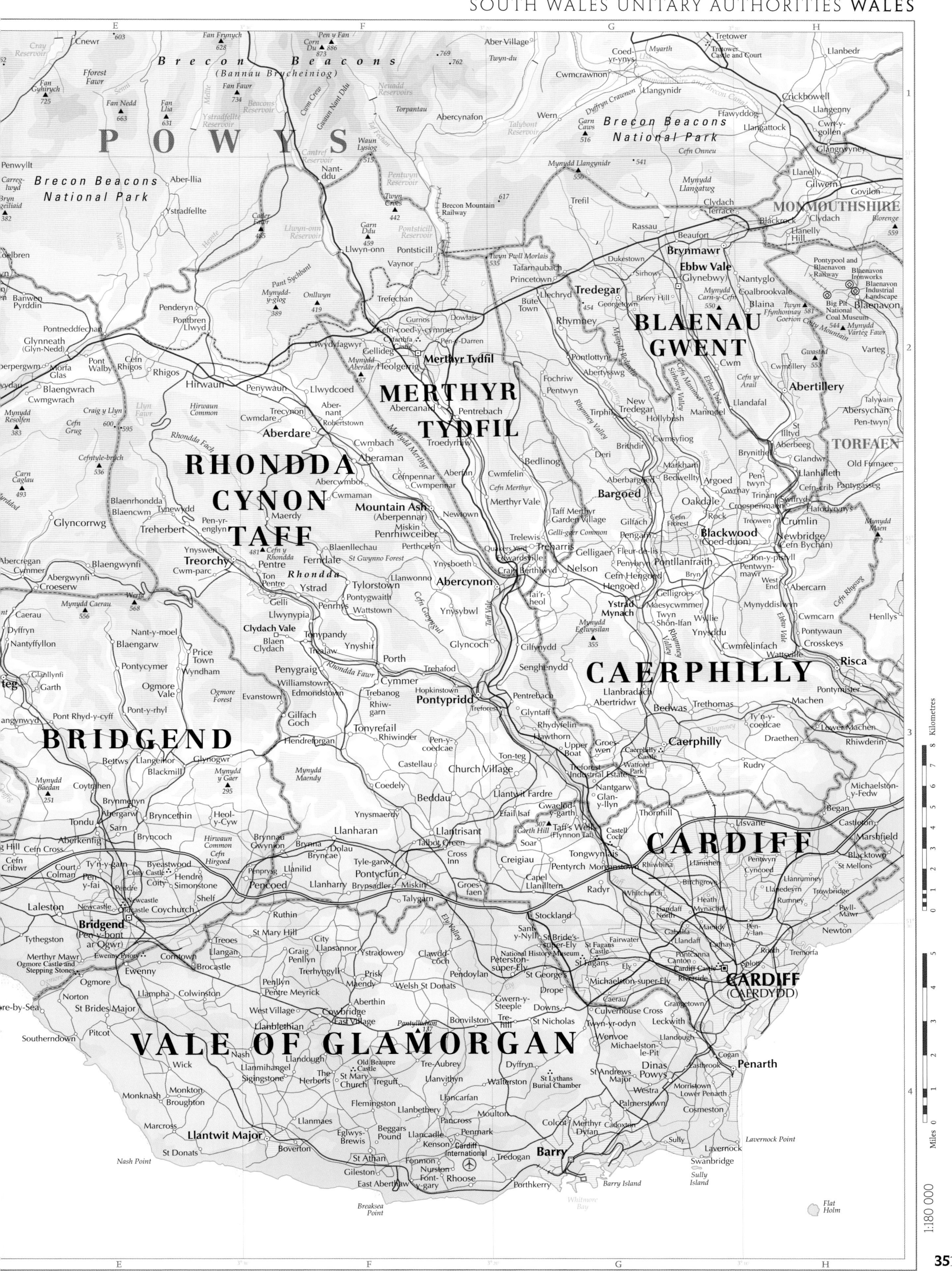

1:180 000

© Collins Bartholomew Ltd

CARMARTHENSHIRE

Area Sq Km   2,439
Area Sq Miles   942
Population   180,500
County town   Carmarthen
Highest point   Fan Foel (781 m) in the Black Mountain

The Welsh *Caerfyrddin* associates *caer* 'fort' with a personal name, and the English is a reference to the fort at *Moridunum*, the town that sprang up around the Roman fort at the fording place of the river Tywi or Towy.

FAMOUS FOR
Carmarthen claims to be the oldest town in Wales, and its Augustinian monastery, founded by the Normans, was home to the **Black Book of Carmarthen**, the earliest surviving manuscript to be written almost entirely in Welsh.

Brynamman is a village that straddles two counties. Upper Brynamman, in Carmarthenshire, is on the western bank of the River Amman, while Lower Brynamman is on the eastern, Neath Port Talbot side.

Laugharne Corporation is the last surviving medieval corporation in Britain. Established by 1291, it still holds a half-yearly Court Leet and a bi-weekly Court Baron.

The Felinfoel Brewery first put its beer in cans in 1935, after much experimentation with linings which would preserve the beer, partly to provide work for local tinplate manufacturing businesses.

The Welsh folk song *Sosban Fach* or 'Little Saucepan' is associated with both the local **Llanelli** Rugby Football Club and the regional Llanelli Scarlets.

FAMOUS PEOPLE
John Lloyd, Principal of Jesus College, Oxford and Bishop of St David's, born Pendine, 1638.
Thomas Brigstocke, portrait painter, born Carmarthen, 1809.
Timothy Richards Lewis, pathologist and parasitologist, born Llanboidy, 1841.
Peter Jones, department store owner, born Newcastle Emlyn, 1843.
Gareth Hughes (William John Hughes), stage and silent film actor, born Dyfen, 1894.
Frederick Elwyn Jones, Baron Elwyn-Jones, Lord Chancellor, born Llanelli, 1909.
Donald Swann, composer and lyricist, born Llanelli, 1923.
Rachel Roberts, actress, born Llanelli, 1927.
Carwyn Rees James, rugby player and coach, born Cefneithin, 1929.
Sir John Cadogan, chemist, former Head of UK Science Research Councils, born Pembrey, 1930.
Barry John, rugby player, born Cefneithin, 1945.

"A rich vale watered by a winding river leads between two woody hills; the distant scene innumerable inclosures [sic]; further still you come to another vale yet richer, the river opening in finer reaches; the declivities bold, and covered with wood, farms, cottages, stacks, a church and village animate the scene."
Arthur Young, describing area around St Clears, 1776

"The manners of the people are considered to be, on the whole, less pleasing than in most parts of Wales: this is more especially remarked at the western extremity of the county, the rudeness of the inhabitants of which is attributed to their habitual jealousy and dislike of their neighbours of Pembrokeshire…"
Samuel Lewis, 1833

Carmarthenshire is a county in southwestern Wales. Sandy beaches along the Bristol Channel rise to upland hills and the mountainous terrain of Black Mountain in the east and Cambrian Mountains to the north. Three rivers flow into Carmarthen Bay, the Gwendraeth, Tywi and Taf, and the river Loughor forms part of the border with Swansea.

One of the historic Welsh counties, Carmarthen was one of three districts of Dyfed after 1975, but was resurrected in the 1996 local government reorganizations as Carmarthenshire. In 2003, further change saw Clunderwen moved to Pembrokeshire. Carmarthenshire's population of 180,500 has risen steadily since 1981, increasing by about 10 per cent. Carmarthen is the administrative centre (14,648), but Llanelli (46,357) is the largest settlement. Other important towns include Ammanford (12,615), Burry Port (7,774) and Cross Hands (4,499).

The lowest fording place on the river Towy, the longest river entirely within Wales, it was considered strategically important by the Romans, who built a fort here. The Roman town, *Moridunum*, had stone walls and an amphitheatre by about AD 220. Pre-Norman Carmarthen has left little apart from legends, especially surrounding the wizard Merlin, but it was in English hands by the 12th century. In 1353 it received a charter giving it the monopoly on wool trading for Wales, granted by Edward III. Despite the introduction of iron smelting in the 18th century and, during the 19th century, tinplate manufacturing, most of the town's prosperity rested on its position as a river port and agricultural marketplace.

The more rural and agricultural areas around Carmarthen in the north and west are sometimes known as the 'Garden of Wales', due to the rolling countryside and many beautiful gardens. Rural Carmarthenshire is traditionally an area of mixed and dairy farming, with sheep farming on the more upland areas. The more industrial areas of the southeast were situated around Llanelli. The growth of Llanelli during the Industrial Revolution was stimulated by the local coalfield, predominantly bearing anthracite, and the invention of steam engines to pump water out of deep mines. These were in use by 1804, and the availability of coal enabled the expansion of nonferrous metal manufacture, initially lead and copper, but later tinplate, for which this area was famous. By the 1870s there were thirty-one tinplate mills in the town, giving rise to its nickname, Tinopolis, but Llanelli also produced pottery, including porcelain, and was a centre for brewing. A network of canals and tramroads, later replaced by rail, and new docks at Llanelli and Burry Port, brought coal down from the upper valleys. The 20th century saw the gradual decline in heavy industry, and coal mining ended, but the Trostre Works has continued Llanelli's tradition of tinplate manufacture.

Many of the outlying towns and villages, including Kidwelly, probably founded earlier than the 9th century, Ammanford, and the villages further up Tywi valley, flourished during the Industrial Revolution, producing tinplate, bricks, iron and, particularly, coal. These industries have declined and they are now dormitory settlements.

Manufacturing remains an important economic sector, and still provides 11 per cent of local employment. Over half of local area employment is in the service sector, particularly in public administration, education and health (35 per cent) and retail, hotels and restaurants (26 per cent). Tourism is also an important local industry providing 8 per cent of jobs, boosted by projects such as the Millennium Coastal Park to reclaim former industrial lands along the coast between Llanelli and Burry Port, where a marina has been built. The National Botanic Garden of Wales at Llanarthney is also very popular with visitors, and the northeastern part of the county includes part of the Brecon Beacons National Park.

The famous poet Dylan Thomas' boathouse at Laugharne, where he lived for the last four years of his life, is now a museum.

The Upper Walled Garden at Aberglasney House, Llangathen.

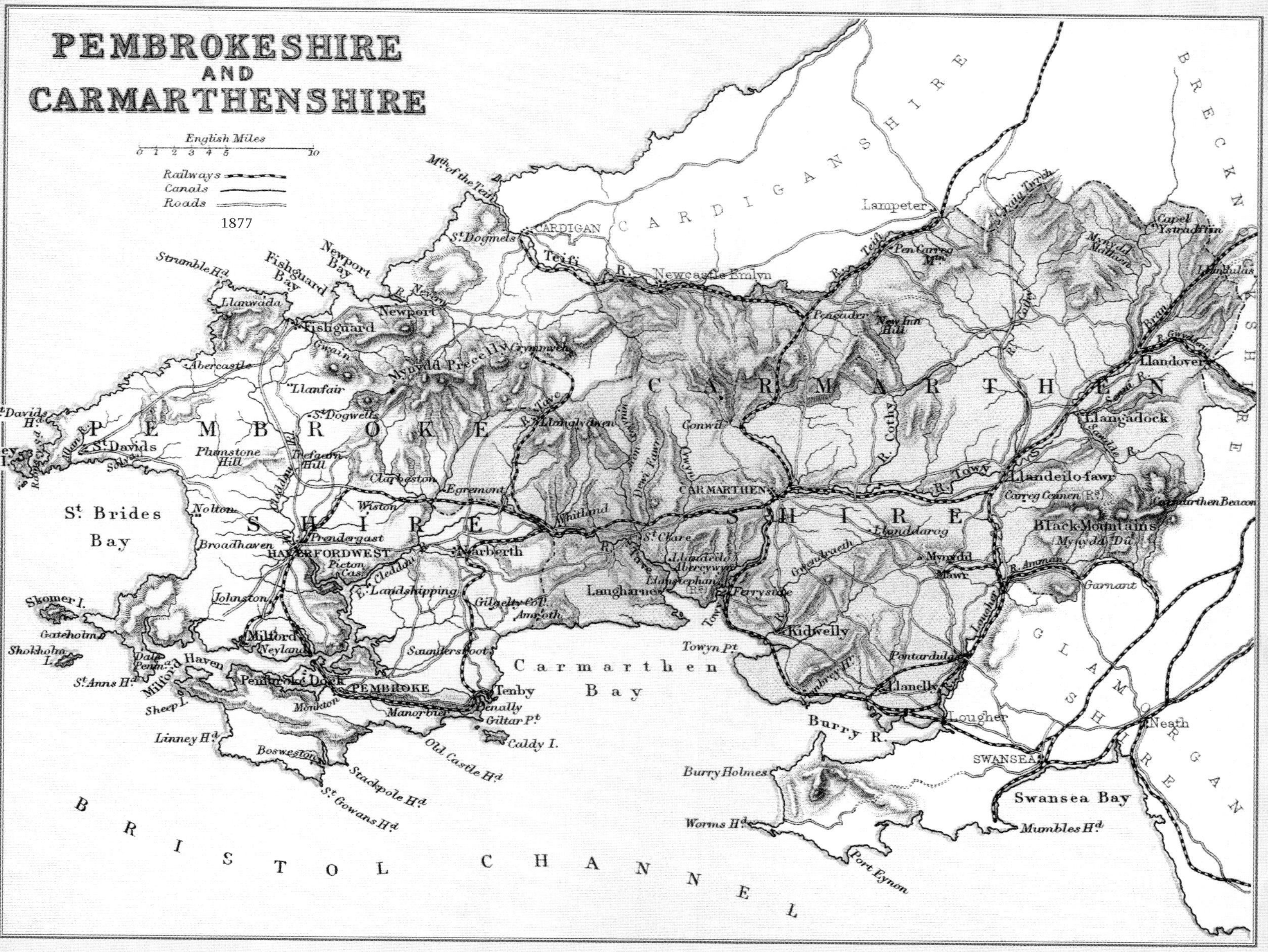

PEMBROKESHIRE AND CARMARTHENSHIRE

English Miles
0 1 2 3 4 5   10

Railways — · · · —
Canals ————
Roads ————

1877

[Map of Pembrokeshire and Carmarthenshire]

Bartholomew Gazetteer of the British Isles, 1887

PEMBROKESHIRE, *a maritime co. of South Wales, washed by the sea on all sides excepting the NE. and E., where it is bounded respectively by Cardiganshire and Carmarthenshire; greatest length, N. to S., about 30 miles; greatest breadth, E. to W., about 25 miles; area, 391,181 ac., pop. 91,824. The coast line, which on the S. is rugged and inhospitable, shows several indentations of more or less importance to mariners; they include St Bride's Bay and Milford Haven in the S., and Newport and Fishguard Bays in the N. Inland the surface of the co. displays a succession of green hills, with fertile valleys intervening. Among the Preseley Hills the highest elevation (1764 ft.) is reached. The chief rivers are the Teifi, which separates the co. from Cardiganshire in the NE., the East Cleddau, and the West Cleddau. Considerable variety characterises the soil; in the S. it is very productive, and in the NW. it is excellently suited for barley growing; but in the hilly and coal districts it is very poor. Owing to the violence of the SW. wind there is comparatively little timber, excepting in sheltered spots. Oats, barley, and potatoes are the chief crops, all being raised under very careful farming. Coal, lead, iron, and slate are the only minerals of the co. having a commercial value. From the number of English-speaking people in Pembrokeshire (chiefly through the settlement of a colony of Flemings, who adopted the English tongue), the co. has been called "Little England beyond Wales." It comprises 7 hundreds, 153 pars, with part of 1 other, and the mun. bors. of Haverfordwest, Pembroke, and Tenby.*

CARMARTHENSHIRE, *a maritime co. of S. Wales, and the largest of all the Welsh counties; is bounded N. by Cardiganshire, E. by Brecknockshire and Glamorgan, S. by the Bristol Channel, and W. by Pembrokeshire; greatest length, NE. and SW., 50 miles; greatest breadth, E. and W., 42 miles; the coast, which is marshy, measures about 35 miles; area, 594,405 ac.; pop. 124,864. The surface generally is upland or mountainous, much of it being waste. The Black Mountains rise on the NE. border, the chief summit, Carmarthen Van, having an alt. of 2596 ft. The vale of the river Towy extends in length about 30 miles NE. and SW. through the middle of the co. The uplands consist chiefly of slate or limestone; old red sandstone occurs about the estuary of the Towy; coal and ironstone are worked in the SE. Good crops of oats, barley, and wheat are produced in the valleys, but the principal industry is stock-raising. The fisheries are of some importance. The co. comprises 5 hundreds, 3 commots, 81 pars., with part of 1 other, and the mun. bors. of Carmarthen and Llandovery. It is entirely in the diocese of St David's.*

dome at the National Botanic Garden of Wales, Llanarthney.

353

The Green Bridge of Wales, near Bosherston, is the largest sea arch in Wales.

A group of puffins on a cliff edge at Skomer Island.

St Govan's Chapel on the South Pembrokeshire Heritage Coast.

Deserted beach at Marloes Sands.

PEMBROKESHIRE

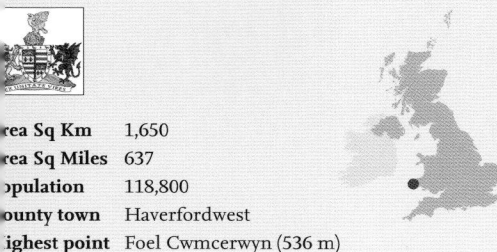

Area Sq Km	1,650
Area Sq Miles	637
Population	118,800
County town	Haverfordwest
Highest point	Foel Cwmcerwyn (536 m)

The county's name is a descriptive one. The old Welsh name for this area is *Penfro* from the Welsh *pen'* and '*brog*', meaning 'land at the end'

FAMOUS FOR

'England to the west of Wales' is not a new concept, first having been recorded in 1594, and the idea had been in circulation since at least 1519, when this part of English-speaking Wales was known as *Ynglond beyond Walys*.

The port of **Milford Haven** handles a quarter of the total British petrol and diesel imports, as well as a growing amount of liquefied natural gas.

Pembrokeshire has the longest coastline of any Welsh county: 230 km.

The Welsh name of the town is *Abergwaun* ('mouth of the marshy river'), but it is the Anglicized Viking name that is most familiar, describing the place they kept their fish catch, *fiskr garthr*: **Fishguard**.

St David's is the smallest city in Britain, the site of St David's Cathedral, built from the 12th century onwards, on the site of St David's 6th century monastery. It has been a place of pilgrimage for 1,400 years.

FAMOUS PEOPLE

Gerald of Wales, author and ecclesiastic, born Manorbier Castle, *c*.1146.
Henry Tudor, Henry VII of England, born Pembroke Castle, 1457.
Robert Recorde, mathematician and royal physician, born Tenby, 1510.
William Evans, grocer and founder of Corona soft drinks brand, born near Fishguard, 1864.
Edgar Evans, polar explorer, born Rhossili, 1876.
Gwen John, painter, born Haverfordwest, 1876.
Augustus Edwin John, painter, born Tenby, 1878.
Waldo Williams, Welsh poet, born Haverfordwest in 1904.
Richard Llewellyn, writer, born St David's in 1907.
Richard (Dick) Francis, jockey and novelist, born Lawrenny, 1920.
Sarah Waters, novelist, born Neyland, 1966.
Christian Bale, actor, born Haverfordwest, 1974.
Claire Jones, royal harpist, born Crymych, 1985.

"The next county west, is Pembrokeshire, which is the most extreme part of Wales on this side, in a rich, fertile, and plentiful country, lying on the sea coast, where it has the benefit of Milford Haven, one of the greatest and best inlets of water in Britain."
Daniel Defoe, 1725

Pembrokeshire is a peninsula of rugged coastlines and several headlands, including St David's Head, the most westerly point in Wales. Much of upland Pembrokeshire lies in the basin of the Eastern and Western Cleddau rivers that form the Daugleddau estuary at Milford Haven. The inland rolling hills and broad plain rise in the north to the Preseli Hills, where Foel Cwmcerwyn (536 m) is the highest point.

The historic country of Pembrokeshire was incorporated as two of six districts of Dyfed in 1975, South Pembrokeshire and Preseli Pembrokeshire. Further local government reorganization in 1996 retained Dyfed as a 'ceremonial county' while restoring Pembrokeshire within its former boundaries. Its population of 118,800 has increased by almost 15 per cent since 1981. Haverfordwest is the administrative centre and largest town (13,367) with Milford Haven running a close second (12,830). Other important towns include Pembroke Dock (8,676), Pembroke (7,214), Tenby (4,934) and Fishguard (3,193).

Haverfordwest is situated at the highest navigable point on the Western Cleddau river, where a castle, much rebuilt, was first constructed around 1110 by Tancred, a Fleming who had been relocated by Henry I from the Scottish borders to control the Welsh. The area became a centre for Flemish migrants who were mainly involved in the wool trade when not soldiering for the English. By the 16th century, Haverfordwest's prosperity was founded on its port, which was accessible to ships up to 40 tonnes, and it was only the coming of the railways in the 19th century that shifted the focus away from the river. Although it lost its parliamentary seat in 1885, four years later the town became the administrative centre of Pembrokeshire County Council, a position it has retained throughout subsequent reorganizations.

Pembrokeshire is a predominantly rural and agricultural county. The south enjoys some of the most fertile soil in Wales as well as an enviably mild climate.

In the past the area has been known for arable crops such as potatoes and, in more modern times, rapeseed, but most of the land is used as pastoral grazing for dairying (producing butter and cheese), beef production and sheep farming. Fishing has contracted since the 1960s, due to over-fishing, regulations and an expansion of other local opportunities. One such is represented by the tea gardens being planted at a site at the foot of the Preseli Hills as well as at Pembroke Dock, where processing and packing also take place. Another, quite different prospect, is the expansion of the oil and gas terminals at Milford Haven, which saw the construction of a controversial 120-km gas pipeline from the port to Aberdulais in the Vale of Neath, which in some places went through the Brecon Beacons National Park. But Pembrokeshire is not without its industrial past: anthracite mining in the south and slate mining in the north brought the area prosperity during the 18th and 19th centuries; modern industry is concentrated at Milford Haven and Pembroke Dock.

As a percentage of employment, manufacturing has declined since 1995, but employment numbers have increased, while jobs in construction have almost doubled in the same time period. Overall, the service sector provides the most significant employment. Public administration, education and health account for 32 per cent of local jobs. Tourism is a major economic sector in Pembrokeshire, responsible for 15 per cent of the local employment. The county's coastline is almost completely incorporated into the Pembrokeshire Coast National Park, established in 1952, which extends inland to include the Preseli Hills. Only the area around the port of Milford Haven is outside the scheme. The impressive 299 km Pembrokeshire Coast Path follows the shoreline from Amroth north of Tenby to St Dogmaels. Ferries run to Rosslare in southern Ireland from Fishguard and Pembroke Dock.

Construction began in 1181 on the present St David's Cathedral.

Tenby Harbour, with the castle and Prince Albert Memorial in the background.

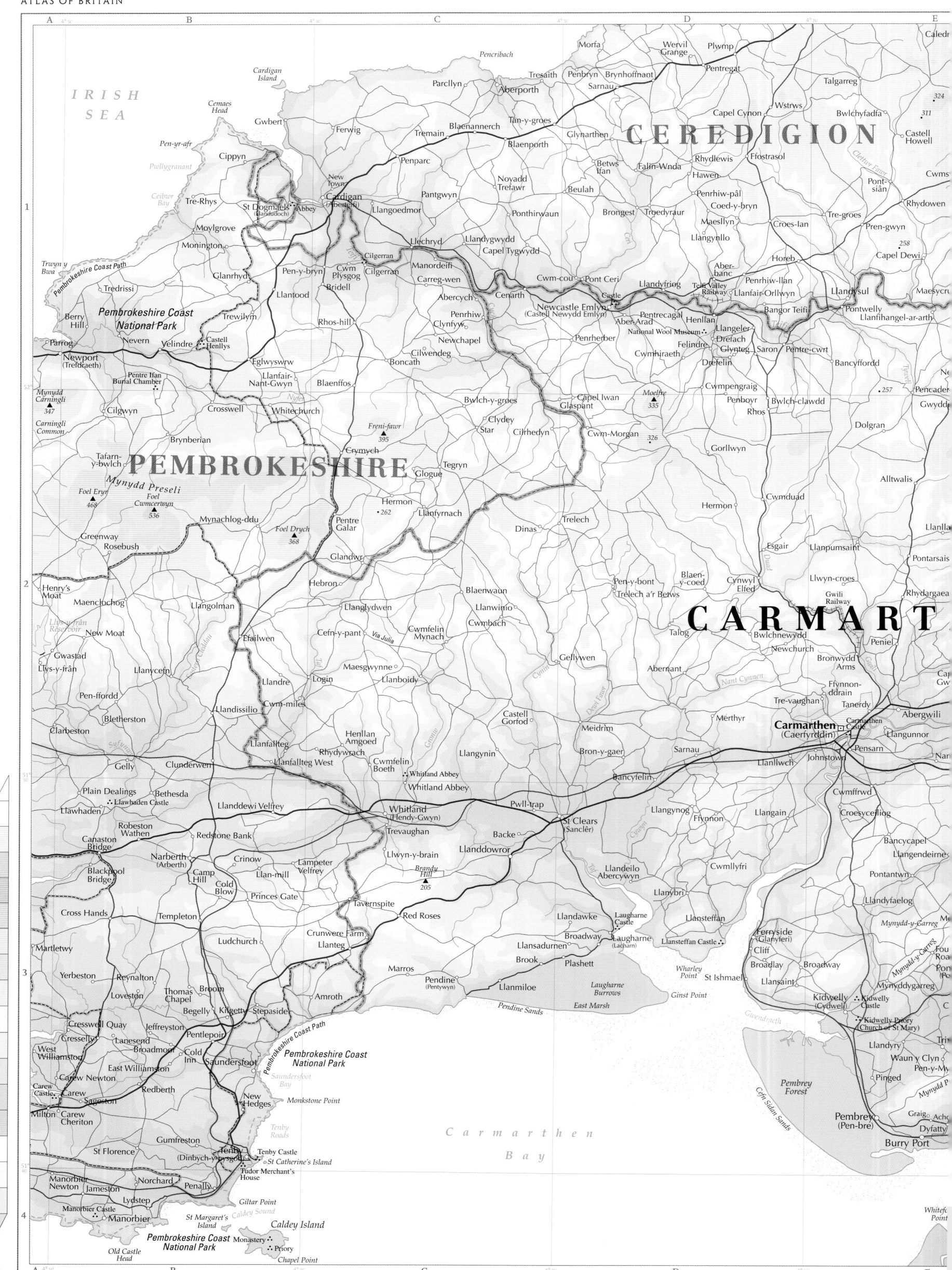

IRISH
SEA

CEREDIGION

PEMBROKESHIRE

CARMART

Pembrokeshire Coast
National Park

Carmarthen
Bay

Caldey Island

Metres
Feet

1000
3280

900
2952

800
2624

700
2296

600
1968

500
1640

400
1312

300
4921

200
656

150
492

100
328

50
164

0
Land
below
sea
level

50
164

200
656

1000
3281

British National Grid projection

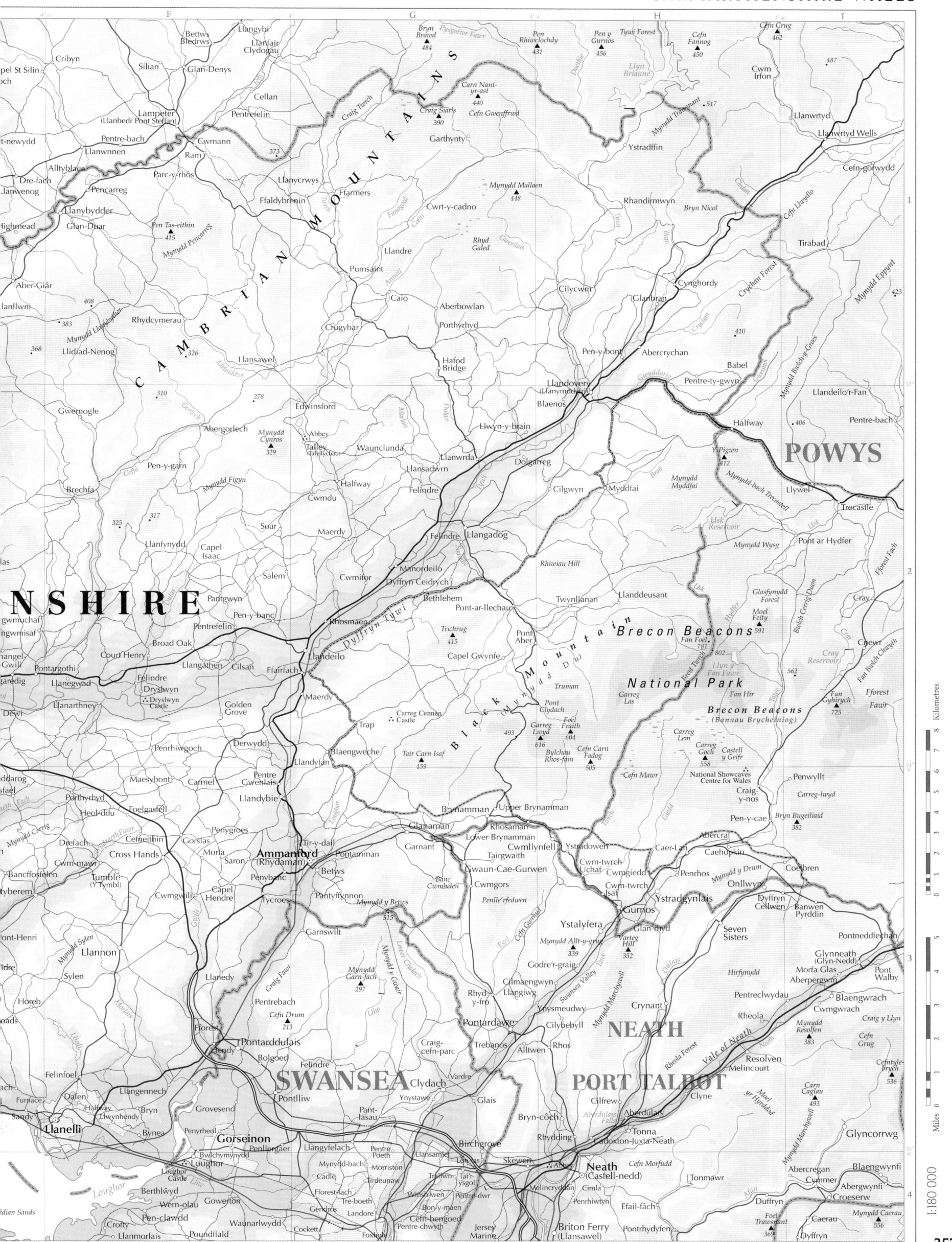

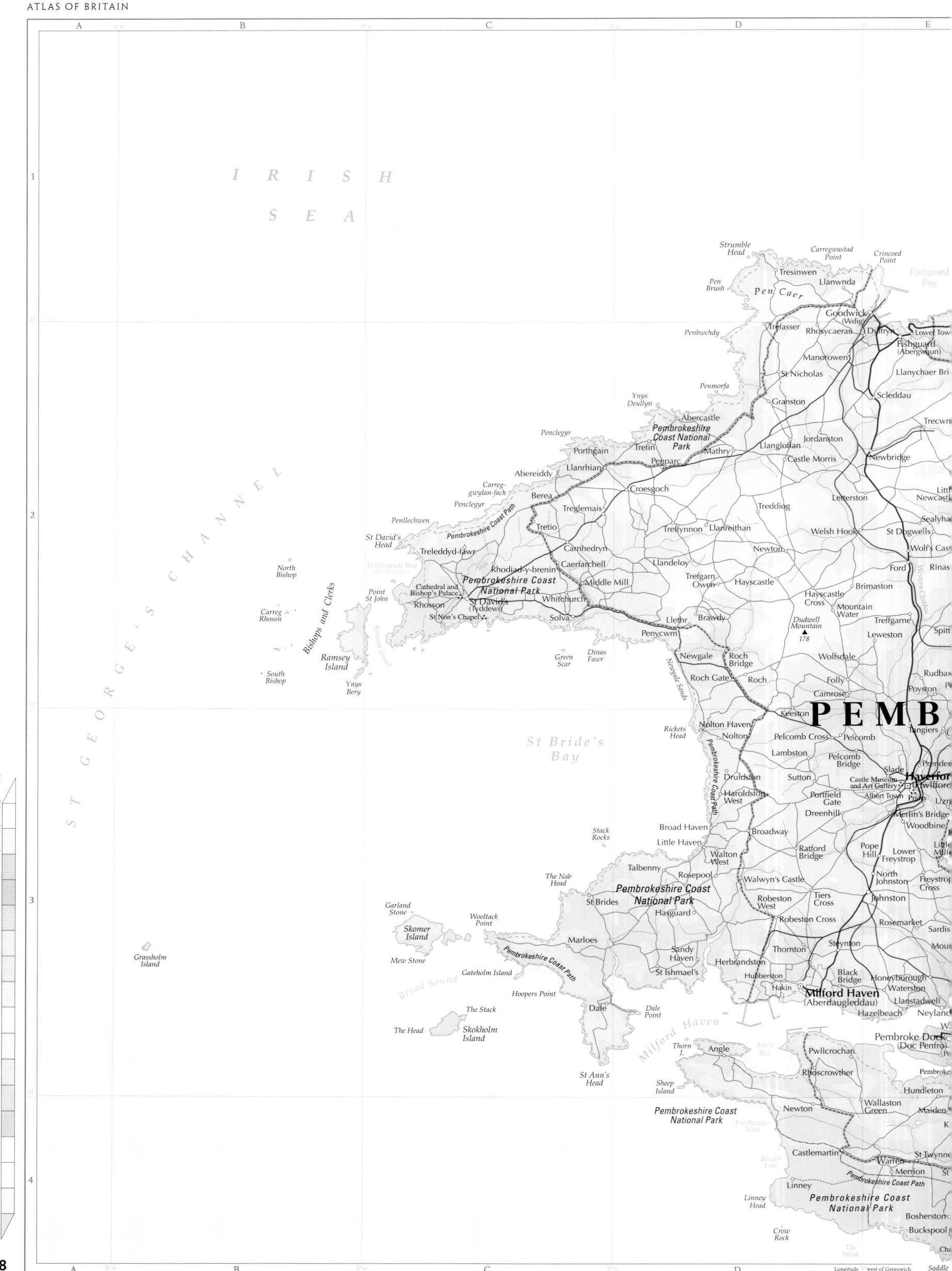

British National Grid projection

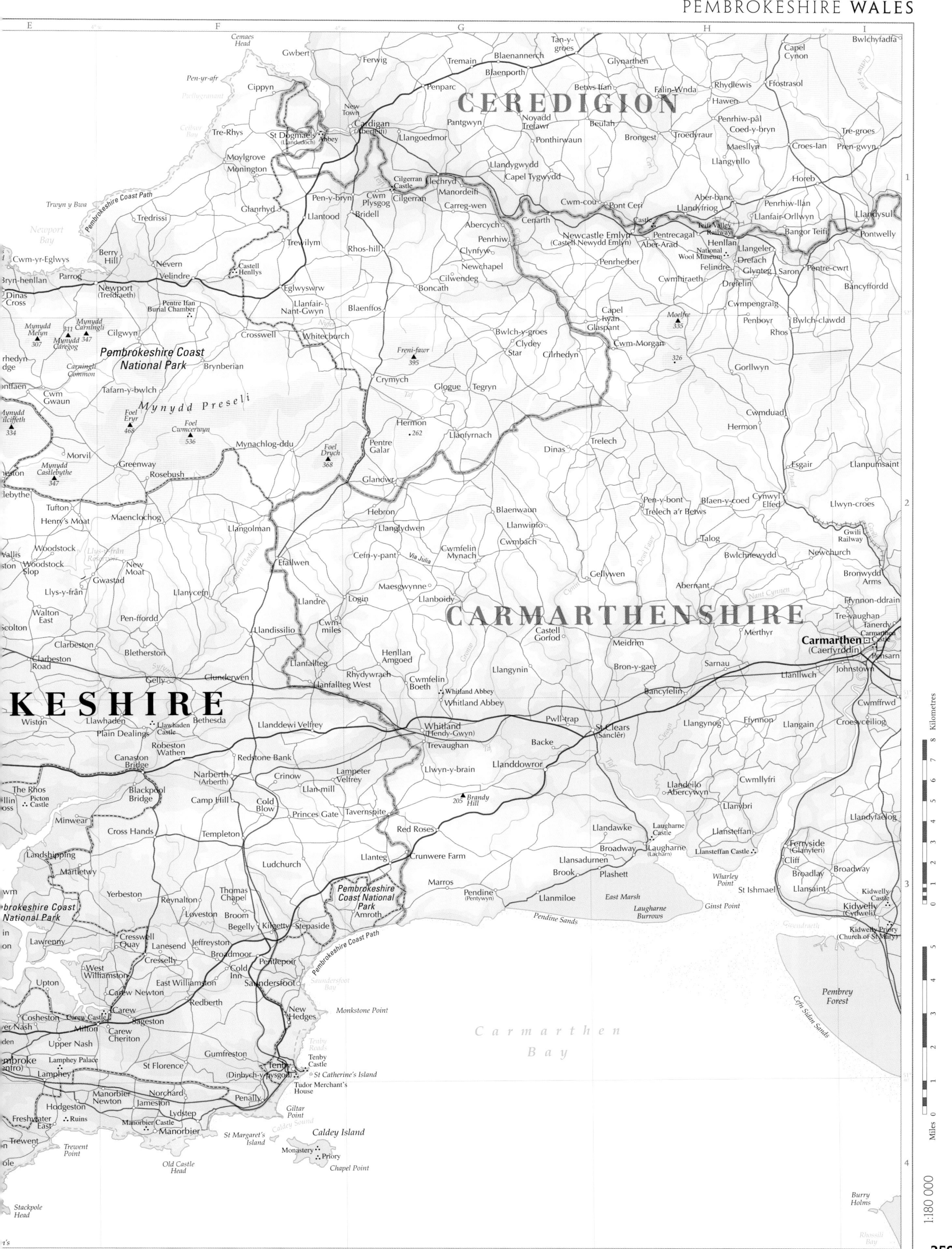

CEREDIGION

CARMARTHENSHIRE

KESHIRE

Pembrokeshire Coast
National Park

Mynydd Preseli

*Carmarthen
Bay*

Caldey Island

1:180 000

© Collins Bartholomew Ltd

CEREDIGION

Area Sq Km	1,806
Area Sq Miles	697
Population	78,000
County town	Aberaeron with offices also in Aberystwyth
Highest point	Pen Pumlumon Fawr (752 m) in the Cambrian Mountains

Ceredigion or 'Land of Ceredig', incorporates the name of a historical person, the son of Cunedda, who established a kingdom here around the 5th century. 'Cardigan' is an Anglicization of the Welsh name following its conquest by Edward I in 1282.

FAMOUS FOR
The **Plynlimon massif** is source of a number of important rivers: the Severn, the Wye and Rheidol rivers. The mountain is reputed to be the home of a sleeping giant.

The waters of **Cardigan Bay** are very clean because there is little in the way of industrial run-off from the land. As a result, a population of around 130 bottlenose dolphins reside here, and their presence is one reason why the bay is now a European Special Area of Conservation.

Considering Ceredigion is one of the least populated counties of Wales, it is home to two of its universities. **Aberystwyth University** is the oldest in Wales. **The University of Wales Trinity Saint David** is the newest, a merger between the University of Wales Lampeter and Trinity University College in Carmarthen.

FAMOUS PEOPLE
Suilien, Bishop of St David's, born Llanbadarn Fawr, c.1012.
Dafydd ap Gwilym, poet, born Brogynin, c.1315.
Moses Williams, Welsh scholar and translator, born Cellan, 1685.
David Jones, missionary in Madagascar, born Penrhiw, Aberaeron, 1796.
Daniel Silvan Evans, lexicographer, born Llannarth, 1818.
Owen Thomas Jones, geologist, born Beulah, 1878.
Evan James Williams, physicist, born Cwmsychbant, 1903.
Morgan Goronwy Rees, writer and University of Aberystwyth principal, born Aberystwyth, 1909.

"This town [Aberystwyth] is enriched by the coals and lead which is found in its neighbourhood, and is a populous, but a very dirty, black, smoky place, and we fancied the people looked as if they lived continually in the coal or lead mines. However, they are rich, and the place is very populous."
Daniel Defoe, 1725

"I should add, that as we passed, we had a sight of the famous Plymlymon-Hill, … and the names of some of these hills seemed as barbarous to us, who spoke no Welsh, as the hills themselves."
Daniel Defoe, 1725

"The gardens produce an abundance of the ordinary kitchen vegetables, but are not distinguished, like those of the eastern parts of South Wales, for their pleasing neatness."
Samuel Lewis, 1833

Ceredigion has an 80 km coastline along Cardigan Bay. Sandy bays and cliffs rise quickly to upland hills and valleys before meeting the Cambrian Mountains in the east. This high peat moorland is often referred to as the 'Welsh Desert'. Pen Pumlumon Fawr (752 m) is the highest point of the Plynlimon massif in the Cambrian Mountains, itself the largest watershed in Wales and the source for (amongst others) the river Rheidol which empties into Cardigan Bay at Aberystwyth. The river Dovey (or Dyfi) forms the county's northern border with Gwynedd. The river Teifi and its tributaries flow into Cardigan Bay just south of Cardigan town.

The historic county of Cardiganshire became one of three districts of Dyfed in 1975. Further local government reorganization in 1996 retained Dyfed as a 'ceremonial county' and restored Cardiganshire within its former boundaries. The day after the Act came into force the council changed its name to Ceredigion. The county's population of 78,000 has risen substantially since 1981 – between 1991 and 2002 alone it had gained 10,000 inhabitants, accounted for by including students at the county's two universities in the 2001 returns. Despite this, it remains one of the smaller Welsh counties. Ancient Aberystwyth (15,935) shares administrative duties with newer Aberaeron (1,520), a variation on the manner in which the area was administered in the 19th century. Other important towns are Cardigan (4,082) and Lampeter (2,894).

Once described as a 'ready-made kingdom' because of its distinct boundaries, Ceredigion expanded in the 8th and 9th centuries, until it was itself incorporated into the larger kingdom of Deheubarth. Briefly drawn into the Marcher lordships of the Clare family, it quickly was restored to Welsh rule. Cardigan, the historic county seat, was an important port throughout the Middle Ages, having been founded in 1093 with the building of a Norman castle here, although it was in Welsh hands within a century, and held by them until the 13th century. By the 15th century it was one of the most important ports in the country, with a thriving shipbuilding trade, and in the 19th century there were 300 sailing vessels registered here. A major export from this port was Cilgerran slate, mined just across the

river Teifi in Pembrokeshire. All this ended by the 20th century as the port gradually silted up and it was not economically viable to dredge it.

Aberystwyth is an ancient site of settlement originally at the mouth of the Ystwyth, as the name suggests, only spreading north when the Norman castle was built in 1277. Later its port was used in the lead and woollen trades, and the town was the last sight of Wales for many immigrants to the United States of America. The railway arrived in the 19th century, undercutting the profits of shipping, but making it possible for the town to reinvent itself as an administrative and educational centre – the University of Wales was founded here in 1872 – and as a seaside resort.

Trade and shipping underpinned the economy of the towns along the Irish Sea coast by the 17th and 18th centuries. Upland farms were famous for their small mountain sheep. During the Industrial Revolution Ceredigion developed into one of the most important Welsh textile regions, exemplified by the mills at Maesllyn in the Teifi valley, which sent cloth as far afield as Middlesbrough. Lead mining in the north of the county was complemented by other mineral extraction, particularly silver. Slate for all purposes was also mined extensively. Railways arrived in the 19th century undercutting the profits of these small ports, and the 'Great Depression' forced the closure of most of the woollen mills.

Today, tourism has replaced most of these industries, providing 13 per cent of local employment. A related economic sector covering retail, hotels and restaurants employed 7,000 people in 2008, a higher percentage (28 per cent) on average than for either Wales or Britain as a whole. Cardigan Bay and the villages along its coastline are very popular holiday destinations and the clean rivers running down from the Cambrian Mountains are notable for brown trout and salmon. Other service industries, particularly public administration, education and health, are major employers (42 per cent). Although relatively small sectors by Welsh standards, even manufacturing (6 per cent) and construction (5 per cent) provide much needed employment.

The north gate of Aberystwyth Castle.

Aberystwyth Promenade stretches for a mile and a half from the harbour to Constitution Hill.

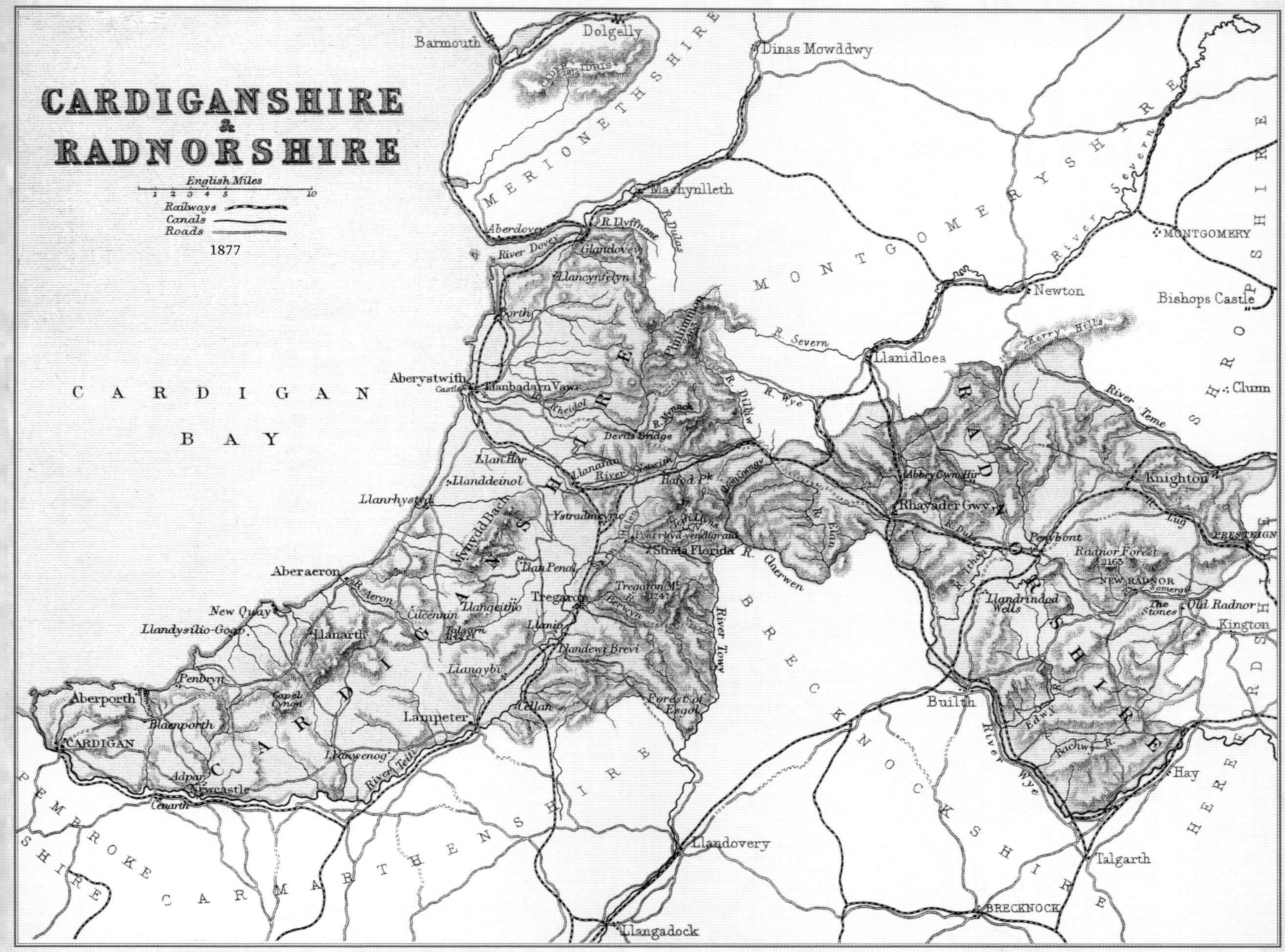

CARDIGANSHIRE & RADNORSHIRE

English Miles

1 2 3 4 5   10

Railways
Canals
Roads

1877

Bartholomew Gazetteer of the British Isles, 1887

CARDIGANSHIRE, *a maritime co. of S. Wales, bounded on the W. by Cardigan Bay, and landward from N. to S. by the cos. of Merioneth, Montgomery, Radnor, Brecknock, Carmarthen, and Pembroke. Its seaboard is in the form of a crescent; coast line, 48 miles; extreme breadth, 22 miles; area, 443,387 ac.; pop. 70,270. Rugged mountains and deep valleys occur in the N. and E. of the co. The summit of Plinlimmon, on the border of Montgomeryshire, has an alt. of 2469 ft. In the SW. the surface is less elevated. The largest streams are the Teifi, Aeron, and Ystwith. The prevailing rocks of the mountains are clay-slate and shale. The soil is either peaty or a sandy loam. The principal crops are oats and barley. Cattle and sheep are reared in great numbers.*

Lead ore is worked. The co. comprises 5 hundreds, 97 pars., the mun. bor. of Aberystwith, and the greater part of the mun. bor. of Cardigan. It is entirely in the diocese of St David's.

RADNORSHIRE, *inland co. of South Wales, bounded N. by Montgomeryshire and Shropshire, E. by Herefordshire, S. and SW. by Brecknockshire, and W. by Cardiganshire; greatest length, N. and S., 30 miles; greatest breadth, E. and W., 34 miles; area, 276,552 ac., pop. 23,528. Radnorshire is the smallest of the 6 counties of South Wales. In the E. and S. are some comparatively level tracts, including the Vale of Radnor, but the greater portion of the surface is hilly, or even mountainous, the Forest of Radnor reaching in its highest summit*

an elevation of 2163 ft. Oats and wheat are grown in the lower parts, but attention is chiefly directed to the rearing of stock; the higher parts serve only for the feeding of sheep and the breeding of Welsh ponies. Butter is made in large quantities. The minerals are of little value, except the limestone which underlies the Vale of Radnor. The mfrs. are very limited, chiefly flannel. The forests, which at one time were of great extent, have long disappeared. There are several medicinal mineral springs, those of Llandrindod being in great repute. None of the rivers (Wye, Elan, Ithon, &c.) are navigable, but the railway communication is good. Radnorshire was made a county by Henry VIII. It comprises 6 hundreds and 60 pars, with part of 1 other. It contains no mun. bor. It is in the dioceses of St David's and Hereford.

Cardigan Bay

A 4°50′   B   4°40′   C   4°30′   D   4°20′   E

1

I R I S H   S E A

52°30′

2

C A R D I G A N   B A Y

(BAE CEREDIGION)

52°20′

3

Aberaeron   Aberarth

Mona

New Quay
Head   Ffos-
New   y-ffin   Llanaeron
New Quay   Quay Bay   Llanere
(Ceinewydd)   Llwyncelyn
Llwyn-onn   Ciliau Aer
Maen-y-   Llaingarreglwyd
Cwmtudu   groes   Gilfachrheda
Cross   Llanarth   Neuadd   Oakford
Nanternis   Inn   Pen-cae   Dihewyd
Ynys-Lochtyn   Caerwedros   Mydroilyn
52°10′   Llwyndafydd
Llangrannog   Blaencelyn   Synod Inn   Caledrhydiau
Pontgarreg   (Post-mawr)
Morfa   Wervil   Plwmp
Pencribach   Grange
Penbryn   Pentregat   Talgarreg   324
Tresaith   Brynhoffnant   Wstrws   311
Parcllyn   Sarnau   Bwlchyfadfa
Aberporth   Capel   Castell
Tan-y-   Cynon   Howell
Cemaes   groes   Glynarthen   Cwrt-newydd   Aber
Head   Gwbert   Ferwig   Blaenannerch   Rhydlewis   Ffostrasol
Tremain   Blaenporth   Betws   Cwmsychbant
Pen-yr-afr   Penparc   Ifan   Falin-Wnda   Hawen   Penrhiw-pâl   Pont-siân   Llanwenog
Cippyn   Noyadd   Penrhiw-pâl   Rhydowen
Pwllygranant   New   Trefawr   Beulah   Troedyraur   Coed-y-bryn   Tre-groes
Town   Pantgwyn   Brongest   Maesllyn   Croes-lan   Pren-gwyn
Tre-Rhys   Abbey   Ponthirwaun   Llangynllo   258
St Dogmaels   Cardigan   Llangoedmor   Capel   Horeb   Capel
Moylgrove   (Llandudoch)   (Aberteifi)   Llandygwydd   Tygwydd   Dewi   Hig
Monington   Llechryd   Aber-banc   Penrhiw-llan
Cilgerran   Llandyfriog   Pontwelly   Maesycrugiau
Glanrhyd   Pen-y-bryn   Castle   Pont Ceri   Teifi Valley   Llanfair-Orllwyn
Cwm   Cilgerran   Manordeifi   Cwm-cou   Railway   Llandysul
Trwyn y   Plysgog   Carreg-wen   Capel   Bangor Teifi   Llanfihangel-ar-arth   Llanfi
Bwa   Clanrhyd   Abercych   Cenarth   Castle   Aber-banc   Llangeler
Tredrissi   Llantood   Penrhiw   Newcastle Emlyn   Pentre-cwrt
Trewilym   Rhos-hill   (Castell Newydd Emlyn)   National   Pentrecagal   Henllan   Drefach
PEMBROKESHIRE   Aber-Arad   Wool Museum
Berry   Newchapel   Clynfyw   Penrherber   Felindre
Hill   Parrog   Nevern   Velindre   Cilwendeg
Newport   Castell
(Trefdraeth)   Henllys

A 4°50′   B   4°40′   C   4°30′   D   4°20′   E

British National Grid projection

Metres
Feet

1000
3280
900
2952
800
2624
700
2296
600
1968
500
1640
400
1312
300
4921
200
656
150
492
100
328
50
164
0
Land
below
sea
level
50
164
200
656
1000
3281

Pembrokeshire Coast Path

Pembrokeshire Coast
National Park

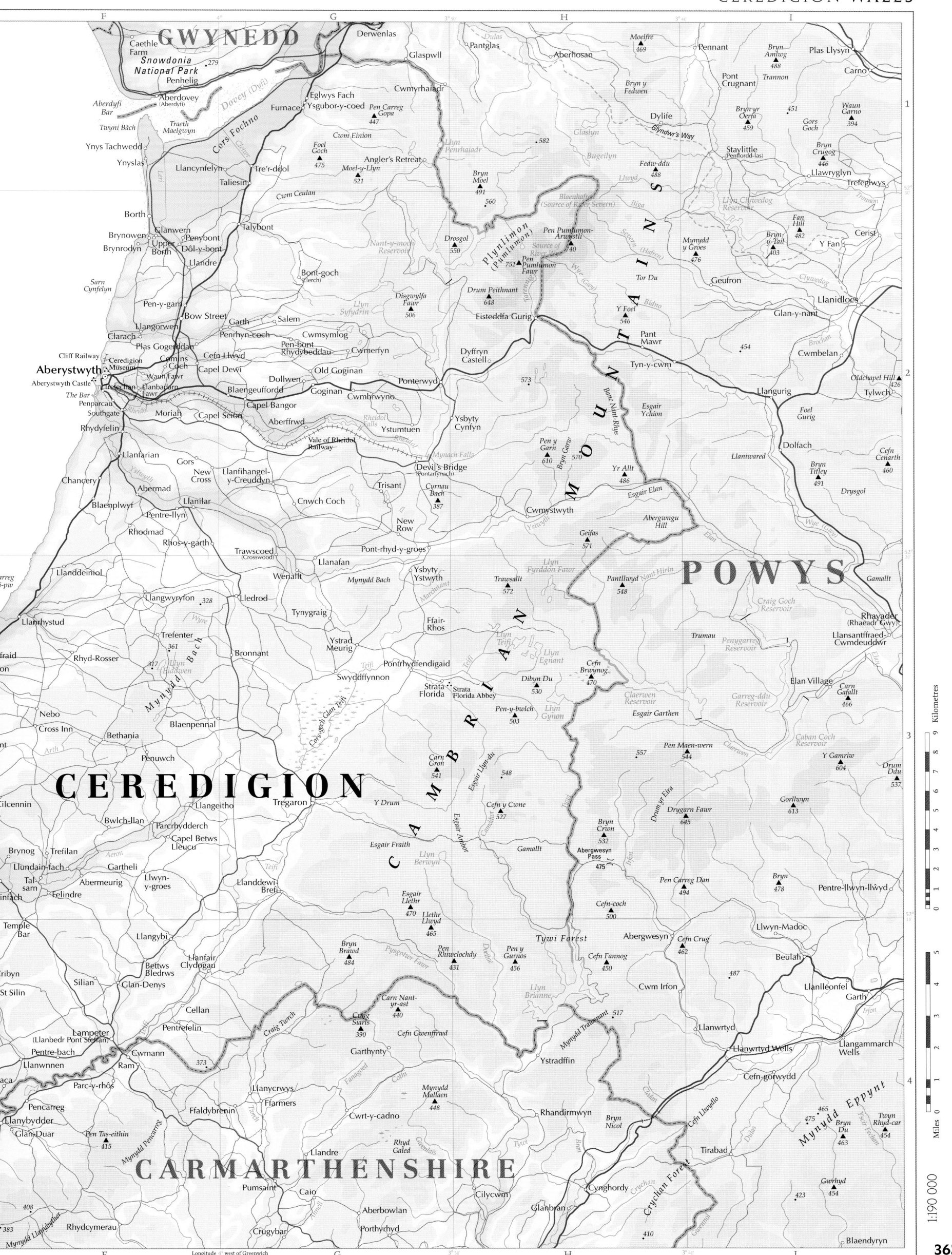

GWYNEDD

Caethle Farm
Snowdonia National Park
Penhelig
Aberdovey (Aberdyfi)
Aberdyfi Bar
Twyni Bâch
Traeth Maelgwyn
Ynys Tachwedd
Ynyslas
Llancynfelyn
Borth
Brynowen
Brynrodyn
Upper Borth
Dôl-y-bont
Llandre
Sarn Cynfelyn
Pen-y-garn
Bow Street
Llangorwen
Clarach
Plas Gogerddan
Cliff Railway
Ceredigion Museum
Aberystwyth
Aberystwyth Castle
Llanbadarn Fawr
The Bar
Penparcau
Southgate
Rhydyfelin
Llanfarian
Chancery
Abermad
Blaenplwyf
Pentre-llyn
Rhodmad
Rhos-y-garth
Llanddeiniol
Llangwyryfon
Llanrhystud
Trefenter
Rhyd-Rosser
Bronnant
Nebo
Cross Inn
Blaenpennal
Bethania
Penuwch
Cilcennin
Llangeitho
Tregaron
Bwlch-llan
Parcrhydderch
Capel Betws Lleucu
Brynog
Trefilan
Llundain-fach
Gartheli
Llwyn-y-groes
Tal-sarn
Abermeurig
Felindre
Temple Bar
Llangybi
Llanddewi-Brefi
Cribyn
Bettws Bledrws
Silian
Glan-Denys
Llanfair Clydogau
Lampeter (Llanbedr Pont Steffan)
Pentre-bach
Llanwnnen
Parc-y-rhôs
Ram
Cwmann
Pencarreg
Llanybydder
Glan-Duar

Derwenlas
Glaspwll
Pantglas
Furnace
Eglwys Fach
Ysgubor-y-coed
Pen Carreg Gopa 447
Cwmyrhaiadr
Aberhosan
Cwm Einion
Foel Goch 475
Angler's Retreat
Moel-y-Llyn 521
Bryn Moel 491
560
Bont-goch (Elerch)
Drosgol 550
Llyn Syfydrin
Disgwylfa Fawr 506
Drum Peithnant 648
Salem
Cwmsymlog
Penrhyn-coch
Pen-bont Rhydybeddau
Cwmerfyn
Capel Dewi
Cefn Llwyd
Dollwen
Old Goginan
Ponterwyd
Comins Coch
Waun Fawr
Goginan
Cwmbrwyno
Capel Bangor
Aberffrwd
Ystumtuen
Ysbyty Cynfyn
Moriah
Capel Seion
Rheidol Falls
Vale of Rheidol Railway
Mynach Falls
Devil's Bridge (Pontarfynach)
New Cross
Llanfihangel-y-Creuddyn
Trisant
Cyrnau Bach 387
New Row
Cnwch Coch
Pont-rhyd-y-groes
Trawscoed (Crosswood)
Llanafan
Wenallt
Mynydd Bach
Ysbyty Ystwyth
Lledrod
Tynygraig
Ffair-Rhos
Ystrad Meurig
Pontrhydfendigaid
Swyddffynnon
Strata Florida
Strata Florida Abbey
Blaenpennal
Y Drum
Esgair Fraith
Esgair Llethr 470
Llethr Llwyd 465
Esgair Llyn-du 548
Carn Gron 541
Cefn y Cwne 527
Esgair Ambor
Pen Rhiwclochdy 431
Bryn Brawd 484
Cefn Gwenffrwd
Pen y Gurnos 456
Carn Nant-yr-ast 440
Craig Starli 390
Craig Twrch
Pentrefelin
Cellan
Llanycrwys
Ffarmers
Cwrt-y-cadno
Llandre
Pumsaint
Caio
Aberbowlan
Crugybar
Mynydd Mallaen 448
Rhyd Galed
Garthynty

Moelfre 469
Aberhosan
Pennant
Bryn Amlwg 488
Plas Llysyn
Carno
Pont Crugnant
Trannon
Bryn y Fedwen
Dylife
Blynwr's Way
Bryn yr Oerfa 459
451
Waun Garno 394
Gors Goch
Staylittle (Penffordd-las)
Bryn Crugog 446
Llawryglyn
Trefeglwys
Fedw-ddu 488
Fan Hill 482
Bryn-y-Tail 403
Cerist
Y Fan
Pen Pumlumon-Arwystli 740
Mynydd y Groes 476
Geufron
Llanidloes
Glan-y-nant
Pen Pumlumon Fawr 752
Tor Du
Y Foel 546
Pant Mawr
Cwmbelan
Eisteddfa Gurig
Tyn-y-cwm
454
Oldchapel Hill 426
Llangurig
Tylwch
Esgair Ychion
Foel Gurig
Dolfach
Dyffryn Castell
573
Cefn Cenarth 460
Bryn Titley 491
Drysgol
Pen y Garn 610
Bryn Caru 570
Yr Allt 486
Llaniwared
Abergwngu Hill
Esgair Elan
Geifas 571
Gamallt
Cwmystwyth
Trawsallt 572
Pantllwyd 548
Craig Goch Reservoir
Rhayader (Rhaeadr Gwy)
Llansantffraed-Cwmdeuddwr
Elan Village
Carn Gafallt 466
Trumau
Penygarreg Reservoir
Dibyn Du 530
Cefn Brwynog 532
Pen-y-bwlch 503
Llyn Egnant
Llyn Gynon
Esgair Garthen
Claerwen Reservoir
Caban Coch Reservoir
557
Pen Maen-wern 544
Drum yr Eira
Y Gamriw 604
Drum Ddu 537
548
Drygarn Fawr 645
Gorllwyn 613
Gamallt
Bryn Crwn 532
Abergwesyn Pass 475
Pen Carreg Dan 494
Bryn 478
Pentre-llwyn-llwyd
Cefn-coch 500
Tywi Forest
Abergwesyn
Cefn Crug 462
Llwyn-Madoc
Cefn Fannog 450
487
Beulah
Cwm Irfon
Llanllèonfel
Garth
Llanwrtyd
Llanwrtyd Wells
Llangammarch Wells
Mynydd Trawsnant
517
Bryn Nicol
Ystradffin
Rhandirmwyn
Cefn Llwydlo
Tirabad
Gwrhyd 454
Mynydd Eppynt
465
475
Bryn Du 463
Twyn Rhyd-car 454
Cynghordy
Glanbran
Crychan Forest
410
Blaendyryn
Cilycwm
Porthyrhyd

POWYS

CAMBRIAN MOUNTAINS

CEREDIGION

CARMARTHENSHIRE

Kilometres
0 1 2 3 4 5 6 7 8 9
Miles
0 1 2 3 4 5

POWYS

Area Sq Km	5,196
Area Sq Miles	2,006
Population	132,600
County town	Llandrindod Wells
Highest point	Pen y Fan (886 m)

Powys stems from the corruption of *pagus* or *pagensis*, a Latin word referring to a province or district, the implication being that the area was a hinterland not necessarily defended by forts.

FAMOUS FOR

A section of Offa's Dyke, built in the 8th century to defend the western boundary of the Mercian kingdom from incursions from the strong Welsh kingdoms to the west, runs north near **Knighton** in Powys.

The **red kite** in Wales was reduced to only 2 breeding pairs in the 1930s, but now there are over 100 pairs in Powys alone, and the raptor is especially strong north of the Brecon Beacons and west of the River Wye.

Hay-on-Wye has become famous as a 'book town' with over 30 second-hand and antiquarian bookshops. The Hay Festival has been held annually since 1988, and is now the largest literary event of its kind in the world.

In 1973 a disused slate quarry near **Machynlleth** was turned into the Centre for Alternative Technology, originally an ecologically aware community experimenting with new technologies and ideas and now a recognized European eco-centre.

FAMOUS PEOPLE

Owain Glyndwr, Welsh prince, leader of last Welsh uprising against English rule, born in Montgomeryshire, *c.*1354.
Hugh Price, lawyer and a founder of Jesus College, Oxford, born Brecon, *c.*1495.
Henry Vaughan, poet, born Newton-on-Usk, 1621
John Lloyd, saint, Catholic priest, born Brecon, *c.*1630.
Sarah Siddons (*born* Sarah Kemble), actress, born Brecon, 1755.
Robert Owen, social reformer, born Newtown, 1771.
Charles Kemble, actor, theatre manager and playwright, born Brecon, 1775.
Richard Roberts, mechanical engineer and machine tool inventor, born Llanymynech, 1789.
Sir George Everest, Surveyor-General of India, born Crickhowell, 1790.
John Evan Thomas, sculptor, born Brecon, 1810.
Hilda Campbell Vaughan, Welsh novelist, born Builth Wells, 1892.

"The general appearance of the county [Montgomeryshire] is mountainous and somewhat dreary, a large portion consisting of moorlands, and the houses are comparatively few and widely separated. There are many fertile spots in the valleys, more especially on the English border, which make up for the barrenness of other parts. The climate is certainly healthy, though considered bleak."
The National Gazetteer, 1868

"The general aspect of this county [Radnorshire] is mountainous, bleak, and dreary, with the exception of the south-eastern districts, which are comparatively level, and producing good crops of corn."
The National Gazetteer, 1868

Powys, with a long border with England, is the largest county by area in Wales. In the south it extends to the Brecon Beacons, where Pen y Fan (886 m) is the highest point. The remainder of the country is predominantly rugged uplands, particularly in the west, which include the Cambrian Mountains, with broad, fertile valleys, especially where the Severn and Wye run roughly on an east–west alignment. The river Usk runs though the southeastern section of the county, and the river Dyfi in the northwest.

Powys was originally created as one of the eight new Welsh authorities in 1974 by combining the traditional counties of Montgomeryshire, Radnorshire, most of Breconshire (the remnants being divided between Merthyr Tydfil and Gwent). Attempts to reconstitute the three original counties as part of the further local government reorganization in 1996 failed. Its population of 132,600 has been rising steadily since 1981. Llandrindod Wells (5,024), situated almost in the middle of the county, is the administrative centre. Other important towns include Newtown (10,358), Brecon (7,901), Welshpool (5,539), Llanidloes (2,807), Crickhowell (2,011), Knighton (2,743), Builth Wells (2,640) and Machynlleth (2,147).

Llandrindod Wells is a very ancient place. The Romans built a fort, Castell Collen, to the northwest of the modern town. Llandrindod appears in the records by the late 13th century as Lando (a corruption of 'Llanddw'), although by 1535 it was no longer the 'Church of God', but the 'Church of the Holy Trinity' (*llan + trindod*). The local chalybeate springs were discovered in 1696, and began to be exploited for their medicinal properties around this time, but it was only in the 19th century, and the coming of the railway, that the town became a spa, and later something of a magnet along the Welsh 'hippy trail'.

The ancient kingdom of Powys was the dominant power in this eastern part of Wales until the 12th century. The development of the Norman lordships along the Welsh border after 1066, and the creation of the 'Welsh March' set the tone for the close, and often uneasy, relationship with neighbouring England. Geography dictated then, as it does today, that communication was easier to the east than to either north or south. Linguistically, the fewest Welsh speakers are still to be found in the east along the English border, and more Welsh is spoken in the northwest and southwest.

Powys has always been primarily an agricultural county, known for its cattle and sheep, and the woollen industry that flourished in the 18th and 19th centuries. This is not to say that the Industrial Revolution had no impact. Lead mining in Montgomeryshire has had a long history, and along the extreme southern fringes of the south Wales coalfields, iron was smelted and coal mined. The Montgomeryshire Canal was designed in the 18th century to service a more rural area, carrying lime to the upper-Severn valley to increase soil fertility, making money for its patrons through increased yields.

Agriculture has contracted in recent times, but remains an important sector of Powys' economy. Welshpool has a large livestock market and is the market town for this northern area. Newtown, south of Welshpool, was designated Wales' second 'new town' in 1967, but its origins are much older. It has a charter dating from 1280, and has links with the Normans, who built a motte and bailey castle southwest of the village. Its situation places it in an enviable position on crossroads heading north–south as well as east–west. Good road links throughout Powys have encouraged tourism, which now accounts for 12 per cent of the area's employment, only slightly behind manufacturing (13 per cent). One famous manufacturer is Laura Ashley – the fabric and clothes company moved from Kent to Carno in 1961 and later to Newtown. Unsurprisingly, it is the service industries that are the main employers, particularly public administration, education and health (33 per cent).

Red Kite conservation is a mid-Wales success story.

The Monmouthshire and Brecon Canal in the Brecon Beacons National Park.

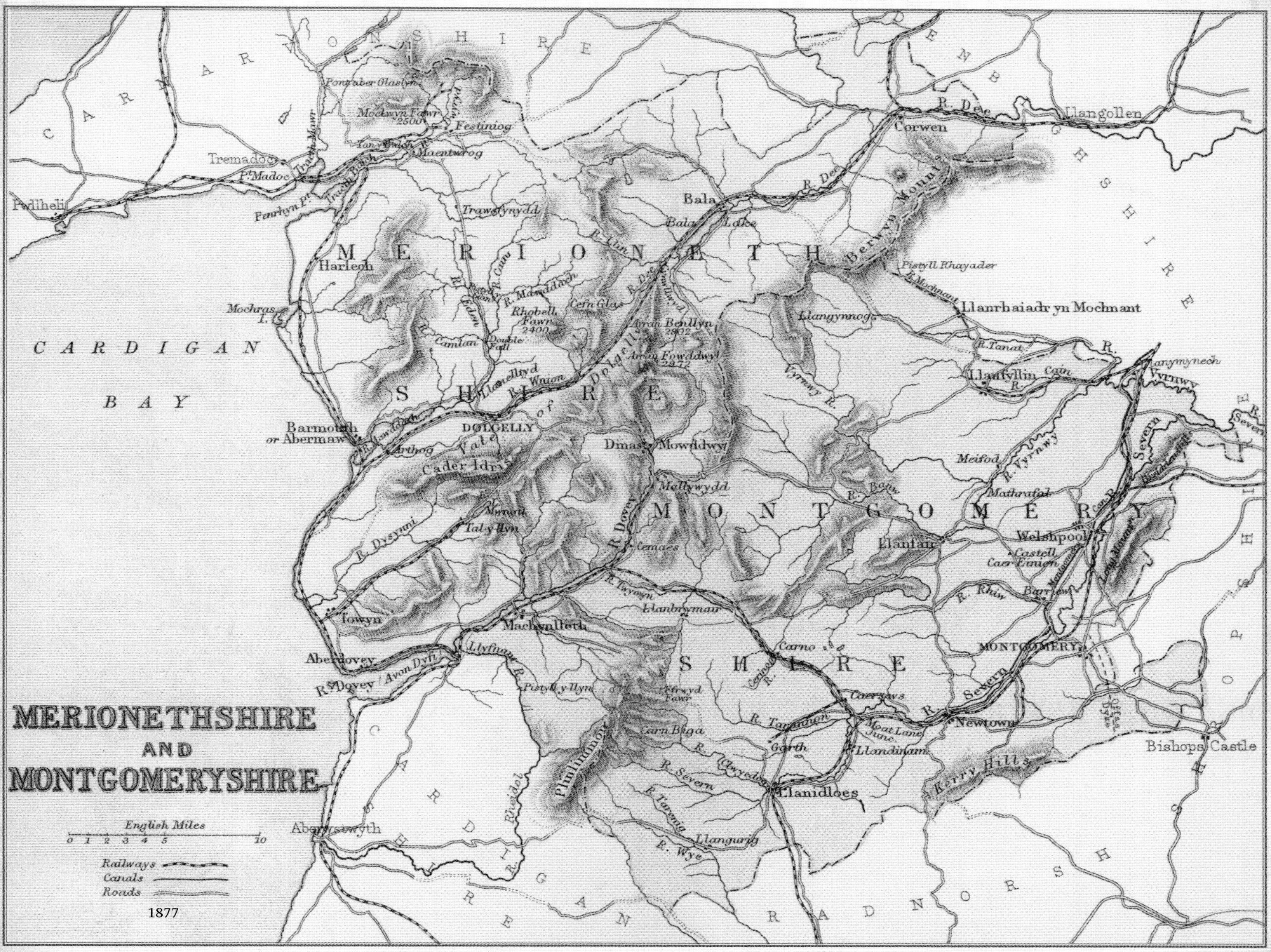

MERIONETHSHIRE
AND
MONTGOMERYSHIRE

English Miles
0 1 2 3 4 5   10

Railways
Canals
Roads

1877

CARDIGAN BAY

Bartholomew Gazetteer of the British Isles, 1887

MERIONETH, *maritime co., N. Wales, bounded N. by Carnarvonshire and Denbighshire, SE. by Denbighshire, Montgomeryshire, and Cardiganshire, and W. by Cardigan Bay; greatest length, NE. to SW., 45 miles; greatest breadth, NW. to SE., 30 miles; area, 384,717 ac., pop. 52,038. The coast-line is alternately cliffs and stretches of sand, and the co. generally is the most mountainous in Wales, although some of the mountains of Carnarvonshire rise to greater elevations. Merioneth abounds in wild and romantic mountain scenery, beautiful and fertile valleys, and fine views of sea and lake and river. The greatest heights are Aran Mowddwy (2970 ft.) and Cader Idris (2929 ft.). The chief rivers are the Dee, the Mawddach, and the Dovey. Waterfalls and small lakes are numerous, the largest of the latter being Bala Lake (4 miles long and 1 mile broad). Having generally a poor soil, with large stretches of moor quite*

beyond a profitable cultivation, Merioneth does not appear as a successful agricultural co., except in the valleys, where there are many fertile tracts. Reclamation of land has been successful in some parts of the co. Mfrs. are insignificant, excepting woollen and flannel goods, which are made chiefly at Dolgelly. Considerable quantities of slate and limestone are quarried, and there is a fair output of lead and copper. Some years ago gold was found to some extent, but the workings proving unprofitable were stopped. Merioneth contains 5 hundreds, 33 pars, and parts of 4 others, and the towns or vils. of Aberdovey, Bala, Barmouth, Corwen, Dolgelly, Festiniog, and Harlech. It contains no mun. boroughs. It is in the dioceses of Bangor and St Asaph.

MONTGOMERYSHIRE, *inland county of North Wales, bounded N. by Denbighshire, E. and SE. by Shropshire, S. by Radnorshire, SW. by Cardiganshire, and W. and*

NW. by Merioneth; greatest length, 37 miles; greatest breadth, 30 miles; area, 495,089 ac., pop. 65,718. Montgomeryshire is almost wholly mountainous and bare, but on the Shropshire side there are some fertile and beautiful valleys. The principal rivers are the Severn (with its affluents the Vyrnwy, Tanat, and Rhiw) and the Dovey. Excellent harvests of wheat, oats, barley, &c., are gathered in the valleys; but in the higher districts the soil is poor, consisting mostly of moorland and sheep-walks. A superior breed of sheep is raised, also the fine description of Welsh ponies known as "Merlins." The principal mineral product is slate. Welsh flannel is the staple mfr. Montgomeryshire contains 9 hundreds, 68 pars, with parts of 3 others, and the mun. bors. of Llanidloes and Welshpool. It is in the dioceses of Bangor, Hereford, and St Asaph.

The Brecon Beacons National Park.

British National Grid projection

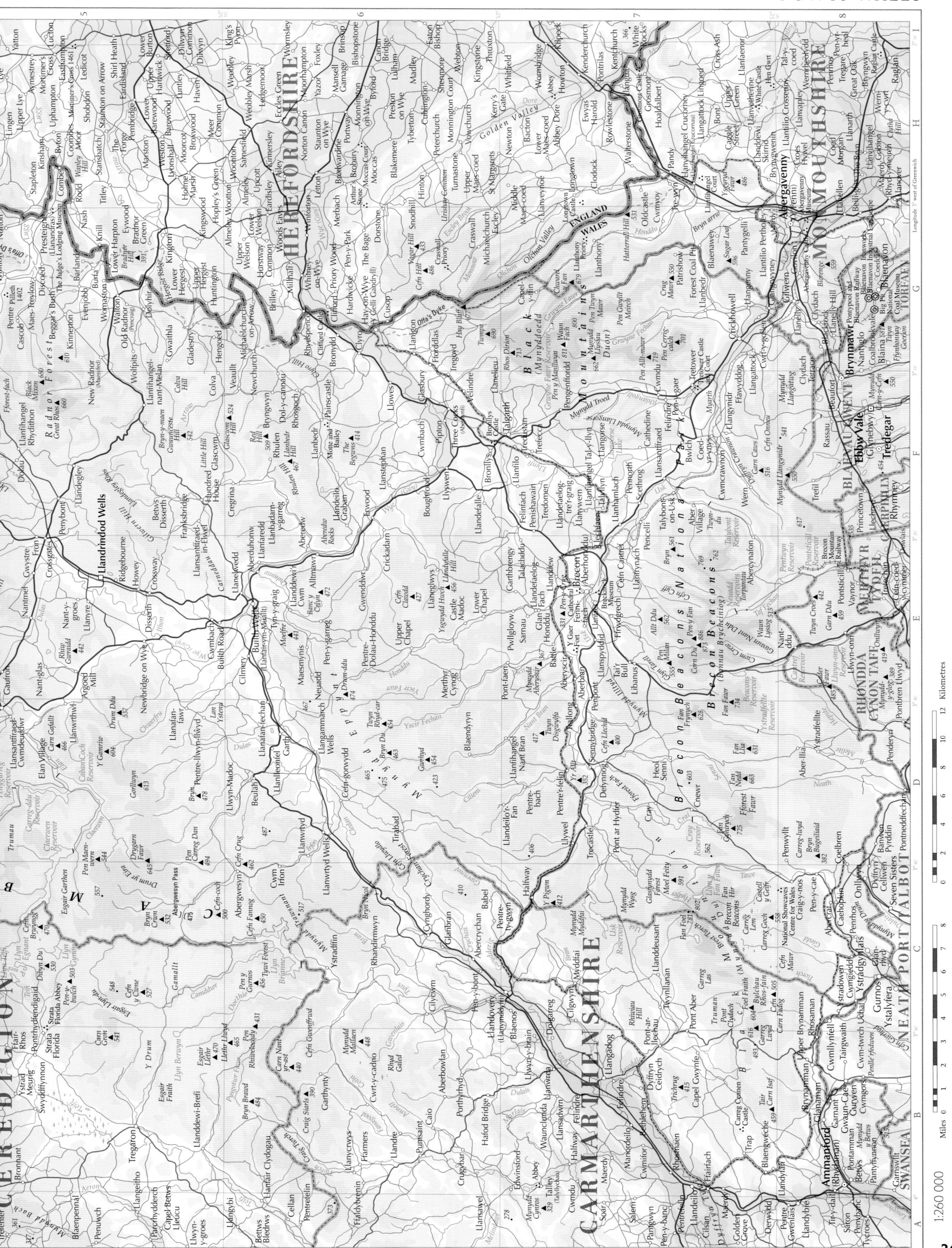

1:260 000

Miles 0 1 2 3 4 5 6 7 8

0 2 4 6 8 10 12 Kilometres

© Collins Bartholomew Ltd

GWYNEDD

Area Sq Km	2,622
Area Sq Miles	1,013
Population	118,200
County town	Caernarfon
Highest point	Snowdon (1,085 m)

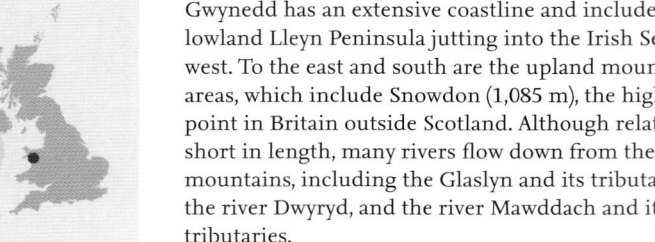

Gwynedd takes its name from the Venedoti tribe, and was the 'territory of the Venedoti'.

FAMOUS FOR
Since Edward I was unable to subdue the mountainous interior of the kingdom of Gwynedd, he set about ringing it with castles, **Caernarfon** and **Harlech** among them.

The well-known song, *Men of Harlech*, commemorating a 15th-century siege, is not only the regimental march of troops associated with the country, but it is said to have been Kaiser Wilhelm II's favourite marching tune.

Bangor University first opened in 1884 in the Penrhyn Arms, an old coaching inn. The funds that supported it were partly raised through subscription by local farmers and quarrymen from their wages.

Portmeirion is a bit of Italy built on the river Dwyryd estuary and designed by Sir Clough Williams-Ellis between 1925 and 1975. Most famously, it served as the set for the Village in the television series *The Prisoner*, as well as the set of other movies.

FAMOUS PEOPLE
Edward II, King of England, born Caernarfon Castle, 1284.
John Jones, regicide, born Llanbedr, *c.* 1597.
Edward Jones 'Bardd y Brenin', harpist and music antiquary, born Llandderfel, 1752.
Robert Foulkes, clergyman and murderer, born Mallwyd, *c.*1634.
Betsi Cadwaladr, nursing pioneer in Crimean War, born Bala, 1789
Sir William Henry Preece, electrical engineer and administrator, born Bryn Helen, Caernarfon, 1834.
Lewis Jones, writer and settler in Patagonia, born Caernarfon, 1837.
Sir Ifor Williams, literary scholar, born Tregarth. Bangor, 1881.
Thomas Edward (TE) Lawrence, soldier and writer, born Tremadoc, 1888.
Christopher Timothy, actor, born Bala, 1940.
Bryn Terfel Jones, bass-baritone opera singer, born Pant Glas, 1965.
Aled Jones, singer and broadcaster, born Bangor, 1970.

"The aspect of the county is for the most part wild and mountainous, and its scenery throughout remarkably various and striking."
Samuel Lewis, 1849

"The beach here [Pwllheli] is admirably adapted for bathing, consisting of fine hard sand, and the respectability of the neighbourhood augments the attraction to bathers."
Tallis's *Topographical Dictionary of England and Wales*, 1860

Gwynedd has an extensive coastline and includes the lowland Lleyn Peninsula jutting into the Irish Sea in the west. To the east and south are the upland mountainous areas, which include Snowdon (1,085 m), the highest point in Britain outside Scotland. Although relatively short in length, many rivers flow down from these high mountains, including the Glaslyn and its tributaries, the river Dwyryd, and the river Mawddach and its tributaries.

Modern Gwynedd, first established in 1975, combined the ancient counties of Anglesey and Caernarfonshire with almost the whole of Merioneth plus Aberconwy in the northeast, divided into five districts. Further local government reorganization in 1996 divested the new authority of both Anglesey (now a county) and Aberconwy (which became part of Conwy). One of the first acts of the new county was to change its name from the unwieldy 'Caernarfonshire and Merionethshire' to Gwynedd. The county has a population of 118,200, a slow but steady rise since 1981. Caernarfon is the administrative centre (9,726) but Bangor is the largest town (15,280). Other important settlements include Bethesda (4,515), Blaenau Ffestiniog (3,961), Pwllheli (3,861), Tywyn (3,085) and Porthmadog (3,008).

Caernarfon's history stretches back at least to the Roman fort, *Segontium*, constructed here in AD 84, and much rebuilt in intervening centuries before being abandoned for a site about 1 km east. It was here that the original Norman castle, and then the huge bulk of Edward I's fortress rose to dominate the surrounding countryside. The town that grew around the castle was initially the seat of the Principality of North Wales, and intended to stamp out the native culture. Much later, it became the county town of Caernarfonshire, and ironically, in 2001, it was one of the most Welsh of towns: over 90 per cent of the inhabitants have some knowledge of the language. Caernarfon's modern heyday was in the first half of the 19th century, when the town became a major port for slate export. The railways soon followed, and at one time four separate newspaper titles were published here, three in Welsh and one in English.

Long the stronghold of the Princes of Gwynedd, an only incorporated into the medieval English state in th 13th century, this part of Wales has a higher proportion of Welsh-speakers than any other county. The upland nature of the landscape, its many small lakes, and the wetness of the climate militate against arable farming. Beef and dairy herds, especially the famous Welsh blac cattle are found in the lowland areas, with sheep in the upland pasturage. Traditionally, a significant industry in this area was slate quarrying, Penrhyn and Dinorwic being the largest of dozens of operations. The expansio of the railways and ports along the coasts were directly connected to the demand for high-quality Welsh slate. Inevitably, alternative materials, requiring less detailed finishing, replaced slate but the Penrhyn quarry continues in operation. Mineral mining, especially for copper and lead, was once carried out here, and gold is still mined at Dolgellau.

Snowdonia National Park, founded in 1951 was the third national park to be formed in Britain. In addition to 60 km of coastline, it covers 2,170 sq km of mainly mountainous terrain, mostly within Gwynedd. Although geographically located in the centre, Blaenau Ffestiniog was excluded from the park in the hopes tha employment from light industries would replace the town's slate mining industry. The Coed y Brenin Forest Park is also part of the national park.

Gwynedd's manufacturing base has shrunk and now provides fewer than 8 per cent of jobs. The county is more heavily dependent on the service sector and tourism than the Welsh average. Over 37 per cent of jobs are in public administration, education and health, while tourism provides 12 per cent of jobs. The attraction of the area for visitors helps to explain why the issue of second homes or holiday residences has been such a contentious subject. In Gwynedd in the 1990s, 33 per cent of the housing in Pwllheli and 37 per cent in Llanegan on the Lleyn Peninsula were holiday homes. In the 1980s there were arson attacks on holiday homes carried out by 'Meibion Glyndŵr' as well as othe nationalist groups.

Snowdonia National Park

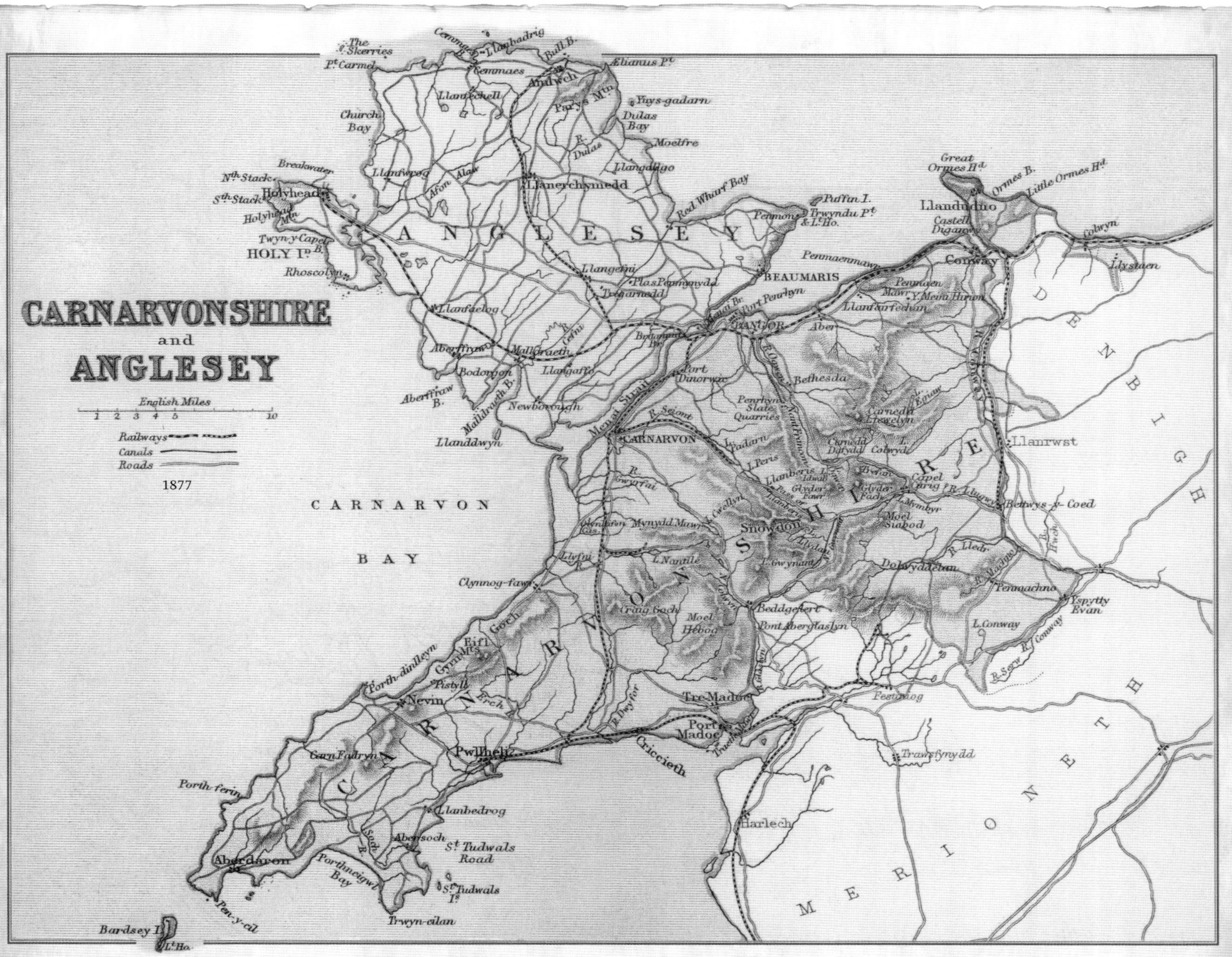

CARNARVONSHIRE and ANGLESEY

English Miles

1 2 3 4 5   10

Railways
Canals
Roads

1877

Bartholomew Gazetteer of the British Isles, 1887

CARNARVONSHIRE, *a maritime co. of North Wales, having the Irish Sea on the N., Denbighshire on the E., Merioneth and Cardigan Bay on the S., and on the W. Carnarvon Bay and the Menai Strait, which separates it from Anglesey; extreme length, NE. and SW., 53 miles; extreme breadth, NW. and SE., 23 miles; average breadth, 9 miles; coast-line, 95 miles; area, 369,477 ac.; pop. 119,349. The surface is grandly mountainous. About the centre of the co. rises Snowdon (3571 ft.), the loftiest mountain in Wales and England. Several other summits are from 1500 to 3000 ft. high. There are fine sea-views along the N. coast, while the interior abounds in grand lake and mountain scenery. A bleak upland peninsula extends from the Snowdon group about 20 miles to the SW., terminating in the prom. of Braich-y-Pwll, off which is Bardsey island. The river Conway flows N. along the E. boundary. The soil in the valleys and along the N. and S. coasts is productive of good crops of oats and barley. Slate is extensively quarried at Penrhyn, Llanberis, and Bethesda. The co. comprises 10 hundreds, 74 pars., with part of 1 other, and the mun. bors. of Carnarvon, Conway, and Pwllheli. It is in the dioceses of St Asaph and Bangor.*

ANGLESEY. *– an insular co. of N. Wales, separated from the mainland by the Menai Strait, over which a suspension bridge was thrown in 1826, and a tubular railway bridge in 1850. The island is about 20 miles long, 16 broad, and 76 in circumference, and is the only co. in Wales that is not mountainous. Area, 193,511 acres; pop. 51,416. The soil is moderately fertile. The rearing of cattle is one of the chief occupations. A considerable trade is also carried on in butter, cheese, hides, honey, wax, and tallow. It contains valuable minerals, and furnishes copper, lead, silver, marble, limestone, coal, and marl. The chief copper mines are at Parys. There are no important mfrs. The Chester and Holyhead Ry., a part of the main route between London and Dublin, traverses the S. of the co. for 23 miles. The distance from Holyhead to Dublin is about 60 miles. Anglesey is generally believed to have been the chief seat of the Druids of the ancient Britons. It was called Mona by the Romans, and Anglesey, or Angle's Eye (that is, island) by the Saxons. Anglesey comprises 6 hundreds, 77 pars., the mun. bor. of Beaumaris, and the towns of Amlwch, Holyhead, and Llangefni. It is in the diocese of Bangor.*

aernarfon Castle viewed across the river Seiont.

The Snowdon Mountain Railway.

ANGLESEY

Area Sq Km	749
Area Sq Miles	289
Population	69,000
County town	Llangefni
Highest point	Holyhead Mountain (220 m)

The Welsh name for the island is *Ynys Môn* derived from British *enisis mona*; the Romans called it *Mona*. The English name, Anglesey is from the Old Norse, from a personal name plus *ey* (island) meaning 'Ongull's Island'.

FAMOUS FOR

South Stack Lighthouse, completed in 1809, was built to protect shipping along the lucrative but dangerous route between Dublin and Liverpool, and was the first light visible along the Anglesey coast for eastbound shipping.

Llanfairpwllgwyngyll, which means St Mary's Church only became well known in the 1860s when its name was deliberately expanded to a total of fifty-eight letters (Llanfairpwllgwyngyllgogerychwyrndrob-wllllantysiliogogogoch) in order that it should be the longest name of a railway station in Britain.

FAMOUS PEOPLE

Robert ap Huw, harpist and manuscript compiler, born Penmynydd, *c.*1580.
Lewes Roberts, merchant and author, born Beaumaris, 1596.
Richard Llwyd, poet born Beaumaris, 1752.
Hugh Owen Thomas, orthopaedic surgeon, born Bodedern, 1834.
Anthony George Lyster, civil engineer, born Porth y Felin, Holyhead, 1852.
Francis Dodd, artist and printmaker, born Holyhead, 1874.
Cledwyn Hughes, Baron Cledwyn of Penrhos, politician, born Holyhead, 1916.
Dawn French, actress and comedienne, born Holyhead, 1957.

"Môn, mam Cymru." (Môn, the mother of Wales.)
Giraldus Cambrensis

"The general aspect and scenery of the island [Anglesey] are uninteresting. It is the only county in Wales that is not mountainous. The surface, which was once covered with forests, is now bare, and it is only along the coast of the Menai Strait, that the scenery becomes pleasing and beautiful."
The National Gazetteer, 1868

Anglesey is separated from the Welsh mainland by the narrow Menai Strait. There are, in fact, two islands: Anglesey and Holy Island, on which is found Holyhead Mountain (220 m), the highest point in an unusually low-lying Welsh landscape. Once part of the ancient Principality of North Wales, by 1975, Anglesey was one of four districts in the newly formed county, Gwynedd. In 1996, the island re-emerged as a county in its own right with a population of 69,000 that has barely altered since 1981. The administrative centre is at Llangefni (4,404), but the largest town is Holyhead (11,237) on Holy Island. Other towns and villages are dotted around the coast, itself designated an Area of Outstanding Natural Beauty, and include Menai Bridge (4,737) and Llanfairpwllgwyngyll (3,040).

Anglesey was the last refuge of the Druids and is replete with Bronze Age monuments, Roman forts and the great Beaumaris Castle, built by Edward I. Considered the centre of power for the kings of Gwynedd, the two islands were coveted for their fertile farmland. Copper mining began in Parys Mountain near Amlwch around 4,000 years ago, and the mines still have workable deposits of copper, lead and zinc. Llangefni, on the river Cefni, is the principal market town on the island and a centre for light industry. Holyhead is the main port, operating ferry services to Ireland. Parliamentary union between Ireland and Britain in 1801 facilitated better communications by road and rail from London through the port, and road and rail bridges across the Menai Strait opened in the 19th century. More recently attempts to bring industry to this area included an aluminium smelter which opened in 1971 (closed in 2009), and the Wylfa nuclear power station which also became operational in 1971, and is due to be decommissioned starting in 2010. Manufacturing sector jobs account for 15 per cent of the area's employment, but the service sector provides most jobs, particularly in public administration, education and health (28 per cent). The tourism industry provides 10 per cent of jobs.

South Stack Lighthouse at sunset.

The old brickworks at Porth Wen, Bull Bay, Anglesey.

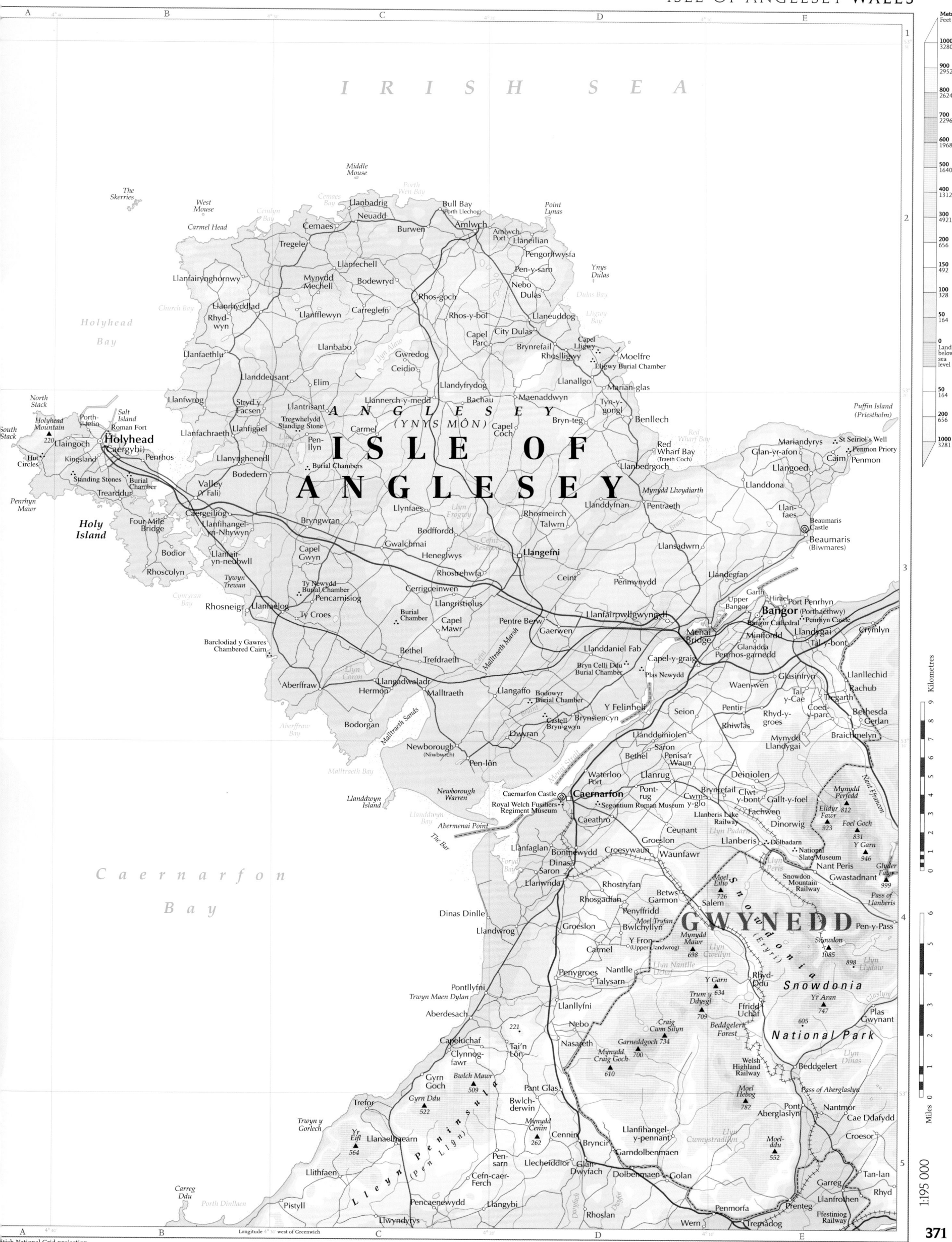

IRISH SEA

Metres Feet
1000 3280
900 2952
800 2624
700 2296
600 1968
500 1640
400 1312
300 4921
200 656
150 492
100 328
50 164
0 Land below sea level
50 164
200 656
1000 3281

The Skerries
West Mouse
Middle Mouse
Porth Wen Bay
Cemaes Bay
Point Lynas
Llanbadrig
Bull Bay (Porth Llechog)
Neuadd
Carmel Head
Cemaes
Amlwch
Amlwch Port
Llaneilian
Tregele
Burwen
Pengorffwysfa
Llanfechell
Pen-y-sarn
Nebo
Mynydd Mechell
Bodewryd
Dulas
Ynys Dulas
Dulas Bay
Rhydwyn
Llanfairynghornwy
Rhos-goch
Holyhead Bay
Llanfflewyn
Carreglefn
Rhos-y-bol
Capel Parc
City Dulas
Llaneuddog
Church Bay
Llanrhyddlad
Capel Llugwy
Ligwy Bay
Brynrefail
Llanbabo
Gwredog
Rhoslligwy
Moelfre
Ceidio
Llanddeusant
Elim
Llandyfrydog
Llanallgo
Ligwy Burial Chamber
Llanfwrog
Llannerch-y-medd
Bachau
Maenaddwyn
Marian-glas
ANGLESEY
(YNYS MÔN)
Carmel
Tyn-y-gongl
Puffin Island (Priestholm)
Styrd y Facsen
Llantrisant
Bryn-teg
Benllech
Tregwhelydd Standing Stone
Penllyn
Capel Coch
North Stack
South Stack
Holyhead Mountain 220
Porth-y-felin
Salt Island Roman Fort
Llaingoch
Holyhead (Caergybi)
Penrhos
ISLE OF ANGLESEY
Red Wharf Bay
Mariandyrys
St Seiriol's Well
Glan-yr-afon
Penmon Priory
Hut Circles
Kingsland
Standing Stones
Llanfachraeth
Llanfigael
Llanynghenedl
Penmon
Caim
Penrhyn Mawr
Treaddur
Burial Chamber
Bodedern
Burial Chambers
Llanbedrgoch
Llangoed
Beaumaris Castle
Beaumaris (Biwmares)
Holy Island
Four Mile Bridge
Caergeiliog
Valley (Y Fali)
Bryngwran
Llynfaes
Mynydd Llwydiarth
Llanddona
Llanfaes
Llanfihangel-yn-Nhywyn
Bodffordd
Rhosmeirch
Talwrn
Rhoscolyn
Llanfair-yn-neubwll
Capel Gwyn
Gwalchmai
Heneglwys
Llangefni
Llansadwrn
Llanddyfnan
Llandegfan
Tywyn Trewan
Ty Newydd Burial Chamber
Pencarnisiog
Rhostrehwfa
Ceint
Penmynydd
Garth
Hirael
Port Penrhyn
Bangor
Cymran Bay
Rhosneigr
Llanfaelog
Ty Croes
Burial Chamber
Cerrigceinwen
Llangristiolus
Pentre Berw
Llanfairpwllgwyngyll
Menai Bridge
Upper Bangor
Bangor Cathedral
Penrhyn Castle
Crymlyn
Barclodiad y Gawres Chambered Cairn
Capel Mawr
Gaerwen
Llanddaniel Fab
Minffordd
Tal-y-bont
Bethel
Trefdraeth
Bryn Celli Ddu Burial Chamber
Capel-y-graig
Glanadda
Penrhos-garnedd
Glasinfryn
Llanllechid
Aberffraw
Hermon
Malltraeth
Llangaffo
Bodowyr Burial Chamber
Plas Newydd
Waen-wen
Tal-y-Cae
Rachub
Tregarth
Bethesda
Ceunan
Aberffraw Bay
Malltraeth Sands
Bodorgan
Y Felinheli
Castell Bryn-gwyn
Brynsiencyn
Pentir
Rhyd-y-groes
Rhiwlas
Coed-y-parc
Braichmelyn
Newborough (Niwbwrch)
Dwyran
Llanddeiniolen
Mynydd Llandygai
Malltraeth Bay
Pen-lôn
Saron
Bethel
Penisa'r Waun
Deiniolen
Llanddwyn Island
Newborough Warren
Caernarfon Castle
Caernarfon
Segontium Roman Museum
Waterloo Port
Llanrug
Pont-rug
Cwm-y-glo
Brynrefail
Clwt-y-bont
Gallt-y-foel
Mynydd Perfedd
Nant Ffrancon
Royal Welch Fusiliers Regiment Museum
Caeathro
Llanberis Lake Railway
Fachwen
Elidir Fawr 812
Foel Goch 831
Llanddwyn Bay
Abermenai Point
The Bar
Bontnewydd
Dinas
Saron
Groeslon
Ceunant
Llanberis
Dinorwig
National Slate Museum
Dolbadarn
Y Garn 946
Nant Peris
Caernarfon Bay
Llanfaglan
Croesywaun
Waunfawr
Llyn Padarn
Gwastadnant
Glyder Fawr 999
Llanwnda
Rhostryfan
Betws Garmon
Salem
Moel Eilio 726
Snowdon Mountain Railway
Pass of Llanberis
Dinas Dinlle
Rhosgadfan
Penyffridd
Moel Trufan
Bwlchyllyn
GWYNEDD
Snowdon 1085
Pen-y-Pass
898
Llyn Llydaw
Llandwrog
Carmel
Y Fron (Upper Llandwrog)
Mynydd Mawr 698
Llyn Cwellyn
Groeslon
Penygroes
Nantlle
Talysarn
Y Garn 633
Rhyd-Ddu
Snowdonia
Yr Aran 747
Plas Gwynant
Pontllyfni
Llanllyfni
Llyn Nantlle Uchaf
Trum y Ddysgl 709
Ffridd Uchaf
605
Trwyn Maen Dylan
Craig Cwm Silyn 734
Beddgelert Forest
Snowdonia
National Park
Aberdesach
221
Nebo
Nasareth
Garneddgoch 700
Welsh Highland Railway
Llyn Dinas
Capelùchaf
Tai'n Lôn
Mynydd Craig Goch 610
Beddgelert
Clynnog-fawr
Bwlch Mawr 509
Pant Glas
Mynydd Cenin 262
Pass of Aberglaslyn
Gyrn Goch
Gyrn Ddu 522
Bwlchderwin
Cennin
Bryncir
Moel Hebog 782
Pont Aberglaslyn
Nantmor
Trefor
Yr Eifl 564
Llanaelhaearn
Pen-sarn
Garndolbenmaen
Cae Ddafydd
Croesor
Trwyn y Gorlech
Llecheiddior
Llanfihangel-y-pennant
Moel-ddu 552
Carreg Ddu
Porth Dinllaen
Llithfaen
Cefn-caer-Ferch
Glan Dwyfach
Dolbenmaen
Penmorfa
Prenteg
Llanfrothen
Rhyd
Pistyll
Llwyndyrys
Pencaenewydd
Llangybi
Rhoslan
Wern
Tremadog
Garreg
Tan-lan
Ffestiniog Railway

Lleyn Peninsula (Pen Llŷn)

Kilometres
Miles
1:195 000

Longitude 4° west of Greenwich

© Collins Bartholomew Ltd

Metres / Feet scale:

Metres	Feet
1000	3280
900	2952
800	2624
700	2296
600	1968
500	1640
400	1312
300	4921
200	656
150	492
100	328
50	164
0	Land below sea level
50	164
200	656
1000	3281

ISLE OF ANGLESEY
(Ynys Môn)

Holy Island
Rhoscolyn
Capel Gwyn
Heneglwys
Llangefni
Llansadwrn
Llandegfan
Port
Penrhyn
Bangor
Bangor Cathedral
Penmynydd
Cerrigceinwen
Llangristiolus
Rhostrehwfa
Ceint
Penmynydd
Trewan
Tywyn
Rhosneigr
Pencarnisiog
Ty Newydd Burial Chamber
Ty Croes
Llanfaelog
Burial Chamber
Capel Mawr
Gaerwen
Llanfairpwllgwyngyll
Menai Bridge (Porthaethwy)
Minffordd
Penrhos-garnedd
Barclodiad y Gawres Chambered Cairn
Aberffraw
Hermon
Bethel
Trefdraeth
Malltraeth
Bryn Celli Ddu Burial Chamber
Plas Newydd
Capel-y-graig
Waen-wen
Glas
Llangadwaladr
Llangaffo
Bodorgan
Burial Chamber
Bodowyr
Castell Bryn-gwyn
Brynsiencyn
Llanddaniel Fab
Llanddeiniolen
Tal-y-C
Rhyd-y-groes
Mynydga
Dwyran
Bryn-gwyn
Saron
Pentir
Rhiwlas
Llandyga
Newborough (Niwbwrch)
Pen-lôn
Waterloo Port
Pont-rug
Llanrug
Penisa'r Waun
Deiniolen
Llanddwyn Island
Caernarfon
Caernarfon Castle
Segontium Roman Museum
Cwm-y-glo
Brynrefail
Llanberis Lake Railway
Fachwen
Newborough Warren
Royal Welch Fusiliers Regiment Museum
Caeathro
Ceunant
Dinorw
Llanberis
Dolbad Castle
Abermenai Point
The Bar
Bontnewydd
Croesywaun
Groeslon
Moel Eilio 726
Nant Gwast
Saron
Dinas
Waunfawr
Snowdon Moun Rails
Llanwnda
Rhostryfan
Betws Garmon
Dinas Dinlle
Moel Tryfan
Penyffridd (Upper Llandwrog)
Mynydd Mawr 698
Llyn Llywelyn
Llandwrog
Groeslon
Carmel
Y Fron
Nantlle
Y Garn 634
Rhyd-Ddu
Ffridd Uchaf
Penygroes
Talysarn
Llanllyfni
Nebo
Trum y Ddysgl 709
Beddgelert Forest
Welsh Highl Railway
Beddg
Pontllyfni
Aberdesach
221
Nasareth
Craig Cwm Silyn 734
Garneddgoch 700
Craig Goch 610
Trwyn Maen Dylan
Capeluchaf
Tai'n Lôn
Clynnog-fawr
Pass of Aberglaslyn
Gyrn Goch
Bwlch Mawr 509
Pant Glas
Moel Hebog 782
Aberglaslyn
Na
Trefor
Gyrn Ddu 522
Bwlch-derwin
Mynydd Cennin 262
Llanfihangel-y-pennant
Carreg Ddu
Porth Dinllaen
Yr Eifl 564
Trwyn y Gorlech
Llanaelhaearn
Bryncir
Garndolbenmaen
Moel-ddu 552
Llyn Cwmystradllyn
Pen-sarn
Cennin
Glan Dwyfach
Llithfaen
Cefn-caer-Ferch
Llecheiddior
Golan
Morfa Nefyn
Nefyn
Pistyll
Llwyndyrys
G W Y
Pencaenewydd
Dolbenmaen
Prentegg
Penmorfa
Pen Y
Tremadog
Carreg Ddu
Garn Boduan
Fron
Llangybi
Rhoslan
Pentrefelin
Wern
Groesffordd
Edern
Tan-y-graig
Y Ffôr
Llanarmon
Gell
Moel-y-Gest 262
Porthmadog
Rhos-y-llan
Ceidio Fawr
Bodfuan
Rhos-fawr
Llanystumdwy
Lloyd George Museum
Chwilog
Borth-y-Gest
Tudweiliog
Hendre
Penarth Fawr Medieval House
Criccieth
Morfa Bychan
Porte
Dinas
Carn Fadryn 371
Llannor
Abererch
Afon Wen
Criccieth Castle
Black Rock Sands
Traeth Bach
Y
Penllech
Garnfadryn
Efailnewydd
Denio
Harlech Point
Bryn-mawr
Sarn Meyllteyrn
Llaniestyn
Rhyd-y-clafdy
Pwllheli
Pen-y-Graig
Llangwnnadl
Nanhoron
Rhedyn
Penrhos
Carreg yr Imbill
Morfa Harlech
Penrhyn Mawr
Bryncroes
Botwnnog
Mynytho
Llanbedrog
Pen-ychain
Tremadog Bay
Harlech Castle
Ty-hen
Rhydlios
Mynydd Rhiw 305
Llandegwning
Trwyn Llanbedrog
Methlem
Plas-yn-Rhiw
Llangian
Abersoch
Y Ganllas
Llandanwg
Porth Oer
Rhoshirwaun
Capel Carmel
Llawr-y-dref
Llanengan
St Tudwal's Road
Pentre Gwy
Braich Anelog
Anelog
Rhiw
Rhydolion
Sarn Bach
Mynydd Anelog 191
Pwlldefaid
Llanfaelrhys
Bwlchtocyn
St Tudwal's Islands
Coed
Braich y Pwll
Aberdaron
Hell's Mouth (Porth Neigwl)
St Tudwal's Islands
Ystumgwen
Llanenddwyn
Dyffryn Burial Chamber
Llanddwyw
Tal-y-bon
Uwchmynydd
Aberdaron Bay
Cilan Uchaf
Porth Ceiriol
Trwyn yr Wylfa
Pen y Cil
Ynys Gwylan-fawr
Trwyn Cilan
Llan
Bardsey Sound (Swnt Enlli)
St Mary's Abbey
Bardsey Island (Ynys Enlli)
Barmout Bay (Bae Bermo)
Fairbourne and Ba R
Llan
CAERNARFON BAY
IRISH SEA
CARDIGAN BAY (BAE CEREDIGION)
Llangelynin
Rhoslefain
Llanfen
Tonfanau
Aber Dysynni
Ty
Aberdy Bay

British National Grid projection

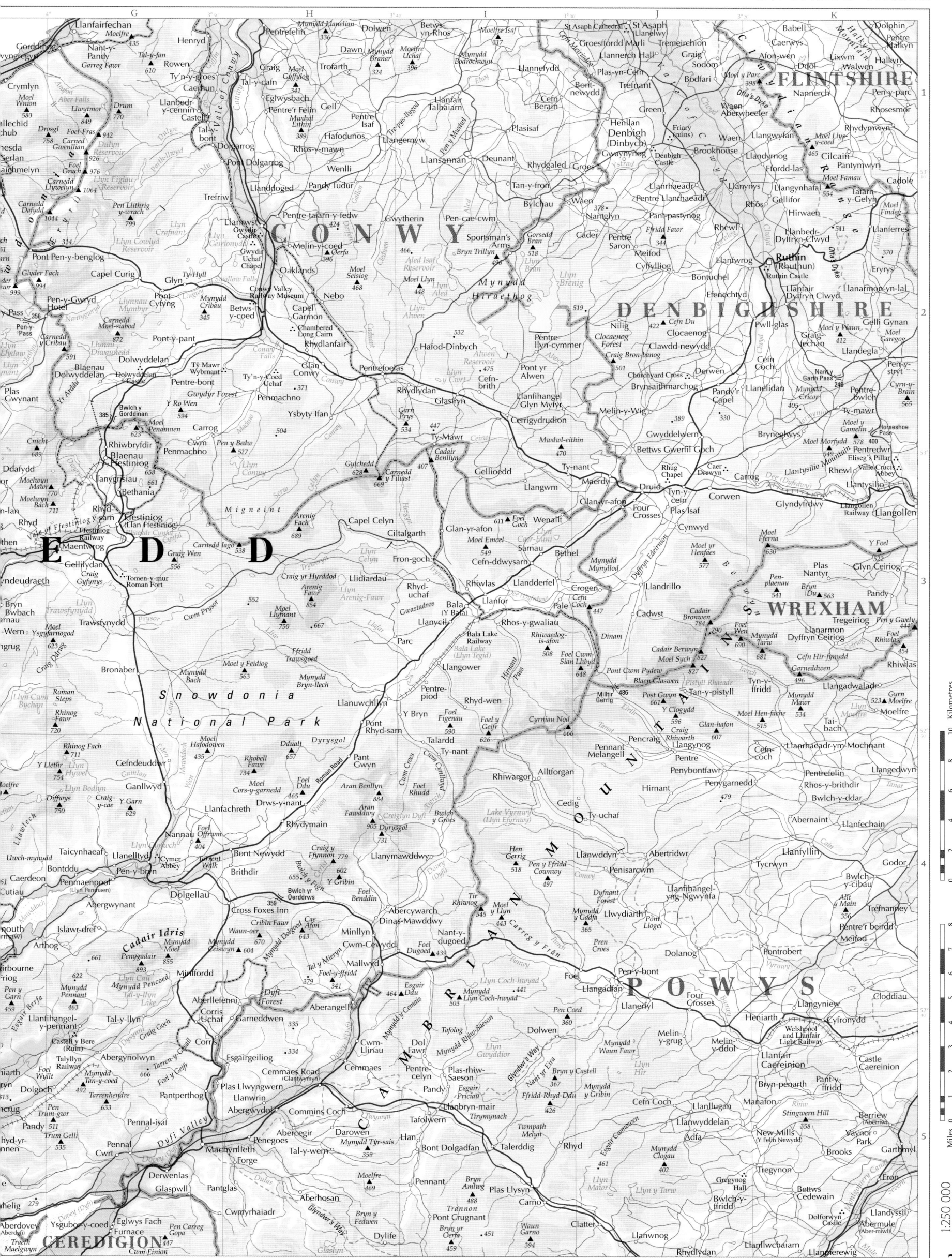

© Collins Bartholomew Ltd

1:250 000

Kilometres

Miles

Longitude 4° west of Greenwich

CONWY

Area Sq Km	1,153
Area Sq Miles	445
Population	112,000
County town	Conwy
Highest point	Carnedd Llewelyn (1,064 m)

The name of the county comes from the eponymous Celtic river name meaning 'reedy one'. It is part of the ceremonial county of Clwyd.

FAMOUS FOR

The stone rabbit checking its watch by the boating pool in **Llandudno** is a reference to *Alice's Adventures in Wonderland*. Henry Liddell, the father of the Alice who was Lewis Carroll's inspiration for the stories, built a holiday home here. The statue was unveiled in 1933 by the Rt. Hon. David Lloyd George.

Thomas Telford's turnpike toll road (now the A5) was the main road from London to Holyhead for stagecoaches going to Ireland. It passed through **Pentrefoelas**, and a plaque records that Queen Victoria stopped here on her way to Ireland.

The medieval merchant's residence of **Aberconwy House** narrowly avoided being dismantled and shipped to the United States when it was bought by the National Trust in 1934.

FAMOUS PEOPLE

John Williams, archbishop of York, born Aberconwy, c.1582.
John Gibson, sculptor, born Gyffin, 1790.
Robert Williams, Celtic scholar and antiquary, born Conwy, 1810.
Llewelyn Wyn Griffith, writer and broadcaster, born Colwyn Bay, 1890.
Hywel David Lewis, theologian and philosopher, born Llandudno, 1910.
Terry Jones, actor and comedian, member of the Monty Python team, born Colwyn Bay, 1942.
Timothy Dalton, actor, born Colwyn Bay, 1946.
Paula Yates, television personality, born Llandudno, 1960.

Conwy is a county borough in northwestern Wales. Its Irish Sea coast includes both spectacular sandy beaches and rugged headlands at Penmaenmawr and the Great Orme at Llandudno. The county is bisected by the river Conwy, still navigable to small craft. To the west rises the mountainous region of Snowdonia, and the location of the area's highest point, Carnedd Llewelyn (1,064 m). The western third of the county lies in the Snowdonia National Park while the eastern areas are mainly moorland and unimproved grasslands.

Local government reorganization in 1996 took the Aberconwy district of Gwynedd and added to it most of the Colwyn district of Clwyd to made the new county borough of Aberconwy and Colwyn, which the new council promptly renamed as Conwy. Its population of 112,00 has risen by around 12 percent since 1981. The administrative centre is in Conwy town (3,847) with some duties shared by the two major seaside resorts of Llandudno (14,872) and Colwyn Bay (30,269).

The majority of remaining population lives in or around the coastal towns of Abergele (17,574), Llanfairfechan (3,653) and Penmaenmawr (2,403) which tend to be Anglocentric, while the inland rural villages, like Llanrwst (3,037) and tiny Llanfair Talhaiarn (980) are home to significant numbers of Welsh speakers.

The town of Conwy's strategic location may have influenced the building of this 'most magnificent' of Edward I's castles simultaneously with its fortified borough, but the area had been settled at least by the 6th century. The coast proved irresistible to the Victorians, with the development of seaside resorts along the coast, well served by railways from northwest England. It is no surprise that tourism is still the main industry in the area, providing employment for almost 17 per cent of the workforce. Public administration, education and health are another vital economic sector in the county (35 per cent) while the services sector as a whole (90 per cent of jobs) is much higher than average.

"This is the poorest but pleasantest town [Conwy] in all this county for the bigness of it; it is seated on the bank of a fine river, which is not only pleasant and beautiful, but is a noble harbour for ships, had they any occasion for them there."
Daniel Defoe, 1725

Bodnant Garden in the Vale of Conwy at Tal-y-cafn.

DENBIGHSHIRE

Area Sq Km	846
Area Sq Miles	327
Population	97,600
County town	Ruthin
Highest point	Cadair Berwyn (827 m) on the border with Powys

Denbigh is from the Welsh *din* and *bach*, meaning 'little fortress', with reference to original fort replaced by the 12th-century castle. It is part of the ceremonial county of Clwyd.

FAMOUS FOR

Archaeologists have found evidence of a Palaeolithic site near **Bont-newydd** including remains of Neanderthals, making Denbighshire the oldest inhabited part of Wales.

The oldest townhouse in Wales, Nantclwyd House, is located in **Ruthin** and was built around 1435. It is one of many houses in the town maintained in the characteristic black and white style.

The international musical Eisteddfod is held annually at **Llangollen**, located on the main route to the mountains of North Wales from England, which also abounds with historical ruins. One of the most unusual is the 9th-century stone cross, Eliseg's Pillar.

FAMOUS PEOPLE

John Jones (bardic name, Talhaiarn), architect and author of the Welsh lyrics to *Men of Harlech*, born Llanfair Talhaearn, 1810.
Sir Henry Morton Stanley (*born* John Rowlands), journalist and explorer, born Denbigh, 1841.
Cyril Radcliffe, Viscount Radcliffe, lawyer and judge, chairman Indian Border Commissions, born Llanychan, 1899.
Sir Huw Weldon, BBC television producer and administrator, born Prestatyn, 1916
Emyr Humphrys, writer, born Prestatyn, 1919.
Ruth Ellis, murderer and last woman to be hanged in Britain, born Rhyl, 1926.
John Prescott, Labour politician, born Prestatyn, 1938.

Denbighshire is situated along the Vale of Clwyd. The land is mainly upland moorland in the west rising to the Clywydian range of hills to the east, with in the far southwest, the Berwyn range. The river Clwyd creates a broad and fertile valley through the centre of the county before flowing into the Irish Sea at Liverpool Bay. The river Dee runs through the south of the county eastward from its headwaters in Snowdonia.

Denbighshire, created in 1536, briefly disappeared from the map when the area was subsumed into Clwyd in 1975. However, the local government reorganization of 1996 combined the districts of Glyndwr, Rhuddlan and part of Colwyn and resurrected the county's name, but in a very different shape. Denbighshire is one of the smaller Welsh counties, but its population of 97,600 has been steadily growing since 1981. The administrative centre is Ruthin (5,218), but the largest town is Rhyl (25,390). Other important towns are Prestatyn (18,496), Denbigh (8,272), Rhuddlan (3,795) and Llangollen (2,930).

Ruthin, in the upper Clwyd valley has an ancient pedigree, and its name reflects the building material of its first forts, red sandstone. It was important enough for Owain Glyndŵr to begin his rebellion here in 1400, by attacking the town and castle. Evidence of human settlement throughout the Vale of Clwyd reaches back to at least the Iron Age, and the Romans are believed to have mined lead here.

Denbighshire's modern economy depends primarily on agriculture, particularly dairying, and tourism. Rhyl, at the mouth of the Clwyd, as well as Prestatyn are well known resorts. Victorian tourists were brought in by rail from Lancashire and the Midlands to enjoy the sandy beaches and the long promenade, pavilions and floral halls. Nowadays, tourism accounts for more than 10 per cent of the workforce. Industrial estates around the towns support a small but healthy manufacturing sector (10 per cent). Unsurprisingly the service sector is the main employer in the county, predominantly in public administration, education and health (45 per cent).

"…descending now from the hills, we came into a most pleasant, fruitful, populous, and delicious vale, full of villages and towns, the fields shining with corn, just ready for the reapers, the meadows green and flowery, and a fine river, with a mild and gentle stream running through it."
Daniel Defoe, 1725

Rhuddlan Castle by the river Clwyd.

FLINTSHIRE

Area Sq Km	489
Area Sq Miles	189
Population	151,000
County town	Mold
Highest point	Moel Famau (554 m) on the border with Denbighshire

Flintshire straightforwardly is named for the predominant stone in the area, and was known as *le Efflynt* or '(place of) hard rock' as early as 1300. It is within the ceremonial county of Clwyd.

FAMOUS FOR

The Mold Cape, now one of the great treasures of the British Museum, is an extraordinary piece of ancient sheet goldwork, fashioned from a single ingot sometime around 1900–1600 BC.

St Deiniol's Library near Hawarden was founded in 1894 by William Gladstone as a residential library with an original donation of 32,000 books. It is the only 'Prime Ministerial' Library in Britain.

The enormous wings for the A380 Airbus built at **Broughton** have to be transported by barge up the River Dee to the Mostyn docks from where they are shipped by sea for assembly in Toulouse.

FAMOUS PEOPLE

John Evans, astrologer and medical practitioner, born Flint, *c*.1594.

Thomas Pennant, naturalist, traveller and writer, born Downing, Holywell, 1726.

John Blackwell, (bardic name Alun), Welsh poet and prose writer, born Mold, 1797.

William Davies, palaeontologist, born Holywell, 1814.

Daniel Owen, Welsh novelist, born Mold, 1836.

George Emlyn Williams, playwright and actor, born Mostyn, 1905.

Jonathan Pryce, actor, born Holywell, 1947.

"Here [Holywell] is a fine chapel … under this chapel the water gushes out in a great stream, and the place where it breaks out, is formed like a basin or cistern, in which they bathe: The water is intensely cold, and indeed there is no great miracle in that point, considering the rocks it flows from, where it is impregnated by divers minerals, the virtue of which, and not of the saint, I suppose, work the greatest part of the cures."
Daniel Defoe, 1725

Flintshire is bounded by the river Dee and its estuary to the northwest and rises to the Clwydian Range to the southeast. The river Alyn, a tributary of the Dee, flows through the southern county.

Modern Flintshire is almost unrecognisable from the 1284 original foundation or even the 1975 restructuring, when it was incorporated into Clwyd. Flintshire reappeared on the map as a result of further local political reorganization in 1996, but was much smaller than the pre-1975 county, including only the districts of Delyn and Alyn and Deeside. The county has a population of 151,000, an increase of 9 per cent since 1981. Mold (9,568) is the administrative centre, but the Shotton/Hawarden conurbation is much bigger (24,751). Buckley (18,268), Connah's Quay (16,526), Flint (11,936) and Holywell (6,983) are the largest towns.

The Romans mined lead here, and the area was once part of the Kingdom of Mercia, which is why many of the placenames are Anglo-Saxon in origin, setting it apart from more western areas of Wales. Mold, the historic county and market town for Flintshire, sits in a small agricultural strip of land sandwiched between industrialized Deeside and Wrexham. Iron and lead were mined here in the 17th century, and the area already enjoyed a reputation for its fire clays for bricks and local pottery. The Industrial Revolution brought shipbuilding and iron and steel manufacturing along the River Dee, powered by coal mined from the north Wales coalfield.

Major manufacturing industries, including aerospace, paper manufacture and the Shotton Steelworks, account for 34 per cent of jobs, with more people employed in the sector significantly outperforming the national average. Only the service sector as a whole provides more employment (59 per cent). It is all a long way from the spring at Holywell, traditionally the place of St Winifred's martyrdom, which gave impetus to the counties first 'tourists'.

Point of Ayr lighthouse in Talacre.

Valle Crucis Abbey, was built in 1201 and dissolved in 1537.

Conwy Castle, built in the 13th century, and the town of Conwy.

WREXHAM

Area Sq Km	504
Area Sq Miles	195
Population	132,900
County town	Wrexham
Highest point	Craig Berwyn (790 m) on the shoulder of Cadair Berwyn in the Berwyn range

The county's name comes from an Old English personal name, *Wryhtel*; *'hamm'* refers to its situation so, rather poetically, 'Wryhtel's water meadow'. It is part of the ceremonial county of Clwyd.

FAMOUS FOR

The **Pontfadog Oak** at approximately 1,500 years old, is said to be the oldest oak tree in Britain, having avoided the axes of Henry II's men in 1165.

The **Bersham Ironworks** produced cannons for the British army during the American War of Independence, as well as cylinders for James Watt's steam engine.

Britain's worst mining accident happened at **Gresford** Colliery, when 266 men died in an underground explosion on 22 September 1934.

One of Britain's newest universities is situated in Wrexham. **Glyndŵr University**, formerly the Northeast Wales Institute of Higher Education, received its charter in 2008.

FAMOUS PEOPLE

George Jeffreys, Baron Jeffreys of Wem, presided over the 'Bloody Assizes' in 1685, born Wrexham, 1645.
Thomas Henry, apothecary and chemist, born Wrexham in 1734.
Philip Yorke, genealogist and writer, born Erddig, Wrexham, 1734.
Robert Waithman, political reformer, born Wrexham in 1764.
Edwin Hughes, 'Balaclava Ned', last survivor (died 1927) of the Charge of the Light Brigade, born Wrexham, 1830.
James Sauvage, baritone singer, born Rhosllanerchrugog in 1849.
John Godfrey Parry-Thomas, engineer and holder of land speed records, born Wrexham, 1884.
Arwel Hughes, conductor and composer, born Rhosllanerchrugog, 1909.
Sir Ewart Jones, chemist, first President of the Royal Society of Chemistry, born Rhostyllen, Wrexham, in 1911.

"Heere is Wrexham to be seene, in the Saxons tongue Writtles-ham, much spoken of for a passing faire towre steeple that the Church hath, and the Musical Organs that be therein."
William Camden, 1610

The County Borough of Wrexham is in the extreme northeast of Wales. The river Dee winds through the country, eventually forming the border with England, in the relatively low-lying and fertile east. In the southwest, the land rises to the Berwyn range near the border with Denbighshire. The river Ceiriog's source is in the Berwyn range, and it flows from the west before joining the river Dee. The Dee and the Clywedog are two other important waterways.

One of the six districts of Clwyd, political reorganization in 1996 combined Wrexham Maelor with four communities of Glyndŵr to which were added Llangollen Rural district in 1998 to form the modern County Borough of Wrexham. Wrexham town (42,576) is by far the largest town and administrative centre. Other important towns include the Brymbo/Gwersyllt conurbation (17,912), Rhosllanerchrugog (13,246), Cefn Mawr (8,098), Coedpoeth (5,783) and Gresford (5,334).

Wrexham first appears in the records in 1161, and developed into a trading centre, but never seems itself to have been of military importance, although a castle was built at Chirk. Early iron works turned this agricultural area into the main commercial centre for the north Wales coalfields during the Industrial Revolution. Ironworks, clay and coal mining formed the backbone of the 19th-century industry in the area, and at Cefn Mawr there were works to extract paraffin oil from local shale.

The late 20th century was a period of decline in the area's fortunes, but enhanced transport links and new industrial estates have successfully transformed the old heavy industrial base to a mainly light and hi-tech one, which includes multinational companies. Manufacturing accounts for 23 per cent of employment in the area while public administration, education and health for 32 per cent. Tourism has received a boost from the granting of UNESCO World Heritage Status in 2009 to the Pontcysyllte Aqueduct and Canal, an 18-km section of canal, with Thomas Telford's showpiece aqueduct, that towers over 38 m above the river Dee.

Chirk Castle was originally the administrative centre for the Marcher Lordship of Chirkland.

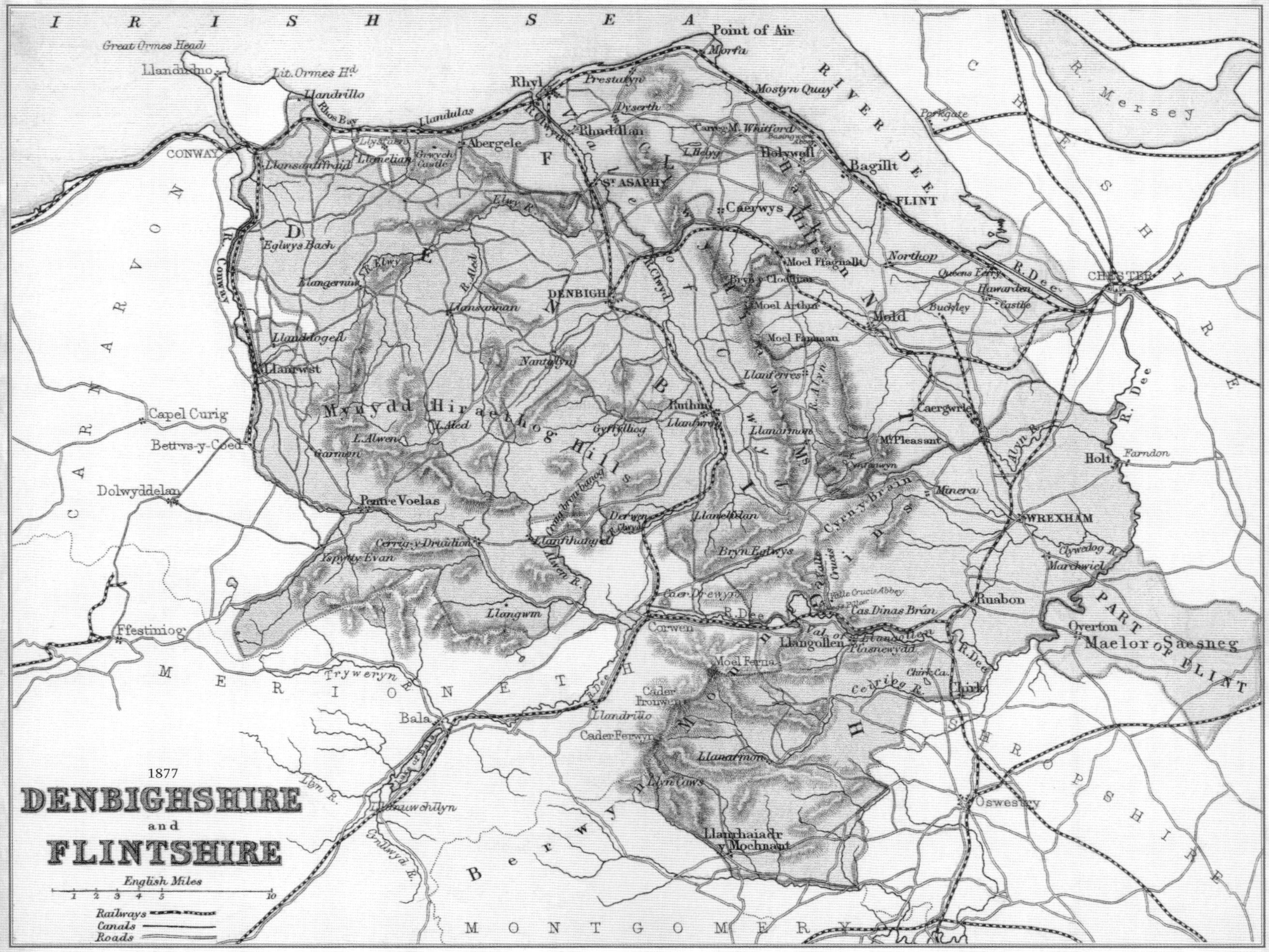

Map labels (Denbighshire and Flintshire):

IRISH SEA
Great Ormes Head
Llandudno
Lit. Ormes Hd.
Llandrillo
Rhos Bay
Llandulas
CONWAY
Llansantffraid
Llanelian
Bryech Castle
Abergele
Rhyl
Prestatyn
Dyserth
Rhuddlan
Point of Air
Morfa
Mostyn Quay
Cwm
M. Whitford
Holywell
Bagillt
FLINT
Parkgate
RIVER DEE
R. Mersey
CHESHIRE
Llangernyw
Eglwys Bach
St ASAPH
Caerwys
Moel Fiagath
Northop
Queens Ferry
Hawarden Castle
Buckley
CHESTER
D
E
Llansannan
DENBIGH
Bryn y Clodian
Moel Arthur
Mold
R. Dee
R. Alod
Llandglogell
Llanrwst
Nantglyn
Moel Fammau
Llanfervis
M. Pleasant
Caergwrle
Holt
Farndon
Capel Curig
Bettws-y-Coed
Mynydd Hiraethog
L. Aled
Ruthin
Llanbedr
Llanarmon
Cyrn-y-Brain
Minera
WREXHAM
Dolwyddelan
L. Alwen
Garnon
Pentre Voelas
Derwen
Llanelidan
Bryn Eglwys
Llansilin
R. Clwyd
Cynwedog R.
Marchwiel
Cerrig-y-Druidion
Ysbyty Evan
Llanfihangel
Caer Drewyn
Valle Crucis Abbey
Cas. Dinas Brân
Ruabon
Overton
Maelor Saesneg
PART OF FLINT
Ffestiniog
Llangwm
Corwen
Llangollen
Chirk Cas.
Chirk
MERIONETH
Tryweryn
Moel Ferna
Cader Ironwen
Cebwr R.
Bala
Llandrillo
Cader Ferwyn
SHROPSHIRE
Llanarmon
Berwyn
Afon Cwm
Oswestry
Llanrhaiadr y Mochnant
MONTGOMERY

1877
DENBIGHSHIRE
and
FLINTSHIRE

English Miles
1 2 3 4 5   10
Railways
Canals
Roads

Bartholomew Gazetteer of the British Isles, 1887

DENBIGHSHIRE, *maritime co. of N. Wales; bounded N. by the Irish Sea, E. by Flintshire, Cheshire, and Shropshire, S. by Montgomeryshire and Merioneth; and W. by Carnarvonshire; length, NW. and SE., 42 miles; breadth, NE. and SW., from 7 to 27 miles; coast-line, about 9 miles; area, 425,038 ac.; pop. 111,740. There is some level ground along the N.; the E. is hilly; and the mountains on the S. and W. rise from 1000 to 2500 ft. high. The principal streams are the Clwyd, Conway, and Dee; their vales are beautiful and fertile. Oats, barley, and rye are grown in the uplands, and wheat in the low grounds of the valleys. Ponies, and small but hardy sheep, are reared on the hills. The mfr. of woollen goods is carried on to some extent, but the chief industry, besides agriculture, is the mining of coal, iron, lead, and slate. The co. comprises (6 hundreds, 90 pars, with parts of 6 others, the Denbigh Boroughs (Denbigh, Holt, Ruthin, and Wrexham), and the mun. bors. of Denbigh, Ruthin, and Wrexham. It is entirely in the diocese of St Asaph.*

FLINTSHIRE, *maritime co. of N. Wales; is bounded N. by the Irish Sea, NE. by the estuary of the Dee, E. by Cheshire, and S. and SW. by Denbighshire; is 26 miles long, and from 10 to 12 miles broad; the detached hundred of Maelor (8 miles to the SE. of the rest of the co., and surrounded by Cheshire, Shropshire, and Denbighshire) is 9 miles long and 5 miles broad; area, 161,807 ac., pop. 80,587. Flintshire is the smallest county of Wales, and, next to Glamorgan, the most populous in proportion to its extent. The coast is generally low, and skirted by sands. A range of hills intersects the county SW. and NE., and there are numerous well-watered and fertile valleys, including a portion of the Vale of Clwyd. Agriculture is advancing. Wheat and oats are grown in the plains and valleys; the uplands afford excellent pasture, and considerable quantities of butter and cheese are made. Flintshire is situated chiefly on the Coal Measures and other members of the Carboniferous rocks group, and is rich in minerals. There are numerous collieries, and the lead mines are the most productive in Britain. Copper, zinc, calamine, and limestone are also worked, and there are some coarse clay potteries. The Chester and Holyhead Ry. runs all along the coast, which is lined by works for coal, iron, copper, lead-smelting, chemicals, shipbuilding, &c. Flintshire comprises 5 hundreds, 37 pars, and parts of 4 others, and the mun. bor. of Flint. It is mostly in the diocese of St Asaph.*

The river Dee flowing through Llangollen, in Denbighshire.

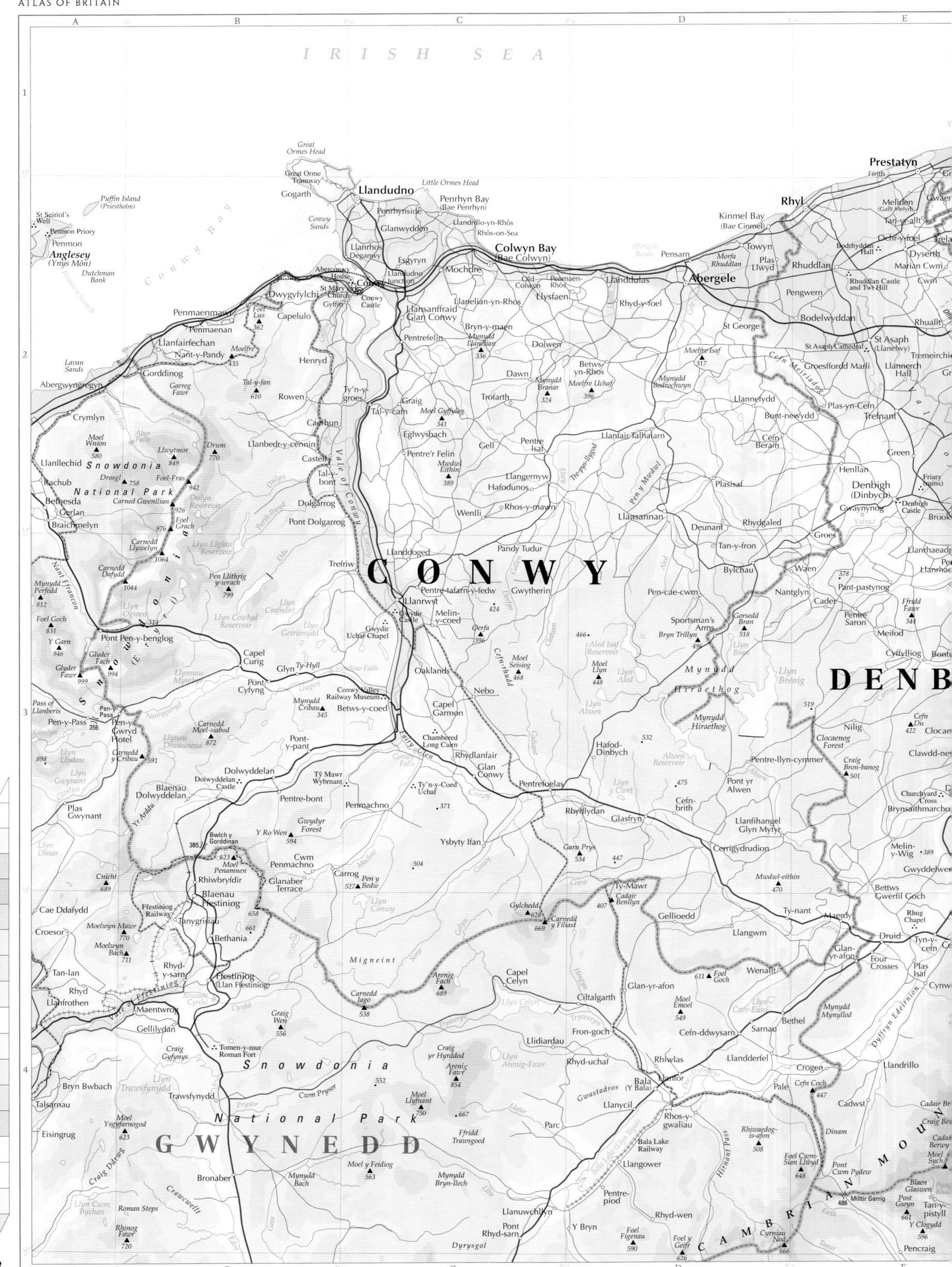

I R I S H   S E A

Great Ormes Head
Great Orme Tramway
Gogarth
Llandudno
Penrhynside
Puffin Island
(Priestholm)
St Seiriol's Well
Penmon Priory
Penmon
Anglesey
(Ynys Môn)
Dutchman Bank
Penmon South
Lavan Sands
Little Ormes Head
Penrhyn Bay
(Bae Penrhyn)
Llandrillo-yn-Rhôs
Rhôs-on-Sea
Conwy Sands
Colwyn Bay
(Bae Colwyn)
Llanrhos
Deganwy
Esgyryn
Mochdre
Old Colwyn
Llanelian-yn-Rhos
Penmaen-Rhôs
Abergele Roads
Pensarn
Rhyl
Kinmel Bay
(Bae Cinmel)
Towyn
Morfa Rhuddlan
Plas Llwyd
Abergele
Llanddulas
Prestatyn
Ffrith
Meliden
(Gallt Melyn)
Tan-yr-allt
Ochr-y-foel
Bodrhyddan Hall
Dyserth
Marian Cwm
Rhuddlan Castle and Twt Hill
Cwm
Rhuddlan
Rhuallt
Bodelwyddan
St George
St Asaph Cathedral
St Asaph
(Llanelwy)
Tremeirchion
Groesffordd Marli
Llannerch Hall
Pengwern
Rhyd-y-foel

Abergwyngregyn
Aberconwy House
St Mary's Church
Conwy
Conwy Castle
Conwy Junction
Llandudno Junction
Gyffin
Llansanffraid Glan Conwy
Llangwstenin
Bryn-y-maen
Mynydd Llanelian
336
Dolwen
Betws-yn-Rhos
Moelfre Uchaf
396
Mynydd Bodrochwyn
Moelfre Isaf
317
Cefn Meiriadog
Llannefydd
Plas-yn-Cefn
Trefnant
Green
Penmaenmawr
Penmaenan
Dwygyfylchi
Capelulo
Foel Lus
362
Moelfre
435
Henryd
Rowen
Pentrefelin
Graig
Moel Gyffylog
341
Eglwysbach
Trofarth
Mynydd Branar
324
Pentre Isaf
Pentre'r Felin
Mwdwl Eithin
389
Llangernyw
Hafodunos
Gell
Rhos-y-mawn
Wenlli
Llanfair Talhaiarn
Cefn Berain
Bont-newydd
Henllan
Plasisaf
Denbigh
(Dinbych)
Gwaenynog
Denbigh Castle
Friary (ruins)
Brook
Llanfairfechan
Gorddinog
Garreg Fawr
Tal-y-fan
610
Aber Falls
Llwytmor
Drum
770
Crymlyn
Moel Wnion
580
Llanllechid
Snowdonia
Drosgl
758
Foel-Fras
942
Rachub
Bethesda
Gerlan
National Park
Carned Gwenllian
926
Foel Grach
Braichmelyn
Carnedd Llywelyn
1064
1044
Carnedd Dafydd
Mynydd Perfedd
812
Foel Goch
831
Y Garn
946
313
Pont Pen-y-benglog
Glyder Fach
994
Glyder Fawr
999
Cae'rhun
Llanbedr-y-cennin
Castell
Tal-y-bont
Dolgarrog
Pont Dolgarrog
Llyn Eigiau Reservoir
Dulyn Reservoir
Llyn Cowlyd Reservoir
Trefriw
Llanddoged
Pentre-tafarn-y-fedw
Gwytherin
Pandy Tudur
378
Waen
Bylchau
Llansannan
Rhydgaled
Deunant
Tan-y-fron
Pen-cae-cwm
Nantglyn
Cader
Pant-pastynog
Pentre Saron
Ffridd Fawr
344
Meifod
Llanthaeadr
Llanrhae
Groes
Vale of Conwy
C O N W Y
D E N B
Llanrwst
Gwydir Castle
Melin-y-coed
424
Oerfa
1396
Nebo
Moel Seisiog
468
Capel Garmon
Llyn Crafnant
Llyn Geirionydd
Gwydir Uchaf Chapel
Cefn-Rhudd
Aled Isaf Reservoir
466
Moel Llyn
448
Sportsman's Arms
Bryn Trillyn
494
Gorsedd Bran
518
Llyn Bran
Cefn Du
422
Mynydd
Moel Aled
Hiraethog
Llyn Brenig
Cyffylliog
Bontuchel
Llanberis
Pass of Llanberis
Pen-y-Pass
356
Pen-y-Gwryd Hotel
Capel Curig
Glyn Ty-Hyll
Pont Cyfyng
Swallow Falls
Oaklands
Conwy Valley Railway Museum
Betws-y-coed
532
519
Hafod-Dinbych
Nilig
Mynydd Hiraethog
Clocaenog Forest
Cefn Du
422
Craig Bron-banog
501
898
Carnedd y Cribau
591
Mynydd Cribau
345
Carnedd Moel-siabod
872
Llynnau Mymbyr
Llynnau Diwaunedd
Pont-y-pant
Chambered Long Cairn
Rhydlanfair
Glan Conwy
Pentrefoelas
Aled Reservoir
475
Pentre-llyn-cymmer
Churchyard Cross
Brynsaithmarchog
Plas Gwynant
Llyn Dinas
Dolwyddelan
Dolwyddelan Castle
Blaenau Dolwyddelan
Pentre-bont
Ty Mawr Wybrnant
Ty'n-y-Coed Uchaf
Penmachno
371
Cefn-brith
Rhyallydan
Glasfryn
Llanfihangel Glyn Myfyr
Pont yr Alwen
Cerrigydrudion
Melin-y-Wig
389
Gwyddelwe
Llyn Llydaw
Llyn Gwynant
Gwydyr Forest
Y Ro Wen
594
Cwm Penmachno
504
Ysbyty Ifan
Garn Prys
534
447
Mwdwl-eithin
470
Bettws Gwerfil Goch
Cnicht
689
Bwlch y Gorddinan
385
623
Moel Penamnen
Rhiwbryfdir
Glanaber Terrace
Carrog
Pen y Bedw
527
Ty-Mawr
Cadair Benllyn
Gellioedd
Ty-nant
Maerdy
Llangwm
Rhug Chapel
Druid
Cae Ddafydd
Ffestiniog Railway
Blaenau Ffestiniog
Tanygrisiau
658
Llyn Conwy
Gylchedd
628
Carnedd y Filiast
669
407
Glan-yr-afon
Mawddwy
Four Crosses
Tyn-y-cefn
Glan-yr-afon
Plas Isaf
Croesor
Moelwyn Mawr
770
661
Migneint
Sarn
Capel Celyn
611
Foel Goch
Wenallt
Moel Emoel
549
Bethania
Moelwyn Bach
711
Arenig Fach
689
Carnedd Iago
538
Llyn Celyn
Ciltalgarth
Glan-yr-afon
Cefn-ddwysarn
Bethel
Mynydd Mynyllod
Tan-lan
Rhyd-y-sarn
Rhyd
Llanfrothen
Ffestiniog
(Llan Ffestiniog)
Graig Wen
556
Fron-goch
Llidiardau
Rhyd-uchaf
Rhiwlas
Sarnau
Llanderfel
Crogen
Maentwrog
Gellilydan
Craig Cwfyms
Tomen-y-mur Roman Fort
Snowdonia
Craig yr Hyrddod
Arenig Fawr
854
Llyn Arenig-Fawr
Ciltalgarth
Llanycil
Bala
(Y Bala)
Llanfor
Pale
Cefn Coch
447
Cadwst
Bryn Bwbach
Talsarnau
Trawsfynydd
552
Moel Llyfnant
750
Cwm Prysor
National Park
Ffridd Trawscoed
Rhos-y-gwaliau
Rhiwaedog-is-afon
508
Foel Cwm-Sian Llwyd
648
Eisingrug
Moel Ysgyfarnogod
623
Bronaber
Mynydd Bach
Moel y Feidiog
563
Craig Durfas
Mynydd Bryn-llech
Llangower
Parc
Dinam
Milltir Gerrig
486
Foel y Geifr
Llyn Cwm Bychan
Roman Steps
Rhinog Fawr
720
Crawcwellt
Llanuwchllyn
Y Bryn
Pont Rhyd-sarn
Dyrysgol
Moel Llyfnant
667
Foel Figenau
590
Cyrniau Nod
666
Hirnant Pass
Bala Lake Railway
Pentre-piod
Pont Cwm Pydew
Llangwm
Rhyd-wen
Foel Cedig
Post Gwyn
665
Cadair Berwyn
Blaen Glaswen
Y Clogydd
596
G W Y N E D D
C A M B R I A N   M O U N
British National Grid projection

Metres / Feet
1000 / 3280
900 / 2952
800 / 2624
700 / 2296
600 / 1968
500 / 1640
400 / 1312
300 / 4921
200 / 656
150 / 492
100 / 328
50 / 164
0 Land below sea level
50 / 164
200 / 656
1000 / 3281

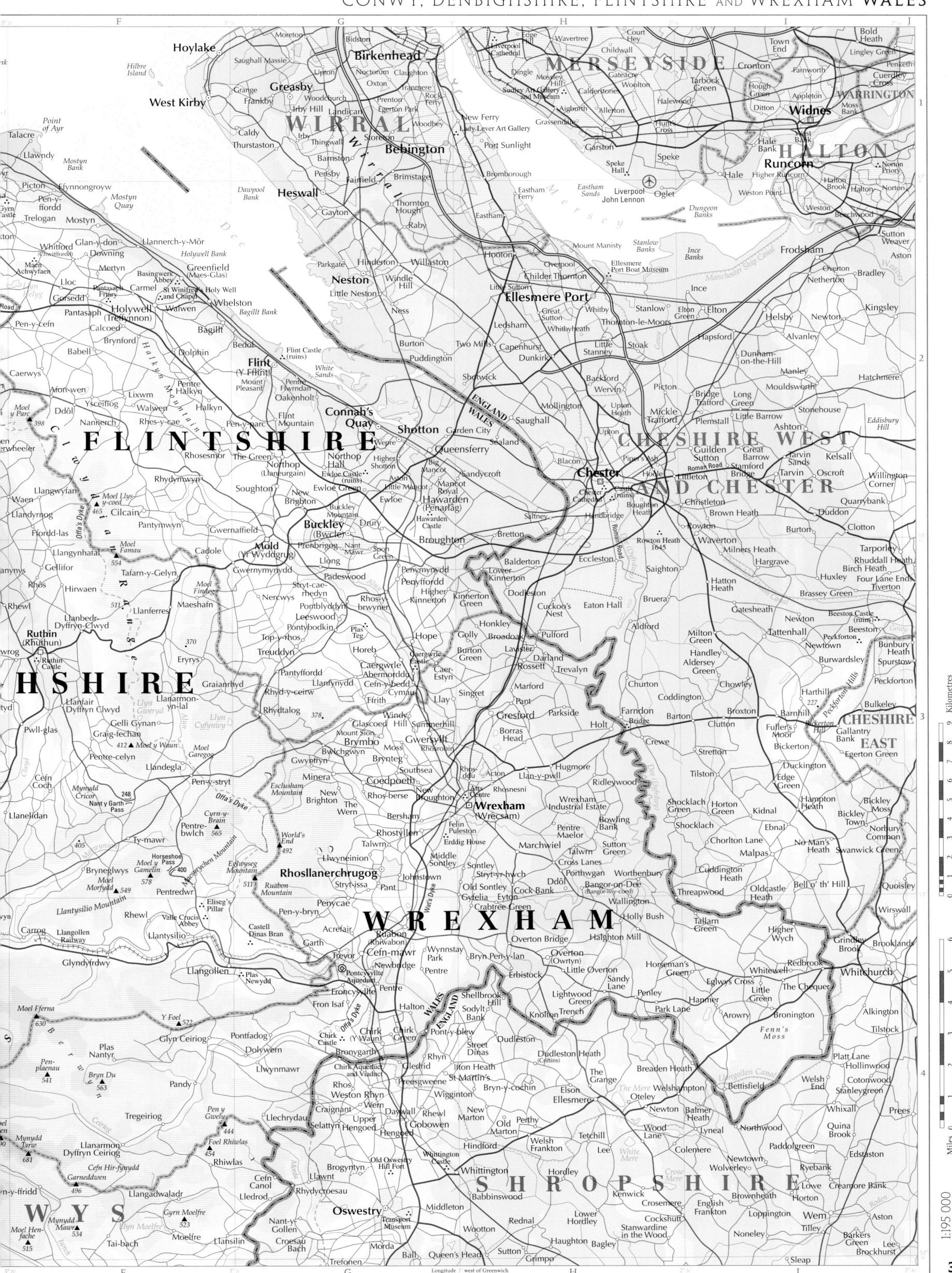

1:195 000

© Collins Bartholomew Ltd

NORTHERN IRELAND

Area Sq Km	13,576
Area Sq Miles	5,242
Population	1,775,000
Capital city	Belfast
Highest point	Slieve Donard (852 m)

County Antrim coastline.

The province of Northern Ireland occupies the northeastern part of the island of Ireland. The remainder of the island forms the Republic of Ireland. Northern Ireland was created by the Government of Ireland Act of 1920 from six out of the nine counties in the historic province of Ulster: Antrim, Armagh, Down, Fermanagh, Londonderry and Tyrone. The remaining counties of Donegal, Cavan and Monaghan are part of the Republic of Ireland, which borders Northern Ireland in the south and west. To the north and east the coast of the province stretches from Lough Foyle east past Rathlin Island to Torr Head, just 20 km from the Mull of Kintyre across the North Channel, then down the coast to Belfast Lough and the Ards Peninsula, ending at Carlingford Loch. The only inhabited island is the improbably L-shaped Rathlin Island around 10 km offshore from Ballycastle in Antrim. The most northerly point in Northen Ireland is Benbane Head in Antrim, the most easterly, Townhead on the Ards peninsula, the most southerly, Cranfield Point in Co. Down and the most westerly is Cornaglah in Fermanagh, just a few kilometres from Donegal Bay on the west coast of Ireland.

The centre of the province is dominated by Lough Neagh, the largest freshwater lake in the United Kingdom, with an area of 382 sq. km. The river Bann flows north out of the lough, draining into the sea by Portstewart. To the east of the Bann valley rise the Antrim Hills whose highest peak is Trostan (554 m). The hills then fall away through the Glens of Antrim to the coast, a dramatic landscape of cliffs and sheltered coves, which are linked by the Antrim Coast Road, one of the most scenic routes in the United Kingdom. On the north Antrim coast, near the town of Portrush and close to Benbane Head, is the Giant's Causeway, an extraordinary collection of over 40,000 polygonal basalt columns, formed during a period of volcanic activity in the early Tertiary period, some 50–60 million years ago. The Causeway and the nearby 'Causeway Coast' form the only UNESCO World Heritage Site in Northern Ireland.

To the west of the Bann rise the Sperrin Mountains that physically separate Londonderry and Strabane from the rest of the province; Sawel Mount at 682 m, is the highest point. The distinctive features of the southwest are the two large freshwater loughs of Upper and Lower Lough Erne, part of the route of the river Erne from Co. Cavan to its outflow into Donegal Bay by Ballyshannon. The town of Enniskillen is positioned between the two loughs. With many islands and a picturesque setting the loughs are popular with pleasure boaters and fishermen. After Lough Neagh, Lower Lough Erne is the second largest lake in the United Kingdom with an area of 105 sq. km. In the southeast of the province are the Mourne Mountains, where nine out of the ten highest peaks in Northern Ireland can be found including the highest, Slieve Donard, at 852 m.

The climate of Northern Ireland is maritime temperate, with average temperatures in January ranging from 1°C to 7°C and in July from 11°C to 18°C. The highest temperature recorded in Northern Ireland was 30.8°C on 30 June 1976 at Knockareven, Co. Fermanagh and on 12 July 1983 at Shaw's Bridge, Belfast. The coldest temperature was −17.5°C on 1 January 1979 at Magherally in Co. Down. The highest daily rainfall recorded was on 31 October 1968 at Tollymore Forest in Co. Down, when 159 mm fell, while average annual rainfall amounts to 1,060 mm, with the west being significantly wetter, up to 2,000 mm, while the east coast can be drier, at 825 mm. Overall, it is wetter than England, which goes some way to explaining why the countryside is so green.

The population of Northern Ireland in 2008 was estimated at 1,775,000, which was just below 3 per cent of the total population of the United Kingdom. Northern Ireland has a younger population than the United Kingdom as a whole, with 21.5 per cent of the population under 16 (compared with the UK figure of just under 19 per cent) and 16.6 per cent over retirement age, compared with 19.2 per cent for the UK overall. In recent years the population of Northern Ireland

Carrick-a-Rede rope bridge.

Casks at Bushmills Irish Whiskey Distillery.

[...] been the fastest growing in the United Kingdom, [...]iven by a rising birth rate and net inward migration, [...]couraged by increased political stability. The districts [...] Craigavon and Dungannon have seen the greatest [...]owth recently (for example, around 2 per cent growth [...]tween 2007 and 2008). Looking forward, this growth [...] expected to continue, with a further increase of 7 per [...]nt expected by 2018 to give a population of 1,896,000, [...]sing to over 2 million in the early 2030s. At the time [...] the 2001 Census, 34 per cent of the population lived [...] the Belfast metropolitan area that stretches around [...]elfast Lough from Carrickfergus to Bangor and a [...]rther 5 per cent of the population lived in the Derry [...]ban area. Overall 65 per cent of the population lived [...] urban settlements of at least 5,000 residents.

The economy of Northern Ireland in the recent past [...]s suffered from problems caused by 'The Troubles' [...]hich were a major disincentive to overseas investment [...] the economy) and by the decline of traditional [...]anufacturing industries, such as shipbuilding in [...]elfast. Overall, however, manufacturing still provides [...] greater percentage of jobs (over 11 per cent) than [...] the UK as a whole, assisted by the aerospace and [...]ectronics industries. The iconic Harland and [...]olff shipyard in Belfast, once the largest shipyard [...] the world, now focuses on ship repair and heavy [...]gineering, particularly for the renewable energy [...]arket, an indication of the need for heavy industry to [...]apt. The largest employment sector, however, is the [...]blic sector (including health and education), which [...]ovides over 35 per cent of the jobs, compared with [...]UK average of 28 per cent. Financial and business [...]rvices, whilst growing, still only provide 13 per cent of [...]bs compared with a UK average approaching [...] per cent. Agriculture remains a vital component of [...]e rural areas of Northern Ireland, with an emphasis [...] livestock farming. With more settled times, tourism [...] becoming an important sector, whether in the form [...] short breaks to the increasingly cosmopolitan Belfast [...] longer trips to the Antrim coast or the loughs of [...]rmanagh.

As in the rest of the United Kingdom, the [...]dministration of local government in the 19th century [...]s through a mixture of parishes and boards. Reform [...]me to Ireland a little later than in England, but in [...]898, new county councils, based on the traditional [...]unties, and county boroughs for the largest [...]ttlements, were created. When Northern Ireland came [...]to existence, this system continued, with two county [...]roughs (Belfast and Londonderry) and six county [...]uncils, each broken down into a number of urban and [...]ral district councils. The system changed completely [...] 1973, when 26 unitary districts were established [...]d the counties ceased to have any local government [...]gnificance. Even so, the county names continued to [...] used to describe the areas of Northern Ireland and [...] use them in the text that follows. The twenty-six [...]stricts are too small to supply all services, and some [...]tivities are shared between a number of districts, [...]hile other functions are retained at national level. [...]owever, it has been recognized that a smaller number [...] districts would be more efficient, and, at the time of [...]riting, the final details of a proposed reform are being [...]scussed, with the number of authorities likely to be [...]duced to eleven in 2011.

The province of Northern Ireland was formally [...]stablished in 1920, when it remained part of the United [...]ingdom while the remainder of Ireland became [...]e independent Irish Free State, later to become the [...]epublic of Ireland. The decision to split the island has [...] origins in events in the 16th and 17th centuries. By [...]e mid-16th century, English authority in Ireland was [...]stricted to the area around Dublin ('the Pale'), with [...]atholic chiefs holding the rest of the country. The [...]rotestant Tudors reasserted English control over all [...] Ireland by the end of the 16th century, amid much [...]pposition from the Catholic population. One means [...] engendering greater Anglicization was to encourage [...]esbyterians, primarily from Scotland, to settle in the

Botanic Gardens, Belfast.

The marina at Bangor, County Down.

northern counties of Ireland. This 'plantation', from the early 17th century, was encouraged by the provision of land confiscated from local Catholics, hardly making the new settlers welcome. Unlike the rest of Ireland, a large resident Protestant population then emerged in the north. This population benefited from the industrialization of the province in the 19th century, gaining most of the skilled work in the booming linen trade and in the shipbuilding and heavy engineering sectors, while Catholic workers tended to receive only the more basic jobs. As the campaign for Irish self-rule developed in the 19th century, so the Protestants in the north started to argue for maintaining the historic ties with Britain. The outcome of the tumultuous and violent early decades of the 20th century, saw the creation of the province of Northern Ireland with a devolved government and parliament, which, from 1932, was based at Stormont, on the outskirts of Belfast. The Protestant majority within Stormont and in most councils ensured that the Catholic minority was discriminated against in many day-to-day matters. In the late 1960s the Civil Rights movement campaigned for equality for Catholics. Their peaceful campaign was quickly overtaken by violent conflict between armed groups from both the Unionist and Nationalist communities. The British Army became involved in maintaining security in 1969 and the Northern Ireland government was suspended in 1972, to be replaced by direct rule from London. After nearly 30 years, during which over 3,500 civilians and security personnel were killed, the Good Friday Agreement of 1998 saw the emergence of a political settlement that has evolved, not always smoothly, over the years that have followed. The 'Peace Dividend' from this settlement has seen Northern Ireland revive its economy, attract tourists and inward investment, and see the fastest population growth in the United Kingdom. There are still many issues to resolve and wounds to heal, but there is a popular will not to return to the bad days of 'The Troubles'.

City Hall, Belfast

HISTORICAL MAPS OF IRELAND

John Speed, Ireland, 1610.

A period of 280 years separates these two maps of the Irish counties. The most striking difference between the two is that the shape of the island of Ireland is drastically different, the earlier map being much more inaccurate even for the time it was published than the maps from a similar era covering England, Wales and much of Scotland, on other pages in this atlas. The least-precisely surveyed part of the Irish coast is the Atlantic seaboard, presumably because surveyors and mariners of the time were more concerned with areas closer to the main shipping routes. In particular the shape of County Mayo, which in fact pushes well out into the Atlantic, is considerably understated.

The older map of the two was drawn by one of the Dutch cartographers called Hondius, and published by the English cartographer John Speed. Illustrations and a large decorative title cartouche are used to add interest and fill space. By modern standards, the categorisation of the inhabitants as either 'gentle', 'civill' or 'wild' would

be highly insensitive. Even so, the map is an appealing and decorative production. An entertaining note is struck by a walrus; it looks bemused to have surfaced just off the Irish coast.

Regarding the mapping of the traditional counties, these can be seen to have changed little over the centuries. County names are not specially emphasised in the older map, and neither are the boundaries, compared with a modern map. These issues apart, the 17th-century map is a thing of some beauty, as well as being a curious snapshot of both the administrative and cartographic history of Ireland.

The English names King's County and Queen's County are used on both maps, for County Offaly and County Laois – these British-orientated names were dropped in the 20th century. Also common to both maps are the traditional four provinces of Ireland – Connaught, Leinster, Munster and Ulster, though again these names are rather clearer on the more recent of the

two, and Munster is 'Mounster' on the older one. After the partition of Ireland in the 20th century, Northern Ireland remained part of the United Kingdom, formed from six of the nine counties which make up Ulster.

Contrasting with practice elsewhere, it is still usual even in our times for the traditional counties of Ireland to be shown on maps, rather than actual local council areas. In the Republic, administration is still based on the old counties, although Tipperary is divided into Ridings, and several urban authorities have been created separately. In Northern Ireland, although public awareness remains strongly with the six counties, administration is based on twenty-six districts created in the 1970s, but this is due to be abandoned in favour of a new arrangement.

IRELAND

English Miles

Railways thus

The Century Atlas & Gazetteer of the World, 1890.

ANTRIM

Area Sq Km	2,844
Area Sq Miles	1,098
Population	616,300
County town	Antrim
Highest point	Trostan (554 m) in the Antrim Hills

Originally *Aontreibh*, from the Gaelic '*aon*' ('one') and '*treabh*' ('house'). Possibly referring to a single isolated dwelling from which the town developed. *Aontroim*, a modern name for the county, is a slight reinterpretation, meaning 'one ridge'.

FAMOUS FOR

The Giant's Causeway is a basalt lava plateau, which cooled into extraordinary (mainly) hexagonal shapes. Some of the columns are 12 m high, and the solidified lava is 28 m thick in many places. Legend has it that the hero, Fionn mac Cumhaill (Finn McCool) built the Causeway in order to walk to Scotland to confront a rival giant.

Samuel Wilson Boyd, the owner of the Old Bushmills Distillery at **Bushmills**, anticipated the eventual end of Prohibition in the United States of America, and rather than cut production, he expanded it. In 1933, the distillery organized the largest shipment of whiskey from an Irish port, bound for Chicago.

La Girona was a damaged galleass of the Spanish Armada which put in for repairs in Donegal during the return voyage to Spain. An additional 800 survivors from two other ships that had come to grief around the Irish coast were taken aboard at Donegal. On 26 October 1588 after setting sail from Donegal, *La Girona* foundered and sank off Lacada Point near Dunluce. Of the 1,300 men on board, 9 survived. It remains the province's only designated wreck site. Many artefacts from *La Girona*, including gold coins and jewellery, are on display in the Ulster Museum in Belfast.

FAMOUS PEOPLE

Sorley Boy Macdonnell (Somhairle Buidhe MacDhomhnaill), chieftain, born Ballycastle, *c.* 1508.
Hugh Boyd, entrepreneur, born Ballycastle, 1690.
George Macartney, Earl Macartney, diplomat, first Envoy of Britain to China (1793), born Lissanoure, Loughguile, 1737.
William Coulson, linen manufacturer, born Lisburn, 1739.
Sir John Jamison, prominent Australian settler, politician, landowner and banker, born Carrickfergus, 1776.
John Bodkin Adams, general practitioner and forger, born Randalstown, 1899.
William Joseph (Joey) Dunlop, world champion motorcyclist, born Ballymoney, 1952.
Liam Neeson, actor, born Ballymena, 1952.
Robert (Bobby) Gerald Sands, Irish Republican and hunger striker, born Newtownabbey, 1954.
James Nesbitt, actor, born Broughshane, 1965.
Antony (Tony) Peter McCoy, champion National Hunt jockey, born Moneyglass, 1974.

"Worth seeing, yes; but not worth going to see."
Samuel Johnson (on the Giant's Causeway)

"It [the Giant's Causeway] looks like the beginning of the world, somehow: the sea looks older than in other places, the hills and rocks strange, and formed differently from other rocks and hills – as those vast dubious monsters were formed who possessed the earth before man. … When the world was moulded and fashioned out of formless chaos, this must have been the bit over – *a remnant of chaos!"*
W M Thackeray, 1843

Antrim is the traditional county on the northeast coast of Northern Ireland. It is hilly, particularly in the east, with a greatly indented coastline, which includes spectacular cliffs and the Antrim Plateau, rising to the highest point at Trostan (550 m) in the Antrim Hills. Rathin Island lies just off the north coast. The Lagan and Larne rivers flow into the Irish Sea, while the Lower river Bann, part of the longest river in Northern Ireland, flows out of Lough Neagh, the star-shaped freshwater lake, the largest in Britain and the third largest in Europe, on its way to the Atlantic at Portstewart. The county's fertile lowlands are found in the valleys of these rivers.

In 1973, local government reorganization divided the six administrative counties and two county boroughs into 26 'single-tier' districts, some of which cut across the old county boundaries. Currently, Ballymena, Ballymoney, Carrickfergus, Larne, Moyle and Newtownabbey Borough Councils as well as part of Belfast and Lisburn City Councils fall within the traditional county borders of Antrim. The former counties are still in use as Lieutenancy areas, as well as for car number plates and passports. Another reorganization is planned to go ahead in 2011, which will reduce the number of districts in Northern Ireland to eleven.

Given the importance of trade to Antrim, it is unsurprising that many of its largest settlements are also along the coast, such as the Newtownabbey urban area (62,056), Carrickfergus (27,201), Larne (18,228) and Ballycastle (5,089). Inland, Lisburn (71,465), granted city status in 2002, Ballymena (28,717), and Antrim (20,001) are the most important towns.

Antrim town is located along the Six Mile Water just northeast of Lough Neagh. Several battles were fought near the town, from the 14th century to the Battle of Antrim in 1798. Its strategic situation was such that Viscount Massereene, who built Antrim castle in 1662, was allowed to maintain a fleet of ships on the lough, and the town returned two Members of Parliament. More recently, Antrim is the location of the province's first technology park.

County Antrim has seen human settlement since around 6000 BC on evidence of flint tools found around Lough Neagh. It is presumed that these people came from across the 21-km North Channel from what is now Scotland, and migration between the two places probably reached a peak in about AD 600, despite a later Scottish (and English) migration in the 16th century. The Vikings made no permanent settlements here, but by the 12th century Anglo-Normans had made inroads. The county was ultimately incorporated into the earldom of Ulster.

Linen and flax growing has been the economic backbone of the inland towns and villages, particularly after the government dropped the tax on plain linens following the Williamite Wars, which encouraged immigration to Ulster from Britain. Huguenot refugees from France were among the immigrants who arrived here in 1698, including skilled weavers as well as 'men of business', such as Louis Crommelin. They established themselves in communities like Lisburn, where there was ready access to ports, water and land for the all-important bleaching greens. They transformed the linen industry, and the Industrial Revolution, particularly the introduction of the 'spinning jenny' was to turn this rural and predominantly agricultural county into one dependent upon textile manufacturing well into the 20th century. The industry has contracted, but is taking advantage of the current demand for natural fibres.

Following 'The Troubles', the 'peace dividend' offered by the 'Good Friday Agreement' (signed in 1998) has attracted investment, and in Antrim (excluding Belfast) manufacturing and construction jobs account for 38,590 jobs, around 22 per cent of the total. Service industries have filled the gap, supplying around 77 per cent of jobs. Tourism-related industries, including 'sustainable tourism', are a growing economic sector, and are exploiting unusual markets – the salmon and eel fisheries along the river Bann are commercially valuable for sportsmen as well as manufacturers. Towns like Portrush and Ballycastle are able to take advantage of their location near the Giant's Causeway UNESCO World Heritage Site and the Antrim Coast and Glens Area of Outstanding Natural Beauty.

North Antrim coastline at White Park Bay.

Carrickfergus Castle

Liam Neeson

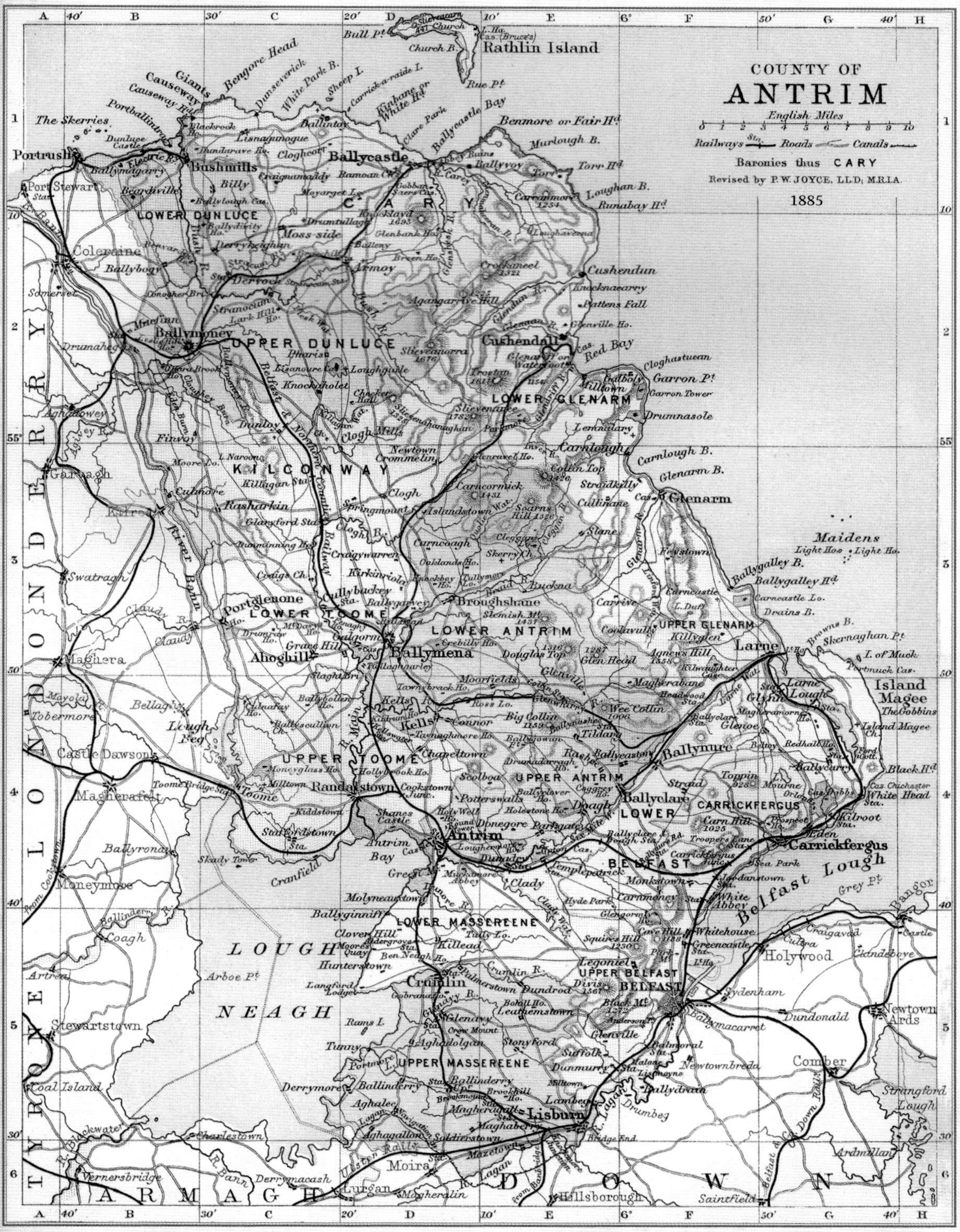
COUNTY OF
ANTRIM
English Miles
Railways Roads Canals
Baronies thus CARY
Revised by P.W. JOYCE, LL.D. M.R.I.A.
1885
Rathlin Island
LOUGH NEAGH
DOWN
ARMAGH
LONDONDERRY
TYRONE
Belfast Lough

Bartholomew Gazetteer of the British Isles,1887

ANTRIM, *a maritime co. in extreme NE. of Ireland, prov. Ulster: bounded N. by the Atlantic, E. by the N. Channel, SE. and S. by Belfast Lough and co. Down, and W. by Lough Neagh and the r. Bann, which separate it from cos. Tyrone and Londonderry. Greatest length, N. and S., 56 m.; greatest breadth, E. and W., 30 m.; coast-line, 90 m. Area, 762,080 ac. (709,832 ac. of land and 52,248 of water). Pop. 421,943, of whom about 190,746 were Presbyterians, 108,344 Roman Catholics, 98,161 Protestant Episcopalians, and 11,842 Methodists. Off the N. coast are Rathlin island and the Skerries; off the E. are the Maiden rocks with 2 lighthouses. The chief headlands are Bengore Head, Fair Head, Garron Point, and Ballygalley Head. The surface consists chiefly of a tableland of basaltic trap, broken by numerous valleys, and presenting on the N. coast the most wonderful columnar formations (see the Giant's Causeway); chief summit, Trostan, 1817 ft. The fisheries on the coast are important. Fine salt is obtained in the district of Carrickfergus. The cultivation of flax and the mfrs. of linen, cotton, and coarse woollens give employment to most of the people. The co. comprises 15 bars., 71 pars., the greater part of the mun. bor. of Belfast, and the towns of Antrim, Ballymena, Ballymoney, Carrickfergus, Larne, and Lisburn (part of).*

ant's Causeway

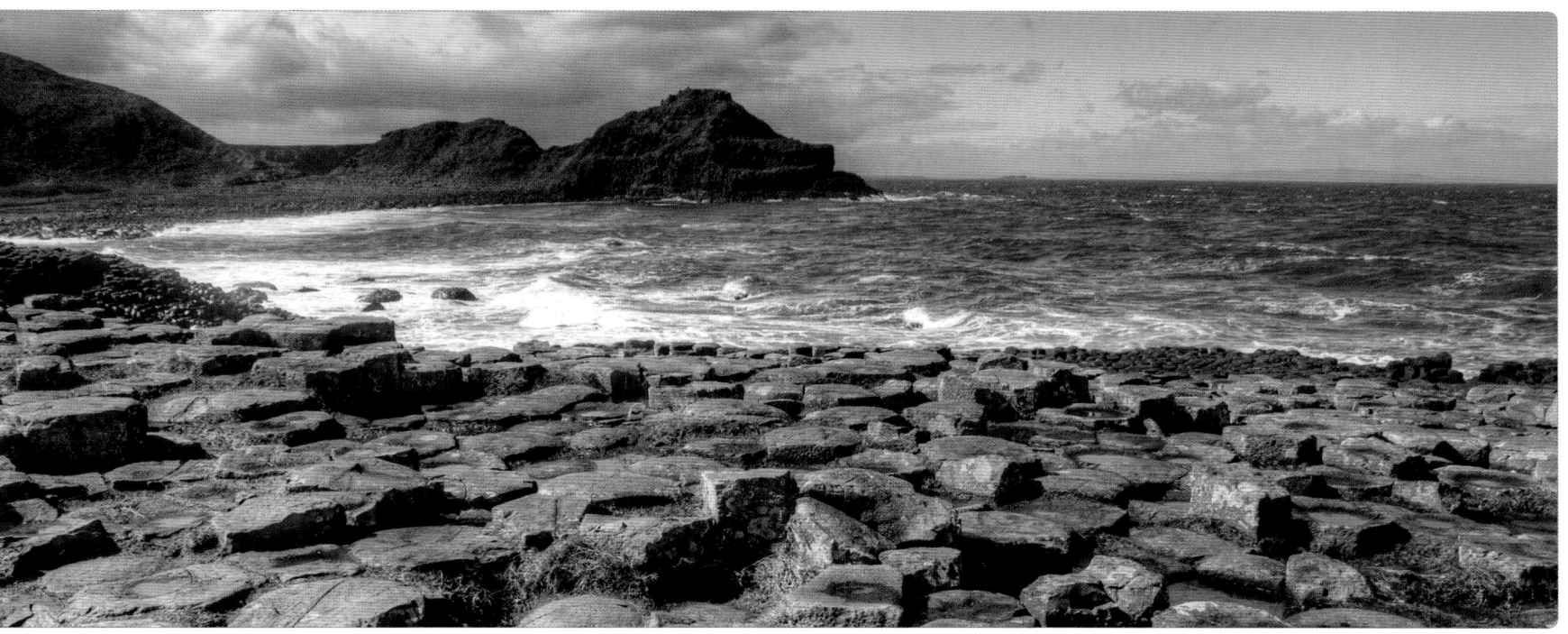

LONDONDERRY (DERRY)

Area Sq Km	2,074
Area Sq Miles	801
Population	233,500
County town	Coleraine
Highest point	Sawel (683 m) in the Sperrin Mountains on the border of County Tyrone

The county takes its name from a landscape description. It was known as *Doire Calgaigh* ('the oak grove') by AD 535, but its original Irish name was *Doire Chalgaigh*, or 'Calgach's oak grove'. Later it was sometimes called *Doire Cholm Cille*, 'Columcille's oak grove', after a monastery founded nearby by St Columba (Columcille). It was renamed Londonderry in 1613.

FAMOUS FOR

In 1689, the city was besieged by the armies of James II wishing to take this stronghold of King William. The Jacobite army was denied entry in December of 1688 by the expedient of thirteen apprentice boys appropriating the city keys and locking the gates. The town was later relieved by the Royal Navy. The town is also known as the **'Maiden City'** because the walls, which still exist, were never breached during the long siege.

The **University of Ulster** has four campuses, two of which are in County Londonderry: its original campus at Coleraine and a second at the Magee Campus in Londonderry, previously the site of Magee College, opened in 1845. The other two campuses are in Belfast and Jordanstown.

The well-known tune, **'Londonderry Air'** was transcribed by Jane Ross of Limavady, who collected it from a local fiddle player.

FAMOUS PEOPLE

George Farquhar, dramatist, born Londonderry, c. 1677.
Denis Hempson, harpist, born near Garvagh, c. 1694.
William Sampson, lawyer, defender of members of the United Irishmen, born Londonderry, 1764.
William McComb, poet, born Coleraine, 1793.
Edward Walsh (Éadbhard Breathnach), poet and translator, born Londonderry, 1805.
John Mitchel, lawyer and Irish nationalist, born Camnish, near Dungiven, 1815.
Thomas Gallaher, tobacco manufacturer, born near Eglinton, 1840.
William James Craig, Shakespearean editor, born Camus-juxta-Bann, Macosquin, 1843.
Sir John Ross, Lord Chancellor of Ireland, born Londonderry, 1853.
William Ferguson Massey, Prime Minister of New Zealand, born Limavady, 1856.
Joyce Cary, novelist, born Londonderry, 1888.
James Chichester-Clark, Baron Moyola, Unionist politician, Prime Minister of Northern Ireland (1969–71), born Moyola Park, Castledawson, 1923.
Sir Eoin Higgins, judge, born Town Parks, Magherafelt, 1927.
John Hume, Social Democratic and Labour Party politician (leader 1979–2001) and Nobel Peace laureate, born Londonderry, 1937.
Seamus Heaney, poet, critic and Nobel laureate, born Castledawson, 1939.
Martin O'Neill, football player and manager, born Kilrea, 1952.

Londonderry is a former county in the northwest of Northern Ireland, and one of six counties that make up the province of Ulster. To the south, along its border with County Tyrone rise the Sperrin Mountains, of which Sawel (678 m) is the highest point. Two of the county's borders are rivers, and their fertile valleys characterize the landscape. The Bann to the east borders Antrim, while the Foyle, with Lough Foyle borders the Republic's county of Donegal. It also has shorelines on Lough Neagh in the south and the Atlantic Ocean, with its spectacular cliffs and beaches, to the north. A maritime temperate climate insures plentiful rainfall but severe temperatures, whether hot or cold, are rare.

In 1973, local government reorganization divided the six administrative counties and two county boroughs into 26 'single-tier' districts, some of which cut across the old county boundaries. Currently, part of Coleraine and all of Limavady Borough Councils, Derry City Council and Magherafelt District Council fall within the traditional county borders of Londonderry. The former counties are still in use as Lieutenancy areas, as well as for car number plates and passports. Another reorganization is planned for 2011, which will reduce the number of districts in Northern Ireland to eleven.

The city of Londonderry (83,652) is the second largest in Northern Ireland, and the fourth largest in Ireland as a whole, and the headquarters of Derry City Council. Coleraine (24,042) is the headquarters of its district, and other important towns are Limavady (12,135) and Magherafelt (39,780).

Settlement in this part of Ireland has a long history, but without significant Viking incursion, and later Norman invasions were only partially successful. The Tudor period saw more determined colonization, and the creation of the 'traditional' counties. County Londonderry did not exist before 1613, so is not a 'traditional' county, usually taken to be those in existence by the 1580s. It was established by combining the former County of Coleraine, some land in the north of County Tyrone as well as a part of County Donegal in order to control the important waterways of the Bann

and Foyle. By the 17th century, land was being given to those Englishmen and Scots who supported the Crown which included merchants, craftsmen and soldiers under a scheme known as the 'Plantation of Ulster', largely displacing the native population.

What to call this county has proved a vexed question, exacerbated in the 20th century by 'The Troubles'. The split remains broadly along sectarian lines: nationalists generally call the city and county 'Derry', while many unionists refer to both as 'Londonderry'. The Irish Republic refers to the place by its Irish name, *Doire*, in English 'Derry', on road signs. It was 'Derrie' that was granted a charter by James I in 1604, but the new walled city which was built during the Plantation of Ulster was on the other side of the River Foyle, and named Londonderry in 1613, a recognition of donations by various liveried companies of the City of London. The county, created at the same time, took the name of this new town.

A predominantly rural county, livestock, especially poultry, cattle and pigs, are raised and the arable crops include oats, barley and potatoes. Linen manufacturing was established, for example, in Limavady, but the industry did not take off the way it did in other parts of Ulster, and now it is a predominantly residential community. Other forms of textile manufacture helped to expand the county's economy, but the relocation of important brands like Viyella have pushed up unemployment, especially in Magherafelt. Manufacturing continues to provide around 14 per cent of employment, but the service sector, which cover a wide spectrum from restaurants to public administration, education and health, provides around 77 per cent of employment. Efforts have also been made to rekindle the tourist industry. Portstewart was a popular Victorian resort, and still attracts holidaymakers – its two-mile sandy beach is a magnet for surfers – and has a large proportion of second-homes. Along with Portrush it is also popular with students attending the nearby Coleraine campus of the University of Ulster.

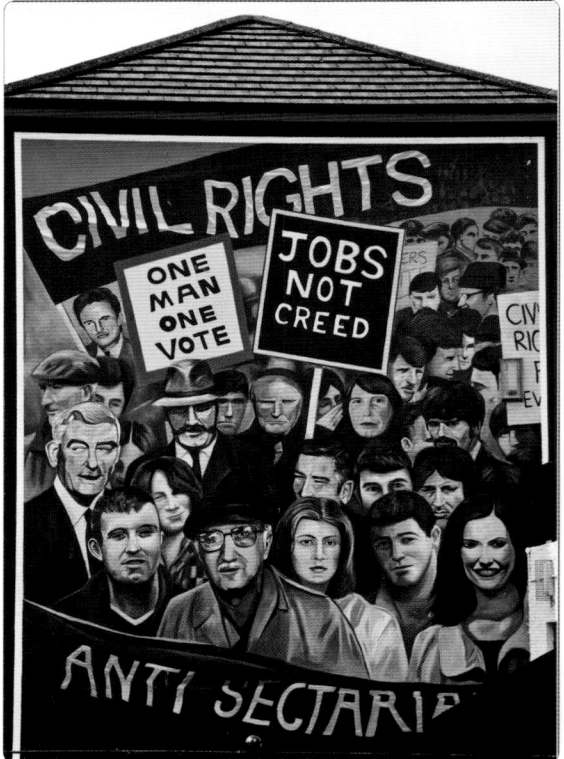

End terrace mural, Londonderry.

Cliffs near Portstewart.

"It was originally and is still popularly called Derry... the English prefix, London, was imposed in 1613, on the incorporation of the Irish Society by charter of Jas. I., and was for a long time retained by the colonists, but has likewise fallen into popular disuse."
Samuel Lewis (1837)

"The public buildings of Derry are, I think, among the best I have seen in Ireland; and the Lunatic Asylum, especially is to be pointed out as a model of neatness and comfort."
William Thackeray

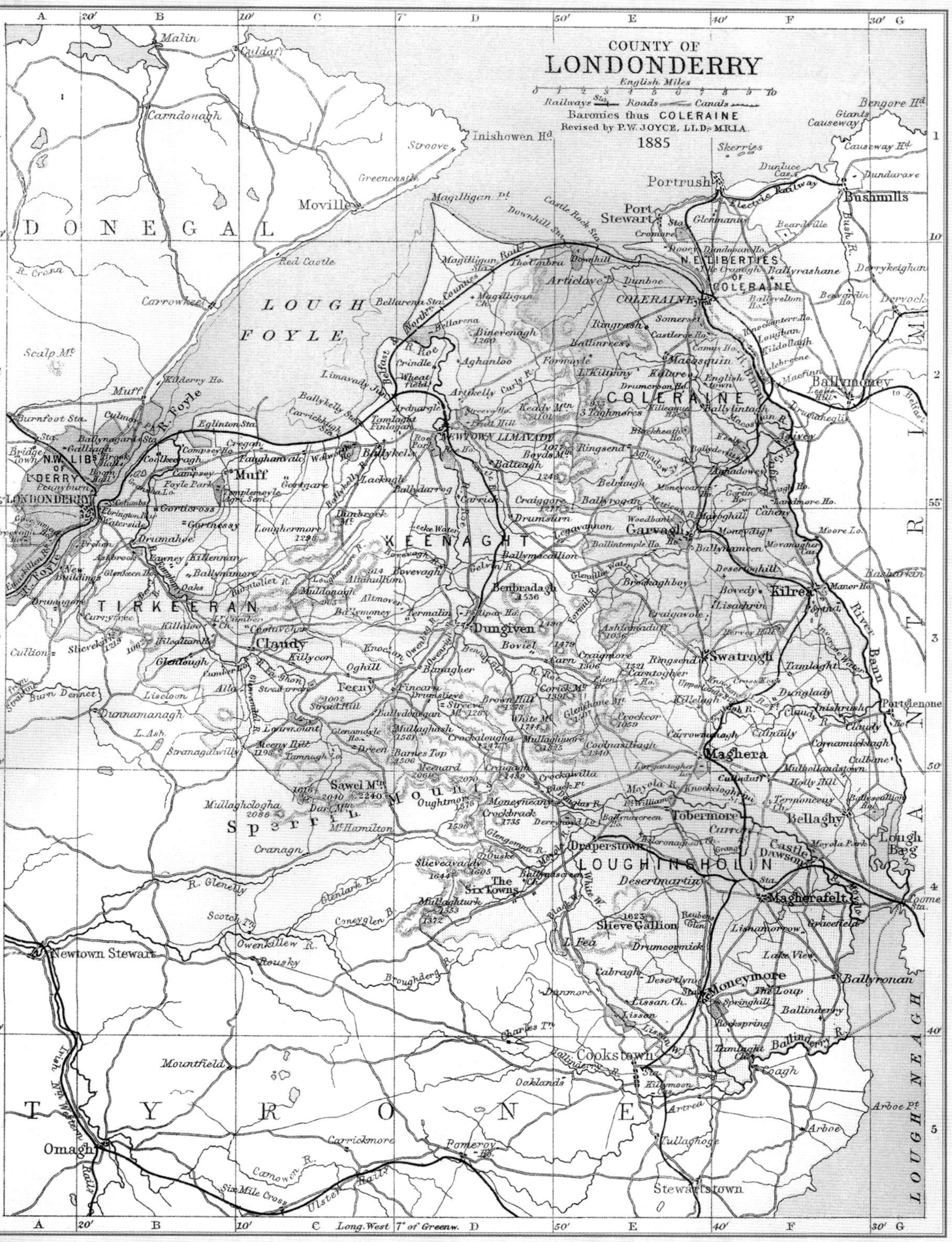

COUNTY OF
LONDONDERRY

English Miles

Railways   Roads   Canals
Baronies thus COLERAINE
Revised by P.W. Joyce, LL.D., M.R.I.A.
1885

Bartholomew Gazetteer of the British Isles, 1887

LONDONDERRY, *a maritime co., Ulster province; bounded N. by Lough Foyle and the Atlantic Ocean, E. by co. Antrim and Lough Neagh, S. by co. Tyrone, and W. by co. Donegal; greatest length, N. and S., 40 miles; greatest breadth, E. and W., 35 miles; average breadth, 20 miles; coast-line, about 30 miles; area, 522,315 ac. (9480 water). or 2.5 per cent. of the total area of Ireland; pop. 164,991, of whom 44.4 per cent. are Roman Catholics, 19.1 Protestant Episcopalians, 33.2 Presbyterians and 0.9 Methodists. The surface is low along the N. and E. for a width of about 6 miles, hilly in the middle, and mountainous in the S., where the highest summit, Sawel, rises to alt. of 2236 ft. The rivers from W. to E. are – Foyle, Faughan, Glen, Roe, Claudy, Moyola, and Bann, the last tracing nearly the whole of the E. boundary. The soil is for the most part fertile; the sub-strata consist of mica-slate, basalt, limestone, and sandstone. The chief crops are flax, oats, barley, and potatoes. The staple mfr. is linen. The fisheries on the coast and inland are important. About three-fourths of the whole county are owned by the Irish Society and the Twelve Trades Companies of the City of London. The co. comprises 6 bars. Coleraine, Keenaght, Loughinsholin, North-East Liberties of Coleraine, North-West Liberties of Londonderry, and Tirkeeran; 43 pars.; the mun. bor. of Londonderry, and the towns of Coleraine and Limavady.*

View from Binevenagh west to Loch Foyle.

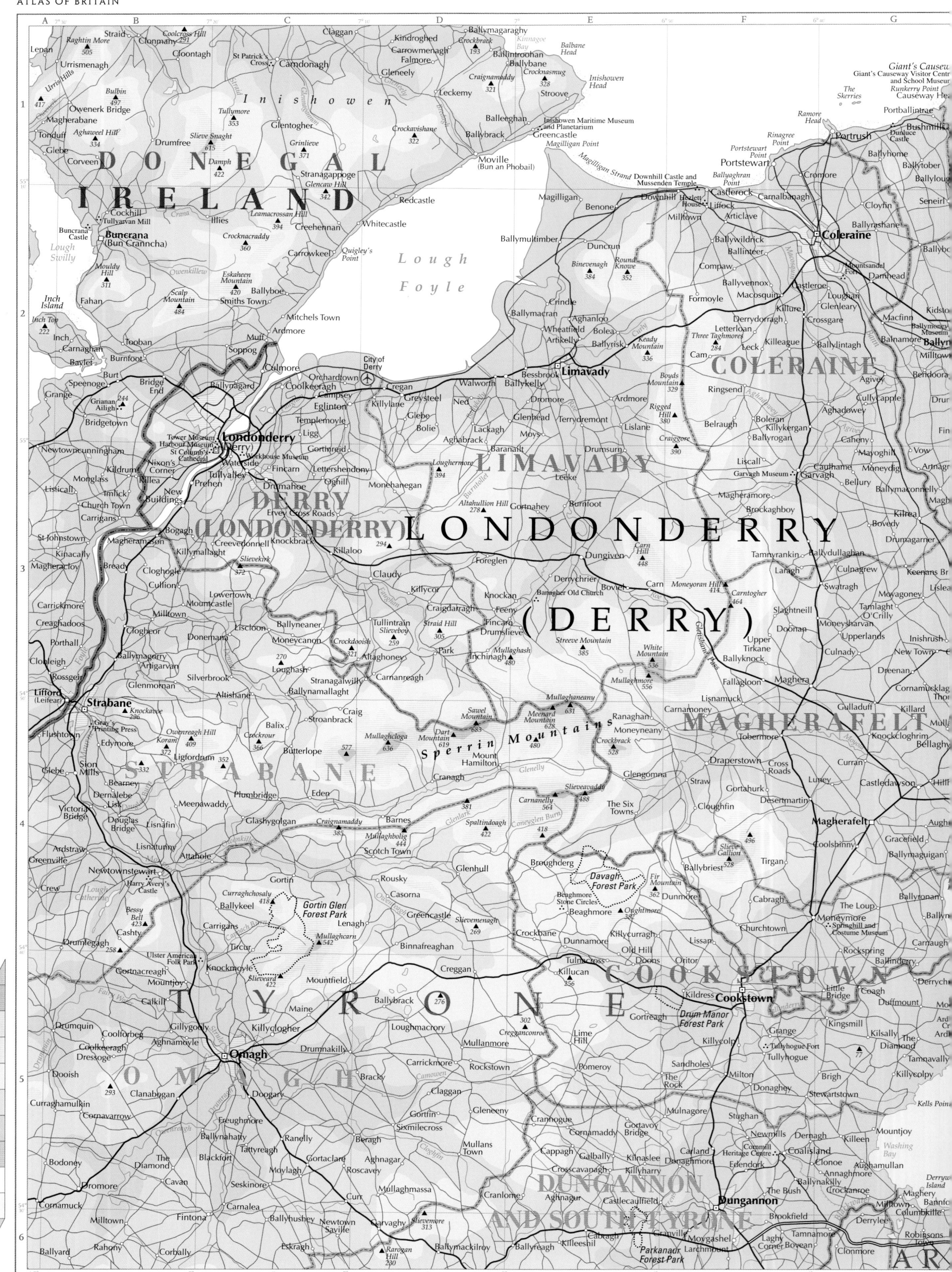

British National Grid projection

Continuation at the same scale

1:275 000

© Collins Bartholomew Ltd

BELFAST

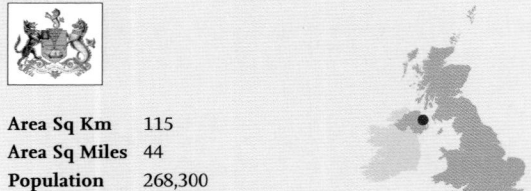

Area Sq Km	115
Area Sq Miles	44
Population	268,300
County town	Belfast
Highest point	Divis Mountain (483 m), in the Belfast Hills

Belfast's name is a descriptive one: *béal feirste*, **or the 'ford-mouth of the sandbank'.**

FAMOUS FOR

Harland and Wolff, the Belfast shipyard on the east bank of the river Lagan that built RMS *Titanic*.

The Stormont Estate is east of Belfast in County Down. The major government buildings are located here, including the Northern Ireland Office, the Northern Ireland Executive and even the Northern Ireland Civil Service Sports and Social Club, but it is the Parliament Building of the Northern Ireland Assembly which is colloquially known as 'Stormont'.

The Belfast Wheel is 60 m high and has 42 pods that allow spectacular views of the surrounding countryside. It is not without controversy, however, as its situation obscures a memorial to the Titanic disaster of 1912. There are ongoing discussions to move the wheel before the centenary.

In 1994, a weir was built across the river Lagan. Costing £14 million it allowed the tidal river to be kept artificially high, stopping the exposure of ugly and occasionally smelly mudflats in the city centre. Two fish passes incorporated into **Lagan Weir** allow salmon to migrate upstream, and other wildlife is once again present in the river.

FAMOUS PEOPLE

Samuel Greg, cotton manufacturer, born 1758.
William Thomson, Baron Kelvin, physicist, born 1824.
Sir John Lavery, painter, born 1856.
Robert Smillie, trade unionist and politician, born 1857.
C S (Clive Staples) Lewis, writer and theologian, born 1898.
Robert Alexander McCance, physician and nutritionist, born 1898.
Louis MacNeice, poet, born 1907.
William John Conway, Roman Catholic cardinal, born 1913.
Brian Moore, novelist, born 1921.
Danny Blanchflower, football player and manager, born 1926
John Stewart Bell, theoretical physicist, born 1928.
Sir James Galway, flautist, born 1939.
Derek Mahon, poet, born 1941.
Anthony (Tony) Louis Banks, Labour politician, born 1942.
David Trimble, Baron Trimble, Unionist politician, Nobel Peace laureate (1998), born 1944.
Van Morrison, singer and songwriter, born 1945.
George Best, football player, born Cregagh (Belfast) in 1946.
Gerry Adams, politician, President of Sinn Féin, born 1948.
Medbh McGuckian, poet, born 1950.
Mary McAleese, lawyer, President of the Republic of Ireland, born 1951.
Kenneth Branagh, actor, born 1960.

Belfast is a city and district in the northeast of Northern Ireland. It is located at the eastern end of Belfast Lough at the mouth of the river Lagan. A tributary to the Lagan, the river Farset (now culverted) was previously another important waterway at this end of the lough. The city is bounded by the Belfast Hills in the west, which includes the highest point in the area, Divis Mountain (478 m). Belfast's climate is broadly temperate, so long periods of either frost or heat are rare, and high levels of rainfall and humidity are characteristic.

In 1973, local government reorganization divided the six administrative counties and two county boroughs into 26 'single-tier' districts, some of which cut across the old county boundaries. Belfast City Council is one of these districts. Whilst it is officially within the traditional borders of County Antrim, physically the city itself – broadly, east Belfast and parts of south Belfast – extends into County Down. The former counties are still in use as Lieutenancy areas, as well as for car number plates and passports. Another reorganization is planned for 2011, which will reduce the number of districts in Northern Ireland to eleven.

Belfast (city population 268,300) is the capital of Northern Ireland and by far its largest city. In 2001, the 'greater Belfast area' had a population of 483,418, almost a quarter of the entire population of the province. The city centre is one of five districts, the other four being north, south, east and west Belfast. These divisions echo the further unhappy segregation of the city into around 14 neighbourhoods, many divided by 'peace lines', erected by the army in 1969 to separate rioting factions during 'The Troubles'. Since 1998, and the 'Good Friday Agreement', the city has also developed cultural 'quarters', such as Cathedral Quarter and Queens Quarter, centred on the university.

There is disagreement about the exact location of the sandy ford of the city's name – whether on the Lagan or the Farset – but settlement here goes back to at least the 7th century, when a battle was recorded between the native Ulidians and the Picts at the ford. Unsurprisingly, the Vikings raided this territory in the 9th century, and

over the centuries no fewer than three castles were built although the most important was at Carrickfergus in Antrim. Belfast's venerable history as a port stretches back to the Middle Ages with trade to Scotland, England and the Continent, but the town's real prosperity began in the 18th century. The Industrial Revolution was to transform a small port into an entrepôt for timber, tobacco and cotton, as well as a town manufacturing rope and, above all, textiles.

Ulster was well known for growing flax and hand weaving the thread into fabric at a time when linen and woollens were the most common cloth in everyday use. Both the Lagan and Farset, as well as other smaller streams, provided water which was essential for processing flax into thread and also for providing the power which ran the looms weaving the thread into linen. The introduction in the late 18th century of 'spinning jennies' revolutionized the manufacture of linen, and by the turn of the century, more than 27,000 people were employed in the production of the fabric, first from locally grown and, later, imported flax, earning the city the reputation as 'Linenopolis'. Belfast also made a name with heavy engineering, particularly shipbuilding – Harland and Wolff was once the largest shipyard in the world – and, in the 20th century, the aerospace industry. The bombings of the city in 1941 and the closure of much heavy industry in the later 20th century was exacerbated by 'The Troubles', and the city's population declined.

Although a smaller sector than in its heyday, manufacturing and ancillary services remain important economically, providing over 10,000 jobs. Belfast is home to Northern Ireland's first science park. Most of the area's employment, however, is in the service industries which account for 90 per cent of employment, ranging widely from public administration, education and health to tourism-related industries, such as hotels and restaurants. By 2004, the regeneration of the riverfront had attracted £800 million of investment, including retail, hotel and office space, another aspect of the 'Peace Dividend'.

Harland and Wolff shipyard cranes.

Parliament Building (Stormont)

Bartholomew Gazetteer of the British Isles, 1887

BELFAST, *mun.bor., manufacturing and seaport town, and the principal town of Ulster, chiefly in Shankhill par., co Antrim, but partly also in Holywood and Knockbreda pars., co Down, at the influx of the Laggan to Belfast Lough, 113 miles N. of Dublin by rail, 129 from Glasgow, and 160 from Liverpool – mun. bor., 5991 ac., pop. 208,122; 6 banks, 11 newspapers. Market-days, Tuesday and Friday. On the land side the city is bounded and sheltered by a lofty and picturesque ridge of hills, which ends abruptly in the basaltic eminence of Cave Hill (1185 ft.). It presents a clean, prosperous, and business-like appearance, and possesses wide and regular streets, elegant and substantial buildings, and beautiful environs. An insignificant vil. in 1612, when Scotch and English colonists first settled there, Belfast is now the chief seat of the trade and mfrs. of Ireland, and the second port next to Dublin. Of its numerous educational institutions, the most important is Queen's College, opened in 1849; it has professorships in arts, law, medicine, and science, including engineering and agriculture. The staple mfrs. are linen and cotton; and bleaching, dyeing, and calico-printing are extensively carried on. Some of the flax-mills are very large. There are flour and oil mills; chemical works; iron foundries; breweries, distilleries; alabaster and barilla mills; ship-building (on Queen's Island), rope, and sailcloth yards. Pork curing is an important branch of trade. The docks and wharfage have become very extensive. Steamers sail daily to and from Liverpool, Glasgow, Fleetwood, Barrow, and Ardrossan; once or twice a week to Dublin, Cork, Bristol, London, Havre, &c.*

Belfast Castle

Queen's University, Belfast.

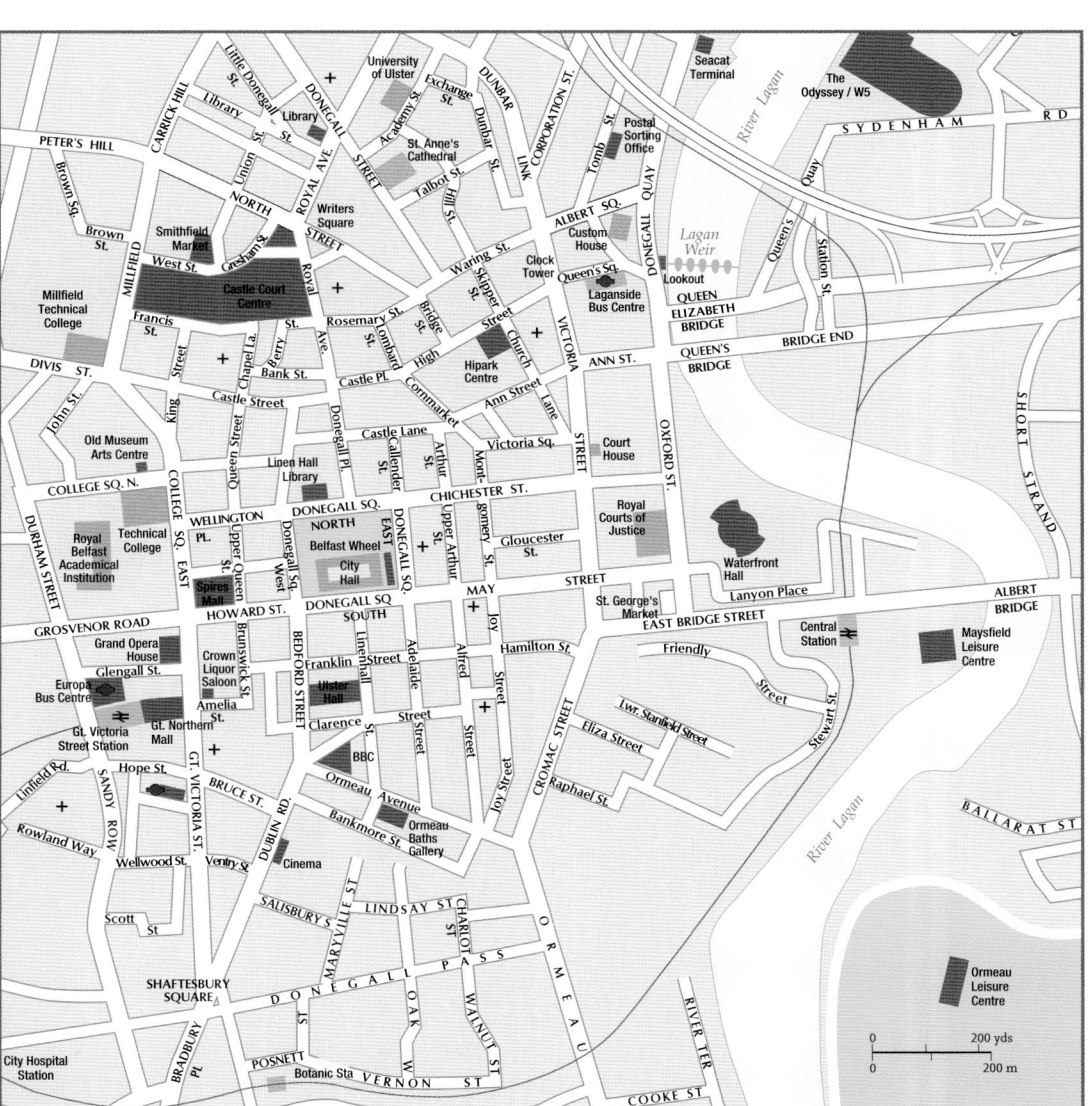

Modern Belfast

DOWN

Area Sq Km	2,448
Area Sq Miles	945
Population	516,000
County town	Downpatrick
Highest point	Slieve Donard (852 m) at the edge of the Mourne Mountains

'Down' comes from the Gaelic word for a fort, '*dún*'. This is in reference to the particular fort at Downpatrick, *Dún Pádraig* or '[St] Patrick's fort'. Prior to AD 496, the Irish name for this place was *Dún Lethghlaisse* or *Lethglasise*, possibly meaning 'the fort of the side of the stream'.

FAMOUS FOR

Bangor and its monastery founded around AD 555, was so influential that it was one of only four places in the whole of Ireland to be found on Hereford Cathedral's *Mappa Mundi* drawn in 1300.

Saint Patrick is reputedly buried in Downpatrick Cathedral, along with two other saints, Brigid and Columcille.

One of the first powered flights took place on the beach at **Newcastle**, when Harry Ferguson flew three miles and won a £100 prize in 1910.

In 2007 a commercial **tidal power station** was installed in the 8 km entrance to Strangford Lough to take advantage of the tidal power of the narrow, fast-flowing channel.

FAMOUS PEOPLE

Sir Hans Sloane, physician, natural historian and collector, born Killyleagh, 1660.
Francis Crozier, naval officer and Arctic and Antarctic explorer, born Banbridge, 1796.
Eldred Pottinger, East India Company army officer and Afghan adventurer, born Mount Pottinger, 1811.
Henry James Campbell, textile merchant and founder of Campbell College, born Newtownards, 1813.
Thomas Ferguson, linen manufacturer, born Clare, Waringstown, 1820.
Sir William Thomson, surgeon, born Downpatrick, 1843.
Henry Bournes Higgins, Australian politician and judge, born Newtownards, 1851.
John Miller Andrews, Prime Minister of Northern Ireland (1940–43), born Comber, 1871.
Sir James Martin, ejector seat designer and manufacturer, born Crossgar, 1893.
Brian Faulkner, Baron Faulkner of Downpatrick, Prime Minister of Northern Ireland (1971–2), born Helen's Bay, 1921.

Down refers to the area demarcating the traditional county on the eastern coast of Northern Ireland. The river Lagan valley borders Antrim to the north, with the Ards peninsula and Strangford Lough to the east. These low-lying lands rise to the west, characterized by glacial hills or 'drumlins' which extend towards the valley of the river Bann, which flows into Lough Neagh from its source in the Mourne Mountains to the south, where Slieve Donard (852 m) is the highest point, not only in the county, but in Northern Ireland. The Newry (or Clanrye) river forms the boundary with Armagh and flows into Carlingford Lough.

In 1973, local government reorganization divided the six administrative counties and two county boroughs into 26 'single-tier' districts, some of which cut across the old county boundaries. Currently, Ards, Down, North Down and Banbridge as well as part of Craigavon and Newry and Mourne Borough Councils, and sections of Belfast and Lisburn City Councils fall within the traditional county borders of Down. The former counties are still in use as Lieutenancy areas, as well as for car number plates and passports. Another reorganization is planned to go ahead in 2011 which will reduce the number of districts in Northern Ireland to eleven.

Downpatrick (10,316) was the county town prior to 1973, although Bangor (76,403) is much larger. Other important settlements in the northeast of the county include Dundonald (20,000), Newtownards (27,821), Holywood (12,037) and Hillsborough (3,400), while more southerly towns include Banbridge (14,744), Newcastle (7,444) and Warrenpoint (6,981). Newry (27,433) is officially included in County Down, despite the fact that half of it physically lies in County Armagh. The Belfast metropolitan area sits astride the old county borders between Down and Antrim, traditionally the line of the river Lagan so that, broadly, east Belfast and parts of south Belfast are also in County Down.

Downpatrick is located at the top of Strangford Lough on the estuary of the river Quoile. The lough, in Irish *Loch Cuan* ('calm lough') provided a secure anchorage and there is evidence of settlement along its shores from the earliest times. However, the town never became a port because the lough is shallow

and characterized by mud flats. Instead, Downpatrick became a place of pilgrimage. St Patrick is reputedly buried on the site of what is now Downpatrick Cathedral.

The Bronze Age Loughbrickland Crannog and the Ballynoe Stone Circle, one of a number of megalithic monuments along the eastern coast of Ireland show that County Down has been occupied since earliest times. St Patrick, who is much connected with the county, began his missionary work at Saul in AD 432. Following the arrival of Christianity towns grew up around the new monasteries and abbeys. Viking invasions in the 8th and 9th centuries had devastating effects on these communities, destroying monastic settlements, including those founded by St Finian near Newtownards and the great abbey at Bangor. Later incursions by Anglo-Normans brought English influence and castle building, the motte and bailey at Dromore being a particularly fine example, but Down was not part of the scheme known as the Plantation of Ulster in the 17th century and actual colonization only occurred in a piecemeal fashion.

County Down's fortunes have much in common with the other Ulster counties. The exploitation of flax growing and linen textile weaving was the basis of local wealth. In 1777, Banbridge was the single largest manufacturer of linen in Ireland, and Thomas Ferguson & Co. is still located in the town, the last to produce traditional damask cloth. In the north and east, Bangor grew as a port and a cotton textile manufacturing centre until the sector collapsed in the 19th century, when it, in common with other coastal towns, was reinvented as a Victorian seaside resort. Shipbuilding on the eastern shore of the river Lagan was exemplified by Harland and Wolff. Nineteenth-century famine and a later collapse of traditional industries saw County Down lose almost half its population between 1841 and 1911. 'The Troubles' also had a significant impact in the county, where HMP Maze was built on a former RAF base outside Belfast. Today, employment in manufacturing and construction sectors have given way to the service sector as the main employers in the area. In 2002, Newry was granted 'city' status by the Queen.

Stepping Stones, Tollymore Forest Park.

"Bangor ... was famous as a seat of learning. ... Its seminary, directed by St Carthagus, is declared to be the germ from which Oxford arose, King Alfred having obtained his professors from Bangor when he founded or restored that university."
Patrick Weston Joyce

"To the south are the holy and curative wells of Struel, with ruins of a chapel and various medieval buildings covering a Drinking Well, an Eye Well, and tanks for the total immersion of men and women. Pilgrims still come here on the night of 23rd June. The wells owe their powers, naturally, to St Patrick."
Brendan Lehane, 1973.

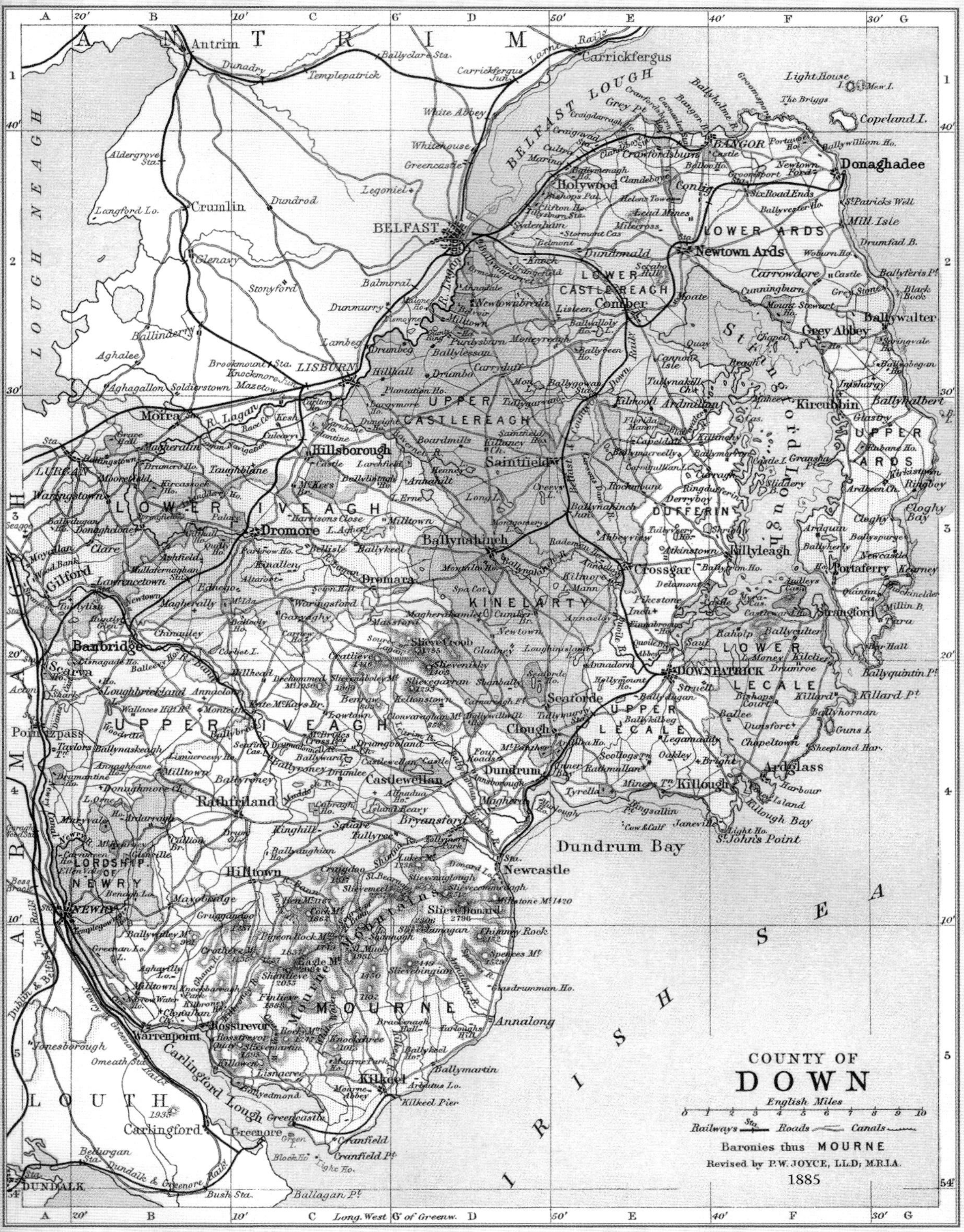

Bartholomew Gazetteer of the British Isles, 1887

Down, *a maritime co. of Ulster province, in the NE. of Ireland, having co. Antrim on the N., co. Armagh on the W., and the sea on all other sides; greatest length, NE. and SW., 50 miles; greatest breadth, NW. and SE., 35 miles; average breadth, 24 miles; coast-line, about 67 miles (or 139 miles including all the inlets); area 612,399 ac. (3004, water), or 2.9 per cent. of the total area of Ireland; pop. 272,107, of whom 29.8 per cent. are Roman Catholics, 23.4 Episcopalians, 40.1 Presbyterians, and 1.9 Methodists. The coast is deeply indented by the spacious inlets of Belfast Lough, Strangford Lough, Dundrum Bay, and Carlingford Lough. There are numerous islands in Strangford Lough, and Copeland Island lies off the entrance to Belfast Lough. The surface on the whole is irregular and hilly. The Mourne Mountains occupy the S., the highest summit of which is Slieve Donard, alt. 2796 ft. The prevailing rock is clay slate; trap and limestone are abundant in the N., and granite occurs among the Mourne Mountains. The mfr. of fine linen fabrics, such as muslin, forms a leading industry. The fisheries are extensive. The co. comprises 12 bars. Ards (Lower and Upper), Castlereagh (Lower and Upper), Dufferin, Iveagh (Lower and Upper), Kinelarty, Lecale (Lower and Upper), Mourne, and Newry lordship; 70 pars.: part of Belfast; the greater part of the parl. bor. of Newry); and the towns of Banbridge, Bangor, Downpatrick, Dromore, Holywood, Lisburn (part of), Newtownards, &c.*

Downpatrick Cathedral

Mourne Mountains

ARMAGH

Area Sq Km	1,254
Area Sq Miles	484
Population	159,000
County town	Armagh
Highest point	Slieve Gullion (577 m)

Ard Mhacha is from the Gaelic *ard*, 'height' or 'high place' and *Macha*, a personal name with reference to either a legendary Celtic goddess or the only High Queen of Ireland.

FAMOUS FOR

The Book of Armagh is a 9th-century codex containing a complete non-Vulgate New Testament as well as documents relating to St Patrick. Rivalling the *Book of Kells* in its richness, it was associated with the saint, although it postdated him.

The Kilnasaggart Stone is a granite pillar covered with crosses as well as Gaelic and Latin inscriptions and thought to date from around AD 700. It is about 2 km from Jonesborough, near the Louth border.

Bessbrook was once known not only for the quality of its linen, but for the fact that it had no pubs, no pawn shops and, therefore, no police station. It is still without a public house.

Armagh's **population** plummeted due to famine, economic contraction and emigration in the century between 1851 and 1951, from its peak of 232,134 in 1841. In fact, the population did not begin to rise until 1951, with another dip in 1981, and it was only in 2001 that the population had nearly matched that recorded in 1881: 163,180.

FAMOUS PEOPLE

Francis Johnston, architect responsible for many buildings in Armagh, born Armagh, 1760/1.
D'Arcy Wentworth, medical practitioner and public servant in Australia, born Portadown, 1762.
James Macartney, anatomist, born Armagh, 1770.
Edward Bunting, collector of folk music, born Armagh, 1773.
Sir Arthur Hunter Palmer, politician in Australia and Premier of Queensland, born Armagh, 1819.
James Breen, astronomer, born Armagh, 1826.
Sir Robert Hart, Inspector General of the Chinese Maritime Customs Bureau (1863–1907), born Portadown, 1835.
Thomas Preston, physicist, born Kilmore, 1860.
Charles Wood, organist and composer, born Armagh, 1866.
George William Russell (*pseudonym* A.E.), poet, painter, writer and economist, born Lurgan, 1867
Eric Mervyn Lindsay, astronomer, born Portadown, 1907.
Patrick McGee, actor, born Armagh, 1922.
Ian Richard Kyle Paisley, church minister and politician, First Minister of Northern Ireland (2007–8), born Armagh, 1926.
Alexander Walker, film critic and biographer, born Portadown, 1930.

"The ride of ten miles from Armagh to Portadown was not the prettiest, but one of the pleasantest drives I have had in Ireland, for the country is well cultivated along the whole of the road, the trees in plenty, and villages and neat houses always in sight. The little farms, with their orchards and comfortable buildings, were as clear and trim as could be wished: they are mostly of one storey, with long thatched roofs and shining windows, such as those that may be seen in Normandy and Picardy."
William Thackeray, 1845

County Armagh is in the southeast of Northern Ireland, bordering the Republic of Ireland. A temperate climate means that generally the county is damp, but rarely freezing. Slieve Gullion (573 m), in the south of the county, is the highest point in the area. It is an extinct volcano, shaped by glaciations, as are many of the rolling hills in the surrounding countryside. In the north, the hills fall away to the relative flat lands around Lough Neagh. The river Blackwater demarcates the border with County Tyrone, and its tributaries include the Callan and the Tall.

In 1973, local government reorganization divided the six administrative counties and two county boroughs into 26 'single-tier' districts, some of which cut across the old county boundaries. Currently, Armagh City and District Council, most of Craigavon Borough Council and the western third of Newry and Mourne District Council fall within the traditional county borders of Armagh. The former counties are still in use as Lieutenancy areas, as well as for car number plates and passports. Another reorganization is planned for 2011, which will reduce the number of districts in Northern Ireland to eleven.

Armagh town (14,590) was the administrative centre of the traditional county of Armagh but both Portadown (32,000) and Lurgan (25,000) are larger. Despite the fact that half of it physically lies in County Armagh, Newry (27,430) is officially included in County Down. Villages include Bessbrook (2,420) and Crossmaglen (1,459).

Armagh played a pivotal role in the Christianization of Ireland in the 5th century, for it was here that St Patrick is said to have converted the local king, created the first diocese, and caused churches and schools to be built. The importance of this ecclesiastical capital was such that the great 11th-century High King Brian Boru left instructions for his burial at the cathedral. It is also home to the internationally renowned Armagh Observatory, founded in 1790 by Archbishop Richard Robinson.

County Armagh was once known as the 'Orchard County' because its land is fertile and traditionally many apple trees were grown here. The Vikings attacked the rich monastic communities in the 9th century, but made no permanent settlements, unlike the Anglo-Normans

"[Portadown] citizens are supposed to be close with their money and have been called 'the Aberdonians of Ireland', a judgment that may have more to do with outside envy than inner character."
Brendan Lehane, 1973

following the Conquest of England. The Plantation of Ulster in the 17th century, saw Armagh colonized mainly by English Protestants at the expense of local, generally perceived as rebellious, Irish.

In common with many other parts of Ulster, flax for linen was grown and woven as a cottage industry, and the prosperity of this rural area was bound up, in part, with the production of linen. Lurgan, founded as part of the Plantation of Ulster, was known for textile manufacturing, especially linen, until the late 20th century decline, although other industries were also part of the industrial mix, including carpet weaving, baking and engineering. Portadown came to prominence as a major junction for the Great North Railway, but was already prosperously situated along the river Bann just north of the Newry Canal, built between 1731 and 1742 to bring coal from the coalfields of Tyrone to port at Carlingford Lough downstream from Newry.

Craigavon was developed as a 'New Town' in 1965 based on an expanding population's need for housing, the pre-existence of local industry and the advantages of spreading development away from Belfast, while keeping the new 'linear city' well connected to the capital by a new motorway link. Unfortunately, the plan encountered two intractable stumbling blocks almost immediately: the closure of the Goodyear factory and 'The Troubles'. Craigavon has given its name to one of the 26 local government districts, which has a population of 90,800.

South Armagh acquired the reputation as 'bandit country' during 'The Troubles', and the consequences of being an IRA stronghold and therefore the most militarised region in the province had deleterious effects, including on its local economy. In 2007, 82 per cent of jobs in Armagh County Council were within the service sector, covering a wide range of employment from public administration, education and health to hotels and restaurants, while only 11 per cent were in manufacturing. Although it is difficult to provide accurate figures because the current districts cross county boundaries, it is clear that the situations are little different in Craigavon and Newry and Mourne districts, but the so-called 'Peace Dividend' is expected to pay out in investment and jobs.

Slieve Gullion Mountain

Statue of Sir John Greer Dill, highly decorated British commander in World War I and II, born Lurgan, 1881.

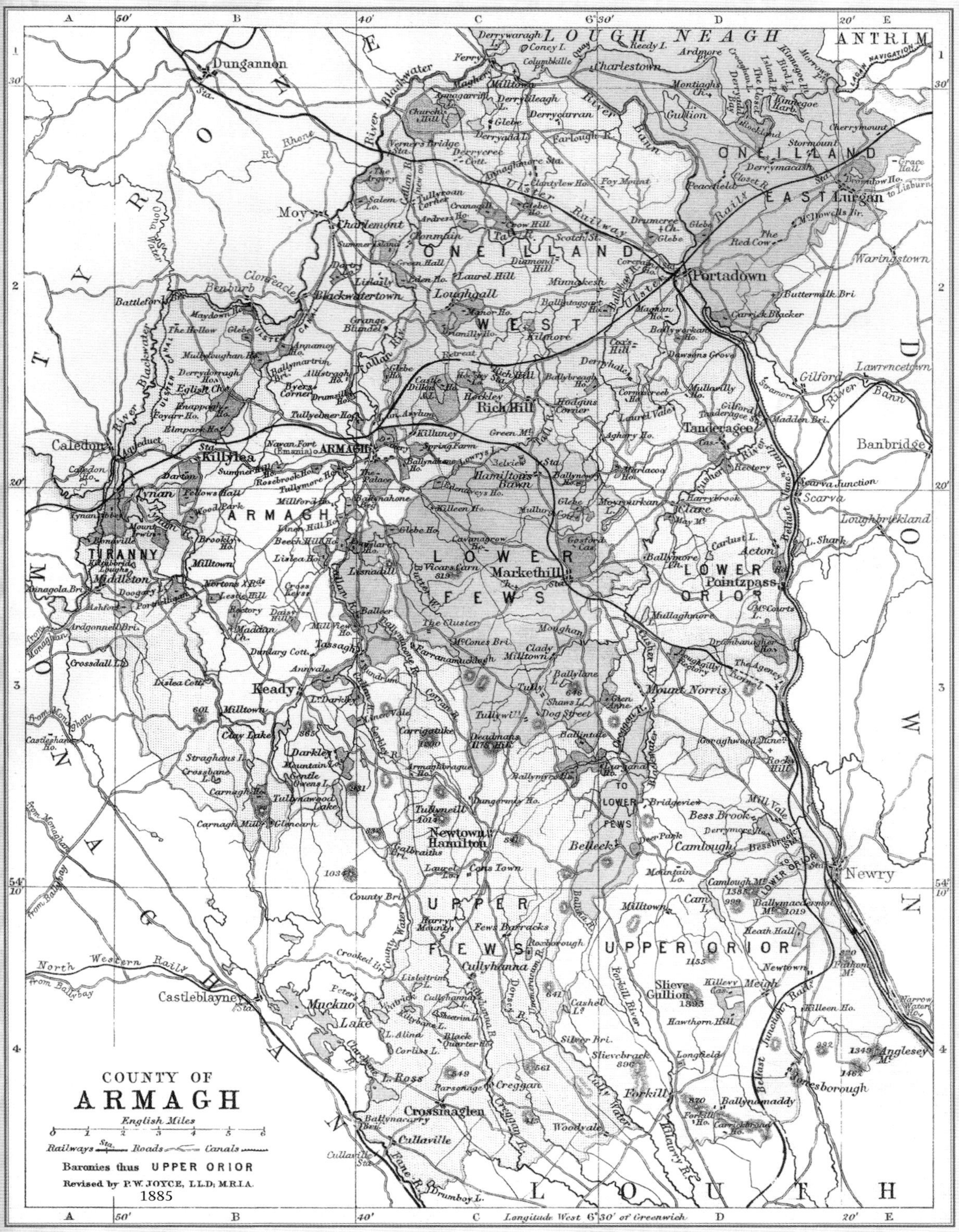

COUNTY OF
ARMAGH
English Miles
Railways ——— Roads ——— Canals ———
Baronies thus UPPER ORIOR
Revised by P.W. Joyce, LL.D., M.R.I.A.
1885

Bartholomew Gazetteer of the British Isles, 1887
ARMAGH, *an inland co., prov. Ulster, bounded N. by co. Tyrone and Lough Neagh, E. by co. Down, S. by Louth, and W. by cos. Monaghan and Tyrone. Greatest length N. and S., 32 miles; greatest breadth E. and W., 20 miles. Area, 328,086 ac. (311,048 ac. land and 17,038 water). Pop 163,177 of whom 75,709 were Roman Catholics, 53,390 Protestant Episcopalians, 26,077 Presbyterians, and 4884 Methodists. The surface rises with gentle undulations from the shores of Lough Neagh to hilly dists. of the S. and SE.; chief summit Slieve Gullion, 1893 ft. The rivers are the Bann, Blackwater, Callan, and Newry. The soil is generally fertile, and there is much bog. Linen is the staple mfr.; there is also cotton. The co. comprises 8 bars., 28 pars. and parts of the pars., part of the parl. bor. of Newry, the city of Armagh, and the towns of Lurgan, Portadown, and Tanderagee.*

Neolithic Court Tomb, Ballymacdermot.

Bluebell wood at the Oxford Island National Nature Reserve on the southern shores of Lough Neagh.

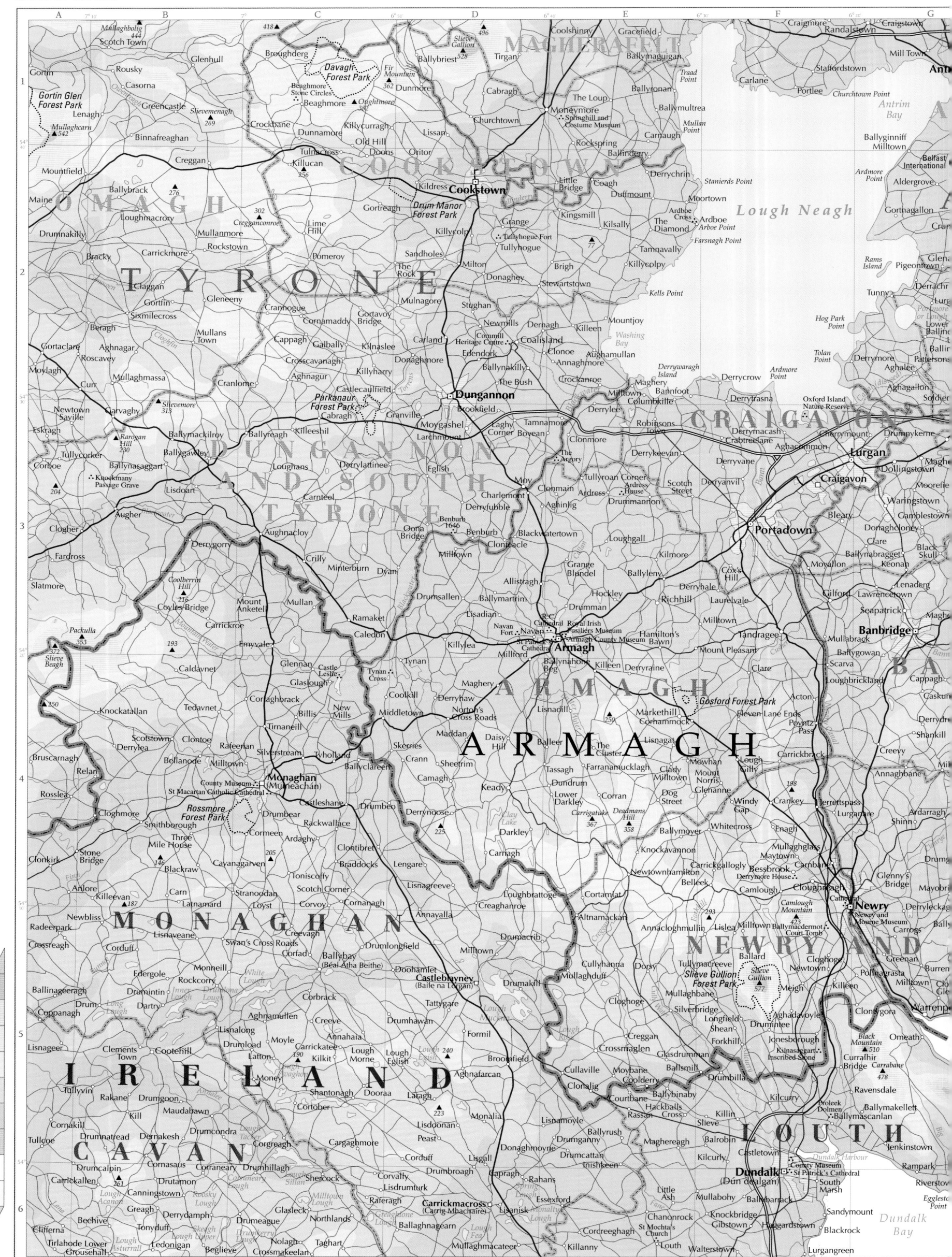

British National Grid projection

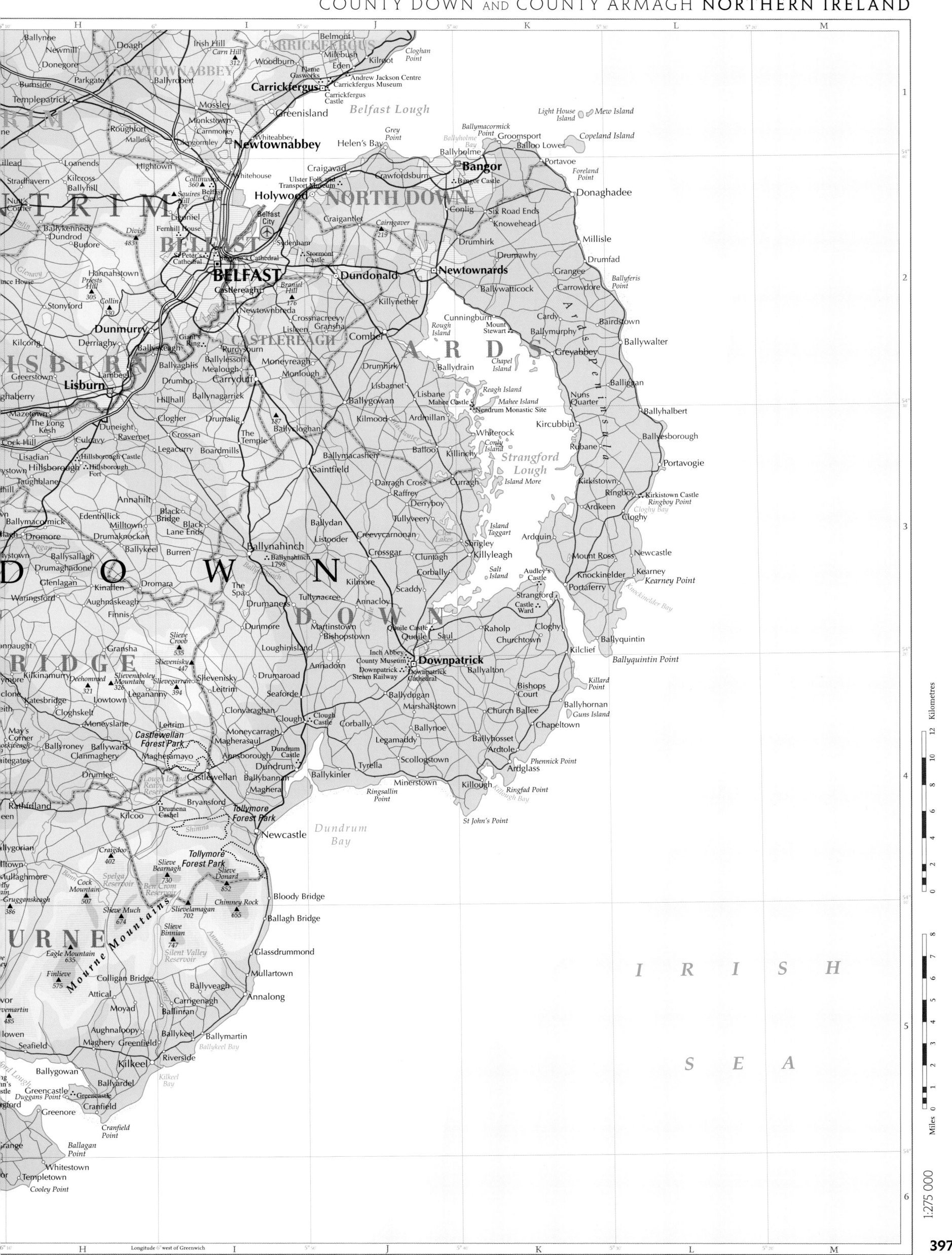

1:275 000

Kilometres

Miles

FERMANAGH

Area Sq Km	1,691
Area Sq Miles	653
Population	57,500
County town	Enniskillen
Highest point	Cuilcagh (667 m)

The county was called Fermanach by 1010, from *Fear Manach*, the 'place of the men of the Manaigh'. There is also the suggestion that the *manach* may refer to monks.

FAMOUS FOR

The Annals of Ulster, a chronicle spanning AD 431 to 1540 and written mainly in Irish, were compiled on Belle Isle in Lough Erne from previously written sources as well as oral history. The original is now in Trinity College Dublin, with a contemporary copy at the Bodleian Library in Oxford.

When Northern Ireland came into being in 1921, Fermanagh County Council declared allegiance to the **Irish Free State**, and was promptly dissolved.

County Fermanagh is the only county in Northern Ireland without a **border** on Lough Neagh.

Belleek porcelain started to be made in the town of Belleek in 1857. The delicate white iridescent pieces are avidly collected, and continue to be made today in Belleek.

The Marble Arch Caves are a series of natural limestone structures first explored in 1895. Ninety years later they were opened to the public, and in 2004 the caves as well as Cuilcagh Mountain Park were combined in the **Marble Arch Caves Global Geopark**, which extends on both sides of the Irish border, and covers thousands of hectares.

FAMOUS PEOPLE

John Armstrong, civil engineer, officer in Continental Army, US Congressman, born Brookeborough, 1717.
William Irvine, American army officer and politician, born near Enniskillen, 1741.
William Plunket, first Baron Plunket, Lord Chancellor of Ireland, born Enniskillen, 1764.
Terence Bellew McManus, Young Irelander leader, born Tempo, 1811/12.
Shan Fadh Bullock (formerly John William Bullock), novelist, born on the Island of Inisherk, Upper Lough Erne, 1865.
Sir (John) Evelyn Leslie Wrench, promoter of the British Empire and author, born Brookeborough, 1882.
Robert (Bobby) Kerr, Olympic 200-m gold medallist, born Enniskillen, 1882.
Basil Stanlake Brooke, Viscount Brookeborough, Prime Minister of Northern Ireland, born Colebrooke Park, Brookeborough, 1888.
Denis Parsons Burkitt, surgeon, first described Burkitt's lymphoma, born Enniskillen, 1911.
Joan Trimble, composer and pianist, born Enniskillen, 1882.

"The whole map of Europe has been changed … but as the deluge subsides and the waters fall short we see the dreary steeples of Fermanagh and Tyrone emerging once again."
Winston Churchill, 1922

"In the highlands to the east [of Upper Lough Erne], as to the west of the lake, are large numbers of prehistoric remains of people who had to stay high above what was, before draining, a large expanse of swampy jungle."
Brendan Lehane, 1973

Fermanagh refers to the traditional county of Ireland situated in the far southwest of the province of Ulster in Northern Ireland. Fermanagh is often referred to as the Irish Lake District. The county is geographically dominated by the basin of the river Erne, its many tributaries and its two loughs, Upper and Lower Lough Erne, which run the diagonal length of the area and are surrounded by drumlins, long, oval hills formed during the retreat of the last Ice Age. Cuilcagh Mountain (665 m) on the border with County Cavan in the Irish Republic is the county's highest point and is set within one of the few intact examples of upland blanket bog in Western Europe. Streams flowing off Cuilcagh's slopes are the source of the river Shannon, the longest river in Ireland. Fermanagh's temperate climate means that rainfall is high, but extremes of temperature are rare.

In 1973, local government reorganization divided the six administrative counties and two county boroughs into 26 'single-tier' districts, some of which cut across the old county boundaries. Currently, Fermanagh Borough Council uniquely lies entirely within its traditional borders. The former counties are still in use as Lieutenancy areas, as well as for car number plates and passports. Another reorganization is planned for 2011, which will reduce the number of districts in Northern Ireland to eleven.

Fermanagh has no cities or large towns. The traditional county town is Enniskillen (13,599), and other important settlements include Lisnaskea (2,739), once the seat of Clan Maguire, Irvinestown (1,801) and Lisbellaw (1,046).

Enniskillen, in the centre of the county, is situated along the river Erne on land called Cethlin's Island, between Upper and Lower Lough Erne. A strategic crossing point of Lough Erne, it was formerly the site of a stronghold of the Maguires. Enniskillen is the largest settlement in the county by some margin, and acts as Fermanagh's market town. It was officially incorporated by James I in the early 17th century, and gained a reputation as a Protestant stronghold, although the 2001 Census records that 60 per cent of the inhabitants of the town today are Roman Catholic. The county town also

became a garrison, and has given its name to two famous British regiments, the Royal Inniskilling Fusiliers and the Inniskilling Dragoons, now amalgamated into the Royal Irish Regiment.

Ancient settlements and religious monuments along the shoreline and on many of the 154 islands of the Erne Loughs include a chain of medieval monasteries. Enniskillen's oldest building, a stone castle built in 1428, was the scene of numerous sieges, finally being captured in 1607. During the Plantation of Ulster in the 17th century, local landowners were supplanted by colonists who were loyal to the Crown, typically English or Scottish and Protestant. Centuries later, 'The Troubles' also left their mark.

The area is predominantly rural, with an emphasis on pastoral farming, especially beef and dairy, sheep and pork. Arable acreage is put to animal feed crops, rather than cereal production, and recently there has been some diversification into growing willow as a fuel source. The Shannon–Erne Waterway, restored for pleasure boats in 1994, was originally one of many canals built during the 18th century to move goods more easily around the country. It was superseded by the railways, and later roads that funnelled traffic through the narrow neck of land between the loughs.

There are a number of thriving industries, such as the world-famous Belleek Pottery, a constructional steel fabrication factory, and knitwear manufacturing at Enniskillen. Manufacturing provides 17 per cent of employment in the area, compared to 12 per cent on average for the Province as a whole.

Fermanagh is consciously developing its reputation as a popular tourist destination, taking advantage of the 'Peace Dividend' offered by the 'Good Friday Agreement'. The waterways have a particularly good reputation for angling and boating. Employment in the marinas, hotels and caravan parks are reflected in the employment rates within the service sector, now the major employer in the county, providing 74 per cent of jobs. This compares to an average in Northern Ireland of 81 per cent in a sector that also includes public administration and 'front-line services' such as education and health.

Enniskillen Castle

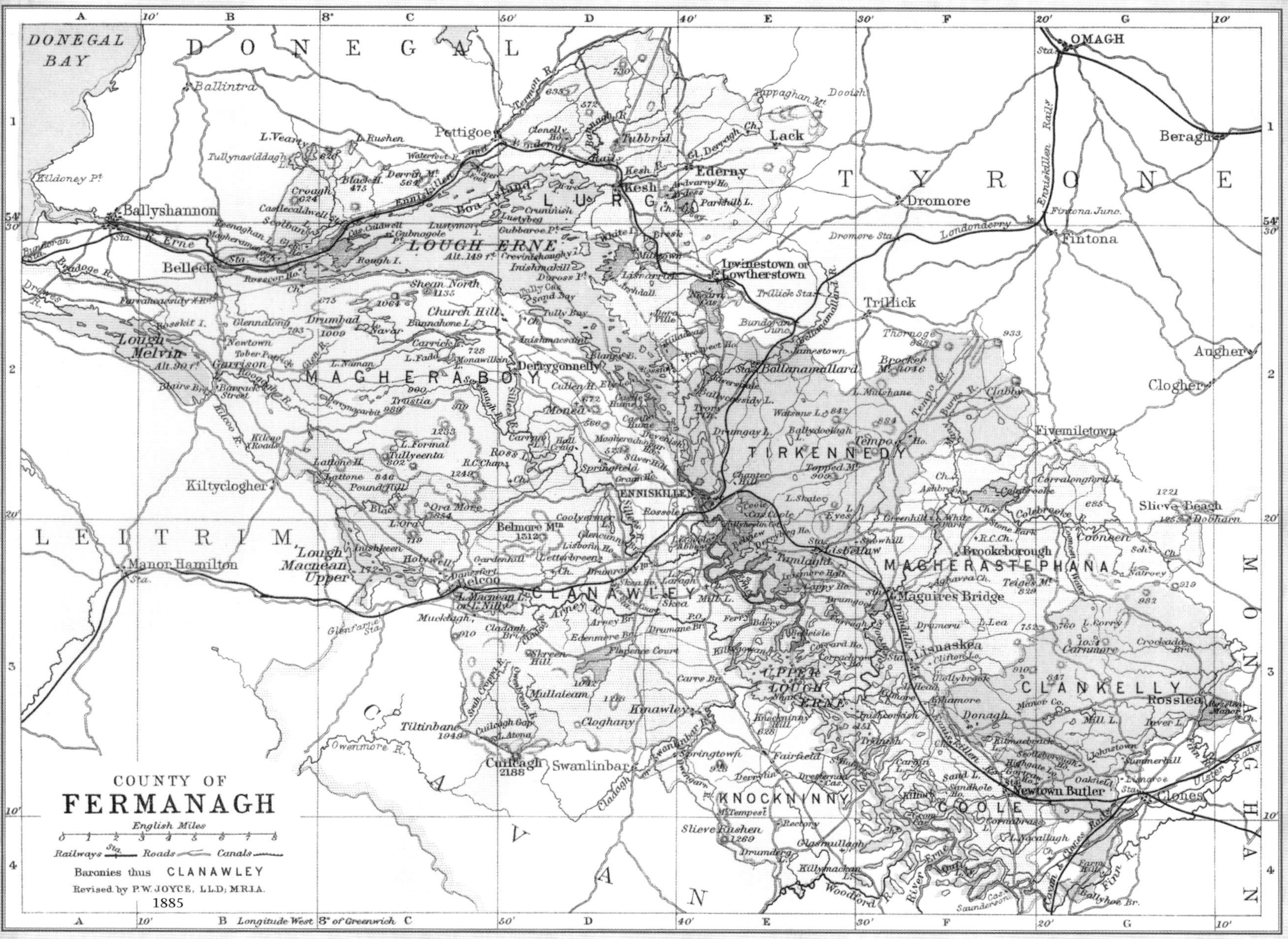

COUNTY OF
FERMANAGH
English Miles

Railways ___Sta.___ Roads ___ Canals ___
Baronies thus CLANAWLEY
Revised by P.W. JOYCE, LL.D. M.R.I.A.
1885

Bartholomew Gazetteer of the British Isles,1887
FERMANAGH, *inland co. of Ulster, Ireland; is surrounded by cos. Donegal, Tyrone, Monaghan, Cavan, and Leitrim; greatest length, NW. and SE., 45 miles; greatest breadth, 18 miles; area 457,369 ac. (46,431 water), or 2.2 per cent. of the total area of Ireland; pop. 84,879, of whom 55.8 per cent. are Roman Catholics, 36.4 Episcopalians,* 2.0 *Presbyterians, and 5.7 Methodists. The surface rises into numerous abrupt eminences of no great elevation; the chief summit is Belmore Mountain, alt. 1312 ft. The great feature of the co. is Lough Erne, which (with the river Erne joining its lower and upper parts) bisects the county throughout its entire length. The loughs are studded with verdant islands, and the whole scenery is picturesque.* *There is abundance of sandstone and limestone; coal and iron occur. The soil is only of middling quality, and there is much bog. The mfr. of coarse linens is carried on. The co. comprises 8 bars. Clanawley, Clankelly, Coole, Knockinny, Lurg, Magheraboy, Magherastephana, and Tirkennedy; 23 pars.; and the town of Enniskillen.*

Marble Arch Caves

Lower Lough Erne

TYRONE

Area Sq Km	3,155
Area Sq Miles	1,218
Population	166,500
County town	Omagh
Highest point	Sawel (683 m) in the Sperrin Mountians

County Tyrone gets its name from the Irish *tír*, meaning 'land' or 'territory' and the personal name, Eoghain. Eoghain was a historical person, the son of King Niall 'of the Nine Hostages'.

FAMOUS FOR

Annaghone near Tullyhogue in County Tyrone claims to sit at the geographical centre of Northern Ireland.

Hugh O'Neill was the last of the chieftains of Ulster to be crowned at **Tullyhogue Fort** in 1593 using the ancient coronation chair with a sacred stone embedded into it, said to have been blessed by St Patrick. The chair was destroyed by the English in 1602, but tales describe how the authentic chair and stone survived, reminiscent of legends surrounding the Scottish Stone of Scone.

The **Ardboe Old Cross** on the shores of Lough Neagh dates from the 10th century. It is made of sandstone with 22 carved panels showing biblical events. It is reputed to be the oldest high cross in Ulster. Unsurprisingly it shows signs of weathering, it is also damaged by emigrants taking small chips with them as keepsakes.

FAMOUS PEOPLE

Hugh O'Neill, second earl of Tyrone, born in the lordship of Tyrone *c.* 1550.
John Dunlap, printer and bookseller in Philadelphia, printer of the first copies of the Declaration of Independence, born Strabane, 1747.
John (Juan) Mackenna, army officer in Chile, born Clogher, 1771.
William Burke, murderer (with William Hare), born Urney, near Strabane, 1792.
Sir Thomas Maclear, astronomer, born Newtownstewart, 1794.
Thomas Mellon, founder of Mellon Bank, Pittsburgh, born Cappagh, 1813.
Joseph Barclay, bishop of Jerusalem, born near Strabane, 1831.
John King, explorer of Australia, born Moy, 1838.
Oliver Sheppard, sculptor, born Cookstown, 1865.
James (Jimmy) Kennedy, popular songwriter, born Omagh, 1902.
Brian O'Nolan (wrote as Flann O'Brien and Myles na gCopaleen), novelist and journalist, born Strabane, 1911.
Sir David Robert Bates, theoretical physicist, born Omagh, 1916.
Brian Friel, dramatist, author and theatre director, born Omagh, 1929.
Josephine Bernadette McAliskey (neé Devlin), political activist, youngest female MP in the House of Commons, born Dungannon, 1947.
Dennis Taylor, international snooker player, born Coalisland, 1949.
Philomena Begley, country music singer, born Pomeroy, 1954.
Darren Clarke, golf professional, born Dungannon, 1968.

"While horses were changed we saw a very dirty town, called Strabane."
William Thackeray, 1845

Tyrone is the name of a traditional county in west central Northern Ireland. Its eastern border along Lough Neagh is flat peatland, rising to moorland toward the Sperrin Mountains in the west, one of the largest upland areas in Ireland, where Sawel (678 m) is the highest point. The river Blackwater rises to the north of Fivemiletown in the south of the county, forming a boundary with both County Armagh and with the Republic of Ireland. The same is true for a short stretch of the river Foyle in the far northwest of the county, where the rivers Finn and Mourne flow through the centre of Strabane, forming the river Foyle. The river Strule flows through Omagh, and has a history of flooding.

In 1973, local government reorganization divided the six administrative counties and two county boroughs into 26 'single-tier' districts, some of which cut across the old county boundaries. Currently, Omagh, Strabane, Cookstown, and Dungannon and South Tyrone Borough Councils fall within the traditional county borders of Tyrone. The former counties are still in use as Lieutenancy areas, as well as for car number plates and passports. Another reorganization is planned for 2011, which will reduce the number of districts in Northern Ireland to eleven.

The population of Tyrone at the time of the 2001 Census was 166,500, with Dungannon District being the most populous. Omagh (19,910) is the largest town and the traditional county town. Other important towns include Strabane (17,000), Dungannon (11,139), Cookstown (10,646) and Coalisland (5,917).

Omagh is probably best known today for the worst bombing of 'The Troubles' in 1998, but its origins are more peaceful and date from the founding of an abbey here in around AD 792. It only became the county town in 1768, prior to which Dungannon was the county seat. Its location was put to good use by the railways, which connected the town to Londonderry, Enniskillen and Belfast between 1852 and 1861. Although the railways are gone, Omagh remains well connected through a series of 'A' roads.

People have made settlements in this part of Ireland for many millennia, as evidenced in the number of standing stones and ancient forts, especially along a line from Omagh to Cookstown. Tyrone was one of the great strongholds of the O'Neills, earls of Ulster until the 17th century, when their power was destroyed in a series of wars with the English. Like neighbouring County Armagh, Tyrone was also caught up in the Plantation of Ulster, which changed land ownership and the religious settlement. Now, however, Tyrone is one of four counties with a majority Catholic population in modern Northern Ireland.

The main occupation in the county, particularly in the west, was the growing of flax and weaving of linen, even before the Linen Board was established in 1711 to regulate quality in this cottage industry, setting stringent standards for the type of seed and the quality of the wheels provided to spin the thread. Later linen and cotton mixes were woven as well as tweed. In the east, coal was mined, although never fully exploited, and a series of canals were built to move this commodity more cheaply to market, including the Coalisland Canal which linked some of the Tyrone coalfields with Loch Neagh. It was last used commercially in 1947.

The 20th century saw the market for linen contract in the face of new, especially man-made, fibres and, combined with 'The Troubles', the county experienced serious unemployment and was considered an area of high deprivation. Dungannon was a centre for linen, before diversifying into glass blowing in the 1960s. Tyrone Crystal traded for 40 years before being closed in June 2010. Investment underwritten by government and regeneration programmes following the 'Good Friday Agreement' have made an impact in the county. Manufacturing jobs account for 20 per cent of employment, and construction another 11 per cent. However, the service industry supplies the lion's share of employment at 63 per cent, and covers public administration, education and health services as well as tourist-related sectors such as hotels and restaurants. An example of these changes can be seen in the conversion of former weaving mills in Cookstown to retail parks and the expansion of Omagh town centre. There have also been countywide initiatives to attract tourists to the area.

Sperrin Mountains

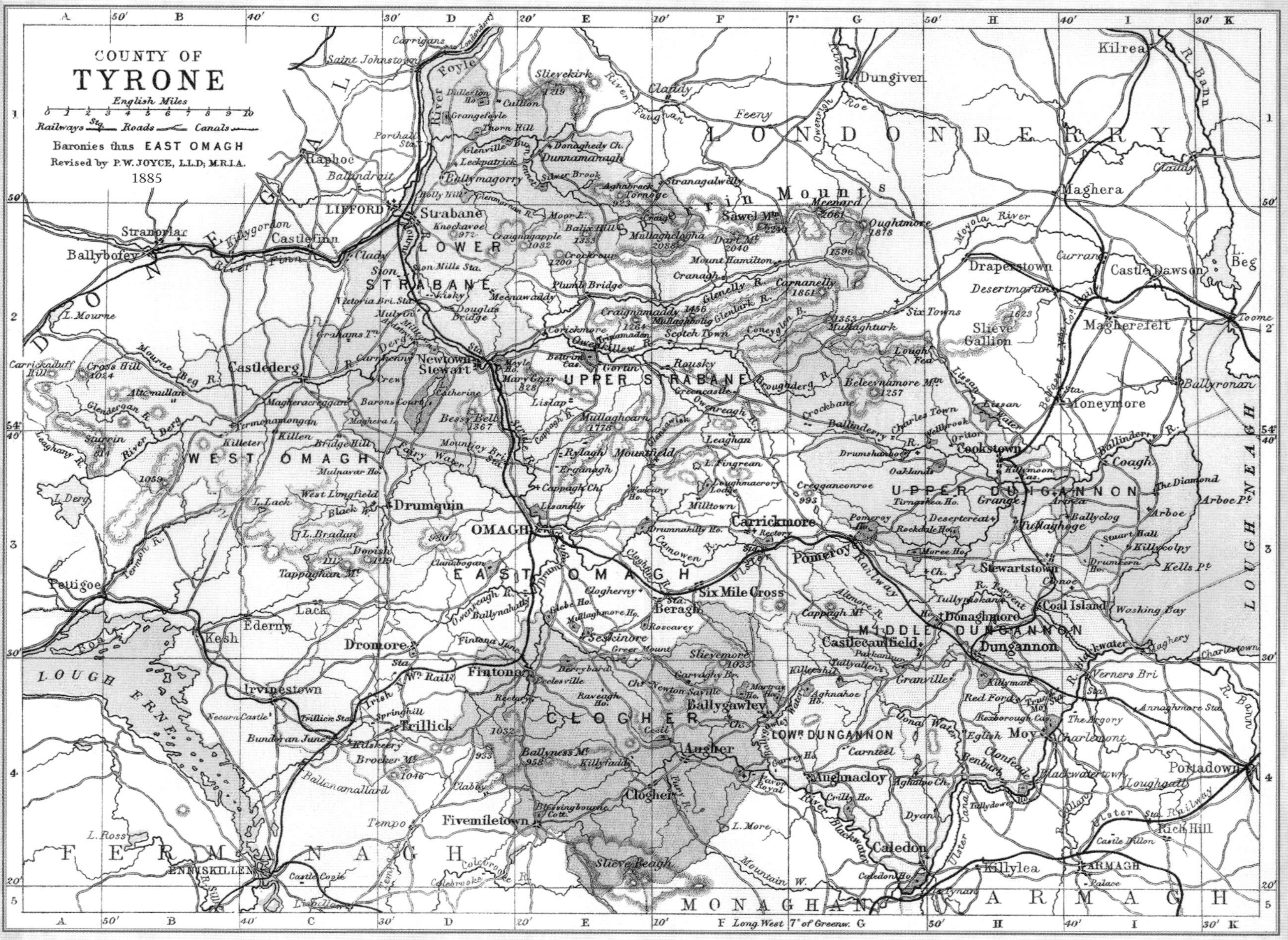

COUNTY OF TYRONE

English Miles

Railways — — — Roads — — — Canals

Baronies thus **EAST OMAGH**

Revised by P.W. JOYCE, LL.D., M.R.I.A.
1885

Bartholomew Gazetteer of the British Isles, 1887

TYRONE, *an inland co. of Ulster province, Ireland; is bounded NE. by co. Londonderry, E. by Lough Neagh, SE. by co. Armagh, S. by co. Monaghan, SW. by co. Fermanagh, and NW. by co. Donegal; greatest length, NW. and SE., 48 miles; greatest breadth, NE. and SW., 38 miles; average breadth, 28 miles; area, 806,658 ac. (31,403 water), or 3.9 per cent. of the total area of Ireland; pop. 197,719, of whom 55.5* per cent. are Roman Catholics, 22.4 Episcopalians, 19.5 Presbyterians, and 1.8 Methodists. The surface in general is hilly and irregular; it rises into mountains of about 2000 ft. on the NE. border, and becomes level towards Lough Neagh on the E. The soil in the lower districts is very fertile and highly cultivated. Coal is worked near Lough Neagh and in the neighbourhood of Dungannon; marble is quarried near the boundary with Monaghan; old red sandstone occurs in the district around Omagh; mica slate and limestone prevail among the mountains. The chief mfrs. are linens, woollens, and coarse earthenware. The principal rivers are the Foyle, the Blackwater, the Mourne, and the Ballinderry. The co. comprises 8 bars. Clogher, Dungannon (Lower, Middle, and Upper), Omagh (East and West), Strabane (Lower and Upper); 46 pars.; and the towns of Omagh (the capital), Strabane, Dungannon, Cookstown, and Aughnacloy.

Ilyhogue Fort

Metres
Feet

700
2296

500
1640

400
1312

300
984

200
656

100
328

0
Land
below
sea
level

50
164

200
656

British National Grid projection

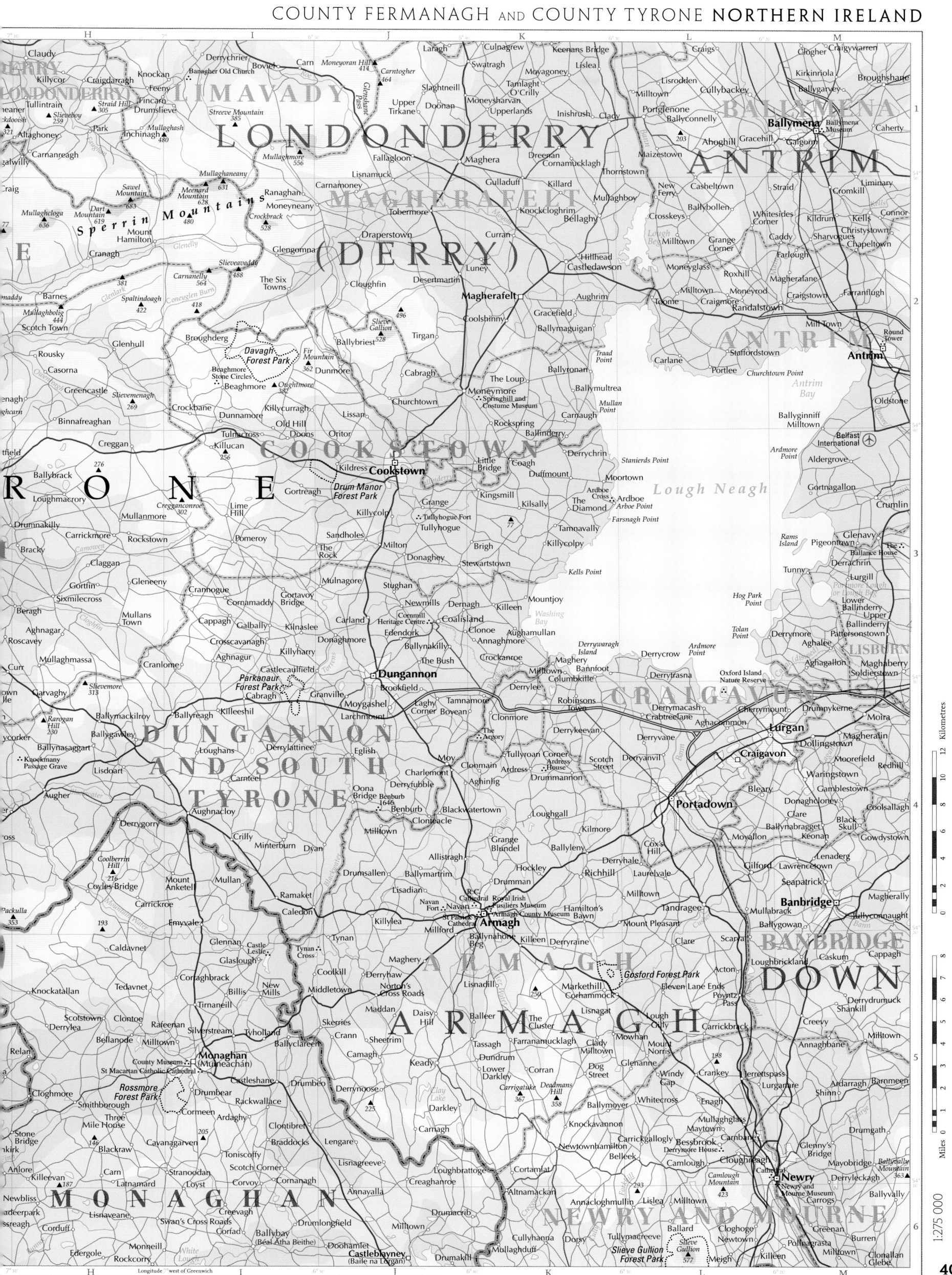

1:275 000

ISLE OF MAN

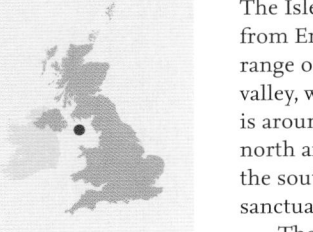

Area Sq Km	572
Area Sq Miles	221
Population	80,000
County town	Douglas
Highest point	Snaefell (621 m)

The origin of the name 'Man' is obscure. In legend it is linked to the Celtic god Manannan mac Lir ('the Son of the Sea') but it may be linked to Môn, the Welsh name for Anglesey. Its Manx name is Ellan Vannam, *Vannam* being a corruption of Manannan mac Lir and *ellan* meaning 'island'.

FAMOUS FOR

The Isle of Man is renowned for the **TT (Tourist Trophy)** motorcycle races that have taken place for over 100 years on the public roads of the island for two weeks around the beginning of June. The current circuit is around 60 km and the races have a reputation for excitement and danger.

At **Laxey** is the world's largest working waterwheel (formally named Lady Isabella after a Lieutenant Governor's wife), designed by the Manxman Robert Casement in 1854 to pump water out of the local mines that produced lead, copper, zinc and silver. The wheel has a diameter of 22 m.

The symbol for the Isle of Man, which appears on its flag, is the **Three Legs of Man** (an example of a triskelion). It has three armoured legs joined at the thigh, bent at the knee and running in a clockwise direction. Its origin is probably linked to the popularity of the triskelion symbol in Celtic and Norse mythology.

The Isle of Man is famous for the breed of tail-less **Manx cats**, which resulted from some genetic anomaly, probably in the late 18th century, that survived because of the island's isolation.

FAMOUS PEOPLE

Archibald Knox, designer, particularly of Liberty fabrics and artefacts, born Cronkbourne, Tromode, 1864.
Sir Frank Kermode, academic and literary critic, born Douglas, 1919.
Randolph Quirk, Baron Quirk, academic and linguistics expert, born Michael, 1920.
Barry Gibb (1946), **Robin Gibb** (1949) and **Maurice Gibb** (1949), musicians, members of the Bee Gees, all born Douglas.
Mark Cavendish, world champion sprint cyclist, born Douglas, 1985.

"There is the natural beauty of the place, its fine adaptation and accommodation for sea bathing, the healthy climate, so grateful to the invalid, and its central situation, like the heart in the system, so well connected in every way with the extremities of the empire, that would make it a desirable residence even for the man of wealth and affluence."
A Six Days' Tour Through the Isle of Man,
by a *stranger*, 1836

The Isle of Man is in the Irish Sea, about equidistant from England and Ireland and closest to Scotland. A range of hills across the island is bisected by a central valley, while the far north is much flatter. The coastline is around 160 km with long sandy beaches in the north and cliffs and sheltered inlets elsewhere. Off the southwestern tip lies the Calf of Man, now a bird sanctuary.

The Isle of Man is a British crown dependency rather than part of the United Kingdom. Apart from defence and foreign policy, it is responsible for its own affairs and is not a member of the European Union. The legislature is the Tynwald, with the Legislative Council and the elected House of Keys. The Tynwald is regarded as the oldest parliament in the world, going back to annual meetings of the Norse settlers held from the 8th century onwards – the legacy continues with an annual outdoor meeting of Tynwald at St John's. The island was under Norse influence until 1266 when Scottish rule was established. Edward II then annexed it in 1333, but it was ruled by the Lords of Man (for most of the period the Earls of Derby) until they sold it to the British government in 1765 and who took full control in 1828.

The population of the Isle of Man in 2006 was 80,000, an increase of over 8,300 in 10 years. The main settlements are Douglas (26,281), Onchan (9,172), Ramse (7,309) and Peel (4,280). The economy was traditionally dependent on agriculture, fishing and tourism. While the latter is still important, offshore banking and hi-tec manufacturing have become key sectors, encouraged by government incentives. Light regulation has also attracted online retailing and gambling operations. There is an airport at Ronaldsway and ferry services from Douglas. On the island itself there are a number of traditional forms of transport, including horsedrawn trams in Douglas, the vintage Manx Electric Railway, the narrow-gauge Steam Railway and the Snaefell Electric Railway.

Peel Bay

Great Laxey Wheel

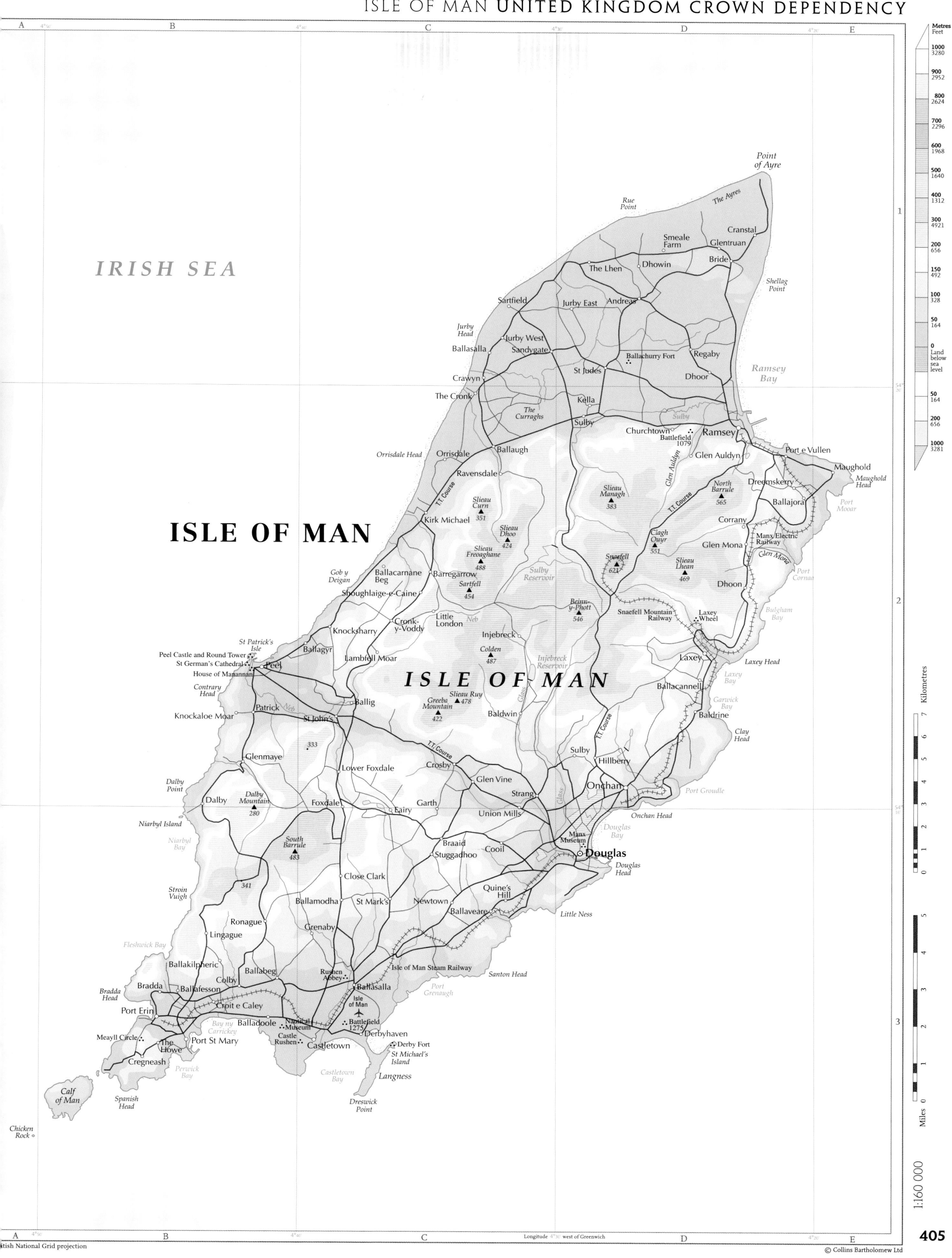

IRISH SEA

ISLE OF MAN

ISLE OF MAN

Point of Ayre

Rue Point

The Ayres

Cranstal

Smeale Farm

Glentruan

The Lhen

Dhowin

Bride

Shellag Point

Sartfield

Jurby East

Andreas

Jurby Head

Jurby West

Sandygate

Ballachurry Fort

Regaby

Ballasalla

St Judes

Dhoor

Ramsey Bay

Crawyn

Kella

The Cronk

The Curraghs

Sulby

Churchtown

Ramsey

Sulby

Port e Vullen

Orrisdale Head

Orrisdale

Ballaugh

Battlefield 1079

Glen Auldyn

Maughold

Ravensdale

Slieau Managh 383

Glen Auldyn

North Barrule 565

Dreemskerry

Maughold Head

Kirk Michael

Slieau Curn 351

T.T. Course

Corrany

Ballajora

Slieau Dhoo 424

Clagh Ouyr 551

Glen Mona

Manx Electric Railway

Port Mooar

Ballacarnane Beg

Slieau Freoaghane 488

Snaefell 621

Slieau Lhean 469

Glen Mona

Gob y Deigan

Barregarrow

Sulby Reservoir

Dhoon

Port Cornaa

Shoughlaige-e-Caine

Sartfell 454

Beinn-y-Phott 546

Snaefell Mountain Railway

Knocksharry

Cronk-y-Voddy

Little London

Neb

Injebreck

Laxey Wheel

Bulgham Bay

St Patrick's Isle

Ballagyr

Lambfell Moar

Colden 487

Injebreck Reservoir

Laxey

Peel Castle and Round Tower

St German's Cathedral

Peel

House of Manannan

Contrary Head

Slieau Ruy 478

Ballacannell

Laxey Bay

Garwick Bay

Knockaloe Moar

Patrick

Neb

St John's

Greeba Mountain 422

Baldwin

Glass

Baldrine

Dalby Point

Ballig

333

Crosby

Sulby

Clay Head

Glenmaye

Glen Vine

Hillberry

Lower Foxdale

Dalby Mountain 280

Foxdale

Garth

Strang

Onchan

Port Groudle

Niarbyl Island

Dalby

Fairy

Union Mills

Onchan Head

Niarbyl Bay

Braaid

Cooil

Manx Museum

Douglas Bay

South Barrule 483

Stuggadhoo

Douglas

Stroin Vuigh

341

Close Clark

Quine's Hill

Douglas Head

Ballamodha

St Mark's

Newtown

Ronague

Grenaby

Ballaveare

Little Ness

Lingague

Fleshwick Bay

Ballakilpheric

Ballabeg

Rushen Abbey

Isle of Man Steam Railway

Santon Head

Ballalpheric

Colby

Ballasalla

Bradda Head

Bradda

Ballafesson

Crpit e Caley

Balladoole

Nautical Museum

Isle of Man

Battlefield 1275

Port Grenaugh

Port Erin

Meayll Circle

Bay ny Carrickey

Derbyhaven

The Howe

Port St Mary

Castle Rushen

Castletown

Derby Fort

St Michael's Island

Cregneash

Perwick Bay

Langness

Calf of Man

Spanish Head

Castletown Bay

Dreswick Point

Chicken Rock

Metres / Feet

1000	3280
900	2952
800	2624
700	2296
600	1968
500	1640
400	1312
300	4921
200	656
150	492
100	328
50	164
0	Land below sea level
50	164
200	656
1000	3281

Kilometres
0 1 2 3 4 5 6 7

Miles
0 1 2 3 4 5

1:160 000

British National Grid projection

Longitude 4°30' west of Greenwich

© Collins Bartholomew Ltd

Bartholomew Gazetteer of the British Isles,1887
ISLE OF MAN, *situated in the Irish Sea, 16 miles S. of Burrow Head, Wigtownshire, 27 miles S.W. of St Bees Head, Cumberland, and 27 miles W. of Strangford Lough, co. Down; greatest length, NE. to SW., 33 miles; greatest breadth, E. to W., 12 and a half miles; area, 145,325 ac., pop. 54,089. A precipitous islet, called the Calf of Man, is situated off the SW. extremity and contains about 800 acres. On the Isle of Man itself a range of mountains runs NE. to SW. – from Maughold Head to the Calf – occupying the greater part of the island, the highest elevation being Snaefell (2034 ft). From the heights may be witnessed scenery which is justly celebrated for its loveliness and its picturesque variety. Amidst the mountains are the sources of the Sulby, Neb, Douglas, and other streams. The island contains no lakes. The coast on the SW. is rugged and precipitous, the cliffs in some places rising sheer from the sea to a height of over 1400 ft.; on the SE. it is generally low, with gradual elevations towards the mountains. On the E. are numerous creeks and bays, including Douglas Bay and Laxey Bay. Clay slate is the formation of the greater part of the island; granite and other eruptive rocks have burst through in one or two localities. Lead, copper, zinc, and iron are the principal minerals; the lead ore especially is rich and plentiful, yielding about 4000 tons a year. The land generally is in a high state of cultivation, scientific farming having greatly increased its richness and fertility. All along the coast sea fishing is actively prosecuted, and gives employment to several thousands of fishermen. For anglers the various streams present exceptional attractions, being well stocked with trout, &c. The shipping is almost wholly connected with coasting trade, which shows a considerable amount of activity. Mfrs. are inconsiderable, and in the main consist of Manx cloth, cordage, nets, and canvas. Railway communication exists between the various towns, and there are numerous excellent roads. Few places can point to more interesting antiquarian features than those found in the Isle of Man. Druidical remains and Runic monuments are numerous; and among ancient buildings special mention should be made of Castle Rushen (947), Rushen Abbey (1154), and Peel Castle. The modern building of Castle Mona (1801) is now used as a hotel. Man has a highly interesting history. In early years it frequently changed hands, passing and repassing at various times under the dominion of the Welsh, the Scots, the Northumbrians, and the Norse. By Magnus VI. of Norway it was ceded to Alexander III. of Scotland in 1266. About the beginning of the 15th century the island was bestowed upon Sir John Stanley, and subsequently remained in the possession of the Derby family- the head being "King of Man"- until it was surrendered to the Parliamentarians in 1651, after the famous and heroic defence attempted by Lady Derby.*

ISLE OF MAN
1892

Thereafter it was granted to General Lord Fairfax, but at the Restoration it again went to the Earl of Derby, in which attachment it remained until 1736. The lordship of Man then fell to the Dukes of Athole, and in 1829 its final reversion to the Crown was effected by purchase. The island has a distinct bishopric, with the designation of Sodor and Man; the former name being derived from the Sudoreys, or Southern Islands, which were at one time politically connected with them. The bishopric is supposed to have been founded by St Patrick in 447.

The island has a government and constitution of its own, also laws, law officers, and courts. The House of Keys, which controls its legislature, is very ancient, and consists of 24 members. Man is divided into 6 sheadings, having 17 parishes, which are subdivided into treens and quarterlands. The principal towns are Douglas, Castletown, Ramsey, and Peel. Castletown is the ancient capital, but Douglas is the chief town and the seat of government.

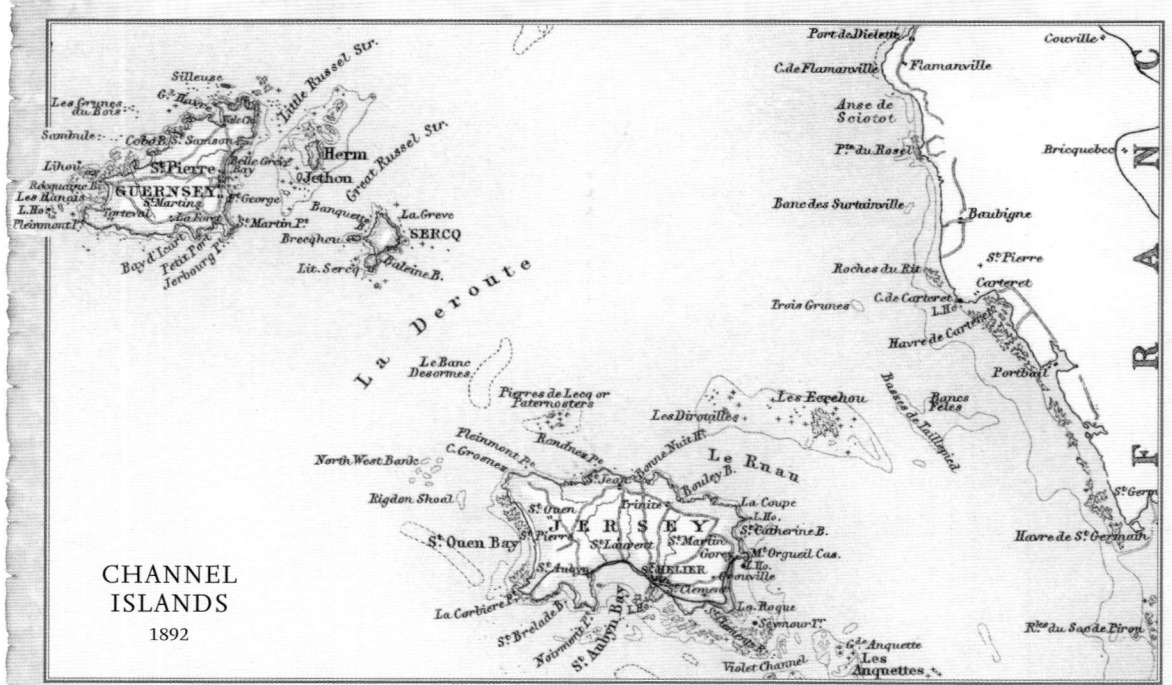

CHANNEL ISLANDS
1892

Bartholomew Gazetteer of the British Isles,1887
THE CHANNEL ISLANDS, *a group of islands, on the S. side of the English Channel, 10 m. W. of coast of France and 80 m. S. of coast of England. The principal members of the group are Jersey, Guernsey, Alderney, and Sark. Geographically connected with France, they have been politically attached to England since the Conquest, and are now all that remain to it of the dukedom of Normandy. The land is parcelled out among a great number of small proprietors, and is carefully cultivated. The language is nearly the same as the old Norman French, but English is taught in all the parochial schools.*

THE CHANNEL ISLANDS

Bailiwick of Jersey
Area sq. km   116
Area sq. miles   45
Population   91,800
County town   St Helier
Highest point   149 m

Bailiwick of Guernsey
Area sq. km   78
Area sq. miles   30
Population   61,700
Capital   St Peter Port
Highest point   Le Moulin, Sark (114 m)

FAMOUS FOR

The Channel Islands are famous for two breeds of cow, the **Jersey** and the **Guernsey**, both prized for the high quality and richness of their milk.

The Channel Islands were occupied during **World War II** by Nazi troops from 1940 to 1945. The Germans established a number of labour camps on the islands, and used slave labour to construct great fortifications. Residents suffered much deprivation and over 2,000 were interned in Germany while a number of Jews were deported to concentration camps.

Victor Hugo lived in exile on Jersey and Guernsey between 1852 and 1870. He spent the first three years on Jersey, until he was expelled for supporting a republican newspaper. On Guernsey he finished three novels including *Les Misérables*.

Sir George Carteret was a staunch royalist and Bailiff of Jersey during the English Civil War. After the execution of Charles I, Jersey became the first place to proclaim Charles II king (on 17 February 1649). During the Restoration Carteret was granted land in America, which he called **New Jersey**.

FAMOUS PEOPLE

James Saumarez, Baron Saumarez, naval commander, victor of Battle of Algeciras (1801), born St Peter Port, Guernsey, 1757.
Sir Isaac Brock, military commander who defended Upper Canada in the War of 1812, born St Peter Port, Guernsey, 1769.
Thomas de la Rue, founder of the De La Rue printers, born La Forêt, Guernsey, 1793.
Lillie Langtry (born Emilie Charlotte Le Breton), society beauty and actress, born St Saviour, Jersey, 1853.
Harry Vardon, golfer, six-time winner of British Open Championship, born Grouville, Jersey, 1870.
Roy Dotrice, actor, born Guernsey, 1923.
Matthew Le Tissier, footballer, born St Peter Port, Guernsey, 1968.

"Sark, fairer than aught in the world that the lit skies cover,
Laughs inly behind her cliffs, and the seafarers mark
As a shrine where the sunlight serves, though the blown
*   clouds hover,*
Sark."
Algernon Charles Swinburne, 1883, 'Insularum Ocelle'

The Channel Islands are a group of islands off the Normandy coast of France and are all that remained when King John lost the Duchy of Normandy in 1204. They are now British crown dependencies. There are two separate administrative jurisdictions – the Bailiwick of Jersey and the Bailiwick of Guernsey. The United Kingdom is responsible for their defence and foreign policy but in all other regards the Bailiwicks are responsible for their own administration. While they are very closely linked to the United Kingdom, neither Bailiwick is a member of the European Union.

Jersey is the larger of the two Bailiwicks with a population of 91,800. Its legislature, the States of Jersey, is headed by the Bailiff. St Helier, the capital, is the largest parish with a population of 28,310. The island consists of a gently rolling plain with some rugged hills along the north coast. The land is fertile, and agricultural exports, particularly of cut flowers and new potatoes were the mainstay of the economy. Tourism, mainly from Britain, continues to be significant. What has changed since the start of the 1980s has been the rapid development of offshore banking and finance, encouraged by a low tax regime. As a result, in 2005 it had the sixth highest Gross Domestic Product per capita in the world (the UK is 34th).

The Bailiwick of **Guernsey** includes the islands of Guernsey, Alderney, Sark, Herm, Jethou, Brecqhou and Lihou. The States of Guernsey has a single chamber, the States of Deliberation. St Peter Port (population 16,488) is the capital and its port was protected by the medieval Castle Cornet. The island of Guernsey is low lying with sandy beaches to the north, rising to higher land in the south. Like Jersey, the contribution of agriculture (particularly cut flowers and tomatoes) to the economy has been declining, while offshore banking and finance make the dominant contribution along with increasing e-commerce activities, all encouraged by the low tax regime. In 2005 it had the 13th highest Gross Domestic Product per capita in the world. Alderney with a population of 2,400 operates semi-independently having its own States of Alderney. Sark, with a population of around 600, is famous for not allowing any cars and for only removing the feudal powers of the Seigneur of Sark in 2008.

St Aubin, Jersey.

Rocky coastline, Guernsey.

Island of Sark

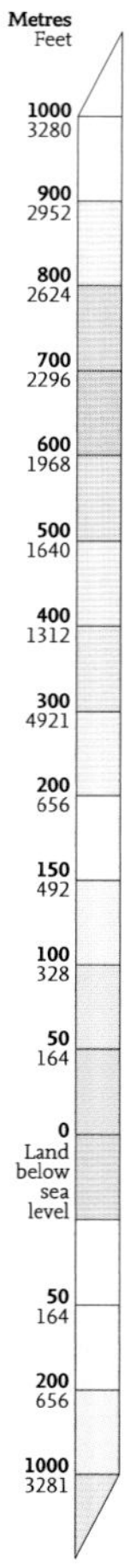

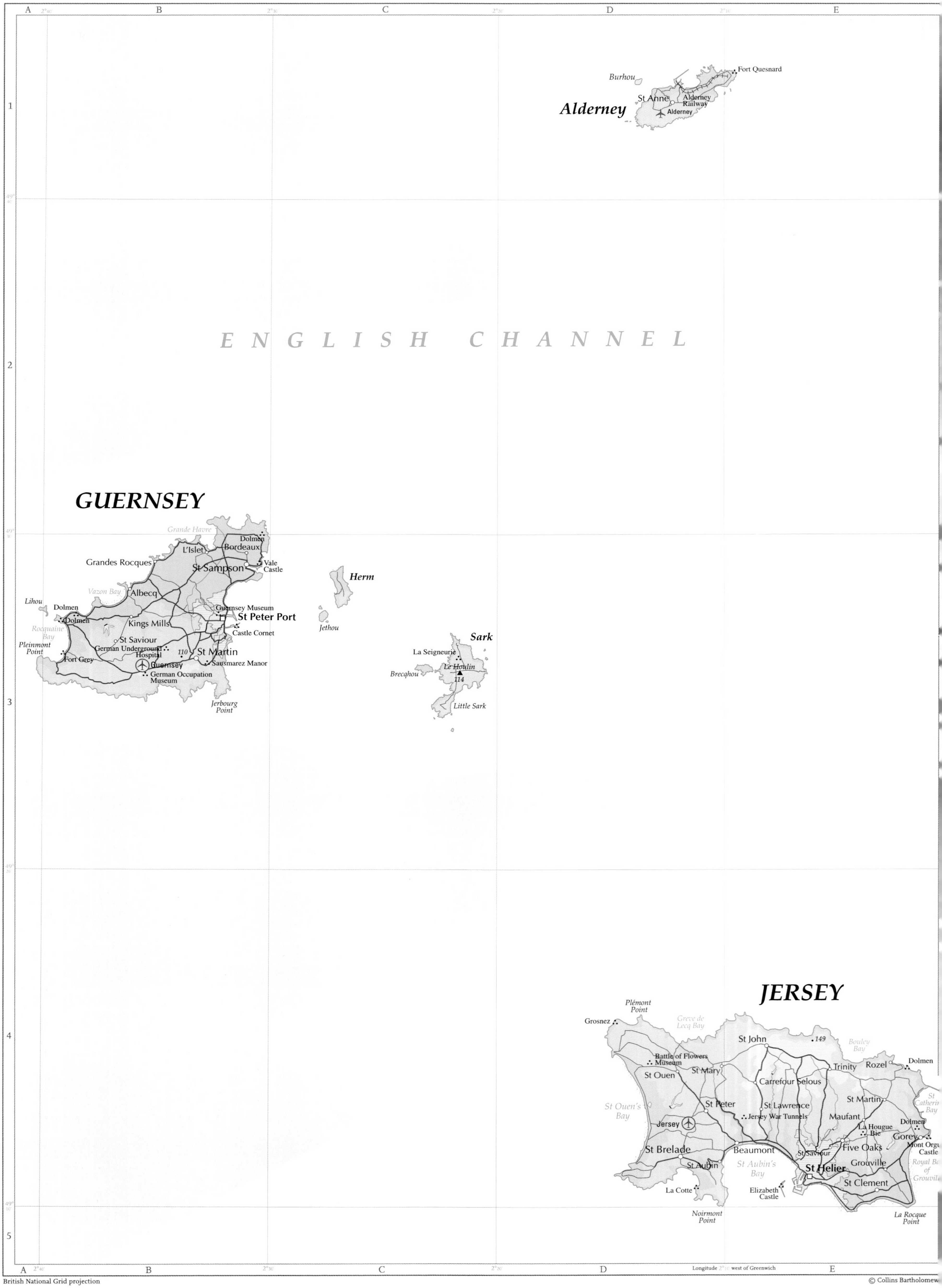

Metres
Feet

1000	3280
900	2952
800	2624
700	2296
600	1968
500	1640
400	1312
300	4921
200	656
150	492
100	328
50	164
0	Land below sea level
50	164
200	656
1000	3281

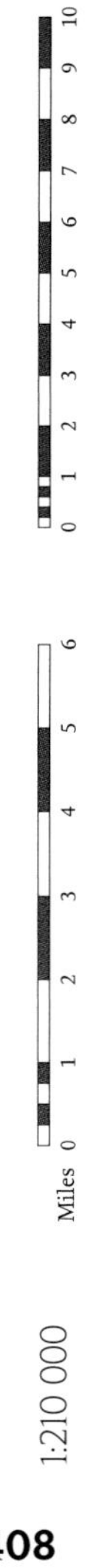

Kilometres

Miles

1:210 000

Alderney

Burhou
Fort Quesnard
St Anne
Alderney Railway
Alderney

ENGLISH CHANNEL

GUERNSEY

Grande Havre
L'Islet
Dolmen
Bordeaux
Grandes Rocques
St Sampson
Vale Castle
Vazon Bay
Albecq
Herm
Lihou
Dolmen
Dolmen
Guernsey Museum
St Peter Port
Rocquaine Bay
Kings Mills
Castle Cornet
Jethou
Pleinmont Point
St Saviour
German Underground Hospital
110
St Martin
Sark
La Seigneurie
Fort Grey
Guernsey
Sausmarez Manor
German Occupation Museum
Brecqhou
Le Houlin
114
Jerbourg Point
Little Sark

JERSEY

Plémont Point
Grève de Lecq Bay
Grosnez
St John
.149
Bouley Bay
Battle of Flowers Museum
Trinity
Rozel
Dolmen
St Ouen
St Mary
Carrefour Selous
St Martin
St Catheri
Bay
St Ouen's Bay
St Peter
St Lawrence
Maufant
Jersey War Tunnels
La Hougue Bie
Dolmen
Jersey
St Saviour
Gorey
Mont Org
Castle
St Brelade
Beaumont
Five Oaks
Royal Ba
of Grouvi
St Aubin
St Aubin's Bay
Grouville
St Helier
St Clement
La Cotte
Elizabeth Castle
Noirmont Point
La Rocque Point

British National Grid projection

Longitude 2° 10' west of Greenwich

© Collins Bartholomew

INTRODUCTION TO THE INDEX

The index includes names shown on the maps in the Times Atlas of Britain. Each entry includes the county/administrative name or geographical area in which the feature is located, a page number and an alphanumeric reference. Additional details within the entries are explained below. Abbreviations used in the index are explained in the table below.

REFERENCING

Names are referenced by page number, the first element of each entry, and by a grid reference. The grid reference correlates to the alphanumeric values which appear within each map frame. These reflect the graticule on the map – the letter relates to longitude divisions, the number to latitude divisions. Entries are referenced to the left-hand-page number though the entry may appear on the right-hand-page. The alphanumeric reference provides guidance.

Settlement names are referenced to the pages where the focus is on their county/administrative area.

A selection of the largest and most important **physical features** are referenced to the small scale national maps on pages 20–27.

Rivers are referenced to their lowest downstream point – either their mouth or their confluence with another river. The river name will generally be positioned as close to this point as possible, but may not necessarily be in the same grid square.

OTHER INFORMATION ABOUT THE INDEX

Alternative names appear as cross-references and refer the user to the entry for the map form of the name.

All **administrative qualifiers** are for the United Kingdom unless otherwise stated at the end of the entry.

Entries, other than those for towns and cities, include a **descriptor** indicating the type of geographical feature. Descriptors are not included where the type of feature is implicit in the name itself, unless there is a town or city of exactly the same name.

Entries relating to names appearing on **insets** are indicated by a small box symbol: □ followed by an inset number if there is more than one inset on the page or by a grid reference if the inset has its own alphanumeric values.

Name forms are as they appear on the maps, with additional alternative forms included as cross-references. Names appear in full in the index, although they may appear in abbreviated form on the maps.

Names beginning with **generic, geographical terms are permuted** – the descriptive term is placed after, and the index alphabetized by, the main part of the name. For example, Strait of Dover is indexed as Dover, Strait of; Firth of Forth as Forth, Firth of.

INDEX ABBREVIATIONS

Aberdeen	Aberdeen City	Herts.	Hertfordshire	R. and C.	Redcar and Cleveland
Abers.	Aberdeenshire	High.	Highland	r. mouth	river mouth
admin. dist.	administrative district	Hull	Kingston upon Hull	r. road	roman road
admin. div.	administrative division	i.	island	r. source	river source
Arg. & B.	Argyll and Bute	I.o.A.	Isle of Anglesey	R.C.T.	Rhondda Cynon Taff
b.	bay	I.o.M.	Isle of Man	reg.	region
B. and H.	Brighton and Hove	I.o.S.	Isles of Scilly	Renf.	Renfrewshire
B. and N.E. Som.	Bath and North East Somerset	I.o.W.	Isle of Wight	resr	reservoir
B'burn	Blackburn with Darwen	is	islands	resrs	reservoirs
B. Gwent	Blaenau Gwent	isth.	isthmus	S. Ayr.	South Ayrshire
Borders	Scottish Borders	l.	lake	S. Glos.	South Gloucestershire
Bourne.	Bournemouth	lag.	lagoon	S. Lanark.	South Lanarkshire
Brack. F.	Bracknell Forest	Lancs.	Lancashire	S. Yorks.	South Yorkshire
Bridg.	Bridgend	Leics.	Leicestershire	Scot.	Scotland
bridge	road bridge	Lincs.	Lincolnshire	sea chan.	sea channel
Bucks.	Buckinghamshire	M. Tyd.	Merthyr Tydfil	Shet.	Shetland
c.	cape	M.K.	Milton Keynes	Shrop.	Shropshire
Caerp.	Caerphilly	met. bor.	metropolitan borough	Som.	Somerset
Cambs.	Cambridgeshire	Middbro.	Middlesbrough	Soton	Southampton
Carmar.	Carmarthenshire	Mon.	Monmouthshire	Staffs.	Staffordshire
Cere.	Ceredigion	mt.	mountain	Stir.	Stirling
Clack.	Clackmannanshire	mts	mountains	Stockton	Stockton-on-Tees
Corn.	Cornwall	N. Ayr.	North Ayrshire	Stoke	Stoke-on-Trent
D. and G.	Dumfries and Galloway	N. Ire.	Northern Ireland	str.	strait
Darl.	Darlington	N. Lanark.	North Lanarkshire	Suff.	Suffolk
Denb.	Denbighshire	N. Lincs.	North Lincolnshire	Surr.	Surrey
Derbys.	Derbyshire	N. Som.	North Somerset	T. and W.	Tyne and Wear
Durham	County Durham	N. Yorks.	North Yorkshire	Telford	Telford and Wrekin
E. Ayr.	East Ayrshire	N.E. Lincs.	North East Lincolnshire	terr.	territory
E. Dun.	East Dunbartonshire	N.P.T.	Neath Port Talbot	Torf.	Torfaen
E. Lothian	East Lothian	nat. park	national park	tun.	tunnel
E. Renf.	East Renfrewshire	nature res.	nature reserve	V. of Glam.	Vale of Glamorgan
E. Riding	East Riding of Yorkshire	Newp.	Newport	val.	valley
E. Sussex	East Sussex	Norf.	Norfolk	W. and M.	Windsor and Maidenhead
Edin.	Edinburgh	Northants.	Northamptonshire	W. Berks.	West Berkshire
Eng.	England	Northumb.	Northumberland	W. Dun.	West Dunbartonshire
est.	estuary	Nott.	Nottingham (City)	W. Isles	Western Isles
Falk.	Falkirk	Notts.	Nottinghamshire	W. Lothian	West Lothian
Flints.	Flintshire	Oxon	Oxfordshire	W. Mids	West Midlands
for.	forest	path	long distance footpath	W. Sussex	West Sussex
Glas.	Glasgow	Pembs.	Pembrokeshire	W. Yorks.	West Yorkshire
Glos.	Gloucestershire	pen.	peninsula	W'ham	Wokingham
Gtr Lon.	Greater London	Perth and Kin.	Perth and Kinross	Warks.	Warwickshire
Gtr Man.	Greater Manchester	Peterb.	Peterborough	Warr.	Warrington
h.	hill	Ports.	Portsmouth	Wilts.	Wiltshire
Hants.	Hampshire	prov.	province	wood.	woodland
hd	headland	pt	point	Worcs.	Worcestershire
Here.	Herefordshire	r.	river	Wrex.	Wrexham

Abbas Combe to Ardochrig

A

94 J4 **Abbas Combe** *Som., Eng.*
136 C2 **Abberley** *Worcs., Eng.*
136 C2 **Abberley Common** *Worcs., Eng.*
116 H2 **Abberton** *Essex, Eng.*
136 E2 **Abberton** *Worcs., Eng.*
26 N4 **Abberton Reservoir** *resr Eng.*
244 G3 **Abberwick** *Northumb., Eng.*
116 D3 **Abbess Roding** *Essex, Eng.*
366 E5 **Abbeycwmhir** *Powys, Wales*
208 C3 **Abbeydale** *S. Yorks., Eng.*
140 B4 **Abbey Dore** *Here., Eng.*
22 I13 **Abbey Head** *hd Scot.*
148 C2 **Abbey Hulton** *Stoke, Eng.*
256 J1 **Abbey St Bathans** *Borders, Scot.*
228 F3 **Abbeystead** *Lancs., Eng.*
232 C3 **Abbeytown** *Cumbria, Eng.*
228 G4 **Abbey Village** *Lancs., Eng.*
74 E3 **Abbey Wood** *Gtr Lon., Eng.*
256 I4 **Abbotrule** *Borders, Scot.*
148 D4 **Abbots Bromley** *Staffs., Eng.*
46 D4 **Abbotsbury** *Dorset, Eng.*
190 E3 **Abbotsfield Farm** *Merseyside, Eng.*
40 D1 **Abbotsham** *Devon, Eng.*
40 F3 **Abbotskerswell** *Devon, Eng.*
110 C5 **Abbots Langley** *Herts., Eng.*
94 I2 **Abbots Leigh** *N. Som., Eng.*
124 C5 **Abbotsley** *Cambs., Eng.*
136 F2 **Abbots Morton** *Worcs., Eng.*
124 C4 **Abbots Ripton** *Cambs., Eng.*
136 A5 **Abbot's Salford** *Warks., Eng.*
52 E4 **Abbotstone** *Hants., Eng.*
78 C2 **Abbotswood** *Surr., Eng.*
52 E4 **Abbots Worthy** *Hants., Eng.*
52 C3 **Abbotts Ann** *Hants., Eng.*
52 E4 **Abbott's Barton** *Hants., Eng.*
52 D4 **Abbottswood** *Hants., Eng.*
94 E5 **Abdon** *Shrop., Eng.*
208 D3 **Abdy** *S. Yorks., Eng.*
98 E2 **Abenhall** *Glos., Eng.*
362 E4 **Aber** *Cere., Wales*
362 E3 **Aberaeron** *Cere., Wales*
350 F2 **Aberaman** *R.C.T., Wales*
372 H4 **Aberangell** *Gwynedd, Wales*
356 D1 **Aber-Arad** *Carmar., Wales*
356 F4 **Aberarder** *High., Scot.*
322 I3 **Aberarder House** *High., Scot.*
304 J5 **Aberargie** *Perth and Kin., Scot.*
362 E3 **Aberarth** *Cere., Wales*
350 D3 **Aberavon** *N.P.T., Wales*
362 D4 **Aber-banc** *Cere., Wales*
350 G2 **Aberbargoed** *Caerp., Wales*
350 H2 **Aberbeeg** *B. Gwent, Wales*
356 G1 **Aberbowlan** *Carmar., Wales*
366 E7 **Aberbran** *Powys, Wales*
350 F2 **Abercanaid** *M. Tyd., Wales*
350 H3 **Abercarn** *Caerp., Wales*
358 D2 **Abercastle** *Pembs., Wales*
366 C3 **Abercegir** *Powys, Wales*
322 G3 **Aberchalder** *High., Scot.*
314 F2 **Aberchirder** *Abers., Scot.*
288 C3 **Abercorn** *W. Lothian, Scot.*
366 C8 **Abercraf** *Powys, Wales*
350 E3 **Abercregan** *N.P.T., Wales*
292 H2 **Abercrombie** *Fife, Scot.*
356 H1 **Abercrychan** *Carmar., Wales*
350 F2 **Abercwmboi** *R.C.T., Wales*
358 G1 **Abercych** *Pembs., Wales*
366 E7 **Abercynafon** *Powys, Wales*
350 G3 **Abercynon** *R.C.T., Wales*
372 H4 **Abercywarch** *Gwynedd, Wales*
304 J4 **Aberdalgie** *Perth and Kin., Scot.*
350 F2 **Aberdare** *R.C.T., Wales*
372 B4 **Aberdaron** *Gwynedd, Wales*
Aberdaugleddau *Pembs., Wales see* **Milford Haven**
314 G3 **Aberdeen** *Aberdeen, Scot.*
314 G3 **Aberdeen** *admin. div. Scot.*
314 G3 **Aberdeen** *airport Scot.*
314 F3 **Aberdeenshire** *admin. div. Scot.*
372 D2 **Aberdesach** *Gwynedd, Wales*
292 E3 **Aberdour** *Fife, Scot.*
372 F5 **Aberdovey** *Gwynedd, Wales*
366 E6 **Aberduhonw** *Powys, Wales*
350 D2 **Aberdulais** *N.P.T., Wales*
Aberdyfi *Gwynedd, Wales see* **Aberdovey**
366 E6 **Aberedw** *Powys, Wales*
358 C2 **Abereiddy** *Pembs., Wales*
372 D3 **Abererch** *Gwynedd, Wales*
350 F2 **Aberfan** *M. Tyd., Wales*
304 G3 **Aberfeldy** *Perth and Kin., Scot.*
371 C3 **Aberffraw** *I.o.A., Wales*
362 G2 **Aberffrwd** *Cere., Wales*
222 F2 **Aberford** *W. Yorks., Eng.*
296 D4 **Aberfoyle** *Stir., Scot.*
350 E3 **Abergarw** *Bridg., Wales*
339 B2 **Abergavenny** *Mon., Wales*
378 D2 **Abergele** *Conwy, Wales*
356 E1 **Aber-Giâr** *Carmar., Wales*
356 F2 **Abergorlech** *Carmar., Wales*
366 C6 **Abergwesyn** *Powys, Wales*
356 E2 **Abergwili** *Carmar., Wales*
366 C3 **Abergwydol** *Powys, Wales*
372 G4 **Abergwynant** *Gwynedd, Wales*
350 E3 **Abergwynfi** *N.P.T., Wales*
372 F1 **Abergwyngregyn** *Gwynedd, Wales*
372 G5 **Abergynolwyn** *Gwynedd, Wales*
366 E3 **Aberhafesp** *Powys, Wales*
366 C3 **Aberhosan** *Powys, Wales*
350 E3 **Aberkenfig** *Bridg., Wales*
288 F2 **Aberlady** *E. Lothian, Scot.*
308 F2 **Aberlemno** *Angus, Scot.*
372 H4 **Aberllefenni** *Gwynedd, Wales*
366 D8 **Aber-llia** *Powys, Wales*
Aberllynfi *Powys, Wales see* **Three Cocks**
314 D2 **Aberlour** *Moray, Scot.*
362 F2 **Abermad** *Cere., Wales*
362 F3 **Abermeurig** *Cere., Wales*
378 G3 **Abermorddu** *Flints., Wales*
366 F3 **Abermule** *Powys, Wales*
366 F2 **Abernaint** *Powys, Wales*
356 D2 **Abernant** *Carmar., Wales*
350 F2 **Aber-nant** *R.C.T., Wales*
304 K4 **Abernethy** *Perth and Kin., Scot.*
304 K4 **Abernyte** *Perth and Kin., Scot.*
Aberpennar *R.C.T., Wales see* **Mountain Ash**
350 E2 **Aberpergwm** *N.P.T., Wales*
362 C4 **Aberporth** *Cere., Wales*
322 I3 **Abersky** *High., Scot.*
372 C4 **Abersoch** *Gwynedd, Wales*
339 B2 **Abersychan** *Torf., Wales*
Aberteifi *Cere., Wales see* **Cardigan**
350 F4 **Aberthin** *V. of Glam., Wales*
350 H2 **Abertillery** *B. Gwent, Wales*
350 G3 **Abertridwr** *Caerp., Wales*
366 E2 **Abertridwr** *Powys, Wales*
350 G2 **Abertysswg** *Caerp., Wales*
304 I5 **Aberuthven** *Perth and Kin., Scot.*
366 F7 **Aber Village** *Powys, Wales*
366 E7 **Aberyscir** *Powys, Wales*
362 F2 **Aberystwyth** *Cere., Wales*
326 D3 **Abhainnsuidhe** *W. Isles, Scot.*
102 D4 **Abingdon** *Oxon, Eng.*
78 D2 **Abinger Common** *Surr., Eng.*
78 D2 **Abinger Hammer** *Surr., Eng.*
268 D4 **Abington** *S. Lanark., Scot.*
124 D6 **Abington Pigotts** *Cambs., Eng.*
58 D3 **Abingworth** *W. Sussex, Eng.*
162 F2 **Ab Kettleby** *Leics., Eng.*
136 F3 **Ab Lench** *Worcs., Eng.*
98 H3 **Ablington** *Glos., Eng.*
86 E4 **Ablington** *Wilts., Eng.*
180 C3 **Abney** *Derbys., Eng.*
148 D2 **Above Church** *Staffs., Eng.*
314 E3 **Aboyne** *Abers., Scot.*
198 B2 **Abram** *Gtr Man., Eng.*
116 C4 **Abridge** *Essex, Eng.*
280 C3 **Abronhill** *N. Lanark., Scot.*
96 E3 **Abson** *S. Glos., Eng.*
128 C5 **Abthorpe** *Northants., Eng.*
329 B3 **Abune-the-Hill** *Orkney, Scot.*
170 G4 **Aby** *Lincs., Eng.*
216 F3 **Acaster Selby** *N. Yorks., Eng.*
228 H4 **Accrington** *Lancs., Eng.*
300 E2 **Accurrach** *Arg. and B., Scot.*
300 □ **Acha** *Arg. and B., Scot.*
300 E2 **Achacha** *Arg. and B., Scot.*
300 E2 **Achadacaie** *Arg. and B., Scot.*
300 D4 **Achadh-chaorrunn** *Arg. and B., Scot.*
322 E2 **Achadh Mòr** *W. Isles, Scot.*
300 F3 **Achadunan** *Arg. and B., Scot.*
300 D5 **Achaglass** *Arg. and B., Scot.*
300 D4 **Achahoish** *Arg. and B., Scot.*
304 J3 **Achalader** *Perth and Kin., Scot.*
300 F2 **Achallader** *Arg. and B., Scot.*
300 C4 **Achamore** *Arg. and B., Scot.*
320 G4 **Achany** *High., Scot.*
322 D4 **Acharacle** *High., Scot.*
320 H2 **Achargary** *High., Scot.*
304 F3 **Acharn** *Perth and Kin., Scot.*
300 B2 **Acharonich** *Arg. and B., Scot.*
300 E4 **Acharosson** *Arg. and B., Scot.*
314 F3 **Achath** *Abers., Scot.*
320 J2 **Achavanich** *High., Scot.*
356 E3 **Achddu** *Carmar., Wales*
Achd-'Ille-Bhuidhe *High., Scot. see* **Achiltibuie**
320 E4 **Achduart** *High., Scot.*
320 I3 **Achentoul** *High., Scot.*
320 K3 **Achfary** *High., Scot.*
320 D4 **Achgarve** *High., Scot.*
320 F2 **Achiemore** *High., Scot.*
320 I2 **Achiemore** *High., Scot.*
322 B3 **A'Chill** *High., Scot.*
A' Chille Mhòr *Arg. and B., Scot. see* **Kilmore**
320 D3 **Achiltibuie** *High., Scot.*
322 J2 **Achindown** *High., Scot.*
320 G4 **Achinduich** *High., Scot.*
322 E2 **Achintee** *High., Scot.*
322 E2 **Achintraid** *High., Scot.*
322 J3 **Achlean** *High., Scot.*
300 E2 **Achlian** *Arg. and B., Scot.*
322 E3 **Achmelvich** *High., Scot.*
320 E4 **Achmore** *High., Scot.*
322 E2 **Achmore** *High., Scot.*
296 E3 **Achmore** *Stir., Scot.*
300 E3 **Achnaba** *Arg. and B., Scot.*
322 I2 **Achnabat** *High., Scot.*
300 D2 **Achnacairn** *Arg. and B., Scot.*
320 D3 **Achnacarnin** *High., Scot.*
322 G2 **Achnaclerach** *High., Scot.*
300 E2 **Achnacloich** *Arg. and B., Scot.*
322 D3 **Achnacloich** *High., Scot.*
320 J3 **Achnaclyth** *High., Scot.*
300 B2 **Achnacraig** *Arg. and B., Scot.*
300 D2 **Achnacroish** *Arg. and B., Scot.*
300 B2 **Achnadrish** *Arg. and B., Scot.*
300 E2 **Achnafalnich** *Arg. and B., Scot.*
304 H3 **Achnafauld** *Perth and Kin., Scot.*
322 H2 **Achnagairn** *High., Scot.*
322 C4 **Achnaha** *High., Scot.*
322 D5 **Achnaha** *High., Scot.*
320 D4 **Achnahanat** *High., Scot.*
320 G3 **Achnairn** *High., Scot.*
300 D3 **Achnamara** *Arg. and B., Scot.*
322 F4 **Achnasaul** *High., Scot.*
322 F2 **Achnasheen** *High., Scot.*
300 D3 **Achnashelloch** *Arg. and B., Scot.*
314 D2 **Achnastank** *Moray, Scot.*
A' Choingheal *Arg. and B., Scot. see* **Connel**
322 C4 **Achosnich** *High., Scot.*
320 F2 **Achriesgill** *High., Scot.*
A' Chrìon-Làraich *Stir., Scot. see* **Crianlarich**
322 H2 **Achterneed** *High., Scot.*
128 G3 **Achurch** *Northants., Eng.*
320 G2 **Achuvoldrach** *High., Scot.*
320 H2 **Achvaich** *High., Scot.*
322 F5 **Achvlair** *High., Scot.*
320 E4 **Achvraie** *High., Scot.*
320 K2 **Ackergill** *High., Scot.*
140 C3 **Ackleton** *Shrop., Eng.*
244 H4 **Acklington** *Northumb., Eng.*
216 F4 **Ackton** *W. Yorks., Eng.*
222 F3 **Ackworth Moor Top** *W. Yorks., Eng.*
166 I3 **Acle** *Norf., Eng.*
154 D3 **Acock's Green** *W. Mids, Eng.*
62 H2 **Acol** *Kent, Eng.*
244 E6 **Acomb** *Northumb., Eng.*
216 F3 **Acomb** *York, Eng.*
140 C3 **Aconbury** *Here., Eng.*
228 I4 **Acre** *Lancs., Eng.*
378 G4 **Acrefair** *Wrex., Wales*
62 G4 **Acrise Place** *Kent, Eng.*
184 D3 **Acton** *Cheshire East, Eng.*
46 G4 **Acton** *Dorset, Eng.*
74 C2 **Acton** *Gtr Lon., Eng.*
144 B5 **Acton** *Shrop., Eng.*
148 B3 **Acton** *Staffs., Eng.*
120 D4 **Acton** *Suff., Eng.*
136 D2 **Acton** *Worcs., Eng.*
396 F4 **Acton** *Armagh, N. Ire.*
378 H3 **Acton** *Wrex., Wales*
140 E3 **Acton Beauchamp** *Here., Eng.*
184 D2 **Acton Bridge** *Cheshire West & Chester, Eng.*
144 D4 **Acton Burnell** *Shrop., Eng.*
140 E3 **Acton Green** *Here., Eng.*
144 D4 **Acton Pigott** *Shrop., Eng.*
144 E4 **Acton Round** *Shrop., Eng.*
144 D4 **Acton Scott** *Shrop., Eng.*
148 C4 **Acton Trussell** *Staffs., Eng.*
98 F4 **Acton Turville** *S. Glos., Eng.*
326 F1 **Adabroc** *W. Isles, Scot.*
262 E3 **Adamhill** *S. Ayr., Scot.*
148 A3 **Adbaston** *Staffs., Eng.*
46 D2 **Adber** *Dorset, Eng.*
102 D2 **Adderbury** *Oxon, Eng.*
144 E2 **Adderley** *Shrop., Eng.*
148 C3 **Adderley Green** *Stoke, Eng.*
244 G2 **Adderstone** *Northumb., Eng.*
288 B3 **Addiewell** *W. Lothian, Scot.*
222 C1 **Addingham** *W. Yorks., Eng.*
106 C3 **Addington** *Bucks., Eng.*
74 D3 **Addington** *Gtr Lon., Eng.*
62 C3 **Addington** *Kent, Eng.*
74 D3 **Addiscombe** *Gtr Lon., Eng.*
78 D1 **Addlestone** *Surr., Eng.*
170 H4 **Addlethorpe** *Lincs., Eng.*
222 E1 **Adel** *W. Yorks., Eng.*
144 F3 **Adeney** *Telford, Eng.*
110 C5 **Adeyfield** *Herts., Eng.*
366 E3 **Adfa** *Powys, Wales*
140 B1 **Adforton** *Here., Eng.*
62 H3 **Adisham** *Kent, Eng.*
98 J2 **Adlestrop** *Glos., Eng.*
210 D4 **Adlingfleet** *E. Riding, Eng.*
184 G2 **Adlington** *Cheshire East, Eng.*
228 G5 **Adlington** *Lancs., Eng.*
148 D4 **Admaston** *Staffs., Eng.*
144 E3 **Admaston** *Telford, Eng.*
132 B5 **Admington** *Warks., Eng.*
94 F4 **Adsborough** *Som., Eng.*
94 E4 **Adscombe** *Som., Eng.*
106 C3 **Adstock** *Bucks., Eng.*
128 C5 **Adstone** *Northants., Eng.*
198 D3 **Adswood** *Gtr Man., Eng.*
58 D3 **Adversane** *W. Sussex, Eng.*
322 K2 **Advie** *High., Scot.*
222 E2 **Adwalton** *W. Yorks., Eng.*
102 F4 **Adwell** *Oxon, Eng.*
208 E2 **Adwick le Street** *S. Yorks., Eng.*
208 E2 **Adwick upon Dearne** *S. Yorks., Eng.*
314 G2 **Adziel** *Abers., Scot.*
26 D3 **Aeron** *r. Wales*
252 F2 **Ae Village** *D. and G., Scot.*
198 C2 **Affetside** *Gtr Man., Eng.*
46 F3 **Affpuddle** *Dorset, Eng.*
22 F8 **Affric, Loch** *l. Scot.*
378 F2 **Afon-wen** *Flints., Wales*
372 E3 **Afon Wen** *Gwynedd, Wales*
52 C6 **Afton** *I.o.W., Eng.*
262 F4 **Afton Bridgend** *E. Ayr., Scot.*
216 D2 **Agglethorpe** *N. Yorks., Eng.*
388 D2 **Aghabrack** *Limavady, N. Ire.*
396 F3 **Aghacommon** *Craigavon, N. Ire.*
388 J3 **Aghacully** *Ballymena, N. Ire.*
396 F5 **Aghadavoyle** *Newry & Mourne, N. Ire.*
388 G2 **Aghadowey** *Coleraine, N. Ire.*
402 G5 **Aghadrumsee** *Fermanagh, N. Ire.*
396 G2 **Aghagallon** *Craigavon, N. Ire.*
402 E5 **Aghakillymaud** *Fermanagh, N. Ire.*
402 E3 **Aghakinmart** *Strabane, N. Ire.*
396 G2 **Aghalee** *Craigavon, N. Ire.*
402 D3 **Aghalunny** *Strabane, N. Ire.*
388 E2 **Aghanloo** *Limavady, N. Ire.*
402 F5 **Aghavea** *Fermanagh, N. Ire.*
396 D3 **Aghinlig** *Armagh, N. Ire.*
402 H3 **Aghnagar** *Omagh, N. Ire.*
402 I3 **Aghnagur** *Dungannon, N. Ire.*
402 F3 **Aghnamoyle** *Omagh, N. Ire.*
402 D2 **Aghyaran** *Strabane, N. Ire.*
388 G2 **Agivey** *Coleraine, N. Ire.*
23 K3 **Agnew's Hill** *hill N. Ire.*
388 H3 **Ahoghill** *Ballymena, N. Ire.*
190 D3 **Aigburth** *Merseyside, Eng.*
210 F3 **Aike** *E. Riding, Eng.*
329 D1 **Aikerness** *Orkney, Scot.*
329 D5 **Aikers** *Orkney, Scot.*
232 F4 **Aiketgate** *Cumbria, Eng.*
232 B4 **Aikshaw** *Cumbria, Eng.*
232 D3 **Aikton** *Cumbria, Eng.*
256 G3 **Aikwood Tower** *Borders, Scot.*
170 G4 **Ailby** *Lincs., Eng.*
140 B3 **Ailey** *Here., Eng.*
22 F12 **Ailsa Craig** *i. Scot.*
132 B5 **Ailstone** *Warks., Eng.*
124 B3 **Ailsworth** *Peterb., Eng.*
116 C3 **Aimes Green** *Essex, Eng.*
216 E2 **Ainderby Steeple** *N. Yorks., Eng.*
116 I2 **Aingers Green** *Essex, Eng.*
190 C2 **Ainsdale** *Merseyside, Eng.*
190 C2 **Ainsdale-on-Sea** *Merseyside, Eng.*
232 F4 **Ainstable** *Cumbria, Eng.*
198 C2 **Ainsworth** *Gtr Man., Eng.*
216 G1 **Ainthorpe** *N. Yorks., Eng.*
190 D3 **Aintree** *Merseyside, Eng.*
326 B4 **Aird** *W. Isles, Scot.*
326 F2 **Aird** *W. Isles, Scot.*
326 B4 **Aird a' Mhachair** *W. Isles, Scot.*
326 D3 **Aird a' Mhulaidh** *W. Isles, Scot.*
326 D3 **Aird Asaig** *W. Isles, Scot.*
326 D3 **Aird Mhige** *W. Isles, Scot.*
326 D3 **Aird Mhighe** *W. Isles, Scot.*
322 D3 **Aird of Sleat** *High., Scot.*
292 H2 **Airdrie** *Fife, Scot.*
280 C3 **Airdrie** *N. Lanark., Scot.*
326 F2 **Aird Thunga** *W. Isles, Scot.*
326 F2 **Aird Uige** *W. Isles, Scot.*
24 N6 **Airedale** *val. Eng.*
326 E2 **Airidh a'Bhruaich** *W. Isles, Scot.*
252 E3 **Airieland** *D. and G., Scot.*
252 A3 **Airies** *D. and G., Scot.*
322 D2 **Airigh-drishaig** *High., Scot.*
210 C4 **Airmyn** *E. Riding, Eng.*
304 J4 **Airntully** *Perth and Kin., Scot.*
322 D3 **Airor** *High., Scot.*
280 D2 **Airth** *Falk., Scot.*
252 C2 **Airyhassen** *D. and G., Scot.*
170 B3 **Aisby** *Lincs., Eng.*
170 D6 **Aisby** *Lincs., Eng.*
Aisgernis *W. Isles, Scot. see* **Askernish**
232 H6 **Aisgill** *Cumbria, Eng.*
40 E3 **Aish** *Devon, Eng.*
40 F3 **Aish** *Devon, Eng.*
94 F4 **Aisholt** *Som., Eng.*
216 E2 **Aiskew** *N. Yorks., Eng.*
216 G1 **Aislaby** *N. Yorks., Eng.*
236 G4 **Aislaby** *Stockton, Eng.*
170 C4 **Aisthorpe** *Lincs., Eng.*
329 B3 **Aith** *Orkney, Scot.*
329 F3 **Aith** *Orkney, Scot.*
331 C3 **Aith** *Shet., Scot.*
331 E2 **Aith** *Shet., Scot.*
331 D3 **Aithsetter** *Shet., Scot.*
322 J2 **Aitnoch** *High., Scot.*
244 E2 **Akeld** *Northumb., Eng.*
106 C2 **Akeley** *Bucks., Eng.*
120 F4 **Akenham** *Suff., Eng.*
216 E3 **Aketon** *N. Yorks., Eng.*
26 D1 **Alaw, Llyn** *resr Wales*
36 G2 **Albaston** *Corn., Eng.*
408 B3 **Albecq** *Guernsey Channel Is*
144 C3 **Alberbury** *Shrop., Eng.*
358 E3 **Albert Town** *Pembs., Wales*
58 E3 **Albourne Green** *W. Sussex, Eng.*
144 D3 **Albrighton** *Shrop., Eng.*
144 G4 **Albrighton** *Shrop., Eng.*
166 G4 **Alburgh** *Norf., Eng.*
166 G4 **Alburgh Street** *Norf., Eng.*
110 F4 **Albury** *Herts., Eng.*
102 E4 **Albury** *Oxon, Eng.*
78 C2 **Albury** *Surr., Eng.*
110 F4 **Albury End** *Herts., Eng.*
78 D2 **Albury Heath** *Surr., Eng.*
232 F3 **Albyfield** *Cumbria, Eng.*
166 G1 **Alby Hill** *Norf., Eng.*
322 H2 **Alcaig** *High., Scot.*
144 D5 **Alcaston** *Shrop., Eng.*
132 A4 **Alcester** *Warks., Eng.*
154 C3 **Alcester Lane's End** *W. Mids, Eng.*
58 G4 **Alciston** *E. Sussex, Eng.*
94 D3 **Alcombe** *Som., Eng.*
124 C4 **Alconbury** *Cambs., Eng.*
124 C4 **Alconbury Hill** *Cambs., Eng.*
124 C4 **Alconbury Weston** *Cambs., Eng.*
166 G1 **Aldborough** *Norf., Eng.*
216 E2 **Aldborough** *N. Yorks., Eng.*
74 E2 **Aldborough Hatch** *Gtr Lon., Eng.*
86 F3 **Aldbourne** *Wilts., Eng.*
210 H4 **Aldbrough** *E. Riding, Eng.*
216 D1 **Aldbrough St John** *N. Yorks., Eng.*
110 B5 **Aldbury** *Herts., Eng.*
228 F2 **Aldcliffe** *Lancs., Eng.*
304 H2 **Aldclune** *Perth and Kin., Scot.*
26 O3 **Alde** *r. Eng.*
120 I4 **Aldeburgh** *Suff., Eng.*
166 I4 **Aldeby** *Norf., Eng.*
110 C5 **Aldenham** *Herts., Eng.*
86 E5 **Alderbury** *Wilts., Eng.*
180 E4 **Aldercar** *Derbys., Eng.*
166 F2 **Alderford** *Norf., Eng.*
198 C3 **Alder Forest** *Gtr Man., Eng.*
388 I5 **Aldergrove** *Antrim, N. Ire.*
46 I2 **Alderholt** *Dorset, Eng.*
98 F4 **Alderley** *Glos., Eng.*
184 F3 **Alderley Edge** *Cheshire East, Eng.*
154 F3 **Alderman's Green** *W. Mids, Eng.*
82 D3 **Aldermaston** *W. Berks., Eng.*
52 F2 **Aldermaston Soke** *Hants., Eng.*
82 D3 **Aldermaston Wharf** *W. Berks., Eng.*
132 C5 **Alderminster** *Warks., Eng.*
408 D1 **Alderney** *airport Guernsey Channel Is*
408 D1 **Alderney** *i. Guernsey Channel Is*
74 E2 **Aldersbrook** *Gtr Lon., Eng.*
140 D3 **Alder's End** *Here., Eng.*
184 C3 **Aldersey Green** *Cheshire West & Chester, Eng.*
52 H3 **Aldershot** *Hants., Eng.*
98 G2 **Alderton** *Glos., Eng.*
128 D5 **Alderton** *Northants., Eng.*
144 D3 **Alderton** *Shrop., Eng.*
120 H4 **Alderton** *Suff., Eng.*
86 B2 **Alderton** *Wilts., Eng.*
180 D4 **Alderwasley** *Derbys., Eng.*
216 E2 **Aldfield** *N. Yorks., Eng.*
184 B3 **Aldford** *Cheshire West & Chester, Eng.*
116 G2 **Aldham** *Essex, Eng.*
120 E4 **Aldham** *Suff., Eng.*
120 E4 **Aldham Street** *Suff., Eng.*
314 H2 **Aldie** *Abers., Scot.*
232 D8 **Aldingham** *Cumbria, Eng.*
62 F4 **Aldington** *Kent, Eng.*
136 F3 **Aldington** *Worcs., Eng.*
314 D3 **Aldivalloch** *Moray, Scot.*
300 G3 **Aldochlay** *Arg. and B., Scot.*
262 C6 **Aldons** *S. Ayr., Scot.*
388 I2 **Aldorough** *Ballymoney, N. Ire.*
120 I2 **Aldous's Corner** *Suff., Eng.*
124 D4 **Aldreth** *Cambs., Eng.*
154 C2 **Aldridge** *W. Mids, Eng.*
120 I3 **Aldringham** *Suff., Eng.*
58 E3 **Aldrington** *B. and H., Eng.*
216 G2 **Aldro** *N. Yorks., Eng.*
98 I3 **Aldsworth** *Glos., Eng.*
58 A3 **Aldsworth** *W. Sussex, Eng.*
314 D3 **Aldunie** *Moray, Scot.*
304 H3 **Aldville** *Perth and Kin., Scot.*
180 D4 **Aldwark** *Derbys., Eng.*
216 F2 **Aldwark** *N. Yorks., Eng.*
58 B4 **Aldwick** *W. Sussex, Eng.*
128 F3 **Aldwincle** *Northants., Eng.*
82 C2 **Aldworth** *W. Berks., Eng.*
276 C2 **Alexandria** *W. Dun., Scot.*
94 F4 **Aley** *Som., Eng.*
110 C4 **Aley Green** *Herts., Eng.*
40 C2 **Alfardisworthy** *Devon, Eng.*
40 G2 **Alfington** *Devon, Eng.*
78 C3 **Alfold** *Surr., Eng.*
78 C3 **Alfold Crossways** *Surr., Eng.*
170 H4 **Alford** *Lincs., Eng.*
94 I4 **Alford** *Som., Eng.*
314 E3 **Alford** *Abers., Scot.*
180 E4 **Alfreton** *Derbys., Eng.*
136 C2 **Alfrick** *Worcs., Eng.*
136 C2 **Alfrick Pound** *Worcs., Eng.*
58 G4 **Alfriston** *E. Sussex, Eng.*
170 F6 **Algarkirk** *Lincs., Eng.*
94 I4 **Alhampton** *Som., Eng.*
170 C1 **Alkborough** *N. Lincs., Eng.*
102 C2 **Alkerton** *Oxon, Eng.*
62 H4 **Alkham** *Kent, Eng.*
144 D2 **Alkington** *Shrop., Eng.*
180 C5 **Alkmonton** *Derbys., Eng.*
40 E3 **Allaleigh** *Devon, Eng.*
314 C3 **Allanaquoich** *Abers., Scot.*
322 I2 **Allanfearn** *High., Scot.*
252 G2 **Allangillfoot** *D. and G., Scot.*
256 K2 **Allanton** *Borders, Scot.*
252 E2 **Allanton** *D. and G., Scot.*
262 F3 **Allanton** *E. Ayr., Scot.*
280 D4 **Allanton** *N. Lanark., Scot.*
268 B2 **Allanton** *S. Lanark., Scot.*
314 G4 **Allardice** *Abers., Scot.*
326 B6 **Allathasdal** *W. Isles, Scot.*
52 D5 **Allbrook** *Hants., Eng.*
86 D3 **All Cannings** *Wilts., Eng.*
244 D6 **Allendale Town** *Northumb., Eng.*
244 D7 **Allenheads** *Northumb., Eng.*
244 F5 **Allensford** *Northumb., Eng.*
110 F5 **Allen's Green** *Herts., Eng.*
140 C3 **Allensmore** *Here., Eng.*
180 E5 **Allenton** *Derby, Eng.*
94 G4 **Aller** *Som., Eng.*
232 B4 **Allerby** *Cumbria, Eng.*
40 G4 **Allerford** *Som., Eng.*
216 G1 **Allerston** *N. Yorks., Eng.*
210 E3 **Allerthorpe** *E. Riding, Eng.*
190 D3 **Allerton** *Merseyside, Eng.*
222 D2 **Allerton** *W. Yorks., Eng.*
222 F2 **Allerton Bywater** *W. Yorks., Eng.*
216 E2 **Allerton Mauleverer** *N. Yorks., Eng.*
154 E3 **Allesley** *W. Mids, Eng.*
180 E5 **Allestree** *Derby, Eng.*
36 D3 **Allet Common** *Corn., Eng.*
162 G3 **Allexton** *Leics., Eng.*
184 G3 **Allgreave** *Cheshire East, Eng.*
62 D2 **Allhallows** *Medway, Eng.*
62 D2 **Allhallows-on-Sea** *Medway, Eng.*
322 E2 **Alligin Shuas** *High., Scot.*
148 B4 **Allimore Green** *Staffs., Eng.*
46 C3 **Allington** *Dorset, Eng.*
62 C3 **Allington** *Kent, Eng.*
170 B6 **Allington** *Lincs., Eng.*
86 C3 **Allington** *Wilts., Eng.*
86 D3 **Allington** *Wilts., Eng.*
86 E5 **Allington** *Wilts., Eng.*
396 D3 **Allistragh** *Armagh, N. Ire.*
232 E7 **Allithwaite** *Cumbria, Eng.*
320 G3 **Allnabad** *High., Scot.*
292 B3 **Alloa** *Clack., Scot.*
232 B4 **Allonby** *Cumbria, Eng.*
184 E2 **Allostock** *Cheshire West & Chester, Eng.*
262 D4 **Alloway** *S. Ayr., Scot.*
94 G5 **Allowenshay** *Som., Eng.*
120 H2 **All Saints South Elmham** *Suff., Eng.*
144 C3 **Allscot** *Shrop., Eng.*
144 E3 **Allscott** *Telford, Eng.*
144 D4 **All Stretton** *Shrop., Eng.*
322 H1 **Alltachonaich** *High., Scot.*
322 E3 **Alltbeithe** *High., Scot.*
366 D2 **Alltforgan** *Powys, Wales*
366 E6 **Alltmawr** *Powys, Wales*
322 H4 **Alltnacaillich** *High., Scot.*
322 H3 **Alltsigh** *High., Scot.*
356 E2 **Alltwalis** *Carmar., Wales*
350 C2 **Alltwen** *N.P.T., Wales*
362 F4 **Alltyblaca** *Cere., Wales*
120 F3 **Allwood Green** *Suff., Eng.*
140 B3 **Almeley** *Here., Eng.*
140 B2 **Almeley Wootton** *Here., Eng.*
46 G3 **Almer** *Dorset, Eng.*
208 F2 **Almholme** *S. Yorks., Eng.*
148 A3 **Almington** *Staffs., Eng.*
40 F2 **Almiston Cross** *Devon, Eng.*
22 J10 **Almond** *r. Scot.*
304 I4 **Almondbank** *Perth and Kin., Scot.*
222 D3 **Almondbury** *W. Yorks., Eng.*
98 D4 **Almondsbury** *S. Glos., Eng.*
216 F2 **Alne** *N. Yorks., Eng.*
320 H4 **Alness** *High., Scot.*
Alness *r. Scot. see* **Averon**
244 E3 **Alnham** *Northumb., Eng.*
244 H3 **Alnmouth** *Northumb., Eng.*
244 G3 **Alnwick** *Northumb., Eng.*
74 C2 **Alperton** *Gtr Lon., Eng.*
116 G2 **Alphamstone** *Essex, Eng.*
120 D4 **Alpheton** *Suff., Eng.*
40 F2 **Alphington** *Devon, Eng.*
166 H3 **Alpington** *Norf., Eng.*
180 D3 **Alport** *Derbys., Eng.*
184 D3 **Alpraham** *Cheshire East, Eng.*
116 I2 **Alresford** *Essex, Eng.*
148 E4 **Alrewas** *Staffs., Eng.*
308 C2 **Alrick** *Angus, Scot.*
184 F2 **Alsager** *Cheshire East, Eng.*
148 B2 **Alsagers Bank** *Staffs., Eng.*
22 E8 **Alsh, Loch** *sea chan. Scot.*
180 C4 **Alsop en le Dale** *Derbys., Eng.*
232 H4 **Alston** *Cumbria, Eng.*
98 G2 **Alstone** *Glos., Eng.*
98 G2 **Alstone** *Glos., Eng.*
94 G3 **Alstone** *Som., Eng.*
148 B4 **Alstone** *Staffs., Eng.*
148 E2 **Alstonefield** *Staffs., Eng.*
94 G3 **Alston Sutton** *Som., Eng.*
40 E2 **Alswear** *Devon, Eng.*
198 E2 **Alt** *Gtr Man., Eng.*
388 D3 **Altaghoney** *Derry, N. Ire.*
402 G5 **Altagoaghan** *Fermanagh, N. Ire.*
320 D3 **Altandhu** *High., Scot.*
320 H3 **Altanduin** *High., Scot.*
36 F2 **Altarnun** *Corn., Eng.*
314 G3 **Altens** *Aberdeen, Scot.*
320 K2 **Alterwall** *High., Scot.*
228 H4 **Altham** *Lancs., Eng.*
116 G4 **Althorne** *Essex, Eng.*
170 B2 **Althorpe** *N. Lincs., Eng.*
252 C3 **Alticry** *D. and G., Scot.*
402 G1 **Altishane** *Strabane, N. Ire.*
402 E4 **Altmartin** *Fermanagh, N. Ire.*
322 G5 **Altnafeadh** *High., Scot.*
320 G3 **Altnaharra** *High., Scot.*
396 E5 **Altnamackan** *Newry & Mourne, N. Ire.*
222 F2 **Altofts** *W. Yorks., Eng.*
180 E3 **Alton** *Derbys., Eng.*
52 G4 **Alton** *Hants., Eng.*
148 D3 **Alton** *Staffs., Eng.*
86 E3 **Alton Barnes** *Wilts., Eng.*
46 E3 **Alton Pancras** *Dorset, Eng.*
86 D3 **Alton Priors** *Wilts., Eng.*
198 C3 **Altrincham** *Gtr Man., Eng.*
154 D3 **Alum Rock** *W. Mids, Eng.*
292 B3 **Alva** *Clack., Scot.*
184 C2 **Alvanley** *Cheshire West & Chester, Eng.*
180 E5 **Alvaston** *Derby, Eng.*
136 F1 **Alvechurch** *Worcs., Eng.*
132 C2 **Alvecote** *Warks., Eng.*
86 C5 **Alvediston** *Wilts., Eng.*
144 F5 **Alveley** *Shrop., Eng.*
40 D1 **Alverdiscott** *Devon, Eng.*
52 F6 **Alverstoke** *Hants., Eng.*
52 E6 **Alverstone** *I.o.W., Eng.*
222 E2 **Alverthorpe** *W. Yorks., Eng.*
176 E5 **Alverton** *Notts., Eng.*
314 C2 **Alves** *Moray, Scot.*
102 B4 **Alvescot** *Oxon, Eng.*
98 D4 **Alveston** *S. Glos., Eng.*
132 C4 **Alveston** *Warks., Eng.*
322 J3 **Alvie** *High., Scot.*
98 D3 **Alvington** *Glos., Eng.*
124 C3 **Alwalton** *Cambs., Eng.*
26 I1 **Alwen Reservoir** *resr Wales*
46 E2 **Alweston** *Dorset, Eng.*
244 E3 **Alwinton** *Northumb., Eng.*
222 E1 **Alwoodley** *W. Yorks., Eng.*
222 E1 **Alwoodley Gates** *W. Yorks., Eng.*
304 K3 **Alyth** *Perth and Kin., Scot.*
Am Barra Calltainn *Arg. and B., Scot. see* **Barcaldine**
180 E5 **Ambaston** *Derbys., Eng.*
180 E4 **Ambergate** *Derbys., Eng.*
170 F5 **Amber Hill** *Lincs., Eng.*
58 C3 **Amberley** *W. Sussex, Eng.*
180 E4 **Amber Row** *Derbys., Eng.*
Am Blàr Dubh *High., Scot. see* **Muir of Ord**
244 H4 **Amble** *Northumb., Eng.*
154 B3 **Amblecote** *W. Mids, Eng.*
232 E6 **Ambleside** *Cumbria, Eng.*
358 E2 **Ambleston** *Pembs., Wales*
300 E4 **Ambrismore** *Arg. and B., Scot.*
102 E3 **Ambrosden** *Oxon, Eng.*
170 B2 **Amcotts** *N. Lincs., Eng.*
82 G3 **Amen Corner** *Brack. F., Eng.*
106 E4 **Amersham** *Bucks., Eng.*
148 C3 **Amerton** *Staffs., Eng.*
86 E4 **Amesbury** *Wilts., Eng.*
46 H3 **Ameysford** *Dorset, Eng.*
A' Mhanachainn *High., Scot. see* **Beauly**
A'Mhormhaich *High., Scot. see* **Morvich**
148 F5 **Amington** *Staffs., Eng.*
252 F2 **Amisfield Town** *D. and G., Scot.*
371 C2 **Amlwch** *I.o.A., Wales*
371 C2 **Amlwch Port** *I.o.A., Wales*
216 G2 **Amotherby** *N. Yorks., Eng.*
52 D4 **Ampfield** *Hants., Eng.*
216 F2 **Ampleforth** *N. Yorks., Eng.*
Am Ploc *High., Scot. see* **Plockton**
98 H3 **Ampney Crucis** *Glos., Eng.*
98 H3 **Ampney St Mary** *Glos., Eng.*
98 H3 **Ampney St Peter** *Glos., Eng.*
52 C3 **Amport** *Hants., Eng.*
110 C3 **Ampthill** *Central Bedfordshire, Eng.*
120 D3 **Ampton** *Suff., Eng.*
358 G3 **Amroth** *Pembs., Wales*
304 H3 **Amulree** *Perth and Kin., Scot.*
322 K2 **Anaboard** *High., Scot.*
322 E4 **Anaheilt** *High., Scot.*
An Apainn *Arg. and B., Scot. see* **Appin**
170 C6 **Ancaster** *Lincs., Eng.*
144 A5 **Anchor** *Shrop., Eng.*
166 E3 **Anchor Corner** *Norf., Eng.*
An Cladach *Arg. and B., Scot. see* **Cladich**
198 D3 **Ancoats** *Gtr Man., Eng.*
244 I2 **Ancroft** *Northumb., Eng.*
256 I3 **Ancrum** *Borders, Scot.*
58 C4 **Ancton** *W. Sussex, Eng.*
170 H4 **Anderby** *Lincs., Eng.*
170 H4 **Anderby Creek** *Lincs., Eng.*
94 G4 **Andersea** *Som., Eng.*
94 F4 **Andersfield** *Som., Eng.*
46 F3 **Anderson** *Dorset, Eng.*
184 D2 **Anderton** *Cheshire West & Chester, Eng.*
An Dòrnaidh *High., Scot. see* **Dornie**
52 D3 **Andover** *Hants., Eng.*
52 D3 **Andover Down** *Hants., Eng.*
98 H2 **Andoversford** *Glos., Eng.*
405 D1 **Andreas** *Isle of Man*
An Drochaid Bhàn *High., Scot. see* **Whitebridge**
372 B4 **Anelog** *Gwynedd, Wales*
74 D3 **Anerley** *Gtr Lon., Eng.*
190 D3 **Anfield** *Merseyside, Eng.*
36 C3 **Angarrack** *Corn., Eng.*
144 E5 **Angelbank** *Shrop., Eng.*
94 F5 **Angersleigh** *Som., Eng.*
232 C3 **Angerton** *Cumbria, Eng.*
358 D3 **Angle** *Pembs., Wales*
362 G1 **Angler's Retreat** *Cere., Wales*
52 F6 **Anglesey** *Hants., Eng.*
26 D1 **Anglesey** *i. Wales*
58 D4 **Angmering** *W. Sussex, Eng.*
216 C1 **Angram** *N. Yorks., Eng.*
216 F3 **Angram** *N. Yorks., Eng.*
318 E2 **Angus** *admin. div. Scot.*
244 E6 **Anick** *Northumb., Eng.*
296 E4 **Anie** *Stir., Scot.*
320 I4 **Ankerville** *High., Scot.*
210 F4 **Anlaby** *E. Riding, Eng.*
An Lagaidh *High., Scot. see* **Loggie**
An Lagaidh *High., Scot. see* **Marybank**
An Lagan *High., Scot. see* **Laggan**
166 C1 **Anmer** *Norf., Eng.*
52 F5 **Anmore** *Hants., Eng.*
396 F5 **Annacloghmullin** *Newry & Mourne, N. Ire.*
396 G4 **Annaclone** *Banbridge, N. Ire.*
396 J3 **Annacloy** *Down, N. Ire.*
396 J4 **Annadorn** *Down, N. Ire.*
396 G4 **Annaghbane** *Newry & Mourne, N. Ire.*
402 K3 **Annaghmore** *Dungannon, N. Ire.*
388 J6 **Annahilt** *Lisburn, N. Ire.*
396 I5 **Annalong** *Newry & Mourne, N. Ire.*
252 G3 **Annan** *D. and G., Scot.*
22 J13 **Annan** *r. Scot.*
22 J12 **Annandale** *val. Scot.*
232 B7 **Annaside** *Cumbria, Eng.*
300 E2 **Annat** *Arg. and B., Scot.*
322 E2 **Annat** *High., Scot.*
280 B3 **Annathill Farm** *N. Lanark., Scot.*
52 C3 **Anna Valley** *Hants., Eng.*
262 D4 **Annbank** *S. Ayr., Scot.*
176 B4 **Annesley** *Notts., Eng.*
176 B4 **Annesley Woodhouse** *Notts., Eng.*
26 □ **Annet** *i. Eng.*
236 E2 **Annfield Plain** *Durham, Eng.*
24 H2 **Annick** *r. Scot.*
276 D2 **Anniesland** *Glas., Scot.*
396 I4 **Annsborough** *Down, N. Ire.*
144 D4 **Annscroft** *Shrop., Eng.*
An Rubha *pen. Scot. see* **Eye Peninsula**
228 E4 **Ansdell** *Lancs., Eng.*
94 I4 **Ansford** *Som., Eng.*
22 I9 **An Sgarsoch** *mt. Scot.*
132 C2 **Ansley** *Warks., Eng.*
148 E4 **Anslow** *Staffs., Eng.*
148 E4 **Anslow Gate** *Staffs., Eng.*
148 E4 **Anslow Leys** *Staffs., Eng.*
78 B3 **Ansteadbrook** *Surr., Eng.*
110 F4 **Anstey** *Herts., Eng.*
162 D2 **Anstey** *Leics., Eng.*
292 H2 **Anstruther** *Fife, Scot.*
132 D3 **Ansty** *Warks., Eng.*
86 C5 **Ansty** *Wilts., Eng.*
58 F3 **Ansty** *W. Sussex, Eng.*
86 C5 **Ansty Coombe** *Wilts., Eng.*
46 E3 **Ansty Cross** *Dorset, Eng.*
26 P2 **Ant** *r. Eng.*
An t-Allt Beithe *High., Scot. see* **Aultbea**
An t-Ath Leathann *High., Scot. see* **Broadford**
22 F7 **An Teallach** *mt. Scot.*
52 E5 **Anthill Common** *Hants., Eng.*
232 C3 **Anthorn** *Cumbria, Eng.*
166 H1 **Antingham** *Norf., Eng.*
An T-Òb *W. Isles, Scot. see* **Leverburgh**
An t-Òban *Arg. and B., Scot. see* **Oban**
An Todhar *High., Scot. see* **Tore**
22 I11 **Antonine Wall** *tourist site Scot.*
170 F5 **Anton's Gowt** *Lincs., Eng.*
36 G2 **Antony** *Corn., Eng.*
388 I4 **Antrim** *Antrim, N. Ire.*
388 I4 **Antrim** *admin. dist. N. Ire.*
399 I3 **Antrim** *county N. Ire.*
23 J2 **Antrim Hills** *hills N. Ire.*
184 D2 **Antrobus** *Cheshire West & Chester, Eng.*
388 J3 **Antynanum** *Ballymena, N. Ire.*
62 G3 **Anvil Green** *Kent, Eng.*
170 E5 **Anwick** *Lincs., Eng.*
252 D3 **Anwoth** *D. and G., Scot.*
22 F8 **Aonach Buidhe** *hill Scot.*
300 A4 **Aoradh** *Arg. and B., Scot.*
128 G2 **Apethorpe** *Northants., Eng.*
148 B4 **Apeton** *Staffs., Eng.*
170 D4 **Apley** *Lincs., Eng.*
180 E3 **Apperknowle** *Derbys., Eng.*
222 D1 **Apperley Bridge** *W. Yorks., Eng.*
216 C2 **Appersett** *N. Yorks., Eng.*
300 D2 **Appin** *Arg. and B., Scot.*
300 D2 **Appin House** *Arg. and B., Scot.*
170 C2 **Appleby** *N. Lincs., Eng.*
232 H5 **Appleby-in-Westmorland** *Cumbria, Eng.*
162 B2 **Appleby Magna** *Leics., Eng.*
162 B2 **Appleby Parva** *Leics., Eng.*
322 D2 **Applecross** *High., Scot.*
40 D1 **Appledore** *Devon, Eng.*
40 G2 **Appledore** *Devon, Eng.*
62 E4 **Appledore** *Kent, Eng.*
62 E4 **Appledore Heath** *Kent, Eng.*
102 D5 **Appleford** *Oxon, Eng.*
52 C3 **Appleshaw** *Hants., Eng.*
232 D5 **Applethwaite** *Cumbria, Eng.*
190 E3 **Appleton** *Halton, Eng.*
102 C4 **Appleton** *Oxon, Eng.*
216 G2 **Appleton-le-Moors** *N. Yorks., Eng.*
216 G2 **Appleton-le-Street** *N. Yorks., Eng.*
216 F3 **Appleton Roebuck** *N. Yorks., Eng.*
190 F3 **Appleton Thorn** *Warr., Eng.*
216 E1 **Appleton Wiske** *N. Yorks., E*
256 H4 **Appletreehall** *Borders, Scot.*
216 D2 **Appletreewick** *N. Yorks., Eng*
94 E5 **Appley** *Som., Eng.*
228 F5 **Appley Bridge** *Lancs., Eng.*
52 E7 **Apse Heath** *I.o.W., Eng.*
120 G3 **Apsey Green** *Suff., Eng.*
110 C5 **Apsley** *Herts., Eng.*
110 C4 **Apsley End** *Central Bedfordshire, Eng.*
58 B4 **Apuldram** *W. Sussex, Eng.*
Arasaig *High., Scot. see* **Arisa**
308 G3 **Arbirlot** *Angus, Scot.*
82 E3 **Arborfield** *W'ham, Eng.*
82 E3 **Arborfield Cross** *W'ham, En*
82 E3 **Arborfield Garrison** *W'ham, Eng.*
208 D3 **Arbourthorne** *S. Yorks., Eng.*
308 G3 **Arbroath** *Angus, Scot.*
314 G4 **Arbuthnott** *Abers., Scot.*
236 F4 **Archdeacon Newton** *Darl., Eng.*
314 D2 **Archiestown** *Moray, Scot.*
184 F3 **Arclid** *Cheshire East, Eng.*
300 E4 **Ard a' Chapuill** *Arg. and B., Scot.*
300 E3 **Ardachearanbeg** *Arg. and B., Scot.*
300 E3 **Ardacheranmor** *Arg. and B., Scot.*
300 C2 **Ardachoil** *Arg. and B., Scot.*
300 C4 **Ardailly** *Arg. and B., Scot.*
300 B3 **Ardalanish** *Arg. and B., Scot.*
314 H2 **Ardallie** *Abers., Scot.*
300 E2 **Ardanaiseig** *Arg. and B., Sco*
322 E2 **Ardaneaskan** *High., Scot.*
300 D3 **Ardanstur** *Arg. and B., Scot.*
396 G4 **Ardarragh** *Newry & Mourne, N. Ire.*
322 E2 **Ardarroch** *High., Scot.*
300 B5 **Ardbeg** *Arg. and B., Scot.*
300 E4 **Ardbeg** *Arg. and B., Scot.*
300 F3 **Ardbeg** *Arg. and B., Scot.*
22 F11 **Ard Bheinn** *hill Scot.*
322 H2 **Ardblair** *High., Scot.*
402 K3 **Ardboe** *Cookstown, N. Ire.*
300 E2 **Ardbrecknish** *Arg. and B., Sc*
320 E4 **Ardcharnich** *High., Scot.*
300 B3 **Ardchiavaig** *Arg. and B., Sco*
300 D2 **Ardchonnel** *Arg. and B., Sco*
300 E3 **Ardchonnell** *Arg. and B., Sc*
300 B2 **Ardchrishnish** *Arg. and B., Scot.*
320 H4 **Ardchronie** *High., Scot.*
322 G2 **Ardchuilk** *High., Scot.*
296 E4 **Ardchullarie More** *Stir., Sco*
296 D3 **Ardchyle** *Stir., Scot.*
366 G2 **Arddlin** *Powys, Wales*
322 F4 **Ardechvie** *High., Scot.*
110 E4 **Ardeley** *Herts., Eng.*
300 E3 **Arden** *Arg. and B., Scot.*
132 B4 **Ardens Grafton** *Warks., Eng.*
300 D2 **Ardentallen** *Arg. and B., Sco*
300 F3 **Ardentinny** *Arg. and B., Scot.*
296 F2 **Ardeonaig** *Stir., Scot.*
322 I2 **Ardersier** *High., Scot.*
322 D4 **Ardery** *High., Scot.*
320 E4 **Ardessie** *High., Scot.*
300 D3 **Ardfad** *Arg. and B., Scot.*
300 D3 **Ardfern** *Arg. and B., Scot.*
300 B4 **Ardfin** *Arg. and B., Scot.*
300 F3 **Ardgartan** *Arg. and B., Scot.*
320 G4 **Ardgay** *High., Scot.*
396 K4 **Ardglass** *Down, N. Ire.*
276 A2 **Ardgowan** *Inverclyde, Scot.*
300 F4 **Ardhallow** *Arg. and B., Scot.*
322 D2 **Ardheslaig** *High., Scot.*
314 E2 **Ardiecow** *Moray, Scot.*
300 D3 **Ardinamar** *Arg. and B., Scot.*
320 E4 **Ardindrean** *High., Scot.*
58 F2 **Ardingly** *W. Sussex, Eng.*
102 C5 **Ardington** *Oxon, Eng.*
102 C5 **Ardington Wick** *Oxon, Eng.*
322 E3 **Ardintoul** *High., Scot.*
22 B8 **Ardivachar Point** *pt Scot.*
396 K3 **Ardkeen** *Ards, N. Ire.*
300 E4 **Ardlamont** *Arg. and B., Scot.*
22 F11 **Ardlamont Point** *pt Scot.*
116 H2 **Ardleigh** *Essex, Eng.*
74 F2 **Ardleigh Green** *Gtr Lon., En*
116 H2 **Ardleigh Heath** *Essex, Eng.*
300 F3 **Ardleish** *Arg. and B., Scot.*
304 K3 **Ardler** *Perth and Kin., Scot.*
102 D3 **Ardley** *Oxon, Eng.*
116 D3 **Ardley End** *Essex, Eng.*
300 C3 **Ardlussa** *Arg. and B., Scot.*
300 E2 **Ardmaddy** *Arg. and B., Scot.*
320 E4 **Ardmair** *High., Scot.*
300 E4 **Ardmaleish** *Arg. and B., Scot*
300 F3 **Ardmay** *Arg. and B., Scot.*
300 C4 **Ardmenish** *Arg. and B., Scot.*
326 B5 **Ardmhòr** *W. Isles, Scot.*
396 J3 **Ardmillan** *Ards, N. Ire.*
300 C4 **Ardminish** *Arg. and B., Scot.*
322 D4 **Ardmolich** *High., Scot.*
388 E2 **Ardmore** *Limavady, N. Ire.*
300 B4 **Ardmore** *Arg. and B., Scot.*
300 D2 **Ardmore** *Arg. and B., Scot.*
300 F4 **Ardmore** *Arg. and B., Scot.*
320 H4 **Ardmore** *High., Scot.*
22 D9 **Ardmore Point** *pt Scot.*
300 C2 **Ardnacross** *Arg. and B., Scot.*
300 F4 **Ardnadam** *Arg. and B., Scot.*
300 C2 **Ardnadrochit** *Arg. and B., Sc*
320 D3 **Ardnagoine** *High., Scot.*
300 E3 **Ardnagowan** *Arg. and B., Sco*
300 F3 **Ardnahein** *Arg. and B., Scot.*
300 B4 **Ardnahoe** *Arg. and B., Scot.*
22 D9 **Ardnamurchan** *pen. Scot.*
22 D9 **Ardnamurchan, Point of** *pt Scot.*
322 E2 **Ardnarff** *High., Scot.*
322 E4 **Ardnastang** *High., Scot.*
300 A4 **Ardnave** *Arg. and B., Scot.*
300 F3 **Ardno** *Arg. and B., Scot.*
314 G2 **Ardo** *Abers., Scot.*
252 E2 **Ardoch** *D. and G., Scot.*
314 C2 **Ardoch** *Moray, Scot.*
304 J3 **Ardoch** *Perth and Kin., Scot.*
268 A2 **Ardochrig** *S. Lanark., Scot.*

Ardpatrick to **Ballymacashen**

D4 **Ardpatrick** Arg. and B., Scot.
E11 **Ardpatrick Point** pt Scot.
F3 **Ardpeaton** Arg. and B., Scot.
K3 **Ardquin** Ards, N. Ire.
F3 **Ardradnaig** Perth and Kin., Scot.
E3 **Ardress** Armagh, N. Ire.
D3 **Ardrishaig** Arg. and B., Scot.
E3 **Ardroe** High., Scot.
H4 **Ardross** High., Scot.
F3 **Ardrossan** N. Ayr., Scot.
K2 **Ards** admin. dist. N. Ire.
E4 **Ardscalpsie** Arg. and B., Scot.
D3 **Ardshellach** Arg. and B., Scot.
D2 **Ardsley** S. Yorks., Eng.
D4 **Ardslignish** High., Scot.
L4 **Ards Peninsula** pen. N. Ire.
F2 **Ardstraw** Strabane, N. Ire.
B4 **Ardtalla** Arg. and B., Scot.
F3 **Ardtalnaig** Perth and Kin., Scot.
E4 **Ardtaraig** Arg. and B., Scot.
E2 **Ardteatle** Arg. and B., Scot.
D4 **Ardtoe** High., Scot.
K4 **Ardtole** Down, N. Ire.
D5 **Ardtornish** High., Scot.
F4 **Ardtrostan** Perth and Kin., Scot.
D2 **Ardtur** Arg. and B., Scot.
D3 **Arduaine** Arg. and B., Scot.
H2 **Ardullie** High., Scot.
C2 **Ardura** Arg. and B., Scot.
E3 **Ardvar** High., Scot.
D3 **Ardvasar** High., Scot.
E3 **Ardveich** Stir., Scot.
F3 **Ardvorlich** Arg. and B., Scot.
E4 **Ardvorlich** Perth and Kin., Scot.
A8 **Ardvule, Rubha** pt Scot.
D3 **Ardwall** D. and G., Scot.
B3 **Ardwell** D. and G., Scot.
B5 **Ardwell** S. Ayr., Scot.
D3 **Ardwick** Gtr Man., Eng.
D1 **Areley Kings** Worcs., Eng.
E2 **Arenig Fawr** hill Wales
H4 **Arford** Hants., Eng.
F4 **Argaty** Stir., Scot.
C3 **Argoed** Shrop., Eng.
G2 **Argoed** Caerp., Wales
E5 **Argoed Mill** Powys, Wales
H2 **Argos Hill** E. Sussex, Eng.
E3 **Argrennan House** D. and G., Scot.
F10 **Argyll** reg. Scot.
C3 **Argyll and Bute** admin. div. Scot.
D3 **Arichamish** Arg. and B., Scot.
F2 **Arichastlich** Arg. and B., Scot.
D3 **Arichonan** Arg. and B., Scot.
E4 **Arienskill** High., Scot.
□ **Arileod** Arg. and B., Scot.
D2 **Arinacrinachd** High., Scot.
D3 **Arinafad Beg** Arg. and B., Scot.
□ **Arinagour** Arg. and B., Scot.
C5 **Arinambane** W. Isles, Scot.
D4 **Arisaig** High., Scot.
E9 **Arisaig, Sound of** sea chan. Scot.
F9 **Arkaig, Loch** l. Scot.
C2 **Arkesden** Essex, Eng.
G2 **Arkholme** Lancs., Eng.
G6 **Arkle** hill Scot.
B4 **Arkleby** Cumbria, Eng.
D2 **Arkleside** N. Yorks., Eng.
H2 **Arkleton** D. and G., Scot.
D1 **Arkle Town** N. Yorks., Eng.
C2 **Arkley** Gtr Lon., Eng.
F2 **Arksey** S. Yorks., Eng.
E3 **Arkwright Town** Derbys., Eng.
J5 **Arlary** Perth and Kin., Scot.
G2 **Arle** Glos., Eng.
B5 **Arlecdon** Cumbria, Eng.
D3 **Arlesey** Central Bedfordshire, Eng.
F3 **Arleston** Telford, Eng.
E2 **Arley** Cheshire East, Eng.
E3 **Arlingham** Glos., Eng.
E1 **Arlington** Devon, Eng.
H3 **Arlington** E. Sussex, Eng.
H3 **Arlington** Glos., Eng.
H2 **Armadale** High., Scot.
D3 **Armadale** High., Scot.
A3 **Armadale** W. Lothian, Scot.
E3 **Armagh** Armagh, N. Ire.
E4 **Armagh** admin. dist. N. Ire.
E4 **Armagh** county N. Ire.
G6 **Armagh County Museum** N. Ire.
F4 **Armathwaite** Cumbria, Eng.
G3 **Arminghall** Norf., Eng.
D4 **Armitage** Staffs., Eng.
D3 **Armitage Bridge** W. Yorks., Eng.
E2 **Armley** W. Yorks., Eng.
I2 **Armoy** Moyle, N. Ire.
C5 **Armscote** Warks., Eng.
C2 **Armshead** Staffs., Eng.
G3 **Armston** Northants., Eng.
F2 **Armthorpe** S. Yorks., Eng.
□ **Arnabost** Arg. and B., Scot.
Arnasdal High., Scot. see **Arnisdale**
C2 **Arncliffe** N. Yorks., Eng.
H2 **Arncroach** Fife, Scot.
G3 **Arne** Dorset, Eng.
E3 **Arnesby** Leics., Eng.
D5 **Arney** Fermanagh, N. Ire.
B2 **Arnfield** Derbys., Eng.
J5 **Arngask** Perth and Kin., Scot.
E5 **Arngibbon** Stir., Scot.
E5 **Arngomery** Stir., Scot.
F4 **Arnhall** Abers., Scot.
D5 **Arnicle** Arg. and B., Scot.
D4 **Arnipol** High., Scot.
E3 **Arnisdale** High., Scot.
C2 **Arnish** High., Scot.
E3 **Arniston Engine** Midlothian, Scot.
E1 **Arnol** W. Isles, Scot.
G3 **Arnold** E. Riding, Eng.
C4 **Arnold** Notts., Eng.
I2 **Arno's Vale** Bristol, Eng.
E5 **Arnprior** Stir., Scot.
F7 **Arnside** Cumbria, Eng.
I4 **Arowry** Wrex., Wales
D7 **Arrad Foot** Cumbria, Eng.
F3 **Arram** E. Riding, Eng.
F11 **Arran** i. Scot.
E3 **Arras** E. Riding, Eng.
G2 **Arrat** Angus, Scot.
E6 **Arreton** I.o.W., Eng.
D6 **Arrington** Cambs., Eng.
F2 **Arrivain** Arg. and B., Scot.
F3 **Arrochar** Arg. and B., Scot.
A4 **Arrow** Warks., Eng.
G3 **Arrow** r. Eng.
F1 **Arrowfield Top** Worcs., Eng.
G3 **Arscaig** High., Scot.
C4 **Arscott** Shrop., Eng.
E1 **Arthington** W. Yorks., Eng.
D3 **Arthingworth** Northants., Eng.
F4 **Arthog** Gwynedd, Wales
G2 **Arthrath** Abers., Scot.
K3 **Arthurstone** Perth and Kin., Scot.
388 F2 **Articlave** Coleraine, N. Ire.
402 F1 **Artigarvan** Strabane, N. Ire.
388 E2 **Artikelly** Limavady, N. Ire.
388 G3 **Artnagross** Ballymoney, N. Ire.
314 H2 **Artrochie** Abers., Scot.
300 A4 **Aruadh** Arg. and B., Scot.
58 C3 **Arundel** W. Sussex, Eng.
322 F4 **Aryhoulan** High., Scot.
232 B5 **Asby** Cumbria, Eng.
300 E4 **Ascog** Arg. and B., Scot.
82 F3 **Ascot** W. and M., Eng.
132 C5 **Ascott** Warks., Eng.
102 B3 **Ascott d'Oyley** Oxon, Eng.
102 B3 **Ascott Earl** Oxon, Eng.
102 B3 **Ascott-under-Wychwood** Oxon, Eng.
308 D2 **Ascreavie** Angus, Scot.
162 F2 **Asfordby** Leics., Eng.
162 F2 **Asfordby Hill** Leics., Eng.
170 D6 **Asgarby** Lincs., Eng.
170 F4 **Asgarby** Lincs., Eng.
46 F2 **Ash** Dorset, Eng.
62 B2 **Ash** Kent, Eng.
62 H3 **Ash** Kent, Eng.
94 H5 **Ash** Som., Eng.
78 B2 **Ash** Surr., Eng.
82 C3 **Ashampstead** W. Berks., Eng.
40 D2 **Ash Barton** Devon, Eng.
120 G4 **Ashbocking** Suff., Eng.
120 G4 **Ashbocking Green** Suff., Eng.
180 C4 **Ashbourne** Derbys., Eng.
94 D5 **Ashbrittle** Som., Eng.
58 I3 **Ashburnham Place** E. Sussex, Eng.
40 E3 **Ashburton** Devon, Eng.
40 D2 **Ashbury** Devon, Eng.
102 B5 **Ashbury** Oxon, Eng.
170 C2 **Ashby** N. Lincs., Eng.
170 G4 **Ashby by Partney** Lincs., Eng.
170 F3 **Ashby cum Fenby** N.E. Lincs., Eng.
170 D5 **Ashby de la Launde** Lincs., Eng.
162 C2 **Ashby de la Zouch** Leics., Eng.
120 J1 **Ashby Dell** Suff., Eng.
162 F2 **Ashby Folville** Leics., Eng.
170 F3 **Ashby Hill** N.E. Lincs., Eng.
162 D3 **Ashby Magna** Leics., Eng.
162 D4 **Ashby Parva** Leics., Eng.
170 F4 **Ashby Puerorum** Lincs., Eng.
128 C4 **Ashby St Ledgers** Northants., Eng.
166 H3 **Ashby St Mary** Norf., Eng.
98 G2 **Ashchurch** Glos., Eng.
40 F3 **Ashcombe** Devon, Eng.
94 G2 **Ashcombe** N. Som., Eng.
94 H4 **Ashcott** Som., Eng.
116 D1 **Ashdon** Essex, Eng.
26 M5 **Ashdown Forest** reg. Eng.
52 E3 **Ashe** Hants., Eng.
116 H3 **Asheldham** Essex, Eng.
116 F1 **Ashen** Essex, Eng.
62 E4 **Ashenden** Kent, Eng.
106 C4 **Ashendon** Bucks., Eng.
300 D4 **Ashens** Arg. and B., Scot.
140 D4 **Ashfield** Here., Eng.
120 G3 **Ashfield** Suff., Eng.
300 D3 **Ashfield** Arg. and B., Scot.
296 G4 **Ashfield** Stir., Scot.
120 C3 **Ashfield Green** Suff., Eng.
120 G3 **Ashfield Green** Suff., Eng.
144 F2 **Ashfields** Shrop., Eng.
58 E2 **Ashfold Crossways** W. Sussex, Eng.
40 D1 **Ashford** Devon, Eng.
52 B5 **Ashford** Hants., Eng.
62 F4 **Ashford** Kent, Eng.
78 D1 **Ashford** Surr., Eng.
144 D6 **Ashford Bowdler** Shrop., Eng.
144 D5 **Ashford Carbonel** Shrop., Eng.
52 E2 **Ashford Hill** Hants., Eng.
180 C3 **Ashford in the Water** Derbys., Eng.
268 C2 **Ashgill** S. Lanark., Scot.
78 B2 **Ash Green** Surr., Eng.
132 C3 **Ash Green** Warks., Eng.
256 G3 **Ashiestiel** Borders, Scot.
40 G2 **Ashill** Devon, Eng.
166 D3 **Ashill** Norf., Eng.
94 G5 **Ashill** Som., Eng.
116 G4 **Ashingdon** Essex, Eng.
244 H4 **Ashington** Northumb., Eng.
94 I5 **Ashington** Som., Eng.
58 D3 **Ashington** W. Sussex, Eng.
256 G4 **Ashkirk** Borders, Scot.
52 D6 **Ashlett** Hants., Eng.
98 F2 **Ashleworth** Glos., Eng.
98 F2 **Ashleworth Quay** Glos., Eng.
124 G5 **Ashley** Cambs., Eng.
184 E1 **Ashley** Cheshire East, Eng.
98 G4 **Ashley** Glos., Eng.
52 C6 **Ashley** Hants., Eng.
52 D4 **Ashley** Hants., Eng.
62 H3 **Ashley** Kent, Eng.
128 D2 **Ashley** Northants., Eng.
148 A3 **Ashley** Staffs., Eng.
86 B3 **Ashley** Wilts., Eng.
94 I2 **Ashley Down** Bristol, Eng.
106 E4 **Ashley Green** Bucks., Eng.
46 H2 **Ashley Heath** Dorset, Eng.
148 A3 **Ashley Heath** Staffs., Eng.
78 D1 **Ashley Park** Surr., Eng.
144 E2 **Ash Magna** Shrop., Eng.
166 H2 **Ashmanhaugh** Norf., Eng.
52 D3 **Ashmansworth** Hants., Eng.
40 C2 **Ashmansworthy** Devon, Eng.
40 E2 **Ash Mill** Devon, Eng.
46 G2 **Ashmore** Dorset, Eng.
304 J3 **Ashmore** Perth and Kin., Scot.
82 C3 **Ashmore Green** W. Berks., Eng.
132 C4 **Ashorne** Warks., Eng.
180 E4 **Ashover** Derbys., Eng.
180 E4 **Ashover Hay** Derbys., Eng.
132 C4 **Ashow** Warks., Eng.
144 E2 **Ash Parva** Shrop., Eng.
140 D3 **Ashperton** Here., Eng.
94 E4 **Ash Priors** Som., Eng.
40 E2 **Ashreigney** Devon, Eng.
120 E4 **Ash Street** Suff., Eng.
78 E2 **Ashtead** Surr., Eng.
40 F2 **Ash Thomas** Devon, Eng.
184 C2 **Ashton** Cheshire West & Chester, Eng.
36 C3 **Ashton** Corn., Eng.
52 E5 **Ashton** Hants., Eng.
140 C2 **Ashton** Here., Eng.
128 D5 **Ashton** Northants., Eng.
128 G3 **Ashton** Northants., Eng.
124 B3 **Ashton** Peterb., Eng.
276 B2 **Ashton** Inverclyde, Scot.
86 C4 **Ashton Common** Wilts., Eng.
198 B3 **Ashton-in-Makerfield** Gtr Man., Eng.
86 D2 **Ashton Keynes** Wilts., Eng.
136 E3 **Ashton under Hill** Worcs., Eng.
198 E3 **Ashton-under-Lyne** Gtr Man., Eng.
198 C3 **Ashton upon Mersey** Gtr Man., Eng.
52 C5 **Ashurst** Hants., Eng.
62 A4 **Ashurst** Kent, Eng.
58 E3 **Ashurst** W. Sussex, Eng.
52 C5 **Ashurst Bridge** Hants., Eng.
58 G2 **Ashurstwood** W. Sussex, Eng.
78 B2 **Ash Vale** Surr., Eng.
40 D2 **Ashwater** Devon, Eng.
110 E3 **Ashwell** Herts., Eng.
162 G2 **Ashwell** Rutland, Eng.
110 D3 **Ashwell End** Herts., Eng.
166 F3 **Ashwellthorpe** Norf., Eng.
94 I3 **Ashwick** Som., Eng.
166 C2 **Ashwicken** Norf., Eng.
256 H4 **Ashybank** Borders, Scot.
232 C7 **Askam in Furness** Cumbria, Eng.
208 F2 **Askern** S. Yorks., Eng.
326 B5 **Askernish** W. Isles, Scot.
46 D3 **Askerswell** Dorset, Eng.
106 D4 **Askett** Bucks., Eng.
232 F5 **Askham** Cumbria, Eng.
176 D3 **Askham** Notts., Eng.
216 F3 **Askham Bryan** York, Eng.
22 D9 **Askival** hill Scot.
300 E3 **Asknish** Arg. and B., Scot.
216 C2 **Askrigg** N. Yorks., Eng.
216 D3 **Askwith** N. Yorks., Eng.
170 D6 **Aslackby** Lincs., Eng.
166 G4 **Aslacton** Norf., Eng.
176 D5 **Aslockton** Notts., Eng.
314 E3 **Asloun** Abers., Scot.
120 G3 **Aspall** Suff., Eng.
232 B4 **Aspatria** Cumbria, Eng.
110 E4 **Aspenden** Herts., Eng.
170 F6 **Asperton** Lincs., Eng.
176 B5 **Aspley** Nott., Eng.
148 B3 **Aspley** Staffs., Eng.
110 B3 **Aspley Guise** Central Bedfordshire, Eng.
110 B3 **Aspley Heath** Central Bedfordshire, Eng.
132 A4 **Aspley Heath** Warks., Eng.
198 B2 **Aspull** Gtr Man., Eng.
198 B3 **Aspull Common** Gtr Man., Eng.
210 C4 **Asselby** E. Riding, Eng.
170 H4 **Asserby** Lincs., Eng.
120 D4 **Assington** Suff., Eng.
120 C4 **Assington Green** Suff., Eng.
22 F6 **Assynt, Loch** l. Scot.
184 F3 **Astbury** Cheshire East, Eng.
128 C4 **Astcote** Northants., Eng.
170 F4 **Asterby** Lincs., Eng.
144 C4 **Asterley** Shrop., Eng.
144 C4 **Asterton** Shrop., Eng.
102 B4 **Asthall** Oxon, Eng.
102 B4 **Asthall Leigh** Oxon, Eng.
184 F2 **Astle** Cheshire East, Eng.
198 C2 **Astley** Gtr Man., Eng.
144 D3 **Astley** Shrop., Eng.
132 C2 **Astley** Warks., Eng.
136 D2 **Astley** Worcs., Eng.
144 F4 **Astley Abbotts** Shrop., Eng.
198 C2 **Astley Bridge** Gtr Man., Eng.
136 D2 **Astley Cross** Worcs., Eng.
198 C3 **Astley Green** Gtr Man., Eng.
144 D3 **Astley Lodge** Shrop., Eng.
184 D3 **Aston** Cheshire East, Eng.
184 D2 **Aston** Cheshire West & Chester, Eng.
180 C2 **Aston** Derbys., Eng.
180 C5 **Aston** Derbys., Eng.
140 C1 **Aston** Here., Eng.
140 C2 **Aston** Here., Eng.
110 E4 **Aston** Herts., Eng.
102 B4 **Aston** Oxon, Eng.
144 D2 **Aston** Shrop., Eng.
144 G4 **Aston** Shrop., Eng.
148 A3 **Aston** Staffs., Eng.
148 C4 **Aston** Staffs., Eng.
208 E3 **Aston** S. Yorks., Eng.
144 E3 **Aston** Telford, Eng.
82 E2 **Aston** W'ham, Eng.
154 C3 **Aston** W. Mids, Eng.
378 G2 **Aston** Flints., Wales
106 D3 **Aston Abbotts** Bucks., Eng.
144 E5 **Aston Botterell** Shrop., Eng.
148 C3 **Aston-by-Stone** Staffs., Eng.
132 B4 **Aston Cantlow** Warks., Eng.
106 D4 **Aston Clinton** Bucks., Eng.
140 E4 **Aston Crews** Here., Eng.
98 G1 **Aston Cross** Glos., Eng.
110 E4 **Aston End** Herts., Eng.
144 E4 **Aston Eyre** Shrop., Eng.
136 E2 **Aston Fields** Worcs., Eng.
162 D3 **Aston Flamville** Leics., Eng.
184 D2 **Aston Heath** Cheshire West & Chester, Eng.
140 E4 **Aston Ingham** Here., Eng.
184 D3 **Aston juxta Mondrum** Cheshire East, Eng.
128 B5 **Aston le Walls** Northants., Eng.
98 I1 **Aston Magna** Glos., Eng.
144 D5 **Aston Munslow** Shrop., Eng.
98 G1 **Aston on Carrant** Glos., Eng.
144 C5 **Aston on Clun** Shrop., Eng.
180 E5 **Aston-on-Trent** Derbys., Eng.
144 C4 **Aston Pigott** Shrop., Eng.
144 C4 **Aston Rogers** Shrop., Eng.
102 F4 **Aston Rowant** Oxon, Eng.
106 C4 **Aston Sandford** Bucks., Eng.
136 F3 **Aston Somerville** Worcs., Eng.
98 I1 **Aston Subedge** Glos., Eng.
102 D5 **Aston Tirrold** Oxon, Eng.
102 D5 **Aston Upthorpe** Oxon, Eng.
128 B5 **Astrop** Northants., Eng.
110 A5 **Astrope** Herts., Eng.
110 D3 **Astwick** Central Bedfordshire, Eng.
180 E3 **Astwith** Derbys., Eng.
106 E2 **Astwood** M.K., Eng.
136 F2 **Astwood Bank** Worcs., Eng.
170 D6 **Aswarby** Lincs., Eng.
170 G4 **Aswardby** Lincs., Eng.
170 F7 **Aswick Grange** Lincs., Eng.
144 D3 **Atcham** Shrop., Eng.
136 F3 **Atch Lench** Worcs., Eng.
46 F3 **Athelhampton** Dorset, Eng.
120 G3 **Athelington** Suff., Eng.
94 G4 **Athelney** Som., Eng.
288 G3 **Athelstaneford** E. Lothian, Scot.
52 D7 **Atherfield Green** I.o.W., Eng.
40 D2 **Atherington** Devon, Eng.
58 C4 **Atherington** W. Sussex, Eng.
208 D2 **Athersley North** S. Yorks., Eng.
94 G5 **Atherstone** Som., Eng.
132 C2 **Atherstone** Warks., Eng.
132 B5 **Atherstone on Stour** Warks., Eng.
198 C2 **Atherton** Gtr Man., Eng.
326 D2 **Ath Linne** W. Isles, Scot.
22 H9 **Atholl, Forest of** reg. Scot.
180 D4 **Atlow** Derbys., Eng.
322 E2 **Attadale** High., Scot.
402 G2 **Attahole** Strabane, N. Ire.
176 B5 **Attenborough** Notts., Eng.
170 C3 **Atterby** Lincs., Eng.
208 D3 **Attercliffe** S. Yorks., Eng.
144 E4 **Atterley** Shrop., Eng.
162 C3 **Atterton** Leics., Eng.
396 H5 **Attical** Newry & Mourne, N. Ire.
166 F3 **Attleborough** Norf., Eng.
132 D2 **Attleborough** Warks., Eng.
166 F2 **Attlebridge** Norf., Eng.
120 C4 **Attleton Green** Suff., Eng.
210 G3 **Atwick** E. Riding, Eng.
86 B3 **Atworth** Wilts., Eng.
140 C3 **Auberrow** Here., Eng.
170 C5 **Aubourn** Lincs., Eng.
300 F2 **Auch** Arg. and B., Scot.
262 B6 **Auchairne** S. Ayr., Scot.
314 C4 **Auchallater** Abers., Scot.
300 D4 **Auchameanach** Arg. and B., Scot.
264 B3 **Auchamore** N. Ayr., Scot.
314 F2 **Aucharnie** Abers., Scot.
320 G4 **Aucharrigill** High., Scot.
308 C2 **Auchavan** Angus, Scot.
300 D4 **Auchbraad** Arg. and B., Scot.
314 D2 **Auchbreck** Moray, Scot.
276 D3 **Auchenback** E. Renf., Scot.
314 F4 **Auchenblae** Abers., Scot.
276 C2 **Auchenbothie** Inverclyde, Scot.
252 E2 **Auchenbrack** D. and G., Scot.
300 E4 **Auchenbreck** Arg. and B., Scot.
252 E3 **Auchencairn** D. and G., Scot.
256 K1 **Auchencrow** Borders, Scot.
288 D3 **Auchendinny** Midlothian, Scot.
252 E3 **Auchendolly** D. and G., Scot.
276 B2 **Auchenfoyle** Inverclyde, Scot.
296 D6 **Auchengillan** Stir., Scot.
268 E2 **Auchengray** S. Lanark., Scot.
314 D2 **Auchenhalrig** Moray, Scot.
268 C2 **Auchenheath** S. Lanark., Scot.
252 E2 **Auchenhessnane** D. and G., Scot.
300 E4 **Auchenlochan** Arg. and B., Scot.
252 B3 **Auchenmalg** D. and G., Scot.
252 H2 **Auchenrivock** D. and G., Scot.
264 G2 **Auchentiber** N. Ayr., Scot.
300 F3 **Auchenvennel** Arg. and B., Scot.
296 C3 **Auchessan** Stir., Scot.
300 D4 **Auchinafaud** Arg. and B., Scot.
262 D4 **Auchincruive** S. Ayr., Scot.
300 D3 **Auchindarrach** Arg. and B., Scot.
300 E3 **Auchindrain** Arg. and B., Scot.
314 F2 **Auchininna** Abers., Scot.
262 F4 **Auchinleck** E. Ayr., Scot.
280 B3 **Auchinloch** N. Lanark., Scot.
304 F5 **Auchinner** Perth and Kin., Scot.
314 D2 **Auchinroath** Moray, Scot.
314 H2 **Auchiries** Abers., Scot.
314 F3 **Auchleven** Abers., Scot.
268 C3 **Auchlochan** S. Lanark., Scot.
314 G3 **Auchlunies** Abers., Scot.
296 D3 **Auchlyne** Stir., Scot.
314 G2 **Auchmacoy** Abers., Scot.
314 D2 **Auchmair** Moray, Scot.
252 B3 **Auchmantle** D. and G., Scot.
308 G3 **Auchmithie** Angus, Scot.
292 E2 **Auchmuirbridge** Fife, Scot.
308 F1 **Auchmull** Angus, Scot.
292 F2 **Auchmuty** Fife, Scot.
252 E3 **Auchnabony** D. and G., Scot.
300 E3 **Auchnabreac** Arg. and B., Scot.
304 G3 **Auchnacloich** Perth and Kin., Scot.
300 C2 **Auchnacraig** Arg. and B., Scot.
308 E2 **Auchnacree** Angus, Scot.
304 G4 **Auchnafree** Perth and Kin., Scot.
322 K2 **Auchnagallin** High., Scot.
314 G2 **Auchnagatt** Abers., Scot.
300 E4 **Auchnaha** Arg. and B., Scot.
314 D3 **Aucholzie** Abers., Scot.
314 F3 **Auchorrie** Abers., Scot.
308 C3 **Auchrannie** Angus, Scot.
296 E3 **Auchraw** Stir., Scot.
296 B3 **Auchreoch** Stir., Scot.
308 E1 **Auchronie** Angus, Scot.
304 H5 **Auchterarder** Perth and Kin., Scot.
292 E3 **Auchterderran** Fife, Scot.
308 D3 **Auchterhouse** Angus, Scot.
292 E2 **Auchtermuchty** Fife, Scot.
292 E3 **Auchtertool** Fife, Scot.
308 D3 **Auchtertyre** Angus, Scot.
322 E3 **Auchtertyre** High., Scot.
314 C2 **Auchtertyre** Moray, Scot.
296 B3 **Auchtertyre** Stir., Scot.
296 D3 **Auchtubh** Stir., Scot.
208 F2 **Auckley** S. Yorks., Eng.
198 E3 **Audenshaw** Gtr Man., Eng.
184 D4 **Audlem** Cheshire East, Eng.
148 B2 **Audley** Staffs., Eng.
116 D1 **Audley End** Essex, Eng.
116 F1 **Audley End** Essex, Eng.
120 D4 **Audley End** Suff., Eng.
148 B4 **Audmore** Staffs., Eng.
388 K3 **Aughaboy** Larne, N. Ire.
402 K3 **Aughamullan** Dungannon, N. Ire.
402 G4 **Aughentaine** Dungannon, N. Ire.
402 H4 **Augher** Dungannon, N. Ire.
402 I4 **Aughnacloy** Dungannon, N. Ire.
396 H5 **Aughnaloopy** Newry & Mourne, N. Ire.
396 H3 **Aughnaskeagh** Banbridge, N. Ire.
388 G4 **Aughrim** Magherafelt, N. Ire.
210 C3 **Aughton** E. Riding, Eng.
228 E5 **Aughton** Lancs., Eng.
228 F2 **Aughton** Lancs., Eng.
208 E3 **Aughton** S. Yorks., Eng.
86 F4 **Aughton** Wilts., Eng.
228 E5 **Aughton Park** Lancs., Eng.
322 J2 **Auldearn** High., Scot.
140 C2 **Aulden** Here., Eng.
252 E2 **Auldgirth** D. and G., Scot.
288 H2 **Auldhame** E. Lothian, Scot.
268 A2 **Auldhouse** S. Lanark., Scot.
304 E2 **Aulich** Perth and Kin., Scot.
322 E3 **Ault a' chruinn** High., Scot.
320 F3 **Aultanrynie** High., Scot.
320 D4 **Aultbea** High., Scot.
320 C4 **Aultgrishan** High., Scot.
180 F3 **Ault Hucknall** Derbys., Eng.
320 J3 **Aultibea** High., Scot.
314 E2 **Aultmore** Moray, Scot.
314 D2 **Aultnapaddock** Abers., Scot.
314 F2 **Aulton** Abers., Scot.
322 H2 **Aultvaich** High., Scot.
170 D7 **Aunby** Lincs., Eng.
322 J3 **Aundorach** High., Scot.
40 F2 **Aunk** Devon, Eng.
170 D6 **Aunsby** Lincs., Eng.
314 G2 **Auquhorthies** Abers., Scot.
22 K4 **Auskerry** i. Scot.
98 D4 **Aust** S. Glos., Eng.
208 F3 **Austerfield** S. Yorks., Eng.
222 F2 **Austhorpe** W. Yorks., Eng.
222 D3 **Austonley** W. Yorks., Eng.
132 C2 **Austrey** Warks., Eng.
216 B2 **Austwick** N. Yorks., Eng.
170 H4 **Authorpe Row** Lincs., Eng.
86 D3 **Avebury** Wilts., Eng.
86 D3 **Avebury Trusloe** Wilts., Eng.
116 D5 **Aveley** Thurrock, Eng.
98 F3 **Avening** Glos., Eng.
176 D4 **Averham** Notts., Eng.
22 H7 **Averon** r. Scot.
74 E3 **Avery Hill** Gtr Lon., Eng.
40 E4 **Aveton Gifford** Devon, Eng.
22 F10 **Avich, Loch** l. Scot.
322 J3 **Avielochan** High., Scot.
322 J3 **Aviemore** High., Scot.
52 E4 **Avington** Hants., Eng.
82 B3 **Avington** W. Berks., Eng.
322 I2 **Avoch** High., Scot.
52 B6 **Avon** Hants., Eng.
26 E7 **Avon** r. Eng.
26 G5 **Avon** r. Eng.
26 H3 **Avon** r. Eng.
26 I6 **Avon** r. Eng.
280 D3 **Avonbridge** Falk., Scot.
86 B3 **Avoncliff** Wilts., Eng.
132 D5 **Avon Dassett** Warks., Eng.
94 H1 **Avonmouth** Bristol, Eng.
40 E3 **Avonwick** Devon, Eng.
52 C4 **Awbridge** Hants., Eng.
22 F10 **Awe, Loch** l. Scot.
252 A3 **Awhirk** D. and G., Scot.
98 D4 **Awkley** S. Glos., Eng.
40 G2 **Awliscombe** Devon, Eng.
98 E3 **Awre** Glos., Eng.
176 B5 **Awsworth** Notts., Eng.
94 H3 **Axbridge** Som., Eng.
26 F6 **Axe** r. Eng.
26 G5 **Axe** r. Eng.
52 F3 **Axford** Hants., Eng.
86 F3 **Axford** Wilts., Eng.
40 H2 **Axminster** Devon, Eng.
40 G2 **Axmouth** Devon, Eng.
378 E2 **Axton** Flints., Wales
236 F4 **Aycliffe** Durham, Eng.
244 F6 **Aydon** Northumb., Eng.
98 D3 **Aylburton** Glos., Eng.
244 C6 **Ayle** Northumb., Eng.
40 F2 **Aylesbeare** Devon, Eng.
106 D4 **Aylesbury** Bucks., Eng.
170 E2 **Aylesby** N.E. Lincs., Eng.
62 C3 **Aylesford** Kent, Eng.
62 H3 **Aylesham** Kent, Eng.
162 E3 **Aylestone** Leicester, Eng.
166 G1 **Aylmerton** Norf., Eng.
166 G2 **Aylsham** Norf., Eng.
140 D3 **Aylton** Here., Eng.
140 B2 **Aymestrey** Here., Eng.
128 B6 **Aynho** Northants., Eng.
110 D5 **Ayot Green** Herts., Eng.
110 D4 **Ayot St Lawrence** Herts., Eng.
110 D5 **Ayot St Peter** Herts., Eng.
262 D4 **Ayr** S. Ayr., Scot.
22 G12 **Ayr** r. Scot.
26 F1 **Ayr, Point of** pt Wales
24 I5 **Ayre, Point of** pt Isle of Man
216 D2 **Aysgarth** N. Yorks., Eng.
232 E7 **Ayside** Cumbria, Eng.
162 G3 **Ayston** Rutland, Eng.
116 D3 **Aythorpe Roding** Essex, Eng.
256 L1 **Ayton** Borders, Scot.
304 J5 **Ayton** Perth and Kin., Scot.
331 D2 **Aywick** Shet., Scot.
216 E2 **Azerley** N. Yorks., Eng.

B

40 F3 **Babbacombe** Torbay, Eng.
26 F6 **Babbacombe Bay** b. Eng.
176 B5 **Babbington** Notts., Eng.
144 C2 **Babbinswood** Shrop., Eng.
110 F5 **Babb's Green** Herts., Eng.
94 I4 **Babcary** Som., Eng.
356 H1 **Babel** Carmar., Wales
120 C4 **Babel Green** Suff., Eng.
378 F2 **Babell** Flints., Wales
40 E3 **Babeny** Devon, Eng.
102 C4 **Bablock Hythe** Oxon, Eng.
124 F6 **Babraham** Cambs., Eng.
176 D3 **Babworth** Notts., Eng.
314 D2 **Baby's Hill** Moray, Scot.
326 F2 **Bac** W. Isles, Scot.
371 C3 **Bachau** I.o.A., Wales
329 E3 **Backaland** Orkney, Scot.
329 D1 **Backaskaill** Orkney, Scot.
232 E7 **Backbarrow** Cumbria, Eng.
356 C3 **Backe** Carmar., Wales
314 H2 **Backfolds** Abers., Scot.
184 B2 **Backford** Cheshire West & Chester, Eng.
314 F2 **Backhill** Abers., Scot.
314 F3 **Backhill of Trustach** Abers., Scot.
320 I4 **Backies** High., Scot.
322 D4 **Back of Keppoch** High., Scot.
314 E2 **Backside** Abers., Scot.
120 C3 **Back Street** Suff., Eng.
22 J9 **Backwater Reservoir** resr Scot.
94 H2 **Backwell** N. Som., Eng.
236 F1 **Backworth** T. and W., Eng.
116 D2 **Bacon End** Essex, Eng.
116 D2 **Baconend Green** Essex, Eng.
166 F1 **Baconsthorpe** Norf., Eng.
140 B4 **Bacton** Here., Eng.
166 H1 **Bacton** Norf., Eng.
120 F3 **Bacton** Suff., Eng.
120 E3 **Bacton Green** Suff., Eng.
228 I4 **Bacup** Lancs., Eng.
320 C4 **Badachro** High., Scot.
22 H6 **Badanloch, Loch** l. Scot.
320 H3 **Badanloch Lodge** High., Scot.
322 F2 **Badavanich** High., Scot.
86 E2 **Badbury** Swindon, Eng.
86 E2 **Badbury Wick** Swindon, Eng.
128 B4 **Badby** Northants., Eng.
320 E2 **Badcall** High., Scot.
320 E3 **Badcall** High., Scot.
320 D4 **Badcaul** High., Scot.
148 C2 **Baddeley Edge** Stoke, Eng.
148 C2 **Baddeley Green** Stoke, Eng.
132 B3 **Baddesley Clinton** Warks., Eng.
132 C2 **Baddesley Ensor** Warks., Eng.
320 E3 **Baddidarach** High., Scot.
22 H9 **Badenoch** reg. Scot.
314 F2 **Badenscoth** Abers., Scot.
314 D3 **Badenyon** Abers., Scot.
36 F2 **Badgall** Corn., Eng.
124 E3 **Badgeney** Cambs., Eng.
144 F4 **Badger** Shrop., Eng.
184 F2 **Badgerbank** Cheshire East, Eng.
62 A2 **Badgers Mount** Kent, Eng.
98 G2 **Badgeworth** Glos., Eng.
94 G3 **Badgworth** Som., Eng.
322 D3 **Badicaul** High., Scot.
120 H3 **Badingham** Suff., Eng.
320 G3 **Badintagairt** High., Scot.
62 F3 **Badlesmere** Kent, Eng.
120 F4 **Badley** Suff., Eng.
320 K2 **Badlipster** High., Scot.
320 D4 **Badluarach** High., Scot.
98 F4 **Badminton** S. Glos., Eng.
320 E3 **Badnaban** High., Scot.
320 E2 **Badnabay** High., Scot.
320 J3 **Badnagie** High., Scot.
304 F1 **Badnambiast** Perth and Kin., Scot.
320 E4 **Badrallach** High., Scot.
136 F3 **Badsey** Worcs., Eng.
78 B2 **Badshot Lea** Surr., Eng.
222 G3 **Badsworth** W. Yorks., Eng.
120 E3 **Badwell Ash** Suff., Eng.
304 I2 **Badyo** Perth and Kin., Scot.
46 E2 **Bagber** Dorset, Eng.
216 F2 **Bagby** N. Yorks., Eng.
98 H3 **Bagendon** Glos., Eng.
144 F5 **Bagginswood** Shrop., Eng.
162 F2 **Baggrave Hall** Leics., Eng.
232 C4 **Baggrow** Cumbria, Eng.
26 D5 **Baggy Point** pt Eng.
Bàgh a'Chaisteil W. Isles, Scot. see **Castlebay**
22 B8 **Baghasdail, Loch** inlet Scot.
326 B5 **Baghasdal** W. Isles, Scot.
326 C4 **Bàgh Mòr** W. Isles, Scot.
378 F2 **Bagillt** Flints., Wales
132 D3 **Baginton** Warks., Eng.
350 D3 **Baglan** N.P.T., Wales
144 C2 **Bagley** Shrop., Eng.
94 H3 **Bagley** Som., Eng.
52 F3 **Bagmore** Hants., Eng.
148 C2 **Bagnall** Staffs., Eng.
82 B3 **Bagnor** W. Berks., Eng.
98 F4 **Bagpath** Glos., Eng.
78 B1 **Bagshot** Surr., Eng.
86 F3 **Bagshot** Wilts., Eng.
198 D2 **Bagslate Moor** Gtr Man., Eng.
166 C1 **Bagthorpe** Norf., Eng.
176 B4 **Bagthorpe** Notts., Eng.
198 D3 **Baguley** Gtr Man., Eng.
162 C2 **Bagworth** Leics., Eng.
140 C4 **Bagwyllydiart** Here., Eng.
222 D1 **Baildon** W. Yorks., Eng.
Baile a'Mhanaich W. Isles, Scot. see **Balivanich**
Baile a' Mhuilinn High., Scot. see **Milton**
322 H3 **Bailebeag** High., Scot.
300 D4 **Baile Boidheach** Arg. and B., Scot.
326 C4 **Baile Glas** W. Isles, Scot.
Baile Mac Ara High., Scot. see **Balmacara**
Baile Mairi High., Scot. see **Maryburgh**
326 B4 **Baile Mhartainn** W. Isles, Scot.
300 A3 **Baile Mòr** Arg. and B., Scot.
326 C3 **Baile-na-Cille** W. Isles, Scot.
326 B4 **Baile Raghaill** W. Isles, Scot.
322 D4 **Bailetonach** High., Scot.
314 E2 **Bailiesward** Abers., Scot.
222 D2 **Bailiff Bridge** W. Yorks., Eng.
276 F2 **Baillieston** Glas., Scot.
24 Q7 **Bain** r. Eng.
216 C2 **Bainbridge** N. Yorks., Eng.
280 D2 **Bainsford** Falk., Scot.
210 E3 **Bainton** E. Riding, Eng.
102 E3 **Bainton** Oxon, Eng.
124 B3 **Bainton** Peterb., Eng.
396 K2 **Bairdstown** Ards, N. Ire.
256 I4 **Bairnkine** Borders, Scot.
314 D2 **Bakebare** Moray, Scot.
110 F4 **Baker's End** Herts., Eng.
116 E4 **Baker Street** Thurrock, Eng.
180 C3 **Bakewell** Derbys., Eng.
322 C2 **Balachuirn** High., Scot.
304 J5 **Balado** Perth and Kin., Scot.
296 E5 **Balafark** Stir., Scot.
26 E2 **Bala Lake** l. Wales
322 J3 **Balavil** High., Scot.
322 H3 **Balbeg** High., Scot.
304 J4 **Balbeggie** Perth and Kin., Scot.
292 F2 **Balbirnie** Fife, Scot.
208 F2 **Balby** S. Yorks., Eng.
22 I13 **Balcary Point** pt Scot.
320 G3 **Balcharn** High., Scot.
314 F2 **Balchers** Abers., Scot.
320 D3 **Balchladich** High., Scot.
322 H2 **Balchraggan** High., Scot.
322 H2 **Balchraggan** High., Scot.
58 F2 **Balcombe** W. Sussex, Eng.
292 F2 **Balcurvie** Fife, Scot.
24 M4 **Balderhead Reservoir** resr Eng.
276 E2 **Baldernock** E. Dun., Scot.
216 E2 **Baldersby** N. Yorks., Eng.
198 E2 **Balderstone** Gtr Man., Eng.
228 G4 **Balderstone** Lancs., Eng.
184 B3 **Balderton** Cheshire West & Chester, Eng.
176 E4 **Balderton** Notts., Eng.
292 G2 **Baldinnie** Fife, Scot.
110 D4 **Baldock** Herts., Eng.
102 D4 **Baldon Row** Oxon, Eng.
308 D3 **Baldovan** Angus, Scot.
308 D2 **Baldovie** Angus, Scot.
308 E4 **Baldovie** Dundee, Scot.
405 D2 **Baldrine** Isle of Man
58 J3 **Baldslow** E. Sussex, Eng.
405 C2 **Baldwin** Isle of Man
148 B3 **Baldwin's Gate** Staffs., Eng.
78 F3 **Baldwins Hill** Surr., Eng.
166 E1 **Bale** Norf., Eng.
300 □ **Balemartine** Arg. and B., Scot.
304 L3 **Balendoch** Perth and Kin., Scot.
300 □ **Balephuil** Arg. and B., Scot.
288 C3 **Balerno** Edin., Scot.
300 F3 **Balernock** Arg. and B., Scot.
300 B3 **Baleromindubh** Arg. and B., Scot.
300 B3 **Balerominmore** Arg. and B., Scot.
22 B7 **Baleshare** i. Scot.
300 B2 **Balevulin** Arg. and B., Scot.
308 F2 **Balfield** Angus, Scot.
329 D3 **Balfour** Orkney, Scot.
296 D5 **Balfron** Stir., Scot.
296 D5 **Balfron Station** Stir., Scot.
292 C3 **Balgonar** Fife, Scot.
314 G2 **Balgove** Abers., Scot.
252 B3 **Balgowan** D. and G., Scot.
322 I3 **Balgowan** High., Scot.
322 B2 **Balgown** High., Scot.
314 F2 **Balgreen** Abers., Scot.
252 B3 **Balgreggan** D. and G., Scot.
322 E2 **Balgy** High., Scot.
296 G4 **Balhaldie** Stir., Scot.
314 F3 **Balhalgardy** Abers., Scot.
74 D3 **Balham** Gtr Lon., Eng.
304 K3 **Balhary** Perth and Kin., Scot.
292 F1 **Balhelvie** Fife, Scot.
292 G2 **Balhousie** Fife, Scot.
331 E1 **Baliasta** Shet., Scot.
308 D2 **Balintore** Angus, Scot.
320 I4 **Balintore** High., Scot.
304 F3 **Balintyre** Perth and Kin., Scot.
326 B4 **Balivanich** W. Isles, Scot.
402 G2 **Balix** Strabane, N. Ire.
308 D3 **Balkeerie** Angus, Scot.
210 D4 **Balkholme** E. Riding, Eng.
262 B6 **Balkissock** S. Ayr., Scot.
144 B2 **Ball** Shrop., Eng.
326 C5 **Balla** W. Isles, Scot.
405 B3 **Ballabeg** Isle of Man
405 D2 **Ballacannell** Isle of Man
405 C2 **Ballacarnane Beg** Isle of Man
405 B3 **Balladoole** Isle of Man
405 B3 **Ballafesson** Isle of Man
402 F5 **Ballagh** Fermanagh, N. Ire.
396 I5 **Ballagh Bridge** Newry & Mourne, N. Ire.
405 C2 **Ballagyr** Isle of Man
405 D2 **Ballajora** Isle of Man
405 B3 **Ballakilpheric** Isle of Man
405 C3 **Ballamodha** Isle of Man
262 A6 **Ballantrae** S. Ayr., Scot.
396 F5 **Ballard** Newry & Mourne, N. Ire.
116 G4 **Ballards Gore** Essex, Eng.
405 C1 **Ballasalla** Isle of Man
405 C3 **Ballasalla** Isle of Man
314 D3 **Ballater** Abers., Scot.
314 E3 **Ballaterach** Abers., Scot.
405 C2 **Ballaugh** Isle of Man
405 C3 **Ballaveare** Isle of Man
304 H3 **Ballechin** Perth and Kin., Scot.
396 E4 **Balleer** Armagh, N. Ire.
296 D4 **Balleich** Stir., Scot.
22 I12 **Ballencleuch Law** hill Scot.
288 G3 **Ballencrieff** E. Lothian, Scot.
388 I2 **Balleny** Moyle, N. Ire.
148 C2 **Ball Green** Stoke, Eng.
148 C2 **Ball Haye Green** Staffs., Eng.
52 D2 **Ball Hill** Hants., Eng.
180 C4 **Ballidon** Derbys., Eng.
264 B3 **Balliekine** N. Ayr., Scot.
300 D2 **Balliemore** Arg. and B., Scot.
300 E3 **Balliemore** Arg. and B., Scot.
405 C2 **Ballig** Isle of Man
396 K2 **Balliggan** Ards, N. Ire.
300 E3 **Ballimeanoch** Arg. and B., Scot.
300 E4 **Ballimore** Arg. and B., Scot.
296 D4 **Ballimore** Stir., Scot.
300 A4 **Ballinaby** Arg. and B., Scot.
402 E4 **Ballinamallard** Fermanagh, N. Ire.
402 F5 **Ballindarragh** Fermanagh, N. Ire.
304 K4 **Ballindean** Perth and Kin., Scot.
402 K3 **Ballinderry** Cookstown, N. Ire.
23 I3 **Ballinderry** r. N. Ire.
120 D4 **Ballingdon** Suff., Eng.
106 D4 **Ballinger Common** Bucks., Eng.
140 D4 **Ballingham** Here., Eng.
292 E3 **Ballingry** Fife, Scot.
388 H1 **Ballinlea** Moyle, N. Ire.
304 I3 **Ballinlick** Perth and Kin., Scot.
304 I3 **Ballinluig** Perth and Kin., Scot.
304 J2 **Ballinluig** Perth and Kin., Scot.
396 I5 **Ballinran** Newry & Mourne, N. Ire.
388 F2 **Ballinteer** Coleraine, N. Ire.
388 H1 **Ballintoy** Moyle, N. Ire.
304 J2 **Ballintuim** Perth and Kin., Scot.
308 D2 **Balloch** Angus, Scot.
322 I2 **Balloch** High., Scot.
280 B3 **Balloch** N. Lanark., Scot.
276 C1 **Balloch** W. Dun., Scot.
314 E3 **Ballochan** Abers., Scot.
300 E4 **Ballochandrain** Arg. and B., Scot.
314 D2 **Ballochford** Moray, Scot.
300 D5 **Ballochgair** Arg. and B., Scot.
264 E2 **Ballochmartin** N. Ayr., Scot.
262 C6 **Ballochmorrie** S. Ayr., Scot.
300 D4 **Ballochroy** Arg. and B., Scot.
314 E3 **Ballogie** Abers., Scot.
396 J3 **Balloo** Ards, N. Ire.
396 K1 **Balloo Lower** North Down, N. Ire.
396 H4 **Balloolymore** Banbridge, N. Ire.
58 C2 **Balls Cross** W. Sussex, Eng.
116 I2 **Balls Green** Essex, Eng.
98 F3 **Ball's Green** Glos., Eng.
154 B2 **Balls Hill** W. Mids, Eng.
396 F5 **Ballsmill** Newry & Mourne, N. Ire.
388 K5 **Ballyaghlis** Lisburn, N. Ire.
396 K4 **Ballyalton** Down, N. Ire.
402 F4 **Ballyard** Omagh, N. Ire.
396 H5 **Ballyardel** Newry & Mourne, N. Ire.
300 D4 **Ballyaurgan** Arg. and B., Scot.
396 I4 **Ballybannan** Down, N. Ire.
388 G2 **Ballybogy** Coleraine, N. Ire.
388 H4 **Ballybollen** Ballymena, N. Ire.
388 H2 **Ballyboyland** Ballymoney, N. Ire.
402 H3 **Ballybrack** Omagh, N. Ire.
402 J2 **Ballybriest** Cookstown, N. Ire.
388 L4 **Ballycarry** Larne, N. Ire.
402 E4 **Ballycassidy** Fermanagh, N. Ire.
388 I1 **Ballycastle** Moyle, N. Ire.
388 I1 **Ballycastle Museum** Moyle, N. Ire.
388 K4 **Ballyclare** Newtownabbey, N. Ire.
396 J3 **Ballycloghan** Down, N. Ire.
388 H3 **Ballyconnelly** Ballymena, N. Ire.
388 L3 **Ballycraigy** Larne, N. Ire.
396 J3 **Ballydan** Down, N. Ire.
388 H2 **Ballydivity** Moyle, N. Ire.
402 E4 **Ballydoolagh** Fermanagh, N. Ire.
396 J2 **Ballydrain** Ards, N. Ire.
396 J4 **Ballydugan** Down, N. Ire.
388 F3 **Ballydullaghan** Coleraine, N. Ire.
388 J4 **Ballyeaston** Newtownabbey, N. Ire.
396 L3 **Ballyesborough** Ards, N. Ire.
388 K3 **Ballygalley** Larne, N. Ire.
388 I3 **Ballygarvey** Ballymena, N. Ire.
402 H4 **Ballygawley** Dungannon, N. Ire.
388 I4 **Ballyginniff Milltown** Antrim, N. Ire.
396 G4 **Ballygorian** Newry & Mourne, N. Ire.
396 J2 **Ballygowan** Ards, N. Ire.
396 G3 **Ballygowan** Banbridge, N. Ire.
396 H5 **Ballygowan** Newry & Mourne, N. Ire.
300 B2 **Ballygown** Arg. and B., Scot.
300 B4 **Ballygrant** Arg. and B., Scot.
396 L3 **Ballyhalbert** Ards, N. Ire.
300 □ **Ballyhaugh** Arg. and B., Scot.
388 J5 **Ballyhill** Antrim, N. Ire.
388 I2 **Ballyhoe Bridge** Ballymoney, N. Ire.
396 K1 **Ballyholme** North Down, N. Ire.
388 G1 **Ballyhome** Coleraine, N. Ire.
396 K4 **Ballyhornan** Down, N. Ire.
396 K4 **Ballyhosset** Down, N. Ire.
402 G4 **Ballyhushey** Omagh, N. Ire.
388 J6 **Ballykeel** Lisburn, N. Ire.
396 I5 **Ballykeel** Newry & Mourne, N. Ire.
402 G2 **Ballykeel** Omagh, N. Ire.
388 D2 **Ballykelly** Limavady, N. Ire.
388 J5 **Ballykennedy** Antrim, N. Ire.
396 J4 **Ballykinler** Down, N. Ire.
388 I2 **Ballyknock** Ballymoney, N. Ire.
388 F3 **Ballyknock** Magherafelt, N. Ire.
396 E3 **Ballyleny** Armagh, N. Ire.
388 K5 **Ballylesson** Lisburn, N. Ire.
388 F2 **Ballylintagh** Coleraine, N. Ire.
388 G1 **Ballyloughbeg** Moyle, N. Ire.
402 E4 **Ballylucas** Fermanagh, N. Ire.
388 L3 **Ballylumford** Larne, N. Ire.
396 J3 **Ballymacashen** Ards, N. Ire.

Ballymackilroy to **Berkshire Downs**

402 H4 **Ballymackilroy** *Dungannon, N. Ire.*
388 G3 **Ballymaconnelly** *Ballymoney, N. Ire.*
396 H3 **Ballymacormick** *Banbridge, N. Ire.*
388 D2 **Ballymacran** *Limavady, N. Ire.*
402 F1 **Ballymagorry** *Strabane, N. Ire.*
388 G4 **Ballymaguigan** *Magherafelt, N. Ire.*
396 I5 **Ballymartin** *Newry & Mourne, N. Ire.*
396 D3 **Ballymartrim** *Armagh, N. Ire.*
300 D3 **Ballymeanoch** *Arg. and B., Scot.*
388 I3 **Ballymena** *Ballymena, N. Ire.*
388 I3 **Ballymena** *admin. dist. N. Ire.*
388 I3 **Ballymena Museum** *N. Ire.*
264 C3 **Ballymichael** *N. Ayr., Scot.*
388 G2 **Ballymoney** *Ballymoney, N. Ire.*
388 H2 **Ballymoney** *admin. dist. N. Ire.*
388 G2 **Ballymoney Museum** *Ballymoney, N. Ire.*
396 E4 **Ballymoyer** *Newry & Mourne, N. Ire.*
388 E2 **Ballymultimber** *Limavady, N. Ire.*
402 K2 **Ballymultrea** *Cookstown, N. Ire.*
396 K2 **Ballymurphy** *Ards, N. Ire.*
396 G3 **Ballynabragget** *Craigavon, N. Ire.*
388 C2 **Ballynagard** *Derry, N. Ire.*
388 K5 **Ballynagarrick** *Lisburn, N. Ire.*
402 G3 **Ballynahatty** *Omagh, N. Ire.*
396 I3 **Ballynahinch** *Down, N. Ire.*
396 E4 **Ballynahone Beg** *Armagh, N. Ire.*
402 J3 **Ballynakilly** *Dungannon, N. Ire.*
402 G1 **Ballynamallaght** *Strabane, N. Ire.*
402 H4 **Ballynasaggart** *Dungannon, N. Ire.*
402 G1 **Ballyneaner** *Strabane, N. Ire.*
388 J4 **Ballynoe** *Antrim, N. Ire.*
396 J4 **Ballynoe** *Down, N. Ire.*
388 K4 **Ballynure** *Larne, N. Ire.*
396 K3 **Ballyquintin** *Ards, N. Ire.*
23 L4 **Ballyquintin Point** *pt N. Ire.*
388 G2 **Ballyrashane** *Coleraine, N. Ire.*
402 I4 **Ballyreagh** *Dungannon, N. Ire.*
402 E4 **Ballyreagh** *Fermanagh, N. Ire.*
388 E2 **Ballyrisk** *Limavady, N. Ire.*
388 J4 **Ballyrobert** *Newtownabbey, N. Ire.*
388 F2 **Ballyrogan** *Coleraine, N. Ire.*
402 K2 **Ballyronan** *Cookstown, N. Ire.*
396 H4 **Ballyroney** *Banbridge, N. Ire.*
396 H3 **Ballysallagh** *Banbridge, N. Ire.*
388 J5 **Ballyskeagh** *Lisburn, N. Ire.*
388 L4 **Ballystrudder** *Larne, N. Ire.*
388 G1 **Ballytober** *Coleraine, N. Ire.*
396 G5 **Ballyvally** *Newry & Mourne, N. Ire.*
396 I5 **Ballyveagh** *Newry & Mourne, N. Ire.*
388 F2 **Ballyvennox** *Coleraine, N. Ire.*
388 I1 **Ballyvoy** *Moyle, N. Ire.*
396 L2 **Ballywalter** *Ards, N. Ire.*
396 H4 **Ballyward** *Banbridge, N. Ire.*
388 H3 **Ballywatermoy** *Ballymena, N. Ire.*
396 K2 **Ballywatticock** *Ards, N. Ire.*
388 F2 **Ballywildrick** *Coleraine, N. Ire.*
322 E3 **Balmacara** *High., Scot.*
252 D2 **Balmaclellan** *D. and G., Scot.*
304 I3 **Balmacneil** *Perth and Kin., Scot.*
308 F3 **Balmadies** *Angus, Scot.*
252 D3 **Balmae** *D. and G., Scot.*
296 C5 **Balmaha** *Stir., Scot.*
292 F2 **Balmalcolm** *Fife, Scot.*
300 B2 **Balmeanach** *Arg. and B., Scot.*
300 C2 **Balmeanach** *Arg. and B., Scot.*
314 G3 **Balmedie** *Abers., Scot.*
144 D2 **Balmer Heath** *Shrop., Eng.*
292 F1 **Balmerino** *Fife, Scot.*
52 C6 **Balmerlawn** *Hants., Eng.*
252 B3 **Balminnoch** *D. and G., Scot.*
276 E2 **Balmore** *E. Dun., Scot.*
322 G2 **Balmore** *High., Scot.*
322 J2 **Balmore** *High., Scot.*
304 F2 **Balmore** *Perth and Kin., Scot.*
292 G1 **Balmullo** *Fife, Scot.*
322 I2 **Balmungie** *High., Scot.*
304 J2 **Balmyle** *Perth and Kin., Scot.*
308 D2 **Balnaboth** *Angus, Scot.*
322 E2 **Balnacra** *High., Scot.*
322 I2 **Balnafoich** *High., Scot.*
304 H3 **Balnaguard** *Perth and Kin., Scot.*
320 H4 **Balnaguisich** *High., Scot.*
300 B2 **Balnahard** *Arg. and B., Scot.*
300 B3 **Balnahard** *Arg. and B., Scot.*
320 F2 **Balnakeil** *High., Scot.*
322 C2 **Balnaknock** *High., Scot.*
308 F2 **Balnamoon** *Angus, Scot.*
388 G2 **Balnamore** *Ballymoney, N. Ire.*
320 H4 **Balnapaling** *High., Scot.*
276 E2 **Balornock** *Glas., Scot.*
296 D3 **Balquhidder** *Stir., Scot.*
154 E3 **Balsall** *W. Mids, Eng.*
154 E3 **Balsall Common** *W. Mids, Eng.*
154 C3 **Balsall Heath** *W. Mids, Eng.*
102 C2 **Balscote** *Oxon, Eng.*
124 F6 **Balsham** *Cambs., Eng.*
22 □O1 **Balta** *i. Scot.*
331 E1 **Baltasound** *Shet., Scot.*
148 A2 **Balterley** *Staffs., Eng.*
148 A2 **Balterley Green** *Staffs., Eng.*
148 A2 **Balterley Heath** *Staffs., Eng.*
252 C3 **Baltersan** *D. and G., Scot.*
304 J4 **Balthayock** *Perth and Kin., Scot.*
94 I4 **Baltonsborough** *Som., Eng.*
300 D3 **Baluachraig** *Arg. and B., Scot.*
300 B4 **Balulive** *Arg. and B., Scot.*
322 H2 **Balvaird** *High., Scot.*
304 I2 **Balvarran** *Perth and Kin., Scot.*
300 D3 **Balvicar** *Arg. and B., Scot.*
322 E3 **Balvraid** *High., Scot.*
322 J2 **Balvraid** *High., Scot.*
228 G4 **Bamber Bridge** *Lancs., Eng.*
116 D2 **Bamber's Green** *Essex, Eng.*
244 G2 **Bamburgh** *Northumb., Eng.*
304 K3 **Bamff** *Perth and Kin., Scot.*
180 C2 **Bamford** *Derbys., Eng.*
198 D2 **Bamford** *Gtr Man., Eng.*
98 G2 **Bamfurlong** *Glos., Eng.*
232 F5 **Bampton** *Cumbria, Eng.*
40 F2 **Bampton** *Devon, Eng.*
102 B4 **Bampton** *Oxon, Eng.*
232 F5 **Bampton Grange** *Cumbria, Eng.*
322 F4 **Banavie** *High., Scot.*
396 G3 **Banbridge** *Banbridge, N. Ire.*
396 H4 **Banbridge** *admin. dist. N. Ire.*
102 C2 **Banbury** *Oxon, Eng.*
356 E3 **Bancffosfelen** *Carmar., Wales*
322 J2 **Banchor** *High., Scot.*
314 F3 **Banchory** *Abers., Scot.*
314 G3 **Banchory Devenick** *Abers., Scot.*
356 E3 **Bancycapel** *Carmar., Wales*
356 D2 **Bancyfelin** *Carmar., Wales*
356 E1 **Bancyffordd** *Carmar., Wales*
292 F2 **Bandon** *Fife, Scot.*
232 D7 **Bandrake Head** *Cumbria, Eng.*
314 F1 **Banff** *Abers., Scot.*
396 J2 **Bangor** *North Down, N. Ire.*
372 F1 **Bangor** *Gwynedd, Wales*
388 L5 **Bangor Castle** *N. Ire.*
Bangor-is-y-coed *Wrex., Wales see* **Bangor-on-Dee**
378 H3 **Bangor-on-Dee** *Wrex., Wales*
228 E5 **Bangor's Green** *Lancs., Eng.*
362 D4 **Bangor Teifi** *Cere., Wales*
166 F4 **Banham** *Norf., Eng.*
52 C5 **Bank** *Hants., Eng.*
252 F2 **Bankend** *D. and G., Scot.*
304 I3 **Bankfoot** *Perth and Kin., Scot.*
262 F4 **Bankglen** *E. Ayr., Scot.*
314 F3 **Bankhead** *Abers., Scot.*
252 E3 **Bankhead** *D. and G., Scot.*
280 C3 **Banknock** *Falk., Scot.*
232 F3 **Banks** *Cumbria, Eng.*
228 E4 **Banks** *Lancs., Eng.*
252 G2 **Bankshill** *D. and G., Scot.*
208 G2 **Bank Side** *S. Yorks., Eng.*
136 B2 **Bank Street** *Worcs., Eng.*
228 F5 **Bank Top** *Lancs., Eng.*
222 C2 **Bank Top** *W. Yorks., Eng.*
222 D2 **Bank Top** *W. Yorks., Eng.*
23 I2 **Bann** *r. N. Ire.*
396 E2 **Bannfoot** *Craigavon, N. Ire.*
166 G2 **Banningham** *Norf., Eng.*
116 E2 **Bannister Green** *Essex, Eng.*
296 G5 **Bannockburn** *Stir., Scot.*
78 E2 **Banstead** *Surr., Eng.*
222 E2 **Bantam Grove** *W. Yorks., Eng.*
40 E4 **Bantham** *Devon, Eng.*
280 B3 **Banton** *N. Lanark., Scot.*
94 G3 **Banwell** *N. Som., Eng.*
350 E2 **Banwen Pyrddin** *N.P.T., Wales*
120 H3 **Banyard's Green** *Suff., Eng.*
62 E3 **Bapchild** *Kent, Eng.*
154 B3 **Baptist End** *W. Mids, Eng.*
296 D5 **Baptiston** *Stir., Scot.*
86 C5 **Bapton** *Wilts., Eng.*
300 E2 **Barachander** *Arg. and B., Scot.*
388 D3 **Baranailt** *Limavady, N. Ire.*
262 D3 **Barassie** *S. Ayr., Scot.*
180 C2 **Barber Booth** *Derbys., Eng.*
232 E7 **Barber Green** *Cumbria, Eng.*
228 F4 **Barber's Moor** *Lancs., Eng.*
232 G7 **Barbon** *Cumbria, Eng.*
184 D3 **Barbridge** *Cheshire East, Eng.*
40 E1 **Barbrook** *Devon, Eng.*
128 B4 **Barby** *Northants., Eng.*
300 E2 **Barcaldine** *Arg. and B., Scot.*
252 D3 **Barcaple** *D. and G., Scot.*
132 C5 **Barcheston** *Warks., Eng.*
232 E3 **Barclose** *Cumbria, Eng.*
58 G3 **Barcombe** *E. Sussex, Eng.*
58 G3 **Barcombe Cross** *E. Sussex, Eng.*
252 D2 **Bardennoch** *D. and G., Scot.*
62 B3 **Barden Park** *Kent, Eng.*
116 E2 **Bardfield End Green** *Essex, Eng.*
116 E2 **Bardfield Saling** *Essex, Eng.*
331 C2 **Bardister** *Shet., Scot.*
170 E4 **Bardney** *Lincs., Eng.*
162 C2 **Bardon** *Leics., Eng.*
314 D2 **Bardon** *Moray, Scot.*
244 D6 **Bardon Mill** *Northumb., Eng.*
276 E2 **Bardowie** *E. Dun., Scot.*
232 D8 **Bardsea** *Cumbria, Eng.*
222 F1 **Bardsey** *W. Yorks., Eng.*
26 C2 **Bardsey Island** *i. Wales*
26 C2 **Bardsey Sound** *sea chan. Wales*
198 E2 **Bardsley** *Gtr Man., Eng.*
120 E3 **Bardwell** *Suff., Eng.*
228 F2 **Bare** *Lancs., Eng.*
52 E4 **Bar End** *Hants., Eng.*
140 B2 **Barewood** *Here., Eng.*
300 D4 **Barfad** *Arg. and B., Scot.*
166 F3 **Barford** *Norf., Eng.*
132 C4 **Barford** *Warks., Eng.*
102 C3 **Barford St John** *Oxon, Eng.*
86 D5 **Barford St Martin** *Wilts., Eng.*
102 C3 **Barford St Michael** *Oxon, Eng.*
236 E4 **Barforth Hall** *Durham, Eng.*
62 H3 **Barfrestone** *Kent, Eng.*
252 C3 **Bargaly** *D. and G., Scot.*
262 C5 **Bargany Mains** *S. Ayr., Scot.*
180 E4 **Bargate** *Derbys., Eng.*
280 B3 **Bargeddie** *N. Lanark., Scot.*
350 G2 **Bargoed** *Caerp., Wales*
252 C2 **Bargrennan** *D. and G., Scot.*
124 B4 **Barham** *Cambs., Eng.*
62 G3 **Barham** *Kent, Eng.*
120 F4 **Barham** *Suff., Eng.*
252 D3 **Barharrow** *D. and G., Scot.*
124 E5 **Bar Hill** *Cambs., Eng.*
170 D7 **Barholm** *Lincs., Eng.*
252 C3 **Barholm Mains** *D. and G., Scot.*
162 E2 **Barkby** *Leics., Eng.*
162 E2 **Barkby Thorpe** *Leics., Eng.*
144 D2 **Barkers Green** *Shrop., Eng.*
162 F1 **Barkestone-le-Vale** *Leics., Eng.*
82 E3 **Barkham** *W'ham, Eng.*
74 E2 **Barking** *Gtr Lon., Eng.*
120 F4 **Barking** *Suff., Eng.*
74 E2 **Barking and Dagenham** *met. bor. Gtr Lon., Eng.*
74 E2 **Barkingside** *Gtr Lon., Eng.*
120 F4 **Barking Tye** *Suff., Eng.*
222 C2 **Barkisland** *W. Yorks., Eng.*
170 C6 **Barkston** *Lincs., Eng.*
216 F3 **Barkston Ash** *N. Yorks., Eng.*
110 F3 **Barkway** *Herts., Eng.*
252 B3 **Barlae** *D. and G., Scot.*
366 G5 **Barland** *Powys, Wales*
148 C3 **Barlaston** *Staffs., Eng.*
180 F3 **Barlborough** *Derbys., Eng.*
216 F3 **Barlby** *N. Yorks., Eng.*
26 E5 **Barle** *r. Eng.*
162 C3 **Barlestone** *Leics., Eng.*
110 F3 **Barley** *Herts., Eng.*
228 I3 **Barley** *Lancs., Eng.*
110 F4 **Barleycroft End** *Herts., Eng.*
120 G3 **Barley Green** *Suff., Eng.*
244 F6 **Barleyhill** *Northumb., Eng.*
162 G2 **Barleythorpe** *Rutland, Eng.*
116 G4 **Barling** *Essex, Eng.*
170 D4 **Barlings** *Lincs., Eng.*
180 E3 **Barlow** *Derbys., Eng.*
216 F3 **Barlow** *N. Yorks., Eng.*
236 E2 **Barlow** *T. and W., Eng.*
198 D3 **Barlow Moor** *Gtr Man., Eng.*
210 D3 **Barmby Moor** *E. Riding, Eng.*
210 C4 **Barmby on the Marsh** *E. Riding, Eng.*
166 D1 **Barmer** *Norf., Eng.*
300 D3 **Barmolloch** *Arg. and B., Scot.*
244 F2 **Barmoor Lane End** *Northumb., Eng.*
372 F4 **Barmouth** *Gwynedd, Wales*
26 D2 **Barmouth Bay** *b. Wales*
236 F4 **Barmpton** *Darl., Eng.*
210 G2 **Barmston** *E. Riding, Eng.*
236 F2 **Barmston** *T. and W., Eng.*
120 I2 **Barnaby Green** *Suff., Eng.*
300 F3 **Barnacabber** *Arg. and B., Scot.*
300 E3 **Barnacarry** *Arg. and B., Scot.*
124 B3 **Barnack** *Peterb., Eng.*
132 D3 **Barnacle** *Warks., Eng.*
236 D4 **Barnard Castle** *Durham, Eng.*
102 C4 **Barnard Gate** *Oxon, Eng.*
120 C4 **Barnardiston** *Suff., Eng.*
136 D3 **Barnard's Green** *Worcs., Eng.*
252 C3 **Barnbarroch** *D. and G., Scot.*
252 E3 **Barnbarroch** *D. and G., Scot.*
208 E2 **Barnburgh** *S. Yorks., Eng.*
120 I2 **Barnby** *Suff., Eng.*
208 F2 **Barnby Dun** *S. Yorks., Eng.*
176 E4 **Barnby in the Willows** *Notts., Eng.*
176 C2 **Barnby Moor** *Notts., Eng.*
252 E2 **Barndennoch** *D. and G., Scot.*
40 D3 **Barne Barton** *Plymouth, Eng.*
74 E3 **Barnehurst** *Gtr Lon., Eng.*
74 C3 **Barnes** *Gtr Lon., Eng.*
402 H2 **Barnes** *Strabane, N. Ire.*
62 C3 **Barnes Street** *Kent, Eng.*
74 C2 **Barnet** *Gtr Lon., Eng.*
74 C2 **Barnet** *met. bor. Gtr Lon., Eng.*
170 D2 **Barnetby le Wold** *N. Lincs., Eng.*
74 C2 **Barnet Gate** *Gtr Lon., Eng.*
166 E1 **Barney** *Norf., Eng.*
120 D2 **Barnham** *Suff., Eng.*
58 C4 **Barnham** *W. Sussex, Eng.*
166 F3 **Barnham Broom** *Norf., Eng.*
308 G2 **Barnhead** *Angus, Scot.*
184 C3 **Barnhill** *Cheshire West & Chester, Eng.*
308 E4 **Barnhill** *Dundee, Scot.*
314 C2 **Barnhill** *Moray, Scot.*
252 A3 **Barnhills** *D. and G., Scot.*
236 D5 **Barningham** *Durham, Eng.*
120 E2 **Barningham** *Suff., Eng.*
166 F1 **Barningham Green** *Norf., Eng.*
396 G4 **Barnmeen** *Newry & Mourne, N. Ire.*
170 F2 **Barnoldby le Beck** *N.E. Lincs., Eng.*
228 I3 **Barnoldswick** *Lancs., Eng.*
74 D2 **Barnsbury** *Gtr Lon., Eng.*
208 E2 **Barnsdale Bar** *S. Yorks., Eng.*
58 D2 **Barns Green** *W. Sussex, Eng.*
98 H3 **Barnsley** *Glos., Eng.*
208 D2 **Barnsley** *S. Yorks., Eng.*
62 H3 **Barnsole** *Kent, Eng.*
40 D1 **Barnstaple** *Devon, Eng.*
26 D5 **Barnstaple Bay** *b. Eng.*
116 E2 **Barnston** *Essex, Eng.*
190 C3 **Barnston** *Merseyside, Eng.*
176 D5 **Barnstone** *Notts., Eng.*
136 F1 **Barnt Green** *Worcs., Eng.*
184 D2 **Barnton** *Cheshire West & Chester, Eng.*
288 D3 **Barnton** *Edin., Scot.*
128 G3 **Barnwell All Saints** *Northants., Eng.*
128 G3 **Barnwell St Andrew** *Northants., Eng.*
140 C2 **Barons' Cross** *Here., Eng.*
94 F4 **Barr** *Som., Eng.*
300 B4 **Barr** *Arg. and B., Scot.*
322 D5 **Barr** *High., Scot.*
262 C5 **Barr** *S. Ayr., Scot.*
22 A9 **Barra** *i. Scot.*
326 B5 **Barra (Tràigh Mhòr)** *airport Scot.*
22 B8 **Barra, Sound of** *sea chan. Scot.*
252 C3 **Barrachan** *D. and G., Scot.*
300 D3 **Barrackan** *Arg. and B., Scot.*
252 C3 **Barraer** *D. and G., Scot.*
326 D2 **Barraglom** *W. Isles, Scot.*
300 C4 **Barrahormid** *Arg. and B., Scot.*
Barraigh *i. Scot. see* **Barra**
300 F2 **Barran** *Arg. and B., Scot.*
300 □ **Barrapoll** *Arg. and B., Scot.*
244 E5 **Barrasford** *Northumb., Eng.*
300 D3 **Barravullin** *Arg. and B., Scot.*
405 C2 **Barregarrow** Isle of Man
184 D3 **Barrets Green** *Cheshire East, Eng.*
116 F2 **Barr Hall** *Essex, Eng.*
276 D3 **Barrhead** *E. Renf., Scot.*
262 C6 **Barrhill** *S. Ayr., Scot.*
124 E6 **Barrington** *Cambs., Eng.*
94 G5 **Barrington** *Som., Eng.*
36 D3 **Barripper** *Corn., Eng.*
322 E3 **Barrisdale** *High., Scot.*
264 G2 **Barrmill** *N. Ayr., Scot.*
300 D2 **Barrnacarry** *Arg. and B., Scot.*
320 K2 **Barrock** *High., Scot.*
98 F2 **Barrow** *Glos., Eng.*
228 H3 **Barrow** *Lancs., Eng.*
162 G2 **Barrow** *Rutland, Eng.*
144 E4 **Barrow** *Shrop., Eng.*
94 I3 **Barrow** *Som., Eng.*
94 J4 **Barrow** *Som., Eng.*
120 C3 **Barrow** *Suff., Eng.*
166 A3 **Barroway Drove** *Norf., Eng.*
198 C2 **Barrow Bridge** *Gtr Man., Eng.*
170 B6 **Barrowby** *Lincs., Eng.*
216 H2 **Barrowcliff** *N. Yorks., Eng.*
162 H3 **Barrowden** *Rutland, Eng.*
228 I3 **Barrowford** *Lancs., Eng.*
94 H2 **Barrow Gurney** *N. Som., Eng.*
170 D1 **Barrow Hann** *N. Lincs., Eng.*
170 D1 **Barrow Haven** *N. Lincs., Eng.*
180 E3 **Barrow Hill** *Derbys., Eng.*
232 C8 **Barrow-in-Furness** *Cumbria, Eng.*
228 E5 **Barrow Nook** *Lancs., Eng.*
232 F7 **Barrows Green** *Cumbria, Eng.*
86 B5 **Barrow Street** *Wilts., Eng.*
170 D1 **Barrow upon Humber** *N. Lincs., Eng.*
162 E2 **Barrow upon Soar** *Leics., Eng.*
180 E5 **Barrow upon Trent** *Derbys., Eng.*
308 F4 **Barry** *Angus, Scot.*
350 G4 **Barry** *V. of Glam., Wales*
162 F2 **Barsby** *Leics., Eng.*
120 I2 **Barsham** *Suff., Eng.*
120 I2 **Barsham Hill** *Suff., Eng.*
262 E4 **Barskimming** *E. Ayr., Scot.*
154 D3 **Barston** *W. Mids, Eng.*
140 D3 **Bartestree** *Here., Eng.*
314 G2 **Barthol Chapel** *Abers., Scot.*
116 E2 **Bartholomew Green** *Essex, Eng.*
184 E3 **Barthomley** *Cheshire East, Eng.*
52 C5 **Bartley** *Hants., Eng.*
154 C3 **Bartley Green** *W. Mids, Eng.*
124 F6 **Bartlow** *Cambs., Eng.*
124 E5 **Barton** *Cambs., Eng.*
184 C3 **Barton** *Cheshire West & Chester, Eng.*
232 F5 **Barton** *Cumbria, Eng.*
98 H2 **Barton** *Glos., Eng.*
228 E5 **Barton** *Lancs., Eng.*
228 F3 **Barton** *Lancs., Eng.*
216 E1 **Barton** *N. Yorks., Eng.*
102 D4 **Barton** *Oxon, Eng.*
40 F3 **Barton** *Torbay, Eng.*
132 A5 **Barton** *Warks., Eng.*
166 C3 **Barton Bendish** *Norf., Eng.*
98 F3 **Barton End** *Glos., Eng.*
102 C3 **Bartongate** *Oxon, Eng.*
148 E4 **Barton Green** *Staffs., Eng.*
106 B3 **Barton Hartshorn** *Bucks., Eng.*
216 G2 **Barton Hill** *N. Yorks., Eng.*
176 B5 **Barton in Fabis** *Notts., Eng.*
162 C3 **Barton in the Beans** *Leics., Eng.*
110 C4 **Barton-le-Clay** *Central Bedfordshire, Eng.*
216 G2 **Barton-le-Willows** *N. Yorks., Eng.*
120 C2 **Barton Mills** *Suff., Eng.*
52 C6 **Barton on Sea** *Hants., Eng.*
132 C6 **Barton-on-the-Heath** *Warks., Eng.*
128 E3 **Barton Seagrave** *Northants., Eng.*
52 D3 **Barton Stacey** *Hants., Eng.*
94 I4 **Barton St David** *Som., Eng.*
40 E1 **Barton Town** *Devon, Eng.*
166 H2 **Barton Turf** *Norf., Eng.*
148 E4 **Barton-under-Needwood** *Staffs., Eng.*
170 D1 **Barton-upon-Humber** *N. Lincs., Eng.*
198 C3 **Barton upon Irwell** *Gtr Man., Eng.*
326 E1 **Barvas** *W. Isles, Scot.*
124 F4 **Barway** *Cambs., Eng.*
162 C3 **Barwell** *Leics., Eng.*
252 D3 **Barwhinnock** *D. and G., Scot.*
110 F4 **Barwick** *Herts., Eng.*
94 I5 **Barwick** *Som., Eng.*
222 F2 **Barwick in Elmet** *W. Yorks., Eng.*
252 C3 **Barwinnock** *D. and G., Scot.*
144 C3 **Baschurch** *Shrop., Eng.*
132 D4 **Bascote** *Warks., Eng.*
120 E3 **Base Green** *Suff., Eng.*
148 B2 **Basford** *Staffs., Eng.*
148 C2 **Basford Green** *Staffs., Eng.*
228 H3 **Bashall Eaves** *Lancs., Eng.*
228 H3 **Bashall Town** *Lancs., Eng.*
52 C6 **Bashley** *Hants., Eng.*
116 E4 **Basildon** *Essex, Eng.*
82 D2 **Basildon** *W. Berks., Eng.*
52 F3 **Basingstoke** *Hants., Eng.*
180 D3 **Baslow** *Derbys., Eng.*
94 G3 **Bason Bridge** *Som., Eng.*
339 B3 **Bassaleg** *Newp., Wales*
232 C4 **Bassenthwaite** *Cumbria, Eng.*
24 K4 **Bassenthwaite Lake** *l. Eng.*
52 D5 **Bassett** *Soton, Eng.*
124 D6 **Bassingbourn** *Cambs., Eng.*
176 C5 **Bassingfield** *Notts., Eng.*
170 C5 **Bassingham** *Lincs., Eng.*
170 C6 **Bassingthorpe** *Lincs., Eng.*
22 K10 **Bass Rock** *i. Scot.*
331 D2 **Basta** *Shet., Scot.*
170 D7 **Baston** *Lincs., Eng.*
136 D3 **Bastonford** *Worcs., Eng.*
166 I2 **Bastwick** *Norf., Eng.*
148 C4 **Baswich** *Staffs., Eng.*
296 C3 **Batavaime** *Stir., Scot.*
94 G3 **Batch** *Som., Eng.*
136 F2 **Batchley** *Worcs., Eng.*
110 C6 **Batchworth** *Herts., Eng.*
110 C6 **Batchworth Heath** *Herts., Eng.*
46 D3 **Batcombe** *Dorset, Eng.*
94 J4 **Batcombe** *Som., Eng.*
184 E2 **Bate Heath** *Cheshire East, Eng.*
166 F2 **Bates Moor Farm** *Norf., Eng.*
94 J2 **Bath** *B. and N.E. Som., Eng.*
94 K2 **Bathampton** *B. and N.E. Som., Eng.*
94 J2 **Bath and North East Somerset** *admin. div. Eng.*
94 E4 **Bathealton** *Som., Eng.*
94 K2 **Batheaston** *B. and N.E. Som., Eng.*
94 K2 **Bathford** *B. and N.E. Som., Eng.*
288 B3 **Bathgate** *W. Lothian, Scot.*
176 D4 **Bathley** *Notts., Eng.*
36 F2 **Bathpool** *Corn., Eng.*
94 I3 **Bathway** *Som., Eng.*
222 E2 **Batley** *W. Yorks., Eng.*
98 I1 **Batsford** *Glos., Eng.*
216 F1 **Battersby** *N. Yorks., Eng.*
74 D3 **Battersea** *Gtr Lon., Eng.*
120 E4 **Battisford** *Suff., Eng.*
120 E4 **Battisford Tye** *Suff., Eng.*
58 I3 **Battle** *E. Sussex, Eng.*
366 E7 **Battle** *Powys, Wales*
98 G2 **Battledown** *Glos., Eng.*
144 D3 **Battlefield** *Shrop., Eng.*
276 E3 **Battlefield** *Glas., Scot.*
396 I3 **Battle of Ballynahinch 1798** *Down, N. Ire.*
402 J4 **Battle of Benburb 1646** *Dungannon, N. Ire.*
116 F4 **Battlesbridge** *Essex, Eng.*
110 B4 **Battlesden** *Central Bedfordshire, Eng.*
94 C4 **Battleton** *Som., Eng.*
52 C6 **Battramsley** *Hants., Eng.*
78 B3 **Batt's Corner** *Surr., Eng.*
314 E1 **Bauds of Cullen** *Moray, Scot.*
300 □ **Baugh** *Arg. and B., Scot.*
136 D3 **Baughton** *Worcs., Eng.*
52 F2 **Baughurst** *Hants., Eng.*
314 F3 **Baulds** *Abers., Scot.*
102 B5 **Baulking** *Oxon, Eng.*
170 E4 **Baumber** *Lincs., Eng.*
98 H3 **Baunton** *Glos., Eng.*
144 F5 **Baveney Wood** *Shrop., Eng.*
86 D5 **Baverstock** *Wilts., Eng.*
166 G3 **Bawburgh** *Norf., Eng.*
166 F2 **Bawdeswell** *Norf., Eng.*
94 G4 **Bawdrip** *Som., Eng.*
120 H4 **Bawdsey** *Suff., Eng.*
120 H5 **Bawdsey Manor** *Suff., Eng.*
166 B2 **Bawsey** *Norf., Eng.*
208 F3 **Bawtry** *S. Yorks., Eng.*
228 H4 **Baxenden** *Lancs., Eng.*
132 C2 **Baxterley** *Warks., Eng.*
120 C3 **Baxter's Green** *Suff., Eng.*
46 F1 **Bay** *Dorset, Eng.*
244 E6 **Baybridge** *Northumb., Eng.*
232 D8 **Baycliff** *Cumbria, Eng.*
86 F2 **Baydon** *Wilts., Eng.*
110 E5 **Bayford** *Herts., Eng.*
94 J4 **Bayford** *Som., Eng.*
110 E5 **Bayfordbury** *Herts., Eng.*
62 C4 **Bayham Abbey** *Kent, Eng.*
326 B6 **Bayherivagh** *W. Isles, Scot.*
232 H4 **Bayles** *Cumbria, Eng.*
120 F4 **Baylham** *Suff., Eng.*
102 D3 **Baynards Green** *Oxon, Eng.*
140 D4 **Baysham** *Here., Eng.*
144 D3 **Bayston Hill** *Shrop., Eng.*
74 C2 **Bayswater** *Gtr Lon., Eng.*
116 F1 **Baythorn End** *Essex, Eng.*
136 C1 **Bayton** *Worcs., Eng.*
102 D4 **Bayworth** *Oxon, Eng.*
98 E5 **Beach** *S. Glos., Eng.*
106 C2 **Beachampton** *Bucks., Eng.*
166 C3 **Beachamwell** *Norf., Eng.*
300 D5 **Beacharr** *Arg. and B., Scot.*
62 G4 **Beachborough** *Kent, Eng.*
98 D4 **Beachley** *Glos., Eng.*
26 M6 **Beachy Head** *hd Eng.*
40 G2 **Beacon** *Devon, Eng.*
116 H2 **Beacon End** *Essex, Eng.*
106 D5 **Beacon Hill** *Bucks., Eng.*
46 G3 **Beacon Hill** *Dorset, Eng.*
116 G3 **Beacon Hill** *Essex, Eng.*
78 B3 **Beacon Hill** *Surr., Eng.*
106 C5 **Beacon's Bottom** *Bucks., Eng.*
106 E5 **Beaconsfield** *Bucks., Eng.*
216 G2 **Beadlam** *N. Yorks., Eng.*
110 C3 **Beadlow** *Central Bedfordshire, Eng.*
244 H2 **Beadnell** *Northumb., Eng.*
24 N2 **Beadnell Bay** *b. Eng.*
40 D2 **Beaford** *Devon, Eng.*
402 E4 **Beagh** *Fermanagh, N. Ire.*
402 I2 **Beaghmore** *Cookstown, N. Ire.*
244 F1 **Beal** *Northumb., Eng.*
216 F3 **Beal** *N. Yorks., Eng.*
184 D3 **Beambridge** *Cheshire East, Eng.*
148 F4 **Beam Hill** *Staffs., Eng.*
148 D3 **Beamhurst** *Staffs., Eng.*
46 C3 **Beaminster** *Dorset, Eng.*
236 F2 **Beamish** *Durham, Eng.*
106 D5 **Beamond End** *Bucks., Eng.*
216 D3 **Beamsley** *N. Yorks., Eng.*
62 B2 **Bean** *Kent, Eng.*
86 C3 **Beanacre** *Wilts., Eng.*
244 F3 **Beanley** *Northumb., Eng.*
262 E3 **Beansburn** *E. Ayr., Scot.*
329 B3 **Beaquoy** *Orkney, Scot.*
228 G4 **Beardwood** *B'burn, Eng.*
78 E2 **Beare Green** *Surr., Eng.*
132 B4 **Bearley** *Warks., Eng.*
Bearnaraigh *i. Scot. see* **Berneray**
Bearnaraigh *i. Scot. see* **Berneray**
402 F2 **Bearney** *Strabane, N. Ire.*
314 G2 **Bearnie** *Abers., Scot.*
300 B2 **Bearnus** *Arg. and B., Scot.*
236 F3 **Bearpark** *Durham, Eng.*
244 C6 **Bearsbridge** *Northumb., Eng.*
276 D2 **Bearsden** *E. Dun., Scot.*
62 D3 **Bearsted** *Kent, Eng.*
144 F2 **Bearstone** *Shrop., Eng.*
46 H3 **Bearwood** *Poole, Eng.*
154 C3 **Bearwood** *W. Mids, Eng.*
252 F2 **Beattock** *D. and G., Scot.*
116 D3 **Beauchamp Roding** *Essex, Eng.*
208 D4 **Beauchief** *S. Yorks., Eng.*
244 F6 **Beauclerc** *Northumb., Eng.*
132 B4 **Beaudesert** *Warks., Eng.*
350 G2 **Beaufort** *B. Gwent, Wales*
52 D6 **Beaulieu** *Hants., Eng.*
322 H2 **Beauly** *High., Scot.*
22 H8 **Beauly** *r. Scot.*
22 H8 **Beauly Firth** *est. Scot.*
371 E3 **Beaumaris** *I.o.A., Wales*
20 E5 **Beaumaris Castle** *tourist site Wales*
408 E4 **Beaumont** *Jersey* Channel Is
232 D3 **Beaumont** *Cumbria, Eng.*
116 I2 **Beaumont** *Essex, Eng.*
236 F4 **Beaumont Hill** *Darl., Eng.*
162 D2 **Beaumont Leys** *Leicester, Eng.*
132 C3 **Beausale** *Warks., Eng.*
176 B4 **Beauvale** *Notts., Eng.*
52 E4 **Beauworth** *Hants., Eng.*
62 F4 **Beaver Green** *Kent, Eng.*
40 D2 **Beaworthy** *Devon, Eng.*
116 F2 **Beazley End** *Essex, Eng.*
190 C3 **Bebington** *Merseyside, Eng.*
244 H5 **Bebside** *Northumb., Eng.*
120 I2 **Beccles** *Suff., Eng.*
228 E4 **Becconsall** *Lancs., Eng.*
144 F4 **Beckbury** *Shrop., Eng.*
74 D3 **Beckenham** *Gtr Lon., Eng.*
170 E4 **Beckering** *Lincs., Eng.*
232 A6 **Beckermet** *Cumbria, Eng.*
216 C2 **Beckermonds** *N. Yorks., Eng.*
166 C3 **Beckett End** *Norf., Eng.*
232 B3 **Beckfoot** *Cumbria, Eng.*
232 C6 **Beckfoot** *Cumbria, Eng.*
232 G6 **Beck Foot** *Cumbria, Eng.*
136 E3 **Beckford** *Worcs., Eng.*
86 D3 **Beckhampton** *Wilts., Eng.*
166 G3 **Beckhithe** *Norf., Eng.*
216 G1 **Beck Hole** *N. Yorks., Eng.*
170 B5 **Beckingham** *Lincs., Eng.*
176 E2 **Beckingham** *Notts., Eng.*
94 K3 **Beckington** *Som., Eng.*
58 J3 **Beckley** *E. Sussex, Eng.*
102 D4 **Beckley** *Oxon, Eng.*
120 B2 **Beck Row** *Suff., Eng.*
120 I2 **Beck's Green** *Suff., Eng.*
232 C7 **Beck Side** *Cumbria, Eng.*
232 E7 **Beck Side** *Cumbria, Eng.*
232 G7 **Beckside** *Cumbria, Eng.*
74 E2 **Beckton** *Gtr Lon., Eng.*
216 E3 **Beckwith** *N. Yorks., Eng.*
216 E3 **Beckwithshaw** *N. Yorks., Eng.*
74 E2 **Becontree** *Gtr Lon., Eng.*
216 E2 **Bedale** *N. Yorks., Eng.*
236 D3 **Bedburn** *Durham, Eng.*
46 F2 **Bedchester** *Dorset, Eng.*
350 F3 **Beddau** *R.C.T., Wales*
372 F2 **Beddgelert** *Gwynedd, Wales*
58 G3 **Beddingham** *E. Sussex, Eng.*
74 D3 **Beddington** *Gtr Lon., Eng.*
74 D3 **Beddington Corner** *Gtr Lon., Eng.*
120 G3 **Bedfield** *Suff., Eng.*
120 G3 **Bedfield Little Green** *Suff., Eng.*
110 C3 **Bedford** *Bedford, Eng.*
110 C2 **Bedford** *admin. div. Eng.*
26 L3 **Bedford Level (Middle Level)** *lowland Eng.*
26 L2 **Bedford Level (North Level)** *lowland Eng.*
26 M3 **Bedford Level (South Level)** *lowland Eng.*
74 C3 **Bedford Park** *Gtr Lon., Eng.*
62 C4 **Bedgebury Cross** *Kent, Eng.*
106 D4 **Bedgrove** *Bucks., Eng.*
58 C3 **Bedham** *W. Sussex, Eng.*
52 F5 **Bedhampton** *Hants., Eng.*
120 G3 **Bedingfield** *Suff., Eng.*
120 G3 **Bedingfield Green** *Suff., Eng.*
166 H4 **Bedingham Green** *Norf., Eng.*
228 H4 **Bedlam** *Lancs., Eng.*
116 D2 **Bedlar's Green** *Essex, Eng.*
244 H5 **Bedlington** *Northumb., Eng.*
350 G2 **Bedlinog** *M. Tyd., Wales*
94 I2 **Bedminster** *Bristol, Eng.*
110 C5 **Bedmond** *Herts., Eng.*
148 C4 **Bednall** *Staffs., Eng.*
378 F2 **Bedol** *Flints., Wales*
256 I4 **Bedrule** *Borders, Scot.*
144 C5 **Bedstone** *Shrop., Eng.*
350 G3 **Bedwas** *Caerp., Wales*
110 D4 **Bedwell** *Herts., Eng.*
350 G2 **Bedwellty** *Caerp., Wales*
132 D3 **Bedworth** *Warks., Eng.*
132 D3 **Bedworth Woodlands** *Warks., Eng.*
22 B8 **Bee, Loch** *l. Scot.*
162 E2 **Beeby** *Leics., Eng.*
52 F4 **Beech** *Hants., Eng.*
148 B3 **Beech** *Staffs., Eng.*
82 D3 **Beech Hill** *W. Berks., Eng.*
86 D4 **Beechingstoke** *Wilts., Eng.*
154 C3 **Beech Lane** *W. Mids, Eng.*
190 E4 **Beechwood** *Halton, Eng.*
339 C3 **Beechwood** *Newp., Wales*
82 C3 **Beedon** *W. Berks., Eng.*
82 C3 **Beedon Hill** *W. Berks., Eng.*
210 G3 **Beeford** *E. Riding, Eng.*
180 D3 **Beeley** *Derbys., Eng.*
170 E2 **Beelsby** *N.E. Lincs., Eng.*
82 D3 **Beenham** *W. Berks., Eng.*
82 F3 **Beenham's Heath** *W. and M., Eng.*
82 D3 **Beenham Stocks** *W. Berks., Eng.*
36 E1 **Beeny** *Corn., Eng.*
40 G2 **Beer** *Devon, Eng.*
94 G5 **Beercrocombe** *Som., Eng.*
46 D2 **Beer Hackett** *Dorset, Eng.*
40 F4 **Beesands** *Devon, Eng.*
170 H4 **Beesby** *Lincs., Eng.*
170 F3 **Beesby** *N.E. Lincs., Eng.*
40 E4 **Beeson** *Devon, Eng.*
110 D3 **Beeston** *Central Bedfordshire, Eng.*
184 C3 **Beeston** *Cheshire West & Chester, Eng.*
166 D2 **Beeston** *Norf., Eng.*
176 B5 **Beeston** *Notts., Eng.*
222 E2 **Beeston** *W. Yorks., Eng.*
166 G1 **Beeston Regis** *Norf., Eng.*
222 E2 **Beeston Royds** *W. Yorks., Eng.*
166 H2 **Beeston St Lawrence** *Norf., Eng.*
252 E2 **Beeswing** *D. and G., Scot.*
232 F7 **Beetham** *Cumbria, Eng.*
94 F5 **Beetham** *Som., Eng.*
166 E2 **Beetley** *Norf., Eng.*
148 B4 **Beffcote** *Staffs., Eng.*
23 J3 **Beg, Lough** *l. N. Ire.*
350 H3 **Began** *Caerp., Wales*
102 D4 **Begbroke** *Oxon, Eng.*
124 E3 **Begdale** *Cambs., Eng.*
358 F3 **Begelly** *Pembs., Wales*
366 G5 **Beggar's Bush** *Powys, Wales*
350 F4 **Beggars Pound** *V. of Glam., Wales*
366 F4 **Beguildy** *Powys, Wales*
166 I3 **Beighton** *Norf., Eng.*
208 D3 **Beighton** *S. Yorks., Eng.*
339 B2 **Beili-glas** *Mon., Wales*
24 F2 **Beinn an Tuirc** *hill Scot.*
22 E8 **Beinn Bhan** *hill Scot.*
22 D11 **Beinn Bheigeir** *hill Scot.*
22 D8 **Beinn Bhreac** *hill Scot.*
22 F10 **Beinn Bhreac** *hill Scot.*
22 F11 **Beinn Bhreac** *hill Scot.*
24 F1 **Beinn Bhreac** *hill Scot.*
22 G10 **Beinn Bhuidhe** *hill Scot.*
22 F10 **Beinn Chapull** *hill Scot.*
22 G7 **Beinn Dearg** *mt. Scot.*
22 I9 **Beinn Dearg** *mt. Scot.*
22 G9 **Beinn Dorain** *mt. Scot.*
20 E3 **Beinn Heasgarnich** *mt. Scot.*
22 G10 **Beinn Ime** *mt. Scot.*
22 G6 **Beinn Leoid** *hill Scot.*
22 C6 **Beinn Mholach** *hill Scot.*
22 B8 **Beinn Mhòr** *hill Scot.*
22 C7 **Beinn Mhòr** *hill Scot.*
22 F10 **Beinn Mhòr** *hill Scot.*
Beinn na Faoghla *i. Scot. see* **Benbecula**
22 G9 **Beinn na Lap** *hill Scot.*
22 E8 **Beinn na Seamraig** *hill Scot.*
22 E9 **Beinn Resipol** *hill Scot.*
22 E8 **Beinn Sgritheall** *hill Scot.*
22 F9 **Beinn Sgulaird** *hill Scot.*
22 H7 **Beinn Tharsuinn** *hill Scot.*
22 H9 **Beinn Udlamain** *mt. Scot.*
264 G2 **Beith** *N. Ayr., Scot.*
62 G3 **Bekesbourne** *Kent, Eng.*
62 G3 **Bekesbourne Hill** *Kent, Eng.*
166 H2 **Belaugh** *Norf., Eng.*
166 H2 **Belaugh Green** *Norf., Eng.*
136 E1 **Belbroughton** *Worcs., Eng.*
46 F2 **Belchalwell** *Dorset, Eng.*
46 F2 **Belchalwell Street** *Dorset, Eng.*
116 F1 **Belchamp St Paul** *Essex, Eng.*
116 F1 **Belchamp Walter** *Essex, Eng.*
170 F4 **Belchford** *Lincs., Eng.*
402 C5 **Belcoo** *Fermanagh, N. Ire.*
388 K5 **Belfast** *Belfast, N. Ire.*
388 K5 **Belfast** *admin. dist. N. Ire.*
388 K5 **Belfast City** *airport N. Ire.*
24 E4 **Belfast International** *airport N. Ire.*
23 K3 **Belfast Lough** *inlet N. Ire.*
198 E2 **Belfield** *Gtr Man., Eng.*
244 G2 **Belford** *Northumb., Eng.*
162 E3 **Belgrave** *Leicester, Eng.*
148 E5 **Belgrave** *Staffs., Eng.*
74 D3 **Belgravia** *Gtr Lon., Eng.*
288 H3 **Belhaven** *E. Lothian, Scot.*
314 E2 **Belhinnie** *Abers., Scot.*
314 D3 **Bellabeg** *Abers., Scot.*
322 H2 **Belladrum** *High., Scot.*
388 G4 **Bellaghy** *Magherafelt, N. Ire.*
276 E2 **Bellahouston** *Glas., Scot.*
402 E5 **Bellanaleck** *Fermanagh, N. Ire.*
300 D3 **Bellanoch** *Arg. and B., Scot.*
210 D4 **Bellasize** *E. Riding, Eng.*
308 C2 **Bellaty** *Angus, Scot.*
110 D5 **Bell Bar** *Herts., Eng.*
216 C2 **Bell Busk** *N. Yorks., Eng.*
170 G4 **Belleau** *Lincs., Eng.*
402 B4 **Belleek** *Fermanagh, N. Ire.*
396 F4 **Belleek** *Newry & Mourne, N. Ire.*
314 C2 **Belleheiglash** *Moray, Scot.*
222 E2 **Belle Isle** *W. Yorks., Eng.*
136 E1 **Bell End** *Worcs., Eng.*
216 D2 **Bellerby** *N. Yorks., Eng.*
154 B3 **Belle Vale** *W. Mids, Eng.*
40 E3 **Bellever** *Devon, Eng.*
232 E3 **Belle Vue** *Cumbria, Eng.*
222 F2 **Belle Vue** *W. Yorks., Eng.*
78 C2 **Bellfields** *Surr., Eng.*
74 D3 **Bell Green** *Gtr Lon., Eng.*
154 F3 **Bell Green** *W. Mids, Eng.*
136 E1 **Bell Heath** *Worcs., Eng.*
52 G4 **Bell Hill** *Hants., Eng.*
308 F2 **Belliehill** *Angus, Scot.*
106 E4 **Bellingdon** *Bucks., Eng.*
74 D3 **Bellingham** *Gtr Lon., Eng.*
244 D5 **Bellingham** *Northumb., Eng.*
300 C5 **Belloch** *Arg. and B., Scot.*
300 C5 **Bellochantuy** *Arg. and B., Scot.*
184 C3 **Bell o' th' Hill** *Cheshire West & Chester, Eng.*
22 L10 **Bell Rock** *i. Scot.*
262 E5 **Bellsbank** *E. Ayr., Scot.*
120 F4 **Bell's Cross** *Suff., Eng.*
244 G2 **Bellshill** *Northumb., Eng.*
280 B4 **Bellshill** *N. Lanark., Scot.*
280 C4 **Bellside** *N. Lanark., Scot.*
276 C2 **Bellsmyre** *W. Dun., Scot.*
288 B3 **Bellsquarry** *W. Lothian, Scot.*
58 H2 **Bells Yew Green** *E. Sussex, Eng.*
388 G3 **Bellury** *Coleraine, N. Ire.*
94 I2 **Belluton** *B. and N.E. Som., Eng.*
162 I2 **Belmesthorpe** *Rutland, Eng.*
228 H5 **Belmont** *B'burn, Eng.*
74 C2 **Belmont** *Gtr Lon., Eng.*
74 C3 **Belmont** *Gtr Lon., Eng.*
388 L4 **Belmont** *Carrickfergus, N. Ire*
262 D4 **Belmont** *S. Ayr., Scot.*
331 E1 **Belmont** *Shet., Scot.*
170 F6 **Belnie** *Lincs., Eng.*
36 E2 **Belowda** *Corn., Eng.*
180 E4 **Belper** *Derbys., Eng.*
180 D4 **Belper Lane End** *Derbys., En*
180 F3 **Belph** *Derbys., Eng.*
388 F2 **Belraugh** *Coleraine, N. Ire.*
244 F5 **Belsay** *Northumb., Eng.*
40 E3 **Belsford** *Devon, Eng.*
110 B5 **Belsize** *Herts., Eng.*
120 F4 **Belstead** *Suff., Eng.*
262 D4 **Belston** *S. Ayr., Scot.*
40 E2 **Belstone** *Devon, Eng.*
40 E2 **Belstone Corner** *Devon, Eng*
288 B3 **Belsyde** *W. Lothian, Scot.*
228 H4 **Belthorn** *B'burn, Eng.*
62 G2 **Beltinge** *Kent, Eng.*
244 D6 **Beltingham** *Northumb., Eng*
170 B2 **Beltoft** *N. Lincs., Eng.*
162 C2 **Belton** *Leics., Eng.*
170 C6 **Belton** *Lincs., Eng.*
170 B2 **Belton** *N. Lincs., Eng.*
166 I3 **Belton** *Norf., Eng.*
162 G3 **Belton** *Rutland, Eng.*
388 L4 **Beltoy** *Larne, N. Ire.*
62 C3 **Beltring** *Kent, Eng.*
74 E3 **Belvedere** *Gtr Lon., Eng.*
162 G1 **Belvoir** *Leics., Eng.*
52 F6 **Bembridge** *I.o.W., Eng.*
148 B2 **Bemersley Green** *Stoke, Eng.*
256 I3 **Bemersyde** *Borders, Scot.*
86 E5 **Bemerton** *Wilts., Eng.*
210 G2 **Bempton** *E. Riding, Eng.*
120 J2 **Benacre** *Suff., Eng.*
22 J7 **Ben Aigan** *hill Scot.*
22 H9 **Ben Alder** *mt. Scot.*
304 D2 **Ben Alder Cottage** *Perth and Kin., Scot.*
322 H4 **Ben Alder Lodge** *High., Scot*
22 J8 **Ben Avon** *mt. Scot.*
23 J2 **Benbane Head** *hd N. Ire.*
326 B4 **Benbecula** *airport Scot.*
22 B8 **Benbecula** *i. Scot.*
252 D2 **Benbuie** *D. and G., Scot.*
396 D3 **Benburb** *Armagh, N. Ire.*
198 D3 **Benchill** *Gtr Man., Eng.*
22 I10 **Ben Chonzie** *hill Scot.*
22 F10 **Ben Cruachan** *mt. Scot.*
300 D2 **Benderloch** *Arg. and B., Scot.*
110 D4 **Bendish** *Herts., Eng.*
388 G2 **Bendooragh** *Ballymoney, N. Ire.*
62 D4 **Benenden** *Kent, Eng.*
252 C3 **Benfield** *D. and G., Scot.*
236 D2 **Benfieldside** *Durham, Eng.*
166 H2 **Bengate** *Norf., Eng.*
22 C7 **Ben Geary** *hill Scot.*
110 E5 **Bengeo** *Herts., Eng.*
136 F3 **Bengeworth** *Worcs., Eng.*
120 H3 **Benhall Green** *Suff., Eng.*
120 H3 **Benhall Street** *Suff., Eng.*
22 G6 **Ben Hee** *hill Scot.*
22 D9 **Ben Hiant** *hill Scot.*
74 C3 **Benhilton** *Gtr Lon., Eng.*
314 G4 **Benholm** *Abers., Scot.*
22 G6 **Ben Hope** *hill Scot.*
22 H6 **Ben Horn** *hill Scot.*
216 F2 **Beningbrough** *N. Yorks., Eng*
110 E4 **Benington** *Herts., Eng.*
170 G6 **Benington** *Lincs., Eng.*
170 G6 **Benington Sea End** *Lincs., Eng.*
22 H6 **Ben Klibreck** *hill Scot.*
22 H9 **Ben Lawers** *mt. Scot.*
22 H10 **Ben Ledi** *hill Scot.*
371 D3 **Benllech** *I.o.A., Wales*
22 G10 **Ben Lomond** *hill Scot.*
22 H6 **Ben Loyal** *hill Scot.*
22 G10 **Ben Lui** *mt. Scot.*
20 F3 **Ben Macdui** *mt. Scot.*
300 F3 **Benmore** *Arg. and B., Scot.*
296 C3 **Benmore** *Stir., Scot.*
22 D10 **Ben More** *hill Scot.*
22 G10 **Ben More** *mt. Scot.*
22 G6 **Ben More Assynt** *hill Scot.*
36 F1 **Bennacott** *Corn., Eng.*
252 D2 **Bennan Cottage** *D. and G., Scot.*
22 F12 **Bennan Head** *hd Scot.*
210 D4 **Bennetland** *E. Riding, Eng.*
106 C4 **Bennett End** *Bucks., Eng.*
232 E5 **Bennett Head** *Cumbria, Eng.*
110 C5 **Bennetts End** *Herts., Eng.*
22 F9 **Ben Nevis** *mt. Scot.*
170 E4 **Benniworth** *Lincs., Eng.*
388 E2 **Benone** *Limavady, N. Ire.*
62 C3 **Benover** *Kent, Eng.*
222 D1 **Ben Rhydding** *W. Yorks., Eng.*
22 J8 **Ben Rinnes** *hill Scot.*
102 E5 **Benson** *Oxon, Eng.*
22 F9 **Ben Starav** *mt. Scot.*
331 D3 **Benston** *Shet., Scot.*
228 I4 **Bent Gate** *Lancs., Eng.*
244 H2 **Benthall** *Northumb., Eng.*
144 F4 **Benthall** *Shrop., Eng.*
98 G2 **Bentham** *Glos., Eng.*
314 G3 **Benthoul** *Aberdeen, Scot.*
22 J9 **Ben Tirran** *hill Scot.*
144 C4 **Bentlawnt** *Shrop., Eng.*
210 F4 **Bentley** *E. Riding, Eng.*
116 D4 **Bentley** *Essex, Eng.*
52 G3 **Bentley** *Hants., Eng.*
120 F5 **Bentley** *Suff., Eng.*
208 F2 **Bentley** *S. Yorks., Eng.*
132 C2 **Bentley** *Warks., Eng.*
154 B2 **Bentley** *W. Mids, Eng.*
222 E2 **Bentley** *W. Yorks., Eng.*
110 D5 **Bentley Heath** *Herts., Eng.*
154 D3 **Bentley Heath** *W. Mids, Eng.*
208 F2 **Bentley Rise** *S. Yorks., Eng.*
236 F1 **Benton Square** *T. and W., En*
252 G2 **Bentpath** *D. and G., Scot.*
208 C3 **Bents Green** *S. Yorks., Eng.*
52 F4 **Bentworth** *Hants., Eng.*
308 D4 **Benvie** *Dundee, Scot.*
46 D3 **Benville Lane** *Dorset, Eng.*
22 G10 **Ben Vorlich** *hill Scot.*
22 H10 **Ben Vorlich** *hill Scot.*
236 F2 **Benwell** *T. and W., Eng.*
124 D4 **Benwick** *Cambs., Eng.*
22 G7 **Ben Wyvis** *mt. Scot.*
136 F2 **Beoley** *Worcs., Eng.*
322 D4 **Beoraidbeg** *High., Scot.*
58 B3 **Bepton** *W. Sussex, Eng.*
402 H3 **Beragh** *Omagh, N. Ire.*
116 C2 **Berden** *Essex, Eng.*
358 C2 **Berea** *Pembs., Wales*
40 D3 **Bere Alston** *Devon, Eng.*
40 D3 **Bere Ferrers** *Devon, Eng.*
36 D3 **Berepper** *Corn., Eng.*
46 F3 **Bere Regis** *Dorset, Eng.*
166 H3 **Bergh Apton** *Norf., Eng.*
102 D5 **Berinsfield** *Oxon, Eng.*
98 E3 **Berkeley** *Glos., Eng.*
110 B5 **Berkhamsted** *Herts., Eng.*
94 K3 **Berkley** *Som., Eng.*
26 J5 **Berkshire Downs** *hills Eng.*

Berkswell to Bossington

4 E3 Berkswell W. Mids, Eng.
4 D3 Bermondsey Gtr Lon., Eng.
0 C5 Bernards Heath Herts., Eng.
2 A9 Berneray i. Scot.
2 B7 Berneray i. Scot.
6 D3 Berners Roding Essex, Eng.
0 F3 Bernice Arg. and B., Scot.
2 C2 Bernisdale High., Scot.
2 E5 Berrick Prior Oxon, Eng.
2 E5 Berrick Salome Oxon, Eng.
0 J3 Berriedale High., Scot.
2 I6 Berriedale Water r. Scot.
4 F1 Berrington Northumb., Eng.
4 D4 Berrington Shrop., Eng.
6 B2 Berrington Worcs., Eng.
6 B2 Berrington Green Worcs., Eng.
4 F3 Berrow Som., Eng.
6 D3 Berrow Worcs., Eng.
6 C2 Berrow Green Worcs., Eng.
2 D3 Berry Brow W. Yorks., Eng.
0 D1 Berry Down Cross Devon, Eng.
6 F7 Berry Head hd Eng.
8 D3 Berry Hill Glos., Eng.
8 F1 Berry Hill Pembs., Wales
4 C3 Berrylands Gtr Lon., Eng.
0 D1 Berrynarbor Devon, Eng.
4 E4 Berry's Green Gtr Lon., Eng.
8 G3 Bersham Wrex., Wales
9 D4 Berstane Orkney, Scot.
0 B3 Berthlŵyd Swansea, Wales
2 L9 Bervie Water r. Scot.
8 G4 Berwick E. Sussex, Eng.
6 D3 Berwick Bassett Wilts., Eng.
4 G5 Berwick Hill Northumb., Eng.
6 D5 Berwick St James Wilts., Eng.
6 C5 Berwick St John Wilts., Eng.
6 C5 Berwick St Leonard Wilts., Eng.
4 E1 Berwick-upon-Tweed Northumb., Eng.
6 F2 Berwyn hills Wales
8 E5 Bescar Lancs., Eng.
4 C2 Bescot W. Mids, Eng.
4 D3 Besford Shrop., Eng.
6 E3 Besford Worcs., Eng.
8 F2 Bessacarr S. Yorks., Eng.
8 E2 Bessbrook Limavady, N. Ire.
6 F4 Bessbrook Newry & Mourne, N. Ire.
2 C4 Bessels Leigh Oxon, Eng.
8 D2 Besses o' th' Barn Gtr Man., Eng.
0 G2 Bessingby E. Riding, Eng.
6 G1 Bessingham Norf., Eng.
8 H2 Best Beech Hill E. Sussex, Eng.
6 F3 Besthorpe Norf., Eng.
6 E3 Besthorpe Notts., Eng.
6 C5 Bestwood Nott., Eng.
0 F3 Beswick E. Riding, Eng.
8 D3 Beswick Gtr Man., Eng.
8 E2 Betchworth Surr., Eng.
2 F3 Bethania Cere., Wales
2 G3 Bethania Gwynedd, Wales
2 E2 Bethel Gwynedd, Wales
2 I3 Bethel Gwynedd, Wales
1 C3 Bethel I.o.A., Wales
2 E4 Bethersden Kent, Eng.
2 F1 Bethesda Gwynedd, Wales
8 F3 Bethesda Pembs., Wales
6 G2 Bethlehem Carmar., Wales
4 D2 Bethnal Green Gtr Lon., Eng.
8 A2 Betley Staffs., Eng.
8 A2 Betley Common Staffs., Eng.
2 B2 Betsham Kent, Eng.
2 H3 Betteshanger Kent, Eng.
6 B3 Bettiscombe Dorset, Eng.
8 I4 Bettisfield Wrex., Wales
4 B4 Betton Shrop., Eng.
4 F2 Betton Shrop., Eng.
4 D3 Betton Strange Shrop., Eng.
0 E3 Bettws Bridg., Wales
6 G3 Bettws Carmar., Wales
9 B3 Bettws Newp., Wales
2 F4 Bettws Bledrws Cere., Wales
6 F3 Bettws Cedewain Powys, Wales
8 E3 Bettws Gwerfil Goch Denb., Wales
9 C2 Bettws Newydd Mon., Wales
4 A5 Bettws-y-crwyn Shrop., Eng.
0 H2 Bettyhill High., Scot.
6 F5 Betws Disserth Powys, Wales
2 E2 Betws Garmon Gwynedd, Wales
2 D4 Betws Ifan Cere., Wales
8 C3 Betws-y-coed Conwy, Wales
8 D2 Betws-yn-Rhos Conwy, Wales
2 D4 Beulah Cere., Wales
6 D6 Beulah Powys, Wales
6 M5 Beult r. Eng.
8 F3 Bevendean B. and H., Eng.
6 D3 Bevercotes Notts., Eng.
0 F3 Beverley E. Riding, Eng.
8 F4 Beverston Glos., Eng.
8 E3 Bevington Glos., Eng.
2 C4 Bewaldeth Cumbria, Eng.
2 F2 Bewcastle Cumbria, Eng.
6 D1 Bewdley Worcs., Eng.
0 G3 Bewholme E. Riding, Eng.
6 C3 Bewley Common Wilts., Eng.
6 M5 Bewl Water resr Eng.
8 I3 Bexhill E. Sussex, Eng.
4 E3 Bexley Gtr Lon., Eng.
4 E3 Bexley met. bor. Gtr Lon., Eng.
4 E3 Bexleyheath Gtr Lon., Eng.
6 B3 Bexwell Norf., Eng.
0 D3 Beyton Suff., Eng.
0 D3 Beyton Green Suff., Eng.
6 E3 Bhalamus W. Isles, Scot.
Bhaleshear i. Scot. see Baleshare
6 D2 Bhaltos W. Isles, Scot.
Bhatarsaigh W. Isles, Scot. see Vatersay
Bhatarsaigh i. Scot. see Vatersay
Bhearnaraigh, Eilean i. Scot. see Berneray
2 I3 Biallaid High., Scot.
8 I3 Bibury Glos., Eng.
2 E3 Bicester Oxon, Eng.
4 F5 Bickenhall Som., Eng.
4 D3 Bickenhill W. Mids, Eng.
0 E6 Bicker Lincs., Eng.
8 B2 Bickershaw Gtr Man., Eng.
8 E5 Bickerstaffe Lancs., Eng.
4 C3 Bickerton Cheshire West & Chester, Eng.
4 E4 Bickerton Northumb., Eng.
6 F3 Bickerton N. Yorks., Eng.
8 B4 Bickford Staffs., Eng.
4 C4 Bickham Som., Eng.
0 D1 Bickington Devon, Eng.
0 D3 Bickleigh Devon, Eng.
0 F2 Bickleigh Devon, Eng.
0 D1 Bickleton Devon, Eng.
4 E3 Bickley Gtr Lon., Eng.
4 C3 Bickley Moss Cheshire West & Chester, Eng.
4 C3 Bickley Town Cheshire West & Chester, Eng.
6 F3 Bicknacre Essex, Eng.
4 E4 Bicknoller Som., Eng.
2 E3 Bicknor Kent, Eng.
52 B5 Bickton Hants., Eng.
140 C2 Bicton Here., Eng.
144 B5 Bicton Shrop., Eng.
144 D3 Bicton Shrop., Eng.
144 D3 Bicton Heath Shrop., Eng.
62 B3 Bidborough Kent, Eng.
62 D4 Biddenden Kent, Eng.
62 E4 Biddenden Green Kent, Eng.
110 C3 Biddenham Bedford, Eng.
86 B3 Biddestone Wilts., Eng.
236 F2 Biddick T. and W., Eng.
94 G3 Biddisham Som., Eng.
106 B2 Biddlesden Bucks., Eng.
244 E3 Biddlestone Northumb., Eng.
148 B2 Biddulph Staffs., Eng.
148 C2 Biddulph Moor Staffs., Eng.
22 F9 Bidean nam Bian mt. Scot.
40 D1 Bideford Devon, Eng.
Bideford Bay b. Eng. see Barnstaple Bay
132 A4 Bidford-on-Avon Warks., Eng.
190 C3 Bidston Merseyside, Eng.
110 B4 Bidwell Central Bedfordshire, Eng.
210 D3 Bielby E. Riding, Eng.
18 G3 Bieldside Aberdeen, Scot.
52 E7 Bierley I.o.W., Eng.
222 D2 Bierley W. Yorks., Eng.
106 D4 Bierton Bucks., Eng.
40 E4 Bigbury Devon, Eng.
26 E7 Bigbury Bay b. Eng.
40 E4 Bigbury-on-Sea Devon, Eng.
170 D2 Bigby Lincs., Eng.
232 C7 Bigert Mire Cumbria, Eng.
232 C8 Biggar Cumbria, Eng.
268 E3 Biggar S. Lanark., Scot.
280 C4 Biggar Road N. Lanark., Scot.
180 C4 Biggin Derbys., Eng.
180 D4 Biggin Derbys., Eng.
216 F3 Biggin N. Yorks., Eng.
331 B3 Biggings Shet., Scot.
74 E4 Biggin Hill Gtr Lon., Eng.
110 D3 Biggleswade Central Bedfordshire, Eng.
252 G2 Bigholms D. and G., Scot.
52 F4 Bighton Hants., Eng.
232 D3 Biglands Cumbria, Eng.
378 G2 Big Mancot Flints., Wales
58 C3 Bignor W. Sussex, Eng.
232 A5 Bigrigg Cumbria, Eng.
320 C4 Big Sand High., Scot.
331 D4 Bigton Shet., Scot.
176 B5 Bilborough Nott., Eng.
94 D4 Bilbrook Som., Eng.
148 B5 Bilbrook Staffs., Eng.
216 F3 Bilbrough N. Yorks., Eng.
176 C2 Bilby Notts., Eng.
236 E4 Bildershaw Durham, Eng.
120 E4 Bildeston Suff., Eng.
116 E4 Billericay Essex, Eng.
162 F3 Billesdon Leics., Eng.
132 B4 Billesley Warks., Eng.
154 C3 Billesley W. Mids, Eng.
252 G2 Billholm D. and G., Scot.
170 D6 Billingborough Lincs., Eng.
190 E3 Billinge Merseyside, Eng.
166 E2 Billingford Norf., Eng.
166 G4 Billingford Norf., Eng.
236 H4 Billingham Stockton, Eng.
170 E5 Billinghay Lincs., Eng.
208 D2 Billingley S. Yorks., Eng.
208 D2 Billingley Green S. Yorks., Eng.
58 D2 Billingshurst W. Sussex, Eng.
144 F5 Billingsley Shrop., Eng.
110 B4 Billington Central Bedfordshire, Eng.
228 H4 Billington Lancs., Eng.
148 B4 Billington Staffs., Eng.
331 D3 Billister Shet., Scot.
166 I3 Billockby Norf., Eng.
26 G6 Bill of Portland hd Eng.
236 F2 Bill Quay T. and W., Eng.
388 H1 Billy Moyle, N. Ire.
236 E3 Billy Row Durham, Eng.
228 F3 Bilsborrow Lancs., Eng.
170 H4 Bilsby Lincs., Eng.
170 H4 Bilsby Field Lincs., Eng.
288 I3 Bilsdean E. Lothian, Scot.
58 C4 Bilsham W. Sussex, Eng.
62 F4 Bilsington Kent, Eng.
98 D3 Bilson Green Glos., Eng.
176 C4 Bilsthorpe Notts., Eng.
176 C4 Bilsthorpe Moor Notts., Eng.
154 B2 Bilston W. Mids, Eng.
288 D3 Bilston Midlothian, Scot.
162 C3 Bilstone Leics., Eng.
62 F3 Bilting Kent, Eng.
210 G4 Bilton E. Riding, Eng.
244 H3 Bilton Northumb., Eng.
132 E3 Bilton Warks., Eng.
216 F3 Bilton-in-Ainsty N. Yorks., Eng.
329 C3 Bimbister Orkney, Scot.
170 E3 Binbrook Lincs., Eng.
236 F3 Binchester Blocks Durham, Eng.
46 E4 Bincombe Dorset, Eng.
94 E4 Bindon Som., Eng.
94 I3 Binegar Som., Eng.
58 E3 Bines Green W. Sussex, Eng.
24 D3 Binevenagh hill N. Ire.
82 F3 Binfield Brack. F., Eng.
102 F6 Binfield Heath Oxon, Eng.
244 E5 Bingfield Northumb., Eng.
176 D5 Bingham Notts., Eng.
46 F3 Bingham's Melcombe Dorset, Eng.
222 D1 Bingley W. Yorks., Eng.
144 D3 Bings Heath Shrop., Eng.
166 E1 Binham Norf., Eng.
52 D3 Binley Hants., Eng.
154 F3 Binley W. Mids, Eng.
402 D4 Binmore Fermanagh, N. Ire.
402 H2 Binnafreaghan Omagh, N. Ire.
22 G9 Binnein Mòr mt. Scot.
280 D3 Binniehill Falk., Scot.
216 E2 Binsoe N. Yorks., Eng.
52 E6 Binstead I.o.W., Eng.
52 G4 Binsted Hants., Eng.
58 C3 Binsted W. Sussex, Eng.
132 B4 Binton Warks., Eng.
166 E2 Bintree Norf., Eng.
144 B4 Binweston Shrop., Eng.
116 G2 Birch Essex, Eng.
198 D2 Birch Gtr Man., Eng.
166 C1 Bircham Newton Norf., Eng.
166 C1 Bircham Tofts Norf., Eng.
116 D2 Birchanger Essex, Eng.
148 E3 Birch Cross Staffs., Eng.
222 D3 Birchencliffe W. Yorks., Eng.
140 C2 Bircher Here., Eng.
140 C2 Bircher Common Here., Eng.
116 G2 Birch Green Essex, Eng.
110 E5 Birch Green Herts., Eng.
58 F2 Birch Grove W. Sussex, Eng.
350 G3 Birchgrove Cardiff, Wales
350 C2 Birchgrove Swansea, Wales
184 C3 Birch Heath Cheshire West & Chester, Eng.
62 H2 Birchington Kent, Eng.
132 C2 Birchmoor Warks., Eng.
180 D4 Birchover Derbys., Eng.
180 B2 Birch Vale Derbys., Eng.
110 D5 Birchwood Herts., Eng.
170 C4 Birchwood Lincs., Eng.
94 F5 Birch Wood Som., Eng.
190 F3 Birchwood Warr., Eng.
176 C2 Bircotes Notts., Eng.
116 E1 Birdbrook Essex, Eng.
86 C5 Birdbush Wilts., Eng.
154 C2 Bird End W. Mids, Eng.
300 E3 Birdfield Arg. and B., Scot.
58 B4 Birdham W. Sussex, Eng.
132 D4 Birdingbury Warks., Eng.
98 G3 Birdlip Glos., Eng.
232 G3 Birdoswald Cumbria, Eng.
216 G2 Birdsall N. Yorks., Eng.
116 D3 Birds Green Essex, Eng.
144 F5 Birdsgreen Shrop., Eng.
46 B3 Birdsmoor Gate Dorset, Eng.
276 F2 Birdston E. Dun., Scot.
120 E4 Bird Street Suff., Eng.
208 D2 Birdwell S. Yorks., Eng.
98 E2 Birdwood Glos., Eng.
256 J3 Birgham Borders, Scot.
228 G5 Birkacre Lancs., Eng.
232 B4 Birkby Cumbria, Eng.
216 E1 Birkby N. Yorks., Eng.
190 C2 Birkdale Merseyside, Eng.
216 C1 Birkdale N. Yorks., Eng.
190 C3 Birkenhead Merseyside, Eng.
314 F2 Birkenhills Abers., Scot.
222 D2 Birkenshaw W. Yorks., Eng.
314 D3 Birkhall Abers., Scot.
308 D4 Birkhill Angus, Scot.
256 E4 Birkhill Borders, Scot.
256 H2 Birkhill Borders, Scot.
170 C7 Birkholme Lincs., Eng.
216 F3 Birkin N. Yorks., Eng.
222 E2 Birks W. Yorks., Eng.
268 C3 Birkwood S. Lanark., Scot.
140 C2 Birley Here., Eng.
208 C3 Birley Carr S. Yorks., Eng.
208 C3 Birley Edge S. Yorks., Eng.
62 C3 Birling Kent, Eng.
244 H3 Birling Northumb., Eng.
58 H4 Birling Gap E. Sussex, Eng.
136 E3 Birlingham Worcs., Eng.
154 C3 Birmingham W. Mids, Eng.
154 D3 Birmingham International airport W. Mids, Eng.
304 I3 Birnam Perth and Kin., Scot.
329 B3 Birsay Orkney, Scot.
314 E3 Birse Abers., Scot.
314 E3 Birsemore Abers., Scot.
162 E2 Birstall Leics., Eng.
222 E2 Birstall Smithies W. Yorks., Eng.
216 E2 Birstwith N. Yorks., Eng.
170 D6 Birthorpe Lincs., Eng.
228 I5 Birtle Lancs., Eng.
140 B2 Birtley Here., Eng.
244 D5 Birtley Northumb., Eng.
236 F2 Birtley T. and W., Eng.
136 B3 Birtsmorton Worcs., Eng.
136 D3 Birts Street Worcs., Eng.
162 G3 Bisbrooke Rutland, Eng.
170 F3 Biscathorpe Lincs., Eng.
110 C4 Biscot Luton, Eng.
82 F2 Bisham W. and M., Eng.
136 E3 Bishampton Worcs., Eng.
236 E4 Bishop Auckland Durham, Eng.
170 D3 Bishopbridge Lincs., Eng.
276 E2 Bishopbriggs E. Dun., Scot.
210 F3 Bishop Burton E. Riding, Eng.
236 G3 Bishop Middleham Durham, Eng.
216 E2 Bishop Monkton N. Yorks., Eng.
170 C3 Bishop Norton Lincs., Eng.
62 G3 Bishopsbourne Kent, Eng.
86 D3 Bishops Cannings Wilts., Eng.
144 C5 Bishop's Castle Shrop., Eng.
46 E2 Bishop's Caundle Dorset, Eng.
98 G2 Bishop's Cleeve Glos., Eng.
396 K4 Bishops Court Down, N. Ire.
140 E3 Bishop's Frome Here., Eng.
78 C1 Bishops Gate Surr., Eng.
116 E2 Bishop's Green Essex, Eng.
52 E2 Bishop's Green Hants., Eng.
94 F4 Bishop's Hull Som., Eng.
132 D4 Bishop's Itchington Warks., Eng.
94 E4 Bishop's Lydeard Som., Eng.
98 F2 Bishop's Norton Glos., Eng.
40 E2 Bishops Nympton Devon, Eng.
148 B3 Bishop's Offley Staffs., Eng.
110 F4 Bishop's Stortford Herts., Eng.
52 F4 Bishop's Sutton Hants., Eng.
132 C4 Bishop's Tachbrook Warks., Eng.
40 D1 Bishop's Tawton Devon, Eng.
40 F3 Bishopsteignton Devon, Eng.
52 D5 Bishopstoke Hants., Eng.
94 I2 Bishopston Bristol, Eng.
350 B3 Bishopston Swansea, Wales
106 C4 Bishopstone Bucks., Eng.
58 G4 Bishopstone E. Sussex, Eng.
140 B3 Bishopstone Here., Eng.
86 E2 Bishopstone Swindon, Eng.
86 D5 Bishopstone Wilts., Eng.
396 J3 Bishopstown Down, N. Ire.
86 C4 Bishopstrow Wilts., Eng.
94 I2 Bishop Sutton B. and N.E. Som., Eng.
52 E5 Bishop's Waltham Hants., Eng.
94 F5 Bishopswood Som., Eng.
148 B4 Bishop's Wood Staffs., Eng.
94 I2 Bishopsworth Bristol, Eng.
216 E2 Bishop Thornton N. Yorks., Eng.
216 F3 Bishopthorpe York, Eng.
236 G4 Bishopton Darl., Eng.
132 B4 Bishopton Warks., Eng.
276 C2 Bishopton Renf., Scot.
210 D3 Bishop Wilton E. Riding, Eng.
339 C3 Bishpool Newp., Wales
339 C3 Bishton Newp., Wales
98 G3 Bisley Glos., Eng.
78 C2 Bisley Surr., Eng.
228 D3 Bispham Blackpool, Eng.
228 F5 Bispham Green Lancs., Eng.
52 B6 Bisterne Hants., Eng.
52 B6 Bisterne Close Hants., Eng.
62 B3 Bitchet Green Kent, Eng.
170 C6 Bitchfield Lincs., Eng.
40 D1 Bittadon Devon, Eng.
40 E3 Bittaford Devon, Eng.
166 E2 Bittering Norf., Eng.
144 E5 Bitterley Shrop., Eng.
52 D5 Bitterne Soton, Eng.
162 D4 Bitteswell Leics., Eng.
98 E5 Bitton S. Glos., Eng.
Biwmares I.o.A., Wales see Beaumaris
102 F5 Bix Oxon, Eng.
331 C3 Bixter Shet., Scot.
22 D8 Bla Bheinn hill Scot.
162 E3 Blaby Leics., Eng.
244 D5 Blackaburn Northumb., Eng.
252 F2 Blackacre D. and G., Scot.
256 K2 Blackadder Borders, Scot.
22 L11 Blackadder Water r. Scot.
40 E3 Blackawton Devon, Eng.
132 D3 Black Bank Warks., Eng.
40 G2 Blackborough Devon, Eng.
166 B2 Blackborough Norf., Eng.
166 B2 Blackborough End Norf., Eng.
102 B4 Black Bourton Oxon, Eng.
314 G3 Blackbraes Abers., Scot.
280 D3 Blackbraes Falk., Scot.
388 K6 Black Bridge Lisburn, N. Ire.
358 D3 Black Bridge Pembs., Wales
180 D4 Blackbrook Derbys., Eng.
162 D2 Blackbrook Leics., Eng.
190 E3 Blackbrook Merseyside, Eng.
148 A3 Blackbrook Staffs., Eng.
228 H4 Blackburn B'burn, Eng.
314 G3 Blackburn Abers., Scot.
288 B3 Blackburn W. Lothian, Scot.
228 H4 Blackburn with Darwen admin. div. Eng.
52 G3 Blackbushe Eng.
236 E1 Black Callerton T. and W., Eng.
166 F3 Black Carr Norf., Eng.
262 C6 Black Clauchrie S. Ayr., Scot.
24 K5 Black Combe hill Eng.
322 G5 Black Corries Lodge High., Scot.
252 C3 Blackcraig D. and G., Scot.
252 D2 Blackcraig D. and G., Scot.
24 I3 Blackcraig Hill hill Scot.
184 F2 Blackden Heath Cheshire East, Eng.
40 E2 Black Dog Devon, Eng.
314 G3 Blackdog Abers., Scot.
46 B3 Blackdown Dorset, Eng.
132 C4 Blackdown Warks., Eng.
26 F6 Black Down Hills hills Eng.
208 D2 Blacker Hill S. Yorks., Eng.
74 E3 Blackfen Gtr Lon., Eng.
52 D6 Blackfield Hants., Eng.
232 E3 Blackford Cumbria, Eng.
94 G3 Blackford Som., Eng.
94 J4 Blackford Som., Eng.
304 H5 Blackford Perth and Kin., Scot.
198 D2 Blackford Bridge Gtr Man., Eng.
162 B2 Blackfordby Leics., Eng.
402 G3 Blackfort Omagh, N. Ire.
52 E7 Blackgang I.o.W., Eng.
288 D3 Blackhall Edin., Scot.
276 D2 Blackhall Renf., Scot.
236 H3 Blackhall Colliery Durham, Eng.
236 E2 Blackhall Mill T. and W., Eng.
236 H3 Blackhall Rocks Durham, Eng.
58 G2 Blackham E. Sussex, Eng.
256 G3 Blackhaugh Borders, Scot.
26 B7 Black Head hd Eng.
23 K3 Black Head hd N. Ire.
116 H2 Blackheath Essex, Eng.
74 E3 Blackheath Gtr Lon., Eng.
120 I3 Blackheath Suff., Eng.
78 C2 Blackheath Surr., Eng.
154 B3 Blackheath W. Mids, Eng.
244 F5 Black Heddon Northumb., Eng.
132 C4 Black Hill Warks., Eng.
314 H2 Blackhill Abers., Scot.
314 H2 Blackhill Abers., Scot.
24 N6 Black Hill hill Eng.
314 D2 Blackhills Moray, Scot.
22 J11 Blackhope Scar hill Scot.
22 H7 Black Isle pen. Scot.
154 B2 Black Lake W. Mids, Eng.
86 D3 Blackland Wilts., Eng.
94 B4 Blacklands Som., Eng.
388 K6 Black Lane Ends Lisburn, N. Ire.
228 F4 Blackleach Lancs., Eng.
198 D2 Blackley Gtr Man., Eng.
222 C2 Blackley W. Yorks., Eng.
304 J2 Blacklunans Perth and Kin., Scot.
144 C4 Black Marsh Shrop., Eng.
350 E3 Blackmill Bridg., Wales
52 G4 Blackmoor Hants., Eng.
94 E5 Blackmoor Som., Eng.
222 E1 Black Moor W. Yorks., Eng.
222 C3 Blackmoorfoot W. Yorks., Eng.
40 E1 Blackmoor Gate Devon, Eng.
116 D3 Blackmore Essex, Eng.
116 F2 Blackmore End Essex, Eng.
110 D4 Blackmore End Herts., Eng.
300 F2 Black Mount Arg. and B., Scot.
26 E4 Black Mountain hills Wales
26 F4 Black Mountains hills Wales
314 F3 Blackness Abers., Scot.
280 E2 Blackness Falk., Scot.
52 G4 Blacknest Hants., Eng.
46 C3 Blackney Dorset, Eng.
116 F2 Black Notley Essex, Eng.
228 I3 Blacko Lancs., Eng.
350 C3 Black Pill Swansea, Wales
136 D2 Blackpole Worcs., Eng.
228 D4 Blackpool Blackpool, Eng.
40 F4 Blackpool Devon, Eng.
228 D4 Blackpool admin. div. Eng.
358 F3 Blackpool Bridge Pembs., Wales
232 F2 Blackpool Gate Cumbria, Eng.
228 D4 Blackpool International airport Eng.
288 A3 Blackridge W. Lothian, Scot.
300 B4 Blackrock Arg. and B., Scot.
339 B2 Blackrock Mon., Wales
198 B2 Blackrod Gtr Man., Eng.
252 F3 Blackshaw D. and G., Scot.
222 B2 Blackshaw Head W. Yorks., Eng.
396 G3 Black Skull Craigavon, N. Ire.
228 H4 Blacksnape B'burn, Eng.
58 E3 Blackstone W. Sussex, Eng.
120 J2 Black Street Suff., Eng.
102 E3 Blackthorn Oxon, Eng.
120 D3 Blackthorpe Suff., Eng.
210 D4 Blacktoft E. Riding, Eng.
314 G3 Blacktop Aberdeen, Scot.
40 D2 Black Torrington Devon, Eng.
402 E3 Blacktown Strabane, N. Ire.
339 B3 Blacktown Newp., Wales
23 I3 Blackwater r. N. Ire./Ireland
36 D3 Blackwater Corn., Eng.
52 H3 Blackwater Hants., Eng.
52 E6 Blackwater I.o.W., Eng.
166 F2 Blackwater Norf., Eng.
94 F5 Blackwater Som., Eng.
120 J2 Blackwater Suff., Eng.
26 N4 Blackwater r. Eng.
22 H6 Black Water r. Scot.
22 H7 Black Water r. Scot.
264 C3 Blackwaterfoot N. Ayr., Scot.
22 G9 Blackwater Reservoir resr Scot.
148 B3 Blackwaters Staffs., Eng.
396 D3 Blackwatertown Armagh, N. Ire.
236 F4 Blackwell Darl., Eng.
180 C3 Blackwell Derbys., Eng.
180 E4 Blackwell Derbys., Eng.
132 C5 Blackwell Warks., Eng.
136 E1 Blackwell Worcs., Eng.
58 F2 Blackwell W. Sussex, Eng.
98 F2 Blackwells End Glos., Eng.
252 E2 Blackwood D. and G., Scot.
268 C2 Blackwood S. Lanark., Scot.
350 G2 Blackwood Caerp., Wales
148 C2 Blackwood Hill Staffs., Eng.
184 B2 Blacon Cheshire West & Chester, Eng.
62 G3 Bladbean Kent, Eng.
252 C3 Bladnoch D. and G., Scot.
102 C4 Bladon Oxon, Eng.
362 C4 Blaenannerch Cere., Wales
378 B3 Blaenau Dolwyddelan Conwy, Wales
372 G3 Blaenau Ffestiniog Gwynedd, Wales
350 G2 Blaenau Gwent admin. div. Wales
339 B2 Blaenavon Torf., Wales
339 B1 Blaenawey Mon., Wales
362 D4 Blaencelyn Cere., Wales
350 F3 Blaen Clydach R.C.T., Wales
350 E2 Blaencwm R.C.T., Wales
366 D6 Blaendyryn Powys, Wales
358 G1 Blaenffos Pembs., Wales
350 E3 Blaengarw Bridg., Wales
362 G2 Blaengeuffordd Cere., Wales
356 G2 Blaengweche Carmar., Wales
350 E2 Blaengwrach N.P.T., Wales
350 E3 Blaengwynfi N.P.T., Wales
350 F3 Blaenllechau R.C.T., Wales
356 H2 Blaenos Carmar., Wales
362 F3 Blaenpennal Cere., Wales
362 F2 Blaenplwyf Cere., Wales
362 C4 Blaenporth Cere., Wales
350 E2 Blaenrhondda R.C.T., Wales
356 C2 Blaenwaun Carmar., Wales
356 D2 Blaen-y-coed Carmar., Wales
94 H3 Blagdon N. Som., Eng.
40 F3 Blagdon Torbay, Eng.
94 F5 Blagdon Hill Som., Eng.
228 F5 Blaguegate Lancs., Eng.
350 H2 Blaina B. Gwent, Wales
264 F2 Blair N. Ayr., Scot.
300 F3 Blairannaich Arg. and B., Scot.
304 G2 Blair Atholl Perth and Kin., Scot.
296 F4 Blair Drummond Stir., Scot.
304 J3 Blairgowrie Perth and Kin., Scot.
292 C3 Blairhall Fife, Scot.
296 E4 Blairhoyle Stir., Scot.
296 C4 Blairhullichan Stir., Scot.
304 I6 Blairingone Perth and Kin., Scot.
262 F3 Blairkip E. Ayr., Scot.
296 G5 Blairlogie Stir., Scot.
300 F3 Blairmore Arg. and B., Scot.
300 F3 Blairnairn Arg. and B., Scot.
314 D3 Blairnamarrow Moray, Scot.
264 F2 Blairpark N. Ayr., Scot.
262 D5 Blairquhan S. Ayr., Scot.
296 D5 Blairquhosh Stir., Scot.
300 E4 Blair's Ferry Arg. and B., Scot.
314 F2 Blairshinnoch Abers., Scot.
296 C4 Blairuskinmore Stir., Scot.
300 F3 Blairvadach Arg. and B., Scot.
314 F3 Blairydryne Abers., Scot.
98 E2 Blaisdon Glos., Eng.
136 D1 Blakebrook Worcs., Eng.
136 D1 Blakedown Worcs., Eng.
116 E2 Blake End Essex, Eng.
236 F2 Blakelaw T. and W., Eng.
256 J3 Blakelaw Borders, Scot.
148 B5 Blakeley Staffs., Eng.
184 E3 Blakelow Cheshire East, Eng.
140 B3 Blakemere Here., Eng.
154 C2 Blakenall Heath W. Mids, Eng.
98 E3 Blakeney Glos., Eng.
166 F1 Blakeney Norf., Eng.
26 N2 Blakeney Point pt Eng.
184 E3 Blakenhall Cheshire East, Eng.
154 B2 Blakenhall W. Mids, Eng.
136 D1 Blakeshall Worcs., Eng.
128 C5 Blakesley Northants., Eng.
244 E6 Blanchland Northumb., Eng.
46 G2 Blandford Camp Dorset, Eng.
46 F2 Blandford Forum Dorset, Eng.
46 F2 Blandford St Mary Dorset, Eng.
216 D3 Bland Hill N. Yorks., Eng.
296 E6 Blanefield Stir., Scot.
256 K2 Blanerne Borders, Scot.
402 D4 Blaney Fermanagh, N. Ire.
170 D5 Blankney Lincs., Eng.
268 B2 Blantyre S. Lanark., Scot.
322 F4 Blar a' Chaorainn High., Scot.
300 G3 Blarglas Arg. and B., Scot.
322 F4 Blarmachfoldach High., Scot.
Blàr na Maigh High., Scot. see Lewiston
52 B5 Blashford Hants., Eng.
162 G3 Blaston Leics., Eng.
326 C4 Blathaisbhal W. Isles, Scot.
128 F2 Blatherwycke Northants., Eng.
Blaven hill Scot. see Bla Bheinn
232 D7 Blawith Cumbria, Eng.
120 H4 Blaxhall Suff., Eng.
208 G3 Blaxton S. Yorks., Eng.
236 E2 Blaydon T. and W., Eng.
94 H3 Bleadney Som., Eng.
94 G3 Bleadon N. Som., Eng.
198 F2 Bleak Hey Nook Gtr Man., Eng.
62 G3 Blean Kent, Eng.
396 F3 Bleary Craigavon, N. Ire.
176 D4 Bleasby Notts., Eng.
170 E3 Bleasby Moor Lincs., Eng.
232 H5 Bleatarn Cumbria, Eng.
140 D2 Bleathwood Common Here., Eng.
292 G2 Blebocraigs Fife, Scot.
366 G5 Bleddfa Powys, Wales
98 J2 Bledington Glos., Eng.
106 C4 Bledlow Bucks., Eng.
106 C4 Bledlow Ridge Bucks., Eng.
232 G4 Blencarn Cumbria, Eng.
24 K4 Blencathra hill Eng.
232 C4 Blencogo Cumbria, Eng.
232 E4 Blencow Cumbria, Eng.
52 G5 Blendworth Hants., Eng.
26 J4 Blenheim Palace tourist site Eng.
232 C4 Blennerhasset Cumbria, Eng.
314 C2 Blervie Castle Moray, Scot.
102 D3 Bletchingdon Oxon, Eng.
78 F2 Bletchingley Surr., Eng.
106 D3 Bletchley M.K., Eng.
144 E2 Bletchley Shrop., Eng.
358 F3 Bletherston Pembs., Wales
110 C2 Bletsoe Bedford, Eng.
102 D5 Blewbury Oxon, Eng.
166 F2 Blickling Norf., Eng.
176 C4 Blidworth Notts., Eng.
176 C4 Blidworth Bottoms Notts., Eng.
244 D3 Blindburn Northumb., Eng.
232 C4 Blindcrake Cumbria, Eng.
78 F2 Blindley Heath Surr., Eng.
36 E2 Blisland Corn., Eng.
52 B5 Blissford Hants., Eng.
136 C1 Bliss Gate Worcs., Eng.
128 D4 Blisworth Northants., Eng.
148 D4 Blithbury Staffs., Eng.
232 B3 Blitterlees Cumbria, Eng.
98 I1 Blockley Glos., Eng.
166 H3 Blofield Norf., Eng.
166 H3 Blofield Heath Norf., Eng.
166 E4 Blo' Norton Norf., Eng.
396 I4 Bloody Bridge Newry & Mourne, N. Ire.
154 B2 Bloomfield W. Mids, Eng.
148 E2 Blore Staffs., Eng.
154 D3 Blossomfield W. Mids, Eng.
148 D3 Blount's Green Staffs., Eng.
190 D2 Blowick Merseyside, Eng.
102 C2 Bloxham Oxon, Eng.
154 B2 Bloxwich W. Mids, Eng.
46 G3 Bloxworth Dorset, Eng.
216 D3 Blubberhouses N. Yorks., Eng.
94 D3 Blue Anchor Som., Eng.
62 D3 Blue Bell Hill Kent, Eng.
190 C3 Blundellsands Merseyside, Eng.
120 J1 Blundeston Suff., Eng.
110 D3 Blunham Central Bedfordshire, Eng.
402 D5 Blunnick Fermanagh, N. Ire.
86 E2 Blunsdon St Andrew Swindon, Eng.
136 E1 Bluntington Worcs., Eng.
124 E4 Bluntisham Cambs., Eng.
36 G2 Blunts Corn., Eng.
148 C3 Blurton Stoke, Eng.
170 C3 Blyborough Lincs., Eng.
120 I2 Blyford Suff., Eng.
148 B4 Blymhill Staffs., Eng.
144 G3 Blymhill Common Shrop., Eng.
148 B4 Blymhill Lawn Staffs., Eng.
244 H5 Blyth Northumb., Eng.
176 C2 Blyth Notts., Eng.
26 P3 Blyth r. Eng.
256 D2 Blyth Bridge Borders, Scot.
120 I3 Blythburgh Suff., Eng.
148 C3 Blythe Bridge Staffs., Eng.
148 C3 Blythe Marsh Staffs., Eng.
132 B2 Blyth End Warks., Eng.
170 B3 Blyton Lincs., Eng.
24 B4 Boa Island i. N. Ire.
388 K6 Boardmills Lisburn, N. Ire.
292 H2 Boarhills Fife, Scot.
52 F5 Boarhunt Hants., Eng.
228 I4 Boarsgreave Lancs., Eng.
58 H2 Boarshead E. Sussex, Eng.
102 D4 Boars Hill Oxon, Eng.
106 B4 Boarstall Bucks., Eng.
58 I2 Boarzell E. Sussex, Eng.
40 D2 Boasley Cross Devon, Eng.
320 G4 Boath High., Scot.
314 D2 Boat o' Brig Moray, Scot.
322 J3 Boat of Garten High., Scot.
62 E2 Bobbing Kent, Eng.
148 B5 Bobbington Staffs., Eng.
116 D3 Bobbingworth Essex, Eng.
36 F2 Bocaddon Corn., Eng.
296 E4 Bochastle Stir., Scot.
82 A2 Bockhampton W. Berks., Eng.
116 F2 Bocking Essex, Eng.
116 F2 Bocking Churchstreet Essex, Eng.
136 B2 Bockleton Worcs., Eng.
36 F2 Boconnoc Corn., Eng.
314 H2 Boddam Abers., Scot.
331 D4 Boddam Shet., Scot.
94 I3 Bodden Som., Eng.
98 G2 Boddington Glos., Eng.
371 C3 Bodedern I.o.A., Wales
378 E2 Bodelwyddan Denb., Wales
140 C3 Bodenham Here., Eng.
86 E5 Bodenham Wilts., Eng.
140 C3 Bodenham Moor Here., Eng.
252 G1 Bodesbeck D. and G., Scot.
371 C2 Bodewryd I.o.A., Wales
378 E2 Bodfari Denb., Wales
371 C3 Bodffordd I.o.A., Wales
372 D3 Bodfuan Gwynedd, Wales
166 F1 Bodham Norf., Eng.
58 J2 Bodiam E. Sussex, Eng.
102 D2 Bodicote Oxon, Eng.
36 E2 Bodieve Corn., Eng.
36 F2 Bodinnick Corn., Eng.
371 B3 Bodior I.o.A., Wales
58 I3 Bodle Street Green E. Sussex, Eng.
36 E2 Bodmin Corn., Eng.
26 C6 Bodmin Moor moorland Eng.
166 D3 Bodney Norf., Eng.
402 F3 Bodoney Omagh, N. Ire.
371 C3 Bodorgan I.o.A., Wales
36 F2 Bodrane Corn., Eng.
62 G3 Bodsham Green Kent, Eng.
132 B2 Bodymoor Heath Warks., Eng.
388 B3 Bogagh Derry, N. Ire.
322 I2 Bogbain High., Scot.
314 H2 Bogbrae Abers., Scot.
262 D3 Bogend S. Ayr., Scot.
314 E3 Bogfern Abers., Scot.
314 G2 Bogfold Abers., Scot.
314 F2 Boghead Abers., Scot.
262 G4 Boghead E. Ayr., Scot.
268 C3 Boghead S. Lanark., Scot.
22 K8 Bogie r. Scot.
314 E2 Bogniebrae Abers., Scot.
58 B4 Bognor Regis W. Sussex, Eng.
292 C3 Bogside Fife, Scot.
314 E3 Bogston Abers., Scot.
314 F2 Bogton Abers., Scot.
252 D2 Bogue D. and G., Scot.
86 E6 Bohemia Wilts., Eng.
402 D4 Boho Fermanagh, N. Ire.
322 G4 Bohuntine High., Scot.
36 E2 Bokiddick Corn., Eng.
236 E4 Bolam Durham, Eng.
244 F5 Bolam Northumb., Eng.
40 E4 Bolberry Devon, Eng.
52 C5 Bolderwood Hants., Eng.
190 E3 Bold Heath Merseyside, Eng.
154 C2 Boldmere W. Mids, Eng.
236 G2 Boldon T. and W., Eng.
236 G2 Boldon Colliery T. and W., Eng.
52 C6 Boldre Hants., Eng.
236 D4 Boldron Durham, Eng.
176 E2 Bole Notts., Eng.
388 E2 Bolea Limavady, N. Ire.
148 E5 Bolehall Staffs., Eng.
180 D4 Bolehill Derbys., Eng.
36 C3 Boleigh Corn., Eng.
36 D3 Bolenowe Corn., Eng.
388 F2 Boleran Coleraine, N. Ire.
256 H3 Boleside Borders, Scot.
304 G3 Bolfracks Perth and Kin., Scot.
350 B2 Bolgoed Swansea, Wales
40 F2 Bolham Devon, Eng.
176 D2 Bolham Notts., Eng.
40 G2 Bolham Water Devon, Eng.
388 D2 Bolie Limavady, N. Ire.
36 D2 Bolingey Corn., Eng.
184 G2 Bollington Cheshire East, Eng.
58 E3 Bolney W. Sussex, Eng.
110 B2 Bolnhurst Bedford, Eng.
308 G3 Bolshan Angus, Scot.
180 F3 Bolsover Derbys., Eng.
222 C3 Bolster Moor W. Yorks., Eng.
208 C3 Bolsterstone S. Yorks., Eng.
140 D4 Bolstone Here., Eng.
216 F2 Boltby N. Yorks., Eng.
106 C5 Bolter End Bucks., Eng.
26 E7 Bolt Head hd Eng.
232 G5 Bolton Cumbria, Eng.
210 D3 Bolton E. Riding, Eng.
198 C2 Bolton Gtr Man., Eng.
244 F3 Bolton Northumb., Eng.
288 G3 Bolton E. Lothian, Scot.
216 D3 Bolton Abbey N. Yorks., Eng.
216 D3 Bolton Bridge N. Yorks., Eng.
228 I3 Bolton by Bowland Lancs., Eng.
232 F2 Boltonfellend Cumbria, Eng.
232 C4 Boltongate Cumbria, Eng.
228 E4 Bolton Houses Lancs., Eng.
228 F2 Bolton-le-Sands Lancs., Eng.
232 C4 Bolton Low Houses Cumbria, Eng.
216 E1 Bolton-on-Swale N. Yorks., Eng.
216 F3 Bolton Percy N. Yorks., Eng.
208 E2 Bolton upon Dearne S. Yorks., Eng.
232 D4 Bolton Wood Lane Cumbria, Eng.
36 F2 Bolventor Corn., Eng.
244 H5 Bomarsund Northumb., Eng.
252 E3 Bombie D. and G., Scot.
144 D3 Bomere Heath Shrop., Eng.
320 G4 Bonar Bridge High., Scot.
300 E2 Bonawe Arg. and B., Scot.
176 B3 Bonbusk Notts., Eng.
170 D2 Bonby N. Lincs., Eng.
358 G1 Boncath Pembs., Wales
256 I4 Bonchester Bridge Borders, Scot.
52 E7 Bonchurch I.o.W., Eng.
40 F2 Bondleigh Devon, Eng.
228 F3 Bonds Lancs., Eng.
148 E5 Bonehill Staffs., Eng.
280 E2 Bo'ness Falk., Scot.
148 D4 Boney Hay Staffs., Eng.
276 C2 Bonhill W. Dun., Scot.
144 G4 Boningale Shrop., Eng.
256 I3 Bonjedward Borders, Scot.
280 C4 Bonkle N. Lanark., Scot.
232 F6 Bonning Gate Cumbria, Eng.
62 F4 Bonnington Kent, Eng.
288 C3 Bonnington Edin., Scot.
292 F2 Bonnybank Fife, Scot.
280 C2 Bonnybridge Falk., Scot.
314 G2 Bonnykelly Abers., Scot.
288 E3 Bonnyrigg Midlothian, Scot.
314 F2 Bonnyton Abers., Scot.
308 D3 Bonnyton Angus, Scot.
308 F3 Bonnyton Angus, Scot.
308 G2 Bonnyton Angus, Scot.
180 D4 Bonsall Derbys., Eng.
339 C1 Bont Mon., Wales
372 G4 Bontddu Gwynedd, Wales
366 D3 Bont Dolgadfan Powys, Wales
362 G2 Bont-goch Cere., Wales
170 H4 Bonthorpe Lincs., Eng.
378 E2 Bont-newydd Denb., Wales
372 E2 Bontnewydd Gwynedd, Wales
372 H4 Bont Newydd Gwynedd, Wales
378 E3 Bontuchel Denb., Wales
350 F4 Bonvilston V. of Glam., Wales
350 C3 Bon-y-maen Swansea, Wales
106 D5 Booker Bucks., Eng.
144 E3 Booley Shrop., Eng.
148 B2 Boon Hill Staffs., Eng.
320 D4 Boor High., Scot.
52 E5 Boorley Green Hants., Eng.
216 G1 Boosbeck R. and C., Eng.
116 G2 Boose's Green Essex, Eng.
232 C6 Boot Cumbria, Eng.
222 C2 Booth W. Yorks., Eng.
222 C3 Booth Bank W. Yorks., Eng.
170 C5 Boothby Graffoe Lincs., Eng.
170 C6 Boothby Pagnell Lincs., Eng.
148 B2 Boothen Stoke, Eng.
184 G2 Booth Green Cheshire East, Eng.
162 B2 Boothorpe Leics., Eng.
198 C2 Boothstown Gtr Man., Eng.
222 C2 Boothtown W. Yorks., Eng.
128 D4 Boothville Northants., Eng.
222 C3 Booth Wood W. Yorks., Eng.
232 B7 Bootle Cumbria, Eng.
190 D3 Bootle Merseyside, Eng.
166 F2 Booton Norf., Eng.
184 E2 Boots Green Cheshire West & Chester, Eng.
120 G4 Boot Street Suff., Eng.
216 D1 Booze N. Yorks., Eng.
296 D5 Boquhan Stir., Scot.
Boraraigh i. Scot. see Boreray
144 E6 Boraston Shrop., Eng.
408 B3 Bordeaux Guernsey Channel Is
62 E3 Borden Kent, Eng.
58 B2 Borden W. Sussex, Eng.
216 C2 Bordley N. Yorks., Eng.
52 G4 Bordon Hants., Eng.
116 F3 Boreham Essex, Eng.
86 C4 Boreham Wilts., Eng.
58 I3 Boreham Street E. Sussex, Eng.
110 D6 Borehamwood Herts., Eng.
252 C3 Boreland D. and G., Scot.
252 G2 Boreland D. and G., Scot.
296 D3 Boreland Stir., Scot.
136 D2 Boreley Worcs., Eng.
322 A2 Boreraig High., Scot.
22 B7 Boreray i. Scot.
22 □1 Boreray i. Scot.
326 B6 Borgh W. Isles, Scot.
326 C3 Borgh W. Isles, Scot.
326 D2 Borghastan W. Isles, Scot.
320 H2 Borgie High., Scot.
22 H5 Borgie r. Scot.
252 D3 Borgue D. and G., Scot.
320 J3 Borgue High., Scot.
116 G1 Borley Essex, Eng.
116 G1 Borley Green Essex, Eng.
120 E3 Borley Green Suff., Eng.
326 B5 Bornais W. Isles, Scot.
252 D3 Borness D. and G., Scot.
322 B2 Bornisketaig High., Scot.
74 D2 Borough Gtr Lon., Eng.
216 E2 Boroughbridge N. Yorks., Eng.
62 B3 Borough Green Kent, Eng.
378 H3 Borras Head Wrex., Wales
180 E5 Borrowash Derbys., Eng.
216 E2 Borrowby N. Yorks., Eng.
232 D5 Borrowdale Cumbria, Eng.
314 G3 Borrowfield Abers., Scot.
62 C2 Borstal Medway, Eng.
362 F2 Borth Cere., Wales
288 E4 Borthwick Midlothian, Scot.
256 G4 Borthwickbrae Borders, Scot.
256 G4 Borthwickshiels Borders, Scot.
372 F3 Borth-y-Gest Gwynedd, Wales
322 C2 Borve High., Scot.
228 F2 Borwick Lancs., Eng.
232 C7 Borwick Rails Cumbria, Eng.
140 E3 Bosbury Here., Eng.
36 E2 Boscarne Corn., Eng.
36 E1 Boscastle Corn., Eng.
46 H3 Boscombe Bourne., Eng.
86 E5 Boscombe Wilts., Eng.
58 A4 Bosham W. Sussex, Eng.
58 A4 Bosham Hoe W. Sussex, Eng.
358 E4 Bosherston Pembs., Wales
184 G2 Bosley Cheshire East, Eng.
62 G3 Bossingham Kent, Eng.
52 C4 Bossington Hants., Eng.

Broomhead to Canfield End

4 G2 Broomhead Abers., Scot.
4 I2 Broomhill Bristol, Eng.
46 H3 Broom Hill Dorset, Eng.
44 H4 Broomhill Northumb., Eng.
8 D2 Broomhill S. Yorks., Eng.
6 E1 Broom Hill Worcs., Eng.
6 H1 Broomholm Norf., Eng.
6 D4 Broomielaw Durham, Eng.
4 F6 Broomley Northumb., Eng.
4 I4 Broom of Dalreoch Perth and Kin., Scot.
6 F3 Broompark Durham, Eng.
8 E2 Broom's Green Glos., Eng.
6 F3 Broomside Durham, Eng.
6 D2 Broomsthorpe Norf., Eng.
0 I3 Brora High., Scot.
2 I6 Brora r. Scot.
2 I6 Brora, Loch l. Scot.
4 F4 Broseley Shrop., Eng.
6 C3 Brotherlee Durham, Eng.
0 F6 Brothertoft Lincs., Eng.
6 G1 Brotton R. and C., Eng.
0 J2 Broubster High., Scot.
2 I5 Brough Cumbria, Eng.
0 C2 Brough Derbys., Eng.
0 E4 Brough E. Riding, Eng.
6 E4 Brough Notts., Eng.
0 K2 Brough High., Scot.
9 B3 Brough Orkney, Scot.
1 D2 Brough Shet., Scot.
1 D2 Brough Shet., Scot.
1 D3 Brough Shet., Scot.
1 D3 Brough Shet., Scot.
1 E2 Brough Shet., Scot.
4 E2 Broughall Shrop., Eng.
2 I2 Broughderg Cookstown, N. Ire.
2 J4 Brough Head hd Scot.
1 E2 Brough Lodge Shet., Scot.
2 K5 Brough Ness pt Scot.
8 I3 Broughshane Ballymena, N. Ire.
2 I5 Brough Sowerby Cumbria, Eng.
6 D4 Broughton Bucks., Eng.
4 D4 Broughton Cambs., Eng.
2 C4 Broughton Hants., Eng.
8 F4 Broughton Lancs., Eng.
6 D2 Broughton M.K., Eng.
0 C2 Broughton N. Lincs., Eng.
8 E3 Broughton Northants., Eng.
6 C3 Broughton N. Yorks., Eng.
6 G2 Broughton N. Yorks., Eng.
2 C2 Broughton Oxon, Eng.
6 D3 Broughton Borders, Scot.
9 D2 Broughton Orkney, Scot.
8 H3 Broughton Flints., Wales
0 E4 Broughton V. of Glam., Wales
2 D3 Broughton Astley Leics., Eng.
2 D7 Broughton Beck Cumbria, Eng.
6 B3 Broughton Common Wilts., Eng.
6 B3 Broughton Gifford Wilts., Eng.
6 E2 Broughton Green Worcs., Eng.
6 E2 Broughton Hackett Worcs., Eng.
2 C7 Broughton in Furness Cumbria, Eng.
2 C7 Broughton Mills Cumbria, Eng.
2 B4 Broughton Moor Cumbria, Eng.
2 B4 Broughton Poggs Oxon, Eng.
9 F2 Broughtown Orkney, Scot.
8 E4 Broughty Ferry Dundee, Scot.
1 C3 Browland Shet., Scot.
2 H6 Brownber Cumbria, Eng.
2 E4 Brown Candover Hants., Eng.
2 E6 Browndown Hants., Eng.
8 E5 Brown Edge Lancs., Eng.
8 C2 Brown Edge Staffs., Eng.
4 C2 Brown Heath Cheshire West & Chester, Eng.
4 D2 Brownheath Shrop., Eng.
4 G2 Brownhill Abers., Scot.
4 C2 Brownhills W. Mids, Eng.
2 H2 Brownhills Fife, Scot.
4 G2 Brownieside Northumb., Eng.
8 B2 Brown Lees Staffs., Eng.
4 F3 Brownlow Cheshire East, Eng.
4 F3 Brownlow Heath Cheshire East, Eng.
4 D4 Brown's Bank Cheshire East, Eng.
4 C2 Brown's Green W. Mids, Eng.
8 F3 Brownshill Glos., Eng.
4 E3 Brownshill Green W. Mids, Eng.
2 E3 Brownsover Warks., Eng.
0 E3 Brownston Devon, Eng.
0 F3 Brown Street Suff., Eng.
6 J3 Browston Green Norf., Eng.
6 H2 Broxa N. Yorks., Eng.
0 E5 Broxbourne Herts., Eng.
8 I3 Broxburn E. Lothian, Scot.
8 C3 Broxburn W. Lothian, Scot.
0 C4 Broxholme Lincs., Eng.
6 D2 Broxted Essex, Eng.
4 C3 Broxton Cheshire West & Chester, Eng.
0 B2 Broxwood Here., Eng.
8 G3 Broyle Side E. Sussex, Eng.
2 J2 Bruachmary High., Scot.
0 K2 Bruan High., Scot.
2 I9 Bruar Water r. Scot.
6 G5 Brue r. Eng.
4 B3 Bruera Cheshire West & Chester, Eng.
2 B3 Bruern Oxon, Eng.
6 B6 Bruernish W. Isles, Scot.
0 A4 Bruichladdich Arg. and B., Scot.
0 H3 Bruisyard Suff., Eng.
0 H3 Bruisyard Street Suff., Eng.
0 C2 Brumby N. Lincs., Eng.
8 D2 Brund Staffs., Eng.
6 H3 Brundall Norf., Eng.
6 I3 Brundish Norf., Eng.
0 G3 Brundish Suff., Eng.
0 G3 Brundish Street Suff., Eng.
2 E3 Brunstock Cumbria, Eng.
2 E3 Bruntingthorpe Leics., Eng.
4 E2 Bruntland Abers., Scot.
4 G2 Brunton Northumb., Eng.
6 F4 Brunton Wilts., Eng.
2 F1 Brunton Fife, Scot.
2 G5 Bruscarnagh Fermanagh, N. Ire.
0 C3 Brushfield Derbys., Eng.
0 E2 Brushford Devon, Eng.
4 C4 Brushford Som., Eng.
4 J4 Bruton Som., Eng.
6 I4 Bryansford Down, N. Ire.
6 F2 Bryanston Dorset, Eng.
6 D4 Bryant's Bottom Bucks., Eng.
2 G2 Brydekirk D. and G., Scot.
6 □ Bryher i. Eng.
8 G3 Brymbo Wrex., Wales
4 H5 Brympton Som., Eng.
4 D2 Bryn Cheshire West & Chester, Eng.
8 B2 Bryn Gtr Man., Eng.
4 B5 Bryn Shrop., Eng.
350 G3 Bryn Caerp., Wales
356 F3 Bryn Carmar., Wales
350 D3 Bryn N.P.T., Wales
356 G3 Brynamman Carmar., Wales
358 F2 Brynberian Pembs., Wales
Brynbuga Mon., Wales see Usk
372 F3 Bryn Bwbach Gwynedd, Wales
350 F3 Bryncae R.C.T., Wales
350 E3 Bryncethin Bridg., Wales
372 E3 Bryncir Gwynedd, Wales
350 E3 Bryncoch Bridg., Wales
350 D2 Bryn-côch N.P.T., Wales
372 C3 Bryncroes Gwynedd, Wales
372 F5 Bryncrug Gwynedd, Wales
378 F3 Bryneglwys Denb., Wales
378 F2 Brynford Flints., Wales
198 B2 Bryn Gates Gtr Man., Eng.
371 C3 Bryngwran I.o.A., Wales
339 C2 Bryngwyn Mon., Wales
366 F6 Bryngwyn Powys, Wales
358 E1 Bryn-henllan Pembs., Wales
362 D4 Brynhoffnant Cere., Wales
228 E4 Bryning Lancs., Eng.
350 H2 Brynithel B. Gwent, Wales
350 G2 Brynmawr B. Gwent, Wales
372 G3 Bryn-mawr Gwynedd, Wales
366 F4 Brynmelyn Powys, Wales
350 E3 Brynmenyn Bridg., Wales
350 C3 Brynmill Swansea, Wales
350 F3 Brynna R.C.T., Wales
350 F3 Brynnau Gwynion R.C.T., Wales
362 F3 Brynog Cere., Wales
362 F2 Brynowen Cere., Wales
366 F3 Bryn-penarth Powys, Wales
378 H4 Bryn Pen-y-lan Wrex., Wales
372 F2 Brynrefail Gwynedd, Wales
371 D2 Brynrefail I.o.A., Wales
362 F2 Brynrodyn Cere., Wales
350 F3 Brynsadler R.C.T., Wales
378 E3 Brynsaithmarchog Denb., Wales
371 D3 Brynsiencyn I.o.A., Wales
371 D3 Bryn-teg I.o.A., Wales
378 G3 Brynteg Wrex., Wales
144 C2 Bryn-y-cochin Shrop., Eng.
339 C1 Brynygwenin Mon., Wales
378 C2 Bryn-y-maen Conwy, Wales
326 B6 Buaile nam Bodach W. Isles, Scot.
322 C3 Bualintur High., Scot.
320 D4 Bualnaluib High., Scot.
132 D3 Bubbenhall Warks., Eng.
180 D3 Bubnell Derbys., Eng.
210 C4 Bubwith E. Riding, Eng.
256 F4 Buccleuch Borders, Scot.
252 E3 Buchan D. and G., Scot.
296 D5 Buchanan Castle Stir., Scot.
314 H2 Buchanhaven Abers., Scot.
304 H4 Buchanty Perth and Kin., Scot.
296 E5 Buchlyvie Stir., Scot.
232 E4 Buckabank Cumbria, Eng.
128 C4 Buckby Wharf Northants., Eng.
124 C5 Buckden Cambs., Eng.
216 C2 Buckden N. Yorks., Eng.
166 H3 Buckenham Norf., Eng.
40 G2 Buckerell Devon, Eng.
40 E3 Buckfast Devon, Eng.
40 E3 Buckfastleigh Devon, Eng.
292 F2 Buckhaven Fife, Scot.
256 H3 Buckholm Borders, Scot.
339 D1 Buckholt Mon., Wales
46 E1 Buckhorn Weston Dorset, Eng.
116 C4 Buckhurst Hill Essex, Eng.
314 E1 Buckie Moray, Scot.
320 J2 Buckies High., Scot.
106 C3 Buckingham Bucks., Eng.
106 C4 Buckinghamshire county Eng.
106 D4 Buckland Bucks., Eng.
98 H1 Buckland Glos., Eng.
52 C6 Buckland Hants., Eng.
140 D2 Buckland Here., Eng.
110 E4 Buckland Herts., Eng.
62 H4 Buckland Kent, Eng.
102 B4 Buckland Oxon, Eng.
78 E2 Buckland Surr., Eng.
40 D2 Buckland Brewer Devon, Eng.
106 E4 Buckland Common Bucks., Eng.
94 J3 Buckland Dinham Som., Eng.
154 D2 Buckland End W. Mids, Eng.
40 D2 Buckland Filleigh Devon, Eng.
40 E3 Buckland in the Moor Devon, Eng.
46 E2 Buckland Newton Dorset, Eng.
46 E4 Buckland Ripers Dorset, Eng.
94 F5 Buckland St Mary Som., Eng.
82 C3 Bucklebury W. Berks., Eng.
308 E3 Bucklerheads Angus, Scot.
52 D6 Bucklers Hard Hants., Eng.
120 G4 Bucklesham Suff., Eng.
378 G2 Buckley Flints., Wales
132 B4 Buckley Green Warks., Eng.
190 D3 Buckley Hill Merseyside, Eng.
378 G2 Buckley Mountain Flints., Wales
184 E1 Bucklow Hill Cheshire East, Eng.
58 D2 Buckman Corner W. Sussex, Eng.
162 G2 Buckminster Leics., Eng.
388 J3 Buckna Ballymena, N. Ire.
170 E4 Bucknall Lincs., Eng.
148 C2 Bucknall Stoke, Eng.
102 D3 Bucknell Oxon, Eng.
144 C5 Bucknell Shrop., Eng.
154 B3 Buckpool W. Mids, Eng.
136 C1 Buckridge Worcs., Eng.
314 G3 Bucksburn Aberdeen, Scot.
40 C2 Buck's Cross Devon, Eng.
58 D2 Bucks Green W. Sussex, Eng.
110 C5 Bucks Hill Herts., Eng.
52 G4 Bucks Horn Oak Hants., Eng.
40 C2 Buck's Mills Devon, Eng.
358 E4 Buckspool Pembs., Wales
210 G2 Buckton E. Riding, Eng.
140 B1 Buckton Here., Eng.
244 F2 Buckton Northumb., Eng.
198 E2 Buckton Vale Gtr Man., Eng.
124 C4 Buckworth Cambs., Eng.
132 C4 Budbrooke Warks., Eng.
176 C3 Budby Notts., Eng.
308 F4 Buddon Angus, Scot.
22 K10 Buddon Ness pt Scot.
36 F1 Bude Corn., Eng.
26 C6 Bude Bay b. Eng.
244 G2 Budle Northumb., Eng.
40 G3 Budleigh Salterton Devon, Eng.
36 D3 Budock Water Corn., Eng.
388 J5 Budore Lisburn, N. Ire.
184 D2 Budworth Heath Cheshire West & Chester, Eng.
198 E2 Buersil Gtr Man., Eng.
184 E4 Buerton Cheshire East, Eng.
128 C4 Bugbrooke Northants., Eng.
402 C4 Buggan Fermanagh, N. Ire.
184 F2 Buglawton Cheshire East, Eng.
36 E2 Bugle Corn., Eng.
210 D2 Bugthorpe E. Riding, Eng.
22 E10 Buie, Loch b. Scot.
116 C1 Building End Essex, Eng.
144 E4 Buildwas Shrop., Eng.
366 E5 Builth Road Powys, Wales
366 E6 Builth Wells Powys, Wales
170 D7 Bulby Lincs., Eng.
176 C5 Bulcote Notts., Eng.
320 I2 Buldoo High., Scot.
86 E4 Bulford Wilts., Eng.
86 E4 Bulford Camp Wilts., Eng.
184 C3 Bulkeley Cheshire East, Eng.
132 D3 Bulkington Warks., Eng.
86 C4 Bulkington Wilts., Eng.
40 D2 Bulkworthy Devon, Eng.
216 E1 Bullamoor N. Yorks., Eng.
371 C2 Bull Bay I.o.A., Wales
180 E4 Bullbridge Derbys., Eng.
82 F3 Bullbrook Brack. F., Eng.
110 D5 Bullen's Green Herts., Eng.
98 E2 Bulley Glos., Eng.
62 E4 Bull Green Kent, Eng.
170 D4 Bullington Lincs., Eng.
23 J2 Bull Point pt N. Ire.
232 G7 Bullpot Farm Cumbria, Eng.
74 D1 Bulls Cross Gtr Lon., Eng.
110 E4 Bull's Green Herts., Eng.
166 I4 Bull's Green Norf., Eng.
300 F4 Bullwood Arg. and B., Scot.
116 E2 Bulmer Essex, Eng.
216 G2 Bulmer N. Yorks., Eng.
116 E2 Bulmer Tye Essex, Eng.
116 E4 Bulphan Thurrock, Eng.
58 J3 Bulverhythe E. Sussex, Eng.
314 G2 Bulwark Abers., Scot.
176 B4 Bulwell Nott., Eng.
128 F2 Bulwick Northants., Eng.
116 C3 Bumble's Green Essex, Eng.
402 F5 Bun Fermanagh, N. Ire.
326 D3 Bun Abhainn Eadarra W. Isles, Scot.
322 D4 Bunacaimb High., Scot.
322 G4 Bunarkaig High., Scot.
Bun Atha Arg. and B., Scot. see Bonawe
184 D3 Bunbury Cheshire East, Eng.
184 D3 Bunbury Heath Cheshire East, Eng.
322 I2 Bunchrew High., Scot.
322 E3 Bundalloch High., Scot.
331 E1 Buness Shet., Scot.
300 B3 Bunessan Arg. and B., Scot.
120 H2 Bungay Suff., Eng.
300 D5 Bunlarie Arg. and B., Scot.
Bun Leothaid High., Scot. see Bunloit
322 H3 Bunloit High., Scot.
322 G3 Bun Loyne High., Scot.
326 C5 Bunmhullin W. Isles, Scot.
300 B4 Bunnahabhain Arg. and B., Scot.
402 F5 Bunneil Fermanagh, N. Ire.
176 C5 Bunny Notts., Eng.
322 H2 Buntait High., Scot.
110 E4 Buntingford Herts., Eng.
166 F4 Bunwell Norf., Eng.
166 F3 Bunwell Street Norf., Eng.
180 B3 Burbage Derbys., Eng.
162 C3 Burbage Leics., Eng.
86 E3 Burbage Wilts., Eng.
82 F2 Burchett's Green W. and M., Eng.
86 D5 Burcombe Wilts., Eng.
102 D5 Burcot Oxon, Eng.
136 E1 Burcot Worcs., Eng.
106 D3 Burcott Bucks., Eng.
216 H2 Burdale N. Yorks., Eng.
288 D3 Burdiehouse Edin., Scot.
58 C3 Burdocks W. Sussex, Eng.
236 G2 Burdon T. and W., Eng.
102 C2 Burdrop Oxon, Eng.
26 P2 Bure r. Eng.
120 D5 Bures Suff., Eng.
120 D5 Bures Green Suff., Eng.
366 G5 Burfa Powys, Wales
102 B4 Burford Oxon, Eng.
144 E6 Burford Shrop., Eng.
94 I3 Burford Som., Eng.
300 B2 Burg Arg. and B., Scot.
120 F2 Burgate Suff., Eng.
52 G4 Burgates Hants., Eng.
110 C4 Burge End Herts., Eng.
58 F3 Burgess Hill W. Sussex, Eng.
120 G4 Burgh Suff., Eng.
232 D3 Burgh by Sands Cumbria, Eng.
166 I3 Burgh Castle Norf., Eng.
52 E2 Burghclere Hants., Eng.
314 C1 Burghead Moray, Scot.
22 I7 Burghead Bay b. Scot.
82 D3 Burghfield W. Berks., Eng.
82 D3 Burghfield Common W. Berks., Eng.
82 D3 Burghfield Hill W. Berks., Eng.
78 E2 Burgh Heath Surr., Eng.
140 C3 Burghill Here., Eng.
170 H5 Burgh le Marsh Lincs., Eng.
166 G2 Burgh next Aylsham Norf., Eng.
170 E3 Burgh on Bain Lincs., Eng.
Burgh St. Margaret Norf., Eng. see Fleggburgh
166 I4 Burgh St Peter Norf., Eng.
208 E2 Burghwallis S. Yorks., Eng.
62 C3 Burham Kent, Eng.
52 G5 Buriton Hants., Eng.
184 D3 Burland Cheshire East, Eng.
36 E2 Burlawn Corn., Eng.
82 F3 Burleigh Brack. F., Eng.
40 G2 Burlescombe Devon, Eng.
46 F3 Burleston Dorset, Eng.
52 B6 Burley Hants., Eng.
162 G2 Burley Rutland, Eng.
222 E2 Burley W. Yorks., Eng.
184 D4 Burleydam Cheshire East, Eng.
140 D3 Burley Gate Here., Eng.
222 D1 Burley in Wharfedale W. Yorks., Eng.
52 B5 Burley Street Hants., Eng.
222 D1 Burley Woodhead W. Yorks., Eng.
166 H3 Burlingham Green Norf., Eng.
58 H3 Burlow E. Sussex, Eng.
144 D3 Burlton Shrop., Eng.
62 G4 Burmarsh Kent, Eng.
132 C5 Burmington Warks., Eng.
198 D3 Burnage Gtr Man., Eng.
180 D5 Burnaston Derbys., Eng.
280 D4 Burnbrae N. Lanark., Scot.
210 D3 Burnby E. Riding, Eng.
208 D3 Burncross S. Yorks., Eng.
58 C4 Burndell W. Sussex, Eng.
198 C2 Burnden Gtr Man., Eng.
198 E2 Burnedge Gtr Man., Eng.
314 G2 Burnend Abers., Scot.
232 F6 Burneside Cumbria, Eng.
329 F2 Burness Orkney, Scot.
94 J2 Burnett B. and N.E. Som., Eng.
388 E3 Burnfoot Limavady, N. Ire.
256 G4 Burnfoot Borders, Scot.
256 H4 Burnfoot Borders, Scot.
320 I3 Burnfoot High., Scot.
304 I5 Burnfoot Perth and Kin., Scot.
106 E5 Burnham Bucks., Eng.
170 D2 Burnham N. Lincs., Eng.
166 D1 Burnham Deepdale Norf., Eng.
110 D4 Burnham Green Herts., Eng.
166 D1 Burnham Market Norf., Eng.
166 D1 Burnham Norton Norf., Eng.
116 G4 Burnham-on-Crouch Essex, Eng.
94 G3 Burnham-on-Sea Som., Eng.
166 D1 Burnham Overy Staithe Norf., Eng.
166 D1 Burnham Overy Town Norf., Eng.
166 D1 Burnham Thorpe Norf., Eng.
314 H2 Burnhaven Abers., Scot.
252 D2 Burnhead D. and G., Scot.
252 E2 Burnhead D. and G., Scot.
314 F3 Burnhervie Abers., Scot.
148 B5 Burnhill Green Staffs., Eng.
236 E3 Burnhope Durham, Eng.
264 G2 Burnhouse N. Ayr., Scot.
216 H2 Burniston N. Yorks., Eng.
228 I4 Burnley Lancs., Eng.
228 I4 Burnley Lane Lancs., Eng.
256 L1 Burnmouth Borders, Scot.
228 D3 Burn Naze Lancs., Eng.
296 F4 Burn of Cambus Stir., Scot.
236 E2 Burnopfield Durham, Eng.
110 E4 Burn's Green Herts., Eng.
388 J4 Burnside Antrim, N. Ire.
388 J4 Burnside Antrim, N. Ire.
314 F3 Burnside Abers., Scot.
308 F3 Burnside Angus, Scot.
262 F4 Burnside E. Ayr., Scot.
292 D2 Burnside Fife, Scot.
331 C2 Burnside Shet., Scot.
288 C3 Burnside W. Lothian, Scot.
308 E3 Burnside of Duntrune Angus, Scot.
244 B6 Burnstones Northumb., Eng.
252 G2 Burnswark D. and G., Scot.
184 G2 Burntcliff Top Cheshire East, Eng.
82 C3 Burnt Hill W. Berks., Eng.
236 E4 Burnt Houses Durham, Eng.
292 E3 Burntisland Fife, Scot.
74 C2 Burnt Oak Gtr Lon., Eng.
262 E4 Burnton E. Ayr., Scot.
262 E5 Burnton E. Ayr., Scot.
148 D4 Burntwood Staffs., Eng.
148 D4 Burntwood Green Staffs., Eng.
216 E2 Burnt Yates N. Yorks., Eng.
94 F5 Burnworthy Som., Eng.
78 C2 Burpham Surr., Eng.
58 C3 Burpham W. Sussex, Eng.
22 □N2 Burra i. Scot.
244 E3 Burradon Northumb., Eng.
236 F1 Burradon T. and W., Eng.
331 E1 Burrafirth Shet., Scot.
331 C2 Burraland Shet., Scot.
36 D3 Burras Corn., Eng.
36 G2 Burraton Corn., Eng.
331 C2 Burravoe Shet., Scot.
331 D2 Burravoe Shet., Scot.
22 K5 Burray i. Scot.
232 H5 Burrells Cumbria, Eng.
304 K3 Burrelton Perth and Kin., Scot.
388 K6 Burren Lisburn, N. Ire.
396 G5 Burren Newry & Mourne, N. Ire.
52 E5 Burridge Hants., Eng.
216 E2 Burrill N. Yorks., Eng.
170 B2 Burringham N. Lincs., Eng.
40 E2 Burrington Devon, Eng.
140 C1 Burrington Here., Eng.
94 H3 Burrington N. Som., Eng.
124 G5 Burrough End Cambs., Eng.
124 G5 Burrough Green Cambs., Eng.
162 F2 Burrough on the Hill Leics., Eng.
94 C3 Burrow Som., Eng.
94 G5 Burrow Som., Eng.
94 G4 Burrow Bridge Som., Eng.
24 I4 Burrow Head hd Scot.
78 C1 Burrowhill Surr., Eng.
78 D2 Burrows Cross Surr., Eng.
350 A3 Burry Swansea, Wales
350 A3 Burry Green Swansea, Wales
26 D4 Burry Inlet inlet Wales
356 E3 Burry Port Carmar., Wales
228 E5 Burscough Lancs., Eng.
228 E5 Burscough Bridge Lancs., Eng.
210 D4 Bursea E. Riding, Eng.
210 D4 Bursea Lane Ends E. Riding, Eng.
210 F3 Burshill E. Riding, Eng.
52 E5 Bursledon Hants., Eng.
148 B2 Burslem Stoke, Eng.
120 F4 Burstall Suff., Eng.
46 C3 Burstock Dorset, Eng.
166 F4 Burston Norf., Eng.
148 C3 Burston Staffs., Eng.
78 F3 Burstow Surr., Eng.
210 H4 Burstwick E. Riding, Eng.
120 C3 Burthorpe Suff., Eng.
232 E3 Burthwaite Cumbria, Eng.
94 G3 Burtle Som., Eng.
94 G3 Burtle Hill Som., Eng.
184 A2 Burton Cheshire West & Chester, Eng.
184 C2 Burton Cheshire West & Chester, Eng.
46 E3 Burton Dorset, Eng.
46 I3 Burton Dorset, Eng.
170 C4 Burton Lincs., Eng.
244 G2 Burton Northumb., Eng.
94 F3 Burton Som., Eng.
86 B2 Burton Wilts., Eng.
86 B5 Burton Wilts., Eng.
358 E3 Burton Pembs., Wales
210 G3 Burton Agnes E. Riding, Eng.
46 C3 Burton Bradstock Dorset, Eng.
170 C7 Burton Coggles Lincs., Eng.
116 D2 Burton End Essex, Eng.
358 E3 Burton Ferry Pembs., Wales
210 F2 Burton Fleming E. Riding, Eng.
132 C3 Burton Green Warks., Eng.
378 H3 Burton Green Wrex., Wales
132 D2 Burton Hastings Warks., Eng.
232 F7 Burton-in-Kendal Cumbria, Eng.
216 B2 Burton in Lonsdale N. Yorks., Eng.
176 C5 Burton Joyce Notts., Eng.
128 E3 Burton Latimer Northants., Eng.
162 F2 Burton Lazars Leics., Eng.
216 E2 Burton Leonard N. Yorks., Eng.
162 E2 Burton on the Wolds Leics., Eng.
162 C3 Burton Overy Leics., Eng.
170 E6 Burton Pedwardine Lincs., Eng.
210 H4 Burton Pidsea E. Riding, Eng.
116 F2 Burton's Green Essex, Eng.
170 B2 Burton Stather N. Lincs., Eng.
170 B2 Burton upon Stather N. Lincs., Eng.
148 H4 Burton upon Trent Staffs., Eng.
190 F3 Burtonwood Warr., Eng.
184 C3 Burwardsley Cheshire West & Chester, Eng.
144 E5 Burwarton Shrop., Eng.
58 I3 Burwash E. Sussex, Eng.
58 I3 Burwash Weald E. Sussex, Eng.
124 F5 Burwell Cambs., Eng.
170 G4 Burwell Lincs., Eng.
371 C2 Burwen I.o.A., Wales
329 D5 Burwick Orkney, Scot.
331 D3 Burwick Shet., Scot.
124 D4 Bury Cambs., Eng.
198 D2 Bury Gtr Man., Eng.
94 C4 Bury Som., Eng.
58 C3 Bury W. Sussex, Eng.
110 C3 Bury End Central Bedfordshire, Eng.
136 F3 Bury End Worcs., Eng.
110 E5 Bury Green Herts., Eng.
110 F4 Bury Green Herts., Eng.
120 D3 Bury St Edmunds Suff., Eng.
216 G2 Burythorpe N. Yorks., Eng.
78 C2 Busbridge Surr., Eng.
276 E3 Busby E. Renf., Scot.
304 I4 Busby Perth and Kin., Scot.
102 B4 Buscot Oxon, Eng.
36 F1 Bush Corn., Eng.
24 D3 Bush r. N. Ire.
140 C3 Bush Bank Here., Eng.
154 B2 Bushbury W. Mids, Eng.
162 E3 Bushby Leics., Eng.
314 D3 Bush Crathie Abers., Scot.
110 C6 Bushey Herts., Eng.
110 C6 Bushey Heath Herts., Eng.
74 C3 Bushey Mead Gtr Lon., Eng.
166 G4 Bush Green Norf., Eng.
120 D3 Bush Green Suff., Eng.
74 D2 Bush Hill Park Gtr Lon., Eng.
136 D3 Bushley Worcs., Eng.
136 D3 Bushley Green Worcs., Eng.
388 G1 Bushmills Moyle, N. Ire.
86 D3 Bushton Wilts., Eng.
166 E2 Bushy Common Norf., Eng.
232 G4 Busk Cumbria, Eng.
198 E2 Busk Gtr Man., Eng.
98 G3 Bussage Glos., Eng.
331 C2 Busta Shet., Scot.
166 G4 Bustard's Green Norf., Eng.
166 H2 Butcher's Common Norf., Eng.
58 H2 Butcher's Cross E. Sussex, Eng.
116 E2 Butcher's Pasture Essex, Eng.
94 H2 Butcombe N. Som., Eng.
22 F11 Bute i. Scot.
22 F11 Bute, Sound of sea chan. Scot.
350 G2 Bute Town Caerp., Wales
314 C1 Buthill Moray, Scot.
94 H4 Butleigh Som., Eng.
94 H4 Butleigh Wootton Som., Eng.
144 E3 Butlersbank Shrop., Eng.
106 D4 Butler's Cross Bucks., Eng.
106 E5 Butler's Cross Bucks., Eng.
176 B4 Butler's Hill Notts., Eng.
132 C5 Butlers Marston Warks., Eng.
120 H4 Butley Suff., Eng.
120 H4 Butley Abbey Suff., Eng.
120 H4 Butley Low Corner Suff., Eng.
120 H3 Butley Mills Suff., Eng.
184 G2 Butley Town Cheshire East, Eng.
52 D5 Butlocks Heath Hants., Eng.
232 G2 Butterburn Cumbria, Eng.
40 F2 Butterleigh Devon, Eng.
180 E4 Butterley Derbys., Eng.
402 F5 Butterlope Strabane, N. Ire.
232 C5 Buttermere Cumbria, Eng.
86 F3 Buttermere Wilts., Eng.
148 B2 Butters Green Staffs., Eng.
222 D2 Buttershaw W. Yorks., Eng.
304 I3 Butterstone Perth and Kin., Scot.
148 B3 Butterton Staffs., Eng.
148 D2 Butterton Staffs., Eng.
236 G4 Butterwick Durham, Eng.
170 G6 Butterwick Lincs., Eng.
216 H2 Butterwick N. Yorks., Eng.
184 E3 Butt Green Cheshire East, Eng.
366 G2 Buttington Powys, Wales
148 B2 Butt Lane Staffs., Eng.
22 D5 Butt of Lewis hd Scot.
144 F5 Buttonbridge Shrop., Eng.
144 F5 Buttonoak Shrop., Eng.
120 D4 Buttons' Green Suff., Eng.
52 D5 Buttsash Hants., Eng.
116 F3 Butt's Green Essex, Eng.
52 C4 Butt's Green Hants., Eng.
58 G3 Buxted E. Sussex, Eng.
180 B3 Buxton Derbys., Eng.
166 G2 Buxton Norf., Eng.
166 G2 Buxton Heath Norf., Eng.
180 B2 Buxworth Derbys., Eng.
Bwcle Flints., Wales see Buckley
366 F7 Bwlch Powys, Wales
356 D2 Bwlch-clawdd Carmar., Wales
372 E2 Bwlch-derwin Gwynedd, Wales
378 G3 Bwlchgwyn Wrex., Wales
362 F3 Bwlch-llan Cere., Wales
356 D2 Bwlchnewydd Carmar., Wales
372 C4 Bwlchtocyn Gwynedd, Wales
366 F2 Bwlch-y-cibau Powys, Wales
366 F2 Bwlch-y-ddar Powys, Wales
362 E4 Bwlchyfadfa Cere., Wales
366 E2 Bwlch-y-ffridd Powys, Wales
358 G2 Bwlch-y-groes Pembs., Wales
372 F2 Bwlchyllyn Gwynedd, Wales
350 B3 Bwlchymynydd Swansea, Wales
366 E4 Bwlch-y-sarnau Powys, Wales
350 E3 Byeastwood Bridg., Wales
106 D4 Bye Green Bucks., Eng.
236 E2 Byermoor T. and W., Eng.
236 F3 Byers Green Durham, Eng.
128 B4 Byfield Northants., Eng.
78 D1 Byfleet Surr., Eng.
140 B3 Byford Here., Eng.
110 E3 Bygrave Herts., Eng.
236 F2 Byker T. and W., Eng.
36 F2 Bylane End Corn., Eng.
378 D3 Bylchau Conwy, Wales
184 E2 Byley Cheshire West & Chester, Eng.
356 F3 Bynea Carmar., Wales
244 C4 Byrness Northumb., Eng.
40 F3 Bystock Devon, Eng.
124 B4 Bythorn Cambs., Eng.
140 B2 Byton Here., Eng.
244 F6 Bywell Northumb., Eng.
58 C3 Byworth W. Sussex, Eng.

C

26 E3 Caban Coch Reservoir resr Wales
170 E2 Cabourne Lincs., Eng.
170 E2 Cabourne Parva Lincs., Eng.
300 B4 Cabrach Arg. and B., Scot.
402 J2 Cabragh Cookstown, N. Ire.
402 I4 Cabragh Dungannon, N. Ire.
228 F3 Cabus Lancs., Eng.
58 G3 Cackle Street E. Sussex, Eng.
58 I3 Cackle Street E. Sussex, Eng.
58 J3 Cackle Street E. Sussex, Eng.
256 F4 Cacrabank Borders, Scot.
26 E2 Cadair Idris hills Wales
320 I4 Cadboll High., Scot.
40 F2 Cadbury Devon, Eng.
98 E5 Cadbury Heath S. Glos., Eng.
276 E2 Cadder E. Dun., Scot.
300 E2 Cadderlie Arg. and B., Scot.
110 C4 Caddington Central Bedfordshire, Eng.
300 D3 Caddleton Arg. and B., Scot.
256 G3 Caddonfoot Borders, Scot.
388 I4 Caddy Antrim, N. Ire.
162 C3 Cadeby Leics., Eng.
208 E3 Cadeby S. Yorks., Eng.
40 F2 Cadeleigh Devon, Eng.
378 E3 Cader Denb., Wales
Cader Idris hills Wales see Cadair Idris
36 D4 Cadgwith Corn., Eng.
292 F2 Cadham Fife, Scot.
198 C3 Cadishead Gtr Man., Eng.
228 F4 Cadley Lancs., Eng.
86 E3 Cadley Wilts., Eng.
106 C5 Cadmore End Bucks., Eng.
52 C5 Cadnam Hants., Eng.
170 D2 Cadney N. Lincs., Eng.
378 F3 Cadole Flints., Wales
350 G4 Cadoxton V. of Glam., Wales
350 D2 Cadoxton-Juxta-Neath N.P.T., Wales
110 D4 Cadwell Herts., Eng.
378 E4 Cadwst Denb., Wales
402 D3 Cady Fermanagh, N. Ire.
268 B2 Cadzow S. Lanark., Scot.
372 E2 Caeathro Gwynedd, Wales
372 F3 Cae Ddafydd Gwynedd, Wales
366 C8 Caehopkin Powys, Wales
170 D3 Caenby Lincs., Eng.
170 C3 Caenby Corner Lincs., Eng.
350 E3 Caerau Bridg., Wales
350 G4 Caerau Cardiff, Wales
372 F4 Caerdeon Gwynedd, Wales
Caerdydd Cardiff, Wales see Cardiff
378 G3 Caer-Estyn Flints., Wales
358 C2 Caerfarchell Pembs., Wales
371 B3 Caergeiliog I.o.A., Wales
378 G3 Caergwrle Flints., Wales
Caergybi I.o.A., Wales see Holyhead
378 B2 Caerhun Conwy, Wales
339 C3 Caerleon Newp., Wales
339 D2 Caer Llan Mon., Wales
372 E2 Caernarfon Gwynedd, Wales
26 C1 Caernarfon Bay b. Wales
350 G3 Caerphilly Caerp., Wales
350 G3 Caerphilly admin. div. Wales
366 E3 Caersws Powys, Wales
362 D3 Caerwedros Cere., Wales
339 D3 Caerwent Mon., Wales
378 F2 Caerwys Flints., Wales
372 F5 Caethle Farm Gwynedd, Wales
322 J3 Caggan High., Scot.
339 C1 Caggle Street Mon., Wales
388 G2 Caheny Coleraine, N. Ire.
388 I3 Caherty Ballymena, N. Ire.
371 E3 Caim I.o.A., Wales
356 G1 Caio Carmar., Wales
Cairinis W. Isles, Scot. see Carinish
326 D2 Cairisiadar W. Isles, Scot.
326 C3 Cairiminis W. Isles, Scot.
300 D3 Cairnbaan Arg. and B., Scot.
314 E3 Cairnbathie Abers., Scot.
314 G3 Cairnbrogie Abers., Scot.
308 F1 Cairncross Angus, Scot.
256 K1 Cairncross Borders, Scot.
276 B2 Cairncurran Inverclyde, Scot.
252 C3 Cairndoon D. and G., Scot.
300 F3 Cairndow Arg. and B., Scot.
314 H2 Cairness Abers., Scot.
292 C3 Cairneyhill Fife, Scot.
292 F1 Cairney Lodge Fife, Scot.
22 I8 Cairn Gorm mt. Scot.
22 I8 Cairngorm Mountains mts Scot.
22 I8 Cairngorms National Park nat. park Scot.
314 G2 Cairnhill Abers., Scot.
314 G3 Cairnie Abers., Scot.
314 G2 Cairnorrie Abers., Scot.
252 A3 Cairnryan D. and G., Scot.
252 C3 Cairnsmore D. and G., Scot.
22 H12 Cairnsmore of Carsphairn hill Scot.
22 H13 Cairnsmore of Fleet hill Scot.
22 I8 Cairn Toul mt. Scot.
22 F11 Caisteal Abhail hill Scot.
166 J3 Caister-on-Sea Norf., Eng.
170 E3 Caistor Lincs., Eng.
166 G3 Caistor St Edmund Norf., Eng.
244 E4 Caistron Northumb., Eng.
22 J6 Caithness reg. Scot.
136 D1 Cakebole Worcs., Eng.
166 F4 Cake Street Norf., Eng.
120 E4 Calais Street Suff., Eng.
Calanais W. Isles, Scot. see Callanish
326 E2 Calbost W. Isles, Scot.
52 D6 Calbourne I.o.W., Eng.
170 G4 Calceby Lincs., Eng.
378 F2 Calcoed Flints., Wales
98 H3 Calcot Glos., Eng.
82 D3 Calcot W. Berks., Eng.
62 G3 Calcott Kent, Eng.
144 D3 Calcott Shrop., Eng.
98 F2 Calcotts Green Glos., Eng.
86 D2 Calcutt Wilts., Eng.
388 H2 Caldanagh Ballymoney, N. Ire.
276 C1 Caldarvan W. Dun., Scot.
331 E1 Caldback Shet., Scot.
232 D4 Caldbeck Cumbria, Eng.
124 C4 Caldecote Cambs., Eng.
124 D5 Caldecote Cambs., Eng.
110 D3 Caldecote Herts., Eng.
128 D5 Caldecote Northants., Eng.
132 D2 Caldecote Warks., Eng.
128 F4 Caldecott Northants., Eng.
102 D5 Caldecott Oxon, Eng.
162 G3 Caldecott Rutland, Eng.
106 D2 Caldecotte M.K., Eng.
22 I5 Calder, Loch l. Scot.
280 C3 Calderbank N. Lanark., Scot.
232 B6 Calder Bridge Cumbria, Eng.
198 E2 Calderbrook Gtr Man., Eng.
280 C3 Caldercruix N. Lanark., Scot.
221 Calderdale met. bor. W. Yorks., Eng.
268 B2 Calderglen S. Lanark., Scot.
222 E3 Calder Grove W. Yorks., Eng.
268 B3 Caldermill S. Lanark., Scot.
190 D3 Calderstones Merseyside, Eng.
228 F3 Calder Vale Lancs., Eng.
268 B2 Calderwood S. Lanark., Scot.
24 L4 Caldew r. Eng.
26 C4 Caldey Island i. Wales
308 E3 Caldhame Angus, Scot.
339 D3 Caldicot Mon., Wales
180 D6 Caldwell Derbys., Eng.
216 D1 Caldwell N. Yorks., Eng.
276 C3 Caldwell E. Renf., Scot.
190 C3 Caldy Merseyside, Eng.
232 D4 Calebreck Cumbria, Eng.
402 I4 Caledon Dungannon, N. Ire.
Caledonia admin. div. see Scotland
362 E4 Caledrhydiau Cere., Wales
24 H5 Calf of Man i. Isle of Man
120 B4 Calford Green Suff., Eng.
329 E2 Calfsound Orkney, Scot.
300 B2 Calgary Arg. and B., Scot.
166 J2 California Norf., Eng.
120 G4 California Suff., Eng.
280 D3 California Falk., Scot.
180 E6 Calke Derbys., Eng.
402 F3 Calkill Omagh, N. Ire.
322 D2 Callakille High., Scot.
244 F3 Callaly Northumb., Eng.
24 D5 Callan r. N. Ire.
296 E4 Callander Stir., Scot.
326 D2 Callanish W. Isles, Scot.
144 E4 Callaughton Shrop., Eng.
236 E1 Callerton Lane End T. and W., Eng.
36 D3 Callestick Corn., Eng.
300 D5 Calliburn Arg. and B., Scot.
322 D3 Calligarry High., Scot.
36 G2 Callington Corn., Eng.
148 E4 Callingwood Staffs., Eng.
252 G2 Callisterhall D. and G., Scot.
140 C3 Callow Here., Eng.
98 F3 Callowell Glos., Eng.
136 D3 Callow End Worcs., Eng.
86 D2 Callow Hill Wilts., Eng.
136 C1 Callow Hill Worcs., Eng.
136 F2 Callow Hill Worcs., Eng.
136 B2 Callows Grave Worcs., Eng.
52 C5 Calmore Hants., Eng.
98 H3 Calmsden Glos., Eng.
86 C3 Calne Wilts., Eng.
180 E3 Calow Derbys., Eng.
52 E6 Calshot Hants., Eng.
36 G2 Calstock Corn., Eng.
86 D3 Calstone Wellington Wilts., Eng.
166 G1 Calthorpe Norf., Eng.
166 I2 Calthorpe Street Norf., Eng.
232 E4 Calthwaite Cumbria, Eng.
216 C2 Calton N. Yorks., Eng.
148 D2 Calton Staffs., Eng.
184 D3 Calveley Cheshire East, Eng.
180 D3 Calver Derbys., Eng.
144 E2 Calverhall Shrop., Eng.
140 C3 Calver Hill Here., Eng.
40 F2 Calverleigh Devon, Eng.
222 D2 Calverley W. Yorks., Eng.
106 C3 Calvert Bucks., Eng.
106 C2 Calverton M.K., Eng.
176 C4 Calverton Notts., Eng.
304 G2 Calvine Perth and Kin., Scot.
232 C3 Calvo Cumbria, Eng.
98 E3 Cam Glos., Eng.
388 F2 Cam Coleraine, N. Ire.
26 M3 Cam r. Eng.
396 D4 Camagh Armagh, N. Ire.
322 E5 Camasnacroise High., Scot.
322 C2 Camastianavaig High., Scot.
322 C3 Camasunary High., Scot.
322 H2 Camault Muir High., Scot.
331 D2 Camb Shet., Scot.
58 K3 Camber E. Sussex, Eng.
78 B1 Camberley Surr., Eng.
74 D3 Camberwell Gtr Lon., Eng.
216 F3 Camblesforth N. Yorks., Eng.
244 F4 Cambo Northumb., Eng.
244 H5 Cambois Northumb., Eng.
36 D3 Camborne Corn., Eng.
124 D5 Cambourne Cambs., Eng.
Cambria admin. div. see Wales
26 E2 Cambrian Mountains hills Wales
124 E5 Cambridge Cambs., Eng.
98 E3 Cambridge Glos., Eng.
124 F5 Cambridge City airport Eng.
124 D4 Cambridgeshire county Eng.
116 G4 Cambridge Town Southend, Eng.
292 A3 Cambus Clack., Scot.
296 G5 Cambusbarron Stir., Scot.
296 G5 Cambuskenneth Stir., Scot.
268 B2 Cambuslang S. Lanark., Scot.
280 C4 Cambusnethan N. Lanark., Scot.
314 E3 Cambus o'May Abers., Scot.
74 D2 Camden met. bor. Gtr Lon., Eng.
74 D2 Camden Town Gtr Lon., Eng.
94 I3 Cameley B. and N.E. Som., Eng.
36 E2 Camelford Corn., Eng.
94 I4 Camel Hill Som., Eng.
280 D2 Camelon Falk., Scot.
78 B3 Camelsdale Surr., Eng.
62 E2 Camer Kent, Eng.
276 C1 Cameron House W. Dun., Scot.
136 D3 Camer's Green Worcs., Eng.
94 J3 Camerton B. and N.E. Som., Eng.
232 B4 Camerton Cumbria, Eng.
210 H4 Camerton E. Riding, Eng.
304 D2 Camghouran Perth and Kin., Scot.
300 F4 Camis Eskan Arg. and B., Scot.
396 F4 Camlough Newry & Mourne, N. Ire.
314 G3 Cammachmore Abers., Scot.
170 C4 Cammeringham Lincs., Eng.
23 H3 Camowen r. N. Ire.
300 F5 Campbeltown Arg. and B., Scot.
300 C5 Campbeltown airport Scot.
236 F1 Camperdown T. and W., Eng.
132 C2 Camp Hill Warks., Eng.
358 F3 Camp Hill Pembs., Wales
304 K3 Campmuir Perth and Kin., Scot.
288 C3 Camps W. Lothian, Scot.
208 E2 Campsall S. Yorks., Eng.
120 H4 Campsea Ashe Suff., Eng.
124 G6 Camps End Cambs., Eng.
388 C2 Campsey Derry, N. Ire.
120 J2 Camps Heath Suff., Eng.
24 I1 Campsie Fells hills Scot.
110 C3 Campton Central Bedfordshire, Eng.
222 E1 Camp Town W. Yorks., Eng.
256 I4 Camptown Borders, Scot.
300 E3 Camquhart Arg. and B., Scot.
358 D2 Camrose Pembs., Wales
304 G3 Camserney Perth and Kin., Scot.
322 D3 Camus Croise High., Scot.
322 E3 Camus-luinie High., Scot.
322 E3 Camusrory High., Scot.
322 D2 Camusteel High., Scot.
322 D2 Camusterrach High., Scot.
296 E3 Camusurich Stir., Scot.
304 E3 Camusvrachan Perth and Kin., Scot.
52 C5 Canada Hants., Eng.
Canaich High., Scot. see Cannich
358 F3 Canaston Bridge Pembs., Wales
314 D3 Candacraig Abers., Scot.
170 H4 Candlesby Lincs., Eng.
268 F3 Candy Mill S. Lanark., Scot.
102 E5 Cane End Oxon, Eng.
116 G4 Canewdon Essex, Eng.
116 D2 Canfield End Essex, Eng.

Canford Bottom to Cheswick Green

46 H3 **Canford Bottom** *Dorset, Eng.*
46 H3 **Canford Cliffs** *Poole, Eng.*
46 H3 **Canford Magna** *Poole, Eng.*
166 H2 **Cangate** *Norf., Eng.*
120 F3 **Canham's Green** *Suff., Eng.*
320 K2 **Canisbay** *High., Scot.*
22 F6 **Canisp** *hill* Scot.
208 D3 **Canklow** *S. Yorks., Eng.*
154 E3 **Canley** *W. Mids, Eng.*
46 F2 **Cann** *Dorset, Eng.*
22 C8 **Canna** *i.* Scot.
22 D8 **Canna, Sound of** *sea chan.* Scot.
94 I3 **Cannard's Grave** *Som., Eng.*
46 G2 **Cann Common** *Dorset, Eng.*
322 G2 **Cannich** *High., Scot.*
94 F4 **Cannington** *Som., Eng.*
74 E2 **Canning Town** *Gtr Lon., Eng.*
148 C4 **Cannock** *Staffs., Eng.*
26 H2 **Cannock Chase** *reg.* Eng.
148 D4 **Cannock Wood** *Staffs., Eng.*
98 D3 **Cannop** *Glos., Eng.*
252 H2 **Canonbie** *D. and G., Scot.*
140 C3 **Canon Bridge** *Here., Eng.*
74 D2 **Canonbury** *Gtr Lon., Eng.*
140 D3 **Canon Frome** *Here., Eng.*
140 C3 **Canon Pyon** *Here., Eng.*
128 C5 **Canons Ashby** *Northants., Eng.*
36 C3 **Canon's Town** *Corn., Eng.*
62 G3 **Canterbury** *Kent, Eng.*
314 E2 **Canterbury** *Abers., Scot.*
166 I3 **Cantley** *Norf., Eng.*
208 F2 **Cantley** *S. Yorks., Eng.*
144 D4 **Cantlop** *Shrop., Eng.*
350 G4 **Canton** *Cardiff, Wales*
322 I2 **Cantray** *High., Scot.*
322 I2 **Cantraydoune** *High., Scot.*
228 G2 **Cantsfield** *Lancs., Eng.*
116 F4 **Canvey Island** *Essex, Eng.*
148 E5 **Canwell Hall** *Staffs., Eng.*
170 C4 **Canwick** *Lincs., Eng.*
36 F1 **Canworthy Water** *Corn., Eng.*
322 F4 **Caol** *High., Scot.*
Caol Acain *High., Scot. see* **Kyleakin**
300 □ **Caolas** *Arg. and B., Scot.*
322 F4 **Caolasnacon** *High., Scot.*
326 B4 **Caolas-Phaibel** *W. Isles, Scot.*
Caolas Scalpaigh *W. Isles, Scot. see* **Kyles Scalpay**
22 E11 **Caolisport, Loch** *inlet* Scot.
Caol Loch Aillse *High., Scot. see* **Kyle of Lochalsh**
62 C3 **Capel** *Kent, Eng.*
78 E3 **Capel** *Surr., Eng.*
362 G2 **Capel Bangor** *Cere., Wales*
362 F3 **Capel Betws Lleucu** *Cere., Wales*
372 B4 **Capel Carmel** *Gwynedd, Wales*
372 H3 **Capel Celyn** *Gwynedd, Wales*
371 D3 **Capel Coch** *I.o.A., Wales*
378 B3 **Capel Curig** *Conwy, Wales*
362 D4 **Capel Cynon** *Cere., Wales*
356 E2 **Capel Dewi** *Carmar., Wales*
362 E4 **Capel Dewi** *Cere., Wales*
362 F2 **Capel Dewi** *Cere., Wales*
378 C3 **Capel Garmon** *Conwy, Wales*
356 E2 **Capel Gwyn** *Carmar., Wales*
371 C3 **Capel Gwyn** *I.o.A., Wales*
356 G2 **Capel Gwynfe** *Carmar., Wales*
356 F3 **Capel Hendre** *Carmar., Wales*
356 F2 **Capel Isaac** *Carmar., Wales*
356 D2 **Capel Iwan** *Carmar., Wales*
62 H4 **Capel le Ferne** *Kent, Eng.*
350 G3 **Capel Llanilltern** *Cardiff, Wales*
371 C3 **Capel Mawr** *I.o.A., Wales*
371 C2 **Capel Parc** *I.o.A., Wales*
120 F4 **Capel St Mary** *Suff., Eng.*
362 F2 **Capel Seion** *Cere., Wales*
120 H4 **Capel St Andrew** *Suff., Eng.*
362 E4 **Capel St Silin** *Cere., Wales*
362 C4 **Capel Tygwydd** *Cere., Wales*
372 D2 **Capeluchaf** *Gwynedd, Wales*
378 B2 **Capelulo** *Conwy, Wales*
366 G7 **Capel-y-ffin** *Powys, Wales*
372 E1 **Capel-y-graig** *Gwynedd, Wales*
184 B2 **Capenhurst** *Cheshire West & Chester, Eng.*
228 F2 **Capernwray** *Lancs., Eng.*
244 F5 **Capheaton** *Northumb., Eng.*
276 D3 **Caplaw** *E. Renf., Scot.*
120 H3 **Capon's Green** *Suff., Eng.*
396 G4 **Cappagh** *Banbridge, N. Ire.*
402 I3 **Cappagh** *Dungannon, N. Ire.*
256 E4 **Cappercleuch** *Borders, Scot.*
252 F1 **Capplegill** *D. and G., Scot.*
62 D2 **Capstone** *Medway, Eng.*
40 F3 **Capton** *Devon, Eng.*
94 E4 **Capton** *Som., Eng.*
304 J3 **Caputh** *Perth and Kin., Scot.*
23 K1 **Cara Island** *i.* Scot.
262 F4 **Carbellow** *E. Ayr., Scot.*
296 D6 **Carbeth** *Stir., Scot.*
322 B3 **Carbost** *High., Scot.*
322 C2 **Carbost** *High., Scot.*
280 C3 **Carbrain** *N. Lanark., Scot.*
208 D3 **Carbrook** *S. Yorks., Eng.*
166 E3 **Carbrooke** *Norf., Eng.*
176 C3 **Carburton** *Notts., Eng.*
308 G2 **Carcary** *Angus, Scot.*
36 D3 **Carclew** *Corn., Eng.*
388 H3 **Carclunty** *Ballymena, N. Ire.*
252 E1 **Carco** *D. and G., Scot.*
176 D5 **Car Colston** *Notts., Eng.*
208 E2 **Carcroft** *S. Yorks., Eng.*
292 E3 **Cardenden** *Fife, Scot.*
144 C3 **Cardeston** *Shrop., Eng.*
232 D3 **Cardew** *Cumbria, Eng.*
350 G4 **Cardiff** *Cardiff, Wales*
110 C3 **Cardiff** *admin. div.* Wales
350 F4 **Cardiff International** *airport* Wales
362 C4 **Cardigan** *Cere., Wales*
26 C2 **Cardigan Bay** *b.* Wales
124 G6 **Cardinal's Green** *Cambs., Eng.*
110 C3 **Cardington** *Bedford, Eng.*
144 D4 **Cardington** *Shrop., Eng.*
36 F2 **Cardinham** *Corn., Eng.*
276 D2 **Cardonald** *Glas., Scot.*
252 D3 **Cardoness** *D. and G., Scot.*
314 C2 **Cardow** *Moray, Scot.*
256 F3 **Cardrona** *Borders, Scot.*
300 G4 **Cardross** *Arg. and B., Scot.*
232 C3 **Cardurnock** *Cumbria, Eng.*
396 K2 **Cardy** *Ards, N. Ire.*
170 D7 **Careby** *Lincs., Eng.*
308 F2 **Careston** *Angus, Scot.*
358 F3 **Carew** *Pembs., Wales*
358 F3 **Carew Cheriton** *Pembs., Wales*
358 F3 **Carew Newton** *Pembs., Wales*
140 D4 **Carey** *Here., Eng.*
280 C4 **Carfin** *N. Lanark., Scot.*
288 G3 **Carfrae** *E. Lothian, Scot.*
256 H2 **Carfraemill** *Borders, Scot.*
388 I3 **Cargan** *Ballymena, N. Ire.*
166 I3 **Cargate Green** *Norf., Eng.*
252 F2 **Cargen** *D. and G., Scot.*
252 F2 **Cargenbridge** *D. and G., Scot.*
304 J3 **Cargill** *Perth and Kin., Scot.*
232 E3 **Cargo** *Cumbria, Eng.*
36 G2 **Cargreen** *Corn., Eng.*
244 D2 **Carham** *Northumb., Eng.*
94 D3 **Carhampton** *Som., Eng.*
36 D3 **Carharrack** *Corn., Eng.*
304 E2 **Carie** *Perth and Kin., Scot.*
304 E3 **Carie** *Perth and Kin., Scot.*
326 C4 **Carinish** *W. Isles, Scot.*
52 E6 **Carisbrooke** *I.o.W., Eng.*
232 E7 **Cark** *Cumbria, Eng.*
Càrlabhagh *W. Isles, Scot. see* **Carloway**
402 J3 **Carland** *Dungannon, N. Ire.*
36 D2 **Carland Cross** *Corn., Eng.*
388 H4 **Carlane** *Antrim, N. Ire.*
232 F3 **Carlatton** *Cumbria, Eng.*
236 E4 **Carlbury** *Darl., Eng.*
170 D7 **Carlby** *Lincs., Eng.*
208 B2 **Carlecotes** *S. Yorks., Eng.*
36 D3 **Carleen** *Corn., Eng.*
232 E3 **Carleton** *Cumbria, Eng.*
232 F5 **Carleton** *Cumbria, Eng.*
228 D3 **Carleton** *Lancs., Eng.*
216 C3 **Carleton** *N. Yorks., Eng.*
222 G2 **Carleton** *W. Yorks., Eng.*
262 B6 **Carleton Fishery** *S. Ayr., Scot.*
166 F3 **Carleton Forehoe** *Norf., Eng.*
166 F4 **Carleton Rode** *Norf., Eng.*
166 H3 **Carleton St Peter** *Norf., Eng.*
94 J3 **Carlingcott** *B. and N.E. Som., Eng.*
23 J4 **Carlingford Lough** *inlet* Ireland/U.K.
216 G1 **Carlin How** *R. and C., Eng.*
232 E3 **Carlisle** *Cumbria, Eng.*
256 D2 **Carlops** *Borders, Scot.*
326 D2 **Carloway** *W. Isles, Scot.*
110 B2 **Carlton** *Bedford, Eng.*
124 G6 **Carlton** *Cambs., Eng.*
162 C3 **Carlton** *Leics., Eng.*
176 C5 **Carlton** *Notts., Eng.*
216 D2 **Carlton** *N. Yorks., Eng.*
216 F2 **Carlton** *N. Yorks., Eng.*
216 F3 **Carlton** *N. Yorks., Eng.*
236 G4 **Carlton** *Stockton, Eng.*
120 H3 **Carlton** *Suff., Eng.*
208 D2 **Carlton** *S. Yorks., Eng.*
222 F2 **Carlton** *W. Yorks., Eng.*
120 J2 **Carlton Colville** *Suff., Eng.*
162 F3 **Carlton Curlieu** *Leics., Eng.*
124 G6 **Carlton Green** *Cambs., Eng.*
216 F1 **Carlton-in-Cleveland** *N. Yorks., Eng.*
176 C2 **Carlton in Lindrick** *Notts., Eng.*
170 C5 **Carlton-le-Moorland** *Lincs., Eng.*
216 E2 **Carlton Miniott** *N. Yorks., Eng.*
176 E3 **Carlton-on-Trent** *Notts., Eng.*
170 C6 **Carlton Scroop** *Lincs., Eng.*
268 C2 **Carluke** *S. Lanark., Scot.*
36 E2 **Carlyon Bay** *Corn., Eng.*
268 C3 **Carmacoup** *S. Lanark., Scot.*
26 C4 **Carmarthen Bay** *b.* Wales
356 E2 **Carmarthenshire** *county* Wales
356 F3 **Carmel** *Carmar., Wales*
378 F2 **Carmel** *Flints., Wales*
372 E2 **Carmel** *Gwynedd, Wales*
371 C3 **Carmel** *I.o.A., Wales*
26 C1 **Carmel Head** *hd* Wales
268 D3 **Carmichael** *S. Lanark., Scot.*
314 G4 **Carmont** *Abers., Scot.*
276 E3 **Carmunnock** *Glas., Scot.*
276 F3 **Carmyle** *Glas., Scot.*
308 F3 **Carmyllie** *Angus, Scot.*
388 E3 **Carn** *Limavady, N. Ire.*
210 G2 **Carnaby** *E. Riding, Eng.*
322 F3 **Carnach** *High., Scot.*
22 G8 **Carn a' Chuilinn** *hill* Scot.
396 D4 **Carnagh** *Armagh, N. Ire.*
388 F2 **Carnalbanagh** *Coleraine, N. Ire.*
402 G3 **Carnalea** *Omagh, N. Ire.*
388 F4 **Carnamoney** *Magherafelt, N. Ire.*
402 H1 **Carnanreagh** *Strabane, N. Ire.*
300 D3 **Carnassarie** *Arg. and B., Scot.*
402 K2 **Carnaugh** *Cookstown, N. Ire.*
396 F4 **Carnbane** *Newry & Mourne, N. Ire.*
292 H2 **Carnbee** *Fife, Scot.*
388 I3 **Carnbeg** *Ballymena, N. Ire.*
304 I5 **Carnbo** *Perth and Kin., Scot.*
36 D3 **Carn Brea Village** *Corn., Eng.*
388 K3 **Carncastle** *Larne, N. Ire.*
22 G7 **Carn Chuinneag** *hill* Scot.
320 C4 **Carn Dearg** *High., Scot.*
22 G8 **Carn Dearg** *hill* Scot.
22 H8 **Carn Dearg** *hill* Scot.
388 I1 **Carnduff** *Moyle, N. Ire.*
36 E3 **Carne** *Corn., Eng.*
22 J8 **Carn Ealasaid** *hill* Scot.
388 I1 **Carneatly** *Moyle, N. Ire.*
26 E1 **Carnedd Llywelyn** *mt.* Wales
26 E2 **Carnedd y Filiast** *hill* Wales
22 F8 **Carn Eige** *mt.* Scot.
22 I8 **Carne na Loine** *hill* Scot.
22 K8 **Carnferg** *hill* Scot.
228 F2 **Carnforth** *Lancs., Eng.*
350 C3 **Carnglas** *Swansea, Wales*
22 I8 **Carn Glas-choire** *hill* Scot.
358 C2 **Carnhedryn** *Pembs., Wales*
36 C3 **Carnhell Green** *Corn., Eng.*
314 G2 **Carnichal** *Abers., Scot.*
36 D3 **Carnkie** *Corn., Eng.*
36 D3 **Carnkie** *Corn., Eng.*
388 K3 **Carnlough** *Larne, N. Ire.*
23 K2 **Carnlough Bay** *b.* N. Ire.
388 K4 **Carnmoney** *Newtownabbey, N. Ire.*
22 J8 **Carn Mòr** *hill* Scot.
300 B5 **Carnmore** *Arg. and B., Scot.*
366 D3 **Carno** *Powys, Wales*
322 G2 **Carnoch** *High., Scot.*
322 G2 **Carnoch** *High., Scot.*
322 J2 **Carnoch** *High., Scot.*
292 C3 **Carnock** *Fife, Scot.*
22 H8 **Carn Odhar** *hill* Scot.
36 D3 **Carnon Downs** *Corn., Eng.*
314 F2 **Carnousie** *Abers., Scot.*
308 F3 **Carnoustie** *Angus, Scot.*
402 I4 **Carnteel** *Dungannon, N. Ire.*
276 E2 **Carntyne** *Glas., Scot.*
276 E3 **Carnwadric** *Glas., Scot.*
268 E2 **Carnwath** *S. Lanark., Scot.*
36 B3 **Carnyorth** *Corn., Eng.*
154 E3 **Carol Green** *W. Mids, Eng.*
216 D2 **Carperby** *N. Yorks., Eng.*
208 E3 **Carr** *S. Yorks., Eng.*
300 D5 **Carradale** *Arg. and B., Scot.*
322 J3 **Carrbridge** *High., Scot.*
228 E5 **Carr Cross** *Lancs., Eng.*
408 E4 **Carrefour Selous** *Jersey* Channel Is
371 C2 **Carreg-lefn** *I.o.A., Wales*
358 G1 **Carreg-wen** *Pembs., Wales*
222 E2 **Carr Gate** *W. Yorks., Eng.*
176 D2 **Carr Hill** *Notts., Eng.*
170 B2 **Carrhouse** *N. Lincs., Eng.*
190 C2 **Carr Houses** *Merseyside, Eng.*
402 E3 **Carrick** *Omagh, N. Ire.*
300 D3 **Carrick** *Arg. and B., Scot.*
22 G12 **Carrick** *reg.* Scot.
396 F4 **Carrickbrack** *Armagh, N. Ire.*
300 F3 **Carrick Castle** *Arg. and B., Scot.*
388 L4 **Carrickfergus** *Carrickfergus, N. Ire.*
388 L4 **Carrickfergus** *admin. dist.* N. Ire.
388 L4 **Carrickfergus Museum** *Carrickfergus, N. Ire.*
396 F4 **Carrickgallogly** *Newry & Mourne, N. Ire.*
402 H3 **Carrickmore** *Omagh, N. Ire.*
280 C3 **Carrickstone** *N. Lanark., Scot.*
402 F5 **Carrickyheenan** *Fermanagh, N. Ire.*
280 E2 **Carriden** *Falk., Scot.*
402 G2 **Carrigans** *Omagh, N. Ire.*
396 I5 **Carrigenagh** *Newry & Mourne, N. Ire.*
300 C6 **Carrine** *Arg. and B., Scot.*
198 C3 **Carrington** *Gtr Man., Eng.*
170 F5 **Carrington** *Lincs., Eng.*
176 C5 **Carrington** *Nott., Eng.*
288 E3 **Carrington** *Midlothian, Scot.*
252 D2 **Carroch** *D. and G., Scot.*
378 B3 **Carrog** *Conwy, Wales*
378 F4 **Carrog** *Denb., Wales*
304 F4 **Carroglen** *Perth and Kin., Scot.*
396 G5 **Carrogs** *Newry & Mourne, N. Ire.*
300 E3 **Carron** *Arg. and B., Scot.*
280 D2 **Carron** *Falk., Scot.*
314 D2 **Carron** *Moray, Scot.*
22 H7 **Carron** *r.* Scot.
22 E8 **Carron, Loch** *inlet* Scot.
252 E2 **Carronbridge** *D. and G., Scot.*
280 B2 **Carron Bridge** *Falk., Scot.*
280 D2 **Carronshore** *Falk., Scot.*
308 E3 **Carrot** *Angus, Scot.*
388 I2 **Carrowcrin** *Ballymoney, N. Ire.*
396 K2 **Carrowdore** *Ards, N. Ire.*
339 D3 **Carrow Hill** *Mon., Wales*
244 D7 **Carr Shield** *Northumb., Eng.*
252 F2 **Carrutherstown** *D. and G., Scot.*
276 C2 **Carruthmuir** *Inverclyde, Scot.*
180 F3 **Carr Vale** *Derbys., Eng.*
236 F3 **Carrville** *Durham, Eng.*
300 E4 **Carry** *Arg. and B., Scot.*
396 I2 **Carryduff** *Castlereagh, N. Ire.*
300 C3 **Carsaig** *Arg. and B., Scot.*
252 B3 **Carscreugh** *D. and G., Scot.*
300 D4 **Carse** *Arg. and B., Scot.*
252 C3 **Carsegowan** *D. and G., Scot.*
252 C3 **Carseriggan** *D. and G., Scot.*
252 F3 **Carsethorn** *D. and G., Scot.*
320 J2 **Carsgoe** *High., Scot.*
74 D3 **Carshalton** *Gtr Lon., Eng.*
74 C3 **Carshalton Beeches** *Gtr Lon., Eng.*
74 D3 **Carshalton on the Hill** *Gtr Lon., Eng.*
304 J3 **Carsie** *Perth and Kin., Scot.*
180 D4 **Carsington** *Derbys., Eng.*
24 N7 **Carsington Water** *resr* Eng.
252 C3 **Carsluith** *D. and G., Scot.*
252 D2 **Carsphairn** *D. and G., Scot.*
268 D2 **Carstairs** *S. Lanark., Scot.*
268 E2 **Carstairs Junction** *S. Lanark., Scot.*
102 B4 **Carswell Marsh** *Oxon, Eng.*
52 C4 **Carter's Clay** *Hants., Eng.*
102 B4 **Carterton** *Oxon, Eng.*
244 F6 **Carterway Heads** *Northumb., Eng.*
36 E2 **Carthew** *Corn., Eng.*
216 E2 **Carthorpe** *N. Yorks., Eng.*
244 F3 **Cartington** *Northumb., Eng.*
268 D2 **Cartland** *S. Lanark., Scot.*
180 D3 **Cartledge** *Derbys., Eng.*
232 E7 **Cartmel** *Cumbria, Eng.*
232 E7 **Cartmel Fell** *Cumbria, Eng.*
222 D3 **Cartworth** *W. Yorks., Eng.*
356 E3 **Carway** *Carmar., Wales*
366 G5 **Cascob** *Powys, Wales*
Cas-gwent *Mon., Wales see* **Chepstow**
296 C5 **Cashel Farm** *Stir., Scot.*
388 H3 **Casheltown** *Ballymena, N. Ire.*
304 D3 **Cashlie** *Perth and Kin., Scot.*
46 G2 **Cashmoor** *Dorset, Eng.*
402 F2 **Cashty** *Strabane, N. Ire.*
292 E2 **Caskieberran** *Fife, Scot.*
396 G4 **Caskum** *Banbridge, N. Ire.*
Casnewydd *Newp., Wales see* **Newport**
402 H2 **Casorna** *Omagh, N. Ire.*
252 C3 **Cassencarie** *D. and G., Scot.*
102 C4 **Cassington** *Oxon, Eng.*
22 G7 **Cassley** *r.* Scot.
236 G3 **Cassop** *Durham, Eng.*
378 B2 **Castell** *Conwy, Wales*
350 F3 **Castellau** *R.C.T., Wales*
356 C2 **Castell Gorfod** *Carmar., Wales*
362 E4 **Castell Howell** *Cere., Wales*
Castell Newydd Emlyn *Cere., Wales see* **Newcastle Emlyn**
350 H3 **Castell-y-bwch** *B. Gwent, Wales*
232 G7 **Casterton** *Cumbria, Eng.*
166 D2 **Castle Acre** *Norf., Eng.*
128 E4 **Castle Ashby** *Northants., Eng.*
148 C4 **Castle Bank** *Staffs., Eng.*
326 B6 **Castlebay** *W. Isles, Scot.*
216 D2 **Castle Bolton** *N. Yorks., Eng.*
154 D2 **Castle Bromwich** *W. Mids, Eng.*
170 C7 **Castle Bytham** *Lincs., Eng.*
358 E2 **Castlebythe** *Pembs., Wales*
366 F3 **Castle Caereinion** *Powys, Wales*
124 G6 **Castle Camps** *Cambs., Eng.*
232 F3 **Castle Carrock** *Cumbria, Eng.*
94 I4 **Castle Cary** *Som., Eng.*
280 C3 **Castlecary** *N. Lanark., Scot.*
402 I3 **Castlecaulfield** *Dungannon, N. Ire.*
86 B3 **Castle Combe** *Wilts., Eng.*
256 D2 **Castlecraig** *Borders, Scot.*
320 I4 **Castlecraig** *High., Scot.*
148 B5 **Castlecroft** *Staffs., Eng.*
388 G4 **Castledawson** *Magherafelt, N. Ire.*
402 E2 **Castlederg** *Strabane, N. Ire.*
162 C1 **Castle Donington** *Leics., Eng.*
252 E3 **Castle Douglas** *D. and G., Scot.*
86 E2 **Castle Eaton** *Swindon, Eng.*
236 G3 **Castle Eden** *Durham, Eng.*
132 C3 **Castle End** *Warks., Eng.*
252 E2 **Castlefairn** *D. and G., Scot.*
222 F2 **Castleford** *W. Yorks., Eng.*
140 E3 **Castle Frome** *Here., Eng.*
36 C3 **Castle Gate** *Corn., Eng.*
58 D3 **Castle Goring** *W. Sussex, Eng.*
78 C1 **Castle Green** *Surr., Eng.*
180 D6 **Castle Gresley** *Derbys., Eng.*
276 D2 **Castlehead** *Renf., Scot.*
244 E1 **Castle Heaton** *Northumb., Eng.*
116 F2 **Castle Hedingham** *Essex, Eng.*
62 C4 **Castle Hill** *Kent, Eng.*
120 F4 **Castle Hill** *Suff., Eng.*
252 B3 **Castle Kennedy** *D. and G., Scot.*
322 H2 **Castle Leod** *High., Scot.*
276 A2 **Castle Levan** *Inverclyde, Scot.*
366 E6 **Castle Madoc** *Powys, Wales*
358 D4 **Castlemartin** *Pembs., Wales*
252 G2 **Castlemilk** *D. and G., Scot.*
276 E3 **Castlemilk** *Glas., Scot.*
358 D2 **Castle Morris** *Pembs., Wales*
136 D3 **Castlemorton** *Worcs., Eng.*
252 G2 **Castle O'er** *D. and G., Scot.*
396 I2 **Castlereagh** *Castlereagh, N. Ire.*
396 I2 **Castlereagh** *admin. dist.* N. Ire.
232 D5 **Castlerigg** *Cumbria, Eng.*
166 B2 **Castle Rising** *Norf., Eng.*
388 F2 **Castlerock** *Coleraine, N. Ire.*
388 G2 **Castleroe** *Coleraine, N. Ire.*
236 D2 **Castleside** *Durham, Eng.*
232 F3 **Castlesteads** *Cumbria, Eng.*
322 I2 **Castle Stuart** *High., Scot.*
106 D2 **Castlethorpe** *M.K., Eng.*
180 C2 **Castleton** *Derbys., Eng.*
198 D2 **Castleton** *Gtr Man., Eng.*
216 G1 **Castleton** *N. Yorks., Eng.*
314 F2 **Castleton** *Abers., Scot.*
308 D3 **Castleton** *Angus, Scot.*
256 H5 **Castleton** *Borders, Scot.*
339 B3 **Castleton** *Newp., Wales*
405 C3 **Castletown** Isle of Man
46 E4 **Castletown** *Dorset, Eng.*
148 C4 **Castletown** *Staffs., Eng.*
236 G2 **Castletown** *T. and W., Eng.*
320 J2 **Castletown** *High., Scot.*
322 I2 **Castletown** *High., Scot.*
154 D2 **Castle Vale** *W. Mids, Eng.*
256 G5 **Castleweary** *Borders, Scot.*
396 I4 **Castlewellan** *Down, N. Ire.*
252 C3 **Castlewigg** *D. and G., Scot.*
216 E3 **Castley** *N. Yorks., Eng.*
166 E3 **Caston** *Norf., Eng.*
124 B3 **Castor** *Peterb., Eng.*
252 D3 **Castramont** *D. and G., Scot.*
350 B3 **Caswell** *Swansea, Wales*
264 C2 **Catacol** *N. Ayr., Scot.*
98 D4 **Catbrain** *S. Glos., Eng.*
339 D2 **Catbrook** *Mon., Wales*
154 E3 **Catchems Corner** *W. Mids, Eng.*
136 D1 **Catchems End** *Worcs., Eng.*
236 E2 **Catchgate** *Durham, Eng.*
244 C4 **Catcleugh** *Northumb., Eng.*
208 D3 **Catcliffe** *S. Yorks., Eng.*
94 G4 **Catcott** *Som., Eng.*
78 F2 **Caterham** *Surr., Eng.*
128 B4 **Catesby** *Northants., Eng.*
166 I2 **Catfield** *Norf., Eng.*
166 I2 **Catfield Common** *Norf., Eng.*
331 D3 **Catfirth** *Shet., Scot.*
74 D3 **Catford** *Gtr Lon., Eng.*
228 F4 **Catforth** *Lancs., Eng.*
350 G4 **Cathays** *Cardiff, Wales*
276 E3 **Cathcart** *Glas., Scot.*
366 F7 **Cathedine** *Powys, Wales*
154 D3 **Catherine-de-Barnes** *W. Mids, Eng.*
52 F5 **Catherington** *Hants., Eng.*
46 B3 **Catherston Leweston** *Dorset, Eng.*
144 E5 **Catherton** *Shrop., Eng.*
208 C2 **Cat Hill** *S. Yorks., Eng.*
268 A2 **Cathkin** *S. Lanark., Scot.*
52 E5 **Catisfield** *Hants., Eng.*
322 I3 **Catlodge** *High., Scot.*
228 I4 **Catlow** *Lancs., Eng.*
232 E2 **Catlowdy** *Cumbria, Eng.*
116 D1 **Catmere End** *Essex, Eng.*
82 B2 **Catmore** *W. Berks., Eng.*
40 E3 **Caton** *Devon, Eng.*
228 F2 **Caton** *Lancs., Eng.*
228 F2 **Caton Green** *Lancs., Eng.*
40 E3 **Cator Court** *Devon, Eng.*
262 F3 **Catrine** *E. Ayr., Scot.*
58 I3 **Catsfield** *E. Sussex, Eng.*
58 I3 **Catsfield Stream** *E. Sussex, Eng.*
94 I4 **Catsham** *Som., Eng.*
208 B2 **Catshaw** *S. Yorks., Eng.*
154 C2 **Catshill** *W. Mids, Eng.*
136 E1 **Catshill** *Worcs., Eng.*
300 B4 **Cattadale** *Arg. and B., Scot.*
216 F3 **Cattal** *N. Yorks., Eng.*
120 F5 **Cattawade** *Suff., Eng.*
40 D3 **Cattedown** *Plymouth, Eng.*
228 F3 **Catterall** *Lancs., Eng.*
216 E1 **Catterick** *N. Yorks., Eng.*
216 E1 **Catterick Bridge** *N. Yorks., Eng.*
216 D1 **Catterick Garrison** *N. Yorks., Eng.*
232 F4 **Catterlen** *Cumbria, Eng.*
314 G4 **Catterline** *Abers., Scot.*
216 F3 **Catterton** *N. Yorks., Eng.*
78 C2 **Catteshall** *Surr., Eng.*
162 D4 **Catthorpe** *Leics., Eng.*
120 D3 **Cattishall** *Suff., Eng.*
46 D3 **Cattistock** *Dorset, Eng.*
128 C5 **Cattle End** *Northants., Eng.*
166 G3 **Catton** *Norf., Eng.*
244 D6 **Catton** *Northumb., Eng.*
216 E2 **Catton** *N. Yorks., Eng.*
180 C6 **Catton Hall** *Derbys., Eng.*
210 G3 **Catwick** *E. Riding, Eng.*
124 B4 **Catworth** *Cambs., Eng.*
98 G3 **Caudle Green** *Glos., Eng.*
110 B3 **Caulcott** *Central Bedfordshire, Eng.*
102 D3 **Caulcott** *Oxon, Eng.*
308 G3 **Cauldcots** *Angus, Scot.*
296 E5 **Cauldhame** *Stir., Scot.*
296 G4 **Cauldhame** *Stir., Scot.*
148 D2 **Cauldon** *Staffs., Eng.*
388 G3 **Caulhame** *Coleraine, N. Ire.*
252 E3 **Caulkerbush** *D. and G., Scot.*
252 H2 **Caulside** *D. and G., Scot.*
46 E2 **Caundle Marsh** *Dorset, Eng.*
136 D1 **Caunsall** *Worcs., Eng.*
176 D4 **Caunton** *Notts., Eng.*
116 E2 **Causeway End** *Essex, Eng.*
228 F5 **Causeway End** *Lancs., Eng.*
252 C3 **Causeway End** *D. and G., Scot.*
154 B3 **Causeway Green** *W. Mids, Eng.*
232 B3 **Causewayhead** *Cumbria, Eng.*
388 G1 **Causeway Head** *Moyle, N. Ire.*
296 G5 **Causewayhead** *Stir., Scot.*
120 E4 **Causeway House Farm** *Suff., Eng.*
388 G1 **Causeway School Museum** *Moyle, N. Ire.*
236 E2 **Causey** *Durham, Eng.*
244 G4 **Causey Park** *Northumb., Eng.*
232 H6 **Cautley** *Cumbria, Eng.*
402 F3 **Cavan** *Omagh, N. Ire.*
402 E4 **Cavanacross** *Fermanagh, N. Ire.*
120 C4 **Cavendish** *Suff., Eng.*
162 C1 **Cavendish Bridge** *Leics., Eng.*
120 C3 **Cavenham** *Suff., Eng.*
252 F3 **Cavens** *D. and G., Scot.*
256 H4 **Cavers** *Borders, Scot.*
102 E3 **Caversfield** *Oxon, Eng.*
82 E3 **Caversham** *Reading, Eng.*
148 C3 **Caverswall** *Staffs., Eng.*
210 C4 **Cavil** *E. Riding, Eng.*
322 J2 **Cawdor** *High., Scot.*
210 F3 **Cawkeld** *E. Riding, Eng.*
170 F4 **Cawkwell** *Lincs., Eng.*
216 F3 **Cawood** *N. Yorks., Eng.*
166 F2 **Cawston** *Norf., Eng.*
132 E3 **Cawston** *Warks., Eng.*
208 C2 **Cawthorne** *S. Yorks., Eng.*
170 D7 **Cawthorpe** *Lincs., Eng.*
124 D5 **Caxton** *Cambs., Eng.*
124 D5 **Caxton End** *Cambs., Eng.*
124 D5 **Caxton Gibbet** *Cambs., Eng.*
144 E5 **Caynham** *Shrop., Eng.*
170 C5 **Caythorpe** *Lincs., Eng.*
176 D4 **Caythorpe** *Notts., Eng.*
216 H2 **Cayton** *N. Yorks., Eng.*
326 C4 **Ceallan** *W. Isles, Scot.*
326 B4 **Ceann a' Bhàigh** *W. Isles, Scot.*
326 D3 **Ceann a' Bhàigh** *W. Isles, Scot.*
Ceann Loch *High., Scot. see* **Lochend**
Ceann Loch Ailleart *High., Scot. see* **Lochailort**
Ceann Loch Èireann *Stir., Scot. see* **Lochearnhead**
Ceann Loch Gilb *Arg. and B., Scot. see* **Lochgilphead**
Ceann Loch Lìobhann *High., Scot. see* **Kinlochleven**
Ceann Lochroag *W. Isles, Scot. see* **Kinlochroag**
326 E2 **Ceann Loch Shiphoirt** *W. Isles, Scot.*
Ceann Loch Shubhairne *High., Scot. see* **Kinloch Hourn**
326 E2 **Cearsiadar** *W. Isles, Scot.*
366 E2 **Cedig** *Powys, Wales*
378 D2 **Cefn Berain** *Conwy, Wales*
378 D3 **Cefn-brith** *Conwy, Wales*
372 D3 **Cefn-caer-Ferch** *Gwynedd, Wales*
366 G1 **Cefn Canol** *Powys, Wales*
366 E7 **Cefn Cantref** *Powys, Wales*
378 F3 **Cefn Coch** *Denb., Wales*
366 F2 **Cefn-coch** *Powys, Wales*
350 F2 **Cefn-coed-y-cymmer** *M. Tyd., Wales*
339 B2 **Cefn-crib** *Torf., Wales*
350 E3 **Cefn Cribwr** *Bridg., Wales*
350 E3 **Cefn Cross** *Bridg., Wales*
372 I3 **Cefn-ddwysarn** *Gwynedd, Wales*
372 G4 **Cefndeuddwr** *Gwynedd, Wales*
144 B5 **Cefn Einion** *Shrop., Eng.*
356 F3 **Cefneithin** *Carmar., Wales*
350 G2 **Cefn Fforest** *Caerp., Wales*
366 D6 **Cefn-gorwydd** *Powys, Wales*
366 F4 **Cefn-gwyn** *Powys, Wales*
350 G3 **Cefn Hengoed** *Caerp., Wales*
350 C3 **Cefn-hengoed** *Swansea, Wales*
362 G2 **Cefn Llwyd** *Cere., Wales*
378 G4 **Cefn-mawr** *Wrex., Wales*
350 F2 **Cefnpennar** *R.C.T., Wales*
350 E2 **Cefn Rhigos** *R.C.T., Wales*
378 G3 **Cefn-y-bedd** *Flints., Wales*
356 C2 **Cefn-y-pant** *Carmar., Wales*
371 C2 **Ceidio** *I.o.A., Wales*
372 C3 **Ceidio Fawr** *Gwynedd, Wales*
Ceinewydd *Cere., Wales see* **New Quay**
371 D3 **Ceint** *I.o.A., Wales*
362 F4 **Cellan** *Cere., Wales*
292 H2 **Cellardyke** *Fife, Scot.*
148 C2 **Cellarhead** *Staffs., Eng.*
20 D6 **Celtic Sea** *sea* Ireland/U.K.
26 E2 **Celyn, Llyn** *l.* Wales
371 C2 **Cemaes** *I.o.A., Wales*
366 C3 **Cemmaes** *Powys, Wales*
356 C1 **Cenarth** *Carmar., Wales*
372 E3 **Cennin** *Gwynedd, Wales*
110 C3 **Central Bedfordshire** *admin. div.* Eng.
Ceol Reatha *High., Scot. see* **Kylerhea**
362 F3 **Ceredigion** *county* Wales
292 G2 **Ceres** *Fife, Scot.*
366 D4 **Cerist** *Powys, Wales*
46 E3 **Cerne Abbas** *Dorset, Eng.*
98 H4 **Cerney Wick** *Glos., Eng.*
371 C3 **Cerrigceinwen** *I.o.A., Wales*
378 D3 **Cerrigydrudion** *Conwy, Wales*
256 J3 **Cessford** *Borders, Scot.*
372 E2 **Ceunant** *Gwynedd, Wales*
98 F2 **Chaceley** *Glos., Eng.*
106 B2 **Chackmore** *Bucks., Eng.*
128 B5 **Chacombe** *Northants., Eng.*
198 E2 **Chadderton** *Gtr Man., Eng.*
198 E2 **Chadderton Fold** *Gtr Man., Eng.*
180 E5 **Chaddesden** *Derby, Eng.*
136 E1 **Chaddesley Corbett** *Worcs., Eng.*
82 B3 **Chaddleworth** *W. Berks., Eng.*
102 B3 **Chadlington** *Oxon, Eng.*
132 D4 **Chadshunt** *Warks., Eng.*
128 E4 **Chadstone** *Northants., Eng.*
154 C3 **Chad Valley** *W. Mids, Eng.*
162 F2 **Chadwell** *Leics., Eng.*
144 G3 **Chadwell** *Shrop., Eng.*
110 C2 **Chadwell End** *Bedford, Eng.*
74 E2 **Chadwell Heath** *Gtr Lon., Eng.*
116 E5 **Chadwell St Mary** *Thurrock, Eng.*
154 D3 **Chadwick End** *W. Mids, Eng.*
190 E3 **Chadwick Green** *Merseyside, Eng.*
94 G5 **Chaffcombe** *Som., Eng.*
116 D5 **Chafford Hundred** *Thurrock, Eng.*
40 E2 **Chagford** *Devon, Eng.*
58 F3 **Chailey** *E. Sussex, Eng.*
62 C3 **Chainhurst** *Kent, Eng.*
46 H2 **Chalbury** *Dorset, Eng.*
46 H2 **Chalbury Common** *Dorset, Eng.*
78 F2 **Chaldon** *Surr., Eng.*
46 F4 **Chaldon Herring** *Dorset, Eng.*
52 E7 **Chale** *I.o.W., Eng.*
52 E7 **Chale Green** *I.o.W., Eng.*
106 E5 **Chalfont Common** *Bucks., Eng.*
106 E5 **Chalfont St Giles** *Bucks., Eng.*
106 E5 **Chalfont St Peter** *Bucks., Eng.*
98 G3 **Chalford** *Glos., Eng.*
86 B4 **Chalford** *Wilts., Eng.*
110 B4 **Chalgrave** *Central Bedfordshire, Eng.*
102 E4 **Chalgrove** *Oxon, Eng.*
62 C2 **Chalk** *Kent, Eng.*
116 E3 **Chalk End** *Essex, Eng.*
102 F5 **Chalkhouse Green** *Oxon, Eng.*
106 D4 **Chalkshire** *Bucks., Eng.*
62 E2 **Chalkwell** *Kent, Eng.*
40 E1 **Challacombe** *Devon, Eng.*
331 E2 **Challister** *Shet., Scot.*
252 C3 **Challoch** *D. and G., Scot.*
62 F3 **Challock** *Kent, Eng.*
46 D3 **Chalmington** *Dorset, Eng.*
110 B4 **Chalton** *Central Bedfordshire, Eng.*
52 G5 **Chalton** *Hants., Eng.*
82 G2 **Chalvey** *Slough, Eng.*
58 G3 **Chalvington** *E. Sussex, Eng.*
280 E3 **Champany** *Falk., Scot.*
362 F2 **Chancery** *Cere., Wales*
110 C5 **Chandler's Cross** *Herts., Eng.*
52 D5 **Chandler's Ford** *Hants., Eng.*
20 F7 **Channel Islands** *is* English Chan.
110 C2 **Channel's End** *Bedford, Eng.*
20 H6 **Channel Tunnel** *tun.* France/U.K.
331 D4 **Channerwick** *Shet., Scot.*
94 J3 **Chantry** *Som., Eng.*
120 F4 **Chantry** *Suff., Eng.*
292 E3 **Chapel** *Fife, Scot.*
94 G3 **Chapel Allerton** *Som., Eng.*
222 E2 **Chapel Allerton** *W. Yorks., Eng.*
36 E2 **Chapel Amble** *Corn., Eng.*
304 I4 **Chapelbank** *Perth and Kin., Scot.*
128 D4 **Chapel Brampton** *Northants., Eng.*
148 B3 **Chapel Chorlton** *Staffs., Eng.*
94 D3 **Chapel Cleeve** *Som., Eng.*
58 H3 **Chapel Cross** *E. Sussex, Eng.*
262 B5 **Chapeldonan** *S. Ayr., Scot.*
110 C2 **Chapel End** *Bedford, Eng.*
124 B4 **Chapel End** *Cambs., Eng.*
110 C3 **Chapel End** *Central Bedfordshire, Eng.*
132 C2 **Chapel End** *Warks., Eng.*
116 E1 **Chapelend Way** *Essex, Eng.*
180 B3 **Chapel-en-le-Frith** *Derbys., Eng.*
24 M4 **Chapelfell Top** *hill* Eng.
198 D2 **Chapel Field** *Gtr Man., Eng.*
154 E3 **Chapel Fields** *W. Mids, Eng.*
170 G7 **Chapelgate** *Lincs., Eng.*
132 C3 **Chapel Green** *Warks., Eng.*
132 E4 **Chapel Green** *Warks., Eng.*
280 C3 **Chapelhall** *N. Lanark., Scot.*
314 H2 **Chapel Hill** *Abers., Scot.*
320 I4 **Chapelhill** *High., Scot.*
304 I4 **Chapelhill** *Perth and Kin., Scot.*
304 K4 **Chapelhill** *Perth and Kin., Scot.*
339 D2 **Chapel Hill** *Mon., Wales*
86 B3 **Chapel Knapp** *Wilts., Eng.*
252 G2 **Chapelknowe** *D. and G., Scot.*
144 B5 **Chapel Lawn** *Shrop., Eng.*
216 B2 **Chapel le Dale** *N. Yorks., Eng.*
94 E4 **Chapel Leigh** *Som., Eng.*
180 B3 **Chapel Milton** *Derbys., Eng.*
314 F3 **Chapel of Garioch** *Abers., Scot.*
252 B3 **Chapel Rossan** *D. and G., Scot.*
116 F3 **Chapel Row** *Essex, Eng.*
82 C3 **Chapel Row** *W. Berks., Eng.*
232 C7 **Chapels** *Cumbria, Eng.*
170 I4 **Chapel St Leonards** *Lincs., Eng.*
232 D6 **Chapel Stile** *Cumbria, Eng.*
222 E3 **Chapelthorpe** *W. Yorks., Eng.*
40 D1 **Chapelton** *Devon, Eng.*
314 G4 **Chapelton** *Abers., Scot.*
308 G3 **Chapelton** *Angus, Scot.*
268 B2 **Chapelton** *S. Lanark., Scot.*
228 H5 **Chapeltown** *B'burn, Eng.*
36 E2 **Chapel Town** *Corn., Eng.*
232 E2 **Chapeltown** *Cumbria, Eng.*
208 D3 **Chapeltown** *S. Yorks., Eng.*
388 I4 **Chapeltown** *Ballymena, N. Ire.*
396 K4 **Chapeltown** *Down, N. Ire.*
314 D3 **Chapeltown** *Moray, Scot.*
86 B4 **Chapmanslade** *Wilts., Eng.*
40 D2 **Chapmans Well** *Devon, Eng.*
110 E5 **Chapmore End** *Herts., Eng.*
116 G2 **Chappel** *Essex, Eng.*
94 G5 **Chard** *Som., Eng.*
94 G5 **Chard Junction** *Som., Eng.*
94 G5 **Chardleigh Green** *Som., Eng.*
40 H2 **Chardstock** *Devon, Eng.*
98 E4 **Charfield** *S. Glos., Eng.*
62 E3 **Charing** *Kent, Eng.*
46 H2 **Charing Cross** *Dorset, Eng.*
62 E3 **Charing Heath** *Kent, Eng.*
98 I1 **Charingworth** *Glos., Eng.*
102 C3 **Charlbury** *Oxon, Eng.*
94 J2 **Charlcombe** *B. and N.E. Som., Eng.*
86 C3 **Charlcutt** *Wilts., Eng.*
132 C4 **Charlecote** *Warks., Eng.*
396 D3 **Charlemont** *Armagh, N. Ire.*
40 E1 **Charles** *Devon, Eng.*
256 I3 **Charlesfield** *Borders, Scot.*
78 B2 **Charleshill** *Surr., Eng.*
308 D3 **Charleston** *Angus, Scot.*
276 D3 **Charleston** *Renf., Scot.*
36 E3 **Charlestown** *Corn., Eng.*
180 B2 **Charlestown** *Derbys., Eng.*
46 E4 **Charlestown** *Dorset, Eng.*
198 D2 **Charlestown** *Gtr Man., Eng.*
222 B2 **Charlestown** *W. Yorks., Eng.*
222 D1 **Charlestown** *W. Yorks., Eng.*
314 G3 **Charlestown** *Aberdeen, Scot.*
292 D3 **Charlestown** *Fife, Scot.*
320 C4 **Charlestown** *High., Scot.*
322 I2 **Charlestown** *High., Scot.*
Charlestown of Aberlour *Moray, Scot. see* **Aberlour**
120 E4 **Charles Tye** *Suff., Eng.*
180 B2 **Charlesworth** *Derbys., Eng.*
292 G2 **Charleton** *Fife, Scot.*
94 F4 **Charlinch** *Som., Eng.*
78 C2 **Charlotteville** *Surr., Eng.*
74 E3 **Charlton** *Gtr Lon., Eng.*
52 D3 **Charlton** *Hants., Eng.*
110 D4 **Charlton** *Herts., Eng.*
128 B5 **Charlton** *Northants., Eng.*
244 D5 **Charlton** *Northumb., Eng.*
102 C5 **Charlton** *Oxon, Eng.*
94 F4 **Charlton** *Som., Eng.*
94 I3 **Charlton** *Som., Eng.*
94 J3 **Charlton** *Som., Eng.*
144 E3 **Charlton** *Telford, Eng.*
86 C2 **Charlton** *Wilts., Eng.*
86 C6 **Charlton** *Wilts., Eng.*
86 E4 **Charlton** *Wilts., Eng.*
136 D1 **Charlton** *Worcs., Eng.*
136 F3 **Charlton** *Worcs., Eng.*
58 B3 **Charlton** *W. Sussex, Eng.*
98 H2 **Charlton Abbots** *Glos., Eng.*
94 I4 **Charlton Adam** *Som., Eng.*
86 E5 **Charlton-All-Saints** *Wilts., Eng.*
46 E3 **Charlton Down** *Dorset, Eng.*
94 J4 **Charlton Horethorne** *Som., Eng.*
98 G2 **Charlton Kings** *Glos., Eng.*
94 H4 **Charlton Mackrell** *Som., Eng.*
46 G3 **Charlton Marshall** *Dorset, Eng.*
94 J4 **Charlton Musgrove** *Som., Eng.*
102 D3 **Charlton-on-Otmoor** *Oxon, Eng.*
46 G2 **Charlton on the Hill** *Dorset, Eng.*
216 G1 **Charltons** *R. and C., Eng.*
78 E3 **Charlwood** *Surr., Eng.*
46 E3 **Charminster** *Dorset, Eng.*
46 B3 **Charmouth** *Dorset, Eng.*
106 B3 **Charndon** *Bucks., Eng.*
102 C5 **Charney Bassett** *Oxon, Eng.*
228 F5 **Charnock Green** *Lancs., Eng.*
228 F5 **Charnock Richard** *Lancs., Eng.*
120 G4 **Charsfield** *Suff., Eng.*
62 D3 **Chart Corner** *Kent, Eng.*
94 H3 **Charterhouse** *Som., Eng.*
102 B4 **Charterville Allotments** *Oxon, Eng.*
62 G3 **Chartham** *Kent, Eng.*
62 G3 **Chartham Hatch** *Kent, Eng.*
106 E4 **Chartridge** *Bucks., Eng.*
62 D3 **Chart Sutton** *Kent, Eng.*
82 E3 **Charvil** *W'ham, Eng.*
128 B4 **Charwelton** *Northants., Eng.*
74 F2 **Chase Cross** *Gtr Lon., Eng.*
136 C3 **Chase End Street** *Worcs., Eng.*
148 D4 **Chase Terrace** *Staffs., Eng.*
148 D4 **Chasetown** *Staffs., Eng.*
102 B3 **Chastleton** *Oxon, Eng.*
40 C2 **Chasty** *Devon, Eng.*
228 H3 **Chatburn** *Lancs., Eng.*
148 B3 **Chatcull** *Staffs., Eng.*
62 D2 **Chatham** *Medway, Eng.*
116 E3 **Chatham Green** *Essex, Eng.*
244 G2 **Chathill** *Northumb., Eng.*
62 D2 **Chattenden** *Medway, Eng.*
116 C2 **Chatter End** *Essex, Eng.*
124 E4 **Chatteris** *Cambs., Eng.*
120 F4 **Chattisham** *Suff., Eng.*
256 J4 **Chatto** *Borders, Scot.*
244 F2 **Chatton** *Northumb., Eng.*
110 B5 **Chaulden** *Herts., Eng.*
110 C4 **Chaul End** *Central Bedfordshire, Eng.*
82 F3 **Chavey Down** *Brack. F., Eng.*
102 D4 **Chawley** *Oxon, Eng.*
110 D2 **Chawston** *Bedford, Eng.*
52 G4 **Chawton** *Hants., Eng.*
102 E6 **Chazey Heath** *Oxon, Eng.*
198 D3 **Cheadle** *Gtr Man., Eng.*
148 D3 **Cheadle** *Staffs., Eng.*
198 D3 **Cheadle Heath** *Gtr Man., Eng.*
198 D3 **Cheadle Hulme** *Gtr Man., Eng.*
74 C3 **Cheam** *Gtr Lon., Eng.*
82 G3 **Cheapside** *W. and M., Eng.*
106 C4 **Chearsley** *Bucks., Eng.*
148 B3 **Chebsey** *Staffs., Eng.*
102 E5 **Checkendon** *Oxon, Eng.*
184 E3 **Checkley** *Cheshire East, Eng.*
140 D3 **Checkley** *Here., Eng.*
148 D3 **Checkley** *Staffs., Eng.*
184 E3 **Checkley Green** *Cheshire East, Eng.*
120 C3 **Chedburgh** *Suff., Eng.*
94 H3 **Cheddar** *Som., Eng.*
106 E3 **Cheddington** *Bucks., Eng.*
148 C2 **Cheddleton** *Staffs., Eng.*
86 C2 **Chedglow** *Wilts., Eng.*
166 H3 **Chedgrave** *Norf., Eng.*
46 C2 **Chedington** *Dorset, Eng.*
120 H2 **Chediston** *Suff., Eng.*
120 H2 **Chediston Green** *Suff., Eng.*
98 H3 **Chedworth** *Glos., Eng.*
94 G4 **Chedzoy** *Som., Eng.*
198 D2 **Cheesden** *Gtr Man., Eng.*
62 F4 **Cheeseman's Green** *Kent, Eng.*
198 D2 **Cheetham Hill** *Gtr Man., Eng.*
198 D2 **Cheetwood** *Gtr Man., Eng.*
40 E2 **Cheldon** *Devon, Eng.*
184 F2 **Chelford** *Cheshire East, Eng.*
180 E5 **Chellaston** *Derby, Eng.*
110 B2 **Chellington** *Bedford, Eng.*
110 E4 **Chells** *Herts., Eng.*
144 F5 **Chelmarsh** *Shrop., Eng.*
26 N4 **Chelmer** *r.* Eng.
120 G5 **Chelmondiston** *Suff., Eng.*
180 B3 **Chelmorton** *Derbys., Eng.*
116 E3 **Chelmsford** *Essex, Eng.*
154 D3 **Chelmsley Wood** *W. Mids, Eng.*
74 C3 **Chelsea** *Gtr Lon., Eng.*
74 E3 **Chelsfield** *Gtr Lon., Eng.*
78 F2 **Chelsham** *Surr., Eng.*
94 E5 **Chelston Heath** *Som., Eng.*
120 E4 **Chelsworth** *Suff., Eng.*
98 G2 **Cheltenham** *Glos., Eng.*
128 F4 **Chelveston** *Northants., Eng.*
94 H2 **Chelvey** *N. Som., Eng.*
94 I2 **Chelwood** *B. and N.E. Som., Eng.*
58 G2 **Chelwood Common** *E. Sussex, Eng.*
58 G2 **Chelwood Gate** *E. Sussex, Eng.*
86 C2 **Chelworth** *Wilts., Eng.*
144 C5 **Cheney Longville** *Shrop., Eng.*
106 E4 **Chenies** *Bucks., Eng.*
339 D3 **Chepstow** *Mon., Wales*
198 C2 **Chequerbent** *Gtr Man., Eng.*
86 D3 **Cherhill** *Wilts., Eng.*
98 G3 **Cherington** *Glos., Eng.*
132 C5 **Cherington** *Warks., Eng.*
40 E1 **Cheriton** *Devon, Eng.*
52 E4 **Cheriton** *Hants., Eng.*
62 G4 **Cheriton** *Kent, Eng.*
358 E4 **Cheriton** *Pembs., Wales*
350 A3 **Cheriton** *Swansea, Wales*
40 E2 **Cheriton Bishop** *Devon, Eng.*
40 E2 **Cheriton Cross** *Devon, Eng.*
40 F2 **Cheriton Fitzpaine** *Devon, Eng.*
144 F3 **Cherrington** *Telford, Eng.*
210 E3 **Cherry Burton** *E. Riding, Eng.*
116 D2 **Cherry Green** *Essex, Eng.*
124 F5 **Cherry Hinton** *Cambs., Eng.*
396 G3 **Cherrymount** *Craigavon, N. Ire.*
228 G4 **Cherry Tree** *B'burn, Eng.*
198 E3 **Cherry Tree** *Gtr Man., Eng.*
170 D4 **Cherry Willingham** *Lincs., Eng.*
78 C1 **Chertsey** *Surr., Eng.*
26 J4 **Cherwell** *r.* Eng.
46 E3 **Cheselbourne** *Dorset, Eng.*
106 E4 **Chesham** *Bucks., Eng.*
198 D2 **Chesham** *Gtr Man., Eng.*
106 E4 **Chesham Bois** *Bucks., Eng.*
26 H1 **Cheshire** *admin. div.* Eng.
184 C2 **Cheshire East** *admin. div.* Eng.
24 L7 **Cheshire Plain** *plain* Eng.
184 C2 **Cheshire West & Chester** *admin. div.* Eng.
110 E5 **Cheshunt** *Herts., Eng.*
26 G6 **Chesil Beach** *coastal area* Eng.
148 C5 **Cheslyn Hay** *Staffs., Eng.*
132 B3 **Chessetts Wood** *Warks., Eng.*
74 C3 **Chessington** *Gtr Lon., Eng.*
148 D4 **Chestall** *Staffs., Eng.*
184 B2 **Chester** *Cheshire West & Chester, Eng.*
94 J3 **Chesterblade** *Som., Eng.*
180 E3 **Chesterfield** *Derbys., Eng.*
148 D5 **Chesterfield** *Staffs., Eng.*
236 F2 **Chester-le-Street** *Durham, Eng.*
236 F2 **Chester Moor** *Durham, Eng.*
256 I3 **Chesters** *Borders, Scot.*
256 I4 **Chesters** *Borders, Scot.*
124 B3 **Chesterton** *Cambs., Eng.*
124 E5 **Chesterton** *Cambs., Eng.*
102 D3 **Chesterton** *Oxon, Eng.*
144 G4 **Chesterton** *Shrop., Eng.*
148 B2 **Chesterton** *Staffs., Eng.*
132 D4 **Chesterton** *Warks., Eng.*
132 D4 **Chesterton Green** *Warks., Eng.*
62 G2 **Chestfield** *Kent, Eng.*
62 E2 **Chestnut Street** *Kent, Eng.*
144 F2 **Cheswardine** *Shrop., Eng.*
144 F3 **Cheswell** *Telford, Eng.*
244 F1 **Cheswick** *Northumb., Eng.*
244 F1 **Cheswick Buildings** *Northumb., Eng.*
154 D3 **Cheswick Green** *W. Mids, Eng.*

Chetnole to Collington

6 D2 Chetnole Dorset, Eng.
0 F2 Chettiscombe Devon, Eng.
4 F4 Chettisham Cambs., Eng.
6 G2 Chettle Dorset, Eng.
4 F4 Chetton Shrop., Eng.
6 B3 Chetwode Bucks., Eng.
4 F3 Chetwynd Aston Telford, Eng.
4 F3 Chetwynd End Telford, Eng.
4 F3 Chetwynd Park Telford, Eng.
4 G5 Cheveley Cambs., Eng.
2 A3 Chevening Kent, Eng.
0 C5 Cheverell's Green Herts., Eng.
0 C3 Chevington Suff., Eng.
4 L3 Cheviot Hills hills Eng.
0 F2 Chevithorne Devon, Eng.
4 I2 Chew Magna B. and N.E. Som., Eng.
8 B2 Chew Moor Gtr Man., Eng.
4 I2 Chew Stoke B. and N.E. Som., Eng.
4 I2 Chewton Keynsham B. and N.E. Som., Eng.
4 I3 Chewton Mendip Som., Eng.
6 G5 Chew Valley Lake resr Eng.
0 E2 Chichacott Devon, Eng.
6 D2 Chicheley M.K., Eng.
8 B3 Chichester W. Sussex, Eng.
2 E2 Chickenley W. Yorks., Eng.
6 D4 Chickerell Dorset, Eng.
0 G2 Chickering Suff., Eng.
6 C5 Chicklade Wilts., Eng.
6 D2 Chickney Essex, Eng.
0 C3 Chicksands Central Bedfordshire, Eng.
2 F5 Chidden Hants., Eng.
2 F5 Chidden Holt Hants., Eng.
8 C3 Chiddingfold Surr., Eng.
8 H3 Chiddingly E. Sussex, Eng.
2 A3 Chiddingstone Kent, Eng.
2 B3 Chiddingstone Causeway Kent, Eng.
2 A4 Chiddingstone Hoath Kent, Eng.
6 C3 Chideock Dorset, Eng.
8 A4 Chidham W. Sussex, Eng.
2 D5 Chidswell W. Yorks., Eng.
2 C3 Chieveley W. Berks., Eng.
6 E3 Chignall Smealy Essex, Eng.
6 E3 Chignall St James Essex, Eng.
6 C4 Chigwell Essex, Eng.
6 C4 Chigwell Row Essex, Eng.
2 D4 Chilbolton Hants., Eng.
2 E4 Chilcomb Hants., Eng.
6 C3 Chilcombe Dorset, Eng.
4 I3 Chilcompton Som., Eng.
2 B2 Chilcote Leics., Eng.
6 D4 Childerditch Essex, Eng.
4 B2 Childer Thornton Cheshire West & Chester, Eng.
6 F2 Child Okeford Dorset, Eng.
2 C5 Childrey Oxon, Eng.
4 F3 Child's Ercall Shrop., Eng.
4 C2 Childs Hill Gtr Lon., Eng.
6 F3 Childswickham Worcs., Eng.
0 D3 Childwall Merseyside, Eng.
0 C5 Childwick Green Herts., Eng.
5 D3 Chilfrome Dorset, Eng.
0 B3 Chilgrove W. Sussex, Eng.
2 F3 Chilham Kent, Eng.
5 D5 Chilhampton Wilts., Eng.
0 D2 Chilla Devon, Eng.
0 D3 Chillaton Devon, Eng.
2 H3 Chillenden Kent, Eng.
2 E7 Chillerton I.o.W., Eng.
0 H4 Chillesford Suff., Eng.
4 F2 Chillingham Northumb., Eng.
4 G5 Chillington Som., Eng.
6 C5 Chilmark Wilts., Eng.
2 B3 Chilson Oxon, Eng.
4 G6 Chilson Som., Eng.
6 G2 Chilsworthy Corn., Eng.
0 C2 Chilsworthy Devon, Eng.
6 K4 Chiltern Hills hills Eng.
4 H5 Chilthorne Domer Som., Eng.
5 B4 Chilton Bucks., Eng.
6 F4 Chilton Durham, Eng.
2 C5 Chilton Oxon, Eng.
0 D4 Chilton Suff., Eng.
4 F3 Chilton Candover Hants., Eng.
4 I5 Chilton Cantelo Som., Eng.
2 B3 Chilton Foliat Wilts., Eng.
4 G4 Chilton Polden Som., Eng.
0 C4 Chilton Street Suff., Eng.
4 F4 Chilton Trinity Som., Eng.
2 D2 Chilvers Coton Warks., Eng.
6 B5 Chilwell Notts., Eng.
2 D3 Chilworth Hants., Eng.
8 B3 Chilworth Surr., Eng.
2 C4 Chimney Oxon, Eng.
0 C4 Chimney Street Suff., Eng.
2 F3 Chineham Hants., Eng.
4 E2 Chingford Gtr Lon., Eng.
4 E2 Chingford Green Gtr Lon., Eng.
4 E2 Chingford Hatch Gtr Lon., Eng.
0 B2 Chinley Derbys., Eng.
0 B2 Chinley Head Derbys., Eng.
2 F4 Chinnor Oxon, Eng.
4 D5 Chipchase Castle Northumb., Eng.
4 E4 Chipley Som., Eng.
4 F2 Chipnall Shrop., Eng.
0 H3 Chippenhall Green Suff., Eng.
4 G5 Chippenham Cambs., Eng.
5 C3 Chippenham Wilts., Eng.
0 C5 Chipperfield Herts., Eng.
0 E4 Chipping Herts., Eng.
3 G3 Chipping Lancs., Eng.
4 C2 Chipping Barnet Gtr Lon., Eng.
8 I1 Chipping Campden Glos., Eng.
5 F3 Chipping Hill Essex, Eng.
2 B3 Chipping Norton Oxon, Eng.
5 D3 Chipping Ongar Essex, Eng.
3 E4 Chipping Sodbury S. Glos., Eng.
3 B5 Chipping Warden Northants., Eng.
4 D4 Chipstable Som., Eng.
2 A3 Chipstead Kent, Eng.
3 F2 Chipstead Surr., Eng.
4 B4 Chirbury Shrop., Eng.
3 G4 Chirk Wrex., Wales
3 G4 Chirk Green Wrex., Wales
2 C6 Chirmorie S. Ayr., Scot.
5 K2 Chirnside Borders, Scot.
5 K2 Chirnsidebridge Borders, Scot.
5 G1 Chirton T. and W., Eng.
5 D4 Chirton Wilts., Eng.
3 F3 Chisbury Wilts., Eng.
0 C5 Chiscan Arg. and B., Scot.
4 H5 Chiselborough Som., Eng.
5 E2 Chiseldon Swindon, Eng.
2 C2 Chiserley W. Yorks., Eng.
2 E4 Chislehampton Oxon, Eng.
4 E3 Chislehurst Gtr Lon., Eng.
3 H2 Chislet Kent, Eng.
2 C5 Chiswell Green Herts., Eng.
4 C3 Chiswick Gtr Lon., Eng.
4 E6 Chiswick End Cambs., Eng.
0 A2 Chisworth Derbys., Eng.
3 B2 Chithurst W. Sussex, Eng.
124 F5 Chittering Cambs., Eng.
86 C4 Chitterne Wilts., Eng.
40 E2 Chittlehamholt Devon, Eng.
40 E1 Chittlehampton Devon, Eng.
86 C3 Chittoe Wilts., Eng.
40 E4 Chivelstone Devon, Eng.
78 C1 Chobham Surr., Eng.
256 J2 Choicelee Borders, Scot.
86 E4 Cholderton Wilts., Eng.
106 E4 Cholesbury Bucks., Eng.
244 E5 Chollerford Northumb., Eng.
244 E5 Chollerton Northumb., Eng.
184 D3 Cholmondeston Cheshire East, Eng.
102 E5 Cholsey Oxon, Eng.
140 C2 Cholstrey Here., Eng.
94 I3 Cholwell B. and N.E. Som., Eng.
244 H5 Choppington Northumb., Eng.
236 E2 Chopwell T. and W., Eng.
184 D3 Chorley Cheshire East, Eng.
228 G5 Chorley Lancs., Eng.
144 F5 Chorley Shrop., Eng.
148 D4 Chorley Staffs., Eng.
184 D3 Chorley Green Cheshire East, Eng.
110 B6 Chorleywood Herts., Eng.
110 B6 Chorleywood Bottom Herts., Eng.
184 E3 Chorlton Cheshire East, Eng.
198 D3 Chorlton-cum-Hardy Gtr Man., Eng.
184 C3 Chorlton Lane Cheshire West & Chester, Eng.
184 C3 Chowley Cheshire West & Chester, Eng.
116 C1 Chrishall Essex, Eng.
124 E6 Chrishall Grange Cambs., Eng.
276 A2 Chrisswell Inverclyde, Scot.
124 F3 Christchurch Cambs., Eng.
46 I3 Christchurch Dorset, Eng.
98 D3 Christchurch Glos., Eng.
339 C3 Christchurch Newp., Wales
86 C2 Christian Malford Wilts., Eng.
184 C2 Christleton Cheshire West & Chester, Eng.
102 F5 Christmas Common Oxon, Eng.
94 G3 Christon N. Som., Eng.
244 G3 Christon Bank Northumb., Eng.
388 I4 Christystown Antrim, N. Ire.
280 B3 Chryston N. Lanark., Scot.
40 F3 Chudleigh Devon, Eng.
40 F3 Chudleigh Knighton Devon, Eng.
40 E2 Chulmleigh Devon, Eng.
180 B2 Chunal Derbys., Eng.
228 H4 Church Lancs., Eng.
98 E2 Churcham Glos., Eng.
144 F3 Church Aston Telford, Eng.
396 K4 Church Ballee Down, N. Ire.
128 D4 Church Brampton Northants., Eng.
148 C4 Churchbridge Staffs., Eng.
232 I5 Church Brough Cumbria, Eng.
180 C5 Church Broughton Derbys., Eng.
128 B4 Church Charwelton Northants., Eng.
120 H3 Church Common Suff., Eng.
52 G3 Church Crookham Hants., Eng.
98 F2 Churchdown Glos., Eng.
148 B4 Church Eaton Staffs., Eng.
110 C2 Church End Bedford, Eng.
106 E4 Church End Bucks., Eng.
124 B4 Church End Cambs., Eng.
124 C4 Church End Cambs., Eng.
124 D4 Church End Cambs., Eng.
124 E3 Church End Cambs., Eng.
124 E5 Church End Cambs., Eng.
124 F5 Church End Cambs., Eng.
110 B3 Church End Central Bedfordshire, Eng.
110 B4 Church End Central Bedfordshire, Eng.
110 B4 Church End Central Bedfordshire, Eng.
110 D3 Church End Central Bedfordshire, Eng.
110 D3 Church End Central Bedfordshire, Eng.
210 F3 Church End E. Riding, Eng.
116 D1 Church End Essex, Eng.
116 E2 Churchend Essex, Eng.
116 F2 Church End Essex, Eng.
116 F3 Church End Essex, Eng.
116 H4 Churchend Essex, Eng.
98 F3 Churchend Glos., Eng.
98 G1 Church End Glos., Eng.
74 C2 Church End Gtr Lon., Eng.
52 F3 Church End Hants., Eng.
110 C5 Church End Herts., Eng.
110 F4 Church End Herts., Eng.
170 E6 Church End Lincs., Eng.
170 G3 Church End Lincs., Eng.
98 E4 Churchend S. Glos., Eng.
132 C2 Church End Warks., Eng.
86 D2 Church End Wilts., Eng.
102 C3 Church Enstone Oxon, Eng.
216 F3 Church Fenton N. Yorks., Eng.
154 C2 Churchfield W. Mids, Eng.
110 E5 Churchgate Herts., Eng.
116 C3 Churchgate Street Essex, Eng.
40 G2 Church Green Devon, Eng.
180 D6 Church Gresley Derbys., Eng.
102 C4 Church Hanborough Oxon, Eng.
184 D2 Church Hill Cheshire West & Chester, Eng.
180 E3 Church Hill Derbys., Eng.
148 D4 Church Hill Staffs., Eng.
402 D4 Church Hill Fermanagh, N. Ire.
216 G1 Church Houses N. Yorks., Eng.
40 H2 Churchill Devon, Eng.
94 H2 Churchill N. Som., Eng.
102 B3 Churchill Oxon, Eng.
136 D1 Churchill Worcs., Eng.
136 E2 Churchill Worcs., Eng.
94 F5 Churchinford Som., Eng.
46 G4 Church Knowle Dorset, Eng.
176 E3 Church Laneham Notts., Eng.
116 C3 Church Langley Essex, Eng.
162 F3 Church Langton Leics., Eng.
132 D3 Church Lawford Warks., Eng.
184 F3 Church Lawton Cheshire East, Eng.
148 D3 Church Leigh Staffs., Eng.
136 F3 Church Lench Worcs., Eng.
148 E2 Church Mayfield Staffs., Eng.
184 D3 Church Minshull Cheshire East, Eng.
58 B4 Church Norton W. Sussex, Eng.
132 E3 Churchover Warks., Eng.
144 D4 Church Preen Shrop., Eng.
144 C4 Church Pulverbatch Shrop., Eng.
94 F5 Churchstanton Som., Eng.
366 G3 Church Stoke Powys, Wales
40 E4 Churchstow Devon, Eng.
128 C4 Church Stowe Northants., Eng.
116 F1 Church Street Essex, Eng.
62 C2 Church Street Kent, Eng.
144 D4 Church Stretton Shrop., Eng.
405 D2 Churchtown Isle of Man
228 D3 Churchtown Blackpool, Eng.
40 E1 Churchtown Devon, Eng.
228 F3 Churchtown Lancs., Eng.
162 C2 Church Town Leics., Eng.
190 D2 Churchtown Merseyside, Eng.
78 F2 Church Town Surr., Eng.
402 J2 Churchtown Cookstown, N. Ire.
396 K3 Churchtown Down, N. Ire.
350 G3 Church Village R.C.T., Wales
176 C3 Church Warsop Notts., Eng.
98 I2 Church Westcote Glos., Eng.
180 E5 Church Wilne Derbys., Eng.
244 B5 Churnsike Lodge Northumb., Eng.
40 F3 Churston Ferrers Torbay, Eng.
78 B3 Churt Surr., Eng.
184 B3 Churton Cheshire West & Chester, Eng.
222 E2 Churwell W. Yorks., Eng.
86 F4 Chute Cadley Wilts., Eng.
86 F4 Chute Standen Wilts., Eng.
372 E3 Chwilog Gwynedd, Wales
Chwitffordd Flints., Wales see Whitford
36 C3 Chysauster Corn., Eng.
372 C4 Cilan Uchaf Gwynedd, Wales
378 F2 Cilcain Flints., Wales
362 F3 Cilcennin Cere., Wales
358 G3 Cilcewydd Powys, Wales
350 G3 Cilfynydd R.C.T., Wales
358 G1 Cilgerran Pembs., Wales
356 H2 Cilgwyn Carmar., Wales
358 F2 Cilgwyn Pembs., Wales
362 E3 Ciliau Aeron Cere., Wales
Cill Chreànain Arg. and B., Scot. see Kilchrenan
326 B5 Cille Bhrighde W. Isles, Scot.
Cille Chuimein High., Scot. see Fort Augustus
350 D2 Cilmaengwyn N.P.T., Wales
366 E6 Cilmery Powys, Wales
358 G2 Cilrhedyn Pembs., Wales
358 E2 Cilrhedyn Bridge Pembs., Wales
356 F2 Cilsan Carmar., Wales
372 I3 Ciltalgarth Gwynedd, Wales
358 G1 Cilwendeg Pembs., Wales
350 D2 Cilybebyll N.P.T., Wales
356 H1 Cilycwm Carmar., Wales
350 D3 Cimla N.P.T., Wales
98 D3 Cinderford Glos., Eng.
176 B5 Cinderhill Nott., Eng.
154 B2 Cinder Hill W. Mids, Eng.
82 G2 Cippenham Slough, Eng.
358 F1 Cippyn Pembs., Wales
326 D2 Cirbhig W. Isles, Scot.
Circebost W. Isles, Scot. see Kirkibost
98 H3 Cirencester Glos., Eng.
74 D2 City Gtr Lon., Eng.
350 F4 City V. of Glam., Wales
371 D2 City Dulas I.o.A., Wales
23 H2 City of Derry airport N. Ire.
74 D2 City of London met. bor. Gtr Lon., Eng.
402 F4 Clabby Fermanagh, N. Ire.
300 □ Clabhach Arg. and B., Scot.
300 E4 Clachaig Arg. and B., Scot.
300 D2 Clachan Arg. and B., Scot.
300 D4 Clachan Arg. and B., Scot.
300 F3 Clachan Arg. and B., Scot.
322 C2 Clachan High., Scot.
326 C4 Clachan-a-Luib W. Isles, Scot.
300 B2 Clachandhu Arg. and B., Scot.
252 C2 Clachaneasy D. and G., Scot.
Clachan Ghairbh High., Scot. see Garve
300 □ Clachan Mòr Arg. and B., Scot.
252 B3 Clachanmore D. and G., Scot.
276 E2 Clachan of Campsie E. Dun., Scot.
300 D3 Clachan-Seil Arg. and B., Scot.
Clachan Strachur Arg. and B., Scot. see Strachur
314 D3 Clachanturn Abers., Scot.
300 D4 Clachbreck Arg. and B., Scot.
308 D2 Clachnabrain Angus, Scot.
320 E3 Clachtoll High., Scot.
292 B3 Clackmannan Clack., Scot.
292 B3 Clackmannanshire admin. div. Scot.
116 I3 Clacton-on-Sea Essex, Eng.
326 B4 Cladach Chircebost W. Isles, Scot.
300 E2 Cladich Arg. and B., Scot.
136 F2 Cladswell Worcs., Eng.
388 G3 Clady Magherafelt, N. Ire.
402 E2 Clady Strabane, N. Ire.
396 E4 Clady Milltown Armagh, N. Ire.
26 E3 Claerwen Reservoir resr Wales
402 H3 Claggan Omagh, N. Ire.
22 C7 Claidh, Loch inlet Scot.
322 B2 Claigan High., Scot.
136 D2 Claines Worcs., Eng.
402 F3 Clanabogan Omagh, N. Ire.
94 J3 Clandown B. and N.E. Som., Eng.
52 F5 Clanfield Hants., Eng.
102 B4 Clanfield Oxon, Eng.
396 H4 Clanmaghery Banbridge, N. Ire.
52 C3 Clanville Hants., Eng.
300 D4 Claonaig Arg. and B., Scot.
300 E3 Claonairigh Arg. and B., Scot.
46 H3 Clapgate Dorset, Eng.
110 F4 Clapgate Herts., Eng.
216 E3 Clap Gate N. Yorks., Eng.
110 C3 Clapham Bedford, Eng.
74 D3 Clapham Gtr Lon., Eng.
216 B2 Clapham N. Yorks., Eng.
58 D3 Clapham W. Sussex, Eng.
110 C3 Clapham Green Bedford, Eng.
62 G2 Clapham Hill Kent, Eng.
244 E1 Clappers Northumb., Eng.
232 E6 Clappersgate Cumbria, Eng.
94 H5 Clapton Som., Eng.
94 I3 Clapton Som., Eng.
94 H2 Clapton-in-Gordano N. Som., Eng.
98 I2 Clapton-on-the-Hill Glos., Eng.
74 D2 Clapton Park Gtr Lon., Eng.
40 E1 Clapworthy Devon, Eng.
22 H6 Clar, Loch nan l. Scot.
362 F2 Clarach Cere., Wales
236 E2 Clara Vale T. and W., Eng.
358 F2 Clarbeston Pembs., Wales
358 E2 Clarbeston Road Pembs., Wales
176 D2 Clarborough Notts., Eng.
320 J2 Clardon High., Scot.
120 C4 Clare Suff., Eng.
396 F4 Clare Armagh, N. Ire.
396 G3 Clare Craigavon, N. Ire.
252 E3 Clarebrand D. and G., Scot.
252 F2 Clarencefield D. and G., Scot.
162 E3 Clarendon Park Leicester, Eng.
256 H4 Clarilaw Borders, Scot.
78 E3 Clark's Green Surr., Eng.
276 E3 Clarkston E. Renf., Scot.
320 H4 Clashban High., Scot.
320 H4 Clashcoig High., Scot.
300 F2 Clashgour Arg. and B., Scot.
314 E2 Clashindarroch Abers., Scot.
320 H4 Clashmore High., Scot.
320 E3 Clashnessie High., Scot.
314 D3 Clashnoir Moray, Scot.
86 E3 Clatford Wilts., Eng.
304 I4 Clathy Perth and Kin., Scot.
314 E3 Clatt Abers., Scot.
366 E3 Clatter Powys, Wales
102 D2 Clattercote Oxon, Eng.
116 D3 Clatterford End Essex, Eng.
116 E3 Clatterford End Essex, Eng.
314 F4 Clatterin Brig Abers., Scot.
252 D2 Clatteringshaws D. and G., Scot.
22 H12 Clatteringshaws Loch l. Scot.
94 D4 Clatworthy Som., Eng.
388 D3 Claudy Derry, N. Ire.
228 F2 Claughton Lancs., Eng.
228 F3 Claughton Lancs., Eng.
190 C3 Claughton Merseyside, Eng.
94 F4 Clavelshay Som., Eng.
132 B4 Claverdon Warks., Eng.
94 H2 Claverham N. Som., Eng.
116 C2 Clavering Essex, Eng.
144 G4 Claverley Shrop., Eng.
94 K2 Claverton B. and N.E. Som., Eng.
94 K2 Claverton Down B. and N.E. Som., Eng.
350 F4 Clawdd-côch V. of Glam., Wales
378 E3 Clawdd-newydd Denb., Wales
262 E4 Clawfin E. Ayr., Scot.
232 F7 Clawthorpe Cumbria, Eng.
40 C2 Clawton Devon, Eng.
170 E3 Claxby Lincs., Eng.
170 G4 Claxby St Andrew Lincs., Eng.
166 H3 Claxton Norf., Eng.
216 G2 Claxton N. Yorks., Eng.
236 H4 Claxton Grange Hartlepool, Eng.
162 D4 Claybrooke Magna Leics., Eng.
162 D4 Claybrooke Parva Leics., Eng.
120 I2 Clay Common Suff., Eng.
128 C3 Clay Coton Northants., Eng.
180 E4 Clay Cross Derbys., Eng.
62 A4 Claydene Kent, Eng.
102 C2 Claydon Oxon, Eng.
120 F4 Claydon Suff., Eng.
110 E4 Clay End Herts., Eng.
62 C3 Claygate Kent, Eng.
78 D1 Claygate Surr., Eng.
62 B3 Claygate Cross Kent, Eng.
74 B2 Clayhall Gtr Lon., Eng.
40 F2 Clayhanger Devon, Eng.
94 G5 Clayhanger Som., Eng.
154 C2 Clayhanger W. Mids, Eng.
24 I5 Clay Head hd Isle of Man
94 I2 Clay Hill Bristol, Eng.
58 J3 Clayhill E. Sussex, Eng.
74 D1 Clay Hill Gtr Lon., Eng.
52 C5 Clayhill Hants., Eng.
124 F5 Clayhithe Cambs., Eng.
170 F7 Clay Lake Lincs., Eng.
320 J2 Clayock High., Scot.
124 D5 Claypit Hill Cambs., Eng.
98 E3 Claypits Glos., Eng.
170 B5 Claypole Lincs., Eng.
170 G4 Claythorpe Lincs., Eng.
198 D3 Clayton Gtr Man., Eng.
148 B3 Clayton Staffs., Eng.
208 E2 Clayton S. Yorks., Eng.
58 F3 Clayton W. Sussex, Eng.
222 D2 Clayton W. Yorks., Eng.
228 G4 Clayton Green Lancs., Eng.
228 H4 Clayton-le-Moors Lancs., Eng.
228 F4 Clayton-le-Woods Lancs., Eng.
222 E3 Clayton West W. Yorks., Eng.
176 D2 Clayworth Notts., Eng.
322 C4 Cleadale High., Scot.
236 G2 Cleadon T. and W., Eng.
40 D3 Clearbrook Devon, Eng.
98 D3 Clearwell Glos., Eng.
216 E1 Cleasby N. Yorks., Eng.
329 D5 Cleat Orkney, Scot.
236 E4 Cleatlam Durham, Eng.
216 C2 Cleatop N. Yorks., Eng.
232 A5 Cleator Cumbria, Eng.
232 A5 Cleator Moor Cumbria, Eng.
222 D2 Cleckheaton W. Yorks., Eng.
144 E5 Cleedownton Shrop., Eng.
144 E5 Cleehill Shrop., Eng.
144 E5 Cleestanton Shrop., Eng.
144 E5 Clee St Margaret Shrop., Eng.
170 F2 Cleethorpes N.E. Lincs., Eng.
144 E5 Cleeton St Mary Shrop., Eng.
94 H2 Cleeve N. Som., Eng.
102 E5 Cleeve Oxon, Eng.
98 G2 Cleeve Hill Glos., Eng.
136 F3 Cleeve Prior Worcs., Eng.
268 D2 Cleghorn S. Lanark., Scot.
140 C3 Clehonger Here., Eng.
300 D2 Cleigh Arg. and B., Scot.
304 J5 Cleish Perth and Kin., Scot.
280 C4 Cleland N. Lanark., Scot.
110 C5 Clement's End Herts., Eng.
58 D2 Clemsfold W. Sussex, Eng.
86 E3 Clench Common Wilts., Eng.
166 B2 Clenchwarton Norf., Eng.
244 E3 Clennell Northumb., Eng.
136 E1 Clent Worcs., Eng.
144 F5 Cleobury Mortimer Shrop., Eng.
144 E5 Cleobury North Shrop., Eng.
74 D2 Clerkenwell Gtr Lon., Eng.
256 H3 Clerklands Borders, Scot.
288 D3 Clermiston Edin., Scot.
329 B4 Clestrain Orkney, Scot.
256 I4 Cleuch Head Borders, Scot.
252 F2 Cleughbrae D. and G., Scot.
86 D3 Clevancy Wilts., Eng.
94 G2 Clevedon N. Som., Eng.
24 O5 Cleveland Hills hills Eng.
216 F1 Cleveland Tontine Inn N. Yorks., Eng.
102 C3 Cleveley Oxon, Eng.
228 D3 Cleveleys Lancs., Eng.
136 D3 Clevelode Worcs., Eng.
86 C2 Cleverton Wilts., Eng.
94 H3 Clewer Som., Eng.
82 G3 Clewer Green W. and M., Eng.
82 G3 Clewer New Town W. and M., Eng.
82 G3 Clewer Village W. and M., Eng.
166 F1 Cley next the Sea Norf., Eng.
232 G5 Cliburn Cumbria, Eng.
52 F3 Cliddesden Hants., Eng.
322 D4 Cliff High., Scot.
356 D3 Cliff Carmar., Wales
236 E4 Cliffe Darl., Eng.
228 H4 Cliffe Lancs., Eng.
62 C2 Cliffe Medway, Eng.
216 G3 Cliffe N. Yorks., Eng.
58 K3 Cliff End E. Sussex, Eng.
62 C2 Cliffe Woods Medway, Eng.
144 E2 Cliff Grange Shrop., Eng.
140 A3 Clifford Here., Eng.
222 F1 Clifford W. Yorks., Eng.
132 B4 Clifford Chambers Warks., Eng.
98 E2 Clifford's Mesne Glos., Eng.
62 I3 Cliffs End Kent, Eng.
94 I2 Clifton Bristol, Eng.
110 D3 Clifton Central Bedfordshire, Eng.
232 F5 Clifton Cumbria, Eng.
180 C4 Clifton Derbys., Eng.
40 D1 Clifton Devon, Eng.
198 C2 Clifton Gtr Man., Eng.
228 F4 Clifton Lancs., Eng.
244 G5 Clifton Northumb., Eng.
176 B5 Clifton Nott., Eng.
216 D3 Clifton N. Yorks., Eng.
102 D3 Clifton Oxon, Eng.
208 D3 Clifton S. Yorks., Eng.
208 E3 Clifton S. Yorks., Eng.
136 D3 Clifton Worcs., Eng.
222 D2 Clifton W. Yorks., Eng.
216 F3 Clifton York, Eng.
296 B3 Clifton Stir., Scot.
148 F4 Clifton Campville Staffs., Eng.
210 C4 Clifton Gardens E. Riding, Eng.
102 D5 Clifton Hampden Oxon, Eng.
46 D2 Clifton Maybank Dorset, Eng.
106 D2 Clifton Reynes M.K., Eng.
132 E3 Clifton upon Dunsmore Warks., Eng.
136 C2 Clifton upon Teme Worcs., Eng.
62 I2 Cliftonville Kent, Eng.
58 C4 Climping W. Sussex, Eng.
268 D2 Climpy S. Lanark., Scot.
94 K3 Clink Som., Eng.
216 E2 Clint N. Yorks., Eng.
314 G3 Clinterty Aberdeen, Scot.
166 E3 Clint Green Norf., Eng.
256 I3 Clintmains Borders, Scot.
166 I2 Clippesby Norf., Eng.
166 F2 Clippings Green Norf., Eng.
162 H2 Clipsham Rutland, Eng.
128 D3 Clipston Northants., Eng.
176 C5 Clipston Notts., Eng.
176 C4 Clipstone Notts., Eng.
22 C7 Clisham hill Scot.
228 H3 Clitheroe Lancs., Eng.
Cliuthar W. Isles, Scot. see Cluer
144 D3 Clive Shrop., Eng.
331 E1 Clivocast Shet., Scot.
170 D2 Clixby Lincs., Eng.
378 E3 Clocaenog Denb., Wales
314 D2 Clochan Moray, Scot.
314 H2 Clochtow Abers., Scot.
190 E3 Clock Face Merseyside, Eng.
314 G2 Clockhill Abers., Scot.
314 C2 Cloddach Moray, Scot.
366 F2 Clodiau Powys, Wales
140 B4 Clodock Here., Eng.
94 J3 Cloford Som., Eng.
388 I3 Clogh Ballymena, N. Ire.
402 F1 Cloghcor Strabane, N. Ire.
388 I3 Clogher Ballymena, N. Ire.
402 G4 Clogher Dungannon, N. Ire.
388 J6 Clogher Lisburn, N. Ire.
402 H5 Cloghmore Fermanagh, N. Ire.
396 E5 Cloghoge Newry & Mourne, N. Ire.
396 F5 Cloghoge Newry & Mourne, N. Ire.
402 F1 Cloghogle Strabane, N. Ire.
396 H4 Cloghskelt Banbridge, N. Ire.
396 L3 Cloghy Ards, N. Ire.
396 K3 Cloghy Down, N. Ire.
296 E3 Cloichran Stir., Scot.
314 H2 Clola Abers., Scot.
396 E5 Clonalig Newry & Mourne, N. Ire.
396 G5 Clonallan Glebe Newry & Mourne, N. Ire.
402 D3 Clonelly Fermanagh, N. Ire.
402 J4 Clonfeacle Dungannon, N. Ire.
402 E5 Clonliff Fermanagh, N. Ire.
396 E3 Clonmain Armagh, N. Ire.
402 K4 Clonmore Dungannon, N. Ire.
402 J3 Clonoe Dungannon, N. Ire.
252 E2 Clonrae D. and G., Scot.
388 H2 Clontyfinnan Ballymoney, N. Ire.
396 G5 Clontygora Newry & Mourne, N. Ire.
396 I4 Clonvaraghan Down, N. Ire.
110 C3 Clophill Central Bedfordshire, Eng.
128 G3 Clopton Northants., Eng.
120 G4 Clopton Corner Suff., Eng.
120 C4 Clopton Green Suff., Eng.
120 E3 Clopton Green Suff., Eng.
120 G4 Clopton Green Suff., Eng.
252 E2 Closeburn D. and G., Scot.
405 C3 Close Clark Isle of Man
94 I5 Closworth Som., Eng.
110 E4 Clothall Herts., Eng.
331 D2 Clothan Shet., Scot.
184 C2 Clotton Cheshire West & Chester, Eng.
232 H7 Clough Cumbria, Eng.
198 E2 Clough Gtr Man., Eng.
198 E2 Clough Gtr Man., Eng.
222 C3 Clough W. Yorks., Eng.
396 J4 Clough Down, N. Ire.
388 F4 Cloughfin Magherafelt, N. Ire.
228 I4 Cloughfold Lancs., Eng.
222 B2 Clough Foot W. Yorks., Eng.
222 C2 Clough Head W. Yorks., Eng.
388 I2 Cloughmills Ballymoney, N. Ire.
396 F4 Cloughreagh Newry & Mourne, N. Ire.
216 H2 Cloughton N. Yorks., Eng.
216 H1 Cloughton Newlands N. Yorks., Eng.
322 E5 Clounlaid High., Scot.
331 C3 Clousta Shet., Scot.
329 B4 Clouston Orkney, Scot.
314 E3 Clova Abers., Scot.
308 D1 Clova Angus, Scot.
40 D1 Clovelly Devon, Eng.
40 C2 Clovelly Cross Devon, Eng.
236 C4 Clove Lodge Durham, Eng.
256 G3 Clovenfords Borders, Scot.
314 F3 Clovenstone Abers., Scot.
314 C2 Cloves Moray, Scot.
322 F4 Clovullin High., Scot.
228 I4 Clow Bridge Lancs., Eng.
180 F3 Clowne Derbys., Eng.
136 C1 Clows Top Worcs., Eng.
388 G2 Cloyfin Coleraine, N. Ire.
262 D5 Cloyntie S. Ayr., Scot.
300 B4 Cluanach Arg. and B., Scot.
22 F8 Cluanie, Loch l. Scot.
190 D3 Clubmoor Merseyside, Eng.
144 E3 Cluddley Telford, Eng.
326 D3 Cluer W. Isles, Scot.
144 B5 Clun Shrop., Eng.
26 G3 Clun r. Eng.
144 C5 Clunbury Shrop., Eng.
356 B2 Clunderwen Carmar., Wales
322 J3 Clune High., Scot.
314 C2 Clune Moray, Scot.
322 G4 Clunes High., Scot.
144 C5 Clungunford Shrop., Eng.
314 F2 Clunie Abers., Scot.
304 J3 Clunie Perth and Kin., Scot.
396 J3 Cluntagh Down, N. Ire.
144 C5 Clunton Shrop., Eng.
292 E3 Cluny Fife, Scot.
94 I3 Clutton B. and N.E. Som., Eng.
184 C3 Clutton Cheshire West & Chester, Eng.
26 F1 Clwydian Range hills Wales
350 F2 Clwydfagwyr M. Tyd., Wales
339 B2 Clydach Mon., Wales
350 C2 Clydach Swansea, Wales
350 G2 Clydach Terrace B. Gwent, Wales
350 F3 Clydach Vale R.C.T., Wales
22 H11 Clyde r. Scot.
22 G12 Clyde, Firth of est. Scot.
276 D2 Clydebank W. Dun., Scot.
22 I11 Clydesdale val. Scot.
358 G2 Clydey Pembs., Wales
86 D3 Clyffe Pypard Wilts., Eng.
300 F3 Clynder Arg. and B., Scot.
358 G1 Clynfyw Pembs., Wales
372 D2 Clynnog-fawr Gwynedd, Wales
366 G6 Clyro Powys, Wales
40 F2 Clyst Hydon Devon, Eng.
40 F2 Clyst St George Devon, Eng.
40 F2 Clyst St Lawrence Devon, Eng.
40 F2 Clyst St Mary Devon, Eng.
40 G2 Clyst William Devon, Eng.
366 D7 Cnewr Powys, Wales
326 F2 Cnoc W. Isles, Scot.
326 F2 Cnoc an t-Solus W. Isles, Scot.
22 I8 Cnoc Fraing hill Scot.
22 E12 Cnoc Moy hill Scot.
362 G2 Cnwch Coch Cere., Wales
Cnwclas Powys, Wales see Knucklas
402 E4 Coa Fermanagh, N. Ire.
402 G4 Coach & Carriage Museum Dungannon, N. Ire.
314 E2 Coachford Abers., Scot.
36 F2 Coad's Green Corn., Eng.
402 K3 Coagh Cookstown, N. Ire.
180 E3 Coal Aston Derbys., Eng.
144 F4 Coalbrookdale Telford, Eng.
350 H2 Coalbrookvale B. Gwent, Wales
268 C3 Coalburn S. Lanark., Scot.
236 E2 Coalburns T. and W., Eng.
244 D7 Coalcleugh Northumb., Eng.
98 F3 Coaley Glos., Eng.
402 J3 Coalisland Dungannon, N. Ire.
144 F4 Coalmoor Telford, Eng.
98 E4 Coalpit Heath S. Glos., Eng.
148 B2 Coalpit Hill Staffs., Eng.
154 C2 Coal Pool W. Mids, Eng.
144 F4 Coalport Shrop., Eng.
292 B3 Coalsnaughton Clack., Scot.
292 F2 Coaltown of Balgonie Fife, Scot.
292 F3 Coaltown of Wemyss Fife, Scot.
162 C2 Coalville Leics., Eng.
98 D3 Coalway Glos., Eng.
244 C6 Coanwood Northumb., Eng.
320 D4 Coast High., Scot.
94 H5 Coat Som., Eng.
280 B3 Coatbridge N. Lanark., Scot.
86 E2 Coate Swindon, Eng.
86 D3 Coate Wilts., Eng.
124 D3 Coates Cambs., Eng.
98 G3 Coates Glos., Eng.
170 C3 Coates Lincs., Eng.
176 E3 Coates Notts., Eng.
58 C3 Coates W. Sussex, Eng.
236 F4 Coatham Mundeville Darl., Eng.
314 E2 Cobairdy Abers., Scot.
40 E1 Cobbaton Devon, Eng.
166 H4 Cobbler's Green Norf., Eng.
339 D2 Cobbler's Plain Mon., Wales
216 D3 Cobby Syke N. Yorks., Eng.
98 G2 Coberley Glos., Eng.
140 C3 Cobhall Common Here., Eng.
62 C2 Cobham Kent, Eng.
78 D2 Cobham Surr., Eng.
296 D5 Cobleland Stir., Scot.
116 E2 Cobler's Green Essex, Eng.
136 F1 Cobley Hill Worcs., Eng.
140 C2 Cobnash Here., Eng.
148 B2 Cobridge Stoke, Eng.
314 G1 Coburty Abers., Scot.
276 D2 Cochno W. Dun., Scot.
180 E3 Cock Alley Derbys., Eng.
216 F1 Cockayne N. Yorks., Eng.
110 E3 Cockayne Hatley Central Bedfordshire, Eng.
378 H3 Cock Bank Wrex., Wales
132 A4 Cock Bevington Warks., Eng.
314 D3 Cock Bridge Abers., Scot.
256 J1 Cockburnspath Borders, Scot.
116 F3 Cock Clarks Essex, Eng.
24 N2 Cockenheugh hill Eng.
288 F3 Cockenzie and Port Seton E. Lothian, Scot.
24 J4 Cocker r. Eng.
228 F4 Cocker Bar Lancs., Eng.
228 F3 Cockerham Lancs., Eng.
232 B5 Cockermouth Cumbria, Eng.
110 C4 Cockernhoe Herts., Eng.
222 E2 Cockersdale W. Yorks., Eng.
236 F4 Cockerton Darl., Eng.
350 C3 Cockett Swansea, Wales
236 E4 Cockfield Durham, Eng.
120 D4 Cockfield Suff., Eng.
74 D2 Cockfosters Gtr Lon., Eng.
116 E2 Cock Green Essex, Eng.
388 J6 Cock Hill Lisburn, N. Ire.
58 B3 Cocking W. Sussex, Eng.
40 F3 Cockington Torbay, Eng.
94 H3 Cocklake Som., Eng.
244 E5 Cocklaw Northumb., Eng.
98 G3 Cockleford Glos., Eng.
244 G4 Cockle Park Northumb., Eng.
232 D6 Cockley Beck Cumbria, Eng.
166 C3 Cockley Cley Norf., Eng.
58 K3 Cock Marling E. Sussex, Eng.
288 E3 Cockpen Midlothian, Scot.
82 E2 Cockpole Green W'ham, Eng.
144 C2 Cockshutt Shrop., Eng.
166 E1 Cockthorpe Norf., Eng.
40 F3 Cockwood Devon, Eng.
94 F3 Cockwood Som., Eng.
180 B3 Cockyard Derbys., Eng.
24 O5 Cod Beck r. Eng.
36 F2 Codda Corn., Eng.
120 F4 Coddenham Suff., Eng.
184 C3 Coddington Cheshire West & Chester, Eng.
140 E3 Coddington Here., Eng.
176 E4 Coddington Notts., Eng.
86 C5 Codford St Mary Wilts., Eng.
86 C5 Codford St Peter Wilts., Eng.
110 D4 Codicote Herts., Eng.
58 D3 Codmore Hill W. Sussex, Eng.
180 E4 Codnor Derbys., Eng.
98 E4 Codrington S. Glos., Eng.
148 B5 Codsall Staffs., Eng.
148 B5 Codsall Wood Staffs., Eng.
339 B2 Coedcae Torf., Wales
350 F3 Coedely R.C.T., Wales
339 B3 Coedkernew Newp., Wales
339 C2 Coed Morgan Mon., Wales
378 G3 Coedpoeth Wrex., Wales
366 H2 Coedway Powys, Wales
362 D4 Coed-y-bryn Cere., Wales
339 C3 Coed-y-caerau Newp., Wales
339 C2 Coed-y-paen Mon., Wales
366 F7 Coed-yr-ynys Powys, Wales
372 F4 Coed Ystumgwern Gwynedd, Wales
366 C8 Coelbren Powys, Wales
40 F3 Cofton Devon, Eng.
136 F1 Cofton Hackett Worcs., Eng.
350 G4 Cogan V. of Glam., Wales
128 E4 Cogenhoe Northants., Eng.
102 C4 Cogges Oxon, Eng.
116 G2 Coggeshall Essex, Eng.
116 G2 Coggeshall Hamlet Essex, Eng.
58 H2 Coggins Mill E. Sussex, Eng.
22 F6 Coigeach, Rubha pt Scot.
326 F1 Còig Peighinnean W. Isles, Scot.
296 E4 Coilantogle Stir., Scot.
322 F5 Coileitir High., Scot.
300 F3 Coilessan Arg. and B., Scot.
300 E2 Coillaig Arg. and B., Scot.
322 C5 Coille Mhorgil High., Scot.
322 B2 Coillore High., Scot.
350 E3 Coity Bridg., Wales
326 F2 Col W. Isles, Scot.
320 G3 Colaboll High., Scot.
36 D2 Colan Corn., Eng.
40 G2 Colaton Raleigh Devon, Eng.
322 B2 Colbost High., Scot.
216 D1 Colburn N. Yorks., Eng.
52 C5 Colbury Hants., Eng.
405 B3 Colby Isle of Man
232 G5 Colby Cumbria, Eng.
166 G1 Colby Norf., Eng.
116 H2 Colchester Essex, Eng.
350 G4 Colcot V. of Glam., Wales
82 C3 Cold Ash W. Berks., Eng.
128 C3 Cold Ashby Northants., Eng.
98 E5 Cold Ashton S. Glos., Eng.
98 I2 Cold Aston Glos., Eng.
320 G2 Coldbackie High., Scot.
74 E3 Coldblow Gtr Lon., Eng.
358 F3 Cold Blow Pembs., Wales
106 E2 Cold Brayfield M.K., Eng.
268 D3 Cold Chapel S. Lanark., Scot.
216 B2 Cold Cotes N. Yorks., Eng.
58 F3 Coldean B. and H., Eng.
40 F3 Coldeast Devon, Eng.
180 C4 Coldeaton Derbys., Eng.
52 E5 Colden Common Hants., Eng.
120 I3 Coldfair Green Suff., Eng.
124 E3 Coldham Cambs., Eng.
170 D3 Cold Hanworth Lincs., Eng.
98 D3 Coldharbour Glos., Eng.
102 E5 Cold Harbour Oxon, Eng.
78 D2 Coldharbour Surr., Eng.
144 E3 Cold Hatton Telford, Eng.
144 E3 Cold Hatton Heath Telford, Eng.
236 G3 Cold Hesledon Durham, Eng.
222 F3 Cold Hiendley W. Yorks., Eng.
128 C4 Cold Higham Northants., Eng.
256 L1 Coldingham Borders, Scot.
358 F3 Cold Inn Pembs., Wales
216 F2 Cold Kirby N. Yorks., Eng.
162 F3 Cold Newton Leics., Eng.
36 F2 Cold Northcott Corn., Eng.
116 G3 Cold Norton Essex, Eng.
162 G2 Cold Overton Leics., Eng.
304 J5 Coldrain Perth and Kin., Scot.
62 H3 Coldred Kent, Eng.
52 G3 Coldrey Hants., Eng.
244 F4 Coldrife Northumb., Eng.
228 E3 Cold Row Lancs., Eng.
256 K3 Coldstream Borders, Scot.
314 H2 Coldwells Abers., Scot.
94 J4 Cole Som., Eng.
144 B5 Colebatch Shrop., Eng.
40 F2 Colebrook Devon, Eng.
40 E2 Colebrooke Devon, Eng.
314 D2 Coleburn Moray, Scot.
170 C5 Coleby Lincs., Eng.
170 C2 Coleby N. Lincs., Eng.
132 B2 Cole End Warks., Eng.
40 E2 Coleford Devon, Eng.
98 D3 Coleford Glos., Eng.
94 J3 Coleford Som., Eng.
166 G4 Colegate End Norf., Eng.
110 E5 Cole Green Herts., Eng.
110 F4 Cole Green Herts., Eng.
52 E3 Cole Henley Hants., Eng.
46 H3 Colehill Dorset, Eng.
110 D5 Coleman Green Herts., Eng.
58 G2 Coleman's Hatch E. Sussex, Eng.
144 C2 Colemere Shrop., Eng.
52 G4 Colemore Hants., Eng.
144 F4 Colemore Green Shrop., Eng.
304 J4 Colenden Perth and Kin., Scot.
162 C2 Coleorton Leics., Eng.
388 G2 Coleraine Coleraine, N. Ire.
388 F2 Coleraine admin. dist. N. Ire.
86 B3 Colerne Wilts., Eng.
98 H3 Colesbourne Glos., Eng.
46 F1 Colesbrook Dorset, Eng.
166 G4 Cole's Common Norf., Eng.
110 C2 Colesden Bedford, Eng.
120 H3 Cole's Green Suff., Eng.
136 C3 Coles Green Worcs., Eng.
106 E5 Coleshill Bucks., Eng.
102 B5 Coleshill Oxon, Eng.
132 B2 Coleshill Warks., Eng.
40 F3 Coleton Devon, Eng.
94 I3 Coley B. and N.E. Som., Eng.
148 D4 Coley Staffs., Eng.
252 A3 Colfin D. and G., Scot.
58 E2 Colgate W. Sussex, Eng.
300 F4 Colgrain Arg. and B., Scot.
22 □O1 Colgrave Sound str. Scot.
74 C2 Colindale Gtr Lon., Eng.
292 G2 Colinsburgh Fife, Scot.
288 D3 Colinton Edin., Scot.
300 E4 Colintraive Arg. and B., Scot.
166 E2 Colkirk Norf., Eng.
22 C9 Coll i. Scot.
304 K4 Collace Perth and Kin., Scot.
331 D2 Collafirth Shet., Scot.
40 F3 Collaton St Mary Torbay, Eng.
292 F2 Collessie Fife, Scot.
136 D3 Collett's Green Worcs., Eng.
74 E2 Collier Row Gtr Lon., Eng.
110 E4 Collier's End Herts., Eng.
62 C3 Collier Street Kent, Eng.
74 C3 Collier's Wood Gtr Lon., Eng.
236 G2 Colliery Row T. and W., Eng.
314 H2 Collieston Abers., Scot.
26 C6 Colliford Reservoir resr Eng.
396 H5 Colligan Bridge Newry & Mourne, N. Ire.
252 F2 Collin D. and G., Scot.
86 F4 Collingbourne Ducis Wilts., Eng.
86 F4 Collingbourne Kingston Wilts., Eng.
176 E4 Collingham Notts., Eng.
222 F1 Collingham W. Yorks., Eng.
140 D2 Collington Here., Eng.

128 D4 Collingtree Northants., Eng.
102 E5 Collins End Oxon, Eng.
190 H4 Collins Green Warr., Eng.
136 C2 Collins Green Worcs., Eng.
308 G3 Colliston Angus, Scot.
40 G2 Colliton Devon, Eng.
132 D3 Collycroft Warks., Eng.
198 D3 Collyhurst Gtr Man., Eng.
128 F2 Collyweston Northants., Eng.
262 B6 Colmonell S. Ayr., Scot.
110 C2 Colmworth Bedford, Eng.
26 I4 Colne r. Eng.
314 D4 Colnabaichin Abers., Scot.
82 G3 Colnbrook W. and M., Eng.
124 E4 Colne Cambs., Eng.
228 I3 Colne Lancs., Eng.
26 N4 Colne r. Eng.
116 G2 Colne Engaine Essex, Eng.
166 G2 Colney Norf., Eng.
110 D5 Colney Heath Herts., Eng.
110 D5 Colney Street Herts., Eng.
98 H3 Coln Rogers Glos., Eng.
98 I3 Coln St Aldwyns Glos., Eng.
98 H3 Coln St Dennis Glos., Eng.
22 D10 Colonsay i. Scot.
256 F3 Colquhar Borders, Scot.
40 D2 Colscott Devon, Eng.
216 D2 Colsterdale N. Yorks., Eng.
170 C7 Colsterworth Lincs., Eng.
176 D5 Colston Bassett Notts., Eng.
314 G2 Coltfield Moray, Scot.
232 E6 Colthouse Cumbria, Eng.
166 H2 Coltishall Norf., Eng.
280 C4 Coltness N. Lanark., Scot.
232 D7 Colton Cumbria, Eng.
166 F3 Colton Norf., Eng.
216 F3 Colton N. Yorks., Eng.
148 D4 Colton Staffs., Eng.
222 F2 Colton W. Yorks., Eng.
326 E2 Col Uarach W. Isles, Scot.
396 E2 Columbkille Craigavon, N. Ire.
366 F5 Colva Powys, Wales
252 E3 Colvend D. and G., Scot.
331 D2 Colvister Shet., Scot.
140 E3 Colwall Here., Eng.
140 E3 Colwall Green Here., Eng.
140 E3 Colwall Stone Here., Eng.
244 E5 Colwell Northumb., Eng.
148 D4 Colwich Staffs., Eng.
176 C5 Colwick Notts., Eng.
350 E4 Colwinston V. of Glam., Wales
58 B4 Colworth W. Sussex, Eng.
40 G2 Colyford Devon, Eng.
40 G2 Colyton Devon, Eng.
102 C3 Combe Oxon, Eng.
94 G4 Combe Som., Eng.
82 B3 Combe W. Berks., Eng.
366 H5 Combe Powys, Wales
78 C3 Combe Common Surr., Eng.
94 J2 Combe Down B. and N.E. Som., Eng.
94 E4 Combe Florey Som., Eng.
94 J2 Combe Hay B. and N.E. Som., Eng.
40 D1 Combe Martin Devon, Eng.
40 F3 Combe Pafford Torbay, Eng.
396 J2 Comber Ards, N. Ire.
40 G2 Combe Raleigh Devon, Eng.
184 D2 Comberbach Cheshire West & Chester, Eng.
148 E5 Comberford Staffs., Eng.
124 E5 Comberton Cambs., Eng.
140 C2 Comberton Here., Eng.
94 G5 Combe St Nicholas Som., Eng.
40 G2 Combpyne Devon, Eng.
148 D3 Combridge Staffs., Eng.
132 C5 Combrook Warks., Eng.
188 B3 Combs Derbys., Eng.
120 E3 Combs Ford Suff., Eng.
94 F3 Combwich Som., Eng.
288 D3 Comely Bank Edin., Scot.
296 C4 Comer Gwyn., Wales
314 F3 Comers Abers., Scot.
136 D2 Comhampton Worcs., Eng.
362 F2 Comins Coch Cere., Wales
124 F5 Commercial End Cambs., Eng.
366 C3 Commins Coch Powys, Wales
216 C3 Commondale N. Yorks., Eng.
228 D4 Common Edge Blackpool, Eng.
36 F2 Common Moor Corn., Eng.
86 D2 Common Platt Wilts., Eng.
180 D3 Commonside Derbys., Eng.
180 E3 Common Side Derbys., Eng.
170 D4 Common Square Lincs., Eng.
388 F2 Compaw Coleraine, N. Ire.
198 E3 Compstall Gtr Man., Eng.
40 F3 Compton Devon, Eng.
52 K5 Compton Hants., Eng.
40 D3 Compton Plymouth, Eng.
148 B6 Compton Staffs., Eng.
78 B3 Compton Surr., Eng.
78 C2 Compton Surr., Eng.
82 C2 Compton W. Berks., Eng.
86 E4 Compton W. Sussex, Eng.
58 A3 Compton W. Sussex, Eng.
222 F1 Compton W. Yorks., Eng.
46 F2 Compton Abbas Dorset, Eng.
98 H2 Compton Abdale Glos., Eng.
86 D3 Compton Bassett Wilts., Eng.
102 B5 Compton Beauchamp Oxon., Eng.
94 G3 Compton Bishop Som., Eng.
86 D5 Compton Chamberlayne Wilts., Eng.
94 I2 Compton Dando B. and N.E. Som., Eng.
94 H4 Compton Dundon Som., Eng.
94 I3 Compton Martin B. and N.E. Som., Eng.
94 I4 Compton Pauncefoot Som., Eng.
46 D3 Compton Valence Dorset, Eng.
132 C4 Compton Verney Warks., Eng.
132 C5 Compton Wynyates Warks., Eng.
322 H4 Comra High., Scot.
292 C3 Comrie Fife, Scot.
304 C2 Comrie Perth and Kin., Scot.
300 E3 Conchra Arg. and B., Scot.
304 D3 Concraigie Perth and Kin., Scot.
228 F3 Conder Green Lancs., Eng.
140 C2 Conderton Worcs., Eng.
98 I2 Condicote Glos., Eng.
280 B3 Condorrat N. Lanark., Scot.
144 D4 Condover Shrop., Eng.
58 D2 Coneyhurst W. Sussex, Eng.
216 D2 Coneythorpe N. Yorks., Eng.
120 E2 Coney Weston Suff., Eng.
52 H4 Conford Hants., Eng.
322 K3 Congash High., Scot.
36 F2 Congdon's Shop Corn., Eng.
162 C3 Congerstone Leics., Eng.
166 G3 Congham Norf., Eng.
184 D3 Congleton Cheshire East, Eng.
94 H2 Congresbury N. Som., Eng.
148 C2 Congreve Staffs., Eng.
314 C2 Conicavel Moray, Scot.
170 E5 Coningsby Lincs., Eng.
124 C4 Conington Cambs., Eng.
124 D5 Conington Cambs., Eng.

208 E3 Conisbrough S. Yorks., Eng.
300 A4 Conisby Arg. and B., Scot.
170 A4 Conisholme Lincs., Eng.
232 D6 Coniston Cumbria, Eng.
210 D3 Coniston E. Riding, Eng.
216 C3 Coniston Cold N. Yorks., Eng.
216 C2 Conistone N. Yorks., Eng.
24 K5 Coniston Water l. Eng.
314 F2 Conland Abers., Scot.
396 J2 Conlig North Down, N. Ire.
378 D2 Connah's Quay Flints., Wales
300 D2 Connel Arg. and B., Scot.
262 F4 Connel Park E. Ayr., Scot.
388 I4 Connor Ballymena, N. Ire.
36 C3 Connor Downs Corn., Eng.
86 D4 Conock Wilts., Eng.
322 H2 Conon Bridge High., Scot.
296 B3 Cononish Stir., Scot.
216 C3 Cononley N. Yorks., Eng.
308 F3 Cononsyth Angus, Scot.
148 C2 Consall Staffs., Eng.
236 E2 Consett Durham, Eng.
216 D2 Constable Burton N. Yorks., Eng.
36 D3 Constantine Corn., Eng.
36 C3 Constantine Bay Corn., Eng.
322 H4 Contin High., Scot.
320 H4 Contullich High., Scot.
378 C2 Conwy Conwy, Wales
378 C3 Conwy admin. div. Wales
26 E1 Conwy r. Wales
62 F2 Conyer Kent, Eng.
120 D3 Conyer's Green Suff., Eng.
40 D2 Cooden E. Sussex, Eng.
58 I3 Coodham S. Ayr., Scot.
262 D3 Coodham S. Ayr., Scot.
40 D2 Cookbury Corn., Eng.
40 D2 Cookbury Wick Devon, Eng.
82 F2 Cookham W. and M., Eng.
82 F2 Cookham Dean W. and M., Eng.
82 F2 Cookham Rise W. and M., Eng.
136 F2 Cookhill Worcs., Eng.
120 H3 Cookley Suff., Eng.
136 D1 Cookley Worcs., Eng.
102 E5 Cookley Green Oxon, Eng.
136 E2 Cookley Green Suff., Eng.
314 G2 Cook's Cairn hill Scot.
136 E2 Cooksey Green Worcs., Eng.
148 C3 Cookshill Staffs., Eng.
116 E4 Cooksmill Green Essex, Eng.
314 G2 Cookston Abers., Scot.
396 E4 Cookstown Cookstown, N. Ire.
388 F5 Cookstown admin. dist. N. Ire.
396 E5 Coolderry Newry & Mourne, N. Ire.
264 C4 Coolforbeg Omagh, N. Ire.
252 D2 Cooldoo D. and G., Scot.
320 F3 Coolham W. Sussex, Eng.
62 D2 Cooling Medway, Eng.
62 D2 Cooling Street Medway, Eng.
170 B3 Coolkeeragh Derry, N. Ire.
402 F3 Coolkeeragh Omagh, N. Ire.
396 C4 Coolkill Armagh, N. Ire.
372 G5 Coolnagoppoge Moyle, N. Ire.
372 G5 Coolsallagh Banbridge, N. Ire.
322 H4 Coolshinny Magherafelt, N. Ire.
300 F3 Coombe Corn., Eng.
322 F3 Coombe Corn., Eng.
300 D5 Coombe Corn., Eng.
304 H4 Coombe Devon, Eng.
86 D5 Coombe Devon, Eng.
94 F4 Coombe Devon, Eng.
94 G5 Coombe Som., Eng.
86 D5 Coombe Wilts., Eng.
320 J2 Coombe Bissett Wilts., Eng.
288 K2 Corsback High., Scot.
94 D4 Coombe End Som., Eng.
46 C2 Coombe Hill Glos., Eng.
98 G2 Coombe Keynes Dorset, Eng.
58 E3 Coombes W. Sussex, Eng.
140 B2 Coombes Moor Here., Eng.
46 E1 Coombe Street Dorset, Eng.
154 B3 Coombeswood W. Mids, Eng.
402 E4 Cooneen Fermanagh, N. Ire.
58 C3 Coopersale Essex, Eng.
116 C3 Coopersale Street Essex, Eng.
62 A3 Cooper's Corner Kent, Eng.
58 E3 Cooper's Green E. Sussex, Eng.
58 C3 Cooper's Green Herts., Eng.
198 B2 Cooper Turning Gtr Man., Eng.
78 C1 Cootham W. Sussex, Eng.
23 L3 Copdock Suff., Eng.
116 E2 Copford Essex, Eng.
216 E2 Copgrove N. Yorks., Eng.
331 D2 Copister Shet., Scot.
110 C3 Cople Bedford, Eng.
236 D4 Copley Durham, Eng.
198 E3 Copley Gtr Man., Eng.
222 E2 Copley W. Yorks., Eng.
162 F3 Copley Hill W. Yorks., Eng.
102 D5 Coplow Dale Derbys., Eng.
216 F3 Copmanthorpe York, Eng.
148 B2 Copmere End Staffs., Eng.
52 F6 Copner Ports., Eng.
36 E1 Coppathorne Corn., Eng.
148 E3 Coppenhall Staffs., Eng.
184 E3 Coppenhall Moss Cheshire East, Eng.
144 F5 Coppicegate Shrop., Eng.
124 C4 Coppingford Cambs., Eng.
40 F1 Copplebridge Devon, Eng.
176 B5 Coppull Lancs., Eng.
228 G5 Coppull Moor Lancs., Eng.
162 E2 Copsale W. Sussex, Eng.
228 G5 Copster Green Lancs., Eng.
198 D2 Copster Hill Gtr Man., Eng.
62 H3 Cop Street Kent, Eng.
116 C3 Copt Green Essex, Eng.
154 C3 Copt Heath W. Mids, Eng.
78 F3 Copthorne Surr., Eng.
162 C3 Copt Oak Leics., Eng.
52 F2 Copythorne Hants., Eng.
162 D2 Coragh Fermanagh, N. Ire.
402 D5 Coragh Glebe Fermanagh, N. Ire.

314 D3 Corgarff Abers., Scot.
402 E2 Corgary Strabane, N. Ire.
396 E4 Corhammock Armagh, N. Ire.
52 F5 Corhampton Hants., Eng.
388 I2 Corkey Ballymoney, N. Ire.
132 C3 Corley Warks., Eng.
132 C3 Corley Ash Warks., Eng.
132 C3 Corley Moor Warks., Eng.
300 B5 Cornabus Arg. and B., Scot.
402 F5 Cornafannoge Fermanagh, N. Ire.
120 D4 Cornard Tye Suff., Eng.
402 F3 Cornavarrow Omagh, N. Ire.
232 B7 Corney Cumbria, Eng.
236 F3 Cornforth Durham, Eng.
314 E2 Cornhill Abers., Scot.
244 D2 Cornhill-on-Tweed Northumb., Eng.
222 B7 Cornholme W. Yorks., Eng.
116 E1 Cornish Hall End Essex, Eng.
136 D2 Cornmeadow Green Worcs., Eng.
329 D4 Cornquoy Orkney, Scot.
128 D4 Cornsay Durham, Eng.
52 D4 Cornsay Colliery Durham, Eng.
322 H2 Corntown High., Scot.
350 E4 Corntown V. of Glam., Wales
314 E2 Cornwall county Eng.
26 □ Cornwall, Cape c. Eng.
26 B7 Cornwall and West Devon Mining Landscape tourist site
102 B3 Cornwell Oxon, Eng.
40 D2 Cornwood Devon, Eng.
40 F3 Cornworthy Devon, Eng.
322 H3 Corpach High., Scot.
166 F3 Corpusty Norf., Eng.
402 D5 Corraghy Fermanagh, N. Ire.
232 A6 Corragole Fermanagh, N. Ire.
314 E2 Corran Armagh, N. Ire.
300 D3 Corran Arg. and B., Scot.
322 E3 Corran High., Scot.
402 G5 Corranbuie Arg. and B., Scot.
396 E4 Corranny Fermanagh, N. Ire.
405 D2 Corrany Isle of Man
22 K8 Correen Hills hills Scot.
322 H4 Corribeg High., Scot.
264 D3 Corrie N. Ayr., Scot.
252 G2 Corrie Common D. and G., Scot.
264 C4 Corriecravie N. Ayr., Scot.
252 D2 Corriedoo D. and G., Scot.
320 F3 Corriekinloch High., Scot.
322 I3 Corrielorne Arg. and B., Scot.
322 I3 Corrievorrie High., Scot.
58 E1 Corrimony High., Scot.
304 K3 Corringham Lincs., Eng.
170 B3 Corringham Thurrock, Eng.
372 G5 Corris Gwyn., Wales
372 G5 Corris Uchaf Gwyn., Wales
62 F4 Corrlarach High., Scot.
350 E3 Corrour Shooting Lodge High., Scot.
128 D4 Corrow Arg. and B., Scot.
300 F3 Corry High., Scot.
304 H4 Corrylach Arg. and B., Scot.
304 H4 Corrymuckloch Perth and Kin., Scot.
116 H4 Corsback High., Scot.
288 E3 Corscombe Dorset, Eng.
58 D2 Corse Glos., Eng.
300 E4 Corse Abers., Scot.
40 F2 Corse Abers., Eng.
252 E2 Corsebank D. and G., Scot.
252 E2 Corsegight Abers., Scot.
314 E2 Corsehill D. and G., Scot.
22 H12 Corse Lawn Worcs., Eng.
314 E2 Corse of Kinnoir Abers., Scot.
322 F2 Corserine hill Scot.
120 J2 Corsewall D. and G., Scot.
148 C5 Corsham Wilts., Eng.
124 F3 Corsindae Abers., Scot.
170 G3 Corsley Wilts., Eng.
86 B4 Corsley Heath Wilts., Eng.
86 B4 Corsock D. and G., Scot.
94 J2 Corston B. and N.E. Som., Eng.
86 C2 Corston Wilts., Eng.
24 N5 Corstorphine Edin., Scot.
36 D3 Corstorphine Hill Edin., Scot.
216 D2 Cortachy Angus, Scot.
396 K4 Cortamlat Newry & Mourne, N. Ire.
120 J1 Corton Suff., Eng.
86 C5 Corton Wilts., Eng.
94 I5 Corton Denham Som., Eng.
26 I5 Corve Dale val. Eng.
262 C6 Corwar House S. Ayr., Scot.
378 C6 Corwen Denb., Wales
74 C3 Coryton Thurrock, Eng.
162 C4 Cosby Leics., Eng.
102 D5 Coscote Oxon, Eng.
154 B2 Coseley W. Mids, Eng.
132 E3 Cosford Warks., Eng.
148 A5 Cosford Shrop., Eng.
128 D5 Cosgrove Northants., Eng.
52 E6 Cosham Ports., Eng.
358 C3 Coshieville Perth and Kin., Scot.
180 D2 Coskills N. Lincs., Eng.
350 E5 Cosmeston V. of Glam., Wales
176 B5 Cossall Notts., Eng.
210 G2 Cossall Marsh Notts., Eng.
162 D2 Cossington Leics., Eng.
94 G3 Cossington Som., Eng.
296 C5 Costa Orkney, Scot.
166 F3 Costessey Norf., Eng.
176 C6 Costock Notts., Eng.
162 E1 Coston Leics., Eng.
166 F3 Coston Norf., Eng.
102 B3 Cote Oxon, Eng.
94 G3 Cote Som., Eng.
184 D3 Cotebrook Cheshire West & Chester, Eng.
236 D2 Cotehill Cumbria, Eng.
232 F7 Cotes Cumbria, Eng.
162 C2 Cotes Leics., Eng.
162 D4 Cotesbach Leics., Eng.
94 D4 Cotford St Luke Som., Eng.
176 C5 Cotgrave Notts., Eng.
314 G2 Cothall Abers., Scot.
176 B5 Cotham Notts., Eng.
94 D3 Cothelstone Som., Eng.
236 C2 Cotherstone Durham, Eng.
102 C5 Cothill Oxon, Eng.
40 G2 Cotleigh Devon, Eng.
176 B5 Cotmanhay Derbys., Eng.
124 D4 Coton Cambs., Eng.
128 B2 Coton Northants., Eng.
148 D3 Coton Staffs., Eng.
148 C3 Coton Staffs., Eng.
148 B4 Coton Clanford Staffs., Eng.

148 C3 Coton Hayes Staffs., Eng.
148 C3 Coton Hill Staffs., Eng.
148 E3 Coton in the Clay Staffs., Eng.
180 D6 Coton in the Elms Derbys., Eng.
144 D3 Cotonwood Shrop., Eng.
148 B4 Cotonwood Staffs., Eng.
378 H4 Cotswold Hills hills Eng.
40 H4 Cott Devon, Eng.
210 F2 Cottam E. Riding, Eng.
228 F4 Cottam Lancs., Eng.
176 C4 Cottam Notts., Eng.
322 K2 Cottartown High., Scot.
36 F1 Cottenham Cambs., Eng.
74 C3 Cottenham Park Gtr Lon., Eng.
110 C1 Cotterdale N. Yorks., Eng.
148 B2 Cottered Herts., Eng.
144 F3 Cotteridge W. Mids, Eng.
216 C3 Cotterstock Northants., Eng.
120 C2 Cottesbrooke Northants., Eng.
40 G2 Cottesmore Rutland, Eng.
140 E3 Cottingham E. Riding, Eng.
154 B3 Cottingham Northants., Eng.
154 B3 Cottingley W. Yorks., Eng.
36 G2 Cottisford Oxon, Eng.
106 D3 Cotton Staffs., Eng.
222 C2 Cotton Suff., Eng.
314 G2 Cotton End Bedford, Eng.
304 G5 Cotton End Northants., Eng.
314 G2 Cottonworth Hants., Eng.
304 F3 Cottown Abers., Scot.
402 F3 Cotwall Telford, Eng.
144 A3 Cotwalton Staffs., Eng.
300 D4 Couch's Mill Corn., Eng.
314 F3 Coughton Here., Eng.
314 G3 Coughton Warks., Eng.
308 F3 Cougie High., Scot.
402 F3 Coughley Arg. and B., Scot.
232 A6 Coulaghailtro Arg. and B., Scot.
314 F3 Coulags High., Scot.
300 F3 Coulderton Cumbria, Eng.
252 D3 Coull Arg. and B., Scot.
314 F3 Coull Abers., Scot.
322 D2 Coulport Arg. and B., Scot.
268 E3 Coulsdon Gtr Lon., Eng.
94 F3 Coulston Wilts., Eng.
268 D5 Coulter S. Lanark., Scot.
94 G3 Coultings Som., Eng.
396 J2 Coultra Fife, Scot.
144 B2 Cound Shrop., Eng.
144 B2 Coundlane Shrop., Eng.
236 F3 Coundon Durham, Eng.
236 F3 Coundon Grange Durham, Eng.
216 C2 Countersett N. Yorks., Eng.
162 E3 Countess Wilts., Eng.
162 E3 Countesthorpe Leics., Eng.
40 E1 Countisbury Devon, Eng.
58 E1 County Oak W. Sussex, Eng.
304 K3 Coupar Angus Perth and Kin., Scot.
252 E2 Coupland Cumbria, Eng.
322 H2 Coupland Northumb., Eng.
300 D4 Cour Arg. and B., Scot.
314 G2 Court-at-Street Kent, Eng.
314 D2 Court Colman Bridg., Wales
252 D2 Courteenhall Northants., Eng.
356 F2 Court Henry Carmar., Wales
190 D3 Court Hey Merseyside, Eng.
154 F3 Court House Green W. Mids, Eng.
116 H4 Courtsend Essex, Eng.
94 F4 Courtway Som., Eng.
300 B4 Cousland Midlothian, Scot.
388 J1 Cousley Wood E. Sussex, Eng.
292 G2 Coustonn Arg. and B., Scot.
296 D5 Cove Devon, Eng.
296 D5 Cove Arg. and B., Scot.
253 D3 Cove Borders, Scot.
304 G3 Cove Hants., Eng.
308 G4 Cove High., Scot.
314 H3 Cove Bay Aberdeen, Scot.
262 D5 Cove Bottom Suff., Eng.
262 E3 Covehithe Suff., Eng.
148 C5 Coven Staffs., Eng.
252 F1 Coveney Cambs., Eng.
304 J3 Covenham St Bartholomew Lincs., Eng.
288 F2 Covenham St Mary Lincs., Eng.
288 E3 Coventry W. Mids, Eng.
288 E3 Coventry airport Warks., Eng.
314 G3 Cover r. Eng.
216 D2 Coverack Corn., Eng.
86 E2 Coverham N. Yorks., Eng.
124 D5 Covington Swindon, Eng.
124 B5 Covington Cambs., Eng.
144 B2 Covington S. Lanark., Scot.
296 E2 Cowan Bridge Lancs., Eng.
262 B6 Cowbeech E. Sussex, Eng.
58 I4 Cowbit Lincs., Eng.
300 C2 Cowbridge V. of Glam., Wales
308 G2 Cowcliffe W. Yorks., Eng.
264 J5 Cowden Kent, Eng.
292 F2 Cowdenbeath Fife, Scot.
314 C2 Cowdenburn Borders, Scot.
46 H2 Cowden Pound Kent, Eng.
296 D3 Cowers Lane Derbys., Eng.
296 E2 Cowes I.o.W., Eng.
296 J3 Cowesby N. Yorks., Eng.
116 E5 Cowesfield Green Wilts., Eng.
162 I4 Cowey Green Essex, Eng.
388 I4 Cowfold W. Sussex, Eng.
314 G2 Cowgill Cumbria, Eng.
308 G2 Cowie Aber., Scot.
210 G5 Cowie Stir., Scot.
276 E2 Cowlam Manor E. Riding, Eng.
40 G2 Cowley Devon, Eng.
98 G2 Cowley Glos., Eng.
74 B2 Cowley Gtr Lon., Eng.
102 D4 Cowley Oxon, Eng.
296 J5 Cowley Devon, Eng.
320 H3 Cowling Lancs., Eng.
228 H4 Cowling N. Yorks., Eng.
388 I3 Cowling N. Yorks., Eng.
256 F4 Cowlinge Suff., Eng.
292 I2 Cowmes W. Yorks., Eng.
256 J3 Cowpe Lancs., Eng.
252 G2 Cowpen Northumb., Eng.
116 F2 Cowpen Bewley Stockton, Eng.
148 B3 Cowplain Hants., Eng.
216 D2 Cowshill Durham, Eng.
236 E3 Cowslip Green N. Som., Eng.
162 C3 Cowstrandburn Fife, Scot.
236 C2 Cowthorpe N. Yorks., Eng.
102 C5 Coxbank Cheshire East, Eng.
166 F2 Coxbench Derbys., Eng.
176 B5 Coxbridge Som., Eng.
350 D2 Coxford Norf., Eng.
116 D5 Coxheath Kent, Eng.
46 H2 Coxhoe Durham, Eng.
94 G3 Coxley Som., Eng.
236 F3 Coxpark Corn., Eng.
222 F3 Coxtie Green Essex, Eng.
102 B2 Coxwold N. Yorks., Eng.
94 G3 Coychurch Bridg., Wales
110 B3 Coylet Arg. and B., Scot.
314 G2 Coylton S. Ayr., Scot.
396 H5 Coylumbridge High., Scot.
23 J4 Coynach Abers., Scot.
74 B3 Coynachie Abers., Scot.

148 C3 Coton Hayes Staffs., Eng.
350 E3 Coytrahen Bridg., Wales
58 F2 Crabbet Park W. Sussex, Eng.
136 F2 Crabbs Cross Worcs., Eng.
40 D3 Crabgate Norf., Eng.
58 E2 Crabtree Plymouth, Eng.
58 E2 Crabtree S. Yorks., Eng.
58 E2 Crabtree W. Sussex, Eng.
378 H4 Crabtree Green Wrex., Eng.
396 H4 Crabtreelane Craigavon, N. Ire.
78 D3 Crackaig Arg. and B., Scot.
120 F3 Crackenedge W. Yorks., Eng.
402 I3 Crackenthorpe Cumbria, Eng.
120 E3 Cranmer Green Suff., Eng.
300 D3 Crackington Corn., Eng.
36 F1 Crackington Haven Corn., Eng.
94 J3 Crackley Staffs., Eng.
144 F3 Crackleybank Shrop., Eng.
216 C2 Crackpot N. Yorks., Eng.
120 C2 Crackthorn Corner Suff., Eng.
40 G2 Cracoe N. Yorks., Eng.
140 E3 Craddock Devon, Eng.
154 B3 Cradley Here., Eng.
154 B3 Cradley W. Mids, Eng.
36 G2 Cradley Heath W. Mids, Eng.
106 D3 Craft Hole Corn., Eng.
222 C2 Cragg W. Yorks., Eng.
314 G2 Craggan Moray, Scot.
304 G5 Craggan Perth, Scot.
314 G2 Cragganmore Moray, Scot.
304 F3 Cragganruar Perth and Kin., Scot.
222 I3 Cragg W. Yorks., Eng.
236 E2 Craggie High., Scot.
144 A3 Craggie High., Scot.
236 F3 Craghead Durham, Eng.
120 H3 Craibstone Aberdeen, Scot.
314 F3 Craibstone Moray, Scot.
314 F3 Craichie Angus, Scot.
402 G2 Craig Strabane, N. Ire.
300 C2 Craig Arg. and B., Scot.
314 F3 Craig Arg. and B., Scot.
252 D3 Craig D. and G., Scot.
322 H2 Craig High., Scot.
322 D2 Craig High., Scot.
262 D5 Craig S. Ayr., Scot.
396 J2 Craigantlet North Down, N. Ire.
396 F3 Craigavon Craigavon, N. Ire.
396 E3 Craigavon admin. dist. N. Ire.
350 G3 Craig Berthlwyd M. Tyd., Wales
350 C2 Craig-cefn-parc Swansea, Wales
252 G2 Craigcleuch D. and G., Scot.
314 G2 Craigculter Abers., Scot.
304 K4 Craigdallie Abers., Scot.
300 B4 Craigdam Abers., Scot.
388 D3 Craigdarragh Derry, N. Ire.
252 E2 Craigdarroch E. Ayr., Scot.
322 H2 Craigdhu D. and G., Scot.
388 J3 Craigdoo Ballymena, N. Ire.
74 F3 Craigearn Abers., Scot.
314 D2 Craigellachie Moray, Scot.
252 C2 Craigencallie D. and G., Scot.
216 F2 Craigend Moray, Scot.
304 J4 Craigend Perth and Kin., Scot.
300 E2 Craigendive Arg. and B., Scot.
262 E5 Craigengillan E. Ayr., Scot.
262 E5 Craigenputtock D. and G., Scot.
304 J3 Craigens Arg. and B., Scot.
300 B4 Crousland Midlothian, Scot.
292 F2 Craigfad Moyle, N. Ire.
292 G2 Craighall Stir., Scot.
252 D3 Craighead Fife, Scot.
300 C4 Craighlaw D. and G., Scot.
308 E4 Craighouse Arg. and B., Scot.
304 G2 Craigie Dundee, Scot.
262 D3 Craigie Perth and Kin., Scot.
262 D3 Craigie S. Ayr., Scot.
296 F2 Craigie S. Ayr., Scot.
252 F1 Craigieburn D. and G., Scot.
304 J3 Craigielaw E. Lothian, Scot.
288 D3 Craigleith Edin., Scot.
288 D3 Craiglockhart Edin., Scot.
288 D3 Craigluig Arg. and B., Scot.
396 J3 Craigmaud Abers., Scot.
388 H4 Craigmillar Edin., Scot.
396 E5 Craigmore Antrim, N. Ire.
144 B2 Craigmore Arg. and B., Scot.
262 B2 Craignant Shrop., Eng.
296 C2 Craignavie Stir., Scot.
280 B2 Craigneil S. Ayr., Scot.
300 C2 Craigneuk N. Lanark., Scot.
308 C2 Craignure Arg. and B., Scot.
262 J5 Craigo Angus, Scot.
262 J5 Craigoch S. Ayr., Scot.
292 F2 Craigrothie Fife, Scot.
314 C2 Craigroy Moray, Scot.
314 C2 Craigroy Farm Moray, Scot.
296 C3 Craigruie Stir., Scot.
252 F1 Craigs Abers., Scot.
262 C5 Craigsanquhar Fife, Scot.
116 I5 Craig's End Essex, Eng.
388 I4 Craigstown Antrim, N. Ire.
388 I4 Craigstown Ballymena, N. Ire.
314 G3 Craigton Aberdeen, Scot.
308 C2 Craigton Angus, Scot.
308 E3 Craigton Angus, Scot.
304 D2 Craigton High., Scot.
320 C2 Craigtown High., Scot.
402 E2 Craig-y-nos Powys, Wales
94 G4 Craig-y-Voddy Isle of Man
388 I3 Crail Fife, Scot.
256 F2 Crailing Borders, Scot.
256 J3 Crailinghall Borders, Scot.
116 F2 Crakehall N. Yorks., Eng.
216 D2 Crakemarsh Staffs., Eng.
148 D2 Crambe N. Yorks., Eng.
216 F2 Cramlington Northumb., Eng.
244 F5 Cramond Edin., Scot.
288 D3 Cramond Bridge Edin., Scot.
184 D3 Cranage Cheshire East, Eng.
148 B3 Cranberry Staffs., Eng.
46 G2 Cranborne Dorset, Eng.
26 H6 Cranborne Chase for. Eng.
82 F3 Cranbourne Brack. F., Eng.
74 C2 Cranbrook Gtr Lon., Eng.
62 E2 Cranbrook Kent, Eng.
62 E2 Cranbrook Common Kent, Eng.
208 C2 Crane Moor S. Yorks., Eng.
116 B3 Cranfield Central Bedfordshire, Eng.
396 H5 Cranfield Newry & Mourne, N. Ire.
74 B3 Cranford Gtr Lon., Eng.
128 F3 Cranford St Andrew Northants., Eng.
128 F3 Cranford St John Northants., Eng.
98 G3 Cranham Glos., Eng.
74 F2 Cranham Gtr Lon., Eng.
190 E3 Crank Merseyside, Eng.
396 F4 Crankey W. Mourne, N. Ire.
78 D3 Cranleigh Surr., Eng.
120 F3 Cranley Suff., Eng.
402 I3 Cranlome Dungannon, N. Ire.
120 E3 Cranmer Green Suff., Eng.
300 D3 Cranmore I.o.W., Eng.
388 E2 Cranna Arg. and B., Scot.
244 A2 Crannach Abers., Scot.
402 I3 Crannogue Dungannon, N. Ire.
162 E3 Cranoe Leics., Eng.
120 H3 Cransford Suff., Eng.
256 F3 Cranshaws Borders, Scot.
22 G6 Cranstackie hill Scot.
405 D1 Cranstal Isle of Man
36 D2 Crantock Corn., Eng.
170 D5 Cranwell Lincs., Eng.
166 C3 Cranwich Norf., Eng.
166 E3 Cranworth Norf., Eng.
300 D3 Craobh Haven Arg. and B., Scot.
40 D3 Crapstone Devon, Eng.
300 D3 Crarae Arg. and B., Scot.
320 G3 Crask Inn High., Scot.
314 E3 Craskins Abers., Scot.
322 H2 Crask of Aigas High., Scot.
244 H3 Craster Northumb., Eng.
140 A3 Craswall Here., Eng.
314 H3 Crateford Staffs., Eng.
120 H3 Cratfield Suff., Eng.
314 F3 Crathes Abers., Scot.
314 D2 Crathie Abers., Scot.
322 H3 Crathie High., Scot.
216 D3 Crathorne N. Yorks., Eng.
144 C5 Craven Arms Shrop., Eng.
264 B2 Craw N. Ayr., Scot.
236 E2 Crawcrook T. and W., Eng.
228 F4 Crawford Lancs., Eng.
268 E4 Crawford S. Lanark., Scot.
396 J2 Crawfordjohn S. Lanark., Scot.
350 H4 Crawfordsburn North Down, N. Ire.
402 E2 Crawfordstown Strabane, N. Ire.
252 E1 Crawforddon D. and G., Scot.
252 E1 Crawick D. and G., Scot.
40 G2 Crawley Devon, Eng.
52 J4 Crawley Hants., Eng.
58 E2 Crawley Oxon, Eng.
58 F2 Crawley Down W. Sussex, Eng.
236 C3 Crawleyside Durham, Eng.
228 I4 Crawshawbooth Lancs., Eng.
405 C1 Crawyn Isle of Man
216 C2 Cray N. Yorks., Eng.
304 J2 Cray Perth and Kin., Scot.
366 G7 Cray Powys, Wales
74 F3 Crayford Gtr Lon., Eng.
216 F2 Crayke N. Yorks., Eng.
116 F4 Crays Hill Essex, Eng.
102 E5 Cray's Pond Oxon, Eng.
82 E2 Crazies Hill W'ham, Eng.
300 E2 Creacombe Devon, Eng.
300 E2 Creagan Arg. and B., Scot.
300 E2 C Creag Ghoraidh W. Isles, Scot. see Creagorry
402 F4 Creagh Fermanagh, N. Ire.
22 G9 Creag Meagaidh mt. Scot.
326 E5 Creagorry W. Isles, Scot.
128 D3 Creamore Bank Shrop., Eng.
128 D3 Creaton Northants., Eng.
252 G2 Creca D. and G., Scot.
140 C3 Credenhill Here., Eng.
40 F2 Crediton Devon, Eng.
252 D2 Creebridge D. and G., Scot.
94 F4 Creech St Michael Som., Eng.
36 E3 Creed Corn., Eng.
74 D2 Creekmouth Gtr Lon., Eng.
120 D7 Creeting St Mary Suff., Eng.
170 D7 Creeton Lincs., Eng.
252 C3 Creetown D. and G., Scot.
405 B1 Cregneash Isle of Man
366 F6 Cregrina Powys, Wales
292 F1 Creich Fife, Scot.
350 G3 Creigau Mon., Wales
350 A5 Creigiau Cardiff, Wales
36 G2 Cremyll Corn., Eng.
166 F2 Crendell Dorset, Eng.
22 F9 Creran, Loch inlet Scot.
180 C3 Cressage Shrop., Eng.
358 F3 Cresselly Pembs., Wales
116 F2 Cressing Essex, Eng.
244 H4 Cresswell Northumb., Eng.
358 F3 Cresswell Quay Pembs., Wales
148 C3 Cresswell Staffs., Eng.
232 F7 Creswell Derbys., Eng.
148 D4 Creswell Green Staffs., Eng.
304 I4 Cretingham Suff., Eng.
300 D4 Cretshengan Arg. and B., Scot.
184 E3 Crewe Cheshire East, Eng.
184 E3 Crewe Cheshire West & Chester, Eng.
184 E3 Crewe Green Cheshire East, Eng.
366 H2 Crewgreen Powys, Wales
94 H5 Crewkerne Som., Eng.
94 I2 Crew's Hole Bristol, Eng.
180 E5 Crewton Derbys., Eng.
296 C3 Crianlarich Stir., Eng.
362 F2 Cribyn Cere., Wales
36 E2 Criccieth Gwynedd, Wales
180 D3 Crich Derbys., Eng.
180 D3 Crich Carr Derbys., Eng.
314 D2 Crich Common Derbys., Eng.
288 D3 Crichie Abers., Scot.
288 D3 Crichton Midlothian, Scot.
128 B3 Crick Northants., Eng.
339 D3 Crick Mon., Wales
366 F6 Crickadarn Powys, Wales
52 H2 Cricket Hill Hants., Eng.
94 G5 Cricket Malherbie Som., Eng.
94 H5 Cricket St Thomas Som., Eng.
144 E3 Crickheath Shrop., Eng.
366 G7 Crickhowell Powys, Wales
86 C2 Cricklade Wilts., Eng.
74 C2 Cricklewood Gtr Lon., Eng.
140 D3 Crick's Green Here., Eng.
52 E3 Criddlestyle Hants., Eng.
304 G4 Crieff Perth and Kin., Scot.
22 I13 Criffel hill Scot.
148 B4 Coton Clanford Staffs., Eng.

Criftins Shrop., Eng. see Dudleston Heath
36 E2 Criggan Corn., Eng.
366 G2 Criggion Powys, Wales
222 E3 Crigglestone W. Yorks., Eng.
402 I4 Crilly Dungannon, N. Ire.
198 D2 Crimble Gtr Man., Eng.
94 G5 Crimchard Som., Eng.
236 H3 Crimdon Park Hartlepool, Eng.
314 H2 Crimond Abers., Scot.
314 H2 Crimonmogate Abers., Scot.
166 D3 Crimplesham Norf., Eng.
300 D3 Crinan Arg. and B., Scot.
388 E2 Crinan Ferry Arg. and B., Scot.
94 J3 Crindle Limavady, N. Ire.
280 C4 Crindledyke N. Lanark., Scot.
166 G3 Cringleford Norf., Eng.
256 F2 Cringletie Borders, Scot.
358 F3 Crinow Pembs., Wales
46 H2 Cripplesease hill Scot.
58 J3 Cripp's Corner E. Sussex, Eng.
116 F3 Crix Essex, Eng.
140 C4 Crizeley Here., Eng.
252 E2 Croachy High., Scot.
232 B5 Croalchapel D. and G., Scot.
402 K3 Croasdale Cumbria, Eng.
62 A2 Crockanroe Dungannon, N. Ire.
402 I2 Crockback Cookstown, N. Ire.
102 F5 Crockenhill Kent, Eng.
52 E5 Crocker End Oxon, Eng.
40 C2 Crockerhill Hants., Eng.
86 B4 Crockernwell Devon, Eng.
252 E2 Crockerton Wilts., Eng.
216 E2 Crockey Hill York, Eng.
62 A3 Crockham Hill Kent, Eng.
116 H2 Crockhurst Street Kent, Eng.
94 G5 Crockleford Heath Essex, Eng.
144 B2 Crock Street Som., Eng.
144 B2 Croesau Bach Shrop., Eng.
350 I3 Croeserw N.P.T., Wales
236 E2 Croesgoch Pembs., Wales
228 F5 Croes Hywel Mon., Wales
268 E4 Croes-Ian Cere., Wales
372 F3 Croesor Gwynedd, Wales
350 H2 Croespenmaen Caerp., Wales
216 B2 Croesyceiliog B. Gwent, Wales
356 E3 Croesyceiliog Carmar., Wales
350 H3 Croes-y-mwyalch B. Gwent, Wales
339 C2 Croes-y-pant Mon., Wales
372 E2 Croesywaun Gwynedd, Wales
140 E4 Croford Som., Eng.
58 F2 Croft Here., Eng.
162 D3 Croft Lincs., Eng.
170 F5 Croft Leics., Eng.
190 F3 Croft Warr., Eng.
232 A2 Croftamie Stir., Scot.
276 E3 Croftfoot Glas., Scot.
232 E2 Crofthead Cumbria, Eng.
304 G2 Croftmore Perth and Kin., Scot.
86 F3 Crofton Wilts., Eng.
74 D3 Crofton W. Yorks., Eng.
198 C3 Crofts Bank Gtr Man., Eng.
320 J3 Crofts of Benachielt High., Scot.
314 G2 Crofts of Haddo Abers., Scot.
350 B3 Crofty Swansea, Wales
372 J3 Crogen Gwynedd, Wales
300 C2 Croggan Arg. and B., Scot.
232 G4 Croglin Cumbria, Eng.
320 H4 Croick High., Scot.
320 I2 Croick High., Scot.
300 B2 Croig Arg. and B., Scot.
326 E5 Crois Dughaill W. Isles, Scot.
405 B3 Croit e Caley Isle of Man
322 K4 Cromarty High., Scot.
22 H7 Cromarty Firth est. Scot.
292 C3 Crombie Fife, Scot.
308 F3 Crombie Mill Angus, Scot.
314 F2 Cromblet Abers., Scot.
322 K2 Cromdale High., Scot.
22 I8 Cromdale, Hills of hills Scot.
110 E4 Cromer Herts., Eng.
166 G1 Cromer Norf., Eng.
110 D5 Cromer Hyde Herts., Eng.
180 D4 Cromford Derbys., Eng.
98 I3 Cromhall S. Glos., Eng.
98 I3 Cromhall Common S. Glos., Eng.
388 I4 Cromkill Ballymena, N. Ire.
326 E3 Cromore Coleraine, N. Ire.
326 E3 Cromore W. Isles, Scot.
198 D2 Crompton Gtr Man., Eng.
198 E2 Crompton Fold Gtr Man., Eng.
176 E4 Cromwell Notts., Eng.
222 D2 Cromwell Bottom W. Yorks., Eng.
262 F4 Cronberry E. Ayr., Scot.
52 G3 Crondall Hants., Eng.
405 C2 Cronk-y-Voddy Isle of Man
190 D3 Cronton Merseyside, Eng.
232 F6 Crook Cumbria, Eng.
236 E3 Crook Durham, Eng.
262 E3 Crookedholm E. Ayr., Scot.
86 F3 Crooked Soley Wilts., Eng.
208 D3 Crookes S. Yorks., Eng.
244 G4 Crookgate Northumb., Eng.
82 C2 Crookham W. Berks., Eng.
244 H3 Crookham Northumb., Eng.
52 G3 Crookham Village Hants., Eng.
232 F7 Crooklands Cumbria, Eng.
304 I5 Crook of Devon Perth and Kin., Scot.
276 D2 Crookston Glas., Scot.
102 C2 Cropredy Oxon, Eng.
162 C2 Cropston Leics., Eng.
136 E3 Cropthorne Worcs., Eng.
216 H2 Cropton N. Yorks., Eng.
176 C5 Cropwell Bishop Notts., Eng.
176 C5 Cropwell Butler Notts., Eng.
326 E2 Cros W. Isles, Scot.
264 C2 Crosbie N. Ayr., Scot.
326 E2 Crosbost W. Isles, Scot.
405 C2 Crosby Isle of Man
232 E4 Crosby Cumbria, Eng.
190 C3 Crosby Merseyside, Eng.
170 L3 Crosby N. Lincs., Eng.
232 H2 Crosby Court N. Yorks., Eng.
232 G5 Crosby Garrett Cumbria, Eng.
232 F3 Crosby-on-Eden Cumbria, Eng.
232 G5 Crosby Ravensworth Cumbria, Eng.
232 D6 Crosby Villa Cumbria, Eng.
94 H3 Croscombe Som., Eng.
144 C2 Crosemere Shrop., Eng.
222 C3 Crosland Hill W. Yorks., Eng.
94 I3 Cross Som., Eng.
326 E2 Cross W. Isles, Scot.
300 D3 Crossaig Arg. and B., Scot.
300 C2 Crossbeg Arg. and B., Scot.
388 K6 Crossan Lisburn, N. Ire.
300 D Crossapol Arg. and B., Scot.
300 C Crossapol Bay b. Scot.
339 C2 Cross Ash Mon., Wales
62 D2 Cross-at-Hand Kent, Eng.
136 G3 Cross Bank Worcs., Eng.
58 J4 Cross Green E. Sussex, Eng.
148 B4 Coton Clanford Staffs., Eng.
232 B4 Crosscanonby Cumbria, Eng.

2 I3 Crosscavanagh Dungannon, N. Ire.
144 C3 Crossdale Shrop., Eng.
6 G1 Crossdale Street Norf., Eng.
0 C2 Cross End Bedford., Eng.
6 E2 Cross End Essex, Eng.
6 E2 Cross End M.K., Eng.
0 D1 Crossens Merseyside, Eng.
4 M4 Cross Fell hill Eng.
2 C1 Crossflatts W. Yorks., Eng.
2 E2 Crossford D. and G., Scot.
2 D3 Crossford Fife, Scot.
8 C2 Crossford S. Lanark., Scot.
2 H4 Cross Foxes Inn Gwynedd, Wales
6 J3 Crossgar Down, N. Ire.
8 F7 Crossgate Coleraine, N. Ire.
0 F7 Crossgate Lincs., Eng.
8 C3 Crossgate Staffs., Eng.
8 L4 Crossgate Larne, N. Ire.
8 E3 Crossgatehall E. Lothian, Scot.
6 H2 Crossgates S. Yorks., Eng.
2 F2 Crossgates W. Yorks., Eng.
2 D3 Crossgates Fife, Scot.
4 I4 Crossgates Perth and Kin., Scot.
6 E5 Crossgates Powys, Wales
8 F2 Crossgill Lancs., Eng.
0 D2 Cross Green Devon, Eng.
8 C5 Cross Green Staffs., Eng.
0 D4 Cross Green Suff., Eng.
0 D4 Cross Green Suff., Eng.
0 E4 Cross Green Suff., Eng.
2 E3 Crosshands E. Ayr., Scot.
6 D3 Cross Hands Carmar., Wales
6 D3 Cross Hands Pembs., Wales
0 E4 Cross Hill Derbys., Eng.
2 D5 Crosshill Fife, Scot.
2 E3 Crosshill S. Ayr., Scot.
4 D4 Crosshouse E. Ayr., Scot.
4 D4 Cross Houses Shrop., Eng.
8 H3 Cross in Hand E. Sussex, Eng.
2 D3 Cross Inn Cere., Wales
0 F3 Cross Inn Cere., Wales
0 F3 Cross Inn R.C.T., Wales
6 B3 Cross Keys Wilts., Eng.
8 H4 Crosskeys Ballymena, N. Ire.
0 H3 Crosskeys Caerp., Wales
0 J2 Crosskirk High., Scot.
2 E6 Cross Lane I.o.W., Eng.
8 F2 Cross Lanes N. Yorks., Eng.
4 B3 Crosslanes Shrop., Eng.
8 H3 Cross Lanes Wrex., Eng.
6 F4 Crosslee Borders, Scot.
6 C2 Crosslee Renf., Scot.
6 E5 Crossmaglen Newry & Mourne, N. Ire.
8 E3 Crossmichael D. and G., Scot.
8 E3 Crossmoor Lancs., Eng.
6 E2 Crossmyloof Glas., Scot.
6 I2 Crossnacreevy Castlereagh, N. Ire.
0 D4 Cross o'th'hands Derbys., Eng.
8 F4 Cross Roads Magherafelt, N. Ire.
2 E3 Crossroads Abers., Scot.
2 E3 Crossroads E. Ayr., Scot.
2 D2 Crossroads Fife, Scot.
8 J2 Cross Skreen Moyle, N. Ire.
0 G2 Cross Street Suff., Eng.
0 D1 Cross Town Cheshire East, Eng.
9 D1 Crossway Mon., Wales
6 E5 Crossway Powys, Wales
0 D3 Crossway Green Worcs., Eng.
9 D3 Crossway Green Mon., Wales
8 Crossways Dorset, Eng.
8 D2 Crossways Glos., Eng.
8 F2 Crosswell Pembs., Wales
Crosswood Cere., Wales see Trawscoed
8 E4 Crosthwaite Cumbria, Eng.
8 F5 Croston Lancs., Eng.
6 H2 Crostwick Norf., Eng.
6 H2 Crostwight Norf., Eng.
2 B3 Crothair W. Isles, Scot.
6 N4 Crouch Kent, Eng.
6 Crouch End Gtr Lon., Eng.
0 D5 Croucheston Wilts., Eng.
6 D5 Crouch Hill Dorset, Eng.
8 B6 Croughton Northants., Eng.
2 B5 Crovie Abers., Scot.
2 B5 Crow Hants., Eng.
8 G2 Crowborough E. Sussex, Eng.
8 G2 Crowborough Warren E. Sussex, Eng.
4 E4 Crowcombe Som., Eng.
0 B3 Crowdecote Derbys., Eng.
2 E5 Crowdhill Hants., Eng.
2 Crow Edge S. Yorks., Eng.
2 F4 Crowell Oxon, Eng.
4 D5 Crow End Cambs., Eng.
8 C5 Crowfield Northants., Eng.
0 D4 Crowfield Suff., Eng.
0 D4 Crow Green Essex, Eng.
0 D4 Crow Hill Here., Eng.
0 Crowhole Derbys., Eng.
8 I3 Crowhurst E. Sussex, Eng.
8 F2 Crowhurst Surr., Eng.
8 F2 Crowhurst Lane End Surr., Eng.
0 E1 Crowland Lincs., Eng.
0 E1 Crowland Suff., Eng.
6 C3 Crowlas Corn., Eng.
0 B2 Crowle N. Lincs., Eng.
6 E3 Crowle Worcs., Eng.
2 E8 Crowlin Islands is Scot.
2 D5 Crowmarsh Gifford Oxon, Eng.
0 F3 Crownthorpe Norf., Eng.
6 C2 Crowntown Corn., Eng.
6 C2 Crows-an-wra Corn., Eng.
6 C2 Crowsnest Shrop., Eng.
2 F3 Crowthorne Brack. F., Eng.
0 Croxall Cheshire West & Chester, Eng.
8 E4 Croxall Staffs., Eng.
8 E3 Croxby Lincs., Eng.
8 D3 Croxdale Durham, Eng.
8 D3 Croxden Staffs., Eng.
0 C6 Croxley Green Herts., Eng.
2 C6 Croxton Cambs., Eng.
0 D4 Croxton N. Lincs., Eng.
0 D4 Croxton Norf., Eng.
8 B3 Croxton Staffs., Eng.
4 D3 Croxtonbank Staffs., Eng.
8 Croxton Green Cheshire East, Eng.
0 C1 Croxton Kerrial Leics., Eng.
2 I2 Croy High., Scot.
0 D1 Croy N. Lanark., Scot.
8 D1 Croyde Devon, Eng.
8 D6 Croyde Bay Devon, Eng.
2 D3 Croydon Cambs., Eng.
0 D3 Croydon Gtr Lon., Eng.
0 D3 Croydon met. bor. Gtr Lon., Eng.

144 C3 Cruckmeole Shrop., Eng.
144 C3 Cruckton Shrop., Eng.
262 D4 Cruden Bay Abers., Scot.
331 D3 Crudgington Telford, Eng.
331 D2 Crudwell Wilts., Eng.
366 F4 Crug Powys, Wales
326 D2 Crugybar Carmar., Wales
388 H5 Crùlabhig W. Isles, Scot.
180 D3 Crumlin Antrim, N. Ire.
148 C4 Crumlin Caerp., Wales
52 E5 Crumpfield Worcs., Eng.
198 D2 Crumpsall Gtr Man., Eng.
144 E5 Crumpsbrook Shrop., Eng.
62 F3 Crundale Kent, Eng.
358 E3 Crundale Pembs., Wales
402 E3 Cruntully Fermanagh, N. Ire.
358 G3 Crunwere Farm Pembs., Wales
268 A2 Crutherland Farm S. Lanark., Scot.
396 J3 Crux Easton Hants., Eng.
402 F3 Crwbin Carmar., Wales
388 G4 Cryers Hill Bucks., Eng.
82 C3 Crymlyn Gwynedd, Wales
288 D3 Crymych Pembs., Wales
94 G5 Crynant N.P.T., Wales
94 G4 Crystal Palace Gtr Lon., Eng.
62 C4 Cuaig High., Scot.
62 C4 Cubbington Warks., Eng.
40 E3 Cubert Corn., Eng.
36 D3 Cubitt Town Gtr Lon., Eng.
36 D3 Cubley S. Yorks., Eng.
388 J2 Cublington Bucks., Eng.
388 J2 Cublington Here., Eng.
94 F4 Cuckfield W. Sussex, Eng.
140 C4 Cucklington Som., Eng.
208 L2 Cuckmere r. Eng.
252 C3 Cuckney Notts., Eng.
94 C4 Cuckold's Green Suff., Eng.
198 D2 Cuckoo Bridge Lincs., Eng.
372 F4 Cuckoo's Corner Hants., Eng.
116 D2 Cuckoo's Nest Cheshire West & Chester, Eng.
216 G1 Cuddesdon Oxon, Eng.
180 D5 Cuddington Bucks., Eng.
331 B3 Cuddington Cheshire West & Chester, Eng.
58 C3 Cuddington Heath Cheshire West & Chester, Eng.
148 B2 Cuddy Hill Lancs., Eng.
331 D3 Cudham Gtr Lon., Eng.
102 E5 Cudliptown Devon, Eng.
62 C2 Cudworth Som., Eng.
170 E3 Cudworth S. Yorks., Eng.
350 G2 Cuerdley Cross Warr., Eng.
378 E2 Cuffley Herts., Eng.
350 D3 Cuidhaseadair W. Isles, Scot.
350 F2 Cuidhir W. Isles, Scot.
356 F1 Cuidhtinis W. Isles, Scot. see Quidinish
366 F6 Cuidrach High., Scot.
366 F6 Cuilcagh Ireland/U.K.
350 F2 Cuillin Hills hills Scot.
366 D4 Cuillin Sound sea chan. Scot.
339 D3 Cuilmuich Arg. and B., Scot.
362 E2 Culag Arg. and B., Scot.
314 H2 Culardoch hill Scot.
208 E3 Culbo High., Scot.
322 J2 Culbone Som., Eng.
252 C3 Culburnie High., Scot.
264 F2 Culcabock High., Scot.
292 D3 Culcharry High., Scot.
262 E2 Culcheth Warr., Eng.
320 H4 Culdrain Abers., Scot.
276 D2 Culduie High., Scot.
304 J2 Culford Suff., Eng.
322 H3 Culfordheath Suff., Eng.
304 I2 Culgaith Cumbria, Eng.
304 J2 Culham Oxon, Eng.
296 D5 Culindrach Arg. and B., Scot.
262 E5 Culkein Arg. and B., Scot.
288 C3 Culkerton Glos., Eng.
320 I3 Cullaville Newry & Mourne, N. Ire.
322 I3 Cullen Moray, Scot.
262 D2 Cullercoats T. and W., Eng.
320 H4 Cullingworth W. Yorks., Eng.
276 D2 Cullion Strabane, N. Ire.
304 J2 Culli, Fermanagh, N. Ire.
314 E2 Cullipool Arg. and B., Scot.
314 F3 Cullivoe Shet., Scot.
304 J2 Culloch Perth and Kin., Scot.
198 C3 Culloden High., Scot.
154 C2 Cullompton Devon, Eng.
232 K7 Cullybackey Ballymena, N. Ire.
236 E4 Cullycapple Coleraine, N. Ire.
40 I3 Cullyhanna Newry & Mourne, N. Ire.
58 F2 Culmalzie D. and G., Scot.
184 F3 Culmington Shrop., Eng.
304 I2 Cul Mòr hill Scot.
288 D3 Culmore Derry, N. Ire.
296 D5 Culnadalloch Arg. and B., Scot.
262 E5 Culnady Magherafelt, N. Ire.
288 C3 Culnagrew Magherafelt, N. Ire.
320 I3 Culnaknock High., Scot.
322 I3 Culpho Suff., Eng.
262 D2 Culquhirk D. and G., Scot.
320 H4 Culrain High., Scot.
276 D2 Culross Fife, Scot.
304 J2 Culroy S. Ayr., Scot.
288 D3 Culsh Abers., Scot.

264 G3 Cunninghamhead N. Ayr., Scot.
300 E2 Cunning Park S. Ayr., Scot.
326 C2 Cunningsburgh Shet., Scot.
Cunnister Shet., Scot.
262 C5 Cunnoquhie Fife, Scot.
326 D2 Cupar Fife, Scot.
292 C1 Cupar Muir Fife, Scot.
180 D3 Curbar Derbys., Eng.
148 C4 Curborough Staffs., Eng.
52 E5 Curbridge Hants., Eng.
102 B4 Curbridge Oxon, Eng.
222 D2 Curdridge Hants., Eng.
222 E2 Curdworth Warks., Eng.
396 D4 Curland Som., Eng.
94 F5 Curland Som., Eng.
120 H3 Curlew Green Suff., Eng.
116 F3 Curling Tye Green Essex, Eng.
94 Curload Som., Eng.
402 G3 Curr Omagh, N. Ire.
396 J3 Curragh Down, N. Ire.
402 F3 Curraghamulkin Omagh, N. Ire.
388 G4 Curran Magherafelt, N. Ire.
82 C3 Curridge W. Berks., Eng.
288 D3 Currie Edin., Scot.
94 G5 Curry Mallet Som., Eng.
94 G4 Curry Rivel Som., Eng.
62 C4 Curteis' Corner Kent, Eng.
62 C4 Curtisden Green Kent, Eng.
40 E3 Curtisknowle Devon, Eng.
36 D3 Cury Corn., Eng.
36 D3 Cusgarne Corn., Eng.
388 J2 Cushendall Moyle, N. Ire.
388 J2 Cushendun Moyle, N. Ire.
94 F4 Cushuish Som., Eng.
140 C4 Cusop Here., Eng.
208 L2 Cusworth S. Yorks., Eng.
252 C3 Cutcloy D. and G., Scot.
94 C4 Cutcombe Som., Eng.
198 D2 Cutgate Gtr Man., Eng.
372 F4 Cutiau Gwynedd, Wales
116 D2 Cutlers Green Essex, Eng.
216 G1 Cutnall Green Worcs., Eng.
180 D5 Cut Moor Derbys., Eng.
331 B3 Cutsdean Glos., Eng.
98 H2 Cutsyke W. Yorks., Eng.
148 B2 Cutthorpe Derbys., Eng.
331 D3 Cutts Shet., Scot.
102 E5 Cuxham Oxon, Eng.
62 C2 Cuxton Medway, Eng.
170 E3 Cuxwold Lincs., Eng.
350 G2 Cwm B. Gwent, Wales
378 E2 Cwm Denb., Wales
350 D3 Cwmafan N.P.T., Wales
350 F2 Cwmaman R.C.T., Wales
356 F1 Cwmann Carmar., Wales
366 F6 Cwmbach Carmar., Wales
350 F2 Cwmbach Powys, Wales
366 D4 Cwmbach R.C.T., Wales
339 D3 Cwmbelan Powys, Wales
362 E2 Cwmbrân Torf., Wales
314 H2 Cwmbrwyno Cere., Wales
208 E3 Cwmcarn Caerp., Wales
322 J2 Cwmcarvan Mon., Wales
372 H4 Cwm-Cewydd Gwynedd, Wales
120 G4 Cwm-cou Cere., Wales
58 I3 Cwmcrawnon Powys, Wales
128 D4 Cwmdare R.C.T., Wales
216 D2 Cwmdu Carmar., Wales
300 F2 Cwmdu Powys, Wales
304 I3 Cwmduad Carmar., Wales
Cwmerfyn Cere., Wales
296 D5 Cwmfelin M. Tyd., Wales
262 E5 Cwmfelin Boeth Carmar., Wales
288 C3 Cwmfelinfach Caerp., Wales
320 I3 Cwmfelin Mynach Carmar., Wales
322 I3 Cwmffrwd Carmar., Wales
262 D2 Cwmfrwd Carmar., Wales
320 H4 Cwm Ffrwd-oer Torf., Wales
276 D2 Cwmgiedd Powys, Wales
304 J2 Cwmgors N.P.T., Wales
Cwm Gwaun Pembs., Wales
322 H3 Cwmgwili Carmar., Wales
304 I2 Cwmgwrach N.P.T., Wales
304 J2 Cwmgwyn Swansea, Wales
300 C4 Cwm Head Shrop., Eng.
322 I3 Cwmhiraeth Carmar., Wales
322 H4 Cwmifor Carmar., Wales
322 H4 Cwm Irfon Powys, Wales
304 H2 Cwmisfael Carmar., Wales
320 H3 Cwm-Llinau Powys, Wales
184 F3 Cwmllyfri Carmar., Wales
304 I2 Cwmllynfell N.P.T., Wales
304 J3 Cwm-mawr Carmar., Wales
288 D3 Cwm-miles Carmar., Wales
304 G4 Cwm-Morgan Carmar., Wales
304 G4 Cwm-parc R.C.T., Wales
288 D3 Cwmpengraig Carmar., Wales
262 D4 Cwm Penmachno Conwy, Wales
128 D4 Cwmpennar R.C.T., Wales
268 C2 Cwm Plysgog Pembs., Wales
252 D2 Cwmsychpant Cere., Wales
252 F2 Cwmsyfiog Caerp., Wales
62 I3 Cwmsymlog Cere., Wales
116 H4 Cwmtillery B. Gwent, Wales
74 D2 Cwm-twrch Uchaf Carmar., Wales
232 B5 Cwm-y-glo Gwynedd, Wales
322 I3 Cwmyoy Mon., Wales
232 F2 Cwm-yr-Eglwys Pembs., Wales
244 A6 Cwmyrhaiadr Powys, Wales
244 G5 Cwmystwyth Cere., Wales
216 D1 Cwrt Gwynedd, Wales
216 E2 Cwrt-newydd Cere., Wales
208 E3 Cwrt-y-cadno Carmar., Wales
252 F2 Cwrt-y-gollen Powys, Wales
378 E3 Cyffylliog Denb., Wales
366 F3 Cyfronydd Powys, Wales
366 F3 Cymau Flints., Wales
350 D1 Cymmer N.P.T., Wales
356 F1 Cymmer R.C.T., Wales
26 D4 Cymru admin. div. see Wales
350 H2 Cyncoed Cardiff, Wales
356 F3 Cynghordy Carmar., Wales
296 E3 Cynheidre Carmar., Wales
262 D4 Cynin r. Wales
322 I4 Cynwyd Denb., Wales
110 D4 Cynwyl Elfed Carmar., Wales
26 D4 Cywyn r. Wales

D

252 D2 Dabton D. and G., Scot.
232 E5 Dacre Cumbria, Eng.
216 D2 Dacre N. Yorks., Eng.
236 D2 Daddry Shield Durham, Eng.
106 B2 Dadford Bucks., Eng.
162 C3 Dadlington Leics., Eng.
356 F3 Dafen Carmar., Wales
166 F3 Daffy Green Norf., Eng.
136 D2 Dagtail End Worcs., Eng.

120 E3 Dagworth Suff., Eng.
300 E2 Dail Arg. and B., Scot.
326 C2 Dail Beag W. Isles, Scot.
Dail Bho Dheas W. Isles, Scot. see South Dell
262 C5 Dailly S. Ayr., Scot.
326 D2 Dail Mòr W. Isles, Scot.
292 G1 Dairsie Fife, Scot.
210 H4 Dairy House E. Riding, Eng.
154 C2 Daisy Bank W. Mids, Eng.
120 E3 Daisy Green Suff., Eng.
222 D2 Daisy Hill W. Yorks., Eng.
222 E2 Daisy Hill W. Yorks., Eng.
190 F3 Daisy Hill Armagh, N. Ire.
396 D4 Dalabrog W. Isles, Scot.
62 F3 Dalavich Arg. and B., Scot.
244 D4 Dalballoch High., Scot.
36 F2 Dalbeattie D. and G., Scot.
252 E3 Dalblair E. Ayr., Scot.
262 G4 Dalbog Angus, Scot.
308 F1 Dalbreck High., Scot.
320 H3 Dalbury Derbys., Eng.
180 D5 Dalby Isle of Man
405 B2 Dalby Lincs., Eng.
170 G4 Dalby N. Yorks., Eng.
216 F2 Dalcairnie E. Ayr., Scot.
262 E5 Dalchalloch Perth and Kin., Scot.
304 F2 Dalchalm High., Scot.
320 I3 Dalchenna Arg. and B., Scot.
300 E4 Dalchreichart High., Scot.
322 G3 Dalchruin Perth and Kin., Scot.
176 D3 Dalderby Lincs., Eng.
314 F2 Daldownie Abers., Scot.
208 D3 Dale Cumbria, Eng.
252 D3 Dale Gtr Man., Eng.
256 H3 Dale Pembs., Wales
366 C3 Dale Abbey Derbys., Eng.
314 F2 Dale End Derbys., Eng.
40 C2 Dale End N. Yorks., Eng.
396 J3 Dale Head Cumbria, Eng.
244 G5 Dalehouse N. Yorks., Eng.
222 E2 Dale Moor Derbys., Eng.
166 G4 Darrow Green Norf., Eng.
120 I3 Darsham Suff., Eng.
170 D6 Dart r. Eng.
208 E3 Dartans Strabane, N. Ire.
314 H2 Dartfield Abers., Scot.
62 B2 Dartford Kent, Eng.
40 E3 Dartington Devon, Eng.
40 E3 Dartmeet Devon, Eng.
26 D6 Dartmoor hills Eng.
26 E6 Dartmoor National Park nat. park Eng.
40 F2 Dartmouth Devon, Eng.
74 D2 Dartmouth Park Gtr Lon., Eng.
208 C2 Darton S. Yorks., Eng.
262 F3 Darvel E. Ayr., Scot.
58 I3 Darwell Hole E. Sussex, Eng.
228 H4 Darwen B'burn., Eng.
82 G3 Datchet W. and M., Eng.
110 C4 Datchworth Herts., Eng.
110 C4 Datchworth Green Herts., Eng.
198 C2 Daubhill Gtr Man., Eng.
314 D2 Daugh of Kinnermony Moray, Scot.
292 G2 Dauntsey Wilts., Eng.
86 C2 Dauntsey Green Wilts., Eng.
86 C2 Dauntsey Lock Wilts., Eng.
314 C2 Dava Moray, Scot.
256 H4 Davenham Cheshire West & Chester, Eng.
184 D2 Davenport Gtr Man., Eng.
198 E3 Davenport Cheshire East, Eng.
184 F2 Davenport Green Gtr Man., Eng.
314 F2 Daventry Northants., Eng.
276 E2 Davidson's Mains Edin., Scot.
280 H4 Davidstow Corn., Eng.
280 D2 Davington D. and G., Scot.
36 F2 Daviot Abers., Scot.
256 E2 Daviot High., Scot.
110 D5 Davoch of Grange Moray, Scot.
362 E3 Davyhulme Gtr Man., Eng.
252 E3 Daw End W. Mids, Eng.
166 H2 Dawley Telford, Eng.
148 C3 Dawley Bank Telford, Eng.
244 E6 Dawlish Devon, Eng.
86 B4 Dawlish Warren Devon, Eng.
140 B3 Dawn Conwy, Wales
198 C2 Daws Heath Essex, Eng.
148 B3 Dawsmere Lincs., Eng.
356 C3 Day Green Cheshire East, Eng.
372 F2 Dayhills Staffs., Eng.
372 F2 Dayhouse Bank Worcs., Eng.
358 G3 Daylesford Glos., Eng.
372 D3 Daddon Oxon, Eng.

166 F3 Danemoor Green Norf., Eng.
180 E4 Danesmoor Derbys., Eng.
314 G3 Danestone Aberdeen, Scot.
62 E4 Daniel's Water Kent, Eng.
288 D3 Danskine E. Lothian, Scot.
210 H4 Danthorpe E. Riding, Eng.
132 B4 Danzey Green Warks., Eng.
78 B2 Darby End W. Mids, Eng.
232 H7 Darby Green Hants., Eng.
216 C2 Darcy Lever Gtr Man., Eng.
62 B2 Darenth Kent, Eng.
170 E7 Daresbury Halton, Eng.
170 E7 Darfield S. Yorks., Eng.
208 D2 Dargate Kent, Eng.
62 F3 Dargues Northumb., Eng.
244 D4 Darite Corn., Eng.
36 F2 Darkley Armagh, N. Ire.
98 F2 Darland Medway, Eng.
98 F2 Darlaston W. Mids, Eng.
136 E3 Darlaston Green W. Mids, Eng.
366 D7 Darley Abbey Derby, Eng.
378 C2 Darley Bridge Derbys., Eng.
300 D3 Darley Dale Derbys., Eng.
216 E1 Darley Head N. Yorks., Eng.
180 D3 Darley Hillside Derbys., Eng.
132 C5 Darlingscott Warks., Eng.
236 F4 Darlington Darl., Eng.
236 F4 Darlington admin. div. Eng.
144 E2 Darliston Shrop., Eng.
176 D3 Darlton Notts., Eng.
314 F2 Darnabo Abers., Scot.
208 D3 Darnall S. Yorks., Eng.
252 D3 Darngarroch D. and G., Scot.
256 H3 Darnick Borders, Scot.
366 C3 Darowen Powys, Wales
314 F2 Darra Abers., Scot.
40 C2 Darracott Devon, Eng.
396 J3 Darragh Cross Down, N. Ire.
244 G5 Darras Hall Northumb., Eng.
222 F2 Darrington W. Yorks., Eng.
116 H2 Dedham Heath Essex, Eng.
82 G3 Dedworth W. and M., Eng.
26 F1 Dee est. Wales
24 K7 Dee r. Eng./Wales
22 L8 Dee r. Scot.
128 F2 Deene Northants., Eng.
128 F2 Deenethorpe Northants., Eng.
208 C3 Deepcar S. Yorks., Eng.
52 H2 Deepcut Surr., Eng.
232 H7 Deepdale Cumbria, Eng.
216 C2 Deepdale N. Yorks., Eng.
170 E2 Deeping Gate Lincs., Eng.
170 E7 Deeping St James Lincs., Eng.
170 E7 Deeping St Nicholas Lincs., Eng.
339 D3 Deepweir Mon., Wales
314 E2 Deerhill Moray, Scot.
98 F2 Deerhurst Glos., Eng.
98 F2 Deerhurst Walton Glos., Eng.
62 E3 Defford Worcs., Eng.
136 E3 Defford Worcs., Eng.
366 D7 Defynnog Powys, Wales
378 C2 Deganwy Conwy, Wales
300 D3 Deighton N. Yorks., Eng.
222 E2 Deighton W. Yorks., Eng.
216 F3 Deighton N. Yorks., Eng.
372 F2 Deiniolen Gwynedd, Wales
36 E2 Delabole Corn., Eng.
184 D2 Delamere Cheshire West & Chester, Eng.
356 C3 Delavorar Moray, Scot.
314 G3 Delfrigs Abers., Scot.
322 K3 Dell Lodge High., Scot.
58 B4 Dell Quay W. Sussex, Eng.
102 C4 Delly End Oxon, Eng.
314 C3 Delnabo Moray, Scot.
320 H4 Delny High., Scot.
366 G2 Delph Gtr Man., Eng.
378 C2 Delphorie Abers., Scot.
236 E1 Delves Durham, Eng.
304 J3 Delvine Perth and Kin., Scot.
170 D6 Dembleby Lincs., Eng.
208 E3 Denaby S. Yorks., Eng.
208 E3 Denaby Main S. Yorks., Eng.
378 E2 Denbigh Denb., Wales
40 E3 Denbighshire county Wales
40 E3 Denbury Devon, Eng.
180 E4 Denby Derbys., Eng.
180 E4 Denby Bottles Derbys., Eng.
222 E3 Denby Dale W. Yorks., Eng.
102 C5 Denchworth Oxon, Eng.
232 D8 Dendron Cumbria, Eng.
314 F2 Denend Abers., Scot.
116 H3 Denford Northants., Eng.
106 F5 Dengie Essex, Eng.
120 E3 Denham Bucks., Eng.
120 E3 Denham Suff., Eng.
120 D3 Denham Suff., Eng.
106 E5 Denham End Suff., Eng.
106 E5 Denham Green Bucks., Eng.
120 E3 Denham Street Suff., Eng.
314 F3 Denhead Abers., Scot.
314 F3 Denhead Abers., Scot.
292 G2 Denhead Fife, Scot.
308 F3 Denhead of Arbirlot Angus, Scot.
308 D4 Denhead of Gray Dundee, Scot.
256 H4 Denholm Borders, Scot.
184 D2 Denholme W. Yorks., Eng.
222 C2 Denholme Clough W. Yorks., Eng.
372 D3 Denio Gwynedd, Wales
52 F5 Denmead Hants., Eng.
314 G3 Denmill Abers., Scot.
314 F3 Denmoss Abers., Scot.
314 F2 Dennington Suff., Eng.
276 E2 Dennistoun Glas., Scot.
288 D3 Denny Falk., Scot.
288 D3 Dennyloanhead Falk., Scot.
198 E2 Denshaw Gtr Man., Eng.
314 G3 Denside Abers., Scot.
128 F2 Densole Kent, Eng.
120 C3 Denston Suff., Eng.
148 D3 Denstone Staffs., Eng.
244 E6 Dent Cumbria, Eng.
86 B4 Denton Cambs., Eng.
140 B3 Denton Darl., Eng.
58 G4 Denton Gtr Man., Eng.
198 E3 Denton Kent, Eng.
62 G3 Denton Lincs., Eng.
148 B2 Denton N. Yorks., Eng.
356 C3 Denton Norf., Eng.
372 F2 Denton Northants., Eng.
372 F2 Denton Oxon, Eng.
358 G3 Denton's Green Merseyside, Eng.
372 H4 Denver Norf., Eng.
350 G4 Denvilles Hants., Eng.
Denwick Northumb., Eng.

388 H2 Derrykeighan Ballymoney, N. Ire.
402 I4 Derrylattinee Dungannon, N. Ire.
402 E5 Derrylea Fermanagh, N. Ire.
396 G4 Derryleckagh Newry & Mourne, N. Ire.
402 K3 Derrylee Dungannon, N. Ire.
402 E5 Derrylin Fermanagh, N. Ire.
396 F3 Derrymacash Craigavon, N. Ire.
396 F2 Derrymore Craigavon, N. Ire.
402 E4 Derrynanny Fermanagh, N. Ire.
402 G5 Derrynoose Armagh, N. Ire.
396 E4 Derryraine Armagh, N. Ire.
170 B2 Derrythorpe N. Lincs., Eng.
396 D4 Derrytvane Craigavon, N. Ire.
166 C1 Dersingham Norf., Eng.
300 B2 Dervaig Arg. and B., Scot.
388 H1 Dervock Ballymoney, N. Ire.
378 E3 Derwen Denb., Wales
366 B3 Derwenlas Powys, Wales
24 P6 Derwent r. Eng.
26 J2 Derwent r. Eng.
24 N4 Derwent Reservoir resr Eng.
24 N7 Derwent Reservoir resr Eng.
24 K4 Derwent Water l. Eng.
356 C3 Derwydd Carmar., Wales
300 C4 Derybruich Arg. and B., Scot.
128 E3 Desborough Northants., Eng.
388 F4 Desertmartin Magherafelt, N. Ire.
162 D3 Desford Leics., Eng.
244 F2 Detchant Northumb., Eng.
180 D4 Detchant Northumb., Eng.
62 C3 Detling Kent, Eng.
366 G2 Deuddwr Powys, Wales
378 G2 Deunant Conwy, Wales
144 F5 Deuxhill Shrop., Eng.
339 D2 Devauden Mon., Wales
22 K7 Devon r. Scot.
362 G4 Devil's Bridge Cere., Wales
132 C2 Devitts Green Warks., Eng.
86 D3 Devizes Wilts., Eng.
40 E2 Devon county Eng.
24 P7 Devon r. Eng.
22 I10 Devon r. Scot.
40 I3 Devonport Plymouth, Eng.
292 B3 Devonside Clack., Scot.
36 D3 Devoran Corn., Eng.
256 F2 Dewar Borders, Scot.
46 F3 Dewlish Dorset, Eng.
140 C3 Dewsall Court Here., Eng.
222 E2 Dewsbury W. Yorks., Eng.
222 E2 Dewsbury Moor W. Yorks., Eng.
300 B2 Dhiseig Arg. and B., Scot.
405 C2 Dhoon Isle of Man
405 D1 Dhoor Isle of Man
405 D1 Dhowin Isle of Man
58 B2 Dial Green W. Sussex, Eng.
58 D3 Dial Post W. Sussex, Eng.
52 D5 Dibden Hants., Eng.
106 E5 Dibden Hants., Eng.
52 D5 Dibden Purlieu Hants., Eng.
154 D3 Dickens Heath W. Mids, Eng.
166 G4 Dickleburgh Moor Norf., Eng.
98 H2 Didbrook Glos., Eng.
102 E3 Didcot Oxon, Eng.
116 H3 Diddington Cambs., Eng.
144 D5 Diddlebury Shrop., Eng.
140 C4 Didley Here., Eng.
58 B3 Didling W. Sussex, Eng.
98 F4 Didmarton Glos., Eng.
198 D3 Didsbury Gtr Man., Eng.
170 D5 Digby Lincs., Eng.
322 C2 Digg High., Scot.
198 F2 Diggle Gtr Man., Eng.
228 F5 Digmoor Lancs., Eng.
110 D5 Digswell Herts., Eng.
362 F3 Dihewyd Cere., Wales
252 E3 Dildawn D. and G., Scot.
166 H2 Dilham Norf., Eng.
148 C3 Dilhorne Staffs., Eng.
244 E6 Dilston Northumb., Eng.
86 B4 Dilton Marsh Wilts., Eng.
140 B3 Dilwyn Here., Eng.
140 B3 Dilwyn Common Here., Eng.
198 C2 Dimple Gtr Man., Eng.
148 B3 Dimsdale Staffs., Eng.
356 C3 Dinas Carmar., Wales
372 F2 Dinas Gwynedd, Wales
372 F2 Dinas Gwynedd, Wales
358 G3 Dinas Pembs., Wales
372 F2 Dinas Cross Pembs., Wales
358 G3 Dinas Dinlle Gwynedd, Wales
26 D3 Dinas Head hd Wales
372 H4 Dinas-Mawddwy Gwynedd, Wales
350 G4 Dinas Powys V. of Glam., Wales
Dinbych Denb., Wales see Denbigh
94 I3 Dinckley Lancs., Eng.
94 I3 Dinder Som., Eng.
140 C3 Dinedor Here., Eng.
339 C2 Dingestow Mon., Wales
190 H3 Dingle Merseyside, Eng.
128 E3 Dingley Northants., Eng.
322 H2 Dingwall High., Scot.
256 H5 Dinlabyre Borders, Scot.
314 E2 Dinnet Abers., Scot.
236 E3 Dinnington S. Yorks., Eng.
236 E3 Dinnington T. and W., Eng.
372 F2 Dinorwig Gwynedd, Wales
106 C4 Dinton Bucks., Eng.
86 C5 Dinton Wilts., Eng.
252 F2 Dinwoodie Mains D. and G., Scot.
94 F5 Dipford Som., Eng.
52 G3 Dipley Hants., Eng.
300 D5 Dippen Arg. and B., Scot.
264 D4 Dippen N. Ayr., Scot.
78 B2 Dippenhall Surr., Eng.
52 E3 Dipple S. Ayr., Scot.
40 E3 Dipple Devon, Eng.
40 E3 Diptford Devon, Eng.
236 E3 Dipton Durham, Eng.
244 E6 Dirdhu High., Scot.
24 M2 Dirleton E. Lothian, Scot.
24 M2 Dirrington Great Law hill Scot.
366 G5 Discoed Powys, Wales
162 D2 Diseworth Leics., Eng.
216 C2 Dishes Orkney, Scot.
216 E2 Dishforth N. Yorks., Eng.
170 E1 Dishley Leics., Eng.
184 G1 Disley Cheshire East, Eng.
120 F2 Diss Norf., Eng.
366 G3 Disserth Powys, Wales
232 A5 Distington Cumbria, Eng.
94 I4 Ditcheat Som., Eng.
166 H4 Ditchingham Norf., Eng.
102 D2 Ditchley Oxon, Eng.
58 F3 Ditchling E. Sussex, Eng.
190 D2 Ditherington Shrop., Eng.
86 B3 Ditteridge Wilts., Eng.
40 I3 Dittisham Devon, Eng.
62 C3 Ditton Kent, Eng.
184 C2 Ditton Halton, Eng.
120 C3 Ditton Green Cambs., Eng.
144 E5 Ditton Priors Shrop., Eng.

Dixton to East Green

98 G2 **Dixton** *Glos., Eng.*
339 D2 **Dixton** *Mon., Wales*
388 J4 **Doagh** *Newtownabbey, N. Ire.*
198 E2 **Dobcross** *Gtr Man., Eng.*
36 F2 **Dobwalls** *Corn., Eng.*
40 E2 **Doccombe** *Devon, Eng.*
22 H10 **Dochart** *r. Scot.*
322 I2 **Dochgarroch** *High., Scot.*
78 B3 **Dockenfield** *Surr., Eng.*
232 F6 **Docker** *Cumbria, Eng.*
228 G2 **Docker** *Lancs., Eng.*
166 C1 **Docking** *Norf., Eng.*
140 D2 **Docklow** *Here., Eng.*
232 D3 **Dockray** *Cumbria, Eng.*
232 E5 **Dockray** *Cumbria, Eng.*
136 C2 **Doddenham** *Worcs., Eng.*
116 D4 **Doddinghurst** *Essex, Eng.*
124 E4 **Doddington** *Cambs., Eng.*
62 E3 **Doddington** *Kent, Eng.*
170 C4 **Doddington** *Lincs., Eng.*
244 E2 **Doddington** *Northumb., Eng.*
144 E5 **Doddington** *Shrop., Eng.*
40 F3 **Doddiscombsleigh** *Devon, Eng.*
36 F2 **Doddycross** *Corn., Eng.*
128 C4 **Dodford** *Northants., Eng.*
136 E1 **Dodford** *Worcs., Eng.*
98 E4 **Dodington** *S. Glos., Eng.*
94 E4 **Dodington** *Som., Eng.*
98 E4 **Dodington Ash** *S. Glos., Eng.*
184 B3 **Dodleston** *Cheshire West & Chester, Eng.*
26 C7 **Dodman Point** *pt Eng.*
140 D3 **Dodmarsh** *Here., Eng.*
148 D3 **Dods Leigh** *Staffs., Eng.*
208 C2 **Dodworth** *S. Yorks., Eng.*
154 C2 **Doe Bank** *W. Mids, Eng.*
180 E4 **Doehole** *Derbys., Eng.*
180 F3 **Doe Lea** *Derbys., Eng.*
198 C2 **Doffcocker** *Gtr Man., Eng.*
170 E5 **Dogdyke** *Lincs., Eng.*
222 D3 **Dogley Lane** *W. Yorks., Eng.*
52 G3 **Dogmersfield** *Hants., Eng.*
124 C3 **Dogsthorpe** *Peterb., Eng.*
396 E4 **Dog Street** *Armagh, N. Ire.*
40 F2 **Dog Village** *Devon, Eng.*
366 E2 **Dolanog** *Powys, Wales*
366 F5 **Dolau** *Powys, Wales*
350 F3 **Dolau** *R.C.T., Wales*
372 E3 **Dolbenmaen** *Gwynedd, Wales*
148 A3 **Doley** *Staffs., Eng.*
366 D4 **Dolfach** *Powys, Wales*
366 D3 **Dol Fawr** *Powys, Wales*
366 F4 **Dolfor** *Powys, Wales*
356 G2 **Dolgarreg** *Carmar., Wales*
378 B2 **Dolgarrog** *Conwy, Wales*
372 G4 **Dolgellau** *Gwynedd, Wales*
372 G5 **Dolgoch** *Gwynedd, Wales*
356 E2 **Dolgran** *Carmar., Wales*
292 B3 **Dollar** *Clack., Scot.*
292 C3 **Dollarbeg** *Clack., Scot.*
396 G3 **Dollingstown** *Craigavon, N. Ire.*
74 C2 **Dollis Hill** *Gtr Lon., Eng.*
362 G2 **Dollwen** *Cere., Wales*
378 F2 **Dolphin** *Flints., Wales*
228 F3 **Dolphinholme** *Lancs., Eng.*
268 F2 **Dolphinton** *S. Lanark., Scot.*
40 D2 **Dolton** *Devon, Eng.*
378 C2 **Dolwen** *Conwy, Wales*
366 D3 **Dolwen** *Powys, Wales*
378 B3 **Dolwyddelan** *Conwy, Wales*
362 F2 **Dôl-y-bont** *Cere., Wales*
366 F6 **Dol-y-cannau** *Powys, Wales*
366 G5 **Dolyhir** *Powys, Wales*
378 G4 **Dolywern** *Wrex., Wales*
366 G2 **Domgay** *Powys, Wales*
22 L8 **Don** *r. Scot.*
402 F5 **Donagh** *Fermanagh, N. Ire.*
396 K2 **Donaghadee** *Ards, N. Ire.*
396 G3 **Donaghcloney** *Craigavon, N. Ire.*
402 J3 **Donaghey** *Cookstown, N. Ire.*
402 J3 **Donaghmore** *Dungannon, N. Ire.*
208 F2 **Doncaster** *S. Yorks., Eng.*
388 J4 **Donegore** *Antrim, N. Ire.*
402 G1 **Donemana** *Strabane, N. Ire.*
86 C5 **Donhead St Andrew** *Wilts., Eng.*
86 C5 **Donhead St Mary** *Wilts., Eng.*
292 D3 **Donibristle** *Fife, Scot.*
94 E3 **Doniford** *Som., Eng.*
170 E6 **Donington** *Lincs., Eng.*
144 G4 **Donington** *Shrop., Eng.*
162 C2 **Donington le Heath** *Leics., Eng.*
170 F4 **Donington on Bain** *Lincs., Eng.*
162 B2 **Donisthorpe** *Leics., Eng.*
78 C1 **Donkey Town** *Surr., Eng.*
170 G3 **Donna Nook** *Lincs., Eng.*
98 I2 **Donnington** *Glos., Eng.*
140 E3 **Donnington** *Here., Eng.*
144 E4 **Donnington** *Shrop., Eng.*
144 F3 **Donnington** *Telford, Eng.*
82 C3 **Donnington** *W. Berks., Eng.*
58 B4 **Donnington** *W. Sussex, Eng.*
94 G5 **Donyatt** *Som., Eng.*
402 G3 **Doogary** *Omagh, N. Ire.*
402 F3 **Dooish** *Omagh, N. Ire.*
402 E5 **Doon** *Fermanagh, N. Ire.*
22 G12 **Doon** *r. Scot.*
22 H12 **Doon, Loch** *l. Scot.*
388 F3 **Doonan** *Magherafelt, N. Ire.*
388 I3 **Doonbought** *Ballymena, N. Ire.*
262 D4 **Doonfoot** *S. Ayr., Scot.*
402 I3 **Doons** *Cookstown, N. Ire.*
46 E3 **Dorchester** *Dorset, Eng.*
102 E5 **Dorchester** *Oxon, Eng.*
132 C2 **Dordon** *Warks., Eng.*
208 C3 **Dore** *S. Yorks., Eng.*
322 I2 **Dores** *High., Scot.*
176 C4 **Dorket Head** *Notts., Eng.*
78 E2 **Dorking** *Surr., Eng.*
120 H3 **Dorley's Corner** *Suff., Eng.*
78 G3 **Dormansland** *Surr., Eng.*
78 F3 **Dormans Park** *Surr., Eng.*
74 B2 **Dormer's Wells** *Gtr Lon., Eng.*
140 D3 **Dormington** *Here., Eng.*
136 E2 **Dormston** *Worcs., Eng.*
98 I1 **Dorn** *Glos., Eng.*
106 E5 **Dorney** *Bucks., Eng.*
106 D5 **Dorney Reach** *Bucks., Eng.*
322 E3 **Dornie** *High., Scot.*
320 H4 **Dornoch** *High., Scot.*
22 H7 **Dornoch Firth** *est. Scot.*
252 G3 **Dornock** *D. and G., Scot.*
154 D3 **Dorridge** *W. Mids, Eng.*
170 D5 **Dorrington** *Lincs., Eng.*
144 D4 **Dorrington** *Shrop., Eng.*
46 H3 **Dorset** *county Eng.*
26 F6 **Dorset and East Devon Coast** *tourist site*
132 B5 **Dorsington** *Warks., Eng.*
140 A3 **Dorstone** *Here., Eng.*
396 E5 **Dorsy** *Newry & Mourne, N. Ire.*
106 B4 **Dorton** *Bucks., Eng.*
144 F4 **Doseley** *Telford, Eng.*
148 E5 **Dosthill** *Staffs., Eng.*
244 E6 **Dotland** *Northumb., Eng.*
46 C3 **Dottery** *Dorset, Eng.*
36 F2 **Doublebois** *Corn., Eng.*
276 E2 **Dougalston** *E. Dun., Scot.*
264 B3 **Dougarie** *N. Ayr., Scot.*
98 F4 **Doughton** *Glos., Eng.*
405 D3 **Douglas** I.o.M.
268 C3 **Douglas** *S. Lanark., Scot.*
308 E4 **Douglas and Angus** *Dundee, Scot.*
402 F2 **Douglas Br.** *Strabane, N. Ire.*
308 E3 **Douglastown** *Angus, Scot.*
268 D3 **Douglas Water** *S. Lanark., Scot.*
94 I3 **Doulting** *Som., Eng.*
329 B3 **Dounby** *Orkney, Scot.*
300 F3 **Doune** *Arg. and B., Scot.*
300 F3 **Doune** *Arg. and B., Scot.*
296 F4 **Doune** *Stir., Scot.*
22 G10 **Doune Hill** *hill Scot.*
314 F2 **Dounepark** *Abers., Scot.*
314 E3 **Douneside** *Abers., Scot.*
320 H4 **Dounie** *High., Scot.*
320 I2 **Dounreay** *High., Scot.*
144 C3 **Dovaston** *Shrop., Eng.*
24 P5 **Dove** *r. Eng.*
26 I2 **Dove** *r. Eng.*
26 O3 **Dove** *r. Eng.*
190 D3 **Dovecot** *Merseyside, Eng.*
180 B3 **Dove Holes** *Derbys., Eng.*
232 B4 **Dovenby** *Cumbria, Eng.*
170 F4 **Dovendale** *Lincs., Eng.*
62 H4 **Dover** *Kent, Eng.*
20 H6 **Dover, Strait of** *str. France/U.K.*
116 J2 **Dovercourt** *Essex, Eng.*
136 D2 **Doverdale** *Worcs., Eng.*
180 C5 **Doveridge** *Derbys., Eng.*
78 E2 **Doversgreen** *Surr., Eng.*
26 E2 **Dovey** *r. Wales*
304 I3 **Dowally** *Perth and Kin., Scot.*
276 E2 **Dowanhill** *Glas., Scot.*
98 G2 **Dowdeswell** *Glos., Eng.*
262 C5 **Dowhill** *S. Ayr., Scot.*
350 F2 **Dowlais** *M. Tyd., Wales*
40 D2 **Dowland** *Devon, Eng.*
94 G5 **Dowlish Ford** *Som., Eng.*
94 G5 **Dowlish Wake** *Som., Eng.*
396 J3 **Down** *admin. dist. N. Ire.*
396 I3 **Down** *county N. Ire.*
98 H3 **Down Ampney** *Glos., Eng.*
396 J4 **Down County Museum** *Down, N. Ire.*
36 F2 **Downderry** *Corn., Eng.*
74 E3 **Downe** *Gtr Lon., Eng.*
52 E6 **Downend** *I.o.W., Eng.*
98 D5 **Downend** *S. Glos., Eng.*
94 G3 **Down End** *Som., Eng.*
82 C3 **Downend** *W. Berks., Eng.*
308 E4 **Downfield** *Dundee, Scot.*
124 G5 **Downfields** *Cambs., Eng.*
36 G2 **Downgate** *Corn., Eng.*
116 E4 **Downham** *Essex, Eng.*
74 E3 **Downham** *Gtr Lon., Eng.*
228 I3 **Downham** *Lancs., Eng.*
244 D2 **Downham** *Northumb., Eng.*
166 B3 **Downham Market** *Norf., Eng.*
98 F2 **Down Hatherley** *Glos., Eng.*
94 I4 **Downhead** *Som., Eng.*
94 J3 **Downhead** *Som., Eng.*
236 G2 **Downhill** *T. and W., Eng.*
388 F1 **Downhill** *Coleraine, N. Ire.*
228 E5 **Downholland Cross** *Lancs., Eng.*
216 D1 **Downholme** *N. Yorks., Eng.*
314 G3 **Downies** *Abers., Scot.*
378 F2 **Downing** *Flints., Wales*
106 D5 **Downley** *Bucks., Eng.*
396 J4 **Downpatrick** *Down, N. Ire.*
350 G4 **Downs** *V. of Glam., Wales*
94 H2 **Downside** *N. Som., Eng.*
94 I3 **Downside** *Som., Eng.*
94 I3 **Downside** *Som., Eng.*
78 D2 **Downside** *Surr., Eng.*
40 E2 **Down St Mary** *Devon, Eng.*
40 D4 **Down Thomas** *Devon, Eng.*
52 C6 **Downton** *Hants., Eng.*
86 E6 **Downton** *Wilts., Eng.*
140 B1 **Downton on the Rock** *Here., Eng.*
170 D6 **Dowsby** *Lincs., Eng.*
148 C4 **Doxey** *Staffs., Eng.*
98 E5 **Doynton** *S. Glos., Eng.*
166 G2 **Drabblegate** *Norf., Eng.*
350 H3 **Draethen** *Caerp., Wales*
268 C2 **Draffan** *S. Lanark., Scot.*
232 D7 **Dragley Beck** *Cumbria, Eng.*
136 D1 **Drakelow** *Worcs., Eng.*
264 F2 **Drakemyre** *N. Ayr., Scot.*
136 E3 **Drakes Broughton** *Worcs., Eng.*
136 F1 **Drakes Cross** *Worcs., Eng.*
388 F4 **Draperstown** *Magherafelt, N. Ire.*
128 D3 **Draughton** *Northants., Eng.*
216 D3 **Draughton** *N. Yorks., Eng.*
132 D4 **Draycote** *Warks., Eng.*
86 E3 **Draycot Foliat** *Swindon, Eng.*
180 E5 **Draycott** *Derbys., Eng.*
98 I1 **Draycott** *Glos., Eng.*
144 G4 **Draycott** *Shrop., Eng.*
94 H3 **Draycott** *Som., Eng.*
136 D3 **Draycott** *Worcs., Eng.*
148 E3 **Draycott in the Clay** *Staffs., Eng.*
148 C3 **Draycott in the Moors** *Staffs., Eng.*
36 F2 **Draynes** *Corn., Eng.*
162 G3 **Drayton** *Leics., Eng.*
170 F6 **Drayton** *Lincs., Eng.*
166 G2 **Drayton** *Norf., Eng.*
102 C2 **Drayton** *Oxon, Eng.*
102 D5 **Drayton** *Oxon, Eng.*
52 F5 **Drayton** *Ports., Eng.*
94 G4 **Drayton** *Som., Eng.*
132 B4 **Drayton** *Warks., Eng.*
136 E1 **Drayton** *Worcs., Eng.*
148 E5 **Drayton Bassett** *Staffs., Eng.*
106 D4 **Drayton Beauchamp** *Bucks., Eng.*
106 D3 **Drayton Parslow** *Bucks., Eng.*
102 E5 **Drayton St Leonard** *Oxon, Eng.*
405 D2 **Dreemskerry** Isle of Man
402 C3 **Dreenan** *Fermanagh, N. Ire.*
388 G3 **Dreenan** *Magherafelt, N. Ire.*
358 D3 **Dreenhill** *Pembs., Wales*
356 D1 **Drefach** *Carmar., Wales*
356 F3 **Drefach** *Carmar., Wales*
362 E4 **Dre-fach** *Cere., Wales*
356 D1 **Drefelin** *Carmar., Wales*
264 G3 **Dreghorn** *N. Ayr., Scot.*
62 H4 **Drellingore** *Kent, Eng.*
288 G2 **Drem** *E. Lothian, Scot.*
148 C3 **Dresden** *Stoke, Eng.*
402 F3 **Dressoge** *Omagh, N. Ire.*
Dreumasdal *W. Isles, Scot. see* **Drimsdale**
40 E2 **Drewsteignton** *Devon, Eng.*
170 G4 **Driby** *Lincs., Eng.*
210 F2 **Driffield** *E. Riding, Eng.*
98 H3 **Driffield** *Glos., Eng.*
232 B6 **Drigg** *Cumbria, Eng.*
222 E2 **Drighlington** *W. Yorks., Eng.*
300 E3 **Drimfern** *Arg. and B., Scot.*
300 E3 **Drimlee** *Arg. and B., Scot.*
322 D5 **Drimnin** *High., Scot.*
46 C2 **Drimpton** *Dorset, Eng.*
326 B5 **Drimsdale** *W. Isles, Scot.*
300 F3 **Drimsynie** *Arg. and B., Scot.*
300 D3 **Drimvore** *Arg. and B., Scot.*
322 C3 **Drinan** *High., Scot.*
326 D3 **Drinisiader** *W. Isles, Scot.*
120 E3 **Drinkstone** *Suff., Eng.*
120 E3 **Drinkstone Green** *Suff., Eng.*
300 F3 **Drishaig** *Arg. and B., Scot.*
300 E3 **Drissaig** *Arg. and B., Scot.*
110 D4 **Driver's End** *Herts., Eng.*
Drochaid Abha *Arg. and B., Scot. see* **Bridge of Awe**
Drochaid an Aonachain *High., Scot. see* **Spean Bridge**
Drochaid Ruaidh *High., Scot. see* **Roybridge**
Drochaid Sgùideil *High., Scot. see* **Conon Bridge**
Drochaid Sheile *High., Scot. see* **Shiel Bridge**
148 D3 **Drointon** *Staffs., Eng.*
136 E2 **Droitwich Spa** *Worcs., Eng.*
396 H3 **Dromara** *Banbridge, N. Ire.*
396 H3 **Dromore** *Banbridge, N. Ire.*
388 E2 **Dromore** *Limavady, N. Ire.*
402 F3 **Dromore** *Omagh, N. Ire.*
402 G4 **Dromore Lower** *Omagh, N. Ire.*
304 J5 **Dron** *Perth and Kin., Scot.*
180 E3 **Dronfield** *Derbys., Eng.*
180 D3 **Dronfield Woodhouse** *Derbys., Eng.*
262 E4 **Drongan** *E. Ayr., Scot.*
308 D3 **Dronley** *Angus, Scot.*
46 E2 **Droop** *Dorset, Eng.*
350 G4 **Drope** *V. of Glam., Wales*
106 D5 **Dropmore** *Bucks., Eng.*
52 F5 **Droxford** *Hants., Eng.*
198 E3 **Droylsden** *Gtr Man., Eng.*
222 D2 **Drub** *W. Yorks., Eng.*
378 E4 **Druid** *Denb., Wales*
154 C2 **Druid's Heath** *W. Mids, Eng.*
358 D3 **Druidston** *Pembs., Wales*
322 F4 **Druimarbin** *High., Scot.*
300 E2 **Druimavuic** *Arg. and B., Scot.*
300 D4 **Druimdrishaig** *Arg. and B., Scot.*
322 D4 **Druimindarroch** *High., Scot.*
Druim na Drochaid *High., Scot. see* **Drumnadrochit**
300 E4 **Drum** *Arg. and B., Scot.*
304 I5 **Drum** *Perth and Kin., Scot.*
300 E4 **Drumachloy** *Arg. and B., Scot.*
388 J1 **Drumadoon** *Moyle, N. Ire.*
388 G3 **Drumagarner** *Coleraine, N. Ire.*
396 H3 **Drumaghadone** *Banbridge, N. Ire.*
388 C3 **Drumahoe** *Derry, N. Ire.*
388 J6 **Drumaknockan** *Lisburn, N. Ire.*
388 K6 **Drumalig** *Lisburn, N. Ire.*
396 I3 **Drumaness** *Down, N. Ire.*
402 D5 **Drumaran** *Fermanagh, N. Ire.*
396 I4 **Drumaroad** *Down, N. Ire.*
396 K2 **Drumawhy** *Ards, N. Ire.*
320 E3 **Drumbeg** *High., Scot.*
314 E2 **Drumblade** *Abers., Scot.*
314 F2 **Drumblair** *Abers., Scot.*
388 K5 **Drumbo** *Lisburn, N. Ire.*
402 D4 **Drumboy** *Fermanagh, N. Ire.*
402 E5 **Drumbrughas** *Fermanagh, N. Ire.*
252 E1 **Drumbuie** *D. and G., Scot.*
322 D3 **Drumbuie** *High., Scot.*
232 D3 **Drumburgh** *Cumbria, Eng.*
402 D5 **Drumcard** *Fermanagh, N. Ire.*
276 D2 **Drumchapel** *Glas., Scot.*
322 H2 **Drumchardine** *High., Scot.*
268 B3 **Drumclog** *S. Lanark., Scot.*
322 I2 **Drumderfit** *High., Scot.*
402 F4 **Drumderg** *Fermanagh, N. Ire.*
402 E4 **Drumduff** *Fermanagh, N. Ire.*
292 G2 **Drumeldrie** *Fife, Scot.*
256 D3 **Drumelzier** *Borders, Scot.*
396 K2 **Drumfad** *Ards, N. Ire.*
322 D3 **Drumfearn** *High., Scot.*
402 E3 **Drumgallan** *Strabane, N. Ire.*
300 D5 **Drumgarve** *Arg. and B., Scot.*
396 G4 **Drumgath** *Newry & Mourne, N. Ire.*
308 E3 **Drumgley** *Angus, Scot.*
322 J3 **Drumguish** *High., Scot.*
402 E4 **Drumharvey** *Fermanagh, N. Ire.*
314 F3 **Drumhead** *Abers., Scot.*
396 J2 **Drumhirk** *Ards, N. Ire.*
396 K2 **Drumhirk** *Ards, N. Ire.*
314 C2 **Drumin** *Moray, Scot.*
396 F5 **Drumintee** *Newry & Mourne, N. Ire.*
252 D2 **Drumjohn** *D. and G., Scot.*
262 C6 **Drumlamford House** *S. Ayr., Scot.*
314 F3 **Drumlasie** *Abers., Scot.*
388 G2 **Drumlee** *Ballymoney, N. Ire.*
396 H4 **Drumlee** *Banbridge, N. Ire.*
402 F3 **Drumlegagh** *Strabane, N. Ire.*
300 C5 **Drumlemble** *Arg. and B., Scot.*
314 F4 **Drumlithie** *Abers., Scot.*
402 D5 **Drummacabranagher** *Fermanagh, N. Ire.*
280 B3 **Drum Mains** *N. Lanark., Scot.*
396 E3 **Drumman** *Armagh, N. Ire.*
396 E3 **Drummannon** *Armagh, N. Ire.*
322 H2 **Drummond** *High., Scot.*
296 F4 **Drummond** *Stir., Scot.*
252 B3 **Drummore** *D. and G., Scot.*
314 D2 **Drummuir** *Moray, Scot.*
322 H2 **Drumnadrochit** *High., Scot.*
314 E2 **Drumnagorrach** *Moray, Scot.*
402 H3 **Drumnakilly** *Omagh, N. Ire.*
396 G3 **Drumnykerne** *Craigavon, N. Ire.*
314 F3 **Drumoak** *Abers., Scot.*
300 D5 **Drumore** *Arg. and B., Scot.*
304 H3 **Drumour** *Perth and Kin., Scot.*
402 F3 **Drumquin** *Omagh, N. Ire.*
252 D2 **Drumrash** *D. and G., Scot.*
320 E3 **Drumrunie** *High., Scot.*
276 D2 **Drumry** *W. Dun., Scot.*
314 G3 **Drums** *Abers., Scot.*
396 D3 **Drumsallen** *Armagh, N. Ire.*
402 G5 **Drumshancorick** *Fermanagh, N. Ire.*
402 D3 **Drumskinny** *Fermanagh, N. Ire.*
388 E3 **Drumslieve** *Limavady, N. Ire.*
308 F3 **Drumsturdy** *Angus, Scot.*
388 E3 **Drumsurn** *Limavady, N. Ire.*
322 C2 **Drumuie** *High., Scot.*
322 J3 **Drumuillie** *High., Scot.*
296 F4 **Drumvaich** *Stir., Scot.*
314 G2 **Drumwhindle** *Abers., Scot.*
252 E2 **Drumwhirn** *D. and G., Scot.*
308 G3 **Drunkendub** *Angus, Scot.*
244 H4 **Druridge** *Northumb., Eng.*
378 G2 **Drury** *Flints., Wales*
372 H4 **Drws-y-nant** *Gwynedd, Wales*
232 G5 **Drybeck** *Cumbria, Eng.*
314 E2 **Drybridge** *Moray, Scot.*
264 G3 **Drybridge** *N. Ayr., Scot.*
98 D2 **Drybrook** *Glos., Eng.*
256 I3 **Dryburgh** *Borders, Scot.*
170 B5 **Dry Doddington** *Lincs., Eng.*
124 E5 **Dry Drayton** *Cambs., Eng.*
26 E3 **Drygarn Fawr** *hill Wales*
256 H3 **Drygrange** *Borders, Scot.*
322 D2 **Dry Harbour** *High., Scot.*
256 F3 **Dryhope** *Borders, Scot.*
288 D3 **Drylaw** *Edin., Scot.*
296 D5 **Drymen** *Stir., Scot.*
322 C3 **Drynoch** *High., Scot.*
102 D4 **Dry Sandford** *Oxon, Eng.*
356 F2 **Dryslwyn** *Carmar., Wales*
116 E4 **Dry Street** *Essex, Eng.*
144 E4 **Dryton** *Shrop., Eng.*
300 D3 **Duachy** *Arg. and B., Scot.*
314 F2 **Dubford** *Abers., Scot.*
22 C10 **Dubh Artach** *i. Scot.*
300 D4 **Dubhchladach** *Arg. and B., Scot.*
304 H4 **Dubheads** *Perth and Kin., Scot.*
120 G3 **Dublin** *Suff., Eng.*
308 F3 **Dubton** *Angus, Scot.*
276 C2 **Duchal** *Inverclyde, Scot.*
320 F3 **Duchally** *High., Scot.*
296 D4 **Duchray** *Stir., Scot.*
300 G3 **Duck Bay** *Arg. and B., Scot.*
110 C3 **Duck End** *Bedford, Eng.*
124 C5 **Duck End** *Cambs., Eng.*
116 E2 **Duck End** *Essex, Eng.*
116 E2 **Duck End** *Essex, Eng.*
116 F2 **Duckend Green** *Essex, Eng.*
184 C3 **Duckington** *Cheshire West & Chester, Eng.*
102 C4 **Ducklington** *Oxon, Eng.*
180 E3 **Duckmanton** *Derbys., Eng.*
110 C2 **Duck's Cross** *Bedford, Eng.*
74 C2 **Ducks Island** *Gtr Lon., Eng.*
52 C3 **Duck Street** *Hants., Eng.*
216 D2 **Duck Street** *N. Yorks., Eng.*
120 E4 **Duck Street** *Suff., Eng.*
228 H4 **Duckworth Hall** *Lancs., Eng.*
116 C1 **Duddenhoe End** *Essex, Eng.*
288 E3 **Duddingston** *Edin., Scot.*
128 F2 **Duddington** *Northants., Eng.*
94 F5 **Duddlestone** *Som., Eng.*
58 G2 **Duddleswell** *E. Sussex, Eng.*
244 E1 **Duddo** *Northumb., Eng.*
184 C2 **Duddon** *Cheshire West & Chester, Eng.*
24 K5 **Duddon** *r. Eng.*
232 C7 **Duddon Bridge** *Cumbria, Eng.*
144 C2 **Dudleston** *Shrop., Eng.*
144 C2 **Dudleston Heath** *Shrop., Eng.*
236 F1 **Dudley** *T. and W., Eng.*
154 B2 **Dudley** *W. Mids, Eng.*
222 D2 **Dudley Hill** *W. Yorks., Eng.*
154 B2 **Dudley Port** *W. Mids, Eng.*
154 B3 **Dudley Wood** *W. Mids, Eng.*
190 F3 **Dudlow's Green** *Warr., Eng.*
46 H3 **Dudsbury** *Dorset, Eng.*
22 L8 **Dudwick, Hill of** *hill Scot.*
180 E5 **Duffield** *Derbys., Eng.*
402 K3 **Duffmount** *Cookstown, N. Ire.*
350 D3 **Duffryn** *N.P.T., Wales*
314 D2 **Dufftown** *Moray, Scot.*
314 C1 **Duffus** *Moray, Scot.*
232 H5 **Dufton** *Cumbria, Eng.*
216 H2 **Duggleby** *N. Yorks., Eng.*
322 K2 **Duiar** *High., Scot.*
320 I3 **Duible** *High., Scot.*
300 F2 **Duiletter** *Arg. and B., Scot.*
304 E2 **Duinish** *Perth and Kin., Scot.*
322 D3 **Duirinish** *High., Scot.*
322 F4 **Duisky** *High., Scot.*
132 B3 **Duke End** *Warks., Eng.*
350 G2 **Dukestown** *B. Gwent, Wales*
198 E3 **Dukinfield** *Gtr Man., Eng.*
371 D2 **Dulas** *I.o.A., Wales*
94 I3 **Dulcote** *Som., Eng.*
Dul Dreagain *High., Scot. see* **Dundreggan**
40 G2 **Dulford** *Devon, Eng.*
304 G3 **Dull** *Perth and Kin., Scot.*
402 E3 **Dullaghan** *Omagh, N. Ire.*
280 B3 **Dullatur** *N. Lanark., Scot.*
124 G5 **Dullingham** *Cambs., Eng.*
124 G5 **Dullingham Ley** *Cambs., Eng.*
22 I8 **Dulnain** *r. Scot.*
322 K3 **Dulnain Bridge** *High., Scot.*
110 D2 **Duloe** *Bedford, Eng.*
36 F2 **Duloe** *Corn., Eng.*
322 J2 **Dulsie** *High., Scot.*
94 C4 **Dulverton** *Som., Eng.*
74 D3 **Dulwich** *Gtr Lon., Eng.*
276 C2 **Dumbarton** *W. Dun., Scot.*
98 H1 **Dumbleton** *Glos., Eng.*
276 E2 **Dumbreck** *Glas., Scot.*
252 F2 **Dumcrieff** *D. and G., Scot.*
300 G3 **Dumfin** *Arg. and B., Scot.*
252 F2 **Dumfries** *D. and G., Scot.*
252 D2 **Dumfries and Galloway** *admin. div. Scot.*
296 D5 **Dumgoyne** *Stir., Scot.*
52 F3 **Dummer** *Hants., Eng.*
308 G2 **Dun** *Angus, Scot.*
300 D2 **Dunach** *Arg. and B., Scot.*
388 H2 **Dunaghy** *Ballymoney, N. Ire.*
304 F2 **Dunalastair** *Perth and Kin., Scot.*
300 F4 **Dunan** *Arg. and B., Scot.*
322 C3 **Dunan** *High., Scot.*
300 E3 **Dunans** *Arg. and B., Scot.*
94 G4 **Dunball** *Som., Eng.*
288 H2 **Dunbar** *E. Lothian, Scot.*
320 J3 **Dunbeath** *High., Scot.*
296 G4 **Dunblane** *Stir., Scot.*
292 F1 **Dunbog** *Fife, Scot.*
52 C4 **Dunbridge** *Hants., Eng.*
22 J5 **Duncansby Head** *hd Scot.*
314 E3 **Duncanston** *Abers., Scot.*
322 H2 **Duncanston** *High., Scot.*
40 F2 **Dunchideock** *Devon, Eng.*
132 E3 **Dunchurch** *Warks., Eng.*
128 C5 **Duncote** *Northants., Eng.*
252 F2 **Duncow** *D. and G., Scot.*
296 D4 **Duncraggan** *Stir., Scot.*
304 J5 **Duncrievie** *Perth and Kin., Scot.*
296 D3 **Duncroist** *Stir., Scot.*
304 I5 **Duncrub** *Perth and Kin., Scot.*
388 E2 **Duncrun** *Limavady, N. Ire.*
276 C1 **Duncryne** *W. Dun., Scot.*
58 C3 **Duncton** *W. Sussex, Eng.*
22 E10 **Dun da Ghaoithe** *hill Scot.*
308 E4 **Dundee** *Dundee, Scot.*
308 E4 **Dundee** *admin. div. Scot.*
304 L4 **Dundee** *airport Scot.*
94 H4 **Dundon** *Som., Eng.*
388 L5 **Dundonald** *Belfast, N. Ire.*
262 D3 **Dundonald** *S. Ayr., Scot.*
94 H4 **Dundon Hayes** *Som., Eng.*
232 C3 **Dundraw** *Cumbria, Eng.*
322 G3 **Dundreggan** *High., Scot.*
252 E3 **Dundrennan** *D. and G., Scot.*
52 E5 **Dundridge** *Hants., Eng.*
388 J5 **Dundrod** *Lisburn, N. Ire.*
396 E4 **Dundrum** *Armagh, N. Ire.*
396 I4 **Dundrum** *Down, N. Ire.*
23 K4 **Dundrum Bay** *b. N. Ire.*
94 I2 **Dundry** *N. Som., Eng.*
388 H3 **Duneany** *Ballymena, N. Ire.*
292 E3 **Dunearn** *Fife, Scot.*
22 I11 **Duneaton Water** *r. Scot.*
314 F3 **Dunecht** *Abers., Scot.*
388 J6 **Duneight** *Lisburn, N. Ire.*
292 D3 **Dunfermline** *Fife, Scot.*
98 I3 **Dunfield** *Glos., Eng.*
208 B2 **Dunford Bridge** *S. Yorks., Eng.*
402 J3 **Dungannon** *Dungannon, N. Ire.*
402 I4 **Dungannon** *admin. dist. N. Ire.*
62 E3 **Dungate** *Kent, Eng.*
26 N6 **Dungeness** *hd Eng.*
388 E3 **Dungiven** *Limavady, N. Ire.*
288 I3 **Dunglass** *E. Lothian, Scot.*
208 C3 **Dungworth** *S. Yorks., Eng.*
176 E3 **Dunham** *Notts., Eng.*
184 C2 **Dunham-on-the-Hill** *Cheshire West & Chester, Eng.*
136 D2 **Dunhampton** *Worcs., Eng.*
198 C3 **Dunham Town** *Gtr Man., Eng.*
198 C3 **Dunham Woodhouses** *Gtr Man., Eng.*
170 D4 **Dunholme** *Lincs., Eng.*
292 H2 **Dunino** *Fife, Scot.*
280 C2 **Dunipace** *Falk., Scot.*
304 F4 **Dunira** *Perth and Kin., Scot.*
304 I3 **Dunkeld** *Perth and Kin., Scot.*
94 J2 **Dunkerton** *B. and N.E. Som., Eng.*
26 E5 **Dunkery Hill** *hill Eng.*
40 G2 **Dunkeswell** *Devon, Eng.*
216 E3 **Dunkeswick** *N. Yorks., Eng.*
184 B2 **Dunkirk** *Cheshire West & Chester, Eng.*
62 F3 **Dunkirk** *Kent, Eng.*
148 B2 **Dunkirk** *Staffs., Eng.*
62 B3 **Dunk's Green** *Kent, Eng.*
308 F2 **Dunlappie** *Angus, Scot.*
52 D3 **Dunley** *Hants., Eng.*
136 D2 **Dunley** *Worcs., Eng.*
262 D2 **Dunlop** *E. Ayr., Scot.*
300 F4 **Dunloskin** *Arg. and B., Scot.*
388 H2 **Dunloy** *Ballymoney, N. Ire.*
20 D4 **Dunluce** *tourist site N. Ire.*
36 E2 **Dunmere** *Corn., Eng.*
388 H3 **Dunminning** *Ballymena, N. Ire.*
402 J2 **Dunmore** *Cookstown, N. Ire.*
396 I3 **Dunmore** *Down, N. Ire.*
300 D4 **Dunmore** *Arg. and B., Scot.*
280 D2 **Dunmore** *Falk., Scot.*
388 J5 **Dunmurry** *Lisburn, N. Ire.*
320 J2 **Dunn** *High., Scot.*
252 G2 **Dunnabie** *D. and G., Scot.*
402 I2 **Dunnamore** *Cookstown, N. Ire.*
320 K2 **Dunnet** *High., Scot.*
22 J5 **Dunnet Bay** *b. Scot.*
22 J5 **Dunnet Head** *hd Scot.*
308 F3 **Dunnichen** *Angus, Scot.*
304 I5 **Dunning** *Perth and Kin., Scot.*
210 G3 **Dunnington** *E. Riding, Eng.*
132 A4 **Dunnington** *Warks., Eng.*
216 G3 **Dunnington** *York, Eng.*
228 I4 **Dunnockshaw** *Lancs., Eng.*
62 D3 **Dunn Street** *Kent, Eng.*
300 F4 **Dunoon** *Arg. and B., Scot.*
252 B3 **Dunragit** *D. and G., Scot.*
22 J11 **Dun Rig** *hill Scot.*
300 D4 **Dunrostan** *Arg. and B., Scot.*
256 J2 **Duns** *Borders, Scot.*
180 D3 **Dunsa** *Derbys., Eng.*
170 D7 **Dunsby** *Lincs., Eng.*
252 E2 **Dunscore** *D. and G., Scot.*
208 F2 **Dunscroft** *S. Yorks., Eng.*
102 F6 **Dunsden Green** *Oxon, Eng.*
388 H1 **Dunseverick** *Moyle, N. Ire.*
78 C3 **Dunsfold** *Surr., Eng.*
40 E2 **Dunsford** *Devon, Eng.*
292 E2 **Dunshalt** *Fife, Scot.*
136 D4 **Dunshill** *Worcs., Eng.*
304 J4 **Dunsinnan** *Perth and Kin., Scot.*
216 G1 **Dunsley** *N. Yorks., Eng.*
148 B6 **Dunsley** *Staffs., Eng.*
106 D4 **Dunsmore** *Bucks., Eng.*
228 G3 **Dunsop Bridge** *Lancs., Eng.*
110 B4 **Dunstable** *Central Bedfordshire, Eng.*
148 E4 **Dunstall** *Staffs., Eng.*
120 C3 **Dunstall Green** *Suff., Eng.*
244 H3 **Dunstan** *Northumb., Eng.*
244 H3 **Dunstan Steads** *Northumb., Eng.*
94 D3 **Dunster** *Som., Eng.*
102 C3 **Duns Tew** *Oxon, Eng.*
170 D5 **Dunston** *Lincs., Eng.*
166 G3 **Dunston** *Norf., Eng.*
148 C4 **Dunston** *Staffs., Eng.*
236 F2 **Dunston** *T. and W., Eng.*
40 E3 **Dunstone** *Devon, Eng.*
148 C4 **Dunston Heath** *Staffs., Eng.*
208 F2 **Dunsville** *S. Yorks., Eng.*
210 F4 **Dunswell** *E. Riding, Eng.*
268 F2 **Dunsyre** *S. Lanark., Scot.*
22 H8 **Duntelchaig, Loch** *l. Scot.*
40 D3 **Dunterton** *Devon, Eng.*
98 G3 **Duntisbourne Abbots** *Glos., Eng.*
98 G3 **Duntisbourne Leer** *Glos., Eng.*
98 G3 **Duntisbourne Rouse** *Glos., Eng.*
46 E2 **Duntish** *Dorset, Eng.*
276 D2 **Duntocher** *W. Dun., Scot.*
106 D3 **Dunton** *Bucks., Eng.*
110 D3 **Dunton** *Central Bedfordshire, Eng.*
166 D1 **Dunton** *Norf., Eng.*
162 D3 **Dunton Bassett** *Leics., Eng.*
62 B3 **Dunton Green** *Kent, Eng.*
116 E4 **Dunton Wayletts** *Essex, Eng.*
320 A4 **Duntulm** *High., Scot.*
262 C4 **Dunure** *S. Ayr., Scot.*
262 C4 **Dunure Mains** *S. Ayr., Scot.*
350 B3 **Dunvant** *Swansea, Wales*
322 B2 **Dunvegan** *High., Scot.*
22 C7 **Dunvegan, Loch** *b. Scot.*
22 C7 **Dunvegan Head** *hd Scot.*
120 I3 **Dunwich** *Suff., Eng.*
292 G2 **Dura** *Fife, Scot.*
Duras *High., Scot. see* **Dores**
232 E3 **Durdar** *Cumbria, Eng.*
36 D3 **Durgan** *Corn., Eng.*
58 H2 **Durgates** *E. Sussex, Eng.*
236 F3 **Durham** *Durham, Eng.*
236 E3 **Durham** *county Eng.*
236 G4 **Durham Tees Valley** *airport Eng.*
252 E2 **Durisdeer** *D. and G., Scot.*
94 F4 **Durleigh** *Som., Eng.*
52 E5 **Durley** *Hants., Eng.*
86 F3 **Durley** *Wilts., Eng.*
52 E5 **Durley Street** *Hants., Eng.*
140 D3 **Durlow Common** *Here., Eng.*
320 F2 **Durness** *High., Scot.*
22 G5 **Durness, Kyle of** *inlet Scot.*
314 F2 **Durno** *Abers., Scot.*
322 F5 **Duror** *High., Scot.*
300 E3 **Durran** *Arg. and B., Scot.*
52 G5 **Durrants** *Hants., Eng.*
86 E4 **Durrington** *Wilts., Eng.*
58 D3 **Durrington** *W. Sussex, Eng.*
98 E3 **Dursley** *Glos., Eng.*
98 E2 **Dursley Cross** *Glos., Eng.*
94 F4 **Durston** *Som., Eng.*
46 F2 **Durweston** *Dorset, Eng.*
331 D3 **Dury** *Shet., Scot.*
22 □N2 **Dury Voe** *inlet Scot.*
128 D4 **Duston** *Northants., Eng.*
322 J3 **Duthil** *High., Scot.*
366 G4 **Dutlas** *Powys, Wales*
116 E2 **Duton Hill** *Essex, Eng.*
36 F2 **Dutson** *Corn., Eng.*
184 D2 **Dutton** *Cheshire West & Chester, Eng.*
124 E6 **Duxford** *Cambs., Eng.*
378 B2 **Dwygyfylchi** *Conwy, Wales*
371 D3 **Dwyran** *I.o.A., Wales*
371 E5 **Dwyryd** *Wales*
402 J4 **Dyan** *Dungannon, N. Ire.*
314 G3 **Dyce** *Aberdeen, Scot.*
356 E3 **Dyfatty** *Carmar., Wales*
350 E3 **Dyffryn** *Bridg., Wales*
358 D2 **Dyffryn** *Pembs., Wales*
350 G4 **Dyffryn** *V. of Glam., Wales*
362 H2 **Dyffryn Castell** *Cere., Wales*
356 G2 **Dyffryn Ceidrych** *Carmar., Wales*
350 D2 **Dyffryn Cellwen** *N.P.T., Wales*
Dyfrdwy *r. Eng./Wales see* **Dee**
170 D7 **Dyke** *Lincs., Eng.*
314 B2 **Dyke** *Moray, Scot.*
308 D2 **Dykehead** *Angus, Scot.*
280 D4 **Dykehead** *N. Lanark., Scot.*
296 E5 **Dykehead** *Stir., Scot.*
314 F4 **Dykelands** *Abers., Scot.*
308 C2 **Dykends** *Angus, Scot.*
314 F2 **Dykeside** *Abers., Scot.*
366 C3 **Dylife** *Powys, Wales*
62 F4 **Dymchurch** *Kent, Eng.*
98 E2 **Dymock** *Glos., Eng.*
98 E5 **Dyrham** *S. Glos., Eng.*
292 F3 **Dysart** *Fife, Scot.*
378 E2 **Dyserth** *Denb., Wales*

E

244 G5 **Eachwick** *Northumb., Eng.*
326 C2 **Eadar dha Fhadhail** *W. Isles, Scot.*
228 E3 **Eagland Hill** *Lancs., Eng.*
170 B4 **Eagle** *Lincs., Eng.*
170 B4 **Eagle Barnsdale** *Lincs., Eng.*
170 B4 **Eagle Moor** *Lincs., Eng.*
236 G4 **Eaglescliffe** *Stockton, Eng.*
232 B5 **Eaglesfield** *Cumbria, Eng.*
252 G2 **Eaglesfield** *D. and G., Scot.*
276 E3 **Eaglesham** *E. Renf., Scot.*
128 G2 **Eaglethorpe** *Northants., Eng.*
198 C2 **Eagley** *Gtr Man., Eng.*
405 C3 **Eairy** Isle of Man
128 E5 **Eakley** *Northants., Eng.*
176 D4 **Eakring** *Notts., Eng.*
170 B2 **Ealand** *N. Lincs., Eng.*
74 C2 **Ealing** *Gtr Lon., Eng.*
74 C2 **Ealing** *met. bor. Gtr Lon., Eng.*
232 F5 **Eamont Bridge** *Cumbria, Eng.*
Earagaidh *High., Scot. see* **Errogie**
22 H9 **Earba, Lochan na h-** *l. Scot.*
228 J3 **Earby** *Lancs., Eng.*
228 H4 **Earcroft** *B'burn, Eng.*
144 F4 **Eardington** *Shrop., Eng.*
140 B2 **Eardisland** *Here., Eng.*
140 A3 **Eardisley** *Here., Eng.*
144 C3 **Eardiston** *Shrop., Eng.*
136 C2 **Eardiston** *Worcs., Eng.*
124 E4 **Earith** *Cambs., Eng.*
244 E2 **Earle** *Northumb., Eng.*
190 F3 **Earlestown** *Merseyside, Eng.*
82 E3 **Earley** *W'ham, Eng.*
166 G3 **Earlham** *Norf., Eng.*
322 B2 **Earlish** *High., Scot.*
128 E4 **Earls Barton** *Northants., Eng.*
116 G2 **Earls Colne** *Essex, Eng.*
136 E2 **Earl's Common** *Worcs., Eng.*
74 C3 **Earl's Court** *Gtr Lon., Eng.*
136 D3 **Earl's Croome** *Worcs., Eng.*
154 E3 **Earlsdon** *W. Mids, Eng.*
292 G2 **Earlsferry** *Fife, Scot.*
74 C3 **Earlsfield** *Gtr Lon., Eng.*
314 G2 **Earlsford** *Abers., Scot.*
120 E3 **Earl's Green** *Suff., Eng.*
222 E2 **Earlsheaton** *W. Yorks., Eng.*
162 D3 **Earl Shilton** *Leics., Eng.*
120 G3 **Earl Soham** *Suff., Eng.*
22 H10 **Earl's Seat** *hill Scot.*
180 B3 **Earl Sterndale** *Derbys., Eng.*
256 H3 **Earlston** *Borders, Scot.*
120 F3 **Earl Stonham** *Suff., Eng.*
78 E2 **Earlswood** *Surr., Eng.*
132 B3 **Earlswood** *Warks., Eng.*
339 D3 **Earlswood** *Mon., Wales*
22 J10 **Earn** *r. Scot.*
58 A4 **Earnley** *W. Sussex, Eng.*
228 F4 **Earnshaw Bridge** *Lancs., Eng.*
326 B6 **Earsairidh** *W. Isles, Scot.*
236 G1 **Earsdon** *T. and W., Eng.*
244 G4 **Earsdon Moor** *Northumb., Eng.*
166 H4 **Earsham** *Norf., Eng.*
120 G2 **Earsham Street** *Suff., Eng.*
58 B3 **Eartham** *W. Sussex, Eng.*
216 F1 **Easby** *N. Yorks., Eng.*
58 B3 **Easebourne** *W. Sussex, Eng.*
132 E3 **Easenhall** *Warks., Eng.*
78 C2 **Eashing** *Surr., Eng.*
106 B4 **Easington** *Bucks., Eng.*
236 G3 **Easington** *Durham, Eng.*
210 I5 **Easington** *E. Riding, Eng.*
244 G2 **Easington** *Northumb., Eng.*
102 C2 **Easington** *Oxon, Eng.*
102 E4 **Easington** *Oxon, Eng.*
216 G1 **Easington** *R. and C., Eng.*
236 H3 **Easington Colliery** *Durham, Eng.*
236 G3 **Easington Lane** *T. and W., Eng.*
216 F2 **Easingwold** *N. Yorks., Eng.*
62 H3 **Easole Street** *Kent, Eng.*
308 D3 **Eassie** *Angus, Scot.*
350 F4 **East Aberthaw** *V. of Glam., Wales*
74 C2 **East Acton** *Gtr Lon., Eng.*
40 E4 **East Allington** *Devon, Eng.*
40 F1 **East Anstey** *Devon, Eng.*
52 D3 **East Anton** *Hants., Eng.*
216 E1 **East Appleton** *N. Yorks., Eng.*
222 E2 **East Ardsley** *W. Yorks., Eng.*
52 E6 **East Ashey** *I.o.W., Eng.*
58 A3 **East Ashling** *W. Sussex, Eng.*
52 D3 **East Aston** *Hants., Eng.*
314 G3 **East Auchronie** *Abers., Scot.*
262 F3 **East Ayrshire** *admin. div. Scot.*
216 H2 **East Ayton** *N. Yorks., Eng.*
170 E4 **East Barkwith** *Lincs., Eng.*
62 C3 **East Barming** *Kent, Eng.*
216 G1 **East Barnby** *N. Yorks., Eng.*
74 D2 **East Barnet** *Gtr Lon., Eng.*
166 E1 **East Barsham** *Norf., Eng.*
166 G1 **East Beckham** *Norf., Eng.*
74 B3 **East Bedfont** *Gtr Lon., Eng.*
120 F5 **East Bergholt** *Suff., Eng.*
222 D2 **East Bierley** *W. Yorks., Eng.*
166 E2 **East Bilney** *Norf., Eng.*
58 G4 **East Blatchington** *E. Sussex, Eng.*
46 G3 **East Bloxworth** *Dorset, Eng.*
236 G2 **East Boldon** *T. and W., Eng.*
52 D6 **East Boldre** *Hants., Eng.*
244 G3 **East Bolton** *Northumb., Eng.*
236 F4 **Eastbourne** *Darl., Eng.*
58 H4 **Eastbourne** *E. Sussex, Eng.*
94 G4 **East Bower** *Som., Eng.*
94 G3 **East Brent** *Som., Eng.*
120 I3 **East Bridge** *Suff., Eng.*
176 D5 **East Bridgford** *Notts., Eng.*
350 G4 **Eastbrook** *V. of Glam., Wales*
40 G3 **East Budleigh** *Devon, Eng.*
210 F3 **Eastburn** *E. Riding, Eng.*
222 C1 **Eastburn** *W. Yorks., Eng.*
106 E5 **East Burnham** *Bucks., Eng.*
331 C3 **East Burrafirth** *Shet., Scot.*
46 F3 **East Burton** *Dorset, Eng.*
110 C6 **Eastbury** *Herts., Eng.*
82 B3 **Eastbury** *W. Berks., Eng.*
236 E3 **East Butsfield** *Durham, Eng.*
170 B2 **East Butterwick** *N. Lincs., Eng.*
216 D3 **Eastby** *N. Yorks., Eng.*
314 F4 **East Cairnbeg** *Abers., Scot.*
288 C3 **East Calder** *W. Lothian, Scot.*
166 G3 **East Carleton** *Norf., Eng.*
128 E3 **East Carlton** *Northants., Eng.*
222 D1 **East Carlton** *W. Yorks., Eng.*
236 E2 **East Castle** *Durham, Eng.*
East Chaldon *Dorset, Eng. see* **Chaldon Herring**
102 C5 **East Challow** *Oxon, Eng.*
46 D2 **East Chelborough** *Dorset, Eng.*
58 F3 **East Chiltington** *E. Sussex, Eng.*
94 H5 **East Chinnock** *Som., Eng.*
86 E4 **East Chisenbury** *Wilts., Eng.*
52 C3 **East Cholderton** *Hants., Eng.*
62 F2 **Eastchurch** *Kent, Eng.*
78 D2 **East Clandon** *Surr., Eng.*
106 C3 **East Claydon** *Bucks., Eng.*
320 I3 **East Clyne** *High., Scot.*
94 I5 **East Coker** *Som., Eng.*
98 G3 **Eastcombe** *Glos., Eng.*
94 E4 **Eastcombe** *Som., Eng.*
46 F2 **East Compton** *Dorset, Eng.*
94 I3 **East Compton** *Som., Eng.*
74 B2 **Eastcote** *Gtr Lon., Eng.*
128 C4 **Eastcote** *Northants., Eng.*
154 D3 **Eastcote** *W. Mids, Eng.*
74 B2 **Eastcote Village** *Gtr Lon., Eng.*
86 D4 **Eastcott** *Wilts., Eng.*
210 C3 **East Cottingwith** *E. Riding, Eng.*
86 C2 **Eastcourt** *Wilts., Eng.*
52 E6 **East Cowes** *I.o.W., Eng.*
210 B4 **East Cowick** *E. Riding, Eng.*
244 H5 **East Cramlington** *Northumb., Eng.*
94 J3 **East Cranmore** *Som., Eng.*
46 G4 **East Creech** *Dorset, Eng.*
300 C5 **East Darlochan** *Arg. and B., Scot.*
314 E3 **East Davoch** *Abers., Scot.*
58 H4 **East Dean** *E. Sussex, Eng.*
52 C4 **East Dean** *Hants., Eng.*
58 B3 **East Dean** *W. Sussex, Eng.*
208 E3 **East Dene** *S. Yorks., Eng.*
236 E2 **East Denton** *T. and W., Eng.*
East Dereham *Norf., Eng. see* **Dereham**
198 D3 **East Didsbury** *Gtr Man., Eng.*
40 F4 **Eastdown** *Devon, Eng.*
176 D3 **East Drayton** *Notts., Eng.*
74 D3 **East Dulwich** *Gtr Lon., Eng.*
276 E2 **East Dunbartonshire** *admin. div. Scot.*
94 I2 **East Dundry** *N. Som., Eng.*
210 F4 **East Ella** *Hull, Eng.*
110 C2 **East End** *Bedford, Eng.*
210 G4 **East End** *E. Riding, Eng.*
210 H4 **East End** *E. Riding, Eng.*
116 C3 **Eastend** *Essex, Eng.*
116 H3 **East End** *Essex, Eng.*
52 D2 **East End** *Hants., Eng.*
52 D6 **East End** *Hants., Eng.*
110 F4 **East End** *Herts., Eng.*
62 D4 **East End** *Kent, Eng.*
62 E2 **East End** *Kent, Eng.*
106 E2 **East End** *M.K., Eng.*
94 H2 **East End** *N. Som., Eng.*
102 B3 **Eastend** *Oxon, Eng.*
102 C4 **East End** *Oxon, Eng.*
46 G3 **East End** *Poole, Eng.*
94 I3 **East End** *Som., Eng.*
120 F3 **East End** *Suff., Eng.*
120 F5 **East End** *Suff., Eng.*
116 I3 **Eastend Green** *Essex, Eng.*
304 J5 **Easter Balgedie** *Perth and Kin., Scot.*
314 D3 **Easter Balmoral** *Abers., Scot.*
296 E4 **Easter Borland** *Stir., Scot.*
296 F5 **Easter Buckieburn** *Stir., Scot.*
98 D4 **Easter Compton** *S. Glos., Eng.*
322 H3 **Easter Drummond** *High., Scot.*
296 E4 **Easter Dullater** *Stir., Scot.*
300 A4 **Easter Ellister** *Arg. and B., Scot.*
320 H4 **Easter Fearn** *High., Scot.*
58 C3 **Eastergate** *W. Sussex, Eng.*
276 F2 **Easterhouse** *Glas., Scot.*
288 D3 **Easter Howgate** *Midlothian, Scot.*
256 J2 **Easter Howlaws** *Borders, Scot.*
322 H2 **Easter Kinkell** *High., Scot.*
308 G3 **Easter Knox** *Angus, Scot.*
308 D2 **Easter Lednathie** *Angus, Scot.*
296 E5 **Easter Poldar** *Stir., Scot.*
22 H7 **Easter Ross** *reg. Scot.*
Easter Skeld *Shet., Scot. see* **Skeld**
322 I2 **Easter Suddie** *High., Scot.*
86 D4 **Easterton** *Wilts., Eng.*
86 D4 **Easterton Sands** *Wilts., Eng.*
94 G3 **Eastertown** *Som., Eng.*
314 F4 **Easter Tulloch** *Abers., Scot.*
314 F1 **Easter Whyntie** *Abers., Scot.*
78 E1 **East Ewell** *Surr., Eng.*
62 C3 **East Farleigh** *Kent, Eng.*
128 D3 **East Farndon** *Northants., Eng.*
24 R7 **East Fen** *reg. Eng.*
170 B3 **East Ferry** *Lincs., Eng.*
94 I2 **Eastfield** *Bristol, Eng.*
216 H2 **Eastfield** *N. Yorks., Eng.*
280 B3 **Eastfield** *N. Lanark., Scot.*
280 D3 **Eastfield** *N. Lanark., Scot.*
244 H3 **Eastfield Hall** *Northumb., Eng.*
170 D3 **East Firsby** *Lincs., Eng.*
244 G2 **East Fleetham** *Northumb., Eng.*
288 G2 **East Fortune** *E. Lothian, Scot.*
222 F2 **East Garforth** *W. Yorks., Eng.*
82 B3 **East Garston** *W. Berks., Eng.*
236 C3 **Eastgate** *Durham, Eng.*
170 D7 **Eastgate** *Lincs., Eng.*
166 G2 **Eastgate** *Norf., Eng.*
102 C5 **East Ginge** *Oxon, Eng.*
162 E2 **East Goscote** *Leics., Eng.*
86 F3 **East Grafton** *Wilts., Eng.*
120 B4 **East Green** *Suff., Eng.*

Farleys End to Gallowhill

98 F2 Farleys End Glos., Eng.
216 F2 Farlington N. Yorks., Eng.
52 F5 Farlington Ports., Eng.
388 I4 Farlough Antrim, N. Ire.
144 E5 Farlow Shrop., Eng.
94 J2 Farmborough B. and N.E. Som., Eng.
116 E3 Farmbridge End Essex, Eng.
98 H2 Farmcote Glos., Eng.
98 I2 Farmington Glos., Eng.
198 A2 Far Moor Gtr Man., Eng.
102 C4 Farmoor Oxon, Eng.
162 C2 Farm Town Leics., Eng.
314 E2 Farmtown Moray, Scot.
180 E4 Farnah Green Derbys., Eng.
74 E3 Farnborough Gtr Lon., Eng.
52 H3 Farnborough Hants., Eng.
132 D5 Farnborough Warks., Eng.
82 B2 Farnborough W. Berks., Eng.
52 H3 Farnborough Street Hants., Eng.
78 C2 Farncombe Surr., Eng.
110 B2 Farndish Bedford, Eng.
184 B3 Farndon Cheshire West & Chester, Eng.
176 D4 Farndon Notts., Eng.
24 N2 Farne Islands is Eng.
308 G2 Farnell Angus, Scot.
46 G2 Farnham Dorset, Eng.
116 C2 Farnham Essex, Eng.
120 H3 Farnham Suff., Eng.
78 B2 Farnham Surr., Eng.
106 E5 Farnham Common Bucks., Eng.
116 C2 Farnham Green Essex, Eng.
106 E5 Farnham Royal Bucks., Eng.
216 D3 Farnhill N. Yorks., Eng.
62 B2 Farningham Kent, Eng.
216 D3 Farnley N. Yorks., Eng.
222 E2 Farnley W. Yorks., Eng.
222 D3 Farnley Tyas W. Yorks., Eng.
176 C4 Farnsfield Notts., Eng.
198 C2 Farnworth Gtr Man., Eng.
190 E3 Farnworth Halton, Eng.
98 G3 Far Oakridge Glos., Eng.
320 H2 Farr High., Scot.
322 I2 Farr High., Scot.
322 J3 Farr High., Scot.
322 H3 Farraline High., Scot.
396 E4 Farranamucklagh Armagh, N. Ire.
402 B4 Farrancassidy Fermanagh, N. Ire.
388 I4 Farranflugh Antrim, N. Ire.
22 G8 Farrar r. Scot.
40 F2 Farringdon Devon, Eng.
94 I3 Farrington Gurney B. and N.E. Som., Eng.
222 E2 Far Royds W. Yorks., Eng.
232 E6 Far Sawrey Cumbria, Eng.
222 D2 Farsley W. Yorks., Eng.
116 F3 Farther Howegreen Essex, Eng.
62 D2 Farthing Corner Medway, Eng.
62 D3 Farthing Green Kent, Eng.
128 B5 Farthinghoe Northants., Eng.
62 H4 Farthingloe Kent, Eng.
128 C4 Farthingstone Northants., Eng.
222 D2 Fartown W. Yorks., Eng.
40 G2 Farway Devon, Eng.
322 E2 Fasag High., Scot.
322 C4 Fascadale High., Scot.
300 F3 Faslane Arg. and B., Scot.
300 E2 Fasnacloich Arg. and B., Scot.
322 G3 Fasnakyle High., Scot.
322 F4 Fassfern High., Scot.
236 F2 Fatfield T. and W., Eng.
232 F3 Faugh Cumbria, Eng.
23 H2 Faughan r. N. Ire.
288 A4 Fauldhouse W. Lothian, Scot.
116 F3 Faulkbourne Essex, Eng.
94 J3 Faulkland Som., Eng.
144 E2 Fauls Shrop., Eng.
86 D5 Faulston Wilts., Eng.
62 F3 Faversham Kent, Eng.
314 D2 Favillar Moray, Scot.
236 F1 Fawdon T. and W., Eng.
148 D1 Fawfieldhead Staffs., Eng.
62 B2 Fawkham Green Kent, Eng.
102 C3 Fawler Oxon, Eng.
106 C5 Fawley Bucks., Eng.
52 D6 Fawley Hants., Eng.
82 B2 Fawley W. Berks., Eng.
140 D4 Fawley Chapel Here., Eng.
314 G4 Fawsyde Abers., Scot.
210 D4 Faxfleet E. Riding, Eng.
128 D3 Faxton Northants., Eng.
58 E2 Faygate W. Sussex, Eng.
190 D3 Fazakerley Merseyside, Eng.
148 E5 Fazeley Staffs., Eng.
320 I4 Fearn High., Scot.
304 F3 Fearnan Perth and Kin., Scot.
322 D2 Fearnbeg High., Scot.
190 F3 Fearnhead Warr., Eng.
322 D2 Fearnmore High., Scot.
300 E4 Fearnoch Arg. and B., Scot.
300 E4 Fearnoch Arg. and B., Scot.
148 C5 Featherstone Staffs., Eng.
222 F2 Featherstone W. Yorks., Eng.
244 B6 Featherstone Castle Northumb., Eng.
136 F2 Feckenham Worcs., Eng.
22 H8 Feehlin r. Scot.
388 D3 Feeny Limavady, N. Ire.
116 G2 Feering Essex, Eng.
216 C1 Feetham N. Yorks., Eng.
314 F2 Feith-hill Abers., Scot.
216 C2 Feizor N. Yorks., Eng.
166 G1 Felbrigg Norf., Eng.
78 F3 Felcourt Surr., Eng.
110 B5 Felden Herts., Eng.
144 D5 Felhampton Shrop., Eng.
356 D1 Felindre Carmar., Wales
356 F2 Felindre Carmar., Wales
356 G2 Felindre Carmar., Wales
356 G2 Felindre Carmar., Wales
362 F3 Felindre Cere., Wales
366 F4 Felindre Powys, Wales
366 F7 Felindre Powys, Wales
350 C2 Felindre Swansea, Wales
362 F3 Felinfach Cere., Wales
366 F7 Felinfach Powys, Wales
356 F3 Felinfoel Carmar., Wales
356 E2 Felingwmisaf Carmar., Wales
356 E2 Felingwmuchaf Carmar., Wales
378 G3 Felin Puleston Wrex., Wales
216 F2 Felixkirk N. Yorks., Eng.
120 H5 Felixstowe Suff., Eng.
120 H5 Felixstowe Ferry Suff., Eng.
244 E1 Felkington Northumb., Eng.
222 F3 Felkirk W. Yorks., Eng.
22 J12 Fell, Loch hill Scot.
236 G2 Fellgate T. and W., Eng.
236 F2 Felling T. and W., Eng.
236 F2 Felling Shore T. and W., Eng.
300 C2 Fellonmore Arg. and B., Scot.
110 B2 Felmersham Bedford, Eng.
166 H2 Felmingham Norf., Eng.
58 C4 Felpham W. Sussex, Eng.
120 E3 Felsham Suff., Eng.
116 E2 Felsted Essex, Eng.
74 B3 Feltham Gtr Lon., Eng.
78 D1 Felthamhill Surr., Eng.
166 G2 Felthorpe Norf., Eng.
140 D3 Felton Here., Eng.
244 G4 Felton Northumb., Eng.
144 C3 Felton Butler Shrop., Eng.
166 C4 Feltwell Norf., Eng.
222 D3 Fenay Bridge W. Yorks., Eng.
228 I3 Fence Lancs., Eng.
236 G2 Fence Houses T. and W., Eng.
102 D3 Fencott Oxon, Eng.
170 G5 Fendike Corner Lincs., Eng.
124 F5 Fen Ditton Cambs., Eng.
124 D5 Fen Drayton Cambs., Eng.
154 D3 Fen End W. Mids, Eng.
166 G2 Fengate Norf., Eng.
244 F2 Fenham Northumb., Eng.
236 F2 Fenham T. and W., Eng.
170 F6 Fenhouses Lincs., Eng.
228 G4 Feniscowles B'burn, Eng.
40 G2 Feniton Devon, Eng.
110 C3 Fenlake Bedford, Eng.
366 E7 Fenni-fach Powys, Wales
62 D2 Fenn Street Medway, Eng.
180 C4 Fenny Bentley Derbys., Eng.
132 D4 Fenny Compton Warks., Eng.
162 C3 Fenny Drayton Leics., Eng.
106 D3 Fenny Stratford M.K., Eng.
244 G4 Fenrother Northumb., Eng.
124 D5 Fenstanton Cambs., Eng.
166 E3 Fen Street Norf., Eng.
166 F4 Fen Street Norf., Eng.
166 F4 Fen Street Norf., Eng.
120 E2 Fen Street Suff., Eng.
120 G3 Fen Street Suff., Eng.
124 D4 Fenton Cambs., Eng.
232 F3 Fenton Cumbria, Eng.
170 B4 Fenton Lincs., Eng.
244 E2 Fenton Northumb., Eng.
176 E2 Fenton Notts., Eng.
148 C3 Fenton Stoke, Eng.
288 G2 Fenton Barns E. Lothian, Scot.
244 F2 Fenwick Northumb., Eng.
244 F5 Fenwick Northumb., Eng.
208 F2 Fenwick S. Yorks., Eng.
262 E3 Fenwick E. Ayr., Scot.
300 D5 Feochaig Arg. and B., Scot.
36 D3 Feock Corn., Eng.
300 C4 Feolin Arg. and B., Scot.
300 B4 Feolin Ferry Arg. and B., Scot.
300 C6 Feorlan Arg. and B., Scot.
300 E3 Feorlin Arg. and B., Scot.
276 D2 Ferguslie Park Renf., Scot.
322 A2 Feriniquarrie High., Scot.
402 D4 Fermanagh admin. dist. N. Ire.
402 E5 Fermanagh county N. Ire.
308 E2 Fern Angus, Scot.
350 F3 Ferndale R.C.T., Wales
46 H3 Ferndown Dorset, Eng.
322 J2 Ferness High., Scot.
102 B5 Fernham Oxon, Eng.
198 D2 Fernhill Gtr Man., Eng.
136 D2 Fernhill Heath Worcs., Eng.
58 B2 Fernhurst W. Sussex, Eng.
292 F2 Fernie Fife, Scot.
322 B3 Fernilea High., Scot.
180 B3 Fernilee Derbys., Eng.
308 F1 Fernybank Angus, Scot.
216 E2 Ferrensby N. Yorks., Eng.
322 D3 Ferrindonald High., Scot.
58 D4 Ferring W. Sussex, Eng.
222 G2 Ferrybridge W. Yorks., Eng.
308 H2 Ferryden Angus, Scot.
124 E4 Ferry Hill Cambs., Eng.
236 F3 Ferryhill Durham, Eng.
356 D3 Ferryside Carmar., Wales
166 F4 Fersfield Norf., Eng.
322 G4 Fersit High., Scot.
362 C4 Ferwig Cere., Wales
322 J3 Feshiebridge High., Scot.
78 D2 Fetcham Surr., Eng.
22 □N1 Fethaland, Point of pt Scot.
331 E2 Fetlar airport Shet., Scot.
22 □O1 Fetlar i. Scot.
314 G2 Fetterangus Abers., Scot.
314 F4 Fettercairn Abers., Scot.
314 F4 Feus of Caldhame Abers., Scot.
102 D3 Fewcott Oxon, Eng.
216 D3 Fewston N. Yorks., Eng.
388 K3 Feystown Larne, N. Ire.
356 G2 Ffairfach Carmar., Wales
362 G3 Ffair-Rhos Cere., Wales
356 G1 Ffaldybrenin Carmar., Wales
356 G1 Ffarmers Carmar., Wales
366 G7 Ffawyddog Powys, Wales
372 G3 Ffestiniog Gwynedd, Wales
378 F2 Ffordd-las Denb., Wales
366 G6 Fforddlas Powys, Wales
356 F3 Fforest Carmar., Wales
350 C3 Fforest-fach Swansea, Wales
362 D4 Ffostrasol Cere., Wales
362 E3 Ffos-y-ffin Cere., Wales
372 F2 Ffridd Uchaf Gwynedd, Wales
378 E1 Ffrith Denb., Wales
378 G3 Ffrith Flints., Wales
366 E7 Ffrwdgrech Powys, Wales
356 D3 Ffynnon Carmar., Wales
356 E2 Ffynnon-ddrain Carmar., Wales
378 F2 Ffynnongroyw Flints., Wales
Ffynnon Taf Cardiff, Wales see Taff's Well
326 D1 Fibhig W. Isles, Scot.
314 E3 Fichlie Abers., Scot.
300 A3 Fidden Arg. and B., Scot.
22 J8 Fiddich r. Scot.
98 G2 Fiddington Glos., Eng.
94 F4 Fiddington Som., Eng.
46 F2 Fiddleford Dorset, Eng.
140 D3 Fiddler's Green Here., Eng.
166 D2 Fiddler's Green Norf., Eng.
166 F3 Fiddler's Green Norf., Eng.
116 C3 Fiddlers Hamlet Essex, Eng.
148 D3 Field Staffs., Eng.
102 B4 Field Assarts Oxon, Eng.
232 E7 Field Broughton Cumbria, Eng.
166 E1 Field Dalling Norf., Eng.
162 D2 Field Head Leics., Eng.
292 F2 Fife admin. div. Scot.
46 F2 Fifehead Magdalen Dorset, Eng.
46 E2 Fifehead Neville Dorset, Eng.
46 F2 Fifehead St Quintin Dorset, Eng.
314 E2 Fife Keith Moray, Scot.
22 K10 Fife Ness pt Scot.
102 B3 Fifield Oxon, Eng.
82 F3 Fifield W. and M., Eng.
86 E4 Fifield Wilts., Eng.
86 D5 Fifield Bavant Wilts., Eng.
86 E4 Figheldean Wilts., Eng.
166 I3 Filby Norf., Eng.
216 I2 Filey N. Yorks., Eng.
106 D2 Filgrave M.K., Eng.
102 B4 Filkins Oxon, Eng.
40 E1 Filleigh Devon, Eng.
170 C3 Fillingham Lincs., Eng.
132 C3 Fillongley Warks., Eng.
52 F4 Filmore Hill Hants., Eng.
98 D4 Filton S. Glos., Eng.
210 E2 Fimber E. Riding, Eng.
308 F2 Finavon Angus, Scot.
388 C3 Fincarn Derry, N. Ire.
388 D3 Fincarn Limavady, N. Ire.
166 B3 Fincham Norf., Eng.
82 E3 Finchampstead W'ham, Eng.
52 G5 Finchdean Hants., Eng.
116 E2 Finchingfield Essex, Eng.
74 C2 Finchley Gtr Lon., Eng.
180 D5 Findern Derbys., Eng.
314 C2 Findhorn Moray, Scot.
22 I7 Findhorn r. Scot.
322 J3 Findhorn Bridge High., Scot.
304 F5 Findhuglen Perth and Kin., Scot.
314 E1 Findochty Moray, Scot.
304 I4 Findo Gask Perth and Kin., Scot.
58 D3 Findon W. Sussex, Eng.
314 G3 Findon Abers., Scot.
322 H2 Findon Mains High., Scot.
58 D3 Findon Valley W. Sussex, Eng.
314 C1 Findrassie Moray, Scot.
314 C3 Findron Moray, Scot.
128 F3 Finedon Northants., Eng.
304 J2 Finegand Perth and Kin., Scot.
120 G3 Fingal Street Suff., Eng.
314 F2 Fingask Abers., Scot.
136 C1 Fingerpost Worcs., Eng.
106 C5 Fingest Bucks., Eng.
216 D2 Finghall N. Yorks., Eng.
232 D3 Fingland Cumbria, Eng.
252 E1 Fingland D. and G., Scot.
252 G2 Fingland D. and G., Scot.
62 I3 Finglesham Kent, Eng.
116 H2 Fingringhoe Essex, Eng.
208 C3 Finkle Street S. Yorks., Eng.
296 E3 Finlarig Stir., Scot.
102 E3 Finmere Oxon, Eng.
300 F3 Finnart Arg. and B., Scot.
304 D2 Finnart Perth and Kin., Scot.
162 D2 Finney Hill Leics., Eng.
276 E2 Finnieston Glas., Scot.
120 F3 Finningham Suff., Eng.
208 G3 Finningley S. Yorks., Eng.
74 D2 Finsbury Gtr Lon., Eng.
74 D2 Finsbury Park Gtr Lon., Eng.
136 E2 Finstall Worcs., Eng.
102 C3 Finstock Oxon, Eng.
329 C3 Finstown Orkney, Scot.
402 G4 Fintona Omagh, N. Ire.
314 F2 Fintry Abers., Scot.
296 E5 Fintry Stir., Scot.
388 H2 Finvoy Ballymoney, N. Ire.
132 B4 Finwood Warks., Eng.
314 E3 Finzean Abers., Scot.
22 F7 Fionn Loch l. Scot.
300 A3 Fionnphort Arg. and B., Scot.
232 G6 Firbank Cumbria, Eng.
208 F3 Firbeck S. Yorks., Eng.
216 G2 Firby N. Yorks., Eng.
198 E2 Firgrove Gtr Man., Eng.
86 E5 Firsdown Wilts., Eng.
198 B3 Firs Lane Gtr Man., Eng.
331 D2 Firth Shet., Scot.
208 D3 Fir Vale S. Yorks., Eng.
52 E6 Fishbourne I.o.W., Eng.
58 B3 Fishbourne W. Sussex, Eng.
236 G3 Fishburn Durham, Eng.
292 B3 Fishcross Clack., Scot.
58 B4 Fisher W. Sussex, Eng.
314 F2 Fisherford Abers., Scot.
58 E3 Fishersgate B. and H., Eng.
52 E5 Fisher's Pond Hants., Eng.
228 E3 Fisher's Row Lancs., Eng.
58 C2 Fisherstreet W. Sussex, Eng.
322 I2 Fisherton High., Scot.
262 C4 Fisherton S. Ayr., Scot.
86 C5 Fisherton de la Mere Wilts., Eng.
26 C3 Fishguard Bay b. Wales
208 F2 Fishlake S. Yorks., Eng.
166 I3 Fishley Norf., Eng.
154 C2 Fishley W. Mids, Eng.
300 C2 Fishnish Arg. and B., Scot.
46 B3 Fishpond Bottom Dorset, Eng.
94 I2 Fishponds Bristol, Eng.
198 D2 Fishpool Gtr Man., Eng.
170 G6 Fishtoft Lincs., Eng.
170 F5 Fishtoft Drove Lincs., Eng.
308 H2 Fishtown of Usan Angus, Scot.
228 G4 Fishwick Lancs., Eng.
256 L2 Fishwick Borders, Scot.
170 D4 Fiskerton Lincs., Eng.
176 D4 Fiskerton Notts., Eng.
22 □N3 Fitful Head hd Scot.
210 H4 Fitling E. Riding, Eng.
86 E4 Fittleton Wilts., Eng.
124 E2 Fitton End Cambs., Eng.
144 D3 Fitz Shrop., Eng.
94 E4 Fitzhead Som., Eng.
94 F4 Fitzroy Som., Eng.
222 F3 Fitzwilliam W. Yorks., Eng.
322 D5 Fiunary High., Scot.
58 G2 Five Ash Down E. Sussex, Eng.
58 H2 Five Ashes E. Sussex, Eng.
140 D3 Five Bridges Here., Eng.
94 G4 Fivehead Som., Eng.
52 D6 Five Houses I.o.W., Eng.
222 D2 Five Lane Ends W. Yorks., Eng.
339 D3 Five Lanes Mon., Wales
402 G4 Fivemiletown Fermanagh, N. Ire.
62 C3 Five Oak Green Kent, Eng.
408 E4 Five Oaks Jersey Channel Is
58 D2 Five Oaks W. Sussex, Eng.
356 E3 Five Roads Carmar., Wales
144 B5 Five Turnings Shrop., Eng.
62 D3 Five Wents Kent, Eng.
116 F3 Flack's Green Essex, Eng.
106 D5 Flackwell Heath Bucks., Eng.
136 E3 Fladbury Worcs., Eng.
331 D3 Fladdabister Shet., Scot.
180 C3 Flagg Derbys., Eng.
210 H2 Flamborough E. Riding, Eng.
24 Q5 Flamborough Head hd Eng.
110 C5 Flamstead Herts., Eng.
110 E5 Flamstead End Herts., Eng.
22 A6 Flannan Isles is Scot.
58 C4 Flansham W. Sussex, Eng.
222 E2 Flanshaw W. Yorks., Eng.
222 C2 Flappit Spring W. Yorks., Eng.
148 D1 Flash Staffs., Eng.
322 B2 Flashader High., Scot.
216 H1 Flask Inn N. Yorks., Eng.
26 F5 Flat Holm i. Wales
110 B5 Flaunden Herts., Eng.
176 D5 Flawborough Notts., Eng.
216 F2 Flawith N. Yorks., Eng.
94 H2 Flax Bourton N. Som., Eng.
216 E2 Flaxby N. Yorks., Eng.
180 E5 Flaxholme Derbys., Eng.
166 F3 Flaxlands Norf., Eng.
98 E3 Flaxley Glos., Eng.
228 I4 Flax Moss Lancs., Eng.
94 E4 Flaxpool Som., Eng.
216 G2 Flaxton N. Yorks., Eng.
162 E3 Fleckney Leics., Eng.
132 E4 Flecknoe Warks., Eng.
176 E3 Fledborough Notts., Eng.
52 G3 Fleet Hants., Eng.
52 G6 Fleet Hants., Eng.
170 G7 Fleet Lincs., Eng.
22 H7 Fleet r. Scot.
22 H7 Fleet, Loch b. Scot.
170 G7 Fleet Hargate Lincs., Eng.
110 D5 Fleetville Herts., Eng.
228 D3 Fleetwood Lancs., Eng.
166 I2 Fleggburgh Norf., Eng.
350 F4 Flemingston V. of Glam., Wales
268 B2 Flemington S. Lanark., Scot.
120 C3 Flempton Suff., Eng.
326 F2 Flesherin W. Isles, Scot.
36 E2 Fletchersbridge Corn., Eng.
232 C4 Fletchertown Cumbria, Eng.
58 G3 Fletching E. Sussex, Eng.
314 D3 Fleuchats Abers., Scot.
350 G3 Fleur-de-lis Caerp., Wales
36 F1 Flexbury Corn., Eng.
78 B2 Flexford Surr., Eng.
232 A4 Flimby Cumbria, Eng.
58 I2 Flimwell E. Sussex, Eng.
378 G2 Flint Flints., Wales
124 E6 Flint Cross Cambs., Eng.
176 D4 Flintham Notts., Eng.
378 G2 Flint Mountain Flints., Wales
210 H4 Flinton E. Riding, Eng.
154 E3 Flint's Green W. Mids, Eng.
378 F2 Flintshire county Wales
62 D4 Flishinghurst Kent, Eng.
166 C2 Flitcham Norf., Eng.
232 H5 Flitholme Cumbria, Eng.
110 C3 Flitton Central Bedfordshire, Eng.
110 C3 Flitwick Central Bedfordshire, Eng.
170 B2 Flixborough N. Lincs., Eng.
198 C3 Flixton Gtr Man., Eng.
216 H2 Flixton N. Yorks., Eng.
120 H2 Flixton Suff., Eng.
222 E3 Flockton W. Yorks., Eng.
222 E3 Flockton Green W. Yorks., Eng.
244 E2 Flodden Northumb., Eng.
322 C2 Flodigarry High., Scot.
124 E3 Flood's Ferry Cambs., Eng.
232 E7 Flookburgh Cumbria, Eng.
128 C4 Flore Northants., Eng.
22 J5 Flotta i. Scot.
244 E4 Flotterton Northumb., Eng.
58 H3 Flowers Green E. Sussex, Eng.
120 F4 Flowton Suff., Eng.
222 E2 Flushdyke W. Yorks., Eng.
36 D3 Flushing Corn., Eng.
36 D3 Flushing Corn., Eng.
314 H2 Flushing Abers., Scot.
402 E2 Flushtown Strabane, N. Ire.
136 E2 Flyford Flavell Worcs., Eng.
120 G3 Foals Green Suff., Eng.
116 E4 Fobbing Thurrock, Eng.
314 D2 Fochabers Moray, Scot.
350 G2 Fochriw Caerp., Wales
170 B2 Fockerby N. Lincs., Eng.
314 C3 Fodderletter Moray, Scot.
322 H2 Fodderty High., Scot.
94 I4 Foddington Som., Eng.
366 E2 Foel Powys, Wales
356 F3 Foelgastell Carmar., Wales
210 C4 Foggathorpe E. Riding, Eng.
198 E3 Foggbrook Gtr Man., Eng.
256 J2 Fogo Borders, Scot.
256 J2 Fogorig Borders, Scot.
314 D2 Fogwatt Moray, Scot.
22 G6 Foinaven hill Scot.
320 E2 Foindle High., Scot.
Foithir High., Scot. see Foyers
308 C2 Folda Angus, Scot.
148 D3 Fole Staffs., Eng.
154 F3 Foleshill W. Mids, Eng.
46 E2 Folke Dorset, Eng.
62 H4 Folkestone Kent, Eng.
170 D6 Folkingham Lincs., Eng.
58 H4 Folkington E. Sussex, Eng.
124 C4 Folksworth Cambs., Eng.
216 H2 Folkton N. Yorks., Eng.
314 F2 Folla Rule Abers., Scot.
216 E3 Follifoot N. Yorks., Eng.
46 E3 Folly Dorset, Eng.
358 D2 Folly Pembs., Wales
40 D2 Folly Gate Devon, Eng.
350 F4 Fonmon V. of Glam., Wales
86 C5 Fonthill Bishop Wilts., Eng.
86 C5 Fonthill Gifford Wilts., Eng.
46 F2 Fontmell Magna Dorset, Eng.
46 F2 Fontmell Parva Dorset, Eng.
58 C3 Fontwell W. Sussex, Eng.
350 F4 Font-y-gary V. of Glam., Wales
180 C3 Foolow Derbys., Eng.
148 D5 Footherley Staffs., Eng.
74 E3 Foots Cray Gtr Lon., Eng.
314 D3 Forbestown Abers., Scot.
232 D7 Force Forge Cumbria, Eng.
62 A3 Force Green Kent, Eng.
216 D1 Forcett N. Yorks., Eng.
106 C4 Ford Bucks., Eng.
180 E3 Ford Derbys., Eng.
40 D2 Ford Devon, Eng.
40 E3 Ford Devon, Eng.
98 H2 Ford Glos., Eng.
190 D3 Ford Merseyside, Eng.
244 E2 Ford Northumb., Eng.
40 D3 Ford Plymouth, Eng.
144 C3 Ford Shrop., Eng.
94 E4 Ford Som., Eng.
148 D2 Ford Staffs., Eng.
86 B3 Ford Wilts., Eng.
58 C4 Ford W. Sussex, Eng.
300 D3 Ford Arg. and B., Scot.
288 F3 Ford Midlothian, Scot.
358 E2 Ford Pembs., Wales
154 D3 Fordbridge W. Mids, Eng.
62 B4 Fordcombe Kent, Eng.
292 D3 Fordell Fife, Scot.
366 G3 Forden Powys, Wales
116 E3 Ford End Essex, Eng.
94 G4 Fordgate Som., Eng.
228 F3 Ford Green Lancs., Eng.
124 G5 Fordham Cambs., Eng.
116 G2 Fordham Essex, Eng.
166 B3 Fordham Norf., Eng.
124 G5 Fordham Abbey Cambs., Eng.
116 G2 Fordham Heath Essex, Eng.
144 C3 Ford Heath Shrop., Eng.
154 B2 Fordhouses W. Mids, Eng.
52 B5 Fordingbridge Hants., Eng.
210 F2 Fordon E. Riding, Eng.
314 F4 Fordoun Abers., Scot.
116 G2 Fordstreet Essex, Eng.
94 E5 Ford Street Som., Eng.
102 B4 Fordwells Oxon, Eng.
62 G3 Fordwich Kent, Eng.
314 E2 Fordyce Abers., Scot.
304 I4 Forebrae Perth and Kin., Scot.
148 C4 Forebridge Staffs., Eng.
388 D3 Foreglen Limavady, N. Ire.
300 A4 Foreland Arg. and B., Scot.
26 J6 Foreland hd Eng.
26 E5 Foreland Point pt Eng.
180 D5 Foremark Derbys., Eng.
216 E1 Forest N. Yorks., Eng.
244 F4 Forestburn Gate Northumb., Eng.
339 B1 Forest Coal Pit Mon., Wales
74 E2 Forest Gate Gtr Lon., Eng.
78 D3 Forest Green Surr., Eng.
232 F6 Forest Hall Cumbria, Eng.
236 F1 Forest Hall T. and W., Eng.
232 G3 Forest Head Cumbria, Eng.
74 D3 Forest Hill Gtr Lon., Eng.
102 E4 Forest Hill Oxon, Eng.
236 B4 Forest-in-Teesdale Durham, Eng.
304 H1 Forest Lodge Perth and Kin., Scot.
292 B3 Forestmill Clack., Scot.
58 G2 Forest Row E. Sussex, Eng.
52 E6 Forest Side I.o.W., Eng.
58 A3 Forestside W. Sussex, Eng.
176 C4 Forest Town Notts., Eng.
308 E3 Forfar Angus, Scot.
304 J4 Forgandenny Perth and Kin., Scot.
366 C3 Forge Powys, Wales
280 B4 Forgewood N. Lanark., Scot.
314 D2 Forgie Moray, Scot.
136 F1 Forhill Worcs., Eng.
396 F5 Forkhill Newry & Mourne, N. Ire.
190 C2 Formby Merseyside, Eng.
388 F2 Formoyle Coleraine, N. Ire.
166 G3 Forncett St Mary Norf., Eng.
304 J3 Forneth Perth and Kin., Scot.
120 D3 Fornham All Saints Suff., Eng.
120 D3 Fornham St Martin Suff., Eng.
322 J2 Fornighty High., Scot.
314 C2 Forres Moray, Scot.
280 D3 Forrest N. Lanark., Scot.
252 D2 Forrest Lodge D. and G., Scot.
148 C3 Forsbrook Staffs., Eng.
320 I2 Forsinain High., Scot.
320 I2 Forsinard High., Scot.
46 E3 Forston Dorset, Eng.
322 G3 Fort Augustus High., Scot.
308 B2 Forter Angus, Scot.
304 I4 Forteviot Perth and Kin., Scot.
322 I2 Fort George High., Scot.
268 D2 Forth S. Lanark., Scot.
20 F3 Forth r. Scot.
22 J10 Forth, Firth of est. Scot.
98 F2 Forthampton Glos., Eng.
304 F3 Fortingall Perth and Kin., Scot.
74 D2 Fortis Green Gtr Lon., Eng.
52 D3 Forton Hants., Eng.
228 F3 Forton Lancs., Eng.
144 C3 Forton Shrop., Eng.
94 G5 Forton Som., Eng.
148 A4 Forton Staffs., Eng.
314 F2 Fortrie Abers., Scot.
322 I2 Fortrose High., Scot.
46 E4 Fortuneswell Dorset, Eng.
106 D5 Forty Green Bucks., Eng.
74 D2 Forty Hill Gtr Lon., Eng.
120 F3 Forward Green Suff., Eng.
86 F4 Fosbury Wilts., Eng.
98 J2 Foscot Glos., Eng.
170 F6 Fosdyke Lincs., Eng.
304 G2 Foss Perth and Kin., Scot.
98 H3 Foss Cross Glos., Eng.
216 C2 Fossdale N. Yorks., Eng.
98 H3 Fossebridge Glos., Eng.
62 F3 Fostall Kent, Eng.
208 F2 Fosterhouses S. Yorks., Eng.
128 C4 Foster's Booth Northants., Eng.
116 C3 Foster Street Essex, Eng.
180 C5 Foston Derbys., Eng.
162 E3 Foston Leics., Eng.
170 B6 Foston Lincs., Eng.
216 G2 Foston N. Yorks., Eng.
210 G3 Foston on the Wolds E. Riding, Eng.
170 F3 Fotherby Lincs., Eng.
128 G2 Fotheringhay Northants., Eng.
329 E4 Foubister Orkney, Scot.
331 A3 Foula airport Scot.
22 □L2 Foula i. Scot.
252 G1 Foulbog D. and G., Scot.
222 F3 Foulby W. Yorks., Eng.
166 C3 Foulden Norf., Eng.
256 L2 Foulden Borders, Scot.
58 H3 Foul Mile E. Sussex, Eng.
26 N4 Foulness Point pt Eng.
58 H4 Foulride Green E. Sussex, Eng.
228 I3 Foulridge Lancs., Eng.
166 F2 Foulsham Norf., Eng.
232 F7 Foulstone Cumbria, Eng.
256 G2 Fountainhall Borders, Scot.
24 N5 Fountains Abbey and Studley Royal Water Garden tourist site Eng.
148 B6 Four Ashes Staffs., Eng.
148 C4 Four Ashes Staffs., Eng.
120 E3 Four Ashes Suff., Eng.
154 D3 Four Ashes W. Mids, Eng.
148 C4 Four Crosses Staffs., Eng.
378 E4 Four Crosses Denb., Wales
366 E2 Four Crosses Powys, Wales
366 G2 Four Crosses Powys, Wales
62 A3 Four Elms Kent, Eng.
94 F4 Four Forks Som., Eng.
124 E2 Four Gotes Cambs., Eng.
208 C2 Four Lane End S. Yorks., Eng.
228 H4 Four Lane Ends B'burn, Eng.
184 D3 Four Lane Ends Cheshire West & Chester, Eng.
180 E4 Fourlane Ends Derbys., Eng.
216 G3 Four Lane Ends York, Eng.
36 D3 Four Lanes Corn., Eng.
184 F3 Fourlanes End Cheshire East, Eng.
52 F4 Four Marks Hants., Eng.
371 B3 Four Mile Bridge I.o.A., Wales
58 J3 Four Oaks E. Sussex, Eng.
98 E2 Four Oaks Glos., Eng.
154 C2 Four Oaks W. Mids, Eng.
154 E3 Four Oaks W. Mids, Eng.
154 C2 Four Oaks Park W. Mids, Eng.
356 E3 Four Roads Carmar., Wales
244 D5 Fourstones Northumb., Eng.
62 D4 Four Throws Kent, Eng.
86 D5 Fovant Wilts., Eng.
36 F2 Fowey Corn., Eng.
26 C7 Fowey r. Eng.
308 D4 Fowlis Angus, Scot.
304 H4 Fowlis Wester Perth and Kin., Scot.
124 E6 Fowlmere Cambs., Eng.
140 D3 Fownhope Here., Eng.
276 D3 Foxbar Renf., Scot.
102 D4 Foxcombe Hill Oxon, Eng.
98 H2 Foxcote Glos., Eng.
94 J3 Foxcote Som., Eng.
52 C3 Foxcotte Hants., Eng.
405 C2 Foxdale Isle of Man
116 G1 Foxearth Essex, Eng.
232 C7 Foxfield Cumbria, Eng.
180 F3 Fox Green Derbys., Eng.
86 C3 Foxham Wilts., Eng.
116 D4 Fox Hatch Essex, Eng.
36 E2 Foxhole Corn., Eng.
322 H2 Foxhole High., Scot.
350 C3 Foxhole Swansea, Wales
216 H2 Foxholes N. Yorks., Eng.
58 H3 Foxhunt Green E. Sussex, Eng.
52 H3 Fox Lane Hants., Eng.
140 B3 Foxley Here., Eng.
166 F2 Foxley Norf., Eng.
128 C5 Foxley Northants., Eng.
86 C2 Foxley Wilts., Eng.
116 H2 Fox Street Essex, Eng.
148 D2 Foxt Staffs., Eng.
124 E6 Foxton Cambs., Eng.
236 G4 Foxton Durham, Eng.
162 F3 Foxton Leics., Eng.
216 C2 Foxup N. Yorks., Eng.
184 D2 Foxwist Green Cheshire West & Chester, Eng.
140 D4 Foy Here., Eng.
322 H3 Foyers High., Scot.
23 H3 Foyle r. Ireland/U.K.
23 H2 Foyle, Lough b. Ireland/U.K.
148 E4 Fradley Staffs., Eng.
148 C3 Fradswell Staffs., Eng.
210 G2 Fraisthorpe E. Riding, Eng.
58 G3 Framfield E. Sussex, Eng.
166 H3 Framingham Earl Norf., Eng.
166 H3 Framingham Pigot Norf., Eng.
120 H3 Framlingham Suff., Eng.
46 D3 Frampton Dorset, Eng.
170 F6 Frampton Lincs., Eng.
98 E4 Frampton Cotterell S. Glos., Eng.
98 G3 Frampton Mansell Glos., Eng.
98 E3 Frampton on Severn Glos., Eng.
170 F6 Frampton West End Lincs., Eng.
120 G3 Framsden Suff., Eng.
236 F3 Framwellgate Moor Durham, Eng.
228 G4 Frances Green Lancs., Eng.
136 D1 Franche Worcs., Eng.
184 D2 Frandley Cheshire West & Chester, Eng.
190 C3 Frankby Merseyside, Eng.
166 H2 Frankfort Norf., Eng.
136 E1 Frankley Worcs., Eng.
136 E1 Frankley Green Worcs., Eng.
366 F5 Franksbridge Powys, Wales
132 D4 Frankton Warks., Eng.
144 D3 Frankwell Shrop., Eng.
58 H2 Frant E. Sussex, Eng.
314 G1 Fraserburgh Abers., Scot.
116 I2 Frating Essex, Eng.
52 F6 Fratton Ports., Eng.
132 C2 Freasley Warks., Eng.
36 G2 Freathy Corn., Eng.
120 B3 Freckenham Suff., Eng.
228 E4 Freckleton Lancs., Eng.
162 G2 Freeby Leics., Eng.
52 E3 Freefolk Hants., Eng.
148 D3 Freehay Staffs., Eng.
102 C4 Freeland Oxon, Eng.
52 D5 Freemantle Soton, Eng.
331 D3 Freester Shet., Scot.
166 I3 Freethorpe Norf., Eng.
166 I3 Freethorpe Common Norf., Eng.
198 D2 Free Town Gtr Man., Eng.
74 D1 Freezy Water Gtr Lon., Eng.
170 G6 Freiston Lincs., Eng.
170 G6 Freiston Shore Lincs., Eng.
40 D1 Fremington Devon, Eng.
94 I2 Frenchay Bristol, Eng.
40 E3 Frenchbeer Devon, Eng.
296 C4 Frenich Stir., Scot.
78 B3 Frensham Surr., Eng.
86 D2 Freshbrook Swindon, Eng.
190 C2 Freshfield Merseyside, Eng.
94 K2 Freshford B. and N.E. Som., Eng.
52 C6 Freshwater I.o.W., Eng.
52 C6 Freshwater Bay I.o.W., Eng.
358 E4 Freshwater East Pembs., Wales
120 G2 Fressingfield Suff., Eng.
120 F4 Freston Suff., Eng.
320 K2 Freswick High., Scot.
98 E3 Fretherne Glos., Eng.
166 G2 Frettenham Norf., Eng.
292 F2 Freuchie Fife, Scot.
402 G3 Freughmore Omagh, N. Ire.
358 E3 Freystrop Cross Pembs., Wales
252 E2 Friars Carse D. and G., Scot.
58 G2 Friar's Gate E. Sussex, Eng.
304 J4 Friarton Perth and Kin., Scot.
124 E3 Friday Bridge Cambs., Eng.
74 E2 Friday Hill Gtr Lon., Eng.
58 H4 Friday Street E. Sussex, Eng.
120 G3 Friday Street Suff., Eng.
120 H3 Friday Street Suff., Eng.
120 H4 Friday Street Suff., Eng.
78 D2 Friday Street Surr., Eng.
210 D2 Fridaythorpe E. Riding, Eng.
74 D2 Friern Barnet Gtr Lon., Eng.
170 D3 Friesthorpe Lincs., Eng.
170 C5 Frieston Lincs., Eng.
106 C5 Frieth Bucks., Eng.
102 C4 Frilford Oxon, Eng.
82 C3 Frilsham W. Berks., Eng.
78 B2 Frimley Surr., Eng.
78 B2 Frimley Green Surr., Eng.
62 D2 Frindsbury Medway, Eng.
166 C1 Fring Norf., Eng.
102 E3 Fringford Oxon, Eng.
62 D3 Friningham Kent, Eng.
62 E3 Frinsted Kent, Eng.
116 J3 Frinton-on-Sea Essex, Eng.
308 F3 Friockheim Angus, Scot.
372 F4 Friog Gwynedd, Wales
22 D9 Frisa, Loch l. Scot.
162 F2 Frisby on the Wreake Leics., Eng.
170 H5 Friskney Lincs., Eng.
170 H5 Friskney Eaudyke Lincs., Eng.
58 H4 Friston E. Sussex, Eng.
120 I3 Friston Suff., Eng.
180 E4 Fritchley Derbys., Eng.
62 E3 Frith Kent, Eng.
52 C5 Fritham Hants., Eng.
170 F5 Frith Bank Lincs., Eng.
136 C2 Frith Common Worcs., Eng.
40 D2 Frithelstock Stone Devon, Eng.
170 F5 Frithville Lincs., Eng.
62 D4 Frittenden Kent, Eng.
166 G4 Fritton Norf., Eng.
166 I3 Fritton Norf., Eng.
102 D3 Fritwell Oxon, Eng.
222 D2 Frizinghall W. Yorks., Eng.
232 B5 Frizington Cumbria, Eng.
98 F3 Frocester Glos., Eng.
366 G2 Frochas Powys, Wales
144 D4 Frodesley Shrop., Eng.
144 D4 Frodesley Lane Shrop., Eng.
170 C2 Frodingham N. Lincs., Eng.
184 C2 Frodsham Cheshire West & Chester, Eng.
256 J3 Frogden Borders, Scot.
124 E6 Frog End Cambs., Eng.
124 E6 Frog End Cambs., Eng.
180 D3 Froggatt Derbys., Eng.
148 D2 Froghall Staffs., Eng.
52 B5 Frogham Hants., Eng.
62 H3 Frogham Kent, Eng.
98 D4 Frogland Cross S. Glos., Eng.
40 E4 Frogmore Devon, Eng.
52 H3 Frogmore Hants., Eng.
110 C5 Frogmore Herts., Eng.
136 D2 Frog Pool Worcs., Eng.
36 G2 Frogwell Corn., Eng.
162 D3 Frolesworth Leics., Eng.
94 K3 Frome Som., Eng.
26 H6 Frome r. Eng.
94 K3 Frome Market Som., Eng.
140 E3 Fromes Hill Here., Eng.
46 D3 Frome St Quintin Dorset, Eng.
46 E3 Frome Whitfield Dorset, Eng.
372 D3 Fron Gwynedd, Wales
366 E5 Fron Powys, Wales
366 F3 Fron Powys, Wales
366 G3 Fron Powys, Wales
378 G4 Froncysyllte Wrex., Wales
372 I3 Fron-goch Gwynedd, Wales
378 G4 Fron Isaf Wrex., Wales
120 I2 Frostenden Suff., Eng.
236 D3 Frosterley Durham, Eng.
86 F3 Froxfield Wilts., Eng.
52 F4 Froxfield Green Hants., Eng.
116 E3 Fryerning Essex, Eng.
216 G2 Fryton N. Yorks., Eng.
22 F9 Fuar Bheinn hill Scot.
22 B8 Fuday i. Scot.
86 D5 Fugglestone St Peter Wilts., Eng.
170 C5 Fulbeck Lincs., Eng.
124 F5 Fulbourn Cambs., Eng.
102 B4 Fulbrook Oxon, Eng.
52 E4 Fulflood Hants., Eng.
94 F4 Fulford Som., Eng.
148 C3 Fulford Staffs., Eng.
74 C3 Fulham Gtr Lon., Eng.
58 E3 Fulking W. Sussex, Eng.
40 E1 Fullaford Devon, Eng.
264 F3 Fullarton N. Ayr., Scot.
154 C2 Fullbrook W. Mids, Eng.
184 C3 Fuller's Moor Cheshire West & Chester, Eng.
116 F3 Fuller Street Essex, Eng.
52 D4 Fullerton Hants., Eng.
170 F4 Fulletby Lincs., Eng.
210 C3 Full Sutton E. Riding, Eng.
74 E2 Fullwell Cross Gtr Lon., Eng.
262 E2 Fullwood E. Ayr., Scot.
106 E5 Fulmer Bucks., Eng.
166 E1 Fulmodeston Norf., Eng.
170 D4 Fulnetby Lincs., Eng.
170 F7 Fulney Lincs., Eng.
132 C5 Fulready Warks., Eng.
222 D3 Fulstone W. Yorks., Eng.
170 F3 Fulstow Lincs., Eng.
102 C3 Fulwell Oxon, Eng.
236 G2 Fulwell T. and W., Eng.
228 F4 Fulwood Lancs., Eng.
208 C3 Fulwood S. Yorks., Eng.
166 G3 Fundenhall Norf., Eng.
166 F3 Fundenhall Street Norf., Eng.
58 A3 Funtington W. Sussex, Eng.
52 E5 Funtley Hants., Eng.
331 E2 Funzie Shet., Scot.
40 G2 Furley Devon, Eng.
300 E3 Furnace Arg. and B., Scot.
320 D4 Furnace High., Scot.
356 E3 Furnace Carmar., Wales
362 G1 Furnace Cere., Wales
132 C2 Furnace End Warks., Eng.
58 E2 Furnace Green W. Sussex, Eng.
58 G2 Furner's Green E. Sussex, Eng.
180 B2 Furness Vale Derbys., Eng.
110 F4 Furneux Pelham Herts., Eng.
94 G5 Furnham Som., Eng.
62 E4 Further Quarter Kent, Eng.
128 D5 Furtho Northants., Eng.
74 D3 Furzedown Gtr Lon., Eng.
40 E1 Furzehill Devon, Eng.
46 H3 Furzehill Dorset, Eng.
52 F5 Furzeley Corner Hants., Eng.
82 F2 Furze Platt W. and M., Eng.
52 D6 Furzey Lodge Hants., Eng.
52 C5 Furzley Hants., Eng.
94 F5 Fyfett Som., Eng.
116 D3 Fyfield Essex, Eng.
98 I3 Fyfield Glos., Eng.
52 C3 Fyfield Hants., Eng.
102 C4 Fyfield Oxon, Eng.
86 E3 Fyfield Wilts., Eng.
86 E3 Fyfield Wilts., Eng.
24 L6 Fylde lowland Eng.
216 H1 Fylingthorpe N. Yorks., Eng.
22 G10 Fyne r. Scot.
22 F11 Fyne, Loch inlet Scot.
58 A2 Fyning W. Sussex, Eng.
314 F2 Fyvie Abers., Scot.

G

350 G3 Gabalfa Cardiff, Wales
326 E1 Gabhsunn Bho Dheas W. Isles, Scot.
326 E1 Gabhsunn Bho Thuath W. Isles, Scot.
52 G6 Gable Head Hants., Eng.
320 H4 Gablon High., Scot.
262 E2 Gabroc Hill E. Ayr., Scot.
162 F2 Gaddesby Leics., Eng.
110 C5 Gaddesden Row Herts., Eng.
110 C5 Gadebridge Herts., Eng.
62 C2 Gadshill Kent, Eng.
339 B3 Gaer Newp., Wales
339 D2 Gaer-fawr Mon., Wales
339 D2 Gaerllwyd Mon., Wales
371 D3 Gaerwen I.o.A., Wales
102 C3 Gagingwell Oxon, Eng.
322 I2 Gaich High., Scot.
322 K3 Gaich High., Scot.
322 I4 Gaick Lodge High., Scot.
264 G3 Gailes N. Ayr., Scot.
148 C4 Gailey Staffs., Eng.
236 E4 Gainford Durham, Eng.
170 B3 Gainsborough Lincs., Eng.
116 F2 Gainsford End Essex, Eng.
320 C4 Gairloch High., Scot.
22 E7 Gair Loch b. Scot.
322 G4 Gairlochy High., Scot.
304 J5 Gairney Bank Perth and Kin., Scot.
22 K4 Gairsay i. Scot.
222 D2 Gaisby W. Yorks., Eng.
232 E4 Gaitsgill Cumbria, Eng.
256 G2 Galabank Borders, Scot.
256 H3 Galashiels Borders, Scot.
24 L2 Gala Water r. Scot.
402 I3 Galbally Dungannon, N. Ire.
388 K2 Galboly Moyle, N. Ire.
252 B3 Galdenoch D. and G., Scot.
198 E2 Gale Gtr Man., Eng.
228 F3 Galgate Lancs., Eng.
388 I3 Galgorm Ballymena, N. Ire.
94 I4 Galhampton Som., Eng.
300 D2 Gallanach Arg. and B., Scot.
184 C3 Gallantry Bank Cheshire East, Eng.
292 F3 Gallatown Fife, Scot.
308 G2 Gallery Angus, Scot.
132 C2 Galley Common Warks., Eng.
116 E3 Galleyend Essex, Eng.
116 E3 Galleywood Essex, Eng.
308 E3 Gallowfauld Angus, Scot.
276 D2 Gallowhill Renf., Scot.

Gallows Green to **Great Bircham**

16 G2 **Gallows Green** *Essex, Eng.*
48 D3 **Gallows Green** *Staffs., Eng.*
02 E5 **Gallowstree Common** *Oxon, Eng.*
48 B6 **Gallowstree Elm** *Staffs., Eng.*
22 E3 **Galltair** *High., Scot.*
Gallt Melyd *Denb., Wales see* **Meliden**
58 G2 **Gallypot Street** *E. Sussex, Eng.*
94 F4 **Galmington** *Som., Eng.*
22 C4 **Galmisdale** *High., Scot.*
40 F3 **Galmpton** *Torbay, Eng.*
40 F3 **Galmpton Warborough** *Torbay, Eng.*
16 E2 **Galphay** *N. Yorks., Eng.*
62 E3 **Galston** *E. Ayr., Scot.*
22 A2 **Galtrigill** *High., Scot.*
32 G4 **Gamblesby** *Cumbria, Eng.*
16 F3 **Gamble's Green** *Essex, Eng.*
96 G3 **Gamblestown** *Craigavon, N. Ire.*
32 D3 **Gamelsby** *Cumbria, Eng.*
80 B2 **Gamesley** *Derbys., Eng.*
24 C6 **Gamlingay** *Cambs., Eng.*
24 C6 **Gamlingay Cinques** *Cambs., Eng.*
24 C6 **Gamlingay Great Heath** *Cambs., Eng.*
40 D1 **Gammaton** *Devon, Eng.*
40 D2 **Gammaton Moor** *Devon, Eng.*
14 F2 **Gamrie** *Abers., Scot.*
76 C5 **Gamston** *Notts., Eng.*
76 D3 **Gamston** *Notts., Eng.*
40 C4 **Ganarew** *Here., Eng.*
26 G3 **Gang** *Corn., Eng.*
72 G4 **Ganllwyd** *Gwynedd, Wales*
08 G2 **Gannochy** *Angus, Scot.*
04 J4 **Gannochy** *Perth and Kin., Scot.*
10 G4 **Ganstead** *E. Riding, Eng.*
16 H2 **Ganton** *N. Yorks., Eng.*
74 E2 **Gantshill** *Gtr Lon., Eng.*
10 D5 **Ganwick Corner** *Herts., Eng.*
00 C2 **Gaodhail** *Arg. and B., Scot.*
00 F3 **Garabal** *Arg. and B., Scot.*
20 D3 **Garadheancal** *High., Scot.*
20 G4 **Garbat** *High., Scot.*
00 E3 **Garbhallt** *Arg. and B., Scot.*
56 E4 **Garboldisham** *Norf., Eng.*
96 E5 **Garden** *Stir., Scot.*
78 G2 **Garden City** *Flints., Wales*
82 F3 **Gardeners Green** *W'ham, Eng.*
14 F1 **Gardenstown** *Abers., Scot.*
08 C3 **Garden Village** *S. Yorks., Eng.*
31 C3 **Garderhouse** *Shet., Scot.*
10 E3 **Gardham** *E. Riding, Eng.*
94 K4 **Gare Hill** *Som., Eng.*
24 H1 **Gare Loch** *inlet Scot.*
00 F3 **Garelochhead** *Arg. and B., Scot.*
02 C5 **Garford** *Oxon, Eng.*
22 F2 **Garforth** *W. Yorks., Eng.*
16 C3 **Gargrave** *N. Yorks., Eng.*
02 D3 **Gargrim** *Strabane, N. Ire.*
32 C3 **Gargunnock** *Stir., Scot.*
22 H10 **Gargunnock Hills** *hills Scot.*
56 G4 **Garlic Street** *Norf., Eng.*
52 C3 **Garlies Castle** *D. and G., Scot.*
52 C3 **Garlieston** *D. and G., Scot.*
62 G3 **Garlinge Green** *Kent, Eng.*
14 F3 **Garlogie** *Abers., Scot.*
48 B3 **Garmelow** *Staffs., Eng.*
14 G2 **Garmond** *Abers., Scot.*
36 G3 **Garmondsway** *Durham, Eng.*
00 C2 **Garmony** *Arg. and B., Scot.*
14 D2 **Garmouth** *Moray, Scot.*
14 E4 **Garmston** *Shrop., Eng.*
56 G3 **Garnant** *Carmar., Wales*
72 E3 **Garndolbenmaen** *Gwynedd, Wales*
72 H5 **Garneddwen** *Gwynedd, Wales*
32 F6 **Garnett Bridge** *Cumbria, Eng.*
72 C3 **Garnfadryn** *Gwynedd, Wales*
50 C2 **Garnswllt** *Swansea, Wales*
26 F2 **Garrabost** *W. Isles, Scot.*
00 E3 **Garrachra** *Arg. and B., Scot.*
14 E2 **Garralburn** *Moray, Scot.*
36 D3 **Garras** *Corn., Eng.*
72 F3 **Garreg** *Gwynedd, Wales*
66 G2 **Garreg Bank** *Powys, Wales*
54 D3 **Garrett's Green** *W. Mids, Eng.*
04 G5 **Garrick** *Perth and Kin., Scot.*
32 H4 **Garrigill** *Cumbria, Eng.*
02 B4 **Garrison** *Fermanagh, N. Ire.*
16 D2 **Garriston** *N. Yorks., Eng.*
52 D2 **Garroch** *D. and G., Scot.*
00 D2 **Garrochty** *Arg. and B., Scot.*
23 K2 **Garron Point** *pt N. Ire.*
22 F2 **Garros** *High., Scot.*
04 G3 **Garrow** *Perth and Kin., Scot.*
22 G8 **Garry** *r. Scot.*
22 G8 **Garry, Loch** *l. Scot.*
88 H2 **Garryduff** *Ballymoney, N. Ire.*
52 D2 **Garryhorn** *D. and G., Scot.*
26 D2 **Garrynahine** *W. Isles, Scot.*
32 H7 **Garsdale** *Cumbria, Eng.*
32 I7 **Garsdale Head** *Cumbria, Eng.*
86 C2 **Garsdon** *Wilts., Eng.*
48 C3 **Garshall Green** *Staffs., Eng.*
02 E4 **Garsington** *Oxon, Eng.*
28 G3 **Garstang** *Lancs., Eng.*
90 D3 **Garston** *Merseyside, Eng.*
90 E3 **Garswood** *Merseyside, Eng.*
96 D5 **Gartachoil** *Stir., Scot.*
04 D4 **Gartavaich** *Arg. and B., Scot.*
00 B4 **Gartbreck** *Arg. and B., Scot.*
80 B3 **Gartcosh** *N. Lanark., Scot.*
05 C2 **Garth** Isle of Man
31 C3 **Garth** *Shet., Scot.*
50 E3 **Garth** *Bridg., Wales*
62 G2 **Garth** *Cere., Wales*
66 D6 **Garth** *Powys, Wales*
78 G4 **Garth** *Wrex., Wales*
76 F2 **Garthamlock** *Glas., Scot.*
66 E7 **Garthbrengy** *Powys, Wales*
14 G3 **Garthdee** *Aberdeen, Scot.*
62 F3 **Gartheli** *Cere., Wales*
66 G3 **Garthmyl** *Powys, Wales*
62 G2 **Garthorpe** *Leics., Eng.*
70 B2 **Garthorpe** *N. Lincs., Eng.*
32 F6 **Garth Row** *Cumbria, Eng.*
56 G1 **Garthynty** *Carmar., Wales*
96 F4 **Gartincaber** *Stir., Scot.*
14 E2 **Gartly** *Abers., Scot.*
96 D5 **Gartmore** *Stir., Scot.*
00 D4 **Gartnagrenach** *Arg. and B., Scot.*
00 B4 **Gartnatra** *Arg. and B., Scot.*
96 D5 **Gartness** *Stir., Scot.*
76 C1 **Gartocharn** *W. Dun., Scot.*
10 H4 **Garton** *E. Riding, Eng.*
24 C3 **Garton End** *Peterb., Eng.*
10 E2 **Garton-on-the-Wolds** *E. Riding, Eng.*
88 F3 **Garvagh** *Coleraine, N. Ire.*
02 H4 **Garvaghy** *Omagh, N. Ire.*
88 H3 **Garvald** *E. Lothian, Scot.*
22 H3 **Garvamore** *High., Scot.*
22 F4 **Garvan** *High., Scot.*
00 B3 **Garvard** *Arg. and B., Scot.*
02 E4 **Garvary** *Fermanagh, N. Ire.*
22 G2 **Garve** *High., Scot.*
00 C6 **Garveld** *Arg. and B., Scot.*
02 E2 **Garvetagh** *Strabane, N. Ire.*
300 E3 **Garvie** *Arg. and B., Scot.*
276 B2 **Garvock** *Inverclyde, Scot.*
304 I5 **Garvock** *Perth and Kin., Scot.*
252 G2 **Garwald** *D. and G., Scot.*
252 G2 **Garwaldwaterfoot** *D. and G., Scot.*
140 C4 **Garway** *Here., Eng.*
140 C4 **Garway Hill** *Here., Eng.*
304 I4 **Gask** *Perth and Kin., Scot.*
322 E4 **Gaskan** *High., Scot.*
22 B7 **Gasker** *i. Scot.*
86 A5 **Gasper** *Wilts., Eng.*
262 D5 **Gass** *S. Ayr., Scot.*
86 B3 **Gastard** *Wilts., Eng.*
166 E4 **Gasthorpe** *Norf., Eng.*
116 D3 **Gaston Green** *Essex, Eng.*
52 E6 **Gatcombe** *I.o.W., Eng.*
190 D3 **Gateacre** *Merseyside, Eng.*
170 B3 **Gate Burton** *Lincs., Eng.*
176 C3 **Gateford** *Notts., Eng.*
216 F3 **Gateforth** *N. Yorks., Eng.*
262 D3 **Gatehead** *E. Ayr., Scot.*
216 G3 **Gate Helmsley** *N. Yorks., Eng.*
300 C4 **Gate House** *Arg. and B., Scot.*
304 G3 **Gatehouse** *Perth and Kin., Scot.*
252 D3 **Gatehouse of Fleet** *D. and G., Scot.*
252 E2 **Gatelawbridge** *D. and G., Scot.*
166 E2 **Gateley** *Norf., Eng.*
216 E2 **Gatenby** *N. Yorks., Eng.*
232 C5 **Gatesgarth** *Cumbria, Eng.*
256 J4 **Gateshaw** *Borders, Scot.*
236 F2 **Gateshead** *T. and W., Eng.*
184 C3 **Gatesheath** *Cheshire West & Chester, Eng.*
308 E3 **Gateside** *Angus, Scot.*
292 E2 **Gateside** *Fife, Scot.*
264 G2 **Gateside** *N. Ayr., Scot.*
252 E2 **Gateslack** *D. and G., Scot.*
198 A2 **Gathurst** *Gtr Man., Eng.*
198 D3 **Gatley** *Gtr Man., Eng.*
256 H3 **Gattonside** *Borders, Scot.*
366 E5 **Gaufron** *Powys, Wales*
162 F3 **Gaulby** *Leics., Eng.*
292 F1 **Gauldry** *Fife, Scot.*
228 H4 **Gaulkthorn** *Lancs., Eng.*
184 D3 **Gauntons Bank** *Cheshire East, Eng.*
46 H2 **Gaunt's Common** *Dorset, Eng.*
98 D4 **Gaunt's Earthcott** *S. Glos., Eng.*
116 D2 **Gaunt's End** *Essex, Eng.*
170 E4 **Gautby** *Lincs., Eng.*
256 J2 **Gavinton** *Borders, Scot.*
208 C2 **Gawber** *S. Yorks., Eng.*
106 B3 **Gawcott** *Bucks., Eng.*
184 G2 **Gawsworth** *Cheshire East, Eng.*
222 D3 **Gawthorpe** *W. Yorks., Eng.*
232 H7 **Gawthrop** *Cumbria, Eng.*
232 D7 **Gawthwaite** *Cumbria, Eng.*
116 F3 **Gay Bowers** *Essex, Eng.*
132 D4 **Gaydon** *Warks., Eng.*
106 D2 **Gayhurst** *M.K., Eng.*
216 C2 **Gayle** *N. Yorks., Eng.*
58 D3 **Gay Street** *W. Sussex, Eng.*
190 C4 **Gayton** *Merseyside, Eng.*
166 C2 **Gayton** *Norf., Eng.*
128 D4 **Gayton** *Northants., Eng.*
148 C3 **Gayton** *Staffs., Eng.*
170 G3 **Gayton le Marsh** *Lincs., Eng.*
170 F3 **Gayton le Wold** *Lincs., Eng.*
166 C2 **Gayton Thorpe** *Norf., Eng.*
166 B2 **Gaywood** *Norf., Eng.*
120 C3 **Gazeley** *Suff., Eng.*
22 H8 **Geal Charn** *hill Scot.*
22 J8 **Geal Charn** *hill Scot.*
22 E11 **Gealldruig Mhòr** *i. Scot.*
320 I4 **Geanies House** *High., Scot.*
300 A4 **Gearach** *Arg. and B., Scot.*
320 H3 **Gearnsary** *High., Scot.*
322 E4 **Gearradh** *High., Scot.*
326 E2 **Gearraidh Bhaird** *W. Isles, Scot.*
Gearraidh na h-Aibhne *W. Isles, Scot. see* **Garrynahine**
326 B5 **Gearraidh na Monadh** *W. Isles, Scot.*
326 D2 **Gearrannan** *W. Isles, Scot.*
Geàrrloch *High., Scot. see* **Gairloch**
322 B2 **Geary** *High., Scot.*
120 E3 **Gedding** *Suff., Eng.*
128 E3 **Geddington** *Northants., Eng.*
120 I4 **Gedgrave Hall** *Suff., Eng.*
322 C2 **Gedintailor** *High., Scot.*
176 C5 **Gedling** *Notts., Eng.*
170 G7 **Gedney** *Lincs., Eng.*
170 G7 **Gedney Broadgate** *Lincs., Eng.*
170 H6 **Gedney Drove End** *Lincs., Eng.*
170 G7 **Gedney Dyke** *Lincs., Eng.*
170 F7 **Gedney Hill** *Lincs., Eng.*
198 E3 **Gee Cross** *Gtr Man., Eng.*
300 G4 **Geilston** *Arg. and B., Scot.*
326 B4 **Geirinis** *W. Isles, Scot.*
326 D2 **Geisiadar** *W. Isles, Scot.*
166 I4 **Geldeston** *Norf., Eng.*
378 C2 **Gell** *Conwy, Wales*
372 E3 **Gell** *Gwynedd, Wales*
350 F3 **Gelli** *R.C.T., Wales*
350 F2 **Gellideg** *M. Tyd., Wales*
378 F3 **Gellifor** *Denb., Wales*
350 G3 **Gelligaer** *Caerp., Wales*
350 G3 **Gelligroes** *Caerp., Wales*
378 F3 **Gelli Gynan** *Denb., Wales*
372 G3 **Gellilydan** *Gwynedd, Wales*
378 D4 **Gellioedd** *Conwy, Wales*
358 F2 **Gelly** *Pembs., Wales*
304 J3 **Gellyburn** *Perth and Kin., Scot.*
356 C2 **Gellywen** *Carmar., Wales*
170 C6 **Gelston** *Lincs., Eng.*
252 E3 **Gelston** *D. and G., Scot.*
210 G3 **Gembling** *E. Riding, Eng.*
350 C3 **Gendros** *Swansea, Wales*
252 C3 **Genoch** *D. and G., Scot.*
252 B3 **Genoch Square** *D. and G., Scot.*
148 D4 **Gentleshaw** *Staffs., Eng.*
326 D3 **Geocrab** *W. Isles, Scot.*
22 D10 **Geodha, Rubh' a'** *pt Scot.*
106 E5 **George Green** *Bucks., Eng.*
40 D1 **Georgeham** *Devon, Eng.*
276 D2 **Georgetown** *Renf., Scot.*
350 G2 **Georgetown** *B. Gwent, Wales*
372 F1 **Gerlan** *Gwynedd, Wales*
40 D2 **Germansweek** *Devon, Eng.*
36 C3 **Germoe** *Corn., Eng.*
36 E3 **Gerrans** *Corn., Eng.*
106 E5 **Gerrards Cross** *Bucks., Eng.*
116 F1 **Gestingthorpe** *Essex, Eng.*
366 F2 **Geuffordd** *Powys, Wales*
366 D4 **Geufron** *Powys, Wales*
23 I2 **Giant's Causeway** *tourist site N. Ire.*
94 J3 **Gibbet Hill** *Som., Eng.*
252 E2 **Gibbshill** *D. and G., Scot.*
154 C2 **Gib Heath** *W. Mids, Eng.*
170 H5 **Gibraltar** *Lincs., Eng.*
120 G4 **Gibraltar** *Suff., Eng.*
24 R7 **Gibraltar Point** *pt Eng.*
86 B3 **Giddeahall** *Wilts., Eng.*
46 F3 **Giddy Green** *Dorset, Eng.*
74 F2 **Gidea Park** *Gtr Lon., Eng.*
40 E2 **Gidleigh** *Devon, Eng.*
276 E3 **Giffnock** *E. Renf., Scot.*
288 G3 **Gifford** *E. Lothian, Scot.*
264 F2 **Giffordland** *N. Ayr., Scot.*
292 F2 **Giffordtown** *Fife, Scot.*
198 D2 **Gigg** *Gtr Man., Eng.*
216 C2 **Giggleswick** *N. Yorks., Eng.*
22 E11 **Gigha** *i. Scot.*
22 E11 **Gigha, Sound of** *sea chan. Scot.*
154 B3 **Gigmill** *W. Mids, Eng.*
198 D3 **Gilbent** *Gtr Man., Eng.*
210 D4 **Gilberdyke** *E. Riding, Eng.*
136 D3 **Gilbert's End** *Worcs., Eng.*
154 D3 **Gilbertstone** *W. Mids, Eng.*
52 F4 **Gilbert Street** *Hants., Eng.*
288 F3 **Gilchriston** *E. Lothian, Scot.*
232 B4 **Gilcrux** *Cumbria, Eng.*
222 E2 **Gildersome** *W. Yorks., Eng.*
208 F3 **Gildingwells** *S. Yorks., Eng.*
236 F3 **Gilesgate Moor** *Durham, Eng.*
350 F4 **Gileston** *V. of Glam., Wales*
350 G2 **Gilfach** *Caerp., Wales*
350 F3 **Gilfach Goch** *R.C.T., Wales*
362 E3 **Gilfachrheda** *Cere., Wales*
396 F3 **Gilford** *Banbridge, N. Ire.*
232 B5 **Gilgarran** *Cumbria, Eng.*
232 E5 **Gill** *Cumbria, Eng.*
216 G2 **Gillamoor** *N. Yorks., Eng.*
190 E3 **Gillar's Green** *Merseyside, Eng.*
322 B2 **Gillen** *High., Scot.*
252 G2 **Gillenbie** *D. and G., Scot.*
252 F2 **Gillfoot** *D. and G., Scot.*
216 F2 **Gilling East** *N. Yorks., Eng.*
46 F1 **Gillingham** *Dorset, Eng.*
62 D2 **Gillingham** *Medway, Eng.*
166 I4 **Gillingham** *Norf., Eng.*
216 D1 **Gilling West** *N. Yorks., Eng.*
320 J2 **Gillock** *High., Scot.*
148 B2 **Gillow Heath** *Staffs., Eng.*
320 K2 **Gills** *High., Scot.*
62 D4 **Gill's Green** *Kent, Eng.*
402 F3 **Gillygooly** *Omagh, N. Ire.*
256 F4 **Gilmanscleuch** *Borders, Scot.*
288 E3 **Gilmerton** *Edin., Scot.*
304 H4 **Gilmerton** *Perth and Kin., Scot.*
262 F3 **Gilmilnscroft** *E. Ayr., Scot.*
236 C4 **Gilmonby** *Durham, Eng.*
162 E4 **Gilmorton** *Leics., Eng.*
244 B6 **Gilsland** *Northumb., Eng.*
232 G2 **Gilsland Spa** *Cumbria, Eng.*
132 B2 **Gilson** *Warks., Eng.*
222 D1 **Gilstead** *W. Yorks., Eng.*
256 G2 **Gilston** *Borders, Scot.*
110 F5 **Gilston Park** *Herts., Eng.*
176 B4 **Giltbrook** *Notts., Eng.*
339 B2 **Gilwern** *Mon., Wales*
166 H1 **Gimingham** *Norf., Eng.*
184 G2 **Ginclough** *Cheshire East, Eng.*
58 H3 **Ginger's Green** *E. Sussex, Eng.*
198 C2 **Gin Pit** *Gtr Man., Eng.*
326 D2 **Giosla** *W. Isles, Scot.*
120 F3 **Gipping** *Suff., Eng.*
170 F5 **Gipsey Bridge** *Lincs., Eng.*
222 D2 **Girlington** *W. Yorks., Eng.*
331 D3 **Girlsta** *Shet., Scot.*
216 E1 **Girsby** *N. Yorks., Eng.*
110 D3 **Girtford** *Central Bedfordshire, Eng.*
252 D3 **Girthon** *D. and G., Scot.*
124 E5 **Girton** *Cambs., Eng.*
176 E3 **Girton** *Notts., Eng.*
262 B5 **Girvan** *S. Ayr., Scot.*
228 I3 **Gisburn** *Lancs., Eng.*
228 I3 **Gisburn Cotes** *Lancs., Eng.*
120 J2 **Gisleham** *Suff., Eng.*
120 F3 **Gislingham** *Suff., Eng.*
166 F4 **Gissing** *Norf., Eng.*
40 G2 **Gittisham** *Devon, Eng.*
78 E2 **Givons Grove** *Surr., Eng.*
320 E4 **Glackour** *High., Scot.*
366 G5 **Gladestry** *Powys, Wales*
288 F3 **Gladsmuir** *E. Lothian, Scot.*
300 E4 **Glaic** *Arg. and B., Scot.*
350 C2 **Glais** *Swansea, Wales*
216 G1 **Glaisdale** *N. Yorks., Eng.*
264 C3 **Glaister** *N. Ayr., Scot.*
322 C2 **Glame** *High., Scot.*
308 E3 **Glamis** *Angus, Scot.*
378 B3 **Glanaber Terrace** *Conwy, Wales*
356 G3 **Glanaman** *Carmar., Wales*
356 H1 **Glanbran** *Carmar., Wales*
378 C3 **Glan Conwy** *Conwy, Wales*
362 F4 **Glan-Denys** *Cere., Wales*
314 E2 **Glanderston** *Abers., Scot.*
166 F1 **Glandford** *Norf., Eng.*
356 F1 **Glan-Duar** *Carmar., Wales*
350 H2 **Glandwr** *B. Gwent, Wales*
358 G2 **Glandwr** *Pembs., Wales*
372 E3 **Glan-Dwyfach** *Gwynedd, Wales*
366 G7 **Glangrwyney** *Powys, Wales*
366 E7 **Glan Honddu** *Powys, Wales*
350 E3 **Glanllynfi** *Bridg., Wales*
366 F3 **Glanmule** *Powys, Wales*
350 D2 **Glan-rhyd** *N.P.T., Wales*
358 F1 **Glanrhyd** *Pembs., Wales*
244 F3 **Glanton** *Northumb., Eng.*
244 F3 **Glanton Pyke** *Northumb., Eng.*
46 E2 **Glanvilles Wootton** *Dorset, Eng.*
362 F2 **Glanwern** *Cere., Wales*
378 C2 **Glanwydden** *Conwy, Wales*
378 F2 **Glan-y-don** *Flints., Wales*
Glanyferi *Carmar., Wales see* **Ferryside**
350 G3 **Glan-y-llyn** *R.C.T., Wales*
366 D4 **Glan-y-nant** *Powys, Wales*
372 I3 **Glan-yr-afon** *Gwynedd, Wales*
372 J3 **Glan-yr-afon** *Gwynedd, Wales*
371 E3 **Glan-yr-afon** *I.o.A., Wales*
372 F3 **Glan-y-Wern** *Gwynedd, Wales*
128 F2 **Glapthorn** *Northants., Eng.*
180 F3 **Glapwell** *Derbys., Eng.*
388 H3 **Glarryford** *Ballymena, N. Ire.*
296 D4 **Glasahoile** *Stir., Scot.*
22 G6 **Glas Bheinn** *hill Scot.*
366 F6 **Glasbury** *Powys, Wales*
22 G7 **Glascarnoch, Loch** *l. Scot.*
Glaschu *Glas., Scot. see* **Glasgow**
339 C2 **Glascoed** *Mon., Wales*
378 G3 **Glascoed** *Wrex., Wales*
314 E3 **Glascorrie** *Abers., Scot.*
148 E5 **Glascote** *Staffs., Eng.*
148 F5 **Glascote Heath** *Staffs., Eng.*
366 F5 **Glascwm** *Powys, Wales*
300 E2 **Glasdrum** *Arg. and B., Scot.*
396 E5 **Glasdrumman** *Newry & Mourne, N. Ire.*
378 D3 **Glasfryn** *Conwy, Wales*
276 E2 **Glasgow** *Glas., Scot.*
276 E2 **Glasgow** *admin. div. Scot.*
276 D2 **Glasgow** *airport Scot.*
262 D3 **Glasgow Prestwick** *airport Scot.*
402 G2 **Glashygolgan** *Strabane, N. Ire.*
372 F1 **Glasinfryn** *Gwynedd, Wales*
22 J9 **Glas Maol** *mt. Scot.*
322 D4 **Glasnacardoch** *High., Scot.*
322 C3 **Glasnakille** *High., Scot.*
356 C2 **Glaspant** *Carmar., Wales*
366 B3 **Glaspwll** *Powys, Wales*
22 G7 **Glass, Loch** *l. Scot.*
396 I5 **Glassdrummond** *Newry & Mourne, N. Ire.*
62 C4 **Glassenbury** *Kent, Eng.*
252 C3 **Glasserton** *D. and G., Scot.*
268 B2 **Glassford** *S. Lanark., Scot.*
98 E2 **Glasshouse** *Glos., Eng.*
216 D2 **Glasshouses** *N. Yorks., Eng.*
296 G4 **Glassingall** *Stir., Scot.*
292 E2 **Glasslie** *Fife, Scot.*
232 D3 **Glasson** *Cumbria, Eng.*
228 E3 **Glasson** *Lancs., Eng.*
232 G4 **Glassonby** *Cumbria, Eng.*
228 E3 **Glasson Dock** *Lancs., Eng.*
308 F3 **Glasterlaw** *Angus, Scot.*
162 G3 **Glaston** *Rutland, Eng.*
94 H4 **Glastonbury** *Som., Eng.*
22 I9 **Glas Tulaichean** *mt. Scot.*
124 C4 **Glatton** *Cambs., Eng.*
190 G3 **Glazebrook** *Warr., Eng.*
190 G3 **Glazebury** *Warr., Eng.*
144 F5 **Glazeley** *Shrop., Eng.*
208 D3 **Gleadless** *S. Yorks., Eng.*
208 D3 **Gleadless Townend** *S. Yorks., Eng.*
184 F2 **Gleadsmoss** *Cheshire East, Eng.*
326 F2 **Gleann Tholastaidh** *W. Isles, Scot.*
232 D8 **Gleaston** *Cumbria, Eng.*
388 D2 **Glebe** *Limavady, N. Ire.*
402 F2 **Glebe** *Strabane, N. Ire.*
300 E4 **Glecknabae** *Arg. and B., Scot.*
222 E2 **Gledhow** *W. Yorks., Eng.*
144 B2 **Gledrid** *Shrop., Eng.*
120 D4 **Glemsford** *Suff., Eng.*
402 B4 **Glen** *Fermanagh, N. Ire.*
402 F4 **Glen** *Fermanagh, N. Ire.*
252 D3 **Glen** *D. and G., Scot.*
252 E2 **Glen** *D. and G., Scot.*
24 F2 **Glenacardoch Point** *pt Scot.*
252 F2 **Glenae** *D. and G., Scot.*
22 F8 **Glen Affric** *val. Scot.*
300 F3 **Glenald** *Arg. and B., Scot.*
300 D2 **Glenamachrie** *Arg. and B., Scot.*
396 F4 **Glenanne** *Armagh, N. Ire.*
262 B6 **Glenapp Castle** *S. Ayr., Scot.*
388 J2 **Glenariff** *Moyle, N. Ire.*
388 K3 **Glenarm** *Larne, N. Ire.*
308 D2 **Glenarm** *Angus, Scot.*
22 H10 **Glen Artney** *val. Scot.*
405 D2 **Glen Auldyn** Isle of Man
22 I8 **Glen Avon** *val. Scot.*
388 I5 **Glenavy** *Lisburn, N. Ire.*
300 C5 **Glenbarr** *Arg. and B., Scot.*
300 C4 **Glenbatrick** *Arg. and B., Scot.*
320 F4 **Glenbeg** *High., Scot.*
322 D4 **Glenbeg** *High., Scot.*
296 E3 **Glenbeich** *Stir., Scot.*
314 F4 **Glenbervie** *Abers., Scot.*
280 C2 **Glenbervie** *Falk., Scot.*
280 B3 **Glenboig** *N. Lanark., Scot.*
322 D4 **Glenborrodale** *High., Scot.*
300 E3 **Glenbranter** *Arg. and B., Scot.*
256 D4 **Glenbreck** *Borders, Scot.*
322 C3 **Glenbrittle** *High., Scot.*
276 D3 **Glenburn** *Renf., Scot.*
300 C2 **Glenbyre** *Arg. and B., Scot.*
22 F8 **Glen Cannich** *val. Scot.*
252 F2 **Glencaple** *D. and G., Scot.*
304 K4 **Glencarse** *Perth and Kin., Scot.*
22 G6 **Glen Cassley** *val. Scot.*
22 J9 **Glen Clova** *val. Scot.*
264 D3 **Glencloy** *N. Ayr., Scot.*
322 F4 **Glencoe** *High., Scot.*
22 F9 **Glen Coe** *val. Scot.*
314 C3 **Glenconglass** *Moray, Scot.*
292 E3 **Glencraig** *Fife, Scot.*
322 D4 **Glencripesdale** *High., Scot.*
252 E2 **Glencrosh** *D. and G., Scot.*
300 D2 **Glencruitten** *Arg. and B., Scot.*
314 E3 **Glencuie** *Abers., Scot.*
22 F10 **Glendaruel** *val. Scot.*
256 H3 **Glendearg** *Borders, Scot.*
252 G2 **Glendearg** *D. and G., Scot.*
22 I8 **Glen Dee** *val. Scot.*
322 F4 **Glendessary** *High., Scot.*
322 H3 **Glendoebeg** *High., Scot.*
304 K4 **Glendoick** *Perth and Kin., Scot.*
262 B5 **Glendoune** *S. Ayr., Scot.*
262 B5 **Glendrissaig** *S. Ayr., Scot.*
292 E1 **Glenduckie** *Fife, Scot.*
262 C6 **Glenduisk** *S. Ayr., Scot.*
23 J2 **Glendun** *r. N. Ire.*
314 F4 **Glendye Lodge** *Abers., Scot.*
304 H5 **Gleneagles** *Perth and Kin., Scot.*
304 H5 **Gleneagles Hotel** *Perth and Kin., Scot.*
304 J5 **Glenearn** *Perth and Kin., Scot.*
402 H3 **Gleneeny** *Omagh, N. Ire.*
300 B4 **Glenegedale** *Arg. and B., Scot.*
304 J5 **Glenfarg** *Perth and Kin., Scot.*
22 I8 **Glen Feshie** *val. Scot.*
162 D3 **Glenfield** *Leicester, Eng.*
304 K5 **Glenfoot** *Perth and Kin., Scot.*
252 D3 **Glengap** *D. and G., Scot.*
264 F2 **Glengarnock** *N. Ayr., Scot.*
300 C3 **Glengarrisdale** *Arg. and B., Scot.*
22 F8 **Glen Garry** *val. Scot.*
22 H9 **Glen Garry** *val. Scot.*
262 C5 **Glengennet** *S. Ayr., Scot.*
388 E4 **Glengomna** *Magherafelt, N. Ire.*
388 K4 **Glengormley** *Newtownabbey, N. Ire.*
322 C2 **Glengrasco** *High., Scot.*
296 C4 **Glengyle** *Stir., Scot.*
388 J4 **Glenhead** *Ballymena, N. Ire.*
388 D2 **Glenhead** *Limavady, N. Ire.*
252 E2 **Glenhead** *D. and G., Scot.*
308 C2 **Glenhead Farm** *Angus, Scot.*
402 H2 **Glenhull** *Omagh, N. Ire.*
256 F4 **Glenkerry** *Borders, Scot.*
264 D3 **Glenkiln** *N. Ayr., Scot.*
300 F4 **Glenkin** *Arg. and B., Scot.*
314 E3 **Glenkindie** *Abers., Scot.*
396 H3 **Glenlagan** *Banbridge, N. Ire.*
252 E2 **Glenlair** *D. and G., Scot.*
314 C2 **Glenlatterach** *Moray, Scot.*
300 E3 **Glenlean** *Arg. and B., Scot.*
388 G2 **Glenleary** *Coleraine, N. Ire.*
308 E1 **Glenlee** *Angus, Scot.*
252 D2 **Glenlee** *D. and G., Scot.*
304 G5 **Glenlichorn** *Perth and Kin., Scot.*
314 C2 **Glenlivet** *Moray, Scot.*
252 E3 **Glenlochar** *D. and G., Scot.*
252 B3 **Glenluce** *D. and G., Scot.*
22 H9 **Glen Lyon** *val. Scot.*
300 F3 **Glenmallan** *Arg. and B., Scot.*
252 E2 **Glenmanna** *D. and G., Scot.*
280 C3 **Glenmavis** *N. Lanark., Scot.*
405 B2 **Glenmaye** Isle of Man
322 G2 **Glenmeanie** *High., Scot.*
300 E4 **Glenmore** *Arg. and B., Scot.*
322 C2 **Glenmore** *High., Scot.*
22 G8 **Glen More** *val. Scot.*
322 J3 **Glenmore Lodge** *High., Scot.*
402 F1 **Glenmornan** *Strabane, N. Ire.*
308 E2 **Glenmoy** *Angus, Scot.*
320 F3 **Glenmuick** *High., Scot.*
22 J9 **Glen Muick** *val. Scot.*
22 F9 **Glen Nevis** *val. Scot.*
300 E2 **Glennoe** *Arg. and B., Scot.*
396 G4 **Glenny's Bridge** *Newry & Mourne, N. Ire.*
268 E4 **Glenochar** *S. Lanark., Scot.*
388 L4 **Glenoe** *Larne, N. Ire.*
308 E2 **Glenogil** *Angus, Scot.*
22 G6 **Glen Oykel** *val. Scot.*
162 E3 **Glen Parva** *Leics., Eng.*
308 D2 **Glenprosen Village** *Angus, Scot.*
308 E2 **Glenquiech** *Angus, Scot.*
300 D5 **Glenramskill** *Arg. and B., Scot.*
252 C3 **Glenrazie** *D. and G., Scot.*
232 E5 **Glenridding** *Cumbria, Eng.*
300 D4 **Glenrisdell** *Arg. and B., Scot.*
320 G4 **Glenrossal** *High., Scot.*
292 F2 **Glenrothes** *Fife, Scot.*
314 F4 **Glensaugh** *Abers., Scot.*
24 D4 **Glenshane Pass** *pass N. Ire.*
22 J9 **Glen Shee** *val. Scot.*
388 I2 **Glenshesk Bridge** *Moyle, N. Ire.*
22 F8 **Glen Shiel** *val. Scot.*
300 E3 **Glensluain** *Arg. and B., Scot.*
22 G9 **Glen Spean** *val. Scot.*
388 I1 **Glenstaghey** *Moyle, N. Ire.*
268 C3 **Glentaggart** *S. Lanark., Scot.*
170 D3 **Glentham** *Lincs., Eng.*
256 F3 **Glentress** *Borders, Scot.*
22 H8 **Glen Tromie** *val. Scot.*
252 C2 **Glentrool** *D. and G., Scot.*
252 C2 **Glen Trool Lodge** *D. and G., Scot.*
405 D1 **Glentruan** Isle of Man
170 C3 **Glentworth** *Lincs., Eng.*
322 C2 **Glenuachdarach** *High., Scot.*
322 D4 **Glenuig** *High., Scot.*
322 I2 **Glenurquhart** *High., Scot.*
280 D3 **Glen Village** *Falk., Scot.*
405 C2 **Glen Vine** Isle of Man
252 B2 **Glenwhilly** *D. and G., Scot.*
268 C3 **Glespin** *S. Lanark., Scot.*
331 D3 **Gletness** *Shet., Scot.*
140 D4 **Glewstone** *Here., Eng.*
124 C3 **Glinton** *Peterb., Eng.*
358 G2 **Glogue** *Pembs., Wales*
162 F3 **Glooston** *Leics., Eng.*
244 G2 **Glororum** *Northumb., Eng.*
180 B2 **Glossop** *Derbys., Eng.*
244 H3 **Gloster Hill** *Northumb., Eng.*
98 F2 **Gloucester** *Glos., Eng.*
26 H4 **Gloucester, Vale of** *val. Eng.*
98 F2 **Gloucestershire** *airport Eng.*
98 F3 **Gloucestershire** *county Eng.*
331 D1 **Gloup** *Shet., Scot.*
36 D3 **Gloweth** *Corn., Eng.*
216 D3 **Glusburn** *N. Yorks., Eng.*
26 D1 **Glyder Fawr** *hill Wales*
102 C3 **Glympton** *Oxon, Eng.*
378 B3 **Glyn** *Conwy, Wales*
362 D4 **Glynarthen** *Cere., Wales*
378 F4 **Glyn Ceiriog** *Wrex., Wales*
350 G3 **Glyncoch** *R.C.T., Wales*
350 E2 **Glyncorrwg** *N.P.T., Wales*
372 F3 **Glyn-Cywarch** *Gwynedd, Wales*
58 G3 **Glynde** *E. Sussex, Eng.*
58 G3 **Glyndebourne** *E. Sussex, Eng.*
378 F4 **Glyndyfrdwy** *Denb., Wales*
388 L4 **Glynn** *Larne, N. Ire.*
350 E2 **Glynneath** *N.P.T., Wales*
Glyn-Nedd *N.P.T., Wales see* **Glynneath**
350 E3 **Glynogwr** *Bridg., Wales*
350 G3 **Glyntaff** *R.C.T., Wales*
356 D1 **Glynteg** *Carmar., Wales*
148 B4 **Gnosall** *Staffs., Eng.*
148 B4 **Gnosall Heath** *Staffs., Eng.*
162 F3 **Goadby** *Leics., Eng.*
162 F2 **Goadby Marwood** *Leics., Eng.*
86 D3 **Goatacre** *Wilts., Eng.*
22 F11 **Goat Fell** *hill Scot.*
300 E3 **Goatfield** *Arg. and B., Scot.*
46 E2 **Goathill** *Dorset, Eng.*
216 G1 **Goathland** *N. Yorks., Eng.*
94 F4 **Goathurst** *Som., Eng.*
320 I3 **Gobernuisgeach** *High., Scot.*
326 C3 **Gobhaig** *W. Isles, Scot.*
144 B2 **Gobowen** *Shrop., Eng.*
78 C2 **Godalming** *Surr., Eng.*
120 H3 **Goddard's Corner** *Suff., Eng.*
58 E3 **Goddards Green** *W. Sussex, Eng.*
62 B3 **Godden Green** *Kent, Eng.*
74 E3 **Goddington** *Gtr Lon., Eng.*
102 E3 **Godington** *Oxon, Eng.*
198 E3 **Godley** *Gtr Man., Eng.*
148 C3 **Godleybrook** *Staffs., Eng.*
124 C5 **Godmanchester** *Cambs., Eng.*
46 E3 **Godmanstone** *Dorset, Eng.*
62 F3 **Godmersham** *Kent, Eng.*
94 H3 **Godney** *Som., Eng.*
36 C3 **Godolphin Cross** *Corn., Eng.*
366 F2 **Godor** *Powys, Wales*
350 D2 **Godre'r-graig** *N.P.T., Wales*
52 B5 **Godshill** *Hants., Eng.*
52 E7 **Godshill** *I.o.W., Eng.*
148 D3 **Godstone** *Staffs., Eng.*
78 F2 **Godstone** *Surr., Eng.*
166 D2 **Godwick** *Norf., Eng.*
339 C2 **Goetre** *Mon., Wales*
110 E5 **Goff's Oak** *Herts., Eng.*
288 D3 **Gogar** *Edin., Scot.*
378 B2 **Gogarth** *Conwy, Wales*
362 G2 **Goginan** *Cere., Wales*
22 G10 **Goil, Loch** *inlet Scot.*
300 E3 **Goirtein** *Arg. and B., Scot.*
372 E3 **Golan** *Gwynedd, Wales*
36 F2 **Golant** *Corn., Eng.*
36 F2 **Golberdon** *Corn., Eng.*
198 B3 **Golborne** *Gtr Man., Eng.*
222 C3 **Golcar** *W. Yorks., Eng.*
339 C3 **Goldcliff** *Newp., Wales*
58 H3 **Golden Cross** *E. Sussex, Eng.*
62 C3 **Golden Green** *Kent, Eng.*
356 F2 **Golden Grove** *Carmar., Wales*
148 B2 **Goldenhill** *Stoke, Eng.*
358 E3 **Golden Hill** *Pembs., Wales*
52 G3 **Golden Pot** *Hants., Eng.*
180 E4 **Golden Valley** *Derbys., Eng.*
98 G2 **Golden Valley** *Glos., Eng.*
26 G3 **Golden Valley** *val. Eng.*
74 C2 **Golders Green** *Gtr Lon., Eng.*
116 G3 **Goldhanger** *Essex, Eng.*
124 F3 **Gold Hill** *Cambs., Eng.*
46 F2 **Gold Hill** *Dorset, Eng.*
252 F2 **Goldielea** *D. and G., Scot.*
144 D4 **Golding** *Shrop., Eng.*
110 C3 **Goldington** *Bedford, Eng.*
216 G1 **Goldsborough** *N. Yorks., Eng.*
154 B2 **Golds Green** *W. Mids, Eng.*
36 C3 **Goldsithney** *Corn., Eng.*
144 F2 **Goldstone** *Shrop., Eng.*
154 B2 **Goldthorn Park** *W. Mids, Eng.*
208 E2 **Goldthorpe** *S. Yorks., Eng.*
40 D2 **Goldworthy** *Devon, Eng.*
62 D4 **Golford** *Kent, Eng.*
322 J2 **Gollanfield** *High., Scot.*
378 H3 **Golly** *Wrex., Wales*
320 I4 **Golspie** *High., Scot.*
320 I2 **Golval** *High., Scot.*
86 E5 **Gomeldon** *Wilts., Eng.*
222 D2 **Gomersal** *W. Yorks., Eng.*
22 D10 **Gometra** *i. Scot.*
300 B2 **Gometra House** *Arg. and B., Scot.*
78 D2 **Gomshall** *Surr., Eng.*
296 E5 **Gonachan Cottage** *Stir., Scot.*
176 D4 **Gonalston** *Notts., Eng.*
170 C6 **Gonerby Hill Foot** *Lincs., Eng.*
331 D2 **Gonfirth** *Shet., Scot.*
116 E3 **Good Easter** *Essex, Eng.*
166 C3 **Gooderstone** *Norf., Eng.*
40 E1 **Goodleigh** *Devon, Eng.*
210 E3 **Goodmanham** *E. Riding, Eng.*
74 E2 **Goodmayes** *Gtr Lon., Eng.*
62 F3 **Goodnestone** *Kent, Eng.*
62 H3 **Goodnestone** *Kent, Eng.*
140 D4 **Goodrich** *Here., Eng.*
40 F3 **Goodrington** *Torbay, Eng.*
228 I4 **Goodshaw** *Lancs., Eng.*
228 I4 **Goodshaw Fold** *Lancs., Eng.*
358 E1 **Goodwick** *Pembs., Wales*
52 D3 **Goodworth Clatford** *Hants., Eng.*
132 C3 **Goodyers End** *Warks., Eng.*
232 B4 **Goodyhills** *Cumbria, Eng.*
210 C4 **Goole** *E. Riding, Eng.*
136 F2 **Goom's Hill** *Worcs., Eng.*
36 D3 **Goonbell** *Corn., Eng.*
36 D2 **Goonhavern** *Corn., Eng.*
36 D3 **Goonvrea** *Corn., Eng.*
116 I2 **Goose Green** *Essex, Eng.*
116 I2 **Goose Green** *Essex, Eng.*
198 B2 **Goose Green** *Gtr Man., Eng.*
62 C3 **Goose Green** *Kent, Eng.*
98 E5 **Goose Green** *S. Glos., Eng.*
36 F1 **Gooseham** *Corn., Eng.*
140 C3 **Goose Pool** *Here., Eng.*
40 D3 **Goosewell** *Plymouth, Eng.*
102 C5 **Goosey** *Oxon, Eng.*
228 F4 **Goosnargh** *Lancs., Eng.*
184 E2 **Goostrey** *Cheshire East, Eng.*
276 E2 **Gorbals** *Glas., Scot.*
136 F2 **Gorcott Hill** *Worcs., Eng.*
372 G1 **Gorddinog** *Gwynedd, Wales*
256 I2 **Gordon** *Borders, Scot.*
320 I3 **Gordonbush** *High., Scot.*
314 C1 **Gordonstoun** *Moray, Scot.*
314 E2 **Gordonstown** *Abers., Scot.*
314 F2 **Gordonstown** *Abers., Scot.*
288 E3 **Gorebridge** *Midlothian, Scot.*
86 D4 **Gore Cross** *Wilts., Eng.*
52 D2 **Gore End** *Hants., Eng.*
124 E2 **Gorefield** *Cambs., Eng.*
116 G2 **Gore Pit** *Essex, Eng.*
86 D4 **Gores** *Wilts., Eng.*
62 H2 **Gore Street** *Kent, Eng.*
408 E4 **Gorey** *Jersey* Channel Is
288 D3 **Gorgie** *Edin., Scot.*
102 E5 **Goring** *Oxon, Eng.*
102 E5 **Goring Heath** *Oxon, Eng.*
166 J3 **Gorleston-on-Sea** *Norf., Eng.*
356 D2 **Gorllwyn** *Carmar., Wales*
22 D11 **Gorm, Loch** *l. Scot.*
154 B2 **Gornalwood** *W. Mids, Eng.*
314 F2 **Gorrachie** *Abers., Scot.*
36 E3 **Gorran Churchtown** *Corn., Eng.*
36 E3 **Gorran Haven** *Corn., Eng.*
362 F2 **Gors** *Cere., Wales*
378 F2 **Gorsedd** *Flints., Wales*
198 D3 **Gorse Hill** *Gtr Man., Eng.*
86 E2 **Gorse Hill** *Swindon, Eng.*
350 B2 **Gorseinon** *Swansea, Wales*
329 C3 **Gorseness** *Orkney, Scot.*
180 D4 **Gorseybank** *Derbys., Eng.*
362 E4 **Gorsgoch** *Cere., Wales*
356 F3 **Gorslas** *Carmar., Wales*
98 E2 **Gorsley** *Glos., Eng.*
98 E2 **Gorsley Common** *Glos., Eng.*
184 D2 **Gorstage** *Cheshire West & Chester, Eng.*
322 G2 **Gorstan** *High., Scot.*
148 D3 **Gorsty Hill** *Staffs., Eng.*
402 G3 **Gortaclare** *Omagh, N. Ire.*
388 F4 **Gortahurk** *Magherafelt, N. Ire.*
402 I3 **Gortavoy Bridge** *Dungannon, N. Ire.*
300 D2 **Gorten** *Arg. and B., Scot.*
300 C2 **Gortenbuie** *Arg. and B., Scot.*
322 D4 **Gorteneorn** *High., Scot.*
402 H3 **Gortfin** *Omagh, N. Ire.*
402 G2 **Gortin** *Omagh, N. Ire.*
388 C3 **Gortinreid** *Derry, N. Ire.*
402 E6 **Gortmullan** *Fermanagh, N. Ire.*
402 F3 **Gortnacreagh** *Omagh, N. Ire.*
388 I5 **Gortnagallon** *Antrim, N. Ire.*
388 E3 **Gortnahey** *Limavady, N. Ire.*
402 B4 **Gortnalee** *Fermanagh, N. Ire.*
198 D3 **Gorton** *Gtr Man., Eng.*
300 □ **Gorton** *Arg. and B., Scot.*
402 I3 **Gortreagh** *Cookstown, N. Ire.*
120 F4 **Gosbeck** *Suff., Eng.*
170 F6 **Gosberton** *Lincs., Eng.*
170 E6 **Gosberton Clough** *Lincs., Eng.*
180 D6 **Goseley Dale** *Derbys., Eng.*
116 F2 **Gosfield** *Essex, Eng.*
140 C2 **Gosford** *Here., Eng.*
102 D4 **Gosford** *Oxon, Eng.*
232 B6 **Gosforth** *Cumbria, Eng.*
236 F1 **Gosforth** *T. and W., Eng.*
184 D3 **Gosland Green** *Cheshire East, Eng.*
110 D4 **Gosmore** *Herts., Eng.*
148 C5 **Gospel End** *Staffs., Eng.*
74 D2 **Gospel Oak** *Gtr Lon., Eng.*
52 D4 **Gosport** *Hants., Eng.*
52 F6 **Gosport** *Hants., Eng.*
331 D2 **Gossabrough** *Shet., Scot.*
110 B3 **Gossard's Green** *Central Bedfordshire, Eng.*
98 E3 **Gossington** *Glos., Eng.*
58 E2 **Gossops Green** *W. Sussex, Eng.*
244 F1 **Goswick** *Northumb., Eng.*
176 B5 **Gotham** *Notts., Eng.*
98 G2 **Gotherington** *Glos., Eng.*
331 D3 **Gott** *Shet., Scot.*
94 F4 **Gotton** *Som., Eng.*
62 C4 **Goudhurst** *Kent, Eng.*
170 F4 **Goulceby** *Lincs., Eng.*
314 G4 **Gourdon** *Abers., Scot.*
276 B2 **Gourock** *Inverclyde, Scot.*
276 E2 **Govan** *Glas., Scot.*
276 E3 **Govanhill** *Glas., Scot.*
176 D4 **Goverton** *Notts., Eng.*
40 E4 **Goveton** *Devon, Eng.*
339 B2 **Govilon** *Mon., Wales*
314 H2 **Gowanhill** *Abers., Scot.*
210 B4 **Gowdall** *E. Riding, Eng.*
396 G3 **Gowdystown** *Banbridge, N. Ire.*
26 D4 **Gower** *pen. Wales*
350 B3 **Gowerton** *Swansea, Wales*
292 C3 **Gowkhall** *Fife, Scot.*
280 C4 **Gowkthrapple** *N. Lanark., Scot.*
210 C3 **Gowthorpe** *E. Riding, Eng.*
24 L7 **Gowy** *r. Eng.*
210 G3 **Goxhill** *E. Riding, Eng.*
170 E1 **Goxhill** *N. Lincs., Eng.*
350 D3 **Goytre** *N.P.T., Wales*
102 D4 **Gozzard's Ford** *Oxon, Eng.*
326 E2 **Grabhair** *W. Isles, Scot.*
170 D6 **Graby** *Lincs., Eng.*
388 G4 **Gracefield** *Magherafelt, N. Ire.*
388 I3 **Gracehill** *Ballymena, N. Ire.*
288 E3 **Gracemount** *Edin., Scot.*
148 C1 **Gradbach** *Staffs., Eng.*
184 D3 **Gradeley Green** *Cheshire East, Eng.*
22 J5 **Graemsay** *i. Scot.*
58 B3 **Graffham** *W. Sussex, Eng.*
124 C5 **Grafham** *Cambs., Eng.*
78 C3 **Grafham** *Surr., Eng.*
26 L3 **Grafham Water** *resr Eng.*
140 C3 **Grafton** *Here., Eng.*
216 E2 **Grafton** *N. Yorks., Eng.*
102 B4 **Grafton** *Oxon, Eng.*
144 C3 **Grafton** *Shrop., Eng.*
136 B2 **Grafton** *Worcs., Eng.*
136 E3 **Grafton** *Worcs., Eng.*
136 E2 **Grafton Flyford** *Worcs., Eng.*
128 D5 **Grafton Regis** *Northants., Eng.*
128 F3 **Grafton Underwood** *Northants., Eng.*
62 E3 **Grafty Green** *Kent, Eng.*
378 F3 **Graianrhyd** *Denb., Wales*
356 E3 **Graig** *Carmar., Wales*
378 C2 **Graig** *Conwy, Wales*
378 E2 **Graig** *Denb., Wales*
378 F3 **Graig-fechan** *Denb., Wales*
350 F4 **Graig Penllyn** *V. of Glam., Wales*
62 E2 **Grain** *Medway, Eng.*
26 N5 **Grain, Isle of** *pen. Eng.*
300 A4 **Grainel** *Arg. and B., Scot.*
314 G2 **Grainhow** *Abers., Scot.*
198 E2 **Grains Bar** *Gtr Man., Eng.*
170 F3 **Grainsby** *Lincs., Eng.*
170 G3 **Grainthorpe** *Lincs., Eng.*
170 A3 **Graizelound** *N. Lincs., Eng.*
22 D4 **Gralisgeir** *i. Scot.*
326 C4 **Gramisdale** *W. Isles, Scot.*
22 G9 **Grampian Mountains** *mts Scot.*
36 E3 **Grampound** *Corn., Eng.*
36 E3 **Grampound Road** *Corn., Eng.*
Gramsdal *W. Isles, Scot. see* **Gramisdale**
106 C3 **Granborough** *Bucks., Eng.*
176 D5 **Granby** *Notts., Eng.*
132 E4 **Grandborough** *Warks., Eng.*
408 B3 **Grandes Rocques** *Guernsey* Channel Is
304 H3 **Grandtully** *Perth and Kin., Scot.*
232 D5 **Grange** *Cumbria, Eng.*
62 D2 **Grange** *Medway, Eng.*
190 C3 **Grange** *Merseyside, Eng.*
216 F1 **Grange** *N. Yorks., Eng.*
402 J3 **Grange** *Cookstown, N. Ire.*
262 D3 **Grange** *E. Ayr., Scot.*
322 G2 **Grange** *High., Scot.*
304 K4 **Grange** *Perth and Kin., Scot.*
396 E3 **Grange Blundel** *Armagh, N. Ire.*
388 H4 **Grange Corner** *Ballymena, N. Ire.*
314 E2 **Grange Crossroads** *Moray, Scot.*
170 C4 **Grange de Lings** *Lincs., Eng.*
396 K2 **Grangee** *Ards, N. Ire.*
116 C4 **Grange Hill** *Essex, Eng.*
180 D4 **Grangemill** *Derbys., Eng.*
222 D3 **Grange Moor** *W. Yorks., Eng.*
280 D2 **Grangemouth** *Falk., Scot.*
292 H2 **Grangemuir** *Fife, Scot.*
292 E1 **Grange of Lindores** *Fife, Scot.*
232 E7 **Grange-over-Sands** *Cumbria, Eng.*
74 D2 **Grange Park** *Gtr Lon., Eng.*
262 C5 **Grangeston** *S. Ayr., Scot.*
216 F1 **Grangetown** *R. and C., Eng.*
350 G4 **Grangetown** *Cardiff, Wales*
236 F2 **Grange Villa** *Durham, Eng.*
396 H3 **Gransha** *Banbridge, N. Ire.*
396 J2 **Gransha** *Castlereagh, N. Ire.*
388 L4 **Gransha** *Larne, N. Ire.*
210 G2 **Gransmoor** *E. Riding, Eng.*
358 D2 **Granston** *Pembs., Wales*
124 E5 **Grantchester** *Cambs., Eng.*
170 C6 **Grantham** *Lincs., Eng.*
216 E2 **Grantley** *N. Yorks., Eng.*
314 F3 **Grantlodge** *Abers., Scot.*
288 D3 **Granton** *Edin., Scot.*
252 F1 **Granton House** *D. and G., Scot.*
322 K3 **Grantown-on-Spey** *High., Scot.*
140 C2 **Grantsfield** *Here., Eng.*
256 K1 **Grantshouse** *Borders, Scot.*
402 J4 **Granville** *Dungannon, N. Ire.*
190 F3 **Grappenhall** *Warr., Eng.*
170 D2 **Grasby** *Lincs., Eng.*
232 D6 **Grasmere** *Cumbria, Eng.*
198 E2 **Grasscroft** *Gtr Man., Eng.*
190 D3 **Grassendale** *Merseyside, Eng.*
232 E6 **Grassgarth** *Cumbria, Eng.*
116 F1 **Grass Green** *Essex, Eng.*
236 C4 **Grassholme** *Durham, Eng.*
216 D2 **Grassington** *N. Yorks., Eng.*
180 E3 **Grassmoor** *Derbys., Eng.*
176 E3 **Grassthorpe** *Notts., Eng.*
52 C3 **Grateley** *Hants., Eng.*
148 C2 **Gratton** *Staffs., Eng.*
148 D3 **Gratwich** *Staffs., Eng.*
124 C5 **Graveley** *Cambs., Eng.*
110 D4 **Graveley** *Herts., Eng.*
106 E5 **Gravel Hill** *Bucks., Eng.*
144 D3 **Gravelhill** *Shrop., Eng.*
154 C2 **Gravelly Hill** *W. Mids, Eng.*
144 C4 **Gravels** *Shrop., Eng.*
331 D2 **Graven** *Shet., Scot.*
62 F3 **Graveney** *Kent, Eng.*
62 C2 **Gravesend** *Kent, Eng.*
170 C3 **Grayingham** *Lincs., Eng.*
232 G6 **Grayrigg** *Cumbria, Eng.*
116 D5 **Grays** *Thurrock, Eng.*
52 H4 **Grayshott** *Hants., Eng.*
78 B3 **Grayswood** *Surr., Eng.*
82 E3 **Grazeley** *W'ham, Eng.*
208 D3 **Greasbrough** *S. Yorks., Eng.*
190 C3 **Greasby** *Merseyside, Eng.*
176 B4 **Greasley** *Notts., Eng.*
124 F6 **Great Abington** *Cambs., Eng.*
128 F3 **Great Addington** *Northants., Eng.*
132 B4 **Great Alne** *Warks., Eng.*
228 D5 **Great Altcar** *Lancs., Eng.*
110 E5 **Great Amwell** *Herts., Eng.*
232 G5 **Great Asby** *Cumbria, Eng.*
120 E3 **Great Ashfield** *Suff., Eng.*
216 F1 **Great Ayton** *N. Yorks., Eng.*
116 F3 **Great Baddow** *Essex, Eng.*
116 E2 **Great Bardfield** *Essex, Eng.*
110 C3 **Great Barford** *Bedford, Eng.*
154 C2 **Great Barr** *W. Mids, Eng.*
98 I3 **Great Barrington** *Glos., Eng.*
184 C2 **Great Barrow** *Cheshire West & Chester, Eng.*
120 D3 **Great Barton** *Suff., Eng.*
216 G2 **Great Barugh** *N. Yorks., Eng.*
244 E5 **Great Bavington** *Northumb., Eng.*
120 G4 **Great Bealings** *Suff., Eng.*
86 F3 **Great Bedwyn** *Wilts., Eng.*
116 I2 **Great Bentley** *Essex, Eng.*
22 C6 **Great Bernera** *i. Scot.*
128 E4 **Great Billing** *Northants., Eng.*
166 C1 **Great Bircham** *Norf., Eng.*

Great Blakenham to Harehills

120 F4 Great Blakenham Suff., Eng.
144 E3 Great Bolas Telford, Eng.
78 D2 Great Bookham Surr., Eng.
102 C2 Great Bourton Oxon, Eng.
162 F4 Great Bowden Leics., Eng.
120 B4 Great Bradley Suff., Eng.
116 G3 Great Braxted Essex, Eng.
106 D3 Great Brickhill Bucks., Eng.
148 B3 Great Bridgeford Staffs., Eng.
128 C4 Great Brington Northants., Eng.
20 G4 Great Britain i.
116 I2 Great Bromley Essex, Eng.
232 B4 Great Broughton Cumbria, Eng.
216 F1 Great Broughton N. Yorks., Eng.
62 C2 Great Buckland Kent, Eng.
184 D2 Great Budworth Cheshire East, Eng.
236 F4 Great Burdon Darl., Eng.
116 E4 Great Burstead Essex, Eng.
124 D5 Great Cambourne Cambs., Eng.
116 D2 Great Canfield Essex, Eng.
116 F3 Great Canney Essex, Eng.
170 G3 Great Carlton Lincs., Eng.
162 H2 Great Casterton Rutland, Eng.
86 B3 Great Chalfield Wilts., Eng.
62 E4 Great Chart Kent, Eng.
144 G3 Great Chatwell Shrop., Eng.
148 B2 Great Chell Stoke, Eng.
116 D1 Great Chesterford Essex, Eng.
86 C4 Great Cheverell Wilts., Eng.
124 E6 Great Chishill Cambs., Eng.
116 I3 Great Clacton Essex, Eng.
222 E3 Great Cliff W. Yorks., Eng.
232 B5 Great Clifton Cumbria, Eng.
170 F2 Great Coates N.E. Lincs., Eng.
136 E3 Great Comberton Worcs., Eng.
232 F3 Great Corby Cumbria, Eng.
120 D4 Great Cornard Suff., Eng.
210 H3 Great Cowden E. Riding, Eng.
102 B5 Great Coxwell Oxon, Eng.
128 E3 Great Cransley Northants., Eng.
166 D3 Great Cressingham Norf., Eng.
190 C3 Great Crosby Merseyside, Eng.
232 D5 Great Crosthwaite Cumbria, Eng.
180 C5 Great Cubley Derbys., Eng.
24 H2 Great Cumbrae i. Scot.
162 F2 Great Dalby Leics., Eng.
24 K4 Great Dodd hill Eng.
128 E4 Great Doddington Northants., Eng.
140 D4 Great Doward Here., Eng.
166 D2 Great Dunham Norf., Eng.
116 E2 Great Dunmow Essex, Eng.
86 E5 Great Durnford Wilts., Eng.
116 E2 Great Easton Essex, Eng.
162 G3 Great Easton Leics., Eng.
228 E3 Great Eccleston Lancs., Eng.
166 E3 Great Ellingham Norf., Eng.
94 J3 Great Elm Som., Eng.
74 D2 Greater London admin. div. Eng.
198 C2 Greater Manchester admin. div. Eng.
124 D5 Great Eversden Cambs., Eng.
216 E1 Great Fencote N. Yorks., Eng.
120 E3 Great Finborough Suff., Eng.
170 D7 Greatford Lincs., Eng.
166 D2 Great Fransham Norf., Eng.
110 B5 Great Gaddesden Herts., Eng.
148 D3 Greatgate Staffs., Eng.
124 B4 Great Gidding Cambs., Eng.
210 D3 Great Givendale E. Riding, Eng.
120 H3 Great Glemham Suff., Eng.
162 E3 Great Glen Leics., Eng.
170 C6 Great Gonerby Lincs., Eng.
124 D5 Great Gransden Cambs., Eng.
124 D6 Great Green Cambs., Eng.
166 H4 Great Green Norf., Eng.
120 E3 Great Green Suff., Eng.
120 F2 Great Green Suff., Eng.
120 F2 Great Green Suff., Eng.
120 G2 Great Green Suff., Eng.
216 G2 Great Habton N. Yorks., Eng.
170 E6 Great Hale Lincs., Eng.
116 D2 Great Hallingbury Essex, Eng.
52 G4 Greatham Hants., Eng.
236 H4 Greatham Hartlepool, Eng.
106 D4 Great Hampden Bucks., Eng.
128 E4 Great Harrowden Northants., Eng.
228 H4 Great Harwood Lancs., Eng.
102 E4 Great Haseley Oxon, Eng.
210 G3 Great Hatfield E. Riding, Eng.
148 D4 Great Haywood Staffs., Eng.
154 E3 Great Heath W. Mids, Eng.
216 F3 Great Heck N. Yorks., Eng.
116 G1 Great Henny Essex, Eng.
86 C4 Great Hinton Wilts., Eng.
166 E4 Great Hockham Norf., Eng.
116 J3 Great Holland Essex, Eng.
116 H2 Great Horkesley Essex, Eng.
110 F4 Great Hormead Herts., Eng.
222 D2 Great Horton W. Yorks., Eng.
106 C3 Great Horwood Bucks., Eng.
128 D4 Great Houghton Northants., Eng.
208 D2 Great Houghton S. Yorks., Eng.
180 C3 Great Hucklow Derbys., Eng.
210 G2 Great Kelk E. Riding, Eng.
106 D4 Great Kimble Bucks., Eng.
106 D4 Great Kingshill Bucks., Eng.
216 E1 Great Langton N. Yorks., Eng.
116 F3 Great Leighs Essex, Eng.
170 E2 Great Limber Lincs., Eng.
106 D2 Great Linford M.K., Eng.
120 D3 Great Livermere Suff., Eng.
180 C3 Great Longstone Derbys., Eng.
236 F2 Great Lumley Durham, Eng.
144 D4 Great Lyth Shrop., Eng.
136 D3 Great Malvern Worcs., Eng.
116 F2 Great Maplestead Essex, Eng.
228 D4 Great Marton Blackpool, Eng.
166 C2 Great Massingham Norf., Eng.
166 F3 Great Melton Norf., Eng.
102 E4 Great Milton Oxon, Eng.
106 D4 Great Missenden Bucks., Eng.
228 H3 Great Mitton Lancs., Eng.
62 I3 Great Mongeham Kent, Eng.
166 G4 Great Moulton Norf., Eng.
110 E4 Great Munden Herts., Eng.
232 H5 Great Musgrave Cumbria, Eng.
62 B3 Greatness Kent, Eng.
144 C3 Great Ness Shrop., Eng.
116 F2 Great Notley Essex, Eng.
94 C4 Great Nurcot Som., Eng.
339 C2 Great Oak Mon., Wales
116 J2 Great Oakley Essex, Eng.
128 E3 Great Oakley Northants., Eng.
110 C4 Great Offley Herts., Eng.
26 E1 Great Ormes Head hd Wales
232 H5 Great Ormside Cumbria, Eng.
232 D3 Great Orton Cumbria, Eng.
26 M2 Great Ouse r. Eng.
216 F2 Great Ouseburn N. Yorks., Eng.
128 D3 Great Oxendon Northants., Eng.
116 E3 Great Oxney Green Essex, Eng.
166 D2 Great Palgrave Norf., Eng.
116 C3 Great Parndon Essex, Eng.
124 C5 Great Paxton Cambs., Eng.
228 E4 Great Plumpton Lancs., Eng.
166 H3 Great Plumstead Norf., Eng.
170 C6 Great Ponton Lincs., Eng.
222 F2 Great Preston W. Yorks., Eng.
128 B5 Great Purston Northants., Eng.
124 D4 Great Raveley Cambs., Eng.
26 F3 Great Rhos hill Wales
98 I2 Great Rissington Glos., Eng.
102 B3 Great Rollright Oxon, Eng.
166 E2 Great Ryburgh Norf., Eng.
244 F3 Great Ryle Northumb., Eng.
144 D4 Great Ryton Shrop., Eng.
116 E2 Great Saling Essex, Eng.
232 F4 Great Salkeld Cumbria, Eng.
116 E2 Great Sampford Essex, Eng.
190 F3 Great Sankey Warr., Eng.
148 C4 Great Saredon Staffs., Eng.
120 C3 Great Saxham Suff., Eng.
116 E3 Great Seabrights Essex, Eng.
82 B3 Great Shefford W. Berks., Eng.
124 E5 Great Shelford Cambs., Eng.
216 E1 Great Smeaton N. Yorks., Eng.
166 E1 Great Snoring Norf., Eng.
86 C2 Great Somerford Wilts., Eng.
236 G4 Great Stainton Darl., Eng.
116 G4 Great Stambridge Essex, Eng.
124 B5 Great Staughton Cambs., Eng.
170 G5 Great Steeping Lincs., Eng.
62 I3 Great Stonar Kent, Eng.
62 F5 Greatstone-on-Sea Kent, Eng.
26 O5 Great Stour r. Eng.
232 F5 Great Strickland Cumbria, Eng.
124 C4 Great Stukeley Cambs., Eng.
170 E4 Great Sturton Lincs., Eng.
184 B2 Great Sutton Cheshire West & Chester, Eng.
144 D5 Great Sutton Shrop., Eng.
244 E5 Great Swinburne Northumb., Eng.
102 C3 Great Tew Oxon, Eng.
116 G2 Great Tey Essex, Eng.
52 D6 Great Thorness I.o.W., Eng.
120 B4 Great Thurlow Suff., Eng.
40 E4 Great Torr Devon, Eng.
40 D2 Great Torrington Devon, Eng.
116 G3 Great Totham Essex, Eng.
116 G3 Great Totham Essex, Eng.
170 F3 Great Tows Lincs., Eng.
232 D8 Great Urswick Cumbria, Eng.
116 G4 Great Wakering Essex, Eng.
120 D4 Great Waldingfield Suff., Eng.
166 E1 Great Walsingham Norf., Eng.
116 E3 Great Waltham Essex, Eng.
116 D4 Great Warley Essex, Eng.
98 G1 Great Washbourne Glos., Eng.
120 D3 Great Welnetham Suff., Eng.
120 F4 Great Wenham Suff., Eng.
24 N5 Great Whernside hill Eng.
244 F5 Great Whittington Northumb., Eng.
116 H3 Great Wigborough Essex, Eng.
58 J2 Great Wigsell E. Sussex, Eng.
124 F5 Great Wilbraham Cambs., Eng.
180 E5 Great Wilne Derbys., Eng.
86 D5 Great Wishford Wilts., Eng.
98 G3 Great Witcombe Glos., Eng.
136 C2 Great Witley Worcs., Eng.
132 C5 Great Wolford Warks., Eng.
128 B5 Greatworth Northants., Eng.
120 B4 Great Wratting Suff., Eng.
110 D4 Great Wymondley Herts., Eng.
148 C5 Great Wyrley Staffs., Eng.
144 E3 Great Wytheford Shrop., Eng.
166 J3 Great Yarmouth Norf., Eng.
116 F1 Great Yeldham Essex, Eng.
198 E3 Greave Gtr Man., Eng.
378 E2 Green Denb., Wales
198 E2 Greenacres Gtr Man., Eng.
396 G5 Greenan Newry & Mourne, N. Ire.
308 E3 Greenburn Angus, Scot.
396 H5 Greencastle Newry & Mourne, N. Ire.
402 H2 Greencastle Omagh, N. Ire.
236 E2 Greencroft Durham, Eng.
78 B3 Green Cross Surr., Eng.
314 F4 Greendams Abers., Scot.
244 F2 Greendykes Northumb., Eng.
110 B3 Green End Bedford, Eng.
110 C2 Green End Bedford, Eng.
110 C2 Green End Bedford, Eng.
110 C3 Green End Bedford, Eng.
106 D3 Green End Bucks., Eng.
124 C4 Green End Cambs., Eng.
124 D5 Green End Cambs., Eng.
124 E5 Green End Cambs., Eng.
110 E4 Green End Herts., Eng.
110 E4 Green End Herts., Eng.
102 B3 Greenend Oxon, Eng.
132 C3 Green End Warks., Eng.
280 B3 Greenfaulds N. Lanark., Scot.
110 C3 Greenfield Central Bedfordshire, Eng.
198 E2 Greenfield Gtr Man., Eng.
170 G4 Greenfield Lincs., Eng.
102 F5 Greenfield Oxon, Eng.
396 H5 Greenfield Newry & Mourne, N. Ire.
322 G3 Greenfield High., Scot.
378 F2 Greenfield Flints., Wales
74 B2 Greenford Gtr Lon., Eng.
280 C3 Greengairs N. Lanark., Scot.
222 D1 Greengates W. Yorks., Eng.
232 B4 Greengill Cumbria, Eng.
106 D4 Green Hailey Bucks., Eng.
228 E4 Greenhalgh Lancs., Eng.
94 E5 Greenham Som., Eng.
82 C3 Greenham W. Berks., Eng.
216 F2 Green Hammerton N. Yorks., Eng.
244 D4 Greenhaugh Northumb., Eng.
244 B6 Greenhead Northumb., Eng.
314 H2 Greenheads Abers., Scot.
148 C4 Green Heath Staffs., Eng.
198 C2 Greenheys Gtr Man., Eng.
74 C2 Greenhill Gtr Lon., Eng.
140 E3 Greenhill Here., Eng.
208 D4 Greenhill S. Yorks., Eng.
86 D2 Green Hill Wilts., Eng.
62 B2 Greenhithe Kent, Eng.
262 E3 Greenholm E. Ayr., Scot.
232 G6 Greenholme Cumbria, Eng.
216 D2 Greenhow Hill N. Yorks., Eng.
329 C4 Greenigo Orkney, Scot.
388 K4 Greenisland Carrickfergus, N. Ire.
208 D3 Greenland S. Yorks., Eng.
106 C5 Greenlands Bucks., Eng.
136 F2 Greenlands Worcs., Eng.
132 A4 Green Lane Warks., Eng.
314 F2 Greenlaw Abers., Scot.
256 J2 Greenlaw Borders, Scot.
304 G5 Greenloaning Perth and Kin., Scot.
22 I12 Green Lowther hill Scot.
339 B3 Greenmeadow Torf., Wales
208 C3 Green Moor S. Yorks., Eng.
102 E5 Greenmoor Hill Oxon, Eng.
198 C2 Greenmount Gtr Man., Eng.
210 D4 Greenoak E. Riding, Eng.
276 B2 Greenock Inverclyde, Scot.
232 D7 Greenodd Cumbria, Eng.
94 I3 Green Ore Som., Eng.
232 F6 Green Quarter Cumbria, Eng.
304 G5 Greenscares Perth and Kin., Scot.
236 E2 Greenside T. and W., Eng.
222 D3 Greenside W. Yorks., Eng.
222 E2 Green Side W. Yorks., Eng.
128 C5 Greens Norton Northants., Eng.
116 H2 Greenstead Essex, Eng.
116 F2 Greenstead Green Essex, Eng.
116 D3 Greensted Essex, Eng.
116 D3 Greensted Green Essex, Eng.
22 E7 Greenstone Point pt Scot.
58 J3 Green Street E. Sussex, Eng.
110 D5 Green Street Herts., Eng.
136 D3 Green Street Worcs., Eng.
58 D3 Green Street W. Sussex, Eng.
74 E3 Green Street Green Gtr Lon., Eng.
62 B2 Green Street Green Kent, Eng.
120 E4 Greenstreet Green Suff., Eng.
110 F4 Green Tye Herts., Eng.
402 F2 Greenville Strabane, N. Ire.
94 G4 Greenway Som., Eng.
358 F2 Greenway Pembs., Wales
232 F3 Greenwell Cumbria, Eng.
74 D3 Greenwich Gtr Lon., Eng.
74 E3 Greenwich met. bor. Gtr Lon., Eng.
388 J5 Greerstown Lisburn, N. Ire.
98 H2 Greet Glos., Eng.
144 E5 Greete Shrop., Eng.
170 F4 Greetham Lincs., Eng.
162 H2 Greetham Rutland, Eng.
222 C2 Greetland W. Yorks., Eng.
222 C2 Greetland Wall Nook W. Yorks., Eng.
228 G4 Gregson Lane Lancs., Eng.
Greinetobht W. Isles, Scot. see Grenitote
94 G4 Greinton Som., Eng.
405 C3 Grenaby Isle of Man
128 E4 Grendon Northants., Eng.
132 E2 Grendon Warks., Eng.
132 C2 Grendon Common Warks., Eng.
140 D2 Grendon Green Here., Eng.
106 B3 Grendon Underwood Bucks., Eng.
326 C4 Grenitote W. Isles, Scot.
40 D3 Grenofen Devon, Eng.
208 D3 Grenoside S. Yorks., Eng.
378 H3 Gresford Wrex., Wales
166 G1 Gresham Norf., Eng.
322 B2 Greshornish High., Scot.
166 E2 Gressenhall Norf., Eng.
228 G2 Gressingham Lancs., Eng.
24 L5 Greta r. Eng.
236 D4 Greta Bridge Durham, Eng.
252 G3 Gretna D. and G., Scot.
252 G3 Gretna Green D. and G., Scot.
98 H2 Gretton Glos., Eng.
128 E2 Gretton Northants., Eng.
144 D4 Gretton Shrop., Eng.
216 E2 Grewelthorpe N. Yorks., Eng.
396 K2 Greyabbey Ards, N. Ire.
94 G4 Greylake Som., Eng.
24 F4 Grey Point pt N. Ire.
102 F5 Greys Green Oxon, Eng.
232 B5 Greysouthen Cumbria, Eng.
244 C4 Greystead Northumb., Eng.
388 D2 Greysteel Limavady, N. Ire.
232 E4 Greystoke Cumbria, Eng.
228 I3 Greystone Lancs., Eng.
314 D3 Greystone Abers., Scot.
308 F3 Greystone Angus, Scot.
208 C3 Greystones S. Yorks., Eng.
52 G3 Greywell Hants., Eng.
210 C4 Gribthorpe E. Riding, Eng.
252 E2 Gribton D. and G., Scot.
132 D3 Griff Warks., Eng.
350 H2 Griffithstown B. Gwent, Wales
162 C2 Griffydam Leics., Eng.
232 F7 Grigghall Cumbria, Eng.
329 C4 Grimbister Orkney, Scot.
228 G5 Grimeford Village Lancs., Eng.
208 D3 Grimesthorpe S. Yorks., Eng.
208 D2 Grimethorpe S. Yorks., Eng.
Griminis W. Isles, Scot. see Griminish
326 B4 Griminish W. Isles, Scot.
22 A7 Griminis Point pt Scot.
331 D2 Grimister Shet., Scot.
136 D2 Grimley Worcs., Eng.
262 D4 Grimmet S. Ayr., Scot.
329 D5 Grimness Orkney, Scot.
170 G3 Grimoldby Lincs., Eng.
144 C2 Grimpo Shrop., Eng.
228 G4 Grimsargh Lancs., Eng.
22 B8 Grimsay i. Scot.
102 D2 Grimsbury Oxon, Eng.
170 F2 Grimsby N.E. Lincs., Eng.
128 C4 Grimscote Northants., Eng.
36 F1 Grimscott Corn., Eng.
326 E2 Grimshader W. Isles, Scot.
228 H4 Grimshaw B'burn, Eng.
228 F5 Grimshaw Green Lancs., Eng.
170 D7 Grimsthorpe Lincs., Eng.
210 H4 Grimston E. Riding, Eng.
162 F2 Grimston Leics., Eng.
166 C2 Grimston Norf., Eng.
46 D3 Grimstone Dorset, Eng.
120 E3 Grimstone End Suff., Eng.
210 G2 Grindale E. Riding, Eng.
331 D3 Grindiscol Shet., Scot.
144 F4 Grindle Shrop., Eng.
180 D3 Grindleford Derbys., Eng.
228 H3 Grindleton Lancs., Eng.
148 D3 Grindley Staffs., Eng.
144 D2 Grindley Brook Shrop., Eng.
180 C3 Grindlow Derbys., Eng.
244 E1 Grindon Northumb., Eng.
148 D2 Grindon Staffs., Eng.
236 G4 Grindon Stockton, Eng.
236 G2 Grindon T. and W., Eng.
176 D2 Gringley on the Hill Notts., Eng.
232 E3 Grinsdale Cumbria, Eng.
144 D3 Grinshill Shrop., Eng.
216 D1 Grinton N. Yorks., Eng.
326 D2 Griomarstaidh W. Isles, Scot.
Griomasaigh i. Scot. see Grimsay
232 H6 Grisdale Cumbria, Eng.
300 □ Grishipoll Arg. and B., Scot.
216 I2 Gristhorpe N. Yorks., Eng.
166 E3 Griston Norf., Eng.
329 E4 Gritley Orkney, Scot.
86 D2 Grittenham Wilts., Eng.
86 B2 Grittleton Wilts., Eng.
232 C7 Grizebeck Cumbria, Eng.
232 D6 Grizedale Cumbria, Eng.
329 F3 Grobister Orkney, Scot.
162 D3 Groby Leics., Eng.
378 E2 Groes Denb., Wales
350 F3 Groes-faen R.C.T., Wales
372 C3 Groesffordd Gwynedd, Wales
378 E2 Groesffordd Marli Denb., Wales
372 E2 Groeslon Gwynedd, Wales
372 E2 Groeslon Gwynedd, Wales
366 F2 Groes-lwyd Powys, Wales
350 G3 Groes-wen Caerp., Wales
300 D5 Grogport Arg. and B., Scot.
326 B5 Groigearraidh W. Isles, Scot.
120 H3 Gromford Suff., Eng.
378 E1 Gronant Flints., Wales
58 H2 Groombridge E. Sussex, Eng.
396 K1 Groomsport North Down, N. Ire.
216 G1 Grosmont N. Yorks., Eng.
339 C1 Grosmont Mon., Wales
256 H4 Groundistone Heights Borders, Scot.
408 E4 Grouville Jersey Channel Is
106 D3 Grove Bucks., Eng.
46 E4 Grove Dorset, Eng.
62 H3 Grove Kent, Eng.
176 D3 Grove Notts., Eng.
102 C5 Grove Oxon, Eng.
358 E3 Grove Pembs., Wales
62 E3 Grove End Kent, Eng.
62 D3 Grove Green Kent, Eng.
110 C5 Grovehill Herts., Eng.
74 C3 Grove Park Gtr Lon., Eng.
74 E3 Grove Park Gtr Lon., Eng.
222 D3 Grove Place W. Yorks., Eng.
98 D4 Grovesend S. Glos., Eng.
350 B2 Grovesend Swansea, Wales
222 G2 Grove Town W. Yorks., Eng.
22 E7 Gruinard Bay b. Scot.
22 D11 Gruinart, Loch inlet Scot.
300 C2 Gruline Arg. and B., Scot.
36 C3 Grumbla Corn., Eng.
304 I4 Grundcruie Perth and Kin., Scot.
120 G4 Grundisburgh Suff., Eng.
331 C3 Gruting Shet., Scot.
331 D4 Grutness Shet., Scot.
322 F5 Gualachulain High., Scot.
292 G1 Guardbridge Fife, Scot.
136 D3 Guarlford Worcs., Eng.
304 I3 Guay Perth and Kin., Scot.
232 B6 Gubbergill Cumbria, Eng.
110 A5 Gubblecote Herts., Eng.
408 B3 Guernsey airport Guernsey Channel Is
408 B2 Guernsey terr. Channel Is
58 J3 Guestling Green E. Sussex, Eng.
58 J3 Guestling Thorn E. Sussex, Eng.
166 F2 Guestwick Norf., Eng.
166 F2 Guestwick Green Norf., Eng.
26 □ Gugh i. Eng.
228 H4 Guide B'burn, Eng.
198 E3 Guide Bridge Gtr Man., Eng.
244 H5 Guide Post Northumb., Eng.
144 B5 Guilden Down Shrop., Eng.
124 D6 Guilden Morden Cambs., Eng.
184 C2 Guilden Sutton Cheshire West & Chester, Eng.
78 C2 Guildford Surr., Eng.
304 J4 Guildtown Perth and Kin., Scot.
128 C3 Guilsborough Northants., Eng.
366 G2 Guilsfield Powys, Wales
208 E3 Guilthwaite S. Yorks., Eng.
62 H3 Guilton Kent, Eng.
216 F1 Guisborough R. and C., Eng.
222 D1 Guiseley W. Yorks., Eng.
166 E2 Guist Norf., Eng.
329 E2 Guith Orkney, Scot.
98 H2 Guiting Power Glos., Eng.
331 D3 Gulberwick Shet., Scot.
388 G3 Gulladuff Magherafelt, N. Ire.
288 G2 Gullane E. Lothian, Scot.
22 F9 Gulvain hill Scot.
36 C3 Gulval Corn., Eng.
358 F3 Gumfreston Pembs., Wales
162 F3 Gumley Leics., Eng.
210 C4 Gunby E. Riding, Eng.
170 C7 Gunby Lincs., Eng.
170 H4 Gunby Lincs., Eng.
52 F4 Gundleton Hants., Eng.
40 E1 Gunn Devon, Eng.
74 C3 Gunnersbury Gtr Lon., Eng.
216 C1 Gunnerside N. Yorks., Eng.
244 E5 Gunnerton Northumb., Eng.
170 B2 Gunness N. Lincs., Eng.
36 G2 Gunnislake Corn., Eng.
331 D3 Gunnista Shet., Scot.
331 C2 Gunnister Shet., Scot.
148 B5 Gunstone Staffs., Eng.
154 B2 Guns Village W. Mids, Eng.
58 C2 Gunter's Bridge W. Sussex, Eng.
166 E1 Gunthorpe Norf., Eng.
176 D5 Gunthorpe Notts., Eng.
124 C3 Gunthorpe Peterb., Eng.
162 G3 Gunthorpe Rutland, Eng.
208 C2 Gunthwaite S. Yorks., Eng.
52 E6 Gunville I.o.W., Eng.
36 D3 Gunwalloe Corn., Eng.
94 D4 Gupworthy Som., Eng.
52 E6 Gurnard I.o.W., Eng.
184 G2 Gurnett Cheshire East, Eng.
94 I3 Gurney Slade Som., Eng.
350 F2 Gurnos M. Tyd., Wales
366 C8 Gurnos Powys, Wales
62 F3 Gushmere Kent, Eng.
46 G2 Gussage All Saints Dorset, Eng.
46 F2 Gussage St Andrew Dorset, Eng.
46 G2 Gussage St Michael Dorset, Eng.
62 H4 Guston Kent, Eng.
331 D1 Gutcher Shet., Scot.
170 E7 Guthram Gowt Lincs., Eng.
308 F3 Guthrie Angus, Scot.
124 E3 Guyhirn Cambs., Eng.
308 F3 Guynd Angus, Scot.
170 H7 Guy's Head Lincs., Eng.
46 F2 Guy's Marsh Dorset, Eng.
244 G4 Guyzance Northumb., Eng.
350 G3 Gwaelod-y-garth Cardiff, Wales
378 E2 Gwaenysgor Flints., Wales
366 G5 Gwaithla Powys, Wales
371 C3 Gwalchmai I.o.A., Wales
358 E2 Gwastad Pembs., Wales
372 F2 Gwastadnant Gwynedd, Wales
350 C2 Gwaun-Cae-Gurwen N.P.T., Wales
378 E2 Gwaynynog Denb., Wales
362 B4 Gwbert Cere., Wales
36 D3 Gweek Corn., Eng.
339 C2 Gwehelog Mon., Wales
366 E6 Gwenddwr Powys, Wales
36 D3 Gwendreath Corn., Eng.
36 D3 Gwennap Corn., Eng.
378 F2 Gwernaffield Flints., Wales
339 C2 Gwernesney Mon., Wales
356 F2 Gwernogle Carmar., Wales
378 F3 Gwernymynydd Flints., Wales
350 F4 Gwern-y-Steeple V. of Glam., Wales
378 G3 Gwersyllt Wrex., Wales
378 E1 Gwespyr Flints., Wales
36 C3 Gwinear Corn., Eng.
36 C3 Gwithian Corn., Eng.
371 C2 Gwredog I.o.A., Wales
350 G2 Gwrhay Caerp., Wales
378 E3 Gwyddelwern Denb., Wales
356 E3 Gwyddgrug Carmar., Wales
372 E3 Gwynedd county Wales
378 G3 Gwynfryn Wrex., Wales
366 E5 Gwystre Powys, Wales
372 G3 Gwytherin Conwy, Wales
378 G3 Gyfelia Wrex., Wales
378 C2 Gyffin Conwy, Wales
329 C4 Gyre Orkney, Scot.
372 D2 Gyrn Goch Gwynedd, Wales

H

144 C4 Habberley Shrop., Eng.
228 I4 Habergham Lancs., Eng.
58 A2 Habin W. Sussex, Eng.
170 E2 Habrough N.E. Lincs., Eng.
170 D7 Hacconby Lincs., Eng.
170 D6 Haceby Lincs., Eng.
120 H3 Hacheston Suff., Eng.
74 D3 Hackbridge Gtr Lon., Eng.
208 D3 Hackenthorpe S. Yorks., Eng.
166 F3 Hackford Norf., Eng.
216 E1 Hackforth N. Yorks., Eng.
329 C3 Hackland Orkney, Scot.
326 C4 Hacklet W. Isles, Scot.
128 E4 Hackleton Northants., Eng.
62 I3 Hacklinge Kent, Eng.
216 H2 Hackness N. Yorks., Eng.
329 C5 Hackness Orkney, Scot.
74 D2 Hackney Gtr Lon., Eng.
74 D2 Hackney met. bor. Gtr Lon., Eng.
74 D2 Hackney Wick Gtr Lon., Eng.
170 C4 Hackthorn Lincs., Eng.
232 F5 Hackthorpe Cumbria, Eng.
Haclait W. Isles, Scot. see Hacklet
74 F2 Hacton Gtr Lon., Eng.
256 J3 Hadden Borders, Scot.
106 C4 Haddenham Bucks., Eng.
124 E4 Haddenham Cambs., Eng.
170 C5 Haddington Lincs., Eng.
288 G3 Haddington E. Lothian, Scot.
166 I3 Haddiscoe Norf., Eng.
124 C3 Haddon Cambs., Eng.
222 D3 Hade Edge W. Yorks., Eng.
148 E3 Hademore Staffs., Eng.
154 B3 Haden Cross W. Mids, Eng.
180 B2 Hadfield Derbys., Eng.
110 F4 Hadham Cross Herts., Eng.
110 F4 Hadham Ford Herts., Eng.
116 F4 Hadleigh Essex, Eng.
120 E4 Hadleigh Suff., Eng.
120 E4 Hadleigh Heath Suff., Eng.
74 C2 Hadley Gtr Lon., Eng.
144 F3 Hadley Telford, Eng.
136 E2 Hadley Worcs., Eng.
148 E4 Hadley End Staffs., Eng.
74 D1 Hadley Wood Gtr Lon., Eng.
62 C3 Hadlow Kent, Eng.
58 H3 Hadlow Down E. Sussex, Eng.
144 D3 Hadnall Shrop., Eng.
24 M3 Hadrian's Wall tourist site Eng.
94 J4 Hadspen Som., Eng.
116 D1 Hadstock Essex, Eng.
244 H4 Hadston Northumb., Eng.
136 E2 Hadzor Worcs., Eng.
62 E4 Haffenden Quarter Kent, Eng.
356 G1 Hafod Bridge Carmar., Wales
378 D3 Hafod-Dinbych Conwy, Wales
378 C2 Hafodunos Conwy, Wales
350 H2 Hafodyrynys Caerp., Wales
228 I4 Haggate Lancs., Eng.
232 F2 Haggbeck Cumbria, Eng.
331 D3 Haggersta Shet., Scot.
74 D2 Haggerston Gtr Lon., Eng.
244 F1 Haggerston Northumb., Eng.
331 C2 Haggrister Shet., Scot.
280 C3 Haggs Falk., Scot.
140 D3 Hagley Here., Eng.
136 E1 Hagley Worcs., Eng.
120 E4 Hagmore Green Suff., Eng.
170 G5 Hagnaby Lincs., Eng.
170 H4 Hagnaby Lincs., Eng.
180 A2 Hague Bar Derbys., Eng.
170 G4 Hagworthingham Lincs., Eng.
198 B2 Haigh Gtr Man., Eng.
228 G4 Haighton Green Lancs., Eng.
232 B6 Haile Cumbria, Eng.
98 H2 Hailes Glos., Eng.
110 E5 Hailey Herts., Eng.
102 C4 Hailey Oxon, Eng.
102 E5 Hailey Oxon, Eng.
58 H3 Hailsham E. Sussex, Eng.
124 C5 Hail Weston Cambs., Eng.
320 J2 Haimer High., Scot.
74 E2 Hainault Gtr Lon., Eng.
62 I2 Haine Kent, Eng.
166 G2 Hainford Norf., Eng.
170 E3 Hainton Lincs., Eng.
222 C1 Hainworth W. Yorks., Eng.
210 G2 Haisthorpe E. Riding, Eng.
358 D3 Hakin Pembs., Wales
176 D4 Halam Notts., Eng.
292 D3 Halbeath Fife, Scot.
40 F2 Halberton Devon, Eng.
320 K2 Halcro High., Scot.
232 F7 Hale Cumbria, Eng.
198 C3 Hale Gtr Man., Eng.
190 E3 Hale Halton, Eng.
52 B5 Hale Hants., Eng.
62 D2 Hale Medway, Eng.
78 B2 Hale Surr., Eng.
190 E3 Hale Bank Halton, Eng.
198 C3 Hale Barns Gtr Man., Eng.
74 E2 Hale End Gtr Lon., Eng.
228 E3 Hale Nook Lancs., Eng.
166 I3 Hales Norf., Eng.
148 A3 Hales Staffs., Eng.
180 C5 Hales Green Derbys., Eng.
154 B3 Halesowen W. Mids, Eng.
62 G3 Hales Place Kent, Eng.
62 C3 Hale Street Kent, Eng.
120 H2 Halesworth Suff., Eng.
190 E3 Halewood Merseyside, Eng.
144 D5 Halford Shrop., Eng.
132 C5 Halford Warks., Eng.
232 F7 Halfpenny Cumbria, Eng.
144 G4 Halfpenny Green Shrop., Eng.
208 D4 Halfway S. Yorks., Eng.
82 B3 Halfway W. Berks., Eng.
356 F3 Halfway Carmar., Wales
356 G3 Halfway Carmar., Wales
366 C7 Halfway Powys, Wales
58 B3 Halfway Bridge W. Sussex, Eng.
144 C3 Halfway House Shrop., Eng.
62 E2 Halfway Houses Kent, Eng.
170 B5 Halfway Houses Lincs., Eng.
40 F2 Half Way Inn Devon, Eng.
378 H4 Halghton Mill Wrex., Wales
222 C2 Halifax W. Yorks., Eng.
322 B2 Halistra High., Scot.
262 D2 Halket E. Ayr., Scot.
320 J2 Halkirk High., Scot.
378 F2 Halkyn Flints., Wales
276 C3 Hall E. Renf., Scot.
20 F2 Halladale r. Scot.
208 C3 Hallam Head S. Yorks., Eng.
58 G3 Halland E. Sussex, Eng.
162 F3 Hallaton Leics., Eng.
94 I3 Hallatrow B. and N.E. Som., Eng.
232 G3 Hallbankgate Cumbria, Eng.
232 G7 Hallbeck Cumbria, Eng.
166 I2 Hall Common Norf., Eng.
228 E4 Hall Cross Lancs., Eng.
232 C6 Hall Dunnerdale Cumbria, Eng.
98 D4 Hallen S. Glos., Eng.
180 E4 Hallfield Gate Derbys., Eng.
236 G3 Hallgarth Durham, Eng.
280 D3 Hallglen Falk., Scot.
184 F3 Hall Green Cheshire East, Eng.
228 F5 Hall Green Lancs., Eng.
166 F4 Hall Green Norf., Eng.
154 C3 Hall Green W. Mids, Eng.
110 D5 Hall Grove Herts., Eng.
322 B2 Hallin High., Scot.
62 C2 Halling Medway, Eng.
170 F3 Hallington Lincs., Eng.
244 E5 Hallington Northumb., Eng.
198 C2 Halliwell Gtr Man., Eng.
144 B5 Hall of the Forest Shrop., Eng.
176 D4 Halloughton Notts., Eng.
136 D2 Hallow Worcs., Eng.
136 D2 Hallow Heath Worcs., Eng.
256 I4 Hallrule Borders, Scot.
288 H3 Halls E. Lothian, Scot.
40 F4 Hallsands Devon, Eng.
116 C3 Halls Green Essex, Eng.
110 E4 Hall's Green Herts., Eng.
232 C7 Hallthwaites Cumbria, Eng.
98 E3 Hallwood Green Glos., Eng.
36 F2 Hallworthy Corn., Eng.
256 G3 Hallyne Borders, Scot.
148 B2 Halmer End Staffs., Eng.
140 C3 Halmond's Frome Here., Eng.
98 E3 Halmore Glos., Eng.
256 E2 Halmyre Mains Borders, Scot.
58 B3 Halnaker W. Sussex, Eng.
228 E5 Halsall Lancs., Eng.
128 B5 Halse Northants., Eng.
94 E4 Halse Som., Eng.
36 C3 Halsetown Corn., Eng.
210 H4 Halsham E. Riding, Eng.
40 D1 Halsinger Devon, Eng.
116 F2 Halstead Essex, Eng.
62 A3 Halstead Kent, Eng.
162 F3 Halstead Leics., Eng.
46 D2 Halstock Dorset, Eng.
94 E4 Halsway Som., Eng.
210 F4 Haltemprice Farm E. Riding, Eng.
170 F5 Haltham Lincs., Eng.
170 G6 Haltoft End Lincs., Eng.
106 D4 Halton Bucks., Eng.
190 E4 Halton Halton, Eng.
228 F2 Halton Lancs., Eng.
244 E5 Halton Northumb., Eng.
222 F2 Halton W. Yorks., Eng.
378 G4 Halton Wrex., Wales
190 E3 Halton admin. div. Eng.
190 E3 Halton Brook Halton, Eng.
216 D3 Halton East N. Yorks., Eng.
216 C2 Halton Gill N. Yorks., Eng.
228 F2 Halton Green Lancs., Eng.
170 G5 Halton Holegate Lincs., Eng.
244 B6 Halton Lea Gate Northumb., Eng.
228 F2 Halton Park Lancs., Eng.
216 C3 Halton West N. Yorks., Eng.
244 C6 Haltwhistle Northumb., Eng.
166 I3 Halvergate Norf., Eng.
40 E3 Halwell Devon, Eng.
40 D2 Halwill Devon, Eng.
40 D2 Halwill Junction Devon, Eng.
98 E3 Ham Glos., Eng.
98 G2 Ham Glos., Eng.
74 C3 Ham Gtr Lon., Eng.
62 H3 Ham Kent, Eng.
94 F4 Ham Som., Eng.
94 F5 Ham Som., Eng.
86 F3 Ham Wilts., Eng.
320 K2 Ham High., Scot.
331 A3 Ham Shet., Scot.
331 D3 Ham Shet., Scot.
106 C5 Hambleden Bucks., Eng.
52 F5 Hambledon Hants., Eng.
78 C3 Hambledon Surr., Eng.
52 E5 Hamble-le-Rice Hants., Eng.
228 E3 Hambleton Lancs., Eng.
216 F3 Hambleton N. Yorks., Eng.
24 O5 Hambleton Hills hills Eng.
228 E3 Hambleton Moss Side Lancs., Eng.
94 G5 Hambridge Som., Eng.
98 D4 Hambrook S. Glos., Eng.
58 A3 Hambrook W. Sussex, Eng.
46 F1 Ham Common Dorset, Eng.
170 F4 Hameringham Lincs., Eng.
124 C4 Hamerton Cambs., Eng.
140 E3 Ham Green Here., Eng.
62 D2 Ham Green Kent, Eng.
62 E4 Ham Green Kent, Eng.
94 H2 Ham Green N. Som., Eng.
136 E2 Ham Green Worcs., Eng.
62 C3 Ham Hill Kent, Eng.
268 B2 Hamilton S. Lanark., Scot.
396 E3 Hamilton's Bawn Armagh, N. Ire.
40 G2 Hamlet Devon, Eng.
46 D2 Hamlet Dorset, Eng.
58 B2 Hammer W. Sussex, Eng.
58 D3 Hammerpot W. Sussex, Eng.
74 C3 Hammersmith Gtr Lon., Eng.
74 C3 Hammersmith and Fulham met. bor. Gtr Lon., Eng.
148 D4 Hammerwich Staffs., Eng.
58 G2 Hammerwood E. Sussex, Eng.
110 E5 Hammond Street Herts., Eng.
46 F2 Hammoon Dorset, Eng.
331 C2 Hamnavoe Shet., Scot.
331 D2 Hamnavoe Shet., Scot.
331 D2 Hamnavoe Shet., Scot.
331 D3 Hamnavoe Shet., Scot.
140 C2 Hamnish Clifford Here., Eng.
94 F4 Hamp Som., Eng.
58 H4 Hampden Park E. Sussex, Eng.
116 D2 Hamperden End Essex, Eng.
98 H3 Hampnett Glos., Eng.
208 E2 Hampole S. Yorks., Eng.
46 H3 Hampreston Dorset, Eng.
52 E3 Hampshire county Eng.
26 I5 Hampshire Downs hills Eng.
74 C2 Hampstead Gtr Lon., Eng.
74 C2 Hampstead Garden Suburb Gtr Lon., Eng.
82 C3 Hampstead Norreys W. Berks., Eng.
74 B3 Hampton Gtr Lon., Eng.
62 G2 Hampton Kent, Eng.
124 C3 Hampton Peterb., Eng.
144 F5 Hampton Shrop., Eng.
86 E2 Hampton Swindon, Eng.
136 F3 Hampton Worcs., Eng.
140 D3 Hampton Bishop Here., Eng.
98 G3 Hampton Fields Glos., Eng.
102 D3 Hampton Gay Oxon, Eng.
184 C3 Hampton Heath Cheshire West & Chester, Eng.
74 B3 Hampton Hill Gtr Lon., Eng.
154 D3 Hampton in Arden W. Mids, Eng.
144 F5 Hampton Loade Shrop., Eng.
136 D2 Hampton Lovett Worcs., Eng.
132 C4 Hampton Lucy Warks., Eng.
132 C4 Hampton on the Hill Warks., Eng.
102 D3 Hampton Poyle Oxon, Eng.
74 C3 Hampton Wick Gtr Lon., Eng.
86 F6 Hamptworth Wilts., Eng.
58 F3 Hamsey E. Sussex, Eng.
148 D4 Hamstall Ridware Staffs., Eng.
52 D6 Hamstead I.o.W., Eng.
154 C2 Hamstead W. Mids, Eng.
82 B3 Hamstead Marshall W. Berks., Eng.
236 E3 Hamsteels Durham, Eng.
236 E2 Hamsterley Durham, Eng.
236 E3 Hamsterley Durham, Eng.
62 F4 Hamstreet Kent, Eng.
94 I4 Ham Street Som., Eng.
46 G3 Hamworthy Poole, Eng.
148 E3 Hanbury Staffs., Eng.
136 E2 Hanbury Worcs., Eng.
148 E3 Hanbury Woodend Staffs., Eng.
170 D6 Hanby Lincs., Eng.
148 B3 Hanchurch Staffs., Eng.
22 F6 Handa Island i. Scot.
184 B2 Handbridge Cheshire West & Chester, Eng.
58 E2 Handcross W. Sussex, Eng.
184 F1 Handforth Cheshire East, Eng.
184 C3 Hand Green Cheshire West & Chester, Eng.
184 C3 Handley Cheshire West & Chester, Eng.
180 E4 Handley Derbys., Eng.
116 E3 Handley Green Essex, Eng.
148 D4 Handsacre Staffs., Eng.
110 D5 Handside Herts., Eng.
208 D3 Handsworth S. Yorks., Eng.
154 C2 Handsworth W. Mids, Eng.
144 D3 Handwoodbank Shrop., Eng.
106 D5 Handy Cross Bucks., Eng.
46 F2 Hanford Dorset, Eng.
148 B3 Hanford Stoke, Eng.
148 E2 Hanging Bridge Staffs., Eng.
128 D3 Hanging Houghton Northants., Eng.
86 D5 Hanging Langford Wilts., Eng.
252 F2 Hangingshaw D. and G., Scot.
58 E3 Hangleton B. and H., Eng.
58 D4 Hangleton W. Sussex, Eng.
98 D5 Hanham S. Glos., Eng.
184 E3 Hankelow Cheshire East, Eng.
86 C2 Hankerton Wilts., Eng.
58 H4 Hankham E. Sussex, Eng.
148 B2 Hanley Stoke, Eng.
136 D3 Hanley Castle Worcs., Eng.
136 D2 Hanley Child Worcs., Eng.
136 D3 Hanley Swan Worcs., Eng.
136 C2 Hanley William Worcs., Eng.
216 C2 Hanlith N. Yorks., Eng.
378 I4 Hanmer Wrex., Wales
170 H4 Hannah Lincs., Eng.
388 J5 Hannahstown Lisburn, N. Ire.
52 E3 Hannington Hants., Eng.
128 E3 Hannington Northants., Eng.
86 E2 Hannington Swindon, Eng.
86 E2 Hannington Wick Swindon, Eng.
106 D2 Hanslope M.K., Eng.
170 D7 Hanthorpe Lincs., Eng.
74 B2 Hanwell Gtr Lon., Eng.
102 C2 Hanwell Oxon, Eng.
144 D3 Hanwood Shrop., Eng.
74 B3 Hanworth Gtr Lon., Eng.
166 G1 Hanworth Norf., Eng.
166 I2 Happisburgh Norf., Eng.
166 I2 Happisburgh Common Norf., Eng.
184 C2 Hapsford Cheshire West & Chester, Eng.
228 I4 Hapton Lancs., Eng.
166 G3 Hapton Norf., Eng.
40 E3 Harberton Devon, Eng.
40 E3 Harbertonford Devon, Eng.
62 G3 Harbledown Kent, Eng.
154 C3 Harborne W. Mids, Eng.
132 E3 Harborough Magna Warks., Eng.
132 E3 Harborough Parva Warks., Eng.
326 F1 Harbost W. Isles, Scot.
244 E3 Harbottle Northumb., Eng.
388 C3 Harbour Museum Derry, N. Ire.
40 E3 Harbourneford Devon, Eng.
52 B5 Harbridge Hants., Eng.
52 B5 Harbridge Green Hants., Eng.
288 B3 Harburn W. Lothian, Scot.
132 D4 Harbury Warks., Eng.
162 F1 Harby Leics., Eng.
176 E3 Harby Notts., Eng.
154 C2 Harden W. Mids, Eng.
222 C1 Harden W. Yorks., Eng.
232 G5 Hardendale Cumbria, Eng.
86 C3 Hardenhuish Wilts., Eng.
314 F3 Hardgate Abers., Scot.
58 C3 Hardham W. Sussex, Eng.
228 E4 Hardhorn Lancs., Eng.
166 F3 Hardingham Norf., Eng.
128 D4 Hardingstone Northants., Eng.
148 B2 Hardings Wood Staffs., Eng.
94 J3 Hardington Som., Eng.
94 H5 Hardington Mandeville Som., Eng.
94 H5 Hardington Marsh Som., Eng.
52 D5 Hardley Hants., Eng.
166 I3 Hardley Street Norf., Eng.
106 E2 Hardmead M.K., Eng.
216 C2 Hardraw N. Yorks., Eng.
180 E4 Hardstoft Derbys., Eng.
52 F6 Hardway Hants., Eng.
94 J4 Hardway Som., Eng.
106 D3 Hardwick Bucks., Eng.
124 E5 Hardwick Cambs., Eng.
170 B4 Hardwick Lincs., Eng.
166 G4 Hardwick Norf., Eng.
128 E4 Hardwick Northants., Eng.
102 C4 Hardwick Oxon, Eng.
102 D3 Hardwick Oxon, Eng.
208 E3 Hardwick S. Yorks., Eng.
154 C2 Hardwick W. Mids, Eng.
98 F3 Hardwicke Glos., Eng.
98 G2 Hardwicke Glos., Eng.
140 A3 Hardwicke Here., Eng.
176 C3 Hardwick Village Notts., Eng.
116 G2 Hardy's Green Essex, Eng.
170 F4 Hareby Lincs., Eng.
222 C1 Harecroft W. Yorks., Eng.
228 G3 Hareden Lancs., Eng.
74 B2 Harefield Gtr Lon., Eng.
116 I2 Hare Green Essex, Eng.
82 E3 Hare Hatch W'ham, Eng.
180 C5 Harehill Derbys., Eng.
24 J2 Hare Hill hill Scot.
222 E2 Harehills W. Yorks., Eng.

Harehope to Highstreet Green

244 F3 Harehope Northumb., Eng.
268 D2 Harelaw S. Lanark., Scot.
62 D4 Hareplain Kent, Eng.
228 G4 Haresceugh Cumbria, Eng.
98 F3 Harescombe Glos., Eng.
98 F3 Haresfield Glos., Eng.
280 C4 Hareshaw N. Lanark., Scot.
268 A3 Hareshaw S. Lanark., Scot.
52 D4 Harestock Hants., Eng.
116 C3 Hare Street Essex, Eng.
110 E4 Hare Street Herts., Eng.
110 F4 Hare Street Herts., Eng.
222 E1 Harewood W. Yorks., Eng.
140 C4 Harewood End Here., Eng.
40 E3 Harford Devon, Eng.
166 F4 Hargate Norf., Eng.
180 C3 Hargatewall Derbys., Eng.
184 C3 Hargrave Cheshire West & Chester, Eng.
128 G4 Hargrave Northants., Eng.
120 C3 Hargrave Suff., Eng.
120 C3 Hargrave Green Suff., Eng.
74 D2 Haringey met. bor. Gtr Lon., Eng.
232 E3 Harker Cumbria, Eng.
120 G5 Harkstead Suff., Eng.
148 E4 Harlaston Staffs., Eng.
170 B6 Harlaxton Lincs., Eng.
372 F3 Harlech Gwynedd, Wales
176 C5 Harlequin Notts., Eng.
144 D3 Harlescott Shrop., Eng.
74 C2 Harlesden Gtr Lon., Eng.
166 G4 Harleston Norf., Eng.
120 E3 Harleston Suff., Eng.
128 D4 Harlestone Northants., Eng.
144 E4 Harley Shrop., Eng.
198 D3 Harley S. Yorks., Eng.
268 D3 Harleyholm S. Lanark., Scot.
110 C4 Harlington Central Bedfordshire, Eng.
74 B3 Harlington Gtr Lon., Eng.
322 B2 Harlosh High., Scot.
116 C3 Harlow Essex, Eng.
244 F5 Harlow Hill Northumb., Eng.
210 C4 Harlthorpe E. Riding, Eng.
124 E6 Harlton Cambs., Eng.
36 E2 Harlyn Corn., Eng.
46 G4 Harman's Cross Dorset, Eng.
216 D2 Harmby N. Yorks., Eng.
110 D5 Harmer Green Herts., Eng.
144 D3 Harmer Hill Shrop., Eng.
74 B3 Harmondsworth Gtr Lon., Eng.
170 C5 Harmston Lincs., Eng.
144 E4 Harnage Shrop., Eng.
86 E5 Harnham Wilts., Eng.
86 E5 Harnham Hill Wilts., Eng.
98 H3 Harnhill Glos., Eng.
74 F2 Harold Hill Gtr Lon., Eng.
74 F2 Harold Park Gtr Lon., Eng.
358 D3 Haroldston West Pembs., Wales
331 E1 Haroldswick Shet., Scot.
74 F2 Harold Wood Gtr Lon., Eng.
216 F2 Harome N. Yorks., Eng.
110 C5 Harpenden Herts., Eng.
40 G2 Harpford Devon, Eng.
210 G2 Harpham E. Riding, Eng.
166 C2 Harpley Norf., Eng.
136 C2 Harpley Worcs., Eng.
128 D4 Harpole Northants., Eng.
232 G7 Harprigg Cumbria, Eng.
102 F5 Harpsden Oxon, Eng.
170 C3 Harpswell Lincs., Eng.
198 D2 Harpurhey Gtr Man., Eng.
180 B3 Harpur Hill Derbys., Eng.
40 D1 Harracott Devon, Eng.
22 J4 Harray, Loch of l. Scot.
304 I4 Harrietfield Perth and Kin., Scot.
62 E3 Harrietsham Kent, Eng.
74 D2 Harringay Gtr Lon., Eng.
232 A5 Harrington Cumbria, Eng.
170 G4 Harrington Lincs., Eng.
128 D3 Harrington Northants., Eng.
128 F2 Harringworth Northants., Eng.
322 B4 Harris High., Scot.
22 C7 Harris reg. Scot.
22 B7 Harris, Sound of sea chan. Scot.
148 B2 Harriseahead Staffs., Eng.
166 G4 Harris Green Norf., Eng.
232 C4 Harriston Cumbria, Eng.
216 E3 Harrogate N. Yorks., Eng.
110 B2 Harrold Bedford, Eng.
228 H3 Harrop Fold Lancs., Eng.
74 B2 Harrow Gtr Lon., Eng.
74 B2 Harrow met. bor. Gtr Lon., Eng.
110 C3 Harrowden Bedford, Eng.
236 F4 Harrowgate Hill Darl., Eng.
120 D4 Harrow Green Suff., Eng.
74 B2 Harrow on the Hill Gtr Lon., Eng.
74 B2 Harrow Weald Gtr Lon., Eng.
98 D4 Harry Stoke S. Glos., Eng.
124 E6 Harston Cambs., Eng.
162 G1 Harston Leics., Eng.
210 D3 Harswell E. Riding, Eng.
236 H3 Hart Hartlepool, Eng.
244 F4 Hartburn Northumb., Eng.
236 G4 Hartburn Stockton, Eng.
198 D2 Hart Common Gtr Man., Eng.
24 L5 Harter Fell hill Eng.
120 D4 Hartest Suff., Eng.
58 G2 Hartfield E. Sussex, Eng.
322 D2 Hartfield High., Scot.
124 D4 Hartford Cambs., Eng.
184 D2 Hartford Cheshire West & Chester, Eng.
94 D4 Hartford Som., Eng.
184 D2 Hartfordbeach Cheshire West & Chester, Eng.
52 G3 Hartfordbridge Hants., Eng.
116 E3 Hartford End Essex, Eng.
216 D1 Hartforth N. Yorks., Eng.
46 F2 Hartgrove Dorset, Eng.
184 C3 Harthill Cheshire West & Chester, Eng.
110 C4 Hart Hill Luton, Eng.
280 D3 Harthill N. Lanark., Scot.
208 E4 Harthill S. Yorks., Eng.
180 C4 Hartington Derbys., Eng.
244 F4 Hartington Hall Northumb., Eng.
40 C2 Hartland Devon, Eng.
26 C5 Hartland Point pt Eng.
136 D1 Hartlebury Worcs., Eng.
236 H3 Hartlepool Hartlepool, Eng.
236 H3 Hartlepool admin. div. Eng.
232 H6 Hartley Cumbria, Eng.
62 B2 Hartley Kent, Eng.
62 D4 Hartley Kent, Eng.
244 I5 Hartley Northumb., Eng.
148 C3 Hartley Green Staffs., Eng.
52 G3 Hartley Wespall Hants., Eng.
52 G3 Hartley Wintney Hants., Eng.
216 D2 Hartlington N. Yorks., Eng.
62 D2 Hartlip Kent, Eng.
62 D2 Hartlip Hill Kent, Eng.
216 G2 Hartoft End N. Yorks., Eng.
216 G2 Harton N. Yorks., Eng.
144 D5 Harton Shrop., Eng.
236 G2 Harton T. and W., Eng.
98 F2 Hartpury Glos., Eng.
256 I4 Hartrigge Borders, Scot.
222 D2 Hartshead W. Yorks., Eng.
132 C2 Hartshill Warks., Eng.
180 D6 Hartshorne Derbys., Eng.
232 E5 Hartsop Cumbria, Eng.
106 C4 Hartwell Bucks., Eng.
58 G2 Hartwell E. Sussex, Eng.
128 D5 Hartwell Northants., Eng.
280 C4 Hartwood N. Lanark., Scot.
62 C2 Harvel Kent, Eng.
154 B2 Harvills Hawthorn W. Mids, Eng.
136 D1 Harvington Worcs., Eng.
136 F3 Harvington Worcs., Eng.
136 F3 Harvington Cross Worcs., Eng.
176 D2 Harwell Notts., Eng.
102 D5 Harwell Oxon, Eng.
116 J2 Harwich Essex, Eng.
236 B3 Harwood Durham, Eng.
198 C2 Harwood Gtr Man., Eng.
244 F4 Harwood Northumb., Eng.
216 H1 Harwood Dale N. Yorks., Eng.
198 C2 Harwood Lee Gtr Man., Eng.
256 G4 Harwood on Teviot Borders, Scot.
176 C2 Harworth Notts., Eng.
154 B3 Hasbury W. Mids, Eng.
78 C3 Hascombe Surr., Eng.
22 □O1 Hascosay i. Scot.
128 D3 Haselbech Northants., Eng.
94 H5 Haselbury Plucknett Som., Eng.
132 C4 Haseley Warks., Eng.
132 C3 Haseley Knob Warks., Eng.
132 B4 Haselor Warks., Eng.
98 F2 Hasfield Glos., Eng.
358 D3 Hasguard Pembs., Wales
228 E5 Haskayne Lancs., Eng.
120 G4 Hasketon Suff., Eng.
180 E3 Hasland Derbys., Eng.
180 E3 Hasland Green Derbys., Eng.
78 B3 Haslemere Surr., Eng.
228 I4 Haslingden Lancs., Eng.
228 H4 Haslingden Grane Lancs., Eng.
124 E6 Haslingfield Cambs., Eng.
184 E3 Haslington Cheshire East, Eng.
154 C3 Hasluck's Green W. Mids, Eng.
184 E3 Hassall Cheshire East, Eng.
184 F3 Hassall Green Cheshire East, Eng.
62 F3 Hassell Street Kent, Eng.
256 H4 Hassendean Borders, Scot.
166 H3 Hassingham Norf., Eng.
58 F3 Hassocks W. Sussex, Eng.
180 D3 Hassop Derbys., Eng.
320 K2 Haster High., Scot.
170 H4 Hasthorpe Lincs., Eng.
320 K2 Hastigrow High., Scot.
62 F4 Hastingleigh Kent, Eng.
58 J3 Hastings E. Sussex, Eng.
94 G5 Hastings Som., Eng.
116 C3 Hastingwood Essex, Eng.
110 A5 Hastoe Herts., Eng.
236 G3 Haswell Durham, Eng.
236 G3 Haswell Plough Durham, Eng.
110 D3 Hatch Central Bedfordshire, Eng.
52 F3 Hatch Hants., Eng.
94 G5 Hatch Beauchamp Som., Eng.
74 B2 Hatch End Gtr Lon., Eng.
94 F5 Hatch Green Som., Eng.
110 C5 Hatching Green Herts., Eng.
184 C2 Hatchmere Cheshire West & Chester, Eng.
170 E3 Hatcliffe N.E. Lincs., Eng.
140 D2 Hatfield Here., Eng.
110 D5 Hatfield Herts., Eng.
208 G2 Hatfield S. Yorks., Eng.
116 D3 Hatfield Broad Oak Essex, Eng.
110 D5 Hatfield Garden Village Herts., Eng.
116 D3 Hatfield Heath Essex, Eng.
110 D5 Hatfield Hyde Herts., Eng.
116 F3 Hatfield Peverel Essex, Eng.
208 G2 Hatfield Woodhouse S. Yorks., Eng.
102 B5 Hatford Oxon, Eng.
52 C3 Hatherden Hants., Eng.
40 D2 Hatherleigh Devon, Eng.
162 D2 Hathern Leics., Eng.
98 I3 Hatherop Glos., Eng.
180 D3 Hathersage Derbys., Eng.
180 D3 Hathersage Booths Derbys., Eng.
198 E2 Hathershaw Gtr Man., Eng.
184 E3 Hatherton Cheshire East, Eng.
148 C4 Hatherton Staffs., Eng.
124 D6 Hatley St George Cambs., Eng.
36 G2 Hatt Corn., Eng.
198 E3 Hattersley Gtr Man., Eng.
52 C4 Hatt Hill Hants., Eng.
52 F4 Hattingley Hants., Eng.
180 C5 Hatton Derbys., Eng.
74 B3 Hatton Gtr Lon., Eng.
170 E4 Hatton Lincs., Eng.
144 D4 Hatton Shrop., Eng.
132 C4 Hatton Warks., Eng.
190 F3 Hatton Warr., Eng.
314 H2 Hatton Abers., Scot.
314 F2 Hatton Castle Abers., Scot.
314 G3 Hattoncrook Abers., Scot.
184 C3 Hatton Heath Cheshire West & Chester, Eng.
314 G3 Hatton of Fintray Abers., Scot.
198 E2 Haugh Gtr Man., Eng.
170 G4 Haugh Lincs., Eng.
244 F2 Haugh Head Northumb., Eng.
276 E2 Haughhead E. Dun., Scot.
120 E3 Haughley Suff., Eng.
120 E3 Haughley Green Suff., Eng.
120 E3 Haughley New Street Suff., Eng.
314 E2 Haugh of Glass Moray, Scot.
252 E3 Haugh of Urr D. and G., Scot.
314 E2 Haughs Abers., Scot.
184 D3 Haughton Cheshire East, Eng.
176 D3 Haughton Notts., Eng.
144 C2 Haughton Shrop., Eng.
144 E3 Haughton Shrop., Eng.
144 F3 Haughton Shrop., Eng.
144 F4 Haughton Shrop., Eng.
148 B4 Haughton Staffs., Eng.
366 G2 Haughton Powys, Wales
198 E3 Haughton Green Gtr Man., Eng.
236 F4 Haughton Le Skerne Darl., Eng.
110 E4 Haultwick Herts., Eng.
326 C5 Haunn W. Isles, Scot.
148 F4 Haunton Staffs., Eng.
124 E6 Hauxton Cambs., Eng.
184 F2 Havannah Cheshire East, Eng.
52 G5 Havant Hants., Eng.
140 B2 Haven Here., Eng.
52 E6 Havenstreet I.o.W., Eng.
222 F3 Havercroft W. Yorks., Eng.
120 B4 Haverhill Suff., Eng.
232 C7 Haverigg Cumbria, Eng.
74 F2 Havering met. bor. Gtr Lon., Eng.
74 F2 Havering-atte-Bower Gtr Lon., Eng.
74 E2 Havering Park Gtr Lon., Eng.
106 D2 Haversham M.K., Eng.
232 D7 Haverthwaite Cumbria, Eng.
236 H4 Haverton Hill Stockton, Eng.
62 C3 Haviker Street Kent, Eng.
94 I4 Havyat Som., Eng.
378 G2 Hawarden Flints., Wales
136 E3 Hawbridge Worcs., Eng.
116 F2 Hawbush Green Essex, Eng.
232 C8 Hawcoat Cumbria, Eng.
362 D4 Hawen Cere., Wales
216 C2 Hawes N. Yorks., Eng.
166 G3 Hawe's Green Norf., Eng.
228 D4 Hawes Side Blackpool, Eng.
24 L4 Haweswater Reservoir resr Eng.
136 D2 Hawford Worcs., Eng.
256 H4 Hawick Borders, Scot.
40 H2 Hawkchurch Devon, Eng.
120 C4 Hawkedon Suff., Eng.
62 B4 Hawkenbury Kent, Eng.
62 D3 Hawkenbury Kent, Eng.
86 B4 Hawkeridge Wilts., Eng.
98 E4 Hawkesbury S. Glos., Eng.
98 F4 Hawkesbury Upton S. Glos., Eng.
154 E3 Hawkes End W. Mids, Eng.
198 E3 Hawk Green Gtr Man., Eng.
244 H3 Hawkhill Northumb., Eng.
208 F2 Hawkhouse Green S. Yorks., Eng.
62 D4 Hawkhurst Kent, Eng.
62 G4 Hawkinge Kent, Eng.
94 C4 Hawkridge Som., Eng.
232 D6 Hawkshead Cumbria, Eng.
232 D6 Hawkshead Hill Cumbria, Eng.
228 F2 Hawksheads Lancs., Eng.
268 D3 Hawksland S. Lanark., Scot.
216 C2 Hawkswick N. Yorks., Eng.
176 D5 Hawksworth Notts., Eng.
222 D1 Hawksworth W. Yorks., Eng.
222 E2 Hawksworth W. Yorks., Eng.
116 F4 Hawkwell Essex, Eng.
244 F5 Hawkwell Northumb., Eng.
52 H3 Hawley Hants., Eng.
62 B2 Hawley Kent, Eng.
74 E4 Hawley's Corner Gtr Lon., Eng.
98 H2 Hawling Glos., Eng.
216 F2 Hawnby N. Yorks., Eng.
222 C2 Haworth W. Yorks., Eng.
120 D3 Hawstead Green Suff., Eng.
236 G3 Hawthorn Durham, Eng.
52 G4 Hawthorn Hants., Eng.
86 B3 Hawthorn Wilts., Eng.
350 G3 Hawthorn R.C.T., Wales
82 F3 Hawthorn Hill Brack. F., Eng.
170 E5 Hawthorn Hill Lincs., Eng.
170 D6 Hawthorpe Lincs., Eng.
176 E4 Hawton Notts., Eng.
216 F2 Haxby York, Eng.
170 A3 Haxey N. Lincs., Eng.
170 A2 Haxey Turbary N. Lincs., Eng.
78 G2 Haxted Surr., Eng.
86 E4 Haxton Wilts., Eng.
144 F3 Haybridge Telford, Eng.
190 F3 Haydock Merseyside, Eng.
46 E2 Haydon Dorset, Eng.
94 F4 Haydon Som., Eng.
86 E2 Haydon Swindon, Eng.
244 D6 Haydon Bridge Northumb., Eng.
86 E2 Haydon Wick Swindon, Eng.
36 F2 Haye Corn., Eng.
74 B2 Hayes Gtr Lon., Eng.
74 E3 Hayes Gtr Lon., Eng.
74 B2 Hayes End Gtr Lon., Eng.
74 B2 Hayes Town Gtr Lon., Eng.
180 B2 Hayfield Derbys., Eng.
300 E2 Hayfield Arg. and B., Scot.
292 E3 Hayfield Fife, Scot.
144 E3 Haygate Telford, Eng.
166 A2 Hay Green Norf., Eng.
94 F4 Haygrove Som., Eng.
308 F3 Hayhillock Angus, Scot.
52 E6 Haylands I.o.W., Eng.
36 C3 Hayle Corn., Eng.
154 B3 Hayley Green W. Mids, Eng.
26 K6 Hayling Island i. Eng.
154 D3 Hay Mills W. Mids, Eng.
184 E3 Haymoor Green Cheshire East, Eng.
40 F2 Hayne Devon, Eng.
110 C3 Haynes Central Bedfordshire, Eng.
110 C3 Haynes Church End Central Bedfordshire, Eng.
110 C3 Haynes West End Central Bedfordshire, Eng.
366 G6 Hay-on-Wye Powys, Wales
52 G4 Hay Place Hants., Eng.
358 D2 Hayscastle Pembs., Wales
358 D2 Hayscastle Cross Pembs., Wales
110 F4 Hay Street Herts., Eng.
232 B4 Hayton Cumbria, Eng.
232 F3 Hayton Cumbria, Eng.
210 D3 Hayton E. Riding, Eng.
176 D2 Hayton Notts., Eng.
144 D5 Hayton's Bent Shrop., Eng.
40 E3 Haytor Vale Devon, Eng.
40 D2 Haytown Devon, Eng.
58 F3 Haywards Heath W. Sussex, Eng.
208 F2 Haywood S. Yorks., Eng.
176 C4 Haywood Oaks Notts., Eng.
58 I3 Hazard's Green E. Sussex, Eng.
300 E3 Hazelbank Arg. and B., Scot.
268 C2 Hazelbank S. Lanark., Scot.
358 E3 Hazelbeach Pembs., Wales
46 E2 Hazelbury Bryan Dorset, Eng.
116 F3 Hazeleigh Essex, Eng.
116 D2 Hazel End Essex, Eng.
52 G3 Hazeley Hants., Eng.
198 E3 Hazel Grove Gtr Man., Eng.
198 C2 Hazelhurst Gtr Man., Eng.
198 D2 Hazelhurst Gtr Man., Eng.
268 C3 Hazelside S. Lanark., Scot.
232 F7 Hazelslack Cumbria, Eng.
148 D4 Hazelslade Staffs., Eng.
62 C4 Hazel Street Kent, Eng.
292 F1 Hazelton Walls Fife, Scot.
180 D4 Hazelwood Derbys., Eng.
74 E3 Hazelwood Gtr Lon., Eng.
252 E3 Hazlefield D. and G., Scot.
208 B2 Hazlehead S. Yorks., Eng.
314 G3 Hazlehead Aberdeen, Scot.
106 D5 Hazlemere Bucks., Eng.
236 F1 Hazlerigg T. and W., Eng.
148 D2 Hazlescross Staffs., Eng.
98 H2 Hazleton Glos., Eng.
244 G3 Hazon Northumb., Eng.
166 B1 Heacham Norf., Eng.
52 E4 Headbourne Worthy Hants., Eng.
62 D3 Headcorn Kent, Eng.
222 E2 Headingley W. Yorks., Eng.
102 D4 Headington Oxon, Eng.
102 D4 Headington Hill Oxon, Eng.
236 E4 Headlam Durham, Eng.
136 F2 Headless Cross Worcs., Eng.
52 E2 Headley Hants., Eng.
52 H4 Headley Hants., Eng.
78 E2 Headley Surr., Eng.
136 F1 Headley Heath Worcs., Eng.
176 D3 Headon Notts., Eng.
232 F3 Heads Nook Cumbria, Eng.
22 G12 Heads of Ayr hd Scot.
198 D2 Heady Hill Gtr Man., Eng.
180 E4 Heage Derbys., Eng.
22 C8 Healabhal Bheag hill Scot.
216 D1 Healaugh N. Yorks., Eng.
216 F3 Healaugh N. Yorks., Eng.
198 D3 Heald Green Gtr Man., Eng.
40 E1 Heale Devon, Eng.
94 G4 Heale Som., Eng.
228 I5 Healey Lancs., Eng.
244 F6 Healey Northumb., Eng.
216 D2 Healey N. Yorks., Eng.
222 E2 Healey W. Yorks., Eng.
236 D3 Healeyfield Durham, Eng.
170 F2 Healing N.E. Lincs., Eng.
36 C3 Heamoor Corn., Eng.
232 E6 Heaning Cumbria, Eng.
300 □ Heanish Arg. and B., Scot.
180 E4 Heanor Derbys., Eng.
40 D1 Heanton Punchardon Devon, Eng.
198 D2 Heap Bridge Gtr Man., Eng.
228 G4 Heapey Lancs., Eng.
170 B3 Heapham Lincs., Eng.
52 H4 Hearn Hants., Eng.
256 D3 Hearthstane Borders, Scot.
40 E1 Heasley Mill Devon, Eng.
322 D3 Heast High., Scot.
180 E3 Heath Derbys., Eng.
222 F2 Heath W. Yorks., Eng.
350 G3 Heath Cardiff, Wales
110 B4 Heath and Reach Central Bedfordshire, Eng.
144 E2 Heathbrook Shrop., Eng.
180 C4 Heathcote Derbys., Eng.
144 E2 Heathcote Shrop., Eng.
128 D5 Heathencote Northants., Eng.
106 D4 Heath End Bucks., Eng.
180 E6 Heath End Derbys., Eng.
52 D2 Heath End Hants., Eng.
52 F2 Heath End Hants., Eng.
98 E4 Heath End S. Glos., Eng.
78 B2 Heath End Surr., Eng.
154 C2 Heath End W. Mids, Eng.
162 C2 Heather Leics., Eng.
184 E3 Heathfield Cheshire East, Eng.
40 F3 Heathfield Devon, Eng.
58 H3 Heathfield E. Sussex, Eng.
216 D2 Heathfield N. Yorks., Eng.
94 E4 Heathfield Som., Eng.
262 D4 Heathfield S. Ayr., Scot.
148 D4 Heath Hayes Staffs., Eng.
144 F3 Heath Hill Shrop., Eng.
94 H3 Heath House Som., Eng.
144 G4 Heathton Shrop., Eng.
154 B2 Heath Town W. Mids, Eng.
190 G3 Heatley Warr., Eng.
198 C2 Heaton Gtr Man., Eng.
228 E2 Heaton Lancs., Eng.
148 C2 Heaton Staffs., Eng.
236 F2 Heaton T. and W., Eng.
222 D2 Heaton W. Yorks., Eng.
198 D3 Heaton Chapel Gtr Man., Eng.
198 D3 Heaton Mersey Gtr Man., Eng.
198 D3 Heaton Moor Gtr Man., Eng.
198 D3 Heaton Norris Gtr Man., Eng.
228 E5 Heaton's Bridge Lancs., Eng.
62 B3 Heaverham Kent, Eng.
198 E3 Heaviley Gtr Man., Eng.
40 F2 Heavitree Devon, Eng.
236 F2 Hebburn T. and W., Eng.
216 D2 Hebden N. Yorks., Eng.
222 B2 Hebden Bridge W. Yorks., Eng.
184 D2 Hebden Green Cheshire West & Chester, Eng.
110 E4 Hebing End Herts., Eng.
22 C9 Hebrides, Sea of the sea Scot.
244 G4 Hebron Northumb., Eng.
356 C2 Hebron Carmar., Wales
252 F2 Heck D. and G., Scot.
52 G2 Heckfield Hants., Eng.
120 G2 Heckfield Green Suff., Eng.
116 G2 Heckfordbridge Essex, Eng.
166 I3 Heckingham Norf., Eng.
170 E6 Heckington Lincs., Eng.
222 D2 Heckmondwike W. Yorks., Eng.
86 C3 Heddington Wilts., Eng.
329 C4 Heddle Orkney, Scot.
244 G5 Heddon-on-the-Wall Northumb., Eng.
166 H4 Hedenham Norf., Eng.
52 E5 Hedge End Hants., Eng.
106 E5 Hedgerley Bucks., Eng.
94 G4 Hedging Som., Eng.
244 F6 Hedley on the Hill Northumb., Eng.
148 D4 Hednesford Staffs., Eng.
210 G4 Hedon E. Riding, Eng.
106 D5 Hedsor Bucks., Eng.
236 G2 Hedworth T. and W., Eng.
208 D3 Heeley S. Yorks., Eng.
331 D3 Heglibister Shet., Scot.
236 F4 Heighington Darl., Eng.
170 D4 Heighington Lincs., Eng.
136 C1 Heightington Worcs., Eng.
320 G2 Heilam High., Scot.
Heisker Islands is Scot. see Monach Islands
252 G2 Heithat D. and G., Scot.
256 J3 Heiton Borders, Scot.
40 D1 Hele Devon, Eng.
40 E3 Hele Devon, Eng.
40 F2 Hele Devon, Eng.
94 F4 Hele Som., Eng.
40 F3 Hele Torbay, Eng.
396 J1 Helen's Bay North Down, N. Ire.
300 F3 Helensburgh Arg. and B., Scot.
36 D3 Helford Corn., Eng.
166 D2 Helhoughton Norf., Eng.
116 E1 Helions Bumpstead Essex, Eng.
208 E3 Hellaby S. Yorks., Eng.
36 E2 Helland Corn., Eng.
94 G4 Helland Som., Eng.
36 E2 Hellandbridge Corn., Eng.
82 B3 Hell Corner W. Berks., Eng.
166 G3 Hellesdon Norf., Eng.
128 B4 Hellidon Northants., Eng.
216 C2 Hellifield N. Yorks., Eng.
58 H3 Hellingly E. Sussex, Eng.
166 H3 Hellington Norf., Eng.
331 D3 Hellister Shet., Scot.
Hell's Mouth b. Wales see Porth Neigwl
128 C5 Helmdon Northants., Eng.
120 G4 Helmingham Suff., Eng.
320 J3 Helmsdale High., Scot.
22 I6 Helmsdale r. Scot.
228 I4 Helmshore Lancs., Eng.
216 F2 Helmsley N. Yorks., Eng.
216 H2 Helperthorpe N. Yorks., Eng.
170 E6 Helpringham Lincs., Eng.
124 B3 Helpston Peterb., Eng.
184 C2 Helsby Cheshire West & Chester, Eng.
170 H4 Helsey Lincs., Eng.
36 D3 Helston Corn., Eng.
36 E2 Helstone Corn., Eng.
232 F5 Helton Cumbria, Eng.
24 K4 Helvellyn hill Eng.
216 D1 Helwith N. Yorks., Eng.
216 C2 Helwith Bridge N. Yorks., Eng.
366 G3 Hem Powys, Wales
166 H3 Hemblington Norf., Eng.
110 C5 Hemel Hempstead Herts., Eng.
216 G3 Hemingbrough N. Yorks., Eng.
170 F4 Hemingby Lincs., Eng.
208 D2 Hemingfield S. Yorks., Eng.
124 D5 Hemingford Abbots Cambs., Eng.
124 D5 Hemingford Grey Cambs., Eng.
120 F4 Hemingstone Suff., Eng.
162 D1 Hemington Leics., Eng.
128 G3 Hemington Northants., Eng.
94 J3 Hemington Som., Eng.
120 G4 Hemley Suff., Eng.
120 H3 Hemp Green Suff., Eng.
210 F3 Hempholme E. Riding, Eng.
166 G3 Hempnall Norf., Eng.
166 G4 Hempnall Green Norf., Eng.
314 C2 Hempriggs Moray, Scot.
116 E1 Hempstead Essex, Eng.
62 D2 Hempstead Medway, Eng.
166 F1 Hempstead Norf., Eng.
166 I2 Hempstead Norf., Eng.
98 F2 Hempsted Glos., Eng.
166 E2 Hempton Norf., Eng.
102 C3 Hempton Oxon, Eng.
166 J2 Hemsby Norf., Eng.
170 C3 Hemswell Lincs., Eng.
170 C3 Hemswell Cliff Lincs., Eng.
222 F3 Hemsworth W. Yorks., Eng.
40 G2 Hemyock Devon, Eng.
94 I1 Henbury Bristol, Eng.
184 F2 Henbury Cheshire East, Eng.
252 E2 Henderland D. and G., Scot.
256 J3 Hendersyde Park Borders, Scot.
40 E3 Hendham Devon, Eng.
74 C2 Hendon Gtr Lon., Eng.
236 G2 Hendon T. and W., Eng.
36 F2 Hendraburnick Corn., Eng.
350 E3 Hendre Bridg., Wales
372 C3 Hendre Gwynedd, Wales
350 F3 Hendreforgan R.C.T., Wales
356 F3 Hendy Carmar., Wales
Hendy-Gwyn Carmar., Wales see Whitland
371 C3 Heneglwys I.o.A., Wales
98 E4 Henfield S. Glos., Eng.
58 E3 Henfield W. Sussex, Eng.
62 E4 Hengherst Kent, Eng.
144 B2 Hengoed Shrop., Eng.
350 G3 Hengoed Caerp., Wales
366 G5 Hengoed Powys, Wales
120 D3 Hengrave Suff., Eng.
116 D2 Henham Essex, Eng.
366 F3 Heniarth Powys, Wales
94 F4 Henlade Som., Eng.
46 E2 Henley Dorset, Eng.
144 D5 Henley Shrop., Eng.
94 H4 Henley Som., Eng.
94 H5 Henley Som., Eng.
120 F4 Henley Suff., Eng.
58 B2 Henley W. Sussex, Eng.
94 H4 Henley Corner Som., Eng.
132 B4 Henley-in-Arden Warks., Eng.
102 F5 Henley-on-Thames Oxon, Eng.
78 C2 Henley Park Surr., Eng.
58 I3 Henley's Down E. Sussex, Eng.
62 C2 Henley Street Kent, Eng.
356 D1 Henllan Carmar., Wales
378 E2 Henllan Denb., Wales
356 C2 Henllan Amgoed Carmar., Wales
350 H3 Henllys B. Gwent, Wales
339 B3 Henllys Vale Torf., Wales
110 D3 Henlow Central Bedfordshire, Eng.
40 F3 Hennock Devon, Eng.
116 G1 Henny Street Essex, Eng.
378 B2 Henryd Conwy, Wales
358 E2 Henry's Moat Pembs., Wales
216 F3 Hensall N. Yorks., Eng.
244 C6 Henshaw Northumb., Eng.
232 A5 Hensingham Cumbria, Eng.
120 J2 Henstead Suff., Eng.
52 E5 Hensting Hants., Eng.
94 J5 Henstridge Som., Eng.
94 J5 Henstridge Ash Som., Eng.
94 J5 Henstridge Bowden Som., Eng.
94 J5 Henstridge Marsh Som., Eng.
102 F4 Henton Oxon, Eng.
94 H3 Henton Som., Eng.
136 D2 Henwick Worcs., Eng.
36 F2 Henwood Corn., Eng.
62 B4 Henwood Green Kent, Eng.
331 D3 Heogan Shet., Scot.
356 F3 Heol-ddu Carmar., Wales
350 F2 Heolgerrig M. Tyd., Wales
366 D7 Heol Senni Powys, Wales
350 E3 Heol-y-Cyw Bridg., Wales
244 F2 Hepburn Northumb., Eng.
244 F2 Hepburn Bell Northumb., Eng.
244 E4 Hepple Northumb., Eng.
244 H5 Hepscott Northumb., Eng.
180 E3 Hepthorne Lane Derbys., Eng.
222 B2 Heptonstall W. Yorks., Eng.
120 E2 Hepworth Suff., Eng.
222 D3 Hepworth W. Yorks., Eng.
120 E3 Hepworth South Common Suff., Eng.
358 D3 Herbrandston Pembs., Wales
140 C3 Hereford Here., Eng.
140 C3 Herefordshire county Eng.
256 G2 Heriot Borders, Scot.
22 □O1 Herma Ness hd Scot.
288 D3 Hermiston Edin., Scot.
46 D2 Hermitage Dorset, Eng.
82 C3 Hermitage W. Berks., Eng.
256 H5 Hermitage Borders, Scot.
252 E3 Hermitage D. and G., Scot.
190 F3 Hermitage Green Warr., Eng.
208 C2 Hermit Hill S. Yorks., Eng.
356 D2 Hermon Carmar., Wales
371 C3 Hermon I.o.A., Wales
358 G2 Hermon Pembs., Wales
62 G2 Herne Kent, Eng.
62 G2 Herne Bay Kent, Eng.
62 G2 Herne Common Kent, Eng.
62 C3 Herne Pound Kent, Eng.
40 D1 Herner Devon, Eng.
62 F3 Hernhill Kent, Eng.
36 F2 Herodsfoot Corn., Eng.
116 E4 Herongate Essex, Eng.
110 B6 Heronsgate Herts., Eng.
58 G2 Heron's Ghyll E. Sussex, Eng.
52 F3 Herriard Hants., Eng.
120 I1 Herringfleet Suff., Eng.
110 C3 Herring's Green Bedford, Eng.
120 C3 Herringswell Suff., Eng.
208 E3 Herringthorpe S. Yorks., Eng.
62 G3 Hersden Kent, Eng.
36 F1 Hersham Corn., Eng.
78 D1 Hersham Surr., Eng.
58 H3 Herstmonceux E. Sussex, Eng.
46 H4 Herston Dorset, Eng.
329 C5 Herston Orkney, Scot.
110 E5 Hertford Herts., Eng.
110 E5 Hertford Heath Herts., Eng.
110 D5 Hertfordshire county Eng.
110 E5 Hertingfordbury Herts., Eng.
228 E4 Hesketh Bank Lancs., Eng.
228 G3 Hesketh Lane Lancs., Eng.
232 D4 Hesket Newmarket Cumbria, Eng.
228 F5 Heskin Green Lancs., Eng.
236 H3 Hesleden Durham, Eng.
244 D5 Hesleyside Northumb., Eng.
216 F3 Heslington York, Eng.
216 F3 Hessay York, Eng.
36 F2 Hessenford Corn., Eng.
120 D3 Hessett Suff., Eng.
210 F4 Hessle E. Riding, Eng.
222 F3 Hessle W. Yorks., Eng.
228 F2 Hest Bank Lancs., Eng.
98 G2 Hester's Way Glos., Eng.
120 F3 Hestley Green Suff., Eng.
74 B3 Heston Gtr Lon., Eng.
190 C4 Heswall Merseyside, Eng.
102 E3 Hethe Oxon, Eng.
98 F2 Hethelpit Cross Glos., Eng.
244 D5 Hetherington Northumb., Eng.
166 G3 Hethersett Norf., Eng.
232 F3 Hethersgill Cumbria, Eng.
244 D2 Hethpool Northumb., Eng.
236 F3 Hett Durham, Eng.
216 C2 Hetton N. Yorks., Eng.
236 G3 Hetton Downs T. and W., Eng.
236 G3 Hetton-le-Hole T. and W., Eng.
244 F5 Heugh Northumb., Eng.
314 D3 Heugh-head Abers., Scot.
120 H3 Heveningham Suff., Eng.
62 A3 Hever Kent, Eng.
232 F7 Heversham Cumbria, Eng.
166 G2 Hevingham Norf., Eng.
136 F2 Hewell Lane Worcs., Eng.
98 D3 Hewelsfield Glos., Eng.
98 D3 Hewelsfield Common Glos., Eng.
94 G2 Hewish N. Som., Eng.
94 H5 Hewish Som., Eng.
46 B3 Hewood Dorset, Eng.
236 F2 Heworth T. and W., Eng.
244 E6 Hexham Northumb., Eng.
62 B2 Hextable Kent, Eng.
208 F2 Hexthorpe S. Yorks., Eng.
110 C4 Hexton Herts., Eng.
40 E3 Hexworthy Devon, Eng.
228 I3 Hey Lancs., Eng.
116 E4 Heybridge Essex, Eng.
116 G3 Heybridge Essex, Eng.
116 G3 Heybridge Basin Essex, Eng.
40 D4 Heybrook Bay Devon, Eng.
124 E6 Heydon Cambs., Eng.
166 F2 Heydon Norf., Eng.
170 D6 Heydour Lincs., Eng.
228 D4 Hey Houses Lancs., Eng.
300 □ Heylipoll Arg. and B., Scot.
331 C2 Heylor Shet., Scot.
366 G4 Heyop Powys, Wales
198 E3 Heyrod Gtr Man., Eng.
228 E2 Heysham Lancs., Eng.
216 D2 Heyshaw N. Yorks., Eng.
58 B3 Heyshott W. Sussex, Eng.
198 E2 Heyside Gtr Man., Eng.
86 C4 Heytesbury Wilts., Eng.
102 C3 Heythrop Oxon, Eng.
198 D2 Heywood Gtr Man., Eng.
86 B4 Heywood Wilts., Eng.
170 C2 Hibaldstow N. Lincs., Eng.
120 D4 Hibb's Green Suff., Eng.
208 E2 Hickleton S. Yorks., Eng.
166 I2 Hickling Norf., Eng.
176 D5 Hickling Notts., Eng.
166 I2 Hickling Green Norf., Eng.
166 I2 Hickling Heath Norf., Eng.
58 E3 Hickstead W. Sussex, Eng.
98 I1 Hidcote Bartrim Glos., Eng.
98 I1 Hidcote Boyce Glos., Eng.
222 F3 High Ackworth W. Yorks., Eng.
180 E4 Higham Derbys., Eng.
62 C2 Higham Kent, Eng.
228 I4 Higham Lancs., Eng.
120 C3 Higham Suff., Eng.
120 E5 Higham Suff., Eng.
208 C2 Higham S. Yorks., Eng.
244 G5 Higham Dykes Northumb., Eng.
128 F4 Higham Ferrers Northants., Eng.
110 C4 Higham Gobion Central Bedfordshire, Eng.
74 D2 Higham Hill Gtr Lon., Eng.
162 C3 Higham on the Hill Leics., Eng.
74 D2 Highams Park Gtr Lon., Eng.
62 B3 Higham Wood Kent, Eng.
244 F5 High Angerton Northumb., Eng.
232 F4 High Bankhill Cumbria, Eng.
74 C2 High Barnet Gtr Lon., Eng.
116 C4 High Beach Essex, Eng.
216 B2 High Bentham N. Yorks., Eng.
40 E2 High Bickington Devon, Eng.
216 C2 High Birkwith N. Yorks., Eng.
268 B2 High Blantyre S. Lanark., Scot.
280 C3 High Bonnybridge Falk., Scot.
252 D3 High Borgue D. and G., Scot.
326 E1 High Borve W. Isles, Scot.
208 C3 High Bradfield S. Yorks., Eng.
216 D3 High Bradley N. Yorks., Eng.
210 G4 High Bransholme Hull, Eng.
232 E4 High Bridge Cumbria, Eng.
52 D5 Highbridge Hants., Eng.
94 G3 Highbridge Som., Eng.
58 F2 Highbrook W. Sussex, Eng.
62 B4 High Brooms Kent, Eng.
40 D2 High Bullen Devon, Eng.
222 D3 Highburton W. Yorks., Eng.
74 D2 Highbury Gtr Lon., Eng.
94 J3 Highbury Som., Eng.
176 B5 Highbury Vale Nott., Eng.
244 H3 High Buston Northumb., Eng.
244 G5 High Callerton Northumb., Eng.
232 G7 High Casterton Cumbria, Eng.
210 C3 High Catton E. Riding, Eng.
244 G5 High Church Northumb., Eng.
52 D2 Highclere Hants., Eng.
46 I3 Highcliffe Dorset, Eng.
236 E4 High Close Durham, Eng.
102 C4 High Cogges Oxon, Eng.
166 G4 High Common Norf., Eng.
236 F4 High Coniscliffe Darl., Eng.
198 E2 High Crompton Gtr Man., Eng.
52 G4 High Cross Hants., Eng.
110 E4 High Cross Herts., Eng.
132 B4 High Cross Warks., Eng.
58 E3 High Cross W. Sussex, Eng.
180 D6 High Cross Bank Derbys., Eng.
232 F4 High Dyke Cumbria, Eng.
116 E3 High Easter Essex, Eng.
94 J3 Higher Alham Som., Eng.
46 F2 Higher Ansty Dorset, Eng.
40 F3 Higher Ashton Devon, Eng.
228 E4 Higher Ballam Lancs., Eng.
228 F4 Higher Bartle Lancs., Eng.
Higher Bentham N. Yorks., Eng. see High Bentham
198 D2 Higher Blackley Gtr Man., Eng.
40 F3 Higher Brixham Torbay, Eng.
198 D2 Higher Broughton Gtr Man., Eng.
144 E3 High Ercall Telford, Eng.
46 D3 Higher Chalmington Dorset, Eng.
94 C4 Higher Combe Som., Eng.
180 B2 Higher Dinting Derbys., Eng.
198 C2 Higher Folds Gtr Man., Eng.
198 C3 Higher Green Gtr Man., Eng.
46 C2 Higher Halstock Leigh Dorset, Eng.
46 D3 Higher Kingcombe Dorset, Eng.
378 G3 Higher Kinnerton Flints., Wales
46 E2 Higher Nyland Dorset, Eng.
190 E3 Higher Runcorn Halton, Eng.
378 G2 Higher Shotton Flints., Wales
184 E2 Higher Shurlach Cheshire West & Chester, Eng.
228 H3 Higher Standen Lancs., Eng.
228 G2 Higher Thrushgill Lancs., Eng.
36 E2 Higher Town Corn., Eng.
36 □ Higher Town I.o.S., Eng.
228 G4 Higher Walton Lancs., Eng.
190 F3 Higher Walton Warr., Eng.
94 F5 Higher Wambrook Som., Eng.
46 F3 Higher Whatcombe Dorset, Eng.
228 G4 Higher Wheelton Lancs., Eng.
36 F1 Higher Whiteleigh Corn., Eng.
184 D2 Higher Whitley Cheshire West & Chester, Eng.
184 E2 Higher Wincham Cheshire West & Chester, Eng.
198 D2 Higher Woodhill Gtr Man., Eng.
46 F3 Higher Woodsford Dorset, Eng.
46 D3 Higher Wraxall Dorset, Eng.
378 I4 Higher Wych Wrex., Wales
236 E4 High Etherley Durham, Eng.
236 F2 High Fell T. and W., Eng.
236 F2 High Felling T. and W., Eng.
170 G5 High Ferry Lincs., Eng.
210 C4 Highfield E. Riding, Eng.
110 C5 Highfield Herts., Eng.
102 D3 Highfield Oxon, Eng.
52 D5 Highfield Soton, Eng.
208 D3 Highfield S. Yorks., Eng.
236 E2 Highfield T. and W., Eng.
264 F2 Highfield N. Ayr., Scot.
124 D5 Highfields Cambs., Eng.
244 E1 Highfields Northumb., Eng.
236 F2 High Flatts Durham, Eng.
222 D3 High Flatts W. Yorks., Eng.
116 F2 High Garrett Essex, Eng.
74 D2 Highgate Gtr Lon., Eng.
222 B2 High Gate W. Yorks., Eng.
236 E3 High Grange Durham, Eng.
166 E2 High Green Norf., Eng.
166 E3 High Green Norf., Eng.
166 F3 High Green Norf., Eng.
216 C1 High Green N. Yorks., Eng.
120 D3 High Green Suff., Eng.
208 D3 High Green S. Yorks., Eng.
136 D3 High Green Worcs., Eng.
244 D4 Highgreen Manor Northumb., Eng.
62 E4 High Halden Kent, Eng.
62 D2 High Halstow Medway, Eng.
94 H4 High Ham Som., Eng.
232 A5 High Harrington Cumbria, Eng.
216 E3 High Harrogate N. Yorks., Eng.
144 E3 High Hatton Shrop., Eng.
244 H4 High Hauxley Northumb., Eng.
216 H1 High Hawsker N. Yorks., Eng.
144 F2 High Heath Shrop., Eng.
154 C2 High Heath W. Mids, Eng.
232 F4 High Hesket Cumbria, Eng.
236 H3 High Hesleden Durham, Eng.
208 C2 High Hoyland S. Yorks., Eng.
210 E4 High Hunsley E. Riding, Eng.
216 G2 High Hutton N. Yorks., Eng.
232 C4 High Ireby Cumbria, Eng.
166 F1 High Kelling Norf., Eng.
216 G2 High Kingthorpe N. Yorks., Eng.
232 F5 High Knipe Cumbria, Eng.
322 F3 Highland admin. div. Scot.
184 F2 Highlane Cheshire East, Eng.
180 E2 Highlane Derbys., Eng.
180 E5 High Lane Derbys., Eng.
198 E3 High Lane Gtr Man., Eng.
148 B2 High Lane Staffs., Eng.
136 C2 High Lane Worcs., Eng.
116 D3 High Laver Essex, Eng.
232 B3 Highlaws Cumbria, Eng.
98 F2 Highleadon Glos., Eng.
184 E1 High Legh Cheshire East, Eng.
58 B4 Highleigh W. Sussex, Eng.
236 H4 High Leven Stockton, Eng.
144 F5 Highley Shrop., Eng.
94 I3 High Littleton B. and N.E. Som., Eng.
232 C5 High Lorton Cumbria, Eng.
216 G2 High Marishes N. Yorks., Eng.
176 E3 High Marnham Notts., Eng.
362 E4 Highmead Cere., Wales
208 E2 High Melton S. Yorks., Eng.
244 F6 High Mickley Northumb., Eng.
180 F3 High Moor Derbys., Eng.
228 F5 High Moor Lancs., Eng.
102 F5 Highmoor Cross Oxon, Eng.
339 D3 Highmoor Hill Mon., Wales
236 G3 High Moorsley T. and W., Eng.
98 F2 Highnam Glos., Eng.
98 F2 Highnam Green Glos., Eng.
232 E7 High Newton Cumbria, Eng.
244 H2 High Newton-by-the-Sea Northumb., Eng.
232 D7 High Nibthwaite Cumbria, Eng.
148 B4 High Offley Staffs., Eng.
116 D3 High Ongar Essex, Eng.
148 B4 High Onn Staffs., Eng.
116 H2 High Park Corner Essex, Eng.
24 N7 High Peak hills Eng.
170 C2 High Risby N. Lincs., Eng.
116 D3 High Roding Essex, Eng.
58 D3 High Salvington W. Sussex, Eng.
24 M5 High Seat hill Eng.
236 E2 High Spen T. and W., Eng.
62 H2 Highstead Kent, Eng.
62 E3 Highsted Kent, Eng.
236 D3 High Stoop Durham, Eng.
62 C4 High Street Kent, Eng.
62 F3 Highstreet Kent, Eng.
120 D4 High Street Suff., Eng.
120 H2 High Street Suff., Eng.
120 I3 High Street Suff., Eng.
120 I4 High Street Suff., Eng.
116 F2 Highstreet Green Essex, Eng.

High Street Green to Ideford

120 E3 **High Street Green** *Suff., Eng.*
78 C3 **Highstreet Green** *Surr., Eng.*
252 F2 **Hightae** *D. and G., Scot.*
154 C3 **Highter's Heath** *W. Mids, Eng.*
236 H3 **High Throston** *Hartlepool, Eng.*
184 F3 **Hightown** *Cheshire East, Eng.*
52 B5 **Hightown** *Hants., Eng.*
190 C2 **Hightown** *Merseyside, Eng.*
148 C4 **High Town** *Staffs., Eng.*
388 K4 **Hightown** *Newtownabbey, N. Ire.*
120 E3 **Hightown Green** *Suff., Eng.*
170 F4 **High Toynton** *Lincs., Eng.*
244 F3 **High Trewhitt** *Northumb., Eng.*
244 E5 **High Warden** *Northumb., Eng.*
86 D3 **Highway** *Wilts., Eng.*
236 E2 **High Westwood** *Durham, Eng.*
236 E4 **High Wham** *Durham, Eng.*
58 J2 **High Wigsell** *E. Sussex, Eng.*
116 E3 **Highwood** *Essex, Eng.*
136 B2 **Highwood** *Worcs., Eng.*
74 C2 **Highwood Hill** *Gtr Lon., Eng.*
98 D3 **High Woolaston** *Glos., Eng.*
86 E2 **Highworth** *Swindon, Eng.*
232 E6 **High Wray** *Cumbria, Eng.*
110 F5 **High Wych** *Herts., Eng.*
106 D5 **High Wycombe** *Bucks., Eng.*
166 D3 **Hilborough** *Norf., Eng.*
180 F4 **Hilcote** *Derbys., Eng.*
86 D4 **Hilcott** *Wilts., Eng.*
62 B3 **Hildenborough** *Kent, Eng.*
216 G2 **Hildenley** *N. Yorks., Eng.*
62 B3 **Hilden Park** *Kent, Eng.*
124 F6 **Hildersham** *Cambs., Eng.*
148 C3 **Hilderstone** *Staffs., Eng.*
210 G2 **Hilderthorpe** *E. Riding, Eng.*
46 D2 **Hilfield** *Dorset, Eng.*
166 B3 **Hilgay** *Norf., Eng.*
98 D4 **Hill** *S. Glos., Eng.*
132 D4 **Hill** *Warks., Eng.*
136 E3 **Hill** *Worcs., Eng.*
216 F3 **Hillam** *N. Yorks., Eng.*
232 I5 **Hillbeck** *Cumbria, Eng.*
405 D2 **Hillberry** Isle of Man
62 H2 **Hillborough** *Kent, Eng.*
102 E5 **Hill Bottom** *Oxon, Eng.*
46 H3 **Hillbourne** *Poole, Eng.*
314 F2 **Hillbrae** *Abers., Scot.*
314 F3 **Hillbrae** *Abers., Scot.*
58 A2 **Hill Brow** *W. Sussex, Eng.*
46 G3 **Hillbutts** *Dorset, Eng.*
148 B3 **Hill Chorlton** *Staffs., Eng.*
180 D4 **Hillclifflane** *Derbys., Eng.*
166 I2 **Hill Common** *Norf., Eng.*
216 G1 **Hill Cottages** *N. Yorks., Eng.*
136 E3 **Hill Croome** *Worcs., Eng.*
86 B5 **Hill Deverill** *Wilts., Eng.*
170 G5 **Hill Dyke** *Lincs., Eng.*
236 D3 **Hill End** *Durham, Eng.*
98 G1 **Hill End** *Glos., Eng.*
74 B2 **Hill End** *Gtr Lon., Eng.*
216 D3 **Hill End** *N. Yorks., Eng.*
314 E2 **Hillend** *Abers., Scot.*
292 C3 **Hill End** *Fife, Scot.*
292 D3 **Hillend** *Fife, Scot.*
288 D3 **Hillend** *Midlothian, Scot.*
280 C3 **Hillend** *N. Lanark., Scot.*
350 A3 **Hillend** *Swansea, Wales*
98 E2 **Hillend Green** *Glos., Eng.*
98 D3 **Hillersland** *Glos., Eng.*
106 B3 **Hillesden** *Bucks., Eng.*
98 E4 **Hillesley** *S. Glos., Eng.*
94 E4 **Hillfarrance** *Som., Eng.*
110 C4 **Hillfoot End** *Central Bedfordshire, Eng.*
116 C2 **Hill Green** *Essex, Eng.*
82 B3 **Hillgreen** *W. Berks., Eng.*
388 J5 **Hillhall** *Lisburn, N. Ire.*
40 F3 **Hillhead** *Devon, Eng.*
52 E6 **Hill Head** *Hants., Eng.*
388 G4 **Hillhead** *Magherafelt, N. Ire.*
276 E2 **Hillhead** *Glas., Scot.*
262 E4 **Hillhead** *S. Ayr., Scot.*
314 G2 **Hillhead of Auchentumb** *Abers., Scot.*
144 E5 **Hill Houses** *Shrop., Eng.*
148 E4 **Hilliard's Cross** *Staffs., Eng.*
320 J2 **Hilliclay** *High., Scot.*
74 B2 **Hillingdon** *Gtr Lon., Eng.*
74 B2 **Hillingdon** *met. bor. Gtr Lon., Eng.*
166 C2 **Hillington** *Norf., Eng.*
276 D2 **Hillington** *Glas., Scot.*
132 E3 **Hillmorton** *Warks., Eng.*
358 E3 **Hill Mountain** *Pembs., Wales*
314 D3 **Hillockhead** *Abers., Scot.*
314 E3 **Hillockhead** *Abers., Scot.*
292 D3 **Hill of Beath** *Fife, Scot.*
252 E3 **Hillowton** *D. and G., Scot.*
52 E5 **Hillpound** *Hants., Eng.*
148 D4 **Hill Ridware** *Staffs., Eng.*
124 E4 **Hill Row** *Cambs., Eng.*
208 C3 **Hillsborough** *S. Yorks., Eng.*
388 J6 **Hillsborough** *Lisburn, N. Ire.*
110 B4 **Hill's End** *Central Bedfordshire, Eng.*
136 C2 **Hillside** *Worcs., Eng.*
222 D3 **Hill Side** *W. Yorks., Eng.*
314 G3 **Hillside** *Abers., Scot.*
308 H2 **Hillside** *Angus, Scot.*
314 C2 **Hillside** *Moray, Scot.*
331 D2 **Hillside** *Shet., Scot.*
180 C5 **Hill Somersal** *Derbys., Eng.*
180 F3 **Hills Town** *Derbys., Eng.*
52 C5 **Hill Street** *Hants., Eng.*
331 C2 **Hillswick** *Shet., Scot.*
198 C2 **Hill Top** *Gtr Man., Eng.*
52 D6 **Hill Top** *Hants., Eng.*
208 C3 **Hill Top** *S. Yorks., Eng.*
208 E3 **Hill Top** *S. Yorks., Eng.*
154 B2 **Hill Top** *W. Mids, Eng.*
222 C3 **Hill Top** *W. Yorks., Eng.*
222 E3 **Hill Top** *W. Yorks., Eng.*
396 H4 **Hilltown** *Newry & Mourne, N. Ire.*
46 G3 **Hill View** *Dorset, Eng.*
52 F6 **Hillway** *I.o.W., Eng.*
331 D4 **Hillwell** *Shet., Scot.*
132 C4 **Hill Wootton** *Warks., Eng.*
52 D5 **Hillyfields** *Hants., Eng.*
86 D3 **Hilmarton** *Wilts., Eng.*
86 B4 **Hilperton** *Wilts., Eng.*
24 K5 **Hilpsford Point** *pt Eng.*
52 F6 **Hilsea** *Ports., Eng.*
210 H4 **Hilston** *E. Riding, Eng.*
124 D5 **Hilton** *Cambs., Eng.*
232 H5 **Hilton** *Cumbria, Eng.*
180 D5 **Hilton** *Derbys., Eng.*
46 F3 **Hilton** *Dorset, Eng.*
236 E4 **Hilton** *Durham, Eng.*
144 G4 **Hilton** *Shrop., Eng.*
148 D5 **Hilton** *Staffs., Eng.*
236 H5 **Hilton** *Stockton, Eng.*
320 I4 **Hilton** *High., Scot.*
314 G2 **Hilton Croft** *Abers., Scot.*
322 J2 **Hilton of Delnies** *High., Scot.*
198 D2 **Hilton Park** *Gtr Man., Eng.*
136 E2 **Himbleton** *Worcs., Eng.*
148 B5 **Himley** *Staffs., Eng.*
232 F7 **Hincaster** *Cumbria, Eng.*
78 D1 **Hinchley Wood** *Surr., Eng.*
162 C3 **Hinckley** *Leics., Eng.*
120 E2 **Hinderclay** *Suff., Eng.*
184 A2 **Hinderton** *Cheshire West & Chester, Eng.*
216 G1 **Hinderwell** *N. Yorks., Eng.*
144 C2 **Hindford** *Shrop., Eng.*
78 B3 **Hindhead** *Surr., Eng.*
228 H4 **Hindle Fold** *Lancs., Eng.*
198 B2 **Hindley** *Gtr Man., Eng.*
244 F6 **Hindley** *Northumb., Eng.*
198 B2 **Hindley Green** *Gtr Man., Eng.*
136 D2 **Hindlip** *Worcs., Eng.*
166 F2 **Hindolveston** *Norf., Eng.*
94 C3 **Hindon** *Som., Eng.*
86 C5 **Hindon** *Wilts., Eng.*
166 E1 **Hindringham** *Norf., Eng.*
166 E3 **Hingham** *Norf., Eng.*
148 B5 **Hinksford** *Staffs., Eng.*
144 F2 **Hinstock** *Shrop., Eng.*
120 F4 **Hintlesham** *Suff., Eng.*
98 E3 **Hinton** *Glos., Eng.*
52 B6 **Hinton** *Hants., Eng.*
140 B3 **Hinton** *Here., Eng.*
128 B4 **Hinton** *Northants., Eng.*
98 E5 **Hinton** *S. Glos., Eng.*
144 C3 **Hinton** *Shrop., Eng.*
52 B6 **Hinton Admiral** *Hants., Eng.*
52 F4 **Hinton Ampner** *Hants., Eng.*
94 I3 **Hinton Blewett** *B. and N.E. Som., Eng.*
94 K3 **Hinton Charterhouse** *B. and N.E. Som., Eng.*
128 B5 **Hinton-in-the-Hedges** *Northants., Eng.*
46 H2 **Hinton Martell** *Dorset, Eng.*
136 F3 **Hinton on the Green** *Worcs., Eng.*
46 G2 **Hinton Parva** *Dorset, Eng.*
86 E2 **Hinton Parva** *Swindon, Eng.*
94 H5 **Hinton St George** *Som., Eng.*
46 F2 **Hinton St Mary** *Dorset, Eng.*
102 C4 **Hinton Waldrist** *Oxon, Eng.*
144 E5 **Hints** *Shrop., Eng.*
148 E5 **Hints** *Staffs., Eng.*
110 B2 **Hinwick** *Bedford, Eng.*
62 F4 **Hinxhill** *Kent, Eng.*
124 F6 **Hinxton** *Cambs., Eng.*
110 D3 **Hinxworth** *Herts., Eng.*
Hiort *i. Scot. see* **St Kilda**
222 D2 **Hipperholme** *W. Yorks., Eng.*
244 H3 **Hipsburn** *Northumb., Eng.*
216 D1 **Hipswell** *N. Yorks., Eng.*
26 E1 **Hiraethog, Mynydd** *hills Wales*
314 F3 **Hirn** *Abers., Scot.*
366 E2 **Hirnant** *Powys, Wales*
244 H4 **Hirst** *Northumb., Eng.*
Hirta *i. Scot. see* **St Kilda**
378 F3 **Hirwaen** *Denb., Wales*
350 E2 **Hirwaun** *R.C.T., Wales*
40 D1 **Hiscott** *Devon, Eng.*
124 E5 **Histon** *Cambs., Eng.*
106 D5 **Hitcham** *Bucks., Eng.*
120 E4 **Hitcham** *Suff., Eng.*
120 E4 **Hitcham Street** *Suff., Eng.*
110 D4 **Hitchin** *Herts., Eng.*
74 D3 **Hither Green** *Gtr Lon., Eng.*
40 E2 **Hittisleigh** *Devon, Eng.*
210 D4 **Hive** *E. Riding, Eng.*
148 D4 **Hixon** *Staffs., Eng.*
62 H3 **Hoaden** *Kent, Eng.*
339 C1 **Hoaldalbert** *Mon., Wales*
148 E4 **Hoar Cross** *Staffs., Eng.*
140 D4 **Hoarwithy** *Here., Eng.*
62 G3 **Hoath** *Kent, Eng.*
144 B5 **Hobarris** *Shrop., Eng.*
329 C4 **Hobbister** *Orkney, Scot.*
120 B4 **Hobbles Green** *Suff., Eng.*
116 C3 **Hobbs Cross** *Essex, Eng.*
124 E3 **Hobbs Lots Bridge** *Cambs., Eng.*
256 I4 **Hobkirk** *Borders, Scot.*
166 J3 **Hobland Hall** *Norf., Eng.*
236 E2 **Hobson** *Durham, Eng.*
162 E2 **Hoby** *Leics., Eng.*
110 F4 **Hockerill** *Herts., Eng.*
166 F2 **Hockering** *Norf., Eng.*
166 F2 **Hockering Heath** *Norf., Eng.*
176 D4 **Hockerton** *Notts., Eng.*
94 E5 **Hockholler** *Som., Eng.*
116 F4 **Hockley** *Essex, Eng.*
148 E5 **Hockley** *Staffs., Eng.*
154 E3 **Hockley** *W. Mids, Eng.*
396 E3 **Hockley** *Armagh, N. Ire.*
154 D3 **Hockley Heath** *W. Mids, Eng.*
110 B4 **Hockliffe** *Central Bedfordshire, Eng.*
166 C4 **Hockwold cum Wilton** *Norf., Eng.*
40 F2 **Hockworthy** *Devon, Eng.*
24 M6 **Hodder** *r. Eng.*
110 E5 **Hoddesdon** *Herts., Eng.*
228 H4 **Hoddlesden** *B'burn, Eng.*
184 F2 **Hodgehill** *Cheshire East, Eng.*
154 D3 **Hodgehill** *W. Mids, Eng.*
358 E4 **Hodgeston** *Pembs., Wales*
144 E2 **Hodnet** *Shrop., Eng.*
144 E2 **Hodnetheath** *Shrop., Eng.*
62 C2 **Hodsoll Street** *Kent, Eng.*
86 E2 **Hodson** *Swindon, Eng.*
180 F3 **Hodthorpe** *Derbys., Eng.*
166 E2 **Hoe** *Norf., Eng.*
52 F5 **Hoe Gate** *Hants., Eng.*
232 G5 **Hoff** *Cumbria, Eng.*
170 F6 **Hoffleet Stow** *Lincs., Eng.*
276 F2 **Hogganfield** *Glas., Scot.*
120 D3 **Hoggard's Green** *Suff., Eng.*
106 D3 **Hoggeston** *Bucks., Eng.*
314 E2 **Hoggie** *Moray, Scot.*
132 B2 **Hoggrill's End** *Warks., Eng.*
326 B4 **Hogha Gearraidh** *W. Isles, Scot.*
228 G4 **Hoghton** *Lancs., Eng.*
180 D4 **Hognaston** *Derbys., Eng.*
110 B5 **Hogpits Bottom** *Herts., Eng.*
170 H4 **Hogsthorpe** *Lincs., Eng.*
170 G7 **Holbeach** *Lincs., Eng.*
170 G7 **Holbeach Bank** *Lincs., Eng.*
170 F7 **Holbeach Drove** *Lincs., Eng.*
170 G7 **Holbeach Hurn** *Lincs., Eng.*
26 M2 **Holbeach Marsh** *marsh Eng.*
170 F7 **Holbeach St Johns** *Lincs., Eng.*
170 G6 **Holbeach St Marks** *Lincs., Eng.*
170 G6 **Holbeach St Matthew** *Lincs., Eng.*
176 B3 **Holbeck** *Notts., Eng.*
176 B3 **Holbeck Woodhouse** *Notts., Eng.*
136 F2 **Holberrow Green** *Worcs., Eng.*
40 E4 **Holbeton** *Devon, Eng.*
62 C2 **Holborough** *Kent, Eng.*
180 E4 **Holbrook** *Derbys., Eng.*
120 F5 **Holbrook** *Suff., Eng.*
180 E4 **Holbrook Moor** *Derbys., Eng.*
154 E3 **Holbrooks** *W. Mids, Eng.*
244 F2 **Holburn** *Northumb., Eng.*
52 D6 **Holbury** *Hants., Eng.*
40 F3 **Holcombe** *Devon, Eng.*
198 D2 **Holcombe** *Gtr Man., Eng.*
94 J3 **Holcombe** *Som., Eng.*
198 D2 **Holcombe Brook** *Gtr Man., Eng.*
40 F2 **Holcombe Burnell Barton** *Devon, Eng.*
40 F2 **Holcombe Rogus** *Devon, Eng.*
128 D4 **Holcot** *Northants., Eng.*
228 H3 **Holden** *Lancs., Eng.*
128 D4 **Holdenby** *Northants., Eng.*
222 B2 **Holden Gate** *W. Yorks., Eng.*
46 I3 **Holdenhurst** *Bourne., Eng.*
24 Q6 **Holderness** *pen. Eng.*
116 E2 **Holder's Green** *Essex, Eng.*
74 C2 **Holders Hill** *Gtr Lon., Eng.*
144 E4 **Holdgate** *Shrop., Eng.*
170 D5 **Holdingham** *Lincs., Eng.*
46 B3 **Holditch** *Dorset, Eng.*
180 B2 **Holehouse** *Derbys., Eng.*
140 D4 **Hole-in-the-Wall** *Here., Eng.*
62 D4 **Hole Park** *Kent, Eng.*
58 D3 **Hole Street** *W. Sussex, Eng.*
94 E4 **Holford** *Som., Eng.*
232 E7 **Holker** *Cumbria, Eng.*
166 D1 **Holkham** *Norf., Eng.*
40 D2 **Hollacombe** *Devon, Eng.*
78 G2 **Holland** *Surr., Eng.*
329 D1 **Holland** *Orkney, Scot.*
329 F3 **Holland** *Orkney, Scot.*
170 F5 **Holland Fen** *Lincs., Eng.*
26 L2 **Holland Fen** *reg. Eng.*
228 F5 **Holland Lees** *Lancs., Eng.*
116 J3 **Holland-on-Sea** *Essex, Eng.*
74 C2 **Holland Park** *Gtr Lon., Eng.*
329 G1 **Hollandstoun** *Orkney, Scot.*
252 G2 **Hollee** *D. and G., Scot.*
120 H4 **Hollesley** *Suff., Eng.*
26 O3 **Hollesley Bay** *b. Eng.*
62 D3 **Hollingbourne** *Kent, Eng.*
58 F3 **Hollingbury** *B. and H., Eng.*
58 I3 **Hollingrove** *E. Sussex, Eng.*
180 D5 **Hollington** *Derbys., Eng.*
58 J3 **Hollington** *E. Sussex, Eng.*
148 D3 **Hollington** *Staffs., Eng.*
198 F3 **Hollingworth** *Gtr Man., Eng.*
180 D3 **Hollins** *Derbys., Eng.*
198 D2 **Hollins** *Gtr Man., Eng.*
148 D1 **Hollinsclough** *Staffs., Eng.*
208 D3 **Hollins End** *S. Yorks., Eng.*
190 G3 **Hollins Green** *Warr., Eng.*
228 F3 **Hollins Lane** *Lancs., Eng.*
222 F2 **Hollinthorpe** *W. Yorks., Eng.*
198 E2 **Hollinwood** *Gtr Man., Eng.*
144 D2 **Hollinwood** *Shrop., Eng.*
40 E2 **Hollocombe** *Devon, Eng.*
180 D4 **Holloway** *Derbys., Eng.*
74 D2 **Holloway** *Gtr Lon., Eng.*
128 D3 **Hollowell** *Northants., Eng.*
208 C3 **Hollow Meadows** *S. Yorks., Eng.*
136 C3 **Hollybush** *Worcs., Eng.*
262 D4 **Hollybush** *E. Ayr., Scot.*
350 G2 **Hollybush** *Caerp., Wales*
378 H4 **Holly Bush** *Wrex., Wales*
82 E2 **Holly Cross** *W'ham, Eng.*
166 A3 **Holly End** *Norf., Eng.*
106 C4 **Holly Green** *Bucks., Eng.*
136 D3 **Holly Green** *Worcs., Eng.*
184 D4 **Hollyhurst** *Cheshire East, Eng.*
210 I4 **Hollym** *E. Riding, Eng.*
52 G4 **Hollywater** *Hants., Eng.*
136 F1 **Hollywood** *Worcs., Eng.*
252 G2 **Holm** *D. and G., Scot.*
222 D3 **Holmbridge** *W. Yorks., Eng.*
78 D2 **Holmbury St Mary** *Surr., Eng.*
58 E2 **Holmbush** *W. Sussex, Eng.*
124 C4 **Holme** *Cambs., Eng.*
232 F7 **Holme** *Cumbria, Eng.*
170 C2 **Holme** *N. Lincs., Eng.*
176 E4 **Holme** *Notts., Eng.*
222 C3 **Holme** *W. Yorks., Eng.*
46 G3 **Holmebridge** *Dorset, Eng.*
228 I4 **Holme Chapel** *Lancs., Eng.*
166 D3 **Holme Hale** *Norf., Eng.*
140 D3 **Holme Lacy** *Here., Eng.*
140 B2 **Holme Marsh** *Here., Eng.*
166 C1 **Holme next the Sea** *Norf., Eng.*
210 D3 **Holme-on-Spalding-Moor** *E. Riding, Eng.*
210 E3 **Holme on the Wolds** *E. Riding, Eng.*
176 C5 **Holme Pierrepont** *Notts., Eng.*
140 C3 **Holmer** *Here., Eng.*
106 D5 **Holmer Green** *Bucks., Eng.*
228 E4 **Holmes** *Lancs., Eng.*
184 E2 **Holmes Chapel** *Cheshire East, Eng.*
180 D3 **Holmesfield** *Derbys., Eng.*
58 H3 **Holme's Hill** *E. Sussex, Eng.*
232 B4 **Holme St Cuthbert** *Cumbria, Eng.*
228 E5 **Holmeswood** *Lancs., Eng.*
78 F2 **Holmethorpe** *Surr., Eng.*
180 E3 **Holmewood** *Derbys., Eng.*
222 C2 **Holmfield** *W. Yorks., Eng.*
222 D3 **Holmfirth** *W. Yorks., Eng.*
252 D2 **Holmhead** *D. and G., Scot.*
262 F4 **Holmhead** *E. Ayr., Scot.*
252 E2 **Holm of Drumlanrig** *D. and G., Scot.*
210 I4 **Holmpton** *E. Riding, Eng.*
232 B6 **Holmrook** *Cumbria, Eng.*
331 D3 **Holmsgarth** *Shet., Scot.*
236 F2 **Holmside** *Durham, Eng.*
262 D4 **Holmston** *S. Ayr., Scot.*
232 F4 **Holmwrangle** *Cumbria, Eng.*
40 E3 **Holne** *Devon, Eng.*
46 E2 **Holnest** *Dorset, Eng.*
94 C3 **Holnicote** *Som., Eng.*
40 C2 **Holsworthy** *Devon, Eng.*
40 D2 **Holsworthy Beacon** *Devon, Eng.*
46 H2 **Holt** *Dorset, Eng.*
190 E3 **Holt** *Merseyside, Eng.*
166 F1 **Holt** *Norf., Eng.*
86 B3 **Holt** *Wilts., Eng.*
136 D2 **Holt** *Worcs., Eng.*
378 H3 **Holt** *Wrex., Wales*
216 G3 **Holtby** *York, Eng.*
52 F4 **Holt End** *Hants., Eng.*
136 F2 **Holt End** *Worcs., Eng.*
136 D2 **Holt Fleet** *Worcs., Eng.*
228 E5 **Holt Green** *Lancs., Eng.*
46 H2 **Holt Heath** *Dorset, Eng.*
136 D2 **Holt Heath** *Worcs., Eng.*
102 E4 **Holton** *Oxon, Eng.*
94 J4 **Holton** *Som., Eng.*
120 I2 **Holton** *Suff., Eng.*
46 G3 **Holton Heath** *Dorset, Eng.*
170 F2 **Holton le Clay** *Lincs., Eng.*
170 D3 **Holton le Moor** *Lincs., Eng.*
120 E5 **Holton St Mary** *Suff., Eng.*
106 D5 **Holtspur** *Bucks., Eng.*
62 H3 **Holt Street** *Kent, Eng.*
46 H2 **Holt Wood** *Dorset, Eng.*
82 B3 **Holtwood** *W. Berks., Eng.*
58 G2 **Holtye** *E. Sussex, Eng.*
94 F4 **Holway** *Som., Eng.*
46 E2 **Holwell** *Dorset, Eng.*
110 D4 **Holwell** *Herts., Eng.*
162 F2 **Holwell** *Leics., Eng.*
102 B4 **Holwell** *Oxon, Eng.*
94 J3 **Holwell** *Som., Eng.*
236 C4 **Holwick** *Durham, Eng.*
46 F4 **Holworth** *Dorset, Eng.*
52 G4 **Holybourne** *Hants., Eng.*
136 E1 **Holy Cross** *Worcs., Eng.*
116 C3 **Holyfield** *Essex, Eng.*
371 B3 **Holyhead** *I.o.A., Wales*
26 C1 **Holyhead Bay** *b. Wales*
244 G1 **Holy Island** *Northumb., Eng.*
24 N2 **Holy Island** *i. Eng.*
22 F11 **Holy Island** *i. Scot.*
26 C1 **Holy Island** *i. Wales*
180 E3 **Holymoorside** *Derbys., Eng.*
82 F3 **Holyport** *W. and M., Eng.*
244 E4 **Holystone** *Northumb., Eng.*
280 C4 **Holytown** *N. Lanark., Scot.*
124 D5 **Holywell** *Cambs., Eng.*
36 D2 **Holywell** *Corn., Eng.*
46 D2 **Holywell** *Dorset, Eng.*
58 H4 **Holywell** *E. Sussex, Eng.*
244 H5 **Holywell** *Northumb., Eng.*
402 C5 **Holywell** *Fermanagh, N. Ire.*
378 F2 **Holywell** *Flints., Wales*
222 C2 **Holywell Green** *W. Yorks., Eng.*
94 E5 **Holywell Lake** *Som., Eng.*
120 C2 **Holywell Row** *Suff., Eng.*
396 J2 **Holywood** *North Down, N. Ire.*
252 F2 **Holywood** *D. and G., Scot.*
144 E4 **Homer** *Shrop., Eng.*
190 C2 **Homer Green** *Merseyside, Eng.*
120 H2 **Homersfield** *Suff., Eng.*
74 D2 **Homerton** *Gtr Lon., Eng.*
140 D4 **Hom Green** *Here., Eng.*
86 E5 **Homington** *Wilts., Eng.*
326 B5 **Homore** *W. Isles, Scot.*
358 E3 **Honeyborough** *Pembs., Wales*
136 F3 **Honeybourne** *Worcs., Eng.*
40 E2 **Honeychurch** *Devon, Eng.*
62 G3 **Honey Hill** *Kent, Eng.*
86 D3 **Honey Street** *Wilts., Eng.*
120 E5 **Honey Tye** *Suff., Eng.*
40 D3 **Honicknowle** *Plymouth, Eng.*
132 C3 **Honiley** *Warks., Eng.*
166 H2 **Honing** *Norf., Eng.*
166 F3 **Honingham** *Norf., Eng.*
170 C6 **Honington** *Lincs., Eng.*
120 D2 **Honington** *Suff., Eng.*
132 C5 **Honington** *Warks., Eng.*
40 G2 **Honiton** *Devon, Eng.*
378 H3 **Honkley** *Wrex., Wales*
222 D3 **Honley** *W. Yorks., Eng.*
144 F3 **Honnington** *Telford, Eng.*
74 D3 **Honor Oak** *Gtr Lon., Eng.*
62 D2 **Hoo** *Medway, Eng.*
120 G3 **Hoo** *Suff., Eng.*
208 C2 **Hood Green** *S. Yorks., Eng.*
208 D3 **Hood Hill** *S. Yorks., Eng.*
58 I3 **Hooe** *E. Sussex, Eng.*
40 D3 **Hooe** *Plymouth, Eng.*
58 I3 **Hooe Common** *E. Sussex, Eng.*
184 E1 **Hoo Green** *Cheshire East, Eng.*
120 G3 **Hoo Green** *Suff., Eng.*
228 D3 **Hoohill** *Blackpool, Eng.*
222 C2 **Hoo Hole** *W. Yorks., Eng.*
124 E3 **Hook** *Cambs., Eng.*
210 C4 **Hook** *E. Riding, Eng.*
74 C3 **Hook** *Gtr Lon., Eng.*
52 E5 **Hook** *Hants., Eng.*
52 G3 **Hook** *Hants., Eng.*
86 D2 **Hook** *Wilts., Eng.*
358 E3 **Hook** *Pembs., Wales*
144 D3 **Hook-a-Gate** *Shrop., Eng.*
46 D3 **Hooke** *Dorset, Eng.*
102 E5 **Hook End** *Oxon, Eng.*
148 A3 **Hookgate** *Staffs., Eng.*
62 B2 **Hook Green** *Kent, Eng.*
62 B2 **Hook Green** *Kent, Eng.*
62 C2 **Hook Green** *Kent, Eng.*
62 C4 **Hook Green** *Kent, Eng.*
102 C3 **Hook Norton** *Oxon, Eng.*
40 F2 **Hookway** *Devon, Eng.*
78 E2 **Hookwood** *Surr., Eng.*
184 B2 **Hoole** *Cheshire West & Chester, Eng.*
78 F2 **Hooley** *Surr., Eng.*
339 D2 **Hoop** *Mon., Wales*
184 B2 **Hooton** *Cheshire West & Chester, Eng.*
208 E3 **Hooton Levitt** *S. Yorks., Eng.*
208 E2 **Hooton Pagnell** *S. Yorks., Eng.*
208 E3 **Hooton Roberts** *S. Yorks., Eng.*
102 D3 **Hopcrofts Holt** *Oxon, Eng.*
180 C2 **Hope** *Derbys., Eng.*
40 E4 **Hope** *Devon, Eng.*
144 C4 **Hope** *Shrop., Eng.*
148 E2 **Hope** *Staffs., Eng.*
378 G3 **Hope** *Flints., Wales*
366 G3 **Hope** *Powys, Wales*
22 G6 **Hope, Loch** *l. Scot.*
144 E5 **Hope Bagot** *Shrop., Eng.*
144 D4 **Hope Bowdler** *Shrop., Eng.*
116 D2 **Hope End Green** *Essex, Eng.*
184 G1 **Hope Green** *Cheshire East, Eng.*
256 F4 **Hopehouse** *Borders, Scot.*
314 C1 **Hopeman** *Moray, Scot.*
140 D4 **Hope Mansell** *Here., Eng.*
144 C5 **Hopesay** *Shrop., Eng.*
116 F4 **Hope's Green** *Essex, Eng.*
222 F2 **Hopetown** *W. Yorks., Eng.*
140 C2 **Hope under Dinmore** *Here., Eng.*
350 F3 **Hopkinstown** *R.C.T., Wales*
140 B2 **Hopley's Green** *Here., Eng.*
128 D4 **Hopping Hill** *Northants., Eng.*
170 E7 **Hop Pole** *Lincs., Eng.*
132 D3 **Hopsford** *Warks., Eng.*
144 G4 **Hopstone** *Shrop., Eng.*
180 D4 **Hopton** *Derbys., Eng.*
166 J3 **Hopton** *Norf., Eng.*
144 C3 **Hopton** *Shrop., Eng.*
144 E2 **Hopton** *Shrop., Eng.*
148 C3 **Hopton** *Staffs., Eng.*
120 E2 **Hopton** *Suff., Eng.*
144 E5 **Hopton Cangeford** *Shrop., Eng.*
144 C5 **Hopton Castle** *Shrop., Eng.*
144 C5 **Hoptonheath** *Shrop., Eng.*
144 E5 **Hopton Wafers** *Shrop., Eng.*
148 E5 **Hopwas** *Staffs., Eng.*
136 F1 **Hopwood** *Worcs., Eng.*
58 H3 **Horam** *E. Sussex, Eng.*
170 D6 **Horbling** *Lincs., Eng.*
222 E3 **Horbury** *W. Yorks., Eng.*
236 H3 **Horden** *Durham, Eng.*
144 C5 **Horderley** *Shrop., Eng.*
52 C6 **Hordle** *Hants., Eng.*
144 C2 **Hordley** *Shrop., Eng.*
356 E3 **Horeb** *Carmar., Wales*
362 D4 **Horeb** *Cere., Wales*
378 G3 **Horeb** *Flints., Wales*
94 I2 **Horfield** *Bristol, Eng.*
120 G3 **Horham** *Suff., Eng.*
116 H2 **Horkesley Heath** *Essex, Eng.*
170 C2 **Horkstow** *N. Lincs., Eng.*
102 C2 **Horley** *Oxon, Eng.*
78 E2 **Horley** *Surr., Eng.*
94 I4 **Hornblotton** *Som., Eng.*
94 I4 **Hornblotton Green** *Som., Eng.*
228 G2 **Hornby** *Lancs., Eng.*
216 E1 **Hornby** *N. Yorks., Eng.*
216 E1 **Hornby** *N. Yorks., Eng.*
170 F4 **Horncastle** *Lincs., Eng.*
74 F2 **Hornchurch** *Gtr Lon., Eng.*
244 E1 **Horncliffe** *Northumb., Eng.*
52 F5 **Horndean** *Hants., Eng.*
256 L2 **Horndean** *Borders, Scot.*
40 D3 **Horndon** *Devon, Eng.*
116 E4 **Horndon on the Hill** *Thurrock, Eng.*
78 F2 **Horne** *Surr., Eng.*
94 C3 **Horner** *Som., Eng.*
116 F3 **Horne Row** *Essex, Eng.*
120 E4 **Horner's Green** *Suff., Eng.*
106 E5 **Horn Hill** *Bucks., Eng.*
308 E2 **Horniehaugh** *Angus, Scot.*
166 H2 **Horning** *Norf., Eng.*
162 G3 **Horninghold** *Leics., Eng.*
148 F4 **Horninglow** *Staffs., Eng.*
124 F5 **Horningsea** *Cambs., Eng.*
86 B4 **Horningsham** *Wilts., Eng.*
166 E2 **Horningtoft** *Norf., Eng.*
36 F2 **Horningtops** *Corn., Eng.*
94 G5 **Hornsbury** *Som., Eng.*
232 F3 **Hornsby** *Cumbria, Eng.*
232 F3 **Hornsby Gate** *Cumbria, Eng.*
40 D2 **Horns Cross** *Devon, Eng.*
58 J3 **Horns Cross** *E. Sussex, Eng.*
210 G3 **Hornsea** *E. Riding, Eng.*
74 D2 **Hornsey** *Gtr Lon., Eng.*
74 E4 **Horns Green** *Gtr Lon., Eng.*
102 C2 **Hornton** *Oxon, Eng.*
40 D3 **Horrabridge** *Devon, Eng.*
120 D3 **Horringer** *Suff., Eng.*
198 C2 **Horrocks Fold** *Gtr Man., Eng.*
40 D3 **Horsebridge** *Devon, Eng.*
52 C4 **Horsebridge** *Hants., Eng.*
148 C2 **Horse Bridge** *Staffs., Eng.*
148 B4 **Horsebrook** *Staffs., Eng.*
94 H2 **Horsecastle** *N. Som., Eng.*
144 F4 **Horsehay** *Telford, Eng.*
124 G6 **Horseheath** *Cambs., Eng.*
216 D2 **Horsehouse** *N. Yorks., Eng.*
78 C2 **Horsell** *Surr., Eng.*
378 I4 **Horseman's Green** *Wrex., Wales*
106 C4 **Horsenden** *Bucks., Eng.*
62 A4 **Horseshoe Green** *Kent, Eng.*
124 E4 **Horseway** *Cambs., Eng.*
166 I2 **Horsey** *Norf., Eng.*
166 I2 **Horsey Corner** *Norf., Eng.*
166 G2 **Horsford** *Norf., Eng.*
222 E1 **Horsforth** *W. Yorks., Eng.*
222 E1 **Horsforth Woodside** *W. Yorks., Eng.*
136 C2 **Horsham** *Worcs., Eng.*
58 E2 **Horsham** *W. Sussex, Eng.*
166 G2 **Horsham St Faith** *Norf., Eng.*
170 E4 **Horsington** *Lincs., Eng.*
94 J4 **Horsington** *Som., Eng.*
94 J4 **Horsington Marsh** *Som., Eng.*
180 E5 **Horsley** *Derbys., Eng.*
98 F3 **Horsley** *Glos., Eng.*
244 D4 **Horsley** *Northumb., Eng.*
244 F6 **Horsley** *Northumb., Eng.*
116 I2 **Horsley Cross** *Essex, Eng.*
116 I2 **Horsleycross Street** *Essex, Eng.*
180 D3 **Horsleygate** *Derbys., Eng.*
236 G2 **Horsley Hill** *T. and W., Eng.*
256 H4 **Horsleyhill** *Borders, Scot.*
106 C5 **Horsleys Green** *Bucks., Eng.*
180 E4 **Horsley Woodhouse** *Derbys., Eng.*
62 C4 **Horsmonden** *Kent, Eng.*
102 D4 **Horspath** *Oxon, Eng.*
166 H2 **Horstead** *Norf., Eng.*
58 F2 **Horsted Keynes** *W. Sussex, Eng.*
106 E3 **Horton** *Bucks., Eng.*
46 H2 **Horton** *Dorset, Eng.*
228 I3 **Horton** *Lancs., Eng.*
128 E4 **Horton** *Northants., Eng.*
98 E4 **Horton** *S. Glos., Eng.*
144 D2 **Horton** *Shrop., Eng.*
94 G5 **Horton** *Som., Eng.*
148 C2 **Horton** *Staffs., Eng.*
144 F3 **Horton** *Telford, Eng.*
82 G3 **Horton** *W. and M., Eng.*
86 D3 **Horton** *Wilts., Eng.*
350 A3 **Horton** *Swansea, Wales*
94 G5 **Horton Cross** *Som., Eng.*
102 E4 **Horton-cum-Studley** *Oxon, Eng.*
236 E1 **Horton Grange** *T. and W., Eng.*
184 C3 **Horton Green** *Cheshire West & Chester, Eng.*
52 E5 **Horton Heath** *Hants., Eng.*
46 H2 **Horton Inn** *Dorset, Eng.*
216 C2 **Horton in Ribblesdale** *N. Yorks., Eng.*
62 B2 **Horton Kirby** *Kent, Eng.*
198 B2 **Horwich** *Gtr Man., Eng.*
180 B3 **Horwich End** *Derbys., Eng.*
40 D1 **Horwood** *Devon, Eng.*
228 F5 **Hoscar** *Lancs., Eng.*
162 F1 **Hose** *Leics., Eng.*
232 C7 **Hoses** *Cumbria, Eng.*
62 A3 **Hosey Hill** *Kent, Eng.*
304 G4 **Hosh** *Perth and Kin., Scot.*
326 B4 **Hosta** *W. Isles, Scot.*
331 D4 **Hoswick** *Shet., Scot.*
210 E4 **Hotham** *E. Riding, Eng.*
62 E4 **Hothfield** *Kent, Eng.*
162 E2 **Hoton** *Leics., Eng.*
331 E2 **Houbie** *Shet., Scot.*
262 C5 **Houdston** *S. Ayr., Scot.*
184 E3 **Hough** *Cheshire East, Eng.*
170 B6 **Hougham** *Lincs., Eng.*
222 E2 **Hough End** *W. Yorks., Eng.*
190 E3 **Hough Green** *Halton, Eng.*
170 C5 **Hough-on-the-Hill** *Lincs., Eng.*
124 D4 **Houghton** *Cambs., Eng.*
232 E3 **Houghton** *Cumbria, Eng.*
52 C4 **Houghton** *Hants., Eng.*
58 C3 **Houghton** *W. Sussex, Eng.*
358 E3 **Houghton** *Pembs., Wales*
236 F4 **Houghton Bank** *Darl., Eng.*
110 C3 **Houghton Conquest** *Central Bedfordshire, Eng.*
190 F3 **Houghton Green** *Warr., Eng.*
236 F4 **Houghton-le-Side** *Darl., Eng.*
236 G2 **Houghton le Spring** *T. and W., Eng.*
162 F3 **Houghton on the Hill** *Leics., Eng.*
110 B4 **Houghton Regis** *Central Bedfordshire, Eng.*
166 E1 **Houghton St Giles** *Norf., Eng.*
216 G1 **Houlsyke** *N. Yorks., Eng.*
52 E5 **Hound** *Hants., Eng.*
256 I2 **Houndslow** *Borders, Scot.*
94 E4 **Houndsmoor** *Som., Eng.*
256 K1 **Houndwood** *Borders, Scot.*
52 D5 **Hounsdown** *Hants., Eng.*
74 B3 **Hounslow** *Gtr Lon., Eng.*
74 B3 **Hounslow** *met. bor. Gtr Lon., Eng.*
22 E8 **Hourn, Loch** *inlet Scot.*
329 F3 **Housebay** *Orkney, Scot.*
322 J2 **Househill** *High., Scot.*
222 D3 **Houses Hill** *W. Yorks., Eng.*
24 M3 **Housesteads** *tourist site Eng.*
331 C2 **Housetter** *Shet., Scot.*
116 D3 **Housham Tye** *Essex, Eng.*
331 D3 **Houss** *Shet., Scot.*
276 C2 **Houston** *Renf., Scot.*
320 J3 **Houstry** *High., Scot.*
320 J2 **Houstry of Dunn** *High., Scot.*
329 B4 **Houton** *Orkney, Scot.*
58 E4 **Hove** *B. and H., Eng.*
222 D2 **Hove Edge** *W. Yorks., Eng.*
176 D4 **Hoveringham** *Notts., Eng.*
166 H2 **Hoveton** *Norf., Eng.*
216 G2 **Hovingham** *N. Yorks., Eng.*
232 F3 **How** *Cumbria, Eng.*
24 O5 **Howardian Hills** *hills Eng.*
208 C3 **Howbrook** *S. Yorks., Eng.*
140 D4 **How Caple** *Here., Eng.*
210 C4 **Howden** *E. Riding, Eng.*
288 B3 **Howden** *W. Lothian, Scot.*
222 E2 **Howden Clough** *W. Yorks., Eng.*
236 F1 **Howdon** *T. and W., Eng.*
232 E7 **Howe** *Cumbria, Eng.*
166 H3 **Howe** *Norf., Eng.*
116 F3 **Howe Green** *Essex, Eng.*
116 F3 **Howegreen** *Essex, Eng.*
170 E5 **Howell** *Lincs., Eng.*
110 C3 **How End** *Central Bedfordshire, Eng.*
314 F2 **Howe of Teuchar** *Abers., Scot.*
22 K9 **Howe of the Mearns** *reg. Scot.*
116 E2 **Howe Street** *Essex, Eng.*
116 E3 **Howe Street** *Essex, Eng.*
366 E5 **Howey** *Powys, Wales*
232 A5 **Howgate** *Cumbria, Eng.*
288 D4 **Howgate** *Midlothian, Scot.*
228 I3 **Howgill** *Lancs., Eng.*
216 D2 **Howgill** *N. Yorks., Eng.*
62 A3 **How Green** *Kent, Eng.*
244 H3 **Howick** *Northumb., Eng.*
144 F3 **Howle** *Telford, Eng.*
140 D4 **Howle Hill** *Here., Eng.*
116 D2 **Howlett End** *Essex, Eng.*
94 F5 **Howley** *Som., Eng.*
232 A6 **How Man** *Cumbria, Eng.*
256 J4 **Hownam** *Borders, Scot.*
256 J4 **Hownam Mains** *Borders, Scot.*
256 F4 **Howpasley** *Borders, Scot.*
170 D2 **Howsham** *N. Lincs., Eng.*
244 E2 **Howtel** *Northumb., Eng.*
62 E2 **Howt Green** *Kent, Eng.*
140 B4 **Howton** *Here., Eng.*
276 C3 **Howwood** *Renf., Scot.*
329 C5 **Hoxa** *Orkney, Scot.*
120 G2 **Hoxne** *Suff., Eng.*
74 D2 **Hoxton** *Gtr Lon., Eng.*
320 J2 **Hoy** *High., Scot.*
22 J5 **Hoy** *i. Scot.*
190 B3 **Hoylake** *Merseyside, Eng.*
208 D3 **Hoyland** *S. Yorks., Eng.*
208 C2 **Hoylandswaine** *S. Yorks., Eng.*
208 D2 **Hoyle Mill** *S. Yorks., Eng.*
216 C2 **Hubberholme** *N. Yorks., Eng.*
358 D3 **Hubberston** *Pembs., Wales*
222 C2 **Hubberton Green** *W. Yorks., Eng.*
170 F6 **Hubbert's Bridge** *Lincs., Eng.*
216 E3 **Huby** *N. Yorks., Eng.*
216 F2 **Huby** *N. Yorks., Eng.*
98 F2 **Hucclecote** *Glos., Eng.*
62 D3 **Hucking** *Kent, Eng.*
176 B4 **Hucknall** *Notts., Eng.*
222 D3 **Huddersfield** *W. Yorks., Eng.*
136 E2 **Huddington** *Worcs., Eng.*
148 E4 **Huddlesford** *Staffs., Eng.*
110 B5 **Hudnall** *Herts., Eng.*
216 D1 **Hudswell** *N. Yorks., Eng.*
210 E3 **Huggate** *E. Riding, Eng.*
162 C2 **Hugglescote** *Leics., Eng.*
106 D5 **Hughenden Valley** *Bucks., Eng.*
144 E4 **Hughley** *Shrop., Eng.*
36 □ **Hugh Town** *I.o.S., Eng.*
378 H3 **Hugmore** *Wrex., Wales*
40 D2 **Huish** *Devon, Eng.*
86 E3 **Huish** *Wilts., Eng.*
94 D4 **Huish Champflower** *Som., Eng.*
94 H4 **Huish Episcopi** *Som., Eng.*
326 C3 **Huisinis** *W. Isles, Scot.*
236 H3 **Hulam** *Durham, Eng.*
110 B3 **Hulcote** *Central Bedfordshire, Eng.*
106 D3 **Hulcott** *Bucks., Eng.*
40 F3 **Hulham** *Devon, Eng.*
Hulin Rocks *is N. Ire. see* **The Maidens**
180 D4 **Hulland** *Derbys., Eng.*
180 D4 **Hulland Ward** *Derbys., Eng.*
86 C2 **Hullavington** *Wilts., Eng.*
116 F4 **Hullbridge** *Essex, Eng.*
148 C2 **Hulme** *Staffs., Eng.*
190 F3 **Hulme** *Warr., Eng.*
148 D2 **Hulme End** *Staffs., Eng.*
184 F2 **Hulme Walfield** *Cheshire East, Eng.*
52 D7 **Hulverstone** *I.o.W., Eng.*
120 I2 **Hulver Street** *Suff., Eng.*
140 C2 **Humber** *Here., Eng.*
24 R6 **Humber, Mouth of the** *r. mouth Eng.*
170 D2 **Humberside** *airport Eng.*
170 F2 **Humberston** *N.E. Lincs., Eng.*
162 E3 **Humberstone** *Leicester, Eng.*
216 E2 **Humberton** *N. Yorks., Eng.*
288 F3 **Humbie** *E. Lothian, Scot.*
236 D4 **Humbleton** *Durham, Eng.*
210 H4 **Humbleton** *E. Riding, Eng.*
244 E2 **Humbleton** *Northumb., Eng.*
170 C6 **Humby** *Lincs., Eng.*
256 J3 **Hume** *Borders, Scot.*
256 J3 **Humehall** *Borders, Scot.*
46 D2 **Hummer** *Dorset, Eng.*
244 E5 **Humshaugh** *Northumb., Eng.*
228 H4 **Huncoat** *Lancs., Eng.*
162 D3 **Huncote** *Leics., Eng.*
256 I4 **Hundalee** *Borders, Scot.*
180 E3 **Hundall** *Derbys., Eng.*
236 C4 **Hunderthwaite** *Durham, Eng.*
358 E3 **Hundleton** *Pembs., Wales*
120 C4 **Hundon** *Suff., Eng.*
52 F5 **Hundred Acres** *Hants., Eng.*
228 E4 **Hundred End** *Lancs., Eng.*
366 F5 **Hundred House** *Powys, Wales*
162 F3 **Hungarton** *Leics., Eng.*
106 C2 **Hungate End** *M.K., Eng.*
52 B5 **Hungerford** *Hants., Eng.*
144 D4 **Hungerford** *Shrop., Eng.*
94 D4 **Hungerford** *Som., Eng.*
82 A3 **Hungerford** *W. Berks., Eng.*
82 B3 **Hungerford Newtown** *W. Berks., Eng.*
170 B6 **Hungerton** *Lincs., Eng.*
22 D7 **Hunish, Rubha** *pt Scot.*
216 I2 **Hunmanby** *N. Yorks., Eng.*
132 D4 **Hunningham** *Warks., Eng.*
132 D4 **Hunningham Hill** *Warks., Eng.*
52 E6 **Hunny Hill** *I.o.W., Eng.*
110 F5 **Hunsdon** *Herts., Eng.*
216 E3 **Hunsingore** *N. Yorks., Eng.*
222 E2 **Hunslet** *W. Yorks., Eng.*
222 E2 **Hunslet Carr** *W. Yorks., Eng.*
232 G4 **Hunsonby** *Cumbria, Eng.*
320 J2 **Hunspow** *High., Scot.*
166 B1 **Hunstanton** *Norf., Eng.*
236 C2 **Hunstanworth** *Durham, Eng.*
120 E3 **Hunston** *Suff., Eng.*
222 D2 **Hunsworth** *W. Yorks., Eng.*
136 F2 **Hunt End** *Worcs., Eng.*
102 E5 **Huntercombe End** *Oxon, Eng.*
62 G2 **Hunters Forstal** *Kent, Eng.*
300 F4 **Hunter's Quay** *Arg. and B., Scot.*
264 E2 **Hunterston** *N. Ayr., Scot.*
256 J4 **Huntford** *Borders, Scot.*
94 G4 **Huntham** *Som., Eng.*
216 G1 **Hunt House** *N. Yorks., Eng.*
124 C5 **Huntingdon** *Cambs., Eng.*
120 H3 **Huntingfield** *Suff., Eng.*
46 F1 **Huntingford** *Dorset, Eng.*
140 A2 **Huntington** *Here., Eng.*
140 C3 **Huntington** *Here., Eng.*
148 C4 **Huntington** *Staffs., Eng.*
144 E4 **Huntington** *Telford, Eng.*
304 J4 **Huntingtower** *Perth and Kin., Scot.*
98 E2 **Huntley** *Glos., Eng.*
314 E2 **Huntly** *Abers., Scot.*
256 I2 **Huntlywood** *Borders, Scot.*
52 E4 **Hunton** *Hants., Eng.*
62 C3 **Hunton** *Kent, Eng.*
216 D2 **Hunton** *N. Yorks., Eng.*
110 C5 **Hunton Bridge** *Herts., Eng.*
94 C3 **Huntscott** *Som., Eng.*
190 D3 **Hunt's Cross** *Merseyside, Eng*
132 B2 **Hunts Green** *Warks., Eng.*
40 F2 **Huntsham** *Devon, Eng.*
40 D2 **Huntshaw** *Devon, Eng.*
106 D5 **Hunt's Hill** *Bucks., Eng.*
94 G3 **Huntspill** *Som., Eng.*
222 F2 **Huntwick Grange Farm** *W. Yorks., Eng.*
94 G4 **Huntworth** *Som., Eng.*
236 E3 **Hunwick** *Durham, Eng.*
166 F1 **Hunworth** *Norf., Eng.*
94 G5 **Hurcott** *Som., Eng.*
94 H4 **Hurcott** *Som., Eng.*
366 G3 **Hurdley** *Powys, Wales*
184 G2 **Hurdsfield** *Cheshire East, Eng*
276 D3 **Hurlet** *Glas., Scot.*
82 F2 **Hurley** *W. and M., Eng.*
132 C2 **Hurley** *Warks., Eng.*
82 F2 **Hurley Bottom** *W. and M., Er*
262 E3 **Hurlford** *E. Ayr., Scot.*
329 B5 **Hurliness** *Orkney, Scot.*
228 E5 **Hurlston Green** *Lancs., Eng.*
46 I3 **Hurn** *Dorset, Eng.*
52 D4 **Hursley** *Hants., Eng.*
198 E3 **Hurst** *Gtr Man., Eng.*
216 D1 **Hurst** *N. Yorks., Eng.*
82 E3 **Hurst** *W'ham, Eng.*
52 D3 **Hurstbourne Priors** *Hants., Eng.*
52 D3 **Hurstbourne Tarrant** *Hants., Eng.*
116 I3 **Hurst Green** *Essex, Eng.*
58 I2 **Hurst Green** *E. Sussex, Eng.*
228 H3 **Hurst Green** *Lancs., Eng.*
78 F2 **Hurst Green** *Surr., Eng.*
154 B3 **Hurst Green** *W. Mids, Eng.*
154 B2 **Hurst Hill** *W. Mids, Eng.*
58 E3 **Hurstpierpoint** *W. Sussex, En*
140 A3 **Hurstway Common** *Here., Er*
58 F3 **Hurst Wickham** *W. Sussex, Eng.*
228 I4 **Hurstwood** *Lancs., Eng.*
78 C2 **Hurtmore** *Surr., Eng.*
236 F5 **Hurworth-on-Tees** *Darl., Eng*
236 C4 **Hury** *Durham, Eng.*
162 E4 **Husbands Bosworth** *Leics., Eng.*
110 B3 **Husborne Crawley** *Central Bedfordshire, Eng.*
216 F2 **Husthwaite** *N. Yorks., Eng.*
40 E3 **Hutcherleigh** *Devon, Eng.*
176 B4 **Huthwaite** *Notts., Eng.*
170 H4 **Huttoft** *Lincs., Eng.*
232 E5 **Hutton** *Cumbria, Eng.*
116 E4 **Hutton** *Essex, Eng.*
228 F4 **Hutton** *Lancs., Eng.*
94 G3 **Hutton** *N. Som., Eng.*
256 L2 **Hutton** *Borders, Scot.*
216 H2 **Hutton Buscel** *N. Yorks., Eng.*
216 E2 **Hutton Conyers** *N. Yorks., En*
210 F3 **Hutton Cranswick** *E. Riding, Eng.*
232 E4 **Hutton End** *Cumbria, Eng.*
236 G3 **Hutton Henry** *Durham, Eng.*
216 G2 **Hutton-le-Hole** *N. Yorks., Eng*
236 E4 **Hutton Magna** *Durham, Eng.*
116 E4 **Hutton Mount** *Essex, Eng.*
216 G1 **Hutton Mulgrave** *N. Yorks., Eng.*
232 E4 **Hutton Roof** *Cumbria, Eng.*
232 G7 **Hutton Roof** *Cumbria, Eng.*
216 F1 **Hutton Rudby** *N. Yorks., Eng.*
216 F2 **Hutton Sessay** *N. Yorks., Eng.*
94 I4 **Huxham Green** *Som., Eng.*
184 C3 **Huxley** *Cheshire West & Cheste Eng.*
331 D3 **Huxter** *Shet., Scot.*
331 E2 **Huxter** *Shet., Scot.*
190 D3 **Huyton** *Merseyside, Eng.*
232 B7 **Hycemoor** *Cumbria, Eng.*
98 G3 **Hyde** *Glos., Eng.*
98 H2 **Hyde** *Glos., Eng.*
198 E3 **Hyde** *Gtr Man., Eng.*
82 C3 **Hyde End** *W. Berks., Eng.*
82 E3 **Hyde End** *W'ham, Eng.*
106 E4 **Hyde Heath** *Bucks., Eng.*
148 C4 **Hyde Lea** *Staffs., Eng.*
78 C3 **Hydestile** *Surr., Eng.*
268 D3 **Hyndford Bridge** *S. Lanark., Scot.*
256 I4 **Hyndlee** *Borders, Scot.*
300 □ **Hynish** *Arg. and B., Scot.*
366 G3 **Hyssington** *Powys, Wales*
52 D5 **Hythe** *Hants., Eng.*
62 G4 **Hythe** *Kent, Eng.*
82 G3 **Hythe End** *W. and M., Eng.*
314 H2 **Hythie** *Abers., Scot.*
232 B7 **Hyton** *Cumbria, Eng.*

I

326 D2 **Iarsiadar** *W. Isles, Scot.*
46 F2 **Ibberton** *Dorset, Eng.*
180 D4 **Ible** *Derbys., Eng.*
276 E2 **Ibrox** *Glas., Scot.*
52 B5 **Ibsley** *Hants., Eng.*
162 C2 **Ibstock** *Leics., Eng.*
106 C5 **Ibstone** *Bucks., Eng.*
52 D3 **Ibthorpe** *Hants., Eng.*
52 E3 **Ibworth** *Hants., Eng.*
94 G2 **Icelton** *N. Som., Eng.*
166 D3 **Ickburgh** *Norf., Eng.*
74 B2 **Ickenham** *Gtr Lon., Eng.*
106 B4 **Ickford** *Bucks., Eng.*
62 H3 **Ickham** *Kent, Eng.*
110 D4 **Ickleford** *Herts., Eng.*
58 K3 **Icklesham** *E. Sussex, Eng.*
124 F6 **Ickleton** *Cambs., Eng.*
120 C3 **Icklingham** *Suff., Eng.*
110 D3 **Ickwell Green** *Central Bedfordshire, Eng.*
98 I2 **Icomb** *Glos., Eng.*
102 B3 **Idbury** *Oxon, Eng.*
40 D2 **Iddesleigh** *Devon, Eng.*
40 F2 **Ide** *Devon, Eng.*
40 F3 **Ideford** *Devon, Eng.*

Ide Hill to Kingsnorth

62 A3 Ide Hill Kent, Eng.
58 K3 Iden E. Sussex, Eng.
62 C4 Iden Green Kent, Eng.
62 D4 Iden Green Kent, Eng.
22 D1 Idle W. Yorks., Eng.
24 P7 Idle r. Eng.
36 D3 Idless Corn., Eng.
32 C5 Idlicote Warks., Eng.
86 E5 Idmiston Wilts., Eng.
80 D4 Idridgehay Derbys., Eng.
80 D4 Idridgehay Green Derbys., Eng.
22 B2 Idrigil High., Scot.
02 B5 Idstone Oxon, Eng.
08 F3 Idvies Angus, Scot.
02 D4 Iffley Oxon, Eng.
58 E2 Ifield W. Sussex, Eng.
58 E2 Ifieldwood W. Sussex, Eng.
58 C2 Ifold W. Sussex, Eng.
46 I3 Iford Bourne., Eng.
58 G3 Iford E. Sussex, Eng.
39 D3 Ifton Mon., Wales
44 B2 Ifton Heath Shrop., Eng.
44 E2 Ightfield Shrop., Eng.
44 E2 Ightfield Heath Shrop., Eng.
62 B3 Ightham Kent, Eng.
20 I4 Iken Suff., Eng.
48 E2 Ilam Staffs., Eng.
94 H4 Ilchester Som., Eng.
44 F3 Ilderton Northumb., Eng.
74 E2 Ilford Gtr Lon., Eng.
94 G5 Ilford Som., Eng.
40 D1 Ilfracombe Devon, Eng.
80 F5 Ilkeston Derbys., Eng.
20 H2 Ilketshall St Andrew Suff., Eng.
20 H2 Ilketshall St Lawrence Suff., Eng.
20 H2 Ilketshall St Margaret Suff., Eng.
22 D1 Ilkley W. Yorks., Eng.
36 F2 Illand Corn., Eng.
44 B3 Illey W. Mids, Eng.
84 F2 Illidge Green Cheshire East, Eng.
66 E4 Illington Norf., Eng.
22 D2 Illingworth W. Yorks., Eng.
36 D3 Illogan Corn., Eng.
62 F3 Illston on the Hill Leics., Eng.
06 C4 Ilmer Bucks., Eng.
32 B5 Ilmington Warks., Eng.
94 G5 Ilminster Som., Eng.
40 E3 Ilsington Devon, Eng.
46 E3 Ilsington Dorset, Eng.
50 B3 Ilston Swansea, Wales
16 D2 Ilton N. Yorks., Eng.
94 G5 Ilton Som., Eng.
64 B3 Imachar N. Ayr., Scot.
86 C4 Imber Wilts., Eng.
02 F4 Imeroo Fermanagh, N. Ire.
96 D4 Immeroin Stir., Scot.
70 E2 Immingham N.E. Lincs., Eng.
70 E2 Immingham Dock N.E. Lincs., Eng.
24 E5 Impington Cambs., Eng.
Inbhir Aora Arg. and B., Scot. see Inveraray
Inbhir Garadh High., Scot. see Invergarry
Inbhir Mhoireasdan High., Scot. see Invermoriston
Inbhir Pheofharain High., Scot. see Dingwall
Inbhir Theòrsa High., Scot. see Thurso
Inbhir Ùige High., Scot. see Wick
84 C2 Ince Cheshire West & Chester, Eng.
90 C2 Ince Blundell Merseyside, Eng.
98 B2 Ince-in-Makerfield Gtr Man., Eng.
88 E3 Inch Edin., Scot.
20 F4 Inchbae Lodge High., Scot.
08 G2 Inchbare Angus, Scot.
14 D2 Inchberry Moray, Scot.
08 H2 Inchbraoch Angus, Scot.
08 E1 Inchgrundle Angus, Scot.
88 D3 Inchinagh Limavady, N. Ire.
20 H4 Inchindown High., Scot.
76 D2 Inchinnan Renf., Scot.
24 K1 Inchkeith i. Scot.
20 G2 Inchkinloch High., Scot.
22 F3 Inchlaggan High., Scot.
20 G4 Inchlumpie High., Scot.
14 D4 Inchnabobart Abers., Scot.
22 G3 Inchnacardoch Hotel High., Scot.
20 F3 Inchnadamph High., Scot.
08 G3 Inchock Angus, Scot.
14 F4 Inch of Arnhall Abers., Scot.
22 F4 Inchree High., Scot.
14 C3 Inchrory Moray, Scot.
04 K4 Inchture Perth and Kin., Scot.
22 C3 Inchvuilt High., Scot.
04 K4 Inchyra Perth and Kin., Scot.
22 D11 Indaal, Loch b. Scot.
36 E2 Indian Queens Corn., Eng.
00 B5 Inerval Arg. and B., Scot.
16 E3 Ingatestone Essex, Eng.
08 C2 Ingbirchworth S. Yorks., Eng.
16 E2 Ingerthorpe N. Yorks., Eng.
48 C4 Ingestre Staffs., Eng.
70 C3 Ingham Lincs., Eng.
66 I2 Ingham Norf., Eng.
20 D3 Ingham Suff., Eng.
66 I2 Ingham Corner Norf., Eng.
66 A2 Ingleborough Norf., Eng.
24 M5 Ingleborough hill Eng.
80 E5 Ingleby Derbys., Eng.
70 C4 Ingleby Lincs., Eng.
36 H4 Ingleby Barwick Stockton, Eng.
16 F1 Ingleby Cross N. Yorks., Eng.
16 F1 Ingleby Greenhow N. Yorks., Eng.
94 J2 Inglesbatch B. and N.E. Som., Eng.
86 E1 Inglesham Swindon, Eng.
36 E4 Ingleton Durham, Eng.
16 B2 Ingleton N. Yorks., Eng.
28 F3 Inglewhite Lancs., Eng.
24 L4 Inglewood Forest for. Eng.
88 C3 Ingliston Edin., Scot.
32 G7 Ingmire Hall Cumbria, Eng.
44 F5 Ingoe Northumb., Eng.
66 C1 Ingoldisthorpe Norf., Eng.
70 I4 Ingoldmells Lincs., Eng.
70 C6 Ingoldsby Lincs., Eng.
32 B4 Ingon Warks., Eng.
44 F3 Ingram Northumb., Eng.
16 E4 Ingrave Essex, Eng.
22 C1 Ingrow W. Yorks., Eng.
36 G3 Ings Cumbria, Eng.
98 D4 Ingst S. Glos., Eng.
66 G2 Ingworth Norf., Eng.
52 E2 Inhurst Hants., Eng.
02 E2 Iniscian Strabane, N. Ire.
88 G3 Inishrush Magherafelt, N. Ire.
00 E2 Inistrynich Arg. and B., Scot.
05 C2 Injebreck Isle of Man
36 F2 Inkberrow Worcs., Eng.
80 E3 Inkersall Derbys., Eng.
80 E3 Inkersall Green Derbys., Eng.
14 G2 Inkhorn Abers., Scot.
82 B3 Inkpen W. Berks., Eng.
320 K2 Inkstack High., Scot.
86 C3 Inmarsh Wilts., Eng.
300 F4 Innellan Arg. and B., Scot.
292 H2 Innergellie Fife, Scot.
304 E2 Innerhadden Perth and Kin., Scot.
256 F3 Innerleithen Borders, Scot.
292 F2 Innerleven Fife, Scot.
252 B3 Innermessan D. and G., Scot.
22 E8 Inner Sound sea chan. Scot.
288 I3 Innerwick E. Lothian, Scot.
304 E3 Innerwick Perth and Kin., Scot.
322 D5 Inninbeg High., Scot.
98 F2 Innsworth Glos., Eng.
314 F2 Insch Abers., Scot.
322 J3 Insh High., Scot.
320 F2 Inshore High., Scot.
228 F3 Inskip Lancs., Eng.
40 D1 Instow Devon, Eng.
208 D3 Intake S. Yorks., Eng.
208 F2 Intake S. Yorks., Eng.
166 G3 Intwood Norf., Eng.
314 D3 Inver Abers., Scot.
300 E2 Inver Arg. and B., Scot.
320 I4 Inver High., Scot.
304 I3 Inver Perth and Kin., Scot.
322 E4 Inverailort High., Scot.
322 E2 Inveralligin High., Scot.
314 H1 Inverallochy Abers., Scot.
320 G4 Inveran High., Scot.
300 E3 Inveraray Arg. and B., Scot.
296 F4 Inverardoch Mains Stir., Scot.
296 C3 Inverardran Stir., Scot.
322 C2 Inverarish High., Scot.
308 E3 Inverarity Angus, Scot.
300 F3 Inverarnan Arg. and B., Scot.
320 D4 Inverasdale High., Scot.
322 D2 Inverbain High., Scot.
300 G3 Inverbeg Arg. and B., Scot.
314 G4 Inverbervie Abers., Scot.
320 E4 Inverbroom High., Scot.
322 J2 Inverbrough High., Scot.
320 G4 Invercassley High., Scot.
300 E4 Inverchaolain Arg. and B., Scot.
322 F5 Invercharnan High., Scot.
300 F3 Inverchorachan Arg. and B., Scot.
322 G2 Inverchoran High., Scot.
276 B2 Inverclyde admin. div. Scot.
322 J3 Inverdruie High., Scot.
314 G2 Inverebrie Abers., Scot.
322 J2 Invereen High., Scot.
314 C2 Inverernie Moray, Scot.
288 E3 Inveresk E. Lothian, Scot.
314 C4 Inverey Abers., Scot.
322 H3 Inverfarigaig High., Scot.
322 G3 Invergarry High., Scot.
304 F4 Invergeldie Perth and Kin., Scot.
322 G4 Invergloy High., Scot.
320 H4 Invergordon High., Scot.
304 L4 Invergowrie Perth and Kin., Scot.
296 C3 Inverherive Stir., Scot.
320 G2 Inverhope High., Scot.
322 D3 Inverie High., Scot.
300 E3 Inverinan Arg. and B., Scot.
322 E3 Inverinate High., Scot.
308 G3 Inverkeilor Angus, Scot.
292 D3 Inverkeithing Fife, Scot.
276 A2 Inverkip Inverclyde, Scot.
320 E3 Inverkirkaig High., Scot.
320 E4 Inverlael High., Scot.
300 F3 Inverlauren Arg. and B., Scot.
300 D3 Inverliever Arg. and B., Scot.
300 E2 Inverliver Arg. and B., Scot.
296 C4 Inverlochlarig Stir., Scot.
300 F2 Inverlochy Arg. and B., Scot.
300 C3 Inverlussa Arg. and B., Scot.
322 F4 Inver Mallie High., Scot.
304 I5 Invermay Perth and Kin., Scot.
388 L3 Invermore Larne, N. Ire.
322 H3 Invermoriston High., Scot.
320 H2 Invernaver High., Scot.
300 F2 Inverneil Arg. and B., Scot.
320 D4 Inverness High., Scot.
322 I2 Inverness (Dalcross) airport Scot.
300 E3 Invernoaden Arg. and B., Scot.
308 E2 Inverquharity Angus, Scot.
322 E4 Inversanda High., Scot.
296 E4 Invertrossachs Stir., Scot.
314 H2 Inverugie Abers., Scot.
300 F3 Inveruglas Arg. and B., Scot.
314 F3 Inverurie Abers., Scot.
304 E3 Invervar Perth and Kin., Scot.
300 E4 Invervegain Arg. and B., Scot.
314 F2 Inverythan Abers., Scot.
40 D2 Inwardleigh Devon, Eng.
116 G3 Inworth Essex, Eng.
326 B4 Iochdar W. Isles, Scot.
22 D10 Iona i. Scot.
22 D10 Iona, Sound of sea chan. Scot.
22 D10 Iona Abbey tourist site Scot.
58 B3 Iping W. Sussex, Eng.
40 E3 Ipplepen Devon, Eng.
102 E5 Ipsden Oxon, Eng.
136 F2 Ipsley Worcs., Eng.
148 D2 Ipstones Staffs., Eng.
120 F4 Ipswich Suff., Eng.
190 C3 Irby Merseyside, Eng.
190 C3 Irby Hill Merseyside, Eng.
170 H5 Irby in the Marsh Lincs., Eng.
170 E2 Irby upon Humber N.E. Lincs., Eng.
128 F4 Irchester Northants., Eng.
232 C4 Ireby Cumbria, Eng.
228 G1 Ireby Lancs., Eng.
329 B4 Ireland Orkney, Scot.
331 D4 Ireland Shet., Scot.
144 F2 Ireland's Cross Shrop., Eng.
232 C7 Ireleth Cumbria, Eng.
236 D3 Ireshopeburn Durham, Eng.
388 K4 Irish Hill Newtownabbey, N. Ire.
20 E5 Irish Sea sea Ireland/U.K.
198 C3 Irlam Gtr Man., Eng.
170 D6 Irnham Lincs., Eng.
98 E4 Iron Acton S. Glos., Eng.
144 F4 Ironbridge Telford, Eng.
132 A4 Iron Cross Warks., Eng.
78 E2 Irons Bottom Surr., Eng.
314 G2 Ironside Abers., Scot.
180 E4 Ironville Derbys., Eng.
166 I2 Irstead Norf., Eng.
24 L4 Irthing r. Eng.
232 F3 Irthington Cumbria, Eng.
128 F4 Irthlingborough Northants., Eng.
264 F3 Irvine N. Ayr., Scot.
22 G11 Irvine Bay b. Scot.
402 E4 Irvinestown Fermanagh, N. Ire.
320 I2 Isauld High., Scot.
329 B3 Isbister Orkney, Scot.
329 C3 Isbister Orkney, Scot.
331 D2 Isbister Shet., Scot.
331 E2 Isbister Shet., Scot.
58 G3 Isfield E. Sussex, Eng.
128 E3 Isham Northants., Eng.
300 C2 Ishriff Arg. and B., Scot.
52 G3 Isington Hants., Eng.
22 J9 Isla r. Scot.
372 G4 Islawr-dref Gwynedd, Wales
300 B4 Islay airport Scot.
22 D11 Islay i. Scot.
22 D11 Islay, Sound of sea chan. Scot.
94 G5 Isle Abbotts Som., Eng.
94 G5 Isle Brewers Som., Eng.
124 G4 Isleham Cambs., Eng.
371 C3 Isle of Anglesey admin. div. Wales
405 C3 Isle of Man airport Isle of Man
252 C3 Isle of Whithorn D. and G., Scot.
52 E6 Isle of Wight county Eng.
52 E7 Isle of Wight (Sandown) airport Eng.
322 D3 Isleornsay High., Scot.
331 C2 Islesburgh Shet., Scot.
36 □ Isles of Scilly Isles of Scilly, England
74 C3 Isleworth Gtr Lon., Eng.
162 C2 Isley Walton Leics., Eng.
326 C2 Islibhig W. Isles, Scot.
74 D2 Islington met. bor. Gtr Lon., Eng.
128 F3 Islip Northants., Eng.
102 D4 Islip Oxon, Eng.
144 E3 Isombridge Telford, Eng.
62 C2 Istead Rise Kent, Eng.
52 D5 Itchen Soton, Eng.
52 E4 Itchen Abbas Hants., Eng.
52 E4 Itchen Stoke Hants., Eng.
58 D2 Itchingfield W. Sussex, Eng.
166 G2 Itteringham Norf., Eng.
40 E2 Itton Devon, Eng.
339 D3 Itton Mon., Wales
339 D3 Itton Common Mon., Wales
106 E5 Iver Bucks., Eng.
106 E5 Iver Heath Bucks., Eng.
236 E2 Iveston Durham, Eng.
148 B4 Ivetsey Bank Staffs., Eng.
106 E3 Ivinghoe Bucks., Eng.
106 E3 Ivinghoe Aston Bucks., Eng.
140 C2 Ivington Here., Eng.
140 C2 Ivington Green Here., Eng.
40 E3 Ivybridge Devon, Eng.
62 E4 Ivychurch Kent, Eng.
62 B3 Ivy Hatch Kent, Eng.
166 D3 Ivy Todd Norf., Eng.
62 E2 Iwade Kent, Eng.
Iwerne Courtney Dorset, Eng. see Shroton
46 F2 Iwerne Minster Dorset, Eng.
120 D3 Ixworth Suff., Eng.
120 D3 Ixworth Thorpe Suff., Eng.

J

144 F4 Jackfield Telford, Eng.
228 G4 Jack Green Lancs., Eng.
216 D3 Jack Hill N. Yorks., Eng.
176 A4 Jacksdale Notts., Eng.
98 G3 Jack's Green Glos., Eng.
314 F2 Jackstown Abers., Scot.
268 A2 Jackton S. Lanark., Scot.
36 F1 Jacobstow Corn., Eng.
40 D2 Jacobstowe Devon, Eng.
78 C2 Jacobswell Surr., Eng.
222 C2 Jagger Green W. Yorks., Eng.
358 F4 Jameston Pembs., Wales
252 G2 Jamestown D. and G., Scot.
276 C2 Jamestown W. Dun., Scot.
322 I2 Janefield High., Scot.
320 K2 Janetstown High., Scot.
236 G2 Jarrow T. and W., Eng.
58 H2 Jarvis Brook E. Sussex, Eng.
116 F2 Jasper's Green Essex, Eng.
280 C3 Jawcraig Falk., Scot.
78 D3 Jayes Park Surr., Eng.
116 I3 Jaywick Essex, Eng.
82 F3 Jealott's Hill Brack. F., Eng.
216 F1 Jeater Houses N. Yorks., Eng.
256 I4 Jedburgh Borders, Scot.
358 F3 Jeffreyston Pembs., Wales
322 I2 Jemimaville High., Scot.
198 D2 Jericho Gtr Man., Eng.
396 F4 Jerrettspass Newry & Mourne, N. Ire.
280 C4 Jersay N. Lanark., Scot.
408 D4 Jersey airport Jersey Channel Is
408 E4 Jersey terr. Channel Is
350 C3 Jersey Marine N.P.T., Wales
268 D2 Jerviswood S. Lanark., Scot.
236 F2 Jesmond T. and W., Eng.
110 C5 Jockey End Herts., Eng.
184 F2 Jodrell Bank Cheshire East, Eng.
232 E4 Johnby Cumbria, Eng.
222 F2 John O' Gaunts W. Yorks., Eng.
320 K2 John o'Groats High., Scot.
58 I3 John's Cross E. Sussex, Eng.
314 F4 Johnshaven Abers., Scot.
358 D3 Johnston Pembs., Wales
276 C2 Johnstone Renf., Scot.
252 F2 Johnstonebridge D. and G., Scot.
276 C3 Johnstone Castle Renf., Scot.
356 E2 Johnstown Carmar., Wales
378 G3 Johnstown Wrex., Wales
396 F5 Jonesborough Newry & Mourne, N. Ire.
288 E3 Joppa Edin., Scot.
262 D4 Joppa S. Ayr., Scot.
166 F2 Jordan Green Norf., Eng.
106 E5 Jordans Bucks., Eng.
358 D2 Jordanston Pembs., Wales
304 K3 Jordanstone Perth and Kin., Scot.
98 D2 Joy's Green Glos., Eng.
208 D2 Jump S. Yorks., Eng.
46 I3 Jumpers Common Dorset, Eng.
288 D3 Juniper Green Edin., Scot.
102 D3 Juniper Hill Oxon, Eng.
22 E10 Jura i. Scot.
22 E11 Jura, Sound of sea chan. Scot.
405 D1 Jurby East Isle of Man
405 C1 Jurby West Isle of Man

K

232 I5 Kaber Cumbria, Eng.
288 E3 Kaimes Edin., Scot.
22 L11 Kale Water r. Scot.
300 D3 Kames Arg. and B., Scot.
300 E4 Kames Arg. and B., Scot.
262 G3 Kames E. Ayr., Scot.
396 H4 Katesbridge Banbridge, N. Ire.
154 B2 Kates Hill W. Mids, Eng.
22 G10 Katrine, Loch l. Scot.
36 D3 Kea Corn., Eng.
170 B2 Keadby N. Lincs., Eng.
396 D4 Keady Armagh, N. Ire.
22 D10 Keal, Loch na b. Scot.
170 G5 Keal Cotes Lincs., Eng.
396 L3 Kearney Ards, N. Ire.
198 C2 Kearsley Gtr Man., Eng.
232 G7 Kearstwick Cumbria, Eng.
216 D1 Kearton N. Yorks., Eng.
320 F2 Kearvaig High., Scot.
216 B2 Keasden N. Yorks., Eng.
314 F2 Kebholes Abers., Scot.
22 D6 Kebock Head hd Scot.
190 F3 Keckwick Halton, Eng.
170 G3 Keddington Lincs., Eng.
170 G3 Keddington Corner Lincs., Eng.
120 B4 Kedington Suff., Eng.
180 D5 Kedleston Derbys., Eng.
170 E2 Keelby Lincs., Eng.
148 B2 Keele Staffs., Eng.
110 B3 Keeley Green Bedford, Eng.
110 B3 Keeley Lane Bedford, Eng.
222 C2 Keelham W. Yorks., Eng.
22 K9 Keen, Mount hill Scot.
402 B4 Keenaghan Fermanagh, N. Ire.
388 G3 Keenans Bridge Coleraine, N. Ire.
94 F4 Keenthorne Som., Eng.
402 E3 Keeran Fermanagh, N. Ire.
116 D3 Keeres Green Essex, Eng.
358 D2 Keeston Pembs., Wales
86 C4 Keevil Wilts., Eng.
162 D1 Kegworth Leics., Eng.
36 C3 Kehelland Corn., Eng.
314 F3 Keig Abers., Scot.
222 C1 Keighley W. Yorks., Eng.
300 D6 Keil Arg. and B., Scot.
314 F2 Keilhill Abers., Scot.
300 C4 Keillmore Arg. and B., Scot.
304 K3 Keillor Perth and Kin., Scot.
304 I4 Keillour Perth and Kin., Scot.
300 B4 Keills Arg. and B., Scot.
300 C4 Keils Arg. and B., Scot.
94 I4 Keinton Mandeville Som., Eng.
296 G5 Keir House Stir., Scot.
252 E2 Keir Mill D. and G., Scot.
170 D6 Keisby Lincs., Eng.
232 H5 Keisley Cumbria, Eng.
320 K2 Keiss High., Scot.
314 E2 Keith Moray, Scot.
304 K3 Keithick Perth and Kin., Scot.
314 D2 Keithmore Moray, Scot.
308 G2 Keithock Angus, Scot.
228 J3 Kelbrook Lancs., Eng.
170 C6 Kelby Lincs., Eng.
232 F5 Keld Cumbria, Eng.
216 C1 Keld N. Yorks., Eng.
216 G2 Keldy Castle N. Yorks., Eng.
170 B2 Kelfield N. Lincs., Eng.
176 D4 Kelham Notts., Eng.
405 D2 Kella Cumbria, Eng.
300 B2 Kellan Arg. and B., Scot.
308 E3 Kellas Angus, Scot.
314 C2 Kellas Moray, Scot.
86 C3 Kellaways Wilts., Eng.
232 G6 Kelleth Cumbria, Eng.
210 F3 Kelleythorpe E. Riding, Eng.
166 F1 Kelling Norf., Eng.
236 G3 Kelloe Durham, Eng.
252 E1 Kelloholm D. and G., Scot.
388 I4 Kells Ballymena, N. Ire.
23 J3 Kells r. N. Ire.
40 D3 Kelly Devon, Eng.
128 D3 Kelmarsh Northants., Eng.
102 B4 Kelmscott Oxon, Eng.
120 H3 Kelsale Suff., Eng.
184 C2 Kelsall Cheshire West & Chester, Eng.
300 A4 Kelsay Arg. and B., Scot.
110 E3 Kelshall Herts., Eng.
232 C3 Kelsick Cumbria, Eng.
256 J3 Kelso Borders, Scot.
180 E3 Kelstedge Derbys., Eng.
170 F3 Kelstern Lincs., Eng.
94 J2 Kelston B. and N.E. Som., Eng.
304 F3 Keltneyburn Perth and Kin., Scot.
252 F2 Kelton D. and G., Scot.
Kelton Hill D. and G., Scot. see Rhonehouse
292 D3 Kelty Fife, Scot.
116 G3 Kelvedon Essex, Eng.
116 D3 Kelvedon Hatch Essex, Eng.
276 E2 Kelvindale Glas., Scot.
276 E2 Kelvinhaugh Glas., Scot.
276 E2 Kelvinside Glas., Scot.
36 B3 Kelynack Corn., Eng.
40 E1 Kemacott Devon, Eng.
292 G2 Kemback Fife, Scot.
144 F4 Kemberton Shrop., Eng.
98 G3 Kemble Glos., Eng.
136 E3 Kemerton Worcs., Eng.
339 C2 Kemeys Commander Mon., Wales
339 C3 Kemeys Inferior Newp., Wales
314 F3 Kemnay Abers., Scot.
62 F3 Kempe's Corner Kent, Eng.
98 E2 Kempley Glos., Eng.
98 E2 Kempley Green Glos., Eng.
136 D3 Kempsey Worcs., Eng.
98 I3 Kempsford Glos., Eng.
132 B3 Kemps Green Warks., Eng.
52 F3 Kempshott Hants., Eng.
110 C3 Kempston Bedford, Eng.
110 B3 Kempston Church End Bedford, Eng.
110 C3 Kempston Hardwick Bedford, Eng.
110 B3 Kempston West End Bedford, Eng.
144 C5 Kempton Shrop., Eng.
58 F4 Kemp Town B. and H., Eng.
62 B3 Kemsing Kent, Eng.
62 E2 Kemsley Kent, Eng.
22 H13 Ken, Loch l. Scot.
62 E4 Kenardington Kent, Eng.
140 C3 Kenchester Here., Eng.
102 B4 Kencot Oxon, Eng.
232 F7 Kendal Cumbria, Eng.
136 F1 Kendal End Worcs., Eng.
140 B4 Kenderchurch Here., Eng.
98 E4 Kendleshire S. Glos., Eng.
350 D3 Kenfig Bridg., Wales
350 D3 Kenfig Hill Bridg., Wales
132 C3 Kenilworth Warks., Eng.
304 D3 Kenknock Perth and Kin., Scot.
296 D2 Kenknock Stir., Scot.
74 D4 Kenley Gtr Lon., Eng.
144 E4 Kenley Shrop., Eng.
300 E3 Kenmore Arg. and B., Scot.
322 D2 Kenmore High., Scot.
304 G3 Kenmore Perth and Kin., Scot.
326 D3 Kenmore W. Isles, Scot.
40 F3 Kenn Devon, Eng.
94 G2 Kenn N. Som., Eng.
300 D4 Kennacraig Arg. and B., Scot.
326 E3 Kennavay W. Isles, Scot.
40 E2 Kennerleigh Devon, Eng.
314 F3 Kennerty Abers., Scot.
292 B3 Kennet Clack., Scot.
26 K5 Kennet r. Eng.
314 E2 Kennethmont Abers., Scot.
124 G5 Kennett Cambs., Eng.
40 F2 Kennford Devon, Eng.
166 F4 Kenninghall Norf., Eng.
74 D3 Kennington Gtr Lon., Eng.
62 F3 Kennington Kent, Eng.
102 D4 Kennington Oxon, Eng.
292 F2 Kennoway Fife, Scot.
94 G5 Kenny Som., Eng.
120 B2 Kennyhill Suff., Eng.
300 □ Kenovay Arg. and B., Scot.
322 C2 Kensaleyre High., Scot.
74 C2 Kensal Green Gtr Lon., Eng.
74 C2 Kensal Rise Gtr Lon., Eng.
74 C2 Kensal Town Gtr Lon., Eng.
74 C2 Kensington Gtr Lon., Eng.
74 C3 Kensington and Chelsea met. bor. Gtr Lon., Eng.
350 F4 Kenson V. of Glam., Wales
144 E2 Kenstone Shrop., Eng.
110 B4 Kensworth Central Bedfordshire, Eng.
110 C4 Kensworth Common Central Bedfordshire, Eng.
62 E3 Kent county Eng.
24 L5 Kent r. Eng.
26 M5 Kent, Vale of val. Eng.
140 B4 Kentchurch Here., Eng.
120 C3 Kentford Suff., Eng.
62 I2 Kent International airport Eng.
40 G2 Kentisbeare Devon, Eng.
40 E1 Kentisbury Devon, Eng.
40 E1 Kentisbury Ford Devon, Eng.
74 D2 Kentish Town Gtr Lon., Eng.
232 E6 Kentmere Cumbria, Eng.
40 F3 Kenton Devon, Eng.
120 G3 Kenton Suff., Eng.
236 F1 Kenton T. and W., Eng.
120 G3 Kenton Corner Suff., Eng.
322 D4 Kentra High., Scot.
232 E7 Kents Bank Cumbria, Eng.
98 E2 Kent's Green Glos., Eng.
52 C4 Kent's Oak Hants., Eng.
58 J3 Kent Street E. Sussex, Eng.
62 C3 Kent Street Kent, Eng.
144 C2 Kenwick Shrop., Eng.
36 D3 Kenwyn Corn., Eng.
198 B3 Kenyon Gtr Man., Eng.
320 F2 Keoldale High., Scot.
396 G3 Keonan Craigavon, N. Ire.
326 E2 Keose W. Isles, Scot.
300 F4 Keppoch Arg. and B., Scot.
322 E3 Keppoch High., Scot.
300 D5 Keprigan Arg. and B., Scot.
216 F2 Kepwick N. Yorks., Eng.
166 F2 Kerdiston Norf., Eng.
154 E3 Keresley W. Mids, Eng.
140 D4 Kerne Bridge Here., Eng.
22 E10 Kerrera i. Scot.
184 G2 Kerridge Cheshire East, Eng.
36 C3 Kerris Corn., Eng.
300 E4 Kerrycroy Arg. and B., Scot.
320 D4 Kerrysdale High., Scot.
140 B4 Kerry's Gate Here., Eng.
176 D4 Kersall Notts., Eng.
120 E4 Kersey Suff., Eng.
120 E4 Kersey Vale Suff., Eng.
232 F2 Kershopefoot Cumbria, Eng.
40 G2 Kerswell Devon, Eng.
136 D3 Kerswell Green Worcs., Eng.
120 G4 Kesgrave Suff., Eng.
402 D3 Kesh Fermanagh, N. Ire.
120 J2 Kessingland Suff., Eng.
120 J2 Kessingland Beach Suff., Eng.
36 E3 Kestle Corn., Eng.
36 D2 Kestle Mill Corn., Eng.
74 E3 Keston Gtr Lon., Eng.
232 D5 Keswick Cumbria, Eng.
166 G3 Keswick Norf., Eng.
166 H1 Keswick Norf., Eng.
144 F3 Ketley Telford, Eng.
144 F3 Ketley Bank Telford, Eng.
170 G4 Ketsby Lincs., Eng.
128 E3 Kettering Northants., Eng.
166 G3 Ketteringham Norf., Eng.
304 K3 Kettins Perth and Kin., Scot.
120 E4 Kettlebaston Suff., Eng.
292 F2 Kettlebridge Fife, Scot.
148 E5 Kettlebrook Staffs., Eng.
120 G3 Kettleburgh Suff., Eng.
62 C3 Kettle Corner Kent, Eng.
292 F2 Kettlehill Fife, Scot.
252 F2 Kettleholm D. and G., Scot.
216 G1 Kettleness N. Yorks., Eng.
184 G2 Kettleshulme Cheshire East, Eng.
216 E2 Kettlesing N. Yorks., Eng.
216 D3 Kettlesing Head N. Yorks., Eng.
166 E1 Kettlestone Norf., Eng.
170 B4 Kettlethorpe Lincs., Eng.
329 F2 Kettletoft Orkney, Scot.
216 C2 Kettlewell N. Yorks., Eng.
162 H3 Ketton Rutland, Eng.
74 E3 Kevingtown Gtr Lon., Eng.
74 C3 Kew Gtr Lon., Eng.
94 G2 Kewstoke N. Som., Eng.
208 C2 Kexbrough S. Yorks., Eng.
170 B3 Kexby Lincs., Eng.
216 G3 Kexby York, Eng.
184 G2 Key Green Cheshire East, Eng.
216 G1 Key Green N. Yorks., Eng.
162 E3 Keyham Leics., Eng.
52 C6 Keyhaven Hants., Eng.
210 H4 Keyingham E. Riding, Eng.
58 F3 Keymer W. Sussex, Eng.
94 I2 Keynsham B. and N.E. Som., Eng.
110 C2 Keysoe Bedford, Eng.
110 C2 Keysoe Row Bedford, Eng.
170 H5 Key's Toft Lincs., Eng.
124 B4 Keyston Cambs., Eng.
62 E2 Key Street Kent, Eng.
176 C5 Keyworth Notts., Eng.
236 F2 Kibblesworth T. and W., Eng.
162 F3 Kibworth Beauchamp Leics., Eng.
162 F3 Kibworth Harcourt Leics., Eng.
74 E3 Kidbrooke Gtr Lon., Eng.
222 F1 Kiddal Lane End W. Yorks., Eng.
148 B4 Kiddemore Green Staffs., Eng.
136 D1 Kidderminster Worcs., Eng.
102 C3 Kiddington Oxon, Eng.
166 F3 Kidd's Moor Norf., Eng.
102 D4 Kidlington Oxon, Eng.
102 F5 Kidmore End Oxon, Eng.
184 C3 Kidnal Cheshire West & Chester, Eng.
252 C3 Kidsdale D. and G., Scot.
148 B2 Kidsgrove Staffs., Eng.
216 C2 Kidstones N. Yorks., Eng.
388 G2 Kidstown Ballymoney, N. Ire.
356 E3 Kidwelly Carmar., Wales
300 D2 Kiel Crofts Arg. and B., Scot.
244 B4 Kielder Northumb., Eng.
24 L3 Kielder Water resr Eng.
276 C2 Kilbarchan Renf., Scot.
322 D3 Kilbeg High., Scot.
300 D4 Kilberry Arg. and B., Scot.
264 F2 Kilbirnie N. Ayr., Scot.
300 E3 Kilblaan Arg. and B., Scot.
276 D2 Kilbowie W. Dun., Scot.
22 F12 Kilbrannan Sound sea chan. Scot.
320 I3 Kilbraur High., Scot.
300 B2 Kilbrennan Arg. and B., Scot.
388 J4 Kilbride Newtownabbey, N. Ire.
300 D2 Kilbride Arg. and B., Scot.
322 D3 Kilbride High., Scot.
300 E4 Kilbride Farm Arg. and B., Scot.
300 E3 Kilbridemore Arg. and B., Scot.
180 E4 Kilburn Derbys., Eng.
74 C2 Kilburn Gtr Lon., Eng.
216 F2 Kilburn N. Yorks., Eng.
162 E3 Kilby Leics., Eng.
300 E4 Kilchattan Bay Arg. and B., Scot.
300 C5 Kilchenzie Arg. and B., Scot.
300 D2 Kilcheran Arg. and B., Scot.
300 A4 Kilchiaran Arg. and B., Scot.
322 C4 Kilchoan High., Scot.
300 A4 Kilchoman Arg. and B., Scot.
300 E2 Kilchrenan Arg. and B., Scot.
396 K3 Kilclief Down, N. Ire.
292 H2 Kilconquhar Fife, Scot.
396 H4 Kilcoo Down, N. Ire.
388 J5 Kilcorig Lisburn, N. Ire.
98 E2 Kilcot Glos., Eng.
322 H2 Kilcoy High., Scot.
300 F4 Kilcreggan Arg. and B., Scot.
388 J5 Kilcross Antrim, N. Ire.
216 F1 Kildale N. Yorks., Eng.
300 D5 Kildavie Arg. and B., Scot.
264 D4 Kildonan N. Ayr., Scot.
320 I3 Kildonan Lodge High., Scot.
322 C4 Kildonnan High., Scot.
402 J3 Kildress Cookstown, N. Ire.
252 B3 Kildrochet House D. and G., Scot.
388 I4 Kildrum Ballymena, N. Ire.
280 C3 Kildrum N. Lanark., Scot.
314 E3 Kildrummy Abers., Scot.
216 D3 Kildwick N. Yorks., Eng.
300 E4 Kilfinan Arg. and B., Scot.
322 G3 Kilfinnan High., Scot.
358 F3 Kilgetty Pembs., Wales
339 D2 Kilgwrrwg Common Mon., Wales
210 F2 Kilham E. Riding, Eng.
244 D2 Kilham Northumb., Eng.
396 I5 Kilkeel Newry & Mourne, N. Ire.
300 □ Kilkenneth Arg. and B., Scot.
98 H2 Kilkenny Glos., Eng.
262 C5 Kilkerran S. Ayr., Scot.
36 F1 Kilkhampton Corn., Eng.
396 H4 Kilkinamurry Banbridge, N. Ire.
402 D4 Killadeas Fermanagh, N. Ire.
388 H2 Killagan Bridge Ballymoney, N. Ire.
388 C3 Killaloo Derry, N. Ire.
180 F3 Killamarsh Derbys., Eng.
402 F4 Killarbran Fermanagh, N. Ire.
388 G4 Killard Magherafelt, N. Ire.
350 B3 Killay Swansea, Wales
300 C2 Killbeg Arg. and B., Scot.
388 I5 Killead Antrim, N. Ire.
388 F2 Killeague Coleraine, N. Ire.
300 D5 Killean Arg. and B., Scot.
300 E3 Killean Arg. and B., Scot.
296 D5 Killearn Stir., Scot.
396 E4 Killeen Armagh, N. Ire.
402 K3 Killeen Dungannon, N. Ire.
396 F5 Killeen Newry & Mourne, N. Ire.
402 I4 Killeeshil Dungannon, N. Ire.
300 D5 Killellan Arg. and B., Scot.
402 E2 Killen Strabane, N. Ire.
322 I2 Killen High., Scot.
236 E4 Killerby Darl., Eng.
40 F2 Killerton Devon, Eng.
402 D2 Killeter Strabane, N. Ire.
304 D2 Killichonan Perth and Kin., Scot.
322 G4 Killiechonate High., Scot.
300 E2 Killiechronan Arg. and B., Scot.
304 H2 Killiecrankie Perth and Kin., Scot.
300 B2 Killiemor Arg. and B., Scot.
322 E3 Killilan High., Scot.
320 I3 Killin High., Scot.
296 E3 Killin Stir., Scot.
300 B4 Killinallan Arg. and B., Scot.
396 K3 Killinchy Ards, N. Ire.
216 E2 Killinghall N. Yorks., Eng.
232 G7 Killington Cumbria, Eng.
236 F1 Killingworth T. and W., Eng.
256 G2 Killochyett Borders, Scot.
300 C5 Killocraw Arg. and B., Scot.
396 K4 Killough Down, N. Ire.
396 G5 Killowen Newry & Mourne, N. Ire.
402 I3 Killucan Cookstown, N. Ire.
300 B2 Killunaig Arg. and B., Scot.
322 D5 Killundine High., Scot.
388 F2 Killure Coleraine, N. Ire.
402 G3 Killyclogher Omagh, N. Ire.
402 J3 Killycolp Cookstown, N. Ire.
402 K3 Killycolpy Cookstown, N. Ire.
388 D3 Killycor Derry, N. Ire.
402 I2 Killycurragh Cookstown, N. Ire.
402 I3 Killyharry Dungannon, N. Ire.
388 F2 Killykergan Coleraine, N. Ire.
388 D2 Killylane Limavady, N. Ire.
396 E4 Killylea Armagh, N. Ire.
396 D3 Killyleagh Down, N. Ire.
388 B3 Killymallaght Derry, N. Ire.
396 J2 Killynether Ards, N. Ire.
388 H2 Killyrammer Ballymoney, N. Ire.
276 C2 Kilmacolm Inverclyde, Scot.
300 E3 Kilmaha Arg. and B., Scot.
388 H1 Kilmahamogue Moyle, N. Ire.
296 E4 Kilmahog Stir., Scot.
322 E5 Kilmalieu High., Scot.
322 C2 Kilmaluag High., Scot.
292 G1 Kilmany Fife, Scot.
322 C3 Kilmarie High., Scot.
262 E3 Kilmarnock E. Ayr., Scot.
300 D3 Kilmartin Arg. and B., Scot.
262 D3 Kilmaurs E. Ayr., Scot.
300 D3 Kilmelford Arg. and B., Scot.
300 B4 Kilmeny Arg. and B., Scot.
94 J3 Kilmersdon Som., Eng.
52 F4 Kilmeston Hants., Eng.
300 D5 Kilmichael Arg. and B., Scot.
40 G2 Kilmington Devon, Eng.
86 B5 Kilmington Wilts., Eng.
86 B5 Kilmington Common Wilts., Eng.
86 B5 Kilmington Street Wilts., Eng.
396 J3 Kilmood Ards, N. Ire.
322 H2 Kilmorack High., Scot.
396 E3 Kilmore Armagh, N. Ire.
396 J3 Kilmore Down, N. Ire.
300 D2 Kilmore Arg. and B., Scot.
322 D3 Kilmore High., Scot.
300 D2 Kilmory Arg. and B., Scot.
300 F6 Kilmory Arg. and B., Scot.
322 B3 Kilmory High., Scot.
322 C4 Kilmory High., Scot.
264 C4 Kilmory N. Ayr., Scot.
320 I3 Kilmote High., Scot.
322 I2 Kilmuir High., Scot.
300 F4 Kilmun Arg. and B., Scot.
292 F2 Kilmux Fife, Scot.
402 I3 Kilnaslee Dungannon, N. Ire.
300 A4 Kilnave Arg. and B., Scot.
268 D2 Kilncadzow S. Lanark., Scot.
62 C4 Kilndown Kent, Eng.
198 F2 Kiln Green Gtr Man., Eng.
140 D4 Kiln Green Here., Eng.
82 F2 Kiln Green W'ham, Eng.
208 E3 Kilnhurst S. Yorks., Eng.
300 B2 Kilninian Arg. and B., Scot.
300 D2 Kilninver Arg. and B., Scot.
244 F6 Kiln Pit Hill Northumb., Eng.
210 I5 Kilnsea E. Riding, Eng.
216 C2 Kilnsey N. Yorks., Eng.
396 G3 Kilntown Banbridge, N. Ire.
210 F3 Kilnwick E. Riding, Eng.
210 D3 Kilnwick Percy E. Riding, Eng.
300 B3 Kiloran Arg. and B., Scot.
264 C4 Kilpatrick N. Ayr., Scot.
140 C4 Kilpeck Here., Eng.
320 I3 Kilphedir High., Scot.
210 D4 Kilpin E. Riding, Eng.
210 C4 Kilpin Pike E. Riding, Eng.
388 H2 Kilraghts Ballymoney, N. Ire.
388 E3 Kilrea Coleraine, N. Ire.
292 H2 Kilrenny Fife, Scot.
388 L4 Kilroot Carrickfergus, N. Ire.
402 K3 Kilsally Cookstown, N. Ire.
128 B3 Kilsby Northants., Eng.
402 E4 Kilskeery Omagh, N. Ire.
304 K4 Kilspindie Perth and Kin., Scot.
252 B3 Kilstay D. and G., Scot.
280 B3 Kilsyth N. Lanark., Scot.
322 H2 Kiltarlity High., Scot.
176 C3 Kilton Notts., Eng.
216 G1 Kilton R. and C., Eng.
94 E3 Kilton Som., Eng.
304 E3 Kiltyrie Perth and Kin., Scot.
322 B2 Kilvaxter High., Scot.
94 E3 Kilve Som., Eng.
166 D4 Kilverstone Norf., Eng.
176 E5 Kilvington Notts., Eng.
388 K3 Kilwaughter Larne, N. Ire.
264 F3 Kilwinning N. Ayr., Scot.
166 F3 Kimberley Norf., Eng.
176 B5 Kimberley Notts., Eng.
166 F3 Kimberley Street Norf., Eng.
208 D3 Kimberworth S. Yorks., Eng.
236 F3 Kimblesworth Durham, Eng.
106 C4 Kimble Wick Bucks., Eng.
124 B5 Kimbolton Cambs., Eng.
140 C2 Kimbolton Here., Eng.
52 C4 Kimbridge Hants., Eng.
162 E4 Kimcote Leics., Eng.
46 G4 Kimmeridge Dorset, Eng.
244 E2 Kimmerston Northumb., Eng.
52 C3 Kimpton Hants., Eng.
110 D4 Kimpton Herts., Eng.
402 E5 Kinakelly Fermanagh, N. Ire.
292 H2 Kinaldy Fife, Scot.
396 H3 Kinallen Banbridge, N. Ire.
402 E5 Kinawley Fermanagh, N. Ire.
308 G3 Kinblethmont Angus, Scot.
320 I3 Kinbrace High., Scot.
322 F3 Kinbreack High., Scot.
296 G4 Kinbuck Stir., Scot.
308 E3 Kincaldrum Angus, Scot.
292 G1 Kincaple Fife, Scot.
292 B3 Kincardine Fife, Scot.
320 G4 Kincardine High., Scot.
314 E3 Kincardine O'Neil Abers., Scot.
304 J3 Kinclaven Perth and Kin., Scot.
314 G3 Kincorth Aberdeen, Scot.
314 G3 Kincraig Abers., Scot.
322 J3 Kincraig High., Scot.
304 I3 Kincraigie Perth and Kin., Scot.
304 I3 Kindallachan Perth and Kin., Scot.
24 N7 Kinder Scout hill Eng.
314 G3 Kinellar Abers., Scot.
98 H2 Kineton Glos., Eng.
132 C5 Kineton Warks., Eng.
154 D3 Kineton Green W. Mids, Eng.
304 J4 Kinfauns Perth and Kin., Scot.
300 E4 Kingarth Arg. and B., Scot.
339 D2 Kingcoed Mon., Wales
102 B3 Kingham Oxon, Eng.
252 F2 Kingholm Quay D. and G., Scot.
292 E3 Kinghorn Fife, Scot.
22 F8 Kingie r. Scot.
292 E2 Kinglassie Fife, Scot.
304 L4 Kingoodie Perth and Kin., Scot.
140 C3 King's Acre Here., Eng.
36 G2 Kingsand Corn., Eng.
58 J3 King's Bank E. Sussex, Eng.
292 I2 Kingsbarns Fife, Scot.
40 E4 Kingsbridge Devon, Eng.
94 D4 Kingsbridge Som., Eng.
148 E4 King's Bromley Staffs., Eng.
322 B2 Kingsburgh High., Scot.
74 C2 Kingsbury Gtr Lon., Eng.
132 B2 Kingsbury Warks., Eng.
94 H5 Kingsbury Episcopi Som., Eng.
140 D4 Kings Caple Here., Eng.
288 B3 Kingscavil W. Lothian, Scot.
52 E3 Kingsclere Hants., Eng.
128 F2 King's Cliffe Northants., Eng.
98 F4 Kingscote Glos., Eng.
132 A4 King's Coughton Warks., Eng.
264 D3 Kingscross N. Ayr., Scot.
292 G1 Kingsdale Fife, Scot.
94 H4 Kingsdon Som., Eng.
62 I3 Kingsdown Kent, Eng.
86 E2 Kingsdown Swindon, Eng.
86 B3 Kingsdown Wilts., Eng.
292 D3 Kingseat Fife, Scot.
106 C4 Kingsey Bucks., Eng.
58 E2 Kingsfold W. Sussex, Eng.
358 E4 Kingsfold Pembs., Wales
136 D1 Kingsford Worcs., Eng.
314 G3 Kingsford Aberdeen, Scot.
314 F2 Kingsford Abers., Scot.
262 E2 Kingsford E. Ayr., Scot.
62 I2 Kingsgate Kent, Eng.
98 E1 King's Green Glos., Eng.
154 C3 King's Heath W. Mids, Eng.
62 C3 Kings Hill Kent, Eng.
132 C3 King's Hill Warks., Eng.
154 B2 King's Hill W. Mids, Eng.
98 F2 Kingsholm Glos., Eng.
296 E3 Kingshouse Stir., Scot.
322 G5 Kingshouse Hotel High., Scot.
154 D3 Kingshurst W. Mids, Eng.
40 F3 Kingskerswell Devon, Eng.
292 F2 Kingskettle Fife, Scot.
74 D2 Kingsland Gtr Lon., Eng.
140 C2 Kingsland Here., Eng.
371 B3 Kingsland I.o.A., Wales
110 C5 Kings Langley Herts., Eng.
184 C2 Kingsley Cheshire West & Chester, Eng.
52 G4 Kingsley Hants., Eng.
148 D2 Kingsley Staffs., Eng.
58 B2 Kingsley Green W. Sussex, Eng.
148 D2 Kingsley Holt Staffs., Eng.
144 G4 Kingslow Shrop., Eng.
166 B2 King's Lynn Norf., Eng.
232 G5 King's Meaburn Cumbria, Eng.
402 K3 Kingsmill Cookstown, N. Ire.
408 B3 Kings Mills Guernsey Channel Is
116 C3 Kingsmoor Essex, Eng.
198 C3 King's Moss Gtr Man., Eng.
308 E3 Kingsmuir Angus, Scot.
256 E3 Kings Muir Borders, Scot.
292 H2 Kingsmuir Fife, Scot.
132 D3 King's Newnham Warks., Eng.
180 E6 Kings Newton Derbys., Eng.
62 F4 Kingsnorth Kent, Eng.

King's Norton to Leck

162 F3 **King's Norton** Leics., Eng.
154 C3 **King's Norton** W. Mids, Eng.
40 E2 **Kings Nympton** Devon, Eng.
276 E3 **King's Park** Glas., Scot.
140 C3 **King's Pyon** Here., Eng.
124 D4 **Kings Ripton** Cambs., Eng.
52 D4 **King's Somborne** Hants., Eng.
46 E2 **King's Stag** Dorset, Eng.
98 F3 **King's Stanley** Glos., Eng.
128 B5 **King's Sutton** Northants., Eng.
40 D3 **King's Tamerton** Plymouth, Eng.
154 C2 **Kingstanding** W. Mids, Eng.
40 F3 **Kingsteignton** Devon, Eng.
322 J2 **Kingsteps** High., Scot.
180 B3 **King Sterndale** Derbys., Eng.
140 C4 **Kingsthorne** Here., Eng.
128 D4 **Kingsthorpe** Northants., Eng.
124 D5 **Kingston** Cambs., Eng.
36 G2 **Kingston** Corn., Eng.
46 E2 **Kingston** Dorset, Eng.
46 G4 **Kingston** Dorset, Eng.
198 E3 **Kingston** Gtr Man., Eng.
52 B6 **Kingston** Hants., Eng.
52 E7 **Kingston** I.o.W., Eng.
62 G3 **Kingston** Kent, Eng.
106 D2 **Kingston** M.K., Eng.
288 G2 **Kingston** E. Lothian, Scot.
314 D1 **Kingston** Moray, Scot.
102 C4 **Kingston Bagpuize** Oxon, Eng.
102 F4 **Kingston Blount** Oxon, Eng.
58 E3 **Kingston by Sea** W. Sussex, Eng.
86 B5 **Kingston Deverill** Wilts., Eng.
140 B3 **Kingstone** Here., Eng.
140 D4 **Kingstone** Here., Eng.
94 G5 **Kingstone** Som., Eng.
148 D3 **Kingstone** Staffs., Eng.
102 B5 **Kingstone Winslow** Oxon, Eng.
58 D4 **Kingston Gorse** W. Sussex, Eng.
102 B5 **Kingston Lisle** Oxon, Eng.
46 E3 **Kingston Maurward** Dorset, Eng.
176 B5 **Kingston on Soar** Notts., Eng.
46 D3 **Kingston Russell** Dorset, Eng.
94 G2 **Kingston Seymour** N. Som., Eng.
102 F4 **Kingston Stert** Oxon, Eng.
94 F4 **Kingston St Mary** Som., Eng.
210 G4 **Kingston upon Hull** Hull, Eng.
219 F4 **Kingston upon Hull** admin. div. Eng.
74 C3 **Kingston upon Thames** Gtr Lon., Eng.
74 C3 **Kingston upon Thames** met. bor. Gtr Lon., Eng.
102 B5 **Kingston Warren** Oxon, Eng.
232 E3 **Kingstown** Cumbria, Eng.
110 D4 **King's Walden** Herts., Eng.
40 F3 **Kingswear** Devon, Eng.
262 E2 **Kingswell** E. Ayr., Scot.
314 G3 **Kingswells** Aberdeen, Scot.
154 A3 **Kingswinford** W. Mids, Eng.
106 C3 **Kingswood** Bucks., Eng.
98 E4 **Kingswood** Glos., Eng.
140 A2 **Kingswood** Here., Eng.
62 D3 **Kingswood** Kent, Eng.
98 D5 **Kingswood** S. Glos., Eng.
94 E4 **Kingswood** Som., Eng.
78 E2 **Kingswood** Surr., Eng.
132 B3 **Kingswood** Warks., Eng.
366 G3 **Kingswood** Powys, Wales
52 E4 **Kings Worthy** Hants., Eng.
170 E4 **Kingthorpe** Lincs., Eng.
140 A2 **Kington** Here., Eng.
136 E2 **Kington** Worcs., Eng.
86 C3 **Kington Langley** Wilts., Eng.
46 F1 **Kington Magna** Dorset, Eng.
86 C3 **Kington St Michael** Wilts., Eng.
322 I3 **Kingussie** High., Scot.
94 H4 **Kingweston** Som., Eng.
314 G2 **Kinharrachie** Abers., Scot.
252 E3 **Kinharvie** D. and G., Scot.
276 E2 **Kinkell** E. Dun., Scot.
304 H5 **Kinkell Bridge** Perth and Kin., Scot.
144 F5 **Kinlet** Shrop., Eng.
292 F2 **Kinloch** Fife, Scot.
320 F3 **Kinloch** High., Scot.
320 G4 **Kinloch** High., Scot.
322 C3 **Kinloch** High., Scot.
322 D5 **Kinloch** High., Scot.
304 J3 **Kinloch** Perth and Kin., Scot.
304 K3 **Kinloch** Perth and Kin., Scot.
322 E4 **Kinlochan** High., Scot.
296 D4 **Kinlochard** Stir., Scot.
322 E4 **Kinlochbeoraid** High., Scot.
320 E2 **Kinlochbervie** High., Scot.
322 F4 **Kinlocheil** High., Scot.
322 F2 **Kinlochewe** High., Scot.
322 E3 **Kinloch Hourn** High., Scot.
322 H4 **Kinloch Laggan** High., Scot.
322 G4 **Kinlochleven** High., Scot.
322 D4 **Kinlochmoidart** High., Scot.
322 E4 **Kinlochmorar** High., Scot.
322 G4 **Kinlochmore** High., Scot.
304 E2 **Kinloch Rannoch** Perth and Kin., Scot.
326 D2 **Kinlochroag** W. Isles, Scot.
300 C2 **Kinlochspelve** Arg. and B., Scot.
314 C2 **Kinloss** Moray, Scot.
378 D2 **Kinmel Bay** Conwy, Wales
308 H2 **Kinnaber** Angus, Scot.
314 G2 **Kinnadie** Abers., Scot.
304 K4 **Kinnaird** Perth and Kin., Scot.
314 G4 **Kinneff** Abers., Scot.
252 F2 **Kinnelhead** D. and G., Scot.
308 G3 **Kinnell** Angus, Scot.
296 E3 **Kinnell** Stir., Scot.
144 C3 **Kinnerley** Shrop., Eng.
140 B3 **Kinnersley** Here., Eng.
136 D3 **Kinnersley** Worcs., Eng.
366 G5 **Kinnerton** Powys, Wales
378 H3 **Kinnerton Green** Flints., Wales
304 K5 **Kinnesswood** Perth and Kin., Scot.
308 E3 **Kinnettles** Angus, Scot.
276 E2 **Kinning Park** Glas., Scot.
236 D4 **Kinninvie** Durham, Eng.
308 D2 **Kinnordy** Angus, Scot.
176 D5 **Kinoulton** Notts., Eng.
304 J5 **Kinross** Perth and Kin., Scot.
304 K4 **Kinrossie** Perth and Kin., Scot.
110 C5 **Kinsbourne Green** Herts., Eng.
140 B2 **Kinsham** Here., Eng.
136 E3 **Kinsham** Worcs., Eng.
222 F3 **Kinsley** W. Yorks., Eng.
46 H3 **Kinson** Bourne., Eng.
326 D2 **Kintarvie** W. Isles, Scot.
82 B3 **Kintbury** W. Berks., Eng.
314 B2 **Kintessack** Moray, Scot.
304 J4 **Kintillo** Perth and Kin., Scot.
140 B1 **Kinton** Here., Eng.
144 C3 **Kinton** Shrop., Eng.
314 F3 **Kintore** Abers., Scot.
300 B4 **Kintour** Arg. and B., Scot.
300 A2 **Kintra** Arg. and B., Scot.
300 B5 **Kintra** Arg. and B., Scot.
320 I3 **Kintradwell** High., Scot.
300 D3 **Kintraw** Arg. and B., Scot.
22 E11 **Kintyre** pen. Scot.
300 C3 **Kinuachdrachd** Arg. and B., Scot.
322 J3 **Kinveachy** High., Scot.
148 B6 **Kinver** Staffs., Eng.
132 A4 **Kinwarton** Warks., Eng.
314 H2 **Kiplaw Croft** Abers., Scot.
216 E1 **Kiplin** N. Yorks., Eng.
210 E3 **Kiplingcotes** E. Riding, Eng.
296 D4 **Kipp** Stir., Scot.
222 F2 **Kippax** W. Yorks., Eng.
304 I5 **Kippen** Perth and Kin., Scot.
296 E5 **Kippen** Stir., Scot.
252 E3 **Kippford** D. and G., Scot.
62 C4 **Kipping's Cross** Kent, Eng.
62 B3 **Kippington** Kent, Eng.
329 C4 **Kirbister** Orkney, Scot.
329 F3 **Kirbister** Orkney, Scot.
329 B3 **Kirbuster** Orkney, Scot.
166 H3 **Kirby Bedon** Norf., Eng.
162 F2 **Kirby Bellars** Leics., Eng.
166 H4 **Kirby Cane** Norf., Eng.
132 C3 **Kirby Corner** Warks., Eng.
116 J2 **Kirby Cross** Essex, Eng.
162 D3 **Kirby Fields** Leics., Eng.
166 H4 **Kirby Green** Norf., Eng.
216 H2 **Kirby Grindalythe** N. Yorks., Eng.
216 D1 **Kirby Hill** N. Yorks., Eng.
216 E2 **Kirby Hill** N. Yorks., Eng.
216 F2 **Kirby Knowle** N. Yorks., Eng.
116 J2 **Kirby le Soken** Essex, Eng.
216 G2 **Kirby Misperton** N. Yorks., Eng.
162 D3 **Kirby Muxloe** Leics., Eng.
166 H4 **Kirby Row** Norf., Eng.
210 D2 **Kirby Underdale** E. Riding, Eng.
396 K3 **Kircubbin** Ards, N. Ire.
58 C2 **Kirdford** W. Sussex, Eng.
320 K2 **Kirk** High., Scot.
331 D3 **Kirkabister** Shet., Scot.
252 D3 **Kirkandrews** D. and G., Scot.
252 F3 **Kirkbean** D. and G., Scot.
208 F2 **Kirk Bramwith** S. Yorks., Eng.
232 C3 **Kirkbride** Cumbria, Eng.
216 E2 **Kirkbridge** N. Yorks., Eng.
308 F3 **Kirkbuddo** Angus, Scot.
210 E3 **Kirkburn** E. Riding, Eng.
256 F3 **Kirkburn** Borders, Scot.
222 D3 **Kirkburton** W. Yorks., Eng.
170 D3 **Kirkby** Lincs., Eng.
190 D3 **Kirkby** Merseyside, Eng.
216 F1 **Kirkby** N. Yorks., Eng.
216 E1 **Kirkby Fleetham** N. Yorks., Eng.
170 D5 **Kirkby Green** Lincs., Eng.
176 B4 **Kirkby in Ashfield** Notts., Eng.
232 C7 **Kirkby-in-Furness** Cumbria, Eng.
170 D5 **Kirkby la Thorpe** Lincs., Eng.
232 G7 **Kirkby Lonsdale** Cumbria, Eng.
216 C2 **Kirkby Malham** N. Yorks., Eng.
162 D3 **Kirkby Mallory** Leics., Eng.
216 E2 **Kirkby Malzeard** N. Yorks., Eng.
216 G2 **Kirkby Mills** N. Yorks., Eng.
216 G2 **Kirkbymoorside** N. Yorks., Eng.
170 F5 **Kirkby on Bain** Lincs., Eng.
216 E3 **Kirkby Overblow** N. Yorks., Eng.
232 H6 **Kirkby Stephen** Cumbria, Eng.
232 G5 **Kirkby Thore** Cumbria, Eng.
170 D6 **Kirkby Underwood** Lincs., Eng.
216 F3 **Kirkby Wharfe** N. Yorks., Eng.
176 B4 **Kirkby Woodhouse** Notts., Eng.
292 F3 **Kirkcaldy** Fife, Scot.
232 F2 **Kirkcambeck** Cumbria, Eng.
252 A3 **Kirkcolm** D. and G., Scot.
252 E1 **Kirkconnel** D. and G., Scot.
252 F3 **Kirkconnell** D. and G., Scot.
252 C3 **Kirkcowan** D. and G., Scot.
252 D3 **Kirkcudbright** D. and G., Scot.
24 I4 **Kirkcudbright Bay** b. Scot.
190 D3 **Kirkdale** Merseyside, Eng.
252 D3 **Kirkdale House** D. and G., Scot.
256 D2 **Kirkdean** Borders, Scot.
210 F4 **Kirk Ella** E. Riding, Eng.
268 D2 **Kirkfieldbank** S. Lanark., Scot.
252 E3 **Kirkgunzeon** D. and G., Scot.
180 F5 **Kirk Hallam** Derbys., Eng.
228 E4 **Kirkham** Lancs., Eng.
222 E2 **Kirkhamgate** W. Yorks., Eng.
216 F3 **Kirk Hammerton** N. Yorks., Eng.
244 F5 **Kirkharle** Northumb., Eng.
244 C6 **Kirkhaugh** Northumb., Eng.
244 F5 **Kirkheaton** Northumb., Eng.
222 D3 **Kirkheaton** W. Yorks., Eng.
308 G2 **Kirkhill** Angus, Scot.
322 H2 **Kirkhill** High., Scot.
314 D2 **Kirkhill** Moray, Scot.
256 G3 **Kirkhope** Borders, Scot.
208 F2 **Kirkhouse Green** S. Yorks., Eng.
326 D2 **Kirkibost** W. Isles, Scot.
308 D3 **Kirkinch** Angus, Scot.
252 C3 **Kirkinner** D. and G., Scot.
388 I3 **Kirkinriola** Ballymena, N. Ire.
276 F2 **Kirkintilloch** E. Dun., Scot.
180 D4 **Kirk Ireton** Derbys., Eng.
396 L3 **Kirkistown** Ards, N. Ire.
232 B5 **Kirkland** Cumbria, Eng.
232 G4 **Kirkland** Cumbria, Eng.
252 D1 **Kirkland** D. and G., Scot.
252 E2 **Kirkland** D. and G., Scot.
252 F2 **Kirkland** D. and G., Scot.
292 F2 **Kirkland** Fife, Scot.
252 C3 **Kirkland of Longcastle** D. and G., Scot.
180 D5 **Kirk Langley** Derbys., Eng.
216 F1 **Kirkleatham** R. and C., Eng.
221 **Kirklees** met. bor. W. Yorks., Eng.
236 G5 **Kirklevington** Stockton, Eng.
120 J2 **Kirkley** Suff., Eng.
184 F2 **Kirkleyditch** Cheshire East, Eng.
176 D4 **Kirklington** Notts., Eng.
216 E2 **Kirklington** N. Yorks., Eng.
232 E3 **Kirklinton** Cumbria, Eng.
288 C3 **Kirkliston** Edin., Scot.
252 B3 **Kirkmaiden** D. and G., Scot.
236 F3 **Kirk Merrington** Durham, Eng.
405 C2 **Kirk Michael** Isle of Man
304 I2 **Kirkmichael** Perth and Kin., Scot.
262 D4 **Kirkmichael** S. Ayr., Scot.
268 C2 **Kirkmuirhill** S. Lanark., Scot.
244 E2 **Kirknewton** Northumb., Eng.
288 C3 **Kirknewton** W. Lothian, Scot.
280 C3 **Kirk of Shotts** N. Lanark., Scot.
232 F4 **Kirkoswald** Cumbria, Eng.
262 C5 **Kirkoswald** S. Ayr., Scot.
252 E2 **Kirkpatrick Durham** D. and G., Scot.
252 G2 **Kirkpatrick-Fleming** D. and G., Scot.
208 F2 **Kirk Sandall** S. Yorks., Eng.
232 C7 **Kirksanton** Cumbria, Eng.
208 E2 **Kirk Smeaton** S. Yorks., Eng.
222 E2 **Kirkstall** W. Yorks., Eng.
170 E5 **Kirkstead** Lincs., Eng.
314 E2 **Kirkstile** Abers., Scot.
252 H2 **Kirkstile** D. and G., Scot.
222 F2 **Kirkthorpe** W. Yorks., Eng.
314 F2 **Kirkton** Abers., Scot.
314 F3 **Kirkton** Abers., Scot.
314 F3 **Kirkton** Abers., Scot.
308 E3 **Kirkton** Angus, Scot.
300 D3 **Kirkton** Arg. and B., Scot.
256 H4 **Kirkton** Borders, Scot.
252 F2 **Kirkton** D. and G., Scot.
292 F1 **Kirkton** Fife, Scot.
320 H4 **Kirkton** High., Scot.
322 E3 **Kirkton** High., Scot.
304 H4 **Kirkton** Perth and Kin., Scot.
314 F4 **Kirktonhill** Abers., Scot.
276 C2 **Kirktonhill** W. Dun., Scot.
256 E3 **Kirkton Manor** Borders, Scot.
308 D3 **Kirkton of Airlie** Angus, Scot.
308 D3 **Kirkton of Auchterhouse** Angus, Scot.
304 K4 **Kirkton of Collace** Perth and Kin., Scot.
308 H2 **Kirkton of Craig** Angus, Scot.
314 F2 **Kirkton of Culsalmond** Abers., Scot.
314 F3 **Kirkton of Durris** Abers., Scot.
314 D3 **Kirkton of Glenbuchat** Abers., Scot.
308 C2 **Kirkton of Glenisla** Angus, Scot.
308 D2 **Kirkton of Kingoldrum** Angus, Scot.
304 J3 **Kirkton of Lethendy** Perth and Kin., Scot.
314 G2 **Kirkton of Logie Buchan** Abers., Scot.
314 G3 **Kirkton of Maryculter** Abers., Scot.
308 F2 **Kirkton of Menmuir** Angus, Scot.
308 F3 **Kirkton of Monikie** Angus, Scot.
314 F2 **Kirkton of Rayne** Abers., Scot.
314 G3 **Kirkton of Skene** Abers., Scot.
308 E3 **Kirkton of Tealing** Angus, Scot.
314 H2 **Kirktown** Abers., Scot.
314 F2 **Kirktown of Alvah** Abers., Scot.
314 F2 **Kirktown of Auchterless** Abers., Scot.
314 G4 **Kirktown of Fetteresso** Abers., Scot.
314 H2 **Kirktown of Slains** Abers., Scot.
329 D4 **Kirkwall** Orkney, Scot.
329 D4 **Kirkwall** airport Scot.
244 E5 **Kirkwhelpington** Northumb., Eng.
256 K3 **Kirk Yetholm** Borders, Scot.
170 E2 **Kirmington** N. Lincs., Eng.
170 E3 **Kirmond le Mire** Lincs., Eng.
300 F4 **Kirn** Arg. and B., Scot.
308 D2 **Kirriemuir** Angus, Scot.
166 H3 **Kirstead Green** Norf., Eng.
252 G2 **Kirtlebridge** D. and G., Scot.
252 G2 **Kirtleton** D. and G., Scot.
124 G5 **Kirtling** Cambs., Eng.
124 G5 **Kirtling Green** Cambs., Eng.
102 D3 **Kirtlington** Oxon, Eng.
320 H2 **Kirtomy** High., Scot.
170 F6 **Kirton** Lincs., Eng.
176 D3 **Kirton** Notts., Eng.
120 G4 **Kirton** Suff., Eng.
170 F6 **Kirton End** Lincs., Eng.
170 F6 **Kirton Holme** Lincs., Eng.
170 C3 **Kirton in Lindsey** N. Lincs., Eng.
264 D4 **Kiscadale** N. Ayr., Scot.
22 E8 **Kishorn, Loch** inlet Scot.
128 D4 **Kislingbury** Northants., Eng.
132 E4 **Kites Hardwick** Warks., Eng.
198 A2 **Kitt Green** Gtr Man., Eng.
94 E5 **Kittisford** Som., Eng.
94 E4 **Kittisford Barton** Som., Eng.
350 B3 **Kittle** Swansea, Wales
110 D5 **Kitt's End** Herts., Eng.
154 D3 **Kitt's Green** W. Mids, Eng.
198 D3 **Kitt's Moss** Gtr Man., Eng.
52 F4 **Kitwood** Hants., Eng.
140 C4 **Kivernoll** Here., Eng.
208 E3 **Kiveton Park** S. Yorks., Eng.
320 G3 **Klibreck** High., Scot.
314 E2 **Knabbygates** Moray, Scot.
170 B3 **Knaith** Lincs., Eng.
170 B3 **Knaith Park** Lincs., Eng.
46 F1 **Knap Corner** Dorset, Eng.
22 E11 **Knapdale** reg. Scot.
78 C2 **Knaphill** Surr., Eng.
94 C4 **Knaplock** Som., Eng.
94 G4 **Knapp** Som., Eng.
304 L4 **Knapp** Perth and Kin., Scot.
176 D4 **Knapthorpe** Notts., Eng.
162 E3 **Knaptoft** Leics., Eng.
166 H1 **Knapton** Norf., Eng.
140 C2 **Knapton Green** Here., Eng.
124 D5 **Knapwell** Cambs., Eng.
216 E2 **Knaresborough** N. Yorks., Eng.
244 B6 **Knarsdale** Northumb., Eng.
329 B3 **Knarston** Orkney, Scot.
314 G2 **Knaven** Abers., Scot.
120 F3 **Knaves' Green** Suff., Eng.
216 F2 **Knayton** N. Yorks., Eng.
110 D4 **Knebworth** Herts., Eng.
210 C4 **Knedlington** E. Riding, Eng.
176 D3 **Kneesall** Notts., Eng.
124 D6 **Kneesworth** Cambs., Eng.
176 D4 **Kneeton** Notts., Eng.
350 A3 **Knelston** Swansea, Wales
148 C3 **Knenhall** Staffs., Eng.
120 E2 **Knettishall** Suff., Eng.
40 E1 **Knightacott** Devon, Eng.
132 D4 **Knightcote** Warks., Eng.
148 B4 **Knightley** Staffs., Eng.
148 B4 **Knightley Dale** Staffs., Eng.
40 D4 **Knighton** Devon, Eng.
46 D2 **Knighton** Dorset, Eng.
162 E3 **Knighton** Leicester, Eng.
46 H3 **Knighton** Poole, Eng.
94 F3 **Knighton** Som., Eng.
148 A3 **Knighton** Staffs., Eng.
148 A3 **Knighton** Staffs., Eng.
86 F3 **Knighton** Wilts., Eng.
366 G4 **Knighton** Powys, Wales
136 B2 **Knighton on Teme** Worcs., Eng.
276 D2 **Knightswood** Glas., Scot.
136 C2 **Knightwick** Worcs., Eng.
140 A2 **Knill** Here., Eng.
300 D2 **Knipoch** Arg. and B., Scot.
162 G1 **Knipton** Leics., Eng.
236 E2 **Knitsley** Durham, Eng.
180 C4 **Kniveton** Derbys., Eng.
232 H5 **Knock** Cumbria, Eng.
300 C2 **Knock** Arg. and B., Scot.
300 D3 **Knockalava** Arg. and B., Scot.
405 B2 **Knockaloe Moar** Isle of Man
388 E3 **Knockan** Limavady, N. Ire.
320 E3 **Knockan** High., Scot.
314 D3 **Knockandhu** Moray, Scot.
314 C2 **Knockando** Moray, Scot.
402 G5 **Knockanorane** Fermanagh, N. Ire.
388 I3 **Knockanully** Ballymena, N. Ire.
402 E6 **Knockarevan** Fermanagh, N. Ire.
320 H3 **Knockarthur** High., Scot.
396 E4 **Knockavannon** Newry & Mourne, N. Ire.
322 G2 **Knockban** High., Scot.
388 C3 **Knockbrack** Derry, N. Ire.
252 D3 **Knockbrex** D. and G., Scot.
388 G4 **Knockcloghrim** Magherafelt, N. Ire.
320 F4 **Knockdamph** High., Scot.
300 E4 **Knockdow** Arg. and B., Scot.
98 F4 **Knockdown** Glos., Eng.
264 D4 **Knockenkelly** N. Ayr., Scot.
262 D3 **Knockentiber** E. Ayr., Scot.
322 G3 **Knockfin** High., Scot.
252 D2 **Knockgray** D. and G., Scot.
22 K7 **Knock Hill** hill Scot.
62 A3 **Knockholt** Kent, Eng.
62 A3 **Knockholt Pound** Kent, Eng.
144 C3 **Knockin** Shrop., Eng.
396 L3 **Knockinelder** Ards, N. Ire.
262 D3 **Knockinlaw** E. Ayr., Scot.
23 J2 **Knocklayd** hill N. Ire.
252 E2 **Knocklearn** D. and G., Scot.
62 B3 **Knockmill** Kent, Eng.
402 G3 **Knockmoyle** Omagh, N. Ire.
388 J2 **Knocknacarry** Moyle, N. Ire.
252 A3 **Knocknain** D. and G., Scot.
252 D2 **Knocknalling** D. and G., Scot.
402 B4 **Knocknashangan** Fermanagh, N. Ire.
300 C4 **Knockrome** Arg. and B., Scot.
402 F5 **Knocks** Fermanagh, N. Ire.
405 C2 **Knocksharry** Isle of Man
252 C2 **Knockville** D. and G., Scot.
300 A3 **Knockvologan** Arg. and B., Scot.
120 I3 **Knodishall** Suff., Eng.
120 I3 **Knodishall Common** Suff., Eng.
120 I3 **Knodishall Green** Suff., Eng.
94 H4 **Knole** Som., Eng.
184 F2 **Knolls Green** Cheshire East, Eng.
378 H4 **Knolton** Wrex., Wales
86 C4 **Knook** Wilts., Eng.
162 G2 **Knossington** Leics., Eng.
228 E3 **Knott End-on-Sea** Lancs., Eng.
110 B2 **Knotting** Bedford, Eng.
110 B2 **Knotting Green** Bedford, Eng.
222 G2 **Knottingley** W. Yorks., Eng.
228 H3 **Knotts** Lancs., Eng.
190 D3 **Knotty Ash** Merseyside, Eng.
106 E5 **Knotty Green** Bucks., Eng.
144 E5 **Knowbury** Shrop., Eng.
252 C2 **Knowe** D. and G., Scot.
396 K2 **Knowehead** Ards, N. Ire.
244 E4 **Knowesgate** Northumb., Eng.
262 C4 **Knoweside** S. Ayr., Scot.
314 F2 **Knowes of Elrick** Abers., Scot.
256 H4 **Knowetownhead** Borders, Scot.
314 G2 **Knowhead** Abers., Scot.
94 I2 **Knowle** Bristol, Eng.
40 D1 **Knowle** Devon, Eng.
40 F3 **Knowle** Devon, Eng.
52 E5 **Knowle** Hants., Eng.
144 E5 **Knowle** Shrop., Eng.
94 D3 **Knowle** Som., Eng.
154 D3 **Knowle** W. Mids, Eng.
228 G3 **Knowle Green** Lancs., Eng.
94 G4 **Knowle Hall** Som., Eng.
94 G5 **Knowle St Giles** Som., Eng.
116 F1 **Knowl Green** Essex, Eng.
82 F2 **Knowl Hill** W. and M., Eng.
46 H2 **Knowlton** Dorset, Eng.
62 H3 **Knowlton** Kent, Eng.
148 B3 **Knowl Wall** Staffs., Eng.
190 D3 **Knowsley** Merseyside, Eng.
40 E2 **Knowstone** Devon, Eng.
62 D4 **Knox Bridge** Kent, Eng.
22 E8 **Knoydart** mts Scot.
366 G4 **Knucklas** Powys, Wales
184 E2 **Knutsford** Cheshire East, Eng.
148 B2 **Knutton** Staffs., Eng.
228 H4 **Knuzden Brook** Lancs., Eng.
148 B2 **Knypersley** Staffs., Eng.
222 C3 **Krumlin** W. Yorks., Eng.
36 D3 **Kuggar** Corn., Eng.
24 O5 **Kyle** r. Eng.
322 D3 **Kyleakin** High., Scot.
322 D3 **Kyle of Lochalsh** High., Scot.
22 H6 **Kyle of Tongue** inlet Scot.
322 D3 **Kylerhea** High., Scot.
322 E4 **Kylesknoydart** High., Scot.
320 E3 **Kylesku** High., Scot.
322 E4 **Kylesmorar** High., Scot.
22 F11 **Kyles of Bute** sea chan. Scot.
326 D3 **Kyles Scalpay** W. Isles, Scot.
320 E3 **Kylestrome** High., Scot.
339 D2 **Kymin** Mon., Wales
144 C3 **Kynaston** Shrop., Eng.
144 F3 **Kynnersley** Telford, Eng.
136 B2 **Kyre Park** Worcs., Eng.
136 B2 **Kyrewood** Worcs., Eng.

L

326 E1 **Labost** W. Isles, Scot.
326 E2 **Lacasaigh** W. Isles, Scot.
170 F2 **Laceby** N.E. Lincs., Eng.
106 D4 **Lacey Green** Bucks., Eng.
184 F1 **Lacey Green** Cheshire East, Eng.
Lacharn Carmar., Wales see **Laugharne**
184 E2 **Lach Dennis** Cheshire West & Chester, Eng.
402 E3 **Lack** Fermanagh, N. Ire.
388 D2 **Lackagh** Limavady, N. Ire.
120 C3 **Lackford** Suff., Eng.
120 C3 **Lackford Green** Suff., Eng.
326 D3 **Lacklee** W. Isles, Scot.
86 C3 **Lacock** Wilts., Eng.
132 D4 **Ladbroke** Warks., Eng.
62 C3 **Laddingford** Kent, Eng.
170 G5 **Lade Bank** Lincs., Eng.
22 E8 **Ladhar Bheinn** mt. Scot.
228 E3 **Ladies Hill** Lancs., Eng.
36 E3 **Ladock** Corn., Eng.
292 F2 **Ladybank** Fife, Scot.
24 N7 **Ladybower Reservoir** resr Eng.
36 F1 **Ladycross** Corn., Eng.
232 C7 **Lady Hall** Cumbria, Eng.
24 H2 **Lady Isle** i. Scot.
256 K2 **Ladykirk** Borders, Scot.
314 G2 **Ladysford** Abers., Scot.
120 C3 **Lady's Green** Suff., Eng.
74 D3 **Ladywell** Gtr Lon., Eng.
154 C3 **Ladywood** W. Mids, Eng.
322 D4 **Laga** High., Scot.
300 D3 **Lagalochan** Arg. and B., Scot.
23 K3 **Lagan** r. N. Ire.
388 H1 **Lagavara** Moyle, N. Ire.
300 B5 **Lagavulin** Arg. and B., Scot.
300 C4 **Lagg** Arg. and B., Scot.
264 C4 **Lagg** N. Ayr., Scot.
262 C4 **Lagg** S. Ayr., Scot.
300 B4 **Laggan** Arg. and B., Scot.
322 G3 **Laggan** High., Scot.
322 I3 **Laggan** High., Scot.
314 D2 **Laggan** Moray, Scot.
296 E4 **Laggan** Stir., Scot.
22 G9 **Laggan, Loch** l. Scot.
24 E2 **Laggan Bay** b. Scot.
300 B2 **Lagganulva** Arg. and B., Scot.
314 C3 **Lagganvoulin** Moray, Scot.
402 J4 **Laghy Corner** Dungannon, N. Ire.
300 E3 **Laglingarten** Arg. and B., Scot.
322 I2 **Lagnalean** High., Scot.
252 D1 **Lagrae** D. and G., Scot.
304 J3 **Laguna** Perth and Kin., Scot.
320 F2 **Laid** High., Scot.
320 D4 **Laide** High., Scot.
22 G9 **Laidon, Loch** l. Scot.
322 C4 **Laig** High., Scot.
262 F4 **Laight** E. Ayr., Scot.
322 K3 **Lainchoil** High., Scot.
116 E4 **Laindon** Essex, Eng.
304 J2 **Lair** Perth and Kin., Scot.
40 D3 **Laira** Plymouth, Eng.
320 G3 **Lairg** High., Scot.
320 G3 **Lairg Lodge** High., Scot.
322 F4 **Lairigmor** High., Scot.
222 D2 **Laisterdyke** W. Yorks., Eng.
314 F2 **Laithers** Abers., Scot.
232 E4 **Laithes** Cumbria, Eng.
52 E7 **Lake** I.o.W., Eng.
86 E5 **Lake** Wilts., Eng.
24 K5 **Lake District National Park** nat. park Eng.
166 G3 **Lakenham** Norf., Eng.
120 C2 **Lakenheath** Suff., Eng.
166 A3 **Lakes End** Norf., Eng.
232 E7 **Lakeside** Cumbria, Eng.
78 D1 **Laleham** Surr., Eng.
350 E3 **Laleston** Bridg., Wales
256 E2 **Lamancha** Borders, Scot.
La Manche str. France/U.K. see **English Channel**
116 G2 **Lamarsh** Essex, Eng.
166 G2 **Lamas** Norf., Eng.
116 H2 **Lamb Corner** Essex, Eng.
256 J2 **Lambden** Borders, Scot.
388 J5 **Lambeg** Lisburn, N. Ire.
62 C4 **Lamberhurst** Kent, Eng.
62 C4 **Lamberhurst Quarter** Kent, Eng.
256 L2 **Lamberton** Borders, Scot.
74 D3 **Lambeth** met. bor. Gtr Lon., Eng.
405 C2 **Lambfell Moar** Isle of Man
276 E2 **Lambhill** Glas., Scot.
244 B6 **Lambley** Northumb., Eng.
176 C4 **Lambley** Notts., Eng.
82 A2 **Lambourn** W. Berks., Eng.
26 I4 **Lambourn Downs** hills Eng.
116 C4 **Lambourne End** Essex, Eng.
82 A3 **Lambourn Woodlands** W. Berks., Eng.
228 H3 **Lamb Roe** Lancs., Eng.
58 E2 **Lambs Green** W. Sussex, Eng.
358 D3 **Lambston** Pembs., Wales
236 F2 **Lambton** T. and W., Eng.
36 F2 **Lamellion** Corn., Eng.
40 D3 **Lamerton** Devon, Eng.
236 F2 **Lamesley** T. and W., Eng.
320 H4 **Lamington** High., Scot.
268 E3 **Lamington** S. Lanark., Scot.
264 D3 **Lamlash** N. Ayr., Scot.
252 D2 **Lamloch** D. and G., Scot.
22 K11 **Lammer Law** hill Scot.
22 K11 **Lammermuir Hills** hills Scot.
232 E4 **Lamonby** Cumbria, Eng.
36 C3 **Lamorna** Corn., Eng.
36 E3 **Lamorran** Corn., Eng.
244 C5 **Lampert** Northumb., Eng.
358 F3 **Lampeter Velfrey** Pembs., Wales
358 E3 **Lamphey** Pembs., Wales
232 B5 **Lamplugh** Cumbria, Eng.
128 D3 **Lamport** Northants., Eng.
74 B3 **Lampton** Gtr Lon., Eng.
94 J4 **Lamyatt** Som., Eng.
40 C2 **Lana** Devon, Eng.
40 C2 **Lana** Devon, Eng.
268 D2 **Lanark** S. Lanark., Scot.
228 F3 **Lancashire** county Eng.
24 K7 **Lancashire Plain** plain Eng.
228 F2 **Lancaster** Lancs., Eng.
24 L6 **Lancaster Canal** canal Eng.
236 E3 **Lanchester** Durham, Eng.
58 E4 **Lancing** W. Sussex, Eng.
124 E5 **Landbeach** Cambs., Eng.
40 D2 **Landcross** Devon, Eng.
314 F3 **Landerberry** Abers., Scot.
36 D4 **Landewednack** Corn., Eng.
86 F6 **Landford** Wilts., Eng.
26 O4 **Landguard Point** pt Eng.
190 C3 **Landican** Merseyside, Eng.
350 A3 **Landimore** Swansea, Wales
40 D1 **Landkey** Devon, Eng.
216 E2 **Landmoth** N. Yorks., Eng.
350 C3 **Landore** Swansea, Wales
52 F6 **Landport** Ports., Eng.
36 G2 **Landrake** Corn., Eng.
36 B3 **Land's End** airport Eng.
26 □ **Land's End** pt Eng.
358 E3 **Landshipping** Pembs., Wales
198 B3 **Land Side** Gtr Man., Eng.
120 B3 **Landwade** Suff., Eng.
148 C5 **Landywood** Staffs., Eng.
222 C3 **Lane** W. Yorks., Eng.
36 F2 **Laneast** Corn., Eng.
228 I4 **Lane Bottom** Lancs., Eng.
106 C5 **Lane End** Bucks., Eng.
232 B7 **Lane End** Cumbria, Eng.
180 E4 **Lane End** Derbys., Eng.
46 F3 **Lane End** Dorset, Eng.
52 E4 **Lane End** Hants., Eng.
140 D4 **Lane End** Here., Eng.
62 B2 **Lane End** Kent, Eng.
86 B4 **Lane End** Wilts., Eng.
180 D5 **Lane Ends** Derbys., Eng.
198 E3 **Lane Ends** Gtr Man., Eng.
228 I4 **Lane Ends** Lancs., Eng.
148 B2 **Lane Ends** Stoke, Eng.
148 B5 **Lane Green** Staffs., Eng.
176 E3 **Laneham** Notts., Eng.
236 B3 **Lanehead** Durham, Eng.
236 D4 **Lane Head** Durham, Eng.
236 E4 **Lane Head** Durham, Eng.
198 B3 **Lane Head** Gtr Man., Eng.
244 D5 **Lanehead** Northumb., Eng.
154 B2 **Lane Head** W. Mids, Eng.
222 D3 **Lane Head** W. Yorks., Eng.
228 E3 **Lane Heads** Lancs., Eng.
358 F3 **Lanesend** Pembs., Wales
154 B2 **Lanesfield** W. Mids, Eng.
228 J3 **Laneshawbridge** Lancs., Eng.
228 I4 **Lane Side** Lancs., Eng.
326 C4 **Langais** W. Isles, Scot.
94 F4 **Langaller** Som., Eng.
300 B2 **Langamull** Arg. and B., Scot.
176 D5 **Langar** Notts., Eng.
22 C6 **Langavat, Loch** l. Scot.
276 C2 **Langbank** Renf., Scot.
216 D3 **Langbar** N. Yorks., Eng.
216 C2 **Langcliffe** N. Yorks., Eng.
216 H2 **Langdale End** N. Yorks., Eng.
36 F1 **Langdon** Corn., Eng.
236 B3 **Langdon Beck** Durham, Eng.
116 E4 **Langdon Hills** Essex, Eng.
292 F2 **Langdyke** Fife, Scot.
116 H3 **Langenhoe** Essex, Eng.
110 D3 **Langford** Central Bedfordshire, Eng.
40 F2 **Langford** Devon, Eng.
116 F3 **Langford** Essex, Eng.
176 E4 **Langford** Notts., Eng.
102 B4 **Langford** Oxon, Eng.
94 F4 **Langford** Som., Eng.
94 E5 **Langford Budville** Som., Eng.
116 H2 **Langham** Essex, Eng.
166 E1 **Langham** Norf., Eng.
162 G2 **Langham** Rutland, Eng.
120 E3 **Langham** Suff., Eng.
116 H2 **Langham Moor** Essex, Eng.
228 H4 **Langho** Lancs., Eng.
252 H2 **Langholm** D. and G., Scot.
350 B3 **Langland** Swansea, Wales
256 I4 **Langlee** Borders, Scot.
244 E3 **Langleeford** Northumb., Eng.
184 G2 **Langley** Cheshire East, Eng.
180 F4 **Langley** Derbys., Eng.
116 C2 **Langley** Essex, Eng.
98 H2 **Langley** Glos., Eng.
198 D2 **Langley** Gtr Man., Eng.
52 D6 **Langley** Hants., Eng.
110 D4 **Langley** Herts., Eng.
62 D3 **Langley** Kent, Eng.
244 D6 **Langley** Northumb., Eng.
102 B3 **Langley** Oxon, Eng.
82 G3 **Langley** Slough, Eng.
94 E4 **Langley** Som., Eng.
132 B4 **Langley** Warks., Eng.
154 B3 **Langley** W. Mids, Eng.
58 A2 **Langley** W. Sussex, Eng.
86 C3 **Langley Burrell** Wilts., Eng.
106 E5 **Langley Corner** Bucks., Eng.
180 D5 **Langley Green** Derbys., Eng.
116 G2 **Langley Green** Essex, Eng.
132 B4 **Langley Green** Warks., Eng.
154 B3 **Langley Green** W. Mids, Eng.
58 E2 **Langley Green** W. Sussex, Eng.
62 D3 **Langley Heath** Kent, Eng.
94 E4 **Langley Marsh** Som., Eng.
180 E4 **Langley Mill** Derbys., Eng.
236 F3 **Langley Moor** Durham, Eng.
236 E3 **Langley Park** Durham, Eng.
166 H3 **Langley Street** Norf., Eng.
166 G4 **Langmere** Norf., Eng.
58 H4 **Langney** E. Sussex, Eng.
176 C2 **Langold** Notts., Eng.
36 F2 **Langore** Corn., Eng.
94 H4 **Langport** Som., Eng.
170 F5 **Langrick** Lincs., Eng.
170 F5 **Langrick Bridge** Lincs., Eng.
94 J2 **Langridge** B. and N.E. Som., Eng.
232 C4 **Langrigg** Cumbria, Eng.
232 H5 **Langrigg** Cumbria, Eng.
52 F4 **Langrish** Hants., Eng.
208 B2 **Langsett** S. Yorks., Eng.
256 H3 **Langshaw** Borders, Scot.
252 G2 **Langshawburn** D. and G., Scot.
276 E3 **Langside** Glas., Scot.
304 G5 **Langside** Perth and Kin., Scot.
329 D2 **Langskaill** Orkney, Scot.
52 G5 **Langstone** Hants., Eng.
339 C3 **Langstone** Newp., Wales
24 M5 **Langstrothdale Chase** hills Eng.
216 E2 **Langthorne** N. Yorks., Eng.
210 F2 **Langtoft** E. Riding, Eng.
170 D7 **Langtoft** Lincs., Eng.
236 E4 **Langton** Durham, Eng.
170 F4 **Langton** Lincs., Eng.
216 G2 **Langton** N. Yorks., Eng.
62 B4 **Langton Green** Kent, Eng.
120 F3 **Langton Green** Suff., Eng.
46 D4 **Langton Herring** Dorset, Eng.
46 G2 **Langton Long Blandford** Dorset, Eng.
46 G4 **Langton Matravers** Dorset, Eng.
40 D2 **Langtree** Devon, Eng.
232 G4 **Langwathby** Cumbria, Eng.
180 F3 **Langwith** Derbys., Eng.
170 D4 **Langworth** Lincs., Eng.
36 E2 **Lanivet** Corn., Eng.
36 E2 **Lank** Corn., Eng.
36 D3 **Lanner** Corn., Eng.
36 F2 **Lanreath** Corn., Eng.
36 F2 **Lansallos** Corn., Eng.
94 J2 **Lansdown** B. and N.E. Som., Eng.
98 G2 **Lansdown** Glos., Eng.
36 E2 **Lanteglos** Corn., Eng.
36 F2 **Lanteglos Highway** Corn., Eng.
244 E2 **Lanton** Northumb., Eng.
256 I4 **Lanton** Borders, Scot.
154 B3 **Lapal** W. Mids, Eng.
40 E2 **Lapford** Devon, Eng.
300 B5 **Laphroaig** Arg. and B., Scot.
148 B4 **Lapley** Staffs., Eng.
132 B3 **Lapworth** Warks., Eng.
322 D5 **Larachbeg** High., Scot.
300 D4 **Larach na Gaibhre** Arg. and B., Scot.
388 F3 **Laragh** Coleraine, N. Ire.
280 C2 **Larbert** Falk., Scot.
228 E3 **Larbreck** Lancs., Eng.
402 J4 **Larchmount** Dungannon, N. Ire.
184 D3 **Larden Green** Cheshire East, Eng.
252 C2 **Larg** D. and G., Scot.
314 F2 **Largie** Abers., Scot.
300 E3 **Largiemore** Arg. and B., Scot.
22 K10 **Largo Bay** b. Scot.
292 G2 **Largoward** Fife, Scot.
264 E2 **Largs** N. Ayr., Scot.
314 F2 **Largue** Abers., Scot.
300 C5 **Largybaan** Arg. and B., Scot.
264 D4 **Largybeg** N. Ayr., Scot.
264 D4 **Largymore** N. Ayr., Scot.
62 C3 **Larkfield** Kent, Eng.
276 B2 **Larkfield** Inverclyde, Scot.
124 F5 **Lark Hall** Cambs., Eng.
268 C2 **Larkhall** S. Lanark., Scot.
86 E4 **Larkhill** Wilts., Eng.
402 C3 **Larkhill** Fermanagh, N. Ire.
180 F5 **Larklands** Derbys., Eng.
166 E4 **Larling** Norf., Eng.
388 L3 **Larne** Larne, N. Ire.
388 K3 **Larne** admin. dist. N. Ire.
23 K3 **Larne Lough** inlet N. Ire.
36 F2 **Larrick** Corn., Eng.
256 H5 **Larriston** Borders, Scot.
236 D4 **Lartington** Durham, Eng.
314 D3 **Lary** Abers., Scot.
98 F4 **Lasborough** Glos., Eng.
52 F3 **Lasham** Hants., Eng.
62 D4 **Lashenden** Kent, Eng.
98 F2 **Lassington** Glos., Eng.
304 F2 **Lassintullich** Perth and Kin., Scot.
292 D3 **Lassodie** Fife, Scot.
288 E3 **Lasswade** Midlothian, Scot.
216 G2 **Lastingham** N. Yorks., Eng.
190 F3 **Latchford** Warr., Eng.
116 G3 **Latchingdon** Essex, Eng.
198 B3 **Lately Common** Gtr Man., Eng.
292 G2 **Lathallan Mill** Fife, Scot.
106 D2 **Lathbury** M.K., Eng.
320 J3 **Latheron** High., Scot.
292 H2 **Lathockar** Fife, Scot.
292 G2 **Lathones** Fife, Scot.
292 E2 **Lathrisk** Fife, Scot.
106 E4 **Latimer** Bucks., Eng.
94 J4 **Lattiford** Som., Eng.
86 D2 **Latton** Wilts., Eng.
116 C3 **Latton Bush** Essex, Eng.
252 D3 **Lauchentyre** D. and G., Scot.
314 F3 **Lauchintilly** Abers., Scot.
256 H2 **Lauder** Borders, Scot.
356 D3 **Laugharne** Carmar., Wales
170 B4 **Laughterton** Lincs., Eng.
58 G3 **Laughton** E. Sussex, Eng.
162 E4 **Laughton** Leics., Eng.
170 B3 **Laughton** Lincs., Eng.
170 D6 **Laughton** Lincs., Eng.
208 E3 **Laughton en le Morthen** S. Yorks., Eng.
36 F1 **Launcells** Corn., Eng.
36 F2 **Launceston** Corn., Eng.
162 G3 **Launde Abbey** Leics., Eng.
102 E3 **Launton** Oxon, Eng.
396 F3 **Laurelvale** Armagh, N. Ire.
314 F4 **Laurencekirk** Abers., Scot.
252 D3 **Laurieston** D. and G., Scot.
280 D3 **Laurieston** Falk., Scot.
106 E1 **Lavendon** M.K., Eng.
120 D4 **Lavenham** Suff., Eng.
252 F2 **Laverhay** D. and G., Scot.
350 G4 **Lavernock** V. of Glam., Wales
26 F5 **Lavernock Point** pt Wales
232 F3 **Laversdale** Cumbria, Eng.
86 E5 **Laverstock** Wilts., Eng.
52 E3 **Laverstoke** Hants., Eng.
98 H1 **Laverton** Glos., Eng.
216 E2 **Laverton** N. Yorks., Eng.
94 K3 **Laverton** Som., Eng.
378 H3 **Lavister** Wrex., Wales
268 C2 **Law** S. Lanark., Scot.
304 F3 **Lawers** Perth and Kin., Scot.
304 G4 **Lawers** Perth and Kin., Scot.
116 I2 **Lawford** Essex, Eng.
94 E4 **Lawford** Som., Eng.
36 G2 **Lawhitton** Corn., Eng.
216 B2 **Lawkland** N. Yorks., Eng.
144 F3 **Lawley** Telford, Eng.
148 B4 **Lawnhead** Staffs., Eng.
222 E2 **Lawns** W. Yorks., Eng.
396 G3 **Lawrencetown** Banbridge, N. Ire.
94 I2 **Lawrence Weston** Bristol, Eng.
358 E3 **Lawrenny** Pembs., Wales
308 F3 **Laws** Angus, Scot.
120 D4 **Lawshall** Suff., Eng.
120 D4 **Lawshall Green** Suff., Eng.
140 C2 **Lawton** Here., Eng.
405 D2 **Laxey** Isle of Man
24 I5 **Laxey Bay** b. Isle of Man
120 H3 **Laxfield** Suff., Eng.
331 D3 **Laxfirth** Shet., Scot.
331 D3 **Laxfirth** Shet., Scot.
22 F6 **Laxford, Loch** inlet Scot.
320 E2 **Laxford Bridge** High., Scot.
331 D2 **Laxo** Shet., Scot.
210 D4 **Laxton** E. Riding, Eng.
128 F2 **Laxton** Northants., Eng.
176 D3 **Laxton** Notts., Eng.
222 C1 **Laycock** W. Yorks., Eng.
388 J2 **Layde** Moyle, N. Ire.
116 G3 **Layer Breton** Essex, Eng.
116 H2 **Layer de la Haye** Essex, Eng.
116 G3 **Layer Marney** Essex, Eng.
120 E4 **Layham** Suff., Eng.
46 B2 **Laymore** Dorset, Eng.
106 E5 **Layter's Green** Bucks., Eng.
210 C3 **Laytham** E. Riding, Eng.
228 D4 **Layton** Blackpool, Eng.
216 F1 **Lazenby** R. and C., Eng.
232 F4 **Lazonby** Cumbria, Eng.
180 D4 **Lea** Derbys., Eng.
140 E4 **Lea** Here., Eng.
170 B3 **Lea** Lincs., Eng.
144 C3 **Lea** Shrop., Eng.
144 C5 **Lea** Shrop., Eng.
86 C2 **Lea** Wilts., Eng.
180 D4 **Lea Bridge** Derbys., Eng.
Leac a' Li W. Isles, Scot. see **Lacklee**
24 E2 **Leacan, Rubha nan** pt Scot.
Leac Mailm High., Scot. see **Leckmelm**
288 D4 **Leadburn** Midlothian, Scot.
170 C5 **Leadenham** Lincs., Eng.
116 D3 **Leaden Roding** Essex, Eng.
256 H3 **Leaderfoot** Borders, Scot.
22 K11 **Leader Water** r. Scot.
232 H4 **Leadgate** Cumbria, Eng.
236 E2 **Leadgate** Durham, Eng.
236 D2 **Leadgate** T. and W., Eng.
268 D4 **Leadhills** S. Lanark., Scot.
62 E3 **Leadingcross Green** Kent, Eng
136 F1 **Lea End** Worcs., Eng.
102 B3 **Leafield** Oxon, Eng.
110 C4 **Leagrave** Luton, Eng.
110 C4 **Leagrave Marsh** Luton, Eng.
140 E2 **Lea Green** Here., Eng.
170 G5 **Leake Commonside** Lincs., Eng.
170 G5 **Leake Hurn's End** Lincs., Eng.
58 H3 **Lealands** E. Sussex, Eng.
216 G1 **Lealholm** N. Yorks., Eng.
300 C3 **Lealt** Arg. and B., Scot.
322 C2 **Lealt** High., Scot.
180 D3 **Leam** Derbys., Eng.
132 B2 **Lea Marston** Warks., Eng.
132 D4 **Leamington Hastings** Warks., Eng.
132 C4 **Leamington Spa, Royal** Warks Eng.
148 D4 **Leamonsley** Staffs., Eng.
144 C5 **Leamoor Common** Shrop., Eng.
236 F3 **Leamside** Durham, Eng.
300 E3 **Leanach** Arg. and B., Scot.
322 H2 **Leanaig** High., Scot.
300 C4 **Leargybreck** Arg. and B., Scot.
232 F7 **Leasgill** Cumbria, Eng.
170 D5 **Leasingham** Lincs., Eng.
236 F4 **Leasingthorne** Durham, Eng.
350 A3 **Leason** Swansea, Wales
190 C3 **Leasowe** Merseyside, Eng.
78 E2 **Leatherhead** Surr., Eng.
216 E3 **Leathley** N. Yorks., Eng.
144 D3 **Leaton** Shrop., Eng.
144 E3 **Leaton** Telford, Eng.
228 F4 **Lea Town** Lancs., Eng.
62 F3 **Leaveland** Kent, Eng.
120 E4 **Leavenheath** Suff., Eng.
216 G2 **Leavening** N. Yorks., Eng.
110 C5 **Leavesden Green** Herts., Eng.
74 E3 **Leaves Green** Gtr Lon., Eng.
232 H7 **Lea Yeat** Cumbria, Eng.
216 H2 **Lebberston** N. Yorks., Eng.
98 I3 **Lechlade-on-Thames** Glos., Eng.
228 G1 **Leck** Lancs., Eng.
388 F2 **Leck** Coleraine, N. Ire.

Leckford to Llaneuddog

52 D4 Leckford Hants., Eng.
300 A4 Leckgruinart Arg. and B., Scot.
106 C2 Leckhampstead Bucks., Eng.
82 B3 Leckhampstead W. Berks., Eng.
82 B3 Leckhampstead Thicket W. Berks., Eng.
98 G2 Leckhampton Glos., Eng.
322 F2 Leckie High., Scot.
296 F5 Leckie Stir., Scot.
320 E4 Leckmelm High., Scot.
322 G4 Leckroy High., Scot.
300 D3 Leckuary Arg. and B., Scot.
350 G4 Leckwith V. of Glam., Wales
210 F3 Leconfield E. Riding, Eng.
300 D2 Ledaig Arg. and B., Scot.
296 D4 Ledard Stir., Scot.
320 F3 Ledbeg High., Scot.
106 D3 Ledburn Bucks., Eng.
140 E3 Ledbury Here., Eng.
296 D3 Ledcharrie Stir., Scot.
140 B3 Ledgemoor Here., Eng.
140 B2 Ledicot Here., Eng.
300 B2 Ledmore Arg. and B., Scot.
320 F3 Ledmore High., Scot.
184 B2 Ledsham Cheshire West & Chester, Eng.
222 G2 Ledsham W. Yorks., Eng.
222 F2 Ledston W. Yorks., Eng.
102 C3 Ledwell Oxon, Eng.
40 D1 Lee Devon, Eng.
52 D5 Lee Hants., Eng.
228 G3 Lee Lancs., Eng.
174 C2 Lee Shrop., Eng.
300 B3 Lee Arg. and B., Scot.
331 D3 Leebotten Shet., Scot.
144 D4 Leebotwood Shrop., Eng.
144 D2 Lee Brockhurst Shrop., Eng.
232 D8 Leece Cumbria, Eng.
116 E4 Lee Chapel Essex, Eng.
106 D4 Lee Clump Bucks., Eng.
62 D3 Leeds Kent, Eng.
222 E2 Leeds W. Yorks., Eng.
222 E1 Leeds Bradford International airport Eng.
36 C3 Leedstown Corn., Eng.
144 F3 Leegomery Telford, Eng.
148 C2 Leek Staffs., Eng.
148 C2 Leekbrook Staffs., Eng.
388 E3 Leeke Limavady, N. Ire.
132 C4 Leek Wootton Warks., Eng.
40 E3 Lee Mill Bridge Devon, Eng.
216 E2 Leeming N. Yorks., Eng.
222 C2 Leeming W. Yorks., Eng.
216 E2 Leeming Bar N. Yorks., Eng.
40 D3 Lee Moor Devon, Eng.
52 E6 Lee-on-the-Solent Hants., Eng.
180 D5 Lees Derbys., Eng.
180 E5 Lees Gtr Man., Eng.
180 D5 Lees Green Derbys., Eng.
378 G3 Leeswood Flints., Wales
304 K4 Leetown Perth and Kin., Scot.
184 D2 Leftwich Cheshire West & Chester, Eng.
388 J6 Legacurry Lisburn, N. Ire.
396 J4 Legamaddy Down, N. Ire.
402 G4 Legamaghery Omagh, N. Ire.
396 H4 Leganamny Banbridge, N. Ire.
256 J3 Legars Borders, Scot.
256 I2 Legerwood Borders, Scot.
402 C3 Leggs Fermanagh, N. Ire.
170 E3 Legsby Lincs., Eng.
162 E3 Leicester Leicester, Eng.
162 E3 Leicester admin. div. Eng.
162 D3 Leicester Forest East Leics., Eng.
162 D2 Leicestershire county Eng.
Leideag Arg. and B., Scot. see Ledaig
46 D2 Leigh Dorset, Eng.
46 H3 Leigh Dorset, Eng.
198 B3 Leigh Gtr Man., Eng.
62 B3 Leigh Kent, Eng.
144 C4 Leigh Shrop., Eng.
78 E2 Leigh Surr., Eng.
86 D2 Leigh Wilts., Eng.
136 D2 Leigh Worcs., Eng.
40 D3 Leigham Plymouth, Eng.
116 F4 Leigh Beck Essex, Eng.
94 J4 Leigh Common Som., Eng.
86 B2 Leigh Delamere Wilts., Eng.
62 E4 Leigh Green Kent, Eng.
94 D4 Leighland Chapel Som., Eng.
116 E4 Leigh-on-Sea Southend, Eng.
52 G5 Leigh Park Hants., Eng.
136 D3 Leigh Sinton Worcs., Eng.
98 F4 Leighterton Glos., Eng.
216 D2 Leighton N. Yorks., Eng.
144 E4 Leighton Shrop., Eng.
94 J3 Leighton Som., Eng.
366 G3 Leighton Powys, Wales
124 B4 Leighton Bromswold Cambs., Eng.
110 B4 Leighton Buzzard Central Bedfordshire, Eng.
94 J3 Leigh upon Mendip Som., Eng.
94 I2 Leigh Woods N. Som., Eng.
140 C2 Leinthall Earls Here., Eng.
140 C2 Leinthall Starkes Here., Eng.
140 B1 Leintwardine Here., Eng.
162 D3 Leire Leics., Eng.
120 I3 Leiston Suff., Eng.
304 K3 Leitfie Perth and Kin., Scot.
288 D3 Leith Edin., Scot.
26 L5 Leith Hill hill Eng.
256 J2 Leitholm Borders, Scot.
Leitir Fheàrna High., Scot. see Letterfearn
396 I4 Leitrim Banbridge, N. Ire.
396 I4 Leitrim Down, N. Ire.
402 G6 Leitrim Fermanagh, N. Ire.
36 C3 Lelant Corn., Eng.
210 G4 Lelley E. Riding, Eng.
136 C1 Lem Hill Worcs., Eng.
136 E2 Lemington T. and W., Eng.
136 G2 Lemnas Abers., Scot.
256 J3 Lempitlaw Borders, Scot.
110 D5 Lemsford Herts., Eng.
396 G3 Lenaderg Banbridge, N. Ire.
402 H2 Lenagh Omagh, N. Ire.
136 F3 Lenchwick Worcs., Eng.
262 B5 Lendalfoot S. Ayr., Scot.
296 D4 Lendrick Lodge Stir., Scot.
62 E3 Lenham Kent, Eng.
62 E3 Lenham Heath Kent, Eng.
322 H3 Lenie High., Scot.
264 B2 Lenimore N. Ayr., Scot.
256 K3 Lennel Borders, Scot.
252 D3 Lennox Plunton D. and G., Scot.
276 E2 Lennoxtown E. Dun., Scot.
106 E5 Lent Bucks., Eng.
170 D6 Lenton Lincs., Eng.
176 B5 Lenton Nott., Eng.
176 B5 Lenton Abbey Nott., Eng.
106 D5 Lent Rise Bucks., Eng.
166 F2 Lenwade Norf., Eng.
276 F2 Lenzie E. Dun., Scot.
280 C3 Lenziemill N. Lanark., Scot.
308 D3 Leoch Angus, Scot.
314 E3 Leochel-Cushnie Abers., Scot.
Leodhais, Eilean i. Scot. see Lewis, Isle of
140 C2 Leominster Here., Eng.
98 F3 Leonard Stanley Glos., Eng.
300 B5 Leorin Arg. and B., Scot.
52 D6 Lepe Hants., Eng.
300 E3 Lephinchapel Arg. and B., Scot.
300 E3 Lephinmore Arg. and B., Scot.
216 G2 Leppington N. Yorks., Eng.
222 D3 Lepton W. Yorks., Eng.
300 D2 Lerags Arg. and B., Scot.
36 F2 Lerryn Corn., Eng.
331 D3 Lerwick Shet., Scot.
244 H3 Lesbury Northumb., Eng.
314 F3 Leschangie Abers., Scot.
314 F3 Leslie Abers., Scot.
292 E2 Leslie Fife, Scot.
268 C3 Lesmahagow S. Lanark., Scot.
36 F1 Lesnewth Corn., Eng.
314 E2 Lessendrum Abers., Scot.
166 I2 Lessingham Norf., Eng.
74 E3 Lessness Heath Gtr Lon., Eng.
232 C3 Lessonhall Cumbria, Eng.
252 A3 Leswalt D. and G., Scot.
110 C5 Letchmore Heath Herts., Eng.
110 D4 Letchworth Garden City Herts., Eng.
102 C5 Letcombe Bassett Oxon, Eng.
102 C5 Letcombe Regis Oxon, Eng.
308 F3 Letham Angus, Scot.
280 D2 Letham Falk., Scot.
292 F2 Letham Fife, Scot.
304 J4 Letham Perth and Kin., Scot.
262 E4 Lethanhill E. Ayr., Scot.
314 G2 Lethenty Abers., Scot.
120 G3 Letheringham Suff., Eng.
166 F1 Letheringsett Norf., Eng.
326 B5 Leth Meadhanach W. Isles, Scot.
402 C3 Letter Fermanagh, N. Ire.
402 D5 Letterbreen Fermanagh, N. Ire.
320 D4 Letterewe High., Scot.
322 E3 Letterfearn High., Scot.
322 G4 Letter Finlay High., Scot.
402 D3 Letterkeen Fermanagh, N. Ire.
388 F2 Letterloan Coleraine, N. Ire.
320 D4 Lettermorar High., Scot.
300 B2 Lettermore Arg. and B., Scot.
320 G2 Lettermore High., Scot.
268 D4 Lettershaws S. Lanark., Scot.
388 C3 Lettershendony Derry, N. Ire.
358 E2 Letterston Pembs., Wales
322 K2 Lettoch High., Scot.
140 B2 Letton Here., Eng.
140 B3 Letton Here., Eng.
110 E5 Letty Green Herts., Eng.
208 F3 Letwell S. Yorks., Eng.
292 G1 Leuchars Fife, Scot.
326 E2 Leumrabhagh W. Isles, Scot.
326 E2 Leurbost W. Isles, Scot.
148 C4 Levedale Staffs., Eng.
116 C2 Level's Green Essex, Eng.
210 G3 Leven E. Riding, Eng.
292 G2 Leven Fife, Scot.
22 F9 Leven, Loch inlet Scot.
22 J10 Leven, Loch l. Scot.
264 D4 Levencorroch N. Ayr., Scot.
288 E3 Levenhall E. Lothian, Scot.
232 F7 Levens Cumbria, Eng.
110 E4 Levens Green Herts., Eng.
198 D3 Levenshulme Gtr Man., Eng.
331 D4 Levenwick Shet., Scot.
326 C3 Leverburgh W. Isles, Scot.
124 E2 Leverington Cambs., Eng.
110 C5 Leverstock Green Herts., Eng.
170 G5 Leverton Lincs., Eng.
170 G5 Leverton Lucasgate Lincs., Eng.
170 G5 Leverton Outgate Lincs., Eng.
120 G4 Levington Suff., Eng.
216 G2 Levisham N. Yorks., Eng.
322 H3 Levishie High., Scot.
102 B4 Lew Oxon, Eng.
36 F2 Lewannick Corn., Eng.
46 C2 Lewcombe Dorset, Eng.
58 G3 Lewes E. Sussex, Eng.
358 E2 Leweston Pembs., Wales
22 C6 Lewis, Isle of i. Scot.
74 D3 Lewisham Gtr Lon., Eng.
74 D3 Lewisham met. bor. Gtr Lon., Eng.
322 H3 Lewiston High., Scot.
102 F4 Lewknor Oxon, Eng.
62 E3 Lewson Street Kent, Eng.
228 F4 Lewth Lancs., Eng.
40 D3 Lewtrenchard Devon, Eng.
36 F2 Ley Corn., Eng.
314 E3 Ley Abers., Scot.
62 C3 Leybourne Kent, Eng.
216 D2 Leyburn N. Yorks., Eng.
148 B2 Leycett Staffs., Eng.
110 D4 Ley Green Herts., Eng.
106 E4 Ley Hill Bucks., Eng.
228 F4 Leyland Lancs., Eng.
222 C3 Leymoor W. Yorks., Eng.
314 H2 Leys Abers., Scot.
304 K3 Leys Perth and Kin., Scot.
62 F2 Leysdown-on-Sea Kent, Eng.
308 G3 Leysmill Angus, Scot.
308 D3 Leys of Cossans Angus, Scot.
110 D2 Leysters Here., Eng.
74 D2 Leyton Gtr Lon., Eng.
74 E2 Leytonstone Gtr Lon., Eng.
36 F2 Lezant Corn., Eng.
314 D2 Lhanbryde Moray, Scot.
22 F7 Liathach mt. Scot.
322 G2 Liatrie High., Scot.
366 E7 Libanus Powys, Wales
268 E2 Libberton S. Lanark., Scot.
136 E2 Libbery Worcs., Eng.
288 E3 Liberton Edin., Scot.
326 D3 Liceasto W. Isles, Scot.
148 E4 Lichfield Staffs., Eng.
136 E1 Lickey Worcs., Eng.
136 E1 Lickey End Worcs., Eng.
58 B2 Lickfold W. Sussex, Eng.
40 D3 Liddaton Green Devon, Eng.
329 D5 Liddel Orkney, Scot.
24 L3 Liddel Water r. Scot.
322 E4 Liddesdale High., Scot.
22 K12 Liddesdale val. Scot.
86 E2 Liddington Swindon, Eng.
180 D3 Lidgate Derbys., Eng.
120 C3 Lidgate Suff., Eng.
176 C3 Lidgett Notts., Eng.
110 B3 Lidlington Central Bedfordshire, Eng.
58 B4 Lidsey W. Sussex, Eng.
62 D3 Lidsing Kent, Eng.
102 C3 Lidstone Oxon, Eng.
320 J2 Lieurary High., Scot.
308 D4 Liff Angus, Scot.
388 F2 Liffock Coleraine, N. Ire.
154 C3 Lifford W. Mids, Eng.
40 D3 Lifton Devon, Eng.
40 D3 Liftondown Devon, Eng.
402 F2 Ligfordrum Strabane, N. Ire.
388 C2 Ligg Derry, N. Ire.
222 D2 Lightcliffe W. Yorks., Eng.
228 F4 Lightfoot Green Lancs., Eng.
132 C4 Lighthorne Warks., Eng.
132 D4 Lighthorne Heath Warks., Eng.
78 C1 Lightwater Surr., Eng.
148 C3 Lightwood Stoke, Eng.
184 D4 Lightwood Green Cheshire East, Eng.
378 H4 Lightwood Green Wrex., Wales
388 K5 Ligoniel Belfast, N. Ire.
128 B3 Lilbourne Northants., Eng.
144 F2 Lilburn Tower Northumb., Eng.
94 G4 Lillesdon Som., Eng.
144 F3 Lilleshall Telford, Eng.
110 C4 Lilley Herts., Eng.
82 B2 Lilley W. Berks., Eng.
256 H3 Lilliesleaf Borders, Scot.
402 F2 Lilling Green N. Yorks., Eng.
106 C2 Lillingstone Dayrell Bucks., Eng.
106 C2 Lillingstone Lovell Bucks., Eng.
46 D2 Lillington Dorset, Eng.
132 C4 Lillington Warks., Eng.
46 H3 Lilliput Poole, Eng.
40 D1 Lilly Devon, Eng.
94 E3 Lilstock Som., Eng.
74 F3 Lilyhurst Shrop., Eng.
388 E2 Limavady Limavady, N. Ire.
388 E3 Limavady admin. dist. N. Ire.
228 G5 Limbrick Lancs., Eng.
110 C4 Limbury Luton, Eng.
198 D2 Limefield Gtr Man., Eng.
402 I3 Lime Hill Cookstown, N. Ire.
74 D2 Limehouse Gtr Lon., Eng.
198 E2 Limehurst Gtr Man., Eng.
268 B2 Limekilnburn S. Lanark., Scot.
292 D3 Limekilns Fife, Scot.
280 D3 Limerigg Falk., Scot.
52 D7 Limerstone I.o.W., Eng.
198 E2 Lime Side Gtr Man., Eng.
388 I3 Liminary Ballymena, N. Ire.
94 I5 Limington Som., Eng.
166 I3 Limpenhoe Norf., Eng.
94 K2 Limpley Stoke B. and N.E. Som., Eng.
78 G2 Limpsfield Surr., Eng.
326 B4 Linaclate W. Isles, Scot.
244 G3 Linbriggs Northumb., Eng.
176 B4 Linby Notts., Eng.
58 B2 Linchmere W. Sussex, Eng.
252 F2 Lincluden D. and G., Scot.
170 C4 Lincoln Lincs., Eng.
170 E5 Lincolnshire county Eng.
24 Q7 Lincolnshire Wolds hills Eng.
136 D2 Lincomb Worcs., Eng.
232 E7 Lindale Cumbria, Eng.
232 D7 Lindal in Furness Cumbria, Eng.
256 H3 Lindean Borders, Scot.
98 F2 Linden Glos., Eng.
308 D3 Lindertis Angus, Scot.
58 F2 Lindfield W. Sussex, Eng.
52 G4 Lindford Hants., Eng.
292 F1 Lindifferon Fife, Scot.
Lindisfarne i. Eng. see Holy Island
216 E3 Lindley N. Yorks., Eng.
222 D3 Lindley W. Yorks., Eng.
292 E1 Lindores Fife, Scot.
184 F2 Lindow End Cheshire East, Eng.
136 C2 Lindridge Worcs., Eng.
116 C2 Lindsell Essex, Eng.
120 E4 Lindsey Suff., Eng.
120 E4 Lindsey Tye Suff., Eng.
216 D3 Lineholt Worcs., Eng.
222 D3 Linfit W. Yorks., Eng.
198 E2 Linfitts Gtr Man., Eng.
52 B5 Linford Hants., Eng.
116 E5 Linford Thurrock, Eng.
106 D2 Linford Wood M.K., Eng.
22 F8 Ling r. Scot.
405 B3 Lingague Isle of Man
222 C3 Lingards Wood W. Yorks., Eng.
216 G1 Lingdale R. and C., Eng.
140 B2 Lingen Here., Eng.
78 F2 Lingfield Surr., Eng.
190 E3 Lingley Green Warr., Eng.
166 H3 Lingwood Norf., Eng.
314 F2 Linhead Abers., Scot.
256 G5 Linhope Borders, Scot.
322 B2 Linicro High., Scot.
136 D4 Linkend Worcs., Eng.
52 D3 Linkenholt Hants., Eng.
62 D4 Linkhill Kent, Eng.
36 F2 Linkinhorne Corn., Eng.
329 D5 Linklater Orkney, Scot.
329 B4 Linksness Orkney, Scot.
329 E4 Linksness Orkney, Scot.
292 F3 Linktown Fife, Scot.
144 C4 Linley Shrop., Eng.
144 F4 Linley Shrop., Eng.
140 E2 Linley Green Here., Eng.
288 B3 Linlithgow W. Lothian, Scot.
288 B3 Linlithgow Bridge W. Lothian, Scot.
244 E6 Linnels Northumb., Eng.
358 D4 Linney Pembs., Wales
26 B4 Linney Head hd Wales
22 E9 Linnhe, Loch inlet Scot.
314 D4 Linn of Muick Cottage Abers., Scot.
244 D3 Linshiels Northumb., Eng.
326 D2 Linsiadar W. Isles, Scot.
322 G4 Linsidemore High., Scot.
110 A4 Linslade Central Bedfordshire, Eng.
120 H2 Linstead Parva Suff., Eng.
232 E3 Linstock Cumbria, Eng.
222 C3 Linthwaite W. Yorks., Eng.
256 K2 Lintlaw Borders, Scot.
314 E1 Lintmill Moray, Scot.
124 F6 Linton Cambs., Eng.
180 D6 Linton Derbys., Eng.
140 E4 Linton Here., Eng.
62 D3 Linton Kent, Eng.
222 F1 Linton W. Yorks., Eng.
256 J3 Linton Borders, Scot.
180 D6 Linton Heath Derbys., Eng.
216 F2 Linton-on-Ouse N. Yorks., Eng.
236 E2 Lintzford T. and W., Eng.
236 E2 Lintz Green Durham, Eng.
52 B5 Linwood Hants., Eng.
170 E3 Linwood Lincs., Eng.
276 D2 Linwood Renf., Scot.
Lionacleit W. Isles, Scot. see Linaclate
326 F1 Lional W. Isles, Scot.
52 H4 Liphook Hants., Eng.
144 F2 Lipley Shrop., Eng.
396 D3 Lisadian Armagh, N. Ire.
388 J6 Lisadian Lisburn, N. Ire.
396 J2 Lisbane Ards, N. Ire.
396 J2 Lisbarnet Ards, N. Ire.
402 E5 Lisbellaw Fermanagh, N. Ire.
388 J5 Lisburn Lisburn, N. Ire.
388 J5 Lisburn admin. dist. N. Ire.
388 F3 Liscall Coleraine, N. Ire.
190 C3 Liscard Merseyside, Eng.
402 G1 Liscloon Strabane, N. Ire.
388 H1 Liscolman Moyle, N. Ire.
94 C4 Liscombe Som., Eng.
402 F4 Lisconrea Omagh, N. Ire.
402 H4 Lisdoart Dungannon, N. Ire.
402 F2 Lisk Strabane, N. Ire.
36 F2 Liskeard Corn., Eng.
388 E2 Lislane Limavady, N. Ire.
388 G3 Lislea Magherafelt, N. Ire.
396 F5 Lislea Newry & Mourne, N. Ire.
396 J2 Lisleen Castlereagh, N. Ire.
408 B3 L'Islet Guernsey Channel Is
22 E10 Lismore i. Scot.
396 E4 Lisnadill Armagh, N. Ire.
402 F2 Lisnafin Strabane, N. Ire.
396 E4 Lisnagat Armagh, N. Ire.
388 H1 Lisnagunogue Moyle, N. Ire.
388 F3 Lisnamuck Magherafelt, N. Ire.
402 D4 Lisnarrick Fermanagh, N. Ire.
402 F5 Lisnaskea Fermanagh, N. Ire.
402 F2 Lisnatunny Strabane, N. Ire.
388 H3 Lisrodden Ballymena, N. Ire.
52 G4 Liss Hants., Eng.
402 J2 Lissan Cookstown, N. Ire.
210 G2 Lissett E. Riding, Eng.
52 G4 Liss Forest Hants., Eng.
170 D3 Lissington Lincs., Eng.
74 C2 Lisson Grove Gtr Lon., Eng.
208 E3 Listerdale S. Yorks., Eng.
116 D1 Liston Essex, Eng.
396 J3 Listooder Down, N. Ire.
350 F4 Lisvane Cardiff, Wales
339 C3 Liswerry Newp., Wales
166 D2 Litcham Norf., Eng.
128 C4 Litchborough Northants., Eng.
52 D3 Litchfield Hants., Eng.
190 D3 Litherland Merseyside, Eng.
124 D6 Litlington Cambs., Eng.
58 G4 Litlington E. Sussex, Eng.
124 F6 Little Abington Cambs., Eng.
128 F3 Little Addington Northants., Eng.
132 B4 Little Alne Warks., Eng.
190 C2 Little Altcar Merseyside, Eng.
110 E5 Little Amwell Herts., Eng.
52 C3 Little Ann Hants., Eng.
232 H6 Little Asby Cumbria, Eng.
86 B3 Little Ashley Wilts., Eng.
320 E3 Little Assynt High., Scot.
148 D5 Little Aston Staffs., Eng.
52 D7 Little Atherfield I.o.W., Eng.
116 F3 Little Baddow Essex, Eng.
98 F4 Little Badminton S. Glos., Eng.
304 H3 Little Ballinluig Perth and Kin., Scot.
232 D3 Little Bampton Cumbria, Eng.
116 D2 Little Bardfield Essex, Eng.
110 D2 Little Barford Bedford, Eng.
166 G1 Little Barningham Norf., Eng.
98 I3 Little Barrington Glos., Eng.
184 C2 Little Barrow Cheshire West & Chester, Eng.
216 G2 Little Barugh N. Yorks., Eng.
244 E5 Little Bavington Northumb., Eng.
120 G4 Little Bealings Suff., Eng.
216 H1 Littlebeck N. Yorks., Eng.
86 E3 Little Bedwyn Wilts., Eng.
162 E3 Little Beeby Leics., Eng.
116 I2 Little Bentley Essex, Eng.
110 E5 Little Berkhamsted Herts., Eng.
128 E4 Little Billing Northants., Eng.
110 B3 Little Billington Central Bedfordshire, Eng.
140 C4 Little Birch Here., Eng.
228 D3 Little Bispham Blackpool, Eng.
120 F4 Little Blakenham Suff., Eng.
154 C2 Little Bloxwich W. Mids, Eng.
144 E4 Little Bolas Shrop., Eng.
184 E1 Little Bollington Cheshire East, Eng.
198 D3 Little Bolton Gtr Man., Eng.
78 D2 Little Bookham Surr., Eng.
198 E2 Littleborough Gtr Man., Eng.
176 E3 Littleborough Notts., Eng.
62 G3 Littlebourne Kent, Eng.
102 D2 Little Bourton Oxon, Eng.
162 F4 Little Bowden Leics., Eng.
144 C5 Little Brampton Shrop., Eng.
116 F3 Little Braxted Essex, Eng.
308 F2 Little Brechin Angus, Scot.
46 D3 Littlebredy Dorset, Eng.
106 D3 Little Brickhill M.K., Eng.
402 K3 Little Bridge Cookstown, N. Ire.
148 B3 Little Bridgeford Staffs., Eng.
128 C4 Little Brington Northants., Eng.
116 I2 Little Bromley Essex, Eng.
154 D3 Little Bromwich W. Mids, Eng.
232 B4 Little Broughton Cumbria, Eng.
184 D2 Little Budworth Cheshire West & Chester, Eng.
236 G4 Little Burdon Darl., Eng.
116 E4 Little Burstead Essex, Eng.
210 G3 Little Burton E. Riding, Eng.
116 D1 Littlebury Essex, Eng.
116 D1 Littlebury Green Essex, Eng.
170 D7 Little Bytham Lincs., Eng.
46 H3 Little Canford Dorset, Eng.
228 D3 Little Carleton Blackpool, Eng.
170 G3 Little Carlton Lincs., Eng.
176 D4 Little Carlton Notts., Eng.
162 I2 Little Casterton Rutland, Eng.
210 G3 Little Catwick E. Riding, Eng.
124 B4 Little Catworth Cambs., Eng.
170 G4 Little Cawthorpe Lincs., Eng.
86 B3 Little Chalfield Wilts., Eng.
106 E4 Little Chalfont Bucks., Eng.
62 E3 Little Chart Kent, Eng.
180 E5 Little Chester Derby, Eng.
116 D1 Little Chesterford Essex, Eng.
102 D3 Little Chesterton Oxon, Eng.
86 C4 Little Cheverell Wilts., Eng.
124 E6 Little Chishill Cambs., Eng.
116 I3 Little Clacton Essex, Eng.
102 B4 Little Clanfield Oxon, Eng.
232 B5 Little Clifton Cumbria, Eng.
170 F2 Little Coates N.E. Lincs., Eng.
22 D10 Little Colonsay i. Scot.
136 E3 Little Comberton Worcs., Eng.
58 I3 Little Common E. Sussex, Eng.
132 C6 Little Compton Warks., Eng.
232 D3 Little Corby Cumbria, Eng.
120 D4 Little Cornard Suff., Eng.
86 E4 Littlecote Wilts., Eng.
140 D3 Little Cowarne Here., Eng.
102 B5 Little Coxwell Oxon, Eng.
216 E2 Little Crakehall N. Yorks., Eng.
128 E3 Little Cransley Northants., Eng.
106 E2 Little Crawley M.K., Eng.
128 D3 Little Creaton Northants., Eng.
166 D3 Little Cressingham Norf., Eng.
190 C2 Little Crosby Merseyside, Eng.
232 C5 Little Crosthwaite Cumbria, Eng.
180 C5 Little Cubley Derbys., Eng.
24 H2 Little Cumbrae i. Scot.
162 F2 Little Dalby Leics., Eng.
26 E6 Little Dart r. Eng.
98 E3 Littledean Glos., Eng.
314 H2 Little Dens Abers., Scot.
140 C4 Little Dewchurch Here., Eng.
124 G5 Little Ditton Cambs., Eng.
140 E4 Little Doward Here., Eng.
52 D3 Little Down Hants., Eng.
124 F4 Little Downham Cambs., Eng.
144 E2 Little Drayton Shrop., Eng.
210 F2 Little Driffield E. Riding, Eng.
166 D2 Little Dunham Norf., Eng.
304 I3 Little Dunkeld Perth and Kin., Scot.
116 E2 Little Dunmow Essex, Eng.
86 E5 Little Durnford Wilts., Eng.
116 D2 Little Easton Essex, Eng.
180 E5 Little Eaton Derbys., Eng.
228 E3 Little Eccleston Lancs., Eng.
216 G2 Little Edstone N. Yorks., Eng.
166 E3 Little Ellingham Norf., Eng.
116 D3 Little End Essex, Eng.
128 C4 Little Everdon Northants., Eng.
124 E6 Little Eversden Cambs., Eng.
102 A4 Little Faringdon Oxon, Eng.
320 H4 Littleferry High., Scot.
82 F3 Littlefield Green W. and M., Eng.
120 E4 Little Finborough Suff., Eng.
166 D2 Little Fransham Norf., Eng.
110 B5 Little Gaddesden Herts., Eng.
140 C4 Little Garway Here., Eng.
124 B4 Little Gidding Cambs., Eng.
120 H3 Little Glemham Suff., Eng.
304 I4 Little Glenshee Perth and Kin., Scot.
140 E4 Little Gorsley Here., Eng.
124 D5 Little Gransden Cambs., Eng.
124 D6 Little Green Cambs., Eng.
176 D5 Little Green Notts., Eng.
120 F3 Little Green Suff., Eng.
120 F3 Little Green Suff., Eng.
378 I4 Little Green Wrex., Wales
170 F3 Little Grimsby Lincs., Eng.
176 D3 Little Gringley Notts., Eng.
320 D4 Little Gruinard High., Scot.
216 G2 Little Habton N. Yorks., Eng.
110 F4 Little Hadham Herts., Eng.
170 E6 Little Hale Lincs., Eng.
180 F5 Little Hallam Derbys., Eng.
116 D2 Little Hallingbury Essex, Eng.
40 D2 Littleham Devon, Eng.
40 F3 Littleham Devon, Eng.
106 D4 Little Hampden Bucks., Eng.
58 C4 Littlehampton W. Sussex, Eng.
98 F3 Little Haresfield Glos., Eng.
128 E3 Little Harrowden Northants., Eng.
102 E4 Little Haseley Oxon, Eng.
210 G3 Little Hatfield E. Riding, Eng.
166 H2 Little Hautbois Norf., Eng.
58 E2 Little Haven W. Sussex, Eng.
358 D3 Little Haven Pembs., Wales
148 E5 Little Hay Staffs., Eng.
180 B2 Little Hayfield Derbys., Eng.
148 D4 Little Haywood Staffs., Eng.
154 F3 Little Heath W. Mids, Eng.
140 D2 Little Hereford Here., Eng.
166 E4 Little Hockham Norf., Eng.
116 H2 Little Horkesley Essex, Eng.
110 F4 Little Hormead Herts., Eng.
58 G3 Little Horsted E. Sussex, Eng.
86 D3 Little Horton Wilts., Eng.
222 D2 Little Horton W. Yorks., Eng.
106 C3 Little Horwood Bucks., Eng.
128 E4 Little Houghton Northants., Eng.
244 H3 Littlehoughton Northumb., Eng.
208 D2 Little Houghton S. Yorks., Eng.
180 C3 Little Hucklow Derbys., Eng.
198 C2 Little Hulton Gtr Man., Eng.
82 C3 Little Hungerford W. Berks., Eng.
128 E4 Little Irchester Northants., Eng.
94 K3 Little Keyford Som., Eng.
106 D4 Little Kimble Bucks., Eng.
132 C5 Little Kineton Warks., Eng.
106 D4 Little Kingshill Bucks., Eng.
232 D6 Little Langdale Cumbria, Eng.
86 D5 Little Langford Wilts., Eng.
116 D3 Little Laver Essex, Eng.
132 E3 Little Lawford Warks., Eng.
228 D3 Little Layton Blackpool, Eng.
184 D2 Little Leigh Cheshire West & Chester, Eng.
116 E3 Little Leighs Essex, Eng.
222 D3 Little Lepton W. Yorks., Eng.
198 C2 Little Lever Gtr Man., Eng.
314 F3 Little Ley Abers., Scot.
106 D2 Little Linford M.K., Eng.
124 F6 Little Linton Cambs., Eng.
22 F7 Little Loch Broom inlet Scot.
405 C2 Little London Isle of Man
106 B4 Little London Bucks., Eng.
124 E3 Little London Cambs., Eng.
116 C2 Little London Essex, Eng.
58 H3 Little London E. Sussex, Eng.
98 E2 Little London Glos., Eng.
52 D3 Little London Hants., Eng.
52 F3 Little London Hants., Eng.
170 E3 Little London Lincs., Eng.
170 F7 Little London Lincs., Eng.
166 A2 Little London Norf., Eng.
166 C3 Little London Norf., Eng.
166 H2 Little London Norf., Eng.
102 D4 Little London Oxon, Eng.
120 E4 Little London Suff., Eng.
222 D1 Little London W. Yorks., Eng.
366 E4 Little London Powys, Wales
180 C3 Little Longstone Derbys., Eng.
144 D4 Little Lyth Shrop., Eng.
136 C3 Little Malvern Worcs., Eng.
378 G2 Little Mancot Flints., Wales
116 F2 Little Maplestead Essex, Eng.
140 E3 Little Marcle Here., Eng.
40 D2 Little Marland Devon, Eng.
106 D5 Little Marlow Bucks., Eng.
228 E4 Little Marsden Lancs., Eng.
166 C2 Little Massingham Norf., Eng.
166 G3 Little Melton Norf., Eng.
358 E3 Little Milford Pembs., Wales
262 E4 Littlemill E. Ayr., Scot.
322 J2 Littlemill High., Scot.
339 C2 Little Mill Mon., Wales
102 E4 Little Milton Oxon, Eng.
22 B7 Little Minch sea chan. Scot.
102 B4 Little Minster Oxon, Eng.
106 D4 Little Missenden Bucks., Eng.
62 I3 Little Mongeham Kent, Eng.
180 E4 Littlemoor Derbys., Eng.
46 E4 Littlemoor Dorset, Eng.
228 H4 Little Moor End Lancs., Eng.
102 D4 Littlemore Oxon, Eng.
198 E3 Littlemoss Gtr Man., Eng.
232 H5 Little Musgrave Cumbria, Eng.
144 C3 Little Ness Shrop., Eng.
184 A2 Little Neston Cheshire West & Chester, Eng.
358 E2 Little Newcastle Pembs., Wales
236 E4 Little Newsham Durham, Eng.
148 D4 Little Norton Staffs., Eng.
116 J2 Little Oakley Essex, Eng.
128 F2 Little Oakley Northants., Eng.
110 B2 Little Odell Bedford, Eng.
110 D4 Little Offley Herts., Eng.
148 B4 Little Onn Staffs., Eng.
232 D3 Little Orton Cumbria, Eng.
162 B3 Little Orton Leics., Eng.
124 G4 Little Ouse Cambs., Eng.
26 M3 Little Ouse r. Eng.
180 D5 Littleover Derby, Eng.
378 H4 Little Overton Wrex., Wales
132 B3 Little Packington Warks., Eng.
116 C3 Little Parndon Essex, Eng.
124 C5 Little Paxton Cambs., Eng.
36 E2 Little Petherick Corn., Eng.
228 E4 Little Plumpton Lancs., Eng.
166 H3 Little Plumstead Norf., Eng.
170 C6 Little Ponton Lincs., Eng.
124 F4 Littleport Cambs., Eng.
52 E5 Little Posbrook Hants., Eng.
40 D2 Little Potheridge Devon, Eng.
128 C4 Little Preston Northants., Eng.
124 D4 Little Raveley Cambs., Eng.
210 D4 Little Reedness E. Riding, Eng.
216 E3 Little Ribston N. Yorks., Eng.
98 I2 Little Rissington Glos., Eng.
102 B3 Little Rollright Oxon, Eng.
166 E2 Little Ryburgh Norf., Eng.
244 F3 Little Ryle Northumb., Eng.
144 D4 Little Ryton Shrop., Eng.
232 F4 Little Salkeld Cumbria, Eng.
116 E2 Little Sampford Essex, Eng.
322 G2 Little Scatwell High., Scot.
124 E6 Little Shelford Cambs., Eng.
144 C3 Little Shrawardine Shrop., Eng.
98 G2 Little Shurdington Glos., Eng.
228 E3 Little Singleton Lancs., Eng.
216 E1 Little Smeaton N. Yorks., Eng.
166 E1 Little Snoring Norf., Eng.
98 E4 Little Sodbury S. Glos., Eng.
98 E4 Little Sodbury End S. Glos., Eng.
52 D4 Little Somborne Hants., Eng.
86 C2 Little Somerford Wilts., Eng.
144 F2 Little Soudley Shrop., Eng.
236 G4 Little Stainton Darl., Eng.
184 B2 Little Stanney Cheshire West & Chester, Eng.
110 C2 Little Staughton Bedford, Eng.
102 F6 Littlestead Green Oxon, Eng.
170 G5 Little Steeping Lincs., Eng.
148 C3 Little Stoke Staffs., Eng.
62 F5 Littlestone-on-Sea Kent, Eng.
120 F3 Little Stonham Suff., Eng.
124 F4 Little Street Cambs., Eng.
162 E3 Little Stretton Leics., Eng.
144 D4 Little Stretton Shrop., Eng.
232 F5 Little Strickland Cumbria, Eng.
124 C4 Little Stukeley Cambs., Eng.
148 B3 Little Sugnall Staffs., Eng.
184 B2 Little Sutton Cheshire West & Chester, Eng.
244 E5 Little Swinburne Northumb., Eng.
140 D3 Little Tarrington Here., Eng.
102 C3 Little Tew Oxon, Eng.
116 G2 Little Tey Essex, Eng.
124 F4 Little Thetford Cambs., Eng.
166 F1 Little Thornage Norf., Eng.
228 E3 Little Thornton Lancs., Eng.
236 G3 Little Thorpe Durham, Eng.
120 B4 Little Thurlow Suff., Eng.
120 B4 Little Thurlow Green Suff., Eng.
116 E5 Little Thurrock Thurrock, Eng.
184 B2 Littleton Cheshire West & Chester, Eng.
52 D4 Littleton Hants., Eng.
94 H4 Littleton Som., Eng.
78 D1 Littleton Surr., Eng.
304 K4 Littleton Perth and Kin., Scot.
86 B2 Littleton Drew Wilts., Eng.
98 D4 Littleton-on-Severn S. Glos., Eng.
86 D4 Littleton Panell Wilts., Eng.
320 H4 Little Torboll High., Scot.
40 D2 Little Torrington Devon, Eng.
244 F4 Little Tosson Northumb., Eng.
116 G3 Little Totham Essex, Eng.
232 C5 Little Town Cumbria, Eng.
236 G3 Littletown Durham, Eng.
52 E6 Littletown I.o.W., Eng.
228 G4 Little Town Lancs., Eng.
190 F3 Little Town Warr., Eng.
162 C3 Little Twycross Leics., Eng.
232 D8 Little Urswick Cumbria, Eng.
116 G4 Little Wakering Essex, Eng.
116 D1 Little Walden Essex, Eng.
120 D4 Little Waldingfield Suff., Eng.
166 E1 Little Walsingham Norf., Eng.
116 E3 Little Waltham Essex, Eng.
116 D4 Little Warley Essex, Eng.
98 G2 Little Washbourne Glos., Eng.
210 E4 Little Weighton E. Riding, Eng.
136 D3 Little Welland Worcs., Eng.
120 D3 Little Welnetham Suff., Eng.
120 F4 Little Wenham Suff., Eng.
144 E4 Little Wenlock Telford, Eng.
94 I4 Little Weston Som., Eng.
244 E5 Little Whittington Northumb., Eng.
82 F5 Littlewick Green W. and M., Eng.
124 F5 Little Wilbraham Cambs., Eng.
46 C2 Littlewindsor Dorset, Eng.
86 E5 Little Wishford Wilts., Eng.
98 G2 Little Witcombe Glos., Eng.
136 C2 Little Witley Worcs., Eng.
102 D5 Little Wittenham Oxon, Eng.
120 H2 Little Wittingham Green Suff., Eng.
132 C5 Little Wolford Warks., Eng.
148 C5 Littlewood Staffs., Eng.
74 D3 Little Woodcote Gtr Lon., Eng.
110 C3 Littleworth Bedford, Eng.
98 I1 Littleworth Glos., Eng.
102 B4 Littleworth Oxon, Eng.
148 C4 Littleworth Staffs., Eng.
148 D4 Littleworth Staffs., Eng.
208 F3 Littleworth S. Yorks., Eng.
136 D3 Littleworth Worcs., Eng.
120 B4 Little Wratting Suff., Eng.
110 B2 Little Wymington Bedford, Eng.
110 D4 Little Wymondley Herts., Eng.
148 D5 Little Wyrley Staffs., Eng.
144 E3 Little Wytheford Shrop., Eng.
116 F1 Little Yeldham Essex, Eng.
116 E3 Littley Green Essex, Eng.
180 C3 Litton Derbys., Eng.
216 C2 Litton N. Yorks., Eng.
94 I3 Litton Som., Eng.
46 D3 Litton Cheney Dorset, Eng.
190 D3 Liverpool Merseyside, Eng.
24 K7 Liverpool Bay b. Eng.
190 D3 Liverpool John Lennon airport Eng.
222 D2 Liversedge W. Yorks., Eng.
40 E3 Liverton Devon, Eng.
216 G1 Liverton R. and C., Eng.
62 E3 Liverton Street Kent, Eng.
288 B3 Livingston W. Lothian, Scot.
288 B3 Livingston Village W. Lothian, Scot.
378 F2 Lixwm Flints., Wales
36 D4 Lizard Corn., Eng.
26 B8 Lizard Point pt Eng.
362 E3 Llaingarreglwyd Cere., Wales
371 B3 Llaingoch I.o.A., Wales
366 E4 Llaithddu Powys, Wales
350 E4 Llampha V. of Glam., Wales
366 D3 Llan Powys, Wales
372 F4 Llanaber Gwynedd, Wales
372 D3 Llanaelhaearn Gwynedd, Wales
362 E3 Llanaeron Cere., Wales
362 G3 Llanafan Cere., Wales
366 D5 Llanafan-fawr Powys, Wales
366 D6 Llanafan-fechan Powys, Wales
371 D2 Llanallgo I.o.A., Wales
Llanandras Powys, Wales see Presteigne
372 D3 Llanarmon Gwynedd, Wales
378 F4 Llanarmon Dyffryn Ceiriog Wrex., Wales
378 F3 Llanarmon-yn-Ial Denb., Wales
362 E3 Llanarth Cere., Wales
339 C2 Llanarth Mon., Wales
356 F2 Llanarthney Carmar., Wales
378 E2 Llanasa Flints., Wales
371 C2 Llanbabo I.o.A., Wales
362 F2 Llanbadarn Fawr Cere., Wales
366 F4 Llanbadarn Fynydd Powys, Wales
366 F6 Llanbadarn-y-garreg Powys, Wales
339 C2 Llanbadoc Mon., Wales
371 C2 Llanbadrig I.o.A., Wales
339 C3 Llanbeder Newp., Wales
372 F4 Llanbedr Gwynedd, Wales
366 F6 Llanbedr Powys, Wales
366 G7 Llanbedr Powys, Wales
378 F3 Llanbedr-Dyffryn-Clwyd Denb., Wales
371 D3 Llanbedrgoch I.o.A., Wales
372 D3 Llanbedrog Gwynedd, Wales
378 B2 Llanbedr-y-cennin Conwy, Wales
372 F2 Llanberis Gwynedd, Wales
350 F4 Llanbethery V. of Glam., Wales
366 F4 Llanbister Powys, Wales
350 F4 Llanblethian V. of Glam., Wales
356 C2 Llanboidy Carmar., Wales
350 G3 Llanbradach Caerp., Wales
366 D3 Llanbryn-mair Powys, Wales
350 F4 Llancadle V. of Glam., Wales
350 F4 Llancarfan V. of Glam., Wales
339 C2 Llancayo Mon., Wales
362 G1 Llancynfelyn Cere., Wales
350 G2 Llandafal B. Gwent, Wales
350 G4 Llandaff Cardiff, Wales
350 G3 Llandaff North Cardiff, Wales
372 F3 Llandanwg Gwynedd, Wales
356 D3 Llandawke Carmar., Wales
371 D3 Llanddaniel Fab I.o.A., Wales
356 E3 Llanddarog Carmar., Wales
362 F3 Llanddeiniol Cere., Wales
372 E1 Llanddeiniolen Gwynedd, Wales
372 I3 Llandderfel Gwynedd, Wales
356 H2 Llanddeusant Carmar., Wales
371 C2 Llanddeusant I.o.A., Wales
366 E7 Llanddew Powys, Wales
350 A3 Llanddewi Swansea, Wales
362 G3 Llanddewi-Brefi Cere., Wales
366 E6 Llanddewi'r Cwm Powys, Wales
339 C2 Llanddewi Rhydderch Mon., Wales
339 C1 Llanddewi Skirrid Mon., Wales
358 F3 Llanddewi Velfrey Pembs., Wales
366 F5 Llanddewi Ystradenni Powys, Wales
378 C3 Llanddoged Conwy, Wales
371 E3 Llanddona I.o.A., Wales
356 C3 Llanddowror Carmar., Wales
378 D2 Llanddulas Conwy, Wales
372 F4 Llanddwywe Gwynedd, Wales
371 D3 Llanddyfnan I.o.A., Wales
366 E7 Llandefaelog Fach Powys, Wales
366 F7 Llandefaelog-tre'r-graig Powys, Wales
366 F6 Llandefalle Powys, Wales
371 E3 Llandegfan I.o.A., Wales
378 F3 Llandegla Denb., Wales
366 F5 Llandegley Powys, Wales
339 C3 Llandegveth Mon., Wales
372 C3 Llandegwning Gwynedd, Wales
356 G2 Llandeilo Carmar., Wales
356 D3 Llandeilo Abercywyn Carmar., Wales
366 F6 Llandeilo Graban Powys, Wales
366 D6 Llandeilo'r-Fan Powys, Wales
358 D2 Llandeloy Pembs., Wales
339 C2 Llandenny Mon., Wales
339 C3 Llandevaud Newp., Wales
339 C3 Llandevenny Mon., Wales
140 C4 Llandinabo Here., Eng.
366 E4 Llandinam Powys, Wales
358 F2 Llandissilio Pembs., Wales
339 D2 Llandogo Mon., Wales
350 F4 Llandough V. of Glam., Wales
350 G4 Llandough V. of Glam., Wales
356 H2 Llandovery Carmar., Wales
350 E4 Llandow V. of Glam., Wales
356 B2 Llandre Carmar., Wales
356 G1 Llandre Carmar., Wales
362 F2 Llandre Cere., Wales
378 E4 Llandrillo Denb., Wales
378 C2 Llandrillo-yn-Rhôs Conwy, Wales
366 E5 Llandrindod Wells Powys, Wales
366 G2 Llandrinio Powys, Wales
378 C2 Llandudno Conwy, Wales
378 C2 Llandudno Junction Conwy, Wales
372 E2 Llandwrog Gwynedd, Wales
356 F3 Llandybie Carmar., Wales
356 E3 Llandyfaelog Carmar., Wales
356 F3 Llandyfan Carmar., Wales
362 D4 Llandyfriog Cere., Wales
371 C2 Llandyfrydog I.o.A., Wales
372 F1 Llandygai Gwynedd, Wales
362 C4 Llandygwydd Cere., Wales
378 E2 Llandyrnog Denb., Wales
356 E3 Llandyry Carmar., Wales
366 G2 Llandysilio Powys, Wales
366 F3 Llandyssil Powys, Wales
362 E4 Llandysul Cere., Wales
350 H3 Llanedeyrn Cardiff, Wales
356 F3 Llanedy Carmar., Wales
366 E6 Llaneglwys Powys, Wales
372 F4 Llanegryn Gwynedd, Wales
356 F2 Llanegwad Carmar., Wales
371 D2 Llaneilian I.o.A., Wales
378 C2 Llanelian-yn-Rhos Conwy, Wales
378 E3 Llanelidan Denb., Wales
366 F6 Llanelieu Powys, Wales
339 B2 Llanellen Mon., Wales
356 F3 Llanelli Carmar., Wales
372 G4 Llanelltyd Gwynedd, Wales
339 B2 Llanelly Mon., Wales
339 B2 Llanelly Hill Mon., Wales
366 E6 Llanelwedd Powys, Wales
Llanelwy Denb., Wales see St Asaph
372 F4 Llanenddwyn Gwynedd, Wales
372 C4 Llanengan Gwynedd, Wales
366 E2 Llanerfyl Powys, Wales
371 D2 Llaneuddog I.o.A., Wales

Llaneurgain to Luddenham Court

Llaneurgain Flints., Wales see Northop
371 B3 Llanfachraeth I.o.A., Wales
372 G4 Llanfachreth Gwynedd, Wales
371 C3 Llanfaelog I.o.A., Wales
372 C4 Llanfaelrhys Gwynedd, Wales
339 D1 Llanfaenor Mon., Wales
371 E3 Llan-faes I.o.A., Wales
366 E7 Llanfaes Powys, Wales
371 B2 Llanfaethlu I.o.A., Wales
372 E2 Llanfaglan Gwynedd, Wales
372 F3 Llanfair Gwynedd, Wales
366 F3 Llanfair Caereinion Powys, Wales
362 F4 Llanfair Clydogau Cere., Wales
378 F3 Llanfair Dyffryn Clwyd Denb., Wales
378 B2 Llanfairfechan Conwy, Wales
358 F1 Llanfair-Nant-Gwyn Pembs., Wales
362 D4 Llanfair-Orllwyn Cere., Wales
371 D3 Llanfairpwllgwyngyll I.o.A., Wales
378 D2 Llanfair Talhaiarn Conwy, Wales
144 B5 Llanfair Waterdine Shrop., Eng.
Llanfair-ym-Muallt Powys, Wales see Builth Wells
371 B2 Llanfairynghornwy I.o.A., Wales
371 B3 Llanfair-yn-neubwll I.o.A., Wales
356 B2 Llanfallteg Carmar., Wales
356 B2 Llanfallteg West Carmar., Wales
366 E6 Llanfaredd Powys, Wales
362 F2 Llanfarian Cere., Wales
366 F2 Llanfechain Powys, Wales
371 C2 Llanfechell I.o.A., Wales
372 F5 Llanfendigaid Gwynedd, Wales
378 F3 Llanferres Denb., Wales
371 C2 Llanfflewyn I.o.A., Wales
371 B3 Llanfigael I.o.A., Wales
356 E1 Llanfihangel-ar-arth Carmar., Wales
Llanfihangel Crucornau Mon., Wales see Llanvihangel Crucorney
378 D3 Llanfihangel Glyn Myfyr Conwy, Wales
366 D6 Llanfihangel Nant Bran Powys, Wales
366 F5 Llanfihangel-nant-Melan Powys, Wales
366 F5 Llanfihangel Rhydithon Powys, Wales
339 D3 Llanfihangel Rogiet Mon., Wales
366 F7 Llanfihangel Tal-y-llyn Powys, Wales
356 E2 Llanfihangel-uwch-Gwili Carmar., Wales
362 G2 Llanfihangel-y-Creuddyn Cere., Wales
366 E2 Llanfihangel-yng-Ngwynfa Powys, Wales
371 B3 Llanfihangel-yn-Nhywyn I.o.A., Wales
372 E3 Llanfihangel-y-pennant Gwynedd, Wales
372 G5 Llanfihangel-y-pennant Gwynedd, Wales
366 F7 Llanfilo Powys, Wales
339 B2 Llanfoist Mon., Wales
372 I3 Llanfor Gwynedd, Wales
98 B4 Llanfrechfa B. Gwent, Wales
372 F3 Llanfrothen Gwynedd, Wales
366 E7 Llanfrynach Powys, Wales
378 F3 Llanfwrog Denb., Wales
371 B3 Llanfwrog I.o.A., Wales
366 F2 Llanfyllin Powys, Wales
356 F2 Llanfynydd Carmar., Wales
378 G3 Llanfynydd Flints., Wales
358 G2 Llanfyrnach Pembs., Wales
366 E2 Llangadfan Powys, Wales
356 G2 Llangadog Carmar., Wales
371 C3 Llangadwaladr I.o.A., Wales
366 F1 Llangadwaladr Powys, Wales
371 D3 Llangaffo I.o.A., Wales
356 D3 Llangain Carmar., Wales
366 D6 Llangammarch Wells Powys, Wales
350 E4 Llangan V. of Glam., Wales
140 C4 Llangarron Here., Eng.
356 F2 Llangathen Carmar., Wales
366 G7 Llangattock Powys, Wales
339 C1 Llangattock Lingoed Mon., Wales
339 D1 Llangattock-Vibon-Avel Mon., Wales
366 F2 Llangedwyn Powys, Wales
371 D3 Llangefni I.o.A., Wales
350 E3 Llangeinor Bridg., Wales
362 F3 Llangeitho Cere., Wales
356 D1 Llangeler Carmar., Wales
372 F5 Llangelynin Gwynedd, Wales
356 E3 Llangendeirne Carmar., Wales
356 E3 Llangennech Carmar., Wales
350 A3 Llangennith Swansea, Wales
366 G7 Llangenny Powys, Wales
378 C2 Llangernyw Conwy, Wales
372 C4 Llangian Gwynedd, Wales
350 C2 Llangiwg N.P.T., Wales
358 D2 Llangloffan Pembs., Wales
356 C2 Llanglydwen Carmar., Wales
371 E3 Llangoed I.o.A., Wales
362 C4 Llangoedmor Cere., Wales
378 F4 Llangollen Denb., Wales
358 F2 Llangolman Pembs., Wales
366 F7 Llangorse Powys, Wales
362 F4 Llangorwen Cere., Wales
339 D2 Llangovan Mon., Wales
372 I3 Llangower Gwynedd, Wales
362 D4 Llangrannog Cere., Wales
371 C3 Llangristiolus I.o.A., Wales
140 C4 Llangrove Here., Eng.
339 C1 Llangua Mon., Wales
366 G4 Llangunllo Powys, Wales
356 E2 Llangunnor Carmar., Wales
366 D4 Llangurig Powys, Wales
378 D4 Llangwm Conwy, Wales
358 E3 Llangwm Pembs., Wales
339 D2 Llangwm-isaf Mon., Wales
372 B3 Llangwnnadl Gwynedd, Wales
378 F2 Llangwyfan Denb., Wales
362 F3 Llangwyryfon Cere., Wales
362 F4 Llangybi Cere., Wales
372 D3 Llangybi Gwynedd, Wales
339 C3 Llangybi Mon., Wales
350 C2 Llangyfelach Swansea, Wales
378 F3 Llangynhafal Denb., Wales
366 F7 Llangynidr Powys, Wales
366 F2 Llangyniew Powys, Wales
356 C2 Llangynin Carmar., Wales
362 D4 Llangynllo Cere., Wales
356 D3 Llangynog Carmar., Wales
366 E2 Llangynog Powys, Wales
350 E3 Llangynwyd Bridg., Wales
366 F7 Llanhamlach Powys, Wales
350 F3 Llanharan R.C.T., Wales
350 F3 Llanharry R.C.T., Wales
339 C3 Llanhennock Mon., Wales
350 H2 Llanhilleth B. Gwent, Wales
366 D4 Llanidloes Powys, Wales
372 C3 Llaniestyn Gwynedd, Wales
366 G6 Llanigon Powys, Wales
362 F2 Llanilar Cere., Wales
350 F3 Llanilid R.C.T., Wales
350 G3 Llanishen Cardiff, Wales
339 D2 Llanishen Mon., Wales
356 E2 Llanllawddog Carmar., Wales
372 F1 Llanllechid Gwynedd, Wales
366 D6 Llanlleonfel Powys, Wales
366 E3 Llanllugan Powys, Wales
356 D2 Llanllwch Carmar., Wales
366 F3 Llanllwchaiarn Powys, Wales
356 E1 Llanllwni Carmar., Wales
372 E2 Llanllyfni Gwynedd, Wales
339 C2 Llanllywel Mon., Wales
350 A3 Llanmadoc Swansea, Wales
350 F4 Llanmaes V. of Glam., Wales
339 C3 Llanmartin Newp., Wales
366 F3 Llanmerewig Powys, Wales
350 F4 Llanmihangel V. of Glam., Wales
358 F3 Llan-mill Pembs., Wales
356 C3 Llanmiloe Carmar., Wales
350 B3 Llanmorlais Swansea, Wales
378 D2 Llannefydd Conwy, Wales
378 E2 Llannerch Hall Denb., Wales
371 C3 Llannerch-y-medd I.o.A., Wales
378 F2 Llannerch-y-Môr Flints., Wales
356 F3 Llannon Carmar., Wales
362 E3 Llan-non Cere., Wales
372 D3 Llannor Gwynedd, Wales
339 C2 Llanover Mon., Wales
356 E2 Llanpumsaint Carmar., Wales
358 D2 Llanreithan Pembs., Wales
378 E3 Llanrhaeadr Denb., Wales
366 F2 Llanrhaeadr-ym-Mochnant Powys, Wales
358 C2 Llanrhian Pembs., Wales
350 A3 Llanrhidian Swansea, Wales
378 C2 Llanrhos Conwy, Wales
371 B2 Llanrhyddlad I.o.A., Wales
362 F3 Llanrhystud Cere., Wales
140 C4 Llanrothal Here., Eng.
372 E2 Llanrug Gwynedd, Wales
350 H3 Llanrumney Cardiff, Wales
378 C3 Llanrwst Conwy, Wales
356 D3 Llansadurnen Carmar., Wales
356 G2 Llansadwrn Carmar., Wales
371 D3 Llansadwrn I.o.A., Wales
356 D3 Llansaint Carmar., Wales
350 C3 Llansamlet Swansea, Wales
362 E3 Llansanffraid Cere., Wales
378 C2 Llansanffraid Glan Conwy Conwy, Wales
378 D2 Llansannan Conwy, Wales
350 F4 Llansannor V. of Glam., Wales
366 F7 Llansantffraed Powys, Wales
366 D5 Llansantffraed-Cwmdeuddwr Powys, Wales
366 F5 Llansantffraed-in-Elwel Powys, Wales
366 G2 Llansantffraid-ym-Mechain Powys, Wales
356 F1 Llansawel Carmar., Wales
366 F1 Llansilin Powys, Wales
339 D2 Llansoy Mon., Wales
366 E7 Llanspyddid Powys, Wales
358 E3 Llanstadwell Pembs., Wales
356 D3 Llansteffan Carmar., Wales
366 F6 Llanstephan Powys, Wales
350 H3 Llantarnam B. Gwent, Wales
358 G3 Llanteg Pembs., Wales
339 B1 Llanthony Mon., Wales
339 C2 Llantilio Crossenny Mon., Wales
339 B1 Llantilio Pertholey Mon., Wales
358 F1 Llantood Pembs., Wales
371 C3 Llantrisant I.o.A., Wales
339 C2 Llantrisant Mon., Wales
350 F3 Llantrisant R.C.T., Wales
350 F4 Llantrithyd V. of Glam., Wales
350 G3 Llantwit Fardre R.C.T., Wales
350 F4 Llantwit Major V. of Glam., Wales
378 F4 Llantysilio Denb., Wales
372 H3 Llanuwchllyn Gwynedd, Wales
339 D3 Llanvaches Newp., Wales
339 D3 Llanvair-Discoed Mon., Wales
339 C2 Llanvapley Mon., Wales
339 C1 Llanvetherine Mon., Wales
140 A4 Llanveynoe Here., Eng.
339 C1 Llanvihangel Crucorney Mon., Wales
339 C2 Llanvihangel Gobion Mon., Wales
339 D2 Llanvihangel-Ystern-Llewern Mon., Wales
350 F4 Llanvithyn V. of Glam., Wales
140 C4 Llanwarne Here., Eng.
366 E2 Llanwddyn Powys, Wales
362 E4 Llanwenog Cere., Wales
339 C3 Llanwern Newp., Wales
356 C2 Llanwinio Carmar., Wales
372 E2 Llanwnda Gwynedd, Wales
358 D1 Llanwnda Pembs., Wales
362 F4 Llanwnnen Cere., Wales
366 E3 Llanwnog Powys, Wales
350 F3 Llanwonno R.C.T., Wales
356 G2 Llanwrda Carmar., Wales
366 C3 Llanwrin Powys, Wales
366 D5 Llanwrthwl Powys, Wales
366 D6 Llanwrtyd Powys, Wales
366 D6 Llanwrtyd Wells Powys, Wales
366 E3 Llanwyddelan Powys, Wales
144 B3 Llanyblodwel Shrop., Eng.
356 D3 Llanybri Carmar., Wales
356 F1 Llanybydder Carmar., Wales
358 F2 Llanycefn Pembs., Wales
358 E2 Llanychaer Bridge Pembs., Wales
372 I3 Llanycil Gwynedd, Wales
356 G1 Llanycrwys Carmar., Wales
372 I4 Llanymawddwy Gwynedd, Wales
366 G2 Llanymynech Powys, Wales
371 B3 Llanynghenedl I.o.A., Wales
378 E3 Llanynys Denb., Wales
378 H3 Llan-y-pwll Wrex., Wales
366 E5 Llanyre Powys, Wales
372 E3 Llanystumdwy Gwynedd, Wales
366 F7 Llanywern Powys, Wales
358 F3 Llawhaden Pembs., Wales
378 F1 Llawndy Flints., Wales
144 B2 Llawnt Shrop., Eng.
372 C4 Llawr-y-dref Gwynedd, Wales
366 D3 Llawryglyn Powys, Wales
378 G3 Llay Wrex., Wales
372 E3 Llecheiddior Gwynedd, Wales
366 E7 Llechfaen Powys, Wales
350 G2 Llechryd Caerp., Wales
362 C4 Llechryd Cere., Wales
378 G4 Llechrydau Wrex., Wales
362 G3 Lledrod Cere., Wales
366 G1 Lledrod Powys, Wales
358 D2 Llethr Pembs., Wales
26 C2 Lleyn Peninsula pen. Wales
356 F1 Llidiad-Nenog Carmar., Wales
372 H3 Llidiardau Gwynedd, Wales
372 D3 Llithfaen Gwynedd, Wales
378 F2 Lloc Flints., Wales
378 G3 Llong Flints., Wales
366 F6 Llowes Powys, Wales
366 G4 Lloyney Powys, Wales
362 F3 Llundain-fach Cere., Wales
350 F2 Llwydcoed R.C.T., Wales
366 E2 Llwydiarth Powys, Wales
144 B5 Llwyn Shrop., Eng.
362 E3 Llwyncelyn Cere., Wales
356 E2 Llwyn-croes Carmar., Wales
362 D3 Llwyndafydd Cere., Wales
366 F3 Llwynderw Powys, Wales
372 D3 Llwyndyrys Gwynedd, Wales
378 G3 Llwyneinion Wrex., Wales
372 F4 Llwyngwril Gwynedd, Wales
356 F3 Llwynhendy Carmar., Wales
366 D6 Llwyn-Madoc Powys, Wales
378 G4 Llwynmawr Wrex., Wales
362 E3 Llwyn-onn Cere., Wales
350 F2 Llwyn-onn M. Tyd., Wales
356 C3 Llwyn-y-brain Carmar., Wales
356 G2 Llwyn-y-brain Carmar., Wales
362 F3 Llwyn-y-groes Cere., Wales
350 F3 Llwynypia R.C.T., Wales
144 B3 Llynclys Shrop., Eng.
26 E3 Llyn Clywedog Reservoir resr Wales
371 C3 Llynfaes I.o.A., Wales
Llyn Tegid l. Wales see Bala Lake
378 D2 Llysfaen Conwy, Wales
366 F6 Llyswen Powys, Wales
350 F4 Llysworney V. of Glam., Wales
358 E2 Llys-y-frân Pembs., Wales
366 D7 Llywel Powys, Wales
208 C3 Load Brook S. Yorks., Eng.
320 I4 Loandhu High., Scot.
388 J5 Loanends Antrim, N. Ire.
314 G2 Loanhead Abers., Scot.
288 E3 Loanhead Midlothian, Scot.
262 D3 Loans S. Ayr., Scot.
40 D1 Lobb Devon, Eng.
22 G9 Lochaber reg. Scot.
326 C4 Loch a Charnain W. Isles, Scot.
322 E4 Lochailort High., Scot.
Loch an Inbhir High., Scot. see Lochinver
252 A3 Lochans D. and G., Scot.
252 F2 Locharbriggs D. and G., Scot.
300 E2 Lochawe Arg. and B., Scot.
22 H10 Lochay r. Scot.
Loch Baghasdail W. Isles, Scot. see Lochboisdale
326 C5 Lochboisdale W. Isles, Scot.
300 C2 Lochbuie Arg. and B., Scot.
Loch Carrann High., Scot. see Lochcarron
322 E2 Lochcarron High., Scot.
320 H3 Loch Choire Lodge High., Scot.
320 I2 Lochdhu Hotel High., Scot.
300 C2 Lochdon Arg. and B., Scot.
320 F4 Lochdrum High., Scot.
296 E3 Lochearnhead Stir., Scot.
308 D4 Lochee Dundee, Scot.
320 K2 Lochend High., Scot.
322 H2 Lochend High., Scot.
326 C4 Locheport W. Isles, Scot.
Locheuphort W. Isles, Scot. see Locheport
252 E2 Lochfoot D. and G., Scot.
300 D3 Lochgair Arg. and B., Scot.
322 H3 Lochgarthside High., Scot.
292 E3 Lochgelly Fife, Scot.
300 D3 Lochgilphead Arg. and B., Scot.
300 F3 Lochgoilhead Arg. and B., Scot.
262 E2 Lochgoyn E. Ayr., Scot.
252 C2 Loch Head D. and G., Scot.
252 C3 Loch Head D. and G., Scot.
262 F4 Lochhill E. Ayr., Scot.
314 D1 Lochhill Moray, Scot.
252 B3 Lochinch Castle D. and G., Scot.
320 E3 Lochinver High., Scot.
308 F3 Lochlair Angus, Scot.
304 G4 Lochlane Perth and Kin., Scot.
262 E3 Lochlea S. Ayr., Scot.
22 G10 Loch Lomond and the Trossachs National Park nat. park Scot.
322 G2 Lochluichart High., Scot.
252 F2 Lochmaben D. and G., Scot.
326 C4 Lochmaddy W. Isles, Scot.
22 J9 Lochnagar mt. Scot.
Loch na Madadh W. Isles, Scot. see Lochmaddy
Loch Obha Arg. and B., Scot. see Lochawe
292 E3 Lochore Fife, Scot.
326 C4 Lochportain W. Isles, Scot.
264 C2 Lochranza N. Ayr., Scot.
326 C5 Loch Sgioport W. Isles, Scot.
320 G2 Lochside High., Scot.
320 I3 Lochside High., Scot.
320 J2 Lochside High., Scot.
320 I4 Lochslin High., Scot.
262 C6 Lochton S. Ayr., Scot.
292 H2 Lochty Fife, Scot.
322 E5 Lochuisge High., Scot.
252 E2 Lochurr D. and G., Scot.
276 C3 Lochwinnoch Renf., Scot.
22 G9 Lochy, Loch l. Scot.
36 E2 Lockengate Corn., Eng.
252 F2 Lockerbie D. and G., Scot.
86 E3 Lockeridge Wilts., Eng.
52 C4 Lockerley Hants., Eng.
232 F4 Lockhills Cumbria, Eng.
94 G3 Locking N. Som., Eng.
210 F3 Lockington E. Riding, Eng.
162 D1 Lockington Leics., Eng.
94 I2 Lockleaze Bristol, Eng.
144 F2 Lockleywood Shrop., Eng.
74 E3 Locksbottom Gtr Lon., Eng.
52 D6 Locksgreen I.o.W., Eng.
52 E5 Locks Heath Hants., Eng.
216 G2 Lockton N. Yorks., Eng.
162 G3 Loddington Leics., Eng.
128 E3 Loddington Northants., Eng.
40 E4 Loddiswell Devon, Eng.
166 H3 Loddon Norf., Eng.
124 F5 Lode Cambs., Eng.
154 D3 Lode Heath W. Mids, Eng.
46 C3 Loders Dorset, Eng.
58 B3 Lodsworth W. Sussex, Eng.
216 D2 Lofthouse N. Yorks., Eng.
222 F2 Lofthouse W. Yorks., Eng.
216 G1 Loftus R. and C., Eng.
252 B3 Logan D. and G., Scot.
262 F4 Logan E. Ayr., Scot.
288 B3 Loganlea W. Lothian, Scot.
148 A3 Loggerheads Staffs., Eng.
320 E4 Loggie High., Scot.
308 D3 Logie Angus, Scot.
308 H2 Logie Angus, Scot.
292 G1 Logie Fife, Scot.
314 C2 Logie Moray, Scot.
314 E3 Logie Coldstone Abers., Scot.
320 H4 Logie Hill High., Scot.
314 F2 Logie Newton Abers., Scot.
308 G2 Logie Pert Angus, Scot.
304 H3 Logierait Perth and Kin., Scot.
356 B2 Login Carmar., Wales
124 E5 Lolworth Cambs., Eng.
22 G10 Lomond, Loch l. Scot.
322 D2 Lonbain High., Scot.
210 D3 Londesborough E. Riding, Eng.
74 D2 London Gtr Lon., Eng.
62 E4 London Beach Kent, Eng.
62 A3 London Biggin Hill airport Eng.
74 E2 London City airport Eng.
110 D5 London Colney Herts., Eng.
154 C3 Londonderry W. Mids, Eng.
388 C3 Londonderry Derry, N. Ire.
388 E3 Londonderry county N. Ire.
154 B2 London Fields W. Mids, Eng.
58 E2 London Gatwick airport Eng.
74 B3 London Heathrow airport Eng.
110 C4 London Luton airport Eng.
52 C5 London Minstead Hants., Eng.
116 G4 London Southend airport Eng.
116 D2 London Stansted airport Eng.
170 C6 Londonthorpe Lincs., Eng.
320 D4 Londubh High., Scot.
22 G10 Long, Loch inlet Scot.
94 I2 Long Ashton N. Som., Eng.
136 C1 Long Bank Worcs., Eng.
170 B6 Long Bennington Lincs., Eng.
236 F1 Longbenton T. and W., Eng.
98 I2 Longborough Glos., Eng.
46 D3 Long Bredy Dorset, Eng.
40 D3 Longbridge Plymouth, Eng.
132 C4 Longbridge Warks., Eng.
154 C3 Longbridge W. Mids, Eng.
86 B4 Longbridge Deverill Wilts., Eng.
148 B2 Longbridge Hayes Staffs., Eng.
128 C4 Long Buckby Northants., Eng.
232 D3 Longburgh Cumbria, Eng.
46 E2 Longburton Dorset, Eng.
162 F1 Long Clawson Leics., Eng.
180 D4 Longcliffe Derbys., Eng.
148 B4 Long Compton Staffs., Eng.
132 C6 Long Compton Warks., Eng.
102 B5 Longcot Oxon, Eng.
106 B4 Long Crendon Bucks., Eng.
46 G2 Long Crichel Dorset, Eng.
280 C3 Longcroft Falk., Scot.
40 D3 Longcross Devon, Eng.
78 C1 Longcross Surr., Eng.
86 B3 Long Dean Wilts., Eng.
144 D4 Longden Shrop., Eng.
78 E1 Long Ditton Surr., Eng.
148 D4 Longdon Staffs., Eng.
136 D3 Longdon Worcs., Eng.
148 D4 Longdon Green Staffs., Eng.
144 E3 Longdon upon Tern Telford, Eng.
40 F2 Longdown Devon, Eng.
36 D3 Long Downs Corn., Eng.
216 G3 Long Drax N. Yorks., Eng.
314 G3 Longdrum Abers., Scot.
180 E3 Long Duckmanton Derbys., Eng.
180 F5 Long Eaton Derbys., Eng.
62 B2 Longfield Kent, Eng.
396 F5 Longfield Newry & Mourne, N. Ire.
62 C2 Longfield Hill Kent, Eng.
46 H3 Longfleet Poole, Eng.
180 C5 Longford Derbys., Eng.
98 F2 Longford Glos., Eng.
74 B3 Longford Gtr Lon., Eng.
144 E2 Longford Shrop., Eng.
144 F3 Longford Telford, Eng.
154 F3 Longford W. Mids, Eng.
304 L4 Longforgan Perth and Kin., Scot.
256 J2 Longformacus Borders, Scot.
244 G4 Longframlington Northumb., Eng.
216 C2 Long Gill N. Yorks., Eng.
184 C2 Long Green Cheshire West & Chester, Eng.
116 G2 Long Green Essex, Eng.
120 F2 Long Green Suff., Eng.
136 D4 Long Green Worcs., Eng.
46 H3 Longham Dorset, Eng.
166 E2 Longham Norf., Eng.
102 C4 Long Hanborough Oxon, Eng.
314 H2 Longhill Abers., Scot.
244 H4 Longhirst Northumb., Eng.
98 E2 Longhope Glos., Eng.
329 B5 Longhope Orkney, Scot.
244 G4 Longhorsley Northumb., Eng.
244 H3 Longhoughton Northumb., Eng.
132 D4 Long Itchington Warks., Eng.
232 D4 Longlands Cumbria, Eng.
74 E3 Longlands Gtr Lon., Eng.
180 D5 Longlane Derbys., Eng.
144 E3 Long Lane Telford, Eng.
82 C3 Longlane W. Berks., Eng.
132 E3 Long Lawford Warks., Eng.
98 F2 Longlevens Glos., Eng.
208 D3 Longley S. Yorks., Eng.
222 C2 Longley W. Yorks., Eng.
222 D3 Longley W. Yorks., Eng.
136 C3 Longley Green Worcs., Eng.
94 H4 Long Load Som., Eng.
314 F2 Longmanhill Abers., Scot.
110 A5 Long Marston Herts., Eng.
216 F3 Long Marston N. Yorks., Eng.
132 B5 Long Marston Warks., Eng.
232 G5 Long Marton Cumbria, Eng.
144 C5 Long Meadowend Shrop., Eng.
120 D4 Long Melford Suff., Eng.
52 G4 Longmoor Camp Hants., Eng.
314 D2 Longmorn Moray, Scot.
98 G4 Long Newnton Glos., Eng.
236 G4 Longnewton Stockton, Eng.
256 I3 Longnewton Borders, Scot.
288 F3 Longniddry E. Lothian, Scot.
144 D4 Longnor Shrop., Eng.
148 D1 Longnor Staffs., Eng.
52 D3 Longparish Hants., Eng.
148 B2 Longport Stoke, Eng.
216 C2 Long Preston N. Yorks., Eng.
228 G4 Longridge Lancs., Eng.
148 C4 Longridge Staffs., Eng.
288 A3 Longridge W. Lothian, Scot.
98 F2 Longridge End Glos., Eng.
244 E1 Longridge Towers Northumb., Eng.
280 C3 Longriggend N. Lanark., Scot.
210 G3 Long Riston E. Riding, Eng.
36 C3 Longrock Corn., Eng.
148 C2 Longsdon Staffs., Eng.
198 A2 Longshaw Gtr Man., Eng.
26 □ Longships is Eng.
314 H2 Longside Abers., Scot.
198 D3 Longsight Gtr Man., Eng.
144 E2 Longslow Shrop., Eng.
232 E3 Longsowerby Cumbria, Eng.
124 E5 Longstanton Cambs., Eng.
52 D4 Longstock Hants., Eng.
288 D3 Longstone Edin., Scot.
124 D5 Longstowe Cambs., Eng.
166 G4 Long Stratton Norf., Eng.
106 C2 Long Street M.K., Eng.
86 E4 Longstreet Wilts., Eng.
52 G3 Long Sutton Hants., Eng.
170 G7 Long Sutton Lincs., Eng.
94 H4 Long Sutton Som., Eng.
124 C3 Longthorpe Peterb., Eng.
120 E3 Long Thurlow Suff., Eng.
228 F4 Longton Lancs., Eng.
148 C3 Longton Stoke, Eng.
232 E2 Longtown Cumbria, Eng.
140 B4 Longtown Here., Eng.
144 D4 Longville in the Dale Shrop., Eng.
144 E3 Long Waste Telford, Eng.
98 E5 Longwell Green S. Glos., Eng.
162 D2 Long Whatton Leics., Eng.
106 C4 Longwick Bucks., Eng.
102 D5 Long Wittenham Oxon, Eng.
244 F4 Longwitton Northumb., Eng.
222 C3 Longwood W. Yorks., Eng.
102 C4 Longworth Oxon, Eng.
288 G3 Longyester E. Lothian, Scot.
314 H2 Lonmay Abers., Scot.
36 F2 Looe Corn., Eng.
62 D3 Loose Kent, Eng.
170 F7 Loosegate Lincs., Eng.
106 D4 Loosley Row Bucks., Eng.
86 F5 Lopcombe Corner Wilts., Eng.
94 H5 Lopen Som., Eng.
144 D2 Loppington Shrop., Eng.
244 F3 Lorbottle Northumb., Eng.
244 F3 Lorbottle Hall Northumb., Eng.
58 A3 Lordington W. Sussex, Eng.
52 D5 Lord's Hill Hants., Eng.
276 C1 Lorn W. Dun., Scot.
22 E10 Lorn, Firth of est. Scot.
304 J3 Lornty Perth and Kin., Scot.
180 E4 Loscoe Derbys., Eng.
46 C3 Loscombe Dorset, Eng.
326 D3 Losgaintir W. Isles, Scot.
22 J7 Lossie r. Scot.
314 D1 Lossiemouth Moray, Scot.
300 A4 Lossit Arg. and B., Scot.
184 E2 Lostock Gralam Cheshire West & Chester, Eng.
184 E2 Lostock Green Cheshire West & Chester, Eng.
198 C2 Lostock Junction Gtr Man., Eng.
36 E2 Lostwithiel Corn., Eng.
329 E2 Loth Orkney, Scot.
320 I3 Lothbeg High., Scot.
320 I3 Lothmore High., Scot.
94 I4 Lottisham Som., Eng.
106 D5 Loudwater Bucks., Eng.
388 G2 Loughan Coleraine, N. Ire.
402 I4 Loughans Dungannon, N. Ire.
402 G1 Loughash Strabane, N. Ire.
162 D2 Loughborough Leics., Eng.
396 G4 Loughbrickland Banbridge, N. Ire.
396 E3 Loughgall Armagh, N. Ire.
396 F4 Lough Gilly Armagh, N. Ire.
388 I2 Loughguile Ballymoney, N. Ire.
396 J3 Loughinisland Down, N. Ire.
402 H3 Loughmacrory Omagh, N. Ire.
350 B3 Loughor Swansea, Wales
26 D4 Loughor r. Wales
116 C4 Loughton Essex, Eng.
106 D2 Loughton M.K., Eng.
144 E5 Loughton Shrop., Eng.
170 D7 Lound Lincs., Eng.
176 D2 Lound Notts., Eng.
120 J1 Lound Suff., Eng.
162 C2 Lount Leics., Eng.
308 E3 Lour Angus, Scot.
170 F3 Louth Lincs., Eng.
228 I4 Love Clough Lancs., Eng.
52 F5 Lovedean Hants., Eng.
86 E6 Lover Wilts., Eng.
208 F3 Loversall S. Yorks., Eng.
116 E3 Loves Green Essex, Eng.
216 E1 Lovesome Hill N. Yorks., Eng.
358 F3 Loveston Pembs., Wales
94 I4 Lovington Som., Eng.
232 F7 Low Cumbria, Eng.
222 G3 Low Ackworth W. Yorks., Eng.
244 F5 Low Angerton Northumb., Eng.
300 C5 Low Ballevain Arg. and B., Scot.
98 F2 Lowbands Glos., Eng.
252 D3 Low Barlay D. and G., Scot.
170 D4 Low Barlings Lincs., Eng.
216 B2 Low Bentham N. Yorks., Eng.
208 C3 Low Bradfield S. Yorks., Eng.
Low Bradley N. Yorks., Eng. see Bradley
232 E4 Low Braithwaite Cumbria, Eng.
244 E5 Low Brunton Northumb., Eng.
170 B2 Low Burnham N. Lincs., Eng.
244 H3 Low Buston Northumb., Eng.
210 C3 Low Catton E. Riding, Eng.
236 F4 Low Coniscliffe Darl., Eng.
262 C5 Low Craighead S. Ayr., Scot.
176 C4 Lowdham Notts., Eng.
236 G5 Low Dinsdale Darl., Eng.
144 D2 Lowe Shrop., Eng.
148 C2 Lowe Hill Staffs., Eng.
216 D2 Low Ellington N. Yorks., Eng.
216 E1 Low Entercommon N. Yorks., Eng.
300 E2 Lower Achachenna Arg. and B., Scot.
94 F4 Lower Aisholt Som., Eng.
46 E3 Lower Ansty Dorset, Eng.
102 E3 Lower Arncott Oxon, Eng.
78 E2 Lower Ashtead Surr., Eng.
102 F5 Lower Assendon Oxon, Eng.
300 D4 Lower Auchalick Arg. and B., Scot.
228 E4 Lower Ballam Lancs., Eng.
388 I5 Lower Ballinderry Lisburn, N. Ire.
140 B2 Lower Barewood Here., Eng.
228 F4 Lower Bartle Lancs., Eng.
326 E1 Lower Barvas W. Isles, Scot.
58 E2 Lower Beeding W. Sussex, Eng.
128 F3 Lower Benefield Northants., Eng.
Lower Bentham N. Yorks., Eng. see Low Bentham
136 E2 Lower Bentley Worcs., Eng.
98 D3 Lower Berry Hill Glos., Eng.
180 E4 Lower Birchwood Derbys., Eng.
46 E3 Lower Bockhampton Dorset, Eng.
128 B4 Lower Boddington Northants., Eng.
78 B2 Lower Bourne Surr., Eng.
132 C5 Lower Brailes Warks., Eng.
322 D3 Lower Breakish High., Scot.
198 E3 Lower Bredbury Gtr Man., Eng.
136 D2 Lower Broadheath Worcs., Eng.
198 D3 Lower Broughton Gtr Man., Eng.
350 C2 Lower Brynamman N.P.T., Wales
140 C3 Lower Bullingham Here., Eng.
52 D4 Lower Bullington Hants., Eng.
184 D3 Lower Bunbury Cheshire East, Eng.
52 B5 Lower Burgate Hants., Eng.
94 H5 Lower Burrow Som., Eng.
140 B2 Lower Burton Here., Eng.
62 C2 Lower Bush Medway, Eng.
110 D3 Lower Caldecote Central Bedfordshire, Eng.
98 E3 Lower Cam Glos., Eng.
124 D5 Lower Cambourne Cambs., Eng.
320 K2 Lower Camster High., Scot.
94 G3 Lower Canada N. Som., Eng.
366 E6 Lower Chapel Powys, Wales
86 C5 Lower Chicksgrove Wilts., Eng.
86 F4 Lower Chute Wilts., Eng.
74 D2 Lower Clapton Gtr Lon., Eng.
136 E1 Lower Clent Worcs., Eng.
180 B3 Lower Crossings Derbys., Eng.
222 E3 Lower Cumberworth W. Yorks., Eng.
396 E4 Lower Darkley Armagh, N. Ire.
228 H4 Lower Darwen B'burn, Eng.
110 C2 Lower Dean Bedford, Eng.
322 D2 Lower Diabaig High., Scot.
144 D5 Lower Dinchope Shrop., Eng.
144 C5 Lower Down Shrop., Eng.
36 C3 Lower Drift Corn., Eng.
82 E3 Lower Earley W'ham, Eng.
74 D2 Lower Edmonton Gtr Lon., Eng.
140 D3 Lower Egleton Here., Eng.
148 D2 Lower Elkstone Staffs., Eng.
106 B4 Lower End Bucks., Eng.
110 B4 Lower End Central Bedfordshire, Eng.
106 E2 Lower End M.K., Eng.
128 E4 Lower End Northants., Eng.
128 E4 Lower End Northants., Eng.
62 F3 Lower Ensden Kent, Eng.
86 E4 Lower Everleigh Wilts., Eng.
62 H3 Lower Eythorne Kent, Eng.
94 H2 Lower Failand N. Som., Eng.
52 G4 Lower Farringdon Hants., Eng.
74 B3 Lower Feltham Gtr Lon., Eng.
58 C3 Lower Fittleworth W. Sussex, Eng.
405 C2 Lower Foxdale Cumbria, Eng.
358 E3 Lower Freystrop Pembs., Wales
52 G3 Lower Froyle Hants., Eng.
94 H3 Lower Godney Som., Eng.
154 B2 Lower Gornal W. Mids, Eng.
110 C3 Lower Gravenhurst Central Bedfordshire, Eng.
116 C2 Lower Green Essex, Eng.
198 C3 Lower Green Gtr Man., Eng.
110 D4 Lower Green Herts., Eng.
62 B4 Lower Green Kent, Eng.
166 E1 Lower Green Norf., Eng.
166 I3 Lower Green Norf., Eng.
148 C5 Lower Green Staffs., Eng.
228 F3 Lower Green Bank Lancs., Eng.
46 C2 Lower Halstock Leigh Dorset, Eng.
62 E2 Lower Halstow Kent, Eng.
62 G3 Lower Hardres Kent, Eng.
140 A2 Lower Harpton Here., Eng.
62 D2 Lower Hartlip Kent, Eng.
180 E4 Lower Hartshay Derbys., Eng.
106 C4 Lower Hartwell Bucks., Eng.
148 B3 Lower Hatton Staffs., Eng.
232 C7 Lower Hawthwaite Cumbria, Eng.
62 B3 Lower Haysden Kent, Eng.
144 D5 Lower Hayton Shrop., Eng.
184 F2 Lower Heath Cheshire East, Eng.
140 A2 Lower Hergest Here., Eng.
102 D3 Lower Heyford Oxon, Eng.
62 C2 Lower Higham Kent, Eng.
120 G5 Lower Holbrook Suff., Eng.
222 D2 Lower Hopton W. Yorks., Eng.
144 C2 Lower Hordley Shrop., Eng.
58 H3 Lower Horsebridge E. Sussex, Eng.
228 I4 Lowerhouse Lancs., Eng.
222 D3 Lower Houses W. Yorks., Eng.
136 D3 Lower Howsell Worcs., Eng.
198 D2 Lower Kersal Gtr Man., Eng.
180 E4 Lower Kilburn Derbys., Eng.
300 B3 Lower Kilchattan Arg. and B., Scot.
98 F4 Lower Kilcott S. Glos., Eng.
300 B5 Lower Killeyan Arg. and B., Scot.
46 D3 Lower Kingcombe Dorset, Eng.
78 E2 Lower Kingswood Surr., Eng.
184 B3 Lower Kinnerton Cheshire West & Chester, Eng.
94 H2 Lower Langford N. Som., Eng.
292 G2 Lower Largo Fife, Scot.
148 D3 Lower Leigh Staffs., Eng.
98 I1 Lower Lemington Glos., Eng.
23 G4 Lower Lough Erne l. N. Ire.
40 E1 Lower Loxhore Devon, Eng.
98 D2 Lower Lydbrook Glos., Eng.
140 B2 Lower Lye Here., Eng.
339 B3 Lower Machen Newp., Wales
140 B4 Lower Maes-coed Here., Eng.
46 H2 Lower Mannington Dorset, Eng.
98 D3 Lower Meend Glos., Eng.
128 B5 Lower Middleton Cheney Northants., Eng.
94 H3 Lower Milton Som., Eng.
136 E3 Lower Moor Worcs., Eng.
98 D4 Lower Morton S. Glos., Eng.
358 E3 Lower Nash Pembs., Wales
116 C3 Lower Nazeing Essex, Eng.
144 E4 Lower Netchwood Shrop., Eng.
106 D4 Lower North Dean Bucks., Eng.
46 E2 Lower Nyland Dorset, Eng.
292 D3 Lower Oakfield Fife, Scot.
98 J2 Lower Oddington Glos., Eng.
350 G4 Lower Penarth V. of Glam., Wales
148 B5 Lower Penn Staffs., Eng.
52 C6 Lower Pennington Hants., Eng.
228 F4 Lower Penwortham Lancs., Eng.
184 E2 Lower Peover Cheshire West & Chester, Eng.
198 E2 Lower Place Gtr Man., Eng.
106 C4 Lower Pollicott Bucks., Eng.
132 B5 Lower Quinton Warks., Eng.
339 B2 Lower Race Torf., Wales
62 D2 Lower Rainham Medway, Eng.
94 D4 Lower Roadwater Som., Eng.
136 C2 Lower Sapey Worcs., Eng.
86 C2 Lower Seagry Wilts., Eng.
110 B3 Lower Shelton Central Bedfordshire, Eng.
102 F5 Lower Shiplake Oxon, Eng.
132 E4 Lower Shuckburgh Warks., Eng.
98 I2 Lower Slaughter Glos., Eng.
222 E2 Lower Soothill W. Yorks., Eng.
98 E3 Lower Soudley Glos., Eng.
228 H3 Lower Standen Lancs., Eng.
86 C2 Lower Stanton St Quintin Wilts., Eng.
62 D2 Lower Stoke Medway, Eng.
110 D3 Lower Stondon Central Bedfordshire, Eng.
98 E4 Lower Stone Glos., Eng.
148 D5 Lower Stonnall Staffs., Eng.
166 E3 Lower Stow Bedon Norf., Eng.
46 F3 Lower Street Dorset, Eng.
58 I3 Lower Street E. Sussex, Eng.
166 G1 Lower Street Norf., Eng.
166 H1 Lower Street Norf., Eng.
120 C4 Lower Street Suff., Eng.
120 F4 Lower Street Suff., Eng.
136 E3 Lower Strensham Worcs., Eng.
190 F3 Lower Stretton Warr., Eng.
110 C4 Lower Sundon Central Bedfordshire, Eng.
98 I2 Lower Swell Glos., Eng.
74 D3 Lower Sydenham Gtr Lon., Eng.
102 C2 Lower Tadmarton Oxon, Eng.
148 D3 Lower Tean Staffs., Eng.
166 I3 Lower Thurlton Norf., Eng.
228 F3 Lower Thurnham Lancs., Eng.
36 D3 Lower Town Corn., Eng.
36 □ Lower Town I.o.S., Eng.
402 G1 Lowertown Strabane, N. Ire.
329 D5 Lowertown Orkney, Scot.
358 E2 Lower Town Pembs., Wales
98 F3 Lower Tuffley Glos., Eng.
132 C5 Lower Tysoe Warks., Eng.
52 E5 Lower Upham Hants., Eng.
62 D2 Lower Upnor Medway, Eng.
94 E4 Lower Vexford Som., Eng.
144 C4 Lower Wallop Shrop., Eng.
190 F3 Lower Walton Warr., Eng.
86 D2 Lower Waterhay Wilts., Eng.
106 C2 Lower Weald M.K., Eng.
94 G3 Lower Weare Som., Eng.
140 A3 Lower Welson Here., Eng.
46 F3 Lower Whatcombe Dorset, Eng.
94 J3 Lower Whatley Som., Eng.
184 D2 Lower Whitley Cheshire West & Chester, Eng.
136 D2 Lower Wick Worcs., Eng.
52 F4 Lower Wield Hants., Eng.
Lower Winchendon Bucks., Eng. see Nether Winchendon
106 D5 Lower Woodend Bucks., Eng.
86 E5 Lower Woodford Wilts., Eng.
46 D3 Lower Wraxall Dorset, Eng.
136 C3 Lower Wyche Worcs., Eng.
222 D2 Lower Wyke W. Yorks., Eng.
162 F3 Lowesby Leics., Eng.
120 J2 Lowestoft Suff., Eng.
120 J2 Lowestoft End Suff., Eng.
232 C5 Loweswater Cumbria, Eng.
236 E4 Low Etherley Durham, Eng.
236 F2 Low Fell T. and W., Eng.
208 D3 Lowfield S. Yorks., Eng.
58 E2 Lowfield Heath W. Sussex, Eng.
244 E6 Low Gate Northumb., Eng.
232 G6 Lowgill Cumbria, Eng.
228 G2 Lowgill Lancs., Eng.
120 D3 Low Green Suff., Eng.
236 E2 Low Greenside T. and W., Eng.
136 D1 Low Habberley Worcs., Eng.
94 H4 Low Ham Som., Eng.
236 G3 Low Haswell Durham, Eng.
244 H4 Low Hauxley Northumb., Eng.
232 H6 Low Haygarth Cumbria, Eng.
232 F4 Low Hesket Cumbria, Eng.
244 F4 Low Hesleyhurst Northumb., Eng.
216 G2 Low Hutton N. Yorks., Eng.
232 D7 Lowick Cumbria, Eng.
128 F3 Lowick Northants., Eng.
244 F2 Lowick Northumb., Eng.
232 D7 Lowick Bridge Cumbria, Eng.
232 D7 Lowick Green Cumbria, Eng.
216 G2 Low Kingthorpe N. Yorks., Eng.
216 D2 Low Laithe N. Yorks., Eng.
170 E4 Low Langton Lincs., Eng.
180 B2 Low Leighton Derbys., Eng.
232 C5 Low Lorton Cumbria, Eng.
216 G2 Low Marishes N. Yorks., Eng.
176 E3 Low Marnham Notts., Eng.
244 G2 Low Middleton Northumb., Eng.
216 G1 Low Mill N. Yorks., Eng.
228 H3 Low Moor Lancs., Eng.
222 D2 Low Moor W. Yorks., Eng.
236 G3 Low Moorsley T. and W., Eng.
232 A5 Low Moresby Cumbria, Eng.
232 E7 Low Newton Cumbria, Eng.
244 H2 Low Newton-by-the-Sea Northumb., Eng.
308 E3 Lownie Moor Angus, Scot.
170 C2 Low Risby N. Lincs., Eng.
232 G3 Low Row Cumbria, Eng.
170 C2 Low Santon N. Lincs., Eng.
132 B4 Lowsonford Warks., Eng.
300 E4 Low Stillaig Arg. and B., Scot.
166 F3 Low Street Norf., Eng.
166 H2 Low Street Norf., Eng.
236 F2 Low Team T. and W., Eng.
166 G3 Low Tharston Norf., Eng.
232 F5 Lowther Cumbria, Eng.
232 F5 Lowther Castle Cumbria, Eng.
22 I12 Lowther Hills hills Scot.
210 F2 Lowthorpe E. Riding, Eng.
198 B3 Lowton Gtr Man., Eng.
94 F5 Lowton Som., Eng.
198 B3 Lowton Common Gtr Man., Eng.
198 B3 Lowton St Mary's Gtr Man., Eng.
292 C3 Low Torry Fife, Scot.
244 G4 Low Town Northumb., Eng.
396 H4 Lowtown Banbridge, N. Ire.
170 F4 Low Toynton Lincs., Eng.
208 D2 Low Valley S. Yorks., Eng.
236 F4 Low Walworth Darl., Eng.
268 B2 Low Waters S. Lanark., Scot.
236 E2 Low Westwood Durham, Eng.
232 D7 Low Wood Cumbria, Eng.
40 F2 Loxbeare Devon, Eng.
74 E2 Loxford Gtr Lon., Eng.
78 C3 Loxhill Surr., Eng.
40 E1 Loxhore Devon, Eng.
132 C4 Loxley Warks., Eng.
148 D3 Loxley Green Staffs., Eng.
94 G3 Loxton N. Som., Eng.
58 C2 Loxwood W. Sussex, Eng.
22 H6 Loyal, Loch l. Scot.
22 F8 Loyne, Loch l. Scot.
116 D3 Loyter's Green Essex, Eng.
154 C3 Lozells W. Mids, Eng.
320 F4 Lubachoinnich High., Scot.
320 F4 Lubcroy High., Scot.
162 F4 Lubenham Leics., Eng.
320 F4 Lubfearn High., Scot.
322 F2 Lubmore High., Scot.
304 C3 Lubreoch Perth and Kin., Scot.
94 C3 Luccombe Som., Eng.
52 E7 Luccombe Village I.o.W., Eng.
22 G13 Luce Bay b. Scot.
244 G2 Lucker Northumb., Eng.
36 G2 Luckett Corn., Eng.
86 B2 Luckington Wilts., Eng.
292 G1 Lucklawhill Fife, Scot.
94 C4 Luckwell Bridge Som., Eng.
140 C2 Lucton Here., Eng.
216 D1 Lucy Cross N. Yorks., Eng.
326 C5 Ludag W. Isles, Scot.
170 F3 Ludborough Lincs., Eng.
358 F3 Ludchurch Pembs., Wales
222 C2 Luddenden W. Yorks., Eng.
222 C2 Luddenden Foot W. Yorks., Eng.
62 F3 Luddenham Court Kent, Eng.

Luddesdown to Merther

62 C2 Luddesdown Kent, Eng.
170 B2 Luddington N. Lincs., Eng.
132 B4 Luddington Warks., Eng.
128 G3 Luddington in the Brook Northants., Eng.
170 E3 Ludford Lincs., Eng.
144 D5 Ludford Shrop., Eng.
106 B3 Ludgershall Bucks., Eng.
86 F4 Ludgershall Wilts., Eng.
36 C3 Ludgvan Corn., Eng.
144 D5 Ludlow Shrop., Eng.
170 G3 Ludney Lincs., Eng.
140 E3 Ludstock Here., Eng.
144 G4 Ludstone Shrop., Eng.
86 C5 Ludwell Wilts., Eng.
236 G3 Ludworth Durham, Eng.
40 C2 Luffincott Devon, Eng.
288 F2 Luffness E. Lothian, Scot.
94 H5 Lufton Som., Eng.
262 F4 Lugar E. Ayr., Scot.
26 G3 Lugg r. Wales
288 H3 Luggate E. Lothian, Scot.
288 H3 Luggate Burn E. Lothian, Scot.
280 C3 Luggiebank N. Lanark., Scot.
262 D2 Lugton E. Ayr., Scot.
140 D3 Lugwardine Here., Eng.
322 D3 Luib High., Scot.
322 G4 Luibeilt High., Scot.
22 G7 Luichart, Loch l. Scot.
22 E10 Luing i. Scot.
22 E10 Luing, Sound of sea chan. Scot.
140 B3 Lulham Here., Eng.
180 D6 Lullington Derbys., Eng.
94 K3 Lullington Som., Eng.
136 C2 Lulsley Worcs., Eng.
46 F4 Lulworth Camp Dorset, Eng.
228 I4 Lumb Lancs., Eng.
222 C2 Lumb W. Yorks., Eng.
222 B2 Lumbutts W. Yorks., Eng.
314 E3 Lumphanan Abers., Scot.
292 E3 Lumphinnans Fife, Scot.
256 K1 Lumsdaine Borders, Scot.
180 D4 Lumsdale Derbys., Eng.
314 E3 Lumsden Abers., Scot.
308 G3 Lunan Angus, Scot.
22 L9 Lunan Bay b. Scot.
308 E3 Lunanhead Angus, Scot.
304 J4 Luncarty Perth and Kin., Scot.
210 E3 Lund E. Riding, Eng.
216 F3 Lund N. Yorks., Eng.
331 E1 Lund Shet., Scot.
326 D2 Lundale W. Isles, Scot.
144 F4 Lundavra High., Scot.
314 H2 Lunderton Abers., Scot.
308 D3 Lundie Angus, Scot.
322 F3 Lundie High., Scot.
292 G2 Lundin Links Fife, Scot.
208 D2 Lundwood S. Yorks., Eng.
26 C5 Lundy i. Eng.
24 L5 Lune r. Eng.
388 G4 Luney Magherafelt, N. Ire.
300 D3 Lunga Arg. and B., Scot.
331 D2 Lunna Shet., Scot.
22 □N2 Lunna Ness hd Scot.
331 D2 Lunning Shet., Scot.
331 C2 Lunnister Shet., Scot.
350 B3 Lunnon Swansea, Wales
58 I3 Lunsford's Cross E. Sussex, Eng.
190 D2 Lunt Merseyside, Eng.
140 B2 Luntley Here., Eng.
40 G2 Luppitt Devon, Eng.
222 E2 Lupset W. Yorks., Eng.
232 F7 Lupton Cumbria, Eng.
22 F6 Lurgainn, Loch l. Scot.
396 G3 Lurgan Craigavon, N. Ire.
396 F4 Lurganare Newry & Mourne, N. Ire.
58 C2 Lurgashall W. Sussex, Eng.
388 I5 Lurgill Lisburn, N. Ire.
300 D2 Lurignich Arg. and B., Scot.
170 G4 Lusby Lincs., Eng.
300 G3 Luss Arg. and B., Scot.
300 C3 Lussagiven Arg. and B., Scot.
24 F2 Lussa Loch l. Scot.
322 B2 Lusta High., Scot.
40 E3 Lustleigh Devon, Eng.
140 C2 Luston Here., Eng.
292 F1 Luthrie Fife, Scot.
40 F3 Luton Devon, Eng.
110 C4 Luton Luton, Eng.
62 D2 Luton Medway, Eng.
110 D5 Luton admin. div. Eng.
162 D4 Lutterworth Leics., Eng.
40 E3 Lutton Devon, Eng.
46 E4 Lutton Dorset, Eng.
170 G7 Lutton Lincs., Eng.
128 G3 Lutton Northants., Eng.
94 D4 Luxborough Som., Eng.
36 E2 Luxulyan Corn., Eng.
198 E2 Luzley Brook Gtr Man., Eng.
320 K3 Lybster High., Scot.
40 D4 Lydacott Devon, Eng.
144 C5 Lydbury North Shrop., Eng.
40 E1 Lydcott Devon, Eng.
62 F5 Lydd Kent, Eng.
62 F5 Lydd (London Ashford) airport Eng.
62 H4 Lydden Kent, Eng.
162 G3 Lyddington Rutland, Eng.
62 F5 Lydd-on-Sea Kent, Eng.
94 E4 Lydeard St Lawrence Som., Eng.
52 G3 Lyde Green Hants., Eng.
98 E5 Lyde Green S. Glos., Eng.
40 D3 Lydford Devon, Eng.
94 I4 Lydford Fair Place Som., Eng.
94 I4 Lydford-on-Fosse Som., Eng.
198 E2 Lydgate Gtr Man., Eng.
198 E2 Lydgate Gtr Man., Eng.
222 B2 Lydgate W. Yorks., Eng.
144 C4 Lydham Shrop., Eng.
86 D2 Lydiard Millicent Wilts., Eng.
86 D2 Lydiard Tregoze Swindon, Eng.
190 D2 Lydiate Merseyside, Eng.
136 E1 Lydiate Ash Worcs., Eng.
46 E2 Lydlinch Dorset, Eng.
98 D3 Lydney Glos., Eng.
358 F4 Lydstep Pembs., Wales
154 B3 Lye W. Mids, Eng.
94 H2 Lye Cross N. Som., Eng.
106 E4 Lye Green Bucks., Eng.
58 G2 Lye Green E. Sussex, Eng.
132 B4 Lye Green Warks., Eng.
136 C1 Lye Head Worcs., Eng.
86 B4 Lye's Green Wilts., Eng.
102 C5 Lyford Oxon, Eng.
62 G4 Lymbridge Green Kent, Eng.
26 G6 Lyme Bay b. Eng.
268 A2 Lymekilns S. Lanark., Scot.
46 B3 Lyme Regis Dorset, Eng.
62 G4 Lyminge Kent, Eng.
52 C6 Lymington Hants., Eng.
58 C3 Lyminster W. Sussex, Eng.
190 G3 Lymm Warr., Eng.
52 C6 Lymore Hants., Eng.
62 G4 Lympne Kent, Eng.
78 G2 Lympsfield Chart Surr., Eng.
94 G3 Lympsham Som., Eng.
40 F3 Lympstone Devon, Eng.
322 I3 Lynaberack High., Scot.
52 E3 Lynch Hants., Eng.
94 C3 Lynch Som., Eng.
322 I3 Lynchat High., Scot.
166 G3 Lynch Green Norf., Eng.
82 G2 Lynch Hill Slough, Eng.
322 B2 Lyndale House High., Scot.
52 C5 Lyndhurst Hants., Eng.
162 H3 Lyndon Rutland, Eng.
154 D3 Lyndon Green W. Mids, Eng.
78 C1 Lyne Surr., Eng.
314 F3 Lyne Abers., Scot.
256 E3 Lyne Borders, Scot.
24 K4 Lyne r. Eng.
144 D2 Lyneal Shrop., Eng.
140 D4 Lyne Down Here., Eng.
102 B3 Lyneham Oxon, Eng.
86 D2 Lyneham Wilts., Eng.
232 F2 Lyneholmeford Cumbria, Eng.
322 K3 Lynemore High., Scot.
314 C2 Lynemore Moray, Scot.
244 H4 Lynemouth Northumb., Eng.
322 H3 Lyne of Gorthleck High., Scot.
314 F3 Lyne of Skene Abers., Scot.
329 B4 Lyness Orkney, Scot.
256 E3 Lyne Station Borders, Scot.
166 D4 Lynford Norf., Eng.
166 F2 Lyng Norf., Eng.
94 F4 Lyng Som., Eng.
166 H2 Lyngate Norf., Eng.
26 D7 Lynher r. Eng.
40 E1 Lynmouth Devon, Eng.
148 D5 Lynn Staffs., Eng.
144 G3 Lynn Telford, Eng.
62 E3 Lynsted Kent, Eng.
36 F1 Lynstone Corn., Eng.
40 E1 Lynton Devon, Eng.
98 G2 Lynworth Glos., Eng.
22 I9 Lyon r. Scot.
22 G9 Lyon, Loch l. Scot.
46 E2 Lyon's Gate Dorset, Eng.
140 B2 Lyonshall Here., Eng.
300 B4 Lyrabus Arg. and B., Scot.
46 G3 Lytchett Matravers Dorset, Eng.
46 G3 Lytchett Minster Dorset, Eng.
320 K2 Lyth High., Scot.
228 E4 Lytham Lancs., Eng.
228 D4 Lytham St Anne's Lancs., Eng.
144 D4 Lythbank Shrop., Eng.
216 G1 Lythe N. Yorks., Eng.
78 B3 Lythe Hill Surr., Eng.
329 D5 Lythes Orkney, Scot.

M

Maaruig W. Isles, Scot. see Maraig
170 H3 Mablethorpe Lincs., Eng.
184 G2 Macclesfield Cheshire East, Eng.
184 G2 Macclesfield Forest Cheshire East, Eng.
314 F1 Macduff Abers., Scot.
292 E2 Macedonia Fife, Scot.
388 G2 Macfinn Ballymoney, N. Ire.
268 C2 Machan S. Lanark., Scot.
304 H5 Machany Perth and Kin., Scot.
300 D6 Macharioch Arg. and B., Scot.
350 H3 Machen Caerp., Wales
22 D11 Machir Bay b. Scot.
300 A4 Machrie Arg. and B., Scot.
300 B5 Machrie Arg. and B., Scot.
264 C3 Machrie N. Ayr., Scot.
300 C5 Machrihanish Arg. and B., Scot.
300 B3 Machrins Arg. and B., Scot.
366 B3 Machynlleth Powys, Wales
402 E5 Mackan Fermanagh, N. Ire.
110 D5 Mackerye End Herts., Eng.
102 E5 Mackney Oxon, Eng.
180 D5 Mackworth Derbys., Eng.
Macleod's Table South hill Scot. see Healabhal Bheag
288 F3 Macmerry E. Lothian, Scot.
23 G4 Macnean Lower, Lough l. N. Ire.
23 G4 Macnean Upper, Lough l. Ireland/U.K.
388 F2 Macosquin Coleraine, N. Ire.
314 F2 Macterry Abers., Scot.
396 D4 Maddan Armagh, N. Ire.
304 H4 Madderty Perth and Kin., Scot.
280 D3 Maddiston Falk., Scot.
58 C3 Madehurst W. Sussex, Eng.
148 A3 Madeley Staffs., Eng.
144 F4 Madeley Telford, Eng.
148 A3 Madeley Heath Staffs., Eng.
40 G2 Madford Devon, Eng.
124 E5 Madingley Cambs., Eng.
46 F1 Madjeston Dorset, Eng.
140 B3 Madley Here., Eng.
136 D3 Madresfield Worcs., Eng.
36 C3 Madron Corn., Eng.
371 D3 Maenaddwyn I.o.A., Wales
358 F2 Maenclochog Pembs., Wales
350 G3 Maendy Cardiff, Wales
350 F4 Maendy V. of Glam., Wales
36 D3 Maenporth Corn., Eng.
372 G3 Maentwrog Gwynedd, Wales
362 D3 Maen-y-groes Cere., Wales
36 F1 Maer Corn., Eng.
148 B3 Maer Staffs., Eng.
356 G2 Maerdy Carmar., Wales
356 G2 Maerdy Carmar., Wales
378 E4 Maerdy Denb., Wales
339 C2 Maerdy Mon., Wales
350 F2 Maerdy R.C.T., Wales
144 B3 Maesbrook Shrop., Eng.
144 B3 Maesbury Marsh Shrop., Eng.
Maes-Glas Flints., Wales see Greenfield
339 B3 Maes-glas Newp., Wales
356 E2 Maesgwynne Carmar., Wales
378 F3 Maeshafn Denb., Wales
362 D4 Maesllyn Cere., Wales
366 E6 Maesmynis Powys, Wales
350 E3 Maesteg Bridg., Wales
366 G5 Maes-Treylow Powys, Wales
356 F3 Maesybont Carmar., Wales
356 E1 Maesycrugiau Carmar., Wales
350 G3 Maesycwmmer Caerp., Wales
Maesyfed Powys, Wales see New Radnor
116 D3 Magdalen Laver Essex, Eng.
23 K3 Magee, Island pen. N. Ire.
314 D2 Maggieknockater Moray, Scot.
116 C2 Maggots End Essex, Eng.
388 I5 Maghaberry Lisburn, N. Ire.
58 H3 Magham Down E. Sussex, Eng.
396 I4 Maghera Down, N. Ire.
388 G3 Maghera Magherafelt, N. Ire.
388 J4 Magherabane Ballymena, N. Ire.
388 H3 Magheraboy Ballymoney, N. Ire.
388 G4 Magherafelt Magherafelt, N. Ire.
388 F4 Magherafelt admin. dist. N. Ire.
388 I4 Magheralane Antrim, N. Ire.
396 G3 Magheralin Craigavon, N. Ire.
396 G3 Magherally Banbridge, N. Ire.
402 E4 Magheralough Omagh, N. Ire.
402 E2 Magheralough Strabane, N. Ire.
402 F1 Magheramason Strabane, N. Ire.
396 H4 Magheramayo Banbridge, N. Ire.
388 F3 Magheramore Coleraine, N. Ire.
388 L4 Magheramorne Larne, N. Ire.
396 I4 Magherasaul Down, N. Ire.
402 G5 Magheraveely Fermanagh, N. Ire.
396 D4 Maghery Armagh, N. Ire.
396 E2 Maghery Craigavon, N. Ire.
396 H5 Maghery Newry & Mourne, N. Ire.
190 D2 Maghull Merseyside, Eng.
388 E2 Magilligan Limavady, N. Ire.
23 I2 Magilligan Point pt N. Ire.
162 D4 Magna Park Leics., Eng.
402 F4 Magonragh Fermanagh, N. Ire.
339 D3 Magor Mon., Wales
120 F2 Magpie Green Suff., Eng.
402 F5 Maguiresbridge Fermanagh, N. Ire.
24 F5 Mahee Island i. N. Ire.
74 C2 Maida Vale Gtr Lon., Eng.
86 B5 Maiden Bradley Wilts., Eng.
40 F3 Maidencombe Torbay, Eng.
40 E3 Maidenhayne Devon, Eng.
94 I2 Maiden Head N. Som., Eng.
82 E2 Maidenhead W. and M., Eng.
236 E2 Maiden Law Durham, Eng.
46 D3 Maiden Newton Dorset, Eng.
262 C4 Maidens S. Ayr., Scot.
82 F3 Maiden's Green Brack. F., Eng.
102 F5 Maidensgrove Oxon, Eng.
36 F2 Maidenwell Corn., Eng.
170 F4 Maidenwell Lincs., Eng.
358 F4 Maiden Wells Pembs., Wales
128 C4 Maidford Northants., Eng.
106 C2 Maids' Moreton Bucks., Eng.
62 D3 Maidstone Kent, Eng.
128 D3 Maidwell Northants., Eng.
331 D3 Mail Shet., Scot.
339 C3 Maindee Newp., Wales
402 G3 Maine Omagh, N. Ire.
22 J4 Mainland i. Scot.
22 □N2 Mainland i. Scot.
236 F3 Mainsforth Durham, Eng.
308 F4 Mains of Ardestie Angus, Scot.
308 F3 Mains of Balgavies Angus, Scot.
308 F2 Mains of Balhall Angus, Scot.
308 E3 Mains of Ballindarg Angus, Scot.
314 C2 Mains of Burgie Moray, Scot.
314 G2 Mains of Culsh Abers., Scot.
314 F4 Mains of Dillavaird Abers., Scot.
314 G3 Mains of Drum Abers., Scot.
322 I2 Mains of Faillie High., Scot.
314 G2 Mains of Fedderate Abers., Scot.
314 D3 Mains of Glenbuchat Abers., Scot.
308 F2 Mains of Melgund Angus, Scot.
314 C2 Mains of Sluie Moray, Scot.
314 F4 Mains of Thornton Abers., Scot.
262 B6 Mains of Tig S. Ayr., Scot.
320 K2 Mains of Watten High., Scot.
252 F3 Mainsriddle D. and G., Scot.
144 B5 Mainstone Shrop., Eng.
98 F2 Maisemore Glos., Eng.
388 H3 Maizestown Ballymena, N. Ire.
136 F1 Major's Green Worcs., Eng.
244 D3 Makendon Northumb., Eng.
180 E5 Makeney Derbys., Eng.
256 I3 Makerstoun Borders, Scot.
Malaig High., Scot. see Mallaig
40 E4 Malborough Devon, Eng.
22 D10 Malcolm's Point pt Scot.
74 C3 Malden Rushett Gtr Lon., Eng.
116 G3 Maldon Essex, Eng.
216 C3 Malham N. Yorks., Eng.
208 C3 Malinbridge S. Yorks., Eng.
144 F3 Malinslee Telford, Eng.
322 D3 Mallaig High., Scot.
322 D3 Mallaigmore High., Scot.
288 D3 Malleny Mills Edin., Scot.
276 D3 Malletsheugh E. Renf., Scot.
296 E4 Malling Stir., Scot.
116 C2 Mallows Green Essex, Eng.
371 C3 Malltraeth I.o.A., Wales
26 D1 Malltraeth Bay b. Wales
388 J4 Mallusk Newtownabbey, N. Ire.
372 H4 Mallwyd Gwynedd, Wales
86 C2 Malmesbury Wilts., Eng.
184 C2 Malpas Cheshire West & Chester, Eng.
36 D3 Malpas Corn., Eng.
339 B3 Malpas Newp., Wales
170 F3 Maltby Lincs., Eng.
236 H4 Maltby Stockton, Eng.
208 E3 Maltby S. Yorks., Eng.
170 H4 Maltby le Marsh Lincs., Eng.
116 H2 Malting Green Essex, Eng.
62 E4 Maltman's Hill Kent, Eng.
216 G2 Malton N. Yorks., Eng.
136 D3 Malvern Link Worcs., Eng.
136 D3 Malvern Wells Worcs., Eng.
300 F3 Mambeg Arg. and B., Scot.
136 C1 Mamble Worcs., Eng.
339 B2 Mamhilad Mon., Wales
24 H5 Man, Isle of i. Irish Sea
405 B2 Man, Isle of terr. Irish Sea
36 D4 Manaccan Corn., Eng.
40 D4 Manadon Plymouth, Eng.
366 F3 Manafon Powys, Wales
Manais W. Isles, Scot. see Manish
40 E3 Manaton Devon, Eng.
170 G3 Manby Lincs., Eng.
132 C2 Mancetter Warks., Eng.
198 D3 Manchester Gtr Man., Eng.
198 D3 Manchester airport Eng.
378 G2 Mancot Royal Flints., Wales
322 G3 Mandally High., Scot.
124 F4 Manea Cambs., Eng.
262 F4 Maneight E. Ayr., Scot.
154 D2 Maney W. Mids, Eng.
331 C2 Mangaster Shet., Scot.
46 C3 Mangerton Dorset, Eng.
110 C4 Mangrove Green Herts., Eng.
326 C2 Mangurstadh W. Isles, Scot.
326 D3 Manish W. Isles, Scot.
222 B2 Mankinholes W. Yorks., Eng.
184 C2 Manley Cheshire West & Chester, Eng.
350 G2 Manmoel Caerp., Wales
300 □ Mannal Arg. and B., Scot.
Manndalaidh High., Scot. see Mandally
86 E4 Manningford Abbots Wilts., Eng.
86 E4 Manningford Bohune Wilts., Eng.
222 D2 Manningham W. Yorks., Eng.
58 E2 Mannings Heath W. Sussex, Eng.
46 H2 Mannington Dorset, Eng.
116 I2 Manningtree Essex, Eng.
314 G3 Mannofield Aberdeen, Scot.
358 F4 Manorbier Pembs., Wales
358 F4 Manorbier Newton Pembs., Wales
358 G1 Manordeifi Pembs., Wales
356 G2 Manordeilo Carmar., Wales
358 D2 Manorowen Pembs., Wales
74 E2 Manor Park Gtr Lon., Eng.
82 G2 Manor Park Slough, Eng.
140 B3 Mansell Gamage Here., Eng.
140 B3 Mansell Lacy Here., Eng.
232 G7 Mansergh Cumbria, Eng.
276 E3 Mansewood Glas., Scot.
176 B3 Mansfield Notts., Eng.
176 B3 Mansfield Woodhouse Notts., Eng.
166 E3 Manson Green Norf., Eng.
232 D7 Mansriggs Cumbria, Eng.
46 F2 Manston Dorset, Eng.
62 I2 Manston Kent, Eng.
222 F2 Manston W. Yorks., Eng.
46 G2 Manswood Dorset, Eng.
170 C6 Manthorpe Lincs., Eng.
170 D7 Manthorpe Lincs., Eng.
170 C2 Manton N. Lincs., Eng.
176 C3 Manton Notts., Eng.
162 G3 Manton Rutland, Eng.
86 E3 Manton Wilts., Eng.
116 D2 Manuden Essex, Eng.
116 D3 Manwood Green Essex, Eng.
300 D3 Maolachy Arg. and B., Scot.
94 J4 Maperton Som., Eng.
176 D4 Maplebeck Notts., Eng.
110 B6 Maple Cross Herts., Eng.
102 E6 Mapledurham Oxon, Eng.
52 F3 Mapledurwell Hants., Eng.
116 D1 Maple End Essex, Eng.
58 E2 Maplehurst W. Sussex, Eng.
62 B2 Maplescombe Kent, Eng.
180 C4 Mapleton Derbys., Eng.
180 E5 Mapperley Derbys., Eng.
176 C5 Mapperley Notts., Eng.
176 C5 Mapperley Park Nott., Eng.
46 C3 Mapperton Dorset, Eng.
46 G3 Mapperton Dorset, Eng.
132 A4 Mappleborough Green Warks., Eng.
210 H3 Mappleton E. Riding, Eng.
208 C2 Mapplewell S. Yorks., Eng.
46 E2 Mappowder Dorset, Eng.
326 D3 Maraig W. Isles, Scot.
36 C3 Marazion Corn., Eng.
326 E2 Marbhig W. Isles, Scot.
184 D3 Marbury Cheshire East, Eng.
124 E3 March Cambs., Eng.
102 C4 Marcham Oxon, Eng.
144 E2 Marchamley Shrop., Eng.
144 E2 Marchamley Wood Shrop., Eng.
148 E3 Marchington Staffs., Eng.
148 E3 Marchington Woodlands Staffs., Eng.
378 H3 Marchwiel Wrex., Wales
52 D5 Marchwood Hants., Eng.
350 E4 Marcross V. of Glam., Wales
308 F2 Marcus Angus, Scot.
140 C3 Marden Here., Eng.
62 D4 Marden Kent, Eng.
236 G1 Marden T. and W., Eng.
86 D4 Marden Wilts., Eng.
116 D3 Marden Ash Essex, Eng.
62 C4 Marden Beech Kent, Eng.
58 G2 Marden's Hill E. Sussex, Eng.
62 D4 Marden Thorn Kent, Eng.
244 E2 Mardon Northumb., Eng.
339 B1 Mardy Mon., Wales
22 F7 Maree, Loch l. Scot.
162 F3 Marefield Leics., Eng.
94 G4 Mare Green Som., Eng.
170 F5 Mareham le Fen Lincs., Eng.
170 F4 Mareham on the Hill Lincs., Eng.
58 G3 Maresfield E. Sussex, Eng.
210 G4 Marfleet Hull, Eng.
378 H3 Marford Wrex., Wales
350 D3 Margam N.P.T., Wales
46 F2 Margaret Marsh Dorset, Eng.
116 E3 Margaret Roding Essex, Eng.
116 E3 Margaretting Essex, Eng.
116 E3 Margaretting Tye Essex, Eng.
62 I2 Margate Kent, Eng.
24 N7 Margery Hill hill Eng.
262 D3 Margnaheglish N. Ayr., Scot.
252 E2 Margreig D. and G., Scot.
166 C3 Marham Norf., Eng.
36 F1 Marhamchurch Corn., Eng.
124 C3 Marholm Peterb., Eng.
378 E2 Marian Cwm Denb., Wales
371 E3 Marianglas I.o.A., Wales
371 D2 Marian-glas I.o.A., Wales
40 E2 Mariansleigh Devon, Eng.
62 E2 Marine Town Kent, Eng.
322 C2 Marishader High., Scot.
94 G3 Mark Som., Eng.
62 A4 Markbeech Kent, Eng.
170 H4 Markby Lincs., Eng.
94 G3 Mark Causeway Som., Eng.
58 H2 Mark Cross E. Sussex, Eng.
252 B2 Markdhu D. and G., Scot.
180 D5 Markeaton Derbys., Eng.
162 C3 Market Bosworth Leics., Eng.
170 E7 Market Deeping Lincs., Eng.
144 F2 Market Drayton Shrop., Eng.
162 F4 Market Harborough Leics., Eng.
396 E4 Markethill Armagh, N. Ire.
304 K3 Markethill Perth and Kin., Scot.
86 D4 Market Lavington Wilts., Eng.
162 G2 Market Overton Rutland, Eng.
170 E3 Market Rasen Lincs., Eng.
170 F4 Market Stainton Lincs., Eng.
166 H2 Market Street Norf., Eng.
176 C3 Market Warsop Notts., Eng.
210 E3 Market Weighton E. Riding, Eng.
120 E2 Market Weston Suff., Eng.
162 D2 Markfield Leics., Eng.
116 C3 Mark Hall South Essex, Eng.
350 G2 Markham Caerp., Wales
176 D3 Markham Moor Notts., Eng.
292 E2 Markinch Fife, Scot.
216 E2 Markington N. Yorks., Eng.
198 C2 Markland Hill Gtr Man., Eng.
94 J2 Marksbury B. and N.E. Som., Eng.
74 E2 Marks Gate Gtr Lon., Eng.
116 G2 Marks Tey Essex, Eng.
110 C4 Markyate Herts., Eng.
198 D2 Marland Gtr Man., Eng.
136 D2 Marl Bank Worcs., Eng.
86 E3 Marlborough Wilts., Eng.
26 I5 Marlborough Downs hills Eng.
136 E1 Marlbrook Worcs., Eng.
132 A5 Marlcliff Warks., Eng.
40 F3 Marldon Devon, Eng.
58 H3 Marle Green E. Sussex, Eng.
120 H3 Marlesford Suff., Eng.
184 D3 Marley Green Cheshire East, Eng.
236 E2 Marley Hill T. and W., Eng.
166 F3 Marlingford Norf., Eng.
314 C4 Mar Lodge Abers., Scot.
358 C3 Marloes Pembs., Wales
106 D5 Marlow Bucks., Eng.
140 B1 Marlow Here., Eng.
62 A3 Marlpit Hill Kent, Eng.
180 E4 Marlpool Derbys., Eng.
46 F2 Marnhull Dorset, Eng.
314 E2 Marnoch Abers., Scot.
198 E3 Marple Gtr Man., Eng.
198 E3 Marple Bridge Gtr Man., Eng.
198 E3 Marpleridge Gtr Man., Eng.
208 E2 Marr S. Yorks., Eng.
216 D1 Marrick N. Yorks., Eng.
331 D2 Marrister Shet., Scot.
356 C3 Marros Carmar., Wales
236 G2 Marsden T. and W., Eng.
222 C3 Marsden W. Yorks., Eng.
216 C2 Marsett N. Yorks., Eng.
40 G2 Marsh Devon, Eng.
222 D2 Marsh W. Yorks., Eng.
222 D3 Marsh W. Yorks., Eng.
244 E1 Marshall Meadows Northumb., Eng.
190 E3 Marshall's Cross Merseyside, Eng.
110 D5 Marshall's Heath Herts., Eng.
396 J4 Marshallstown Down, N. Ire.
46 B3 Marshalsea Dorset, Eng.
110 D5 Marshalswick Herts., Eng.
166 G2 Marsham Norf., Eng.
228 G3 Marshaw Lancs., Eng.
102 D4 Marsh Baldon Oxon, Eng.
82 B3 Marsh Benham W. Berks., Eng.
62 H3 Marshborough Kent, Eng.
144 D4 Marshbrook Shrop., Eng.
170 G3 Marshchapel Lincs., Eng.
98 F5 Marshfield S. Glos., Eng.
339 B3 Marshfield Newp., Wales
36 F1 Marshgate Corn., Eng.
106 B3 Marsh Gibbon Bucks., Eng.
198 A2 Marsh Green Gtr Man., Eng.
62 A4 Marsh Green Kent, Eng.
144 E3 Marsh Green Telford, Eng.
166 A3 Marshland St James Norf., Eng.
180 E3 Marsh Lane Derbys., Eng.
190 D1 Marshside Merseyside, Eng.
94 D3 Marsh Street Som., Eng.
40 H2 Marshwood Devon, Eng.
216 D1 Marske N. Yorks., Eng.
216 F1 Marske-by-the-Sea R. and C., Eng.
198 C3 Marsland Green Gtr Man., Eng.
184 E2 Marston Cheshire West & Chester, Eng.
140 B2 Marston Here., Eng.
170 B6 Marston Lincs., Eng.
102 D4 Marston Oxon, Eng.
148 B4 Marston Staffs., Eng.
148 C3 Marston Staffs., Eng.
132 B2 Marston Warks., Eng.
86 C4 Marston Wilts., Eng.
132 E4 Marston Doles Warks., Eng.
154 D3 Marston Green W. Mids, Eng.
94 I4 Marston Magna Som., Eng.
86 E1 Marston Meysey Wilts., Eng.
180 C5 Marston Montgomery Derbys., Eng.
110 B3 Marston Moretaine Central Bedfordshire, Eng.
180 D5 Marston on Dove Derbys., Eng.
140 D2 Marston Stannett Here., Eng.
128 B5 Marston St Lawrence Northants., Eng.
128 D3 Marston Trussell Northants., Eng.
140 D4 Marstow Here., Eng.
106 E4 Marsworth Bucks., Eng.
86 F3 Marten Wilts., Eng.
184 F2 Marthall Cheshire East, Eng.
166 I2 Martham Norf., Eng.
52 A5 Martin Hants., Eng.
62 I3 Martin Kent, Eng.
170 E5 Martin Lincs., Eng.
170 F4 Martin Lincs., Eng.
22 F7 Martin, Isle i. Scot.
52 A5 Martin Drove End Hants., Eng.
40 E1 Martinhoe Devon, Eng.
136 D2 Martin Hussingtree Worcs., Eng.
190 F3 Martinscroft Warr., Eng.
46 D3 Martinstown Dorset, Eng.
388 I3 Martinstown Ballymena, N. Ire.
396 J3 Martinstown Down, N. Ire.
120 G4 Martlesham Suff., Eng.
120 G4 Martlesham Heath Suff., Eng.
358 E3 Martletwy Pembs., Wales
136 C2 Martley Worcs., Eng.
94 H5 Martock Som., Eng.
184 F2 Marton Cheshire East, Eng.
184 D2 Marton Cheshire West & Chester, Eng.
232 D7 Marton Cumbria, Eng.
210 G3 Marton E. Riding, Eng.
210 H2 Marton E. Riding, Eng.
170 B4 Marton Lincs., Eng.
216 E3 Marton N. Yorks., Eng.
216 G2 Marton N. Yorks., Eng.
144 B4 Marton Shrop., Eng.
144 D3 Marton Shrop., Eng.
132 D4 Marton Warks., Eng.
216 F2 Marton Abbey N. Yorks., Eng.
216 E2 Marton-le-Moor N. Yorks., Eng.
228 D4 Marton Moss Side Blackpool, Eng.
78 D2 Martyr's Green Surr., Eng.
52 E4 Martyr Worthy Hants., Eng.
329 A3 Marwick Orkney, Scot.
40 D1 Marwood Devon, Eng.
322 H2 Marybank High., Scot.
326 E2 Marybank W. Isles, Scot.
322 H2 Maryburgh High., Scot.
331 D3 Maryfield Shet., Scot.
256 K2 Marygold Borders, Scot.
314 G2 Maryhill Abers., Scot.
276 E2 Maryhill Glas., Scot.
314 F4 Marykirk Abers., Scot.
74 D2 Marylebone Gtr Lon., Eng.
198 B2 Marylebone Gtr Man., Eng.
314 C1 Marypark Moray, Scot.
232 B4 Maryport Cumbria, Eng.
252 B3 Maryport D. and G., Scot.
40 D3 Marystow Devon, Eng.
40 D3 Mary Tavy Devon, Eng.
308 G2 Maryton Angus, Scot.
314 E3 Marywell Abers., Scot.
314 G3 Marywell Abers., Scot.
308 G3 Marywell Angus, Scot.
216 E2 Masham N. Yorks., Eng.
116 E3 Mashbury Essex, Eng.
216 B2 Masongill N. Yorks., Eng.
396 H3 Massford Banbridge, N. Ire.
180 E3 Mastin Moor Derbys., Eng.
314 G3 Mastrick Aberdeen, Scot.
136 D2 Matchborough Worcs., Eng.
116 D3 Matching Essex, Eng.
116 D3 Matching Green Essex, Eng.
116 D3 Matching Tye Essex, Eng.
244 F5 Matfen Northumb., Eng.
62 C4 Matfield Kent, Eng.
339 D3 Mathern Mon., Wales
140 E3 Mathon Here., Eng.
358 D2 Mathry Pembs., Wales
166 G1 Matlaske Norf., Eng.
180 D4 Matlock Derbys., Eng.
180 D4 Matlock Bank Derbys., Eng.
180 D4 Matlock Bath Derbys., Eng.
180 D4 Matlock Dale Derbys., Eng.
98 F2 Matson Glos., Eng.
232 E5 Matterdale End Cumbria, Eng.
176 D2 Mattersey Notts., Eng.
176 D2 Mattersey Thorpe Notts., Eng.
52 G3 Mattingley Hants., Eng.
166 F3 Mattishall Norf., Eng.
166 F3 Mattishall Burgh Norf., Eng.
262 E3 Mauchline E. Ayr., Scot.
314 G2 Maud Abers., Scot.
408 E4 Maufant Jersey Channel Is
98 I2 Maugersbury Glos., Eng.
405 E2 Maughold Isle of Man
24 I5 Maughold Head hd Isle of Man
322 H2 Mauld High., Scot.
110 C3 Maulden Central Bedfordshire, Eng.
232 G5 Maulds Meaburn Cumbria, Eng.
216 E2 Maunby N. Yorks., Eng.
140 D3 Maund Bryan Here., Eng.
94 D4 Maundown Som., Eng.
166 I3 Mautby Norf., Eng.
148 D4 Mavesyn Ridware Staffs., Eng.
170 G4 Mavis Enderby Lincs., Eng.
22 □N2 Mavis Grind isth. Scot.
232 B4 Mawbray Cumbria, Eng.
228 F5 Mawdesley Lancs., Eng.
350 D3 Mawdlam Bridg., Wales
36 D3 Mawgan Corn., Eng.
36 D2 Mawgan Porth Corn., Eng.
184 E3 Maw Green Cheshire East, Eng.
154 C2 Maw Green W. Mids, Eng.
36 D3 Mawla Corn., Eng.
36 D3 Mawnan Corn., Eng.
36 D3 Mawnan Smith Corn., Eng.
128 E3 Mawsley Northants., Eng.
170 H4 Mawthorpe Lincs., Eng.
124 B3 Maxey Peterb., Eng.
132 C3 Maxstoke Warks., Eng.
62 G4 Maxted Street Kent, Eng.
62 H4 Maxton Kent, Eng.
256 I3 Maxton Borders, Scot.
256 J3 Maxwellheugh Borders, Scot.
252 F2 Maxwelltown D. and G., Scot.
36 F1 Maxworthy Corn., Eng.
22 K10 May, Isle of i. Scot.
350 B3 Mayals Swansea, Wales
22 J9 Mayar hill Scot.
148 B2 May Bank Staffs., Eng.
262 C4 Maybole S. Ayr., Scot.
78 C2 Maybury Surr., Eng.
314 E2 Mayen Moray, Scot.
74 D2 Mayfair Gtr Lon., Eng.
58 H2 Mayfield E. Sussex, Eng.
148 E2 Mayfield Staffs., Eng.
288 E3 Mayfield Midlothian, Scot.
78 C2 Mayford Surr., Eng.
98 E2 May Hill Glos., Eng.
116 G3 Mayland Essex, Eng.
116 G3 Maylandsea Essex, Eng.
58 H3 Maynard's Green E. Sussex, Eng.
396 G4 Mayobridge Newry & Mourne, N. Ire.
388 G3 Mayoghill Coleraine, N. Ire.
36 □ Maypole I.o.S., Eng.
62 G2 Maypole Kent, Eng.
339 D1 Maypole Mon., Wales
116 H2 Maypole Green Essex, Eng.
166 I3 Maypole Green Norf., Eng.
120 D3 Maypole Green Suff., Eng.
120 G3 Maypole Green Suff., Eng.
396 H4 May's Corner Banbridge, N. Ire.
94 G2 May's Green N. Som., Eng.
102 F5 Mays Green Oxon, Eng.
396 F4 Maytown Newry & Mourne, N. Ire.
331 D3 Maywick Shet., Scot.
388 J6 Mazetown Lisburn, N. Ire.
388 I3 McGregor's Corner Ballymena, N. Ire.
276 A2 McInroy's Point Inverclyde, Scot.
40 C2 Mead Devon, Eng.
Meadarloch Arg. and B., Scot. see Benderloch
86 D5 Mead End Wilts., Eng.
94 J3 Meadgate B. and N.E. Som., Eng.
106 C4 Meadle Bucks., Eng.
236 F3 Meadowfield Durham, Eng.
140 E2 Meadow Green Here., Eng.
208 D3 Meadowhall S. Yorks., Eng.
288 F3 Meadowmill E. Lothian, Scot.
144 B4 Meadowtown Shrop., Eng.
40 D3 Meadwell Devon, Eng.
148 C3 Meaford Staffs., Eng.
326 C2 Mealasta W. Isles, Scot.
22 B6 Mealasta Island i. Scot.
232 F6 Meal Bank Cumbria, Eng.
22 G8 Meal Fuar-mhonaidh hill Scot.
222 D3 Meal Hill W. Yorks., Eng.
22 B6 Mealisval hill Scot.
22 H9 Meall Chuaich hill Scot.
22 G8 Meall Dubh hill Scot.
388 K5 Mealough Lisburn, N. Ire.
170 G3 Meals Lincs., Eng.
232 C4 Mealsgate Cumbria, Eng.
228 H3 Meanley Lancs., Eng.
222 E1 Meanwood W. Yorks., Eng.
94 H3 Meare Som., Eng.
94 F5 Meare Green Som., Eng.
276 E3 Mearns E. Renf., Scot.
128 E4 Mears Ashby Northants., Eng.
26 I2 Mease r. Eng.
162 B2 Measham Leics., Eng.
78 E2 Meath Green Surr., Eng.
232 E7 Meathop Cumbria, Eng.
40 D3 Meavy Devon, Eng.
162 G3 Medbourne Leics., Eng.
40 C2 Meddon Devon, Eng.
24 P7 Meden r. Eng.
176 C3 Meden Vale Notts., Eng.
228 E4 Medlar Lancs., Eng.
106 C5 Medmenham Bucks., Eng.
236 E2 Medomsley Durham, Eng.
52 F4 Medstead Hants., Eng.
62 D2 Medway admin. div. Eng.
26 M5 Medway r. Eng.
402 F2 Meenawaddy Strabane, N. Ire.
402 D3 Meentullyclogh Fermanagh, N. Ire.
148 C2 Meerbrook Staffs., Eng.
140 B2 Meer Common Here., Eng.
154 E3 Meer End W. Mids, Eng.
110 F4 Meesden Herts., Eng.
144 E3 Meeson Telford, Eng.
40 D2 Meeth Devon, Eng.
166 H2 Meeting House Hill Norf., Eng.
388 J6 Megarrystown Lisburn, N. Ire.
256 E4 Meggethead Borders, Scot.
356 D2 Meidrim Carmar., Wales
378 E3 Meifod Denb., Wales
366 F2 Meifod Powys, Wales
396 F5 Meigh Newry & Mourne, N. Ire.
304 L3 Meigle Perth and Kin., Scot.
24 I1 Meikle Bin hill Scot.
268 B2 Meikle Earnock S. Lanark., Scot.
300 E4 Meikle Grenach Arg. and B., Scot.
300 E4 Meikle Kilmory Arg. and B., Scot.
304 J3 Meikleour Perth and Kin., Scot.
300 F3 Meikle Rahane Arg. and B., Scot.
22 K11 Meikle Says Law hill Scot.
314 G2 Meikle Tarty Abers., Scot.
314 F2 Meikle Wartle Abers., Scot.
262 E3 Meikleyard E. Ayr., Scot.
356 E3 Meinciau Carmar., Wales
148 C3 Meir Stoke, Eng.
148 C3 Meirheath Staffs., Eng.
22 D9 Meirleach, Rubha nam pt Scot.
326 E1 Melbost Borve W. Isles, Scot.
124 E6 Melbourn Cambs., Eng.
180 E6 Melbourne Derbys., Eng.
210 C3 Melbourne E. Riding, Eng.
46 G2 Melbury Abbas Dorset, Eng.
46 D2 Melbury Bubb Dorset, Eng.
46 D2 Melbury Osmond Dorset, Eng.
46 D2 Melbury Sampford Dorset, Eng.
331 C3 Melby Shet., Scot.
110 C2 Melchbourne Bedford, Eng.
46 E3 Melcombe Bingham Dorset, Eng.
46 E4 Melcombe Regis Dorset, Eng.
40 D2 Meldon Devon, Eng.
244 G5 Meldon Northumb., Eng.
124 E6 Meldreth Cambs., Eng.
300 D3 Melfort Arg. and B., Scot.
322 H3 Melgarve High., Scot.
378 E2 Meliden Denb., Wales
350 D2 Melincourt N.P.T., Wales
350 D3 Melincryddan N.P.T., Wales
378 C3 Melin-y-coed Conwy, Wales
366 E3 Melin-y-ddol Powys, Wales
366 E3 Melin-y-grug Powys, Wales
378 E3 Melin-y-Wig Denb., Wales
232 F5 Melkinthorpe Cumbria, Eng.
244 C6 Melkridge Northumb., Eng.
86 C3 Melksham Wilts., Eng.
86 C3 Melksham Forest Wilts., Eng.
300 E4 Melldalloch Arg. and B., Scot.
228 G2 Melling Lancs., Eng.
190 D3 Melling Merseyside, Eng.
190 D2 Melling Mount Merseyside, Eng.
120 F3 Mellis Suff., Eng.
320 D4 Mellon Charles High., Scot.
320 D4 Mellon Udrigle High., Scot.
198 E3 Mellor Gtr Man., Eng.
228 G4 Mellor Lancs., Eng.
228 G4 Mellor Brook Lancs., Eng.
94 J3 Mells Som., Eng.
26 E4 Mellte r. Wales
232 G4 Melmerby Cumbria, Eng.
216 D2 Melmerby N. Yorks., Eng.
216 E2 Melmerby N. Yorks., Eng.
120 D3 Melon Green Suff., Eng.
46 C3 Melplash Dorset, Eng.
314 F1 Melrose Abers., Scot.
256 H3 Melrose Borders, Scot.
329 B5 Melsetter Orkney, Scot.
216 D1 Melsonby N. Yorks., Eng.
222 C3 Meltham W. Yorks., Eng.
210 E4 Melton E. Riding, Eng.
120 G4 Melton Suff., Eng.
210 D3 Meltonby E. Riding, Eng.
166 F1 Melton Constable Norf., Eng.
162 F2 Melton Mowbray Leics., Eng.
170 D2 Melton Ross N. Lincs., Eng.
320 C4 Melvaig High., Scot.
144 C3 Melverley Shrop., Eng.
144 C3 Melverley Green Shrop., Eng.
320 I2 Melvich High., Scot.
23 F4 Melvin, Lough l. Ireland/U.K.
40 G2 Membury Devon, Eng.
314 G2 Memsie Abers., Scot.
308 E2 Memus Angus, Scot.
36 E3 Menabilly Corn., Eng.
371 E3 Menai Bridge I.o.A., Wales
26 D1 Menai Strait sea chan. Wales
120 G2 Mendham Suff., Eng.
26 G5 Mendip Hills hills Eng.
120 F3 Mendlesham Suff., Eng.
120 F3 Mendlesham Green Suff., Eng.
52 G6 Mengham Hants., Eng.
36 F2 Menheniot Corn., Eng.
136 C2 Menithwood Worcs., Eng.
252 E1 Mennock D. and G., Scot.
222 D1 Menston W. Yorks., Eng.
292 A3 Menstrie Clack., Scot.
22 H10 Menteith, Lake of l. Scot.
216 G3 Menthorpe N. Yorks., Eng.
106 D3 Mentmore Bucks., Eng.
322 E4 Meoble High., Scot.
144 D3 Meole Brace Shrop., Eng.
52 E6 Meon Hants., Eng.
52 F5 Meonstoke Hants., Eng.
62 C2 Meopham Kent, Eng.
62 C2 Meopham Green Kent, Eng.
124 E4 Mepal Cambs., Eng.
110 C3 Meppershall Central Bedfordshire, Eng.
140 A3 Merbach Here., Eng.
180 D5 Mercaston Derbys., Eng.
288 D3 Merchiston Edin., Scot.
184 E2 Mere Cheshire East, Eng.
86 B5 Mere Wilts., Eng.
228 E5 Mere Brow Lancs., Eng.
228 I4 Mereclough Lancs., Eng.
154 C2 Mere Green W. Mids, Eng.
184 D2 Mere Heath Cheshire West & Chester, Eng.
228 E4 Mereside Blackpool, Eng.
144 F3 Meretown Telford, Eng.
62 C3 Mereworth Kent, Eng.
314 G4 Mergie Abers., Scot.
154 E3 Meriden W. Mids, Eng.
322 C3 Merkadale High., Scot.
322 I2 Merkinch High., Scot.
252 E2 Merkland D. and G., Scot.
46 H3 Merley Poole, Eng.
358 E3 Merlin's Bridge Pembs., Wales
22 H12 Merrick hill Scot.
94 F4 Merridge Som., Eng.
40 E4 Merrifield Devon, Eng.
144 D3 Merrington Shrop., Eng.
358 E4 Merrion Pembs., Wales
94 H5 Merriott Som., Eng.
40 D3 Merrivale Devon, Eng.
78 C2 Merrow Surr., Eng.
110 C6 Merry Hill Herts., Eng.
154 A2 Merry Hill W. Mids, Eng.
36 F2 Merrymeet Corn., Eng.
26 N4 Mersea Island i. Eng.
24 L7 Mersey est. Eng.
190 D3 Merseyside admin. div. Eng.
62 F4 Mersham Kent, Eng.
78 F2 Merstham Surr., Eng.
52 E7 Merstone I.o.W., Eng.
36 D3 Merther Corn., Eng.

Merthyr to Much Hoole

356 D2 Merthyr Carmar., Wales
366 E6 Merthyr Cynog Powys, Wales
350 G4 Merthyr Dyfan V. of Glam., Wales
350 E4 Merthyr Mawr Bridg., Wales
350 F2 Merthyr Tydfil M. Tyd., Wales
350 F2 Merthyr Tydfil admin. div. Wales
350 F2 Merthyr Vale M. Tyd., Wales
40 D2 Merton Devon, Eng.
166 D3 Merton Norf., Eng.
102 D3 Merton Oxon, Eng.
74 C3 Merton met. bor. Gtr Lon., Eng.
378 F2 Mertyn Flints., Wales
256 I4 Mervinslaw Borders, Scot.
40 E2 Meshaw Devon, Eng.
116 G2 Messing Essex, Eng.
170 C2 Messingham N. Lincs., Eng.
120 H2 Metfield Suff., Eng.
36 G2 Metherell Corn., Eng.
170 D5 Metheringham Lincs., Eng.
292 F2 Methil Fife, Scot.
292 F2 Methilhill Fife, Scot.
372 B3 Methlem Gwynedd, Wales
222 F2 Methley W. Yorks., Eng.
222 F2 Methley Junction W. Yorks., Eng.
222 F2 Methley Lanes W. Yorks., Eng.
314 G2 Methlick Abers., Scot.
304 I4 Methven Perth and Kin., Scot.
166 C3 Methwold Norf., Eng.
166 C3 Methwold Hythe Norf., Eng.
120 H2 Mettingham Suff., Eng.
166 G1 Metton Norf., Eng.
36 E3 Mevagissey Corn., Eng.
216 B2 Mewith Head N. Yorks., Eng.
208 E3 Mexborough S. Yorks., Eng.
320 K2 Mey High., Scot.
98 I3 Meysey Hampton Glos., Eng.
22 D11 Mhàil, Rubh' a' pt Scot.
22 H8 Mhòr, Loch l. Scot.
326 D3 Miabhag W. Isles, Scot.
326 D3 Miabhag W. Isles, Scot.
Miabhaig W. Isles, Scot. see Miavaig
326 D2 Miavaig W. Isles, Scot.
140 C4 Michaelchurch Here., Eng.
140 A3 Michaelchurch Escley Here., Eng.
366 G6 Michaelchurch-on-Arrow Powys, Wales
350 G4 Michaelston-le-Pit V. of Glam., Wales
350 G4 Michaelston-super-Ely Cardiff, Wales
339 B3 Michaelston-y-Fedw Newp., Wales
36 E2 Michaelstow Corn., Eng.
52 E4 Micheldever Hants., Eng.
52 C4 Michelmersh Hants., Eng.
120 F3 Mickfield Suff., Eng.
208 E3 Micklebring S. Yorks., Eng.
216 G1 Mickleby N. Yorks., Eng.
222 G2 Micklefield W. Yorks., Eng.
110 C5 Micklefield Green Herts., Eng.
78 E2 Mickleham Surr., Eng.
198 E2 Micklehurst Gtr Man., Eng.
180 D5 Micklemeadow Derbys., Eng.
180 D5 Mickleover Derby, Eng.
232 D3 Micklethwaite Cumbria, Eng.
222 C1 Micklethwaite W. Yorks., Eng.
236 C4 Mickleton Durham, Eng.
98 I1 Mickleton Glos., Eng.
222 F2 Mickletown W. Yorks., Eng.
184 B2 Mickle Trafford Cheshire West & Chester, Eng.
180 D3 Mickley Derbys., Eng.
216 E2 Mickley N. Yorks., Eng.
120 D3 Mickley Green Suff., Eng.
244 F6 Mickley Square Northumb., Eng.
314 G2 Mid Ardlaw Abers., Scot.
329 D2 Midbea Orkney, Scot.
314 F3 Mid Beltie Abers., Scot.
288 C3 Mid Calder W. Lothian, Scot.
102 F5 Middle Assendon Oxon, Eng.
102 D3 Middle Aston Oxon, Eng.
102 C3 Middle Barton Oxon, Eng.
154 D3 Middle Bickenhill W. Mids, Eng.
252 G2 Middlebie D. and G., Scot.
46 I3 Middle Bockhampton Dorset, Eng.
94 H5 Middle Chinnock Som., Eng.
106 C3 Middle Claydon Bucks., Eng.
208 D2 Middlecliff S. Yorks., Eng.
180 E3 Middlecroft Derbys., Eng.
308 F2 Middle Drums Angus, Scot.
98 G3 Middle Duntisbourne Glos., Eng.
106 E5 Middle Green Bucks., Eng.
120 C3 Middle Green Suff., Eng.
216 D2 Middleham N. Yorks., Eng.
180 E3 Middle Handley Derbys., Eng.
166 E4 Middle Harling Norf., Eng.
314 G2 Middlehill Abers., Scot.
144 D5 Middlehope Shrop., Eng.
300 D3 Middle Kames Arg. and B., Scot.
136 F3 Middle Littleton Worcs., Eng.
148 A2 Middle Madeley Staffs., Eng.
140 B4 Middle Maes-coed Here., Eng.
46 E2 Middlemarsh Dorset, Eng.
148 E2 Middle Mayfield Staffs., Eng.
358 C2 Middle Mill Pembs., Wales
62 E4 Middle Quarter Kent, Eng.
236 G3 Middle Rainton T. and W., Eng.
170 D3 Middle Rasen Lincs., Eng.
304 I5 Middle Rigg Perth and Kin., Scot.
228 G2 Middle Salter Lancs., Eng.
216 F1 Middlesbrough Middbro., Eng.
216 F1 Middlesbrough admin. div. Eng.
232 E4 Middlesceugh Cumbria, Eng.
232 F7 Middleshaw Cumbria, Eng.
216 D2 Middlesmoor N. Yorks., Eng.
378 G3 Middle Sontley Wrex., Wales
94 E5 Middle Stoford Som., Eng.
236 F3 Middlestone Durham, Eng.
236 F3 Middlestone Moor Durham, Eng.
94 H3 Middle Stoughton Som., Eng.
222 E3 Middlestown W. Yorks., Eng.
36 F2 Middle Taphouse Corn., Eng.
232 G7 Middleton Cumbria, Eng.
180 C4 Middleton Derbys., Eng.
180 D4 Middleton Derbys., Eng.
116 G1 Middleton Essex, Eng.
198 D2 Middleton Gtr Man., Eng.
52 D3 Middleton Hants., Eng.
140 C2 Middleton Here., Eng.
228 E2 Middleton Lancs., Eng.
166 B2 Middleton Norf., Eng.
128 E2 Middleton Northants., Eng.
244 F2 Middleton Northumb., Eng.
244 F5 Middleton Northumb., Eng.
216 G2 Middleton N. Yorks., Eng.
144 B2 Middleton Shrop., Eng.
144 B4 Middleton Shrop., Eng.
144 D5 Middleton Shrop., Eng.
120 I3 Middleton Suff., Eng.
132 B2 Middleton Warks., Eng.
222 D1 Middleton W. Yorks., Eng.
222 E2 Middleton W. Yorks., Eng.
308 F3 Middleton Angus, Scot.
300 □ Middleton Arg. and B., Scot.
288 E4 Middleton Midlothian, Scot.
304 J3 Middleton Perth and Kin., Scot.
304 J5 Middleton Perth and Kin., Scot.
350 A3 Middleton Swansea, Wales
144 E4 Middleton Baggot Shrop., Eng.
244 F5 Middleton Bank Top Northumb., Eng.
128 B5 Middleton Cheney Northants., Eng.
148 C3 Middleton Green Staffs., Eng.
244 E2 Middleton Hall Northumb., Eng.
236 C4 Middleton in Teesdale Durham, Eng.
120 I3 Middleton Moor Suff., Eng.
236 G4 Middleton One Row Darl., Eng.
216 F1 Middleton-on-Leven N. Yorks., Eng.
58 C4 Middleton-on-Sea W. Sussex, Eng.
140 C2 Middleton on the Hill Here., Eng.
210 E3 Middleton-on-the-Wolds E. Riding, Eng.
144 E4 Middleton Priors Shrop., Eng.
236 G4 Middleton St George Darl., Eng.
144 F5 Middleton Scriven Shrop., Eng.
102 D3 Middleton Stoney Oxon, Eng.
216 E1 Middleton Tyas N. Yorks., Eng.
232 A6 Middletown Cumbria, Eng.
36 □ Middle Town I.o.S., Eng.
396 C4 Middletown Armagh, N. Ire.
366 G2 Middletown Powys, Wales
132 C5 Middle Tysoe Warks., Eng.
52 C4 Middle Wallop Hants., Eng.
106 C2 Middle Weald M.K., Eng.
184 E2 Middlewich Cheshire East, Eng.
86 F5 Middle Winterslow Wilts., Eng.
184 G1 Middlewood Cheshire East, Eng.
36 F2 Middlewood Corn., Eng.
208 C3 Middlewood S. Yorks., Eng.
86 E5 Middle Woodford Wilts., Eng.
120 F3 Middlewood Green Suff., Eng.
98 F3 Middleyard Glos., Eng.
94 G4 Middlezoy Som., Eng.
236 F4 Middridge Durham, Eng.
320 G2 Midfield High., Scot.
94 J2 Midford B. and N.E. Som., Eng.
228 F4 Midge Hall Lancs., Eng.
232 G3 Midgeholme Cumbria, Eng.
82 C3 Midgham W. Berks., Eng.
222 C2 Midgley W. Yorks., Eng.
222 E3 Midgley W. Yorks., Eng.
208 C3 Midhopestones S. Yorks., Eng.
58 B3 Midhurst W. Sussex, Eng.
94 H5 Mid Lambrook Som., Eng.
58 B3 Mid Lavant W. Sussex, Eng.
256 H3 Midlem Borders, Scot.
300 E3 Mid Letter Arg. and B., Scot.
292 C3 Mid Lix Stir., Scot.
124 C5 Midloe Grange Cambs., Eng.
288 E3 Midlothian admin. div. Scot.
216 C2 Mid Mossdale N. Yorks., Eng.
300 E4 Midpark Arg. and B., Scot.
94 J3 Midsomer Norton B. and N.E. Som., Eng.
170 F4 Midthorpe Lincs., Eng.
276 B2 Midton Inverclyde, Scot.
320 D4 Midtown High., Scot.
320 G2 Midtown High., Scot.
314 G4 Midtown of Barras Abers., Scot.
170 G5 Midville Lincs., Eng.
180 D6 Midway Derbys., Eng.
331 D2 Mid Yell Shet., Scot.
320 H4 Migdale High., Scot.
314 E3 Migvie Abers., Scot.
296 C5 Milarrochy Stir., Scot.
314 F2 Milbethill Abers., Scot.
94 J5 Milborne Port Som., Eng.
46 F3 Milborne St Andrew Dorset, Eng.
94 J5 Milborne Wick Som., Eng.
244 G5 Milbourne Northumb., Eng.
86 C2 Milbourne Wilts., Eng.
232 G5 Milburn Cumbria, Eng.
98 E4 Milbury Heath S. Glos., Eng.
102 C2 Milcombe Oxon, Eng.
120 E4 Milden Suff., Eng.
120 C2 Mildenhall Suff., Eng.
86 E3 Mildenhall Wilts., Eng.
366 G4 Milebrook Powys, Wales
62 D3 Milebush Kent, Eng.
388 L4 Milebush Carrickfergus, N. Ire.
86 C3 Mile Elm Wilts., Eng.
116 H2 Mile End Essex, Eng.
98 D3 Mile End Glos., Eng.
74 D2 Mile End Gtr Lon., Eng.
166 E2 Mileham Norf., Eng.
58 E3 Mile Oak B. and H., Eng.
62 C4 Mile Oak Kent, Eng.
148 B2 Miles Green Staffs., Eng.
140 D2 Miles Hope Here., Eng.
292 D3 Milesmark Fife, Scot.
198 D3 Miles Platting Gtr Man., Eng.
82 C3 Miles's Green W. Berks., Eng.
62 E2 Mile Town Kent, Eng.
244 E2 Milfield Northumb., Eng.
180 E4 Milford Derbys., Eng.
40 C2 Milford Devon, Eng.
144 C3 Milford Shrop., Eng.
148 C4 Milford Staffs., Eng.
78 C2 Milford Surr., Eng.
358 D3 Milford Haven Pembs., Wales
52 C6 Milford on Sea Hants., Eng.
98 D3 Milkwall Glos., Eng.
86 C5 Milkwell Wilts., Eng.
58 B2 Milland W. Sussex, Eng.
276 D2 Millarston Renf., Scot.
222 C2 Mill Bank W. Yorks., Eng.
314 H2 Millbank Abers., Scot.
388 L4 Millbay Larne, N. Ire.
232 D5 Millbeck Cumbria, Eng.
329 E2 Millbounds Orkney, Scot.
314 H2 Millbreck Abers., Scot.
78 B2 Millbridge Surr., Eng.
110 B3 Millbrook Central Bedfordshire, Eng.
36 G2 Millbrook Corn., Eng.
198 E3 Millbrook Gtr Man., Eng.
52 D5 Millbrook Soton, Eng.
388 K3 Millbrook Larne, N. Ire.
198 E3 Mill Brow Gtr Man., Eng.
22 I7 Mill Buie hill Scot.
314 E3 Millburn Abers., Scot.
58 J3 Millcorner E. Sussex, Eng.
148 E2 Milldale Staffs., Eng.
314 G3 Millden Abers., Scot.
308 F3 Milldens Angus, Scot.
304 H4 Millearne Perth and Kin., Scot.
106 C5 Mill End Bucks., Eng.
124 G5 Mill End Cambs., Eng.
110 B6 Mill End Herts., Eng.
110 E4 Mill End Herts., Eng.
102 B3 Millend Oxon, Eng.
136 E3 Mill End Worcs., Eng.
116 E2 Mill End Green Essex, Eng.
144 E2 Millenheath Shrop., Eng.
288 E3 Millerhill Midlothian, Scot.
180 C3 Miller's Dale Derbys., Eng.
180 D4 Millers Green Derbys., Eng.
116 D3 Miller's Green Essex, Eng.
22 F12 Milleur Point pt Scot.
396 D4 Millford Armagh, N. Ire.
228 I4 Millgate Lancs., Eng.
124 G6 Mill Green Cambs., Eng.
116 E3 Mill Green Essex, Eng.
110 D5 Mill Green Herts., Eng.
166 F4 Mill Green Norf., Eng.
144 F2 Mill Green Shrop., Eng.
148 D4 Mill Green Staffs., Eng.
120 E3 Mill Green Suff., Eng.
120 E4 Mill Green Suff., Eng.
120 F3 Mill Green Suff., Eng.
120 H3 Mill Green Suff., Eng.
154 C2 Mill Green W. Mids, Eng.
140 A3 Millhalf Here., Eng.
40 G2 Millhayes Devon, Eng.
228 G4 Mill Hill B'burn, Eng.
124 C6 Mill Hill Cambs., Eng.
74 C2 Mill Hill Gtr Lon., Eng.
232 F7 Millholme Cumbria, Eng.
232 E4 Millhouse Cumbria, Eng.
300 E4 Millhouse Arg. and B., Scot.
252 F2 Millhousebridge D. and G., Scot.
208 C2 Millhouse Green S. Yorks., Eng.
228 G2 Mill Houses Lancs., Eng.
208 C3 Millhouses S. Yorks., Eng.
208 D2 Millhouses S. Yorks., Eng.
276 C3 Millikenpark Renf., Scot.
358 E3 Millin Cross Pembs., Wales
210 D3 Millington E. Riding, Eng.
180 D4 Millington Green Derbys., Eng.
396 K2 Millisle Ards, N. Ire.
52 G3 Mill Lane Hants., Eng.
148 B3 Millmeece Staffs., Eng.
322 G2 Millness High., Scot.
300 F4 Mill of Camsail Arg. and B., Scot.
304 G4 Mill of Fortune Perth and Kin., Scot.
314 G4 Mill of Uras Abers., Scot.
232 C7 Millom Cumbria, Eng.
110 D3 Millow Central Bedfordshire, Eng.
36 F2 Millpool Corn., Eng.
264 E2 Millport N. Ayr., Scot.
232 E7 Mill Side Cumbria, Eng.
62 C3 Mill Street Kent, Eng.
166 F2 Mill Street Norf., Eng.
120 F3 Mill Street Suff., Eng.
180 D3 Millthorpe Derbys., Eng.
232 G7 Millthrop Cumbria, Eng.
314 G3 Milltimber Aberdeen, Scot.
36 F2 Milltown Corn., Eng.
180 E4 Milltown Derbys., Eng.
40 D1 Milltown Devon, Eng.
388 H4 Milltown Antrim, N. Ire.
388 I4 Mill Town Antrim, N. Ire.
396 D3 Milltown Armagh, N. Ire.
396 E3 Milltown Armagh, N. Ire.
388 H3 Milltown Ballymena, N. Ire.
388 H4 Milltown Ballymena, N. Ire.
388 G2 Milltown Ballymoney, N. Ire.
388 F2 Milltown Coleraine, N. Ire.
396 E2 Milltown Craigavon, N. Ire.
402 D4 Milltown Fermanagh, N. Ire.
388 J6 Milltown Lisburn, N. Ire.
396 F5 Milltown Newry & Mourne, N. Ire.
396 G4 Milltown Newry & Mourne, N. Ire.
396 G5 Milltown Newry & Mourne, N. Ire.
402 F4 Milltown Omagh, N. Ire.
402 F1 Milltown Strabane, N. Ire.
314 D3 Milltown Abers., Scot.
252 G2 Milltown D. and G., Scot.
322 J2 Milltown High., Scot.
304 J4 Milltown of Aberdalgie Perth and Kin., Scot.
314 D2 Milltown of Edinvillie Moray, Scot.
314 E2 Milltown of Rothiemay Moray, Scot.
314 E3 Milltown of Towie Abers., Scot.
74 D3 Millwall Gtr Lon., Eng.
304 J5 Milnathort Perth and Kin., Scot.
184 C3 Milners Heath Cheshire West & Chester, Eng.
276 E2 Milngavie E. Dun., Scot.
198 E2 Milnrow Gtr Man., Eng.
222 D3 Milnsbridge W. Yorks., Eng.
232 F7 Milnthorpe Cumbria, Eng.
222 F3 Milnthorpe W. Yorks., Eng.
322 A2 Milovaig High., Scot.
262 E3 Milrig E. Ayr., Scot.
144 E5 Milson Shrop., Eng.
62 E3 Milstead Kent, Eng.
86 E4 Milston Wilts., Eng.
128 C5 Milthorpe Northants., Eng.
124 E5 Milton Cambs., Eng.
232 F7 Milton Cumbria, Eng.
180 D5 Milton Derbys., Eng.
62 C2 Milton Kent, Eng.
176 D3 Milton Notts., Eng.
94 G2 Milton N. Som., Eng.
102 B3 Milton Oxon, Eng.
102 D5 Milton Oxon, Eng.
52 F6 Milton Ports., Eng.
94 H5 Milton Som., Eng.
148 C2 Milton Stoke, Eng.
402 J3 Milton Cookstown, N. Ire.
308 D3 Milton Angus, Scot.
252 B3 Milton D. and G., Scot.
252 E2 Milton D. and G., Scot.
252 E2 Milton D. and G., Scot.
276 E2 Milton Glas., Scot.
320 H4 Milton High., Scot.
322 D2 Milton High., Scot.
322 G2 Milton High., Scot.
322 H2 Milton High., Scot.
322 H2 Milton High., Scot.
322 J2 Milton High., Scot.
314 E2 Milton Moray, Scot.
304 H3 Milton Perth and Kin., Scot.
296 D4 Milton Stir., Scot.
276 C2 Milton W. Dun., Scot.
339 C3 Milton Newp., Wales
358 E3 Milton Pembs., Wales
46 F3 Milton Abbas Dorset, Eng.
40 D3 Milton Abbot Devon, Eng.
288 D3 Milton Bridge Midlothian, Scot.
110 B4 Milton Bryan Central Bedfordshire, Eng.
94 J4 Milton Clevedon Som., Eng.
40 D3 Milton Combe Devon, Eng.
314 C2 Miltonduff Moray, Scot.
98 E3 Milton End Glos., Eng.
110 B2 Milton Ernest Bedford, Eng.
184 C3 Milton Green Cheshire West & Chester, Eng.
102 D5 Milton Hill Oxon, Eng.
252 B2 Miltonise D. and G., Scot.
106 D2 Milton Keynes M.K., Eng.
106 D2 Milton Keynes admin. div. Eng.
106 D2 Milton Keynes Village M.K., Eng.
86 E3 Milton Lilbourne Wilts., Eng.
268 C2 Milton-Lockhart S. Lanark., Scot.
128 D4 Milton Malsor Northants., Eng.
304 E3 Milton Morenish Perth and Kin., Scot.
292 F2 Milton of Balgonie Fife, Scot.
296 C5 Milton of Buchanan Stir., Scot.
314 E2 Milton of Cairnborrow Abers., Scot.
296 E4 Milton of Callander Stir., Scot.
314 F3 Milton of Campfield Abers., Scot.
276 F2 Milton of Campsie E. Dun., Scot.
304 I2 Milton of Dalcapon Perth and Kin., Scot.
314 E2 Milton of Noth Abers., Scot.
314 D3 Milton of Tullich Abers., Scot.
46 F1 Milton on Stour Dorset, Eng.
62 E3 Milton Regis Kent, Eng.
58 H4 Milton Street E. Sussex, Eng.
102 B3 Milton-under-Wychwood Oxon, Eng.
94 E4 Milverton Som., Eng.
132 C4 Milverton Warks., Eng.
148 C3 Milwich Staffs., Eng.
78 C1 Mimbridge Surr., Eng.
300 E3 Minard Arg. and B., Scot.
300 E3 Minard Castle Arg. and B., Scot.
46 G2 Minchington Dorset, Eng.
98 F3 Minchinhampton Glos., Eng.
22 J11 Minch Moor hill Scot.
244 D2 Mindrum Northumb., Eng.
244 D2 Mindrummill Northumb., Eng.
94 D3 Minehead Som., Eng.
378 G3 Minera Wrex., Wales
396 J4 Minerstown Down, N. Ire.
86 D2 Minety Wilts., Eng.
86 D2 Minety Lower Moor Wilts., Eng.
372 F1 Minffordd Gwynedd, Wales
372 E3 Minffordd Gwynedd, Wales
372 G4 Minffordd Gwynedd, Wales
22 A9 Mingulay i. Scot.
170 F5 Miningsby Lincs., Eng.
36 F2 Minions Corn., Eng.
262 D4 Minishant S. Ayr., Scot.
52 H3 Minley Manor Hants., Eng.
372 H4 Minllyn Gwynedd, Wales
326 B5 Minngearraidh W. Isles, Scot.
252 C3 Minnigaff D. and G., Scot.
314 F2 Minnonie Abers., Scot.
216 E2 Minskip N. Yorks., Eng.
52 C5 Minstead Hants., Eng.
58 B3 Minsted W. Sussex, Eng.
62 E2 Minster Kent, Eng.
62 H2 Minster Kent, Eng.
244 F6 Minsteracres Northumb., Eng.
144 C4 Minsterley Shrop., Eng.
102 B4 Minster Lovell Oxon, Eng.
98 F2 Minsterworth Glos., Eng.
402 I4 Minterburn Dungannon, N. Ire.
46 E2 Minterne Magna Dorset, Eng.
46 E3 Minterne Parva Dorset, Eng.
170 E4 Minting Lincs., Eng.
314 H2 Mintlaw Abers., Scot.
256 H4 Minto Borders, Scot.
144 D4 Minton Shrop., Eng.
358 E3 Minwear Pembs., Wales
154 D2 Minworth W. Mids, Eng.
300 □ Miodar Arg. and B., Scot.
329 B3 Mirbister Orkney, Scot.
232 A5 Mirehouse Cumbria, Eng.
222 D2 Mirfield W. Yorks., Eng.
98 G3 Miserden Glos., Eng.
350 F2 Miskin R.C.T., Wales
350 F3 Miskin R.C.T., Wales
86 D5 Misselfore Wilts., Eng.
176 D2 Misson Notts., Eng.
162 D4 Misterton Leics., Eng.
176 D2 Misterton Notts., Eng.
94 H5 Misterton Som., Eng.
116 I2 Mistley Essex, Eng.
74 D3 Mitcham Gtr Lon., Eng.
98 E2 Mitcheldean Glos., Eng.
36 D2 Mitchell Corn., Eng.
232 E6 Mitchelland Cumbria, Eng.
339 D2 Mitchel Troy Mon., Wales
339 D2 Mitcheltroy Common Mon., Wales
244 G4 Mitford Northumb., Eng.
36 D3 Mithian Corn., Eng.
148 B4 Mitton Staffs., Eng.
228 H3 Mitton Green Lancs., Eng.
Miughalaigh i. Scot. see Mingulay
102 E2 Mixbury Oxon, Eng.
222 C2 Mixenden W. Yorks., Eng.
304 D3 Moar Perth and Kin., Scot.
232 E2 Moat Cumbria, Eng.
120 E4 Moats Tye Suff., Eng.
184 F2 Mobberley Cheshire East, Eng.
148 D3 Mobberley Staffs., Eng.
140 B3 Moccas Here., Eng.
378 C2 Mochdre Conwy, Wales
366 E4 Mochdre Powys, Wales
252 C3 Mochrum D. and G., Scot.
52 B5 Mockbeggar Hants., Eng.
62 D3 Mockbeggar Kent, Eng.
232 B5 Mockerkin Cumbria, Eng.
40 E3 Modbury Devon, Eng.
148 C3 Moddershall Staffs., Eng.
184 G2 Mode Hill Cheshire East, Eng.
320 H2 Modsarie High., Scot.
26 F1 Moel Famau hill Wales
371 D2 Moelfre I.o.A., Wales
366 F1 Moelfre Powys, Wales
26 F2 Moel Sych hill Wales
252 F1 Moffat D. and G., Scot.
110 D3 Mogerhanger Central Bedfordshire, Eng.
22 E9 Moidart reg. Scot.
300 B4 Moin'a'choire Arg. and B., Scot.
162 B2 Moira Leics., Eng.
388 I6 Moira Lisburn, N. Ire.
62 F3 Molash Kent, Eng.
322 C3 Mol-chlach High., Scot.
378 G2 Mold Flints., Wales
222 D3 Moldgreen W. Yorks., Eng.
26 E6 Mole r. Eng.
116 E2 Molehill Green Essex, Eng.
116 E2 Molehill Green Essex, Eng.
210 F3 Molescroft E. Riding, Eng.
244 G5 Molesden Northumb., Eng.
124 B4 Molesworth Cambs., Eng.
252 E3 Mollance D. and G., Scot.
40 E1 Molland Devon, Eng.
184 B2 Mollington Cheshire West & Chester, Eng.
102 C2 Mollington Oxon, Eng.
280 B3 Mollinsburn N. Lanark., Scot.
22 A7 Monach, Sound of sea chan. Scot.
22 A7 Monach Islands is Scot.
362 E3 Monachty Cere., Wales
296 D3 Monachyle Stir., Scot.
22 G8 Monadhliath Mountains mts Scot.
388 I2 Monanclogh Moyle, N. Ire.
22 F8 Monar, Loch l. Scot.
304 J4 Moncreiffe Perth and Kin., Scot.
402 D4 Monea Fermanagh, N. Ire.
388 D3 Monehanegan Derry, N. Ire.
300 F3 Monevechadan Arg. and B., Scot.
120 G3 Monewden Suff., Eng.
402 G1 Moneycanon Strabane, N. Ire.
396 I4 Moneycarragh Down, N. Ire.
304 I4 Moneydie Perth and Kin., Scot.
388 G3 Moneydig Coleraine, N. Ire.
388 H4 Moneyglass Antrim, N. Ire.
402 J2 Moneymore Cookstown, N. Ire.
388 E4 Moneyneany Magherafelt, N. Ire.
396 J2 Moneyreagh Castlereagh, N. Ire.
388 H4 Moneyrod Antrim, N. Ire.
82 F3 Moneyrow Green W. and M., Eng.
388 F3 Moneysharvan Magherafelt, N. Ire.
396 H4 Moneyslane Banbridge, N. Ire.
22 L9 Mongour hill Scot.
252 E2 Moniaive D. and G., Scot.
308 F4 Monifieth Angus, Scot.
308 F3 Monikie Angus, Scot.
292 F2 Monimail Fife, Scot.
358 F1 Monington Pembs., Wales
208 D2 Monk Bretton S. Yorks., Eng.
74 C2 Monken Hadley Gtr Lon., Eng.
216 F3 Monk Fryston N. Yorks., Eng.
236 H3 Monk Hesleden Durham, Eng.
140 D3 Monkhide Here., Eng.
144 E4 Monkhopton Shrop., Eng.
140 C2 Monkland Here., Eng.
40 D2 Monkleigh Devon, Eng.
350 E4 Monknash V. of Glam., Wales
40 D2 Monkokehampton Devon, Eng.
236 G1 Monkseaton T. and W., Eng.
120 E4 Monks Eleigh Suff., Eng.
58 E2 Monk's Gate W. Sussex, Eng.
184 F2 Monks' Heath Cheshire East, Eng.
52 F3 Monk Sherborne Hants., Eng.
62 D4 Monk's Hill Kent, Eng.
94 E4 Monksilver Som., Eng.
132 E3 Monks Kirby Warks., Eng.
120 G3 Monk Soham Suff., Eng.
120 G3 Monk Soham Green Suff., Eng.
74 D3 Monks Orchard Gtr Lon., Eng.
106 D4 Monks Risborough Bucks., Eng.
322 B2 Monkstadt High., Scot.
388 K4 Monkstown Newtownabbey, N. Ire.
116 E2 Monk Street Essex, Eng.
339 C2 Monkswood Mon., Wales
40 G2 Monkton Devon, Eng.
62 H2 Monkton Kent, Eng.
236 G2 Monkton T. and W., Eng.
262 D3 Monkton S. Ayr., Scot.
358 E3 Monkton Pembs., Wales
350 E4 Monkton V. of Glam., Wales
94 K2 Monkton Combe B. and N.E. Som., Eng.
86 B5 Monkton Deverill Wilts., Eng.
86 B3 Monkton Farleigh Wilts., Eng.
288 E3 Monktonhall E. Lothian, Scot.
94 F4 Monkton Heathfield Som., Eng.
46 H2 Monkton Up Wimborne Dorset, Eng.
46 B3 Monkton Wyld Dorset, Eng.
236 G2 Monkwearmouth T. and W., Eng.
52 F4 Monkwood Hants., Eng.
396 I2 Monlough Castlereagh, N. Ire.
154 B2 Monmore Green W. Mids, Eng.
339 D2 Monmouth Mon., Wales
339 C2 Monmouthshire county Wales
140 B3 Monnington Court Here., Eng.
140 B3 Monnington on Wye Here., Eng.
26 G4 Monnow r. Eng./Wales
252 C3 Monreith D. and G., Scot.
94 H5 Montacute Som., Eng.
396 G4 Monteith Banbridge, N. Ire.
144 C3 Montford Shrop., Eng.
144 C3 Montford Bridge Shrop., Eng.
314 E3 Montgarrie Abers., Scot.
264 G3 Montgreenan N. Ayr., Scot.
292 F2 Montrave Fife, Scot.
308 H2 Montrose Angus, Scot.
52 C3 Monxton Hants., Eng.
180 C3 Monyash Derbys., Eng.
314 F3 Monymusk Abers., Scot.
304 H4 Monzie Perth and Kin., Scot.
280 B3 Moodiesburn N. Lanark., Scot.
136 F2 Moons Moat North Worcs., Eng.
136 F2 Moons Moat South Worcs., Eng.
292 F1 Moonzie Fife, Scot.
222 E1 Moor Allerton W. Yorks., Eng.
170 F5 Moorby Lincs., Eng.
228 H2 Moor Cock Lancs., Eng.
140 B2 Moorcot Here., Eng.
46 G2 Moor Crichel Dorset, Eng.
46 H3 Moordown Bourne., Eng.
190 F3 Moore Halton, Eng.
396 G3 Moorefield Craigavon, N. Ire.
110 B2 Moor End Bedford, Eng.
124 E6 Moor End Cambs., Eng.
110 B4 Moor End Central Bedfordshire, Eng.
232 D3 Moorend Cumbria, Eng.
232 G7 Moor End Cumbria, Eng.
210 D4 Moor End E. Riding, Eng.
98 E3 Moorend Glos., Eng.
228 E3 Moor End Lancs., Eng.
216 F3 Moor End N. Yorks., Eng.
222 C2 Moor End W. Yorks., Eng.
208 G2 Moorends S. Yorks., Eng.
180 B2 Moorfield Derbys., Eng.
388 J4 Moorfields Ballymena, N. Ire.
22 J11 Moorfoot Hills hills Scot.
52 E5 Moorgreen Hants., Eng.
176 B4 Moorgreen Notts., Eng.
86 B3 Moor Green Wilts., Eng.
154 C3 Moor Green W. Mids, Eng.
180 D3 Moorhall Derbys., Eng.
140 B3 Moorhampton Here., Eng.
222 D2 Moor Head W. Yorks., Eng.
232 D3 Moorhouse Cumbria, Eng.
176 D3 Moorhouse Notts., Eng.
208 E2 Moorhouse S. Yorks., Eng.
Moorland Som., Eng. see Northmoor Green
94 G4 Moorlinch Som., Eng.
402 F5 Moorlough Lake N. Ire.
228 G3 Moor Nook Lancs., Eng.
232 A5 Moor Row Cumbria, Eng.
216 G1 Moorsholm R. and C., Eng.
232 C7 Moor Side Cumbria, Eng.
46 F2 Moorside Dorset, Eng.
198 C2 Moorside Gtr Man., Eng.
198 E2 Moorside Gtr Man., Eng.
228 E4 Moor Side Lancs., Eng.
228 F4 Moor Side Lancs., Eng.
170 F5 Moor Side Lincs., Eng.
222 D2 Moor Side W. Yorks., Eng.
222 E2 Moorside W. Yorks., Eng.
62 D2 Moor Street Medway, Eng.
154 B3 Moor Street W. Mids, Eng.
222 G3 Moorthorpe W. Yorks., Eng.
52 D7 Moortown I.o.W., Eng.
170 D3 Moortown Lincs., Eng.
144 E3 Moortown Telford, Eng.
402 K3 Moortown Cookstown, N. Ire.
320 H4 Morangie High., Scot.
322 D4 Morar High., Scot.
22 E9 Morar hills Scot.
22 E9 Morar, Loch l. Scot.
314 D2 Moray admin. div. Scot.
22 H7 Moray Firth b. Scot.
124 C3 Morborne Cambs., Eng.
40 E2 Morchard Bishop Devon, Eng.
46 B3 Morcombelake Dorset, Eng.
162 H3 Morcott Rutland, Eng.
144 B2 Morda Shrop., Eng.
46 G3 Morden Dorset, Eng.
74 C3 Morden Gtr Lon., Eng.
74 C3 Morden Park Gtr Lon., Eng.
140 D3 Mordiford Here., Eng.
256 L2 Mordington Holdings Borders, Scot.
236 G4 Mordon Durham, Eng.
144 C4 More Shrop., Eng.
22 G6 More, Loch l. Scot.
22 I6 More, Loch l. Scot.
40 F1 Morebath Devon, Eng.
256 J3 Morebattle Borders, Scot.
228 E2 Morecambe Lancs., Eng.
24 K5 Morecambe Bay b. Eng.
86 E2 Moredon Swindon, Eng.
288 E3 Moredun Edin., Scot.
40 E3 Moreleigh Devon, Eng.
304 E4 Morenish Perth and Kin., Scot.
232 A5 Moresby Parks Cumbria, Eng.
52 E4 Morestead Hants., Eng.
46 F3 Moreton Dorset, Eng.
116 D3 Moreton Essex, Eng.
140 C2 Moreton Here., Eng.
190 C3 Moreton Merseyside, Eng.
102 F4 Moreton Oxon, Eng.
148 B4 Moreton Staffs., Eng.
148 E3 Moreton Staffs., Eng.
144 E3 Moreton Corbet Shrop., Eng.
40 E3 Moretonhampstead Devon, Eng.
98 I2 Moreton-in-Marsh Glos., Eng.
140 D3 Moreton Jeffries Here., Eng.
144 E3 Moreton Mill Shrop., Eng.
132 C4 Moreton Morrell Warks., Eng.
140 C3 Moreton on Lugg Here., Eng.
132 C4 Moreton Paddox Warks., Eng.
128 C5 Moreton Pinkney Northants., Eng.
144 E2 Moreton Say Shrop., Eng.
98 F3 Moreton Valence Glos., Eng.
356 F3 Morfa Carmar., Wales
362 D4 Morfa Cere., Wales
372 F3 Morfa Bychan Gwynedd, Wales
350 E2 Morfa Glas N.P.T., Wales
372 D3 Morfa Nefyn Gwynedd, Wales
350 G3 Morganstown Cardiff, Wales
86 E6 Morgan's Vale Wilts., Eng.
362 F2 Moriah Cere., Wales
24 K4 Moricambe b. Eng.
22 G8 Moriston r. Scot.
98 D3 Mork Glos., Eng.
232 G5 Morland Cumbria, Eng.
180 E5 Morley Derbys., Eng.
236 E4 Morley Durham, Eng.
222 E2 Morley W. Yorks., Eng.
184 F1 Morley Green Cheshire East, Eng.
166 F3 Morley St Botolph Norf., Eng.
288 E3 Morningside Edin., Scot.
280 C4 Morningside N. Lanark., Scot.
166 G4 Morningthorpe Norf., Eng.
244 G4 Morpeth Northumb., Eng.
314 F4 Morphie Abers., Scot.
148 E4 Morrey Staffs., Eng.
148 D2 Morridge Side Staffs., Eng.
148 C3 Morrilow Heath Staffs., Eng.
262 C4 Morriston S. Ayr., Scot.
350 C3 Morriston Swansea, Wales
350 G4 Morristown V. of Glam., Wales
166 E1 Morston Norf., Eng.
26 D5 Morte Bay b. Eng.
40 D1 Mortehoe Devon, Eng.
208 E3 Morthen S. Yorks., Eng.
82 D3 Mortimer W. Berks., Eng.
140 B2 Mortimer's Cross Here., Eng.
52 F2 Mortimer West End Hants., Eng.
74 C3 Mortlake Gtr Lon., Eng.
180 E4 Morton Derbys., Eng.
170 B3 Morton Lincs., Eng.
170 B5 Morton Lincs., Eng.
170 D7 Morton Lincs., Eng.
176 D4 Morton Notts., Eng.
98 D4 Morton S. Glos., Eng.
144 B3 Morton Shrop., Eng.
132 B4 Morton Bagot Warks., Eng.
166 F2 Morton on the Hill Norf., Eng.
236 E4 Morton Tinmouth Durham, Eng.
36 C3 Morvah Corn., Eng.
22 I6 Morven hill Scot.
22 J8 Morven hill Scot.
22 E9 Morvern reg. Scot.
320 H4 Morvich High., Scot.
322 E3 Morvich High., Scot.
358 E2 Morvil Pembs., Wales
144 F4 Morville Shrop., Eng.
40 D3 Morwellham Devon, Eng.
36 F1 Morwenstow Corn., Eng.
244 H4 Morwick Hall Northumb., Eng.
208 D4 Mosborough S. Yorks., Eng.
262 E3 Moscow E. Ayr., Scot.
232 D4 Mosedale Cumbria, Eng.
222 C3 Moselden Height W. Yorks., Eng.
148 C5 Moseley Staffs., Eng.
154 B2 Moseley W. Mids, Eng.
154 C3 Moseley W. Mids, Eng.
136 D2 Moseley Worcs., Eng.
198 C2 Moses Gate Gtr Man., Eng.
208 F2 Moss S. Yorks., Eng.
300 □ Moss Arg. and B., Scot.
378 G3 Moss Wrex., Wales
314 E3 Mossat Abers., Scot.
190 E3 Moss Bank Halton, Eng.
190 E3 Moss Bank Merseyside, Eng.
331 D2 Mossbank Shet., Scot.
262 D4 Mossblown S. Ayr., Scot.
256 I4 Mossburnford Borders, Scot.
252 D2 Mossdale D. and G., Scot.
280 B4 Mossend N. Lanark., Scot.
232 B5 Mosser Cumbria, Eng.
262 E3 Mossgiel E. Ayr., Scot.
184 G2 Moss Houses Cheshire East, Eng.
308 E3 Mosside of Ballinshoe Angus, Scot.
184 F3 Mossley Cheshire East, Eng.
198 E2 Mossley Gtr Man., Eng.
388 K4 Mossley Newtownabbey, N. Ire.
190 D3 Mossley Hill Merseyside, Eng.
198 D3 Moss Nook Gtr Man., Eng.
314 D2 Moss of Barmuckity Moray, Scot.
276 E2 Mosspark Glas., Scot.
252 H2 Mosspaul Hotel D. and G., Scot.
198 D3 Moss Side Gtr Man., Eng.
228 E4 Moss Side Lancs., Eng.
190 D2 Moss Side Merseyside, Eng.
388 H2 Moss-side Moyle, N. Ire.
322 J2 Moss-side High., Scot.
314 D2 Mosstodloch Moray, Scot.
308 F3 Mosston Angus, Scot.
244 F6 Mosswood Northumb., Eng.
228 F5 Mossy Lea Lancs., Eng.
46 C2 Mosterton Dorset, Eng.
198 D2 Moston Gtr Man., Eng.
144 E2 Moston Shrop., Eng.
184 E3 Moston Green Cheshire East, Eng.
378 F2 Mostyn Flints., Wales
46 F1 Motcombe Dorset, Eng.
40 E4 Mothecombe Devon, Eng.
232 E5 Motherby Cumbria, Eng.
280 C4 Motherwell N. Lanark., Scot.
74 C3 Motspur Park Gtr Lon., Eng.
74 E3 Mottingham Gtr Lon., Eng.
52 C4 Mottisfont Hants., Eng.
52 D7 Mottistone I.o.W., Eng.
198 E3 Mottram in Longdendale Gtr Man., Eng.
184 F2 Mottram St Andrew Cheshire East, Eng.
184 C2 Mouldsworth Cheshire West & Chester, Eng.
304 H2 Moulin Perth and Kin., Scot.
58 F3 Moulsecoomb B. and H., Eng.
102 E5 Moulsford Oxon, Eng.
116 E3 Moulsham Essex, Eng.
106 D2 Moulsoe M.K., Eng.
184 D2 Moulton Cheshire West & Chester, Eng.
170 F7 Moulton Lincs., Eng.
128 D4 Moulton Northants., Eng.
216 E1 Moulton N. Yorks., Eng.
120 B3 Moulton Suff., Eng.
350 F4 Moulton V. of Glam., Wales
170 F7 Moulton Chapel Lincs., Eng.
170 F7 Moulton Seas End Lincs., Eng.
166 I3 Moulton St Mary Norf., Eng.
36 F2 Mount Corn., Eng.
62 G4 Mount Kent, Eng.
222 C3 Mount W. Yorks., Eng.
222 C2 Mountain W. Yorks., Eng.
350 F2 Mountain Ash R.C.T., Wales
256 D2 Mountain Cross Borders, Scot.
358 D2 Mountain Water Pembs., Wales
36 D3 Mount Ambrose Corn., Eng.
256 F3 Mountbenger Borders, Scot.
276 D2 Mountblow W. Dun., Scot.
116 G2 Mount Bures Essex, Eng.
402 F1 Mountcastle Strabane, N. Ire.
58 I3 Mountfield E. Sussex, Eng.
402 G3 Mountfield Omagh, N. Ire.
276 E3 Mount Florida Glas., Scot.
322 H2 Mountgerald High., Scot.
388 H2 Mount Hamilton Ballymoney, N. Ire.
402 H2 Mount Hamilton Strabane, N. Ire.
36 D3 Mount Hawke Corn., Eng.
402 K3 Mountjoy Dungannon, N. Ire.
402 F3 Mountjoy Omagh, N. Ire.
184 B2 Mount Manisty Cheshire West & Chester, Eng.
116 E4 Mountnessing Essex, Eng.
396 F4 Mount Norris Armagh, N. Ire.
262 D4 Mount Oliphant S. Ayr., Scot.
339 D3 Mounton Mon., Wales
106 C3 Mount Pleasant Bucks., Eng.
184 F3 Mount Pleasant Cheshire East, Eng.
180 D6 Mount Pleasant Derbys., Eng.
180 E4 Mount Pleasant Derbys., Eng.
236 F3 Mount Pleasant Durham, Eng.
74 B2 Mount Pleasant Gtr Lon., Eng.
52 C6 Mount Pleasant Hants., Eng.
166 E3 Mount Pleasant Norf., Eng.
236 H4 Mount Pleasant Stockton, Eng.
148 B3 Mount Pleasant Stoke, Eng.
120 C4 Mount Pleasant Suff., Eng.
120 J2 Mount Pleasant Suff., Eng.
236 F2 Mount Pleasant T. and W., Eng.
154 A3 Mount Pleasant W. Mids, Eng.
222 E2 Mount Pleasant W. Yorks., Eng.
396 E3 Mount Pleasant Armagh, N. Ire.
378 G2 Mount Pleasant Flints., Wales
396 L3 Mount Ross Ards, N. Ire.
26 B7 Mount's Bay b. Eng.
378 G3 Mount Sion Wrex., Wales
162 E2 Mountsorrel Leics., Eng.
86 D5 Mount Sorrel Wilts., Eng.
222 C2 Mount Tabor W. Yorks., Eng.
276 F2 Mount Vernon Glas., Scot.
24 C4 Mourne r. N. Ire.
23 J4 Mourne Mountains hills N. Ire.
22 □N2 Mousa i. Scot.
36 C3 Mousehole Corn., Eng.
132 B4 Mousley End Warks., Eng.
252 F2 Mouswald D. and G., Scot.
148 B2 Mow Cop Staffs., Eng.
236 F4 Mowden Darl., Eng.
396 E4 Mowhan Armagh, N. Ire.
256 K4 Mowhaugh Borders, Scot.
162 E4 Mowsley Leics., Eng.
314 G4 Mowtie Abers., Scot.
154 B2 Moxley W. Mids, Eng.
396 D3 Moy Armagh, N. Ire.
322 F4 Moy High., Scot.
322 H4 Moy High., Scot.
322 I2 Moy High., Scot.
396 H5 Moyad Newry & Mourne, N. Ire.
388 G3 Moyagoney Magherafelt, N. Ire.
396 F3 Moyallon Craigavon, N. Ire.
388 I1 Moyarget Moyle, N. Ire.
402 D4 Moybane Fermanagh, N. Ire.
396 E5 Moybane Newry & Mourne, N. Ire.
402 J4 Moygashel Dungannon, N. Ire.
402 G3 Moylagh Omagh, N. Ire.
388 I2 Moyle admin. dist. N. Ire.
52 B5 Moyles Court Hants., Eng.
358 F1 Moylgrove Pembs., Wales
24 D4 Moyola r. N. Ire.
388 E2 Moys Limavady, N. Ire.
300 C5 Muasdale Arg. and B., Scot.
314 G3 Muchalls Abers., Scot.
140 C4 Much Birch Here., Eng.
140 D3 Much Cowarne Here., Eng.
140 C4 Much Dewchurch Here., Eng.
94 H4 Muchelney Som., Eng.
94 H4 Muchelney Ham Som., Eng.
110 F4 Much Hadham Herts., Eng.
228 F4 Much Hoole Lancs., Eng.

Much Hoole Town to Nidd

228 F4 Much Hoole Town Lancs., Eng.
36 F2 Muchlarnick Corn., Eng.
140 E4 Much Marcle Here., Eng.
256 E4 Muchra Borders, Scot.
322 G2 Muchrachd High., Scot.
144 E4 Much Wenlock Shrop., Eng.
22 D9 Muck i. Scot.
116 E4 Mucking Thurrock, Eng.
22 □O1 Muckle Flugga i. Scot.
46 D3 Muckleford Dorset, Eng.
22 □N2 Muckle Roe i. Scot.
148 A3 Mucklestone Staffs., Eng.
144 E3 Muckleton Shrop., Eng.
314 E3 Muckletown Abers., Scot.
144 E4 Muckley Shrop., Eng.
148 D5 Muckley Corner Staffs., Eng.
170 G4 Muckton Lincs., Eng.
320 G3 Mudale High., Scot.
198 E3 Mudd Gtr Man., Eng.
40 D1 Muddiford Devon, Eng.
58 H3 Muddles Green E. Sussex, Eng.
58 E3 Muddleswood W. Sussex, Eng.
46 I3 Mudeford Dorset, Eng.
94 I5 Mudford Som., Eng.
94 I5 Mudford Sock Som., Eng.
94 H3 Mudgley Som., Eng.
296 E6 Mugdock Stir., Scot.
322 C2 Mugeary High., Scot.
180 D5 Mugginton Derbys., Eng.
180 D4 Muggintonlane End Derbys., Eng.
236 D2 Muggleswick Durham, Eng.
78 E2 Mugswell Surr., Eng.
320 H3 Muie High., Scot.
314 C4 Muir Abers., Scot.
314 F2 Muirden Abers., Scot.
308 F3 Muirdrum Angus, Scot.
292 F2 Muiredge Fife, Scot.
276 E3 Muirend Glas., Scot.
314 E3 Muirhead Abers., Scot.
308 D4 Muirhead Angus, Scot.
292 F2 Muirhead Fife, Scot.
276 F2 Muirhead Glas., Scot.
314 C2 Muirhead Moray, Scot.
280 B3 Muirhead N. Lanark., Scot.
288 D3 Muirhouse Edin., Scot.
280 E2 Muirhouses Falk., Scot.
262 G3 Muirkirk E. Ayr., Scot.
296 F5 Muirmill Stir., Scot.
22 D6 Muirneag hill Scot.
314 E3 Muir of Fowlis Abers., Scot.
322 H2 Muir of Ord High., Scot.
314 G2 Muirtack Abers., Scot.
314 G2 Muirtack Abers., Scot.
304 H5 Muirton Perth and Kin., Scot.
304 J4 Muirton Perth and Kin., Scot.
304 J3 Muirton of Ardblair Perth and Kin., Scot.
308 G2 Muirton of Ballochy Angus, Scot.
314 F2 Muiryfold Abers., Scot.
216 C1 Muker N. Yorks., Eng.
166 G3 Mulbarton Norf., Eng.
314 D2 Mulben Moray, Scot.
326 E3 Mulhagery W. Isles, Scot.
22 E10 Mull i. Scot.
22 D9 Mull, Sound of sea chan. Scot.
396 F3 Mullabrack Banbridge, N. Ire.
40 D1 Mullacott Cross Devon, Eng.
396 F5 Mullaghbane Newry & Mourne, N. Ire.
388 I3 Mullaghboy Larne, N. Ire.
388 G4 Mullaghboy Magherafelt, N. Ire.
23 H3 Mullaghcarn hill N. Ire.
23 H3 Mullaghcloga hill N. Ire.
396 E5 Mullaghduff Newry & Mourne, N. Ire.
396 F4 Mullaghglass Newry & Mourne, N. Ire.
402 H3 Mullaghmassa Omagh, N. Ire.
396 G4 Mullaghmore Newry & Mourne, N. Ire.
402 D5 Mullan Fermanagh, N. Ire.
402 H3 Mullanmore Omagh, N. Ire.
402 H3 Mullans Town Omagh, N. Ire.
22 F8 Mullardoch, Loch l. Scot.
396 I5 Mullartown Newry & Mourne, N. Ire.
22 K5 Mull Head hd Scot.
36 D3 Mullion Corn., Eng.
36 D3 Mullion Cove Corn., Eng.
20 E4 Mull of Galloway c. Scot.
22 E12 Mull of Kintyre hd Scot.
22 D11 Mull of Oa hd Scot.
402 J3 Mulnagore Dungannon, N. Ire.
26 E4 Mumbles Head hd Wales
170 H4 Mumby Lincs., Eng.
140 D3 Munderfield Row Here., Eng.
140 D3 Munderfield Stocks Here., Eng.
166 H1 Mundesley Norf., Eng.
166 C3 Mundford Norf., Eng.
166 H3 Mundham Norf., Eng.
116 G3 Mundon Essex, Eng.
314 G3 Mundurno Aberdeen, Scot.
322 G3 Munerigie High., Scot.
288 G2 Mungoswells E. Lothian, Scot.
232 E5 Mungrisdale Cumbria, Eng.
322 I2 Munlochy High., Scot.
264 F2 Munnoch N. Ayr., Scot.
140 E3 Munsley Here., Eng.
144 D5 Munslow Shrop., Eng.
140 C3 Munstone Here., Eng.
40 E2 Murchington Devon, Eng.
102 E3 Murcott Oxon, Eng.
86 C2 Murcott Wilts., Eng.
280 C4 Murdostoun N. Lanark., Scot.
288 B3 Murieston W. Lothian, Scot.
296 D3 Murlaganmore Stir., Scot.
322 F4 Murlaggan High., Scot.
322 G4 Murlaggan High., Scot.
402 G4 Murley Dungannon, N. Ire.
329 A4 Murra Orkney, Scot.
288 D3 Murrayfield Edin., Scot.
52 G3 Murrell Green Hants., Eng.
308 E3 Murroes Angus, Scot.
124 E3 Murrow Cambs., Eng.
106 D3 Mursley Bucks., Eng.
62 E2 Murston Kent, Eng.
308 F2 Murthill Angus, Scot.
304 J3 Murthly Perth and Kin., Scot.
232 H5 Murton Cumbria, Eng.
236 G3 Murton Durham, Eng.
244 E1 Murton Northumb., Eng.
216 F3 Murton York, Eng.
350 B3 Murton Swansea, Wales
40 G2 Musbury Devon, Eng.
46 H3 Muscliff Bourne., Eng.
Musdàl Arg. and B., Scot. see Musdale
300 D2 Musdale Arg. and B., Scot.
288 E3 Musselburgh E. Lothian, Scot.
166 I2 Mustard Hyrn Norf., Eng.
162 G1 Muston Leics., Eng.
216 I2 Muston N. Yorks., Eng.
136 D1 Mustow Green Worcs., Eng.
74 D2 Muswell Hill Gtr Lon., Eng.
120 I2 Mutford Suff., Eng.
304 G5 Muthill Perth and Kin., Scot.
40 D3 Mutley Plymouth, Eng.
144 F3 Muxton Telford, Eng.
320 J2 Mybster High., Scot.
356 H2 Myddfai Carmar., Wales
144 D3 Myddle Shrop., Eng.
144 D3 Myddlewood Shrop., Eng.
362 E3 Mydroilyn Cere., Wales
228 F3 Myerscough College Lancs., Eng.
36 D3 Mylor Corn., Eng.
36 D3 Mylor Bridge Corn., Eng.
350 G3 Mynachdy Cardiff, Wales
358 F2 Mynachlog-ddu Pembs., Wales
144 C4 Myndtown Shrop., Eng.
339 D3 Mynydd-bach Mon., Wales
350 C3 Mynydd-bach Swansea, Wales
350 H3 Mynyddislwyn Caerp., Wales
372 F1 Mynydd Llandygai Gwynedd, Wales
371 C2 Mynyddmechell I.o.A., Wales
356 E3 Mynyddygarreg Carmar., Wales
372 C3 Mynytho Gwynedd, Wales
314 F3 Myrebird Abers., Scot.
78 B2 Mytchett Surr., Eng.
228 B2 Mytholm W. Yorks., Eng.
222 C2 Mytholmroyd W. Yorks., Eng.
228 E4 Mythop Lancs., Eng.
216 F2 Myton-on-Swale N. Yorks., Eng.
144 D3 Mytton Shrop., Eng.

N

320 D4 Naast High., Scot.
228 G4 Nab's Head Lancs., Eng.
326 D3 Na-Buirgh W. Isles, Scot.
216 F3 Naburn York, Eng.
222 D2 Nab Wood W. Yorks., Eng.
62 G3 Nackington Kent, Eng.
120 G4 Nacton Suff., Eng.
26 I5 Nadder r. Eng.
210 F2 Nafferton E. Riding, Eng.
98 D2 Nailbridge Glos., Eng.
94 F4 Nailsbourne Som., Eng.
94 H2 Nailsea N. Som., Eng.
162 C3 Nailstone Leics., Eng.
98 F3 Nailsworth Glos., Eng.
322 J2 Nairn High., Scot.
22 I7 Nairn r. Scot.
36 C3 Nancledra Corn., Eng.
372 C3 Nanhoron Gwynedd, Wales
372 G4 Nannau Gwynedd, Wales
372 F4 Nannerch Flints., Wales
162 D2 Nanpantan Leics., Eng.
36 E2 Nanpean Corn., Eng.
36 E2 Nanstallon Corn., Eng.
26 F4 Nant Bran r. Wales
366 E8 Nant-ddu Powys, Wales
350 D2 Nanternis Cere., Wales
356 E2 Nantgaredig Carmar., Wales
350 G3 Nantgarw R.C.T., Wales
366 F5 Nant-glas Powys, Wales
372 E3 Nantglyn Denb., Wales
366 D4 Nantgwyn Powys, Wales
372 E2 Nantlle Gwynedd, Wales
144 B3 Nantmawr Shrop., Eng.
378 G3 Nant Mawr Flints., Wales
366 E5 Nantmel Powys, Wales
372 F3 Nantmor Gwynedd, Wales
372 F2 Nant Peris Gwynedd, Wales
184 D3 Nantwich Cheshire East, Eng.
356 E2 Nantycaws Carmar., Wales
339 C2 Nant-y-derry Mon., Wales
366 D2 Nant-y-dugoed Powys, Wales
350 E3 Nantyffyllon Bridg., Wales
350 G2 Nantyglo B. Gwent, Wales
144 B2 Nant-y-Gollen Shrop., Eng.
366 E5 Nant-y-groes Powys, Wales
26 E3 Nant-y-moch Reservoir resr Wales
350 E3 Nant-y-moel Bridg., Wales
378 B2 Nant-y-Pandy Conwy, Wales
106 D5 Naphill Bucks., Eng.
148 A3 Napley Heath Staffs., Eng.
216 C3 Nappa N. Yorks., Eng.
132 E4 Napton on the Hill Warks., Eng.
358 F3 Narberth Pembs., Wales
162 D3 Narborough Leics., Eng.
166 C2 Narborough Norf., Eng.
300 D3 Narrachan Arg. and B., Scot.
372 E2 Nasareth Gwynedd, Wales
128 D3 Naseby Northants., Eng.
106 C3 Nash Bucks., Eng.
140 A2 Nash Here., Eng.
62 H3 Nash Kent, Eng.
144 E5 Nash Shrop., Eng.
339 C3 Nash Newp., Wales
350 F4 Nash V. of Glam., Wales
106 D4 Nash Lee Bucks., Eng.
62 C2 Nash Street Kent, Eng.
128 G2 Nassington Northants., Eng.
110 E4 Nasty Herts., Eng.
232 H6 Nateby Cumbria, Eng.
228 F3 Nateby Lancs., Eng.
52 G3 Nately Scures Hants., Eng.
232 F7 Natland Cumbria, Eng.
120 E4 Naughton Suff., Eng.
98 I2 Naunton Glos., Eng.
136 D3 Naunton Worcs., Eng.
136 E2 Naunton Beauchamp Worcs., Eng.
396 D3 Navan Armagh, N. Ire.
24 E2 Nave Island i. Scot.
170 C5 Navenby Lincs., Eng.
22 H5 Naver r. Scot.
22 H6 Naver, Loch l. Scot.
116 D4 Navestock Essex, Eng.
116 D4 Navestock Side Essex, Eng.
320 J3 Navidale High., Scot.
322 I2 Navity High., Scot.
120 E5 Nayland Suff., Eng.
116 C3 Nazeing Essex, Eng.
116 C3 Nazeing Gate Essex, Eng.
52 B6 Neacroft Hants., Eng.
23 J3 Neagh, Lough l. N. Ire.
132 C3 Neal's Green Warks., Eng.
331 D3 Neap Shet., Scot.
170 B2 Neap House N. Lincs., Eng.
232 E6 Near Sawrey Cumbria, Eng.
106 D3 Nearton End Bucks., Eng.
74 C2 Neasden Gtr Lon., Eng.
236 G5 Neasham Darl., Eng.
102 C3 Neat Enstone Oxon, Eng.
26 E4 Neath r. Wales
52 G4 Neatham Hants., Eng.
350 D2 Neath Port Talbot admin. div. Wales
166 H2 Neatishead Norf., Eng.
362 F3 Nebo Cere., Wales
378 C3 Nebo Conwy, Wales
372 E2 Nebo Gwynedd, Wales
371 D2 Nebo I.o.A., Wales
154 C2 Nechells W. Mids, Eng.
166 D3 Necton Norf., Eng.
388 D2 Ned Limavady, N. Ire.
320 E3 Nedd High., Scot.
244 H5 Nedderton Northumb., Eng.
120 E4 Nedging Suff., Eng.
120 E4 Nedging Tye Suff., Eng.
166 G4 Needham Norf., Eng.
120 F4 Needham Market Suff., Eng.
120 C3 Needham Street Suff., Eng.
124 D5 Needingworth Cambs., Eng.
148 E4 Needwood Staffs., Eng.
144 F5 Neen Savage Shrop., Eng.
144 F5 Neen Sollars Shrop., Eng.
144 E5 Neenton Shrop., Eng.
372 C3 Nefyn Gwynedd, Wales
94 I3 Neighbourne Som., Eng.
276 D3 Neilston E. Renf., Scot.
102 C2 Neithrop Oxon, Eng.
402 E3 Nelsherry Fermanagh, N. Ire.
228 I3 Nelson Lancs., Eng.
350 G3 Nelson Caerp., Wales
244 H5 Nelson Village Northumb., Eng.
268 D2 Nemphlar S. Lanark., Scot.
94 H2 Nempnett Thrubwell B. and N.E. Som., Eng.
26 M2 Nene r. Eng.
232 H4 Nenthall Cumbria, Eng.
232 H4 Nenthead Cumbria, Eng.
256 I3 Nenthorn Borders, Scot.
22 J4 Neolithic Orkney tourist site Scot.
20 F2 Neolithic Orkney tourist site Scot.
300 A4 Nerabus Arg. and B., Scot.
378 G3 Nercwys Flints., Wales
300 B4 Neriby Arg. and B., Scot.
268 B2 Nerston S. Lanark., Scot.
256 E2 Nesbit Northumb., Eng.
216 D3 Nesfield N. Yorks., Eng.
184 A2 Ness Cheshire West & Chester, Eng.
22 H8 Ness r. Scot.
22 G8 Ness, Loch l. Scot.
144 C3 Nesscliffe Shrop., Eng.
329 B3 Ness of Tenston Orkney, Scot.
184 A2 Neston Cheshire West & Chester, Eng.
86 B3 Neston Wilts., Eng.
184 F2 Nether Alderley Cheshire East, Eng.
262 D4 Nether Auchendrane S. Ayr., Scot.
86 E4 Netheravon Wilts., Eng.
252 C3 Nether Barr D. and G., Scot.
256 H2 Nether Blainslie Borders, Scot.
314 F2 Netherbrae Abers., Scot.
329 B3 Netherbrough Orkney, Scot.
162 F2 Nether Broughton Leics., Eng.
268 C2 Netherburn S. Lanark., Scot.
228 G1 Nether Burrow Lancs., Eng.
46 C3 Netherbury Dorset, Eng.
232 E2 Netherby Cumbria, Eng.
216 E3 Netherby N. Yorks., Eng.
46 E3 Nether Cerne Dorset, Eng.
46 D2 Nether Compton Dorset, Eng.
102 D3 Nethercott Oxon, Eng.
256 F4 Nether Dalgliesh Borders, Scot.
314 D2 Nether Dallachy Moray, Scot.
308 D3 Nether Edge S. Yorks., Eng.
180 D3 Nether End Derbys., Eng.
222 E3 Nether End W. Yorks., Eng.
58 I3 Netherfield E. Sussex, Eng.
170 F5 Netherfield Notts., Eng.
268 B2 Netherfield S. Lanark., Scot.
314 G2 Nether Glasslaw Abers., Scot.
264 E2 Netherhall N. Ayr., Scot.
86 D5 Netherhampton Wilts., Eng.
180 E3 Nether Handley Derbys., Eng.
308 D3 Nether Handwick Angus, Scot.
208 D3 Nether Haugh S. Yorks., Eng.
46 C2 Netherhay Dorset, Eng.
176 D3 Nether Headon Notts., Eng.
180 E4 Nether Heage Derbys., Eng.
216 C2 Nether Heselden N. Yorks., Eng.
128 C4 Nether Heyford Northants., Eng.
228 F2 Nether Kellet Lancs., Eng.
314 H2 Nether Kinmundy Abers., Scot.
148 D3 Netherland Green Staffs., Eng.
180 F3 Nether Langwith Derbys., Eng.
314 F2 Nether Lenshie Abers., Scot.
314 G3 Netherley Abers., Scot.
180 D2 Nether Loads Derbys., Eng.
252 F2 Nethermill D. and G., Scot.
180 E3 Nether Moor Derbys., Eng.
314 G2 Nethermuir Abers., Scot.
222 D2 Netheroyd Hill W. Yorks., Eng.
180 D3 Nether Padley Derbys., Eng.
314 G4 Nether Pitforthie Abers., Scot.
216 F3 Nether Poppleton York, Eng.
180 D6 Netherseal Derbys., Eng.
262 F3 Nethershield E. Ayr., Scot.
144 B5 Nether Skyborry Shrop., Eng.
94 F4 Nether Stowey Som., Eng.
86 C3 Netherstreet Wilts., Eng.
252 D3 Netherthird D. and G., Scot.
262 F4 Netherthird E. Ayr., Scot.
222 D3 Netherthong W. Yorks., Eng.
180 E3 Netherthorpe Derbys., Eng.
208 E4 Netherthorpe S. Yorks., Eng.
184 C2 Netherton Cheshire West & Chester, Eng.
232 B4 Netherton Cumbria, Eng.
40 F3 Netherton Devon, Eng.
52 D3 Netherton Hants., Eng.
190 D3 Netherton Merseyside, Eng.
244 E3 Netherton Northumb., Eng.
102 D4 Netherton Oxon, Eng.
154 B3 Netherton W. Mids, Eng.
136 E3 Netherton Worcs., Eng.
222 D3 Netherton W. Yorks., Eng.
222 E3 Netherton W. Yorks., Eng.
308 F2 Netherton Angus, Scot.
280 C4 Netherton N. Lanark., Scot.
304 J3 Netherton Perth and Kin., Scot.
268 D2 Netherton S. Lanark., Scot.
244 E3 Netherton Burnfoot Northumb., Eng.
244 E3 Netherton Northside Northumb., Eng.
232 A6 Nethertown Cumbria, Eng.
148 D4 Nethertown Staffs., Eng.
329 C5 Nethertown Orkney, Scot.
292 E2 Nether Urquhart Fife, Scot.
52 C4 Nether Wallop Hants., Eng.
232 B6 Nether Wasdale Cumbria, Eng.
262 G3 Nether Wellwood E. Ayr., Scot.
232 D4 Nether Welton Cumbria, Eng.
98 I2 Nether Westcote Glos., Eng.
132 C2 Nether Whitacre Warks., Eng.
106 C4 Nether Winchendon Bucks., Eng.
244 F4 Netherwitton Northumb., Eng.
252 F2 Netherwood D. and G., Scot.
262 G3 Netherwood E. Ayr., Scot.
102 D3 Nether Worton Oxon, Eng.
322 K3 Nethy Bridge High., Scot.
52 D5 Netley Abbey Hants., Eng.
52 C5 Netley Marsh Hants., Eng.
102 F5 Nettlebed Oxon, Eng.
94 I3 Nettlebridge Som., Eng.
46 C3 Nettlecombe Dorset, Eng.
52 E7 Nettlecombe I.o.W., Eng.
94 D4 Nettlecombe Som., Eng.
110 B5 Nettleden Herts., Eng.
170 D4 Nettleham Lincs., Eng.
62 C3 Nettlestead Kent, Eng.
120 F4 Nettlestead Suff., Eng.
62 C3 Nettlestead Green Kent, Eng.
52 F6 Nettlestone I.o.W., Eng.
116 C3 Nettleswell Essex, Eng.
236 F3 Nettlesworth Durham, Eng.
170 D3 Nettleton Lincs., Eng.
86 B2 Nettleton Wilts., Eng.
222 C3 Nettleton Hill W. Yorks., Eng.
86 E5 Netton Wilts., Eng.
362 E3 Neuadd Cere., Wales
371 C2 Neuadd I.o.A., Wales
366 E6 Neuadd Powys, Wales
116 F4 Nevendon Essex, Eng.
358 F1 Nevern Pembs., Wales
162 G3 Nevill Holt Leics., Eng.
22 E8 Nevis, Loch inlet Scot.
252 F3 New Abbey D. and G., Scot.
314 G2 New Aberdour Abers., Scot.
74 D3 New Addington Gtr Lon., Eng.
222 D1 Newall W. Yorks., Eng.
198 D3 Newall Green Gtr Man., Eng.
52 F4 New Alresford Hants., Eng.
304 K3 New Alyth Perth and Kin., Scot.
124 C3 Newark Peterb., Eng.
329 G2 Newark Orkney, Scot.
176 E4 Newark-on-Trent Notts., Eng.
132 C2 New Arley Warks., Eng.
210 F3 New Arram E. Riding, Eng.
280 C4 Newarthill N. Lanark., Scot.
62 B2 New Ash Green Kent, Eng.
176 E4 New Balderton Notts., Eng.
170 D4 Newball Lincs., Eng.
62 B2 New Barn Kent, Eng.
62 G4 Newbarn Kent, Eng.
74 C2 New Barnet Gtr Lon., Eng.
232 C8 Newbarns Cumbria, Eng.
128 E4 New Barton Northants., Eng.
288 E3 Newbattle Midlothian, Scot.
74 D3 New Beckenham Gtr Lon., Eng.
256 H3 New Belses Borders, Scot.
244 F3 New Bewick Northumb., Eng.
232 B6 Newbiggin Cumbria, Eng.
232 D8 Newbiggin Cumbria, Eng.
232 F3 Newbiggin Cumbria, Eng.
232 F5 Newbiggin Cumbria, Eng.
232 G5 Newbiggin Cumbria, Eng.
236 C4 Newbiggin Durham, Eng.
244 E6 Newbiggin Northumb., Eng.
216 C2 Newbiggin N. Yorks., Eng.
216 D2 Newbiggin N. Yorks., Eng.
244 H4 Newbiggin-by-the-Sea Northumb., Eng.
314 C4 Newbigging Abers., Scot.
314 G3 Newbigging Abers., Scot.
308 D3 Newbigging Angus, Scot.
308 E3 Newbigging Angus, Scot.
308 F3 Newbigging Angus, Scot.
268 E2 Newbigging S. Lanark., Scot.
232 H6 Newbiggin-on-Lune Cumbria, Eng.
180 E3 Newbold Derbys., Eng.
162 C2 Newbold Leics., Eng.
132 E3 Newbold on Avon Warks., Eng.
132 C5 Newbold on Stour Warks., Eng.
132 C4 Newbold Pacey Warks., Eng.
162 C3 Newbold Verdon Leics., Eng.
170 F5 New Bolingbroke Lincs., Eng.
180 F3 New Bolsover Derbys., Eng.
124 C3 Newborough Peterb., Eng.
148 E4 Newborough Staffs., Eng.
371 C4 Newborough I.o.A., Wales
190 F3 New Boston Merseyside, Eng.
128 B5 Newbottle Northants., Eng.
236 G2 Newbottle T. and W., Eng.
120 G4 Newbourne Suff., Eng.
106 D2 New Bradwell M.K., Eng.
236 F3 New Brancepeth Durham, Eng.
36 C3 Newbridge Corn., Eng.
36 G2 Newbridge Corn., Eng.
58 G2 Newbridge E. Sussex, Eng.
52 C5 Newbridge Hants., Eng.
52 D6 Newbridge I.o.W., Eng.
216 G2 Newbridge N. Yorks., Eng.
102 C4 Newbridge Oxon, Eng.
252 F2 New Bridge D. and G., Scot.
288 C3 Newbridge Edin., Scot.
358 E2 Newbridge Pembs., Wales
378 G4 Newbridge Wrex., Wales
136 D3 Newbridge Green Worcs., Eng.
339 C3 Newbridge-on-Usk Mon., Wales
366 E5 Newbridge on Wye Powys, Wales
52 G5 New Brighton Hants., Eng.
190 C3 New Brighton Merseyside, Eng.
222 E2 New Brighton W. Yorks., Eng.
378 G2 New Brighton Flints., Wales
378 G3 New Brighton Wrex., Wales
180 E3 New Brimington Derbys., Eng.
176 B4 New Brinsley Notts., Eng.
244 D5 Newbrough Northumb., Eng.
378 G3 New Broughton Wrex., Wales
166 F4 New Buckenham Norf., Eng.
388 B3 New Buildings Derry, N. Ire.
228 F5 Newburgh Lancs., Eng.
314 G2 Newburgh Abers., Scot.
314 G3 Newburgh Abers., Scot.
256 F4 Newburgh Borders, Scot.
292 E1 Newburgh Fife, Scot.
236 F2 Newburn T. and W., Eng.
94 J3 Newbury Som., Eng.
82 C3 Newbury W. Berks., Eng.
86 B4 Newbury Wilts., Eng.
Newbury admin. div. Eng. see West Berkshire
74 E2 Newbury Park Gtr Lon., Eng.
232 G5 Newby Cumbria, Eng.
228 H3 Newby Lancs., Eng.
216 B2 Newby N. Yorks., Eng.
216 F1 Newby N. Yorks., Eng.
232 E7 Newby Bridge Cumbria, Eng.
216 E3 Newby Cote N. Yorks., Eng.
232 E3 Newby Cross Cumbria, Eng.
232 F3 Newby East Cumbria, Eng.
314 G2 New Byth Abers., Scot.
232 E3 Newby West Cumbria, Eng.
144 B5 Newcastle Shrop., Eng.
396 L3 Newcastle Ards, N. Ire.
396 I4 Newcastle Down, N. Ire.
292 E2 Newcastle Fife, Scot.
350 E3 Newcastle Bridg., Wales
339 D1 Newcastle Mon., Wales
362 D4 Newcastle Emlyn Carmar., Wales
236 E1 Newcastle International airport Eng.
256 H5 Newcastleton Borders, Scot.
148 B2 Newcastle-under-Lyme Staffs., Eng.
236 F2 Newcastle upon Tyne T. and W., Eng.
166 G3 New Catton Norf., Eng.
148 B2 Newchapel Stoke, Eng.
78 E3 Newchapel Surr., Eng.
358 G1 Newchapel Pembs., Wales
74 E3 New Charlton Gtr Lon., Eng.
52 F4 New Cheriton Hants., Eng.
124 E5 New Chesterton Cambs., Eng.
52 E6 Newchurch I.o.W., Eng.
62 F4 Newchurch Kent, Eng.
228 I3 Newchurch Lancs., Eng.
228 I4 Newchurch Lancs., Eng.
148 E4 Newchurch Staffs., Eng.
356 D2 Newchurch Carmar., Wales
339 D2 Newchurch Mon., Wales
366 G6 Newchurch Powys, Wales
166 G3 New Costessey Norf., Eng.
236 F4 New Coundon Durham, Eng.
288 E3 Newcraighall Edin., Scot.
74 D3 New Cross Gtr Lon., Eng.
94 H5 New Cross Som., Eng.
362 F2 New Cross Cere., Wales
132 C4 New Cubbington Warks., Eng.
262 F4 New Cumnock E. Ayr., Scot.
314 G2 New Deer Abers., Scot.
244 H5 New Delaval Northumb., Eng.
198 E2 New Delph Gtr Man., Eng.
78 E3 Newdigate Surr., Eng.
128 D4 New Duston Northants., Eng.
208 E3 New Edlington S. Yorks., Eng.
314 D2 New Elgin Moray, Scot.
210 G3 New Ellerby E. Riding, Eng.
82 F3 Newell Green Brack. F., Eng.
74 E3 New Eltham Gtr Lon., Eng.
136 F2 New End Worcs., Eng.
62 D4 Newenden Kent, Eng.
124 C3 New England Peterb., Eng.
98 E2 Newent Glos., Eng.
98 D3 Newerne Glos., Eng.
222 E2 New Farnley W. Yorks., Eng.
190 D3 New Ferry Merseyside, Eng.
388 H4 New Ferry Ballymena, N. Ire.
236 E3 Newfield Durham, Eng.
236 F2 Newfield Durham, Eng.
124 C3 New Fletton Peterb., Eng.
26 I6 New Forest National Park nat. park Eng.
52 F3 Newfound Hants., Eng.
222 G2 New Fryston W. Yorks., Eng.
358 D2 Newgale Pembs., Wales
252 D2 New Galloway D. and G., Scot.
166 F1 Newgate Norf., Eng.
110 E5 Newgate Street Herts., Eng.
292 G2 New Gilston Fife, Scot.
331 E1 Newgord Shet., Scot.
110 C5 New Greens Herts., Eng.
36 □ New Grimsby I.o.S., Eng.
184 D3 Newhall Cheshire East, Eng.
180 D6 Newhall Derbys., Eng.
244 G2 Newham Northumb., Eng.
74 E2 Newham met. bor. Gtr Lon., Eng.
244 G2 Newham Hall Northumb., Eng.
244 H5 New Hartley Northumb., Eng.
58 G4 Newhaven E. Sussex, Eng.
288 D3 Newhaven Edin., Scot.
78 D1 New Haw Surr., Eng.
102 D4 New Headington Oxon, Eng.
244 D2 New Heaton Northumb., Eng.
358 F3 New Hedges Pembs., Wales
236 G2 New Herrington T. and W., Eng.
198 E2 Newhey Gtr Man., Eng.
208 D3 Newhill S. Yorks., Eng.
102 D4 New Hinksey Oxon, Eng.
170 D1 New Holland N. Lincs., Eng.
180 F3 New Houghton Derbys., Eng.
166 C2 New Houghton Norf., Eng.
280 C3 Newhouse N. Lanark., Scot.
216 C2 New Houses N. Yorks., Eng.
162 E3 New Humberstone Leicester, Eng.
236 E3 New Hunwick Durham, Eng.
232 F7 New Hutton Cumbria, Eng.
62 C3 New Hythe Kent, Eng.
58 G3 Newick E. Sussex, Eng.
62 G4 Newingreen Kent, Eng.
74 D2 Newington Gtr Lon., Eng.
62 E2 Newington Kent, Eng.
62 G4 Newington Kent, Eng.
176 D2 Newington Notts., Eng.
102 E5 Newington Oxon, Eng.
288 D3 Newington Edin., Scot.
98 F4 Newington Bagpath Glos., Eng.
292 F2 New Inn Fife, Scot.
350 H2 New Inn B. Gwent, Wales
356 E1 New Inn Carmar., Wales
339 D2 New Inn Mon., Wales
144 B5 New Invention Shrop., Eng.
154 B2 New Invention W. Mids, Eng.
322 E2 New Kelso High., Scot.
236 F2 New Kyo Durham, Eng.
236 F2 New Lambton T. and W., Eng.
268 D3 New Lanark S. Lanark., Scot.
22 I11 New Lanark World Heritage Site tourist site Scot.
232 D7 Newland Cumbria, Eng.
210 D4 Newland E. Riding, Eng.
98 D3 Newland Glos., Eng.
210 F4 Newland Hull, Eng.
216 G3 Newland N. Yorks., Eng.
102 C4 Newland Oxon, Eng.
136 D3 Newland Worcs., Eng.
222 F2 Newland Hall W. Yorks., Eng.
288 E3 Newlandrig Midlothian, Scot.
232 D4 Newlands Cumbria, Eng.
116 F4 Newlands Essex, Eng.
244 F6 Newlands Northumb., Eng.
256 H5 Newlands Borders, Scot.
276 E3 Newlands Glas., Scot.
78 C2 Newland's Corner Surr., Eng.
320 J2 Newlands of Geise High., Scot.
228 E5 New Lane Lancs., Eng.
228 F4 New Lane End Warr., Eng.
170 G5 New Leake Lincs., Eng.
314 G2 New Leeds Abers., Scot.
314 E3 New Leslie Abers., Scot.
208 D2 New Lodge S. Yorks., Eng.
228 F4 New Longton Lancs., Eng.
252 B3 New Luce D. and G., Scot.
36 C3 Newlyn Corn., Eng.
314 G3 Newmachar Abers., Scot.
280 C4 Newmains N. Lanark., Scot.
268 D3 New Mains S. Lanark., Scot.
314 G4 New Mains of Ury Abers., Scot.
74 C3 New Malden Gtr Lon., Eng.
116 D3 Newman's End Essex, Eng.
120 D4 Newman's Green Suff., Eng.
120 B3 Newmarket Suff., Eng.
326 E2 Newmarket W. Isles, Scot.
216 F1 New Marske R. and C., Eng.
144 C2 New Marton Shrop., Eng.
36 C3 New Mill Corn., Eng.
110 B5 New Mill Herts., Eng.
222 D3 New Mill W. Yorks., Eng.
388 J4 Newmill Antrim, N. Ire.
314 F4 Newmill Abers., Scot.
314 G2 Newmill Abers., Scot.
314 G3 Newmill Abers., Scot.
256 G4 Newmill Borders, Scot.
314 E2 Newmill Moray, Scot.
110 C4 New Mill End Central Bedfordshire, Eng.
222 E3 Newmillerdam W. Yorks., Eng.
308 E2 Newmill of Inshewan Angus, Scot.
36 E3 New Mills Corn., Eng.
180 B2 New Mills Derbys., Eng.
98 D3 New Mills Glos., Eng.
402 J3 Newmills Dungannon, N. Ire.
322 I3 Newmills High., Scot.
339 D2 New Mills Mon., Wales
366 F3 New Mills Powys, Wales
304 I4 Newmiln Perth and Kin., Scot.
304 J4 Newmiln Perth and Kin., Scot.
262 E3 Newmilns E. Ayr., Scot.
52 B6 New Milton Hants., Eng.
116 I2 New Mistley Essex, Eng.
358 F2 New Moat Pembs., Wales
116 E3 Newney Green Essex, Eng.
98 E3 Newnham Glos., Eng.
52 G3 Newnham Hants., Eng.
110 D3 Newnham Herts., Eng.
62 E3 Newnham Kent, Eng.
128 C4 Newnham Northants., Eng.
136 B2 Newnham Bridge Worcs., Eng.
132 E3 Newnham Paddox Warks., Eng.
314 E2 Newnoth Abers., Scot.
176 C3 New Ollerton Notts., Eng.
300 D5 New Orleans Arg. and B., Scot.
154 C2 New Oscott W. Mids, Eng.
36 F2 New Park Corn., Eng.
216 E2 New Park N. Yorks., Eng.
162 D3 New Parks Leicester, Eng.
314 G2 New Pitsligo Abers., Scot.
36 E2 New Polzeath Corn., Eng.
40 D1 Newport Devon, Eng.
210 D4 Newport E. Riding, Eng.
116 D2 Newport Essex, Eng.
98 E3 Newport Glos., Eng.
52 E6 Newport I.o.W., Eng.
166 J2 Newport Norf., Eng.
94 G4 Newport Som., Eng.
144 F3 Newport Telford, Eng.
320 J3 Newport High., Scot.
339 C3 Newport Newp., Wales
339 C3 Newport admin. div. Wales
26 C3 Newport Bay b. Wales
292 G1 Newport-on-Tay Fife, Scot.
106 D2 Newport Pagnell M.K., Eng.
58 D2 Newpound Common W. Sussex, Eng.
262 D4 New Prestwick S. Ayr., Scot.
36 D2 Newquay Corn., Eng.
362 D3 New Quay Cere., Wales
36 D2 Newquay Cornwall International airport Eng.
166 H3 New Rackheath Norf., Eng.
366 G5 New Radnor Powys, Wales
232 E4 New Rent Cumbria, Eng.
244 F6 New Ridley Northumb., Eng.
222 D2 New Road Side W. Yorks., Eng.
62 F5 New Romney Kent, Eng.
208 F3 New Rossington S. Yorks., Eng.
228 G3 New Row Lancs., Eng.
362 G2 New Row Cere., Wales
396 G4 Newry Newry & Mourne, N. Ire.
396 G5 Newry and Mourne admin. dist. N. Ire.
23 J4 Newry Canal canal N. Ire.
222 F2 Newsam Green W. Yorks., Eng.
180 F5 New Sawley Derbys., Eng.
184 F2 Newsbank Cheshire East, Eng.
314 F2 Newseat Abers., Scot.
110 F3 Newsells Herts., Eng.
228 F4 Newsham Lancs., Eng.
244 H5 Newsham Northumb., Eng.
216 D1 Newsham N. Yorks., Eng.
216 E2 Newsham N. Yorks., Eng.
210 C4 Newsholme E. Riding, Eng.
228 I3 Newsholme Lancs., Eng.
222 C1 Newsholme W. Yorks., Eng.
244 G2 New Shoreston Northumb., Eng.
236 G2 New Silksworth T. and W., Eng.
222 D3 Newsome W. Yorks., Eng.
166 G3 New Sprowston Norf., Eng.
244 G2 Newstead Northumb., Eng.
176 B4 Newstead Notts., Eng.
256 H3 Newstead Borders, Scot.
280 C4 New Stevenston N. Lanark., Scot.
162 C2 New Swannington Leics., Eng.
176 B4 Newthorpe Notts., Eng.
216 F3 Newthorpe N. Yorks., Eng.
170 D3 Newtoft Lincs., Eng.
124 E2 Newton Cambs., Eng.
124 E6 Newton Cambs., Eng.
184 C2 Newton Cheshire West & Chester, Eng.
184 C3 Newton Cheshire West & Chester, Eng.
232 C8 Newton Cumbria, Eng.
180 E4 Newton Derbys., Eng.
198 E3 Newton Gtr Man., Eng.
140 B2 Newton Here., Eng.
140 B4 Newton Here., Eng.
140 C2 Newton Here., Eng.
228 E4 Newton Lancs., Eng.
228 G1 Newton Lancs., Eng.
228 H3 Newton Lancs., Eng.
170 D6 Newton Lincs., Eng.
166 D2 Newton Norf., Eng.
128 E3 Newton Northants., Eng.
244 E3 Newton Northumb., Eng.
244 F6 Newton Northumb., Eng.
176 D5 Newton Notts., Eng.
98 D4 Newton S. Glos., Eng.
144 C2 Newton Shrop., Eng.
94 E4 Newton Som., Eng.
148 D4 Newton Staffs., Eng.
120 D4 Newton Suff., Eng.
208 F2 Newton S. Yorks., Eng.
132 E3 Newton Warks., Eng.
86 F5 Newton Wilts., Eng.
154 C2 Newton W. Mids, Eng.
222 G2 Newton W. Yorks., Eng.
314 E2 Newton Abers., Scot.
314 H2 Newton Abers., Scot.
300 E3 Newton Arg. and B., Scot.
256 I4 Newton Borders, Scot.
252 F2 Newton D. and G., Scot.
320 E3 Newton High., Scot.
320 H5 Newton High., Scot.
322 H2 Newton High., Scot.
322 I2 Newton High., Scot.
314 D2 Newton Moray, Scot.
264 C2 Newton N. Ayr., Scot.
304 H4 Newton Perth and Kin., Scot.
268 D3 Newton S. Lanark., Scot.
288 C3 Newton W. Lothian, Scot.
350 D4 Newton Bridg., Wales
350 H4 Newton Cardiff, Wales
358 D2 Newton Pembs., Wales
358 D4 Newton Pembs., Wales
350 B3 Newton Swansea, Wales
40 F3 Newton Abbot Devon, Eng.
252 E2 Newtonairds D. and G., Scot.
232 C3 Newton Arlosh Cumbria, Eng.
236 F4 Newton Aycliffe Durham, Eng.
236 H4 Newton Bewley Hartlepool, Eng.
106 E2 Newton Blossomville M.K., Eng.
128 F4 Newton Bromswold Northants., Eng.
162 C2 Newton Burgoland Leics., Eng.
40 D4 Newton Ferrers Devon, Eng.
166 G3 Newton Flotman Norf., Eng.
288 E3 Newtongrange Midlothian, Scot.
339 D3 Newton Green Mon., Wales
162 E3 Newton Harcourt Leics., Eng.
198 D2 Newton Heath Gtr Man., Eng.
314 G3 Newtonhill Abers., Scot.
190 F3 Newton-le-Willows Merseyside, Eng.
216 D2 Newton-le-Willows N. Yorks., Eng.
106 D3 Newton Longville Bucks., Eng.
276 D3 Newton Mearns E. Renf., Scot.
308 G2 Newtonmill Angus, Scot.
322 I3 Newtonmore High., Scot.
102 E3 Newton Morrell Oxon, Eng.
358 E3 Newton Mountain Pembs., Wales
308 F3 Newton of Affleck Angus, Scot.
304 J5 Newton of Balcanquhal Perth and Kin., Scot.
314 C2 Newton of Dalvey Moray, Scot.
292 E2 Newton of Falkland Fife, Scot.
322 I2 Newton of Leys High., Scot.
262 D4 Newton on Ayr S. Ayr., Scot.
216 F2 Newton-on-Ouse N. Yorks., Eng.
216 G2 Newton-on-Rawcliffe N. Yorks., Eng.
144 D3 Newton on the Hill Shrop., Eng.
244 G3 Newton-on-the-Moor Northumb., Eng.
170 B4 Newton on Trent Lincs., Eng.
40 G2 Newton Poppleford Devon, Eng.
102 E3 Newton Purcell Oxon, Eng.
132 C2 Newton Regis Warks., Eng.
232 F4 Newton Reigny Cumbria, Eng.
40 F2 Newton St Cyres Devon, Eng.
180 D6 Newton Solney Derbys., Eng.
52 D4 Newton Stacey Hants., Eng.
252 C3 Newton Stewart D. and G., Scot.
166 G2 Newton St Faith Norf., Eng.
94 J2 Newton St Loe B. and N.E. Som., Eng.
40 D2 Newton St Petrock Devon, Eng.
86 E5 Newton Tony Wilts., Eng.
40 D1 Newton Tracey Devon, Eng.
216 F1 Newton under Roseberry R. and C., Eng.
244 G4 Newton Underwood Northumb., Eng.
210 C3 Newton upon Derwent E. Riding, Eng.
52 G4 Newton Valence Hants., Eng.
228 E4 Newton with Scales Lancs., Eng.
198 E3 Newton Wood Gtr Man., Eng.
208 C4 New Totley S. Yorks., Eng.
405 C3 Newtown Isle of Man
106 E4 Newtown Bucks., Eng.
110 D3 New Town Central Bedfordshire, Eng.
184 C3 Newtown Cheshire West & Chester, Eng.
232 E3 Newtown Cumbria, Eng.
232 F3 Newtown Cumbria, Eng.
180 A2 Newtown Derbys., Eng.
46 C3 Newtown Dorset, Eng.
46 G2 New Town Dorset, Eng.
46 G2 New Town Dorset, Eng.
98 E3 Newtown Glos., Eng.
98 H2 New Town Glos., Eng.
198 B2 Newtown Gtr Man., Eng.
198 C2 Newtown Gtr Man., Eng.
52 C4 Newtown Hants., Eng.
52 C5 Newtown Hants., Eng.
52 D5 Newtown Hants., Eng.
52 E2 Newtown Hants., Eng.
52 E5 Newtown Hants., Eng.
52 F5 Newtown Hants., Eng.
140 C2 Newtown Here., Eng.
140 D3 Newtown Here., Eng.
140 E3 Newtown Here., Eng.
52 D6 Newtown I.o.W., Eng.
110 C4 New Town Luton, Eng.
244 F2 Newtown Northumb., Eng.
244 F4 Newtown Northumb., Eng.
102 F5 Newtown Oxon, Eng.
46 H3 Newtown Poole, Eng.
144 D2 Newtown Shrop., Eng.
94 F4 Newtown Som., Eng.
94 F5 Newtown Som., Eng.
148 C2 Newtown Staffs., Eng.
148 C5 Newtown Staffs., Eng.
148 D1 Newtown Staffs., Eng.
236 G2 New Town T. and W., Eng.
86 C5 Newtown Wilts., Eng.
86 F3 New Town Wilts., Eng.
86 F3 Newtown Wilts., Eng.
136 C2 Newtown Worcs., Eng.
136 D1 Newtown Worcs., Eng.
388 G3 New Town Magherafelt, N. Ire.
396 F5 Newtown Newry & Mourne, N. Ire.
288 F3 New Town E. Lothian, Scot.
322 G3 Newtown High., Scot.
350 G2 Newtown B. Gwent, Wales
362 C4 New Town Cere., Wales
366 F3 Newtown Powys, Wales
350 F4 Newtown R.C.T., Wales
388 K5 Newtownabbey Newtownabbey, N. Ire.
388 K4 Newtownabbey admin. dist. N. Ire.
396 J2 Newtownards Ards, N. Ire.
396 I2 Newtownbreda Castlereagh, N. Ire.
402 F5 Newtownbutler Fermanagh, N. Ire.
388 I3 Newtown Crommelin Ballymena, N. Ire.
396 E4 Newtownhamilton Newry & Mourne, N. Ire.
36 D3 Newtown-in-St-Martin Corn., Eng.
162 D2 Newtown Linford Leics., Eng.
256 H3 Newtown St Boswells Borders, Scot.
402 G4 Newtown Saville Omagh, N. Ire.
402 F2 Newtownstewart Strabane, N. Ire.
162 D3 Newtown Unthank Leics., Eng.
350 G2 New Tredegar Caerp., Wales
180 E3 New Tupton Derbys., Eng.
308 D3 Newtyle Angus, Scot.
300 C4 New Ulva Arg. and B., Scot.
326 E2 New Valley W. Isles, Scot.
208 F2 New Village S. Yorks., Eng.
124 F3 New Walsoken Cambs., Eng.
170 F2 New Waltham N.E. Lincs., Eng.
180 E3 New Whittington Derbys., Eng.
288 F3 New Winton E. Lothian, Scot.
124 E4 New World Cambs., Eng.
102 C4 New Yatt Oxon, Eng.
74 B2 Newyears Green Gtr Lon., Eng.
170 F5 New York Lincs., Eng.
236 G1 New York T. and W., Eng.
180 D5 New Zealand Derby, Eng.
358 E3 Neyland Pembs., Wales
98 E3 Nibley Glos., Eng.
98 E4 Nibley S. Glos., Eng.
98 E3 Nibley Green Glos., Eng.
40 G2 Nicholashayne Devon, Eng.
350 B3 Nicholaston Swansea, Wales
216 E2 Nidd N. Yorks., Eng.

Nidd to Otter

24 O5 Nidd r. Eng.
24 N5 Nidderdale val. Eng.
288 E3 Niddrie Edin., Scot.
314 G3 Nigg Aberdeen, Scot.
320 H4 Nigg High., Scot.
22 H7 Nigg Bay b. Scot.
94 C4 Nightcott Som., Eng.
378 E3 Nilig Denb., Wales
244 D6 Nilston Rigg Northumb., Eng.
98 E5 Nimlet S. Glos., Eng.
116 D3 Nine Ashes Essex, Eng.
244 C6 Ninebanks Northumb., Eng.
74 D3 Nine Elms Gtr Lon., Eng.
78 D2 Nine Elms Swindon, Eng.
288 D4 Nine Mile Burn Midlothian, Scot.
136 B2 Nineveh Worcs., Eng.
58 I3 Ninfield E. Sussex, Eng.
52 D6 Ningwood I.o.W., Eng.
256 I3 Nisbet Borders, Scot.
22 I12 Nith r. Scot.
22 I12 Nithsdale val. Scot.
252 F2 Nithside D. and G., Scot.
52 E7 Niton I.o.W., Eng.
276 D3 Nitshill Glas., Scot.
Niwbwrch I.o.A., Wales see Newborough
388 B3 Nixon's Corner Derry, N. Ire.
62 B3 Nizels Kent, Eng.
62 B3 Noah's Ark Kent, Eng.
116 E4 Noak Bridge Essex, Eng.
74 F2 Noak Hill Gtr Lon., Eng.
252 F2 Noblehill D. and G., Scot.
208 C2 Noblethorpe S. Yorks., Eng.
144 D3 Nobold Shrop., Eng.
128 C4 Nobottle Northants., Eng.
170 D4 Nocton Lincs., Eng.
190 C3 Noctorum Merseyside, Eng.
264 E2 Noddsdale N. Ayr., Scot.
74 D2 Noel Park Gtr Lon., Eng.
166 I3 Nogdam End Norf., Eng.
102 D4 Noke Oxon, Eng.
358 D3 Nolton Pembs., Wales
358 D3 Nolton Haven Pembs., Wales
184 C3 No Man's Heath Cheshire West & Chester, Eng.
132 C1 No Man's Heath Warks., Eng.
36 F2 No Man's Land Corn., Eng.
40 F2 Nomansland Devon, Eng.
86 F6 Nomansland Wilts., Eng.
144 D2 Noneley Shrop., Eng.
62 H3 Nonington Kent, Eng.
128 B4 Nook Cumbria, Eng.
232 F7 Nook Cumbria, Eng.
331 C3 Noonsbrough Shet., Scot.
308 E2 Noranside Angus, Scot.
74 C3 Norbiton Gtr Lon., Eng.
228 D3 Norbreck Blackpool, Eng.
184 D3 Norbury Cheshire East, Eng.
180 C5 Norbury Derbys., Eng.
74 D3 Norbury Gtr Lon., Eng.
144 C4 Norbury Shrop., Eng.
148 B4 Norbury Staffs., Eng.
184 C3 Norbury Common Cheshire East, Eng.
148 B4 Norbury Junction Staffs., Eng.
198 E3 Norbury Moor Gtr Man., Eng.
136 D2 Norchard Worcs., Eng.
358 F4 Norchard Pembs., Wales
184 D2 Norcott Brook Cheshire West & Chester, Eng.
166 A3 Nordelph Norf., Eng.
46 G4 Norden Dorset, Eng.
198 D2 Norden Gtr Man., Eng.
144 F4 Nordley Shrop., Eng.
166 D2 Norfolk county Eng.
244 E1 Norham Northumb., Eng.
78 E2 Nork Surr., Eng.
222 C2 Norland Town W. Yorks., Eng.
184 D2 Norley Cheshire West & Chester, Eng.
52 D6 Norleywood Hants., Eng.
58 G3 Norlington E. Sussex, Eng.
148 C3 Normacot Stoke, Eng.
170 C2 Normanby N. Lincs., Eng.
170 D3 Normanby-by-Spital Lincs., Eng.
170 B3 Normanby by Stow Lincs., Eng.
170 E3 Normanby le Wold Lincs., Eng.
124 C3 Norman Cross Cambs., Eng.
Normandes, Îles is English Chan. see Channel Islands
78 B2 Normandy Surr., Eng.
300 B2 Normann's Ruh Arg. and B., Scot.
58 I4 Norman's Bay E. Sussex, Eng.
120 J2 Normanston Suff., Eng.
180 E5 Normanton Derby, Eng.
162 G1 Normanton Leics., Eng.
170 C5 Normanton Lincs., Eng.
176 D4 Normanton Notts., Eng.
162 H3 Normanton Rutland, Eng.
86 E5 Normanton Wilts., Eng.
222 F2 Normanton W. Yorks., Eng.
162 C2 Normanton le Heath Leics., Eng.
176 B6 Normanton on Soar Notts., Eng.
176 C5 Normanton-on-the-Wolds Notts., Eng.
176 E3 Normanton on Trent Notts., Eng.
208 D3 Normanton Spring S. Yorks., Eng.
228 E4 Normoss Lancs., Eng.
86 B3 Norrington Common Wilts., Eng.
190 D3 Norris Green Merseyside, Eng.
162 B2 Norris Hill Leics., Eng.
222 D2 Norristhorpe W. Yorks., Eng.
166 E3 Northacre Norf., Eng.
74 C2 North Acton Gtr Lon., Eng.
106 E3 Northall Bucks., Eng.
216 E1 Northallerton N. Yorks., Eng.
166 E2 Northall Green Norf., Eng.
40 D1 Northam Devon, Eng.
52 D5 Northam Soton, Eng.
128 D4 Northampton Northants., Eng.
128 D3 Northamptonshire county Eng.
208 E3 North Anston S. Yorks., Eng.
82 F3 North Ascot Brack. F., Eng.
102 D3 North Aston Oxon, Eng.
110 E5 Northaw Herts., Eng.
94 F5 Northay Som., Eng.
264 D3 North Ayrshire admin. dist. Scot.
52 D5 North Baddesley Hants., Eng.
262 D5 North Balloch S. Ayr., Scot.
94 I4 North Barrow Som., Eng.
166 E1 North Barsham Norf., Eng.
170 D6 Northbeck Lincs., Eng.
116 F4 North Benfleet Essex, Eng.
58 B4 North Bersted W. Sussex, Eng.
288 G2 North Berwick E. Lothian, Scot.
236 E3 North Bitchburn Durham, Eng.
52 F5 North Boarhunt Hants., Eng.
46 I3 North Bockhampton Dorset, Eng.
314 D2 North Bogbain Moray, Scot.
124 C3 Northborough Peterb., Eng.
62 I3 Northbourne Kent, Eng.
102 D5 Northbourne Oxon, Eng.
40 E3 North Bovey Devon, Eng.
86 B4 North Bradley Wilts., Eng.
40 D3 North Brentor Devon, Eng.
94 J4 North Brewham Som., Eng.
78 C3 North Bridge Surr., Eng.
58 I3 Northbridge Street E. Sussex, Eng.
52 E4 Northbrook Hants., Eng.
102 D3 Northbrook Oxon, Eng.
124 D6 North Brook End Cambs., Eng.
280 C2 North Broomage Falk., Scot.
40 D1 North Buckland Devon, Eng.
166 H3 North Burlingham Norf., Eng.
94 I4 North Cadbury Som., Eng.
252 A3 North Cairn D. and G., Scot.
52 H3 North Camp Hants., Eng.
170 C4 North Carlton Lincs., Eng.
176 C2 North Carlton Notts., Eng.
210 E4 North Cave E. Riding, Eng.
98 H3 North Cerney Glos., Eng.
58 F3 North Chailey E. Sussex, Eng.
22 D12 North Channel str. Scot.
58 C2 Northchapel W. Sussex, Eng.
52 B5 North Charford Hants., Eng.
244 G3 North Charlton Northumb., Eng.
74 C3 North Cheam Gtr Lon., Eng.
94 J4 North Cheriton Som., Eng.
46 C3 North Chideock Dorset, Eng.
110 B5 Northchurch Herts., Eng.
210 D4 North Cliffe E. Riding, Eng.
176 E3 North Clifton Notts., Eng.
236 F3 North Close Durham, Eng.
170 G3 North Cockerington Lincs., Eng.
94 I5 North Coker Som., Eng.
331 C2 North Collafirth Shet., Scot.
98 E5 North Common S. Glos., Eng.
120 E2 North Common Suff., Eng.
300 D2 North Connel Arg. and B., Scot.
350 D3 North Cornelly Bridg., Wales
170 G3 North Cotes Lincs., Eng.
102 D4 Northcourt Oxon, Eng.
120 I2 North Cove Suff., Eng.
216 E1 North Cowton N. Yorks., Eng.
106 E2 North Crawley M.K., Eng.
74 E3 North Cray Gtr Lon., Eng.
166 D1 North Creake Norf., Eng.
94 G4 North Curry Som., Eng.
300 D2 North Dallens Arg. and B., Scot.
210 E3 North Dalton E. Riding, Eng.
329 D4 North Dawn Orkney, Scot.
26 G6 North Dorset Downs hills Eng.
62 I2 Northdown Kent, Eng.
396 J2 North Down admin. dist. N. Ire.
26 K5 North Downs hills Eng.
216 G3 North Duffield N. Yorks., Eng.
329 A3 Northdyke Orkney, Scot.
170 F2 North East Lincolnshire county Eng.
180 E3 Northedge Derbys., Eng.
62 G4 North Elham Kent, Eng.
170 F3 North Elkington Lincs., Eng.
166 E2 North Elmham Norf., Eng.
222 G3 North Elmsall W. Yorks., Eng.
94 K2 Northend B. and N.E. Som., Eng.
106 C5 Northend Bucks., Eng.
106 D3 North End Bucks., Eng.
46 F1 North End Dorset, Eng.
210 G3 North End E. Riding, Eng.
210 G3 North End E. Riding, Eng.
210 H4 North End E. Riding, Eng.
116 E2 North End Essex, Eng.
116 H4 Northend Essex, Eng.
52 A5 North End Hants., Eng.
52 D2 North End Hants., Eng.
162 E2 North End Leics., Eng.
170 G3 North End Lincs., Eng.
166 E4 North End Norf., Eng.
244 G4 North End Northumb., Eng.
94 G2 North End N. Som., Eng.
52 F6 North End Ports., Eng.
132 D4 Northend Warks., Eng.
58 D3 North End W. Sussex, Eng.
198 D3 Northenden Gtr Man., Eng.
23 I3 Northern Ireland prov.
198 D3 Northern Moor Gtr Man., Eng.
320 C4 North Erradale High., Scot.
22 L9 North Esk r. Scot.
314 H2 North Essie Abers., Scot.
162 E3 North Evington Leicester, Eng.
116 G4 North Fambridge Essex, Eng.
210 E4 North Ferriby E. Riding, Eng.
210 F4 Northfield Hull, Eng.
154 C3 Northfield W. Mids, Eng.
314 G1 Northfield Abers., Scot.
256 L1 Northfield Borders, Scot.
162 I3 Northfield Rutland, Eng.
62 C2 Northfleet Kent, Eng.
62 C2 Northfleet Green Kent, Eng.
26 O5 North Foreland c. Eng.
210 G3 North Frodingham E. Riding, Eng.
58 E2 Northgate W. Sussex, Eng.
331 C2 North Gluss Shet., Scot.
52 B5 North Gorley Hants., Eng.
166 G4 North Green Norf., Eng.
120 H2 North Green Suff., Eng.
120 H3 North Green Suff., Eng.
120 I3 North Green Suff., Eng.
216 G2 North Grimston N. Yorks., Eng.
62 C2 North Halling Medway, Eng.
176 E3 North Harby Notts., Eng.
74 B2 North Harrow Gtr Lon., Eng.
236 H3 North Hart Hartlepool, Eng.
52 G6 North Hayling Hants., Eng.
244 F2 North Hazelrigg Northumb., Eng.
82 B3 North Heath W. Berks., Eng.
58 D3 North Heath W. Sussex, Eng.
36 F2 North Hill Corn., Eng.
74 B2 North Hillingdon Gtr Lon., Eng.
102 D4 North Hinksey Oxon, Eng.
216 G2 North Holme N. Yorks., Eng.
78 E2 North Holmwood Surr., Eng.
52 C4 North Houghton Hants., Eng.
256 G4 Northhouse Borders, Scot.
40 E3 North Huish Devon, Eng.
74 B3 North Hyde Gtr Lon., Eng.
170 C4 North Hykeham Lincs., Eng.
236 G2 North Hylton T. and W., Eng.
58 J3 Northiam E. Sussex, Eng.
110 D3 Northill Central Bedfordshire, Eng.
98 E3 Northington Glos., Eng.
52 E4 Northington Hants., Eng.
358 E3 North Johnston Pembs., Wales
170 D3 North Kelsey Lincs., Eng.
74 C2 North Kensington Gtr Lon., Eng.
322 I2 North Kessock High., Scot.
170 E2 North Killingholme N. Lincs., Eng.
162 E4 North Kilworth Leics., Eng.
52 B6 North Kingston Hants., Eng.
170 E5 North Kyme Lincs., Eng.
280 C3 North Lanarkshire admin. dist. Scot.
58 E3 North Lancing W. Sussex, Eng.
170 G5 Northlands Lincs., Eng.
98 H3 Northleach Glos., Eng.
236 E4 North Leazes Durham, Eng.
106 D4 North Lee Bucks., Eng.
40 G2 Northleigh Devon, Eng.
102 C4 North Leigh Oxon, Eng.
176 E3 North Leverton with Habblesthorpe Notts., Eng.
40 D2 Northlew Devon, Eng.
170 C2 North Lincolnshire county Eng.
136 F3 North Littleton Worcs., Eng.
166 E4 North Lopham Norf., Eng.
162 H3 North Luffenham Rutland, Eng.
58 A3 North Marden W. Sussex, Eng.
106 C3 North Marston Bucks., Eng.
244 E2 North Middleton Northumb., Eng.
288 E4 North Middleton Midlothian, Scot.
216 F3 North Milford N. Yorks., Eng.
314 G2 North Millbrex Abers., Scot.
40 E1 North Molton Devon, Eng.
102 C4 Northmoor Oxon, Eng.
94 G4 Northmoor Green Som., Eng.
102 D5 North Moreton Oxon, Eng.
308 D2 Northmuir Angus, Scot.
58 B4 North Mundham W. Sussex, Eng.
176 E4 North Muskham Notts., Eng.
210 E4 North Newbald E. Riding, Eng.
102 C2 North Newington Oxon, Eng.
86 E4 North Newnton Wilts., Eng.
94 F4 North Newton Som., Eng.
52 G6 Northney Hants., Eng.
98 E4 North Nibley Glos., Eng.
52 E3 North Oakley Hants., Eng.
116 D4 North Ockendon Thurrock, Eng.
74 B2 Northolt Gtr Lon., Eng.
378 G2 Northop Flints., Wales
378 G2 Northop Hall Flints., Wales
170 F3 North Ormsby Lincs., Eng.
170 C3 Northorpe Lincs., Eng.
170 D7 Northorpe Lincs., Eng.
170 E6 Northorpe Lincs., Eng.
216 E2 North Otterington N. Yorks., Eng.
94 H4 Northover Som., Eng.
170 D3 North Owersby Lincs., Eng.
222 D2 Northowram W. Yorks., Eng.
94 H5 North Perrott Som., Eng.
94 F4 North Petherton Som., Eng.
36 F1 North Petherwin Corn., Eng.
166 D3 North Pickenham Norf., Eng.
136 E2 North Piddle Worcs., Eng.
232 C3 North Plain Cumbria, Eng.
46 C3 North Poorton Dorset, Eng.
46 G3 Northport Dorset, Eng.
52 B5 North Poulner Hants., Eng.
331 D4 Northpunds Shet., Scot.
94 C4 North Quarme Som., Eng.
292 D3 North Queensferry Fife, Scot.
40 E1 North Radworthy Devon, Eng.
170 D5 North Rauceby Lincs., Eng.
166 H1 Northrepps Norf., Eng.
170 G4 North Reston Lincs., Eng.
216 E3 North Rigton N. Yorks., Eng.
52 B6 North Ripley Hants., Eng.
184 F2 North Rode Cheshire East, Eng.
331 D2 North Roe Shet., Scot.
North Rona i. Scot. see Rona
329 G1 North Ronaldsay airport Scot.
22 L4 North Ronaldsay i. Scot.
22 L4 North Ronaldsay Firth sea chan. Scot.
166 B2 North Runcton Norf., Eng.
331 E2 North Sandwick Shet., Scot.
232 C8 North Scale Cumbria, Eng.
170 B4 North Scarle Lincs., Eng.
244 H4 North Seaton Northumb., Eng.
74 C3 North Sheen Gtr Lon., Eng.
236 G1 North Shields T. and W., Eng.
116 G4 North Shoebury Southend, Eng.
124 D3 North Side Peterb., Eng.
170 G3 North Somercotes Lincs., Eng.
94 H2 North Somerset admin. div. Eng.
216 E2 North Stainley N. Yorks., Eng.
232 I5 North Stainmore Cumbria, Eng.
116 D5 North Stifford Thurrock, Eng.
94 J2 North Stoke B. and N.E. Som., Eng.
102 E5 North Stoke Oxon, Eng.
58 C3 North Stoke W. Sussex, Eng.
52 D5 North Stoneham Hants., Eng.
52 B5 North Street Hants., Eng.
62 F3 North Street Kent, Eng.
62 D2 North Street Medway, Eng.
82 D3 North Street W. Berks., Eng.
244 H2 North Sunderland Northumb., Eng.
36 F1 North Tamerton Corn., Eng.
40 E2 North Tawton Devon, Eng.
296 F5 North Third Stir., Scot.
170 F3 North Thoresby Lincs., Eng.
86 E4 North Tidworth Wilts., Eng.
244 H4 North Togston Northumb., Eng.
326 C3 Northton W. Isles, Scot.
52 H3 North Town Hants., Eng.
82 F2 North Town W. and M., Eng.
329 D4 Northtown Orkney, Scot.
166 F2 North Tuddenham Norf., Eng.
24 M4 North Tyne r. Eng.
242 North Tyneside met. bor. T. and W., Eng.
22 M7 North Ugie r. Scot.
22 B7 North Uist i. Scot.
244 E4 Northumberland county Eng.
74 E3 Northumberland Heath Gtr Lon., Eng.
24 M3 Northumberland National Park nat. park Eng.
236 E1 North Walbottle T. and W., Eng.
166 H2 North Walsham Norf., Eng.
52 E3 North Waltham Hants., Eng.
52 G3 North Warnborough Hants., Eng.
314 F4 North Water Bridge Abers., Scot.
98 G1 Northway Glos., Eng.
94 E4 Northway Som., Eng.
116 C3 North Weald Bassett Essex, Eng.
74 C2 North Wembley Gtr Lon., Eng.
102 E4 North Weston Oxon, Eng.
176 D2 North Wheatley Notts., Eng.
184 D2 Northwich Cheshire West & Chester, Eng.
94 I2 North Wick B. and N.E. Som., Eng.
98 D4 Northwick S. Glos., Eng.
94 G3 Northwick Som., Eng.
136 D2 Northwick Worcs., Eng.
94 I3 North Widcombe B. and N.E. Som., Eng.
170 E3 North Willingham Lincs., Eng.
180 E3 North Wingfield Derbys., Eng.
170 C7 North Witham Lincs., Eng.
166 C3 Northwold Norf., Eng.
74 B2 Northwood Gtr Lon., Eng.
52 E6 Northwood I.o.W., Eng.
62 I2 Northwood Kent, Eng.
190 D3 Northwood Merseyside, Eng.
144 D2 Northwood Shrop., Eng.
148 B3 Northwood Staffs., Eng.
148 C2 Northwood Stoke, Eng.
98 E2 Northwood Green Glos., Eng.
74 B2 Northwood Hills Gtr Lon., Eng.
74 E2 North Woolwich Gtr Lon., Eng.
46 E2 North Wootton Dorset, Eng.
166 B2 North Wootton Norf., Eng.
94 I3 North Wootton Som., Eng.
86 B3 North Wraxall Wilts., Eng.
86 E2 North Wroughton Swindon, Eng.
244 E4 North Yardhope Northumb., Eng.
24 P5 North York Moors moorland Eng.
24 P5 North York Moors National Park nat. park Eng.
216 E2 North Yorkshire county Eng.
98 F2 Norton Glos., Eng.
190 F4 Norton Halton, Eng.
110 D4 Norton Herts., Eng.
52 C6 Norton I.o.W., Eng.
128 C4 Norton Northants., Eng.
176 C3 Norton Notts., Eng.
94 G2 Norton N. Som., Eng.
216 G2 Norton N. Yorks., Eng.
144 D5 Norton Shrop., Eng.
144 E3 Norton Shrop., Eng.
144 F4 Norton Shrop., Eng.
120 E3 Norton Suff., Eng.
208 D4 Norton S. Yorks., Eng.
208 E2 Norton S. Yorks., Eng.
86 C2 Norton Wilts., Eng.
154 B3 Norton W. Mids, Eng.
136 D3 Norton Worcs., Eng.
136 F3 Norton Worcs., Eng.
58 B3 Norton W. Sussex, Eng.
58 B4 Norton W. Sussex, Eng.
339 D1 Norton Mon., Wales
366 G5 Norton Powys, Wales
350 B3 Norton Swansea, Wales
350 E4 Norton V. of Glam., Wales
86 C4 Norton Bavant Wilts., Eng.
148 B3 Norton Bridge Staffs., Eng.
148 D4 Norton Canes Staffs., Eng.
140 D3 Norton Canon Here., Eng.
170 B5 Norton Disney Lincs., Eng.
86 B5 Norton Ferris Wilts., Eng.
94 F4 Norton Fitzwarren Som., Eng.
110 D4 Norton Green Herts., Eng.
52 C6 Norton Green I.o.W., Eng.
148 C2 Norton Green Stoke, Eng.
116 D3 Norton Heath Essex, Eng.
144 F2 Norton in Hales Shrop., Eng.
148 C2 Norton in the Moors Stoke, Eng.
162 B3 Norton-Juxta-Twycross Leics., Eng.
216 E2 Norton-le-Clay N. Yorks., Eng.
132 C4 Norton Lindsey Warks., Eng.
120 E3 Norton Little Green Suff., Eng.
94 I2 Norton Malreward B. and N.E. Som., Eng.
116 D3 Norton Mandeville Essex, Eng.
396 D4 Norton's Cross Roads Armagh, N. Ire.
94 K3 Norton St Philip Som., Eng.
94 H5 Norton-sub-Hamdon Som., Eng.
140 B3 Norton Wood Here., Eng.
208 D3 Norton Woodseats S. Yorks., Eng.
176 D4 Norwell Notts., Eng.
176 D4 Norwell Woodhouse Notts., Eng.
166 G3 Norwich Norf., Eng.
166 G2 Norwich International airport Eng.
331 E1 Norwick Shet., Scot.
180 F3 Norwood Derbys., Eng.
74 D3 Norwood Gtr Lon., Eng.
208 D3 Norwood S. Yorks., Eng.
116 D3 Norwood End Essex, Eng.
74 B3 Norwood Green Gtr Lon., Eng.
222 D2 Norwood Green W. Yorks., Eng.
78 E2 Norwood Hill Surr., Eng.
94 H4 Norwood Park Som., Eng.
124 E3 Norwoodside Cambs., Eng.
162 F3 Noseley Leics., Eng.
22 □N2 Noss, Isle of i. Scot.
22 J6 Noss Head hd Scot.
40 D4 Noss Mayo Devon, Eng.
124 G6 Nosterfield End Cambs., Eng.
322 E3 Nostie High., Scot.
98 H2 Notgrove Glos., Eng.
350 D4 Nottage Bridg., Wales
176 C5 Nottingham Nott., Eng.
320 K3 Nottingham High., Scot.
176 B5 Nottingham county Eng.
176 C4 Nottinghamshire county Eng.
74 C2 Notting Hill Gtr Lon., Eng.
46 E4 Nottington Dorset, Eng.
86 C3 Notton Wilts., Eng.
222 F3 Notton W. Yorks., Eng.
98 E2 Nottswood Hill Glos., Eng.
116 F3 Nounsley Essex, Eng.
22 J4 Noup Head hd Scot.
136 D2 Noutard's Green Worcs., Eng.
120 D3 Nowton Suff., Eng.
144 C3 Nox Shrop., Eng.
362 C4 Noyadd Trefawr Cere., Wales
102 E5 Nuffield Oxon, Eng.
216 F3 Nun Appleton N. Yorks., Eng.
210 D3 Nunburnholme E. Riding, Eng.
176 B4 Nuncargate Notts., Eng.
132 D2 Nuneaton Warks., Eng.
102 D4 Nuneham Courtenay Oxon, Eng.
102 E5 Nuney Green Oxon, Eng.
74 D3 Nunhead Gtr Lon., Eng.
216 F2 Nun Monkton N. Yorks., Eng.
94 J3 Nunney Som., Eng.
140 D3 Nunnington Here., Eng.
216 G2 Nunnington N. Yorks., Eng.
94 E4 Nunnington Park Som., Eng.
244 F4 Nunnykirk Northumb., Eng.
396 K3 Nuns Quarter Ards, N. Ire.
170 F3 Nunsthorpe N.E. Lincs., Eng.
86 E5 Nunton Wilts., Eng.
244 D5 Nunwick Northumb., Eng.
216 E2 Nunwick N. Yorks., Eng.
106 D3 Nup End Bucks., Eng.
98 F2 Nup End Glos., Eng.
98 F3 Nupend Glos., Eng.
110 D4 Nup End Herts., Eng.
52 D5 Nursling Hants., Eng.
52 G5 Nursted Hants., Eng.
350 F4 Nurston V. of Glam., Wales
148 B5 Nurton Staffs., Eng.
58 A3 Nutbourne W. Sussex, Eng.
78 F2 Nutfield Surr., Eng.
176 B5 Nuthall Notts., Eng.
110 F4 Nuthampstead Herts., Eng.
132 B3 Nuthurst Warks., Eng.
58 E2 Nuthurst W. Sussex, Eng.
58 G2 Nutley E. Sussex, Eng.
52 F3 Nutley Hants., Eng.
388 J5 Nutt's Corner Antrim, N. Ire.
208 F2 Nutwell S. Yorks., Eng.
296 F5 Nyadd Stir., Scot.
320 K2 Nybster High., Scot.
58 B4 Nyetimber W. Sussex, Eng.
58 A3 Nyewood W. Sussex, Eng.
98 F3 Nympsfield Glos., Eng.
94 E5 Nynehead Som., Eng.
94 H4 Nythe Som., Eng.
58 C3 Nyton W. Sussex, Eng.

O

162 E3 Oadby Leics., Eng.
62 E3 Oad Street Kent, Eng.
148 D2 Oakamoor Staffs., Eng.
300 C2 Oakbank Arg. and B., Scot.
288 C3 Oakbank W. Lothian, Scot.
40 D2 Oak Cross Devon, Eng.
46 H3 Oakdale Poole, Eng.
350 G2 Oakdale Caerp., Wales
94 E4 Oake Som., Eng.
94 E4 Oake Green Som., Eng.
148 B5 Oaken Staffs., Eng.
228 F3 Oakenclough Lancs., Eng.
144 F3 Oakengates Telford, Eng.
314 D1 Oakenhead Moray, Scot.
378 G2 Oakenholt Flints., Wales
236 E3 Oakenshaw Durham, Eng.
222 D2 Oakenshaw W. Yorks., Eng.
180 E4 Oakerthorpe Derbys., Eng.
222 D3 Oakes W. Yorks., Eng.
52 F6 Oakfield I.o.W., Eng.
339 B3 Oakfield Torf., Wales
40 F2 Oakford Devon, Eng.
362 E3 Oakford Cere., Wales
184 G2 Oakgrove Cheshire East, Eng.
162 G2 Oakham Rutland, Eng.
52 G4 Oakhanger Hants., Eng.
94 I3 Oakhill Som., Eng.
148 B3 Oak Hill Stoke, Eng.
124 E5 Oakington Cambs., Eng.
110 D4 Oaklands Herts., Eng.
378 C3 Oaklands Conwy, Wales
74 C2 Oakleigh Park Gtr Lon., Eng.
98 E2 Oakle Street Glos., Eng.
110 B2 Oakley Bedford, Eng.
106 B4 Oakley Bucks., Eng.
52 E3 Oakley Hants., Eng.
102 F4 Oakley Oxon, Eng.
46 H3 Oakley Poole, Eng.
120 G2 Oakley Suff., Eng.
292 C3 Oakley Fife, Scot.
82 F3 Oakley Green W. and M., Eng.
366 E4 Oakley Park Powys, Wales
144 C4 Oaks Shrop., Eng.
86 C2 Oaksey Wilts., Eng.
180 C5 Oaks Green Derbys., Eng.
232 F2 Oakshaw Ford Cumbria, Eng.
52 G4 Oakshott Hants., Eng.
162 B2 Oakthorpe Leics., Eng.
236 G4 Oak Tree Darl., Eng.
74 D2 Oakwood Gtr Lon., Eng.
78 D3 Oakwoodhill Surr., Eng.
222 C1 Oakworth W. Yorks., Eng.
62 F3 Oare Kent, Eng.
94 B3 Oare Som., Eng.
86 E3 Oare Wilts., Eng.
170 C6 Oasby Lincs., Eng.
300 D5 Oatfield Arg. and B., Scot.
94 G4 Oath Som., Eng.
308 E2 Oathlaw Angus, Scot.
216 E3 Oatlands N. Yorks., Eng.
276 E2 Oatlands Glas., Scot.
78 D1 Oatlands Park Surr., Eng.
300 D2 Oban Arg. and B., Scot.
144 C5 Obley Shrop., Eng.
46 E2 Oborne Dorset, Eng.
170 D7 Obthorpe Lincs., Eng.
216 F2 Occaney N. Yorks., Eng.
184 E3 Occlestone Green Cheshire East, Eng.
120 F3 Occold Suff., Eng.
320 K3 Occumster High., Scot.
22 I10 Ochil Hills hills Scot.
262 E4 Ochiltree E. Ayr., Scot.
378 E2 Ochr-y-foel Denb., Wales
304 G5 Ochtermuthill Perth and Kin., Scot.
304 G4 Ochtertyre Perth and Kin., Scot.
296 F5 Ochtertyre Stir., Scot.
180 E5 Ockbrook Derbys., Eng.
154 B2 Ocker Hill W. Mids, Eng.
136 D2 Ockeridge Worcs., Eng.
78 D2 Ockham Surr., Eng.
322 D4 Ockle High., Scot.
78 D3 Ockley Surr., Eng.
140 D3 Ocle Pychard Here., Eng.
210 F2 Octon E. Riding, Eng.
94 H5 Odcombe Som., Eng.
94 J2 Odd Down B. and N.E. Som., Eng.
232 G5 Oddendale Cumbria, Eng.
136 E2 Oddingley Worcs., Eng.
102 D4 Oddington Oxon, Eng.
331 E2 Oddsta Shet., Scot.
110 B2 Odell Bedford, Eng.
329 F3 Odie Orkney, Scot.
52 G3 Odiham Hants., Eng.
110 E3 Odsey Herts., Eng.
86 E5 Odstock Wilts., Eng.
162 C2 Odstone Leics., Eng.
132 D4 Offchurch Warks., Eng.
136 F3 Offenham Worcs., Eng.
198 E3 Offerton Gtr Man., Eng.
236 G2 Offerton T. and W., Eng.
198 E3 Offerton Green Gtr Man., Eng.
58 F3 Offham E. Sussex, Eng.
62 C3 Offham Kent, Eng.
58 C3 Offham W. Sussex, Eng.
148 B3 Offleyhay Staffs., Eng.
110 D4 Offley Hoo Herts., Eng.
148 B3 Offleymarsh Staffs., Eng.
124 C5 Offord Cluny Cambs., Eng.
124 C5 Offord D'Arcy Cambs., Eng.
120 F4 Offton Suff., Eng.
40 G2 Offwell Devon, Eng.
86 E3 Ogbourne Maizey Wilts., Eng.
86 E3 Ogbourne St Andrew Wilts., Eng.
86 E3 Ogbourne St George Wilts., Eng.
222 C2 Ogden W. Yorks., Eng.
388 C3 Oghill Derry, N. Ire.
308 E2 Ogil Angus, Scot.
244 G5 Ogle Northumb., Eng.
190 D4 Oglet Merseyside, Eng.
222 F1 Oglethorpe Hall Farm W. Yorks., Eng.
350 E4 Ogmore V. of Glam., Wales
350 E4 Ogmore-by-Sea V. of Glam., Wales
350 E3 Ogmore Vale Bridg., Wales
22 G8 Oich r. Scot.
22 G8 Oich, Loch l. Scot.
22 C9 Oigh-sgeir is Scot.
46 F2 Okeford Fitzpaine Dorset, Eng.
40 D2 Okehampton Devon, Eng.
40 E2 Okehampton Camp Devon, Eng.
26 D6 Okement r. Eng.
331 D3 Okraquoy Shet., Scot.
40 F3 Olchard Devon, Eng.
350 B3 Olchfa Swansea, Wales
128 D3 Old Northants., Eng.
314 G3 Old Aberdeen Aberdeen, Scot.
52 F4 Old Alresford Hants., Eng.
132 C2 Old Arley Warks., Eng.
176 B5 Old Basford Nott., Eng.
52 F3 Old Basing Hants., Eng.
256 H3 Old Belses Borders, Scot.
132 B4 Oldberrow Warks., Eng.
244 F3 Old Bewick Northumb., Eng.
304 G2 Old Blair Perth and Kin., Scot.
170 G5 Old Bolingbroke Lincs., Eng.
40 E2 Oldborough Devon, Eng.
222 E1 Old Bramhope W. Yorks., Eng.
180 E3 Old Brampton Derbys., Eng.
252 E3 Old Bridge of Urr D. and G., Scot.
166 F4 Old Buckenham Norf., Eng.
236 G2 Old Burdon T. and W., Eng.
52 E3 Old Burghclere Hants., Eng.
62 B3 Oldbury Kent, Eng.
144 F4 Oldbury Shrop., Eng.
132 C2 Oldbury Warks., Eng.
154 B2 Oldbury W. Mids, Eng.
98 D4 Oldbury Naite S. Glos., Eng.
98 D4 Oldbury-on-Severn S. Glos., Eng.
98 F4 Oldbury on the Hill Glos., Eng.
216 F2 Old Byland N. Yorks., Eng.
236 G3 Old Cassop Durham, Eng.
350 E3 Oldcastle Bridg., Wales
339 C1 Oldcastle Mon., Wales
184 C3 Oldcastle Heath Cheshire West & Chester, Eng.
366 G3 Old Church Stoke Powys, Wales
170 F2 Old Clee N.E. Lincs., Eng.
94 D3 Old Cleeve Som., Eng.
176 C3 Old Clipstone Notts., Eng.
378 C2 Old Colwyn Conwy, Wales
176 C2 Oldcotes Notts., Eng.
314 G3 Old Craig Abers., Scot.
288 E3 Old Craighall E. Lothian, Scot.
98 D3 Oldcroft Glos., Eng.
314 E2 Old Crombie Abers., Scot.
262 C5 Old Dailly S. Ayr., Scot.
262 C5 Old Dailly S. Ayr., Scot.
162 E2 Old Dalby Leics., Eng.
180 C3 Old Dam Derbys., Eng.
314 G2 Old Deer Abers., Scot.
86 B4 Old Dilton Wilts., Eng.
222 C2 Old Dolphin W. Yorks., Eng.
98 D4 Old Down S. Glos., Eng.
94 I3 Old Down Som., Eng.
124 D3 Oldeamere Cambs., Eng.
208 E3 Old Edlington S. Yorks., Eng.
236 F4 Old Eldon Durham, Eng.
210 G4 Old Ellerby E. Riding, Eng.
148 C4 Oldfallow Staffs., Eng.
120 H5 Old Felixstowe Suff., Eng.
136 D2 Oldfield Worcs., Eng.
222 C1 Oldfield W. Yorks., Eng.
222 D3 Oldfield W. Yorks., Eng.
198 C3 Oldfield Brow Gtr Man., Eng.
124 C3 Old Fletton Peterb., Eng.
74 D2 Old Ford Gtr Lon., Eng.
94 K3 Oldford Som., Eng.
339 B2 Old Furnace Torf., Wales
362 G3 Old Goginan Cere., Wales
210 C4 Old Goole E. Riding, Eng.
140 D4 Old Gore Here., Eng.
102 D2 Old Grimsbury Oxon, Eng.
36 □ Old Grimsby I.o.S., Eng.
210 H5 Old Hall E. Riding, Eng.
314 E3 Oldhall Abers., Scot.
276 D2 Oldhall Renf., Scot.
110 E4 Old Hall Green Herts., Eng.
166 H1 Old Hall Street Norf., Eng.
198 E2 Oldham Gtr Man., Eng.
198 E2 Oldham Edge Gtr Man., Eng.
288 I3 Oldhamstocks E. Lothian, Scot.
116 C3 Old Harlow Essex, Eng.
116 H2 Old Heath Essex, Eng.
154 B3 Old Hill W. Mids, Eng.
402 I2 Old Hill Cookstown, N. Ire.
124 D4 Old Hurst Cambs., Eng.
232 G7 Old Hutton Cumbria, Eng.
276 D2 Old Kilpatrick W. Dun., Scot.
314 F3 Old Kinnernie Abers., Scot.
110 D4 Old Knebworth Herts., Eng.
98 E5 Oldland S. Glos., Eng.
170 G5 Old Leake Lincs., Eng.
314 F3 Old Leslie Abers., Scot.
74 C3 Old Malden Gtr Lon., Eng.
216 G2 Old Malton N. Yorks., Eng.
144 C2 Old Marton Shrop., Eng.
314 G2 Oldmeldrum Abers., Scot.
388 K3 Old Mill Larne, N. Ire.
52 C6 Old Milton Hants., Eng.
132 C4 Old Milverton Warks., Eng.
116 H4 Old Montsale Essex, Eng.
52 E5 Old Netley Hants., Eng.
120 E3 Old Newton Suff., Eng.
144 F3 Oldpark Telford, Eng.
288 B3 Old Philpstoun W. Lothian, Scot.
236 F3 Old Quarrington Durham, Eng.
366 G5 Old Radnor Powys, Wales
236 F2 Old Ravensworth T. and W., Eng.
40 F2 Oldridge Devon, Eng.
62 F5 Old Romney Kent, Eng.
304 J4 Old Scone Perth and Kin., Scot.
280 C3 Old Shields N. Lanark., Scot.
320 E2 Oldshoremore High., Scot.
222 F2 Old Snydale W. Yorks., Eng.
98 E4 Old Sodbury S. Glos., Eng.
170 C6 Old Somerby Lincs., Eng.
378 H3 Old Sontley Wrex., Wales
216 F2 Oldstead N. Yorks., Eng.
388 I4 Oldstone Antrim, N. Ire.
128 D5 Old Stratford Northants., Eng.
210 F3 Old Sunderlandwick E. Riding, Eng.
190 D3 Old Swan Merseyside, Eng.
244 G4 Old Swarland Northumb., Eng.
154 B3 Old Swinford W. Mids, Eng.
232 G7 Old Town Cumbria, Eng.
36 □ Old Town I.o.S., Eng.
222 B2 Old Town W. Yorks., Eng.
244 D4 Old Town Farm Northumb., Eng.
314 F2 Oldtown of Ord Abers., Scot.
198 D3 Old Trafford Gtr Man., Eng.
180 E3 Old Tupton Derbys., Eng.
110 C3 Old Warden Central Bedfordshire, Eng.
40 F1 Oldways End Devon, Eng.
124 B4 Old Weston Cambs., Eng.
180 E3 Old Whittington Derbys., Eng.
154 D3 Oldwich Lane W. Mids, Eng.
82 G3 Old Windsor W. and M., Eng.
62 F3 Old Wives Lees Kent, Eng.
78 C2 Old Woking Surr., Eng.
106 D2 Old Wolverton M.K., Eng.
170 E4 Old Woodhall Lincs., Eng.
144 D3 Old Woods Shrop., Eng.
256 D3 Oliver Borders, Scot.
52 D4 Oliver's Battery Hants., Eng.
331 D2 Ollaberry Shet., Scot.
184 E2 Ollerton Cheshire East, Eng.
176 C3 Ollerton Notts., Eng.
144 E3 Ollerton Shrop., Eng.
124 G6 Olmstead Green Cambs., Eng.
106 D2 Olney M.K., Eng.
154 D3 Olton W. Mids, Eng.
98 D4 Olveston S. Glos., Eng.
402 G3 Omagh Omagh, N. Ire.
402 G3 Omagh admin. dist. N. Ire.
136 D2 Ombersley Worcs., Eng.
176 D3 Ompton Notts., Eng.
405 D2 Onchan Isle of Man
148 D2 Onecote Staffs., Eng.
120 E3 Onehouse Suff., Eng.
166 B2 Ongar Hill Norf., Eng.
140 B2 Ongar Street Here., Eng.
144 D5 Onibury Shrop., Eng.
350 D2 Onllwyn N.P.T., Wales
148 A3 Onneley Staffs., Eng.
116 E2 Onslow Green Essex, Eng.
78 C2 Onslow Village Surr., Eng.
402 J4 Oona Bridge Dungannon, N. Ire.
198 D3 Openshaw Gtr Man., Eng.
180 E4 Openwoodgate Derbys., Eng.
320 C4 Opinan High., Scot.
320 D4 Opinan High., Scot.
256 J2 Orange Lane Borders, Scot.
326 E2 Orasaigh W. Isles, Scot.
314 D2 Orbliston Moray, Scot.
322 B2 Orbost High., Scot.
170 H4 Orby Lincs., Eng.
300 E4 Orcadia Arg. and B., Scot.
388 C2 Orchardtown Derry, N. Ire.
86 D4 Orcheston Wilts., Eng.
22 F10 Orchy r. Scot.
140 C4 Orcop Here., Eng.
140 C4 Orcop Hill Here., Eng.
322 D3 Ord High., Scot.
314 F3 Ordhead Abers., Scot.
314 E3 Ordie Abers., Scot.
314 D2 Ordiequish Moray, Scot.
198 D3 Ordsall Gtr Man., Eng.
176 D3 Ordsall Notts., Eng.
58 J3 Ore E. Sussex, Eng.
58 E3 Oreham Common W. Sussex, Eng.
40 D3 Oreston Plymouth, Eng.
144 E5 Oreton Shrop., Eng.
120 I4 Orford Suff., Eng.
190 F3 Orford Warr., Eng.
26 P3 Orford Ness hd Eng.
46 G3 Organford Dorset, Eng.
148 E4 Orgreave Staffs., Eng.
402 J3 Oritor Cookstown, N. Ire.
329 C3 Orkney admin. div. Scot.
20 F2 Orkney Islands is Scot.
62 F4 Orlestone Kent, Eng.
140 C2 Orleton Here., Eng.
136 C2 Orleton Worcs., Eng.
140 C2 Orleton Common Here., Eng.
128 E3 Orlingbury Northants., Eng.
326 B5 Ormacleit W. Isles, Scot.
166 J2 Ormesby St Margaret Norf., Eng.
166 I2 Ormesby St Michael Norf., Eng.
300 E4 Ormidale Arg. and B., Scot.
288 F3 Ormiston E. Lothian, Scot.
322 C4 Ormsaigmore High., Scot.
300 D4 Ormsary Arg. and B., Scot.
228 E5 Ormskirk Lancs., Eng.
22 D10 Oronsay i. Scot.
329 C4 Orphir Orkney, Scot.
74 E3 Orpington Gtr Lon., Eng.
198 A2 Orrell Gtr Man., Eng.
190 D3 Orrell Merseyside, Eng.
22 H7 Orrin r. Scot.
22 G7 Orrin Reservoir resr Scot.
405 C2 Orrisdale Isle of Man
252 E3 Orroland D. and G., Scot.
116 E5 Orsett Thurrock, Eng.
116 E5 Orsett Heath Thurrock, Eng.
148 B4 Orslow Staffs., Eng.
176 D5 Orston Notts., Eng.
232 G6 Orton Cumbria, Eng.
128 E3 Orton Northants., Eng.
124 C3 Orton Longueville Peterb., Eng.
162 B3 Orton-on-the-Hill Leics., Eng.
232 D3 Orton Rigg Cumbria, Eng.
124 C3 Orton Waterville Peterb., Eng.
124 D6 Orwell Cambs., Eng.
26 O3 Orwell r. Eng.
228 G4 Osbaldeston Lancs., Eng.
228 G4 Osbaldeston Green Lancs., Eng.
216 F3 Osbaldwick York, Eng.
162 C3 Osbaston Leics., Eng.
144 B3 Osbaston Shrop., Eng.
144 E3 Osbaston Telford, Eng.
162 C3 Osbaston Hollow Leics., Eng.
52 E6 Osborne I.o.W., Eng.
170 D6 Osbournby Lincs., Eng.
184 C2 Oscroft Cheshire West & Chester, Eng.
322 B2 Ose High., Scot.
162 C2 Osgathorpe Leics., Eng.
170 D3 Osgodby Lincs., Eng.
216 H2 Osgodby N. Yorks., Eng.
74 D2 Osidge Gtr Lon., Eng.
322 C2 Oskaig High., Scot.
180 D5 Osleston Derbys., Eng.
180 E5 Osmaston Derby, Eng.
180 C5 Osmaston Derbys., Eng.
46 E4 Osmington Dorset, Eng.
46 E4 Osmington Mills Dorset, Eng.
222 E2 Osmondthorpe W. Yorks., Eng.
216 F1 Osmotherley N. Yorks., Eng.
Osnaburgh Fife, Scot. see Dairsie
102 D4 Osney Oxon, Eng.
62 F3 Ospringe Kent, Eng.
222 E2 Ossett W. Yorks., Eng.
222 E2 Ossett Street Side W. Yorks., Eng.
176 D3 Ossington Notts., Eng.
116 G4 Ostend Essex, Eng.
74 B3 Osterley Gtr Lon., Eng.
228 H4 Oswaldtwistle Lancs., Eng.
144 B2 Oswestry Shrop., Eng.
144 C2 Oteley Shrop., Eng.
62 B3 Otford Kent, Eng.
62 D3 Otham Kent, Eng.
148 C4 Otherton Staffs., Eng.
94 G4 Othery Som., Eng.
120 G4 Otley Suff., Eng.
222 D1 Otley W. Yorks., Eng.
120 G4 Otley Green Suff., Eng.
300 E4 Otter Arg. and B., Scot.

Otter to Pipewell

26 F6 Otter r. Eng.
52 D4 Otterbourne Hants., Eng.
244 D4 Otterburn Northumb., Eng.
216 C2 Otterburn N. Yorks., Eng.
244 E4 Otterburn Camp Northumb., Eng.
62 E3 Otterden Place Kent, Eng.
300 E3 Otter Ferry Arg. and B., Scot.
36 F1 Otterham Corn., Eng.
94 F3 Otterhampton Som., Eng.
62 D2 Otterham Quay Medway, Eng.
326 C3 Otternish W. Isles, Scot.
78 C1 Ottershaw Surr., Eng.
331 D2 Otterswick Shet., Scot.
40 G3 Otterton Devon, Eng.
52 D6 Otterwood Hants., Eng.
26 D6 Ottery r. Eng.
40 G2 Ottery St Mary Devon, Eng.
62 G4 Ottinge Kent, Eng.
210 H4 Ottringham E. Riding, Eng.
232 D3 Oughterby Cumbria, Eng.
216 C2 Oughtershaw N. Yorks., Eng.
232 B4 Oughterside Cumbria, Eng.
208 C3 Oughtibridge S. Yorks., Eng.
216 F2 Oulston N. Yorks., Eng.
232 C3 Oulton Cumbria, Eng.
166 F2 Oulton Norf., Eng.
148 B4 Oulton Staffs., Eng.
148 C3 Oulton Staffs., Eng.
120 J2 Oulton Suff., Eng.
222 F2 Oulton W. Yorks., Eng.
120 J2 Oulton Broad Suff., Eng.
148 C3 Oultoncross Staffs., Eng.
148 C3 Oulton Grange Staffs., Eng.
148 C3 Oulton Heath Staffs., Eng.
166 G2 Oulton Street Norf., Eng.
128 G3 Oundle Northants., Eng.
232 G4 Ousby Cumbria, Eng.
320 J3 Ousdale High., Scot.
120 C3 Ousden Suff., Eng.
24 P6 Ouse r. Eng.
26 M6 Ouse r. Eng.
210 D4 Ousefleet E. Riding, Eng.
236 F2 Ouston Durham, Eng.
244 F5 Ouston Northumb., Eng.
232 D7 Outcast Cumbria, Eng.
244 G2 Outchester Northumb., Eng.
22 B7 Outer Hebrides is Scot.
329 A4 Outertown Orkney, Scot.
232 E6 Outgate Cumbria, Eng.
232 I6 Outhgill Cumbria, Eng.
148 A3 Outlands Staffs., Eng.
222 C3 Outlane W. Yorks., Eng.
210 I4 Out Newton E. Riding, Eng.
228 E3 Out Rawcliffe Lancs., Eng.
331 E2 Out Skerries airport Scot.
22 □O2 Out Skerries is Scot.
166 A3 Outwell Norf., Eng.
78 F2 Outwood Surr., Eng.
222 E2 Outwood W. Yorks., Eng.
148 B4 Outwoods Staffs., Eng.
26 K3 Ouzel r. Eng.
222 F2 Ouzlewell Green W. Yorks., Eng.
222 C2 Ovenden W. Yorks., Eng.
124 E5 Over Cambs., Eng.
184 D2 Over Cheshire West & Chester, Eng.
98 F2 Over Glos., Eng.
98 D4 Over S. Glos., Eng.
329 F2 Overbister Orkney, Scot.
180 D5 Over Burrows Derbys., Eng.
136 E3 Overbury Worcs., Eng.
46 E4 Overcombe Dorset, Eng.
46 D2 Over Compton Dorset, Eng.
216 E1 Over Dinsdale N. Yorks., Eng.
124 B3 Over End Cambs., Eng.
180 D3 Over End Derbys., Eng.
180 D3 Overgreen Derbys., Eng.
132 B2 Over Green Warks., Eng.
180 C3 Over Haddon Derbys., Eng.
198 C2 Over Hulton Gtr Man., Eng.
228 F2 Over Kellet Lancs., Eng.
102 C3 Over Kiddington Oxon, Eng.
94 H4 Overleigh Som., Eng.
148 E4 Overley Staffs., Eng.
339 D2 Over Monnow Mon., Wales
102 B3 Over Norton Oxon, Eng.
184 F2 Over Peover Cheshire East, Eng.
184 B2 Overpool Cheshire West & Chester, Eng.
292 F2 Over Rankeilour Fife, Scot.
320 F3 Overscaig Hotel High., Scot.
180 D6 Overseal Derbys., Eng.
216 F2 Over Silton N. Yorks., Eng.
132 E3 Overslade Warks., Eng.
62 F3 Oversland Kent, Eng.
132 A4 Oversley Green Warks., Eng.
128 E4 Overstone Northants., Eng.
94 F4 Over Stowey Som., Eng.
166 H1 Overstrand Norf., Eng.
94 H5 Over Stratton Som., Eng.
184 E2 Over Tabley Cheshire East, Eng.
128 B5 Overthorpe Northants., Eng.
184 C2 Overton Cheshire West & Chester, Eng.
52 E3 Overton Hants., Eng.
228 E2 Overton Lancs., Eng.
216 F3 Overton N. Yorks., Eng.
144 D5 Overton Shrop., Eng.
222 E3 Overton W. Yorks., Eng.
314 F3 Overton Abers., Scot.
350 A3 Overton Swansea, Wales
378 H4 Overton Wrex., Wales
378 H4 Overton Bridge Wrex., Wales
228 G1 Overtown Lancs., Eng.
86 E2 Overtown Swindon, Eng.
280 C4 Overtown N. Lanark., Scot.
52 C4 Over Wallop Hants., Eng.
132 C2 Over Whitacre Warks., Eng.
Over Winchendon Bucks., Eng. see Upper Winchendon
102 C3 Over Worton Oxon, Eng.
102 E5 Overy Oxon, Eng.
106 C3 Oving Bucks., Eng.
58 F4 Ovingdean B. and H., Eng.
244 F6 Ovingham Northumb., Eng.
236 E4 Ovington Durham, Eng.
116 F1 Ovington Essex, Eng.
52 E4 Ovington Hants., Eng.
166 E3 Ovington Norf., Eng.
244 F6 Ovington Northumb., Eng.
23 H3 Owenreagh r. N. Ire.
52 C5 Ower Hants., Eng.
52 E6 Ower Hants., Eng.
46 F4 Owermoigne Dorset, Eng.
180 E3 Owlcotes Derbys., Eng.
180 D3 Owler Bar Derbys., Eng.
208 D3 Owlerton S. Yorks., Eng.
98 F3 Owlpen Glos., Eng.
120 H3 Owl's Green Suff., Eng.
106 C4 Owlswick Bucks., Eng.
208 D4 Owlthorpe S. Yorks., Eng.
170 D2 Owmby Lincs., Eng.
170 D3 Owmby-by-Spital Lincs., Eng.
52 E4 Owslebury Hants., Eng.
162 F3 Owston Leics., Eng.
208 F2 Owston S. Yorks., Eng.
170 B3 Owston Ferry N. Lincs., Eng.
210 H4 Owstwick E. Riding, Eng.
176 C5 Owthorpe Notts., Eng.
166 C3 Oxborough Norf., Eng.
228 E2 Oxcliffe Hill Lancs., Eng.
170 F4 Oxcombe Lincs., Eng.
180 F3 Oxcroft Derbys., Eng.
40 F3 Oxencombe Devon, Eng.
116 E2 Oxen End Essex, Eng.
98 E2 Oxenhall Glos., Eng.
232 F7 Oxenholme Cumbria, Eng.
222 C2 Oxenhope W. Yorks., Eng.
232 D7 Oxen Park Cumbria, Eng.
94 H3 Oxenpill Som., Eng.
98 G2 Oxenton Glos., Eng.
86 F4 Oxenwood Wilts., Eng.
102 D4 Oxford Oxon, Eng.
102 C4 Oxfordshire county Eng.
288 D3 Oxgangs Edin., Scot.
110 C6 Oxhey Herts., Eng.
236 E2 Oxhill Durham, Eng.
132 C5 Oxhill Warks., Eng.
110 D5 Oxlease Herts., Eng.
154 B2 Oxley W. Mids, Eng.
116 G3 Oxley Green Essex, Eng.
58 I3 Oxley's Green E. Sussex, Eng.
256 J4 Oxnam Borders, Scot.
166 G2 Oxnead Norf., Eng.
78 D1 Oxshott Surr., Eng.
208 C2 Oxspring S. Yorks., Eng.
78 F2 Oxted Surr., Eng.
190 C3 Oxton Merseyside, Eng.
176 C4 Oxton Notts., Eng.
216 F3 Oxton N. Yorks., Eng.
256 H2 Oxton Borders, Scot.
350 A3 Oxwich Swansea, Wales
350 A3 Oxwich Green Swansea, Wales
166 E2 Oxwick Norf., Eng.
22 H7 Oykel r. Scot.
320 F4 Oykel Bridge High., Scot.
314 F3 Oyne Abers., Scot.
350 B3 Oystermouth Swansea, Wales
98 F4 Ozleworth Glos., Eng.

P

Pabaigh i. Scot. see Pabbay
22 A9 Pabbay i. Scot.
22 B7 Pabbay i. Scot.
162 C2 Packington Leics., Eng.
132 C4 Packmores Warks., Eng.
132 B3 Packwood Warks., Eng.
308 E3 Padanaram Angus, Scot.
106 C3 Padbury Bucks., Eng.
74 C2 Paddington Gtr Lon., Eng.
190 F3 Paddington Warr., Eng.
62 G4 Paddlesworth Kent, Eng.
62 F3 Paddock Kent, Eng.
222 D3 Paddock W. Yorks., Eng.
252 G2 Paddockhole D. and G., Scot.
62 C3 Paddock Wood Kent, Eng.
144 D2 Paddolgreen Shrop., Eng.
378 G3 Padeswood Flints., Wales
180 B2 Padfield Derbys., Eng.
190 F3 Padgate Warr., Eng.
228 I4 Padiham Lancs., Eng.
216 D2 Padside N. Yorks., Eng.
36 E2 Padstow Corn., Eng.
82 D3 Padworth W. Berks., Eng.
98 F3 Paganhill Glos., Eng.
236 F3 Page Bank Durham, Eng.
190 D3 Page Moss Merseyside, Eng.
58 B4 Pagham W. Sussex, Eng.
116 G4 Paglesham Churchend Essex, Eng.
116 G4 Paglesham Eastend Essex, Eng.
326 C3 Paible W. Isles, Scot.
40 F3 Paignton Torbay, Eng.
132 E3 Pailton Warks., Eng.
58 H3 Paine's Corner E. Sussex, Eng.
148 D3 Painleyhill Staffs., Eng.
366 F6 Painscastle Powys, Wales
244 F6 Painshawfield Northumb., Eng.
210 D2 Painsthorpe E. Riding, Eng.
98 F3 Painswick Glos., Eng.
326 D2 Pairc W. Isles, Scot.
276 D2 Paisley Renf., Scot.
120 J2 Pakefield Suff., Eng.
120 D3 Pakenham Suff., Eng.
372 I3 Pale Gwynedd, Wales
58 G3 Palehouse Common E. Sussex, Eng.
52 C3 Palestine Hants., Eng.
82 F3 Paley Street W. and M., Eng.
154 C2 Palfrey W. Mids, Eng.
252 C2 Palgowan D. and G., Scot.
120 F2 Palgrave Suff., Eng.
244 E2 Pallinsburn House Northumb., Eng.
62 G4 Palmarsh Kent, Eng.
78 C3 Palmers Cross Surr., Eng.
74 D2 Palmers Green Gtr Lon., Eng.
350 G4 Palmerstown V. of Glam., Wales
252 E3 Palnackie D. and G., Scot.
252 C3 Palnure D. and G., Scot.
180 F3 Palterton Derbys., Eng.
52 F3 Pamber End Hants., Eng.
52 F2 Pamber Green Hants., Eng.
52 F2 Pamber Heath Hants., Eng.
46 G3 Pamphill Dorset, Eng.
124 F6 Pampisford Cambs., Eng.
329 C5 Pan Orkney, Scot.
94 H3 Panborough Som., Eng.
308 F3 Panbride Angus, Scot.
40 C2 Pancrasweek Devon, Eng.
350 F4 Pancross V. of Glam., Wales
372 F5 Pandy Gwynedd, Wales
339 C1 Pandy Mon., Wales
366 D3 Pandy Powys, Wales
378 F4 Pandy Wrex., Wales
378 E3 Pandy'r Capel Denb., Wales
378 C3 Pandy Tudur Conwy, Wales
116 F2 Panfield Essex, Eng.
82 D3 Pangbourne W. Berks., Eng.
216 E3 Pannal N. Yorks., Eng.
144 B5 Panpunton Shrop., Eng.
110 D5 Panshanger Herts., Eng.
144 B3 Pant Shrop., Eng.
378 G3 Pant Wrex., Wales
378 H3 Pant Wrex., Wales
26 N4 Pant r. Eng.
378 F2 Pantasaph Flints., Wales
339 C2 Panteg Torf., Wales
372 E2 Pant Glas Gwynedd, Wales
366 C3 Pantglas Powys, Wales
356 F2 Pantgwyn Carmar., Wales
362 C4 Pantgwyn Cere., Wales
372 H4 Pant Gwyn Gwynedd, Wales
350 C2 Pant-lasau Swansea, Wales
366 C4 Pant Mawr Powys, Wales
170 E4 Panton Lincs., Eng.
378 E3 Pant-pastynog Denb., Wales
372 G5 Pantperthog Gwynedd, Wales
366 E4 Pant-y-dwr Powys, Wales
378 G3 Pantyffordd Flints., Wales
366 F3 Pant-y-ffridd Powys, Wales
356 G3 Pantyffynnon Carmar., Wales
339 B2 Pantygasseg Torf., Wales
339 B1 Pantygelli Mon., Wales
378 F2 Pantymwyn Flints., Wales
166 H3 Panxworth Norf., Eng.
331 B3 Papa Stour airport Scot.
22 □M2 Papa Stour i. Scot.
22 K4 Papa Stronsay i. Scot.
329 D1 Papa Westray airport Scot.
22 K4 Papa Westray i. Scot.
Papay i. Scot. see Papa Westray
232 B4 Papcastle Cumbria, Eng.
331 C3 Papil Shet., Scot.
288 H3 Papple E. Lothian, Scot.
176 B4 Papplewick Notts., Eng.
22 D11 Paps of Jura hills Scot.
124 D5 Papworth Everard Cambs., Eng.
124 D5 Papworth St Agnes Cambs., Eng.
36 E2 Par Corn., Eng.
228 F5 Parbold Lancs., Eng.
58 D2 Parbrook W. Sussex, Eng.
372 H3 Parc Gwynedd, Wales
362 C4 Parcllyn Cere., Wales
362 F3 Parcrhydderch Cere., Wales
339 C3 Parc-Seymour Newp., Wales
356 F1 Parc-y-rhôs Carmar., Wales
232 B5 Pardshaw Cumbria, Eng.
120 H3 Parham Suff., Eng.
268 C3 Parish Holm S. Lanark., Scot.
388 D3 Park Derry, N. Ire.
314 E2 Park Abers., Scot.
198 E2 Park Bridge Gtr Man., Eng.
232 E3 Parkbroom Cumbria, Eng.
228 I3 Park Close Lancs., Eng.
58 H2 Park Corner E. Sussex, Eng.
102 E5 Park Corner Oxon, Eng.
232 D4 Parkend Cumbria, Eng.
98 D3 Parkend Glos., Eng.
244 D5 Park End Northumb., Eng.
148 B2 Park End Staffs., Eng.
136 C1 Park End Worcs., Eng.
62 B3 Parker's Green Kent, Eng.
116 J2 Parkeston Essex, Eng.
106 C4 Parkfield Bucks., Eng.
36 F2 Parkfield Corn., Eng.
98 E5 Parkfield S. Glos., Eng.
154 B2 Parkfield W. Mids, Eng.
308 E2 Parkford Angus, Scot.
184 A2 Parkgate Cheshire West & Chester, Eng.
52 E5 Park Gate Hants., Eng.
62 D4 Parkgate Kent, Eng.
78 E2 Parkgate Surr., Eng.
208 D3 Parkgate S. Yorks., Eng.
136 E1 Park Gate Worcs., Eng.
222 D1 Park Gate W. Yorks., Eng.
222 E3 Park Gate W. Yorks., Eng.
388 J4 Parkgate Antrim, N. Ire.
120 F3 Park Green Suff., Eng.
276 D2 Parkhall W. Dun., Scot.
40 D2 Parkham Devon, Eng.
180 E4 Park Head Derbys., Eng.
208 C3 Parkhead S. Yorks., Eng.
222 D3 Park Head W. Yorks., Eng.
276 E2 Parkhead Glas., Scot.
208 D3 Park Hill S. Yorks., Eng.
308 G3 Parkhill Angus, Scot.
304 K3 Parkhill Perth and Kin., Scot.
339 D2 Parkhouse Mon., Wales
180 E3 Parkhouse Green Derbys., Eng.
52 E6 Parkhurst I.o.W., Eng.
378 H4 Park Lane Wrex., Wales
74 D3 Park Langley Gtr Lon., Eng.
350 B3 Parkmill Swansea, Wales
314 F4 Parkneuk Abers., Scot.
292 D3 Parkneuk Fife, Scot.
74 C2 Park Royal Gtr Lon., Eng.
378 H3 Parkside Wrex., Wales
46 H3 Parkstone Poole, Eng.
110 C5 Park Street Herts., Eng.
102 D4 Park Town Oxon, Eng.
154 B2 Park Village W. Mids, Eng.
94 I5 Parkway Som., Eng.
208 D3 Parkwood Springs S. Yorks., Eng.
46 H3 Parley Cross Dorset, Eng.
46 H3 Parley Green Dorset, Eng.
222 F2 Parlington W. Yorks., Eng.
26 F5 Parrett r. Eng.
358 E1 Parrog Pembs., Wales
116 E3 Parsonage Green Essex, Eng.
232 C4 Parsonby Cumbria, Eng.
208 D3 Parson Cross S. Yorks., Eng.
124 E3 Parson Drove Cambs., Eng.
74 C3 Parsons Green Gtr Lon., Eng.
276 E2 Partick Glas., Scot.
198 C3 Partington Gtr Man., Eng.
170 G4 Partney Lincs., Eng.
232 A5 Parton Cumbria, Eng.
252 D2 Parton D. and G., Scot.
58 E3 Partridge Green W. Sussex, Eng.
180 C4 Parwich Derbys., Eng.
Pas de Calais str. France/U.K. see Dover, Strait of
116 D3 Paslow Wood Common Essex, Eng.
128 D5 Passenham Northants., Eng.
52 H4 Passfield Hants., Eng.
116 D4 Passingford Bridge Essex, Eng.
166 H1 Paston Norf., Eng.
124 C3 Paston Peterb., Eng.
166 H1 Paston Green Norf., Eng.
166 H1 Paston Street Norf., Eng.
148 C4 Pasturefields Staffs., Eng.
40 D2 Patchacott Devon, Eng.
58 F3 Patcham B. and H., Eng.
110 C6 Patchetts Green Herts., Eng.
58 D3 Patching W. Sussex, Eng.
98 D4 Patchway S. Glos., Eng.
216 D2 Pateley Bridge N. Yorks., Eng.
94 G4 Pathe Som., Eng.
40 F2 Pathfinder Village Devon, Eng.
314 F4 Pathhead Abers., Scot.
262 F4 Pathhead E. Ayr., Scot.
292 F3 Pathhead Fife, Scot.
288 F3 Pathhead Midlothian, Scot.
132 B4 Pathlow Warks., Eng.
304 J5 Path of Condie Perth and Kin., Scot.
110 F4 Patmore Heath Herts., Eng.
262 D4 Patna E. Ayr., Scot.
86 D4 Patney Wilts., Eng.
405 B2 Patrick Isle of Man
216 E2 Patrick Brompton N. Yorks., Eng.
198 C3 Patricroft Gtr Man., Eng.
210 H4 Patrington E. Riding, Eng.
210 H4 Patrington Haven E. Riding, Eng.
366 G7 Patrishow Powys, Wales
62 G3 Patrixbourne Kent, Eng.
232 E5 Patterdale Cumbria, Eng.
388 I5 Pattersonstown Lisburn, N. Ire.
148 B5 Pattingham Staffs., Eng.
128 C4 Pattishall Northants., Eng.
116 F2 Pattiswick Essex, Eng.
36 C3 Paul Corn., Eng.
128 D5 Paulerspury Northants., Eng.
210 G4 Paull E. Riding, Eng.
210 G4 Paull Holme E. Riding, Eng.
94 I3 Paulton B. and N.E. Som., Eng.
244 F4 Pauperhaugh Northumb., Eng.
144 F3 Pave Lane Telford, Eng.
110 B2 Pavenham Bedford, Eng.
94 F3 Pawlett Som., Eng.
244 D2 Pawston Northumb., Eng.
98 I1 Paxford Glos., Eng.
58 F2 Paxhill Park W. Sussex, Eng.
256 L2 Paxton Borders, Scot.
62 E3 Payden Street Kent, Eng.
40 G2 Payhembury Devon, Eng.
110 E5 Paynes Hall Herts., Eng.
228 I3 Paythorne Lancs., Eng.
58 F4 Peacehaven E. Sussex, Eng.
46 F1 Peacemarsh Dorset, Eng.
136 D2 Peachley Worcs., Eng.
180 B3 Peak Dale Derbys., Eng.
24 N7 Peak District National Park nat. park Eng.
180 C3 Peak Forest Derbys., Eng.
124 C3 Peakirk Peterb., Eng.
62 G3 Pean Hill Kent, Eng.
308 D2 Pearsie Angus, Scot.
62 C4 Pearson's Green Kent, Eng.
180 E5 Pear Tree Derby, Eng.
110 D5 Peartree Herts., Eng.
116 D4 Peartree Green Essex, Eng.
140 D4 Peartree Green Here., Eng.
94 J3 Peasedown St John B. and N.E. Som., Eng.
180 E4 Peasehill Derbys., Eng.
166 F2 Peaseland Green Norf., Eng.
82 B3 Peasemore W. Berks., Eng.
120 H3 Peasenhall Suff., Eng.
58 E2 Pease Pottage W. Sussex, Eng.
78 D2 Peaslake Surr., Eng.
190 E3 Peasley Cross Merseyside, Eng.
58 K3 Peasmarsh E. Sussex, Eng.
94 G5 Peasmarsh Som., Eng.
78 C2 Peasmarsh Surr., Eng.
288 F3 Peaston E. Lothian, Scot.
288 F3 Peastonbank E. Lothian, Scot.
314 G1 Peathill Abers., Scot.
236 E4 Peathrow Durham, Eng.
292 G2 Peat Inn Fife, Scot.
162 E3 Peatling Magna Leics., Eng.
162 E3 Peatling Parva Leics., Eng.
144 D5 Peaton Shrop., Eng.
78 E2 Pebble Coombe Surr., Eng.
116 G2 Pebmarsh Essex, Eng.
136 G3 Pebworth Worcs., Eng.
222 B2 Pecket Well W. Yorks., Eng.
184 C3 Peckforton Cheshire East, Eng.
74 D3 Peckham Gtr Lon., Eng.
162 D3 Peckleton Leics., Eng.
154 B3 Pedmore W. Mids, Eng.
94 H4 Pedwell Som., Eng.
256 E3 Peebles Borders, Scot.
405 B2 Peel Isle of Man
228 E4 Peel Lancs., Eng.
198 C3 Peel Green Gtr Man., Eng.
62 E4 Peening Quarter Kent, Eng.
162 C2 Peggs Green Leics., Eng.
110 C4 Pegsdon Central Bedfordshire, Eng.
244 H4 Pegswood Northumb., Eng.
62 I3 Pegwell Kent, Eng.
26 O5 Pegwell Bay b. Eng.
322 C3 Peinchorran High., Scot.
322 C2 Peinmore High., Scot.
236 F2 Pelaw T. and W., Eng.
358 D3 Pelcomb Pembs., Wales
358 D3 Pelcomb Bridge Pembs., Wales
358 D3 Pelcomb Cross Pembs., Wales
116 H3 Peldon Essex, Eng.
58 I2 Pell Green E. Sussex, Eng.
222 C2 Pellon W. Yorks., Eng.
154 C2 Pelsall W. Mids, Eng.
154 C2 Pelsall Wood W. Mids, Eng.
236 F2 Pelton Durham, Eng.
232 B4 Pelutho Cumbria, Eng.
36 F2 Pelynt Corn., Eng.
198 A2 Pemberton Gtr Man., Eng.
140 B2 Pembridge Here., Eng.
358 E3 Pembroke Dock Pembs., Wales
358 E3 Pembrokeshire county Wales
26 B4 Pembrokeshire Coast National Park nat. park Wales
62 B4 Pembury Kent, Eng.
339 D2 Penallt Mon., Wales
358 F4 Penally Pembs., Wales
140 D4 Penalt Here., Eng.
36 E3 Penare Corn., Eng.
Penarlâg Flints., Wales see Hawarden
366 F4 Penarran Powys, Wales
350 G4 Penarth V. of Glam., Wales
362 G2 Pen-bont Rhydybeddau Cere., Wales
356 D1 Penboyr Carmar., Wales
362 D4 Penbryn Cere., Wales
356 E1 Pencader Carmar., Wales
362 E3 Pen-cae Cere., Wales
378 D3 Pen-cae-cwm Conwy, Wales
372 D3 Pencaenewydd Gwynedd, Wales
288 F3 Pencaitland E. Lothian, Scot.
371 C3 Pencarnisiog I.o.A., Wales
356 F1 Pencarreg Carmar., Wales
36 E2 Pencarrow Corn., Eng.
366 F7 Pencelli Powys, Wales
350 B3 Pen-clawdd Swansea, Wales
350 F3 Pencoed Bridg., Wales
140 D2 Pencombe Here., Eng.
140 C4 Pencoyd Here., Eng.
140 D4 Pencraig Here., Eng.
366 E1 Pencraig Powys, Wales
Pencraig Powys, Wales see Old Radnor
36 C3 Pendeen Corn., Eng.
350 E2 Penderyn R.C.T., Wales
356 C3 Pendine Carmar., Wales
198 D2 Pendlebury Gtr Man., Eng.
24 M6 Pendle Hill hill Eng.
198 D3 Pendleton Gtr Man., Eng.
228 H3 Pendleton Lancs., Eng.
136 D4 Pendock Worcs., Eng.
36 E2 Pendoggett Corn., Eng.
94 H5 Pendomer Som., Eng.
350 F4 Pendoylan V. of Glam., Wales
350 E3 Pendre Bridg., Wales
366 C3 Penegoes Powys, Wales
36 D3 Penelewey Corn., Eng.
358 F2 Pen-ffordd Pembs., Wales
350 G2 Pengam Caerp., Wales
74 D3 Penge Gtr Lon., Eng.
366 F7 Pengenffordd Powys, Wales
371 D2 Pengorffwysfa I.o.A., Wales
36 F2 Pengover Green Corn., Eng.
339 C2 Pen-groes-oped Mon., Wales
378 E2 Pengwern Denb., Wales
36 D3 Penhale Corn., Eng.
36 D3 Penhallow Corn., Eng.
372 F5 Penhelig Gwynedd, Wales
86 E2 Penhill Swindon, Eng.
339 C3 Penhow Newp., Wales
58 I3 Penhurst E. Sussex, Eng.
372 F5 Peniarth Gwynedd, Wales
288 D4 Penicuik Midlothian, Scot.
356 E2 Peniel Carmar., Wales
322 C2 Penifiler High., Scot.
300 D5 Peninver Arg. and B., Scot.
366 E2 Penisarcwm Powys, Wales
372 E2 Penisa'r Waun Gwynedd, Wales
366 F7 Penishawain Powys, Wales
208 C2 Penistone S. Yorks., Eng.
190 F3 Penketh Warr., Eng.
148 C4 Penkridge Staffs., Eng.
36 F1 Penlean Corn., Eng.
378 H4 Penley Wrex., Wales
372 C3 Penllech Gwynedd, Wales
350 B2 Penllergaer Swansea, Wales
371 C3 Pen-llyn I.o.A., Wales
350 F4 Penllyn V. of Glam., Wales
371 C4 Pen-lôn I.o.A., Wales
378 C3 Penmachno Conwy, Wales
350 B3 Penmaen Swansea, Wales
378 B2 Penmaenan Conwy, Wales
378 B2 Penmaenmawr Conwy, Wales
372 G4 Penmaenpool Gwynedd, Wales
378 C2 Penmaen-Rhôs Conwy, Wales
350 F4 Penmark V. of Glam., Wales
371 E3 Penmon I.o.A., Wales
372 F3 Penmorfa Gwynedd, Wales
371 D3 Penmynydd I.o.A., Wales
106 D5 Penn Bucks., Eng.
154 B2 Penn W. Mids, Eng.
372 G5 Pennal Gwynedd, Wales
372 G5 Pennal-isaf Gwynedd, Wales
314 G1 Pennan Abers., Scot.
36 D3 Pennance Corn., Eng.
362 E3 Pennant Cere., Wales
366 D3 Pennant Powys, Wales
366 E2 Pennant Melangell Powys, Wales
358 E3 Pennar Pembs., Wales
350 B3 Pennard Swansea, Wales
144 C4 Pennerley Shrop., Eng.
24 M5 Pennines hills Eng.
252 C3 Penninghame D. and G., Scot.
232 D7 Pennington Cumbria, Eng.
52 C6 Pennington Hants., Eng.
198 B2 Pennington Green Gtr Man., Eng.
366 F7 Pennorth Powys, Wales
106 E5 Penn Street Bucks., Eng.
98 E5 Pennsylvania S. Glos., Eng.
232 D7 Penny Bridge Cumbria, Eng.
40 D3 Pennycross Plymouth, Eng.
300 D2 Pennyfuir Arg. and B., Scot.
166 H2 Pennygate Norf., Eng.
300 B2 Pennyghael Arg. and B., Scot.
262 C4 Pennyglen S. Ayr., Scot.
300 C2 Pennygown Arg. and B., Scot.
180 F3 Penny Green Derbys., Eng.
40 F2 Pennymoor Devon, Eng.
166 G3 Penny's Green Norf., Eng.
262 E4 Pennyvenie E. Ayr., Scot.
362 C4 Penparc Cere., Wales
358 D2 Penparc Pembs., Wales
362 F2 Penparcau Cere., Wales
339 C2 Penpedairheol Mon., Wales
339 C2 Penperlleni Mon., Wales
36 F2 Penpoll Corn., Eng.
36 D3 Penponds Corn., Eng.
252 E2 Penpont D. and G., Scot.
366 E7 Penpont Powys, Wales
350 F3 Penprysg Bridg., Wales
40 E3 Penquit Devon, Eng.
36 F2 Penrest Corn., Eng.
356 D1 Penrherber Carmar., Wales
358 G1 Penrhiw Pembs., Wales
350 F2 Penrhiwceiber R.C.T., Wales
356 F2 Penrhiwgoch Carmar., Wales
362 D4 Penrhiw-llan Cere., Wales
362 D4 Penrhiw-pâl Cere., Wales
350 D3 Penrhiwtyn N.P.T., Wales
372 D3 Penrhos Gwynedd, Wales
371 B3 Penrhos I.o.A., Wales
339 C2 Penrhos Mon., Wales
366 C8 Penrhos Powys, Wales
372 F1 Penrhos-garnedd Gwynedd, Wales
378 C2 Penrhyn Bay Conwy, Wales
362 F2 Penrhyn-coch Cere., Wales
372 F3 Penrhyndeudraeth Gwynedd, Wales
26 C2 Penrhyn Mawr pt Wales
378 C2 Penrhyn-side Conwy, Wales
350 F3 Penrhys R.C.T., Wales
350 A3 Penrice Swansea, Wales
232 F5 Penrith Cumbria, Eng.
36 E2 Penrose Corn., Eng.
232 E5 Penruddock Cumbria, Eng.
36 D3 Penryn Corn., Eng.
356 E2 Pensarn Carmar., Wales
378 D2 Pensarn Conwy, Wales
372 E3 Pen-sarn Gwynedd, Wales
372 F4 Pen-sarn Gwynedd, Wales
136 C2 Pensax Worcs., Eng.
190 C3 Pensby Merseyside, Eng.
94 J4 Penselwood Som., Eng.
94 I2 Pensford B. and N.E. Som., Eng.
136 E3 Pensham Worcs., Eng.
236 G2 Penshaw T. and W., Eng.
62 B3 Penshurst Kent, Eng.
36 F2 Pensilva Corn., Eng.
154 B2 Pensnett W. Mids, Eng.
288 F3 Penston E. Lothian, Scot.
36 E3 Pentewan Corn., Eng.
372 F1 Pentir Gwynedd, Wales
36 D2 Pentire Corn., Eng.
26 B6 Pentire Point pt Eng.
22 J5 Pentland Firth sea chan. Scot.
22 I11 Pentland Hills hills Scot.
358 F3 Pentlepoir Pembs., Wales
116 F1 Pentlow Essex, Eng.
116 F1 Pentlow Street Essex, Eng.
166 C2 Pentney Norf., Eng.
52 C3 Penton Grafton Hants., Eng.
52 C3 Penton Mewsey Hants., Eng.
74 D2 Pentonville Gtr Lon., Eng.
371 D3 Pentraeth I.o.A., Wales
144 B5 Pentre Shrop., Eng.
144 C3 Pentre Shrop., Eng.
366 E2 Pentre Powys, Wales
366 E4 Pentre Powys, Wales
366 F4 Pentre Powys, Wales
366 G3 Pentre Powys, Wales
366 G5 Pentre Powys, Wales
350 F3 Pentre R.C.T., Wales
378 G4 Pentre Wrex., Wales
378 G4 Pentre Wrex., Wales
362 F4 Pentre-bach Cere., Wales
350 F2 Pentrebach M. Tyd., Wales
366 D7 Pentre-bach Powys, Wales
350 G3 Pentrebach R.C.T., Wales
350 B2 Pentrebach Swansea, Wales
371 D3 Pentre Berw I.o.A., Wales
378 B3 Pentre-bont Conwy, Wales
378 F3 Pentre-bwlch Denb., Wales
356 D1 Pentrecagal Carmar., Wales
378 F3 Pentre-celyn Denb., Wales
366 D3 Pentre-celyn Powys, Wales
350 C3 Pentre-chwyth Swansea, Wales
350 E2 Pentreclwydau N.P.T., Wales
356 D1 Pentre-cwrt Carmar., Wales
366 E6 Pentre-Dolau-Honddu Powys, Wales
378 F3 Pentredwr Denb., Wales
350 C3 Pentre-dwr Swansea, Wales
356 F2 Pentrefelin Carmar., Wales
362 F4 Pentrefelin Cere., Wales
378 C2 Pentrefelin Conwy, Wales
372 E3 Pentrefelin Gwynedd, Wales
366 F2 Pentrefelin Powys, Wales
378 G2 Pentre Ffwrndan Flints., Wales
378 C3 Pentrefoelas Conwy, Wales
358 G2 Pentre Galar Pembs., Wales
362 D4 Pentregat Cere., Wales
356 F3 Pentre Gwenlais Carmar., Wales
372 F4 Pentre Gwynfryn Gwynedd, Wales
378 F2 Pentre Halkyn Flints., Wales
144 B4 Pentreheyling Shrop., Eng.
378 C2 Pentre Isaf Conwy, Wales
378 E3 Pentre Llanrhaeadr Denb., Wales
366 D5 Pentre-llwyn-llŵyd Powys, Wales
362 F2 Pentre-llyn Cere., Wales
378 D3 Pentre-llyn-cymmer Conwy, Wales
378 H3 Pentre Maelor Wrex., Wales
350 F4 Pentre Meyrick V. of Glam., Wales
372 I3 Pentre-piod Gwynedd, Wales
339 B3 Pentre-poeth Newp., Wales
350 C2 Pentre Poeth Swansea, Wales
366 F2 Pentre'r beirdd Powys, Wales
378 C2 Pentre'r Felin Conwy, Wales
366 D7 Pentre'r-felin Powys, Wales
378 E3 Pentre Saron Denb., Wales
378 C3 Pentre-tafarn-y-fedw Conwy, Wales
356 H1 Pentre-ty-gwyn Carmar., Wales
180 E4 Pentrich Derbys., Eng.
46 H2 Pentridge Dorset, Eng.
350 G2 Pentwyn Caerp., Wales
350 H2 Pen-twyn Caerp., Wales
350 H3 Pentwyn Cardiff, Wales
339 D2 Pen-twyn Mon., Wales
339 B2 Pen-twyn Torf., Wales
350 G3 Pentwyn-mawr Caerp., Wales
350 G3 Pentyrch Cardiff, Wales
Pentywyn Carmar., Wales see Pendine
362 F3 Penuwch Cere., Wales
36 E2 Penwithick Corn., Eng.
52 D2 Penwood Hants., Eng.
228 F4 Penwortham Lancs., Eng.
228 F4 Penwortham Lane Lancs., Eng.
366 D8 Penwyllt Powys, Wales
356 F2 Pen-y-banc Carmar., Wales
356 F3 Penybanc Carmar., Wales
356 D2 Pen-y-bont Carmar., Wales
356 H1 Pen-y-bont Carmar., Wales
362 F2 Penybont Cere., Wales
366 E2 Pen-y-bont Powys, Wales
366 F2 Pen-y-bont Powys, Wales
366 F5 Penybont Powys, Wales
366 E2 Penybontfawr Powys, Wales
350 G3 Penybryn Caerp., Wales
372 G4 Pen-y-bryn Gwynedd, Wales
358 G1 Pen-y-bryn Pembs., Wales
378 G4 Pen-y-bryn Wrex., Wales
366 C8 Pen-y-cae Powys, Wales
378 G3 Penycae Wrex., Wales
339 C3 Pen-y-cae-mawr Mon., Wales
378 F2 Pen-y-cefn Flints., Wales
339 D2 Pen-y-clawdd Mon., Wales
350 F3 Pen-y-coedcae R.C.T., Wales
358 D2 Penycwm Pembs., Wales
350 F2 Pen-y-Darren M. Tyd., Wales
350 E3 Pen-y-fai Bridg., Wales
378 F2 Pen-y-ffordd Flints., Wales
378 G3 Penyffordd Flints., Wales
372 E2 Penyffridd Gwynedd, Wales
26 E2 Penygadair hill Wales
366 F7 Pen-y-gaer Powys, Wales
356 F2 Pen-y-garn Carmar., Wales
362 F2 Pen-y-garn Cere., Wales
339 B2 Penygarn Torf., Wales
366 F2 Penygarnedd Powys, Wales
366 E6 Pen-y-garreg Powys, Wales
24 M5 Pen-y-Ghent hill Eng.
372 B3 Pen-y-Graig Gwynedd, Wales
350 F3 Penygraig R.C.T., Wales
356 F3 Penygroes Carmar., Wales
372 E2 Penygroes Gwynedd, Wales
372 F2 Pen-y-Gwryd Hotel Gwynedd, Wales
350 H3 Pen-y-lan Cardiff, Wales
356 E3 Pen-y-Mynydd Carmar., Wales
378 G3 Penymynydd Flints., Wales
378 F2 Pen-y-parc Flints., Wales
140 A3 Pen-y-Park Here., Eng.
372 F2 Pen-y-Pass Gwynedd, Wales
350 E2 Pen-yr-englyn R.C.T., Wales
339 D2 Pen-yr-heol Mon., Wales
350 B2 Penyrheol Swansea, Wales
371 D2 Pen-y-sarn I.o.A., Wales
378 F3 Pen-y-stryt Denb., Wales
350 F2 Penywaun R.C.T., Wales
36 C3 Penzance Corn., Eng.
136 E3 Peopleton Worcs., Eng.
184 F2 Peover Heath Cheshire East, Eng.
78 C2 Peper Harow Surr., Eng.
144 E3 Peplow Shrop., Eng.
216 E1 Pepper Arden N. Yorks., Eng.
116 E3 Pepper's Green Essex, Eng.
110 C4 Pepperstock Central Bedfordshire, Eng.
264 G3 Perceton N. Ayr., Scot.
314 E3 Percie Abers., Scot.
314 G1 Percyhorner Abers., Scot.
236 G2 Percy Main T. and W., Eng.
86 F4 Perham Down Wilts., Eng.
94 D3 Periton Som., Eng.
74 C2 Perivale Gtr Lon., Eng.
314 E3 Perkhill Abers., Scot.
144 C4 Perkins Beach Shrop., Eng.
176 C3 Perlethorpe Notts., Eng.
36 D3 Perranarworthal Corn., Eng.
36 D2 Perranporth Corn., Eng.
36 C3 Perranuthnoe Corn., Eng.
36 D3 Perranzabuloe Corn., Eng.
98 H3 Perrott's Brook Glos., Eng.
154 C2 Perry W. Mids, Eng.
154 C2 Perry Barr W. Mids, Eng.
148 E5 Perry Crofts Staffs., Eng.
116 F2 Perry Green Essex, Eng.
110 F4 Perry Green Herts., Eng.
86 C2 Perry Green Wilts., Eng.
94 J2 Perrymead B. and N.E. Som., Eng.
62 C2 Perry Street Kent, Eng.
148 B3 Pershall Staffs., Eng.
136 E3 Pershore Worcs., Eng.
304 J2 Persie House Perth and Kin., Scot.
308 G2 Pert Angus, Scot.
110 C2 Pertenhall Bedford, Eng.
304 G2 Perth and Kinross admin. div. Scot.
350 F3 Perthcelyn R.C.T., Wales
144 C2 Perthy Shrop., Eng.
148 B5 Perton Staffs., Eng.
58 J3 Pestalozzi Children's Village E. Sussex, Eng.
124 C3 Peterborough Peterb., Eng.
124 C3 Peterborough admin. div. Eng.
320 C4 Peterburn High., Scot.
140 B3 Peterchurch Here., Eng.
314 G3 Peterculter Aberdeen, Scot.
314 H2 Peterhead Abers., Scot.
236 H3 Peterlee Durham, Eng.
52 G4 Petersfield Hants., Eng.
86 E5 Petersfinger Wilts., Eng.
110 C4 Peter's Green Herts., Eng.
326 C4 Peters Port W. Isles, Scot.
339 B3 Peterstone Wentlooge Newp., Wales
350 G4 Peterston-super-Ely V. of Glam., Wales
140 D4 Peterstow Here., Eng.
40 D3 Peter Tavy Devon, Eng.
62 G3 Petham Kent, Eng.
40 D2 Petrockstowe Devon, Eng.
58 J3 Pett E. Sussex, Eng.
120 F3 Pettaugh Suff., Eng.
232 F4 Petteril Green Cumbria, Eng.
402 D3 Pettigo Fermanagh, N. Ire.
268 E2 Pettinain S. Lanark., Scot.
120 H4 Pettistree Suff., Eng.
40 F1 Petton Devon, Eng.
144 D3 Petton Shrop., Eng.
74 E3 Petts Wood Gtr Lon., Eng.
314 F2 Petty Abers., Scot.
292 E3 Pettycur Fife, Scot.
98 F4 Petty France S. Glos., Eng.
314 G3 Pettymuick Abers., Scot.
58 C3 Petworth W. Sussex, Eng.
58 I4 Pevensey E. Sussex, Eng.
58 I4 Pevensey Bay E. Sussex, Eng.
26 M6 Pevensey Levels lowland Eng.
40 D3 Peverell Plymouth, Eng.
86 E3 Pewsey Wilts., Eng.
26 I5 Pewsey, Vale of val. Eng.
388 H2 Pharis Ballymoney, N. Ire.
106 C5 Pheasant's Hill Bucks., Eng.
314 F4 Phesdo Abers., Scot.
40 C2 Philham Devon, Eng.
256 G3 Philiphaugh Borders, Scot.
36 C3 Phillack Corn., Eng.
36 E3 Philleigh Corn., Eng.
288 B3 Philpstoun W. Lothian, Scot.
140 D4 Phocle Green Here., Eng.
52 G3 Phoenix Green Hants., Eng.
322 I3 Phones High., Scot.
314 C2 Phorp Moray, Scot.
94 H4 Pibsbury Som., Eng.
232 A5 Pica Cumbria, Eng.
166 H4 Piccadilly Corner Norf., Eng.
110 C5 Piccotts End Herts., Eng.
208 E2 Pickburn S. Yorks., Eng.
116 D3 Pickerells Essex, Eng.
216 G2 Pickering N. Yorks., Eng.
24 P5 Pickering, Vale of val. Eng.
236 E2 Pickering Nook Durham, Eng.
52 D3 Picket Piece Hants., Eng.
52 B5 Picket Post Hants., Eng.
154 E3 Pickford W. Mids, Eng.
154 E3 Pickford Green W. Mids, Eng.
144 D4 Picklescott Shrop., Eng.
292 G1 Pickletillem Fife, Scot.
184 E2 Pickmere Cheshire East, Eng.
94 F4 Pickney Som., Eng.
144 F3 Pickstock Telford, Eng.
304 I4 Pickston Perth and Kin., Scot.
228 H4 Pickup Bank B'burn, Eng.
40 D1 Pickwell Devon, Eng.
162 F2 Pickwell Leics., Eng.
170 D6 Pickworth Lincs., Eng.
162 H2 Pickworth Rutland, Eng.
184 B2 Picton Cheshire West & Chester, Eng.
216 E1 Picton N. Yorks., Eng.
378 F2 Picton Flints., Wales
58 G4 Piddinghoe E. Sussex, Eng.
106 C5 Piddington Bucks., Eng.
128 E4 Piddington Northants., Eng.
102 E3 Piddington Oxon, Eng.
26 H6 Piddle r. Eng.
46 E3 Piddlehinton Dorset, Eng.
46 E3 Piddletrenthide Dorset, Eng.
124 D4 Pidley Cambs., Eng.
329 D2 Pierowall Orkney, Scot.
244 G4 Pigdon Northumb., Eng.
388 I5 Pigeontown Antrim, N. Ire.
180 C4 Pikehall Derbys., Eng.
228 I4 Pike Hill Lancs., Eng.
52 C5 Pikeshill Hants., Eng.
46 H3 Pilford Dorset, Eng.
116 D4 Pilgrims Hatch Essex, Eng.
170 B3 Pilham Lincs., Eng.
94 H2 Pill N. Som., Eng.
24 K5 Pillar hill Eng.
36 G2 Pillaton Corn., Eng.
148 C4 Pillaton Staffs., Eng.
132 C5 Pillerton Hersey Warks., Eng.
132 C5 Pillerton Priors Warks., Eng.
366 G5 Pilleth Powys, Wales
98 G2 Pilley Glos., Eng.
52 C6 Pilley Hants., Eng.
208 D3 Pilley S. Yorks., Eng.
339 C3 Pillgwenlly Newp., Wales
228 E3 Pilling Lancs., Eng.
228 E3 Pilling Lane Lancs., Eng.
98 D3 Pillowell Glos., Eng.
98 D4 Pilning S. Glos., Eng.
180 C4 Pilsbury Derbys., Eng.
46 C3 Pilsdon Dorset, Eng.
124 B3 Pilsgate Peterb., Eng.
180 D3 Pilsley Derbys., Eng.
180 E4 Pilsley Derbys., Eng.
166 I2 Pilson Green Norf., Eng.
128 G3 Pilton Northants., Eng.
162 H3 Pilton Rutland, Eng.
94 I4 Pilton Som., Eng.
288 D3 Pilton Edin., Scot.
350 A3 Pilton Swansea, Wales
350 A3 Pilton Green Swansea, Wales
198 D2 Pimhole Gtr Man., Eng.
74 D3 Pimlico Gtr Lon., Eng.
110 C5 Pimlico Herts., Eng.
46 G2 Pimperne Dorset, Eng.
170 F7 Pinchbeck Lincs., Eng.
170 E7 Pinchbeck Bars Lincs., Eng.
170 E7 Pinchbeck West Lincs., Eng.
208 F2 Pincheon Green S. Yorks., Eng.
216 F1 Pinchinthorpe R. and C., Eng.
62 B2 Pinden Kent, Eng.
106 C2 Pindon End M.K., Eng.
62 H4 Pineham Kent, Eng.
86 E2 Pinehurst Swindon, Eng.
228 E5 Pinfold Lancs., Eng.
120 D3 Pinford End Suff., Eng.
356 E3 Pinged Carmar., Wales
110 D4 Pin Green Herts., Eng.
40 F2 Pinhoe Devon, Eng.
82 F2 Pinkneys Green W. and M., Eng.
132 B4 Pinley Green Warks., Eng.
120 G5 Pin Mill Suff., Eng.
262 B5 Pinminnoch S. Ayr., Scot.
262 C5 Pinmore S. Ayr., Scot.
74 B2 Pinner Gtr Lon., Eng.
74 B2 Pinner Green Gtr Lon., Eng.
136 E3 Pinvin Worcs., Eng.
262 C6 Pinwherry S. Ayr., Scot.
180 F4 Pinxton Derbys., Eng.
140 C3 Pipe and Lyde Here., Eng.
144 F2 Pipe Gate Shrop., Eng.
148 D4 Pipehill Staffs., Eng.
300 E4 Piperhall Arg. and B., Scot.
148 D4 Pipe Ridware Staffs., Eng.
184 B2 Piper's Ash Cheshire West & Chester, Eng.
36 F2 Pipers Pool Corn., Eng.
128 E3 Pipewell Northants., Eng.

Pippacott to Raunds

40 D1 Pippacott Devon, Eng.
366 F6 Pipton Powys, Wales
78 C2 Pirbright Surr., Eng.
264 B3 Pirnmill N. Ayr., Scot.
110 C4 Pirton Herts., Eng.
136 D3 Pirton Worcs., Eng.
296 G4 Pisgah Stir., Scot.
102 F5 Pishill Oxon, Eng.
208 D3 Pismire Hill S. Yorks., Eng.
372 D3 Pistyll Gwynedd, Wales
304 G2 Pitagowan Perth and Kin., Scot.
304 I4 Pitcairngreen Perth and Kin., Scot.
304 I5 Pitcairns Perth and Kin., Scot.
314 F3 Pitcaple Abers., Scot.
98 F3 Pitchcombe Glos., Eng.
106 C3 Pitchcott Bucks., Eng.
144 D4 Pitchford Shrop., Eng.
106 C4 Pitch Green Bucks., Eng.
78 B3 Pitch Place Surr., Eng.
78 C2 Pitch Place Surr., Eng.
94 J4 Pitcombe Som., Eng.
350 E4 Pitcot V. of Glam., Wales
288 H3 Pitcox E. Lothian, Scot.
304 K3 Pitcur Perth and Kin., Scot.
314 F3 Pitfichie Abers., Scot.
314 F2 Pitinnan Abers., Scot.
308 F2 Pitkennedy Angus, Scot.
292 E2 Pitkevy Fife, Scot.
292 F2 Pitlessie Fife, Scot.
304 H2 Pitlochry Perth and Kin., Scot.
314 F2 Pitmachie Abers., Scot.
120 F3 Pitman's Corner Suff., Eng.
314 G2 Pitmedden Abers., Scot.
94 F5 Pitminster Som., Eng.
308 F3 Pitmuies Angus, Scot.
314 F3 Pitmunie Abers., Scot.
304 H3 Pitnacree Perth and Kin., Scot.
94 H4 Pitney Som., Eng.
304 K4 Pitroddie Perth and Kin., Scot.
292 G2 Pitscottie Fife, Scot.
116 F4 Pitsea Essex, Eng.
128 D4 Pitsford Northants., Eng.
94 E4 Pitsford Hill Som., Eng.
26 K3 Pitsford Reservoir resr Eng.
208 D3 Pitsmoor S. Yorks., Eng.
106 E4 Pitstone Bucks., Eng.
52 D4 Pitt Hants., Eng.
320 H4 Pittentrail High., Scot.
292 H2 Pittenweem Fife, Scot.
292 E2 Pitteuchar Fife, Scot.
236 G3 Pittington Durham, Eng.
86 E5 Pitton Wilts., Eng.
350 A3 Pitton Swansea, Wales
148 B2 Pitts Hill Stoke, Eng.
314 G1 Pittulie Abers., Scot.
98 G2 Pittville Glos., Eng.
36 E2 Pityme Corn., Eng.
236 F3 Pity Me Durham, Eng.
120 G3 Pixey Green Suff., Eng.
140 E3 Pixley Here., Eng.
314 F2 Plaidy Abers., Scot.
358 F3 Plain Dealings Pembs., Wales
244 E4 Plainfield Northumb., Eng.
280 C3 Plains N. Lanark., Scot.
94 F4 Plainsfield Som., Eng.
144 D4 Plaish Shrop., Eng.
74 E2 Plaistow Gtr Lon., Eng.
74 E3 Plaistow Gtr Lon., Eng.
58 C2 Plaistow W. Sussex, Eng.
86 F6 Plaitford Wilts., Eng.
52 C5 Plaitford Green Hants., Eng.
198 B3 Plank Lane Gtr Man., Eng.
356 E2 Plas Carmar., Wales
362 F2 Plas Gogerddan Cere., Wales
372 F2 Plas Gwynant Gwynedd, Wales
356 D3 Plashett Carmar., Wales
378 D2 Plasisaf Conwy, Wales
378 E4 Plas Isaf Denb., Wales
378 D2 Plas Llwyd Conwy, Wales
366 B3 Plas Llwyngwern Powys, Wales
366 D3 Plas Llysyn Powys, Wales
378 F4 Plas Nantyr Wrex., Wales
366 D3 Plas-rhiw-Saeson Powys, Wales
52 E2 Plastow Green Hants., Eng.
378 E2 Plas-yn-Cefn Denb., Wales
62 B3 Platt Kent, Eng.
198 B2 Platt Bridge Gtr Man., Eng.
144 D2 Platt Lane Shrop., Eng.
62 E3 Platt's Heath Kent, Eng.
236 F3 Plawsworth Durham, Eng.
62 B3 Plaxtol Kent, Eng.
58 K3 Playden E. Sussex, Eng.
120 G4 Playford Suff., Eng.
102 F6 Play Hatch Oxon, Eng.
36 D3 Playing Place Corn., Eng.
98 E2 Playley Green Glos., Eng.
144 C4 Plealey Shrop., Eng.
296 G5 Plean Stir., Scot.
292 E2 Pleasance Fife, Scot.
116 D1 Pleasant Valley Essex, Eng.
228 G4 Pleasington B'burn, Eng.
180 F3 Pleasley Derbys., Eng.
176 B3 Pleasleyhill Notts., Eng.
46 E2 Pleck Dorset, Eng.
154 B2 Pleck W. Mids, Eng.
116 D2 Pledgdon Green Essex, Eng.
222 F3 Pledwick W. Yorks., Eng.
184 C2 Plemstall Cheshire West & Chester, Eng.
244 C6 Plenmeller Northumb., Eng.
116 E3 Pleshey Essex, Eng.
322 E2 Plockton High., Scot.
326 D3 Plocropol W. Isles, Scot.
106 D5 Plomer's Hill Bucks., Eng.
94 I4 Plot Gate Som., Eng.
94 I4 Plot Street Som., Eng.
132 C2 Plough Hill Warks., Eng.
144 C5 Plowden Shrop., Eng.
144 C4 Ploxgreen Shrop., Eng.
62 E3 Pluckley Kent, Eng.
62 E3 Pluckley Thorne Kent, Eng.
62 H3 Plucks Gutter Kent, Eng.
232 C4 Plumbland Cumbria, Eng.
208 D4 Plumbley S. Yorks., Eng.
402 G2 Plumbridge Strabane, N. Ire.
184 E2 Plumley Cheshire East, Eng.
232 F4 Plumpton Cumbria, Eng.
58 F3 Plumpton E. Sussex, Eng.
128 C5 Plumpton Northants., Eng.
128 D5 Plumpton End Northants., Eng.
58 F3 Plumpton Green E. Sussex, Eng.
232 F4 Plumpton Head Cumbria, Eng.
74 E3 Plumstead Gtr Lon., Eng.
166 F1 Plumstead Norf., Eng.
166 F1 Plumstead Green Norf., Eng.
176 C5 Plumtree Notts., Eng.
162 F1 Plungar Leics., Eng.
46 E3 Plush Dorset, Eng.
362 D4 Plwmp Cere., Wales
26 D7 Plym r. Eng.
40 D3 Plym Bridge Plymouth, Eng.
40 D3 Plymouth Plymouth, Eng.
40 D3 Plymouth admin. div. Eng.
40 D3 Plymouth City airport Eng.
40 D3 Plympton Plymouth, Eng.
40 D3 Plymstock Plymouth, Eng.
40 F2 Plymtree Devon, Eng.
26 E3 Plynlimon hill Wales
216 F2 Pockley N. Yorks., Eng.
210 D3 Pocklington E. Riding, Eng.
166 F2 Pockthorpe Norf., Eng.
166 F2 Pockthorpe Norf., Eng.
170 E7 Pode Hole Lincs., Eng.
94 I4 Podimore Som., Eng.
110 B2 Podington Bedford, Eng.
148 B3 Podmore Staffs., Eng.
98 F2 Podsmead Glos., Eng.
102 C4 Poffley End Oxon, Eng.
116 I3 Point Clear Essex, Eng.
170 D6 Pointon Lincs., Eng.
46 I3 Pokesdown Bourne., Eng.
252 B2 Polbae D. and G., Scot.
320 D3 Polbain High., Scot.
36 G2 Polbathic Corn., Eng.
288 B3 Polbeth W. Lothian, Scot.
252 F2 Poldean D. and G., Scot.
128 G3 Polebrook Northants., Eng.
136 D3 Pole Elm Worcs., Eng.
58 H4 Polegate E. Sussex, Eng.
222 C3 Pole Moor W. Yorks., Eng.
320 H4 Poles High., Scot.
132 C2 Polesworth Warks., Eng.
320 D3 Polglass High., Scot.
36 E3 Polgooth Corn., Eng.
252 D2 Polgown D. and G., Scot.
58 C3 Poling W. Sussex, Eng.
58 C3 Poling Corner W. Sussex, Eng.
36 E2 Polkerris Corn., Eng.
320 F2 Polla High., Scot.
322 F4 Polldubh High., Scot.
320 H3 Pollie High., Scot.
210 B4 Pollington E. Riding, Eng.
396 G5 Pollnagrasta Newry & Mourne, N. Ire.
322 E4 Polloch High., Scot.
276 D2 Pollok Glas., Scot.
276 E3 Pollokshaws Glas., Scot.
276 E2 Pollokshields Glas., Scot.
276 E2 Polmadie Glas., Scot.
36 E3 Polmassick Corn., Eng.
280 D3 Polmont Falk., Scot.
276 E3 Polnoon E. Renf., Scot.
36 F3 Polperro Corn., Eng.
36 F3 Polruan Corn., Eng.
94 H3 Polsham Som., Eng.
120 E4 Polstead Suff., Eng.
120 E4 Polstead Heath Suff., Eng.
300 D3 Poltalloch Arg. and B., Scot.
36 D4 Poltesco Corn., Eng.
288 E3 Polton Midlothian, Scot.
256 J2 Polwarth Borders, Scot.
36 F2 Polyphant Corn., Eng.
36 E2 Polzeath Corn., Eng.
402 I3 Pomeroy Cookstown, N. Ire.
40 D3 Pomphlett Plymouth, Eng.
124 D3 Pondersbridge Cambs., Eng.
74 D2 Ponders End Gtr Lon., Eng.
116 C1 Pond Street Essex, Eng.
36 D3 Ponsanooth Corn., Eng.
232 B6 Ponsonby Cumbria, Eng.
36 D3 Ponsongath Corn., Eng.
40 E3 Ponsworthy Devon, Eng.
356 G2 Pont Aber Carmar., Wales
372 F3 Pont Aberglaslyn Gwynedd, Wales
356 G3 Pontamman Carmar., Wales
356 E3 Pontantwn Carmar., Wales
350 C2 Pontardawe N.P.T., Wales
350 B2 Pontarddulais Swansea, Wales
Pontarfynach Cere., Wales see Devil's Bridge
356 E2 Pontargothi Carmar., Wales
366 D7 Pont ar Hydfer Powys, Wales
356 G2 Pont-ar-llechau Carmar., Wales
356 E2 Pontarsais Carmar., Wales
378 G3 Pontblyddyn Flints., Wales
350 E2 Pontbren Llwyd R.C.T., Wales
350 G4 Pontcanna Cardiff, Wales
362 D4 Pont Ceri Cere., Wales
366 D3 Pont Crugnant Powys, Wales
378 B3 Pont Cyfyng Conwy, Wales
378 C2 Pont Dolgarrog Conwy, Wales
222 G2 Pontefract W. Yorks., Eng.
244 G5 Ponteland Northumb., Eng.
362 G2 Ponterwyd Cere., Wales
144 C4 Pontesbury Shrop., Eng.
144 C4 Pontesbury Hill Shrop., Eng.
144 C4 Pontesford Shrop., Eng.
378 G4 Pontfadog Wrex., Wales
358 E2 Pontfaen Pembs., Wales
366 E7 Pont-faen Powys, Wales
362 D4 Pontgarreg Cere., Wales
356 E3 Pont-Henri Carmar., Wales
98 B4 Ponthir B. Gwent, Wales
362 C4 Ponthirwaun Cere., Wales
350 G3 Pontllanfraith Caerp., Wales
350 B2 Pontlliw Swansea, Wales
372 D2 Pontllyfni Gwynedd, Wales
350 G2 Pontlottyn Caerp., Wales
366 D8 Pontneddfechan Powys, Wales
350 H3 Pontnewydd B. Gwent, Wales
339 B2 Pontnewynydd Torf., Wales
378 A3 Pont Pen-y-benglog Conwy, Wales
362 G3 Pontrhydfendigaid Cere., Wales
372 H3 Pont Rhyd-sarn Gwynedd, Wales
350 E3 Pont Rhyd-y-cyff Bridg., Wales
350 D3 Pontrhydyfen N.P.T., Wales
362 G2 Pont-rhyd-y-groes Cere., Wales
350 H3 Pontrhydyrun B. Gwent, Wales
140 B4 Pontrilas Here., Eng.
366 F2 Pontrobert Powys, Wales
372 E2 Pont-rug Gwynedd, Wales
58 I3 Ponts Green E. Sussex, Eng.
140 D4 Pontshill Here., Eng.
362 E4 Pont-siân Cere., Wales
350 F2 Pontsticill M. Tyd., Wales
26 F4 Pontsticill Reservoir resr Wales
350 E2 Pont Walby N.P.T., Wales
356 E1 Pontwelly Carmar., Wales
356 E3 Pontyates Carmar., Wales
356 E3 Pontyberem Carmar., Wales
378 G4 Pont-y-blew Wrex., Wales
378 G3 Pontybodkin Flints., Wales
350 F3 Pontyclun R.C.T., Wales
350 E3 Pontycymer Bridg., Wales
350 F3 Pontygwaith R.C.T., Wales
350 H3 Pontymister Caerp., Wales
339 B2 Pontymoel Torf., Wales
378 B3 Pont-y-pant Conwy, Wales
339 B2 Pontypool Torf., Wales
350 F3 Pontypridd R.C.T., Wales
378 D3 Pont yr Alwen Conwy, Wales
350 E3 Pont-y-rhyl Bridg., Wales
350 H3 Pontywaun Caerp., Wales
52 D5 Pooksgreen Hants., Eng.
36 D3 Pool Corn., Eng.
222 E1 Pool W. Yorks., Eng.
232 E7 Pool Bank Cumbria, Eng.
216 F3 Poole N. Yorks., Eng.
46 H3 Poole Poole, Eng.
46 H3 Poole admin. div. Eng.
26 I6 Poole Bay b. Eng.
98 G4 Poole Keynes Glos., Eng.
148 C2 Poolend Staffs., Eng.
320 D4 Poolewe High., Scot.
232 F5 Pooley Bridge Cumbria, Eng.
166 F4 Pooley Street Norf., Eng.
148 C2 Poolfold Staffs., Eng.
154 C2 Pool Green W. Mids, Eng.
140 D3 Pool Head Here., Eng.
228 E5 Pool Hey Lancs., Eng.
98 E2 Poolhill Glos., Eng.
292 C2 Pool of Muckhart Clack., Scot.
366 G2 Pool Quay Powys, Wales
180 E3 Poolsbrook Derbys., Eng.
198 B2 Poolstock Gtr Man., Eng.
116 F1 Pool Street Essex, Eng.
170 D2 Poolthorne Farm N. Lincs., Eng.
358 E3 Pope Hill Pembs., Wales
82 F3 Popeswood Brack. F., Eng.
52 E3 Popham Hants., Eng.
74 D2 Poplar Gtr Lon., Eng.
176 C5 Porchester Notts., Eng.
52 D6 Porchfield I.o.W., Eng.
322 G2 Porin High., Scot.
166 H3 Poringland Norf., Eng.
36 D3 Porkellis Corn., Eng.
94 C3 Porlock Som., Eng.
94 C3 Porlock Weir Som., Eng.
300 D4 Portachoillan Arg. and B., Scot.
396 F3 Portadown Craigavon, N. Ire.
396 K3 Portaferry Ards, N. Ire.
304 K4 Port Allen Perth and Kin., Scot.
300 D2 Port Appin Arg. and B., Scot.
300 B4 Port Askaig Arg. and B., Scot.
300 E4 Portavadie Arg. and B., Scot.
396 K2 Portavoe North Down, N. Ire.
396 L3 Portavogie Ards, N. Ire.
388 G1 Portballintrae Coleraine, N. Ire.
300 E4 Port Bannatyne Arg. and B., Scot.
388 H1 Portbraddan Moyle, N. Ire.
94 H2 Portbury N. Som., Eng.
232 C3 Port Carlisle Cumbria, Eng.
300 A4 Port Charlotte Arg. and B., Scot.
52 F5 Portchester Hants., Eng.
236 H4 Port Clarence Stockton, Eng.
300 E4 Port Driseach Arg. and B., Scot.
300 B5 Port Ellen Arg. and B., Scot.
314 F3 Port Elphinstone Abers., Scot.
264 E2 Portencross N. Ayr., Scot.
405 B3 Port Erin Isle of Man
314 H2 Port Erroll Abers., Scot.
46 D3 Portesham Dorset, Eng.
405 D2 Port e Vullen Isle of Man
350 A3 Port Eynon Swansea, Wales
300 C2 Portfield Arg. and B., Scot.
358 D3 Portfield Gate Pembs., Wales
40 D3 Portgate Devon, Eng.
36 E2 Port Gaverne Corn., Eng.
276 B2 Port Glasgow Inverclyde, Scot.
388 H3 Portglenone Ballymena, N. Ire.
314 D2 Portgordon Moray, Scot.
320 I3 Portgower High., Scot.
36 D2 Porth Corn., Eng.
350 F3 Porth R.C.T., Wales
Porthaethwy I.o.A., Wales see Menai Bridge
36 D3 Porthallow Corn., Eng.
36 F2 Porthallow Corn., Eng.
350 D4 Porthcawl Bridg., Wales
372 B3 Porth Colmon Gwynedd, Wales
36 D2 Porthcothan Corn., Eng.
36 C3 Porthcurno Corn., Eng.
320 C4 Port Henderson High., Scot.
358 C2 Porthgain Pembs., Wales
148 B2 Porthill Staffs., Eng.
350 G4 Porthkerry V. of Glam., Wales
36 D3 Porthleven Corn., Eng.
Porth Llechog I.o.A., Wales see Bull Bay
372 F3 Porthmadog Gwynedd, Wales
36 C3 Porthmeor Corn., Eng.
36 D3 Porth Navas Corn., Eng.
26 C2 Porth Neigwl b. Wales
36 E3 Portholland Corn., Eng.
36 D3 Porthoustock Corn., Eng.
36 E3 Porthpean Corn., Eng.
36 D3 Porthtowan Corn., Eng.
378 H3 Porthwgan Wrex., Wales
371 B3 Porth-y-felin I.o.A., Wales
356 F3 Porthyrhyd Carmar., Wales
356 G1 Porthyrhyd Carmar., Wales
144 B3 Porth-y-waen Shrop., Eng.
300 F3 Portincaple Arg. and B., Scot.
210 D4 Portington E. Riding, Eng.
300 E3 Portinnisherrich Arg. and B., Scot.
232 D5 Portinscale Cumbria, Eng.
36 E2 Port Isaac Corn., Eng.
26 C6 Port Isaac Bay b. Eng.
94 H2 Portishead N. Som., Eng.
314 E1 Portknockie Moray, Scot.
26 H6 Portland, Isle of pen. Eng.
Portland Bill hd Eng. see Bill of Portland
26 H6 Portland Harbour inlet Eng.
388 H4 Portlee Antrim, N. Ire.
314 G3 Portlethen Abers., Scot.
36 E3 Portloe Corn., Eng.
252 B3 Port Logan D. and G., Scot.
36 F2 Portlooe Corn., Eng.
320 I4 Portmahomack High., Scot.
372 F3 Portmeirion Gwynedd, Wales
36 E3 Portmellon Corn., Eng.
322 C4 Port Mòr High., Scot.
52 C6 Portmore Hants., Eng.
388 L3 Portmuck Larne, N. Ire.
216 G1 Port Mulgrave N. Yorks., Eng.
320 F2 Port-na-Con High., Scot.
304 H2 Port na Craig Perth and Kin., Scot.
Port na Croise Arg. and B., Scot. see Portnacroish
300 D2 Portnacroish Arg. and B., Scot.
Port na h-Apainn Arg. and B., Scot. see Port Appin
300 A4 Portnahaven Arg. and B., Scot.
322 B3 Portnalong High., Scot.
322 D4 Portnaluchaig High., Scot.
326 C3 Port nan Long W. Isles, Scot.
154 B2 Portobello W. Mids, Eng.
296 E4 Port of Menteith Stir., Scot.
86 E5 Porton Wilts., Eng.
252 E3 Port o' Warren D. and G., Scot.
252 A3 Portpatrick D. and G., Scot.
372 F1 Port Penrhyn Gwynedd, Wales
Port Pheadair W. Isles, Scot. see Peters Port
36 E2 Port Quin Corn., Eng.
300 D2 Port Ramsay Arg. and B., Scot.
36 D3 Portreath Corn., Eng.
322 C2 Portree High., Scot.
Port Righ High., Scot. see Portree
388 G1 Portrush Coleraine, N. Ire.
405 B3 Port St Mary Isle of Man
36 E3 Portscatho Corn., Eng.
52 F6 Portsea Ports., Eng.
320 I2 Portskerra High., Scot.
339 D3 Portskewett Mon., Wales
58 E3 Portslade B. and H., Eng.
58 E4 Portslade-by-Sea B. and H., Eng.
252 A3 Portslogan D. and G., Scot.
52 F6 Portsmouth Ports., Eng.
52 F6 Portsmouth admin. div. Eng.
52 F5 Port Solent Ports., Eng.
314 E1 Portsoy Abers., Scot.
388 F1 Portstewart Coleraine, N. Ire.
190 D3 Port Sunlight Merseyside, Eng.
52 D5 Portswood Soton, Eng.
350 D3 Port Talbot N.P.T., Wales
350 C3 Port Tennant Swansea, Wales
322 C4 Portuairk High., Scot.
326 F2 Portvoller W. Isles, Scot.
140 B3 Portway Here., Eng.
140 C3 Portway Here., Eng.
140 C3 Portway Here., Eng.
136 F1 Portway Worcs., Eng.
300 A4 Port Wemyss Arg. and B., Scot.
252 C3 Port William D. and G., Scot.
36 G2 Portwrinkle Corn., Eng.
252 C3 Portyerrock D. and G., Scot.
144 E4 Posenhall Shrop., Eng.
120 C4 Poslingford Suff., Eng.
276 E2 Possil Park Glas., Scot.
40 E3 Postbridge Devon, Eng.
102 F4 Postcombe Oxon, Eng.
62 G4 Postling Kent, Eng.
Post-mawr Cere., Wales see Synod Inn
166 H3 Postwick Norf., Eng.
314 F3 Potarch Abers., Scot.
110 B4 Potsgrove Central Bedfordshire, Eng.
110 B5 Potten End Herts., Eng.
170 D4 Potterhanworth Lincs., Eng.
170 D4 Potterhanworth Booths Lincs., Eng.
166 I2 Potter Heigham Norf., Eng.
86 C4 Potterne Wilts., Eng.
86 D4 Potterne Wick Wilts., Eng.
222 E2 Potternewton W. Yorks., Eng.
110 D5 Potters Bar Herts., Eng.
148 B6 Potter's Cross Staffs., Eng.
110 C5 Potters Crouch Herts., Eng.
154 F3 Potter's Green W. Mids, Eng.
94 H2 Potters Hill N. Som., Eng.
162 D3 Potters Marston Leics., Eng.
180 C5 Potter Somersal Derbys., Eng.
128 D5 Potterspury Northants., Eng.
116 C3 Potter Street Essex, Eng.
222 F1 Potterton W. Yorks., Eng.
314 G3 Potterton Abers., Scot.
86 B5 Pottle Street Wilts., Eng.
216 F1 Potto N. Yorks., Eng.
110 D3 Potton Central Bedfordshire, Eng.
166 C2 Pott Row Norf., Eng.
116 G2 Pott's Green Essex, Eng.
184 G2 Pott Shrigley Cheshire East, Eng.
36 F1 Poughill Corn., Eng.
40 F2 Poughill Devon, Eng.
52 B5 Poulner Hants., Eng.
86 C4 Poulshot Wilts., Eng.
98 H3 Poulton Glos., Eng.
190 C3 Poulton Merseyside, Eng.
228 E3 Poulton-le-Fylde Lancs., Eng.
136 C1 Pound Bank Worcs., Eng.
136 D3 Pound Bank Worcs., Eng.
46 E3 Poundbury Dorset, Eng.
350 B3 Poundffald Swansea, Wales
58 H2 Poundfield E. Sussex, Eng.
58 G2 Poundgate E. Sussex, Eng.
52 C6 Pound Green I.o.W., Eng.
120 C4 Pound Green Suff., Eng.
136 C1 Pound Green Worcs., Eng.
58 F2 Pound Hill W. Sussex, Eng.
262 B6 Poundland S. Ayr., Scot.
106 B3 Poundon Bucks., Eng.
62 B4 Poundsbridge Kent, Eng.
36 F1 Poundstock Corn., Eng.
52 D2 Pound Street Hants., Eng.
78 E3 Povey Cross Surr., Eng.
244 F3 Powburn Northumb., Eng.
40 F3 Powderham Devon, Eng.
46 C3 Powerstock Dorset, Eng.
252 G3 Powfoot D. and G., Scot.
140 E3 Pow Green Here., Eng.
136 D3 Powick Worcs., Eng.
40 D2 Powler's Piece Devon, Eng.
304 I6 Powmill Perth and Kin., Scot.
366 E4 Powys county Wales
46 E4 Poxwell Dorset, Eng.
82 G3 Poyle Slough, Eng.
110 D4 Poynders End Herts., Eng.
58 E3 Poynings W. Sussex, Eng.
46 E2 Poyntington Dorset, Eng.
184 G1 Poynton Cheshire East, Eng.
144 E3 Poynton Telford, Eng.
144 E3 Poynton Green Telford, Eng.
396 F4 Poyntz Pass Armagh, N. Ire.
120 H3 Poys Street Suff., Eng.
358 E2 Poyston Pembs., Wales
358 E2 Poyston Cross Pembs., Wales
120 E3 Poystreet Green Suff., Eng.
36 C3 Praa Sands Corn., Eng.
292 F2 Pratis Fife, Scot.
180 D3 Pratthall Derbys., Eng.
74 E3 Pratt's Bottom Gtr Lon., Eng.
26 E7 Prawle Point pt Eng.
36 D3 Praze-an-Beeble Corn., Eng.
36 D4 Predannack Wollas Corn., Eng.
144 E2 Prees Shrop., Eng.
228 E3 Preesall Lancs., Eng.
144 E2 Prees Green Shrop., Eng.
144 B2 Preesgweene Shrop., Eng.
144 E2 Prees Heath Shrop., Eng.
144 E2 Prees Higher Heath Shrop., Eng.
144 E2 Prees Lower Heath Shrop., Eng.
388 B3 Prehen Derry, N. Ire.
378 G2 Prenbrigog Flints., Wales
358 E3 Prendergast Pembs., Wales
244 F3 Prendwick Northumb., Eng.
362 E4 Pren-gwyn Cere., Wales
372 F3 Prenteg Gwynedd, Wales
190 C3 Prenton Merseyside, Eng.
Prescelly Mts hills Wales see Preseli, Mynydd
190 E3 Prescot Merseyside, Eng.
144 C3 Prescott Shrop., Eng.
26 C4 Preseli, Mynydd hills Wales
314 C2 Presley Moray, Scot.
180 E3 Press Derbys., Eng.
244 D2 Pressen Northumb., Eng.
378 E1 Prestatyn Denb., Wales
184 G2 Prestbury Cheshire East, Eng.
98 G2 Prestbury Glos., Eng.
366 G5 Presteigne Powys, Wales
144 E4 Presthope Shrop., Eng.
94 I4 Prestleigh Som., Eng.
198 C2 Prestolee Gtr Man., Eng.
58 F3 Preston B. and H., Eng.
40 F3 Preston Devon, Eng.
46 E4 Preston Dorset, Eng.
210 G4 Preston E. Riding, Eng.
98 E1 Preston Glos., Eng.
98 H3 Preston Glos., Eng.
74 C2 Preston Gtr Lon., Eng.
110 D4 Preston Herts., Eng.
62 F3 Preston Kent, Eng.
62 H3 Preston Kent, Eng.
228 F4 Preston Lancs., Eng.
244 G2 Preston Northumb., Eng.
162 G3 Preston Rutland, Eng.
144 D3 Preston Shrop., Eng.
94 E4 Preston Som., Eng.
120 E4 Preston Suff., Eng.
236 G1 Preston T. and W., Eng.
86 D2 Preston Wilts., Eng.
256 J2 Preston Borders, Scot.
288 H3 Preston E. Lothian, Scot.
132 B4 Preston Bagot Warks., Eng.
106 B3 Preston Bissett Bucks., Eng.
94 E4 Preston Bowyer Som., Eng.
144 D3 Preston Brockhurst Shrop., Eng.
190 F4 Preston Brook Halton, Eng.
52 F3 Preston Candover Hants., Eng.
128 C4 Preston Capes Northants., Eng.
128 D4 Preston Deanery Northants., Eng.
288 E3 Prestonfield Edin., Scot.
132 B4 Preston Green Warks., Eng.
144 D3 Preston Gubbals Shrop., Eng.
236 F4 Preston-le-Skerne Durham, Eng.
144 C3 Preston Montford Shrop., Eng.
132 B5 Preston on Stour Warks., Eng.
190 F4 Preston on the Hill Halton, Eng.
140 B3 Preston on Wye Here., Eng.
288 F3 Prestonpans E. Lothian, Scot.
94 I5 Preston Plucknett Som., Eng.
216 D2 Preston-under-Scar N. Yorks., Eng.
144 F3 Preston upon the Weald Moors Telford, Eng.
140 D3 Preston Wynne Here., Eng.
198 D2 Prestwich Gtr Man., Eng.
244 G5 Prestwick Northumb., Eng.
262 D4 Prestwick S. Ayr., Scot.
162 E2 Prestwold Leics., Eng.
106 D4 Prestwood Bucks., Eng.
148 D3 Prestwood Staffs., Eng.
350 E3 Price Town Bridg., Wales
124 G4 Prickwillow Cambs., Eng.
94 H3 Priddy Som., Eng.
180 C3 Priestcliffe Derbys., Eng.
228 G3 Priest Hill Lancs., Eng.
Priestholm i. Wales see Puffin Island
228 F2 Priest Hutton Lancs., Eng.
262 F3 Priestland E. Ayr., Scot.
222 D2 Priestley Green W. Yorks., Eng.
402 E2 Priestsessagh Strabane, N. Ire.
222 D1 Priestthorpe W. Yorks., Eng.
144 B4 Priest Weston Shrop., Eng.
62 C2 Priestwood Kent, Eng.
62 C2 Priestwood Green Kent, Eng.
162 D3 Primethorpe Leics., Eng.
236 G2 Primrose T. and W., Eng.
166 F2 Primrose Green Norf., Eng.
74 D2 Primrose Hill Gtr Lon., Eng.
154 B3 Primrose Hill W. Mids, Eng.
222 D2 Prince Royd W. Yorks., Eng.
154 B2 Princes End W. Mids, Eng.
358 F3 Princes Gate Pembs., Wales
106 C4 Princes Risborough Bucks., Eng.
132 D3 Princethorpe Warks., Eng.
40 E3 Princetown Devon, Eng.
350 G2 Princetown Caerp., Wales
292 H2 Prior Muir Fife, Scot.
140 D3 Prior's Frome Here., Eng.
144 D5 Priors Halton Shrop., Eng.
132 E4 Priors Hardwick Warks., Eng.
144 F3 Priorslee Telford, Eng.
132 E4 Priors Marston Warks., Eng.
98 F2 Prior's Norton Glos., Eng.
98 G2 Priors Park Glos., Eng.
140 A3 Priory Wood Here., Eng.
350 F4 Prisk V. of Glam., Wales
94 J2 Priston B. and N.E. Som., Eng.
116 G4 Prittlewell Southend, Eng.
52 F4 Privett Hants., Eng.
40 D1 Prixford Devon, Eng.
300 B4 Proaig Arg. and B., Scot.
36 E3 Probus Corn., Eng.
22 K9 Prosen Water r. Scot.
314 G2 Protstonhill Abers., Scot.
276 E2 Provanmill Glas., Scot.
244 F6 Prudhoe Northumb., Eng.
304 D3 Pubil Perth and Kin., Scot.
94 I2 Publow B. and N.E. Som., Eng.
110 F4 Puckeridge Herts., Eng.
94 G5 Puckington Som., Eng.
98 E5 Pucklechurch S. Glos., Eng.
52 D4 Pucknall Hants., Eng.
98 F1 Puckrup Glos., Eng.
184 E2 Puddinglake Cheshire East, Eng.
184 A2 Puddington Cheshire West & Chester, Eng.
40 F2 Puddington Devon, Eng.
98 D2 Puddlebrook Glos., Eng.
166 F4 Puddledock Norf., Eng.
46 E3 Puddletown Dorset, Eng.
140 D2 Pudleston Here., Eng.
222 E2 Pudsey W. Yorks., Eng.
26 D1 Puffin Island i. Wales
58 C3 Pulborough W. Sussex, Eng.
320 K2 Puldagon High., Scot.
144 F3 Puleston Telford, Eng.
184 B3 Pulford Cheshire West & Chester, Eng.
46 E2 Pulham Dorset, Eng.
166 G4 Pulham Market Norf., Eng.
166 G4 Pulham St Mary Norf., Eng.
144 D3 Pulley Shrop., Eng.
110 C4 Pulloxhill Central Bedfordshire, Eng.
144 C4 Pulverbatch Shrop., Eng.
288 C3 Pumpherston W. Lothian, Scot.
356 G1 Pumsaint Carmar., Wales
358 E2 Puncheston Pembs., Wales
46 D3 Puncknowle Dorset, Eng.
26 H6 Purbeck, Isle of pen. Eng.
52 F5 Purbrook Hants., Eng.
388 K5 Purdysburn Lisburn, N. Ire.
46 I3 Purewell Dorset, Eng.
116 D5 Purfleet Thurrock, Eng.
94 G3 Puriton Som., Eng.
116 F3 Purleigh Essex, Eng.
74 D3 Purley Gtr Lon., Eng.
82 D3 Purley on Thames W. Berks., Eng.
144 B5 Purlogue Shrop., Eng.
86 B3 Purlpit Wilts., Eng.
124 F4 Purls Bridge Cambs., Eng.
46 E2 Purse Caundle Dorset, Eng.
136 E1 Purshull Green Worcs., Eng.
144 C5 Purslow Shrop., Eng.
222 F2 Purston Jaglin W. Yorks., Eng.
94 G5 Purtington Som., Eng.
98 E3 Purton Glos., Eng.
98 E3 Purton Glos., Eng.
86 D2 Purton Wilts., Eng.
86 D2 Purton Stoke Wilts., Eng.
256 J2 Purves Hall Borders, Scot.
128 D5 Pury End Northants., Eng.
102 C4 Pusey Oxon, Eng.
140 D3 Putley Here., Eng.
140 D3 Putley Green Here., Eng.
98 F3 Putloe Glos., Eng.
74 C3 Putney Gtr Lon., Eng.
110 A5 Puttenham Herts., Eng.
78 C2 Puttenham Surr., Eng.
40 G2 Putts Corner Devon, Eng.
94 G2 Puxton N. Som., Eng.
356 E3 Pwll Carmar., Wales
358 D3 Pwllcrochan Pembs., Wales
372 B4 Pwlldefaid Gwynedd, Wales
378 F3 Pwll-glas Denb., Wales
366 E7 Pwllgloyw Powys, Wales
372 D3 Pwllheli Gwynedd, Wales
350 H3 Pwll-Mawr Cardiff, Wales
339 D3 Pwllmeyric Mon., Wales
356 C3 Pwll-trap Carmar., Wales
350 D3 Pwll-y-glaw N.P.T., Wales
58 E3 Pyecombe W. Sussex, Eng.
110 F5 Pye Corner Herts., Eng.
62 D3 Pye Corner Kent, Eng.
339 C3 Pye Corner Newp., Wales
148 C4 Pye Green Staffs., Eng.
52 E7 Pyle I.o.W., Eng.
350 D3 Pyle Bridg., Wales
94 E4 Pyleigh Som., Eng.
94 I4 Pylle Som., Eng.
Pymoor Cambs., Eng. see Pymore
124 F4 Pymore Cambs., Eng.
46 C3 Pymore Dorset, Eng.
78 C2 Pyrford Surr., Eng.
78 D2 Pyrford Green Surr., Eng.
102 E5 Pyrton Oxon, Eng.
128 E3 Pytchley Northants., Eng.
40 C2 Pyworthy Devon, Eng.

Q

144 A5 Quabbs Shrop., Eng.
170 E6 Quadring Lincs., Eng.
170 F6 Quadring Eaudike Lincs., Eng.
22 I9 Quaich r. Scot.
106 C3 Quainton Bucks., Eng.
350 G3 Quakers Yard M. Tyd., Wales
26 F5 Quantock Hills hills Eng.
331 D3 Quarff Shet., Scot.
52 C3 Quarley Hants., Eng.
222 D3 Quarmby W. Yorks., Eng.
180 D5 Quarndon Derbys., Eng.
276 C2 Quarrelton Renf., Scot.
52 E6 Quarr Hill I.o.W., Eng.
276 C2 Quarrier's Village Inverclyde, Scot.
170 D6 Quarrington Lincs., Eng.
236 G3 Quarrington Hill Durham, Eng.
184 C2 Quarrybank Cheshire West & Chester, Eng.
154 B3 Quarry Bank W. Mids, Eng.
268 B2 Quarter S. Lanark., Scot.
144 F4 Quatford Shrop., Eng.
144 F5 Quatt Shrop., Eng.
236 E3 Quebec Durham, Eng.
98 F3 Quedgeley Glos., Eng.
124 F4 Queen Adelaide Cambs., Eng.
62 E2 Queenborough Kent, Eng.
94 I4 Queen Camel Som., Eng.
94 I2 Queen Charlton B. and N.E. Som., Eng.
46 F1 Queen Oak Dorset, Eng.
52 E7 Queen's Bower I.o.W., Eng.
74 C2 Queensbury Gtr Lon., Eng.
222 C2 Queensbury W. Yorks., Eng.
378 G2 Queensferry Flints., Wales
144 C2 Queen's Head Shrop., Eng.
228 D4 Queenstown Blackpool, Eng.
62 C3 Queen Street Kent, Eng.
120 C4 Queen Street Suff., Eng.
148 C4 Queensville Staffs., Eng.
280 B3 Queenzieburn N. Lanark., Scot.
86 D3 Quemerford Wilts., Eng.
331 D4 Quendale Shet., Scot.
116 D2 Quendon Essex, Eng.
162 E2 Queniborough Leics., Eng.
98 I3 Quenington Glos., Eng.
228 F2 Quernmore Lancs., Eng.
154 C2 Queslett W. Mids, Eng.
36 F2 Quethiock Corn., Eng.
329 B4 Quholm Orkney, Scot.
82 D3 Quick's Green W. Berks., Eng.
166 E4 Quidenham Norf., Eng.
52 E3 Quidhampton Hants., Eng.
86 D5 Quidhampton Wilts., Eng.
326 D3 Quidinish W. Isles, Scot.
314 G2 Quilquox Abers., Scot.
144 D2 Quina Brook Shrop., Eng.
22 F6 Quinag hill Scot.
329 D5 Quindry Orkney, Scot.
405 C3 Quine's Hill Isle of Man
300 D4 Quinhill Arg. and B., Scot.
128 D4 Quinton Northants., Eng.
154 B3 Quinton W. Mids, Eng.
128 D4 Quinton Green Northants., Eng.
36 D2 Quintrell Downs Corn., Eng.
148 D3 Quixhill Staffs., Eng.
40 D2 Quoditch Devon, Eng.
22 F8 Quoich, Loch l. Scot.
304 G4 Quoig Perth and Kin., Scot.
304 G5 Quoiggs House Perth and Kin., Scot.
396 J3 Quoile Down, N. Ire.
23 K4 Quoile r. N. Ire.
184 C3 Quoisley Cheshire East, Eng.
162 E2 Quorn Leics., Eng.
Quorndon Leics., Eng. see Quorn
268 E3 Quothquan S. Lanark., Scot.
329 B3 Quoyloo Orkney, Scot.
331 E1 Quoys Shet., Scot.

R

22 D8 Raasay i. Scot.
22 D8 Raasay, Sound of sea chan. Scot.
190 C4 Raby Merseyside, Eng.
388 J3 Racavan Ballymena, N. Ire.
256 D3 Rachan Borders, Scot.
372 F1 Rachub Gwynedd, Wales
40 F2 Rackenford Devon, Eng.
58 C3 Rackham W. Sussex, Eng.
166 H2 Rackheath Norf., Eng.
252 F2 Racks D. and G., Scot.
329 A4 Rackwick Orkney, Scot.
329 D1 Rackwick Orkney, Scot.
180 D5 Radbourne Derbys., Eng.
198 D2 Radcliffe Gtr Man., Eng.
244 H4 Radcliffe Northumb., Eng.
176 C5 Radcliffe on Trent Notts., Eng.
106 B2 Radclive Bucks., Eng.
102 B4 Radcot Oxon, Eng.
94 D4 Raddington Som., Eng.
292 G2 Radernie Fife, Scot.
94 J3 Radford B. and N.E. Som., Eng.
176 B5 Radford Nott., Eng.
102 C3 Radford Oxon, Eng.
154 E3 Radford W. Mids, Eng.
132 D4 Radford Semele Warks., Eng.
46 E4 Radipole Dorset, Eng.
110 D5 Radlett Herts., Eng.
102 D4 Radley Oxon, Eng.
116 E3 Radley Green Essex, Eng.
184 D3 Radmore Green Cheshire East, Eng.
106 C4 Radnage Bucks., Eng.
276 D2 Radnor Park W. Dun., Scot.
94 J3 Radstock B. and N.E. Som., Eng.
128 C5 Radstone Northants., Eng.
132 D5 Radway Warks., Eng.
184 E3 Radway Green Cheshire East, Eng.
110 B2 Radwell Bedford, Eng.
110 D3 Radwell Herts., Eng.
116 E1 Radwinter Essex, Eng.
350 G3 Radyr Cardiff, Wales
244 E4 Raechester Northumb., Eng.
320 D3 Raffin High., Scot.
314 C2 Rafford Moray, Scot.
396 J3 Raffrey Down, N. Ire.
162 E2 Ragdale Leics., Eng.
52 C3 Ragged Appleshaw Hants., Eng.
339 C2 Raglan Mon., Wales
176 E3 Ragnall Notts., Eng.
396 K3 Raholp Down, N. Ire.
402 F4 Rahony Omagh, N. Ire.
322 D5 Rahoy High., Scot.
190 E2 Rainford Merseyside, Eng.
74 F2 Rainham Gtr Lon., Eng.
62 D2 Rainham Medway, Eng.
190 E3 Rainhill Merseyside, Eng.
190 E3 Rainhill Stoops Merseyside, Eng.
184 G2 Rainow Cheshire East, Eng.
198 D2 Rain Shore Gtr Man., Eng.
198 D2 Rainsough Gtr Man., Eng.
216 E2 Rainton N. Yorks., Eng.
176 C4 Rainworth Notts., Eng.
232 G6 Raisbeck Cumbria, Eng.
232 H4 Raise Cumbria, Eng.
304 K4 Rait Perth and Kin., Scot.
170 F3 Raithby Lincs., Eng.
170 G4 Raithby Lincs., Eng.
58 A2 Rake W. Sussex, Eng.
148 D4 Rake End Staffs., Eng.
148 D3 Rakeway Staffs., Eng.
94 D4 Raleigh's Cross Som., Eng.
388 K4 Raloo Larne, N. Ire.
356 F1 Ram Carmar., Wales
402 I4 Ramaket Dungannon, N. Ire.
402 F4 Ramaley Fermanagh, N. Ire.
86 E3 Ram Alley Wilts., Eng.
322 A2 Ramasaig High., Scot.
36 D3 Rame Corn., Eng.
36 G3 Rame Corn., Eng.
26 D7 Rame Head hd Eng.
62 E3 Ram Lane Kent, Eng.
46 D3 Rampisham Dorset, Eng.
232 C8 Rampside Cumbria, Eng.
124 E5 Rampton Cambs., Eng.
176 E3 Rampton Notts., Eng.
198 D2 Ramsbottom Gtr Man., Eng.
86 F3 Ramsbury Wilts., Eng.
52 G5 Ramsdean Hants., Eng.
52 F3 Ramsdell Hants., Eng.
102 C3 Ramsden Oxon, Eng.
116 E4 Ramsden Bellhouse Essex, Eng.
116 E4 Ramsden Heath Essex, Eng.
405 D2 Ramsey Isle of Man
124 D4 Ramsey Cambs., Eng.
116 J2 Ramsey Essex, Eng.
24 I5 Ramsey Bay b. Isle of Man
124 D4 Ramsey Forty Foot Cambs., Eng.
124 D4 Ramsey Heights Cambs., Eng.
116 G3 Ramsey Island Essex, Eng.
26 B4 Ramsey Island i. Wales
124 D4 Ramsey Mereside Cambs., Eng.
124 D4 Ramsey St Mary's Cambs., Eng.
62 I2 Ramsgate Kent, Eng.
166 F1 Ramsgate Street Norf., Eng.
216 D2 Ramsgill N. Yorks., Eng.
120 H4 Ramsholt Suff., Eng.
148 D2 Ramshorn Staffs., Eng.
78 C3 Ramsnest Common Surr., Eng.
388 E4 Ranaghan Magherafelt, N. Ire.
170 F4 Ranby Lincs., Eng.
176 C3 Ranby Notts., Eng.
170 D4 Rand Lincs., Eng.
388 I4 Randalstown Antrim, N. Ire.
98 F3 Randwick Glos., Eng.
402 G3 Ranelly Omagh, N. Ire.
148 E4 Rangemore Staffs., Eng.
98 E4 Rangeworthy S. Glos., Eng.
262 E4 Rankinston E. Ayr., Scot.
116 F3 Rank's Green Essex, Eng.
208 C3 Ranmoor S. Yorks., Eng.
228 H4 Rann B'burn, Eng.
22 H9 Rannoch, Loch l. Scot.
22 G9 Rannoch Moor moorland Scot.
304 E2 Rannoch School Perth and Kin., Scot.
322 E4 Ranochan High., Scot.
94 C3 Ranscombe Som., Eng.
176 C2 Ranskill Notts., Eng.
148 B4 Ranton Staffs., Eng.
148 B4 Ranton Green Staffs., Eng.
166 H2 Ranworth Norf., Eng.
296 G5 Raploch Stir., Scot.
329 D2 Rapness Orkney, Scot.
94 G5 Rapps Som., Eng.
252 E3 Rascarrel D. and G., Scot.
232 G7 Rash Cumbria, Eng.
388 H3 Rasharkin Ballymoney, N. Ire.
388 J4 Rashee Newtownabbey, N. Ire.
136 E2 Rashwood Worcs., Eng.
216 F2 Raskelf N. Yorks., Eng.
350 G2 Rassau B. Gwent, Wales
222 D2 Rastrick W. Yorks., Eng.
322 E3 Ratagan High., Scot.
162 D3 Ratby Leics., Eng.
162 B3 Ratcliffe Culey Leics., Eng.
176 B5 Ratcliffe on Soar Notts., Eng.
162 E2 Ratcliffe on the Wreake Leics., Eng.
358 D3 Ratford Bridge Pembs., Wales
86 E4 Ratfyn Wilts., Eng.
314 H2 Rathen Abers., Scot.
396 H4 Rathfriland Newry & Mourne, N. Ire.
292 F1 Rathillet Fife, Scot.
388 J3 Rathkeel Ballymena, N. Ire.
23 J2 Rathlin Island i. N. Ire.
216 C2 Rathmell N. Yorks., Eng.
288 C3 Ratho Edin., Scot.
288 C3 Ratho Station Edin., Scot.
314 E1 Rathven Moray, Scot.
132 D5 Ratley Warks., Eng.
62 H3 Ratling Kent, Eng.
144 C4 Ratlinghope Shrop., Eng.
40 F2 Ratsloe Devon, Eng.
232 E3 Ratten Row Cumbria, Eng.
228 E3 Ratten Row Lancs., Eng.
40 E3 Rattery Devon, Eng.
120 E3 Rattlesden Suff., Eng.
304 J3 Rattray Perth and Kin., Scot.
22 M7 Rattray Head hd Scot.
232 E4 Raughton Head Cumbria, Eng.
128 F3 Raunds Northants., Eng.

Ravenfield to Saighdinis

208 E3 Ravenfield S. Yorks., Eng.
232 B6 Ravenglass Cumbria, Eng.
166 I3 Raveningham Norf., Eng.
216 H1 Ravenscar N. Yorks., Eng.
405 C2 Ravensdale Isle of Man
110 C2 Ravensden Bedford, Eng.
116 I2 Raven's Green Essex, Eng.
40 F2 Ravenshayes Devon, Eng.
176 B4 Ravenshead Notts., Eng.
184 D3 Ravensmoor Cheshire East, Eng.
128 C4 Ravensthorpe Northants., Eng.
222 E2 Ravensthorpe W. Yorks., Eng.
162 C2 Ravenstone Leics., Eng.
106 D2 Ravenstone M.K., Eng.
232 H6 Ravenstonedale Cumbria, Eng.
268 D2 Ravenstruther S. Lanark., Scot.
216 D1 Ravensworth N. Yorks., Eng.
388 J6 Ravernet Lisburn, N. Ire.
216 H1 Raw N. Yorks., Eng.
402 F5 Raw Fermanagh, N. Ire.
210 C4 Rawcliffe E. Riding, Eng.
210 C4 Rawcliffe Bridge E. Riding, Eng.
222 D1 Rawdon W. Yorks., Eng.
208 C2 Raw Green S. Yorks., Eng.
208 D3 Rawmarsh S. Yorks., Eng.
148 D4 Rawnsley Staffs., Eng.
116 F4 Rawreth Essex, Eng.
40 G2 Rawridge Devon, Eng.
180 E4 Rawson Green Derbys., Eng.
228 I4 Rawtenstall Lancs., Eng.
280 C3 Rawyards N. Lanark., Scot.
314 G2 Raxton Abers., Scot.
244 E4 Raylees Northumb., Eng.
116 F4 Rayleigh Essex, Eng.
40 H2 Raymond's Hill Devon, Eng.
116 F2 Rayne Essex, Eng.
74 B2 Rayners Lane Gtr Lon., Eng.
74 C3 Raynes Park Gtr Lon., Eng.
26 G3 Rea Brook r. Eng.
124 F5 Reach Cambs., Eng.
228 H4 Read Lancs., Eng.
82 E3 Reading Reading, Eng.
82 E3 Reading admin. div. Eng.
120 G3 Reading Green Suff., Eng.
62 E4 Reading Street Kent, Eng.
62 I2 Reading Street Kent, Eng.
232 G5 Reagill Cumbria, Eng.
320 H4 Rearquhar High., Scot.
162 E2 Rearsby Leics., Eng.
184 D3 Rease Heath Cheshire East, Eng.
320 K2 Reaster High., Scot.
244 F3 Reaveley Northumb., Eng.
331 C3 Reawick Shet., Scot.
320 I2 Reay High., Scot.
62 H2 Reculver Kent, Eng.
358 F3 Redberth Pembs., Wales
110 C5 Redbourn Herts., Eng.
170 C5 Redbourne N. Lincs., Eng.
52 D5 Redbridge Soton, Eng.
74 E2 Redbridge met. bor. Gtr Lon., Eng.
98 C3 Redbrook Glos., Eng.
378 I4 Redbrook Wrex., Wales
62 E4 Redbrook Street Kent, Eng.
184 F3 Red Bull Cheshire East, Eng.
244 C6 Redburn Northumb., Eng.
320 G4 Redburn High., Scot.
322 J2 Redburn High., Scot.
216 F1 Redcar R. and C., Eng.
216 F1 Redcar and Cleveland admin. div. Eng.
308 G3 Redcastle Angus, Scot.
94 H2 Redcliff Bay N. Som., Eng.
314 G4 Redcloak Abers., Scot.
124 E5 Red Cross Cambs., Eng.
232 D4 Red Dial Cumbria, Eng.
280 D3 Redding Falk., Scot.
280 D3 Reddingmuirhead Falk., Scot.
198 E3 Reddish Gtr Man., Eng.
136 F2 Redditch Worcs., Eng.
120 C3 Rede Suff., Eng.
24 M3 Rede r. Eng.
166 G4 Redenhall Norf., Eng.
52 C3 Redenham Hants., Eng.
244 D5 Redesmouth Northumb., Eng.
236 D3 Redford Durham, Eng.
58 B2 Redford W. Sussex, Eng.
314 F4 Redford Abers., Scot.
308 F3 Redford Angus, Scot.
120 F2 Redgrave Suff., Eng.
308 E2 Redheugh Angus, Scot.
52 G5 Red Hill Hants., Eng.
176 C4 Redhill Notts., Eng.
94 H2 Redhill N. Som., Eng.
78 E2 Redhill Surr., Eng.
144 F3 Redhill Telford, Eng.
132 B4 Red Hill Warks., Eng.
388 I6 Redhill Lisburn, N. Ire.
314 F2 Redhill Abers., Scot.
300 D4 Redhouse Arg. and B., Scot.
300 B4 Redhouses Arg. and B., Scot.
120 I2 Redisham Suff., Eng.
94 I2 Redland Bristol, Eng.
329 C3 Redland Orkney, Scot.
120 G3 Redlingfield Suff., Eng.
120 B3 Red Lodge Suff., Eng.
198 D2 Red Lumb Gtr Man., Eng.
94 J4 Redlynch Som., Eng.
86 E6 Redlynch Wilts., Eng.
98 E2 Redmarley D'Abitot Glos., Eng.
236 G4 Redmarshall Stockton, Eng.
162 G1 Redmile Leics., Eng.
216 D2 Redmire N. Yorks., Eng.
36 E2 Redmoor Corn., Eng.
144 C2 Rednal Shrop., Eng.
154 C3 Rednal W. Mids, Eng.
116 D1 Red Oaks Hill Essex, Eng.
256 I3 Redpath Borders, Scot.
322 D2 Red Point High., Scot.
36 F1 Red Post Corn., Eng.
40 F3 Red Post Devon, Eng.
140 D4 Red Rail Here., Eng.
198 B2 Red Rock Gtr Man., Eng.
356 C3 Red Roses Carmar., Wales
244 H4 Red Row Northumb., Eng.
36 D3 Redruth Corn., Eng.
256 E2 Redscarhead Borders, Scot.
268 D3 Redshaw S. Lanark., Scot.
358 F3 Redstone Bank Pembs., Wales
148 B2 Red Street Staffs., Eng.
371 D3 Red Wharf Bay I.o.A., Wales
26 D1 Red Wharf Bay b. Wales
98 D4 Redwick S. Glos., Eng.
339 C3 Redwick Newp., Wales
236 F4 Redworth Darl., Eng.
110 E3 Reed Herts., Eng.
110 E3 Reed End Herts., Eng.
166 I3 Reedham Norf., Eng.
228 I4 Reedley Lancs., Eng.
210 D4 Reedness E. Riding, Eng.
326 D2 Reef W. Isles, Scot.
170 D4 Reepham Lincs., Eng.
166 F2 Reepham Norf., Eng.
216 D1 Reeth N. Yorks., Eng.
405 D1 Regaby Isle of Man
94 I2 Regil N. Som., Eng.
322 J2 Regoul High., Scot.
22 E7 Reidh, Rubha pt Scot.
320 D3 Reiff High., Scot.
78 E2 Reigate Surr., Eng.
216 I2 Reighton N. Yorks., Eng.
Reinigeadal W. Isles, Scot. see Rhenigidale
320 K2 Reiss High., Scot.
36 D2 Rejerrah Corn., Eng.
402 H5 Relan Fermanagh, N. Ire.
36 D3 Releath Corn., Eng.
36 C3 Relubbus Corn., Eng.
314 B2 Relugas Moray, Scot.
82 E2 Remenham W'ham, Eng.
82 E2 Remenham Hill W'ham, Eng.
304 F3 Remony Perth and Kin., Scot.
176 C6 Rempstone Notts., Eng.
98 H3 Rendcomb Glos., Eng.
120 H3 Rendham Suff., Eng.
120 H4 Rendlesham Suff., Eng.
276 D2 Renfrew Renf., Scot.
276 C2 Renfrewshire admin. div. Scot.
110 C3 Renhold Bedford, Eng.
180 F3 Renishaw Derbys., Eng.
22 C7 Renish Point pt Scot.
244 G3 Rennington Northumb., Eng.
276 C2 Renton W. Dun., Scot.
232 G4 Renwick Cumbria, Eng.
166 I2 Repps Norf., Eng.
180 D5 Repton Derbys., Eng.
308 F3 Rescobie Angus, Scot.
322 D4 Resipole High., Scot.
322 I2 Resolis High., Scot.
350 D2 Resolven N.P.T., Wales
22 B6 Resort, Loch inlet Scot.
322 E4 Resourie High., Scot.
36 E2 Respryn Corn., Eng.
283 E2 Restalrig Edin., Scot.
256 K1 Reston Borders, Scot.
36 F2 Restormel Corn., Eng.
308 F3 Reswallie Angus, Scot.
116 F4 Rettendon Essex, Eng.
116 F4 Rettendon Place Essex, Eng.
170 F5 Revesby Lincs., Eng.
170 F5 Revesby Bridge Lincs., Eng.
40 F2 Rewe Devon, Eng.
52 E6 Rew Street I.o.W., Eng.
86 C3 Reybridge Wilts., Eng.
120 I2 Reydon Suff., Eng.
120 J2 Reydon Smear Suff., Eng.
166 E3 Reymerston Norf., Eng.
358 F3 Reynalton Pembs., Wales
350 A3 Reynoldston Swansea, Wales
36 G2 Rezare Corn., Eng.
339 C2 Rhadyr Mon., Wales
356 H1 Rhandirmwyn Carmar., Wales
320 H3 Rhaoine High., Scot.
366 D5 Rhayader Powys, Wales
372 C3 Rhedyn Gwynedd, Wales
320 E3 Rhegreanoch High., Scot.
26 D3 Rheidol r. Wales
322 D5 Rhemore High., Scot.
326 D3 Rhenigidale W. Isles, Scot.
350 D2 Rheola N.P.T., Wales
378 F2 Rhes-y-cae Flints., Wales
144 B2 Rhewl Shrop., Eng.
378 E3 Rhewl Denb., Wales
378 F4 Rhewl Denb., Wales
320 G3 Rhian High., Scot.
320 E3 Rhicarn High., Scot.
320 F2 Rhiconich High., Scot.
320 E4 Rhidorroch High., Scot.
320 H2 Rhifail High., Scot.
350 E2 Rhigos R.C.T., Wales
22 H12 Rhinns of Kells hills Scot.
366 G3 Rhiston Powys, Wales
372 C4 Rhiw Gwynedd, Wales
366 D2 Rhiwargor Powys, Wales
350 G3 Rhiwbina Cardiff, Wales
372 E3 Rhiwbryfdir Gwynedd, Wales
339 B3 Rhiwderin Newp., Wales
350 F3 Rhiw-garn R.C.T., Wales
350 F3 Rhiwinder R.C.T., Wales
372 F1 Rhiwlas Gwynedd, Wales
372 I3 Rhiwlas Gwynedd, Wales
366 F1 Rhiwlas Powys, Wales
94 F4 Rhode Som., Eng.
198 D2 Rhodes Gtr Man., Eng.
176 C3 Rhodesia Notts., Eng.
62 G4 Rhodes Minnis Kent, Eng.
358 C2 Rhodiad-y-brenin Pembs., Wales
362 F2 Rhodmad Cere., Wales
300 D5 Rhonadale Arg. and B., Scot.
26 F4 Rhondda reg. Wales
339 F2 Rhondda Cynon Taff admin. div. Wales
252 E3 Rhonehouse D. and G., Scot.
350 F4 Rhoose V. of Glam., Wales
144 B2 Rhos Shrop., Eng.
356 D2 Rhos Carmar., Wales
378 F3 Rhôs Denb., Wales
350 D2 Rhos N.P.T., Wales
356 G3 Rhosaman Carmar., Wales
378 G3 Rhos-berse Wrex., Wales
371 B3 Rhoscolyn I.o.A., Wales
366 G2 Rhos Common Powys, Wales
358 D3 Rhoscrowther Pembs., Wales
378 H3 Rhos-ddu Wrex., Wales
378 F2 Rhosesmor Flints., Wales
372 D3 Rhos-fawr Gwynedd, Wales
372 E2 Rhosgadfan Gwynedd, Wales
371 C2 Rhos-goch I.o.A., Wales
366 F6 Rhosgoch Powys, Wales
358 E3 Rhos-hill Pembs., Wales
372 B4 Rhoshirwaun Gwynedd, Wales
372 E3 Rhoslan Gwynedd, Wales
372 F5 Rhoslefain Gwynedd, Wales
378 G3 Rhosllanerchrugog Wrex., Wales
371 D2 Rhoslligwy I.o.A., Wales
356 G2 Rhosmaen Carmar., Wales
371 D3 Rhosmeirch I.o.A., Wales
371 B3 Rhosneigr I.o.A., Wales
378 H3 Rhosnesni Wrex., Wales
378 C2 Rhôs-on-Sea Conwy, Wales
378 G3 Rhosrobin Wrex., Wales
350 A3 Rhossili Swansea, Wales
358 C2 Rhosson Pembs., Wales
371 C3 Rhostrehwfa I.o.A., Wales
372 E2 Rhostryfan Gwynedd, Wales
378 G3 Rhostyllen Wrex., Wales
371 C2 Rhos-y-bol I.o.A., Wales
366 F2 Rhos-y-brithdir Powys, Wales
378 G3 Rhos-y-brwyner Flints., Wales
358 D1 Rhosycaerau Pembs., Wales
362 F2 Rhos-y-garth Cere., Wales
372 I3 Rhos-y-gwaliau Gwynedd, Wales
372 C3 Rhos-y-llan Gwynedd, Wales
378 C2 Rhos-y-mawn Conwy, Wales
366 G5 Rhos-y-Meirch Powys, Wales
300 F3 Rhu Arg. and B., Scot.
378 E2 Rhuallt Denb., Wales
300 E4 Rhubodach Arg. and B., Scot.
184 D3 Rhuddall Heath Cheshire West & Chester, Eng.
378 E2 Rhuddlan Denb., Wales
366 F6 Rhulen Powys, Wales
Rhum i. Scot. see Rum
322 D4 Rhumach High., Scot.
300 D4 Rhunahaorine Arg. and B., Scot.
372 F3 Rhyd Gwynedd, Wales
366 D3 Rhyd Powys, Wales
356 E2 Rhydargaeau Carmar., Wales
356 F1 Rhydcymerau Carmar., Wales
136 D3 Rhydd Worcs., Eng.
372 F2 Rhyd-Ddu Gwynedd, Wales
350 D2 Rhydding N.P.T., Wales
378 D2 Rhydgaled Conwy, Wales
378 C3 Rhydlanfair Conwy, Wales
362 D4 Rhydlewis Cere., Wales
372 B3 Rhydlios Gwynedd, Wales
378 D3 Rhydlydan Conwy, Wales
366 E3 Rhydlydan Powys, Wales
372 C4 Rhydolion Gwynedd, Wales
362 E4 Rhydowen Cere., Wales
362 F3 Rhyd-Rosser Cere., Wales
140 A3 Rhydspence Here., Eng.
378 G3 Rhydtalog Flints., Wales
372 I3 Rhyd-uchaf Gwynedd, Wales
366 D1 Rhyd-wen Wales
371 B2 Rhydwyn I.o.A., Wales
378 G3 Rhyd-y-ceirw Flints., Wales
372 D3 Rhyd-y-clafdy Gwynedd, Wales
366 G1 Rhydycroesau Powys, Wales
362 F2 Rhydyfelin Cere., Wales
350 G3 Rhydyfelin R.C.T., Wales
378 D2 Rhyd-y-foel Conwy, Wales
350 C2 Rhyd-y-fro N.P.T., Wales
372 F1 Rhyd-y-groes Gwynedd, Wales
372 H4 Rhydymain Gwynedd, Wales
339 C2 Rhyd-y-meirch Mon., Wales
378 F2 Rhydymwyn Flints., Wales
372 F5 Rhyd-yr-onnen Gwynedd, Wales
372 G3 Rhyd-y-sarn Gwynedd, Wales
356 C2 Rhydywrach Carmar., Wales
378 E2 Rhyl Denb., Wales
350 G2 Rhymney Caerp., Wales
144 B2 Rhyn Shrop., Eng.
304 J4 Rhynd Perth and Kin., Scot.
314 E3 Rhynie Abers., Scot.
320 I4 Rhynie High., Scot.
136 D1 Ribbesford Worcs., Eng.
24 L6 Ribble r. Eng.
24 M5 Ribblesdale val. Eng.
228 F4 Ribbleton Lancs., Eng.
228 F4 Ribby Lancs., Eng.
228 G4 Ribchester Lancs., Eng.
320 G2 Ribigill High., Scot.
170 E2 Riby Lincs., Eng.
24 P5 Riccal r. Eng.
216 H5 Riccall N. Yorks., Eng.
262 D3 Riccarton E. Ayr., Scot.
144 D6 Richards Castle Shrop., Eng.
396 E3 Richhill Armagh, N. Ire.
106 E5 Richings Park Bucks., Eng.
216 D1 Richmond N. Yorks., Eng.
208 D3 Richmond S. Yorks., Eng.
74 C3 Richmond upon Thames Gtr Lon., Eng.
74 C3 Richmond upon Thames met. bor. Gtr Lon., Eng.
94 E4 Rich's Holford Som., Eng.
314 G4 Rickarton Abers., Scot.
148 C4 Rickerscote Staffs., Eng.
94 H3 Rickford N. Som., Eng.
120 E2 Rickinghall Suff., Eng.
236 F2 Rickleton T. and W., Eng.
116 D2 Rickling Essex, Eng.
116 D2 Rickling Green Essex, Eng.
110 C6 Rickmansworth Herts., Eng.
256 H3 Riddell Borders, Scot.
180 E4 Riddings Derbys., Eng.
40 E2 Riddlecombe Devon, Eng.
222 C1 Riddlesden W. Yorks., Eng.
276 E2 Riddrie Glas., Scot.
46 G3 Ridge Dorset, Eng.
110 D5 Ridge Herts., Eng.
86 C5 Ridge Wilts., Eng.
366 E5 Ridgebourne Powys, Wales
78 F2 Ridge Green Surr., Eng.
198 E3 Ridge Hill Gtr Man., Eng.
132 C2 Ridge Lane Warks., Eng.
180 E3 Ridgeway Derbys., Eng.
180 E4 Ridgeway Derbys., Eng.
148 C2 Ridgeway Staffs., Eng.
140 E3 Ridgeway Cross Here., Eng.
180 E3 Ridgeway Moor Derbys., Eng.
116 F1 Ridgewell Essex, Eng.
58 G3 Ridgewood E. Sussex, Eng.
110 B3 Ridgmont Central Bedfordshire, Eng.
62 E2 Ridham Dock Kent, Eng.
94 J4 Riding Gate Som., Eng.
244 F6 Riding Mill Northumb., Eng.
62 B2 Ridley Kent, Eng.
378 H3 Ridleywood Wrex., Wales
166 H2 Ridlington Norf., Eng.
162 G3 Ridlington Rutland, Eng.
166 H2 Ridlington Street Norf., Eng.
244 E5 Ridsdale Northumb., Eng.
304 I3 Riechip Perth and Kin., Scot.
216 F2 Rievaulx N. Yorks., Eng.
252 G3 Rigg D. and G., Scot.
322 C2 Rigg High., Scot.
280 C3 Riggend N. Lanark., Scot.
22 E11 Righ Mòr, Loch l. Scot.
232 G7 Rigmaden Park Cumbria, Eng.
170 G4 Rigsby Lincs., Eng.
268 D3 Rigside S. Lanark., Scot.
228 G4 Riley Green Lancs., Eng.
148 E4 Rileyhill Staffs., Eng.
36 F2 Rilla Mill Corn., Eng.
216 G2 Rillington N. Yorks., Eng.
292 E2 Rimbleton Fife, Scot.
228 I3 Rimington Lancs., Eng.
94 I5 Rimpton Som., Eng.
210 H4 Rimswell E. Riding, Eng.
358 E2 Rinaston Pembs., Wales
396 L3 Ringboy Ards, N. Ire.
252 D3 Ringford D. and G., Scot.
208 C3 Ringinglow S. Yorks., Eng.
166 F2 Ringland Norf., Eng.
58 G3 Ringles Cross E. Sussex, Eng.
58 G4 Ringmer E. Sussex, Eng.
40 E4 Ringmore Devon, Eng.
228 F5 Ring o' Bells Lancs., Eng.
124 E3 Ring's End Cambs., Eng.
388 F2 Ringsend Coleraine, N. Ire.
120 I2 Ringsfield Suff., Eng.
120 I2 Ringsfield Corner Suff., Eng.
110 B5 Ringshall Herts., Eng.
120 E4 Ringshall Stocks Suff., Eng.
166 C1 Ringstead Norf., Eng.
128 F3 Ringstead Northants., Eng.
52 B5 Ringwood Hants., Eng.
62 I3 Ringwould Kent, Eng.
314 D3 Rinloan Abers., Scot.
314 E3 Rinmore Abers., Scot.
329 B5 Rinnigill Orkney, Scot.
22 D11 Rinns of Islay pen. Scot.
22 D11 Rinns Point pt Scot.
36 C3 Rinsey Corn., Eng.
Riof W. Isles, Scot. see Reef
58 G3 Ripe E. Sussex, Eng.
180 E4 Ripley Derbys., Eng.
52 B6 Ripley Hants., Eng.
216 E2 Ripley N. Yorks., Eng.
78 D2 Ripley Surr., Eng.
210 E4 Riplingham E. Riding, Eng.
216 E2 Ripon N. Yorks., Eng.
170 D6 Rippingale Lincs., Eng.
62 I3 Ripple Kent, Eng.
136 D3 Ripple Worcs., Eng.
222 C2 Ripponden W. Yorks., Eng.
300 B5 Risabus Arg. and B., Scot.
140 D2 Risbury Here., Eng.
210 F4 Risby E. Riding, Eng.
120 C3 Risby Suff., Eng.
350 H3 Risca Caerp., Wales
210 G3 Rise E. Riding, Eng.
62 C4 Riseden Kent, Eng.
170 E6 Risegate Lincs., Eng.
170 C4 Riseholme Lincs., Eng.
110 C2 Riseley Bedford, Eng.
82 E3 Riseley W'ham, Eng.
120 F3 Rishangles Suff., Eng.
228 H4 Rishton Lancs., Eng.
222 C3 Rishworth W. Yorks., Eng.
102 D3 Risinghurst Oxon, Eng.
180 F5 Risley Derbys., Eng.
190 F3 Risley Warr., Eng.
320 G2 Rispond High., Scot.
86 F3 Rivar Wilts., Eng.
116 F3 Rivenhall Essex, Eng.
116 G3 Rivenhall End Essex, Eng.
62 H4 River Kent, Eng.
58 C3 River W. Sussex, Eng.
124 F5 River Bank Cambs., Eng.
94 G3 River Bridge Som., Eng.
82 B3 Riverhead Kent, Eng.
396 I5 Riverside Newry & Mourne, N. Ire.
350 G4 Riverside Cardiff, Wales
62 C5 Riverview Park Kent, Eng.
222 B8 Rivington Lancs., Eng.
128 D5 Roade Northants., Eng.
26 D6 Roadford Reservoir resr Eng.
166 G4 Road Green Norf., Eng.
232 F2 Roadhead Cumbria, Eng.
320 J2 Roadside High., Scot.
329 F2 Roadside Orkney, Scot.
94 D4 Roadwater Som., Eng.
128 C4 Road Weedon Northants., Eng.
322 B2 Roag High., Scot.
232 C8 Roa Island Cumbria, Eng.
22 K12 Roan Fell hill Scot.
116 C2 Roast Green Essex, Eng.
350 H4 Roath Cardiff, Wales
256 G4 Roberton Borders, Scot.
268 D3 Roberton S. Lanark., Scot.
58 I3 Robertsbridge E. Sussex, Eng.
350 F3 Robertstown R.C.T., Wales
222 D3 Roberttown W. Yorks., Eng.
358 D3 Robeston Cross Pembs., Wales
358 F3 Robeston Wathen Pembs., Wales
358 D3 Robeston West Pembs., Wales
180 D3 Robin Hood Derbys., Eng.
228 F5 Robin Hood Lancs., Eng.
222 E2 Robin Hood W. Yorks., Eng.
208 F3 Robin Hood Doncaster Sheffield airport S. Yorks., Eng.
116 E1 Robinhood End Essex, Eng.
216 H1 Robin Hood's Bay N. Yorks., Eng.
58 B2 Robins W. Sussex, Eng.
396 E3 Robinsons Town Craigavon, N. Ire.
40 D2 Roborough Devon, Eng.
190 D3 Roby Merseyside, Eng.
228 F5 Roby Mill Lancs., Eng.
148 D3 Rocester Staffs., Eng.
358 D2 Roch Pembs., Wales
304 J3 Rochallie Perth and Kin., Scot.
358 D2 Roch Bridge Pembs., Wales
198 E2 Rochdale Gtr Man., Eng.
36 E2 Roche Corn., Eng.
62 D2 Rochester Medway, Eng.
244 D4 Rochester Northumb., Eng.
116 G4 Rochford Essex, Eng.
136 B2 Rochford Worcs., Eng.
358 D2 Roch Gate Pembs., Wales
36 E2 Rock Corn., Eng.
244 G3 Rock Northumb., Eng.
136 C1 Rock Worcs., Eng.
350 G2 Rock Caerp., Wales
20 □ Rockall i. N. Atlantic Ocean
40 F2 Rockbeare Devon, Eng.
52 A5 Rockbourne Hants., Eng.
232 D3 Rockcliffe Cumbria, Eng.
252 E3 Rockcliffe D. and G., Scot.
232 D3 Rockcliffe Cross Cumbria, Eng.
190 C3 Rock Ferry Merseyside, Eng.
300 D4 Rockfield Arg. and B., Scot.
320 I4 Rockfield High., Scot.
339 D2 Rockfield Mon., Wales
52 B5 Rockford Hants., Eng.
98 E4 Rockhampton S. Glos., Eng.
36 E2 Rockhead Corn., Eng.
128 E2 Rockingham Northants., Eng.
26 K2 Rockingham Forest for. Eng.
166 E3 Rockland All Saints Norf., Eng.
166 H3 Rockland St Mary Norf., Eng.
166 E3 Rockland St Peter Norf., Eng.
176 D3 Rockley Notts., Eng.
86 E3 Rockley Wilts., Eng.
300 A4 Rockside Arg. and B., Scot.
402 K2 Rockspring Cookstown, N. Ire.
402 H3 Rockstown Omagh, N. Ire.
106 C5 Rockwell End Bucks., Eng.
94 E5 Rockwell Green Som., Eng.
98 F3 Rodborough Glos., Eng.
86 E2 Rodbourne Swindon, Eng.
86 C2 Rodbourne Wilts., Eng.
120 D4 Rodbridge Corner Suff., Eng.
140 B2 Rodd Here., Eng.
244 F3 Roddam Northumb., Eng.
46 D4 Rodden Dorset, Eng.
228 G4 Roddlesworth Lancs., Eng.
94 K3 Rode Som., Eng.
184 F2 Rodeheath Cheshire East, Eng.
184 F2 Rode Heath Cheshire East, Eng.
326 D3 Rodel W. Isles, Scot.
144 E3 Roden Telford, Eng.
26 G2 Roden r. Eng.
94 D4 Rodhuish Som., Eng.
144 E3 Rodington Telford, Eng.
144 E3 Rodington Heath Telford, Eng.
98 E3 Rodley Glos., Eng.
98 G3 Rodmarton Glos., Eng.
58 G3 Rodmell E. Sussex, Eng.
62 E3 Rodmersham Kent, Eng.
62 E3 Rodmersham Green Kent, Eng.
94 H3 Rodney Stoke Som., Eng.
180 D4 Rodsley Derbys., Eng.
94 F4 Rodway Som., Eng.
98 E5 Rodway Hill S. Glos., Eng.
24 D3 Roe r. N. Ire.
216 E2 Roecliffe N. Yorks., Eng.
198 E3 Roe Cross Gtr Man., Eng.
110 D5 Roe Green Herts., Eng.
110 E4 Roe Green Herts., Eng.
74 C3 Roehampton Gtr Lon., Eng.
228 H4 Roe Lee B'burn, Eng.
331 C2 Roesound Shet., Scot.
110 D5 Roestock Herts., Eng.
58 E2 Roffey W. Sussex, Eng.
320 H3 Rogart High., Scot.
58 A2 Rogate W. Sussex, Eng.
339 B3 Rogerstone Newp., Wales
Roghadal W. Isles, Scot. see Rodel
339 D2 Rogiet Mon., Wales
22 E9 Rois-Bheinn hill Scot.
102 E5 Rokemarsh Oxon, Eng.
236 G2 Roker T. and W., Eng.
166 I2 Rollesby Norf., Eng.
162 F3 Rolleston Leics., Eng.
176 D4 Rolleston Notts., Eng.
86 D4 Rollestone Wilts., Eng.
148 F3 Rolleston-on-Dove Staffs., Eng.
210 H3 Rolston E. Riding, Eng.
94 G2 Rolstone N. Som., Eng.
62 D4 Rolvenden Kent, Eng.
62 D4 Rolvenden Layne Kent, Eng.
236 C4 Romaldkirk Durham, Eng.
26 N4 Roman r. Eng.
256 D2 Romannobridge Borders, Scot.
40 E2 Romansleigh Devon, Eng.
322 C2 Romesdal High., Scot.
46 H2 Romford Dorset, Eng.
74 F2 Romford Gtr Lon., Eng.
198 E3 Romiley Gtr Man., Eng.
26 N5 Romney Marsh reg. Eng.
62 B3 Romney Street Kent, Eng.
52 D5 Romsey Hants., Eng.
144 G5 Romsley Shrop., Eng.
136 E1 Romsley Worcs., Eng.
22 E4 Rona i. Scot.
22 E7 Rona i. Scot.
300 D4 Ronachan Arg. and B., Scot.
405 B3 Ronague Isle of Man
Ronaigh i. Scot. see Ronay
329 D5 Ronaldsvoe Orkney, Scot.
22 □N1 Ronas Hill hill Scot.
22 B8 Ronay i. Scot.
136 D2 Ronkswood Worcs., Eng.
300 B4 Ronnachmore Arg. and B., Scot.
154 C3 Rood End W. Mids, Eng.
236 C3 Rookhope Durham, Eng.
52 E7 Rookley I.o.W., Eng.
52 E7 Rookley Green I.o.W., Eng.
94 G3 Rooks Bridge Som., Eng.
94 E4 Rook's Nest Som., Eng.
210 H4 Roos E. Riding, Eng.
232 C8 Roose Cumbria, Eng.
232 D8 Roosebeck Cumbria, Eng.
232 C8 Roosecote Cumbria, Eng.
110 C2 Rootham's Green Bedford, Eng.
268 D2 Rootpark S. Lanark., Scot.
52 F4 Ropley Hants., Eng.
52 F4 Ropley Dean Hants., Eng.
52 F4 Ropley Soke Hants., Eng.
170 C6 Ropsley Lincs., Eng.
314 H2 Rora Abers., Scot.
314 F3 Rorandle Abers., Scot.
144 B4 Rorrington Shrop., Eng.
314 B2 Rosarie Moray, Scot.
402 G3 Roscavey Omagh, N. Ire.
36 D2 Rose Corn., Eng.
62 D3 Roseacre Kent, Eng.
228 E4 Roseacre Lancs., Eng.
40 E2 Rose Ash Devon, Eng.
268 C2 Rosebank S. Lanark., Scot.
24 O4 Roseberry Topping hill Eng.
244 G2 Rosebrough Northumb., Eng.
358 F2 Rosebush Pembs., Wales
36 F1 Rosecare Corn., Eng.
36 D2 Rosecliston Corn., Eng.
216 G1 Rosedale Abbey N. Yorks., Eng.
244 F3 Roseden Northumb., Eng.
116 G2 Rose Green Essex, Eng.
120 E4 Rose Green Suff., Eng.
58 B4 Rose Green W. Sussex, Eng.
314 G1 Rosehearty Abers., Scot.
58 G3 Rose Hill E. Sussex, Eng.
228 I4 Rose Hill Lancs., Eng.
102 D4 Rose Hill Oxon, Eng.
144 D3 Rosehill Shrop., Eng.
144 E2 Rosehill Shrop., Eng.
236 F2 Rosehill T. and W., Eng.
314 C1 Roseisle Moray, Scot.
58 H4 Roselands E. Sussex, Eng.
358 E3 Rosemarket Pembs., Wales
322 I2 Rosemarkie High., Scot.
402 G4 Rosemeilan Dungannon, N. Ire.
304 K3 Rosemount Perth and Kin., Scot.
262 D3 Rosemount S. Ayr., Scot.
36 E2 Rosenannon Corn., Eng.
22 K5 Rose Ness hd Scot.
36 D3 Rosenithon Corn., Eng.
358 D3 Rosepool Pembs., Wales
154 B2 Roseville W. Mids, Eng.
283 E3 Rosewell Midlothian, Scot.
232 F5 Rosgill Cumbria, Eng.
322 D4 Roshven High., Scot.
322 B2 Roskhill High., Scot.
232 D4 Rosley Cumbria, Eng.
283 E3 Roslin Midlothian, Scot.
180 D6 Rosliston Derbys., Eng.
300 F3 Rosneath Arg. and B., Scot.
244 G2 Ross Northumb., Eng.
252 D3 Ross D. and G., Scot.
304 F4 Ross Perth and Kin., Scot.
402 B4 Rosscor Fermanagh, N. Ire.
378 H3 Rossett Wrex., Wales
216 E3 Rossett Green N. Yorks., Eng.
232 D7 Rosside Cumbria, Eng.
308 G2 Rossie Farm School Angus, Scot.
304 J5 Rossie Ochill Perth and Kin., Scot.
304 L4 Rossie Priory Perth and Kin., Scot.
208 F3 Rossington S. Yorks., Eng.
402 H5 Rosslea Fermanagh, N. Ire.
46 H3 Rossmore Poole, Eng.
140 D4 Ross-on-Wye Here., Eng.
276 C1 Ross Priory W. Dun., Scot.
320 K2 Roster High., Scot.
184 E1 Rostherne Cheshire East, Eng.
208 F2 Rostholme S. Yorks., Eng.
232 C7 Rosthwaite Cumbria, Eng.
232 D5 Rosthwaite Cumbria, Eng.
180 C5 Roston Derbys., Eng.
396 G5 Rostrevor Newry & Mourne, N. Ire.
36 C3 Rosudgeon Corn., Eng.
292 D3 Rosyth Fife, Scot.
244 F4 Rothbury Northumb., Eng.
24 N3 Rothbury Forest for. Eng.
26 K6 Rother r. Eng.
162 E2 Rotherby Leics., Eng.
58 H2 Rotherfield E. Sussex, Eng.
102 F5 Rotherfield Greys Oxon, Eng.
102 F5 Rotherfield Peppard Oxon, Eng.
208 D3 Rotherham S. Yorks., Eng.
74 D3 Rotherhithe Gtr Lon., Eng.
128 D4 Rothersthorpe Northants., Eng.
52 G3 Rotherwick Hants., Eng.
314 D2 Rothes Moray, Scot.
300 E4 Rothesay Arg. and B., Scot.
314 F2 Rothienorman Abers., Scot.
329 F3 Rothiesholm Orkney, Scot.
162 E2 Rothley Leics., Eng.
244 F4 Rothley Northumb., Eng.
314 F2 Rothney Abers., Scot.
170 E3 Rothwell Lincs., Eng.
128 E3 Rothwell Northants., Eng.
222 E2 Rothwell W. Yorks., Eng.
222 F2 Rothwell Haigh W. Yorks., Eng.
210 F3 Rotsea E. Riding, Eng.
308 D2 Rottal Angus, Scot.
106 C5 Rotten Row Bucks., Eng.
154 D3 Rotten Row W. Mids, Eng.
58 F4 Rottingdean B. and H., Eng.
232 A5 Rottington Cumbria, Eng.
52 E7 Roud I.o.W., Eng.
166 E4 Roudham Norf., Eng.
166 D2 Rougham Norf., Eng.
120 D3 Rougham Suff., Eng.
322 H4 Roughburn High., Scot.
148 C3 Rough Close Staffs., Eng.
62 G3 Rough Common Kent, Eng.
388 J4 Roughfort Newtownabbey, N. Ire.
228 I3 Roughlee Lancs., Eng.
154 D2 Roughley W. Mids, Eng.
170 F4 Roughton Lincs., Eng.
166 G1 Roughton Norf., Eng.
144 F4 Roughton Shrop., Eng.
110 C5 Round Bush Herts., Eng.
116 D3 Roundbush Green Essex, Eng.
110 C4 Round Green Luton, Eng.
94 H5 Roundham Som., Eng.
222 F2 Roundhay W. Yorks., Eng.
24 O5 Round Hill hill Eng.
58 C2 Roundstreet Common W. Sussex, Eng.
198 D3 Roundthorn Gtr Man., Eng.
86 D3 Roundway Wilts., Eng.
22 J4 Rousay i. Scot.
40 H2 Rousdon Devon, Eng.
102 D3 Rousham Oxon, Eng.
102 D3 Rousham Gap Oxon, Eng.
402 G2 Rousky Omagh, N. Ire.
136 F2 Rous Lench Worcs., Eng.
264 E2 Routenburn N. Ayr., Scot.
210 F3 Routh E. Riding, Eng.
106 C4 Rout's Green Bucks., Eng.
36 E2 Row Corn., Eng.
232 E7 Row Cumbria, Eng.
232 G4 Row Cumbria, Eng.
252 H2 Rowanburn D. and G., Scot.
98 G2 Rowanfield Glos., Eng.
296 C5 Rowardennan Lodge Stir., Scot.
180 B2 Rowarth Derbys., Eng.
94 F4 Rowbarton Som., Eng.
94 H3 Rowberrow Som., Eng.
296 B4 Rowchoish Stir., Scot.
86 C3 Rowde Wilts., Eng.
216 E2 Rowden N. Yorks., Eng.
378 B2 Rowen Conwy, Wales
180 C4 Rowfields Derbys., Eng.
244 C6 Rowfoot Northumb., Eng.
116 I3 Row Heath Essex, Eng.
116 H2 Rowhedge Essex, Eng.
58 D2 Rowhook W. Sussex, Eng.
132 B4 Rowington Warks., Eng.
132 B4 Rowington Green Warks., Eng.
180 C3 Rowland Derbys., Eng.
52 G5 Rowland's Castle Hants., Eng.
236 E2 Rowlands Gill T. and W., Eng.
78 B2 Rowledge Surr., Eng.
140 B4 Rowlestone Here., Eng.
236 D3 Rowley Durham, Eng.
210 E4 Rowley E. Riding, Eng.
144 B4 Rowley Shrop., Eng.
148 C4 Rowley Park Staffs., Eng.
154 B3 Rowley Regis W. Mids, Eng.
154 E3 Rowley's Green W. Mids, Eng.
78 C3 Rowly Surr., Eng.
52 E6 Rowner Hants., Eng.
136 F1 Rowney Green Worcs., Eng.
52 D5 Rownhams Hants., Eng.
232 B5 Rowrah Cumbria, Eng.
106 D3 Rowsham Bucks., Eng.
102 D5 Rowstock Oxon, Eng.
170 D5 Rowston Lincs., Eng.
180 F3 Rowthorne Derbys., Eng.
184 C2 Rowton Cheshire West & Chester, Eng.
144 C3 Rowton Shrop., Eng.
144 E3 Rowton Telford, Eng.
78 C1 Row Town Surr., Eng.
256 J3 Roxburgh Borders, Scot.
170 C2 Roxby N. Lincs., Eng.
216 G1 Roxby N. Yorks., Eng.
74 B2 Roxeth Gtr Lon., Eng.
388 H4 Roxhill Antrim, N. Ire.
110 D2 Roxton Bedford, Eng.
116 E3 Roxwell Essex, Eng.
22 G9 Roy r. Scot.
62 C3 Royal British Legion Village Kent, Eng.
396 E3 Royal Irish Fusiliers Museum Armagh, N. Ire.
228 E5 Royal Oak Lancs., Eng.
322 G4 Roybridge High., Scot.
222 D3 Roydhouse W. Yorks., Eng.
208 C2 Royd Moor S. Yorks., Eng.
116 C3 Roydon Essex, Eng.
166 C2 Roydon Norf., Eng.
166 F4 Roydon Norf., Eng.
116 C3 Roydon Hamlet Essex, Eng.
110 E3 Royston Herts., Eng.
208 D2 Royston S. Yorks., Eng.
198 E2 Royton Gtr Man., Eng.
408 E4 Rozel Jersey Channel Is
378 G4 Ruabon Wrex., Wales
300 □ Ruaig Arg. and B., Scot.
300 A3 Ruanaich Arg. and B., Scot.
36 D3 Ruan Major Corn., Eng.
36 D4 Ruan Minor Corn., Eng.
98 D2 Ruardean Glos., Eng.
98 D2 Ruardean Hill Glos., Eng.
98 D2 Ruardean Woodside Glos., Eng.
396 L3 Rubane Ards, N. Ire.
154 B3 Rubery W. Mids, Eng.
Rubha an t-Siumpain hd Scot. see Tiumpan Head
Rubha Robhanais hd Scot. see Butt of Lewis
276 F2 Ruchazie Glas., Scot.
232 F4 Ruckcroft Cumbria, Eng.
62 F4 Ruckinge Kent, Eng.
110 C5 Rucklers Lane Herts., Eng.
144 D4 Ruckley Shrop., Eng.
358 E2 Rudbaxton Pembs., Wales
244 G5 Rudchester Northumb., Eng.
176 C5 Ruddington Notts., Eng.
98 F2 Rudford Glos., Eng.
94 K3 Rudge Som., Eng.
58 D2 Rudgwick W. Sussex, Eng.
140 D4 Rudhall Here., Eng.
184 E2 Rudheath Cheshire West & Chester, Eng.
116 F3 Rudley Green Essex, Eng.
86 B3 Rudloe Wilts., Eng.
350 G3 Rudry Caerp., Wales
210 G2 Rudston E. Riding, Eng.
148 C2 Rudyard Staffs., Eng.
228 F5 Rufford Lancs., Eng.
216 F3 Rufforth York, Eng.
236 C2 Ruffside Durham, Eng.
132 E3 Rugby Warks., Eng.
148 D4 Rugeley Staffs., Eng.
94 F4 Ruishton Som., Eng.
326 C3 Ruisigearraidh W. Isles, Scot.
74 B2 Ruislip Gtr Lon., Eng.
74 B2 Ruislip Gardens Gtr Lon., Eng.
74 B2 Ruislip Manor Gtr Lon., Eng.
22 D9 Rum i. Scot.
22 D9 Rum, Sound of sea chan. Scot.
304 I5 Rumbling Bridge Perth and Kin., Scot.
120 H2 Rumburgh Suff., Eng.
120 H2 Rumburgh Street Suff., Eng.
36 E2 Rumford Corn., Eng.
40 D3 Rumleigh Devon, Eng.
350 H3 Rumney Cardiff, Wales
94 F4 Rumwell Som., Eng.
23 J2 Runabay Head hd N. Ire.
296 E4 Runacraig Stir., Scot.
190 E4 Runcorn Halton, Eng.
58 B4 Runcton W. Sussex, Eng.
166 B3 Runcton Holme Norf., Eng.
40 D3 Rundlestone Devon, Eng.
78 B2 Runfold Surr., Eng.
166 F3 Runhall Norf., Eng.
166 I3 Runham Norf., Eng.
166 J3 Runham Norf., Eng.
94 E5 Runnington Som., Eng.
236 G3 Running Waters Durham, Eng.
116 F3 Runsell Green Essex, Eng.
228 F4 Runshaw Moor Lancs., Eng.
216 G1 Runswick Bay N. Yorks., Eng.
308 C2 Runtaleave Angus, Scot.
116 F4 Runwell Essex, Eng.
98 F3 Ruscombe Glos., Eng.
82 E3 Ruscombe W'ham, Eng.
140 D3 Rushall Here., Eng.
166 G4 Rushall Norf., Eng.
86 E4 Rushall Wilts., Eng.
154 C2 Rushall W. Mids, Eng.
120 D3 Rushbrooke Suff., Eng.
144 D4 Rushbury Shrop., Eng.
110 E4 Rushden Herts., Eng.
128 F4 Rushden Northants., Eng.
40 D3 Rushford Devon, Eng.
166 D4 Rushford Norf., Eng.
74 F2 Rush Green Gtr Lon., Eng.
110 D4 Rush Green Herts., Eng.
166 F3 Rush Green Norf., Eng.
190 G3 Rushgreen Warr., Eng.
58 H3 Rushlake Green E. Sussex, Eng.
120 J2 Rushmere Suff., Eng.
120 G4 Rushmere St Andrew Suff., Eng.
78 B3 Rushmoor Surr., Eng.
144 E3 Rushmoor Telford, Eng.
136 D1 Rushock Worcs., Eng.
198 D3 Rusholme Gtr Man., Eng.
184 D2 Rushton Cheshire West & Chester, Eng.
128 E3 Rushton Northants., Eng.
144 E3 Rushton Shrop., Eng.
148 C2 Rushton Spencer Staffs., Eng.
136 D2 Rushwick Worcs., Eng.
236 F4 Rushyford Durham, Eng.
58 G3 Rushy Green E. Sussex, Eng.
296 E4 Ruskie Stir., Scot.
170 D5 Ruskington Lincs., Eng.
252 D3 Rusko D. and G., Scot.
232 D7 Rusland Cumbria, Eng.
58 E2 Rusper W. Sussex, Eng.
98 D3 Ruspidge Glos., Eng.
322 E2 Russel High., Scot.
116 F3 Russell Green Essex, Eng.
58 I3 Russell's Green E. Sussex, Eng.
102 F5 Russell's Water Oxon, Eng.
120 G3 Russel's Green Suff., Eng.
78 E3 Russ Hill Surr., Eng.
62 B4 Rusthall Kent, Eng.
58 C4 Rustington W. Sussex, Eng.
210 F2 Ruston Parva E. Riding, Eng.
216 H1 Ruswarp N. Yorks., Eng.
268 B2 Rutherend S. Lanark., Scot.
256 I3 Rutherford Borders, Scot.
268 A2 Rutherglen S. Lanark., Scot.
36 E2 Ruthernbridge Corn., Eng.
320 K2 Ruthers of Howe High., Scot.
350 F3 Ruthin V. of Glam., Wales
314 G3 Ruthrieston Aberdeen, Scot.
314 E2 Ruthven Abers., Scot.
308 D3 Ruthven Angus, Scot.
322 I3 Ruthven High., Scot.
322 J2 Ruthven High., Scot.
36 E2 Ruthvoes Corn., Eng.
232 C4 Ruthwaite Cumbria, Eng.
252 F3 Ruthwell D. and G., Scot.
162 H2 Rutland county Eng.
26 K2 Rutland Water resr Eng.
140 C4 Ruxton Green Here., Eng.
144 C3 Ruyton-XI-Towns Shrop., Eng.
244 F5 Ryal Northumb., Eng.
228 G4 Ryal Fold B'burn, Eng.
46 B3 Ryall Dorset, Eng.
136 D3 Ryall Worcs., Eng.
22 F12 Ryan, Loch b. Scot.
62 C3 Ryarsh Kent, Eng.
232 E6 Rydal Cumbria, Eng.
52 F6 Ryde I.o.W., Eng.
58 K3 Rye E. Sussex, Eng.
24 P5 Rye r. Eng.
144 D2 Ryebank Shrop., Eng.
26 N6 Rye Bay b. Eng.
222 C1 Ryecroft W. Yorks., Eng.
140 D4 Ryeford Here., Eng.
58 K3 Rye Foreign E. Sussex, Eng.
58 K3 Rye Harbour E. Sussex, Eng.
210 H4 Ryehill E. Riding, Eng.
110 E5 Rye Park Herts., Eng.
136 D3 Rye Street Worcs., Eng.
162 I2 Ryhall Rutland, Eng.
222 F3 Ryhill W. Yorks., Eng.
236 G3 Ryhope T. and W., Eng.
236 G2 Ryhope Colliery T. and W., Eng.
180 F3 Rylah Derbys., Eng.
170 D4 Ryland Lincs., Eng.
176 B5 Rylands Notts., Eng.
216 C3 Rylstone N. Yorks., Eng.
46 D2 Ryme Intrinseca Dorset, Eng.
216 F3 Ryther N. Yorks., Eng.
98 F2 Ryton Glos., Eng.
144 F4 Ryton Shrop., Eng.
236 E2 Ryton T. and W., Eng.
132 D3 Ryton Warks., Eng.
132 D3 Ryton-on-Dunsmore Warks., Eng.
236 E2 Ryton Woodside T. and W., Eng.

S

228 I3 Sabden Lancs., Eng.
228 I3 Sabden Fold Lancs., Eng.
120 D4 Sackers Green Suff., Eng.
110 E4 Sacombe Herts., Eng.
110 E4 Sacombe Green Herts., Eng.
236 F3 Sacriston Durham, Eng.
236 G4 Sadberge Darl., Eng.
300 D5 Saddell Arg. and B., Scot.
162 E3 Saddington Leics., Eng.
Saddleback hill Eng. see Blencathra
166 B2 Saddle Bow Norf., Eng.
232 F6 Sadgill Cumbria, Eng.
116 D1 Saffron Walden Essex, Eng.
358 F3 Sageston Pembs., Wales
166 D3 Saham Hills Norf., Eng.
166 D3 Saham Toney Norf., Eng.
326 C4 Saighdinis W. Isles, Scot.

Shelswell to South Tyne

102 E3 Shelswell Oxon, Eng.
162 D2 Shelthorpe Leics., Eng.
110 C2 Shelton Bedford, Eng.
166 G4 Shelton Norf., Eng.
176 D5 Shelton Notts., Eng.
144 D3 Shelton Shrop., Eng.
180 E5 Shelton Lock Derby, Eng.
144 C4 Shelve Shrop., Eng.
140 C3 Shelwick Here., Eng.
140 C3 Shelwick Green Here., Eng.
116 D4 Shenfield Essex, Eng.
102 C2 Shenington Oxon, Eng.
110 D5 Shenley Herts., Eng.
106 D2 Shenley Brook End M.K., Eng.
110 D5 Shenleybury Herts., Eng.
106 D2 Shenley Church End M.K., Eng.
154 C3 Shenley Fields W. Mids, Eng.
140 B3 Shenmore Here., Eng.
252 C3 Shennanton D. and G., Scot.
148 D5 Shenstone Staffs., Eng.
136 D1 Shenstone Worcs., Eng.
148 D5 Shenstone Woodend Staffs., Eng.
162 C3 Shenton Leics., Eng.
314 D2 Shenval Moray, Scot.
170 F7 Shepeau Stow Lincs., Eng.
110 D4 Shephall Herts., Eng.
74 C2 Shepherd's Bush Gtr Lon., Eng.
102 F5 Shepherd's Green Oxon, Eng.
98 E3 Shepherd's Patch Glos., Eng.
62 H3 Shepherdswell Kent, Eng.
222 D3 Shepley W. Yorks., Eng.
98 D4 Shepperdine S. Glos., Eng.
78 D1 Shepperton Surr., Eng.
26 N5 Sheppey, Isle of i. Eng.
124 E6 Shepreth Cambs., Eng.
162 D2 Shepshed Leics., Eng.
94 G5 Shepton Beauchamp Som., Eng.
94 I3 Shepton Mallet Som., Eng.
94 J4 Shepton Montague Som., Eng.
62 D3 Shepway Kent, Eng.
236 H3 Sheraton Hartlepool, Eng.
46 D2 Sherborne Dorset, Eng.
98 I3 Sherborne Glos., Eng.
52 F3 Sherborne St John Hants., Eng.
132 C4 Sherbourne Warks., Eng.
120 E4 Sherbourne Street Suff., Eng.
236 F3 Sherburn Durham, Eng.
216 H2 Sherburn N. Yorks., Eng.
236 G3 Sherburn Hill Durham, Eng.
216 F3 Sherburn in Elmet N. Yorks., Eng.
78 D2 Shere Surr., Eng.
166 D2 Shereford Norf., Eng.
52 C5 Sherfield English Hants., Eng.
52 F3 Sherfield on Loddon Hants., Eng.
40 E4 Sherford Devon, Eng.
94 F4 Sherford Som., Eng.
144 F3 Sheriffhales Shrop., Eng.
216 F2 Sheriff Hutton N. Yorks., Eng.
166 G1 Sheringham Norf., Eng.
106 D2 Sherington M.K., Eng.
166 C1 Shernborne Norf., Eng.
322 H3 Sherramore High., Scot.
86 C5 Sherrington Wilts., Eng.
86 B2 Sherston Wilts., Eng.
176 C5 Sherwood Nott., Eng.
24 O7 Sherwood Forest reg. Eng.
40 D2 Sherwood Green Devon, Eng.
331 C3 Shetland admin. div. Scot.
20 G1 Shetland Islands is Scot.
276 F2 Shettleston Glas., Scot.
198 A2 Shevington Gtr Man., Eng.
198 A2 Shevington Moor Gtr Man., Eng.
36 G2 Sheviock Corn., Eng.
22 D7 Shiant, Sound of str. Scot.
22 D7 Shiant Islands is Scot.
222 C2 Shibden Head W. Yorks., Eng.
52 E6 Shide I.o.W., Eng.
22 E9 Shiel, Loch l. Scot.
322 E3 Shiel Bridge High., Scot.
320 C4 Shieldaig High., Scot.
322 E2 Shieldaig High., Scot.
276 D2 Shieldhall Glas., Scot.
280 D3 Shieldhill Falk., Scot.
236 E2 Shield Row Durham, Eng.
322 D4 Shielfoot High., Scot.
308 E2 Shielhill Angus, Scot.
102 C4 Shifford Oxon, Eng.
144 F3 Shifnal Shrop., Eng.
244 G3 Shilbottle Northumb., Eng.
236 F4 Shildon Durham, Eng.
388 J3 Shillanavogy Ballymena, N. Ire.
22 B7 Shillay i. Scot.
40 F1 Shillingford Devon, Eng.
102 E5 Shillingford Oxon, Eng.
40 F2 Shillingford Abbot Devon, Eng.
40 F2 Shillingford St George Devon, Eng.
46 F2 Shillingstone Dorset, Eng.
110 C4 Shillington Central Bedfordshire, Eng.
244 D3 Shillmoor Northumb., Eng.
102 B4 Shilton Oxon, Eng.
132 D3 Shilton Warks., Eng.
166 F4 Shimpling Norf., Eng.
120 D4 Shimpling Suff., Eng.
120 D4 Shimpling Street Suff., Eng.
22 G6 Shin, Loch l. Scot.
236 F3 Shincliffe Durham, Eng.
236 G2 Shiney Row T. and W., Eng.
82 E3 Shinfield W'ham, Eng.
124 D6 Shingay Cambs., Eng.
166 C3 Shingham Norf., Eng.
120 H4 Shingle Street Suff., Eng.
24 M7 Shining Tor hill Eng.
396 G4 Shinn Newry & Mourne, N. Ire.
62 B3 Shipbourne Kent, Eng.
184 E2 Shipbrookhill Cheshire West & Chester, Eng.
166 E3 Shipdham Norf., Eng.
94 H3 Shipham Som., Eng.
40 F3 Shiphay Torbay, Eng.
102 F5 Shiplake Oxon, Eng.
102 F5 Shiplake Row Oxon, Eng.
244 G3 Shipley Northumb., Eng.
144 G4 Shipley Shrop., Eng.
58 D3 Shipley W. Sussex, Eng.
222 D1 Shipley W. Yorks., Eng.
40 E3 Shipley Bridge Devon, Eng.
78 F3 Shipley Bridge Surr., Eng.
180 F5 Shipley Common Derbys., Eng.
120 H2 Shipmeadow Suff., Eng.
124 G4 Shippea Hill Cambs., Eng.
102 D4 Shippon Oxon, Eng.
132 C5 Shipston on Stour Warks., Eng.
98 H2 Shipton Glos., Eng.
216 F2 Shipton N. Yorks., Eng.
144 E4 Shipton Shrop., Eng.
52 C3 Shipton Bellinger Hants., Eng.
46 C3 Shipton Gorge Dorset, Eng.
58 A4 Shipton Green W. Sussex, Eng.
98 G4 Shipton Moyne Glos., Eng.
98 H2 Shipton Oliffe Glos., Eng.
102 D3 Shipton-on-Cherwell Oxon, Eng.
98 H2 Shipton Solers Glos., Eng.
210 D3 Shiptonthorpe E. Riding, Eng.
102 B3 Shipton-under-Wychwood Oxon, Eng.
300 F3 Shira Arg. and B., Scot.
22 F10 Shira r. Scot.
102 F5 Shirburn Oxon, Eng.
228 E5 Shirdley Hill Lancs., Eng.
180 F3 Shirebrook Derbys., Eng.
208 D3 Shirecliffe S. Yorks., Eng.
208 D3 Shiregreen S. Yorks., Eng.
94 H2 Shirehampton Bristol, Eng.
236 F1 Shiremoor T. and W., Eng.
339 D3 Shirenewton Mon., Wales
154 C2 Shire Oak W. Mids, Eng.
176 B3 Shireoaks Notts., Eng.
180 E4 Shirland Derbys., Eng.
180 C5 Shirley Derbys., Eng.
74 D3 Shirley Gtr Lon., Eng.
52 B6 Shirley Hants., Eng.
52 D5 Shirley Soton, Eng.
154 D3 Shirley W. Mids, Eng.
154 D3 Shirley Heath W. Mids, Eng.
52 D5 Shirley Warren Soton, Eng.
148 C4 Shirleywich Staffs., Eng.
140 C2 Shirl Heath Here., Eng.
52 E5 Shirrell Heath Hants., Eng.
40 D1 Shirwell Cross Devon, Eng.
264 C3 Shiskine N. Ayr., Scot.
236 D3 Shittlehope Durham, Eng.
140 B2 Shobdon Here., Eng.
52 B5 Shobley Hants., Eng.
40 F2 Shobrooke Devon, Eng.
184 B3 Shocklach Cheshire West & Chester, Eng.
184 B3 Shocklach Green Cheshire West & Chester, Eng.
116 G4 Shoeburyness Southend, Eng.
62 I3 Sholden Kent, Eng.
52 D5 Sholing Soton, Eng.
22 E9 Shona, Eilean i. Scot.
74 E3 Shooter's Hill Gtr Lon., Eng.
144 C3 Shoot Hill Shrop., Eng.
36 E2 Shop Corn., Eng.
36 F1 Shop Corn., Eng.
120 G5 Shop Corner Suff., Eng.
94 E4 Shopnoller Som., Eng.
120 G3 Shop Street Suff., Eng.
388 J4 Shoptown Ballymena, N. Ire.
198 E2 Shore Gtr Man., Eng.
74 D2 Shoreditch Gtr Lon., Eng.
62 B3 Shoreham Kent, Eng.
58 E4 Shoreham airport Eng.
58 E3 Shoreham-by-Sea W. Sussex, Eng.
244 E1 Shoresdean Northumb., Eng.
244 G2 Shoreston Hall Northumb., Eng.
244 E1 Shoreswood Northumb., Eng.
322 I2 Shoreton High., Scot.
52 E4 Shorley Hants., Eng.
98 H4 Shorncote Glos., Eng.
62 C2 Shorne Kent, Eng.
62 C2 Shorne Ridgeway Kent, Eng.
58 G3 Shortbridge E. Sussex, Eng.
366 G3 Short Cross Powys, Wales
78 B2 Shortfield Common Surr., Eng.
58 G3 Shortgate E. Sussex, Eng.
166 F4 Short Green Norf., Eng.
116 D2 Shortgrove Essex, Eng.
102 B3 Shorthampton Oxon, Eng.
180 D6 Short Heath Derbys., Eng.
154 C2 Short Heath W. Mids, Eng.
74 E3 Shortlands Gtr Lon., Eng.
36 D3 Shortlanesend Corn., Eng.
40 F3 Shorton Torbay, Eng.
276 D2 Shortroods Renf., Scot.
98 D3 Shortstanding Glos., Eng.
52 D7 Shorwell I.o.W., Eng.
94 J3 Shoscombe B. and N.E. Som., Eng.
144 C3 Shotatton Shrop., Eng.
166 G3 Shotesham Norf., Eng.
116 F4 Shotgate Essex, Eng.
128 F2 Shotley Northants., Eng.
120 G5 Shotley Suff., Eng.
236 D2 Shotley Bridge Durham, Eng.
244 F6 Shotleyfield Northumb., Eng.
120 G5 Shotley Gate Suff., Eng.
120 G5 Shotley Street Suff., Eng.
62 F3 Shottenden Kent, Eng.
78 B3 Shottermill Surr., Eng.
132 B4 Shottery Warks., Eng.
132 D5 Shotteswell Warks., Eng.
120 H4 Shottisham Suff., Eng.
180 D4 Shottle Derbys., Eng.
180 D4 Shottlegate Derbys., Eng.
236 G3 Shotton Durham, Eng.
236 G4 Shotton Durham, Eng.
244 D2 Shotton Northumb., Eng.
244 H5 Shotton Northumb., Eng.
378 G2 Shotton Flints., Wales
236 G3 Shotton Colliery Durham, Eng.
280 D4 Shotts N. Lanark., Scot.
184 B2 Shotwick Cheshire West & Chester, Eng.
405 C2 Shoughlaige-e-Caine Isle of Man
166 B3 Shouldham Norf., Eng.
166 B3 Shouldham Thorpe Norf., Eng.
136 D2 Shoulton Worcs., Eng.
58 I2 Shover's Green E. Sussex, Eng.
148 B2 Shraleybrook Staffs., Eng.
144 C3 Shrawardine Shrop., Eng.
136 D2 Shrawley Worcs., Eng.
106 E5 Shreding Green Bucks., Eng.
132 B4 Shrewley Warks., Eng.
144 D3 Shrewsbury Shrop., Eng.
86 D4 Shrewton Wilts., Eng.
396 K3 Shrigley Down, N. Ire.
58 B4 Shripney W. Sussex, Eng.
102 B5 Shrivenham Oxon, Eng.
166 E4 Shropham Norf., Eng.
144 D4 Shropshire county Eng.
46 F2 Shroton Dorset, Eng.
116 H2 Shrub End Essex, Eng.
140 D3 Shucknall Here., Eng.
124 G6 Shudy Camps Cambs., Eng.
98 G2 Shurdington Glos., Eng.
82 F3 Shurlock Row W. and M., Eng.
136 F2 Shurnock Worcs., Eng.
320 J2 Shurrery High., Scot.
94 F3 Shurton Som., Eng.
132 C2 Shustoke Warks., Eng.
40 F2 Shute Devon, Eng.
102 C2 Shutford Oxon, Eng.
148 B4 Shut Heath Staffs., Eng.
98 F1 Shuthonger Glos., Eng.
148 B3 Shutlanehead Staffs., Eng.
128 D5 Shutlanger Northants., Eng.
148 B4 Shutt Green Staffs., Eng.
132 C2 Shuttington Warks., Eng.
180 F3 Shuttlewood Derbys., Eng.
198 D2 Shuttleworth Gtr Man., Eng.
Siabost W. Isles, Scot. see Shawbost
326 E1 Siadar Iarach W. Isles, Scot.
326 E1 Siadar Uarach W. Isles, Scot.
252 F2 Sibbaldbie D. and G., Scot.
128 C3 Sibbertoft Northants., Eng.
144 C5 Sibdon Carwood Shrop., Eng.
Sibertswold Kent, Eng. see Shepherdswell
102 C2 Sibford Ferris Oxon, Eng.
102 C2 Sibford Gower Oxon, Eng.
116 F2 Sible Hedingham Essex, Eng.
116 E2 Sibley's Green Essex, Eng.
170 G5 Sibsey Lincs., Eng.
124 B3 Sibson Cambs., Eng.
162 C3 Sibson Leics., Eng.
176 D4 Sibthorpe Notts., Eng.
120 H3 Sibton Suff., Eng.
120 H3 Sibton Green Suff., Eng.
120 D3 Sicklesmere Suff., Eng.
216 E3 Sicklinghall N. Yorks., Eng.
40 G2 Sidbury Devon, Eng.
144 F5 Sidbury Shrop., Eng.
94 H3 Sidcot N. Som., Eng.
74 E3 Sidcup Gtr Lon., Eng.
222 C2 Siddal W. Yorks., Eng.
184 F2 Siddington Cheshire East, Eng.
98 H3 Siddington Glos., Eng.
136 E1 Sidemoor Worcs., Eng.
166 H1 Sidestrand Norf., Eng.
40 G2 Sidford Devon, Eng.
22 J10 Sidlaw Hills hills Scot.
58 B4 Sidlesham W. Sussex, Eng.
58 I3 Sidley E. Sussex, Eng.
78 E2 Sidlow Surr., Eng.
40 G2 Sidmouth Devon, Eng.
40 E3 Sigford Devon, Eng.
210 G3 Sigglesthorne E. Riding, Eng.
288 D3 Sighthill Edin., Scot.
350 F4 Sigingstone V. of Glam., Wales
102 B4 Signet Oxon, Eng.
52 F2 Silchester Hants., Eng.
326 E2 Sildinis W. Isles, Scot.
162 E2 Sileby Leics., Eng.
232 C7 Silecroft Cumbria, Eng.
166 F3 Silfield Norf., Eng.
362 F4 Silian Cere., Wales
52 D4 Silkstead Hants., Eng.
208 C2 Silkstone S. Yorks., Eng.
208 C2 Silkstone Common S. Yorks., Eng.
236 G2 Silksworth T. and W., Eng.
170 D6 Silk Willoughby Lincs., Eng.
232 F7 Sill Field Cumbria, Eng.
232 B3 Silloth Cumbria, Eng.
244 D4 Sills Northumb., Eng.
216 H2 Silpho N. Yorks., Eng.
222 C1 Silsden W. Yorks., Eng.
110 C3 Silsoe Central Bedfordshire, Eng.
46 F1 Silton Dorset, Eng.
396 E5 Silverbridge Newry & Mourne, N. Ire.
402 G1 Silverbrook Strabane, N. Ire.
288 D4 Silverburn Midlothian, Scot.
300 D3 Silvercraigs Arg. and B., Scot.
228 F1 Silverdale Lancs., Eng.
148 B2 Silverdale Staffs., Eng.
110 C3 Silver End Central Bedfordshire, Eng.
116 F2 Silver End Essex, Eng.
166 G2 Silvergate Norf., Eng.
166 G4 Silver Green Norf., Eng.
58 I2 Silver Hill E. Sussex, Eng.
58 J3 Silverhill E. Sussex, Eng.
402 D4 Silver Hill Fermanagh, N. Ire.
288 D3 Silverknowes Edin., Scot.
120 H3 Silverlace Green Suff., Eng.
120 H2 Silverley's Green Suff., Eng.
314 G2 Silvermoss Abers., Scot.
128 C5 Silverstone Northants., Eng.
62 E3 Silver Street Kent, Eng.
94 I4 Silver Street Som., Eng.
40 F2 Silverton Devon, Eng.
74 E2 Silvertown Gtr Lon., Eng.
144 E5 Silvington Shrop., Eng.
331 C3 Silwick Shet., Scot.
198 D2 Simister Gtr Man., Eng.
180 B2 Simmondley Derbys., Eng.
244 D5 Simonburn Northumb., Eng.
94 B4 Simonsbath Som., Eng.
236 G2 Simonside T. and W., Eng.
228 H4 Simonstone Lancs., Eng.
350 E3 Simonstone Bridg., Wales
256 K2 Simprim Borders, Scot.
106 D2 Simpson M.K., Eng.
222 D1 Simpson Green W. Yorks., Eng.
22 J5 Sinclair's Bay b. Scot.
256 K2 Sinclair's Hill Borders, Scot.
262 E4 Sinclairston E. Ayr., Scot.
292 F3 Sinclairtown Fife, Scot.
216 E2 Sinderby N. Yorks., Eng.
244 D6 Sinderhope Northumb., Eng.
82 E3 Sindlesham W'ham, Eng.
180 E5 Sinfin Derby, Eng.
256 I5 Singdean Borders, Scot.
74 E4 Single Street Gtr Lon., Eng.
228 E3 Singleton Lancs., Eng.
58 B3 Singleton W. Sussex, Eng.
62 C2 Singlewell Kent, Eng.
378 H3 Singret Wrex., Wales
62 D4 Sinkhurst Green Kent, Eng.
314 E3 Sinnahard Abers., Scot.
216 G2 Sinnington N. Yorks., Eng.
136 D2 Sinton Green Worcs., Eng.
22 F6 Sionascaig, Loch l. Scot.
402 F2 Sion Mills Strabane, N. Ire.
74 B3 Sipson Gtr Lon., Eng.
350 G2 Sirhowy B. Gwent, Wales
166 H3 Sisland Norf., Eng.
62 D4 Sissinghurst Kent, Eng.
98 E5 Siston S. Glos., Eng.
36 D3 Sithney Corn., Eng.
62 E2 Sittingbourne Kent, Eng.
326 F2 Siulaisiadar W. Isles, Scot.
144 G5 Six Ashes Shrop., Eng.
162 E2 Six Hills Leics., Eng.
170 E3 Sixhills Lincs., Eng.
62 G4 Sixmile Kent, Eng.
124 F5 Six Mile Bottom Cambs., Eng.
402 H3 Sixmilecross Omagh, N. Ire.
46 G2 Sixpenny Handley Dorset, Eng.
396 K2 Six Road Ends Ards, N. Ire.
148 E3 Six Roads End Staffs., Eng.
120 I3 Sizewell Suff., Eng.
320 H2 Skail High., Scot.
329 B3 Skaill Orkney, Scot.
329 D3 Skaill Orkney, Scot.
329 E4 Skaill Orkney, Scot.
22 J4 Skara Brae tourist site Scot.
314 F2 Skares Abers., Scot.
262 F4 Skares E. Ayr., Scot.
331 C3 Skarpigarth Shet., Scot.
288 I3 Skateraw E. Lothian, Scot.
331 E2 Skaw Shet., Scot.
322 C2 Skeabost High., Scot.
329 B3 Skeabrae Orkney, Scot.
216 D1 Skeeby N. Yorks., Eng.
162 F3 Skeffington Leics., Eng.
210 I5 Skeffling E. Riding, Eng.
176 B4 Skegby Notts., Eng.
170 I5 Skegness Lincs., Eng.
331 D2 Skelberry Shet., Scot.
331 D4 Skelberry Shet., Scot.
320 H4 Skelbo High., Scot.
320 H4 Skelbo Street High., Scot.
208 E2 Skelbrooke S. Yorks., Eng.
331 C3 Skeld Shet., Scot.
22 □N2 Skelda Ness hd Scot.
262 D4 Skeldon E. Ayr., Scot.
170 F6 Skeldyke Lincs., Eng.
170 C4 Skellingthorpe Lincs., Eng.
331 D3 Skellister Shet., Scot.
208 E2 Skellow S. Yorks., Eng.
222 E3 Skelmanthorpe W. Yorks., Eng.
228 F5 Skelmersdale Lancs., Eng.
314 G2 Skelmonae Abers., Scot.
264 E1 Skelmorlie N. Ayr., Scot.
314 G2 Skelmuir Abers., Scot.
320 H2 Skelpick High., Scot.
232 E4 Skelton Cumbria, Eng.
210 C4 Skelton E. Riding, Eng.
216 D1 Skelton N. Yorks., Eng.
216 G1 Skelton R. and C., Eng.
216 F3 Skelton York, Eng.
Skelton-in-Cleveland R. and C., Eng. see Skelton
329 D2 Skelwick Orkney, Scot.
232 D6 Skelwith Bridge Cumbria, Eng.
170 G4 Skendleby Lincs., Eng.
170 G4 Skendleby Psalter Lincs., Eng.
339 D1 Skenfrith Mon., Wales
210 F3 Skerne E. Riding, Eng.
300 D5 Skeroblingarry Arg. and B., Scot.
396 D4 Skerries Armagh, N. Ire.
228 F2 Skerton Lancs., Eng.
162 C3 Sketchley Leics., Eng.
350 C3 Sketty Swansea, Wales
350 C3 Skewen N.P.T., Wales
166 G2 Skeyton Norf., Eng.
166 H2 Skeyton Corner Norf., Eng.
170 G3 Skidbrooke Lincs., Eng.
170 H3 Skidbrooke North End Lincs., Eng.
210 F4 Skidby E. Riding, Eng.
24 K4 Skiddaw hill Eng.
94 D4 Skilgate Som., Eng.
170 B7 Skillington Lincs., Eng.
232 B3 Skinburness Cumbria, Eng.
280 D2 Skinflats Falk., Scot.
216 G1 Skinningrove R. and C., Eng.
300 D4 Skipness Arg. and B., Scot.
228 E3 Skippool Lancs., Eng.
210 G3 Skipsea E. Riding, Eng.
210 G3 Skipsea Brough E. Riding, Eng.
216 C3 Skipton N. Yorks., Eng.
216 G3 Skipwith N. Yorks., Eng.
170 F6 Skirbeck Lincs., Eng.
216 C2 Skirethorns N. Yorks., Eng.
210 G3 Skirlaugh E. Riding, Eng.
256 D3 Skirling Borders, Scot.
106 C5 Skirmett Bucks., Eng.
210 C2 Skirpenbeck E. Riding, Eng.
232 G4 Skirwith Cumbria, Eng.
320 K2 Skirza High., Scot.
106 C4 Skittle Green Bucks., Eng.
26 B4 Skokholm Island i. Wales
26 B4 Skomer Island i. Wales
144 B5 Skyborry Green Shrop., Eng.
22 D8 Skye i. Scot.
116 G2 Skye Green Essex, Eng.
180 D4 Slack Derbys., Eng.
222 B2 Slack W. Yorks., Eng.
314 E2 Slack Abers., Scot.
198 E2 Slackcote Gtr Man., Eng.
180 B2 Slackhall Derbys., Eng.
314 E2 Slackhead Moray, Scot.
170 H4 Slackholme End Lincs., Eng.
222 D2 Slack Side W. Yorks., Eng.
98 F3 Slad Glos., Eng.
40 D1 Slade Devon, Eng.
40 G2 Slade Devon, Eng.
358 E3 Slade Pembs., Wales
350 A3 Slade Swansea, Wales
74 F3 Slade Green Gtr Lon., Eng.
208 E3 Slade Hooton S. Yorks., Eng.
36 E2 Sladesbridge Corn., Eng.
136 D3 Slades Green Worcs., Eng.
244 B6 Slaggyford Northumb., Eng.
388 F3 Slaghtneill Magherafelt, N. Ire.
228 H3 Slaidburn Lancs., Eng.
314 G4 Slains Park Abers., Scot.
222 C3 Slaithwaite W. Yorks., Eng.
180 D4 Slaley Derbys., Eng.
244 E6 Slaley Northumb., Eng.
280 D3 Slamannan Falk., Scot.
388 J3 Slane Ballymena, N. Ire.
106 E3 Slapton Bucks., Eng.
40 F4 Slapton Devon, Eng.
128 C5 Slapton Northants., Eng.
314 E2 Slate Haugh Moray, Scot.
180 E3 Slatepit Dale Derbys., Eng.
402 G4 Slatmore Dungannon, N. Ire.
320 D4 Slattadale High., Scot.
198 D2 Slattocks Gtr Man., Eng.
58 E2 Slaugham W. Sussex, Eng.
120 I4 Slaughden Suff., Eng.
86 B3 Slaughterford Wilts., Eng.
162 F3 Slawston Leics., Eng.
24 Q7 Slea r. Eng.
52 G4 Sleaford Hants., Eng.
170 D5 Sleaford Lincs., Eng.
232 G5 Sleagill Cumbria, Eng.
144 D3 Sleap Shrop., Eng.
144 E3 Sleapford Telford, Eng.
110 D5 Sleapshyde Herts., Eng.
22 E8 Sleat pen. Scot.
22 D8 Sleat, Point of pt Scot.
22 E8 Sleat, Sound of sea chan. Scot.
136 D3 Sledge Green Worcs., Eng.
210 E2 Sledmere E. Riding, Eng.
216 H1 Sleights N. Yorks., Eng.
46 G3 Slepe Dorset, Eng.
40 C2 Slerra Devon, Eng.
320 K2 Slickly High., Scot.
264 C4 Sliddery N. Ayr., Scot.
322 K3 Sliemore High., Scot.
23 H4 Slieve Beagh hill Ireland/U.K.
23 K4 Slieve Donard hill N. Ire.
24 D4 Slieve Gallion hill N. Ire.
23 H3 Slievekirk hill N. Ire.
396 I4 Slievenisky Banbridge, N. Ire.
24 B5 Slieve Rushen hill N. Ire.
322 C3 Sligachan High., Scot.
98 E3 Slimbridge Glos., Eng.
148 B3 Slindon Staffs., Eng.
58 C3 Slindon W. Sussex, Eng.
58 D2 Slinfold W. Sussex, Eng.
98 D3 Sling Glos., Eng.
236 G3 Slingley Hill T. and W., Eng.
216 G2 Slingsby N. Yorks., Eng.
22 F7 Slioch hill Scot.
110 C4 Slip End Central Bedfordshire, Eng.
110 E3 Slip End Herts., Eng.
128 F3 Slipton Northants., Eng.
148 D4 Slitting Mill Staffs., Eng.
322 J3 Slochd High., Scot.
300 D3 Slockavullin Arg. and B., Scot.
252 D3 Slogarie D. and G., Scot.
166 H2 Sloley Norf., Eng.
252 E2 Slongaber D. and G., Scot.
170 H4 Sloothby Lincs., Eng.
82 G2 Slough Slough, Eng.
82 G2 Slough admin. div. Eng.
94 F5 Slough Green Som., Eng.
58 E2 Slough Green W. Sussex, Eng.
82 G2 Slough Trading Estate Slough, Eng.
322 J3 Sluggan High., Scot.
228 F2 Slyne Lancs., Eng.
256 I3 Smailholm Borders, Scot.
198 E2 Smallbridge Gtr Man., Eng.
166 H2 Smallburgh Norf., Eng.
262 G3 Smallburn E. Ayr., Scot.
180 B3 Smalldale Derbys., Eng.
58 E3 Small Dole W. Sussex, Eng.
180 E5 Smalley Derbys., Eng.
78 F2 Smallfield Surr., Eng.
110 D5 Smallford Herts., Eng.
154 C3 Small Heath W. Mids, Eng.
62 E4 Small Hythe Kent, Eng.
40 H2 Smallridge Devon, Eng.
148 B2 Smallthorne Stoke, Eng.
166 E4 Smallworth Norf., Eng.
52 D3 Smannell Hants., Eng.
232 H6 Smardale Cumbria, Eng.
62 E4 Smarden Kent, Eng.
300 A4 Smaull Arg. and B., Scot.
405 D1 Smeale Farm Isle of Man
40 G2 Smeatharpe Devon, Eng.
62 F4 Smeeth Kent, Eng.
162 E3 Smeeton Westerby Leics., Eng.
320 J3 Smerral High., Scot.
148 B5 Smestow Staffs., Eng.
154 C3 Smethwick W. Mids, Eng.
184 F2 Smethwick Green Cheshire East, Eng.
322 D4 Smirisary High., Scot.
180 E6 Smisby Derbys., Eng.
136 D3 Smith End Green Worcs., Eng.
232 E3 Smithfield Cumbria, Eng.
228 F3 Smith Green Lancs., Eng.
208 D2 Smithies S. Yorks., Eng.
40 G2 Smithincott Devon, Eng.
208 D2 Smithley S. Yorks., Eng.
110 F3 Smith's End Herts., Eng.
116 D2 Smith's Green Essex, Eng.
116 E1 Smith's Green Essex, Eng.
322 I2 Smithton High., Scot.
184 E2 Smithy Green Cheshire East, Eng.
198 D3 Smithy Green Gtr Man., Eng.
180 E4 Smithy Houses Derbys., Eng.
228 E5 Smithy Lane Ends Lancs., Eng.
162 C3 Smockington Leics., Eng.
110 C5 Smug Oak Herts., Eng.
262 B6 Smyrton S. Ayr., Scot.
116 G3 Smythe's Green Essex, Eng.
24 I5 Snaefell hill Isle of Man
144 C4 Snailbeach Shrop., Eng.
124 G5 Snailwell Cambs., Eng.
216 H2 Snainton N. Yorks., Eng.
210 B4 Snaith E. Riding, Eng.
216 E2 Snape N. Yorks., Eng.
120 H3 Snape Suff., Eng.
228 E5 Snape Green Lancs., Eng.
120 I3 Snape Street Suff., Eng.
120 H3 Snape Watering Suff., Eng.
74 E2 Snaresbrook Gtr Lon., Eng.
162 C2 Snarestone Leics., Eng.
170 D4 Snarford Lincs., Eng.
62 F4 Snargate Kent, Eng.
339 B2 Snatchwood Torf., Wales
62 F4 Snave Kent, Eng.
136 E2 Sneachill Worcs., Eng.
366 G3 Snead Powys, Wales
136 D2 Snead's Green Worcs., Eng.
166 G4 Sneath Common Norf., Eng.
216 H1 Sneaton N. Yorks., Eng.
170 D4 Snelland Lincs., Eng.
232 A6 Snellings Cumbria, Eng.
180 C5 Snelston Derbys., Eng.
166 E4 Snetterton Norf., Eng.
166 C1 Snettisham Norf., Eng.
94 I2 Sneyd Park Bristol, Eng.
162 C2 Snibston Leics., Eng.
62 E2 Snipeshill Kent, Eng.
Sniseabhal W. Isles, Scot. see Snishival
326 B5 Snishival W. Isles, Scot.
244 F4 Snitter Northumb., Eng.
170 C3 Snitterby Lincs., Eng.
132 B4 Snitterfield Warks., Eng.
180 D4 Snitterton Derbys., Eng.
232 C4 Snittlegarth Cumbria, Eng.
144 E5 Snitton Shrop., Eng.
22 D7 Snizort, Loch b. Scot.
140 B3 Snodhill Here., Eng.
62 C3 Snodland Kent, Eng.
208 C2 Snowden Hill S. Yorks., Eng.
26 D1 Snowdon mt. Wales
26 E2 Snowdonia National Park nat. park Wales
110 F4 Snow End Herts., Eng.
98 H1 Snowshill Glos., Eng.
Soaigh i. Scot. see Soay
22 D10 Soa Island i. Scot.
40 E4 Soar Devon, Eng.
350 G3 Soar Cardiff, Wales
356 F2 Soar Carmar., Wales
22 D8 Soay i. Scot.
22 □1 Soay i. Scot.
52 F5 Soberton Hants., Eng.
52 F5 Soberton Heath Hants., Eng.
288 C3 Society W. Lothian, Scot.
236 G5 Sockburn Darl., Eng.
378 E2 Sodom Denb., Wales
144 C2 Sodylt Bank Shrop., Eng.
236 D4 Softley Durham, Eng.
124 G4 Soham Cambs., Eng.
124 F4 Soham Cotes Cambs., Eng.
Solas W. Isles, Scot. see Sollas
388 I5 Soldierstown Lisburn, N. Ire.
40 C2 Soldon Cross Devon, Eng.
52 F4 Soldridge Hants., Eng.
252 A3 Soleburn D. and G., Scot.
62 C2 Sole Street Kent, Eng.
62 G3 Sole Street Kent, Eng.
154 D3 Solihull W. Mids, Eng.
154 C3 Solihull Lodge W. Mids, Eng.
326 B4 Sollas W. Isles, Scot.
140 B2 Sollers Dilwyn Here., Eng.
140 D4 Sollers Hope Here., Eng.
228 F5 Sollom Lancs., Eng.
98 E2 Solomon's Tump Glos., Eng.
304 I6 Solsgirth Perth and Kin., Scot.
358 C2 Solva Pembs., Wales
26 B4 Solva r. Wales
252 G2 Solwaybank D. and G., Scot.
22 I13 Solway Firth est. Scot.
162 F2 Somerby Leics., Eng.
170 D2 Somerby Lincs., Eng.
180 E4 Somercotes Derbys., Eng.
148 C4 Somerford Staffs., Eng.
98 H4 Somerford Keynes Glos., Eng.
58 A4 Somerley W. Sussex, Eng.
120 I1 Somerleyton Suff., Eng.
180 C5 Somersal Herbert Derbys., Eng.
170 G4 Somersby Lincs., Eng.
94 F4 Somerset county Eng.
124 E4 Somersham Cambs., Eng.
120 F4 Somersham Suff., Eng.
74 D2 Somers Town Gtr Lon., Eng.
102 D3 Somerton Oxon, Eng.
94 H4 Somerton Som., Eng.
120 C4 Somerton Suff., Eng.
339 C3 Somerton Newp., Wales
58 D4 Sompting W. Sussex, Eng.
58 D3 Sompting Abbotts W. Sussex, Eng.
82 E3 Sonning W'ham, Eng.
102 F5 Sonning Common Oxon, Eng.
102 F6 Sonning Eye Oxon, Eng.
378 H3 Sontley Wrex., Wales
176 B3 Sookholme Notts., Eng.
52 B6 Sopley Hants., Eng.
86 B2 Sopworth Wilts., Eng.
252 C3 Sorbie D. and G., Scot.
320 J2 Sordale High., Scot.
300 A1 Sorisdale Arg. and B., Scot.
262 F3 Sorn E. Ayr., Scot.
262 E3 Sornhill E. Ayr., Scot.
300 D2 Soroba Arg. and B., Scot.
170 E4 Sotby Lincs., Eng.
170 E4 Sots Hole Lincs., Eng.
120 I2 Sotterley Suff., Eng.
144 F2 Soudley Shrop., Eng.
378 G2 Soughton Flints., Wales
106 D3 Soulbury Bucks., Eng.
232 H6 Soulby Cumbria, Eng.
102 D3 Souldern Oxon, Eng.
110 B2 Souldrop Bedford, Eng.
184 D3 Sound Cheshire East, Eng.
331 D3 Sound Shet., Scot.
331 D3 Sound Shet., Scot.
98 E5 Soundwell S. Glos., Eng.
256 K4 Sourhope Borders, Scot.
329 C3 Sourin Orkney, Scot.
40 D2 Sourton Devon, Eng.
232 C7 Soutergate Cumbria, Eng.
166 D2 South Acre Norf., Eng.
74 C2 South Acton Gtr Lon., Eng.
62 H4 South Alkham Kent, Eng.
74 B2 Southall Gtr Lon., Eng.
280 D2 South Alloa Falk., Scot.
98 G2 Southam Glos., Eng.
132 D4 Southam Warks., Eng.
58 B3 South Ambersham W. Sussex, Eng.
52 D5 Southampton Soton, Eng.
52 D5 Southampton admin. div. Eng.
52 D5 Southampton airport Eng.
26 J6 Southampton Water est. Eng.
208 E3 South Anston S. Yorks., Eng.
82 F3 South Ascot W. and M., Eng.
94 H5 Southay Som., Eng.
262 D5 South Ayrshire admin. div. Scot.
52 C6 South Baddesley Hants., Eng.
262 D5 South Balloch S. Ayr., Scot.
276 D2 Southbar Renf., Scot.
94 I4 South Barrow Som., Eng.
74 D3 South Beddington Gtr Lon., Eng.
280 D2 South Bellsdyke Falk., Scot.
116 F4 South Benfleet Essex, Eng.
46 I3 South Bockhampton Dorset, Eng.
74 E3 Southborough Gtr Lon., Eng.
62 B4 Southborough Kent, Eng.
46 I3 Southbourne Bourne., Eng.
58 A3 Southbourne W. Sussex, Eng.
46 C3 South Bowood Dorset, Eng.
208 F2 South Bramwith S. Yorks., Eng.
40 E3 South Brent Devon, Eng.
94 J4 South Brewham Som., Eng.
244 H4 South Broomhill Northumb., Eng.
166 E3 Southburgh Norf., Eng.
166 I3 South Burlingham Norf., Eng.
210 F3 Southburn E. Riding, Eng.
94 I4 South Cadbury Som., Eng.
252 A3 South Cairn D. and G., Scot.
170 C4 South Carlton Lincs., Eng.
176 C2 South Carlton Notts., Eng.
210 E4 South Cave E. Riding, Eng.
98 H3 South Cerney Glos., Eng.
94 G5 South Chard Som., Eng.
244 G3 South Charlton Northumb., Eng.
94 J4 South Cheriton Som., Eng.
236 E4 South Church Durham, Eng.
116 G4 Southchurch Southend, Eng.
210 D4 South Cliffe E. Riding, Eng.
176 E3 South Clifton Notts., Eng.
331 C2 South Collafirth Shet., Scot.
176 E4 South Collingham Notts., Eng.
58 F3 South Common E. Sussex, Eng.
350 D3 South Cornelly Bridg., Wales
264 D3 South Corriegills N. Ayr., Scot.
110 A4 Southcott Central Bedfordshire, Eng.
86 E3 Southcott Wilts., Eng.
106 D4 Southcourt Bucks., Eng.
120 J2 South Cove Suff., Eng.
300 E2 South Creagan Arg. and B., Scot.
166 D1 South Creake Norf., Eng.
222 D3 South Crosland W. Yorks., Eng.
162 F2 South Croxton Leics., Eng.
74 D3 South Croydon Gtr Lon., Eng.
210 E3 South Dalton E. Riding, Eng.
62 B2 South Darenth Kent, Eng.
256 I4 Southdean Borders, Scot.
326 F1 South Dell W. Isles, Scot.
190 D3 Southdene Merseyside, Eng.
26 G6 South Dorset Downs hills Eng.
26 L6 South Downs hills Eng.
216 G3 South Duffield N. Yorks., Eng.
58 G4 Southease E. Sussex, Eng.
170 F3 South Elkington Lincs., Eng.
222 G3 South Elmsall W. Yorks., Eng.
110 C3 South End Bedford, Eng.
106 C5 Southend Bucks., Eng.
106 D3 South End Bucks., Eng.
232 C8 South End Cumbria, Eng.
74 D3 Southend Gtr Lon., Eng.
52 A5 South End Hants., Eng.
170 E1 South End N. Lincs., Eng.
166 E4 South End Norf., Eng.
86 E3 Southend Wilts., Eng.
300 D6 Southend Arg. and B., Scot.
116 G4 Southend admin. div. Eng.
116 G4 Southend-on-Sea Southend, Eng.
232 C4 Southerfield Cumbria, Eng.
40 D2 Southerly Devon, Eng.
58 E3 Southern Cross B. and H., Eng.
350 E4 Southerndown V. of Glam., Wales
252 F3 Southerness D. and G., Scot.
110 E4 Southern Green Herts., Eng.
22 G12 Southern Uplands hills Scot.
320 C4 South Erradale High., Scot.
166 B3 Southery Norf., Eng.
22 K9 South Esk r. Scot.
208 D3 Southey Green S. Yorks., Eng.
116 G4 South Fambridge Essex, Eng.
82 B2 South Fawley W. Berks., Eng.
170 C1 South Ferriby N. Lincs., Eng.
210 F4 South Field E. Riding, Eng.
292 E2 Southfield Fife, Scot.
74 C3 Southfields Gtr Lon., Eng.
62 B2 Southfleet Kent, Eng.
26 O5 South Foreland pt Eng.
331 E1 South Garth Shet., Scot.
74 D2 Southgate Gtr Lon., Eng.
166 C1 Southgate Norf., Eng.
166 F2 Southgate Norf., Eng.
58 E2 Southgate W. Sussex, Eng.
362 F2 Southgate Cere., Wales
350 B3 Southgate Swansea, Wales
98 E4 South Gloucestershire admin. div. Eng.
78 F2 South Godstone Surr., Eng.
52 B5 South Gorley Hants., Eng.
116 E4 South Green Essex, Eng.
116 H2 South Green Essex, Eng.
166 F3 South Green Norf., Eng.
166 G4 South Green Norf., Eng.
120 G3 South Green Suff., Eng.
288 D3 South Gyle Edin., Scot.
74 D2 South Hackney Gtr Lon., Eng.
300 E4 South Hall Arg. and B., Scot.
74 C2 South Hampstead Gtr Lon., Eng.
116 F4 South Hanningfield Essex, Eng.
74 B2 South Harefield Gtr Lon., Eng.
74 B2 South Harrow Gtr Lon., Eng.
58 A3 South Harting W. Sussex, Eng.
110 D5 South Hatfield Herts., Eng.
52 G6 South Hayling Hants., Eng.
244 F2 South Hazelrigg Northumb., Eng.
106 D4 South Heath Bucks., Eng.
58 G4 South Heighton E. Sussex, Eng.
236 G3 South Hetton Durham, Eng.
222 F3 South Hiendley W. Yorks., Eng.
36 F2 South Hill Corn., Eng.
102 D4 South Hinksey Oxon, Eng.
216 G2 South Holme N. Yorks., Eng.
78 E2 South Holmwood Surr., Eng.
74 F2 South Hornchurch Gtr Lon., Eng.
264 F2 South Hourat N. Ayr., Scot.
170 C4 South Hykeham Lincs., Eng.
236 G2 South Hylton T. and W., Eng.
110 D3 Southill Central Bedfordshire, Eng.
52 E3 Southington Hants., Eng.
170 D3 South Kelsey Lincs., Eng.
74 C3 South Kensington Gtr Lon., Eng.
170 E2 South Killingholme N. Lincs., Eng.
162 E4 South Kilworth Leics., Eng.
222 G3 South Kirkby W. Yorks., Eng.
314 F3 South Kirkton Abers., Scot.
170 E5 South Kyme Lincs., Eng.
268 D3 South Lanarkshire admin. div. Scot.
58 E4 South Lancing W. Sussex, Eng.
300 D2 South Ledaig Arg. and B., Scot.
40 G2 Southleigh Devon, Eng.
102 C4 South Leigh Oxon, Eng.
176 E3 South Leverton Notts., Eng.
136 F3 South Littleton Worcs., Eng.
166 E4 South Lopham Norf., Eng.
162 H3 South Luffenham Rutland, Eng.
94 J4 Southmarsh Som., Eng.
86 E2 South Marston Swindon, Eng.
244 E2 South Middleton Northumb., Eng.
216 F3 South Milford N. Yorks., Eng.
110 D5 South Mimms Herts., Eng.
116 G4 Southminster Essex, Eng.
40 E1 South Molton Devon, Eng.
236 E2 South Moor Durham, Eng.
102 C4 Southmoor Oxon, Eng.
102 D5 South Moreton Oxon, Eng.
308 E2 Southmuir Angus, Scot.
176 E4 South Muskham Notts., Eng.
22 □N2 South Nesting Bay b. Scot.
210 E4 South Newbald E. Riding, Eng.
102 C3 South Newington Oxon, Eng.
86 D5 South Newton Wilts., Eng.
180 E4 South Normanton Derbys., Eng.
74 D3 South Norwood Gtr Lon., Eng.
78 F2 South Nutfield Surr., Eng.
116 D4 South Ockendon Thurrock, Eng.
124 C5 Southoe Cambs., Eng.
120 G3 Southolt Suff., Eng.
170 G4 South Ormsby Lincs., Eng.
124 B3 Southorpe Peterb., Eng.
222 E2 South Ossett W. Yorks., Eng.
216 E2 South Otterington N. Yorks., Eng.
170 D3 South Owersby Lincs., Eng.
222 D2 Southowram W. Yorks., Eng.
110 C6 South Oxhey Herts., Eng.
78 E2 South Park Surr., Eng.
292 E2 South Parks Fife, Scot.
46 C2 South Perrott Dorset, Eng.
94 H5 South Petherton Som., Eng.
36 F2 South Petherwin Corn., Eng.
166 D3 South Pickenham Norf., Eng.
40 E4 South Pool Devon, Eng.
46 C3 South Poorton Dorset, Eng.
190 C2 Southport Merseyside, Eng.
94 C4 South Quarme Som., Eng.
40 E1 South Radworthy Devon, Eng.
170 D5 South Rauceby Lincs., Eng.
166 D2 South Raynham Norf., Eng.
314 F2 South Redbriggs Abers., Scot.
166 H1 Southrepps Norf., Eng.
170 G4 South Reston Lincs., Eng.
170 E4 Southrey Lincs., Eng.
South Rona i. Scot. see Rona
22 K5 South Ronaldsay i. Scot.
98 I3 Southrop Glos., Eng.
52 F3 Southrope Hants., Eng.
74 B2 South Ruislip Gtr Lon., Eng.
166 B3 South Runcton Norf., Eng.
176 E3 South Scarle Notts., Eng.
52 F6 Southsea Ports., Eng.
378 G3 Southsea Wrex., Wales
236 G2 South Shields T. and W., Eng.
170 G3 South Somercotes Lincs., Eng.
170 G3 South Somercotes Fen Houses Lincs., Eng.
216 E2 South Stainley N. Yorks., Eng.
94 J2 South Stoke B. and N.E. Som., Eng.
102 E5 South Stoke Oxon, Eng.
58 C3 South Stoke W. Sussex, Eng.
58 F3 South Street E. Sussex, Eng.
74 E4 South Street Gtr Lon., Eng.
62 C2 South Street Kent, Eng.
62 D3 South Street Kent, Eng.
62 F3 South Street Kent, Eng.
62 G2 South Street Kent, Eng.
40 E2 South Tawton Devon, Eng.
170 G4 South Thoresby Lincs., Eng.
236 D4 Souththorpe Farm Durham, Eng.
86 F4 South Tidworth Wilts., Eng.
74 D2 South Tottenham Gtr Lon., Eng.
52 F4 South Town Hants., Eng.
166 J3 Southtown Norf., Eng.
94 G5 Southtown Som., Eng.
329 D4 Southtown Orkney, Scot.
24 M4 South Tyne r. Eng.

South Tyneside to Strubby

242 **South Tyneside** met. bor. T. and W., Eng.
22 B8 **South Uist** i. Scot.
52 F3 **South View** Hants., Eng.
232 E4 **Southwaite** Cumbria, Eng.
232 I6 **Southwaite** Cumbria, Eng.
22 J5 **South Walls** pen. Scot.
166 H3 **South Walsham** Norf., Eng.
74 D3 **Southwark** met. bor. Gtr Lon., Eng.
52 G3 **South Warnborough** Hants., Eng.
58 D2 **Southwater** W. Sussex, Eng.
58 D2 **Southwater Street** W. Sussex, Eng.
94 H3 **Southway** Som., Eng.
116 D4 **South Weald** Essex, Eng.
46 E4 **Southwell** Dorset, Eng.
176 D4 **Southwell** Notts., Eng.
102 F4 **South Weston** Oxon, Eng.
36 F1 **South Wheatley** Corn., Eng.
176 D2 **South Wheatley** Notts., Eng.
331 D3 **South Whiteness** Shet., Scot.
52 F5 **Southwick** Hants., Eng.
128 G2 **Southwick** Northants., Eng.
94 G3 **Southwick** Som., Eng.
236 G2 **Southwick** T. and W., Eng.
86 B4 **Southwick** Wilts., Eng.
58 E3 **Southwick** W. Sussex, Eng.
252 F3 **Southwick** D. and G., Scot.
94 I3 **South Widcombe** B. and N.E. Som., Eng.
162 E3 **South Wigston** Leics., Eng.
62 F4 **South Willesborough** Kent, Eng.
170 E3 **South Willingham** Lincs., Eng.
74 C3 **South Wimbledon** Gtr Lon., Eng.
236 G3 **South Wingate** Durham, Eng.
180 E4 **South Wingfield** Derbys., Eng.
170 C7 **South Witham** Lincs., Eng.
120 J3 **Southwold** Suff., Eng.
52 D4 **South Wonston** Hants., Eng.
166 I3 **Southwood** Norf., Eng.
94 I4 **Southwood** Som., Eng.
74 E2 **South Woodford** Gtr Lon., Eng.
116 F4 **South Woodham Ferrers** Essex, Eng.
166 B2 **South Wootton** Norf., Eng.
86 B3 **South Wraxall** Wilts., Eng.
154 D3 **South Yardley** W. Mids, Eng.
208 D3 **South Yorkshire** admin. div. Eng.
40 E2 **South Zeal** Devon, Eng.
216 E2 **Sowerby** N. Yorks., Eng.
222 C2 **Sowerby** W. Yorks., Eng.
222 C2 **Sowerby Bridge** W. Yorks., Eng.
232 E4 **Sowerby Row** Cumbria, Eng.
228 E3 **Sower Carr** Lancs., Eng.
94 C4 **Sowerhill** Som., Eng.
120 B4 **Sowley Green** Suff., Eng.
222 C3 **Sowood** W. Yorks., Eng.
222 C3 **Sowood Green** W. Yorks., Eng.
40 F2 **Sowton** Devon, Eng.
222 C2 **Soyland Town** W. Yorks., Eng.
166 H2 **Spa Common** Norf., Eng.
232 G2 **Spadeadam** Cumbria, Eng.
170 F7 **Spalding** Lincs., Eng.
210 C4 **Spaldington** E. Riding, Eng.
124 B4 **Spaldwick** Cambs., Eng.
292 H2 **Spalefield** Fife, Scot.
176 E3 **Spalford** Notts., Eng.
402 E2 **Spamount** Strabane, N. Ire.
170 D6 **Spanby** Lincs., Eng.
26 E5 **Span Head** hill Eng.
166 F2 **Sparham** Norf., Eng.
166 F2 **Sparhamhill** Norf., Eng.
232 D7 **Spark Bridge** Cumbria, Eng.
94 I4 **Sparkford** Som., Eng.
154 C3 **Sparkhill** W. Mids, Eng.
40 E3 **Sparkwell** Devon, Eng.
166 E2 **Sparrow Green** Norf., Eng.
180 B3 **Sparrowpit** Derbys., Eng.
58 H2 **Sparrow's Green** E. Sussex, Eng.
52 D4 **Sparsholt** Hants., Eng.
102 B5 **Sparsholt** Oxon, Eng.
244 D6 **Spartylea** Northumb., Eng.
148 D3 **Spath** Staffs., Eng.
94 F4 **Spaxton** Som., Eng.
322 G4 **Spean Bridge** High., Scot.
58 D3 **Spear Hill** W. Sussex, Eng.
252 E2 **Speddoch** D. and G., Scot.
94 I2 **Speedwell** Bristol, Eng.
106 D4 **Speen** Bucks., Eng.
82 B3 **Speen** W. Berks., Eng.
216 I2 **Speeton** N. Yorks., Eng.
190 D3 **Speke** Merseyside, Eng.
62 B4 **Speldhurst** Kent, Eng.
110 F4 **Spellbrook** Herts., Eng.
102 C3 **Spelsbury** Oxon, Eng.
22 E10 **Spelve, Loch** inlet Scot.
222 D2 **Spen** W. Yorks., Eng.
82 E3 **Spencers Wood** W'ham, Eng.
184 F3 **Spen Green** Cheshire East, Eng.
236 F3 **Spennymoor** Durham, Eng.
132 A4 **Spernall** Warks., Eng.
23 H3 **Sperrin Mountains** hills N. Ire.
136 E2 **Spetchley** Worcs., Eng.
46 G3 **Spetisbury** Dorset, Eng.
120 H2 **Spexhall** Suff., Eng.
22 J7 **Spey** r. Scot.
314 D1 **Spey Bay** Moray, Scot.
314 D2 **Speyview** Moray, Scot.
170 G4 **Spilsby** Lincs., Eng.
244 G2 **Spindlestone** Northumb., Eng.
180 F3 **Spinkhill** Derbys., Eng.
162 E3 **Spinney Hills** Leicester, Eng.
320 H4 **Spinningdale** High., Scot.
86 C3 **Spirthill** Wilts., Eng.
82 G3 **Spital** W. and M., Eng.
110 E5 **Spitalbrook** Herts., Eng.
170 C3 **Spital in the Street** Lincs., Eng.
58 G3 **Spithurst** E. Sussex, Eng.
210 C3 **Spittal** E. Riding, Eng.
244 F1 **Spittal** Northumb., Eng.
252 C3 **Spittal** D. and G., Scot.
252 C3 **Spittal** D. and G., Scot.
288 F3 **Spittal** E. Lothian, Scot.
320 J2 **Spittal** High., Scot.
358 E2 **Spittal** Pembs., Wales
304 J3 **Spittalfield** Perth and Kin., Scot.
314 D4 **Spittal of Glenmuick** Abers., Scot.
304 J2 **Spittal of Glenshee** Perth and Kin., Scot.
166 G2 **Spixworth** Norf., Eng.
58 G3 **Splayne's Green** E. Sussex, Eng.
350 H4 **Splott** Cardiff, Wales
216 E3 **Spofforth** N. Yorks., Eng.
180 E5 **Spondon** Derby, Eng.
378 G3 **Spon Green** Flints., Wales
166 F3 **Spooner Row** Norf., Eng.
144 E2 **Spoonley** Shrop., Eng.
166 D2 **Sporle** Norf., Eng.
378 D3 **Sportsman's Arms** Denb., Wales
288 H3 **Spott** E. Lothian, Scot.
128 D4 **Spratton** Northants., Eng.
78 B2 **Spreakley** Surr., Eng.
40 E2 **Spreyton** Devon, Eng.
170 D3 **Spridlington** Lincs., Eng.
276 F2 **Springboig** Glas., Scot.
276 E2 **Springburn** Glas., Scot.
116 F3 **Springfield** Essex, Eng.
154 B3 **Springfield** W. Mids, Eng.
154 C3 **Springfield** W. Mids, Eng.
402 D4 **Springfield** Fermanagh, N. Ire.
300 E4 **Springfield** Arg. and B., Scot.
252 G2 **Springfield** D. and G., Scot.
292 F2 **Springfield** Fife, Scot.
304 K3 **Springfield** Perth and Kin., Scot.
74 B3 **Spring Grove** Gtr Lon., Eng.
148 C5 **Springhill** Staffs., Eng.
148 D5 **Springhill** Staffs., Eng.
154 A2 **Spring Hill** W. Mids, Eng.
252 E2 **Springholm** D. and G., Scot.
252 G2 **Springkell** D. and G., Scot.
314 F2 **Springleys** Abers., Scot.
264 G3 **Springside** N. Ayr., Scot.
170 B3 **Springthorpe** Lincs., Eng.
52 F6 **Spring Vale** I.o.W., Eng.
236 F2 **Springwell** T. and W., Eng.
210 G4 **Sproatley** E. Riding, Eng.
184 E2 **Sproston Green** Cheshire West & Chester, Eng.
208 E2 **Sprotbrough** S. Yorks., Eng.
120 F4 **Sproughton** Suff., Eng.
256 J3 **Sprouston** Borders, Scot.
166 G3 **Sprowston** Norf., Eng.
162 G2 **Sproxton** Leics., Eng.
216 F2 **Sproxton** N. Yorks., Eng.
106 D4 **Spurlands End** Bucks., Eng.
24 R6 **Spurn Head** hd Eng.
184 D3 **Spurstow** Cheshire East, Eng.
46 C3 **Spyway** Dorset, Eng.
252 E2 **Square Point** D. and G., Scot.
228 D4 **Squires Gate** Blackpool, Eng.
22 G8 **Sròn a' Choire Ghairbh** hill Scot.
300 D4 **Sròndoire** Arg. and B., Scot.
304 F1 **Sronphadruig Lodge** Perth and Kin., Scot.
144 F4 **Stableford** Shrop., Eng.
148 B3 **Stableford** Staffs., Eng.
208 C3 **Stacey Bank** S. Yorks., Eng.
358 E4 **Stackpole** Pembs., Wales
228 I4 **Stacksteads** Lancs., Eng.
22 F6 **Stac Pollaidh** hill Scot.
Stac Polly hill Scot. see **Stac Pollaidh**
210 D4 **Staddlethorpe** E. Riding, Eng.
180 B3 **Staden** Derbys., Eng.
102 E4 **Stadhampton** Oxon, Eng.
22 D10 **Staffa** i. Scot.
232 F4 **Staffield** Cumbria, Eng.
322 C2 **Staffin** High., Scot.
22 D7 **Staffin Bay** b. Scot.
148 C4 **Stafford** Staffs., Eng.
148 C3 **Staffordshire** county Eng.
388 H4 **Staffordstown** Antrim, N. Ire.
116 E3 **Stagden Cross** Essex, Eng.
110 B3 **Stagsden** Bedford, Eng.
244 E5 **Stagshaw Bank** Northumb., Eng.
232 A5 **Stainburn** Cumbria, Eng.
170 C7 **Stainby** Lincs., Eng.
208 C2 **Staincross** S. Yorks., Eng.
236 E4 **Staindrop** Durham, Eng.
78 C1 **Staines-upon-Thames** Surr., Eng.
170 D4 **Stainfield** Lincs., Eng.
170 D7 **Stainfield** Lincs., Eng.
216 C2 **Stainforth** N. Yorks., Eng.
208 F2 **Stainforth** S. Yorks., Eng.
228 E4 **Staining** Lancs., Eng.
222 C2 **Stainland** W. Yorks., Eng.
180 E3 **Stainsby** Derbys., Eng.
170 F4 **Stainsby** Lincs., Eng.
232 F5 **Stainton** Cumbria, Eng.
232 F7 **Stainton** Cumbria, Eng.
236 D4 **Stainton** Durham, Eng.
216 F1 **Stainton** Middbro., Eng.
216 D1 **Stainton** N. Yorks., Eng.
208 E3 **Stainton** S. Yorks., Eng.
170 D4 **Stainton by Langworth** Lincs., Eng.
216 H1 **Staintondale** N. Yorks., Eng.
170 E3 **Stainton le Vale** Lincs., Eng.
232 D8 **Stainton with Adgarley** Cumbria, Eng.
232 C5 **Stair** Cumbria, Eng.
262 E4 **Stair** E. Ayr., Scot.
208 D2 **Stairfoot** S. Yorks., Eng.
216 G1 **Staithes** N. Yorks., Eng.
22 G11 **Stake, Hill of** hill Scot.
244 H5 **Stakeford** Northumb., Eng.
228 E3 **Stake Pool** Lancs., Eng.
52 F5 **Stakes** Hants., Eng.
46 E2 **Stalbridge** Dorset, Eng.
46 E2 **Stalbridge Weston** Dorset, Eng.
166 I2 **Stalham** Norf., Eng.
166 I2 **Stalham Green** Norf., Eng.
62 E3 **Stalisfield Green** Kent, Eng.
170 E2 **Stallingborough** N.E. Lincs., Eng.
148 C3 **Stallington** Staffs., Eng.
228 E3 **Stalmine** Lancs., Eng.
198 E3 **Stalybridge** Gtr Man., Eng.
116 F1 **Stambourne** Essex, Eng.
170 D8 **Stamford** Lincs., Eng.
244 H3 **Stamford** Northumb., Eng.
184 C2 **Stamford Bridge** Cheshire West & Chester, Eng.
210 C3 **Stamford Bridge** E. Riding, Eng.
244 F5 **Stamfordham** Northumb., Eng.
74 D2 **Stamford Hill** Gtr Lon., Eng.
228 E3 **Stanah** Lancs., Eng.
110 D5 **Stanborough** Herts., Eng.
110 B4 **Stanbridge** Central Bedfordshire, Eng.
46 H3 **Stanbridge** Dorset, Eng.
52 C4 **Stanbridge Earls** Hants., Eng.
222 C2 **Stanbury** W. Yorks., Eng.
280 C3 **Stand** N. Lanark., Scot.
280 D3 **Standburn** Falk., Scot.
148 C5 **Standeford** Staffs., Eng.
62 D4 **Standen** Kent, Eng.
62 D4 **Standen Street** Kent, Eng.
94 K3 **Standerwick** Som., Eng.
52 G4 **Standford** Hants., Eng.
144 F3 **Standford Bridge** Telford, Eng.
98 F3 **Standish** Glos., Eng.
198 B2 **Standish** Gtr Man., Eng.
102 C4 **Standlake** Oxon, Eng.
52 D4 **Standon** Hants., Eng.
110 F4 **Standon** Herts., Eng.
148 B3 **Standon** Staffs., Eng.
110 E4 **Standon Green End** Herts., Eng.
280 D4 **Stane** N. Lanark., Scot.
264 G3 **Stanecastle** N. Ayr., Scot.
166 E2 **Stanfield** Norf., Eng.
148 B2 **Stanfield** Stoke, Eng.
110 D3 **Stanford** Central Bedfordshire, Eng.
62 G4 **Stanford** Kent, Eng.
144 C3 **Stanford** Shrop., Eng.
140 E3 **Stanford Bishop** Here., Eng.
136 C2 **Stanford Bridge** Worcs., Eng.
82 C3 **Stanford Dingley** W. Berks., Eng.
82 E3 **Stanford End** W'ham, Eng.
102 B5 **Stanford in the Vale** Oxon, Eng.
116 E4 **Stanford-le-Hope** Thurrock, Eng.
128 C3 **Stanford on Avon** Northants., Eng.
176 B6 **Stanford on Soar** Notts., Eng.
136 C2 **Stanford on Teme** Worcs., Eng.
116 D3 **Stanford Rivers** Essex, Eng.
180 F3 **Stanfree** Derbys., Eng.
124 C3 **Stanground** Peterb., Eng.
166 D1 **Stanhoe** Norf., Eng.
236 C3 **Stanhope** Durham, Eng.
256 D3 **Stanhope** Borders, Scot.
128 F3 **Stanion** Northants., Eng.
232 C8 **Stank** Cumbria, Eng.
136 D1 **Stanklyn** Worcs., Eng.
222 F2 **Stanks** W. Yorks., Eng.
180 E5 **Stanley** Derbys., Eng.
236 E2 **Stanley** Durham, Eng.
176 B4 **Stanley** Notts., Eng.
148 C2 **Stanley** Staffs., Eng.
86 C3 **Stanley** Wilts., Eng.
222 F2 **Stanley** W. Yorks., Eng.
304 J4 **Stanley** Perth and Kin., Scot.
180 E5 **Stanley Common** Derbys., Eng.
236 E3 **Stanley Crook** Durham, Eng.
228 E5 **Stanley Gate** Lancs., Eng.
144 D2 **Stanleygreen** Shrop., Eng.
140 E3 **Stanley Hill** Here., Eng.
148 C2 **Stanley Moor** Staffs., Eng.
184 B2 **Stanlow** Cheshire West & Chester, Eng.
144 G4 **Stanlow** Shrop., Eng.
58 F3 **Stanmer** B. and H., Eng.
74 C2 **Stanmore** Gtr Lon., Eng.
82 C2 **Stanmore** W. Berks., Eng.
244 C4 **Stannersburn** Northumb., Eng.
120 D3 **Stanningfield** Suff., Eng.
222 E2 **Stanningley** W. Yorks., Eng.
244 H5 **Stannington** Northumb., Eng.
208 C3 **Stannington** S. Yorks., Eng.
46 I3 **Stanpit** Dorset, Eng.
140 B2 **Stansbatch** Here., Eng.
148 E2 **Stanshope** Staffs., Eng.
120 D4 **Stanstead** Suff., Eng.
110 F5 **Stanstead Abbotts** Herts., Eng.
62 B2 **Stansted** Kent, Eng.
116 D2 **Stansted Mountfitchet** Essex, Eng.
180 D6 **Stanton** Derbys., Eng.
98 H1 **Stanton** Glos., Eng.
244 G4 **Stanton** Northumb., Eng.
148 E2 **Stanton** Staffs., Eng.
120 E3 **Stanton** Suff., Eng.
124 C4 **Stanton Butts** Cambs., Eng.
180 E5 **Stanton by Bridge** Derbys., Eng.
180 F5 **Stanton by Dale** Derbys., Eng.
94 I2 **Stanton Drew** B. and N.E. Som., Eng.
86 E2 **Stanton Fitzwarren** Swindon, Eng.
102 C4 **Stanton Harcourt** Oxon, Eng.
176 B4 **Stanton Hill** Notts., Eng.
180 D3 **Stanton in Peak** Derbys., Eng.
144 D5 **Stanton Lacy** Shrop., Eng.
180 D4 **Stanton Lees** Derbys., Eng.
144 E4 **Stanton Long** Shrop., Eng.
176 C5 **Stanton-on-the-Wolds** Notts., Eng.
86 D3 **Stanton St Bernard** Wilts., Eng.
102 D4 **Stanton St John** Oxon, Eng.
86 C2 **Stanton St Quintin** Wilts., Eng.
120 E3 **Stanton Street** Suff., Eng.
162 D2 **Stanton under Bardon** Leics., Eng.
144 E3 **Stanton upon Hine Heath** Shrop., Eng.
94 I2 **Stanton Wick** B. and N.E. Som., Eng.
144 C3 **Stanwardine in the Fields** Shrop., Eng.
144 C2 **Stanwardine in the Wood** Shrop., Eng.
116 G2 **Stanway** Essex, Eng.
98 H2 **Stanway** Glos., Eng.
116 H2 **Stanway Green** Essex, Eng.
78 D1 **Stanwell** Surr., Eng.
78 D1 **Stanwell Moor** Surr., Eng.
128 F4 **Stanwick** Northants., Eng.
198 D2 **Stanycliffe** Gtr Man., Eng.
331 C3 **Stanydale** Shet., Scot.
326 B5 **Staoinebrig** W. Isles, Scot.
216 G2 **Stape** N. Yorks., Eng.
46 H3 **Stapehill** Dorset, Eng.
184 E3 **Stapeley** Cheshire East, Eng.
148 F4 **Stapenhill** Staffs., Eng.
62 H3 **Staple** Kent, Eng.
94 E4 **Staple** Som., Eng.
58 J3 **Staplecross** E. Sussex, Eng.
58 E2 **Staplefield** W. Sussex, Eng.
94 F5 **Staple Fitzpaine** Som., Eng.
124 E6 **Stapleford** Cambs., Eng.
110 E4 **Stapleford** Herts., Eng.
162 G2 **Stapleford** Leics., Eng.
170 B5 **Stapleford** Lincs., Eng.
176 B5 **Stapleford** Notts., Eng.
86 D5 **Stapleford** Wilts., Eng.
116 C4 **Stapleford Abbotts** Essex, Eng.
116 D3 **Stapleford Tawney** Essex, Eng.
94 F4 **Staplegrove** Som., Eng.
94 F5 **Staplehay** Som., Eng.
98 E5 **Staple Hill** S. Glos., Eng.
62 D4 **Staplehurst** Kent, Eng.
52 E6 **Staplers** I.o.W., Eng.
62 F3 **Staplestreet** Kent, Eng.
232 F2 **Stapleton** Cumbria, Eng.
140 B2 **Stapleton** Here., Eng.
162 C3 **Stapleton** Leics., Eng.
216 E1 **Stapleton** N. Yorks., Eng.
144 D4 **Stapleton** Shrop., Eng.
94 H5 **Stapleton** Som., Eng.
94 F5 **Stapley** Som., Eng.
110 D2 **Staploe** Bedford, Eng.
140 E3 **Staplow** Here., Eng.
94 H3 **Star** Som., Eng.
292 F2 **Star** Fife, Scot.
358 G2 **Star** Pembs., Wales
216 C2 **Starbotton** N. Yorks., Eng.
40 F3 **Starcross** Devon, Eng.
132 C3 **Stareton** Warks., Eng.
180 D4 **Starkholmes** Derbys., Eng.
198 C2 **Starling** Gtr Man., Eng.
116 C2 **Starling's Green** Essex, Eng.
262 E5 **Starr** E. Ayr., Scot.
166 G4 **Starston** Norf., Eng.
26 E7 **Start Bay** b. Eng.
236 D4 **Startforth** Durham, Eng.
86 C2 **Startley** Wilts., Eng.
106 E4 **Startop's End** Bucks., Eng.
26 E7 **Start Point** pt Eng.
190 G3 **Statham** Warr., Eng.
94 G4 **Stathe** Som., Eng.
162 F1 **Stathern** Leics., Eng.
236 G3 **Station Town** Durham, Eng.
124 B5 **Staughton Green** Cambs., Eng.
124 B5 **Staughton Highway** Cambs., Eng.
98 D3 **Staunton** Glos., Eng.
98 F2 **Staunton** Glos., Eng.
162 C2 **Staunton Harold Hall** Leics., Eng.
176 E5 **Staunton in the Vale** Notts., Eng.
140 B2 **Staunton on Arrow** Here., Eng.
140 B3 **Staunton on Wye** Here., Eng.
232 F6 **Staveley** Cumbria, Eng.
180 E3 **Staveley** Derbys., Eng.
216 E2 **Staveley** N. Yorks., Eng.
232 E7 **Staveley-in-Cartmel** Cumbria, Eng.
40 E3 **Staverton** Devon, Eng.
98 G2 **Staverton** Glos., Eng.
128 B4 **Staverton** Northants., Eng.
86 B3 **Staverton** Wilts., Eng.
98 G2 **Staverton Bridge** Glos., Eng.
94 G4 **Stawell** Som., Eng.
94 D5 **Stawley** Som., Eng.
320 K2 **Staxigoe** High., Scot.
216 H2 **Staxton** N. Yorks., Eng.
366 D3 **Staylittle** Powys, Wales
228 E3 **Staynall** Lancs., Eng.
176 D4 **Staythorpe** Notts., Eng.
216 D2 **Stean** N. Yorks., Eng.
128 B5 **Steane** Northants., Eng.
216 F2 **Stearsby** N. Yorks., Eng.
94 F3 **Steart** Som., Eng.
116 E2 **Stebbing** Essex, Eng.
116 E2 **Stebbing Green** Essex, Eng.
154 D3 **Stechford** W. Mids, Eng.
58 B3 **Stedham** W. Sussex, Eng.
208 C3 **Steel Bank** S. Yorks., Eng.
58 H2 **Steel Cross** E. Sussex, Eng.
256 H5 **Steele Road** Borders, Scot.
232 C7 **Steel Green** Cumbria, Eng.
140 C2 **Steen's Bridge** Here., Eng.
52 G4 **Steep** Hants., Eng.
26 F5 **Steep Holm** i. Eng.
24 R7 **Steeping** r. Eng.
222 C2 **Steep Lane** W. Yorks., Eng.
46 G4 **Steeple** Dorset, Eng.
116 G3 **Steeple** Essex, Eng.
86 C4 **Steeple Ashton** Wilts., Eng.
102 D3 **Steeple Aston** Oxon, Eng.
102 C3 **Steeple Barton** Oxon, Eng.
116 E1 **Steeple Bumpstead** Essex, Eng.
106 C3 **Steeple Claydon** Bucks., Eng.
124 C4 **Steeple Gidding** Cambs., Eng.
86 D5 **Steeple Langford** Wilts., Eng.
124 D6 **Steeple Morden** Cambs., Eng.
52 G4 **Steep Marsh** Hants., Eng.
144 E3 **Steeraway** Telford, Eng.
222 C1 **Steeton** W. Yorks., Eng.
322 B2 **Stein** High., Scot.
314 F2 **Steinmanhill** Abers., Scot.
236 E2 **Stella** T. and W., Eng.
62 G3 **Stelling Minnis** Kent, Eng.
94 H5 **Stembridge** Som., Eng.
36 E2 **Stenalees** Corn., Eng.
288 D3 **Stenhouse** Edin., Scot.
280 D2 **Stenhousemuir** Falk., Scot.
331 C2 **Stenness** Shet., Scot.
22 J4 **Stenness, Loch of** l. Scot.
322 C2 **Stenscholl** High., Scot.
180 D5 **Stenson** Derbys., Eng.
288 H3 **Stenton** E. Lothian, Scot.
304 I3 **Stenton** Perth and Kin., Scot.
358 F3 **Stepaside** Pembs., Wales
366 E4 **Stepaside** Powys, Wales
74 D2 **Stepney** Gtr Lon., Eng.
110 B3 **Steppingley** Central Bedfordshire, Eng.
280 B3 **Stepps** N. Lanark., Scot.
120 H3 **Sternfield** Suff., Eng.
40 D1 **Sterridge** Devon, Eng.
86 D3 **Stert** Wilts., Eng.
124 G5 **Stetchworth** Cambs., Eng.
124 G5 **Stetchworth Ley** Cambs., Eng.
110 D4 **Stevenage** Herts., Eng.
264 F3 **Stevenston** N. Ayr., Scot.
52 E3 **Steventon** Hants., Eng.
102 D5 **Steventon** Oxon, Eng.
116 E1 **Steventon End** Essex, Eng.
110 B2 **Stevington** Bedford, Eng.
116 C3 **Stewards** Essex, Eng.
110 B3 **Stewartby** Bedford, Eng.
252 C3 **Stewarton** D. and G., Scot.
262 D2 **Stewarton** E. Ayr., Scot.
402 J3 **Stewartstown** Cookstown, N. Ire.
106 D3 **Stewkley** Bucks., Eng.
94 G5 **Stewley** Som., Eng.
170 G3 **Stewton** Lincs., Eng.
58 E3 **Steyning** W. Sussex, Eng.
358 D3 **Steynton** Pembs., Wales
36 F1 **Stibb** Corn., Eng.
166 E2 **Stibbard** Norf., Eng.
86 E3 **Stibb Green** Wilts., Eng.
124 B3 **Stibbington** Cambs., Eng.
256 J3 **Stichill** Borders, Scot.
36 E3 **Sticker** Corn., Eng.
170 G5 **Stickford** Lincs., Eng.
94 G5 **Sticklepath** Som., Eng.
116 C2 **Stickling Green** Essex, Eng.
170 G5 **Stickney** Lincs., Eng.
166 E1 **Stiffkey** Norf., Eng.
140 E3 **Stifford's Bridge** Here., Eng.
62 E3 **Stiff Street** Kent, Eng.
94 H3 **Stileway** Som., Eng.
216 F3 **Stillingfleet** N. Yorks., Eng.
216 F2 **Stillington** N. Yorks., Eng.
236 G4 **Stillington** Stockton, Eng.
124 C4 **Stilton** Cambs., Eng.
98 E3 **Stinchcombe** Glos., Eng.
46 E3 **Stinsford** Dorset, Eng.
144 F4 **Stirchley** Telford, Eng.
154 C3 **Stirchley** W. Mids, Eng.
320 K2 **Stirkoke House** High., Scot.
314 H2 **Stirling** Abers., Scot.
296 G5 **Stirling** Stir., Scot.
296 D4 **Stirling** admin. div. Scot.
116 F2 **Stisted** Essex, Eng.
86 F3 **Stitchcombe** Wilts., Eng.
36 D3 **Stithians** Corn., Eng.
154 E3 **Stivichall** W. Mids, Eng.
304 G3 **Stix** Perth and Kin., Scot.
170 E4 **Stixwould** Lincs., Eng.
184 B2 **Stoak** Cheshire West & Chester, Eng.
22 G9 **Stob Choire Claurigh** mt. Scot.
22 G9 **Stob Ghabhar** mt. Scot.
256 E3 **Stobo** Borders, Scot.
46 G3 **Stoborough** Dorset, Eng.
46 G3 **Stoborough Green** Dorset, Eng.
268 D2 **Stobwood** S. Lanark., Scot.
116 E4 **Stock** Essex, Eng.
52 D4 **Stockbridge** Hants., Eng.
58 B4 **Stockbridge** W. Sussex, Eng.
296 G4 **Stockbridge** Stir., Scot.
62 D3 **Stockbury** Kent, Eng.
82 B3 **Stockcross** W. Berks., Eng.
36 D3 **Stockdale** Corn., Eng.
232 E4 **Stockdalewath** Cumbria, Eng.
162 G3 **Stockerston** Leics., Eng.
136 E2 **Stock Green** Worcs., Eng.
170 A2 **Stockholes Turbary** N. Lincs., Eng.
132 C2 **Stockingford** Warks., Eng.
116 D1 **Stocking Green** Essex, Eng.
106 D2 **Stocking Green** M.K., Eng.
110 F4 **Stocking Pelham** Herts., Eng.
40 G2 **Stockland** Devon, Eng.
350 G3 **Stockland** Cardiff, Wales
94 F3 **Stockland Bristol** Som., Eng.
86 F3 **Stock Lane** Wilts., Eng.
40 F2 **Stockleigh Pomeroy** Devon, Eng.
86 D3 **Stockley** Wilts., Eng.
94 G5 **Stocklinch** Som., Eng.
198 E3 **Stockport** Gtr Man., Eng.
208 C3 **Stocksbridge** S. Yorks., Eng.
244 F6 **Stocksfield** Northumb., Eng.
24 M5 **Stocks Reservoir** resr Eng.
140 C2 **Stockton** Here., Eng.
166 I4 **Stockton** Norf., Eng.
144 B4 **Stockton** Shrop., Eng.
144 F4 **Stockton** Shrop., Eng.
144 F3 **Stockton** Telford, Eng.
132 D4 **Stockton** Warks., Eng.
86 C5 **Stockton** Wilts., Eng.
190 F3 **Stockton Heath** Warr., Eng.
236 H4 **Stockton-on-Tees** Stockton, Eng.
236 H4 **Stockton-on-Tees** admin. div. Eng.
136 C2 **Stockton on Teme** Worcs., Eng.
216 G3 **Stockton on the Forest** York, Eng.
98 G3 **Stockwell** Glos., Eng.
74 D3 **Stockwell** Gtr Lon., Eng.
148 D4 **Stockwell Heath** Staffs., Eng.
94 I2 **Stockwood** Bristol, Eng.
46 D2 **Stockwood** Dorset, Eng.
136 F2 **Stock Wood** Worcs., Eng.
228 F2 **Stodday** Lancs., Eng.
62 H3 **Stodmarsh** Kent, Eng.
166 F1 **Stody** Norf., Eng.
320 E3 **Stoer** High., Scot.
22 F6 **Stoer, Point of** pt Scot.
94 I5 **Stoford** Som., Eng.
86 D5 **Stoford** Wilts., Eng.
94 E4 **Stogumber** Som., Eng.
94 F3 **Stogursey** Som., Eng.
40 C2 **Stoke** Devon, Eng.
52 D3 **Stoke** Hants., Eng.
52 G6 **Stoke** Hants., Eng.
62 D2 **Stoke** Medway, Eng.
40 D3 **Stoke** Plymouth, Eng.
154 F3 **Stoke** W. Mids, Eng.
46 C3 **Stoke Abbott** Dorset, Eng.
128 E3 **Stoke Albany** Northants., Eng.
120 F3 **Stoke Ash** Suff., Eng.
176 C5 **Stoke Bardolph** Notts., Eng.
94 I2 **Stoke Bishop** Bristol, Eng.
136 B2 **Stoke Bliss** Worcs., Eng.
128 D5 **Stoke Bruerne** Northants., Eng.
120 C4 **Stoke by Clare** Suff., Eng.
120 E5 **Stoke-by-Nayland** Suff., Eng.
40 F2 **Stoke Canon** Devon, Eng.
52 E4 **Stoke Charity** Hants., Eng.
78 D2 **Stoke D'Abernon** Surr., Eng.
128 G3 **Stoke Doyle** Northants., Eng.
162 G3 **Stoke Dry** Rutland, Eng.
140 D3 **Stoke Edith** Here., Eng.
86 D5 **Stoke Farthing** Wilts., Eng.
166 C3 **Stoke Ferry** Norf., Eng.
40 F4 **Stoke Fleming** Devon, Eng.
46 F3 **Stokeford** Dorset, Eng.
40 F3 **Stoke Gabriel** Devon, Eng.
98 D4 **Stoke Gifford** S. Glos., Eng.
162 C3 **Stoke Golding** Leics., Eng.
106 D2 **Stoke Goldington** M.K., Eng.
106 E5 **Stoke Green** Bucks., Eng.
176 E3 **Stokeham** Notts., Eng.
106 D3 **Stoke Hammond** Bucks., Eng.
144 E2 **Stoke Heath** Shrop., Eng.
136 E2 **Stoke Heath** Worcs., Eng.
166 G3 **Stoke Holy Cross** Norf., Eng.
40 F3 **Stokeinteignhead** Devon, Eng.
140 D3 **Stoke Lacy** Here., Eng.
102 D3 **Stoke Lyne** Oxon, Eng.
106 D4 **Stoke Mandeville** Bucks., Eng.
106 C5 **Stokenchurch** Bucks., Eng.
74 D2 **Stoke Newington** Gtr Lon., Eng.
40 E4 **Stokenham** Devon, Eng.
144 E2 **Stoke on Tern** Shrop., Eng.
148 B2 **Stoke-on-Trent** Stoke, Eng.
148 C3 **Stoke-on-Trent** admin. div. Eng.
98 G2 **Stoke Orchard** Glos., Eng.
94 C3 **Stoke Pero** Som., Eng.
106 E5 **Stoke Poges** Bucks., Eng.
136 E2 **Stoke Pound** Worcs., Eng.
140 C2 **Stoke Prior** Here., Eng.
136 E2 **Stoke Prior** Worcs., Eng.
40 E1 **Stoke Rivers** Devon, Eng.
170 C6 **Stoke Rochford** Lincs., Eng.
102 E5 **Stoke Row** Oxon, Eng.
144 D5 **Stokesay** Shrop., Eng.
166 I3 **Stokesby** Norf., Eng.
216 F1 **Stokesley** N. Yorks., Eng.
94 G4 **Stoke St Gregory** Som., Eng.
94 F5 **Stoke St Mary** Som., Eng.
94 J3 **Stoke St Michael** Som., Eng.
144 E5 **Stoke St Milborough** Shrop., Eng.
94 H5 **Stoke sub Hamdon** Som., Eng.
102 E4 **Stoke Talmage** Oxon, Eng.
94 J4 **Stoke Trister** Som., Eng.
94 I2 **Stoke Villice** B. and N.E. Som., Eng.
46 E2 **Stoke Wake** Dorset, Eng.
94 F3 **Stolford** Som., Eng.
62 I3 **Stonar Cut** Kent, Eng.
116 D3 **Stondon Massey** Essex, Eng.
106 C4 **Stone** Bucks., Eng.
98 E4 **Stone** Glos., Eng.
62 B2 **Stone** Kent, Eng.
62 E4 **Stone** Kent, Eng.
94 I4 **Stone** Som., Eng.
148 C3 **Stone** Staffs., Eng.
208 E3 **Stone** S. Yorks., Eng.
136 D1 **Stone** Worcs., Eng.
124 E3 **Stonea** Cambs., Eng.
94 G3 **Stone Allerton** Som., Eng.
94 I3 **Ston Easton** Som., Eng.
58 G3 **Stonebridge** E. Sussex, Eng.
94 G3 **Stonebridge** N. Som., Eng.
132 B3 **Stonebridge** Warks., Eng.
180 E4 **Stonebroom** Derbys., Eng.
198 C2 **Stoneclough** Gtr Man., Eng.
236 D4 **Stone Cross** Durham, Eng.
58 G2 **Stone Cross** E. Sussex, Eng.
58 H4 **Stone Cross** E. Sussex, Eng.
62 B4 **Stone Cross** Kent, Eng.
62 F4 **Stone Cross** Kent, Eng.
62 I3 **Stone Cross** Kent, Eng.
210 G4 **Stoneferry** Hull, Eng.
148 C3 **Stonefield** Staffs., Eng.
300 D4 **Stonefield** Arg. and B., Scot.
228 I4 **Stone Fold** Lancs., Eng.
58 I2 **Stonegate** E. Sussex, Eng.
216 G1 **Stonegate** N. Yorks., Eng.
216 G2 **Stonegrave** N. Yorks., Eng.
244 C5 **Stonehaugh** Northumb., Eng.
314 G4 **Stonehaven** Abers., Scot.
26 I5 **Stonehenge** tourist site Eng.
78 C1 **Stonehill** Surr., Eng.
208 G2 **Stone Hill** S. Yorks., Eng.
184 C2 **Stonehouse** Cheshire West & Chester, Eng.
232 H7 **Stone House** Cumbria, Eng.
98 F3 **Stonehouse** Glos., Eng.
244 C6 **Stonehouse** Northumb., Eng.
40 D3 **Stonehouse** Plymouth, Eng.
252 E3 **Stonehouse** D. and G., Scot.
268 C2 **Stonehouse** S. Lanark., Scot.
78 E1 **Stoneleigh** Surr., Eng.
132 C3 **Stoneleigh** Warks., Eng.
184 D3 **Stoneley Green** Cheshire East, Eng.
124 B5 **Stonely** Cambs., Eng.
52 G4 **Stoner Hill** Hants., Eng.
162 B2 **Stone Rows** Leics., Eng.
222 B2 **Stones** W. Yorks., Eng.
162 G2 **Stonesby** Leics., Eng.
102 C3 **Stonesfield** Oxon, Eng.
116 I2 **Stones Green** Essex, Eng.
62 B3 **Stone Street** Kent, Eng.
120 E4 **Stone Street** Suff., Eng.
120 H2 **Stone Street** Suff., Eng.
62 F4 **Stonestreet Green** Kent, Eng.
232 D5 **Stonethwaite** Cumbria, Eng.
288 B3 **Stoneyburn** W. Lothian, Scot.
52 C5 **Stoney Cross** Hants., Eng.
162 E3 **Stoneygate** Leicester, Eng.
116 G4 **Stoneyhills** Essex, Eng.
252 B3 **Stoneykirk** D. and G., Scot.
180 D3 **Stoney Middleton** Derbys., Eng.
162 D3 **Stoney Stanton** Leics., Eng.
94 J4 **Stoney Stoke** Som., Eng.
94 J4 **Stoney Stratton** Som., Eng.
144 C3 **Stoney Stretton** Shrop., Eng.
314 G3 **Stoneywood** Aberdeen, Scot.
331 D1 **Stonganess** Shet., Scot.
120 F3 **Stonham Aspal** Suff., Eng.
148 D5 **Stonnall** Staffs., Eng.
102 F5 **Stonor** Oxon, Eng.
162 F3 **Stonton Wyville** Leics., Eng.
331 □ **Stonybreck** Shet., Scot.
388 J5 **Stonyford** Lisburn, N. Ire.
236 G2 **Stony Gate** T. and W., Eng.
236 E2 **Stony Heap** Durham, Eng.
180 F3 **Stony Houghton** Derbys., Eng.
106 C2 **Stony Stratford** M.K., Eng.
40 E1 **Stoodleigh** Devon, Eng.
40 F2 **Stoodleigh** Devon, Eng.
58 C3 **Stopham** W. Sussex, Eng.
110 C4 **Stopsley** Luton, Eng.
190 C3 **Storeton** Merseyside, Eng.
304 J4 **Stormontfield** Perth and Kin., Scot.
326 E2 **Stornoway** airport Scot.
140 E3 **Storridge** Here., Eng.
58 D3 **Storrington** W. Sussex, Eng.
208 C3 **Storrs** S. Yorks., Eng.
26 M4 **Stort** r. Eng.
232 F7 **Storth** Cumbria, Eng.
210 C3 **Storwood** E. Riding, Eng.
314 D1 **Stotfield** Moray, Scot.
110 D3 **Stotfold** Central Bedfordshire, Eng.
144 F5 **Stottesdon** Shrop., Eng.
162 E3 **Stoughton** Leics., Eng.
78 C2 **Stoughton** Surr., Eng.
58 A3 **Stoughton** W. Sussex, Eng.
94 H3 **Stoughton Cross** Som., Eng.
322 D4 **Stoul** High., Scot.
136 E3 **Stoulton** Worcs., Eng.
26 I3 **Stour** r. Eng.
26 I6 **Stour** r. Eng.
26 O4 **Stour** r. Eng.
26 O5 **Stour** r. Eng.
154 B3 **Stourbridge** W. Mids, Eng.
46 F2 **Stourpaine** Dorset, Eng.
136 D1 **Stourport-on-Severn** Worcs., Eng.
46 F2 **Stour Provost** Dorset, Eng.
46 F2 **Stour Row** Dorset, Eng.
148 B6 **Stourton** Staffs., Eng.
132 C5 **Stourton** Warks., Eng.
86 B5 **Stourton** Wilts., Eng.
46 E2 **Stourton Caundle** Dorset, Eng.
329 E2 **Stove** Orkney, Scot.
120 I2 **Stoven** Suff., Eng.
170 B4 **Stow** Lincs., Eng.
256 G2 **Stow** Borders, Scot.
166 B3 **Stow Bardolph** Norf., Eng.
166 E3 **Stow Bedon** Norf., Eng.
166 B3 **Stowbridge** Norf., Eng.
124 F5 **Stow cum Quy** Cambs., Eng.
98 D3 **Stowe** Glos., Eng.
144 B5 **Stowe** Shrop., Eng.
148 E4 **Stowe** Staffs., Eng.
148 D3 **Stowe-by-Chartley** Staffs., Eng.
128 C4 **Stowehill** Northants., Eng.
98 H3 **Stowell** Glos., Eng.
94 J5 **Stowell** Som., Eng.
94 I2 **Stowey** B. and N.E. Som., Eng.
40 D3 **Stowford** Devon, Eng.
40 E1 **Stowford** Devon, Eng.
40 G2 **Stowford** Devon, Eng.
120 E3 **Stowlangtoft** Suff., Eng.
124 B5 **Stow Longa** Cambs., Eng.
116 F4 **Stow Maries** Essex, Eng.
120 E3 **Stowmarket** Suff., Eng.
98 I2 **Stow-on-the-Wold** Glos., Eng.
62 G4 **Stowting** Kent, Eng.
62 G4 **Stowting Common** Kent, Eng.
120 F3 **Stowupland** Suff., Eng.
300 E4 **Straad** Arg. and B., Scot.
402 F2 **Strabane** Strabane, N. Ire.
402 G2 **Strabane** admin. dist. N. Ire.
308 G2 **Stracathro** Angus, Scot.
314 F3 **Strachan** Abers., Scot.
300 E3 **Strachur** Arg. and B., Scot.
120 G3 **Stradbroke** Suff., Eng.
388 J5 **Stradhavern** Antrim, N. Ire.
120 C4 **Stradishall** Suff., Eng.
166 B3 **Stradsett** Norf., Eng.
170 C5 **Stragglethorpe** Lincs., Eng.
388 I4 **Straid** Ballymena, N. Ire.
388 H1 **Straid** Moyle, N. Ire.
388 K4 **Straid** Newtownabbey, N. Ire.
388 H1 **Straidbilly** Moyle, N. Ire.
388 K3 **Straidkilly** Larne, N. Ire.
86 F3 **Straight Soley** Wilts., Eng.
288 E3 **Straiton** Edin., Scot.
262 D5 **Straiton** S. Ayr., Scot.
304 I2 **Straloch** Perth and Kin., Scot.
148 D3 **Stramshall** Staffs., Eng.
402 H1 **Stranagalwilly** Strabane, N. Ire.
232 C7 **Strands** Cumbria, Eng.
405 C2 **Strang** Isle of Man
198 D3 **Strangeways** Gtr Man., Eng.
140 D4 **Strangford** Here., Eng.
396 K3 **Strangford** Down, N. Ire.
23 K4 **Strangford Lough** inlet N. Ire.
326 D3 **Strannda** W. Isles, Scot.
388 H2 **Stranocum** Ballymoney, N. Ire.
252 A3 **Stranraer** D. and G., Scot.
362 G3 **Strata Florida** Cere., Wales
82 D3 **Stratfield Mortimer** W. Berks., Eng.
52 F2 **Stratfield Saye** Hants., Eng.
52 F2 **Stratfield Turgis** Hants., Eng.
110 D3 **Stratford** Central Bedfordshire, Eng.
98 F1 **Stratford** Glos., Eng.
74 D2 **Stratford** Gtr Lon., Eng.
120 H3 **Stratford St Andrew** Suff., Eng.
120 E5 **Stratford St Mary** Suff., Eng.
86 E5 **Stratford sub Castle** Wilts., Eng.
86 D5 **Stratford Tony** Wilts., Eng.
132 B4 **Stratford-upon-Avon** Warks., Eng.
320 K2 **Strath** High., Scot.
320 E3 **Strathan** High., Scot.
322 F4 **Strathan** High., Scot.
268 B2 **Strathaven** S. Lanark., Scot.
296 E6 **Strathblane** Stir., Scot.
22 K8 **Strathbogie** reg. Scot.
320 E4 **Strathcanaird** High., Scot.
322 E2 **Strathcarron** High., Scot.
22 G7 **Strathcarron** val. Scot.
22 G7 **Strathconon** val. Scot.
22 H8 **Strath Dearn** val. Scot.
22 H10 **Strath Earn** val. Scot.
22 H6 **Strath Fleet** val. Scot.
314 D3 **Strathgirnock** Abers., Scot.
22 G8 **Strathglass** val. Scot.
22 I6 **Strath Halladale** val. Scot.
292 G1 **Strathkinness** Fife, Scot.
292 E2 **Strathmiglo** Fife, Scot.
22 G5 **Strathmore** r. Scot.
22 H6 **Strathnaver** val. Scot.
22 I6 **Strath of Kildonan** val. Scot.
322 H2 **Strathpeffer** High., Scot.
Strath Pheofhair High., Scot. see **Strathpeffer**
320 F4 **Strathrannoch** High., Scot.
22 I8 **Strathspey** val. Scot.
304 H3 **Strathtay** Perth and Kin., Scot.
22 I9 **Strath Tay** val. Scot.
264 D3 **Strathwhillan** N. Ayr., Scot.
320 I2 **Strathy** High., Scot.
22 H5 **Strathy Point** pt Scot.
296 E4 **Strathyre** Stir., Scot.
36 F1 **Stratton** Corn., Eng.
46 E3 **Stratton** Dorset, Eng.
98 H3 **Stratton** Glos., Eng.
102 E3 **Stratton Audley** Oxon, Eng.
120 G4 **Stratton Hall** Suff., Eng.
94 J3 **Stratton-on-the-Fosse** Som., Eng.
86 E2 **Stratton St Margaret** Swindon, Eng.
166 G4 **Stratton St Michael** Norf., Eng.
166 G2 **Stratton Strawless** Norf., Eng.
300 E4 **Stravanan** Arg. and B., Scot.
292 H2 **Stravithie** Fife, Scot.
388 F4 **Straw** Magherafelt, N. Ire.
74 B3 **Strawberry Hill** Gtr Lon., Eng.
94 D4 **Stream** Som., Eng.
58 F3 **Streat** E. Sussex, Eng.
74 D3 **Streatham** Gtr Lon., Eng.
74 D3 **Streatham Hill** Gtr Lon., Eng.
74 D3 **Streatham Park** Gtr Lon., Eng.
74 D3 **Streatham Vale** Gtr Lon., Eng.
110 C4 **Streatley** Central Bedfordshire, Eng.
82 D2 **Streatley** W. Berks., Eng.
40 G2 **Street** Devon, Eng.
228 F3 **Street** Lancs., Eng.
216 G1 **Street** N. Yorks., Eng.
94 G5 **Street** Som., Eng.
94 H4 **Street** Som., Eng.
132 E3 **Street Ashton** Warks., Eng.
144 C2 **Street Dinas** Shrop., Eng.
62 G3 **Street End** Kent, Eng.
58 B4 **Street End** W. Sussex, Eng.
236 E2 **Street Gate** T. and W., Eng.
148 E4 **Streethay** Staffs., Eng.
222 F2 **Streethouse** W. Yorks., Eng.
216 F3 **Street Houses** N. Yorks., Eng.
216 E1 **Streetlam** N. Yorks., Eng.
180 E4 **Street Lane** Derbys., Eng.
148 D5 **Streetly** Staffs., Eng.
124 G6 **Streetly End** Cambs., Eng.
94 I4 **Street on the Fosse** Som., Eng.
144 D5 **Strefford** Shrop., Eng.
176 B5 **Strelley** Notts., Eng.
216 F2 **Strensall** York, Eng.
136 E3 **Strensham** Worcs., Eng.
94 F3 **Stretcholt** Som., Eng.
40 F4 **Strete** Devon, Eng.
198 D3 **Stretford** Gtr Man., Eng.
140 C2 **Stretford** Here., Eng.
140 C2 **Stretford** Here., Eng.
116 C1 **Strethall** Essex, Eng.
124 F4 **Stretham** Cambs., Eng.
58 B3 **Strettington** W. Sussex, Eng.
184 C3 **Stretton** Cheshire West & Chester, Eng.
180 E4 **Stretton** Derbys., Eng.
162 H2 **Stretton** Rutland, Eng.
148 B4 **Stretton** Staffs., Eng.
148 F3 **Stretton** Staffs., Eng.
190 F3 **Stretton** Warr., Eng.
162 B2 **Stretton en le Field** Leics., Eng.
140 D3 **Stretton Grandison** Here., Eng.
144 C3 **Stretton Heath** Shrop., Eng.
132 D3 **Stretton-on-Dunsmore** Warks., Eng.
132 B5 **Stretton-on-Fosse** Warks., Eng.
140 C3 **Stretton Sugwas** Here., Eng.
132 D3 **Stretton under Fosse** Warks., Eng.
144 E4 **Stretton Westwood** Shrop., Eng.
232 E7 **Stribers** Cumbria, Eng.
314 G2 **Strichen** Abers., Scot.
198 E3 **Strines** Gtr Man., Eng.
94 E3 **Stringston** Som., Eng.
24 G2 **Striven, Loch** inlet Scot.
128 E4 **Strixton** Northants., Eng.
402 G2 **Stroanbrack** Strabane, N. Ire.
98 D3 **Stroat** Glos., Eng.
22 J5 **Stroma, Island of** i. Scot.
322 E2 **Stromeferry** High., Scot.
322 E2 **Stromemore** High., Scot.
329 B4 **Stromness** Orkney, Scot.
296 C4 **Stronachlachar** Stir., Scot.
300 F4 **Strone** Arg. and B., Scot.
322 F4 **Strone** High., Scot.
322 H3 **Strone** High., Scot.
296 C4 **Strone** Stir., Scot.
320 F3 **Stronechrubie** High., Scot.
300 E3 **Stronlonag** Arg. and B., Scot.
300 F2 **Stronmilchan** Arg. and B., Scot.
329 F3 **Stronsay** airport Scot.
22 K4 **Stronsay** i. Scot.
22 K4 **Stronsay Firth** sea chan. Scot.
300 D2 **Strontoiller** Arg. and B., Scot.
296 D3 **Stronvar** Stir., Scot.
62 C2 **Strood** Medway, Eng.
78 E2 **Strood Green** Surr., Eng.
58 C2 **Strood Green** W. Sussex, Eng.
58 D2 **Strood Green** W. Sussex, Eng.
252 E2 **Stroquhan** D. and G., Scot.
98 F3 **Stroud** Glos., Eng.
52 G4 **Stroud** Hants., Eng.
78 C2 **Stroud Common** Surr., Eng.
78 C1 **Stroude** Surr., Eng.
116 G4 **Stroud Green** Essex, Eng.
98 F3 **Stroud Green** Glos., Eng.
74 D2 **Stroud Green** Gtr Lon., Eng.
300 F3 **Stroul** Arg. and B., Scot.
170 C6 **Stroxton** Lincs., Eng.
304 G2 **Struan** Perth and Kin., Scot.
170 E4 **Strubby** Lincs., Eng.
170 H4 **Strubby** Lincs., Eng.

Strule to Thornham

23 H3 **Strule** *r. N. Ire.*
26 B3 **Strumble Head** *hd Wales*
66 H3 **Strumpshaw** *Norf., Eng.*
92 F2 **Struthers** *Fife, Scot.*
22 H2 **Struy** *High., Scot.*
71 B3 **Stryd y Facsen** *I.o.A., Wales*
78 G3 **Stryt-cae-rhedyn** *Flints., Wales*
78 G3 **Stryt-issa** *Wrex., Wales*
78 H3 **Stryt-yr-hwch** *Wrex., Wales*
14 G2 **Stuartfield** *Abers., Scot.*
66 I2 **Stubb** *Norf., Eng.*
54 C2 **Stubber's Green** *W. Mids, Eng.*
52 E6 **Stubbington** *Hants., Eng.*
28 I5 **Stubbins** *Lancs., Eng.*
66 G3 **Stubb's Green** *Norf., Eng.*
46 G2 **Stubhampton** *Dorset, Eng.*
80 E3 **Stubley** *Derbys., Eng.*
32 B7 **Stub Place** *Cumbria, Eng.*
98 B3 **Stubshaw Cross** *Gtr Man., Eng.*
70 B5 **Stubton** *Lincs., Eng.*
00 F3 **Stuck** *Arg. and B., Scot.*
00 F3 **Stuckbeg** *Arg. and B., Scot.*
00 F3 **Stuckgowan** *Arg. and B., Scot.*
00 F3 **Stuckindroin** *Arg. and B., Scot.*
00 E3 **Stuckreoch** *Arg. and B., Scot.*
52 B5 **Stuckton** *Hants., Eng.*
62 H3 **Studdal** *Kent, Eng.*
44 D6 **Studdon** *Northumb., Eng.*
16 C2 **Studfold** *N. Yorks., Eng.*
82 F3 **Stud Green** *W. and M., Eng.*
10 B5 **Studham** *Central Bedfordshire, Eng.*
32 D3 **Studholme** *Cumbria, Eng.*
46 H4 **Studland** *Dorset, Eng.*
32 A4 **Studley** *Warks., Eng.*
86 C3 **Studley** *Wilts., Eng.*
32 A4 **Studley Common** *Warks., Eng.*
06 C5 **Studley Green** *Bucks., Eng.*
16 E2 **Studley Roger** *N. Yorks., Eng.*
05 C3 **Stuggadhoo** Isle of Man
02 J3 **Stughan** *Dungannon, N. Ire.*
16 D1 **Stump Cross** *Essex, Eng.*
28 G3 **Stump Cross** *Lancs., Eng.*
24 F4 **Stuntney** *Cambs., Eng.*
58 H3 **Stunts Green** *E. Sussex, Eng.*
48 B3 **Sturbridge** *Staffs., Eng.*
70 B3 **Sturgate** *Lincs., Eng.*
16 E1 **Sturmer** *Essex, Eng.*
46 F2 **Sturminster Common** *Dorset, Eng.*
46 G3 **Sturminster Marshall** *Dorset, Eng.*
46 F2 **Sturminster Newton** *Dorset, Eng.*
62 G3 **Sturry** *Kent, Eng.*
70 C4 **Sturton by Stow** *Lincs., Eng.*
22 F2 **Sturton Grange** *W. Yorks., Eng.*
76 E2 **Sturton le Steeple** *Notts., Eng.*
20 F2 **Stuston** *Suff., Eng.*
16 F3 **Stutton** *N. Yorks., Eng.*
20 F5 **Stutton** *Suff., Eng.*
84 F1 **Styal** *Cheshire East, Eng.*
28 G4 **Stydd** *Lancs., Eng.*
76 C2 **Styrrup** *Notts., Eng.*
Suainebost *W. Isles, Scot. see* **Swainbost**
26 F2 **Suardail** *W. Isles, Scot.*
14 E2 **Succoth** *Abers., Scot.*
00 F3 **Succoth** *Arg. and B., Scot.*
36 C3 **Suckley** *Worcs., Eng.*
36 C2 **Suckley Green** *Worcs., Eng.*
36 C2 **Suckley Knowl** *Worcs., Eng.*
28 F3 **Sudborough** *Northants., Eng.*
20 I4 **Sudbourne** *Suff., Eng.*
70 C6 **Sudbrook** *Lincs., Eng.*
39 D3 **Sudbrook** *Mon., Wales*
70 D4 **Sudbrooke** *Lincs., Eng.*
80 C5 **Sudbury** *Derbys., Eng.*
74 C2 **Sudbury** *Gtr Lon., Eng.*
20 D4 **Sudbury** *Suff., Eng.*
98 D2 **Sudden** *Gtr Man., Eng.*
98 G3 **Sudgrove** *Glos., Eng.*
66 G1 **Suffield** *Norf., Eng.*
16 H2 **Suffield** *N. Yorks., Eng.*
20 E4 **Suffolk** *county Eng.*
62 F4 **Sugarloaf** *Kent, Eng.*
44 E3 **Sugdon** *Telford, Eng.*
48 B3 **Sugnall** *Staffs., Eng.*
40 C3 **Sugwas Pool** *Here., Eng.*
22 F6 **Suilven** *hill Scot.*
22 D3 **Suisnish** *High., Scot.*
22 D4 **Sula Sgeir** *i. Scot.*
05 D2 **Sulby** Isle of Man
05 D2 **Sulby** *Cumbria, Eng.*
22 H4 **Sule Skerry** *i. Scot.*
22 G4 **Sule Stack** *i. Scot.*
28 B5 **Sulgrave** *Northants., Eng.*
82 D3 **Sulham** *W. Berks., Eng.*
82 D3 **Sulhamstead** *W. Berks., Eng.*
82 D3 **Sulhamstead Abbots** *W. Berks., Eng.*
58 D3 **Sullington** *W. Sussex, Eng.*
31 C2 **Sullom** *Shet., Scot.*
22 □N2 **Sullom Voe** *inlet Scot.*
50 G4 **Sully** *V. of Glam., Wales*
31 D4 **Sumburgh** *Shet., Scot.*
31 D4 **Sumburgh** *airport Scot.*
22 □N3 **Sumburgh Head** *hd Scot.*
16 D2 **Summer Bridge** *N. Yorks., Eng.*
36 E2 **Summercourt** *Corn., Eng.*
66 C1 **Summerfield** *Norf., Eng.*
36 D1 **Summerfield** *Worcs., Eng.*
54 B2 **Summer Hill** *W. Mids, Eng.*
36 D1 **Summerhill** *Worcs., Eng.*
52 F2 **Summerhill** *D. and G., Scot.*
78 G3 **Summerhill** *Wrex., Wales*
22 E6 **Summer Isles** *is Scot.*
32 F7 **Summerlands** *Cumbria, Eng.*
39 D3 **Summerleaze** *Newp., Wales*
16 C1 **Summer Lodge** *N. Yorks., Eng.*
98 D2 **Summerseat** *Gtr Man., Eng.*
74 C3 **Summerstown** *Gtr Lon., Eng.*
02 D4 **Summertown** *Oxon, Eng.*
98 E1 **Summit** *Gtr Man., Eng.*
16 C3 **Sumners** *Essex, Eng.*
00 D5 **Sunadale** *Arg. and B., Scot.*
22 E9 **Sunart, Loch** *inlet Scot.*
32 G6 **Sunbiggin** *Cumbria, Eng.*
78 D1 **Sunbury** *Surr., Eng.*
52 E2 **Sundaywell** *D. and G., Scot.*
32 C4 **Sunderland** *Cumbria, Eng.*
28 E3 **Sunderland** *Lancs., Eng.*
36 G2 **Sunderland** *T. and W., Eng.*
36 F3 **Sunderland Bridge** *Durham, Eng.*
56 F3 **Sundhope** *Borders, Scot.*
10 C4 **Sundon Park** *Luton, Eng.*
74 E3 **Sundridge** *Gtr Lon., Eng.*
62 A3 **Sundridge** *Kent, Eng.*
62 D4 **Sundrum Mains** *S. Ayr., Scot.*
98 E3 **Sun Green** *Gtr Man., Eng.*
98 I3 **Sunhill** *Glos., Eng.*
00 B2 **Sunipol** *Arg. and B., Scot.*
10 H5 **Sunk Island** *E. Riding, Eng.*
82 G3 **Sunningdale** *W. and M., Eng.*
82 G3 **Sunninghill** *W. and M., Eng.*
02 D4 **Sunningwell** *Oxon, Eng.*
36 E3 **Sunniside** *Durham, Eng.*
36 E2 **Sunniside** *T. and W., Eng.*
232 D7 **Sunny Bank** *Cumbria, Eng.*
180 E5 **Sunny Hill** *Derby, Eng.*
296 G5 **Sunnylaw** *Stir., Scot.*
102 D4 **Sunnymead** *Oxon, Eng.*
116 E4 **Sunnymede** *Essex, Eng.*
244 E6 **Sunnyside** *Northumb., Eng.*
208 E3 **Sunnyside** *S. Yorks., Eng.*
86 F4 **Sunton** *Wilts., Eng.*
256 L2 **Sunwick** *Borders, Scot.*
74 C3 **Surbiton** *Gtr Lon., Eng.*
170 F6 **Surfleet** *Lincs., Eng.*
170 F6 **Surfleet Seas End** *Lincs., Eng.*
166 H3 **Surlingham** *Norf., Eng.*
78 D2 **Surrey** *county Eng.*
166 G1 **Sustead** *Norf., Eng.*
170 B2 **Susworth** *Lincs., Eng.*
40 C2 **Sutcombe** *Devon, Eng.*
22 H6 **Sutherland** *reg. Scot.*
166 F3 **Suton** *Norf., Eng.*
320 I4 **Sutors of Cromarty** *High., Scot.*
170 G4 **Sutterby** *Lincs., Eng.*
170 F6 **Sutterton** *Lincs., Eng.*
124 E4 **Sutton** *Cambs., Eng.*
110 D3 **Sutton** *Central Bedfordshire, Eng.*
74 C3 **Sutton** *Gtr Lon., Eng.*
62 I3 **Sutton** *Kent, Eng.*
170 B5 **Sutton** *Lincs., Eng.*
166 I2 **Sutton** *Norf., Eng.*
176 D2 **Sutton** *Notts., Eng.*
176 D5 **Sutton** *Notts., Eng.*
216 F3 **Sutton** *N. Yorks., Eng.*
102 C4 **Sutton** *Oxon, Eng.*
124 B3 **Sutton** *Peterb., Eng.*
144 C2 **Sutton** *Shrop., Eng.*
144 D3 **Sutton** *Shrop., Eng.*
144 F2 **Sutton** *Shrop., Eng.*
144 F5 **Sutton** *Shrop., Eng.*
148 A4 **Sutton** *Staffs., Eng.*
120 H4 **Sutton** *Suff., Eng.*
208 E2 **Sutton** *S. Yorks., Eng.*
58 C3 **Sutton** *W. Sussex, Eng.*
358 D3 **Sutton** *Pembs., Wales*
74 C3 **Sutton** *met. bor. Gtr Lon., Eng.*
78 D2 **Sutton Abinger** *Surr., Eng.*
62 B2 **Sutton at Hone** *Kent, Eng.*
128 D2 **Sutton Bassett** *Northants., Eng.*
86 C2 **Sutton Benger** *Wilts., Eng.*
94 I5 **Sutton Bingham** *Som., Eng.*
176 B6 **Sutton Bonington** *Notts., Eng.*
170 H7 **Sutton Bridge** *Lincs., Eng.*
162 C3 **Sutton Cheney** *Leics., Eng.*
154 D2 **Sutton Coldfield** *W. Mids, Eng.*
102 D5 **Sutton Courtenay** *Oxon, Eng.*
170 G7 **Sutton Crosses** *Lincs., Eng.*
216 E2 **Sutton Grange** *N. Yorks., Eng.*
102 C4 **Sutton Green** *Oxon, Eng.*
78 C2 **Sutton Green** *Surr., Eng.*
378 H3 **Sutton Green** *Wrex., Wales*
190 E3 **Sutton Heath** *Merseyside, Eng.*
46 H2 **Sutton Holms** *Dorset, Eng.*
216 E2 **Sutton Howgrave** *N. Yorks., Eng.*
176 B4 **Sutton in Ashfield** *Notts., Eng.*
216 D3 **Sutton-in-Craven** *N. Yorks., Eng.*
210 G4 **Sutton Ings** *Hull, Eng.*
162 D3 **Sutton in the Elms** *Leics., Eng.*
184 G2 **Sutton Lane Ends** *Cheshire East, Eng.*
190 E3 **Sutton Leach** *Merseyside, Eng.*
170 H4 **Sutton le Marsh** *Lincs., Eng.*
144 F4 **Sutton Maddock** *Shrop., Eng.*
94 G4 **Sutton Mallet** *Som., Eng.*
86 C5 **Sutton Mandeville** *Wilts., Eng.*
190 E3 **Sutton Manor** *Merseyside, Eng.*
140 D3 **Sutton Marsh** *Here., Eng.*
94 I4 **Sutton Montis** *Som., Eng.*
210 G4 **Sutton-on-Hull** *Hull, Eng.*
170 H4 **Sutton on Sea** *Lincs., Eng.*
216 F2 **Sutton-on-the-Forest** *N. Yorks., Eng.*
180 D5 **Sutton on the Hill** *Derbys., Eng.*
176 E3 **Sutton on Trent** *Notts., Eng.*
46 E4 **Sutton Poyntz** *Dorset, Eng.*
180 E3 **Sutton Scarsdale** *Derbys., Eng.*
52 D4 **Sutton Scotney** *Hants., Eng.*
170 G7 **Sutton St Edmund** *Lincs., Eng.*
170 G7 **Sutton St James** *Lincs., Eng.*
140 C3 **Sutton St Michael** *Here., Eng.*
140 C3 **Sutton St Nicholas** *Here., Eng.*
132 C5 **Sutton-under-Brailes** *Warks., Eng.*
210 C3 **Sutton upon Derwent** *E. Riding, Eng.*
62 D3 **Sutton Valence** *Kent, Eng.*
86 C4 **Sutton Veny** *Wilts., Eng.*
46 F2 **Sutton Waldron** *Dorset, Eng.*
52 G3 **Sutton Warblington** *Hants., Eng.*
184 C2 **Sutton Weaver** *Cheshire West & Chester, Eng.*
94 I3 **Sutton Wick** *B. and N.E. Som., Eng.*
102 D5 **Sutton Wick** *Oxon, Eng.*
170 G4 **Swaby** *Lincs., Eng.*
180 D6 **Swadlincote** *Derbys., Eng.*
166 D3 **Swaffham** *Norf., Eng.*
124 F5 **Swaffham Bulbeck** *Cambs., Eng.*
124 F5 **Swaffham Prior** *Cambs., Eng.*
166 H1 **Swafield** *Norf., Eng.*
326 F1 **Swainbost** *W. Isles, Scot.*
140 C3 **Swainshill** *Here., Eng.*
94 J2 **Swainswick** *B. and N.E. Som., Eng.*
208 D2 **Swaithe** *S. Yorks., Eng.*
102 C2 **Swalcliffe** *Oxon, Eng.*
24 O5 **Swale** *r. Eng.*
62 G2 **Swalecliffe** *Kent, Eng.*
170 E2 **Swallow** *Lincs., Eng.*
170 C4 **Swallow Beck** *Lincs., Eng.*
86 C5 **Swallowcliffe** *Wilts., Eng.*
82 E3 **Swallowfield** *W'ham, Eng.*
116 D4 **Swallows Cross** *Essex, Eng.*
236 E2 **Swalwell** *T. and W., Eng.*
52 D3 **Swampton** *Hants., Eng.*
46 H4 **Swanage** *Dorset, Eng.*
184 D4 **Swanbach** *Cheshire East, Eng.*
106 C3 **Swanbourne** *Bucks., Eng.*
350 G4 **Swanbridge** *V. of Glam., Wales*
144 F4 **Swancote** *Shrop., Eng.*
184 E2 **Swan Green** *Cheshire West & Chester, Eng.*
120 H3 **Swan Green** *Suff., Eng.*
210 F4 **Swanland** *E. Riding, Eng.*
256 J4 **Swanlaws** *Borders, Scot.*
62 B2 **Swanley** *Kent, Eng.*
62 B2 **Swanley Village** *Kent, Eng.*
52 E5 **Swanmore** *Hants., Eng.*
52 E6 **Swanmore** *I.o.W., Eng.*
162 C2 **Swannington** *Leics., Eng.*
166 F2 **Swannington** *Norf., Eng.*
62 B2 **Swanscombe** *Kent, Eng.*
350 C3 **Swansea** *Swansea, Wales*
350 C3 **Swansea** *admin. div. Wales*
26 E4 **Swansea Bay** *b. Wales*
288 D3 **Swanston** *Edin., Scot.*
116 G2 **Swan Street** *Essex, Eng.*
166 H2 **Swanton Abbot** *Norf., Eng.*
166 E2 **Swanton Morley** *Norf., Eng.*
166 F1 **Swanton Novers** *Norf., Eng.*
62 E3 **Swanton Street** *Kent, Eng.*
154 B2 **Swan Village** *W. Mids, Eng.*
180 E4 **Swanwick** *Derbys., Eng.*
52 E5 **Swanwick** *Hants., Eng.*
184 C3 **Swanwick Green** *Cheshire East, Eng.*
170 D6 **Swarby** *Lincs., Eng.*
166 G3 **Swardeston** *Norf., Eng.*
180 E5 **Swarkestone** *Derbys., Eng.*
244 G4 **Swarland** *Northumb., Eng.*
52 E4 **Swarraton** *Hants., Eng.*
170 E6 **Swaton** *Lincs., Eng.*
388 G3 **Swatragh** *Magherafelt, N. Ire.*
124 D5 **Swavesey** *Cambs., Eng.*
52 C6 **Sway** *Hants., Eng.*
170 C7 **Swayfield** *Lincs., Eng.*
52 D5 **Swaythling** *Soton, Eng.*
210 F2 **Swaythorpe** *E. Riding, Eng.*
40 F2 **Sweetham** *Devon, Eng.*
94 F5 **Sweethay** *Som., Eng.*
36 E2 **Sweetshouse** *Corn., Eng.*
120 H3 **Sweffling** *Suff., Eng.*
94 G4 **Swell** *Som., Eng.*
162 C2 **Swepstone** *Leics., Eng.*
102 C3 **Swerford** *Oxon, Eng.*
350 H2 **Swffryd** *B. Gwent, Wales*
58 I2 **Swiftsden** *E. Sussex, Eng.*
62 E3 **Swift's Green** *Kent, Eng.*
120 G4 **Swilland** *Suff., Eng.*
228 F4 **Swillbrook** *Lancs., Eng.*
222 F2 **Swillington** *W. Yorks., Eng.*
40 E1 **Swimbridge** *Devon, Eng.*
102 B4 **Swinbrook** *Oxon, Eng.*
216 C3 **Swinden** *N. Yorks., Eng.*
170 B5 **Swinderby** *Lincs., Eng.*
148 B5 **Swindon** *Staffs., Eng.*
86 E2 **Swindon** *Swindon, Eng.*
86 E2 **Swindon** *admin. div. Eng.*
98 G2 **Swindon Village** *Glos., Eng.*
210 G4 **Swine** *E. Riding, Eng.*
210 C4 **Swinefleet** *E. Riding, Eng.*
98 E5 **Swineford** *S. Glos., Eng.*
110 C2 **Swineshead** *Bedford, Eng.*
170 F6 **Swineshead** *Lincs., Eng.*
170 E6 **Swineshead Bridge** *Lincs., Eng.*
162 E4 **Swinford** *Leics., Eng.*
102 C4 **Swinford** *Oxon, Eng.*
176 B5 **Swingate** *Notts., Eng.*
62 G4 **Swingfield Minnis** *Kent, Eng.*
120 E4 **Swingleton Green** *Suff., Eng.*
268 C2 **Swinhill** *S. Lanark., Scot.*
244 G2 **Swinhoe** *Northumb., Eng.*
170 E3 **Swinhope** *Lincs., Eng.*
331 D2 **Swining** *Shet., Scot.*
216 D2 **Swinithwaite** *N. Yorks., Eng.*
222 E2 **Swinnow** *W. Yorks., Eng.*
148 E2 **Swinscoe** *Staffs., Eng.*
256 J4 **Swinside Hall** *Borders, Scot.*
170 D7 **Swinstead** *Lincs., Eng.*
198 C2 **Swinton** *Gtr Man., Eng.*
216 D2 **Swinton** *N. Yorks., Eng.*
208 E3 **Swinton** *S. Yorks., Eng.*
256 K2 **Swinton** *Borders, Scot.*
256 K2 **Swintonmill** *Borders, Scot.*
256 K2 **Swinton Quarter** *Borders, Scot.*
162 D2 **Swithland** *Leics., Eng.*
Swnt Enlli *sea chan. Wales see* **Bardsey Sound**
322 E4 **Swordland** *High., Scot.*
322 C4 **Swordle** *High., Scot.*
184 E1 **Sworton Heath** *Cheshire East, Eng.*
362 G3 **Swyddffynnon** *Cere., Wales*
102 E5 **Swyncombe** *Oxon, Eng.*
148 B3 **Swynnerton** *Staffs., Eng.*
46 D3 **Swyre** *Dorset, Eng.*
366 D4 **Sychnant** *Powys, Wales*
98 G3 **Syde** *Glos., Eng.*
74 D3 **Sydenham** *Gtr Lon., Eng.*
102 F4 **Sydenham** *Oxon, Eng.*
94 G4 **Sydenham** *Som., Eng.*
388 K5 **Sydenham** *Belfast, N. Ire.*
40 D3 **Sydenham Damerel** *Devon, Eng.*
166 D1 **Syderstone** *Norf., Eng.*
46 D3 **Sydling St Nicholas** *Dorset, Eng.*
52 E3 **Sydmonton** *Hants., Eng.*
184 E3 **Sydney** *Cheshire East, Eng.*
176 D4 **Syerston** *Notts., Eng.*
198 E2 **Syke** *Gtr Man., Eng.*
208 F2 **Sykehouse** *S. Yorks., Eng.*
228 G3 **Sykes** *Lancs., Eng.*
356 F3 **Sylen** *Carmar., Wales*
331 D2 **Symbister** *Shet., Scot.*
262 D3 **Symington** *S. Ayr., Scot.*
268 E3 **Symington** *S. Lanark., Scot.*
46 C3 **Symondsbury** *Dorset, Eng.*
140 D4 **Symonds Yat** *Here., Eng.*
362 D4 **Synod Inn** *Cere., Wales*
320 H2 **Syre** *High., Scot.*
98 H2 **Syreford** *Glos., Eng.*
128 C5 **Syresham** *Northants., Eng.*
162 E2 **Syston** *Leics., Eng.*
170 C6 **Syston** *Lincs., Eng.*
136 D2 **Sytchampton** *Worcs., Eng.*
128 E4 **Sywell** *Northants., Eng.*

T

322 F2 **Taagan** *High., Scot.*
184 E2 **Tableyhill** *Cheshire East, Eng.*
326 E2 **Tabost** *W. Isles, Scot.*
Tabost *W. Isles, Scot. see* **Harbost**
132 C4 **Tachbrook Mallory** *Warks., Eng.*
320 J2 **Tacher** *High., Scot.*
102 D3 **Tackley** *Oxon, Eng.*
166 F3 **Tacolneston** *Norf., Eng.*
216 F3 **Tadcaster** *N. Yorks., Eng.*
46 G3 **Tadden** *Dorset, Eng.*
180 C3 **Taddington** *Derbys., Eng.*
98 H2 **Taddington** *Glos., Eng.*
52 F2 **Tadley** *Hants., Eng.*
124 D6 **Tadlow** *Cambs., Eng.*
102 C2 **Tadmarton** *Oxon, Eng.*
102 B4 **Tadpole Bridge** *Oxon, Eng.*
78 E2 **Tadworth** *Surr., Eng.*
26 D4 **Taf** *r. Wales*
350 G2 **Tafarnaubach** *B. Gwent, Wales*
358 F2 **Tafarn-y-bwlch** *Pembs., Wales*
378 F3 **Tafarn-y-Gelyn** *Denb., Wales*
26 F4 **Taff** *r. Wales*
350 G2 **Taff Merthyr Garden Village** *M. Tyd., Wales*
350 G3 **Taff's Well** *Cardiff, Wales*
366 D3 **Tafolwern** *Powys, Wales*
350 D3 **Taibach** *N.P.T., Wales*
366 F1 **Tai-bach** *Powys, Wales*
372 G4 **Taicynhaeaf** *Gwynedd, Wales*
Taigh an Droma *Stir., Scot. see* **Tyndrum**
Taigh an Uillt *Arg. and B., Scot. see* **Taynuilt**
320 H4 **Tain** *High., Scot.*
372 E2 **Tai'n Lôn** *Gwynedd, Wales*
Tairbeart *W. Isles, Scot. see* **Tarbert**
Tairbhidh *High., Scot. see* **Tarvie**
366 E7 **Tai'r Bull** *Powys, Wales*
350 C2 **Tairgwaith** *N.P.T., Wales*
350 G3 **Tai'r-heol** *Caerp., Wales*
262 D5 **Tairlaw** *S. Ayr., Scot.*
350 C3 **Tai'r-ysgol** *Swansea, Wales*
116 D2 **Takeley** *Essex, Eng.*
116 D2 **Takeley Street** *Essex, Eng.*
366 E7 **Talachddu** *Powys, Wales*
378 F1 **Talacre** *Flints., Wales*
372 I4 **Talardd** *Gwynedd, Wales*
40 G2 **Talaton** *Devon, Eng.*
358 D3 **Talbenny** *Pembs., Wales*
350 F3 **Talbot Green** *R.C.T., Wales*
46 H3 **Talbot Village** *Bourne., Eng.*
366 D3 **Talerddig** *Powys, Wales*
362 E4 **Talgarreg** *Cere., Wales*
366 F7 **Talgarth** *Powys, Wales*
362 G1 **Taliesin** *Cere., Wales*
322 B3 **Talisker** *High., Scot.*
148 B2 **Talke** *Staffs., Eng.*
148 B2 **Talke Pits** *Staffs., Eng.*
232 F3 **Talkin** *Cumbria, Eng.*
320 D4 **Talladale** *High., Scot.*
304 D2 **Talladh-a-Bheithe** *Perth and Kin., Scot.*
256 D4 **Talla Linnfoots** *Borders, Scot.*
36 F2 **Talland** *Corn., Eng.*
378 I4 **Tallarn Green** *Wrex., Wales*
232 B4 **Tallentire** *Cumbria, Eng.*
356 G2 **Talley** *Carmar., Wales*
170 D8 **Tallington** *Lincs., Eng.*
320 G2 **Talmine** *High., Scot.*
356 D2 **Talog** *Carmar., Wales*
362 F3 **Tal-sarn** *Cere., Wales*
372 F3 **Talsarnau** *Gwynedd, Wales*
36 E2 **Talskiddy** *Corn., Eng.*
371 D3 **Talwrn** *I.o.A., Wales*
378 G3 **Talwrn** *Wrex., Wales*
378 H3 **Talwrn** *Wrex., Wales*
362 G2 **Talybont** *Cere., Wales*
378 B2 **Tal-y-bont** *Conwy, Wales*
372 F1 **Tal-y-bont** *Gwynedd, Wales*
372 F4 **Tal-y-bont** *Gwynedd, Wales*
366 F7 **Talybont-on-Usk** *Powys, Wales*
372 F1 **Tal-y-Cae** *Gwynedd, Wales*
378 C2 **Tal-y-cafn** *Conwy, Wales*
339 C2 **Tal-y-coed** *Mon., Wales*
350 F3 **Talygarn** *R.C.T., Wales*
372 G4 **Tal-y-llyn** *Gwynedd, Wales*
366 F7 **Talyllyn** *Powys, Wales*
372 E2 **Talysarn** *Gwynedd, Wales*
339 B2 **Talywain** *Torf., Wales*
366 C3 **Tal-y-wern** *Powys, Wales*
26 D7 **Tamar** *r. Eng.*
296 E5 **Tamavoid** *Stir., Scot.*
40 D3 **Tamerton Foliot** *Plymouth, Eng.*
197 **Tameside** *met. bor. Gtr Man., Eng.*
388 H3 **Tamlaght** *Ballymoney, N. Ire.*
402 E5 **Tamlaght** *Fermanagh, N. Ire.*
388 G3 **Tamlaght O'Crilly** *Magherafelt, N. Ire.*
402 K4 **Tamnamore** *Dungannon, N. Ire.*
402 K3 **Tamnavally** *Cookstown, N. Ire.*
388 F3 **Tamnyrankin** *Coleraine, N. Ire.*
148 E5 **Tamworth** *Staffs., Eng.*
170 G6 **Tamworth Green** *Lincs., Eng.*
26 F2 **Tanat** *r. Wales*
216 F2 **Tancred** *N. Yorks., Eng.*
222 D3 **Tandem** *W. Yorks., Eng.*
396 F3 **Tandragee** *Armagh, N. Ire.*
78 F2 **Tandridge** *Surr., Eng.*
356 E2 **Tanerdy** *Carmar., Wales*
236 E2 **Tanfield** *Durham, Eng.*
236 E2 **Tanfield Lea** *Durham, Eng.*
216 E2 **Tang** *N. Yorks., Eng.*
358 E3 **Tangiers** *Pembs., Wales*
314 G2 **Tanglandford** *Abers., Scot.*
52 C3 **Tangley** *Hants., Eng.*
58 B3 **Tangmere** *W. Sussex, Eng.*
331 C2 **Tangwick** *Shet., Scot.*
300 C5 **Tangy** *Arg. and B., Scot.*
329 D4 **Tankerness** *Orkney, Scot.*
208 D3 **Tankersley** *S. Yorks., Eng.*
62 G2 **Tankerton** *Kent, Eng.*
372 F3 **Tan-lan** *Gwynedd, Wales*
308 E2 **Tannadice** *Angus, Scot.*
136 F1 **Tanners Green** *Worcs., Eng.*
120 G3 **Tannington** *Suff., Eng.*
280 B3 **Tannochside** *N. Lanark., Scot.*
120 C3 **Tan Office Green** *Suff., Eng.*
292 E2 **Tanshall** *Fife, Scot.*
180 D4 **Tansley** *Derbys., Eng.*
180 D4 **Tansley Knoll** *Derbys., Eng.*
128 G2 **Tansor** *Northants., Eng.*
236 E2 **Tantobie** *Durham, Eng.*
216 F1 **Tanton** *N. Yorks., Eng.*
132 A4 **Tanworth in Arden** *Warks., Eng.*
378 D3 **Tan-y-fron** *Conwy, Wales*
372 C3 **Tan-y-graig** *Gwynedd, Wales*
372 G3 **Tanygrisiau** *Gwynedd, Wales*
362 C4 **Tan-y-groes** *Cere., Wales*
366 E1 **Tan-y-pistyll** *Powys, Wales*
378 E2 **Tan-yr-allt** *Denb., Wales*
326 C5 **Taobh a' Deas Loch Baghasdail** *W. Isles, Scot.*
326 D3 **Taobh Siar** *W. Isles, Scot.*
Taobh Tuath *W. Isles, Scot. see* **Northton**
106 D5 **Taplow** *Bucks., Eng.*
22 K8 **Tap o' Noth** *hill Scot.*
180 E3 **Tapton** *Derbys., Eng.*
180 E3 **Tapton Grove** *Derbys., Eng.*
22 B7 **Taransay** *i. Scot.*
Tarasaigh *i. Scot. see* **Taransay**
22 I7 **Tarbat Ness** *pt Scot.*
300 C4 **Tarbert** *Arg. and B., Scot.*
300 C4 **Tarbert** *Arg. and B., Scot.*
300 D4 **Tarbert** *Arg. and B., Scot.*
322 D4 **Tarbert** *High., Scot.*
326 D3 **Tarbert** *W. Isles, Scot.*
22 D11 **Tarbert, Loch** *inlet Scot.*
300 F3 **Tarbet** *Arg. and B., Scot.*
320 E2 **Tarbet** *High., Scot.*
322 E4 **Tarbet** *High., Scot.*
190 E3 **Tarbock Green** *Merseyside, Eng.*
262 E3 **Tarbolton** *S. Ayr., Scot.*
268 E2 **Tarbrax** *S. Lanark., Scot.*
136 E2 **Tardebigge** *Worcs., Eng.*
228 F4 **Tardy Gate** *Lancs., Eng.*
308 F1 **Tarfside** *Angus, Scot.*
314 E3 **Tarland** *Abers., Scot.*
228 E4 **Tarleton** *Lancs., Eng.*
228 E5 **Tarlscough** *Lancs., Eng.*
98 G3 **Tarlton** *Glos., Eng.*
228 G3 **Tarnbrook** *Lancs., Eng.*
94 G3 **Tarnock** *Som., Eng.*
184 C3 **Tarporley** *Cheshire West & Chester, Eng.*
94 E4 **Tarr** *Som., Eng.*
46 G3 **Tarrant Crawford** *Dorset, Eng.*
46 G2 **Tarrant Gunville** *Dorset, Eng.*
46 G2 **Tarrant Hinton** *Dorset, Eng.*
46 G2 **Tarrant Keyneston** *Dorset, Eng.*
46 G2 **Tarrant Launceston** *Dorset, Eng.*
46 G2 **Tarrant Monkton** *Dorset, Eng.*
46 G2 **Tarrant Rawston** *Dorset, Eng.*
46 G2 **Tarrant Rushton** *Dorset, Eng.*
320 I4 **Tarrel** *High., Scot.*
58 G4 **Tarring Neville** *E. Sussex, Eng.*
140 D3 **Tarrington** *Here., Eng.*
264 C3 **Tarrnacraig** *N. Ayr., Scot.*
304 J4 **Tarsappie** *Perth and Kin., Scot.*
322 D3 **Tarskavaig** *High., Scot.*
314 G2 **Tarves** *Abers., Scot.*
322 H2 **Tarvie** *High., Scot.*
304 I2 **Tarvie** *Perth and Kin., Scot.*
184 C2 **Tarvin** *Cheshire West & Chester, Eng.*
184 C2 **Tarvin Sands** *Cheshire West & Chester, Eng.*
144 F4 **Tasley** *Shrop., Eng.*
396 D4 **Tassagh** *Armagh, N. Ire.*
102 C3 **Taston** *Oxon, Eng.*
148 E4 **Tatenhill** *Staffs., Eng.*
106 D2 **Tathall End** *M.K., Eng.*
228 G2 **Tatham** *Lancs., Eng.*
170 F4 **Tathwell** *Lincs., Eng.*
78 G2 **Tatsfield** *Surr., Eng.*
184 C3 **Tattenhall** *Cheshire West & Chester, Eng.*
106 D3 **Tattenhoe** *M.K., Eng.*
166 D2 **Tatterford** *Norf., Eng.*
166 D1 **Tattersett** *Norf., Eng.*
170 E5 **Tattershall** *Lincs., Eng.*
170 E5 **Tattershall Bridge** *Lincs., Eng.*
170 E5 **Tattershall Thorpe** *Lincs., Eng.*
120 F5 **Tattingstone** *Suff., Eng.*
402 F4 **Tattinweer** *Fermanagh, N. Ire.*
402 G3 **Tattyreagh** *Omagh, N. Ire.*
94 G5 **Tatworth** *Som., Eng.*
314 D2 **Tauchers** *Moray, Scot.*
388 J6 **Taughblane** *Lisburn, N. Ire.*
198 E2 **Taunton** *Gtr Man., Eng.*
94 F4 **Taunton** *Som., Eng.*
314 F3 **Tavelty** *Abers., Scot.*
166 G2 **Taverham** *Norf., Eng.*
358 G3 **Tavernspite** *Pembs., Wales*
40 D3 **Tavistock** *Devon, Eng.*
26 D7 **Tavy** *r. Eng.*
26 D5 **Taw** *r. Eng.*
26 E4 **Tawe** *r. Wales*
40 E2 **Taw Green** *Devon, Eng.*
40 D1 **Tawstock** *Devon, Eng.*
180 B3 **Taxal** *Derbys., Eng.*
22 J10 **Tay** *r. Scot.*
22 J10 **Tay, Firth of** *est. Scot.*
22 H10 **Tay, Loch** *l. Scot.*
262 E3 **Tayburn** *E. Ayr., Scot.*
300 D5 **Tayinloan** *Arg. and B., Scot.*
300 E3 **Taynafead** *Arg. and B., Scot.*
300 D4 **Taynish** *Arg. and B., Scot.*
98 E2 **Taynton** *Glos., Eng.*
102 B4 **Taynton** *Oxon, Eng.*
300 E2 **Taynuilt** *Arg. and B., Scot.*
308 H2 **Tayock** *Angus, Scot.*
300 A4 **Tayovullin** *Arg. and B., Scot.*
292 G1 **Tayport** *Fife, Scot.*
300 D3 **Tayvallich** *Arg. and B., Scot.*
110 C4 **Tea Green** *Herts., Eng.*
170 E3 **Tealby** *Lincs., Eng.*
308 E3 **Tealing** *Angus, Scot.*
326 B4 **Teanamachar** *W. Isles, Scot.*
322 D3 **Teangue** *High., Scot.*
292 G2 **Teasses** *Fife, Scot.*
232 G6 **Tebay** *Cumbria, Eng.*
110 B4 **Tebworth** *Central Bedfordshire, Eng.*
40 E2 **Tedburn St Mary** *Devon, Eng.*
402 E3 **Tedd** *Fermanagh, N. Ire.*
98 G2 **Teddington** *Glos., Eng.*
74 C3 **Teddington** *Gtr Lon., Eng.*
140 E2 **Tedstone Delamere** *Here., Eng.*
140 E2 **Tedstone Wafre** *Here., Eng.*
402 E6 **Teemore** *Fermanagh, N. Ire.*
24 O4 **Tees** *r. Eng.*
24 O4 **Tees Bay** *b. Eng.*
24 M4 **Teesdale** *val. Eng.*
216 F1 **Teesville** *R. and C., Eng.*
128 D4 **Teeton** *Northants., Eng.*
86 C5 **Teffont Evias** *Wilts., Eng.*
86 C5 **Teffont Magna** *Wilts., Eng.*
358 G2 **Tegryn** *Pembs., Wales*
26 C3 **Teifi** *r. Wales*
162 G2 **Teigh** *Rutland, Eng.*
26 E6 **Teign** *r. Eng.*
40 F3 **Teigngrace** *Devon, Eng.*
40 F3 **Teignmouth** *Devon, Eng.*
144 F3 **Telford** *Telford, Eng.*
144 F3 **Telford and Wrekin** *admin. div. Eng.*
58 J3 **Telham** *E. Sussex, Eng.*
94 K3 **Tellisford** *Som., Eng.*
58 F4 **Telscombe** *E. Sussex, Eng.*
58 F4 **Telscombe Cliffs** *E. Sussex, Eng.*
26 H3 **Teme** *r. Eng.*
304 F2 **Tempar** *Perth and Kin., Scot.*
252 F2 **Templand** *D. and G., Scot.*
36 F2 **Temple** *Corn., Eng.*
276 D2 **Temple** *Glas., Scot.*
288 E4 **Temple** *Midlothian, Scot.*
154 D3 **Temple Balsall** *W. Mids, Eng.*
362 F4 **Temple Bar** *Cere., Wales*
94 I3 **Temple Cloud** *B. and N.E. Som., Eng.*
94 J5 **Templecombe** *Som., Eng.*
102 D4 **Temple Cowley** *Oxon, Eng.*
120 B4 **Temple End** *Suff., Eng.*
62 H4 **Temple Ewell** *Kent, Eng.*
116 C3 **Temple Fields** *Essex, Eng.*
132 B4 **Temple Grafton** *Warks., Eng.*
98 H2 **Temple Guiting** *Glos., Eng.*
132 D5 **Temple Herdewyke** *Warks., Eng.*
216 F3 **Temple Hirst** *N. Yorks., Eng.*
388 C2 **Templemoyle** *Derry, N. Ire.*
180 E3 **Temple Normanton** *Derbys., Eng.*
388 J4 **Templepatrick** *Antrim, N. Ire.*
232 G5 **Temple Sowerby** *Cumbria, Eng.*
40 F2 **Templeton** *Devon, Eng.*
358 F3 **Templeton** *Pembs., Wales*
308 G2 **Templewood** *Angus, Scot.*
402 F4 **Tempo** *Fermanagh, N. Ire.*
110 D2 **Tempsford** *Central Bedfordshire, Eng.*
136 B2 **Tenbury Wells** *Worcs., Eng.*
358 F3 **Tenby** *Pembs., Wales*
116 I2 **Tendring** *Essex, Eng.*
116 I2 **Tendring Green** *Essex, Eng.*
300 B2 **Tenga** *Arg. and B., Scot.*
166 B3 **Ten Mile Bank** *Norf., Eng.*
62 E4 **Tenterden** *Kent, Eng.*
252 B3 **Terally** *D. and G., Scot.*
116 F3 **Terling** *Essex, Eng.*
144 E3 **Tern** *Telford, Eng.*
26 G2 **Tern** *r. Eng.*
144 E2 **Ternhill** *Shrop., Eng.*
252 E2 **Terregles** *D. and G., Scot.*
106 D4 **Terrick** *Bucks., Eng.*
106 D5 **Terriers** *Bucks., Eng.*
216 G2 **Terrington** *N. Yorks., Eng.*
166 A2 **Terrington St Clement** *Norf., Eng.*
166 A2 **Terrington St John** *Norf., Eng.*
388 E2 **Terrydremont** *Limavady, N. Ire.*
132 A3 **Terry's Green** *Warks., Eng.*
314 D2 **Tervieside** *Moray, Scot.*
300 E2 **Tervine** *Arg. and B., Scot.*
26 J6 **Test** *r. Eng.*
62 C3 **Teston** *Kent, Eng.*
52 C5 **Testwood** *Hants., Eng.*
98 G4 **Tetbury** *Glos., Eng.*
98 F4 **Tetbury Upton** *Glos., Eng.*
144 C2 **Tetchill** *Shrop., Eng.*
40 C2 **Tetcott** *Devon, Eng.*
170 F4 **Tetford** *Lincs., Eng.*
170 B2 **Tetley** *N. Lincs., Eng.*
170 F3 **Tetney** *Lincs., Eng.*
170 G2 **Tetney Lock** *Lincs., Eng.*
102 E4 **Tetsworth** *Oxon, Eng.*
154 B2 **Tettenhall** *W. Mids, Eng.*
154 A2 **Tettenhall Wood** *W. Mids, Eng.*
124 C6 **Tetworth** *Cambs., Eng.*
314 H2 **Teuchan** *Abers., Scot.*
176 B4 **Teversal** *Notts., Eng.*
124 F5 **Teversham** *Cambs., Eng.*
22 L11 **Teviot** *r. Scot.*
22 K12 **Teviotdale** *val. Scot.*
256 G4 **Teviothead** *Borders, Scot.*
314 G4 **Tewel** *Abers., Scot.*
110 E5 **Tewin** *Herts., Eng.*
228 F2 **Tewitfield** *Lancs., Eng.*
98 G2 **Tewkesbury** *Glos., Eng.*
22 D11 **Texa** *i. Scot.*
62 E3 **Teynham** *Kent, Eng.*
222 D1 **Thackley** *W. Yorks., Eng.*
314 F4 **Thainston** *Abers., Scot.*
314 F3 **Thainstone** *Abers., Scot.*
58 D3 **Thakeham** *W. Sussex, Eng.*
102 F4 **Thame** *Oxon, Eng.*
26 J4 **Thame** *r. Eng.*
26 N5 **Thames** *est. Eng.*
26 M5 **Thames** *r. Eng.*
78 D1 **Thames Ditton** *Surr., Eng.*
Thamesdown *admin. div. Eng. see* **Swindon**
116 F4 **Thames Haven** *Thurrock, Eng.*
74 E2 **Thamesmead** *Gtr Lon., Eng.*
26 O5 **Thanet, Isle of** *pen. Eng.*
62 G3 **Thanington** *Kent, Eng.*
268 E3 **Thankerton** *S. Lanark., Scot.*
166 G3 **Tharston** *Norf., Eng.*
82 C3 **Thatcham** *W. Berks., Eng.*
190 E3 **Thatto Heath** *Merseyside, Eng.*
116 E2 **Thaxted** *Essex, Eng.*
216 E2 **Theakston** *N. Yorks., Eng.*
170 C2 **Thealby** *N. Lincs., Eng.*
94 H3 **Theale** *Som., Eng.*
82 D3 **Theale** *W. Berks., Eng.*
124 F4 **The Apes Hall** *Cambs., Eng.*
210 F4 **Thearne** *E. Riding, Eng.*
140 A3 **The Bage** *Here., Eng.*
304 G4 **The Balloch** *Perth and Kin., Scot.*
314 F2 **The Banking** *Abers., Scot.*
58 D2 **The Bar** *W. Sussex, Eng.*
388 J4 **The Battery** *Ballymena, N. Ire.*
132 B2 **The Belfry** *Warks., Eng.*
120 I3 **Theberton** *Suff., Eng.*
314 F3 **The Birks** *Abers., Scot.*
144 C4 **The Bog** *Shrop., Eng.*
78 B2 **The Bourne** *Surr., Eng.*
148 B5 **The Bratch** *Staffs., Eng.*
140 C2 **The Broad** *Here., Eng.*
26 P2 **The Broads** *nat. park Eng.*
339 C2 **The Bryn** *Mon., Wales*
136 D2 **The Burf** *Worcs., Eng.*
314 F4 **The Burn** *Abers., Scot.*
402 J3 **The Bush** *Dungannon, N. Ire.*
94 J3 **The Butts** *Som., Eng.*
24 L5 **The Calf** *hill Eng.*
98 G3 **The Camp** *Glos., Eng.*
110 D5 **The Camp** *Herts., Eng.*
378 I4 **The Chequer** *Wrex., Wales*
24 M3 **The Cheviot** *hill Eng.*
154 C2 **The Chuckery** *W. Mids, Eng.*
106 C5 **The City** *Bucks., Eng.*
120 I2 **The City** *Suff., Eng.*
396 E4 **The Cluster** *Armagh, N. Ire.*
86 D2 **The Common** *Wilts., Eng.*
86 F5 **The Common** *Wilts., Eng.*
144 D5 **The Corner** *Shrop., Eng.*
388 H2 **The Craigs** *Ballymoney, N. Ire.*
405 C2 **The Cronk** Isle of Man
52 F4 **Thedden Grange** *Hants., Eng.*
162 E4 **Theddingworth** *Leics., Eng.*
170 H3 **Theddlethorpe All Saints** *Lincs., Eng.*
170 H3 **Theddlethorpe St Helen** *Lincs., Eng.*
154 C2 **The Delves** *W. Mids, Eng.*
264 F2 **The Den** *N. Ayr., Scot.*
402 K3 **The Diamond** *Cookstown, N. Ire.*
402 F3 **The Diamond** *Omagh, N. Ire.*
58 H3 **The Dicker** *E. Sussex, Eng.*
144 F4 **The Down** *Shrop., Eng.*
388 H2 **The Drones** *Ballymoney, N. Ire.*
308 D2 **The Drums** *Angus, Scot.*
98 D3 **The Eaves** *Glos., Eng.*
22 □M1 **The Faither** *stack Scot.*
26 L2 **The Fens** *reg. Eng.*
402 E4 **The Fingerpost** *Omagh, N. Ire.*
232 F2 **The Flatt** *Cumbria, Eng.*
110 D5 **The Folly** *Herts., Eng.*
140 B2 **The Forge** *Here., Eng.*
58 H2 **The Forstal** *E. Sussex, Eng.*
62 F4 **The Forstal** *Kent, Eng.*
22 H12 **The Glenkens** *val. Scot.*
144 C2 **The Grange** *Shrop., Eng.*
78 F2 **The Grange** *Surr., Eng.*
232 C7 **The Green** *Cumbria, Eng.*
116 F2 **The Green** *Essex, Eng.*
166 F1 **The Green** *Norf., Eng.*
86 B5 **The Green** *Wilts., Eng.*
300 □ **The Green** *Arg. and B., Scot.*
378 G2 **The Green** *Flints., Wales*
136 D3 **The Grove** *Worcs., Eng.*
58 D2 **The Haven** *W. Sussex, Eng.*
236 H3 **The Headland** *Hartlepool, Eng.*
166 G2 **The Heath** *Norf., Eng.*
148 D3 **The Heath** *Staffs., Eng.*
350 F4 **The Herberts** *V. of Glam., Wales*
78 E2 **The Hermitage** *Surr., Eng.*
232 C7 **The Hill** *Cumbria, Eng.*
216 D2 **The Holme** *N. Yorks., Eng.*
405 B3 **The Howe** Isle of Man
74 C2 **The Hyde** *Gtr Lon., Eng.*
144 D3 **The Isle** *Shrop., Eng.*
62 C4 **The Knowle** *Kent, Eng.*
166 H3 **The Laurels** *Norf., Eng.*
62 E4 **The Leacon** *Kent, Eng.*
106 D4 **The Lee** *Bucks., Eng.*
98 F2 **The Leigh** *Glos., Eng.*
405 D1 **The Lhen** Isle of Man
120 E2 **Thelnetham** *Suff., Eng.*
300 F3 **The Lodge** *Arg. and B., Scot.*
388 J6 **The Long Kesh** *Lisburn, N. Ire.*
26 G2 **The Long Mynd** *hills Eng.*
402 K2 **The Loup** *Cookstown, N. Ire.*
166 G4 **Thelveton** *Norf., Eng.*
190 F3 **Thelwall** *Warr., Eng.*
22 H13 **The Machars** *reg. Scot.*
23 K3 **The Maidens** *is N. Ire.*
184 F3 **The Marsh** *Cheshire East, Eng.*
366 G3 **The Marsh** *Powys, Wales*
166 F2 **Themelthorpe** *Norf., Eng.*
22 D6 **The Minch** *sea chan. Scot.*
124 E6 **The Moor** *Cambs., Eng.*
58 J3 **The Moor** *E. Sussex, Eng.*
62 D4 **The Moor** *Kent, Eng.*
350 B3 **The Mumbles** *Swansea, Wales*
268 A2 **The Murray** *S. Lanark., Scot.*
98 G1 **The Mythe** *Glos., Eng.*
339 D2 **The Narth** *Mon., Wales*
26 O4 **The Naze** *pt Eng.*
26 I6 **The Needles** *stack Eng.*
128 B5 **Thenford** *Northants., Eng.*
110 D4 **The Node** *Herts., Eng.*
22 K4 **The North Sound** *sea chan. Scot.*
22 D11 **The Oa** *pen. Scot.*
86 D3 **Theobald's Green** *Wilts., Eng.*
24 K5 **The Old Man of Coniston** *hill Eng.*
322 J3 **The Polchar** *High., Scot.*
62 E4 **The Quarter** *Kent, Eng.*
98 G2 **The Reddings** *Glos., Eng.*
110 E3 **Therfield** *Herts., Eng.*
358 E3 **The Rhos** *Pembs., Wales*
22 F13 **The Rinns of Galloway** *pen. Scot.*
402 I3 **The Rock** *Cookstown, N. Ire.*
62 C3 **The Rocks** *Kent, Eng.*
148 B2 **The Rookery** *Staffs., Eng.*
148 B3 **The Rowe** *Staffs., Eng.*
110 D5 **The Ryde** *Herts., Eng.*
148 E4 **The Sale** *Staffs., Eng.*
78 B2 **The Sands** *Surr., Eng.*
388 J3 **The Sheddings** *Ballymena, N. Ire.*
86 B3 **The Shoe** *Wilts., Eng.*
388 E4 **The Six Towns** *Magherafelt, N. Ire.*
82 C3 **The Slade** *W. Berks., Eng.*
144 F4 **The Smithies** *Shrop., Eng.*
22 □L2 **The Sneug** *hill Scot.*
26 J6 **The Solent** *str. Eng.*
396 I3 **The Spa** *Down, N. Ire.*
62 E4 **The Stocks** *Kent, Eng.*
86 C3 **The Stocks** *Wilts., Eng.*
22 D7 **The Storr** *hill Scot.*
26 N5 **The Swale** *sea chan. Eng.*
110 B6 **The Swillett** *Herts., Eng.*
26 N3 **Thet** *r. Eng.*
388 K6 **The Temple** *Lisburn, N. Ire.*
170 D7 **Thetford** *Lincs., Eng.*
166 D4 **Thetford** *Norf., Eng.*
110 E3 **The Thrift** *Herts., Eng.*
232 E4 **Thethwaite** *Cumbria, Eng.*
22 H10 **The Trossachs** *hills Scot.*
140 C3 **The Vauld** *Here., Eng.*
26 M2 **The Wash** *b. Eng.*
26 M5 **The Weald** *reg. Eng.*
378 G3 **The Wern** *Wrex., Wales*
74 C3 **The Wrythe** *Gtr Lon., Eng.*
144 F4 **The Wyke** *Shrop., Eng.*
116 C3 **Theydon Bois** *Essex, Eng.*
116 C3 **Theydon Garnon** *Essex, Eng.*
116 C3 **Theydon Mount** *Essex, Eng.*
86 B3 **Thickwood** *Wilts., Eng.*
170 F4 **Thimbleby** *Lincs., Eng.*
216 F1 **Thimbleby** *N. Yorks., Eng.*
86 C3 **Thingley** *Wilts., Eng.*
190 C3 **Thingwall** *Merseyside, Eng.*
216 F2 **Thirkleby** *N. Yorks., Eng.*
216 F2 **Thirlby** *N. Yorks., Eng.*
256 H2 **Thirlestane** *Borders, Scot.*
24 K4 **Thirlmere** *resr Eng.*
216 E2 **Thirn** *N. Yorks., Eng.*
216 E2 **Thirsk** *N. Yorks., Eng.*
244 G4 **Thirston New Houses** *Northumb., Eng.*
210 G4 **Thirtleby** *E. Riding, Eng.*
228 E3 **Thistleton** *Lancs., Eng.*
162 H2 **Thistleton** *Rutland, Eng.*
120 B2 **Thistley Green** *Suff., Eng.*
216 G2 **Thixendale** *N. Yorks., Eng.*
244 E5 **Thockrington** *Northumb., Eng.*
124 E3 **Tholomas Drove** *Cambs., Eng.*
358 F3 **Thomas Chapel** *Pembs., Wales*
232 E4 **Thomas Close** *Cumbria, Eng.*
314 E2 **Thomastown** *Abers., Scot.*
166 D3 **Thompson** *Norf., Eng.*
402 E5 **Thompson's Bridge** *Fermanagh, N. Ire.*
314 D2 **Thomshill** *Moray, Scot.*
62 C2 **Thong** *Kent, Eng.*
222 D3 **Thongsbridge** *W. Yorks., Eng.*
216 D2 **Thoralby** *N. Yorks., Eng.*
176 C3 **Thoresby** *Notts., Eng.*
170 H4 **Thoresthorpe** *Lincs., Eng.*
170 E3 **Thoresway** *Lincs., Eng.*
170 E3 **Thorganby** *Lincs., Eng.*
216 G3 **Thorganby** *N. Yorks., Eng.*
216 G1 **Thorgill** *N. Yorks., Eng.*
120 I3 **Thorington** *Suff., Eng.*
120 E5 **Thorington Street** *Suff., Eng.*
216 C3 **Thorlby** *N. Yorks., Eng.*
110 F4 **Thorley** *Herts., Eng.*
110 F4 **Thorley Houses** *Herts., Eng.*
110 F4 **Thorley Street** *Herts., Eng.*
52 D6 **Thorley Street** *I.o.W., Eng.*
216 F2 **Thormanby** *N. Yorks., Eng.*
236 H4 **Thornaby-on-Tees** *Stockton, Eng.*
166 F1 **Thornage** *Norf., Eng.*
106 C3 **Thornborough** *Bucks., Eng.*
216 E2 **Thornborough** *N. Yorks., Eng.*
216 E2 **Thornbrough** *N. Yorks., Eng.*
40 D2 **Thornbury** *Devon, Eng.*
140 D2 **Thornbury** *Here., Eng.*
98 D4 **Thornbury** *S. Glos., Eng.*
222 D2 **Thornbury** *W. Yorks., Eng.*
128 C3 **Thornby** *Northants., Eng.*
222 D3 **Thorncliff** *W. Yorks., Eng.*
148 D2 **Thorncliffe** *Staffs., Eng.*
46 B3 **Thorncombe** *Dorset, Eng.*
78 C2 **Thorncombe Street** *Surr., Eng.*
110 D3 **Thorncote Green** *Central Bedfordshire, Eng.*
52 D7 **Thorncross** *I.o.W., Eng.*
120 F3 **Thorndon** *Suff., Eng.*
40 D2 **Thorndon Cross** *Devon, Eng.*
208 G2 **Thorne** *S. Yorks., Eng.*
222 F1 **Thorner** *W. Yorks., Eng.*
148 D5 **Thornes** *Staffs., Eng.*
222 E2 **Thornes** *W. Yorks., Eng.*
94 E5 **Thorne St Margaret** *Som., Eng.*
106 F5 **Thorney** *Bucks., Eng.*
176 E3 **Thorney** *Notts., Eng.*
124 D3 **Thorney** *Peterb., Eng.*
94 H4 **Thorney** *Som., Eng.*
236 G2 **Thorney Close** *T. and W., Eng.*
52 B6 **Thorney Hill** *Hants., Eng.*
176 C5 **Thorneywood** *Notts., Eng.*
46 D2 **Thornford** *Dorset, Eng.*
244 D6 **Thorngrafton** *Northumb., Eng.*
94 G4 **Thorngrove** *Som., Eng.*
210 G4 **Thorngumbald** *E. Riding, Eng.*
166 C1 **Thornham** *Norf., Eng.*

Thornham Magna to Tullintrain

120 F3 Thornham Magna Suff., Eng.
120 F3 Thornham Parva Suff., Eng.
124 B3 Thornhaugh Peterb., Eng.
232 A6 Thornhill Cumbria, Eng.
180 C2 Thornhill Derbys., Eng.
52 E5 Thornhill Soton, Eng.
222 E3 Thornhill W. Yorks., Eng.
252 E2 Thornhill D. and G., Scot.
296 F4 Thornhill Stir., Scot.
350 G3 Thornhill Cardiff, Wales
222 E2 Thornhill Lees W. Yorks., Eng.
222 D2 Thornhills W. Yorks., Eng.
210 G2 Thornholme E. Riding, Eng.
46 F3 Thornicombe Dorset, Eng.
236 E3 Thornley Durham, Eng.
236 G3 Thornley Durham, Eng.
244 D6 Thornley Gate Northumb., Eng.
276 E3 Thornliebank E. Renf., Scot.
276 D3 Thornly Park Renf., Scot.
314 G2 Thornroan Abers., Scot.
120 C3 Thorns Suff., Eng.
180 B2 Thornsett Derbys., Eng.
180 D3 Thorns Green Gtr Man., Eng.
388 H3 Thornstown Magherafelt, N. Ire.
232 C5 Thornthwaite Cumbria, Eng.
106 C2 Thornton Bucks., Eng.
210 C3 Thornton E. Riding, Eng.
228 D3 Thornton Lancs., Eng.
162 D3 Thornton Leics., Eng.
176 F4 Thornton Lincs., Eng.
190 C2 Thornton Merseyside, Eng.
244 E1 Thornton Northumb., Eng.
222 C2 Thornton W. Yorks., Eng.
308 E3 Thornton Angus, Scot.
292 F2 Thornton Fife, Scot.
304 I3 Thornton Perth and Kin., Scot.
358 D3 Thornton Pembs., Wales
216 E2 Thornton Bridge N. Yorks., Eng.
170 D2 Thornton Curtis N. Lincs., Eng.
216 G2 Thornton Dale N. Yorks., Eng.
268 A2 Thorntonhall S. Lanark., Scot.
74 D3 Thornton Heath Gtr Lon., Eng.
190 C4 Thornton Hough Merseyside, Eng.
216 B2 Thornton in Lonsdale N. Yorks., Eng.
216 E2 Thornton-le-Beans N. Yorks., Eng.
170 D3 Thornton le Moor Lincs., Eng.
184 B2 Thornton-le-Moors Cheshire West & Chester, Eng.
216 E2 Thornton-le-Street N. Yorks., Eng.
288 I3 Thorntonloch E. Lothian, Scot.
244 E1 Thornton Park Northumb., Eng.
216 C2 Thornton Rust N. Yorks., Eng.
216 D2 Thornton Steward N. Yorks., Eng.
216 E2 Thornton Watlass N. Yorks., Eng.
116 C3 Thornwood Essex, Eng.
314 F4 Thornyhill Abers., Scot.
256 G3 Thornylee Borders, Scot.
176 D5 Thoroton Notts., Eng.
222 F1 Thorp Arch W. Yorks., Eng.
180 C4 Thorpe Derbys., Eng.
210 F3 Thorpe E. Riding, Eng.
170 H4 Thorpe Lincs., Eng.
166 I3 Thorpe Norf., Eng.
176 D4 Thorpe Notts., Eng.
216 D2 Thorpe N. Yorks., Eng.
78 C1 Thorpe Surr., Eng.
166 G4 Thorpe Abbotts Norf., Eng.
162 D2 Thorpe Acre Leics., Eng.
162 F2 Thorpe Arnold Leics., Eng.
222 G3 Thorpe Audlin W. Yorks., Eng.
216 G2 Thorpe Bassett N. Yorks., Eng.
116 G4 Thorpe Bay Southend, Eng.
162 G3 Thorpe by Water Rutland, Eng.
148 F4 Thorpe Constantine Staffs., Eng.
170 H5 Thorpe Culvert Lincs., Eng.
166 H3 Thorpe End Norf., Eng.
216 E2 Thorpefield N. Yorks., Eng.
116 I2 Thorpe Green Essex, Eng.
228 G4 Thorpe Green Lancs., Eng.
120 D4 Thorpe Green Suff., Eng.
78 C1 Thorpe Green Surr., Eng.
166 G3 Thorpe Hamlet Norf., Eng.
208 D3 Thorpe Hesley S. Yorks., Eng.
208 F2 Thorpe in Balne S. Yorks., Eng.
170 C4 Thorpe in the Fallows Lincs., Eng.
162 F3 Thorpe Langton Leics., Eng.
236 G4 Thorpe Larches Durham, Eng.
78 C1 Thorpe Lea Surr., Eng.
116 I2 Thorpe-le-Soken Essex, Eng.
210 D3 Thorpe le Street E. Riding, Eng.
128 E3 Thorpe Malsor Northants., Eng.
128 B5 Thorpe Mandeville Northants., Eng.
166 G1 Thorpe Market Norf., Eng.
120 E4 Thorpe Morieux Suff., Eng.
120 I3 Thorpeness Suff., Eng.
170 C4 Thorpe on the Hill Lincs., Eng.
222 E2 Thorpe on the Hill W. Yorks., Eng.
166 E3 Thorpe Row Norf., Eng.
166 H3 Thorpe St Andrew Norf., Eng.
208 E4 Thorpe Salvin S. Yorks., Eng.
162 F2 Thorpe Satchville Leics., Eng.
170 H5 Thorpe St Peter Lincs., Eng.
120 E2 Thorpe Street Suff., Eng.
236 G4 Thorpe Thewles Stockton, Eng.
170 E5 Thorpe Tilney Dales Lincs., Eng.
128 D3 Thorpe Underwood Northants., Eng.
216 F2 Thorpe Underwood N. Yorks., Eng.
128 G3 Thorpe Waterville Northants., Eng.
216 F3 Thorpe Willoughby N. Yorks., Eng.
166 B3 Thorpland Norf., Eng.
116 I2 Thorrington Essex, Eng.
40 F2 Thorverton Devon, Eng.
128 F3 Thrapston Northants., Eng.
232 C4 Threapland Cumbria, Eng.
184 B3 Threapwood Cheshire West & Chester, Eng.
148 D3 Threapwood Head Staffs., Eng.
94 I3 Three Ashes Som., Eng.
58 E2 Three Bridges W. Sussex, Eng.
36 D3 Three Burrows Corn., Eng.
58 H4 Three Chimneys Kent, Eng.
366 F6 Three Cocks Powys, Wales
350 B3 Three Crosses Swansea, Wales
58 H3 Three Cups Corner E. Sussex, Eng.
36 F2 Three Hammers Corn., Eng.
166 A3 Three Holes Norf., Eng.
170 D6 Threekingham Lincs., Eng.
58 I2 Three Leg Cross E. Sussex, Eng.
46 H2 Three Legged Cross Dorset, Eng.
82 E3 Three Mile Cross W'ham, Eng.
36 D3 Threemilestone Corn., Eng.
58 J3 Three Oaks E. Sussex, Eng.
232 D5 Threlkeld Cumbria, Eng.
116 D3 Threshers Bush Essex, Eng.
216 C2 Threshfield N. Yorks., Eng.
166 D3 Threxton Hill Norf., Eng.
308 D3 Thriepley Angus, Scot.
166 I3 Thrigby Norf., Eng.
236 C4 Thringarth Durham, Eng.
162 C2 Thringstone Leics., Eng.
124 E6 Thriplow Cambs., Eng.
208 E3 Throapham S. Yorks., Eng.
124 D3 Throckenholt Cambs., Eng.
110 E4 Throcking Herts., Eng.
236 E2 Throckley T. and W., Eng.
136 E3 Throckmorton Worcs., Eng.
46 F3 Throop Dorset, Eng.
244 G4 Throphill Northumb., Eng.
244 F4 Thropton Northumb., Eng.
98 G3 Througham Glos., Eng.
40 E2 Throwleigh Devon, Eng.
62 F3 Throwley Kent, Eng.
116 E2 Throws Essex, Eng.
176 B5 Thrumpton Notts., Eng.
176 D3 Thrumpton Notts., Eng.
320 K2 Thrumster High., Scot.
170 F2 Thrunscoe N.E. Lincs., Eng.
244 F3 Thrunton Northumb., Eng.
98 F3 Thrupp Glos., Eng.
102 B4 Thrupp Oxon, Eng.
102 D3 Thrupp Oxon, Eng.
216 D2 Thruscross N. Yorks., Eng.
40 D2 Thrushelton Devon, Eng.
162 E2 Thrussington Leics., Eng.
52 C3 Thruxton Hants., Eng.
140 C3 Thruxton Here., Eng.
208 E3 Thrybergh S. Yorks., Eng.
180 E5 Thulston Derbys., Eng.
222 D3 Thunder Bridge W. Yorks., Eng.
264 B2 Thundergay N. Ayr., Scot.
116 F4 Thundersley Essex, Eng.
314 H2 Thunderton Abers., Scot.
110 E4 Thundridge Herts., Eng.
162 E2 Thurcaston Leics., Eng.
208 E3 Thurcroft S. Yorks., Eng.
36 F1 Thurdon Corn., Eng.
166 G1 Thurgarton Norf., Eng.
176 D4 Thurgarton Notts., Eng.
208 C2 Thurgoland S. Yorks., Eng.
162 D3 Thurlaston Leics., Eng.
132 E3 Thurlaston Warks., Eng.
94 F5 Thurlbear Som., Eng.
170 C5 Thurlby Lincs., Eng.
170 D7 Thurlby Lincs., Eng.
170 H4 Thurlby Lincs., Eng.
110 C2 Thurleigh Bedford, Eng.
40 E4 Thurlestone Devon, Eng.
94 F4 Thurloxton Som., Eng.
208 C2 Thurlstone S. Yorks., Eng.
166 I3 Thurlton Norf., Eng.
184 F3 Thurlwood Cheshire East, Eng.
162 E2 Thurmaston Leics., Eng.
162 E3 Thurnby Leics., Eng.
166 I2 Thurne Norf., Eng.
62 D3 Thurnham Kent, Eng.
166 F2 Thurning Norf., Eng.
128 G3 Thurning Northants., Eng.
208 E2 Thurnscoe S. Yorks., Eng.
116 E4 Thurrock admin. div. Eng.
232 D3 Thursby Cumbria, Eng.
228 J4 Thursden Lancs., Eng.
166 E1 Thursford Norf., Eng.
78 B3 Thursley Surr., Eng.
320 J2 Thurso High., Scot.
22 I5 Thurso r. Scot.
22 I5 Thurso Bay b. Scot.
190 C3 Thurstaston Merseyside, Eng.
120 D3 Thurston Suff., Eng.
198 E2 Thurston Clough Gtr Man., Eng.
232 D3 Thurstonfield Cumbria, Eng.
222 D3 Thurstonland W. Yorks., Eng.
120 D3 Thurston Planch Suff., Eng.
166 H3 Thurton Norf., Eng.
180 C5 Thurvaston Derbys., Eng.
180 D5 Thurvaston Derbys., Eng.
166 E3 Thuxton Norf., Eng.
216 C1 Thwaite N. Yorks., Eng.
120 F3 Thwaite Suff., Eng.
232 D7 Thwaite Head Cumbria, Eng.
222 C1 Thwaites W. Yorks., Eng.
222 C1 Thwaites Brow W. Yorks., Eng.
166 H4 Thwaite St Mary Norf., Eng.
210 F2 Thwing E. Riding, Eng.
304 I4 Tibbermore Perth and Kin., Scot.
98 E2 Tibberton Glos., Eng.
144 F3 Tibberton Telford, Eng.
136 E2 Tibberton Worcs., Eng.
256 E4 Tibbie Shiels Inn Borders, Scot.
166 F4 Tibenham Norf., Eng.
300 D3 Tibertich Arg. and B., Scot.
180 E4 Tibshelf Derbys., Eng.
210 E3 Tibthorpe E. Riding, Eng.
58 I2 Ticehurst E. Sussex, Eng.
52 E4 Tichborne Hants., Eng.
162 H2 Tickencote Rutland, Eng.
94 H2 Tickenham N. Som., Eng.
106 D2 Tickford End M.K., Eng.
208 F3 Tickhill S. Yorks., Eng.
144 D4 Ticklerton Shrop., Eng.
180 E6 Ticknall Derbys., Eng.
210 F3 Tickton E. Riding, Eng.
154 C3 Tidbury Green W. Mids, Eng.
86 F4 Tidcombe Wilts., Eng.
102 E4 Tiddington Oxon, Eng.
132 B4 Tiddington Warks., Eng.
86 B3 Tiddleywink Wilts., Eng.
58 H2 Tidebrook E. Sussex, Eng.
36 G2 Tideford Corn., Eng.
36 F2 Tideford Cross Corn., Eng.
98 D4 Tidenham Glos., Eng.
98 D3 Tidenham Chase Glos., Eng.
180 C3 Tideswell Derbys., Eng.
82 D3 Tidmarsh W. Berks., Eng.
132 C5 Tidmington Warks., Eng.
52 A5 Tidpit Hants., Eng.
86 F4 Tidworth Wilts., Eng.
358 D3 Tiers Cross Pembs., Wales
128 D5 Tiffield Northants., Eng.
314 F2 Tifty Abers., Scot.
308 F2 Tigerton Angus, Scot.
322 D5 Tighachnoic High., Scot.
304 G5 Tighnablair Perth and Kin., Scot.
300 E4 Tighnabruaich Arg. and B., Scot.
40 E3 Tigley Devon, Eng.
124 B5 Tilbrook Cambs., Eng.
116 E5 Tilbury Thurrock, Eng.
116 F1 Tilbury Green Essex, Eng.
388 J4 Tildarg Ballymena, N. Ire.
154 D3 Tile Cross W. Mids, Eng.
116 D3 Tilegate Green Essex, Eng.
154 E3 Tile Hill W. Mids, Eng.
82 D3 Tilehurst Reading, Eng.
78 B2 Tilford Surr., Eng.
58 E2 Tilgate W. Sussex, Eng.
58 E2 Tilgate Forest Row W. Sussex, Eng.
24 M2 Till r. Eng.
314 E2 Tillathrowie Abers., Scot.
98 E2 Tillers' Green Glos., Eng.
144 D2 Tilley Shrop., Eng.
292 B3 Tillicoultry Clack., Scot.
268 C2 Tillietudlem S. Lanark., Scot.
116 H3 Tillingham Essex, Eng.
140 C3 Tillington Here., Eng.
58 C3 Tillington W. Sussex, Eng.
140 C3 Tillington Common Here., Eng.
308 F2 Tillyarblet Angus, Scot.
314 F3 Tillybirloch Abers., Scot.
314 G3 Tillycorthie Abers., Scot.
314 G2 Tillyfar Abers., Scot.
314 F3 Tillyfour Abers., Scot.
314 F3 Tillyfourie Abers., Scot.
314 G3 Tillygreig Abers., Scot.
314 E3 Tillypronie Abers., Scot.
62 H3 Tilmanstone Kent, Eng.
176 D2 Tiln Notts., Eng.
166 A2 Tilney All Saints Norf., Eng.
166 A2 Tilney Fen End Norf., Eng.
166 A2 Tilney High End Norf., Eng.
166 A2 Tilney St Lawrence Norf., Eng.
86 D4 Tilshead Wilts., Eng.
144 D2 Tilstock Shrop., Eng.
184 C3 Tilston Cheshire West & Chester, Eng.
184 D3 Tilstone Bank Cheshire West & Chester, Eng.
184 D3 Tilstone Fearnall Cheshire West & Chester, Eng.
110 B4 Tilsworth Central Bedfordshire, Eng.
22 I9 Tilt r. Scot.
162 F3 Tilton on the Hill Leics., Eng.
208 F2 Tilts S. Yorks., Eng.
98 F3 Tiltups End Glos., Eng.
116 D2 Tilty Essex, Eng.
170 E5 Timberland Lincs., Eng.
170 E5 Timberland Dales Lincs., Eng.
184 G3 Timbersbrook Cheshire East, Eng.
94 D3 Timberscombe Som., Eng.
216 D3 Timble N. Yorks., Eng.
198 D3 Timperley Gtr Man., Eng.
94 J3 Timsbury B. and N.E. Som., Eng.
52 C4 Timsbury Hants., Eng.
326 C2 Timsgearraidh W. Isles, Scot.
120 D3 Timworth Suff., Eng.
120 D3 Timworth Green Suff., Eng.
46 F3 Tincleton Dorset, Eng.
232 G3 Tindale Cumbria, Eng.
236 E4 Tindale Crescent Durham, Eng.
116 E2 Tindon End Essex, Eng.
106 B3 Tingewick Bucks., Eng.
222 E2 Tingley W. Yorks., Eng.
110 B4 Tingrith Central Bedfordshire, Eng.
329 C3 Tingwall Orkney, Scot.
331 D3 Tingwall airport Scot.
222 E1 Tinshill W. Yorks., Eng.
208 D3 Tinsley S. Yorks., Eng.
58 F2 Tinsley Green W. Sussex, Eng.
36 E2 Tintagel Corn., Eng.
339 D2 Tintern Parva Mon., Wales
94 H5 Tintinhull Som., Eng.
24 J2 Tinto hill Scot.
180 B2 Tintwistle Derbys., Eng.
252 F2 Tinwald D. and G., Scot.
162 H3 Tinwell Rutland, Eng.
40 E1 Tippacott Devon, Eng.
314 F4 Tipperty Abers., Scot.
314 G3 Tipperty Abers., Scot.
124 F3 Tipps End Cambs., Eng.
52 C6 Tiptoe Hants., Eng.
154 B2 Tipton W. Mids, Eng.
116 G3 Tiptree Essex, Eng.
116 G3 Tiptree Heath Essex, Eng.
366 D6 Tirabad Powys, Wales
402 E5 Tiraroe Fermanagh, N. Ire.
402 G2 Tircur Omagh, N. Ire.
300 □ Tiree airport Scot.
22 C10 Tiree i. Scot.
22 C7 Tirga Mòr hill Scot.
388 F4 Tirgan Magherafelt, N. Ire.
98 F2 Tirley Glos., Eng.
350 G2 Tirphil Caerp., Wales
232 F5 Tirril Cumbria, Eng.
356 G3 Tir-y-dail Carmar., Wales
86 C5 Tisbury Wilts., Eng.
58 D2 Tisman's Common W. Sussex, Eng.
180 C4 Tissington Derbys., Eng.
40 C1 Titchberry Devon, Eng.
52 E5 Titchfield Hants., Eng.
128 G3 Titchmarsh Northants., Eng.
166 C1 Titchwell Norf., Eng.
176 D5 Tithby Notts., Eng.
140 B2 Titley Here., Eng.
244 F5 Titlington Northumb., Eng.
110 D4 Titmore Green Herts., Eng.
78 D2 Titsey Surr., Eng.
36 F1 Titson Corn., Eng.
148 B3 Tittensor Staffs., Eng.
166 D2 Tittleshall Norf., Eng.
22 D6 Tiumpan Head hd Scot.
184 C3 Tiverton Cheshire West & Chester, Eng.
40 F2 Tiverton Devon, Eng.
166 G4 Tivetshall St Margaret Norf., Eng.
166 G4 Tivetshall St Mary Norf., Eng.
154 B2 Tividale W. Mids, Eng.
94 C3 Tivington Som., Eng.
148 C4 Tixall Staffs., Eng.
162 H3 Tixover Rutland, Eng.
329 D4 Toab Orkney, Scot.
331 D4 Toab Shet., Scot.
120 J2 Toad Row Suff., Eng.
388 H2 Toberdoney Moyle, N. Ire.
388 H1 Toberkeagh Moyle, N. Ire.
388 F4 Tobermore Magherafelt, N. Ire.
300 B2 Tobermory Arg. and B., Scot.
300 D3 Toberonochy Arg. and B., Scot.
Tobha Mòr W. Isles, Scot. see Homore
326 D2 Tobson W. Isles, Scot.
314 F2 Tocher Abers., Scot.
86 D2 Tockenham Wilts., Eng.
86 D2 Tockenham Wick Wilts., Eng.
228 G4 Tockholes B'burn, Eng.
98 D4 Tockington S. Glos., Eng.
216 F3 Tockwith N. Yorks., Eng.
46 F2 Todber Dorset, Eng.
110 B4 Toddington Central Bedfordshire, Eng.
98 H2 Toddington Glos., Eng.
98 J1 Todenham Glos., Eng.
232 E3 Todhills Cumbria, Eng.
308 E3 Todhills Angus, Scot.
314 F3 Todlachie Abers., Scot.
222 B2 Todmorden W. Yorks., Eng.
208 E3 Todwick S. Yorks., Eng.
22 B7 Toe Head hd Scot.
124 D5 Toft Cambs., Eng.
170 D7 Toft Lincs., Eng.
331 D2 Toft Shet., Scot.
320 K2 Toftcarl High., Scot.
236 E4 Toft Hill Durham, Eng.
166 I4 Toft Monks Norf., Eng.
170 D3 Toft next Newton Lincs., Eng.
166 D2 Toftrees Norf., Eng.
320 K2 Tofts High., Scot.
166 E3 Toftwood Norf., Eng.
244 H4 Togston Northumb., Eng.
322 D3 Tokavaig High., Scot.
102 F6 Tokers Green Oxon, Eng.
74 C2 Tokyngton Gtr Lon., Eng.
326 F1 Tolastadh W. Isles, Scot.
326 D2 Tolastadh a' Chaolais W. Isles, Scot.
326 F1 Tolastadh Ùr W. Isles, Scot.
94 E4 Tolland Som., Eng.
46 G2 Tollard Farnham Dorset, Eng.
86 C6 Tollard Royal Wilts., Eng.
208 F2 Toll Bar S. Yorks., Eng.
132 D3 Tollbar End Warks., Eng.
276 E2 Tollcross Glas., Scot.
154 B2 Toll End W. Mids, Eng.
46 C3 Toller Down Gate Dorset, Eng.
46 D3 Toller Fratrum Dorset, Eng.
46 D3 Toller Porcorum Dorset, Eng.
176 C5 Tollerton Notts., Eng.
216 F2 Tollerton N. Yorks., Eng.
46 C3 Toller Whelme Dorset, Eng.
116 H3 Tollesbury Essex, Eng.
116 G3 Tolleshunt D'Arcy Essex, Eng.
116 G3 Tolleshunt Knights Essex, Eng.
116 G3 Tolleshunt Major Essex, Eng.
314 H2 Toll of Birness Abers., Scot.
326 D3 Tolmachan W. Isles, Scot.
46 F3 Tolpuddle Dorset, Eng.
22 D6 Tolsta Head hd Scot.
322 J3 Tolvah High., Scot.
74 C3 Tolworth Gtr Lon., Eng.
326 E2 Tom an Fhuadain W. Isles, Scot.
322 J2 Tomatin High., Scot.
322 I2 Tombreck High., Scot.
Tom Chrasgaidh High., Scot. see Tomchrasky
322 G3 Tomchrasky High., Scot.
322 F3 Tomdoun High., Scot.
314 C2 Tomdow Moray, Scot.
320 G3 Tomich High., Scot.
322 G3 Tomich High., Scot.
314 C3 Tomintoul Moray, Scot.
314 E2 Tomnaven Moray, Scot.
314 D3 Tomnavoulin Moray, Scot.
62 B3 Tonbridge Kent, Eng.
350 E3 Tondu Bridg., Wales
26 G5 Tone r. Eng.
94 E5 Tonedale Som., Eng.
402 D4 Toneel Fermanagh, N. Ire.
372 F5 Tonfanau Gwynedd, Wales
62 D3 Tong Kent, Eng.
144 G4 Tong Shrop., Eng.
222 D2 Tong W. Yorks., Eng.
162 C2 Tonge Leics., Eng.
198 C2 Tonge Fold Gtr Man., Eng.
78 B2 Tongham Surr., Eng.
252 D3 Tongland D. and G., Scot.
144 G3 Tong Norton Shrop., Eng.
222 D1 Tong Park W. Yorks., Eng.
222 D2 Tong Street W. Yorks., Eng.
320 G2 Tongue High., Scot.
320 G2 Tongue House High., Scot.
350 G3 Tongwynlais Cardiff, Wales
350 D3 Tonmawr N.P.T., Wales
350 D3 Tonna N.P.T., Wales
402 F5 Tonnaboy Fermanagh, N. Ire.
350 F3 Ton Pentre R.C.T., Wales
350 F3 Ton-teg R.C.T., Wales
110 E4 Tonwell Herts., Eng.
402 F4 Tonyglaskan Fermanagh, N. Ire.
350 F3 Tonypandy R.C.T., Wales
350 H3 Ton-y-pistyll Caerp., Wales
350 F3 Tonyrefail R.C.T., Wales
402 E5 Tonyteige Fermanagh, N. Ire.
402 E5 Tonyvarnog Fermanagh, N. Ire.
388 H4 Toome Antrim, N. Ire.
102 D4 Toot Baldon Oxon, Eng.
116 D3 Toot Hill Essex, Eng.
52 D5 Toothill Hants., Eng.
86 E2 Toothill Swindon, Eng.
74 C3 Tooting Graveney Gtr Lon., Eng.
216 E2 Topcliffe N. Yorks., Eng.
166 G4 Topcroft Norf., Eng.
166 G4 Topcroft Street Norf., Eng.
110 C2 Top End Bedford, Eng.
208 F2 Topham S. Yorks., Eng.
198 D2 Top of Hebers Gtr Man., Eng.
228 G4 Top of Ramsgreave Lancs., Eng.
198 E2 Top o' th' Meadows Gtr Man., Eng.
116 F1 Toppesfield Essex, Eng.
198 C2 Toppings Gtr Man., Eng.
166 G3 Toprow Norf., Eng.
40 F2 Topsham Devon, Eng.
378 G3 Top-y-rhos Flints., Wales
300 A2 Torastan Arg. and B., Scot.
314 C3 Torbain Moray, Scot.
40 F3 Torbay admin. div. Eng.
26 E7 Tor Bay b. Eng.
314 D3 Torbeg Abers., Scot.
264 C3 Torbeg N. Ayr., Scot.
280 D4 Torbothie N. Lanark., Scot.
40 E4 Torcross Devon, Eng.
322 I2 Tordarroch High., Scot.
322 I2 Tore High., Scot.
314 C2 Toreduff Moray, Scot.
320 J3 Toremore High., Scot.
322 K2 Toremore High., Scot.
339 B2 Torfaen admin. div. Wales
198 E3 Torkington Gtr Man., Eng.
170 B4 Torksey Lincs., Eng.
326 B4 Torlum W. Isles, Scot.
322 F4 Torlundy High., Scot.
98 E4 Tormarton S. Glos., Eng.
300 A4 Tormisdale Arg. and B., Scot.
264 B3 Tormore N. Ayr., Scot.
320 J2 Tormsdale High., Scot.
322 I2 Tornagrain High., Scot.
314 D3 Tornahaish Abers., Scot.
314 F3 Tornaveen Abers., Scot.
24 P6 Torne r. Eng.
322 H3 Torness High., Scot.
236 E3 Toronto Durham, Eng.
232 C4 Torpenhow Cumbria, Eng.
288 B3 Torphichen W. Lothian, Scot.
314 F3 Torphins Abers., Scot.
36 G2 Torpoint Corn., Eng.
40 F3 Torquay Torbay, Eng.
256 G2 Torquhan Borders, Scot.
388 J1 Torr Moyle, N. Ire.
300 D3 Torran Arg. and B., Scot.
320 H4 Torran High., Scot.
322 C2 Torran High., Scot.
276 E2 Torrance E. Dun., Scot.
268 B2 Torrance House S. Lanark., Scot.
314 D3 Torrancroy Abers., Scot.
94 D4 Torre Som., Eng.
40 F3 Torre Torbay, Eng.
26 D6 Torridge r. Eng.
322 E2 Torridon High., Scot.
22 E7 Torridon, Loch b. Scot.
322 C3 Torrin High., Scot.
300 D5 Torrisdale Arg. and B., Scot.
320 H2 Torrisdale High., Scot.
228 F2 Torrisholme Lancs., Eng.
314 G3 Torry Aberdeen, Scot.
314 E2 Torry Abers., Scot.
292 C3 Torryburn Fife, Scot.
256 G2 Torsonce Borders, Scot.
314 H2 Torterston Abers., Scot.
252 F2 Torthorwald D. and G., Scot.
58 C3 Tortington W. Sussex, Eng.
136 D1 Torton Worcs., Eng.
98 E4 Tortworth S. Glos., Eng.
322 C2 Torvaig High., Scot.
232 D6 Torver Cumbria, Eng.
280 C2 Torwood Falk., Scot.
176 C2 Torworth Notts., Eng.
40 C2 Tosberry Devon, Eng.
322 D2 Toscaig High., Scot.
124 C5 Toseland Cambs., Eng.
228 H2 Tosside Lancs., Eng.
120 E3 Tostock Suff., Eng.
322 A2 Totaig High., Scot.
300 □ Totamore Arg. and B., Scot.
320 H2 Totegan High., Scot.
58 B2 Tote Hill W. Sussex, Eng.
52 E4 Totford Hants., Eng.
116 G3 Totham Hill Essex, Eng.
116 G3 Totham Plains Essex, Eng.
170 G4 Tothill Lincs., Eng.
52 C6 Totland I.o.W., Eng.
208 C4 Totley S. Yorks., Eng.
208 C4 Totley Brook S. Yorks., Eng.
208 C4 Totley Rise S. Yorks., Eng.
40 E3 Totnes Devon, Eng.
176 B5 Toton Notts., Eng.
300 □ Totronald Arg. and B., Scot.
322 B2 Totscore High., Scot.
74 D2 Tottenham Gtr Lon., Eng.
74 D2 Tottenham Hale Gtr Lon., Eng.
166 B2 Tottenhill Norf., Eng.
166 B2 Tottenhill Row Norf., Eng.
106 D5 Totteridge Bucks., Eng.
74 C2 Totteridge Gtr Lon., Eng.
110 B4 Totternhoe Central Bedfordshire, Eng.
198 C2 Tottington Gtr Man., Eng.
166 D3 Tottington Norf., Eng.
228 H4 Tottleworth Lancs., Eng.
52 D5 Totton Hants., Eng.
82 F3 Touchen-End W. and M., Eng.
216 F3 Toulston N. Yorks., Eng.
94 F4 Toulton Som., Eng.
320 D4 Tournaig High., Scot.
26 K3 Tove r. Eng.
62 D3 Tovil Kent, Eng.
36 D3 Towan Cross Corn., Eng.
300 F4 Toward Arg. and B., Scot.
128 D5 Towcester Northants., Eng.
36 C3 Towednack Corn., Eng.
166 B2 Tower End Norf., Eng.
62 H4 Tower Hamlets Kent, Eng.
74 D2 Tower Hamlets met. bor. Gtr Lon., Eng.
388 C2 Tower Museum Derry, N. Ire.
102 F4 Towersey Oxon, Eng.
314 G2 Towie Abers., Scot.
314 D2 Towiemore Moray, Scot.
236 E3 Tow Law Durham, Eng.
106 C4 Town End Bucks., Eng.
124 E4 Town End Cambs., Eng.
232 E7 Town End Cumbria, Eng.
232 E7 Town End Cumbria, Eng.
190 E3 Town End Merseyside, Eng.
236 C3 Townfield Durham, Eng.
184 D2 Town Fields Cheshire West & Chester, Eng.
228 E5 Town Green Lancs., Eng.
166 H3 Town Green Norf., Eng.
208 B2 Townhead S. Yorks., Eng.
252 D3 Townhead D. and G., Scot.
252 E3 Townhead of Greenlaw D. and G., Scot.
292 D3 Townhill Fife, Scot.
350 C3 Townhill Swansea, Wales
236 G3 Town Kelloe Durham, Eng.
198 B3 Town of Lowton Gtr Man., Eng.
58 H2 Town Row E. Sussex, Eng.
106 C4 Townsend Bucks., Eng.
52 E3 Towns End Hants., Eng.
110 C5 Townsend Herts., Eng.
184 D3 Towns Green Cheshire West & Chester, Eng.
36 C3 Townshend Corn., Eng.
120 C2 Town Street Suff., Eng.
256 K3 Town Yetholm Borders, Scot.
210 E2 Towthorpe E. Riding, Eng.
216 F2 Towthorpe York, Eng.
216 F3 Towton N. Yorks., Eng.
378 D2 Towyn Conwy, Wales
170 G5 Toynton All Saints Lincs., Eng.
170 G5 Toynton Fen Side Lincs., Eng.
170 G5 Toynton St Peter Lincs., Eng.
62 A3 Toy's Hill Kent, Eng.
262 E4 Trabboch E. Ayr., Scot.
322 J2 Tradespark High., Scot.
329 D4 Tradespark Orkney, Scot.
Traeth Coch I.o.A., Wales see Red Wharf Bay
197 Trafford met. bor. Gtr Man., Eng.
198 D3 Trafford Park Gtr Man., Eng.
22 E11 Tràille, Rubha na pt Scot.
366 D7 Trallong Powys, Wales
350 C3 Trallwn Swansea, Wales
140 C4 Tram Inn Here., Eng.
339 B2 Tranch Torf., Wales
288 F3 Tranent E. Lothian, Scot.
190 C3 Tranmere Merseyside, Eng.
320 I2 Trantlebeg High., Scot.
244 G5 Tranwell Northumb., Eng.
356 G2 Trap Carmar., Wales
288 H3 Traprain E. Lothian, Scot.
132 A4 Trap's Green Warks., Eng.
184 F2 Trap Street Cheshire East, Eng.
256 F3 Traquair Borders, Scot.
228 J3 Trawden Lancs., Eng.
362 G2 Trawscoed Cere., Wales
372 G3 Trawsfynydd Gwynedd, Wales
372 G3 Trawsfynydd, Llyn resr Wales
350 F3 Trealaw R.C.T., Wales
228 E4 Treales Lancs., Eng.
371 B3 Trearddur I.o.A., Wales
322 B2 Treaslane High., Scot.
350 F4 Tre-Aubrey V. of Glam., Wales
350 F3 Trebanog R.C.T., Wales
350 C2 Trebanos N.P.T., Wales
36 F1 Trebarrow Corn., Eng.
36 E2 Trebetherick Corn., Eng.
331 D3 Trebister Shet., Scot.
94 E4 Treble's Holford Som., Eng.
350 C3 Tre-boeth Swansea, Wales
94 D4 Treborough Som., Eng.
36 E2 Trebudannon Corn., Eng.
36 F2 Trebullett Corn., Eng.
36 G2 Treburley Corn., Eng.
36 D2 Treburrick Corn., Eng.
36 E2 Trebyan Corn., Eng.
366 D7 Trecastle Powys, Wales
36 F2 Trecrogo Corn., Eng.
358 E2 Trecwn Pembs., Wales
350 F2 Trecynon R.C.T., Wales
36 C3 Tredavoe Corn., Eng.
358 D2 Treddiog Pembs., Wales
350 G2 Tredegar B. Gwent, Wales
98 G2 Tredington Glos., Eng.
132 C5 Tredington Warks., Eng.
36 F2 Tredinnick Corn., Eng.
350 F4 Tredogan V. of Glam., Wales
366 F7 Tredomen Powys, Wales
358 F1 Tredrissi Pembs., Wales
36 E2 Tredrizzick Corn., Eng.
339 C3 Tredunnock Mon., Wales
366 F7 Tredustan Powys, Wales
98 F2 Tredworth Glos., Eng.
36 G3 Treen Corn., Eng.
36 C3 Treen Corn., Eng.
36 E2 Treesmill Corn., Eng.
208 D3 Treeton S. Yorks., Eng.
358 D1 Trefasser Pembs., Wales
371 C3 Trefdraeth I.o.A., Wales
366 F7 Trefecca Powys, Wales
362 E3 Trefechan Cere., Wales
350 F2 Trefechan M. Tyd., Wales
366 D3 Trefeglwys Powys, Wales
362 F3 Trefenter Cere., Wales
358 E2 Treffgarne Pembs., Wales
Treffynnon Flints., Wales see Holywell
358 D2 Treffynnon Pembs., Wales
358 D2 Trefgarn Owen Pembs., Wales
350 G2 Trefil B. Gwent, Wales
362 F3 Trefilan Cere., Wales
358 D2 Trefin Pembs., Wales
144 B3 Treflach Shrop., Eng.
366 F2 Trefnanney Powys, Wales
378 F2 Trefnant Denb., Wales
144 B3 Trefonen Shrop., Eng.
372 E3 Trefor Gwynedd, Wales
371 C3 Trefor I.o.A., Wales
350 F3 Treforest R.C.T., Wales
350 G3 Treforest Industrial Estate R.C.T., Wales
378 C3 Trefriw Conwy, Wales
Tref-y-clawdd Powys, Wales see Knighton
Trefynwy Mon., Wales see Monmouth
36 F2 Tregadillett Corn., Eng.
339 C2 Tregare Mon., Wales
36 D3 Tregarne Corn., Eng.
362 G3 Tregaron Cere., Wales
372 F3 Tregarth Gwynedd, Wales
36 E3 Tregear Corn., Eng.
36 F2 Tregeare Corn., Eng.
378 F4 Tregeiriog Wrex., Wales
371 C2 Tregele I.o.A., Wales
36 D3 Tregidden Corn., Eng.
358 C2 Treglemais Pembs., Wales
36 E2 Tregolds Corn., Eng.
36 F2 Tregole Corn., Eng.
36 E2 Tregonetha Corn., Eng.
36 E2 Tregony Corn., Eng.
36 F2 Tregoodwell Corn., Eng.
366 F6 Tregoyd Powys, Wales
36 E3 Tregrehan Mills Corn., Eng.
362 E4 Tre-groes Cere., Wales
350 F4 Treguff V. of Glam., Wales
36 E2 Tregullon Corn., Eng.
36 D2 Tregurrian Corn., Eng.
366 F3 Tregynon Powys, Wales
350 F3 Trehafod R.C.T., Wales
350 G2 Treharris M. Tyd., Wales
350 E2 Treherbert R.C.T., Wales
350 F4 Tre-hill V. of Glam., Wales
22 G9 Treig, Loch l. Scot.
36 E2 Treknow Corn., Eng.
36 D3 Trelan Corn., Eng.
36 F1 Trelash Corn., Eng.
378 E2 Trelawnyd Flints., Wales
356 C2 Trelech Carmar., Wales
356 C2 Trelech a'r Betws Carmar., Wales
358 C2 Treleddyd-fawr Pembs., Wales
350 G2 Trelewis M. Tyd., Wales
36 E2 Treligga Corn., Eng.
36 E2 Trelights Corn., Eng.
36 E2 Trelill Corn., Eng.
36 D3 Trelissick Corn., Eng.
339 D2 Trelleck Mon., Wales
339 D2 Trelleck Grange Mon., Wales
378 F2 Trelogan Flints., Wales
36 F2 Trelowla Corn., Eng.
366 G3 Trelystan Powys, Wales
372 F3 Tremadog Gwynedd, Wales
26 D2 Tremadog Bay b. Wales
36 F2 Tremail Corn., Eng.
362 C4 Tremain Cere., Wales
36 F1 Tremaine Corn., Eng.
36 F2 Tremar Corn., Eng.
36 G2 Trematon Corn., Eng.
378 E2 Tremeirchion Denb., Wales
36 E2 Tremore Corn., Eng.
350 H4 Tremorfa Cardiff, Wales
36 D2 Trenance Corn., Eng.
36 E2 Trenance Corn., Eng.
36 E2 Trenarren Corn., Eng.
144 F3 Trench Telford, Eng.
378 H4 Trench Wrex., Wales
102 E6 Trench Green Oxon, Eng.
36 D2 Trencreek Corn., Eng.
36 D3 Trenear Corn., Eng.
36 F2 Treneglos Corn., Eng.
36 E2 Trengune Corn., Eng.
46 D2 Trent Dorset, Eng.
24 P6 Trent r. Eng.
Trent r. Eng. see Piddle
148 B3 Trentham Stoke, Eng.
40 E1 Trentishoe Devon, Eng.
170 B4 Trent Port Lincs., Eng.
148 B3 Trent Vale Stoke, Eng.
36 C3 Trenwheal Corn., Eng.
350 E4 Treoes V. of Glam., Wales
350 F3 Treorchy R.C.T., Wales
350 H2 Treowen Caerp., Wales
36 E2 Trequite Corn., Eng.
362 G1 Tre'r-ddol Cere., Wales
350 F4 Trerhyngyll V. of Glam., Wales
358 F1 Tre-Rhys Pembs., Wales
36 F2 Trerulefoot Corn., Eng.
362 C4 Tresaith Cere., Wales
26 □ Tresco i. Eng.
148 B5 Trescott Staffs., Eng.
36 C3 Trescowe Corn., Eng.
98 F4 Tresham Glos., Eng.
300 B2 Treshnish Arg. and B., Scot.
22 D10 Treshnish Isles is Scot.
36 E3 Tresillian Corn., Eng.
36 E2 Tresinney Corn., Eng.
358 D1 Tresinwen Pembs., Wales
36 F1 Treskinnick Cross Corn., Eng.
36 E3 Treslea Corn., Eng.
36 F2 Tresmeer Corn., Eng.
36 F1 Tresparrett Corn., Eng.
36 F1 Tresparrett Posts Corn., Eng.
304 G2 Tressait Perth and Kin., Scot.
331 C3 Tresta Shet., Scot.
331 E2 Tresta Shet., Scot.
176 E3 Treswell Notts., Eng.
36 C3 Trethewey Corn., Eng.
350 G3 Trethomas Caerp., Wales
36 E2 Trethurgy Corn., Eng.
358 C2 Tretio Pembs., Wales
140 C4 Tretire Here., Eng.
366 F7 Tretower Powys, Wales
378 G3 Treuddyn Flints., Wales
36 E1 Trevalga Corn., Eng.
378 H3 Trevalyn Wrex., Wales
36 C3 Trevarrack Corn., Eng.
36 D2 Trevarrian Corn., Eng.
36 E3 Trevarrick Corn., Eng.
356 C3 Trevaughan Carmar., Wales
356 E2 Tre-vaughan Carmar., Wales
36 E2 Treveighan Corn., Eng.
36 D3 Trevellas Corn., Eng.
36 F2 Trevelmond Corn., Eng.
36 D3 Trevenen Corn., Eng.
36 D3 Treverva Corn., Eng.
339 B2 Trevethin Torf., Wales
36 F2 Trevigro Corn., Eng.
36 E2 Treviscoe Corn., Eng.
36 E2 Trevone Corn., Eng.
378 G4 Trevor Wrex., Wales
26 B6 Trevose Head hd Eng.
36 E2 Trewalder Corn., Eng.
36 E2 Trewarmett Corn., Eng.
36 E3 Trewarthenick Corn., Eng.
36 B3 Trewellard Corn., Eng.
36 F2 Trewen Corn., Eng.
140 C4 Trewen Here., Eng.
36 D3 Trewennack Corn., Eng.
358 E4 Trewent Pembs., Wales
366 G2 Trewern Powys, Wales
358 F1 Trewilym Pembs., Wales
36 F2 Trewint Corn., Eng.
36 E3 Trewithian Corn., Eng.
36 E2 Trewoon Corn., Eng.
36 E3 Treworga Corn., Eng.
36 E3 Treworlas Corn., Eng.
339 C1 Tre-wyn Mon., Wales
36 D2 Treyarnon Corn., Eng.
58 B3 Treyford W. Sussex, Eng.
222 C2 Triangle W. Yorks., Eng.
46 H3 Trickett's Cross Dorset, Eng.
232 G3 Triermain Cumbria, Eng.
402 F4 Trillick Omagh, N. Ire.
236 G3 Trimdon Durham, Eng.
236 G3 Trimdon Colliery Durham, Eng.
236 G3 Trimdon Grange Durham, Eng.
166 H1 Trimingham Norf., Eng.
120 G5 Trimley Lower Street Suff., Eng.
120 G5 Trimley St Mary Suff., Eng.
120 G5 Trimley St Martin Suff., Eng.
136 D1 Trimpley Worcs., Eng.
356 E3 Trimsaran Carmar., Wales
304 F2 Trinafour Perth and Kin., Scot.
350 H2 Trinant Caerp., Wales
110 B5 Tring Herts., Eng.
408 E4 Trinity Jersey Channel Is
308 G2 Trinity Angus, Scot.
288 D3 Trinity Edin., Scot.
232 D7 Trinkeld Cumbria, Eng.
362 G2 Trisant Cere., Wales
94 C4 Triscombe Som., Eng.
94 E4 Triscombe Som., Eng.
36 D3 Trispen Corn., Eng.
244 G4 Tritlington Northumb., Eng.
304 I3 Trochry Perth and Kin., Scot.
362 D4 Troedyraur Cere., Wales
350 F2 Troedyrhiw M. Tyd., Wales
378 C2 Trofarth Conwy, Wales
22 H8 Tromie r. Scot.
331 D2 Trondavoe Shet., Scot.
26 E6 Troney r. Eng.
36 D3 Troon Corn., Eng.
262 D3 Troon S. Ayr., Scot.
402 E4 Trory Fermanagh, N. Ire.
326 B5 Trosairidh W. Isles, Scot.
23 J2 Trostan hill N. Ire.
120 D3 Troston Suff., Eng.
22 D7 Trotternish hills Scot.
308 E4 Trottick Dundee, Scot.
62 C3 Trottiscliffe Kent, Eng.
58 B3 Trotton W. Sussex, Eng.
244 D4 Troughend Northumb., Eng.
228 I4 Trough Gate Lancs., Eng.
22 L7 Troup Head hd Scot.
300 E4 Troustan Arg. and B., Scot.
232 E5 Troutbeck Cumbria, Eng.
232 E6 Troutbeck Cumbria, Eng.
232 E6 Troutbeck Bridge Cumbria, Eng.
180 E3 Troway Derbys., Eng.
86 B4 Trowbridge Wilts., Eng.
350 H3 Trowbridge Cardiff, Wales
176 B5 Trowell Notts., Eng.
98 D3 Trow Green Glos., Eng.
86 B4 Trowle Common Wilts., Eng.
110 C5 Trowley Bottom Herts., Eng.
256 J3 Trows Borders, Scot.
166 G3 Trowse Newton Norf., Eng.
222 E1 Troy W. Yorks., Eng.
300 B4 Trudernish Arg. and B., Scot.
94 J3 Trudoxhill Som., Eng.
136 F1 Trueman's Heath Worcs., Eng.
94 F5 Trull Som., Eng.
326 C4 Trumaisgearraidh W. Isles, Scot.
208 F2 Trumfleet S. Yorks., Eng.
322 B2 Trumpan High., Scot.
140 D3 Trumpet Here., Eng.
124 E5 Trumpington Cambs., Eng.
78 C1 Trumps Green Surr., Eng.
166 H1 Trunch Norf., Eng.
228 D3 Trunnah Lancs., Eng.
36 D3 Truro Corn., Eng.
36 F2 Truscott Corn., Eng.
180 D5 Trusley Derbys., Eng.
170 H4 Trusthorpe Lincs., Eng.
36 D3 Truthan Corn., Eng.
148 B5 Trysull Staffs., Eng.
22 D9 Tuath, Loch sea chan. Scot.
22 D6 Tuath, Loch a' b. Scot.
102 C4 Tubney Oxon, Eng.
144 G5 Tuckhill Shrop., Eng.
36 D3 Tuckingmill Corn., Eng.
86 C5 Tuckingmill Wilts., Eng.
46 I3 Tuckton Bourne., Eng.
120 C3 Tuddenham Suff., Eng.
120 G4 Tuddenham Suff., Eng.
62 B3 Tudeley Kent, Eng.
62 B3 Tudeley Hale Kent, Eng.
236 F3 Tudhoe Durham, Eng.
372 C3 Tudweiliog Gwynedd, Wales
208 G2 Tudworth Green Farm S. Yorks., Eng.
190 D3 Tuebrook Merseyside, Eng.
78 C2 Tuesley Surr., Eng.
98 F3 Tuffley Glos., Eng.
74 D2 Tufnell Park Gtr Lon., Eng.
52 D3 Tufton Hants., Eng.
358 E2 Tufton Pembs., Wales
162 F3 Tugby Leics., Eng.
144 E5 Tugford Shrop., Eng.
244 G2 Tughall Northumb., Eng.
304 H4 Tulchan Perth and Kin., Scot.
292 A3 Tullibody Clack., Scot.
300 D3 Tullich Arg. and B., Scot.
300 E3 Tullich Arg. and B., Scot.
314 D2 Tullich Moray, Scot.
296 D2 Tullich Stir., Scot.
304 I3 Tulliemet Perth and Kin., Scot.
388 D3 Tullintrain Derry, N. Ire.

Tulloch to Wardley

14 G2 Tulloch Abers., Scot.
14 G2 Tulloch Moray, Scot.
00 E3 Tullochgorm Arg. and B., Scot.
14 E3 Tullochvenus Abers., Scot.
08 F3 Tulloes Angus, Scot.
02 F5 Tully Fermanagh, N. Ire.
88 C3 Tullyalley Derry, N. Ire.
02 E3 Tullyard Omagh, N. Ire.
04 F4 Tullybannocher Perth and Kin., Scot.
04 I4 Tullybelton Perth and Kin., Scot.
23 G4 Tullybrack hill N. Ire.
02 D2 Tullycar Strabane, N. Ire.
96 G3 Tullyconnaught Banbridge, N. Ire.
02 G4 Tullycorker Dungannon, N. Ire.
04 K3 Tullyfergus Perth and Kin., Scot.
02 J3 Tullyhogue Cookstown, N. Ire.
02 D5 Tullyhona Fermanagh, N. Ire.
96 E5 Tullymacreeve Newry & Mourne, N. Ire.
04 K3 Tullymurdoch Perth and Kin., Scot.
96 J3 Tullynacree Down, N. Ire.
96 E3 Tullyroan Corner Armagh, N. Ire.
02 C4 Tullyrossmearn Fermanagh, N. Ire.
96 J3 Tullyveery Down, N. Ire.
02 I3 Tulnacross Cookstown, N. Ire.
74 D3 Tulse Hill Gtr Lon., Eng.
56 F3 Tumble Carmar., Wales
70 F5 Tumby Lincs., Eng.
22 I9 Tummel, Loch l. Scot.
04 F2 Tummel Bridge Perth and Kin., Scot.
02 E3 Tummery Omagh, N. Ire.
52 B4 Tunbridge Wells, Royal Kent, Eng.
52 G2 Tundergarth Mains D. and G., Scot.
26 E2 Tunga W. Isles, Scot.
66 H2 Tungate Norf., Eng.
94 J2 Tunley B. and N.E. Som., Eng.
96 G2 Tunny Craigavon, N. Ire.
10 H4 Tunstall E. Riding, Eng.
62 E3 Tunstall Kent, Eng.
28 D2 Tunstall Lancs., Eng.
66 I3 Tunstall Norf., Eng.
16 E1 Tunstall N. Yorks., Eng.
48 A3 Tunstall Staffs., Eng.
58 D2 Tunstall Stoke, Eng.
20 H4 Tunstall Suff., Eng.
36 G2 Tunstall T. and W., Eng.
98 F2 Tunstead Gtr Man., Eng.
56 H2 Tunstead Norf., Eng.
80 B3 Tunstead Milton Derbys., Eng.
52 F3 Tunworth Hants., Eng.
70 E4 Tupholme Lincs., Eng.
40 C3 Tupsley Here., Eng.
80 E3 Tupton Derbys., Eng.
00 D3 Turbiskill Arg. and B., Scot.
52 F3 Turgis Green Hants., Eng.
08 F2 Turin Angus, Scot.
98 H2 Turkdean Glos., Eng.
62 F3 Tur Langton Leics., Eng.
86 B3 Turleigh Wilts., Eng.
28 I5 Turn Lancs., Eng.
40 B3 Turnastone Here., Eng.
62 C5 Turnberry S. Ayr., Scot.
36 B2 Turnchapel Plymouth, Eng.
80 D4 Turnditch Derbys., Eng.
58 H3 Turner's Green E. Sussex, Eng.
32 B4 Turner's Green Warks., Eng.
58 F2 Turners Hill W. Sussex, Eng.
46 F3 Turners Puddle Dorset, Eng.
10 E5 Turnford Herts., Eng.
46 F2 Turnworth Dorset, Eng.
22 G4 Turret Bridge High., Scot.
14 F2 Turriff Abers., Scot.
28 H5 Turton Bottoms B'burn, Eng.
54 C3 Turves Green W. Mids, Eng.
10 B3 Turvey Bedford, Eng.
06 C5 Turville Bucks., Eng.
06 C5 Turville Heath Bucks., Eng.
06 B2 Turweston Bucks., Eng.
48 B3 Tutbury Staffs., Eng.
36 E2 Tutnall Worcs., Eng.
98 D4 Tutshill Glos., Eng.
66 G2 Tuttington Norf., Eng.
06 B3 Tutts Clump W. Berks., Eng.
36 G2 Tutwell Corn., Eng.
76 D3 Tuxford Notts., Eng.
29 B3 Twatt Orkney, Scot.
31 C3 Twatt Shet., Scot.
76 F2 Twechar E. Dun., Scot.
24 M2 Tweed r. Scot.
22 J11 Tweeddale val. Scot.
44 E1 Tweedmouth Northumb., Eng.
56 D3 Tweedsmuir Borders, Scot.
36 D3 Twelveheads Corn., Eng.
58 H3 Twelve Oaks E. Sussex, Eng.
84 F2 Twemlow Green Cheshire East, Eng.
70 E7 Twenty Lincs., Eng.
94 J2 Twerton B. and N.E. Som., Eng.
74 B3 Twickenham Gtr Lon., Eng.
98 F2 Twigworth Glos., Eng.
58 E3 Twineham W. Sussex, Eng.
58 E3 Twineham Green W. Sussex, Eng.
94 J2 Twinhoe B. and N.E. Som., Eng.
16 G2 Twinstead Essex, Eng.
16 G2 Twinstead Green Essex, Eng.
90 F3 Twiss Green Warr., Eng.
28 I3 Twiston Lancs., Eng.
40 E1 Twitchen Devon, Eng.
44 C5 Twitchen Shrop., Eng.
62 B3 Twitton Kent, Eng.
44 G2 Twizell House Northumb., Eng.
40 E3 Two Bridges Devon, Eng.
98 E3 Two Bridges Glos., Eng.
80 D4 Two Dales Derbys., Eng.
48 E5 Two Gates Staffs., Eng.
84 B2 Two Mills Cheshire West & Chester, Eng.
62 B3 Twycross Leics., Eng.
06 B3 Twyford Bucks., Eng.
80 D5 Twyford Derbys., Eng.
46 F2 Twyford Dorset, Eng.
52 E4 Twyford Hants., Eng.
62 F2 Twyford Leics., Eng.
66 E2 Twyford Norf., Eng.
02 D2 Twyford Oxon, Eng.
82 E3 Twyford W'ham, Eng.
40 C3 Twyford Common Here., Eng.
52 D3 Twynholm D. and G., Scot.
98 G1 Twyning Glos., Eng.
98 G1 Twyning Green Glos., Eng.
56 H2 Twynllanan Carmar., Wales
50 G3 Twyn Shôn-Ifan Caerp., Wales
50 G4 Twyn-yr-odyn V. of Glam., Wales
39 C2 Twyn-y-Sheriff Mon., Wales
28 F3 Twywell Northants., Eng.
40 B3 Tyberton Here., Eng.
54 D2 Tyburn W. Mids, Eng.
56 F3 Tycroes Carmar., Wales
74 C3 Ty Croes I.o.A., Wales
66 F2 Tycrwyn Powys, Wales
Tyddewi Pembs., Wales see St David's
170 G7 Tydd Gote Lincs., Eng.
124 E2 Tydd St Giles Cambs., Eng.
170 G7 Tydd St Mary Lincs., Eng.
52 G6 Tye Hants., Eng.
116 E4 Tye Common Essex, Eng.
166 H3 Tyegate Green Norf., Eng.
116 C3 Tye Green Essex, Eng.
116 D2 Tye Green Essex, Eng.
116 E3 Tye Green Essex, Eng.
116 F2 Tye Green Essex, Eng.
222 D2 Tyersal W. Yorks., Eng.
222 D2 Tyersal Gate W. Yorks., Eng.
372 B3 Ty-hen Gwynedd, Wales
198 C2 Tyldesley Gtr Man., Eng.
350 F3 Tyle-garw R.C.T., Wales
62 G3 Tyler Hill Kent, Eng.
106 D5 Tylers Green Bucks., Eng.
116 D3 Tyler's Green Essex, Eng.
350 F3 Tylorstown R.C.T., Wales
366 D4 Tylwch Powys, Wales
378 D3 Ty-Mawr Conwy, Wales
378 F3 Ty-mawr Denb., Wales
396 D4 Tynan Armagh, N. Ire.
378 D4 Ty-nant Conwy, Wales
372 I4 Ty-nant Gwynedd, Wales
296 B3 Tyndrum Stir., Scot.
22 K10 Tyne r. Scot.
236 F2 Tyne and Wear admin. div. Eng.
288 F4 Tynehead Midlothian, Scot.
236 G1 Tynemouth T. and W., Eng.
350 E2 Tynewydd R.C.T., Wales
288 H2 Tyninghame E. Lothian, Scot.
252 E2 Tynron D. and G., Scot.
372 H2 Tyntesfield N. Som., Eng.
378 E4 Tyn-y-cefn Denb., Wales
350 H3 Ty'n-y-coedcae Caerp., Wales
366 C4 Tyn-y-cwm Powys, Wales
366 F1 Tyn-y-ffridd Powys, Wales
350 E3 Ty'n-y-garn Bridg., Wales
371 D3 Ty'n-y-gongl I.o.A., Wales
362 G3 Tynygraig Cere., Wales
366 E6 Tyn-y-graig Powys, Wales
378 B2 Ty'n-y-groes Conwy, Wales
396 J4 Tyrella Down, N. Ire.
314 G2 Tyrie Abers., Scot.
106 D2 Tyringham M.K., Eng.
402 H3 Tyrone county N. Ire.
154 C3 Tyseley W. Mids, Eng.
350 E4 Tythegston Bridg., Wales
184 G2 Tytherington Cheshire East, Eng.
98 E4 Tytherington S. Glos., Eng.
94 K3 Tytherington Som., Eng.
86 C4 Tytherington Wilts., Eng.
86 C3 Tytherton Lucas Wilts., Eng.
110 D5 Tyttenhanger Herts., Eng.
366 E2 Ty-uchaf Powys, Wales
36 E2 Tywardreath Corn., Eng.
26 D4 Tywi r. Wales
372 F5 Tywyn Gwynedd, Wales

U

326 B4 Uachdar W. Isles, Scot.
Uachdar Thire High., Scot. see Auchtertyre
322 D2 Uags High., Scot.
148 C2 Ubberley Stoke, Eng.
120 H3 Ubbeston Green Suff., Eng.
94 H3 Ubley B. and N.E. Som., Eng.
216 E1 Uckerby N. Yorks., Eng.
58 G3 Uckfield E. Sussex, Eng.
136 D3 Uckinghall Worcs., Eng.
98 G2 Uckington Glos., Eng.
268 B2 Uddingston S. Lanark., Scot.
268 D3 Uddington S. Lanark., Scot.
58 J3 Udimore E. Sussex, Eng.
94 H2 Udley N. Som., Eng.
314 G3 Udny Green Abers., Scot.
268 B2 Udston S. Lanark., Scot.
268 B2 Udstonhead S. Lanark., Scot.
86 E3 Uffcott Wilts., Eng.
40 G2 Uffculme Devon, Eng.
170 D8 Uffington Lincs., Eng.
102 B5 Uffington Oxon, Eng.
144 D3 Uffington Shrop., Eng.
120 H4 Ufford Suff., Eng.
132 D4 Ufton Warks., Eng.
82 D3 Ufton Green W. Berks., Eng.
82 D3 Ufton Nervet W. Berks., Eng.
40 E3 Ugborough Devon, Eng.
86 D5 Ugford Wilts., Eng.
120 I2 Uggeshall Suff., Eng.
216 H1 Ugglebarnby N. Yorks., Eng.
116 D2 Ugley Essex, Eng.
116 D2 Ugley Green Essex, Eng.
216 G1 Ugthorpe N. Yorks., Eng.
Uibhist a' Deas i. Scot. see South Uist
Uibhist a' Tuath i. Scot. see North Uist
326 B6 Uidh W. Isles, Scot.
300 F3 Uig Arg. and B., Scot.
300 □ Uig Arg. and B., Scot.
322 B2 Uig High., Scot.
Uige High., Scot. see Uig
322 B2 Uiginish High., Scot.
322 C2 Uigshader High., Scot.
Uisgebhagh W. Isles, Scot. see Uiskevagh
300 B3 Uisken Arg. and B., Scot.
326 C4 Uiskevagh W. Isles, Scot.
320 K2 Ulbster High., Scot.
232 E5 Ulcat Row Cumbria, Eng.
170 G4 Ulceby Lincs., Eng.
170 E2 Ulceby N. Lincs., Eng.
170 E4 Ulceby Cross Lincs., Eng.
170 E2 Ulceby Skitter N. Lincs., Eng.
62 D3 Ulcombe Kent, Eng.
232 D4 Uldale Cumbria, Eng.
232 H6 Uldale House Cumbria, Eng.
98 F3 Uley Glos., Eng.
244 H4 Ulgham Northumb., Eng.
320 E4 Ullapool High., Scot.
Ullapul High., Scot. see Ullapool
132 B4 Ullenhall Warks., Eng.
98 G2 Ullenwood Glos., Eng.
162 D4 Ullesthorpe Leics., Eng.
208 E3 Ulley S. Yorks., Eng.
140 D3 Ullingswick Here., Eng.
322 B2 Ullinish High., Scot.
232 B5 Ullock Cumbria, Eng.
24 L4 Ullswater l. Eng.
232 C7 Ulpha Cumbria, Eng.
232 E7 Ulpha Cumbria, Eng.
170 D3 Ulrome E. Riding, Eng.
331 D2 Ulsta Shet., Scot.
23 H3 Ulster reg. Ireland/U.K.
396 J2 Ulster Folk & Transport Museum North Down, N. Ire.
116 F3 Ulting Essex, Eng.
300 C2 Uluvalt Arg. and B., Scot.
22 D10 Ulva i. Scot.
154 D3 Ulverley Green W. Mids, Eng.
232 D7 Ulverston Cumbria, Eng.
46 H4 Ulwell Dorset, Eng.
252 E1 Ulzieside D. and G., Scot.
40 E2 Umberleigh Devon, Eng.
402 F4 Ummer Fermanagh, N. Ire.
320 E3 Unapool High., Scot.
210 D2 Uncleby E. Riding, Eng.
232 F7 Underbarrow Cumbria, Eng.
222 D2 Undercliffe W. Yorks., Eng.
144 D3 Underdale Shrop., Eng.
74 C2 Underhill Gtr Lon., Eng.
331 E1 Underhoull Shet., Scot.
62 D3 Underling Green Kent, Eng.
62 B3 Underriver Kent, Eng.
176 B4 Underwood Notts., Eng.
40 D3 Underwood Plymouth, Eng.
339 C3 Underwood Newp., Wales
120 B2 Undley Suff., Eng.
339 D3 Undy Mon., Wales
326 D2 Ungisiadar W. Isles, Scot.
331 C3 Unifirth Shet., Scot.
405 C2 Union Mills Isle of Man
58 I2 Union Street E. Sussex, Eng.
331 E1 Unst airport Scot.
22 □O1 Unst i. Scot.
180 E3 Unstone Derbys., Eng.
180 E3 Unstone Green Derbys., Eng.
198 D2 Unsworth Gtr Man., Eng.
232 E4 Unthank Cumbria, Eng.
180 D3 Unthank Derbys., Eng.
86 E4 Upavon Wilts., Eng.
46 E3 Up Cerne Dorset, Eng.
62 D2 Upchurch Kent, Eng.
40 D1 Upcott Devon, Eng.
140 B3 Upcott Here., Eng.
94 C4 Upcott Som., Eng.
94 F4 Upcott Som., Eng.
124 G5 Upend Cambs., Eng.
166 G2 Upgate Norf., Eng.
166 F4 Upgate Street Norf., Eng.
166 H4 Upgate Street Norf., Eng.
40 G3 Uphall Dorset, Eng.
288 B3 Uphall W. Lothian, Scot.
288 B3 Uphall Station W. Lothian, Scot.
40 F2 Upham Devon, Eng.
52 E5 Upham Hants., Eng.
140 B2 Uphampton Here., Eng.
136 D2 Uphampton Worcs., Eng.
98 G2 Up Hatherley Glos., Eng.
94 G3 Uphill N. Som., Eng.
228 F5 Up Holland Lancs., Eng.
98 F3 Uplands Glos., Eng.
350 C3 Uplands Swansea, Wales
276 D3 Uplawmoor E. Renf., Scot.
98 E2 Upleadon Glos., Eng.
62 F2 Uplees Kent, Eng.
46 C3 Uploders Dorset, Eng.
40 H2 Uplyme Devon, Eng.
58 A3 Up Marden W. Sussex, Eng.
74 F2 Upminster Gtr Lon., Eng.
94 I5 Up Mudford Som., Eng.
52 F3 Up Nately Hants., Eng.
40 G2 Upottery Devon, Eng.
144 D5 Upper Affcot Shrop., Eng.
300 E4 Upper Ardroscadale Arg. and B., Scot.
136 C1 Upper Arley Worcs., Eng.
102 E3 Upper Arncott Oxon, Eng.
144 D3 Upper Astley Shrop., Eng.
144 G4 Upper Aston Shrop., Eng.
128 B5 Upper Astrop Northants., Eng.
388 I5 Upper Ballinderry Lisburn, N. Ire.
326 E1 Upper Barvas W. Isles, Scot.
82 D3 Upper Basildon W. Berks., Eng.
58 E3 Upper Beeding W. Sussex, Eng.
128 F3 Upper Benefield Northants., Eng.
136 E2 Upper Bentley Worcs., Eng.
144 D3 Upper Berwick Shrop., Eng.
350 G3 Upper Boat R.C.T., Wales
128 B4 Upper Boddington Northants., Eng.
362 F2 Upper Borth Cere., Wales
132 C5 Upper Brailes Warks., Eng.
322 D3 Upper Breakish High., Scot.
140 C3 Upper Breinton Here., Eng.
136 D2 Upper Broadheath Worcs., Eng.
176 D6 Upper Broughton Notts., Eng.
356 G3 Upper Brynamman Carmar., Wales
82 C3 Upper Bucklebury W. Berks., Eng.
52 B5 Upper Burgate Hants., Eng.
232 E3 Upperby Cumbria, Eng.
110 D3 Upper Caldecote Central Bedfordshire, Eng.
94 G3 Upper Canada N. Som., Eng.
128 B4 Upper Catesby Northants., Eng.
136 E1 Upper Catshill Worcs., Eng.
366 E6 Upper Chapel Powys, Wales
86 C5 Upper Chicksgrove Wilts., Eng.
86 F4 Upper Chute Wilts., Eng.
74 D2 Upper Clapton Gtr Lon., Eng.
52 C4 Upper Clatford Hants., Eng.
98 G2 Upper Coberley Glos., Eng.
140 E3 Upper Colwall Here., Eng.
148 D2 Upper Cotton Staffs., Eng.
144 E4 Upper Cound Shrop., Eng.
222 D3 Upper Cumberworth W. Yorks., Eng.
350 H3 Upper Cwmbran B. Gwent, Wales
110 C2 Upper Dean Bedford, Eng.
222 E3 Upper Denby W. Yorks., Eng.
232 G3 Upper Denton Cumbria, Eng.
322 K2 Upper Derraid High., Scot.
322 E2 Upper Diabaig High., Scot.
58 H3 Upper Dicker E. Sussex, Eng.
116 J2 Upper Dovercourt Essex, Eng.
216 F2 Upper Dunsforth N. Yorks., Eng.
110 B5 Upper Dunsley Herts., Eng.
154 E3 Upper Eastern Green W. Mids, Eng.
322 I2 Upper Eathie High., Scot.
74 D2 Upper Edmonton Gtr Lon., Eng.
140 D3 Upper Egleton Here., Eng.
148 D2 Upper Elkstone Staffs., Eng.
74 D3 Upper Elmers End Gtr Lon., Eng.
180 B3 Upper End Derbys., Eng.
52 D3 Upper Enham Hants., Eng.
52 G4 Upper Farringdon Hants., Eng.
98 E3 Upper Framilode Glos., Eng.
52 G3 Upper Froyle Hants., Eng.
94 H3 Upper Godney Som., Eng.
154 B2 Upper Gornal W. Mids, Eng.
110 C3 Upper Gravenhurst Central Bedfordshire, Eng.
116 C2 Upper Green Essex, Eng.
116 D2 Upper Green Essex, Eng.
120 C3 Upper Green Suff., Eng.
82 B3 Upper Green W. Berks., Eng.
339 C1 Upper Green Mon., Wales
140 D4 Upper Grove Common Here., Eng.
300 D2 Upper Gylen Arg. and B., Scot.
180 D4 Upper Hackney Derbys., Eng.
78 D1 Upper Halliford Surr., Eng.
62 C2 Upper Halling Medway, Eng.
162 G3 Upper Hambleton Rutland, Eng.
62 G3 Upper Harbledown Kent, Eng.
62 G3 Upper Hardres Court Kent, Eng.
140 B2 Upper Hardwick Here., Eng.
58 G2 Upper Hartfield E. Sussex, Eng.
180 E4 Upper Hartshay Derbys., Eng.
148 B3 Upper Hatton Staffs., Eng.
208 D3 Upper Haugh S. Yorks., Eng.
62 B3 Upper Hayesden Kent, Eng.
144 D5 Upper Hayton Shrop., Eng.
144 E5 Upper Heath Shrop., Eng.
222 D2 Upper Heaton W. Yorks., Eng.
166 G3 Upper Hellesdon Norf., Eng.
144 B2 Upper Hengoed Shrop., Eng.
140 A2 Upper Hergest Here., Eng.
128 C4 Upper Heyford Northants., Eng.
102 D3 Upper Heyford Oxon, Eng.
140 C2 Upper Hill Here., Eng.
98 D3 Upper Hill S. Glos., Eng.
74 D2 Upper Holloway Gtr Lon., Eng.
222 D3 Upper Hopton W. Yorks., Eng.
58 H3 Upper Horsebridge E. Sussex, Eng.
136 D3 Upper Howsell Worcs., Eng.
148 D2 Upper Hulme Staffs., Eng.
86 E2 Upper Inglesham Swindon, Eng.
300 B3 Upper Kilchattan Arg. and B., Scot.
350 B3 Upper Killay Swansea, Wales
82 A2 Upper Lambourn W. Berks., Eng.
388 G3 Upperlands Magherafelt, N. Ire.
148 C5 Upper Landywood Staffs., Eng.
94 H3 Upper Langford N. Som., Eng.
180 F3 Upper Langwith Derbys., Eng.
292 G2 Upper Largo Fife, Scot.
148 D3 Upper Leigh Staffs., Eng.
98 E2 Upper Ley Glos., Eng.
180 D3 Upper Loads Derbys., Eng.
314 F3 Upper Lochton Abers., Scot.
148 D4 Upper Longdon Staffs., Eng.
144 E4 Upper Longwood Shrop., Eng.
23 G4 Upper Lough Erne l. N. Ire.
144 G4 Upper Ludstone Shrop., Eng.
98 D2 Upper Lydbrook Glos., Eng.
140 C3 Upper Lyde Here., Eng.
140 B2 Upper Lye Here., Eng.
140 B3 Upper Maes-coed Here., Eng.
208 B3 Upper Midhope S. Yorks., Eng.
198 E2 Uppermill Gtr Man., Eng.
102 B3 Upper Milton Oxon, Eng.
94 I3 Upper Milton Som., Eng.
86 D2 Upper Minety Wilts., Eng.
136 D1 Upper Mitton Worcs., Eng.
136 D3 Upper Moor Worcs., Eng.
98 D4 Upper Morton S. Glos., Eng.
314 G3 Upper Muirskie Abers., Scot.
358 E3 Upper Nash Pembs., Wales
180 E3 Upper Newbold Derbys., Eng.
148 B3 Upper Nobut Staffs., Eng.
106 D4 Upper North Dean Bucks., Eng.
74 D3 Upper Norwood Gtr Lon., Eng.
304 I3 Upper Obney Perth and Kin., Scot.
98 I2 Upper Oddington Glos., Eng.
322 C2 Upper Ollach High., Scot.
180 D3 Upper Padley Derbys., Eng.
52 C6 Upper Pennington Hants., Eng.
106 C4 Upper Pollicott Bucks., Eng.
216 F3 Upper Poppleton York, Eng.
132 B5 Upper Quinton Warks., Eng.
52 C4 Upper Ratley Hants., Eng.
314 H2 Upper Ridinghill Abers., Scot.
98 I2 Upper Rissington Glos., Eng.
136 B2 Upper Rochford Worcs., Eng.
329 E4 Upper Sanday Orkney, Scot.
140 E2 Upper Sapey Here., Eng.
358 E2 Upper Scolton Pembs., Wales
86 C2 Upper Seagry Wilts., Eng.
110 B3 Upper Shelton Central Bedfordshire, Eng.
166 G1 Upper Sheringham Norf., Eng.
52 D5 Upper Shirley Soton, Eng.
132 E4 Upper Shuckburgh Warks., Eng.
98 H3 Upper Siddington Glos., Eng.
264 E1 Upper Skelmorlie N. Ayr., Scot.
98 I2 Upper Slaughter Glos., Eng.
300 E2 Upper Sonachan Arg. and B., Scot.
98 E3 Upper Soudley Glos., Eng.
110 D2 Upper Staploe Bedford, Eng.
166 G3 Upper Stoke Norf., Eng.
154 F3 Upper Stoke W. Mids, Eng.
110 D3 Upper Stondon Central Bedfordshire, Eng.
128 C4 Upper Stowe Northants., Eng.
52 B5 Upper Street Hants., Eng.
166 G4 Upper Street Norf., Eng.
166 H2 Upper Street Norf., Eng.
120 F4 Upper Street Suff., Eng.
120 F5 Upper Street Suff., Eng.
120 H4 Upper Street Suff., Eng.
136 E3 Upper Strensham Worcs., Eng.
110 C4 Upper Sundon Central Bedfordshire, Eng.
52 E5 Upper Swanmore Hants., Eng.
98 I2 Upper Swell Glos., Eng.
74 D3 Upper Sydenham Gtr Lon., Eng.
166 G3 Upper Tasburgh Norf., Eng.
148 D3 Upper Tean Staffs., Eng.
222 D3 Upperthong W. Yorks., Eng.
180 F3 Upperthorpe Derbys., Eng.
228 F3 Upper Thurnham Lancs., Eng.
304 J5 Upper Tillyrie Perth and Kin., Scot.
388 F3 Upper Tirkane Magherafelt, N. Ire.
58 C3 Upperton W. Sussex, Eng.
74 D3 Upper Tooting Gtr Lon., Eng.
180 D3 Uppertown Derbys., Eng.
180 D4 Upper Town Derbys., Eng.
180 D4 Upper Town Derbys., Eng.
140 D3 Upper Town Here., Eng.
120 D3 Upper Town Suff., Eng.
388 H3 Uppertown Ballymoney, N. Ire.
329 C5 Uppertown Orkney, Scot.
329 C5 Uppertown Orkney, Scot.
132 C5 Upper Tysoe Warks., Eng.
86 E3 Upper Upham Wilts., Eng.
62 D2 Upper Upnor Medway, Eng.
308 F3 Upper Victoria Angus, Scot.
94 J3 Upper Vobster Som., Eng.
74 D2 Upper Walthamstow Gtr Lon., Eng.
102 D2 Upper Wardington Oxon, Eng.
86 D2 Upper Waterhay Wilts., Eng.
106 D2 Upper Weald M.K., Eng.
128 C4 Upper Weedon Northants., Eng.
140 A3 Upper Welson Here., Eng.
94 J2 Upper Weston B. and N.E. Som., Eng.
120 G2 Upper Weybread Suff., Eng.
208 E3 Upper Whiston S. Yorks., Eng.
136 D2 Upper Wick Worcs., Eng.
52 F4 Upper Wield Hants., Eng.
106 C4 Upper Winchendon Bucks., Eng.
154 C2 Upper Witton W. Mids, Eng.
86 E5 Upper Woodford Wilts., Eng.
82 C3 Upper Woolhampton W. Berks., Eng.
52 E3 Upper Wootton Hants., Eng.
86 B3 Upper Wraxall Wilts., Eng.
162 G3 Uppingham Rutland, Eng.
46 H2 Uppington Dorset, Eng.
144 E3 Uppington Shrop., Eng.
256 K2 Upsettlington Borders, Scot.
116 C3 Upshire Essex, Eng.
52 D4 Up Somborne Hants., Eng.
62 H3 Upstreet Kent, Eng.
46 D3 Up Sydling Dorset, Eng.
120 E3 Upthorpe Suff., Eng.
106 C4 Upton Bucks., Eng.
124 C4 Upton Cambs., Eng.
184 B2 Upton Cheshire West & Chester, Eng.
36 F1 Upton Corn., Eng.
36 F2 Upton Corn., Eng.
46 E4 Upton Dorset, Eng.
46 G3 Upton Dorset, Eng.
210 G3 Upton E. Riding, Eng.
74 E2 Upton Gtr Lon., Eng.
52 D3 Upton Hants., Eng.
52 D5 Upton Hants., Eng.
162 C3 Upton Leics., Eng.
170 B3 Upton Lincs., Eng.
190 C3 Upton Merseyside, Eng.
166 I3 Upton Norf., Eng.
128 D4 Upton Northants., Eng.
176 D3 Upton Notts., Eng.
176 D4 Upton Notts., Eng.
102 B4 Upton Oxon, Eng.
102 D5 Upton Oxon, Eng.
124 B3 Upton Peterb., Eng.
82 G2 Upton Slough, Eng.
94 D4 Upton Som., Eng.
94 H4 Upton Som., Eng.
132 B4 Upton Warks., Eng.
86 B5 Upton Wilts., Eng.
222 G3 Upton W. Yorks., Eng.
358 E3 Upton Pembs., Wales
140 D4 Upton Bishop Here., Eng.
98 E5 Upton Cheyney S. Glos., Eng.
144 E4 Upton Cressett Shrop., Eng.
140 D4 Upton Crews Here., Eng.
110 C3 Upton End Central Bedfordshire, Eng.
166 I3 Upton Green Norf., Eng.
52 F3 Upton Grey Hants., Eng.
184 B2 Upton Heath Cheshire West & Chester, Eng.
40 F2 Upton Hellions Devon, Eng.
86 C4 Upton Lovell Wilts., Eng.
144 E3 Upton Magna Shrop., Eng.
94 J4 Upton Noble Som., Eng.
74 E2 Upton Park Gtr Lon., Eng.
40 F2 Upton Pyne Devon, Eng.
98 F2 Upton St Leonards Glos., Eng.
86 B4 Upton Scudamore Wilts., Eng.
136 E2 Upton Snodsbury Worcs., Eng.
136 D3 Upton upon Severn Worcs., Eng.
136 E2 Upton Warren Worcs., Eng.
58 C3 Upwaltham W. Sussex, Eng.
124 F5 Upware Cambs., Eng.
166 A3 Upwell Norf., Eng.
46 E4 Upwey Dorset, Eng.
110 F4 Upwick Green Herts., Eng.
124 D4 Upwood Cambs., Eng.
331 D3 Uradale Shet., Scot.
331 C2 Urafirth Shet., Scot.
322 J2 Urchany High., Scot.
86 D4 Urchfont Wilts., Eng.
140 C3 Urdimarsh Here., Eng.
331 C2 Ure Shet., Scot.
24 O5 Ure r. Eng.
326 D3 Urgha W. Isles, Scot.
22 L8 Urie r. Scot.
236 G4 Urlay Nook Stockton, Eng.
198 C3 Urmston Gtr Man., Eng.
236 F2 Urpeth Durham, Eng.
322 H2 Urquhart High., Scot.
314 D2 Urquhart Moray, Scot.
216 F1 Urra N. Yorks., Eng.
322 H2 Urray High., Scot.
236 F3 Ushaw Moor Durham, Eng.
339 C2 Usk Mon., Wales
26 G4 Usk r. Wales
26 E4 Usk Reservoir resr Wales
170 D3 Usselby Lincs., Eng.
236 F2 Usworth T. and W., Eng.
222 C1 Utley W. Yorks., Eng.
40 F2 Uton Devon, Eng.
170 F3 Utterby Lincs., Eng.
148 D3 Uttoxeter Staffs., Eng.
372 B4 Uwchmynydd Gwynedd, Wales
74 B2 Uxbridge Gtr Lon., Eng.
22 □O1 Uyea i. Scot.
331 E1 Uyeasound Shet., Scot.
358 E3 Uzmaston Pembs., Wales

V

22 □M2 Vaila i. Scot.
350 F4 Vale of Glamorgan admin. div. Wales
22 B7 Vallay i. Scot.
371 B3 Valley I.o.A., Wales
252 D3 Valleyfield D. and G., Scot.
292 C3 Valleyfield Fife, Scot.
36 E2 Valley Truckle Corn., Eng.
331 E1 Valsgarth Shet., Scot.
116 E4 Vange Essex, Eng.
350 C3 Vardre Swansea, Wales
339 B2 Varteg Torf., Wales
22 C7 Vaternish Point pt Scot.
326 B6 Vatersay W. Isles, Scot.
22 A9 Vatersay i. Scot.
331 D2 Vatsetter Shet., Scot.
322 B2 Vatten High., Scot.
300 □ Vaul Arg. and B., Scot.
74 D3 Vauxhall Gtr Lon., Eng.
154 C3 Vauxhall W. Mids, Eng.
350 F2 Vaynor M. Tyd., Wales
366 F3 Vaynor Park Powys, Wales
366 F6 Veaullt Powys, Wales
331 D3 Veensgarth Shet., Scot.
358 F1 Velindre Pembs., Wales
366 F6 Velindre Powys, Wales
94 E4 Vellow Som., Eng.
329 E3 Veness Orkney, Scot.
144 C3 Vennington Shrop., Eng.
40 G2 Venn Ottery Devon, Eng.
36 G2 Venterdon Corn., Eng.
52 E7 Ventnor I.o.W., Eng.
Vercovicium tourist site Eng. see Housesteads
52 C3 Vernham Dean Hants., Eng.
52 C3 Vernham Street Hants., Eng.
144 D5 Vernolds Common Shrop., Eng.
46 H2 Verwood Dorset, Eng.
36 E3 Veryan Corn., Eng.
232 C8 Vickerstown Cumbria, Eng.
36 E2 Victoria Corn., Eng.
402 F2 Victoria Bridge Strabane, N. Ire.
331 D2 Vidlin Shet., Scot.
320 J2 Viewfield High., Scot.
280 B4 Viewpark N. Lanark., Scot.
154 C2 Vigo W. Mids, Eng.
62 C3 Vigo Village Kent, Eng.
58 J3 Vinehall Street E. Sussex, Eng.
58 H3 Vine's Cross E. Sussex, Eng.
98 E3 Viney Hill Glos., Eng.
402 F5 Vintage Cycle Museum Fermanagh, N. Ire.
78 C1 Virginia Water Surr., Eng.
40 D2 Virginstow Devon, Eng.
116 G3 Virley Essex, Eng.
94 J3 Vobster Som., Eng.
331 C2 Voe Shet., Scot.
331 D2 Voe Shet., Scot.
388 G3 Vow Ballymoney, N. Ire.
140 B3 Vowchurch Here., Eng.
329 B3 Voy Orkney, Scot.
144 C3 Vron Gate Shrop., Eng.
190 F3 Vulcan Village Merseyside, Eng.
26 F2 Vyrnwy, Lake l. Wales

W

232 B6 Waberthwaite Cumbria, Eng.
236 E4 Wackerfield Durham, Eng.
166 G4 Wacton Norf., Eng.
331 D3 Wadbister Shet., Scot.
136 E3 Wadborough Worcs., Eng.
106 C3 Waddesdon Bucks., Eng.
190 D3 Waddicar Merseyside, Eng.
170 C3 Waddingham Lincs., Eng.
228 H3 Waddington Lancs., Eng.
170 C4 Waddington Lincs., Eng.
170 E4 Waddingworth Lincs., Eng.
74 D3 Waddon Gtr Lon., Eng.
36 E2 Wadebridge Corn., Eng.
94 G5 Wadeford Som., Eng.
128 F3 Wadenhoe Northants., Eng.
110 E4 Wadesmill Herts., Eng.
58 I2 Wadhurst E. Sussex, Eng.
180 D3 Wadshelf Derbys., Eng.
208 C3 Wadsley S. Yorks., Eng.
208 F3 Wadworth S. Yorks., Eng.
210 H4 Wadworth Hill E. Riding, Eng.
378 D3 Waen Denb., Wales
378 E2 Waen Denb., Wales
378 E2 Waen Aberwheeler Denb., Wales
366 F2 Waen-fâch Powys, Wales
372 F1 Waen-wen Gwynedd, Wales
320 I3 Wag High., Scot.
170 H5 Wainfleet All Saints Lincs., Eng.
170 H5 Wainfleet Bank Lincs., Eng.
170 H5 Wainfleet St Mary Lincs., Eng.
166 H4 Wainford Norf., Eng.
36 F1 Wainhouse Corner Corn., Eng.
62 D2 Wainscott Medway, Eng.
222 C2 Wainstalls W. Yorks., Eng.
232 H6 Waitby Cumbria, Eng.
222 E2 Wakefield W. Yorks., Eng.
154 C3 Wake Green W. Mids, Eng.
128 F2 Wakerley Northants., Eng.
116 G2 Wakes Colne Essex, Eng.
120 I3 Walberswick Suff., Eng.
58 C3 Walberton W. Sussex, Eng.
236 E2 Walbottle T. and W., Eng.
170 D6 Walcot Lincs., Eng.
170 E5 Walcot Lincs., Eng.
170 B1 Walcot N. Lincs., Eng.
144 C5 Walcot Shrop., Eng.
144 E3 Walcot Telford, Eng.
162 D4 Walcote Leics., Eng.
132 B4 Walcote Warks., Eng.
166 F4 Walcot Green Norf., Eng.
166 I1 Walcott Norf., Eng.
216 D2 Walden N. Yorks., Eng.
216 C2 Walden Head N. Yorks., Eng.
216 F4 Walden Stubbs N. Yorks., Eng.
62 D2 Walderslade Medway, Eng.
58 A3 Walderton W. Sussex, Eng.
46 C3 Walditch Dorset, Eng.
180 C5 Waldley Derbys., Eng.
26 D6 Waldon r. Eng.
236 F2 Waldridge Durham, Eng.
120 G4 Waldringfield Suff., Eng.
58 H3 Waldron E. Sussex, Eng.
94 I4 Wales Som., Eng.
208 E3 Wales S. Yorks., Eng.
26 E3 Wales admin. div.
208 E3 Wales Bar S. Yorks., Eng.
170 E3 Walesby Lincs., Eng.
176 D3 Walesby Notts., Eng.
208 E3 Waleswood S. Yorks., Eng.
140 B1 Walford Here., Eng.
140 D4 Walford Here., Eng.
144 D3 Walford Shrop., Eng.
94 F4 Walford Som., Eng.
148 B3 Walford Staffs., Eng.
144 D3 Walford Heath Shrop., Eng.
184 E3 Walgherton Cheshire East, Eng.
128 E3 Walgrave Northants., Eng.
74 C3 Walham Green Gtr Lon., Eng.
52 C6 Walhampton Hants., Eng.
198 C2 Walkden Gtr Man., Eng.
236 F2 Walker T. and W., Eng.
256 F3 Walkerburn Borders, Scot.
228 G3 Walker Fold Lancs., Eng.
176 D2 Walkeringham Notts., Eng.
170 B3 Walkerith Lincs., Eng.
110 E4 Walkern Herts., Eng.
140 C3 Walker's Green Here., Eng.
154 C3 Walker's Heath W. Mids, Eng.
46 I3 Walkford Dorset, Eng.
40 D3 Walkhampton Devon, Eng.
210 F4 Walkington E. Riding, Eng.
208 D3 Walkley S. Yorks., Eng.
228 I4 Walk Mill Lancs., Eng.
136 F2 Walkwood Worcs., Eng.
36 C3 Wall Corn., Eng.
244 E5 Wall Northumb., Eng.
148 D5 Wall Staffs., Eng.
252 G2 Wallacehall D. and G., Scot.
262 C5 Wallacetown S. Ayr., Scot.
262 D4 Wallacetown S. Ayr., Scot.
190 C3 Wallasey Merseyside, Eng.
358 D4 Wallaston Green Pembs., Wales
144 D4 Wall Bank Shrop., Eng.
154 B2 Wallbrook W. Mids, Eng.
232 C7 Wall End Cumbria, Eng.
140 C2 Wall End Here., Eng.
62 E2 Wallend Medway, Eng.
140 E3 Waller's Green Here., Eng.
154 A2 Wall Heath W. Mids, Eng.
198 E2 Wall Hill Gtr Man., Eng.
244 F5 Wall Houses Northumb., Eng.
102 E5 Wallingford Oxon, Eng.
74 D3 Wallington Gtr Lon., Eng.
52 E5 Wallington Hants., Eng.
110 E4 Wallington Herts., Eng.
378 H3 Wallington Wrex., Wales
154 B2 Wallington Heath W. Mids, Eng.
176 C2 Wallingwells Notts., Eng.
358 E2 Wallis Pembs., Wales
46 H3 Wallisdown Bourne., Eng.
78 D3 Walliswood Surr., Eng.
236 E3 Wall Nook Durham, Eng.
331 C3 Walls Shet., Scot.
236 F2 Wallsend T. and W., Eng.
144 D4 Wall under Heywood Shrop., Eng.
288 E3 Wallyford E. Lothian, Scot.
62 I3 Walmer Kent, Eng.
228 F4 Walmer Bridge Lancs., Eng.
198 D2 Walmersley Gtr Man., Eng.
154 D2 Walmley W. Mids, Eng.
170 G4 Walmsgate Lincs., Eng.
24 K5 Walney, Isle of i. Eng.
120 H3 Walpole Suff., Eng.
166 A2 Walpole Cross Keys Norf., Eng.
166 A2 Walpole Highway Norf., Eng.
166 A2 Walpole Marsh Norf., Eng.
166 A2 Walpole St Andrew Norf., Eng.
166 A2 Walpole St Peter Norf., Eng.
94 G5 Walrond's Park Som., Eng.
94 G3 Walrow Som., Eng.
154 C2 Walsall W. Mids, Eng.
154 C2 Walsall Wood W. Mids, Eng.
222 B2 Walsden W. Yorks., Eng.
154 F3 Walsgrave on Sowe W. Mids, Eng.
120 E3 Walsham le Willows Suff., Eng.
216 E3 Walshford N. Yorks., Eng.
124 F2 Walsoken Cambs., Eng.
268 F2 Walston S. Lanark., Scot.
110 D4 Walsworth Herts., Eng.
106 D4 Walter's Ash Bucks., Eng.
350 F4 Walterston V. of Glam., Wales
140 B4 Walterstone Here., Eng.
62 G3 Waltham Kent, Eng.
170 F2 Waltham N.E. Lincs., Eng.
116 C3 Waltham Abbey Essex, Eng.
52 E5 Waltham Chase Hants., Eng.
110 E5 Waltham Cross Herts., Eng.
74 D2 Waltham Forest met. bor. Gtr Lon., Eng.
162 G2 Waltham on the Wolds Leics., Eng.
116 E2 Waltham's Cross Essex, Eng.
82 F3 Waltham St Lawrence W. and M., Eng.
74 D2 Walthamstow Gtr Lon., Eng.
106 D4 Walton Bucks., Eng.
232 F3 Walton Cumbria, Eng.
180 E3 Walton Derbys., Eng.
162 E4 Walton Leics., Eng.
190 D3 Walton Merseyside, Eng.
106 D2 Walton M.K., Eng.
124 C3 Walton Peterb., Eng.
144 D5 Walton Shrop., Eng.
94 H4 Walton Som., Eng.
148 C3 Walton Staffs., Eng.
120 H5 Walton Suff., Eng.
144 E3 Walton Telford, Eng.
132 C4 Walton Warks., Eng.
222 F3 Walton W. Yorks., Eng.
222 G1 Walton W. Yorks., Eng.
366 G5 Walton Powys, Wales
98 G2 Walton Cardiff Glos., Eng.
358 E2 Walton East Pembs., Wales
46 F2 Walton Elm Dorset, Eng.
166 A2 Walton Highway Norf., Eng.
94 H2 Walton-in-Gordano N. Som., Eng.
228 F4 Walton-le-Dale Lancs., Eng.
120 G5 Walton Lower Street Suff., Eng.
78 D1 Walton-on-Thames Surr., Eng.
148 C4 Walton-on-the-Hill Staffs., Eng.
78 E2 Walton on the Hill Surr., Eng.
116 J2 Walton on the Naze Essex, Eng.
162 E3 Walton on the Wolds Leics., Eng.
180 C6 Walton-on-Trent Derbys., Eng.
94 G2 Walton Park N. Som., Eng.
252 E2 Walton Park D. and G., Scot.
358 D3 Walton West Pembs., Wales
378 F2 Walwen Flints., Wales
378 F2 Walwen Flints., Wales
244 E5 Walwick Northumb., Eng.
236 F4 Walworth Darl., Eng.
74 D3 Walworth Gtr Lon., Eng.
388 D2 Walworth Limavady, N. Ire.
236 F4 Walworth Gate Darl., Eng.
358 D3 Walwyn's Castle Pembs., Wales
94 F5 Wambrook Som., Eng.
78 C2 Wanborough Surr., Eng.
86 E2 Wanborough Swindon, Eng.
268 E3 Wandel S. Lanark., Scot.
244 F2 Wandon Northumb., Eng.
110 C4 Wandon End Herts., Eng.
74 C3 Wandsworth Gtr Lon., Eng.
74 C3 Wandsworth met. bor. Gtr Lon., Eng.
244 G2 Wandylaw Northumb., Eng.
120 C2 Wangford Suff., Eng.
120 I2 Wangford Suff., Eng.
162 E2 Wanlip Leics., Eng.
252 E1 Wanlockhead D. and G., Scot.
210 F3 Wansford E. Riding, Eng.
124 B3 Wansford Peterb., Eng.
62 D3 Wanshurst Green Kent, Eng.
74 E2 Wanstead Gtr Lon., Eng.
94 J3 Wanstrow Som., Eng.
98 E3 Wanswell Glos., Eng.
102 C5 Wantage Oxon, Eng.
98 E4 Wapley S. Glos., Eng.
132 D4 Wappenbury Warks., Eng.
128 C5 Wappenham Northants., Eng.
74 D2 Wapping Gtr Lon., Eng.
232 D4 Warblebank Cumbria, Eng.
58 H3 Warbleton E. Sussex, Eng.
52 G5 Warblington Hants., Eng.
102 E5 Warborough Oxon, Eng.
124 D4 Warboys Cambs., Eng.
228 D3 Warbreck Blackpool, Eng.
36 F1 Warbstow Corn., Eng.
198 C3 Warburton Gtr Man., Eng.
198 D3 Warburton Green Gtr Man., Eng.
232 H5 Warcop Cumbria, Eng.
62 F2 Warden Kent, Eng.
244 E6 Warden Northumb., Eng.
154 D3 Ward End W. Mids, Eng.
98 G2 Warden Hill Glos., Eng.
110 C3 Warden Street Central Bedfordshire, Eng.
120 E3 Ward Green Suff., Eng.
22 J5 Ward Hill hill Scot.
102 D2 Wardington Oxon, Eng.
184 D3 Wardle Cheshire East, Eng.
198 E2 Wardle Gtr Man., Eng.
198 E2 Wardley Gtr Man., Eng.
162 G3 Wardley Rutland, Eng.

Wardley to Whateley

236 F2 Wardley T. and W., Eng.
180 C3 Wardlow Derbys., Eng.
22 □N2 Ward of Bressay hill Scot.
184 G1 Wardsend Cheshire East, Eng.
24 L5 Ward's Stone hill Eng.
124 E4 Wardy Hill Cambs., Eng.
110 E5 Ware Herts., Eng.
62 H3 Ware Kent, Eng.
46 G3 Wareham Dorset, Eng.
62 F4 Warehorne Kent, Eng.
244 G2 Warenford Northumb., Eng.
244 G2 Waren Mill Northumb., Eng.
244 G2 Warenton Northumb., Eng.
110 F5 Wareside Herts., Eng.
124 C5 Waresley Cambs., Eng.
136 D2 Waresley Worcs., Eng.
62 D3 Ware Street Kent, Eng.
82 F3 Warfield Brack., Eng.
190 F3 Wargrave Merseyside, Eng.
82 E2 Wargrave W'ham, Eng.
140 C3 Warham Here., Eng.
166 E1 Warham Norf., Eng.
396 H3 Waringsford Banbridge, N. Ire.
132 B3 Waring's Green Warks., Eng.
396 G3 Waringstown Craigavon, N. Ire.
244 D2 Wark Northumb., Eng.
244 D5 Wark Northumb., Eng.
40 E3 Warkleigh Devon, Eng.
128 C3 Warkton Northants., Eng.
128 B5 Warkworth Northants., Eng.
244 H3 Warkworth Northumb., Eng.
216 E2 Warlaby N. Yorks., Eng.
222 B2 Warland W. Yorks., Eng.
36 F2 Warleggan Corn., Eng.
116 D4 Warley Essex, Eng.
154 C3 Warley W. Mids, Eng.
222 C3 Warley Town W. Yorks., Eng.
78 F2 Warlingham Surr., Eng.
222 F2 Warmfield W. Yorks., Eng.
184 E3 Warmingham Cheshire East, Eng.
128 G2 Warmington Northants., Eng.
132 D5 Warmington Warks., Eng.
86 B4 Warminster Wilts., Eng.
62 D3 Warmlake Kent, Eng.
98 E3 Warmley S. Glos., Eng.
98 E5 Warmley Hill S. Glos., Eng.
208 E3 Warmsworth S. Yorks., Eng.
46 E3 Warmwell Dorset, Eng.
136 E2 Warndon Worcs., Eng.
110 C5 Warners End Herts., Eng.
58 D2 Warnford Hants., Eng.
58 D2 Warningcamp W. Sussex, Eng.
58 E2 Warninglid W. Sussex, Eng.
184 F2 Warren Cheshire East, Eng.
358 E4 Warren Pembs., Wales
216 F1 Warrenby R. and C., Eng.
40 E3 Warren House Devon, Eng.
396 G5 Warrenpoint Newry & Mourne, N. Ire.
82 F2 Warren Row W. and M., Eng.
110 E4 Warren's Green Herts., Eng.
62 E3 Warren Street Kent, Eng.
106 D1 Warrington M.K., Eng.
190 F3 Warrington Warr., Eng.
190 F3 Warrington admin. div. Eng.
288 D3 Warriston Edin., Scot.
304 I5 Warroch Perth and Kin., Scot.
52 E5 Warsash Hants., Eng.
148 D2 Warslow Staffs., Eng.
176 B3 Warsop Vale Notts., Eng.
210 D3 Warter E. Riding, Eng.
314 E3 Wartle Abers., Scot.
58 I3 Wartling E. Sussex, Eng.
162 F2 Wartnaby Leics., Eng.
228 E4 Warton Lancs., Eng.
228 F2 Warton Lancs., Eng.
244 F4 Warton Northumb., Eng.
132 C2 Warton Warks., Eng.
228 E4 Warton Bank Lancs., Eng.
132 C4 Warwick Warks., Eng.
232 F3 Warwick Bridge Cumbria, Eng.
132 C4 Warwickshire county Eng.
78 F2 Warwick Wold Surr., Eng.
329 C2 Wasbister Orkney, Scot.
232 C6 Wasdale Head Cumbria, Eng.
180 B2 Wash Derbys., Eng.
110 F4 Washall Green Herts., Eng.
36 E2 Washaway Corn., Eng.
40 H5 Washbourne Devon, Eng.
94 H3 Washbrook Suff., Eng.
120 F4 Washbrook Suff., Eng.
82 B3 Wash Common W. Berks., Eng.
148 C2 Washerwall Staffs., Eng.
216 D1 Washfold N. Yorks., Eng.
94 B3 Washford Som., Eng.
132 A4 Washford Warks., Eng.
170 C4 Washingborough Lincs., Eng.
236 F2 Washington T. and W., Eng.
58 D3 Washington W. Sussex, Eng.
120 D4 Washmere Green Suff., Eng.
154 C3 Washwood Heath W. Mids, Eng.
82 C3 Wasing W. Berks., Eng.
236 B3 Waskerley Durham, Eng.
132 C4 Wasperton Warks., Eng.
170 D4 Wasps Nest Lincs., Eng.
24 K5 Wast Water l. Eng.
94 B3 Watchet Som., Eng.
102 B5 Watchfield Oxon, Eng.
94 C3 Watchfield Som., Eng.
232 F6 Watchgate Cumbria, Eng.
40 I4 Watcombe Torbay, Eng.
232 D5 Watendlath Cumbria, Eng.
228 I4 Water Lancs., Eng.
124 F5 Waterbeach Cambs., Eng.
252 E2 Waterbeck D. and G., Scot.
46 E4 Watercombe Dorset, Eng.
106 D3 Water Eaton M.K., Eng.
102 D4 Water Eaton Oxon, Eng.
110 C3 Water End Bedford, Eng.
106 C5 Waterend Bucks., Eng.
110 C3 Water End Central Bedfordshire, Eng.
110 E3 Water End Central Bedfordshire, Eng.
210 D3 Water End E. Riding, Eng.
116 C1 Water End Essex, Eng.
110 C5 Water End Herts., Eng.
110 D5 Water End Herts., Eng.
148 D2 Waterfall Staffs., Eng.
228 I4 Waterfoot Lancs., Eng.
250 B2 Waterfoot E. Renf., Scot.
26 B7 Watergate Bay b. Eng.
94 H5 Watergore Som., Eng.
232 E6 Waterhead Cumbria, Eng.
252 E2 Waterhead D. and G., Scot.
166 I1 Waterheath Norf., Eng.
236 E3 Waterhouses Durham, Eng.
148 D2 Waterhouses Staffs., Eng.
62 C3 Wateringbury Kent, Eng.
98 G3 Waterlane Glos., Eng.
180 B3 Waterloo Derbys., Eng.
198 E2 Waterloo Gtr Man., Eng.
190 C3 Waterloo Merseyside, Eng.
166 G2 Waterloo Norf., Eng.
46 H3 Waterloo Poole, Eng.
314 H2 Waterloo Abers., Scot.
322 C3 Waterloo High., Scot.
280 C4 Waterloo N. Lanark., Scot.
304 I3 Waterloo Perth and Kin., Scot.

358 E3 Waterloo Pembs., Wales
372 E2 Waterloo Port Gwynedd, Wales
52 F5 Waterlooville Hants., Eng.
222 C2 Waterlow Norf., Eng.
268 E4 Watermeetings S. Lanark., Scot.
232 E6 Watermillock Cumbria, Eng.
124 B3 Water Newton Cambs., Eng.
24 K2 Water of Leith r. Scot.
22 G9 Water of Tulla r. Scot.
132 B2 Water Orton Warks., Eng.
102 E4 Waterperry Oxon, Eng.
94 D4 Waterrow Som., Eng.
58 C3 Watersfield W. Sussex, Eng.
198 E2 Watersheddings Gtr Man., Eng.
228 H4 Waterside B'burn, Eng.
106 E4 Waterside Bucks., Eng.
208 G2 Waterside E. Ayr., Scot.
388 C3 Waterside Derry, N. Ire.
314 D3 Waterside Abers., Scot.
314 H2 Waterside Abers., Scot.
262 E4 Waterside E. Ayr., Scot.
262 E4 Waterside E. Ayr., Scot.
276 E4 Waterside E. Dun., Scot.
102 E4 Waterstock Oxon, Eng.
358 E3 Waterston Pembs., Wales
106 B2 Water Stratford Bucks., Eng.
144 E3 Waters Upton Telford, Eng.
208 D3 Waterthorpe S. Yorks., Eng.
232 D7 Water Yeat Cumbria, Eng.
110 C6 Watford Herts., Eng.
128 C4 Watford Northants., Eng.
106 C4 Watford Park Caerp., Wales
216 D2 Wath N. Yorks., Eng.
216 E2 Wath N. Yorks., Eng.
232 A5 Wath Brow Cumbria, Eng.
208 D3 Wath upon Dearne S. Yorks., Eng.
98 E4 Watley's End S. Glos., Eng.
166 B2 Watlington Norf., Eng.
102 E5 Watlington Oxon, Eng.
176 B4 Watnall Notts., Eng.
320 K2 Watten High., Scot.
22 J6 Watten, Loch l. Scot.
120 E4 Wattisfield Suff., Eng.
120 E4 Wattisham Suff., Eng.
402 F6 Wattlebridge Fermanagh, N. Ire.
46 C3 Watton Dorset, Eng.
210 F3 Watton E. Riding, Eng.
166 D3 Watton Norf., Eng.
110 E4 Watton at Stone Herts., Eng.
94 F4 Watton Green Norf., Eng.
116 D4 Watton's Green Essex, Eng.
280 C3 Wattston N. Lanark., Scot.
350 F3 Wattstown R.C.T., Wales
350 H3 Wattsville Caerp., Wales
350 B3 Waunarlwydd Swansea, Wales
356 G2 Waunclunda Carmar., Wales
362 F2 Waun Fawr Cere., Wales
372 E2 Waun Fawr Gwynedd, Wales
356 E3 Waun y Clyn Carmar., Wales
106 D2 Wavendon M.K., Eng.
232 C4 Waverbridge Cumbria, Eng.
184 C2 Waverton Cheshire West & Chester, Eng.
232 C4 Waverton Cumbria, Eng.
190 D3 Wavertree Merseyside, Eng.
210 F4 Wawne E. Riding, Eng.
166 I2 Waxham Norf., Eng.
210 I4 Waxholme E. Riding, Eng.
94 G5 Wayford Som., Eng.
216 C2 Way Gill N. Yorks., Eng.
46 C3 Waytown Dorset, Eng.
40 F2 Way Village Devon, Eng.
94 Q2 Way Wick N. Som., Eng.
314 F2 Weachyburn Abers., Scot.
94 E4 Weacombe Som., Eng.
102 B4 Weald Oxon, Eng.
74 B2 Wealdstone Gtr Lon., Eng.
24 O4 Wear r. Eng.
222 E1 Weardley W. Yorks., Eng.
94 A3 Weare Som., Eng.
40 D2 Weare Giffard Devon, Eng.
236 B3 Wearhead Durham, Eng.
94 H4 Weare Som., Eng.
166 D2 Weasenham All Saints Norf., Eng.
166 D2 Weasenham St Peter Norf., Eng.
198 D3 Weaste Gtr Man., Eng.
136 F1 Weatheroak Hill Worcs., Eng.
184 D2 Weaverham Cheshire West & Chester, Eng.
62 D3 Weaving Street Kent, Eng.
98 E5 Webb's Heath S. Glos., Eng.
136 F2 Webheath Worcs., Eng.
140 B3 Webton Here., Eng.
132 D2 Weddington Warks., Eng.
86 D4 Wedhampton Wilts., Eng.
94 B2 Wedmore Som., Eng.
154 B2 Wednesbury W. Mids, Eng.
154 B2 Wednesfield W. Mids, Eng.
176 E3 Weecar Notts., Eng.
106 D3 Weedon Bucks., Eng.
128 C4 Weedon Bec Northants., Eng.
128 C5 Weedon Lois Northants., Eng.
148 E5 Weeford Staffs., Eng.
40 E2 Week Devon, Eng.
94 C4 Week Som., Eng.
52 E4 Weeke Hants., Eng.
128 E3 Weekley Northants., Eng.
36 F1 Week St Mary Corn., Eng.
210 F4 Weel E. Riding, Eng.
116 I2 Weeley Essex, Eng.
116 I2 Weeley Heath Essex, Eng.
304 G3 Weem Perth and Kin., Scot.
148 C4 Weeping Cross Staffs., Eng.
132 A4 Weethley Warks., Eng.
166 C4 Weeting Norf., Eng.
210 I5 Weeton E. Riding, Eng.
228 E4 Weeton Lancs., Eng.
222 E4 Weeton N. Yorks., Eng.
222 E2 Weetwood W. Yorks., Eng.
116 F4 Weir Essex, Eng.
228 I4 Weir Lancs., Eng.
144 C3 Weirbrook Shrop., Eng.
40 D3 Weir Quay Devon, Eng.
331 D3 Weisdale Shet., Scot.
176 B3 Welbeck Abbey Notts., Eng.
166 F3 Welborne Norf., Eng.
170 C5 Welbourn Lincs., Eng.
216 G2 Welburn N. Yorks., Eng.
216 G2 Welburn N. Yorks., Eng.
170 C6 Welby Lincs., Eng.
40 C2 Welcombe Devon, Eng.
128 F3 Weldon Northants., Eng.
128 C3 Welford Northants., Eng.
82 B3 Welford W. Berks., Eng.
132 A4 Welford-on-Avon Warks., Eng.
162 F3 Welham Leics., Eng.
176 D3 Welham Notts., Eng.
110 D5 Welham Green Herts., Eng.
52 F4 Welhams Hants., Eng.
170 Q4 Well Lincs., Eng.
216 E2 Well N. Yorks., Eng.
26 L2 Welland r. Eng.
308 D3 Wellbank Angus, Scot.

106 D5 Well End Bucks., Eng.
110 D6 Well End Herts., Eng.
132 C4 Wellesbourne Warks., Eng.
222 C2 Well Heads W. Yorks., Eng.
62 A2 Well Hill Kent, Eng.
314 B2 Wellhill Moray, Scot.
82 C3 Wellhouse W. Berks., Eng.
222 C3 Wellhouse W. Yorks., Eng.
74 E3 Welling Gtr Lon., Eng.
128 F4 Wellingborough Northants., Eng.
166 D2 Wellingham Norf., Eng.
170 C5 Wellingore Lincs., Eng.
232 B6 Wellington Cumbria, Eng.
140 C3 Wellington Here., Eng.
94 C5 Wellington Som., Eng.
144 E3 Wellington Telford, Eng.
140 C3 Wellington Heath Here., Eng.
86 B3 Wellington Marsh Here., Eng.
94 I2 Wellow B. and N.E. Som., Eng.
52 D6 Wellow I.o.W., Eng.
176 C3 Wellow Notts., Eng.
94 I3 Wells Som., Eng.
162 C5 Wellsborough Leics., Eng.
184 E3 Wells Green Cheshire East, Eng.
154 D3 Wells Green W. Mids, Eng.
166 E1 Wells-next-the-Sea Norf., Eng.
62 C3 Wells Street Kent, Eng.
116 C2 Wellstye Green Essex, Eng.
288 B3 Wellwood Fife, Scot.
166 A3 Welney Norf., Eng.
144 C2 Welshampton Shrop., Eng.
144 C2 Welsh Bicknor Glos., Eng.
144 C2 Welsh End Shrop., Eng.
144 C2 Welsh Frankton Shrop., Eng.
358 D4 Welsh Hook Pembs., Wales
140 C4 Welsh Newton Here., Eng.
366 G3 Welshpool Powys, Wales
350 F4 Welsh St Donats V. of Glam., Wales
94 J3 Welton B. and N.E. Som., Eng.
232 D4 Welton Cumbria, Eng.
210 E4 Welton E. Riding, Eng.
170 C4 Welton Lincs., Eng.
128 C4 Welton Northants., Eng.
170 F3 Welton le Marsh Lincs., Eng.
170 F3 Welton le Wold Lincs., Eng.
210 I4 Welwick E. Riding, Eng.
110 D4 Welwyn Herts., Eng.
110 D5 Welwyn Garden City Herts., Eng.
144 C2 Wem Shrop., Eng.
94 F4 Wembdon Som., Eng.
74 B2 Wembley Gtr Lon., Eng.
74 B2 Wembley Park Gtr Lon., Eng.
40 D4 Wembury Devon, Eng.
40 F2 Wembworthy Devon, Eng.
94 I3 Wembworthy Devon, Eng.
102 B5 Wemyss Bay Inverclyde, Scot.
78 D2 Wenallt Cere., Wales
102 D2 Wendens Ambo Essex, Eng.
86 E3 Wendlebury Oxon, Eng.
210 B4 Wendling Norf., Eng.
106 D2 Wendover Bucks., Eng.
350 B3 Wendover Dean Bucks., Eng.
36 F1 Wendron Corn., Eng.
124 D6 Wendy Cambs., Eng.
36 E2 Wenfordbridge Corn., Eng.
120 I3 Wenhaston Suff., Eng.
378 C2 Wenlli Conwy, Wales
26 Wenlock Edge ridge Eng.
170 D7 Wennington Cambs., Eng.
190 D3 Wennington Gtr Lon., Eng.
166 B3 Wennington Lancs., Eng.
198 D3 Wensley Derbys., Eng.
244 G3 Wensley N. Yorks., Eng.
40 D1 Wensleydale val. Eng.
74 B2 Wensum r. Eng.
176 B2 Went r. Eng.
222 G3 Wentbridge W. Yorks., Eng.
144 C4 Wentnor Shrop., Eng.
124 F4 Wentworth Cambs., Eng.
208 D3 Wentworth S. Yorks., Eng.
208 C2 Wentworth Castle S. Yorks., Eng.
350 G4 Wenvoe V. of Glam., Wales
140 B3 Weobley Here., Eng.
140 B3 Weobley Marsh Here., Eng.
154 C3 Weoley Castle W. Mids, Eng.
58 C3 Wepham W. Sussex, Eng.
378 G2 Wepre Flints., Wales
166 B3 Wereham Norf., Eng.
154 A2 Wergs W. Mids, Eng.
144 B2 Wern Shrop., Eng.
372 F3 Wern Gwynedd, Wales
366 F7 Wern Powys, Wales
366 G2 Wern Powys, Wales
350 B3 Wernffrwd Swansea, Wales
350 H3 Wern-olau Swansea, Wales
339 C2 Wernrheolydd Mon., Wales
339 C2 Wern-y-cwrt Mon., Wales
124 C3 Werrington Peterb., Eng.
148 C2 Werrington Staffs., Eng.
362 D4 Wervil Grange Cere., Wales
184 B2 Wervin Cheshire West & Chester, Eng.
228 E4 Wesham Lancs., Eng.
180 E4 Wessington Derbys., Eng.
350 F4 Wesseral V. of Glam., Wales
166 C2 West Acre Norf., Eng.
74 C2 West Acton Gtr Lon., Eng.
244 E1 West Allerdean Northumb., Eng.
40 E4 West Alvington Devon, Eng.
86 E4 West Amesbury Wilts., Eng.
40 F1 West Anstey Devon, Eng.
170 F4 West Ashby Lincs., Eng.
58 A3 West Ashling W. Sussex, Eng.
86 B4 West Ashton Wilts., Eng.
236 E4 West Auckland Durham, Eng.
216 H2 West Ayton N. Yorks., Eng.
94 H4 West Bagborough Som., Eng.
320 J2 West Balk Halton, Eng.
170 B4 West Barkwith Lincs., Eng.
288 H3 West Barns E. Lothian, Scot.
166 D1 West Barsham Norf., Eng.
46 C3 West Bay Dorset, Eng.
166 G1 West Beckham Norf., Eng.
280 D3 West Benhar N. Lanark., Scot.
62 G3 West Bergholt Essex, Eng.
116 D2 West Bergholt Essex, Eng.
82 C3 West Berkshire admin. div. Eng.
46 D3 West Bexington Dorset, Eng.
166 C2 West Bilney Norf., Eng.
58 D3 West Blatchington B. and H., Eng.
236 G2 West Boldon T. and W., Eng.
170 B6 Westborough Lincs., Eng.
52 E5 Westbourne Bourne., Eng.
58 A4 Westbourne W. Sussex, Eng.
74 C2 Westbourne Green Gtr Lon., Eng.

94 I4 West Bradley Som., Eng.
222 E3 West Bretton W. Yorks., Eng.
176 C5 West Bridgford Notts., Eng.
154 C2 West Bromwich W. Mids, Eng.
62 I2 Westbrook Kent, Eng.
82 B3 Westbrook W. Berks., Eng.
86 C3 Westbrook Wilts., Eng.
40 E1 West Buckland Devon, Eng.
94 E5 West Buckland Som., Eng.
78 C2 West Burra r. Scot. see Burra
331 C3 West Burrafirth Shet., Scot.
216 D2 West Burton N. Yorks., Eng.
58 C3 West Burton W. Sussex, Eng.
320 J2 Westburton High., Scot.
280 B3 Westburton W. Lanark., Scot.
98 E4 Westbury Shrop., Eng.
144 C3 Westbury Shrop., Eng.
86 B4 Westbury Wilts., Eng.
98 E4 Westbury Leigh Wilts., Eng.
98 E3 Westbury-on-Severn Glos., Eng.
94 E5 Westbury on Trym Bristol, Eng.
94 H3 Westbury-sub-Mendip Som., Eng.
236 D3 West Butsfield Durham, Eng.
170 B2 West Butterwick N. Lincs., Eng.
166 C1 Westby Lancs., Eng.
170 C6 Westby Lincs., Eng.
222 D3 Westgate Hill W. Yorks., Eng.
78 C1 West Cairncake Abers., Scot.
314 D4 West Caister Norf., Eng.
300 E4 West Calder W. Lothian, Scot.
102 C3 West Carbeth Stir., Scot.
74 D1 West Carlton York., Eng.
58 C2 West Carr N. Lincs., Eng.
170 A2 West Carr Houses N. Lincs., Eng.
268 B3 West Cauldcoats S. Lanark., Scot.
46 F4 West Chaldon Dorset, Eng.
102 C5 West Challow Oxon, Eng.
46 D2 West Charleton Devon, Eng.
46 D2 West Chelborough Dorset, Eng.
244 H4 West Chevington Northumb., Eng.
58 D3 West Chiltington Common W. Sussex, Eng.
94 H5 West Chinnock Som., Eng.
86 H4 West Chisenbury Wilts., Eng.
78 C2 West Clandon Surr., Eng.
62 I4 West Cliffe Kent, Eng.
116 G4 Westcliff-on-Sea Southend, Eng.
94 H5 West Coker Som., Eng.
94 J4 Westcombe Som., Eng.
102 E3 Westcote Glos., Eng.
94 I3 West Compton Dorset, Eng.
102 B5 Westcot Oxon, Eng.
106 C3 Westcott Bucks., Eng.
78 D2 Westcott Devon, Eng.
102 C3 Westcott Barton Oxon, Eng.
86 E3 Westcourt Wilts., Eng.
210 B4 West Cowick E. Riding, Eng.
106 D2 Westcroft M.K., Eng.
350 B3 West Cross Swansea, Wales
86 C5 West Crudwell Wilts., Eng.
36 F1 West Curry Corn., Eng.
232 D4 West Curthwaite Cumbria, Eng.
58 G4 Westdean E. Sussex, Eng.
86 F5 West Dean Wilts., Eng.
58 B3 West Dean W. Sussex, Eng.
170 D7 West Deeping Lincs., Eng.
190 D3 West Derby Merseyside, Eng.
166 B3 West Dereham Norf., Eng.
198 D3 West Didsbury Gtr Man., Eng.
244 G3 West Ditchburn Northumb., Eng.
40 D1 West Down Devon, Eng.
74 B2 West Drayton Gtr Lon., Eng.
176 D3 West Drayton Notts., Eng.
74 D1 West Dudley Stir., Scot.
314 C3 West Dulwich Gtr Lon., Eng.
276 C2 West Dunbartonshire admin. div. Eng.
244 G5 West Edington Northumb., Eng.
210 F4 West Ella E. Riding, Eng.
110 D3 West End Bedford, Eng.
82 E3 West End F., Brack., Eng.
124 E3 West End Cambs., Eng.
210 F2 West End E. Riding, Eng.
180 E3 Westend Glos., Eng.
52 E5 West End Hants., Eng.
110 D5 West End Herts., Eng.
62 G2 West End Kent, Eng.
228 H2 West End Lancs., Eng.
170 C2 West End Lincs., Eng.
78 E1 West End Norf., Eng.
78 C1 West End S. Yorks., Eng.
208 E2 West End S. Yorks., Eng.
208 E2 West End S. Yorks., Eng.
86 D5 West End Wilts., Eng.
86 C5 West End Wilts., Eng.
58 A4 West End Wilts., Eng.
58 A4 West End Wilts., Eng.
268 E2 West End S. Lanark., Scot.
350 H3 West End Caerp., Wales
52 F2 West End Green Hants., Eng.
98 E5 Westend Town Northumb., Eng.
62 F2 West Farleigh Kent, Eng.
128 B5 West Farndon Northants., Eng.
144 C3 West Felton Shrop., Eng.
22 C6 West Fen reg. Eng.
170 D2 West Fen reg. Eng.
232 A5 Westfield Cumbria, Eng.
58 J3 Westfield E. Sussex, Eng.
166 F3 Westfield Norf., Eng.
78 C2 Westfield Surr., Eng.
300 D2 Westfield W. Lothian, Scot.
222 D2 Westfield W. Yorks., Eng.
320 J2 Westfield High., Scot.
280 B3 Westfield S. Lanark., Scot.
288 A3 Westfield W. Lothian, Scot.
62 D3 Westfield Sole Kent, Eng.
86 B4 West Firle E. Sussex, Eng.
244 G2 West Fleetham Northumb., Eng.
94 E5 Westford Som., Eng.
222 F2 West Garforth W. Yorks., Eng.
236 C3 Westgate Durham, Eng.
166 E1 Westgate N. Lincs., Eng.
216 C3 Westgate N. Lincs., Eng.
222 D3 Westgate Hill W. Yorks., Eng.
62 I2 Westgate on Sea Kent, Eng.
102 C5 West Ginge Oxon, Eng.
102 C3 West Glen Arg. and B., Scot.
74 F3 West Gorton Gtr Man., Eng.
86 D5 West Grafton Wilts., Eng.
74 D2 West Green Gtr Lon., Eng.
52 G3 West Green Hants., Eng.
58 E2 West Green W. Sussex, Eng.
58 E3 West Grimstead Wilts., Eng.
58 E3 West Grinstead W. Sussex, Eng.
176 C3 West Haddlesey N. Yorks., Eng.
128 C3 West Haddon Northants., Eng.
102 D5 West Hagbourne Oxon, Eng.
136 E1 West Hagley Worcs., Eng.
94 H4 West Hall Cumbria, Eng.
120 I2 Westhall Suff., Eng.
314 E3 Westhall Abers., Scot.
180 E5 West Hallam Derbys., Eng.
170 C1 West Halton N. Lincs., Eng.
46 E3 Westham Dorset, Eng.
58 H4 Westham E. Sussex, Eng.
74 E2 West Ham Gtr Lon., Eng.
94 I5 Westham Som., Eng.
308 F2 Westmuir Angus, Scot.
58 B3 Westhampnett W. Sussex, Eng.
216 G2 West Hampstead Gtr Lon., Eng.
180 E3 West Handley Derbys., Eng.
102 C5 West Hanney Oxon, Eng.
116 E3 West Hanningfield Essex, Eng.
222 F3 West Hardwick W. Yorks., Eng.
74 B2 West Harnham Gtr Lon., Eng.
236 G2 West Harton T. and W., Eng.
94 F5 West Hatch Som., Eng.
86 C5 West Hatch Wilts., Eng.
94 H3 Westhay Som., Eng.
228 G2 West Head Norf., Eng.
166 A3 West Head Norf., Eng.
184 F3 West Heath Cheshire East, Eng.
58 C2 West Heath Gtr Lon., Eng.
52 D3 West Heath Hants., Eng.
52 F3 West Heath Hants., Eng.
154 C3 West Heath W. Mids, Eng.
74 C2 West Hendon Gtr Lon., Eng.
102 C5 West Hendred Oxon, Eng.
216 H2 West Heslerton N. Yorks., Eng.
94 H3 West Hewish N. Som., Eng.
140 D3 Westhide Here., Eng.
46 H3 West Hill Devon, Eng.
210 G2 West Hill E. Riding, Eng.
46 H3 West Hill E. Riding, Eng.
98 E4 Westhill Abers., Scot.
322 I2 Westhill Abers., Scot.
52 F2 West Hoathly W. Sussex, Eng.
46 E3 West Holme Dorset, Eng.
236 F3 West Holywell T. and W., Eng.
210 F4 Westhope Here., Eng.
144 D5 Westhope Shrop., Eng.
128 G6 West Hornfon Essex, Eng.
180 F3 Westhorpe Derbys., Eng.
170 E6 Westhorpe Lincs., Eng.
120 E3 Westhorpe Suff., Eng.
78 E2 West Horrington Som., Eng.
94 I3 West Horsley Surr., Eng.
62 H4 West Horton Northumb., Eng.
244 F2 West Hougham Kent, Eng.
198 D2 Westhoughton Gtr Man., Eng.
180 B3 Westhouses Derbys., Eng.
46 H3 West Howe Bourne., Eng.
52 E5 West Howetown Corn., Eng.
94 D4 Westhumble Surr., Eng.
78 E2 West Huntspill Som., Eng.
94 H3 West Hyde Herts., Eng.
110 B6 West Hythe Kent, Eng.
62 G4 West Ilsley W. Berks., Eng.
82 C2 Westing Shet., Scot.
331 E1 West Itchenor W. Sussex, Eng.
58 A4 West Keal Lincs., Eng.
170 C5 West Kennett Wilts., Eng.
86 E3 West Kilbride N. Ayr., Scot.
264 C2 West Kilburn Gtr Lon., Eng.
74 C2 West Kingsdown Kent, Eng.
62 B2 West Kington Wilts., Eng.
86 B3 West Kington Wick Wilts., Eng.
98 E5 West Kirby Merseyside, Eng.
190 B3 West Knapton N. Yorks., Eng.
216 H2 West Knighton Dorset, Eng.
46 E3 West Knoyle Wilts., Eng.
86 B5 West Kyloe Northumb., Eng.
244 F2 West Kyo Durham, Eng.
236 F2 Westlake Devon, Eng.
40 E4 West Lambrook Som., Eng.
94 H5 Westlands High., Scot.
148 B3 Westlands High., Scot.
62 H3 West Langdon Kent, Eng.
320 H3 West Langwell High., Scot.
216 G2 West Lavington W. Sussex, Eng.
58 B3 West Lavington Wilts., Eng.
86 D4 West Layton N. Yorks., Eng.
216 D1 West Lea N. Yorks., Eng.
94 H3 Westlea Swindon, Eng.
86 E2 Westleigh Devon, Eng.
86 E2 West Leigh Devon, Eng.
40 E2 West Leigh Devon, Eng.
40 E2 Westleigh Gtr Man., Eng.
198 D2 Westleigh Som., Eng.
120 I3 Westleton Suff., Eng.
94 E4 West Lexham Norf., Eng.
166 D2 Westley Shrop., Eng.
144 C4 Westley Suff., Eng.
120 C3 Westley Waterless Cambs., Eng.
124 F6 Westley Waterless Cambs., Eng.
86 E2 West Lilling N. Yorks., Eng.
216 G1 West Lingo Fife, Scot.
331 C3 West Linton Notts., Eng.

331 C3 Westerwick Shet., Scot.
256 D2 West Linton Borders, Scot.
52 G4 West Liss Hants., Eng.
98 E5 Westloch Borders, Scot.
144 C3 West Loch Roag b. Scot.
22 C6 West Loch Tarbert inlet Scot.
102 C5 West Looe Corn., Eng.
36 F2 Westlooe Corn., Eng.
288 B3 West Lothian admin. div. Scot.
46 F4 West Lulworth Dorset, Eng.
331 D2 West Lydford Som., Eng.
40 E1 West Lyn Devon, Eng.
94 G4 West Lyng Som., Eng.
166 B2 West Lynn Norf., Eng.
244 F1 West Mains Northumb., Eng.
136 C3 West Malling Kent, Eng.
136 C3 West Malvern Worcs., Eng.
58 A3 Westmancote Worcs., Eng.
46 F1 West Marden W. Sussex, Eng.
62 H3 West Markham Notts., Eng.
52 E4 West Marsh N.E. Lincs., Eng.
216 C3 West Marton N. Yorks., Eng.
208 D2 West Melbury Dorset, Eng.
58 A3 West Melton S. Yorks., Eng.
52 F4 West Meon Hants., Eng.
52 F4 West Meon Hut Hants., Eng.
58 A3 West Meon Woodlands Hants., Eng.
116 H3 West Mersea Essex, Eng.
58 F3 West Meston E. Sussex, Eng.
154 C2 West Midlands admin. div. Eng.
110 C4 Westmill Herts., Eng.
46 E4 West Milton Dorset, Eng.
74 D2 West Minster Kent, Eng.
74 D2 West Molesey Surr., Eng.
94 H4 West Monkton Som., Eng.
46 H3 West Moors Dorset, Eng.
46 F4 West Morden Dorset, Eng.
256 I2 West Morriston Borders, Scot.
222 C1 West Morton W. Yorks., Eng.
176 B4 West Mostard Cumbria, Eng.
166 A2 West Walton Norf., Eng.
232 D4 West Ward Cumbria, Eng.
40 E1 Westward Ho! Devon, Eng.
62 H4 West Ness N. Yorks., Eng.
329 C3 Westness Orkney, Scot.
62 E5 West Newbiggin Darl., Eng.
232 B4 West Newton Cumbria, Eng.
216 H3 West Newton E. Riding, Eng.
166 C3 West Newton Norf., Eng.
244 E2 Westnewton Northumb., Eng.
94 G4 West Newton Som., Eng.
94 E2 West Norwood Gtr Lon., Eng.
236 G2 Westoe T. and W., Eng.
184 E3 Weston Cheshire East, Eng.
40 G2 Weston Devon, Eng.
40 H4 Weston Devon, Eng.
46 F4 Weston Dorset, Eng.
190 E4 Weston Halton, Eng.
52 G3 Weston Hants., Eng.
58 A4 Weston Here., Eng.
216 D2 Weston Here., Eng.
86 E5 Weston Herts., Eng.
170 F7 Weston Lincs., Eng.
124 C3 Weston N. Yorks., Eng.
144 D5 Weston Shrop., Eng.
144 E4 Weston Shrop., Eng.
148 C3 Weston Staffs., Eng.
82 B3 Weston W. Berks., Eng.
314 E4 Weston Moray, Scot.
40 E2 Weston Bampfylde Som., Eng.
140 D3 Weston Beggard Here., Eng.
98 F4 Weston-by-Welland Northants., Eng.
86 B3 Weston Colville Cambs., Eng.
124 G6 Weston Corbett Hants., Eng.
148 C3 Weston Coyney Stoke, Eng.
128 G6 Weston Favell Northants., Eng.
128 G6 Weston Green Cambs., Eng.
232 F3 Weston Green Norf., Eng.
166 F3 Weston Green Surr., Eng.
144 G3 Weston Heath Shrop., Eng.
170 F7 Weston Hills Lincs., Eng.
132 D3 Weston in Arden Warks., Eng.
110 C4 Westoning Central Bedfordshire, Eng.
94 H2 Weston-in-Gordano N. Som., Eng.
148 A4 Weston Jones Staffs., Eng.
166 F2 Weston Longville Norf., Eng.
144 C3 Weston Lullingfields Shrop., Eng.
40 H2 Weston Mill Plymouth, Eng.
132 B5 Weston-on-Avon Warks., Eng.
102 D3 Weston-on-the-Green Oxon, Eng.
180 E5 Weston-on-Trent Derbys., Eng.
52 E5 Weston Patrick Hants., Eng.
190 E2 Weston Point Halton, Eng.
144 B2 Weston Rhyn Shrop., Eng.
94 G2 Weston Subedge Glos., Eng.
94 I1 Weston-super-Mare N. Som., Eng.
94 J3 Weston Town Som., Eng.
106 C3 Weston Turville Bucks., Eng.
148 B4 Weston-under-Lizard Staffs., Eng.
140 D3 Weston under Penyard Here., Eng.
132 D4 Weston under Wetherley Warks., Eng.
180 D5 Weston Underwood Derbys., Eng.
106 D2 Weston Underwood M.K., Eng.
94 I4 Westonzoyland Som., Eng.
46 F2 West Orchard Dorset, Eng.
86 E3 West Overton Wilts., Eng.
216 G2 Westow N. Yorks., Eng.
190 E3 West Park Merseyside, Eng.
314 F3 West Park Abers., Scot.
331 C2 West Parley Dorset, Eng.
62 G3 West Peckham Kent, Eng.
236 F2 West Pelton Durham, Eng.
94 I4 West Pennard Som., Eng.
36 D2 West Pentire Corn., Eng.
124 C5 West Perry Cambs., Eng.
170 F7 West Porlock Som., Eng.
216 C2 West Putford Devon, Eng.
24 N5 West Pulham Dorset, Eng.
228 E4 West Quantoxhead Som., Eng.
350 G4 Westra V. of Glam., Wales
208 C3 West Rainton Durham, Eng.
170 D3 West Rasen Lincs., Eng.
329 C1 West Rasen Lincs., Eng.
22 J4 Westray i. Scot.
184 D2 Wharton Cheshire West & Chester, Eng.

82 C2 Westridge Green W. Berks., Eng.
288 A3 Westrigg W. Lothian, Scot.
86 C5 Westrop Wilts., Eng.
216 E1 West Rounton N. Yorks., Eng.
120 B2 West Row Suff., Eng.
166 G1 West Rudham Norf., Eng.
166 I1 West Runton Norf., Eng.
256 I2 Struther Borders, Scot.
288 B3 Westry Cambs., Eng.
244 F4 Westruther Borders, Scot.
288 E3 West Saltoun E. Lothian, Eng.
244 A3 Westward Shet., Scot.
40 E1 West Shepton Som., Eng.
94 I3 West Shepton Som., Eng.
166 I2 West Somerton Norf., Eng.
46 F3 West Stafford Dorset, Eng.
176 D4 West Stockwith Notts., Eng.
216 C1 West Stonesdale N. Yorks., Eng.
94 H3 West Stoughton Som., Eng.
46 F3 West Stour Dorset, Eng.
62 H3 West Stourmouth Kent, Eng.
120 D3 West Stow Suff., Eng.
86 E4 West Stowell Wilts., Eng.
52 E4 West Stratton Hants., Eng.
62 H3 West Street Kent, Eng.
52 F4 West Street Medway, Eng.
58 F4 West Street Suff., Eng.
58 F4 West Sussex county Eng.
216 E2 West Tanfield N. Yorks., Eng.
300 D4 West Tarbert Arg. and B., Scot.
244 G4 West Thirston Northumb., Eng.
58 A4 West Thorney W. Sussex, Eng.
116 D5 West Thurrock Thurrock, Eng.
52 F4 West Tilbury Thurrock, Eng.
52 F4 West Tisted Hants., Eng.
166 D3 West Tofts Norf., Eng.
170 E4 West Tofts Perth and Kin., Scot.
304 J4 West Torrington Lincs., Eng.
94 H2 West Town B. and N.E. Som., Eng.
52 G6 West Town Hants., Eng.
52 F4 West Town N. Som., Eng.
94 I4 West Town Som., Eng.
94 I4 Westvale Merseyside, Eng.
190 D3 Westville V. of Glam., Wales
350 F4 Westville Notts., Eng.
176 B4 Westward Cumbria, Eng.
232 D4 Westward Cumbria, Eng.
40 E1 Westwell Kent, Eng.
62 F3 Westwell Kent, Eng.
62 A4 Westwell Leacon Kent, Eng.
52 G5 West Wellow Hants., Eng.
292 F3 West Wemyss Fife, Scot.
124 E5 Westwick Cambs., Eng.
236 D1 Westwick Durham, Eng.
166 H2 Westwick Norf., Eng.
124 G6 West Wick N. Som., Eng.
124 F6 West Wickham Cambs., Eng.
74 D2 West Wickham Gtr Lon., Eng.
110 C5 Westwick Row Herts., Eng.
358 E3 West Williamston Pembs., Wales
166 B2 West Winch Norf., Eng.
86 E5 West Winterslow Wilts., Eng.
58 A4 West Wittering W. Sussex, Eng.
216 D2 West Witton N. Yorks., Eng.
176 B4 Westwood Peterb., Eng.
124 C3 Westwood Peterb., Eng.
268 A2 Westwood S. Lanark., Scot.
244 D4 West Woodburn Northumb., Eng.
88 B3 West Woodhay W. Berks., Eng.
132 C4 Westwood Heath Warks., Eng.
94 K3 West Woodlands Som., Eng.
170 A3 Westwoodside N. Lincs., Eng.
94 I2 West Worldham Hants., Eng.
40 E2 West Worlington Devon, Eng.
58 D4 West Worthing W. Sussex, Eng.
124 G6 West Wratting Cambs., Eng.
106 C5 West Wycombe Bucks., Eng.
244 F6 West Wylam Northumb., Eng.
86 B3 West Yatton Wilts., Eng.
22 C6 West Yell Shet., Scot.
331 C4 West Yorkshire admin. div. Eng.
222 D2 West Youlstone Corn., Eng.
148 C3 Wetham Green Kent, Eng.
232 F3 Wetheral Cumbria, Eng.
216 G2 Wetherby W. Yorks., Eng.
216 G2 Wether Cote Fm N. Yorks., Eng.
120 E3 Wetherden Suff., Eng.
120 F3 Wetheringsett Suff., Eng.
116 B1 Wethersfield Essex, Eng.
331 C2 Wethersta Shet., Scot.
78 F1 Wetherup Street Suff., Eng.
148 C2 Wetley Abbey Staffs., Eng.
148 C2 Wetley Rocks Staffs., Eng.
184 D3 Wettenhall Cheshire East, Eng.
184 D3 Wettenhall Green Cheshire East, Eng.
148 D2 Wetton Staffs., Eng.
210 E2 Wetwang E. Riding, Eng.
148 A4 Wetwood Staffs., Eng.
86 F4 Wexcombe Wilts., Eng.
106 C5 Wexham Street Bucks., Eng.
166 F1 Weybourne Norf., Eng.
52 F3 Weybourne Surr., Eng.
120 G2 Weybread Suff., Eng.
120 G2 Weybread Street Suff., Eng.
78 D1 Weybridge Surr., Eng.
40 B5 Weycroft Devon, Eng.
320 K4 Weydale High., Scot.
52 D4 Weyhill Hants., Eng.
46 E4 Weymouth Dorset, Eng.
106 D2 Whaddon Bucks., Eng.
124 D6 Whaddon Cambs., Eng.
98 F3 Whaddon Glos., Eng.
98 E2 Whaddon Glos., Eng.
86 E5 Whaddon Wilts., Eng.
86 C3 Whaddon Wilts., Eng.
216 E2 Whaddon Gap Cambs., Eng.
232 F5 Whale Cumbria, Eng.
180 B3 Whaley Bridge Derbys., Eng.
180 B3 Whaley Thorns Notts., Eng.
228 H4 Whalley Lancs., Eng.
228 H4 Whalley Banks Lancs., Eng.
190 F3 Whalley Range Gtr Man., Eng.
331 C3 Whalsay airport Shet., Scot.
22 □Q2 Whalsay i. Scot.
244 G5 Wham N. Yorks., Eng.
216 B3 Wham N. Yorks., Eng.
170 F7 Whaplode Lincs., Eng.
170 F7 Whaplode Drove Lincs., Eng.
170 F7 Whaplode St Catherine Lincs., Eng.
216 C2 Wharfe r. Eng.
24 O6 Wharfe r. Eng.
216 B3 Wharfe N. Yorks., Eng.
228 E4 Wharles Lancs., Eng.
148 C2 Wharncliffe Side S. Yorks., Eng.
216 G2 Wharram le Street N. Yorks., Eng.
184 D2 Wharton Cheshire West & Chester, Eng.
140 C2 Wharton Here., Eng.
236 D1 Whashton N. Yorks., Eng.
132 C5 Whatcote Warks., Eng.
132 B2 Whateley Warks., Eng.

Whatfield to Woodwalton

20 E4 Whatfield Suff., Eng.
94 J3 Whatley Som., Eng.
58 I3 Whatlington E. Sussex, Eng.
62 G4 Whatsole Street Kent, Eng.
80 E4 Whatstandwell Derbys., Eng.
76 D5 Whatton Notts., Eng.
52 C3 Whauphill D. and G., Scot.
16 C1 Whaw N. Yorks., Eng.
66 I4 Wheatacre Norf., Eng.
80 E4 Wheatcroft Derbys., Eng.
98 E3 Wheatenhurst Glos., Eng.
02 E4 Wheatfield Oxon, Eng.
88 E2 Wheatfield Limavady, N. Ire.
10 D5 Wheathampstead Herts., Eng.
44 E5 Wheathill Shrop., Eng.
94 I4 Wheathill Som., Eng.
02 D5 Wheathill Fermanagh, N. Ire.
52 G4 Wheatley Hants., Eng.
02 E4 Wheatley Oxon, Eng.
22 C2 Wheatley W. Yorks., Eng.
36 G3 Wheatley Hill Durham, Eng.
08 F2 Wheatley Hills S. Yorks., Eng.
28 I3 Wheatley Lane Lancs., Eng.
08 F2 Wheatley Park S. Yorks., Eng.
48 B4 Wheaton Aston Staffs., Eng.
94 C4 Wheddon Cross Som., Eng.
14 E3 Wheedlemont Abers., Scot.
78 C3 Wheelerstreet Surr., Eng.
84 E3 Wheelock Cheshire East, Eng.
84 E3 Wheelock Heath Cheshire East, Eng.
28 G4 Wheelton Lancs., Eng.
08 D2 Wheen Angus, Scot.
22 G2 Wheldale W. Yorks., Eng.
16 G3 Wheldrake York, Eng.
98 I3 Whelford Glos., Eng.
98 B2 Whelley Gtr Man., Eng.
10 B5 Whelpley Hill Herts., Eng.
32 D4 Whelpo Cumbria, Eng.
78 F2 Whelston Flints., Wales
16 F2 Whenby N. Yorks., Eng.
20 D3 Whepstead Suff., Eng.
24 M5 Whernside hill Eng.
20 F4 Wherstead Suff., Eng.
52 D3 Wherwell Hants., Eng.
36 F4 Whessoe Darl., Eng.
80 C3 Wheston Derbys., Eng.
46 C2 Whetley Cross Dorset, Eng.
62 C3 Whetsted Kent, Eng.
74 C2 Whetstone Gtr Lon., Eng.
62 D3 Whetstone Leics., Eng.
32 C7 Whicham Cumbria, Eng.
32 C5 Whichford Warks., Eng.
36 E2 Whickham T. and W., Eng.
40 E2 Whiddon Down Devon, Eng.
80 B3 Whifflet N. Lanark., Scot.
08 E3 Whigstreet Angus, Scot.
28 C4 Whilton Northants., Eng.
56 E2 Whim Borders, Scot.
40 F2 Whimple Devon, Eng.
66 I2 Whimpwell Green Norf., Eng.
66 E3 Whinburgh Norf., Eng.
28 E3 Whin Lane End Lancs., Eng.
14 H2 Whinnyfold Abers., Scot.
28 H4 Whinny Heights B'burn, Eng.
36 G4 Whinny Hill Stockton, Eng.
52 E6 Whippingham I.o.W., Eng.
10 B4 Whipsnade Central Bedfordshire, Eng.
40 F2 Whipton Devon, Eng.
08 C3 Whirlow S. Yorks., Eng.
70 C4 Whisby Lincs., Eng.
62 G2 Whissendine Rutland, Eng.
66 E2 Whissonsett Norf., Eng.
84 F2 Whisterfield Cheshire East, Eng.
82 E3 Whistley Green W'ham, Eng.
90 E3 Whiston Merseyside, Eng.
28 E4 Whiston Northants., Eng.
48 C4 Whiston Staffs., Eng.
48 D2 Whiston Staffs., Eng.
08 E3 Whiston S. Yorks., Eng.
90 E3 Whiston Cross Merseyside, Eng.
44 G4 Whiston Cross Shrop., Eng.
48 D2 Whiston Eaves Staffs., Eng.
32 C2 Whitacre Fields Warks., Eng.
32 B2 Whitacre Heath Warks., Eng.
32 B7 Whitbeck Cumbria, Eng.
40 E2 Whitbourne Here., Eng.
36 G2 Whitburn T. and W., Eng.
88 A3 Whitburn W. Lothian, Scot.
84 B2 Whitby Cheshire West & Chester, Eng.
16 H1 Whitby N. Yorks., Eng.
84 B2 Whitbyheath Cheshire West & Chester, Eng.
94 I2 Whitchurch B. and N.E. Som., Eng.
06 C3 Whitchurch Bucks., Eng.
40 D3 Whitchurch Devon, Eng.
52 D3 Whitchurch Hants., Eng.
40 D4 Whitchurch Here., Eng.
44 D2 Whitchurch Shrop., Eng.
32 B5 Whitchurch Warks., Eng.
50 G3 Whitchurch Cardiff, Wales
58 C2 Whitchurch Pembs., Wales
46 B3 Whitchurch Canonicorum Dorset, Eng.
02 E5 Whitchurch Hill Oxon, Eng.
02 E6 Whitchurch-on-Thames Oxon, Eng.
46 E3 Whitcombe Dorset, Eng.
44 B5 Whitcott Keysett Shrop., Eng.
88 K4 Whiteabbey Newtownabbey, N. Ire.
14 D2 Whiteacen Moray, Scot.
24 M2 Whiteadder Water r. Scot.
16 F2 Whiteash Green Essex, Eng.
94 E5 White Ball Som., Eng.
28 H4 Whitebirk B'burn, Eng.
14 G2 Whitebog Abers., Scot.
22 H3 Whitebridge High., Scot.
39 D2 Whitebrook Mon., Wales
56 I2 Whiteburn Borders, Scot.
52 B3 Whitecairn D. and G., Scot.
14 G3 Whitecairns Abers., Scot.
68 E3 Whitecastle S. Lanark., Scot.
74 D2 Whitechapel Gtr Lon., Eng.
28 F3 Whitechapel Lancs., Eng.
94 J5 Whitechurch Som., Eng.
58 F2 Whitechurch Pembs., Wales
16 G2 White Colne Essex, Eng.
22 J12 White Coomb hill Scot.
28 G4 White Coppice Lancs., Eng.
22 E2 Whitecote W. Yorks., Eng.
88 E3 Whitecraig E. Lothian, Scot.
98 D3 Whitecroft Glos., Eng.
52 B3 Whitecrook D. and G., Scot.
76 D2 Whitecrook W. Dun., Scot.
36 E2 Whitecross Corn., Eng.
36 E2 White Cross Corn., Eng.
40 F2 White Cross Devon, Eng.
46 C3 Whitecross Dorset, Eng.
40 C3 White Cross Here., Eng.
86 B5 White Cross Wilts., Eng.
96 F4 Whitecross Newry & Mourne, N. Ire.
80 E3 Whitecross Falk., Scot.
98 F2 White End Glos., Eng.
62 C4 Whitefaulds S. Ayr., Scot.
46 G3 Whitefield Dorset, Eng.
198 D2 Whitefield Gtr Man., Eng.
314 F2 Whitefield Abers., Scot.
320 K2 Whitefield High., Scot.
322 H3 Whitefield High., Scot.
304 J3 Whitefield Perth and Kin., Scot.
184 D2 Whitegate Cheshire West & Chester, Eng.
396 H4 Whitegates Banbridge, N. Ire.
52 G3 Whitehall Hants., Eng.
58 D3 Whitehall W. Sussex, Eng.
329 F3 Whitehall Orkney, Scot.
232 A5 Whitehaven Cumbria, Eng.
388 L4 Whitehead Carrickfergus, N. Ire.
52 G4 Whitehill Hants., Eng.
62 F3 Whitehill Kent, Eng.
86 B5 White Hill Wilts., Eng.
402 E4 Whitehill Fermanagh, N. Ire.
314 G2 Whitehill Abers., Scot.
288 E3 Whitehill Midlothian, Scot.
314 E2 Whitehill Moray, Scot.
264 F2 Whitehill N. Ayr., Scot.
314 F1 Whitehills Abers., Scot.
26 I4 White Horse, Vale of val. Eng.
180 B2 Whitehough Derbys., Eng.
388 K5 Whitehouse Belfast, N. Ire.
314 F3 Whitehouse Abers., Scot.
300 D4 Whitehouse Arg. and B., Scot.
154 D2 Whitehouse Common W. Mids, Eng.
176 D3 White Houses Notts., Eng.
276 D2 Whiteinch Glas., Scot.
288 H2 Whitekirk E. Lothian, Scot.
236 D3 White Kirkley Durham, Eng.
46 E3 White Lackington Dorset, Eng.
94 G5 Whitelackington Som., Eng.
136 E2 White Ladies Aston Worcs., Eng.
256 K2 Whitelaw Borders, Scot.
320 K2 Whiteleen High., Scot.
262 D3 Whitelees S. Ayr., Scot.
52 E5 Whiteley Hants., Eng.
52 E7 Whiteley Bank I.o.W., Eng.
184 G2 Whiteley Green Cheshire East, Eng.
252 A3 Whiteleys D. and G., Scot.
78 D1 Whiteley Village Surr., Eng.
228 E2 White Lund Lancs., Eng.
339 D2 Whitelye Mon., Wales
58 F2 Whitemans Green W. Sussex, Eng.
356 E2 White Mill Carmar., Wales
314 B2 Whitemire Moray, Scot.
180 E4 White Moor Derbys., Eng.
176 B5 Whitemoor Nott., Eng.
331 D3 Whiteness Shet., Scot.
22 G5 Whiten Head hd Scot.
116 F2 White Notley Essex, Eng.
102 B4 Whiteoak Green Oxon, Eng.
86 F5 Whiteparish Wilts., Eng.
170 G4 White Pit Lincs., Eng.
314 G3 Whiterashes Abers., Scot.
396 K3 Whiterock Ards, N. Ire.
140 C4 White Rocks Here., Eng.
116 D3 White Roding Essex, Eng.
98 F3 Whiteshill Glos., Eng.
244 C5 Whiteside Northumb., Eng.
288 B3 Whiteside W. Lothian, Scot.
388 H4 Whitesides Corner Ballymena, N. Ire.
58 H3 Whitesmith E. Sussex, Eng.
40 F2 Whitestone Devon, Eng.
314 F3 Whitestone Abers., Scot.
300 D5 Whitestone Arg. and B., Scot.
120 E4 Whitestreet Green Suff., Eng.
314 G2 Whitestripe Abers., Scot.
82 F3 White Waltham W. and M., Eng.
98 G3 Whiteway Glos., Eng.
228 G3 Whitewell Lancs., Eng.
378 I4 Whitewell Wrex., Wales
40 E3 Whiteworks Devon, Eng.
314 D2 Whitewreath Moray, Scot.
140 B4 Whitfield Here., Eng.
62 H4 Whitfield Kent, Eng.
128 C5 Whitfield Northants., Eng.
244 C6 Whitfield Northumb., Eng.
98 E4 Whitfield S. Glos., Eng.
40 G2 Whitford Devon, Eng.
378 F2 Whitford Flints., Wales
26 D4 Whitford Point pt Wales
210 D4 Whitgift E. Riding, Eng.
148 C3 Whitgreave Staffs., Eng.
252 C3 Whithorn D. and G., Scot.
264 D4 Whiting Bay N. Ayr., Scot.
222 F2 Whitkirk W. Yorks., Eng.
314 G3 Whitlam Abers., Scot.
356 C3 Whitland Carmar., Wales
356 C3 Whitland Abbey Carmar., Wales
40 D3 Whitleigh Plymouth, Eng.
262 D4 Whitletts S. Ayr., Scot.
216 F3 Whitley N. Yorks., Eng.
82 E3 Whitley Reading, Eng.
86 C3 Whitley Wilts., Eng.
154 F3 Whitley W. Mids, Eng.
236 G1 Whitley Bay T. and W., Eng.
244 E6 Whitley Chapel Northumb., Eng.
148 B3 Whitley Heath Staffs., Eng.
222 E3 Whitley Lower W. Yorks., Eng.
62 A3 Whitley Row Kent, Eng.
154 C3 Whitlock's End W. Mids, Eng.
98 F3 Whitminster Glos., Eng.
46 H2 Whitmore Dorset, Eng.
148 B3 Whitmore Staffs., Eng.
132 C4 Whitnash Warks., Eng.
94 F4 Whitnell Som., Eng.
140 A3 Whitney-on-Wye Here., Eng.
232 C4 Whitrigg Cumbria, Eng.
26 D7 Whitsand Bay b. Eng.
52 B5 Whitsbury Hants., Eng.
256 K2 Whitsome Borders, Scot.
339 C3 Whitson Newp., Wales
62 G2 Whitstable Kent, Eng.
36 F1 Whitstone Corn., Eng.
244 F3 Whittingham Northumb., Eng.
144 D5 Whittingslow Shrop., Eng.
180 E3 Whittington Derbys., Eng.
98 H2 Whittington Glos., Eng.
228 G1 Whittington Lancs., Eng.
166 C3 Whittington Norf., Eng.
144 B2 Whittington Shrop., Eng.
148 B6 Whittington Staffs., Eng.
148 E4 Whittington Staffs., Eng.
136 D2 Whittington Worcs., Eng.
128 D5 Whittlebury Northants., Eng.
132 C2 Whittleford Warks., Eng.
228 G4 Whittle-le-Woods Lancs., Eng.
124 D3 Whittlesey Cambs., Eng.
124 E6 Whittlesford Cambs., Eng.
228 H4 Whittlestone Head B'burn, Eng.
74 B3 Whitton Gtr Lon., Eng.
170 C1 Whitton N. Lincs., Eng.
244 F4 Whitton Northumb., Eng.
144 E5 Whitton Shrop., Eng.
236 G4 Whitton Stockton, Eng.
120 F4 Whitton Suff., Eng.
366 G5 Whitton Powys, Wales
86 F3 Whittonditch Wilts., Eng.
244 F6 Whittonstall Northumb., Eng.
52 D3 Whitway Hants., Eng.
180 F3 Whitwell Derbys., Eng.
110 D4 Whitwell Herts., Eng.
52 E7 Whitwell I.o.W., Eng.
162 H2 Whitwell Rutland, Eng.
166 F2 Whitwell Street Norf., Eng.
162 C2 Whitwick Leics., Eng.
222 F2 Whitwood W. Yorks., Eng.
228 I5 Whitworth Lancs., Eng.
144 D2 Whixall Shrop., Eng.
236 D4 Whorlton Durham, Eng.
216 F1 Whorlton N. Yorks., Eng.
244 C5 Whygate Northumb., Eng.
58 B4 Whyke W. Sussex, Eng.
140 D2 Whyle Here., Eng.
78 F2 Whyteleafe Surr., Eng.
22 B8 Wiay i. Scot.
98 D3 Wibdon Glos., Eng.
222 D2 Wibsey W. Yorks., Eng.
162 D4 Wibtoft Leics., Eng.
136 D2 Wichenford Worcs., Eng.
62 E3 Wichling Kent, Eng.
46 I3 Wick Bourne., Eng.
98 E5 Wick S. Glos., Eng.
94 F3 Wick Som., Eng.
94 H4 Wick Som., Eng.
86 E6 Wick Wilts., Eng.
136 E3 Wick Worcs., Eng.
58 C4 Wick W. Sussex, Eng.
320 K2 Wick High., Scot.
350 E4 Wick V. of Glam., Wales
320 K2 Wick airport Scot.
22 J6 Wick r. Scot.
124 F5 Wicken Cambs., Eng.
128 D5 Wicken Northants., Eng.
116 D2 Wicken Bonhunt Essex, Eng.
170 D4 Wickenby Lincs., Eng.
232 G5 Wickerslack Cumbria, Eng.
208 E3 Wickersley S. Yorks., Eng.
176 C5 Wicketwood Hill Notts., Eng.
116 F4 Wickford Essex, Eng.
52 E5 Wickham Hants., Eng.
82 B3 Wickham W. Berks., Eng.
116 F3 Wickham Bishops Essex, Eng.
62 H3 Wickhambreaux Kent, Eng.
120 C4 Wickhambrook Suff., Eng.
136 F3 Wickhamford Worcs., Eng.
120 F3 Wickham Green Suff., Eng.
82 B3 Wickham Green W. Berks., Eng.
82 B3 Wickham Heath W. Berks., Eng.
120 H4 Wickham Market Suff., Eng.
166 I3 Wickhampton Norf., Eng.
120 F3 Wickham Skeith Suff., Eng.
116 G2 Wickham St Paul Essex, Eng.
120 C4 Wickham Street Suff., Eng.
120 F3 Wickham Street Suff., Eng.
62 D4 Wick Hill Kent, Eng.
82 E3 Wick Hill W'ham, Eng.
166 F3 Wicklewood Norf., Eng.
166 G1 Wickmere Norf., Eng.
94 G2 Wick St Lawrence N. Som., Eng.
58 H3 Wickstreet E. Sussex, Eng.
98 E4 Wickwar S. Glos., Eng.
116 D2 Widdington Essex, Eng.
222 B2 Widdop W. Yorks., Eng.
244 H4 Widdrington Northumb., Eng.
244 H4 Widdrington Station Northumb., Eng.
22 J4 Wide Firth sea chan. Scot.
36 F2 Widegates Corn., Eng.
36 F1 Widemouth Bay Corn., Eng.
236 F1 Wide Open T. and W., Eng.
329 D5 Widewall Orkney, Scot.
116 E3 Widford Essex, Eng.
110 F5 Widford Herts., Eng.
102 B4 Widford Oxon, Eng.
124 G5 Widgham Green Cambs., Eng.
106 D5 Widmer End Bucks., Eng.
176 C5 Widmerpool Notts., Eng.
74 E3 Widmore Gtr Lon., Eng.
190 E3 Widnes Halton, Eng.
198 B2 Wigan Gtr Man., Eng.
94 H5 Wigborough Som., Eng.
40 G2 Wiggaton Devon, Eng.
166 B2 Wiggenhall St Germans Norf., Eng.
166 B2 Wiggenhall St Mary Magdalen Norf., Eng.
166 B2 Wiggenhall St Mary the Virgin Norf., Eng.
166 B2 Wiggenhall St Peter Norf., Eng.
116 E1 Wiggens Green Essex, Eng.
110 B5 Wigginton Herts., Eng.
102 C3 Wigginton Oxon, Eng.
144 C2 Wigginton Shrop., Eng.
148 E5 Wigginton Staffs., Eng.
216 F2 Wigginton York, Eng.
216 C2 Wigglesworth N. Yorks., Eng.
232 D3 Wiggonby Cumbria, Eng.
216 F3 Wighill N. Yorks., Eng.
20 G6 Wight, Isle of i. Eng.
166 E1 Wighton Norf., Eng.
208 C3 Wightwizzle S. Yorks., Eng.
52 C5 Wigley Hants., Eng.
140 B2 Wigmore Here., Eng.
62 D2 Wigmore Medway, Eng.
176 E3 Wigsley Notts., Eng.
128 G3 Wigsthorpe Northants., Eng.
162 E3 Wigston Leics., Eng.
162 D3 Wigston Parva Leics., Eng.
176 C2 Wigthorpe Notts., Eng.
232 D4 Wigton Cumbria, Eng.
252 C3 Wigtown D. and G., Scot.
22 H13 Wigtown Bay b. Scot.
222 F1 Wike W. Yorks., Eng.
128 E3 Wilbarston Northants., Eng.
210 C3 Wilberfoss E. Riding, Eng.
166 E4 Wilby Norf., Eng.
128 E4 Wilby Northants., Eng.
120 G3 Wilby Suff., Eng.
120 G3 Wilby Green Suff., Eng.
86 E3 Wilcot Wilts., Eng.
144 C3 Wilcott Shrop., Eng.
339 C3 Wilcrick Newp., Wales
180 D3 Wilday Green Derbys., Eng.
184 G2 Wildboarclough Cheshire East, Eng.
110 C2 Wilden Bedford, Eng.
136 D1 Wilden Worcs., Eng.
120 C2 Wilde Street Suff., Eng.
52 D3 Wildhern Hants., Eng.
110 D5 Wildhill Herts., Eng.
268 C2 Wildmanbridge S. Lanark., Scot.
52 F3 Wildmoor Hants., Eng.
136 E1 Wildmoor Worcs., Eng.
170 B3 Wildsworth Lincs., Eng.
176 C5 Wilford Nott., Eng.
184 D4 Wilkesley Cheshire East, Eng.
320 I4 Wilkhaven High., Scot.
288 C3 Wilkieston W. Lothian, Scot.
170 F5 Wilksby Lincs., Eng.
228 F4 Willacy Lane End Lancs., Eng.
40 F2 Willand Devon, Eng.
94 F5 Willand Som., Eng.
184 E3 Willaston Cheshire East, Eng.
184 A2 Willaston Cheshire West & Chester, Eng.
144 E2 Willaston Shrop., Eng.
106 D2 Willen M.K., Eng.
154 B2 Willenhall W. Mids, Eng.
154 F3 Willenhall W. Mids, Eng.
210 F4 Willerby E. Riding, Eng.
98 H1 Willersey Glos., Eng.
140 A3 Willersley Here., Eng.
62 F4 Willesborough Kent, Eng.
62 F4 Willesborough Lees Kent, Eng.
74 C2 Willesden Gtr Lon., Eng.
74 C2 Willesden Green Gtr Lon., Eng.
86 B2 Willesley Wilts., Eng.
94 E4 Willett Som., Eng.
144 F4 Willey Shrop., Eng.
132 E3 Willey Warks., Eng.
78 C2 Willey Green Surr., Eng.
102 D2 Williamscot Oxon, Eng.
120 E4 William's Green Suff., Eng.
350 F3 Williamstown R.C.T., Wales
180 E3 Williamthorpe Derbys., Eng.
110 D4 Willian Herts., Eng.
244 C6 Willimontswick Northumb., Eng.
116 D3 Willingale Essex, Eng.
58 H4 Willingdon E. Sussex, Eng.
124 E5 Willingham Cambs., Eng.
170 B3 Willingham by Stow Lincs., Eng.
124 G6 Willingham Green Cambs., Eng.
110 C3 Willington Bedford, Eng.
180 D5 Willington Derbys., Eng.
236 E3 Willington Durham, Eng.
62 D3 Willington Kent, Eng.
236 F1 Willington T. and W., Eng.
132 C5 Willington Warks., Eng.
184 C2 Willington Corner Cheshire West & Chester, Eng.
236 G2 Willington Quay T. and W., Eng.
210 C4 Willitoft E. Riding, Eng.
94 E4 Williton Som., Eng.
402 E3 Willmount Omagh, N. Ire.
148 A3 Willoughbridge Staffs., Eng.
170 H4 Willoughby Lincs., Eng.
132 E4 Willoughby Warks., Eng.
176 C6 Willoughby-on-the-Wolds Notts., Eng.
162 E3 Willoughby Waterleys Leics., Eng.
170 C3 Willoughton Lincs., Eng.
184 D2 Willow Green Cheshire West & Chester, Eng.
116 E2 Willows Green Essex, Eng.
98 E5 Willsbridge S. Glos., Eng.
148 D3 Willslock Staffs., Eng.
40 D3 Willsworthy Devon, Eng.
94 G4 Willtown Som., Eng.
132 B4 Wilmcote Warks., Eng.
94 J2 Wilmington B. and N.E. Som., Eng.
40 G2 Wilmington Devon, Eng.
58 H4 Wilmington E. Sussex, Eng.
62 B2 Wilmington Kent, Eng.
184 F2 Wilmslow Cheshire East, Eng.
148 E5 Wilnecote Staffs., Eng.
166 F4 Wilney Green Norf., Eng.
228 H4 Wilpshire Lancs., Eng.
222 C2 Wilsden W. Yorks., Eng.
170 C6 Wilsford Lincs., Eng.
86 D4 Wilsford Wilts., Eng.
86 E5 Wilsford Wilts., Eng.
40 E1 Wilsham Devon, Eng.
222 D3 Wilshaw W. Yorks., Eng.
216 D2 Wilsill N. Yorks., Eng.
62 D4 Wilsley Green Kent, Eng.
62 D4 Wilsley Pound Kent, Eng.
162 C2 Wilson Leics., Eng.
110 C3 Wilstead Bedford, Eng.
210 G2 Wilsthorpe E. Riding, Eng.
170 D7 Wilsthorpe Lincs., Eng.
110 A5 Wilstone Herts., Eng.
110 A5 Wilstone Green Herts., Eng.
232 B6 Wilton Cumbria, Eng.
140 D4 Wilton Here., Eng.
86 D5 Wilton Wilts., Eng.
86 F3 Wilton Wilts., Eng.
256 H4 Wilton Borders, Scot.
40 G2 Wiltown Devon, Eng.
86 D4 Wiltshire county Eng.
116 D1 Wimbish Essex, Eng.
116 E2 Wimbish Green Essex, Eng.
26 F5 Wimbleball Lake l. Eng.
148 D4 Wimblebury Staffs., Eng.
74 C3 Wimbledon Gtr Lon., Eng.
124 E3 Wimblington Cambs., Eng.
46 H3 Wimborne Minster Dorset, Eng.
46 H2 Wimborne St Giles Dorset, Eng.
166 B3 Wimbotsham Norf., Eng.
124 D6 Wimpole Cambs., Eng.
124 D6 Wimpole Lodge Cambs., Eng.
132 B5 Wimpstone Warks., Eng.
94 J4 Wincanton Som., Eng.
170 F4 Winceby Lincs., Eng.
184 E2 Wincham Cheshire West & Chester, Eng.
288 C3 Winchburgh W. Lothian, Scot.
98 H2 Winchcombe Glos., Eng.
58 K3 Winchelsea E. Sussex, Eng.
58 K3 Winchelsea Beach E. Sussex, Eng.
52 E4 Winchester Hants., Eng.
62 C4 Winchet Hill Kent, Eng.
52 G3 Winchfield Hants., Eng.
106 E5 Winchmore Hill Bucks., Eng.
74 D2 Winchmore Hill Gtr Lon., Eng.
184 G2 Wincle Cheshire East, Eng.
208 D3 Wincobank S. Yorks., Eng.
232 E6 Windermere Cumbria, Eng.
24 L5 Windermere l. Eng.
132 C5 Winderton Warks., Eng.
322 H2 Windhill High., Scot.
184 A2 Windle Hill Cheshire West & Chester, Eng.
198 E3 Windlehurst Gtr Man., Eng.
78 C1 Windlesham Surr., Eng.
22 K11 Windlestraw Law hill Scot.
180 D4 Windley Derbys., Eng.
180 C3 Windmill Derbys., Eng.
94 I2 Windmill Hill Bristol, Eng.
58 I3 Windmill Hill E. Sussex, Eng.
228 G4 Windmill Hill Lancs., Eng.
94 G5 Windmill Hill Som., Eng.
136 E3 Windmill Hill Worcs., Eng.
98 I3 Windrush Glos., Eng.
26 J4 Windrush r. Eng.
82 G3 Windsor W. and M., Eng.
82 F3 Windsor and Maidenhead admin. div. Eng.
396 F4 Windy Gap Newry & Mourne, N. Ire.
292 F2 Windygates Fife, Scot.
378 G3 Windy Hill Wrex., Wales
236 F2 Windy Nook T. and W., Eng.
262 E2 Windy-Yett E. Ayr., Scot.
58 E3 Wineham W. Sussex, Eng.
210 H4 Winestead E. Riding, Eng.
228 J3 Winewall Lancs., Eng.
166 F4 Winfarthing Norf., Eng.
52 E7 Winford I.o.W., Eng.
94 I2 Winford N. Som., Eng.
140 A3 Winforton Here., Eng.
46 F4 Winfrith Newburgh Dorset, Eng.
106 D3 Wing Bucks., Eng.
162 G3 Wing Rutland, Eng.
236 G3 Wingate Durham, Eng.
198 B2 Wingates Gtr Man., Eng.
244 F4 Wingates Northumb., Eng.
180 E3 Wingerworth Derbys., Eng.
110 B4 Wingfield Central Bedfordshire, Eng.
120 G2 Wingfield Suff., Eng.
86 B4 Wingfield Wilts., Eng.
180 E4 Wingfield Park Derbys., Eng.
62 H3 Wingham Kent, Eng.
62 H3 Wingham Green Kent, Eng.
62 H3 Wingham Well Kent, Eng.
62 G3 Wingmore Kent, Eng.
106 D3 Wingrave Bucks., Eng.
176 D4 Winkburn Notts., Eng.
82 F3 Winkfield Brack. F., Eng.
82 F3 Winkfield Row Brack. F., Eng.
148 D2 Winkhill Staffs., Eng.
40 E2 Winkleigh Devon, Eng.
216 E2 Winksley N. Yorks., Eng.
46 I3 Winkton Dorset, Eng.
236 E2 Winlaton T. and W., Eng.
236 E2 Winlaton Mill T. and W., Eng.
320 K2 Winless High., Scot.
228 F3 Winmarleigh Lancs., Eng.
36 E2 Winnard's Perch Corn., Eng.
82 E3 Winnersh W'ham, Eng.
184 D2 Winnington Cheshire West & Chester, Eng.
148 D3 Winnothdale Staffs., Eng.
94 G3 Winscombe N. Som., Eng.
184 D2 Winsford Cheshire West & Chester, Eng.
94 C4 Winsford Som., Eng.
94 G5 Winsham Som., Eng.
148 F4 Winshill Staffs., Eng.
350 C3 Winsh-wen Swansea, Wales
232 G4 Winskill Cumbria, Eng.
52 F3 Winslade Hants., Eng.
86 B3 Winsley Wilts., Eng.
106 C3 Winslow Bucks., Eng.
98 H3 Winson Glos., Eng.
154 C3 Winson Green W. Mids, Eng.
52 C5 Winsor Hants., Eng.
232 E6 Winster Cumbria, Eng.
180 D4 Winster Derbys., Eng.
236 E4 Winston Durham, Eng.
120 G3 Winston Suff., Eng.
98 G3 Winstone Glos., Eng.
120 G3 Winston Green Suff., Eng.
40 D2 Winswell Devon, Eng.
46 E3 Winterborne Came Dorset, Eng.
46 F3 Winterborne Clenston Dorset, Eng.
46 E3 Winterborne Herringston Dorset, Eng.
46 F2 Winterborne Houghton Dorset, Eng.
46 F3 Winterborne Kingston Dorset, Eng.
46 E3 Winterborne Monkton Dorset, Eng.
46 F3 Winterborne Muston Dorset, Eng.
46 F2 Winterborne Stickland Dorset, Eng.
46 F3 Winterborne Whitechurch Dorset, Eng.
46 G3 Winterborne Zelston Dorset, Eng.
98 D4 Winterbourne S. Glos., Eng.
82 B3 Winterbourne W. Berks., Eng.
46 D3 Winterbourne Abbas Dorset, Eng.
86 D3 Winterbourne Bassett Wilts., Eng.
86 E5 Winterbourne Dauntsey Wilts., Eng.
86 E5 Winterbourne Earls Wilts., Eng.
86 E5 Winterbourne Gunner Wilts., Eng.
86 D3 Winterbourne Monkton Wilts., Eng.
46 D3 Winterbourne Steepleton Dorset, Eng.
86 D4 Winterbourne Stoke Wilts., Eng.
102 E5 Winterbrook Oxon, Eng.
216 C2 Winterburn N. Yorks., Eng.
268 E4 Wintercleugh S. Lanark., Scot.
170 C1 Winteringham N. Lincs., Eng.
184 E3 Winterley Cheshire East, Eng.
222 F3 Wintersett W. Yorks., Eng.
52 E5 Wintershill Hants., Eng.
86 E5 Winterslow Wilts., Eng.
170 C2 Winterton N. Lincs., Eng.
166 J2 Winterton-on-Sea Norf., Eng.
170 I5 Winthorpe Lincs., Eng.
176 E4 Winthorpe Notts., Eng.
46 H3 Winton Bourne., Eng.
232 I6 Winton Cumbria, Eng.
216 E1 Winton N. Yorks., Eng.
216 H2 Wintringham N. Yorks., Eng.
124 B4 Winwick Cambs., Eng.
128 C3 Winwick Northants., Eng.
190 F3 Winwick Warr., Eng.
180 D4 Wirksworth Derbys., Eng.
180 D4 Wirksworth Moor Derbys., Eng.
189 Wirral met. bor. Merseyside, Eng.
24 K7 Wirral pen. Eng.
184 C4 Wirswall Cheshire East, Eng.
124 E3 Wisbech Cambs., Eng.
124 E3 Wisbech St Mary Cambs., Eng.
58 C2 Wisborough Green W. Sussex, Eng.
176 D2 Wiseton Notts., Eng.
132 B2 Wishaw Warks., Eng.
280 C4 Wishaw N. Lanark., Scot.
24 O5 Wiske r. Eng.
78 D2 Wisley Surr., Eng.
170 E4 Wispington Lincs., Eng.
120 H2 Wissett Suff., Eng.
120 E5 Wissington Suff., Eng.
144 C5 Wistanstow Shrop., Eng.
144 E2 Wistanswick Shrop., Eng.
184 E3 Wistaston Cheshire East, Eng.
184 E3 Wistaston Green Cheshire East, Eng.
58 D3 Wiston W. Sussex, Eng.
268 E3 Wiston S. Lanark., Scot.
358 E3 Wiston Pembs., Wales
124 D4 Wistow Cambs., Eng.
216 F3 Wistow N. Yorks., Eng.
228 H4 Wiswell Lancs., Eng.
124 E4 Witcham Cambs., Eng.
46 G2 Witchampton Dorset, Eng.
300 D5 Witchburn Arg. and B., Scot.
124 F4 Witchford Cambs., Eng.
94 H5 Witcombe Som., Eng.
116 F3 Witham Essex, Eng.
26 M2 Witham r. Eng.
94 J4 Witham Friary Som., Eng.
170 D7 Witham on the Hill Lincs., Eng.
170 F3 Withcall Lincs., Eng.
162 G3 Withcote Leics., Eng.
58 F3 Withdean B. and H., Eng.
58 I2 Witherenden Hill E. Sussex, Eng.
166 H2 Withergate Norf., Eng.
58 I3 Witherhurst E. Sussex, Eng.
40 E2 Witheridge Devon, Eng.
162 B3 Witherley Leics., Eng.
170 G4 Withern Lincs., Eng.
210 I4 Withernsea E. Riding, Eng.
210 G3 Withernwick E. Riding, Eng.
120 G2 Withersdale Street Suff., Eng.
120 B4 Withersfield Suff., Eng.
232 E7 Witherslack Cumbria, Eng.
232 E7 Witherslack Hall Cumbria, Eng.
36 E2 Withiel Corn., Eng.
94 D4 Withiel Florey Som., Eng.
36 E2 Withielgoose Corn., Eng.
184 F2 Withington Cheshire East, Eng.
98 H2 Withington Glos., Eng.
198 D3 Withington Gtr Man., Eng.
140 D3 Withington Here., Eng.
144 E3 Withington Shrop., Eng.
148 D3 Withington Staffs., Eng.
184 F2 Withington Green Cheshire East, Eng.
140 D3 Withington Marsh Here., Eng.
40 F2 Withleigh Devon, Eng.
228 G4 Withnell Lancs., Eng.
228 G4 Withnell Fold Lancs., Eng.
94 J3 Withybrook Som., Eng.
132 D3 Withybrook Warks., Eng.
94 D4 Withycombe Som., Eng.
40 F3 Withycombe Raleigh Devon, Eng.
58 G2 Withyham E. Sussex, Eng.
94 C4 Withypool Som., Eng.
78 C3 Witley Surr., Eng.
120 G4 Witnesham Suff., Eng.
102 C4 Witney Oxon, Eng.
116 D3 Witney Green Essex, Eng.
124 B3 Wittering Peterb., Eng.
62 E4 Wittersham Kent, Eng.
166 H3 Witton Norf., Eng.
154 C2 Witton W. Mids, Eng.
136 E2 Witton Worcs., Eng.
308 F2 Witton Angus, Scot.
236 F3 Witton Gilbert Durham, Eng.
236 E3 Witton-le-Wear Durham, Eng.
236 E4 Witton Park Durham, Eng.
94 E4 Wiveliscombe Som., Eng.
58 F3 Wivelsfield E. Sussex, Eng.
58 F3 Wivelsfield Green E. Sussex, Eng.
116 H2 Wivenhoe Essex, Eng.
166 F1 Wiveton Norf., Eng.
116 I2 Wix Essex, Eng.
132 A4 Wixford Warks., Eng.
144 E2 Wixhill Shrop., Eng.
120 B4 Wixoe Suff., Eng.
110 B4 Woburn Central Bedfordshire, Eng.
106 E2 Woburn Sands M.K., Eng.
82 D3 Wokefield Park W. Berks., Eng.
78 C2 Woking Surr., Eng.
82 E3 Wokingham W'ham, Eng.
82 E3 Wokingham admin. div. Eng.
78 F2 Woldingham Surr., Eng.
210 F2 Wold Newton E. Riding, Eng.
170 F3 Wold Newton N.E. Lincs., Eng.
256 I4 Wolfelee Borders, Scot.
140 E2 Wolferlow Here., Eng.
166 B2 Wolferton Norf., Eng.
132 E4 Wolfhampcote Warks., Eng.
304 J4 Wolfhill Perth and Kin., Scot.
366 G5 Wolfpits Powys, Wales
358 E2 Wolf's Castle Pembs., Wales
358 D2 Wolfsdale Pembs., Wales
256 G4 Woll Borders, Scot.
128 E4 Wollaston Northants., Eng.
144 C3 Wollaston Shrop., Eng.
154 B3 Wollaston W. Mids, Eng.
176 B5 Wollaton Nott., Eng.
144 E2 Wollerton Shrop., Eng.
154 B3 Wollescote W. Mids, Eng.
236 D3 Wolsingham Durham, Eng.
198 D2 Wolstenholme Gtr Man., Eng.
132 D3 Wolston Warks., Eng.
232 B3 Wolsty Cumbria, Eng.
102 D4 Wolvercote Oxon, Eng.
154 B2 Wolverhampton W. Mids, Eng.
144 D2 Wolverley Shrop., Eng.
136 D1 Wolverley Worcs., Eng.
94 G2 Wolvers Hill N. Som., Eng.
52 E3 Wolverton Hants., Eng.
106 D2 Wolverton M.K., Eng.
132 B4 Wolverton Warks., Eng.
86 B5 Wolverton Wilts., Eng.
52 E2 Wolverton Common Hants., Eng.
339 D2 Wolvesnewton Mon., Wales
132 D3 Wolvey Warks., Eng.
132 D3 Wolvey Heath Warks., Eng.
236 H4 Wolviston Stockton, Eng.
366 G5 Womaston Powys, Wales
148 B5 Wombourne Staffs., Eng.
144 F3 Wombridge Telford, Eng.
208 D2 Wombwell S. Yorks., Eng.
62 H3 Womenswold Kent, Eng.
339 D2 Wonastow Mon., Wales
78 C2 Wonersh Surr., Eng.
52 E4 Wonston Hants., Eng.
106 D5 Wooburn Bucks., Eng.
106 D5 Wooburn Green Bucks., Eng.
40 D2 Woodacott Devon, Eng.
216 D2 Woodale N. Yorks., Eng.
208 E4 Woodall S. Yorks., Eng.
166 H2 Woodbastwick Norf., Eng.
176 D3 Woodbeck Notts., Eng.
132 A4 Wood Bevington Warks., Eng.
358 E3 Woodbine Pembs., Wales
176 C4 Woodborough Notts., Eng.
86 D3 Woodborough Wilts., Eng.
46 E2 Woodbridge Dorset, Eng.
120 G4 Woodbridge Suff., Eng.
78 C2 Woodbridge Hill Surr., Eng.
128 D5 Wood Burcote Northants., Eng.
388 K4 Woodburn Carrickfergus, N. Ire.
40 F2 Woodbury Devon, Eng.
94 I3 Woodbury Som., Eng.
98 F3 Woodchester Glos., Eng.
62 E4 Woodchurch Kent, Eng.
190 C3 Woodchurch Merseyside, Eng.
94 D3 Woodcombe Som., Eng.
74 D3 Woodcote Gtr Lon., Eng.
102 E5 Woodcote Oxon, Eng.
144 F3 Woodcote Telford, Eng.
136 E1 Woodcote Green Worcs., Eng.
52 D3 Woodcott Hants., Eng.
98 D4 Woodcroft Glos., Eng.
46 G2 Woodcutts Dorset, Eng.
166 F2 Wood Dalling Norf., Eng.
124 G5 Woodditton Cambs., Eng.
102 D4 Woodeaton Oxon, Eng.
148 B4 Wood Eaton Staffs., Eng.
110 B3 Wood End Bedford, Eng.
110 C2 Wood End Bedford, Eng.
106 C3 Wood End Bucks., Eng.
232 C6 Woodend Cumbria, Eng.
110 E4 Wood End Herts., Eng.
228 I4 Wood End Lancs., Eng.
128 C5 Woodend Northants., Eng.
132 A3 Wood End Warks., Eng.
132 C2 Wood End Warks., Eng.
132 C3 Wood End Warks., Eng.
154 B2 Wood End W. Mids, Eng.
58 A3 Woodend W. Sussex, Eng.
322 E4 Woodend High., Scot.
304 F3 Woodend Perth and Kin., Scot.
170 F5 Wood Enderby Lincs., Eng.
116 D2 Woodend Green Essex, Eng.
86 E6 Woodfalls Wilts., Eng.
102 E3 Woodfield Oxon, Eng.
262 D4 Woodfield S. Ayr., Scot.
232 G5 Woodfoot Cumbria, Eng.
36 F1 Woodford Corn., Eng.
40 E3 Woodford Devon, Eng.
98 E4 Woodford Glos., Eng.
74 E2 Woodford Gtr Lon., Eng.
198 E3 Woodford Gtr Man., Eng.
128 F3 Woodford Northants., Eng.
94 D4 Woodford Som., Eng.
74 E2 Woodford Bridge Gtr Lon., Eng.
74 E2 Woodford Green Gtr Lon., Eng.
128 B4 Woodford Halse Northants., Eng.
166 E2 Woodgate Norf., Eng.
154 B3 Woodgate W. Mids, Eng.
136 E2 Woodgate Worcs., Eng.
74 D2 Wood Green Gtr Lon., Eng.
52 B5 Woodgreen Hants., Eng.
166 G4 Wood Green Norf., Eng.
110 D5 Woodhall Herts., Eng.
276 C2 Woodhall Inverclyde, Scot.
222 D2 Woodhall Hills W. Yorks., Eng.
170 E5 Woodhall Spa Lincs., Eng.
106 C3 Woodham Bucks., Eng.
236 F4 Woodham Durham, Eng.
78 C1 Woodham Surr., Eng.
116 F4 Woodham Ferrers Essex, Eng.
116 F3 Woodham Mortimer Essex, Eng.
116 F3 Woodham Walter Essex, Eng.
292 G1 Woodhaven Fife, Scot.
154 B2 Wood Hayes W. Mids, Eng.
148 D3 Woodhead Staffs., Eng.
314 F2 Woodhead Abers., Scot.
190 C3 Woodhey Merseyside, Eng.
184 D3 Woodhey Green Cheshire East, Eng.
144 F5 Woodhill Shrop., Eng.
94 G4 Woodhill Som., Eng.
244 H4 Woodhorn Northumb., Eng.
232 F7 Woodhouse Cumbria, Eng.
162 D2 Woodhouse Leics., Eng.
170 B2 Woodhouse N. Lincs., Eng.
208 D3 Woodhouse S. Yorks., Eng.
222 D2 Woodhouse W. Yorks., Eng.
222 E2 Woodhouse W. Yorks., Eng.
222 F2 Woodhouse W. Yorks., Eng.
162 D2 Woodhouse Eaves Leics., Eng.
148 C2 Woodhouse Green Staffs., Eng.
208 D3 Woodhouse Mill S. Yorks., Eng.
198 C3 Woodhouses Gtr Man., Eng.
198 E2 Woodhouses Gtr Man., Eng.
148 D4 Woodhouses Staffs., Eng.
148 E4 Woodhouses Staffs., Eng.
124 D4 Woodhurst Cambs., Eng.
58 F3 Woodingdean B. and H., Eng.
52 C5 Woodington Hants., Eng.
40 E3 Woodland Devon, Eng.
236 D4 Woodland Durham, Eng.
62 G4 Woodland Kent, Eng.
40 E2 Woodland Head Devon, Eng.
46 H2 Woodlands Dorset, Eng.
74 B3 Woodlands Gtr Lon., Eng.
52 C5 Woodlands Hants., Eng.
144 F5 Woodlands Shrop., Eng.
94 E4 Woodlands Som., Eng.
82 F2 Woodlands Park W. and M., Eng.
82 A3 Woodlands St Mary W. Berks., Eng.
144 C2 Wood Lane Shrop., Eng.
148 B2 Wood Lane Staffs., Eng.
148 E4 Woodlane Staffs., Eng.
222 F2 Woodlesford W. Yorks., Eng.
198 E3 Woodley Gtr Man., Eng.
82 E3 Woodley W'ham, Eng.
98 E3 Woodmancote Glos., Eng.
98 G2 Woodmancote Glos., Eng.
98 H3 Woodmancote Glos., Eng.
58 A3 Woodmancote W. Sussex, Eng.
58 E3 Woodmancote W. Sussex, Eng.
52 E3 Woodmancott Hants., Eng.
210 F4 Woodmansey E. Riding, Eng.
78 E2 Woodmansterne Surr., Eng.
148 E4 Woodmill Staffs., Eng.
86 D5 Woodminton Wilts., Eng.
144 B4 Woodmoor Shrop., Eng.
62 H3 Woodnesborough Kent, Eng.
128 G2 Woodnewton Northants., Eng.
166 E2 Wood Norton Norf., Eng.
102 D4 Woodperry Oxon, Eng.
228 F4 Woodplumpton Lancs., Eng.
166 E3 Woodrising Norf., Eng.
46 E2 Woodrow Dorset, Eng.
136 F2 Woodrow Worcs., Eng.
154 B2 Woods Bank W. Mids, Eng.
58 I3 Wood's Corner E. Sussex, Eng.
180 A2 Woodseats Derbys., Eng.
208 D3 Wood Seats S. Yorks., Eng.
140 A3 Woods Eaves Here., Eng.
144 F2 Woodseaves Shrop., Eng.
148 B4 Woodseaves Staffs., Eng.
86 E3 Woodsend Wilts., Eng.
208 E3 Woodsetts S. Yorks., Eng.
46 E3 Woodsford Dorset, Eng.
58 I2 Wood's Green E. Sussex, Eng.
82 G3 Woodside Brack. F., Eng.
110 C4 Woodside Central Bedfordshire, Eng.
232 B4 Woodside Cumbria, Eng.
180 E5 Woodside Derbys., Eng.
74 D3 Woodside Gtr Lon., Eng.
52 C6 Woodside Hants., Eng.
110 D5 Woodside Herts., Eng.
144 B5 Woodside Shrop., Eng.
154 B3 Woodside W. Mids, Eng.
252 F2 Woodside D. and G., Scot.
292 F2 Woodside Fife, Scot.
292 G2 Woodside Fife, Scot.
264 G2 Woodside N. Ayr., Scot.
304 K3 Woodside Perth and Kin., Scot.
62 E3 Woodside Green Kent, Eng.
198 E3 Woods Moor Gtr Man., Eng.
98 H2 Wood Stanway Glos., Eng.
102 C3 Woodstock Oxon, Eng.
358 E2 Woodstock Pembs., Wales
358 E2 Woodstock Slop Pembs., Wales
166 I2 Wood Street Norf., Eng.
78 C2 Wood Street Village Surr., Eng.
180 F3 Woodthorpe Derbys., Eng.
162 D2 Woodthorpe Leics., Eng.
170 G4 Woodthorpe Lincs., Eng.
208 D3 Woodthorpe S. Yorks., Eng.
166 H4 Woodton Norf., Eng.
190 C2 Woodvale Merseyside, Eng.
180 D6 Woodville Derbys., Eng.
148 B3 Woodwall Green Staffs., Eng.
124 C4 Woodwalton Cambs., Eng.

Woodwick to **Zouch**

329 C3 **Woodwick** *Orkney, Scot.*
184 D3 **Woodworth Green** *Cheshire East, Eng.*
46 H2 **Woodyates** *Dorset, Eng.*
144 D6 **Woofferton** *Shrop., Eng.*
94 H3 **Wookey** *Som., Eng.*
94 H3 **Wookey Hole** *Som., Eng.*
46 F3 **Wool** *Dorset, Eng.*
40 D1 **Woolacombe** *Devon, Eng.*
62 H3 **Woolage Green** *Kent, Eng.*
62 H3 **Woolage Village** *Kent, Eng.*
98 D3 **Woolaston** *Glos., Eng.*
98 D3 **Woolaston Slade** *Glos., Eng.*
94 G3 **Woolavington** *Som., Eng.*
58 B2 **Woolbeding** *W. Sussex, Eng.*
94 D4 **Woolcotts** *Som., Eng.*
222 D3 **Wooldale** *W. Yorks., Eng.*
244 E2 **Wooler** *Northumb., Eng.*
190 D3 **Woolfall Heath** *Merseyside, Eng.*
40 C2 **Woolfardisworthy** *Devon, Eng.*
40 F2 **Woolfardisworthy** *Devon, Eng.*
198 D2 **Woolfold** *Gtr Man., Eng.*
268 E2 **Woolfords Cottages** *S. Lanark., Scot.*
46 G4 **Woolgarston** *Dorset, Eng.*
222 F3 **Woolgreaves** *W. Yorks., Eng.*
82 C3 **Woolhampton** *W. Berks., Eng.*
140 D3 **Woolhope** *Here., Eng.*
46 F2 **Woolland** *Dorset, Eng.*
40 D2 **Woollaton** *Devon, Eng.*
110 E5 **Woollensbrook** *Herts., Eng.*
94 J2 **Woolley** *B. and N.E. Som., Eng.*
124 C4 **Woolley** *Cambs., Eng.*
36 F1 **Woolley** *Corn., Eng.*
180 E4 **Woolley** *Derbys., Eng.*
222 E3 **Woolley** *W. Yorks., Eng.*
198 F3 **Woolley Bridge** *Gtr Man., Eng.*
82 F2 **Woolley Green** *W. and M., Eng.*
86 B3 **Woolley Green** *Wilts., Eng.*
136 E2 **Woolmere Green** *Worcs., Eng.*
110 D4 **Woolmer Green** *Herts., Eng.*
94 F4 **Woolmersdon** *Som., Eng.*
120 E3 **Woolpit** *Suff., Eng.*
120 E3 **Woolpit Green** *Suff., Eng.*
132 E4 **Woolscott** *Warks., Eng.*
144 D4 **Woolstaston** *Shrop., Eng.*
170 B6 **Woolsthorpe** *Lincs., Eng.*
170 C7 **Woolsthorpe by Colsterworth** *Lincs., Eng.*
40 E4 **Woolston** *Devon, Eng.*
144 B3 **Woolston** *Shrop., Eng.*
144 C5 **Woolston** *Shrop., Eng.*
52 D5 **Woolston** *Soton, Eng.*
190 F3 **Woolston** *Warr., Eng.*
98 G2 **Woolstone** *Glos., Eng.*
106 D2 **Woolstone** *M.K., Eng.*
102 B5 **Woolstone** *Oxon, Eng.*
190 D3 **Woolton** *Merseyside, Eng.*
52 D2 **Woolton Hill** *Hants., Eng.*
120 G4 **Woolverstone** *Suff., Eng.*
94 K3 **Woolverton** *Som., Eng.*
74 E3 **Woolwich** *Gtr Lon., Eng.*
140 B3 **Woonton** *Here., Eng.*
244 F3 **Wooperton** *Northumb., Eng.*
144 F2 **Woore** *Shrop., Eng.*
120 G3 **Wootten Green** *Suff., Eng.*
110 B3 **Wootton** *Bedford, Eng.*
52 C6 **Wootton** *Hants., Eng.*
52 E6 **Wootton** *I.o.W., Eng.*
62 H3 **Wootton** *Kent, Eng.*
170 D2 **Wootton** *N. Lincs., Eng.*
128 D4 **Wootton** *Northants., Eng.*
102 C3 **Wootton** *Oxon, Eng.*
102 D4 **Wootton** *Oxon, Eng.*
144 C2 **Wootton** *Shrop., Eng.*
144 D5 **Wootton** *Shrop., Eng.*
148 B3 **Wootton** *Staffs., Eng.*
148 D2 **Wootton** *Staffs., Eng.*
86 D2 **Wootton Bassett** *Wilts., Eng.*
52 E6 **Wootton Bridge** *I.o.W., Eng.*
52 E6 **Wootton Common** *I.o.W., Eng.*
94 C3 **Wootton Courtenay** *Som., Eng.*
46 B3 **Wootton Fitzpaine** *Dorset, Eng.*
110 B3 **Wootton Green** *Bedford, Eng.*
86 E3 **Wootton Rivers** *Wilts., Eng.*
52 F3 **Wootton St Lawrence** *Hants., Eng.*
132 B4 **Wootton Wawen** *Warks., Eng.*
136 D2 **Worcester** *Worcs., Eng.*
74 C3 **Worcester Park** *Gtr Lon., Eng.*
136 D2 **Worcestershire** *county Eng.*
154 B3 **Wordsley** *W. Mids, Eng.*
120 D3 **Wordwell** *Suff., Eng.*
144 F4 **Worfield** *Shrop., Eng.*
46 G3 **Worgret** *Dorset, Eng.*
329 D3 **Work** *Orkney, Scot.*
110 C3 **Workhouse End** *Bedford, Eng.*
388 C3 **Workhouse Museum** *Derry, N. Ire.*
232 A5 **Workington** *Cumbria, Eng.*
176 C3 **Worksop** *Notts., Eng.*
170 G4 **Worlaby** *Lincs., Eng.*
170 D2 **Worlaby** *N. Lincs., Eng.*
106 D4 **World's End** *Bucks., Eng.*
74 D2 **World's End** *Gtr Lon., Eng.*
52 F5 **Worlds End** *Hants., Eng.*
82 C3 **World's End** *W. Berks., Eng.*
154 D3 **Worlds End** *W. Mids, Eng.*
94 G2 **Worle** *N. Som., Eng.*
184 D3 **Worleston** *Cheshire East, Eng.*
120 I2 **Worlingham** *Suff., Eng.*
120 B2 **Worlington** *Suff., Eng.*
120 G3 **Worlingworth** *Suff., Eng.*
216 E2 **Wormald Green** *N. Yorks., Eng.*
140 B4 **Wormbridge** *Here., Eng.*
166 B2 **Wormegay** *Norf., Eng.*
140 C4 **Wormelow Tump** *Here., Eng.*
180 C3 **Wormhill** *Derbys., Eng.*
116 G2 **Wormingford** *Essex, Eng.*
106 B4 **Worminghall** *Bucks., Eng.*
98 H1 **Wormington** *Glos., Eng.*
94 I3 **Worminster** *Som., Eng.*
292 I2 **Wormiston** *Fife, Scot.*
292 G1 **Wormit** *Fife, Scot.*
132 D4 **Wormleighton** *Warks., Eng.*
110 E5 **Wormley** *Herts., Eng.*
78 C3 **Wormley** *Surr., Eng.*
208 G2 **Wormley Hill** *S. Yorks., Eng.*
110 E5 **Wormley West End** *Herts., Eng.*
26 D4 **Worms Head** *hd Wales*
62 E3 **Wormshill** *Kent, Eng.*
140 B3 **Wormsley** *Here., Eng.*
78 C2 **Worplesdon** *Surr., Eng.*
208 C3 **Worrall** *S. Yorks., Eng.*
208 D2 **Worsbrough** *S. Yorks., Eng.*
198 C2 **Worsley** *Gtr Man., Eng.*
198 B2 **Worsley Mesnes** *Gtr Man., Eng.*
166 H2 **Worstead** *Norf., Eng.*
124 F6 **Worsted Lodge** *Cambs., Eng.*
228 I4 **Worsthorne** *Lancs., Eng.*
228 H3 **Worston** *Lancs., Eng.*
62 I3 **Worth** *Kent, Eng.*
94 H3 **Worth** *Som., Eng.*
58 F2 **Worth** *W. Sussex, Eng.*
120 F2 **Wortham** *Suff., Eng.*
144 C4 **Worthen** *Shrop., Eng.*
378 H3 **Worthenbury** *Wrex., Wales*
166 E2 **Worthing** *Norf., Eng.*
58 D4 **Worthing** *W. Sussex, Eng.*
162 C2 **Worthington** *Leics., Eng.*
46 G4 **Worth Matravers** *Dorset, Eng.*
52 F3 **Worting** *Hants., Eng.*
98 E4 **Wortley** *Glos., Eng.*
208 C3 **Wortley** *S. Yorks., Eng.*
222 E2 **Wortley** *W. Yorks., Eng.*
216 C2 **Worton** *N. Yorks., Eng.*
86 C4 **Worton** *Wilts., Eng.*
166 H4 **Wortwell** *Norf., Eng.*
222 F1 **Wothersome** *W. Yorks., Eng.*
144 B4 **Wotherton** *Shrop., Eng.*
40 D3 **Wotter** *Devon, Eng.*
78 D2 **Wotton** *Surr., Eng.*
98 E4 **Wotton-under-Edge** *Glos., Eng.*
106 C3 **Wotton Underwood** *Bucks., Eng.*
106 D2 **Woughton on the Green** *M.K., Eng.*
62 C2 **Wouldham** *Kent, Eng.*
116 J2 **Wrabness** *Essex, Eng.*
314 F2 **Wrae** *Abers., Scot.*
40 D1 **Wrafton** *Devon, Eng.*
170 E4 **Wragby** *Lincs., Eng.*
222 F3 **Wragby** *W. Yorks., Eng.*
166 F3 **Wramplingham** *Norf., Eng.*
222 G3 **Wrangbrook** *W. Yorks., Eng.*
314 F2 **Wrangham** *Abers., Scot.*
170 G5 **Wrangle** *Lincs., Eng.*
170 G5 **Wrangle Lowgate** *Lincs., Eng.*
94 E5 **Wrangway** *Som., Eng.*
94 G5 **Wrantage** *Som., Eng.*
22 F5 **Wrath, Cape** *c. Scot.*
170 D2 **Wrawby** *N. Lincs., Eng.*
94 H2 **Wraxall** *N. Som., Eng.*
94 I4 **Wraxall** *Som., Eng.*
228 G2 **Wray** *Lancs., Eng.*
232 E6 **Wray Castle** *Cumbria, Eng.*
78 E2 **Wrays** *Surr., Eng.*
82 G3 **Wraysbury** *W. and M., Eng.*
228 G2 **Wrayton** *Lancs., Eng.*
228 E4 **Wrea Green** *Lancs., Eng.*
26 J2 **Wreake** *r. Eng.*
232 E4 **Wreay** *Cumbria, Eng.*
232 E5 **Wreay** *Cumbria, Eng.*
78 B2 **Wrecclesham** *Surr., Eng.*
Wrecsam *Wrex., Wales see* **Wrexham**
236 F2 **Wrekenton** *T. and W., Eng.*
216 G2 **Wrelton** *N. Yorks., Eng.*
184 D3 **Wrenbury** *Cheshire East, Eng.*
216 H2 **Wrench Green** *N. Yorks., Eng.*
166 G3 **Wreningham** *Norf., Eng.*
120 J2 **Wrentham** *Suff., Eng.*
222 E2 **Wrenthorpe** *W. Yorks., Eng.*
144 C4 **Wrentnall** *Shrop., Eng.*
210 C4 **Wressle** *E. Riding, Eng.*
170 C2 **Wressle** *N. Lincs., Eng.*
110 E3 **Wrestlingworth** *Central Bedfordshire, Eng.*
166 D4 **Wretham** *Norf., Eng.*
166 B3 **Wretton** *Norf., Eng.*
378 H3 **Wrexham** *Wrex., Wales*
378 H4 **Wrexham** *admin. div. Wales*
378 H3 **Wrexham Industrial Estate** *Wrex., Wales*
136 D1 **Wribbenhall** *Worcs., Eng.*
228 F5 **Wrightington Bar** *Lancs., Eng.*
296 E5 **Wrightpark** *Stir., Scot.*
116 D2 **Wright's Green** *Essex, Eng.*
148 A2 **Wrinehill** *Staffs., Eng.*
94 H2 **Wrington** *N. Som., Eng.*
94 J3 **Writhlington** *B. and N.E. Som., Eng.*
116 E3 **Writtle** *Essex, Eng.*
144 E3 **Wrockwardine** *Telford, Eng.*
170 A2 **Wroot** *N. Lincs., Eng.*
222 D2 **Wrose** *W. Yorks., Eng.*
62 B3 **Wrotham** *Kent, Eng.*
62 C3 **Wrotham Heath** *Kent, Eng.*
62 B3 **Wrotham Hill Park** *Kent, Eng.*
110 D5 **Wrotham Park** *Herts., Eng.*
148 B5 **Wrottesley** *Staffs., Eng.*
86 E2 **Wroughton** *Swindon, Eng.*
52 E7 **Wroxall** *I.o.W., Eng.*
132 B3 **Wroxall** *Warks., Eng.*
144 E3 **Wroxeter** *Shrop., Eng.*
166 H2 **Wroxham** *Norf., Eng.*
102 C2 **Wroxton** *Oxon, Eng.*
362 D4 **Wstrws** *Cere., Wales*
180 C5 **Wyaston** *Derbys., Eng.*
170 F6 **Wyberton** *Lincs., Eng.*
110 D2 **Wyboston** *Bedford, Eng.*
184 E3 **Wybunbury** *Cheshire East, Eng.*
136 E2 **Wychbold** *Worcs., Eng.*
58 G2 **Wych Cross** *E. Sussex, Eng.*
148 E4 **Wychnor** *Staffs., Eng.*
148 E4 **Wychnor Bridges** *Staffs., Eng.*
52 G4 **Wyck** *Hants., Eng.*
98 I2 **Wyck Rissington** *Glos., Eng.*
236 E4 **Wycliffe** *Durham, Eng.*
228 J3 **Wycoller** *Lancs., Eng.*
162 F2 **Wycomb** *Leics., Eng.*
106 D5 **Wycombe Marsh** *Bucks., Eng.*
110 E4 **Wyddial** *Herts., Eng.*
94 C3 **Wydon** *Som., Eng.*
62 F3 **Wye** *Kent, Eng.*
24 N7 **Wye** *r. Eng.*
26 G4 **Wye** *r. Eng./Wales*
339 D2 **Wyesham** *Mon., Wales*
162 G2 **Wyfordby** *Leics., Eng.*
46 F1 **Wyke** *Dorset, Eng.*
144 E4 **Wyke** *Shrop., Eng.*
78 B2 **Wyke** *Surr., Eng.*
222 D2 **Wyke** *W. Yorks., Eng.*
94 J4 **Wyke Champflower** *Som., Eng.*
216 H2 **Wykeham** *N. Yorks., Eng.*
144 F4 **Wyken** *Shrop., Eng.*
154 F3 **Wyken** *W. Mids, Eng.*
46 E4 **Wyke Regis** *Dorset, Eng.*
144 C3 **Wykey** *Shrop., Eng.*
162 C3 **Wykin** *Leics., Eng.*
244 G6 **Wylam** *Northumb., Eng.*
154 D2 **Wylde Green** *W. Mids, Eng.*
350 G3 **Wyllie** *Caerp., Wales*
86 D5 **Wylye** *Wilts., Eng.*
26 I5 **Wylye** *r. Eng.*
52 F5 **Wymering** *Ports., Eng.*
162 E2 **Wymeswold** *Leics., Eng.*
110 B2 **Wymington** *Bedford, Eng.*
162 G2 **Wymondham** *Leics., Eng.*
166 F3 **Wymondham** *Norf., Eng.*
350 E3 **Wyndham** *Bridg., Wales*
46 D3 **Wynford Eagle** *Dorset, Eng.*
378 G4 **Wynnstay Park** *Wrex., Wales*
236 G4 **Wynyard** *Stockton, Eng.*
22 K4 **Wyre** *i. Scot.*
24 L6 **Wyre** *r. Eng.*
136 E3 **Wyre Piddle** *Worcs., Eng.*
228 G3 **Wyresdale Tower** *Lancs., Eng.*
176 C5 **Wysall** *Notts., Eng.*
144 D6 **Wyson** *Shrop., Eng.*
136 F1 **Wythall** *Worcs., Eng.*
102 D4 **Wytham** *Oxon, Eng.*
232 D5 **Wythburn** *Cumbria, Eng.*
198 D3 **Wythenshawe** *Gtr Man., Eng.*
124 D4 **Wyton** *Cambs., Eng.*
210 G4 **Wyton** *E. Riding, Eng.*
120 E3 **Wyverstone** *Suff., Eng.*
170 B6 **Wyville** *Lincs., Eng.*
320 G4 **Wyvis Lodge** *High., Scot.*

Y

170 C2 **Yaddlethorpe** *N. Lincs., Eng.*
52 D7 **Yafford** *I.o.W., Eng.*
216 E1 **Yafforth** *N. Yorks., Eng.*
40 F3 **Yalberton** *Torbay, Eng.*
62 C3 **Yalding** *Kent, Eng.*
94 I2 **Yanley** *N. Som., Eng.*
232 F5 **Yanwath** *Cumbria, Eng.*
98 H3 **Yanworth** *Glos., Eng.*
210 D3 **Yapham** *E. Riding, Eng.*
58 C4 **Yapton** *W. Sussex, Eng.*
170 G3 **Yarburgh** *Lincs., Eng.*
40 G2 **Yarcombe** *Devon, Eng.*
154 D3 **Yardley** *W. Mids, Eng.*
128 D5 **Yardley Gobion** *Northants., Eng.*
128 E4 **Yardley Hastings** *Northants., Eng.*
154 C3 **Yardley Wood** *W. Mids, Eng.*
26 P3 **Yare** *r. Eng.*
94 F4 **Yarford** *Som., Eng.*
140 D3 **Yarkhill** *Here., Eng.*
148 C3 **Yarlet** *Staffs., Eng.*
94 H3 **Yarley** *Som., Eng.*
94 J4 **Yarlington** *Som., Eng.*
236 G4 **Yarm** *Stockton, Eng.*
52 D6 **Yarmouth** *I.o.W., Eng.*
40 E1 **Yarnacott** *Devon, Eng.*
86 B4 **Yarnbrook** *Wilts., Eng.*
40 E3 **Yarner** *Devon, Eng.*
148 B3 **Yarnfield** *Staffs., Eng.*
40 D2 **Yarnscombe** *Devon, Eng.*
102 D4 **Yarnton** *Oxon, Eng.*
140 C2 **Yarpole** *Here., Eng.*
94 G3 **Yarrow** *Som., Eng.*
256 F3 **Yarrow** *Borders, Scot.*
256 F3 **Yarrow Feus** *Borders, Scot.*
256 G3 **Yarrowford** *Borders, Scot.*
140 B3 **Yarsop** *Here., Eng.*
128 G2 **Yarwell** *Northants., Eng.*
98 E4 **Yate** *S. Glos., Eng.*
184 E2 **Yatehouse Green** *Cheshire West & Chester, Eng.*
52 H2 **Yateley** *Hants., Eng.*
86 D3 **Yatesbury** *Wilts., Eng.*
82 C3 **Yattendon** *W. Berks., Eng.*
140 B2 **Yatton** *Here., Eng.*
94 H2 **Yatton** *N. Som., Eng.*
86 B3 **Yatton Keynell** *Wilts., Eng.*
52 F7 **Yaverland** *I.o.W., Eng.*
166 E3 **Yaxham** *Norf., Eng.*
124 C3 **Yaxley** *Cambs., Eng.*
120 F3 **Yaxley** *Suff., Eng.*
140 B3 **Yazor** *Here., Eng.*
372 H3 **Y Bryn** *Gwynedd, Wales*
94 H5 **Yeabridge** *Som., Eng.*
74 B2 **Yeading** *Gtr Lon., Eng.*
222 D1 **Yeadon** *W. Yorks., Eng.*
228 F2 **Yealand Conyers** *Lancs., Eng.*
228 F1 **Yealand Redmayne** *Lancs., Eng.*
228 F1 **Yealand Storrs** *Lancs., Eng.*
40 E3 **Yealmpton** *Devon, Eng.*
216 F1 **Yearby** *R. and C., Eng.*
216 F2 **Yearsley** *N. Yorks., Eng.*
144 C3 **Yeaton** *Shrop., Eng.*
180 C5 **Yeaveley** *Derbys., Eng.*
244 E2 **Yeavering** *Northumb., Eng.*
216 H2 **Yedingham** *N. Yorks., Eng.*
102 C4 **Yelford** *Oxon, Eng.*
22 □N1 **Yell** *i. Scot.*
40 D1 **Yelland** *Devon, Eng.*
40 D2 **Yelland** *Devon, Eng.*
124 D5 **Yelling** *Cambs., Eng.*
22 □N1 **Yell Sound** *str. Scot.*
128 C3 **Yelvertoft** *Northants., Eng.*
40 D3 **Yelverton** *Devon, Eng.*
166 H3 **Yelverton** *Norf., Eng.*
94 J5 **Yenston** *Som., Eng.*
26 E6 **Yeo** *r. Eng.*
40 E2 **Yeoford** *Devon, Eng.*
36 F2 **Yeolmbridge** *Corn., Eng.*
94 I5 **Yeovil** *Som., Eng.*
94 I5 **Yeovil Marsh** *Som., Eng.*
94 I4 **Yeovilton** *Som., Eng.*
358 F3 **Yerbeston** *Pembs., Wales*
329 A3 **Yesnaby** *Orkney, Scot.*
26 D6 **Yes Tor** *hill Eng.*
256 K3 **Yetholm Mains** *Borders, Scot.*
244 F3 **Yetlington** *Northumb., Eng.*
46 D2 **Yetminster** *Dorset, Eng.*
40 F3 **Yettington** *Devon, Eng.*
292 C2 **Yetts o'Muckhart** *Clack., Scot.*
132 C4 **Yew Green** *Warks., Eng.*
Y Fali *I.o.A., Wales see* **Valley**
366 D4 **Y Fan** *Powys, Wales*
372 E1 **Y Felinheli** *Gwynedd, Wales*
Y Fenni *Mon., Wales see* **Abergavenny**
Y Fflint *Flints., Wales see* **Flint**
372 D3 **Y Ffôr** *Gwynedd, Wales*
372 E2 **Y Fron** *Gwynedd, Wales*
Y Gelli Gandryll *Powys, Wales see* **Hay-on-Wye**
110 B2 **Yielden** *Bedford, Eng.*
268 D2 **Yieldshields** *S. Lanark., Scot.*
74 B2 **Yiewsley** *Gtr Lon., Eng.*
26 E2 **Y Llethr** *hill Wales*
372 F3 **Ynys** *Gwynedd, Wales*
350 F3 **Ynysboeth** *R.C.T., Wales*
350 G3 **Ynysddu** *Caerp., Wales*
Ynys Enlli *i. Wales see* **Bardsey Island**
350 F3 **Ynyshir** *R.C.T., Wales*
362 F1 **Ynyslas** *Cere., Wales*
350 F3 **Ynysmaerdy** *R.C.T., Wales*
350 C2 **Ynysmeudwy** *N.P.T., Wales*
Ynys Môn *i. Wales see* **Anglesey**
362 F1 **Ynys Tachwedd** *Cere., Wales*
350 C2 **Ynystawe** *Swansea, Wales*
350 E2 **Ynyswen** *R.C.T., Wales*
350 F3 **Ynysybwl** *R.C.T., Wales*
144 C3 **Yockleton** *Shrop., Eng.*
210 D4 **Yokefleet** *E. Riding, Eng.*
276 D2 **Yoker** *Glas., Scot.*
314 F2 **Yonder Bognie** *Abers., Scot.*
46 C3 **Yondover** *Dorset, Eng.*
216 F3 **York** *York, Eng.*
216 F3 **York** *admin. div. Eng.*
24 N5 **York, Vale of** *val. Eng.*
62 F3 **Yorkletts** *Kent, Eng.*
98 D3 **Yorkley** *Glos., Eng.*
24 M5 **Yorkshire Dales National Par** *nat. park Eng.*
24 P6 **Yorkshire Wolds** *hills Eng.*
78 B1 **York Town** *Surr., Eng.*
144 D3 **Yorton** *Shrop., Eng.*
144 D3 **Yorton Heath** *Shrop., Eng.*
180 C3 **Youlgreave** *Derbys., Eng.*
210 D3 **Youlthorpe** *E. Riding, Eng.*
148 E4 **Yoxall** *Staffs., Eng.*
120 I3 **Yoxford** *Suff., Eng.*
Yr Wyddfa *mt. Wales see* **Snowdon**
Yr Wyddgrug *Flints., Wales see* **Mold**
362 G2 **Ysbyty Cynfyn** *Cere., Wales*
378 C3 **Ysbyty Ifan** *Conwy, Wales*
362 G3 **Ysbyty Ystwyth** *Cere., Wales*
378 F2 **Ysceifiog** *Flints., Wales*
362 G1 **Ysgubor-y-coed** *Cere., Wales*
350 D2 **Ystalyfera** *N.P.T., Wales*
350 F3 **Ystrad** *R.C.T., Wales*
26 F1 **Ystrad** *r. Wales*
362 F3 **Ystrad Aeron** *Cere., Wales*
366 D8 **Ystradfellte** *Powys, Wales*
356 H1 **Ystradffin** *Carmar., Wales*
366 C8 **Ystradgynlais** *Powys, Wales*
362 G3 **Ystrad Meurig** *Cere., Wales*
350 G3 **Ystrad Mynach** *Caerp., Wales*
350 D2 **Ystradowen** *N.P.T., Wales*
350 F4 **Ystradowen** *V. of Glam., Wales*
362 G2 **Ystumtuen** *Cere., Wales*
26 D3 **Ystwyth** *r. Wales*
22 L8 **Ythan** *r. Scot.*
314 F2 **Ythanwells** *Abers., Scot.*
314 G2 **Ythsie** *Abers., Scot.*

Z

40 E2 **Zeal Monachorum** *Devon, Eng*
86 B5 **Zeals** *Wilts., Eng.*
36 D3 **Zelah** *Corn., Eng.*
36 C3 **Zennor** *Corn., Eng.*
176 B6 **Zouch** *Notts., Eng.*

ACKNOWLEDGEMENTS

TIMES ATLAS OF BRITAIN

Concept, design, maps, editorial and project management by the staff at CollinsBartholomew, Glasgow:

Vaila Alexander, David Alford, John Allen, Craig Balfour, Sheena Barclay, Amanda Berry, Craig Blackwood, Carol Cumming, John Downs, Elizabeth Donald, Sarah Garner, Kenneth Gibson, Graham Gill, Nichola Goodliffe, Helen Gordon, Graham Howse, Jim Irvine, Ed James, David Jamieson, Kathryn Kelly, Jethro Lennox, Iain MacDonald, Rosemary MacLeod, Nina MacVinish, Anne Mahon, Jackie McGeough, Alistair McKnight, Elizabeth McLachlan, Keith Moore, Stuart Morton, David Mumford, Roger Pountain, Selvaraj Rajendran, Donald Ralston, Kevin Robbins, Kate Rogers, Ewan Ross, Norman Samuels, Rob Schouppe, Liz Scott, Robin Scrimgeour, Sheena Shanks, Amanda Sim, Andy Slater, Jenny Slater, Katie Spike, Mark Steward, Julie Surman, Alex Wallace, David White, Sarah Woods, Susan Wright.

Text compiled and written by:

Christopher Riches, Nancy E M Bailey and Catherine Gaunt.

Additional contributions by:

William Watt, David Maltby, Alison Davies, Neil Forrest, Gordon MacGilp, Karen Midgely, Sonia Dawkins, Ruth Hall, Belinda Kane, Mick Ashworth, Jennifer Ashworth, Mapseeker Archive Publishing (Paul Line and Steve Toulouse), Christopher Fleet at the National Library of Scotland, and Davidsons Pre Press Solutions, Glasgow (Evelyn Sword, Karen Stewart, Scott Campbell, Margaret Walker and Robert Campbell).

HISTORICAL COUNTY MAPS

County maps of England and Wales:
Collins County Atlas of England and Wales, 1877.

County maps of Scotland:
Phillips Handy Atlas of the Counties of Scotland, 1882. Mapping by J. Bartholomew except:
Aberdeenshire, Scottish Borders, Dumfries and Galloway, Edinburgh Environs and The Highlands:
Maps of Scotland,
J. Bartholomew 1885.

Northern Ireland:
Phillips Handy Atlas of the Counties of Ireland, 1885.

Isle of Man and the Channel Islands:
Handy Atlas of England and Wales, J. Bartholomew. A.& C. Black, 1892.

HISTORICAL INNER CITY MAPS

Bristol, Leicester, Liverpool, Leeds:
Survey Atlas of England and Wales. Edinburgh Geographical Institute, J. Bartholomew, 1903.

Birmingham, Nottingham, Manchester, Sheffield, Hull, Newcastle and York:
The Royal Atlas of England and Wales, J.G. Bartholomew 1898/1900.

Coventry: *Shakespeare's land: being a description of central and southern Warwickshire*, C. J. Ribton-Turner ; maps by John Bartholomew and Co., 1893.

Glasgow and Edinburgh: The Royal Scottish Geographical Society's *Atlas of Scotland* produced by J.G.Bartholomew, 1895.

Inner London: A. Fullarton & Company. Engraved by J Bartholomew, c.1870.

Belfast: *Black's Guide to Ireland*, 1891.

Cardiff: *Black's Guide to South Wales*, 1896.

HISTORICAL NATIONAL MAPS

England (p33), Scotland (p249), Wales (p335) and Ireland (p383): *Century Atlas and Gazatteer of the World*, John Walker and Co., 1890. Maps by John Bartholomew.

England (p32): Willem and Johan Blau's map of England and Wales, 1635

Scotland (p248), Wales (p334) and Ireland (p382): Maps by John Speed, 1610.

STATISTICS

Office for National Statistics
http://www.statistics.gov.uk/default.asp
Country, county and administrative division statistics all 2008 estimates unless otherwise indicated.
City and town populations all from the 2001 census unless otherwise indicated.

NOMIS: official labour market
statistics.*https://www.nomisweb.co.uk/Default.asp*

Northern Ireland Statistics and Research Agency.
http://www.nisra.gov.uk/

General Register Office for Scotland.
http://www.gro-scotland.gov.uk/statistics/

OTHER REFERENCES

Met Office
http://www.metoffice.gov.uk/climate/uk/

Tourism
http://www.alva.org.uk/

Department of Energy and Climate change
http://www.decc.gov.uk/

PHOTO CREDITS

The letters in bold refer to the photograph's position on the page: T, B, M, L, R, i.e. top, bottom, middle, left and right respectively.

All images from www.shutterstock.co.uk unless otherwise noted with an asterisk. All photographers credited unless unknown.

Cover image St Ives, Cornwall, satellite image. North is at top. Water is dark green, land is green, brown and grey. Sand is white/pale green. *©GETMAPPING PLC/ SCIENCE PHOTO LIBRARY;

10 T ©stewyphoto; **10 B** ©Brendan Howard; **12 T** ©Ewen Cameron; **12 B** ©David Woods; **14 T** ©r.nagy; **14 M** ©Ian Bracegirdle; **14 B** ©r.nagy; **16 T** ©Darren Baker; **16 B** ©Amy Johansson; **17 T** ©David Hughes; **17 M** ©Dmitry Chernobrov; **17 B** ©Chris Harvey; **18 T** ©TVR; **18 M** ©Graham Lumsden; **18 B** *© (by CC 2.0) Jim Linwood; **18** *©ETSU for the DTI 1999; **18–19** Energy icons ©SimonasP; **18–19** Power icon ©Colorlife; **18–19** Electricity icon ©Yury Kosourov; **18–19** Energy icons ©Kar; **18–19** Refinery icon ©Charmaine Paulson; **28 TL** ©Clive Chilvers; **28 BL** ©Karen Gentry; **28 BR** ©David Hughes; **29** ©vitek12; **30 L** ©David Hughes; **30 R** ©Douglas Freer; **31 TL** ©Patrick Wang; **31 TR** ©vitek12; **31 M** ©Ulrich Mueller; **31 ML** ©Samot; **31 B** ©vitek12; **34 T** ©Joe Gough; **34 B** ©Mike Graham; **35** ©Stephen Aaron Rees; **38 TL** ©Nikki Bidgood; **38 TR** ©Neil Lang; **38 ML** ©Juneisy Q. Hawkins; **38 B** ©jennyt; **42 T** ©Stephen Meese; **42 B** ©jennyt; **43 TL** ©DavidYoung; **43 TR** ©ND Johnston; **43 B** ©Philip Lange; **44** ©Horia Bogdan; **45 T** ©Leslie Budzynski; **45 B** ©Becky Stares; **48 L** ©Dave Coadwell; **48 R** ©Richard Melichar; **49** ©Joe Gough; **50 TL** ©4361000358; **50 TR** ©Steeve Roche; **50 B** ©Jane Rix; **51 T** ©duriantree; **51 ML** ©shaun sadler; **51 MR** ©stocker1970; **51 B** ©Hicki; **54 L** ©Lance Bellers; **54 TR** ©Chester Tugwell;

54 BR ©David Peta; **55** ©Chris Mole; **56 T** ©chamomille; **56 B** ©David Hughes; **57 T** ©Chris Mole; **57 M** ©Christopher Dodge; **57 B** ©Markus Gann; **60 T** ©John Hemmings; **60 B** ©Gyrohype; **65** ©yampi; **66 T** ©jan kranendonk; **66 B** ©Monkey Business Images; **67 T** ©Mike Liu; **67 B** ©andrew chambers; **68** ©Lee Torrens; **69** ©Marc Pinter; **72 L** *© (by CC 2.0) JamesZ; **72 R** ©Neil Balderson; **73 L** ©David Peta; **73 R** ©David Peta; **76 L** ©Lesley Rigg; **76 R** ©Alex Brown; **77** ©Stephen Mulligan; **80** *© (GNU Free Documentation License) Mark S Jobling; **81 L** ©Entertainment Press; **81 R** ©Chrislofoto; **84 TL** ©FrankfurtDave; **84 TR** ©Jane Rix; **84 B** ©stocker1970; **85** *© (by CC 2.0) Marcin Wichary; **88 L** ©Chris Loneragan; **88 R** ©rtguest; **89 L** ©Matthew Collingwood; **89 R** *© (by CC 2.0) Rob Young; **90 TL** *©London Red carpet/Alamy; **90 TR** *© (by CC 3.0) Bedford Lemere; **90 BL** ©Christopher Poe; **90 BR** ©Pres Panayotov; **91 T** ©godrick; **91 B** ©Jane Rix; **92 T** ©willmetts; **92 BL** ©Slavko Sereda; **92 BR** ©David Woolfenden; **93** ©Mohd Yusri b. Mohamad Yusoff; **96 T** *© (by CC 2.0) flickr (unknown); **96 B** ©stocker1970; **97** ©Joe Gough; **100 TL** ©Doctor Jools; **100 TR** ©Andrei Nekrassov; **100 B** ©David Peta; **101** ©Rachael Russell; **104 T** ©Patrick Wang; **104 B** ©David Hughes; **105** ©Terence Mendoza; **108 TL** *© (by CC 2.0) Fabio Veronesi; **108 TR** *© (by CC 2.0) Le Scribbler; **108 B** *© (by CC 2.0) Martin Pettitt; **109 L** *© (by CC 2.0) Dave Hamster; **109 R** *© (by CC 2.0) greenacre8; **112** ©mjt; **113 L** ©Brigida Soriano; **113 R** ©CarbonSilver Photography (Greg Benz); **114 T** *© (by CC 2.0) Jim Linwood; **114 B** ©Rui Saraiva; **115 L** ©Tom Curtis; **115 R** *© (by CC 2.0) Jim Linwood; **118 TL** ©Mike J Roberts; **118 R** ©Richard Bowden; **118 BL** ©Len Green; **119** ©joingate; **122 T** ©Benson HE; **122 B** *© (by CC 2.0) DavidHBolton; **123** *© (by CC 2.0) Acradenia; **126 L** ©Awe Inspiring Images; **126 R** ©Tony Carr; **127 L** ©Graham Taylor; **127 R** ©Rachael Russell; **130 T** ©David Hughes; **130 B** ©David Hughes; **131 L** ©James Kingman; **131 R** ©Graham Taylor;

134 T ©David Benton; **134 B** ©Robert Hackett; **135** ©David Hughes; **138 L** *© (by CC 2.0) PhillipC; **138 R** ©C Berry Ottaway; **139 T** ©C Berry Ottaway; **139 B** ©dcwcreations; **142 T** ©David Hughes; **142 B** ©Peter R Foster IDMA; **146 T** ©Andy Linden; **146 B** *© (by CC 2.0) dullhunk; **150** ©Dainis Derics; **151 T** ©Lesley Rigg; **151 B** ©Feraru Nicolae; **152** ©Paul Matthew Photography; **153** *© (by CC 2.0) Jim Linwood; **156 T** *© (by CC 2.0) stevecadman; **156 M** ©Monkey Business Images; **156 BL** *© (by CC 2.0) Lee Jordan; **156 BR** *© (by CC 2.0) RATAEDL; **157 T** *© (by CC 2.0) ahisgett; **157 M** *© (by CC 2.0) jo-h; **157 BL** *© (by CC 2.0) wwarby; **157 BR** *© (by CC 2.0) ahisgett; **158 T** *© (by CC 2.0) Jams 123; **158 B** *© (by CC 2.0) ahisgett; **159 T** *© (by CC 2.0) jlastras; **159 M** *©Jams 123; **159 B** *© (by CC 2.0) sashafatcat; **160 T** *© (by CC 2.0) u07ch; **160 M** ©WojciechKozlowski; **160 B** *©Dave Porter/Alamy; **161 T** *© (by CC 2.0) andy.v; **161 B** *© (by CC 2.0) davidfullerdaniel; **164** ©David Hughes; **165 L** ©David Hughes; **165 R** *© (by CC 2.0) Charlie Dave; **168 L** ©Artur Bogacki; **168 R** ©Guy Erwood; **169 L** ©Artur Bogacki; **169 R** ©Dean Mitchell; **172 TL** *© (by CC 2.0) Ratherbewalking; **172 TR** *© (by CC 2.0) D H Wright; **172 B** *© (by CC 2.0) D H Wright; **173 T** ©mitzy; **173 B** ©Ingvar Tjostheim; **174** ©Entertainment Press; **175 T** ©Mark William Richardson; **175 B** ©Mark Burrows (Nottingham, UK) ; **178 T** ©Robert Ford; **178 B** *© (by CC 2.0) Jonathan Gill; **179** ©Jane McIlroy; **182** ©Chris Green; **183 L** ©Entertainment Press; **183 R** ©David Woods; **186** ©Dave McAleavy; **187** *© (GNU1.3) Stefan Bernd; **188 T** *© (by CC 2.0) Ben Sutherland; **188 M** ©Gail Johnson; **188 B** ©Peter R Foster IDMA; **189** ©Matt Hart; **192** ©David Peta; **193** ©Guy Erwood; **194 T** ©Samot; **194 B** *© (by CC 2.0) terry6082 Books; **195 TL** *© (by CC 2.0) Gene Hunt; **195 TR** *©Andy Marshall/Alamy; **195 B** ©Paul Reid; **196 L** ©Paul Reid; **196 R** *© (by CC 2.0) Tim Green aka atoach; **197 T** ©Tom Plesnik; **197 B** *© (by CC 2.0) Paolo Camera; **200** *© (by CC 2.0) kT LindSAy;

447

ACKNOWLEDGEMENTS (CONTINUED)

202 TL *© (by CC 2.0) Lighthelper; 202 TR ©Mark William Richardson; 202 BR *© (by CC 2.0) Peter Meade; 203 T ©Tom Curtis;203 M ©Tom Curtis; 203 B *© (by CC 2.0) ell brown; 206 T ©Gordon Ball LRPS; 206 BL ©Gordon Ball LRPS; 206 BR ©Quayside; 207 T ©chris2766; 207 B ©MalcolmC; 212 TL ©cinemafestival; 212 TR ©David Hughes; 212 BL ©Atlaspix; 212 BR ©4745052183; 213 ©ronfromyork; 214 TL ©cinemafestival; 214 TR ©redjar; 214 BL ©Dale Mitchell; 214 BR ©Doctor Jools; 215 T ©Awe Inspiring Images; 215 B ©Tom Curtis; 218 ©WH CHOW; 219 ©WH CHOW; 220 BL *© (by CC 2.0) Tim Green aka atoach; 220 BR *© (by CC 2.0) Tim Green aka atoach; 220 ML *© (by CC 2.0) Tim Green aka atoach; 220 MR *© (by CC 2.0) stevecadman; 221 TL ©Mountain Light Studios; 221 TR *© (by CC 2.0) Jordanhill School D&T Dept; 221 BL ©cinemafestival; 221 BR ©Christian Wilkinson; 224 ©Jane McIlroy; 225 L ©Tom Curtis; 225 R *© (by CC 2.0) Melanie-m; 226 B ©george green; 226 T ©albinoni; 227 TL ©Pefkos; 227 TR ©CaptureLight; 227 ML ©Mark Bolton; 227 B ©Dave McAleavy; 230 ©stewyphoto; 234 T ©Gail Johnson; 234 B ©Paul Gregory; 238 T *© (by CC 2.0) Victoria Reay; 238 B ©Tom Curtis; 239 T ©verityjohnson; 239 B ©SueC; 240 ©Darren Turner; 241 T ©CJ08; 241 M ©Gail Johnson; 241 B ©Darren Turner; 242 ©Darren Turner; 243 L ©Tony Brindley; 243 R *© (by CC 2.0) Gaspa; 246 TL ©Anyka; 246 M ©John A Cameron; 246 B ©Daniele Silva; 247 TL ©John A Cameron; 247 R ©Gordon Saunders; 247 BL ©Merlindo; 250 TL ©Dave McAleavy; 250 TR ©Terry Kettlewell; 250 B ©Peter Guess; 254 TL ©Jule Berlin; 254 TR ©Gail Johnson; 254 B ©Kevin Eaves; 258 T *© (by CC 2.0) gee; 258 B *©Robert Murray/Alamy; 259 T ©Marianna Raszkowska; 259 M ©David Woods; 259 BL ©rubiphoto; 259 BR ©Monkey Business Images; 260 TL ©Kristofer Keane; 260 TR ©Bill McKelvie; 260 ML ©Jeff Banke; 260 B ©Matt Hart; 261 ©Gordon Saunders; 266 TL ©IgorGolovniov; 266 TR ©Bill McKelvie; 266 B *© (by CC 2.0) SeaDave; 267 *©Craig Balfour; 271 L ©Bill McKelvie;

271 M ©antoninaart; 271 R *© (by CC 2.0) ; 272 T ©Iain McGillivray; 272 B ©Bill McKelvie; 273 ©Bertrand Collet; 275 L ©Bill McKelvie; 275 R ©David Woods; 278 T ©Ian D Walker; 278 BL *© (by CC 2.0) Gone-Walkabout; 278 BR *©Mark Steward; 279 T ©Terry Kettlewell; 279 B ©Ross Wallace; 282 L ©Tamara Kulikova; 282 R ©Christopher Walker; 283 ©David Lochhead; 284 T ©Piotr Peszko; 284 B ©roger pilkington; 285 ©Sandy Stupart; 287 TL ©Aitor Bouzo Ateca; 287 TR ©Bill McKelvie; 287 B ©leonardo da gressignanto; 290 T *©Mark Steward; 290 B *©Mark Steward; 291 ©Andrew West; 294 L ©Creative Hearts; 294 R ©Terry Kettlewell; 295 ©Mark Steward; 298 L ©Alf Thomas; 298 R ©Stephen Finn; 299 ©Julietphotography; 302 T ©jean morrison; 302 B ©Richard Melichar; 303 ©Brendan Howard; 306 ©Palis Michalis; 307 L ©Adrian T Jones; 307 R ©Creative Hearts; 307 M *© (by CC 2.0) Flickr (unknown); 310 T ©Damian Gil; 310 B *©Mark Steward; 312 T ©Paula Gent; 312 BL *© (by CC 2.0) Harb; 312 BR ©Creative Hearts; 313 T ©Paul Butchard; 313 B ©jean morrison; 316 T ©Gail Johnson; 316 B *©Mark Steward; 317 TR ©Jason Ho; 317 L ©Lance Bellers; 317 BR ©Morag Fleming; 319 ©stewyphoto; 324 T ©Joe Gough; 324 B ©Joe Gough; 325 ©Roberto Cerruti; 328 ©karin claus; 330 ©Paula Gent; 332 TL ©Darryl Sleath; 332 BL ©Carlos Neto; 332 BR ©Len Green; 333 TL ©Neil Wigmore; 333 BL ©Gail Johnson; 333 R ©Len Green; 336 L ©David Hughes; 336 R ©Lesley Rigg; 338 T ©Mike Price; 338 CL *© (by CC 3.0) Joe D; 338 CR *© (by CC 2.0) jonworth-eu; 338 BL *© (by CC 2.0) hha124l; 338 BR ©Luká? Hejtman; 340 T ©Bryce Newell; 340 B ©david lehner; 341 ©Becky Stares; 343 TL *©Adrian Sherratt/Alamy; 343 TR *© (PDPhoto.org) Jon Sullivan; 343 B ©eldo; 345 TL ©David Peta; 345 TR *©Colin Palmer Photography/Alamy; 345 CL ©Nicholas Peter Gavin Davies; 345 BL *©david martyn hughes/Alamy; 345 B ©David Hughes; 346 ©Nicholas Peter Gavin Davies; 347 TL ©jon le-bon; 347 TR ©Adrian Phillips; 347 B ©jon le-bon; 348 T ©Entertainment Press;

348 M ©Michael Pemberton; 348 B *© (by CC 2.0) moleitau; 352 L ©Mark William Penny; 352 R ©Christina Richards; 353 ©marilyn barbone; 354 T ©Merlindo; 354 CL ©Ewen Cameron; 354 CR ©Brian A Jackson; 354 B ©Chris Pole; 355 T ©Will Iredale; 355 B ©Adrian Phillips; 360 L ©Stephen Aaron Rees; 360 R ©Stephen Aaron Rees; 361 ©Joe Goodson; 364 T ©marilyn barbone; 364 B ©David Hughes; 365 ©David Hughes; 368 ©David Hughes; 369 L ©Gail Johnson; 369 R ©Brynteg; 370 T ©Gail Johnson; 370 B ©Gail Johnson; 374 T ©Gail Johnson; 374 B *© (by CC 2.0) Richard0; 375 TL ©Steve Wilson; 375 TR ©Adrian Phillips; 375 B ©Gail Johnson; 376 ©Tom Curtis; 377 ©Steven Paul Pepper; 380 T ©stenic56; 380 T ©Qing Ding; 380 M *© (by CC 2.0) Supermac1961; 380 B *© (by CC 2.0) yvescosentino; 381 T stenic56; 381 M *© (by CC 2.0) Margaret Anne Clarke; 381 B ©Tomasz Szymanski; 384 T ©RexRover; 384 BL ©walshphotos; 384 BR *© (by CC 2.0) karen in toronto; 385 ©Josemaria Toscano; 386 L *© (by CC 2.0) LaRsNoW; 386 R ©ZDreamer; 387 *© (by CC 2.0) Carisenda; 390 T ©gabo; 390 B ©Josemaria Toscano; 391 T ©Josemaria Toscano; 391 B ©John Gordon; 392 ©Chrismoira; 393 L ©Jane McIlroy; 393 R ©RexRover; 394 L ©M Reel; 394 R *© (by CC 2.0) cliff1066™; 395 L ©Jane McIlroy; 395 R ©Martin Heaney; 398 *© (by CC 2.0) Jule Berlin; 399 L *© (by CC 2.0) andrewmuir.net; 399 R *© (by CC 2.0) walshphotos; 400 ©PHB.cz (Richard Semik); 401 *©Christopher Hill/Alamy; 404 T ©Graham Taylor; 404 ©Graham Taylor; 406 T ©MarilynJane; 406 M ©Alan Jeffery; 407 B *© (by CC 2.0) PhillipC.

CC by 2.0
These works are licensed under the Creative Commons 2.0 Attribution License. To view a copy of this license, visit *http://creativecommons.org/licenses/by/2.0/*

CC by sa 3.0
These works are licensed under the Creative Commons Attribution Share Alike 3.0 License. To view a copy of this license, visit *http://creativecommons.org/licenses/by-sa/3.0/*

KEY: SCOTLAND AND NORTHERN IRELAND

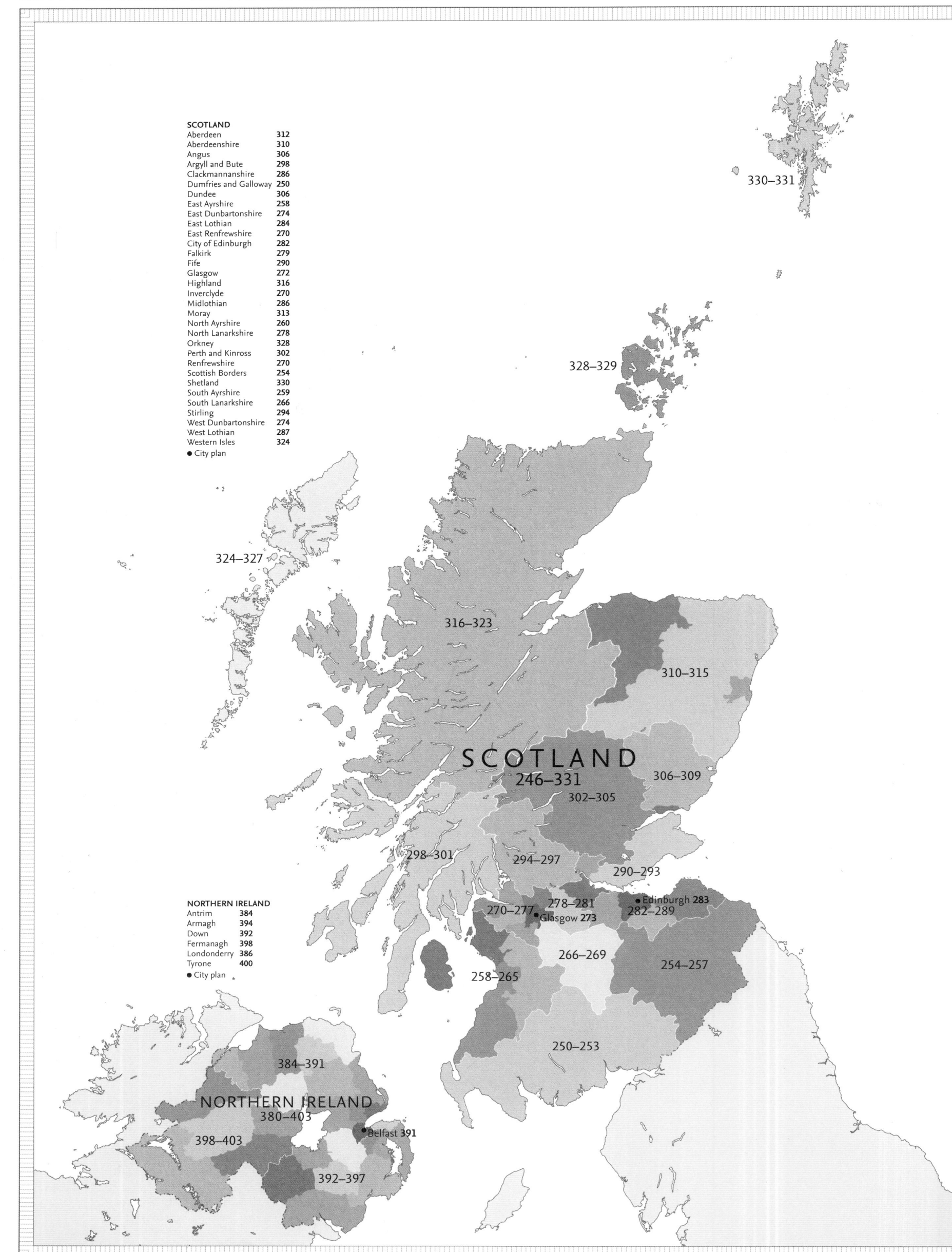

SCOTLAND

Aberdeen	312
Aberdeenshire	310
Angus	306
Argyll and Bute	298
Clackmannanshire	286
Dumfries and Galloway	250
Dundee	306
East Ayrshire	258
East Dunbartonshire	274
East Lothian	284
East Renfrewshire	270
City of Edinburgh	282
Falkirk	279
Fife	290
Glasgow	272
Highland	316
Inverclyde	270
Midlothian	286
Moray	313
North Ayrshire	260
North Lanarkshire	278
Orkney	328
Perth and Kinross	302
Renfrewshire	270
Scottish Borders	254
Shetland	330
South Ayrshire	259
South Lanarkshire	266
Stirling	294
West Dunbartonshire	274
West Lothian	287
Western Isles	324
● City plan	

NORTHERN IRELAND

Antrim	384
Armagh	394
Down	392
Fermanagh	398
Londonderry	386
Tyrone	400
● City plan	

330–331

328–329

324–327

316–323

310–315

SCOTLAND
246–331

306–309

302–305

298–301

294–297

290–293

278–281

270–277

● Edinburgh **283**

282–289

● Glasgow **273**

266–269

254–257

258–265

250–253

384–391

NORTHERN IRELAND
380–403

398–403

● Belfast **391**

392–397